THE WORLD'S BEST ORATIONS

David J. Brewer
Editor

Edward A. Allen & William Schuyler
Associate Editors

Volumes 1 - 5

Mini-Print™ Corporation
Metuchen, N.J.   1970

The World's Best Orations
was originally published
in 10 Volumes by
Ferd P. Kaiser, St. Louis
c. 1901

ISBN 0-8108-0341-0

TABLE OF CONTENTS

VOL. I

TABLE OF CONTENTS

VOL. II

TABLE OF CONTENTS

VOL. III

TABLE OF CONTENTS

VOL. IV

TABLE OF CONTENTS

VOLUME V

TABLE OF CONTENTS

VOLUME VI

TABLE OF CONTENTS

VOLUME VII

TABLE OF CONTENTS

VOL. VIII

———

TABLE OF CONTENTS

VOLUME IX

TABLE OF CONTENTS

VOLUME X

————

THE ADVISORY COUNCIL

---

cruel dissecting knife of the critic. It is the marvelous light flashing out in the intellectual heavens which no Franklin has yet or may ever draw and tie to earth by string of kite.

But while there is a living something which no human art has yet been able to grasp and preserve, there is a wonderful joy and comfort in the record of that which the orator said. As we read we see the very picture, though inarticulate, of the living orator. We may never know all the marvelous power of Demosthenes, yet Πρωτον, μὲγ, ὦ ἄνδρες Ἀθηναίοι, suggests something of it. Cicero's silver speech may never reach our ears, and yet who does not love to read *Quousque tandem abutere, O Catilina, patientia nostra?* So if on the printed page we may not see the living orator, we may look upon his picture—the photograph of his power. And it is this which it is the thought and purpose of this work to present. We mean to photograph the orators of the world, reproducing the words which they spake, and trusting to the vivid imagination of the thoughtful reader to put behind the recorded words the living force and power. In this we shall fill a vacant place in literature. There are countless books of poetry in which the gems of the great poets of the world have been preserved, but oratory has not been thus favored. We have many volumes which record the speeches of different orators, sometimes connected with a biography of their lives and sometimes as independent gatherings of speeches. We have also single books, like Goodrich's 'British Eloquence,' which give us partial selections of the great orations. But this is intended to be universal in its reach, a complete encyclopedia of oratory. The purpose is to present the best efforts of the world's greatest orators in all ages; and with this purpose kept in view as the matter of primary importance, to supplement the great orations with others that are representative and historically important—especially with those having a fundamental connection with the most important events in the development of Anglo-Saxon civilization. The greatest attention has been given to the representative orators of England and America, so that the work includes all that is most famous or most necessary to be known in the oratory of the Anglo-Saxon race. Wherever possible, addresses have been published *in extenso.* This has been the rule

PREFACE

ORATORY is the masterful art. Poetry, painting, music, sculpture, architecture please, thrill, inspire; but oratory rules. The orator dominates those who hear him, convinces their reason, controls their judgment, compels their action. For the time being he is master. Through the clearness of his logic, the keenness of his wit, the power of his appeal, or that magnetic something which is felt and yet cannot be defined, or through all together, he sways his audience as the storm bends the branches of the forest. Hence it is that in all times this wonderful power has been something longed for and striven for. Demosthenes, on the beach, struggling with the pebbles in his mouth to perfect his articulation, has been the great example. Yet it is often true of the orator, as of the poet; *nascitur non fit.* Patrick Henry seemed to be inspired as "Give me liberty or give me death" rolled from his lips. The untutored savage has shown himself an orator.

Who does not delight in oratory? How we gather to hear even an ordinary speaker! How often is a jury swayed and controlled by the appeals of counsel! Do we not all feel the magic of the power, and when occasionally we are permitted to listen to a great orator how completely we lose ourselves and yield in willing submission to the imperious and impetuous flow of his speech! It is said that after Webster's great reply to Hayne every Massachusetts man walking down Pennsylvania Avenue seemed a foot taller.

This marvelous power is incapable of complete preservation on the printed page. The presence, the eye, the voice, the magnetic touch, are beyond record. The phonograph and kinetoscope may some day seize and perpetuate all save the magnetic touch, but that weird, illusive, indefinable yet wonderfully real power by which the orator subdues may never be caught by science or preserved for the

followed in giving the great orations. In dealing with minor orators, the selections made are considerable enough to show the style, method, and spirit. Where it has been necessary to choose between two orations of equal merit, the one having the greater historical significance has been selected. Of course it would not be possible, keeping within reasonable limits, to give every speech of every one worthy to be called an orator. Indeed, the greatest of orators sometimes failed. So we have carefully selected only those speeches which manifest the power of eloquence; and this selection, we take pleasure in assuring our readers, has been made by the most competent critics of the country.

We have not confined ourselves to any one profession or field of eloquence. The pulpit, the bar, the halls of legislation, and the popular assembly have each and all been called upon for their best contributions. The single test has been, is it oratory? the single question, is there eloquence? The reader and student of every class will therefore find within these pages that which will satisfy his particular taste and desire in the matter of oratory.

As this work is designed especially for the American reader, we have deemed it proper to give prominence to Anglo-Saxon orators; and yet this prominence has not been carried so far as to make the work a one-sided collection. It is not a mere presentation of American or even of English-speaking orators. We submit the work to the American public in the belief that all will find pleasure, interest, and instruction in its pages, and in the hope that it will prove an inspiration to the growing generation to see to it that oratory be not classed among the "lost arts," but that it shall remain an ever-present and increasing power and blessing to the world.

David J. Brewer.

THE ORATORY OF ANGLO-SAXON COUNTRIES

BY EDWARD A. ALLEN

Professor of Anglo-Saxon and English Literature in the University of Missouri

NGLISH-SPEAKING people have always been the freest people, the greatest lovers of liberty, the world has ever seen. Long before English history properly begins, the pen of Tacitus reveals to us our forefathers in their old home-land in North Germany beating back the Roman legions under Varus, and staying the progress of Rome's triumphant car whose mighty wheels had crushed Hannibal, Jugurtha, Vercingetorix, and countless thousands in every land. The Germanic ancestors of the English nation were the only people who did not bend the neck to these lords of all the world besides. In the year 9, when the Founder of Christianity was playing about his humble home at Nazareth, or watching his father at work in his shop, our forefathers dealt Rome a blow from which she never recovered. As Freeman, late professor of history at Oxford, said in one of his lectures: "In the blow by the Teutoburg wood was the germ of the Declaration of Independence, the germ of the surrender of Yorktown." Arminius was our first Washington, "*haud dubie liberator*," as Tacitus calls him,—the savior of his country.

When the time came for expansion, and our forefathers in the fifth century began the conquest and settlement of the island that was to become their New England, they pushed out the Celts, the native inhabitants of the island, just as their descendants, about twelve hundred years later, were to push out the indigenous people of this continent, to make way for a higher civilization, a larger destiny. No Englishman ever saw an armed Roman in England, and though traces of the Roman conquest may be seen everywhere in that country to-day, it is sometimes forgotten that it was the

Britain of the Celts, not the England of the English, which was held for so many centuries as a province of Rome.

The same love of freedom that resisted the Roman invasion in the first home of the English was no less strong in their second home, when Alfred with his brave yeomen withstood the invading Danes at Ashdown and Edington, and saved England from becoming a Danish province. It is true that the Normans, by one decisive battle, placed a French king on the throne of England, but the English spirit of freedom was never subdued; it rose superior to the conquerors of Hastings, and in the end English speech and English freedom gained the mastery.

The sacred flame of freedom has burned in the hearts of the Anglo-Saxon race through all the centuries of our history, and this spirit of freedom is reflected in our language and in our oratory. There never have been wanting English orators when English liberty seemed to be imperiled; indeed, it may be said that the highest oratory has always been coincident with the deepest aspirations of freedom.

It is said of Pitt,—the younger, I believe,—that he was fired to oratory by reading the speeches in Milton's 'Paradise Lost.' These speeches—especially those of Satan, the most human of the characters in this noble epic,—when analyzed and traced to their source, are neither Hebrew nor Greek, but English to the core. They are imbued with the English spirit, with the spirit of Cromwell, with the spirit that beat down oppression at Marston Moor, and ushered in a freer England at Naseby. In the earlier Milton of a thousand years before, whether the work of Cædmon or of some other English muse, the same spirit is reflected in Anglo-Saxon words. Milton's Satan is more polished, better educated, thanks to Oxford and Cambridge, but the spirit is essentially one with that of the ruder poet; and this spirit, I maintain, is English.

The dry annals of the Anglo-Saxon Chronicle are occasionally lighted up with a gleam of true eloquence, as in the description of the battle of Brunanburh, which breaks forth into a pean of victory. Under the year 991, there is mention of a battle at Maldon, between the English and the Danes, in which great heroism must have been

displayed, for it inspired at the time one of the most patriotic outbursts of song to be found in the whole range of English literature. During an enforced truce, because of a swollen stream that separated the two armies, a messenger is sent from the Danes to Byrhtnoth, leader of the English forces, with a proposition to purchase peace with English gold. Byrhtnoth, angry and resolute, gave him this answer:—

"Hearest thou, pirate, what this folk sayeth? They will give you spears for tribute, weapons that will avail you nought in battle. Messenger of the vikings, get thee back. Take to thy people a sterner message, that here stands a fearless earl, who with his band will defend this land, the home of Æthelred, my prince, folk and fold. Too base it seems to me that ye go without battle to your ships with our money, now that ye have come thus far into our country. Ye shall not so easily obtain treasure. Spear and sword, grim battle-play, shall decide between us ere we pay tribute."

Though the battle was lost and Byrhtnoth slain, the spirit of the man is an English inheritance. It is the same spirit that refused ship-money to Charles I., and tea-money to George III.

The encroachments of tyranny and the stealthier step of royal prerogative have shrunk before this spirit which through the centuries has inspired the noblest oratory of England and America. It not only inspired the great orators of the mother country, it served at the same time as a bond of sympathy with the American colonies in their struggle for freedom. Burke, throughout his great speech on Conciliation, never lost sight of this idea:—

"This fierce spirit of liberty is stronger in the English colonies probably than in any other people of the earth. The people of the colonies are descendants of Englishmen. England, sir, is a nation which still, I hope, respects, and formerly adored, her freedom. The colonists emigrated from you when this part of your character was most predominant; and they took this bias and direction the moment they parted from your hands. They are therefore not only devoted to liberty, but to liberty according to English ideas and our English principles. . . . The temper and character which prevail in our colonies are, I am afraid, unalterable by any human art. We cannot, I fear, falsify the pedigree of this fierce people, and persuade them that they are not sprung from a nation in whose veins the blood of freedom circulates. The language in which they would hear you tell them this tale would detect the imposition; your speech would betray you. . . . In order to prove that Americans have no right to their liberties, we are every day endeavoring to subvert the maxims which preserve the whole spirit of our own. To prove

that the Americans ought not to be free, we are obliged to depreciate the value of freedom itself; and we never gain a paltry advantage over them in debate without attacking some of those principles, or deriding some of those feelings, for which our ancestors have shed their blood. . . . As long as you have the wisdom to keep the sovereign authority of this country as the sanctuary of liberty, the sacred temple consecrated to our common faith, wherever the chosen race and sons of England worship freedom they will turn their faces towards you. The more ardently they love liberty the more perfect will be their obedience. Slavery they can have anywhere—it is a weed that grows in every soil. They can have it from Spain; they may have it from Prussia. But until you become lost to all feeling of your true interest and your natural dignity, freedom they can have from none but you."

So, too, in the speeches of Chatham, the great Commoner, whose eloquence has never been surpassed, an intense spirit of liberty, the animating principle of his life, shines out above all things else. Though opposed to the independence of the colonies, he could not restrain his admiration for the spirit they manifested:—

"The Americans contending for their rights against arbitrary exactions I love and admire. It is the struggle of free and virtuous patriots. . . . My Lords, you cannot conquer America. You may swell every expense and every effort still more extravagantly; pile and accumulate every assistance you can buy or borrow; traffic and barter with every pitiful little German prince that sells and sends his subjects to the shambles of a foreign prince; your efforts are forever vain and impotent. If I were an American as I am an Englishman, while a foreign troop was landed in my country I would never lay down my arms—never—never—never!"

Wherever the principle of Anglo-Saxon freedom and the rights of man have been at stake, the all-animating voice of the orator has kept alive the sacred flame. In the witenagemote of the earlier kings, in the parliament of the later kings, in the Massachusetts town-meeting and in the Virginia House of Burgesses, in the legislature of every State, and in the Congress of the United States, wherever in Anglo-Saxon countries the torch of liberty seemed to burn low, the breath of the orator has fanned it into flame. It fired the eloquence of Sheridan pleading against Warren Hastings for the down-trodden natives of India in words that have not lost their magnetic charm:—

"My Lords, do you, the judges of this land and the expounders of its rightful laws, do you approve of this mockery and call that the character of justice which takes the form of right to execute wrong? No, my Lords, justice is not this halt and miserable object; it is not the ineffective bauble of an Indian pagoda; it is not the portentous phantom of despair; it is not like any fabled monster, formed in the eclipse of reason and found in some unhallowed grove of superstitious darkness and political dismay. No, my Lords! In the happy reverse of all this I turn from the disgusting caricature to the real image. Justice I have now before me, august and pure, the abstract ideal of all that would be perfect in the spirits and aspirings of men — where the mind rises; where the heart expands; where the countenance is ever placid and benign; where the favorite attitude is to stoop to the unfortunate, to hear their cry, and help them; to rescue and relieve, to succor and save; majestic from its mercy, venerable from its utility, uplifted without pride, firm without obduracy, beneficent in each preference, lovely though in her frown.»

This same spirit fired the enthusiasm of Samuel Adams and James Otis to such a pitch of eloquence that «every man who heard them went away ready to take up arms.» It inspired Patrick Henry to hurl his defiant alternative of «liberty or death» in the face of unyielding despotism. It inspired that great-hearted patriot and orator, Henry Clay, in the first quarter of this century, to plead, single-handed and alone, in the Congress of the United States, session after session before the final victory was won, for the recognition of the provinces of South America in their struggle for independence.

«I may be accused of an imprudent utterance of my feelings on this occasion. I care not: when the independence, the happiness, the liberty of a whole people is at stake, and that people our neighbors, our brethren, occupying a portion of the same continent, imitating our example, and participating in the same sympathies with ourselves, I will boldly avow my feelings and my wishes in their behalf, even at the hazard of such an imputation. I maintain that an oppressed people are authorized, whenever they can, to rise and break their fetters. This was the great principle of the English revolution. It was the great principle of our own. Spanish-America has been doomed for centuries to the practical effects of an odious tyranny. If we were justified, she is more than justified. I am no propagandist. I would not seek to force upon other nations our principles and our liberty, if they do not want them. But if an abused and oppressed people will their freedom; if they seek to establish it; if, in truth, they have established it. we have a right, as a sovereign power, to notice the fact, and to act as circumstances and our interest require. I will say in the language of the venerated father of my country, 'born in a land of liberty, my anxious recollections, my sympathetic feelings, and my best wishes, are irresistibly excited, whensoever, in any country, I see an oppressed nation unfurl the banners of freedom.'»

1—2

This same spirit loosed the tongue of Wendell Phillips to plead the cause of the enslaved African in words that burned into the hearts of his countrymen. It emboldened George William Curtis to assert the right to break the shackles of party politics and follow the dictates of conscience:—

«I know,—no man better,—how hard it is for earnest men to separate their country from their party, or their religion from their sect. But, nevertheless, the welfare of the country is dearer than the mere victory of party, as truth is more precious than the interest of any sect. You will hear this patriotism scorned as an impracticable theory, as the dream of a cloister, as the whim of a fool. But such was the folly of the Spartan Leonidas, staying with his three hundred the Persian horde, and teaching Greece the self-reliance that saved her. Such was the folly of the Swiss Arnold von Winkelried, gathering into his own breast the points of Austrian spears, making his dead body the bridge of victory for his countrymen. Such was the folly of the American Nathan Hale, gladly risking the seeming disgrace of his name, and grieving that he had but one life to give for his country. Such are the beacon-lights of a pure patriotism that burn forever in men's memories and answer each other through the illuminated ages.»

So long as there are wrongs to be redressed, so long as the strong oppress the weak, so long as injustice sits in high places, the voice of the orator will be needed to plead for the rights of man. He may not, at this stage of the republic, be called upon to sound a battle cry to arms, but there are bloodless victories to be won as essential to the stability of a great nation and the uplifting of its millions of people as the victories of the battlefield.

When the greatest of modern political philosophers, the author of the Declaration of Independence, urged that, if men were left free to declare the truth the effect of its great positive forces would overcome the negative forces of error, he seems to have hit the central fact of civilization. Without freedom of thought and absolute freedom to speak out the truth as one sees it, there can be no advancement, no high civilization. To the orator who has heard the call of humanity, what nobler aspiration than to enlarge and extend the freedom we have inherited from our Anglo-Saxon forefathers, and to defend the hope of the world?

Edward A. Allen

PIERRE ABELARD

(1079–1142)

ABÉLARD'S reputation for oratory and for scholarship was so great that he attracted hearers and disciples from all quarters. They encamped around him like an army and listened to him with such eagerness that the jealousy of some and the honest apprehension of others were excited by the boldness with which he handled religious subjects. He has been called the originator of modern rationalism, and though he was apparently worsted in his contest with his great rival, St. Bernard, he remains the most real and living personality among the great pulpit orators of the Middle Ages. This is due in large part, no doubt, to his connection with the unfortunate Héloise. That story, one of the most romantic, as it is one of the saddest of human history, must be passed over with a mere mention of the fact that it gave occasion for a number of the sermons of Abélard which have come down to us. Several of those were preached in the convent of the Paraclete of which Héloise became abbess,— where, in his old age, her former lover, broken with the load of a life of most extraordinary sorrows, went to die. These sermons do not suggest the fire and force with which young Abélard appealed to France, compelling its admiration even in exciting its alarm, but they prevent him from being a mere name as an orator.

He was born near Nantes, A. D. 1079. At his death in 1142, he was buried in the convent of the Paraclete, where the body of Héloise was afterwards buried at his side.

The extracts from his sermons here given were translated by Rev. J. M. Neale, of Sackville College, from the first collected edition of the works of Abélard, published at Paris in 1616. There are thirty-two such sermons extant. They were preached in Latin, or, at least, they have come down to us in that language.

him that by which he ought to avoid sin, and then restores the same thing, and by it retains him in sin. His captive fears temporal, and not spiritual, evil; he is ashamed before men and he despises God. He is ashamed that things should come to the knowledge of men which he was not ashamed to commit in the sight of God, and of the whole heavenly host. He trembles at the judgment of man, and he has no respect to that of God. Of which the Apostle says: "It is a fearful thing to fall into the hands of the living God"; and the Truth saith himself, "Fear not them that kill the body, and after that have no more that they can do; but fear him rather who can cast body and soul into hell."

There are diseases of the soul, as there are of the body; and therefore the Divine mercy has provided beforehand physicians for both. Our Lord Jesus Christ saith, "I came not to call the righteous, but sinners to repentance." His priests now hold his place in the Church, to whom, as unto physicians of the soul, we ought to confess our sins, that we may receive from them the plaister of satisfaction. He that fears the death of the body, in whatever part of the body he may suffer, however much he may be ashamed of the disease, makes no delay in revealing it to the physician, and setting it forth, so that it may be cured. However rough, however hard may be the remedy, he avoids it not, so that he may escape death. Whatever he has that is most precious, he makes no hesitation in giving it, if only for a little while he may put off the death of the body. What, then, ought we to do for the death of the soul? For this, however terrible, may be forever prevented, without such great labor, without such great expense. The Lord seeks us ourselves, and not what is ours. He stands in no need of our wealth who bestows all things. For it is he to whom it is said, "My goods are nothing unto thee." With him a man is by so much the greater, as, in his own judgment, he is less. With him a man is as much the more righteous, as in his own opinion he is the more guilty. In his eyes we hide our faults all the more, the more that here by confession we manifest them.

THE RESURRECTION OF LAZARUS

THE Lord performed that miracle once for all in the body which much more blessedly he performs every day in the souls of penitents. He restored life to Lazarus, but it was a temporal life, one that would die again. He bestows life on the penitent; life, but it is life that will remain, world without end. The one is wonderful in the eyes of men; the other is far more wonderful in the judgment of the faithful; and in that it is so much the greater, by so much the more is it to be sought. This is written of Lazarus, not for Lazarus himself, but for us and to us. "Whatsoever things," saith the Apostle, "were written of old, were written for our learning." The Lord called Lazarus once, and he was raised from temporal death. He calls us often, that we may rise from the death of the soul. He said to him once, "Come forth!" and immediately he came forth at one command of the Lord. The Lord every day invites us by Scripture to confession, exhorts us to amendment, promises the life which is prepared for us by him who willeth not the death of a sinner. We neglect his call, we despise his invitation, we contemn his promise. Placed between God and the devil, as between a father and a foe, we prefer the enticement of the enemy to a father's warning. "We are not ignorant," says the Apostle, "of the devices of Satan,"—the devices, I say, by which he induces us to sin, and keeps us back from repentance. Suggesting sin, he deprives us of two things by which the best assistance might be offered to us, namely, shame and fear. For that which we avoid, we avoid either through fear of some loss, or through the reverence of shame. . . . When, therefore, Satan impels any one to sin, he easily accomplishes the object, if, as we have said, he first deprives him of fear and shame. And when he has effected that, he restores the same things, but in another sense, which he has taken away; that so he may keep back the sinner from confession, and make him die in his sin. Then he secretly whispers into his soul: "Priests are light-minded, and it is a difficult thing to check the tongue. If you tell this or that to them, it cannot remain a secret; and when it shall have been published abroad, you will incur the danger of losing your good character, or bearing some injury, and being confounded from your own vileness." Thus the devil deceives that wretched man; he first takes from

THE LAST ENTRY INTO JERUSALEM

"HE CAME unto his own, and his own received him not." That is, he entered Jerusalem. Yet now he entered, not Jerusalem, which by interpretation is "The Vision of Peace," but the home of tyranny. For now the elders of the city have so manifestly conspired against him, that he can no longer find a place of refuge within it. This is not to be attributed to his helplessness but to his patience. He could be harbored there securely, seeing that no one can do him harm by violence, and that he has the power to incline the hearts of men whither he wills. For in that same city he freely did whatever he willed to do; and when he sent his disciples thither, and commanded them that they should loose the ass and the colt, and bring them to him, and said that no man would forbid them, he accomplished that which he said, although he was not ignorant of the conspiracy against himself. Of which he saith to his disciples whom he sends, "Go ye into the castle over against you"; that is, to the place which is equally opposed to God and to you; no longer to be called a city, an assembly of men living under the law, but a castle of tyrannical fortification. Go confidently, saith he, into the place, though such it is, and though it is therefore opposed to you, and do with all security that which I command you. Whence he adds, also: "And if any man say aught unto you, say that the Lord hath need of them, and he will straightway send them away." A wonderful confidence of power! As if the Lord, using his own right of command, lays his own injunction on those whom he knows already to have conspired for his death. Thus he commands, thus he enjoins, thus he compels obedience. Nor do they who are sent hesitate in accomplishing that which is laid upon them, confident as they are in the strength of the power of him who sends them. By that power they who were chiefly concerned in this conspiracy had been more than once ejected from the Temple, where many were not able to resist one. And they, too, after this ejection and conspiracy, as we have said, when he was daily teaching in the Temple, knew how intrepid he showed himself to be, into whose hands the Father had given all things. And last of all, when he desired to celebrate the Passover in the same night in which he had foreordained to be betrayed, he again sent his Disciples whither he willed, and prepared a home for himself in the city itself, wherein he might keep the feast. He, then, who so often showed his power in such things as these, now also, if he had desired it, could have prepared a home wherever he would, and had no need to return to Bethany. Therefore, he did these two things intentionally: he showed that they whom he avoided were unworthy of his dwelling among them; and he gave himself, in the last hours of his life, to his beloved hosts, that they might have their own reception of him as the reward of their hospitality.

THE DIVINE TRAGEDY

WHETHER, therefore, Christ is spoken of as about to be crowned or about to be crucified, it is said that he "went forth"; to signify that the Jews, who were guilty of so great wickedness against him, were given over to reprobation, and that his grace would now pass to the vast extent of the Gentiles, where the salvation of the Cross, and his own exaltation by the gain of many peoples, in the place of the one nation of the Jews, has extended itself. Whence, also, to-day we rightly go forth to adore the Cross in the open plain; showing mystically that both glory and salvation had departed from the Jews, and had spread themselves among the Gentiles. But in that we afterwards returned (in procession) to the place whence we had set forth, we signify that in the end of the world the grace of God will return to the Jews; namely, when, by the preaching of Enoch and Elijah, they shall be converted to him. Whence the Apostle: "I would not, brethren, that ye should be ignorant of this mystery, that blindness in part has fallen upon Israel, until the fullness of the Gentiles shall be come, and so all Israel shall be saved." Whence the place itself of Calvary, where the Lord was crucified, is now, as we know, contained in the city; whereas formerly it was without the walls. "The crown wherewith his Mother crowned him in the day of his espousals, and in the day of the gladness of his heart." For thus kings are wont to exhibit their glory when they betroth queens to themselves, and celebrate the solemnities of their nuptials. Now the day of the Lord's crucifixion was, as it were, the day of his betrothal; because it was then that he associated the Church to himself as his bride, and

on the same day descended into Hell, and, setting free the souls of the faithful, accomplished in them that which he had promised to the thief: "Verily I say unto thee, to-day shalt thou be with me in Paradise."

"To-day," he says, of the gladness of his heart; because in his body he suffered the torture of pain; but while the flesh inflicted on him torments through the outward violence of men, his soul was filled with joy on account of our salvation, which he thus brought to pass. Whence, also, when he went forth to his crucifixion, he stilled the women that were lamenting him, and said, "Daughters of Jerusalem, weep not for me, but weep for yourselves and your children." As if he said, "Grieve not for me in these my sufferings, as if by their means I should fall into any real destruction; but rather lament for that heavy vengeance which hangs over you and your children, because of that which they have committed against me." So we, also, brethren, should rather weep for ourselves than for him; and for the faults which we have committed, not for the punishments which he bore. Let us so rejoice with him and for him, as to grieve for our own offenses, and for that the guilty servant committed the transgression, while the innocent Lord bore the punishment. He taught us to weep who is never said to have wept for himself, though he wept for Lazarus when about to raise him from the dead.

CHARLES FRANCIS ADAMS

(1807–1886)

THE son of one President of the United States and the grandson of another, Charles Francis Adams won for himself in his own right a position of prominence in the history of his times. He studied law in the office of Daniel Webster, and after beginning practice was drawn into public life by his election to the Massachusetts legislature in which he served from 1831 to 1838. A Whig in politics until the slavery issue became prominent, he was nominated for Vice-President on the Free Soil ticket with Van Buren in 1848. The Republican party which grew out of the Free Soil movement elected him to Congress as a representative of the third Massachusetts district in 1858 and re-elected him in 1860. In 1861 President Lincoln appointed him minister to England, and he filled with credit that place which had been filled by his father and grandfather before him. He died November 21st, 1886, leaving besides his own speeches and essays an edition of the works of John and John Quincy Adams in twenty-two volumes octavo.

THE STATES AND THE UNION

(Delivered in the House of Representatives, January 31st, 1861)

I CONFESS, Mr. Speaker, that I should be very jealous, as a citizen of Massachusetts, of any attempt on the part of Virginia, for example, to propose an amendment to the Constitution designed to rescind or abolish the bill of rights prefixed to our own form of government. Yet I cannot see why such a proposition would be more unjustifiable than any counter proposition to abolish slavery in Virginia, as coming from Massachusetts. If I have in any way succeeded in mastering the primary elements of our forms of government, the first and fundamental idea is, the reservation to the people of the respective States of every power of regulating their own affairs not specifically surrendered in the Constitution. The security of the State governments depends upon the fidelity with which this principle is observed.

Even the intimation of any such interference as I have mentioned by way of example could not be made in earnest without at once shaking the entire foundation of the whole confederated Union. No man shall exceed me in jealousy of affection for the State rights of Massachusetts. So far as I remember, nothing of this kind was ever thought of heretofore; and I see no reason to apprehend that what has not happened thus far will be more likely to happen hereafter. But if the time ever come when it does occur, I shall believe the dissolution of the system to be much more certain than I do at this moment.

For these reasons, I cannot imagine that there is the smallest foundation for uneasiness about the intentions of any considerable number of men in the free States to interfere in any manner whatever with slavery in the States, much less by the hopeless mode of amending the Constitution. To me it looks like panic, pure panic. How, then, is it to be treated? Is it to be neglected or ridiculed? Not at all. If a child in the nursery be frightened by the idea of a spectre, common humanity would prompt an effort by kindness to assuage the alarm. But in cases where the same feeling pervades the bosoms of multitudes of men, this imaginary evil grows up at once into a gigantic reality, and must be dealt with as such. It is at all times difficult to legislate against a possibility. The committee have reported a proposition intended to meet this case. It is a form of amendment of the Constitution which, in substance, takes away no rights whatever which the free States ever should attempt to use, whilst it vests exclusively in the slave States the right to use them or not, as they shall think proper, the whole treatment of the subject to which they relate being conceded to be a matter of common interest to them, exclusively within their jurisdiction, and subject to their control. A time may arrive, in the course of years, when they will themselves desire some act of interference in a friendly and beneficent spirit. If so, they have the power reserved to them of initiating the very form in which it would be most welcome. If not, they have a security, so long as this government shall endure, that no sister State shall dictate any change against their will.

I have now considered all the alleged grievances which have thus far been brought to our attention. 1. The personal liberty laws, which never freed a slave. 2. Exclusion from a Territory which slaveholders will never desire to occupy. 3. Apprehension of an event which will never take place. For the sake of these three causes of complaint, all of them utterly without practical result, the slaveholding States, unquestionably the weakest section of this great Confederacy, are voluntarily and precipitately surrendering the realities of solid power woven into the very texture of a government that now keeps nineteen million freemen, willing to tolerate, and, in one sense, to shelter, institutions which, but for that, would meet with no more sympathy among them than they now do in the remainder of the civilized world.

For my own part, I must declare that, even supposing these alleged grievances to be more real than I represent them, I think the measures of the committee dispose of them effectually and forever. They contribute directly all that can be legitimately done by Congress, and they recommend it to the legislatures of the States to accomplish the remainder. Why, then, is it that harmony is not restored? The answer is, that you are not satisfied with this settlement, however complete. You must have more guarantees in the Constitution. You must make the protection and extension of slavery in the Territories now existing, and hereafter to be acquired, a cardinal doctrine of our great charter. Without that, you are determined to dissolve the Union. How stands the case, then? We offer to settle the question finally in all of the present territory that you claim, by giving you every chance of establishing slavery that you have any right to require of us. You decline to take the offer, because you fear it will do you no good. Slavery will not go there. But, if that be true, what is the use of asking for the protection anyhow, much less in the Constitution? Why require protection where you will have nothing to protect? All you appear to desire it for is New Mexico. Nothing else is left. Yet, you will not accept New Mexico at once, because ten years of experience have proved to you that protection has been of no use thus far. But, if so, how can you expect that it will be of so much more use hereafter as to make it worth dissolving the Union?

But, if we pass to the other condition, is it any more reasonable? Are we going to fight because we cannot agree upon the mode of disposing of our neighbor's lands? Are we to break up the Union of these States, cemented by so many years of common sufferings, and resplendent with so many years of common glory, because it is insisted that we should incorporate into what we regard as the charter of our freedom a proclamation to the

civilized world that we intend to grasp the territory of other nations whenever we can do it, for the purpose of putting into it certain institutions which some of us disapprove, and that, too, whether the people inhabiting that territory themselves approve of it or not?

I am almost inclined to believe that they who first contrived this demand must have done so for the sake of presenting a condition which they knew beforehand must be rejected, or which, if accepted, must humiliate us in the dust forever. In point of fact, this proposal covers no question of immediate moment which may not be settled by another and less obnoxious one. Why is it, then, persevered in, and the other rejected? The answer is obvious. You want the Union dissolved. You want to make it impossible for honorable men to become reconciled. If it be, indeed, so, then on you, and you alone, shall rest the responsibility of what may follow. If the Union be broken up, the reason why it happened shall remain on record forever. It was because you rejected one form of settling a question which might be offered and accepted with honor, in order to insist upon another which you knew we could not accept without disgrace. I answer for myself only when I say that, if the alternative to the salvation of the Union be only that the people of the United States shall, before the Christian nations of the earth, print in broad letters upon the front of their charter of republican government the dogma of slave propagandism over the remainder of the countries of the world, I will not consent to brand myself with what I deem such disgrace, let the consequences be what they may.

But it is said that this answer closes the door of reconciliation. The slaveholding States will secede, and what then?

This brings me to the last point which I desire to touch today, the proper course for the government to pursue in the face of these difficulties. Some of the friends with whom I act have not hesitated to express themselves in favor of coercion; and they have drawn very gloomy pictures of the fatal consequences to the prosperity and security of the whole Union that must ensue. For my own sake, I am glad that I do not partake so largely in these fears. I see no obstacle to the regular continuance of the government in not less than twenty States, and perhaps more, the inhabitants of which have not in a moment been deprived of that peculiar practical wisdom in the management

of their affairs which is the secret of their past success. Several new States will, before long, be ready to take their places with us, and make good, in part, the loss of the old ones. The mission of furnishing a great example of free government to the nations of the earth will still be in our hands, impaired, I admit, but not destroyed; and I doubt not our power to accomplish it yet, in spite of the temporary drawback. Even the problem of coercion will go on to solve itself without our aid. For if the sentiment of disunion become so far universal and permanent in the dissatisfied States as to show no prospect of good from resistance, and there be no acts of aggression attempted on their part, I will not say that I may not favor the idea of some arrangement of a peaceful character, though I do not now see the authority under which it can be originated. The new Confederacy can scarcely be other than a secondary Power. It can never be a maritime State. It will begin with the necessity of keeping eight millions of its population to watch four millions, and with the duty of guarding, against the egress of the latter, several thousand miles of an exposed border, beyond which there will be no right of reclamation. Of the ultimate result of a similar experiment, I cannot, in my own mind, have a moment's doubt. At the last session I ventured to place on record, in this House, a prediction by which I must abide, let the effect of the future on my sagacity be what it may. I have not yet seen any reason to doubt its accuracy. I now repeat it. The experiment will ignominiously fail.

But there are exceptions to the adoption of this peaceful policy which it will not be wise to overlook. If there be violent and wanton attacks upon the persons or the property of the citizens of the United States or of their government, I see not how demands for immediate redress can be avoided. If any interruptions should be attempted of the regular channels of trade on the great water-courses or on the ocean, they cannot long be permitted. And if any considerable minorities of citizens should be persecuted or proscribed on account of their attachment to the Union, and should call for protection, I cannot deny the obligation of this government to afford it. There are persons in many of the States whose patriotic declarations and honorable pledges of support of the Union may bring down upon them more than the ill-will of their infatuated fellow-citizens. It would be impossible for the people of the United States to look upon

any proscription of them with indifference. These are times which should bring together all men, by whatever party name they may have been heretofore distinguished, upon common ground.

When I heard the gentlemen from Virginia the other day so bravely and so forcibly urging their manly arguments in support of the Union, the Constitution, and the enforcement of the laws, my heart involuntarily bounded towards them as brethren sacredly engaged in a common cause. Let them, said I to myself, accept the offered settlement of the differences that remain between us, on some fair basis like that proposed by the committee, and then, what is to prevent us all, who yet believe that the Union must be preserved, from joining heart and hand our common forces to effect it? When the cry goes out that the ship is in danger of sinking, the first duty of every man on board, no matter what his particular vocation, is to lend all the strength he has to the work of keeping her afloat. What! shall it be said that we waver in the view of those who begin by trying to expunge the sacred memory of the fourth of July? Shall we help them to obliterate the associations that cluster around the glorious struggle for independence, or stultify the labors of the patriots who erected this magnificent political edifice upon the adamantine base of human liberty? Shall we surrender the fame of Washington and Laurens, of Gadsden and the Lees, of Jefferson and Madison, and of the myriads of heroes whose names are imperishably connected with the memory of a united people? Never, never!

CHARLES FRANCIS ADAMS, JUNIOR

HARLES FRANCIS ADAMS, JR., son of Charles Francis Adams, keeps up the tradition of his family so well that, unless it is John Adams himself, no other member of the family surpasses him as an orator. He was born in Boston, May 27th, 1835; graduating at Harvard and studying law in the office of R. H. Dana, Jr. His peaceful pursuits were interrupted by the Civil War which he entered a first lieutenant, coming out a brevet-brigadier general. He was a chief of squadron in the Gettysburg campaign and served in Virginia afterwards. He was for six years president of the Union Pacific railroad and is well known both as a financier and as an author. The address on the Battle of Gettysburg is generally given as his masterpiece, but he has delivered a number of other orations of high and well-sustained eloquence.

THE BATTLE OF GETTYSBURG

(Delivered at Quincy, Mass., July 4th, 1869)

SIX years ago this anniversary, we, and not only we who stood upon the sacred and furrowed field of battle, but you and our whole country, were drawing breath after the struggle of Gettysburg. For three long days we had stood the strain of conflict, and now, at last, when the nation's birthday dawned, the shattered rebel columns had suddenly withdrawn from our front, and we drew that long breath of deep relief which none have ever drawn who have not passed in safety through the shock of doubtful battle. Nor was our country gladdened then by news from Gettysburg alone. The army that day twined noble laurel garlands round the proud brow of the motherland. Vicksburg was, thereafter, to be forever associated with the Declaration of Independence, and the glad anniversary rejoicings, as they rose from every town and village and city of the loyal North, mingled with the last sullen echoes that died away from our cannon over Cemetery Ridge, and were answered by glad shouts of victory from the far Southwest. To all of us of this generation,—and especially to such of us as were ourselves part

of those great events,—this celebration, therefore, now has and must ever retain a special significance. It belonged to us, as well as to our fathers. As upon this day ninety-three years ago this nation was brought into existence through the efforts of others, so upon this day six years ago I am disposed to believe, through our own efforts, it dramatically touched the climax of its great argument.

The time that has since elapsed enables us now to look back and to see things in their true proportions. We begin to realize that the years we have so recently passed through, though we did not appreciate it at the time, were the heroic years of American history. Now that their passionate excitement is over, it is pleasant to dwell upon them; to recall the rising of a great people; the call to arms as it boomed from our hilltops and clashed from our steeples; the eager patriotism of that fierce April which kindled new sympathies in every bosom, which caused the miser to give freely of his wealth, the wife with eager hands to pack the knapsack of her husband, and mothers, with eyes glistening with tears of pride, to look out upon the shining bayonets of their boys; then came the frenzy of impatience and the defeat entailed upon us by rashness and inexperience, before our nation settled down, solidly and patiently, to its work, determined to save itself from destruction; and then followed the long weary years of doubt and mingled fear and hope, until at last that day came six years ago which we now celebrate—the day which saw the flood tide of rebellion reach the high-water mark, whence it never after ceased to recede. At the moment, probably, none of us, either at home or at the seat of war, realized the grandeur of the situation, the dramatic power of the incidents, or the Titanic nature of the conflict. To you who were at home, mothers, fathers, wives, sisters, brothers, citizens of the common country, if nothing else, the agony of suspense, the anxiety, the joy, and, too often, the grief which was to know no end, which marked the passage of those days, left little either of time or inclination to dwell upon aught save the horrid reality of the drama. To others who more immediately participated in those great events, the daily vexations and annoyances—the hot and dusty day—the sleepless, anxious night—the rain upon the unsheltered bivouac—the dead lassitude which succeeded the excitement of action—the cruel orders which recognized no fatigue and made no allowance for

labors undergone—all these small trials of the soldier's life made it possible to but few to realize the grandeur of the drama in which they were playing a part. Yet we were not wholly oblivious of it. Now and then I come across strange evidences of this in turning over the leaves of the few weather-stained, dog-eared volumes which were the companions of my life in camp. The title page of one bears witness to the fact that it was my companion at Gettysburg, and in it I recently found some lines of Browning's noble poem of 'Saul' marked and altered to express my sense of our situation, and bearing date upon this very fifth of July. The poet had described in them the fall of snow in the springtime from a mountain, under which nestled a valley; the altering of a few words made them well describe the approach of our army to Gettysburg.

"Fold on fold, all at once, we crowded thundrously down to your
        feet;
And there fronts you, stark black but alive yet, your army of old
With its rents, the successive bequeathing of conflicts untold.
Yea, each harm got in fighting your battles, each furrow and scar
Of its head thrust twixt you and the tempest—all hail, here we
        are."

And there we were, indeed, and then and there was enacted such a celebration as I hope may never again be witnessed there or elsewhere on another fourth of July. Even as I stand here before you, through the lapse of years and the shifting experiences of the recent past, visions and memories of those days rise thick and fast before me. We did, indeed, crowd thundrously down to their feet. Of the events of those three terrible days I may speak with feeling and yet with modesty, for small, indeed, was the part which those with whom I served were called upon to play. When those great bodies of infantry drove together in the crash of battle, the clouds of cavalry which had hitherto covered up their movements were swept aside to the flanks. Our work for the time was done, nor had it been an easy or a pleasant work. The road to Gettysburg had been paved with our bodies and watered with our blood. Three weeks before, in the middle days of June, I, a captain of cavalry, had taken the field at the head of one hundred mounted men, the joy and pride of my life. Through twenty days of almost incessant conflict the hand of death had been heavy upon us, and now, upon

the eve of Gettysburg, thirty-four of the hundred only remained, and our comrades were dead on the field of battle, or languishing in hospitals, or prisoners in the hands of the enemy. Six brave young fellows we had buried in one grave where they fell on the heights of Aldie. It was late on the evening of the first of July, that there came to us rumors of heavy fighting at Gettysburg, nearly forty miles away. The regiment happened then to be detached, and its orders for the second were to move in the rear of Sedgwick's corps and see that no man left the column. All that day we marched to the sound of the cannon. Sedgwick, very grim and stern, was pressing forward his tired men, and we soon saw that for once there would be no stragglers from the ranks. As the day grew old and as we passed rapidly up from the rear to the head of the hurrying column, the roar of battle grew more distinct, until at last we crowned a hill, and the contest broke upon us. Across the deep valley, some two miles away, we could see the white smoke of the bursting shells, while below the sharp incessant rattle of the musketry told of the fierce struggle that was going on. Before us ran the straight, white, dusty road, choked with artillery, ambulances, caissons, ammunition trains, all pressing forward to the field of battle, while mixed among them, their bayonets gleaming through the dust like wavelets on a river of steel, tired, foot-sore, hungry, thirsty, begrimed with sweat and dust, the gallant infantry of Sedgwick's corps hurried to the sound of the cannon as men might have flocked to a feast. Moving rapidly forward, we crossed the brook which ran so prominently across the map of the field of battle, and halted on its further side to await our orders. Hardly had I dismounted from my horse when, looking back, I saw that the head of the column had reached the brook and deployed and halted on its other bank, and already the stream was filled with naked men shouting with pleasure as they washed off the sweat of their long day's march. Even as I looked, the noise of the battle grew louder, and soon the symptoms of movement were evident. The rappel was heard, the bathers hurriedly clad themselves, the ranks were formed, and the sharp, quick snap of the percussion caps told us the men were preparing their weapons for action. Almost immediately a general officer rode rapidly to the front of the line, addressed to it a few brief, energetic words, the short sharp order to move by the flank was given, followed immediately by the "double-quick"; the officer placed himself at the head of the column, and that brave infantry which had marched almost forty miles since the setting of yesterday's sun,—which during that day had hardly known either sleep, or food, or rest, or shelter from the July heat,—now, as the shadows grew long, hurried forward on the run to take its place in the front of battle and to bear up the reeling fortunes of the day.

It is said that at the crisis of Solferino, Marshal McMahon appeared with his corps upon the field of battle, his men having run for seven miles. We need not go abroad for examples of endurance and soldierly bearing. The achievement of Sedgwick and the brave Sixth Corps, as they marched upon the field of Gettysburg on that second day of July, far excels the vaunted efforts of the French Zouaves.

Twenty-four hours later we stood on that same ground. Many dear friends had yielded up their young lives during the hours which had elapsed, but, though twenty thousand fellow-creatures were wounded or dead around us, though the flood gates of heaven seemed opened and the torrents fell upon the quick and the dead, yet the elements seemed electrified with a certain magic influence of victory, and as the great army sank down over-wearied in its tracks it felt that the crisis and danger was passed,—that Gettysburg was immortal.

May I not, then, well express the hope that never again may we or ours be called upon so to celebrate this anniversary? And yet now that the passionate hopes and fears of those days are all over,—now that the grief which can never be forgotten is softened and modified by the soothing hand of time,—now that the distracting doubts and untold anxieties are buried and almost forgotten,—we love to remember the gathering of the hosts, to hear again in memory the shock of battle, and to wonder at the magnificence of the drama. The passion and the excitement are gone, and we can look at the work we have done and pronounce upon it. I do not fear the sober second judgment. Our work was a great work,—it was well done, and it was done thoroughly. Some one has said, "Happy is the people which has no history." Not so! As it is better to have loved and lost than never to have loved at all, so it is better to have lived greatly, even though we have suffered greatly, than to have passed a long life of inglorious ease. Our generation,— yes, we ourselves have been a part of great things. We have suffered

greatly and greatly rejoiced; we have drunk deep of the cup of joy and of sorrow; we have tasted the agony of defeat, and we have supped full with the pleasures of victory. We have proved ourselves equal to great deeds, and have learnt what qualities were in us, which in more peaceful times we ourselves did not suspect.

And, indeed, I would here in closing fain address a few words to such of you, if any such are here, who like myself may have been soldiers during the War of the Rebellion. We should never more be partisans. We have been a part of great events in the service of the common country, we have worn her uniform, we have received her pay and devoted ourselves to the death, if need be, in her service. When we were blackened by the smoke of Antietam, we did not ask or care whether those who stood shoulder to shoulder beside us, whether he who led us, whether those who sustained us, were Democrats or Republicans, conservatives or radicals; we asked only that they might prove as true as was the steel we grasped, and as brave as we ourselves would fain have been. When we stood like a wall of stone vomiting fire from the heights of Gettysburg,—nailed to our position through three long days of mortal Hell,—did we ask each other whether that brave officer who fell while gallantly leading the counter-charge—whether that cool gunner steadily serving his piece before us amid the storm of shot and shell—whether the poor wounded, mangled, gasping-comrades, crushed and torn, and dying in agony around us—had voted for Lincoln or Douglas, for Breckenridge or Bell? We then were full of other thoughts. We prized men for what they were worth to the common country of us all, and recked not of empty words. Was the man true, was he brave, was he earnest, was all we thought of then; —not, did he vote or think with us, or label himself with our party name? This lesson let us try to remember. We cannot give to party all that we once offered to country, but our duty is not yet done. We are no longer, what we have been, the young guard of the Republic; we have earned an exemption from the dangers of the field and camp, and the old musket or the crossed sabres hang harmless over our winter fires, never more to be grasped in these hands henceforth devoted to more peaceful labors; but the duties of the citizen, and of the citizen who has received his baptism in fire, are still incumbent upon us. Though young in years, we should remember that hence-

forth, and as long as we live in the land, we are the ancients,— the veterans of the Republic. As such, it is for us to protect in peace what we preserved in war; it is for us to look at all things with a view to the common country and not to the exigencies of party politics; it is for us ever to bear in mind the higher allegiance we have sworn, and to remember that he who has once been a soldier of the motherland degrades himself forever when he becomes the slave of faction. Then at last, if through life we ever bear these lessons freshly in mind, will it be well for us, will it be well for our country, will it be well for those whose names we bear, that our bones also do not molder with those of our brave comrades beneath the sods of Gettysburg, or that our graves do not look down on the swift-flowing Mississippi from the historic heights of Vicksburg?

JOHN ADAMS

(1735–1826)

JOHN ADAMS, second President of the United States, was not a man of the strong emotional temperament which so often characterizes the great orator. He was fitted by nature for a student and scholar rather than to lead men by the direct appeal the orator makes to their emotions, their passions, or their judgment. His inclinations were towards the Church; but after graduating from Harvard College, which he entered at the age of sixteen, he had a brief experience as a school-teacher and found it so distasteful to him that he adopted the law as a relief, without waiting to consult his inclinations further. "Necessity drove me to this determination," he writes, "but my inclination was to preach." He began the practice of law in his native village of Braintree, Massachusetts, and took no prominent part in public affairs until 1765, when he appeared as counsel for the town of Boston in proceedings growing out of the Stamp Act difficulties.

From this time on, his name is constantly associated with the great events of the Revolution. That he never allowed his prejudices as a patriot to blind him to his duties as a lawyer, he showed by appearing as counsel for the British soldiers who killed Crispus Attucks, Samuel Gray, and others, in the Boston riot of 1770. He was associated in this case with Josiah Quincy, and the two distinguished patriots conducted the case with such ability that the soldiers were acquitted—as no doubt they should have been.

Elected a member of the Continental Congress, Mr. Adams did work in it which identified him in an enduring way with the formative period of republican institutions in America. This must be remembered in passing upon his acts when as President, succeeding Washington, he is brought into strong contrast with the extreme republicans of the French school. In the Continental Congress, contrasted with English royalists and conservatives Mr. Adams himself appeared an extremist, as later on, under the same law of contrast, he appeared conservative when those who were sometimes denounced as "Jacobins" and "Levellers" were fond of denouncing him as a disguised royalist.

Prior to his administration as President, he had served as commissioner to the court of France, "Minister Plenipotentiary for the

Purpose of Negotiating a Treaty of Peace and Commerce with Great Britain"; commissioner to conclude a treaty with the States-General of Holland; minister to England after the conclusion of peace, and finally as Vice-President under Washington. His services in every capacity in which he was engaged for his country showed his great ability and zeal; but in the struggle over the Alien and Sedition Laws his opponents gave him no quarter and when he retired from the Presidency it was with the feeling, shared to some extent by his great opponent Jefferson, that republics never have a proper regard for the services and sacrifices of statesmen, though they are only too ready to reward military heroes beyond their deserts. The author of 'Familiar Letters on Public Affairs' writes of Mr. Adams:—

"He was a man of strong mind, great learning, and eminent ability to use knowledge both in speech and writing. He was ever a firm believer in Christianity, not from habit and example but from a diligent investigation of its proofs. He had an uncompromising regard for his own opinion and was strongly contrasted with Washington in this respect. He seemed to have supposed that his opinions could not have been corrected by those of other men or bettered by any comparison."

It might be inferred from this that Mr. Adams was as obstinate in prejudice as in opinion, but as he had demonstrated to the contrary in taking the unpopular cause of the British soldiers at the beginning of his public career, he showed it still more strikingly by renewing and continuing until his death a friendship with Jefferson which had been interrupted by the fierce struggle over the Alien and Sedition Act.

INAUGURAL ADDRESS

(March 4th, 1797)

WHEN it was first perceived, in early times, that no middle course for America remained, between unlimited submission to a foreign legislature and a total independence of its claims, men of reflection were less apprehensive of danger from the formidable powers of fleets and armies they must determine to resist, than from those contests and dissensions which would certainly arise concerning the forms of government to be instituted over the whole and over the parts of this extensive country. Relying, however, on the purity of their intentions, the justice of their cause, and the integrity and intelligence of the people, under an over-ruling Providence, which

had so signally protected this country from the first, the representatives of this nation, then consisting of little more than half its present numbers, not only broke to pieces the chains which were forging, and the rod of iron that was lifted up, but frankly cut asunder the ties which had bound them, and launched into an ocean of uncertainty.

The zeal and ardor of the people during the Revolutionary War, supplying the place of government, commanded a degree of order, sufficient, at least, for the temporary preservation of society. The confederation, which was early felt to be necessary, was prepared from the models of the Bavarian and Helvetic confederacies, the only examples which remain, with any detail and precision, in history, and certainly the only ones which the people at large had ever considered. But, reflecting on the striking difference, in so many particulars, between this country and those where a courier may go from the seat of government to the frontier in a single day, it was then certainly foreseen by some who assisted in Congress at the formation of it, that it could not be durable.

Negligence of its regulations, inattention to its recommendations, if not disobedience to its authority, not only in individuals but in States, soon appeared with their melancholy consequences—universal languor, jealousies, rivalries of States, decline of navigation and commerce, discouragement of necessary manufactures, universal fall in the value of lands and their produce, contempt of public and private faith, loss of consideration and credit with foreign nations; and, at length, in discontents, animosities, combinations, partial conventions, and insurrection, threatening some great national calamity.

In this dangerous crisis, the people of America were not abandoned by their usual good sense, presence of mind, resolution, or integrity. Measures were pursued to concert a plan to form a more perfect union, establish justice, ensure domestic tranquillity, provide for the common defense, promote the general welfare, and secure the blessings of liberty. The public disquisitions, discussions, and deliberations issued in the present happy constitution of government.

Employed in the service of my country abroad during the whole course of these transactions, I first saw the Constitution of the United States in a foreign country. Irritated by no literary altercation, animated by no public debate, heated by no party

animosity, I read it with great satisfaction, as the result of good heads, prompted by good hearts; as an experiment better adapted to the genius, character, situation, and relations of this nation and country than any which had ever been proposed or suggested. In its general principles and great outlines, it was conformable to such a system of government as I had ever most esteemed, and in some States, my own native State in particular, had contributed to establish. Claiming a right of suffrage common with my fellow-citizens in the adoption or rejection of a constitution, which was to rule me and my posterity, as well as them and theirs, I did not hesitate to express my approbation of it on all occasions, in public and in private. It was not then, nor has been since, any objection to it, in my mind, that the Executive and Senate were not more permanent. Nor have I entertained a thought of promoting any alteration in it, but such as the people themselves, in the course of their experience, should see and feel to be necessary or expedient, and by their representatives in Congress and the State legislature, according to the constitution itself, adopt and ordain.

Returning to the bosom of my country, after a painful separation from it for ten years, I had the honor to be elected to a station under the new order of things; and I have repeatedly laid myself under the most serious obligations to support the constitution. The operation of it has equaled the most sanguine expectations of its friends; and from an habitual attention to it, satisfaction in its administration, and delight in its effects upon the peace, order, prosperity, and happiness of the nation, I have acquired an habitual attachment to it, and veneration for it. What other form of government, indeed, can so well deserve our esteem and love?

There may be little solidity in an ancient idea that congregations of men into cities and nations are the most pleasing objects in the sight of superior intelligences; but this is very certain, that to a benevolent human mind there can be no spectacle presented by any nation more pleasing, more noble, majestic, or august, than an assembly like that which has so often been seen in this and the other chamber of Congress—of a government in which the executive authority, as well as that of all the branches of the legislature, are exercised by citizens selected at regular periods by their neighbors, to make and execute laws for the general good. Can any thing essential, any thing more than

mere ornament and decoration be added to this by robes or diamonds? Can authority be more amiable or respectable when it descends from accident or institutions established in remote antiquity than when it springs fresh from the hearts and judgments of an honest and enlightened people? For it is the people that are represented; it is their power and majesty that is reflected, and only for their good, in every legitimate government, under whatever form it may appear. The existence of such a government as ours for any length of time is a full proof of a general dissemination of knowledge and virtue throughout the whole body of the people. And what object of consideration more pleasing than this can be presented to the human mind? If natural pride is ever justifiable or excusable, it is when it springs, not from power or riches, grandeur or glory, but from conviction of national innocence, information, and benevolence.

In the midst of these pleasing ideas, we should be unfaithful to ourselves if we should ever lose sight of the danger to our liberties—if anything partial or extraneous should infect the purity of our free, fair, virtuous, and independent elections. If an election is to be determined by a majority of a single vote, and that can be procured by a party through artifice or corruption, the government may be the choice of a party, for its own ends, not of the nation for the national good. If that solitary suffrage can be obtained by foreign nations by flattery or menaces, by fraud or violence, by terror, intrigue, or venality, the government may not be the choice of the American people, but of foreign nations. It may be foreign nations who govern us, and not we, the people, who govern ourselves; and candid men will acknowledge that, in such cases, choice would have little advantage to boast of over lot or chance.

Such is the amiable and interesting system of government (and such are some of the abuses to which it may be exposed) which the people of America have exhibited to the admiration and anxiety of the wise and virtuous of all nations for eight years, under the administration of a citizen, who, by a long course of great actions, regulated by prudence, justice, temperance, and fortitude, conducting a people inspired with the same virtues, and animated with the same ardent patriotism and love of liberty, to independence and peace, to increasing wealth and unexampled prosperity, has merited the gratitude of his fellow-citizens, commanded the highest praises of foreign nations, and secured immortal glory with posterity.

In that retirement, which is his voluntary choice, may he long live to enjoy the delicious recollection of his services—the gratitude of mankind; the happy fruits of them to himself and the world, which are daily increasing, and that splendid prospect of the future fortunes of his country, which is opening from year to year. His name may be still a rampart and the knowledge that he lives a bulwark against all open or secret enemies of his country's peace.

This example has been recommended to the imitation of his successors, by both houses of Congress, and by the voice of the legislatures and the people, throughout the nation.

On this subject it might become me better to be silent, or to speak with diffidence; but as something may be expected, the occasion, I hope, will be admitted as an apology, if I venture to say, that if a preference upon principle, of a free republican government, formed upon long and serious reflection, after a diligent and impartial inquiry after truth; if an attachment to the Constitution of the United States, and a conscientious determination to support it, until it shall be altered by the judgments and wishes of the people, expressed in the mode prescribed in it; if a respectful attention to the constitution of the individual States, and a constant caution and delicacy towards the State governments; if an equal and impartial regard to the rights, interests, honor, and happiness of all the States in the Union, without preference or regard to a northern or southern, eastern or western position, their various political opinions on essential points, or their personal attachments; if a love of virtuous men, of all parties and denominations; if a love of science or letters and a wish to patronize every rational effort to encourage schools, colleges, universities, academies, and every institution of propagating knowledge, virtue, and religion among all classes of people, not only for their benign influence on the happiness of life, in all its stages and classes, and of society in all its forms, but as the only means of preserving our constitution from its natural enemies, the spirit of sophistry, the spirit of party, the spirit of intrigue, profligacy, and corruption, and the pestilence of foreign influence, which is the angel of destruction to elective governments, if a love of equal laws, of justice and humanity, in the interior administration; if an inclination to improve agriculture,

commerce, and manufactures for necessity, convenience, and defense; if a spirit of equity and humanity towards the aboriginal nations of America, and a disposition to ameliorate their condition by inclining them to be more friendly to us, and our citizens to be more friendly to them; if an inflexible determination to maintain peace and inviolable faith with all nations, and the system of neutrality and impartiality among the belligerent powers of Europe which has been adopted by the government, and so solemnly sanctioned by both houses of Congress, and applauded by the legislatures of the States and by public opinion, until it shall be otherwise ordained by Congress; if a personal esteem for the French nation, formed in a residence of seven years chiefly among them, and a sincere desire to preserve the friendship, which has been so much for the honor and interest of both nations; if, while the conscious honor and integrity of the people of America and the internal sentiment of their own power and energies must be preserved, an earnest endeavor to investigate every just cause, and remove every colorable pretense of complaint; if an intention to pursue, by amicable negotiation, a reparation for the injuries that have been committed on the commerce of our fellow-citizens, by whatever nation; and, if success cannot be obtained, to lay the facts before the legislature, that they may consider what further measures the honor and interest of the government and its constituents demand; if a resolution to do justice, as far as may depend upon me, at all times and to all nations, and maintain peace, friendship, and benevolence with all the world; if an unshaken confidence in the honor, spirit, and resources of the American people, on which I have so often hazarded my all, and never been deceived; if elevated ideas of the high destinies of this country, and of my own duties towards it, founded on a knowledge of the moral principles and intellectual improvements of the people, deeply engraven on my mind in early life, and not obscured, but exalted, by experience and age; and with humble reverence, I feel it my duty to add, if a veneration for the religion of the people who profess and call themselves Christians, and a fixed resolution to consider a decent respect for Christianity among the best recommendations for the public service, can enable me, in any degree, to comply with your wishes, it shall be my strenuous endeavor that this sagacious injunction of the two houses shall not be without effect.

With this great example before me—with the sense and spirit, the faith and honor, the duty and interest of the same American people, pledged to support the Constitution of the United States, I entertain no doubt of its continuance in all its energy; and my mind is prepared, without hesitation, to lay myself under the most solemn obligations to support it to the utmost of my power.

And may that Being who is supreme over all, the patron of order, the fountain of justice, and the protector, in all ages of the world, of virtuous liberty, continue his blessing upon this nation and its government, and give it all possible success and duration, consistent with the ends of his providence!

THE BOSTON MASSACRE

(First Day's Speech in Defense of the British Soldiers Accused of Murdering Attucks, Gray and Others, in the Boston Riot of 1770)

May It Please Your Honor, and You, Gentlemen of the Jury:—

I AM for the prisoners at the bar, and shall apologize for it only in the words of the Marquis Beccaria:—

"If I can but be the instrument of preserving one life, his blessings and tears of transport shall be a sufficient consolation for me for the contempt of all mankind."

As the prisoners stand before you for their lives, it may be proper to recollect with what temper the law requires we should proceed to this trial. The form of proceeding at their arraignment has discovered that the spirit of the law upon such occasions is conformable to humanity, to common sense and feeling; that it is all benignity and candor. And the trial commences with the prayer of the court, expressed by the clerk, to the Supreme Judge of judges, empires, and worlds, "God send you a good deliverance."

We find in the rules laid down by the greatest English judges, who have been the brightest of mankind: We are to look upon it as more beneficial that many guilty persons should escape unpunished than one innocent should suffer. The reason is, because it is of more importance to the community that innocence should be protected than it is that guilt should be punished; for guilt and crimes are so frequent in the world that all

of them cannot be punished; and many times they happen in such a manner that it is not of much consequence to the public whether they are punished or not. But when innocence itself is brought to the bar and condemned, especially to die, the subject will exclaim, "It is immaterial to me whether I behave well or ill, for virtue itself is no security." And if such a sentiment as this should take place in the mind of the subject, there would be an end to all security whatsoever. I will read the words of the law itself.

The rules I shall produce to you from Lord Chief-Justice Hale, whose character as a lawyer, a man of learning and philosophy, and a Christian, will be disputed by nobody living; one of the greatest and best characters the English nation ever produced. His words are these:—

(2 H. H. P. C.): *Tutius semper est errare, in acquietando quam in puniendo, ex parte misericordiæ quam ex parte justitiæ.*—"It is always safer to err in acquitting than punishing, on the part of mercy than the part of justice."

The next is from the same authority, 305:—

Tutius erratur ex parte mitiori.—"It is always safer to err on the milder side, the side of mercy."

(H. H. P. C. 509): "The best rule in doubtful cases is rather to incline to acquittal than conviction."

And on page 300:—

Quod dubitas, ne feceris.—"Where you are doubtful, never act; that is, if you doubt of the prisoner's guilt, never declare him guilty."

This is always the rule, especially in cases of life. Another rule from the same author, 289, where he says:—

"In some cases presumptive evidences go far to prove a person guilty, though there is no express proof of the fact to be committed by him; but then it must be very warily expressed, for it is better five guilty persons should escape unpunished than one innocent person should die."

The next authority shall be from another judge of equal character, considering the age wherein he lived; that is, Chancellor Fortescue in 'Praise of the Laws of England,' page 59.

This is a very ancient writer on the English law. His words are:—

"Indeed, one would rather, much rather, that twenty guilty persons escape punishment of death, than one innocent person be condemned and suffer capitally."

Lord Chief-Justice Hale says:—

"It is better five guilty persons escape, than one innocent person suffer."

Lord Chancellor Fortescue, you see, carries the matter further, and says:—

"Indeed, one had rather, much rather, that twenty guilty persons should escape than one innocent person suffer capitally."

Indeed, this rule is not peculiar to the English law; there never was a system of laws in the world in which this rule did not prevail. It prevailed in the ancient Roman law, and, which is more remarkable, it prevails in the modern Roman law. Even the judges in the Courts of Inquisition, who with racks, burnings, and scourges examine criminals,—even there they preserve it as a maxim, that it is better the guilty should escape punishment than the innocent suffer. *Satius esse nocentem absolvi quam innocentem damnari.* This is the temper we ought to set out with, and these the rules we are to be governed by. And I shall take it for granted, as a first principle, that the eight prisoners at the bar had better be all acquitted, though we should admit them all to be guilty, than that any one of them should, by your verdict, be found guilty, being innocent.

I shall now consider the several divisions of law under which the evidence will arrange itself.

The action now before you is homicide; that is, the killing of one man by another. The law calls it homicide; but it is not criminal in all cases for one man to slay another. Had the prisoners been on the Plains of Abraham and slain a hundred Frenchmen apiece, the English law would have considered it as a commendable action, virtuous and praiseworthy; so that every instance of killing a man is not a crime in the eye of the law. There are many other instances which I cannot enumerate—an officer that executes a person under sentence of death, etc. So that, gentlemen, every instance of one man's killing another is

not a crime, much less a crime to be punished with death. But to descend to more particulars.

The law divides homicide into three branches; the first is "justifiable," the second "excusable," and the third "felonious." Felonious homicide is subdivided into two branches; the first is murder, which is killing with malice aforethought; the second is manslaughter, which is killing a man on a sudden provocation. Here, gentlemen, are four sorts of homicide; and you are to consider whether all the evidence amounts to the first, second, third, or fourth of these heads. The fact was the slaying five unhappy persons that night. You are to consider whether it was justifiable, excusable, or felonious; and if felonious, whether it was murder or manslaughter. One of these four it must be. You need not divide your attention to any more particulars. I shall, however, before I come to the evidence, show you several authorities which will assist you and me in contemplating the evidence before us.

I shall begin with justifiable homicide. If an officer, a sheriff, execute a man on the gallows, draw and quarter him, as in case of high treason, and cut off his head, this is justifiable homicide. It is his duty. So also, gentlemen, the law has planted fences and barriers around every individual; it is a castle round every man's person, as well as his house. As the love of God and our neighbor comprehends the whole duty of man, so self-love and social comprehend all the duties we owe to mankind; and the first branch is self-love, which is not only our indisputable right, but our clearest duty. By the laws of nature, this is interwoven in the heart of every individual. God Almighty, whose law we cannot alter, has implanted it there, and we can annihilate ourselves as easily as root out this affection for ourselves. It is the first and strongest principle in our nature. Justice Blackstone calls it "The primary canon in the law of nature." That precept of our holy religion which commands us to love our neighbor as ourselves does not command us to love our neighbor better than ourselves, or so well. No Christian divine has given this interpretation. The precept enjoins that our benevolence to our fellow-men should be as real and sincere as our affection to ourselves, not that it should be as great in degree. A man is authorized, therefore, by common sense and the laws of England, as well as those of nature, to love himself better than his fellow-subject. If two persons are cast away at sea, and get on a

plank (a case put by Sir Francis Bacon), and the plank is insufficient to hold them both, the one has a right to push the other off to save himself. The rules of the common law, therefore, which authorize a man to preserve his own life at the expense of another's, are not contradicted by any divine or moral law. We talk of liberty and property, but if we cut up the law of self-defense, we cut up the foundations of both; and if we give up this, the rest is of very little value, and therefore this principle must be strictly attended to; for whatsoever the law pronounces in the case of these eight soldiers will be the law to other persons and after ages. All the persons that have slain mankind in this country from the beginning to this day had better have been acquitted than that a wrong rule and precedent should be established.

I shall now read to you a few authorities on this subject of self-defense. Foster, 273 (in the case of justifiable self-defense):

"The injured party may repel force with force in defense of person, habitation, or property, against one who manifestly intendeth and endeavoreth with violence or surprise to commit a known felony upon either. In these cases he is not obliged to retreat, but may pursue his adversary till he finds himself out of danger; and if in a conflict between them he happeneth to kill, such killing is justifiable."

I must entreat you to consider the words of this authority. The injured person may repel force by force against any who endeavoreth to commit any kind of felony on him or his. Here the rule is, I have a right to stand on my own defense, if you intend to commit felony. If any of the persons made an attack on these soldiers, with an intention to rob them, if it was but to take their hats feloniously, they had a right to kill them on the spot, and had no business to retreat. If a robber meet me in the street and command me to surrender my purse, I have a right to kill him without asking any questions. If a person commit a bare assault on me, this will not justify killing; but if he assault me in such a manner as to discover an intention to kill me, I have a right to destroy him, that I may put it out of his power to kill me. In the case you will have to consider, I do not know there was any attempt to steal from these persons; however, there were some persons concerned who would, probably enough, have stolen, if there had been anything to

steal, and many were there who had no such disposition. But this is not the point we aim at. The question is, Are you satisfied the people made the attack in order to kill the soldiers? If you are satisfied that the people, whoever they were, made that assault with a design to kill or maim the soldiers, this was such an assault as will justify the soldiers killing in their own defense. Further, it seems to me, we may make another question, whether you are satisfied that their real intention was to kill or maim, or not? If any reasonable man in the situation of one of these soldiers would have had reason to believe in the time of it, that the people came with an intention to kill him, whether you have this satisfaction now or not in your own minds, they were justifiable, at least excusable, in firing. You and I may be suspicious that the people who made this assault on the soldiers did it to put them to flight, on purpose that they might go exulting about the town afterwards in triumph; but this will not do. You must place yourselves in the situation of Weems and Killroy—consider yourselves as knowing that the prejudice of the world about you thought you came to dragoon them into obedience, to statutes, instructions, mandates, and edicts, which they thoroughly detested—that many of these people were thoughtless and inconsiderate, old and young, sailors and landsmen, negroes and mulattoes—that they, the soldiers, had no friends about them, the rest were in opposition to them; with all the bells ringing to call the town together to assist the people in King Street, for they knew by that time that there was no fire; the people shouting, huzzaing, and making the mob whistle, as they call it, which, when a boy makes it in the street is no formidable thing, but when made by a multitude is a most hideous shriek, almost as terrible as an Indian yell; the people crying, "Kill them, kill them." Knock them over, heaving snowballs, oyster shells, clubs, white-birch sticks three inches and a half in diameter; consider yourselves in this situation, and then judge whether a reasonable man in the soldiers' situation would not have concluded they were going to kill him. I believe if I were to reverse the scene, I should bring it home to our own bosoms. Suppose Colonel Marshall when he came out of his own door and saw these grenadiers coming down with swords, etc., had thought it proper to have appointed a military watch; suppose he had assembled Gray and Attucks that were killed, or any other person in town, and appointed them in that situation as a military watch, and there had come from Murray's barracks thirty or forty soldiers with no other arms than snowballs, cakes of ice, oyster shells, cinders, and clubs, and attacked this military watch in this manner, what do you suppose would have been the feelings and reasonings of any of our householders? I confess, I believe they would not have borne one-half of what the witnesses have sworn the soldiers bore, till they had shot down as many as were necessary to intimidate and disperse the rest; because the law does not oblige us to bear insults to the danger of our lives, to stand still with such a number of people around us, throwing such things at us, and threatening our lives, until we are disabled to defend ourselves.

(Foster, 274): "Where a known felony is attempted upon the person, be it to rob or murder, here the party assaulted may repel force with force, and even his own servant, then attendant on him, or any other person present, may interpose for preventing mischief, and if death ensue, the party so interposing will be justified. In this case nature and social duty co-operate."

Hawkins, P. C., Chapter 28, Section 25, towards the end:—"Yet it seems that a private person, a fortiori, an officer of justice, who happens unavoidably to kill another in endeavoring to defend himself from or suppress dangerous rioters, may justify the fact in as much as he only does his duty in aid of the public justice."

Section 24:—"And I can see no reason why a person, who, without provocation, is assaulted by another, in any place whatsoever, in such a manner as plainly shows an intent to murder him, as by discharging a pistol, or pushing at him with a drawn sword, etc., may not justify killing such an assailant, as much as if he had attempted to rob him. For is not he who attempts to murder me more injurious than he who barely attempts to rob me? And can it be more justifiable to fight for my goods than for my life?"

And it is not only highly agreeable to reason that a man in such circumstances may lawfully kill another, but it seems also to be confirmed by the general tenor of our books, which, speaking of homicide se defendo, suppose it done in some quarrel or affray.

(Hawkins, p. 71, § 14); "And so, perhaps, the killing of dangerous rioters may be justified by any private persons, who cannot otherwise suppress them or defend themselves from them, inasmuch as every

private person seems to be authorized by the law to arm himself for the purposes aforesaid."

Here every private person is authorized to arm himself; and on the strength of this authority I do not deny the inhabitants had a right to arm themselves at that time for their defense, not for offense. That distinction is material, and must be attended to.

(Hawkins, p. 75, § 14): "And not only he who on an assault retreats to the wall, or some such strait, beyond which he can go no further before he kills the other, is judged by the law to act upon unavoidable necessity; but also he who being assaulted in such a manner and in such a place that he cannot go back without manifestly endangering his life, kills the other without retreating at all."

(Section 16): "And an officer who kills one that insults him in the execution of his office, and where a private person that kills one who feloniously assaults him in the highway, may justify the fact without ever giving back at all."

There is no occasion for the magistrate to read the riot act. In the case before you, I suppose you will be satisfied when you come to examine the witnesses and compare it with the rules of the common law, abstracted from all mutiny acts and articles of war, that these soldiers were in such a situation that they could not help themselves. People were coming from Royal Exchange Lane, and other parts of the town, with clubs and cord-wood sticks; the soldiers were planted by the wall of the Customhouse; they could not retreat; they were surrounded on all sides, for there were people behind them as well as before them; there were a number of people in the Royal Exchange Lane; the soldiers were so near to the Customhouse that they could not retreat, unless they had gone into the brick wall of it. I shall show you presently that all the party concerned in this unlawful design were guilty of what any one of them did; if anybody threw a snowball it was the act of the whole party; if any struck with a club or threw a club, and the club had killed anybody, the whole party would have been guilty of murder in the law. Lord Chief-Justice Holt, in Mawgrige's case (Keyling, 128), says:—

"Now, it has been held, that if A of his malice prepense assaults B to kill him, and B draws his sword and attacks A and pursues him, then A, for his safety, gives back and retreats to a wall, and B

still pursuing him with his drawn sword, A in his defense kills B; this is murder in A. For A having malice against B, and in pursuance thereof endeavoring to kill him, is answerable for all the consequences of which he was the original cause. It is not reasonable for any man that is dangerously assaulted, and when he perceives his life in danger from his adversary, but to have liberty for the security of his own life, to pursue him that maliciously assaulted him; for he that has manifested that he has malice against another is not fit to be trusted with a dangerous weapon in his hand. And so resolved by all the judges when they met at Seargeant's Inn, in preparation for my Lord Morley's trial."

In the case here we will take Montgomery, if you please, when he was attacked by the stout man with a stick, who aimed it at his head, with a number of people round him crying out, "Kill them, kill them." Had he not a right to kill the man? If all the party were guilty of the assault made by the stout man, and all of them had discovered malice in their hearts, had not Montgomery a right, according to Lord Chief-Justice Holt, to put it out of their power to wreak their malice upon him? I will not at present look for any more authorities in the point of self-defense; you will be able to judge from these how far the law goes in justifying or excusing any person in defense of himself, or taking away the life of another who threatens him in life or limb. The next point is this: that in case of an unlawful assembly, all and every one of the assembly is guilty of all and every unlawful act committed by any one of that assembly in prosecution of the unlawful design set out upon.

Rules of law should be universally known, whatever effect they may have on politics; they are rules of common law, the law of the land; and it is certainly true, that wherever there is an unlawful assembly, let it consist of many persons or of a few, every man in it is guilty of every unlawful act committed by any one of the whole party, be they more or be they less, in pursuance of their unlawful design. This is the policy of the law; to discourage and prevent riots, insurrections, turbulence, and tumults.

In the continual vicissitudes of human things, amidst the shocks of fortune and the whirls of passion that take place at certain critical seasons, even in the mildest government, the people are liable to run into riots and tumults. There are Church-quakes and State-quakes in the moral and political world,

as well as earthquakes, storms, and tempests in the physical. Thus much, however, must be said in favor of the people and of human nature, that it is a general, if not a universal truth, that the aptitude of the people to mutinies, seditions, tumults, and insurrections, is in direct proportion to the despotism of the government. In governments completely despotic,—that is, where the will of one man is the only law, this disposition is most prevalent. In aristocracies next; in mixed monarchies, less than either of the former; in complete republics the least of all, and under the same form of governments as in a limited monarchy, for example, the virtue and wisdom of the administrations may generally be measured by the peace and order that are seen among the people. However this may be, such is the imperfection of all things in this world, that no form of government, and perhaps no virtue or wisdom in the administration, can at all times avoid riots and disorders among the people.

Now, it is from this difficulty that the policy of the law has framed such strong discouragements to secure the people against tumults; because, when they once begin, there is danger of their running to such excesses as will overturn the whole system of government. There is the rule from the reverend sage of the law, so often quoted before:—

(1 H. H. P. C. 437): "All present, aiding and assisting, are equally principal with him that gave the stroke whereof the party died. For though one gave the stroke, yet in interpretation of law it is the stroke of every person that was present, aiding and assisting."

(1 H. H. P. C. 440): "If divers come with one assent to do mischief, as to kill, to rob or beat, and one doeth it, they are all principals in the felony. If many be present and one only give the stroke whereof the party dies, they are all principal, if they came for that purpose."

Now, if the party at Dock Square came with an intention only to beat the soldiers, and began to affray with them, and any of them had been accidentally killed, it would have been murder, because it was an unlawful design they came upon. If but one does it they are all considered in the eye of the law guilty; if any one gives the mortal stroke, they are all principals here, therefore there is a reversal of the scene. If you are satisfied that these soldiers were there on a lawful design, and it should be proved any of them shot without provocation, and killed anybody, he only is answerable for it.

(First Hale's Pleas of the Crown, 1 H. H. P. C. 444): "Although if many come upon an unlawful design, and one of the company kill one of the adverse party in pursuance of that design, all are principals; yet if many be together upon a lawful account, and one of the company kill another of the adverse party, without any particular abetment of the rest to this fact of homicide, they are not all guilty that are of the company, but only those that gave the stroke or actually abetted him to do it."

(1 H. H. P. C. 445): "In case of a riotous assembly to rob or steal deer, or to do any unlawful act of violence, there the offense of one is the offense of all the company."

(In another place, 1 H. H. P. C. 439): "The Lord Dacre and divers others went to steal deer in the park of one Pellham. Raydon, one of the company, killed the keeper in the park, the Lord Dacre and the rest of the company being in the other part of the park. Yet it was adjudged murder in them all, and they died for it." (And he quotes Crompton 25, Dalton 93, p. 241.) "So that in so strong a case as this, where this nobleman set out to hunt deer in the ground of another, he was in one part of the park and his company in another part, yet they were all guilty of murder."

The next is:—

(Hale's Pleas of the Crown, 1 H. H. P. C. 440): "The case of Drayton Bassit; divers persons doing an unlawful act, all are guilty of what is done by one."

(Foster 353, 354): "A general resolution against all opposers, whether such resolution appears upon evidence to have been actually and implicitly entered into by the confederates, or may reasonably be collected from their number, arms or behavior, at or before the scene of action, such resolutions so proved have always been considered as strong ingredients in cases of this kind. And in cases of homicide committed in consequence of them, every person present, in the sense of the law, when the homicide has been involved in the guilt of him that gave the mortal blow."

(Foster): "The cases of Lord Dacre, mentioned by Hale, and of Pudsey, reported by Crompton and cited by Hale, turned upon this point. The offenses they respectively stood charged with, as principals, were committed far out of their sight and hearing, and yet both were held to be present. It was sufficient that at the instant the facts were committed, they were of the same party and upon the

same pursuit, and under the same engagements and expectations of mutual defense and support with those that did the facts."

Thus far I have proceeded, and I believe it will not be hereafter disputed by anybody, that this law ought to be known to every one who has any disposition to be concerned in an unlawful assembly, whatever mischief happens in the prosecution of the design they set out upon, all are answerable for it. It is necessary we should consider the definitions of some other crimes as well as murder; sometimes one crime gives occasion to another. An assault is sometimes the occasion of manslaughter, sometimes of excusable homicide. It is necessary to consider what is a riot. (1 Hawkins, ch. 65, § 2): I shall give you the definition of it:—

"Wheresoever more than three persons use force or violence, for the accomplishment of any design whatever, all concerned are rioters."

Were there not more than three persons in Dock Square? Did they not agree to go to King Street, and attack the main guard? Where, then, is the reason for hesitation at calling it a riot? If we cannot speak the law as it is, where is our liberty? And this is law, that wherever more than three persons are gathered together to accomplish anything with force, it is a riot.

(1 Hawkins, ch. 65, § 2): "Wherever more than three persons use force and violence, all who are concerned therein are rioters. But in some cases wherein the law authorizes force, it is lawful and commendable to use it. As for a sheriff [2 And. 67 Poph. 121], or constable [3 H. 7, 10, 6], or perhaps even for a private person [Poph. 121, Moore 656], to assemble a competent number of people, in order with force to oppose rebels or enemies or rioters, and afterwards, with such force actually to suppress them."

I do not mean to apply the word rebel on this occasion; I have no reason to suppose that ever there was one in Boston, at least among the natives of the country; but rioters are in the same situation, as far as my argument is concerned, and proper officers may suppress rioters, and so may even private persons.

If we strip ourselves free from all military laws, mutiny acts, articles of war and soldiers' oaths, and consider these prisoners as neighbors, if any of their neighbors were attacked in King Street, they had a right to collect together to suppress this riot and combination. If any number of persons meet together at a fair or market, and happen to fall together by the ears, they are

not guilty of a riot, but of a sudden affray. Here is another paragraph, which I must read to you:—

(1 Hawkins, ch. 65, § 3): "If a number of persons being met together at a fair or market, or on any other lawful or innocent occasion, happen, on a sudden quarrel, to fall together by the ears, they are not guilty of a riot, but of a sudden affray only, of which none are guilty but those who actually began it," etc.

It would be endless, as well as superfluous, to examine whether every particular person engaged in a riot were in truth one of the first assembly or actually had a previous knowledge of the design thereof. I have endeavored to produce the best authorities, and to give you the rules of law in their words, for I desire not to advance anything of my own. I choose to lay down the rules of law from authorities which cannot be disputed. Another point is this, whether and how far a private person may aid another in distress? Suppose a press-gang should come on shore in this town and assault any sailor or householder in King Street, in order to carry him on board one of his Majesty's ships, and impress him without any warrant as a seaman in his Majesty's service; how far do you suppose the inhabitants would think themselves warranted by law to interpose against that lawless press-gang? I agree that such a press-gang would be as unlawful an assembly as that was in King Street. If they were to press an inhabitant and carry him off for a sailor, would not the inhabitants think themselves warranted by law to interpose in behalf of their fellow-citizen? Now, gentlemen, if the soldiers had no right to interpose in the relief of the sentry, the inhabitants would have no right to interpose with regard to the citizen, for whatever is law for a soldier is law for a sailor and for a citizen. They all stand upon an equal footing in this respect. I believe we shall not have it disputed that it would be lawful to go into King Street and help an honest man there against the press-master. We have many instances in the books which authorize it.

Now, suppose you should have a jealousy in your minds that the people who made this attack upon the sentry had nothing in their intention more than to take him off his post, and that was threatened by some. Suppose they intended to go a little further, and tar and feather him, or to ride him (as the phrase is in Hudibras), he would have had a good right to have stood

upon his defense—the defense of his liberty; and if he could not preserve that without the hazard of his own life, he would have been warranted in depriving those of life who were endeavoring to deprive him of his. That is a point I would not give up for my right hand—nay, for my life.

Well, I say, if the people did this, or if this was only their intention, surely the officers and soldiers had a right to go to his relief; and therefore they set out upon a lawful errand. They were, therefore, a lawful assembly, if we only consider them as private subjects and fellow-citizens, without regard to mutiny acts, articles of war, or soldiers' oaths. A private person, or any number of private persons, has a right to go to the assistance of a fellow-subject in distress or danger of his life, when assaulted and in danger from a few or a multitude.

(Keyl. 136): "If a man perceives another by force to be injuriously treated, pressed, and restrained of his liberty, though the person abused doth not complain or call for aid or assistance, and others, out of compassion, shall come to his rescue, and kill any of those that shall so restrain him, that is manslaughter."

Keyl.: "A and others without any warrant impress B to serve the king at sea. B quietly submitted, and went off with the pressmaster. Hugett and the others pursued them, and required a sight of their warrant; but they showing a piece of paper that was not a sufficient warrant, thereupon Hugett with the others drew their swords, and the pressmasters theirs, and so there was a combat, and those who endeavored to rescue the pressed man killed one of the pretended pressmasters. This was but manslaughter; for when the liberty of one subject is invaded, it affects all the rest. It is a provocation to all people, as being of ill example and pernicious consequences."

Lord Raymond, 1301. The Queen *versus* Tooley *et al.* Lord Chief-Justice Holt says: "The prisoner (*i. e.* Tooley) in this had sufficient provocation; for if one be impressed upon an unlawful authority, it is a sufficient provocation to all people out of compassion; and where the liberty of the subject is invaded, it is a provocation to all the subjects of England, etc.; and surely a man ought to be concerned for Magna Charta and the laws; and if any one, against the law, imprisons a man, he is an offender against Magna Charta."

I am not insensible to Sir Michael Foster's observations on these cases, but apprehend they do not invalidate the authority of them as far as I now apply them to the purposes of my argument. If a stranger, a mere fellow-subject, may interpose to defend the liberty, he may, too, defend the life of another individual. But, according to the evidence, some imprudent people, before the sentry, proposed to take him off his post; others threatened his life; and intelligence of this was carried to the main guard before any of the prisoners turned out. They were then ordered out to relieve the sentry; and any of our fellow-citizens might lawfully have gone upon the same errand. They were, therefore, a lawful assembly.

I have but one point of law more to consider, and that is this: In the case before you I do not pretend to prove that every one of the unhappy persons slain was concerned in the riot. The authorities read to you just now say it would be endless to prove whether every person that was present and in a riot was concerned in planning the first enterprise or not. Nay, I believe it but justice to say some were perfectly innocent of the occasion. I have reason to suppose that one of them was—Mr. Maverick. He was a very worthy young man, as he has been represented to me, and had no concern in the rioters' proceedings of that night; and I believe the same may be said in favor of one more at least, Mr. Caldwell, who was slain; and, therefore, many people may think that as he and perhaps another was innocent, therefore innocent blood having been shed, that must be expiated by the death of somebody or other. I take notice of this, because one gentleman was nominated by the sheriff for a juryman upon this trial, because he had said he believed Captain Preston was innocent, but innocent blood had been shed, and therefore somebody ought to be hanged for it, which he thought was indirectly giving his opinion in this cause. I am afraid many other persons have formed such an opinion. I do not take it to be a rule, that where innocent blood is shed the person must die. In the instance of the Frenchmen on the Plains of Abraham, they were innocent, fighting for their king and country; their blood is as innocent as any. There may be multitudes killed, when innocent blood is shed on all sides; so that it is not an invariable rule. I will put a case in which, I dare say, all will agree with me. Here are two persons, the father and the son, go out a-hunting. They take different roads. The father hears a rushing among the bushes, takes it to be game, fires, and kills his son, through a mistake. Here is innocent blood shed, but yet nobody will say the father ought to die for it. So that the general rule of law is, that whenever one

person has a right to do an act, and that act, by any accident, takes away the life of another, it is excusable. It bears the same regard to the innocent as to the guilty. If two men are together, and attack me, and I have a right to kill them, I strike at them, and by mistake strike a third and kill him, as I had a right to kill the first, my killing the other will be excusable, as it happened by accident. If I, in the heat of passion, aim a blow at the person who has assaulted me, and aiming at him I kill another person, it is but manslaughter.

(Foster, 261, § 3): "If an action unlawful in itself is done deliberately, and with intention of mischief, or great bodily harm to particulars, or of mischief indiscriminately, fall it where it may, and death ensues, against or beside the original intention of the party, it will be murder. But if such mischievous intention doth not appear, which is matter of fact, and to be collected from circumstances, and the act was done heedlessly and inconsiderately, it will be manslaughter, not accidental death; because the act upon which death ensued was unlawful."

Suppose, in this case, the mulatto man was the person who made the assault; suppose he was concerned in the unlawful assembly, and this party of soldiers, endeavoring to defend themselves against him, happened to kill another person, who was innocent—though the soldiers had no reason, that we know of, to think any person there, at least of that number who were crowding about them, innocent; they might, naturally enough, presume all to be guilty of the riot and assault, and to come with the same design—I say, if on firing on those who were guilty, they accidentally killed an innocent person, it was not their fault. They were obliged to defend themselves against those who were pressing upon them. They are not answerable for it with their lives; for on supposition it was justifiable or excusable to kill Attucks, or any other person, it will be equally justifiable or excusable if in firing at him they killed another, who was innocent; or if the provocation was such as to mitigate the guilt of manslaughter, it will equally mitigate the guilt, if they killed an innocent man undesignedly, in aiming at him who gave the provocation, according to Judge Foster; and as this point is of such consequence, I must produce some more authorities for it:

(1 Hawkins, 84): "Also, if a third person accidentally happen to be killed by one engaged in a combat, upon a sudden quarrel, it seems

that he who killed him is guilty of manslaughter only," etc. (H. H. P. C., 442, to the same point; and 1 H. H. P. C. 484, and 4 Black, 27.)

I shall now consider one question more, and that is concerning provocation. We have hitherto been considering self-defense, and how far persons may go in defending themselves against aggressors, even by taking away their lives, and now proceed to consider such provocations as the law allows to mitigate or extenuate the guilt of killing, where it is not justifiable or excusable. An assault and battery committed upon a man in such a manner as not to endanger his life is such a provocation as the law allows to reduce killing down to the crime of manslaughter. Now, the law has been made on more considerations than we are capable of making at present; the law considers a man as capable of bearing anything and everything but blows. I may reproach a man as much as I please; I may call him a thief, robber, traitor, scoundrel, coward, lobster, bloody-back, etc., and if he kill me it will be murder, if nothing else but words precede; but if from giving him such kind of language I proceed to take him by the nose, or fillip him on the forehead, that is an assault; that is a blow. The law will not oblige a man to stand still and bear it; there is the distinction. Hands off; touch me not. As soon as you touch me, if I run you through the heart, it is but manslaughter. The utility of this distinction, the more you think of it the more you will be satisfied with it. It is an assault whenever a blow is struck, let it be ever so slight, and sometimes even without a blow. The law considers man as frail and passionate. When his passions are touched, he will be thrown off his guard, and therefore the law makes allowance for this frailty—considers him as in a fit of passion, not having the possession of his intellectual faculties, and therefore does not oblige him to measure out his blows with a yard-stick, or weigh them in a scale. Let him kill with a sword, gun, or hedge-stake, it is not murder, but only manslaughter.

(Keyling's Report, 135. Regina *versus* Mawgrige.) "Rules supported by authority and general consent, showing what are always allowed to be sufficient provocations. First, if one man upon any words shall make an assault upon another, either by pulling him by the nose or filliping him on the forehead, and he that is so assaulted shall draw his sword and immediately run the other through, that

is but manslaughter, for the peace is broken by the person killed, and with an indignity to him that received the assault. Besides, he that was so affronted might reasonably apprehend that he that treated him in that manner might have some further design upon him."

So that here is the boundary, when a man is assaulted and kills in consequence of that assault, it is but manslaughter. I will just read as I go along the definition of assault:—

(1 Hawkins, ch. 62, § 1): "An assault is an attempt or offer, with force or violence, to do a corporal hurt to another, as by striking at him with or without a weapon, or presenting a gun at him at such a distance to which the gun will carry, or pointing a pitchfork at him, or by any other such like act done in angry, threatening manner, etc.; but no words can amount to an assault."

Here is the definition of an assault, which is a sufficient provocation to soften killing down to manslaughter:—

(1 Hawkins, ch. 31, § 36): "Neither can he be thought guilty of a greater crime than manslaughter, who, finding a man in bed with his wife, or being actually struck by him, or pulled by the nose or filliped upon the forehead, immediately kills him, or in the defense of his person from an unlawful arrest, or in the defense of his house from those who, claiming a title to it, attempt forcibly to enter it, and to that purpose shoot at it," etc.

Every snowball, oyster shell, cake of ice, or bit of cinder, that was thrown that night at the sentinel, was an assault upon him; every one that was thrown at the party of soldiers was an assault upon them, whether it hit any of them or not. I am guilty of an assault if I present a gun at any person; and if I insult him in that manner and he shoots me, it is but manslaughter.

(Foster, 295, 296): "To what I have offered with regard to sudden rencounters let me add, that the blood already too much heated, kindleth afresh at every pass or blow. And in the tumult of the passions, in which the mere instinct of self-preservation has no inconsiderable share, the voice of reason is not heard; and therefore the law, in condescension to the infirmities of flesh and blood, doth extenuate the offense."

Insolent, scurrilous, or slanderous language, when it precedes an assault, aggravates it.

(Foster, 316): "We all know that words of reproach, how grating and offensive soever, are in the eye of the law no provocation in the case of voluntary homicide; and yet every man who hath considered the human frame, or but attended to the workings of his own heart, knoweth that affronts of that kind pierce deeper and stimulate in the veins more effectually than a slight injury done to a third person, though under the color of justice, possibly can."

I produce this to show the assault in this case was aggravated by the scurrilous language which preceded it. Such words of reproach stimulate in the veins and exasperate the mind, and no doubt if an assault and battery succeeds them, killing under such provocation is softened to manslaughter, but killing without such provocation makes it murder.

End of the first day's speech

JOHN QUINCY ADAMS
(1767–1848)

No OTHER American President, not even Thomas Jefferson, has equaled John Quincy Adams in literary accomplishments. His orations and public speeches will be found to stand for a tradition of painstaking, scholastic finish hardly to be found elsewhere in American orations, and certainly not among the speeches of any other President. As a result of the pains he took with them, they belong rather to literature than to politics, and it is possible that they will not be generally appreciated at their real worth for several generations still to come. If, as is sometimes alleged in such cases, they gain in literary finish at the expense of force, it is not to be forgotten that the forcible speech which, ignoring all rules, carries its point by assault, may buy immediate effect at the expense of permanent respectability. And if John Quincy Adams, who labored as Cicero did to give his addresses the greatest possible literary finish, does not rank with Cicero among orators, it is certain that respectability will always be willingly conceded him by every generation of his countrymen.

Some idea of the extent of his early studies may be gained from his father's letter to Benjamin Waterhouse, written from Auteuil, France, in 1785. John Quincy Adams being then only in his eighteenth year, the elder Adams said of him:—

"If you were to examine him in English and French poetry, I know not where you would find anybody his superior; in Roman and English history few persons of his age. It is rare to find a youth possessed of such knowledge. He has translated Virgil's 'Æneid,' 'Suetonius,' the whole of 'Sallust'; 'Tacitus,' 'Agricola'; his 'Germany' and several other books of his 'Annals,' a great part of Horace, some of Ovid, and some of Cæsar's 'Commentaries,' in writing, besides a number of Tully's orations. . . . In Greek his progress has not been equal, yet he has studied morsels in Aristotle's 'Poetics,' in Plutarch's 'Lives,' and Lucian's 'Dialogues,' 'The Choice of Hercules,' in Xenophon, and lately he has gone through several books of Homer's 'Iliad.'"

The elder Adams concludes the list of his son's accomplishments with a catalogue of his labors in mathematics hardly inferior in length to that cited in the classics. Even if it were true, as has been urged by the political opponents of the Adams family, that no one of its members has ever shown more than respectable natural talent,

it would add overwhelming weight to the argument in favor of the laborious habits of study which have characterized them to the third and fourth generations, and, from the time of John Adams until our own, have made them men of mark and far-reaching national influence.

In national politics, John Quincy Adams, the last of the line of colonial gentlemen who achieved the presidency, stood for education, for rigid ideas of moral duty, for dignity, for patriotism, for all the virtues which are best cultivated through processes of segregation. He ended an epoch in which it was possible for a man who, as he did, wrote 'Poems on Religion and Society' and paraphrased the Psalms into English verse to be elected President. It has hardly been possible since his day.

Chosen as a Democrat in 1825, Mr. Adams was really the first Whig President. His speeches are important, historically, because they define political tendencies as a result of which the Whig party took the place of the Federalist.

ORATION AT PLYMOUTH

(Delivered at Plymouth on the Twenty-Second Day of December, 1802, in Commemoration of the Landing of the Pilgrims)

AMONG the sentiments of most powerful operation upon the human heart, and most highly honorable to the human character, are those of veneration for our forefathers, and of love for our posterity. They form the connecting links between the selfish and the social passions. By the fundamental principle of Christianity, the happiness of the individual is interwoven, by innumerable and imperceptible ties, with that of his contemporaries. By the power of filial reverence and parental affection, individual existence is extended beyond the limits of individual life, and the happiness of every age is chained in mutual dependence upon that of every other. Respect for his ancestors excites, in the breast of man, interest in their history, attachment to their characters, concern for their errors, involuntary pride in their virtues. Love for his posterity spurs him to exertion for their support, stimulates him to virtue for their example, and fills him with the tenderest solicitude for their welfare. Man, therefore, was not made for himself alone. No, he was made for his country, by the obligations of the social compact; he was made for his species, by the Christian duties of

universal charity; he was made for all ages past, by the sentiment of reverence for his forefathers; and he was made for all future times, by the impulse of affection for his progeny. Under the influence of these principles,

"Existence sees him spurn her bounded reign."

They redeem his nature from the subjection of time and space; he is no longer a "puny insect shivering at a breeze"; he is the glory of creation, formed to occupy all time and all extent; bounded, during his residence upon earth, only to the boundaries of the world, and destined to life and immortality in brighter regions, when the fabric of nature itself shall dissolve and perish.

The voice of history has not, in all its compass, a note but answers in unison with these sentiments. The barbarian chieftain, who defended his country against the Roman invasion, driven to the remotest extremity of Britain, and stimulating his followers to battle by all that has power of persuasion upon the human heart, concluded his persuasion by an appeal to these irresistible feelings: "Think of your forefathers and of your posterity." The Romans themselves, at the pinnacle of civilization, were actuated by the same impressions, and celebrated, in anniversary festivals, every great event which had signalized the annals of their forefathers. To multiply instances where it were impossible to adduce an exception would be to waste your time and abuse your patience; but in the sacred volume, which contains the substance of our firmest faith and of our most precious hopes, these passions not only maintain their highest efficacy, but are sanctioned by the express injunctions of the Divine Legislator to his chosen people.

The revolutions of time furnish no previous example of a nation shooting up to maturity and expanding into greatness with the rapidity which has characterized the growth of the American people. In the luxuriance of youth, and in the vigor of manhood, it is pleasing and instructive to look backwards upon the helpless days of infancy; but in the continual and essential changes of a growing subject, the transactions of that early period would be soon obliterated from the memory but for some periodical call of attention to aid the silent records of the historian. Such celebrations arouse and gratify the kindliest emotions of the bosom. They are faithful pledges of the respect we bear to the memory of our ancestors and of the tenderness with which we cherish the rising generation. They introduce the sages and heroes of ages past to the notice and emulation of succeeding times; they are at once testimonials of our gratitude, and schools of virtue to our children.

These sentiments are wise; they are honorable; they are virtuous; their cultivation is not merely innocent pleasure, it is incumbent duty. Obedient to their dictates, you, my fellow-citizens, have instituted and paid frequent observance to this annual solemnity. And what event of weightier intrinsic importance, or of more extensive consequences, was ever selected for this honorary distinction?

In reverting to the period of our origin, other nations have generally been compelled to plunge into the chaos of impenetrable antiquity, or to trace a lawless ancestry into the caverns of ravishers and robbers. It is your peculiar privilege to commemorate, in this birthday of your nation, an event ascertained in its minutest details; an event of which the principal actors are known to you familiarly, as if belonging to your own age; an event of a magnitude before which imagination shrinks at the imperfection of her powers. It is your further happiness to behold, in those eminent characters, who were most conspicuous in accomplishing the settlement of your country, men upon whose virtue you can dwell with honest exultation. The founders of your race are not handed down to you, like the father of the Roman people, as the sucklings of a wolf. You are not descended from a nauseous compound of fanaticism and sensuality, whose only argument was the sword, and whose only paradise was a brothel. No Gothic scourge of God, no Vandal pest of nations, no fabled fugitive from the flames of Troy, no bastard Norman tyrant, appears among the list of worthies who first landed on the rock, which your veneration has preserved as a lasting monument of their achievement. The great actors of the day we now solemnize were illustrious by their intrepid valor no less than by their Christian graces, but the clarion of conquest has not blazoned forth their names to all the winds of heaven. Their glory has not been wafted over oceans of blood to the remotest regions of the earth. They have not erected to themselves colossal statues upon pedestals of human bones, to provoke and insult the tardy hand of heavenly retribution. But theirs was "the better fortitude of patience and heroic martyrdom." Theirs was the gentle temper of Christian kindness; the rigorous observance of

reciprocal justice; the unconquerable soul of conscious integrity. Worldly fame has been parsimonious of her favor to the memory of those generous companions. Their numbers were small; their stations in life obscure; the object of their enterprise unostentatious; the theatre of their exploits remote; how could they possibly be favorites of worldly Fame—that common crier, whose existence is only known by the assemblage of multitudes; that pander of wealth and greatness, so eager to haunt the palaces of fortune, and so fastidious to the houseless dignity of virtue; that parasite of pride, ever scornful to meekness, and ever obsequious to insolent power; that heedless trumpeter, whose ears are deaf to modest merit, and whose eyes are blind to bloodless, distant excellence?

When the persecuted companions of Robinson, exiles from their native land, anxiously sued for the privilege of removing a thousand leagues more distant to an untried soil, a rigorous climate, and a savage wilderness, for the sake of reconciling their sense of religious duty with their affections for their country, few, perhaps none of them, formed a conception of what would be, within two centuries, the result of their undertaking. When the jealous and niggardly policy of their British sovereign denied them even that humblest of requests, and instead of liberty would barely consent to promise connivance, neither he nor they might be aware that they were laying the foundations of a power, and that he was sowing the seeds of a spirit, which, in less than two hundred years, would stagger the throne of his descendants, and shake his united kingdoms to the centre. So far is it from the ordinary habits of mankind to calculate the importance of events in their elementary principles, that had the first colonists of our country ever intimated as a part of their designs the project of founding a great and mighty nation, the finger of scorn would have pointed them to the cells of bedlam as an abode more suitable for hatching vain empires than the solitude of a transatlantic desert.

These consequences, then so little foreseen, have unfolded themselves, in all their grandeur, to the eyes of the present age. It is a common amusement of speculative minds to contrast the magnitude of the most important events with the minuteness of their primeval causes, and the records of mankind are full of examples for such contemplations. It is, however, a more profitable employment to trace the constituent principles of future

greatness in their kernel; to detect in the acorn at our feet the germ of that majestic oak, whose roots shoot down to the centre, and whose branches aspire to the skies. Let it be, then, our present occupation to inquire and endeavor to ascertain the causes first put in operation at the period of our commemoration, and already productive of such magnificent effects; to examine with reiterated care and minute attention the characters of those men who gave the first impulse to a new series of events in the history of the world; to applaud and emulate those qualities of their minds which we shall find deserving of our admiration; to recognize with candor those features which forbid approbation or even require censure, and, finally, to lay alike their frailties and their perfections to our own hearts, either as warning or as example.

Of the various European settlements upon this continent, which have finally merged in one independent nation, the first establishments were made at various times, by several nations, and under the influence of different motives. In many instances, the conviction of religious obligation formed one and a powerful inducement of the adventures; but in none, excepting the settlement at Plymouth, did they constitute the sole and exclusive actuating cause. Worldly interest and commercial speculation entered largely into the views of other settlers, but the commands of conscience were the only stimulus to the emigrants from Leyden. Previous to their expedition hither, they had endured a long banishment from their native country. Under every species of discouragement, they undertook the vogage; they performed it in spite of numerous and almost insuperable obstacles; they arrived upon a wilderness bound with frost and hoary with snow, without the boundaries of their charter, outcasts from all human society, and coasted five weeks together, in the dead of winter, on this tempestuous shore, exposed at once to the fury of the elements, to the arrows of the native savage, and to the impending horrors of famine.

Courage and perseverance have a magical talisman, before which difficulties disappear and obstacles vanish into air. These qualities have ever been displayed in their mightiest perfection, as attendants in the retinue of strong passions. From the first discovery of the Western Hemisphere by Columbus until the settlement of Virginia which immediately preceded that of Plymouth, the various adventurers from the ancient world had

exhibited upon innumerable occasions that ardor of enterprise and that stubbornness of pursuit which set all danger at defiance, and chained the violence of nature at their feet. But they were all instigated by personal interests. Avarice and ambition had tuned their souls to that pitch of exaltation. Selfish passions were the parents of their heroism. It was reserved for the first settlers of New England to perform achievements equally arduous, to trample down obstructions equally formidable, to dispel dangers equally terrific, under the single inspiration of conscience. To them even liberty herself was but a subordinate and secondary consideration. They claimed exemption from the mandates of human authority, as militating with their subjection to a superior power. Before the voice of heaven they silenced even the calls of their country.

Yet, while so deeply impressed with the sense of religious obligation, they felt, in all its energy, the force of that tender tie which binds the heart of every virtuous man to his native land. It was to renew that connection with their country which had been severed by their compulsory expatriation, that they resolved to face all the hazards of a perilous navigation and all the labors of a toilsome distant settlement. Under the mild protection of the Batavian government, they enjoyed already that freedom of religious worship, for which they had resigned so many comforts and enjoyments at home; but their hearts panted for a restoration to the bosom of their country. Invited and urged by the open-hearted and truly benevolent people who had given them an asylum from the persecution of their own kindred to form their settlement within the territories then under their jurisdiction, the love of their country predominated over every influence save that of conscience alone, and they preferred the precarious chance of relaxation from the bigoted rigor of the English government to the certain liberality and alluring offers of the Hollanders. Observe, my countrymen, the generous patriotism, the cordial union of soul, the conscious yet unaffected vigor which beam in their application to the British monarch:—

"They were well weaned from the delicate milk of their mother country, and inured to the difficulties of a strange land. They were knit together in a strict and sacred bond, to take care of the good of each other and of the whole. It was not with them as with other men, whom small things could discourage, or small discontents cause to wish themselves again at home."

Children of these exalted Pilgrims! Is there one among you who can hear the simple and pathetic energy of these expressions without tenderness and admiration? Venerated shades of our forefathers! No, ye were, indeed, not ordinary men! That country which had ejected you so cruelly from her bosom you still delighted to contemplate in the character of an affectionate and beloved mother. The sacred bond which knit you together was indissoluble while you lived; and oh, may it be to your descendants the example and the pledge of harmony to the latest period of time! The difficulties and dangers, which so often had defeated attempts of similar establishments, were unable to subdue souls tempered like yours. You heard the rigid interdictions; you saw the menacing forms of toil and danger, forbidding your access to this land of promise; but you heard without dismay; you saw and disdained retreat. Firm and undaunted in the confidence of that sacred bond; conscious of the purity, and convinced of the importance of your motives, you put your trust in the protecting shield of Providence, and smiled defiance at the combining terrors of human malice and of elemental strife. These, in the accomplishment of your undertaking, you were summoned to encounter in their most hideous forms; these you met with that fortitude, and combatted with that perseverance, which you had promised in their anticipation; these you completely vanquished in establishing the foundations of New England, and the day which we now commemorate is the perpetual memorial of your triumph.

It were an occupation peculiarly pleasing to cull from our early historians, and exhibit before you every detail of this transaction; to carry you in imagination on board their bark at the first moment of her arrival in the bay; to accompany Carver, Winslow, Bradford, and Standish, in all their excursions upon the desolate coast; to follow them into every rivulet and creek where they endeavored to find a firm footing, and to fix, with a pause of delight and exultation, the instant when the first of these heroic adventurers alighted on the spot where you, their descendants, now enjoy the glorious and happy reward of their labors. But in this grateful task, your former orators, on this anniversary, have anticipated all that the most ardent industry could collect, and gratified all that the most inquisitive curiosity could desire. To you, my friends, every occurrence of that momentous period is already familiar. A transient allusion to a few characteristic instances, which mark the peculiar history of the

Plymouth settlers, may properly supply the place of a narrative, which, to this auditory, must be superfluous.

One of these remarkable incidents is the execution of that instrument of government by which they formed themselves into a body politic, the day after their arrival upon the coast, and previous to their first landing. This is, perhaps, the only instance in human history of that positive, original social compact, which speculative philosophers have imagined as the only legitimate source of government. Here was a unanimous and personal assent, by all the individuals of the community, to the association by which they became a nation. It was the result of circumstances and discussions which had occurred during their passage from Europe, and is a full demonstration that the nature of civil government, abstracted from the political institutions of their native country, had been an object of their serious meditation. The settlers of all the former European colonies had contented themselves with the powers conferred upon them by their respective charters, without looking beyond the seal of the royal parchment for the measure of their rights and the rule of their duties. The founders of Plymouth had been impelled by the peculiarities of their situation to examine the subject with deeper and more comprehensive research. After twelve years of banishment from the land of their first allegiance, during which they had been under an adoptive and temporary subjection to another sovereign, they must naturally have been led to reflect upon the relative rights and duties of allegiance and subjection. They had resided in a city, the seat of a university, where the polemical and political controversies of the time were pursued with uncommon fervor. In this period they had witnessed the deadly struggle between the two parties, into which the people of the United Provinces, after their separation from the crown of Spain, had divided themselves. The contest embraced within its compass not only theological doctrines, but political principles, and Maurice and Barnevelt were the temporal leaders of the same rival factions, of which Episcopius and Polyander were the ecclesiastical champions.

That the investigation of the fundamental principles of government was deeply implicated in these dissensions is evident from the immortal work of Grotius, upon the rights of war and peace, which undoubtedly originated from them. Grotius himself had been a most distinguished actor and sufferer in those

important scenes of internal convulsion, and his work was first published very shortly after the departure of our forefathers from Leyden. It is well known that in the course of the contest Mr. Robinson more than once appeared, with credit to himself, as a public disputant against Episcopius; and from the manner in which the fact is related by Governor Bradford, it is apparent that the whole English Church at Leyden took a zealous interest in the religious part of the controversy. As strangers in the land, it is presumable that they wisely and honorably avoided entangling themselves in the political contentions involved with it. Yet the theoretic principles, as they were drawn into discussion, could not fail to arrest their attention, and must have assisted them to form accurate ideas concerning the origin and extent of authority among men, independent of positive institutions. The importance of these circumstances will not be duly weighed without taking into consideration the state of opinion then prevalent in England. The general principles of government were there little understood and less examined. The whole substance of human authority was centred in the simple doctrine of royal prerogative, the origin of which was always traced in theory to divine institution. Twenty years later, the subject was more industriously sifted, and for half a century became one of the principal topics of controversy between the ablest and most enlightened men in the nation. The instrument of voluntary association executed on board the Mayflower testifies that the parties to it had anticipated the improvement of their nation.

Another incident, from which we may derive occasion for important reflections, was the attempt of these original settlers to establish among them that community of goods and of labor, which fanciful politicians, from the days of Plato to those of Rousseau, have recommended as the fundamental law of a perfect republic. This theory results, it must be acknowledged, from principles of reasoning most flattering to the human character. If industry, frugality, and disinterested integrity were alike the virtues of all, there would, apparently, be more of the social spirit, in making all property a common stock, and giving to each individual a proportional title to the wealth of the whole. Such is the basis upon which Plato forbids, in his Republic, the division of property. Such is the system upon which Rousseau pronounces the first man who enclosed a field with a fence, and, said, "This is mine," a traitor to the human species. A wiser

and more useful philosophy, however, directs us to consider man according to the nature in which he was formed; subject to infirmities, which no wisdom can remedy; to weaknesses, which no institution can strengthen; to vices, which no legislation can correct. Hence, it becomes obvious that separate property is the natural and indisputable right of separate exertion; that community of goods without community of toil is oppressive and unjust; that it counteracts the laws of nature, which prescribe that he only who sows the seed shall reap the harvest; that it discourages all energy, by destroying its rewards; and makes the most virtuous and active members of society the slaves and drudges of the worst. Such was the issue of this experiment among our forefathers, and the same event demonstrated the error of the system in the elder settlement of Virginia. Let us cherish that spirit of harmony which prompted our forefathers to make the attempt, under circumstances more favorable to its success than, perhaps, ever occurred upon earth. Let us no less admire the candor with which they relinquished it, upon discovering its irremediable inefficacy. To found principles of government upon too advantageous an estimate of the human character is an error of inexperience, the source of which is so amiable that it is impossible to censure it with severity. We have seen the same mistake, committed in our own age, and upon a larger theatre. Happily for our ancestors, their situation allowed them to repair it before its effects had proved destructive. They had no pride of vain philosophy to support, no perfidious rage of faction to glut, by persevering in their mistakes until they should be extinguished in torrents of blood.

As the attempt to establish among themselves the community of goods was a seal of that sacred bond which knit them so closely together, so the conduct they observed towards the natives of the country displays their steadfast adherence to the rules of justice and their faithful attachment to those of benevolence and charity.

No European settlement ever formed upon this continent has been more distinguished for undeviating kindness and equity towards the savages. There are, indeed, moralists who have questioned the right of the Europeans to intrude upon the possessions of the aboriginals in any case, and under any limitations whatsoever. But have they maturely considered the whole subject? The Indian right of possession itself stands, with regard to the greatest part of the country, upon a questionable foundation. Their cultivated fields; their constructed habitations; a space of ample sufficiency for their subsistence, and whatever they had annexed to themselves by personal labor, was undoubtedly, by the laws of nature, theirs. But what is the right of a huntsman to the forest of a thousand miles over which he has accidentally ranged in quest of prey? Shall the liberal bounties of Providence to the race of man be monopolized by one of ten thousand for whom they were created? Shall the exuberant bosom of the common mother, amply adequate to the nourishment of millions, be claimed exclusively by a few hundreds of her offspring? Shall the lordly savage not only disdain the virtues and enjoyments of civilization himself, but shall he control the civilization of a world? Shall he forbid the wilderness to blossom like a rose? Shall he forbid the oaks of the forest to fall before the ax of industry, and to rise again, transformed into the habitations of ease and elegance? Shall he doom an immense region of the globe to perpetual desolation, and to hear the howlings of the tiger and the wolf silence forever the voice of human gladness? Shall the fields and the valleys, which a beneficent God has formed to teem with the life of innumerable multitudes, be condemned to everlasting barrenness? Shall the mighty rivers, poured out by the hand of nature, as channels of communication between numerous nations, roll their waters in sullen silence and eternal solitude to the deep? Have hundreds of commodious harbors, a thousand leagues of coast, and a boundless ocean, been spread in the front of this land, and shall every purpose of utility to which they could apply be prohibited by the tenant of the woods? No, generous philanthropists! Heaven has not been thus inconsistent in the works of its hands. Heaven has not thus placed at irreconcilable strife its moral laws with its physical creation. The Pilgrims of Plymouth obtained their right of possession to the territory on which they settled, by titles as fair and unequivocal as any human property can be held. By their voluntary association they recognized their allegiance to the government of Britain, and in process of time received whatever powers and authorities could be conferred upon them by a charter from their sovereign. The spot on which they fixed had belonged to an Indian tribe, totally extirpated by that devouring pestilence which had swept the country shortly before their arrival. The territory, thus free from all exclusive possession,

they might have taken by the natural right of occupancy. Desirous, however, of giving ample satisfaction to every pretense of prior right, by formal and solemn conventions with the chiefs of the neighboring tribes, they acquired the further security of a purchase. At their hands the children of the desert had no cause of complaint. On the great day of retribution, what thousands, what millions of the American race will appear at the bar of judgment to arraign their European invading conquerors! Let us humbly hope that the fathers of the Plymouth Colony will then appear in the whiteness of innocence. Let us indulge in the belief that they will not only be free from all accusation of injustice to these unfortunate sons of nature, but that the testimonials of their acts of kindness and benevolence towards them will plead the cause of their virtues, as they are now authenticated by the record of history upon earth.

Religious discord has lost her sting; the cumbrous weapons of theological warfare are antiquated; the field of politics supplies the alchemists of our times with materials of more fatal explosion, and the butchers of mankind no longer travel to another world for instruments of cruelty and destruction. Our age is too enlightened to contend upon topics which concern only the interests of eternity; the men who hold in proper contempt all controversies about trifles, except such as inflame their own passions, have made it a commonplace censure against your ancestors, that their zeal was enkindled by subjects of trivial importance; and that however aggrieved by the intolerance of others, they were alike intolerant themselves. Against these objections, your candid judgment will not require an unqualified justification; but your respect and gratitude for the founders of the State may boldly claim an ample apology. The original grounds of their separation from the Church of England were not objects of a magnitude to dissolve the bonds of communion, much less those of charity, between Christian brethren of the same essential principles. Some of them, however, were not inconsiderable, and numerous inducements concurred to give them an extraordinary interest in their eyes. When that portentous system of abuses, the Papal dominion, was overturned, a great variety of religious sects arose in its stead in the several countries, which for many centuries before had been screwed beneath its subjection. The fabric of the reformation, first undertaken in England upon a contracted basis, by a capricious and sanguinary tyrant, had been

successively overthrown and restored, renewed and altered, according to the varying humors and principles of four successive monarchs. To ascertain the precise point of division between the genuine institutions of Christianity and the corruptions accumulated upon them in the progress of fifteen centuries, was found a task of extreme difficulty throughout the Christian world.

Men of the profoundest learning, of the sublimest genius, and of the purest integrity, after devoting their lives to the research, finally differed in their ideas upon many great points, both of doctrine and discipline. The main question, it was admitted on all hands, most intimately concerned the highest interests of man, both temporal and eternal. Can we wonder that men who felt their happiness here and their hopes of hereafter, their worldly welfare and the kingdom of heaven at stake, should sometimes attach an importance beyond their intrinsic weight to collateral points of controversy, connected with the all-involving object of the reformation? The changes in the forms and principles of religious worship were introduced and regulated in England by the hand of public authority. But that hand had not been uniform or steady in its operations. During the persecutions inflicted in the interval of Popish restoration under the reign of Mary, upon all who favored the reformation, many of the most zealous reformers had been compelled to fly their country. While residing on the continent of Europe, they had adopted the principles of the most complete and rigorous reformation, as taught and established by Calvin. On returning afterwards to their native country, they were dissatisfied with the partial reformation, at which, as they conceived, the English establishment had rested; and claiming the privilege of private conscience, upon which alone any departure from the Church of Rome could be justified, they insisted upon the right of adhering to the system of their own preference, and, of course, upon that of nonconformity to the establishment prescribed by the royal authority. The only means used to convince them of error and reclaim them from dissent was force, and force served but to confirm the opposition it was meant to suppress. By driving the founders of the Plymouth Colony into exile, it constrained them to absolute separation from the Church of England; and by the refusal afterwards to allow them a positive toleration, even in this American wilderness, the council of James I. rendered that separation irreconcilable. Viewing their religious liberties here,

as held only by sufferance, yet bound to them by all the ties of conviction, and by all their sufferings for them, could they forbear to look upon every dissenter among themselves with a jealous eye? Within two years after their landing, they beheld a rival settlement attempted in their immediate neighborhood; and not long after, the laws of self-preservation compelled them to break up a nest of revelers, who boasted of protection from the mother country, and who had recurred to the easy but pernicious resource of feeding their wanton idleness, by furnishing the savages with the means, the skill, and the instruments of European destruction. Toleration, in that instance, would have been self-murder, and many other examples might be alleged, in which their necessary measures of self-defense have been exaggerated into cruelty, and their most indispensable precautions distorted into persecution. Yet shall we not pretend that they were exempt from the common laws of mortality, or entirely free from all the errors of their age. Their zeal might sometimes be too ardent, but it was always sincere. At this day, religious indulgence is one of our clearest duties, because it is one of our undisputed rights. While we rejoice that the principles of genuine Christianity have so far triumphed over the prejudices of a former generation, let us fervently hope for the day when it will prove equally victorious over the malignant passions of our own.

In thus calling your attention to some of the peculiar features in the principles, the character, and the history of our forefathers, it is as wide from my design, as I know it would be from your approbation, to adorn their memory with a chaplet plucked from the domain of others. The occasion and the day are more peculiarly devoted to them, and let it never be dishonored with a contracted and exclusive spirit. Our affections as citizens embrace the whole extent of the Union, and the names of Raleigh, Smith, Winthrop, Calvert, Penn, and Oglethorpe, excite in our minds recollections equally pleasing and gratitude equally fervent with those of Carver and Bradford. Two centuries have not yet elapsed since the first European foot touched the soil which now constitutes the American Union. Two centuries more and our numbers must exceed those of Europe itself. The destinies of this empire, as they appear in prospect before us, disdain the powers of human calculation. Yet, as the original founder of the Roman state is said once to have lifted upon his shoulders the fame and fortunes of all his posterity, so let us never forget that the glory and greatness of all our descendants is in our hands. Preserve in all their purity, refine, if possible, from all their alloy, those virtues which we this day commemorate as the ornament of our forefathers. Adhere to them with inflexible resolution, as to the horns of the altar; instill them with unwearied perseverance into the minds of your children; bind your souls and theirs to the national Union as the chords of life are centred in the heart, and you shall soar with rapid and steady wing to the summit of human glory. Nearly a century ago, one of those rare minds to whom it is given to discern future greatness in its seminal principles upon contemplating the situation of this continent, pronounced, in a vein of poetic inspiration, "Westward the star of empire takes its way." Let us unite in ardent supplication to the Founder of nations and the Builder of worlds, that what then was prophecy may continue unfolding into history,—that the dearest hopes of the human race may not be extinguished in disappointment, and that the last may prove the noblest empire of time.

LAFAYETTE

(Delivered in Congress, December 31st, 1834)

ON THE sixth of September, 1757, Lafayette was born. The kings of France and Britain were seated upon their thrones by virtue of the principle of hereditary succession, variously modified and blended with different forms of religious faith, and they were waging war against each other, and exhausting the blood and treasure of their people for causes in which neither of the nations had any beneficial or lawful interest.

In this war the father of Lafayette fell in the cause of his king but not of his country. He was an officer of an invading army, the instrument of his sovereign's wanton ambition and lust of conquest. The people of the electorate of Hanover had done no wrong to him or to his country. When his son came to an age capable of understanding the irreparable loss that he had suffered, and to reflect upon the causes of his father's fate, there was no drop of consolation mingled in the cup from the consideration that he had died for his country. And when the youthful mind was awakened to meditation upon the rights of mankind,

In entering upon the threshold of life, a career was to open before him. He had the option of the court and the camp. An office was tendered to him in the household of the King's brother, the Count de Provence, since successively a royal exile and a reinstated king. The servitude and inaction of a court had no charms for him; he preferred a commission in the army, and, at the time of the Declaration of Independence, was a captain of dragoons in garrison at Metz.

There, at an entertainment given by his relative, the Marechal de Broglie, the commandant of the place, to the Duke of Gloucester, brother to the British king, and then a transient traveler through that part of France, he learns, as an incident of intelligence received that morning by the English Prince from London, that the congress of rebels at Philadelphia had issued a Declaration of Independence. A conversation ensues upon the causes which have contributed to produce this event, and upon the consequences which may be expected to flow from it. The imagination of Lafayette has caught across the Atlantic tide the spark emitted from the Declaration of Independence; his heart has kindled at the shock, and, before he slumbers upon his pillow, he has resolved to devote his life and fortune to the cause.

You have before you the cause and the man. The self-devotion of Lafayette was twofold. First to the people, maintaining a bold and seemingly desperate struggle against oppression, and for national existence. Secondly, and chiefly, to the principles of their declaration, which then first unfurled before his eyes the consecrated standard of human rights. To that standard, without an instant of hesitation, he repaired. Where it would lead him, it is scarcely probable that he himself then foresaw. It was then identical with the Stars and Stripes of the American Union, floating to the breeze from the Hall of Independence, at Philadelphia. Nor sordid avarice, nor vulgar ambition, could point his footsteps to the pathway leading to that banner. To the love of ease or pleasure nothing could be more repulsive. Something may be allowed to the beatings of the youthful breast, which make ambition virtue, and something to the spirit of military adventure, imbibed from his profession, and which he felt in common with many others. France, Germany, Poland, furnished to the armies of this Union, in our revolutionary struggle, no inconsiderable number of officers of high rank and distinguished merit. The names of Pulaski and De Kalb are numbered among

I—6

the principles of freedom, and theories of government, it cannot be difficult to perceive in the illustrations of his own family records the source of that aversion to hereditary rule, perhaps the most distinguishing feature of his own political opinions, and to which he adhered through all the vicissitudes of his life. . . .

Lafayette was born a subject of the most absolute and most splendid monarchy of Europe, and in the highest rank of her proud and chivalrous nobility. He had been educated at a college of the University of Paris, founded by the royal munificence of Louis XIV., or Cardinal Richelieu. Left an orphan in early childhood, with the inheritance of a princely fortune, he had been married, at sixteen years of age, to a daughter of the house of Noailles, the most distinguished family of the kingdom, scarcely deemed in public consideration inferior to that which wore the crown. He came into active life, at the change from boy to man, a husband and a father, in the full enjoyment of everything that avarice could covet, with a certain prospect before him of all that ambition could crave. Happy in his domestic affections, incapable, from the benignity of his nature, of envy, hatred, or revenge, a life of "ignoble ease and indolent repose" seemed to be that which nature and fortune had combined to prepare before him. To men of ordinary mold this condition would have led to a life of luxurious apathy and sensual indulgence. Such was the life into which, from the operation of the same causes, Louis XV. had sunk, with his household and court, while Lafayette was rising to manhood surrounded by the contamination of their example. Had his natural endowments been even of the higher and nobler order of such as adhere to virtue, even in the lap of prosperity, and in the bosom of temptation, he might have lived and died a pattern of the nobility of France, to be classed, in aftertimes, with the Turennes and the Montausiers of the age of Louis XIV., or with the Villars or the Lamoignons of the age immediately preceding his own.

But as, in the firmament of heaven that rolls over our heads, there is, among the stars of the first magnitude, one so pre-eminent in splendor as, in the opinion of astronomers, to constitute a class by itself, so in the fourteen hundred years of the French monarchy, among the multitudes of great and mighty men which it has evolved, the name of Lafayette stands unrivaled in the solitude of glory.

the martyrs of our freedom, and their ashes repose in our soil side by side with the canonized bones of Warren and of Montgomery. To the virtues of Lafayette, a more protracted career and happier earthly destinies were reserved. To the moral principle of political action, the sacrifices of no other man were comparable to his. Youth, health, fortune; the favor of his king; the enjoyment of ease and pleasure; even the choicest blessings of domestic felicity—he gave them all for toil and danger in a distant land, and an almost hopeless cause; but it was the cause of justice, and of the rights of human kind. . . .

Pronounce him one of the first men of his age, and you have not yet done him justice. Try him by that test to which he sought in vain to stimulate the vulgar and selfish spirit of Napoleon; class him among the men who, to compare and seat themselves, must take in the compass of all ages; turn back your eyes upon the records of time, summon from the creation of the world to this day the mighty dead of every age and every clime —and where, among the race of merely mortal men, shall one be found, who, as the benefactor of his kind, shall claim to take precedence of Lafayette?

There have doubtless been, in all ages, men whose discoveries or inventions, in the world of matter or of mind, have opened new avenues to the dominion of man over the material creation; have increased his means or his faculties of enjoyment; have raised him in nearer approximation to that higher and happier condition, the object of his hopes and aspirations in his present state of existence.

Lafayette discovered no new principle of politics or of morals. He invented nothing in science. He disclosed no new phenomenon in the laws of nature. Born and educated in the highest order of feudal nobility, under the most absolute monarchy of Europe, in possession of an affluent fortune, and master of himself and of all his capabilities, at the moment of attaining manhood the principle of republican justice and of social equality took possession of his heart and mind, as if by inspiration from above. He devoted himself, his life, his fortune, his hereditary honors, his towering ambition, his splendid hopes, all to the cause of liberty. He came to another hemisphere to defend her. He became one of the most effective champions of our independence; but, that once achieved, he returned to his own country, and thenceforward took no part in the controversies which have divided us. In the events of our revolution, and in the forms of policy which we have adopted for the establishment and perpetuation of our freedom, Lafayette found the most perfect form of government. He wished to add nothing to it. He would gladly have abstracted nothing from it. Instead of the imaginary republic of Plato, or the Utopia of Sir Thomas Moore, he took a practical existing model, in actual operation here, and never attempted or wished more than to apply it faithfully to his own country.

It was not given to Moses to enter the promised land; but he saw it from the summit of Pisgah. It was not given to Lafayette to witness the consummation of his wishes in the establishment of a republic and the extinction of all hereditary rule in France. His principles were in advance of the age and hemisphere in which he lived. A Bourbon still reigns on the throne of France, and it is not for us to scrutinize the title by which he reigns. The principles of elective and hereditary power, blended in reluctant union in his person, like the red and white roses of York and Lancaster, may postpone to aftertime the last conflict to which they must ultimately come. The life of the patriarch was not long enough for the development of his whole political system. Its final accomplishment is in the womb of time.

The anticipation of this event is the more certain, from the consideration that all the principles for which Lafayette contended were practical. He never indulged himself in wild and fanciful speculations. The principle of hereditary power was, in his opinion, the bane of all republican liberty in Europe. Unable to extinguish it in the Revolution of 1830, so far as concerned the chief magistracy of the nation, Lafayette had the satisfaction of seeing it abolished with reference to the peerage. An hereditary crown, stript of the support which it may derive from an hereditary peerage, however compatible with Asiatic despotism, is an anomaly in the history of the Christian world, and in the theory of free government. There is no argument producible against the existence of an hereditary peerage but applies with aggravated weight against the transmission, from sire to soh, of an hereditary crown. The prejudices and passions of the people of France rejected the principle of inherited power, in every station of public trust, excepting the first and highest of them all;

but there they clung to it, as did the Israelites of old to the savory deities of Egypt.

This is not the time nor the place for a disquisition upon the comparative merits, as a system of government, of a republic, and a monarchy surrounded by republican institutions. Upon this subject there is among us no diversity of opinion; and if it should take the people of France another half century of internal and external war, of dazzling and delusive glories; of unparalleled triumphs, humiliating reverses, and bitter disappointments, to settle it to their satisfaction, the ultimate result can only bring them to the point where we have stood from the day of the Declaration of Independence—to the point where Lafayette would have brought them, and to which he looked as a consummation devoutly to be wished.

Then, too, and then only, will be the time when the character of Lafayette will be appreciated at its true value throughout the civilized world. When the principle of hereditary dominion shall be extinguished in all the institutions of France; when government shall no longer be considered as property transmissible from sire to son, but as a trust committed for a limited time, and then to return to the people whence it came; as a burdensome duty to be discharged, and not as a reward to be abused; when a claim, any claim, to political power by inheritance shall, in the estimation of the whole French people, be held as it now is by the whole people of the North American Union—then will be the time for contemplating the character of Lafayette, not merely in the events of his life, but in the full development of his intellectual conceptions, of his fervent aspirations, of the labors and perils and sacrifices of his long and eventful career upon earth; and thenceforward, till the hour when the trump of the Archangel shall sound to announce that Time shall be no more, the name of Lafayette shall stand enrolled upon the annals of our race, high on the list of the pure and disinterested benefactors of mankind.

THE JUBILEE OF THE CONSTITUTION

(Delivered at New York, April 30th, 1839)

Fellow-Citizens and Brethren, Associates of the New York Historical Society:—

WOULD it be an unlicensed trespass of the imagination to conceive that on the night preceding the day of which you now commemorate the fiftieth anniversary—on the night preceding that thirtieth of April, 1789, when from the balcony of your city hall the chancellor of the State of New York administered to George Washington the solemn oath faithfully to execute the office of President of the United States, and to the best of his ability to preserve, protect, and defend the Constitution of the United States—that in the visions of the night the guardian angel of the Father of our country had appeared before him, in the venerated form of his mother, and, to cheer and encourage him in the performance of the momentous and solemn duties that he was about to assume, had delivered to him a suit of celestial armor—a helmet, consisting of the principles of piety, of justice, of honor, of benevolence, with which from his earliest infancy he had hitherto walked through life, in the presence of all his brethren; a spear, studded with the self-evident truths of the Declaration of Independence; a sword, the same with which he had led the armies of his country through the war of freedom to the summit of the triumphal arch of independence; a corslet and cuishes of long experience and habitual intercourse in peace and war with the world of mankind, his contemporaries of the human race, in all their stages of civilization; and, last of all, the Constitution of the United States, a shield, embossed by heavenly hands with the future history of his country.

Yes, gentlemen, on that shield the Constitution of the United States was sculptured (by forms unseen, and in characters then invisible to mortal eye), the predestined and prophetic history of the one confederated people of the North American Union.

They had been the settlers of thirteen separate and distinct English colonies, along the margin of the shore of the North American continent; contiguously situated, but chartered by adventurers of characters variously diversified, including sectarians, religious and political, of all the classes which for the two preceding centuries had agitated and divided the people of the

British islands—and with them were intermingled the descendants of Hollanders, Swedes, Germans, and French fugitives from the persecution of the revoker of the Edict of Nantes.

In the bosoms of this people, thus heterogeneously composed, there was burning, kindled at different furnaces, but all furnaces of affliction, one clear, steady flame of liberty. Bold and daring enterprise, stubborn endurance of privation, unflinching intrepidity in facing danger, and inflexible adherence to conscientious principle, had steeled to energetic and unyielding hardihood the characters of the primitive settlers of all these colonies. Since that time two or three generations of men had passed away, but they had increased and multiplied with unexampled rapidity; and the land itself had been the recent theatre of a ferocious and bloody seven-years' war between the two most powerful and most civilized nations of Europe contending for the possession of this continent.

Of that strife the victorious combatant had been Britain. She had conquered the provinces of France. She had expelled her rival totally from the continent, over which, bounding herself by the Mississippi, she was thenceforth to hold divided empire only with Spain. She had acquired undisputed control over the Indian tribes still tenanting the forests unexplored by the European man. She had established an uncontested monopoly of the commerce of all her colonies. But forgetting all the warnings of preceding ages—forgetting the lessons written in the blood of her own children, through centuries of departed time, she undertook to tax the people of the colonies without their consent.

Resistance, instantaneous, unconcerted, sympathetic, inflexible resistance, like an electric shock, startled and roused the people of all the English colonies on this continent.

This was the first signal of the North American Union. The struggle was for chartered rights—for English liberties—for the cause of Algernon Sidney and John Hampden—for trial by jury —the Habeas Corpus and Magna Charta.

But the English lawyers had decided that Parliament was omnipotent—and Parliament, in its omnipotence, instead of trial by jury and the Habeas Corpus, enacted admiralty courts in England to try Americans for offenses charged against them as committed in America; instead of the privileges of Magna Charta, nullified the charter itself of Massachusetts Bay; shut up the port of Boston; sent armies and navies to keep the peace and teach the colonies that John Hampden was a rebel and Algernon Sidney a traitor.

English liberties had failed them. From the omnipotence of Parliament the Colonists appealed to the rights of man and the omnipotence of the God of battles. Union! Union! was the instinctive and simultaneous cry throughout the land. Their congress, assembled at Philadelphia, once — twice — had petitioned the king; had remonstrated to Parliament; had addressed the people of Britain, for the rights of Englishmen — in vain. Fleets and armies, the blood of Lexington, and the fires of Charlestown and Falmouth, had been the answer to petition, remonstrance, and address. . . .

The dissolution of allegiance to the British crown, the severance of the colonies from the British empire, and their actual existence as independent States, were definitively established in fact, by war and peace. The independence of each separate State had never been declared of right. It never existed in fact. Upon the principles of the Declaration of Independence, the dissolution of the ties of allegiance, the assumption of sovereign power, and the institution of civil government, are all acts of transcendent authority, which the people alone are competent to perform; and, accordingly, it is in the name and by the authority of the people, that two of these acts — the dissolution of allegiance, with the severance from the British empire, and the declaration of the United Colonies, as free and independent States, were performed by that instrument.

But there still remained the last and crowning act, which the people of the Union alone were competent to perform — the institution of civil government, for that compound nation, the United States of America.

At this day it cannot but strike us as extraordinary, that it does not appear to have occurred to any one member of that assembly, which had laid down in terms so clear, so explicit, so unequivocal, the foundation of all just government, in the imprescriptible rights of man, and the transcendent sovereignty of the people, and who in those principles had set forth their only personal vindication from the charges of rebellion against their king, and of treason to their country, that their last crowning act was still to be performed upon the same principles. That is, the institution, by the people of the United States, of a civil government, to guard and protect and defend them all. On the

contrary, that same assembly which issued the Declaration of Independence, instead of continuing to act in the name and by the authority of the good people of the United States, had, immediately after the appointment of the committee to prepare the Declaration, appointed another committee, of one member from each colony, to prepare and digest the form of confederation to be entered into between the colonies.

That committee reported on the twelfth of July, eight days after the Declaration of Independence had been issued, a draft of articles of confederation between the colonies. This draft was prepared by John Dickinson, then a delegate from Pennsylvania, who voted against the Declaration of Independence, and never signed it, having been superseded by a new election of delegates from that State, eight days after his draft was reported.

There was thus no congeniality of principle between the Declaration of Independence and the articles of confederation. The foundation of the former was a superintending Providence — the rights of man, and the constituent revolutionary power of the people. That of the latter was the sovereignty of organized power, and the independence of the separate or dis-united States. The fabric of the Declaration and that of the confederation were each consistent with its own foundation, but they could not form one consistent, symmetrical edifice. They were the productions of different minds and of adverse passions; one, ascending for the foundation of human government to the laws of nature and of God, written upon the heart of man; the other, resting upon the basis of human institutions, and prescriptive law, and colonial charter. The corner stone of the one was right, that of the other was power. . . .

Where, then, did each State get the sovereignty, freedom, and independence, which the articles of confederation declare it retains? — not from the whole people of the whole Union — not from the Declaration of Independence — not from the people of the State itself. It was assumed by agreement between the legislatures of the several States, and their delegates in Congress, without authority from or consultation of the people at all.

In the Declaration of Independence, the enacting and constituent party dispensing and delegating sovereign power is the whole people of the United Colonies. The recipient party, invested with power, is the United Colonies, declared United States.

In the articles of confederation, this order of agency is inverted. Each State is the constituent and enacting party, and the United States in Congress assembled the recipient of delegated power — and that power delegated with such a penurious and carking hand that it had more the aspect of a revocation of the Declaration of Independence than an instrument to carry it into effect.

None of these indispensably necessary powers were ever conferred by the State legislatures upon the Congress of the federation; and well was it that they never were. The system itself was radically defective. Its incurable disease was an apostasy from the principles of the Declaration of Independence. A substitution of separate State sovereignties, in the place of the constituent sovereignty of the people, was the basis of the Confederate Union.

In the Congress of the confederation, the master minds of James Madison and Alexander Hamilton were constantly engaged through the closing years of the Revolutionary War and those of peace which immediately succeeded. That of John Jay was associated with them shortly after the peace, in the capacity of secretary to the Congress for foreign affairs. The incompetency of the articles of confederation for the management of the affairs of the Union at home and abroad was demonstrated to them by the painful and mortifying experience of every day. Washington, though in retirement, was brooding over the cruel injustice suffered by his associates in arms, the warriors of the Revolution; over the prostration of the public credit and the faith of the nation, in the neglect to provide for the payment even of the interest upon the public debt; over the disappointed hopes of the friends of freedom; in the language of the address from Congress to the States of the eighteenth of April, 1783 — "the pride and boast of America, that the rights for which she contended were the rights of human nature."

At his residence at Mount Vernon, in March 1785, the first idea was started of a revisal of the articles of confederation, by an organization, of means differing from that of a compact between the State legislatures and their own delegates in Congress. A convention of delegates from the State legislatures, independent of the Congress itself, was the expedient which presented itself for effecting the purpose, and an augmentation of the powers of Congress for the regulation of commerce, as the

object for which this assembly was to be convened. In January 1786 the proposal was made and adopted in the legislature of Virginia, and communicated to the other State legislatures.

The convention was held at Annapolis, in September of that year. It was attended by delegates from only five of the central States, who, on comparing their restricted powers with the glaring and universally acknowledged defects of the confederation, reported only a recommendation for the assemblage of another convention of delegates to meet at Philadelphia, in May 1787, from all the States, and with enlarged powers.

The Constitution of the United States was the work of this convention. But in its construction the convention immediately perceived that they must retrace their steps, and fall back from a league of friendship between sovereign States to the constituent sovereignty of the people; from power to right — from the irresponsible despotism of State sovereignty to the self-evident truths of the Declaration of Independence. In that instrument, the right to institute and to alter governments among men was ascribed exclusively to the people — the ends of government were declared to be to secure the natural rights of man; and that when the government degenerates from the promotion to the destruction of that end, the right and the duty accrues to the people to dissolve this degenerate government and to institute another. The signers of the Declaration further averred, that the one people of the United Colonies were then precisely in that situation — with a government degenerated into tyranny, and called upon by the laws of nature and of nature's God to dissolve that government and to institute another. Then, in the name and by the authority of the good people of the colonies, they pronounced the dissolution of their allegiance to the king, and their eternal separation from the nation of Great Britain — and declared the United Colonies independent States. And here as the representatives of the one people they had stopped. They did not require the confirmation of this act, for the power to make the declaration had already been conferred upon them by the people, delegating the power, indeed, separately in the separate colonies, not by colonial authority, but by the spontaneous revolutionary movement of the people in them all.

From the day of that Declaration, the constituent power of the people had never been called into action. A confederacy had been substituted in the place of a government.

sovereignty had usurped the constituent sovereignty of the people.

The convention assembled at Philadelphia had themselves no direct authority from the people. Their authority was all derived from the State legislatures. But they had the articles of confederation before them, and they saw and felt the wretched condition into which they had brought the whole people, and that the Union itself was in the agonies of death. They soon perceived that the indispensably needed powers were such as no State government, no combination of them, was by the principles of the Declaration of Independence competent to bestow. They could emanate only from the people. A highly respectable portion of the assembly, still clinging to the confederacy of States, proposed, as a substitute for the Constitution, a mere revival of the articles of confederation, with a grant of additional powers to the Congress. Their plan was respectfully and thoroughly discussed, but the want of a government and of the sanction of the people to the delegation of powers happily prevailed. A constitution for the people, and the distribution of legislative, executive, and judicial powers was prepared. It announced itself as the work of the people themselves; and as this was unquestionably a power assumed by the convention, not delegated to them by the people, they religiously confined it to a simple power to propose, and carefully provided that it should be no more than a proposal until sanctioned by the confederation Congress, by the State legislatures, and by the people of the several States, in conventions specially assembled, by authority of their legislatures, for the single purpose of examining and passing upon it.

And thus was consummated the work commenced by the Declaration of Independence — a work in which the people of the North American Union, acting under the deepest sense of responsibility to the Supreme Ruler of the universe, had achieved the most transcendent act of power that social man in his mortal condition can perform — even that of dissolving the ties of allegiance by which he is bound to his country; of renouncing that country itself; of demolishing its government; of instituting another government; and of making for himself another country in its stead.

And on that day, of which you now commemorate the fiftieth anniversary, — on that thirtieth day of April, 1789, — was this mighty revolution, not only in the affairs of our own country,

but in the principles of government over civilized man, accomplished.

The revolution itself was a work of thirteen years — and had never been completed until that day. The Declaration of Independence and the Constitution of the United States are parts of one consistent whole, founded upon one and the same theory of government, then new in practice, though not as a theory, for it had been working itself into the mind of man for many ages, and had been especially expounded in the writings of Locke, though it had never before been adopted by a great nation in practice.

There are yet, even at this day, many speculative objections to this theory. Even in our own country, there are still philosophers who deny the principles asserted in the Declaration, as self-evident truths — who deny the natural equality and inalienable rights of man — who deny that the people are the only legitimate source of power — who deny that all just powers of government are derived from the consent of the governed. Neither your time, nor perphaps the cheerful nature of this occasion, permit me here to enter upon the examination of this anti-revolutionary theory, which arrays State sovereignty against the constituent sovereignty of the people, and distorts the Constitution of the United States into a league of friendship between confederate corporations. I speak to matters of fact. There is the Declaration of Independence, and there is the Constitution of the United States — let them speak for themselves. The grossly immoral and dishonest doctrine of despotic State sovereignty, the exclusive judge of its own obligations, and responsible to no power on earth or in heaven, for the violation of them, is not there. The Declaration says, it is not in me. The Constitution says, it is not in me.

SAMUEL ADAMS

(1722–1803)

SAMUEL ADAMS, called by his contemporaries, "the Father of the American Revolution," drew up in 1764 the instructions of the people of Boston to their representatives in the Massachusetts general assembly, containing what is said to be the first official denial of the right of the British Parliament to tax the Colonists.

Deeply religious by nature, having what Everett calls "a most angelic voice," studying sacred music as an avocation, and exhibiting through life the fineness of nerve and sensitiveness of temperament which gave him his early disposition to escape the storms of life by a career in the pulpit, circumstances, or rather his sense of fitness, dominating his physical weakness, imposed on him the work of leading in what results have shown to be the greatest revolution of history. So sensitive, physically, that he had "a tremulous motion of the head when speaking," his intellectual force was such that he easily became a leader of popular opposition to royal authority in New England. Unlike Jefferson in being a fluent public speaker, he resembled him in being the intellectual heir of Sidney and Locke. He showed very early in life the bent which afterwards forced him, as it did the naturally timid and retiring Jefferson, to take the leadership of the uneducated masses of the people against the wealth, the culture, and the conservatism of the colonial aristocracy.

After passing through the Lovell School he graduated at Harvard College, and on proposing a thesis for his second degree, as college custom required, he defended the proposition that "it is lawful to resist the supreme authority, if the commonwealth cannot otherwise be preserved." Like questions had been debated during the Middle Ages from the time returning Crusaders brought back with them copies of Aristotle and other great Greek philosophers whose authority was still reverenced at Byzantium and Bagdad when London and Paris knew nothing of them. Out of the denial of one set of schoolmen that a divine right to rule, greater than that derived from the people, could exist in kings, grew the political controversy which preceded the English revolution against the Stuarts. Our revolution grew out of the English as the French grew out of ours, and in putting on his seal Cromwell's motto, "Rebellion to tyrants is obedience to God," Jefferson, the Virginian, illustrated the same intellectual

heredity which Samuel Adams, the New Englander, showed in asserting the right of the people composing the Commonwealth to resist the supreme authority when in their judgment its exercise had become prejudicial to their rights or their interests.

From 1764 when he was chosen to present the denial made by the people of Boston of the English Parliament's right to tax them, until he joined Jefferson in forcing on the then unprepared mind of the public the idea of a complete and final separation from the "Mother Country," his aggressive denunciations of the English government's attempts at absolutism made him so hated by the English administration and its colonial representatives that, with John Hancock, he was specially exempted from General Gage's amnesty proclamation of June 1775, as "having committed offenses of too flagitious a nature to admit of any other consideration than that of condign punishment."

Joining with John Adams, Franklin, and Jefferson in forcing issues for complete separation from England and for the formal Declaration of Independence, Samuel Adams was himself the author of the celebrated circular letter addressed by the assembly of Massachusetts to the speakers of the several assemblies in other colonies. In 1774 he was chosen a member of the Continental Congress, where he took a prominent part in preventing the possibility of compromise with England. In 1794 he succeeded Hancock as governor of Massachusetts, retiring in 1797 because of "the increasing infirmities of age."

Like many other statesmen of his time he lived the greater part of his life in poverty, but his only son, dying before him, left him a property which supported him in his old age.

It is said that his great oration on American Independence, delivered at Philadelphia in August 1776, and published here, is the only complete address of his which has come down to us. It was translated into French and published in Paris, and it is believed that Napoleon borrowed from it the phrase, "A Nation of Shopkeepers," to characterize the English.

AMERICAN INDEPENDENCE

Countrymen and Brethren:—

I WOULD gladly have declined an honor to which I find myself unequal. I have not the calmness and impartiality which the infinite importance of this occasion demands. I will not deny the charge of my enemies, that resentment for the accumulated injuries of our country, and an ardor for her glory, rising to enthusiasm, may deprive me of that accuracy of judgment and expression which men of cooler passions may possess. Let me beseech you, then, to hear me with caution, to examine your prejudice, and to correct the mistakes into which I may be hurried by my zeal.

Truth loves an appeal to the common sense of mankind. Your unperverted understandings can best determine on subjects of a practical nature. The positions and plans which are said to be above the comprehension of the multitude may be always suspected to be visionary and fruitless. He who made all men hath made the truths necessary to human happiness obvious to all.

Our forefathers threw off the yoke of Popery in religion; for you is reserved the honor of leveling the popery of politics. They opened the Bible to all, and maintained the capacity of every man to judge for himself in religion. Are we sufficient for the comprehension of the sublimest spiritual truths, and unequal to material and temporal ones?

Heaven hath trusted us with the management of things for eternity, and man denies us ability to judge of the present, or to know from our feelings the experience that will make us happy. "You can discern," they say, objects distant and remote, but cannot perceive those within your grasp. Let us have the distribution of present goods, and cut out and manage as you please the interests of futurity." This day, I trust, the reign of political protestantism will commence. We have explored the temple of royalty, and found that the idol we have bowed down to has eyes which see not, ears that hear not our prayers, and a heart like the nether millstone. We have this day restored the Sovereign to whom alone men ought to be obedient. He reigns in Heaven, and with a propitious eye beholds his subjects assuming that freedom of thought and dignity of self-direction which he bestowed on them. From the rising to the setting sun, may his kingdom come!

Having been a slave to the influence of opinion early acquired, and distinctions generally received, I am ever inclined not to despise but pity those who are yet in darkness. But to the eye of reason what can be more clear than that all men have an equal right to happiness? Nature made no other distinction than that of higher and lower degrees of power of mind and body. But what mysterious distribution of character has the craft of statesmen, more fatal than priestcraft, introduced?

According to their doctrine, the offspring of perhaps the lewd embraces of a successful invader shall, from generation to generation, arrogate the right of lavishing on their pleasures a proportion of the fruits of the earth, more than sufficient to supply the wants of thousands of their fellow-creatures; claim authority to manage them like beasts of burthen, and, without superior industry, capacity, or virtue, nay, though disgraceful to humanity, by their ignorance, intemperance, and brutality, shall be deemed best calculated to frame laws and to consult for the welfare of society.

Were the talents and virtues which heaven has bestowed on men given merely to make them more obedient drudges, to be sacrificed to the follies and ambition of a few? Or, were not the noble gifts so equally dispensed with a divine purpose and law, that they should as nearly as possible be equally exerted, and the blessings of Providence be equally enjoyed by all? Away, then, with those absurd systems which to gratify the pride of a few debase the greater part of our species below the order of men. What an affront to the King of the universe, to maintain that the happiness of a monster, sunk in debauchery and spreading desolation and murder among men, of a Caligula, a Nero, or a Charles, is more precious in his sight than that of millions of his suppliant creatures, who do justice, love mercy, and walk humbly with their God! No, in the judgment of heaven there is no other superiority among men than a superiority in wisdom and virtue. And can we have a safer model in forming ours? The Deity, then, has not given any order or family of men authority over others; and if any men have given it, they only could give it for themselves. Our forefathers, 'tis said, consented to be subject to the laws of Great Britain. I will not, at present, dispute it, nor mark out the limits and conditions of their submission; but will it be denied that they contracted to pay obedience and to be under the control of Great Britain because it appeared to them most beneficial in their then present circumstances and situations? We, my countrymen, have the same right to consult and provide for our happiness which they had to promote theirs. If they had a view to posterity in their contracts, it must have been to advance the felicity of their descendants. If they erred in their expectations and prospects, we can never be condemned for a conduct which they would have recommended had they foreseen our present condition.

Ye darkeners of counsel, who would make the property, lives, and religion of millions depend on the evasive interpretations of musty parchments; who would send us to antiquated charters of uncertain and contradictory meaning, to prove that the present generation are not bound to be victims to cruel and unforgiving despotism, tell us whether our pious and generous ancestors bequeathed to us the miserable privilege of having the rewards of our honesty, industry, the fruits of those fields which they purchased and bled for, wrested from us at the will of men over whom we have no check. Did they contract for us that, with folded arms, we should expect that justice and mercy from brutal and inflamed invaders which have been denied to our supplications at the foot of the throne? Were we to hear our character as a people ridiculed with indifference? Did they promise for us that our meekness and patience should be insulted; our coasts harassed, our towns demolished and plundered, and our wives and offspring exposed to nakedness, hunger, and death, without our feeling the resentment of men, and exerting those powers of self-preservation which God has given us? No man had once a greater veneration for Englishmen than I entertained. They were dear to me as branches of the same parental trunk, and partakers of the same religion and laws; I still view with respect the remains of the constitution as I would a lifeless body, which had once been animated by a great and heroic soul. But when I am aroused by the din of arms; when I behold legions of foreign assassins, paid by Englishmen to imbrue their hands in our blood; when I tread over the uncoffined bodies of my countrymen, neighbors, and friends; when I see the locks of a venerable father torn by savage hands, and a feeble mother, clasping her infants to her bosom, and on her knees imploring their lives from her own slaves, whom Englishmen have allured to treachery and murder; when I behold my country, once the seat of industry, peace, and plenty, changed by Englishmen to a theatre of blood and misery, Heaven forgive me, if I cannot root out those passions which it has implanted in my bosom, and detest submission to a people who have either ceased to be human, or have not virtue enough to feel their own wretchedness and servitude!

Men who content themselves with the semblance of truth, and a display of words, talk much of our obligations to Great Britain for protection. Had she a single eye to our advantage?

A nation of shopkeepers are very seldom so disinterested. Let us not be so amused with words; the extension of her commerce was her object. When she defended our coasts, she fought for her customers, and convoyed our ships loaded with wealth, which we had acquired for her by our industry. She has treated us as beasts of burthen, whom the lordly masters cherish that they may carry a greater load. Let us inquire also against whom she has protected us? Against her own enemies with whom we had no quarrel, or only on her account, and against whom we always readily exerted our wealth and strength when they were required. Were these colonies backward in giving assistance to Great Britain, when they were called upon in 1739 to aid the expedition against Carthagena? They at that time sent three thousand men to join the British army, although the war commenced without their consent. But the last war, 'tis said, was purely American. This is a vulgar error, which, like many others, has gained credit by being confidently repeated. The dispute between the courts of Great Britain and France related to the limits of Canada and Nova Scotia. The controverted territory was not claimed by any in the colonies, but by the crown of Great Britain. It was therefore their own quarrel. The infringement of a right which England had, by the treaty of Utrecht, of trading in the Indian country of Ohio, was another cause of the war. The French seized large quantities of British manufacture and took possession of a fort which a company of British merchants and factors had erected for the security of their commerce. The war was therefore waged in defense of lands claimed by the crown, and for the protection of British property. The French at that time had no quarrel with America, and, as appears by letters sent from their commander-in-chief, to some of the colonies, wished to remain in peace with us. The part, therefore, which we then took, and the miseries to which we exposed ourselves, ought to be charged to our affection to Britain. These colonies granted more than their proportion to the support of the war. They raised, clothed, and maintained nearly twenty-five thousand men, and so sensible were the people of England of our great exertions, that a message was annually sent to the House of Commons purporting, "that his Majesty, being highly satisfied with the zeal and vigor with which his faithful subjects in North America had exerted themselves in defense of his Majesty's just rights and possessions, recommend it to the House to take the same into consideration, and enable him to give them a proper compensation."

But what purpose can arguments of this kind answer? Did the protection we received annul our rights as men, and lay us under an obligation of being miserable?

Who among you, my countrymen, that is a father, would claim authority to make your child a slave because you had nourished him in infancy?

'Tis a strange species of generosity which requires a return infinitely more valuable than anything it could have bestowed; that demands as a reward for a defense of our property a surrender of those inestimable privileges, to the arbitrary will of vindictive tyrants, which alone give value to that very property.

Political right and public happiness are different words for the same idea. They who wander into metaphysical labyrinths, or have recourse to original contracts, to determine the rights of men, either impose on themselves or mean to delude others. Public utility is the only certain criterion. It is a test which brings disputes to a speedy decision, and makes its appeal to the feelings of mankind. The force of truth has obliged men to use arguments drawn from this principle who were combating it, in practice and speculation. The advocates for a despotic government and nonresistance to the magistrate employ reasons in favor of their systems drawn from a consideration of their tendency to promote public happiness.

The Author of Nature directs all his operations to the production of the greatest good, and has made human virtue to consist in a disposition and conduct which tends to the common felicity of his creatures. An abridgement of the natural freedom of men, by the institutions of political societies, is vindicable only on this foot. How absurd, then, is it to draw arguments from the nature of civil society for the annihilation of those very ends which society was intended to procure! Men associate for their mutual advantage. Hence, the good and happiness of the members, that is, the majority of the members, of any State, is the great standard by which everything relating to that State must finally be determined; and though it may be supposed that a body of people may be bound by a voluntary resignation (which they have been so infatuated as to make) of all their interests to a

single person, or to a few, it can never be conceived that the resignation is obligatory to their posterity; because it is manifestly contrary to the good of the whole that it should be so.

These are the sentiments of the wisest and most virtuous champions of freedom. Attend to a portion on this subject from a book in our own defense, written, I had almost said, by the pen of inspiration. "I lay no stress," says he, "on charters; they derive their rights from a higher source. It is inconsistent with common sense to imagine that any people would ever think of settling in a distant country on any such condition, or that the people from whom they withdrew should forever be masters of their property, and have power to subject them to any modes of government they pleased. And had there been expressed stipulations to this purpose in all the charters of the colonies, they would, in my opinion, be no more bound by them, than if it had been stipulated with them that they should go naked, or expose themselves to the incursions of wolves and tigers."

Such are the opinions of every virtuous and enlightened patriot in Great Britain. Their petition to heaven is, "That there may be one free country left upon earth, to which they may fly, when venality, luxury, and vice shall have completed the ruin of liberty there."

Courage, then, my countrymen, our contest is not only whether we ourselves shall be free, but whether there shall be left to mankind an asylum on earth for civil and religious liberty. Dismissing, therefore, the justice of our cause, as incontestable, the only question is, What is best for us to pursue in our present circumstances?

The doctrine of dependence on Great Britain is, I believe, generally exploded; but as I would attend to the honest weakness of the simplest of men, you will pardon me if I offer a few words on that subject.

We are now on this continent, to the astonishment of the world, three millions of souls united in one cause. We have large armies, well disciplined and appointed, with commanders inferior to none in military skill, and superior in activity and zeal. We are furnished with arsenals and stores beyond our most sanguine expectations, and foreign nations are waiting to crown our success by their alliances. There are instances of, I would say, an almost astonishing Providence in our favor; our

success has staggered our enemies, and almost given faith to infidels; so we may truly say it is not our own arm which has saved us.

The hand of heaven appears to have led us on to be, perhaps, humble instruments and means in the great Providential dispensation which is completing. We have fled from the political Sodom; let us not look back, lest we perish and become a monument of infamy and derision to the world. For can we ever expect more unanimity and a better preparation for defense; more infatuation of counsel among our enemies, and more valor and zeal among ourselves? The same force and resistance which are sufficient to procure us our liberties will secure us a glorious independence and support us in the dignity of free, imperial States. We cannot suppose that our opposition has made a corrupt and dissipated nation more friendly to America, or created in them a greater respect for the rights of mankind. We can therefore expect a restoration and establishment of our privileges, and a compensation for the injuries we have received from their want of power, from their fears, and not from their virtues. The unanimity and valor which will effect an honorable peace can render a future contest for our liberties unnecessary. He who has strength to chain down the wolf is a madman if he let him loose without drawing his teeth and paring his nails.

From the day on which an accommodation takes place between England and America, on any other terms than as independent States, I shall date the ruin of this country. A politic minister will study to lull us into security, by granting us the full extent of our petitions. The warm sunshine of influence would melt down the virtue, which the violence of the storm rendered more firm and unyielding. In a state of tranquillity, wealth, and luxury, our descendants would forget the arts of war and the noble activity and zeal which made their ancestors invincible. Every art of corruption would be employed to loosen the bond of union which renders our resistance formidable. When the spirit of liberty which now animates our hearts and gives success to our arms is extinct, our numbers will accelerate our ruin and render us easier victims to tyranny. Ye abandoned minions of an infatuated ministry, if peradventure any should yet remain among us, remember that a Warren and Montgomery are numbered among the dead. Contemplate the mangled bodies of your countrymen, and then say, What should be the reward of

such sacrifices? Bid us and our posterity bow the knee, supplicate the friendship, and plough, and sow, and reap, to glut the avarice of the men who have let loose on us the dogs of war to riot in our blood and hunt us from the face of the earth? If ye love wealth better than liberty, the tranquillity of servitude than the animating contest of freedom,—go from us in peace. We ask not your counsels or arms. Crouch down and lick the hands which feed you. May your chains sit lightly upon you, and may posterity forget that ye were our countrymen!

To unite the supremacy of Great Britain and the liberty of America is utterly impossible. So vast a continent, and of such a distance from the seat of empire, will every day grow more unmanageable. The motion of so unwieldy a body cannot be directed with any dispatch and uniformity without committing to the Parliament of Great Britain powers inconsistent with our freedom. The authority and force which would be absolutely necessary for the preservation of the peace and good order of this continent would put all our valuable rights within the reach of that nation.

As the administration of government requires firmer and more numerous supports in proportion to its extent, the burdens imposed on us would be excessive, and we should have the melancholy prospect of their increasing on our posterity. The scale of officers, from the rapacious and needy commissioner to the haughty governor, and from the governor, with his hungry train, to perhaps a licentious and prodigal viceroy, must be upheld by you and your children. The fleets and armies which will be employed to silence your murmurs and complaints must be supported by the fruits of your industry.

And yet with all this enlargement of the expense and powers of government, the administration of it at such a distance, and over so extensive a territory, must necessarily fail of putting the laws into vigorous execution, removing private oppressions, and forming plans for the advancement of agriculture and commerce, and preserving the vast empire in any tolerable peace and security. If our posterity retain any spark of patriotism, they can never tamely submit to such burthens. This country will be made the field of bloody contention till it gain that independence for which nature formed it. It is, therefore, injustice and cruelty to our offspring, and would stamp us with the character of baseness and cowardice, to leave the salvation of this country to be worked out by them with accumulated difficulty and danger.

Prejudice, I confess, may warp our judgments. Let us hear the decision of Englishmen on this subject, who cannot be suspected of partiality. "The Americans," they say, "are but little short of half our number. To this number they have grown from a small body of original settlers by a very rapid increase. The probability is that they will go on to increase, and that in fifty or sixty years they will be double our number, and form a mighty empire, consisting of a variety of States, all equal or superior to ourselves in all the arts and accomplishments which give dignity and happiness to human life. In that period will they be still bound to acknowledge that supremacy over them which we now claim? Can there be any person who will assert this, or whose mind does not revolt at the idea of a vast continent holding all that is valuable to it at the discretion of a handful of people on the other side of the Atlantic? But if at that period this would be unreasonable, what makes it otherwise now? Draw the line if you can. But there is still a greater difficulty."

Britain is now, I will suppose, the seat of liberty and virtue, and its legislature consists of a body of able and independent men, who govern with wisdom and justice. The time may come when all will be reversed; when its excellent constitution of government will be subverted; when, pressed by debts and taxes, it will be greedy to draw to itself an increase of revenue from every distant province, in order to ease its own burdens; when the influence of the crown, strengthened by luxury and a universal profligacy of manners, will have tainted every heart, broken down every fence of liberty, and rendered us a nation of tame and contented vassals; when a general election will be nothing but a general auction of boroughs, and when the Parliament, the grand council of the nation, and once the faithful guardian of the State, and a terror to evil ministers, will be degenerated into a body of sycophants, dependent and venal, always ready to confirm any measures, and little more than a public court for registering royal edicts. Such, it is possible, may, some time or other, be the state of Great Britain. What will, at that period, be the duty of the colonies? Will they be still bound to unconditional submission? Must they always continue an appendage to our government and follow it implicitly through every change

that can happen to it? Wretched condition, indeed, of millions of freemen as good as ourselves! Will you say that we now govern equitably, and that there is no danger of such revolution? Would to God that this were true! But you will not always say the same. Who shall judge whether we govern equitably or not? Can you give the colonies any security that such a period will never come? No. THE PERIOD, COUNTRYMEN, IS ALREADY COME! The calamities were at our door. The rod of oppression was raised over us. We were roused from our slumbers, and may we never sink into repose until we can convey a clear and undisputed inheritance to our posterity! This day we are called upon to give a glorious example of what the wisest and best of men were rejoiced to view, only in speculation. This day presents the world with the most august spectacle that its annals ever unfolded,—millions of freemen, deliberately and voluntarily forming themselves into a society for their common defense and common happiness. Immortal spirits of Hampden, Locke, and Sidney, will it not add to your benevolent joys to behold your posterity rising to the dignity of men, and evincing to the world the reality and expediency of your systems, and in the actual enjoyment of that equal liberty, which you were happy, when on earth, in delineating and recommending to mankind?

Other nations have received their laws from conquerors; some are indebted for a constitution to the suffering of their ancestors through revolving centuries. The people of this country, alone, have formally and deliberately chosen a government for themselves, and with open and uninfluenced consent bound themselves into a social compact. Here no man proclaims his birth or wealth as a title to honorable distinction, or to sanctify ignorance and vice with the name of hereditary authority. He who has most zeal and ability to promote public felicity, let him be the servant of the public. This is the only line of distinction drawn by nature. Leave the bird of night to the obscurity for which nature intended him, and expect only from the eagle to brush the clouds with his wings and look boldly in the face of the sun.

Some who would persuade us that they have tender feelings for future generations, while they are insensible to the happiness of the present, are perpetually foreboding a train of dissensions under our popular system. Such men's reasoning amounts to this: Give up all that is valuable to Great Britain and then you will have no inducements to quarrel among yourselves; or, suffer

yourselves to be chained down by your enemies that you may not be able to fight with your friends.

This is an insult on your virtue as well as your common sense. Your unanimity this day and through the course of the war is a decisive refutation of such invidious predictions. Our enemies have already had evidence that our present constitution contains in it the justice and ardor of freedom and the wisdom and vigor of the most absolute system. When the law is the will of the people, it will be uniform and coherent; but fluctuation, contradiction, and inconsistency of councils must be expected under those governments where every revolution in the ministry of a court produces one in the State — such being the folly and pride of all ministers, that they ever pursue measures directly opposite to those of their predecessors.

We shall neither be exposed to the necessary convulsions of elective monarchies, nor to the want of wisdom, fortitude, and virtue, to which hereditary succession is liable. In your hands it will be to perpetuate a prudent, active, and just legislature, and which will never expire until you yourselves loose the virtues which give it existence.

And, brethren and fellow-countrymen, if it was ever granted to mortals to trace the designs of Providence, and interpret its manifestations in favor of their cause, we may, with humility of soul, cry out, "Not unto us, not unto us, but to thy Name be the praise!" The confusion of the devices among our enemies, and the rage of the elements against them, have done almost as much towards our success as either our councils or our arms.

The time at which this attempt on our liberty was made, when we were ripened into maturity, had acquired a knowledge of war, and were free from the incursions of enemies in this country; the gradual advances of our oppressors enabling us to prepare for our defense; the unusual fertility of our lands and clemency of the seasons; the success which at first attended our feeble arms, producing unanimity among our friends and reducing our internal foes to acquiescence — these are all strong and palpable marks and assurances that Providence is yet gracious unto Zion, that it will turn away the captivity of Jacob.

Our glorious reformers when they broke through the fetters of superstition effected more than could be expected from an

age so darkened. But they left much to be done by their posterity. They lopped off, indeed, some of the branches of Popery, but they left the root and stock when they left us under the domination of human systems and decisions, usurping the infallibility which can be attributed to Revelation alone. They dethroned one usurper only to raise up another; they refused allegiance to the Pope only to place the civil magistrate in the throne of Christ, vested with authority to enact laws and inflict penalties in his kingdom. And if we now cast our eyes over the nations of the earth, we shall find that, instead of possessing the pure religion of the Gospel, they may be divided either into infidels, who deny the truth; or politicians who make religion a stalking horse for their ambition; or professors, who walk in the trammels of orthodoxy, and are more attentive to traditions and ordinances of men than to the oracles of truth.

The civil magistrate has everywhere contaminated religion by making it an engine of policy; and freedom of thought and the right of private judgment, in matters of conscience, driven from every other corner of the earth, direct their course to this happy country as their last asylum. Let us cherish the noble guests, and shelter them under the wings of a universal toleration! Be this the seat of unbounded religious freedom. She will bring with her in her train, industry, wisdom, and commerce. She thrives most when left to shoot forth in her natural luxuriance, and asks from human policy only not to be checked in her growth by artificial encouragements.

Thus, by the beneficence of Providence, we shall behold our empire arising, founded on justice and the voluntary consent of the people, and giving full scope to the exercise of those faculties and rights which most ennoble our species. Besides the advantages of liberty and the most equal constitution, Heaven has given us a country with every variety of climate and soil, pouring forth in abundance whatever is necessary for the support, comfort, and strength of a nation. Within our own borders we possess all the means of sustenance, defense, and commerce; at the same time, these advantages are so distributed among the different States of this continent, as if nature had in view to proclaim to us: Be united among yourselves and you will want nothing from the rest of the world.

The more northern States most amply supply us with every necessary, and many of the luxuries of life; with iron, timber, and masts for ships of commerce or of war; with flax for the manufacture of linen, and seed either for oil or exportation.

So abundant are our harvests, that almost every part raises more than double the quantity of grain requisite for the support of the inhabitants. From Georgia and the Carolinas we have, as well for our own wants as for the purpose of supplying the wants of other powers, indigo, rice, hemp, naval stores, and lumber.

Virginia and Maryland teem with wheat, Indian corn, and tobacco. Every nation whose harvest is precarious, or whose lands yield not those commodities which we cultivate, will gladly exchange their superfluities and manufactures for ours.

We have already received many and large cargoes of clothing, military stores, etc., from our commerce with foreign powers, and, in spite of the efforts of the boasted navy of England, we shall continue to profit by this connection.

The want of our naval stores has already increased the price of these articles to a great height, especially in Britain. Without our lumber, it will be impossible for those haughty islanders to convey the products of the West Indies to their own ports; for a while they may with difficulty effect it, but, without our assistance, their resources soon must fail. Indeed, the West India Islands appear as the necessary appendages to this our empire. They must owe their support to it, and ere long, I doubt not, some of them will, from necessity, wish to enjoy the benefit of our protection.

These natural advantages will enable us to remain independent of the world, or make it the interest of European powers to court our alliance, and aid in protecting us against the invasion of others. What argument, therefore, do we want to show the equity of our conduct; or motive of interest to recommend it to our prudence? Nature points out the path, and our enemies have obliged us to pursue it.

If there is any man so base or so weak as to prefer a dependence on Great Britain to the dignity and happiness of living a member of a free and independent nation, let me tell him that necessity now demands what the generous principle of patriotism should have dictated.

We have no other alternative than independence, or the most ignominious and galling servitude. The legions of our enemies thicken on our plains; desolation and death mark their bloody

career; whilst the mangled corpses of our countrymen seem to cry out to us as a voice from heaven: —

"Will you permit our posterity to groan under the galling chains of our murderers? Has our blood been expended in vain? Is the only benefit which our constancy till death has obtained for our country, that it should be sunk into a deeper and more ignominious vassalage? Recollect who are the men that demand your submission, to whose decrees you are invited to pay obedience. Men who, unmindful of their relation to you as brethren; of your long implicit submission to their laws; of the sacrifice which you and your forefathers made of your natural advantages for commerce to their avarice; formed a deliberate plan to wrest from you the small pittance of property which they had permitted you to acquire. Remember that the men who wish to rule over you are they who, in pursuit of this plan of despotism, annulled the sacred contracts which they had made with your ancestors; conveyed into your cities a mercenary soldiery to compel you to submission by insult and murder; who called your patience cowardice, your piety hypocrisy."

Countrymen, the men who now invite you to surrender your rights into their hands are the men who have let loose the merciless savages to riot in the blood of their brethren; who have dared to establish Popery triumphant in our land; who have taught treachery to your slaves, and courted them to assassinate your wives and children.

These are the men to whom we are exhorted to sacrifice the blessings which Providence holds out to us; the happiness, the dignity, of uncontrolled freedom and independence.

Let not your generous indignation be directed against any among us who may advise so absurd and maddening a measure. Their number is but few, and daily decreases; and the spirit which can render them patient of slavery will render them contemptible enemies.

Our Union is now complete; our constitution composed, established, and approved. You are now the guardians of your own liberties. We may justly address you, as the *decemviri* did the Romans, and say, "Nothing that we propose can pass into a law without your consent. Be yourselves, O Americans, the authors of those laws on which your happiness depends."

You have now in the field armies sufficient to repel the whole force of your enemies and their base and mercenary auxiliaries. The hearts of your soldiers beat high with the spirit of freedom;

they are animated with the justice of their cause, and while they grasp their swords can look up to Heaven for assistance. Your adversaries are composed of wretches who laugh at the rights of humanity, who turn religion into derision, and would, for higher wages, direct their swords against their leaders or their country. Go on, then, in your generous enterprise with gratitude to Heaven for past success, and confidence of it in the future. For my own part, I ask no greater blessing than to share with you the common danger and common glory. If I have a wish dearer to my soul than that my ashes may be mingled with those of a Warren and Montgomery, it is that these American States may never cease to be free and independent.

ÆLRED

(1109–1166)

SAINT ÆLRED, EALRED, or ETHELRED, was abbot of the Cistercian monastery at Rievaulx, Yorkshire, in the twelfth century. Thirty-two of his sermons, collected and published by Richard Gibbon, remain as examples of the pulpit eloquence of his age; but not very much is remembered of Ælred himself except that he was virtuous enough to be canonized, and was held in high estimation as a preacher during the Middle Ages. He died in 1166.

His command of language is extraordinary, and he is remarkable for the cumulative power with which he adds clause to clause and sentence to sentence, in working towards a climax.

A FAREWELL

IT is time that I should begin the journey to which the law of our order compels me, desire incites me, and affection calls me. But how, even for so short a time, can I be separated from my beloved ones? Separated, I say, in body, and not in spirit; and I know that in affection and spirit I shall be so much the more present by how much in body I am the more absent. I speak after the manner of men because of the infirmity of my flesh; my wish is, that I may lay down among you the tabernacle of my flesh, that I may breathe forth my spirit in your hands, that ye may close the eyes of your father, and that all my bones should be buried in your sight! Pray, therefore, O my beloved ones, that the Lord may grant me the desire of my soul. Call to mind, dearest brethren, that it is written of the Lord Jesus, when he was about to remove his presence from his Disciples, that he, being assembled together with them, commanded them that they should not depart from Jerusalem. Following, therefore, his example, since, after our sweet banquet, we have now risen from the table, I, who in a little while am about to go away, command you, beseech you, warn you, not to depart from Jerusalem. For Jerusalem signifies peace. Therefore, we commend peace to you, we enjoin peace to you. Now, Christ himself, our Peace, who hath united us, keep you in the unity of the spirit and in the bond of peace; to whose protection and consolation I commend you under the wings of the Holy Ghost; that he may return you to me, and me to you in peace and with safety. Approach now, dearest sons, and in sign of the peace and love which I have commended to you, kiss your father; and let us all pray together that the Lord may make our way prosperous, and grant us when we return to find you in the same peace, who liveth and reigneth one God, through all ages of ages. Amen.

A SERMON AFTER ABSENCE

BEHOLD, I have returned, my beloved sons, my joy and my crown in the Lord! Behold! I have returned after many labors, after a dangerous journey; I am returned to you, I am returned to your love. This day is the day of exultation and joy, which, when I was in a foreign land, when I was struggling with the winds and with the sea, I so long desired to behold; and the Lord hath heard the desire of the poor. O love, how sweetly thou inflamest those that are absent! How deliciously thou feedest those that are present; and yet dost not satisfy the hungry till thou makest Jerusalem to have peace and fillest it with the flour of wheat! This is the peace which, as you remember, I commended to you when the law of our order compelled me for a time to be separated from you; the peace which, now I have returned, I find (Thanks be to God!) among you; the peace of Christ, which, with a certain foretaste of love, feeds you in the way that shall satisfy you with the plentitude of the same love in your country. Well, beloved brethren, all that I am, all that I have, all that I know, I offer to your profit, I devote to your advantage. Use me as you will; spare not my labor if it can in any way serve to your benefit. Let us return, therefore, if you please, or rather because you please, to the work which we have intermitted; and let us examine the Holy Ghost enduing us with the light of truth, the heavenly treasures which holy Isaiah has laid up under the guise of parables, when he writes that parable which the people, freed from his tyranny, shall take up against the king of Babylon. "And it shall come to pass in the day that the Lord shall give thee rest from thy sorrow, and from thy

fear, and from the hard bondage wherein thou wast made to serve, that thou shalt take up this parable against the king of Babylon." Let us, therefore, understand the parable as a parable. Not imagining that it was spoken against Nebuchadnezzar, the prince of that earthly Babylon, but rather against him who is from the North, the prince of confusion. . . . If any one of us, then, who was once set in the confusion of vices, and oppressed by the yoke of iniquity, now rejoices that he rests from his labors, and is without confusion for that which is past, and has cast off the yoke of that worst of slaveries, let him take up this parable against the king of Babylon. There is labor in vice, there is rest in virtue; there is confusion in lust, there is security in chastity; there is servitude in covetousness, there is liberty in charity. Now, there is a labor in vice, and labor for vice, and labor against vice. A labor in vice, when, for the sake of fulfilling our evil desires, the ancient enemy inflicts hard labor upon us. There is a labor for vice, when any one is either afflicted against his will, for the evil which he has done, or of his will is troubled by the labor of penance. There is a labor against vice, when he that is converted to God is troubled with divers temptations. There is also a confusion in vice, when a man, distracted by most evil passions, is not ruled by reason, but hurried along confusedly by the tumult of vices; a confusion for vice, when a man is found out and convicted of any crime, and is therefore confounded, or when a man repenting and confessing what he has done is purified by healthful confusion and confession; and there is a confusion against vice, when a man, converted to God, resists the temptation from which he suffers, by the recollection of former confusion.

Wonder not if I have kept you longer to-day than my wont is, because desirous of you, after so long a hunger, I could not be easily satiated with your presence. Think not, indeed, that even now I am satiated; I leave off speaking because I am weary, not because I am satisfied. But I shall be satisfied when the glory of Christ shall appear, in whom I now embrace you with delight, you, with whom I hope that I shall be happily found in him, to whom is honor and glory to ages of ages. Amen.

ON MANLINESS

FORTITUDE comes next, which is necessary in temptation, since perfection of sanctity cannot be so uninterruptedly maintained in this life that its serenity will be disturbed by no temptations. But as our Lord God seems to us, in times when everything appears peaceful and tranquil, to be merciful and loving and the giver of joy, thus when he exposes us either to the temptations of the flesh, or to the suggestions of demons, or when he afflicts us with the troubles, or wears us out with the persecutions of this world, he seems, as it were, a hard and angry master. And happy is he who becomes valiant in this his anger, now resisting, now fighting, now flying, so as to be found neither infirm through consenting, nor weak through despairing. Therefore, brethren, whoever is not found valiant in his anger cannot exult in his glory. If we have passed through fire and water, so that neither did the fire consume us, nor the water drown us, whose is the glory? Is it ours, so that we should exult in it as if it belonged to us? God forbid! How many exult, brethren, when they are praised by men, taking the glory of the gifts of God as if it were their own and not exulting in the honor of Christ, who, while they seek that which is their own and not the things of Jesus Christ, both lose that which is their own and do not gain that which is Christ's! He then exults in Christ's glory, who seeks not his glory but Christ's, and he understands that, in ourselves, there is nothing of which we can boast, since we have nothing that is our own. And this is the way in which, in individual men, the City of Confusion is overthrown, when chastity expels luxury, fortitude overthrows temptations, humility excludes vanity. Furthermore, we have sanctification from the faith and sacraments of Christ, fortitude from the love of Christ, exultation in the hope of the promises of Christ. Let us each do what we can, that faith may sanctify us, love strengthen us, and hope make us joyful in Christ Jesus our Lord, to whom be honor and glory forever and forever. Amen.

1—8

ÆSCHINES

(389–314 B. C.)

PROFESSOR R. C. JEBB says of Æschines, the rival of Demosthenes for supremacy at Athens, that when the Rhodians asked him to teach them oratory, he replied that he did not know it himself. He took pride in being looked upon as a representative of natural oratorical genius who had had little help from the traditions of the schools. "If, however, Æschines was no rhetorical artist," writes Doctor Jebb, "he brought to public speaking the twofold training of the actor and the scribe. He had a magnificent voice under perfect musical control. 'He compares me to the sirens,' says Æschines of his rival."

First known as an actor, playing "tritagonist" in the tragedies of Sophocles and the other great Athenian dramatists, Æschines was afterwards clerk to one of the minor officials at Athens; then secretary to Aristophon and Eubulos, well-known public men, and later still secretary of the ekklesia or assembly.

The greatest event of his life was his contest with Demosthenes 'De Corona' (Over the Crown). When Ktesiphon proposed that Athens should bestow a wreath of gold on Demosthenes for his public services, Æschines, after the bill proposing it had come before the assembly, challenged it and gave notice of his intention to proceed against Ktesiphon for proposing an unconstitutional measure. One of the allegations in support of its unconstitutionality was that "to record a bill describing Demosthenes as a public benefactor was to deposit a lying document among the public archives." The issues were thus joined between Æschines and Demosthenes for one of the most celebrated forensic contests in history. Losing the case Æschines went into banishment. He died at Samos, B. C. 314, in his seventy-fifth year. He is generally ranked next to Demosthenes among Greek orators. For the following from the oration of Æschines, the reader is under obligations to Professor Jebb's admirable translation.

AGAINST CROWNING DEMOSTHENES
(Against Ktesiphon)

OUR days have not fallen on the common chances of mortal life. We have been set to bequeath a story of marvels to posterity. Is not the king of Persia, he who cut through Athos, and bridged the Hellespont, he who demands earth and water from the Greeks, he who in his letters presumes to style himself lord of all men from the sunrise to the sunset, is he not struggling at this hour, no longer for authority over others, but for his own life? Do you not see the men who delivered the Delphian temple invested not only with that glory but with the leadership against Persia? While Thebes — Thebes, our neighbor city — has been in one day swept from the face of Greece — justly it may be in so far as her general policy was erroneous, yet in consequence of a folly which was no accident, but the judgment of heaven. The unfortunate Lacedæmonians, though they did but touch this affair in its first phase by the occupation of the temple, — they who once claimed the leadership of Greece, — are now to be sent to Alexander in Asia to give hostages, to parade their disasters, and to hear their own and their country's doom from his lips, when they have been judged by the clemency of the master they provoked. Our city, the common asylum of the Greeks, from which, of old, embassies used to come from all Greece to obtain deliverance for their several cities at our hands, is now battling, no more for the leadership of Greece, but for the ground on which it stands. And these things have befallen us since Demosthenes took the direction of our policy. The poet Hesiod will interpret such a case. There is a passage meant to educate democracies and to counsel cities generally, in which he warns us not to accept dishonest leaders. I will recite the lines myself, the reason, I think, for our learning the maxims of the poets in boyhood being that we may use them as men: —

"Oft hath the bad man been the city's bane;
Oft hath his sin brought to the sinless pain;
Oft hath all-seeing Heaven sore vexed the town
With dearth and death and brought the people down;
Cast down their walls and their most valiant slain,
And on the seas made all their navies vain!"

small. Now, however, the flood of royal gold has floated his extravagance. But not even this will suffice. No wealth could ever hold out long against vice. In a word, he draws his livelihood not from his own resources but from your dangers. What, however, are his qualifications in respect to sagacity and to power of speech? A clever speaker, an evil liver! And what is the result to Athens? The speeches are fair; the deeds are vile! Then as to courage I have a word to say. If he denied his cowardice or if you were not aware of it, the topic might have called for discussion, but since he himself admits in the assemblies and you know it, it remains only to remind you of the laws on the subject. Solon, our ancient lawgiver, thought the coward should be liable to the same penalties as the man who refuses to serve or who has quitted his post. Cowardice, like other offenses, is indictable.

Some of you will, perhaps, ask in amazement: Is a man to be indicted for his temperament? He is. And why? In order that every one of us fearing the penalties of the law more than the enemy may be the better champion of his country. Accordingly, the lawgiver excludes alike the man who declines service, the coward, and the deserter of his post, from the lustral limits in the market place, and suffers no such person to receive a wreath of honor or to enter places of public worship. But you, Ktesiphon, exhort us to set a crown on the head to which the laws refuse it. You by your private edict call a forbidden guest into the forefront of our solemn festival, and invite into the temple of Dionysos that dastard by whom all temples have been betrayed. . . . Remember then, Athenians, that the city whose fate rests with you is no alien city, but your own. Give the prizes of ambition by merit, not by chance. Reserve your rewards for those whose manhood is truer, whose characters are worthier. Look at each other and judge not only with your ears but with your eyes who of your number are likely to support Demosthenes. His young companions in the chase or the gymnasium? No, by the Olympian Zeus! He has not spent his life in hunting or in any healthful exercise, but in cultivating rhetoric to be used against men of property. Think of his boastfulness when he claims by his embassy to have snatched Byzantium out of the hands of Philip, to have thrown the Acharnians into revolt, to have astonished the Thebans with his harangue! He thinks that you have reached the point of fatuity at which you

Strip these lines of their poetic garb, look at them closely, and I think you will say these are no mere verses of Hesiod — that they are a prophecy of the administration of Demosthenes, for by the agency of that administration our ships, our armies, our cities have been swept from the earth. . . . "O yes," it will be replied, "but then he is a friend of the constitution." If, indeed, you have a regard only to his delicacy you will be deceived as you were before, but not if you look at his character and at the facts. I will help you to estimate the characteristics which ought to be found in a friend of the constitution; in a sober-minded citizen. I will oppose to them the character that may be looked for in an unprincipled revolutionist. Then you shall draw your comparison and consider on which part he stands — not in his language, remember, but in his life. Now all, I think, will allow that these attributes should belong to a friend of the constitution: First, that he should be of free descent by both parents so that the disadvantage of birth may not embitter him against those laws which preserve the democracy. Second, that he should be able to show that some benefit has been done to the people by his ancestors; or, at the worst, that there had been no enmity between them which would prompt him to revenge the misfortunes of his fathers on the State. Third, he should be virtuous and temperate in his private life, so that no profligate expense may lead him into taking bribes to the hurt of the people. Next, he should be sagacious and able to speak — since our ideal is that the best course should be chosen by the intelligence and then commended to his hearers by the trained eloquence of the orator, — though, if we cannot have both, sagacity must needs take rank before eloquence. Lastly, he must have a stout heart or he may play the country false in the crisis of danger or of war. The friend of oligarchy must be the opposite of all this. I need not repeat the points. Now, consider: How does Demosthenes answer to these conditions?

[After accusing Demosthenes of being by parentage half a Scythian, Greek in nothing but language, the orator proceeds:] —

In his private life, what is he? The tetrarch sank to rise a pettifogger, a spendthrift, ruined by his own follies. Then having got a bad name in this trade, too, by showing his speeches to the other side, he bounded on the stage of public life, where his profits out of the city were as enormous as his savings were

can be made to believe even this — as if your citizen were the deity of persuasion instead of a pettifogging mortal! And when, at the end of his speech, he calls as his advocates those who shared his bribes, imagine that you see upon this platform, where I now speak before you, an array drawn up to confront their profligacy — the benefactors of Athens: Solon, who set in order the Democracy by his glorious laws, the philosopher, the good legislator, entreating you with the gravity which so well became him never to set the rhetoric of Demosthenes above your oaths and above the laws; Aristides, who assessed the tribute of the Confederacy, and whose daughters after his death were dowered by the State — indignant at the contumely threatened to justice and asking: Are you not ashamed? When Arthmios of Zeleia brought Persian gold to Greece and visited Athens, our fathers well-nigh put him to death, though he was our public guest, and proclaimed him expelled from Athens and from all territory that the Athenians rule; while Demosthenes, who has not brought us Persian gold but has taken bribes for himself and has kept them to this day, is about to receive a golden wreath from you! And Themistokles, and they who died at Marathon and Platæa, aye, and the very graves of our forefathers — do you not think they will utter a voice of lamentation, if he who covenants with barbarians to work against Greece shall be — crowned!

FREDERICK A. AIKEN

(1810–1878)

N DEFENDING the unpopular cause of the British soldiers who were engaged in the Boston Massacre, John Adams said:—

    "May it please your honor and you, gentlemen of the jury, I am for the prisoner at the bar, and shall apologize for it only in the words of the Marquis of Beccaria: 'If I can but be the instrument of preserving one life, his blessings and tears of transport shall be a sufficient compensation to me for the contempt of all mankind.'"

Something of the same idea inspires the fine opening of Aiken's defense of Mrs. Surratt. It lacks the sinewy assertiveness of Adams's terse and almost defiant apology for doing his duty as a lawyer in spite of public opinion, but it justifies itself and the plea it introduces.

Until within the recent past, political antagonisms have been too strong to allow fair consideration for such orations as that of Aiken at the Surratt trial. But this is no longer the case. It can now be considered on its merits as an oration, without the assumption that it is necessary in connection with it to pass on the evidence behind it.

The assassins of President Lincoln were tried by military commission under the War Department's order of May 6th, 1865. The prosecution was conducted by Brigadier-General Joseph Holt, as judge advocate-general, with Brevet-Colonel H. L. Burnett, of Indiana, and Hon. John A. Bingham, of Ohio, assisting him. The attorneys for the defense were Reverdy Johnson, of Maryland; Thomas Ewing, of Kansas; W. E. Doster, of Pennsylvania; Frederick A. Aiken, of the District of Columbia; Walter S. Cox, John W. Clampit, and F. Stone, of Maryland. The fault of the Adams oration in the case of the Boston Massacre is one of excessive severity of logic. Aiken errs in the direction of excessive ornament, but, considering the importance of the occasion and the great stress on all engaged in the trial as well as on the public, the florid style may have served better than the force of severe logic could have done.

DEFENSE OF MRS. MARY E. SURRATT

FOR the lawyer as well as the soldier, there is an equally pleasant duty—an equally imperative command. That duty is to shelter the innocent from injustice and wrong, to protect the weak from oppression, and to rally at all times and all occasions, when necessity demands it, to the special defense of those whom nature, custom, or circumstance may have placed in dependence upon our strength, honor, and cherishing regard. That command emanates and reaches each class from the same authoritative and omnipotent source. It comes from a superior, whose right to command none dare question, and none dare disobey. In this command there is nothing of that *lex talionis* which nearly two thousand years ago nailed to the cross its Divine Author.

"Therefore all things whatsoever ye would that men should do to you, do ye even so unto them; for this is the law and the prophets."

God has not only given us life, but he has filled the world with everything to make life desirable; and when we sit down to determine the taking away of that which we did not give, and which, when taken away, we cannot restore, we consider a subject the most solemn and momentous within the range of human thought and human action.

Profoundly impressed with the innocence of our client, we enter upon the last duty in her case with the heartfelt prayer that her honorable judges may enjoy the satisfaction of not having a single doubt left on their minds in granting her an acquittal, either as to the testimony affecting her, or by the surrounding circumstances of the case.

The first point that naturally arises in the presentation of the defense of our client is that which concerns the plea that has been made to the jurisdiction of the commission to try her—a plea which by no means implies anything against the intelligence, fairness, or integrity of the brilliant and distinguished officers who compose the court, but merely touches the question of the right of this tribunal, under the authority by which it is convoked. This branch of her case is left to depend upon the argument already submitted by her senior counsel, the *grande decus columenque* of his profession, and which is exhaustive

of the subject on which it treats. Therefore, in proceeding to the discussion of the merits of the case against her, the jurisdiction of the court, for the sake of argument, may be taken as conceded.

But, if it be granted that the jurisdiction is complete, the next preliminary inquiry naturally is as to the principles of evidence by which the great mass of accumulated facts is to be analyzed and weighed in the scales of justice and made to bias the minds of her judges; and it may be here laid down as a *concessum* in the case, that we are here in this forum, constrained and concluded by the same process, in this regard, that would bind and control us in any other court of civil origin having jurisdiction over a crime such as is here charged. For it is asserted in all the books that court-martial must proceed, so far as the acceptance and the analysis of evidence is concerned, upon precisely those reasonable rules of evidence which time and experience, *ab antiquo*, surviving many ages of judicial wisdom, have unalterably fixed as unerring guides in the administration of the criminal law. Upon this conceded proposition it is unnecessary to consume time by the multiplication of references. We are content with two brief citations from works of acknowledged authority.

In Greenleaf it is laid down:—

"That courts-martial are bound, *in general*, to observe the rules of the law of evidence by which the courts of criminal jurisdiction are governed." (3 Greenleaf, § 467.)

This covers all the great *general* principles of evidence, the points of difference being wholly as to minor matters.

And it is also affirmed in Benet:—

"That it has been laid down as an indisputable principle, that whenever a legislative act erects a new jurisdiction, without prescribing any particular rules of evidence to it, the common law will supply its own rules, from which it will not allow such newly-erected court to depart. The rules of evidence, then, that obtain in the criminal courts of the country must be the guides for the courts-martial; the end sought for being the truth, these rules laid down for the attainment of that end must be intrinsically the same in both cases. These rules constitute the law of evidence, and involve the quality, admissibility, and effect of evidence and its application to the purposes of truth." (Benet, pp. 226, 227.)

Therefore, all the facts that tend against the accused, and all those that make for her, are to be weighed and are to operate upon her conviction or acquittal precisely as they would in a court of law. If they present a case such as would there convict her, she may be found guilty here; and if, on the other hand, the rules of law upon these facts would raise any presumption or create any doubt, or force any conclusions that would acquit her in a court of law, then she must be discharged, upon the same principles by the commission. This is a point which, in our judgment, we cannot too strongly impress upon the minds of her judges. The extraordinary character of the crime—the assassination that removed from us the President of the United States—makes it most desirable that the findings of this tribunal shall be so well founded in reason as to satisfy and secure public confidence and approval; for many of the most material objects of the prosecution, and some of the most important ends of justice, will be defeated and frustrated if convictions and acquittals, and more especially the former, shall be adjudged upon the grounds that are notoriously insufficient.

Such a course of action would have a tendency to draw sympathy and support to the parties thus adjudged guilty, and would rob the result of this investigation of the wholesome support of professional and public opinion. The jurisdiction of the commission, for example, is a matter that has already provoked considerable criticism and much warm disapproval; but in the case of persons clearly found to be guilty, the public mind would easily overlook any doubts that might exist as to the regularity of the court in the just sentence that would overtake acknowledged criminals. Thus, if Booth himself and a party of men clearly proved, by ocular evidence or confession, to have aided him, were here tried and condemned, and, as a consequence, executed, not much stress, we think, would be laid by many upon the irregularity of the mode by which they should reach that just death which all good citizens would affirm to be their deserts. But the case is far different when it affects persons who are only suspected, or against whom the evidence is weak and imperfect; for, if citizens may be arraigned and convicted for so grievous an offense as this upon insufficient evidence, every one will feel his own personal safety involved, and the tendency would be to intensify public feelings against the whole process of the trial. It would be felt and argued that they had been condemned upon evidence that would not have convicted them in a civil court, and that they had been deprived, therefore, of the advantages which they would have had for their defense. Reproach and contumely upon the government would be the natural result, and the first occasion would arise in all history for such demonstrations as would be sure to follow the condemnation of mere citizens, and particularly of a woman, upon evidence on which an acquittal would follow in a civil court. It is, therefore, not only a matter of the highest concern to the accused themselves, as a question of personal and private right, but also of great importance upon considerations of general public utility and policy, that the results of this trial, as affecting each of the accused, among them Mrs. Surratt, shall be rigidly held within the bounds and limitations that would control in the premises, if the parties were on trial in a civil court upon an indictment equivalent to the charges and specifications here. Conceding, as we have said, the jurisdiction for the purpose of this branch of the argument, we hold to the principle first enunciated as the one great, all-important, and controlling rule that is to guide the commission in the findings they are now about to make. In order to apply this principle to the case of our client, we do not propose to range through the general rules of evidence with a view to seeing how they square with the facts as proven against her. In the examination of the evidence in detail, many of these must from necessity be briefly alluded to; but there is only one of them to which we propose in this place to advert specifically, and that is the principle that may be justly said to lie at the foundation of all the criminal law—a principle so just, that it seems to have sprung from the brain of Wisdom herself, and so undoubted and universal as to stand upon the recognition of all the times and all the mighty intellects through and by which the common law has been built up. We allude, of course, to that principle which declares that "every man is held to be innocent until he shall be proven guilty"—a principle so natural that it has fastened itself upon the common reason of mankind, and been immemorially adopted as a cardinal doctrine in all courts of justice worthy of the name. It is by reason of this great underlying legal tenet that we are in possession of the rule of law, administered by all the courts, which, in mere technical expression, may be termed "the presumption of innocence in favor of the accused." And it is from hence that we derive

that further application of the general principle, which has also become a rule of law, and of universal application wherever the common law is respected (and with which we have more particularly to deal), by which it is affirmed, in common language, that in any prosecution for crime "the accused must be acquitted where there is a reasonable doubt of his guilt." We hardly think it necessary to adduce authorities for this position before any tribunal. In a civil court we certainly should waive the citations, for the principle as stated would be assumed by any civil judge, and would, indeed, be the starting point for any investigation whatever. Though a maxim so common and conceded, it is fortified by the authority of all the great lights of the law. Before reference is made to them, however, we wish to impress upon the minds of the court another and important rule to which we shall have occasion to refer:—

"The evidence in support of a conspiracy is generally *circumstantial.*" (Russell on Crimes, Vol. ii., 698.)

In regard to circumstantial evidence, all the best and ablest writers, ancient and modern, agree in treating it as wholly inferior in cogency, force, and effect, to *direct* evidence. And now for the rule that must guide the jury in all cases of reasonable doubt:—

"If evidence leave reasonable ground for doubt, the conclusion cannot be morally certain, however great may be the preponderance of probability in its favor." (Wills on Circumstantial Evidence. Law Library, Vol. xli.)

"The burden of proof in every criminal case is on the government to prove all the material allegations in the indictment; and if, on the whole evidence, the jury have a reasonable doubt whether the defendant is guilty of the crime charged, they are bound to acquit him. If the evidence lead to a reasonable doubt, that doubt will avail in favor of the prisoner." (1 Greenleaf, § 34—Note.)

Perhaps one of the best and clearest definitions of the meaning of a "reasonable doubt" is found in an opinion given in Dr. Webster's case by the learned and accurate Chief-Justice of Massachusetts. He said:—

"The evidence must establish the truth of the fact to a reasonable and moral certainty; a certainty that convinces and directs the

understanding and satisfies the reason and judgment of those who are bound to act conscientiously upon it." (Commonwealth *versus* Webster, 5 Cush., 320.)

Far back in the early history of English jurisprudence we find that it was considered a most serious abuse of the common law, "that justices and their officers, who kill people by false judgment, be not destroyed as other murderers, which King Alfred caused to be done, who caused forty-four justices in one year to be hanged for their false judgment. He hanged Freburne because he judged Harpin to die, whereas the jury were in doubt of their verdict; for in doubtful cases we ought rather to save than to condemn."

The spirit of the Roman law partook of the same care and caution in the condemnation of those charged with crime. The maxim was:—

"*Satius est, impunitum relinqui facinus nocentis, quam innocentem damnare.*"

That there may be no mistake concerning the fact that this commission is bound as a jury by these rules, the same as juries in civil courts, we again quote from Benet:—

"It is in the province of the court (court-martial) to decide all questions on the admissibility of evidence. Whether there is any evidence is a question for the court as judges, but whether the evidence is sufficient is a question for the court as jury to determine, and this rule applies to the admissibility of every kind of evidence, written as well as oral." (Benet, pp. 225, 226.)

These citations may be indefinitely multiplied, for this principle is as true in the law as any physical fact in the exact sciences. It is not contended, indeed, that any degree of doubt must be of a reasonable nature, so as to overset the moral evidence of guilt. A mere possibility of innocence will not suffice, for, upon human testimony, no case is free from possible innocence. Even the more direct evidence of crime may be possibly mistaken. But the doubt required by the law must be consonant with reason and of such a nature that in analogous circumstances it would affect the action of a reasonable creature concerning his own affairs. We may make the nature of such a doubt clearer to the court by alluding to a very common rule in the application

tion of the general principle in certain cases, and the rule will readily appeal to the judgment of the court as a remarkable and singularly beautiful example of the inexorable logic with which the law applies its own unfailing reason.

Thus, in case of conspiracy, and some others, where many persons are charged with joint crime, and where the evidence against most of them must, of necessity, be circumstantial, the plea of "reasonable doubt" becomes peculiarly valuable to the separate accused, and the mode in which it is held it can best be applied is the test whether the facts as proved, circumstantial, as supposed, can be made to consist just as reasonably with a theory that is essentially different from the theory of guilt.

If, therefore, in the developments of the whole facts of a conspiracy, all the particular facts against a particular person can be taken apart and shown to support a reasonable theory that excludes the theory of guilt, it cannot be denied that the moral proof of the latter is so shaken as to admit the rule concerning the presumption of innocence. For surely no man should be made to suffer because certain facts are proved against him, which are consistent with guilt, when it can be shown that they are also, and more reasonably, consistent with innocence. And, as touching the conspiracy here charged, we suppose there are hundreds of innocent persons, acquaintances of the actual assassin, against whom, on the social rule of *noscitur a sociis*, mercifully set aside in law, many facts might be elicited that would corroborate a suspicion of participation in his crime; but it would be monstrous that they should suffer from that theory when the same facts are rationally explainable on other theories.

The distinguished assistant judge advocate, Mr. Bingham, who has brought to the aid of the prosecution, in this trial, such ready and trenchant astuteness in the law, has laid the following down as an invariable rule, and it will pass into the books as such:—

"A party who conspires to do a crime may approach the most upright man in the world with whom he had been, before the criminality was known to the world, on terms of intimacy, and whose position in the world was such that he might be on terms of intimacy with reputable gentlemen. It is the misfortune of a man that is approached in that way; it is not his crime, and it is not colorably his crime either."

This rule of construction, we humbly submit, in connection with the question of doubt, has a direct and most weighty bearing upon the case of our client. Some indication of the mode in which we propose to apply it may be properly stated here. Now, in all the evidence, there is not a shadow of direct and positive proof which connects Mrs. Surratt with a participation in this conspiracy alleged, or with any knowledge of it. Indeed, considering the active part she is charged with taking, and the natural communicativeness of her sex, the case is most singularly and wonderfully barren of even circumstantial facts concerning her. But all there is, is circumstantial. Nothing is proved against her except some few detached facts and circumstances lying around the outer circle of the alleged conspiracy, and by no means necessarily connected with guilty intent or guilty knowledge.

It becomes our duty to see:—

1. What these facts are.

2. The character of the evidence in support of them, and of the witnesses by whom they are said to be proven. And,

3. Whether they are consistent with a reasonable theory by which guilt is excluded.

We assume, of course, as a matter that does not require argument, that she has committed no crime at all, even if these facts be proved, unless there is the necessary express or implied criminal intent, for guilty knowledge and guilty intent are the constituent elements, the principles of all crime. The intent and malice, too, in her case, must be express, for the facts proved against her, taken in themselves, are entirely and perfectly innocent, and are not such as give rise to a necessary implication of malice. This will not be denied. Thus, when one commits a violent homicide, the law will presume the requisite malice; but when one only delivers a message, which is an innocent act in itself, the guilty knowledge, malice, and intent, that are absolutely necessary to make it criminal, must be expressly proven before any criminal consequences can attach to it. And, to quote:—

"Knowledge and intent, when material, must be shown by the prosecutor." (Wharton's American Criminal Law, § 631.)

The intent to do a criminal act as defined by Bouvier implies and means a preconceived purpose and resolve and determination to commit the crime alleged. To quote again:—

"But the intent or guilty knowledge must be brought directly home to the defendant." (Wharton's American Criminal Law, § 635.)

"When an act, in itself indifferent, becomes criminal, if done with a particular intent, then the intent must be proved and found." (3 Greenleaf, § 13.)

In the light of these principles, let us examine the evidence as it affects Mrs. Surratt. 1. What are the acts she has done? The specification against her, in the general charge, is as follows:—

"And in further prosecution of the said conspiracy, Mary E. Surratt did, at Washington City, and within the military department and military lines aforesaid, on or before the sixth day of March, A. D. 1865, and on divers other days and times between that day and the twentieth of April, A. D. 1865, receive and entertain, harbor and conceal, aid and assist, the said John Wilkes Booth, David E. Herold, Lewis Payne, John H. Surratt, Michael O'Laughlin, George A. Atzerodt, Samuel Arnold, and their confederates, with knowledge of the murderous and traitorous conspiracy aforesaid, and with intent to aid, abet, and assist them in the execution thereof, and in escaping from justice after the murder of the said Abraham Lincoln, as aforesaid."

The first striking fact proved is her acquaintance with John Wilkes Booth—that he was an occasional visitor at her house. From the evidence, if it can be relied on, it distinctly appears that this acquaintance commenced the latter part of January, in the vicinage of three months only before the assassination of the President, and, with slight interruptions, it was continued down to the day of the assassination of the President. Whether he was first invited to the house and introduced to the family by Weichmann, John H. Surratt, or some other person, the evidence does not disclose. When asked by the judge advocate, "Whom did he call to see," the witness, Weichmann, responded, "He generally called for Mr. Surratt—John H. Surratt—and, in the absence of John H. Surratt, he would call for Mrs. Surratt."

Before calling the attention of the commission to the next evidence of importance against Mrs. Surratt, we desire to refresh the recollection of the court as to the time and manner, and by whom, according to the testimony of Lloyd, the carbines were first brought to his (Lloyd's) house.

From the official record the following is taken:—

Question.—Will you state whether or not some five or six weeks before the assassination of the President, any or all of these men about whom I have inquired came to your house?

Answer.—They were there.

Q.—All three together?

A.—Yes; John H. Surratt, Herold, and Atzerodt were there together.

Q.—What did they bring to your house, and what did they do there?

A.—When they drove up there in the morning, John H. Surratt and Atzerodt came first; they went from my house and went toward T. B., a post office kept about five miles below here. They had not been gone more than half an hour when they returned with Herold; then the three were together—Herold, Surratt, and Atzerodt.

Q.—What did they bring to your house?

A.—I saw nothing until they all three came into the bar-room. I noticed one of the buggies—the one I supposed Herold was driving or went down in—standing at the front gate. All three of them, when they came into the bar-room, drank, I think, and then John Surratt called me into the front parlor, and on the sofa were two carbines, with ammunition. I think he told me they were carbines.

Q.—Anything besides the carbines and ammunition?

A.—There was also a rope and a monkey-wrench.

Q.—How long a rope?

A.—I cannot tell. It was a coil—a right smart bundle—probably sixteen to twenty feet.

Q.—Were those articles left at your house?

A.—Yes, sir; Surratt asked me to take care of them, to conceal the carbines. I told him that there was no place to conceal them, and I did not wish to keep such things in the house.

Q.—You say that he asked you to conceal those articles for him?

A.—Yes, sir; he asked me to conceal them. I told him there was no place to conceal them. He then carried me into a room that I had never been in, which was just immediately above the store room, as it were, in the back building of the house. I had never been in that room previous to that time. He showed me where I could put them, underneath the joists of the house—the joists of the second floor of the main building. This little unfinished room will admit of anything between the joists.

Q.—Were they put in that place?

A.—They were put in there according to his directions.

1—9

Q.—Were they concealed in that condition?

A.—Yes, sir; I put them in there. I stated to Colonel Wells through mistake that Surratt put them there; but I put them in there myself, I carried the arms up myself.

Q.—How much ammunition was there?

A.—One cartridge box.

Q.—For what purpose, and for how long, did he ask you to keep these articles?

A.—I am very positive that he said that he would call for them in a few days. He said that he just wanted them to stay for a few days and he would call for them.

It also appears in evidence against Mrs. Surratt, if the testimony is to be relied on, that on the Tuesday previous to the murder of the President, the eleventh of April, she met John M. Lloyd, a witness for the prosecution, at Uniontown, when the following took place:—

Question by the judge advocate:—Did she say anything to you in regard to those carbines?

Answer.—When she first broached the subject to me, I did not know what she had reference to; then she came out plainer, and I am quite positive she asked me about the "shooting irons." I am quite positive about that, but not altogether positive. I think she named "shooting irons" or something to call my attention to those things, for I had almost forgot about their being there. I told her that they were hid away far back—that I was afraid that the house would be searched, and they were shoved far back. She told me to get them out ready; they would be wanted soon.

Q.—Was her question to you first, whether they were still there, or what was it?

A.—Really, I cannot recollect the first question she put to me. I could not do it to save my life.

On the afternoon of the fourteenth of April, at about half-past five Lloyd again met Mrs. Surratt, at Surrattsville, at which time, according to his version, she met him by the woodpile near the house and told him to have those shooting irons ready that night as there would be some parties calling for them, and that she gave him something wrapped in a piece of paper, and asked him to get two bottles of whisky ready also. This message to Mr. Lloyd is the second item of importance against Mrs. Surratt, and in support of the specification against her. The third and last fact that makes against her in the minds of the court is the one narrated by Major H. W. Smith, a witness for the prosecution, who states that while at the house of Mrs. Surratt, on the night of the seventeenth of April, assisting in making arrest of its inmates, the prisoner, Payne, came in. He (Smith) stepped to the door of the parlor and said, "Mrs. Surratt, will you step here a minute?" As Mrs. Surratt came forward, he asked her this question, "Do you know this man?" She replied, quoting the witness's language, "Before God, sir, I do not know this man, and I have never seen him." An addition to this is found in the testimony of the same witness, as he was drawn out by the judge advocate. The witness repeats the language of Mrs. Surratt, "Before God, sir, I do not know this man, and I have never seen him, and did not hire him to dig a gutter for me." The fact of the photographs and card of the State arms of Virginia have ceased to be of the slightest importance, since the explanations given in evidence concerning them, and need not be alluded to. If there is any doubt as to whom they all belonged, reference to the testimony of Misses Surratt and Fitzpatrick will settle it.

These three circumstances constitute the part played by the accused, Mary E. Surratt, in this great conspiracy. They are the acts she has done. They are all that two months of patient and unwearying investigation, and the most thorough search for evidence that was probably ever made, have been able to develop against her. The acquaintance with Booth, the message to Lloyd, the nonrecognition of Payne, constitute the sum total of her receiving, entertaining, harboring and concealing, aiding and assisting those named as conspirators and their confederates, with knowledge of the murderous and traitorous conspiracy; and with intent to aid, abet, and assist them in the execution thereof, and in escaping from justice. The acts she has done, in and of themselves are perfectly innocent. Of themselves they constitute no crime. They are what you or I or any of us might have done. She received and entertained Booth, the assassin, and so did a hundred others. She may have delivered a message to Lloyd—so have a hundred others. She might have said she did not know Payne—and who within the sound of my voice can say they know him now? They are ordinary and commonplace transactions, such as occur every day and to almost everybody. But as all the case against her must consist in the guilty intent that will be attempted to be connected with these facts, we now

propose to show that they are not so clearly proven as to free them from great doubt, and, therefore, we will inquire:—

2. How are these acts proven? Solely by the testimony of Louis J. Weichmann and John M. Lloyd. Here let us state that we have no malice toward either of them, but if in the analysis of their evidence we should seem to be severe, it is that error and duplicity may be exposed and innocence protected.

We may start out with the proposition that a body of men banded together for the consummation of an unlawful act against the government, naturally would not disclose their purpose and hold suspicious consultations concerning it in the presence continually of an innocent party. In the light of this fair presumption let us look at the acts of Weichmann, as disclosed by his own testimony. Perhaps the most singular and astonishing fact that is made to appear is his omnipresence and co-action with those declared to be conspirators, and his professed and declared knowledge of all their plans and purposes. His acquaintance with John H. Surratt commenced in the fall of 1859, at St. Charles, Maryland. In January 1863 he renewed his acquaintance with him in this city. On the first of November, 1864, he took board and lodging with Mrs. Surratt at her house, No. 541 H. Street, in this city. If this testimony is correct, he was introduced to Booth on the fifteenth day of January, 1865. At this first, very first meeting, he was invited to Booth's room at the National, where he drank wine and took cigars at Booth's expense. After consultation about something in an outer passage between Booth and the party alleged to be with him by Weichmann, they all came into the room, and for the first time business was proceeded with in his presence. After that he met Booth in Mrs. Surratt's parlor and in his own room, and had conversations with him. As near as Weichmann recollects, about three weeks after his introduction he met the prisoner, Atzerodt, at Mrs. Surratt's. (How Atzerodt was received at the house will be referred to.) About the time that Booth played Pescara in the 'Apostate' at Ford's Theatre, Weichmann attended the theatre in company with Surratt and Atzerodt. At the theatre they were joined by Herold. John T. Holohan, a gentleman not suspected of complicity in the great tragedy, also joined the company at the theatre. After the play was over, Surratt, Holohan, and himself went as far as the corner of Tenth and E Streets, when Surratt, noticing that Atzerodt and Herold were

not with them, sent Weichmann back for them. He found them in a restaurant with Booth, by whose invitation Weichmann took a drink. After that the entire party went to Kloman's, on Seventh Street, and had some oysters. The party there separated, Surratt, Weichmann, and Holohan going home. In the month of March last the prisoner, Payne, according to Weichmann, went to Mrs. Surratt's house and inquired for John H. Surratt. "I, myself," says Weichmann, "went to open the door, and he inquired for Mr. Surratt. I told him Mr. Surratt was not at home; but I would introduce him to the family, and did introduce him to Mrs. Surratt—under the name of Wood." What more? By Weichmann's request Payne remained in the house all night. He had supper served him in the privacy of Weichmann's own room. More than that, Weichmann went down into the kitchen and got the supper and carried it up to him himself, and as nearly as he recollects, it was about eight weeks previous to the assassination; Payne remained as Weichmann's guest until the next morning, when he left on the early train for Baltimore.

About three weeks after that Payne called again. Says Weichmann, "I again went to the door, and I again ushered him into the parlor." But he adds that he had forgotten his name, and only recollected that he had given the name of Wood on the former visit, when one of the ladies called Payne by that name. He who had served supper to Payne in his own room, and had spent a night with him, could not recollect for three weeks the common name of "Wood," but recollects with such distinctness and particularity scenes and incidents of much greater age, and by which he is jeopardizing the lives of others. Payne remained that time about three days, representing himself to the family as a Baptist preacher; claiming that he had been in prison in Baltimore for about a week; that he had taken the oath of allegiance and was going to become a good loyal citizen. To Mrs. Surratt this seemed eccentric, and she said "he was a great-looking Baptist preacher." "They looked upon it as odd and laughed about it." It seemed from Weichmann's testimony that he again shared his room with Payne. Returning from his office one day, and finding a false mustache on the table in his room, he took it and threw it into his toilet box, and afterward put it with a box of paints into his trunk. The mustache was subsequently found in Weichmann's baggage. When Payne, according to Weichmann's testimony, inquired, "Where is my mustache?" Weichmann said

nothing, but "thought it rather queer that a Baptist preacher should wear a false mustache." He says that he did not want it about his room—"thought no honest person had any reason to wear a false mustache," and as no "honest person" should be in possession of it, he locked it up in his own trunk. Weichmann professes throughout his testimony the greatest regard and friendship for Mrs. Surratt and her son. Why did he not go to Mrs. Surratt and communicate his suspicions at once? She, an innocent and guileless woman, not knowing what was occurring in her own house; he, the friend, coming into possession of important facts, and not making them known to her, the head of the household, but claiming now, since this overwhelming misfortune has fallen upon Mrs. Surratt, that, while reposing in the very bosom of the family as a friend and confidant, he was a spy and an informer, and, that, we believe, is the best excuse the prosecution is able to make for him. His account and explanation of the mustache would be treated with contemptuous ridicule in a civil court.

But this is not all. Concede Weichmann's account of the mustache to be true, and if it was not enough to rouse his suspicions that all was not right, he states that, on the same day, he went to Surratt's room and found Payne seated on the bed with Surratt, playing with bowie knives, and surrounded with revolvers and spurs. Miss Honora Fitzpatrick testifies that Weichmann was treated by Mrs. Surratt "more like a son than a friend." Poor return for motherly care! Guilty knowledge and participation in crime or in wild schemes for the capture of the President would be a good excuse for not making all this known to Mrs. Surratt. In speaking of the spurs and pistols, Weichmann knew that there were just eight spurs and two long navy revolvers. Bear in mind, we ask you, gentlemen of the commission, that there is no evidence before you showing that Mrs. Surratt knew anything about these things. It seems farther on, about the nineteenth of March, that Weichmann went to the Herndon House with Surratt to engage a room. He says that he afterwards learned from Atzerodt that it was for Payne, but contradicts himself in the same breath by stating that he inquired of Atzerodt if he were going to see Payne at the Herndon House. His intimate knowledge of Surratt's movements between Richmond and Washington, fixing the dates of the trips with great exactitude; of Surratt's bringing gold back; of Surratt's leaving on the evening of the third of April for Canada, spending his last moments here with Weichmann; of Surratt's telling Weichmann about his interview with Davis and Benjamin—in all this knowledge concerning himself and his associations with those named as conspirators he is no doubt truthful, as far as his statements extend; but when he comes to apply some of this knowledge to others, he at once shakes all faith in his testimony bearing upon the accused.

"Do you remember," the question was asked him, "early in the month of April, of Mrs. Surratt having sent for you and asking you to give Mr. Booth notice that she wished to see him?"

Weichmann stated in his reply that she did, that it was on the second of April, and that he found in Mr. Booth's room John McCullough, the actor, when he delivered the message. One of two things to which he swears in this statement cannot be true; 1. That he met John McCullough in Booth's room, for we have McCullough's sworn statement that at that time he was not in the city of Washington, and if, when he delivered the message to Booth, McCullough was in the room, it could not have been the second of April.

St. Lawrence Hall, Montreal, June 3, 1865.

I am an actor by profession, at present fulfilling an engagement at Mr. Buckland's theatre, in this city. I arrived here on the twelfth of May. I performed two engagements at Ford's Theatre in Washington, during the past winter, the last one closing on Saturday evening, twenty-fifth of March. I left Washington Sunday evening, twenty-sixth of March, and have not been there since. I have no recollection of meeting any person by the name of Weichmann.

JOHN McCULLOUGH.

Sworn to and before me, at the United States Consulate General's, in Montreal, this third day of June, A. D. 1865.

C. H. POWERS, U. S. Vice Consul-General.

If he can be so mistaken about those facts, may he not be in regard to that whole transaction? It is also proved by Weichmann that before Mrs. Surratt started for the country, on the fourteenth of April, Booth called; that he remained three or four minutes, and then Weichmann and Mrs. Surratt started for the country.

All this comes out on his first examination in chief. The following is also told in his first cross-examination: Mrs. Surratt

There was no intimacy with Booth, as Mrs. Surratt has proved, but only common acquaintance, and such as would warrant only occasional calls on Booth's part, and only intimacy would have excused Mrs. Surratt to herself in accepting such a favor, had it been made known to her. Moreover, Miss Surratt has attested to remarks of her brother, which prove that intimacy of Booth with his sister and mother were not considered desirable by him.

The preceding facts are proven by statements made by Weichmann during his first examination. But, as though the commission had not sufficiently exposed the character of one of its chief witnesses in the rôle of grand conspirator, Weichmann is recalled and further attests to the genuineness of the following telegram:

New York, March 23d, 1865.— To Weichmann, Esq., 541 H St.— Tell John telegraph number and street at once.

[Signed] J. Booth.

What additional proof of confidential relations between Weichmann and Booth could the court desire? If there was a conspiracy planned and maintained among the persons named in the indictment, Weichmann must have had entire knowledge of the same, else he had not been admitted to that degree of knowledge to which he testifies; and in such case, and in the alleged case of Mrs. Surratt's complicity, Weichmann must have known the same by circumstances strong enough to exclude doubt, and in comparison with which all present facts of accusation would sink into insignificance.

We proceed to the notice and review of the second chief witness of the prosecution against Mrs. Surratt, John M. Lloyd. He testifies to the fact of a meeting with Mrs. Surratt at Uniontown on the eleventh of April, 1865, and to a conversation having occurred between Mrs. Surratt and himself in regard to which he states: "I am quite positive she asked me about the 'shooting irons'; I am quite positive about that, but not altogether positive. I think she named shooting irons, or something to call my attention to those things, for I had almost forgotten about their being there." Question.— "Was her question to you first, whether they were there, or what was it?" Answer.— "Really, I cannot recollect the first question she put to me—I could not do it to save my life." The question was asked Lloyd, "During this conversation, was the word 'carbine' mentioned?" He answered, "No. She finally came out (but I cannot be determined

keeps a boarding house in this city, and was in the habit of renting out her rooms, and that he was upon very intimate terms with Surratt; that they occupied the same room; that when he and Mrs. Surratt went to Surrattsville on the fourteenth, she took two packages, one of papers, the contents of the other were not known. That persons have been in the habit of going to Mrs. Surratt's and staying a day or two; that Atzerodt stopped in the house only one night; that the first time Payne came to the house he was dressed genteelly, like a gentleman; that he heard both Mrs. Surratt and her daughter say that they did not care about having Atzerodt brought to the house; and at the conclusion, in swearing as to Mrs. Surratt's character, he said it was exemplary and lady-like in every respect, and apparently, as far as he could judge, she was all the time, from the first of November up to the fourteenth of April, "doing her duties to God and man." It also distinctly appears that Weichmann never had any conversation with Mrs. Surratt touching any conspiracy. One thing is apparent to our minds, and it is forced upon us, as it must be upon every reasonable mind, that in order to have gained all this knowledge Weichmann must have been within the inner circle of the conspiracy. He knows too much for an innocent man, and the conclusion is perfectly irresistible that if Mrs. Surratt had knowledge of what was going on, and had been, with others, a *particeps criminis* in the great conspiracy, she certainly would have done more than she did or has been shown against her, and Weichmann would have known it. How does her nonrecognition of Payne, her acquaintance with Booth, and the delivery of the message to Lloyd, compare with the long and startling array of facts proved against Weichmann out of his own mouth? All the facts point strongly to him as a co-conspirator.

Is there a word on record of conversation between Booth and Mrs. Surratt? That they did converse together, we know; but if anything treasonable had passed between them, would not the quick ears of Weichmann have caught it, and would not he have recited it to this court?

When Weichmann went, on Tuesday, the eleventh of April, to get Booth's buggy, he was not asked by Mrs. Surratt to get ten dollars. It was proffered by Booth, according to Weichmann, and he took it. If Mrs. Surratt ever got money from Booth she paid it back to him. It is not her character to be in any one's debt.

about it, that she said shooting irons), and asked me in relation to them." The question was then asked, "Can you swear on your oath, that Mrs. Surratt mentioned the words 'shooting irons' to you at all?" A.— "I am very positive she did." Q.— "Are you certain?" A.— "I am very positive that she named shooting irons on both occasions. Not so positive as to the first as I am about the last."

Here comes in the plea of "reasonable doubt." If the witness himself is not absolutely positive as to what occurred, and as to the conversation that took place, how can the jury assume to act upon it as they would upon a matter personally concerning themselves?

On this occasion of Mrs. Surratt's visit to Uniontown, three days before the assassination, where she met Lloyd, and where this conversation occurred between them, at a time when Lloyd was, by presumption, sober and not intoxicated, he declares definitely before the commission that he is unable to recollect the conversation, or parts of it, with distinctness. But on the fourteenth of April, and at a time when, as testified by his sister-in-law, he was more than ordinarily affected by intoxicating drink,— and Captain Gwynn, James Lusby, Knott, the barkeeper, and others, corroborate the testimony as to his absolute inebriation— he attests that he positively remembers that Mrs. Surratt said to him, "'Mr. Lloyd, I want you to have those shooting irons ready. That a person would call for them.' That was the language she made use of, and she gave me this other thing to give to whoever called."

In connection with the fact that Lloyd cannot swear positively that Mrs. Surratt mentioned "shooting irons" to him at Uniontown, bear in mind the fact that Weichmann sat in the buggy on the same seat with Mrs. Surratt, and he swears that he heard nothing about "shooting irons." Would not the quick ears of Weichmann have heard the remark had it been made?

The gentlemen of the commission will please recollect that these statements were rendered by a man addicted to excessive use of intoxicating liquors; that he was even inordinately drunk at the time referred to; that he had voluntarily complicated himself in the concealment of the arms by John H. Surratt and his friends; that he was in a state of maudlin terror when arrested and when forced to confess; that for two days he maintained denial of all knowledge that Booth and Herold had been at his house; and that at last, and in the condition referred to, he was coerced by threats to confess, and into a weak and common effort to exculpate himself by the accusation of another and by statements of conversation already cited. Notwithstanding his utter denial of all knowledge of Booth and Herold having called at his house, it afterward appears, by his own testimony, that immediately Herold commanded him (Lloyd) "For God's sake, make haste and get those things," he comprehended what "things" were indicated, without definition, and brought forth both carbines and whisky. He testifies that John H. Surratt had told him, when depositing the weapons in concealment in his house, that they would soon be called for, but did not instruct him, it seems, by whom they would be demanded.

All facts connecting Lloyd with the case tend to his implication and guilt, and to prove that he adopted the *dernier ressort* of guilt — accusation and inculpation of another. In case Lloyd were innocent and Mrs. Surratt the guilty coadjutrix and messenger of the conspirators, would not Lloyd have been able to cite so many open and significant remarks and acts of Mrs. Surratt that he would not have been obliged to recall, in all perversion and weakness of uncertainty, deeds and speech so common and unmeaning as his testimony includes?

It is upon these considerations that we feel ourselves safe and reasonable in the position that there are facts and circumstances, both external and internal, connected with the testimony of Weichmann and Lloyd, which, if they do not destroy, do certainly greatly shake their credibility, and which, under the rule that will give Mrs. Surratt the benefit of all reasonable doubts, seem to forbid that she should be convicted upon the unsupported evidence of these two witnesses. But even admitting the facts to be proven as above recited, it remains to be seen where is the guilty knowledge of the contemplated assassination; and this brings us to the inquiry whether these facts are not explainable so as to exclude guilt.

From one of the most respected of legal authorities the following is taken: —

"Whenever, therefore, the evidence leaves it indifferent which of several hypotheses is true, or merely establishes some finite probability in favor of one hypothesis rather than another, such evidence cannot amount to proof. The maxim of the law is that it is better

that ninety-nine offenders should escape than that one innocent man should be condemned." (Starkie on Evidence.)

The acts of Mrs. Surratt must have been accompanied with criminal intent in order to make them criminal. If any one supposes that any such intent existed, the supposition comes alone from inference. If disloyal acts and constant disloyal practices, if overt and open action against the government, on her part, had been shown down to the day of the murder of the President, it would do something toward establishing the inference of criminal intent. On the other hand, just the reverse is shown. The remarks here of the learned and honorable judge advocate are peculiarly appropriate to this branch of the discussion, and, with his authority, we waive all others.

"If the court please, I will make a single remark. I think the testimony in this case has proved, what I believe history sufficiently attests, how kindred to each other are the crimes of treason against a nation and the assassination of its chief magistrate. As I think of those crimes, the one seems to be, if not the necessary consequence, certainly a logical sequence from the other. The murder of the President of the United States, as alleged and shown, was pre-eminently a political assassination. Disloyalty to the government was its sole, its only inspiration. When, therefore, we shall show, on the part of the accused, acts of intense disloyalty, bearing arms in the field against that government, we show, with him, the presence of an *animus* toward the government which relieves this accusation of much, if not all, of its improbability. And this course of proof is constantly resorted to in criminal courts. I do not regard it as in the slightest degree a departure from the usages of the profession in the administration of public justice. The purpose is to show that the prisoner, in his mind and course of life, was prepared for the commission of this crime; that the tendencies of his life, as evidenced by open and overt acts, lead and point to this crime, if not as a necessary, certainly as a most probable, result, and it is with that view, and that only, that the testimony is offered."

Is there anything in Mrs. Surratt's mind and course of life to show that she was prepared for the commission of this crime? The business transaction by Mrs. Surratt at Surrattsville, on the fourteenth, clearly discloses her only purpose in making this visit. Calvert's letters, the package of papers relating to the estate, the business with Nothe, would be sufficiently clear to most minds, when added to the fact that the other unknown

package had been handed to Mrs. Offutt; that, while at Surrattsville, she made an inquiry for, or an allusion to, Mr. Lloyd, and was ready to return to Washington when Lloyd drove up to the house. Does not this open wide the door for the admission of the plea of "reasonable doubt"? Had she really been engaged in assisting in the great crime, which makes an epoch in our country's history, her only object and most anxious wish would have been to see Lloyd. It was no ruse to transact important business there to cover up what the uncharitable would call the real business. Calvert's letter was received by her on the forenoon of the fourteenth, and long before she saw Booth that day, or even before Booth knew that the President would be at the theatre that night, Mrs. Surratt had disclosed her intention to go to Surrattsville, and had she been one moment earlier in her start she would not have seen Booth at all. All these things furnish powerful presumptions in favor of the theory that, if she delivered the message at all, it was done innocently.

In regard to the nonrecognition of Payne, the third fact adduced by the prosecution against Mrs. Surratt, we incline to the opinion that, to all minds not forejudging, the testimony of Miss Anna E. Surratt, and various friends and servants of Mrs. Surratt, relative to physical causes, might fully explain and account for such ocular remissness and failure. In times and on occasions of casual meeting of intimate acquaintances on the street, and of common need for domestic uses, the eyesight of Mrs. Surratt had proved treacherous and failing. How much more liable to fail her was her imperfect vision on an occasion of excitement and anxiety, like the night of her arrest and the disturbance of her household by military officers, and when the person with whom she was confronted was transfigured by a disguise which varied from the one in which she had previously met him, with all the wide difference between a Baptist parson and an earth-soiled, uncouthly-dressed digger of gutters! Anna E. Surratt, Emma Offutt, Anna Ward, Elize Holohan, Honora Fitzpatrick, and a servant, attest to all the visual incapacity of Mrs. Surratt, and the annoyance she experienced therefrom in passing friends without recognition in the daytime, and from inability to sew or read even on a dark day, as well as at night. The priests of her church, and gentlemen who have been friendly and neighborhood acquaintances of Mrs. Surratt for many years, bear witness to her untarnished name, to her discreet and Christian character, to

the absence of all imputation of disloyalty, to her character for patriotism. Friends and servants attest to her voluntary and gratuitous beneficence to our soldiers stationed near her; and, "in charges for high treason, it is pertinent to inquire into the humanity of the prisoner toward those representing the government," is the maxim of the law; and, in addition, we invite your attention to the singular fact that of the two officers who bore testimony in this matter, one asserts that the hall wherein Payne sat was illuminated with a full head of gas; the other, that the gaslight was purposely dimmed. The uncertainty of the witness who gave the testimony relative to the coat of Payne may also be called to your notice.

Should not this valuable testimony of loyal and moral character shield a woman from the ready belief, on the part of judges who judge her worthiness in every way, that during the few moments Booth detained Mrs. Surratt from her carriage, already waiting, when he approached and entered the house, she became so converted to diabolical evil as to hail with ready assistance his terrible plot, which must have been framed (if it were complete in his intent at that hour, half-past two o'clock), since the hour of eleven that day?

If any part of Lloyd's statements is true, and Mrs. Surratt did verily bear to his or Mrs. Offutt's hands the field glass, enveloped in paper, by the evidence itself we may believe she knew not the nature of the contents of the package; and had she known, what evil could she or any other have attached to a commission of so common a nature? No evidence of individual or personal intimacy with Booth has been adduced against Mrs. Surratt; no long and apparently confidential interviews; no indications of a private comprehension mutual between them; only the natural and not frequent custom on the part of Booth — as any other associate of her son might and doubtless did do — of inquiring through the mother, whom he would request to see, of the son, who, he would learn, was absent from home. No one has been found who could declare any appearance of the nursing or mysteriously discussing of anything like conspiracy within the walls of Mrs. Surratt's house. Even if the son of Mrs. Surratt, from the significancies of associations, is to be classed with the conspirators, if such a body existed, it is monstrous to suppose that the son would weave a net of circumstantial evidences around the dwelling of his widowed mother, were he never so reckless and sin-determined; and that they (the mother and the son) joined hands in such dreadful pact, is a thought more monstrous still!

A mother and son associate in crime, and such a crime as this, which half of the civilized world never saw matched in all its dreadful bearings! Our judgments can have hardly recovered their unprejudiced poise since the shock of the late horror, if we can contemplate with credulity such a picture, conjured by the unjust spirits of indiscriminate accusation and revenge. A crime which, in its public magnitude, added to its private misery, would have driven even the Atis-haunted heart of a Medici, a Borgia, or a Madame Bocarme to wild confession before its accomplishment, and daunted even that soul, of all the recorded world the most eager for novelty in license, and most unshrinking in sin — the indurated soul of Christina of Sweden; such a crime the profoundest plotters within padded walls would scarcely dare whisper; the words forming the expression of which, spoken aloud in the upper air, would convert all listening boughs to aspens, and all glad sounds of nature to shuddering wails. And this made known, even surmised, to a woman a *materfamilias*, the good genius, the *placens uxor* of a home where children had gathered all the influences of purity and the reminiscences of innocence, where religion watched, and the Church was minister and teacher!

Who — were circumstantial evidence strong and conclusive, such as only time and the slow-weaving fates could elucidate and deny — who will believe, when the mists of uncertainty which cloud the present shall have dissolved, that a woman born and bred in respectability and competence — a Christian mother, and a citizen who never offended the laws of civil propriety; whose unfailing attention to the most sacred duties of life has won for her the name of "a proper Christian matron"; whose heart was ever warmed by charity; whose door unbarred to the poor; and whose Penates had never cause to veil their faces — who will believe that she could so suddenly and so fully have learned the intricate arts of sin? A daughter of the South, her life associations confirming her natal predilections, her individual preferences inclined, without logic or question, to the Southern people, but with no consciousness nor intent of disloyalty to her

government, and causing no exclusion from her friendship and active favors of the people of the loyal North, nor repugnance in the distribution among our Union soldiery of all needed comforts, and on all occasions.

A strong but guileless-hearted woman, her maternal solicitude would have been the first denouncer, even the abrupt betrayer, of a plotted crime in which one companion of her son could have been implicated, had cognizance of such reached her. Her days would have been agonized, and her nights sleepless, till she might have exposed and counteracted that spirit of defiant hate which watched its moment of vantage to wreak an immortal wrong — till she might have sought the intercession and absolution of the Church, her refuge, in behalf of those she loved. The brains which were bold and crafty and couchant enough to dare the world's opprobrium in the conception of a scheme which held as naught the lives of men in highest places, would never have imparted it to the intelligence, nor sought the aid nor sympathy, of any living woman who had not, like Lady Macbeth, "unsexed herself" — not though she were wise and discreet as Maria Theresa or the Castilian Isabella. This woman knew it not. This woman, who, on the morning preceding that blackest day in our country's annals, knelt in the performance of her most sincere and sacred duty at the confessional, and received the mystic rite of the Eucharist, knew it not. Not only would she have rejected it with horror, but such a proposition, presented by the guest who had sat at her hearth as the friend and convive of the son upon whose arm and integrity her widowed womanhood relied for solace and protection, would have roused her maternal wits to some sure cunning which would have contravened the crime and sheltered her son from the evil influences and miserable results of such companionship.

The mothers of Charles IX. and of Nero could harbor underneath their terrible smiles schemes for the violent and unshriven deaths, or the moral vitiation and decadence which would painfully and gradually remove lives sprung from their own, were they obstacles to their demoniac ambition. But they wrought their awful romances of crime in lands where the sun of supreme civilization, through a gorgeous evening of Sybaritic luxury, was sinking, with red tints of revolution, into the night of anarchy and national caducity. In our own young nation, strong in its morality, energy, freedom, and simplicity, assassination can never

be indigenous. Even among the desperadoes and imported lazzaroni of our largest cities, it is comparatively an infrequent cause of fear.

The daughters of women to whom, in their yet preserved abodes, the noble mothers who adorned the days of our early independence are vividly remembered realities and not haunting shades — the descendants of earnest seekers for liberty, civil and religious, of rare races, grown great in heroic endurance, in purity which comes of trial borne, and in hope born of conscious right, whom the wheels of fortune sent hither to transmit such virtues — the descendants of these have no heart, no ear for the diabolisms born in hotbeds of tyranny and intolerance. No descendant of these — no woman of this temperate land — could have seen, much less joined, her son, descending the sanguinary and irrepassable ways of treason and murder to an ignominious death, or an expatriated and attainted life, worse than the punishing wheel and bloody pool of the poets' hell.

In our country, where reason and moderation so easily quench the fires of insane hate, and where the vendetta is so easily overcome by the sublime grace of forgiveness, no woman could have been found so desperate as to sacrifice all spiritual, temporal, and social good, self, offspring, fame, honor, and all the *desiderata* of life, and time, and immortality, to the commission, or even countenance, of such a deed of horror, as we have been compelled to contemplate during the two months past.

In a Christian land, where all records and results of the world's intellectual, civil, and moral advancement mold the human heart and mind to highest impulses, the theory of old Helvétius is more probable than desirable.

The natures of all born in equal station are not so widely varied as to present extremes of vice and goodness, but by the effects of rarest and severest experience. Beautiful fairies and terrible gnomes do not stand by each infant's cradle, sowing the nascent mind with tenderest graces or vilest errors. The slow attrition of vicious associations and law-defying indulgences, or the sudden impetus of some terribly multiplied and social disaster, must have worn away the susceptibility of conscience and self-respect, or dashed the mind from the height of these down to the depths of despair and recklessness, before one of ordinary life could take counsel with violence and crime. In no such manner was the life of our client marked. It was the

parallel of nearly all the competent masses. Surrounded by the scenes of her earliest recollections, independent in her condition, she was satisfied with the *mundus* of her daily pursuits, and the maintenance of her own and children's status in society and her Church.

Remember your wives, mothers, sisters, and gentle friends, whose graces, purity, and careful affection, ornament and cherish and strengthen your lives. Not widely different from their natures and spheres have been the nature and sphere of the woman who sits in the prisoner's dock to-day, mourning with the heart of Alcestis her children and her lot; by whose desolated hearthstone a solitary daughter wastes her uncomforted life away in tears and prayers and vigils for the dawn of hope; and this wretchedness and unpitied despair have closed like a shadow around one of earth's common pictures of domestic peace and social comfort, destroyed by the one sole cause — suspicion fastened and fed upon the facts of acquaintance and mere fortuitous intercourse with that man in whose name so many miseries gather, the assassin of the President.

Since the days when Christian teachings first elevated woman to her present free, refined, and refining position, man's power and honoring regard have been the palladium of her sex.

Let no stain of injustice, eager for a sacrifice to revenge, rest upon the reputation of the men of our country and time!

This woman, who, widowed of her natural protectors, who, in helplessness and painfully severe imprisonment, in sickness and in grief ineffable, sues for mercy and justice from your hands, may leave a legacy of blessings, sweet as fruition-hastening showers, for those you love and care for, in return for the happiness of fame and home restored, though life be abbreviated and darkened through this world by the miseries of this unmerited and woeful trial. But long and chilling is the shade which just retribution, slow creeping on, *pede claudo*, casts around the fate of him whose heart is merciless to his fellows bowed low in misfortune.

ALBERTUS MAGNUS

(1205–1280)

ALBERT THE GREAT (Albertus Magnus), teacher of St. Thomas Aquinas, was one of the most celebrated orators and theologians of the Church in the thirteenth century. He was born at Lauingen on the Danube in 1205 (according to some in 1193), and, becoming a Dominican at the age of twenty-nine, he taught in various German cities with continually increasing celebrity, until finally the Pope called him to preach in Rome. In 1260 he was made Bishop of Ratisbon, but after three years resigned the bishopric and returned to his work in the ranks of the clergy. While teaching at Cologne he suddenly lost his memory, probably as a result of his excessive studies. He died November 15th, 1280. He was placed on the calendar of saints in 1615. His works, collected by Peter Jammy, and published at Lyons in 1651, make twenty-one volumes, folio.

THE MEANING OF THE CRUCIFIXION

IT WAS surrounded by the thick wreath of thorns even to the tender brain. Whence in the Prophet,— the people hath surrounded me with the thorns of sin. And why was this, save that thine own head might not suffer — thine own conscience might not be wounded? His eyes grew dark in death; and those lights, which give light to the world, were for a time extinguished. And when they were clouded, there was darkness over all the earth, and with them the two great lights of the firmament were moved, to the end that thine eyes might be turned away, lest they should behold vanity; or, if they chance to behold it, might for his sake condemn it. Those ears, which in heaven unceasingly hear "Holy, Holy, Holy," vouchsafed on earth to be filled with: "Thou hast a devil,— Crucify him, Crucify him!" to the intent that thine ears might not be deaf to the cry of the poor, nor, open to idle tales, should readily receive the poison of detraction or of adulation. That fair face of him that was fairer than the children of men, yea, than

the petition, "Let him kiss me with the kisses of his mouth"; also that he might ask permission of his bride to leave her. Of great virtue is the memory of the Lord's passion, which, if it be firmly held in the mind, every cloud of error and sin is dispersed. Whence the blessed Bernard says: "Always having Christ, and him crucified, in the heart."

THE BLESSED DEAD

THEY who die in the Lord are blessed, on account of two things which immediately follow. For they enter into most sweet rest, and enjoy most delicate refreshment. Concerning their rest, it immediately follows. "Even so saith the spirit" (that is, says the gloss, the whole Trinity), for they rest from their labors. "And it is a pleasant bed on which they take their rest, who, as is aforesaid, die in the Lord." For this bed is none other than the sweet consolation of the Creator. Of this consolation he speaks himself by the Prophet Isaiah: "As one whom his mother comforteth, so will I comfort you, and ye shall be comforted in Jerusalem." Of the second,— that is, the delicate refreshment of those that die in Christ,— it is immediately subjoined, and their works do follow them. For every virtue which a man has practiced by good works in this world will bring a special cup of recompense, and offer it to the soul that has entered into rest. Thus, purity of body and mind will bring one cup, justice another, which also is to be said concerning truth, love, gentleness, humility, and the other virtues. Of this holy refreshment it is written in Isaiah: "Kings shall be thy nursing fathers, and queens thy nursing mothers." By kings we understand the Father, the Son, and the Holy Ghost, who, in inseparable unity, possess the kingdom of heaven; by queens, the virtues are expressed, which, as has been said, receive the cups of refreshment from the storehouse of the Trinity, and offer them to the happy souls. Pray, therefore, dearly beloved, to the Lord, that he would so grant us to live according to his will, that we may die in him, and may evermore be comforted and refreshed by him

thousands of angels, was bedaubed with spitting, afflicted with blows, given up to mockery, to the end that thy face might be enlightened, and, being enlightened, might be strengthened, so that it might be said of thee, "His countenance is no more changed." That mouth, which teaches angels and instructs men, "which spake and it was done," was fed with gall and vinegar, that thy mouth might speak the truth, and might be opened to the praise of the Lord; and it was silent, lest thou shouldst lightly lend thy tongue to the expression of anger.

Those hands, which stretched abroad the heavens, were stretched out on the cross and pierced with most bitter nails; as saith Isaiah, "I have stretched forth my hands all the day to an unbelieving people." And David, "They pierced my hands and my feet; I may tell all my bones." And Saint Jerome says, "We may, in the stretching forth of his hands, understand the liberality of the giver, who denieth nothing to them that ask lovingly; who restored health to the leper that requested it of him; enlightened him that was blind from his birth; fed the hungry multitude in the wilderness." And again he says, "The stretched-out hands denote the kindness of the parent, who desires to receive his children to his breast." And thus let thy hands be so stretched out to the poor that thou mayest be able to say, "My soul is always in my hand." For that which is held in the hand is not easily forgotten. So he may be said to call his soul to memory, who carries it, as it were, in his hands through the good opinion that men conceive of it. His hands were fixed, that they may instruct thee to hold back thy hands, with the nails of fear, from unlawful or harmful works.

That glorious breast, in which are hidden all the treasures of wisdom and knowledge, is pierced with the lance of a soldier, to the end that thy heart might be cleansed from evil thoughts, and being cleansed might be sanctified, and being sanctified might be preserved. The feet, whose footstool the Prophets commanded to be sanctified, were bitterly nailed to the cross, lest thy feet should sustain evil, or be swift to shed blood; but, running in the way of the Lord, stable in his path, and fixed in his road, might not turn aside to the right hand nor to the left. "What could have been done more?"

Why did Christ bow his head on the cross? To teach us that by humility we must enter into Heaven. Also, to show that we must rest from our own work. Also, that he might comply with

ETHAN ALLEN

ETHAN ALLEN, of New York, a descendant of the Revolutionary hero made famous by the capture of Ticonderoga, has never been a professional public speaker, but from time to time, when stirred by some cause which appealed to him strongly, he has shown great power as an orator. His address of 1861, delivered in New York city, is here republished from a contemporaneous report, preserved among the papers of Mr. Enos Clarke. It was described in the newspapers of the day as "thrilling eloquence," and perhaps it is the best expression extant of the almost inconceivable excitement of the opening months of the war.

In 1872 Mr. Allen joined the Liberal Republicans and made earnest pleas for reconciliation with the South. In 1897 he took a prominent part in supporting the Cubans in their struggle for independence.

A CALL TO ARMS

(Delivered in New York city in 1861)

Fellow-Citizens: —

ONCE more the country is aroused by a call to arms. It is now nearly a century ago that our fathers assembled in mass meetings in this city to devise ways and means for this very flag which to-day we give to the winds of heaven, bearing defiance from every star. Fired, then, with the same spirit of freedom that kindles on this spot to-day, for the time throwing aside the habiliments of peace, our fathers armed themselves for vengeance and for war. The history of that war, read it in the hearts of the American people; the trials and struggles of that war, mark them in the teardrops which the very allusion brings to every eye; the blessings from that war, count them in the temples of industry and trade that arise everywhere around us; the wisdom of that war, and the honor and the perpetuity of its triumphs, behold the one in our unexampled prosperity as a nation, and the other in the impulses that, like an electric flash, bind heart to heart, throughout this vast assemblage, in the firm resolve that, cost what it may, rebellion shall go down. Again, the American people are assembled in mass meetings throughout the nation, while the States once more rock in the throes of revolution. Once more the cry to arms reverberates throughout the land; but this time we war against domestic foes. Treason has raised its black flag near the tomb of Washington, and the Union of our States hangs her fate upon the bayonet and the sword. Accursed be the hand that would not seize the bayonet; withered the arm that would not wield the sword in such a cause! Everything that the American citizen holds dear hangs upon the issue of this contest. Our national honor and reputation demand that rebellion shall not triumph on our soil. In the name of our heroic dead, in the name of our numberless victories, in the name of our thousand peaceful triumphs, our Union shall and must be preserved! Our peaceful triumphs? These are the victories we should be jealous to guard. Let others recount their martial glories; they shall be eclipsed by the charity and the grace of the triumphs which have been won in peace. "Peace hath her victories not less renowned than war," and the hard-earned fruits of these victories rebellion shall not take from us. Our peaceful triumphs? Who shall enumerate their value to the millions yet unborn? What nation in so short a time has seen so many? On the land and on the sea, in the realms of science and in the world of art, we have everywhere gathered our honors and won our garlands. Upon the altars of the States they yet lie, fresh from gathering, while their happy influence fills the land. Of the importance and value of our thousand peaceful triumphs time will permit me to mention only one. It is now just two years ago when up the waters of the Potomac sailed the representatives of an empire till then shut out from intercourse with all Christian nations. In the Eastern seas there lay an empire of islands which had hitherto enjoyed no recognition in the Christian world other than its name upon the map. No history, as far as we know, illuminated it; no ancient time-marks told of its advancement, step by step, in the march of improvement. There it has rested for thousands of years, wrapped in the mysteries of its own exclusiveness—gloomy, dark, peculiar. It has been supposed to possess great powers; and vague rumors have attributed to it arts to us unknown. Against nearly all the world, for thousands of years, Japan has obstinately shut her doors; the wealth of the Christian

world could not tempt her cupidity; the wonders of the Christian world could not excite her curiosity. There she lay, sullen and alone, the phenomenon of nations. England and France and the other powerful governments of Europe have at various times tried to conquer this Oriental exclusiveness, but the Portuguese only partly succeeded, while all the rest have signally failed. At length we, bearing at our masthead the glorious old Stars and Stripes, approach the mysterious portals and seek an entrance. Not with cannon and the implements of death do we demand admission, but, appreciating the saying of Euripides, that

"Resistless eloquence shall open
The gates that steel exclude,"

we peacefully appeal to that sense of justice which is the "touch of nature that makes the whole world kin," and behold! the interdiction is removed; the doors of the mysterious empire fly open, and a new garland is added to our commercial conquests! Who shall set limits to the gain that shall follow this one victory of peace, if our government shall be perpetuated so as to gather it for the generations? Who shall say that in an unbroken, undivided union, the opening of the empire of Japan shall not accomplish for the present era all that the Reformation, the art of printing, steam, and the telegraph have done within the last three hundred years? New avenues of wealth are thrown open; new fields are to be occupied; arts new to us, perhaps, are to be studied; and science, doubtless, has revelations to make us, from that arcana of nations, equal to anything we have ever learned before. Fifty millions of people are to be enlightened; the printing press is yet to catch the daily thought and stamp it on the page; the magnetic wire must yet tremble along her highways, and Niphon yet tremble to her very centre at each heart-beat of our ocean steamers, as they sweep through her waters and thunder round her island homes. All hail, all hail, to these children of the morning; all hail, all hail, to the Great Republic of the West that calls them into life! From every age that has passed there comes a song of praise for the treaty that has been consummated. The buried masters of three thousand years start again to life and march in solemn and grand procession before the eyes of the new-found empire. Homer with his songs, Greece with her arts, Rome with her legions, and America with her heroes, all come to us with the

freshness and novelty of the newly born. Wipe off the mold that time has gathered upon their tombs, and let them all come forth and answer, at the summons of a new-born nation that calls them again to life!

Tell to these strangers the story of the resurrection. Clutching in their hands their dripping blades, the warriors recount their conquests, and joined at last in harmonious brotherhood, Copernicus, with bony fingers pointing upward, tells to Confucius his story of the stars!

Fellow-citizens, I have recounted but one of our many peaceful triumphs. Shall all these hopes of the future, shall all these peaceful victories of our people, shall all these struggles of the past be swept away by the dissolution of this Union and the destruction of the government? Forbid it, Almighty God! Rather perish a thousand times the cause of the rebellion, and over the ruins of slavery let peace once more resume her sway, and let the cannon's lips grow cold. *Delenda est Carthago*, said the old Roman patriot, when gloom settled upon his State. The rebellion must go down in the same spirit, say we all to-day. Down with party, sect, and class, and up with a sentiment of unanimity when our country calls to arms! New England leads us in the contest. The legions of Vermont are now *en route* for the field. Again, she can say with truth that "the bones of her sons lie mingling and bleaching with the soil of every State from Maine to Georgia, and there they will lie forever." New York must not be behind the Old Bay State which led a year ago. In the spirit world, Warren calls to Hamilton, and Hamilton calls back to Warren, that hand in hand their mortal children go on together to fame, to victory, or to the grave. Where the ranks are full, let us catch an inspiration from the past, and with it upon us go forth to conflict. Go call the roll on Saratoga, Bunker Hill, and Yorktown, that the sheeted dead may rise as witnesses, and tell your legions of the effort to dissolve their Union, and there receive their answer. Mad with frenzy, burning with indignation at the thought, all ablaze for vengeance upon the traitors, such shall be the fury and impetuosity of the onset that all opposition shall be swept away before them, as the pigmy yields to the avalanche that comes tumbling, rumbling, thundering from its Alpine home! Let us gather at the tomb of Washington and invoke his immortal spirit to direct us in the combat. Rising again incarnate from the tomb, in one hand he

holds that same old flag, blackened and begrimed with the smoke of a seven-years' war, and with the other hand he points us to the foe. Up and at them! Let immortal energy strengthen our arms, and infernal fury thrill us to the soul. One blow,—deep, effectual, and forever,—one crushing blow upon the rebellion, in the name of God, Washington, and the Republic!

FISHER AMES

(1758–1808)

FISHER AMES is easily first among the New England Federalist orators of the first quarter of a century of the Republic. He was greatly, sometimes extravagantly, admired by his contemporaries, and his addresses are studied as models by eminent public speakers of our own day. Dr. Charles Caldwell in his autobiography calls Ames "one of the most splendid rhetoricians of his age." . . . "Two of his speeches," writes Doctor Caldwell, "that on Jay's Treaty and that usually called his Tomahawk speech, because it included some resplendent passages on Indian massacre, were the most brilliant and fascinating specimens of eloquence I have ever heard, though I have listened to some of the most eloquent speakers in the British Parliament,—among others to Wilberforce and Mackintosh, Plunkett, Brougham, and Canning. Doctor Priestly who was familiar with the oratory of Pitt the father, and Pitt the son, as also with that of Burke and Fox, made to myself the acknowledgment that the speech of Ames on the British treaty was 'the most bewitching piece of eloquence' to which he had ever listened."

Ames was born at Dedham, Massachusetts, on April 9th, 1758. His father, Nathaniel Ames, a physician, had the "honorable family standing" which was so important in the life of most of the colonies. He had scientific tendencies and published an "Astronomical Diary," or nautical almanac, which was in considerable vogue. The son, however, developed at the early age of six years a fondness for classical literature, which led him to undertake to master Latin. He made such progress that he was admitted to Harvard when but twelve years old. While there, it "was observed that he coveted the glory of eloquence," showing his fondness for oratory not merely in the usual debating society declamation, but by the study of classical models and of such great English poets as Shakespeare and Milton. To this, no doubt correctly, has been attributed his great command of language and his fertility in illustration. After graduating from Harvard in 1774, he studied law in Boston, served in the Massachusetts legislature, in the convention for ratifying the Federal constitution, and in the first Congress elected under the constitution. After retiring, he was called in 1804 to the presidency of Harvard. He declined

the honor, however, on account of diffidence and failing health. His death occurred on the fourth of July, 1808, in the fiftieth year of his age.

After the treaty with Great Britain (Jay's), concluded in 1794, had been ratified and proclaimed by the President, he communicated it to the House of Representatives, "in order that the necessary appropriations might be made to carry it into effect." The speech on the Treaty, delivered by Ames, was on a resolution in favor of making the appropriations thus called for, the House being in committee of the whole April 28th, 1796.

ON THE BRITISH TREATY

(Delivered in the House of Representatives, April 28, 1796)

Mr. Chairman:—

I ENTERTAIN the hope, perhaps a rash one, that my strength will hold me out to speak a few minutes.

In my judgment, a right decision will depend more on the temper and manner with which we may prevail upon ourselves to contemplate the subject than upon the development of any profound political principles, or any remarkable skill in the application of them. If we could succeed to neutralize our inclinations, we should find less difficulty than we have to apprehend in surmounting all our objections.

The suggestion, a few days ago, that the House manifested symptoms of heat and irritation, was made and retorted as if the charge ought to create surprise, and would convey reproach. Let us be more just to ourselves and to the occasion. Let us not affect to deny the existence and the intrusion of some portion of prejudice and feeling into the debate, when, from the very structure of our nature, we ought to anticipate the circumstance as a probability, and when we are admonished by the evidence of our senses that it is the fact.

How can we make professions for ourselves, and offer exhortations to the House, that no influence should be felt but that of duty, and no guide respected but that of the understanding, while the peal to rally every passion of man is continually ringing in our ears?

Our understandings have been addressed, it is true, and with ability and effect; but, I demand, has any corner of the heart been left unexplored? It has been ransacked to find auxiliary

arguments, and, when that attempt failed, to awaken the sensibilities that would require none. Every prejudice and feeling has been summoned to listen to some peculiar style of address; and yet we seem to believe and to consider as an affront a doubt that we are strangers to any influence but that of unbiased reason.

It would be strange that a subject which has aroused in turn all the passions of the country should be discussed without the interference of any of our own. We are men, and, therefore, not exempt from those passions; as citizens and representatives we feel the interests that must excite them. The hazard of great interests cannot fail to agitate strong passions. We are not disinterested; it is impossible we should be dispassionate. The warmth of such feelings may becloud the judgment, and, for a time, pervert the understanding. But the public sensibility, and our own, has sharpened the spirit of inquiry, and given an animation to the debate. The public attention has been quickened to mark the progress of the discussion, and its judgment, often hasty and erroneous on first impressions, has become solid and enlightened at last. Our result will, I hope, on that account, be the safer and more mature, as well as more accordant with that of the nation. The only constant agents in political affairs are the passions of men. Shall we complain of our nature—shall we say that man ought to have been made otherwise? It is right already, because he, from whom we derive our nature, ordained it so; and because thus made and thus acting, the cause of truth and the public good is the more surely promoted.

But an attempt has been made to produce an influence of a nature more stubborn and more unfriendly to truth. It is very unfairly pretended, that the constitutional right of this house is at stake, and to be asserted and preserved only by a vote in the negative. We hear it said that this is a struggle for liberty, a manly resistance against the design to nullify this assembly and to make it a cipher in the government; that the President and Senate, the numerous meetings in the cities, and the influence of the general alarm of the country, are the agents and instruments of a scheme of coercion and terror, to force the treaty down our throats, though we loathe it, and in spite of the clearest convictions of duty and conscience.

It is necessary to pause here and inquire whether suggestions of this kind be not unfair in their very texture and fabric, and

pernicious in all their influences. They oppose an obstacle in the path of inquiry, not simply discouraging, but absolutely insurmountable. They will not yield to argument; for as they were not reasoned up, they cannot be reasoned down. They are higher than a Chinese wall in truth's way, and built of materials that are indestructible. While this remains, it is vain to argue; it is vain to say to this mountain, Be thou cast into the sea. For, I ask of the men of knowledge of the world whether they would not hold him for a blockhead that should hope to prevail in an argument whose scope and object is to mortify the self-love of the expected proselyte? I ask, further, when such attempts have been made, have they not failed of success? The indignant heart repels a conviction that is believed to debase it.

The self-love of an individual is not warmer in its sense, nor more constant in its action, than what is called in French, *l'esprit du corps*, or the self-love of an assembly; that jealous affection which a body of men is always found to bear towards its own prerogatives and power. I will not condemn this passion. Why should we urge an unmeaning censure or yield to groundless fears that truth and duty will be abandoned, because men in a public assembly are still men, and feel that *esprit du corps* which is one of the laws of their nature? Still less should we despond or complain, if we reflect that this very spirit is a guardian instinct that watches over the life of this assembly. It cherishes the principle of self-preservation, and without its existence, and its existence with all the strength we see it possess, the privileges of the representatives of the people, and mediately the liberties of the people, would not be guarded, as they are, with a vigilance that never sleeps and an unrelaxed constancy and courage.

If the consequences, most unfairly attributed to the vote in the affirmative, were not chimerical, and worse, for they are deceptive, I should think it a reproach to be found even moderate in my zeal to assert the constitutional powers of this assembly; and whenever they shall be in real danger, the present occasion affords proof that there will be no want of advocates and champions.

Indeed, so prompt are these feelings, and, when once roused, so difficult to pacify, that if we could prove the alarm was groundless, the prejudice against the appropriations may remain on the mind, and it may even pass for an act of prudence and duty to negative a measure which was lately believed by our-selves, and may hereafter be misconceived by others, to encroach upon the powers of the House. Principles that bear a remote affinity with usurpation on those powers will be rejected, not merely as errors, but as wrongs. Our sensibilities will shrink from a post where it is possible they may be wounded, and be inflamed by the slightest suspicion of an assault.

While these prepossessions remain, all argument is useless. It may be heard with the ceremony of attention, and lavish its own resources, and the patience it wearies, to no manner of purpose. The ears may be open; but the mind will remain locked up, and every pass to the understanding guarded.

Unless, therefore, this jealous and repulsive fear for the rights of the House can be allayed, I will not ask a hearing.

I cannot press this topic too far; I cannot address myself with too much emphasis to the magnanimity and candor of those who sit here, to suspect their own feelings, and, while they do, to examine the grounds of their alarm. I repeat it, we must con-quer our persuasion that this body has an interest in one side of the question more than the other, before we attempt to sur-mount our objections. On most subjects, and solemn ones too, perhaps in the most solemn of all, we form our creed more from inclination than evidence.

Let me expostulate with gentlemen to admit, if it be only by way of supposition, and for a moment, that it is barely possible they have yielded too suddenly to their alarms for the powers of this House; that the addresses which have been made with such variety of forms and with so great dexterity in some of them, to all that is prejudice and passion in the heart, are either the effects or the instruments of artifice and deception, and then let them see the subject once more in its singleness and simplicity.

It will be impossible, on taking a fair review of the subject, to justify the passionate appeals that have been made to us to struggle for our liberties and rights, and the solemn exhortations to reject the proposition, said to be concealed in that on your table, to surrender them forever. In spite of this mock solem-nity, I demand, if the House will not concur in the measure to execute the treaty, what other course shall we take? How many ways of proceeding lie open before us?

In the nature of things there are but three; we are either to make the treaty, to observe it, or break it. It would be absurd

to say we will do neither. If I may repeat a phrase already so much abused, we are under coercion to do one of them; and we have no power, by the exercise of our discretion, to prevent the consequences of a choice.

By refusing to act, we choose. The treaty will be broken and fall to the ground. Where is the fitness, then, of replying to those who urge upon the House the topics of duty and policy, that they attempt to force the treaty down, and to compel this assembly to renounce its discretion, and to degrade itself to the rank of a blind and passive instrument in the hands of the treaty-making power? In case we reject the appropriation, we do not secure any greater liberty of action; we gain no safer shelter than before from the consequences of the decision. In-deed, they are not to be evaded. It is neither just nor manly to complain that the treaty-making power has produced this coercion to act. It is not the act or the despotism of that power — it is the nature of things that compels. Shall we, dreading to become the blind instruments of power, yield ourselves the blinder dupes of mere sounds of imposture? Yet that word, that empty word, coercion, has given scope to an eloquence that, one would imag-ine, could not be tired and did not choose to be quieted.

Let us examine still more in detail the alternatives that are before us, and we shall scarcely fail to see, in still stronger lights, the futility of our apprehensions for the power and liberty of the House.

If, as some have suggested, the thing called a treaty is in-complete, — if it has no binding force or obligation, — the first question is, Will this House complete the instrument, and, by concurring, impart to it that force which it wants?

The doctrine has been avowed that the treaty, though form-ally ratified by the executive power of both nations, though pub-lished as a law for our own by the President's proclamation, is still a mere proposition submitted to this assembly, no way dis-tinguishable, in point of authority or obligation, from a motion for leave to bring in a bill, or any other original act of ordinary legislation. This doctrine, so novel in our country, yet so dear to many, precisely for the reason that, in the contention for power, victory is always dear, is obviously repugnant to the very terms as well as the fair interpretation of our own resolutions (Mr. Blount's). We declare that the treaty-making power is exclusively vested in the President and Senate, and not in this

House. Need I say that we fly in the face of that resolution when we pretend that the acts of that power are not valid until we have concurred in them? It would be nonsense, or worse, to use the language of the most glaring contradiction, and to claim a share in a power which we at the same time disdain as exclu-sively vested in other departments.

What can be more strange than to say that the compacts of the President and Senate with foreign nations are treaties, with-out our agency, and yet those compacts want all power and obligation, until they are sanctioned by our concurrence? It is not my design, in this place, if at all, to go into the discussion of this part of the subject. I will, at least for the present, take it for granted, that this monstrous opinion stands in little need of remark, and if it does, lies almost out of the reach of refu-tation.

But, say those who hide the absurdity under the cover of ambiguous phrases, Have we no discretion? And if we have, are we not to make use of it in judging of the expediency or inex-pediency of the treaty? Our resolution claims that privilege, and we cannot surrender it without equal inconsistency and breach of duty.

If there be any inconsistency in the case, it lies, not in mak-ing the appropriations for the treaty, but in the resolution itself (Mr. Blount's). Let us examine it more nearly. A treaty is a bargain between nations, binding in good faith; and what makes a bargain? The assent of the contracting parties. We allow that the treaty power is not in this House; this House has no share in contracting, and is not a party; of consequence, the President and Senate alone may make a treaty that is binding in good faith. We claim, however, say the gentlemen, a right to judge of the expediency of treaties; that is the constitutional province of our discretion. Be it so. What follows? Treaties, when adjudged by us to be inexpedient, fall to the ground, and the public faith is not hurt. This, incredible and extravagant as it may seem, is asserted. The amount of it, in plainer language, is this — the President and Senate are to make national bargains, and this House has nothing to do in making them. But bad bargains do not bind this House, and, of inevitable consequence, do not bind the nation. When a national bargain, called a treaty, is made, its binding force does not depend upon the making, but upon our opinion that it is good. . . .

To expatiate on the value of public faith may pass with some men for declamation — to such men I have nothing to say. To others I will urge, Can any circumstance mark upon a people more turpitude and debasement? Can anything tend more to make men think themselves mean, or degrade to a lower point their estimation of virtue and their standard of action?

It would not merely demoralize mankind; it tends to break all the ligaments of society, to dissolve that mysterious charm which attracts individuals to the nation, and to inspire in its stead a repulsive sense of shame and disgust.

What is patriotism? Is it a narrow affection for the spot where a man was born? Are the very clods where we tread entitled to this ardent preference because they are greener? No, sir; this is not the character of the virtue, and it soars higher for its object. It is an extended self-love, mingling with all the enjoyments of life, and twisting itself with the minutest filaments of the heart. It is thus we obey the laws of society, because they are the laws of virtue. In their authority we see, not the array of force and terror, but the venerable image of our coun-try's honor. Every good citizen makes that honor his own, and cherishes it not only as precious, but as sacred. He is willing to risk his life in its defense, and is conscious that he gains pro-tection while he gives it. For what rights of a citizen will be deemed inviolable when a State renounces the principles that constitute their security? Or, if his life should not be invaded, what would its enjoyments be in a country odious in the eyes of strangers and dishonored in his own? Could he look with affec-tion and veneration to such a country as his parent? The sense of having one would die within him; he would blush for his patriotism, if he retained any, and justly, for it would be a vice. He would be a banished man in his native land.

I see no exception to the respect that is paid among nations to the law of good faith. If there are cases in this enlightened period when it is violated, there are none when it is decried. It is the philosophy of politics, the religion of governments. It is observed by barbarians — a whiff of tobacco smoke, or a string of beads, gives not merely binding force, but sanctity to treaties. Even in Algiers a truce may be bought for money; but, when ratified, even Algiers is too wise, or too just, to disown and annul its obligation. Thus, we see neither the ignorance of sav-ages nor the principles of an association for piracy and rapine, permit a nation to despise its engagements. If, sir, there could be a resurrection from the foot of the gallows, if the victims of justice could live again, collect together and form a society, they would, however loath, soon find themselves obliged to make justice, that justice under which they fell, the fundamental law of their state. They would perceive it was their interest to make others respect, and they would therefore soon pay some respect themselves to the obligations of good faith.

It is painful, I hope it is superfluous, to make even the supposition, that America should furnish the occasion of this opprobrium. No, let me not even imagine that a republican government, sprung as our own is, from a people enlightened and uncorrupted, a government whose origin is right, and whose daily discipline is duty, can, upon solemn debate, make its option to be faithless — can dare to act what despots dare not avow, what our own example evinces, the states of Barbary are unsuspected of. No, let me rather make the supposition that Great Britain refuses to execute the treaty, after we have done everything to carry it into effect. Is there any language of reproach pungent enough to express your commentary on the fact? What would you say, or rather what would you not say? Would you not tell them, wherever an Englishman might travel, shame would stick to him — he would disown his country. You would exclaim, England, proud of your wealth, and arrogant in the possession of power — blush for these distinctions, which become the vehicles of your dishonor. Such a nation might truly say to corruption, Thou art my father, and to the worm, Thou art my mother and my sister. We should say of such a race of men, their name is a heavier burden than their debt.

I can scarcely persuade myself to believe that the consideration I have suggested requires the aid of any auxiliary. But, unfortunately, auxiliary arguments are at hand. Five millions of dollars, and probably more, on the score of spoliations committed on our commerce, depend upon the treaty. The treaty offers the only prospect of indemnity. Such redress is promised as the merchants place some confidence in. Will you interpose and frustrate that hope, leaving to many families nothing but beggary and despair? It is a smooth proceeding to take a vote in this body; it takes less than half an hour to call the yeas and nays and reject the treaty. But what is the effect of it? What, but this? The very men formerly so loud for redress, such fierce

champions that even to ask for justice was too mean and too slow, now turn their capricious fury upon the sufferers and say, by their vote, to them and their families, No longer eat bread; petitioners, go home and starve; we can not satisfy your wrongs and our resentments.

Will you pay the sufferers out of the treasury? No. The answer was given two years ago, and appears on our journals. Will you give them letters of marque and reprisal to pay themselves by force? No; that is war. Besides, it would be an opportunity for those who have already lost much to lose more. Will you go to war to avenge their injury? If you do, the war will leave you no money to indemnify them. If it should be unsuccessful, you will aggravate existing evils; if successful, your enemy will have no treasure left to give our merchants; the first losses will be confounded with much greater, and be forgotten. At the end of a war there must be a negotiation, which is the very point we have already gained; and why relinquish it? And who will be confident that the terms of the negotiation, after a desolating war, would be more acceptable to another House of Representatives than the treaty before us? Members and opinions may be so changed that the treaty would then be rejected for being what the present majority say it should be. Whether we shall go on making treaties and refusing to execute them, I know not. Of this I am certain, it will be very difficult to exercise the treaty-making power on the new principles, with much reputation or advantage to the country.

The refusal of the posts (inevitable if we reject the treaty) is a measure too decisive in its nature to be neutral in its consequences. From great causes we are to look for great effects. A plain and obvious one will be the price of the western lands will fall. Settlers will not choose to fix their habitation on a field of battle. Those who talk so much of the interest of the United States should calculate how deeply it will be affected by rejecting the treaty; how vast a tract of wild land will almost cease to be property. The loss, let it be observed, will fall upon a fund expressly devoted to sink the national debt. What, then, are we called upon to do? However the form of the vote and the protestations of many may disguise the proceeding, our resolution is in substance, and it deserves to wear the title of a resolution to prevent the sale of the western lands and the discharge of the public debt.

Will the tendency to Indian hostilities be contested by any one? Experience gives the answer. The frontiers were scourged with war till the negotiation with Great Britain was far advanced, and then the state of hostility ceased. Perhaps the public agents of both nations are innocent of fomenting the Indian war, and perhaps they are not. We ought not, however, to expect that neighboring nations, highly irritated against each other, will neglect the friendship of the savages; the traders will gain an influence and will abuse it; and who is ignorant that their passions are easily raised, and hardly restrained from violence? Their situation will oblige them to choose between this country and Great Britain, in case the treaty should be rejected. They will not be our friends, and at the same time the friends of our enemies.

But am I reduced to the necessity of proving this point? Certainly the very men who charged the Indian war on the detention of the posts, will call for no other proofs than the recital of their own speeches. It is remembered with what emphasis, with what acrimony, they expatiated on the burden of taxes, and the drain of blood and treasure into the western country, in consequence of Britain's holding the posts. Until the posts are restored, they exclaimed, the treasury and the frontiers must bleed.

If any, against all these proofs, should maintain that the peace with the Indians will be stable without the posts, to them I will urge another reply. From arguments calculated to produce conviction, I will appeal directly to the hearts of those who hear me, and ask whether it is not already planted there. I resort especially to the convictions of the western gentlemen, whether, supposing no posts and no treaty, the settlers will remain in security. Can they take it upon them to say that an Indian peace, under these circumstances, will prove firm? No, sir; it will not be peace, but a sword; it will be no better than a lure to draw victims within the reach of the tomahawk.

On this theme, my emotions are unutterable. If I could find words for them — if my powers bore any proportion to my zeal — I would swell my voice to such a note of remonstrance, it should reach every log house beyond the mountains. I would say to the inhabitants, Wake from your false security; your cruel dangers, your more cruel apprehensions, are soon to be renewed; the wounds, yet unhealed, are to be torn open again; in the day-

time, your path through the woods will be ambushed; the darkness of midnight will glitter with the blaze of your dwellings. You are a father — the blood of your sons shall fatten your corn-field; you are a mother — the war-whoop shall wake the sleep of the cradle.

On this subject you need not suspect any deception on your feelings. It is a spectacle of horror which can not be overdrawn. If you have nature in your hearts, it will speak a language compared with which all I have said or can say will be poor and frigid.

Will it be whispered that the treaty has made a new champion for the protection of the frontiers? It is known that my voice as well as vote has been uniformly given in conformity with the ideas I have expressed. Protection is the right of the frontiers; it is our duty to give it.

Who will accuse me of wandering out of the subject? Who will say that I exaggerate the tendencies of our measures? Will any one answer by a sneer, that all this is idle preaching? Will any one deny that we are bound, and I would hope to good purpose, by the most solemn sanctions of duty, for the vote we give? Are despots alone to be approached for unfeeling indifference to the tears and blood of their subjects? Are republicans unresponsible? Have the principles, on which you ground the reproach upon cabinets and kings, no practical influence, no binding force? Are they merely themes of idle declamation, introduced to decorate the morality of a newspaper essay, or to furnish pretty topics of harangue from the windows of that state house? I trust it is neither too presumptuous nor too late to ask, Can you put the dearest interest of society at risk without guilt, and without remorse?

It is vain to offer as an excuse, that public men are not to be reproached for the evils that may happen to ensue from their measures. This is very true, where they are unforeseen or inevitable. Those I have depicted are not unforeseen; they are so far from inevitable, we are going to bring them into being by our vote. We choose the consequences, and become as justly answerable for them as for the measure that we know will produce them.

By rejecting the posts, we light the savage fires — we bind the victims. This day we undertake to render account to the widows and orphans whom our decision will make, to the wretches that

will be roasted at the stake, to our country, and I do not deem
it too serious to say, to conscience and to God. We are answerable, and if duty be anything more than a word of imposture,
if conscience be not a bugbear, we are preparing to make ourselves as wretched as our country.

There is no mistake in this case; there can be none. Experience has already been the prophet of events, and the cries of
our future victims have already reached us. The western inhabitants are not a silent and uncomplaining sacrifice. The voice of
humanity issues from the shade of their wilderness. It exclaims,
that while one hand is held up to reject this treaty, the other
grasps a tomahawk. It summons our imagination to the scenes
that will open. It is no great effort to the imagination to conceive that events so near are already begun. I can fancy that I
listen to the yells of savage vengeance and the shrieks of torture. Already they seem to sigh in the west wind — already they
mingle with every echo from the mountains.

It is not the part of prudence to be inattentive to the tendencies of measures. Where there is any ground to fear that
these will be pernicious, wisdom and duty forbid that we should
underrate them. If we reject the treaty, will our peace be as
safe as if we executed it with good faith? I do honor to the intrepid spirit of those who say it will. It was formerly understood to constitute the excellence of a man's faith to believe
without evidence and against it.

But as opinions on this article are changed, and we are called
to act for our country, it becomes us to explore the dangers that
will attend its peace, and to avoid them if we can.

Few of us here, and fewer still in proportion of our constituents, will doubt that, by rejecting, all those dangers will be
aggravated. . . .

ST. ANSELM

(1032–1109)

ST. ANSELM, who has been called the acutest thinker and profoundest theologian of his day, was born in Piedmont about
1032. Educated under the celebrated Lanfranc, he went to
England in 1093 and became Archbishop of Canterbury. He was
banished by William Rufus as a result of a conflict between royal
and ecclesiastical prerogative. He died in 1109. Neale calls him the
last of the great fathers except St. Bernard, and adds that «he probably possessed the greatest genius of all except St. Augustine.»

The sermon here given, the third of the sixteen extant, is given
entire from Neale's translation. It is one of the best examples of
the Middle-Age style of interpreting all Scripture as metaphor and
parable. It contains, moreover, a number of striking passages, such
as, «It is a proof of great virtue to struggle with happiness.»

THE SEA OF LIFE

«AND straightway Jesus constrained his disciples to get into a
ship, and to go before him to the other side, while he
sent the multitude away.» (Matt. xiv. 22.)

In this section, according to its mystical interpretation, we
have a summary description of the state of the Church, from the
coming of the Savior to the end of the world. For the Lord
constrained his Disciples to get into a ship, when he committed
the Church to the government of the Apostles and their followers. And thus to go before him unto the other side, — that
is, to bear onwards towards the haven of the celestial country,
before he himself should entirely depart from the world. For,
with his elect, and on account of his elect, he ever remains here
until the consummation of all things; and he is preceded to the
other side of the sea of this world by those who daily pass hence
to the Land of the Living. And when he shall have sent all
that are his to that place, then, leaving the multitude of the

reprobate, and no longer warning them to be converted, but giving them over to perdition, he will depart hence that he may be
with his elect alone in the kingdom.

Whence it is added, «while he sent the multitude away.» For
in the end of the world he will «send away the multitude» of
his enemies, that they may then be hurried by the Devil to
everlasting damnation. «And when he had sent the multitude
away, he went up in a mountain to pray.» He will not send
away the multitude of the Gentiles till the end of the world;
but he did dismiss the multitude of the Jewish people at the time
when, as saith Isaiah, «He commanded his clouds that they
should rain no rain upon it»; that is, he commanded his Apostles
that they should preach no longer to the Jews, but should go to
the Gentiles. Thus, therefore, he sent away that multitude, and
«went up into a mountain»; that is, to the height of the celestial kingdom, of which it had been written, «Who shall ascend
into the hill of the Lord, or who shall rise up in his holy place?»
For a mountain is a height, and what is higher than heaven?
There the Lord ascended. And he ascended alone, «for no man
hath ascended up into heaven save he that came down from
heaven, even the Son of Man which is in heaven.» And even
when he shall come at the end of the world, and shall have collected all of us, his members, together, and shall have raised us
into heaven, he will also ascend alone, because Christ, the head,
is one with his body. But now the Head alone ascends, — the
Mediator of God and man — the man Christ Jesus. And he goes
up to pray, because he went to the Father to intercede for us.
«For Christ is not entered into holy places made with hands,
which are figures of the true, but into heaven itself, now to
appear in the presence of God for us.»

It follows: «And when the evening was come, he was there
alone.» This signifies the nearness of the end of the world, concerning which John also speaks: «Little children, it is the last
time.» Therefore it is said that, «when the evening was come,
he was there alone,» because, when the world was drawing to its
end, he by himself, as the true high priest, entered into the holy
of holies, and is there at the right hand of God, and also maketh
intercession for us. But while he prays on the mountain, the
ship is tossed with waves in the deep. For, since the billows
arise, the ship may be tossed; but since Christ prays, it cannot
be overwhelmed.

We may notice, also, that this commotion of the waves, and
tottering or half-sinking of Peter, takes place even in our time,
according to the spiritual sense daily. For every man's own be-
setting sin is the tempest. You love God; you walk upon the
sea; the swellings of this world are under your feet. You love
the world; it swallows you up; its wont is to devour, not to
bear up, its lovers. But when your heart fluctuates with the
desire of sin, call on the divinity of Christ, that you may conquer that desire. You think that the wind is then contrary when
the adversity of this world rises against you, and not also when
its prosperity fawns upon you. For when wars, when tumults,
when famine, when pestilence comes, when any private calamity
happens even to individual men, then the wind is thought adverse, and then it is held right to call upon God; but when the
world smiles with temporal felicity, then, forsooth, the wind is
not contrary. Do not, by such tokens as these, judge of the
tranquillity of the time; but judge of it by your own temptations. See if you are tranquil within yourself; see if no internal
tempest is overwhelming you. It is a proof of great virtue to
struggle with happiness, so that it shall not seduce, corrupt, subvert. Learn to trample on this world; remember to trust in
Christ. And if your foot be moved, — if you totter, — if there
be some temptations that you cannot overcome, — if you begin
to sink, cry out to Jesus, Lord, save me. In Peter, therefore,
the common condition of all of us is to be considered; so that,
if the wind of temptation endeavor to upset us in any matter,
or its billows to swallow us up, we may cry to Christ. He shall
stretch forth his hand, and preserve us from the deep.

It follows: «And when he was come into the ship, the wind
ceased.» In the last day he shall ascend into the ship of the
Church, because then he shall sit upon the throne of his glory;
which throne may not unfitly be understood of the Church. For
he who by faith and good works now and always dwells in the
Church shall then, by the manifestation of his glory, enter into it.
And then the wind shall cease, because evil spirits shall no more
have the power of sending forth against it the flames of temptation or the commotions of troubles; for then all things shall be
at peace and at rest.

It follows: «Then they that were with him in the ship came
and worshipped him, saying, Of a truth thou art the Son of
God.» They who remain faithfully in the Church amidst the

tempests of temptations will approach to him with joy, and, entering into his kingdom with him, will worship him; and, praising him perpetually, will affirm him of a truth to be the Son of God. Then, also, that will happen which is written concerning the elect raised from death: "All flesh shall come and shall worship before my face," saith the Lord. And again: "Blessed are they that dwell in thy house; they will always be praising thee." For him, whom with their heart they believe unto righteousness, and with their mouth confess to salvation, him they shall see with their heart to light, and with their mouth shall praise to glory, when they behold how ineffably he is begotten of the Father, with whom he liveth and reigneth, in the unity of the Holy Ghost, God to all ages of ages. Amen.

THOMAS ARNOLD

(1795-1842)

DOCTOR THOMAS ARNOLD, the celebrated head master of Rugby, was born June 13th, 1795, at West Cowes, in the Isle of Wight, where his father, William Arnold, was a Collector of Customs. After several years at Winchester school, he went to Oxford where in 1815 he was elected a fellow of Oriel College. His intellectual bent showed at Oxford, on the one hand, in fondness for Aristotle and Thucydides, and on the other in what one of his friends has described as "an earnest, penetrating, and honest examination of Christianity." As a result of this honesty and earnestness, he became and remains a great force wherever English is spoken. Elected head master of Rugby in December 1827, and remaining in charge of that school for nearly fourteen years, he almost revolutionized and did much to civilize the English system of public education. When he left Rugby, in December 1841, it was to go to Oxford as professor of Modern History, but his death, June 12th, 1842, left him remembered by the English-speaking world as "Arnold of Rugby." He left five volumes of sermons, an edition of 'Thucydides,' a 'History of Rome' in three volumes, and other works, but his greatest celebrity has been given him by the enthusiastic love which his manly Christian character inspired in his pupils and acquaintances, furnishing as it did the master motive of 'Tom Brown at Rugby,' a book which is likely to hold the place it has taken next to 'Robinson Crusoe' among English classics for the young.

The sermon here republished from the text given in 'Simons's Sermons of Great Preachers,' is an illustration of the eloquence which appeals to the mind of others, not through musical and beautiful language so much as through deep thought and compact expression.

THE REALITIES OF LIFE AND DEATH

"God is not the God of the dead, but of the living."— Matt. xxii. 32

WE HEAR these words as a part of our Lord's answer to the Sadducees; and, as their question was put in evident profaneness, and the answer to it is one which to our minds is quite obvious and natural, so we are apt to think that in this particular story there is less than usual that particularly concerns us. But it so happens, that our Lord, in answering the Sadducees, has brought in one of the most universal and most solemn of all truths,— which is indeed implied in many parts of the Old Testament, but which the Gospel has revealed to us in all its fullness,— the truth contained in the words of the text, that "God is not the God of the dead, but of the living."

I would wish to unfold a little what is contained in these words, which we often hear even, perhaps, without quite understanding them; and many times oftener without fully entering into them. And we may take them, first, in their first part, where they say that "God is not the God of the dead."

The word "dead," we know, is constantly used in Scripture in a double sense, as meaning those who are dead spiritually, as well as those who are dead naturally. And, in either sense, the words are alike applicable: "God is not the God of the dead."

God's not being the God of the dead signifies two things: that they who are without him are dead, as well as that they who are dead are also without him. So far as our knowledge goes respecting inferior animals, they appear to be examples of this truth. They appear to us to have no knowledge of God; and we are not told that they have any other life than the short one of which our senses inform us. I am well aware that our ignorance of their condition is so great that we may not dare to say anything of them positively; there may be a hundred things true respecting them which we neither know nor imagine. I would only say that, according to that most imperfect light in which we see them, the two points of which I have been speaking appear to meet in them: we believe that they have no consciousness of God, and we believe that they will die. And so far, therefore, they afford an example of the agreement, if I may so speak, between these two points; and were intended, perhaps, to be to our view a continual image of it. But we had far better speak

of ourselves. And here, too, it is the case that "God is not the God of the dead." If we are without him we are dead; and if we are dead we are without him: in other words, the two ideas of death and absence from God are in fact synonymous.

Thus, in the account given of the fall of man, the sentence of death and of being cast out of Eden go together; and if any one compares the description of the second Eden in the Revelation, and recollects how especially it is there said, that God dwells in the midst of it, and is its light by day and night, he will see that the banishment from the first Eden means a banishment from the presence of God. And thus, in the day that Adam sinned, he died; for he was cast out of Eden immediately, however long he may have moved about afterwards upon the earth where God was not. And how very strong to the same point are the words of Hezekiah's prayer, "The grave cannot praise thee, Death cannot celebrate thee; they that go down into the pit cannot hope for thy truth"; words which express completely the feeling that God is not the God of the dead. This, too, appears to be the sense generally of the expression used in various parts of the Old Testament, "Thou shalt surely die." It is, no doubt, left purposely obscure; nor are we ever told, in so many words, all that is meant by death; but, surely, it always implies a separation from God, and the being— whatever the notion may extend to— the being dead to him. Thus, when David had committed his great sin, and had expressed his repentance for it, Nathan tells him, "The Lord also hath put away thy sin; thou shalt not die": which means, most expressively, thou shalt not die to God. In one sense David died, as all men die; nor was he by any means freed from the punishment of his sin: he was not, in that sense, forgiven; but he was allowed still to regard God as his God; and, therefore, his punishments were but fatherly chastisements from God's hand, designed for his profit, that he might be partaker of God's holiness. And thus, although Saul was sentenced to lose his kingdom, and although he was killed with his sons on Mount Gilboa, yet I do not think that we find the sentence passed upon him, "Thou shalt surely die;" and, therefore, we have no right to say that God had ceased to be his God, although he visited him with severe chastisements, and would not allow him to hand down to his sons the crown of Israel. Observe, also, the language of the eighteenth chapter of Ezekiel, where the expressions occur so often, "He shall surely live," and "He shall surely die." We have no right to refer these to a mere extension on the one hand, or a cutting short on the other, of the term of earthly existence. The promise of living long in the land, or, as in Hezekiah's case, of adding to his days fifteen years, is very different from the full and unreserved blessing, "Thou shalt surely live." And we know, undoubtedly, that both the good and the bad to whom Ezekiel spoke died alike the natural death of the body. But the peculiar force of the promise, and of the threat, was, in the one case, Thou shalt belong to God; in the other, Thou shalt cease to belong to him; although the veil was not yet drawn up which concealed the full import of those terms, "belonging to God," and "ceasing to belong to him": nay, can we venture to affirm that it is fully drawn aside even now?

I have dwelt on this at some length, because it really seems to place the common state of the minds of too many amongst us in a light which is exceedingly awful; for if it be true, as I think the Scripture implies, that to be dead, and to be without God, are precisely the same thing, then can it be denied that the symptoms of death are strongly marked upon many of us? Are there not many who never think of God or care about his service? Are there not many who live, to all appearances, as unconscious of his existence as we fancy the inferior animals to be? And is it not quite clear, that to such persons, God cannot be said to be their God? He may be the God of heaven and earth, the God of the universe, the God of Christ's Church; but he is not their God, for they feel to have nothing at all to do with him; and, therefore, as he is not their God, they are, and must be, according to the Scripture, reckoned among the dead.

But God is the God "of the living." That is, as before, all who are alive, live unto him; all who live unto him are alive. "God said, I am the God of Abraham, and the God of Isaac, and the God of Jacob;" and, therefore, says our Lord, "Abraham, and Isaac, and Jacob are not and cannot be dead." They cannot be dead because God owns them; he is not ashamed to be called their God; therefore, they are not cast out from him; therefore, by necessity, they live. Wonderful, indeed, is the truth here implied, in exact agreement, as we have seen, with the general language of Scripture; that, as she who but touched the hem of Christ's garment was, in a moment, relieved from her infirmity, so great was the virtue which went out from him; so they who are not cast out from God, but have anything whatever to do

with him, feel the virtue of his gracious presence penetrating their whole nature; because he lives, they must live also.

Behold, then, life and death set before us; not remote (if a few years be, indeed, to be called remote), but even now present before us; even now suffered or enjoyed. Even now we are alive unto God or dead unto God; and, as we are either the one or the other, so we are, in the highest possible sense of the terms, alive or dead. In the highest possible sense of the terms; but who can tell what that highest possible sense of the terms is? So much has, indeed, been revealed to us, that we know now that death means a conscious and perpetual death, as life means a conscious and perpetual life. But greatly, indeed, do we deceive ourselves, if we fancy that, by having thus much told us, we have also risen to the infinite heights, or descended to the infinite depths, contained in those little words, life and death. They are far higher, and far deeper, than ever thought or fancy of man has reached to. But, even on the first edge of either, at the visible beginnings of that infinite ascent or descent, there is surely something which may give us a foretaste of what is beyond. Even to us in this mortal state, even to you advanced but so short a way on your very earthly journey, life and death have a meaning: to be dead unto God or to be alive to him, are things perceptibly different.

For, let me ask of those who think least of God, who are most separate from him, and most without him, whether there is not now actually, perceptibly, in their state, something of the coldness, the loneliness, the fearfulness of death? I do not ask them whether they are made unhappy by the fear of God's anger; of course they are not: for they who fear God are not dead to him, nor he to them. The thought of him gives them no disquiet at all; this is the very point we start from. But I would ask them whether they know what it is to feel God's blessing. For instance: we all of us have our troubles of some sort or other, our disappointments, if not our sorrows. In these troubles, in these disappointments,—I care not how small they may be,—have they known what it is to feel that God's hand is over them; that these little annoyances are but his fatherly correction; that he is all the time loving us, and supporting us? In seasons of joy, such as they taste very often, have they known what it is to feel that they are tasting the kindness of their heavenly Father, that their good things come from his hand, and are but an infinitely

slight foretaste of his love? Sickness, danger,—I know that they come to many of us but rarely; but if we have known them, or at least sickness, even in its lighter form, if not in its graver,—have we felt what it is to know that we are in our Father's hands, that he is with us, and will be with us to the end; that nothing can hurt those whom he loves? Surely, then, if we have never tasted anything of this: if in trouble, or in joy, or in sickness, we are left wholly to ourselves, to bear as we can, and enjoy as we can; if there is no voice that ever speaks out of the heights and the depths around us, to give any answer to our own; if we are thus left to ourselves in this vast world,—there is in this a coldness and a loneliness; and whenever we come to be, of necessity, driven to be with our own hearts alone, the coldness and the loneliness must be felt. But consider that the things which we see around us cannot remain with us, nor we with them. The coldness and loneliness of the world, without God, must be felt more and more as life wears on: in every change of our own state, in every separation from or loss of a friend, in every more sensible weakness of our own bodies, in every additional experience of the uncertainty of our own counsels,—the deathlike feeling will come upon us more and more strongly: we shall gain more of that fearful knowledge which tells us that "God is not the God of the dead."

And so, also, the blessed knowledge that he is the God "of the living" grows upon those who are truly alive. Surely he "is not far from every one of us." No occasion of life fails to remind those who live unto him, that he is their God, and that they are his children. On light occasions or on grave ones, in sorrow and in joy, still the warmth of his love is spread, as it were, all through the atmosphere of their lives: they for ever feel his blessing. And if it fills them with joy unspeakable even now, when they so often feel how little they deserve it; if they delight still in being with God, and in living to him, let them be sure that they have in themselves the unerring witness of life eternal:—God is the God of the living, and all who are with him must live.

Hard it is, I well know, to bring this home, in any degree, to the minds of those who are dead: for it is of the very nature of the dead that they can hear no words of life. But it has happened that, even whilst writing what I have just been uttering to you, the news reached me that one, who two months ago was

one of your number, who this very half-year has shared in all the business and amusements of this place, is passed already into that state where the meanings of the terms life and death are become fully revealed. He knows what it is to live unto God, and what it is to die to him. Those things which are to us unfathomable mysteries, are to him all plain: and yet but two months ago he might have thought himself as far from attaining this knowledge as any of us can do. Wherefore it is clear, that these things, life and death, may hurry their lesson upon us sooner than we deem of, sooner than we are prepared to receive it. And that were indeed awful, if, being dead to God, and yet little feeling it, because of the enjoyments of our worldly life these enjoyments were of a sudden to be struck away from us, and we should find then that to be dead to God is death indeed, a death from which there is no waking and in which there is no sleeping forever.

CHESTER ALAN ARTHUR

(1830–1886)

F "ELOQUENCE consists in saying all that is necessary and no more," President Arthur's inaugural address is one of its best examples. He was placed in a position of the gravest difficulty. He had been nominated for Vice-President as a representative of the "Stalwart" Republicans when that element of the party had been defeated in National convention by the element then described as "Half-Breeds." After the assassination of President Garfield by the "paranoiac" Guiteau, the country waited with breathless interest to hear what the Vice-President would say in taking the Presidency. With a tact which amounted to genius, which never failed him during his administration, which in its results showed itself equivalent to the highest statesmanship, Mr. Arthur, a man to whom his opponents had been unwilling to concede more than mediocre abilities, rose to the occasion, disarmed factional oppositions, mitigated the animosity of partisanship, and during his administration did more than had been done before him to re-unite the sections divided by Civil War.

He was born in Fairfield, Vermont, October 5th, 1830. His father, Rev. William Arthur, a Baptist clergyman, born in Ireland, gave him a good education, sending him to Union College where he graduated in 1848. After teaching school in Vermont, he studied law and began practice in New York city. Entering politics as a Henry Clay Whig, and casting his first vote in 1852 for Winfield Scott, he was active as a Republican in the Fremont campaign of 1856 and from that time until elected to the Vice-Presidency took that strong interest in public affairs which led his opponents to class him as a "professional politician." During the Civil War he was inspector-general and quarter-master general of New York troops. In 1871 President Grant appointed him collector of the port of New York and he held the office until July 1878, when he was suspended by President Hayes. Taking an active part in the movement to nominate General Grant for the Presidency to succeed Mr. Hayes, he attended the Republican convention of 1880, and after the defeat of the Grant forces, he was nominated as their representative for the Vice-Presidency. He died suddenly in New York city, November 18th, 1886, having won for himself during his administration as President

anxiety which have enshrouded the country must make repose especially welcome now. No demand for speedy legislation has been heard; no adequate occasion is apparent for an unusual session of Congress. The constitution defines the functions and powers of the executive as clearly as those of either of the other two departments of the government, and he must answer for the just exercise of the discretion it permits and the performance of the duties it imposes. Summoned to these high duties and responsibilities, and profoundly conscious of their magnitude and gravity, I assume the trust imposed by the constitution, relying for aid on divine guidance and on the virtue, patriotism, and intelligence of the American people.

the good-will of so many of his political opponents that the future historian will probably study his administration as that during which the most notable changes of the decade were made from the politics of the Civil War period.

INAUGURAL ADDRESS

(Delivered September 22d, 1881)

FOR the fourth time in the history of the Republic its chief magistrate has been removed by death. All hearts are filled with grief and horror at the hideous crime which has darkened our land, and the memory of the murdered President, his protracted sufferings, his unyielding fortitude, the example and achievements of his life and the pathos of his death will forever illumine the pages of our history.

For the fourth time, the officer elected by the people and ordained by the constitution to fill a vacancy so created, is called to assume the executive chair. The wisdom of our fathers, foreseeing even the most dire possibilities, made sure that the government should never be imperiled because of the uncertainty of human life. Men may die but the fabric of our free institutions remains unshaken. No higher or more assuring proof could exist of the strength and permanence of popular government than the fact that though the chosen of the people be struck down, his constitutional successor is peacefully installed without shock or strain except that of the sorrow which mourns the bereavement. All the noble aspirations of my lamented predecessor, which found expression during his life, the measures devised and suggested during his brief administration to correct abuses, to enforce economy, to advance prosperity, to promote the general welfare, to insure domestic security and maintain friendly and honorable relations with the nations of the earth, will be garnered in the hearts of the people and it will be my earnest endeavor to profit and to see that the nation shall profit by his example and experience.

Prosperity blesses our country. Our fiscal policy as fixed by law is well-grounded and generally approved. No threatening issue mars our foreign intercourse and the wisdom, integrity, and thrift of our people may be trusted to continue undisturbed the present career of peace, tranquillity, and welfare. The gloom and

ATHANASIUS

(298–373)

ATHANASIUS, patriarch of Alexandria, owes his great celebrity chiefly to the controversy with the Arians, in which for half a century he was at the head of the orthodox party in the Church. He was born at Alexandria in the year 298, and was ordained a priest at the age of twenty-one. He accompanied his bishop, Alexander, to the Council of Nice in 325, and when under thirty years old succeeded to the bishopric, on the death of Alexander. His success in the Arian controversy was not achieved without cost, since, as an incident of it, he spent twenty years in banishment. His admirers credit him with "a deep mind, invincible courage, and living faith," but as his orations and discourses were largely controversial, the interest which now attaches to them is chiefly historical. The following was preached from the seventh and eighth verses of the Forty-Fifth Psalm.

THE DIVINITY OF CHRIST

BEHOLD, O ye Arians, and acknowledge hence the truth. The Psalmist speaks of us all as fellows or partakers of the Lord, but were he one of things which come out of nothing and of things generated he himself had been one of those who partake. But since he hymned him as the eternal God, saying, "Thy throne, O God, is forever and ever," and has declared that all other things partake of him, what conclusion must we draw, but that he is distinct from generated things, and he only the Father's veritable word, radiance, and wisdom, which all things generate partake, being sanctified by him in the Spirit? And, therefore, he is here "anointed," not that he may become God, for he was so even before; nor that he may become king, for he had the kingdom eternally, existing as God's image, as the sacred oracle shows; but in our behalf is this written, as before. For the Israelitish kings, upon their being anointed, then became kings, not being so before, as David, as Ezekias, as Josias, and the rest; but the Savior, on the contrary, being God, and ever ruling in the Father's kingdom, and being himself the Dispenser of the Holy Ghost, nevertheless is here said to be anointed, that, as before, being said as man to be anointed with the Spirit, he might provide for us more, not only exaltation and resurrection, but the indwelling and intimacy of the Spirit. And signifying this, the Lord himself hath said by his own mouth, in the Gospel according to John: "I have sent them into the world, and for their sakes do I sanctify myself, that they may be sanctified in the truth." In saying this, he has shown that he is not the sanctified, but the Sanctifier; for he is not sanctified by other, but himself sanctifies himself, that we may be sanctified in the truth. He who sanctifies himself is Lord of sanctification. How, then, does this take place? What does he mean but this? "I, being the Father's Word, I 'give to myself, when become man, the Spirit; and myself, become man, do I sanctify in him, that henceforth in me, who am truth (for "Thy Word is Truth"), all may be sanctified."

If, then, for our sake, he sanctifies himself, and does this when he becomes man, it is very plain that the Spirit's descent on him in Jordan was a descent upon us, because of his bearing our body. And it did not take place for promotion to the Word, but again for our sanctification, that we might share his anointing, and of us it might be said, Know ye not that ye are God's temple, and the Spirit of God dwelleth in you? For when the Lord, as man, was washed in Jordan, it was we who were washed in him and by him. And when he received the Spirit, we it was who, by him, were made recipients of it. And, moreover, for this reason, not as Aaron, or David, or the rest, was he anointed with oil, but in another way, above all his fellows, "with the oil of gladness," which he himself interprets to be the Spirit, saying by the prophet, "The Spirit of the Lord is upon me, because the Lord hath anointed me"; as also the Apostle has said, "How God anointed him with the Holy Ghost." When, then, were these things spoken of him, but when he came in the flesh, and was baptized in Jordan, and the spirit descended on him? And, indeed, the Lord himself said, "The Spirit shall take of mine," and "I will send him"; and to his Disciples, "Receive ye the Holy Ghost." And, notwithstanding, he who, as the word and radiance of the Father, gives to others, now is said to be sanctified, because now he has become Man, and the Body that is sanctified is his. From him, then, we have begun to receive the unction and the

seal, John saying, "And ye have an unction from the Holy One"; and the Apostle, "And ye were sealed with the Holy Spirit of promise." Therefore, because of us, and for us, are these words.

What advance, then, of promotion, and reward of virtue, or generally of conduct, is proved from this in our Lord's instance? For if he was not God, and then had become God — if, not being king, he was preferred to the kingdom, your reasoning would have had some faint plausibility. But if he is God, and the throne of his kingdom is everlasting, in what way could God advance? Or what was there wanting to him who was sitting on his Father's throne? And if, as the Lord himself has said, the Spirit is his, and takes of his, and he sends it, it is not the Word, considered as the Word and Wisdom, who is anointed with the Spirit, which he himself gives, but the flesh assumed by him, which is anointed in him and by him; that the sanctification coming to the Lord as man, may come to all men from him. For, not of itself, saith he, doth the Spirit speak, but the word is he who gives it to the worthy. For this is like the passage considered above; for, as the Apostle hath written, "Who, existing in form of God, thought it not robbery to be equal with God, but humbled himself, and took a servant's form," so David celebrates the Lord, as the everlasting God and king, but sent to us, and assuming our body, which is mortal. For this is his meaning in the Psalm, "All thy garments smell of myrrh, aloes, and cassia"; and it is represented by Nicodemus's and by Mary's company, when he came, bringing a mixture of myrrh and aloes, about an hundred pounds weight; and they took the spices which they had prepared for the burial of the Lord's body.

What advancement, then, was it to the Immortal to have assumed the mortal? Or what promotion is it to the Everlasting to have put on the temporal? What reward can be great to the Everlasting God and King, in the bosom of the Father? See ye not, that this, too, was done and written because of us and for us, that us who are mortal and temporal, the Lord, become man, might make immortal, and bring into the everlasting kingdom of heaven? Blush ye not, speaking lies against the divine oracles? For when our Lord Jesus Christ had been among us, we, indeed, were promoted, as rescued from sin; but he is the same, nor did he alter when he became man (to repeat what I have said), but, as has been written, "The word of God abideth forever." Surely as, before his becoming man, he, the Word, dispensed to the saints

the Spirit as his own; so also, when made man, he sanctifies all by the Spirit, and says to his Disciples, "Receive ye the Holy Ghost." And he gave to Moses and the other seventy; and through him David prayed to the Father, saying, "Take not thy Holy Spirit from me." On the other hand, when made man, he said, "I will send to you the Paraclete, the Spirit of Truth"; and he sent him, he, the Word of God, as being faithful.

Therefore "Jesus Christ is the same yesterday, to-day, and forever," remaining unalterable, and at once gives and receives, giving as God's Word, receiving as man. It is not the Word then, viewed as the Word, that is promoted,—for he had all things and has had them always,—but men, who have in him and through him their origin of receiving them. For, when he is now said to be anointed in a human respect, we it is who in him are anointed; since also, when he is baptized, we it is who in him are baptized. But on all these things the Savior throws much light, when he says to the Father, "And the glory which thou gavest me, I have given to them, that they may be one, even as we are one." Because of us, then, he asked for glory, and the words occur, "took" and "gave" and "highly exalted," that we might take, and to us might be given, and we might be exalted, in him; as also for us he sanctifies himself, that we might be sanctified in him.

But if they take advantage of the word "wherefore," as connected with the passage in the Psalm, "Wherefore God, even thy God, hath anointed thee," for their own purposes, let these novices in Scripture and masters in irreligion know that, as before, the word "wherefore" does not imply reward of virtue or conduct in the Word, but the reason why he came down to us, and of the Spirit's anointing, which took place in him for our sakes. For he says not, "Wherefore he anointed thee in order to thy being God or King or Son or Word,"—for so he was before, and is forever, as has been shown,—but rather, "Since thou art God and king, therefore thou wast anointed, since none but thou couldst unite man to the Holy Ghost, thou the image of the Father, in which we were made in the beginning; for thine is even the Spirit." For the nature of things generate could give no warranty for this, angels having transgressed, and men disobeyed. Wherefore there was need of God; and the Word is God; that those who had become under a curse, he himself might set free. If then he was of nothing, he would not

have been the Christ or Anointed, being one among others and having fellowship as the rest. But, whereas he is God, as being the Son of God, and is everlasting King, and exists as radiance and expression of the Father, wherefore fitly is he the expected Christ, whom the Father announces to mankind, by revelation to his holy prophets; that as through him we have come to be, so also in him all men might be redeemed from their sins, and by him all things might be ruled. And this is the cause of the anointing which took place in him, and of the incarnate presence of the Word; which the Psalmist foreseeing, celebrates, first his Godhead and kingdom, which is the Father's, in these tones, "Thy throne, O God, is forever and ever; a sceptre of righteousness is the sceptre of thy kingdom"; then announces his descent to us thus: "Wherefore God, even thy God, hath anointed thee with the oil of gladness above thy fellows."

SAINT AUGUSTINE

(354–430)

SAINT AUGUSTINE who is always classed as one of the four great Latin fathers is generally conceded to be chief among them in natural strength of intellect. Saint Jerome, who excelled him in knowledge of classical literature, is his inferior in intellectual acuteness; and certainly no other theologian of the earlier ages of the Church has done so much as has Saint Augustine to influence the thought of its strongest minds.

Augustine (Aurelius Augustinus) was a Numidian by birth. He had a Christian mother, whose devotion resulted in his conversion, as well as in that of his father, who seems to have been a man of liberal mind, aware of the value of literary education. Augustine was well versed in the Latin classics. The extent of his knowledge of Greek literature has been questioned, but it is conceded that he knew the language, at least well enough for purposes of comparative study of the Scripture text.

As a young man, his ideas of morality, as we know from his 'Confessions,' were not severe. He was not extraordinarily licentious, but he had the introspective sensitiveness which seems to characterize great genius wherever it is found, and in his later life he looked with acute pain on the follies of his youth.

Becoming a Christian at the age of twenty-three, he was ordained a priest four years later, and in 395 became Bishop of Hippo. Of his literary works, his book 'The City of God' is accounted his masterpiece, though it is not so generally read as his 'Confessions.' The sermon on the Lord's Prayer here given as an illustration of his style in the pulpit, is from his 'Homilies on the New Testament,' as translated in Parker's 'Library of the Fathers.'

THE LORD'S PRAYER

THE order established for your edification requires that ye learn first what to believe, and afterwards what to ask. For so saith the Apostle, "Whosoever shall call upon the name of the Lord shall be saved." This testimony blessed Paul cited out of the Prophet; for by the Prophet were those times foretold, when all men should call upon God; "Whosoever shall call upon the name of the Lord shall be saved." And he added, "How then shall they call on him in whom they have not believed? And how shall they believe in him of whom they have not heard? Or how shall they hear without a preacher? Or how shall they preach except they be sent?" Therefore were preachers sent. They preached Christ. As they preached, the people heard; by hearing they believed, and by believing called upon him. Because then it was most rightly and most truly said, "How shall they call on him in whom they have not believed?" therefore have ye first learned what to believe: and to-day have learned to call on him in whom ye have believed.

The Son of God, our Lord Jesus Christ, hath taught us a prayer; and though he be the Lord himself, as ye have heard and repeated in the Creed, the Only Son of God, yet he would not be alone. He is the Only Son, and yet would not be alone; he hath vouchsafed to have brethren. For to whom doth he say, "Say, Our Father, which art in heaven?" Whom did he wish us to call our father, save his own father? Did he grudge us this? Parents sometimes when they have gotten one, or two, or three children, fear to give birth to any more, lest they reduce the rest to beggary. But because the inheritance which he promised us is such as many may possess, and no one be straitened, therefore hath he called into his brotherhood the peoples of the nations; and the only son hath numberless brethren, who say, "Our Father, which art in heaven." So said they who have been before us; and so shall say those who will come after us. See how many brethren the only son hath in his grace, sharing his inheritance with those for whom he suffered death. We had a father and mother on earth, that we might be born to labors and to death; but we have found other parents, God our father and the Church our mother, by whom we are born unto life eternal. Let us then consider,

beloved, whose children we have begun to be; and let us live so as becomes those who have such a father. See, how that our Creator hath condescended to be our Father.

We have heard whom we ought to call upon, and with what hope of an eternal inheritance we have begun to have a father in heaven; let us now hear what we must ask of him. Of such a father what shall we ask? Do we not ask rain of him, to-day, and yesterday, and the day before? This is no great thing to have asked of such a father, and yet ye see with what sighings, and with what great desire we ask for rain, when death is feared,—when that is feared which none can escape. For sooner or later every man must die, and we groan, and pray, and travail in pain, and cry to God, that we may die a little later. How much more ought we to cry to him, that we may come to that place where we shall never die!

Therefore it is said, "Hallowed be thy name." This we also ask of him that his name may be hallowed in us; for holy is it always. And how is his name hallowed in us, except while it makes us holy? For once we were not holy, and we are made holy by his name, but he is always holy, and his name always holy. It is for ourselves, not for God, that we pray. For we do not wish well to God, to whom no ill can ever happen. But we wish what is good for ourselves, that his holy name may be hallowed, that that which is always holy, may be hallowed in us.

"Thy kingdom come." Come it surely will, whether we ask or no. Indeed, God hath an eternal kingdom. For when did he not reign? When did he begin to reign? For his kingdom hath no beginning, neither shall it have any end. But that ye may know that in this prayer also we pray for ourselves, and not for God (For we do not say, "Thy kingdom come," as though we were asking that God may reign); we shall be ourselves his kingdom, if believing in him we make progress in this faith. All the faithful, redeemed by the blood of his only son, will be his kingdom. And this his kingdom will come, when the resurrection of the dead shall have taken place; for then he will come himself. And when the dead are risen, he will divide them, as he himself saith, "and he shall set some on the right hand, and some on the left." To those who shall be on the right hand he will say, "Come, ye blessed of my Father, receive the kingdom." This is what we wish and pray for when we say, "Thy kingdom come"; that it may come to us. For if we shall be reprobates, that

kingdom shall come to others, but not to us. But if we shall be of that number, who belong to the members of his only-begotten son, his kingdom will come to us, and will not tarry. For are there as many ages yet remaining as have already passed away? The Apostle John hath said, "My little children, it is the last hour." But it is a long hour proportioned to this long day; and see how many years this last hour lasteth. But, nevertheless, be ye as those who watch, and so sleep, and rise again, and reign. Let us watch now, let us sleep in death; at the end we shall rise again, and shall reign without end.

"Thy will be done as in heaven, so in earth." The third thing we pray for is, that his will may be done as in heaven so in earth. And in this, too, we wish well for ourselves. For the will of God must necessarily be done. It is the will of God that the good should reign, and the wicked be damned. Is it possible that this will should not be done? But what good do we wish for ourselves, when we say, "Thy will be done as in heaven, so in earth?" Give ear. For this petition may be understood in many ways, and many things are to be in our thoughts in this petition, when we pray God, "Thy will be done as in heaven, so in earth." As thy angels offend thee not, so may we also not offend thee. Again, how is "Thy will be done as in heaven, so in earth," understood? All the holy Patriarchs, all the Prophets, all the Apostles, all the spiritual are, as it were, God's heaven; and we in comparison of them are earth. "Thy will be done in heaven, so in earth"; as in them, so in us also. Again, "Thy will be done as in heaven, so in earth"; the Church of God is heaven, his enemies are earth. So we wish well for our enemies, that they too may believe and become Christians, and so the will of God be done as in heaven, so also in earth. Again, "Thy will be done as in heaven, so in earth." Our spirit is heaven, and the flesh earth. As our spirit is renewed by believing, so may our flesh be renewed by rising again; and "the will of God be done as in heaven, so in earth." Again, our mind whereby we see truth, and delight in this truth, is heaven; as, "I delight in the law of God, after the inward man." What is the earth? "I see another law in my members, warring against the law of my mind?" When this strife shall have passed away, and a full concord be brought about of the flesh and spirit, the will of God will be done as in heaven, so also in earth. When we repeat this petition, let us think of all these things, and ask them all of the Father. Now all these things which we have mentioned, these three petitions, beloved, have respect to the life eternal. For if the name of our God is sanctified in us, it will be for eternity. If his kingdom come, where we shall live forever, it will be for eternity. If his will be done as in heaven, so in earth, in all the ways which I have explained, it will be for eternity.

There remain now the petitions for this life of our pilgrimage; therefore follows, "Give us this day our daily bread." Give us eternal things, give us things temporal. Thou hast promised a kingdom, deny us not the means of subsistence. Thou wilt give everlasting glory with thyself hereafter, give us in this earth temporal support. Therefore is it day by day, and to-day, that is, in this present time. For when this life shall have passed away, shall we ask for daily bread then? For then it will not be called day by day, but to-day. Now it is called day by day, when one day passes away, and another day succeeds. Will it be called day by day when there will be one eternal day? This petition for daily bread is doubtless to be understood in two ways, both for the necessary supply of our bodily food, and for the necessities of our spiritual support. There is a necessary supply of bodily food, for the preservation of our daily life, without which we cannot live. This is food and clothing, but the whole is understood in a part. When we ask for bread, we thereby understand all things. There is a spiritual food, also, which the faithful know, which ye, too, will know when ye shall receive it at the altar of God. This also is "daily bread," necessary only for this life. For shall we receive the Eucharist when we shall have come to Christ himself, and begun to reign with him forever? So then the Eucharist is our daily bread; but let us in such wise receive it, that we be not refreshed in our bodies only, but in our souls. For the virtue which is apprehended there, is unity, that gathered together into his body, and made his members, we may be what we receive. Then will it be, indeed, our daily bread. Again, what I am handling before you now is "daily bread"; and the daily lessons which ye hear in church are daily bread, and the hymns ye hear and repeat are daily bread. For all these are necessary in our state of pilgrimage. But when we shall have got to heaven, shall we hear the Word, we who shall see the Word himself, and hear the Word himself, and eat and drink him as the angels do

now? Do the angels need books, and interpreters, and readers? Surely not. They read in seeing, for the truth itself they see, and are abundantly satisfied from that fountain, from which we obtain some few drops. Therefore has it been said touching our daily bread, that this petition is necessary for us in this life.

"Forgive us our debts, as we forgive our debtors." Is this necessary except in this life? For in the other we shall have no debts. For what are debts, but sins? See, ye are on the point of being baptized, then all your sins will be blotted out, none whatever will remain. Whatever evil ye have ever done, in deed, or word, or desire, or thought, all will be blotted out. And yet if in the life which is after baptism there were security from sin, we should not learn such a prayer as this, "Forgive us our debts." Only let us by all means do what comes next, "As we forgive our debtors." Do ye then, who are about to enter in to receive a plenary and entire remission of your debts, do ye above all things see that ye have nothing in your hearts against any other, so as to come forth from baptism secure, as it were, free and discharged of all debts, and then begin to purpose to avenge yourselves on your enemies, who in time past have done you wrong. Forgive, as ye are forgiven. God can do no one wrong, and yet he forgiveth who oweth nothing. How then ought he to forgive who is himself forgiven, when he forgiveth all who oweth nothing that can be forgiven him?

"Lead us not into temptation, but deliver us from evil." Will this again be necessary in the life to come? "Lead us not into temptation," will not be said except where there can be temptation. We read in the book of holy Job, "Is not the life of man upon earth a temptation?" What, then, do we pray for? Hear what. The Apostle James saith, "Let no man say when he is tempted, I am tempted of God." He spoke of those evil temptations whereby men are deceived, and brought under the yoke of the devil. This is the kind of temptation he spoke of. For there is another sort of temptation which is called a proving; of this kind of temptation it is written, "The Lord your God tempteth [proveth] you to know whether ye love him." What means "to know"? "To make you know," for he knoweth already. With that kind of temptation whereby we are deceived and seduced, God tempteth no man. But undoubtedly in his deep and hidden judgment he abandons some. And when he hath abandoned them, the tempter finds his opportunity. For he finds in him no

resistance against his power, but forthwith presents himself to him as his possessor, if God abandon him. Therefore, that he may not abandon us, do we say, "Lead us not into temptation." "For every one is tempted," says the same Apostle James, "when he is drawn away of his own lust and enticed. Then lust, when it hath conceived, bringeth forth sin; and sin, when it is finished, bringeth forth death." What, then, has he hereby taught us? To fight against our lusts. For ye are about to put away your sins in holy baptism; but lusts will still remain, wherewith ye must fight after that ye are regenerate. For a conflict with your own selves still remains. Let no enemy from without be feared; conquer thine own self, and the whole world is conquered. What can any tempter from without, whether the devil or the devil's minister, do against thee? Whosoever sets the hope of gain before thee to seduce thee, let him only find no covetousness in thee; and what can he who would tempt thee by gain effect? Whereas, if covetousness be found in thee, thou takest fire at the sight of gain, and art taken by the bait of this corrupt food. But if we find no covetousness in thee, the trap remains spread in vain. Or should the tempter set before thee some woman of surpassing beauty; if chastity be within, iniquity from without is overcome. Therefore, that he may not take thee with the bait of a strange woman's beauty, fight with thine own lust within; thou hast no sensible perception of thine enemy, but of thine own concupiscence thou hast. Thou dost not see the devil, but the object that engageth thee thou dost see. Get the mastery then over that of which thou art sensible within. Fight valiantly, for he who hath regenerated thee is thy judge; he hath arranged the lists, he is making ready the crown. But because thou wilt without doubt be conquered, if thou have not him to aid thee, if he abandon thee, therefore dost thou say in the prayer, "Lead us not into temptation." The judge's wrath hath given over some to their own lusts; and the Apostle says, "God gave them over to the lusts of their hearts." How did he give them up? Not by forcing, but by forsaking them.

"Deliver us from evil," may belong to the same sentence. Therefore, that thou mayst understand it to be all one sentence, it runs thus, "Lead us not into temptation, but deliver us from evil." Therefore, he added "but," to show that all this belongs to one sentence, "Lead us not into temptation, but deliver us from evil." How is this? I will propose them singly. "Lead

us not into temptation, but deliver us from evil." By delivering us from evil, he leadeth us not into temptation; by not leading us into temptation, he delivereth us from evil.

And, truly, it is a great temptation, dearly beloved, it is a great temptation in this life, when that in us is the subject of temptation whereby we attain pardon if, in any of our temptations, we have fallen. It is a frightful temptation when that is taken from us whereby we may be healed from the wounds of other temptations. I know that ye have not yet understood me. Give me your attention, that ye may understand. Suppose, avarice tempts a man, and he is conquered in any single temptation (for sometimes even a good wrestler and fighter may get roughly handled): avarice, then, has got the better of a man, good wrestler though he be, and he has done some avaricious act. Or there has been a passing lust; it has not brought the man to fornication, nor reached unto adultery—for when this does take place, the man must at all events be kept back from the criminal act. But he "hath seen a woman to lust after her"; he has let his thoughts dwell on her with more pleasure than was right; he has admitted the attack; excellent combatant though he be, he has been wounded, but he has not consented to it; he has beaten back the motion of his lust, has chastised it with the bitterness of grief, he has beaten it back; and has prevailed. Still, in the very fact that he had slipped, has he ground for saying, "Forgive us our debts." And so of all other temptations, it is a hard matter that in them all there should not be occasion for saying, "Forgive us our debts." What, then, is that frightful temptation which I have mentioned, that grievous, that tremendous temptation, which must be avoided with all our strength, with all our resolution; what is it? When we go about to avenge ourselves. Anger is kindled, and the man burns to be avenged. O frightful temptation! Thou art losing that, whereby thou hadst to attain pardon for other faults. If thou hadst committed any sin as to other senses, and other lusts, hence mightest thou have had thy cure, in that thou mightest say, "Forgive us our debts, as we also forgive our debtors." But whoso instigateth thee to take vengeance will lose for thee the power thou hadst to say, "As we also forgive our debtors." When that power is lost, all sins will be retained; nothing at all is remitted.

Our Lord and Master, and Savior, knowing this dangerous temptation in this life, when he taught us six or seven petitions in this prayer, took none of them for himself to treat of, and to commend to us with greater earnestness, than this one. Have we not said, "Our Father, which art in heaven," and the rest which follows? Why after the conclusion of the prayer, did he not enlarge upon it to us, either as to what he had laid down in the beginning, or concluded with at the end, or placed in the middle? For why said he not, if the name of God be not hallowed in you, or if ye have no part in the kingdom of God, or if the will of God be not done in you, as in heaven, or if God guard you not, that ye enter not into temptation; why none of all these? but what saith he? "Verily I say unto you, that if ye forgive men their trespasses," in reference to that petition, "Forgive us our debts, as we also forgive our debtors." Having passed over all the other petitions which he taught us, this he taught us with an especial force. There was no need of insisting so much upon those sins in which if a man offend, he may know the means whereby he may be cured: need of it there was with regard to that sin in which, if thou sin, there is no means whereby the rest can be cured. For this thou oughtest to be ever saying, "Forgive us our debts." What debts? There is no lack of them, for we are but men; I have talked somewhat more than I ought, have said something I ought not, have laughed more than I ought, have eaten more than I ought, have listened with pleasure to what I ought not, have drunk more than I ought, have seen with pleasure what I ought not, have thought with pleasure on what I ought not; "Forgive us our debts, as we also forgive our debtors." This if thou hast lost, thou art lost thyself.

Take heed, my brethren, my sons, sons of God, take heed, I beseech you, in that I am saying to you. Fight to the uttermost of your powers with your own hearts. And if ye shall see your anger making a stand against you, pray to God against it, that God may make thee conqueror of thyself, that God may make thee conqueror, I say, not of thine enemy without, but of thine own soul within. For he will give thee his present help, and will do it. He would rather that we ask this of him, than rain. For ye see, beloved, how many petitions the Lord Christ hath taught us; and there is scarce found among them one which speaks of daily bread, that all our thoughts may be molded after the life to come. For what can we fear that he will not give us, who hath promised and said, "Seek ye first the kingdom of God

and his righteousness, and all these things shall be added unto you; for your Father knoweth that ye have need of these things before ye ask him." "Seek ye first the kingdom of God and his righteousness, and all these things shall be added unto you." For many have been tried even with hunger, and have been found gold, and have not been forsaken by God. They would have perished with hunger, if the daily inward bread were to leave their heart. After this let us chiefly hunger. For, "Blessed are they who hunger and thirst after righteousness, for they shall be filled." But he can in mercy look upon our infirmity, and see us, as it is said, "Remember that we are dust." He who from the dust made and quickened man, for that his work of clay's sake, gave his only son to death. Who can explain, who can worthily so much as conceive, how much he loveth us?

FRANCIS BACON

(1561-1626)

FRANCIS BACON, Baron Verulam and Viscount St. Albans, is called by one of his contemporaries, "the eloquentest man in England." Perhaps those who read his legal arguments before the Star Chamber may not see this eloquence so fully exemplified in them as in his incomparable essays; but wherever he speaks, it is Francis Bacon speaking. It is doubtful if any other man ever lived who has even approached him in the power of controlling his own and subsequent times by purely intellectual means. Until his time, Aristotle had no rival in the domain of pure intellect. Since he lived, the higher mind of the world has owned his mastery and has shown the results of the inspiration of his intellectual daring in following, regardless of consequences, the "inductive method," the determination to make truth fruitful through experiment, which has resulted in the scientific accomplishments of the modern world. Lucretius writes of the pleasure of knowing truth as like that a man on shore in a storm has in seeing the struggles of those who are about to be shipwrecked:—

"'Tis sweet when the seas are roughened by violent winds to view on land the toils of others; not that there is pleasure in seeing others in distress, but because man is glad to know himself secure. It is pleasant, too, to look with no share of peril on the mighty contests of war; but nothing is sweeter than to reach those calm, undisturbed temples, raised by the wisdom of philosophers, whence thou mayst look down on poor, mistaken mortals, wandering up and down in life's devious ways."—(Lucretius ii. 1, translated by Ramage.)

"Suave mari magno turbantibus æquora ventis,
E terra magnum alterius spectare laborem;
Non quia vexari quenquam est jucunda voluptas,
Sed quibus ipse malis careas, quia cernere suave est," etc.

Perhaps the spirit of the ancient learning was never so well expressed elsewhere as in these lines. In what may be called a plea for the possibilities of the nineteenth and twentieth centuries Bacon answered it.

"Is there any such happiness for a man's mind to be raised above the confusion of things where he may have the prospect of the order of nature

and error of man? But is this view of delight only and not of discovery? of contentment, and not of benefit? Shall he not as well discern the riches of Nature's warehouse as the beauties of her shop? Is truth ever barren? Shall he not be able thereby to produce worthy effects and to endow the life of man with infinite commodities?"

Among the "infinite commodities" already developed from the thought flowing into and out of the mind which framed these sublime sentences are the steam engine, the electric motor, the discoveries of the microscope in the treatment of disease, the wonders of chemistry, working out practical results to alleviate human misery, and to increase steadily from year to year, and from century to century, the sum of human comfort. Looking forward to this, Bacon worked for it until his whole life became a manifestation of his master-thought. It may be said with literal truth that he died of it, for the cold which brought him his death resulted from his rashness in leaving his carriage, when sick, to experiment on the arrest of putrefaction by freezing. The idea came to him. It was winter and the ground was covered with snow. He was feeble, but he left his carriage to stuff snow into the carcass of a chicken he had procured for the experiment. The experiment succeeded, and centuries later, as a result of it, England is fed with the meat of America and Australia. But Bacon died after it, leaving behind him ideas which stamp him as the greatest and brightest, whether or not he was also "the meanest of mankind." On this latter point, he may speak for himself, as he does thus in the volume 'State Trials' from which his speech on Dueling, before the Star Chamber, here used, is extracted:—

(Howell's, Vol. ii.): "Upon advised consideration of the charge, descending into my own conscience and calling my memory to account, as far as I am able, I do plainly and ingenuously confess that I am guilty of corruption, and do renounce all defense and put myself upon the grace and mercy of your lordships. . . . To the nineteenth article, viz., 'That in the cause between Reynell and Peacock, he received from Reynell two hundred pounds and a diamond ring worth four or five hundred pounds,' I confess and declare that on my first coming to the Seal when I was at Whitehall, my servant Hunt delivered me two hundred pounds from Sir George Reynell, my near ally, to be bestowed upon furniture of my house, adding further that he had received divers former favors from me. And this was, as I verily think, before any suit was begun. The ring was received certainly pendente lite, and though it was at New Year's tide it was too great a value for a New Year's gift, though, I take it, nothing near the value mentioned in the article."

That while Lord Chancellor of England he took gifts intended to corrupt justice, he confessed to his shame, but he does not seem to have been wholly able to decide whether in doing so he broke faith with those who wished to corrupt him, or with the kingdom and constitution of England he represented, against their desire to purchase justice. He seems to have believed that though his conduct was corrupt, his decisions were honest. He says, indeed, that in spite of his bribe-taking, « he never had bribe or reward in his eye or thought when he pronounced any sentence or order. »

This cannot be admitted in excuse even for Bacon, but his moral weakness, if it obscure for the time the splendor of his intellect, died with him, while his genius, marvelously radiant above that of any other of the last ten centuries, still illuminates the path of every pioneer of progress.

His address to the Star Chamber on Dueling was delivered in the proceedings against Mr. William Priest for writing and sending a challenge, and Mr. Richard Wright for carrying it, January 26th, 1615, Bacon being then the King's attorney-general. The text is from T. B. Howell's 'State Trials,' London 1816.

SPEECH AGAINST DUELING

MY LORDS, I thought it fit for my place, and for these times, to bring to hearing before your lordships some cause touching private duels, to see if this court can do any good to tame and reclaim that evil, which seems unbridled. And I could have wished that I had met with some greater persons, as a subject for your censure; both because it had been more worthy of this presence, and also the better to have shown the resolution I myself have to proceed without respect of persons in this business. But finding this cause on foot in my predecessor's time, I thought to lose no time in a mischief that groweth every day; and besides, it passes not amiss sometimes in government, that the greater sort be admonished by an example made in the meaner, and the dog to be eaten before the lion. Nay, I should think, my lords, that men of birth and quality will leave the practice, when it begins to be vilified, and come so low as to barber-surgeons and butchers, and such base mechanical persons. And for the greatness of this presence, in which I take much comfort, both as I consider it in itself, and much more in respect it is by his Majesty's direction, I will supply the meanness of the particular cause, by handling of the general point: to the end that by the occasion of this present cause, both my purpose of prosecution against duels and the opinion of the court, without

receive them, and not keep the people in conflict and distraction between two laws. Again, my lords, it is a miserable effect, when young men full of towardness and hope, such as the poets call "*Auroræ filii*," sons of the morning, in whom the expectation and comfort of their friends consisteth, shall be cast away and destroyed in such a vain manner. But much more it is to be deplored when so much noble and genteel blood should be spilt upon such follies, as, if it were adventured in the field in service of the King and realm, were able to make the fortune of a day and change the future of a kingdom. So your lordships see what a desperate evil this is; it troubleth peace; it disfurnisheth war; it bringeth calamity upon private men, peril upon the State, and contempt upon the law.

Touching the causes of it: the first motive, no doubt, is a false and erroneous imagination of honor and credit; and therefore the King, in his last proclamation, doth most aptly and excellently call them bewitching duels. For, if one judge of it truly, it is no better than a sorcery that enchanteth the spirits of young men, that bear great minds with a false show, *species falsa;* and a kind of satanical illusion and apparition of honor against religion, against law, against moral virtue, and against the precedents and examples of the best times and valiantest nations; as I shall tell you by and by, when I shall show you that the law of England is not alone in this point. But then the seed of this mischief being such, it is nourished by vain discourses and green and unripe conceits, which, nevertheless, have so prevailed as though a man were staid and sober-minded and a right believer touching the vanity and unlawfulness of these duels; yet the stream of vulgar opinion is such, as it imposeth a necessity upon men of value to conform themselves, or else there is no living or looking upon men's faces; so that we have not to do, in this case, so much with particular persons as with unsound and depraved opinions, like the dominations and spirits of the air which the Scripture speaketh of. Hereunto may be added that men have almost lost the true notion and understanding of fortitude and valor. For fortitude distinguisheth of the grounds of quarrels whether they be just; and not only so, but whether they be worthy; and setteth a better price upon men's lives than to bestow them idly. Nay, it is weakness and disesteem of a man's self, to put a man's life upon such ledger performances. A man's life is not to be trifled away; it is to be offered up and

which I am nothing, for the censure of them may appear, and thereby offenders in that kind may read their own case, and know what they are to expect; which may serve for a warning until example may be made in some greater person, which I doubt the times will but too soon afford.

Therefore, before I come to the particular, whereof your lordships are now to judge, I think the time best spent to speak somewhat of (1) of the nature and greatness of this mischief; (2) of the causes and remedies; (3) of the justice of the law of England, which some stick not to think defective in this matter; (4) of the capacity of this court, where certainly the remedy of this mischief is best to be found; (5) touching mine own purpose and resolution, wherein I shall humbly crave your lordships' aid and assistance.

For the mischief itself, it may please your lordships to take into your consideration that, when revenge is once extorted out of the magistrate's hands, contrary to God's ordinance, *mihi vindicta, ego retribuam*, and every man shall bear the sword, not to defend, but to assail, and private men begin once to presume to give law to themselves and to right their own wrongs, no man can foresee the danger and inconveniences that may arise and multiply thereupon. It may cause sudden storms in court, to the disturbance of his Majesty and unsafety of his person. It may grow from quarrels to bandying, and from bandying to trooping, and so to tumult and commotion; from particular persons to dissension of families and alliances; yea, to national quarrels, according to the infinite variety of accidents, which fall not under foresight. So that the State by this means shall be like to a distempered and imperfect body, continually subject to inflammations and convulsions. Besides, certainly both in divinity and in policy, offenses of presumption are the greatest. Other offenses yield and consent to the law that it is good, not daring to make defense, or to justify themselves; but this offense expressly gives the law an affront, as if there were two laws, one a kind of gown law and the other a law of reputation, as they term it. So that Paul's and Westminster, the pulpit and the courts of justice, must give place to the law, as the King speaketh in his proclamation, of ordinary tables, and such reverend assemblies; the Yearbooks, and statute books must give place to some French and Italian pamphlets, which handle the doctrines of duels, which, if they be in the right, *transeamus ad illa*, let us

sacrificed to honorable services, public merits, good causes, and noble adventures. It is in expense of blood as it is in expense of money. It is no liberality to make a profusion of money upon every vain occasion; nor no more is it fortitude to make effusion of blood, except the cause be of worth. And thus much for the cause of this evil.

For the remedies. I hope some great and noble person will put his hand to this plough, and I wish that my labors of this day may be but forerunners to the work of a higher and better hand. But yet to deliver my opinion as may be proper for this time and place, there be four things that I have thought on, as the most effectual for the repressing of this depraved custom of particular combats.

The first is, that there do appear and be declared a constant and settled resolution in the State to abolish it. For this is a thing, my lords, must go down at once or not at all; for then every particular man will think himself acquitted in his reputation, when he sees that the State takes it to heart, as an insult against the King's power and authority, and thereupon hath absolutely resolved to master it; like unto that which we set down in express words in the edict of Charles IX. of France, touching duels, that the King himself took upon him the honor of all that took themselves grieved or interested for not having performed the combat. So must the State do in this business; and in my conscience there is none that is but of a reasonable sober disposition, be he never so valiant, except it be some furious person that is like a firework, but will be glad of it, when he shall see the law and rule of State disinterest him of a vain and unnecessary hazard.

Secondly, care must be taken that this evil be no more cockered, nor the humor of it fed; wherein I humbly pray your lordships, that I may speak my mind freely, and yet be understood aright. The proceedings of the great and noble commissioners martial I honor and reverence much, and of them I speak not in any sort. But I say the compounding of quarrels, which is otherwise in use by private noblemen and gentlemen, is so punctual, and hath such reference and respect unto the received conceits, what is beforehand, and what is behindhand, and I cannot tell what, as without all question it doth, in a fashion, countenance and authorize this practice of duels, as if it had in it somewhat of right.

Thirdly, I must acknowledge that I learned out of the King's last proclamation, the most prudent and best applied remedy for this offense, if it shall please his Majesty to use it, that the wit of man can devise. This offense, my lords, is grounded upon a false conceit of honor; and therefore it would be punished in the same kind, *in eo quis rectissime plectitur, in quo peccat.* The fountain of honor is the King and his aspect, and the access to his person continueth honor in life, and to be banished from his presence is one of the greatest eclipses of honor that can be. If his Majesty shall be pleased that when this court shall censure any of these offenses in persons of eminent quality, to add this out of his own power and discipline, that these persons shall be banished and excluded from his court for certain years, and the courts of his queen and prince, I think there is no man that hath any good blood in him will commit an act that shall cast him into that darkness that he may not behold his sovereign's face.

Lastly, and that which more properly concerneth this court. We see, my lords, the root of this offense is stubborn; for it despiseth death, which is the utmost of punishments; and it were a just but a miserable severity to execute the law without all remission or mercy, where the case proveth capital. And yet the late severity in France was more, where by a kind of martial law, established by ordinance of the King and Parliament, the party that had slain another was presently had to the gibbet, insomuch as gentlemen of great quality were hanged, their wounds bleeding, lest a natural death should prevent the example of justice. But, my lords, the course which we shall take is of far greater lenity, and yet of no less efficacy; which is to punish, in this court, all the middle acts and proceedings which tend to the duel, which I will enumerate to you anon, and so to hew and vex the root in the branches, which, no doubt, in the end will kill the root, and yet prevent the extremity of law.

Now for the law of England, I see it excepted to, though ignorantly, in two points. The one, that it should make no difference between an insidious and foul murder, and the killing of a man upon fair terms, as they now call it. The other, that the law hath not provided sufficient punishment and reparations for contumely of words, as the lie, and the like. But these are no better than childish novelties against the divine law, and against

all laws in effect, and against the examples of all the bravest and most virtuous nations of the world.

For first, for the law of God, there is never to be found any difference made in homicide, but between homicide voluntary and involuntary, which we term misadventure. And for the case of misadventure itself, there were cities of refuge; so that the offender was put to his flight, and that flight was subject to accident, whether the revenger of blood should overtake him before he had gotten sanctuary or no. It is true that our law hath made a more subtle distinction between the will inflamed and the will advised, between manslaughter in heat and murder upon prepensed malice or cold blood, as the soldiers call it; an indulgence not unfit for a choleric and warlike nation; for it is true, *ira furor brevis,* a man in fury is not himself. This privilege of passion the ancient Roman law restrained, but to a case; that was, if the husband took the adulterer in the manner. To that rage and provocation only it gave way, that a homicide was justifiable. But for a difference to be made in killing and destroying man, upon a forethought purpose, between foul and fair, and, as it were, between single murder and vied murder, it is but a monstrous child of this latter age, and there is no shadow of it in any law, divine or human. Only it is true, I find in the Scripture that Cain enticed his brother into the field and slew him treacherously; but Lamech vaunted of his manhood, that he would kill a young man, and if it were to his hurt; so as I see no difference between an insidious murder and a braving or presumptuous murder, but the difference between Cain and Lamech.

As for examples in civil states, all memory doth consent, that Græcia and Rome were the most valiant and generous nations of the world; and that, which is more to be noted, they were free estates, and not under a monarchy; whereby a man would think it a great deal the more reason that particular persons should have righted themselves. And yet they had not this practice of duels, nor anything that bare show thereof; and sure they would have had it, if there had been any virtue in it. Nay, as he saith, *"Fas est et ab hoste doceri."* It is memorable, that which is reported by a counsel or ambassador of the emperor, touching the censure of the Turks of these duels. There was a combat of this kind performed by two persons of quality of the Turks, wherein one of them was slain, and the other party was converted before the council of bashaws. The manner of the reprehension was in

these words: " How durst you undertake to fight one with the other? Are there not Christians enough to kill? Did you not know that whether of you shall be slain, the loss would be the great seignor's? " So, as we may see, the most warlike nations, whether generous or barbarous, have ever despised this wherein now men glory.

It is true, my lords, that I find combats of two natures authorized, how justly I will not dispute as to the latter of them. The one, when upon the approaches of armies in the face one of the other, particular persons have made challenges for trial of valors in the field upon the public quarrel. This the Romans called *"pugna per provocationem."* And this was never, but either between the generals themselves, who were absolute, or between particulars by license of the generals; never upon private authority. So you see David asked leave when he fought with Goliath; and Joab, when the armies were met, gave leave, and said " Let the young man play before us. " And of this kind was that famous example in the wars of Naples, between twelve Spaniards and twelve Italians, where the Italians bore away the victory; besides other infinite like examples worthy and laudable, sometimes by singles, sometimes by numbers.

The second combat is a judicial trial of right, where the right is obscure, introduced by the Goths and the northern nations, but more anciently entertained in Spain. And this yet remains in some cases as a divine lot of battle, though controverted by divines, touching the lawfulness of it; so that a wise writer saith: " *Taliter pugnantes videntur tentare Deum, quia hoc volunt ut Deus ostendat et faciat miraculum, ut justam causam habens victor efficiatur, quod sæpe contra accidit.* " But whosoever it be, this kind of fight taketh its warrant from law. Nay, the French themselves, whence this folly seemeth chiefly to have flown, never had it but only in practice and toleration, and never as authorized by law; and yet now of late they have been fain to purge their folly with extreme rigor, in so much as many gentlemen left between death and life in the duels, as I spake before, were hastened to hanging with their wounds bleeding. For the State found it had been neglected so long, as nothing could be thought cruelty which tended to the putting of it down. As for the second defect, pretended in our law, that it hath provided no remedy for lies and fillips, it may receive like answer. It would have been thought a madness amongst the ancient lawgivers to

have set a punishment upon the lie given, which in effect is but a word of denial, a negative of another's saying. Any lawgiver, if he had been asked the question, would have made Solon's answer: That he had not ordained any punishment for it, because he never imagined the world would have been so fantastical as to take it so highly. The civilians dispute whether an action of injury lie for it, and rather resolve the contrary. And Francis I. of France, who first set on and stamped this disgrace so deep, is taxed by the judgment of all wise writers for beginning the vanity of it; for it was he, that when he had himself given the lie and defy to the Emperor, to make it current in the world, said in a solemn assembly, " that he was no honest man that would bear the lie, " which was the fountain of this new learning.

As for the words of approach and contumely, whereof the lie was esteemed none, it is not credible, but that the orations themselves are extant, what extreme and exquisite reproaches were tossed up and down in the Senate of Rome and the places of assembly, and the like in Græcia, and yet no man took himself fouled by them, but took them but for breath, and the style of an enemy, and either despised them or returned them, but no blood was spilt about them.

So of every touch or light blow of the person, they are not in themselves considerable, save that they have got them upon the stamp of a disgrace, which maketh these light things pass for great matters. The law of England and all laws hold these degrees of injury to the person, slander, battery, mayhem, death; and if there be extraordinary circumstances of despite and contumely, as in case of libels and bastinadoes and the like, this court taketh them in hand and punisheth them exemplarily. But for this apprehension of a disgrace that a fillip to the person should be a mortal wound to the reputation, it were good that men did hearken unto the saying of Gonsalvo, the great and famous commander, that was wont to say a gentleman's honor should be *de tela crassiore,* of a good strong warp or web, that every little thing should not catch in it; when as now it seems they are but of cobweb-lawn or such light stuff, which certainly is weakness, and not true greatness of mind, but like a sick man's body, that is so tender that it feels everything. And so much in maintenance and demonstration of the wisdom and justice of the law of the land.

For the capacity of this court, I take this to be a ground infallible, that wheresoever an offense is capital, or matter of felony, though it be not acted, there the combination or practice tending to the offense is punishable in this court as high misdemeanor. So practice to imprison, though it took no effect; waylaying to murder, though it took no effect; and the like; have been adjudged heinous misdemeanors punishable in this court. Nay, inceptions and preparations in inferior crimes, that are not capital, as suborning and preparing of witnesses that were never deposed, or deposed nothing material, have likewise been censured in this court, as appeareth by the decree in Garnon's case.

Why, then, the major proposition being such, the minor cannot be denied, for every appointment of the field is but combination and plotting of murder. Let them gild it how they list, they shall never have fairer terms of me in a place of justice. Then the conclusion followeth, that it is a case fit for the censure of the court. And of this there be precedents in the very point of challenge. It was the case of Wharton, plaintiff, against Ellekar and Acklam, defendants, where Acklam, being a follower of Ellekar's, was censured for carrying a challenge from Ellekar to Wharton, though the challenge was not put in writing, but delivered only by word of message; and there are words in the decree, that such challenges are to the subversion of government. These things are well known, and therefore I needed not so much to have insisted upon them, but that in this case I would be thought not to innovate anything of my own head, but to follow the former precedents of the court, though I mean to do it more thoroughly, because the time requires it more.

Therefore now to come to that which concerneth my part, I say that by the favor of the king and the court, I will prosecute in this court in the cases following: If any man shall appoint the field, though the fight be not acted or performed. If any man shall send any challenge in writing, or any message of challenge. If any man carry or deliver any writing or message of challenge. If any man shall accept to be second in a challenge of either side. If any man shall depart the realm, with intention and agreement to perform the fight beyond the seas. If any man shall revive a quarrel by any scandalous bruits or writings, contrary to former proclamation published by his Majesty in that behalf.

Nay, I hear there be some counsel learned of duels, that tell young men when they are beforehand, and when they are otherwise, and thereby incense and incite them to the duel, and make an art of it. I hope I shall meet with some of them too; and I am sure, my lords, this course of preventing duels, in nipping them in the bud, is fuller of clemency and providence than the suffering them to go on, and hanging men with their wounds bleeding, as they did in France.

To conclude, I have some petitions to make first to your lordship, my lord chancellor, that in case I be advertised of a purpose in any to go beyond the sea to fight, I may have granted his Majesty's writ of *ne exeat regnum* to stop him, for this giant bestrideth the sea, and I would take and snare him by the foot on this side; for the combination and plotting is on this side, though it should be acted beyond the sea. And your lordship said notably the last time I made a motion in this business, that a man may be as well *fur de se* as *felo de se*, if he steal out of the realm for a bad purpose. As for the satisfying of the words of the writ, no man will doubt but he does *machinari contra coronam*, as the words of the writ be, seeking to murder a subject; for that is ever *contra coronam et dignitatem*. I have also a suit to your lordships all in general, that for justice's sake, and for true honor's sake, honor of religion, law, and the King our master, against this fond and false disguise or puppetry of honor. I may, in my prosecution, which, it is like enough, may sometimes stir coals, which I esteem not for my particular, but as it may hinder the good service, I may, I say, be countenanced and assisted from your lordships. Lastly, I have a petition to the nobles and gentlemen of England, that they would learn to esteem themselves at a just price. *Non hos quæsitum munus in usus*—their blood is not to be spilt like water or a vile thing; therefore, that they would rest persuaded there cannot be a form of honor, except it be upon a worthy matter. But this, *ipsi viderunt*, I am resolved.

JAMES BARBOUR

(1775–1842)

ENATOR JAMES BARBOUR'S speech on the treaty-making power, made in the United States Senate in January 1816, is one of the ablest and most concise presentations of the Virginia view of the Federal constitution represented by Madison before he came under Jefferson's influence. The speech itself, here reproduced from Benton's 'Debates,' sufficiently explains all that is of permanent importance in the question presented to the Senate. If, under the Federal constitution, it was necessary after the ratification of a treaty to specially repeal laws in conflict with it, then such laws and "municipal regulations" as remained unrepealed by special act would be in force in spite of the treaty. Arguing against this as it affected the treaty-making power of the Senate from which the House of Representatives was excluded by the constitution, Senator Barbour declared the treaty-making power supreme over commerce, and incidentally asserted that unless there is such a supremacy lodged somewhere in the government, the condition would be as anomalous as that of Christendom when it had three Popes.

Mr. Barbour was born in 1775 and educated for the bar. He served in the Virginia legislature, was twice governor of the State, and twice elected to represent it in the United States Senate. He was Secretary of War in 1825 under John Quincy Adams, who sent him as minister to England—a post from which he was recalled by President Jackson. He presided over the national convention which nominated William Henry Harrison for the presidency, dying in 1842.

TREATIES AS SUPREME LAWS

MR. PRESIDENT, as it seems to be the wish of the Senate to pass upon this subject without debate, it adds to the reluctance I always feel when compelled, even by a sense of duty, to intrude on their attention. Yet, as I feel myself obliged, under the solemn responsibility attached to the station I hold here, to vote against the bill under consideration—as I

think, also, it is but a due respect to the other branch of the legislature, from whom it is my misfortune to differ, and but an act of justice to myself to state the grounds of my opinion, I must be pardoned for departing from the course which seemed to be desired by the Senate.

In the exercise of this privilege, with a view to promote the wishes of the Senate as far as a sense of duty will permit, I will confine myself to a succinct view of the most prominent objections which lie against its passage, rather than indulge in the extensive range of which the subject is susceptible. Before I enter into the discussion of the merits of the question, I beg leave to call the attention of the Senate to the course which was adopted by us in relation to this subject. A bill, brought in by the Committee on Foreign Relations, passed the Senate unanimously, declaring that all laws in opposition to the convention between the United States and Great Britain, concluded on the third of July last, should be held as null and void. The principle on which this body acted was, that the treaty, upon the exchange of its ratification, did, of itself, repeal any commercial regulation, incompatible with its provisions, existing in our municipal code; it being by us believed at the time that such a bill was not necessary, but by a declaratory act, it was supposed, all doubts and difficulties, should any exist, might be removed. This bill is sent to the House of Representatives, who, without acting thereon, send us the one under consideration, but differing materially from ours. Far from pretending an intimate knowledge of the course of business pursued by the two houses, I do not say that the mode adopted in this particular case is irregular, but if it has not the sanction of precedent, it appears to me to be wanting in that courtesy which should be perpetually cherished between the two houses. It would have been more decorous to have acted on our bill, to have agreed to it if it were approved, to reject or amend it. In the latter case, upon its being returned to the Senate, the views of the other body would have been contrasted with our own, and we might then have regularly passed upon the subject. A different course, however, has been adopted; and if a regard to etiquette had been the only obstacle to my support to the bill, it would have been readily given; for it is the substance, and not the shadow, which weighs with me. The difference between the two bills is rendered important by its involving a constitutional question.

It is my misfortune, for such I certainly esteem it, to differ from the other branch of the legislature on that question; were it a difference of opinion on the expediency of a measure, it might readily be obviated, as being entirely free, or at least I hope so, from pride of opinion. My disposition is to meet, by mutual concession, those with whom I am in the habit of acting; but when a principle of the constitution is involved, concession and compromise are out of the question. With one eye on the sacred charter of our liberties, and the other on the solemn sanction under which I act here, I surrender myself to the dictates of my best judgment (weak enough God knows), and fearlessly pursue the course pointed out by these guides. My regret is certainly greatly lessened by the reflection that there is no difference of opinion with any one on the propriety of executing the treaty with good faith — we differ only as to the manner in which our common purpose shall be effected.

The difference between the friends of the bill, and those opposed to it is, as I understand it, this: the former contend, that the law of Congress, discriminating between American and British tonnage, is not abrogated by the treaty, although its provisions conflict with the treaty, but that to effect its repeal, the bill in question, a mere echo of the treaty, must pass; the latter, among whom I wish to be considered, on the contrary say, that the law above alluded to was annulled upon the ratification of the treaty. I hope I have succeeded in stating the question fairly, for that certainly was my wish, and it is also my determination to discuss it in the same spirit.

This, then, is the issue which is made up between the friends and the opponents of the bill; and although in its practical effects I cannot believe it would be of consequence which way it is decided, yet, as the just interpretation of the constitution is the pivot on which it turns, from that consideration alone the question becomes an interesting one.

Fortunately for us we have a written constitution to recur to, dictated with the utmost precision of which our language is susceptible — it being the work of whatsoever of wisdom, of experience, and of foresight, united America possessed.

To a just understanding of this instrument, it will be essential to recur to the object of its adoption; in this there can be no difference of opinion. The old band of union had been literally dissolved in its own imbecility; to remedy this serious evil, an

increase of the powers of the general government was indispensable.

To draw the line of demarcation between the powers thus granted to the general government, and those retained by the States, was the primary and predominating object. In conformity with this view, we find a general enumeration of the powers assigned the former, of which Congress is made the depository; which powers, although granted to Congress in the first instance, are, in the same instrument, subsequently distributed among the other branches of the government. Various examples might be adduced in support of this position. The following for the present will suffice: Article i., § 1, of the constitution declares, that "all legislative powers herein granted shall be vested in a Congress of the United States, which shall consist of a Senate and House of Representatives." Yet we find, by the seventh section of the same article, the President invested with a large share of legislative power, and, in fact, constituting an integral branch of the legislature; in addition to this, I will here barely add, that the grant of the very power to regulate the exercise of which gave birth to this bill, furnishes, by the admission of the friends of the bill, another evidence of the truth of this position, as I shall show hereafter; and, therefore, to comprehend the true meaning of the constitution, an isolated view of a particular clause or section will involve you in error, while a comprehensive one, both of its spirit and letter, will conduct you to a just result; when apparent collisions will be removed, and vigor and effect will be given to every part of the instrument. With this principle as our guide, I come directly to that part of the constitution which recognizes the treaty-making power. In the second clause, second section, second article, are the following plain and emphatic words: "He [the President] shall have power, by and with the advice and consent of the Senate, to make treaties, provided two-thirds of the Senators present concur." Two considerations here irresistibly present themselves — first, there is no limitation to the exercise of the power, save such restrictions as arise from the constitution, as to the subjects on which it is to act; nor is there any participation of the power, with any other branch of the government, in any way alluded to.

Am I borne out in this declaration by the clause referred to? That I am, seems to me susceptible of demonstration. To the President and Senate has been imparted the power of making

treaties. Well, what is a treaty? If a word have a known signification by the common consent of mankind, and it be used without any qualification in a law, constitution, or otherwise, the fair inference is that the received import of such word is intended to be conveyed. If so, the extent of the power intended to be granted admits of no difficulty. It reaches to those acts of courtesy and kindness, which philanthropy has established in the intercourse of nations, as well as to treaties of commerce, of boundaries, and, in fine, to every international subject whatsoever. This exposition is supported by such unequivocal authority, that it is believed it will not be questioned. I, therefore, infer that it will be readily yielded, that in regard to the treaty, in aid of which this bill is exhibited, the treaty-making power has not exceeded its just limits. So far we have proceeded on sure ground; we now come to the pith of the question. Is the legislative sanction necessary to give it effect? I answer in the negative. Why? Because, by the second clause of the sixth article of the constitution, it is declared that all treaties made or which shall be made, under the authority of the United States, shall be the supreme law of the land. If this clause means anything, it is conclusive of the question.

If the treaty be a supreme law, then whatsoever municipal regulation comes within its provisions must *ipso facto* be annulled — unless gentlemen contend there can be at the same time two supreme laws, emanating from the same authority, conflicting with each other, and still both in full vigor and effect. This would indeed produce a state of things without a parallel in human affairs, unless indeed its like might be found in the history of the Popes. In one instance, we are told, there were three at one time roaming over the Christian world, all claiming infallibility, and denouncing their anathemas against all who failed to yield implicit obedience to their respective mandates, when to comply with the one was to disobey the other. A result like this, so monstrous in its aspect, excludes the interpretation which produces it. It is a safe course in attempting to ascertain the meaning of a law or constitution to connect different clauses (no matter how detached) upon the same subject together. Let us do it in this case. The President shall have power, by and with the advice and consent of the Senate, to make treaties, which treaties shall be the supreme law of the land. I seek to gain no surreptitious advantage from the word

supreme, because I frankly admit that it is used in the constitution, in relation to the laws and constitutions of the States; but I appeal to it merely to ascertain the high authority intended to be imparted by the framers of the constitution to a ratified treaty. It is classed in point of dignity with the laws of the United States. We ask for no superiority, but equality; and as the last law made annuls a former one, where they conflict, so we contend that a subsequent treaty, as in the present case, revokes a former law in opposition thereto. But the other side contend that it is inferior to the law in point of authority, which continues in full force despite of a treaty, and to its repeal the assent of the whole legislature is necessary. Our claims rest on the expressed words of the constitution — the opposite on implication; and if the latter be just, I cannot forbear to say that the framers of the constitution would but ill deserve what I have heretofore thought a just tribute to their meritorious services. If they really designed to produce the effect contended for, instead of so declaring by a positive provision, they have used a language which, to my mind, operates conclusively against it. Under what clause of the constitution is the right to exercise this power set up? The reply is, the third clause of eighth section, first article — Congress shall have power to regulate commerce with foreign nations, etc. I immediately inquire to what extent does the authority of Congress, in relation to commercial treaties, reach? Is the aid of the legislature necessary in all cases whatsoever, to give effect to a commercial treaty? It is readily admitted that it is not. That a treaty, whose influence is extraterritorial, becomes obligatory the instant of its ratification. That, as the aid of the legislature is not necessary to its execution, the legislature has no right to interpose. It is then admitted that while a general power on the subject of commerce is given to Congress, that yet important commercial regulations may be adopted by treaty, without the co-operation of the legislature, notwithstanding the generality of the grant of power on commercial subjects to Congress. If it be true that the President and Senate have, in their treaty-making power, an exclusive control over part and not over the whole, I demand to know at what point that exclusive control ceases? In the clause relied upon, there is no limitation. The fact is, sir, none exists. The treaty-making power over commerce is supreme. No legislative sanction is necessary, if the treaty be capable of self-execution, and when a legislative sanction is necessary, as I shall more at large hereafter show, such sanction, when given, adds nothing to the validity of the treaty, but enables the proper authority to execute it; and when the legislature do act in this regard, it is under such obligation as the necessity of fulfilling a moral contract imposes.

If it be inquired of me what I understand by the clause in question, in answer I refer to the principle with which I set out; that this was a grant of power to the general government of which Congress was in the first instance merely the depository, which power, had not a portion thereof been transferred to another branch of the government, would have been exclusively exercised by Congress, but that a distribution of this power has been made by the constitution; as a portion thereof has been given to the treaty-making power, and that which is not transferred is left in the possession of Congress. Hence, to Congress it is competent to act in this grant in its proper character by establishing municipal regulations. The President and the Senate, on the other hand, have the same power within their sphere, that is, by a treaty or convention with a foreign nation, to establish such regulations in regard to commerce, as to them may seem friendly to the public interest. Thus each department moves in its own proper orbit, nor do they come in collision with each other. If they have exercised their respective powers on the same subject, the last act, whether by the legislature or the treaty-making power, abrogates a former one. The legislature of the nation may, if a cause exist in their judgment sufficient to justify it, abrogate a treaty, as has been done; so the President and Senate by a treaty may abrogate a pre-existing law containing interfering provisions, as has been done heretofore (without the right being questioned), and as we say in the very case under consideration. I will endeavor to make myself understood by examples; Congress has power, under the clause in question, to lay embargoes, to pass nonintercourse, or nonimportation, or countervailing laws, and this power they have frequently exercised. On the other hand, if the nation against whom one of those laws is intended to operate is made sensible of her injustice and tenders reparation, the President and Senate have power by treaty to restore the amicable relations between the two nations, and the law directing otherwise, upon the ratification of the treaty, is forthwith annulled. Again, if Congress should be of

the contrary, the treaty from its nature cannot be carried into effect but by the agency of the legislature, that is, if some municipal regulation be necessary, then the legislature must act not as participating in the treaty-making power, but in its proper character as a legislative body.

opinion that the offending nation had not complied with their engagements, they might by law revoke the treaty, and place the relation between the two nations upon such footing as they approved. Where is the collision here? I see none. This view of the subject presents an aspect as innocent as that which is produced when a subsequent law repeals a former one. By this interpretation you reconcile one part of the constitution with another, giving to each a proper effect, a result always desirable, and in rules of construction claiming a precedence to all others. Indeed, sir, I do not see how the power in question could have been otherwise arranged. The power which has been assigned to Congress was indispensable; without it we should have been at the mercy of a foreign government, who, knowing the incompetency of Congress to act, would have subjected our commerce to the most injurious regulations, as was actually the case before the adoption of the constitution, when it was managed by the States, by whom no regular system could be established; indeed, we all know this very subject was among the most prominent of the causes which produced the constitution. Had this state of things continued, no nation which could profit by a contrary course would have treated. On the other hand, had not a power been given to some branch of the government to treat, whatever might have been the friendly dispositions of other powers, or however desirous to reciprocate beneficial arrangements, they could not, without a treaty-making power lodged somewhere, be realized.

I therefore contend, that although to Congress a power is given in the clause alluded to, to regulate commerce, yet this power is in part, as I have before endeavored to show, given to the President and Senate in their treaty-making capacity—the truth of which position is admitted by the friends of the bill to a certain extent. The fact is, that the only difference between us is to ascertain the precise point where legislative aid is necessary to the execution of the treaty, and where not. To fix this point is to settle the question. After the most mature reflection which I have been able to give this subject, my mind has been brought to the following results: Whenever the President and Senate, within the acknowledged range of their treaty-making power, ratify a treaty upon extraterritorial subjects, then it is binding without any auxiliary law. Again, if from the nature of the treaty it is self-executory, no legislative aid is necessary. If, on

BARNAVE

(1761–1793)

ANTOINE PIERRE JOSEPH MARIE BARNAVE was born at Grenoble, France, in 1761. He was the son of an advocate, who gave him a careful education. His first work of a public character, a pamphlet against the Feudal system, led to his election to the States-General in 1789. He advocated the Proclamation of the Rights of Man and identified himself with those enthusiastic young Republicans of whom Lafayette is the best type. The emancipation of the Jews from all civil and religious disabilities and the abolition of slavery throughout French territory owed much to his efforts. He also opposed the Absolute Veto and led the fight for the sequestration of the property of the Church. This course made him a popular idol and in the early days of the Revolution he was the leader of the extreme wing of the Republicans. When he saw, however, that mob law was about to usurp the place of the Republican institutions for which he had striven, he leaned towards the court and advocated the sacrosanctity of the King's person. Denounced as a renegade, with his life threatened and his influence lost, he retired to his native province. In August 1792 he was impeached for correspondence with the King, and on November 26th, 1793, he was guillotined. The specimens of his eloquence here given were translated for this Library from the Paris edition of his works, published in 1843.

REPRESENTATIVE DEMOCRACY AGAINST MAJORITY ABSOLUTISM

(Delivered in the National Assembly, August 11th, 1791)

IT IS not enough to desire to be free—one must know how to be free. I shall speak briefly on this subject, for after the success of our deliberations, I await with confidence the spirit and action of this Assembly. I only wish to announce my opinions on a question, the rejection of which would sooner or later mean the loss of our liberties. This question leaves no doubt in the minds of those who reflect on governments and are guided by impartial judgments. Those who have combatted the committee have made a fundamental error. They have confounded democratic government with representative government; they have confounded the rights of the people with the qualifications of an elector, which society dispenses for its well understood interest. Where the government is representative, where there exists an intermediary degree of electors, society which elects them has essentially the right to determine the conditions of their eligibility. There is one right existing in our constitution, that of the active citizen, but the function of an elector is not a right. I repeat, society has the right to determine its conditions. Those who misunderstand the nature as they do the advantages of representative government, remind us of the governments of Athens and Sparta, ignoring the differences that distinguish them from France, such as extent of territory, population, etc. Do they forget that they interdicted representative government? Have they forgotten that the Lacedemonians had the right to vote in the assemblies only when they held helots? And only by sacrifice of individual rights did the Lacedemonians, Athenians, and Romans possess any democratic governments! I ask those who remind us of them, if it is at such government they would arrive? I ask those who profess here metaphysical ideas, because they have no practical ideas, those who envelop the question in clouds of theory, because they ignore entirely the fundamental facts of a positive government—I ask is it forgotten that the democracy of a portion of a people would exist but by the entire enslavement of the other portion of the people? A representative government has but one evil to fear, that of corruption. That such a government shall be good, there must be guaranteed the purity and incorruptibility of the electorate. This body needs the union of three eminent guarantees. First, the light of a fair education and broadened views. Second, an interest in things, and still better if each had a particular and considerable interest at stake to defend. Third, such condition of fortune as to place the elector above attack from corruption.

These advantages I do not look for in the superior class of the rich, for they undoubtedly have too many special and individual interests, which they separate from the general interests. But if it is true that we must not look for the qualifications of the pure elector among the eminently rich, neither should I look for it among those whose lack of fortune has prevented their

If you would have liberty subsist do not hesitate because of specious arguments which will be presented to you by those who, if they reflect, will recognize the purity of our intentions and the resultant advantages of our plans. I add to what I have already said that the system will diminish many existing inconveniences, and the proposed law will not have its full effect for two years. They tell us we are taking from the citizen a right which elevated him by the only means through which he can acquire it. I reply that if it was an honor the career which you will open for them will imprint them with character greater and more in conformity with true equality. Our opponents have not failed either to magnify the inconveniences of changing the constitution. Nor do I desire its change. For that reason we should not introduce imprudent discussions to create the necessity of a national convention. In one word, the advice and conclusions of the committee are the sole guarantees for the prosperity and peaceable condition of the nation.

COMMERCIAL POLITICS

COMMERCE forms a numerous class, friends of external peace and internal tranquillity, who attach themselves to the established government.

It creates great fortunes, which in republics become the origin of the most forceful aristocracies. As a rule commerce enriches the cities and their inhabitants, and increases the laboring and mechanical classes, in opening more opportunities for the acquirement of riches. To an extent it fortifies the democratic element in giving the people of the cities greater influence in the government. It arrives at nearly the same result by impoverishing the peasant and land owner, by the many new pleasures offered him and by displaying to him the ostentation and voluptuousness of luxury and ease. It tends to create bands of mercenaries rather than those capable of worthy personal service. It introduces into the nation luxury, ease, and avarice at the same time as labor.

The manners and morals of a commercial people are not the manners of the merchant. He individually is economical, while the general mass are prodigal. The individual merchant is conservative and moral, while the general public are rendered dissolute.

enlightenment; among such, unceasingly feeling the touches of want, corruption too easily can find its means. It is, then, in the middle class that we find the qualities and advantages I have cited. And, I ask, is it the demand that they contribute five to ten francs that causes the assertion that we would throw elections into the hands of the rich? You have established the usage that the electors receive nothing; if it were otherwise their great number would make an election most expensive. From the instant that the voter has not means enough to enable him to sacrifice a little time from his daily labor, one of three things would occur. The voter would absent himself, or insist on being paid by the State, else he would be rewarded by the one who wanted to obtain his suffrage. This does not occur when a comfortable condition is necessary to constitute an elector. As soon as the government is established, when the constitution is guaranteed, there is but a common interest for those who live on their property, and those who toil honestly. Then can be distinguished those who desire a stable government and those who seek but revolution and change, since they increase in importance in the midst of trouble as vermin in the midst of corruption.

If it is true, then, that under an established constitutional government all its well-wishers have the same interest, the power of the same must be placed in the hands of the enlightened who can have no interest pressing on them, greater than the common interest of all the citizens. Depart from these principles and you fall into the abuses of representative government. You would have extreme poverty in the electorate and extreme opulence in the legislature. You would see soon in France what you see now in England, the purchase of voters in the boroughs not with money even, but with pots of beer. Thus incontestably are elected many of their parliamentary members. Good representation must not be sought in either extreme, but in the middle class. The committee have thus placed it by making it incumbent that the voter shall possess an accumulation the equivalent of, say forty days of labor. This would unite the qualities needed to make the elector exercise his privilege with an interest in the same. It is necessary that he own from one hundred and twenty to two hundred and forty livres, either in property or chattels. I do not think it can seriously be said that this qualification is fixed too high, unless we would introduce among our electors men who would beg or seek improper recompense.

The mixture of riches and pleasures which commerce produces, joined to freedom of manners, leads to excesses of all kinds, at the same time that the nation may display the perfection of elegance and taste that one noticed in Rome, mistress of the world, or in France before the Revolution. In Rome the wealth was the inflow of the whole world, the product of the hardiest ambition, producing the deterioration of the soldier and the indifference of the patrician. In France the wealth was the accumulation of an immense commerce and the varied labors of the most industrious nation on the earth diverted by a brilliant and corrupt court, a profligate and chivalrous nobility, and a rich and voluptuous capital.

Where a nation is exclusively commercial, it can make an immense accumulation of riches without sensibly altering its manners. The passion of the trader is avarice and the habit of continuous labor. Left alone to his instincts he amasses riches to possess them, without designing or knowing how to use them. Examples are needed to conduct him to prodigality, ostentation, and moral corruption. As a rule the merchant opposes the soldier. One desires the accumulations of industry, the other of conquest. One makes of power the means of getting riches, the other makes of riches the means of getting power. One is disposed to be economical, a taste due to his labor. The other is prodigal, the instinct of his valor. In modern monarchies these two classes form the aristocracy and the democracy. Commerce in certain republics forms an aristocracy, or rather an "extra aristocracy in the democracy." These are the directing forces of such democracies, with the addition of two other governing powers, which have come in, the clergy and the legal fraternity, who assist largely in shaping the course of events.

ISAAC BARROW

(1630–1677)

IT is not often that a sermon, however eloquent it may be, becomes a literary classic, as has happened to those preached by Barrow against Evil Speaking. Literature—that which is expressed in letters—has its own method, foreign to that of oratory—the art of forcing one mind on another by word of mouth. Literature can rely on suggestion, since it leaves those who do not comprehend at once free to read over again what has attracted their attention without compelling their understanding. All great literature relies mostly on suggestion. This is the secret of Shakespeare's strength in 'Hamlet,' as it is the purpose of Burke's in such speeches as that at the trial of Hastings, to compel immediate comprehension by crowding his meaning on the hearer in phalanxed sentences, moving to the attack, rank on rank, so that the first are at once supported and compelled by those which succeed them.

It is not easy to find the secret by virtue of which sermons that made Barrow his reputation for eloquence escaped the fate of most eloquent sermons so far as to find a place in the standard "Libraries of English Classics," but it lies probably in their compactness, clearness, and simplicity. Barrow taught Sir Isaac Newton mathematics, and his style suggests the method of thought which Newton illustrated in such great results.

Born in London in 1630, Barrow was educated at the Charterhouse School, at Felstead, and at Cambridge. Belonging to a Royalist family, under Cromwell, he left England after his graduation and traveled abroad, studying the Greek fathers in Constantinople. After the Restoration he became Lucasian professor of mathematics at Cambridge and chaplain to Charles II., who called him the best scholar in England. Celebrated for the length of his sermons, Barrow had nevertheless a readiness at sharp repartee which made him formidable on occasion. "I am yours, Doctor, to the knee-strings," said the Earl of Rochester, meeting him at court and seeking amusement at his expense. "I am yours, my lord, to the shoe-tie," answered the Doctor, bowing still lower than the Earl had done. "Yours, Doctor, to the ground," said Rochester. "Yours, my lord, to the centre of the earth," answered Barrow with another bow. "Yours, Doctor, to the lowest pit of hell," said Rochester, as he imagined, in conclusion. "There, my lord, I must leave you!" was the immediate answer.

ISAAC BARROW 225

But from especial causes our age peculiarly doth abound in this practice; for, besides the common dispositions inclining thereto, there are conceits newly coined, and greedily entertained by many, which seem purposely leveled at the disparagement of piety, charity, and justice, substituting interest in the room of conscience, authorizing and commending for good and wise, all ways serving to private advantage. There are implacable dissensions, fierce animosities, and bitter zeals sprung up; there is an extreme curiosity, niceness, and delicacy of judgment; there is a mighty affectation of seeming wise and witty by any means; there is a great unsettlement of mind, and corruption of manners, generally diffused over people; from which sources it is no wonder that this flood hath so overflown, that no banks can restrain it, no fences are able to resist it; so that ordinary conversation is full of it, and no demeanor can be secure from it.

If we do mark what is done in many (might I not say, in most?) companies, what is it but one telling malicious stories of, or fastening odious characters upon, another? What do men commonly please themselves in so much as in carping and harshly censuring, in defaming and abusing their neighbors? Is it not the sport and divertisement of many to cast dirt in the faces of all they meet with? to bespatter any man with foul imputations? Doth not in every corner a Momus lurk, from the venom of whose spiteful or petulant tongue no eminency of rank, dignity of place, or sacredness of office, no innocence or integrity of life, no wisdom or circumspection in behavior, no good-nature or benignity in dealing and carriage, can protect any person? Do not men assume to themselves a liberty of telling romances, and framing characters concerning their neighbors, as freely as a poet doth about Hector or Turnus, Thersites or Draucus? Do they not usurp a power of playing with, or tossing about, of tearing in pieces their neighbor's good name, as if it were the veriest toy in the world? Do not many having a form of godliness (some of them demurely, others confidently, both without any sense of, or remorse for, what they do) backbite their brethren? Is it not grown so common a thing to asperse causelessly that no man wonders at it, that few dislike, that scarce any detest it? that most notorious calumniators are heard, not only with patience, but with pleasure; yea, are even held in vogue and reverence as men of a notable talent, and very serviceable to their party? so that slander seemeth to have lost its nature and not to

I—15

SLANDER

GENERAL declamations against vice and sin are indeed excellently useful, as rousing men to consider and look about them; but they do often want effect, because they only raise confused apprehensions of things, and indeterminate propensions to action, which usually, before men thoroughly perceive or resolve what they should practice, do decay and vanish. As he that cries out "Fire!" doth stir up people, and inspireth them with a kind of hovering tendency every way, yet no man thence to purpose moveth until he be distinctly informed where the mischief is; then do they, who apprehend themselves concerned, run hastily to oppose it: so, till we particularly discern where our offenses lie (till we distinctly know the heinous nature and the mischievous consequences of them), we scarce will effectually apply ourselves to correct them. Whence it is requisite that men should be particularly acquainted with their sins, and by proper arguments be dissuaded from them.

In order whereto I have now selected one sin to describe, and dissuade from, being in nature as vile, and in practice as common, as any other whatever that hath prevailed among men. It is slander, a sin which in all times and places hath been epidemical and rife, but which especially doth seem to reign and rage in our age and country.

There are principles innate to men, which ever have, and ever will, incline them to this offense. Eager appetites to secular and sensual goods; violent passions, urging the prosecution of what men affect; wrath and displeasure against those who stand in the way of compassing their desires; emulation and envy towards those who happen to succeed better, or to attain a greater share in such things; excessive self-love; unaccountable malignity and vanity are in some degrees connatural to all men, and ever prompt them to this dealing, as appearing the most efficacious, compendious, and easy way of satisfying such appetites, of promoting such designs, of discharging such passions. Slander thence hath always been a principal engine whereby covetous, ambitious, envious, ill-natured, and vain persons have striven to supplant their competitors and advance themselves; meaning thereby to procure, what they chiefly prize and like, wealth, or dignity, or reputation, favor and power in the court, respect and interest with the people.

---

be now an odious sin, but a fashionable humor, a way of pleasing entertainment, a fine knack, or curious feat of policy; so that no man at least taketh himself or others to be accountable for what is said in this way? Is not, in fine, the case become such, that whoever hath in him any love of truth, any sense of justice or honesty, any spark of charity towards his brethren, shall hardly be able to satisfy himself in the conversations he meeteth; but will be tempted, with the holy prophet, to wish himself sequestered from society, and cast into solitude; repeating those words of his, "Oh, that I had in the wilderness a lodging-place of wayfaring men, that I might leave my people, and go from them: for they are . . . an assembly of treacherous men, and they bend their tongues like their bow for lies"? This he wished in an age so resembling ours, that I fear the description with equal patness may suit both: "Take ye heed" (said he then, and may we not advise the like now?) "every one of his neighbor, and trust ye not in any brother: for every brother will utterly supplant, and every neighbor will walk with slanders. They will deceive every one his neighbor, and will not speak the truth; they have taught their tongue to speak lies, and weary themselves to commit iniquity."

Such being the state of things, obvious to experience, no discourse may seem more needful, or more useful, than that which serveth to correct or check this practice: which I shall endeavor to do (1) by describing the nature, (2) by declaring the folly of it: or showing it to be very true which the wise man here asserteth, "He that uttereth slander is a fool." Which particulars I hope so to prosecute, that any man shall be able easily to discern, and ready heartily to detest this practice.

1. For explication of its nature, we may describe slander to be the uttering false (or equivalent to false, morally false) speech against our neighbor, in prejudice to his fame, his safety, his welfare, or concernment in any kind, out of malignity, vanity, rashness, ill-nature, or bad design. That which is in Holy Scripture forbidden and reproved under several names and notions: of bearing false witness, false accusation, railing censure, sycophantry, talebearing, whispering, backbiting, supplanting, taking up reproach: which terms some of them do signify the nature, others denote the special kinds, others imply the manners, others suggest the ends of this practice. But it seemeth most fully intelligible by observing the several kinds and degrees thereof;

as also by reflecting on the divers ways and manners of practicing it.

The principal kinds thereof I observe to be these:—

1. The grossest kind of slander is that which in the Decalogue is called, bearing false testimony against our neighbor; that is, flatly charging him with acts which he never committed, and is nowise guilty of. As in the case of Naboth, when men were suborned to say, "Naboth did blaspheme God and the king," and as was David's case, when he thus complained, "False witnesses did rise up, they laid to my charge things that I knew not of." This kind in the highest way (that is, in judicial proceedings) is more rare; and of all men, they who are detected to practice it are held most vile and infamous, as being plainly the most pernicious and perilous instruments of injustice, the most desperate enemies of all men's right and safety that can be. But also out of the court there are many knights-errant of the poet, whose business it is to run about scattering false reports; sometimes loudly proclaiming them in open companies, sometimes closely whispering them in dark corners; thus infecting conversation with their poisonous breath: these no less notoriously are guilty of this kind, as bearing always the same malice and sometimes breeding as ill effects.

2. Another kind is, affixing scandalous names, injurious epithets, and odious characters upon persons, which they deserve not. As when Corah and his accomplices did accuse Moses of being ambitious, unjust, and tyrannical; when the Pharisees called our Lord an impostor, a blasphemer, a sorcerer, a glutton and wine-bibber, an incendiary and perverter of the people, one that spake against Cæsar, and forbade to give tribute; when the Apostles were charged with being pestilent, turbulent, factious, and seditious fellows. This sort being very common, and thence in ordinary repute not so bad, yet in just estimation may be judged even worse than the former, as doing to our neighbor more heavy and more irreparable wrong. For it imposeth on him really more blame, and that such which he can hardly shake off; because the charge signifies habits of evil, and includeth many acts; then, being general and indefinite, can scarce be disproved. He, for instance, that calleth a sober man drunkard doth impute to him many acts of such intemperance (some really past, others probably future), and no particular time or place being specified, how can a man clear himself of that imputation,

especially with those who are not thoroughly acquainted with his conversation? So he that calleth a man unjust, proud, perverse, hypocritical, doth load him with most grievous faults, which it is not possible that the most innocent person should discharge himself from.

3. Like to that kind is this: aspersing a man's actions with harsh censures and foul terms, importing that they proceed from ill principles, or tend to bad ends; so as it doth not or cannot appear. Thus, when we say of him that is generously hospitable, that he is profuse; of him that is prudently frugal, that he is niggardly; of him that is cheerful and free in his conversation, that he is vain or loose; of him that is serious and resolute in a good way, that he is sullen or morose; of him that is conspicuous and brisk in virtuous practice, that it is ambition or ostentation which prompts him; of him that is close and bashful in the like good way, that it is sneaking stupidity, or want of spirit; of him that is reserved, that it is craft; of him that is open, that it is simplicity in him; when we ascribe a man's liberality and charity to vainglory or popularity; his strictness of life, and constancy in devotion, to superstition, or hypocrisy. When, I say, we pass such censures, or impose such characters on the laudable or innocent practice of our neighbors, we are indeed slanderers, imitating therein the great calumniator, who thus did slander even God himself, imputing his prohibition of the fruit unto envy towards men; "God," said he, "doth know that in the day ye eat thereof, your eyes shall be opened, and ye shall be as gods, knowing good and evil;" who thus did ascribe the steady piety of Job, not to a conscientious love and fear of God, but to policy and selfish design: "Doth Job fear God for naught?"

Whoever, indeed, pronounceth concerning his neighbor's intentions otherwise than as they are evidently expressed by words, or signified by overt actions, is a slanderer; because he pretendeth to know, and dareth to aver, that which he nowise possibly can tell whether it be true; because the heart is exempt from all jurisdiction here, is only subject to the government and trial of another world; because no man can judge concerning the truth of such accusations, because no man can exempt or defend himself from them: so that apparently such practice doth thwart all course of justice and equity.

4. Another kind is, perverting a man's words or actions disadvantageously by affected misconstruction. All words are

ambiguous, and capable of different senses, some fair, some more foul; all actions have two handles, one that candor and charity will, another that disingenuity and spite may lay hold on; and in such cases to misapprehend is a calumnious procedure, arguing malignant disposition and mischievous design. Thus, when two men did witness that our Lord affirmed, he "could demolish the Temple, and rear it again in three days"—although he did, indeed, speak words to that purpose, meaning them in a figurative sense, discernible enough to those who would candidly have minded his drift and way of speaking—yet they who crudely alleged them against him are called false witnesses. "At last," saith the Gospel, "came two false witnesses, and said, This fellow said, I am able to destroy the temple," etc. Thus, also, when some certified of St. Stephen, as having said that "Jesus of Nazareth should destroy this place, and change the customs that Moses delivered"; although probably he did speak words near to that purpose, yet are those men called false witnesses. "And," saith St. Luke, "they set up false witnesses, which said, This man ceaseth not to speak blasphemous words," etc. Which instances do plainly show, if we would avoid the guilt of slander, how careful we should be to interpret fairly and favorably the words and actions of our neighbor.

5. Another sort of this practice is, partial and lame representation of men's discourse, or their practice, suppressing some part of the truth in them, or concealing some circumstances about them which might serve to explain, to excuse, or to extenuate them. In such a manner easily, without uttering any logical untruth, one may yet grievously calumniate. Thus, suppose a man speaketh a thing upon supposition, or with exception, or in way of objection, or merely for disputation's sake, in order to the discussion or clearing of truth; he that should report him asserting it absolutely, unlimitedly, positively, and peremptorily, as his own settled judgment, would notoriously calumniate. If one should be inveigled by fraud, or driven by violence, or slip by chance into a bad place or bad company, he that should so represent the gross of that accident, as to breed an opinion of that person, that out of pure disposition and design he did put himself there, doth slanderously abuse that innocent person. The reporter in such cases must not think to defend himself by pretending that he spake nothing false; for such propositions, however true in logic, may justly be deemed lies in morality, being

uttered with a malicious and deceitful (that is, with a calumnious) mind, being apt to impress false conceits and to produce hurtful effects concerning our neighbor. There are slanderous truths as well as slanderous falsehoods; when truth is uttered with a deceitful heart, and to a base end, it becomes a lie. "He that speaketh truth," saith the wise man, "showeth forth righteousness, but a false witness deceit." Deceiving is the proper work of slander; and truth abused to that end putteth on its nature, and will engage into like guilt.

6. Another kind of calumny is, by instilling sly suggestions, which although they do not downrightly assert falsehoods, yet they breed sinister opinions in the hearers, especially in those who, from weakness or credulity, from jealousy or prejudice, from negligence or inadvertency, are prone to entertain them. This is done in many ways: by propounding wily suppositions, shrewd insinuations, crafty questions, and specious comparisons, intimating a possibility, or inferring some likelihood of, and thence inducing to believe the fact. "Doth not," saith this kind of slanderer, "his temper incline him to do thus? may not his interest have swayed him thereto? had he not fair opportunity and strong temptation to it? hath he not acted so in like cases? Judge you, therefore, whether he did it not." Thus the close slanderer argueth; and a weak or prejudiced person is thereby so caught, that he presently is ready thence to conclude the thing done. Again: "He doeth well," saith the sycophant, "it is true; but why, and to what end? Is it not, as most men do, out of ill design? may he not dissemble now? may he not recoil hereafter? have not others made as fair a show? yet we know what came of it." Thus do calumnious tongues pervert the judgments of men to think ill of the most innocent, and meanly of the worthiest actions. Even commendation itself is often used calumniously, with intent to breed dislike and ill-will towards a person commended in envious or jealous ears; or so as to give passage to dispraises, and render the accusations following more credible. 'Tis an artifice commonly observed to be much in use there, where the finest tricks of supplanting are practiced, with greatest effect; so that *pessimum inimicorum genus, laudantes;* there is no more pestilent enemy than a malevolent praiser. All these kinds of dealing, as they issue from the principles of slander, and perform its work, so they deservedly bear the guilt thereof.

7. A like kind is that of oblique and covert reflections; when a man doth not directly or expressly charge his neighbor with faults, but yet so speaketh that he is understood, or reasonably presumed to do it. This is a very cunning and very mischievous way of slandering; for therein the skulking calumniator keepeth a reserve for himself, and cutteth off from the person concerned the means of defense. If he goeth to clear himself from the matter of such aspersions: "What need," saith this insidious speaker, "of that? must I needs mean you? did I name you? why do you then assume it to yourself? do you not prejudice yourself guilty? I did not, but your own conscience, it seemeth, doth accuse you. You are so jealous and suspicious, as persons overwise or guilty use to be." So meaneth this serpent out of the hedge securely and unavoidably to bite his neighbor, and is in that respect more base and more hurtful than the most flat and positive slanderer.

8. Another kind is that of magnifying and aggravating the faults of others; raising any small miscarriage into a heinous crime, any slender defect into an odious vice, and any common infirmity into a strange enormity; turning a small "mote in the eye" of our neighbor into a huge "beam," a little dimple in his face into a monstrous wen. This is plainly slander, at least in degree, and according to the surplusage whereby the censure doth exceed the fault. As he that, upon the score of a small debt, doth extort a great sum, is no less a thief, in regard to what amounts beyond his due, than if without any pretense he had violently or fraudulently seized on it, so he is a slanderer that, by heightening faults or imperfections, doth charge his neighbor with greater blame, or load him with more disgrace than he deserves. 'Tis not only slander to pick a hole where there is none, but to make that wider which is, so that it appeareth more ugly, and cannot so easily be mended. For charity is wont to extenuate faults, justice doth never exaggerate them. As no man is exempt from some defects, or can live free from some misdemeanors, so by this practice every man may be rendered very odious and infamous.

9. Another kind of slander is, imputing to our neighbor's practice, judgment, or profession, evil consequences (apt to render him odious, or despicable) which have no dependence on them, or connection with them. There do in every age occur disorders and mishaps, springing from various complications of causes,

working some of them in a more open and discernible, others in a more secret and subtle way (especially from Divine judgment and providence checking or chastising sin); from such occurrences it is common to snatch occasion and matter of calumny. Those who are disposed this way are ready peremptorily to charge them upon whomsoever they dislike or dissent from, although without any apparent cause, or upon most frivolous and senseless pretenses; yea, often when reason showeth quite the contrary, and they who are so charged are in just esteem of all men the least obnoxious to such accusations. So, usually, the best friends of mankind, those who most heartily wish the peace and prosperity of the world and most earnestly to their power strive to promote them, have all the disturbances and disasters happening charged on them by those fiery vixens, who (in pursuance of their base designs, or gratification of their wild passions) really do themselves embroil things, and raise miserable combustions in the world. So it is that they who have the conscience to do mischief will have the confidence also to disavow the blame and the iniquity, to lay the burden of it on those who are most innocent. Thus, whereas nothing more disposeth men to live orderly and peaceably, nothing more conduceth to the settlement and safety of the public, nothing so much draweth blessings down from heaven upon the commonwealth, as true religion, yet nothing hath been more ordinary than to attribute all the miscarriages and mischiefs that happened unto it; even those are laid at his door, which plainly do arise from the contempt or neglect of it, being the natural fruits or the just punishments of irreligion. King Ahab, by forsaking God's commandments and following wicked superstitions, had troubled Israel, drawing sore judgments and calamities thereon; yet had he the heart and the face to charge those events on the great assertor of piety, Elias: "Art thou he that troubleth Israel?" The Jews by provocation of Divine justice had set themselves in a fair way towards desolation and ruin; this event to come they had the presumption to lay upon the faith of our Lord's doctrine. "If," said they, "we let him alone, all men will believe on him, and the Romans shall come, and take away our place and nation," whereas, in truth, a compliance with his directions and admonitions had been the only means to prevent those presaged mischiefs. And, *si Tibris ascenderit in mœnia*, if any public calamity did appear, then *Christianos ad leones*, Christians

must be charged and persecuted as the causes thereof. To them it was that Julian and other pagans did impute all the discussions, confusions, and devastations falling upon the Roman Empire. The sacking of Rome by the Goths they cast upon Christianity; for the vindication of it from which reproach St. Augustine did write those renowned books 'De Civitate Dei.' So liable are the best and most innocent sort of men to be calumniously accused in this manner.

Another practice (worthily bearing the guilt of slander) is, aiding and being accessory thereto, by anywise furthering, cherishing, abetting it. He that by crafty significations of ill-will doth prompt the slanderer to vent his poison; he that by a willing audience and attention doth readily suck it up, or who greedily swalloweth it down by credulous approbation and assent; he that pleasingly relisheth and smacketh at it, or expresseth a delightful complacence therein: as he is a partner in the fact, so he is a sharer in the guilt. There are not only slanderous throats, but slanderous ears also; not only wicked inventions, which engender and brood lies, but wicked assents, which hatch and foster them. Not only the spiteful mother that conceiveth such spurious brats, but the midwife that helpeth to bring them forth, the nurse that feedeth them, the guardian that traineth them up to maturity, and setteth them forth to live in the world; as they do really contribute to their subsistence, so deservedly they partake in the blame due to them, and must be responsible for the mischief they do.

BASIL THE GREAT

(329-379)

BASIL THE GREAT, born at Cæsarea in Cappadocia A. D. 329, was one of the leading orators of the Christian Church in the fourth century. He was a friend of the famous Gregory of Nazianzus, and Gregory of Nyssa was his brother.

The spirit of his time was one of change. The foundations of the Roman world were undermined. The old classical civilization of beauty and order had reached its climax and reacted on itself; the Greek worship of the graceful; the Roman love of the regular, the strong, the martial, the magnificent, had failed to save the world from a degradation which, under the degeneracy of the later Cæsars, had become indescribable. The early Christians, filled with a profound conviction of the infernal origin of the corruption of the decaying civilization they saw around them, were moved by such a compelling desire to escape it as later times can never realize and hardly imagine. Moved by this spirit, the earnest young men of the time, educated as Basil was in the philosophy, the poetry, and the science of the classical times, still felt that having this they would lose everything unless they could escape the influences of the world around them. They did not clearly discriminate between what was within and without themselves. It was not clear to them whether the corruption of an effete civilization was not the necessary corruption of all human nature including their own. This doubt sent men like Basil to the desert to attempt, by fasting and scourging, to get such mastery over their bodies as to compel every rebellious nerve and stubborn muscle to yield instant obedience to their aspirations after a more than human perfection. If they never attained their ideal; if we find them coming out of the desert, as they sometimes did, to engage in controversies, often fierce and unsaintly enough, we can see, nevertheless, how the deep emotions of their struggle after a higher life made them the great orators they were. Their language came from profound depths of feeling. Often their very earnestness betrays them into what for later ages is unintelligibility. Only antiquarians now can understand how deeply the minds of the earlier centuries of the New Order, which saved progress from going down into the bottomless pit of classical decadence, were stirred by controversies over prepositions and conjunctions. But if we remember that in all of it, the men who are sometimes ridiculed as mere ascetics, mere pedants, were moved by a profound sense of their duty to save a world so demoralized, so shameless in the pursuit of everything sensual and base, that nothing short of their sublime enthusiasm, their very madness of contempt for the material and the sensual, could have saved it.

After studying in Constantinople and in Athens, the spirit of the Reformers of his time took hold on Basil and, under the ascetic impulse, he visited the hermits of Arabia and Asia Minor, hoping to learn sanctity from them. He founded a convent in Pontus, which his mother and sister entered. After his ordination as "Presbyter," he was involved in the great Arian controversy, and the ability he showed as a disputant probably had much to do with his promotion to the bishopric of Cæsarea. In meeting the responsibilities of that office, his courage and eloquence made him famous. When threatened by the Emperor Valens, he replied that having nothing but a few books and his cloak, he did not fear confiscation of his goods; that he could not be exiled, since the whole earth was the Lord's; that torture and death would merely put an end to his labors and bring him nearer to the God for whom he longed. He died at Cæsarea A. D. 379. Such men must be judged from their own standpoints. It is worth much to understand them.

The sermon 'To the Fallen,' here used from Fish's translation, was greatly admired by Fenelon, who calls it a masterpiece. It was occasioned by a nun's breaking a vow of perpetual virginity.

ON A RECREANT NUN

IT is time, now, to take up the exclamation of the Prophet: "O that my head were waters, and mine eyes a fountain of tears, that I might weep for the wounded of the daughter of my people!"—Jer. ix. 1.

For, although they are wrapped in profound silence, and lie quite stupefied by their calamity, and deprived, by their deadly wound, even of the very sense of suffering, yet it does not become us to withhold our tears over so sad a fall. For if Jeremiah deemed those worthy of countless lamentations who had received bodily wounds in battle, what shall we say when souls are involved in so great a calamity? "Thy wounded," says the Prophet, "are not wounded with the sword, and thy dead are not the dead of war." But my lamentation is for grievous sin, the sting of the true death, and for the fiery darts of the wicked,

which have cruelly kindled a flame in both body and soul. Well might the laws of God groan within themselves, beholding such pollution on earth, those laws which always utter their loud prohibition, saying in olden time, "Thou shalt not covet thy neighbor's wife"; and in the Gospels, "That whosoever looketh on a woman to lust after her, hath committed adultery with her already in his heart." But now they behold the very bride of the Lord —her of whom Christ is the head—committing adultery without fear or shame. Yes, the very spirits of departed saints may well groan, the zealous Phineas, that it is not permitted to him now to snatch the spear and to punish the loathsome sin with a summary corporeal vengeance; and John the Baptist, that he cannot now leave the celestial abodes, as he once left the wilderness, and hasten to rebuke the transgression, and if the sacrifice were called for, to lay down his head sooner than abate the severity of his reproof. Nay, let us rather say that, like blessed Abel, John "being dead yet speaketh," and now lifts up his voice with a yet louder cry than in the case of Herodias, saying, "It is not lawful for thee to have her." For, although the body of John, yielding to the inevitable sentence of God, has paid the debt of nature, and his tongue is silent, yet "the word of God is not bound." And he who, when the marriage covenant had been violated in the case of a fellow-servant, was faithful even unto death with his stern reproofs, what must he have felt if he had seen the holy bride-chamber of the Lord thus wantonly outraged?

But as for thee, O thou who hast thus cast off the yoke of that divine union, and deserted the undefiled chamber of the true King, and shamefully fallen into this disgraceful and impious defilement, since thou hast no way of evading this bitter charge, and no method or artifice can avail to conceal thy fearful crime, thou boldly hardenest thyself in guilt. And as he who has once fallen into the abyss of crime becomes henceforth an impious despiser, so thou deniest thy very covenant with the true bridegroom; alleging that thou wast not a virgin, and hadst never taken the vow, although thou hast both received and given many pledges of virginity. Remember the good confession which thou hast made before God and angels and men. Remember that venerable assembly, and the sacred choir of virgins, and the congregation of the Lord, and the Church of the saints. Remember thy aged grandmother in Christ, whose Christian virtues still

flourish in the vigor of youth; and thy mother in the Lord, who vies with the former, and strives by new and unwonted endeavors to dissolve the bands of custom; and thy sister likewise, in some things their imitator, and in some aspiring to excel them, and to surpass in the merits of virginity the attainments of her progenitors, and both in word and deed diligently inviting thee, her sister, as is meet, to the same competition. Remember these, and the angelic company associated with them in the service of the Lord, and the spiritual life though yet in the flesh, and the heavenly converse upon earth. Remember the tranquil days and the luminous nights, and the spiritual songs, and the melodious psalmody, and the holy prayers, and the chaste and undefiled couch, and the progress in virginal purity, and the temperate diet so helpful in preserving thy virginity uncontaminated. And where is now that grave deportment, and that modest mien, and that plain attire which so become a virgin, and that beautiful blush of bashfulness, and that comely paleness—the delicate bloom of abstinence and vigils, that outshines every ruddier glow. How often in prayer that thou mightest keep unspotted thy virginal purity hast thou poured forth thy tears! How many letters hast thou indited to holy men, imploring their prayers, not that thou mightest obtain these human—nuptials, shall I call them? rather this dishonorable defilement—but that thou mightest not fall away from the Lord Jesus? How often hast thou received the gifts of the spouse! And why should I mention also the honors accorded for his sake by those who are his—the companionship of the virgins, journeyings with them, welcomes from them, encomiums on virginity, blessings bestowed by virgins, letters addressed to thee as to a virgin! But now, having been just breathed upon by the aërial spirit that worketh in the children of disobedience, thou hast denied all these, and hast bartered that precious and enviable possession for a brief pleasure, which is sweet to thy taste for a moment, but which afterward thou wilt find bitterer than gall.

Besides all this, who can avoid exclaiming with grief, "How is Zion, the faithful city, become an harlot!" Nay, does not the Lord himself say to some who now walk in the spirit of Jeremiah, "Hast thou seen what the virgin of Israel hath done unto me?" "I betrothed her unto me in faith and purity, in righteousness and in judgment, and in loving-kindness and in mercies," even as I promised her by Hosea, the prophet. But she has loved

strangers; and even while I her husband lived, she has made herself an adulteress, and has not feared to become the wife of another husband. And what would the bride's guardian and conductor say, the divine and blessed Paul? Both the ancient Apostle, and this modern one, under whose auspices and instruction thou didst leave thy father's house, and join thyself to the Lord? Would not each, filled with grief at the great calamity, say, "The thing which I greatly feared has come upon me, and that which I was afraid of is come unto me," for "I espoused you unto one husband, that I might present you as a chaste virgin to Christ"; and I was always fearful, lest in some way as the serpent beguiled Eve by his subtilty, so thy mind should sometime be corrupted. And on this account I always endeavored, like a skillful charmer, by innumerable incantations, to suppress the tumult of the passions, and by a thousand safeguards to secure the bride of the Lord, rehearsing again and again the manner of her who is unmarried, how that she only "careth for the things of the Lord, that she may be holy both in body and in spirit"; and I set forth the honor of virginity, calling thee the temple of God, that I might add wings to thy zeal, and help thee upward to Jesus; and I also had recourse to the fear of evil, to prevent thee from falling, telling thee that "if any man defile the temple of God, him shall God destroy." I also added the assistance of my prayers, that, if possible, "thy whole body, and soul, and spirit might be preserved blameless unto the coming of our Lord Jesus Christ." But all this labor I have spent in vain upon thee; and those sweet toils have ended in a bitter disappointment; and now I must again groan over her of whom I ought to have joy. For lo, thou hast been beguiled by the serpent more bitterly than Eve; for not only has thy mind become defiled, but with it thy very body also, and what is still more horrible—I dread to say it, but I cannot suppress it; for it is as fire burning and blazing in my bones, and I am dissolving in every part and cannot endure it—thou hast taken the members of Christ, and made them the members of a harlot. This is incomparably the greatest evil of all. This is a new crime in the world, to which we may apply the words of the Prophet, "Pass over the isles of Chittim, and see; and send unto Kedar, and consider diligently, and see if there be such a thing. Hath a nation changed their gods, which are yet no gods?" For the virgin hath changed her glory, and now glories in her shame. The heavens are astonished at this, and the earth trembleth very exceedingly. Now, also, the Lord says, the virgin hath committed two evils, she hath forsaken me, the true and holy bridegroom of sanctified souls, and hath fled to an impious and lawless polluter of the body, and corrupter of the soul. She hath turned away from God her Savior, and hath yielded her members servants to impurity and iniquity; she hath forgotten me, and gone after her lover, by whom she shall not profit.

It were better for him that a millstone were hanged about his neck, and he cast into the sea, than that he should cause one of the Lord's virgins to offend. What impudent servant ever carried his insane audacity so far as to fling himself upon the couch of his lord? Or what robber has ever become so madly hardened as to lay hands upon the very offerings devoted to God?—but here it is not inanimate vessels, but living bodies, inhabited by souls made in the image of God. Since the beginning of the world was any one ever heard of, who dared, in the midst of a great city, in broad midday, to deface the likeness of a king by inscribing upon it the forms of filthy swine? He that despises human nuptials dies without mercy under two or three witnesses; of how much sorer punishment, suppose ye, shall he be thought worthy who hath trodden under foot the Son of God, and defiled his espoused wife, and done despite to the spirit of virginity? . . .

But, after all this, "shall they fall and not arise? shall he turn away and not return?" Why hath the virgin turned away in so shameless an apostasy?—and that, too, after having heard Christ, the bridegroom, saying by Jeremiah, "And I said, after she had lewdly done all these things, turn thou unto me. But she returned not." "Is there no balm in Gilead? Is there no physician there? Why, then, is not the health of the daughter of my people recovered?" Truly thou mightest find in the Divine Scriptures many remedies for such an evil—many medicines that recover from perdition and restore to life; mysterious words about death and resurrection, a dreadful judgment, and everlasting punishment; the doctrines of repentance and remission of sins; those innumerable examples of conversion—the piece of silver, the lost sheep, the son that had devoured his living with harlots, that was lost and found, that was dead and alive again. Let us use these remedies for the evil; with these let us heal our souls. Think, too, of thy last day (for thou art not to live always, more than

---

others), of the distress, and the anguish, as the hour of death draws nearer, of the impending sentence of God, of the angels moving on rapid wing, of the soul fearfully agitated by all these things, and bitterly tormented by a guilty conscience, and clinging pitifully to the things here below, and still under the inevitable necessity of taking its departure. Picture to thy mind the final dissolution of all that belongs to our present life, when the Son of Man shall come in his glory, with his holy angels; for he "shall come, and shall not keep silence," when he shall come to judge the living and the dead, and to render to every man according to his work; when the trumpet, with its loud and terrible echo, shall awaken those who have slept from the beginning of the world, and they shall come forth, they that have done good to the resurrection of the life, and they that have done evil to the resurrection of damnation. Remember the divine vision of Daniel, how he brings the judgment before our eyes. "I beheld," says he, "till the thrones were placed, and the Ancient of days did sit, whose garment was white as snow, and the hair of his head like the pure wool; his throne was like the fiery flame, and his wheels as burning fire. A fiery stream issued and came forth from before him; thousand thousands ministered unto him, and ten thousand times ten thousand stood before him; the judgment was set, and the books were opened," revealing all at once in the hearing of all men and all angels, all things, whether good or bad, open or secret, deeds, words, thoughts. What effect must all these things have on those who have lived viciously? Where, then, shall the soul, thus suddenly revealed in all the fullness of its shame in the eyes of such a multitude of spectators—Oh, where shall it hide itself? In what body can it endure those unbounded and intolerable torments of the unquenchable fire, and the tortures of the undying worm, and the dark and frightful abyss of hell, and the bitter howlings, and woeful wailings, and weeping, and gnashing of teeth; and all these dire woes without end? Deliverance from these after death there is none; neither is there any device, nor contrivance, for escaping these bitter torments.

But now it is possible to escape them. Now, then, while it is possible, let us recover ourselves from our fall, let us not despair of restoration, if we break loose from our vices. Jesus Christ came into the world to save sinners. "Oh, come, let us worship and bow down," let us weep before him. His word, calling us to repentance, lifts up its voice and cries aloud, "Come unto me

---

all ye that labor and are heavy laden, and I will give you rest." There is, then, a way to be saved, if we will. Death has prevailed and swallowed us up; but be assured, that God will wipe away every tear from the face of every penitent. The Lord is faithful in all his words. He does not lie, when he says, "Though your sins be as scarlet, they shall be as white as snow; though they be red like crimson, they shall be as wool." The great Physician of souls is ready to heal thy disease; he is the prompt Deliverer, not of thee alone, but of all who are in bondage to sin. These are his words,—his sweet and life-giving lips pronounced them,—"They that be whole need not a physician, but they that are sick. I am not come to call the righteous, but sinners to repentance." What excuse, then, remains to thee, or to any one else, when he utters such language as this? The Lord is willing to heal thy painful wound, and to enlighten thy darkness. The Good Shepherd leaves the sheep who have not strayed, to seek for thee. If thou give thyself up to him, he will not delay, he in his mercy will not disdain to carry thee upon his own shoulders, rejoicing that he has found his sheep which was lost. The Father stands waiting thy return from thy wanderings. Only arise and come, and whilst thou art yet a great way off he will run and fall upon thy neck; and, purified at once by thy repentance, thou shalt be enfolded in the embraces of his friendship. He will put the best robe on thy soul, when it has put off the old man with his deeds; he will put a ring on thy hands when they have been washed from the blood of death; he will put shoes on thy feet, when they have turned from the evil way to the path of the Gospel of peace; and he will proclaim a day of joy and gladness to the whole family of both angels and men, and will celebrate thy salvation with every form of rejoicing. For he himself says, "Verily I say unto you, that joy shall be in heaven before God over one sinner that repenteth." And if any of those that stand by should seem to find fault, because thou art so quickly received, the good Father himself will plead for thee, saying, "It was meet that we should make merry and be glad; for this my daughter was dead, and is alive again; and was lost, and is found."

1—16

RICHARD BAXTER

(1615–1691)

ICHARD BAXTER, author of 'The Saints' Everlasting Rest' and of other works to the extent of sixty octavo volumes, was called by Doddridge "the English Demosthenes." He was born November 12th, 1615, in Shropshire, England, and was admitted to orders in the English Church in 1638. He refused, however, to take the oath of "Submission to Archbishops, Bishops," etc., and established himself as the pastor of a dissenting church in Kidderminster. He was twice imprisoned for refusing to conform to the requirements of the Established Church. He died in 1691. One of his critics says of him:—

"The leading characteristics of Baxter are, eminent piety and vigor of intellect, keenness of logic, burning power and plainness of language, melting pathos, cloudless perspicuity, graceful description, and a certain vehemence of feeling which brings home his words with an irresistible force."

The sermon here extracted from was preached first at Kidderminster and afterwards at London, and it is said it produced "a profound sensation." As published entire, under the title 'Making Light of Christ and Salvation,' it makes a considerable volume.

UNWILLINGNESS TO IMPROVE

BELOVED hearers, the office that God hath called us to, is by declaring the glory of his grace, to help under Christ to the saving of men's souls. I hope you think not that I come hither to-day on any other errand. The Lord knows I had not set a foot out of doors but in hope to succeed in this work for your souls. I have considered, and often considered, what is the matter that so many thousands should perish when God hath done so much for their salvation; and I find this that is mentioned in my text is the cause. It is one of the wonders of the world, that when God hath so loved the world as to send his Son, and Christ hath made a satisfaction by his death sufficient for them

all, and offereth the benefits of it so freely to them, even without
money or price, that yet the most of the world should perish;
yea, the most of those that are thus called by his word! Why,
here is the reason, when Christ hath done all this, men make
light of it. God hath showed that he is not unwilling; and Christ
hath showed that he is not unwilling that men should be restored
to God's favor and be saved; but men are actually unwilling
themselves. God takes not pleasure in the death of sinners, but
rather that they return and live. But men take such pleasure
in sin that they will die before they will return. The Lord
Jesus was content to be their Physician, and hath provided them
a sufficient plaster of his own blood: but if men make light of
it, and will not apply it, what wonder if they perish after all?
The Scripture giveth us the reason of their perdition. This, sad
experience tells us, the most of the world is guilty of. It is a
most lamentable thing to see how most men do spend their care,
their time, their pains, for known vanities, while God and glory
are cast aside; that he who is all should seem to them as nothing,
and that which is nothing should seem to them as good as all;
that God should set mankind in such a race where heaven or
hell is their certain end, and that they should sit down, and
loiter, or run after the childish toys of the world, and so much
forget the prize that they should run for. Were it but possible
for one of us to see the whole of this business as the all-seeing
God doth; to see at one view both heaven and hell, which men
are so near; and see what most men in the world are minding,
and what they are doing every day, it would be the saddest sight
that could be imagined. Oh how should we marvel at their
madness, and lament their self-delusion! Oh poor distracted
world! what is it you run after? and what is it that you neglect? If God had never told them what they were sent into the
world to do, or whither they are going, or what was before them
in another world, then they had been excusable; but he hath
told them over and over, till they were weary of it. Had he left
it doubtful, there had been some excuse; but it is his sealed
word, and they profess to believe it, and would take it ill of us
if we should question whether they do believe it or not.

Beloved, I come not to accuse any of you particularly of this
crime; but seeing it is the commonest cause of men's destruction, I suppose you will judge it the fittest matter for our inquiry, and deserving our greatest care for the cure. To which

Do not those men make light of Christ and salvation that
shun the mention of his name, unless it be in a vain or sinful
use? Those that love not the company where Christ and salvation is much talked of, but think it troublesome, precise discourse; that had rather hear some merry jests, or idle tales, or
talk of their riches or business in the world? When you may
follow them from morning to night, and scarce have a savory
word of Christ; but, perhaps, some slight and weary mention of
him sometimes; judge whether these make not light of Christ
and salvation. How seriously do they talk of the world and
speak vanity! but how heartlessly do they make mention of
Christ and salvation!

3. The things that we highly value we would secure the possession of, and, therefore, would take any convenient course to
have all doubts and fears about them well resolved. Do not
those men then make light of Christ and salvation that have
lived twenty or thirty years in uncertainty whether they have
any part in these or not, and yet never seek out for the right
resolution of their doubts? Are all that hear me this day certain they shall be saved? Oh that they were! Oh, had you not
made light of salvation, you could not so easily bear such doubting of it; you could not rest till you had made it sure, or done
your best to make it sure. Have you nobody to inquire of, that
might help you in such a work? Why, you have ministers that
are purposely appointed to that office. Have you gone to them,
and told them the doubtfulness of your case, and asked their
help in the judging of your condition? Alas, ministers may sit
in their studies from one year to another, before ten persons
among a thousand will come to them on such an errand! Do
not these make light of Christ and salvation? When the Gospel
pierceth the heart indeed, they cry out, "Men and brethren,
what shall we do to be saved?" Trembling and astonished, Paul
cries out, "Lord, what wilt thou have me to do?" And so did
the convinced Jews to Peter. But when hear we such questions?

4. The things that we value do deeply affect us, and some
motions will be in the heart according to our estimation of them.
O sirs, if men made not light of these things, what working
would there be in the hearts of all our hearers! What strange
affections would it raise in them to hear of the matters of the
world to come! How would their hearts melt before the power
of the Gospel! What sorrow would be wrought in the discovery

end I shall, 1. Endeavor the conviction of the guilty. 2. Shall
give them such considerations as may tend to humble and reform
them. 3. I shall conclude with such direction as may help them
that are willing to escape the destroying power of this sin. And
for the first, consider: —

1. It is the case of most sinners to think themselves freest
from those sins that they are most enslaved to; and one reason
why we cannot reform them, is because we cannot convince them
of their guilt. It is the nature of sin so far to blind and befool
the sinner, that he knoweth not what he doth, but thinketh he
is free from it when it reigneth in him, or when he is committing it; it bringeth men to be so much unacquainted with
themselves that they know not what they think, or what they
mean and intend, nor what they love or hate, much less what
they are habituated and disposed to. They are alive to sin, and
dead to all the reason, consideration, and resolution that should
recover them, as if it were only by their sinning that we must
know they are alive. May I hope that you that hear me to-day
are but willing to know the truth of your case, and then I shall
be encouraged to proceed to an inquiry. God will judge impartially; why should not we do so? Let me, therefore, by these
following questions, try whether none of you are slighters of
Christ and your own salvation. And follow me, I beseech you,
by putting them close to your own hearts, and faithfully answering them.

1. Things that men highly value will be remembered; they
will be matter of their freest and sweetest thoughts. This is a
known case.

Do not those then make light of Christ and salvation that
think of them so seldom and coldly in comparison of other
things? Follow thy own heart, man, and observe what it daily
runneth after; and then judge whether it make not light of
Christ.

We cannot persuade men to one hour's sober consideration
what they should do for an interest in Christ, or in thankfulness
for his love, and yet they will not believe that they make light
of him.

2. Things that we highly value will be matter of our discourse; the judgment and heart will command the tongue.
Freely and delightfully will our speech run after them. This
also is a known case.

of their sins! What astonishment at the consideration of their
misery! What unspeakable joy at the glad tidings of salvation
by the blood of Christ! What resolution would be raised in
them upon the discovery of their duty! Oh what hearers should
we have, if it were not for this sin! Whereas, now we are liker
to weary them, or preach them asleep with matters of this unspeakable moment. We talk to them of Christ and salvation till
we make their heads ache; little would one think by their careless carriage that they heard and regarded what we said, or
thought we spoke at all to them.

5. Our estimation of things will be seen in the diligence of
our endeavors. That which we highliest value, we shall think no
pains too great to obtain. Do not those men then make light of
Christ and salvation that think all too much that they do for
them; that murmur at his service, and think it too grievous for
them to endure? that ask of his service as Judas of the ointment, What need this waste? Cannot men be saved without so
much ado? This is more ado than needs. For the world they
will labor all the day, and all their lives; but for Christ and
salvation they are afraid of doing too much. Let us preach to
them as long as we will, we cannot bring them to relish or
resolve upon a life of holiness. Follow them to their houses,
and you shall not hear them read a chapter, nor call upon God
with their families once a day; nor will they allow him that one
day in seven which he hath separated to his service. But pleasure, or worldly business, or idleness, must have a part. And
many of them are so far hardened as to reproach them that will
not be as mad as themselves. And is not Christ worth the seeking? Is not everlasting salvation worth more than all this?
Doth not that soul make light of all these that thinks his ease
more worth than they? Let but common sense judge.

6. That which we most highly value, we think we cannot buy
too dear: Christ and salvation are freely given, and yet the most
of men go without them because they cannot enjoy the world and
them together. They are called but to part with that which
would hinder them from Christ, and they will not do it. They
are called but to give God his own, and to resign all to his will,
and let go the profits and pleasures of this world, when they
must let go either Christ or them, and they will not. They
think this too dear a bargain, and say they cannot spare these
things; they must hold their credit with men; they must look to

their estates: how shall they live else? They must have their pleasure, whatsoever becomes of Christ and salvation: as if they could live without Christ better than without these: as if they were afraid of being losers by Christ or could make a saving match by losing their souls to gain the world. Christ hath told us over and over that if we will not forsake all for him we cannot be his disciples. Far are these men from forsaking all, and yet will needs think that they are his disciples indeed.

7. That which men highly esteem, they would help their friends to as well as themselves. Do not those men make light of Christ and salvation that can take so much care to leave their children portions in the world, and do so little to help them to heaven? that provide outward necessaries so carefully for their families, but do so little to the saving of their souls? Their neglected children and friends will witness that either Christ, or their children's souls, or both, were made light of.

8. That which men highly esteem, they will so diligently seek after that you may see it in the success, if it be a matter within their reach. You may see how many make light of Christ, by the little knowledge they have of him, and the little communion with him, and communication from him; and the little, yea, none of his special grace in them. Alas! how many ministers can speak it to the sorrow of their hearts, that many of their people know almost nothing of Christ, though they hear of him daily! Nor know they what they must do to be saved: if we ask them an account of these things, they answer as if they understood not what we say to them, and tell us they are no scholars, and therefore think they are excusable for their ignorance. Oh if these men had not made light of Christ and their salvation, but had bestowed but half as much pains to know and enjoy him as they have done to understand the matters of their trades and callings in the world, they would not have been so ignorant as they are: they make light of these things, and therefore will not be at the pains to study or learn them. When men that can learn the hardest trade in a few years have not learned a catechism, nor how to understand their creed, under twenty or thirty years' preaching, nor can abide to be questioned about such things, doth not this show that they have slighted them in their hearts? How will these despisers of Christ and salvation be able one day to look him in the face, and to give an account of these neglects? . . .

After the success of that mission, he was appointed minister to Russia, but declined saying that he had "no wish to serve the administration except when his services were necessary for the public good." He died in August 1815.

His speeches show a strong and comprehensive grasp of facts, a power to present them in logical sequence, and an apprehension of principle which is not often seen in public speeches. They were addressed, however, only to the few who will take the pains to do severe and connected thinking and they are never likely to become extensively popular.

THE FEDERAL JUDICIARY

(Delivered on the Judiciary Bill, in the House of Representatives, on the Nineteenth of February, 1802)

Mr. Chairman:—

I MUST be allowed to express my surprise at the course pursued by the honorable gentleman from Virginia, Mr. Giles, in the remarks which he has made on the subject before us. I had expected that he would have adopted a different line of conduct. I had expected it as well from that sentiment of magnanimity which ought to have been inspired by a sense of the high ground he holds on the floor of this House, as from the professions of a desire to conciliate, which he has so repeatedly made during the session. We have been invited to bury the hatchet, and brighten the chain of peace. We were disposed to meet on middle-ground. We had assurances from the gentleman that he would abstain from reflections on the past, and that his only wish was that we might unite in future in promoting the welfare of our common country. We confided in the gentleman's sincerity, and cherished the hope, that if the divisions of party were not banished from the House, its spirit would be rendered less intemperate. Such were our impressions, when the mask was suddenly thrown aside, and we saw the torch of discord lighted and blazing before our eyes. Every effort has been made to revive the animosities of the House and inflame the passions of the nation. I am at no loss to perceive why this course has been pursued. The gentleman has been unwilling to rely upon the strength of his subject, and has, therefore, determined to make the measure a party question. He has probably secured success, but would it not

JAMES A. BAYARD

(1767–1815)

DURING the first decade of the nineteenth century, a most important formative period of American history, James A. Bayard was the recognized leader of the Federalists in the Senate. They had lost the presidential election of 1800, and their party had been so completely disorganized by the defeat that they never recovered from it, nor won, as a party, another victory. Defeat, however, did not prevent them from making a stubborn fight for principle—from filing, as it were, an appeal from the first to the third quarter of the century. In this James A. Bayard was their special advocate and representative. The pleas he made in his celebrated speech on the Judiciary, delivered in the House of Representatives, and in similar speeches in the Senate, defined as they had not been defined before, the views of that body of Conservatives whose refusal to accept the defeat of 1800 as anything more than an ephemeral incident, led to the far-reaching results achieved by other parties which their ideas brought into existence. It was said of Bayard, as their representative and leader, that "he was distinguished for the depth of his knowledge, the solidity of his reasoning, and the perspicuity of his illustration." He was called "the Goliath of Federalism," and "the high priest of the constitution," by the opponents of "Jacobinism," as Federalists often termed Jeffersonian democracy.

Mr. Bayard was born in Philadelphia, July 28th, 1767. His father, Dr. James A. Bayard, claimed his descent from the celebrated "Chevalier" Bayard,—a fact which greatly influenced the son as it has others of the family who have succeeded him in public life. Thus when offered the French mission James A. Bayard declined it, fearing that it might involve the suspicion of a bargain. "My ambitions," he wrote in a letter to a relative, "shall never be gratified at the expense of a suspicion. I shall never lose sight of the motto of the great original of our name."

After preparing for the bar, Bayard settled in Delaware and in 1796 that State elected him to the lower house of Congress, promoting him in 1804 to the Senate and re-electing him at the expiration of his first term. In 1813, President Madison appointed him one of the Commissioners to conclude the treaty of peace with England.

have been more honorable and more commendable to have left the decision of a great constitutional question to the understanding, and not to the prejudices of the House? It was my ardent wish to discuss the subject with calmness and deliberation, and I did intend to avoid every topic which could awaken the sensibility of party. This was my temper and design when I took my seat yesterday. It is a course at present we are no longer at liberty to pursue. The gentleman has wandered far, very far, from the points of the debate, and has extended his animadversions to all the prominent measures of the former administrations. In following him through his preliminary observations, I necessarily lose sight of the bill upon your table.

The gentleman commenced his strictures with the philosophic observation, that it was the fate of mankind to hold different opinions as to the form of government which was preferable; that some were attached to the monarchical, while others thought the republican more eligible. This, as an abstract remark, is certainly true, and could have furnished no ground of offense, if it had not evidently appeared that an allusion was designed to be made to the parties in this country. Does the gentleman suppose that we have a less lively recollection than himself, of the oath which we have taken to support the constitution; that we are less sensible of the spirit of our government, or less devoted to the wishes of our constituents? Whatever impression it might be the intention of the gentleman to make, he does not believe that there exists in the country an anti-republican party. He will not venture to assert such an opinion on the floor of this House. That there may be a few individuals having a preference for monarchy is not improbable; but will the gentleman from Virginia, or any other gentleman, affirm in his place, that there is a party in the country who wish to establish monarchy? Insinuations of this sort belong not to the legislature of the Union. Their place is an election ground, or an alehouse. Within these walls they are lost; abroad, they have had an effect, and I fear are still capable of abusing popular credulity.

We were next told of the parties which have existed, divided by the opposite views of promoting executive power and guarding the rights of the people. The gentleman did not tell us in plain language, but he wished it to be understood, that he and his friends were the guardians of the people's rights, and that we were the advocates of executive power.

I know that this is the distinction of party which some gentlemen have been anxious to establish; but it is not the ground on which we divide. I am satisfied with the constitutional powers of the executive, and never wished nor attempted to increase them; and I do not believe, that gentlemen on the other side of the House ever had a serious apprehension of danger from an increase of executive authority. No, sir, our views, as to the powers which do and ought to belong to the general and State governments, are the true sources of our divisions. I co-operate with the party to which I am attached, because I believe their true object and end is an honest and efficient support of the general government, in the exercise of the legitimate powers of the constitution.

I pray to God I may be mistaken in the opinion I entertain as to the designs of gentlemen to whom I am opposed. Those designs I believe hostile to the powers of this government. State pride extinguishes a national sentiment. Whatever power is taken from this government is given to the States.

The ruins of this government aggrandize the States. There are States which are too proud to be controlled; whose sense of greatness and resource renders them indifferent to our protection, and induces a belief that if no general government existed, their influence would be more extensive, and their importance more conspicuous. There are gentlemen who make no secret of an extreme point of depression, to which the government is to be sunk. To that point we are rapidly progressing. But I would beg gentlemen to remember that human affairs are not to be arrested in their course, at artificial points. The impulse now given may be accelerated by causes at present out of view. And when those, who now design well, wish to stop, they may find their powers unable to resist the torrent. It is not true, that we ever wished to give a dangerous strength to executive power. While the government was in our hands, it was our duty to maintain its constitutional balance, by preserving the energies of each branch. There never was an attempt to vary the relation of its powers. The struggle was to maintain the constitutional powers of the executive. The wild principles of French liberty were scattered through the country. We had our Jacobins and disorganizers. They saw no difference between a king and a president, and as the people of France had put down their King, they thought the people of America ought to put down

their President. They, who considered the constitution as securing all the principles of rational and practicable liberty, who were unwilling to embark upon the tempestuous sea of revolution in pursuit of visionary schemes, were denounced as monarchists. A line was drawn between the government and the people, and the friends of the government were marked as the enemies of the people. I hope, however, that the government and the people are now the same; and I pray to God, that what has been frequently remarked, may not, in this case, be discovered to be true, that they, who have the name of the people the most often in their mouths, have their true interests the most seldom at their hearts.

The honorable gentleman from Virginia wandered to the very confines of the federal administration, in search of materials the most inflammable and most capable of kindling the passions of his party. . . .

I did suppose, sir, that this business was at an end; and I did imagine, that as gentlemen had accomplished their object, they would have been satisfied. But as the subject is again renewed, we must be allowed to justify our conduct. I know not what the gentleman calls an expression of the public will. There were two candidates for the office of President, who were presented to the House of Representatives with equal suffrages. The constitution gave us the right and made it our duty to elect that one of the two whom we thought preferable. A public man is to notice the public will as constitutionally expressed. The gentleman from Virginia, and many others, may have had their preference; but that preference of the public will not appear by its constitutional expression. Sir, I am not certain that either of those candidates had a majority of the country in his favor. Excluding the State of South Carolina, the country was equally divided. We know that parties in that State were nearly equally balanced, and the claims of both the candidates were supported by no other scrutiny into the public will than our official return of votes. Those votes are very imperfect evidence of the true will of a majority of the nation. They resulted from political intrigue and artificial arrangement.

When we look at the votes, we must suppose that every man in Virginia voted the same way. These votes are received as a correct expression of the public will. And yet we know that if the votes of that State were apportioned according to the several

voices of the people, that at least seven out of twenty-one would have been opposed to the successful candidate. It was the suppression of the will of one-third of Virginia, which enables gentlemen now to say that the present chief magistrate is the man of the people. I consider that as the public will, which is expressed by constitutional organs. To that will I bow and submit. The public will, thus manifested, gave to the House of Representatives the choice of the two men for President. Neither of them was the man whom I wished to make President; but my election was confined by the constitution to one of the two, and I gave my vote to the one whom I thought was the greater and better man. That vote I repeated, and in that vote I should have persisted, had I not been driven from it by imperious necessity. The prospect ceased of the vote being effectual, and the alternative only remained of taking one man for President, or having no President at all. I chose, as I then thought, the lesser evil.

From the scene in this House, the gentleman carried us to one in the Senate. I should blush, sir, for the honor of the country, could I suppose that the law, designed to be repealed, owed its support in that body to the motives which have been indicated. The charge designed to be conveyed, not only deeply implicates the integrity of individuals of the Senate, but of the person who was then the chief magistrate. The gentleman, going beyond all precedent, has mentioned the names of members of that body, to whom commissions issued for offices not created by the bill before them, but which that bill, by the promotions it afforded, was likely to render vacant. He has considered the scandal of the transaction as aggravated by the issuing of commissions for offices not actually vacant, upon the bare presumption that they would become vacant by the incumbents accepting commissions for higher offices which were issued in their favor. The gentleman has particularly dwelt upon the indecent appearance of the business, from two commissions being held by different persons at the same time for the same office.

I beg that it will be understood that I mean to give no opinion as to the regularity of granting a commission for a judicial office, upon the probability of a vacancy before it is actually vacant; but I shall be allowed to say that so much doubt attends the point, that an innocent mistake might be made on the subject. I believe, sir, it has been the practice to consider the acceptance of an office as relating to the date of the commission.

The officer is allowed his salary from that date, upon the principle that the commission is a grant of the office, and the title commences with the date of the grant. This principle is certainly liable to abuse, but where there was a suspicion of abuse, I presume the government would depart from it. Admitting the office to pass by the commission, and the acceptance to relate to its date, it then does not appear very incorrect, in the case of a commission for the office of a circuit judge, granted to a district judge, as the acceptance of the commission for the former office relates to the date of the commission, to consider the latter office as vacant from the same time. The offices are incompatible. You cannot suppose the same person in both offices at the same time. From the moment, therefore, that you consider the office of circuit judge as filled by a person who holds the commission of district judge, you must consider the office of district judge as vacated. The grant is contingent. If the contingency happen, the office vests from the date of the commission; if the contingency does not happen, the grant is void. If this reasoning be sound, it was not irregular, in the late administration, after granting a commission to a district judge, for the place of a circuit judge, to make a grant of the office of the district judge, upon the contingency of his accepting the office of circuit judge.

. . . .

The legislative power of the government is not absolute, but limited. If it be doubtful whether the legislature can do what the constitution does not explicitly authorize, yet there can be no question, that they cannot do what the constitution expressly prohibits. To maintain, therefore, the constitution, the judges are a check upon the legislature. The doctrine, I know, is denied, and it is, therefore, incumbent upon me to show that it is sound.

It was once thought by gentlemen, who now deny the principle, that the safety of the citizen and of the States rested upon the power of the judges to declare an unconstitutional law void. How vain is a paper restriction if it confers neither power nor right. Of what importance is it to say, Congress are prohibited from doing certain acts, if no legitimate authority exists in the country to decide whether an act done is a prohibited act? Do gentlemen perceive the consequences which would follow from establishing the principle, that Congress have the exclusive right to decide upon their own powers? This principle admitted, does any constitution remain? Does not the power of the legislature become absolute and omnipotent? Can you talk to them of transgressing their powers, when no one has a right to judge of those powers but themselves? They do what is not authorized, they do what is inhibited, nay, at every step, they trample the' constitution under foot; yet their acts are lawful and binding, and it is treason to resist them. How ill, sir, do the doctrines and professions of these gentlemen agree. They tell us they are friendly to the existence of the States; that they are the friends of federative, but the enemies of a consolidated general government, and yet, sir, to accomplish a paltry object, they are willing to settle a principle which, beyond all doubt, would eventually plant a consolidated government, with unlimited power, upon the ruins of the State governments.

Nothing can be more absurd than to contend that there is a practical restraint upon a political body, who are answerable to none but themselves for the violation of the restraint, and who can derive, from the very act of violation, undeniable justification of their conduct.

If, Mr. Chairman, you mean to have a constitution, you must discover a power to which the acknowledged right is attached of pronouncing the invalidity of the acts of the legislature, which contravened the instrument.

Does the power reside in the States? Has the legislature of a State a right to declare an act of Congress void? This would be erring upon the opposite extreme. It would be placing the general government at the feet of the State governments. It would be allowing one member of the Union to control all the rest. It would inevitably lead to civil dissension and a dissolution of the general government. Will it be pretended that the State courts have the exclusive right of deciding upon the validity of our laws?

I admit they have the right to declare an act of Congress void. But this right they enjoy in practice, and it ever essentially must exist, subject to the revision and control of the courts of the United States. If the State courts definitely possessed the right of declaring the invalidity of the laws of this government, it would bring us in subjection to the States. The judges of those courts, being bound by the laws of the State, if a State declared an act of Congress unconstitutional, the law of the State would oblige its courts to determine the law invalid. This

principle would also destroy the uniformity of obligation upon all the States, which should attend every law of this government. If a law were declared void in one State, it would exempt the citizens of that State from its operation, whilst obedience was yielded to it in the other States. I go further, and say, if the States or State courts had a final power of annulling the acts of this government, its miserable and precarious existence would not be worth the trouble of a moment to preserve. It would endure but a short time, as a subject of derision, and, wasting into an empty shadow, would quickly vanish from our sight.

Let me now ask, if the power to decide upon the validity of our laws resides with the people. Gentlemen cannot deny this right to the people. I admit they possess it. But if, at the same time, it does not belong to the courts of the United States, where does it lead the people? It leads them to the gallows. Let us suppose that Congress, forgetful of the limits of their authority, pass an unconstitutional law. They lay a direct tax upon one State and impose none upon the others. The people of the State taxed contest the validity of the law. They forcibly resist its execution. They are brought by the executive authority before the courts upon charges of treason. The law is unconstitutional, the people have done right, but the court are bound by the law, and obliged to pronounce upon them the sentence which it inflicts. Deny to the courts of the United States the power of judging upon the constitutionality of our laws, and it is vain to talk of its existing elsewhere. The infractors of the laws are brought before these courts, and if the courts are implicitly bound, the invalidity of the laws can be no defense. There is, however, Mr. Chairman, still a stronger ground of argument upon this subject. I shall select one or two cases to illustrate it. Congress are prohibited from passing a bill of attainder; it is also declared in the constitution, that "no attainder of treason shall work corruption of blood or forfeiture, except during the life of the party attainted." Let us suppose that Congress pass a bill of attainder, or they enact, that any one attainted of treason shall forfeit, to the use of the United States, all the estate which he held in any lands or tenements.

The party attainted is seized and brought before a federal court, and an award of execution passed against him. He opens the constitution and points to this line, "no bill of attainder or

ex post facto law shall be passed." The attorney for the United States reads the bill of attainder.

The courts are bound to decide, but they have only the alternative of pronouncing the law or the constitution invalid. It is left to them only to say that the law vacates the constitution, or the constitution voids the law. So, in the other case stated, the heir, after the death of his ancestor, brings his ejectment in one of the courts of the United States to recover his inheritance. The law by which it is confiscated is shown. The constitution gave no power to pass such a law. On the contrary, it expressly denied it to the government. The title of the heir is rested on the constitution, the title of the government on the law. The effect of one destroys the effect of the other; the court must determine which is effectual.

There are many other cases, Mr. Chairman, of a similar nature to which I might allude. There is the case of the privilege of *habeas corpus*, which cannot be suspended but in times of rebellion or invasion. Suppose a law prohibiting the issue of the writ at a moment of profound peace! If, in such case, the writ were demanded of a court, could they say, it is true the legislature were restrained from passing the law suspending the privilege of this writ, at such a time as that which now exists, but their mighty power has broken the bonds of the constitution, and fettered the authority of the court? I am not, sir, disposed to vaunt, but standing on this ground, I throw the gauntlet to any champion upon the other side. I call upon them to maintain, that, in a collision between a law and the constitution, the judges are bound to support the law, and annul the constitution. Can the gentlemen relieve themselves from this dilemma? Will they say, though a judge has no power to pronounce a law void, he has a power to declare the constitution invalid?

The doctrine for which I am contending, is not only clearly inferable from the plain language of the constitution, but by law has been expressly declared and established in practice since the existence of the government.

The second section of the third article of the constitution expressly extends the judicial power to all cases arising under the constitution, laws, etc. The provision in the second clause of the sixth article leaves nothing to doubt. "This constitution and the laws of the United States, which shall be made in pursuance

thereof, etc., shall be the supreme law of the land." The constitution is absolutely the supreme law. Not so the acts of the legislature! Such only are the law of the land as are made in pursuance of the constitution.

I beg the indulgence of the committee one moment, while I read the following provision from the twenty-fifth section of the judicial act of the year 1789: "A final judgment or decree in any suit in the highest court of law or equity of a state, in which a decision in the suit could be had, where is drawn in question the validity of a treaty or statute of, or an authority exercised under, the United States, and the decision is against their validity, etc., may be re-examined and reversed or affirmed in the Supreme Court of the United States, upon a writ of error." Thus, as early as the year 1789, among the first acts of the government, the legislature explicitly recognized the right of a State court to declare a treaty, a statute, and an authority exercised under the United States, void, subject to the revision of the Supreme Court of the United States; and it has expressly given the final power to the Supreme Court to affirm a judgment which is against the validity, either of a treaty, statute, or an authority of the government.

I humbly trust, Mr. Chairman, that I have given abundant proofs from the nature of our government, from the language of the constitution, and from legislative acknowledgment, that the judges of our courts have the power to judge and determine upon the constitutionality of our laws.

Let me now suppose that, in our frame of government, the judges are a check upon the legislature; that the constitution is deposited in their keeping. Will you say afterwards that their existence depends upon the legislature? That the body whom they are to check has the power to destroy them? Will you say that the constitution may be taken out of their hands by a power the most to be distrusted, because the only power which could violate it with impunity? Can anything be more absurd than to admit that the judges are a check upon the legislature, and yet to contend that they exist at the will of the legislature? A check must necessarily imply a power commensurate to its end. The political body, designed to check another, must be independent of it, otherwise there can be no check. What check can there be when the power designed to be checked can annihilate the body which is to restrain?

I go further, Mr. Chairman, and take a stronger ground. I say, in the nature of things, the dependence of the judges upon the legislature, and their right to declare the acts of the legislature void, are repugnant, and cannot exist together. The doctrine, sir, supposes two rights — first, the right of the legislature to destroy the office of the judge, and the right of the judge to vacate the act of the legislature. You have a right to abolish by a law the offices of the judges of the circuit courts; they have a right to declare the law void. It unavoidably follows, in the exercise of these rights, either that you destroy their rights, or that they destroy yours. This doctrine is not a harmless absurdity, it is a most dangerous heresy. It is a doctrine which cannot be practiced without producing not discord only, but bloodshed. If you pass the bill upon your table, the judges have a constitutional right to declare it void. I hope they will have courage to exercise that right; and if, sir, I am called upon to take my side, standing acquitted in my conscience, and before my God, of all motives but the support of the constitution of my country, I shall not tremble at the consequences.

The constitution may have its enemies, but I know that it has also its friends. I beg gentlemen to pause, before they take this rash step. There are many, very many, who believe, if you strike this blow, you inflict a mortal wound on the constitution. There are many now willing to spill their blood to defend that constitution. Are gentlemen disposed to risk the consequences? Sir, I mean no threats, I have no expectation of appalling the stout hearts of my adversaries; but if gentlemen are regardless of themselves, let them consider their wives and children, their neighbors and their friends. Will they risk civil dissension, will they hazard the welfare, will they jeopardize the peace of the country, to save a paltry sum of money, less than thirty thousand dollars?

Mr. Chairman, I am confident that the friends of this measure are not apprised of the nature of its operation, nor sensible of the mischievous consequences which are likely to attend it. Sir, the morals of your people, the peace of the country, the stability of the government, rest upon the maintenance of the independence of the judiciary. It is not of half the importance in England, that the judges should be independent of the crown, as it is with us that they should be independent of the legislature.

Am I asked, would you render the judges superior to the legislature? I answer, no, but co-ordinate. Would you render them independent of the legislature? I answer, yes, independent of every power on earth, while they behave themselves well. The essential interests, the permanent welfare of society, require this independence; not, sir, on account of the judge; that is a small consideration, but on account of those between whom he is to decide. You calculate on the weaknesses of human nature, and you suffer the judge to be dependent on no one, lest he should be partial to those on whom he depends. Justice does not exist where partiality prevails. A dependent judge cannot be impartial. Independence is, therefore, essential to the purity of your judicial tribunals.

Let it be remembered, that no power is so sensibly felt by society, as that of the judiciary. The life and property of every man is liable to be in the hands of the judges. Is it not our great interest to place our judges upon such high ground that no fear can intimidate, no hope seduce them? The present measure humbles them in the dust, it prostrates them at the feet of faction, it renders them the tools of every dominant party. It is this effect which I deprecate, it is this consequence which I deeply deplore. What does reason, what does argument avail, when party spirit presides? Subject your bench to the influence of this spirit, and justice bids a final adieu to your tribunals. We are asked, sir, if the judges are to be independent of the people? The question presents a false and delusive view. We are all the people. We are, and as long as we enjoy our freedom, we shall be divided into parties. The true question is, shall the judiciary be permanent, or fluctuate with the tide of public opinion? I beg, I implore gentlemen to consider the magnitude and value of the principle which they are about to annihilate. If your judges are independent of political changes, they may have their preferences, but they will not enter into the spirit of party. But let their existence depend upon the support of the power of a certain set of men, and they cannot be impartial. Justice will be trodden under foot. Your courts will lose all public confidence and respect.

The judges will be supported by their partisans, who, in their turn, will expect impunity for the wrongs and violence they commit. The spirit of party will be inflamed to madness: and the

moment is not far off, when this fair country is to be desolated by a civil war.

Do not say that you render the judges dependent only on the people. You make them dependent on your President. This is his measure. The same tide of public opinion which changes a President will change the majorities in the branches of the legislature. The legislature will be the instrument of his ambition, and he will have the courts as the instruments of his vengeance. He uses the legislature to remove the judges, that he may appoint creatures of his own. In effect, the powers of the government will be concentrated in the hands of one man, who will dare to act with more boldness, because he will be sheltered from responsibility. The independence of the judiciary was the felicity of our constitution. It was this principle which was to curb the fury of party on sudden changes. The first movements of power gained by a struggle are the most vindictive and intemperate. Raised above the storm it was the judiciary which was to control the fiery zeal, and to quell the fierce passions of a victorious faction.

We are standing on the brink of that revolutionary torrent, which deluged in blood one of the fairest countries of Europe.

France had her national assembly, more numerous than, and equally popular with, our own. She had her tribunals of justice, and her juries. But the legislature and her courts were but the instruments of her destruction. Acts of proscription and sentences of banishment and death were passed in the cabinet of a tyrant. Prostrate your judges at the feet of party, and you break down the mounds which defend you from this torrent.

I am done. I should have thanked my God for greater power to resist a measure so destructive to the peace and happiness of the country. My feeble efforts can avail nothing. But it was my duty to make them. The meditated blow is mortal, and from the moment it is struck, we may bid a final adieu to the constitution.

COMMERCE AND NAVAL POWER

(United States Senate, February 12th, 1810)

God has decided that the people of this country should be a commercial people. You read that decree in the seacoast of seventeen hundred miles which he has given you; in the numerous navigable waters which penetrate the interior of the country; in the various ports and harbors scattered along your shores; in your fisheries; in the redundant productions of your soil; and, more than all, in the enterprising and adventurous spirit of your people. It is no more a question whether the people of this country shall be allowed to plough the ocean, than it is whether they shall be permitted to plough the land. It is not in the power of this government, nor would it be if it were as strong as the most despotic upon the earth, to subdue the commercial spirit, or to destroy the commercial habits of the country.

Young as we are, our tonnage and commerce surpass those of every nation upon the globe but one, and if not wasted by the deprivations to which they were exposed by their defenseless situation, and the more ruinous restrictions to which this government subjected them, it would require not many more years to have made them the greatest in the world. Is this immense wealth always to be exposed as a prey to the rapacity of free-booters? Why will you protect your citizens and their property upon land, and leave them defenseless upon the ocean? As your mercantile property increases, the prize becomes more tempting to the cupidity of foreign nations. In the course of things, the ruins and aggressions which you have experienced will multiply, nor will they be restrained while we have no appearance of a naval force.

I have always been in favor of a naval establishment — not from the unworthy motives attributed by the gentleman from Georgia to a former administration, in order to increase patronage, but from a profound conviction that the safety of the Union and the prosperity of the nation depended greatly upon its commerce, which never could be securely enjoyed without the protection of naval power. I offer, sir, abundant proof for the satisfaction of the liberal mind of that gentleman, that patronage was not formerly a motive in voting an increase in the navy, when I give now the same vote, when surely I and my friends have nothing to hope, and for myself, I thank God, nothing to wish from the patronage it may confer.

You must and will have a navy; but it is not to be created in a day, nor is it to be expected that, in its infancy, it will be able to cope, foot to foot with the full-grown vigor of the navy of England. But we are even now capable of maintaining a naval force formidable enough to threaten the British commerce, and to render this nation an object of more respect and consideration.

In another point of view, the protection of commerce has become more indispensable. The discovery is completely made, that it is from commerce that the revenue is to be drawn which is to support this government. A direct tax, a stamp act, a carriage tax, and an excise, have been tried; and I believe, sir, after the lesson which experience has given on the subject, no set of men in power will ever repeat them again, for all they are likely to produce. The burden must be pretty light upon the people of this country, or the rider is in great danger. You may be allowed to sell your back lands for some time longer, but the permanent fund for the support of this government is the imports.

If the people were willing to part with commerce, can the government dispense with it? But when it belongs equally to the interest of the people and of the government to encourage and protect it, will you not spare a few of those dollars which it brings into your treasury, to defend and protect it?

In relation to the increase of a permanent military force, a free people cannot cherish too great a jealousy. An army may wrest the power from the hands of the people, and deprive them of their liberty. It becomes us, therefore, to be extremely cautious how we augment it. But a navy of any magnitude can never threaten us with the same danger. Upon land, at this time, we have nothing — and probably, at any future time, we shall have but little — to fear from any foreign power. It is upon the ocean we meet them; it is there our collisions arise; it is there we are most feeble, most vulnerable, and most exposed; it is there by consequence, that our safety and prosperity must require an augmented force.

THOMAS F. BAYARD

(1828–1898)

IN 1876, when the country was in imminent danger of the renewal of civil war as a result of the contested presidential election, the conservative element of the Democratic party, advised by Mr. Tilden himself, determined to avoid anything which might result in extreme measures. The masses of the people were excited as they had not been since the close of the Civil War, and the great majority of the Democrats of the country were undoubtedly opposed to making concessions. Thomas F. Bayard, who took the lead in the Senate as the representative of the moderate policy favored by Mr. Tilden, met the reproaches sure to be visited in such cases on the peacemaker. Nevertheless, he advocated the Electoral Commission as a method of settling the contest, and his speech in supporting it, without doubt one of the best as it was certainly the most important of his life, paved the way for the final adoption of the bill. It is no more than justice to say that the speech is worthy of the dignity of that great occasion.

Mr. Bayard inherited the equable temperament shown by his father and his grandfather. He was a warm-hearted man with a long memory for services done him, but he had a faculty of containing himself which few men exercise to the degree that he exercised it habitually, both in his public and private life. The habit was so strong, in fact, that he indulged only on rare occasions that emotion which is necessary for the highest success as an orator. The calmness of his thought shows itself in logic which, while it may invite confidence, does not compel admiration. When he is moved, however, the freedom of his utterances from exaggeration and from that tendency to rant which mars many orations makes such periods as those with which he closes his speech on the Electoral Bill models of expression for all who wish to realize the highest possibilities of cumulative force.

The son of one United States Senator, James A. Bayard, of Delaware, and the grandson of another, Mr. Bayard represented well the family tradition of integrity. Born in 1828, he succeeded to his father's place in the Senate when forty-one years of age, and remained in the public service until within a short time of his death. He was Secretary of State under the first Cleveland administration and ambassador

to England under the second. In the convention which nominated Mr. Cleveland in 1884, Mr. Bayard, who had been strongly supported for the Democratic presidential nomination in 1880, was so close to the presidency at the beginning of the balloting that his managers confidently expected his success. He became much attached to President Cleveland, and in 1896 he took a course on the financial issue then uppermost, which alienated many of his friends, as far as friends could be alienated by the political action of a man whose public and private life were so full of dignity, simplicity, and the qualities which result from habitual good faith. Mr. Bayard survived almost into the twentieth century as a last representative of the colonial gentlemen who debated the Federal Constitution. Supposed to be cold and unapproachable, he was really warm in his friendships, with a memory which never allowed an act of service done him to escape it. Few better men have had anything to do with the politics of the second half of the century. He died in 1898.

W. V. B.

A PLEA FOR CONCILIATION IN 1876

("Counting the Electoral Votes," United States Senate, January 24th, 1877)

MR. PRESIDENT, I might have been content as a friend of this measure to allow it to go before the Senate and the country unaccompanied by any remarks of mine had it not been the pleasure of the Senate to assign me as one of the minority in this Chamber to a place upon the select committee appointed for the purpose of reporting a bill intended to meet the exigencies of the hour in relation to the electoral votes. There is for every man in a matter of such gravity his own measure of responsibility, and that measure I desire to assume. Nothing less important than the decision, into whose hands the entire executive power of this government shall be vested in the next four years, is embraced in the provisions of this bill. The election for President and Vice-President has been held, but as to the results of that election the two great political parties of the country stand opposed in serious controversy. Each party claims success for its candidate and insists that he and he alone shall be declared by the two houses of Congress entitled to exercise the executive power of this government for the next four years. The canvass was prolonged and unprecedented in its

excitement and even bitterness. The period of advocacy of either candidate has passed, and the time for judgment has almost come. How shall we who purpose to make laws for others do better than to exhibit our own reverence for law and set the example here of subordination to the spirit of law?

It cannot be disguised that an issue has been sought, if not actually raised, in this country, between a settlement of this great question by sheer force and arbitrary exercise of power or by the peaceful, orderly, permanent methods of law and reason. Ours is, as we are wont to boast, a government of laws, and not of will; and we must not permit it to pass away from us by changing its nature.

"O, yet a nobler task awaits thy hand,
For what can war but endless war still breed?"

By this measure now before the Senate it is proposed to have a peaceful conquest over partisan animosity and lawless action, to procure a settlement grounded on reason and justice, and not upon force. Therefore, it is meant to lift this great question of determining who has been lawfully elected President and Vice-President of these United States out of the possibility of popular broils and tumult, and elevate it with all dignity to the higher atmosphere of legal and judicial decision. In such a spirit I desire to approach the consideration of the subject and shall seek to deal with it at least worthily, with a sense of public duty unobstructed, I trust, by prejudice or party animosity. The truth of Lord Bacon's aphorism that "great empire and little minds go ill together," should warn us now against the obtrusion of narrow or technical views in adjusting such a question and at such a time in our country's history.

Mr. President, from the very commencement of the attempt to form the government under which we live, the apportionment of power in the executive branch and the means of choosing the chief magistrate have been the subject of the greatest difficulty. Those who founded this government and preceded us in its control had felt the hand of kingly power, and it was from the abuse of executive power that they dreaded the worst results. Therefore it was that when the Constitution came to be framed that was the point upon which they met and upon which they parted, less able to agree than upon almost all others combined,

A glance at the history of the convention that met at Philadelphia on the fourteenth day of May, 1787, but did not organize until the twenty-fifth day of the same month, will show that three days after the convention assembled two plans of a Constitution were presented, respectively, by Mr. Edmund Randolph, of Virginia, and Mr. Charles Pinckney, of South Carolina. The first proposed the election of the executive by the legislature, as the two houses were then termed, for a term of seven years, with ineligibility for re-election. The other proposed an election, but left the power to elect or the term of office in blank. Both of these features in the schemes proposed came up early for consideration, and, as I have said before, as the grave and able minds of that day approached this subject they were unable to agree, and accordingly, from time to time, the question was postponed and no advance whatever made in the settlement of the question. Indeed, so vital and wide was the difference that each attempt made during the course of the five months in which that convention was assembled only seemed to result in renewed failure. So it stood until the fourth day of September had arrived. The labors of the convention by that time had resulted in the framing of a Constitution, wise and good and fairly balanced, calculated to preserve power sufficient in the government, and yet leaving that individual freedom and liberty essential for the protection of the States and their citizens. Then it was that this question, so long postponed, came up for consideration and had to be decided. As it was decided then, it appears in the Constitution as submitted to the States in 1787; but an amendment of the second article was proposed in 1804, which, meeting the approval of the States, became part of the Constitution.

I must be pardoned if I repeat something of what has preceded in this debate, by way of citation from the Constitution of the United States, in order that we may find there our warrant for the present measure. There were difficulties of which these fathers of our government were thoroughly conscious. The very difficulties that surround the question to-day are suggested in the debates of 1800, in which the history of double returns is foretold by Mr. Pinckney in his objections to the measure then before the Senate. The very title of that act, "A Bill Prescribing a Mode of Deciding Disputed Elections of President and Vice-President of the United States," will show the difficulties which they then perceived and of which they felt the future was to be

The electors shall meet in their respective States and vote by ballot for President and Vice-President, one of whom, at least, shall not be an inhabitant of the same State with themselves; they shall name in their ballots the person voted for as President, and in distinct ballots the person voted for as Vice-President, and they shall make distinct lists of all persons voted for as President, and of all persons voted for as Vice-President, and of the number of votes for each; which lists they shall sign and certify, and transmit sealed to the seat of government of the United States, directed to the President of the Senate. The President of the Senate shall, in the presence of the Senate and House of Representatives, open all the certificates, and the votes shall then be counted.

Then follows the duty and power of Congress in connection with this subject to determine the time of choosing the electors and the day on which they shall give their votes, which day shall be the same throughout the United States. The next clause provides for the qualifications of the candidates for the presidency and vice-presidency. The next clause gives power to the Congress of the United States to provide for filling the office of President and Vice-President in the event of the death, resignation, or inability of the incumbents to vest the powers and duties of the said office. The other clause empowers Congress thus to designate a temporary President. The other clauses simply relate to the compensation of the President and the oath he shall take to perform the duties of the office. Connected with that delegation of power is to be considered the eighth section of the first article which gives to the Congress of the United States power "to make all laws which shall be necessary and proper for carrying into execution the foregoing powers, and all other powers vested by this Constitution in the government of the United States, or in any department or officer thereof."

It will be observed, so far, that the Constitution has provided the power but has not provided the regulations for carrying that power into effect. The Supreme Court of the United States sixty-odd years ago defined so well the character of that power and the method of its use that I will quote it from the first volume of Wheaton's Reports, page 326:—

Leaving it to the legislature from time to time to adopt its own means to effectuate, legitimate, and mold and model the exercise of its powers as its own wisdom and public interest should require.

so full. They made the attempt in 1800 to meet those difficulties. They did not succeed. Again and again the question came before them. In 1824 a second attempt was made at legislation. It met the approval of the Senate. It seemed to meet the approval of the Committee on the Judiciary of the House, by whom it was reported without amendment, but never was acted upon in that body, and failed to become a law. This all shows to us that there has been a postponement from generation to generation of a subject of great difficulty that we of to-day are called upon to meet under circumstances of peculiar and additional disadvantage; for while in the convention of 1787 there was a difference arising from interest, from all the infinite variances of prejudice and opinion upon subjects of local, geographical, and pecuniary interests, and making mutual concessions and patriotic considerations necessary at all times, yet they were spared the most dangerous of all feelings under which our country has suffered of late; for, amid all the perturbing causes to interfere with and distract their counsels, partisan animosity was at least unknown. There was in that day no such thing as political party in the United States:—

"Then none were for a party,
But all were for the State."

Political parties were formed afterward and have grown in strength since, and to-day the troubles that afflict our country chiefly may be said to arise from the dangerous excess of party feeling in our councils.

But I propose to refer to the condition of the law and the Constitution as we now find it. The second article of the first section of the Constitution provides for the vesting of the executive power in the President and also for the election of a Vice-President. First it provides that "each State" shall, through its legislature, appoint the number of electors to which it is entitled, which shall be the number of its Representatives in Congress and its Senators combined. The power there is to the State to appoint. The grant is as complete and perfect that the State shall have that power as is another clause of the Constitution giving to "each State" the power to be represented by the Senators in this branch of Congress. There is given to the electors prescribed duties, which I will read:—

In less than four years, in March 1792, after the first Congress had assembled there was legislation upon this subject, carrying into execution the power vested by this second article of the Constitution in a manner which will leave no doubt of what the men of that day believed was competent and proper. Here let me advert to that authority which must ever attach to the contemporaneous exposition of historical events. The men who sat in the Congress of 1792 had many of them been members of the convention that framed the Federal Constitution. All were its contemporaries and closely were they considering with master-minds the consequences of that work. Not only may we gather from the manner in which they treated this subject when they legislated upon it in 1792 what were their views of the powers of Congress on the subject of where the power was lodged and what was the proper measure of its exercise, but we can gather equally well from the inchoate and imperfect legislation of 1800 what those men also thought of their power over this subject, because, although differing as to details, there were certain conceded facts as to jurisdiction quite as emphatically expressed as if their propositions had been enacted into law. Likewise in 1824 the same instruction is afforded. If we find the Senate of the United States without division pass bills which, although not passed by the co-ordinate branch of Congress, are received by them and reported back from the proper committees after examination and without amendment to the committee of the whole House, we may learn with equal authority what was conceded by those houses as to the question of power over the subject. In a compilation made at the present session by order of the House Committee, co-ordinate with the Senate Committee, will be found at page 129 a debate containing expressions by the leading men of both parties in 1857 of the lawfulness of the exercise of the legislative power of Congress over this subject. I venture to read here from the remarks of Mr. Hunter, of Virginia, one of the most respected and conservative minds of his day in the Congress of the United States:—

The Constitution evidently contemplated a provision to be made by law to regulate the details and the mode of counting the votes for President and Vice-President of the United States. The President of the Senate shall, in the presence of the Senate and House of Representatives, open all the certificates, and the votes shall then be counted. By whom, and how to be counted, the Constitution does not say. But Congress has power to make all laws which shall be necessary and proper for carrying into execution the foregoing powers, and all other powers vested by this Constitution in the government of the United States, or in any department or officer thereof. Congress, therefore, has the power to regulate by law the details of the mode in which the votes are to be counted. As yet, no such law has been found necessary. The cases, happily, have been rare in which difficulties have occurred in the count of the electoral votes. All difficulties of this sort have been managed heretofore by the consent of the two houses — a consent either implied at the time or declared by joint resolutions adopted by the houses on the recommendation of the joint committee which is usually raised to prescribe the mode in which the count is to be made. In the absence of law, the will of the two houses thus declared has prescribed the rule under which the President of the Senate and the tellers have acted. It was by this authority, as I understand it, that the President of the Senate acted yesterday. The joint resolution of the two houses prescribed the mode in which the tellers were to make the count and also required him to declare the result, which he did. It was under the authority, therefore, and by the direction of the two houses that he acted. The resolutions by which the authority was given were according to unbroken usage and established precedent.

Mr. President, the debate from which I have read took place in 1857 and was long and able, the question there arising upon the proposed rejection of the vote of the State of Wisconsin, because of the delay of a single day in the meeting of the electors. A violent snowstorm having prevented the election on the third of December, it was held on the fourth, which was clearly in violation of the law of Congress passed in pursuance of the Constitution requiring that the votes for the electors should be cast on the same day throughout the Union. That debate will disclose the fact that the danger then became more and more realized of leaving this question unsettled as to who should determine whether the electoral votes of a State should be received or rejected when the two houses of Congress should differ upon that subject. There was no arbiter between them. This new-fangled idea of the present hour, that the presiding officer of the Senate should decide that question between the two disagreeing houses, had not yet been discovered in the fertility of political invention, or born perhaps of party necessity. The question has challenged all along through our country's history

I—18

the ablest minds of the country; but at last we have reached a point when under increased difficulties we are bound to settle it. It arose in 1817 in the case of the State of Indiana, the question being whether Indiana was a State in the Union at the time of the casting of her vote. The two houses disagreed upon that subject; but by a joint resolution, which clearly assumed the power of controlling the subject, as the vote of Indiana did not if cast either way control the election, the difficulty was tided over by an arrangement for that time and that occasion only. In 1820 the case of the State of Missouri arose and contained the same question. There again came the difficulty when the genius and patriotism of Henry Clay were brought into requisition and a joint resolution introduced by him and adopted by both houses was productive of a satisfactory solution for the time being. The remedy was merely palliative; the permanent character of the difficulty was confessed and the fact that it was only a postponement to men of a future generation of a question still unsettled.

It is not necessary, and would be fatiguing to the Senate and to myself, to give anything like a sketch of the debate which followed, of the able and eminent men on both sides who considered the question, arriving, however, at one admitted conclusion, that the remedy was needed and that it did lie in the law-making power of the government to furnish it.

Thus, Mr. President, the unbroken line of precedent, the history of the usage of this government from 1789 at the first election of President and Vice-President until 1873, when the last count of electoral votes was made for the same offices, exhibits this fact, that the control of the count of the electoral votes, the ascertainment and declaration of the persons who were elected President and Vice-President, has been under the co-ordinate power of the two houses of Congress, and under no other power at any time or in any instance. The claim is now gravely made for the first time, in 1877, that in the event of disagreement of the two houses the power to count the electoral votes and decide upon their validity under the Constitution and law is vested in a single individual, an appointee of one of the houses of Congress, the presiding officer of the Senate. In the event of a disagreement between the two houses, we are now told, he is to assume the power, in his sole discretion, to count the vote, to ascertain and declare what persons have been elected; and this, too, in the face of an act of Congress, passed in 1792, unrepealed, always

recognized, followed in every election from the time it was passed until the present day. Section 5 of the act of 1792 declares: —

That Congress shall be in session on the second Wednesday in February 1793, and on the second Wednesday in February succeeding every meeting of the electors; and the said certificates, or so many of them as shall have been received, shall then be opened, the votes counted, and the persons who shall fill the offices of President and Vice-President ascertained and declared agreeably to the Constitution.

Let it be noted that the words "President of the Senate" nowhere occur in the section.

But we are now told that though "Congress shall be in session," that though these two great bodies duly organized, each with its presiding officer, accompanied by all its other officers, shall meet to perform the duty of ascertaining and declaring the true result of the action of the electoral colleges and what persons are entitled to these high executive offices, in case they shall not agree in their decisions there shall be interposed the power of the presiding officer of one of the houses to control the judgment of either and become the arbiter between them. Why, Mr. President, how such a claim can be supposed to rest upon authority is more than I can imagine. It is against all history. It is against the meaning of laws. It is not consistent with the language of the Constitution. It is in the clearest violation of the whole scheme of this popular government of ours, that one man should assume a power in regard to which the convention hung for months undecided, and carefully and grudgingly bestowing that power even when they finally disposed of it. Why, sir, a short review of history will clearly show how it was that the presiding officer of the Senate became even the custodian of the certificates of the electors.

On the fourth of September, 1787, when approaching the close of their labors, the convention discovered that they must remove this obstacle, and they must come to an agreement in regard to the deposit of this grave power. When they were scrupulously considering that no undue grant of power should be made to either branch of Congress, and when no one dreamed of putting it in the power of a single hand, the proposition was made by Hon. Mr. Brearly, from a committee of eleven, of alterations in

the former schemes of the convention, which embraced this subject. It provided: —

5. Each State shall appoint, in such manner as its legislature may direct, a number of electors equal to the whole number of Senators and Members of the House of Representatives to which the State may be entitled in the legislature.

6. The electors shall meet in their respective States and vote by ballot for two persons, one of whom at least shall not be an inhabitant of the same State with themselves; and they shall make a list of all the persons voted for, and of the number of votes for each, which list they shall sign and certify, and transmit sealed to the seat of the general government, directed to the President of the Senate.

7. The President of the Senate shall, in that house, open all the certificates; and the votes shall be then and there counted. The person having the greatest number of votes shall be the President, if such number shall be a majority of the whole number of the electors appointed; and if there be more than one who have such majority and have an equal number of votes, then the Senate shall choose by ballot one of them for President; but if no person have a majority, then from the five highest on the list the Senate shall choose by ballot the President. And in every case after the choice of the President the person having the greatest number of votes shall be Vice-President. But if there should remain two or more who shall equal votes, the Senate shall choose from them the Vice-President. (See 'Madison Papers,' page 506, etc.)

Here we discover the reason why the President of the Senate was made the custodian of these certificates. It was because in that plan of the Constitution the Senate was to count the votes alone; the House was not to be present; and in case there was a tie or failure to find a majority the Senate was to elect the President and Vice-President. The presiding officer of the body that was to count the votes alone, of the body that alone was to elect the President in default of a majority — the presiding officer of that body was naturally the proper person to hold the certificates until the Senate should do its duty. It might as well be said that because certificates and papers of various kinds are directed to the President of this Senate to be laid before the Senate that he should have the control to enact those propositions into law, as to say that because the certificates of these votes were handed to him he should have the right to count them and ascertain and declare what persons had been chosen President and Vice-President of the United States.

But the scheme reported by Mr. Brearly met with no favor. In the first place, it was moved and seconded to insert the words "in the presence of the Senate and House of Representatives" after the word "counted." That was passed in the affirmative. Next it was moved to strike out the words "the Senate shall immediately choose by ballot" and insert the words "and House of Representatives shall immediately choose by ballot one of them for President, and the members of each State shall have one vote," and this was adopted by ten States in the affirmative to one State in the negative.

Then came another motion to agree to the following paragraph, giving to the Senate the right to choose the Vice-President in case of the failure to find a majority, which was agreed to by the convention; so that the amendment as agreed to read as follows:—

The President of the Senate, in the presence of the Senate and House of Representatives, shall open all the certificates, and the votes shall then be counted. The person having the greatest number of votes shall be President, if such number be a majority of the whole number of electors appointed; and if there be more than one who have such majority, and have an equal number of votes, then the House of Representatives shall immediately choose by ballot one of them for President, the representation from each State having one vote; but if no person have a majority, then from the five highest on the list the House of Representatives shall in like manner choose by ballot the President.

And then follows that if there should remain two candidates voted for as Vice-President having an equal vote the Senate shall choose from them the Vice-President. Mr. President, is it not clear that the Constitution directed that the certificates should be deposited with the presiding officer of that body which was alone to count the votes and elect both the President and Vice-President in case there was a failure to find a majority of the whole number of electors appointed? There is a maxim of the law, that where the reason ceases the law itself ceases. It is not only a maxim of common law, but equally of common sense. The history of the manner in which and the reason for which the certificates were forwarded to the President of the Senate completely explains why he was chosen as the depositary and just what connection he had with and power over those certificates. After the power had been vested in the House of

Representatives to ballot for the President, voting by States, after the presence of the House of Representatives was made equally necessary before the count could begin or proceed at all, the President of the Senate was still left as the officer designated to receive the votes. Why? Because the Senate is a continuing body, because the Senate always has a quorum. Divided into three classes, there never is a day or a time when a quorum of the Senate of the United States is not elected and cannot be summoned to perform its functions under the Constitution. Therefore you had the officer of a continuing body, and as the body over which he presided and by whom he is chosen was one of the two co-ordinate bodies to perform the great function of counting the votes and of ascertaining and declaring the result of the electoral vote, he was left in charge of the certificates.

You also find in the sixth section of the act of 1792 that Congress exercised its regulating power and declared "that in case there shall be no President of the Senate at the seat of government on the arrival of the persons intrusted with the lists of votes of the electors, then such persons shall deliver the lists of votes in their custody into the office of the Secretary of State to be safely kept and delivered over as soon as may be to the President of the Senate."

What does this signify? That it was a simple question of custody, of safe and convenient custody, and there is just as much reason to say that the Secretary of State being the recipient of those votes had a right to count them as to say that the other officer designated as the recipient of the votes, the President of the Senate, had a right to count them.

Now, here is another fact a denial of which cannot be safely challenged. Take the history of these debates upon the formation of the Federal Constitution from beginning to end, search them, and no line or word can be discovered that even suggests any power whatever in any one man over the subject, much less in the President of the Senate, in the control of the election of the President or the Vice-President. Why, sir, there is the invariable rule of construction in regard to which there can be no dispute, that the express grant of one thing excludes any other. Here you have the direction to the President of the Senate that he shall receive these certificates, or if absent that another custodian shall receive them, hold them during his absence, and pass them over to him as soon as may be, and that then he shall in

the presence of the two houses of Congress "open all the certificates." There is his full measure of duty; it· is clearly expressed; and then after that follows the totally distinct duty, not confided to him, that "the votes shall then be counted."

I doubt very much whether any instrument not written by an inspired hand was more clear, terse, frugal of all words except those necessary to express its precise meaning, than the Constitution of the United States. It would require the greatest ingenuity to discover where fewer words could be used to accomplish a plain end. How shall it be that in this closely considered charter, where every word, every punctuation was carefully weighed and canvassed, they should employ seven words out of place when two words in place would have fulfilled their end? If it had been intended to give this officer the power to count, how easy to read, "The President of the Senate shall, in the presence of the Senate and House of Representatives, open and count the votes." Why resort to this other, strained, awkward, ungrammatical, unreasonable transposition of additional words to grant one power distinctly and leave the other to be grafted upon it by an unjust implication? No, Mr. President, if it were a deed of bargain and sale, or any question of private grant, if it did not touch the rights of a great people, there would be but one construction given to this language, that the expression of one grant excluded the other. It was a single command to the President of the Senate that, as the custodian, he should honestly open those certificates and lay them before the two houses of Congress who were to act, and then his duty was done, and that was the belief of the men who sat in that convention, many of whom joined in framing the law of 1792 which directed Congress to be in session on a certain day and that the votes should be counted and the persons who should fill the office of President and Vice-President ascertained and declared agreeably to the Constitution.

The certificates are to be opened by their custodian, the President of the Senate, in the presence of the Senate and the House of Representatives. Let it be noted this is not in the presence of the Senators and Representatives, but it is in the presence of two organized bodies who cannot be present except as a Senate and as a House of Representatives, each with its own organization, its own presiding officer and all adjuncts, each organized for the performance of a great duty.

When the first drafts of the Constitution were made, instead of saying "in the presence of the Senate and the House of Representatives," they called it "the Legislature." What is a Legislature? A law-making body organized, not a mob, but an organized body to make laws; and so the law-making power of this Union, consisting of these two houses, is brought together. But it seems to me a most unreasonable proposition to withhold from the law-making power of this government the authority to regulate this subject and yet be willing to intrust it to a single hand. There is not a theory of this government that will support such a construction. It is contrary to the whole genius of the government; it is contrary to everything in the history of the formation of the government; it is contrary to the usage of the government since its foundation.

The President of the Senate is commanded by the Constitution to open the votes in the presence of the two houses. He does not summon them to witness his act, but they summon him by appointing a day and hour when he is to produce and open in their presence all the certificates he may have received, and only then and in their presence can he undertake to open them at all. If he was merely to summon them as witnesses of his act it would have been so stated. But when did the President of the Senate ever·undertake to call the two houses together to witness the opening and counting of the votes? No, sir; he is called at their will and pleasure to bring with him the certificates which he has received, and open them before them and under their inspection, and not his own. When the certificates have been opened, when the votes have been counted, can the President of the Senate declare the result? No, sir, he has never declared a result except as the mouthpiece and the organ of the two houses authorizing and directing him what to declare, and what he did declare was what they had ascertained and in which ascertainment he had never interfered by word or act.

Suppose there shall be an interruption in the count, as has occurred in our history, can the President of the Senate do it? Did he ever do it? Is such an instance to be found? Every interruption in the count comes from some Member of the House or of the Senate, and upon that the pleasure of the two houses is considered, the question put to them to withdraw if they desire, and the count is arrested until they shall order it to recommence. The proceeding in the count, the commencement of the count is not in any degree under his control. It is and ever was in the two houses, and in them alone. They are not powerless spectators; they do not sit "state statues only," but they are met as a legislature in organized bodies to insure a correct result of the popular election, to see to it that "the votes shall then be counted" agreeably to the Constitution.

In 1792 when some of the men who sat in the convention that framed the Constitution enacted into law the powers given in relation to the count of the electoral votes, they said, as I have read, that the certificates then received shall be opened and the votes counted, "and the persons to fill the offices of President and Vice-President ascertained agreeably to the Constitution," and that direction is contained in the same section of the law that commands Congress to be in session on that day. It is the law-making power of the nation, the legislature, that is to perform this solemn and important duty, and not a single person who is selected by one branch of Congress and who is removable at their will, according to a late decision of the Senate.

Yes, Mr. President, the power contended for by some Senators, that the President of the Senate can, in the contingency of a disagreement between the two houses, from the necessity of the case, open and count the vote, leads to this: that upon every disputed vote and upon every decision a new President of the Senate could be elected; that one man could be selected in the present case to count the vote of Florida; another, of South Carolina; another, of Oregon; another, of Louisiana; and the Senate could fill those four offices with four different men, each chosen for that purpose, and when that purpose was over to be displaced by the same breath that set them up for the time being.

Now, sir, if, as has been claimed, the power of counting the votes is deposited equally in both houses, does not this admission exclude the idea of any power to count the votes being deposited in the presiding officer of one of those houses, who is, as I say, eligible and removable by a bare majority of the Senate, and at will? If the presiding officer of the Senate can thus count the vote, the Senate can control him. Then the Senate can control the count and, the Senate appointing their President, become the sole controllers of the vote in case of disagreement. What then becomes of the equal measure of power in the two houses over this subject? If the power may be said to exist only in case of disagreement, and then *ex necessitate rei*, all that remains for the

Senate is to disagree, and they themselves have created the very contingency that gives them the power, through their President, to have the vote counted or not counted, as they may desire. Why, sir, such a statement destroys all idea of equality of power between the two houses in regard to this subject.

When the President of the Senate has opened the certificates and handed them over to the tellers of the two houses, in the presence of the two houses, his functions and powers have ended. He cannot repossess himself of those certificates or papers. He can no longer control their custody. They are then and thereafter in the possession and under the control of the two houses, who shall alone dispose of them.

Why, sir, what a spectacle would it be, some ambitious and unscrupulous man the presiding officer of the Senate, as was once Aaron Burr, assuming the power to order the tellers to count the vote of this State and reject the vote of that, and so boldly and shamelessly reverse the action of the people expressed at the polls, and step into the presidency by force of his own decision. Sir, this is a reduction of the thing to an absurdity never dreamed of until now, and impossible while this shall remain a free government of law.

Now, Mr. President, as to the measure before us a few words.

It will be observed that this bill is enacted for the present year, and no longer.

This is no answer to an alleged want of constitutional power to pass it, but it is an answer in great degree where the mere policy and temporary convenience of the act are to be considered.

In the first place, the bill gives to each house of Congress equal power over the question of counting, at every stage.

It preserves intact the prerogatives, under the Constitution, of each house.

It excludes any possibility of judicial determination by the presiding officer of the Senate upon the reception and exclusion of a vote.

The certificates of the electoral colleges will be placed in the possession and subject to the disposition of both houses of Congress in joint session.

The two houses are co-ordinate and separate and distinct. Neither can dominate the other. They are to ascertain whether the electors have been validly appointed, and whether they have validly performed their duties as electors. The two houses must,

under the act of 1792, "ascertain and declare" whether there has been a valid election, according to the Constitution and laws of the United States. The votes of the electors and the declaration of the result by the two houses give a valid title, and nothing else can, unless no majority has been disclosed by the count; in which case the duty of the House is to be performed by electing a President, and of the Senate by electing a Vice-President.

If it be the duty of the two houses "to ascertain" whether the action of the electors has been in accordance with the Constitution, they must inquire. They exercise supervisory power over every branch of public administration and over the electors. The methods they choose to employ in coming to a decision are such as the two houses, acting separately or together, may lawfully employ. Sir, the grant of power to the commission is in just that measure, no more and no less. The decision they render can be overruled by the concurrent votes of the two houses. Is it not competent for the two houses of Congress to agree that a concurrent majority of the two houses is necessary to reject the electoral vote of a State? If so, may they not adopt means which they believe will tend to produce a concurrence? Finally, sir, this bill secures the great object for which the two houses were brought together: the counting of the votes of the electoral college; not to elect a President by the two houses, but to determine who has been elected agreeably to the Constitution and the laws. It provides against the failure to count the electoral vote of a State in event of disagreement between the two houses, in case of single returns, and, in cases of contest and double returns, furnishes a tribunal whose composition secures a decision of the question in disagreement, and whose perfect justice and impartiality cannot be gainsaid or doubted.

The tribunal is carved out of the body of the Senate and out of the body of the House by their vote *viva voce*. No man can sit upon it from either branch without the choice, openly made, by a majority of the body of which he is a member, that he shall go there. The five judges who are chosen are from the court of last resort in this country, men eminent for learning, selected for their places because of the virtues and the capacities that fit them for this high station. . . . Mr. President, objection has been made to the employment of the commission at all, to the creation of this committee of five senators, five representatives, and five judges of the Supreme Court, and the reasons for the

objection have not been distinctly stated. The reasons for the appointment I will dwell upon briefly.

Sir, how has the count of the vote of every President and Vice-President, from the time of George Washington and John Adams, in 1789, to the present day, been made? Always and without exception by tellers appointed by the two houses. This is without exception, even in the much commented case of Mr. John Langdon, who, before the government was in operation, upon the recommendation of the constitutional convention, was appointed by the Senate its President, for the sole purpose of opening and counting these votes. He did it, as did every successor to him, under the motion and authority of the two houses of Congress, who appointed their own agents, called tellers to conduct the count, and whose count, being reported to him, was by him declared.

From 1793 to 1865 the count of votes was conducted under concurrent resolutions of the two houses, appointing their respective committees to join "in ascertaining and reporting a mode of examining the votes for President and Vice-President."

The respective committees reported resolutions fixing the time and place for the assembling of the two houses, and appointing tellers to conduct the examination on the part of each house respectively.

Mr. President, the office of teller, or the word "teller," is unknown to the Constitution, and yet each house has appointed tellers, and has acted upon their report, as I have said, from the very foundation of the government. The present commission is more elaborate, but its objects and its purposes are the same, the information and instruction of the two houses who have a precisely equal share in its creation and organization; they are the instrumentalities of the two houses for performing the high constitutional duty of ascertaining whom the electors in the several States have duly chosen President and Vice-President of the United States. Whatever is the jurisdiction and power of the two houses of Congress over the votes, and the judgment of either reception or rejection, is by this law wholly conferred upon this commission of fifteen. The bill presented does not define what that jurisdiction and power is, but it leaves it all as it is, adding nothing, subtracting nothing. Just what power the Senate by itself, or the House by itself, or the Senate and the House acting together, have over the subject of counting, admitting, or rejecting an electoral vote, in case of double returns from the same State, that power is by this act, no more and no less, vested in the commission of fifteen men; reserving, however, to the two houses the power of overruling the decision of the commission by their concurrent action.

The delegation to masters in chancery of the consideration and adjustments of questions of mingled law and fact is a matter of familiar and daily occurrence in the courts of the States and of the United States.

The circuit court of the United States is composed of the district judge and the circuit judge, and the report to them of a master is affirmed unless both judges concur in overruling it.

Under the present bill the decision of the commission will stand unless overruled by the concurrent votes of the two houses.

I do not propose to follow the example which has been set here in the Senate by some of the advocates as well as the opponents of this measure, and discuss what construction is to be given and what definition may be applied or ought to be applied in the exercise of this power by the commission under this law. Let me read the bill:—

All the certificates and papers purporting to be certificates of the electoral votes of each State shall be opened, in the alphabetical order of the States, as provided in Section 1 of this act; and when there shall be more than one such certificate or paper, as the certificates and papers from such State shall so be opened (excepting duplicates of the same return), they shall be read by the tellers, and thereupon the President of the Senate shall call for objections, if any. Every objection shall be made in writing, and shall state clearly and concisely, and without argument, the ground thereof, and shall be signed by at least one Senator and one Member of the House of Representatives before the same shall be received. When all such objections so made to any certificate, vote, or paper from a State shall have been received and read, all such certificates, votes, and papers so objected to, and all papers accompanying the same, together with such objections, shall be forthwith submitted to said commission, which shall proceed to consider the same, with the same powers, if any, now possessed for that purpose by the two houses acting separately or together, and, by a majority of votes, decide whether any and what votes from such States are the votes provided for by the Constitution of the United States, and how many and what persons were duly appointed electors in such State, and may therein take into view such petitions, depositions, and other papers, if any,

as shall, by the Constitution and now existing law, be competent and pertinent in such consideration; which decision shall be made in writing.

It will be observed that all the questions to be decided by this commission are to be contained in the written objections. Until those objections are read and filed, their contents must be unknown, and the issues raised by them undescribed. But whatever they are, they are submitted to the decision of the commission. The duty of interpreting this law and of giving a construction to the Constitution and existing laws is vested in the commission; and I hold that we have no right or power to control in advance, by our construction, their sworn judgment as to the matters which they are to decide. We would defeat the very object of the bill should we invade the essential power of judgment of this commission and establish a construction in advance and bind them to it. It would, in effect, be giving to them a mere mock power to decide by leaving them nothing to decide.

.   .   .   .

Mr. President, there are certainly very good reasons why the concurrent action of both houses should be necessary to reject a vote. It is that feature of this bill which has my heartiest concurrence; for I will frankly say that the difficulties which have oppressed me most in considering this question a year or more ago, before any method had been devised, arose from my apprehensions of the continued absorption of undue power over the affairs of the States; and I here declare that the power and the sole power of appointing the electors is in the State, and nowhere else. The power of ascertaining whether the State has executed that power justly and according to the Constitution and laws is the duty which is cast upon the two houses of Congress. Now, if, under the guise or pretext of judging of the regularity of the action of a State or its electors, the Congress or either house may interpose the will of its members in opposition to the will of the State, the act will be one of usurpation and wrong, although I do not see where is the tribunal to arrest and punish it except the great tribunal of an honest public opinion. But, sir, that tribunal, though great, though in the end certain, is yet ofttimes slow to be awakened to action; and therefore I rejoice when the two houses agree that neither of them shall be able to reject the vote of a State which is without contest arising within that

State itself, but that the action of both shall be necessary to concur in the rejection.

If either house may reject, or by dissenting cause a rejection, then it is in the power of either house to overthrow the electoral colleges or the popular vote, and throw the election upon the House of Representatives. This, it is clear to me, cannot be lawfully done unless no candidate has received a majority of the votes of all the electors appointed. The sworn duty is to ascertain what persons have been chosen by the electors, and not to elect by Congress.

It may be said that the Senate would not be apt to throw the election into the House. Not so, Mr. President; look at the relative majorities of the two houses of Congress as they will be after the fourth of March next. It is true there will be a numerical majority of the members of the Democratic party in the House of Representatives, but the States represented will have a majority as States of the Republican party. If the choice were to be made after March 4th, then a Republican Senate, by rejecting or refusing to count votes, could of its own motion throw the election into the House; which, voting by States, would be in political accord with the Senate. The House of Representatives, like the present House in its political complexion, composed of a numerical majority, and having also a majority of the States of the same party, would have the power then to draw the election into its own hands. Mr. President, either of these powers would be utterly dangerous and in defeat of the object and intent of the constitutional provisions on this subject.

Sir, this was my chief objection to the twenty-second joint rule. Under that rule either house of Congress, without debate, without law, without reason, without justice, could, by the sheer exercise of its will or its caprice, disfranchise any State in the electoral college. Under that rule we lived and held three presidential elections.

In January 1873, under a resolution introduced by the honorable Senator from Ohio [Mr. Sherman] and adopted by the Senate, the Committee on Privileges and Elections, presided over by the honorable Senator from Indiana [Mr Morton], proceeded to investigate the elections held in the States of Louisiana and Arkansas, and inquired whether these elections had been held in accordance with the Constitution and laws of the United States and the laws of said States, and sent for persons and papers and

made thorough investigation, which resulted in excluding the electoral votes of Louisiana from the count. (See Report No. 417, third session Forty-Second Congress.)

The popular vote was then cast, and it was cast at the mercy of a majority in either branch of Congress, who claimed the right to annul it by casting out States until they should throw the election into a Republican House of Representatives. I saw that dangerous power then, and, because I saw it then, am I so blind, am I so without principle in my action, that I should ask for myself a dangerous power that I refused to those who differ from me in opinion? God forbid.

This concurrence of the two houses to reject the electoral votes of a State was the great feature that John Marshall sought for in 1800. The Senate then proposed that either house should have power to reject a vote. The House of Representatives, under the lead of John Marshall, declared that they should concur to reject the vote, and upon that difference of opinion the measure fell and was never revived. In 1824 the bill prepared by Mr. Van Buren contained the same wholesome principle and provided that the two houses must concur in the rejection of a vote. Mr. Van Buren reported this bill in 1824. It was amended and passed, and, as far as I can find from the record, without a division of the Senate. It was referred in the House of Representatives to the Committee on the Judiciary, and it was reported back by Mr. Daniel Webster, without amendment, to the Committee of the Whole House, showing their approval of the bill; and that principle is thoroughly incorporated in the present measure and gives to me one of the strong reasons for my approval.

Mr. President, this bill is not the product of any one man's mind, but it is the result of careful study and frequent amendment. Mutual concessions, modifications of individual preferences, were constantly and necessarily made in the course of framing such a measure as it now stands. My individual opinions might lead me to object to the employment of the judicial branch at all, of ingrafting even to any extent political power upon the judicial branch or its members, or confiding to them any question even quasi-political in its character To this I have expressed and still have disinclination, but my sense of the general value of this measure and the necessity for the adoption of a plan outweighed my disposition to insist upon my own preferences as to this feature. At first I was disposed to question the constitutional power to call in the five justices of the Supreme Court, but the duty of ascertaining what are the votes, the true votes, under the Constitution, having been imposed upon the commission, the methods were necessarily discretionary with the two houses. Any and every aid that intelligence and skill combined can furnish may be justly used when it is appropriate to the end in view.

Why, sir, the members of the Supreme Court have in the history of this country been employed in public service entirely distinct from judicial function. Here lately the treaty of Washington was negotiated by a member of the Supreme Court of the United States; the venerable and learned Mr. Justice Nelson, of New York, was nominated by the President and confirmed by the Senate as one of the Joint High Commission. Chief-Justice Jay was sent in 1794, while he was chief-justice of the United States, as minister plenipotentiary to England, and negotiated a treaty of permanent value and importance to both countries. He was holding court in the city of Philadelphia at the time that he was nominated and confirmed, as is found by reference to his biography, and —

Without vacating his seat upon the bench he went to England, negotiated the treaty which has since borne his name, and returned to this country in the spring of the following year.

His successor was Chief-Justice Rutledge, and the next to him was Chief-Justice Oliver Ellsworth. He, while holding the high place of chief-justice, was nominated and confirmed as minister plenipotentiary to Spain. By a law of Congress the chief-justice of the United States is *ex officio* the president of the Board of Regents of the Smithsonian Institution.

Mr. Morton — I should like to ask the Senator, if it does not interrupt him, whether he regards the five judges acting on this commission as acting in their character as judges of the Supreme Court, if that is their official character, and that this bill simply enlarges their jurisdiction in that respect?

Mr. Bayard — Certainly not, Mr. President. They are not acting as judges of the Supreme Court, and their powers and their jurisdiction as judges of the Supreme Court are not in any degree involved; they are simply performing functions under the government not inconsistent, by the Constitution, or the law, or the policy of the law, with the stations which they now hold. So I

hold that the employment of one or more of the Supreme Court judges in the matter under discussion was appropriate legislation. We have early and high authority in the majorities in both House and Senate in the bill of 1800, in both of which houses a bill was passed creating a commission similar to that proposed by this bill and calling in the chief-justice of the United States as the chairman of the grand committee, as they called it then, a commission as we term it now.

As has been said before, many of the Senators and members of the Congress of 1800 had taken part in the convention that framed the Constitution, and all were its contemporaries, and one of the chief actors in the proceedings on the part of the House of Representatives was John Marshall, of Virginia, who one year afterward became the chief-justice of the United States, whose judicial interpretations have since that time clad the skeleton of the Constitution with muscles of robust power. Is it not safe to abide by such examples? And I could name many more, and some to whom my respect is due for other and personal reasons.

In the debate of 1817, in the case of the disputed vote of Indiana; in 1820, in the case of Missouri; and again in 1857, in the case of Wisconsin, I find an array of constitutional lawyers who took part in those debates, among them the most distinguished members of both political parties, concurring in the opinion that by appropriate legislation all causes of dispute on this all-important matter of counting the electoral vote could be and ought to be adjusted satisfactorily. Why, sir, even the *dictum* of Chancellor Kent, that has been read here with so much apparent confidence by the honorable Senator from Indiana, is itself expressed to be his opinion of the law "in the absence of legislation on the subject."

Mr. President, there were other objections to this bill; one by the honorable Senator from Indiana. He denounced it as "a compromise." I have gone over its features and I have failed to discover, nor has the fact yet been stated in my hearing, wherein anything is compromised. What power of the Senate is relinquished? What power of the House is relinquished? What power that both should possess is withheld? I do not know where the compromise can be, what principle is surrendered. This bill intends to compromise nothing in the way of principle, to compromise no right, but to provide an honest adjudication for the rights of all. Where is it unjust? Whose rights are

endangered by it? Who can foretell the judgment of this commission upon any question of law or fact? Sir, there is no compromise in any sense of the word, but there is a blending of feeling, a blending of opinions in favor of right and justice.

But, sir, if it were a compromise, what is there in compromise that is discreditable either to men or to nations? This very charter of government under which we live was created in a spirit of compromise and mutual concession. Without that spirit it never would have been made, and without a continuance of that spirit it will not be prolonged. Sir, when the Committee on Style and Revision of the Federal convention of 1787 had prepared a digest of their plan, they reported a letter to accompany the plan to Congress, from which I take these words as being most applicable to the bill under consideration: —

And thus the Constitution which we now present is the result of a spirit of amity and of that mutual deference and concession which the peculiarity of our political situation rendered indispensable.

The language of that letter may well be applied to the present measure; and had the words been recalled to my memory before the report was framed I cannot doubt that they would have been adopted as part of it to be sent here to the Senate as descriptive of the spirit and of the object with which the committee had acted.

But, sir, the honorable Senator also stated, as a matter deterring us from our proper action on this bill, that the shadow of intimidation had entered the halls of Congress, and that members of this committee had joined in this report and presented this bill under actual fear of personal violence. Such a statement seems to me almost incredible. I may not read other men's hearts and know what they have felt, nor can I measure the apprehension of personal danger felt by the honorable Senator. It seems to me incredible. Fear, if I had it, had been the fear of doing wrong in this great juncture of public affairs, not the fear of the consequences of doing right. Had there been this intimidation tenfold repeated to which the Senator has alluded, and of which I have no knowledge, I should have scorned myself had I hesitated one moment in my onward march of duty on this subject.

"Hate's yell, or envy's hiss, or folly's bray" —

what are they to a man who, in the face of events such as now confront us, is doing that which his conscience dictates to him to do? It has been more than one hundred years since a great judgment was delivered in Westminster Hall in England by one of the great judges of our English-speaking people. Lord Mansfield, when delivering judgment in the case of the King against John Wilkes, was assailed by threats of popular violence of every description, and he has placed upon record how such threats should be met by any public man who sees before him the clear star of duty and trims his bark only that he may follow it through darkness and through light. I will ask my friend from Missouri if he will do me the favor to read the extract to which I have alluded.

Mr. Cockrell read as follows: —

But here, let me pause.

It is fit to take some notice of the various terrors hung out; the numerous crowds which have attended and now attend in and about the hall, out of all reach of hearing what passes in court, and the tumults which, in other places, have shamefully insulted all order and government. Audacious addresses in print dictate to us from those they call the people, the judgment to be given now and afterward upon the conviction. Reasons of policy are urged from danger to the kingdom by commotion and general confusion.

Give me leave to take the opportunity of this great and respectable audience to let the whole world know all such attempts are vain.

I pass over many anonymous letters I have received. Those in print are public; and some of them have been brought judicially before the court. Whoever the writers are, they take the wrong way. I will do my duty, unawed. What am I to fear? That *mendax infamia* from the press, which daily coins false facts and false motives? The lies of calumny carry no terror to me. I trust that my temper of mind, and the color and conduct of my life, have given me a suit of armor against these arrows. If, during this king's reign, I have ever supported his government, and assisted his measures, I have done it without any other reward than the consciousness of doing what I thought right. If I have ever opposed, I have done it upon the points themselves, without mixing in party or faction, and without any collateral views. I honor the king, and respect the people; but many things acquired by force of either, are, in my account, objects not worth ambition. I wish popularity; but it is that popularity which follows, not that which is run after. It is that popularity which, sooner or later, never fails to do justice to the pursuit of noble ends by noble means. I will not do that which my conscience tells me is wrong upon this occasion to gain the huzzas of thousands, or the daily praise of all the papers which come from the press; I will not avoid doing what I think is right, though it should draw on me the whole artillery of libel, all that falsehood and malice can invent or the credulity of a deluded populace can swallow. I can say, with a great magistrate, upon an occasion and under circumstances not unlike, "*Ego hoc animo semper fui, ut invidiam virtute partam gloriam, non invidiam putarem.*"

The threats go further than abuse; personal violence is denounced. I do not believe it; it is not the genius of the worst men of this country in the worst of times. But I have set my mind at rest. The last end that can happen to any man never comes too soon, if he falls in support of the law and liberty of his country (for liberty is synonymous to law and government). Such a shock, too, might be productive of public good; it might awake the better part of the kingdom out of that lethargy which seems to have benumbed them; and bring the mad part back to their senses, as men intoxicated are sometimes stunned into sobriety.—Burrows's Reports No. 4, pp. 2561-3.

Mr. Bayard—Mr. President, in the course of my duty here as a representative of the rights of others, as a chosen and sworn public servant, I feel that I have no right to give my individual wishes, prejudices, interests, undue influence over my public action. To do so would be to commit a breach of trust in the powers confided to me. It is true I was chosen a Senator by a majority only, but not for a majority only. I was chosen by a party, but not for a party. I represent all the good people of the State which has sent me here. In my office as a Senator I recognize no claim upon my action in the name and for the sake of party. The oath I have taken is to support the Constitution of my country's government, not the fiat of any political organization, even could its will be ascertained. In sessions preceding the present I have adverted to the difficulty attending the settlement of this great question, and have urgently besought action in advance at a time when the measure adopted could not serve to predicate its results to either party. My failure then gave me great uneasiness, and filled me with anxiety; and yet I can now comprehend the wisdom concealed in my disappointment, for in the very emergency of this hour, in the shadow of the danger that has drawn so nigh to us, has been begotten in the hearts of

American Senators and Representatives and the American people a spirit worthy of the occasion — born to meet these difficulties, to cope with them, and, God willing, to conquer them.

Animated by this spirit the partisan is enlarged into the patriot. Before it the lines of party sink into hazy obscurity; and the horizon which bounds our view reaches on every side to the uttermost verge of the great Republic. It is a spirit that exalts humanity, and imbued with it the souls of men soar into the pure air of unselfish devotion to the public welfare. It lighted with a smile the cheek of Curtius as he rode into the gulf; it guided the hand of Aristides as he sadly wrote upon the shell the sentence of his own banishment; it dwelt in the frozen earthworks of Valley Forge; and from time to time it has been an inmate of these halls of legislation. I believe it is here to-day, and that the present measure was born under its influence.

LORD BEACONSFIELD

(BENJAMIN DISRAELI)

(1804-1881)

WHEN, at the age of thirty-three, Benjamin Disraeli entered the House of Commons, he was flushed with his first literary successes and inclined perhaps to take parliamentary popularity by storm. It was the first year of Victoria's reign (1837) and the fashions of the times allowed great latitude for the display of idiosyncracies in dress. It seems that Disraeli pushed this advantage to the point of license. We hear much of the amount of jewelry he wore and of the gaudiness of his waistcoats. This may or may not have had a deciding influence in determining the character of his reception by the house, but at any rate it was a tempestuous one. He was repeatedly interrupted, and when he attempted to proceed the uproar of cries and laughter finally overpowered him and he abandoned for the time being the attempt to speak — not, however, until he had served on the house due notice of his great future, expressed in the memorable words — thundered, we are told, at the top of his voice, and audible still in English history — "You *shall* hear me!"

Not ten years later, the young man with the gaudy waistcoats had become the leading Conservative orator of the campaign against the Liberals on their Corn Law policy and so great was the impression produced by his speeches that in 1852, when the Derby ministry was formed, he was made Chancellor of the Exchequer.

The secret of his success is the thorough-going way in which he identified himself with the English aristocracy. Where others had apologized for aristocracy as a method of government, he justified. Instead of excusing and avoiding, he assumed that a government of privilege rather than that based on rights or the assumption of their existence is the best possible government, the only natural one, the only one capable of perpetuating itself without constant and violent changes. Kept on the defensive by the forward movement of the people, as well as by the tendency towards Liberalism or Radicalism shown by the men of highest education among the aristocratic classes themselves, the English Conservatives were delighted to find a man

of great ability and striking eloquence, who seemed to have a religious conviction that "Toryism" was the only means of saving society and ensuring progress. It is characteristic of his mind and his methods, that he does not shrink from calling himself a Tory. He is as proud of bearing that reproach as Camille Desmoulins was of being called a Sansculotte. When a man is thus "for thorough," he becomes representative of all who have his aspirations or share his tendencies without his aggressiveness. No doubt Disraeli's speeches are the best embodiment of Tory principle, the most attractive presentation of aristocratic purposes in government made in the nineteenth century. No member of the English peerage to the "manner born" has approached him in this respect. It is not a question of whether others have equaled or exceeded him in ability or statesmanship. On that point there may be room for difference of opinion, but to read any one of his great speeches is to see at once that he has the infinite advantage of the rest in being the strenuous and faith-inspired champion of aristocracy and government by privilege — not the mere defender and apologist for it.

In the extent of his information, the energy and versatility of his intellect, and the boldness of his methods, he had no equal among the Conservative leaders of the Victorian reign. His audacity was well illustrated when, after the great struggle over the reform measures of 1866 which he opposed, the Conservatives succeeded to power, and he, as their representative, advanced a measure "more sweeping in its nature as a reform bill than that he had successfully opposed" when it was advocated by Gladstone. In foreign affairs, he showed the same boldness, working to check the Liberal advance at home by directing public attention away from domestic grievances to brilliant achievements abroad. This policy which his opponents resented the more bitterly because they saw it to be the only one by which they could be held in check, won him the title of "Jingo," and made him the leading representative of British imperialism abroad as he was of English aristocracy at home.

THE ASSASSINATION OF LINCOLN
(From a Speech in Parliament, 1865)

THERE are rare instances when the sympathy of a nation approaches those tenderer feelings which are generally supposed to be peculiar to the individual and to be the happy privilege of private life; and this is one. Under any circumstances we should have bewailed the catastrophe at Washington; under any circumstances we should have shuddered at the means by which it was accomplished. But in the character of the victim, and even in the accessories of his last moments, there is something so homely and innocent that it takes the question, as it were, out of all the pomp of history and the ceremonial of diplomacy,—it touches the heart of nations and appeals to the domestic sentiment of mankind. Whatever the various and varying opinions in this house, and in the country generally, on the policy of the late President of the United States, all must agree that in one of the severest trials which ever tested the moral qualities of man he fulfilled his duty with simplicity and strength. Nor is it possible for the people of England at such a moment to forget that he sprang from the same fatherland and spoke the same mother tongue. When such crimes are perpetrated the public mind is apt to fall into gloom and perplexity, for it is ignorant alike of the causes and the consequences of such deeds. But it is one of our duties to reassure them under unreasoning panic and despondency. Assassination has never changed the history of the world. I will not refer to the remote past, though an accident has made the most memorable instance of antiquity at this moment fresh in the minds and memory of all around me. But even the costly sacrifice of a Cæsar did not propitiate the inexorable destiny of his country. If we look to modern times, to times at least with the feelings of which we are familiar, and the people of which were animated and influenced by the same interests as ourselves, the violent deaths of two heroic men, Henry IV. of France and the Prince of Orange, are conspicuous illustrations of this truth. In expressing our unaffected and profound sympathy with the citizens of the United States on this untimely end of their elected chief, let us not, therefore, sanction any feeling of depression, but rather let us express a fervent hope that from out of the awful trials of the last four

years, of which the least is not this violent demise, the various populations of North America may issue elevated and chastened, rich with the accumulated wisdom and strong in the disciplined energy which a young nation can only acquire in a protracted and perilous struggle. Then they will be enabled not merely to renew their career of power and prosperity, but they will renew it to contribute to the general happiness of mankind. It is with these feelings that I second the address to the crown.

AGAINST DEMOCRACY FOR ENGLAND
(Delivered in 1865)

SIR, I could have wished, and once I almost believed, that it was not necessary for me to take part in this debate. I look on this discussion as the natural epilogue of the Parliament of 1859; we remember the prologue. I consider this to be a controversy between the educated section of the Liberal party and that section of the Liberal party, according to their companions and colleagues, not entitled to an epithet so euphuistic and complimentary. But after the speech of the minister, I hardly think it would become me, representing the opinions of the gentlemen with whom I am acting on this side of the house, entirely to be silent. We have a measure before us to-night which is to increase the franchise in boroughs. Without reference to any other circumstances I object to that measure. I object to it because an increase of the franchise in boroughs is a proposal to redistribute political power in the country. I do not think political power in the country ought to be treated partially; from the very nature of things it is impossible, if there is to be a redistribution of political power, that you can only regard the suffrage as it affects one section of the constituent body. Whatever the proposition of the honorable gentleman, whether abstractedly it may be expedient or not, this is quite clear, that it must be considered not only in relation to the particular persons with whom it will deal, but to other persons with whom it does not deal, though it would affect them. And therefore it has always been quite clear that if you deal with the subject popularly called Parliamentary Reform, you must deal with it comprehensively. The arrangements you may make with reference to one part of

the community may not be objectionable in themselves, but may be extremely objectionable if you consider them with reference to other parts. Consequently it has been held—and the more we consider the subject the more true and just appears to be the conclusion—that if you deal with the matter you must deal with it comprehensively. You must not only consider borough constituencies, you must consider county constituencies: and when persons rise up and urge their claims to be introduced into the constituent body, even if you think there is a plausible claim substantiated on their part, you are bound in policy and justice to consider also the claims of other bodies not in possession of the franchise, but whose right to consideration may be equally great. And so clear is it when you come to the distribution of power that you must consider the subject in all its bearings, that even honorable gentlemen who have taken part in this debate have not been able to avoid the question of what they call the redistribution of seats—a very important part of the distribution of power. It is easy for the honorable member for Liskeard, for example, to rise and say, in supporting this measure for the increase of the borough franchise, that it is impossible any longer to conceal the anomalies of our system in regard to the distribution of seats. "Is it not monstrous," he asks, "that Calne, with 173 voters, should return a member, while Glasgow returns only two, with a constituency of 20,000?" Well, it may be equally monstrous that Liskeard should return one member, and that Birkenhead should only make a similar return. The distribution of seats, as any one must know who has ever considered the subject deeply and with a sense of responsibility towards the country, is one of the most profound and difficult questions that can be brought before the house. It is all very well to treat it in an easy, offhand manner; but how are you to reconcile the case of North Cheshire, of North Durham, of West Kent, and many other counties, where you find four or six great towns, with a population, perhaps, of 100,000, returning six members to this house, while the rest of the population of the county, though equal in amount, returns only two members? How are you to meet the case of the representation of South Lancashire in reference to its boroughs? Why, those are more anomalous than the case of Calne.

Then there is the question of Scotland. With a population hardly equal to that of the metropolis, and with wealth greatly

inferior—probably not more than two-thirds of the amount—Scotland yet possesses forty-eight members, while the metropolis has only twenty. Do you Reformers mean to say that you are prepared to disfranchise Scotland; or that you are going to develop the representation of the metropolis in proportion to its population and property; and so allow a country like England, so devoted to local government and so influenced by local feeling, to be governed by London? And, therefore, when those speeches are made which gain a cheer for the moment, and are supposed to be so unanswerable as arguments in favor of parliamentary change, I would recommend the house to recollect that this, as a question, is one of the most difficult and one of the deepest that can possibly engage the attention of the country. The fact is this—in the representation of this country you do not depend on population or on property merely, or on both conjoined; you have to see that there is something besides population and property—you have to take care that the country itself is represented. That is one reason why I am opposed to the second reading of the bill. There is another objection which I have to this bill brought forward by the honorable member for Leeds, and that is, that it is brought forward by the member for Leeds. I do not consider this a subject which ought to be intrusted to the care and guidance of any independent member of this house. If there be one subject more than another that deserves the consideration and demands the responsibility of the government, it certainly is the reconstruction of our parliamentary system; and it is the government or the political party candidates for power, who recommend a policy, and who will not shrink from the responsibility of carrying that policy into effect if the opportunity be afforded to them, who alone are qualified to deal with a question of this importance. But, sir, I shall be told, as we have been told in a previous portion of the adjourned debate, that the two great parties of the State cannot be trusted to deal with this question, because they have both trifled with it. That is a charge which has been made repeatedly during this discussion and on previous occasions, and certainly a graver one could not be made in this house. I am not prepared to admit that even our opponents have trifled with this question. We have had a very animated account by the right honorable gentleman who has just addressed us as to what may be called the Story of the Reform Measures. It was animated, but it was not accurate. Mine will be accurate, though I fear it will not be animated. I am not prepared to believe that English statesmen, though they be opposed to me in politics, and may sit on opposite benches, could ever have intended to trifle with this question. I think that possibly they may have made great mistakes in the course which they took; they may have miscalculated, they may have been misled; but I do not believe that any men in this country, occupying the posts, the eminent posts, of those who have recommended any reconstruction of our parliamentary system in modern days, could have advised a course which they disapproved. They may have thought it perilous, they may have thought it difficult, but though they may have been misled I am convinced they must have felt that it was necessary. Let me say a word in favor of one with whom I have had no political connection, and to whom I have been placed in constant opposition in this house when he was an honored member of it — I mean Lord Russell. I cannot at all agree with the lively narrative of the right honorable gentleman, according to which Parliamentary Reform was but the creature of Lord John Russell, whose cabinet, controlled by him with the vigor of a Richelieu, at all times disapproved his course; still less can I acknowledge that merely to amuse himself, or in a moment of difficulty to excite some popular sympathy, Lord John Russell was a statesman always with Reform in his pocket, ready to produce it and make a display. How different from that astute and sagacious statesman now at the head of her Majesty's government, whom I almost hoped to have seen in his place this evening. I am sure it would have given the house great pleasure to have seen him here, and the house itself would have assumed a more good-humored appearance. I certainly did hope that the noble lord would have been enabled to be in his place and prepared to support his policy. According to the animated but not quite accurate account of the right honorable gentleman who has just sat down, all that Lord Derby did was to sanction the humor and caprice of Lord John Russell. It is true that Lord John Russell when prime minister recommended that her Majesty in the speech from the throne should call the attention of Parliament to the expediency of noticing the condition of our representative system; but Lord John Russell unfortunately shortly afterwards retired from his eminent position.

He was succeeded by one of the most considerable statesmen of our days, a statesman not connected with the political school

of Lord John Russell, who was called to power not only with the assistance of Lord John Russell and the leading members of the Whig party, but supported by the whole class of eminent statesmen who had been educated in the same school and under the same distinguished master. This eminent statesman, however, is entirely forgotten. The right honorable gentleman overlooks the fact that Lord Aberdeen, when prime minister, and when all the principal places in his cabinet were filled with the disciples of Sir Robert Peel, did think it his duty to recommend the same counsel to her Majesty. But this is an important, and not the only important, item in the history of the Reform Bill which has been ignored by the right honorable gentleman. The time, however, came when Lord Aberdeen gave place to another statesman, who has been complimented on his sagacity in evading the subject, as if such a course would be a subject for congratulation. Let me vindicate the policy of Lord Palmerston in his absence. He did not evade the question. Lord Palmerston followed the example of Lord John Russell. He followed the example also of Lord Aberdeen, and recommended her Majesty to notice the subject in the speech from the throne. What becomes, then, of the lively narrative of the right honorable gentleman, and what becomes of the inference and conclusions which he drew from it? Not only is his account inaccurate, but it is injurious, as I take it, to the course of sound policy and the honor of public men. Well, now you have three prime ministers bringing forward the question of Parliamentary Reform; you have Lord John Russell, Lord Aberdeen, and you have even that statesman who, according to the account of the right honorable gentleman, was so eminent for his sagacity in evading the subject altogether. Now, let me ask the house to consider the position of Lord Derby when he was called to power, a position which you cannot rightly understand if you accept as correct the fallacious statements of the right honorable gentleman. I will give the house an account of this subject, the accuracy of which I believe neither side will impugn. It may not possibly be without interest, and will not, I am sure, be without significance. Lord Derby was sent for by her Majesty — an unwilling candidate for office, for let me remind the house that at that moment there was an adverse majority of 140 in the House of Commons, and I therefore do not think that Lord Derby was open to any imputation in hesitating to accept political responsibility under such circumstances. Lord Derby

laid these considerations before her Majesty. I speak, of course, with reserve. I say nothing now which I have not said before on the discussion of political subjects in this house. But when a government comes in on Reform and remains in power six years without passing any measure of the kind, it is possible that these circumstances, too, may be lost sight of. Lord Derby advised her Majesty not to form a government under his influence, because there existed so large a majority against him in the House of Commons, and because this question of Reform was placed in such a position that it was impossible to deal with it as he should wish. But it should be remembered that Lord Derby was a member of the famous Cabinet which carried the Reform Bill in 1832. Lord Derby, as Lord Stanley, was in the House of Commons one of the most efficient promoters of the measure. Lord Derby believed that the bill had tended to effect the purpose for which it was designed, and although no man superior to prejudices could fail to see that some who were entitled to the exercise of the franchise were still debarred from the privilege, yet he could not also fail to perceive the danger which would arise from our tampering with the franchise. On these grounds Lord Derby declined the honor which her Majesty desired to confer upon him, but the appeal was repeated. Under these circumstances it would have been impossible for any English statesman longer to hesitate; but I am bound to say that there was no other contract or understanding further than that which prevails among men, however different their politics, who love their country and wish to maintain its greatness. I am bound to add that there was an understanding at the time existing among men of weight on both sides of the house that the position in which the Reform question was placed was one embarrassing to the crown and not creditable to the house, and that any minister trying his best to deal with it under these circumstances would receive the candid consideration of the house. It was thought, moreover, that a time might possibly arrive when both parties would unite in endeavoring to bring about a solution which would tend to the advantage and benefit of the country. And yet, says the right honorable gentleman, it was only in 1860 that the portentous truth flashed across the mind of the country — only in 1860, after so many ministers had been dealing with the question for so many years. All I can say is that this was the question, and the only question, which engaged the attention of Lord

Derby's cabinet. The question was whether they could secure the franchise for a certain portion of the working classes, who, by their industry, their intelligence, and their integrity, showed that they were worthy of such a possession, without at the same time overwhelming the rest of the constituency by the numbers of those whom they admitted. That, sir, was the only question which occupied the attention of the government of Lord Derby, and yet the right honorable gentleman says that it was in 1860 that the attention of the public was first called to the subject, when, in fact, the question of Parliamentary Reform had been before them for ten years, and on a greater, scale than that embraced by the measure under consideration this evening.

I need not remind the house of the reception which Lord Derby's Bill encountered. It is neither my disposition, nor, I am sure, that of any of my colleagues, to complain of the votes of this house on that occasion. Political life must be taken as you find it, and as far as I am concerned not a word shall escape me on the subject. But from the speeches made the first night, and from the speech made by the right honorable gentleman this evening, I believe I am right in vindicating the conduct pursued by the party with which I act. I believe that the measure which we brought forward was the only one which has tended to meet the difficulties which beset this question. Totally irrespective of other modes of dealing with the question, there were two franchises especially proposed on this occasion, which, in my mind, would have done much towards solving the difficulty. The first was the franchise founded upon personal property, and the second the franchise founded upon partial occupation. Those two franchises, irrespective of other modes by which we attempted to meet the want and the difficulty — these two franchises, had they been brought into committee of this house, would, in my opinion, have been so shaped and adapted that they would have effected those objects which the majority of the house desire. We endeavored in that bill to make proposals which were in the genius of the English constitution. We did not consider the constitution a mere phrase. We knew that the constitution of this country is a monarchy tempered by co-ordinate estates of the realm. We knew that the House of Commons is an estate of the realm; we knew that the estates of the realm form a political body, invested with political power for the government of the country and for the public good; yet we thought that it was a body founded upon privilege and not upon right. It is, therefore, in the noblest and properest sense of the word, an aristocratic body, and from that characteristic the Reform Bill of 1832 did not derogate; and if at this moment we could contrive, as we did in 1859, to add considerably to the number of the constituent body, we should not change that characteristic, but it would still remain founded upon an aristocratic principle. Well, now the Secretary of State [Sir G. Grey] has addressed us to-night in a very remarkable speech. He also takes up the history of Reform, and before I touch upon some of the features of that speech it is my duty to refer to the statements which he made with regard to the policy which the government of Lord Derby was prepared to assume after the general election. By a total misrepresentation of the character of the amendment proposed by Lord John Russell, which threw the government of 1858 into a minority, and by quoting a passage from a very long speech of mine in 1859, the right honorable gentleman most dexterously conveyed these two propositions to the house — first, that Lord John Russell had proposed an amendment to our Reform Bill, by which the house declared that no bill could be satisfactory by which the working classes were not admitted to the franchise — one of our main objects being that the working classes should in a great measure be admitted to the franchise; and, secondly, that after the election I was prepared, as the organ of the government, to give up all the schemes for those franchises founded upon personal property, partial occupation, and other grounds, and to substitute a bill lowering the borough qualification. That conveyed to the house a totally inaccurate idea of the amendment of Lord John Russell. There was not a single word in that amendment about the working classes. There was not a single phrase upon which that issue was raised, nor could it have been raised, because our bill, whether it could have effected the object or not, was a bill which proposed greatly to enfranchise the working classes. And as regards the statement I made, it simply was this. The election was over — we were still menaced, but we, still acting according to our sense of duty, recommended in the royal speech that the question of a reform of Parliament should be dealt with; because I must be allowed to remind the house that whatever may have been our errors, we proposed a bill which we intended to carry. And having once taken up the question as a matter of duty, no doubt greatly influenced by what

we considered the unhappy mistakes of our predecessors, and the difficult position in which they had placed Parliament and the country, we determined not to leave the question until it had been settled. But although still menaced, we felt it to be our duty to recommend to her Majesty to introduce the question of Reform when the Parliament of 1859 met; and how were we, except in that spirit of compromise which is the principal characteristic of our political system, how could we introduce a Reform Bill after that election, without in some degree considering the possibility of lowering the borough franchise? But it was not a franchise of £6, but it was an arrangement that was to be taken with the rest of the bill, and if it had been met in the same spirit we might have retained our places. But, says the right honorable gentleman, pursuing his history of the Reform question, when the government of Lord Derby retired from office "we came in, and we were perfectly sincere in our intentions to carry a Reform Bill; but we experienced such opposition, and never was there such opposition. There was the right honorable gentleman," meaning myself, "he absolutely allowed our bill to be read a second time."

That tremendous reckless opposition to the right honorable gentleman, which allowed the bill to be read a second time, seems to have laid the government prostrate. If he had succeeded in throwing out the bill, the right honorable gentleman and his friends would have been relieved from great embarrassment. But the bill having been read a second time, the government were quite overcome, and it appears they never have recovered from the paralysis up to this time. The right honorable gentleman was good enough to say that the proposition of his government was rather coldly received upon his side of the house, but he said "nobody spoke against it." Nobody spoke against the bill on this side, but I remember some most remarkable speeches from the right honorable gentleman's friends. There was the great city of Edinburgh, represented by acute eloquence of which we never weary, and which again upon the present occasion we have heard; there was the great city of Bristol, represented on that occasion among the opponents, and many other constituencies of equal importance. But the most remarkable speech, which "killed cock robin" was absolutely delivered by one who might be described as almost a member of the government — the chairman of ways and means [Mr. Massey], who, I

believe, spoke from immediately behind the prime minister. Did the government express any disapprobation of such conduct? They have promoted him to a great post, and have sent him to India with an income of fabulous amount. And now they are astonished they cannot carry a Reform Bill. If they removed all those among their supporters who oppose such bills by preferring them to posts of great confidence and great lucre, how can they suppose that they will ever carry one? Looking at the policy of the government, I am not at all astonished at the speech which the right honorable gentleman, the Secretary of State, has made this evening. Of which speech I may observe, that although it was remarkable for many things, yet there were two conclusions at which the right honorable gentleman arrived. First, the repudiation of the rights of man, and, next, the repudiation of the £6 franchise. The first is a great relief, and, remembering what the feeling of the house was only a year ago, when, by the dangerous but fascinating eloquence of the Chancellor of the Exchequer, we were led to believe that the days of Tom Paine had returned, and that Rousseau was to be rivaled by a new social contract, it must be a great relief to every respectable man here to find that not only are we not to have the rights of man, but we are not even to have the 1862 franchise. It is a matter, I think, of great congratulation, and I am ready to give credit to the Secretary of State for the honesty with which he has expressed himself, and I only wish we had had the same frankness, the same honesty we always have, arising from a clear view of his subject, in the first year of the Parliament as we have had in the last. I will follow the example of the right honorable gentleman and his friends. I have not changed my opinions upon the subject of what is called Parliamentary Reform. All that has occurred, all that I have observed, all the results of my reflections, lead me to this more and more — that the principle upon which the constituencies of this country should be increased is one not of radical, but I may say of lateral reform — the extension of the franchise, not its degradation. And although I do not wish in any way to deny that we were in the most difficult position when the Parliament of 1859 met, being anxious to assist the crown and the Parliament by proposing some moderate measure which men on both sides might support, we did, to a certain extent, agree to some modification of the £10 franchise — to what extent no one knows; but I may say that it would have been one which would

not at all have affected the character of the franchise, such as I and my colleagues wished to maintain. Yet I confess that my opinion is opposed, as it originally was, to any course of the kind. I think that it would fail in its object, that it would not secure the introduction of that particular class which we all desire to introduce, but that it would introduce many others who are totally unworthy of the suffrage. But I think it is possible to increase the electoral body of the country by the introduction of voters upon principles in unison with the principles of the constitution, so that the suffrage should remain a privilege, and not a right — a privilege to be gained by virtue, by intelligence, by industry, by integrity, and to be exercised for the common good of the country. I think if you quit that ground — if you once admit that every man has a right to vote whom you cannot prove to be disqualified — you would change the character of the constitution, and you would change it in a manner which will tend to lower the importance of this country. Between the scheme we brought forward and the measure brought forward by the honorable member for Leeds, and the inevitable conclusion which its principal supporters acknowledge it must lead to, it is a question between an aristocratic government in the proper sense of the term — that is, a government by the best men of all classes — and a democracy. I doubt very much whether a democracy is a government that would suit this country; and it is just as well that the house, when coming to a vote on this question, should really consider if that be the real issue, between retaining the present constitution — not the present constitutional body, but between the present constitution and a democracy.

It is just as well for the house to recollect that what is at issue is of some price. You must remember, not to use the word profanely, that we are dealing really with a peculiar people. There is no country at the present moment that exists under the circumstances and under the same conditions as the people of this realm. You have, for example, an ancient, powerful, richly-endowed Church, and perfect religious liberty. You have unbroken order and complete freedom. You have estates as large as the Romans; you have a commercial system of enterprise such as Carthage and Venice united never equaled. And you must remember that this peculiar country with these strong contrasts is governed not by force; it is not governed by standing armies — it is governed by a most singular series of traditionary influences, which generation after generation cherishes and preserves because they know that they embalm customs and represent the law. And, with this, what have you done? You have created the greatest empire that ever existed in modern times. You have amassed a capital of fabulous amount. You have devised and sustained a system of credit still more marvelous, and above all, you have established and maintained a scheme, so vast and complicated, of labor and industry, that the history of the world offers no parallel to it. And all these mighty creations are out of all proportion to the essential and indigenous elements and resources of the country. If you destroy that state of society, remember this — England cannot begin again. There are countries which have been in great peril and gone through great suffering; there are the United States, which in our own immediate day have had great trials; you have had — perhaps even now in the States of America you have — a protracted and fratricidal civil war which has lasted for four years; but if it lasted for four years more, vast as would be the disaster and desolation, when ended the United States might begin again, because the United States would only be in the same condition that England was at the end of the War of the Roses, and probably she had not even 3,000,000 of population, with vast tracts of virgin soil and mineral treasures, not only undeveloped but undiscovered. Then you have France. France had a real revolution in our days and those of our predecessors — a real revolution, not merely a political and social revolution. You had the institutions of the country uprooted, the orders of society abolished — you had even the landmarks and local names removed and erased. But France could begin again. France had the greatest spread of the most exuberant soil in Europe; she had, and always had, a very limited population, living in a most simple manner. France, therefore, could begin again. But England — the England we know, the England we live in, the England of which we are proud — could not begin again. I don't mean to say that after great troubles England would become a howling wilderness. No doubt the good sense of the people would to some degree prevail, and some fragments of the national character would survive; but it would not be the old England — the England of power and tradition, of credit and capital, that now exists. That is not in the nature of things, and, under these circumstances, I hope the house will, when the

question before us is one impeaching the character of our constitution, sanction no step that has a preference for democracy, but that they will maintain the ordered state of free England in which we live. I do not think that in this country generally there is a desire at this moment for any further change in this matter. I think the general opinion of the country on the subject of Parliamentary Reform is that our views are not sufficiently matured on either side. Certainly, so far as I can judge, I cannot refuse the conclusion that such is the condition of honorable gentlemen opposite. We all know the paper circulated among us before Parliament met, on which the speech of the honorable member from Maidstone commented this evening. I quite sympathize with him; it was one of the most interesting contributions to our elegiac literature I have heard for some time. But is it in this house only that we find these indications of the want of maturity in our views upon this subject? Our tables are filled at this moment with propositions of eminent members of the Liberal party — men eminent for character or talent, and for both — and what are these propositions? All devices to counteract the character of the Liberal Reform Bill, to which they are opposed: therefore, it is quite clear, when we read these propositions and speculations, that the mind and intellect of the party have arrived at no conclusions on the subject. I do not speak of honorable gentlemen with disrespect; I treat them with the utmost respect; I am prepared to give them the greatest consideration; but I ask whether these publications are not proofs that the active intelligence of the Liberal party is itself entirely at sea on the subject?

I may say there has been more consistency, more calmness, and consideration on this subject on the part of gentlemen on this side than on the part of those who seem to arrogate to themselves the monopoly of treating this subject. I can, at least, in answer to those who charge us with trifling with the subject, appeal to the recollection of every candid man, and say that we treated it with sincerity — we prepared our measure with care, and submitted it to the house, trusting to its candid consideration — we spared no pains in its preparation: and at this time I am bound to say, speaking for my colleagues, in the main principles on which that bill was founded — namely, the extension of the franchise, not its degradation, will be found the only solution that will ultimately be accepted by the country. Therefore, I cannot

say that I look to this question, or that those with whom I act look to it, with any embarrassment. We feel we have done our duty; and it is not without some gratification that I have listened to the candid admissions of many honorable gentlemen who voted against it, that they feel the defeat of that measure by the Liberal party was a great mistake. So far as we are concerned, I repeat, we, as a party, can look to Parliamentary Reform not as an embarrassing subject; but that is no reason why we should agree to the measure of the honorable member for Leeds. It would reflect no credit on the House of Commons. It is a mean device. I give all credit to the honorable member for Leeds for his conscientious feeling; but it would be a mockery to take this bill; from the failures of the government and the whole of the circumstances that attended it, it is of that character that I think the house will best do its duty to the country, and will best meet the constituencies with a very good understanding, if they reject the measure by a decided majority.

THE MEANING OF «CONSERVATISM»
(Manchester, April 3d, 1872)

Gentlemen: —

THE chairman has correctly reminded you that this is not the first time that my voice has been heard in this hall. But that was an occasion very different from that which now assembles us together — was nearly thirty years ago, when I endeavored to support and stimulate the flagging energies of an institution in which I thought there were the germs of future refinement and intellectual advantage to the rising generation of Manchester, and since I have been here on this occasion I have learned with much gratification that it is now counted among your most flourishing institutions. There was also another and more recent occasion when the gracious office fell to me to distribute among the members of the Mechanics' Institution those prizes which they had gained through their study in letters and in science. Gentlemen, these were pleasing offices, and if life consisted only of such offices you would not have to complain of it. But life has its masculine duties, and we are assembled here to fulfill some of the most important of these, when, as citizens of a free country, we are assembled together to declare our

determination to maintain, to uphold the constitution to which we are debtors, in our opinion, for our freedom and our welfare.

Gentlemen, there seems at first something incongruous that one should be addressing the population of so influential and intelligent a county as Lancashire who is not locally connected with them, and, gentlemen, I will frankly admit that this circumstance did for a long time make me hesitate in accepting your cordial and generous invitation. But, gentlemen, after what occurred yesterday, after receiving more than two hundred addresses from every part of this great county, after the welcome which then greeted me, I feel that I should not be doing justice to your feelings, I should not do my duty to myself, if I any longer consider my presence here to-night to be an act of presumption. Gentlemen, though it may not be an act of presumption, it still is, I am told, an act of great difficulty. Our opponents assure us that the Conservative party has no political program; and, therefore, they must look with much satisfaction to one whom you honor to-night by considering him the leader and representative of your opinions when he comes forward, at your invitation, to express to you what that program is. The Conservative party are accused of having no program of policy. If by a program is meant a plan to despoil churches and plunder landlords, I admit we have no program. If by a program is meant a policy which assails or menaces every institution and every interest, every class and every calling in the country, I admit we have no program. But if to have a policy with distinct ends, and these such as most deeply interest the great body of the nation, be a becoming program for a political party, then I contend we have an adequate program, and one which, here or elsewhere, I shall always be prepared to assert and to vindicate.

Gentlemen, the program of the Conservative party is to maintain the constitution of the country. I have not come down to Manchester to deliver an essay on the English constitution; but when the banner of Republicanism is unfurled — when the fundamental principles of our institutions are controverted — I think, perhaps, it may not be inconvenient that I should make some few practical remarks upon the character of our constitution — upon that monarchy limited by the co-ordinate authority of the estates of the realm, which, under the title of Queen, Lords, and Commons, has contributed so greatly to the prosperity of this country, and with the maintenance of which I believe that prosperity is bound up.

Gentlemen, since the settlement of that constitution, now nearly two centuries ago, England has never experienced a revolution, though there is no country in which there has been so continuous and such considerable change. How is this? Because the wisdom of your forefathers placed the prize of supreme power without the sphere of human passions. Whatever the struggle of parties, whatever the strife of factions, whatever the excitement and exaltation of the public mind, there has always been something in this country round which all classes and parties could rally, representing the majesty of the law, the administration of justice, and involving, at the same time, the security for every man's rights and the fountain of honor. Now, gentlemen, it is well clearly to comprehend what is meant by a country not having a revolution for two centuries. It means, for that space, the unbroken exercise and enjoyment of the ingenuity of man. It means for that space the continuous application of the discoveries of science to his comfort and convenience. It means the accumulation of capital, the elevation of labor, the establishment of those admirable factories which cover your district; the unwearied improvement of the cultivation of the land, which has extracted from a somewhat churlish soil harvests more exuberant than those furnished by lands nearer to the sun. It means the continuous order which is the only parent of personal liberty and political right. And you owe all these, gentlemen, to the throne.

There is another powerful and most beneficial influence which is also exercised by the crown. Gentlemen, I am a party man. I believe that, without party, parliamentary government is impossible. I look upon parliamentary government as the noblest government in the world, and certainly the one most suited to England. But without the discipline of political connection, animated by the principle of private honor, I feel certain that a popular assembly would sink before the power or the corruption of a minister. Yet, gentlemen, I am not blind to the faults of party government. It has one great defect. Party has a tendency to warp the intelligence, and there is no minister, however resolved he may be in treating a great public question, who does not find some difficulty in emancipating himself from

the traditionary prejudice on which he has long acted. It is, therefore, a great merit in our constitution, that before a minister introduces a measure to Parliament, he must submit it to an intelligence superior to all party, and entirely free from influences of that character.

I know it will be said, gentlemen, that, however beautiful in theory, the personal influence of the sovereign is now absorbed in the responsibility of the minister. Gentlemen, I think you will find there is great fallacy in this view. The principles of the English constitution do not contemplate the absence of personal influence on the part of the sovereign; and if they did, the principles of human nature would prevent the fulfillment of such a theory. Gentlemen, I need not tell you that I am now making on this subject abstract observations of general application to our institutions and our history. But take the case of a sovereign of England, who accedes to his throne at the earliest age the law permits, and who enjoys a long reign,—take an instance like that of George III. From the earliest moment of his accession that sovereign is placed in constant communication with the most able statesmen of the period, and of all parties. Even with average ability it is impossible not to perceive that such a sovereign must soon attain a great mass of political information and political experience. Information and experience, gentlemen, whether they are possessed by a sovereign or by the humblest of his subjects, are irresistible in life. No man with the vast responsibility that devolves upon an English minister can afford to treat with indifference a suggestion that has not occurred to him, or information with which he had not been previously supplied. But, gentlemen, pursue this view of the subject. The longer the reign, the influence of that sovereign must proportionately increase. All the illustrious statesmen who served his youth disappear. A new generation of public servants rises up, there is a critical conjunction in affairs—a moment of perplexity and peril. Then it is that the sovereign can appeal to a similar state of affairs that occurred perhaps thirty years before. When all are in doubt among his servants, he can quote the advice that was given by the illustrious men of his early years, and, though he may maintain himself within the strictest limits of the constitution, who can suppose, when such information and such suggestions are made by the most exalted person in the country, that they can

be without effect? No, gentlemen; a minister who could venture to treat such influence with indifference would not be a constitutional minister, but an arrogant idiot.

Gentlemen, the influence of the crown is not confined merely to political affairs. England is a domestic country. Here the home is revered and the hearth is sacred. The nation is represented by a family—the royal family; and if that family is educated with a sense of responsibility and a sentiment of public duty, it is difficult to exaggerate the salutary influence they may exercise over a nation. It is not merely an influence upon manners; it is not merely that they are a model for refinement and for good taste—they affect the heart as well as the intelligence of the people; and in the hour of public adversity, or in the anxious conjuncture of public affairs, the nation rallies round the family and the throne, and its spirit is animated and sustained by the expression of public affection. Gentlemen, there is yet one other remark that I would make upon our monarchy, though had it not been for recent circumstances, I should have refrained from doing so. An attack has recently been made upon the throne on account of the costliness of the institution. Gentlemen, I shall not dwell upon the fact that if the people of England appreciate the monarchy, as I believe they do, it would be painful to them that their royal and representative family should not be maintained with becoming dignity, or fill in the public eye a position inferior to some of the nobles of the land. Nor will I insist upon what is unquestionably the fact, that the revenues of the crown estates, on which our sovereign might live with as much right as the Duke of Bedford, or the Duke of Northumberland, has to his estates, are now paid into the public exchequer. All this, upon the present occasion, I am not going to insist upon. What I now say is this: that there is no sovereignty of any first-rate State which costs so little to the people as the sovereignty of England. I will not compare our civil list with those of European empires, because it is known that in amount they treble and quadruple it; but I will compare it with the cost of sovereignty in a republic, and that a republic with which you are intimately acquainted—the republic of the United States of America.

Gentlemen, there is no analogy between the position of our sovereign, Queen Victoria, and that of the President of the United States. The President of the United States is not the

sovereign of the United States. There is a very near analogy between the position of the President of the United States and that of the prime minister of England, and both are paid at much the same rate—the income of a second-class professional man. The sovereign of the United States is the people; and I will now show you what the sovereignty of the United States costs. Gentlemen, you are aware of the Constitution of the United States. There are thirty-seven independent States, each with a sovereign legislature. Besides these, there is a Confederation of States, to conduct their external affairs, which consists of the House of Representatives and a Senate. There are two hundred and eighty-five members of the House of Representatives, and there are seventy-four members of the Senate, making altogether three hundred and fifty-nine members of Congress. Now each member of Congress receives £1,000 sterling per annum. In addition to this he receives an allowance called "mileage," which varies according to the distance which he travels, but the aggregate cost of which is about £30,000 per annum. That makes £389,000, almost the exact amount of our civil list.

But this, gentlemen, will allow you to make only a very imperfect estimate of the cost of sovereignty in the United States. Every member of every legislature in the thirty-seven States is also paid. There are, I believe, five thousand and ten members of State legislatures, who receive about $350 per annum each. As some of the returns are imperfect, the average which I have given of expenditure may be rather high, and therefore I have not counted the mileage, which is also universally allowed. Five thousand and ten members of State legislatures at $350 each make $1,753,500, or £350,700 sterling a year. So you see, gentlemen, that the immediate expenditure for the sovereignty of the United States is between £700,000 and £800,000 a year. Gentlemen, I have not time to pursue this interesting theme, otherwise I could show that you have still but imperfectly ascertained the cost of sovereignty in a republic. But, gentlemen, I cannot resist giving you one further illustration.

The government of this country is considerably carried on by the aid of royal commissions. So great is the increase of public business that it would be probably impossible for a minister to carry on affairs without this assistance. The Queen of England can command for these objects the services of the most experienced statesmen, and men of the highest position in society. If necessary, she can summon to them distinguished scholars or men most celebrated in science and in arts; and she receives from them services that are unpaid. They are only too proud to be described in the commission as her Majesty's "trusty councilors"; and if any member of these commissions performs some transcendent services, both of thought and of labor, he is munificently rewarded by a public distinction conferred upon him by the fountain of honor. Gentlemen, the government of the United States, has, I believe, not less availed itself of the services of commissions than the government of the United Kingdom; but in a country where there is no fountain of honor, every member of these commissions is paid.

Gentlemen, I trust I have now made some suggestions to you respecting the monarchy of England which at least may be so far serviceable that when we are separated they may not be altogether without advantage; and now, gentlemen, I would say something on the subject of the House of Lords. It is not merely the authority of the throne that is now disputed, but the character and the influence of the House of Lords that are held up by some to public disregard. Gentlemen, I shall not stop for a moment to offer you any proofs of the advantage of a second chamber; and for this reason. That subject has been discussed now for a century, ever since the establishment of the government of the United States, and all great authorities, American, German, French, Italian, have agreed in this, that a representative government is impossible without a second chamber. And it has been, especially of late, maintained by great political writers in all countries, that the repeated failure of what is called the French republic is mainly to be ascribed to its not having a second chamber.

But, gentlemen, however anxious foreign countries have been to enjoy this advantage, that anxiety has only been equaled by the difficulty which they have found in fulfilling their object. How is a second chamber to be constituted? By nominees of the sovereign power? What influence can be exercised by a chamber of nominees? Are they to be bound by popular election? In what manner are they to be elected? If by the same constituency as the popular body, what claim have they, under such circumstances, to criticize or to control the decisions of that body? If they are to be elected by a more select body, qualified by a higher franchise, there immediately occurs the objection,

why should the majority be governed by the minority? The United States of America were fortunate in finding a solution of this difficulty; but the United States of America had elements to deal with which never occurred before, and never probably will occur again, because they formed their illustrious Senate from materials that were offered them by the thirty-seven States. We, gentlemen, have the House of Lords, an assembly which has historically developed and periodically adapted itself to the wants and necessities of the times.

What, gentlemen, is the first quality which is required in a second chamber? Without doubt, independence. What is the best foundation of independence? Without doubt, property. The prime minister of England has only recently told you, and I believe he spoke quite accurately, that the average income of the members of the House of Lords is £20,000 per annum. Of course there are some who have more, and some who have less; but the influence of a public assembly, so far as property is concerned, depends upon its aggregate property, which, in the present case, is a revenue of £9,000,000 a year. But, gentlemen, you must look to the nature of this property. It is visible property, and therefore it is responsible property, which every rate-payer in the room knows to his cost. But, gentlemen, it is not only visible property; it is, generally speaking, territorial property; and one of the elements of territorial property is, that it is representative. Now, for illustration, suppose—which God forbid—there was no House of Commons, and any Englishman,—I will take him from either end of the island,—a Cumberland, or a Cornish man, finds himself aggrieved, the Cumbrian says: "This conduct I experience is most unjust. I know a Cumberland man in the House of Lords, the Earl of Carlisle or the Earl of Lonsdale; I will go to him; he will never see a Cumberland man ill-treated." The Cornish man will say: "I will go to the Lord of Port Eliot; his family have sacrificed themselves before this for the liberties of Englishmen, and he will get justice done me."

But, gentlemen, the charge against the House of Lords is that the dignities are hereditary, and we are told that if we have a House of Peers they should be peers for life. There are great authorities in favor of this, and even my noble friend near me [Lord Derby], the other day, gave in his adhesion to a limited application of this principle. Now, gentlemen, in the first place,

let me observe that every peer is a peer for life, as he cannot be a peer after his death; but some peers for life are succeeded in their dignities by their children. The question arises, who is most responsible—a peer for life whose dignities are not descendible, or a peer for life whose dignities are hereditary? Now, gentlemen, a peer for life is in a very strong position. He says: "Here I am; I have got power and I will exercise it." I have no doubt that, on the whole, a peer for life would exercise it for what he deemed was the public good. Let us hope that. But, after all, he might and could exercise it according to his own will. Nobody can call him to account; he is independent of everybody. But a peer for life whose dignities descend is in a very different position. He has every inducement to study public opinion, and, when he believes it just, to yield; because he naturally feels that if the order to which he belongs is in constant collision with public opinion, the chances are that his dignities will not descend to his posterity.

Therefore, gentlemen, I am not prepared myself to believe that a solution of any difficulties in the public mind on this subject is to be found by creating peers for life. I know there are some philosophers who believe that the best substitute for the House of Lords would be an assembly formed of ex-governors of colonies. I have not sufficient experience on that subject to give a decided opinion upon it. When the Muse of Comedy threw her frolic grace over society, a retired governor was generally one of the characters in every comedy; and the last of our great actors,—who, by the way, was a great favorite at Manchester,—Mr. Farren, was celebrated for his delineation of the character in question. Whether it be the recollection of that performance or not, I confess I am inclined to believe that an English gentleman—born to business, managing his own estate, administering the affairs of his county, mixing with all classes of his fellowmen, now in the hunting field, now in the railway direction, unaffected, unostentatious, proud of his ancestors, if they have contributed to the greatness of our common country—is, on the whole, more likely to form a Senator agreeable to English opinion and English taste than any substitute that has yet been produced.

Gentlemen, let me make one observation more on the subject of the House of Lords before I conclude. There is some advantage in political experience. I remember the time when there was a similar outcry against the House of Lords, but much more

intense and powerful; and, gentlemen, it arose from the same cause. A Liberal government had been installed in office, with an immense Liberal majority. They proposed some violent measures. The House of Lords modified some, delayed others, and some they threw out. Instantly there was a cry to abolish or to reform the House of Lords, and the greatest popular orator [Daniel O'Connell] that probably ever existed was sent on a pilgrimage over England to excite the people in favor of this opinion. What happened? That happened, gentlemen, which may happen to-morrow. There was a dissolution of Parliament. The great Liberal majority vanished. The balance of parties was restored. It was discovered that the House of Lords had behind them at least half of the English people. We heard no more cries for their abolition or their reform, and before two years more passed England was really governed by the House of Lords, under the wise influence of the Duke of Wellington and the commanding eloquence of Lyndhurst; and such was the enthusiasm of the nation in favor of the second chamber that at every public meeting its health was drunk, with the additional sentiment, for which we are indebted to one of the most distinguished members that ever represented the House of Commons: "Thank God, there is the House of Lords."

Gentlemen, you will, perhaps, not be surprised that, having made some remarks upon the monarchy and the House of Lords, I should say something respecting that house in which I have literally passed the greater part of my life, and to which I am devotedly attached. It is not likely, therefore, that I should say anything to depreciate the legitimate position and influence of the House of Commons. Gentlemen, it is said that the diminished power of the throne and the assailed authority of the House of Lords are owing to the increased power of the House of Commons, and the new position which of late years, and especially during the last forty years, it has assumed in the English constitution. Gentlemen, the main power of the House of Commons depends upon its command over the public purse, and its control of the public expenditure; and if that power is possessed by a party which has a large majority in the House of Commons, the influence of the House of Commons is proportionately increased, and, under some circumstances, becomes more predominant. But, gentlemen, this power of the House of Commons is not a power which has been created by any reform act, from the days of Lord Grey, in 1832, to 1867. It is the power which the House of Commons has enjoyed for centuries, which it has frequently asserted and sometimes even tyrannically exercised. Gentlemen, the House of Commons represents the constituencies of England, and I am here to show you that no addition to the elements of that constituency has placed the House of Commons in a different position with regard to the throne and the House of Lords from that it has always constitutionally occupied.

Gentlemen, we speak now on this subject with great advantage. We recently have had published authentic documents upon this matter which are highly instructive. We have, for example, just published the census of Great Britain, and we are now in possession of the last registration of voters for the United Kingdom. Gentlemen, it appears that by the census the population at this time is about 32,000,000. It is shown by the last registration that, after making the usual deductions for deaths, removals, double entries, and so on, the constituency of the United Kingdom may be placed at 2,200,000. So, gentlemen, it at once appears that there are 30,000,000 people in this country who are as much represented by the House of Lords as by the House of Commons, and who, for the protection of their rights, must depend upon them and the majesty of the throne. And now, gentlemen, I will tell you what was done by the last reform act.

Lord Grey, in his measure of 1832, which was no doubt a statesmanlike measure, committed a great, and for a time it appeared an irretrievable, error. By that measure he fortified the legitimate influence of the aristocracy, and accorded to the middle classes great and salutary franchises; but he not only made no provision for the representation of the working classes in the constitution, but he absolutely abolished those ancient franchises which the working classes had peculiarly enjoyed and exercised from time immemorial. Gentlemen, that was the origin of Chartism, and of that electoral uneasiness which existed in this country more or less for thirty years.

The Liberal party, I feel it my duty to say, had not acted fairly by this question. In their adversity they held out hopes to the working classes, but when they had a strong government they laughed their vows to scorn. In 1848 there was a French revolution, and a republic was established. No one can have forgotten what the effect was in this country. I remember the day

when not a woman could leave her house in London, and when cannon were planted on Westminster Bridge. When Lord Derby became prime minister affairs had arrived at such a point that it was of the first moment that the question should be sincerely dealt with. He had to encounter great difficulties, but he accomplished his purpose with the support of a united party. And, gentlemen, what has been the result? A year ago there was another revolution in France, and a republic was again established of the most menacing character. What happened in this country? You could not get half a dozen men to assemble in a street and grumble. Why? Because the people had got what they wanted. They were content, and they were grateful.

But, gentlemen, the constitution of England is not merely a constitution in State, it is a constitution in Church and State. The wisest sovereigns and statesmen have ever been anxious to connect authority with religion — some to increase their power, some, perhaps, to mitigate its exercise. But the same difficulty has been experienced in effecting this union which has been experienced in forming a second chamber — either the spiritual power has usurped upon the civil, and established a sacerdotal society, or the civil power has invaded successfully the rights of the spiritual, and the ministers of religion have been degraded into stipendiaries of the state and instruments of the government. In England we accomplish this great result by an alliance between Church and State, between two originally independent powers. I will not go into the history of that alliance, which is rather a question for those archæological societies which occasionally amuse and instruct the people of this city. Enough for me that this union was made and has contributed for centuries to the civilization of this country. Gentlemen, there is the same assault against the Church of England and the union between the State and the Church as there is against the monarchy and against the House of Lords. It is said that the existence of nonconformity proves that the Church is a failure. I draw from these premises an exactly contrary conclusion; and I maintain that to have secured a national profession of faith with the unlimited enjoyment of private judgment in matters spiritual, is the solution of the most difficult problem, and one of the triumphs of civilization.

It is said that the existence of parties in the Church also proves its incompetence. On that matter, too, I entertain a con-

trary opinion. Parties have always existed in the Church; and some have appealed to them as arguments in favor of its divine institution, because, in the services and doctrines of the Church have been found representatives of every mood in the human mind. Those who are influenced by ceremonies find consolation in forms which secure to them the beauty of holiness. Those who are not satisfied except with enthusiasm find in its ministrations the exaltation they require, while others who believe that the "anchor of faith" can never be safely moored except in the dry sands of reason find a religion within the pale of the Church which can boast of its irrefragable logic and its irresistible evidence.

Gentlemen, I am inclined sometimes to believe that those who advocate the abolition of the union between Church and State have not carefully considered the consequences of such a course. The Church is a powerful corporation of many millions of her Majesty's subjects, with a consummate organization and wealth which in its aggregate is vast. Restricted and controlled by the State, so powerful a corporation may be only fruitful of public advantage, but it becomes a great question what might be the consequences of the severance of the controlling tie between these two bodies. The State would be enfeebled, but the Church would probably be strengthened. Whether that is a result to be desired is a grave question for all men. For my own part, I am bound to say that I doubt whether it would be favorable to the cause of civil and religious liberty. I know that there is a common idea that if the union between Church and State was severed, the wealth of the Church would revert to the State; but it would be well to remember that the great proportion of ecclesiastical property is the property of individuals. Take, for example, the fact that the great mass of Church patronage is patronage in the hands of private persons. That you could not touch without compensation to the patrons. You have established that principle in your late Irish Bill, where there was very little patronage. And in the present state of the public mind on the subject, there is very little doubt that there would be scarcely a patron in England — irrespective of other aid the Church would receive — who would not dedicate his compensation to the spiritual wants of his neighbors.

It was computed some years ago that the property of the Church in this manner, if the union was terminated, would not

be less than between £80,000,000 and £90,000,000, and since that period the amount of private property dedicated to the purposes of the Church has very largely increased. I therefore trust that when the occasion offers for the country to speak out, it will speak out in an unmistakable manner on this subject; and recognizing the inestimable services of the Church, that it will call upon the government to maintain its union with the State. Upon this subject there is one remark I would make. Nothing is more surprising to me than the plea on which the present outcry is made against the Church of England. I could not believe that in the nineteenth century the charge against the Church of England should be that churchmen, and especially the clergy, had educated the people. If I were to fix upon one circumstance more than another which redounded to the honor of churchmen, it is that they should fulfill this noble office; and, next to being "the stewards of divine mysteries," I think the greatest distinction of the clergy is the admirable manner in which they have devoted their lives and their fortunes to this greatest of national objects.

Gentlemen, you are well acquainted in this city with this controversy. It was in this city — I don't know whether it was not in this hall — that that remarkable meeting was held of the Nonconformists to effect important alterations in the Education Act, and you are acquainted with the discussion in Parliament which arose in consequence of that meeting. Gentlemen, I have due and great respect for the Nonconformist body. I acknowledge their services to their country, and though I believe that the political reasons which mainly called them into existence have entirely ceased, it is impossible not to treat with consideration a body which has been eminent for its conscience, its learning, and its patriotism; but I must express my mortification that, from a feeling of envy or of pique, the Nonconformist body, rather than assist the Church in its great enterprise, should absolutely have become the partisans of a merely secular education. I believe myself, gentlemen, that without the recognition of a superintending Providence in the affairs of this world all national education will be disastrous, and I feel confident that it is impossible to stop at that mere recognition. Religious education is demanded by the nation generally and by the instincts of human nature. I should like to see the Church and the Nonconformists work together; but I trust, whatever may be the result, the country will stand by the Church in its efforts to maintain the religious education of the people. Gentlemen, I foresee yet trials for the Church of England; but I am confident in its future. I am confident in its future because I believe there is now a very general feeling that to be national it must be comprehensive. I will not use the word "broad," because it is an epithet applied to a system with which I have no sympathy. But I would wish churchmen, and especially the clergy, always to remember that in our "Father's home there are many mansions," and I believe that comprehensive spirit is perfectly consistent with the maintenance of formularies and the belief in dogmas without which I hold no practical religion can exist.

Gentlemen, I have now endeavored to express to you my general views upon the most important subjects that can interest Englishmen. They are subjects upon which, in my mind, a man should speak with frankness and clearness to his countrymen, and although I do not come down here to make a party speech, I am bound to say that the manner in which those subjects are treated by the leading subject of this realm is to me most unsatisfactory. Although the prime minister of England is always writing letters and making speeches, and particularly on these topics, he seems to me ever to send forth an "uncertain sound." If a member of Parliament announces himself a Republican, Mr. Gladstone takes the earliest opportunity of describing him as a "fellow-worker" in public life. If an inconsiderate multitude calls for the abolition or reform of the House of Lords, Mr. Gladstone says that it is no easy task, and that he must think once or twice, or perhaps even thrice, before he can undertake it. If your neighbor, the member for Bradford, Mr. Miall, brings forward a motion in the House of Commons for the severance of Church and State, Mr. Gladstone assures Mr. Miall with the utmost courtesy that he believes the opinion of the House of Commons is against him, but that if Mr. Miall wishes to influence the House of Commons he must address the people out of doors; whereupon Mr. Miall immediately calls a public meeting, and alleges as its cause the advice he has just received from the prime minister.

But, gentlemen, after all, the test of political institutions is the condition of the country whose fortunes they regulate; and I do not mean to evade that test. You are the inhabitants of an island of no colossal size; which, geographically speaking, was

intended by nature as the appendage of some continental empire — either of Gauls and Franks on the other side of the Channel, or of Teutons and Scandinavians beyond the German Sea. Such, indeed, and for a long period, was your early history. You were invaded; you were pillaged and you were conquered; yet amid all these disgraces and vicissitudes there was gradually formed that English race which has brought about a very different state of affairs. Instead of being invaded, your land is proverbially the only "inviolate land"—"the inviolate land of the sage and free." Instead of being plundered, you have attracted to your shores all the capital of the world. Instead of being conquered, your flag floats on many waters, and your standard waves in either zone. It may be said that these achievements are due to the race that inhabited the land, and not to its institutions. Gentlemen, in political institutions are the embodied experiences of a race. You have established a society of classes which give vigor and variety to life. But no class possesses a single exclusive privilege, and all are equal before the law. You possess a real aristocracy, open to all who desire to enter it. You have not merely a middle class, but a hierarchy of middle classes, in which every degree of wealth, refinement, industry, energy, and enterprise is duly represented.

And now, gentlemen, what is the condition of the great body of the people? In the first place, gentlemen, they have for centuries been in the full enjoyment of that which no other country in Europe has ever completely attained — complete rights of personal freedom. In the second place, there has been a gradual, and therefore a wise, distribution on a large scale of political rights. Speaking with reference to the industries of this great part of the country, I can personally contrast it with the condition of the working classes forty years ago. In that period they have attained two results — the raising of their wages and the diminution of their toil. Increased means and increased leisure are the two civilizers of man. That the working classes of Lancashire and Yorkshire have proved not unworthy of these boons may be easily maintained; but their progress and elevation have been during this interval wonderfully aided and assisted by three causes, which are not so distinctively attributable to their own energies. The first is the revolution in locomotion, which has opened the world to the working man, which has enlarged the horizon of his experience, increased his knowledge of nature and

of art, and added immensely to the salutary recreation, amusement, and pleasure of his existence. The second cause is the cheap postage, the moral benefits of which cannot be exaggerated. And the third is that unshackled press which has furnished him with endless sources of instruction, information, and amusement.

Gentlemen, if you would permit me, I would now make an observation upon another class of the laboring population. This is not a civic assembly, although we meet in a city. That was for convenience, but the invitation which I received was to meet the county and all the boroughs of Lancashire; and I wish to make a few observations upon the condition of the agricultural laborer. That is a subject which now greatly attracts public attention. And, in the first place, to prevent any misconception, I beg to express my opinion that an agricultural laborer has as much right to combine for the bettering of his condition as a manufacturing laborer or a worker in metals. If the causes of his combination are natural — that is to say, if they arise from his own feelings and from the necessities of his own condition — the combination will end in results mutually beneficial to employers and employed. If, on the other hand, it is factitious and he is acted upon by extraneous influences and extraneous ideas, the combination will produce, I fear, much loss and misery both to employers and employed; and after a time he will find himself in a similar, or in a worse, position.

Gentlemen, in my opinion, the farmers of England cannot, as a body, afford to pay higher wages than they do, and those who will answer me by saying that they must find their ability by the reduction of rents are, I think, involving themselves with economic laws which may prove too difficult for them to cope with. The profits of a farmer are very moderate. The interest upon capital invested in land is the smallest that any property furnishes. The farmer will have his profits and the investor in land will have his interest, even though they may be obtained at the cost of changing the mode of the cultivation of the country. Gentlemen, I should deeply regret to see the tillage of this country reduced, and a recurrence to pasture take place. I should regret it principally on account of the agricultural laborers themselves. Their new friends call them Hodge, and describe them as a stolid race. I must say that, from my experience of them,

they are sufficiently shrewd and open to reason. I would say to them with confidence, as the great Athenian said to the Spartan who rudely assailed him: "Strike, but hear me."

First, a change in the cultivation of the soil of this country would be very injurious to the laboring class; and second, I am of opinion that that class instead of being stationary has made, if not as much progress as the manufacturing class, very considerable progress during the last forty years. Many persons write and speak about the agricultural laborer with not so perfect a knowledge of his condition as is desirable. They treat him always as a human being who in every part of the country finds himself in an identical condition. Now, on the contrary, there is no class of laborers in which there is greater variety of condition than that of the agricultural laborers. It changes from north to south, from east to west, and from county to county. It changes even in the same county, where there is an alteration of soil and of configuration. The hind in Northumberland is in a very different condition from the famous Dorsetshire laborer; the tiller of the soil in Lincolnshire is different from his fellow-agriculturalist in Sussex. What the effect of manufactures is upon the agricultural districts in their neighborhood it would be presumption in me to dwell upon; your own experience must tell you whether the agricultural laborer in North Lancashire, for example, has had no rise in wages and no diminution in toil. Take the case of the Dorsetshire laborer — the whole of the agricultural laborers on the southwestern coast of England for a very long period worked only half the time of the laborers in other parts of England, and received only half the wages. In the experience of many, I dare say, who are here present, even thirty years ago a Dorsetshire laborer never worked after three o'clock in the day; and why? Because the whole of that part of England was demoralized by smuggling. No one worked after three o'clock in the day, for a very good reason — because he had to work at night. No farmer allowed his team to be employed after three o'clock, because he reserved his horses to take his illicit cargo at night and carry it rapidly into the interior. Therefore, as the men were employed and remunerated otherwise, they got into a habit of half work and half play so far as the land was concerned, and when smuggling was abolished — and it has only been abolished for thirty years — these imperfect habits of labor continued, and do even now continue to a great extent. That is the origin of the condition of the agricultural laborer in the southwestern part of England.

But now, gentlemen, I want to test the condition of the agricultural laborer generally; and I will take a part of England with which I am familiar, and can speak as to the accuracy of the facts — I mean the group described as the south-midland counties. The conditions of labor there are the same, or pretty nearly the same, throughout. The group may be described as a strictly agricultural community, and they embrace a population of probably a million and a half. Now, I have no hesitation in saying that the improvement in their lot during the last forty years has been progressive and is remarkable. I attribute it to three causes. In the first place, the rise in their money wages is no less than fifteen per cent. The second great cause of their improvement is the almost total disappearance of excessive and exhausting toil, from the general introduction of machinery. I don't know whether I could get a couple of men who could or, if they could, would thresh a load of wheat in my neighborhood. The third great cause which has improved their condition is the very general, not to say universal, institution of allotment grounds. Now, gentlemen, when I find that this has been the course of affairs in our very considerable and strictly agricultural portion of the country, where there have been no exceptional circumstances, like smuggling, to degrade and demoralize the race, I cannot resist the conviction that the condition of the agricultural laborers, instead of being stationary, as we are constantly told by those not acquainted with them, has been one of progressive improvement, and that in those counties — and they are many — where the stimulating influence of a manufacturing neighborhood acts upon the land, the general conclusion at which I arrive is that the agricultural laborer has had his share in the advance of national prosperity. Gentlemen, I am not here to maintain that there is nothing to be done to increase the well-being of the working classes of this country, generally speaking. There is not a single class in the country which is not susceptible of improvement; and that makes the life and animation of our society. But in all we do we must remember, as my noble friend told them at Liverpool, that much depends upon the working classes themselves; and what I know of the working classes in Lancashire makes me sure that they will respond to

minister should be the health of the people. A land may be covered with historic trophies, with museums of science and galleries of art, with universities and with libraries; the people may be civilized and ingenious; the country may be even famous in the annals and action of the world, but, gentlemen, if the population every ten years decreases, and the stature of the race every ten years diminishes, the history of that country will soon be the history of the past.

Gentlemen, I said I had not come here to make a party speech. I have addressed you upon subjects of grave, and I will venture to believe of general, interest; but to be here and altogether silent upon the present state of public affairs would not be respectful to you, and, perhaps, on the whole, would be thought incongruous. Gentlemen, I cannot pretend that our position either at home or abroad is in my opinion satisfactory. At home, at a period of immense prosperity, with a people contented and naturally loyal, we find to our surprise the most extravagant doctrines professed and the fundamental principles of our most valuable institutions impugned, and that, too, by persons of some authority. Gentlemen, this startling inconsistency is accounted for, in my mind, by the circumstances under which the present administration was formed. It is the first instance in my knowledge of a British administration being avowedly formed on a principle of violence. It is unnecessary for me to remind you of the circumstances which preceded the formation of that government. You were the principal scene and theatre of the development of statesmanship that then occurred. You witnessed the incubation of the portentous birth. You remember when you were informed that the policy to secure the prosperity of Ireland and the content of Irishmen was a policy of sacrilege and confiscation. Gentlemen, when Ireland was placed under the wise and able administration of Lord Abercorn, Ireland was prosperous, and I may say content. But there happened at that time a very peculiar conjuncture in politics. The Civil War in America had just ceased; and a band of military adventurers — Poles, Italians, and many Irishmen — concocted in New York a conspiracy to invade Ireland, with the belief that the whole country would rise to welcome them. How that conspiracy was baffled — how those plots were confounded, I need not now remind you. For that we were mainly indebted to the eminent qualities of a great man who has just left us. You remember how the constituencies

this appeal. Much, also, may be expected from that sympathy between classes which is a distinctive feature of the present day; and, in the last place, no inconsiderable results may be obtained by judicious and prudent legislation. But, gentlemen, in attempting to legislate upon social matters, the great object is to be practical — to have before us some distinct aims and some distinct means by which they can be accomplished.

Gentlemen, I think public attention as regards these matters ought to be concentrated upon sanitary legislation. That is a wide subject, and, if properly treated, comprises almost every consideration which has a just claim upon legislative interference. Pure air, pure water, the inspection of unhealthy habitations, the adulteration of food, — these and many kindred matters may be legitimately dealt with by the legislature; and I am bound to say the legislature is not idle upon them; for we have at this time two important measures before Parliament on the subject. One — by a late colleague of mine, Sir Charles Adderley — is a large and comprehensive measure, founded upon a sure basis, for it consolidates all existing public acts, and improves them. A prejudice has been raised against that proposal, by stating that it interferes with the private acts of the great towns. I take this opportunity of contradicting that. The bill of Sir Charles Adderley does not touch the acts of the great towns. It only allows them, if they think fit, to avail themselves of its new provisions.

The other measure by the government is of a partial character. What it comprises is good, so far as it goes, but it shrinks from that bold consolidation of existing acts which I think one of the great merits of Sir Charles Adderley's bill, which permits us to become acquainted with how much may be done in favor of sanitary improvement by existing provisions. Gentlemen, I cannot impress upon you too strongly my conviction of the importance of the legislature and society uniting together in favor of these important results. A great scholar and a great wit, three hundred years ago, said that, in his opinion, there was a great mistake in the Vulgate, which, as you all know, is the Latin translation of the Holy Scriptures, and that, instead of saying "Vanity of vanities, all is vanity" — *Vanitas vanitatum, omnia vanitas* — the wise and witty king really said: "*Sanitas sanitatum, omnia sanitas.*" Gentlemen, it is impossible to overrate the importance of the subject. After all the first consideration of a

were appealed to to vote against the government which had made so unfit an appointment as that of Lord Mayo to the viceroyalty of India. It was by his great qualities when Secretary for Ireland, by his vigilance, his courage, his patience, and his perseverance that this conspiracy was defeated. Never was a minister better informed. He knew what was going on at New York just as well as what was going on in the city of Dublin.

When the Fenian conspiracy had been entirely put down, it became necessary to consider the policy which it was expedient to pursue in Ireland; and it seemed to us at that time that what Ireland required after all the excitement which it had experienced was a policy which should largely develop its material resources. There were one or two subjects of a different character, which, for the advantage of the State, it would have been desirable to have settled, if that could have been effected with a general concurrence of both the great parties in that country. Had we remained in office, that would have been done. But we were destined to quit it, and we quitted it without a murmur. The policy of our successors was different. Their specific was to despoil churches and plunder landlords, and what has been the result? Sedition rampant, treason thinly veiled, and whenever a vacancy occurs in the representation a candidate is returned pledged to the disruption of the realm. Her Majesty's new ministers proceeded in their career like a body of men under the influence of some delirious drug. Not satiated with the spoliation and anarchy of Ireland, they began to attack every institution and every interest, every class and calling in the country.

It is curious to observe their course. They took into hand the army. What have they done? I will not comment on what they have done. I will historically state it, and leave you to draw the inference. So long as constitutional England has existed there has been a jealousy among all classes against the existence of a standing army. As our empire expanded, and the existence of a large body of disciplined troops became a necessity, every precaution was taken to prevent the danger to our liberties which a standing army involved.

It was a first principle not to concentrate in the island any overwhelming number of troops, and a considerable portion was distributed in the colonies. Care was taken that the troops generally should be officered by a class of men deeply interested in the property and the liberties of England. So extreme was the jealousy that the relations between that once constitutional force, the militia, and the sovereign were rigidly guarded, and it was carefully placed under local influences. All this is changed. We have a standing army of large amount, quartered and brigaded and encamped permanently in England, and fed by a considerable and constantly increasing reserve.

It will in due time be officered by a class of men eminently scientific, but with no relations necessarily with society; while the militia is withdrawn from all local influences, and placed under the immediate command of the Secretary of War. Thus, in the nineteenth century, we have a large standing army established in England, contrary to all the traditions of the land, and that by a Liberal government, and with the warm acclamations of the Liberal party.

Let us look what they have done with the Admiralty. You remember, in this country especially, the denunciations of the profligate expenditure of the Conservative government, and you have since had an opportunity of comparing it with the gentler burden of Liberal estimates. The navy was not merely an instance of profligate expenditure, but of incompetent and inadequate management. A great revolution was promised in its administration. A gentleman [Mr. Childers], almost unknown to English politics, was strangely preferred to one of the highest places in the councils of her Majesty. He set to at his task with ruthless activity. The Consultative Council, under which Nelson had gained all his victories, was dissolved. The secretaryship of the Admiralty, an office which exercised a complete supervision over every division of that great department,—an office which was to the Admiralty what the Secretary of State is to the kingdom,—which, in the qualities which it required and the duties which it fulfilled, was rightly a stepping-stone to the cabinet, as in the instances of Lord Halifax, Lord Herbert, and many others,—was reduced to absolute insignificance. Even the office of Control, which of all others required a position of independence, and on which the safety of the navy mainly depended, was deprived of all its important attributes. For two years the opposition called the attention of Parliament to these destructive changes, but Parliament and the nation were alike insensible. Full of other business, they could not give a thought to what they looked upon merely as captious criticism. It requires a great disaster to command the attention of England; and when

the Captain was lost, and when they had the detail of the perilous voyage of the Megara, then public indignation demanded a complete change in this renovating administration of the navy.

And what has occurred? It is only a few weeks since that in the House of Commons I heard the naval statement made by a new First Lord [Mr. Goschen], and it consisted only of the rescinding of all the revolutionary changes of his predecessor, the mischief of every one of which during the last two years has been pressed upon the attention of Parliament and the country by that constitutional and necessary body, the Opposition. Gentlemen, it will not do for me—considering the time I have already occupied, and there are still some subjects of importance that must be touched—to dwell upon any of the other similar topics, of which there is a rich abundance. I doubt not there is in this hall more than one farmer who has been alarmed by the suggestion that his agricultural machinery should be taxed.

I doubt not there is in this hall more than one publican who remembers that last year an act of Parliament was introduced to denounce him as a "sinner." I doubt not there are in this hall a widow and an orphan who remember the profligate proposition to plunder their lonely heritage. But, gentlemen, as time advanced it was not difficult to perceive that extravagance was being substituted for energy by the government. The unnatural stimulus was subsiding. Their paroxysms ended in prostration. Some took refuge in melancholy, and their eminent chief alternated between a menace and a sigh. As I sat opposite the treasury bench the ministers reminded me of one of those marine landscapes not very unusual on the coast of South America. You behold a range of exhausted volcanoes. Not a flame flickers on a single pallid crest. But the situation is still dangerous. There are occasional earthquakes, and ever and anon the dark rumbling of the sea.

But, gentlemen, there is one other topic on which I must touch. If the management of our domestic affairs has been founded upon a principle of violence, that certainly cannot be alleged against the management of our external relations. I know the difficulty of addressing a body of Englishmen on these topics. The very phrase "Foreign Affairs" makes an Englishman convinced that I am about to treat of subjects with which he has no concern. Unhappily the relations of England to the rest of the world, which are "Foreign Affairs," are the matters which

most influence his lot. Upon them depends the increase or reduction of taxation. Upon them depends the enjoyment or the embarrassment of his industry. And yet, though so momentous are the consequences of the mismanagement of our foreign relations, no one thinks of them till the mischief occurs and then it is found how the most vital consequences have been occasioned by mere inadvertence.

I will illustrate this point by two anecdotes. Since I have been in public life there has been for this country a great calamity and there is a great danger, and both might have been avoided. The calamity was the Crimean War. You know what were the consequences of the Crimean War: A great addition to your debt, an enormous addition to your taxation, a cost more precious than your treasure—the best blood of England. Half a million of men, I believe, perished in that great undertaking. Nor are the evil consequences of that war adequately described by what I have said. All the disorders and disturbances of Europe, those immense armaments that are an incubus on national industry and the great obstacle to progressive civilization, may be traced and justly attributed to the Crimean War. And yet the Crimean War need never have occurred.

When Lord Derby acceded to office, against his own wishes, in 1852, the Liberal party most unconstitutionally forced him to dissolve Parliament at a certain time by stopping the supplies, or at least by limiting the period for which they were voted. There was not a single reason to justify that course, for Lord Derby had only accepted office, having once declined it, on the renewed application of his sovereign. The country, at the dissolution, increased the power of the Conservative party, but did not give to Lord Derby a majority, and he had to retire from power. There was not the slightest chance of a Crimean War when he retired from office; but the Emperor of Russia, believing that the successor of Lord Derby was no enemy to Russian aggression in the East, commenced those proceedings, with the result of which you are familiar. I speak of what I know, not of what I believe, but of what I have evidence in my possession to prove—that the Crimean War never would have happened if Lord Derby had remained in office.

The great danger is the present state of our relations with the United States. When I acceded to office I did so, so far as regarded the United States of America, with some advantage.

During the whole of the Civil War in America both my noble friend near me and I had maintained a strict and fair neutrality. This was fully appreciated by the government of the United States, and they expressed their wish that with our aid the settlement of all differences between the two governments should be accomplished. They sent here a plenipotentiary, an honorable gentleman, very intelligent and possessing general confidence. My noble friend near me, with great ability, negotiated a treaty for the settlement of all these claims. He was the first minister who proposed to refer them to arbitration, and the treaty was signed by the American government. It was signed, I think, on November 10th, on the eve of the dissolution of Parliament. The borough elections that first occurred proved what would be the fate of the ministry, and the moment they were known in America the American government announced that Mr. Reverdy Johnson, the American minister, had mistaken his instructions, and they could not present the treaty to the Senate for its sanction—the sanction of which there had been previously no doubt.

But the fact is that, as in the case of the Crimean War, it was supposed that our successors would be favorable to Russian aggression, so it was supposed that by the accession to office of Mr. Gladstone and a gentleman you know well, Mr. Bright, the American claims would be considered in a very different spirit. How they have been considered is a subject which, no doubt, occupies deeply the minds of the people of Lancashire. Now, gentlemen, observe this—the question of the Black Sea involved in the Crimean War, the question of the American claims involved in our negotiations with Mr. Johnson, are the two questions that have again turned up, and have been the two great questions that have been under the management of his government.

How have they treated them? Prince Gortschakoff, thinking he saw an opportunity, announced his determination to break from the Treaty of Paris, and terminate all the conditions hostile to Russia which had been the result of the Crimean War. What was the first movement on the part of our government is at present a mystery. This we know, that they selected the most rising diplomatist of the day and sent him to Prince Bismarck with a declaration that the policy of Russia, if persisted in, was war with England. Now, gentlemen, there was not the slightest chance of Russia going to war with England, and no necessity, as I shall always maintain, of England going to war with Russia. I believe I am not wrong in stating that the Russian government was prepared to withdraw from the position they had rashly taken; but suddenly her Majesty's government, to use a technical phrase, threw over the plenipotentiary, and, instead of threatening war, if the Treaty of Paris were violated, agreed to arrangements by which the violation of that treaty should be sanctioned by England, and, in the form of a congress, showed themselves guaranteeing their own humiliation. That Mr. Odo Russell made no mistake is quite obvious, because he has since been selected to be her Majesty's ambassador at the most important court of Europe. Gentlemen, what will be the consequence of this extraordinary weakness on the part of the British government it is difficult to foresee. Already we hear that Sebastopol is to be refortified, nor can any man doubt that the entire command of the Black Sea will soon be in the possession of Russia. The time may not be distant when we may hear of the Russian power in the Persian Gulf, and what effect that may have upon the dominions of England and upon those possessions on the productions of which you every year more and more depend, are questions upon which it will be well for you on proper occasions to meditate.

I come now to that question which most deeply interests you at this moment, and that is our relations with the United States. I approved the government referring this question to arbitration. It was only following the policy of Lord Stanley. My noble friend disapproved the negotiations being carried on at Washington. I confess that I would willingly have persuaded myself that this was not a mistake, but reflection has convinced me that my noble friend was right. I remember the successful negotiation of the Clayton-Bulwer treaty by Sir Henry Bulwer. I flattered myself that treaties at Washington might be successfully negotiated; but I agree with my noble friend that his general view was far more sound than my own. But no one, when that commission was sent forth, for a moment could anticipate the course of its conduct under the strict injunctions of the government. We believed that commission was sent to ascertain what points should be submitted to arbitration, to be decided by the principles of the law of nations. We had not the slightest idea that that commission was sent with power and instructions to alter the law of nations itself. When that result was announced, we expressed our entire disapprobation; and yet

trusting to the representations of the government that matters were concluded satisfactorily, we had to decide whether it were wise, if the great result was obtained, to wrangle upon points, however important, such as those to which I have referred.

Gentlemen, it appears that, though all parts of England were ready to make those sacrifices, the two negotiating States—the government of the United Kingdom and the government of the United States—placed a different interpretation upon the treaty when the time had arrived to put its provisions into practice. Gentlemen, in my mind, and in the opinion of my noble friend near me, there was but one course to take under the circumstances, painful as it might be, and that was at once to appeal to the good feeling and good sense of the United States, and, stating the difficulty, to invite confidential conference whether it might not be removed. But her Majesty's government took a different course. On December 15th her Majesty's government were aware of a contrary interpretation being placed on the Treaty of Washington by the American government. The prime minister received a copy of their counter case, and he confessed he had never read it. He had a considerable number of copies sent to him to distribute among his colleagues, and you remember, probably, the remarkable statement in which he informed the house that he had distributed those copies to everybody except those for whom they were intended.

Time went on, and the adverse interpretation of the American government oozed out, and was noticed by the press. Public alarm and public indignation were excited; and it was only seven weeks afterward, on the very eve of the meeting of Parliament,—some twenty-four hours before the meeting of Parliament,—that her Majesty's government felt they were absolutely obliged to make a "friendly communication" to the United States that they had arrived at an interpretation of the treaty the reverse of that of the American government. What was the position of the American government? Seven weeks had passed without their having received the slightest intimation from her Majesty's ministers. They had circulated their case throughout the world. They had translated it into every European language. It had been sent to every court and cabinet, to every sovereign and prime minister. It was impossible for the American government to recede from their position, even if they had believed it to be an erroneous one. And then, to aggravate the difficulty,

the prime minister goes down to Parliament, declares that there is only one interpretation to be placed on the treaty, and defies and attacks everybody who believes it susceptible of another.

Was there ever such a combination of negligence and blundering? And now, gentlemen, what is about to happen? All we know is that her Majesty's ministers are doing everything in their power to evade the cognizance and criticism of Parliament. They have received an answer to their "friendly communication"; of which, I believe, it has been ascertained that the American government adhere to their interpretation; and yet they prolong the controversy. What is about to occur it is unnecessary for one to predict; but if it be this—if after a fruitless ratiocination worthy of a schoolman, we ultimately agree so far to the interpretation of the American government as to submit the whole case to arbitration, with feeble reservation of a protest, if it be decided against us, I venture to say that we shall be entering on a course not more distinguished by its feebleness than by its impending peril. There is before us every prospect of the same incompetence that distinguished our negotiations respecting the independence of the Black Sea; and I fear that there is every chance that this incompetence will be sealed by our ultimately acknowledging these direct claims of the United States, which, both as regards principle and practical results, are fraught with the utmost danger to this country. Gentlemen, don't suppose, because I counsel firmness and decision at the right moment, that I am of that school of statesmen who are favorable to a turbulent and aggressive diplomacy. I have resisted it during a great part of my life. I am not unaware that the relations of England to Europe have undergone a vast change during the century that has just elapsed. The relations of England to Europe are not the same as they were in the days of Lord Chatham or Frederick the Great. The Queen of England has become the sovereign of the most powerful of Oriental States. On the other side of the globe there are now establishments belonging to her, teeming with wealth and population, which will, in due time, exercise their influence over the distribution of power. The old establishments of this country, now the United States of America, throw their lengthening shades over the Atlantic, which mix with European waters. These are vast and novel elements in the distribution of power. I acknowledge that the policy of England with respect to Europe should be

a policy of reserve, but proud reserve; and in answer to those statesmen—those mistaken statesmen who have intimated the decay of the power of England and the decline of its resources, I express here my confident conviction that there never was a moment in our history when the power of England was so great and her resources so vast and inexhaustible.

And yet, gentlemen, it is not merely our fleets and armies, our powerful artillery, our accumulated capital, and our unlimited credit on which I so much depend, as upon that unbroken spirit of her people, which I believe was never prouder of the imperial country to which they belong. Gentlemen, it is to that spirit that I above all things trust. I look upon the people of Lancashire as fairly representative of the people of England. I think the manner in which they have invited me here, locally a stranger, to receive the expression of their cordial sympathy, and only because they recognize some effort on my part to maintain the greatness of their country, is evidence of the spirit of the land. I must express to you again my deep sense of the generous manner in which you have welcomed me, and in which you have permitted me to express to you my views upon public affairs. Proud of your confidence, and encouraged by your sympathy, I now deliver to you, as my last words, the cause of the Tory party, of the English constitution, and of the British empire.

THE VENERABLE BEDE

(672–735)

THE VENERABLE BEDE, "The father of English literature," was born about 672 in the county of Durham. The Anglo-Saxons, whose earliest historian he was, had been converted by St. Austin and others by the then not unusual process of preaching to the king until he was persuaded to renounce heathenism both for himself and his subjects. Bede, though born among a people not greatly addicted either to religion or letters, became a remarkable preacher, scholar, and thinker. Professionally a preacher, his sermons are interesting, chiefly because they are the earliest specimens of oratory extant from any Anglo-Saxon public speaker.

Best known as the author of the 'Ecclesiastical History of England,' Bede was a most prolific writer. He left a very considerable collection of sermons or homilies, many of which are still extant. He also wrote on science, on poetic art, on medicine, philosophy, and rhetoric, not to mention his hymns and his 'Book of Epigrams in Heroic and Elegaic Verse'—all very interesting and some of them valuable, as any one may see who will take the trouble to read them in his simple and easily understood Latin. It is a pity, however, that they are not adequately translated and published in a shape which would make the father of English eloquence the first English rhetorician, as he was the first English philosopher, poet, and historian, more readily accessible to the general public.

Bede's sermons deal very largely in allegory, and though he may have been literal in his celebrated suggestions of the horrors of hell—which were certainly literally understood by his hearers—it is pertinent to quote in connection with them his own assertion, that "he who knows how to interpret allegorically will see that the inner sense excels the simplicity of the letter as apples do leaves."

Bede's reputation spread not only through England but throughout Western Europe and to Rome. Attempts were made to thrust honors on him, but he refused them for fear they would prevent him from learning. He taught in a monastery at Jarrow where at one time he had six hundred monks and many strangers attending on his discourses.

He died in 735, just as he had completed the first translation of the Gospel of John ever made into any English dialect. The present

Anglo-Saxon version, generally in use among English students, is supposed to include that version if not actually to present its exact language. The King James version comes from Bede's in a direct line of descent through Wycliff and Tyndale.

THE MEETING OF MERCY AND JUSTICE

THERE was a certain father of a family, a powerful king, who had four daughters, of whom one was called Mercy, the second Truth, the third Justice, the fourth Peace; of whom it is said, "Mercy and Truth are met together; Justice and Peace have kissed each other." He had also a certain most wise son, to whom no one could be compared in wisdom. He had, also, a certain servant, whom he had exalted and enriched with great honor: for he had made him after his own likeness and similitude, and that without any preceding merit on the servant's part. But the Lord, as is the custom with such wise masters, wished prudently to explore, and to become acquainted with, the character and the faith of his servant, whether he were trustworthy towards himself or not; so he gave him an easy commandment, and said, "If you do what I tell you, I will exalt you to further honors; if not, you shall perish miserably."

The servant heard the commandment, and without any delay went and broke it. Why need I say more? Why need I delay you by my words and by my tears? This proud servant, stiff-necked, full of contumely, and puffed up with conceit, sought an excuse for his transgression, and retorted the whole fault on his Lord. For when he said, "the woman whom thou gavest to be with me, she deceived me," he threw all the fault on his Maker. His Lord, more angry for such contumelious conduct than for the transgression of his command, called four most cruel executioners, and commanded one of them to cast him into prison, another to afflict him with grievous torments; the third to strangle him, and the fourth to behead him. By and by, when occasion offers, I will give you the right name of these tormentors.

These torturers, then, studying how they might carry out their own cruelty, took the wretched man and began to afflict him with all manner of punishments. But one of the daughters of the King, by name Mercy, when she had heard of this punishment of the servant, ran hastily to the prison, and looking in and

seeing the man given over to the tormentors, could not help having compassion upon him, for it is the property of Mercy to have pity. She tore her garments and struck her hands together, and let her hair fall loose about her neck, and crying and shrieking, ran to her father, and kneeling before his feet began to say with an earnest and sorrowful voice: "My beloved father, am not I thy daughter Mercy? and art not thou called merciful? If thou art merciful, have mercy upon thy servant; and if thou wilt not have mercy upon him, thou canst not be called merciful; and if thou art not merciful, thou canst not have me, Mercy, for thy daughter." While she was thus arguing with her father, her sister Truth came up, and demanded why it was that Mercy was weeping. "Your sister Mercy," replied the father, "wishes me to have pity upon that proud transgressor whose punishment I have appointed." Truth, when she heard this, was excessively angry, and looking sternly at her father, "Am not I," said she, "thy daughter Truth? art not thou called true? Is it not true that thou didst fix a punishment for him, and threaten him with death by torments? If thou art true, thou wilt follow that which is true; if thou art not true, thou canst not have me, Truth, for thy daughter." Here, you see, Mercy and Truth are met together. The third sister, namely, Justice, hearing this strife, contention, quarreling, and pleading, and summoned by the outcry, began to inquire the cause from Truth. And Truth, who could only speak that which was true, said, "This sister of ours, Mercy, if she ought to be called a sister who does not agree with us, desires that our father should have pity on that proud transgressor." Then Justice, with an angry countenance, and meditating on a grief which she had not expected, said to her father, "Am not I thy daughter Justice? are thou not called just? If thou art just, thou wilt exercise justice on the transgressor; if thou dost not exercise that justice, thou canst not be just; if thou art not just, thou canst not have me, Justice, for thy daughter." So here were Truth and Justice on the one side, and Mercy on the other. *Ultima coelicolum terras Astræa reliquit ;* this means, that Peace fled into a far distant country. For where there is strife and contention, there is no peace; and by how much greater the contention, by so much further peace is driven away.

Peace, therefore, being lost, and his three daughters in warm discussion, the King found it an extremely difficult matter to determine what he should do, or to which side he should lean.

For, if he gave ear to Mercy, he would offend Truth and Justice; if he gave ear to Truth and Justice, he could not have Mercy for his daughter; and yet it was necessary that he should be both merciful and just, and peaceful and true. There was great need then of good advice. The father, therefore, called his wise son, and consulted him about the affair. Said the son, "Give me, my father, this present business to manage, and I will both punish the transgressor for thee, and will bring back to thee in peace thy four daughters." "These are great promises," replied the father, "if the deed only agrees with the word. If thou canst do that which thou sayest, I will act as thou shalt exhort me."

Having, therefore, received the royal mandate, the son took his sister Mercy along with him, and leaping upon the mountains, passing over the hills, came to the prison, and looking through the windows, looking through the lattice, he beheld the imprisoned servant, shut out from the present life, devoured of affliction, and from the sole of his foot even to the crown there was no soundness in him. He saw him in the power of death, because through him death entered into the world. He saw him devoured, because, when a man is once dead he is eaten of worms. And because I now have the opportunity of telling you, you shall hear the names of the four tormentors. The first, who put him in prison, is the Prison of the Present Life, of which it is said, "Woe is me that I am constrained to dwell in Mesech"; the second, who tormented him, is the Misery of the World, which besets us with all kinds of pain and wretchedness; the third, who was putting him to death, conquered death, bound the strong man, took his goods, and distributed the spoils; and ascending up on high, led captivity captive and gave gifts for men, and brought back the servant into his country, crowned with double honor, and endued with a garment of immortality. When Mercy beheld this, she had no grounds for complaint, Truth found no cause of discontent, because her father was found true. The servant had paid all his penalties. Justice in like manner complained not, because justice had been executed on the transgressor; and thus he who had been lost was found. Peace, therefore, when she saw her sisters at concord, came back and united them. And now, behold, Mercy and Truth are met together, Justice and Peace have kissed each other. Thus, therefore, by the Mediator of man and angels, man was purified and reconciled, and the hundredth sheep was brought back to the fold of God. To which

fold Jesus Christ brings us, to whom is honor and power everlasting. Amen.

A SERMON FOR ANY DAY

BELOVED BRETHREN, it is time to pass from evil to good, from
darkness to light, from this most unfaithful world to everlasting joys, lest that day take us unawares in which our
Lord Jesus Christ shall come to make the round world a desert,
and to give over to everlasting punishment sinners who would
not repent of the sins which they did. There is a great sin in
lying, as saith Solomon, "The lips which lie slay the soul. The
wrath of man worketh not the righteousness of God," no more
doth his covetousness. Whence the Apostle saith, "The love of
money and pride are the root of all evil." Pride, by which that
apostate angel fell, who, as it is read in the prophecy, "despised
the beginning of the ways of God. How art thou fallen from
heaven!" We must avoid pride, which had power to deceive
angels; how much more will it have power to deceive men! And
we ought to fear envy, by which the devil deceived the first
man, as it is written, "Christ was crucified through envy, therefore he that envieth his neighbor crucifieth Christ."

See that ye always expect the advent of the Judge with fear
and trembling, lest he should find us unprepared; because the
Apostle saith, "My days shall come as a thief in the night."
Woe to them whom it shall find sleeping in sins, for "then," as
we read in the Gospel, "He shall gather all nations, and shall
separate them one from the other, as a shepherd divideth the
sheep from the goats. Then shall the King say unto them on
his right hand, Come, ye blessed of my Father," where there
is no grief nor sorrow; where there is no other sound but love,
and peace, and everlasting gladness with all the elect of God;
where no good thing can be wanting. Then shall the righteous
answer and say, Lord, why hast thou prepared such glory and
such good things? He shall answer, for mercy, for faith, for
piety, and truth and the like. Lord, when didst thou see these
good things in us? The Lord shall answer, "Verily, I say unto
you, Inasmuch as ye have done it unto one of the least of these,
my brethren, ye have done it unto me, and what ye did in secret,
I will reward openly." Then shall the King say unto them
on his left hand, "Depart from me, ye cursed, into everlasting

fire, prepared for the devil and his angels, where shall be weeping and gnashing of teeth," and tears of eyes; where death is
desired and comes not; where the worm dieth not and the fire
is not quenched; where is no joy, but sorrow; where is no rest,
except pain; where nothing is heard but lamentations. Then
they also shall answer and say, Lord, why hast thou prepared
such punishments for us? For your iniquity and malignity, the
Lord shall say.

Therefore, my brethren, I beseech you, that they who are in
the habits of good works would persevere in every good work;
and that they who are evil would amend themselves quickly, before sudden death come upon them. While, therefore, we have
time, let us do good to all men, and let us leave off doing ill,
that we may attain to eternal life.

THE TORMENTS OF HELL

THE Sunday is a chosen day, in which the angels rejoice. We
must ask who was the first to request that souls might (on
Sunday) have rest in hell; and the answer is that Paul the
Apostle and Michael the Archangel besought the Lord when
they came back from hell; for it was the Lord's will that Paul
should see the punishments of that place. He beheld trees all
on fire, and sinners tormented on those trees; and some were
hung by the feet, some by the hands, some by the hair, some
by the neck, some by the tongue, and some by the arm. And
again, he saw a furnace of fire burning with seven flames, and
many were punished in it; and there were seven plagues round
about this furnace; the first, snow; the second, ice; the third,
fire, the fourth, blood; the fifth, serpents; the sixth, lightning;
the seventh, stench; and in that furnace itself were the souls of
the sinners who repented not in this life. There they are tormented, and every one receiveth according to his works; some
weep, some howl, some groan; some burn and desire to have
rest, but find it not, because souls can never die. Truly we
ought to fear that place in which is everlasting dolor, in which
is groaning, in which is sadness without joy, in which are abundance of tears on account of the tortures of souls; in which a
fiery wheel is turned a thousand times a day by an evil angel,
and at each turn a thousand souls are burnt upon it. After this
he beheld a horrible river, in which were many diabolic beasts,

like fishes in the midst of the sea, which devour the souls of sinners; and over that river there is a bridge, across which righteous souls pass without dread, while the souls of sinners suffer
each one according to its merits.

There Paul beheld many souls of sinners plunged, some to
the knees, some to the loins, some to the mouth, some to the
eyebrows; and every day and eternally they are tormented. And
Paul wept, and asked who they were that were therein plunged
to the knees. And the angel said, These are detractors and evil
speakers; and those up to the loins are fornicators and adulter-
ers, who returned not to repentance; and those to the mouth are
they who went to Church, but they heard not the word of God;
and those to the eyebrows are they who rejoiced in the wickedness of their neighbor. And after this, he saw between heaven
and earth the soul of a sinner, howling betwixt seven devils, that
had on that day departed from the body. And the angels cried
out against it and said, Woe to thee, wretched soul! What hast
thou done upon earth? Thou hast despised the commandments
of God, and hast done no good works; and therefore thou shalt
be cast into outer darkness, where shall be weeping and gnashing of teeth. And after this, in one moment, angels carried a
soul from its body to heaven; and Paul heard the voice of a
thousand angels rejoicing over it, and saying, O most happy and
blessed soul! rejoice to-day, because thou hast done the will of
God. And they set it in the presence of God. . . . And
the angel said, Whoso keepeth the Sunday shall have his part
with the angels of God. And Paul demanded of the angel, how
many kinds of punishment there were in hell. And the angel
said, there are a hundred and forty-four thousand, and if there
were a hundred eloquent men, each having four iron tongues,
that spoke from the beginning of the world, they could not reckon
up the torments of hell. But let us, beloved brethren, hearing
of these so great torments, be converted to our Lord that we
may be able to reign with the angels.

HENRY WARD BEECHER

(1813–1887)

 VERY great orator must be a thoroughly representative man,
sensitive enough to be moved to the depths of his nature
by the master-passions of his time. Henry Ward Beecher
was a very great orator,—one of the greatest the country has produced,—and in his speeches and orations inspired by the feelings
which evolved the Civil War and were themselves exaggerated by it
to tenfold strength, we feel all the volcanic forces which buried the
primitive political conditions of the United States deep under the
ashes and lava of their eruption. Words are feeble in the presence
of the facts of such a war. But what more could words do to suggest its meaning than they do in Mr. Beecher's oration on the raising of the flag at Fort Sumter, April 14th, 1865:—

"The soil has drunk blood and is glutted. Millions mourn for myriads
slain, or, envying the dead, pray for oblivion. Towns and villages have been
razed. Fruitful fields have been turned back to wilderness. It came to pass
as the prophet had said: 'The sun was turned to darkness and the moon to
blood.' The course of the law was ended. The sword sat chief magistrate
in half the nation; industry was paralyzed; morals corrupted; the public weal
invaded by rapine and anarchy; whole States were ravaged by avenging
armies. The world was amazed. The earth reeled."

In such passages, Mr. Beecher has something of the force which
immortalized the "Voluspa." The "bardic inspiration," which moved
the early Norse poets to sing the bloody results of the "Berserker
fury," peculiar to the Teutonic and Norse peoples, seems to control
him as he recounts the dreadful features of the war and reminds
the vanquished of the meaning of defeat.

In considering the oratory inspired by the passions which found
their climax in the destructiveness of civil war,—and especially in
considering such magnificent outbursts as Mr. Beecher's oration at
Fort Sumter, intelligence will seek to free itself alike from sympathy and from prejudice that it may the better judge the effect of the
general mind of the people on the orator, and the extent to which
that general mind as he voiced it, was influenced by the strength
of his individuality. If when we ourselves are moved by no passion
we judge with critical calmness the impassioned utterances of the

orators of any great epoch of disturbance, we can hardly fail to be repelled by much that the critical faculties will reject as exaggeration. But taking into account the environment, the traditions, the public opinion, the various general or individual impulses which influenced the oratory of one side or the other, we can the better determine its true relation to the history of the human intellect and that forward movement of the world which is but a manifestation of the education of intellect.

Mr. Beecher had the temperament, the habits, the physique of the orator. His ancestry, his intellectual training, his surroundings, fitted him to be a prophet of the crusade against slavery. Of those names which for a time were bruited everywhere as a result of the struggles of the three decades from 1850 to 1880, a majority are already becoming obscure, and in another generation most of the rest will be "names only" to all who are not students of history as a specialty. But the mind in Henry Ward Beecher was so representative, he was so fully mastered by the forces which sent Sherman on his march to the sea and Grant to his triumph at Appomattox, that he will always be remembered as one of the greatest orators of the Civil War period. Perhaps when the events of the war are so far removed in point of time as to make a critical judgment really possible, he may even rank as the greatest.

RAISING THE FLAG OVER FORT SUMTER

(Delivered April 14th, 1865, by request of President Lincoln)

ON THIS solemn and joyful day we again lift to the breeze our fathers' flag, now again the banner of the United States, with the fervent prayer that God will crown it with honor, protect it from treason, and send it down to our children, with all the blessings of civilization, liberty, and religion. Terrible in battle, may it be beneficent in peace. Happily, no bird or beast of prey has been inscribed upon it. The stars that redeem the night from darkness, and the beams of red light that beautify the morning, have been united upon its folds. As long as the sun endures, or the stars, may it wave over a nation neither enslaved nor enslaving! Once, and but once, has treason dishonored it. In that insane hour when the guiltiest and bloodiest rebellion of all time hurled their fires upon this fort, you, sir [turning to General Anderson], and a small, heroic band, stood within these now crumbled walls, and did gallant and just battle for the honor and defense of the nation's banner. In that cope of fire,

that glorious flag still peacefully waved to the breeze above your head, unconscious of harm as the stars and skies above it. Once it was shot down. A gallant hand, in whose care this day it has been, plucked it from the ground, and reared it again—"cast down, but not destroyed." After a vain resistance, with trembling hand and sad heart, you withdrew it from its height, closed its wings, and bore it far away, sternly to sleep amid the tumults of rebellion, and the thunder of battle. The first act of war had begun. The long night of four years had set in. While the giddy traitors whirled in a maze of exhilaration, dim horrors were already advancing, that were ere long to fill the land with blood. To-day you are returned again. We devoutly join with you in thanksgiving to Almighty God that he has spared your honored life, and vouchsafed to you the glory of this day. The heavens over you are the same, the same shores are here, morning comes, and evening, as they did. All else, how changed! What grim batteries crowd the burdened shores! What scenes have filled this air, and disturbed these waters! These shattered heaps of shapeless stone are all that is left of Fort Sumter. Desolation broods in yonder city—solemn retribution hath avenged our dishonored banner! You have come back with honor, who departed hence four years ago, leaving the air sultry with fanaticism. The surging crowds that rolled up their frenzied shouts as the flag came down, are dead, or scattered, or silent, and their habitations are desolate. Ruin sits in the cradle of treason. Rebellion has perished. But there flies the same flag that was insulted. With starry eyes it looks over this bay for the banner that supplanted it, and sees it not. You that then, for the day, were humbled, are here again, to triumph once and forever. In the storm of that assault this glorious ensign was often struck; but, memorable fact, not one of its stars was torn out by shot or shell. It was a prophecy. It said: "Not a State shall be struck from this nation by treason!" The fulfillment is at hand. Lifted to the air to-day, it proclaims that after four years of war, "Not a State is blotted out." Hail to the flag of our fathers, and our flag! Glory to the banner that has gone through four years black with tempests of war, to pilot the nation back to peace without dismemberment! And glory be to God, who, above all hosts and banners, hath ordained victory, and shall ordain peace. Wherefore have we come hither, pilgrims from distant places? Are we come to exult that Northern hands are stronger than Southern?

No; but to rejoice that the hands of those who defend a just and beneficent government are mightier than the hands that assaulted it. Do we exult over fallen cities? We exult that a nation has not fallen. We sorrow with the sorrowful. We sympathize with the desolate. We look upon this shattered fort and yonder dilapidated city with sad eyes, grieved that men should have committed such treason, and glad that God hath set such a mark upon treason that all ages shall dread and abhor it. We exult, not for a passion gratified, but for a sentiment victorious; not for temper, but for conscience; not, as we devoutly believe, that our will is done, but that God's will hath been done. We should be unworthy of that liberty intrusted to our care, if, on such a day as this, we sullied our hearts by feelings of aimless vengeance; and equally unworthy if we did not devoutly thank him who hath said: "Vengeance is mine, I will repay, saith the Lord," that he hath set a mark upon arrogant rebellion, ineffaceable while time lasts.

Since this flag went down on that dark day, who shall tell the mighty woes that have made this land a spectacle to angels and men? The soil has drunk blood and is glutted. Millions mourn for myriads slain, or, envying the dead, pray for oblivion. Towns and villages have been razed. Fruitful fields have been turned back to wilderness. It came to pass, as the prophet said: "The sun was turned to darkness and the moon to blood." The course of law was ended. The sword sat chief magistrate in half the nation; industry was paralyzed; morals corrupted; the public weal invaded by rapine and anarchy; whole States ravaged by avenging armies. The world was amazed. The earth reeled. When the flag sunk here, it was as if political night had come, and all beasts of prey had come forth to devour. That long night is ended. And for this returning day we have come from afar to rejoice and give thanks. No more war. No more accursed secession. No more slavery, that spawned them both. Let no man misread the meaning of this unfolding flag! It says: "Government has returned hither." It proclaims, in the name of vindicated government, peace and protection to loyalty, humiliation and pains to traitors. This is the flag of sovereignty. The nation, not the States, is sovereign. Restored to authority, this flag commands, not supplicates. There may be pardon, but no concession. There may be amnesty and oblivion, but no honeyed compromises. The nation to-day has peace for the peaceful, and

war for the turbulent. The only condition to submission is to submit! There is the Constitution, there are the laws, there is the government. They rise up like mountains of strength that shall not be moved. They are the conditions of peace. One nation, under one government, without slavery, has been ordained, and shall stand. There can be peace on no other basis. On this basis reconstruction is easy, and needs neither architect nor engineer. Without this basis no engineer nor architect shall ever reconstruct these rebellious States. We do not want your cities or your fields. We do not envy you your prolific soil, nor heavens full of perpetual summer. Let agriculture revel here; let manufactures make every stream twice musical; build fleets in every port; inspire the arts of peace with genius second only to that of Athens, and we shall be glad in your gladness, and rich in your wealth. All that we ask is unswerving loyalty and universal liberty. And that, in the name of this high sovereignty of the United States of America, we demand; and that, with the blessing of Almighty God, we will have! We raise our fathers' banner that it may bring back better blessings than those of old; that it may cast out the devil of discord; that it may restore lawful government, and a prosperity purer and more enduring than that which it protected before; that it may win parted friends from their alienation; that it may inspire hope, and inaugurate universal liberty; that it may say to the sword, "Return to thy sheath"; and to the plow and sickle, "Go forth"; that it may heal all jealousies, unite all policies, inspire a new national life, compact our strength, purify our principles, ennoble our national ambitions, and make this people great and strong, not for agression and quarrelsomeness, but for the peace of the world, giving to us the glorious prerogative of leading all nations to juster laws, to more humane policies, to sincerer friendship, to rational, instituted civil liberty, and to universal Christian brotherhood. Reverently, piously, in hopeful patriotism, we spread this banner on the sky, as of old the bow was painted on the cloud, and, with solemn fervor, beseech God to look upon it, and make it a memorial of an everlasting covenant and decree that never again on this fair land shall a deluge of blood prevail. Why need any eye turn from this spectacle? Are there not associations which, overleaping the recent past, carry us back to times when, over North and South, this flag was honored alike by all? In all our colonial days we were one; in the long revolutionary struggle, and in the scores of prosperous years succeeding, we were united. When the passage of the Stamp Act in 1765 aroused the colonies, it was Gadsden, of South Carolina, that cried, with prescient enthusiasm, "We stand on the broad common ground of those natural rights that we all feel and know as men. There ought to be no New England man, no New Yorker, known on this continent, but all of us," said he, "Americans." That was the voice of South Carolina. That shall be the voice of South Carolina. Faint is the echo; but it is coming. We now hear it sighing sadly through the pines; but it shall yet break in thunder upon the shore. No North, no West, no South, but the United States of America. There is scarcely a man born in the South who has lifted his hand against this banner but had a father who would have died for it. Is memory dead? Is there no historic pride? Has a fatal fury struck blindness or hate into eyes that used to look kindly towards each other, that read the same Bible, that hung over the historic pages of our national glory, that studied the same Constitution? Let this uplifting bring back all of the past that was good, but leave in darkness all that was bad. It was never before so wholly unspotted; so clear of all wrong, so purely and simply the sign of justice and liberty. Did I say that we brought back the same banner that you bore away, noble and heroic sir? It is not the same. It is more and better than it was. The land is free from slavery since that banner fell.

When God would prepare Moses for emancipation, he overthrew his first steps and drove him for forty years to brood in the wilderness. When our flag came down, four years it lay brooding in darkness. It cried to the Lord, "Wherefore am I deposed?" Then arose before it a vision of its sin. It had strengthened the strong, and forgotten the weak. It proclaimed liberty, but trod upon slaves. In that seclusion it dedicated itself to liberty. Behold, to-day, it fulfills its vows! When it went down four million people had no flag. To-day it rises, and four million people cry out, "Behold our flag!" Hark! they murmur. It is the Gospel that they recite in sacred words: "It is a Gospel to the poor, it heals our broken hearts, it preaches deliverance to captives, it gives sight to the blind, it sets at liberty them that are bruised." Rise up then, glorious Gospel banner, and roll out these messages of God. Tell the air that not a spot now sullies thy whiteness. Thy red is not the blush of shame, but the flush of joy. Tell the dews that wash thee that thou art as pure as

you that the State, by a mere amnesty and benevolence of government, can be put again, by a mere decree, in its old place. It would not be honest, it would not be kind or fraternal, for me to pretend that Southern revolution against the Union has not reacted, and wrought revolution in the Southern States themselves, and inaugurated a new dispensation. Society here is like a broken loom, and the piece which Rebellion put in, and was weaving, has been cut, and every thread broken. You must put in new warp and new woof, and weaving anew, as the fabric slowly unwinds we shall see in it no Gorgon figures, no hideous grotesques of the old barbarism, but the figures of liberty, vines, and golden grains, framing in the heads of justice, love, and liberty. The august convention of 1787 formed the Constitution with this memorable preamble: "We, the people of the United States, in order to form a more perfect union, establish justice, insure domestic tranquillity, provide for the common defense, promote the general welfare, and secure the blessings of liberty to ourselves and our posterity, do ordain this Constitution for the United States of America." Again, in the awful convention of war, the people of the United States, for the very ends just recited, have debated, settled, and ordained certain fundamental truths, which must henceforth be accepted and obeyed. Nor is any State nor any individual wise who shall disregard them. They are to civil affairs what the natural laws are to health—indispensable conditions of peace and happiness. What are the ordinances given by the people, speaking out of fire and darkness of war, with authority inspired by that same God who gave the law from Sinai amid thunders and trumpet voices? 1. That these United States shall be one and indivisible. 2. That States have not absolute sovereignty, and have no right to dismember the Republic. 3. That universal liberty is indispensable to republican government, and that slavery shall be utterly and forever abolished.

Such are the results of war! These are the best fruits of the war. They are worth all they have cost. They are foundations of peace. They will secure benefits to all nations as well as to ours. Our highest wisdom and duty is to accept the facts as the decrees of God. We are exhorted to forget all that has happened. Yes, the wrath, the conflict, the cruelty, but not those overruling decrees of God which this war has pronounced. As solemnly as on Mount Sinai, God says, "Remember! remember!" Hear it to-day. Under this sun, under that bright child of the

they. Say to the night that thy stars lead toward the morning; and to the morning, that a brighter day arises with healing in its wings. And then, O glowing flag, bid the sun pour light on all thy folds with double brightness while thou art bearing round and round the world the solemn joy—a race set free! a nation redeemed! The mighty hand of government, made strong in war by the favor of the God of Battles, spreads wide to-day the banner of liberty that went down in darkness, that arose in light; and there it streams, like the sun above it, neither parceled out nor monopolized, but flooding the air with light for all mankind. Ye scattered and broken, ye wounded and dying, bitten by the fiery serpents of oppression, everywhere, in all the world, look upon this sign, lifted up, and live! And ye homeless and houseless slaves, look, and ye are free! At length you, too, have part and lot in this glorious ensign that broods with impartial love over small and great, the poor and the strong, the bond and the free. In this solemn hour, let us pray for the quick coming of reconciliation and happiness under this common flag. But we must build again, from the foundations, in all these now free Southern States. No cheap exhortations "to forgetfulness of the past, to restore all things as they were," will do. God does not stretch out his hand, as he has for four dreadful years, that men may easily forget the might of his terrible acts. Restore things as they were! What, the alienations and jealousies, the discords and contentions, and the causes of them? No. In that solemn sacrifice on which a nation has offered for its sins so many precious victims, loved and lamented, let our sins and mistakes be consumed utterly and forever. No, never again shall things be restored as before the war. It is written in God's decree of events fulfilled, "Old things are passed away." That new earth, in which dwelleth righteousness, draws near. Things as they were! Who has an omnipotent hand to restore a million dead, slain in battle or wasted by sickness, or dying of grief, broken-hearted? Who has omniscience to search for the scattered ones? Who shall restore the lost to broken families? Who shall bring back the squandered treasure, the years of industry wasted, and convince you that four years of guilty rebellion and cruel war are no more than dirt upon the hand, which a moment's washing removes and leaves the hand clean as before? Such a war reaches down to the very vitals of society. Emerging from such a prolonged rebellion, he is blind who tells

sun, our banner, with the eyes of this nation and of the world upon us, we repeat the syllables of God's providence and recite the solemn decrees: No more Disunion! No more Secession! No more Slavery! Why did this civil war begin? We do not wonder that European statesmen failed to comprehend this conflict, and that foreign philanthropists were shocked at a murderous war that seemed to have no moral origin, but, like the brutal fights of beasts of prey, to have sprung from ferocious animalism. This great nation, filling all profitable latitudes, cradled between two oceans, with inexhaustible resources, with riches increasing in an unparalleled ratio, by agriculture, by manufactures, by commerce, with schools and churches, with books and newspapers thick as leaves in our own forests, with institutions sprung from the people, and peculiarly adapted to their genius; a nation not sluggish, but active, used to excitement, practiced in political wisdom, and accustomed to self-government, and all its vast outlying parts held together by the Federal government, mild in temper, gentle in administration, and beneficent in results, seemed to have been formed for peace. All at once, in this hemisphere of happiness and hope, there came trooping clouds with fiery bolts, full of death and desolation. At a cannon shot upon this fort, all the nation, as if it had been a trained army lying on its arms, awaiting a signal, rose up and began a war which, for awfulness, rises into the front rank of bad eminence. The front of the battle, going with the sun, was twelve hundred miles long; and the depth, measured along a meridian, was a thousand miles. In this vast area more than two million men, first and last, for four years, have, in skirmish, fight, and battle, met in more than a thousand conflicts; while a coast and river line, not less than four thousand miles in length, has swarmed with fleets freighted with artillery. The very industry of the country seemed to have been touched by some infernal wand, and, with sudden wheel, changed its front from peace to war. The anvils of the land beat like drums. As out of the ooze emerge monsters, so from our mines and foundries uprose new and strange machines of war, ironclad. And so, in a nation of peaceful habits, without external provocation, there arose such a storm of war as blackened the whole horizon and hemisphere. What wonder that foreign observers stood amazed at this fanatical fury, that seemed without Divine guidance, but inspired wholly with infernal frenzy. The explosion was sudden, but the train had long been laid. We must consider the condition of Southern society, if we would understand the mystery of this iniquity. Society in the South resolves itself into three divisions, more sharply distinguished than in any other part of the nation. At the base is the laboring class, made up of slaves. Next is the middle class, made up of traders, small farmers, and poor men. The lower edge of this class touches the slave, and the upper edge reaches up to the third and ruling class. This class was a small minority in numbers, but in practical ability they had centred in their hands the whole government of the South, and had mainly governed the country. Upon this polished, cultured, exceedingly capable, and wholly unprincipled class, rests the whole burden of this war. Forced up by the bottom heat of slavery, the ruling class in all the disloyal States arrogated to themselves a superiority not compatible with republican equality, nor with just morals. They claimed a right of pre-eminence. An evil prophet arose who trained these wild and luxuriant shoots of ambition to the shapely form of a political philosophy. By its reagents they precipitated drudgery to the bottom of society, and left at the top what they thought to be a clarified fluid. In their political economy, labor was to be owned by capital; in their theory of government, the few were to rule the many. They boldly avowed, not the fact alone, that, under all forms of government, the few rule the many, but their right and duty to do so. Set free from the necessity of labor, they conceived a contempt for those who felt its wholesome regimen. Believing themselves foreordained to supremacy, they regarded the popular vote, when it failed to register their wishes, as an intrusion and a nuisance. They were born in a garden, and popular liberty, like freshets overswelling their banks, but covered their dainty walks and flowers with slime and mud — of democratic votes. When, with shrewd observation, they saw the growth of the popular element in the Northern States, they instinctively took in the inevitable events. It must be controlled or cut off from a nation governed by gentlemen! Controlled, less and less, could it be in every decade; and they prepared secretly, earnestly, and with wide conference and mutual connivance, to separate the South from the North. We are to distinguish between the pretenses and means, and the real causes of this war. To inflame and unite the great middle class of the South, who had no interest in separation and no business with war, they alleged grievances that never existed, and employed

arguments which they, better than all other men, knew to be specious and false.

Slavery itself was cared for only as an instrument of power or of excitement. They had unalterably fixed their eye upon empire, and all was good which would secure that, and bad which hindered it. Thus, the ruling class of the South — an aristocracy as intense, proud, and inflexible as ever existed — not limited either by customs or institutions, not recognized and adjusted in the regular order of society, playing a reciprocal part in its machinery, but secret, disowning its own existence, baptized with ostentatious names of democracy, obsequious to the people for the sake of governing them; this nameless, lurking aristocracy, that ran in the blood of society like a rash not yet come to the skin; this political tapeworm, that produced nothing, but lay coiled in the body, feeding on its nutriment, and holding the whole structure to be but a servant set up to nourish it — this aristocracy of the plantation, with firm and deliberate resolve, brought on the war, that they might cut the land in two, and, clearing themselves from an incorrigibly free society, set up a sterner, statelier empire, where slaves worked that gentlemen might live at ease. Nor can there be any doubt that though, at first, they meant to erect the form of republican government, this was but a device, a step necessary to the securing of that power by which they should be able to change the whole economy of society. That they never dreamed of such a war, we may well believe. That they would have accepted it, though twice as bloody, if only thus they could rule, none can doubt that knows the temper of these worst men of modern society. But they miscalculated. They understood the people of the South; but they were totally incapable of understanding the character of the great working classes of the loyal States. That industry, which is the foundation of independence, and so of equity, they stigmatized as stupid drudgery, or as mean avarice. That general intelligence and independence of thought which schools for the common people and newspapers breed, they reviled as the incitement of unsettled zeal, running easily into fanaticism. They more thoroughly misunderstood the profound sentiment of loyalty, the deep love of country, which pervaded the common people. If those who knew them best had never suspected the depth and power of that love of country which threw it into an agony of grief when the flag was here humbled,

how should they conceive of it who were wholly disjoined from them in sympathy? The whole land rose up, you remember, when the flag came down, as if inspired unconsciously by the breath of the Almighty, and the power of omnipotence. It was as when one pierces the banks of the Mississippi for a rivulet, and the whole raging stream plunges through with headlong course. There they calculated, and miscalculated! And more than all, they miscalculated the bravery of men who have been trained under law, who are civilized and hate personal brawls, who are so protected by society as to have dismissed all thought of self-defense, the whole force of whose life is turned to peaceful pursuits. These arrogant conspirators against government, with Chinese vanity, believed that they could blow away these self-respecting citizens as chaff from the battlefield. Few of them are left alive to ponder their mistake! Here, then, are the roots of this civil war. It was ·not a quarrel of wild beasts, it was an inflection of the strife of ages, between power and right, between ambition and equity. An armed band of pestilent conspirators sought the nation's life. Her children rose up and fought at every door and room and hall, to thrust out the murderers and save the house and household. It was not legitimately a war between the common people of the North and South. The war was set on by the ruling class, the aristocratic conspirators of the South. They suborned the common people with lies, with sophistries, with cruel deceits and slanders, to fight for secret objects which they abhorred, and against interests as dear to them as their own lives. I charge the whole guilt of this war upon the ambitious, educated, plotting, political leaders of the South. They have shed this ocean of blood. They have desolated the South. They have poured poverty through all her towns and cities. They have bewildered the imagination of the people with phantasms, and led them to believe that they were fighting for their homes and liberty, whose homes were unthreatened, and whose liberty was in no jeopardy. These arrogant instigators of civil war have renewed the plagues of Egypt, not that the oppressed might go free, but that the free might be oppressed. A day will come when God will reveal judgment, and arraign at his bar these mighty miscreants; and then, every orphan that their bloody game has made, and every widow that sits sorrowing, and every maimed and wounded sufferer, and every bereaved heart in all the wide regions of this

land, will rise up and come before the Lord to lay upon these chief culprits of modern history their awful witness. And from a thousand battlefields shall rise up armies of airy witnesses, who, with the memory of their awful sufferings, shall confront the miscreants with shrieks of fierce accusation; and every pale and starved prisoner shall raise his skinny hand in judgment. Blood shall call out for vengeance, and tears shall plead for justice, and grief shall silently beckon, and love, heart-smitten, shall wail for justice. Good men and angels will cry out: "How long, O Lord, how long, wilt thou not avenge?" And, then, these guiltiest and most remorseless traitors, these high and cultured men, — with might and wisdom, used for the destruction of their country, — the most accursed and detested of all criminals, that have drenched a continent in needless blood, and moved the foundations of their times with hideous crimes and cruelty, caught up in black clouds, full of voices of vengeance and lurid with punishment, shall be whirled aloft and plunged downwards forever and forever in an endless retribution; while God shall say, "Thus shall it be to all who betray their country"; and all in heaven and upon the earth will say "Amen!"

But for the people misled, for the multitudes drafted and driven into this civil war, let not a trace of animosity remain. The moment their willing hand drops the musket, and they return to their allegiance, then stretch out your own honest right hand to greet them. Recall to them the old days of kindness. Our hearts wait for their redemption. All the resources of a renovated nation shall be applied to rebuild their prosperity, and smooth down the furrows of war. Has this long and weary period of strife been an unmingled evil? Has nothing been gained? Yes, much. This nation has attained to its manhood. Among Indian customs is one which admits young men to the rank of warriors only after severe trials of hunger, fatigue, pain, endurance. They reach their station, not through years, but ordeals. Our nation has suffered, but now is strong. The sentiment of loyalty and patriotism, next in importance to religion, has been rooted and grounded. We have something to be proud of, and pride helps love. Never so much as now did we love our country. But four such years of education in ideas, in the knowledge of political truth, in the love of history, in the geography of our own country, almost every inch of which we have probed with the bayonet, have never passed before. There is half a hundred years' advance in four. We believed in our institutions and principles before; but now we know their power. It is one thing to look upon artillery, and be sure that it is loaded; it is another thing to prove its power in battle! We believe in the hidden power stored in our institutions; we had never before seen this nation thundering like Mount Sinai at all those that worshiped the calf at the base of the mountain. A people educated and moral are competent to all the exigencies of national life. A vote can govern better than a crown. We have proved it. A people intelligent and religious are strong in all economic elements. They are fitted for peace and competent to war. They are not easily inflamed, and, when justly incensed, not easily extinguished. They are patient in adversity, endure cheerfully needful burdens, tax themselves to meet real wants more royally than any prince would dare to tax his people. They pour forth without stint relief for the sufferings of war, and raise charity out of the realm of a dole into a munificent duty of beneficence. The habit of industry among free men prepares them to meet the exhaustion of war with increase of productiveness commensurate with the need that exists. Their habits of skill enable them at once to supply such armies as only freedom can muster, with arms and munitions such as only free industry can create. Free society is terrible in war, and afterwards repairs the mischief of war with celerity almost as great as that with which the ocean heals the seams gashed in it by the keel of ploughing ships. Free society is fruitful of military genius. It comes when called; when no longer needed, it falls back as waves do to the level of the common sea, that no wave may be greater than the undivided water. With proof of strength so great, yet in its infancy, we stand up among the nations of the world, asking no privileges, asserting no rights, but quietly assuming our place, and determined to be second to none in the race of civilization and religion. Of all nations we are the most dangerous and the least to be feared. We need not expound the perils that wait upon enemies that assault us. They are sufficiently understood! But we are not a dangerous people because we are warlike. All the arrogant attitudes of this nation, so offensive to foreign governments, were inspired by slavery, and under the administration of its minions. Our tastes, our habits, our interests, and our principles, incline us to the arts of peace. This nation was founded by the common people for the

common people. We are seeking to embody in public economy more liberty, with higher justice and virtue, than have been organized before. By the necessity of our doctrines, we are put in sympathy with the masses of men in all nations. It is not our business to subdue nations, but to augment the powers of the common people. The vulgar ambition of mere domination, as it belongs to universal human nature, may tempt us; but it is withstood by the whole force of our principles, our habits, our precedents, and our legends. We acknowledge the obligation which our better political principles lay upon us, to set an example more temperate, humane, and just, than monarchical governments can. We will not suffer wrong, and still less will we inflict it upon other nations. Nor are we concerned that so many, ignorant of our conflict, for the present, misconceive the reasons of our invincible military zeal. "Why contend," say they, "for a little territory that you do not need?" Because it is ours! Because it is the interest of every citizen to save it from becoming a fortress and refuge of iniquity. This nation is our house, and our fathers' house; and accursed be the man who will not defend it to the uttermost. More territory than we need! England, that is not large enough to be our pocket, may think that it is more than we need, because it is more than it needs; but we are better judges of what we need than others are.

Shall a philanthropist say to a banker, who defends himself against a robber, "Why do you need so much money?" But we will not reason with such questions. When any foreign nation willingly will divide its territory and give it cheerfully away, we will answer the question why we are fighting for territory! At present—for I pass to the consideration of benefits that accrue to the South in distinction from the rest of the nation—the South reaps only suffering; but good seed lies buried under the furrows of war, that peace will bring to harvest. 1. Deadly doctrines have been purged away in blood. The subtle poison of secession was a perpetual threat of revolution. The sword has ended that danger. That which reason had affirmed as a philosophy, that people have settled as a fact. Theory pronounces, "There can be no permanent government where each integral particle has liberty to fly off." Who would venture upon a voyage in a ship each plank and timber of which might withdraw at its pleasure? But the people have reasoned by the logic of the sword and of the ballot, and they have declared that States

are inseparable parts of the national government. They are not sovereign. State rights remain; but sovereignty is a right higher than all others; and that has been made into a common stock for the benefit of all. All further agitation is ended. This element must be cast out of political problems. Henceforth that poison will not rankle in the blood. 2. Another thing has been learned: the rights and duties of minorities. The people of the whole nation are of more authority than the people of any section. These United States are supreme over Northern, Western, and Southern States. It ought not to have required the awful chastisement of this war to teach that a minority must submit the control of the nation's government to a majority. The army and navy have been good political schoolmasters. The lesson is learned. Not for many generations will it require further illustration. 3. No other lesson will be more fruitful of peace than the dispersion of those conceits of vanity, which, on either side, have clouded the recognition of the manly courage of all Americans. If it be a sign of manhood to be able to fight, then Americans are men. The North certainly is in no doubt whatever of the soldierly qualities of Southern men. Southern soldiers have learned that all latitudes breed courage on this continent. Courage is a passport to respect. The people of all the regions of this nation are likely hereafter to cherish a generous admiration of each other's prowess. The war has bred respect, and respect will breed affection, and affection peace and unity. 4. No other event of the war can fill an intelligent Southern man, of candid nature, with more surprise than the revelation of the capacity, moral and military, of the black race. It is a revelation indeed. No people were ever less understood by those most familiar with them. They were said to be lazy, lying, impudent, and cowardly wretches, driven by the whip alone to the tasks needful to their own support and the functions of civilization. They were said to be dangerous, bloodthirsty, liable to insurrection; but four years of tumultuous distress and war have rolled across the area inhabited by them, and I have yet to hear of one authentic instance of the misconduct of a colored man. They have been patient and gentle and docile, and full of faith and hope and piety; and, when summoned to freedom, they have emerged with all the signs and tokens that freedom will be to them what it was to us, the swaddling-band that shall bring them to manhood. And after the government, honoring them as

men, summoned them to the field, when once they were disciplined, and had learned the arts of war, they have proved themselves to be not second to their white brethren in arms. And when the roll of men that have shed their blood is called in the other land, many and many a dusky face will rise, dark no more when the light of eternal glory shall shine upon it from the throne of God! 5. The industry of the Southern States is regenerated, and now rests upon a basis that never fails to bring prosperity. Just now industry is collapsed; but it is not dead; it sleepeth. It is vital yet. It will spring like mown grass from the roots that need but showers and heat and time to bring them forth. Though in many districts not a generation will see wanton wastes of self-invoked war repaired, and many portions may lapse again to wilderness, yet, in our lifetime, we shall see States, as a whole, raised to a prosperity, vital, wholesome, and immovable. 6. The destruction of class interests, working with a religion which tends toward true democracy, in proportion as it is pure and free, will create a new era of prosperity for the common laboring people of the South. Upon them have come the labor, the toil, and the loss of this war. They have fought blindfolded. They have fought for a class that sought their degradation, while they were made to believe that it was for their own homes and altars. Their leaders meant a supremacy which would not long have left them political liberty, save in name. But their leaders are swept away. The sword has been hungry for the ruling classes. It has sought them out with remorseless zeal. New men are to rise up; new ideas are to bud and blossom; and there will be men with different ambition and altered policy. 7. Meanwhile, the South, no longer a land of plantations, but of farms; no longer tilled by slaves, but by freedmen, will find no hindrance to the spread of education. Schools will multiply. Books and papers will spread. Churches will bless every hamlet. There is a good day coming for the South. Through darkness and tears and blood she has sought it. It has been an unconscious *via dolorosa*. But in the end it will be worth all that it has cost. Her institutions before were deadly. She nourished death in her bosom. The greater her secular prosperity, the more sure was her ruin. Every year of delay but made the change more terrible. Now, by an earthquake, the evil is shaken down. And her own historians, in a better day, shall write, that from the day the sword cut off the cancer, she began to find her health. What, then, shall hinder the rebuilding of the Republic? The evil spirit is cast out: why should not this nation cease to wander among tombs, cutting itself? Why should it not come, clothed and in its right mind, to "sit at the feet of Jesus"? Is it feared that the government will oppress the conquered States? What possible motive has the government to narrow the base of that pyramid on which its own permanence depends? Is it feared that the rights of the States will be withheld? The South is not more jealous of State rights than the North. State rights from the earliest colonial days have been the peculiar pride and jealousy of New England. In every stage of national formation, it was peculiarly Northern, and not Southern, statesmen that guarded State rights as we were forming the Constitution. But once united, the loyal States gave up forever that which had been delegated to the national government. And now, in the hour of victory, the loyal States do not mean to trench upon Southern State rights. They will not do it, nor suffer it to be done. There is not to be one rule for high latitudes and another for low. We take nothing from the Southern States that has not already been taken from the Northern. The South shall have just those rights that every eastern, every middle, every western State has—no more, no less. We are not seeking our own aggrandizement by impoverishing the South. Its prosperity is an indispensable element of our own.

We have shown, by all that we have suffered in war, how great is our estimate of the Southern States of this Union; and we will measure that estimate, now, in peace, by still greater exertions for their rebuilding. Will reflecting men not perceive, then, the wisdom of accepting established facts, and, with alacrity of enterprise, begin to retrieve the past? Slavery cannot come back. It is the interest, therefore, of every man to hasten its end. Do you want more war? Are you not yet weary of contest? Will you gather up the unexploded fragments of this prodigious magazine of all mischief, and heap them up for continued explosions? Does not the South need peace? And, since free labor is inevitable, will you have it in its worst forms or in its best? Shall it be ignorant, impertinent, indolent, or shall it be educated, self-respecting, moral, and self-supporting? Will you have men as drudges, or will you have them as citizens? Since they have vindicated the government, and cemented its

foundation stones with their blood, may they not offer the tribute of their support to maintain its laws and its policy? It is better for religion; it is better for political integrity; it is better for industry; it is better for money—if you will have that ground motive—that you should educate the black man, and, by education, make him a citizen. They who refuse education to the black man would turn the South into a vast poorhouse, and labor into a pendulum, incessantly vibrating between poverty and indolence. From this pulpit of broken stone we speak forth our earnest greeting to all our land. We offer to the President of these United States our solemn congratulations that God has sustained his life and health under the unparalleled burdens and sufferings of four bloody years, and permitted him to behold this auspicious consummation of that national unity for which he has waited with so much patience and fortitude, and for which he has labored with such disinterested wisdom. To the members of the government associated with him in the administration of perilous affairs in critical times; to the senators and representatives of the United States, who have eagerly fashioned the instruments by which the popular will might express and enforce itself, we tender our grateful thanks. To the officers and men of the army and navy, who have so faithfully, skillfully, and gloriously upheld their country's authority, by suffering, labor, and sublime courage, we offer a heart-tribute beyond the compass of words. Upon those true and faithful citizens, men and women, who have borne up with unflinching hope in the darkest hour, and covered the land with their labor of love and charity, we invoke the divinest blessing of him whom they have so truly imitated. But chiefly to thee, God of our fathers, we render thanksgiving and praise for that wondrous Providence that has brought forth from such a harvest of war the seed of so much liberty and peace! We invoke peace upon the North. Peace be to the West! Peace be upon the South! In the name of God we lift up our banner, and dedicate it to peace, union, and liberty, now and for evermore! Amen.

EFFECT OF THE DEATH OF LINCOLN

(Delivered in Brooklyn, April 16th, 1865)

AGAIN a great leader of the people has passed through toil, sorrow, battle, and war, and come near to the promised land of peace, into which he might not pass over. Who shall recount our martyr's sufferings for this people? Since the November of 1860, his horizon has been black with storms. By day and by night, he trod a way of danger and darkness. On his shoulders rested a government dearer to him than his own life. At its integrity millions of men were striking at home. Upon this government foreign eyes lowered. It stood like a lone island in a sea full of storms, and every tide and wave seemed eager to devour it. Upon thousands of hearts great sorrows and anxieties have rested, but not on one such, and in such measure, as upon that simple, truthful, noble soul, our faithful and sainted Lincoln. Never rising to the enthusiasm of more impassioned natures in hours of hope, and never sinking with the mercurial in hours of defeat to the depths of despondency, he held on with unmovable patience and fortitude, putting caution against hope, that it might not be premature, and hope against caution, that it might not yield to dread and danger. He wrestled ceaselessly, through four black and dreadful purgatorial years, wherein God was cleansing the sin of his people as by fire.

At last, the watcher beheld the gray dawn for the country. The mountains began to give forth their forms from out the darkness, and the East came rushing toward us with arms full of joy for all our sorrows. Then it was for him to be glad exceedingly that had sorrowed immeasurably. Peace could bring to no other heart such joy, such rest, such honor, such trust, such gratitude. But he looked upon it as Moses looked upon the promised land. Then the wail of a nation proclaimed that he had gone from among us. Not thine the sorrow, but ours, sainted soul. Thou hast, indeed, entered the promised land, while we are yet on the march. To us remains the rocking of the deep, the storm upon the land, days of duty and nights of watching; but thou art sphered high above all darkness and fear, beyond all sorrow and weariness. Rest, O weary heart! Rejoice exceedingly, thou that hast enough suffered! Thou hast beheld him who invisibly led thee in this great wilderness. Thou standest

among the elect. Around thee are the royal men that have ennobled human life in every age. Kingly art thou, with glory on thy brow as a diadem. And joy is upon thee for evermore. Over all this land, over all the little cloud of years that now from thine infinite horizon moves back as a speck, thou art lifted up as high as the star is above the clouds that hide us, but never reach it. In the goodly company of Mount Zion thou shalt find that rest which thou hast sorrowing sought in vain; and thy name, an everlasting name in heaven, shall flourish in fragrance and beauty as long as men shall last upon the earth, or hearts remain, to revere truth, fidelity, and goodness.

Never did two such orbs of experience meet in one hemisphere, as the joy and the sorrow of the same week in this land. The joy was as sudden as if no man had expected it, and as entrancing as if it had fallen a sphere from heaven. It rose up over sobriety, and swept business from its moorings, and ran down through the land in irresistible course. Men embraced each other in brotherhood that were strangers in the flesh. They sang, or prayed, or, deeper yet, many could only think thanksgiving and weep gladness. That peace was sure; that government was firmer than ever; that the land was cleansed of plague; that the ages were opening to our footsteps, and we were to begin a march of blessings; that blood was staunched, and scowling enmities were sinking like storms beneath the horizon; that the dear fatherland, nothing lost, much gained, was to rise up in unexampled honor among the nations of the earth—these thoughts, and that undistinguishable throng of fancies, and hopes, and desires, and yearnings, that filled the soul with tremblings like the heated air of midsummer days—all these kindled up such a surge of joy as no words may describe.

In one hour joy lay without a pulse, without a gleam or breath. A sorrow came that swept through the land as huge storms sweep through the forest and field, rolling thunder along the sky, disheveling the flowers, daunting every singer in thicket or forest, and pouring blackness and darkness across the land and up the mountains. Did ever so many hearts, in so brief a time, touch two such boundless feelings? It was the uttermost of joy; it was the uttermost of sorrow—noon and midnight, without a space between.

The blow brought not a sharp pang. It was so terrible that at first it stunned sensibility. Citizens were like men awakened at midnight by an earthquake and bewildered to find everything that they were accustomed to trust wavering and falling. The very earth was no longer solid. The first feeling was the least. Men waited to get straight to feel. They wandered in the streets as if groping after some impending dread, or undeveloped sorrow, or some one to tell them what ailed them. They met each other as if each would ask the other, "Am I awake, or do I dream?" There was a piteous helplessness. Strong men bowed down and wept. Other and common griefs belonged to some one in chief; this belonged to all. It was each and every man's. Every virtuous household in the land felt as if its first-born were gone. Men were bereaved and walked for days as if a corpse lay unburied in their dwellings. There was nothing else to think of. They could speak of nothing but that; and yet of that they could speak only falteringly. All business was laid aside. Pleasure forgot to smile. The city for nearly a week ceased to roar. The great Leviathan lay down, and was still. Even avarice stood still, and greed was strangely moved to generous sympathy and universal sorrow. Rear to his name monuments, found charitable institutions, and write his name above their lintels; but no monument will ever equal the universal, spontaneous, and sublime sorrow that in a moment swept down lines and parties, and covered up animosities, and in an hour brought a divided people into unity of grief and indivisible fellowship of anguish. . . .

This nation has dissolved — but in tears only. It stands four-square, more solid to-day than any pyramid in Egypt. This people are neither wasted, nor daunted, nor disordered. Men hate slavery and love liberty with stronger hate and love to-day than ever before. The government is not weakened, it is made stronger. How naturally and easily were the ranks closed! Another steps forward, in the hour that the one fell, to take his place and his mantle; and I avow my belief that he will be found a man true to every instinct of liberty; true to the whole trust that is reposed in him; vigilant of the Constitution; careful of the laws; wise for liberty, in that he himself, through his life, has known what it was to suffer from the stings of slavery, and to prize liberty from bitter personal experiences.

Where could the head of government in any monarchy be smitten down by the hand of an assassin, and the funds not quiver or fall one-half of one per cent? After a long period of

national disturbance, after four years of drastic war, after tremendous drafts on the resources of the country, in the height and top of our burdens, the heart of this people is such that now, when the head of government is stricken down, the public funds do not waver, but stand as the granite ribs in our mountains.

Republican institutions have been vindicated in this experience as they never were before; and the whole history of the last four years, rounded up by this cruel stroke, seems, in the providence of God, to have been clothed, now, with an illustration, with a sympathy, with an aptness, and with a significance, such as we never could have expected nor imagined. God, I think, has said, by the voice of this event, to all nations of the earth, "Republican liberty, based upon true Christianity, is firm as the foundation of the globe."

Even he who now sleeps has, by this event, been clothed with new influence. Dead, he speaks to men who now willingly hear what before they refused to listen to. Now his simple and weighty words will be gathered like those of Washington, and your children and your children's children shall be taught to ponder the simplicity and deep wisdom of utterances which, in their time, passed, in party heat, as idle words. Men will receive a new impulse of patriotism for his sake and will guard with zeal the whole country which he loved so well. I swear you, on the altar of his memory, to be more faithful to the country for which he has perished. They will, as they follow his hearse, swear a new hatred to that slavery against which he warred, and which, in vanquishing him, has made him a martyr and a conqueror. I swear you, by the memory of this martyr, to hate slavery with an unappeasable hatred. They will admire and imitate the firmness of this man, his inflexible conscience for the right, and yet his gentleness, as tender as a woman's, his moderation of spirit, which not all the heat of party could inflame, nor all the jars and disturbances of his country shake out of place. I swear you to an emulation of his justice, his moderation, and his mercy.

You I can comfort; but how can I speak to that twilight million to whom his name was as the name of an angel of God? There will be wailing in places which no minister shall be able to reach. When, in hovel and in cot, in wood and in wilderness, in the field throughout the South, the dusky children, who looked upon him as that Moses whom God sent before them to lead them out of the land of bondage, learn that he has fallen, who

shall comfort them? O, thou Shepherd of Israel, that didst comfort thy people of old, to thy care we commit the helpless, the long-wronged, and grieved.

And now the martyr is moving in triumphal march, mightier than when alive. The nation rises up at every stage of his coming. Cities and States are his pallbearers, and the cannon beats the hours with solemn progression. Dead, dead, dead, he yet speaketh. Is Washington dead? Is Hampden dead? Is David dead? Is any man that ever was fit to live dead? Disenthralled of flesh, and risen in the unobstructed sphere where passion never comes, he begins his illimitable work. His life now is grafted upon the infinite, and will be fruitful as no earthly life can be. Pass on, thou that hast overcome. Your sorrows, O people, are his peace. Your bells and bands and muffled drums sound triumph in his ear. Wail and weep here; God made it echo joy and triumph there. Pass on.

Four years ago, O Illinois, we took from your midst an untried man and from among the people. We return him to you a mighty conqueror. Not thine any more, but the nation's; not ours, but the world's. Give him place, O ye prairies. In the midst of this great continent his dust shall rest, a sacred treasure to myriads who shall pilgrim to that shrine to kindle anew their zeal and patriotism. Ye winds that move over the mighty places of the West, chant his requiem. Ye people, behold a martyr whose blood, as so many articulate words, pleads for fidelity, for law, for liberty.

1—24

LORD BELHAVEN

(1656–1708)

SCOTLAND ceased to exist as a nation by the act of union, May 1st, 1707. As occasions have been so rare in the world's history when a nation has voluntarily abdicated its sovereignty and ceased to exist by its own free act, it would be too much to say that Lord Belhaven's speech against surrendering Scotch nationality was worthy of so remarkable a scene as that presented in the Scotch Parliament when, soon after its opening, November 1st, 1706, he rose to make the protest which immortalized him.

Smollet belongs more properly to another generation, but the feeling against the union was rather exaggerated than diminished between the date of its adoption and that of his poem, 'The Tears of Scotland,' into the concluding stanza of which he has condensed the passion which prompted Belhaven's protest:—

> "While the warm blood bedews my veins
> And unimpaired remembrance reigns,
> Resentment of my country's fate
> Within my filial heart shall beat,
> And spite of her insulting foe,
> My sympathizing verse shall flow:—
> 'Mourn, helpless Caledonia, mourn,
> Thy banished peace, thy laurels torn!'"

If there is nothing in Belhaven's oration which equals this in intensity, there is power and pathos, as well as Ciceronian syntax, in the period: "Hannibal, my lord, is at our gates; Hannibal is come within our gates; Hannibal is come the length of this table; he is at the foot of this throne; if we take not notice he'll seize upon these regalia, he'll take them as our *spolia opima*, and whip us out of this house, never to return."

It is unfortunate for Belhaven's fame as an orator that his most effective passages are based on classical allusions intelligible at once to his audience then, but likely to appear pedantic in times when Latin has ceased to be the "vulgar tongue" of the educated, as it still was in the Scotland of Queen Anne's time.

The text of his speech here used is from 'The Parliamentary Debates,' London 1741.

A PLEA FOR THE NATIONAL LIFE OF SCOTLAND

(Delivered 1706 in the Scotch Parliament)

My Lord Chancellor:—

WHEN I consider the affair of a union betwixt the two nations, as it is expressed in the several articles thereof, and now the subject of our deliberation at this time, I find my mind crowded with a variety of melancholy thoughts, and I think it my duty to disburden myself of some of them, by laying them before, and exposing them to, the serious consideration of this honorable house.

I think I see a free and independent kingdom delivering up that which all the world hath been fighting for since the days of Nimrod; yea, that for which most of all the empires, kingdoms, states, principalities, and dukedoms of Europe, are at this very time engaged in the most bloody and cruel wars that ever were, to-wit, a power to manage their own affairs by themselves, without the assistance and counsel of any other.

I think I see a national church, founded upon a rock, secured by a claim of right, hedged and fenced about by the strictest and most pointed legal sanction that sovereignty could contrive, voluntarily descending into a plain, upon an equal level with Jews, Papists, Socinians, Arminians, Anabaptists, and other sectaries, etc.

I think I see the noble and honorable peerage of Scotland, whose valiant predecessors led armies against their enemies, upon their own proper charges and expenses, now divested of their followers and vassalages, and put upon such an equal foot with their vassals, that I think I see a petty English exciseman receive more homage and respect than what was paid formerly to their quondam Mackallamores.

I think I see the present peers of Scotland, whose noble ancestors conquered provinces, over-run countries, reduced and subjected towns and fortified places, exacted tribute through the greatest part of England, now walking in the court of requests like so many English attorneys, laying aside their walking swords when in company with the English peers, lest their self-defense should be found murder.

I think I see the honorable estate of barons, the bold assertors of the nation's rights and liberties in the worst of times, now

setting a watch upon their lips and a guard upon their tongues, lest they be found guilty of *scandalum magnatum.*

I think I see the royal state of boroughs walking their desolate streets, hanging down their heads under disappointments, wormed out of all the branches of their old trade, uncertain what hand to turn to, necessitate to become 'prentices to their unkind neighbors; and yet, after all, finding their trade so fortified by companies, and secured by prescriptions, that they despair of any success therein.

I think I see our learned judges laying aside their practiques and decisions, studying the common law of England, graveled with *certiories, nisi prius's,* writs of error, *verdicts indovar, ejectione firmæ,* injunctions, demurs, etc., and frighted with appeals and avocations, because of the new regulations and rectifications they may meet with.

I think I see the valiant and gallant soldiery either sent to learn the plantation-trade abroad; or at home petitioning for a small subsistence, as the reward of their honorable exploits; while their old corps are broken, the common soldiers left to beg, and the youngest English corps kept standing.

I think I see the honest, industrious tradesman loaded with new taxes and impositions, disappointed of the equivalents, drinking water in place of ale, eating his saltless pottage, petitioning for encouragement to his manufactories, and answered by counter-petitions.

In short, I think I see the laborious plowman, with his corn spoiling upon his hands, for want of sale, cursing the day of his birth, dreading the expense of his burial, and uncertain whether to marry or do worse.

I think I see the incurable difficulties of the landed men, fettered under the golden chain of equivalents, their pretty daughters petitioning for want of husbands, and their sons for want of employment.

I think I see our mariners delivering up their ships to their Dutch partners, and what through presses and necessity, earning their bread as underlings in the royal English navy.

But above all, my lord, I think I see our ancient mother Caledonia, like Cæsar, sitting in the midst of our senate, ruefully looking round about her, covering herself with her royal garment, attending the fatal blow, and breathing out her last with an *Et tu quoque, mi fili.*

Are not these, my lord, very afflicting thoughts? And yet they are but the least part suggested to me by these dishonorable articles. Should not the consideration of these things vivify these dry bones of ours? Should not the memory of our noble predecessors' valor and constancy rouse up our drooping spirits? Are our noble predecessors' souls got so far into the English cabbage stock and cauliflowers that we should show the least inclination that way? Are our eyes so blinded? Are our ears so deafened? Are our hearts so hardened? Are our tongues so faltered? Are our hands so fettered that in this our day, I say, my lord, that in this our day, we should not mind the things that concern the very being and well-being of our ancient kingdom, before the day be hid from our eyes?

No, my lord, God forbid! man's extremity is God's opportunity; he is a present help in time of need, and a deliverer, and that right early. Some unforeseen Providence will fall out, that may cast the balance; some Joseph or other will say, "Why do ye strive together, since ye are brethren?" None can destroy Scotland, save Scotland itself; hold your hands from the pen, you are secure. Some Judah or other will say, "Let not our hands be upon the lad, he is our brother." There will be a Jehovah-Jireh, and some ram will be caught in the thicket, when the bloody knife is at our mother's throat. Let us up then, my lord, and let our noble patriots behave themselves like men, and we know not how soon a blessing may come.

My lord, I wish from my heart, that this my vision prove not as true as my reasons for it are probable. I design not at this time to enter into the merits of any one particular article; I intend this discourse as an introduction to what I may afterwards say upon the whole debate as it falls in before this honorable house; and therefore, in the farther prosecution of what I have to say, I shall insist upon few particulars, very necessary to be understood, before we enter into the detail of so important a matter.

I shall, therefore, in the first place, endeavor to encourage a free and full deliberation, without animosities and heats. In the next place I shall endeavor to make an inquiry into the nature and source of the unnatural and dangerous divisions that are now on foot within this isle, with some motives showing that it is our interest to lay them aside at this time. Then I shall inquire into the reasons which have induced the two nations to

enter into a treaty of union at this time, with some considerations and meditations with relation to the behavior of the lord's commissioners of the two kingdoms in the management of this great concern. And lastly, I shall propose a method, by which we shall most distinctly, and without confusion, go through the several articles of this treaty, without unnecessary repetitions or loss of time. And all this with all deference, and under the correction of this honorable house.

My lord chancellor, the greatest honor that was done unto a Roman was to allow him the glory of a triumph; the greatest and most dishonorable punishment was that of *parricide.* He that was guilty of *parricide* was beaten with rods upon his naked body till the blood gushed out of all the veins of his body; then he was sewed up in a leathern sack, called a *culeus,* with a cock, a viper, and an ape, and thrown headlong into the sea.

My lord, *patricide* is a greater crime than *parricide,* all the world over.

In a triumph, my lord, when the conqueror was riding in his triumphal chariot, crowned with laurels, adorned with trophies, and applauded with huzzas, there was a monitor appointed to stand behind him, to warn him not to be high-minded, not puffed up with overweening thoughts of himself; and to his chariot were tied a whip and a bell, to mind him that for all his glory and grandeur he was accountable to the people for his administration, and would be punished as other men, if found guilty.

The greatest honor amongst us, my lord, is to represent the sovereign's sacred person in Parliament; and in one particular it appears to be greater than that of a triumph, because the whole legislative power seems to be wholly intrusted with him. If he give the royal assent to an act of the estates, it becomes a law obligatory upon the subject, though contrary or without any instructions from the sovereign. If he refuse the royal assent to a vote in Parliament, it cannot be a law, though he has the Sovereign's particular and positive instructions for it.

His Grace, the Duke of Queensbury, who now presents her Majesty in this session of Parliament, hath had the honor of that great trust, as often, if not more, than any Scotchman ever had. He hath been the favorite of two successive sovereigns; and I cannot but commend his constancy and perseverance, that notwithstanding his former difficulties and unsuccessful attempts, and maugre some other specialties not yet determined, that his

Grace has yet had the resolution to undertake the most unpopular measures last. If his Grace succeed in this affair of a union, and that it prove for the happiness and welfare of the nation, then he justly merits to have a statue of gold erected for himself; but if it shall tend to the entire destruction and abolition of our nation, and that we the nation's trustees will go into it, then I must say that a whip and a bell, a cock and a viper and an ape, are but too small punishments for any such bold, unnatural undertaking and complaisance.

That I may pave a way, my lord, to a full, calm, and free reasoning upon this affair, which is of the last consequence unto this nation, I shall mind this honorable house, that we are the successors of our noble predecessors, who founded our monarchy, framed our laws, amended, altered, and corrected them from time to time, as the affairs and circumstances of the nation did require, without the assistance or advice of any foreign power or potentate, and who, during the time of 2,000 years, have handed them down to us, a free independent nation, with the hazard of their lives and fortunes. Shall not we then argue for that which our progenitors have purchased for us at so dear a rate, and with so much immortal honor and glory? God forbid. Shall the hazard of a father unbind the ligaments of a dumb son's tongue; and shall we hold our peace, when our *patria* is in danger? I speak this, my lord, that I may encourage every individual member of this house to speak his mind freely. There are many wise and prudent men amongst us, who think it not worth their while to open their mouths; there are others, who can speak very well, and to good purpose, who shelter themselves under the shameful cloak of silence, from a fear of the frowns of great men and parties. I have observed, my lord, by my experience, the greatest number of speakers in the most trivial affairs; and it will always prove so, while we come not to the right understanding of the oath *de fideli*, whereby we are bound not only to give our vote, but our faithful advice in Parliament, as we should answer to God; and in our ancient laws, the representatives of the honorable barons and the royal boroughs are termed spokesmen. It lies upon your lordships, therefore, particularly to take notice of such whose modesty makes them bashful to speak. Therefore, I shall leave it upon you, and conclude this point with a very memorable saying of an honest private gentleman to a great queen, upon occasion of a State

project, contrived by an able statesman, and the favorite to a great king, against a peaceable, obedient people, because of the diversity of their laws and constitutions: "If at this time thou hold thy peace, salvation shall come to the people from another place, but thou and thy house shall perish." I leave the application to each particular member of this house.

My lord, I come now to consider our divisions. We are under the happy reign (blessed be God) of the best of queens, who has no evil design against the meanest of her subjects, who loves all her people, and is equally beloved by them again; and yet that under the happy influence of our most excellent Queen there should be such divisions and factions more dangerous and threatening to her dominions than if we were under an arbitrary government, is most strange and unaccountable. Under an arbitrary prince all are willing to serve because all are under a necessity to obey, whether they will or not. He chooses therefore whom he will, without respect to either parties or factions; and if he think fit to take the advices of his councils or parliaments, every man speaks his mind freely, and the prince receives the faithful advice of his people without the mixture of self-designs. If he prove a good prince, the government is easy; if bad, either death or a revolution brings a deliverance. Whereas here, my lord, there appears no end of our misery, if not prevented in time; factions are now become independent, and have got footing in councils, in parliaments, in treaties, armies, in incorporations, in families, among kindred, yea, man and wife are not free from their political jars.

It remains therefore, my lord, that I inquire into the nature of these things; and since the names give us not the right idea of the thing, I am afraid I shall have difficulty to make myself well understood.

The names generally used to denote the factions are Whig and Tory, as obscure as that of Guelfs and Gibelins. Yea, my lord, they have different significations, as they are applied to factions in each kingdom; a Whig in England is a heterogeneous creature, in Scotland he is all of a piece; a Tory in England is all of a piece, and a statesman in Scotland, he is quite otherways, an anti-courtier and anti-statesman.

A Whig in England appears to be somewhat like Nebuchadnezzar's image, of different metals, different classes, different principles, and different designs; yet take the Whigs all together, they

are like a piece of fine mixed drugget of different threads, some finer, some coarser, which, after all, make a comely appearance and an agreeable suit. Tory is like a piece of loyal-made English cloth, the true staple of the nation, all of a thread; yet, if we look narrowly into it, we shall perceive diversity of colors, which, according to the various situations and positions, make various appearances. Sometimes Tory is like the moon in its full, as appeared in the affair of the bill of occasional conformity; upon other occasions it appears to be under a cloud, and as if it were eclipsed by a greater body, as it did in the design of calling over the illustrious Princess Sophia. However, by this we may see their designs are to outshoot Whig in his own bow.

Whig in Scotland is a true blue Presbyterian, who, without considering time or power, will venture their all for the Kirk, but something less for the State. The greatest difficulty is how to describe a Scots Tory. Of old, when I knew them first, Tory was an honest-hearted comradish fellow, who, provided he was maintained and protected in his benefices, titles, and dignities by the State, was the less anxious who had the government and management of the Church. But now what he is since *jure divino* came in fashion, and that Christianity, and, by consequence, salvation comes to depend upon episcopal ordination, I profess I know not what to make of him; only this I must say for him, that he endeavors to do by opposition that which his brother in England endeavors by a more prudent and less scrupulous method.

Now, my lord, from these divisions there has got up a kind of aristocracy something like the famous triumvirate at Rome; they are a kind of undertakers and pragmatic statesmen, who, finding their power and strength great, and answerable to their designs, will make bargains with our gracious sovereign; they will serve her faithfully, but upon their own terms; they must have their own instruments, their own measures; this man must be turned out, and that man put in, and then they will make her the most glorious queen in Europe.

Where will this end, my lord? Is not her Majesty in danger by such a method? Is not the monarchy in danger? Is not the nation's peace and tranquillity in danger? Will a change of parties make the nation more happy? No, my lord, the seed is sown that is like to afford us a perpetual increase; it is not an annual herb, it takes deep root; it seeds and breeds; and, if not

timely prevented by her Majesty's royal endeavors, will split the whole island in two.

My lord, I think, considering our present circumstances at this time, the Almighty God has reserved this great work for us. We may bruise this Hydra of division, and crush this Cockatrice's egg. Our neighbors in England are not yet fitted for any such thing; they are not under the afflicting hand of Providence, as we are; their circumstances are great and glorious; their treaties are prudently managed, both at home and abroad; their generals brave and valorous; their armies successful and victorious; their trophies and laurels memorable and surprising; their enemies subdued and routed; their strongholds besieged and taken, sieges relieved, marshals killed and taken prisoners; provinces and kingdoms are the results of their victories; their royal navy is the terror of Europe; their trade and commerce extended through the universe, encircling the whole habitable world and rendering their own capital city the emporium for the whole inhabitants of the earth. And, which is yet more than all these things, the subjects freely bestow their treasure upon their sovereign! And, above all, these vast riches, the sinews of war, and without which all the glorious success had proved abortive—these treasures are managed with such faithfulness and nicety, that they answer seasonably all their demands, though at never so great a distance. Upon these considerations, my lord, how hard and difficult a thing will it prove to persuade our neighbors to a self-denying bill.

'Tis quite otherwise with us, my lord; we are an obscure poor people, though formerly of better account, removed to a remote corner of the world, without name, and without alliances, our posts mean and precarious, so that I profess I don't think any one post of the kingdom worth the briguing after, save that of being commissioner to a long session of a factious Scotch Parliament, with an antedated commission, and that yet renders the rest of the ministers more miserable. What hinders us then, my lord, to lay aside our divisions, to unite cordially and heartily together in our present circumstances, when our all is at stake? Hannibal, my lord, is at our gates; Hannibal is come within our gates; Hannibal is come the length of this table; he is at the foot of this throne; he will demolish this throne; if we take not notice, he'll seize upon these regalia, he'll take them as our *spolia opima*, and whip us out of this house, never to return again.

For the love of God then, my lord, for the safety and welfare of our ancient kingdom, whose sad circumstances, I hope, we shall yet convert into prosperity and happiness, we want no means, if we unite. God blessed the peacemakers; we want neither men, nor sufficiency of all manner of things necessary, to make a nation happy; all depends upon management, *Concordia res parvæ crescunt.* I fear not these articles, though they were ten times worse than they are, if we once cordially forgive one another, and that, according to our proverb, bygones be bygones, and fair play for time to come. For my part, in the sight of God, and in the presence of this honorable house, I heartily forgive every man, and beg that they may do the same to me; and I do most humbly propose that his grace, my lord commissioner, may appoint an Agape, may order a love feast for this honorable house, that we may lay aside all self-designs, and after our fasts and humiliations may have a day of rejoicing and thankfulness, may eat our meat with gladness, and our bread with a merry heart; then shall we sit each man under his own fig-tree, and the voice of the turtle shall be heard in our land, a bird famous for constancy and fidelity.

My lord, I shall make a pause here, and stop going on further in my discourse, till I see further, if his grace, my lord commissioner, receive any humble proposals for removing misunderstandings among us, and putting an end to our fatal divisions; upon honor, I have no other design, and I am content to beg the favor upon my bended knees. (No answer.) My lord chancellor, I am sorry that I must pursue the thread of my sad and melancholy story. What remains, I am afraid may prove as afflicting as what I have said; I shall therefore consider the motives which have engaged the two nations to enter upon a treaty of union at this time. In general, my lord, I think both of them had in their view to better themselves by the treaty; but before I enter upon the particular motives of each nation, I must inform this honorable house that since I can remember, the two nations have altered their sentiments upon that affair, even almost to downright contradiction — they have changed head-bands, as we say; for the English, till of late, never thought it worth their pains of treating with us; the good bargain they made at the beginning they resolve to keep, and that which we call an incorporating union was not so much as in their

thoughts. The first notice they seemed to take of us was in our affair of Caledonia, when they had most effectually broken off that design in a manner very well known to the world, and unnecessary to be repeated here; they kept themselves quiet during the time of our complaints upon that head. In which time our sovereign, to satisfy the nation, and allay their heats, did condescend to give us some good laws, and amongst others that of personal liberties; but they having declared their succession, and extended their entail, without ever taking notice of us, our gracious sovereign Queen Anne was graciously pleased to give the royal assent to our act of security, to that of peace and war after the decease of her Majesty, and the heirs of her body, and to give us a hedge to all our sacred and civil interests, by declaring it high treason to endeavor the alteration of them, as they were then established. Thereupon did follow the threatening and minatory laws against us by the Parliament of England, and the unjust and unequal character of what her Majesty had so graciously condescended to in our favors. Now, my lord, whether the desire they had to have us engaged in the same succession with them, or whether they found us like a free and independent people, breathing after more liberty than what formerly was looked after, or whether they were afraid of our act of security, in case of her Majesty's decease; which of all these motives has induced them to a treaty I leave it to themselves. This I must say only, they have made a good bargain this time also.

For the particular motives that induced us, I think they are obvious to be known, we found by sad experience, that every man hath advanced in power and riches, as they have done in trade, and at the same time considering that nowhere through the world slaves are found to be rich, though they should be adorned with chains of gold, we thereupon changed our notion of an incorporating union to that of a federal one; and being resolved to take this opportunity to make demands upon them, before we enter into the succession, we were content to empower her Majesty to authorize and appoint commissioners to treat with the commissioners of England, with as ample powers as the lords commissioners from England had from their constituents, that we might not appear to have less confidence in her Majesty, nor more narrow-heartedness in our act, than our neighbors of England. And thereupon last Parliament, after her Majesty's

gracious letter was read, desiring us to declare the succession in the first place, and afterwards to appoint commissioners to treat, we found it necessary to renew our former resolve, which I shall read to this honorable house. The resolve presented by the Duke of Hamilton last session of Parliament: —

«That this Parliament will not proceed to the nomination of a successor till we have had a previous treaty with England, in relation to our commerce, and other concerns with that nation. And further, it is resolved that this Parliament will proceed to make such limitations and conditions of government, for the rectification of our constitution, as may secure the liberty, religion, and independency of this kingdom, before they proceed to the said nomination.»

Now, my lord, the last session of Parliament having, before they would enter into any treaty with England, by a vote of the house, passed both an act for limitations and an act for rectification of our constitution, what mortal man has reason to doubt the design of this treaty was only federal?

My lord chancellor, it remains now, that we consider the behavior of the lords commissioners at the opening of this treaty. And before I enter upon that, allow me to make this meditation, that if our posterity, after we are all dead and gone, shall find themselves under an ill-made bargain, and shall have recourse unto our records, and see who have been the managers of that treaty, by which they have suffered so much; when they read the names, they will certainly conclude, and say, Ah! our nation has been reduced to the last extremity, at the time of this treaty; all our great chieftains, all our great peers and considerable men, who used formerly to defend the rights and liberties of the nation, have been all killed and dead in the bed of honor, before ever the nation was necessitated to condescend to such mean and contemptible terms. Where are the names of the chief men, of the noble families of Stuarts, Hamiltons, Grahams, Campbels, Gordons, Johnstons, Humes, Murrays, Kers? Where are the two great officers of the crown, the constables and marshals of Scotland? They have certainly all been extinguished, and now we are slaves forever.

Whereas the English records will make their posterity reverence the memory of the honorable names who have brought under their fierce, warlike, and troublesome neighbors, who had struggled so long for independence, shed the best blood of their

nation, and reduced a considerable part of their country to become waste and desolate.

I am informed, my lord, that our commissioners did indeed frankly tell the lords commissioners for England that the inclinations of the people of Scotland were much altered of late, in relation to an incorporating union; and that, therefore, since the entail was to end with her Majesty's life (whom God long preserve), it was proper to begin the treaty upon the foot of the treaty of 1604, year of God, the time when we came first under one sovereign; but this the English commissioners would not agree to, and our commissioners, that they might not seem obstinate, were willing to treat and conclude in the terms laid before this honorable house and subjected to their determination.

If the lords commissioners for England had been as civil and complaisant, they should certainly have finished a federal treaty likewise, that both nations might have the choice which of them to have gone into as they thought fit; but they would hear of nothing but an entire and complete union, a name which comprehends a union, either by incorporation, surrender, or conquest, whereas our commissioners thought of nothing but a fair, equal, incorporating union. Whether this be so or not I leave it to every man's judgment; but as for myself I must beg liberty to think it no such thing; for I take an incorporating union to be, where there is a change both in the material and formal points of government, as if two pieces of metal were melted down into one mass, it can neither be said to retain its former form or substance as it did before the mixture. But now, when I consider this treaty, as it hath been explained and spoke to before us this three weeks by past, I see the English constitution remaining firm, the same two houses of Parliament, the same taxes, the same customs, the same excises, the same trading companies, the same municipal laws and courts of judicature; and all ours either subject to regulations or annihilations, only we have the honor to pay their old debts and to have some few persons present for witnesses to the validity of the deed when they are pleased to contract more.

Good God! What, is this an entire surrender!

My lord, I find my heart so full of grief and indignation that I must beg pardon not to finish the last part of my discourse, that I may drop a tear as the prelude to so sad a story.

JOHN BELL

(1797–1869)

JOHN BELL, of Tennessee, who was a candidate with Edward Everett on the "Constitutional Union" ticket of 1860, when Virginia, Kentucky, and Tennessee gave him their thirty-nine electoral votes in favor of a hopeless peace, will always seem one of the most respectable figures in the politics of a time when calmness and conservatism, such as characterized him and his co-adjutor, Mr. Everett, of Massachusetts, had ceased to be desired by men who wished immediate success in public life. He was one of the founders of the Whig party, and by demonstrating himself to be one of the very few men who could win against Andrew Jackson's opposition in Tennessee, he acquired, under Jackson and Van Buren, a great influence with the Whigs of the country at large. He was a member of Congress from Tennessee for fourteen years dating from 1827, when he won by a single vote against Felix Grundy, one of the strongest men in Tennessee and a special favorite with General Jackson. Disagreeing with Jackson on the removal of the deposits, Bell was elected Speaker of the House over Jackson's protégé, James K. Polk, in 1834, and in 1841 he entered the Whig cabinet as Secretary of War under Harrison who had defeated another of Jackson's protégés, Van Buren. In 1847 and again in 1853, he was elected United States Senator from Tennessee and he did his best to prevent secession. He had opposed Calhoun's theories of the right of a State to nullify a Federal act if unconstitutional, and in March 1858, in the debate over the Lecompton constitution, he opposed Toombs in a speech which probably made him the candidate of the Constitutional Unionists two years later. Another notable speech, of even more far-reaching importance, he had delivered in 1853 in favor of opening up the West by building the Pacific Railroad, a position in which he was supported by Jefferson Davis.

Mr. Bell was for the Union in 1861, denying the right of secession, but he opposed the coercion of the Southern States, and when the fighting actually began he sided with Tennessee, and took little or no part in public affairs thereafter. He died in 1869.

AGAINST EXTREMISTS, NORTH AND SOUTH

(From a Speech in the Senate, March 18th, 1858, on the Lecompton Constitution)

THE honorable Senator from Georgia, Mr. Toombs, announced some great truths to-day. He said that mankind made a long step, a great stride, when they declared that minorities should not rule; and that a still higher and nobler advance had been made when it was decided that majorities could only rule through regular and legal forms. He asserted this general doctrine with reference to the construction he proposed to give to the Lecompton constitution; and to say that the people of Kansas, unless they spoke through regular forms, cannot speak at all. He will allow me to say, however, that the forms through which a majority speaks must be provided and established by competent authority, and his doctrine can have no application to the Lecompton constitution, unless he can first show that the legislature of Kansas was vested with legal authority to provide for the formation of a State constitution; for, until that can be shown, there could be no regular and legal forms through which the majority could speak. But how does that Senator reconcile his doctrine with that avowed by the President, as to the futility of attempting, by constitutional provisions, to fetter the power of the people in changing their constitution at pleasure? In no States of the Union so much as in some of the slaveholding States would such a doctrine as that be so apt to be abused by incendiary demagogues, disappointed and desperate politicians, in stirring up the people to assemble voluntarily in convention — disregarding all the restrictions in their constitution — and strike at the property of the slaveholder.

The honorable Senator from Kentucky inquired what, under this new doctrine, would prevent the majority of the people of the States of the Union from changing the present Federal Constitution, and abrogating all existing guarantees for the protection of the small States, and any peculiar or particular interest confined to a minority of the States of the Union. The analogy, I admit, is not complete between the Federal Constitution and a constitution of a State; but the promulgation of the general principle, that a majority of the people are fettered by no constitutional restrictions in the exercise of their right to change their

form of government, is dangerous. That is quite enough for the purposes of demagogues and incendiary agitators. When I read the special message of the President, I said to some friends that the message, taking it altogether, was replete with more dangerous heresies than any paper I had ever seen emanating, not from a President of the United States, but from any political club in the country, and calculated to do more injury. I consider it in effect, and in its tendencies, as organizing anarchy.

We are told that if we shall admit Kansas with the Lecompton constitution, this whole difficulty will soon be settled by the people of Kansas. How? By disregarding the mode and forms prescribed by the constitution for amending it? No. I am not sure that the President, after all the lofty generalities announced in his message, in regard to the inalienable rights of the people, intended to sanction the idea that all the provisions of the Lecompton constitution in respect to the mode and form of amending it should be set aside. He says the legislature now elected may, at its first meeting, call a convention to amend the constitution; and in another passage of his message he says that this inalienable power of the majority must be exercised in a lawful manner. This is perplexing. Can there be any lawful enactment of the legislature in relation to the call of a convention, unless it be in conformity with the provisions of the constitution? They require that two-thirds of the members of the legislature shall concur in passing an act to take the sense of the people upon the call of a convention, and that the vote shall be taken at the next regular election, which cannot be held until two years afterwards. How can this difficulty be got over? The truth is, that unless all constitutional impediments in respect to forms be set aside, and the people take it in hand to amend the constitution on revolutionary principles, there can be no end of agitation on this subject in less than three years. I long since ventured the prediction that there would be no settlement of the difficulties in Kansas until the next presidential election. To continue the agitation is too important to the interests of both the great parties of the country to dispense with it, as long as any pretext can be found for prolonging it. In the closing debate on the Kansas-Nebraska Bill, I told its supporters that they could do nothing more certain to disturb the composure of the two Senators who sat on the opposite side of the chamber, the one from Massachusetts [Mr. Sumner] and the other from Ohio [Mr. Chase], than to

reject that bill. Its passage was the only thing in the range of possible events by which their political fortunes could be resuscitated, so completely had the Free-Soil movement at the North been paralyzed by the compromise measures of 1850. I say now to the advocates of this measure, if they want to strengthen the Republican party, and give the reins of government into their hands, pass this bill. If they desire to weaken the power of that party, and arrest the progress of slavery agitation, reject it. And if it is their policy to put an end to the agitation connected with Kansas affairs at the earliest day practicable, as they say it is, then let them remit this constitution back to the people of Kansas, for their ratification or rejection. In that way the whole difficulty will be settled before the adjournment of the present session of Congress, without the violation of any sound principle, or the sacrifice of the rights of either section of the Union.

But the President informs us that threatening and ominous clouds impend over the country; and he fears that if Kansas is not admitted under the Lecompton constitution, slavery agitation will be revived in a more dangerous form than it has ever yet assumed. There may be grounds for that opinion, for aught I know; but it seems to me that if any of the States of the South have taken any position on this question which endangers the peace of the country, they could not have been informed of the true condition of affairs in Kansas, and of the strong objections which may be urged on principle against the acceptance by Congress of the Lecompton constitution. And I have such confidence in the intelligence of the people of the whole South, that when the history and character of this instrument shall be known, even those who would be glad to find some plausible pretext for dissolving the Union will see that its rejection by Congress would not furnish them with such a one as they could make available for their purposes.

When the Kansas-Nebraska Bill was under discussion, in 1854, in looking to all the consequences which might follow the adoption of that measure, I could not overlook the fact that a sentiment of hostility to the Union was widely diffused in certain States of the South; and that that sentiment was only prevented from assuming an organized form of resistance to the authority of the Federal government, at least in one of the States, in 1851, by the earnest remonstrance of a sister State, that was supposed to sympathize with her in the project of establishing a southern republic. Nor could I fail to remember that the project—I speak of the convention held in South Carolina, in pursuance of an act of the legislature—was then postponed, not dropped. The argument was successfully urged that an enterprise of such magnitude ought not to be entered upon without the co-operation of a greater number of States than they could then certainly count upon. It was urged that all the cotton-planting States would, before a great while, be prepared to unite in the movement, and that they, by the force of circumstances, would bring in all the slaveholding States. The ground was openly taken, that separation was an inevitable necessity. It was only a question of time. It was said that no new aggression was necessary on the part of the North to justify such a step. It was said that the operation of this government from its foundation had been adverse to southern interests; and that the admission of California as a free State, and the attempt to exclude the citizens of the South, with their property, from all the territory acquired from Mexico, was a sufficient justification for disunion. It was not a mere menace to deter the North from further aggressions. These circumstances made a deep impression on my mind at the time, and from a period long anterior to that I had known that it was a maxim with the most skillful tacticians among those who desire separation, that the slaveholding States must be united—consolidated into one party. That object once effected, disunion, it was supposed, would follow without difficulty.

I had my fears that the Kansas-Nebraska Bill was expected to consolidate the South, and to pave the way for the accomplishment of ulterior plans by some of the most active supporters of that measure from the South; and these fears I indicated in the closing debate on that subject. Some of the supporters of that measure, I fear, are reluctant now to abandon the chances of finding some pretext for agitating the subject of separation in the South in the existing complications of the Kansas embroilment.

To what extent the idea of disunion is entertained in some of the Southern States, and what importance is attached to the policy of uniting the whole South in one party as a preliminary step, may be inferred from a speech delivered before the Southern convention lately held in Knoxville, Tenn., by Mr. De Bow, the president of the convention, and the editor of a popular Southern review. I will only refer now to the fate to which the author resigns those who dare to break the ranks of that solid phalanx

in which he thinks the South should be combined—that is, to be "held up to public scorn and public punishment as traitors and Tories, more steeped in guilt than those of the Revolution itself."

The honorable Senator from New York further announced to us, in exultant tones, that "at last there was a North side of this Chamber, a North side of the Chamber of the House of Representatives, and a North side of the Union, as well as a South side of all these"; and he admonished us that the time was at hand when freedom would assert its influence in the regulation of the domestic and foreign policy of the country.

When was there a time in the history of the government that there was no North side of this Chamber and of the other? When was there a time that there was not a proud array of Northern men in both Chambers, distinguished by their genius and ability, devoted to the interests of the North, and successful in maintaining them?

Though it may be true that Southern men have filled the executive chair for much the larger portion of the time that has elapsed since the organization of the government, yet when, in what instance was it, that a Southerner has been elevated to that high station without the support of a majority of the freemen of the North?

Do you of the North complain that the policy of the government, under the long-continued influence of Southern Presidents, has been injurious or fatal to your interests? Has it paralyzed your industry? Has it crippled your resources? Has it impaired your energies? Has it checked your progress in any one department of human effort? Let your powerful mercantile marine, your ships whitening every sea—the fruit of wise commercial regulations and navigation laws; let your flourishing agriculture, your astonishing progress in manufacturing skill, your great canals, your thousands of miles of railroads, your vast trade, internal and external, your proud cities, and your accumulated millions of moneyed capital, ready to be invested in profitable enterprises in any part of the world, answer that question. Do you complain of a narrow and jealous policy under Southern rule, in extending and opening new fields of enterprise to your hardy sons in the great West, along the line of the great chain of American lakes, even to the head waters of the Father of Rivers, and over the rich and fertile plains stretching southward from the lake shores? Let the teeming populations—let the hundreds of millions of annual

products that have succeeded to the but recent dreary and unproductive haunts of the red man—answer that question. That very preponderance of free States which the Senator from New York contemplates with such satisfaction, and which has moved him exultingly to exclaim that there is at last a North side of this Chamber, has been hastened by the liberal policy of Southern Presidents and Southern statesmen; and has it become the ambition of that Senator to unite and combine all this great, rich, and powerful North in the policy of crippling the resources and repressing the power of the South? Is this to be the one idea which is to mold the policy of the government, when that gentleman and his friends shall control it? If it be, then I appeal to the better feelings and the better judgment of his followers to arrest him in his mad career. Sir, let us have some brief interval of repose at least from this eternal agitation of the slavery question. Let power go into whatever hands it may, let us save the Union!

I have all the confidence other gentlemen can have in the extent to which this Union is intrenched in the hearts of the great mass of the people of the North and South; but when I reflect upon and consider the desperate and dangerous extremes to which ambitious party leaders are often prepared to go, without meaning to do the country any mischief, in the struggle for the imperial power, the crown of the American presidency, I sometimes tremble for its fate.

Two great parties are now dividing the Union on this question. It is evident to every man of sense, who examines it, that practically, in respect to slavery, the result will be the same both to North and South; Kansas will be a free State, no matter what may be the decision on this question. But how that decision may affect the fortunes of those parties, is not certain; and there is the chief difficulty. But the greatest question of all is, How will that decision affect the country as a whole?

Two adverse yet concurrent and mighty forces are driving the vessel of State towards the rocks upon which she must split, unless she receives timely aid—a paradox, yet expressive of a momentous and perhaps a fatal truth.

There is no hope of rescue unless the sober-minded men, both of the North and South, shall, by some sufficient influence, be brought to adopt the wise maxims and sage counsels of the great founders of our government.

TRANS-CONTINENTAL RAILROADS

(Delivered in the United States Senate, February 17th, 1858, in Support of the Pacific Railroad Bill)

AN OBJECTION made to this bill is, the gigantic scale of the projected enterprise. A grand idea it is. A continent of three thousand miles in extent from east to west, reaching from the Atlantic to the Pacific, is to be connected by a railway! Honorable Senators will remember, that over one thousand miles—one-third of this whole expanse of the continent—the work is already accomplished, and that chiefly by private enterprise. I may, as a safe estimate, say, that a thousand miles of this railroad leading from the Atlantic to the West, upon the line of the lakes, and nearly as much upon a line further south, are either completed, or nearly so. We have two thousand miles yet to compass, in the execution of a work which it is said has no parallel in the history of the world. No, sir; it has no parallel in the history of the world, ancient or modern, either as to its extent and magnitude, or to its consequences, beneficent and benignant in all its bearings on the interests of all mankind. It is in these aspects, and in the contemplation of these consequences, that it has no parallel in the history of the world—changing the course of the commerce of the world—bringing the West almost in contact, by reversing the ancient line of communication, with the gorgeous East, and all its riches, the stories of which, in our earlier days we regarded as fabulous; but now, sir, what was held to be merely fictions of the brain in former times, in regard to the riches of Eastern Asia, is almost realized on our own western shores. Sir, these are some of the inducements to the construction of this great road, besides its importance to the military defenses of the country, and its mail communications. Sir, it is a magnificent and splendid project in every aspect in which you can view it. One-third of this great railway connection is accomplished; two-thirds remain to be. Shall we hesitate to go forward with the work?

Now, with regard to the means provided for the construction of the road. It is said, here is an enormous expenditure of the public money proposed. We propose to give twenty millions of dollars in the bonds of the government, bearing five per cent.

interest, and fifteen millions of acres of land, supposed to be worth as much more, on the part of the government. This is said to be enormous, and we are reminded that we ought to look at what the people will say, and how they will feel when they come to the knowledge that twenty millions in money and twenty millions in land have been given for the construction of a railway! Some doubtless there are in this chamber who are ready to contend that we had better give these fifteen millions of acres of land to become homesteads for the landless and homeless. What is this twenty millions in money, and how is it to be paid? It is supposed that the road cannot be constructed in less than five years. In that event, bonds of the government to the amount of four millions of dollars will issue annually. Probably the road will not be built in less than ten years, and that will require an issue of bonds amounting to two millions a year; and possibly the road may not be finished in less than twenty years, which would limit the annual issue of bonds to one million. The interest upon these bonds, at five per cent., will of course have to be paid out of the treasury, a treasury in which there is now a surplus of twelve or fourteen millions of dollars. When the road is completed and the whole amount of twenty millions in lands is paid, making the whole sum advanced by the government forty millions, the annual interest upon them will only be two millions. And what is that? Why, sir, the donations and benevolences, the allowances of claims upon flimsy and untenable grounds, and other extravagant and unnecessary expenditures that are granted by Congress and the executive departments, while you have an overflowing treasury, will amount to the half of that sum annually. The enormous sum of two millions is proposed to be paid out of the treasury annually, when this great road shall be completed! It is a tremendous undertaking, truly! What a scheme! What extravagance! I understand the cost of the New York and Erie road alone, constructed principally by private enterprise, has been not less than thirty millions — between thirty and thirty-three millions of dollars. That work was constructed by a single State giving aid occasionally to a company, which supplied the balance of the cost. I understand that the road from Baltimore to Wheeling, when it shall have been finished, and its furniture placed upon it, will have cost at least thirty millions. What madness, what extravagance, then, is it for the government of the United States to

undertake to expend forty millions for a road from the Mississippi to the Pacific.

Mr. President, one honorable Senator says the amount is not sufficient to induce a capitalist to invest his money in the enterprise. Others, again, say it is far too much; more than we can afford to give for the construction of the work. Let us see which is right. The government is to give twenty millions in all out of the treasury for the road; or we issue bonds and pay five per cent. interest annually upon them, and twenty millions in lands, which, if regarded as money, amounts to a cost to the government of two millions per annum.

What are the objects to be accomplished? A daily mail from the valley of the Mississippi to the Pacific; the free transportation of all troops and munitions of war required for the protection and defense of our possessions on the Pacific; which we could not hold three months in a war either with England or France, without such a road. By building this road we accomplish this further object: This road will be the most effective and powerful check that can be interposed by the government upon Indian depredations and aggressions upon our frontiers or upon each other; the northern tribes upon the southern, and the southern upon the northern. You cut them in two. You will be constantly in their midst, and cut off their intercommunication and hostile depredations. You will have a line of *quasi* fortifications, a line of posts and stations, with settlements on each side of the road. Every few miles you will thus have settlements strong enough to defend themselves against inroads of the Indians, and so constituting a wall of separation between the Indian tribes, composed of a white population, with arms in their hands. This object alone would, perhaps, be worth as much as the road will cost; and when I speak of what the road will be worth in this respect, I mean to say, that besides the prevention of savage warfare, the effusion of blood, it will save millions of dollars to the treasury annually, in the greater economy attained in moving troops and military supplies and preventing hostilities.

.   .   .   .

I have been thus particular in noting these things because I want to show where or on which side the balance will be found in the adjustment of the responsibility account between the friends and the opponents of this measure — which will have the heaviest account to settle with the country.

For myself, I am not wedded to this particular scheme. Rather than have no road, I would prefer to adopt other projects. I am now advocating one which I supposed would meet the views of a greater number of Senators than any other. I think great honor is due to Mr. Whitney for having originated the scheme, and having obtained the sanction of the legislatures of seventeen or eighteen States of the Union. Rather than have the project altogether fail, I would be willing to adopt this plan. It may not offer the same advantages for a speedy consummation of the work; but still, we would have a road in prospect, and that would be a great deal. But if gentlemen are to rise here in their places year after year — and this is the fifth year from the time we ought to have undertaken this work — and tell us it is just time to commence a survey, we will never have a road. The honorable Senator from South Carolina [Mr. Butler] says there ought to be some limitation in this idea of progress, when regarded as a spur to great activity and energy, as to what we shall do in our day. He says we have acquired California; we have opened up those rich regions on our western borders, which promises such magnificent results; and he asks, is not that enough for the present generation? Leave it to the next generation to construct a work of such magnitude as this — requiring forty millions of dollars from the government. Mr. President, I have said that if the condition was a road or no road, I would regard one hundred and fifty millions of dollars as well laid out by the government for the work; though I have no idea that it will take such an amount. Eighty or one hundred millions of dollars will build the road.

But with regard to what is due from this generation to itself, or what may be left to the next generation, I say it is for the present generation that we want the road. As to our having acquired California, and opened this new world of commerce and enterprise, and as to what we shall leave to the next generation, I say that, after we of this generation shall have constructed this road, we will, perhaps, not even leave to the next generation the construction of a second one. The present generation, in my opinion, will not pass away until it shall have seen two great lines of railroads in prosperous operation between the Atlantic and Pacific Oceans, and within our own territory, and still leave quite enough to the next generation — the third and fourth great lines of communication between the two extremes of the

continent. One, at least, is due to ourselves, and to the present generation; and I hope there are many within the sound of my voice who will live to see it accomplished. We want that new Dorado, the new Ophir of America, to be thrown open and placed within the reach of the whole people. We want the great cost, the delays, as well as the privations and risks of a passage to California, by the malarious Isthmus of Panama, or any other of the routes now in use, to be mitigated, or done away with. There will be some greater equality in the enjoyment and advantages of these new acquisitions upon the Pacific coast when this road shall be constructed. The inexhaustible gold mines, or placers of California, will no longer be accessible only to the more robust, resolute, or desperate part of our population, and who may be already well enough off to pay their passage by sea, or provide an outfit for an overland travel of two and three thousand miles. Enterprising young men all over the country, who can command the pittance of forty or fifty dollars to pay their railroad fare; heads of families who have the misfortune to be poor, but spirit and energy enough to seek comfort and independence by labor, will no longer be restrained by the necessity of separating themselves from their families, but have it in their power, with such small means as they may readily command, in eight or ten days, to find themselves with their whole households transported and set down in the midst of the gold regions of the West, at full liberty to possess and enjoy whatever of the rich harvest spread out before them their industry and energy shall entitle them to. It will be theirs by as good a title as any can boast who have had the means to precede them. We hear much said of late of the justice and policy of providing a homestead, a quarter section of the public land, to every poor and landless family in the country. Make this road, and you enable every poor man in the country to buy a much better homestead, and retain all the pride and spirit of independence. Gentlemen here may say that the region of California, so inviting, and abundant in gold now, will soon be exhausted, and all these bright prospects for the enterprising poor pass away. No, sir; centuries will pass — ages and ages must roll away before those goldbearing mountains shall all have been excavated — those auriferous sands and alluvial deposits shall give out all their wealth; and even after all these shall have failed, the beds of the rivers will yield a generous return to the toil of the laborer. . . .

Mr. President, I alluded to the importance of having a communication by railway between the Mississippi River and the Pacific Ocean, in the event of war with any great maritime Power. I confess that the debates upon the subject of our foreign relations within the last few weeks, if all that was said had commanded my full assent, would have dissipated very much the force of any argument which I thought might be fairly urged in favor of this road as a necessary work for the protection and security of our possessions on the Pacific coast. We now hear it stated, and reiterated by grave and respectable and intelligent Senators, that there is no reason that any one should apprehend a war with either Great Britain or France. Not now, nor at any time in the future; at all events, unless there shall be a total change in the condition, social, political, and economical, of those Powers, and especially as regards Great Britain. All who have spoken agree that there is no prospect of war. None at all. I agree that I can see nothing in the signs of the times which is indicative of immediate and certain war. Several gentlemen have thrown out the idea that we hold the bond of Great Britain to keep the peace, with ample guarantees and sureties, not only for the present time, but for an indefinite time; and as long as Great Britain stands as an independent monarchy. These sureties and guarantees are said to consist in the discontented and destitute class of her population, of her operatives and laborers, and the indispensable necessity of the cotton crop of the United States in furnishing them with employment and subsistence, without which it is said she would be torn with internal strife.

I could tell gentlemen who argue in that way, that we have another guarantee that Great Britain will not break with the United States for any trivial cause, which they have not thought proper to raise. We may threaten and denounce and bluster as much as we please about British violations of the Clayton and Bulwer treaty, and the Mosquito protectorate, about the assumption of territorial dominion over the Balize or British Honduras, and the new colony of the Bay Islands; and Great Britain will negotiate, explain, treat, and transgress, and negotiate again, and resort to any device, before she will go to war with us, as long as she can hope to prolong the advantages to herself of the free-trade policy now established with the United States. It is not only the cotton crop of America which she covets, but it is the

rich market for the products of her manufacturing industry, which she finds in the United States; and this has contributed as much as any other cause to improve the condition of her operatives, and impart increased prosperity to her trade and revenue. As long as we think proper to hold to our present commercial regulations, I repeat that it will require very great provocation on our part to force Great Britain into a war with the United States. . . .

As for this road, we are told at every turn that it is ridiculous to talk of war in connection with it, for we will have no wars except those with the Indians. Both England and France dare not go to war with us. I say this course of argument is not only unwise and delusive, but if such sentiments take hold on the country, they will be mischievous; they will almost to a certainty lead to a daring and reckless policy on our part; and as each government labors under a similar delusion as to what the other will not dare to do, what is more probable than that both may get into such a position—the result of a mutual mistake—that war must ensue? It is worth while to reflect upon the difference between the policy of Great Britain and this country in her diplomatic correspondence and debates in Parliament. When we make a threat, Great Britain does not threaten in turn. We hear of no gasconade on her part. If we declare that we have a just right to latitude 54° 40′, and will maintain our right at all hazard, she does not bluster, and threaten, and declare what she will do, if we dare to carry out our threat. When we talk about the Mosquito king, of Balize, and of the Bay Islands, and declare our determination to drive her from her policy and purposes in regard to them, we do not hear of an angry form of expression from her. We employed very strong language last year in regard to the rights of American fishermen; but the reply of Great Britain scarcely assumed the tone of remonstrance against the intemperate tone of our debates. Her policy upon all such occasions is one of wisdom. Her strong and stern purpose is seldom to be seen in her diplomatic intercourse, or in the debates of her leading statesmen; but if you were about her dock-yards, or in her foundries, or her timber-yards, and her great engine manufactories, and her armories, you would find some bustle and stir. There, all is life and motion.

I have always thought that the proper policy of this country is to make no threats—to make no parade of what we intend to

do. Let us put the country in a condition to defend its honor and interests; to maintain them successfully whenever they may be assailed; no matter by what Power, whether by Great Britain, or France, or both combined. Make this road; complete the defenses of the country, of your harbors, and navy yards; strengthen your navy—put it upon an efficient footing; appropriate ample means for making experiments to ascertain the best model of ships-of-war, to be driven by steam or any other motive power; the best models of the engines to be employed in them; to inquire whether a large complement of guns, or a few guns of great calibre, is the better plan. We may well, upon such questions, take a lesson from England. At a recent period she has been making experiments of this nature, in order to give increased efficiency to her naval establishment. How did she set about it? Her Admiralty Board gave orders for eleven of the most perfect engines that could be built by eleven of the most skillful and eminent engine-builders in the United Kingdom, without limit as to the cost, or any other limitation, except as to class or size. At the same time orders were issued for the building of thirteen frigates of a medium class by thirteen of the most skillful shipbuilders in the kingdom, in order to ascertain the best models, the best running lines, and the best of every other quality desirable in a war vessel. This is the mode in which Great Britain prepares for any contingencies which may arise. She cannot tell when they may occur, yet she knows that she has no immunity from those chances which, at some time or other, are seen to happen to all nations. In my opinion, the construction of this road from the Mississippi to the Pacific is essential to the protection and safety of this country, in the event of a war with any great maritime Power. It may take ten years to complete it; but every hundred miles of it, which may be finished before the occurrence of war, will be just so much gained—so much added to our ability to maintain our honor in that war. In every view of this question I can take, I am persuaded that we ought at least prepare to commence the work, and do it immediately.

JUDAH PHILIP BENJAMIN

(1811–1884)

JUDAH P. BENJAMIN, the "Beaconsfield of the Confederacy," was born at St. Croix in the West Indies, where his parents, a family of English-Jews, on their way to settle in New Orleans, were delayed by the American measures against intercourse with England. In 1816 his parents brought him to Wilmington, North Carolina, where, and at Yale College, he was educated. Not until after he was ready to begin life at the bar, did he reach New Orleans, the destination for which his parents had set out before he was born. In New Orleans, after a severe struggle, he rose to eminence as a lawyer, and his firm, of which Mr. Slidell was a partner, was the leading law firm of the State. He was elected to the United States Senate as a Whig in 1852 and re-elected as a Democrat in 1859. With Mr. Slidell, who was serving with him in the Senate, he withdrew in 1861 and became Attorney-General in the Confederate cabinet. He was afterwards made Secretary of War, but as the Confederate congress censured him in that position he resigned it and Mr. Davis immediately appointed him Secretary of State. After the close of the war, when pursuit after members of the Confederate cabinet was active, he left the coast of Florida in an open boat and landed at the Bahamas, taking passage thence to London where he rose to great eminence as a lawyer. He was made Queen's Counsel, and on his retirement from practice, because of ill health, in 1883, a farewell banquet was given him by the bar in the hall of the Inner Temple, probably the most notable compliment paid in England to any orator since the banquet to Berryer. He died in 1884.

Benjamin was called the "brains of the Confederacy" and in acuteness of intellect he probably surpassed most men of his time. He resembled Disraeli in this as well as in being a thorough-going believer in an aristocratic method of government rather than in one based on universal suffrage and the will of the masses determined by majority vote.

FAREWELL TO THE UNION

(On Leaving the United States Senate in 1861)

MR. PRESIDENT, if we were engaged in the performance of our accustomed legislative duties, I might well rest content with the simple statement of my concurrences in the remarks just made by my colleague [Mr. Slidell]. Deeply impressed, however, with the solemnity of the occasion, I cannot remain insensible to the duty of recording, among the authentic reports of your proceedings, the expression of my conviction that the State of Louisiana has judged and acted well and wisely in this crisis of her destiny.

Sir, it has been urged, on more than one occasion, in the discussions here and elsewhere, that Louisiana stands on an exceptional footing. It has been said that whatever may be the rights of the States that were original parties to the Constitution,—even granting their right to resume, for sufficient cause, those restricted powers which they delegated to the general government in trust for their own use and benefit,—still Louisiana can have no such right, because she was acquired by purchase. Gentlemen have not hesitated to speak of the sovereign States formed out of the territory ceded by France as property bought with the money of the United States, belonging to them as purchasers; and, although they have not carried their doctrine to its legitimate results, I must conclude that they also mean to assert, on the same principle, the right of selling for a price that which for a price was bought.

I shall not pause to comment on this repulsive dogma of a party which asserts the right of property in free-born white men, in order to reach its cherished object of destroying the right of property in slave-born black men — still less shall I detain the Senate in pointing out how shadowy the distinction between the condition of the servile African and that to which the white freeman of my State would be reduced, if it, indeed, be true that they are bound to this government by ties that cannot be legitimately dissevered without the consent of that very majority which wields its powers for their oppression. I simply deny the fact on which the argument is founded. I deny that the province of Louisiana, or the people of Louisiana, were ever

conveyed to the United States for a price as property that could be bought or sold at will. Without entering into the details of the negotiation, the archives of our State Department show the fact to be, that although the domain, the public lands, and other property of France in the ceded province, were conveyed by absolute title to the United States, the sovereignty was not conveyed otherwise than in trust.

A hundredfold, sir, has the Government of the United States been reimbursed by the sales of public property, of public lands, for the price of the acquisition; but not with the fidelity of the honest trustee has it discharged the obligations as regards the sovereignty.

I have said that the government assumed to act as trustee or guardian of the people of the ceded province, and covenanted to transfer to them the sovereignty thus held in trust for their use and benefit, as soon as they were capable of exercising it. What is the express language of the treaty?

"The inhabitants of the ceded territory shall be incorporated in the Union of the United States, and admitted as soon as possible, according to the principles of the Federal Constitution, to the enjoyments of all rights, advantages, and immunities of citizens of the United States; and in the meantime they shall be maintained and protected in the enjoyment of their liberty, property, and the religion which they profess."

And, sir, as if to mark the true nature of the cession in a manner too significant to admit of misconstruction, the treaty stipulates no price; and the sole consideration for the conveyance, as stated on its face, is the desire to afford a strong proof of the friendship of France for the United States. By the terms of a separate convention stipulating the payment of a sum of money, the precaution is again observed of stating that the payment is to be made, not as a consideration or a price or a condition precedent of the cession, but it is carefully distinguished as being a consequence of the cession. It was by words thus studiously chosen, sir, that James Monroe and Thomas Jefferson marked their understanding of a contract now misconstrued as being a bargain and sale of sovereignty over freemen. With what indignant scorn would those stanch advocates of the inherent right of self-government have repudiated the slavish doctrine now deduced from their action!

How were the obligations of this treaty fulfilled? That Louisiana at that date contained slaves held as property by her people through the whole length of the Mississippi Valley, that those people had an unrestricted right of settlement with their slaves under legal protection throughout the entire ceded province, no man has ever yet had the hardihood to deny. Here is a treaty promise to protect their property — their slave property — in that Territory, before it should become a State. That this promise was openly violated, in the adjustment forced upon the South at the time of the admission of Missouri, is a matter of recorded history. The perspicuous and unanswerable exposition of Mr. Justice Catron, in the opinion delivered by him in the Dred Scott case, will remain through all time as an ample vindication of this assertion.

If then, sir, the people of Louisiana had a right, which Congress could not deny, of the admission into the Union with all the rights of all the citizens of the United States, it is in vain that the partisans of the right of the majority to govern the minority with despotic control, attempt to establish a distinction, to her prejudice, between her rights and those of any other State. The only distinction which really exists is this, that she can point to a breach of treaty stipulations expressly guaranteeing her rights, as a wrong superadded to those which have impelled a number of her sister States to the assertion of their independence.

The rights of Louisiana as a sovereign State are those of Virginia; no more, no less. Let those who deny her right to resume delegated powers successfully refute the claim of Virginia to the same right, in spite of her express reservation made and notified to her sister States when she consented to enter the Union! And, sir, permit me to say that, of all the causes which justify the action of the Southern States, I know none of greater gravity and more alarming magnitude than that now developed of the right of secession. A pretension so monstrous as that which perverts a restricted agency constituted by sovereign States for common purposes, into the unlimited despotism of the majority, and denies all legitimate escape from such despotism, when powers not delegated are usurped, converts the whole constitutional fabric into the secure abode of lawless tyranny, and degrades sovereign States into provincial dependencies.

It is said that the right of secession, if conceded, makes of our government a mere rope of sand; that to assert its existence

imputes to the framers of the Constitution the folly of planting the seeds of death in that which was designed for perpetual existence. If this imputation were true, sir, it would merely prove that their offspring was not exempt from that mortality which is the common lot of all that is not created by higher than human power. But it is not so, sir. Let facts answer theory. For two-thirds of a century this right has been known by many of the States to be, at all times, within their power. Yet, up to the present period, when its exercise has become indispensable to a people menaced with absolute extermination, there have been but two instances in which it has been even threatened seriously; the first, when Massachusetts led the New England States in an attempt to escape from the dangers of our last war with Great Britain; the second, when the same State proposed to secede on account of the admission of Texas as a new State into the Union.

Sir, in the language of our declaration of secession from Great Britain, it is stated as an established truth, that "all experience has shown that mankind are more disposed to suffer while evils are sufferable than to right themselves by abolishing the forms to which they have been accustomed"; and nothing can be more obvious to the calm and candid observer of passing events than that the disruption of the Confederacy has been due, in a great measure, not to the existence, but to the denial of this right. Few candid men would refuse to admit that the Republicans of the North would have been checked in their mad career had they been convinced of the existence of this right, and the intention to assert it. The very knowledge of its existence by preventing occurrences which alone could prompt its exercise would have rendered it a most efficient instrument in the preservation of the Union. But, sir, if the fact were otherwise — if all the teachings of experience were reversed — better, far better, a rope of sand, aye, the flimsiest gossamer that ever glistened in the morning dew, than chains of iron and shackles of steel; better the wildest anarchy, with the hope, the chance, of one hour's inspiration of the glorious breath of freedom, than ages of the hopeless bondage and oppression to which our enemies would reduce us.

We are told that the laws must be enforced; that the revenues must be collected; that the South is in rebellion without cause, and that her citizens are traitors.

Rebellion! the very word is a confession; an avowal of tyranny, outrage, and oppression. It is taken from the despot's code, and has no terror for others than slavish souls. When, sir, did millions of people, as a single man, rise in organized, deliberate, unimpassioned rebellion against justice, truth, and honor? Well did a great Englishman exclaim on a similar occasion:—

"You might as well tell me that they rebelled against the light of heaven, that they rejected the fruits of the earth. Men do not war against their benefactors; they are not mad enough to repel the instincts of self-preservation. I pronounce fearlessly that no intelligent people ever rose, or ever will rise, against a sincere, rational, and benevolent authority. No people were ever born blind. Infatuation is not a law of human nature. When there is a revolt by a free people, with the common consent of all classes of society, there must be a criminal against whom that revolt is aimed."

Traitors! Treason! Ay, sir, the people of the South imitate and glory in just such treason as glowed in the soul of Hampden; just such treason as leaped in living flame from the impassioned lips of Henry; just such treason as encircles with a sacred halo the undying name of Washington.

You will enforce the laws. You want to know if we have a government; if you have any authority to collect revenue; to wring tribute from an unwilling people? Sir, humanity desponds, and all the inspiring hopes of her progressive improvement vanish into empty air at the reflections which crowd on the mind at hearing repeated, with aggravated enormity, the sentiments against which a Chatham launched his indignant thunders nearly a century ago. The very words of Lord North and his royal master are repeated here in debate, not as quotations, but as the spontaneous outpourings of a spirit the counterpart of theirs.

In Lord North's speech on the destruction of the tea in Boston harbor, he said:—

"We are no longer to dispute between legislation and taxation; we are now only to consider whether or not we have any authority there. It is very clear we have none, if we suffer the property of our subjects to be destroyed. We must punish, control, or yield to them."

And thereupon he proposed to close the port of Boston, just as the representatives of Massachusetts now propose to close the port of Charleston, in order to determine whether or not you have any authority there. It is thus that, in 1861, Boston is to pay her debt of gratitude to Charleston, which, in the days of

her struggle, proclaimed the generous sentiment that "the cause of Boston was the cause of Charleston." Who, after this, will say that republicans are ungrateful? Well, sir, the statesmen of Great Britain answered to Lord North's appeal, "yield." The courtiers and the politicians said, "punish," "control." The result is known. History gives you the lesson. Profit by its teachings!

So, sir, in the address sent under the royal sign-manual to Parliament, it was invoked to take measures "for better securing the execution of the laws," and it acquiesced in the suggestion. Just as now, a senile executive, under the sinister influence of insane counsels, is proposing, with your assent, "to secure the better execution of the laws," by blockading ports and turning upon the people of the States the artillery which they provided at their own expense for their own defense, and intrusted to you and to him for that and for no other purpose—nay, even in States that are now exercising the undoubted and most precious rights of a free people; where there is no secession; where the citizens are assembling to hold peaceful elections for considering what course of action is demanded in this dread crisis by a due regard for their own safety and their own liberty; aye, even in Virginia herself, the people are to cast their suffrages beneath the undisguised menaces of a frowning fortress. Cannon are brought to bear on their homes, and parricidal hands are preparing weapons for rending the bosom of the mother of Washington.

Sir, when Great Britain proposed to exact tribute from your fathers against their will, Lord Chatham said:—

"Whatever is a man's own is absolutely his own; no man has a right to take it from him without his consent. Whoever attempts to do it attempts an injury. Whoever does it commits a robbery. You have no right to tax America. I rejoice that America has resisted.

"Let the sovereign authority of this country over the colonies be asserted in as strong terms as can be devised, and be made to extend to every point of legislation whatever, so that we may bind their trade, confine their manufactures, and exercise every power, except that of taking money out of their own pockets without their consent."

It was reserved for the latter half of the nineteenth century, and for the Congress of a Republic of free men, to witness the willing abnegation of all power, save that of exacting tribute.

What imperial Britain, with the haughtiest pretensions of unlimited power over dependent colonies, could not even attempt without the vehement protest of her greatest statesmen, is to be enforced in aggravated form, if you can enforce it, against independent States.

Good God, sir! since when has the necessity arisen of recalling to American legislators the lessons of freedom taught in lisping childhood by loving mothers; that pervade the atmosphere we have breathed from infancy; that so form part of our very being, that in their absence we would lose the consciousness of our own identity? Heaven be praised that not all have forgotten them; that when we shall have left these familiar halls, and when force bills, blockades, armies, navies, and all the accustomed coercive appliances of despots shall be proposed and advocated, voices shall be heard from this side of the chamber that will make its very roof resound with the indignant clamor of outraged freedom. Methinks I still hear ringing in my ears the appeal of the eloquent Representative [Hon. George H. Pendleton, of Ohio], whose Northern home looks down on Kentucky's fertile borders: "Armies, money, blood cannot maintain this Union; justice, reason, peace may."

And now to you, Mr. President, and to my brother Senators, on all sides of this chamber, I bid a respectful farewell; with many of those from whom I have been radically separated in political sentiment, my personal relations have been kindly, and have inspired me with a respect and esteem that I shall not willingly forget; with those around me from the Southern States I part as men part from brothers on the eve of a temporary absence, with a cordial pressure of the hand and a smiling assurance of the speedy renewal of sweet intercourse around the family hearth. But to you, noble and generous friends, who, born beneath other skies, possess hearts that beat in sympathy with ours; to you, who, solicited and assailed by motives the most powerful that could appeal to selfish natures, have nobly spurned them all; to you, who, in our behalf, have bared your breasts to the fierce beatings of the storm, and made willing sacrifice of life's most glittering prizes in your devotion to constitutional liberty; to you, who have made our cause your cause, and from many of whom I feel I part forever, what shall I, can I say? Naught, I know and feel, is needed for myself; but this I will say for the people in whose name I speak to-day:

whether prosperous or adverse fortunes await you, one priceless treasure is yours—the assurance that an entire people honor your names, and hold them in grateful and affectionate memory. But with still sweeter and more touching return shall your unselfish devotion be rewarded. When, in after days, the story of the present shall be written, when history shall have passed her stern sentence on the erring men who have driven their unoffending brethren from the shelter of their common home, your names will derive fresh lustre from the contrast; and when your children shall hear repeated the familiar tale, it will be with glowing cheek and kindling eye; their very souls will stand a-tiptoe as their sires are named, and they will glory in their lineage from men of spirit as generous and of patriotism as high-hearted as ever illustrated or adorned the American Senate.

SLAVERY AS ESTABLISHED BY LAW

(Delivered in the United States Senate, March 11th, 1858)

EXAMINE your Constitution; are slaves the only species of property there recognized as requiring peculiar protection? Sir, the inventive genius of our brethren of the North is a source of vast wealth to them and vast benefit to the nation. I saw a short time ago in one of the New York journals, that the estimated value of a few of the patents now before us in this capitol for renewal was $40,000,000. I cannot believe that the entire capital invested in inventions of this character in the United States can fall short of one hundred and fifty or two hundred million dollars. On what protection does this vast property rest? Just upon that same constitutional protection which gives a remedy to the slave-owner when his property is also found outside of the limits of the State in which he lives.

Without this protection what would be the condition of the Northern inventor? Why, sir, the Vermont inventor protected by his own law would come to Massachusetts, and there say to the pirate who had stolen his property, "Render me up my property, or pay me value for its use." The Senator from Vermont would receive for answer, if he were the counsel of this Vermont inventor: "Sir, if you want protection for your property go to your own State; property is governed by the laws of the State within whose jurisdiction it is found; you have no property in your invention outside of the limits of your State; you cannot go an inch beyond it." Would not this be so? Does not every man see at once that the right of the inventor to his discovery, that the right of the poet to his inspiration, depends upon those principles of eternal justice which God has implanted in the heart of man; and that wherever he cannot exercise them, it is because man, faithless to the trust that he has received from God, denies them the protection to which they are entitled?

Sir, follow out the illustration which the Senator from Vermont himself has given; take his very case of the Delaware owner of a horse riding him across the line into Pennsylvania. The Senator says, "Now you see that slaves are not property, like other property; if slaves were property like other property, why have you this special clause in your Constitution to protect a slave? You have no clause to protect a horse, because horses are recognized as property everywhere." Mr. President, the same fallacy lurks at the bottom of this argument, as of all the rest. Let Pennsylvania exercise her undoubted jurisdiction over persons and things within her own boundary, let her do as she has a perfect right to do — declare that hereafter, within the State of Pennsylvania, there shall be no property in horses, and that no man shall maintain a suit in her courts for the recovery of property in a horse, and where will your horse owner be then? Just where the English poet is now; just where the slaveholder and the inventor would be if the Constitution, foreseeing a difference of opinion in relation to rights in these subject-matters, had not provided the remedy in relation to such property as might easily be plundered. Slaves, if you please, are not property like other property in this, that you can easily rob us of them; but as to the right in them, that man has to overthrow the whole history of the world, he has to overthrow every treatise on jurisprudence, he has to ignore the common sentiment of mankind, he has to repudiate the authority of all that is considered sacred with man, ere he can reach the conclusion that the person who owns a slave, in a country where slavery has been established for ages, has no other property in that slave than the mere title which is given by the statute law of the land where it is found.

THOMAS H. BENTON

(1782-1858)

N JANUARY 19th, 1830, when Mr. Foot's innocent resolution to inquire into the sales of public lands was before the United States Senate, Thomas H. Benton turned several of his stately periods by an attack on Massachusetts, which precipitated one of the greatest parliamentary debates of modern times—that in which Hayne and Webster were pitted against each other on the right of a State to declare null a Federal statute.

Benton himself believed in what he called "the Virginia idea" of Nullification—which, as he defined it, was that an unconstitutional act is "null and void, as being against the Constitution, but is to be obeyed while it remains unrepealed and that its repeal is to be effected constitutionally."

Though he never succeeded in making this definition part of the creed of any political party, Benton held it himself to the end of his life, and after agreeing with Jackson that Calhoun was guilty of treason, he opposed Fremont, his own son-in-law, for the presidency, and so maintained his consistency to the last.

With Webster, Clay, and Calhoun, he stands as one of the most remarkable group of statesmen and orators of modern times. It happened more than once that he was opposed on questions of vital public policy to all three of the others of the great quartet and that he won against them as he did on what was once the burning question of the removal of the Indians beyond the Mississippi.

Differing from each other in so many other respects, Webster, Clay, and Calhoun occupied common ground in their dissent from Benton's theory that the "better element" of the community is apt to give the worst results when it is trusted to govern the rest. This theory was involved in Jefferson's teachings, but it did not come into actual and rude collision with the stately patriotism of the gentlemen of the colonial and revolutionary period until such of them as survived in 1828 saw Jackson with Benton at his back ready to force issues in its behalf as they had never been forced before in any English-speaking country. The shock produced was so profound that, becoming cumulative from year to year, it resulted finally in the great panic and prostration of business under Van Buren. In his war against the United States Bank, in his detestation of Calhoun and Nullification, in his long fight for vindication under the "Expunging

resolution," Jackson had Benton for his real prime minister and parliamentary leader. Among the American statesmen of the nineteenth century, only Jefferson, Jackson, Webster, Clay, Calhoun, and Lincoln can be conceded to have influenced the history of their country more deeply than did the great Missourian. What his intellect lacked in flexibility it gained in force. The country can never produce his like again. Men may be greater in other ways hereafter, but no one else will ever be great in Benton's way. Such desperate brawls as that in which he and his brother Jesse worsted Jackson's superior forces in Nashville were common enough in 1813, but it is characteristic of Benton, and only of Benton, that the incident was merely an incident with him. He had somehow got into a world which required, or seemed to require, of him to hold his own life and that of others cheap where the alternative was retreat or surrender. But that, after the Nashville fight, he should have been Jackson's lifelong and strongest friend,—that is so much a part of the individuality peculiar to two men, each of whom was in his own way unique, that it is useless to try to explain it.

Benton was born in Hillsborough, North Carolina, March 14th, 1782. The removal of his family to Tennessee interrupted his studies at the University of North Carolina, but in one way and another he managed to continue them though life; and, as his speeches show, he had at his command such a stock of information on public affairs as few other statesmen of his time possessed. After his quarrel with Jackson who had been his friend and patron in Tennessee, he removed to St. Louis where for a time he edited the Missouri Enquirer. According to one version of the Lucas duel, he was involved in that tragedy by an article which appeared in the Enquirer while it was under his charge. He was elected Senator from Missouri in 1820 and held the place for thirty years. After his defeat for the Senate he was elected to the House of Representatives in 1852. In 1856 he ran for governor of the State to vindicate the democracy of Andrew Jackson's time against the school of Calhoun, but he was defeated. In the presidential campaign of 1856 he supported Buchanan and opposed Fremont, who as the nominee of the Republican party stood for constitutional views to which Benton was not less opposed than to those of Calhoun. He died April 10th, 1858, at Washington.

It is a noteworthy fact that Benton's influence survives the struggle over slavery and the Civil War to a much greater extent than does that of any other statesman of his time, Clay only excepted. As "Old Bullion," and the stalwart advocate of a currency of the precious metals issued only by the government, he is identified with a permanent question of public policy much as Clay by his advocacy of the "American System" is with that of indirect taxation.

THE POLITICAL CAREER OF ANDREW JACKSON

(United States Senate, January 12th, 1837)

THE Expunging resolution and preamble having been read, Mr. Benton said: Mr. President, it is now near three years since the resolve was adopted by the Senate, which it is my present motion to expunge from the journal. At the moment that this resolve was adopted, I gave notice of my intention to move to expunge it, and then expressed my confident belief that the motion would eventually prevail. That expression of confidence was not an ebullition of vanity, nor a presumptuous calculation, intended to accelerate the event it affected to foretell. It was not a vain boast, nor an idle assumption, but was the result of a deep conviction of the injustice done President Jackson, and a thorough reliance upon the justice of the American people. I felt that the President had been wronged, and my heart told me that this wrong would be redressed. The event proves that I was not mistaken. The question of expunging this resolution has been carried to the people, and their decision has been had upon it. They decide in favor of the expurgation; and their decision has been both made and manifested, and communicated to us in a great variety of ways. A great number of States have expressly instructed their Senators to vote for this expurgation. A very great majority of the States have elected Senators and Representatives to Congress, upon the express ground of favoring this expurgation. The Bank of the United States, which took the initiative in the accusation against the President, and furnished the material and worked the machinery which was used against him, and which was then so powerful on this floor, has become more and more odious to the public mind, and musters now but a slender phalanx of friends in the two houses of Congress. The late presidential election furnishes additional evidence of public sentiment. The candidate who was the friend of President Jackson, the supporter of his administration, and the avowed advocate for the expurgation, has received a large majority of the suffrages of the whole Union, and that after an express declaration of his sentiments on this precise point. The evidence of the public will, exhibited in all these forms, is too manifest to be mistaken, too explicit to require illustration, and too imperative to be disregarded. Omitting

details and specific enumeration of proofs, I refer to our own files for the instructions to expunge—to the complexion of the two houses for the temper of the people—to the denationalized condition of the Bank of the United States for the fate of the imperious accuser—and to the issue of the presidential election for the answer of the Union. All these are pregnant proofs of the public will; and the last pre-eminently so, because both the question of the expurgation and the form of the process were directly put in issue upon it. A representative of the people from the State of Kentucky formally interrogated a prominent candidate for the presidency on these points, and required from him a public answer, for the information of the public mind. The answer was given, and published, and read by all the voters before the election; and I deem it right to refer to that answer in this place, not only as evidence of the points put in issue, but also for the purpose of doing more ample justice to President Jackson, by incorporating into the legislative history of this case the high and honorable testimony in his favor of the eminent citizen who has just been exalted to the lofty honors of the American presidency:—

"Your last question seeks to know 'my' opinion as to the constitutional power of the Senate or House of Representatives to expunge or obliterate from the journals the proceedings of a previous session.

"You will, I am sure, be satisfied, upon further consideration, that there are but few questions of a political character less connected with the duties of the office of President of the United States, or that might not with equal propriety be put by an elector to a candidate for that station, than this. With the journals of neither house of Congress can he properly have anything to do. But as your question has doubtless been induced by the pendency of Colonel Benton's resolutions to expunge from the journals of the Senate certain other resolutions touching the official conduct of President Jackson, I prefer to say that I regard the passage of Colonel Benton's preamble and resolutions to be an act of justice to a faithful and greatly injured public servant, not only constitutional in itself but imperiously demanded by a proper respect for the well-known will of the people."

I do not propose, sir, to draw violent, unwarranted, or strained inferences. I do not assume to say that the question of this expurgation was a leading or controlling point in the issue of this election. I do not assume to say or insinuate that every individual and every voter delivered his suffrage with reference to this question. Doubtless there were many exceptions. Still, the triumphant election of the candidate who had expressed himself in the terms just quoted, and who was, besides, the personal and political friend of President Jackson, and the avowed approver of his administration, must be admitted to a place among the proofs in this case, and ranked among the high concurring evidences of the public sentiment in favor of the motion which I make.

Assuming, then, that we have ascertained the will of the people on this great question, the inquiry presents itself, how far the expression of that will ought to be conclusive of our action here. I hold that it ought to be binding and obligatory upon us; and that, not only upon the principles of representative government, which require obedience to the known will of the people, but also in conformity to the principles upon which the proceeding against President Jackson was conducted, when the sentence against him was adopted. Then, everything was done with special reference to the will of the people. Their impulsion was assumed to be the sole motive to action, and to them the ultimate verdict was expressly referred. The whole machinery of alarm and pressure, every engine of political and moneyed power was put in motion, and worked for many months, to excite the people against the President, and to stir up meetings, memorials, petitions, traveling committees, and distress deputations against him; and each symptom of popular discontent was hailed as an evidence of public will, and quoted here as proof that the people demanded the condemnation of the President. Not only legislative assemblies and memorials from large assemblies were then produced here as evidence of public opinion, but the petitions of boys under age, the remonstrances of a few signers, and the results of the most inconsiderable elections, were ostentatiously paraded and magnified as the evidence of the sovereign will of our constituents. Thus, sir, the public voice was everything, while that voice partially obtained through political and pecuniary machinations was adverse to the President. Then the popular will was the shrine at which all worshiped. Now, when that will is regularly, soberly, repeatedly, and almost universally expressed through the ballot boxes, at the various elections, and turns out to be in favor of the President, certainly no one can disregard it, nor otherwise look at it than as the solemn verdict of the competent and ultimate tribunal, upon an issue

fairly made up, fully argued, and duly submitted for decision. As such verdict I receive it. As the deliberate verdict of the sovereign people I bow to it. I am content. I do not mean to reopen the case, nor to recommence the argument. I leave that work to others, if any others choose to perform it. For myself, I am content; and, dispensing with further argument, I shall call for judgment, and ask to have execution done upon that unhappy journal, which the verdict of millions of freemen finds guilty of bearing on its face an untrue, illegal, and unconstitutional sentence of condemnation against the approved President of the republic.

But, while declining to reopen the argument of this question, and refusing to tread over again the ground already traversed, there is another and a different task to perform; one which the approaching termination of President Jackson's administration makes peculiarly proper at this time, and which it is my privilege, and perhaps my duty, to execute, as being the suitable conclusion to the arduous contest in which we have been so long engaged. I allude to the general tenor of his administration, and to its effect, for good or for evil, upon the condition of his country. This is the proper time for such a view to be taken. The political existence of this great man now draws to a close. In little more than forty days he ceases to be a public character. In a few brief weeks he ceases to be an object of political hope to any, and should cease to be an object of political hate or envy to all. Whatever of motive the servile and time-serving might have found in his exalted station for raising the altar of adulation, and burning the incense of praise before him, that motive can no longer exist. The dispenser of the patronage of an empire — the chief of this great confederacy of States — is soon to be a private individual, stripped of all power to reward or to punish. His own thoughts, as he has shown us in the concluding paragraph of that message, which is to be the last of its kind that we shall ever receive from him, are directed to that beloved retirement from which he was drawn by the voice of millions of freemen, and to which he now looks for that interval of repose which age and infirmities require. Under these circumstances he ceases to be a subject for the ebullition of the passions, and passes into a character for the contemplation of history. Historically, then, shall I view him; and, limiting this **view to his civil administration, I demand where is there a chief**

magistrate of whom so much evil has been predicted, and from whom so much good has come? Never has any man entered upon the chief magistracy of a country under such appalling predictions of ruin and woe! Never has any one been so pursued with direful prognostications! Never has any one been so beset and impeded by a powerful combination of political and moneyed confederates! Never has any one in any country, where the administration of justice has risen above the knife or the bowstring, been so lawlessly and shamelessly tried and condemned by rivals and enemies, without hearing, without defense, without the forms of law or justice! History has been ransacked to find examples of tyrants sufficiently odious to illustrate him by comparison. Language has been tortured to find epithets sufficiently strong to paint him in description. Imagination has been exhausted in her efforts to deck him with revolting and inhuman attributes. Tyrant, despot, usurper; destroyer of the liberties of his country; rash, ignorant, imbecile; endangering the public peace with all foreign nations; destroying domestic prosperity at home; ruining all industry, all commerce, all manufactories; annihilating confidence between man and man; delivering up the streets of populous cities to grass and weeds, and the wharves of commercial towns to the incumbrance of decaying vessels; depriving labor of all reward; depriving industry of all employment; destroying the currency; plunging an innocent and happy people from the summit of felicity to the depths of misery, want, and despair. Such is the faint outline, followed up by actual condemnation, of the appalling denunciations daily uttered against this one man, from the moment he became an object of political competition, down to the concluding moment of his political existence.

The sacred voice of inspiration has told us that there is a time for all things. There certainly has been a time for every evil that human nature admits of to be vaticinated of President Jackson's administration; equally certain the time has now come for all rational and well-disposed people to compare the predictions with the facts, and to ask themselves if these calamitous prognostications have been verified by events. Have we peace, or war, with foreign nations? Certainly, we have peace! peace with all the world! peace with all its benign and felicitous and beneficent influences! Are we respected or despised abroad? Certainly the American name never was more honored throughout the four quarters of the globe than in this very moment. Do

we hear of indignity or outrage in any quarter, of merchants robbed in foreign ports, of vessels searched on the high seas, of American citizens impressed into foreign service, of the national flag insulted anywhere? On the contrary, we see former wrongs repaired; no new ones inflicted. France pays twenty-five millions of francs for spoliations committed thirty years ago; Naples pays two millions one hundred thousand ducats for wrongs of the same date; Denmark pays six hundred and fifty thousand rix-dollars for wrongs done a quarter of a century ago; Spain engages to pay twelve millions of reals velon for injuries of fifteen years' date; and Portugal, the last in the list of former aggressors, admits her liability, and only waits the adjustment of details to close her account by adequate indemnity. So far from war, insult, contempt, and spoliation from abroad, this denounced administration has been the season of peace and good will, and the auspicious era of universal reparation. So far from suffering injury at the hands of foreign powers, our merchants have received indemnities for all former injuries. It has been the day of accounting, of settlement, and of retribution. The long list of arrearages, extending through four successive previous administrations, has been closed and settled up. The wrongs done to commerce for thirty years back, and under so many different Presidents, and indemnities withheld from all, have been repaired and paid over under the beneficent and glorious administration of President Jackson. But one single instance of outrage has occurred, and that at the extremities of the world, and by a piratical horde, amenable to no law but the law of force. The Malays of Sumatra committed a robbery and massacre upon an American vessel. Wretches! they did not then know that Jackson was President of the United States, and that no distance, no time, no idle ceremonial of treating with robbers and assassins, was to hold back the arm of justice. Commodore Downes went out. His cannon and his bayonets struck the outlaws in their den. They paid in terror and in blood for the outrage which was committed; and the great lesson was taught to these distant pirates — to our antipodes themselves — that not even the entire diameter of this globe could protect them, and that the name of American citizen, like that of Roman citizen in the great days of the republic and of the empire, was to be the inviolable passport of all that wore it throughout the whole extent of the habitable world.

At home the most gratifying picture presents itself to the view: the public debt paid off; taxes reduced one-half; the completion of the public defenses systematically commenced; the compact with Georgia, uncomplied with since 1802, now carried into effect, and her soil ready to be freed, as her jurisdiction has been delivered from the presence and incumbrance of an Indian population. Mississippi and Alabama, Georgia, Tennessee, and North Carolina, Ohio, Indiana, Illinois, Missouri, and Arkansas— in a word, all the States incumbered with an Indian population— have been relieved from that incumbrance; and the Indians themselves have been transferred to new and permanent homes, every way better adapted to the enjoyment of their existence, the preservation of their rights, and the improvement of their condition.

The currency is not ruined! On the contrary, seventy-five millions of specie in the country is a spectacle never seen before, and is the barrier of the people against the designs of any banks which may attempt to suspend payments and to force a dishonored paper currency upon the community. These seventy-five millions are the security of the people against the dangers of a depreciated and inconvertible paper money. Gold, after a disappearance of thirty years, is restored to our country. All Europe beholds with admiration the success of our efforts, in three years, to supply ourselves with the currency which our Constitution guarantees, and which the example of France and Holland shows to be so easily attainable, and of such incalculable value to industry, morals, economy, and solid wealth. The success of these efforts is styled, in the best London papers, not merely a reformation, but a revolution, in the currency—a revolution by which our America is now regaining from Europe the gold and silver which she has been sending to them for thirty years past.

Domestic industry is not paralyzed; confidence is not destroyed; factories are not stopped; workmen are not mendicants for bread and employment; credit is not extinguished; prices have not sunk; grass is not growing in the streets of populous cities; the wharves are not lumbered with decaying vessels; columns of curses, rising from the bosoms of a ruined and agonized people, are not ascending to heaven against the destroyer of a nation's felicity and prosperity. On the contrary, the reverse of all this is true, and true to a degree that astonishes and bewilders the

11—27

senses. I know that all is not gold that glitters, that there is a difference between a specious and a solid prosperity. I know that a part of the present prosperity is apparent only, the effect of an increase of fifty millions of paper money forced into circulation by one thousand banks; but, after making due allowance for this fictitious and delusive excess, the real prosperity of the country is still unprecedently and transcendently great. I know that every flow must be followed by its ebb, that every expansion must be followed by its contraction. I know that a revulsion in the paper system is inevitable; but I know, also, that these seventy-five millions of gold and silver are the bulwark of the country, and will enable every honest bank to meet its liabilities, and every prudent citizen to take care of himself.

Turning to some points in the civil administration of President Jackson, and how much do we not find to admire! The great cause of the Constitution has been vindicated from an imputation of more than forty years' duration. He has demonstrated, by the fact itself, that a national bank is not "necessary" to the fiscal operations of the Federal government, and in that demonstration he has upset the argument of General Hamilton, and the decision of the Supreme Court of the United States, and all that ever has been said in favor of the constitutionality of a national bank. All this argument and decision rested upon the single assumption of the "necessity" of that institution to the Federal government. He has shown it is not "necessary"; that the currency of the Constitution, and especially a gold currency, is all that the Federal government wants, and that she can get that whenever she pleases. In this single act he has vindicated the Constitution from an unjust imputation, and knocked from under the decision of the Supreme Court the assumed fact on which it rested. He has prepared the way for the reversal of that decision; and it is a question for lawyers to answer, whether the case is not ripe for the application of that writ of most remedial nature, as Lord Coke calls it, and which was invented lest in any case there should be an oppressive defect of justice— the venerable writ of *audita querela defendentis*—to ascertain the truth of a fact happening since the judgment, and upon the due finding of which the judgment will be vacated. Let the lawyers bring their books, and answer us if there is not a case here presented for the application of that ancient and most remedial writ.

From President Jackson the country has first learned the true theory and practical intent of the Constitution, in giving to the Executive a qualified negative on the legislative power of Congress. Far from being an odious, dangerous, or kingly prerogative, this power, as vested in the President, is nothing but a qualified copy of the famous veto power vested in the tribunes of the people among the Romans, and intended to suspend the passage of a law until the people themselves should have time to consider it. The qualified veto of the President destroys nothing; it only delays the passage of a law, and refers it to the people for their consideration and decision. It is the reference of the law, not to a committee of the House, or of the whole House, but to the committee of the whole Union. It is a recommitment of the bill to the people, for them to examine and consider; and if, upon this examination, they are content to pass it, it will pass at the next session. The delay of a few months is the only effect of a veto in a case where the people shall ultimately approve a law; where they do not approve it, the interposition of the veto is the barrier which saves them the infliction of a law, the repeal of which might afterwards be almost impossible. The qualified negative is, therefore, a beneficent power, intended, as General Hamilton expressly declares in the Federalist, to protect, first, the executive department from the encroachments of the legislative department; and, secondly, to preserve the people from hasty, dangerous, or criminal legislation on the part of their representatives. This is the design and intention of the veto power; and the fear expressed by General Hamilton was, that Presidents, so far from exercising it too often, would not exercise it as often as the safety of the people required; they might lack the moral courage to stake themselves in opposition to a favorite measure of the majority of the two houses of Congress, and thus deprive the people, in many instances, of their right to pass upon a bill before it becomes a final law. The cases in which President Jackson has exercised the veto power has shown the soundness of these observations. No ordinary President would have staked himself against the Bank of the United States and the two houses of Congress in 1832. It required President Jackson to confront that power, to stem that torrent, to stay the progress of that charter, and to refer it to the people for their decision. His moral courage was equal to the crisis. He arrested the charter until it could go to the people, and they have arrested it forever.

Had he not done so, the charter would have become law, and its repeal almost impossible. The people of the whole Union would now have been in the condition of the people of Pennsylvania, bestrode by the monster, in daily conflict with him, and maintaining a doubtful contest for supremacy between the government of a State and the directory of a moneyed corporation.

To detail specific acts which adorn the administration of President Jackson, and illustrate the intuitive sagacity of his intellect, the firmness of his mind, his disregard of personal popularity, and his entire devotion to the public good, would be inconsistent with this rapid sketch, intended merely to present general views, and not to detail single actions, howsoever worthy they may be of a splendid page in the volume of history. But how can we pass over the great measure of the removal of the public moneys from the Bank of the United States in the autumn of 1833?—that wise, heroic, and masterly measure of prevention, which has rescued an empire from the fangs of a merciless, revengeful, greedy, insatiate, implacable, moneyed power. It is a remark for which I am indebted to the philosophic observation of my most esteemed colleague and friend [pointing to Dr. Linn], that, while it requires far greater talent to foresee an evil before it happens, and to arrest it by precautionary measures, than it requires to apply an adequate remedy to the same evil after it has happened, yet the applause bestowed by the world is always greatest in the latter case. Of this the removal of the public moneys from the Bank of the United States is an eminent instance. The veto of 1832, which arrested the charter which Congress had granted, immediately received the applause and approbation of a majority of the Union; the removal of the deposits, which prevented the bank from forcing a recharter, was disapproved by a large majority of the country, and even of his own friends; yet the veto would have been unavailing, and the bank would inevitably have been rechartered, if the deposits had not been removed. The immense sums of public money since accumulated would have enabled the bank, if she had retained the possession of it, to have coerced a recharter. Nothing but the removal could have prevented her from extorting a recharter from the sufferings and terrors of the people. If it had not been for that measure, the previous veto would have been unavailing; the bank would have been again installed in power, and this entire Federal government would have been held as an appendage to that bank, and administered according to her directions and by her nominees. That great measure of prevention, the removal of the deposits, though feebly and faintly supported by friends at first, has expelled the bank from the field, and driven her into abeyance under a State charter. She is not dead, but, holding her capital and stockholders together under a State charter, she has taken a position to watch events and to profit by them. The royal tiger has gone into the jungle, and, crouched on his belly, he awaits the favorable moment for emerging from his cover and springing on the body of the unsuspicious traveler!

The Treasury order for excluding paper money from the land offices is another wise measure, originating in an enlightened forecast and preventing great mischiefs. The President foresaw the evils of suffering a thousand streams of paper money, issuing from a thousand different banks, to discharge themselves on the national domain. He foresaw that, if these currents were allowed to run their course, the public lands would be swept away, the treasury would be filled with irredeemable paper, a vast number of banks must be broken by their folly, and the cry set up that nothing but a national bank could regulate the currency. He stopped the course of these streams of paper, and, in so doing, has saved the country from a great calamity, and excited anew the machinations of those whose schemes of gain and mischief have been disappointed, and who had counted on a new edition of panic and pressure, and again saluting Congress with the old story of confidence destroyed, currency ruined, prosperity annihilated, and distress produced, by the tyranny of one man. They began their lugubrious song; but ridicule and contempt have proved too strong for money and insolence, and the panic letter of the ex-president of the denationalized bank, after limping about for a few days, has shrunk from the lash of public scorn, and disappeared from the forum of public debate.

The difficulty with France: what an instance it presents to the superior sagacity of President Jackson over all the commonplace politicians who beset and impede his administration at home! That difficulty, inflamed and aggravated by domestic faction, wore, at one time, a portentous aspect; the skill, firmness, elevation of purpose, and manly frankness of the President avoided the danger, accomplished the object, commanded the admiration of Europe, and retained the friendship of France. He

conducted the delicate affair to a successful and mutually honorable issue. All is amicably and happily terminated, leaving not a wound, nor even a scar, behind; leaving the Frenchman and American on the ground on which they have stood for fifty years, and should forever stand—the ground of friendship, respect, good will, and mutual wishes for the honor, happiness, and prosperity of each other.

But why this specification? So beneficent and so glorious has been the administration of this President, that where to begin and where to end, in the enumeration of great measures, would be the embarrassment of him who has his eulogy to make. He came into office the first of generals; he goes out the first of statesmen. His civil competitors have shared the fate of his military opponents; and Washington city has been to the American politicians who have assailed him what New Orleans was to the British generals who attacked his lines. Repulsed! driven back! discomfited! crushed! has been the fate of all assailants, foreign and domestic, civil and military. At home and abroad the impress of his genius and of his character is felt. He has impressed upon the age in which he lives the stamp of his arms, of his diplomacy, and of his domestic policy. In a word, so transcendent have been the merits of his administration that they have operated a miracle upon the minds of his most inveterate opponents. He has expunged their objections to military chieftains! He has shown them that they were mistaken; that military men were not the dangerous rulers they had imagined, but safe and prosperous conductors of the vessel of State. He has changed their fear into love. With visible signs they admit their error, and, instead of deprecating, they now invoke the reign of chieftains. They labored hard to procure a military successor to the present incumbent; and if their love goes on increasing at the same rate, the Republic may be put to the expense of periodical wars, to breed a perpetual succession of these chieftains to rule over them and their posterity forever.

To drop this irony, which the inconsistency of mad opponents has provoked, and to return to the plain delineations of historical painting, the mind instinctively dwells on the vast and unprecedented popularity of this President. Great is the influence, great the power, greater than any man ever before possessed in our America, which he has acquired over the public mind. And how has he acquired it? Not by the arts of intrigue, or the

juggling tricks of diplomacy; not by undermining rivals, or sacrificing public interests for the gratification of classes or individuals. But he has acquired it, first, by the exercise of an intuitive sagacity which, leaving all book learning at an immeasurable distance behind, has always enabled him to adopt the right remedy at the right time and to conquer soonest when the men of forms and office thought him most near to ruin and despair. Next, by a moral courage which knew no fear when the public good beckoned him to go on. Last and chiefest, he has acquired it by an open honesty of purpose, which knew no concealments; by a straightforwardness of action, which disdained the forms of office and the arts of intrigue; by a disinterestedness of motive, which knew no selfish or sordid calculation; a devotedness of patriotism, which staked everything personal on the issue of every measure which the public welfare required him to adopt. By these qualities and these means he has acquired his prodigious popularity and his transcendent influence over the public mind; and if there are any who envy that influence and popularity, let them envy also, and emulate, if they can, the qualities and means by which they were acquired.

Great has been the opposition to President Jackson's administration; greater, perhaps, than ever has been exhibited against any government, short of actual insurrection and forcible resistance. Revolution has been proclaimed, and everything has been done that could be expected to produce revolution. The country has been alarmed, agitated, convulsed. From the Senate chamber to the village barroom, from one end of the continent to the other, denunciation, agitation, excitement has been the order of the day. For eight years the President of this republic has stood upon a volcano, vomiting fire and flames upon him, and threatening the country itself with ruin and desolation, if the people did not expel the usurper, despot, and tyrant, as he was called, from the high place to which the suffrages of millions of freemen had elevated him.

Great is the confidence which he has always reposed in the discernment and equity of the American people. I have been accustomed to see him for many years, and under many discouraging trials, but never saw him doubt, for an instant, the ultimate support of the people. It was my privilege to see him often, and during the most gloomy period of the panic conspiracy, when the whole earth seemed to be in commotion against

him, and when many friends were faltering, and stout hearts were quailing before the raging storm which bank machination and senatorial denunciation had conjured up to overwhelm him. I saw him in the darkest moments of this gloomy period; and never did I see his confidence in the ultimate support of his fellow-citizens forsake him for an instant. He always said the people would stand by those who stand by them; and nobly have they justified that confidence! That verdict, the voice of millions, which now demands the expurgation of that sentence which the Senate and the bank then pronounced upon him, is the magnificent response of the people's hearts to the implicit confidence which he then reposed in them. But it was not in the people only that he had confidence; there was another, and a far higher power, to which he constantly looked to save the country, and its defenders, from every danger; and signal events prove that he did not look to that high power in vain.

Sir, I think it right, in approaching the termination of this great question, to present this faint and rapid sketch of the brilliant, beneficent, and glorious administration of President Jackson. It is not for me to attempt to do it justice; it is not for ordinary men to attempt its history. His military life, resplendent with dazzling events, will demand the pen of a nervous writer; his civil administration, replete with scenes which have called into action so many and such various passions of the human heart, and which has given to native sagacity so many victories over practiced politicians, will require the profound, luminous, and philosophical conceptions of a Livy, a Plutarch, or a Sallust. This history is not to be written in our day. The contemporaries of such events are not the hands to describe them. Time must first do its office—must silence the passions, remove the actors, develop consequences, and canonize all that is sacred to honor, patriotism, and glory. In after ages the historic genius of our America shall produce the writers which the subject demands—men far removed from the contests of this day, who will know how to estimate this great epoch, and how to acquire an immortality for their own names by painting, with a master's hand, the immortal events of the patriot President's life.

And now, sir, I finish the task which, three years ago, I imposed on myself. Solitary and alone, and amidst the jeers and taunts of my opponents, I put this ball in motion. The people have taken it up, and rolled it forward, and I am no longer anything but a unit in the vast mass which now propels it. In the name of that mass I speak. I demand the execution of the edict of the people; I demand the expurgation of that sentence which the voice of a few Senators, and the power of their confederate, the Bank of the United States, has caused to be placed on the journal of the Senate, and which the voice of millions of freemen has ordered to be expunged from it.

AGAINST THE UNITED STATES BANK

(United States Senate, Wednesday, February 2d, 1831)

Mr. President:—

I OBJECT to the renewal of the charter of the Bank of the United States, because I look upon the bank as an institution too great and powerful to be tolerated in a government of free and equal laws. Its power is that of a purse—a power more potent than that of the sword; and this power it possesses to a degree and extent that will enable the bank to draw to itself too much of the political power of this Union, and too much of the individual property of the citizens of these States. The money power of the bank is both direct and indirect.

The direct power of the bank is now prodigious, and, in the event of the renewal of the charter, must speedily become boundless and uncontrollable. The bank is now authorized to own effects, lands inclusive, to the amount of fifty-five millions of dollars, and to issue notes to the amount of thirty-five millions more. This makes ninety millions; and, in addition to this vast sum, there is an opening for an unlimited increase; or, there is a dispensation in the charter to issue as many more notes as Congress, by law, may permit. This opens the door to boundless emissions; for what can be more unbounded than the will and pleasure of successive Congresses? The indirect power of the bank cannot be stated in figures; but it can be shown to be immense. In the first place, it has the keeping of the public moneys, now amounting to twenty-six millions per annum (the Post Office Department included), and the gratuitous use of the undrawn balances, large enough to constitute in themselves the capital of a great State bank. In the next place, its promissory notes are receivable, by law, in purchase of all property owned by the United States, and in payment of all debts due them; and

this may increase its power to the amount of the annual revenue, by creating a demand for its notes to that amount. In the third place, it wears the name of the United States, and has the Federal government for a partner; and this name and this partnership identify the credit of the bank with the credit of the Union. In the fourth place, it is armed with authority to disparage and discredit the notes of other banks, by excluding them from all payments to the United States; and this, added to all its other powers, direct and indirect, makes this institution the uncontrollable monarch of the moneyed system of the Union. To whom is all this power granted? To a company of private individuals, many of them foreigners, and the mass of them residing in a remote and narrow corner of the Union, unconnected by any sympathy with the fertile regions of the great valley, in which the natural power of this Union—the power of numbers—will be found to reside long before the renewed term of a second charter would expire. By whom is all this power to be exercised? By a directory of seven (it may be), governed by a majority of four (it may be); and none of these elected by the people, or responsible to them. Where is it to be exercised? At a single city, distant a thousand miles from some of the States, receiving the produce of none of them (except one); no interest in the welfare of any of them (except one); no commerce with the people; with branches in every State; and every branch subject to the secret and absolute orders of the supreme central head, thus constituting a system of centralism, hostile to the federative principle of our Union, encroaching upon the wealth and power of the States, and organized upon a principle to give the highest effect to the greatest power. This mass of power, thus concentrated, thus ramified, and thus directed, must necessarily become, under a prolonged existence, the absolute monopolist of American money, the sole manufacturer of paper currency, and the sole authority (for authority it will be) to which the Federal government, the State governments, the great cities, corporate bodies, merchants, traders, and every private citizen, must, of necessity, apply, for every loan which their exigencies may demand. . . .

What are the tendencies of a great moneyed power, connected with the government, and controlling its fiscal operations? Are they not dangerous to every interest, public and private, political as well as pecuniary? I say they are, and briefly enumerate the heads of each mischief:—

1. Such a bank tends to subjugate the government, as I have already shown in the history of what happened to the British minister in the year 1795.

2. It tends to collusions between the government and the bank in the terms of the loans, as has been fully experienced in England in those frauds upon the people, and insults upon the understanding, called three per cent. loans, in which the government for about £50 borrowed became liable to pay £100.

3. It tends to create public debt, by facilitating public loans and substituting unlimited supplies of paper for limited supplies of coin. The British debt is born of the Bank of England. That bank was chartered in 1694, and was nothing more nor less in the beginning than an act of Parliament for the incorporation of a company of subscribers to a government loan. The loan was £1,200,000, the interest £80,000, and the expenses of management £4,000. And this is the birth and origin, the germ and nucleus of that debt, which is now £900,000,000 (the unfunded items included), which bears an interest of £30,000,000, and costs £260,000 for annual management.

4. It tends to beget and prolong unnecessary wars, by furnishing the means of carrying them on without recurrence to the people. England is the ready example for this calamity. Her wars for the restoration of the Capet Bourbons were kept up by loans and subsidies created out of bank paper. The people of England had no interest in these wars, which cost them about £600,000,000 of debt in twenty-five years, in addition to the supplies raised within the year. The kings she put back upon the French throne were not able to sit on it. Twice she put them on; twice they tumbled off in the mud; and all that now remains of so much sacrifice of life and money is the debt, which is eternal; the taxes, which are intolerable; the pensions and titles of some warriors, and the keeping of the Capet Bourbons, who are returned upon their hands.

5. It tends to aggravate the inequality of fortunes; to make the rich richer, and the poor poorer; to multiply nabobs and paupers, and to deepen and widen the gulf which separates Dives from Lazarus. A great moneyed power is favorable to great capitalists, for it is the principle of money to favor money. It is unfavorable to small capitalists, for it is the principle of money to eschew the needy and unfortunate. It is injurious to the laboring classes, because they receive no favors and have the price

of the property they wish to acquire raised to the paper maximum, while wages remain at the silver minimum.

6. It tends to make and to break fortunes, by the flux and reflux of paper. Profuse issues and sudden contractions perform this operation, which can be repeated, like planetary and pestilential visitations, in every cycle of so many years; at every periodical return, transferring millions from the actual possessors of property to the Neptunes who preside over the flux and reflux of paper. The last operation of this kind performed by the Bank of England, about five years ago, was described by Mr. Alexander Baring, in the House of Commons, in terms which are entitled to the knowledge and remembrance of American citizens. I will read his description, which is brief but impressive. After describing the profuse issues of 1823–24, he painted the reaction in the following terms:—

"They, therefore, all at once, gave a sudden jerk to the horse on whose neck they had before suffered the reins to hang loose. They contracted their issues to a considerable extent. The change was at once felt throughout the country. A few days before that no one knew what to do with his money; now no one knew where to get it. . . . The London bankers found it necessary to follow the same course towards their country correspondents, and these again towards their customers, and each individual towards his debtor. The consequence was obvious in the late panic. Every one desirous to obtain what was due to him ran to his banker, or to any other on whom he had a claim; and even those who had no immediate use for their money took it back and let it lie unemployed in their pockets, thinking it unsafe in others' hands. The effect of this alarm was that houses which were weak went immediately. Then went second-rate houses; and, lastly, houses which were solvent went, because their securities were unavailable. The daily calls to which each individual was subject put it out of his power to assist his neighbor. Men were known to seek for assistance, and that, too, without finding it, who, on examination of their affairs, were proved to be worth £200,000— men, too, who held themselves so secure that if asked six months before whether they could contemplate such an event, they would have said it would be impossible, unless the sky should fall, or some other event equally improbable should occur."

This is what was done in England five years ago; it is what may be done here in every five years to come, if the bank charter is renewed. Sole dispenser of money, it cannot omit the oldest and most obvious means of amassing wealth by the flux and reflux of paper. The game will be in its own hands, and the only answer to be given is that to which I have alluded: "The Sultan is too just and merciful to abuse his power."

"THERE IS EAST: THERE IS INDIA"

(From a Speech Delivered in St. Louis in 1849)

WE LIVE in extraordinary times and are called upon to elevate ourselves to the grandeur of the occasion. Three and a half centuries ago the great Columbus, the man who afterwards was carried home in chains from the New World which he discovered, this great Columbus, in the year 1492, departed from Europe to arrive in the east by going to the west. It was a sublime conception, he was in the line of success, when the intervention of two continents, not dreamed of before, stopped his progress. Now in the nineteenth century mechanical genius enables his great design to be fulfilled. In the beginning and in barbarous ages, the sea was a barrier to the intercourse of nations. It separated nations. Mechanical genius invented the ship, which converted the barrier into a facility. Then land and continents became an obstruction. The two Americas intervening have prevented Europe and Asia from communicating on a straight line. For three centuries and a half this obstacle has frustrated the grand design of Columbus. Now in our day, mechanical genius has again triumphed over the obstacles of nature and converted into a facility what had so long been an impassable obstacle. The steam car has worked upon the land among enlightened nations to a degree far transcending the miracle which the ship in barbarous ages worked upon the ocean. The land has now become a facility for the most distant communication. A conveyance being invented which annihilated both time and space, we hold the intervening land; we hold the obstacle which stopped Columbus; we are in the line between Europe and Asia; we have it in our power to remove that obstacle; to convert it into a facility to carry him on to this land of promise and of hope with a rapidity and precision and a safety unknown to all ocean navigation. A king and queen started him upon this grand enterprise. It lies in the hands of a republic to complete it. It is in our hands, in the hands of us, the people of the United States, of the first half of the nineteenth century. Let us raise ourselves up.

Let us rise to the grandeur of the occasion. Let us complete the grand design of Columbus by putting Europe and Asia into communication and that to our advantage, through the heart of our country. Let us give to his ships a continued course unknown to all former times. Let us make an iron road, and make it from sea to sea, States and individuals making it east of the Mississippi and the Nation making it west. Let us now, in this convention rise above everything sectional, personal, local. Let us beseech the national legislature to build a great road upon the great national line which unites Europe and Asia—the line which will find on our continent the Bay of San Francisco on one end, St. Louis in the middle, and the great national metropolis and emporium at the other, and which shall be adorned with its crowning honor, the colossal statue of the great Columbus, whose design it accomplishes, hewn from a granite mass of a peak of the Rocky Mountains, the mountain itself the pedestal, and the statue a part of the mountain, pointing with outstretched arm to the western horizon, and saying to the flying passengers, "There is East: there is India!"

ST. BERNARD OF CLAIRVAUX

(1091-1153)

SAINT BERNARD is one of the few great orators of the Middle Ages whose eloquence is still self-explanatory. Often, if not generally, in reading addresses, sermons, and homilies translated from Middle Age Latin into modern languages, we wonder what it is in them that could so have moved men as we know they were moved by them. St. Bernard excites no such wonder, but rather moves us first to assent and then to admiration. He is one of the few great orators and writers whose power can be transferred from one language to another. To read ten sentences of one of the sermons in which he preached the twelfth-century Crusade is to be able to understand the otherwise unaccountable enthusiasm he never failed to excite in his hearers. Other orators of the Middle Ages may have been more admired in their time, but Bernard seems more worthy than any of the rest to rank with the great classical and modern masters of eloquence whose utterances are for all time.

He was born in Burgundy in 1091, and at twenty-two joined a small monastery near Citeaux, being even then so eloquent that he persuaded his two elder brothers to give up the military life they had chosen and follow him into the monastery. What is more remarkable, one of them had a wife and children whom he abandoned in leaving the world, and so many others imitated his sacrifice that it is said "mothers hid their sons, wives their husbands, and companions their friends" to prevent them from following Bernard to become monks.

In 1115 he left the monastery at Citeaux and founded a new one at Clairvaux, which soon became famous throughout Europe. The most notable events in his career of remarkable achievement were the controversy in which he worsted Abélard, his support of Pope Innocent II. against the rival pope, Anacletus II., and his 'Preaching the Crusade.' He died August 20th, 1153.

PREACHING THE CRUSADE

(From Michaud's 'History of the Crusades')

YOU cannot but know that we live in a period of chastisement and ruin; the enemy of mankind has caused the breath of corruption to fly over all regions; we behold nothing but unpunished wickedness. The laws of men or the laws of religion have no longer sufficient power to check depravity of manners and the triumph of the wicked. The demon of heresy has taken possession of the chair of truth, and God has sent forth his malediction upon his sanctuary. Oh, ye who listen to me, hasten then to appease the anger of heaven, but no longer implore his goodness by vain complaints; clothe not yourselves in sackcloth, but cover yourselves with your impenetrable bucklers; the din of arms, the dangers, the labors, the fatigues of war are the penances that God now imposes upon you. Hasten then to expiate your sins by victories over the infidels, and let the deliverance of holy places be the reward of your repentance.

If it were announced to you that the enemy had invaded your cities, your castles, your lands; had ravished your wives and your daughters, and profaned your temples, which among you would not fly to arms? Well, then, all these calamities, and calamities still greater, have fallen upon your brethren, upon the family of Jesus Christ, which is yours. Why do you hesitate to repair so many evils—to revenge so many outrages? Will you allow the infidels to contemplate in peace the ravages they have committed on Christian people? Remember that their triumph will be a subject for grief to all ages, and an eternal opprobrium upon the generation that has endured it. Yes, the living God has charged me to announce to you that he will punish them who shall not have defended him against his enemies. Fly then to arms; let a holy rage animate you in the fight, and let the Christian world resound with these words of the prophet, "Cursed be he who does not stain his sword with blood!" If the Lord calls you to the defense of his heritage, think not that his hand has lost its power. Could he not send twelve legions of angels, or breathe one word, and all his enemies would crumble away into dust? But God has considered the sons of men, to open for them the road to his mercy. His goodness has caused to dawn

for you a day of safety, by calling on you to avenge his glory
and his name. Christian warriors, he who gave his life for you,
to-day demands yours in return. These are combats worthy of
you, combats in which it is glorious to conquer and advantageous
to die. Illustrious knights, generous defenders of the cross, remember the example of your fathers who conquered Jerusalem,
and whose names are inscribed in heaven; abandon then the
things that perish to gather unfading palms, and conquer a kingdom which has no end.

ADVICE TO YOUNG MEN

D O NOT put forward the empty excuse of your rawness or
want of experience; for barren modesty is not pleasing,
nor is that humility praiseworthy that passes the bounds
of moderation. Attend to your work; drive out bashfulness by
a sense of duty, and act as like master. You are young, yet
you are a debtor; you must know that you were a debtor from
the day you were born. Will youth be an excuse to a creditor
for the loss of his profits? Does the usurer expect no interest
at the beginning of his loan? "But," you say, "I am not sufficient for these things." As if your offering were not accepted
from what you have, and not from what you have not! Be prepared to answer for the single talent committed to your charge,
and take no thought for the rest. "If thou hast much, give
plenteously; if thou hast little, do thy diligence gladly to give
of that little." For he that is unjust in the least is also unjust in much. Give all, as assuredly you shall pay to the uttermost farthing; but, of a truth, out of what you possess, not out
of what you possess not.

Take heed to give to your words the voice of power. You
ask, What is that? It is that your words harmonize with your
works, that you be careful to do before you teach. It is a most
beautiful and salutary order of things that you should first bear
the burden you place on others, and learn from yourself how
men should be ruled. Otherwise the wise man will mock you, as
that lazy one to whom it is labor to lift his hand to his mouth.
The Apostle also will reprove you, saying: "Thou who teachest
another, teachest thou not thyself?" . . . That speech, also,
which is full of life and power is an example of work, as it

11—28

makes easy what it speaks persuasively, while it shows that can
be done which it advises. Understand, therefore, to the quieting
of your conscience, that in these two commandments,—of precept and example, the whole of your duty resides. You, however,
if you be wise, will add a third, namely, a zeal for prayer, to
complete that treble repetition of the Gospel in reference to
"feeding the sheep." You will know that no sacrament of that
Trinity is in any wise broken by you, if you feed them by word,
by example, and by the fruit of holy prayers. Now abideth
speech, example, prayer, these three; but the greatest of these is
prayer. For although, as has been said, the strength of speech
is work, yet prayer wins grace and efficacy for both work and
speech.

AGAINST LUXURY IN THE CHURCH

I AM astonished to see among churchmen such excess in eating,
in drinking, in clothes, in bed-covering, in horse-trappings, in
buildings. Economy is now stigmatized as avarice, soberness
as austerity, silence as sullenness. On the other hand, laxity is
called discretion, extravagance liberality, talkativeness affability,
silly laughter a happy wit, pomp and luxury in horses and clothing, respectability; superfluous attention to the building is called
cleanliness; and when you countenance one another in these
trifles, that forsooth is charity. So ingeniously do ye lay out
your money, that it returns with a manifold increase. It is spent
that it may be doubled, and plenty is born of profusion. By the
exhibition of wonderful and costly vanities, men are excited to
give rather than to pray. Some beautiful picture of a saint is
shown, and the brighter its coloring the greater is the holiness
attributed to it; men run eager to kiss; they are invited to give,
and the beautiful is more admired than the sacred is revered.
In the churches are placed, not *coronæ*, but wheels studded with
gems and surrounded by lights, which are not less glittering than
the precious stones inserted among them. Instead of candle-
sticks, we see great and heavy trees of brass, wonderfully fashioned by the skill of the artificer, and radiant as much through
their jewels as through their own lights. What do you imagine
to be the object of all this? The repentance of the contrite, or
the admiration of the spectators? O vanity of vanities! But not
greater vanity than folly.

ON THE CANTICLES

R EMEMBER that no spirit can by itself reach unto our minds—
that is, supposing it to have no assistance from our body or
its own. No spirit can so mingle with us, and be poured
into us, that we become in consequence either good or learned.
No angel, no spirit can comprehend me; none can I comprehend
in this manner. Even angels themselves cannot seize each others'
thoughts without bodily organs. This prerogative is reserved for
the highest, the unbounded spirit, who alone, when he imparts
knowledge either to angel or to man, needs not that we should
have ears to hear, or that we should have a mouth to speak. By
himself he is poured in; by himself he is made manifest. Pure
himself, he is understood by the pure. He alone needs nothing;
alone is sufficient to himself and to all by his sole omnipotent will.

I could not pass over in silence those spiritual feet of God,
which, in the first place, it behooves the penitent to kiss in a
spiritual manner. I well know your curiosity, which does not
willingly allow anything obscure to pass by it; nor indeed is it
a contemptible thing to know what are those feet which the
Scripture so frequently mentions in connection with God. Sometimes he is spoken of as standing on them, as "We will worship
in the place where thy feet have stood." Sometimes as walking,
as "I will dwell in them and will walk in them." Sometimes
even as running, as "He rejoiceth as a strong man to run a
race." If it appear right to the Apostle to call the head of
Christ God it appears to me as not unnatural to consider his feet
as representing man; one of which I shall name mercy and the
other judgment. Those two words are known to you, and the
Scripture repeats them in many places. On those feet, fitly
moving under one divine head, Christ, born of a woman, he who
was invisible under the law, then made Emmanuel ("God with
us"), was seen on the earth, and conversed with men.

As regards creatures devoid of sense and reason, who can
doubt that God needs them much less? but when they concur in
the performance of a good work, then it appears how all things
serve him who can justly say: "The world is mine, and the fullness thereof." Assuredly, seeing that he knows the means best
adapted to ends, he does not in the service of his creatures seek
efficacy, but suitability.

JOHN M. BERRIEN

(1781–1856)

J OHN M. BERRIEN was Attorney-General in Andrew Jackson's
first cabinet and he was identified with the public life of
the country during three of the most important decades of
its history. His public service began with his appointment as Judge
of the Eastern District of Georgia. He served in the Georgia legislature and was elected to the United States Senate from that State.
After his retirement from the cabinet, he was again elected to the
United States Senate and in 1846 was re-elected. He was born in
New Jersey in 1781 and died in 1856. His speeches still extant contain passages of great, if not of sustained force. He was much admired in his own State and in the South at large, and his utterances
will always have a historical interest as reflexes of the feelings of
his time.

CONQUEST AND TERRITORIAL ORGANIZATION

(United States Senate, 1850)

W ITH respect to the war-making power, unquestionably territory might be acquired by conquest, not conveyed by
treaty. There may be a continued hostile occupation unsupported by a treaty of cession, which may, by lapse of time,
destroy the right of the conquered party, the right of *postlimi-
nium*, and therefore the fruits of the conquest may be enjoyed
without treaty. In that state of things, unquestionably, as to
territory acquired by the exercise of the war-making power, the
power to govern that territory would be deduced from the same
source.

But, sir, speaking generally, almost universally, wars are terminated by treaty, and the conquests are transferred to the
acquiring power by cession. The real source and origin of this
power, therefore, are to be found in the treaty-making power,
and its derivatives. It might be implied as a necessary incident
to the power to make treaties, but it is more generally the result

of express stipulations made in the exercise of that power. I shall be understood by a brief explanation, and by the application of it to the case before us. By the power which you have to enter into treaties with foreign nations, you have acquired this Mexican territory. If it were indispensable to you to resort to the principle that the right to acquire gives you the right to govern, I agree that the right might be deduced from that source. But this is not necessary; for there is in the treaty an express stipulation for the exercise of the power, which is equivalent to a grant, under which we are not only authorized, but bound to exercise it, since treaties, when they are not in conflict with the Constitution, and when they are ratified by the competent authorities of the nation, become the supreme law of the land. In those treaties — in all of those which are treaties of cession — the right to receive the ceded territories is accompanied by the express stipulation to govern, by the stipulation to protect them in their persons and in their property, which can alone be done by government. The power, then, to govern a territory which is acquired by cession from a foreign nation is a power deduced from the treaty by which that territory is acquired; which treaty, upon its ratification, becomes the supreme law of the land.

And now, sir, I think you may see what is the reason that there is no express grant in the Constitution to organize Territorial Governments. That reason may be found in the fact that there was no necessity for its existence there. Cast your recollection back to the period when the Constitution was adopted — consider what were the objects upon which this power to organize territorial governments could be exercised. They were, first, the unlocated territory of the United States. And what was that? The great Northwestern Territory, the subject of the famous ordinance of 1787. Now, in respect to that territory, it was a portion of the State of Virginia, subject to the sovereign law of Virginia. While Virginia held it, it was competent for her to organize a government there; and when the sovereignty of Virginia was transferred to the Confederation, if the Confederation had had the power to receive the transfer, the sovereign power which had been theretofore in Virginia might have been exercised by the Confederation. There is, I presume, scarcely a lawyer of the present day, who supposes that the Congress of the Confederation had the power to do what they did. But validity was given to their act — not by the act of Congress adapting the

mere agency provided by the ordinance to the state of things which existed under the new Constitution — not by that, or any other act of Congress, but by the clause of the Constitution which declares that contracts and engagements entered into by the government of the Confederation should be obligatory upon the government of the United States established by the Constitution. Here, then, was a contract entered into between Virginia and the Federal Congress, which was rendered valid by a stipulation of the Constitution of the United States. From that transfer of the sovereignty by Virginia, and this recognition of it by the Constitution of the United States, is derived the authority to organize governments in these territories. When, therefore, Congress have organized governments for the several territories parcelled out of the Northwestern Territory, they have not acted under the power which you are now calling into exercise, but under the power derived from the transfer of the sovereignty of Virginia, and the provision of the Constitution of the United States which gave validity to that act.

That disposes of the first class of territorial governments organized by the United States — those in the Northwestern Territory. Now, with regard to the second: that is, governments which have been organized in territories which were heretofore portions of different States of this Union, which were unlocated at the time of the adoption of the Constitution, and which have, by subsequent cession, been transferred to the United States, precisely the same principle was applicable to them, as in the case which I have been considering. Georgia ceded to the United States an extent of territory which now constitutes the two great States of Alabama and Mississippi. While they remained under the sovereignty of Georgia it was competent to her to have organized territorial governments within their limits; but she ceded them to the United States, and transferred, not merely the soil, but, by the express terms of the articles of cession, the sovereignty and jurisdiction. She did more. She stipulated for the organization of territorial governments within those territories. This was therefore sufficient authority for establishing territorial governments in the Territories of Mississippi and Alabama. Tennessee was territory ceded from North Carolina to the United States, and was in like condition.

Then there remains the other class of territorial governments, organized upon territory acquired by the United States from

foreign powers: and for the organization of governments within those territories it was always competent to the United States to do whatever was necessary for the fulfillment of its treaty stipulations, which, by the act of ratification, became the supreme law of the land.

I suggest to you, then, sir, that this alone furnishes a sufficient explanation (without resorting to the supposition that our ancestors did not anticipate the future extension of the limits of the Republic) why there was no express power to organize territorial governments contained in the Constitution — namely, that the grant of such power was wholly unnecessary; that with regard to the unlocated territory of the United States — that which was within its limits at the time of the formation of the Constitution — it was competent for the government of the United States to establish governments by virtue of the transfer of the sovereignty of Virginia, and the recognition of the validity of that transfer as an engagement of the former government, by the Constitution of the United States; that in relation to territory within the limits of particular States, the same power was acquired by the cession and transfer of sovereignty of the ceding States. And with regard to such territory as should be acquired from foreign nations, it was competent to the government of the United States to establish territorial governments, in virtue of treaty stipulations which they were authorized to make, and bound to execute.

EFFECT OF THE MEXICAN CONQUEST

(United States Senate, February 11th, 1850)

I HAVE united, heretofore — at some personal hazard of popularity and station — I have united with my friends of the free States; foreseeing the consequences of the measures which were then in operation — foreseeing the evils which they would bring upon us, I have joined with them at some such hazard in the effort to prevent it. We failed. The evil is upon us. The territory which we have acquired by an expenditure of blood and treasure is about to subject us — unless under the mercy of Providence, we are guided by wiser counsels than those we have exhibited — to an expenditure, in comparison with which the blood and treasure expended upon the Mexican conquest would sink into insignificance. I have united with the representatives

of the free States in the effort to prevent the occurrence of this difficulty. Nay, sir, if some two or three of them could have remained firm upon the ground they had occupied, it would have been prevented. I am desirous now to unite in averting, if it be possible, the dangers which are threatened. It may require some self-sacrifice: it may require the sacrifice of popularity or official station. I am willing to make it, if you will present to me any ground upon which an honest man may unite with you in giving peace to the country. I know, sir, that in making this offer the sacrifice upon my part would be comparatively trifling with those of men in the earlier stages of life, with more extended prospects for the future, and with greater political aspirations. But I am willing to give you all I have. It may be less than the widow's mite, but it is all that I have to give, for the first desire of my heart is that to which you cannot minister.

I have endeavored thus to present to the consideration of the Senate the impressions of my own mind, in relation to the magnitude and difficulty of this subject, for the purpose of urging upon them the truth of the conviction, which I feel, that if these difficulties can indeed be surmounted, it is only by a calm, dispassionate, and, as far as may be, impartial consideration of them, under a full sense of the duties which we owe to each other as members of this great society of States. And I derive something of hope — oh, no, sir, that falls far short of conveying what I would express — I derive a hope amounting almost to confidence, from the cheering recollection that these difficulties, these self-same difficulties, existed at the time of the adoption of our Constitution, and that they were then surmounted by the patriotism of our fathers.

There are other difficulties which have been connected with this subject. They have been generated by the madness of fanaticism; by the colder, more calculating, more selfish spirit of political demagogues; by the excitable and excited feelings of a wronged and insulted people. These may be surmounted, if we resolve to meet them in the unselfish, self-sacrificing spirit which our duty demands from all and from each of us, with a determination, on every side of this great question, to yield whatever may be yielded without a sacrifice, not of mere speculative opinion, but of constitutional principle. Sir, there have been many crises in the brief history of this Republic — appalling dangers have often menaced us — and we have more than once stood upon the brink of a precipice from which one advancing step would have plunged us into the fathomless abyss of anarchy, with all its countless horrors. At least such has been the picture presented to us by our political orators and political essayists, from the rostrum and from the press. And yet, sir, in the deepest hour of gloom, there has ever been found some auspicious moment in which the light of truth has penetrated the clouds of folly and passion, of fanaticism and selfishness; has dissipated the mists of error; has awakened the slumbering patriotism of our countrymen, and has revealed to us our glorious charter, unscathed amid the tumult, in all its original strength and vigor. So may it ever be! In the darkest hour of our national fortunes let us never despair — no, sir, let us never despair. For myself, though age has somewhat checked the current of my blood, I would still cling to this hope with all the hopefulness of youth.

.   .   .   .

I have an abiding confidence that the God of our fathers will be the God of their children — that he will be our God; that he will graciously enable us to preserve that glorious fabric, which his mercy and his goodness, not the might and strength of our ancestors, enabled them to construct; and that countless generations, enjoying the rich heritage which they have transmitted to us, and which, by his blessing, we will transmit to them, will in distant ages unite in the tribute of gratitude to their memories, which, in this our day, it is our privilege to offer.

Yet, sir, we must not forget in indulging in this hope that the providence of God is often exerted through the agency of man, and that we must be mindful of our own duties if we would hope for his mercy. I ask of my honorable associates in this chamber, then, to come to the consideration of this subject in that spirit of conciliation which can alone lead to a propitious result. I ask them to remember that we are brethren of a common family, united by a thousand social as well as political ties. I ask them especially to remember, that in such a conflict as that which menaces us, the splendor of victory would be dimmed by the unnatural character of the strife in which it was achieved.

PIERRE ANTOINE BERRYER

(1790–1868)

PIERRE ANTOINE BERRYER, one of the most noted parliamentary orators of France during the second quarter of the nineteenth century, was born at Paris, January 4th, 1790. He was the son of an eminent advocate of Paris who educated him for his own profession. He joined his father in supporting the Bourbons against Napoleon I., and in the Hundred Days' campaign he followed Louis XVIII. to Ghent as a volunteer. He was one of the counsel for the defense at the trial of Marshal Ney. He took part in many of the most important trials of his time, especially in the defense of the Press when the Police Department undertook to enforce the censorship against Parisian newspapers. In 1830 he was elected a member of the French Chamber of Deputies, retaining his seat after the revolution of July, when the other Legitimists withdrew in a body. He resisted unsuccessfully the abolition of the peerage, and advocated trial by jury in the prosecution of newspaper editors for libel. In the troubles of 1832 he was arrested, but was acquitted on his trial, for organizing an insurrection in favor of the Count of Chambord. He was a member of the National Assembly which was called after the Revolution of February 1848. His parliamentary career closed with his protest against the *coup d'état* of 1851. Twelve years later he reappeared as a deputy to the Corps Legislatif. He was elected a member of the French Academy in 1854. In 1865 he visited Lord Brougham, and the benchers of the Temple and of Lincoln's Inn gave him a banquet. He died in November 1868 at his country seat at Augerville.

CENSORSHIP OF THE PRESS

(Delivered February 15th, 1868)

I HAVE but few words to say in presenting a brief amendment to the Press law now under discussion. This paragraph was suggested to me by the grave circumstances now existing which have a profound influence on private rights.

The principle of the matter now under consideration is this: Private life should be walled in and sacred, but public life has no such right. All public existence created by great public interests and all variations of these interests create a responsibility, and this responsibility is moral as well as material. There is no gainsaying this, and all public functionaries admit they are responsible for their personal actions. But in opposition to them we find a body of men occupying an anomalous position. Immense establishments have been founded, which have attained such exaggerated proportions in their influence on public and private life that the men responsible for their direction are more powerful than even public characters. I speak particularly of the directors of the great corporate companies and financial institutions who are irresponsible, or at least their acts are impersonal and official and free from direct responsibility.

What have we seen and what do we still see? A large number of such establishments are founded; they develop and some crumble. Values or their equivalents have been emitted by these concerns under the direction of men responsible for nothing. They are issued in enormous proportions up to the hundreds of millions, even to the billion mark. What is the character of many of these values created by establishments calling themselves French? What social, business, and political calamities have resulted? You have seen shares issued at five hundred francs sold for one thousand nine hundred francs and then fall, carrying ruin to the citizens to whom they had been transferred under the faith of the government, since the authorization of the government was necessary to the foundation of such establishments. And have any of them a censor placed near or over them? There should be rigorous censorship over all stock companies. They are freed from all supervision now, and I believe it an error. Well, I ask when private fortune in such colossal proportions is exposed to disaster: Is this not a public danger?

Is it not for the general interest that the actions of such societies, the commerce of their directors and administrators, should be called to public attention, that every one may know what is occurring?

If, in reviewing the deeds of these gentlemen, we find that these deeds are criminal in character, and worthy of condemnation, is it well that the publisher of such news to the public should be prosecuted for defamation, because he makes known to his fellow-citizens fraudulent manœuvres and irregular operations, when in so doing he acts from an evident general interest of honesty against men who have in their hands the fate of interests so vast that it is really the cause of administrative justice to make public the lies, falsities, and perils which are evident in much of the certificate values in circulation? The Lord knows how, when one has had the courage to say, " Here are their practices, here are the secret acts, here is what menaces you," shall he be censured and punished for defamation as having brought disgrace to or soiled the dignity of such corporate administrators. I repeat that the proof of facts which interest private fortunes in such degree may be said to be public facts, and their free publication should be authorized. With this view I present the amendment to make such officials subject to the Press censures applicable to political and public functionaries.

JOHN A. BINGHAM

(1815-)

THE trial of the assassins of President Lincoln was, in many respects, the most important State case in the history of English-speaking peoples since the discovery of America. As often happens where the occasion demands much, its very dignity may excite disappointment with the result, but it would be hard to overestimate the importance of such arguments as those of Bingham, Reverdy Johnson, and others, who handled the law and the evidence before the military commission which tried the conspirators. However great the disadvantage under which the attorneys for the defense were placed their arguments lose nothing in value with the passage of time, while on several points the argument for the prosecution has been outlawed by time. When Guiteau murdered President Garfield no one questioned the genuineness of the indignation of those he insanely claimed to represent, and the murderers of President Lincoln have long ago come to be regarded not as traitors but merely as assassins. The charges and the arguments supporting them as far as they are intended to suggest treason rather than murder are now universally looked upon as the result of a mistake of judgment excusable enough in the excitement of the times, but not justified by any evidence or any argument presented in connection with the evidence.

AGAINST THE ASSASSINS OF PRESIDENT LINCOLN

MAY it please the Court: It only remains for me to sum up the evidence, and present my views of the law arising upon the facts in the case on trial. The questions of fact involved in the issue are:—

First, did the accused, or any two of them, confederate and conspire together, as charged? and,

Second, did the accused, or any of them, in pursuance of such conspiracy, and with the intent alleged, commit either or all of the several acts specified?

In the United States *versus* Cole *et al.*, 5 McLean, 601, Mr. Justice McLean says:—

"A conspiracy is rarely, if ever, proved by positive testimony. When a crime of high magnitude is about to be perpetrated by a combination of individuals, they do not act openly, but covertly and secretly. The purpose formed is known only to those who enter into it. Unless one of the original conspirators betray his companions and give evidence against them, their guilt can be proved only by circumstantial evidence. It is said by some writers on evidence that such circumstances are stronger than positive proof. A witness swearing positively, it is said, may misapprehend the facts or swear falsely, but that circumstances cannot lie.

"The common design is the essence of the charge; and this may be made to appear when the defendants steadily pursue the same object, whether acting separately or together, by common or different means, all leading to the same unlawful result. And where *prima facie* evidence has been given of a combination, the acts or confessions of one are evidence against all. It is reasonable that where a body of men assume the attribute of individuality, whether for commercial business or for the commission of a crime, that the association should be bound by the acts of one of its members in carrying out the design."

It is a rule of the law, not to be overlooked in this connection, that the conspiracy or agreement of the parties, or some of them, to act in concert to accomplish the unlawful act charged, may be established either by direct evidence of a meeting or consultation for the illegal purpose charged, or more usually, from the very nature of the case, by circumstantial evidence. (2 Starkie, 232.)

Lord Mansfield ruled that it was not necessary to prove the actual fact of a conspiracy; but that it might be collected from collateral circumstances. (Parson's Case, 1 W. Blackstone, 392.)

"If," says a great authority on the law of evidence, "on a charge of conspiracy, it appear that two persons by their acts are pursuing the same object, and often by the same means, or one performing part of the act, and the other completing it, for the attainment of the same object, the jury may draw the conclusion there is a conspiracy. If a conspiracy be formed, and a person join in it afterward, he is equally guilty with the original conspirators." (Roscoe, 415.)

"The rule of the admissibility of the acts and declarations of any one of the conspirators, said or done in furtherance of the common

If the conspiracy be established, as charged, it results that whatever was said or done by either of the parties thereto, in the furtherance or execution of the common design, is the declaration or act of all the other parties to the conspiracy; and this, whether the other parties, at the time such words were uttered or such acts done by their confederates, were present or absent—here, within the entrenched lines of your capital, or crouching behind the entrenched lines of Richmond, or awaiting the results of their murderous plot against their country, its Constitution and laws, across the border, under the shelter of the British flag.

The declared and accepted rule of law in cases of conspiracy is that:—

"In prosecutions for conspiracy it is an established rule that where several persons are proved to have combined together for the same illegal purpose, any act done by one of the party, in pursuance of the original concerted plan, and in reference to the common object, is, in the contemplation of law as well as in sound reason, the act of the whole party; and, therefore, the proof of the act will be evidence against any of the others who were engaged in the same general conspiracy, without regard to the question whether the prisoner is proved to have been concerned in the particular transaction." (Phillips on Evidence, p. 210.)

The same rule obtains in cases of treason:—

"If several persons agree to levy war, some in one place and some in another, and one party do actually appear in arms, this is a levying of war by all, as well those who were not in arms as those who were, if it were done in pursuance of the original concert, for those who made the attempt were emboldened by the confidence inspired by the general concert, and, therefore, these particular acts are in justice imputable to all the rest." (1 East., Pleas of the Crown, p. 97; Roscoe 84.)

In *Ex parte* Bollman and Swartwout, 4 Cranch, 126, Marshall, Chief-Justice, rules:—

"If war be actually levied—that is, if a body of men be actually assembled for the purpose of effecting by force a treasonable purpose—all those who perform any part, however minute, or however remote from the scene of action, and who are actually leagued in the general conspiracy, are to be considered as traitors."

design, applies in cases as well where only part of the conspirators are indicted, or upon trial, as where all are indicted and upon trial. Thus, upon an indictment for murder, if it appear that others, together with the prisoner, conspired to commit the crime, the act of one done in pursuance of that intention will be evidence against the rest." (2 Starkie, 237.)

They are all alike guilty as principals. (Commonwealth *versus* Knapp, 9 Pickering, 496; 10 Pickering, 477; 6 Term Reports, 528; 11 East. 584.) . . .

Was there co-operation between the several accused in the execution of this conspiracy? That there was is as clearly established by the testimony as is the fact that Abraham Lincoln was killed and murdered by John Wilkes Booth. The evidence shows that all of the accused, save Mudd and Arnold, were in Washington on April 14th, the day of the assassination, together with John Wilkes Booth and John H. Surratt; that on that day Booth had a secret interview with the prisoner, Mary E. Surratt; that immediately thereafter she went to Surrattsville to perform her part of the preparation necessary to the successful execution of the conspiracy, and did make that preparation; that John H. Surratt had arrived here from Canada, notifying the parties that the price to be paid for this great crime had been provided for, at least in part, by the deposit receipts of April 6th, for $180,000, procured by Thompson, of the Ontario Bank, Montreal, Canada; that he was also prepared to keep watch, or strike a blow, and ready for the contemplated flight; that Atzerodt, on the afternoon of that day, was seeking to obtain a horse, the better to secure his own safety by flight, after he should have performed the task which he had voluntarily undertaken by contract in the conspiracy—the murder of Andrew Johnson, then Vice-President of the United States; that he did procure a horse for that purpose at Naylor's and was seen about nine o'clock in the evening to ride to the Kirkwood House, where the Vice-President then was, dismount, and enter. At a previous hour Booth was in the Kirkwood House, and left his card, now in evidence, doubtless intended to be sent to the room of the Vice-President, and which was in these words: "Don't wish to disturb you. Are you at home? J. Wilkes Booth." Atzerodt, when he made application at Brooks's in the afternoon for the horse, said to Weichmann, who was there, he was going to ride in the country, and that "he was going to get a horse and send for

Payne." He did get a horse for Payne, as well as for himself; for it is proven that on the twelfth he was seen in Washington, riding the horse which had been procured by Booth, in company with Mudd, last November, from Gardner. A similar horse was tied before the door of Mr. Seward on the night of the murder, was captured after the flight of Payne, who was seen to ride away, and which horse is now identified as the Gardner horse. Booth also procured a horse on the same day, took it to his stable in the rear of the theatre, where he had an interview with Spangler, and where he concealed it. Herold, too, obtained a horse in the afternoon, and was seen between nine and ten o'clock riding with Atzerodt down the avenue from the Treasury, then up Fourteenth and down F Street, passing close by Ford's Theatre.

O'Laughlin had come to Washington the day before, had sought out his victim, General Grant, at the house of the Secretary of War, that he might be able with certainty to identify him, and at the very hour when these preparations were going on was lying in wait at Rullman's, on the avenue, keeping watch, and declaring as he did, at about ten o'clock P. M., when told that the fatal blow had been struck by Booth, "I don't believe Booth did it." During the day, and the night before, he had been visiting Booth, and doubtless encouraging him, and at that very hour was in position, at a convenient distance, to aid and protect him in his flight, as well as to execute his own part of the conspiracy by inflicting death upon General Grant, who happily was not at the theatre nor in the city, having left the city that day. Who doubts that Booth having ascertained in the course of the day that General Grant would not be present at the theatre, O'Laughlin, who was to murder General Grant, instead of entering the box with Booth was detailed to lie in wait, and watch and support him?

His declarations of his reasons for changing his lodgings here and in Baltimore, after the murder, so ably and so ingeniously presented in the argument of his learned counsel [Mr. Cox], avail nothing before the blasting fact that he did change his lodgings, and declared "he knew nothing of the affair whatever." O'Laughlin, who lurked here, conspiring daily with Booth and Arnold for six weeks to do this murder, declares "he knew nothing of the affair." O'Laughlin, who said he was "in the oil business," which Booth and Surratt, and Payne and Arnold, have

II—29

all declared meant this conspiracy, says he "knew nothing of the affair." O'Laughlin, to whom Booth sent the dispatches of the thirteenth and twenty-seventh of March—O'Laughlin, who is named in Arnold's letter as one of the conspirators; who searched for General Grant on Thursday night, and laid in wait for him on Friday; who was defeated by that Providence "which shapes our ends," and laid in wait to aid Booth and Payne,—this man declares "he knows nothing of the matter." Such a denial is as false and inexcusable as Peter's denial of our Lord.

Mrs. Surratt had arrived at home, from the completion of her part of the plot, about half-past eight o'clock in the evening. A few moments afterwards she was called to the parlor, and there had a private interview with some one unseen, but whose retreating footsteps were heard by the witness, Weichmann. This was doubtless the secret and last visit of John H. Surratt to his mother, who had instigated and encouraged him to strike his traitorous and murderous blow against his country.

While all these preparations were going on, Mudd was awaiting the execution of the plot, ready to faithfully perform his part in securing the safe escape of the murderers. Arnold was at his post at Fortress Monroe, awaiting the meeting referred to in his letter of March 27th, wherein he says they were not "to meet for a month or so," which month had more than expired on the day of the murder, for his letter and the testimony disclose that this month of suspension began to run from about the first week in March. He stood ready with the arms which Booth had furnished him to aid the escape of the murderers by that route, and secure their communication with their employers. He had given the assurance in that letter to Booth, that although the government "suspicioned them," and the undertaking was "becoming complicated," yet "a time more propitious would arrive" for the consummation of this conspiracy in which he "was one" with Booth, and when he would "be better prepared to again be with him."

Such were the preparations. The horses were in readiness for the flight; the ropes were procured, doubtless, for the purpose of tying the horses at whatever point they might be constrained to delay, and to secure their boats to their moorings in making their way across the Potomac. The five murderous camp knives, the two carbines, the eight revolvers, the Deringer, in court and identified, all were ready for the work of death.

The part that each had played has already been in part stated in this argument, and needs no repetition.

Booth proceeded to the theatre about nine o'clock in the evening, at the same time that Atzerodt, Payne, and Herold were riding the streets, while Surratt, having parted with his mother at the brief interview in her parlor, from which his retreating steps were heard, was walking the avenue, booted and spurred, and doubtless consulting with O'Laughlin. When Booth reached the rear of the theatre, he called Spangler to him (whose denial of that fact, when charged with it, as proven by three witnesses, is very significant), and received from Spangler his pledge to help him all he could, when with Booth he entered the theatre by the stage door, doubtless to see that the way was clear from the box to the rear door of the theatre, and look upon their victim, whose exact position they could study from the stage. After this view, Booth passes to the street in front of the theatre, where, on the pavement, with other conspirators yet unknown, among them one described as a low-browed villain, he awaits the appointed moment. Booth himself, impatient, enters the vestibule of the theatre from the front and asks the time. He is referred to the clock and returns. Presently, as the hour of ten approached, one of his guilty associates called the time; they wait; again, as the moments elapsed, this conspirator upon watch called the time; again, as the appointed hour draws nigh, he calls the time; and, finally, when the fatal moment arrives, he repeats in a louder tone, "Ten minutes past ten o'clock." Ten minutes past ten o'clock! The hour has come when the red right hand of these murderous conspirators should strike, and the dreadful deed of assassination be done.

Booth, at the appointed moment, entered the theatre, ascended to the dress circle, passed to the right, paused a moment, looking down, doubtless to see if Spangler is at his post, and approached the outer door of the close passage leading to the box occupied by the President, pressed it open, passed in, and closed the passage door behind him. Spangler's bar was in its place, and was readily adjusted by Booth in the mortise, and pressed against the inner side of the door, so that he was secure from interruption from without. He passes on to the next door, immediately behind the President, and there stopping, looks through the aperture in the door into the President's box and deliberately observes the precise position of his victim, seated in the chair which had

been prepared by the conspirators as the altar for the sacrifice, looking calmly and quietly down upon the glad and grateful people whom, by his fidelity, he had saved from the peril which had threatened the destruction of their government, and all they held dear this side of the grave—whom he had come upon invitation to greet with his presence, with the words still lingering upon his lips which he had uttered with uncovered head and uplifted hand before God and his country, when on the fourth of last March he took again the oath to preserve, protect, and defend the Constitution, declaring that he entered upon the duties of his great office "with malice toward none, with charity for all." In a moment more, strengthened by the knowledge that his co-conspirators were all at their posts, seven at least of them present in the city, two of them, Mudd and Arnold, at their appointed places, watching for his coming, this hired assassin moves stealthily through the door, the fastenings of which had been removed to facilitate his entrance, fires upon his victim, and the martyr spirit of Abraham Lincoln ascends to God.

> "Treason has done his worst; nor steel nor poison,
> Malice domestic, foreign levy, nothing
> Can touch him further."

At the same hour when these accused and their co-conspirators in Richmond and Canada, by the hand of John Wilkes Booth, inflicted this mortal wound which deprived the Republic of its defender, and filled this land from ocean to ocean with a strange, great sorrow, Payne, a very demon in human form, with the words of falsehood upon his lips, that he was the bearer of a message from the physician of the venerable Secretary of State, sweeps by his servant, encounters his son, who protests that the assassin shall not disturb his father, prostrate on a bed of sickness, and receives for answer the assassin's blow from the revolver in his hand, repeated again and again; rushes into the room, is encountered by Major Seward, inflicts wound after wound upon him with his murderous knife; is encountered by Hansell and Robinson, each of whom he also wounds; springs upon the defenseless and feeble Secretary of State, stabs him first on one side of his throat, then on the other, again in the face, and is only prevented from literally hacking out his life by the persistence and courage of the attendant Robinson. He turns to flee; and his giant arm and murderous hand for a moment paralyzed by the consciousness of guilt, he drops his weapons of death, one in the house, the other at the door, where they were taken up, and are here now to bear witness against him. He attempts escape on the horse which Booth and Mudd had procured of Gardner — with what success has already been stated. . . .

If this conspiracy was thus entered into by the accused; if John Wilkes Booth did kill and murder Abraham Lincoln in pursuance thereof; if Lewis Payne did, in pursuance of said conspiracy, assault, with intent to kill and murder, William H. Seward, as stated, and if the several parties accused did commit the several acts alleged against them, in the prosecution of the said conspiracy, then it is the law that all the parties to that conspiracy, whether present at the time of its execution or not, whether on trial before this court or not, are alike guilty of the several acts done by each in the execution of the common design. What these conspirators did in the execution of this conspiracy by the hand of one of their co-conspirators they did themselves; his act, done in the prosecution of the common design, was the act of all the parties to the treasonable combination, because done in execution and furtherance of their guilty and treasonable agreement.

As we have seen, this is the rule, whether all the conspirators are indicted or not, whether they are all on trial or not. "It is not material what the nature of the indictment is, provided the offense involve a conspiracy. Upon indictment for murder, for instance, if it appear that others, together with the prisoner, conspired to perpetrate the crime, the act of one, done in pursuance of that intention, would be evidence against the rest." (1 Wharton, 706.) To the same effect are the words of Chief-Justice Marshall, before cited, that whoever leagued in a general conspiracy, performed any part, however minute, or however remote, from the scene of action, are guilty as principals. In this treasonable conspiracy to aid the existing armed rebellion by murdering the executive officers of the United States and the commander of the armies, all the parties to it must be held as principals, and the act of one in the prosecution of the common design the act of all.

I leave the decision of this dread issue with the court, to which alone it belongs. It is for you to say, upon your oaths, whether the accused are guilty.

I am not conscious that in this argument I have made any erroneous statement of the evidence, or drawn any erroneous

conclusions; yet I pray the court, out of tender regard and jealous care for the rights of the accused, to see that no error of mine, if any there be, shall work them harm. The past services of the members of this honorable court give assurance that without fear, favor, or affection, they will discharge with fidelity the duty enjoined upon them by their oaths. Whatever else may befall, I trust in God that in this, as in every other American court, the rights of the whole people will be respected, and that the Republic in this its supreme hour of trial will be true to itself and just to all, ready to protect the rights of the humblest, to redress every wrong, to avenge every crime, to vindicate the majesty of law, and to maintain inviolate the Constitution, whether assailed secretly or openly, by hosts armed with gold or armed with steel.

BISMARCK

(1815–1898)

N DELIVERING his great speech on the Army Bill (February 1888) which, in the opinion of his enemies, was the most powerful reactionary utterance of the second half of the century, Bismarck showed himself a consummate master of that art which conceals itself so thoroughly that it requires a laborious collection of evidence to demonstrate its existence. He did not care at all to be considered an orator. His whole mind was centred on carrying his point. In this he succeeded so well on that occasion, and on almost every other, that though he probably made more public speeches and carried more points than any other man in Germany during his day, he is seldom thought of as an eloquent man or as an orator and is rarely classed among the great speakers of his country. In delivering his speech on the Army Bill, he talked to the German Reichstag in what was apparently a bluff, off-hand, jovial style, very much as if he were talking to half a dozen companions around a table over beer and pipes. Now, he stopped to jest with the opposition, now he grew confidential as if he were revealing State secrets to trusted friends, now he appealed as a German to Germans in behalf of the Fatherland, now he spoke for the sacred interests of peace and philanthropy — always with the easy, assured assumption that every one must agree with him as a matter of course without the necessity for anything more than this conversational style of putting things among friends.

His mastery of German is phenomenal. Though his language is simplicity itself, his sentences grow on him until no one of less mental power could have emerged from their labyrinths. He does emerge, however, and that so easily and naturally that their involved nature only becomes remarkable when the attempt is made to transfer his thought to another language.

Bismarck (Otto Edward Leopold, Prince von Bismarck-Schönhausen), was born April 1st, 1815, and died July 30th, 1898. He was the greatest "Conservative" of his age and one of the greatest of any age. Among the public men with whom he was matched in Europe only Gladstone equaled him in intellect and, lacking his intense force of prejudice, Gladstone himself was never anything like his equal in effectiveness. To Bismarck more than to any other one

man, probably more than to any other ten men, was due the gradual but sure growth of the feeling which at his death had turned Europe into an "armed camp." When he first entered politics, as a representative of the extreme royalists of the German land-holding nobility in their opposition to the parliamentary movement of 1848-49, he showed the same tendencies which appear in his speech on the Army Bill of 1888. He was disturbed by the evident tendency of the world to grow into cities, which he regarded as hotbeds of treason and disorder. To check this he believed "blood and iron" were necessary in both domestic and foreign politics. This and his intense devotion to the royal family of Prussia are the mainsprings of his politics. He opposed the "United Germany," proposed by the Frankfort Parliament of 1849, because he thought it gave too much recognition to the people at the expense of the crown. He fought for royal prerogative at every point in the history of Germany until the empire was established at Versailles after France had submitted on terms he had dictated. In 1884 he achieved his greatest triumph against the "Liberals" of Germany by committing the empire to the colonial policy, which it has since pursued in antagonism to England. His quarrel with the present emperor which resulted in his retirement from court did not retire him from the public affairs of Germany and, up to the time of his death, he remained one of the greatest individual forces in the politics of Europe.

His speech on the Army Bill, here given as an illustration of his oratory, was translated for this work from the Stuttgart edition of his speeches published by authority in 1894.

A PLEA FOR IMPERIAL ARMAMENT

(Delivered in the Reichstag, February 6th, 1888)

IF I RISE to speak to-day it is not to urge on your acceptance the measure the President has mentioned (the army appropriation). I do not feel anxious about its adoption, and I do not believe that I can do anything to increase the majority by which it will be adopted — by which it is all-important at home and abroad that it should be adopted. Gentlemen of all parties have made up their minds how they will vote and I have the fullest confidence in the German Reichstag that it will restore our armament to the height from which we reduced it in the period between 1867 and 1882; and this not with respect to the conditions of the moment, not with regard to the apprehensions which may excite the stock exchanges and the mind of the public; but with a considerate regard for the general condition of Europe. In speaking, I will have more to say of this than of the immediate question.

I do not speak willingly, for under existing conditions a word unfortunately spoken may be ruinous, and the multiplication of words can do little to explain the situation, either to our own people or to foreigners. I speak unwillingly, but I fear that if I kept silent there would be an increase rather than a diminution of the expectations which have attached themselves to this debate, of unrest in the public mind, of the disposition to nervousness at home and abroad. The public might believe the question to be so difficult and critical that a minister for foreign affairs would not dare to touch upon it. I speak, therefore, but I can say truly that I speak with reluctance. I might limit myself to recalling expressions to which I gave utterance from this same place a year and a day ago. Little change has taken place in the situation since then. I chanced to-day on a clipping from the Liberal Gazette, a paper which I believe stands nearer to my friend, Representative Richter, than it does to me. It pictures one difficult situation to elucidate another, but I can take only general notice of the main points there touched on, with the explanation that if the situation has since altered, it is for the better rather than for the worse.

We had then our chief apprehension because of a war which might come to us from France. Since then, one peace-loving President has retired from administration in France, and another peace-loving President has succeeded him. It is certainly a favorable symptom that in choosing its new chief executive France has not put its hand into Pandora's box, but that we have assurance of a continuation under President Carnot of the peaceful policy represented by President Grévy. We have, moreover, other changes in the French administration whose peaceful significance is even stronger than that of the change in the presidency—an event which involved other causes. Such members of the ministry as were disposed to subordinate the peace of France and of Europe to their personal interests have been shoved out, and others, of whom we have not this to fear, have taken their places. I think I can state, also—and I do it with pleasure, because I do not wish to excite but to calm the public mind—that our relations with France are more peaceful, much less explosive than a year ago.

whether we will have war and of the success with which we shall have it (it was a representative of the Centre who upbraided me with it in the Reichstag) depends to-day only on Russia. Russia alone has the decision in her hands."

Perhaps I will return to this question later. In the meantime, I will continue the pictures of these forty years and recall that in 1876 a war-cloud gathered in the South; that in 1877, the Balkan War was only prevented by the Berlin Congress from putting the whole of Europe in a blaze, and that quite suddenly after the Congress a new vision of danger was disclosed to us in the East because Russia was offended by our action at the conference. Perhaps, later on, I will recur to this also if my strength will permit.

Then followed a certain reaction in the intimate relations of the three emperors which allowed us to look for some time into the future with more assurance; yet on the first signs of uncertainty in their relations, or because of the lapsing of the agreements they had made with each other, our public opinion showed the same nervous and, I think, exaggerated excitement with which we had to contend last year—which, at the present time, I hold to be specially uncalled for. But because I think this nervousness uncalled for now, I am far from concluding that we do not need an increase of our war-footing. On the contrary! Therefore, I have unrolled before you this tableau of forty years— perhaps not to your amusement! If not, I beg your pardon, but had I omitted a year from that which you yourselves had experienced with shuddering, the impression might have been lost that the state of anxiety before wars, before continually extending complications, the entanglements of which no one can anticipate,—that this condition is permanent with us; that we must reckon upon it as a permanency; and that independently of the circumstances of the moment, with the self-confidence of a great nation which is strong enough under any circumstances to take its fate into its own hands against any coalition; with the confidence in itself and in God which its own power and the righteousness of its cause, a righteousness which the care of the government will always keep with Germany—that we shall be able to foresee every possibility and, doing so, to look forward to peace.

The long and the short of it is that in these days we must be as strong as we can; and if we will, we can be stronger than

The fears which have been excited during the year have been occasioned more by Russia than by France, or I may say that the occasion was rather the exchange of mutual threats, excitement, reproaches, and provocations which have taken place during the summer between the Russian and the French press. But I do not believe that the situation in Russia is materially different now from what it was a year ago. The Liberal Gazette has printed in display type what I said then:—" Our friendship with Russia sustained no interruption during our war and it is elevated above all doubt to-day. We expect neither assault nor attack nor unfriendliness from Russia." Perhaps this was printed in large letters to make it easier to attack it. Perhaps also with the hope that I had reached a different conclusion in the meantime and had become convinced that my confidence in the Russian policy of last year was erroneous. This is not the case. The grounds which gave occasion for it lie partly in the Russian press and partly in the mobilization of Russian troops. I cannot attach decided importance to the attitude of the press. They say that it means more in Russia than it does in France. I am of the contrary opinion. In France the press is a power which influences the conclusions of the administration. It is not such a power in Russia, nor can it be; but in both cases the press is only spots of printer's ink on paper against which we have no war to wage. There can be no ground of provocation for us in it. Behind each article is only one man—the man who has guided the pen to send the article into the world. Even in a Russian paper, we may say in an independent Russian paper, secretly supported by French subsidies, the case is not altered. The pen which has written in such a paper an article hostile to Germany has no one behind it but the man whose hand held the pen, the man who in his cabinet produced the lucubration and the protector which every Russian newspaper is wont to have— that is to say the official more or less important in Russian party politics who gives such a paper his protection. But both of them do not weigh a feather against the authority of his Majesty, the Czar of Russia. . . .

Since the great war of 1870 was concluded, has there been any year, I ask you, without its alarm of war? Just as we were returning, at the beginning of the seventies, they said: When will we have the next war? When will the Revanche be fought? In five years at latest. They said to us then: "The question of

any other country of equal resources in the world. I will return to that. And it would be a crime not to use our resources. If we do not need an army prepared for war, we do not need to call for it. It depends merely on the not very important question of the cost—and it is not very important, though I mention it incidentally. I have no mind to go into figures, financial or military, but France during the last few years has spent in improving her forces three thousand millions, while we have spent hardly fifteen hundred millions including that we are now asking for. But I leave the ministers of war and of finance to deal with that. When I say that we must strive continually to be ready for all emergencies, I advance the proposition that, on account of our geographical position, we must make greater efforts than other powers would be obliged to make in view of the same ends. We lie in the middle of Europe. We have at least three fronts on which we can be attacked. France has only an eastern boundary; Russia only its western, exposed to assault. We are, moreover, more exposed than any other people to the danger of hostile coalition because of our geographical position, and because, perhaps, of the feeble power of cohesion which, until now, the German people has exhibited when compared with others. At any rate, God has placed us in a position where our neighbors will prevent us from falling into a condition of sloth —of wallowing in the mire of mere existence. On one side of us he has set the French, a most warlike and restless nation; and he has allowed to become exaggerated in the Russians fighting tendencies which had not become apparent in them during the earlier part of the century. So we are spurred forward on both sides to endeavors which perhaps we would not make otherwise. The pikes in the European carp-pond will not allow us to become carp, because they make us feel their stings in both our sides. They force us to an effort which, perhaps, we would not make otherwise, and they force us also to a cohesion among ourselves as Germans which is opposed to our innermost nature; otherwise we would prefer to struggle with each other. But when we are enfiladed by the press of France and Russia, it compels us to stand together, and through such compression it will so increase our fitness for cohesion that we may finally come into the same condition of indivisibility which is natural to other people—which thus far we have lacked. We must respond to this dispensation of Providence, however, by making ourselves so strong that the pike can do nothing more than encourage us to exert ourselves. We had, years ago, in the times of the Holy Alliance (I recall an old American song which I learned from my dead friend, Motley:—

In good old colonial times
When we lived under a king!)

We had then patriarchal times and with them a multitude of balustrades on which we could support ourselves, and a multitude of dykes to protect us from the wild European floods. That was the German confederation, and the true beginning, and continuance, and conclusion of the German confederation was the Holy Alliance, for whose service it was made. We depended on Russia and Austria, and, above everything, we relied on our own modesty, which did not allow us to speak before the rest of the company had spoken. We have lost all that, and we must help ourselves. The Holy Alliance was shipwrecked in the Crimean War—through no fault of ours! The German confederation has been destroyed by us because our existence under it was neither tolerable for us nor for the German people. Both have ceased to exist. After the dissolution of the German confederation, after the war of 1866, we would have been obliged to reckon on isolation for Prussia or North Germany, had we been obliged to stop at reckoning with the fact that, on no side would they forgive us the new and great successes which we had obtained. Never do other powers look with pleasure on the triumphs of a neighbor.

Our connection with Russia was not disturbed, however, by the events of 1866. In 1866 the memory of the politics of Count von Buol and of Austrian politics during the Crimean War was too fresh in Russia to allow them to think of supporting the Austrian against the Prussian monarchy, or of renewing the campaign which Czar Nicholas had conducted for Austria in 1849. For us, therefore, there remained a natural inclination towards Russia, which, foreseen in the last century, had in this its recognized origin in the politics of Czar Alexander I. To him Prussia owes thanks indeed. In 1813 he could easily have turned on the Polish frontiers and concluded peace. Later he could have brought about the fall of Prussia. We have then, as a fact, to thank, for the restoration of the old footing, the good will of Czar Alexander I.; or, if you are inclined to be skeptical, say to the need felt in Russian politics for Prussia. This feeling of

gratitude has controlled the administration of Frederick William the Third.

The balance which Russia had on its account with Prussia was used up through the friendship, I may say through the serviceability of Prussia during the entire reign of Czar Nicholas and, I may add, settled at Olmutz. At Olmutz, Czar Nicholas did not take the part of Prussia, did not shield us from adverse experience, did not guard us against humiliation; for, on the whole, he leaned towards Austria more than towards Prussia. The idea that during his administration we owed thanks to Russia results from a historical legend. But while Czar Nicholas lived, we, on our side, did not violate the tradition with Russia. During the Crimean War, as I have already told you, we stood by Russia in spite of threats and of some hazard. His Majesty, the late King, had no desire to play a decided part in the war with a strong army, as I think he could easily have done. We had concluded treaties by which we were bound to put a hundred thousand men in the field by a set time. I advised his Majesty that we should put not a hundred thousand but two hundred thousand in the field and to put them there *à cheval* so that we could use them right and left; so that his Majesty would have been the final arbiter of the fortunes of the Crimean War. But his late Majesty was not inclined to warlike undertakings, and the people ought to be grateful to him for it. I was younger and less experienced then than I am now. We bore no malice for Olmutz, however, during the Crimean War. We came out of the Crimean War as a friend of Russia, and while I was ambassador to Russia I enjoyed the fruit of this friendship in a very favorable reception at court and in Russian society. Our attitude towards Austria in the Italian War was not to the taste of the Russian cabinet, but it had no unfavorable consequences. Our Austrian War of 1866 was looked upon with a certain satisfaction. No one in Russia then grudged Austria what she got. In the year 1870 we had, in taking our stand and making our defense, the satisfaction of coincidently rendering a service to our Russian friends in the Black Sea. The opening of the Black Sea by the contracting powers would never have been probable if the Germans had not been victorious in the neighborhood of Paris. Had we been defeated, for example, I think the conclusion of the London agreement would not have been so easily in Russia's favor. So the war of 1870 left no ill humor between us and Russia. . . .

The bill will bring us an increase of troops capable of bearing arms—a possible increase, which if we do not need it, we need not call out, but can leave the men at home. But we will have it ready for service if we have arms for it. And that is a matter of primary importance. I remember the carbine which was furnished by England to our Landwehr in 1813, and with which I had some practice as a huntsman—that was no weapon for a soldier! We can get arms suddenly for an emergency, but if we have them ready for it, then this bill will count for a strengthening of our peace forces and a reinforcement of the peace league as great as if a fourth great power had joined the alliance with an army of seven hundred thousand men—the greatest yet put in the field.

I think, too, that this powerful reinforcement of the army will have a quieting effect on our own people, and will in some measure relieve the nervousness of our exchanges, of our press, and of our public opinion. I hope they all will be comforted if they make it clear to themselves that after this reinforcement and from the moment of the signature and publication of the bill, the soldiers are there! But arms are necessary, and we must provide better ones if we wish to have an army of triarians—of the best manhood that we have among our people; of fathers of family over thirty years old! And we must give them the best arms that can be had! We must not send them into battle with what we have not thought good enough for our young troops of the line. But our steadfast men, our fathers of family, our Samsons, such as we remember seeing hold the bridge at Versailles, must have the best arms on their shoulders, and the best clothing to protect them against the weather, which can be had from anywhere. We must not be niggardly in this. And I hope it will reassure our countrymen if they think now it will be the case—as I do not believe—that we are likely to be attacked on both sides at once. There is a possibility of it, for, as I have explained to you in the history of the Forty Years' War, all manner of coalitions may occur. But if it should occur we could hold the defensive on our borders with a million good soldiers. At the same time, we could hold in reserve a half million or more, almost a million, indeed; and send them forward as they were needed. Some one has said to me: "The only result of that will be that the others will increase their forces also." But they cannot. They have long ago reached the maximum. We

lowered it in 1867 because we thought that, having the North-German confederation, we could make ourselves easier and exempt men over thirty-two. In consequence our neighbors have adopted a longer term of service—many of them a twenty-year term. They have a maximum as high as ours, but they cannot touch us in quality. Courage is equal in all civilized nations. The Russians or the French acquit themselves as bravely as the Germans. But our people, our seven hundred thousand men, are veterans trained in service, tried soldiers who have not yet forgotten their training. And no people in the world can touch us in this, that we have the material for officers and under-officers to command this army. That is what they cannot imitate. The whole tendency of popular education leads to that in Germany as it does in no other country. The measure of education necessary to fit an officer or under-officer to meet the demands which the soldier makes on him, exists with us to a much greater extent than with any other people. We have more material for officers and under-officers than any other country, and we have a corps of officers that no other country can approach. In this and in the excellence of our corps of under-officers, who are really the pupils of our officers' corps, lies our superiority. The course of education which fits an officer to meet the strong demands made on his position for self-denial, for the duty of comradeship, and for fulfilling the extraordinarily difficult social duties whose fulfillment is made necessary among us by the comradeship which, thank God, exists in the highest degree among officers and men without the least detriment to discipline—they cannot imitate us in that —that relationship between officers and men which, with a few unfortunate exceptions, exists in the German army. But the exceptions confirm the rule, and so we can say that no German officer leaves his soldiers under fire, but brings them out even at the risk of his own life; while, on the other hand, no German soldier, as we know by experience, forsakes his officer.

If other armies intend to supply with officers and sub-officers as many troops as we intend to have at once, then they must educate the officers, for no untaught fool is fit to command a company, and much less is he fit to fulfill the difficult duties which an officer owes to his men, if he is to keep their love and respect. The measure of education which is demanded for that, and the qualities which, among us especially, are expressed in comradeship and sympathy by the officer,—*that* no rule and no regulation in the world can impress on the officers of other countries. In *that* we are superior to all, and in that they cannot imitate us! On that point I have no fear.

But there is still another advantage to be derived from the adoption of this bill: The very strength for which we strive shows our peaceful disposition. That sounds paradoxical, but still it is true.

No man would attack us when we have such a powerful war-machine as we wish to make the German army. If I were to come before you to-day and say to you — supposing me to be convinced that the conditions are different from what they are — if I were to say to you: "We are strongly threatened by France and Russia; it is evident that we will be attacked; my conviction as a diplomat, considering the military necessities of the case, is that it is expedient for us to take the defensive by striking the first blow, as we are now in a position to do; an aggressive war is to our advantage, and I beg the Reichstag for a milliard or half a milliard to begin it at once against both our neighbors" — indeed, gentlemen, I do not know that you would have sufficient confidence in me to consent! I hope you would not.

But if you were to do it, it would not satisfy me. If we in Germany should wish to wage war with the full exertion of our national strength, it must be a war with which all who engage in it, all who offer themselves as sacrifices in it — in short, the whole nation takes part as one man; it must be a people's war; it must be a war carried on with the enthusiasm of 1870, when we were ruthlessly attacked. I well remember the ear-splitting, joyful shouts at the Cologne railway station; it was the same from Berlin to Cologne; and it was the same here in Berlin. The waves of public feeling in favor of war swept us into it whether we wished or not. It must always be so if the power of a people such as ours is to be exerted to the full. It will be very difficult, however, to make it clear to the provinces and states of the confederation and to their peoples, that war is now unavoidably necessary. They would ask: "Are you sure of that? Who knows?" In short, when we came to actual hostilities, the weight of such imponderable considerations would be much heavier against us than the material opposition we would meet from our enemies. "Holy Russia" would be irritated; France would bristle with bayonets as far as the Pyrenees. It would be

the same everywhere. A war which was not decreed by the popular will could be carried on if once the constituted authorities had finally decided on it as a necessity; it would be carried on vigorously, and perhaps successfully, after the first fire and the sight of blood. But it would not be a finish fight in its spirit with such fire and *élan* behind it as we would have in a war in which we were attacked. Then all Germany from Memel to Lake Constance would flame out like a powder mine; the country would bristle with arms, and no enemy would be rash enough to join issues with the *furor Teutonicus* (Berserker madness) thus roused by attack.

We must not lose sight of such considerations, even if we are now superior to our future opponents, as many military critics besides our own consider us to be. All our own critics are convinced of our superiority. Naturally every soldier believes it. He would come very near to being a failure as a soldier if he did not wish for war and feel full assurance of victory. If our rivals sometimes suspect that it is fear of the result which makes us peaceful, they are grievously in error. We believe as thoroughly in the certainty of our victory in a righteous cause as any lieutenant in a foreign garrison can believe in his third glass of champagne — and perhaps we have more ground for our assurance! It is not fear which makes us peaceable, but the consciousness of our strength — the consciousness that if we were attacked at the most unfavorable time, we are strong enough for defense and for keeping in view the possibility of leaving it to the providence of God to remove in the meantime the necessity for war.

I am never for an offensive war, and if war can come only through our initiative, it will not begin. Fire must be kindled by some one before it can burn, and we will not kindle it. Neither the consciousness of our strength, as I have just represented it, nor the trust in our alliances will prevent us from continuing with our accustomed zeal our accustomed efforts to keep the peace. We will not allow ourselves to be led by bad temper; we will not yield to prejudice. It is undoubtedly true that the threats, the insults, the provocations which have been directed against us, have aroused great and natural animosities on our side. And it is hard to rouse such feelings in the Germans, for they are less sensitive to the dislike of others towards them than any other nation. We are taking pains, however, to

soften these animosities, and in the future as in the past we will strive to keep the peace with our neighbors — especially with Russia. When I say "especially with Russia," I mean that France offers us no security for the success of our efforts, though I will not say that it does not help. We will never seek occasion to quarrel. We will never attack France. In the many small occasions for trouble which the disposition of our neighbors to spy and to bribe has given us, we have made pleasant and amicable settlements. I would hold it grossly criminal to allow such trifles either to occasion a great national war or to make it probable. There are occasions when it is true that the "more reasonable gives way." I name Russia especially, and I have the same confidence in the result I had a year ago when my expression gave this "Liberal" paper here occasion for black type. But I have it without running after — or, as a German paper expressed it, "grovelling before Russia." That time has gone by. We no longer sue for favor either in France or in Russia. The Russian press and Russian public opinion have shown the door to an old, powerful, and attached friend as we were. We will not force ourselves upon them. We have sought to regain the old confidential relationship, but we will run after no one. But that does not prevent us from observing — it rather spurs us on to observe with redoubled care — the treaty rights of Russia. Among these treaty rights are some which are not conceded by all our friends: I mean the rights which at the Berlin Congress Russia won in the matter of Bulgaria. . . .

In consequence of the resolution of the Congress, Russia, up to 1885, chose as prince a near relative of the Czar concerning whom no one asserted or could assert that he was anything else than a Russian dependent. It appointed the minister of war and a greater part of the officials. In short, it governed Bulgaria. There is no possible doubt of it. The Bulgarians, or a part of them, or their prince, — I do not know which, — were not satisfied. There was a *coup d'état* and there has been a defection from Russia. This has created a situation which we have no call to change by force of arms — though its existence does not change theoretically the rights which Russia gained from the conference. But if Russia should seek to establish its rights forcibly I do not know what difficulties might arise and it does not concern us to know. We will not support forcible measures and will not advise them. I do not believe there is any disposition towards them. I

am sure no such inclination exists. But if through diplomatic means, through the intervention of the Sultan as the suzerain of Bulgaria, Russia seeks its rights, then I assume that it is the province of loyal German statesmanship to give an unmistakable support to the provisions of the Berlin Treaty, and to stand by the interpretation which without exception we gave it — an interpretation on which the voice of the Bulgarians cannot make me err. Bulgaria, the Statelet between the Danube and the Balkans, is certainly not of sufficient importance to justify plunging Europe into war from Moscow to the Pyrenees, from the North Sea to Palermo — a war the issue of which no one could foresee, at the end of which no one could tell what the fighting had been about.

So I can say openly that the position of the Russian press, the unfriendliness we have experienced from Russian public opinion, will not prevent us from supporting Russia in a diplomatic attempt to establish its rights as soon as it makes up its mind to assert them in Bulgaria. I say deliberately — "As soon as Russia expresses the wish." We have put ourselves to some trouble heretofore to meet the views of Russia on the strength of reliable hints, but we have lived to see the Russian press attacking, as hostile to Russia, the very things in German politics which were prompted by a desire to anticipate Russia's wishes. We did that at the Congress, but it will not happen again. If Russia officially asks us to support measures for the restoration in Bulgaria of the situation approved by the Congress with the Sultan as suzerain, I would not hesitate to advise his Majesty, the Emperor, that it should be done. This is the demand which the treaties make on our loyalty to a neighbor, with whom, be the mood what it will, we have to maintain neighborly relations and defend great common interests of monarchy, such as the interests of order against its antagonists in all Europe, with a neighbor, I say, whose sovereign has a perfect understanding in this regard with the allied sovereigns. I do not doubt that when the Czar of Russia finds that the interests of his great empire of a hundred million people requires war, he will make war. But his interests cannot possibly prompt him to make war against us. I do not think it at all probable that such a question of interest is likely to present itself. I do not believe that a disturbance of the peace is imminent — if I may recapitulate — and I beg that you will consider the pending measure without regard to that thought or that apprehension, looking on it rather as a full restoration of the mighty power which God has created in the German people — a power to be used if we need it! If we do not need it, we will not use it and we will seek to avoid the necessity for its use. This attempt is made somewhat more difficult by threatening articles in foreign newspapers and I may give special admonition to the outside world against the continuance of such articles. They lead to nothing. The threats made against us, not by the government but in the newspapers, are incredibly stupid, when it is remembered that they assume that a great and proud power such as the German Empire is capable of being intimidated by an array of black spots made by a printer on paper, a mere marshalling of words. If they would give up that idea, we could reach a better understanding with both our neighbors. Every country is finally answerable for the wanton mischief done by its newspapers, and the reckoning is liable to be presented some day in the shape of a final decision from some other country. We can be bribed very easily — perhaps too easily — with love and good-will. But with threats, never!

We Germans fear God, and nothing else in the world!

It is the fear of God which makes us love peace and keep it. He who breaks it against us ruthlessly will learn the meaning of the warlike love of the Fatherland which in 1813 rallied to the standard the entire population of the then small and weak kingdom of Prussia; he will learn, too, that this patriotism is now the common property of the entire German nation, so that whoever attacks Germany will find it unified in arms, every warrior having in his heart the steadfast faith that God will be with us.

JEREMIAH SULLIVAN BLACK

(1810–1883)

JEREMIAH SULLIVAN BLACK was born January 10th, 1810, in Somerset County, Pennsylvania. In the public affairs of the United States before and after the Civil War, from the time he entered politics as a supporter of Andrew Jackson until his death in August 1883, he stood for one of the great forces of minority opinion, seldom strong enough to control by mere weight of its impact, but always liable to assert itself in every great emergency as a controlling balance of power. When attacked by his last illness he was writing a reply to Jefferson Davis, suggested by a somewhat heated attack made upon him by Mr. Davis, because while declaring that "the States have rights carefully reserved and as sacred as the life, liberty, and property of the private citizen," he held Andrew Jackson's view of secession. If this closing incident of his career is kept in mind and brought to bear on his grim jest that "next to the original Fall of Man the landing of the Mayflower was the greatest misfortune that ever happened to the human race," the illustration will give a better idea than could be given by any definition of his attitude during the Civil War and Reconstruction periods. Judge Black served on the supreme bench of Pennsylvania and in the cabinet of President Buchanan, but his great influence was never an incident of official prominence. As a man and as a lawyer he showed an individuality so marked, and in certain ways so representative, that men of all parties listened to him with an attention they seldom give the official utterance of any public man. When, in 1883, he went before the judiciary committee of the Pennsylvania senate and delivered an address on the State's power of eminent domain, and on the duties of corporations as public servants, the effect was felt throughout the country. It is doubtful if any other speech on a technical question of law and industrial economy ever produced effects so profound and so far-reaching. It is believed that the forces set in motion by sympathy with Judge Black's views thus expressed decided more than one presidential election and did more than anything else to make possible the radical changes which took place in the politics of the Northwestern States between 1883 and 1892.

CORPORATIONS UNDER EMINENT DOMAIN

(Delivered before the Judiciary Committee of the Pennsylvania Senate, at the Session of 1883)

Mr. Chairman:—

THE irrepressible conflict between the rights of the people and the interests of railroad corporations does not seem likely to terminate immediately. I beg your permission to put our case on your record somewhat more distinctly than heretofore.

Why do I give myself this trouble? My great and good friend, the President of the Reading Railroad Company, expresses the suspicion that I am quietly acting in the interest of some anonymous corporation. I wish to contradict that as flatly as I can.

The charge that I am communist enough to wish the destruction of all corporate property is equally untrue. I think myself the most conservative of citizens. I believe with my whole heart in the rights of life, liberty, and property, and if anybody has struggled more faithfully, through good report and evil, to maintain them inviolate, I do not know who he is. I respect the State constitution. Perhaps I am prejudiced in favor of natural justice and equality. I am convinced that without the enforcement of the fundamental law honest government cannot be expected.

These considerations, together with the request of many friends, would be sufficient reason for doing all the little I can to get "appropriate legislation." At all events, it is unfair to charge me with any motive of lucre or malice.

It is not proposed by those who think as I do that any corporation shall lose one atom of its property. A lawful contract between a railroad company and the State is inviolable, and must not be touched by hostile hands, however bad the bargain may have been for the people. Mr. Gowen and all others with similar contracts on their hands are entitled each to his pound of flesh, and if it be "so nominated in the bond" the Commonwealth must bare her bosom to all their knives and let them "cut nearest the heart."

But we, the people, have rights of property as well as the corporations, and ours are — or ought to be — as sacred as theirs. Between the great domain which we have ceded to them and that which still belongs to us the line is plainly and distinctly

marked, and if they cross it for purposes of plunder they should be driven back under the lash of the law. It is not the intent of the amended Constitution, nor the desire of those who demand its enforcement, to do them the slightest injury. We only ask for that impartial and just protection which the State, as *parens patriæ*, owes to us not less than to them.

In the first place, it will, I think, be admitted by all impartial persons of average intelligence, that the companies are not the owners of the railroads. The notion that they are is as silly as it is pernicious. It is the duty of every commercial, manufacturing, or agricultural State, to open thoroughfares of trade and travel through her territory. For that purpose she may take the property of citizens and pay for the work out of her own treasury. When it is done she may make it free to all comers, or she may reimburse the cost by levying a special tax upon those who use it; or she may get the road built and opened by a corporation or an individual, and pay for it by permitting the builder to collect tolls or taxes from those who carry and travel on it. Pennsylvania has tried all these methods with her turnpikes, canals, and railroads. Some have been made at her own cost and thrown open; on others made by herself she placed officers to collect a special tax; others have been built for her by contract, in which some natural or artificial person agreed to do the work for the privilege of appropriating the taxes which she authorized to be levied.

But in all these cases the proprietary right remained in the State and was held by her in trust for the use of the people. Those who run the railroads and canals are always public agents. It is impossible to look at them in any other light or to conceive how a different relation could exist, because a railroad which is not managed by public agents cannot be a public highway. The character of their appointment, even upon the same work, has differed materially. The Columbia Railroad and all the canals were for a time under the management of officers appointed by the governor, or elected by the people, and paid out of the State treasury. Afterwards the duty was devolved by the State upon the persons associated together under acts of incorporation, who contracted to perform it upon certain terms. The Erie and Northeast Railroad was at first run for the State by a company; the company was removed from its trust for misbehavior; the governor then took it and appointed an officer to superintend the work; later the governor's appointee was displaced, with the consent of the legislature, and the duty was again confided to a corporation newly chartered.

None of these agents — neither the canal commissioner nor the State receiver, nor any corporation that went before or came after — had the slightest proprietary right or title to the railroads themselves. To say that they had would be as preposterous as to assert that township roads are the private property of the supervisors.

The legal relations existing between the State and the persons whom she authorizes to supervise her highways were somewhat elaborately discussed by the supreme court of Pennsylvania in the case of the Erie and N. E. R. R. Co. *versus* Casey. (2 Casey, pp. 307–24.) It was there determined that a railroad built by authority of the State for the general purposes of commerce is a public highway and in no sense private property; that a corporation authorized to run it is a servant of the State as much as an officer legally appointed to do any other public duty; as strictly confined by the laws and as liable to be removed for transgressing them.

All the judges concurred in this opinion. The two who dissented from the judgment did so on the technical ground that certain circumstances, which would have estopped the State in a judicial proceeding, disarmed the legislature of the power to repeal. Neither they nor any other judge in the country whose authority is worth a straw ever denied the doctrine for which I have here cited that case, though it may have been sometimes overlooked, ignored, or perchance evaded. This principle and no other was the basis of the decision in Pennsylvania and all the other States that cities and counties might issue bonds, or their money, and tax their people to aid in building railways. The Supreme Court of the United States has affirmed it in scores of cases. It was so universally acknowledged that the convention of 1873 incorporated it into the Constitution as a part of the fundamental law. I do not know upon what foundation more solid than this any great principle of jurisprudence was ever established in a free country. When in addition you consider the reason of the thing, and the supreme necessity of it for the purposes of common justice, it seems like a sin, a shame, a scandal to oppose it.

that this odious and demoralizing theory has made a strong lodgment in the minds of disinterested, upright, and high-placed men. Two members of the Senate judiciary — I do not say they are the ablest, because comparisons are odious, but they are both of them among the foremost men of the country for talents and integrity — these gentlemen emphatically dissented from me when I asserted that the management of the railroads was not a matter of business to be conducted like a private enterprise merely for the profit of the directors or stockholders. A heresy so supported is entitled to serious refutation, however absurd it may seem on its face.

I aver that a man or corporation appointed to do a public duty must perform it with an eye single to the public interest. If he perverts his authority to purposes of private gain he is guilty of corruption, and all who aid and abet him are his accomplices in crime. He defiles himself if he mingles his own business with that intrusted to him by the government and uses one to promote the other. If a judge excuse himself for a false decision by saying that he sold his judgment for the highest price he could get, you cover his character with infamy. A ministerial officer, like a sheriff, for instance, who extorts from a defendant, or even from a convict in his custody, what the law does not allow him to collect, and puts the surplus in his pocket, is a knave upon whom you have no mercy. You send county commissioners to the penitentiary for consulting their own financial advantage to the injury of the general weal. When the officers of a city corporation make a business of running it to enrich themselves, at the expense of the public, you can see at a glance that they are the basest of criminals. Why, then, can you not see that the officers of a railway corporation are equally guilty when they pervert the authority with which they are clothed to purposes purely selfish? A railroad corporation is a part of the civil government as much as a city corporation. The officers of the former, as much as the latter, are agents and trustees of the public, and the public has an interest precisely similar in the fidelity of both. Why, then, should partiality or extortion be condemned as criminal in one if it be tolerated as fair business when practiced by the other? Yet there are virtuous and disinterested statesmen among us, who think that faithful service ought not to be enforced against the railroad companies, however loudly it may be claimed by the body of the people as their just

It being settled that the railroads and canals belong of right to the State for the use of the people, and that the corporations who have them in charge are mere agents to run them for the owners, it will surely not be denied that all proper regulations should be made to prevent those agents from betraying their trust. The wisdom is very plain of those provisions in our Constitution which put them on a level with other public servants and forbid them to prostitute their functions for purposes merely mercenary or to engage in any business which necessarily brings their private interests into conflict with their public duty. Seeing the vast magnitude of the affairs intrusted to them, and the terrible temptation to which their cupidity is exposed, it is certainly necessary that you should hold them to their responsibilities, and hold them hard.

But, on the other hand, the corporations deny that they owe any responsibility to the State more than individuals engaged in private business. They assert that the management of the railroads, being a mere speculation of their own, these thoroughfares of trade and travel must be run for their interests, without regard to public right. If they take advantage of their power to oppress the labor and overtax the land of the State; if they crush the industry of one man or place to build up the prosperity of another; if they plunder the rich by extortion, or deepen the distress of the poor by discriminating against them, they justify themselves by showing that all this was in the way of business; that their interest required them to do it; that if they had done otherwise their fortunes would not have been so great as they are; that it was the prudent, proper, and successful method of managing their own affairs. This is their universal answer to all complaints. Their protests against legislative intervention to protect the public always takes this shape, with more or less distinctness of outline. In whatever language they clothe their argument it is the same in substance as that with which Demetrius, the silversmith, defended the sanctity of the temple for which he made shrines: "Sirs, ye know that by this craft we have our wealth."

That railroad corporations and their paid adherents should take this view of the subject is perhaps not surprising, nor does it excite our special wonder to see them supported by the subsidiary rings whom they patronize; but it is amazing to find

due, and no matter how distinctly it may be commanded by the Constitution itself.

I am able to maintain that all the corruption and misgovernment with which the earth is cursed grows out of this fatal proclivity of public servants to make a business of their duty. Recall the worst cases that have occurred in our history and see if every one of them does not finally resolve itself into that. Tweed and his associates, the Philadelphia rings, the carpet-bag thieves, the Star Route conspirators, all went into business for themselves while pretending to be engaged in the public service. Oakes Ames distributed the stock of the Credit Mobilier where he thought it would "do the most good" to himself and others with whom he was connected, and that was the business in him who gave and in them that took his bribes. Madison Wells, when he proposed to Mr. Kenner that he would make a true return of the election if he could be assured of getting "two hundred thousand dollars apiece for himself and Jim Anderson, and a less sum for the niggers," had as keen an eye to business as if he had been president of a railroad company instead of a returning board. Certain greedy adventurers made it a business to rob the nation of its lands, and, uniting with Congress, carried it on so magnificently, that they got away with an area nearly equal to nine States as large as Pennsylvania. The imposition of the whisky tax, excluding what was held on speculation, was business to the officers and legislators who were sharp enough to anticipate their own votes. You will see on reflection that every base combination which officers have made with one another or with outside parties has been a business arrangement, precisely like that which the railroads justify on the sole ground that it is business. The effect is not only to corrupt those who engage in such transactions, but to demoralize all who are tempted by personal and party attachments to apologize for it.

When the officers of the Pennsylvania Railroad Company corruptly bought the remission of the tonnage tax, and thereby transferred to their own pockets an incalculable sum justly due to the State, it was business, rich to them and profitable beyond the dreams of avarice, while to the swindled taxpayers it was proportionately disastrous. The nine million steal of later date was a business enterprise which failed, because Governor Geary most unexpectedly put his veto upon it. Still more recently the same organization undertook to get from the treasury of the

State four millions of dollars to which it had no decent pretense of a claim. Never was any affair conducted in a more business-like way. The appointed agents of the corporation came to Harrisburg when the legislature was in session and regularly set up a shop for the purchase of members at prearranged and specified prices. You condemn this piece of business because it was dishonest, but was it more dishonest than that which the same corporation habitually does when it stands on the highway and by fraud or force extorts from individual citizens a much larger sum in excessive tolls, to which its right is no better than to the money it tried to get by bribery?

The functions of railroad corporations are clearly defined and ought to be as universally understood as those of any servant which the State or general government employs. Without proprietary right in the highways, they are appointed to superintend them for the owners. They are charged with the duty of seeing that every needed facility for the use of those thoroughfares shall be furnished to all citizens, like the justice promised in Magna Charta, without sale, denial, or delay. Such services, if faithfully performed, are important and valuable, and the compensation ought to be a full equivalent; accordingly they are authorized to pay themselves, by levying upon all who use the road, a tax, or toll, or freight, sufficient for that purpose.

But this tax must be reasonable, fixed, certain, and uniform, otherwise it is a fraud upon the people, which no department of the State government, nor all of them combined, has power to legalize.

It is much easier to see the nature and character of the mischief wrought by the present practices of the railroad companies than it is to calculate its extent. If your action depends in any degree upon the amount of the spoliation which the people of the State have suffered and are now suffering for want of just laws to protect them, you certainly ought to direct an official inquiry into the subject and ascertain the whole truth as nearly as possible.

But investigations have already taken place in Congress and the legislatures of several States; complaints founded upon specified facts come up from every quarter; verified accusations are made by some of the companies against others; railroad men have openly confessed their fraudulent practices, and sometimes boasted of the large sums they accumulate by them. Putting

these together you can make at least an approximate calculation. I doubt not you will find the sum total of the plunder they have taken in the shape of excessive charges to be frightful.

Three or four years ago a committee of the United States Senate collected the materials and made a report upon this general subject, in which they showed that an excess of five cents per hundredweight, charged on the whole agricultural crop of the then current year, would amount to seventy millions of dollars. Upon the crop of the last year it would doubtless come nearer a hundred millions. The railroads would not get this sum, because not nearly all of it is carried, but it would operate as an export tax operates; that is to say, the producer, the consumer, or the intermediate dealer, would lose that amount on the whole crop, carried or not carried. In 1880 the charges from Chicago to the eastern markets were raised from ten cents per hundredweight to thirty-five cents, the latter rate being unquestionably twice as high as a fair one. You can count from these data the terrible loss sustained by the land, labor, and trade of the country. It was the end and the attainment of a combination still subsisting between the great trunk lines, as they are called, to pool their receipts, to stop all competition, to unite the stealing power of all into one grand monopoly and put the whole people at their mercy. It was a criminal conspiracy by the common and statute laws of all the States. . . .

We are often told that in this struggle for honest government against the power of the railroad corporations the just cause has no chance of success. We do seem to be out on a forlorn hope. The little finger of monopoly is thicker than the loins of the law.

The influence of our enemies over the legislature is mysterious, incalculable, and strong enough to make the Constitution a dead letter in spite of oaths to obey it, and a popular demand, almost universal, to enforce it. There is no other subject upon which the press is so shy as upon this, the most important of all. Afraid to oppose the corrupt corporations, and ashamed to defend them, it sinks into neutrality. Prudent politicians always want a smooth road to run on, and the right path here is full of impediments. In this state of things we seem weaker than we really are; for the unbroken heart of the people is on the side of justice, equality, and truth. Monopolists may sneer at our blundering leadership and the unorganized condition of our common file, but they had better bethink them that when the worst comes

to the worst, our raw militia is numerous enough to overwhelm their regulars, well paid and well drilled as they are. They have destroyed the business of hundreds for one that they have favored. For every millionaire they have made ten thousand paupers, and the injured parties lack no gall to make oppression bitter.

The people, certainly, got one immense advantage over the carrying corporations when they adopted the seventeenth article of the Constitution. That concedes to us all the rights we ask, puts the flag of the commonwealth into our hands and consecrates our warfare. The malign influence that heretofore has palsied the legislative arm cannot last forever. We will continue to elect representatives again and again, and every man shall swear upon the Gospel of God that he will do us the full and perfect justice which the Constitution commands. At last we will rouse the "conscience of a majority, screw their courage to the sticking place, and get the appropriate legislation" which we need so sorely.

Whenever a majority in both houses becomes independent enough to throw off the chains which now bind them to the service of monopoly; when frequent repetitions of the oath to obey the Constitution shall impress its obligation upon their hearts; when admonition and reproof from within and without — "line upon line, precept upon precept, here a little and there a little" — shall have taught them that fidelity to the rights of the people is a higher virtue than subserviency to the mere interests of a corrupt corporation; when the seventeenth article shall have been read and reread in their hearing often enough to make them understand the import of its plain and simple words, then, without further delay and with no more paltry excuses, they will give us legislation appropriate, just, and effective. A tolerably clear perception of their duty, coupled with a sincere desire to do it, will enable them to catch the shortest and easiest way. All trifling with the subject will cease at once; all modes of evading this great point will go out of fashion; no contrivance will be resorted to of ways not to do it while professing to be in favor of it; our common sense will not be insulted by the offer of a civil remedy to each individual for public offenses which affect the whole body of the people and diminish the security of all men's rights at once. The legislative vision, relieved from the moral strabismus which makes it crooked now, will see straight through the folly of trying to correct the general evil except by the one

appropriate means of regular punishment at the suit of the State. Does this seem harsh? Certainly not more severe than any other criminal law on our statute book which applies to railway managers as well as to everybody else. They need not suffer the penalty unless they commit the crime; and they will not commit the crime if you make a just penalty the legal consequence. Pass a proper law to-day and they will be as honest as you are to-morrow. Every one of them can be trusted to keep clear of acts which may take him to the penitentiary. They have been guilty in their past lives, and will continue in evil doing for some time to come because the present state of your laws assures them that they shall go "unwhipped of justice." But threaten them with a moderate term of imprisonment and a reasonable fine, and they will no more rob a shipper on the railroad than they will pick your pocket at a prayer meeting. Your law will do its work without a single prosecution. Thus you could, if you would, effect a perfect reform, and yet not hurt a hair on any head — "a consummation most devoutly to be wished."

But it is not to be expected that such good will come immediately. Nearly ten years ago the legislature was commanded to carry out the beneficent measure of the Constitution. For nine years that illustrious body was a dumb impediment to the course of justice — all its faculties paralyzed by some inscrutable influence — dead — devoid of sense and motion, as if its only function was to "lie in cold obstruction and to rot." At last, when it was wakened up by the present governor, and reminded of the seventeenth article, it opened its mouth and spoke as one who did not know whether he was sworn to oppose the Constitution or to obey it. Some members have shown their utter hostility to it, some have been willing to defend small portions of it, and one Senator discovered that it was all equally sacred. But his plan meets no favor. Still, we need not despair. The people and the Constitution, mutually supporting one another, will be triumphant yet. Meanwhile let all the railroad rings rejoice. This is their day; ours is to come.

JAMES G. BLAINE

(1830-1893)

MR. BLAINE'S great strength lies in his naturalness and in his perfect control of himself. In his studied efforts he strains after effect seldomer than almost any other man in American history who has exercised great power over popular assemblies. Burke goes from one climax to another in rapid succession, regardless of the risk of bathos. Blaine rises steadily to his final climax as if it were part of his nature to increase his strength at every step of his progress. He described himself and his own naturalness of method in saying of Garfield: "He never did so well but that it seemed he could easily have done better." Whether he rises with the first impetus of his subject, or circles with easy grace and assured wing-sweep after having risen, we see that what he does is essentially part of his nature.

It is said that Whitefield once preached to an audience of sailors in New York city and described the wreck of a vessel on a lee shore with such effect that at the climax the entire audience rose to its feet crying, "The long boat—take to the long boat!" Blaine had something of the same faculty of compelling his audience to forget him, to lose sight of his individuality, to cease to hear his voice, and to become wholly engrossed in the subject itself. This and his intense nervous energy, so controlled that it does not display itself in passion, show in his greatest oratorical efforts as the probable secret of what was called his "magnetism." In his oration over Garfield he sinks himself wholly in the character of the man he eulogizes, and without once confessing himself voices his own deepest nature in defining the intellectual and moral nature of his friend. The rapid flow of its limpid sentences make the oration over Garfield a model for all who hate exaggeration and love above everything else the simplicity of that continuous and sustained statement which feels no need of tropes and metaphors. Mr. Blaine's great strength is the purity of his English, the power of sustained effort, the ability to keep the end in view from the beginning, and the power to make every subordinate part fit into the whole. Lacking this faculty, the greatest orator of England, forgetting in his own strength the weakness of his audiences, made almost as great a reputation for emptying the benches before the close of his speeches as he did for the

II—31

intellectual freedom and ecclesiastical independence, rather than for worldly honor and profit, the emigration naturally ceased when the contest for religious liberty began in earnest at home. The man who struck his most effective blow for freedom of conscience, by sailing for the colonies in 1620, would have been accounted a deserter to leave after 1640. The opportunity had then come on the soil of England for that great contest which established the authority of Parliament, gave religious freedom to the people, sent Charles to the block, and committed to the hands of Oliver Cromwell the supreme executive authority of England. The English emigration was never renewed, and from these twenty thousand men, with a small emigration from Scotland and from France, are descended the vast numbers who have New England blood in their veins.

In 1685 the revocation of the Edict of Nantes by Louis XVI., scattered to other countries four hundred thousand Protestants, who were among the most intelligent and enterprising of French subjects — merchants of capital, skilled manufacturers, and handicraftsmen superior at the time to all others in Europe. A considerable number of these Huguenot French came to America; a few landed in New England and became honorably prominent in its history. Their names have in large part become Anglicized, or have disappeared, but their blood is traceable in many of the most reputable families and their fame is perpetuated in honorable memorials and useful institutions.

From these two sources, the English-Puritan and the French-Huguenot, came the late President — his father, Abram Garfield, being descended from the one, and his mother, Eliza Ballou, from the other.

It was good stock on both sides — none better, none braver, none truer. There was in it an inheritance of courage, of manliness, of imperishable love of liberty, of undying adherence to principle. Garfield was proud of his blood; and, with as much satisfaction as if he were a British nobleman reading his stately ancestral record in Burke's 'Peerage,' he spoke of himself as ninth in descent from those who would not endure the oppression of the Stuarts, and seventh in descent from the brave French Protestants who refused to submit to tyranny even from the Grand Monarque.

General Garfield delighted to dwell on these traits, and during his only visit to England he busied himself in discovering every

genius which filled them at his openings. But Blaine never failed to control the attention of his audience. The expectation he excited at the beginning he knew how to sustain to the close, gratifying it finally in such bursts of poetry as that which forms the climax of the oration over Garfield.

Henry Clay was the model on whom Blaine formed himself. His admiration for the great Kentuckian shaped his political course in early life and remained strong in his maturity. His admirers loved to call him "a second Clay," and it is not at all improbable that when the passage of time has been great enough to make possible the true perspective of history, the best examples of Blaine's eloquence will be ranked with those of Clay as powerful factors in changing the general trend of American oratory from the mere imitation of the Latin style to the development of the Anglo-Saxon.

ORATION ON GARFIELD

(In the Hall of the House of Representatives, February 27th, 1882)

Mr. President:—

FOR the second time in this generation the great departments of the Government of the United States are assembled in the Hall of Representatives, to do honor to the memory of a murdered President. Lincoln fell at the close of a mighty struggle, in which the passions of men had been deeply stirred. The tragical termination of his great life added but another to the lengthened succession of horrors which had marked so many lintels with the blood of the firstborn. Garfield was slain in a day of peace, when brother had been reconciled to brother, and when anger and hate had been banished from the land.

"Whoever shall hereafter draw a portrait of murder, if he will show it as it has been exhibited where such example was last to have been looked for, let him not give it the grim visage of Moloch, the brow knitted by revenge, the face black with settled hate. Let him draw, rather, a decorous, smooth-faced, bloodless demon; not so much an example of human nature in its depravity and in its paroxysms of crime, as an infernal being, a fiend in the ordinary display and development of his character."

From the landing of the Pilgrims at Plymouth till the uprising against Charles I., about twenty thousand emigrants came from old England to New England. As they came in pursuit of

trace of his forefathers in parish registers and on ancient army rolls. Sitting with a friend in the gallery of the House of Commons one night after a long day's labor in this field of research, he said with evident elation that in every war in which for three centuries patriots of English blood had struck sturdy blows for constitutional government and human liberty, his family had been represented. They were at Marston Moor, at Naseby, and at Preston; they were at Bunker Hill, at Saratoga, and at Monmouth, and in his own person had battled for the same great cause in the war which preserved the Union of the States.

Losing his father before he was two years old, the early life of Garfield was one of privation, but its poverty has been made indelicately and unjustly prominent. Thousands of readers have imagined him as the ragged, starving child, whose reality too often greets the eye in the squalid sections of our large cities. General Garfield's infancy and youth had none of their destitution, none of their pitiful features appealing to the tender heart and to the open hand of charity. He was a poor boy in the same sense in which Henry Clay was a poor boy; in which Andrew Jackson was a poor boy; in which Daniel Webster was a poor boy; in the sense in which the large majority of the eminent men of America in all generations have been poor boys. Before a great multitude of men, in a public speech, Mr. Webster bore this testimony:—

"It did not happen to me to be born in a log cabin, but my elder brothers and sisters were born in a log cabin raised amid the snowdrifts of New Hampshire, at a period so early that when the smoke rose first from its rude chimney and curled over the frozen hills, there was no similar evidence of a white man's habitation between it and the settlements on the rivers of Canada. Its remains still exist. I make to it an annual visit. I carry my children to it to teach them the hardships endured by the generations which have gone before them. I love to dwell on the tender recollections, the kindred ties, the early affections, and the touching narratives and incidents which mingle with all I know of this primitive family abode."

With the requisite change of scene the same words would aptly portray the early days of Garfield. The poverty of the frontier, where all are engaged in a common struggle, and where a common sympathy and hearty co-operation lighten the burdens of each, is a very different poverty—different in kind, different in influence and effect—from that conscious and humiliating indigence which is every day forced to contrast itself with neighboring wealth on which it feels a sense of grinding dependence. The poverty of the frontier is, indeed, no poverty. It is but the beginning of wealth, and has the boundless possibilities of the future always opening before it. No man ever grew up in the agricultural regions of the West, where a house-raising, or even a corn-husking, is a matter of common interest and helpfulness, with any other feeling than that of broad-minded, generous independence. This honorable independence marked the youth of Garfield as it marks the youth of millions of the best blood and brain now training for the future citizenship and future government of the Republic. Garfield was born heir to land, to the title of freeholder which has been the patent and passport of self-respect with the Anglo-Saxon race ever since Hengist and Horsa landed on the shores of England. His adventure on the canal—an alternative between that and the deck of a Lake Erie schooner—was a farmer boy's device for earning money, just as the New England lad begins a possibly great career by sailing before the mast on a coasting vessel or on a merchantman bound to the farther India or to the China Seas.

No manly man feels anything of shame in looking back to early struggles with adverse circumstances, and no man feels a worthier pride than when he has conquered the obstacles to his progress. But no one of noble mold desires to be looked upon as having occupied a menial position, as having been repressed by a feeling of inferiority, or as having suffered the evils of poverty until relief was found at the hand of charity. General Garfield's youth presented no hardships which family love and family energy did not overcome, subjected him to no privations which he did not cheerfully accept, and left no memories save those which were recalled with delight, and transmitted with profit and with pride.

Garfield's early opportunities for securing an education were extremely limited, and yet were sufficient to develop in him an intense desire to learn. He could read at three years of age, and each winter he had the advantage of the district school. He read all the books to be found within the circle of his acquaintance; some of them he got by heart. While yet in childhood he was a constant student of the Bible, and became familiar with its literature. The dignity and earnestness of his speech in his

maturer life gave evidence of this early training. At eighteen years of age he was able to teach school, and thenceforward his ambition was to obtain a college education. To this end he bent all his efforts, working in the harvest field, at the carpenter's bench, and in the winter season teaching the common schools of the neighborhood. While thus laboriously occupied he found time to prosecute his studies, and was so successful that at twenty-two years of age he was able to enter the junior class at Williams College, then under the presidency of the venerable and honored Mark Hopkins, who, in the fullness of his powers, survives the eminent pupil to whom he was of inestimable service.

The history of Garfield's life to this period presents no novel features. He had undoubtedly shown perseverance, self-reliance, self-sacrifice, and ambition—qualities which, be it said for the honor of our country, are everywhere to be found among the young men of America. But from his graduation at Williams onward, to the hour of tragical death, Garfield's career was eminent and exceptional. Slowly working through his educational period, receiving his diploma when twenty-four years of age, he seemed at one bound to spring into conspicuous and brilliant success. Within six years he was successively president of a college, State senator of Ohio, Major-General of the Army of the United States, and Representative-Elect to the national Congress. A combination of honors so varied, so elevated, within a period so brief and to a man so young, is without precedent or parallel in the history of the country.

Garfield's army life was begun with no other military knowledge than such as he had hastily gained from books in the few months preceding his march to the field. Stepping from civil life to the head of a regiment, the first order he received when ready to cross the Ohio was to assume command of a brigade, and to operate as an independent force in Eastern Kentucky. His immediate duty was to check the advance of Humphrey Marshall, who was marching down the Big Sandy with the intention of occupying in connection with other Confederate forces the entire territory of Kentucky, and of precipitating the State into secession. This was at the close of the year 1861. Seldom, if ever, has a young college professor been thrown into a more embarrassing and discouraging position. He knew just enough of military science, as he expressed it himself, to measure the extent of his ignorance, and with a handful of men he was

marching, in rough winter weather, into a strange country, among a hostile population, to confront a largely superior force under the command of a distinguished graduate of West Point, who had seen active and important service in two preceding wars.

The result of the campaign is matter of history. The skill, the endurance, the extraordinary energy shown by Garfield, the courage imparted to his men, raw and untried as himself, the measures he adopted to increase his force and to create in the enemy's mind exaggerated estimates of his numbers, bore perfect fruit in the routing of Marshall, the capture of his camp, the dispersion of his force, and the emancipation of an important territory from the control of the rebellion. Coming at the close of a long series of disasters to the Union arms, Garfield's victory had an unusual and an extraneous importance, and in the popular judgment elevated the young commander to the rank of a military hero. With less than two thousand men in his entire command, with a mobilized force of only eleven hundred, without cannon, he had met an army of five thousand and defeated them, driving Marshall's forces successively from two strongholds of their own selection, fortified with abundant artillery. Major-General Buell, commanding the Department of the Ohio, an experienced and able soldier of the regular army, published an order of thanks and congratulation on the brilliant result of the Big Sandy campaign which would have turned the head of a less cool and sensible man than Garfield. Buell declared that his services had called into action the highest qualities of a soldier, and President Lincoln supplemented these words of praise by the more substantial reward of a brigadier-general's commission, to bear date from the day of his decisive victory over Marshall.

The subsequent military career of Garfield fully sustained its brilliant beginning. With his new commission he was assigned to the command of a brigade in the Army of the Ohio, and took part in the second decisive day's fight in the great battle of Shiloh. The remainder of the year 1862 was not especially eventful to Garfield, as it was not to the armies with which he was serving. His practical sense was called into exercise in completing the task assigned him by General Buell, of reconstructing bridges and re-establishing lines of railway communication for the army. His occupation in this useful but not brilliant field was varied by service on courts-martial of importance, in which

department of duty he won a valuable reputation, attracting the notice and securing the approval of the able and eminent judge-advocate-general of the army. That of itself was a warrant to honorable fame; for among the great men who in those trying days gave themselves, with entire devotion, to the service of their country, one who brought to that service the ripest learning, the most fervid eloquence, the most varied attainments, who labored with modesty and shunned applause, who in the day of triumph sat reserved and silent and grateful—as Francis Deak in the hour of Hungary's deliverance—was Joseph Holt, of Kentucky, who in his honorable retirement enjoys the respect and veneration of all who love the Union of the States.

Early in 1863 Garfield was assigned to the highly important and responsible post of chief of staff to General Rosecrans, then at the head of the Army of the Cumberland. Perhaps in a great military campaign no subordinate officer requires sounder judgment and quicker knowledge of men than the chief of staff to the commanding general. An indiscreet man in such a position can sow more discord, breed more jealousy, and disseminate more strife than any other officer in the entire organization. When General Garfield assumed his new duties he found various troubles already well developed and seriously affecting the value and efficiency of the Army of the Cumberland. The energy, the impartiality, and the tact with which he sought to allay these dissensions, and to discharge the duties of his new and trying position, will always remain one of the most striking proofs of his great versatility. His military duties closed on the memorable field of Chickamauga, a field which however disastrous to the Union arms gave to him the occasion of winning imperishable laurels. The very rare distinction was accorded him of great promotion for his bravery on a field that was lost. President Lincoln appointed him a major-general in the Army of the United States for gallant and meritorious conduct in the battle of Chickamauga.

The Army of the Cumberland was reorganized under the command of General Thomas, who promptly offered Garfield one of its divisions. He was extremely desirous to accept the position, but was embarrassed by the fact that he had, a year before, been elected to Congress, and the time when he must take his seat was drawing near. He preferred to remain in the military service, and had within his own breast the largest confidence of success in the wider field which his new rank opened to him. Balancing the arguments on the one side and the other, anxious to determine what was for the best, desirous, above all things, to do his patriotic duty, he was decisively influenced by the advice of President Lincoln and Secretary Stanton, both of whom assured him that he could, at that time, be of especial value in the House of Representatives. He resigned his commission of major-general on the fifth day of December, 1863, and took his seat in the House of Representatives on the seventh. He had served two years and four months in the army, and had just completed his thirty-second year.

The Thirty-Eighth Congress is pre-eminently entitled in history to the designation of the War Congress. It was elected while the war was flagrant, and every Member was chosen upon the issues involved in the continuance of the struggle. The Thirty-Seventh Congress had, indeed, legislated to a large extent on war measures, but it was chosen before any one believed that secession of the States would be actually attempted. The magnitude of the work which fell upon its successor was unprecedented, both in respect to the vast sums of money raised for the support of the army and navy, and of the new and extraordinary powers of legislation which it was forced to exercise. Only twenty-four States were represented, and one hundred and eighty-two members were upon its roll. Among these were many distinguished party leaders on both sides, veterans in the public service with established reputations for ability and with that skill which comes only from parliamentary experience. Into this assemblage of men Garfield entered without special preparation, and it might almost be said unexpectedly. The question of taking command of a division of troops under General Thomas, or taking his seat in Congress, was kept open till the last moment; so late, indeed, that the resignation of his military commission and his appearance in the House were almost contemporaneous. He wore the uniform of a major-general of the United States army on Saturday, and on Monday, in civilian's dress, he answered to the roll call as a Representative in Congress from the State of Ohio.

He was especially fortunate in the constituency which elected him. Descended almost entirely from New England stock, the men of the Ashtabula district were intensely radical on all questions relating to human rights. Well educated, thrifty, thoroughly

intelligent in affairs, acutely discerning of character, not quick to bestow confidence, and slow to withdraw it, they were at once the most helpful and most exacting of supporters. Their tenacious trust in men in whom they have once confided is illustrated by the unparalleled fact that Elisha Whittlesey, Joshua R. Giddings, and James A. Garfield represented the district for fifty-four years.

There is no test of man's ability in any department of public life more severe than service in the House of Representatives; there is no place where so little deference is paid to reputation previously acquired or to eminence won outside; no place where so little consideration is shown for the feelings or failures of beginners. What a man gains in the House he gains by sheer force of his own character, and if he loses and falls back he must expect no mercy and will receive no sympathy. It is a field in which the survival of the strongest is the recognized rule and where no pretense can deceive and no glamour can mislead. The real man is discovered, his worth is impartially weighed, his rank is irreversibly decreed.

With possibly a single exception, Garfield was the youngest Member in the House when he entered, and was but seven years from his college graduation. But he had not been in his seat sixty days before his ability was recognized and his place conceded. He stepped to the front with the confidence of one who belonged there. The House was crowded with strong men of both parties; nineteen of them have since been transferred to the Senate, and many of them have served with distinction in the gubernatorial chairs of their respective States and on foreign missions of great consequence; but among them all none grew so rapidly, none so firmly, as Garfield. As is said by Trevelyan of his parliamentary hero, Garfield succeeded "because all the world in concert could not have kept him in the background, and because when once in the front he played his part with a prompt intrepidity and a commanding ease that were but the outward symptoms of the immense reserves of energy on which it was in his power to draw." Indeed, the apparently reserved force which Garfield possessed was one of his great characteristics. He never did so well but that it seemed he could easily have done better. He never expended so much strength but that he seemed to be holding additional power to call. This is one of the happiest and rarest distinctions of an effective debater,

and often counts for as much in persuading an assembly as the eloquent and elaborate argument.

The great measure of Garfield's fame was filled by his service in the House of Representatives. His military life, illustrated by honorable performance, and rich in promise, was, as he himself felt, prematurely terminated and necessarily incomplete. Speculation as to what he might have done in the field, where the great prizes are so few, cannot be profitable. It is sufficient to say that as a soldier he did his duty bravely; he did it intelligently; he won an enviable fame, and he retired from the service without blot or breath against him. As a lawyer, though admirably equipped for the profession, he can scarcely be said to have entered on its practice. The few efforts that he made at the bar were distinguished by the same high order of talent which he exhibited on every field where he was put to test, and if a man may be accepted as a competent judge of his own capacities and adaptation, the law was the profession to which Garfield should have devoted himself. But fate ordained it otherwise, and his reputation in history will rest largely upon his service in the House of Representatives. That service was exceptionally long. He was nine times consecutively chosen to the House, an honor enjoyed by not more than six other Representatives of the more than five thousand who have been elected from the organization of the government to this hour.

As a parliamentary orator, as a debater on an issue squarely joined, where the position had been chosen and the ground laid out, Garfield must be assigned a very high rank. More, perhaps, than any man with whom he was associated in public life he gave careful and systematic study to public questions, and he came to every discussion in which he took part with elaborate and complete preparation. He was a steady and indefatigable worker. Those who imagine that talent or genius can supply the place or achieve the results of labor will find no encouragement in Garfield's life. In preliminary work he was apt, rapid, and skillful. He possessed in a high degree the power of readily absorbing ideas and facts, and, like Dr. Johnson, had the art of getting from a book all that was of value in it by a reading apparently so quick and cursory that it seemed like a mere glance at the table of contents. He was a pre-eminently fair and candid man in debate, took no petty advantage, stooped to no unworthy methods, avoided personal allusions, rarely appealed

to prejudice, did not seek to inflame passion. He had a quicker eye for the strong point of his adversary than for his weak point, and on his own side he so marshaled his weighty arguments as to make his hearers forget any possible lack in the complete strength of his position. He had a habit of stating his opponent's side with such amplitude of fairness and such liberality of concession that his followers often complained that he was giving his case away. But never in his prolonged participation in the proceedings of the House did he give his case away, or fail in the judgment of competent and impartial listeners to gain the mastery.

These characteristics, which marked Garfield as a great debater, did not, however, make him a great parliamentary leader. A parliamentary leader, as that term is understood wherever free representative government exists, is necessarily and very strictly the organ of his party. An ardent American defined the instinctive warmth of patriotism when he offered the toast, "Our country always right; but, right or wrong, our country." The parliamentary leader who has a body of followers that will do and dare and die for the cause is one who believes his party always right, but, right or wrong, is for his party. No more important or exacting duty devolves upon him than the selection of the field and the time of the contest. He must know not merely how to strike, but where to strike and when to strike. He often skillfully avoids the strength of his opponent's position and scatters confusion in his ranks by attacking an exposed point, when really the righteousness of the cause and the strength of logical intrenchment are against him. He conquers often both against the right and the heavy battalions; as when young Charles Fox, in the days of his Toryism, carried the House of Commons against justice, against immemorial rights, against his own convictions,—if, indeed, at that period Fox had convictions,—and in the interest of a corrupt administration, in obedience to a tyrannical sovereign, drove Wilkes from the seat to which the electors of Middlesex had chosen him and installed Luttrell in defiance, not merely of law, but of public decency. For an achievement of that kind Garfield was disqualified—disqualified by the texture of his mind, by the honesty of his heart, by his conscience, and by every instinct and aspiration of his nature.

The three most distinguished parliamentary leaders hitherto developed in this country are Mr. Clay, Mr. Douglas, and Mr.

Thaddeus Stevens. Each was a man of consummate ability, of great earnestness, of intense personality, differing widely each from the others, and yet with a signal trait in common—the power to command. In the "give and take" of daily discussion; in the art of controlling and consolidating reluctant and refractory followers; in the skill to overcome all forms of opposition, and to meet with competency and courage the varying phases of unlooked-for assault or unsuspected defection, it would be difficult to rank with these a fourth name in all our Congressional history. But of these Mr. Clay was the greatest. It would, perhaps, be impossible to find in the parliamentary annals of the world a parallel to Mr. Clay, in 1841, when at sixty-four years of age he took the control of the Whig party from the President who had received their suffrages, against the power of Webster in the Cabinet, against the eloquence of Choate in the Senate, against the Herculean efforts of Caleb Cushing and Henry A. Wise in the House. In unshared leadership, in the pride and plentitude of power he hurled against John Tyler with deepest scorn the mass of that conquering column which had swept over the land in 1840, and drove his administration to seek shelter behind the lines of his political foes. Mr. Douglas achieved a victory scarcely less wonderful when, in 1854, against the secret desires of a strong administration, against the wise counsel of the older chiefs, against the conservative instincts and even the moral sense of the country, he forced a reluctant Congress into a repeal of the Missouri Compromise. Mr. Thaddeus Stevens, in his contests from 1865 to 1868, actually advanced his parliamentary leadership until Congress tied the hands of the President and governed the country by its own will, leaving only perfunctory duties to be discharged by the Executive. With two hundred millions of patronage in his hands at the opening of the contest, aided by the active force of Seward in the Cabinet, and the moral power of Chase on the Bench, Andrew Johnson could not command the support of one-third in either house against the parliamentary uprising of which Thaddeus Stevens was the animating spirit and the unquestioned leader.

From these three great men Garfield differed radically; differed in the quality of his mind, in temperament, in the form and phase of ambition. He could not do what they did, but he could do what they could not, and in the breadth of his Congressional

work he left that which will longer exert a potential influence among men, and which, measured by the severe test of posthumous criticism, will secure a more enduring and more enviable fame.

Those unfamiliar with Garfield's industry, and ignorant of the details of his work, may in some degree measure them by the annals of Congress. No one of the generation of public men to which he belonged has contributed so much that will be valuable for future reference. His speeches are numerous, many of them brilliant, all of them well studied, carefully phrased, and exhaustive of the subject under consideration. Collected from the scattered pages of ninety royal octavo volumes of the Congressional Record, they would present an invaluable compendium of the political history of the most important era through which the national government has ever passed. When the history of this period shall be impartially written, when war legislation, measures of reconstruction, protection of human rights, amendments to the Constitution, maintenance of public credit, steps toward specie resumption, true theories of revenue may be reviewed, unsurrounded by prejudice and disconnected from partisanism, the speeches of Garfield will be estimated at their true value and will be found to comprise a vast magazine of fact and argument, of clear analysis and sound conclusion. Indeed, if no other authority were accessible, his speeches in the House of Representatives, from December 1863, to June 1880, would give a well connected history and complete defense of the important legislation of the seventeen eventful years that constitute his parliamentary life. Far beyond that, his speeches would be found to forecast many great measures yet to be completed—measures which he knew were beyond the public opinion of the hour, but which he confidently believed would secure popular approval within the period of his own lifetime, and by the aid of his own efforts.

Differing, as Garfield does, from the brilliant parliamentary leaders, it is not easy to find his counterpart anywhere in the record of American public life. He perhaps more nearly resembles Mr. Seward in his supreme faith in the all-conquering power of a principle. He had the love of learning and the patient industry of investigation to which John Quincy Adams owes his prominence and his presidency. He had some of those ponderous elements of mind which distinguished Mr. Webster, and

which indeed, in all our public life, have left the great Massachusetts Senator without an intellectual peer.

In English parliamentary history, as in our own, the leaders in the House of Commons present points of essential difference from Garfield. But some of his methods recall the best features in the strong, independent course of Sir Robert Peel, and striking resemblances are discernable in that most promising of modern conservatives, who died too early for his country and his fame, the Lord George Bentinck. He had all of Burke's love for the sublime and the beautiful, with, possibly, something of his superabundance, and in his faith and his magnanimity, in his power of statement, in his subtle analysis, in his faultless logic, in his love of literature, in his wealth and world of illustration, one is reminded of that great English statesman of to-day, who, confronted with obstacles that would daunt any but the dauntless, reviled by those whom he would relieve as bitterly as by those whose supposed rights he is forced to invade, still labors with serene courage for the amelioration of Ireland and for the honor of the English name.

Garfield's nomination to the presidency, while not predicted or anticipated, was not a surprise to the country. His prominence in Congress, his solid qualities, his wide reputation, strengthened by his then recent election as Senator from Ohio, kept him in the public eye as a man occupying the very highest rank among those entitled to be called statesmen. It was not mere chance that brought him this high honor. "We must," says Mr. Emerson, "reckon success a constitutional trait. If Eric is in robust health, and has slept well and is at the top of his condition, and thirty years old at his departure from Greenland, he will steer west and his ships will reach Newfoundland. But take Eric out and put in a stronger and bolder man and the ships will sail six hundred, one thousand, fifteen hundred miles farther and reach Labrador and New England. There is no chance in results."

As a candidate Garfield steadily grew in public favor. He was met with a storm of detraction at the very hour of his nomination, and it continued with increasing volume and momentum until the close of his victorious campaign:—

> "No might nor greatness in mortality
> Can censure 'scape; backwounding calumny
> The whitest virtue strikes. What king so strong
> Can tie the gall up in the slanderous tongue?"

Under it all he was calm, strong, and confident; never lost his self-possession, did no unwise act, spoke no hasty or ill-considered word. Indeed, nothing in his whole life is more remarkable or more creditable than his bearing through those five full months of vituperation—a prolonged agony of trial to a sensitive man, a constant and cruel draft upon the powers of moral endurance. The great mass of these unjust imputations passed unnoticed, and, with the general *débris* of the campaign, fell into oblivion. But in a few instances the iron entered his soul and he dies with the injury unforgotten if not unforgiven.

One aspect of Garfield's candidacy was unprecedented. Never before in the history of partisan contests in this country had a successful presidential candidate spoken freely on passing events and current issues. To attempt anything of the kind seemed novel, rash, and even desperate. The older class of voters recalled the unfortunate Alabama letter, in which Mr. Clay was supposed to have signed his political death warrant. They remembered also the hot-tempered effusion by which General Scott lost a large share of his popularity before his nomination, and the unfortunate speeches which rapidly consumed the remainder. The younger voters had seen Mr. Greeley in a series of vigorous and original addresses preparing the pathway for his own defeat. Unmindful of these warnings, unheeding the advice of friends, Garfield spoke to large crowds as he journeyed to and from New York in August, to a great multitude in that city, to delegations and to deputations of every kind that called at Mentor during the summer and autumn. With innumerable critics, watchful and eager to catch a phrase that might be turned into odium or ridicule, or a sentence that might be distorted to his own or his party's injury, Garfield did not trip or halt in any one of his seventy speeches. This seems all the more remarkable when it is remembered that he did not write what he said, and yet spoke with such logical consecutiveness of thought and such admirable precision of phrase as to defy the accident of misreport and the malignity of misrepresentation.

In the beginning of his presidential life Garfield's experience did not yield him pleasure or satisfaction. The duties that engross so large a portion of the President's time were distasteful to him, and were unfavorably contrasted with his legislative work. "I have been dealing all these years with ideas," he impatiently exclaimed one day, "and here I am dealing only with persons. I have been heretofore treating of the fundamental principles of government, and here I am considering all day whether A or B shall be appointed to this or that office." He was earnestly seeking some practical way of correcting the evils arising from the distribution of overgrown and unwieldy patronage — evils always appreciated and often discussed by him, but whose magnitude had been more deeply impressed upon his mind since his accession to the presidency. Had he lived, a comprehensive improvement in the mode of appointment and in the tenure of office would have been proposed by him, and, with the aid of Congress, no doubt perfected.

But, while many of the executive duties were not grateful to him, he was assiduous and conscientious in their discharge. From the very outset he exhibited administrative talent of a high order. He grasped the helm of office with the hand of a master. In this respect, indeed, he constantly surprised many who were most intimately associated with him in the government, and especially those who had feared that he might be lacking in the executive faculty. His disposition of business was orderly and rapid. His power of analysis and his skill in classification enabled him to dispatch a vast mass of detail with singular promptness and ease. His cabinet meetings were admirably conducted. His clear presentation of official subjects, his well-considered suggestion of topics on which discussion was invited, his quick decision when all had been heard, combined to show a thoroughness of mental training as rare as his natural ability and his facile adaptation to a new and enlarged field of labor.

With perfect comprehension of all the inheritances of the war, with a cool calculation of the obstacles in his way, impelled always by a generous enthusiasm, Garfield conceived that much might be done by his administration towards restoring harmony between the different sections of the Union. He was anxious to go South and speak to the people. As early as April he had ineffectually endeavored to arrange for a trip to Nashville, whither he had been cordially invited, and he was again disappointed a few weeks later to find that he could not go to South Carolina to attend the centennial celebration of the victory of the Cowpens. But for the autumn he definitely counted on being present at the three memorable assemblies in the South, the celebration at Yorktown, the opening of the Cotton

Exposition at Atlanta, and the meeting of the Army of the Cumberland at Chattanooga. He was already turning over in his mind his address for each occasion, and the three taken together, he said to a friend, gave him the exact scope and verge which he needed. At Yorktown he would have before him the association of a hundred years that bound the South and the North in the sacred memory of a common danger and a common victory. At Atlanta he would present the material interests and the industrial development which appealed to the thrift and independence of every household, and which should unite the two sections by the instinct of self-interest and self-defense. At Chattanooga he would revive memories of the war only to show that after all its disaster and all its suffering the country was stronger and greater, the Union rendered indissoluble, and the future, through the agony and blood of one generation, made brighter and better for all.

Garfield's ambition for the success of his administration was high. With strong caution and conservatism in his nature, he was in no danger of attempting rash experiments or of resorting to the empiricism of statesmanship. But he believed that renewed and closer attention should be given to questions affecting the material interests and commercial prospects of fifty millions of people. He believed that our continental relations, extensive and undeveloped as they are, involved responsibility and could be cultivated into profitable friendship or be abandoned to harmful indifference or lasting enmity. He believed with equal confidence that an essential forerunner to a new era of national progress must be a feeling of contentment in every section of the Union and a generous belief that the benefits and burdens of government would be common to all. Himself a conspicuous illustration of what ability and ambition may do under republican institutions, he loved his country with a passion of patriotic devotion, and every waking thought was given to her advancement. He was an American in all his aspirations, and he looked to the destiny and influence of the United States with the philosophic composure of Jefferson and the demonstrative confidence of John Adams.

The political events which disturbed the President's serenity for many weeks before that fatal day in July, form an important chapter in his career, and, in his own judgment, involved questions of principle and right which are vitally essential to the

constitutional administration of the Federal Government. It would be out of place here and now to speak the language of controversy, but the events referred to, however they may continue to be a source of contention with others, have become, as far as Garfield is concerned, as much a matter of history as his heroism at Chickamauga or his illustrious service in the House. Detail is not needful, and personal antagonism shall not be rekindled by any word uttered to-day. The motives of those opposing him are not to be here adversely interpreted nor their course harshly characterized. But of the dead President this is to be said, and said because his own speech is forever silenced and he can be no more heard except through the fidelity and the love of surviving friends. From the beginning to the end of the controversy he so much deplored, the President was never for one moment actuated by any motive of gain to himself or of loss to others. Least of all men did he harbor revenge, rarely did he even show resentment, and malice was not in his nature. He was congenially employed only in the exchange of good offices and the doing of kindly deeds.

There was not an hour, from the beginning of the trouble till the fatal shot entered his body, when the President would not gladly, for the sake of restoring harmony, have retracted any step he had taken if such retracting had merely involved consequences personal to himself. The pride of consistency, or any supposed sense of humiliation that might result from surrendering his position, had not a feather's weight with him. No man was ever less subject to such influences from within or from without. But after the most anxious deliberation and the coolest survey of all the circumstances, he solemnly believed that the true prerogatives of the Executive were involved in the issue which had been raised and that he would be unfaithful to his supreme obligation if he failed to maintain, in all their vigor, the constitutional rights and dignities of his great office. He believed this in all the convictions of conscience when in sound and vigorous health, and he believed it in his suffering and prostration in the last conscious thought which his wearied mind bestowed on the transitory struggles of life.

More than this need not be said. Less than this could not be said. Justice to the dead, the highest obligation that devolves upon the living, demands the declaration that in all the bearings of the subject, actual or possible, the President was content

in his mind, justified in his conscience, immovable in his conclusions.

The religious element in Garfield's character was deep and earnest. In his early youth he espoused the faith of the Disciples, a sect of that great Baptist Communion which in different ecclesiastical establishments is so numerous and so influential throughout all parts of the United States. But the broadening tendency of his mind and his active spirit of inquiry were early apparent, and carried him beyond the dogmas of sect and the restraints of association. In selecting a college in which to continue his education he rejected Bethany, though presided over by Alexander Campbell, the greatest preacher of his church. His reasons were characteristic: First, that Bethany leaned too heavily toward slavery; and, second, that being himself a Disciple, and the son of Disciple parents, he had little acquaintance with people of other beliefs, and he thought it would make him more liberal, quoting his own words, both in his religious and general views, to go into a new circle and be under new influences.

The liberal tendency which he had anticipated as the result of wider culture was fully realized. He was emancipated from mere sectarian belief, and with eager interest pushed his investigations in the direction of modern progressive thought. He followed with quickening steps in the paths of exploration and speculation so fearlessly trodden by Darwin, by Huxley, by Tyndall, and by other living scientists of the radical and advanced type. His own church, binding its disciples by no formulated creed, but accepting the Old and New Testaments as the word of God, with unbiased liberality of private interpretation, favored, if it did not stimulate, the spirit of investigation. Its members profess with sincerity, and profess only, to be of one mind and one faith with those who immediately followed the Master and who were first called Christians at Antioch.

But however high Garfield reasoned of "fixed fate, freewill, foreknowledge absolute," he was never separated from the Church of the Disciples in his affections and in his associations. For him it held the Ark of the Covenant. To him it was the gate of heaven. The world of religious belief is full of solecisms and contradictions. A philosophic observer declares that men by the thousand will die in defense of a creed whose doctrines they do not comprehend and whose tenets they habitually violate. It is equally true that men by the thousand will cling to church organizations with instinctive and undenying fidelity when their belief in maturer years is radically different from that which inspired them as neophytes.

But after this range of speculation and this latitude of doubt, Garfield came back always with freshness and delight to the simpler instincts of religious faith, which, earliest implanted, longest survive. Not many weeks before his assassination, walking on the banks of the Potomac with a friend, and conversing on those topics of personal religion concerning which noble natures have unconquerable reserve, he said that he found the Lord's Prayer and the simple petitions learned in infancy infinitely restful to him, not merely in their stated repetition, but in their casual and frequent recall as he went about the daily duties of life. Certain texts of Scripture had a very strong hold on his memory and his heart. He heard, while in Edinburgh some years ago, an eminent Scotch preacher, who prefaced his sermon with reading the eighth chapter of the Epistle to the Romans, which book had been the subject of careful study with Garfield during his religious life. He was greatly impressed by the elocution of the preacher and declared that it had imparted a new and deeper meaning to the majestic utterances of Saint Paul. He referred often in after years to that memorable service, and dwelt with exaltation of feeling upon the radiant promise and the assured hope with which the great Apostle of the Gentiles was "persuaded that neither death, nor life, nor principalities, nor powers, nor things present, nor things to come, nor height, nor depth, nor any other creature, shall be able to separate us from the love of God, which is in Christ Jesus our Lord."

The crowning characteristic of Garfield's religious opinions, as, indeed, of all his opinons, was his liberality. In all things he had charity. Tolerance was of his nature. He respected in others the qualities which he possessed himself — sincerity of conviction and frankness of expression. With him inquiry was not so much what a man believes, but Does he believe it? The lines of his friendship and his confidence encircled men of every creed and men of no creed, and, to the end of his life, on his ever lengthening list of friends were to be found the names of a pious Catholic priest and of an honest-minded and generous-hearted freethinker.

On the morning of Saturday, July 2d, the President was a contented and happy man — not in an ordinary degree, but joyfully,

almost boyishly, happy. On his way to the railroad station, to which he drove slowly, in conscious enjoyment of the beautiful morning, with an unwonted sense of leisure and a keen anticipation of pleasure, his talk was all in the grateful and gratulatory vein. He felt that, after four months of trial, his administration was strong in its grasp of affairs, strong in popular favor, and destined to grow stronger; that grave difficulties confronting him at his inauguration had been safely passed; that troubles lay behind him, and not before him; that he was soon to meet the wife whom he loved, now recovering from an illness which had but lately disquieted and at times almost unnerved him; that he was going to his Alma Mater to renew the most cherished associations of his young manhood, and to exchange greetings with those whose deepening interest had followed every step of his upward progress, from the day he entered upon his college course until he had attained the loftiest elevation in the gift of his countrymen.

Surely, if happiness can ever come from the honors or triumphs of this world, on that quiet July morning James A. Garfield may well have been a happy man. No foreboding of evil haunted him; no slightest premonition of danger clouded his sky. His terrible fate was upon him in an instant. One moment he stood erect, strong, confident in the years stretching peacefully out before him. The next he lay wounded, bleeding, helpless, doomed to weary weeks of torture, to silence and the grave.

Great in life, he was surpassingly great in death. For no cause, in the very frenzy of wantonness and wickedness, by the red hand of murder, he was thrust from the full tide of this world's interest, from its hopes, its aspirations, its victories, into the visible presence of death — and he did not quail. Not alone for one short moment in which, stunned and dazed, he could give up life, hardly aware of its relinquishment, but through days of deadly languor, through weeks of agony, that was not less agony because silently borne, with clear sight and calm courage he looked into his open grave. What blight and ruin met his anguished eyes, whose lips may tell — what brilliant, broken plans, what baffled, high ambitions, what sundering of strong, warm, manhood's friendship, what bitter rending of sweet household ties! Behind him a proud, expectant nation, a great host of sustaining friends, a cherished and happy mother, wearing the full, rich honors of her early toil and tears; the wife of his youth,

whose whole life lay in his; the little boys not yet emerged from childhood's day of frolic; the fair, young daughter; the sturdy sons just springing into closest companionship, claiming every day and every day rewarding a father's love and care; and in his heart the eager, rejoicing power to meet all demands. And his soul was not shaken. His countrymen were thrilled with instant, profound, and universal sympathy. Masterful in his mortal weakness, he became the centre of a nation's love, enshrined in the prayers of a world. But all the love and all the sympathy could not share with him his suffering. He trod the wine press alone. With unfaltering front he faced death. With unfailing tenderness he took leave of life. Above the demoniac hiss of the assassin's bullet he heard the voice of God. With simple resignation he bowed to the Divine decree.

As the end drew near his early craving for the sea returned. The stately mansion of power had been to him the wearisome hospital of pain, and he begged to be taken from his prison walls, from its oppressive, stifling air, from its homelessness and its hopelessness. Gently, silently, the love of a great people bore the pale sufferer to the longed-for healing of the sea, to live or to die, as God should will, within sight of the heaving billows, within sound of its manifold voices. With a wan, fevered face, tenderly lifted to the cooling breeze, he looked out wistfully upon the ocean's changing wonders; on its far sails; on its restless waves, rolling shoreward to break and die beneath the noonday sun; on the red clouds of evening, arching low to the horizon; on the serene and shining pathway of the stars. Let us think that his dying eyes read a mystic meaning which only the rapt and parting soul may know. Let us believe that in the silence of the receding world he heard the great waves breaking on a farther shore and felt already upon his wasted brow the breath of the eternal morning.

AUSTIN BLAIR

(1818–1894)

AUSTIN BLAIR, the "War-Governor of Michigan," was one of the most prominent organizers of the Republican party in the Northwest, an aggressive abolitionist and a "Radical" under Andrew Johnson, whose impeachment he supported. In 1872, he made a number of strong speeches for civil as against military government, which were widely read throughout the country. The following on "Military Government" is from a report preserved in the collection of Mr. Enos Clark.

MILITARY GOVERNMENT

(Delivered in Michigan, July 4th, 1872)

THE habits of military government are not easily laid aside. The soldier naturally has much greater faith in the efficiency of his sword to maintain public order and due respect for law than in the slower process of the court and the sheriff. He is apt to feel a certain contempt for the arrest that cannot be made without a demand based on affidavit, and for the imprisonment that may rapidly be terminated by an action of *habeas corpus* and the technicalities of the civil law. The arguments of the lawyer are to him little better than jargon — at the best, cunning devices to defeat justice. Tell him that the great reliance of good government must be upon the good judgment and patriotism of the people, and if he does not contradict you, he will still believe that it would be better if his sword could somehow be thrown into the scale. For some years after the close of the Rebellion it seemed necessary to continue the military occupation of the lately insurrectionary States, and it has been continued in a greater or less degree until this time. During those years we have learned to believe that the use of military force is the most summary and convenient method of putting down those evils which exist there, and very many no doubt seriously believe that there is no other efficient way. Their faith in the people is entirely lost, and they will struggle to keep up that system. Those portions of the people who may consider themselves oppressed and wronged fly to the military for protection, because they have found it efficient heretofore. The general government is constantly importuned to interfere upon every sort of pretext, and many statutes have been enacted to make such interference legal, until there is a danger that it may be drawn into precedent and become a common recourse. The great constitutional barriers which our fathers erected with such painstaking care and foresight, against the encroachments of power upon the liberties of the people, have been more or less arrested, one after another, until the time has arrived when it is necessary to look into these assumptions and consider whither they tend. None of the safeguards of liberty which experience has proved to be essential can safely be set aside for any cause not of the most serious nature, and then only in pursuance of settled laws. The Constitution of the United States has declared in section nine of the first article, that "the privilege of the Habeas Corpus shall not be suspended unless when in case of rebellion or invasion the public safety may require it." And yet a proposition has lately been made in Congress in a time of profound peace to authorize the President at his discretion to suspend the writ until the fourth of March next. The proposition passed the Senate, and was only defeated in the House by the most strenuous exertions. It seemed to me a very startling proposition considering all the circumstances that surrounded it. The President of the United States, with the power in his hands to suspend that writ at his pleasure, is a dictator in fact, whatever he may be called. It is in the power of his single will to shut up all the courts in the country, to arrest every person in the land by armed soldiery, without a warrant, and to imprison at discretion any citizen who may have incurred the displeasure of the government. This power is so vast and so dangerous that nothing short of the actual existence of the emergencies contemplated by the constitution could for a moment justify it. That it should have been contemplated at all is an evidence of the great progress made within the last four years in those principles and practices which easily justify the use of arbitrary power. There has been no invasion or rebellion, and there is no reason to apprehend either. What, then, was the purpose of this attempt to authorize the suspension of the writ in time of peace? Was it any well-grounded fear that the occasion might occur in which it might lawfully be done, or was it intended to exercise the power against the law

in a certain event? Whatever may have been the design of those who set the scheme on foot, it was frustrated altogether, and the result has been anything but satisfactory to them, as I believe every such effort in the future will be. It is now several years since the war closed. The States have all been restored and are represented in Congress. Is it not time that war legislation should cease? If it is not, when will it be? Are we to go on forever, as if a new rebellion was just about to break out? Shall we never again trust the people with the control of their own affairs? Has local self-government already failed, and must we bring in the mailed Cæsar at once? Perhaps these are vain questions, as I know many regard them, but with very many others they are of the most serious import, and surely it will never be out of order for the American people to consider carefully the drift of public affairs. It is their especial duty to know just what is the meaning of public acts which are in themselves unusual and which seem to lead us in the wrong direction.

What remains for us is restoration. We need to clear away all the rubbish of the war; to put behind us all old conflicts which have no longer any meaning. Why nurse the enmities which grew out of slavery after slavery itself is dead? Why continue to indulge the spirit of war long after war has ceased? Why enact laws of doubtful constitutionality in hope of accomplishing by intimidation what could be much more easily done by conciliation and good will? Why maintain exasperating disabilities after all occasion for them has passed away? A union that rests upon force is not the union established by our forefathers. Force was necessary for a temporary object, but cannot, must not, take the place of statesmanship in our institutions. Reason is the power on which we must rely, with patriotism for the motive to give it direction. Our government is one of the people, and its appeal is always to the good sense and patriotism of the people. Let no man doubt the safety of that appeal in every part of the land. Interest, hopes, ambition, all combine to unite our whole population in one vast National Commonwealth under a Constitution which secures abundantly the rights of all. We want peace, indeed, real, enduring peace, based on mutual interests and common respect. We want order secured by the institution of peace; the court and jury and not the soldier with his bayonet, who never did and never can secure it — not the peace of a desert made by fear, but the blooming, wholesome peace that respects the rights and liberties of all men!

FRANCIS PRESTON BLAIR

(1821–1875)

DURING and after the Civil War the decisive balance of power was held in a territory extending from the eastern line of Ohio to the western line of Missouri and from the latitude of Springfield, Illinois, on the north to the southern boundary of Kentucky.

The question of keeping Missouri and Kentucky in the Union was the vital question of 1861, and it was decided when Frank P. Blair, with characteristic force, rallied the supporters of the Union in Missouri for the defense of the St. Louis arsenal and its 65,000 stands of arms. When, as major-general in the army of General Sherman, he led the Seventeenth army corps on the march to the sea, his services were more brilliant without being more important. The control of the Mississippi and its great confluent streams, the Ohio, the Missouri, and especially the Tennessee, was the decisive factor of the struggle in the Mississippi Valley, and hence in the entire country. The final result was really involved as a logical necessity at the very beginning when the arsenal at St. Louis was held and the State of Missouri kept in the Union.

Once more, after the close of the war, it fell to Blair to lead men whose influence conclusively and unmistakably determined the course of events, though they were in a minority, representing the views of the masses of neither of the great parties as they then were. He stood in the politics of that period for devotion to the Union, and for strong objection to the reconstruction of the government on a basis which was not contemplated during the progress of the war. In his speech on the Fifteenth Amendment he expressed the idea which controlled not only his own course after the war but that of the powerful element he represented as the Democratic nominee for vice-president on the ticket with Seymour. "Have we a Federal Union on a constitutional basis?" he asked. "Are the States equal in political rights? Is the central government acting within constitutional limitations? What is the whole system of reconstruction as it is called, this exclusion of States from their inherent and guaranteed rights? Taxation without representation, their fundamental laws set aside, the popular will suppressed, the right of suffrage taken from the States by an usurping fragment of Congress, the Federal

Constitution itself changed in its character by the same usurping fragment and in defiance of the known and expressed will of the people?"

The politics of more than a decade were directly determined by the idea which is condensed into these sentences. The Liberal Republican movement which began in Missouri and in one way or another decided the course of events until it forced the nomination of Garfield, had its real beginnings when Blair came home after the march to the sea and refused to follow the Republican party beyond the surrender at Appomattox.

In considering the work of men so earnest in their purposes and so reckless of personal considerations in carrying them out as Blair was, the critical faculties refuse to respond to the demand made upon them. We do not ask "Is he right? Is he wrong? Is he for us or against us?" but rather how he came by the intense and fiery energy which compels him in his action as it gives him strength for the struggle.

His characteristic energy showed itself when he took the lead in the fight against the test oaths which were proposed immediately after the close of the war. The case of Blair *versus* Ridgely, one of the most important in American history, was brought by him on the theory that the constitutional clauses and enactments requiring test oaths and providing punishments for refusal to comply with such requirement were in the nature of a bill of attainder and *ex post facto*. This case and others of the same nature were carried to the United States Supreme Court which upheld the theories of those who opposed test oaths as in violation of the Federal Constitution.

Blair was born in Lexington, Kentucky, February 19th, 1821. A graduate of Princeton, educated for the bar in Washington, he located in St. Louis, but ill-health and the necessity for the open air sent him to lead the life of a trapper in the Rocky Mountains. He enlisted as a private in the Mexican War and, after his return, edited the Missouri Democrat in St. Louis. From the campaign in 1848, when he sided with the Free Soil Democrats until after the close of the Civil War, he held the middle ground between the extreme South and the extreme North. Elected to Congress as a Republican in 1856, he advocated colonizing the negroes of the South under an arrangement with Spanish-American countries. In 1866, when nominated for Collector of Internal Revenue at St. Louis, and for Minister to Russia, he was rejected by the Senate for both offices — a fact which probably helped to secure his nomination on the Democratic National ticket in 1868. He was elected United States Senator from Missouri in 1871, and died July 10th, 1875.

THE CHARACTER AND WORK OF BENTON
(Delivered at the Unveiling of the Benton Statue in St. Louis)

People of Missouri:—

THE highest honor ever conferred on me is that of being called on by you to speak on this occasion. To express the gratitude of a great State to its greatest public benefactor; to represent a generous, proud-spirited, yet fond, affectionate community, paying its homage to the exalted genius that cherished its own infancy with a devoted feeling exceeding the instinct which attaches the parent to its new-born offspring; to express the sentiment that swells the heart of Missouri, now elevating to the view of the whole country the imperishable form of her statesman who gave his whole career to her faithful service in the most trying times,—this to me is a most grateful duty, however impossible it may be to discharge it adequately. Your indulgence in assigning me to this honor I know proceeds from the partial kindness always extended to me by the man whose memory your present ceremonies and the monument they consecrate are designed to perpetuate. It is a recollection of this, his personal partiality, that clothes me with your favor, and his great merits will, in your eyes, cover all the imperfection of my efforts to body them forth again. A keynote from my feeble voice will strike the chord in your bosoms requiring no pathos from mine.

All nations, especially free and highly-endowed, cultivated commonwealths, have raised monuments to such of their children as distinguished them by illustrious labors elevating their country to renown. The bond which leads to this so-called "hero-worship" emanates from the sort of self-love which, spreading among a whole people endued with like sympathies, converges in the individual in whose character they perceive the exalted elements that signalize their own genius as a people. Hero-worship in enlightened nations is directly the reverse of the idolatry that springs up in savage ignorance and supplants intelligence by superstition. The Christian religion, in its magnificent monuments and emblems, gives the senses clear conceptions of the life, the body, the moral excellence, and even the sufferings of the Savior. By addressing the senses as well as the reasoning faculties and the sympathies of our nature, it gives embodiment to the thought and feeling which arise from our devotion, with the aspiration which enables it to incorporate with itself the

excellence by which it is impressed. It is so, but in a less degree, of the excellencies of our fellow-men who are commemorated in history, whose forms and lineaments living in marble and painting are presented through successive ages, to animate posterity, to perpetuate virtue by example—by the presentment of the very form and features of the illustrious men who are crowned with national honors, and so to inspire the noble few in every generation to become public benefactors.

To-day, you raise from the grave and give to the light the form, the features of that model of an American Senator, whose patriotism entitled him to all the honors that the Roman Cato merited in the eyes of his countrymen. There never lived a man with more instinctive patriotism than Benton. He was a man of strong, sometimes of unruly passions, but his paramount passion was love of country. Let me open my reminiscences of this strong man of intellect and impulses with a proof of his title to this proud position. I will first touch on an important transaction with which his public life commenced.

After glorious service in the war with Great Britain, in which Benton acted as the aid of General Jackson, a bloody feud arose between them, growing out of a duel in which the brother of the former was wounded by a friend of Jackson, whom he attended as a second. This resulted in hatred, which time made inveterate. With men of such determination, who had refused all explanation at first, who would have no arbitrators but their weapons, no approach to reconciliation seemed possible. The thought of it was not welcome to either until a conjuncture arose which threatened the safety of the country. Both then perceived that their joint efforts were essential to the good of the country, and without a word spoken, without the slightest intimation from either that friendly relations would be welcomed, the Senator began his labors in the service of the President and went to him to know how his co-operation could be made most effective in defense of the Union. Not a word about bygones passed between them. The memory of the quarrel was blotted out by the danger which menaced the country. The old intimacy was revived in their devotion to the public cause. Cordial, unaffected, mutual attachment sprung up, and not a cloud remained of the black storm where rage was once welcomed as promising to end all differences in a common destruction. Patriotism, the ruling passion in both bosoms, exorcised from both every particle of anger, pride, and

the cherished antagonism of years. Benton belonged to the generation of statesmen who followed the founders of the government; when he entered Congress, Monroe was still President, and some few of the framers of the Constitution were Members of the Senate and House. He admired the form of government which these men had assisted in making, and regarded them with a profound veneration which extended to and embraced those who belonged to the Federal school of politics as well as those who belonged to the Democratic school, to which he himself was attached. Nothing better could exemplify his respect for, his deference to these men than the account he gives in a letter to his wife of the "reproof" administered to him by Mr. Rufus King, of New York. He had made a speech in reply to some Member and had spoken with force and animation. "When it was over," he says in his letter, "Mr. King, of New York, came and sat down beside me, on a chair, and took hold of my hand and said he would speak to me as a father; that I had great powers, and that he felt a sincere pleasure in seeing me advance and rise in the world and that he would take the liberty of warning me against an effect of my temperament when heated by opposition; that under those circumstances I took an authoritative manner and a look and tone of defiance which sat ill even on the older Members; and advised me to moderate my manner." "This," says Benton, "was real friendship, enhanced by kindness of manner, and it had its effect." Twenty years afterwards, Benton met two sons of Rufus King in Congress, and he relates "that he was glad to let them both see the sincere respect he had for the memory of their father."

He not only admired and believed in our form of government, but he was of that Democratic school which insisted on restraining the government in the exercise of its powers to a strict and literal interpretation of the Constitution, not only because they believed the framers of the government were wise and sagacious men and knew how to employ language to describe the powers which they sought to confer on the government, but they were upon principles opposed to a strong government and sought in every way to limit its powers and to make each of the different branches a check upon the others. They were profoundly convinced that "the world was governed too much," and that the best government was that which least intermeddled with the affairs of the citizens.

These men believed that the world owed but little to its statesmen and rulers who paid themselves so well, who monopolized the glory, the wealth, and the fame, and whose acts, even when they sought to do good, as a general thing, resulted in obstruction to the progress of mankind. It is sad to reflect that those whose position gives them the greatest power and ability to benefit the human race have been those who have done the least for its advancement. Why is this? What is the explanation? It is found in the fact that power almost invariably corrupts those who are clothed with it; and no class of men have been intrusted with authority who have not abused it. How much greater is our debt to the humble ministers of that science which enables us to encounter disease and disarm pestilence! How much more does the world owe to those who have gained for us the knowledge of the forces of nature and brought them under control, and made them minister to the comfort and happiness of man! How infinitely greater should be our gratitude to those whose inventions in machinery have cheapened the articles of indispensable necessity to the poor than that which we owe to the mightiest potentates of the world! In those countries in which freedom is allowed and where the least intermeddling on the part of the government with the private pursuits is permitted, the greatest success has attended moral and intellectual culture and industrial enterprise. The most meritorious legislation is now confessedly that which has undone the errors of past legislation. Whenever the interests of religion even have been protected by legislation it has led to the persecution of those who have dissented from it and the corruption of those who have conformed to the protective system. Where laws have been made to protect against usury, it has invariably increased the usury and produced crime in the evasion of the laws. And so of every species of protective legislation, a system through which, as it has been well said by one of the most philosophical writers of modern times, "the industrious classes were robbed in order that industry might thrive."

It is in precisely the same sense that the Democratic school, of which Benton was such a profound and faithful expositor, desired to restrict the powers of our government within the narrowest limits, believing that to be the best government which gives to the individual the most complete control of his own actions, and that every restraint upon the freedom of thought and of actions which do not injure others is not only oppressive to the individual but is also an obstruction to progress and an injury to civilization; that national character improves and becomes vigorous and powerful as free scope is given to the masses of the people to think and act for themselves; and that it deteriorates into feebleness and routine in the degree in which the government assumes to act for them.

Deeply imbued with the political philosophy of Jefferson, the founder of the Democratic school of statesmen, Benton was, moreover, the very personification of the rugged energy and genius of the West, where these theories had taken deepest root. He knew better than any one who preceded him or has followed him its wants, its capabilities, and its destiny. He gave himself with his whole strength and with all the ardor of his mind to the duty of supplying these wants, to the development of its capabilities, and to preparing the way for the accomplishment of its destiny. His task was to undo the vicious legislation by which the energy of the giant West had been chained — legislation the result of the jealous rivalry of other sections, and of that ignorance of our true interests which attaches itself like a fungus to every object from which it can draw strength and life. He well understood that the West only needed to be left free to work out its own prosperity; that all sections would share in this prosperity and that it most wanted the reversal of those laws by which its strength and energy were trammeled; by which its lands were withheld from cultivation to be sold to speculators; by which its mines were leased by the government without gain to any one; by which the necessaries of life were taxed to pay bounty to some losing trade in another section. All such laws were odious to Benton because repugnant to his democratic convictions; especially odious, because burdensome to the young States of the West; and he resolved to attack and overthrow them. The greatness and prosperity of the West are the fitting monuments of him whose labor, energy, and unflagging zeal, unchained her strength, gave homes to her people, fought to death the hydra-headed monopoly which had made her a spoil, and beckoned her to extend her empire to that remote West which blends with the East.

11—33

THE DEATHBED OF BENTON
(Peroration of the Benton Monument Address)

WHEN Colonel Benton was on his deathbed, my father and mother both hastened from the country to be by his side. When they arrived his articulation was almost lost; but his mind was clear and his features gave it expression. After some motion of his lips, he drew my father's face close to his and said "Kiss me," and spoke of their long and unbroken friendship. He then uttered Clay's name and with repeated efforts gave my father to understand that he wished him to get the last of his compilation of 'The Debates of Congress' which he prepared a few days before, — the last effort of his feeble hand. It contained Mr. Clay's pregnant reply to Senator Barnwell, of South Carolina, who had vindicated Mr. Rhett's secession pronunciamento for the South. Mr. Clay, in the passage preserved by Colonel Benton, proclaimed the course which should be taken against the attempt indicated by Rhett and advocated by Mr. Barnwell, and my father expressed his satisfaction that this was given prominence as the work of his last moments, since there were then strong symptoms of the revolutionary movement which culminated in the last war. Colonel Benton's countenance, as he recognized that the sense of the manuscript was understood, evidenced his gratification. The scene was reported to Mr. Crittenden and other Union men who had power to impress it on the public mind. It had its efficacy. In 1858 at the epoch of Benton's death, the country and its loyal sons were struggling, like Laocoon and his offspring, with the two great serpents crushing them in their fatal coils. Benton, in his dying hour, seemed in his agonies concerned alone for those which he foresaw awaited the country.

The page to which he pointed my father's eye contained Mr. Clay's last appeal intended to arouse the people to support the government against impending convulsions. Colonel Benton adopted his life-long rival's last appeal as his own, and made it speak when he could no longer utter the counsel which had healed the bitter enmity between him and his great political opponent. And he left that fact as a dissuasive command to the ambitious factions that would rend the country into hostile sections and submerge its glorious institutions to subserve views of personal aggrandizement or gratify a vindictive hatred. The last labors of this great man's life exhibited its great moral attributes

under these most striking circumstances. All the prejudice born of the rivalry of his personal and party ambitions was forgotten Benton forgot even himself, he almost forgot that he had a soul to save or that he had a suffering body bleeding to death. His bodily pangs at the moment of dissolution seemed to be lost in the thoughts fixed sadly on the ruin portending the grand commonwealth to which he gave a homage that was almost worship. He was like a soldier battling earnestly for the cause that tasked all his powers. He does not feel the bullet that carries his life's blood away in its flight. He remembered that his efforts combined with those of his great party-antagonist had once contributed to save the Union and he was unwilling to lay down his head in the peace of death until he tried to repel another similar but more appalling danger.

It was Woolsey's praise that he was the founder of Oxford University.

> "——so famous,
> So excellent in art and still so rising
> That Christendom shall ever speak his virtue."

It is a larger merit in our Democratic statesman that he aided in the noble system of public schools in our city and he was, as I am informed, the first secretary of its board. I have often heard him say that he had mistaken his vocation — that he would have accomplished more as a schoolmaster than he had done — that he would have trained many to greatness. It is certain that this was genuine feeling, for he found time amid labors which would have overwhelmed almost any other man, to become the successful instructor of his own children.

I trust that I may not be thought to tread on ground too holy in alluding to the gentle care, the touching solicitude with which he guarded the last feeble pulses of life in her who was the pride and glory of his young ambition, the sweet ornament of his mature fame, and best love of his ripened age. These are the complete qualities which enables us to know him as he was: —

> "Lofty and sour to those who loved him not,
> But to those men who sought him, sweet as summer."

ON THE FIFTEENTH AMENDMENT
(In the United States Senate, February 15th, 1871)

The Senate having under consideration the joint resolution of the legislature of Indiana withdrawing its assent to the ratification of the fifteenth article of amendment to the Constitution —

Mr. President : —

I DID not intend to take part in this discussion, and I shall be very brief in the expression of my views now, and endeavor not to trespass too long on the indulgence of the Senate.

The Senator from Indiana [Mr. Morton], with his usual ability, which marks him as the leader of the administration party on this floor, — there being many of the old leaders of the Republicans who cannot be claimed for the administration, — has opened the discussion of questions which I regard as of paramount importance to the country. These are the questions involved in the reconstruction acts of Congress. Other questions which attract much attention and employ some of the best minds of our country do not, in my opinion, deserve the prominence which has been given them at this juncture. I do not undervalue the great advantages to the people of low taxes and a sound system of finance; but these are only incidents to the great question beyond, as to the government itself. We might have free trade and a good financial system under a despotism; but a Federal Union of free States, coequal in political rights, with a general government of limited and clearly defined powers, is the opposite of despotism. The two cannot exist together.

Have we a Federal Union on the constitutional basis? Are the States equal in political rights? Is the central government acting within constitutional limitations? What is this whole system of reconstruction, as it is called; this exclusion of States from their inherent and guaranteed rights? Taxation without representation, their fundamental laws set aside, the popular will suppressed, the right of suffrage taken from the States by a usurping fragment of Congress, the Federal Constitution itself changed in its character by the same usurping fragment, and, in defiance of the known and expressed will of the people, the government is literally, practically subverted, and the paramount issue now is to bring back the central government to its legitimate powers, and the restoration of the States to their reserved and undoubted rights, instead of expending argument and effort on minor questions of expediency, touching the affairs of finance and free trade, questions which will become great and important when we shall have succeeded in rescuing the government itself from the perils which threaten its existence. Democrats may honestly differ on these minor matters, and so may radicals. But on the subject of a consolidated empire or a federal union there can be no division among those who prefer the one or the other system.

If the central government can make and unmake States at pleasure; can reconstruct them, displace the duly elected authorities chosen by the people, and put others in their places by edicts to be executed by the military arm, then we are under a consolidated government without limitation of power. Such has been, and is, the action of Congress and of the administration of General Grant.

The Senator from Indiana fitly represents the administration in the bold, open, and outspoken expression of contempt for representative government. Sir, during the last summer the news was brought to us that the Senator had been appointed to a high mission abroad, the mission to England. It was very gratifying to me. Knowing well his ability and courage, and confiding in his patriotism upon questions pending between his own and a foreign country, I believed our affairs at the English court would be conducted by the honorable Senator with ability, courage, and decorum, and that the honor of the country would be safe in his hands.

But, sir, an election took place during the autumn, in the State of Indiana, and the Democratic party succeeded in electing a majority of the legislature of that State. The Senator at once renounced the mission which he had so recently accepted, and assigned as his reason that he would not have his State send a Senator here in his place to represent the political sentiments of the people of Indiana.

Mr. Morton — Misrepresent?

Mr. Blair — We need not quarrel about that. I shall not use so harsh a term toward him as to say he misrepresents the State of Indiana. He may, and doubtless does, believe that he represents the people of the State, but if there was a Senator to be chosen by the legislature just elected no one doubts that a Democrat would be chosen; and this fact would furnish the best evidence of the political sentiment of the people.

If the distinguished Senator had gone abroad upon the mission to which he was appointed, he would have learned in the royal court to which he was accredited a greater deference for the popular will than he seems to have attained in the party to which he belongs at home. He would have discovered there, in monarchical England, that no minister or public servant can hold office against the popular sentiment; but the Senator holds his place, although the people of his State have condemned him in the only form and manner in which public sentiment is ascertained in our country. He openly avows, moreover, that he continues so to hold it to prevent the election of one who more nearly represents the opinions of that body whose duty it is to select a Senator in his place.

The Senator has gone somewhat into the history of the Fifteenth Amendment, the rightful adoption of which is controverted by his State in the concurrent resolutions passed by the legislature of Indiana, and which are now under consideration by the Senate. I shall also refer to some historical matters pertaining to that measure. I remember very well that the Congress which proposed that amendment to the States failed to do so until after the presidential election, and that their nominating convention, which sat in Chicago, held out the promise to the people that no such amendment should be proposed, declaring in emphatic terms that, while they claimed the right to regulate the suffrage by Congress in the States lately in revolt, the States that had not been in rebellion should have, and of right ought to have, the power to regulate suffrage for themselves. This was a trick to avoid an issue which would have been fatal to them in the presidential election. But when, after the election, the party to which the Senator belongs had secured another lease of power, they then proposed to the States this amendment, refusing and voting down a proposition made, I think, in both houses of Congress, certainly in one of the houses, that the amendment should be submitted to legislatures of the States, elected after the amendment was submitted by Congress to the States for ratification. This was promptly refused. They did not intend that the people should have anything to do with framing their own organic law. This measure, the Senator declares, had become "a political necessity" for his party, and could not be trusted to the people.

What further? The two Senators who sat here from my own State, neither of whom sit here now, voted for this amendment

after the people of Missouri, in the election immediately preceding, had voted down negro suffrage by thirty thousand majority, and the legislature, elected by that very vote, ratified the amendment, in defiance of this overwhelming expression of public sentiment.

A similar state of facts occurred in Kansas, where, in the election preceding, negro suffrage had been defeated by fifteen thousand majority. In the State of Ohio the majority against negro suffrage was fifty thousand, and yet her Republican Senators and Representatives, and her Republican legislature, promptly disregarded the public will by proposing and ratifying this amendment. In the State of Michigan the people refused to give suffrage to the negroes by a majority of thirty-four thousand. Her Senators and Representatives were equally regardless of the wishes of their people, and hastened to fasten upon them an organic law for which they had proclaimed their detestation. I could go on and enumerate many more of' the Northern States in which the people had expressed their will with equal emphasis, and were treated with equal contempt by their Republican Senators and Representatives. Among the number were the States of New York, Connecticut, and New Jersey; and, indeed, I think that none of the Northern States can be excepted,— not one!

Now, sir, I do not know a single northern State outside of New England in which the people, whenever the question has been submitted to them, have not rejected the proposition to allow negro suffrage; and yet these gentlemen hurried the matter through without a constitutional quorum in the State of the Senator from Indiana; and in my State, after the people had condemned it by thirty thousand majority six months previous, the radical legislature adopted one-half of it on a telegram, not waiting to receive an official and authentic copy, such was their haste to show contempt for the popular will of the State.

Then the question is raised by the State of Indiana in these resolutions in reference to the ratification of Virginia, Mississippi, Texas, and Georgia, without the ratification of which States the amendment was not adopted. If adopted at all, we have seen that it was adopted against the remonstrance of all the people of the North, and simply by coercion in the States of the South; and yet that amendment is now to be considered as one of those sacred things upon which no man must lay his hands. Because the perfidious representatives of the people have betrayed their

trust and fixed a yoke upon their necks, they are not to wince when they are galled; and if some States, by a fraud obtaining the signatures of the presiding officers of the two houses, enact into a law that which they had no right to enact, and contrary to the forms ordained in their own constitution, we have no right to examine it or hold to proper accountability those who have committed fraud and perverted the forms of law to give effect to their crime.

Sir, if constitutional amendments can be adopted in that way we might well have constitutional amendments here that would create what the gentleman pretends so much to apprehend. If constitutional amendments can be adopted in this mode, against the remonstrance of the entire body of the people of the North, or a vast majority of them, as indicated by the facts to which I have referred, and which are not contradicted in the Senate, and cannot be contradicted, why may we not soon have one declared adopted which provides for a President and Senate for life, and why may not other aristocratic and monarchical institutions be fixed upon us by coercing these carpet-bag States, or, in the congressional slang, requiring them to adopt another fundamental condition, and by misrepresenting and defying the will of the people in the States of the North? And then we shall be told, in the language of the Senator, that we have no right to say a word; we have no right even to expose the perfidy by which the people have been betrayed; and we shall be denounced as revolutionists if we do.

This is no idle apprehension. Each day ushers in some new and monstrous usurpation of power on the part of the dominant party. One aggression is but the stepping-stone of another. The indignation excited by each successive infringement of the rights of the people is a pretext for still further encroachments. The plea of "political necessity," by which the Senator justifies the adoption of the Fifteenth Amendment, is always ready, and has become the law of the existence of that party which, having forfeited the confidence of the people, is now compelled to retain power by fraud and force. Hence the bill to employ the army to enforce the Fifteenth Amendment, which has grown out of that measure, and the bill now pending in the other house enlarging the powers of the President for the same purpose. It is the fungus growth from a rotten system, more poisonous than that which produced it.

Sir, I had occasion to be very grateful to the Senator from Wisconsin who sits nearest to me [Mr. Carpenter] for the speech which he made in this hall the other day, able and learned as it was, vindicating the position which the Democratic party have taken upon this subject. The argument is one which is familiar to us in Missouri. We have there labored under disqualifications and disabilities fixed upon us by a constitution of our State by which more than one-half the citizens were deprived of the right of suffrage and the right to hold office, and even to practice professions by which they earned their bread.

The Democratic party in the convention at New York made this issue broadly and unmistakably: that the reconstruction acts of Congress were unconstitutional, null, and void. That is the very language of their resolution, and because in these acts Congress sought and did inflict punishments upon a whole people, which the Constitution prohibits and declares shall never be inflicted except after a judicial trial and conviction by due process of law. This legislative trial, conviction, and punishment is known to every lawyer to be a bill of attainder prohibited by the Constitution of the United States. Congress has no power not given by that instrument, and when it inflicts punishment without its authority it is no more than a mere mob of lynchers. It has no more rightful power than a body of conspirators against the government. It is the Constitution that gives life and vigor to the resolutions of Congress; and, when it attempts to exercise powers not delegated to it, its edicts ought to be void and of no more effect than the resolutions of a mass meeting held in the streets of a city.

What were the punishments which Congress in the reconstruction acts sought to inflict upon the people of the South? Instead of proceeding to punish those who had been in rebellion according to law, by indictment, trial, and conviction, they declared by act of Congress that certain classes had been guilty of treason, and condemned the community en masse, forfeiting their rights as citizens, depriving them of the right of suffrage, and declaring them ineligible to office. The persons upon whom these punishments were inflicted were citizens of the States recently in rebellion. The fact that they were States in the Union cannot be denied, because all of them had voted to ratify the Thirteenth Amendment to the Constitution, emancipating the slaves, and their votes upon this amendment had already been

counted and accepted by Congress. They were thus recognized as States, capable of performing the highest functions of the States, capable of acting upon amendments to the organic law of the Republic proposed by Congress to the States; not proposed to Territories or conquered provinces, but proposed to the States in the Union.

And unless they had thus been recognized and regarded as States in the Union they could not have voted for the ratification of that amendment, fixing the organic law of the Republic, not alone for themselves, but all the other States. This is a higher function, a more important office than that of participating by their representatives in the legislation of Congress. Without the votes of these States the Thirteenth Amendment was not adopted and is not a part of the Constitution. If it is valid, and no one denies its validity, then they were States at that time, and Congress could not expel them or reconstruct them. It was after this recognition that Congress proceeded to displace their constituted authorities, place them under martial law, disfranchise their citizens, and disqualify them from the exercise of all civil rights, transferring the political power to the hands of the ignorant and vicious part of the population, who had hitherto been slaves, thus inflicting punishment without judicial trial. This brings me to the point put so strongly to the Senate the other day by the Senator from Wisconsin [Mr. Carpenter], that no man can be punished by an act of Congress or by the act of any legislative body; that such an act is a bill of attainder, and is denounced and prohibited by the Constitution, and especially as against a whole community, confounding the innocent with the guilty, if guilt could be attached to any individual under such circumstances.

Again, this disfranchisement was the operative part of the machinery of these reconstruction acts. Without it they would have had no effect in the South. The effective machinery was the deprivation of classes of citizens of their right of suffrage and conferring that same right upon others who never had been entitled to it, in violation of another plain provision of the Constitution, which reserves to the States themselves the right to regulate their own suffrage. The reconstruction acts go still further, giving to the military authorities the power to enforce their provisions by arrest, by imprisonment, by punishment of any person resisting them, thus depriving those charged with the

commission of crime of the right of trial by jury and the other safeguards which the Constitution has thrown over all the citizens of the country, its humblest and highest, its best and worst. I believe there is scarcely a single article or paragraph of the Constitution which was not violated by the reconstruction acts. The command of the troops who were to put the acts into execution was taken away from the constitutional commander-in-chief of the Army and Navy of the United States and conferred upon another individual. You can hardly put your hand on a single sentence of these abominations, called the reconstruction acts, without encountering some violation of the Constitution, in its letter or principle, of the United States; and the difficulty is to find any one of its articles which they do not violate. These gentlemen themselves knew these acts to be in violation of the Constitution.

I do not hesitate to say that the conduct of Congress betrayed their own knowledge of the fact that they were violating the Constitution. Not only were the principles which they violated plain and unmistakable, but they had been decided by the Supreme Court in the case of Milligan and others in Indiana, the Senator's own State,—and he at least must have been familiar with it,—where an attempt was made to punish a citizen of the United States, alleged to be guilty of crime, by a military commission. The Supreme Court delivered him from their hands. He was condemned to death by the commission. But he is still alive, and lives in the gentleman's State.

In Milligan's case the Supreme Court of the United States said:—

"Another guarantee of freedom was broken when Milligan was denied a trial by jury. The great minds of the country have differed on the correct interpretation to be given to various provisions of the Federal Constitution, and judicial decision has been often invoked to settle their true meaning; but until recently no one ever doubted that the right of trial by jury was fortified in the organic law against the power of attack. It is now assailed; but if ideas can be expressed by words, and language has any meaning, this right, one of the most valuable in a free country, is preserved to every one accused of crime who is not attached to the army or navy or militia in actual service." (4 Wallace's Supreme Court Reports, page 122.)

In the case of Cummings versus The State of Missouri, the question involved was the right of a State to pass an ex post

facto law, or bill of attainder, disqualifying citizens from practicing particular professions and disqualifying persons from the exercise of the right of suffrage; and such an attempt was pronounced by the Supreme Court of the United States to be unconstitutional, null, and void.

Both of these decisions were prior to the reconstruction acts. But after the reconstruction acts were passed the McCardle case, which arose under those acts, came up by appeal to the Supreme Court; and what was the conduct of the Republican party in Congress?

First, an attempt was made to get the court to dismiss the case for want of jurisdiction; but when the Republican majority of Congress ascertained that the court had taken jurisdiction of the McCardle case, they unhesitatingly passed an act taking away the right of appeal which theretofore had been given to people suffering deprivation of personal liberty under color of a law of Congress. They thus took away the jurisdiction of the Supreme Court, thinking they rescued their acts from condemnation in that way. Surely this was a most unparalleled occurrence. If they had desired that the first court of the land should have an opportunity to pass upon the constitutionality or unconstitutionality of their acts, they would unhesitatingly have abided the decision of the Supreme Court; but as they knew that the Supreme Court had decided to take jurisdiction, they knew from its decision in the case of Milligan what would be the result in the case of McCardle, and they immediately passed a bill taking away the right of appeal, which had been given by previous legislation. I say this act betrays their own guilty knowledge that they were violating the Constitution. I do not think so meanly of the intelligence of the Republicans in Congress as not to believe that they knew these acts were unconstitutional, that they were without a vestige of authority.

Now, if the crime committed by the Southern men in going into the rebellion deserved punishment, they should have been punished according to the Constitution. That was the only way in which we could punish their crime without committing on our part as great a crime, the crime of destroying our own government and overthrowing our own Constitution. Sir, in overthrowing our Constitution, in violating its sacred guarantees, we committed the same crime with which we had charged the rebels of the South and of which they undoubtedly had been guilty.

That was my view of the case, and believing that these acts of Congress were unconstitutional, null, and void, I believe that the President of the United States, who was sworn to maintain the Constitution, ought not to allow it to be trampled under foot; that your conscience, sir, and the conscience of the majority in these two houses, should not dictate to the President what he should do in a case of this kind. He had his own conscience to keep clear and spotless, he had sworn an oath himself, and I remember right well that it was not the Democratic convention which sat in New York two years ago that first gave utterance to this doctrine, that the President of the United States was bound by his oath to maintain the Constitution, and not to allow it to be violated in any way or by anybody, neither by Congress nor by his own act, nor by the act of any one else.

Mr. Jefferson, who founded the Democratic party, held and declared this doctrine not only as a matter of theory, but he acted upon it on a memorable occasion when President of the United States. I prefer to quote his own language. In a letter to Mr. Adams, dated the eleventh of September, 1804, he says:—

" You seem to think it devolved on the judges to decide on the validity of the Sedition Law. But nothing in the Constitution has given them a right to decide for the Executive, more than to the Executive to decide for them. Both magistracies are equally independent in the sphere of action assigned to them."

And again, in a letter to George Hay, dated Washington, June 2d, 1807, in reference to the action of the Executive on the Sedition Act, he says:—

" The judges determined the Sedition Act was valid under the Constitution." . . . " But the Executive determined that the Sedition Act was a nullity under the Constitution, and exercised his regular power of prohibiting the execution of the sentence."

General Jackson was equally explicit, both in the declaration of the principle and its exemplification in his official action. In his protest against the resolution of censure adopted by the Senate, December 26th, 1833, he says:—

" Each of the three great departments is independent of the other in its sphere of action, and when it deviates from that sphere is not responsible to the others further than it is especially made so in the

Constitution. In every other respect each of them is the coequal of the other two, and all are the servants of the American people, without power or right to control or censure each other in the service of their common superiors save only in the manner and to the degree which that superior has prescribed."

In the bank veto, July 10th, 1832, are these words:—

" The Congress, the Executive, and the court must each for itself be guided by its own opinion of the Constitution. Each public officer who takes an oath to support the Constitution swears that he will support it as he understands it, and not as it is understood by others."

And this construction of the Constitution, so manifestly true, so far from being revolutionary, is demonstrated by recent events to be essential to secure the people in the enjoyment of their rights and protect them from usurpation by Congress, the strongest and least responsible and most dangerous department of the government. We have seen this body not only denying representation to the people of eleven States, but foisting governments upon those States and putting its own creatures into the halls of Congress as Representatives of those States, merely to strengthen the hands of the dominant party. Thus re-enforced, it was enabled to override the President's veto and to withdraw from the courts all power to revise its action. Coercing the President to execute its behests by the fear of impeachment, its power has been unlimited. In this way it has carried out reconstruction acts and constitutional amendments, and intends to perpetuate its power in defiance of the popular will.

The danger which now menaces the liberties of the people could never have occurred if by refusing to execute its revolutionary program the people could have been called on to decide between the Congress and the President. There would have been no delay by adjourning the question over for the popular umpirage in the settlement of the questions at issue, and the only difference would be that the questions would have been fairly presented to and decided by the proper tribunal, with no possible danger to the public peace in the meantime.

This view proceeds upon and accords with the theory that the people — not the Congress, or the President, or the courts — are to govern. Radicalism proceeds upon the reverse of this. None of the measures of reconstruction, so called, would have been

adopted if they had been submitted to the people in this manner. They have been forced in, *seriatim*, by fraud, by denying persistently that it was the purpose to impose such measures upon the country, and using the power obtained by such denials to press upon the country the very measures disavowed before the people. The constitutional amendments have been obtained by coercion in the South, and in defiance of the known will of the people of the North.

This, sir, is simply and without any concealment my view of the theory of our government. That Congress has been usurping the powers which belong to the President and to other co-ordinate branches of the government I have not a particle of doubt. The overwhelming majority obtained by the Republicans in Congress during the Rebellion and afterward, by bringing unauthorized persons into Congress to increase that majority, has sent them headlong upon their career; and they have been and are grasping at every power which was placed by our ancestors in the hands of the President and the courts. Our fathers defined and divided the powers of the government, to prevent all power being grasped and concentrated in the hands of any one of the different branches of government. I believe that the reckless legislation of which the Republican party have been guilty are flagitous violations of the Constitution; and in it the gentleman has been a leader, though he did not begin early to lead in this direction. He began, if I am not mistaken, with the same views of reconstruction as those now held by the Democratic party. But having been converted to this doctrine, he has out-Heroded Herod, and, with the proverbial zeal of a new convert, has gone further than any one else, and signalized himself by the boldness and audacity of his assaults upon the Constitution. What is there in our government now that we can recognize as the government which descended to us from our fathers? I remember reading one of the first contested-election cases which occurred in Congress. It was the case of Mr. Preston, of western Virginia, and he was expelled from his seat because his brother marched a company of troops through the streets of the town on the day of the election. Such was the jealousy with which even the appearance of employing force in our elections was regarded by our ancestors. Now an election is not valid unless it is superintended by the bayonets of the regular army. Our army moves wherever there is an election. They no longer make war upon

the camps of the enemies of the government, but they make war upon the political opponents of the administration, and charge upon the ballot boxes and the polls.

Mr. President, I was perfectly well aware that this practice, although it commenced at the South, would not end there. The party in power commenced using the bayonets to set up the carpet-baggers in the Southern States, in the reconstructed States. Although those States were at peace, and desired peace more than any other part of our country, still they were not allowed to hold an election without the presence of the army. I knew very well that when the Republican party had accustomed the people of this country to hold elections under the superintendence of military officers and armed troops it would not be a great while before the " political necessity " of the party would extend that practice into the Northern States; and from having originated in the South, in those States which had been in rebellion, it has recently gone into the States which furnished the most powerful aid and the largest number of men to overthrow the rebellion.

Mr. Morton — Will the Senator allow me to ask him a question?

Mr. Blair — Certainly.

Mr. Morton — I ask the Senator whether he regards the Fifteenth Amendment as having been adopted, and as now being a part of the fundamental law of the land?

Mr. Blair — I should think the gentleman ought to have got my opinion of the Fifteenth Amendment by this time. [Laughter.] I think that the ratification of my own State, for instance, was in legal form, although that ratification was obtained by the most infamous perfidy. General Grant carried the State of Missouri by twenty-five thousand majority, and at the same election the negro suffrage amendment to the Constitution was voted down by thirty thousand majority, and not one-half of the people of Missouri were allowed to vote. The majority in the State of Missouri against that amendment was known to the Senators who sat upon this floor, and the Representatives who sat in the other house, to be probably two-thirds of the entire population of the State; and yet, without any sort of consideration or regard for the will of that immense and overwhelming majority, the Senators and Representatives of the State and the Members of the Legislature hurried to give effect and vitality to this Fifteenth Amendment.

The very gentlemen who claim that the ballot is necessary to protect the negro, who attach such immense importance to the ballot, when the ballot has been exercised by their own constituents adverse to their wishes and party interests, disregard it as if it were no more than waste paper. That shows the real opinion of those gentlemen in regard to the suffrage. How much protection did the suffrage afford the people of Missouri, Ohio, Kansas, Michigan, New York, Connecticut, and the other Northern States also, that voted by immense majorities against negro suffrage, against the perfidy and misrepresentation of their Representatives in Congress and the State legislatures which have saddled them with the Fifteenth Amendment, and which the Senator from Indiana well says became a "political necessity" to his party at this crisis?

I have enumerated already other States, and I do not wish to call the roll again to show the gentleman from Indiana what my opinion of the adoption of the Fifteenth Amendment is. I do not controvert the fact that even the fraud which was successfully practiced in his own State has been placed beyond the reach of any other correction than the rebuke administered by the people in the election of a Democratic legislature, whose resolutions are now under consideration, placing its perpetrators in the pillory of public opinion, and depriving us of the Senator's services as minister to the Court of St. James. This act has probably reached a point where it cannot now, according to the rules of law, be investigated; but I wish to be understood as saying that the people of this country have a right to hold those who have perpetrated these infamies to responsibility.

II—34

RICHARD P. BLAND

(1835-1899)

IT IS generally believed that what is known as the "Parting of the Ways" speech, delivered by Richard P. Bland, of Missouri, in the House of Representatives, resulted in what were to many the surprising political changes of the presidential campaign of 1896. Soon after his inauguration in 1893, President Cleveland called an extra session of Congress to repeal the clauses of the Sherman Act which required the purchase and coinage of silver bullion. It was in protesting against the policy suggested by this recommendation that Mr. Bland spoke of the "Parting of the Ways." In copying his speech from the official report, only the argument bearing on abstract questions of political economy has been omitted, while that which explains subsequent political history has been given verbatim.

THE PARTING OF THE WAYS

(Delivered in the House of Representatives, August 11th, 1893)

IT IS said that history repeats itself, and it seems that the Democratic party is especially the victim of history repeated in some way. When the people intrusted our party in 1884 with the administration of the government, when the Democratic House of Representatives was chosen, I remember full well, and I see around me gentlemen who remember it as I do, for they were here at that time, that before the inauguration of the President of the United States whom we had elected, the emissaries of Wall Street swarmed the lobbies of the House and this capitol, just as they did last winter, demanding—what? Demanding the repeal of the so-called Bland Act.

Precisely the same proceedings that we had here last winter! We were told then that it was the wish of the Executive-Elect that that act be repealed, as we were told the same thing last winter. We were told that it was his opinion and the opinion of his advisers that this country was coming then to the single silver standard. If we did not repeal that law, we were threatened

---

with a panic, with gold going to a premium. The House was forced to a vote upon that subject before we were adjourned at that time, as we were practically last winter; but it voted the proposition down by a tremendous majority. During the following summer, the New York papers, as they have been this summer, were filled with predictions of gold premiums and panics.

The New York Herald, one of their leading papers, had every day in its columns, "We are still coining the 70 and 75 cent dollar," as a standing advertisement of a panic.

Some time in September or October, before the meeting of Congress, these generous bankers in New York, who say that they control the finances of this country and that what they demand must be acceded, made arrangement with the then Secretary of the Treasury by which they were to withdraw $10,000,000 of subsidiary silver coin and to place in the Treasury of the United States $10,000,000 of gold, in order to secure and maintain gold payments, advertising to all the country that the bankers of New York had come to the relief of the Federal Treasury with $10,000,000 of gold to maintain the public credit.

It was done, Mr. Speaker, to terrorize the people of this country and, if possible, to bring about a panic such as you have to-day, and they know it. And we met in something of a financial panic; not so severe as it is now, however. The whole country was stirred on the silver question. We met in Congress and the question was debated. The result of it all was the refusal to repeal the silver law by over a two-thirds' vote of that House; and the panic vanished. That was the end of it. When they ascertained that the free people of this country, through their representatives, could not be driven as a herd of buffaloes on the Western plains into a panic, to trample themselves and those depending upon them, they ceased.

The howl against silver and the panic stopped. The country continued in its usual prosperity, whatever that may be. We kept on winning these seventy-cent dollars, and no disturbance was made of it, practically, for four years. The Democratic party in the House maintained it against all assaults. But when, unfortunately, our friends on the other side got the power, they enacted another law, repealing the law of 1878. . . .

Now, sir, we are asked here deliberately to repeal that law, and I want to call the attention of my friends on this side of the House, who proclaim themselves to be friends of free coinage

---

at a reasonable ratio—I want to call their attention to this point and to ask them this question: Why do you gentlemen insist that you will repeal this law and send silver down probably fifteen cents an ounce before you fix the ratio? Is that an act friendly to silver? Can any gentleman here fail his free coinage constituency and defend his vote subtracting from the value of silver fifteen cents an ounce before he votes to fix the ratio? I dare him to undertake it. He cannot do it.

It may be convenient to follow the recommendations of the President, but the President does not elect the Members of this House. We do not hold our commissions from the Executive, and I am afraid that if some of us undertake to act here upon that line, when our present commissions expire we shall have all the leisure that we want to study the silver question in peace and quietness at home. For myself I feel it to be a conscientious duty to carry out my convictions on this subject, and I owe it to my constituents to represent what I believe to be their interests. Why are we rushed in here and asked to repeal the only law that sustains, for the moment, at least, the value of silver, before we fix the ratio?

There is no consistency in it; none whatever! The claim is not sincere that the President expects hereafter to recommend bimetallism, for he does not do it in his message, and that claim misrepresents his position. He recommends the reverse. The concluding paragraph of the message means, if it means anything, that after you shall have totally demonetized silver by repealing this Sherman Act, you will be required to go further in the same direction; and I make a prediction here and now, and, my friends, I want you to watch the proceedings of Congress in these coming weeks of this extra session, or of the next regular session, to see whether I am right or not.

My prediction is that in order to carry out the recommendations of that message we shall be called upon to sell bonds to procure gold. For what? To redeem all our pecuniary obligations, according to the very language of that message, in that money which is recognized by the principal nations of the world. Why did not the President say "gold"? We know what his language means. You are asked to load up the Federal Treasury with gold, to redeem every pecuniary obligation to the government with gold, although the standard silver dollar is the identical dollar on which bond obligations were based when they were issued, because they called for coin of the standard value at the time of their issue, and that was the standard.

But now, I repeat, we shall have to redeem all this bullion, all these Sherman notes in gold; we shall have to sell bonds to get gold to redeem all our greenbacks, all our silver certificates, and we will be compelled to carry our silver dollars as so much dead weight of bullion in the Treasury, so that we might as well dump them into the Potomac. That is what all this means. In other words, every piece of paper money issued in this country to-day, every silver certificate, every greenback, every bond, every Sherman note, is to be redeemed in gold, and we must procure the gold for their redemption.

What, then, are you to do with your silver bullion and with all your silver dollars, together about $500,000,000? They are to be demonetized as a base metal, and you know it. I am talking to intelligent gentlemen here who have read it; who can understand it. Why should you go on, then, to try to deceive yourselves and your constituents on this subject? There is no silver in that message, and gentlemen on the other side will simply do themselves and the subject justice if hereafter, in the course of their debate, they will leave silver out of it, because they are proposing a measure in which there is no consideration whatever for silver.

Mr. Speaker, it may be necessary, and probably is, that I go somewhat into the discussion of the silver question on its merits. I have alluded to these preliminary matters which have been thrown in, and have tried to state that no legislation which we can enact here is going to relieve the panic. This panic has been brought about for the express purpose of repealing this law; there is no question about that. We were threatened last winter with a gold premium. I stated, then, on this floor, and I state now, that there is no gold premium.

On the contrary, I believe the people are now paying a premium for silver and silver certificates. We were urged that we must issue more bonds, that if we did not we were to have a panic. All the newspapers, of the East especially, were advertising a panic if we did not issue bonds. We did not issue them. The Secretary of the Treasury was threatened with a panic if he did not comply with the demand, and he refused. Those who were interested in getting up this panic began to refuse loans, to cramp, to draw in currency. Many of the banks which had been

engaged in booming real estate, or in other questionable transactions, and were consequently weak, began to fail.

Stocks called "industrial stocks," that had been watered in Wall Street, cordage trusts, lead trusts, whisky trusts, railroad stocks that had been watered, began to tumble down to something like natural rates, and you had a panic. Banks which were weak began to fail, and the people began a run on banks which were strong. The whole country became alarmed. People began to take their money out of the banks and put it into safe-deposit vaults or into their safes at home. It is said they ought to let their money remain in the banks. Well, probably they ought to do so; but what is the difference? The banks are afraid to let the money go out if they have it. Now, the panic has come; and those who conspired to bring it about have got more than they bargained for. The idea is that we can relieve this panic by the repeal of the Sherman law.

Why, Mr. Speaker, I say right here (and history will bear me out in the statement) that while there was some alarm in the country before, yet the moment the British government demonetized silver in India, then the panic began in earnest — not before! That precipitated this panic in its present shape. We all understand that. In this way desolation was brought into many of the States of this Union, and men who had before been prosperous and happy were by the thousands sent as tramps throughout the land.

All parts of the country have felt its effects. It is this fight upon silver that has precipitated this panic; and the repeal of the Sherman law will only intensify it, not relieve it. The panic will be relieved when everything gets so low that people see they can make money by buying; when they begin to buy, prices will go up; and when everybody is buying money will come from its hoarding places and you will have some relief. In no other way will relief come.

Gold is coming to us to-day. Notwithstanding we are told the people across the water are afraid to invest here for fear that we will not pay in gold, yet these people are sustaining prices to-day and sending here all the money that they can spare. There was a panic in gold-using Australia that has bankrupted that whole people and sent terror to the banks all over England. We know that gold cannot be obtained there except by paying for it; yet it is coming here.

Talk about a premium on gold! Here is the Treasury of the United States that is open to the plunder of every speculator in the civilized world. He can take his Sherman note or his greenback or any other government currency there and get gold without cost. Did you ever notice the names of the gentlemen in New York who are shipping gold abroad, or bringing it back? Every one of those names that I have seen has a foreign termination; every one of those gentlemen, so far as I am advised, is an agent for or conducts a branch bank of some bank across the water.

If you go to the Bank of England to get gold for export you must pay a premium on it; if you go to the Bank of France to get gold for export you must pay a premium on it. The case is the same with every other banking house in Europe; no gold can be obtained there without paying a premium. But here is the Treasury of the United States professing to be so helpless that it cannot prevent every gold speculator from robbing the government of its gold. Our Treasury will not pay out the silver which it might pay.

The Bank of France will pay out silver, or will charge a premium on gold if it is wanted for anything but domestic use. But the Treasury of the United States, instead of paying out gold and silver in equal quantities and thus preserving its gold (if it is necessary to preserve it, — though I see no necessity of preserving it, for all our money is at a premium to-day), lets everybody go there and get as much gold as he pleases. Why not pay out the silver when we have more of it than we have of gold, or pay out gold when we have more of it than silver, and thus protect ourselves?

It is because the administration is hostile to silver; and thus it is surrendering this country to the Shylocks of the Old World who have made war upon it. The aristocracy of Western Europe has absolutely tabooed silver in those countries and driven it away from there. Here it finds its only resting place. The last fight for the white metal is to be made here in this country and in this House, my friends. Will you stand by it now, or will you let the Shylocks come and have their way? It is for you to determine.

I think, Mr. Speaker, that we can trust the people of this country on a question of as vital importance as this. The question is now before us. This is its last resort. Will you virtually

demonetize the money of nearly 70,000,000 of people, with a vast empire of 3,000,000 of square miles, a people thirsting for money to open up new railroads, to establish new factories, to operate new places of business, to inaugurate new industries; 70,000,000 people demanding money, twice what we have to-day, a new people, a new country, a free people, — or they ought to be free whether they are or not.

Are you to give up the fight and let this vast body of our wealth go to ruin? I do not believe it. We know well enough that if we repeal this law and give nothing for it, the people of this country will regard it as a total demonetization of silver, which it will be, so far as this Congress is concerned, without any question.

Now, my friends, — and I do not care whether you are Democrats or Republicans, or who you are, but I appeal to you, especially as Democrats, — when in 1890 in nearly every State of this Union the Democratic party in its platforms demanded free and unlimited coinage of silver, when you embodied it in your great Chicago national platform, when the Democratic party has for years stood before the House and the country as the bulwark in defense of the white metal, — in the face of all these things are you now to desert the cause and surrender the fight? Can you afford to do it? Will you go to your people and tell them that you are not able to carry out the pledges of your platform, the promises upon which you were sent here, or any part of it, except that which resulted in the total demonetization of silver and the sacrifice of their interests?

What does free coinage of silver mean? It means that the holders of silver bullion, at some ratio to be fixed in the bill, may go to the mints of the government and have it struck into legal-tender money of the government and deposit the dollars so coined, if the holder so desires, and have a certificate issued to him in place of it. What is the effect of unlimited coinage of silver in this country? and I invite your attention to this particularly, because it is a question of vital importance. It means that the silver coins of the United States at whatever ratio is fixed, and I want the present ratio that we have now, 16 to 1, maintained precisely as it is — it means that the silver of the world can come here in exchange for what we have to sell.

Yes, it means that the silver of the whole world can come here. But they say that we will be flooded with the world's silver, that it will be dumped down upon us. Now, let us see about that for a moment. It means that any one with sixteen ounces of silver can come here from any part of the world, or with one ounce of gold, and he can buy your grain, he can buy your house and lot, he can buy your manufactured product, and buy the property and commodities of all sorts that you have to sell with either the one or the other; that is to say, he can buy just as much with his sixteen ounces of silver as with his one ounce of gold.

With the billions upon billions of property existing in this country to-day and being produced in this country every year, we simply offer to exchange that which we have in abundance on a basis of one pound of gold as the equivalent of sixteen pounds of silver. We invite, then, the world to come with its silver and make the exchange. No nation now, it is true, offers in exchange for silver the gold at any fixed ratio; consequently, all the silver that is coined is used in the countries where it is coined. And why? Because no great power offers to exchange commodities for one metal or the other at any fixed ratio. That is the only trouble with silver to-day.

Now, it must be remembered that France gave an example to the world in this regard, having kept its silver on a parity with gold for a period of seventy years, on a ratio of 15½ to 1. It said to the nations of the world, "Come with your gold and your silver, fifteen and one-half ounces of silver or one ounce of gold, and you can buy all of our salable property in France and you can pay us in silver or in gold, just as you choose, on that basis." And, according to the report of the British royal commission of 1888 on that subject, France was enabled to maintain the parity of the two metals at that ratio, for the reason that she had property enough to effect exchanges on that basis. We are in the same condition.

What is it, then, that you are asked to do? It is that we, the Government of the United States, we as a people say to all the world, especially the silver-using people, all of the Asiatic nations and the Great Indies, come here with your white metal, if you choose to come, and trade with us on the basis of 16 to 1, and buy your commodities from us at that ratio. When you do that, will not the silver-using people come to our shores to make their purchases rather than go to the European powers, where they demand a ratio of 22 to 25? There can be no doubt of the answer to that question.

bimetallism instead of gold monometallism. They know that, and hence their eagerness and determination to prevent it.

It is a fight between the standards, and this great country must settle it; and you, my friends, must think about settling it here. It is a serious question. It is not only a serious question for the American people, but we are appealed to by the oppressed in the Old World, those who have not the voice that our people in their sovereignty have.

The oppressed of the Old World are appealing to us to settle for the world this great question, and to settle for men who are seeking advantages in the stock markets, not for men who are seeking advantages in bond holding, in interest drawing, in money lending, in seeking to have money increase in value every day and every year, but for the great toiling and producing masses of the other countries as well as our own, for whom it is our proud province here to think and to legislate. They are in a panic, my friends. I want to remind you of that, and they will remind you of it when you go home, if you are not reminded of it now.

The people are watching this thing. They understand that the battle to be fought here is the battle of the standards the world over, and the man who fails now they will brand as a traitor to the cause which is intrusted to his hands. . . .

Now, I say, Mr. Speaker, the contention that we lose our gold, and that we have got to exchange gold for silver, does not hold good. It is put on the broad proposition of a nation which produces enough wealth; and where is the nation under the shining sun that compares with this growing country of ours in population and increasing development? I believe that I may yet live to see this country with nearly one hundred million inhabitants, increasing, as it does, at the rate of over a million and a half annually.

Many now born, by the time they are voters will compose part of a nation containing perhaps one hundred and twenty-five millions of people, with unsurpassed energies, with a genius nowhere equaled, and with a vast territory upon which those energies and that genius can operate. But a short time ago when you looked across the Alleghany Mountains you beheld the Western wilderness roamed only by the savage and wild beast. To-day it is teeming with its millions of civilized people, and when you cross the Mississippi you just begin to enter the great domain of this country of ours, for more than two-thirds of it lies beyond the Father of Waters.

You at once undermine and sap the prosperity ot Western Europe. You will divert from them all the trade of every silver-using country in the world, because you offer to sell those people property and commodities here that are better, and on better terms, than they can get anywhere else in the world. You say their silver will come here. Suppose it does. It will go back again, because here is the flood gate that is opened for gold and silver to come and to go with the tides of trade, of free exchange, in this the greatest country the world ever saw. It will come and it will go, and so it will continue; because we have opened up the mint, we have opened a sluice for the dam that now blockades the silver tide.

Do you suppose that England could stand that for a moment? Certainly not. What has made the manufacturers in Manchester, England, the strongest bimetallists in the world to-day? Simply the fact that they must sell their commodities in India for the India rupee. They are thus interested in the value of that silver rupee. They want to maintain it; and if all the manufacturing products of Western Europe that are sent here and sold to us are sold for silver, as they must be, or gold at our ratio, do you not see how quickly you will convert them to bimetallism? Thus you will segregate all the industrial inhabitants of Western Europe from those who live on fixed incomes,— the aristocracy, the bond holders, and the coupon clippers. That is all there is about it and we want to segregate them.

You see, then, that when we do this in this country, Western Europe must come to our standard or abandon commerce with all silver-using countries and with us. Mark that. We are the best market in the world for manufactured European products. They cannot live without this market, and they cannot keep this market unless they recognize and take our silver at the same value we take it; and they know it.

I know that the gold owners in that country and this, the bond holders and bankers, those who are living on fixed incomes, and who are living on interest, and whose business it is to loan money and to have that money increase in value from year to year—they fight this proposition as a matter of course; but I do not think they ought to do it, for ultimately I think they would be benefited, as would the industrial people of the world. They ought not to fight it. They know what I state is truth, that if this country gives free coinage of gold and silver at a fair ratio it settles the question for the world and drives the world to

And, Mr. Speaker, it is that two-thirds of our territory, rich as it is in gold and silver, embedded together in the same deposits, in the same mountains, so that you cannot extract the one without extracting the other,—it is that portion of our territory that would give us the money that we need, the money of the world, good money, hard money, Democratic money,—a country that the civilized world must look to for its future monetary supply if it is to continue on what is called the hard-money basis. And yet we are to-day asked to do what? To lay the blighting hand of confiscation upon the millions of people inhabiting that country, to turn them out as tramps upon the land, merely to satisfy the greed of English gold.

Oh, my God, shall we do such a thing as that? Will you crush the people of your own land and send them abroad as tramps? Will you kill and destroy your own industries, and especially the production of your precious metals that ought to be sent abroad everywhere,—will you do this simply to satisfy the greed of Wall Street, the mere agent of Lombard Street, in oppressing the people of Europe and of this country? It cannot be done, it shall not be done! I speak for the great masses of the Mississippi Valley, and those west of it, when I say you shall not do it!

Any political party that undertakes to do it will, in God's name, be trampled, as it ought to be trampled, into the dust of condemnation, now and in the future. Speaking as a Democrat, all my life battling for what I conceived to be Democracy, and what I conceived to be right, I am yet an American above Democracy. I do not intend, we do not intend, that any party shall survive, if we can help it, that will lay the confiscating hand upon Americans in the interest of England or of Europe. Now, mark it. This may be strong language, but heed it. The people mean it, and, my friends of the Eastern Democracy, we bid farewell when you do that thing.

Now, you can take your choice of sustaining America against England, American interests, and American laborers and producers, or you can go out of power. We have come to the Parting of the Ways. I do not pretend to speak for anybody but myself and my constituents, but I believe that I do speak for the great masses of the great Mississippi Valley when I say that we will not submit to the domination of any political party, however much we may love it, that lays the sacrificing hand upon silver and will demonetize it in this country.

LORD BOLINGBROKE

(1678-1751)

ENRY ST. JOHN (Viscount Bolingbroke), the friend of Pope, and the most admired orator of his day in England, was born at Battersea in 1678. His great reputation as an orator is now completely beyond the reach of criticism since, according to the British Encyclopedia, not one of his speeches has come down to us. When for the purposes of this work a search was made through the parliamentary debates to test this statement, only a report attributed to him and a few sentences of debate in the third person were found to represent him. His prose writings, however, were numerous and they are still readily accessible. Professor Morley recently republished a number of his letters. He died in 1751. Heading the Tories successfully under Queen Anne, Bolingbroke, an adherent of the Stuarts, was out-generaled by the Whigs after her death, and learning that they intended to impeach him he left England, remaining abroad from 1715 to 1723. This experience suggested his celebrated 'Reflections upon Exile,' from which an extract is taken to illustrate his admirable prose style, on which it is said that Edmund Burke formed his style as an orator.

MISFORTUNE AND EXILE

DISSIPATION of mind and length of time are remedies to which the greatest part of mankind trust in their afflictions. But the first of these works a temporary, the second a slow effect; and such are unworthy of a wise man. Are we to fly from ourselves that we may fly from our misfortunes, and only to imagine that the disease is cured because we find means to get some moments of respite from pain? Or shall we expect from time, the physician of brutes, a lingering and uncertain deliverance? Shall we wait to be happy till we can forget that we are miserable, and owe to the weakness of our faculties a tranquillity which ought to be the effect of their strength? Far otherwise. Let us set all our past and present afflictions at once before our eyes. Let us resolve to overcome them, instead of

are perpetually to remain with us, if we lean upon them, and expect to be considered for them, we shall sink into all the bitterness of grief, as soon as our vain and childish minds, unfraught with solid pleasures, become destitute even of those which are imaginary. But if we do not suffer ourselves to be transported by prosperity, neither shall we be reduced by adversity. Our souls will be proof against the dangers of both these states; and, having explored our strength, we shall be sure of it; for, in the midst of felicity, we shall have tried how we can bear misfortune.

It is much harder to examine and judge than to take up opinions on trust; and, therefore, the far greatest part of the world borrow from others those which they entertain concerning all the affairs of life and death. Hence, it proceeds that men are so unanimously eager in the pursuit of things which, far from having any inherent real good, are varnished over with a specious and deceitful gloss, and contain nothing answerable to their appearances. Hence, it proceeds, on the other hand, that in those things which are called evils there is nothing so hard and terrible as the general cry of the world threatens. The word "exile" comes, indeed, harsh to the ear, and strikes us like a melancholy and execrable sound, through a certain persuasion which men have habitually concurred in. Thus, the multitude has ordained. But the greatest part of their ordinances are abrogated by the wise.

Rejecting, therefore, the judgment of those who determine according to popular opinions, or the first appearances of things, let us examine what exile really is. It is, then, a change of place; and, lest you should say that I diminish the object, and conceal the most shocking parts of it, I add, that this change of place is frequently accompanied by some or all of the following inconveniences: by the loss of the estate we have enjoyed, and the rank which we held; by the loss of that consideration and power which we were in possession of; by a separation from our family and our friends; by the contempt we may fall into; by the ignominy with which those who have driven us abroad will endeavor to sully the innocence of our characters, and to justify the injustice of their own conduct.

All these shall be spoken to hereafter. In the meanwhile let us consider what evil there is in change of place, abstractedly and by itself.

flying from them, or wearing out the sense of them by long and ignominious patience. Instead of palliating remedies, let us use the incisive knife and the caustic, search the wound to the bottom, and work an immediate and radical cure.

The recalling of former misfortunes serves to fortify the mind against later. He must blush to sink under the anguish of one wound, who survives a body seamed over with the scars of many, and who has come victorious out of all the conflicts wherein he received them. Let sighs and tears, and fainting under the slightest stroke of adverse fortune be the portion of those unhappy people whose tender minds a long course of felicity has enervated; while such as have passed through years of calamity bear up, with a noble and immovable constancy, against the heaviest. Uninterrupted misery has this good effect,—as it continually torments, it finally hardens.

Such is the language of philosophy; and happy is the man who acquires the right of holding it. But this right is not to be acquired by pathetic discourse. Our comfort can alone give it to us; and, therefore, instead of presuming on our strength, the surest method is to confess our weakness, and, without the loss of time, to apply ourselves to the study of wisdom. This was the advice which the oracle gave to Zeno, and there is no other way of securing our tranquillity amidst all the accidents to which human life is exposed.

In order to which great end, it is necessary that we stand watchful, as sentinels, to discover the secret wiles and open attacks of the capricious goddess, Fortune, before they reach us. Where she falls upon us unexpectedly, it is hard to resist; but those who wait for her will repel her with ease. The sudden invasion of an enemy overthrows such as are not on their guard; but they who foresee war, and prepare themselves for it before it breaks out, they stand, without difficulty, the first and fiercest onset. I learned this important lesson long ago, and never trusted to Fortune even while she seemed to be at peace with me. The riches, the honors, the reputations, and all the advantages which her treacherous indulgence poured upon me, I placed so that she might snatch them away, without giving me any disturbance. I kept a great interval between me and them. She took them, but she could not tear them from me. No man suffers by bad fortune, but he who has been deceived by good. If we grow fond of her gifts, fancy that they belong to us, and

To live deprived of one's country is intolerable. Is it so? How comes it, then, to pass, that such numbers of men live out of their country by choice? Observe how the streets of London and Paris are crowded. Call over those millions by name, and ask them, one by one, of what country they are; how many will you find, who, from different parts of the earth, come to inhabit these great cities, which afford the largest opportunities, and the largest encouragement to virtue and vice. Some are drawn by ambition, and some are sent by duty; many resort thither to improve their minds, and many to improve their fortunes; others bring their beauty, and others their eloquence, to market. Remove from hence, and go to the utmost extremities of the East or West; visit the barbarous nations of Africa, or the inhospitable regions of the North; you will find no climate so bad, no country so savage, as not to have some people who come from abroad and inhabit there by choice.

Among numberless extravagances which have passed through the minds of men, we may justly reckon for one that notion of a secret affection, independent of our reason, and superior to our reason, which we are supposed to have for our country; as if there were some physical virtue in every spot of ground, which necessarily produced this effect in every one born upon it. . . .

There is nothing surely more groundless than the notion here advanced, nothing more absurd. We love the country in which we were born, because we receive particular benefits from it, and because we have particular obligations to it; which ties we may have to another country, as well as to that we are born in; to our country by election, as well as to our country by birth. In all other respects, a wise man looks on himself as a citizen of the world; and, when you ask him where his country lies, points, like Anaxagoras, with his finger to the heavens. . . .

Varro, the most learned of the Romans, thought, since nature is the same wherever we go, that this single circumstance was sufficient to remove all objections to change of place, taken by itself, and stripped of the other inconveniences which attend exile. M. Brutus thought it enough that those who go into banishment cannot be hindered from carrying their virtue along with them. Now, if any one judge that each of these comforts is in itself insufficient, he must, however, confess that both of them, joined together, are able to remove the terrors of the exile. For what trifles must all we leave behind us be esteemed, in comparison of the two most precious things which men can enjoy, and which, we are sure, will follow us wherever we turn our steps—the same nature and our proper virtue. Believe me, the Providence of God has established such an order in the world, that of all which belongs to us the least valuable parts can alone fall under the will of others. Whatever is best is safest; lies out of the reach of human power; can neither be given nor taken away. Such is this great and beautiful work of nature, the world. Such is the mind of man, which contemplates and admires the world whereof it makes the noblest part. These are inseparably ours, and as long as we remain in one we shall enjoy the other. Let us march, therefore, intrepidly wherever we are led by the force of human accidents. Wherever they lead us, on what coast soever we are thrown by them, we shall not find ourselves absolutely strangers. We shall meet with men and women, creatures of the same figure, endowed with the same faculties, and born under the same laws of nature. We shall see the same virtues and vices, flowing from the same general principles, but varied in a thousand different and contrary modes, according to that infinite variety of laws and customs which is established for the same universal end —the preservation of society. We shall feel the same revolution of the seasons, and the same sun and moon will guide the course of our year. The same azure vault, bespangled with stars, will be everywhere spread over our heads. There is no part of the world from whence we may not admire those planets which roll, like ours, in different orbits around the same central sun; from whence we may not discover an object still more stupendous, that army of fixed stars hung up in the immense space of the universe, innumerable suns whose beams enlighten and cherish the unknown worlds which roll around them; and whilst I am ravished by such contemplations as these, whilst my soul is thus raised up in heaven, it imports me little what ground I tread upon.

Change of place, then, may be borne by every man. It is the delight of many. But who can bear the evils which accompany exile? You who ask the question can bear them. Every one who considers them as they are in themselves, instead of looking at them through the false optic which prejudice holds before our eyes. For what? You have lost your estate; reduce your desires, and you will perceive yourself to be as rich as ever, with this considerable advantage to boot, that your cares will be diminished. Our natural and real wants are confined to narrow

II—35

bounds, whilst those which fancy and custom create are confined to none. Truth lies within a little and certain compass, but error is immense. If we suffer our desires, therefore, to wander beyond these bounds, they wander eternally. We become necessitous in the midst of plenty, and our poverty increases with our riches. Reduce our desires, be able to say with the apostle of Greece, to whom Erasmus was ready to address his prayers, *quam multis ipse non egeo*, banish out of your exile all imaginary, and you will suffer no real wants. The little stream which is left will suffice to quench the thirst of nature, and that which cannot be quenched by it is not your thirst but your distemper; a distemper formed by the vicious habits of your mind, and not the effects of exile. How great a part of mankind bear poverty with cheerfulness, because they have been bred in it, and are accustomed to it. Shall we not be able to acquire, by reason and by reflection, what the meanest artisan possesses by habit? Shall those who have so many advantages over him be slaves to wants and necessities of which he is ignorant? The rich, whose wanton appetites neither the produce of one country nor of one part of the world can satisfy, for whom the whole habitable globe is ransacked, for whom the caravans of the East are continually in march, and the remotest seas are covered with ships; these pampered creatures, sated with superfluity, are often glad to inhabit a humble cot, and to make a homely meal. They run for refuge into the arm of frugality. Madmen that they are, to live always in fear of what they sometimes wish for, and to fly from that life which they find it luxury to imitate. Let us cast our eyes backwards on those great men who lived in the ages of virtue, of simplicity, of frugality, and let us blush to think that we enjoy in banishment more than they were masters of in the midst of their glory, in the utmost affluence of their fortune. Let us imagine that we behold a great dictator giving audience to the Samnite ambassadors, and preparing on the hearth his mean repast with the same hand that had so often subdued the enemies of the commonwealth, and borne the triumphal laurel to the capitol. Let us remember that Plato had but three servants, and that Zeno had none. Socrates, the reformer of his country, was maintained, as Menenius Agrippa, the arbiter of his country, was buried, by contribution. While Attilius Regulus beat the Carthaginians in Africa, the flight of his plowman reduced his family to distress at home, and the tillage of his little farm

became the public care. Scipio died without leaving enough to marry his daughters, and their portions were paid out of the treasures of the State; for surely it was just that the people of Rome should once pay tribute to him who had established a perpetual tribute on Carthage. After such examples, shall we be afraid of poverty? Shall we disdain to be adopted into a family which has so many illustrious ancestors? Shall we complain of banishment for taking from us what the greatest philosophers and the greatest heroes of antiquity never enjoyed?

You will find fault, perhaps, and attribute to artifice, that I consider singly misfortunes which come altogether on the banished man, and overbear him with their united weight; you could support change of place if it was not accompanied with poverty, or poverty if it was not accompanied with the separation from your family and your friends, with the loss of your rank, consideration, and power, with contempt and ignominy. Whoever he be who reasons in this manner, let him take the following answer. The least of these circumstances is singly sufficient to render the man miserable who is not prepared for it, he who has not divested himself of that passion upon which it is directed to work. But he who has got the mastery of all his passions, who has foreseen all these accidents, and prepared his mind to endure them all, will be superior to all of them, and to all of them at once as well as singly. He will not bear the loss of his rank, because he can bear the loss of his estate; but he will bear both, because he is prepared for both; because he is free from pride as much as he is from avarice.

You are separated from your family and your friends. Take the list of them, and look it well over. How few of your family will you find who deserve the name of friends. And how few among those who are really such. Erase the names of such as ought not to stand on the roll, and the voluminous catalogue will soon dwindle into a narrow compass. Regret, if you please, your separation from this small remnant. Far be it from me, whilst I declaim against a shameful and vicious weakness of mind, to proscribe the sentiments of a virtuous friendship. Regret your separation from your friends, but regret it like a man who deserves to be theirs. This is strength, not weakness of mind; it is virtue, not vice.

But the least uneasiness under the loss of the rank which we held is ignominious. There is no valuable rank among men,

but that which real merit assigns. The princes of the earth may give names, and institute ceremonies, and exact the observation of them; their imbecility and their wickedness may prompt them to clothe fools and knaves with robes of honor, and emblems of wisdom and virtue; but no man will be in truth superior to another, without superior merit; and that rank can no more be taken from us than the merit which establishes it. The supreme authority gives a fictitious and arbitrary value to coin, which is therefore not current alike at all times and in all places; but the real value remains invariable, and the provident man, who gets rid as soon as he can of the drossy piece, hoards up the good silver. This merit will not procure the same consideration universally. But what then? the title to this consideration is the same, and will be found alike in every circumstance by those who are wise and virtuous themselves. If it is not owned by such as are otherwise, nothing is, however, taken from us; we have no reason to complain. They considered us for a rank which we had; for our denomination, not for our intrinsic value. We have that rank, that denomination no longer; and they consider us no longer; they admire in us what we admire not in ourselves. If they learn to neglect, let us learn to pity them. Their assiduity was importunate; let us not complain of the ease which this change procures us; let us rather apprehend the return of that rank and that power, which, like a sunny day, would bring back these little insects, and make them swarm once more about us. I know how apt we are, under specious pretenses, to disguise our weaknesses and our vices, and how often we succeed, not only in deceiving the world, but even in deceiving ourselves. An inclination to do good is inseparable from a virtuous mind, and, therefore, the man who cannot bear with patience the loss of that rank and power which he enjoyed may be willing to attribute his regrets to the impossibility which he supposes himself reduced to of satisfying this inclination. But let such an one know that a wise man contents himself with doing as much good as his situation allows him to do; that there is no situation wherein we may not do a great deal; and that, when we were deprived of greater powers to do more good, we escape at the same time the temptation of doing some evil.

The inconveniences which we have mentioned carry nothing along with them difficult to be borne by a wise and virtuous man; and those which remained to be mentioned, contempt and ignominy, can never fall to his lot. It is impossible that he who reverences himself should be despised by others, and how can ignominy affect the man who collects all his strength within himself, who appeals from the judgment of the multitude to another tribunal, and lives independent of mankind and the accidents of life? Cato lost the election of prætor, and that of consul; but is any one blind enough to truth to imagine that these repulses reflected any disgrace on him? The dignity of those two magistracies would have been increased by his wearing them. They suffered, not Cato. . . .

Ignominy can take no hold upon virtue; for virtue is in every condition the same, and challenges the same respect. We applaud the world when she prospers, and when she falls into adversity we still applaud her. Like the temples of the gods she is venerable even in her ruins. After this, must it not appear a degree of madness to defer one moment acquiring the only arms capable of defending us against the attacks which at every moment we are exposed to? Our being miserable, or not miserable, when we fall into misfortunes, depends on the manner in which we have enjoyed prosperity. If we have applied ourselves betimes to the study of wisdom, and to the practice of virtue, these evils become indifferent; but if we have neglected to do so they become necessary. In one case they are evils, in the other they are remedies for greater evils than themselves. Zeno rejoiced that a shipwreck had thrown him on the Athenian coast, and he owed to the loss of his fortune the acquisition which he made of virtue, of wisdom, of immortality. There are good and bad airs for the mind as well as the body. Prosperity often irritates our chronical distempers, and leaves no hopes of finding any specific but in adversity. In such cases banishment is like change of air, and the evils we suffer are like rough medicines applied to inveterate diseases. What Anacharsis said of the vine may aptly enough be said of prosperity. She bears the three grapes of drunkenness, of pleasure, and of sorrow; and happy it is if the last can cure the mischief which the former work. When afflictions fail to have their due effect, the case is desperate. They are the last remedy which indulgent Providence uses; and, if they fail, we must languish and die in misery and contempt. Vain men, how seldom do we know what to wish or to pray for. When we pray against misfortunes, and when we fear them most we want them most. It was for this reason that

will not say, like Seneca, that the noblest spectacle which God can behold is a virtuous man suffering, and struggling with afflictions; but this I will say, that the second Cato, driven out of the forum and dragged to prison, enjoyed more inward pleasure, and maintained more outward dignity, than they who insulted him, and who triumphed in the ruin of their country.

Pythagoras forbade his disciples to ask anything in particular of God. The shortest and best prayer which we can address to him, who knows our wants and our ignorance in asking, is this: Thy will be done.

PATRIOTISM

NEITHER Montaigne in writing his 'Essays,' nor Descartes in building new worlds, not Burnet in framing an antediluvian earth, no, nor Newton in discovering and establishing the true laws of nature on experiment and a sublimer geometry, felt more intellectual joys than he feels who is a real patriot, who bends all the force of his understanding, and directs all his thoughts and actions to the good of his country. When such a man forms a political scheme, and adjusts various and seemingly independent parts in it to one great and good design, he is transported by imagination, or absorbed in meditation, as much and as agreeable as they; and the satisfaction that arises from the different importance of these objects, in every step of the work, is vastly in his favor. It is here that the speculative philosopher's labor and pleasure end. But he who speculates in order to act, goes on and carries his scheme into execution. His labor continues, it varies, it increases; but so does his pleasure, too. The execution, indeed, is often traversed by unforeseen and untoward circumstances, by the perverseness and treachery of friends, and by the power and malice of enemies; but the first and last of these animate, and the docility and fidelity of some men make amends for the perverseness and treachery of others. Whilst a great event is in suspense, the action warms, and the very suspense, made up of hope and fear, maintains no unpleasing agitation in the mind. If the event is decided successfully, such a man enjoys pleasure proportionable to the good he has done—a pleasure like to that which is attributed to the Supreme Being on a survey of his works. If the event is decided otherwise, and usurping courts or overbearing parties prevail, such a man has still the testimony of his conscience, and a sense of the honor he has acquired, to soothe his mind and support his courage. For although the course of State affairs be to those who meddle in them like a lottery, yet it is a lottery wherein no good man can be a loser; he may be reviled, it is true, instead of being applauded, and may suffer violence of many kinds. I

ST. BONAVENTURA

(1221–1274)

ST. BONAVENTURA, celebrated as one of the great preachers of the Franciscan order and one of the greatest doctors of the Western church, was born in Tuscany in 1221. He studied under St. Francis and, on going to Paris, under the "Irrefragable Doctor," Alexander Hales, who said of him, "I think Adam could not have sinned in that young man." Entering the Franciscan order at twenty-three years of age, he was promoted step by step until he became Cardinal Bishop of Albano. In the Council of Lyons and thereafter he did much to effect the union of the Eastern and Western churches, attempted with some promise of permanent success at that time. He died in June 1274. The celebrity which his sermons gave him during the Middle Ages makes them interesting as examples of the style and taste of his time.

THE LIFE OF SERVICE

WE MAY notice that Jesus Christ proposed to us in the Gospel four very notable things to be received, namely: the Cross, in the chastisement of our evil natures; his Body in Sacramental Communion; the Holy Ghost in mental unction; the Penny in eternal remuneration.

The Cross is the mortification of the flesh; they that are Christ's have crucified the flesh with its affections and lusts. He takes up the Cross who accepts a penance, who enters into religion, who determines to pass through the sea of this world into the Holy Land, that is, the Land of the Living; and he receives the remission of all his sins. There are four things which urge us to take up this Cross. The first is the irrefutable example of our Lord Jesus Christ; "If any man will come after me, let him deny himself and take up his Cross." For it is a glorious thing that the servants should be configured to the likeness of their Lord. The second is invincible help; for the Lord is the helper of them that are signed with the Cross. The Psalmist says: "Thou, Lord, hast holden me and comforted me." Thou hast holden me against the evil of sin, and hast comforted me against the evil of punishment. Wherefore, when the sign of the Cross appears in a church, there also has been the anointing with oil, because there ought to be in ourselves external triumph and internal unction. Many see our Cross, but see not our unction.

The third is inviolable privilege. For the privilege of them that have taken the Cross is to be in the special guardianship of the Pope. But this is often violated; it is not so in our Cross; stay not the men on whom ye find the sign Tau. From henceforth, let no man trouble me, for I bear in my body the marks of the Lord Jesus. The fourth is a reward that cannot be lost. Many return from the Holy Land, who, by negligence and evil living, lose their reward. It is not so with those that are here signed; they that were sealed out of every people stood before the throne. On this Cross, O Christian soul, thou must hang without intermission, as Christ did, who would not be taken down from the Cross while he lived. So neither must thou be from thy life of penitence or of religion. Let us listen to no one, brethren, neither to man nor to spirit, who would persuade us to come down from the Cross; let us persist in remaining on the Cross, let us die on the Cross, let us be taken down by the hands of others and not by our own, after his example who said on the Cross, "It is finished." So do thou also remain to the end on the Cross, and thus at the termination of thy life, when thou art about to give up the ghost, thou mayest say: "It is finished; I have kept the rule which I vowed, obedience, penitence, the commandments of God, I have kept them all, I have fought a good fight, I have finished my course."

Of the second: Take, eat, this is my body. But in what manner we are to receive the body of Jesus, we read: and when Joseph had received the body, he wrapped it in a clean linen cloth. Thou must, therefore, receive from the altar the body of Jesus with the same fervor and devotion with which Joseph received it from the Cross. The altar, by its four corners, sets forth the Cross. Thus do thou wrap our Lord's body in clean linen. "He wraps Jesus in clean linen, who receives him with a pure mind." Now purity is well set forth by linen, which is in its nature most white, and thereby sets forth how pure we should be in our souls. It is written: "Her Nazarites were purer than snow, they were whiter than milk." Purity of heart is the milk, by which God and the angels are delighted. A fly or dust shows itself at once in milk; so in a pure conscience, any, the smallest stain, cannot be hid. And, as a fly is quickly cast forth by any

one who is drinking milk, so the busy fly of impure thought is cast out from a pure conscience. Much it displeases the devil, much it pleases God and the angels, when you eject the fly of the devil from the milk of the heart. "It is the part of demons to inject evil thoughts; it is our part not to consent to them." For, as often as we resist, we conquer the devil, we glorify the angels, we honor God; it is impossible to say how great is the joy of the angels when one heart is converted to God; so on the other hand, neither can we express the grief with which demons are then afflicted, they, who are ever lying in ambush to deprive us of our salvation.

Of the third it is thus written: Receive the Holy Ghost. The Holy Ghost is here given to the Disciples when the doors were shut, as the oil was multiplied in the vessels borrowed from the neighbors when the doors were also shut. Note the history. The oil is the grace of the Holy Ghost. In the Psalm it is said: "God, even thy God, hath anointed thee with the oil of gladness." Vessels which are lifted by the hand are the virtue and examples for which we look in the saints who now dwell in this world, and which we collect into the house of our soul, as if we borrowed vessels from our neighbors; but those vessels are empty, so far as we are concerned, if we imitate not those examples of the saints by the grace of the Holy Ghost. Whereas, on the other hand, the virgins that were wise took oil in their lamps, as it is written. "The doors of our senses are sight, taste, hearing, touch, smell, and thy mouth is the gate." Unless these doors be cleansed against unlawful thoughts, the oil of grace will not be multiplied in the house of thy soul. Enter into the closet of thy mind and shut the door on all things except the Lord, and that which assists in seeking him.

Of the fourth: They likewise received every man a penny. The penny is eternal life, which is not given save to those who labor in the vineyard, that is in penitence or religion; in which vineyard we must not only labor, but also triumph over that lion the devil, which is prefigured in Samson; then Samson came to the vineyard of Timnath, and behold a young lion roared against him. That lion he conquered, and afterwards found honey in his mouth. Honey is the sweetness of the consolation of the Holy Ghost. "My spirit is sweeter than honey." You see then that the honey of grace is not given save to them that fight, nor is the penny of glory bestowed save on them who labor in the vineyard.

JACQUES BÉNIGNE BOSSUET

(1627-1704)

AMONG the funeral orations of Bossuet, who is sometimes ranked with Mirabeau at the head of the list of French orators, two are most admired — that over the great Prince of Condé, and that which he delivered on the death of Henrietta of England. "As the orator advances," says one of his critics, speaking of the former oration, "he gathers strength by the force of his movements; his thoughts bound and leap like the quick, impetuous sallies of the warrior whom he describes; his language glows and sparkles, rushes and rejoices like a free and bounding river, sweeping in beauty through the open champaign, gathering volume and strength from tributary streams, glancing through green meadows and dark woodlands, rushing through forests and mountains, and finally plunging with resistless force and majesty into the open sea."

It does not seem that oratory worthy to inspire so magnificent an eulogy as this could have higher merits than those thus marshalled and brought to climax. But the compliment, high as it is, fails to do justice to that which is greatest in Bossuet — to that which can follow him into every language into which he is translated, and so make him a model for the writers as well as for the speakers of every country. This supreme merit is his delicacy. "All great art is delicate art," writes John Ruskin, and Bossuet illustrates the meaning of this profound law of effectiveness in saying of the Prince of Condé: "When a favor was asked of him, it was he that appeared obliged." It is easy enough for one who has mastered the first secrets of language to imitate the Ciceronian array of clauses in which one phalanx of words after another moves forward to complete an already assured conquest. It is not wholly impossible even for one who is not great to attain something of the style by virtue of which Taine commands words with the same perfect mastery of rank on rank, corps on corps, which Napoleon showed in the handling of men. And this is art. But it is not the greatest art. We may be awed by the storm into fear and contempt of self; but after the hurricane is stilled, after the clouds have passed, after the night has grown silent — it is then that the sublimity of the stars can appeal to us to recognize in ourselves our kinship with all that is best and highest in the universe. And it is to this highest quality in us that Bossuet

appeals with the wonderful delicacy of genius in saying of Condé: "When a favor was asked of him, it was *he* that appeared obliged." We feel at once that if this had not been true, it could not have been imagined as possible, and that it could have been possible only in a life of the highest order.

It is remarkable that France should have had as contemporaries three such orators as Bossuet, Fénelon, and Bourdaloue. It has been said in comparing them that Bourdaloue spoke to the understanding, Bossuet to the imagination, and Fénelon to the heart. If this were true, it would give the palm of highest effectiveness to Fénelon who, indeed, is still known to thousands of actual readers where Bossuet is known to hundreds. But to Bossuet the palm of art would remain, for it was only Bossuet who could have said of such a man as Condé, so as to make us think it of Condé himself and yet recognize the propriety of not having so sublime a compliment paid directly to any man, that his glory followed him everywhere, and that when all alone, he appeared as great and as worthy of respect as when he gave the word of command to vast armies.

Bossuet was born at Dijon, September 27th, 1627, of a respectable family of bourgeois rank. He was educated from his earliest years for the Church. He learned the art of expression from its greatest master, Homer, for whose poems and those of Virgil he developed a fondness in youth which he never lost. His love for Homer was exceeded only by that which made him so great a student of the Bible that Lamartine says he had it "transfused into him." A man of many books, it was to these three that he reverted always, and they made him great, as they have made so many others. It is strange that men as diverse as Bossuet and Samuel Houston, the one speaking in full canonicals to French nobles and court beauties; the other, in his hunting shirt, haranguing American frontiersmen, should have been governed by the same taste in literature, and should have been formed so largely on the same models.

Bossuet began to be celebrated as soon as he began to preach. In his thirty-fifth year he appeared before Louis XIV., who immediately after the close of the sermon sent a messenger to congratulate the elder Bossuet "on having such a son." He became tutor to the Dauphin, and wrote for his use the 'Discourse on Universal History' and several other works of minor importance. His 'Exposition of Catholic Doctrine' was published about 1671, and his 'Defense of the Doctrine of the Clergy of France' was written some ten years later, though not published until 1735. His celebrated controversy with Fénelon is thought by some even of his admirers to have added less to his credit than to that of his great rival. He died at Paris, April 12th, 1704.   W. V. B.

FUNERAL ORATION OVER THE PRINCE OF CONDÉ

(Delivered before Louis XIV.)

AT THE moment that I open my lips to celebrate the undying glory of Louis Bourbon, Prince of Condé, I find myself equally overwhelmed by the greatness of the subject, and, if permitted to avow it, by the uselessness of the task. What part of the habitable world has not heard of the victories of the Prince of Condé, and the wonders of his life? Everywhere they are rehearsed. The Frenchman, in extolling them, can give no information to the stranger. And although I may remind you of them to-day, yet, always anticipated by your thoughts, I shall have to suffer your secret reproach for falling so far below them. We feeble orators can add nothing to the glory of extraordinary souls. Well has the sage remarked that their actions alone praise them; all other praise languishes by the side of their great names. The simplicity of a faithful narrative alone can sustain the glory of the Prince of Condé. But expecting that history, which owes such a narrative to future ages, will make this appear, we must satisfy, as we can, the gratitude of the public, and the commands of the greatest of kings. What does the empire not owe to a prince who has honored the house of France, the whole French name, and, so to speak, mankind at large! Louis the Great himself has entered into these sentiments. After having mourned that great man, and given by his tears, in the presence of his whole court, the most glorious eulogy which he could receive, he gathers together in this illustrious temple whatever is most august in his kingdom, to render public acknowledgments to the memory of the Prince; and he desires that my feeble voice should animate all these mournful signs—all this funeral array. Let us then subdue our grief and make the effort.

But here a greater object, and one more worthy of the pulpit, presents itself to my thoughts. God it is who makes warriors and conquerors. "Thou," said David, "hast taught my hands to war, and my fingers to fight." If he inspires courage he gives no less other great qualities, natural and supernatural, both of the mind and heart. Everything comes from his powerful hand, from heaven he sends all generous sentiments, wise counsels, and good thoughts. But he would have us to distinguish between the

gifts which he abandons to his enemies and those which he reserves for his servants. What distinguishes his friends from all others is piety; until that gift of heaven is received, all others are not only useless, but aid the ruin of those whom they adorn. Without this inestimable gift of piety, what were the Prince of Condé, with all his great heart and lofty genius? No, my brethren, if piety had not consecrated his other virtues, neither these princes would have found any solace for their grief, nor that venerable prelate any confidence in his prayers, nor myself any support for the praises which are due to so great a man. Under the influence of such an example, let us lose sight of all human glory! Destroy the idol of the ambitious! Let it fall prostrate before these altars! On this occasion, group together—for we can do it with propriety—the highest qualities of an excellent nature, and to the glory of truth exhibit in a prince universally admired whatever constitutes the hero and carries the glory of the world to the loftiest eminence, valor, magnanimity, and natural goodness—qualities of the heart; vivacity and penetration, grandeur of thought, and sublimity of genius—qualities of the intellect; all would be nothing but an illusion, if piety were not added—piety, which indeed is the whole of man! This it is, messieurs, which you see in the life, eternally memorable, of the high and illustrious Prince Louis Bourbon, Prince of Condé, Prince of the blood!

God has revealed to us that he alone makes conquerors, that he alone causes them to subserve his designs. Who made Cyrus but God, who, in the prophecies of Isaiah, named him two hundred years before his birth? "Thou hast not known me," said he to him, "but I have even called thee by thy name, and surnamed thee. I will go before thee and make the crooked places straight; I will break in pieces the gates of brass, and cut in sunder the bars of iron. I am the Lord, and there is none else, there is no God beside me. I form the light and create darkness"; as if he had said, "I the Lord do everything, and from eternity know everything that I do." Who could have formed an Alexander but the same God who made him visible from afar to the prophet Daniel, and revealed by such vivid images his unconquerable ardor? "See," said he, "that conqueror, with what rapidity he advances from the west, as it were by bounds and without touching the earth." Resembling, in his bold movements and rapid march, certain vigorous and bounding animals, he advances, only by quick and impetuous attacks, and is arrested

neither by mountains nor precipices. Already the King of Persia falls into his power. At sight of him, he is "moved with anger—rushes upon him, stamps him under his feet; none can defend him from his attacks, or deliver him out of his hand." Listening only to these words of Daniel, whom do you expect to see under that image—Alexander or the Prince of Condé? God had given him that indomitable valor for the salvation of France during the minority of a king of four years. But let that king, cherished of heaven, advance in life, everything will yield to his exploits. Equally superior to his friends and his enemies, he will hasten now to employ, now to surpass his most distinguished generals; and under the hand of God, who will ever befriend him, he will be acknowledged the firm bulwark of his kingdom. But God had chosen the Duke d'Enghien to defend him in his childhood. Thus, during the first years of his reign, the duke conceived a design which the most experienced veterans could not achieve; but victory justified it before Rocroy! True, the hostile army is the stronger. It is composed of those old bands of Valonnaise, Italians, and Spaniards, which never till then were broken. But how much could be counted on the courage which inspired our troops, the pressing necessity of the State, past advantages, and a prince of the blood who carried victory in his eyes! Don Francisco de Mellos steadily waits his approach; and, without the possibility of retreating, the two generals and their armies had chosen to shut themselves in by woods and marshes, in order to decide their quarrels like two warriors, in close combat. Then, what was seen? The young Prince appeared another man! Moved by so great an object, his mighty soul revealed itself entire; his courage increased with his peril, his sagacity with his ardor. During the night, which must be spent in presence of the enemy, like a vigilant general, he was the last to retire; yet never did he repose more peacefully. In the prospect of so great a day, and his first battle, he is tranquil; so much is he in his element; for well is it known that on the morrow, at the appointed time, he must awake from his profound slumber—another Alexander! See him, as he flies, either to victory or to death. As soon as he has conveyed from rank to rank the ardor which animates himself, he is seen, almost at the same time, attacking the right wing of the enemy; sustaining ours about to give way; now rallying the half-subdued Frenchman, now putting to flight the victorious Spaniard; carrying

terror everywhere, and confounding with his lightning glance those who had escaped his blows. But that formidable infantry of the Spanish army, whose heavy and wedged battalions, resembling so many towers,—towers which had succeeded in repairing their breaches,—remained immovable in the midst of all others in disorder, and from all sides kept up a steady fire. Thrice the young conqueror attempted to break these intrepid warriors; thrice was he repulsed by the valorous Count de Fontaine, who was borne in his carriage, and, notwithstanding his infirmities, proved that the warrior spirit is master of the body which it animates. In vain does Bek, with his fresh cavalry, endeavor to rush through the wood to fall on our exhausted soldiers; the Prince has prevented him; the routed battalions demand quarter; but victory is more disastrous to the Duke d'Enghien than conflict itself. As he advances with an assured air to receive the parole of those brave men, they, ever on their guard, are seized with the fear of being surprised by a new attack; their terrible discharge renders our army furious; nothing is seen but carnage; blood maddens the soldier; until that great Prince, who could not slaughter those lions like timid sheep, calmed their excited courage, and joined to the pleasure of conquering that of pardoning his enemies. What then was the astonishment of those veteran troops and their brave officers when they saw that there was no safety but in the arms of the conqueror! With what wonder did they look upon that young Prince, whose victory had enhanced his lofty bearing, and whose clemency added to it a new charm! Ah, how willingly would he have saved the brave Duke de Fontaine! But he was found prostrate among thousands of the dead, of whom Spain yet feels the loss. She knew not that the Prince who had destroyed so many of her veteran regiments on the field of Rocroy would complete their subjugation on the plains of Lens. Thus the first victory was the pledge of many more. The Prince bends the knee, and on the battlefield renders back to the God of armies the glory which he had conferred. There they celebrated Rocroy delivered, the threatenings of a formidable army turned to shame, the regency established, France in repose, and a reign, destined to such prosperity, begun by an omen so happy. The army commenced the thanksgiving: all France followed. The first achievement of the Duke d'Enghien was extolled to the skies. Such an event was enough to render illustrious any other life; but in his case, it was but the first step in his career.

From that first campaign, after the taking of Thionville, noble fruit of the victory at Rocroy, he passed for a general equally invincible in sieges and battles. But observe in this young Prince what is not less beautiful than victory. The court, which had prepared for him the applause which he merited, was astonished at the manner in which he received it. The queen-regent testified to him that the king was satisfied with his services. In the mouth of the sovereign, that was a recompense worthy of his toils. But if others ventured to praise him, he rejected their praises as offensive. Intractable to flattery, he dreaded its very appearance. Such was the delicacy, or rather such was the good sense of the Prince. His maxim was — and you will please to notice it, for it is the maxim which makes great men — that in great actions our only care ought to be to perform well our part, and let glory follow virtue. This he inspired in others, this he *followed* himself, so that he was never tempted by false glory; everything in him tended to the true and the great. Whence it followed that he placed his glory in the service of the king and the prosperity of the State. This was the fundamental principle of his life — this engrossed his last and most cherished feelings. The court could scarcely hold him, though he was the object of its admiration. He must show himself everywhere, to Germany as to Flanders, the intrepid defender given us by God. Here direct your special attention. A contest awaits the Prince more formidable than Rocroy: to prove his virtue, war is about to exhaust all its inventions, all its efforts. What object presents itself to my eyes? Not only men to combat, but inaccessible mountains, ravines, and precipices on one side; on the other an impenetrable wood, the bottom of which is a marsh; behind, streams and prodigious intrenchments; everywhere lofty forts, and leveled forests traversed by frightful roads; in the midst Merci with his brave Bavarians, flushed with such distinguished success, and the taking of Fribourg; — Merci, whom the Prince of Condé and the vigilant Turenne had never surprised in an irregular movement, and to whom they rendered the distinguished testimony that he never lost a favorable opportunity, and never failed to foresee their plans, as if he had assisted at their councils. Here, during eight days, and in four different attacks, was seen all that could be endured and undertaken in war. Our troops seemed disheartened as much by the resistance of the enemy as by the frightful disposition of the ground; and the

11—36

Prince at times saw himself almost abandoned. But like another Maccabeus, "his own arm never failed him"; and his courage, excited by so many perils, "brought him succor." No sooner was he seen the first to force those inaccessible heights, than his ardor drew all others after him. Merci sees his destruction certain: his best regiments are defeated; the night saves the remains of his army. But what excessive rains also come to the enemy's aid, so that we have at once not only courage and art, but all nature to contend with; what advantage of this is taken by a bold and dexterous enemy, and in what frightful mountain does he anew intrench himself! But, beaten on all sides, he must leave, as booty to the Duke d'Enghien, not only his cannon and baggage, but also all the regions bordering on the Rhine. See how the whole gives way. In ten days Philisbourg is reduced, notwithstanding the approach of winter, Philisbourg, which so long held the Rhine captive under our laws, and whose loss the most illustrious of kings has so gloriously repaired. Worms, Spire, Mayence, Landau, and twenty other places of note open their gates. Merci can not defend them, and no longer appears before his conqueror. But this is not enough; he must fall at his feet, a victim worthy of his valor: Nordlingen shall see his fall; — then shall it be decided that their enemies cannot stand before the French, either in Germany or Flanders; and there shall it be seen, that to the Prince all these advantages are due. God, the Protector of France and of a king, whom he has destined for his mighty works, ordains it thus.

By such arrangements, everything appeared safe under the conduct of the Duke d'Enghien; and without wishing to spend the day in recounting his other exploits, you know that among so many places attacked not one escaped his hands; and thus the glory of the Prince continued to rise. Europe, which admired the noble ardor by which he was animated in his battles, was astonished to perceive that he had perfect self-control; and that at the age of twenty-six years, he was as capable of managing his troops as of urging them into perils; of yielding to fortune as of causing it to subserve his designs. In all situations he appears to us one of those extraordinary men who force all obstacles. The promptitude of his action leaves no time for its contravention. Such is the character of conquerors. When David, himself a great warrior, deplored the death of two captains, he gave them this eulogy: "They were swifter than eagles, they

were stronger than lions." Such is the very image of the Prince whom we deplore. Like lightning, he appeared at the same time in different and distant places. He was seen in all attacks, in all quarters. When occupied on one side, he sends to reconnoitre the other; the active officer who conveys his orders is anticipated, and finds all reanimated by the presence of the Prince. He seems to multiply himself in action; neither fire nor steel arrests his progress. No need has he to arm his head exposed to so many perils; God is his assured armor; blows lose their force as they reach him, and leave behind only the tokens of his courage and of the protection of heaven. Tell him not that the life of the first prince of the blood, so necessary to the State, ought to be spared; he answers that such a prince, more interested by his birth in the glory of the king and crown, ought, in the extremity of the State, more readily than all others to devote himself to its recovery. After having made his enemies, during so many years, feel the invincible power of the king, were it asked, What did he do to sustain it at home? I would answer, in a word, he made the regent respected. And since it is proper for me once for all to speak of those things respecting which I desire to be forever silent, it may be stated that up to the time of that unfortunate imprisonment, he had never dreamed that it was possible for him to attempt anything against the State; and to his honor be it said, if he desired to secure a recompense, he desired still more to merit it. It was this which caused him to say — and here I can confidently repeat his words, which I received from his own lips, and which so strikingly indicate his true disposition — that "he had entered that prison the most innocent of men, and that he had issued from it the most culpable. Alas!" said he, "I lived only for the service of the king, and the honor of the State." Words which indicate a sincere regret for having been carried so far by his misfortunes. But without excusing what he himself so strongly condemned, let us say, so that it may never again be mentioned, that as in celestial glory the faults of holy penitents, covered by what they have done to repair them, and the infinite compassion of God, never more appear, so in the faults so sincerely acknowledged, and in the end so gloriously repaired by faithful services, nothing ought to be remembered but the penitence of the Prince, and the clemency of his sovereign who has forgotten them.

However much he was involved in those unfortunate wars, he has at least this glory, never to have permitted the grandeur of his house to be tarnished among strangers. Notwithstanding the majesty of the empire, the pride of Austria, and the hereditary crowns attached to that house, particularly in the branch which reigns in Germany, even when a refugee at Namur, and sustained only by his courage and reputation, he urged the claims of a Prince of France and of the first family in the world so far that all that could be obtained from him was his consent to treat upon equality with the archduke, through a brother of the emperor, and the descendant of so many emperors, on condition that the prince in the third degree should wear the honors of the "Low Countries." The same treatment was secured to the Duke d'Enghien; and the house of France maintained its rank over that of Austria even in Brussels. But mark what constitutes true courage. While the Prince bore himself so loftily with the archduke who governed, he rendered to the King of England and the Duke of York, now so great a monarch, but then unfortunate, all the honors which were their due; and finally he taught Spain, too disdainful, what that majesty was which misfortune could not tear from princes. The rest of his conduct was not less distinguished. Amid the difficulties which his interests introduced into the treaty of the Pyrenees, hear what were his orders, and see whether any one ever acted so nobly, with reference to his own interests. He wrote to his agents in the conference, that it was not right that the peace of Christendom should be postponed for his sake; that they might take care of his friends, but must leave him to his fate. Ah, what a noble victim thus sacrificed himself for the public good! But when things changed, and Spain was willing to give him either Cambray and its environs, or Luxembourg in full sovereignty, he declared that to these advantages, and all others, however great, which they could give him, he preferred — what? His duty and the good-will of the king! This formed the ruling passion of his heart. This he was incessantly repeating to the Duke d'Enghien, his son. Thus did he appear himself! France beheld him, in these last traits, returning to her bosom with a character ennobled by suffering, and more than ever devoted to his king and country. But in those first wars he had but one life to offer; now he has another which is dearer to him than his own. After having, under his father's example, nobly finished his studies, the Duke d'Enghien is ready to follow him to the battlefield. Not content with teaching him the art of war by his instructions, he conducts him to living lessons and actual practice. Leave we the passage of the Rhine, the wonder of our age, and the life of Louis the Great. In the field of Senef, although he commanded, as he had already done in other campaigns, he learned war by the side of his father, in the most terrible conflicts. In the midst of so many perils, he sees the Prince thrown down in a trench, under a horse covered with blood. While offering him his own and raising him from the trench, he is wounded in the arms of his affectionate father, but without discontinuing his kind offices, delighted with the opportunity of satisfying at once his filial piety and love of glory. How could the Prince fail to think that nothing was wanting to that noble son but opportunities, to achieve the greatest things. Moreover his tenderness increased with his esteem.

But not only for his son and his family did he cherish such tender sentiments. I have seen him (and do not imagine that I exaggerate here) deeply moved with the perils of his friends; I have seen him, simple and natural, change color at the recital of their misfortunes, entering into their minutest as well as most important affairs, reconciling contending parties, and calming angry spirits with a patience and gentleness which could never have been expected from a temper so sensitive, and a rank so high. Far from us be heroes without humanity! As in the case of all extraordinary things, they might force our respect and seduce our admiration, but they could never win our love. When God formed the heart of man he planted goodness there, as the proper characteristic of the Divine nature, and the mark of that beneficent hand from which we sprang. Goodness, then, ought to be the principal element of our character, and the great means of attracting the affection of others. Greatness, which supervenes upon this, so far from diminishing goodness, ought only to enable it, like a public fountain, to diffuse itself more extensively. This is the price of hearts! For the great whose goodness is not diffusive, as a just punishment of their haughty indifference, remain forever deprived of the greatest good of life, the fellowship of kindred souls. Never did man enjoy this more than the Prince of whom we are speaking. Never did one less fear that familiarity would diminish respect. Is this the man that stormed cities and gained battles? Have I forgotten

the high rank he knew so well to defend. Let us acknowledge the hero, who, always equal to himself, without rising to appear great, or descending to be civil and kind, naturally appeared everything that he ought to be toward all men, like a majestic and beneficent river, which peacefully conveys from city to city the abundance which it has spread through the countries it waters; which flows for the benefit of all, and rises and swells only when some violent opposition is made to the gentle current which bears it on its tranquil course. Such was the gentleness and such the energy of the Prince of Condé. Have you an important secret? Confide it freely to that noble heart; your affair becomes his by that confidence. Nothing was more inviolable to that Prince than the rights of friendship. When a favor was asked of him, it was he that appeared obliged; and never was his joy so natural or lively as when he conferred pleasure upon others. The first money which, by the permission of the king, he received from Spain, notwithstanding the necessities of his exhausted house, was given to his friends, although he had nothing to hope from their friendship after the peace. Four hundred thousand crowns, distributed by his orders — rare instance of generosity — showed that gratitude was as powerful in the Prince of Condé as selfishness is in most men. With him virtue was ever its own reward. He praised it even in his enemies. Whenever he had occasion to speak of his actions, and even in the communications which he sent to the court, he extolled the wise counsels of one and the courage of another; the merits of none were overlooked; and in his anxiety to do others justice he never seemed to find a place for what he had done himself. Without envy, without disguise or pretension; equally great in action and in repose, he appeared at Chantilly as he did at the head of his troops. Whether he embellished that magnificent and charming home, whether he planted his camp, or fortified a place in the midst of a hostile country — whether he marched with an army amid perils, or conducted his friends through superb alleys to the noise of falling fountains silent neither by day nor night, he was always the same man; his glory followed him everywhere. How delightful, after the contest and tumult of arms, to be able to relish those peaceful virtues and that tranquil glory which none can share with the soldier more than with fortune; where one can pursue the great end of life without being stunned with the noise of trumpets, the roar of cannons, or the cries of the

wounded; and when all alone, man appears as great, and as worthy of respect as when he gives the word of command, and whole armies do his bidding.

Let us now look at the qualities of his intellect; and since, alas! that which is most fatal to human life, namely, the military art, admits of the greatest genius and talent, let us in the first place consider the great genius of the Prince with reference to that department. And in the first place what general ever displayed such far-reaching foresight? One of his maxims was, that we ought to fear enemies at a distance, in order not to fear them near at hand — nay more, to rejoice in their approach. See, as he considers all the advantages which he can give or take, with what rapidity he comprehends times, places, persons, and not only their interests and talents, but even their humors and caprices! See how he estimates the cavalry and infantry of his enemies, by the nature of the country, or the resources of the confederated princes! Nothing escapes his penetration. With what prodigious comprehension of the entire details and general plan of the war, he is ever awake to the occurrence of the slightest incident; drawing from a deserter, a prisoner, a passer-by, what he wishes him to say or to conceal, what he knows, and, so to speak, what he does not know, so certain is he in his conclusions. His patrols repeat to him the slightest things: he is ever on the watch, for he holds it as a maxim, that an able general may be vanquished, but ought never to suffer himself to be surprised. And it is due to him to say that this never occurred in his case. At whatever, or from whatever quarter his enemies come, they find him on his guard, always ready to fall upon them and take advantage of their position; like an eagle, which, whether soaring in mid air, or perched upon the summit of some lofty rock, sweeps the landscape with his piercing eyes, and falls so surely upon his prey, that it can neither escape his talons nor his lightning glance. So keen his perception, so quick and impetuous his attack, so strong and irresistible the hands of the Prince of Condé. In his camp vain terrors, which fatigue and discourage more than real ones, are unknown. All strength remains entire for true perils; all is ready at the first signal, and, as saith the prophet, "All arrows are sharpened, all bows bent." While waiting, he enjoys as sound repose as he would under his own roof. Repose, did I say? At Pieton, in the presence of that formidable army which three united powers had assembled, our

troops indulged in constant amusements, the whole army was rejoicing, and never for a moment felt that it was weaker than the enemy. The Prince, by the disposition of his army, had put in safety, not only our whole frontier and all our stations, but also our soldiers; he watches — that is enough! At last the enemy moves off — precisely what the Prince expected. At their first movement he starts; the army of Holland, with its proud standards, is already in his power — blood flows everywhere — the whole becomes his prey. But God knows how to limit the best formed plans. The enemy is everywhere scattered. Oudenarde is delivered out of their hands; but they themselves are saved out of those of the Prince by a dense cloud, which covers the heavens; terror and desertion enter the troops; none can tell what has become of that formidable army. Then it was that Louis, after having accomplished the rude siege of Besançon, and once more reduced Franche Comté, with unparalleled rapidity, returned, irradiated with glory, to profit by the action of his armies in Flanders and Germany, and commanded the army which performed such prodigies in Alsace; thus appearing the greatest of heroes, as much by his personal exploits as by those of his generals.

While a happy disposition imparted such noble traits to our Prince, he never ceased to enrich it by reflection. The campaigns of Cæsar formed the subject of his study. Well do I recollect how much he interested us by indicating, with all the precision of a catalogue, the place where that celebrated general, by the advantageous nature of his positions, compelled five Roman legions and two experienced leaders to lay down their arms without a struggle. He himself had explored the rivers and mountains, which aided in the accomplishment of that grand result; and never before had so accomplished a teacher explained the 'Commentaries' of Cæsar. The generals of a future age will render him the same homage. They will be seen studying in the places where it took place, what history will relate of the encampment of Pieton, and the wonders that followed. They will notice, in that of Chatenoy, the eminence occupied by that great captain, and the stream where he covered himself from the cannon of the intrenchments of Selestad. Then will they see him putting Germany to shame — now pursuing his enemies, though stronger; now counteracting their schemes, and now causing them to raise the siege of Saverne, as he had that of Haguenau a little while before. It was by strokes like these, of which his life is full, that he carried his fame to such a height that, in the present day, it is one of the highest honors to have served in the army of the Prince of Condé, and even a title to command to have seen him perform that duty.

But if ever he appeared great, and by his wondrous self-possession, superior to all exigencies, it was in these critical moments upon which victory turns, and in the deepest ardor of battle. In all other circumstances he deliberates — docile, he lends an ear to the counsels of all; but here everything is presented to him at once; the multiplicity of objects confounds him not; in an instant his part is taken; he commands, he acts together; everything is made to subserve his purpose. Shall I add, (for why fear the reputation of so great a man should be diminished by the acknowledgment?) that he was distinguished not only by his quick sallies which he knew so promptly and agreeably to repair, but that he sometimes appeared, on ordinary occasions, as if he had in him another nature, to which his great soul abandoned minor details, in which he himself deigned not to mingle. In the fire, the shock, the confusion of battle, all at once sprung up in him — I know not what firmness and clearness, what ardor and grace — so attractive to his friends, so terrible to his enemies — a combination of qualities and contrasts, at once singular and striking. In that terrible engagement, when before the gates of the city, and in the sight of the citizens, heaven seemed to decide the fate of the Prince; when he had against him choice troops and a powerful general — when, more than once he saw himself exposed to the caprices of fortune — when, in a word, he was attacked on every side, those who were fighting near him have told us that if they had an affair of importance to transact with him, they would have chosen for it that very moment when the fires of battle were raging around him; so much did his spirit appear elevated above them, and, as it were, inspired in such terrible encounters; like those lofty mountains, whose summits, rising above clouds and storms, find their serenity in their elevation, and lose not a single ray of the light by which they are enveloped. Thus on the plains of Lens, name agreeable to France! the Archduke, drawn contrary to his design from an advantageous position, through the influence of a false success, is forced, by a sudden movement of the Prince, who opposes fresh troops to those already exhausted, to take flight. His veteran troops perish; his

disports itself in the universe, would show us under what perfect forms, and with what excellent qualities he can endow men. What encampments and what marches! what hazards and precautions! what perils and resources! Were ever in two men seen the same virtues with such diverse not to say contrary characteristics! The one seemed to act from profound reflection; the other from sudden illumination; the latter consequently was more ardent, though by no means precipitate, while the former, with an appearance of greater coolness, never exhibited anything like languor — ever more ready to act than to speak, resolute and determined within, even when he seemed hesitating and cautious without. The one, as soon as he appeared in the army, gave a high idea of his valor, and caused an expectation of something extraordinary; nevertheless he advanced systematically, and by degrees reached the prodigies which crowned his life; the other, like a man inspired, from his first battle equaled the most consummate masters. The one by his rapid and constant efforts won the admiration of the world, and silenced all envy; the other, at the very first, reflected such a vivid light that none dared to attack him. The one, in fine, by the depth of his genius and the incredible resources of his courage, rose superior to the greatest dangers, and profited even by the infelicities of fortune; the other, at once by the advantages of his elevated birth, and the lofty thoughts by which he was inspired from heaven, and especially by an admirable instinct of which men know not the secret, seemed born to draw fortune into his plans, and to force destiny itself. And as in their life, those great men were seen distinguished by diverse characteristics, so the one, cut down by a sudden blow, like a Judas Macabeus, dies for his country; the army mourns him as a father; the court and country are covered with tears; his piety is praised with his courage, and his memory fades not with time; the other, raised, like a David, by his arms to the summit of glory, like him also dies in his bed, celebrating the praises of God and giving instructions to his family, and thus leaves all hearts filled as much with the splendor of his life as the serenity of his death. What a privilege to see and to study these great men, and learn from each the esteem which the other merits. This has been the spectacle of our age; but what is greater still, we have seen a king making use of these great generals, and enjoying the succor of heaven; and being deprived of the one by death, and of the other by his

cannon, which he relied on, falls into our hands; and Bek, who had flattered himself with certain victory, taken and wounded in the battle, renders, by his dying despair, a mournful homage to his conqueror. Is it necessary to relieve or besiege a city? The Prince knows how to profit by every opportunity. Thus, being suddenly informed of an important siege, he passes, at once, by a rapid march, to the place, and discovers a safe passage through which to give relief, at a spot not sufficiently fortified by the enemy. Does he lay siege to a place? Each day he invents some new means of advancing its conquest. Some have thought that he exposed his troops; but he protected them by abridging the time of peril through the vigor of his attacks. Amid so many surprising blows the most courageous governors cannot make good their promises to their generals. Dunkirk is taken in thirteen days amid the rains of autumn; and those ships, so renowned among our allies, all at once appear upon the ocean with our flags.

But what a wise general ought especially to know, is his soldiers and officers. For thence comes that perfect concert which enables armies to act as one body, or to use the language of Scripture, "as one man." But how as one man? Because under one chief, that knows both soldiers and officers, as if they were his arms and hands, all is equally animated, all is equally moved. This it is which secures victory; for I have heard our great Prince say that, in the battle of Nordlingen, what gained success was his knowledge of M. de Turenne, whose consummate genius needed no order to perform whatever was necessary. The latter, on his side, declared that he acted without anxiety, because he knew the Prince, and his directions which were always safe. Thus they imparted to each other a mutual confidence which enabled them to apply themselves wholly to their respective parts; and thus happily ended the most hazardous and keenly contested battle that was ever fought.

That was a noble spectacle in our day to behold, at the same time, and in the same campaign, these two men, whom the common voice of all Europe equaled to the greatest generals of past ages — now at the head of separate troops, now united, yet more by the concurrence of the same thoughts, than by the orders which the inferior received from the other; now opposed front to front, and redoubling the one in the other activity and vigilance; — as if the Deity, whose wisdom, according to the Scriptures,

maladies, conceiving the greatest plans, and performing the noblest deeds, rising above himself, surpassing the hopes of his friends and the expectations of the world; so lofty is his courage, so vast his intelligence, so glorious his destiny.

Such, messieurs, are the spectacles which God gives to the world, and the men whom he sends into it, to illustrate, now in one nation, now in another, according to his eternal counsels, his power and his wisdom. For, do his Divine attributes discover themselves more clearly in the heavens which his fingers have formed, than in the rare talents which he has distributed, as it pleases him, to extraordinary men? What star shines more brilliantly in the firmament than the Prince de Condé has done in Europe? Not war alone gave him renown; but his resplendent genius which embraced everything, ancient as well as modern, history, philosophy, theology the most sublime, the arts and the sciences. None possessed a book which he had not read; no man of excellence existed, with whom he had not, in some speculation or in some work, conversed; all left him instructed by his penetrating questions or judicious reflections. His conversation, too, had a charm, because he knew how to speak to every one according to his talents; not merely to warriors on their enterprises, to courtiers on their interests, to politicans on their negotiations, but even to curious travelers on their discoveries in nature, government, or commerce; to the artisan on his inventions, and in fine to the learned of all sorts, on their productions. That gifts like these come from God, who can doubt? That they are worthy of admiration, who does not see? But to confound the human spirit which prides itself upon these gifts, God hesitates not to confer them upon his enemies. St. Augustine considers among the heathen, so many sages, so many conquerors, so many grave legislators, so many excellent citizens — a Socrates, a Marcus Aurelius, a Scipio, a Cæsar, an Alexander, all deprived of the knowledge of God, and excluded from his eternal kingdom. Is it not God then who has made them? Who else could do so but he who made everything in heaven, and in the earth? But why has he done so? what in this case are the particular designs of that infinite wisdom which makes nothing in vain? Hear the response of St. Augustine. "He has made them," says he, "that they might adorn the present world." He has made the rare qualities of those great men, as he made the sun. Who admires not that splendid luminary; who is not ravished with his midday radiance, and the gorgeous beauty of his rising or decline? But as God has made it to shine upon the evil and upon the good, such an object, beautiful as it is, cannot render us happy; God has made it to embellish and illumine this great theatre of the universe. So, also, when he has made, in his enemies as well as in his servants, those beautiful lights of the mind, those rays of his intelligence, those images of his goodness; it is not that these alone can secure our happiness. They are but a decoration of the universe, an ornament of the age. See, moreover, the melancholy destiny of those men who are chosen to be the ornaments of their age. What do such rare men desire but the praise and the glory which men can give? God, perhaps to confound them, will refuse that glory to their vain desires! No:—he confounds them rather by giving it to them, and even beyond their expectation.

That Alexander, who desired only to make a noise in the world, has made it even more than he dared to hope. Thus he must find himself in all our panegyrics, and by a species of glorious fatality, so to speak, partake of all the praises conferred upon every prince. If the great actions of the Romans required a recompense, God knows how to bestow one correspondent to their merits as well as their desires. For a recompense he gives them the empire of the world, as a thing of no value. O kings! humble yourselves in your greatness: conquerors, boast not your victories! He gives them, for recompense, the glory of men; a recompense which never reaches them; a recompense which we endeavor to attach to—what? To their medals or their statues disinterred from the dust, the refuse of years and barbarian violence; to the ruins of their monuments and works, which contend with time, or rather to their idea, their shadow, or what they call their name. Such is the glorious prize of all their labors; such, in the very attainment of their wishes, is the conviction of their error. Come, satisfy yourselves, ye great men of earth! Grasp, if you can, that phantom of glory, after the example of the great men whom ye admire. God who punishes their pride in the regions of despair, envies them not, as St. Augustine says, that glory so much desired; "vain, they have received a recompense as vain as their desires."

But not thus shall it be with our illustrious Prince. The hour of God is come; hour anticipated, hour desired, hour of mercy and of grace. Without being alarmed by disease, or pressed by

time, he executes what he designed. A judicious ecclesiastic, whom he had expressly called, performs for him the offices of religion; he listens, humble Christian, to his instructions; indeed, no one ever doubted his good faith. From that time he is seen seriously occupied with the care of vanquishing himself; rising superior to his insupportable pains, making, by his submission, a constant sacrifice. God, whom he invoked by faith, gave him a relish for the Scriptures; and in that Divine Book he found the substantial nurture of piety. His counsels were more and more regulated by justice; he solaced the widow and orphan, the poor approached him with confidence. A serious as well as an affectionate father, in the pleasant intercourse which he enjoyed with his children, he never ceased to inspire them with sentiments of true virtue; and that young prince, his grandchild, will forever feel himself indebted to his training. His entire household profited by his example. . . . These, messieurs, these simple things — governing his family, edifying his domestics, doing justice and mercy, accomplishing the good which God enjoins, and suffering the evils which he sends — these are the common practices of the Christian life which Jesus Christ will applaud before his Father and the holy angels. But histories will be destroyed with empires; no more will they speak of the splendid deeds with which they are filled. While he passed his life in such occupations, and carried beyond that of his most famous actions the glory of a retreat so good and pious, the news of the illness of the Duchess de Bourbon reached Chantilly, like a clap of thunder. Who was not afraid to see that rising light extinguished? It was apprehended that her condition was worse than it proved. What, then, were the feelings of the Prince of Condé, when he saw himself threatened with the loss of that new tie of his family to the person of the king? Was it on such an occasion that the hero must die? Must he who had passed through so many sieges and battles perish through his tenderness? Overwhelmed by anxieties produced by so frightful a calamity, his heart, which so long sustained itself alone, yields to the blow; his strength is exhausted. If he forgets all his feebleness at the sight of the king approaching the sick princess; if transported by his zeal, he runs, without assistance, to avert the perils which that great king does not fear, by preventing his approach, he falls exhausted before he has taken four steps — a new and affecting way of exposing his life for the king. Although the Duchess d'Enghien, a

princess, whose virtue never feared to perform her duty to her family and friends, had obtained leave to remain with him, to solace him, she did not succeed in assuaging his anxieties; and after the young princess was beyond danger, the malady of the king caused new troubles to the Prince. . . . The Prince of Condé grew weaker, but death concealed his approach. When he seemed to be somewhat restored, and the Duke d'Enghien, ever occupied between his duties as a son and his duties as a subject, had returned by his order to the king, in an instant all was changed, and his approaching death was announced to the Prince. Christians, give attention, and here learn to die, or rather learn not to wait for the last hour, to begin to live well. What! expect to commence a new life when, seized by the freezing grasp of death, ye know not whether ye are among the living or the dead? Ah! prevent, by penitence, that hour of trouble and darkness! Thus, without being surprised at that final sentence communicated to him, the Prince remains for a moment in silence, and then all at once exclaims: "Thou dost will it, O my God; thy will be done! Give me grace to die well!" What more could you desire? In that brief prayer you see submission to the will of God, reliance on his Providence, trust in his grace, and all devotion.

From that time, such as he had been in all combats, serene, self-possessed, and occupied without anxiety, only with what was necessary to sustain them — such also he was in that last conflict. Death appeared to him no more frightful, pale, and languishing, than amid the fires of battle and in the prospect of victory. While sobbings were heard all around him, he continued, as if another than himself were their object, to give his orders; and if he forbade them weeping, it was not because it was a distress to him, but simply a hinderance. At that time, he extended his cares to the least of his domestics. With a liberality worthy of his birth and of their services, he loaded them with gifts, and honored them still more with mementos of his regard. . . .

The manner in which he began to acquit himself of his religious duties deserves to be recounted throughout the world; not because it was particularly remarkable, but rather because it was, so to speak, not such — for it seemed singular that a Prince so much under the eye of the world should furnish so little to spectators. Do not, then, expect those magniloquent words which serve to reveal, if not a concealed pride, at least an agitated

soul, which combats or dissembles its secret trouble. The Prince of Condé knew not how to utter such pompous sentences; in death, as in life, truth ever formed his true grandeur. His confession was humble, full of penitence and trust. He required no long time to prepare it; the best preparation for such a confession is not to wait for it as a last resort. But give attention to what follows. At the sight of the holy Viaticum, which he so much desired, see how deeply he is affected. Then he remembers the irreverence with which, alas! he had sometimes dishonored that Divine mystery. . . . Calling to mind all the sins which he had committed, but too feeble to give utterance to his intense feelings, he borrowed the voice of his confessor to ask pardon of the world, of his domestics, and of his friends. They replied with their tears. Ah! reply ye now, profiting by that example! The other duties of religion were performed with the same devotion and self-possession. With what faith and frequency did he, kissing the cross, pray the Savior of the world that his blood, shed for him, might not prove in vain! This it is which justifies the sinner, which sustains the righteous, which reassures the Christian. . . . Three times did he cause the prayers for those in anguish to be repeated, and ever with renewed consolation. In thanking his physicians, "See," said he, "my true physicians," pointing to the ecclesiastics to whose teachings he had listened, and in whose prayers he joined. The Psalms were always upon his lips, and formed the joy of his heart. If he complained, it was only that he suffered so little in reparation for his sins. Sensible to the last of the tenderness of his friends, he never permitted himself to be overcome by it; on the contrary, he was afraid of yielding too much to nature. What shall I say of his last interview with the Duke d'Enghien? What colors are vivid enough to represent to you the constancy of the father, the extreme grief of the son? Bathed in tears, his voice choked with sobs, he clasps his dying father, then falls back, then again rushes into his arms, as if by such means he would retain that dear object of his affection; his strength gives way, and he falls at his feet. The Prince, without being moved, waits for his recovery; then calling the Duchess, his daughter-in-law, whom he also sees speechless, and almost without life, with a tenderness in which nothing of weakness is visible, he gives them his last commands, all of which are instinct with piety. He closes with those prayers which God ever hears, like Jacob,

invoking a blessing upon them, and upon each of their children
in particular. Nor shall I forget thee, O Prince, his dear
nephew, nor the glorious testimony which he constantly tendered
to your merit, nor his tender zeal on your behalf, nor the letter
which he wrote, when dying, to reinstate you in the favor of the
king,—the dearest object of your wishes,—nor the noble qualities which made you worthy to occupy, with so much interest,
the last hours of so good a life. Nor shall I forget the goodness
of the King, which anticipated the desires of the dying Prince;
nor the generous cares of the Duke d'Enghien, who promoted
that favor; nor the satisfaction which he felt in fulfilling the
wishes of his dying father. While his heart is expanded, and his
voice animated in praising the king, the Prince de Conti arrives,
penetrated with gratitude and grief. His sympathies are renewed afresh; and the two princes hear what they will never
permit to escape from their heart. The Prince concludes, by
assuring them that they could never be great men, nor great
princes, nor honorable persons, except so far as they possessed
real goodness, and were faithful to God and the king. These
were the last words which he left engraven on their memory—
this was the last token of his affection—the epitome of their
duties.

All were in tears, and weeping aloud. The Prince alone was
unmoved; trouble came not into that asylum where he had cast
himself. O God, thou wert his strength and his refuge, and, as
David says, the immovable rock upon which he placed his confidence. . . .

Tranquil in the arms of his God, he waited for his salvation,
and implored his support, until he finally ceased to breathe.
And here our lamentations ought to break forth at the loss of so
great a man. But for the love of the truth, and the shame of
those who despise it, listen once more to that noble testimony
which he bore to it in dying. Informed by his confessor that if
our heart is not entirely right with God, we must, in our addresses, ask God himself to make it such as he pleases, and
address him in the affecting language of David, "O God, create in
me a clean heart." Arrested by these words, the Prince pauses,
as if occupied with some great thought; then calling the ecclesiastic who had suggested the idea, he says: "I have never
doubted the mysteries of religion, as some have reported."
Christians, you ought to believe him; for in the state he then

II—37

was, he owed to the world nothing but truth. "But," added he,
"I doubt them less than ever. May these truths," he continued,
"reveal and develop themselves more and more clearly in my
mind. Yes!" says he, "we shall see God as he is, face to face!"
With a wonderful relish he repeated in Latin those lofty words—
"As he is—face to face!" Nor could those around him grow
weary of seeing him in so sweet a transport. What was then
taking place in that soul? What new light dawned upon him?
What sudden ray pierced the cloud, and instantly dissipated, not
only all the darkness of sense, but the very shadows, and if I
dare to say it, the sacred obscurities of faith? What then became of those splendid titles by which our pride is flattered?
On the very verge of glory, and in the dawning of a light so
beautiful, how rapidly vanish the phantoms of the world! How
dim appears the splendor of the most glorious victory! How
profoundly we despise the glory of the world, and how deeply
regret that our eyes were ever dazzled by its radiance. Come,
ye people, come now—or rather ye princes and lords, ye judges
of the earth, and ye who open to man the portals of heaven;
and more than all others, ye princes and princesses, nobles descended from a long line of kings, lights of France, but to-day
in gloom, and covered with your grief, as with a cloud, come
and see how little remains of a birth so august, a grandeur so
high, a glory so dazzling. Look around on all sides, and see all
that magnificence and devotion can do to honor so great a hero;
titles and inscriptions, vain signs of that which is no more—
shadows which weep around a tomb, fragile images of a grief
which time sweeps away with everything else; columns which
appear as if they would bear to heaven the magnificent evidence
of our emptiness; nothing, indeed, is wanting in all these honors
but he to whom they are rendered! Weep then over these feeble
remains of human life; weep over that mournful immortality we
give to heroes. But draw near, especially ye who run, with such
ardor, the career of glory, intrepid and warrior spirits! Who was
more worthy to command you, and in whom did ye find command more honorable? Mourn then that great Captain, and
weeping, say: "Here is the man that led us through all hazards,
under whom were formed so many renowned captains, raised by
his example, to the highest honors of war; his shadow might yet
gain battles, and lo! in his silence, his very name animates us,
and at the same time warns us, that to find, at death, some rest

from our toils, and not arrive unprepared at our eternal dwelling,
we must, with an earthly king, yet serve the King of Heaven."
Serve then that immortal and ever merciful King, who will value
a sigh or a cup of cold water, given in his name, more than all
others will value the shedding of your blood. And begin to
reckon the time of your useful services from the day on which
you gave yourselves to so beneficent a Master. Will not ye too
come, ye whom he honored by making you his friends? To
whatever extent you enjoyed this confidence, come all of you,
and surround this tomb. Mingle your prayers with your tears;
and while admiring, in so great a prince, a friendship so excellent, an intercourse so sweet, preserve the remembrance of a hero
whose goodness equaled his courage. Thus may he ever prove
your cherished instructor; thus may you profit by his virtues;
and may his death, which you deplore, serve you at once for
consolation and example. For myself, if permitted, after all
others, to render the last offices at this tomb, O Prince, the worthy subject of our praises and regrets, thou wilt live forever in
my memory. There will thy image be traced, but not with that
bold aspect which promises victory. No, I would see in you
nothing which death can efface. You will have in that image
only immortal traits. I shall behold you such as you were in
your last hours under the hand of God, when his glory began to
dawn upon you. There shall I see you more triumphant than
at Fribourg and at Rocroy; and ravished by so glorious a triumph, I shall give thanks in the beautiful words of the well-
beloved disciple, "This is the victory that overcometh the world,
even our faith." Enjoy, O Prince, this victory, enjoy it forever,
through the everlasting efficacy of that sacrifice. Accept these
last efforts of a voice once familiar to you. With you these discourses shall end. Instead of deploring the death of others,
great Prince, I would henceforth learn from you to render my
own holy, happy, if reminded by these white locks of the account
which I must give of my ministry, I reserve for the flock, which
I have to feed with the word of life, the remnants of a voice
which falters, and an ardor which is fading away.

ELIAS BOUDINOT

(1740–1821)

As "President of Congress," Elias Boudinot signed the treaty
of peace with England which gave the United States their
independence. This fact no doubt led to his selection by
the Order of the Cincinnati to deliver one of the very earliest of
those set Fourth of July orations which moved our ancestors to admiration, inspired them with pride in the institutions of the country,
and encouraged in them that readiness for self-sacrifice without which,
when the emergency calls for it, the "American idea" must become
a demonstrated impossibility.

If, as a result of changing tastes, the patriotic orations of the first
quarter of a century under the Constitution no longer stir the responsive emotions they once did, the zeal which inspired, the hope
which animated, the earnestness which compelled them, can never be
otherwise than admirable to all who are still in sympathy with the
ideal towards which these men strove. For it must be remembered
always in judging them that their hopes were lofty and that they
had a faith as deep as the hope was high. They believed that they
and their descendants had been chosen by heaven to set the world an
example, the force of which would finally establish liberty and justice
as the directing impulses of the whole earth. In order to understand
them, it is necessary to keep this in view. There is an intense earnestness behind such words as these of Boudinot:—

"It is our duty, then, as a people acting on principles of universal application, to convince mankind of the truth and practicability of them by carrying
them into actual exercise for the happiness of our fellow-men, without suffering
them to be perverted to oppression and licentiousness."

The idea which animated Boudinot, as it did so many others of
his time, was that it is the destiny of America to demonstrate to
all men that moral force is the true basis of government, and that
physical force must, "in the long run," give way before it. "The
eyes of the nations of the world are fast opening," says Boudinot,
"and the inhabitants of this globe, notwithstanding it is three thousand years since the promulgation of the precept, 'Thou shalt love
thy neighbor as thyself,' are just beginning to discover their brotherhood to each other, and that all men, however different as regards

nation or color, have an essential interest in each other's welfare. Let it then be our peculiar constant care to inculcate this sacred principle.»

The Order of the Cincinnati having resolved to encourage the celebration of the Fourth of July «as a festival to be sacredly observed by every true American,» Mr. Boudinot was invited to speak before the New Jersey branch of the order, and his «Cincinnati oration» was accordingly delivered at Elizabethton, July 4th, 1793. When published it was dedicated to Washington.

Boudinot was born in Philadelphia, May 2d, 1740, of a French-Huguenot family which came to America after the revocation of the Edict of Nantes. He «received a classical and legal education,» and began the practice of law in New Jersey with Richard Stockton, at that time a famous lawyer, who stood at the head of the New Jersey bar. Active in the agitation which brought on the Revolution, Boudinot was first appointed «commissary general of prisoners» and afterwards elected to the Continental Congress,—of which, in November 1782, he was chosen president. After the adoption of the Constitution he served six years in Congress, and in 1796 became director of the mint under President Washington.

Retiring from politics he was chosen president of the American Bible Society at its organization,—an honor he esteemed above that conferred by any political position he had ever held. He took a great interest in the education of the Indians, and the «Boudinots» who have been prominent in the affairs of the Cherokees belong to a family which adopted his name. He died in 1821.

THE MISSION OF AMERICA

(Oration before the «Cincinnati,» Elizabethton, New Jersey, July 4th, 1793)

Gentlemen, Brethren, and Fellow-Citizens:—

HAVING devoutly paid the sacrifice of prayer and praise to that Almighty Being, by whose favor and mercy this day is peculiarly dedicated to the commemoration of events which fill our minds with joy and gladness, it becomes me, in obedience to the resolutions of our society, to aim at a further improvement of this festival, by leading your reflections to the contemplation of those special privileges which attend the happy and important situation you now enjoy among the nations of the earth.

Is there any necessity, fellow-citizens, to spend your time in attempting to convince you of the policy and propriety of setting

apart this anniversary, for the purpose of remembering, with gratitude, the unexampled event of our political salvation?

The cordial testimony you have borne to this institution for seventeen years past supersedes the necessity of an attempt of this kind; and, indeed, if this had been the first instance of our commemorating the day, the practice of all nations and of all ages would have given a sanction to the measure.

The history of the world, as well sacred as profane, bears witness to the use and importance of setting apart a day as a memorial of great events, whether of a religious or political nature.

No sooner had the great Creator of the heavens and the earth finished his almighty work, and pronounced all very good, but he set apart (not an anniversary, or one day in a year, but) one day in seven, for the commemoration of his inimitable power in producing all things out of nothing.

The deliverance of the children of Israel from a state of bondage to an unreasonable tyrant was perpetuated by the eating of the Paschal Lamb and enjoining it to their posterity as an annual festival forever, with a «Remember this day, in which ye came out of Egypt, out of the house of bondage.»

The resurrection of the Savior of mankind is commemorated by keeping the first day of the week, not only as a certain memorial of his first coming in a state of humiliation, but the positive evidence of his future coming in glory.

Let us then, my friends and fellow-citizens, unite all our endeavors this day, to remember, with reverential gratitude to our supreme benefactor, all the wonderful things he has done for us, in a miraculous deliverance from a second Egypt—another house of bondage. «And thou shalt show thy son on this day, saying this day is kept as a day of joy and gladness, because of the great things the Lord has done for us, when we were delivered from the threatening power of an invading foe. And it shall be a sign unto thee, upon thine hand, and for a memorial between thine eyes, that the law of the Lord may be in thy mouth, for with a strong hand hast thou been delivered from thine enemies: Thou shalt therefore keep this ordinance in its season, from year to year, forever.»

When great events are to be produced in this our world, great exertions generally become necessary; men are, therefore, usually raised up, with talents and powers peculiarly adapted to

the purposes intended by Providence, who often, by their disinterested services and extreme sufferings, become the wonder as well as the examples of their generation.

The obligations of mankind to these worthy characters increase in proportion to the importance of the blessings purchased by their labors.

It is not, then, an unreasonable expectation which, I well know, generally prevails, that this day should be usually devoted to perpetuating and respectfully remembering the dignified characters of those great men, with whom it has been our honor to claim the intimate connection of fellow-citizens,—men who have purchased our present joyful circumstances at the invaluable price of their blood.

But you must also acknowledge with me, that this subject has been so fully considered, and so ably handled by those eloquent and enlightened men who have gone before me in this honorable path, that had their superior abilities fallen to my lot, I could do but little more than repeat the substance of their observations and vary their language.

Forgive me, ye spirits of my worthy departed fellow-citizens! Patriots of the first magnitude, whose integrity no subtle arts of bribery and corruption could successfully assail, and whose fortitude and perseverance no difficulties or dangers could intimidate! Whose labors and sufferings in the common cause of our country, whose exploits in the field and wisdom in the cabinet, I have often been witness to, during a cruel and distressing war! Forgive, O Warren, Montgomery, and all the nameless heroes of your illustrious group! Forgive, that I omit on the present occasion to follow the steps of those compatriots who have preceded me, but had rather spend this sacred hour in contemplating those great purposes which animated your souls in the severe conflict, and for which you fought and bled!

Were you present to direct this day's meditations, would you not point to your scarred limbs and bleeding breasts, and loudly call upon us to reward your toils and sufferings, by forcibly inculcating and improving those patriotic principles and practices which led you to those noble achievements that secured the blessings we now enjoy?

Yes, ye martyrs to liberty! ye band of heroes! ye once worthy compatriots and fellow-citizens! We will obey your friendly suggestion, and greatly prize that freedom and independence,

purchased by your united exertions, as the most invaluable gem of our earthly crown.

The late revolution, my respected audience, in which we this day rejoice, is big with events that are daily unfolding themselves and pressing in thick succession, to the astonishment of a wondering world.

It has been marked with the certain characteristic of a Divine overruling hand, in that it was brought about and perfected against all human reasoning, and apparently against all human hope; and that in the very moment of time when all Europe seemed ready to be plunged into commotion and distress.

Divine Providence, throughout the government of this world, appears to have impressed many great events with the undoubted evidence of his own almighty arm. He putteth down kingdoms and he setteth up whom he pleaseth, and it has been literally verified in us that «no king prevaileth by the power of his own strength.»

The first great principle established and secured by our revolution, and which since seems to be pervading all the nations of the earth, and which should be most zealously and carefully improved and gloried in by us, is the rational equality and rights of men, as men and citizens.

I do not mean to hold up the absurd idea charged upon us, by the enemies of this valuable principle, and which contains in it inevitable destruction to every government, «that all men are equal as to acquired or adventitious rights.» Men must and do continually differ in their genius, knowledge, industry, integrity, and activity.

Their natural and moral characters; their virtues and vices; their abilities, natural and acquired, together with favorable opportunities for exertion, will always make men different among themselves, and of course create a pre-eminency and superiority one over another. But the equality and rights of men here contemplated are natural, essential, and unalienable, such as the security of life, liberty, and property. These should be the firm foundation of every good government, as they will apply to all nations, at all times, and may properly be called a universal law. It is apparent that every man is born with the same right to improve the talent committed to him, for the use and benefit of society, and to be respected accordingly.

We are all the workmanship of the same Divine hand. With our Creator, abstractly considered, there are neither kings nor subjects, masters nor servants, otherwise than stewards of his appointment, to serve each other according to our different opportunities and abilities, and of course accountable for the manner in which we perform our duty; he is no respecter of persons; he beholds all with an equal eye, and although "order is heaven's first law," and he has made it essential to every good government, and necessary for the welfare of every community, that there should be distinctions among members of the same society, yet this difference is originally designed for the service, benefit, and best good of the whole, and not for their oppression or destruction.

It is our duty then, as a people, acting on principles of universal application, to convince mankind of the truth and practicability of them, by carrying them into actual exercise for the happiness of our fellow-men, without suffering them to be perverted to, oppression or licentiousness.

The eyes of the nations of the earth are fast opening, and the inhabitants of this globe, notwithstanding it is three thousand years since the promulgation of the precept, "Thou shalt love thy neighbor as thyself," are but just beginning to discover their brotherhood to each other, and that all men, however different with regard to nation or color, have an essential interest in each other's welfare.

Let it then be our peculiar constant care and vigilant attention to inculcate this sacred principle and to hand it down to posterity, improved by every generous and liberal practice, that while we are rejoicing in our own political and religious privileges, we may with pleasure contemplate the happy period, when all the nations of the earth shall join in the triumph of this day and one universal anthem of praise shall arise to the Universal Creator in return for the general joy.

Another essential ingredient in the happiness we enjoy as a nation, and which arises from the principles of the revolution, is the right that every people have to govern themselves in such manner as they judge best calculated for the common benefit.

It is a principle interwoven with our Constitution, and not one of the least blessings purchased by that glorious struggle, to the commemoration of which this day is specially devoted, that every man has a natural right to be governed by laws of his

own making, either in person or by his representative, and that no authority ought justly to be exercised over him, that is not derived from the people, of whom he is one.

This, fellow-citizens, is a most important practical principle, first carried into complete execution by the United States of America.

I tremble for the event, while I glory in the subject.

To you, ye citizens of America, do the inhabitants of the earth look with eager attention for the success of a measure on which their happiness and prosperity so manifestly depend.

To use the words of a famous foreigner: "You are become the hope of human nature, and ought to become its great example. The asylum opened in your land for the oppressed of all nations must console the earth."

On your virtue, patriotism, integrity, and submission to the laws of your own making, and the government of your own choice, do the hopes of men rest with prayers and supplications for a happy issue.

Be not, therefore, careless, indolent, or inattentive, in the exercise of any right of citizenship. Let no duty, however small, or seemingly of little importance, be neglected by you.

Ever keep in mind that it is parts that form the whole, and fractions constitute the unit. Good government generally begins in the family, and if the moral character of a people once degenerates, their political character must soon follow.

A friendly consideration of our fellow-citizens, who by our free choice become the public servants and manage the affairs of our common country, is but a reasonable return for their diligence and care in our service.

The most enlightened and zealous of our public servants can do little without the exertions of private citizens to perfect what they do but form, as it were, in embryo. The highest officers of our government are but the first servants of the people and always in their power; they have, therefore, a just claim to a fair and candid experiment of the plans they form and the laws they enact for the public weal. Too much should not be expected from them; they are but men and of like passions and of like infirmities with ourselves; they are liable to err, though exercising the purest motives and best abilities required for the purpose.

Times and circumstances may change and accidents intervene to disappoint the wisest measures. Mistaken and wicked men

(who cannot live but in troubled waters) are often laboring with indefatigable zeal, which sometimes proves but too successful, to sour our minds and derange the best-formed systems. Plausible pretensions and censorious insinuations are always at hand to transfer the deadly poison of jealousy, by which the best citizens may for a time be deceived.

These considerations should lead to an attentive solicitude to keep the pure unadulterated principles of our Constitution always in view; to be religiously careful in our choice of public officers; and as they are again in our power at very short periods, lend not too easily a patient ear to every invidious insinuation or improbable story, but prudently mark the effects of their public measures and judge of the tree by its fruits.

I do not wish to discourage a constant and lively attention to the conduct of our rulers. A prudent suspicion of public measures is a great security to a republican government; but a line should be drawn between a careful and critical examination into the principles and effects of regular systems after a fair and candid trial and a captious, discontented, and censorious temper, which leads to find fault with every proposition in which we have not an immediate hand, and raises obstacles to rational plans of government, without waiting a fair experiment. It is generally characteristic of this disposition to find fault without proposing a better plan for consideration.

We should not forget that our country is large and our fellow-citizens of different manners, interests, and habits—that our laws to be right must be equal and general. Of course the differing interests must be combined, and brotherly conciliation and forbearance continually exercised, if we will judge with propriety of those measures that respect a nation at large.

While we thus enjoy as a community the blessings of the social compact in its purity, and are all endeavoring to secure the invaluable privileges purchased by the blood of thousands of our brethren who fell in the dreadful conflict, let us also be careful to encourage and promote a liberality and benevolence of mind towards those whom they have left behind, and whose unhappy fate it has been to bear a heavier proportion of the expensive purchase, in the loss of husbands, parents, or children, perhaps their only support and hope in life. . . .

Do you, my worthy fellow-citizens, of every description, wish for more lasting matter of pleasure and satisfaction in

contemplating the great events brought to your minds this day? Extend, then, your views to a distant period of future time. Look forward a few years, and behold our extended forests (now a pathless wilderness) converted into fruitful fields and busy towns. Take into view the pleasing shores of our immense lakes, united to the Atlantic States by a thousand winding canals, and beautified with rising cities, crowned with innumerable peaceful fleets, transporting the rich produce from one coast to another.

Add to all this, what must most please every humane and benevolent mind, the ample provision thus made by the God of all flesh, for the reception of the despots of the earth, flying from the tyranny and oppression of the despots of the Old World, and say, if the prophecies of ancient times are not hastening to a fulfillment, when this wilderness shall blossom as a rose, the heathen be given to the Great Redeemer as his inheritance, and these uttermost parts of the earth for his possession.

Who knows but the country for which we have fought and bled may hereafter become a theatre of greater events than yet have been known to mankind?

May these invigorating prospects lead us to the exercise of every virtue, religious, moral, and political. May we be roused to a circumspect conduct,—to an exact obedience to the laws of our own making,—to the preservation of the spirit and principles of our truly invaluable Constitution,—to respect and attention to magistrates of our own choice; and finally, by our example as well as precept, add to the real happiness of our fellow-men and the particular glory of our common country.

And may these great principles in the end become instrumental in bringing about that happy state of the world, when, from every human breast, joined by the grand chorus of the skies, shall arise with the profoundest reverence, that divinely celestial anthem of universal praise,—"Glory to God in the highest; peace on earth; good will towards men."

LOUIS BOURDALOUE

(1632-1704)

THE member of the old French nobility who is reported to have doubted heaven's ability to damn a gentleman of his quality was not one of Bourdaloue's audience when he preached before Louis XIV. what Madame de Sévigné called his «beautiful, his noble, his astonishing» sermons. But there were present many such, and their presence served to give the great preacher habits of thought and expression which distinguish his style from that of the modern pulpit. He belonged to an aristocratic age, and while he rebukes its vices his sympathy with its habits of thought makes it impossible to judge him by the standard we apply in criticizing a modern pulpit orator who addresses himself not to a select court circle, but to the largest possible number of the people. What is considered Bourdaloue's greatest sermon on the sufferings of Christ was preached before the King whom it so charmed that after the close of the series he said he «loved better to hear the repetition of Bourdaloue than the novelties of any one else.» The style which characterizes sermons worthy of this compliment from a king is nobly persuasive; full of dignity, elegance, and sweetness. The worst that can be said in criticism of it is that it is controlled by courtesy,—that even in rebuking the vices of the court the preacher himself is a courtier still. But this does not prevent so poor a courtier as Lord Brougham from ranking Bourdaloue above Bossuet and next to Massillon. We may not accept that judgment as it applies against Bossuet, but no one who reads Bourdaloue's masterly periods will wish to question his place as one of the three great pulpit orators of the French classical period.

He was born at Bourges in 1632, and educated a Jesuit. His genius showed itself in his earliest discourses, and in 1669 his superiors sent him to Paris where for thirty years he kept his place in the affections of the polite world. In his old age, after doing the King's pleasure in preaching in the provinces to reconcile the Protestants after the revocation of the Edict of Nantes, he abandoned his pulpit and worked as what would now be called «a city missionary,» in Paris. It is said that his persuasiveness and pathos affected the people as powerfully as the court had been affected by his sermons before the King. He died in 1704.

LOUIS BOURDALOUE

see in the Passion of Jesus Christ? A Divine Savior betrayed and abandoned by cowardly disciples, persecuted by pontiffs and hypocritical priests, ridiculed and mocked in the palace of Herod by impious courtiers, placed upon a level with Barabbas, and to whom Barabbas is preferred by a blind and inconstant people, exposed to the insults of libertinism, and treated as a mock-king by a troop of soldiers equally barbarous and insolent; in fine, crucified by merciless executioners! Behold, in a few words, what is most humiliating and most cruel in the death of the Savior of the world! Then tell me if this is not precisely what we now see, of what we are every day called to be witnesses. Let us resume; and follow me.

Betrayed and abandoned by cowardly disciples: such, O divine Savior, has been thy destiny. But it was not enough that the Apostles, the first men whom thou didst choose for thine own, in violation of the most holy engagement, should have forsaken thee in the last scene of thy life; that one of them should have sold thee, another renounced thee, and all disgraced themselves by a flight which was, perhaps, the most sensible of all the wounds that thou didst feel in dying. This wound must be again opened by a thousand acts of infidelity yet more scandalous. Even in the Christian ages we must see men bearing the character of thy disciples, and not having the resolution to sustain it; Christians, prevaricators, and deserters from their faith; Christians ashamed of declaring themselves for thee, not daring to appear what they are, renouncing at least in the exterior what they have professed, flying when they ought to fight; in a word, Christians in form, ready to follow thee even to the Supper when in prosperity, and while it required no sacrifice, but resolved to abandon thee in the moment of temptation. It is on your account, and my own, my dear hearers, that I speak, and behold what ought to be the subject of our sorrow.

A Savior mortally persecuted by pontiffs and hypocritical priests. Let us not enter, Christians, into the discussion of this article, at which your piety would, perhaps, be offended, and which would weaken or prejudice the respect which you owe to the ministers of the Lord. It belongs to us, my brethren, to meditate to-day on this fact in the spirit of holy compunction; to us consecrated to the ministry of the altars, to us priests of Jesus Christ, whom God has chosen in his church to be the dispensers of his sacraments. It does not become me to remonstrate in

---

THE PASSION OF CHRIST

THE Passion of Jesus Christ, however sorrowful and ignominious it may appear to us, must nevertheless have been to Jesus Christ himself an object of delight, since this God-man, by a wonderful secret of his wisdom and love, has willed that the mystery of it shall be continued and solemnly renewed in his Church until the final consummation of the world. For what is the Eucharist but a perpetual repetition of the Savior's Passion, and what has the Savior supposed in instituting it, but that whatever passed at Calvary is not only represented but consummated on our altars? That is to say, that he is still performing the functions of the victim anew, and is every moment virtually sacrificed, as though it were not sufficient that he should have suffered once. At least that his love, as powerful as it is free, has given to his adorable sufferings that character of perpetuity which they have in the Sacrament, and which renders them so salutary to us. Behold, Christians, what the love of a God has devised; but behold, also, what has happened through the malice of men! At the same time that Jesus Christ, in the sacrament of his body, repeats his holy Passion in a manner altogether mysterious, men, the false imitators, or rather base corruptors of the works of God, have found means to renew this same Passion, not only in a profane, but in a criminal, sacrilegious, and horrible manner!

Do not imagine that I speak figuratively. Would to God, Christians, that what I am going to say to you were only a figure, and that you were justified in vindicating yourselves to-day against the horrible expressions which I am obliged to employ! I speak in the literal sense; and you ought to be more affected with this discourse, if what I advance appears to you to be overcharged; for it is by your excesses that it is so, and not by my words. Yes, my dear hearers, the sinners of the age, by the disorders of their lives, renew the bloody and tragic Passion of the Son of God in the world; I will venture to say that the sinners of the age cause to the Son of God, even in the state of glory, as many new passions as they have committed outrages against him by their actions! Apply yourselves to form an idea of them; and in this picture, which will surprise you, recognize what you are, that you may weep bitterly over yourselves! What do we

---

this place. God forbid that I should undertake to judge those who sustain the sacred office! This is not the duty of humility to which my condition calls me. Above all, speaking as I do, before many ministers, the irreprehensible life of whom contributes so much to the edification of the people, I am not yet so infatuated as to make myself the judge, much less the censor of their conduct. But though it should induce you only to acknowledge the favors with which God prevents you, as a contrast, from the frightful blindness into which he permits others to fall, remember that the priests, and the princes of the priests, are those whom the Evangelist describes as the authors of the conspiracy formed against the Savior of the world, and of the wickedness committed against him. Remember that this scandal is notoriously public, and renewed still every day in Christianity. Remember, but with fear and horror, that the greatest persecutors of Jesus Christ are not lay libertines, but wicked priests; and that among the wicked priests, those whose corruption and iniquity are covered with the vail of hypocrisy are his most dangerous and most cruel enemies. A hatred, disguised under the name of zeal, and covered with the specious pretext of observance of the law, was the first movement of the persecution which the Pharisees and the priests raised against the Son of God. Let us fear lest the same passion should blind us! Wretched passion, exclaims St. Bernard, which spreads the venom of its malignity even over the most lovely of the children of men, and which could not see a God upon earth without hating him! A hatred not only of the prosperity and happiness, but what is yet more strange, of the merit and perfection of others! A cowardly and shameful passion, which, not content with having caused the death of Jesus Christ, continues to persecute him by rending his mystical body, which is the Church; dividing his members, which are believers; and stifling in their hearts that charity which is the spirit of Christianity! Behold, my brethren, the subtle temptation against which we have to defend ourselves, and under which it is but too common for us to fall!

A Redeemer reviled and mocked in the palace of Herod by the impious creatures of his court! This was, without doubt, one of the most sensible insults which Jesus Christ received. But do not suppose, Christians, that this act of impiety ended there. It has passed from the court of Herod, from that prince destitute of religion, into those even of Christian princes. And is not the Savior still a subject of ridicule to the libertine spirits which compose them? They worship him externally, but internally how do they regard his maxims? What idea have they of his humility, of his poverty, of his sufferings? Is not virtue either unknown or despised? It is not a rash zeal which induces me to speak in this manner; it is what you too often witness, Christians; it is what you perhaps feel in yourselves; and a little reflection upon the manners of the court will convince you that there is nothing that I say which is not confirmed by a thousand examples, and that you yourselves are sometimes unhappy accomplices in these crimes.

Herod had often earnestly wished to see Jesus Christ. The reputation which so many miracles had given him excited the curiosity of this prince, and he did not doubt but that a man who commanded all nature might strike some wonderful blow to escape from the persecution of his enemies. But the Son of God, who had not been sparing of his prodigies for the salvation of others, spared them for himself, and would not say a single word about his own safety. He considered Herod and his people as profane persons, with whom he thought it improper to hold any intercourse, and he preferred rather to pass for a fool than to satisfy the false wisdom of the world. As his kingdom was not of this world, as he said to Pilate, it was not at the court that he designed to establish himself. He knew too well that his doctrine could not be relished in a place where the rules of worldly wisdom only were followed, and where all the miracles which he had performed had not been sufficient to gain men full of love for themselves and intoxicated with their greatness. In this corrupted region they breathe only the air of vanity; they esteem only that which is splendid; they speak only of preferment: and on whatever side we cast our eyes, we see nothing but what either flatters or inflames the ambitious desires of the heart of man.

What probability, then, was there that Jesus Christ, the most humble of all men, should obtain a hearing where only pageantry and pride prevail? If he had been surrounded with honors and riches, he would have found partisans near Herod and in every other place. But as he preached a renunciation of the world both to his disciples and to himself, let us not be astonished that they treated him with so much disdain. Such is the

11—38

prediction of the holy man Job, and which after him must be accomplished in the person of all the righteous; "the upright man is laughed to scorn." In fact, my dear hearers, you know that, whatever virtue and merit we may possess, they are not enough to procure us esteem at court. Enter it, and appear only like Jesus Christ clothed with the robe of innocence; only walk with Jesus Christ in the way of simplicity; only speak as Jesus Christ to render testimony to the truth, and you will find that you meet with no better treatment there than Jesus Christ. To be well received there, you must have pomp and splendor. To keep your station there, you must have artifice and intrigue. To be favorably heard there, you must have complaisance and flattery. Then all this is opposed to Jesus Christ; and the court being what it is, that is to say, the kingdom of the prince of this world, it is not surprising that the kingdom of Jesus Christ cannot be established there. But woe to you, princes of the earth! Woe to you, men of the world, who despise this incarnate wisdom, for you shall be despised in your turn, and the contempt which shall fall upon you shall be much more terrible than the contempt which you manifest can be prejudicial.

A Savior placed upon a level with Barabbas, and to whom Barabbas is preferred by a blind and fickle rabble! How often have we been guilty of the same outrage against Jesus Christ as the blind and fickle Jews! How often, after having received him in triumph in the sacrament of the Communion, seduced by cupidity, have we not preferred either a pleasure or interest after which we sought, in violation of his law, to this God of glory! How often, divided between conscience which governed us, and passion which corrupted us, have we not renewed this abominable judgment, this unworthy preference of the creature even above our God! Christians, observe this application; it is that of St. Chrysostom, and if you properly understand it, you must be affected by it. Conscience, which, in spite of ourselves, presides in us as judge, said inwardly to us, "What art thou going to do? Behold thy pleasure on the one hand, and thy God on the other: for which of the two dost thou declare thyself? for thou canst not save both; thou must either lose thy pleasure or thy God; and it is for thee to decide." And the passion, which by a monstrous infidelity had acquired the influence over our hearts, made us conclude—I will keep my pleasure. "But what then will become of thy God," replied conscience secretly, "and what must I

do, I, who cannot prevent myself from maintaining his interests against thee?" I care not what will become of my God, answered passion insolently; I will satisfy myself, and the resolution is taken. "But dost thou know," proceeded conscience by its remorse, "that in indulging thyself in this pleasure it will at last submit thy Savior to death and crucifixion for thee?" It is of no consequence if he be crucified, provided I can have my enjoyments. "But what evil has he done, and what reason hast thou to abandon him in this manner?" My pleasure is my reason; and since Christ is the enemy of my pleasure, and my pleasure crucifies him, I say it again, let him be crucified.

Behold, my dear hearers, what passes every day in the consciences of men, and what passes in you and in me, every time that we fall into sin, which causes death to Jesus Christ, as well as to our souls! Behold what makes the enormity and wickedness of this sin! I know that we do not always speak, that we do not always explain ourselves in such express terms and in so perceptible a manner; but after all, without explaining ourselves so distinctly and so sensibly, there is a language of the heart which says all this. For, from the moment that I know that this pleasure is criminal and forbidden of God, I know that it is impossible for me to desire it, impossible to seek it, without losing God; and consequently I prefer this pleasure to God in the desire that I form of it, and in the pursuit that I make after it. This, then, is sufficient to justify the thought of St. Chrysostom and the doctrine of the theologians upon the nature of deadly sin.

A Savior exposed to insults, and treated as a mock-king by a troop of feigned worshipers! What a spectacle, Christians! Jesus Christ, the eternal Word, covered with a pitiful, purple robe, a reed in his hand, a crown of thorns upon his head, delivered to an insolent soldiery, who, according to the expression of Clement Alexandrine, made a theatrical king of him whom the angels adore with trembling! They bowed the knee before him, and, with the most cutting derision, they snatched from him the reed which he held, to strike him on the head. An act too much resembling the impieties which are every day committed, during the celebration of our most august mysteries! Were he to appear in all his majesty, such as he will display at his second coming, you would be seized with fear. But, says St. Bernard, the more he is little, the more worthy is he of our respects; since it is his love, and not necessity, which reduces him to his state of

abasement. But it appears that you take pleasure in destroying his work, by opposing your malice to his goodness. You insult him, even on the throne of his grace; and, to use the words of the Apostle, you do not fear to trample under foot the blood of the New Testament! For, indeed, what else do you do by so many acts of irreverence, and so many scandals which equally dishonor the sanctuary which you enter and the God which it contains?

Ah, my brethren, I might well ask the greater part of the Christians of the present day, what St. Bernard asked them in his time: What do you think of your God, and what idea have you conceived of him? If he occupied the rank which he ought to occupy in your minds, would you proceed to such extremes in his presence? Would you go to his feet to insult him? for I call it insulting Jesus Christ to come before the altars to unbend ourselves, to amuse ourselves, to speak, to converse, to trouble the sacred mysteries by immodest smiles and laughter. I call it insulting the majesty of Jesus Christ to remain in his presence in indecent postures and with as little decorum as in a public place. I call it insulting the humility of Jesus Christ to make an ostentatious display before his eyes, of all the luxury and all the vanities of the world. I call it insulting the holiness of Jesus Christ to bring near his tabernacle, and into his holy house, a shameful passion which we entertain and kindle afresh there, by bold looks, by sensual desires, by the most dissolute discourses, and sometimes by the most sacrilegious abominations. God formerly complained of the infidelity of his people, addressing them by the mouth of his prophet—"Thou hast profaned my holy name." But it is not only his name that we profane, it is his body; it is his blood; it is his infinite merits; it is even his divinity; it is all that he possesses that is venerable and great. Nevertheless, do not deceive yourselves; for the Lord will have a day of reckoning; and, justly incensed at so many injuries, he will not allow you to escape with impunity; but he will know how to avenge himself by covering you with eternal confusion!

In fine, Christians, a Savior crucified by merciless executioners, the last effect of the cruelty of men upon the innocent person of the Son of God. It was at the foot of that cross, where we see him suspended, that the justice of the Father waited for him during four thousand years. Thus he regarded it, however frightful it might seem, as an object of delight; because he there found the reparation of the Divine glory and the punishment of our offenses. But in proportion as this first cross had charms for him, in that same proportion does he feel horror at that which our sins prepare for him every day. It is not, said St. Augustine, the rigor of that of which he complains, but the cruelty and the weight of this appear to him insupportable! He knew that his cross, ignominious as it was, would be transferred from Calvary, as speaks St. Augustine, to the heads of the emperors. He foresaw that his death would be the salvation of the world, and that his Father would one day render his ignominy so glorious, that it would become the hope and the happiness of all nations. But in this other cross, where we fasten him ourselves by sin, what is there, and what can there be to console him? Nothing but his love despised! His favors rejected! Unworthy creatures preferred to the Creator!

If, then, the sun concealed himself that he might not give his light to the barbarous action of his enemies who crucified him, sinner, what darkness ought not to cover from view thy wanderings and thy excesses? For it is by these,—understand it yet once more, if you have not sufficiently understood it,—it is by these, my dear hearers, that you incessantly renew all the passion of Jesus Christ. It is not I who say it, it is Saint Paul in the Epistle to the Hebrews: "They crucify to themselves the Son of God afresh, and put him to an open shame." As if this great Apostle would explain himself thus. Do not think, my brethren, that they were the Jews only who imbrued their hands in the blood of the Savior. Ye are accomplices in this deicide. And by what means? By your impieties, your sacrileges, your obscenities, your jealousies, your resentments, your antipathies, your revenge, and whatever corrupts your heart and excites it to revolt against God! Is it not then just, that while you weep over Jesus Christ you should yet weep more over yourselves, since ye are not only the authors of his death, but your sins destroy all the merit of it, as it respects yourselves, and render it useless and even prejudicial to you; as it remains for me to prove in the third part.

That there are men, and Christian men, to whom, by a secret judgment of God, the Passion of Jesus Christ, salutary as it is, may become useless, is a truth too essential in our religion to be unknown, and too sorrowful not to be the subject of our grief. When the Savior from the height of his cross. ready to give up

his spirit, raised this cry toward heaven, "My God, my God, why hast thou forsaken me?" there was no one who did not suppose but that the violence of his torments forced from him this complaint, and perhaps we ourselves yet believe it. But the great Bishop Arnauld de Chartres, penetrating deeper into the thoughts and affections of this dying Savior, says, with much more reason, that the complaint of Christ Jesus to his Father proceeded from the sentiment with which he was affected, in representing to himself the little fruit which his death would produce; in considering the small number of the elect who would profit by it; in foreseeing with horror the infinite number of the reprobate, for whom it would be useless: as if he had wished to proclaim that his merits were not fully enough, nor worthily enough remunerated; and that after having done so much work he had a right to promise to himself a different success in behalf of men. The words of this author are admirable: Jesus Christ complains, says this learned prelate, but of what does he complain? That the wickedness of sinners makes him lose what ought to be the reward of the conflicts which he has maintained. That millions of the human race for whom he suffers will, nevertheless, be excluded from the benefit of redemption. And because he regards himself in them as their head, and themselves, in spite of their worthlessness, as the members of his mystical body; seeing them abandoned by God, he complains of being abandoned himself; "My God, my God, why hast thou forsaken me?" He complains of what made St. Paul groan when transported with an apostolic zeal, he said to the Galatians: "What, my brethren, is Jesus Christ then dead in vain? Is the mystery of the cross then nothing to you? Will not this blood which he has so abundantly shed have the virtue to sanctify you?"

But here, Christians, I feel myself affected with a thought which, contrary as it appears to that of the Apostle, only serves to strengthen and confirm it. For it appears that St. Paul is grieved because Jesus Christ has suffered in vain; but I, I should almost console myself if he had only suffered in vain, and if his passion was only rendered useless to us. That which fills me with consternation is, that at the same time that we render it useless to ourselves, by an inevitable necessity it must become pernicious: for this passion, says St. Gregory of Nazianzen, "partakes of the nature of those remedies which kill if they do not heal, and of which the effect is either to give life or to convert

itself into poison; lose nothing of this, I beseech you." Remember, then, Christians, what happened during the judgment and at the moment of the condemnation of the Son of God.

When Pilate washed his hands before the Jews and declared to them that there was nothing worthy of death in this righteous man, but that the crime from which he freed himself rested upon them, and that they would have to answer for it, they all cried with one voice that they consented to it, and that they readily agreed that the blood of this just man should fall upon them and upon their children. You know what this cry has cost them. You know the curses which one such imprecation has drawn upon them, the anger of heaven which began from that time to burst upon this nation, the ruin of Jerusalem which followed soon after,—the carnage of their citizens, the profanation of their temple, the destruction of their republic, the visible character of their reprobation which their unhappy posterity bear to this day, that universal banishment, that exile of sixteen hundred years, that slavery through all the earth,—and all in consequence of the authentic prediction which Jesus Christ made to them of it when going to Calvary, and with circumstances which incontestably prove that a punishment as exemplary as this cannot be imputed but to the deicide which they had committed in the person of the Savior; since it is evident, says St. Augustine, that the Jews were never further from idolatry, nor more religious observers of their law than they were then, and that, excepting the crime of the death of Jesus Christ, God, very far from punishing them, would, it seems, rather have loaded them with his blessings. You know all this, I say; and all this is a convincing proof that the blood of this God-man is virtually fallen upon these sacrilegious men, and that God, in condemning them by their own mouth, although in spite of himself, employs that to destroy them which was designed for their salvation.

But, Christians, to speak with the Holy Spirit, this has happened to the Jews only as a figure; it is only the shadow of the fearful curses of which the abuse of the merits and passion of the Son of God must be to us the source and the measure. I will explain myself. What do we, my dear hearers, when borne away by the immoderate desires of our hearts to a sin against which our consciences protest? And what do we, when, possessed of the spirit of the world, we resist a grace which solicits us, which presses us to obey God? Without thinking upon it,

and without wishing it, we secretly pronounce the same sentence of death which the Jews pronounced against themselves before Pilate, when they said to him, "His blood be upon us." For this grace which we despise is the price of the blood of Jesus Christ, and the sin that we commit is an actual profanation of this very blood. It is, then, as if we were to say to God: "Lord, I clearly see what engagement I make, and I know what risk I run, but rather than not satisfy my own desires, I consent that the blood of thy Son shall fall upon me. This will be to bear the chastisement of it, but I will indulge my passion; thou hast a right to draw forth from it a just indignation, but nevertheless I will complete my undertaking."

Thus we condemn ourselves. And here, Christians, is one of the essential foundations of this terrible mystery of the eternity of the punishments with which faith threatens us, and against which our reason revolts. We suppose that we cannot have any knowledge of it in this life, and we are not aware, says St. Chrysostom, that we find it completely in the blood of the Savior, or rather in our profanation of it every day. For this blood, my brethren, adds this holy doctor, is enough to make eternity, not less frightful, but less incredible. And behold the reason, This blood is of an infinite dignity; it can therefore be avenged only by an infinite punishment. This blood, if we destroy ourselves, will cry eternally against us at the tribunal of God. It will eternally excite the wrath of God against us. This blood, falling upon lost souls, will fix a stain upon them, which shall never be effaced. Their torments must consequently never end. A reprobate in hell will always appear in the eyes of God stained with that blood which he has so basely treated. God will then always abhor him; and, as the aversion of God from his creature is that which makes hell, it must be inferred that hell will be eternal. And in this, O my God, thou art sovereignly just, sovereignly holy, and worthy of our praise and adoration. It is in this way that the beloved Disciple declared it even to God himself in the Apocalypse. Men, said he, have shed the blood of thy servants and of thy prophets; therefore they deserve to drink it, and to drink it from the cup of thine indignation. "For they have shed the blood of saints and prophets, and thou hast given them blood to drink." An expression which the Scripture employs to describe the extreme infliction of Divine vengeance. Ah! if the blood of the prophets has drawn down the scourge of God upon men, what may we not expect from the blood of Jesus Christ? If the blood of martyrs is heard crying out in heaven against the persecutors of the faith, how much more will the blood of the Redeemer be heard!

Then once more, Christians, behold the deplorable necessity to which we are reduced. This blood which flows from Calvary either demands grace for us, or justice against us. When we apply ourselves to it by a lively faith and a sincere repentance, it demands grace; but when by our disorders and impieties we check its salutary virtue, it demands justice, and it infallibly obtains it. It is in this blood, says St. Bernard, that all righteous souls are purified; but by a prodigy exactly opposite, it is also in this same blood that all the sinners of the land defile themselves, and render themselves, if I may use the expression, more hideous in the sight of God.

Ah! my God, shall I eternally appear in thine eyes polluted with that blood which washes away the crimes of others? If I had simply to bear my own sins, I might promise myself a punishment less rigorous, considering my sins as my misfortune, my weakness, my ignorance. Then, perhaps, thou wouldst be less offended on account of them. But when these sins with which I shall be covered shall present themselves before me as so many sacrileges with respect to the blood of thy Son; when the abuse of this blood shall be mixed and confounded with all the disorders of my life; when there shall not be one of them against which this blood shall not cry louder than the blood of Abel against Cain; then, O God of my soul! what will become of me in thy presence? No, Lord, cries the same St. Bernard, affectionately, suffer not the blood of my Savior to fall upon me in this manner. Let it fall upon me to sanctify, but let it not fall upon me to destroy. Let it fall upon me in a right use of the favors which are the Divine overflowings of it, and not through the blindness of mind and hardness of heart, which are the most terrible punishments of it. Let it fall upon me by the participation of the sacred Eucharist, which is the precious source of it, and not by the maledictions attached to the despisers of thy sacraments. In fine, let it fall upon me by influencing my conduct and inducing the practice of good works and let it not fall upon me for my wanderings, my infidelities, my obstinacy, and my impenitence. This, my brethren, is what we ought to ask to-day from Jesus Christ crucified. It is with these views that we

ought to go to the foot of the cross and catch the blood as it flows. He was the Savior of the Jews as well as ours, but this Savior, St. Augustine says, the Jews have converted into their judge. Avert from us such an evil. May he who died to save us, be our Savior. May he be our Savior during all the days of our lives. And may his merits shed upon us abundantly, lose none of their efficacy in our hands, but be preserved entire by the fruits we produce from them. May he be our Savior in death. And at the last moment may the cross be our support, and thus may he consummate the work of our salvation which he has begun. May he be our Savior in a blessed eternity, where we shall be as much the sharer in his glory as we have been in his sufferings.

GEORGE S. BOUTWELL

(1818–)

THERE were eleven articles in the bill of impeachment brought against President Andrew Johnson, but the realities of the proceeding were summed in the last—that on which he was arraigned for his hostility to the reconstruction program of Congress.

The impeachment resolutions having been introduced in the House, the leading speech in support of them was made by Hon. George Sewall Boutwell, of Massachusetts, who, as one of the managers of the impeachment proceedings, made an argument which, especially as it bears on the eleventh article, is of enduring historical importance. He was chairman of the committee which drafted the articles of impeachment, and as he afterwards drafted the fifteenth amendment and led the debate on it in the House, he may be considered as fairly representative of that great and determined constituency which forced the acceptance of the Civil War amendments and the reconstruction acts in spite of the desperate resistance of a minority as skillful and as uncompromising as ever opposed the inevitable in the history of the world.

Mr. Boutwell had been a Democrat before issues were forced on the slavery question. He represented in Massachusetts a class analogous to that from which Andrew Johnson sprang in Tennessee. He was a self-made man as Johnson was, though his disadvantages had not been as great as those overcome by the Tennessee tailor. Born in Brookline, Massachusetts, January 28th, 1818, Mr. Boutwell began life as a clerk in a country store at Groton Centre. While working in the store he studied law, but though admitted to the bar, he never practiced his profession until after his election to Congress. In 1849 he supported Van Buren for the presidency, and two years later he was elected to the Massachusetts legislature as a Democrat. While he was still keeping his country store at Groton Centre, the Democrats nominated him for Governor of Massachusetts. He was much ridiculed by what its enemies have called the "Brahmin class," but in spite of this ridicule,—perhaps because of it,—he was triumphantly elected Governor in his third race.

Harvard vindicated his scholarship by giving him the degree of LL.D., and the "store-keeper of Groton Centre," from the time he

finally left his counter for the Massachusetts Statehouse, was one of the most prominent men of the most important period in American history. He was re-elected Governor of Massachusetts as a Democrat in 1852, but in 1856 he joined the Republican party. He was a member of the Peace Congress of 1861, and President Lincoln appointed him Commissioner of Internal Revenue. Elected to the House of Representatives in 1864, he served three terms and was elected to the Senate in 1873. His service as Secretary of the Treasury under President Grant was his last in appointive office, and, after his retirement from public life, he devoted himself to the practice of law in Washington city.

PRESIDENT JOHNSON'S "HIGH CRIMES AND MISDEMEANORS"

(In the House of Representatives, Proposing the Impeachment of the President, 1868)

IF THE position I have taken is sound, that the meaning of the phrase "high crimes and misdemeanors" is to be ascertained by reference to the principles of the English common law of crimes, Blackstone's definition, "that a crime or misdemeanor is an act committed or omitted in violation of a public law either forbidding or commanding it," becomes important. I stand upon this definition of the great writer upon English law as the connecting link between the theory of the law that I maintain and the facts which in this case are proved.

It is to be observed in connection with Blackstone's definition that in our system the Constitution and the statutes are the "public law" of which he speaks, and any act done by the President which is forbidden by the law or by the Constitution, or the omission by him to do what is by the law or the Constitution commanded, is a "high crime and misdemeanor," and renders him liable to impeachment and removal from office.

He is amenable to the House and the Senate in accordance with the great principles of public law of which the Constitution of the United States is the foundation. And it is true, in a higher and better sense than it is true of the statutes, that the President of the United States is bound to support the Constitution, the vital part of which, in reference to the public affairs of the country, is that he shall take care that the laws be faithfully executed, and he violates that great provision of the Constitution, especially when he himself disregards the law either by doing that which is forbidden or neglecting that which he is commanded to do.

Sir, in approaching the discussion of the transactions of which we complain, I labor under great difficulties, such as are incident to the case. The President has in his hands the immense patronage of the government. Its influence is all-pervading. The country was disappointed, no doubt, in the report of the committee, and very likely this House participated in the disappointment, that there was no specific, heinous, novel offense charged upon and proved against the President of the United States. It is in the very nature of the case that no such heinous offense could be proved. If we understand the teachings of the successive acts which are developed in the voluminous report of the testimony, and if we understand the facts which are there developed, they all point to one conclusion, and that is that the offense with which the President is charged, and of which I believe by history he will ultimately be convicted, is that he used as he had the opportunity, and misused as necessity and circumstances dictated, the great powers of the nation with which he was intrusted, for the purpose of reconstructing this government in the rebellion, so that henceforth this Union, in its legitimate connection, in its relations, in its powers, in its historical character, should be merely the continuation of the government which was organized at Montgomery and transferred to Richmond.

If, sir, this statement unfolds the nature of the case, there would not be found any particular specific act which would disclose the whole of the transaction. It was only by a series of acts, by a succession of events, by participation direct or indirect in numerous transactions, some of them open and some of them secret, that this great scheme was carried on and far on toward its final consummation. Hence, it happens that when we present a particular charge, it is one which for a long time has been before the public. The country has heard of it again and again. Men do not see in that particular offense any great enormity. Then we are told that this particular act was advised by this cabinet officer, and that act assented to by another cabinet officer. This matter was discussed in cabinet meeting, the other was considered in a side-chamber, and, therefore, the President is not alone responsible for anything that has been done. But, sir, I

assert that, whoever else may be responsible with him, he is responsible for himself. Any other theory is destructive to public liberty. We understand the relations which subsisted between the President and his cabinet officers. The tenure-of-office act gave the latter a degree of independence. But, whatever were the subsisting relations, the President cannot shield himself by their counsel, and claim immunity for open, known, and willful violations of the laws of the land. I do not speak now of the errors of judgment, but of open and avowed illegal acts personally done or authorized by himself. But he has not always had even the countenance of his cabinet officers. The test-oath was suspended by the President against the opinion of Attorney-General Speed. If cabinet officers have been concerned in these illegal transactions, I have for them, to a large extent, the same excuse that I have for myself, the same that I have for the members of this House and for the people of this country. In the beginning they did not understand the President's character, capacity, and purposes.

His capacity has not been comprehended by the country. Violent sometimes in language, indiscreet in manner, impulsive in action, unwise in declamation, he is still animated by a persistency of purpose which never yields under any circumstances, but seeks by means covert and tortuous, as well as open and direct, the accomplishment of the purpose of his life.

I care not to go into an examination—indeed, I have neither the time nor the taste for it now—of the tortuous ways by which he has controlled men who in the public estimation are superior to himself. But my excuse for cabinet officers, for members of Congress, for the country, is that in 1865, when he issued his proclamation for the reorganization of North Carolina, no one understood him. General Grant in his testimony says that he considered the plan temporary, to be approved or annulled when Congress should meet in December. But when Congress assembled the President told us that the work was ended; that the rebellious States were restored to the Union. He then planted himself firmly upon the proposition laid down in his North Carolina proclamation in defiance of the decision of the Supreme Court of the United States that the power was in Congress to decide whether the government of a State was republican or not; in defiance of the cardinal principle of the sovereignty of the people through Congress. He ratified substantially in his

message that which he had assumed merely in the proclamation of the twenty-ninth of May, that he was the United States for the purpose of deciding whether the government of a State was republican or not.

Sir, if this whole case rested merely upon that assumption, that exercise of power, I maintain that it would bring him specifically and exactly within control of this House, for the purpose of arraigning him before the Senate upon the charge of seizing and usurping the greatest power of the legislative department of the government, unless it be that of taxation, which he has also usurped and exercised in defiance of the Constitution. But even then the nature of the proceedings was not fully understood and his motives were only partially disclosed. The public mind did not comprehend the character and extent of the usurpation.

Thus it was that his motive was concealed. He was not understood, and the charity of the country silenced suspicions of evil. But he moved on step by step. The country in the meanwhile was under the influence of his bold declarations, made frequently from the fourteenth of April to about the first of July 1865; declarations which, even in the coldest of us, made the blood kindle in our veins, as he set forth the punishment to which the rebels were entitled. Even the most violent of the Northern people, they who had suffered from the war, those who had offered their sons, their brothers, and their husbands in sacrifice for the Republic, shuddered when they listened to his declamation as to the power and duty of this government to punish those who had been engaged in the rebellion. But from July 1865 his conduct and his policy have been entirely opposed to the declarations made in the spring and early summer of that year. I see in those declarations only this: that they were designed and intended, when they were uttered, to conceal from the public the great purpose he had in view, which was to wrest this government from the power of the loyal people of the North and turn it over to the tender mercies of those who had brought upon this country all the horrors of civil war.

I pass, sir, to the testimony of Judge Mathews, of Ohio, a person whom I never saw but once, and of whom I know nothing except what the record discloses. He was an officer of the Northern army, and he has been a judge of some of the courts in Cincinnati or vicinity. He says that, in the month of February 1865, when Mr. Johnson was passing from Tennessee to

Washington, to take the oath of office as Vice-President, he called upon him at the Burnett House. The conversation was apparently unimportant, but it discloses a purpose on the part of Mr. Johnson. He said to Judge Mathews, "You and I were old Democrats." "Yes," replied Judge Mathews. Says Mr. Johnson, "I will tell you what it is: if the country is ever to be saved, it is to be done through the old Democratic party." That was in February 1865. He had then received the suffrages of a free and generous people. They had taken him from Tennessee, where he would have had no abiding-place but with the armies of the Republic that protected him in his person and property. He was then entering upon the second office in the gift of the people, chosen by the great party of power and of progress in the country, which had saved the Union in its days of peril. No act had been by them done which could possibly have alienated him from them. Jefferson Davis was still at Richmond. The armies of Lee menaced the capital of his country. Andrew Johnson was approaching that capital for the purpose of taking the oath of office. That capital was merely a fortified garrison. He then declares that the country cannot be saved except by the old Democratic party.

What was the old Democratic party? It was the party of the South; it was made up of those men in the southern country who entered into the rebellion. That casual expression, dropped at the Burnett House in Cincinnati in February 1865, discloses his mysterious course from that day to this. I do not speak now of those Democrats of the North who stood by the flag of the country, who maintained the cause of the Union, but I speak of that old Democratic party of which he spoke, whose inspiring principle was devotion to slavery, hatred to republican institutions and the cause of the Union and of liberty. It was to them that Mr. Johnson, in February 1865, turned his eyes for the salvation of the country. He was then Vice-President only, but his career as President illustrates his devotion to the purpose he then entertained.

I come now to a brief statement of those acts of the President which disclose his motives and establish his guilt. First, he and his friends sedulously promulgated the idea that what he did in the year 1865 was temporary.

Then came his message of December 1865, which disclosed more fully his ulterior purpose.

Then came the speech of February 22d, 1866, in which he arraigned the Congress of the United States collectively and individually, and, as I believe, made use of expressions which, uttered by a sovereign of Great Britain in reference to Parliament and to individual members of Parliament, would have led to most serious consequences, if not to the overthrow of the government.

Then came his vetoes of the various reconstruction measures. I know very well that it will be said that the President has the veto power in his hands. To be sure he has; but it is a power to be exercised like the discretion of a court, in good faith, for proper purposes, in honest judgment and good conscience, and not persistently in the execution of a scheme which is in contravention of the just authority of the legislative branch of the government. It was exercised, however, by the President for the purpose of preventing reconstruction by congressional agency and by authority of law.

Then came his interference by his message of the twenty-second of June, 1866, and by other acts, all disclosing and furthering a purpose to prevent the ratification of the pending constitutional amendment, a matter with which, as the Executive of the country, he had no concern whatever. The Constitution provides that the House and the Senate, by specified means, may propose amendments to the Constitution; and if any subject is wholly separated from executive authority or control, it is this power to amend the Constitution of the United States. The Constitution reserves this power to Congress, and to the people, excluding the President. In the same year he suspended the test-oath, against the advice of the Attorney-General, and appointed men to office who, as he well knew, could not take that oath. The oath was prescribed for the purpose of protecting the country against the presence of disloyal persons in office — a measure necessary to the public safety. Can any act be more reprehensible? Can any act be more criminal? Can any act be more clearly within Blackstone's definition of "crimes and misdemeanors"?

Then follows his surrender of abandoned lands. In 1865 we passed the first Freedman's Bureau bill, in which we set apart the abandoned lands for the negroes and refugees of the South. In violation of law and without authority of law he has restored them to their former rebel owners. This class of property was of the value of many millions of money.

11—39

We had captured in the South vast amounts of railway property. All these millions of property he had turned over to their former rebel proprietors. In many instances, as in the case of one railway, the government itself, under his special direction and control, in the State of Tennessee, constructed fifty-four miles of railway at an expense of more than two million dollars. This railway, with others, was turned over without consideration, without power to make reclamation, or to obtain compensation, and all without authority of law.

We possessed a vast amount of rolling-stock used on Southern roads during the war, some it captured from the enemy. The rolling-stock captured he restored without money and without price. Other portions of it, constructed by the Government of the United States, or purchased of manufacturers or of the railroad companies, he sold without authority of law to corporations that, according to the principles of law, were insolvent. When the time arrived for payment to the government many of them neglected to comply with the conditions of sale. One of those corporations, the Nashville and Chattanooga Railroad, Tennessee, made an exhibit by which it appeared they had money on hand to pay the government what they owed it. The officers of the government demanded payment, and threatened to take possession of the road in case of further neglect. President Johnson, by his simple order, and that, as far as is known, without consultation with any member of the cabinet, authorized, or rather directed, a delay or postponement in the collection of this debt. Agreeably to a previous order which he had issued, the interest on the bonds guaranteed by the State of Tennessee to this road, which had been due three or four years, were then paid out of money which, upon every principle of reason, equity, and law, belonged to the government. The money had been earned by the use of the rolling-stock which the government had furnished.

Mr. Johnson's order was in utter disregard of the great principle that of all creditors the government is to be paid first. Under no circumstances does the law concede to the citizen the right of payment until the claim of the sovereign is satisfied.

One important fact in connection with this transaction is, that the President himself was the holder of these Tennessee State bonds, issued for the benefit of this road, to the amount of either nineteen thousand or thirty thousand dollars; and that of that money, which upon the contract and by every principle of law

was due to the United States, he received past interest for about four years. A small matter, you may say; a small matter, the country may say; but in a public trust he had no right, in the first place, to make sale of this property; secondly, he had no right to postpone payment; and above all, he had no right to delay payment for the purpose of receiving to himself that which belonged to the government. Nor is it any excuse for him that there were other holders, whether loyal or rebel, who shared the benefits of this transaction.

Then there are connected with these proceedings other public acts, such as the appointment of provisional governors for North Carolina and the other nine States without any authority of law. Not only that, but he authorized the payment from the War Department of those salaries, notwithstanding there had been no appropriation by law, and notwithstanding the Constitution of the United States says that no money shall be drawn from the Treasury but in consequence of an appropriation by law.

When you bring all these acts together; when you consider what he has said; when you consider what he has done; when you consider that he has appropriated the public property for the benefit of the rebels; when you consider that in every public act, as far as we can learn, from May 1865 to the present time, all has tended to this great result, the restoration of the rebels to power under and in the government of the country; when you consider all these things, can there be any doubt as to his purpose, or doubt as to the criminality of his purpose, and his responsibility under the Constitution.

It may not be possible, by specific charge, to arraign him for this great crime, but is he therefore to escape? These offenses which I have enumerated, which are impeachable — and I have enumerated but a part of them — are the acts, the individual acts, the subordinate crimes, the tributary offenses to the accomplishment of the great object which he had in view. But if, upon the body of the testimony, you are satisfied of his purpose, and if you are satisfied that these tributary offenses were committed as the means of enabling him to accomplish this great crime, will you hesitate to try him and convict him upon those charges of which he is manifestly guilty, even if they appear to be of inferior importance, knowing that they were in themselves misdemeanors, that they were tributary offenses, and that in this way, and in this way only, can you protect the State against the

final consummation of his crime? We have not yet seen the end of this contest.

I am not disposed to enter into the region of prophecy, but we can understand the logic of propositions. The propositions which the President has laid down in his last message, and elsewhere, will lead to certain difficulty if they are acted upon. Whether they will be acted upon I cannot say. The first proposition is, that under some circumstances, an act of Congress may be, in his judgment, so unconstitutional that he will violate the law and utterly disregard legislative authority. This is an assumption of power which strikes at the foundation of the government. The Constitution authorizes Congress to pass bills. When they have been passed, they are presented to the President for his approval or objection. If he objects to a bill for constitutional or other reason, he returns it to the House in which it originated; and then and there his power over the subject is exhausted. If the House and the Senate by a two-thirds, vote pass a bill, it becomes a law, and, until it is repealed by the same authority or annulled by the Supreme Court, the President has but one duty, and that is to obey it; and no consideration or opinion of his as to its constitutionality will defend or protect him in any degree. The opposite doctrine is fraught with evils of the most alarming character to the country. If the President may refuse to execute or may violate a law because he thinks it unconstitutional in a certain particular, another President may disregard it for another reason; and thus the government becomes not a government of laws, but a government of men. Every civil officer has the same right in this respect as the President. If the latter has the right to disregard a law because he thinks it unconstitutional, the Secretary of the Treasury and every subordinate have the same right. Is that doctrine to prevail in this country?

But coupled with that declaration is another declaration, that the negroes of the South have no right whatever to vote. Our whole plan of reconstruction is based upon the doctrine that the loyal people of the South, black and white, are to vote. Now, while there is no evidence conclusively establishing the fact, it is still undoubtedly true that thousands and tens of thousands of white men in the States recently in rebellion have abstained from participation in the work of calling the conventions, because they have been stimulated by the conduct of the President to believe that they will ultimately be able to secure governments from which the negro population will be excluded. What is our condition to-day? Governments are being set up in the ten States largely by the black people, and without the concurrence of the whites, that concurrence being refused, to a large extent, through the influence of the President. Are we to leave this officer, if we judge him guilty of high crimes and misdemeanors, in control of the army and navy, with his declaration upon the record that under certain circumstances he will not execute the laws? He has the control of the army. Do you not suppose that next November a single soldier at each polling-place in the Southern country, aided by the whites, could prevent the entire negro population from voting? And, if it is for the interest of the President to do so, have we any reason to anticipate a different course of conduct? At any rate, such is the logic of the propositions which he has presented to us. If that logic be followed, the next presidential election will be heralded by a civil war, or the next inauguration of a President of the United States will be the occasion for the renewal of fratricidal strife.

Mr. Speaker, we are at present involved in financial difficulties. I see no way of escape while Mr. Johnson is President of the United States. I assent to much of what he has in his message concerning the effects of the tenure-of-office act. From my experience in the internal revenue office, I reach the conclusion that it is substantially impossible to collect the taxes while the tenure-of-office act is in force; and I have no doubt that whenever a new administration is organized, of whatever party it may be, some of the essential provisions of that act will be changed. The reason, Mr. Speaker, of the present difficulty is due to the fact that the persons engaged in plundering the revenues of the country are more or less associated criminally with public officers. The character of those public officers can be substantially known in the internal revenue office and in the treasury department; but if the Secretary of the Treasury and the President, before they can remove officers against whom probable cause exists, are obliged to wait until they have evidence which will satisfy the Senate of their guilt, the very process of waiting for that evidence to be procured exhausts the public revenues. There is but one way of overcoming this difficulty. When the President, the Secretary of the Treasury, and the Commissioner of Internal Revenue, are in harmony, and the commissioner is

satisfied from the circumstances existing that an officer is in collusion with thieves, he can ask the President for the removal of that man: and then and there should exist the power of removal by a stroke of the pen. Neither the official nor his friends should know the reason thereof. Nothing so inspires officials with zeal in the discharge of their duties as to feel that if they are derelict their commissions may at any moment he taken from them.

But what is our position to-day? Can this House and the Senate, with the knowledge that they have of the President's purposes and of the character of the men who surround him, give him the necessary power? Do they not feel that, if he be allowed such power, these places will be given to worse men? Hence I say that with Mr. Johnson in office from this time until the fourth of March, 1869, there is no remedy for these grievances. These are considerations only why we should not hesitate to do that which justice authorizes us to do if we believe that the President has been guilty of impeachable offenses.

Mr. Speaker, all rests here. To this House is given under the Constitution the sole power of impeachment; and this power of impeachment furnishes the only means by which we can secure the execution of the laws. And those of our fellow-citizens who desire the administration of the law ought to sustain this House while it executes that great law which is in its hands and which is nowhere else, while it performs a high and solemn duty resting upon it by which that man who has been the chief violator of the law shall be removed, and without which there can be no execution of the law anywhere. Therefore the whole responsibility, whatever it may be, for the nonexecution of the laws of the country is, in the presence of these great facts, upon this House. If this House believes that the President has executed the laws of the country, that he has obeyed the provision of the Constitution to take care that the laws be faithfully executed, then it is our duty to sustain him, to lift up his hands, to strengthen his arms; but if we believe, as upon this record I think we cannot do otherwise than believe, that he has disregarded that great injunction of the Constitution to take care that the laws be faithfully executed, there is but one remedy. The remedy is with this House, and it is nowhere else. If we neglect or refuse to use our powers when the case arises demanding decisive action, the government ceases to be a government of laws and becomes a government of men.

JOHN C. BRECKENRIDGE

(1821–1875)

JOHN CABELL BRECKENRIDGE was born in Kentucky in 1821. After graduating at Transylvania University and studying law, he settled at Lexington. Using his power as an orator in the discussion of the slavery issue, he became popular as a radical opponent of the radical enemies of slavery. Elected Vice-President on the ticket with Buchanan in 1856, the events which culminated in the John Brown raid of 1859 increased his popularity, and in 1860 he was nominated for 'the presidency by one wing of the Democratic party. After the election of Lincoln, Kentucky sent Breckenridge to the United States Senate, from which he retired to become a major-general in the Confederate army. After the fall of the Confederacy he spent several years abroad, but finally returned to Kentucky. He died in 1875.

THE DRED SCOTT DECISION

(Delivered before the Kentucky Legislature, December 1859)

GENTLEMEN, I bow to the decision of the Supreme Court of the United States upon every question within its proper jurisdiction, whether it corresponds with my private opinion or not; only, I bow a trifle lower when it happens to do so, as the decision in this Dred Scott case does. I approve it in all its parts as a sound exposition of the law and constitutional rights of the States, and citizens that inhabit them. . . .

I was in the Congress of the United States when that Missouri line was repealed. I never would have voted for any bill organizing the Territory of Kansas as long as that odious stigma upon our institutions remained in the statute book. I voted cheerfully for its repeal, and in doing that I cast no reflection upon the wise patriots who acquiesced in it at the time it was established. It was repealed, and we passed the act known as

the Kansas-Nebraska Bill. The Abolition, or *quasi* Abolition, party of the United States were constantly contending that it was the right of Congress to prohibit slavery in the common Territories of the Union. The Democratic party, aided by most of the gentlemen from the South, took the opposite view of the case. . . . A considerable portion of the Northern Democracy held that slavery was in derogation of common right and could only exist by force of positive law. They contended that the Constitution did not furnish that law, and that the slaveholder could not go into the Territories with his slaves with the Constitution to authorize him in holding his slaves as property, or to protect him. The South generally, without distinction of party, held the opposite view. They held that the citizens of all the States may go with whatever was recognized by the Constitution as property, and enjoy it. That did not seem to be denied to any article of property except slaves. Accordingly, the bill contained the provision that any question in reference to slavery should be referred to the courts of the United States, and the understanding was that, whatever the judicial decision should be, it would be binding upon all parties, not only by virtue of the agreement, but under the obligation of the citizen, to respect the authority of the legally constituted courts of the country. . . .

The view that we in the Southern States took of it was sustained—that in the Territories, the common property of the Union, pending their Territorial condition, neither Congress nor the Territorial government had the power to confiscate any description of property recognized in the States of the Union. The court drew no distinction between slaves and other property. It is true some foreign philanthropists and some foreign writers do undertake to draw this distinction, but these distinctions have nothing to do with our system of government. Our government rests not upon the speculations of philanthropic writers, but upon the plain understanding of a written constitution which determines it, and upon that alone. It is the result of positive law; therefore we are not to look to the analogy of the supposed law of nations, but to regard the Constitution itself, which is the written expression of the respective powers of the government and the rights of the States.

Well, that being the case, and it having been authoritatively determined by the very tribunal to which it was referred, that Congress had no power to exclude slavery from the Territories, and judicially determined that the Territorial legislatures, authorities created by Congress, had not the power to exclude or confiscate slave property, I confess that I had not anticipated that the doctrine of "unfriendly legislation" would be set up. Hence, I need not say to you that I do not believe in the doctrine of unfriendly legislation; that I do not believe in the authority of the Territorial legislatures to do by indirection what they cannot do directly. I repose upon the decision of the Supreme Court of the United States, as to the point that neither Congress nor the Territorial legislature has the right to obstruct or confiscate the property of any citizen, slaves included, pending the Territorial condition. I do not see any escape from that decision, if you admit that the question was a judicial one; if you admit the decision of the Supreme Court; and if you stand by the decision of the highest court of the country. . . .

JOHN BRIGHT

(1811–1889)

JOHN BRIGHT has been called the most eloquent of the Liberal orators of his day, and he was certainly the most strenuous, the most forcible, as he was no doubt the most effective of them all.

To appreciate his relations to the England of his time, to the British empire, and to the movement of the world in general, it is necessary to keep in view the fact that he stood for the largest possible measure of free intercourse and uncoerced co-operation among all men in all countries, and conversely for the minimum of forcible interference of nation with nation, class with class, individual with individual.

This idea gave him his strength in politics, and it also fixed his limitations. The England of his day was engaging more and more actively in "world-politics," while he preached nonintervention. His opposition to the Crimean War defeated him for Parliament in 1857 when he sought re-election before a Manchester constituency. Vindicated by election from Birmingham, he remained in Parliament for more than thirty years. In 1882, when a member of the Gladstone cabinet, he had presented to him the question of the coercive extension of "spheres of influence," as it was involved in the bombardment of Alexandria. However easily other Liberals might find reasons reconciling such aggressive acts to their party principles and to their ideas of public policy, the habits and tendencies of his lifetime governed him and compelled his resignation from the cabinet.

If honesty, strength of purpose, and courage to hold a predetermined course regardless of the opinions of others, constitute the chief grounds for respecting the character of a public man, then John Bright, regardless of the nature of his opinions, is one of the most respectable public men of his century. Perhaps it is true that a party under his leadership would have been reduced to a mere balance of power, but it is probable that the force he stands for would make such a balance of power the controlling factor in every real crisis. Mr. Gladstone was an organizer, because with many of the same qualities which made Bright admirable, and illustrating the same tendencies almost to the point of parallelism, he was more capable of looking into the immediate future and seeing all that in

looking to the long run Bright was likely to pass over as immaterial or even as contemptible. It would not be just or historical to call Gladstone an opportunist, but he was a party leader, a great organizer, a man who, while he was directed throughout his life by principle, had that desire for immediate practical results which increases political effectiveness in a given case, but often works to prevent the most effective operation of principle in shaping the course of events in that higher domain of politics where the forces which govern are too manifold and involved to be comprehended by any mind, however great. It is in this domain that men like Bright are most effective. It is not the fault of Bright that a strong conservative reaction has overtaken the English world at the close of the nineteenth century. He asked no quarter, and on questions of principle conceded nothing; yet few men have been really more conservative in method than he. It is not necessary to assume him correct in his methods of applying his theories, but if we look into his general plan of work in public affairs we cannot fail to see that he is, above everything, the advocate of quiet and peaceful growth,—of development through natural processes of education and evolution. He most ardently desired that the world should grow better, and, being an optimist by nature, he was fully convinced that, if given an opportunity to do so in peace, it would develop to the extent of the removal of those oppressive restrictions which check its progress.

He was the son of a Quaker cotton spinner of Lancashire, and the influence of this heredity affected him deeply, showing itself constantly in his work for the peaceful extension of industrial helpfulness and coöperation throughout the world, regardless of national boundaries. Born near Rochdale, in Lancashire, in 1811, he grew up at a time when the condition of manufacturing operatives was often miserable in the extreme. From his entrance into public life, in 1843, when he took his seat in Parliament, until within a short time of his death, he was at the front in every fight for reform. He worked with Cobden against the corn laws, and was himself the moving spirit in the agitation against the game laws, under which a man's liberty, or even his life, had often been accounted less important than the security of a rabbit warren. In all questions which concerned the United States, his principles almost inevitably carried him to the defense of American institutions. He dissented from Gladstone on Irish Home Rule,—for the same reason, no doubt, which led him to sympathize with the side of the Union in the American Civil War. He died March 27th, 1889.

WILL THE UNITED STATES SUBJUGATE CANADA?

(Delivered in the House of Commons on the Defense of Canada in 1865)

I HOPE the debate on the defense of Canada will be useful, though I am obliged to say, while I admit the importance of the question brought before the House, that I think it is one of some delicacy. Its importance is great, because it refers to the possibility of a war with the United States, and its delicacy arises from this, that it is difficult to discuss the question without saying things which tend rather in the direction of war than of peace. The difficulty now before us is that there is an extensive colony or dependency of this country adjacent to the United States, and if there be a war party in the United States,—a party hostile to this country,—that circumstance affords it a very strong temptation to enter without much hesitation into a war with England, because it feels that through Canada it can inflict a great humiliation on this country. At the same time, it is perfectly well known to all intelligent men, and especially to all statesmen and public men of the United States,—it is as well known to them as it is to us,—that there is no power whatever in this United Kingdom to defend successfully the territory of Canada against the United States. We ought to know that in order to put ourselves right upon the question, and that we may not be called upon to talk folly and to act folly. The noble lord at the head of the government—or his government, at least—is responsible for having compelled this discussion; because if a vote is to be asked from the House of Commons—and it will only be the beginning of votes—it is clearly the duty of the House to bring the matter under discussion. That is perfectly clear for many reasons, but especially since we have heard from the Governor-General of Canada that in the North American provinces they are about to call into existence a new nationality; and I, for one, should certainly object to the taxation of this country being expended needlessly on behalf of any nationality but our own. What I should like to ask the House first of all is this: Will Canada attack the States? Certainly not. Next, will the States attack Canada, keeping England out of view altogether? Certainly not. There is not a man in the United States, probably, whose voice or opinion would have the smallest influence who would recommend or desire that an attack should be made by the United States on Canada with a view to its forcible annexation to the Union. There have been dangers, as we know, on the frontier lately. The Canadian people have been no wiser than some Members of this House, or a great many men among the richer classes in this country. When the refugees from the South,—I am not speaking of the respectable, honorable men from the South, many of whom have left that country during their troubles, and for whom I feel the greatest commiseration, but I mean the ruffians from the South, who in large numbers have entered Canada, and who have employed themselves there in a course of policy likely to embroil us with the United States,—when they entered Canada the Canadians treated them with far too much consideration. They expressed very openly opinions hostile to the United States, whose power lay close to them. I will not go into details with which we are all acquainted: the seizing of the American ships on the lakes, the raid into the State of Vermont, the robbery of a bank, the killing of a man in his own shop, the stealing of horses in open day, nor the transaction, of which there is strong proof, that men of this class conspired to set fire to the greatest cities of the Union. All these things have taken place, and the Canadian government made scarcely any sign. I believe an application was made to the noble lord at the head of the foreign office a year ago to stimulate the Canadian government to take some steps to avoid the dangers which have since arisen; but with that sort of negligence which has been seen so much here, nothing was done until the American government, roused by these transactions, showed that they were no longer going to put up with them. Then the Canadian government and people took a little notice. I have heard a good many people complain of Lord Monck's appointment; that he was a follower of the noble lord who had lost his election, and therefore must be sent out to govern a province; but I will say of him that from all I have heard from Canada he has conducted himself there in a manner very serviceable to the colony, and with the greatest possible propriety as representing the sovereign. He was all along favorable to the United States; his cabinet, I believe, has always been favorable, and I know that at least the most important newspaper there has always been favorable to the North. But still nothing was done until these troubles began, and then everything was done. Volunteers were

sent to the frontier, the trial of the raiders was proceeded with, and probably they may be surrendered; and the Canadian Chancellor of the Exchequer has proposed a vote in the new Parliament to restore to the persons at St. Alban's who were robbed, the fifty thousand dollars which were taken from them. What is the state of things now? There is the greatest possible calm on the frontier. The United States have not a syllable to say against Canada. The Canadian people found they were wrong; they have now returned to their right minds, and there is not a man in Canada at this moment, I believe, who has any kind of idea that the United States government has the smallest notion of attacking them, now or at any future time, on account of anything which has transpired between Canada and the United States. If there comes a war in which Canada may be made a victim, it will be a war got up between the government in Washington and the government in London, and it becomes us to inquire whether that is at all probable. Is there anybody in the House in favor of such a war? I notice with the greatest delight a change which I said would some day come—and I was not a false prophet—in the line taken here with regard to the American question. Even the noble lord, the member for Stamford, spoke to-night without anger, and without any of that ill feeling which, I am sorry to say, on previous occasions he has manifested in discussing this question. I hope there is no man out of bedlam, or, at least, who ought to be out,—nay, I suspect there are few men in bedlam, who are in favor of our going to war with the United States.

In taking this view I am not arguing that we regard the vast naval and military power and the apparently boundless resources of that country. I will assume that you, my countrymen, have come to the conclusion that it is better for us not to make war with the United States, not because they are strong, but on the higher ground that we are against wars. Our history for the last two hundred years and more has recorded sufficient calamitous and, for the most part, unnecessary wars. We have had enough of whatever a nation can gain from military success and glory. I will not speak of the disasters which might follow to our commerce and the widespread ruin that might be caused by a war. We are a wiser and better people than we were in this respect, and we should regard a war with the United States as even a greater crime, if needlessly entered into, than a war with almost

any other nation in the world. Well, then, as to our government, with a great many blunders, one or two of which I will comment on by-and-by, they have preserved neutrality during this great struggle. We have had it stated in the House, and there has been in the House a motion, that the blockade was ineffectual and ought to be broken. Bad men of various classes, and, perhaps, agents of the Richmond conspiracy, and persons, it is said, of influence from France,—all these are stated to have brought pressure to bear on the noble lord and his colleagues with a view of inducing them to take part in this quarrel, but all this has failed to break our neutrality. Therefore, I say, we may very fairly come to the conclusion that England is not for war. If anything arises on any act of aggression out of which Canada might suffer, I believe the fault is not with this country. That is a matter which gives me great satisfaction; and I believe the House will agree with me that I am not misstating the case. But, let me ask, are the United States for war? because, after all, I know the noble lord, the member for Stamford, has a lurking idea that there is some danger from that quarter, and I am afraid the same feeling prevails in minds not so acute as that which the noble lord possesses. Now, if we could have at the bar of the House Earl Russell, as representing her Majesty's government, and Mr. Adams, as representing the government of President Lincoln, and ask them their opinions, I think they would tell us what the Secretary for the Colonies has told us to-night: that the relations between those governments are peaceable; and I know, from the communications between the minister of the United States and our minister for foreign affairs, that our relations with the United States are perfectly amicable and have been growing more and more amicable for many months past. And I will take the liberty of expressing this opinion, that there has never been an administration in the United States since the time of the Revolutionary War up to this hour more entirely favorable to peace with all foreign countries, and more especially favorable to peace with this country, than the government of which President Lincoln is the head. I will undertake to say that the most exact investigator of what has taken place will be unable to point to a single word he, President Lincoln, has said, or a single line he has written, or a single act he has done, since his first accession to power, that betrays that anger or passion or ill feeling towards this country which some

people here imagine influences the breasts of his cabinet. If, then, Canada is not for war, if England is not for war, if the United States are not for war, whence is the war to come? I should like to ask—I wish the noble lord, the member for Stamford, had been a little more frank—whence comes that anxiety which to some extent prevails? It may even be assumed that the government is not free from it, though it has shown it in the ridiculous form of proposing a vote of fifty thousand pounds. It is said that the newspapers have got into a sort of panic. Well, they can do that every night between twelve and six, when they write these articles; they can be very courageous or very panic-stricken. It is said that "the City,"—we know what "the City" means, the right honorable gentleman alluded to it to-night; they are persons who deal in shares, though that does not describe the whole of them,—it is said that what they call the "money interests" are alarmed. Well, I never knew the City to be right. Men who are deep in great monetary transactions, and steeped to the lips sometimes in perilous speculations, they are not able to take a broad, dispassionate view of questions of this nature; and as to the newspapers, I agree with my honorable friend, the Member for Bradford, who, referring to one of them in particular, said the course it took indicated its wishes to cover its own confusion. Surely, after four years of uninterrupted publication of lies with regard to America, it has done much to destroy its influence in foreign questions forever. I must now mention a much higher authority, the authority of the Peers. I don't know why we should be so much restricted here with regard to the House of Lords. I think this House must have observed that the other house is not always so squeamish in what they say about us. It appeared to me that in this debate the right honorable gentleman [Mr. Disraeli] felt it necessary to get up and endeavor to excuse his chief.

Now, if I were to give advice to the honorable gentleman opposite, it would be this,—for while stating that during the last four years many noble lords in the other House have said foolish things, I think I should be uncandid if I did not say that you also have said foolish things,—learn from the example set you by the right honorable gentleman. He, with a thoughtfulness and statesmanship which you do not all acknowledge, did not say a word from that bench likely to create difficulty with the United States. I think his chief and his followers might learn something from his example. Not long ago, I think, a panic was raised by what was said in another place about France; and now an attempt is made there to create a panic on this question. In the reform club there is fixed to the wall a paper giving a telegraphic account of what is done in this House every night, and also of what is done in the other House; and I find that the only words required to describe what is done in the other House are the words, "Lords adjourned." The noble lord at the head of the government is responsible for that. He has brought this House to very nearly the same condition; because we do very little, and they absolutely nothing. All of us, no doubt, in our young days were taught a verse intended to inculcate virtue and industry, a couplet of which runs thus:—

« For Satan still some mischief finds
    For idle hands to do.»

I don't believe that many here are afflicted with any disease arising from a course of continued idleness; but I should like to ask the House, in a more serious mood, what is the reason that any man in this country has now any more anxiety with regard to the preservation of peace with the United States than he had five years ago? Is there not a consciousness in your heart of hearts that you have not behaved generously towards your neighbor? Do we not feel in some way or other a reproving of conscience? And in ourselves are we not sensible of this, that conscience tends to make us cowards at this particular juncture? Well, I shall not revive past transactions with anger, but with a feeling of sorrow, for I maintain, and I think history will bear out what I say, that there is no generous and high-minded Englishman who can look back on the transactions of the last four years without a feeling of sorrow at the course that we have pursued in some particulars; and as I am anxious to speak with the view to a better state of feeling both in this country and the United States, I shall take the liberty, if the House will allow me, for a few minutes, to refer to two or three of those transactions, regarding which, though not in the main greatly wrong, in some circumstances we were so unfortunate as to create the irritation that at this moment we wish did not exist. The honorable Member for Horsham referred to the course taken by the government with regard to acknowledging the belligerent rights of the South. Now, I have never been one to condemn

II—40

the government for acknowledging the South as belligerents then, except on this ground. I think it might be logically contended that it might possibly become necessary to take that step, but I think the time and the manner of the act were most unfortunate, and could not but have produced very evil effects. Why, going back four years ago, we recollect what occurred when the news arrived here of the first shot fired at Fort Sumter. I think that was about the fourth of April, and immediately after it was announced that a new minister was coming from the United States to this country. Mr. Dallas had represented that, as he did not represent the new government, nor the new President, he would rather not undertake anything of importance. It was announced that his successor had left New York on a certain day; and we know that when we have the date of a departure from New York for this country we can calculate the time of arrival here to within twelve hours. Mr. Adams arrived in London on the thirteenth of May, and when he opened his newspaper the next morning he found it contained the proclamation of neutrality and the acknowledgment of the belligerent rights of the South. In my opinion the proper course would have been to have waited until Mr. Adams arrived, and to have discussed the matter with him in a friendly manner, when an explanation might have been given of the grounds upon which the English government felt themselves bound to issue it. But everything was done in an unfriendly manner, and the effect was to afford great comfort at Richmond, and generally to grieve those people of America who were most anxious for the continuance of the friendly and amicable relations between that country and England. To illustrate the point, allow me to suppose that a great revolt having taken place in Ireland, that we within a fortnight after the outbreak sent over a new minister to the United States, and that on the morning of his arrival he found that government had, without consulting him, taken such a hasty step as to acknowledge the belligerent rights of the Irish. I ask whether, under such circumstances, a feeling of irritation would not have been expressed by every man in Great Britain? I will not argue this question further, as to do so would be simply to depreciate the intellect of the honorable gentlemen listening to me. But seven or eight months after that event another transaction, of a very different and of a very unfortunate nature, took place, namely, that which arose out of

the seizure of the two Southern envoys on board an English ship called the Trent.

I recollect at that time making a speech at Rochdale entirely in favor of the United States government and people, but I did not then, nor do I now, attempt to defend the seizure of those persons. I said that, although precedents for such an action might possibly be found to have occurred in what I may call the evil days of our history, they were totally opposed to the maxims of the United States government, and that it was most undoubtedly a bad act. I do not complain of the demand that the men should be given up. I only complain of the manner in which the demand was made and the menaces by which it was accompanied. I think it was absurd and wrong, and was not statesmanlike, when there was not the least foundation for supposing the United States government was aware of the act, or had in the slightest degree sanctioned it, immediately to get ships ready, and to make other offensive preparations, and to allow the Press, who is always ready to inflame the passions of the people to frenzy, to prepare their minds for war. That was not the whole of the transaction, however, for the United States, before they heard a word from this country on the subject, sent a dispatch to Mr. Adams, which was shown to our government, stating that the act had not been done by their orders,—that it was a pure accident, and that they should regard the matter with the most friendly disposition towards this country. How came it that this dispatch was never published for the information of the people of this country? How came it that the flame of war was fanned by the newspapers supposed to be devoted to the government, and that one of them, said to be peculiarly devoted to the prime minister, had the audacity—I know not whence it obtained its instructions—flatly and emphatically to deny that such a dispatch had ever been received? How is it possible to maintain amicable relations with any great country, or even with any small one, unless government will manage these transactions in what I may call a more courteous and a more honorable manner? I received a letter from a most eminent gentleman resident in the United States, dated only two days before the Southern envoys were given up, in which he stated that the real difficulty encountered by the President in the matter was that the menaces of the English government had made it almost impossible for him to concede the point, and he asked whether the

English government was intending to seek a cause of quarrel or not. I am sure that the noble lord at the head of the government would himself feel more disposed to yield, and would find it more easy to grant a demand of the kind if made in a courteous and friendly manner than if accompanied by manners such as this government had offered to that of the United States. The House will observe that I am not condemning the government of this country on the main point, but that I am complaining merely because they did not do what they had to do in that manner which was most likely to remove difficulties and to preserve a friendly feeling between the two nations. The last point to which I shall direct your attention is with respect to the ships which have been sent out to prey upon the commerce of the United States, and in doing so I shall confine myself to the Alabama. This vessel was built in this country, all her munitions of war were obtained from this country, and almost every man on board was a subject of the Queen. She sailed from one of our chief ports, and she was built by a firm in which a Member of this House was, and I presume is still, interested. I don't complain now, neither did I two years ago, when the matter was brought before the House by the honorable Member for Bradford, that the Member for Birkenhead struck up a friendship with Captain Semmes, who, perhaps, in the words applied to another person under somewhat similar circumstances, "was the mildest mannered man that ever scuttled ship." I don't complain, and I have never done so, that the Member for Birkenhead looks admiringly upon what has been called the greatest example that man has ever seen of the greatest crime that man has ever committed. And I should not complain even had he entered into that gigantic traffic in flesh and blood which no subject of this realm can enter into without being deemed a felon in the eyes of our law and punished as such; but what I do complain of is that a magistrate of a county, a deputy-lieutenant, whatever that may be, and a representative of the constituency of the country, having sat in this ancient and honorable assembly, did, as I believe he did with regard to this ship, break the laws of this country, drive us into an infraction of international law, and treat with undeserved disrespect the proclamation of neutrality of the Queen. But I have another cause of complaint, though not against the honorable gentleman this time, for he having, on a previous occasion, declared that he would rather be the builder of a dozen Alabamas than do something which nobody else had done, his language was received with repeated cheers from the other side of the House.

I think that that was a very unfortunate circumstance, and I beg to tell honorable gentlemen that at the end of last session, when there was a great debate on the Denmark question, there were many men on this side of the House who had no objection whatever to see the present government turned out of office,—for they had many grounds of complaint against them,—but they felt it impossible to take upon themselves the responsibility of bringing into office and power a party who could cheer such sentiments. But turning from the honorable Member for Birkenhead to the noble lord at the head of the Foreign Office, he, who in the case of the acknowledgment of belligerent rights had proceeded with such remarkable celerity, amply compensated for it by the slowness which he displayed in the case of the Alabama. And another curious thing, which even the noble lord's colleagues have never been able to explain, is that, although he sent after the Alabama to Cork to stop her, notwithstanding she had gone out of our jurisdiction, still she was permitted subsequently to go into a dozen or a score of ports belonging to this country in various parts of the world. Now, it seems to me that this is rather a special instance of that feebleness of purpose on the part of the noble lord which has done much to mar what would otherwise have been a great political career. Well, then, the honorable Member for Birkenhead, or his firm, or his family, or whoever it is that does these things, after having seen the peril into which the country was drifting on account of the Alabama, proceeded at once to build the two rams, and it was only at the very last moment, when we were on the eve of a war with the United States, that the government had the courage to seize these vessels. There are shipowners here, and I ask them what would be the feelings of the people of this country if they had suffered as the shipowners of America have suffered? As a rule, all their ships have been driven from the ocean. Mr. Lowe, an influential shipowner of New York, has had three very large ships destroyed by the Alabama. The George Griswold, a ship of two thousand tons, that came to this country with a heavy cargo of provisions of various kinds for the suffering people of Lancashire, that very ship was destroyed on her return passage, and the ship that destroyed her may have been, and I believe

was, built by these patriotic shipbuilders of Birkenhead. Well, sir, these are things to rankle in the breast of the country that is subjected to these losses and indignities. To-day you may see by the papers that one vessel has destroyed between twelve and thirteen ships, between the Cape of Good Hope and Australia. If I had, as some honorable Members have done, thought it necessary to bring American questions before this House three or four times during the session, I should have asked questions about these ships; but no! You who were in favor of the disruption of the States do not ask questions of this kind, but refer to other points that may embarrass the government or make their difficulties greater with the United States. But the members of the government itself have not been very wise, and I shall not be thought unnecessarily critical if I say that governments generally are not very wise. Two years ago, in that very debate, the noble lord at the head of the government and the Attorney-General addressed the House. I besought the noble lord—and I do not ask favors from him very often—only to speak for five minutes words of generosity and sympathy for the government and people of the United States. He did not do it, and perhaps it was foolish to expect it. The Attorney-General made a most able speech, but it was the only time I ever listened to him with pain, for I thought his speech full of bad morals and bad law; and I am quite certain that he gave an account of the facts which was not so ingenuous or fair as the House had a right to expect at his hands. Next session the noble lord and the Attorney-General turned right round and had a different story to tell, and as the aspect of things changed on the other side they gradually returned to good sense and fairness. They were not the only members of the government who have spoken on this subject. The noble lord the Secretary of State for Foreign Affairs and the Chancellor of the Exchequer have also made speeches. Every one will feel that I would not willingly say a word against either of them, because I do not know among the official statesmen of this country two men for whom I feel greater sympathy or more respect, but I have to complain of them that they should both go to Newcastle, a town in which I feel great interest, and there give forth their words of offense and unwisdom. The noble lord, we all know very well, can say very good and very smart things, but I regret to say that what he said was not true, and I, for one, have not much respect for things that

are smart but not true. The Chancellor of the Exchequer appeared from the papers to have spoken in a tone of exultation and to have made a speech which I undertake to say he wishes he had never made. But the House must bear in mind that these gentlemen are set on a hill. They are not obscure men, making speeches in a public house or in some mechanics' institute, but they are men whose voices are heard wherever the English language is known; and, knowing what effect their eloquence produced in Lancashire,—how they affected prices, and the profits and losses of every one, and changed the course of business,—I can form an idea of the irritation that these speeches caused in the United States. Then, I must refer to the unwise abuse of the learned gentleman, the Member for Sheffield, and, I may add to that, the unsleeping ill-will of the noble lord the Member for Stamford. I am not sure that either of them is converted, for I thought I heard something from the honorable and learned Member that shows he retains his sentiments. [Mr. Roebuck—"Exactly."]

I hope that these things are regretted and repented, and that any one who is thus ungenerous to the United States and the people of that country will never fall into trouble of any kind. But if you do, you will find your countrymen are more generous to you than you have been to the people of the United States. And now as to the Press. I think it unnecessary to say much about that, because now every night these unfortunate writers are endeavoring to back out of everything they have been saying. I only hope that their power for evil in future will be greatly lessened by the stupendous exhibition of ignorance and folly that they have made to the world. Having made this statement, I must expect that if the noble lord the Member for Stamford could get up again he would say, if all this be true, and if these speeches created all this irritation in the United States, is there not reason to fear that this irritation will provoke a desire for vengeance, and that the chances of war will be increased by it? I say that war from such a course is to the last degree improbable. There has been another side to this expression of opinion. All England is not included in the rather general condemnation I have thought it my duty to express. What have the millions been saying and doing?—those whom you have been so very much afraid of, especially the noble lord the Member for Stamford, who objects to the transfer of power into

their hands. I beg leave to tell the House that, taking the counties of Lancaster and York, your two greatest counties, there are millions of men there who, by their industry, not only have created but sustain the fabric of our national power, who have had no kind of sympathy with the men whom I am condemning. They are more generous and wise. They have shown that magnanimity and love of freedom are not extinct among us. I speak of the county from which I come,—a county of many sorrows, that have hung like a dark cloud over almost every home during the last three years. In the country all attempts of the agents of the Confederacy, by money, by printing, by platform speaking, and by agitation, have utterly failed to elicit any expression of sympathy with the American insurrection; and if the bond of union and friendship between England and the United States remain unbroken, we have not to thank the wealthy and the cultivated, but the laborious millions, whom statesmen and historians too frequently make little account of. They know something of the United States that the honorable gentlemen opposite and some on this side of the House do not know—that every man of them would be welcome on the American continent if they chose to go there, that every right and privilege which the greatest and highest in that country enjoy would be theirs, and that every man would have given to him by the United States a free gift of one hundred and sixty acres of the most fertile land in the world. Honorable gentlemen may laugh, but that is a good deal to a man who has no land, and I can assure them that this Homestead Act has a great effect on the population of the north of England. I can tell them, too, that the laboring population of these counties, the artisans and the mechanics, will give you no encouragement to any policy that is intended to estrange the people of the United States from the people of the United Kingdom. But, sir, we have other securities for peace not less than these, and I find them in the character of the government and people of the American Union. Now, I think the right honorable gentleman, the Member for Bucks, referred to what might reasonably be supposed to happen in case the rebellion was suppressed. He did not think when a nation was exhausted that it would rush rashly into a new struggle. The loss of life has been great, the loss of treasure enormous. Happily for them, it was not to keep a Bourbon on the throne of France, or to keep the Turks in Europe. It was for an object which every man can comprehend who examines it by the light of his own intelligence and his own conscience; and if men have given their lives and possessions for the attainment of the great end of maintaining the integrity and unity of a great country, the history of the future must be written in a different spirit from the history of the past, if she expresses any condemnation of that temper. But Mr. Lincoln is President of the United States,—President now for the second term; he was elected exclusively at first by what was termed the Republican party, and he has been elected now by what may be called the great Union party of the nation. But Mr. Lincoln's party has always been for peace. That party in the North has never carried on any war of aggression, and has never desired one. Now, speaking only of the North,—of the free States,—let the House remember that landed property, and, indeed, property of all kinds, is more universally diffused there than in any other nation, and that instruction and school education are also more widely diffused. Well, I say they have never hitherto carried on a war for aggression or for vengeance, and I believe they will not begin one now. Canada is, indeed, a tempting bait. The noble lord agrees in that—it is a very tempting bait, not for purposes of annexation, but of humiliating this country. I agree with honorable gentlemen who have said that it would be discreditable to England in the light of her past history that she should leave any portion of her empire undefended which she could defend. But still it is admitted,—and I think the speech of the right honorable gentleman, the Member for Calne, produced a great effect upon those who heard it,—that once at war with the United States for any cause, Canada cannot be defended by any power on land or at sea which this country could raise or spare for that purpose.

I am very sorry, not that we cannot defend Canada, understand, but that any portion of the dominions of the British crown is in such circumstances that it might tempt an evil-disposed people to attack it with a view to humiliate us, because I believe that transactions which humiliate a government and a nation are not only discreditable, but do great national harm. Is there a war party, then, in America? I believe there is, and it is the same party which was a war party eighty years ago. It is the party represented by a number of gentlemen who sit on that bench, and by some who sit here. They, sir, in the United

States who are hostile to this country are those who were recently the malcontent subjects of the right honorable gentleman, the Member for Tamworth. They are those and such as those to whom the noble lord at the head of the government offers consolation, only in such a shape as this, when he tells them that the rights of the tenant are the wrongs of the landlord. Sir, that is the only war party in the United States, and it was a war party in the days of Lord North. But the real power of the United States does not reside in that class. You talk of American mobs. Excepting some portion of the population of New York,—and I would not apply the word even to them,—such things as mobs in the United States for the sake of forcing either Congress or the Executive to a particular course of action are altogether unknown. The real mob in your sense is that party of chivalrous gentlemen in the South who have received, I am sorry to say, so much sympathy from some persons in this country and in this House. But the real power is in the hands of another class,—the landowners throughout the country,—and there are millions of them. Why, in this last election for the presidency of the United States I was told by a citizen of New York, who took a most active part in the election, that in that State alone 100,000 Irish votes were given "solidly," as it is called, for General McClellan, and that not more than 2,000 were given for President Lincoln. You see the preponderance of that party in the city of New York, and its vast influence in the State of New York; but throughout the whole of the United States they form but a very small percentage, which has no sensible effect upon the legislation of Congress or the Constitution of the government. My honorable friend, the Member for Bradford, referred to a point which, I suppose, has really been the cause of this debate, and that was the temper of the United States in making some demands upon our government. Well, I asked a question the other evening, after one that had been put by the noble lord [Lord R. Cecil], whether we had not claims upon them. I understand the claims made by the United States may amount to £300,000 or £400,000, and probably the sum of our claims may amount to as much as that. But if any man has a right to go to law with another, he is obliged to go into court and the case must be heard before the proper tribunal. And why should it not be so between two great nations and two free governments? If one has claims against the other, the other has claims

against it, and nothing can be more fair than that those claims should be courteously and honestly considered. It is quite absurd to suppose that the English government and the government at Washington could have a question about half a million of money which they could not settle. I think the noble lord considers it a question of honor. But all questions of property are questions of law, and you go to a lawyer to settle them. Assuredly, this would be a fit case for the Senate of Hamburg, just as much as the case between this country and Brazil. Well, then, I rest in the most perfect security that as the war in America draws to a close, if happily we shall become more generous to them, they will become less irritated against us; and when passions have cooled down, I don't see why Lord Russell and Mr. Seward, Mr. Adams, and I hope, Sir F. Bruce, should not be able to settle these matters between the two nations. I have only one more observation to make. I apprehend that the root of all the unfortunate circumstances that have arisen is a feeling of jealousy which we have cherished with regard to the American Union. It was very much shown at the beginning of this war when an honorable Member whom I will not name, for he would not like it now, spoke of "the bursting of the bubble republic." Well, I recollect that Lord John Russell, as he then was, turned round and rebuked him in language worthy of his name, character, and position. I beg to tell that gentleman and any one else who talks about bubble republics that I have a great suspicion that a great many bubbles will burst before that bubble bursts. Why should we fear a great nation on the American continent? Some fear that a great nation would be arrogant and aggressive. But that does not at all follow. It does not depend altogether upon the size of a nation, but upon its qualities, and upon the intelligence, instruction, and morals of its people. You fancy that the supremacy of the sea will pass away from you; and the noble lord, though wiser than many others, will lament that 'Rule Britannia,' that noble old song, should become antiquated at last. Well, but if the supremacy of the sea excites the arrogance of this country, the sooner it becomes obsolete the better. I don't believe it to be for the advantage of this country or of any other that any one nation should pride itself upon what it terms the supremacy of the sea, and I hope the time is come—and I believe it is—when we shall find that law and justice shall guide the councils and direct the policy of the Christian nations of the world.

Now, nature will not be baffled because we are jealous of the United States. The laws of nature will not be overthrown. At this moment the population of the United States is not less than 35,000,000 souls. If the next Parliament live to the age of the present, the population of the United States will be 40,000,000, and you may calculate that the rate of increase will be at rather more than a million per year. Who is to gainsay this; who is to contradict it? Will constant snarling at a great republic alter the state of things, or swell us islanders to 40,000,000 or 50,000,000, and bring them down to 20,000,000 or 30,000,000? Honorable Members should consider these facts and should learn from them that it is the interest of this nation to be one in perfect courtesy and perfect amity with the English nation on the other side of the Atlantic. I am certain that the longer the nation exists, the less will our people be disposed to sustain you in any needless hostility against them, or in any jealousy of them; and I am the more convinced of this from what I have seen of their conduct in the north of England during the last four years. I believe, on the other hand, that the American people, when this excitement is over, will be willing, so far as regards any aggressive acts against us, to bury in oblivion transactions which have given them much pain, and they will probably make an allowance which they may fairly make,—that the people of this country, even those high in rank and distinguished in culture, have had a very inadequate knowledge of the transactions which have really taken place in that country since the beginning of the war. Now, it is on record that when the author of 'The Decline and Fall of the Roman Empire' was about beginning his great work, David Hume wrote a letter to him, urging him not to employ the French, but the English tongue, because, he said, "our establishments in America promise a superior stability and duration to the English language." How far the promise has been in part fulfilled, we who are living now can tell. But how far it will be more largely and more completely fulfilled in after times, we must leave for after times to tell. I believe, however, that in the centuries which are to come it will be the greatest pride and the highest renown of England that from her loins have sprung a hundred—it may be two hundred—millions of men to dwell and to prosper on the continent which the old Genoese gave to Europe. Now, sir, if the sentiment which I have heard to-night shall become the sentiment of the Parliament and people of the

United Kingdom, and if the moderation which I have described shall mark the course of the government and people of the United States, then, notwithstanding some present irritation and some fresh distrust,—and I have faith, mind, both in us and in them,—I believe that these two great commonwealths may march on abreast, parents and guardians of freedom and justice, wheresoever their language shall be spoken and their power shall extend.

MORALITY AND MILITARY GREATNESS

(Delivered at Birmingham, October 29th, 1858)

WE ALL know and deplore that at the present moment a larger number of the grown men of Europe are employed, and a larger portion of the industry of Europe is absorbed, to provide for and maintain the enormous armaments which are now on foot in every considerable continental State. Assuming, then, that Europe is not much better in consequence of the sacrifices we have made, let us inquire what has been the result in England, because, after all, that is the question which it becomes us most to consider. I believe that I understate the sum when I say that, in pursuit of this will-o'-the-wisp (the liberties of Europe and the balance of power), there has been extracted from the industry of the people of this small island no less an amount than £2,000,000,000. I cannot imagine how much £2,000,000,000 is, and therefore I shall not attempt to make you comprehend it.

I presume it is something like those vast and incomprehensible astronomical distances with which we have been lately made familiar; but, however familiar, we feel that we do not know one bit more about them than we did before. When I try to think of that sum of £2,000,000,000 there is a sort of vision passes before my mind's eye. I see your peasant laborer delve and plough, sow and reap, sweat beneath the summer's sun, or grow prematurely old before the winter's blast. I see your noble mechanic with his manly countenance and his matchless skill, toiling at his bench or his forge. I see one of the workers in our factories in the North, a woman,—a girl it may be, gentle and good, as many of them are, as your sisters and daughters are,—I see her intent upon the spindle, whose

more freedom to write or speak, or politically to act, than there is now in the most despotic country of Europe.

But, it may be asked, did nobody gain? If Europe is no better, and the people of England have been so much worse, who has benefited by the new system of foreign policy? What has been the fate of those who were enthroned at the Revolution, and whose supremacy has been for so long a period undisputed among us? Mr. Kinglake, the author of an interesting book on Eastern travel, describing the habits of some acquaintances that he made in the Syrian deserts, says that the jackals of the desert follow their prey in families, like the place-hunters of Europe. I will reverse, if you like, the comparison, and say that the great territorial families of England, which were enthroned at the Revolution, have followed their prey like the jackals of the desert. Do you not observe at a glance that, from the time of William III., by reason of the foreign policy which I denounce, wars have been multiplied, taxes increased, loans made, and the sums of money which every year the government has to expend augmented, and that so the patronage at the disposal of ministers must have increased also, and the families who were enthroned and made powerful in the legislation and administration of the country must have had the first pull at, and the largest profit out of, that patronage? There is no actuary in existence who can calculate how much of the wealth, of the strength, of the supremacy of the territorial families of England has been derived from an unholy participation in the fruits of the industry of the people, which have been wrested from them by every device of taxation, and squandered in every conceivable crime of which a government could possibly be guilty.

The more you examine this matter, the more you will come to the conclusion which I have arrived at, that this foreign policy, this regard for the "liberties of Europe," this care at one time for "the Protestant interests," this excessive love for "the balance of power," is neither more nor less than a gigantic system of out-door relief for the aristocracy of Great Britain. [Great laughter.] I observe that you receive that declaration as if it were some new and important discovery. In 1815, when the great war with France was ended, every Liberal in England whose politics, whose hopes, and whose faith had not been crushed out of him by the tyranny of the time of that war, was fully aware of this, and openly admitted it; and up to 1832, and for

revolutions are so rapid that the eye fails altogether to detect them, or to watch the alternating flight of the unresting shuttle. I turn again to another portion of your population, which, "plunged in mines, forgets a sun was made," and I see the man who brings up from the secret chambers of the earth the elements of the riches and greatness of his country. When I see all this I have before me a mass of produce and of wealth which I am no more able to comprehend than I am that £2,000,000,000 of which I have spoken, but I behold in its full proportions the hideous error of your governments, whose fatal policy consumes in some cases a half, never less than a third, of all the results of that industry which God intended should fertilize and bless every home in England, but the fruits of which are squandered in every part of the surface of the globe, without producing the smallest good to the people of England.

We have, it is true, some visible results that are of a more positive character. We have that which some people call a great advantage,—the national debt,—a debt which is now so large that the most prudent, the most economical, and the most honest have given up all hope, not of its being paid off, but of its being diminished in amount.

We have, too, taxes which have been during many years so onerous that there have been times when the patient beasts of burden threatened to revolt,—so onerous that it has been utterly impossible to levy them with any kind of honest equality, according to the means of the people to pay them. We have that, moreover, which is a standing wonder to all foreigners who consider our condition,—an amount of apparently immovable pauperism which to strangers is wholly irreconcilable with the fact that we, as a nation, produce more of what should make us all comfortable than is produced by any other nation of similar numbers on the face of the globe. Let us likewise remember that during the period of those great and so-called glorious contests on the continent of Europe, every description of home reform was not only delayed, but actually crushed out of the minds of the great bulk of the people. There can be no doubt whatever that in 1793 England was about to realize political changes and reforms, such as did not appear again until 1830, and during the period of that war, which now almost all men agree to have been wholly unnecessary, we were passing through a period which may be described as the dark age of English politics; when there was no

some years afterward, it was the fixed and undoubted creed of the great Liberal party. But somehow all is changed. We who stand upon the old landmarks, who walk in the old paths, who would conserve what is wise and prudent, are hustled and shoved about as if we were come to turn the world upside down. The change which has taken place seems to confirm the opinion of a lamented friend of mine, who, not having succeeded in all his hopes, thought that men made no progress whatever, but went round and round like a squirrel in a cage. The idea is now so general that it is our duty to meddle everywhere, that it really seems as if we had pushed the Tories from the field, expelling them by our competition. . . .

It is for you to decide whether our greatness shall be only temporary, or whether it shall be enduring. When I am told that the greatness of our country is shown by the £100,000,000 of revenue produced, may I not also ask how it is that we have 1,100,000 paupers in this kingdom, and why it is that £7,000,000 should be taken from the industry chiefly of the laboring classes to support a small nation, as it were, of paupers? Since your legislation upon the corn laws, you have not only had nearly £20,000,000 of food brought into the country annually, but such an extraordinary increase of trade that your exports are about doubled, and yet I understand that in the year 1856, for I have no later return, there were no less than 1,100,000 paupers in the United Kingdom, and the sum raised in poor-rates was not less than £7,200,000. And that cost of pauperism is not the full amount, for there is a vast amount of temporary, casual, and vagrant pauperism that does not come in to swell that sum.

Then do not you well know—I know it, because I live among the population of Lancashire, and I doubt not the same may be said of the population of this city and county—that just above the level of the 1,100,000 there is at least an equal number who are ever oscillating between independence and pauperism, who, with a heroism which is not the less heroic because it is secret and unrecorded, are doing their very utmost to maintain an honorable and independent position before their fellow-men?

While Irish labor, notwithstanding the improvement which has taken place in Ireland, is only paid at the rate of about one shilling a day; while in the straths and glens of Scotland there are hundreds of shepherd families whose whole food almost consists of oatmeal porridge from day to day, and from week to week; while these things continue, I say that we have no reason to be self-satisfied and contented with our position, but that we who are in Parliament and are more directly responsible for affairs, and you who are also responsible though in a lesser degree, are bound by the sacred duty which we owe our country to examine why it is that with all this trade, all this industry, and all this personal freedom, there is still so much that is unsound at the base of our social fabric? . . .

I have been already told by a very eminent newspaper publisher in Calcutta, who, commenting on a speech I made at the close of the session with regard to the condition of India and our future policy in that country, said that the policy I recommended was intended to strike at the root of the advancement of the British empire, and that its advancement did not necessarily involve the calamities which I pointed out as likely to occur.

My Calcutta critic assured me that Rome pursued a similar policy for a period of eight centuries, and that for those eight centuries she remained great. Now, I do not think that examples taken from pagan, sanguinary Rome are proper models for the imitation of a Christian country, nor would I limit my hopes of the greatness of England even to the long duration of eight hundred years.

But what is Rome now? The great city is dead. A poet has described her as "the lone mother of dead empires." Her language even is dead. Her very tombs are empty; the ashes of her most illustrious citizens are dispersed.

"The Scipios' tomb contains no ashes now." Yet I am asked, I, who am one of the legislators of a Christian country, to measure my policy by the policy of ancient and pagan Rome!

I believe there is no permanent greatness to a nation except it be based upon morality. I do not care for military greatness or military renown. I care for the condition of the people among whom I live. There is no man in England who is less likely to speak irreverently of the crown and monarchy of England than I am; but crowns, coronets, mitres, military display, the pomp of war, wide colonies, and a huge empire are, in my view, all trifles, light as air, and not worth considering, unless with them you can have a fair share of comfort, contentment, and happiness among the great body of the people. Palaces, baronial castles, great halls, stately mansions, do not make a

II—41

nation. The nation in every country dwells in the cottage; and unless the light of your constitution can shine there, unless the beauty of your legislation and the excellence of your statesmanship are impressed there on the feelings and condition of the people, rely upon it you have yet to learn the duties of government.

I have not, as you have observed, pleaded that this country should remain without adequate and scientific means of defense. I acknowledge it to be the duty of your statesmen, acting upon the known opinions and principles of ninety-nine out of every hundred persons in the country, at all times, with all possible moderation, but with all possible efficiency, to take steps which shall preserve order within and on the confines of your kingdom. But I shall repudiate and denounce the expenditure of every shilling, the engagement of every man, the employment of every ship, which has no object but intermeddling in the affairs of other countries, and endeavoring to extend the boundaries of an empire which is already large enough to satisfy the greatest ambition, and I fear is much too large for the highest statesmanship to which any man has yet attained.

The most ancient of profane historians has told us that the Scythians of his time were a very warlike people, and that they elevated an old cimeter upon a platform as a symbol of Mars,— for to Mars alone, I believe, they built altars and offered sacrifices. To this cimeter they offered sacrifices of horses and cattle, the main wealth of the country, and more costly sacrifices than to all the rest of their gods. I often ask myself whether we are at all advanced in one respect beyond those Scythians. What are our contributions to charity, to education, to morality, to religion, to justice, and to civil government, when compared with the wealth we expend in sacrifices to the old cimeter? Two nights ago I addressed in this hall a vast assembly composed to a great extent of your countrymen who have no political power, who are at work from the dawn of the day to the evening, and who have therefore limited means of informing themselves on these great subjects. Now I am privileged to speak to a somewhat different audience. You represent those of your great community who have a more complete education, who have on some points greater intelligence, and in whose hands reside the power and influence of the district. I am speaking, too, within the hearing of those whose gentle nature, whose finer instincts, whose purer

minds, have not suffered as some of us have suffered in the turmoil and strife of life. You can mold opinion, you can create political power;—you cannot think a good thought on this subject and communicate it to your neighbors, you cannot make these points topics of discussion in your social circles and more general meetings, without affecting sensibly and speedily the course which the government of your country will pursue.

May I ask you, then, to believe, as I do most devoutly believe, that the moral law was not written for men alone in their individual character, but that it was written as well for nations, and for nations great as this of which we are citizens. If nations reject and deride that moral law, there is a penalty which will inevitably follow. It may not come at once, it may not come in our lifetime; but rely upon it, the great Italian is not a poet only, but a prophet, when he says:—

"The sword of heaven is not in haste to smite,
Nor yet doth linger."

We have experience, we have beacons, we have landmarks enough. We know what the past has cost us, we know how much and how far we have wandered, but we are not left without a guide. It is true we have not, as an ancient people, had Urim and Thummim,—those oraculous gems on Aaron's breast,— from which to take counsel, but we have the unchangeable and eternal principles of the moral law to guide us, and only so far as we walk by that guidance can we be permanently a great nation, or our people a happy people.

PHILLIPS BROOKS

(1835-1893)

PHILLIPS BROOKS ranks with Henry Ward Beecher as one of the most admired pulpit orators of the latter half of the nineteenth century. He was less popular than Beecher because he was less emotional and more polished. His style approximates the simplicity of conversation even when it is most artistic. It has an Attic severity, which, while it ennobles the successful expression of a great thought, requires great thoughts to make it tolerable. And the underlying thoughts which shaped the life of Brooks and made him an orator were great. He sympathized at once with what is weakest and what is strongest in human nature. He is remarkable for restrained force, which, in spite of restraint and the better because of it, moves irresistibly forward, drawing the mind of the hearer with it.

He was born December 13th, 1835. His father, a Boston merchant, educated him at Harvard. After studying theology for four years in an Episcopal seminary, he entered the ministry of that church. After ten years in Philadelphia, he became rector of Trinity Church, Boston, assuming thus the cure of the souls of the "largest and wealthiest Episcopal congregation in Massachusetts." He was elected bishop of Massachusetts in 1891 and died January 23d, 1893.

LINCOLN AS A TYPICAL AMERICAN

(Delivered in Philadelphia as a Funeral Oration)

WHILE I speak to you to-day, the body of the President who ruled this people, is lying, honored and loved, in our city. It is impossible with that sacred presence in our midst for me to stand and speak of ordinary topics which occupy the pulpit. I must speak of him to-day; and I therefore undertake to do what I had intended to do at some future time, to invite you to study with me the character of Abraham Lincoln, the impulses of his life and the causes of his death. I know how hard it is to do it rightly, how impossible it is to do it worthily.

But I shall speak with confidence, because I speak to those who love him, and whose ready love will fill out the deficiencies in a picture which my words will weakly try to draw.

We take it for granted, first of all, that there is an essential connection between Mr. Lincoln's character and his violent and bloody death. It is no accident, no arbitrary decree of Providence. He lived as he did, and he died as he did, because he was what he was. The more we see of events, the less we come to believe in any fate or destiny except the destiny of character. It will be our duty, then, to see what there was in the character of our great President that created the history of his life, and at last produced the catastrophe of his cruel death. After the first trembling horror, the first outburst of indignant sorrow, has grown calm, these are the questions which we are bound to ask and answer.

It is not necessary for me even to sketch the biography of Mr. Lincoln. He was born in Kentucky fifty-six years ago, when Kentucky was a pioneer State. He lived, as a boy and man, the hard and needy life of a backwoodsman, a farmer, a river boatman, and, finally, by his own efforts at self-education, of an active, respected, influential citizen, in the half-organized and manifold interests of a new and energetic community. From his boyhood up he lived in direct and vigorous contact with men and things, not as in older States and easier conditions with words and theories; and both his moral convictions and intellectual opinions gathered from that contact a supreme degree of that character by which men knew him, that character which is the most distinctive possession of the best American nature, that almost indescribable quality which we call, in general, clearness or truth, and which appears in the physical structure as health, in the moral constitution as honesty, in the mental structure as sagacity, and in the region of active life as practicalness. This one character, with many sides, all shaped by the same essential force and testifying to the same inner influences, was what was powerful in him and decreed for him the life he was to live and the death he was to die. We must take no smaller view than this of what he was. Even his physical conditions are not to be forgotten in making up his character. We make too little always of the physical; certainly we make too little of it here if we lose out of sight the strength and muscular activity, the power of doing and enduring, which the backwoods boy inherited from

generations of hard-living ancestors, and appropriated for his own by a long discipline of bodily toil. He brought to the solution of the question of labor in this country not merely a mind, but a body thoroughly in sympathy with labor, full of the culture of labor, bearing witness to the dignity and excellence of work in every muscle that work had toughened and every sense that work had made clear and true. He could not have brought the mind for his task so perfectly, unless he had first brought the body whose rugged and stubborn health was always contradicting to him the false theories of labor, and always asserting the true.

As to the moral and mental powers which distinguished him, all embraceable under this general description of clearness of truth, the most remarkable thing is the way in which they blend with one another, so that it is next to impossible to examine them in separation. A great many people have discussed very crudely whether Abraham Lincoln was an intellectual man or not; as if intellect were a thing always of the same sort, which you could precipitate from the other constituents of a man's nature and weigh by itself, and compare by pounds and ounces in this man with another. The fact is, that in all the simplest characters that line between the mental and moral natures is always vague and indistinct. They run together, and in their best combinations you are unable to discriminate, in the wisdom which is their result, how much is moral and how much is intellectual. You are unable to tell whether in the wise acts and words which issue from such a life there is more of the righteousness that comes of a clear conscience, or of the sagacity that comes of a clear brain. In more complex characters and under more complex conditions, the moral and the mental lives come to be less healthily combined. They co-operate, they help each other less. They come even to stand over against each other as antagonists; till we have that vague but most melancholy notion which pervades the life of all elaborate civilization, that goodness and greatness, as we call them, are not to be looked for together; till we expect to see and so do see a feeble and narrow conscientiousness on the one hand, and a bad, unprincipled intelligence on the other, dividing the suffrages of men.

It is the great boon of such characters as Mr. Lincoln's, that they reunite what God has joined together and man has put asunder. In him was vindicated the greatness of real goodness

and the goodness of real greatness. The twain were one flesh. Not one of all the multitudes who stood and looked up to him for direction with such a loving and implicit trust can tell you to-day whether the wise judgments that he gave came most from a strong head or a sound heart. If you ask them, they are puzzled. There are men as good as he, but they do bad things. There are men as intelligent as he, but they do foolish things. In him goodness and intelligence combined and made their best result of wisdom. For perfect truth consists not merely in the right constituents of character, but in their right and intimate conjunction. This union of the mental and moral into a life of admirable simplicity is what we most admire in children; but in them .t is unsettled and unpractical. But when it is preserved into manhood, deepened into reliability and maturity, it is that glorified childlikeness, that high and reverend simplicity, which shames and baffles the most accomplished astuteness, and is chosen by God to fill his purposes when he needs a ruler for his people, of faithful and true heart, such as he had who was our President.

Another evident quality of such a character as this will be its freshness or newness, if we may so speak. Its freshness or readiness,—call it what you will,—its ability to take up new duties and do them in a new way, will result of necessity from its truth and clearness. The simple natures and forces will always be the most pliant ones. Water bends and shapes itself to any channel. Air folds and adapts itself to each new figure. They are the simplest and the most infinitely active things in nature. So this nature, in very virtue of its simplicity, must be also free, always fitting itself to each new need. It will always start from the most fundamental and eternal conditions, and work in the straightest even although they be the newest ways, to the present prescribed purpose. In one word, it must be broad and independent and radical. So that freedom and radicalness in the character of Abraham Lincoln were not separate qualities, but the necessary results of his simplicity and childlikeness and truth.

Here then we have some conception of the man. Out of this character came the life which we admire and the death which we lament to-day. He was called in that character to that life and death. It was just the nature, as you see, which a new nation such as ours ought to produce. All the conditions of his

birth, his youth, his manhood, which made him what he was, were not irregular and exceptional, but were the normal conditions of a new and simple country. His pioneer home in Indiana was a type of the pioneer land in which he lived. If ever there was a man who was a part of the time and country he lived in, this was he. The same simple respect for labor won in the school of work and incorporated into blood and muscle; the same unassuming loyalty to the simple virtues of temperance and industry and integrity; the same sagacious judgment which had learned to be quick-eyed and quick-brained in the constant presence of emergency; the same direct and clear thought about things, social, political, and religious, that was in him supremely, was in the people he was sent to rule. Surely, with such a typeman for ruler, there would seem to be but a smooth and even road over which he might lead the people whose character he represented into the new region of national happiness and comfort and usefulness, for which that character had been designed.

But then we come to the beginning of all trouble. Abraham Lincoln was the type-man of the country, but not of the whole country. This character which we have been trying to describe was the character of an American under the discipline of freedom. There was another American character which had been developed under the influence of slavery. There was no one American character embracing the land. There were two characters, with impulses of irrepressible and deadly conflict. This citizen whom we have been honoring and praising represented one. The whole great scheme with which he was ultimately brought in conflict, and which has finally killed him, represented the other. Beside this nature, true and fresh and new, there was another nature, false and effete and old. The one nature found itself in a new world, and set itself to discover the new ways for the new duties that were given it. The other nature, full of the false pride of blood, set itself to reproduce in a new world the institutions and the spirit of the old, to build anew the structure of the feudalism which had been corrupt in its own day, and which had been left far behind by the advancing conscience and needs of the progressing race. The one nature magnified labor, the other nature depreciated and despised it. The one honored the laborer, and the other scorned him. The one was simple and direct; the other complex, full of sophistries and self-excuses. The one was free to look all that claimed to be truth in the face, and separate the error from the truth that might be in it; the other did not dare to investigate, because its own established prides and systems were dearer to it than the truth itself, and so even truth went about in it doing the work of error. The one was ready to state broad principles, of the brotherhood of man, the universal fatherhood and justice of God, however imperfectly it might realize them in practice; the other denied even the principles, and so dug deep and laid below its special sins the broad foundation of a consistent, acknowledged sinfulness. In a word, one nature was full of the influences of freedom, the other nature was full of the influences of slavery. . . .

The cause that Abraham Lincoln died for shall grow stronger by his death,—stronger and sterner. Stronger to set its pillars deep into the structure of our nation's life; sterner to execute the justice of the Lord upon his enemies. Stronger to spread its arms and grasp our whole land into freedom; sterner to sweep the last poor ghost of Slavery out of our haunted homes. But while we feel the folly of this act, let not its folly hide its wickedness. It was the wickedness of Slavery putting on a foolishness for which its wickedness and that alone is responsible, that robbed the nation of a President and the people of a father. And remember this, that the folly of the Slave power in striking the representative of Freedom, and thinking that thereby it killed Freedom itself, is only a folly that we shall echo if we dare to think that in punishing the representatives of Slavery who did this deed, we are putting Slavery to death. Dispersing armies and hanging traitors, imperatively as justice and necessity may demand them both, are not killing the spirit out of which they sprang. The traitor must die because he has committed treason. The murderer must die because he has committed murder. Slavery must die, because out of it, and it alone, came forth the treason of the traitor and the murder of the murderer. Do not say that it is dead. It is not, while its essential spirit lives. While one man counts another man his born inferior for the color of his skin, while both in North and South prejudices and practices, which the law cannot touch, but which God hates, keep alive in our people's hearts the spirit of the old iniquity, it is not dead. The new American nature must supplant the old. We must grow like our President, in his truth, his independence, his religion, and his wide humanity. Then the character by which he died shall be in us, and by it we shall live. Then

peace shall come that knows no war, and law that knows no treason; and full of his spirit a grateful land shall gather round his grave, and, in the daily psalm of prosperous and righteous living, thank God forever for his life and death.

So let him lie here in our midst to-day, and let our people go and bend with solemn thoughtfulness and look upon his face and read the lessons of his burial. As he paused here on his journey from the Western home and told us what by the help of God he meant to do, so let him pause upon his way back to his Western grave and tell us, with a silence more eloquent than words, how bravely, how truly, by the strength of God, he did it. God brought him up as he brought David up from the sheepfolds to feed Jacob, his people, and Israel, his inheritance. He came up in earnestness and faith, and he goes back in triumph. As he pauses here to-day, and from his cold lips bids us bear witness how he has met the duty that was laid on him, what can we say out of our full hearts but this—"He fed them with a faithful and true heart, and ruled them prudently with all his power."

The *Shepherd of the People!* that old name that the best rulers ever craved. What ruler ever won it like this dead President of ours? He fed us faithfully and truly. He fed us with counsel when we were in doubt, with inspiration when we sometimes faltered, with caution when we would be rash, with calm, clear, trustful cheerfulness through many an hour when our hearts were dark. He fed hungry souls all over the country with sympathy and consolation. He spread before the whole land feasts of great duty and devotion and patriotism, on which the land grew strong. He fed us with solemn, solid truths. He taught us the sacredness of government, the wickedness of treason. He made our souls glad and vigorous with the love of liberty that was in his. He showed us how to love truth and yet be charitable—how to hate wrong and all oppression, and yet not treasure one personal injury or insult. He fed *all* his people, from the highest to the lowest, from the most privileged down to the most enslaved. Best of all, he fed us with a reverent and genuine religion. He spread before us the love and fear of God just in that shape in which we need them most, and out of his faithful service of a higher Master who of us has not taken and eaten and grown strong? "He fed them with a faithful and true heart." Yes, till the last. For at the last, behold him

standing with hand reached out to feed the South with mercy, and the North with charity, and the whole land with peace, when the Lord who had sent him called him, and his work was done!

He stood once on the battlefield of our own State, and said of the brave men who had saved it words as noble as any countryman of ours ever spoke. Let us stand in the country he has saved, and which is to be his grave and monument, and say of Abraham Lincoln what he said of the soldiers who had died at Gettysburg. He stood there with their graves before him, and these are the words he said:—

"We cannot dedicate, we cannot consecrate, we cannot hallow this ground. The brave men who struggled here have consecrated it far beyond our power to add or detract. The world will little note nor long remember what we say here, but it can never forget what they did here. It is for us the living rather to be dedicated to the unfinished work which they who fought here have thus far so nobly advanced. It is rather for us to be here dedicated to the great task remaining before us, that from these honored dead we take increased devotion to that cause for which they gave the last full measure of devotion; that we here highly resolve that these dead shall not have died in vain; and this nation, under God, shall have a new birth of freedom; and that government of the people, by the people, and for the people, shall not perish from the earth."

May God make us worthy of the memory of Abraham Lincoln!

POWER OVER THE LIVES OF OTHERS

TELL me you have a sin that you mean to commit this evening that is going to make this night black. What can keep you from committing that sin? Suppose you look into its consequences. Suppose the wise man tells you what will be the physical consequences of that sin. You shudder and you shrink, and, perhaps, you are partially deterred. Suppose you see the glory that might come to you, physical, temporal, spiritual, if you do not commit that sin. The opposite of it shows itself to you—the blessing and the richness in your life. Again there comes a great power that shall control your lust and wickedness. Suppose there comes to you something even deeper than that, no consequence on consequence at all, but simply an abhorrence for

the thing, so that your whole nature shrinks from it as the nature of God shrinks from a sin that is polluting and filthy and corrupt and evil. They are all great powers. Let us thank God for them all. He knows that we are weak enough to need every power that can possibly be brought to bear upon our feeble lives; but if, along with all of them, there could come this other power, if along with them there could come the certainty that if you refrain from that sin to-night you make the sum of sin that is in the world, and so the sum of all temptation that is in the world, and so the sum of future evil that is to spring out of temptation in the world, less, shall there not be a nobler impulse rise up in your heart, and shall you not say: "I will not do it; I will be honest, I will be sober, I will be pure, at least, to-night"? I dare to think that there are men here to whom that appeal can come, men, who, perhaps, will be all dull and deaf if one speaks to them about their personal salvation; who, if one dares to picture to them, appealing to their better nature, trusting to their nobler soul, that there is in them the power to save other men from sin, and to help the work of God by the control of their own passions and the fulfillment of their own duty, will be stirred to the higher life. Men—very often we do not trust them enough—will answer to the higher appeal that seems to be beyond them when the poor, lower appeal that comes within the region of their selfishness is cast aside, and they will have nothing to do with it.

Oh, this marvelous, this awful power that we have over other people's lives! Oh, the power of the sin that you have done years and years ago! It is awful to think of it. I think there is hardly anything more terrible to the human thought than this—the picture of a man who, having sinned years and years ago in a way that involved other souls in his sin, and then, having repented of his sin and undertaken another life, knows certainly that the power, the consequence of that sin is going on outside of his reach, beyond even his ken and knowledge. He cannot touch it. You wronged a soul ten years ago. You taught a boy how to tell his first mercantile lie; you degraded the early standards of his youth. What has become of that boy to-day? You may have repented. He has passed out of your sight. He has gone years and years ago. Somewhere in this great, multitudinous mass of humanity he is sinning and sinning, and reduplicating and extending the sin that you did. You touched the faith of some believing soul years ago with some miserable sneer of yours, with some cynical and skeptical disparagement of God and of the man who is the utterance of God upon the earth. You taught the soul that was enthusiastic to be full of skepticisms and doubts. You wronged a woman years ago, and her life has gone out from your life, you cannot begin to tell where. You have repented of your sin. You have bowed yourself, it may be, in dust and ashes. You have entered upon a new life. You are pure to-day. But where is the skeptical soul? Where is the ruined woman whom you sent forth into the world out of the shadow of your sin years ago? You cannot touch that life. You cannot reach it. You do not know where it is. No steps of yours, quickened with all your earnestness, can pursue it. No contrition of yours can draw back its consequences. Remorse cannot force the bullet back again into the gun from which it once has gone forth. It makes life awful to the man who has ever sinned, who has ever wronged and hurt another life because of this sin, because no sin ever was done that did not hurt another life. I know the mercy of our God, that while he has put us into each other's power to a fearful extent, he never will let any soul absolutely go to everlasting ruin for another's sin; and so I dare to see the love of God pursuing that lost soul where you cannot pursue it. But that does not for one moment lift the shadow from your heart, or cease to make you tremble when you think of how your sin has outgrown itself and is running far, far away where you can never follow it.

Thank God the other thing is true as well. Thank God that when a man does a bit of service, however little it may be, of that, too, he can never trace the consequences. Thank God that that which in some better moment, in some nobler inspiration, you did ten years ago to make your brother's faith a little more strong, to let your shop boy confirm and not doubt the confidence in man which he had brought into his business, to establish the purity of a soul instead of staining it and shaking it, thank God, in this quick, electric atmosphere in which we live, that, too, runs forth.

PRESTON S. BROOKS

(1819–1857)

THE address in which Preston S. Brooks, of South Carolina, explained his motives for the assault on Senator Sumner is a historical document rather than an oration, but its importance in its bearing on the history of the time is too great to allow its omission. It was delivered July 14th, 1856. Brooks, in the controversy of which this speech was a part, challenged Congressman Burlingame, of Massachusetts, who accepted and named for the duel a place near Niagara Falls. Brooks did not approve the location which he believed involved an unfair hazard for himself, and the duel never took place. According to biographers, who were his contemporaries, Burlingame's popularity was greatly increased by the affair.

THE ASSAULT ON SUMNER

(Delivered in the House of Representatives, July 14th, 1856)

Mr. Speaker:—

SOME time since a Senator from Massachusetts allowed himself, in an elaborately prepared speech, to offer a gross insult to my State, and to a venerable friend, who is my State representative, and who was absent at the time.

Not content with that, he published to the world, and circulated extensively, this uncalled-for libel on my State and my blood. Whatever insults my State insults me. Her history and character have commanded my pious veneration; and in her defense I hope I shall always be prepared, humbly and modestly, to perform the duty of a son. I should have forfeited my own self-respect and perhaps the good opinion of my countrymen, if I had failed to resent such an injury by calling the offender in question to a personal account. It was a personal affair, and in taking redress into my own hands I meant no disrespect to the Senate of the United States or to this House. Nor, sir, did I design insult or disrespect to the State of Massachusetts. I was aware of the personal responsibilities I incurred, and was willing

to meet them. I knew, too, that I was amenable to the laws of the country, which afford the same protection to all, whether they be members of Congress or private citizens. I did not, and do not now believe, that I could be properly punished, not only in a court of law, but here also, at the pleasure and discretion of the House. I did not then, and do not now, believe that the spirit of American freemen would tolerate slander in high places, and permit a Member of Congress to publish and circulate a libel on another, and then call upon either House to protect him against the personal responsibilities which he had thus incurred.

But if I had committed a breach of privilege, it was the privilege of the Senate, and not of this House, which was violated. I was answerable there, and not here. They had no right, as it seems to me, to prosecute me in these Halls, nor have you the right in law or under the Constitution, as I respectfully submit, to take jurisdiction over offenses committed against them. The Constitution does not justify them in making such a request, nor this House in granting it. If, unhappily, the day should ever come when sectional or party feeling should run so high as to control all other considerations of public duty or justice, how easy it will be to use such precedents for the excuse of arbitrary power, in either House, to expel Members of the minority who may have rendered themselves obnoxious to the prevailing spirit in the House to which they belong.

Matters may go smoothly enough when one House asks the other to punish a Member who is offensive to a majority of its own body; but how will it be when, upon a pretense of insulted dignity, demands are made of this House to expel a Member who happens to run counter to its party predilections, or other demands which it may not be so agreeable to grant? It could never have been designed by the Constitution of the United States to expose the two Houses to such temptations to collision, or to extend so far the discretionary power which was given to either House to punish its own Members for the violation of its rules and orders. Discretion has been said to be the law of the tyrant, and when exercised under the color of the law, and under the influence of party dictation, it may and will become a terrible and insufferable despotism.

This House, however, it would seem, from the unmistakable tendency of its proceedings, takes a different view from that which I deliberately entertain in common with many others.

So far as public interests or constitutional rights are involved, I have now exhausted my means of defense. I may, then, be allowed to take a more personal view of the question at issue. The further prosecution of this subject, in the shape it has now assumed, may not only involve my friends, but the House itself, in agitations which might be unhappy in their consequences to the country. If these consequences could be confined to myself individually, I think I am prepared and ready to meet them, here or elsewhere; and when I use this language I mean what I say. But others must not suffer for me. I have felt more on account of my two friends who have been implicated, than for myself, for they have proven that "there is a friend that sticketh closer than a brother." I will not constrain gentlemen to assume a responsibility on my account, which, possibly, they would not assume on their own.

Sir, I cannot, on my own account, assume the responsibility, in the face of the American people, of commencing a line of conduct which in my heart of hearts I believe would result in subverting the foundations of this government and in drenching this hall in blood. No act of mine, on my personal account, shall inaugurate revolution; but when you, Mr. Speaker, return to your own home and hear the people of the great North — and they are a great people — speak of me as a bad man, you will do me the justice to say that a blow struck by me at this time would be followed by revolution — and this I know.

If I desired to kill the Senator, why did not I do it? You all admit that I had him in my power. Let me tell the Member from New Jersey that it was expressly to avoid taking life that I used an ordinary cane, presented to me by a friend in Baltimore, nearly three months before its application to the "bare head" of the Massachusetts Senator. I went to work very deliberately, as I am charged, — and this is admitted, — and speculated somewhat as to whether I should employ a horsewhip or a cowhide; but, knowing that the Senator was my superior in strength, it occurred to me that he might wrest it from my hand, and then — for I never attempt anything I do not perform — I might have been compelled to do that which I would have regretted the balance of my natural life.

The question has been asked in certain newspapers, why I did not invite the Senator to personal combat in the mode usually adopted. Well, sir, as I desire the whole truth to be known about the matter, I will for once notice a newspaper article on the floor of the House, and answer here.

My answer is, that the Senator would not accept a message; and, having formed the unalterable determination to punish him, I believed that the offense of "sending a hostile message," superadded to the indictment for assault and battery, would subject me to legal penalties more severe than would be imposed for a simple assault and battery. That is my answer.

Now, Mr. Speaker, I have nearly finished what I intended to say. If my opponents, who have pursued me with unparalleled bitterness, are satisfied with the present condition of this affair, I am. I return my thanks to my friends, and especially to those who are from non-slave-owning States, who have magnanimously sustained me, and felt that it was a higher honor to themselves to be just in their judgment of a gentleman than to be a Member of Congress for life. In taking my leave, I feel that it is proper that I should say that I believe that some of the votes that have been cast against me have been extorted by an outside pressure at home, and that their votes do not express the feelings or opinions of the Members who gave them.

To such of these as have given their votes and made their speeches on the constitutional principles involved, and without indulging in personal vilification, I owe my respect. But, sir, they have written me down upon the history of the country as worthy of expulsion, and in no unkindness I must tell them that, for all future time, my self-respect requires that I shall pass them as strangers.

And now, Mr. Speaker, I announce to you and to this House, that I am no longer a Member of the Thirty-Fourth Congress.

II—42

LORD BROUGHAM

(1778–1868)

N NOVEMBER 22d, 1830, Henry Brougham, still a commoner, took his seat as Speaker of the House of Lords, Keeper of the Great Seal, and Lord High Chancellor of England.

Nothing could be more characteristic than this of the system which has given England its greatness. It is a system which, during the last two hundred years at least, has made possible the highest promotion for every man with the intellect and strength of will to force himself forward and keep his position at the front in spite of the determined opposition of all whom hereditary rank, privilege, or fortune have made powerful without effort of their own.

To promote every such strong and persistent "upstart" is the studied policy which has steadied and perpetuated English aristocracy against the powerful attacks of such men as Brougham. It does not buy them. It could not have bought Brougham. It honors them and so disarms them. "You are one of us," it says to them, "and even if you are against us, we are for you!" So we have two Broughams—both great, but one with an increasing, the other with a waning greatness. It is Henry Brougham, commoner, plain barrister, champion of popular liberties, the greatest Liberal orator of his day, who takes his seat as presiding officer of the chamber which represents hereditary privilege against those very rights as the champion of which he had risen to greatness. A day later the patent of his peerage had been made out. He is "Baron Brougham and Vaux" and is introduced among the peers as one of them—as, indeed, from that time, he never ceased to be. He still fought strenuously the battles of his youth, and the Reform Bill of 1832 had no more ardent champion than he. But he fought as "Baron Brougham," and every day of his life brought him closer to the old age he spent in prattling of his associations with the royal family and of ancestors in the ancient peerage—of ancestors who existed, as even his friendly biographers fear, only in his always active and at last uncontrolled imagination. He had not been bought with honors and titles. could not have been purchased. He was merely assimilated, but in the end his power went out from him completely. Henry Brougham, the greatest mind of England, showing in statesmanship, in oratory,

---

in literature, in mathematics, in science, the manifold talents which delighted while they controlled the England of 1830, came at last to be merely a member of the peerage, outliving himself and surviving into a later generation as a memento of his own inconsistencies.

If this will explain or suggest why the judgments passed upon a most extraordinary man have been so diverse, it will have its own excuse for attempting to take its place with other explanations where none are adequate. It is impossible to judge such a man as Brougham by ordinary standards. Except Benjamin Franklin, no statesman of modern times has had such a diversity of gifts or has shown such an easy mastery of the agencies through which mind controls other minds and the material world around it. He had Franklin's strong love for science. The two men illustrate the same astonishing versatility, the same strong desire to apply knowledge so as to make it of immediate practical advantage; the same ability in public affairs, the same determination so to live as to leave the world after them better, freer, and more comfortable than they found it. Yet Brougham invented no bedroom stoves and sent no kites to heaven to call down social, political, and economic revolutions out of the clouds. Lacking this gift of Franklin's, he had others which Franklin had not. He set himself to become the greatest orator in the public life of England, and succeeded. He worked as deliberately to acquire a "genius for oratory" as Franklin worked to make his open stove ventilate a bedroom. He succeeded as well. When he "learned by heart" the great orations of men whose eloquence had swayed crowds with the masterful power which mind when freely expressed always exerts, it was not to imitate but to assimilate. When he defended Queen Caroline, when he denounced the lash in the British army, when he plead for the liberation of British slaves, when he opposed himself to every enemy of progress, making himself the mouthpiece of the aspiration of the Wilberforces and the Howards, surrendering his voice to be the voice of those who are themselves speechless because of oppression, it was not Cicero, not Demosthenes, not any framer of classical periods, speaking to times of which classical modes are no longer a part, but the very deepest aspiration of the times themselves, the very highest inspiration which the present can catch from the future it is to achieve by its struggles and its sacrifices.

In the noble climax of his speech at Liverpool in 1812, after having denounced Pitt for the war upon America, Brougham said that his own proudest ambition was to be looked upon by posterity as the friend of liberty and peace.

This ambition he has realized. From 1808, when he was admitted to the bar of England, until after the struggle over the Reform Bill

---

of 1832, he was a great and growing force for the progress of England, not merely in power, but in all that makes civilization. He forced the fighting for the abolition of degrading punishments in the army and navy; he compelled public attention to English slaveholding and English complicity in the slave trade until the demand for action could not be evaded; he dared the displeasure of the court and won the lasting enmity of the King by taking the part of the unfortunate Queen Caroline, and at the same time he was experimenting in optics, studying mathematics, and writing scientific papers for the English Royal Society or the French Academy of Sciences.

Seeing him passing in a carriage one of his acquaintances said of him, with that resentment genius often challenges from those it seeks to benefit: "There go Solon, Lycurgus, Demosthenes, Archimedes, Sir Isaac Newton, Lord Chesterfield, and a great many more, all in one post-chaise."

If he invited such scoffs by the very eagerness of his intellectual grasp, if finally through the arrogance of attempting everything, he lost the substance for the shadow of attainment, he had achieved in the meantime more in his own lifetime than it could happen to men of normally active intellect to achieve if they lived to double his great age. It has been said that he left nothing of permanent value in literature, but his 'Statesmen of the Time of George IV.' has the rare power of compelling the reader who begins it to go on. The sketches, though they may be called nothing but sketches, have in them the life of times of which Brougham was a part, and they go with his speeches to make his intellect intelligible, not merely in its methods, but in its essence. At his best, when he was doing the work which made him great, he was not critical but constructive in his processes. His mind was creative, assimilative, ready to take from every source, no matter how humble, that which gives strength and originality. The same quality made Burke a great orator as it made Shakespeare a great poet. In spite of such weaknesses as grew on Brougham until they made him powerless to realize himself in action, it made him great—so great that when his detractors call him a failure in all the climaxes of his efforts, it is enough to answer that the world has grown more through such failures than it has through the best successes of those who dared not take such risks as he dared at the expense of failure.

W. V. B.

AGAINST PITT AND WAR WITH AMERICA

(Delivered at the Liverpool Election, Friday, October 8th, 1812)

GENTLEMEN, I told you last night when we were near the head of the poll, that I, for one at least, would neither lose heart in the conflict, nor lower my courage in fighting your battles, nor despair of the good cause although we should be fifty, a hundred, or even two hundred behind our enemies. It has happened this day that we have fallen short of them, not quite by two hundred, but we have lost one hundred and seventy votes. I tell you this with the deepest concern, with feelings of pain and sorrow which I dare not trust myself in attempting to express. But I tell it you without any sensation approaching to despondency. This is the only feeling which I have not now present in my breast. I am overcome with your unutterable affection towards me and my cause. I feel a wonder mingled with gratitude, which no language can even attempt to describe, at your faithful, unwearied, untamable exertions in my behalf of our common object. I am penetrated with an anxiety for its success, if possible more lively than any of yourselves can know who are my followers in this mighty struggle — an anxiety cruelly increased by that which as yet you are ignorant of, though you are this night to hear it. To my distinguished friends who surround me, and connect me more closely with you, I am thankful beyond all expression. I am lost in admiration of the honest and courageous men amongst you who have resisted all threats as well as all bribes, and persevered in giving me their free unbought voices. For those unhappy persons who have been scared by imminent fear on their own and their children's behalf from obeying the impulse of their conscience, I feel nothing of resentment — nothing but pity and compassion. Of those who have thus opposed us, I think as charitably as a man can think in such circumstances. For this great town (if it is indeed to be defeated in the contest, which I will not venture to suppose), for the country at large whose cause we are upholding — whose fight we are fighting — for the whole manufacturing and trading interests — for all who love peace — all who have no profit in war — I feel moved by the deepest alarm lest our grand attempt may not prosper. All these feelings are in my heart at this moment — they are various, they are conflicting, they are painful, they are

burthensome, but they are not overwhelming, and amongst them all — and I have swept round the whole range of which the human mind is susceptible — there is not one that bears the slightest resemblance to despair. I trust myself once more in your faithful hands; I fling myself again on you for protection; I call aloud to you to bear your own cause in your hearts; I implore of you to come forth in your own defense, for the sake of this vast town and its people, for the salvation of the middle and lower orders, for the whole industrial part of the whole country; I entreat you by your love of peace, by your hatred of oppression, by your weariness of burthensome and useless taxation, by yet another appeal to which those must lend an ear who have been deaf to all the rest; I ask it for your families, for your infants, if you would avoid such a winter of horrors as the last. It is coming fast upon us; already it is near at hand; yet a few short weeks and we may be in the midst of those unspeakable miseries, the recollection of which now rends your very souls. If there is one freeman amongst this immense multitude who has not tendered his voice, and if he can be deaf to this appeal, if he can suffer the threats of our antagonists to frighten him away from the recollection of the last dismal winter, that man will not vote for me. But if I have the happiness of addressing one honest man amongst you, who has a care left for his wife and children, or for other endearing ties of domestic tenderness (and which of us is altogether without them?), that man will lay his hand on his heart when I now bid him do so, and with those little threats of present spite ringing in his ear, he will rather consult his fears of greater evil by listening to the dictates of his heart, when he casts a look towards the dreadful season through which he lately passed, and will come bravely forward to place those men in Parliament whose whole efforts have been directed towards the restoration of peace and the revival of trade.

Do not, gentlemen, listen to those who tell you the cause of freedom is desperate; they are the enemies of that cause and of you, but listen to me, — and I am one who has never yet deceived you, — I say, then, that it will be desperate if you make no exertions to retrieve it. I tell you that your language alone can betray it, that it can only be made desperate through your despair. I am not a man to be cast down by temporary reverses, let them come upon me as thick and as swift and as

sudden as they may. I am not he who is daunted by majorities in the outset of a struggle for worthy objects, — else I should not now stand here before you to boast of triumphs won in your cause. If your champions had yielded to the force of numbers, of gold, of power, — if defeat could have dismayed them, then would the African slave trade never have been abolished, then would the cause of reform, which now bids fair to prevail over its enemies, have been long ago sunk amidst the desertions of its friends; then would those prospects of peace have been utterly benighted, which I still devoutly cherish, and which even now brighten in our eyes; then would the orders in council which I overthrew by your support, have remained a disgrace to the British name, and an eternal obstacle to our best interests. I no more despond now than I have done in the course of those sacred and glorious contentions, but it is for you to say whether to-morrow shall not make it my duty to despair. To-morrow is your last day; your last efforts must then be made; if you put forth your strength the day is your own; if you desert it, it is lost. To win it, I shall be the first to lead you on and the last to forsake you.

Gentlemen, when I told you a little while ago that there were new and powerful reasons to-day for ardently desiring that our cause might succeed, I did not sport with you; yourselves shall now judge of them. I ask you, — Is the trade with America of any importance to this great and thickly peopled town? [Cries of, "Yes, yes!"] Is a continuance of the rupture with America likely to destroy that trade? [Loud cries of, "It is, it is!"] Is there any man who would deeply feel it, if he heard that the rupture was at length converted into open war? Is there a man present who would not be somewhat alarmed if he supposed that we should have another year without the American trade? Is there any one of nerves so hardy, as calmly to hear that our government has given up all negotiation, abandoned all hopes of speedy peace with America? Then I tell that man to brace up his nerves; I bid you all be prepared to hear what touches you all equally. We are by this day's intelligence at war with America in good earnest; our government has at length issued letters of marque and reprisal against the United States. [Universal cries of, "God help us, God help us!"] Aye, God help us! God of his infinite compassion take pity on us! God help and protect this poor town, and this whole trading country!

Now I ask you whether you will be represented in Parliament by the men who have brought this grievous calamity on your heads, or by those who have constantly opposed the mad career which was plunging us into it? Whether you will trust the revival of your trade — the restoration of your livelihood — to them who have destroyed it, or to me whose counsels, if followed in time, would have averted this unnatural war, and left Liverpool flourishing in opulence and peace? Make your choice, for it lies with yourselves which of us shall be commissioned to bring back commerce and plenty, — they whose stubborn infatuation has chased those blessings away, or we, who are only known to you as the strenuous enemies of their miserable policy, the fast friends of your best interests.

Gentlemen, I stand up in this conquest against the friends and followers of Mr. Pitt, or, as they partially designate him, the immortal statesman, now no more. Immortal in the miseries of his devoted country! Immortal in the wounds of her bleeding liberties! Immortal in the cruel wars which sprang from his cold miscalculating ambition! Immortal in the intolerable taxes, the countless loads of debt which these wars have flung upon us — which the youngest man among us will not live to see the end of! Immortal in the triumph of our enemies, and the ruin of our allies, the costly purchase of so much blood and treasure! Immortal in the afflictions of England, and the humiliations of her friends, through the whole results of his twenty years' reign, from the first rays of favor with which a delighted court gilded his early apostasy, to the deadly glare which is at this instant cast upon his name by the burning metropolis of our last ally. But may no such immortality ever fall to my lot; let me rather live innocent and inglorious; and when at last I cease to serve you, and to feel for your wrongs, may I have an humble monument in some nameless stone, to tell that beneath it there rests from his labors in your service "an enemy of the immortal statesman — a friend of peace and of the people."

Friends, you must now judge for yourselves, and act accordingly. Against us and against you stand those who call themselves the successors of that man. They are the heirs of his policy; and if not of his immortality, too, it is only because their talents for the work of destruction are less transcendent than his. They are his surviving colleagues. His fury survives in them, if not his fire; and they partake of all his infatuated principles, if they have lost the genius that first made those principles triumphant. If you choose them for your delegates you know to what policy you lend your sanction — what men you exalt to power. Should you prefer me, your choice falls upon one who. if obscure and unambitious, will at least give his own age no reason to fear him, or posterity to curse him, — one whose proudest ambition it is to be deemed the friend of liberty and of peace.

CLOSING ARGUMENT FOR QUEEN CAROLINE

MY LORDS, I have another remark to make before I leave this case. I have heard it said by some acute sifters of evidence: "Oh! you have damaged the witnesses, but only by proving falsehoods, by proving perjury indeed, in unimportant particulars." I need but remind your lordships that this is an observation which can only come from the lay part of the community. Any lawyer at once will see how ridiculous, if I may so speak, such an objection must always be. It springs from an entire confusion of ideas, a heedless confounding together of different things. If I am to confirm the testimony of an accomplice — if I am to set up an informer — no doubt my confirmation ought to extend to matters connected with the crime — no doubt it must be an important particular, else it will avail me nothing to prove it by way of confirmation. But it is quite the reverse in respect to pulling down a perjured witness, or a witness suspected of swearing falsely. It is quite enough if he perjure himself in any part to take away all credit from the whole of his testimony. Can it be said that you are to pick and choose; that you are to believe in part, and reject the rest as false? You may, indeed, be convinced that a part is true, notwithstanding other parts are false — provided these parts are not falsely and willfully sworn to by the witness, but parts which he may have been ignorant of, or may have forgotten, or may have mistaken. In this sense, you may choose — culling the part you believe and separating the part you think contradicted. But if one part is not only not true — is not only not consistent with the fact, but is falsely and willfully sworn to on his part — if you are satisfied that one part of his story is an invention, to use the plain word, a lie, and that he is a forsworn man — good God!

have you acquitted, if the villain, who has immovably told a consistent, firm tale (though not contradicted, though not touched, upon the story itself), tells the least falsehood upon the most unimportant particulars on which your advocate shall examine him. My lords, I ask for the Queen no other justice than this upon which you rely, and must needs rely, for your own escape from the charge of such crimes! I desire she may have no other safety than that which forms the only safety to any of your lordships in such cases, before any court that deserved the name of a court of justice, where it might be your lot to be dragged and tried!

I am told that the sphere of life in which Bergami, afterwards promoted to be the Queen's chamberlain, originally moved compared with the fortune which has since attended him in her service, is of itself matter of suspicion. I should be sorry, my lords, to have lived to see the day when nothing more was required to ruin any exalted character in this free country than the having shown favor to a meritorious servant, by promoting him above his rank in society, the rank of his birth. It is a lot which has happened to many a great man — which has been that of those who have been the ornaments of their country. God forbid that we should ever see the time when all ranks, all stations in this community, except the highest, were not open to all men, and that we should ever reckon it of itself a circumstance even of suspicion in any person (for neither sex can be exempt from an inference of such a nature if it is once made general and absolute) that he has promoted an inferior to be his equal! Let me, however, remind your lordships, that the rapidity of the promotion of Bergami has been greatly overstated; and the manner in which it took place is a convincing proof that the story of love having been the cause of it is inconsistent with the fact. Now, this I state, from a distinct recollection of the dates in the evidence before you. Believe Majocchi or Dement, and three weeks after Bergami's arrival in the household, he was promoted to the Queen's bed. How was it with respect to her board? Because, after that, he continued in the situation of courier; he dined with the servants, and lived not even with the chamberlains; certainly not with those gentlemen, for they were at her table, as usual. He continued to dine with the servants at Genoa; there, withstanding Majocchi's story, it is proved to your lordships that he did not dine with her Majesty.

my lords, what safety is there for human kind against the malice of their enemies — what chance of innocence escaping from the toils of the perjured and unprincipled conspirator, if you are to believe part of a tale, even though ten witnesses swear to it, all of whom you convict of lying and perjury in some other part of the story? I only pray your lordships to consider what it is that forms the safeguard of each and every one of you against the arts of the mercenary or the spiteful conspirator. Suppose any one man, — and let each of your lordships lay this to his mind before you dismiss the mighty topic, — suppose any one of your lordships were to meet with a misfortune, the greatest that can befall a human being, and the greater in proportion as he is of an honorable mind, whose soul is alien even to any idea or glance of suspicion of such a case being possible to himself, whose feelings shudder at the bare thought of his name even being accidentally coupled with a charge at which his nature revolts — suppose that mischance, which has happened to the best and purest of men, which may happen to any of you to-morrow, and which, if it does happen, must succeed against you to-morrow, if you adopt the principle I am struggling against — suppose any one of your lordships charged by a mere mercenary scoundrel with the perpetration of a crime at which we show in this country our infinite horror, by almost, and with singular injustice, considering the bare charge to stand in place of proof — suppose this plot laid to defame the fairest reputation in England — I say, that reputation must be saved, if escape it may, only by one means. No perjury can be expected to be exposed in the main, the principal part of the fabric; that can be easily defended from any attack against it; all the arts of the defendant's counsel, and all his experience, will be exhausted in vain: the plotter knows full well (as these conspirators have here done) how to take care that only one person shall swear to a fact — to lay no others present — to choose the time and select the place when contradiction cannot be given, by knowing the time and the place where any one of your lordships, whom he marks for his prey, may have chanced to be alone at any moment of time. Contradiction is not here to be expected, — refutation is impossible. Prevarication of the witness upon the principal part of his case, beyond all doubt, by every calculation of chances, there will not be. But you will be defended by counsel; and the court before whom you are tried will assuredly

He continued as courier, even after he had once sat at her Majesty's table by accident, by one of the accidents usual in traveling. It appears even in the evidence (believing it to be true), that the Queen sat at the table where he was for the space of one day. He, however, continued as courier; and it was only on the eve of the long voyage that he was admitted to her table, commencing with the journey to Mount St. Gothard. He continued in his situation as courier, still in livery, until, by degrees, he was promoted, first to travel in a carriage of his own, instead of riding on horseback. Then he was promoted occasionally to sit at the same table with the Queen, and at last he was appointed a chamberlain generally. My lords, this is not consistent with the story told of Naples. Show me the woman, particularly the amorous, the imprudent, the insane woman her Majesty is described to be by those perjured witnesses, who would have allowed her paramour, after indulging in all the gratifications described at Naples, for weeks and months, to continue for months, and almost for years, in an apparent menial capacity! My lords, this is not the rapidity of pace with which love promotes his favorite votaries; it much more resembles the sluggish progress with which merit wends its ways in the world, and in courts. He was a man of merit, as you will hear in evidence, — if you put me on calling any. He was not of the low origin he has been described to be. He was a person whose father held the situation of a landed proprietor, though of moderate income, in the north of Italy. He had got into difficulties as has happened to many of the Italian gentry of late years; and his son, if I mistake not, had sold the family estate, in order to pay his father's debts. He was reduced — but he was a reduced gentleman. When he was in the service of General Pino, he was recognized as such. The General repeatedly favored him as such: he has dined at his table, General Pino being the commander-in-chief in the Milanese. He thus sat at the table of an Italian noble in the highest station. He has dined at his table during the Spanish campaigns. He was respected in his station — he was esteemed by those whom he served at that time. They encouraged him, as knowing his former pretensions and his present merits; and when he was hired, he was proposed by a gentleman who desired to befriend and promote him, an Austrian nobleman, then living in Italy, in the Austrian service — he was proposed to the Queen's chamberlain as a courier, there being a vacancy, and was hired without the knowledge of her Majesty, and before she had even seen him. The Austrian nobleman, when he offered him as a courier, said, he fairly confessed he hoped, if Bergami behaved well, he might be promoted, because he was a man whose family had seen better days, because he was a faithful servant, and because he had ideas belonging rather to his former than to his present situation. It was almost a condition of his going, that he should go for the present as courier, with the expectation of soon filling some other and higher place.

I do not dwell on this, my lords, as of any importance to the case; for whether I shall think it necessary to prove what I have just stated or not, I consider that I have already disposed of the case in the comments which I have made upon the evidence, and in the appeal which I have made to the general principles of criminal justice. But, as the conduct of her Majesty has been so unsparingly scrutinized, and as it is important to show that not even impropriety existed, where I utterly defy guilt to be proved, I thought it requisite to dwell on this prominent feature in the cause. If the Queen had frequented companies below her station — if she had lowered her dignity — if she had followed the courses which, though not guilty ones, might be deemed improper in themselves and inconsistent with her high station — if she had been proved guilty of any unworthiness, I could have trod upon high ground still. But I have no occasion to occupy it. I say, guilt there is none — levity there is none — unworthiness there is none. But, if there had been any of the latter, while I dared her accusers to the proof of guilt, admitting levity and even indecorum, I might still have appealed to that which always supports virtue in jeopardy, the course of her former life at home, among her own relations, before she was frowned upon here — while she had protection among you — while she had the most powerful of all protection, that of our late venerable monarch. I hold in my hand a testimonial — which cannot be read, and which I am sure will not be weighed, without the deepest sense of importance; above all, without a feeling of sorrow when we reflect upon the reign that has passed, and compare it with the rule we live under. It is a melancholy proof, — more melancholy because we no longer have him who furnishes it amongst us, — but it is a proof how that illustrious sovereign viewed her, whom he knew better than all others — whom he loved more than all the rest of her family did — even than those upon whose affection she had a

greater claim; nay, whom he loved better than he did almost any child of his own. The plainness, the honesty, the intelligible, and manly sense of this letter are such that I cannot refrain from the gratification of reading it. It was written in 1804: —

WINDSOR CASTLE, November 13th, 1804.

My Dearest Daughter-in-Law and Niece: —

Yesterday I and the rest of my family had an interview with the Prince of Wales, at Kew. Care was taken on all sides to avoid all subjects of altercation or explanation, consequently the conversation was neither instructive nor entertaining; but it leaves the Prince of Wales in a situation to show whether his desire to return to his family is only verbal or real (a difference which George III. never knew, except in others), which time alone can show. I am not idle in my endeavors to make inquiries that may enable me to communicate some plan for the advantage of the dear child you and I, with so much reason, must interest ourselves in, and its effecting my having the happiness of living more with you is no small incentive to my forming some ideas on the subject; but you may depend on their being not decided upon without your thorough and cordial concurrence, for your authority as mother it is my object to support.

Believe me at all times, my dearest daughter-in-law and niece,

Your most affectionate father-in-law and uncle,

GEORGE R.

Such, my lords, was the opinion which this good man, not ignorant of human affairs, no ill judge of human character, had formed of this near and cherished relation, and upon which, in the most delicate particulars, the care of his granddaughter and the heir of his crown, he honestly, really, and not in mere words, always acted.

I might now read to your lordships a letter from his illustrious successor, not written in the same tone of affection — not indicative of the same feelings of regard — but by no means indicative of any want of confidence, or at least of any desire harshly to trammel his royal consort's conduct. I allude to a letter which has been so often before your lordships in other shapes, that I may not think it necessary to repeat it here. It is a permission to live apart, and a desire never to come together again; the expression of an opinion, that their happiness was better consulted, and pursued asunder; and a very plain indication, that her Majesty's conduct should at least not be watched with all the scrupulousness, all the rigor, all the scrutinizing agency which

has resulted in bringing the present Bill of Pains and Penalties before your lordships. [Cries of "Read, read!" Mr. Brougham accordingly read the letter, as follows:]

WINDSOR CASTLE, April 30th, 1796.

Madam: —

As Lord Cholmondely informs me that you wish I would define, in writing, the terms upon which we are to live, I shall endeavor to explain with as much clearness and with as much propriety as the nature of the subject will admit. Our inclinations are not in our power, nor should either of us be held answerable to the other, because nature has not made us suitable to each other. Tranquil and comfortable society is, however, in our power; let our intercourse, therefore, be restricted to that, and I will distinctly subscribe to the condition which you required, through Lady Cholmondely, that even in the event of any accident happening to my daughter, which I trust Providence in its mercy will avert, I shall not infringe the terms of the restriction, by proposing at any period, a connexion of more particular nature. I shall finally close this disagreeable correspondence, trusting that, as we have completely explained ourselves to each other, the rest of our lives will be passed in uninterrupted tranquillity. I am, Madam, with great truth, very sincerely yours,

GEORGE P.

My lords, I do not call this, as it has been termed, a Letter of License; such was the term applied to it, on the former occasion, by those who are now, unhappily for the Queen, no more, — those who were the colleagues and coadjutors of the present ministers, — but I think it such an epistle as would make it a matter of natural wonderment to the person who received it, that her conduct should ever after — and especially the more rigorously the older the parties were growing — become the subject of the most unceasing and unscrupulous watching, prying, spying, and investigation.

Such then, my lords, is this case. And again let me call on you, even at the risk of repetition, never to dismiss for a moment from your minds the two great points upon which I rest my attack upon the evidence: — first, that the accusers have not proved the facts by the good witnesses who were within their reach, whom they had no shadow of pretext for not calling; and secondly, that the witnesses whom they have ventured to call are, every one of them, irreparably damaged in their credit. How, I again ask, is a plot ever to be discovered, except by the

means of these two principles? Nay, there are instances, in which plots have been discovered, through the medium of the second principle, when the first had happened to fail. When venerable witnesses have been brought forward — when persons above all suspicion have lent themselves for a season to impure plans — when no escape for the guiltless seemed open, no chance of safety to remain — they have almost providentially escaped from the snare by the second of those two principles; by the evidence breaking down where it was not expected to be sifted; by a weak point being found, where no provision, from the attack being unforeseen, had been made to support it. Your lordships recollect that great passage — I say great, for it is poetically just and eloquent, even were it not inspired — in the Sacred Writings, where the Elders had joined themselves in a plot which appeared to have succeeded "for that," as the Book says, "they had hardened their hearts, and had turned away their eyes, that they might not look at heaven, and that they might do the purposes of unjust judgment." But they, though giving a clear, consistent, uncontradicted story, were disappointed, and their victim was wrested from their grip, by the trifling circumstance of a contradiction about a tamarisk tree. Let not man call those contradictions or those falsehoods which false witnesses swear to from needless and heedless falsehood, such as Sacchi about his changing his name — or such as Demont about changing her letters — such as Majocchi about the banker's clerk — or such as all the other contradictions and falsehoods not going to the main body of the case, but to the main body of the credit of the witnesses — let no man rashly and blindly call these accidents. They are just rather than merciful dispensations of that Providence, which wills not that the guilty should triumph, and which favorably protects the innocent!

Such, my lords, is the case now before you! Such is the evidence in support of this measure — evidence inadequate to prove a debt; impotent to deprive of a civil right; ridiculous to convict of the lowest offense; scandalous if brought forward to support a charge of the highest nature which the law knows; monstrous to ruin the honor, to blast the name of an English Queen! What shall I say, then, if this is the proof by which an act of judicial legislation, a parliamentary sentence, an *ex post facto* law, is sought to be passed against this defenseless woman? My lords, I pray you to pause. I do earnestly beseech you to take heed!

You are standing on the brink of a precipice — then beware! It will go forth as your judgment, if sentence shall go against the Queen. But it will be the only judgment you ever pronounced, which, instead of reaching its object, will return and bound back upon those who give it. Save the country, my lords, from the horrors of this catastrophe; save yourselves from this peril; rescue that country, of which you are the ornaments, but in which you can flourish no longer, when severed from the people, than the blossom when cut off from the roots and the stem of the tree. Save that country, that you may continue to adorn it; save the crown, which is in jeopardy; the aristocracy which is shaken; save the altar, which must stagger with the blow that rends its kindred throne! You have said, my lords, you have willed — the Church and the King have willed — that the Queen should be deprived of its solemn service! She has instead of that solemnity, the heartfelt prayers of the people. She wants no prayers of mine. But I do here pour forth my humble supplications at the throne of mercy, that that mercy may be poured down upon the people, in a larger measure than the merits of its rulers may deserve, and that your hearts may be turned to justice!

II—43

A PROPHECY

(United States Senate, March 8th, 1864)

THE supreme democracy, which has been smothered so long under names and parties and cunning issues, has in these disturbed times recognized itself, and demands as its exponent a political form coextensive with the country, and imperial as itself. It does not need to tread back into the old exploded days to tell how unutterably the slave system that stained our name and wrecked our Federal unity has ever held in dread the undefiled democratic principle; how it has sought under a like nomenclature to palm off something other in its stead; how it has labored to divert it into other channels of foreign conquest rather than home assertion; how it has manacled it with chains of local organization and demoralized it with the spoils of office. The recorded debates of this Senate will show far back how such fear ever haunted those leaders who have now taken a last appeal from democracy to war. At the point where rebellion began, they recognized perfectly that if they were to preserve intact the slave system from being obliterated by the progress of a plebeian public will, it must be done by a resort to violence and terror. They chose that resort deliberately, not foolishly, and have stood to it with conviction and courage. It was the irrepressible conflict. And the antagonism is manifest now in the throes of an unparalleled struggle still more than in the plastic days of peace; for with them development has shaped their slavery into confederate despotism, while here revolution uprises into nationality. The latent force of this American people, the feeling of brotherhood, the need of unity, at length demands and will have clear, emphatic type as a nation. What other is the meaning of this so rapid resumption of sovereign right in all departments of the government? Drawing a sustenance no longer from the customs but from the firesides, substituting national paper-credits for all other currencies, levying armies directly by conscriptions, not remotely by contingents, organizing vast industries, mortgaging the next age to its debt, and enforcing its law as highest law even in matters of personal liberty — these are but as outer garments of an inner form already instinct with life. Nor is this a completion. So much has been realized, while in the

B. GRATZ BROWN

(1826–1885)

B. GRATZ BROWN who, in the presidential campaign of 1872, led the Liberal Republican movement in the West, was born in Kentucky in 1826. He was a graduate of Yale College and a lawyer by profession. His ability at the bar was notable, but it is as a representative of the Liberal Republican movement in the North after the close of the Civil War that he is apt to be longest remembered. He became a resident of St. Louis in 1852, and not long afterwards was elected to the State legislature. In 1854 he founded the Missouri Democrat, and gave it marked influence in the politics of the period. During the Civil War he commanded a brigade in the Union army. In 1863 he was elected to the United States Senate from Missouri, and in 1872 was nominated for Vice-President on the Liberal Republican ticket with Horace Greeley.

Though defeated by an electoral vote which seemed to be overwhelming, Greeley and Brown succeeded during that campaign in giving direction to the politics of the next fifteen years. They represented the increasing desire at the North and West to divert the country as a whole from the issues of the Civil War. They believed that this could not be done unless the movement for it began in the section which had won in the contest, and hence at a time when it subjected them to violent attack they led a Republican minority to co-operate with the Northern Democrats and the combination of Whigs and Democrats at the South, which was then contesting every presidential election, with a remote chance of winning through the electoral votes of the South, New York, and some State of the central West. Some of these Republicans who returned to their party helped to influence it towards the policies which under Hayes, Garfield, and Arthur, altered completely the political alignment of the States, and caused the great changes, which, though they were potentially in existence at the close of Arthur's term, did not fully manifest themselves until the campaign of 1892.

future still more impends. The industrial relations of reconquered territories, inauguration of majestic commercial ways, settlements affecting multitudes of people, and vast undeveloped wealth, are in its hands. Again, consider the changed relations of heretofore self-styled sovereign States. Much has been said during the shadowing forth of this new phase of our political life of the "Suicide of States," and in groping down into the rubbish of the time it has been deemed needful to affix names and hypotheses to ascertain results. But what needs? That no authority has been asked or resistance heeded from any State in enforcing national policies is literally true, and that such enforcement is inconsistent with any recognized vitality in State organization other than a strictly subordinate one, none will controvert. Call it, then, suicide or subordination, the implication is the same. Indeed, it is realized on every side that what was heretofore held up as "State," with assumption of a coequal or antagonistic control as such, is gone down in the mighty tread of this people marching on to deliverance. Commonwealths may exist, may be revived, may do functional work, may co-operate in subordinate orbits, but their so-called sovereignty assuredly is suicide. State sovereignty, the least sought to be put on the democracy of the nation; State sovereignty, the banner of the oligarchs in their war on freedom; State sovereignty, the archetype of disunion and disintegration, has become a myth and a fable, and in the stead of its many idols there shines forth the one splendor and power of a national sovereignty foreordained to conquest. Such is the outgrowth. Substantially it is the expression in advance of that which is to follow in due time by its appointed courses — the continental republic. It is the highest type of nationality, bounded by no mixed frontier of impassable prejudice, but representative of whoever may assimilate under its standard; for while European rulers are seeking to bolster themselves with nativisms, and to render synonymous nationalities and races, it is ours to assert the larger and truer nationality of free principles and free men. Nor does this connect simply with geographical progress or endanger compactness of guidance and control; for as its birth is from the people, so will it reflect their positioning. Democracy is its parent, — democracy that asserts and recognizes itself again in the lusty turmoil of our great commotions, — and democracy means numbers, and numbers govern from the centre outward, and not jug handle wise from any remote source. Thus we see, and the fact is significant, in the vast impulses given to freedom policies, war policies, and national policies in the great basin of the Mississippi, with its fifteen millions of population, new illustration of the democratic force and faith of the people. Go forward furthermore, make dense that population, intensify the life of the recovered States, enumerate fifty millions instead of fifteen millions, and consider of the result. Power there, government there, democratic organism there, reposing on rural and industrial masses, will abjure the monarchies of special interests that have sat around the edges clutching at control, and coerce the Republic into healthy action throughout.

Originating thus, this new development of a national unity will require no after-molding to make it representative in its promptings. It will be a form of organized popular thought that will dictate to cabinets and administrations other policies than those of this hour; that will look outward as well as inward, and if it accept its mission of a continental republic will be prompt to recognize the antagonisms erecting beyond and around us, no less than the incongruities abolishing within our present confines. Be sure it will prove no respecter of diplomatic connection that looks ever backward and never forward; that multiplies its ambassadors and its plenipotentiaries, tailed out a hundredfold by suits and attachés, and numberless commercial agents, to connect a shipping interest with twenty million artisans of Europe; but apologizes through a couple of ministers and half a dozen consuls for its failure to unite our vast production and manufacture with three hundred million machineless consumers around the Pacific circle. Be sure likewise it will not fail to note and resent the intrusion of trans-Atlantic monarchies to crush out a republic in Mexico, seize on the islands of the Gulf, and fortify a thousand miles of seacoast threatening the line of our interoceanic communication. France, Spain, England, a triple alliance, eager and watchful for the death of discordant belligerent States, will have to confront for their conquests a nation rising as a phœnix, writing freedom on its flag, and fraternizing with liberty in all lands.

And with equal, if not still greater scrutiny, will the newborn aspiration for national life look within to shape the expression and the correlations on which its future must repose. The fact that we have never been a nation heretofore, that in three

quarters of a century we have achieved no individuality, that our civilization has been insignificant and transient and barren, only sharpens the zest for a future of enduring accomplishment. That such a future cannot be predicated on distinctions of race, on subordination of classes, on the accidents of lineage or tongue or clime, neither upon enslavement in any name or wealth or caste or condition — all this is certain, for it has been tried and failed; has once been inoculated into the system to cure our social disease, but instead of healing has run into this putrid eruption that threatens us with anarchic death. That new life must be founded on assimilation, not antagonisms; on an ingrown unity, not an irreconcilable contradiction. The lowly must be exalted, the slave freed, the chattel humanized, and a democratic equality before the law must obtain for all men. The people must have fraternity as well as solidarity; each must be a multiple of the whole. Just now amalgamation is the ghost in grave clothes that walks to terrify and affright, as if the very nation were not already an amalgam of all peoples, as if for generations heretofore there had not been this same dwelling together side by side that is to be hereafter. Slavery feared not amalgamation; shall freedom, then, be a greater coward? Neither skins, nor colors, nor castes can determine here. The body politic that shall sustain such nationality as ours is foreordained to be must furthermore absorb all increments as they come, and not allow an anaconda torpor of five or seven or twenty years to determine the natural rights of man, his right to be one in any aggregate of many. All such limitation on citizenship will pass away under attrition of growth. The open door of the Republic will invite the oppressed of every land to seek asylum and enter upon the enjoyment of liberty. Impartial justice will stand ready to succor and to aid all who shall appeal from wrong or violence or intimidation. And that grand future of democratic unity will arrive when our people of every lineage and every type shall meet on the plane of equal rights to attest a nationality that will stand out a waymark to the centuries.

The third and completing symbol of the outcome of these times will be found to indicate the instauration here of Christian government, founded upon, indwelling with, and springing out of the divine justices — government recognizing that in the affairs of nations, as in those of individuals, there is one equality that comes of the equality of creation; there is one right, avenger on

compromises, which is the supreme right; there is one law, which ever must be, as it ever has been, a higher law. And they are to become practice, not merely theory. These are earnest days in the experiences of our people, and in this Senate, as abroad throughout the land, the most important fact around and about you is not always your law of yesterday or your tax of to-morrow, or your conscription of a month hence; it is not the vote here, or the battle yonder, but it is the spirit of this nation that upholds these things, and out of which they flow — the spirit that buoys you, Senators, into this upper air, and without which, or false to which, you will sink as empty, collapsed bladders. It is in obedience to such recognition that now you hasten to do that which but lately you refused to do — nay, declared by resolution just repealed that you never would do. These are earnest days, let me repeat it, but of which are coming convictions that will not bear to be trifled with; and as it has become an accepted faith, the idea of nationality, that our being and the being of the nation are one and inseparable for good and for evil, so it will further appear that the existence on which we are entering as a great people is no half life, made up only of the vicissitudes of protection and the exaction of revenues, but must be blended in with those deeper feelings and outlooks and co-workings that ennoble and make sublime communities of men and that entwine enduring hopes with cheering duties.

Nor is this simply affirmation, unsupported by substantial experiences of history. On the contrary, it is the very epitome of what is memorable and held in veneration out of all annals. Never yet at any time have the aspirations of a whole people after enlarged liberties been dissociate from the yearning for a more clear affinity between God and government. And can any fail to see the clear evidence of the same gleamings along our horizon? The voices now that are touched with truest eloquence are those that have come up out of tribulation for conscience's sake in the past. From the pulpit, as in all periods of unrest, proceed the foremost words of guidance — from the pulpit that preaches politics, as some have it; that preaches rather our God-wrought relations to fellow-men equally with those to a future state, as others more clearly interpret. Those grand old mother words of justice and truth and brotherhood begin to have meaning anew kindled up in them by the light that is breaking out around. The nation is putting on its Puritanism. Thanksgivings

appoint themselves unitedly. Days of supplication are become somewhat more than holidays. The bowing down has ceased to be a mockery in the presence of the multitudinous dead; and even they who have heretofore been accounted most indifferent begin to hold to a realizing conviction that God does direct the affairs of a nation by his special providence. The scoffers have had their generation, and we are returned upon a period of faith; these things are plain before us, to be seen of all. Have they, then, no significance? Do they point to no new time? Are they to be swallowed up in reactions as godless as the past in our government? Will the endurances through which we have just passed leave no moral impress? Is there to be no higher record of the deliverances from the great perils than that of the statute book? Can it be possible that the deep moving of the spirit of this people which has accomplished so much of work and worship shall take no permanent form that may transmit it to posterity? No! it cannot be thus — it never has been thus. It will not be in vain that we have learned so many lessons of humiliation, as well as experienced so many signal mercies. The scarlet sins of the past stand revealed and abashed. Is it presumptuous, pharisaical vanity of race — how has it been cast down in the necessity of resort to the armed intervention of another and much discredited race to assist in final suppression of the rebellion! Is it pride of civilization, — how has it been at fault in the presence of so great perils and the appeal for solution to the barbarisms of force, the coarsest methods of untutored nature! Is it reliance upon complex machinery of government, the balances of political science, the trick of names and forms, — how brief has been the delusion, and how complete and undeceiving, showing that all votings and ballotings and adjustings of powers and solemn constitution-making will never naturalize a received falsehood, or equalize the scale of right and wrong! Turn where you will, the lesson is the same, that it is not in departure from, but in conformity to, divine precept that a nation will find its prosperity; that there is a law of retribution for the sin of a people as of a person, and that it is only by cleaving to the right at every sacrifice that any hope of a broad, enduring unity can be justified.

It was a declaration that led to much thought and was significant of much which has since transpired, that this nation could not endure half free and half slave, that one or the other would be supreme. But it is a truth of far deeper significance that this nation will not long survive with no God anywhere in its Constitution, with policies shamelessly substituted for duties, and with a government the antithesis rather than the exponent of any aspiration of the people for higher development as a free Christian State. The end of such conjunctions must be desolating anarchy, which will be fatal to all respect for authority. What other is the meaning of that strange and stupendous demoralization which has characterized the administration of public affairs in these United States as the result of three quarters of a century's growth? Without doubt ours has been for many years the worst-governed community on the face of the globe, in all aspects of official conduct. Fraud and speculation and neglect and waste and indulgence and nepotism and intrigue and time-serving and all the calendar of crimes do our governing. Towns and cities and States, with multiplied charters and checks, have all taken the same character, fallen to a large extent under sinister control, become asylums of corruption, and are a jeer and a byword of reproach. Names of policemen, aldermen, Congressmen, bear a stain. When quit of his vocation the curious ask, "Is he honest?" Politics has become a filthy pool, in whose waters the good and brave shrink to be immersed. And this in its entirety is the result of practical atheism in government. The ignoring of any moral responsibility in the State entails the absence of any practical morality in its administration. What other could be the outcome of such national apostasy than the national demoralization upon which we have fallen? And from whence are we to expect any reform? Be sure it will not be from continuance in such courses. Half a century more of like degeneration, and what of good is left in the land will revolt from such dominion, preferring death to abject disgrace. Human nature cannot stand it. This, then, is the momentous question of our people in the present hour, and how best to return to other ideas of government, and other bases of public administration, challenges all their forethought and endeavor, all their humility and entreaty. And it is because the evil lies deeper than men or offices that it demands such inquest. It is not only that pure men shall be put in office, or that there be pure offices to put them in; but the controlling thought over men and offices must be that of purity which recognizes a tribunal before which no deceit prospereth. Indeed, there is no refuge for any nation out

of such a low estate but in despotism to constrain probity, or Christianity to inspire purity; and for democracy, such as ours, where the rule is with the many, the latter is the only safety. And how true is this, as in all things else, in the instinct of peoples; how clearly does this great heart of the multitudes in this day of revolution recognize such dependence, and how sternly is it putting on the armor of faith for the conflict with corruption, and bowing down before God to search out conformity to his eternal laws! The many are not blinded, but clearly see irrepressible conflict between a nation to be saved and a government to be damned. Not that the obsolete type of Church and State will be revived in our Republic, not that formalisms of creed and ritual shall be enacted or set up in the stead of departed convictions, but something more and other than all this, in the repudiation of those falsities that are the parlance of cabinets and the resorts of administrations, in the absolute reception and enforcement of that impartial justice and brotherhood which makes the true social state, and in the elevation to control and authority in the nation of the same moralities and Christianized public thought, which is ever the highest and last appeal among the consciences of men.

HENRY ARMITT BROWN

(1844–1878)

THE oration delivered by Henry Armitt Brown, of the Philadelphia bar, at the Valley Forge Centennial, has been greatly admired. He was born in Philadelphia in 1844 and educated at Yale. His greatest reputation was made as a political orator in presidential campaigns, and in such movements as that for municipal reform in Philadelphia. He died in 1878, and two years later a number of his speeches were collected and published.

ONE CENTURY'S ACHIEVEMENT

(Delivered at the Valley Forge Centennial)

My Countrymen:—

THE century that has gone by has changed the face of nature and wrought a revolution in the habits of mankind. We stand to-day at the dawn of an extraordinary age. Freed from the chains of ancient thought and superstition, man has begun to win the most extraordinary victories in the domain of science. One by one he has dispelled the doubts of the ancient world. Nothing is too difficult for his hand to attempt — no region too remote — no place too sacred for his daring eye to penetrate. He has robbed the earth of her secrets and sought to solve the mysteries of the heavens! He has secured and chained to his service the elemental forces of nature — he has made the fire his steed — the winds his ministers — the seas his pathway — the lightning his messenger. He has descended into the bowels of the earth, and walked in safety on the bottom of the sea. He has raised his head above the clouds, and made the impalpable air his resting-place. He has tried to analyze the stars, count the constellations, and weigh the sun. He has advanced with such astounding speed that, breathless, we have reached a moment when it seems as if distance has been annihilated, time made as naught, the invisible seen, the inaudible heard, the unspeakable spoken, the intangible felt, the impossible accomplished. And already we knock at the door of a new century which promises

to be infinitely brighter and more enlightened and happier than this. But in all this blaze of light which illuminates the present and casts its reflection into the distant recesses of the past, there is not a single ray that shoots into the future. Not one step have we taken toward the solution of the mystery of life. That remains to-day as dark and unfathomable as it was ten thousand years ago.

We know that we are more fortunate than our fathers. We believe that our children shall be happier than we. We know that this century is more enlightened than the last. We believe that the time to come will be better and more glorious than this. We think, we believe, we hope, but we do not know. Across that threshold we may not pass: behind that veil we may not penetrate. Into that country it may not be for us to go. It may be vouchsafed to us to behold it, wonderingly, from afar, but never to enter in. It matters not. The age in which we live is but a link in the endless and eternal chain. Our lives are like the sands upon the shore; our voices like the breath of this summer breeze that stirs the leaf for a moment and is forgotten. Whence we have come and whither we shall go, not one of us can tell. And the last survivor of this mighty multitude shall stay but a little while.

But in the impenetrable To Be, the endless generations are advancing to take our places as we fall. For them, as for us, shall the earth roll on and the seasons come and go, the snowflakes fall, the flowers bloom, and the harvests be gathered in. For them as for us shall the sun, like the life of man, rise out of darkness in the morning and sink into darkness in the night. For them as for us shall the years march by in the sublime procession of the ages. And here, in this place of sacrifice, in this vale of humiliation, in this valley of the shadow of that death out of which the life of America arose, regenerate and free, let us believe with an abiding faith that, to them, union will seem as dear, and liberty as sweet, and progress as glorious, as they were to our fathers, and are to you and me, and that the institutions which have made us happy, preserved by the virtue of our children, shall bless the remotest generations of the time to come. And unto him who holds in the hollow of his hand the fate of nations, and yet marks the sparrow's fall, let us lift up our hearts this day, and into his eternal care commend ourselves, our children, and our country.

THE DANGERS OF THE PRESENT

(Delivered at the Centennial of the First Colonial Congress)

THE conditions of life are always changing, and the experience of the fathers is rarely the experience of the sons. The temptations which are trying us are not the temptations which beset their footsteps, nor the dangers which threaten our pathway the dangers which surrounded them. These men were few in number; we are many. They were poor, but we are rich. They were weak, but we are strong. What is it, countrymen, that we need to-day? Wealth? Behold it in your hands. Power? God has given it to you. Liberty? It is your birthright. Peace? It dwells amongst you. You have a government founded in the hearts of men, built by the people for the common good. You have a land flowing with milk and honey; your homes are happy, your workshops busy, your barns are full. The school, the railway, the telegraph, the printing press, have welded you together into one. Descend those mines that honeycomb the hills! Behold that commerce whitening the sea! Stand by yon gates and see that multitude pour through them from the corners of the earth, grafting the qualities of older stocks upon one stem, mingling the blood of many races in a common stream, and swelling the rich volume of our English speech with varied music from an hundred tongues. You have a long and glorious history, a past glittering with heroic deeds, an ancestry full of lofty and imperishable examples. You have passed through danger, endured privation, been acquainted with sorrow, been tried by suffering. You have journeyed in safety through the wilderness and crossed in triumph the Red Sea of civil strife, and the foot of him who led you hath not faltered, nor the light of his countenance been turned away.

It is a question for us now, not of founding a new government, but of the preservation of one already old; not of the formation of an independent power, but of the purification of a nation's life; not of the conquest of a foreign foe, but of the subjection of ourselves. The capacity of man to rule himself is to be proven in the days to come, not by the greatness of his wealth, nor by his valor in the field; not by the extent of his dominion, nor by the splendor of his genius. The dangers of to-day come from within. The worship of self, the love of power,

the lust for gold, the weakening of faith, the decay of public virtue, the lack of private worth—these are the perils which threaten our future; these are the enemies we have to fear; these are the traitors which infest the camp; and the danger was far less when Cataline knocked with his army at the gates of Rome, than when he sat smiling in the Senate House. We see them daily face to face; in the walk of virtue; in the road to wealth; in the path of honor; on the way to happiness. There is no peace between them and our safety. Nor can we avoid them and turn back. It is not enough to rest upon the past. No man or nation can stand still. We must mount upward or go down. We must grow worse or better. It is the eternal law— we cannot change it. . . .

My countrymen, this anniversary has gone by forever, and my task is done. While I have spoken the hour has passed from us, the hand has moved upon the dial, and the old century is dead. The American Union has endured an hundred years! Here on the threshold of the future the voice of humanity shall not plead to us in vain. There shall be darkness in the days to come; danger for our courage; temptation for our virtue; doubt for our faith; suffering for our fortitude. A thousand shall fall before us, and tens of thousands at our right hand. The years shall pass beneath our feet, and century follow century in quick succession. The generations of men shall come and go; the greatness of yesterday shall be forgotten to-day, and the glories of this noon shall vanish before to-morrow's sun; yet America shall not perish, but endure while the spirit of our fathers animates their sons.

THE PLEA OF THE FUTURE

My Countrymen:—

THE moments are quickly passing, and we stand like some traveler upon a lofty crag that separates two boundless seas. The century that is closing is complete. "The past," said your great statesman, "is secure." It is finished and beyond our reach. The hand of detraction cannot dim its glories, nor the tears of repentance wipe away its stains. Its good and evil, its joy and sorrow, its truth and falsehood, its honor and its shame we cannot touch. Sigh for them, blush for them, weep for them if we will, we cannot change them now. The old century is dying

and they are to be buried with him; his history is finished and they will stand upon its roll forever.

The century that is opening is all our own. The years that are before us are a virgin page. We can inscribe them as we will. The future of our country rests upon us. The happiness of posterity depends on us. The fate of humanity may be in our hands. That pleading voice, choked with the sobs of ages, which has so often spoken to deaf ears, is lifted up to us. It asks us to be brave, benevolent, consistent, true to the teachings of our history, proving "divine descent by worth divine." It asks us to be virtuous, building up public virtue upon private worth; seeking that righteousness that exalteth nations. It asks us to be patriotic, loving our country before all other things; making her happiness our happiness, her honors ours, her fame our own. It asks us in the name of charity, in the name of freedom, in the name of God!

WILLIAM GANNAWAY BROWNLOW

(1805-1877)

THE volcanic passion of the Civil War period found, no doubt, its most nearly adequate verbal expression in the vehement speeches, addresses, letters, and editorials of William G. Brownlow, called "the Fighting Parson" from the aggressiveness of his utterances. He ranks with David Crockett as one of the most remarkable products of his native State, and the future historian will study him with curious interest. He is important to the history, both of politics and of oratory, because of his entire lack of reservation in his utterances. Where others were restrained by the fear of incongruity, or by past habits of self-repression, he voiced without restraint the feelings which on one side and the other expressed themselves in the fierce antagonisms of debate as a prelude to the scarcely fiercer struggles of the battlefield. During the contest which led to the secession of Tennessee,—or rather to its direct rebellion, as it waived in express terms all discussion of the Constitutional "Right of Secession" and revolted in due form,—Parson Brownlow kept a United States flag flying over his house in Knoxville, and, on threats being made to pull it down, issued the following address, which not only illustrates his style, but is of great historical value as an expression of the feeling which resulted in the Civil War:—

It is known to this community and to the people of this county that I have had the Stars and Stripes, in the character of a small flag, floating over my dwelling, in East Knoxville, since February. This flag has become very offensive to certain leaders of the Secession party in this town, and to certain would-be leaders, and the more so as it is about the only one of the kind floating in the city. Squads of troops, from three to twenty, have come over to my house, within the last several days, cursing the flag in front of my house, and threatening to take it down, greatly to the annoyance of my wife and children. No attack has been made upon it, and consequently we have had no difficulty. It is due to the Tennessee troops to say that they have never made any such demonstrations. Other troops from the Southern States, passing on to Virginia, have been induced to do so, by certain cowardly, sneaking, white-livered scoundrels, residing here, who have not the *melt* to undertake what they urge strangers to do. One of the Louisiana squads proclaimed in front of my house, on Thursday, that they were told to take it down by citizens of Knoxville. . . .

If these God-forsaken scoundrels and hell-deserving assassins want satisfaction out of me for what I have said about them,—and it has been no little,—they can find me on these streets every day of my life but Sunday. I am at all times prepared to give them satisfaction. I take back nothing I have ever said against the corrupt and unprincipled villains, but reiterate all, cast it in their dastardly faces, and hurl down their lying throats their own infamous calumnies.

Finally, the destroying of my small flag or of my town property is a small matter. The carrying out of the State upon the mad wave of Secession is also a small matter, compared with the great PRINCIPLE involved. Sink or swim, live or die, survive or perish, I am a Union man, and owe my allegiance to the Stars and Stripes of my country. Nor can I, in any possible contingency, have any respect for the Government of the Confederated States, originating as it did with, and being controlled by, the worst men in the South. And any man saying—whether of high or low degree—that I am an Abolitionist or a Black Republican, is a liar and a scoundrel.

Brownlow was born in Virginia in 1805. He was bred a carpenter but educated himself until he thought himself ready for the ministry. He began preaching as a Methodist circuit-rider in 1826 and about the same time entered politics as a Whig, supporting Adams in 1828. In 1839 he became the editor of the Knoxville (Tennessee) Whig through which he gave vehement expression to his views on the issues of the day—especially on slavery and disunion. He opposed the coercive Abolition of Slavery and with even greater aggressiveness denounced the advocates of secession. As a result, he was arrested after the war began and, after imprisonment in the Knoxville jail, was sent beyond the Confederate lines by order of the Confederate War Department. Returning to the State after it was occupied by the Union forces, he was elected Governor in 1865 and to the United States Senate in 1869. He died in 1877.

East Tennessee was almost as strongly Union in sentiment as the rest of the State was for the Confederacy. Brownlow, like Andrew Johnson and others, represented the East Tennessee Union sentiment, but historically he is of far more importance as a representative of the modes of thought and expression of the pioneer class which produced Houston, Crockett, Lincoln, and so many other remarkable men. With a few such exceptions as Brownlow and Crockett, those who went into public life to represent this class assimilated enough of the habits of culture to become conventional and so, to a great extent, unrepresentative. But Brownlow never did. He speaks the feelings of the men in the ranks in their own language and with their own habits of unreserved expression. In this view of his relations to history, no orator of his times surpasses him in importance.

II—44

THE VALUE OF THE AMERICAN UNION
(From the Philadelphia Debate with Rev. Mr. Pryne)

WHO can estimate the value of the American Union? Proud, happy, thrice-happy America! The home of the oppressed, the asylum of the emigrant! where the citizen of every clime, and the child of every creed, roam free and untrammeled as the wild winds of heaven! Baptized at the fount of Liberty in fire and blood, cold must be the heart that thrills not at the name of the American Union!

When the Old World, with "all its pomp, and pride, and circumstance," shall be covered with oblivion,—when thrones shall have crumbled and dynasties shall have been forgotten,—may this glorious Union, despite the mad schemes of Southern fire-eaters and Northern Abolitionists, stand amid regal ruin and national desolation, towering sublime, like the last mountain in the Deluge—majestic, immutable, and magnificent!

In pursuance of this, let every conservative Northern man, who loves his country and her institutions, shake off the trammels of Northern fanaticism, and swear upon the altar of his country that he will stand by her Constitution and laws. Let every Southern man shake off the trammels of disunion and nullification, and pledge his life and his sacred honor to stand by the Constitution of his country as it is, the laws as enacted by Congress and interpreted by the Supreme Court. Then we shall see every heart a shield, and a drawn sword in every hand, to preserve the ark of our political safety! Then we shall see reared a fabric upon our national Constitution which time cannot crumble, persecution shake, fanaticism disturb, nor revolution change, but which shall stand among us like some lofty and stupendous Apennine, while the earth rocks at its feet, and the thunder peals above its head!

GRAPE SHOT AND HEMP
(Delivered at Nashville in 1862)

Gentlemen:—

I AM in a sad plight to say much of interest,—too thoroughly incapacitated to do justice to you or myself. My throat has been disordered for the past three years, and I have been compelled to almost abandon public speaking. Last December

I was thrust into an uncomfortable and disagreeable jail,—for what? *Treason!* Treason to the bogus Confederacy; and the proofs of that treason were articles which appeared in the Knoxville Whig in May last, when the State of Tennessee was a member of the imperishable Union. At the expiration of four weeks I became a victim of the typhoid fever, and was removed to a room in a decent dwelling, and a guard of seven men kept me company. I subsequently became so weak that I could not turn over in my bed, and the guard was increased to twelve men, for fear I should suddenly recover and run away to Kentucky. But I never had any intention to run, and if I had, I was not able to escape. My purpose was to make them send me out of their infamous government, according to contract, or to hang me, if they thought proper. I was promised passports by their Secretary of War, a little Jew, late of New Orleans; and upon the faith of that promise, and upon the invitation of General Crittenden, then in command at Knoxville, I reported myself and demanded my passports. They gave me passports, but they were from my house to the Knoxville jail, and the escort was a deputy marshal of Jeff Davis. But I served my time out, and have landed here at last, through much tribulation. When I started on this perilous journey, I was sore distressed both in mind and body, being weak from disease and confinement. I expected to meet with insults and indignities at every point from the blackguard portion of the Rebel soldiers and citizens, and in this I was not disappointed. It was fortunate, indeed, that I was not mobbed. This would have been done, but for the vigilance and fidelity of the officers having me in charge. These were Adjutant-General Young and Lieutenant O'Brien, clever men, high-minded, and honorable; and they were of my own selection. They had so long been Union men that I felt assured they had not lost the instincts of gentlemen and patriots, afflicted as they were with the incurable disease of Secession!

But, gentlemen, some three or four days ago I landed in this city, as you are aware. Five miles distant I encountered the Federal pickets. Then it was that I felt like a new man. My depression ceased, and returning life and health seemed suddenly to invigorate my system and to arouse my physical constitution. I had been looking at soldiers in uniform for twelve months, and to me they appeared as hateful as their Confederacy and their

infamous flag. But these Federal pickets, who received me kindly and shook me cordially by the hand, looked like angels of light, compared with the insulting blackguards who had been groaning and cursing around my house.

Why, my friends, these demagogues actually boast that the Lord is upon their side, and declare that God Almighty is assisting them in the furtherance of their nefarious project. In Knoxville and surrounding localities, a short time since, daily prayer-meetings were held, wherein the Almighty was beseeched to raise Lincoln's blockade and to hurl destruction against the Burnside Expedition. Their prayers were partly answered: the blockade at Roanoke Island was most effectually raised!

Gentlemen, I am no Abolitionist; I applaud no sectional doctrines. I am a Southern man, and all my relatives and interests are thoroughly identified with the South and Southern institutions. I was born in the Old Dominion; my parents were born in Virginia, and they and their ancestors were all slave-holders. Let me assure you that the South has suffered no infringement upon her institutions; the Slavery question was actually *no* pretext for this unholy, unrighteous conflict. Twelve Senators from the Cotton States, who had sworn to preserve inviolate the Constitution framed by our forefathers, plotted treason at night,—a fit time for such a crime,—and telegraphed to their States dispatches advising them to pass ordinances of secession. Yes, gentlemen, twelve Senators swore allegiance in the daytime, and unswore it at night.

Soldiers and citizens! Secession is well-nigh played out,—the dog is dead,—and their demoralized army is on its way to the Cotton States, where they can look back at you, as you approach their scattered lines. I have been detained among them for ten days, General Hardee refusing to let me pass. This was only fifty-five miles from here, in the sound Union town of Shelbyville. They were pushing off their bacon and flour and their demoralized men; and I hope you will follow them up. You will overtake them at the Tennessee River,—sooner, if they come up with new supplies of mean whisky.

But, gentlemen, you see that I am growing hoarse in this fierce wind. I am otherwise feeble, not having attempted to make a speech in months. Excuse me, therefore, and join me in this sentiment, should this wicked and unholy war continue,—
"Grape for the Rebel masses, and hemp for their leaders!"

WILLIAM J. BRYAN

(1860-)

HAT is known as «The Cross of Gold» speech, delivered by William J. Bryan in the Chicago convention of 1896, is generally believed to have caused his nomination — which by the general public at least was wholly unexpected. The speech attained immediate and wide celebrity. Perhaps no other single speech ever delivered in the country was read in the first month after its delivery by so many people, or when read was so strongly debated as this. The text here used is that authorized by Mr. Bryan and published in his book, 'The First Battle; a Story of the Campaign of 1896.' It is used by his permission, and in connection with it the following, written by him for 'The First Battle,' will be found of interest:—

«In view of the wide publication of this speech, I may be pardoned for making some reference to it. While a member of the Committee on Resolutions, in the Chicago convention, I was prevented from attending the first sessions of the committee owing to our contest, and was not a member of the sub-committee which drafted the platform. As soon as our contest was settled, I met with the committee and took part in the final discussion and adoption of the platform. Just before the platform was reported to the convention, Senator Jones sent for me and asked me to take charge of the debate. In dividing the time I was to have twenty minutes to close, but as the minority used ten minutes more than the time allotted, my time was extended ten minutes. The concluding sentence of my speech was criticized both favorably and unfavorably. I had used the idea in substantially the same form in a speech in Congress, but did not recall the fact when I used it in the convention. A portion of the speech was extemporaneous, and its arrangement entirely so, but parts of it had been prepared for another occasion. Next to the conclusion, the part most quoted was the definition of the term 'business men.' Since I became interested in the discussion of monetary questions, I have often had occasion to note and comment upon the narrowness of some of the terms used, and nowhere is this narrowness more noticeable than in the attempt to ignore the most important business men of the country, the real creators of wealth.»

THE «CROSS OF GOLD»

(Concluding the Debate on the Chicago Platform of 1896)

Mr. Chairman and Gentlemen of the Convention:—

I WOULD be presumptuous, indeed, to present myself against the distinguished gentlemen to whom you have listened if this were a mere measuring of abilities; but this is not a contest between persons. The humblest citizen in all the land, when clad in the armor of a righteous cause, is stronger than all the hosts of error. I come to speak to you in defense of a cause as holy as the cause of liberty — the cause of humanity.

When this debate is concluded, a motion will be made to lay upon the table the resolution offered in commendation of the administration, and also the resolution offered in condemnation of the administration. We object to bringing this question down to the level of persons. The individual is but an atom; he is born, he acts, he dies; but principles are eternal; and this has been a contest over a principle.

Never before in the history of this country has there been witnessed such a contest as that through which we have just passed. Never before in the history of American politics has a great issue been fought out as this issue has been, by the voters of a great party. On the fourth of March, 1895, a few Democrats, most of them Members of Congress, issued an address to the Democrats of the nation, asserting that the money question was the paramount issue of the hour; declaring that a majority of the Democratic party had the right to control the action of the party on this paramount issue; and concluding with the request that the believers in the free coinage of silver in the Democratic party should organize, take charge of, and control the policy of the Democratic party. Three months later, at Memphis, an organization was perfected, and the silver Democrats went forth openly and courageously proclaiming their belief, and declaring that, if successful, they would crystallize into a platform the declaration which they had made. Then began the conflict. With a zeal approaching the zeal which inspired the crusaders who followed Peter the Hermit, our silver Democrats went forth from victory unto victory until they are now assembled, not to discuss, not to debate, but to enter up the judgment already

rendered by the plain people of this country. In this contest brother has been arrayed against brother, father against son. The warmest ties of love, acquaintance, and association have been disregarded; old leaders have been cast aside when they have refused to give expression to the sentiments of those whom they would lead, and new leaders have sprung up to give direction to this cause of truth. Thus has the contest been waged, and we have assembled here under as binding and solemn instructions as were ever imposed upon representatives of the people.

We do not come as individuals. As individuals we might have been glad to compliment the gentleman from New York [Senator Hill], but we know that the people for whom we speak would never be willing to put him in a position where he could thwart the will of the Democratic party. I say it was not a question of persons; it was a question of principle, and it is not with gladness, my friends, that we find ourselves brought into conflict with those who are now arrayed on the other side.

The gentleman who preceded me [ex-Governor Russell] spoke of the State of Massachusetts; let me assure him that not one present in all this convention entertains the least hostility to the people of the State of Massachusetts, but we stand here representing people who are the equals, before the law, of the greatest citizens in the State of Massachusetts. When you [turning to the gold delegates] come before us and tell us that we are about to disturb your business interests, we reply that you have disturbed our business interests by your course.

We say to you that you have made the definition of a business man too limited in its application. The man who is employed for wages is as much a business man as his employer; the attorney in a country town is as much a business man as the corporation counsel in a great metropolis; the merchant at the cross-roads store is as much a business man as the merchant of New York; the farmer who goes forth in the morning and toils all day, who begins in spring and toils all summer, and who by the application of brain and muscle to the natural resources of the country creates wealth, is as much a business man as the man who goes upon the Board of Trade and bets upon the price of grain; the miners who go down a thousand feet into the earth, or climb two thousand feet upon the cliffs, and bring forth from their hiding places the precious metals to be poured into the channels of trade are as much business men as the few financial

magnates who, in a back room, corner the money of the world. We come to speak of this broader class of business men.

Ah, my friends, we say not one word against those who live upon the Atlantic Coast, but the hardy pioneers who have braved all the dangers of the wilderness, who have made the desert to blossom as the rose,—the pioneers away out there [pointing to the West], who rear their children near to Nature's heart, where they can mingle their voices with the voices of the birds,—out there where they have erected schoolhouses for the education of their young, churches where they praise their Creator, and cemeteries where rest the ashes of their dead — these people, we say, are as deserving of the consideration of our party as any people in this country. It is for these that we speak. We do not come as aggressors. Our war is not a war of conquest; we are fighting in the defense of our homes, our families, and posterity. We have petitioned, and our petitions have been scorned; we have entreated, and our entreaties have been disregarded; we have begged, and they have mocked when our calamity came. We beg no longer; we entreat no more; we petition no more. We defy them!

The gentleman from Wisconsin has said that he fears a Robespierre. My friends, in this land of the free you need not fear that a tyrant will spring up from among the people. What we need is an Andrew Jackson to stand, as Jackson stood, against the encroachments of organized wealth.

They tell us that this platform was made to catch votes. We reply to them that changing conditions make new issues; that the principles upon which Democracy rests are as everlasting as the hills, but that they must be applied to new conditions as they arise. Conditions have arisen, and we are here to meet those conditions. They tell us that the income tax ought not to be brought in here; that it is a new idea. They criticize us for our criticism of the Supreme Court of the United States. My friends, we have not criticized; we have simply called attention to what you already know. If you want criticisms, read the dissenting opinions of the court. There you will find criticisms. They say that we passed an unconstitutional law; we deny it. The income tax law was not unconstitutional when it was passed; it was not unconstitutional when it went before the Supreme Court for the first time; it did not become unconstitutional until one of the judges changed his mind, and we cannot be expected to know when a judge will change his mind. The income tax is just. It simply intends to put the burdens of government justly upon the backs of the people. I am in favor of an income tax. When I find a man who is not willing to bear his share of the burdens of the government which protects him, I find a man who is unworthy to enjoy the blessings of a government like ours.

They say that we are opposing national bank currency; it is true. If you will read what Thomas Benton said, you will find he said that, in searching history, he could find but one parallel to Andrew Jackson; that was Cicero, who destroyed the conspiracy of Cataline and saved Rome. Benton said that Cicero only did for Rome what Jackson did for us when he destroyed the bank conspiracy and saved America. We say in our platform that we believe that the right to coin and issue money is a function of government. We believe it. We believe that it is a part of sovereignty, and can no more with safety be delegated to private individuals than we could afford to delegate to private individuals the power to make penal statutes or levy taxes. Mr. Jefferson, who was once regarded as good Democratic authority, seems to have differed in opinion from the gentleman who has addressed us on the part of the minority. Those who are opposed to this proposition tell us that the issue of paper money is a function of the bank, and that the government ought to go out of the banking business. I stand with Jefferson rather than with them, and tell them, as he did, that the issue of money is a function of government, and that the banks ought to go out of the governing business.

They complain about the plank which declares against life tenure in office. They have tried to strain it to mean that which it does not mean. What we oppose by that plank is the life tenure which is being built up in Washington, and which excludes from participation in official benefits the humbler members of society.

Let me call your attention to two or three important things. The gentleman from New York says that he will propose an amendment to the platform providing that the proposed change in our monetary system shall not affect contracts already made. Let me remind you that there is no intention of affecting those contracts which, according to present laws, are made payable in gold; but if he means to say that we cannot change our monetary system without protecting those who have loaned money

before the change was made, I desire to ask him where, in law or in morals, he can find justification for not protecting the debtors when the act of 1873 was passed, if he now insists that we must protect the creditors.

He says he will also propose an amendment which will provide for the suspension of free coinage if we fail to maintain the parity within a year. We reply that when we advocate a policy which we believe will be successful, we are not compelled to raise a doubt as to our own sincerity by suggesting what we shall do if we fail. I ask him, if he would apply his logic to us, why he does not apply it to himself. He says he wants this country to try to secure an international agreement. Why does he not tell us what he is going to do if he fails to secure an international agreement? There is more reason for him to do that than there is for us to provide against the failure to maintain the parity. Our opponents have tried for twenty years to secure an international agreement, and those are waiting for it most patiently who do not want it at all.

And now, my friends, let me come to the paramount issue. If they ask us why it is that we say more on the money question than we say upon the tariff question, I reply that, if protection has slain its thousands, the gold standard has slain its tens of thousands. If they ask us why we do not embody in our platform all the things that we believe in, we reply that when we have restored the money of the Constitution all other necessary reforms will be possible; but that until this is done there is no other reform that can be accomplished.

Why is it that within three months such a change has come over the country? Three months ago when it was confidently asserted that those who believe in the gold standard would frame our platform and nominate our candidates, even the advocates of the gold standard did not think that we could elect a President. And they had good reason for their doubt, because there is scarcely a State here to-day asking for the gold standard which is not in the absolute control of the Republican party. But note the change. Mr. McKinley was nominated at St. Louis upon a platform which declared for the maintenance of the gold standard until it can be changed into bimetallism by international agreement. Mr. McKinley was the most popular man among the Republicans, and three months ago everybody in the Republican party prophesied his election. How is it to-day? Why, the

man who was once pleased to think that he looked like Napoleon—that man shudders to-day when he remembers that he was nominated on the anniversary of the battle of Waterloo. Not only that, but as he listens he can hear with ever-increasing distinctness the sound of the waves as they beat upon the lonely shores of St. Helena.

Why this change? Ah, my friends, is not the reason for the change evident to any one who will look at the matter? No private character, however pure, no personal popularity, however great, can protect from the avenging wrath of an indignant people a man who will declare that he is in favor of fastening the gold standard upon this country, or who is willing to surrender the right of self-government and place the legislative control of our affairs in the hands of foreign potentates and powers.

We go forth confident that we shall win. Why? Because upon the paramount issue of this campaign there is not a spot of ground upon which the enemy will dare to challenge battle. If they tell us that the gold standard is a good thing, we shall point to their platform and tell them that their platform pledges the party to get rid of the gold standard and substitute bimetallism. If the gold standard is a good thing, why try to get rid of it? I call your attention to the fact that some of the very people who are in this convention to-day and who tell us that we ought to declare in favor of international bimetallism,—thereby declaring that the gold standard is wrong and that the principle of bimetallism is better,—these very people four months ago were open and avowed advocates of the gold standard, and were then telling us that we could not legislate two metals together, even with the aid of all the world. If the gold standard is a good thing, we ought to declare in favor of its retention and not in favor of abandoning it; and if the gold standard is a bad thing why should we wait until other nations are willing to help us to let go? Here is the line of battle, and we care not upon which issue they force the fight; we are prepared to meet them on either issue or on both. If they tell us that the gold standard is the standard of civilization, we reply to them that this, the most enlightened of all the nations of the earth, has never declared for a gold standard and that both the great parties this year are declaring against it. If the gold standard is the standard of civilization, why, my friends, should we not have it? If they come to meet us on that issue we can present the history of our

nation. More than that; we can tell them that they will search the pages of history in vain to find a single instance where the common people of any land have ever declared themselves in favor of the gold standard. They can find where the holders of fixed investments have declared for a gold standard, but not where the masses have.

Mr. Carlisle said in 1878 that this was a struggle between "the idle holders of idle capital" and "the struggling masses, who produce the wealth and pay the taxes of the country"; and, my friends, the question we are to decide is: Upon which side will the Democratic party fight; upon the side of "the idle holders of idle capital" or upon the side of "the struggling masses"? That is the question which the party must answer first, and then it must be answered by each individual hereafter. The sympathies of the Democratic party, as shown by the platform, are on the side of the struggling masses who have ever been the foundation of the Democratic party. There are two ideas of government. There are those who believe that, if you will only legislate to make the well-to-do prosperous, their prosperity will leak through on those below. The Democratic idea, however, has been that if you legislate to make the masses prosperous, their prosperity will find its way up through every class which rests upon them.

You come to us and tell us that the great cities are in favor of the gold standard; we reply that the great cities rest upon our broad and fertile prairies. Burn down your cities and leave our farms, and your cities will spring up again as if by magic; but destroy our farms and the grass will grow in the streets of every city in the country.

My friends, we declare that this nation is able to legislate for its own people on every question, without waiting for the aid or consent of any other nation on earth; and upon that issue we expect to carry every State in the Union. I shall not slander the inhabitants of the fair State of Massachusetts nor the inhabitants of the State of New York by saying that, when they are confronted with the proposition, they will declare that this nation is not able to attend to its own business. It is the issue of 1776 over again. Our ancestors, when but three millions in number, had the courage to declare their political independence of every other nation; shall we, their descendants, when we have grown to seventy millions, declare that we are less independent than our forefathers? No, my friends, that will never be the verdict of our people. Therefore, we care not upon what lines the battle is fought. If they say bimetallism is good, but that we cannot have it until other nations help us, we reply that, instead of having a gold standard because England has, we will restore bimetallism, and then let England have bimetallism because the United States has it. If they dare to come out in the open field and defend the gold standard as a good thing, we will fight them to the uttermost. Having behind us the producing masses of this nation and the world, supported by the commercial interests, the laboring interests, and the toilers everywhere, we will answer their demand for a gold standard by saying to them: You shall not press down upon the brow of labor this crown of thorns, you shall not crucify mankind upon a cross of gold.

WILLIAM CULLEN BRYANT
(1794–1878)

THE poet Bryant was the favorite after-dinner speaker of New York city for years, not merely because of his reputation as a poet, but because of his genuine eloquence and the importance of the position in politics given him by the editorship of the New York Evening Post. He was at his best when speaking on such topics as the poetry of Burns or the influence of the Press, but he spoke with equal facility on the political issues of the day, and his collected orations make a volume of more literary merit than can be found in most volumes of speeches. He was born in Massachusetts in 1794. Showing extraordinary precocity in writing verse, as he did in developing a love for politics, he was encouraged by his parents, who allowed the publication of one of his metrical productions against the Embargo, written when he was thirteen years old. He had begun writing verse at ten, and his finest poem, 'Thanatopsis,' was produced while he was still in his minority. He became editor of the New York Evening Post in 1827, after a year's work as editorial assistant. This connection was continued during the rest of his life. He gave the paper strong Democratic tendencies, but used it in 1856 in helping to organize the Republican party whose policies during the war it supported. He was a strong advocate of free trade, and made a number of speeches in favor of it. He died in 1878. His address on Burns was delivered at the Burns banquet in New York in 1859, and the text here given is from a contemporaneous report preserved by Mr. Enos Clark.

THE GREATNESS OF BURNS
(Delivered at the Burns Centennial Banquet, New York, 1859)

ON RISING to begin the announcement of the regular toasts for this evening, my first duty is to thank my excellent friends of the Burns Club, with whom I do not now meet for the first time, and whose annual festivities are among the pleasantest I ever attended, for the honor they have done me

in calling me to the chair I occupy,—an honor the more to be prized on account of the rare occasion on which it is bestowed. An honor which can be conferred but once in a century is an honor indeed. This evening the memory of Burns will be celebrated as it never was before. His fame, from the time when he first appeared before the world as a poet, has been growing and brightening as the morning brightens into the perfect day. There never was a time when his merits were so freely acknowledged as now; when the common consent of the literary world placed him so high, or spoke his praises with so little intermixture of disparagement; when the anniversary of his birth could have awakened so general and fervent an enthusiasm. If we could imagine a human being endowed with the power of making himself, through the medium of his senses, a witness of whatever is passing on the face of the globe, what a series of festivities, what successive manifestations of the love and admiration which all who speak our language bear to the great Scottish poet, would present themselves to his observation, accompanying the shadow of this night in its circuit round the earth! Some twelve hours before this time he would have heard the praises of Burns recited and the songs of Burns sung on the banks of the Ganges, the music flowing out at the open windows on the soft evening air of that region, and mingling with the murmurs of the sacred river. A little later, he might have heard the same sounds from the mouth of the Euphrates; later still, from the southern extremity of Africa, under constellations strange to our eyes,—the stars of the Southern Hemisphere,—and almost at the same moment from the rocky shores of the Ionian Isles. Next they would have been heard from the orange groves of Malta, and from the winter colony of English and Americans on the banks of the Tiber. Then, in its turn, the Seine takes up the strain; and what a chorus rises from the British Isles—from every ocean mart, and river, and mountain side, with a distant response from the rock of Gibraltar! Last, in the Old World, on the westernmost verge, the observer whom I have imagined would have heard the voice of song and of gladness from the coasts of Liberia and Sierra Leone, among a race constitutionally and passionately fond of music, and to which we have given our language and literature. In the New World, frozen Newfoundland has already led in the festival of this night; and next, those who dwell where the St. Lawrence holds an icy mirror to the

stars; thence it has passed to the hills and valleys of New England; and it is now our turn, on the lordly Hudson. The Schuylkill will follow, the Potomac, the rivers of the Carolinas; the majestic St. John's, drawing his dark, deep waters from the Everglades; the borders of our mighty lakes; the beautiful Ohio; the great Mississippi, with its fountains gushing under fields of snow, and its mouth among flowers that fear not the frost. Then will our festival, in its westward course, cross the Rocky Mountains, gather in joyous assemblies those who pasture their herds on the Columbia and those who dig for gold on the Sacramento. By a still longer interval it will pass to Australia, lying in her distant solitude of waters, and now glowing with the heats of midsummer, where I fear the zealous countrymen of Burns will find the short night of the season too short for their festivities. And thus will this commemoration pursue the sunset round the globe, and follow the journey of the evening star till that gentle planet shines on the waters of China. Well has our great poet deserved this universal commemoration,—for who has written like him? What poem descriptive of rural manners and virtues, rural life in its simplicity and dignity,—yet without a single false outline or touch of false coloring,—clings to our memories and lives in our bosoms like his 'Cotter's Saturday Night'? What humorous narrative in verse can be compared with his 'Tam O'Shanter'? From the fall of Adam to his time, I believe, there was nothing written in the vein of his 'Mountain Daisy'; others have caught his spirit from that poem, but who among them all has excelled him? Of all the convivial songs I have ever seen in any language, there is none so overflowing with the spirit of conviviality, so joyous, so contagious, as his song of 'Willie Brewed a Peck o' Maut.' What love songs are sweeter and tenderer than those of Burns? What song addresses itself so movingly to our love of old friends and our pleasant recollection of old days as his 'Auld Lang Syne,' or to the domestic affections so powerfully as his 'John Anderson'? You heard yesterday, my friends, and will hear again to-day, better things said of the genius of Burns than I can say. That will be your gain and mine. But there is one observation which, if I have not already tried your patience too far, I would ask your leave to make. If Burns was thus great among poets, it was not because he stood higher than they by any pre-eminence of a creative and fertile imagination. Original, affluent, and active his imagination certainly was, and it was always kept under the guidance of a masculine and vigorous understanding; but it is the feeling which lives in his poems that gives them their supreme mastery over the minds of men. Burns was thus great, because, whatever may have been the errors of his after life, when he came from the hand that formed him,—I say it with the profoundest reverence,—God breathed into him, in larger measure than into other men, the spirit of that love which constitutes his own essence, and made him more than other men—a living soul. Burns was great by the greatness of his sympathies,—sympathies acute and delicate, yet large, comprehensive, boundless. They were warmest and strongest toward those of his own kin, yet they overflowed upon all sentient beings,—upon the animals in his stall; upon the 'wee, sleekit, cowerin,' tim'rous beastie' dislodged from her autumnal covert; upon the hare wounded by the sportsman; upon the very field flower, overturned by his share and crushed among the stubble. And in all this we feel that there is nothing strained or exaggerated, nothing affected or put on, nothing childish or silly, but that all is true, genuine, manly, noble; we honor, we venerate the poet while we read; we take the expression of these sympathies to our hearts, and fold it in our memory forever.

II—45

JAMES BUCHANAN

(1791-1868)

THE fact that the long sectional quarrel over slavery culminated during the administration of President Buchanan has almost completely obscured the intimate connection of his administration with an industrial and commercial revolution which is already showing itself greater in potentiality, if not in actual results, than the Civil War itself.

In his Inaugural Address President Buchanan defined the policy which resulted in the Pacific Railroad and the enormous development of the trans-Mississippi West. If, reading his Inaugural Address in this later time, we are more impressed by the ingenuity which enables him to reconcile this policy with his views as a strict Constructionist, than we are by the eloquence of his expression, or the method of his argument, we will not forget on that account how enormous were the forces he helped to set in motion, nor will we fail to be impressed with the operation of that great power of conservation of energy in society which at the beginning of a most destructive civil war had already prepared in embryo the growth of a then unimaginable system, through whose constructive development the destructive effects of civil war were to be compensated.

In view of the beginning of railroad development to the Pacific coast, and of the Atlantic cable to Europe, Buchanan's administration is, altogether aside from its bearing on the Civil War, one of the most revolutionary periods of our history. It would be idle to attempt to guess how much of this future President Buchanan may have had in view, when in his Inaugural Address he expressed his "humble confidence that the kind Providence which inspired our fathers with wisdom to frame the most perfect form of government and union ever devised by man will not suffer it to perish until it shall have been peacefully instrumental, by its example, in the extension of civil and religious liberty throughout the world."

But, however little it may have then been possible to foresee the industrial development of the last quarter of the nineteenth century, it is certain enough already that the twentieth century will study the Buchanan administration for something more important than the mere politics of Sectionalism. The mistakes on one side and the other, resulting from that Sectionalism, are apparent enough now, and perhaps

they are nowhere more apparent than in Mr. Buchanan's statement of what he conceived to be the results of diplomacy and attempts at compromise. When compromise fails, it can never assert an allowable claim to respectability. Except to the historian and the antiquary, Mr. Buchanan's utterances, as one of the diplomats and compromisers of a period of storm and stress, will not hereafter seem important; but it is true, nevertheless, that to understand the present of the United States, as it involves the future and the past, it is necessary to study such utterances as Buchanan's Inaugural Address until their connection with the forces of development inherent in the country makes them eloquent with presages of its progress.

Mr. Buchanan was born near Mercersburg, Pennsylvania, April 23d, 1791, from a Scotch-Irish family in moderate circumstances. Educated for the law, he entered politics as a Federalist at an early age, and from October 1814, when he was elected to the legislature of Pennsylvania, until March 4th, 1861, when he retired from the presidency, he was in office almost continuously. He served ten years in the House of Representatives, and, becoming a warm personal friend and supporter of President Jackson, lost altogether his early affiliations with Federalism, and became a strict Constructionist. President Jackson appointed him minister to Russia. Returning in 1834 he was elected to the United States Senate, where he served until the administration of President Polk, in whose cabinet he was Secretary of State. Retired temporarily from public life by the Whig victory which followed the Mexican War, he was an unsuccessful candidate for the presidency before the Democratic national convention of 1852. President Pierce appointed him minister to England, and, returning in 1855, he was nominated and elected to the presidency by the Democrats. After his retirement he took no part in public affairs, and preserved an almost unbroken silence concerning them. He died June 1st, 1868, at his home, Wheatland, near Lancaster, Pennsylvania.

INAUGURAL ADDRESS

Fellow-Citizens :—

I APPEAR before you this day to take the solemn oath "that I will faithfully execute the office of President of the United States and will to the best of my ability preserve, protect, and defend the Constitution of the United States."

In entering upon this great office I must humbly invoke the God of our fathers for wisdom and firmness to execute its high and responsible duties in such a manner as to restore harmony

and ancient friendship among the people of the several States, and to preserve our free institutions throughout many generations. Convinced that I owe my election to the inherent love for the Constitution and the Union which still animates the hearts of the American people, let me earnestly ask their powerful support in sustaining all just measures calculated to perpetuate these, the richest political blessings which heaven has ever bestowed upon any nation. Having determined not to become a candidate for re-election, I shall have no motive to influence my conduct in administering the government, except the desire ably and faithfully to serve my country and to live in the grateful memory of my countrymen.

We have recently passed through a presidential contest in which the passions of our fellow-citizens were excited to the highest degree by questions of deep and vital importance; but when the people proclaimed their will the tempest at once subsided and all was calm.

The voice of the majority, speaking in the manner prescribed by the Constitution, was heard, and instant submission followed. Our own country could alone have exhibited so grand and striking a spectacle of the capacity of man for self-government.

What a happy conception, then, was it for Congress to apply this simple rule, that the will of the majority shall govern, to the settlement of the question of domestic slavery in the Territories! Congress is neither "to legislate slavery into any Territory or State, nor to exclude it therefrom, but to leave the people thereof perfectly free to form and regulate their domestic institutions in their own way, subject only to the Constitution of the United States."

As a natural consequence, Congress has also prescribed that when the Territory of Kansas shall be admitted as a State it "shall be received into the Union with or without slavery, as their constitution may prescribe at the time of their admission."

A difference of opinion has arisen in regard to the point of time when the people of a Territory shall decide this question for themselves.

This is, happily, a matter of but little practical importance. Besides, it is a judicial question, which legitimately belongs to the Supreme Court of the United States, before whom it is now pending, and will, it is understood, be speedily and finally settled. To their decision, in common with all good citizens, I shall cheerfully submit, whatever this may be, though it has ever been my individual opinion that under the Nebraska-Kansas act the appropriate period will be when the number of actual residents in the Territory shall justify the formation of a constitution with a view to its admission as a State into the Union. But be this as it may, it is the imperative and indispensable duty of the Government of the United States to secure to every resident inhabitant the free and independent expression of his opinion by his vote. This sacred right of each individual must be preserved. That being accomplished, nothing can be fairer than to leave the people of a Territory free from all foreign interference, to decide their own destiny for themselves, subject only to the Constitution of the United States.

The whole Territorial question being settled upon the principle of popular sovereignty,—a principle as ancient as free government itself,—everything of a practical nature has been decided. No other question remains for adjustment, because all agree that under the Constitution slavery in the States is beyond any human power except that of the respective States themselves wherein it exists. May we not, then, hope that the long agitation on this subject is approaching its end, and that the geographical parties to which it has given birth, so much dreaded by the Father of his Country, will speedily become extinct? Most happy will it be for the country when the public mind shall be diverted from this question to others of more pressing and practical importance. Throughout the whole progress of this agitation, which has scarcely known any intermission for more than twenty years, while it has been productive of no positive good to any human being, it has been the prolific source of great evils to the master, to the slave, and to the whole country. It has alienated and estranged the people of the sister States from each other, and has even seriously endangered the very existence of the Union. Nor has the danger yet entirely ceased. Under our system there is a remedy for all mere political evils in the sound sense and sober judgment of the people. Time is a great corrective. Political subjects which but a few years ago excited and exasperated the public mind have passed away and are now entirely forgotten. But this question of domestic slavery is of far graver importance than any mere political question, because should the agitation continue it may eventually endanger the personal safety of a large portion of our countrymen where the institution exists. In

that event no form of government, however admirable in itself, and however productive of material benefits, can compensate for the loss of peace and domestic security around the family altar. Let every Union-loving man, therefore, exert his best influence to suppress this agitation, which, since the recent legislation of Congress, is without any legitimate object.

It is an evil omen of the times that men have undertaken to calculate the mere material value of the Union. Reasoned estimates have been presented of the pecuniary profits and local advantages which would result to the different States and sections from its dissolution and of the comparative injuries which such an event would inflict on other States and sections. Even descending to this low and narrow view of the mighty question, all such calculations are at fault. The bare reference to a single consideration will be conclusive on this point. We at present enjoy a free trade throughout our extensive and expanding country such as the world has never witnessed. This trade is conducted on railroads and canals, on noble rivers and arms of the sea, which bind together the North and South, the East and West, of our Confederacy. Annihilate this trade, arrest its free progress by the geographical lines of jealous and hostile States, and you destroy the prosperity and onward march of the whole and every part, and involve all in a common ruin. But such considerations, important as they are in themselves, sink into insignificance when we reflect upon the terrific evils which would result from disunion to every portion of the Confederacy,—to the North not more than to the South, to the East not more than to the West. These I shall not attempt to portray, because I feel a humble confidence that the kind Providence which inspired our fathers with wisdom to frame the most perfect form of government and union ever devised by man will not suffer it to perish until it shall have been peacefully instrumental by its example in the extension of civil and religious liberty throughout the world.

Next in importance to the maintenance of the Constitution and the Union is the duty of preserving the government free from the taint or even the suspicion of corruption. Public virtue is the vital spirit of republics, and history proves that when this has decayed and the love of money has usurped its place, although the forms of free government may remain for a season, the substance has departed forever.

Our present financial condition is without parallel in history. No nation has ever before been embarrassed from too large a surplus in its Treasury. This almost necessarily gives birth to extravagant legislation. It produces wild schemes of expenditure, and begets a race of speculators and jobbers, whose ingenuity is exerted in contriving and promoting expedients to obtain public money. The purity of official agents, whether rightfully or wrongfully, is suspected, and the character of the government suffers in the estimation of the people. This is in itself a very great evil.

The natural mode of relief from this embarrassment is to appropriate the surplus in the Treasury to great national objects for which a clear warrant can be found in the Constitution. Among these I might mention the extinguishment of the public debt, a reasonable increase of the navy, which is at present inadequate to the protection of our vast tonnage afloat, now greater than any other nation, as well as the defense of our extended seacoast.

It is beyond all question the true principle that no more revenue ought to be collected from the people than the amount necessary to defray the expense of a wise, economical, and efficient administration of the government. To reach this point it was necessary to resort to a modification of the tariff, and this has, I trust, been accomplished in such a manner as to do as little injury as may have been practicable to our domestic manufactures, especially those necessary for the defense of the country. Any discrimination against a particular branch for the purpose of benefiting favored corporations, individuals, or interests, would have been unjust to the rest of the community and inconsistent with that spirit of fairness and equality which ought to govern in the adjustment of a revenue tariff.

But the squandering of the public money sinks into comparative insignificance as a temptation to corruption when compared with the squandering of the public lands.

No nation in the tide of time has ever been blessed with so rich and noble an inheritance as we enjoy in the public lands. In administering this important trust, while it may be wise to grant portions of them for the improvement of the remainder, yet we should never forget that it is our cardinal policy to reserve these lands, as much as may be, for actual settlers, and this at moderate prices. We shall thus not only best promote the prosperity of the new States and Territories, by furnishing

them a hardy and independent race of honest and industrious citizens, but shall secure homes for our children and our children's children, as well as for those exiles from foreign shores who may seek in this country to improve their condition and to enjoy the blessings of civil and religious liberty. Such immigrants have done much to promote the growth and prosperity of the country. They have proved faithful both in peace and in war. After becoming citizens they are entitled, under the Constitution and laws, to be placed on a perfect equality with native-born citizens, and in this character they should ever be kindly recognized.

The Federal Constitution is a grant from the States to Congress of certain specific powers, and the question whether this grant should be liberally or strictly construed has more or less divided political parties from the beginning. Without entering into the argument, I desire to state at the commencement of my administration that long experience and observation have convinced me that a strict construction of the powers of the government is the only true, as well as the only safe, theory of the Constitution. Whenever in our past history doubtful powers have been exercised by Congress, these have never failed to produce injurious and unhappy consequences. Many such instances might be adduced if this were the proper occasion. Neither is it necessary for the public service to strain the language of the Constitution, because all the great and useful powers required for a successful administration of the government, both in peace and in war, have been granted, either in express terms or by the plainest implication.

While deeply convinced of these truths, I yet consider it clear that under the war-making power Congress may appropriate money toward the construction of a military road when this is absolutely necessary for the defense of any State or Territory of the Union against foreign invasion. Under the Constitution Congress has power "to declare war," "to raise and support armies," "to provide and maintain a navy," and to call forth the militia to "repel invasions." Thus endowed, in an ample manner, with the war-making power, the corresponding duty is required that "the United States shall protect each of them [the States] against invasion." Now, how is it possible to afford this protection to California and our Pacific possessions, except by means of a military road through the Territories of the United States, over which men and munitions of war may be speedily transported from the Atlantic States to meet and to repel the invader? In the event of a war with a naval power much stronger than our own, we should then have no other available access to the Pacific coast, because such a power would instantly close the route across the isthmus of Central America. It is impossible to conceive that while the Constitution has expressly required Congress to defend all the States, it should yet deny to them, by any fair construction, the only possible means by which one of these States can be defended. Besides, the government, ever since its origin, has been in the constant practice of constructing military roads. It might also be wise to consider whether the love for the Union which now animates our fellow-citizens on the Pacific coast may not be impaired by our neglect or refusal to provide for them, in their remote and isolated condition, the only means by which the power of the States on this side of the Rocky Mountains can reach them in sufficient time to "protect" them "against invasion." I forbear for the present from expressing an opinion as to the wisest and most economical mode in which the government can lend its aid in accomplishing this great and necessary work. I believe that many of the difficulties in the way, which now appear formidable, will in a great degree vanish as soon as the nearest and best route shall have been satisfactorily ascertained.

It may be proper that on this occasion I should make some brief remarks in regard to our rights and duties as a member of the great family of nations. In our intercourse with them there are some plain principles, approved by our own experience, from which we should never depart. We ought to cultivate peace, commerce, and friendship with all nations, and this not merely as the best means of promoting our own material interests, but in a spirit of Christian benevolence toward our fellow-men, wherever their lot may be cast. Our diplomacy should be direct and frank, neither seeking to obtain more nor accepting less than is due. We ought to cherish a sacred regard for the independence of all nations, and never attempt to interfere in the domestic concerns of any unless this shall be imperatively required by the great law of self-preservation. To avoid entangling alliances has been a maxim of our policy ever since the days of Washington, and its wisdom no one will attempt to dispute. In short, we

ought to do justice in a kindly spirit to all nations, and require justice from them in return.

It is our glory that while other nations have extended their dominions by the sword, we have never acquired any territory except by fair purchase or, in the case of Texas, by the voluntary determination of a brave, kindred, and independent people to blend their destinies with our own. Even our acquisitions from Mexico form no exception. Unwilling to take advantage of the fortune of war against a sister republic, we purchased these possessions under the treaty of peace for a sum which was considered at the time a fair equivalent. Our past history forbids that we shall in the future acquire territory unless this be sanctioned by the laws of justice and honor. Acting on this principle, no nation will have a right to interfere or to complain if, in the progress of events, we shall still further extend our possessions. Hitherto in all our acquisitions the people, under the protection of the American flag, have enjoyed civil and religious liberty as well as equal and just laws, and have been contented, prosperous, and happy. Their trade with the rest of the world has rapidly increased, and thus every commercial nation has shared largely in their successful progress.

I shall now proceed to take the oath prescribed by the Constitution, while humbly invoking the blessing of Divine Providence on this great people.

March 4th, 1857.

JOHN BUNYAN

(1628–1688)

REMEMBERED, and, while the English language lasts, always to be remembered, as the author of 'Pilgrim's Progress,' John Bunyan is almost forgotten as the inspired orator whose voice so swayed the English Commons away from the "established order" of the State religion that he was locked up for more than twelve years in Bedford jail.

To understand the power wielded by such a speaker as Bunyan it is necessary to forget dissent from his opinions and to enter with him into the spirit of his theme. Those who do this, either to understand his unconscious art,—and he was a great if an untrained artist,—or for the nobler purpose of understanding both the man and his message, will be richly rewarded. Most of the great English orators, whether of the forum or the pulpit, are Roman in their habit of expression. Bunyan is eminently English. He speaks the language of Alfred the Great,—a language of short sentences, compact, earnest, decisive. The orator, trained in the school of Cicero, may expand a single idea from sentence to sentence, from period to period; but if he is speaking the English of Alfred with the syntax of Bunyan, he must put an idea into every clause. "I will assure you," says Bunyan, "the devil is nimble, he can run apace; he is light of foot; he hath overtaken many; he hath turned up their heels and given them an everlasting fall." Here, in thirty words, we are compelled to witness every stage of what in the mind of Bunyan was the infinite tragedy of the attempted escape of a soul from hell; of the pursuit by the fiend; the loss of ground by the panting fugitive; and finally the very movement of his body as his feet are tripped from under him and he falls,—an everlasting fall. Dante could not have bettered that sentence. Not once, but continually, Bunyan shows this same mastery of English, compelling the unwilling language to accept and bear the burden of his cumulative ideas. "I have married a wife; I have a farm; I shall offend my landlord; I shall offend my master; I shall lose my trading; I shall lose my pride; I shall be mocked and scoffed at: therefore I dare not come!" It is thus that he crowds on the mind the excuses of those he was calling to better their lives—groaning in himself that they would not because each one

had "his vile sins, his bosom sins, his beloved, pleasant, darling sins that stick as close to him as the flesh sticks to the bones."

Perhaps it is fortunate that no one can have such a control of English who has not with it the earnestness which gave this tinker speaking before street crowds a greater power than Bourdaloue ever had speaking before princes. In oratory as in poetry, the first canon of art is that every idea which comes from the intellect of the speaker must rise through his heart to his lips if it is to reach the hearts of others. Always Bunyan spoke from the heart. He is the prose Dante of England. W. V. B.

THE HEAVENLY FOOTMAN

"So run that ye may obtain."—1 Cor. ix. 24

HEAVEN and happiness is that which everyone desireth, insomuch that wicked Balaam could say: "Let me die the death of the righteous, and let my last end be like his." Yet, for all this, there are but very few that do obtain that ever-to-be-desired glory, insomuch that many eminent professors drop short of a welcome from God into this pleasant place. The Apostle, therefore, because he did desire the salvation of the souls of the Corinthians, to whom he writes this epistle, layeth them down in these words such counsel which, if taken, would be for their help and advantage.

Firstly, not to be wicked, and sit still, and wish for heaven; but to run for it.

Secondly, not to content themselves with every kind of running, but, saith he, "So run that ye may obtain." As if he should say, some, because they would not lose their souls, they begin to run betimes, they run apace, they run with patience, they run the right way. Do you so run. Some run from both father and mother, friends and companions, and thus, that they may have the crown. Do you so run. Some run through temptations, afflictions, good report, evil report, that they may win the pearl. Do you so run. "So run that ye may obtain."

These words they are taken from men's running for a wager: a very apt similitude to set before the eyes of the saints of the Lord. "Know you not that they which run in a race run all, but one obtains the prize? So run that ye may obtain." That is, do not only run, but be sure you win as well as run. "So run that ye may obtain."

I shall not need to make any great ado in opening the words at this time, but shall rather lay down one doctrine that I do find in them; and in prosecuting that, I shall show you, in some measure, the scope of the words.

The doctrine is this: They that will have heaven must run for it; I say, they that will have heaven, they must run for it. I beseech you to heed it well. "Know ye not that they which run in a race run all, but one obtaineth the prize? So run ye." The prize is heaven, and if you will have it you must run for it. You have another Scripture for this in the twelfth of the Hebrews, the first, second, and third verses: "Wherefore seeing also," saith the Apostle, "that we are compassed about with so great a cloud of witnesses, let us lay aside every weight, and the sin which doth so easily beset us, and let us run with patience the race that is set before us." And let us run, saith he.

Again, saith Paul, "I so run, not as uncertainly: so fight I," etc.

But before I go any further: —

1. Fleeing. Observe, that this running is not an ordinary, or any sort of running, but it is to be understood of the swiftest sort of running; and, therefore, in the sixth of the Hebrews, it is called a fleeing: "That we might have strong consolation, who have fled for refuge, to lay hold on the hope set before us." Mark, who have fled. It is taken from that twentieth of Joshua, concerning the man that was to flee to the city of refuge, when the avenger of blood was hard at his heels, to take vengeance on him for the offense he had committed; therefore it is a running or fleeing for one's life: A running with all might and main, as we used to say. So run.

2. Pressing. Secondly, this running in another place is called a pressing. "I press toward the mark"; which signifieth that they that will have heaven, they must not stick at any difficulties they meet with; but press, crowd, and thrust through all that may stand between heaven and their souls. So run.

3. Continuing. Thirdly, this running is called in another place, a continuing in the way of life. "If you continue in the faith grounded, and settled, and be not moved away from the hope of the Gospel of Christ." Not to run a little now and

then, by fits and starts, or halfway, or almost thither, but to run for my life, to run through all difficulties, and to continue therein to the end of the race, which must be to the end of my life. "So run that ye may obtain." And the reasons for this point are these : —

1. Because all or every one that runneth doth not obtain the prize; there may be many that do run, yea, and run far too, who yet miss of the crown that standeth at the end of the race. You know that all that run in a race do not obtain the victory; they all run, but one wins. And so it is here; it is not every one that runneth, nor every one that seeketh, nor every one that striveth for the mastery, that hath it. "Though a man do strive for the mastery," saith Paul, "yet he is not crowned, unless he strive lawfully"; that is, unless he so run, and so strive, as to have God's approbation. What, do ye think that every heavy-heeled professor will have heaven? What, every lazy one? every wanton and foolish professor, that will be stopped by anything, kept back by anything, that scarce runneth so fast heavenward as a snail creepeth on the ground? Nay, there are some professors that do not go on so fast in the way of God as a snail doth go on the wall, and yet these think that heaven and happiness are for them. But stay, there are many more that run than there be that obtain; therefore he that will have heaven must run for it.

2. Because you know, that though a man do run, yet if he do not overcome, or win, as well as run, what will they be the better for their running? They will get nothing. You know the man that runneth, he doth do it that he may win the prize; but if he doth not obtain it, he doth lose his labor, spend his pains and time, and that to no purpose; I say, he getteth nothing. And ah! how many such runners will there be found in the day of judgment? Even multitudes, multitudes that have run, yea, run so far as to come to heaven-gates, and not able to get any further, but there stand knocking, when it is too late, crying, Lord, Lord, when they have nothing but rebukes for their pains. Depart from me, you come not here, you come too late, you run too lazily; the door is shut. "When once the master of the house is risen up," saith Christ, "and hath shut to the door, and ye begin to stand without, and to knock, saying, Lord, Lord, open to us, I will say, I know you not, Depart!" O sad will the state of those be that run and miss; therefore, if you

will have heaven, you must run for it; and "so run that ye may obtain."

3. Because the way is long (I speak metaphorically), and there is many a dirty step, many a high hill, much work to do, a wicked heart, world, and devil to overcome; I say, there are many steps to be taken by those that intend to be saved, by running or walking in the steps of that faith of our father Abraham. Out of Egypt thou must go through the Red Sea; thou must run a long and tedious journey, through the vast howling wilderness, before thou come to the land of promise.

4. They that will go to heaven they must run for it; because, as the way is long, so the time in which they are to get to the end of it is very uncertain; the time present is the only time; thou hast no more time allotted thee than that thou now enjoyest: "Boast not thyself of to-morrow, for thou knowest not what a day may bring forth." Do not say, I have time enough to get to heaven seven years hence, for, I tell thee, the bell may toll for thee before seven days more be ended; and when death comes, away thou must go, whether thou art provided or not; and therefore look to it; make no delays; it is not good dallying with things of so great concernment as the salvation or damnation of thy soul. You know he that hath a great way to go in a little time, and less by half than he thinks of, he had need to run for it.

5. They that will have heaven, they must run for it; because the devil, the law, sin, death, and hell follow them. There is never a poor soul that is going to heaven, but the devil, the law, sin, death, and hell make after that soul. "The devil, your adversary, as a roaring lion, goeth about, seeking whom he may devour." And I will assure you, the devil is nimble, he can run apace, he is light of foot, he hath overtaken many, he hath turned up their heels, and hath given them an everlasting fall. Also the law, that can shoot a great way, have a care thou keep out of the reach of those great guns, the Ten Commandments. Hell also hath a wide mouth; it can stretch itself further than you are aware of. And as the angel said to Lot: "Take heed, look not behind thee, neither tarry thou in all the plain" (that is, anywhere between this and heaven), "lest thou be consumed"; so say I to thee, Take heed, tarry not, lest either the devil, hell, death, or the fearful curses of the law of God, do overtake thee, and throw thee down in the midst of thy sins, so as never

to rise and recover again. If this were well considered, then thou, as well as I, wouldst say, They that will have heaven must run for it.

6. They that will go to heaven must run for it; because perchance the gates of heaven may be shut shortly. Sometimes sinners have not heaven-gates open to them so long as they suppose; and if they be once shut against a man, they are so heavy, that all the men in the world, nor all the angels in heaven, are not able to open them. "I shut, and no man can open," saith Christ. And how if thou shouldst come but one quarter of an hour too late? I tell thee, it will cost thee an eternity to bewail thy misery in. Francis Spira can tell thee what it is to stay till the gate of mercy be quite shut; or to run so lazily, that they be shut before thou get within them. What, to be shut out! what, out of heaven! Sinner, rather than lose it, run for it; yea, and "so run that thou mayest obtain."

7. Lastly, because if thou lose, thou losest all, thou losest soul, God, Christ, heaven, ease, peace! Besides, thou layest thyself open to all the shame, contempt, and reproach, that either God, Christ, saints, the world, sin, the devil, and all, can lay upon thee. As Christ saith of the foolish builder, so will I say of thee, if thou be such a one who runs and misses; I say, even all that go by will begin to mock at thee, saying, This man began to run well, but was not able to finish. . . .

In the next place, be not daunted though thou meetest with never so many discouragements in thy journey thither. That man that is resolved for heaven, if Satan cannot win him by flatteries, he will endeavor to weaken him by discouragements, saying: "Thou art a sinner, thou hast broken God's law, thou art not elected, thou comest too late, the day of grace is passed, God doth not care for thee, thy heart is naught, thou art lazy," with a hundred other discouraging suggestions. And thus it was with David, where he saith: "I had fainted, unless I had believed to see the loving-kindness of the Lord in the land of the living." As if he should say, the devil did so rage, and my heart was so base, that had I judged according to my own sense and feeling, I had been absolutely distracted; but I trusted to Christ in the promise, and looked that God would be as good as his promise, in having mercy upon me, an unworthy sinner; and this is that which encouraged me and kept me from fainting. And thus must thou do when Satan, or the law, or thy own conscience, do go about to dishearten thee, either by the greatness of thy sins, the wickedness of thy heart, the tediousness of the way, the loss of outward enjoyments, the hatred that thou wilt procure from the world, or the like; then thou must encourage thyself with the freeness of the promises, the tender-heartedness of Christ, the merits of his blood, the freeness of his invitations to come in, the greatness of the sin of others that have been pardoned, and that the same God, through the same Christ, holdeth forth the same grace as free as ever. If these be not thy meditations, thou wilt draw very heavily in the way to heaven, if thou do not give up all for lost, and so knock off from following any further; therefore, I say, take heart in thy journey, and say to them that seek thy destruction: "Rejoice not against me, O my enemy, for when I fall I shall arise, when I sit in darkness the Lord shall be a light unto me." So run.

Take heed of being offended at the cross that thou must go by before thou come to heaven. You must understand (as I have already touched) that there is no man that goeth to heaven but he must go by the cross. The cross is the standing way-mark by which all they that go to glory must pass.

"We must through much tribulation enter into the kingdom of heaven." "Yea, and all that will live godly in Christ Jesus shall suffer persecution." If thou art in thy way to the kingdom, my life for thine thou wilt come at the cross shortly (the Lord grant thou dost not shrink at it, so as to turn thee back again). "If any man will come after me," saith Christ, "let him deny himself, and take up his cross daily, and follow me." The cross it stands, and hath stood, from the beginning, as a way-mark to the kingdom of heaven. You know, if one ask you the way to such and such a place, you, for the better direction, do not only say, "This is the way," but then also say, "You must go by such a gate, by such a stile, such a bush, tree, bridge," or such like; why, so it is here; art thou inquiring the way to heaven? Why, I tell thee, Christ is the way; into him thou must get—into his righteousness—to be justified; and if thou art in him, thou wilt presently see the cross; thou must go close by it, thou must touch it,—nay, thou must take it up, or else thou wilt quickly go out of the way that leads to heaven, and turn up some of those crooked lanes that lead down to the chambers of death.

Now thou mayest know the cross by these six things:—

1. It is known in the doctrine of justification.

11—46

2. In the doctrine of mortification.
3. In the doctrine of perseverance.
4. In self-denial.
5. Patience.
6. Communion with poor saints.

1. In the doctrine of justification, there is a great deal of the cross in that a man is forced to suffer the destruction of his own righteousness for the righteousness of another. This is no easy matter for a man to do; I assure to you it stretcheth every vein in his heart, before he will be brought to yield to it. What, for a man to deny, reject, abhor, and throw away all his prayers, tears, alms, keeping of Sabbaths, hearing, reading, with the rest, in the point of justification, and to count them accursed; and to be willing, in the very midst of the sense of his sins, to throw himself wholly upon the righteousness and obedience of another man, abhorring his own, counting it as deadly sin, as the open breach of the law,—I say, to do this in deed and in truth is the biggest piece of the cross; and, therefore, Paul calleth this very thing a suffering, where he saith: "And I have suffered the loss of all things (which principally was his righteousness) that I might win Christ, and be found in him, not having (but rejecting) my own righteousness." That is the first.

2. In the doctrine of mortification is also much of the cross. Is it nothing for a man to lay hands on his vile opinions, on his vile sins, on his bosom sins, on his beloved, pleasant, darling sins, that stick as close to him as the flesh sticks to the bones? What, to lose all these brave things that my eyes behold, for that which I never saw with my eyes? What, to lose my pride, my covetousness, my vain company, sports and pleasures, and the rest? I tell you, this is no easy matter: if it were, what need all those prayers, sighs, watchings? What need we be so backward to it? Nay, do you not see that some men, before they will set about this work, they will even venture the loss of their souls, heaven, God, Christ, and all? What means else all those delays and put-offs, saying, "Stay a little longer, I am loth to leave my sins while I am so young, and in health"? Again, what is the reason else that others do it so by the halves, coldly and seldom. notwithstanding they are convinced over and over; nay, and also promise to amend, and yet all's in vain? I will assure you, to cut off right hands, and to pluck out right eyes, is no pleasure to the flesh.

3. The doctrine of perseverance is also cross to the flesh; which is not only to begin but to hold out, not only to bid fair, and to say: "Would I had heaven," but so to know Christ, put on Christ, and walk with Christ, so as to come to heaven. Indeed, it is no great matter to begin to look for heaven, to begin to seek the Lord, to begin to shun sin; O but it is a very great matter to continue with God's approbation: "My servant Caleb," saith God, "is a man of another spirit, he hath followed me (followed me always, he hath continually followed me) fully, he shall possess the land." Almost all the many thousands of the children of Israel in their generation fell short of perseverance when they walked from Egypt towards the land of Canaan. Indeed, they went to work at first pretty willingly, but they were very short-winded, they were quickly out of breath, and in their hearts they turned back again into Egypt.

It is an easy matter for a man to run hard for a spurt, for a furlong, for a mile or two: O, but to hold out for a hundred, for a thousand, for ten thousand miles, that man that doth this, he must look to meet with cross, pain, and wearisomeness to the flesh, especially if, as he goeth, he meeteth with briars and quagmires, and other incumbrances, that make his journey so much the more painful.

Nay, do you not see with your eyes daily, that perseverance is a very great part of the cross? Why else do men so soon grow weary? I could point out a many, that after they have followed the ways of God about a twelvemonth, others it may be two, three, or four (some more, and some less) years, they have been beat out of wind, have taken up their lodging and rest before they have gotten half-way to heaven, some in this, some in that sin, and have secretly, nay, sometimes openly, said that the way is too straight, the race too long, the religion too holy,—I cannot hold out, I can go no further.

And so likewise of the other three, to-wit: patience, self-denial, communion, and communication with and to the poor saints: How hard are these things? It is an easy matter to deny another man, but it is not so easy a matter to deny one's self; to deny myself out of love to God, to his Gospel, to his saints, of this advantage, and of that gain; nay, of that which otherwise I might lawfully do, were it not for offending them. That Scripture is but seldom read, and seldomer put in practice, which saith, "I will eat no flesh while the world standeth, if it make my brother to

offend"; again, "We that are strong ought to bear the infirmities of the weak, and not to please ourselves." But how froward, how hasty, how peevish, and self-resolved are the generality of professors at this day! Also how little considering the poor, unless it be to say, "Be thou warmed and filled!" But to give is a seldom work; also especially to give to any poor. I tell you all things are cross to flesh and blood; and that man that hath but a watchful eye over the flesh, and also some considerable measure of strength against it, he shall find his heart in these things like unto a starting horse, that is rode without a curbing bridle, ready to start at everything that is offensive to him—yea, and ready to run away, too, do what the rider can.

It is the cross which keepeth those that are kept from heaven. I am persuaded, were it not for the cross, where we have one professor we should have twenty; but this cross, that is it which spoileth all.

Some men, as I said before, when they come at the cross they can go no further, but back again to their sins they must go. Others they stumble at it, and break their necks; others again, when they see the cross is approaching, they turn aside to the left hand, or to the right hand, and so think to get to heaven another way; but they will be deceived. "For all that will live godly in Christ Jesus shall," mark, "shall be sure to suffer persecution." There are but few when they come at the cross, cry, "Welcome cross!" as some of the martyrs did to the stake they were burned at. Therefore, if you meet with the cross in thy journey, in what manner soever it be, be not daunted, and say, "Alas, what shall I do now!" But rather take courage, knowing that by the cross is the way to the kingdom. Can a man believe in Christ, and not be hated by the devil? Can he make a profession of this Christ, and that sweetly and convincingly, and the children of satan hold their tongues? Can darkness agree with light, or the devil endure that Christ Jesus should be honored both by faith and a heavenly conversation, and let that soul alone at quiet? Did you never read that "the dragon persecuted the woman"? And that Christ saith, "In the world you shall have tribulations"?

Beg of God that he would do these two things for thee: First, enlighten thine understanding; and, second, inflame thy will. If these two be but effectually done, there is no fear but thou wilt go safe to heaven.

One of the great reasons why men and women do so little regard the other world is because they see so little of it; and the reason why they see so little of it is because they have their understanding darkened. And, therefore, saith Paul, "Do not you believers walk as do other Gentiles, even in the vanity of their minds having their understanding darkened, being alienated from the life of God through the ignorance (or foolishness) that is in them, because of the blindness of their heart." Walk not as those, run not with them: alas, poor souls, they have their understandings darkened, their hearts blinded, and that is the reason they have such undervaluing thoughts of the Lord Jesus Christ and the salvation of their souls. For when men do come to see the things of another world, what a God, what a Christ, what a heaven, and what an eternal glory there is to be enjoyed; also, when they see that it is possible for them to have a share in it, I tell you it will make them run through thick and thin to enjoy it. Moses, having a sight of this, because his understanding was enlightened, "He feared not the wrath of the king, but chose rather to suffer afflictions with the people of God than to enjoy the pleasures of sin for a season. He refused to be called the son of the king's daughter," accounting it wonderful riches to be accounted worthy of so much as to suffer for Christ, with the poor despised saints; and that was because he saw him who was invisible, and had respect unto the recompense of reward. And this is that which the Apostle usually prayeth for in his epistles for the saints, namely, "That they might know what is the hope of God's calling, and the riches of the glory of his inheritance in the saints; and that they might be able to comprehend with all saints what is the breadth, and length, and depth, and height, and know the love of Christ, which passeth knowledge." Pray, therefore, that God would enlighten thy understanding; that will be a very great help unto thee. It will make thee endure many a hard brunt for Christ; as Paul saith, "After you were illuminated ye endured a great sight of afflictions; you took joyfully the spoiling of your goods, knowing in yourselves that ye have in heaven a better and an enduring substance." If there be never such a rare jewel lie just in a man's way, yet if he sees it not he will rather trample upon it than stoop for it, and it is because he sees it not. Why, so it is here, though heaven be worth never so much, and thou hast never so much need of it, yet if thou see it not,—that is, have not thy

understanding opened or enlightened to see,—thou wilt not regard at all: therefore cry to the Lord for enlightening grace, and say, "Lord, open my blind eyes; Lord, take the veil off my dark heart," show me the things of the other world, and let me see the sweetness, the glory, and excellency of them for Christ's sake. This is the first.

Cry to God that he would inflame thy will also with the things of the other world. For when a man's will is fully set to do such or such a thing, then it must be a very hard matter that shall hinder that man from bringing about his end. When Paul's will was set resolvedly to go up to Jerusalem, though it was signified to him before what he should there suffer, he was not daunted at all; nay, saith he, "I am ready [or willing] not only to be bound, but also to die at Jerusalem for the name of the Lord Jesus." His will was inflamed with love to Christ; and therefore all the persuasions that could be used wrought nothing at all.

Your self-willed people, nobody knows what to do with them: we used to say, "He will have his own will, do all what you can." Indeed, to have such a will for heaven is an admirable advantage to a man that undertaketh a race thither; a man that is resolved, and hath his will fixed; saith he: "I will do my best to advantage myself, I will do my worst to hinder my enemies, I will not give out as long as I can stand, I will have it or I will lose my life; though he slay me, yet will I trust in him. I will not let thee go except thou bless me." I will, I will, I will, O this blessed inflamed will for heaven! What is it like? If a man be willing, then any argument shall be matter of encouragement; but if unwilling, then any argument shall give discouragement. This is seen both in saints and sinners; in them that are the children of God, and also those that are the children of the devil. As,

1. The saints of old, they being willing and resolved for heaven, what could stop them? Could fire and faggot, sword or halter, stinking dungeons, whips, bears, bulls, lions, cruel rackings, stoning, starving, nakedness; "and in all these things they were more than conquerors, through him that loved them," who had also made them "willing in the day of his power."

2. See again, on the other side, the children of the devil, because they are not willing, how many shifts and starting-holes they will have. I have married a wife; I have a farm; I shall

offend my landlord; I shall offend my master; I shall lose my trading; I shall lose my pride, my pleasures; I shall be mocked and scoffed: therefore I dare not come. I, saith another, will stay till I am older, till my children are out, till I am got a little aforehand in the world, till I have done this and that, and the other business: but, alas! the thing is, they are not willing; for, were they but soundly willing, these, and a thousand such as these, would hold them no faster than the cords held Samson, when he broke them like burnt flax. I tell you the will is all: that is one of the chief things which turns the wheel either backwards or forwards; and God knoweth that full well, and so likewise doth the devil, and therefore they both endeavor very much to strengthen the will of their servants. God, he is for making of his a willing people to serve him; and the devil, he doth what he can to possess the will and affection of those that are his with love to sin; and therefore when Christ comes close to the matter, indeed, saith he, "You will not come to me. How often would I have gathered you as a hen doth her chickens, but you would not." The devil had possessed their wills, and so long he was sure enough of them. O, therefore, cry hard to God to inflame thy will for heaven and Christ: thy will, I say, if that be rightly set for heaven, thou wilt not be beat off with discouragements; and this was the reason that when Jacob wrestled with the angel, though he lost a limb, as it were, and the hollow of his thigh was put out of joint as he wrestled with him, yet, saith he, "I will not," mark, "I will not let thee go except thou bless me." Get thy will tipt with the heavenly grace, and resolution against all discouragements, and then thou goest full speed for heaven; but if thou falter in thy will, and be not found there, thou wilt run hobbling and halting all the way thou runnest, and also to be sure thou wilt fall short at last. The Lord give thee a will and courage.

TRISTAM BURGES

(1770–1853)

THE speech on the Judiciary delivered by Tristam Burges soon after he entered Congress in 1825 attracted the immediate attention of the country. The greater genius of Webster had not then fully asserted itself, and there was a sort of interregnum between the New England orators of the Revolutionary epoch and those who were developed later on by the struggle over slavery. As a representative of the Federalists and Whigs, Burges was welcomed to "the first rank of the orators and statesmen of his country," while his speech on the Judiciary Bill was classed as "one of the greatest displays of eloquence ever made in the House of Representatives."

He had already established a reputation for eloquence at the bar, and it is said that the "power of his oratory was supreme over judges, juries, and spectators." His career in Congress was brief. After a single term he retired to private life, but while representing Rhode Island in Washington, he made several addresses which greatly added to the fame he had won by his first. Among them was his reply to John Randolph, who loved to make New England the butt of the saturnine humor he illustrated in his desire "to go a mile out of his way to kick a sheep" every time he thought of the demand for a high tariff on wool and woolens. Exasperated by Randolph's taunts, Burges closed his defense of New England with the celebrated period:—

"Sir, Divine Providence takes care of his own Universe. Moral monsters cannot propagate. Impotent of everything but malevolence of purpose, they can no otherwise multiply miseries than by blaspheming all that is pure and prosperous and happy. Could demon propagate demon, the earth might become a pandemonium; but I rejoice that the father of lies cannot become also a father of liars. One adversary of God and man is enough for one Universe. Too much—O how much too much for one nation!"

Born at Rochester, Massachusetts, February 26th, 1770, Burges was bred to his father's trade,—that of a cooper,—but having his mind stirred to activity by reading the 'Pilgrim's Progress,' and several other books which fell into his hands when he was young, he made a brave struggle for higher education, winning it by graduating from Rhode Island College (now Brown University) in 1793. After teaching school in Providence, Rhode Island, while educating himself for the bar, he began the practice of law in 1799, and through his eloquence won prominence so soon, that in 1811 he was appointed Chief-Justice of Rhode Island. He served also for a short time as professor of Oratory and Belles-Lettres in Brown University. After his retirement from Congress and until his death, October 13th, 1853, he "devoted his time chiefly to rural and literary occupations free from any participation in public affairs."

THE SUPREME COURT

(From the Speech Delivered in the House of Representatives, December 1825)

THIS bill proposes to increase the Supreme Court, originally six, but now seven, by adding three new judges, and making the whole number ten. Can this, sir, be constitutionally done? All supreme judicial power is now lodged in the Supreme Court. What judicial power have you then, sir, to confer on your three new judges? Circuit Court power you certainly have, for all inferior courts are within your control; but all the supreme judicial power is already vested, and no part of it can be taken away. The Supreme Court is a whole, in all its parts, its properties, its extension, its relations. Have you the power to alter it? How, then, can you add to it? Or is it that wonderful entity which addition to it does not increase, or which, multiplied any number of times by itself, would continue to be the same? We shall all acknowledge, sir, that Congress cannot require, by law, the President to select a judge of the Supreme Court from any particular district or part of the United States; but Congress can create a court inferior to the Supreme Court, and among the legal qualifications of the judge insert an inhabitancy or residence within his territorial jurisdiction. This may be the Circuit Court. If, sir, you then annex the office of such a Circuit judge to that of a judge of the Supreme Court, you require, by law, the President to select a judge of the Supreme Court from a limited and designated district of the United States; that is to say, from the territorial jurisdiction of such Circuit judge. The constitutional power of the Supreme Court is vested in the majority of that court; whatever shall change this

relative proportion to the whole number of the number creating that majority must change the vested power of that court, and must, for that reason, be unconstitutional; but four, the majority of six, is two-thirds of that court; whereas six, the majority of ten, is less than two-thirds of that court. Making the number of judges ten is therefore altering the power of the court, vested in two-thirds thereof, and giving it to a lesser proportionate number.

It may, sir, be set down as a political axiom, that, when you shall have added so many judges to the original number of the Supreme Court as will make a majority or constitutional quorum of that court, the judicial article of the Constitution will have been expunged. Add your three new judges, it makes ten. This is four more than the original number; six is a constitutional quorum of ten: but four is a majority of that quorum, and may reverse all the decisions of the original court.

All decisions of the Supreme Court, on the Constitution, on treaties, and on laws, not enacted by Congress, are beyond the control of the National Legislature; but if we can send into the Supreme Court an overruling majority, whenever the united ambition of Congress and the Executive may choose to do it, we place the Constitution, and all treaties, and all constitutions and laws of all the States, in the power of two branches of the government, and thus erect ourselves into a complete tyranny; and, that, too, as the advocates of the bill must contend, upon perfectly constitutional principles. Does the Constitution, sir, thus place the Judiciary at the good will and pleasure of the other two branches of the government? No, sir; the patriots who built, and the people who consecrated that glorious fabric, did not intend to devote their temple to the polluted oblations of legislative ambition, or the unhallowed rites of executive subserviency.

The wisdom of legislation, sir, should look to the durability of her works. How long, sir, will the Judiciary, as amended by the provisions of the bill, continue to subserve and satisfy the wants of the country? Some of its advocates say twenty, some fifty, and some one hundred years. Yes, sir, those gentlemen, who have, with all the force of facts, and all the resistless conclusions of reason, pressed on this House the unparalleled growth of Western wealth and Western population, do say that new States will not, in less than one hundred years, have been added to this Union in such a number as to require even one additional

judicial circuit. Have they duly considered the various expansive principles of production and population in this country? A prescient policy should look to the future under the lights of the past. In twice that period, a few scattered families have augmented to more than ten millions of people, covering eight hundred and forty-seven thousand one hundred and eighteen square miles of territory, arranged into twenty-four United States, and requiring ten judicial circuits. Through this whole course, the people and the country seem to have multiplied and extended in nearly a geometrical ratio. Ten millions of people not quite five years ago; five millions of couples for heads of families; and, at this moment, not less than two millions five hundred thousand of the whole number placed in that relation. Ordinary calculation may, under ordinary prosperity, expect to find in each family eight children. This will, in less than twenty years, give to our population twenty additional millions of people. Will not new States arise? Already, sir, you have three new territories. Florida is spreading her population down to the very margin of her waters, and enriching her cultivation from the "cane-bearing isles of the West." Arkansas is looking up the channel of her long rivers, towards the mountains of Mexico, and will soon become rich, populous, and highly cultivated. The tide of migration is setting up the grand canal towards Michigan, and that peninsula will, in a short period, be located and peopled from lake to lake. These three, sir, in less than five years, with due courtesy, and fair cause for admission, will knock at your door, and propose to sit down in the family circle of political union. This is not all, sir. Population is traveling up the latitude, across your northwestern territory, towards the great Caspian of our continent; and when they shall have heard of your ships on the waters of the Oregon, and of your colonies along the rich valley of that river,—as from the able report of the gentleman from Massachusetts, whose mind is capacious of such things, we may predict they will very soon hear, —these people will then, sir, with the rapidity of a deep sealead, thrown from the chains of a seventy-four, plunge down the longitude to meet and to mingle with their countrymen on the waters of the Pacific.

Twenty years, sir! Are we told the system of the bill will accommodate and satisfy the judicial wants of this country for twenty years? In twenty years you will have ten new States

and thirty millions of people! Why, sir, in such a country— such a sun-bright region of hill and vale, mountain and moor, river, plain, lake, and all of boundless fertility—where population is busy on land and on ocean; where, from the plough, the loom, and the soil, are continually drawn the materials of food, clothing, habitation; where the human arteries swell and pulsate with teeming existence; where the human bosom heaves and palpitates with the fostering current of incipient life—what calculation will you make? What calculation can you make, approximating in any reasonable degree towards reality?

What then, sir, the advocates of the system of the bill may ask—what shall be done? The opposers of it are prepared for the interrogatory: Adopt the system recommended by the resolution. Restore the Constitution. Trace out and fill up the great judiciary map of 1789, revise and correct and establish the constitutional lines of the law of 1801. We are told, sir, by the gentleman from Illinois, that the experience of a single year overthrew that system. Was, then, the system of 1801 overthrown by experience? As well might the honorable gentleman tell us that brick and granite and marble are improper materials for houses and palaces and temples, because experience has taught us that, at some times, and in some places, earthquakes have overthrown and demolished such buildings. "It was," says the honorable gentleman from Massachusetts, chairman of the Judiciary Committee, "repealed in one year *in toto.*" Was it because that, or the law on which it was founded, was "enacted in the hurried session of the summer of 1789"? Because it was built on false analogies, or contained awkward provisions? That session, sir, was begun on the fourth of March, and ended on the twenty-fourth of September. In this session of somewhat more than six months, those illustrious men enacted twenty-seven laws, and passed three resolutions. Was this hurried legislation? Why, sir, many a Congress, since that period, putting no extraordinary vigor or hasty effort to the work, has, in less time, sent into the world a legislative progeny of from two to three hundred laws, great and little. What have we now, sir, valuable, or of probable durability, and which was not produced by that Congress, at that session? The fiscal, the foreign, the war, the naval, and the judicial departments, were then, and by those men, founded, erected, and finished. These great national edifices have stood, and I trust will continue to stand; for, when the vandalism of faction shall demolish them, we shall cease to be a nation. Later times, it is true, have added, now and then, a piece of tiling, or a patch of paint; and the nation has put itself to costs upon the interior garniture of them, the drapery, and other various ornament and accommodation; but, otherwise, these valuable edifices are as old, as unaltered, and quite as venerable as the Constitution itself. "Awkward provisions and false analogies," do we call any part of the Judiciary Act of that session? It was, sir, indited by the Ellsworths and Hamiltons of those times,—men, whose political little finger was larger than the loins of politicians in these degenerate days. Why, sir, do not men who know tell us boldly for what cause the judiciary law of 1801 was repealed? Men of candor, and I trust, sir, such men are in great numbers here, will all agree that party overthrew that system. Why disguise it? Those unhappy days are past, and we are indeed now all "brothers of the same principle." What was not demolished in those inconsiderate times? The national bank, the army, the navy, fortifications,—almost all that told the understanding, or the eye, that we are one,—tumbled into ruins in the shock of that tremendous political earthquake. Coming years brought better feelings and sounder reasonings; and men have profited by their experience, and re-edified all that was most valuable: the bank, the army, the navy, the system of fortifications; and we are again a nation. Our fortresses on the ocean and on the land look out from many a hundred iron eyes, ready with indignation to blaze annoyance and destruction against hostile approach. Why, sir, do you not follow this enlightened experience in your Judiciary? The very Turk or Tartar, though he demolish the palace and temple of classical antiquity, yet will he draw from the ruins materials for his stable and his seraglio. He who does not profit by that of others stands in the next rank of fatuity to him who is a fool in spite of his own experience.

EDMUND BURKE

(1729–1797)

DMUND BURKE has been called the Shakespeare of English orators, and certainly no one else so well deserves the title. His mind never acknowledges limitation. His thoughts are multitudinous, succeeding each other, flowing into each other, impelling each other with that ever-changing unity which, when seen in the waves of the sea, with the sun shining upon it, at once delights and dazzles.

"Possessed," says Brougham, "of most extensive knowledge and of learning of the most various description; acquainted alike with what different classes of men knew, each in his own province, and with much that hardly any one else ever thought of learning, he could either bring his masses of information to bear directly upon the subjects to which they severally belonged, or he could avail himself of them generally to strengthen his faculties and enlarge his views, or he could turn any portion of them to account for the purpose of enlarging his theme and enriching his diction. Hence, when he is handling any one matter, we perceive that we are conversing with a reasoner or a teacher to whom almost every other branch of knowledge is familiar. His views range over all cognate subjects; his reasonings are derived from principles applicable to other matters, as well as to the one in hand; arguments pour in from all sides, as well as those which start up under our feet, the natural growth of the path he is leading us; while to throw light round our steps and either explore its darker places or serve for our recreation, illustrations are fetched from a thousand quarters; and an imagination marvelously quick to descry unthought-of resemblances pours forth the stores which a lore yet more marvelous has gathered from all ages and nations and arts and tongues."

That this tribute of one great orator to the powers of a greater is not exaggerated, we know from the effects often produced by Burke upon his audiences. "In the Hastings trial," writes Doctor Matthews, "it is said that when Burke, with an imagination almost as Oriental as the scenes he depicted, described, in words that will live as long as the English language, the cruelties inflicted upon the natives of India by Debi Sing, one of Hastings's agents, a convulsive shudder ran through the whole assembly; indignation and rage filled the breasts

of his hearers; some of the ladies "swooned away"; and Hastings himself, though he had protested his innocence, was utterly overwhelmed. "For half an hour," he said afterwards, in describing the scene, "I looked on the orator in a reverie of wonder, and actually thought myself the most culpable man on earth."

That the ability to produce this profound impression on others was not merely intellectual but constitutional with Burke, we know from his defense of himself when his 'Reflections on the French Revolution' alienated many who had been his friends,—among them Philip Francis, who, seeing the proof sheets of the work, tried to dissuade Burke from publishing it.

Speaking of Marie Antoinette, Burke had written the memorable comparison: "And surely never lighted on this orb, which she hardly seemed to touch, a more delightful vision. I saw her just above the horizon, decorating and cheering the elevated sphere she had just begun to move in, glittering like the morning star, full of life and splendor and joy."

When Francis called this a piece of foppery, asking Burke if Marie Antoinette were not a jade, a mere Messalina, Burke replied indignantly: "I know nothing of your Messalinas. Am I obliged to prove judicially the virtues of those I see suffering every kind of wrong? . . . . I tell you again that the recollection of the manner in which I saw the Queen of France in 1774 and the contrast between that brilliancy, splendor, and beauty, with the prostrate homage of a nation to her, and the abominable scene of 1789, which I was describing, did draw tears from me and wetted the paper. Those tears came again into my eyes almost as often as I looked at the description. They may again. You do not believe this fact nor that these are my real feelings, but that the whole is affected or, as you express it, 'downright foppery.' My friend, I tell you it is truth and that it is true and will be true when you and I are no more, and will exist as long as men with their natural feelings shall exist."

Undoubtedly it was this deep emotional earnestness which gave Burke's magnificent intellect its effectiveness. We can see what this effectiveness means and how completely it depends on his sympathies when we undertake to read those speeches where, without being "keyed up" to his highest nervous possibilities, he is using his intellect merely. Such passages are frequent in his speeches; often when he is reasoning well and consecutively, they are prosy; and sometimes when he is relaxed after the strain of intellectual and emotional exaltation, they are dull. Reading them and searching for the secret of the power which has gone out from them and left them thus lifeless, we see that it is the same which controlled Burke when he wetted his paper with tears for Marie Antoinette. No man who attains the sublime as often as he did can keep his

position of costly eminence, and in his reactions he must pay the price for it Burke paid in acquiring habits through which he won the ability to make the most wonderful speeches ever made in England, and joined with it a more extraordinary faculty for emptying benches under the sound of his voice than any other great orator had ever demonstrated. This seems largely due to his very greatness. His own intellectual strength made him forget the intellectual weaknesses of others. Standing unwearied before people of ordinary minds, pouring out not one oration, a perfect whole, but one after another, each dealing with some thought which, for the time, mastered him,—each with its own perfection of art, its own rapid development of thought,—he could not carry his audience with him, because he alone had the intellectual strength to keep the thread of the argument so as to be able to join the splendid parts into an intelligible and concordant whole. His speeches at the trial of Hastings are as Homeric in quantity as in quality. Few will even attempt to keep the connection from their beginning to the end. But no one could be so obtuse as to miss the point of the fiery periods in which his immortal indignation blazed out against Hastings and conquest as a commercial method, when he came to describe the atrocities of Debi Sing.

Burke was born in Dublin, January 12th, 1729 N. S.,—the second of the fifteen children of an Irish attorney, most of whom were delicate and died young. Burke himself was never strong, and the great results he achieved were in spite of physical weakness. His education which received its greatest impetus at Trinity College, Dublin, never ceased during his lifetime. He seems to have had one of those peculiar minds which retain in mature life the childish ability to learn easily,—the puerile habit, so soon lost and with most never regained, of welcoming information regardless of the quarter it comes from.

Burke's biography is the history of the most important period in modern politics. It would be presumption to attempt it here. It is enough to add that when he died, July 9th, 1797, he left a world which his genius and his sympathy for the suffering he saw everywhere around him had made more fit for his successor, when he comes to pay with his own emotion the price of the sympathy every great mind feels as the secret of its ability to champion the weak and to win the battles of helplessness against power. But his successor has not yet come nor do those who would welcome him most, expect him soon.   W. V. B.

As the most nearly adequate introduction possible for Burke's unapproachable oration of February 18th and 19th, 1788, opening the charge of bribery against Hastings, Macaulay's description of the trial is subjoined.

THE TRIAL OF WARREN HASTINGS

(From Macaulay's 'Essay on Warren Hastings,' Edinburgh Review, October 1841)

THERE have been spectacles more dazzling to the eye, more gorgeous with jewelry and cloth of gold, more attractive to grown-up children, than that which was exhibited at Westminster; but, perhaps, there never was a spectacle so well calculated to strike a highly cultivated, a reflecting, an imaginative mind. All the various kinds of interest which belong to the near and to the distant, to the present and to the past, were collected on one spot and in one hour. All the talents and all the accomplishments which are developed by liberty and civilization were now displayed, with every advantage that could be derived both from co-operation and from contrast. Every step in the proceedings carried the mind either backward, through many troubled centuries, to the days when the foundations of the Constitution were laid; or far away over boundless seas and deserts, to dusky nations living under strange stars, worshiping strange gods, and writing strange characters from right to left. The High Court of Parliament was to sit, according to forms handed down from the days of the Plantagenets, on an Englishman accused of exercising tyranny over the lord of the holy city of Benares, and the ladies of the princely house of Oude.

The place was worthy of such a trial. It was the great hall of William Rufus; the hall which had resounded with acclamations at the inauguration of thirty kings; the hall which had witnessed the just sentence of Bacon and the just absolution of Somers; the hall where the eloquence of Strafford had for a moment awed and melted a victorious party inflamed with just resentment; the hall where Charles had confronted the High Court of Justice with the placid courage which has half redeemed his fame. Neither military nor civil pomp was wanting. The avenues were lined with grenadiers. The streets were kept clear by cavalry. The peers, robed in gold and ermine, were marshaled by the heralds under Garter-King-at-Arms. The judges, in their vestments of state, attended to give advice on points of law. Nearly a hundred and seventy lords, three-fourths of the Upper House, as the Upper House then was, walked in solemn order from their

II—47

usual place of assembling to the tribunal. The junior baron present led the way,—Lord Heathfield, recently ennobled for his memorable defense of Gibraltar against the fleets and armies of France and Spain. The long procession was closed by the Duke of Norfolk, earl marshal of the realm, by the great dignitaries, and by the brothers and sons of the king. Last of all came the Prince of Wales, conspicuous by his fine person and noble bearing. The gray old walls were hung with scarlet. The long galleries were crowded by such an audience as had rarely excited the fears or the emulation of an orator. There were gathered together, from all parts of a great, free, enlightened, and prosperous realm, grace and female loveliness, wit and learning, the representatives of every science and of every art. There were seated around the Queen the fair-haired young daughters of the house of Brunswick. There the ambassadors of great kings and commonwealths gazed with admiration on a spectacle which no other country in the world could present. There Siddons, in the prime of her majestic beauty, looked with emotion on a scene surpassing all the imitations of the stage. There the historian of the Roman Empire thought of the days when Cicero pleaded the cause of Sicily against Verres, and when, before a senate which had still some show of freedom, Tacitus thundered against the oppressor of Africa. There were seen, side by side, the greatest painter and the greatest scholar of the age. The spectacle had allured Reynolds from that easel which has preserved to us the thoughtful foreheads of so many writers and statesmen and the sweet smiles of so many noble matrons. It had induced Parr to suspend his labors in that dark and profound mine from which he had extracted a vast treasure of erudition,—a treasure too often buried in the earth, too often paraded with injudicious and inelegant ostentation, but still precious, massive, and splendid. There appeared the voluptuous charms of her to whom the heir of the throne had in secret plighted his faith. There, too, was she, the beautiful mother of a beautiful race, the Saint Cecilia, whose delicate features, lighted up by love and music, art has rescued from the common decay. There were the members of that brilliant society which quoted, criticized, and exchanged repartees, under the rich peacock hangings of Mrs. Montague. And here the ladies, whose lips, more persuasive than those of Fox himself, had carried the Westminster election against palace and treasury, shone round Georgiana, Duchess of Devonshire.

The Sergeants made proclamation. Hastings advanced to the bar and bent his knee. The culprit was indeed not unworthy of that great presence. He had ruled an extensive and populous country, had made laws and treaties, had sent forth armies, had set up and pulled down princes. And in his high place he had so borne himself, that all had feared him, that most had loved him, and that hatred itself could deny him no title to glory, except virtue. He looked like a great man and not like a bad man. A person small and emaciated, yet deriving dignity from a carriage which, while it indicated deference to the court, indicated also habitual self-possession and self-respect; a high and intellectual forehead; a brow pensive, but not gloomy; a mouth of inflexible decision; a face pale and worn, but serene, on which was written, as legibly as under the great picture in the council chamber at Calcutta, *Mens æqua in arduis.* Such was the aspect with which the great proconsul presented himself to the judges.

His counsel accompanied him, men all of whom were afterwards raised by their talents and learning to the highest posts in their profession,—the bold and strong-minded Law, afterwards chief-justice of the king's bench; the more humane and eloquent Dallas, afterwards chief-justice of the common pleas; and Plomer, who, nearly twenty years later, successfully conducted in the same high court the defense of Lord Melville, and subsequently became vice-chancellor and master of the rolls.

But neither the culprit nor his advocates attracted so much notice as the accusers. In the midst of the blaze of red drapery, a space had been fitted up with green benches and tables for the Commons. The managers, with Burke at their head, appeared in full dress. The collectors of gossip did not fail to remark that even Fox, generally so regardless of his appearance, had paid to the illustrious tribunal the compliment of wearing a bag and sword. Pitt had refused to be one of the conductors of the impeachment; and his commanding, copious, and sonorous eloquence was wanting to that great muster of various talents. Age and blindness had unfitted Lord North for the duties of a public prosecutor, and his friends were left without the help of his excellent sense, his tact, and his urbanity. But, in spite of the absence of these two distinguished members of the Lower House, the box in which the managers stood contained an array of speakers such as perhaps had not appeared together since the great age of Athenian eloquence. There stood Fox and Sheridan,

the English Demosthenes and the English Hyperides. There was Burke, ignorant, indeed, or negligent of the art of adapting his reasonings and his style to the capacity and taste of his hearers, but in aptitude of comprehension and richness of imagination superior to every orator, ancient or modern. There, with eyes reverentially fixed on Burke, appeared the finest gentleman of the age,—his form developed by every manly exercise, his face beaming with intelligence and spirit,—the ingenious, the chivalrous, the high-souled Windham. Nor, though surrounded by such men, did the youngest manager pass unnoticed. At an age when most of those who distinguish themselves in life are still contending for prizes and fellowships at college, he had won for himself a conspicuous place in Parliament. No advantage of fortune or connection was wanting that could set off to the height his splendid talents and his unblemished honor. At twenty-three he had been thought worthy to be ranked with the veteran statesmen who appeared as the delegates of the British Commons, at the bar of the British nobility. All who stood at that bar, save him alone, are gone,—culprit, advocates, accusers. To the generation which is now in the vigor of life, he is the sole representative of a great age which has passed away. But those who, within the last ten years, have listened with delight, till the morning sun shone on the tapestries of the House of Lords, to the lofty and animated eloquence of Charles Earl Grey, are able to form some estimate of the powers of a race of men among whom he was not the foremost.

The charges and the answers of Hastings were first read. This ceremony occupied two whole days, and was rendered less tedious than it would otherwise have been, by the silver voice and just emphasis of Cowper, the clerk of the court, a near relation of the amiable poet. On the third day Burke rose. Four sittings of the court were occupied by his opening speech, which was intended to be a general introduction to all the charges. With an exuberance of thought and a splendor of diction which more than satisfied the highly-raised expectation of the audience, he described the character and institutions of the natives of India, recounted the circumstances in which the Asiatic empire of Britain had originated, and set forth the constitution of the company and of the English presidencies. Having thus attempted to communicate to his hearers an idea of Eastern society, as vivid as that which existed in his own mind, he proceeded to arraign the administration of Hastings, as systematically conducted in defiance of morality and public law. The energy and pathos of the great orator extorted expressions of unwonted admiration even from the stern and hostile chancellor, and for a moment seemed to pierce even the resolute heart of the defendant. The ladies in the galleries, unaccustomed to such displays of eloquence, excited by the solemnity of the occasion, and perhaps not unwilling to display their taste and sensibility, were in a state of uncontrollable emotion. Handkerchiefs were pulled out, smelling bottles were handed round, hysterical sobs and screams were heard, and Mrs. Sheridan was carried out in a fit. At length the orator concluded. Raising his voice till the old arches of Irish oak resounded—"Therefore," said he, "hath it with all confidence been ordered by the Commons of Great Britain, that I impeach Warren Hastings of high crimes and misdemeanors. I impeach him in the name of the Commons House of Parliament, whose trust he has betrayed. I impeach him in the name of the English nation, whose ancient honor he has sullied. I impeach him in the name of the people of India, whose rights he has trodden under foot, and whose country he has turned into a desert. Lastly, in the name of human nature itself, in the name of both sexes, in the name of every age, in the name of every rank, I impeach the common enemy and oppressor of all!"

When the deep murmur of various emotions had subsided, Mr. Fox rose to address the lords respecting the course of proceedings to be followed. The wish of the accuser was, that the court would bring to a close the investigation of the first charge before the second was opened. The wish of Hastings and his counsel was, that the managers should open all the charges, and produce all the evidence for the prosecution, before the defense began. The lords retired to their own house, to consider the question. The Chancellor took the side of Hastings. Lord Loughborough, who was now in opposition, supported the demand of the managers. The division showed which way the inclination of the tribunal leaned. A majority of nearly three to one decided in favor of the course for which Hastings contended.

When the court sat again, Mr. Fox, assisted by Mr. Grey, opened the charge respecting Cheyte Sing, and several days were spent in reading papers and hearing witnesses. The next article was that relating to the Princesses of Oude. The conduct

season. But in the following year, the King's illness, the debates on the regency, the expectation of a change of ministry, completely diverted public attention from Indian affairs; and within a fortnight after George III. had returned thanks in St. Paul's for his recovery, the States-General of France met at Versailles. In the midst of the agitation produced by those events, the impeachment was for a time almost forgotten.

SPEECH OF BURKE

(On the Impeachment of Warren Hastings, Opening the Charge of Bribery, February 18th and 19th, 1788)

My Lords:—

THE gentlemen who are appointed by the Commons to manage this prosecution have directed me to inform your lordships that they have very carefully and attentively weighed the magnitude of the subject, which they bring before you, with the time which the nature and circumstances of affairs allows for their conducting it.

My lords, on that comparison they are very apprehensive, that, if I should go very largely into a preliminary explanation of the several matters in charge, it might be to the prejudice of an early trial of the substantial merits of each article. We have weighed and considered this maturely. We have compared exactly the time with the matter, and we have found that we are obliged to do, as all men must do who would manage their affairs practicably, to make our opinion of what might be most advantageous to the business conform to the time that is left to perform it in. We must, as all men must, submit affairs to time, and not think of making time conform to our wishes; and therefore, my lords, I very willingly fall in with the inclinations of the gentlemen, with whom I have the honor to act, to come as soon as possible to close fighting, and to grapple immediately and directly with the corruptions of India; to bring before your lordships the direct articles; to apply the evidence to the articles, and to bring the matter forward for your lordships' decision in that manner which the confidence we have in the justice of our cause demands from the Commons of Great Britain.

My lords, these are the opinions of those with whom I have the honor to act, and in their opinions I readily acquiesce. For

of this part of the case was intrusted to Sheridan. The curiosity of the public to hear him was unbounded. The sparkling and highly-finished declamation lasted two days, but the hall was crowded to suffocation during the whole time. It was said that fifty guineas had been paid for a single ticket. Sheridan, when he concluded, contrived, with a knowledge of stage effect which his father might have envied, to sink back, as if exhausted, into the arms of Burke, who hugged him with the energy of generous admiration.

June was now far advanced. The session could not last much longer, and the progress which had been made in the impeachment was not very satisfactory. There were twenty charges. On two only of these had even the case for the prosecution been heard, and it was now a year since Hastings had been admitted to bail.

The interest taken by the public in the trial was great when the court began to sit, and rose to the height when Sheridan spoke on the charges relating to the Begums. From that time the excitement went down fast. The spectacle had lost the attraction of novelty. The great displays of rhetoric were over. What was behind was not of a nature to entice men of letters from their books in the morning, or to tempt ladies who had left the masquerade at two, to be out of bed before eight. There remained examinations and cross-examinations. There remained statements of accounts. There remained the reading of papers, filled with words unintelligible to English ears — with lacs and crores, zemindars and aumils, sunnuds and perwannahs, jagnires and nuzzurs. There remained bickerings, not always carried on with the best taste or with the best temper, between the managers of the impeachment and the counsel for the defense, particularly between Mr. Burke and Mr. Law. There remained the endless marches and countermarches of the peers between their house and the hall, for as often as a point of law was to be discussed their lordships retired to discuss it apart; and the consequence was, as the late Lord Stanhope wittily said, that the judges walked and the trial stood still.

It is to be added, that in the spring of 1788, when the trial commenced, no important question, either of domestic or foreign policy, excited the public mind. The proceeding in Westminster Hall, therefore, naturally excited most of the attention of Parliament and of the public. It was the one great event of that

I am far from wishing to waste any of your lordships' time upon any matter merely through any opinion I have of the nature of the business, when at the same time I find that in the opinion of others it might militate against the production of its full, proper, and, if I may so say, its immediate effect.

It was my design to class the crimes of the late governor of Bengal — to show their mutual bearings — how they were mutually aided, and grew and were formed out of each other. I proposed first of all to show your lordships that they have their root in that, which is the origin of all evil, avarice, and rapacity; to show how that led to prodigality of the public money, and how prodigality of the public money, by wasting the treasures of the East India Company, furnished an excuse to the governor-general to break its faith, to violate all its most solemn engagements, and to fall with a hand of stern, ferocious, and unrelenting rapacity upon all the allies and dependencies of the company. But I shall be obliged in some measure to abridge this plan; and as your lordships already possess, from what I had the honor to state on Saturday, a general view of this matter, you will be in a condition to pursue it when the several articles are presented.

My lords, I have to state to-day the root of all these misdemeanors; namely, the pecuniary corruption and avarice which gave rise and primary motion to all the rest of the delinquencies charged to be committed by the governor-general.

My lords, pecuniary corruption forms not only, as your lordships will observe in the charges before you, an article of charge by itself, but likewise so intermixes with the whole, that it is necessary to give, in the best manner I am able, a history of that corrupt system, which brought on all the subsequent acts of corruption. I will venture to say, there is no one act, in which tyranny, malice, cruelty, and oppression can be charged, that does not at the same time carry evident marks of pecuniary corruption.

I stated to your lordships, on Saturday last, the principles upon which Mr. Hastings governed his conduct in India, and upon which he grounds his defense. These may all be reduced to one short word, *arbitrary power*. My lords, if Mr. Hastings had contended as other men have often done, that the system of government which he patronizes, and on which he acted, was a system tending on the whole to the blessing and benefit of mankind, possibly something might be said for him for setting up so wild, absurd, irrational, and wicked a system. Something might be said to qualify the act from the intention; but it is singular in this man, that, at the time he tells you he acted on the principles of arbitrary power, he takes care to inform you that he was not blind to the consequences. Mr. Hastings foresaw that the consequence of this system was corruption. An arbitrary system, indeed, must always be a corrupt one. My lords, there never was a man who thought he had no law but his own will, who did not soon find that he had no end but his own profit. Corruption and arbitrary power are of natural unequivocal generation, necessarily producing one another. Mr. Hastings foresees the abusive and corrupt consequences, and then he justifies his conduct upon the necessities of that system. These are things which are new in the world: for there never was a man, I believe, who contended for arbitrary power,—and there have been persons wicked and foolish enough to contend for it,—who did not pretend, either that the system was good in itself, or that by his conduct he had mitigated or had purified it, and that the poison by passing through his constitution had acquired salutary properties. But if you look at his defense before the House of Commons, you will see that that very system upon which he governed, and under which he now justifies his actions, did appear to himself a system pregnant with a thousand evils and a thousand mischiefs.

The next thing that is remarkable and singular in the principles upon which the governor-general acted is that when he is engaged in a vicious system which clearly leads to evil consequences, he thinks himself bound to realize all the evil consequences involved in that system. All other men have taken a directly contrary course; they have said, I have been engaged in an evil system, that led, indeed, to mischievous consequences, but I have taken care by my own virtues to prevent the evils of the system under which I acted.

We say, then, not only that he governed arbitrarily, but corruptly; that is to say, that he was a giver and receiver of bribes, and formed a system for the purpose of giving and receiving them. We wish your lordships distinctly to consider, that he did not only give and receive bribes accidentally, as it happened, without any system and design, merely as the opportunity or momentary temptation of profit urged him to it, but that he has

formed plans and systems of government for the very purpose of accumulating bribes and presents to himself. This system of Mr. Hastings's government is such a one, I believe, as the British nation in particular will disown, for I will venture to say that, if there is any one thing which distinguishes this nation eminently above another, it is, that in its offices at home, both judicial and in the State, there is less suspicion of pecuniary corruption attaching to them than to any similar offices in any part of the globe, or that have existed at any time; so that he, who would set up a system of corruption, and attempt to justify it upon the principle of utility, that man is staining not only the nature and character of office, but that which is the peculiar glory of the official and judicial character of this country; and therefore in this house, which is eminently the guardian of the purity of all the offices of this kingdom, he ought to be called eminently and peculiarly to account. There are many things, undoubtedly, in crimes, which make them frightful and odious; but bribery, filthy hands, a chief governor of a great empire receiving bribes from poor, miserable, indigent people, this is what makes government itself base, contemptible, and odious in the eyes of mankind.

My lords, it is certain that even tyranny itself may find some specious color, and appear as a more severe and rigid execution of justice. Religious persecution may shield itself under the guise of a mistaken and over-zealous piety. Conquest may cover its baldness with its own laurels, and the ambition of the conqueror may be hid in the secrets of his own heart under a veil of benevolence, and make him imagine he is bringing temporary desolation upon a country only to promote its ultimate advantage and his own glory. But in the principles of that governor, who makes nothing but money his object, there can be nothing of this. There are here none of those specious delusions that look like virtues, to veil either the governed or the governor. If you look at Mr. Hastings's merits, as he calls them, what are they? Did he improve the internal state of the government by great reforms? No such thing. Or by a wise and incorrupt administration of justice? No. Has he enlarged the boundary of our government? No; there are but too strong proofs of his lessening it. But his pretensions to merit are, that he squeezed more money out of the inhabitants of the country than other persons could have done,—money got by oppression, violence

extortion from the poor, or the heavy hand of power upon the rich and great.

These are his merits. What we charge as his demerits are all of the same nature; for though there is undoubtedly oppression, breach of faith, cruelty, perfidy, charged upon him, yet the great ruling principle of the whole, and that from which you can never have an act free, is money. It is the vice of base avarice, which never is, nor ever appears even to the prejudices of mankind to be anything like a virtue. Our desire of acquiring sovereignty in India undoubtedly originated first in ideas of safety and necessity; its next step was a step of ambition. That ambition, as generally happens in conquest, was followed by gains of money; but afterwards there was no mixture at all; it was, during Mr. Hastings's time, altogether a business of money. If he has extirpated a nation, I will not say whether properly or improperly, it is because, says he, you have all the benefit of conquest without expense, you have got a large sum of money from the people, and you may leave them to be governed by whom, and as they will. This is directly contrary to the principles of conquerors. If he has at any time taken any money from the dependencies of the company, he does not pretend that it was obtained from their zeal and affection to our cause, or that it made their submission more complete; very far from it. He says they ought to be independent, and all that you have to do is to squeeze money from them. In short, money is the beginning, the middle, and the end of every kind of act done by Mr. Hastings,—pretendedly for the company, but really for himself.

Having said so much about the origin, the first principle both of that which he makes his merit, and which we charge as his demerit, the next step is, that I should lay open to your lordships, as clearly as I can, what the sense of his employers, the East India Company, and what the sense of the legislature itself has been upon those merits and demerits of money.

My lords, the company, knowing that these money transactions were likely to subvert that empire which was first established upon them, did, in the year 1765, send out a body of the strongest and most solemn covenants to their servants, that they should take no presents from the country powers under any name or description, except those things which were publicly and openly taken for the use of the company, namely, territories or sums of

money, which might be obtained by treaty. They distinguished such presents as were taken from any persons privately and unknown to them, and without their authority, from subsidies; and that this is the true nature and construction of their order, I shall contend and explain afterwards to your lordships. They have said nothing shall be taken for their private use; for though in that and in every State there may be subsidiary treaties by which sums of money may be received, yet they forbid their servants, their governors,—whatever application they might pretend to make of them,—to receive, under any other name or pretense, more than a certain marked simple sum of money, and this not without the consent and permission of the presidency to which they belong. This is the substance, the principle, and the spirit of the covenants, and will show your lordships how radicated an evil this of bribery and presents was judged to be.

When these covenants arrived in India, the servants refused at first to execute them, and suspended the execution of them till they had enriched themselves with presents. Eleven months elapsed, and it was not till Lord Clive reached the place of his destination, that the covenants were executed; and they were not executed then without some degree of force. Soon afterwards the treaty was made with the country powers, by which Shuja ul Dowla was re-established in the province of Oude, and paid a sum of £500,000 to the company for it. It was a public payment, and there was not a suspicion that a single shilling of private emolument attended it. But whether Mr. Hastings had the example of others or not, their example could not justify his briberies. He was sent there to put an end to all those examples. The company did expressly vest him with that power. They declared at that time, that the whole of their service was totally corrupted by bribes and presents, and by extravagance and luxury, which partly gave rise to them; and these in their turn enabled them to pursue those excesses. They not only reposed trust in the integrity of Mr. Hastings, but reposed trust in his remarkable frugality and order in his affairs, which they considered as things that distinguished his character. But in his defense we have him in quite another character, no longer the frugal, attentive servant bred to business, bred to bookkeeping, as all the company's servants are; he now knows nothing of his own affairs, knows not whether he is rich or poor, knows not what he has in the world. Nay, people are brought forward to say that they know better than he does what his affairs are. He is not like a careful man bred in a countinghouse, and by the directors put into an office of the highest trust on account of the regularity of his affairs; he is like one buried in the contemplation of the stars, and knows nothing of the things in this world. It was then on account of an idea of his great integrity that the company put him into this situation. Since that he has thought proper to justify himself, not by clearing himself of receiving bribes, but by saying that no bad consequences resulted from it, and that, if any such evil consequences did arise from it, they arose rather from his inattention to money than from his desire of acquiring it.

I have stated to your lordships the nature of the covenants, which the East India Company sent out. Afterwards, when they found their servants had refused to execute these covenants, they not only very severely reprehended even a moment's delay in their execution, and threatened the exacting and the most strict and rigorous performance of them, but they sent a commission to enforce the observance of them more strongly; and that commission had it specially in charge never to receive presents. They never sent out a person to India without recognizing the grievance, and without ordering that presents should not be received, as the main fundamental part of their duty, and upon which all the rest depended, as it certainly must; for persons at the head of government should not encourage that by example, which they ought by precept, authority, and force, to restrain in all below them. That commission failing, another commission was preparing to be sent out with the same instructions, when an act of Parliament took it up; and that act, which gave Mr. Hastings power, did mold in the very first stamina of his power this principle, in words the most clear and forcible that an act of Parliament could possibly devise upon the subject. And that act was made not only upon a general knowledge of the grievance, but your lordships will see in the reports of that time that Parliament had directly in view before them the whole of that monstrous head of corruption under the name of presents, and all the monstrous consequences that followed it.

Now, my lords, every office of trust, in its very nature, forbids the receipt of bribes. But Mr. Hastings was forbidden it, first, by his official situation; next by covenant; and, lastly, by act of Parliament; that is to say, by all the things that bind

mankind, or that can bind them,—first, moral obligation inherent in the duty of their office; next, the positive injunctions of the legislature of the country; and, lastly, a man's own private, particular, voluntary act and covenant. These three, the great and only obligations that bind mankind, all united in the focus of this single point—that they should take no presents.

I am to mark to your lordships, that this law and this covenant did consider indirect ways of taking presents—taking them by others, and such like—directly in the very same light as they considered taking them by themselves. It is perhaps a much more dangerous way, because it adds to the crime a false prevaricating mode of concealing it, and makes it much more mischievous by admitting others into the participation of it. Mr. Hastings has said, and it is one of the general complaints of Mr. Hastings, that he is made answerable for the acts of other men. It is a thing inherent in the nature of his situation. All those who enjoy a great superintending trust, which is to regulate the whole affairs of an empire, are responsible for the acts and conduct of other men, so far as they had anything to do with appointing them, or holding them in their places, or having any sort of inspection into their conduct.

But when a governor presumes to remove from their situations those persons whom the public authority and sanction of the company have appointed, and obtrudes upon them by violence other persons, superseding the orders of his masters, he becomes doubly responsible for their conduct. If the persons he names should be of notorious evil character and evil principles, and if this should be perfectly known to himself, and of public notoriety to the rest of the world, then another strong responsibility attaches on him for the acts of those persons.

Governors, we know very well, cannot, with their own hands, be continually receiving bribes; for then they must have as many hands as one of the idols in an Indian temple in order to receive all the bribes which a governor-general may receive; but they have them vicariously. As there are many offices, so he has had various officers for receiving and distributing his bribes; he has had a great many, some white and some black agents. The white men are loose and licentious; they are apt to have resentments, and to be bold in revenging them. The black men are very secret and mysterious; they are not apt to have very quick resentments; they have not the same liberty and boldness

of language which characterize Europeans; and they have fears, too, for themselves, which makes it more likely that they will conceal anything committed to them by Europeans. Therefore, Mr. Hastings had his black agents, not one, two, three, but many, disseminated through the country; no two of them hardly appear to be in the secret of any one bribe. He has had likewise his white agents,—they were necessary,—a Mr. Larkins and a Mr. Crofts. Mr. Crofts was sub-treasurer, and Mr. Larkins accountant-general. These were the last persons of all others, that should have had anything to do with bribes; yet these were some of his agents in bribery. There are few instances in comparison of the whole number of bribes, but there are some, where two men are in the secret of the same bribe. Nay, it appears that there was one bribe divided into different payments at different times,—that one part was committed to one black secretary, another part to another black secretary. So that it is almost impossible to make up a complete body of all his bribery; you may find the scattered limbs, some here, and others there, and while you are employed in picking them up, he may escape entirely in a prosecution for the whole.

The first act of his government in Bengal was the most bold and extraordinary that I believe ever entered into the head of any man,—I will say, of any tyrant. It was no more or less than a general, almost exceptionless, confiscation, in time of profound peace, of all the landed property in Bengal, upon most extraordinary pretenses. Strange as this may appear, he did so confiscate it; he put it up to a pretended public, in reality to a private, corrupt auction, and such favored landowners as came to it were obliged to consider themselves as not any longer proprietors of the estates, but to recognize themselves as farmers under government; and even those few that were permitted to remain on their estates had their payments raised at his arbitrary discretion, and the rest of the lands were given to farmers-general, appointed by him and his committee, at a price fixed by the same arbitrary discretion.

It is necessary to inform your lordships that the revenues of Bengal are, for the most part, territorial revenues, great quitrents issuing out of lands. I shall say nothing either of the nature of this property, of the rights of the people to it, or of the mode of exacting the rents, till that great question of revenues, one of the greatest which we shall have to lay before you, shall be

brought before your lordships particularly and specially as an article of charge. I only mention it now as an exemplification of the great principle of corruption which guided Mr. Hastings's conduct.

When the ancient nobility, the great princes,—for such I may call them,—a nobility, perhaps, as ancient as that of your lordships, and a more truly noble body never existed in that character; my lords, when all the nobility, some of whom have borne the rank and port of princes, all the gentry, all the freeholders of the country, had their estates in that manner confiscated, that is, either given to themselves to hold on the footing of farmers, or totally confiscated; when such an act of tyranny was done, no doubt some good was pretended. This confiscation was made by Mr. Hastings, and the lands let to these farmers for five years, upon an idea, which always accompanies his acts of oppression,—the idea of moneyed merit. He adopted this mode of confiscating the estates, and letting them to farmers, for the avowed purpose of seeing how much it was possible to take out of them. Accordingly, he set them up to this wild and wicked auction, as it would have been, if it had been a real one,—corrupt and treacherous, as it was. He set these lands up for the purpose of making that discovery, and pretended that the discovery would yield a most amazing increase of rent. And for some time it appeared so to do, till it came to the touchstone of experience; and then it was found that there was a defalcation from these monstrous raised revenues, which were to cancel in the minds of the directors the wickedness of so atrocious, flagitious, and horrid an act of treachery. At the end of five years, what do you think was the failure?—No less than £2,050,000. Then a new source of corruption was opened, that is, how to deal with the balances, for every man who had engaged in these transactions was a debtor to government, and the remission of that debt depended upon the discretion of the governor-general. Then the persons, who were to settle the composition of that immense debt, who were to see how much was recoverable, and how much not, were able to favor, or to exact to the last shilling; and there never existed a doubt but that, not only upon the original, cruel exaction, but upon the remission afterwards, immense gains were derived. This will account for the manner in which those stupendous fortunes, which astonish the world, have been made. They have been made, first, by a tyrannous exaction from the people, who were suffered to remain in possession of their own land as farmers, then by selling the rest to farmers at rents and under hopes which could never be realized, and then getting money for the relaxation of their debts. But whatever excuse, and however wicked, there might have been for this wicked act, namely, that it carried upon the face of it some sort of appearance of public good, that is to say, that sort of public good which Mr. Hastings so often professed, of ruining the country for the benefit of the company, yet, in fact, this business of balances is that *nidus* in which have been nestled and bred and born all the corruption of India,—first, by making extravagant demands, and afterwards by making corrupt relaxations of them.

Besides this monstrous failure in consequence of a miserable exaction, by which more was attempted to be forced from the country than it was capable of yielding, and this by way of experiment, when your lordships come to inquire who the farmers-general of the revenue were, you would naturally expect to find them to be the men in the several countries, who had the most interest, the greatest wealth, the best knowledge of the revenue and resources of the country in which they lived. These would be thought the natural proper farmers-general of each district. No such thing, my lords. They are found in the body of people, whom I have mentioned to your lordships. They were almost all let to Calcutta banyans. Calcutta banyans were the farmers of almost the whole. They sub-delegated to others, who sometimes had sub-delegates under them *ad infinitum*. The whole formed a system together through the succession of black tyrants scattered through the country, in which you at last find the European at the end, sometimes, indeed, not hid very deep, not above one between him and the farmer, namely, his banyan directly, or some other black person to represent him. But some have so managed the affair, that when you inquire who the farmer is,—Was such a one farmer? No. Cantoo Baboo? No. Another? No. At last you find three deep of fictitious farmers, and you find the European gentlemen, high in place and authority, the real farmers of the settlement. So that the zemindars were dispossessed, the country racked and ruined for the benefit of a European, under the name of a farmer; for you will easily judge whether these gentlemen had fallen so deeply in love with

11—48

the banyans, and thought so highly of their merits and services, as to reward them with all the possessions of the great landed interest of the country. Your lordships are too grave, wise, and discerning, to make it necessary for me to say more upon that subject. Tell me, that the banyans of English gentlemen, dependents on them at Calcutta, were the farmers throughout, and I believe I need not tell your lordships for whose benefit they were farmers.

But there is one of these, who comes so nearly, indeed so precisely, within this observation, that it is impossible for me to pass him by. Whoever has heard of Mr. Hastings's name with any knowledge of Indian connections has heard of his banyan Cantoo Baboo. This man is well known in the records of the company as his agent for receiving secret gifts, confiscations, and presents. You would have imagined that he would at least have kept him out of these farms, in order to give the measure a color at least of disinterestedness and to show that this whole system of corruption and pecuniary oppression was carried on for the benefit of the company. The governor-general and council made an ostensible order, by which no collector or person concerned in the revenue should have any connection with these farms. This order did not include the governor-general in the words of it, but more than included him in the spirit of it; because his power to protect a farmer-general in the person of his own servant was infinitely greater than that of any subordinate person. Mr. Hastings, in breach of this order, gave farms to his own banyan. You find him the farmer of great, of vast, and extensive farms.

Another regulation that was made on that occasion was that no farmer should have, except in particular cases, which were marked, described, and accurately distinguished, a greater farm than what paid £10,000 a year to government. Mr. Hastings, who had broken the first regulation by giving any farm at all to his banyan, finding himself bolder, broke the second, too, and, instead of £10,000, gave him farms paying a revenue of £130,000 a year to the government. Men undoubtedly have been known to be under the dominion of their domestics; such things have happened to great men; they never have happened justifiably, in my opinion. They have never happened excusably; but we are acquainted sufficiently with the weakness of human nature

to know that a domestic, who has served you in a near office long, and in your opinion faithfully, does become a kind of relation; it brings on a great affection and regard for his interest. Now was this the case with Mr. Hastings and Cantoo Baboo? Mr. Hastings was just arrived at his government, and Cantoo Baboo had been but a year in his service; so that he could not in that time have contracted any great degree of friendship for him. These people do not live in your house; the Hindoo servants never sleep in it; they cannot eat with your servants; they have no second table, in which they can be continually about you, to be domesticated with yourself, a part of your being, as people's servants are to a certain degree. These persons live all abroad; they come at stated hours upon matters of business, and nothing more. But if it had been otherwise, Mr. Hastings's connection with Cantoo Baboo had been but of a year's standing; he had before served in that capacity Mr. Sykes, who recommended him to Mr. Hastings. Your lordships, then, are to judge whether such outrageous violations of all the principles, by which Mr. Hastings pretended to be guided in the settlement of these farms, were for the benefit of this old, decayed, affectionate servant of one year's standing—your lordships will judge of that.

I have here spoken only of the beginning of a great notorious system of corruption, which branched out so many ways, and into such a variety of abuses, and has afflicted that kingdom with such horrible evils from that day to this, that I will venture to say it will make one of the greatest, weightiest, and most material parts of the charge, that is now before you; as I believe I need not tell your lordships, that an attempt to set up the whole landed interest of a kingdom to auction must be attended, not only in that act, but every consequential act, with most grievous and terrible consequences.

My lords, I will now come to a scene of peculation of another kind; namely, a peculation by the direct sale of offices of justice; by the direct sale of the successions of families; by the sale of guardianships and trusts, held most sacred among the people of India; by the sale of them, not as before to farmers, not as you might imagine to near relations of the families, but a sale of them to the unfaithful servants of those families, their own perfidious servants, who had ruined their estates, who, if any balances had accrued to the government, had been the cause

ot those debts. Those very servants were put in power over their estates, their persons, and their families by Mr. Hastings for a shameful price. It will be proved to your lordships in the course of this business, that Mr. Hastings has done this in another sacred trust, the most sacred trust a man can have; that is, in the case of those vackiels,—as they call them,—agents, or attorneys, who had been sent to assert and support the rights of their miserable masters before the council-general. It will be proved that these vackiels were by Mr. Hastings, for a price to be paid for it, put in possession of the very power, situation, and estates of those masters who sent them to Calcutta to defend them from wrong and violence. The selling offices of justice, the sale of succession in families, of guardianships and other sacred trusts, the selling masters to their servants, and principals to the attorneys they employed to defend themselves, were all parts of the same system; and these were the horrid ways in which he received bribes beyond any common rate.

When Mr. Hastings was appointed in the year 1773 to be governor-general of Bengal, together with Mr. Barwell, General Clavering, Colonel Monson, and Mr. Francis, the company, knowing the former corrupt state of their service,—but the whole corrupt system of Mr. Hastings at that time not being known, or even suspected at home,—did order them, in discharge of the spirit of the act of Parliament, to make an inquiry into all manner of corruptions and malversations in office, without the exception of any persons whatever. Your lordships are to know, that the act did expressly authorize the court of directors to frame a body of instructions, and to give orders to their new servants, appointed under the act of Parliament, lest it should be supposed that they, by their appointment under the act, could supersede the authority of the directors.

The directors, sensible of the power left in them over their servants by the act of Parliament, though their nomination was taken from them, did, agreeably to the spirit and power of that act, give this order.

The council consisted of two parties: Mr. Hastings and Mr. Barwell, who were chosen, and kept there, upon the idea of their local knowledge; and the other three, who were appointed on account of their great parts and known integrity. And I will venture to say, that those three gentlemen did so execute their duty in India in all the substantial parts of it, that they will serve as a shield to cover the honor of England, whenever this country is upbraided in India.

They found a rumor running through the country of great peculations and oppressions. Soon after, when it was known what their instructions were, and that the council was ready, as is the first duty of all governors, even when there is no express order, to receive complaints against the oppressions and corruptions of government in any part of it, they found such a body—and that body shall be produced to your lordships—of corruption and peculation in every walk, in every department, in every situation of life, in the sale of the most sacred trusts, and in the destruction of the most ancient families of the country, as I believe in so short a time never was unveiled since the world began.

Your lordships would imagine that Mr. Hastings would at least ostensibly have taken some part in endeavoring to bring these corruptions before the public, or that he would, at least, have acted with some little management in his opposition. But alas! it was not in his power; there was not one, I think, but I am sure very few, of these general articles of corruption, in which the most eminent figure in the crowd, the principal figure, as it were, in the piece, was not Mr. Hastings himself. There were a great many others involved, for all departments were corrupted and vitiated. But you could not open a page, in which you did not see Mr. Hastings, or in which you did not see Cantoo Baboo. Either the black or white side of Mr. Hastings constantly was visible to the world in every part of these transactions.

With the other gentlemen, who were visible too, I have at present no dealing. Mr. Hastings, instead of using any management on that occasion, instantly set up his power and authority, directly against the majority of the council, directly against his colleagues, directly against the authority of the East India Company and the authority of the act of Parliament, to put a dead stop to all these inquiries. He broke up the council the moment they attempted to perform this part of their duty. As the evidence multiplied upon him, the daring exertions of his power in stopping all inquiries increased continually. But he gave a credit and authority to the evidence by these attempts to suppress it.

Your lordships have heard that among the body of the accusers of this corruption there was a principal man in the country, a man of the first rank and authority in it, called Nundcomar, who had the management of revenues amounting to £150,000 a year, and who had, if really inclined to play the small game with which he has been charged by his accusers, abundant means to gratify himself in playing great ones; but Mr. Hastings has himself given him, upon the records of the company, a character, which would at least justify the council in making some inquiry into charges made by him.

First, he was perfectly competent to make them, because he was in the management of those affairs, from which Mr. Hastings is supposed to have received corrupt emolument. He and his son were the chief managers in those transactions. He was, therefore, perfectly competent to it. Mr. Hastings has cleared his character; for, though it is true in the contradictions, in which Mr. Hastings has entangled himself, he has abused and insulted him, and particularly after his appearance as an accuser, yet before this he has given this testimony of him, that the hatred that had been drawn upon him, and the general obloquy of the English nation, was on account of his attachment to his own prince and the liberties of his country. Be he what he might, I am not disposed, nor have I the least occasion, to defend either his conduct or his memory.

It is to no purpose for Mr. Hastings to spend time in idle objections to the character of Nundcomar. Let him be as bad as Mr. Hastings represents him. I suppose he was a caballing, bribing, intriguing politician, like others in that country, both black and white. We know that associates in dark and evil actions are not generally the best of men; but be that as it will, it generally happens that they are the best of all discoverers. If Mr. Hastings were the accuser of Nundcomar, I should think the presumptions equally strong against Nundcomar, if he had acted as Mr. Hastings has acted. He was not competent, but the most competent of all men to be Mr. Hastings's accuser. But Mr. Hastings has himself established both his character, and his competency, by employing him against Mahomed Reza Khân. He shall not blow hot and cold. In what respect was Mr. Hastings better than Mahomed Reza Khân, that the whole rule, principle, and system of accusation and inquiry should be totally reversed in general, nay, reversed in the particular instance, the

moment he became accuser against Mr. Hastings. Such was the accuser. He was the man that gave the bribes, and, in addition to his own evidence, offers proof by other witnesses.

What was the accusation? Was the accusation improbable, either on account of the subject-matter, or the actor in it? Does such an appointment as that of Munny Begum in the most barefaced evasion of his orders appear to your lordships a matter that contains no just presumptions of guilt, so that when a charge of bribery comes upon it, you are prepared to reject it, as if the action were so clear and proper that no man could attribute it to an improper motive? And, as to the man, is Mr. Hastings a man against whom a charge of bribery is improbable? Why, he owns it. He is a professor of it. He reduces it into scheme and system. He glories in it. He turns it to merit, and declares it is the best way of supplying the exigencies of the company. Why, therefore, should it be held improbable?—But I cannot mention this proceeding without shame and horror.

My lords, when this man appeared as an accuser of Mr. Hastings, if he was a man of bad character, it was a great advantage to Mr. Hastings to be accused by a man of that description. There was no likelihood of any great credit being given to him.

This person, who, in one of those sales, of which I have already given you some account in the history of the last period of the revolutions of Bengal, had been, or thought he had been, cheated of his money, had made some discoveries, and been guilty of that great irremissible sin in India, the disclosure of peculation. He afterwards came with a second disclosure, and was likely to have odium enough upon the occasion. He directly charged Mr. Hastings with the receipt of bribes amounting together to about £40,000 sterling, given by himself, on his own account, and that of Munny Begum. The charge was accompanied with every particular, which could facilitate proof or detection, time, place, persons, species, to whom paid, by whom received. Here was a fair opportunity for Mr. Hastings at once to defeat the malice of his enemies, and to clear his character to the world. His course was different. He railed much at the accuser, but did not attempt to refute the accusation. He refuses to permit the inquiry to go on, attempts to dissolve the council, commands his banyan not to attend. The council, however, goes on, examines to the bottom, and resolves that the charge was

proved, and that the money ought to go to the company. Mr. Hastings then broke up the council, I will not say whether legally or illegally. The company's law counsel thought he might legally do it; but he corruptly did it, and left mankind no room to judge but that it was done for the screening of his own guilt; for a man may use a legal power corruptly, and for the most shameful and detestable purposes. And thus matters continued, till he commenced a criminal prosecution against this man,—this man whom he dared not meet as a defendant.

Mr. Hastings, instead of answering the charge, attacks the accuser. Instead of meeting the man in front, he endeavored to go round, to come upon his flanks and rear, but never to meet him in the face upon the ground of his accusation, as he was bound by the express authority of law, and the express injunctions of the directors, to do. If the bribery is not admitted on the evidence of Nundcomar, yet his suppressing it is a crime—a violation of the orders of the court of directors. He disobeyed those instructions; and if it be only for disobedience, for rebellion against his masters, putting the corrupt motive out of the question, I charge him for this disobedience, and especially on account of the principles, upon which he proceeded in it.

Then he took another step; he accused Nundcomar of a conspiracy, which was a way he then and ever since has used, whenever means were taken to detect any of his own iniquities.

And here it becomes necessary to mention another circumstance of history, that the legislature, not trusting entirely to the governor-general and council, had sent out a court of justice to be a counter-security against these corruptions, and to detect and punish any such misdemeanors as might appear. And this court, I take for granted, has done great services.

Mr. Hastings flew to this court, which was meant to protect in their situations informers against bribery and corruption rather than to protect the accused from any of the preliminary methods, which must indispensably be used for the purpose of detecting their guilt; he flew to this court, charging this Nundcomar and others with being conspirators.

A man might be convicted as a conspirator, and yet afterwards live; he might put the matter into other hands, and go on with his information; nothing less than stone-dead would do the business. And here happened an odd concurrence of circumstances. Long before Nundcomar preferred his charge he knew that Mr. Hastings was plotting his ruin, and that for this purpose he had used a man, whom he, Nundcomar, had turned out of doors, called Mohun Persaud. Mr. Hastings had seen papers put upon the board, charging him with this previous plot for the destruction of Nundcomar; and this identical person, Mohun Persaud, whom Nundcomar had charged as Mr. Hastings's associate in plotting his ruin, was now again brought forward, as the principal evidence against him. I will not enter (God forbid I should!) into the particulars of the subsequent trial of Nundcomar; but you will find the marks and characters of it to be these. You will find a close connection between Mr. Hastings and the chief-justice, which we shall prove. We shall prove that one of the witnesses who appeared there was a person who had been before, or has since been, concerned with Mr. Hastings in his most iniquitous transactions. You will find what is very odd, that in this trial for forgery, with which this man stood charged, forgery in a private transaction, all the persons who were witnesses, or parties to it, had been, before or since, the particular friends of Mr. Hastings,—in short, persons from that rabble, with whom Mr. Hastings was concerned, both before and since, in various transactions and negotiations of the most criminal kind. But the law took its course. I have nothing more to say than that the man is gone—hanged justly if you please; and that it did so happen luckily for Mr. Hastings,—it so happened, that the relief of Mr. Hastings and the justice of the court, and the resolution never to relax its rigor, did all concur just at a happy nick of time and moment; and Mr. Hastings accordingly had the full benefit of them all.

His accuser was supposed to be what men may be, and yet very competent for accusers,—namely, one of his accomplices in guilty actions, one of those persons who may have a great deal to say of bribes. All that I contend for is that he was in the closest intimacy with Mr. Hastings, was in a situation for giving bribes, and that Mr. Hastings was proved afterwards to have received a sum of money from him, which may be well referred to bribes.

This example had its use in the way in which it was intended to operate and in which alone it could operate. It did not discourage forgeries; they went on at their usual rate, neither more nor less. But it put an end to all accusations against all persons in power for any corrupt practice. Mr. Hastings observes, that

no man in India complains of him. It is generally true. The voice of all India is stopped. All complaint was strangled with the same cord that strangled Nundcomar. This murdered not only that accuser, but all future accusation; and not only defeated, but totally vitiated and reversed, all the ends for which this country, to its eternal and indelible dishonor, had sent out a pompous embassy of justice to the remotest parts of the globe.

But though Nundcomar was put out of the way by the means by which he was removed, a part of the charge was not strangled with him. Whilst the process against Nundcomar was carrying on before Sir Elijah Impey, the process was continuing against Mr. Hastings in other modes; the receipt of a part of those bribes from Munny Begum to the amount of £15,000 was proved against him; and that a sum, to the same amount, was to be paid to his associate, Mr. Middleton, as it was proved at Calcutta, so it will be proved at your lordships' bar, to your entire satisfaction, by records and living testimony now in England. It was, indeed, obliquely admitted by Mr. Hastings himself.

The excuse for this bribe, fabricated by Mr. Hastings, and taught to Munny Begum, when he found that she was obliged to prove it against him, was, that it was given to him for his entertainment, according to some pretended custom, at the rate of £200 a day, whilst he remained at Moorshedabad. My lords, this leads me to a few reflections on the apology or defense of this bribe. We shall certainly, I hope, render it clear to your lordships, that it was not paid in this manner, as a daily allowance, but given in a gross sum. But take it in his own way, it was no less illegal, and no less contrary to his covenant; but if true under the circumstances, it was a horrible aggravation of his crime. The first thing that strikes is that visits from Mr. Hastings are pretty severe things; and hospitality at Moorshedabad is an expensive virtue, though for provision it is one of the cheapest countries in the universe. No wonder that Mr. Hastings lengthened his visit, and made it extend nearly three months. Such hosts and such guests cannot be soon parted. Two hundred pounds a day for a visit! It is at the rate of £73,000 a year for himself; and, as I find his companion was put on the same allowance, it will be £146,000 a year for hospitality to two English gentlemen.

I believe that there is not a prince in Europe who goes to such expensive hospitality of splendor. But that you may judge

of the true nature of this hospitality of corruption, I must bring before you the business of the visitor, and the condition of the host, as stated by Mr. Hastings himself, who best knows what he was doing.

He was then at the old capital of Bengal, at the time of this expensive entertainment, on a business of retrenchment, and for the establishment of a most harsh, rigorous, and oppressive economy. He wishes the task were assigned to spirits of a less gentle kind. By Mr. Hastings's account, he was giving daily and hourly wounds to his humanity, in depriving of their sustenance hundreds of persons of the ancient nobility of a great fallen kingdom. Yet it was in the midst of this galling duty, it was at that very moment of his tender sensibility, that from the collected morsels plucked from the famished mouths of hundreds of decayed, indigent, and starving nobility, he gorged his ravenous maw with £200 a day for his entertainment. In the course of all this proceeding, your lordships will not fail to observe, he is never corrupt, but he is cruel; he never dines with comfort, but where he is sure to create a famine. He never robs from the loose superfluity of standing greatness; he devours the fallen, the indigent, the necessitous. His extortion is not like the generous rapacity of the princely eagle, who snatches away the living, struggling prey; he is a vulture, who feeds upon the prostrate, the dying, and the dead. As his cruelty is more shocking than his corruption, so his hypocrisy has something more frightful than his cruelty. For whilst his bloody and rapacious hand signs proscriptions, and now sweeps away the food of the widow and the orphan, his eyes overflow with tears, and he converts the healing balm, that bleeds from wounded humanity, into a rancorous and deadly poison to the race of man.

Well, there was an end to this tragic entertainment, this feast of Tantalus. The few left on the pension list, the poor remnants that had escaped, were they paid by his administratrix and deputy, Munny Begum? Not a shilling. No fewer than forty-nine petitions, mostly from the widows of the greatest and most splendid houses of Bengal, came before the council, praying in the most deplorable manner for some sort of relief out of the pittance assigned them. His colleagues, General Clavering, Colonel Monson, and Mr. Francis, men, who, when England is reproached for the government of India, will, I repeat it, as a shield be held up between this nation and infamy, did, in conformity to the

strict orders of the directors, appoint Mahomed Reza Khân to his old offices, that is, to the general superintendency of the household and the administration of justice, a person, who, by his authority, might keep some order in the ruling family and in the State. The court of directors authorized them to assure those offices to him, with a salary reduced, indeed, to £30,000 a year, during his good behavior. But Mr. Hastings, as soon as he obtained a majority by the death of the two best men ever sent to India, notwithstanding the orders of the court of directors, in spite of the public faith solemnly pledged to Mahomed Reza Khân, without a shadow of complaint, had the audacity to dispossess him of all his offices, and appoint his bribing patroness, the old dancing girl, Munny Begum, once more to the viceroyalty and all its attendant honors and functions.

The pretense was more insolent and shameless than the act. Modesty does not long survive innocence. He brings forward the miserable pageant of the nabob, as he called him, to be the instrument of his own disgrace and the scandal of his family and government. He makes him to pass by his mother, and to petition us to appoint Munny Begum once more to the administration of the viceroyalty. He distributed Mahomed Reza Khân's salary as a spoil.

When the orders of the court to restore Mahomed Reza Khân, with their opinion on the corrupt cause of his removal, and a second time to pledge to him the public faith for his continuance, were received, Mr. Hastings, who had been just before a pattern of obedience, when the despoiling, oppressing, imprisoning, and persecuting this man was the object, yet when the order was of a beneficial nature, and pleasant to a well-formed mind, he at once loses all his old principles, he grows stubborn and refractory, and refuses obedience. And in this sullen, uncomplying mood he continues, until, to gratify Mr. Francis in an agreement on some of their differences, he consented to his proposition of obedience to the appointment of the court of directors. He grants to his arrangement of convenience what he had refused to his duty, and replaces that magistrate. But mark the double character of the man, never true to anything but fraud and duplicity. At the same time that he publicly replaces this magistrate, pretending compliance with his colleague, and obedience to his masters, he did, in defiance of his own and the public faith, privately send an assurance to the nabob, that is, to

Munny Begum, informing her that he was compelled by necessity to the present arrangement in favor of Mahomed Reza Khân, but that on the first opportunity he would certainly displace him again. And he kept faith with his corruption; and to show how vainly any one sought protection in the lawful authority of this kingdom, he displaced Mahomed Reza Khân from the lieutenancy and controllership, leaving him only the judicial department miserably curtailed.

But does he adhere to his old pretense of freedom to the nabob? No such thing. He appoints an absolute master to him under the name of resident, a creature of his personal favor, Sir J. Doiley, from whom there is not one syllable of correspondence, and not one item of account. How grievous this yoke was to that miserable captive appears by a paper of Mr. Hastings, in which he acknowledges that the nabob had offered, out of the £160,000 payable to him yearly, to give up to the company no less than £40,000 a year, in order to have the free disposal of the rest. On this all comment is superfluous. Your lordships are furnished with a standard, by which you may estimate his real receipt from the revenue assigned to him, the nature of the pretended residency, and its predatory effects. It will give full credit to what was generally rumored and believed, that substantially and beneficially the nabob never received £50 out of the £160,000; which will account for his known poverty and wretchedness, and that of all about him.

Thus, by his corrupt traffic of bribes with one scandalous woman, he disgraced and enfeebled the native Mahomedan government, captived the person of the sovereign, and ruined and subverted the justice of the country. What is worse, the steps taken for the murder of Nundcomar, his accuser, have confirmed and given sanction not only to the corruptions then practiced by the governor-general, but to all of which he has since been guilty. This will furnish your lordships with some general idea, which will enable you to judge of the bribe for which he sold the country government.

Under this head you will have produced to you full proof of his sale of a judicial office to a person called Khân Jehân Khân and the modes he took to frustrate all inquiry on that subject upon a wicked and false pretense, that according to his religious scruples he could not be sworn.

The great end and object I have in view is to show the criminal tendency, the mischievous nature, of these crimes, and the means taken to elude their discovery. I am now giving your lordships that general view, which may serve to characterize Mr. Hastings's administration in all the other parts of it.

It was not true in fact, as Mr. Hastings gives out, that there was nothing now against him, and that when he had got rid of Nundcomar and his charge, he got rid of the whole. No such thing. An immense load of charges of bribery remained. They were coming afterwards from every part of the province, and there was no office in the execution of justice which he was not accused of having sold in the most flagitious manner.

After all this thundering, the sky grew calm and clear, and Mr. Hastings sat with recorded peculation, with peculation proved upon oath on the minutes of that very council; he sat at the head of that council and that board where his peculations were proved against him. These were afterwards transmitted, and recorded in the registers of his masters, as an eternal monument of his corruption and of his high disobedience and flagitious attempts to prevent a discovery of the various peculations of which he had been guilty, to the disgrace and ruin of the country committed to his care.

Mr. Hastings, after the execution of Nundcomar, if he had intended to make even a decent and commonly sensible use of it, would naturally have said: "This man is justly taken away, who has accused me of these crimes; but as there are other witnesses, as there are other means of a further inquiry, as the man is gone, of whose perjuries I might have reason to be afraid, let us now go into the inquiry." I think he did very ill not to go into the inquiry, when the man was alive; but be it so that he was afraid of him, and waited till he was removed, why not afterwards go into such an inquiry? Why not go into an inquiry of all the other peculations and charges upon him, which were innumerable, one of which I have just mentioned in particular, the charge of Munny Begum,—of having received from her, or her adopted son, a bribe of £40,000?

Is it fit for a governor to say,—will Mr. Hastings say before this august assembly: "I may be accused in a court of justice, I am upon my defense, let all charges remain against me, I will not give you an account"? Is it fit that a governor should sit

with recorded bribery upon him at the head of a public board, and the government of a great kingdom, when it is in his power by inquiry to do it away? No; the chastity of character of a man in that situation ought to be as dear to him as his innocence. Nay, more depended upon it. His innocence regarded himself, his character regarded the public justice, regarded his authority, and the respect due to the English in that country. I charge it upon him, that not only did he suppress the inquiry to the best of his power, and it shall be proved, but he did not in any one instance endeavor to clear off that imputation and reproach from the English government. He went further, he never denied hardly any of those charges at the time. They are so numerous, that I cannot be positive; some of them he might meet with some sort of denial, but the most part he did not.

The first thing a man under such an accusation owes to the world is to deny the charge; next to put it to the proof; and lastly to let inquiry freely go on. He did not permit this, but stopped it all in his power. I am to mention some exceptions perhaps hereafter, which will tend to fortify the principle tenfold.

He promised, indeed, the court of directors, to whom he never denied the facts, a full and liberal explanation of these transactions; which full and liberal explanation he never gave. Many years passed; even Parliament took notice of it; and he never gave a liberal explanation, or any explanation at all, of them. A man may say, I am threatened with a suit in a court, and it may be very disadvantageous to me, if I disclose my defense. That is a proper answer for a man in common life, who has no particular character to sustain; but is that a proper answer for a governor accused of bribery? that accusation transmitted to his masters, and his masters giving credit to it? Good God! is that a state in which a man is to say: "I am upon the defensive? I am on my guard? I will give you no satisfaction? I have promised it, but I have already deferred it for seven or eight years?" Is not this tantamount to a denial?

Mr. Hastings, with this great body of bribery against him, was providentially freed from Nundcomar, one of his accusers; and as good events do not come alone,—I think there is some such proverb,—it did so happen that all the rest, or a great many of them, ran away. But, however, the recorded evidence of the former charges continued, no new evidence came in, and Mr. Hastings enjoyed that happy repose, which branded peculation,

fixed and eternized upon the records of the company, must leave upon a mind conscious of its own integrity.

My lords, I will venture to say there is no man but owes something to his character. It is the grace, undoubtedly, of a virtuous, firm mind often to despise common vulgar calumny; but if there is an occasion in which it does become such a mind to disprove it, it is the case of being charged in high office with pecuniary malversation, pecuniary corruption. There is no case, in which it becomes an honest man—much less a great man—to leave upon record specific charges against him of corruption in his government, without taking any one step whatever to refute them.

Though Mr. Hastings took no step to refute the charges, he took many steps to punish the authors of them; and those miserable people, who had the folly to make complaints against Mr. Hastings, to make them under the authority of an act of Parliament, under every sanction of public faith, yet in consequence of those charges every person concerned in them has been, as your lordships will see, since his restoration to power, absolutely undone; brought from the highest situation to the lowest misery, so that they may have good reason to repent they ever trusted an English council, that they ever trusted a court of directors, that they ever trusted an English act of Parliament, that they ever dared to make their complaints.

And here I charge upon Mr. Hastings, that by never taking a single step to defeat, or detect the falsehood of, any of those charges against him, and by punishing the authors of them, he has been guilty of such a subversion of all the principles of British government, as will deserve, and will, I dare say, meet, your lordships' most severe animadversion.

In the course of this inquiry we find a sort of pause in his peculations, a sort of gap in the history, as if pages were torn out. No longer we meet with the same activity in taking money, that was before found; not even a trace of complimentary presents is to be found in the records during the time, whilst General Clavering, Colonel Monson, and Mr. Francis formed the majority of the council. There seems to have been a kind of truce with that sort of conduct for a while, and Mr. Hastings rested upon his arms. However, the very moment Mr. Hastings returned to power, peculation began again just at the same instant; the moment we find him free from the compulsion and terror of a majority of persons otherwise disposed than himself, we find him at his peculation again.

My lords, at this time very serious inquiries had begun in the House of Commons concerning peculation. They did not go directly to Bengal, but they began upon the coast of Coromandel, and with the principal governors there. There was, however, a universal opinion—and justly founded—that these inquiries would go to far greater lengths. Mr. Hastings was resolved then to change the whole course and order of his proceeding. Nothing could persuade him upon any account to lay aside his system of bribery; that he was resolved to persevere in. The point was now to reconcile it with his safety. The first thing he did was to attempt to conceal it, and accordingly we find him depositing very great sums of money in the public treasury through the means of the two persons I have already mentioned, namely, the deputy treasurer and the accountant, paying them in and taking bonds for them as money of his own, and bearing legal interest.

This was his method of endeavoring to conceal some, at least, of his bribes, for I would not suggest, nor have your lordships to think, that I believe that these were his only bribes, for there is reason to think there was an infinite number besides; but it did so happen, that they were those bribes which he thought might be discovered, some of which he knew were discovered, and all of which he knew might become the subject of a parliamentary inquiry.

Mr. Hastings said he might have concealed them forever. Every one knows the facility of concealing corrupt transactions everywhere, in India particularly. But this is by himself proved not to be universally true, at least not to be true in his own opinion. For he tells you in his letter from Cheltenham, that he would have concealed the nabob's £100,000 but that the magnitude rendered it easy of discovery. He, therefore, avows an intention of concealment.

But it happens here very singularly, that this sum, which his fears of discovery by others obliged him to discover himself, happens to be one of those of which no trace whatsoever appears, except merely from the operation of his own apprehensions. There is no collateral testimony; Middleton knew nothing of it; Anderson knew nothing of it. It was not directly communicated to the faithful Larkins, or the trusty Crofts,—which proves, indeed, the facility of concealment. The fact is, you find

II—49

the application always upon the discovery. But concealment or discovery is a thing of accident.

The bribes which I have hitherto brought before your lordships belong to the first period of his bribery, before he thought of the doctrine, on which he has since defended it. There are many other bribes, which we charge him with having received during this first period, before an improving conversation and close virtuous connection with great lawyers had taught him how to practice bribes in such a manner as to defy detection, and, instead of punishment, to plead merit. I am not bound to find order and consistency in guilt; it is the reign of disorder. The order of the proceeding, as far as I am able to trace such a scene of prevarication, direct fraud, falsehood, and falsification of the public accounts, was this: From bribes he knew he could never abstain; and his then precarious situation made him the more rapacious. He knew that a few of his former bribes had been discovered, declared, recorded; that for the moment, indeed, he was secure, because all informers had been punished and all concealers rewarded. He expected hourly a total change in the council, and that men like Clavering and Monson might be again joined to Francis; that some great avenger should arise from their ashes,—*Exoriare aliquis nostris ex ossibus ultor*,—and that a more severe investigation, and an infinitely more full display, would be made of his robbery than hitherto had been done. He therefore began, in the agony of his guilt, to cast about for some device by which he might continue his offense, if possible, with impunity, and possibly make a merit of it. He therefore first carefully perused the act of Parliament, forbidding bribery, and his old covenant engaging him not to receive presents. And here he was more successful than upon former occasions. If ever an act was studiously and carefully framed to prevent bribery, it is that law of the thirteenth of the king, which he well observes admits no latitudes of construction, no subterfuge, no escape, no evasion. Yet has he found a defense of his crimes even in the very provisions which were made for their prevention and their punishment. Besides the penalty which belongs to every informer, the East India Company was invested with a fiction of property in all such bribes, in order to drag them with more facility out of the corrupt hands which held them. The covenant, with an exception of £100, and the act of Parliament without any exception, declared that the governor-general and

council should receive no presents for their own use. He therefore concluded that the system of bribery and extortion might be clandestinely and safely carried on, provided the party taking the bribes had an inward intention and mental reservation that they should be privately applied to the company's service, in any way the briber should think fit, and that on many occasions this would prove the best method of supply for the exigencies of their service.

He accordingly formed, or pretended to form, a private bribe exchequer, collateral with, and independent of, the company's public exchequer, though in some cases administered by those whom for his purposes he had placed in the regular official department. It is no wonder that he has taken to himself an extraordinary degree of merit. For surely such an invention of finance I believe never was heard of,—an exchequer wherein extortion was the assessor, fraud the cashier, confusion the accountant, concealment the reporter, and oblivion the remembrancer; in short, such as I believe no man, but one driven by guilt into frenzy, could ever have dreamed of.

He treats the official and regular directors with just contempt, as a parcel of mean, mechanical bookkeepers. He is an eccentric bookkeeper, a Pindaric accountant. I have heard of "the poet's eye in a fine frenzy rolling." Here was a revenue, exacted from whom he pleased, at what times he pleased, in what proportions he pleased, through what persons he pleased, by what means he pleased, to be accounted for or not, at his discretion, and to be applied to what service he thought proper. I do believe your lordships stand astonished at this scheme; and, indeed, I should be very loth to venture to state such a scheme at all, however I might have credited it myself, to any sober ears, if, in his defense before the House of Commons and before the lords, he had not directly admitted the fact of taking the bribes or forbidden presents, and had not in those defenses, and much more fully in his correspondence with the directors, admitted the fact, and justified it upon these very principles.

As this is a thing so unheard of and unexampled in the world, I shall first endeavor to account, as well as I can, for his motives to it, which your lordships will receive or reject, just as you shall find them tally with the evidence before you. I say, his motives to it, because I contend that public valid reasons for it he could have none, and the idea of making the corruption of

the governor-general a resource to the company never did nor could for a moment enter into his thoughts. I shall then take notice of the judicial constructions upon which he justifies his acting in this extraordinary manner. And, lastly, show you the concealments, prevarications, and falsehoods with which he endeavors to cover it, because wherever you find a concealment you make a discovery. Accounts of money received and paid ought to be regular and official.

He wrote over to the court of directors that there were certain sums of money he had received, and which were not his own, but that he had received them for their use. By this time, his intercourse with gentlemen of the law became more considerable than it had been before. When first attacked for presents, he never denied the receipt of them, or pretended to say they were for public purposes; but on looking more into the covenants, and probably with better legal advice, he found that no money could be legally received for his own use; but as these bribes were directly given and received, as for his own use, yet, says he, there was an inward destination of them in my own mind to your benefit, and to your benefit have I applied them.

Now here is a new system of bribery, contrary to law, very ingenious in the contrivance, but, I believe, as unlikely to produce its intended effect upon the mind of man as any pretense that was ever used. Here Mr. Hastings changes his ground. Before, he was accused as a peculator; he did not deny the fact; he did not refund the money; he fought it off, he stood upon the defensive, and used all the means in his power to prevent the inquiry. That was the first era of his corruption, a bold, ferocious, plain, downright use of power. In the second he is grown a little more careful and guarded, the effect of subtility. He appears no longer as a defendant, he holds himself up with a firm, dignified, and erect countenance, and says, I am not here any longer as a delinquent, a receiver of bribes, to be punished for what I have done wrong, or at least to suffer in my character for it. No, I am a great inventive genius, who have gone out of all the ordinary roads of finance, have made great discoveries in the unknown regions of that science, and have for the first time established the corruption of the supreme magistrate as a principle of resource for government.

There are crimes, undoubtedly, of great magnitude, naturally fitted to create horror, and that loudly call for punishment, that have yet no idea of turpitude annexed to them; but unclean hands, bribery, venality, and peculation are offenses of turpitude, such as, in a governor, at once debase the person, and degrade the government itself, making it not only horrible, but vile and contemptible in the eyes of all mankind. In this humiliation and abjectness of guilt, he comes here not as a criminal on his defense, but as a vast fertile genius, who has made astonishing discoveries in the art of government,—*Dicam insigne, recens, alio indictum ore,*—who, by his flaming zeal and the prolific ardor and energy of his mind, has boldly dashed out of the common path, and served his country by new and untrodden ways; and now he generously communicates, for the benefit of all future governors, and all future governments, the grand arcanum of his long and toilsome researches. He is the first, but if we do not take good care he will not be the last, that has established the corruption of the supreme magistrate among the settled resources of the State; and he leaves this principle as a bountiful donation, as the richest deposit that ever was made in the treasury of Bengal. He claims glory and renown from that, by which every other person since the beginning of time has been dishonored and disgraced. It has been said of an ambassador, that he is a person employed to tell lies for the advantage of the court that sends him. His is patriotic bribery and public-spirited corruption. He is a peculator for the good of his country. It has been said that private vices are public benefits. He goes the full length of that position, and turns his private peculation into a public good. This is what you are to thank him for. You are to consider him as a great inventor upon this occasion. Mr. Hastings improves on this principle. He is a robber in gross, and a thief in detail; he steals, he filches, he plunders, he oppresses, he extorts,—all for the good of the dear East India Company,—all for the advantage of his honored masters, the proprietors,—all in gratitude to the dear perfidious court of directors, who have been in a practice to heap "insults on his person, slanders on his character, and indignities on his station; who never had the confidence in him that they had in the meanest of his predecessors."

If you sanction this practice, if, after all you have exacted from the people by your taxes and public imposts, you are to let loose your servants upon them to extort by bribery and peculation what they can from them, for the purpose of applying it

to the public service only whenever they please,—this shocking consequence will follow from it. If your governor is discovered in taking a bribe, he will say, "What is that to you? Mind your business, I intend it for the public service." The man who dares to accuse him loses the favor of the governor-general and the India Company. They will say the governor has been doing a meritorious action, extorting bribes for our benefit, and you have the impudence to think of prosecuting him. So that the moment the bribe is detected, it is instantly turned into a merit; and we shall prove that this is the case with Mr. Hastings, whenever a bribe has been discovered.

I am now to inform your lordships that when he made these great discoveries to the court of directors he never tells them who gave him the money, upon what occasion he received it, by what hands, or to what purposes he applied it.

When he can himself give no account of his motives, and even declares that he cannot assign any cause, I am authorized and required to find motives for him,—corrupt motives for a corrupt act. There is no one capital act of his administration that did not strongly imply corruption. When a man is known to be free from all imputation of taking money, and it becomes an established part of his character, the errors, or even crimes, of his administration ought to be, and are in general, traced to other sources. You know it is a maxim. But once convict a man of bribery in any instance, and once by direct evidence, and you are furnished with a rule of irresistible presumption, that every other irregular act, by which unlawful gain may arise, is done upon the same corrupt motive. *Semel malus praesumitur semper malus.* As for good acts, candor, charity, justice oblige me not to assign evil motives, unless they serve some scandalous purpose, or terminate in some manifest evil end, so justice, reason, and common sense compel me to suppose that wicked acts have been done upon motives correspondent to their nature. Otherwise, I reverse all the principles of judgment, which can guide the human mind, and accept even the symptoms, the marks, and criteria of guilt, as presumptions of innocence. One that confounds good and evil is an enemy to the good.

His conduct upon these occasions may be thought irrational. But, thank God, guilt was never a rational thing; it distorts all the faculties of the mind, it perverts them, it leaves a man no longer in the free use of his reason, it puts him into confusion.

He has recourse to such miserable and absurd expedients for covering his guilt as all those who are used to sit in the seat of judgment know have been the cause of detection of half the villainies in the world. To argue that these could not be his reasons, because they were not wise, sound, and substantial, would be to suppose what is not true, that bad men were always discreet and able. But I can very well from the circumstances discover motives, which may affect a giddy, superficial, shattered, guilty, anxious, restless mind, full of the weak resources of fraud, craft, and intrigue, that might induce him to make these discoveries, and to make them in the manner he has done. Not rational and well-fitted for their purposes, I am very ready to admit. For God forbid that guilt should ever leave a man the free undisturbed use of his faculties. For as guilt never rose from a true use of our rational faculties, so it is very frequently subversive of them. God forbid that prudence, the first of all the virtues, as well as the supreme director of them all, should ever be employed in the service of any of the vices. No, it takes the lead, and is never found where justice does not accompany it; and if ever it is attempted to bring it into the service of the vices, it immediately subverts their cause. It tends to their discovery, and, I hope and trust, finally to their utter ruin and destruction.

In the first place I am to remark to your lordships, that the accounts he has given of one of these sums of money are totally false and contradictory. Now, there is not a stronger presumption, nor can one want more reason, to judge a transaction fraudulent, than that the accounts given of it are contradictory; and he has given three accounts utterly irreconcilable with each other. He is asked, "How came you to take bonds for this money, if it was not your own? How came you to vitiate and corrupt the state of the company's records, and to state yourself a lender to the company, when in reality you were its debtor?" His answer was, "I really cannot tell; I have forgot my reasons; the distance of time is so great [namely, a time of about two years, or not so long] I cannot give an account of the matter; perhaps I had this motive, perhaps I had another [but what is the most curious], perhaps I had none at all, which I can now recollect." You shall hear the account which Mr. Hastings himself gives, his own fraudulent representation of these corrupt transactions. "For my motives for withholding the several receipts from the

knowledge of the council, or of the court of directors, and for taking bonds for part of these sums, and paying others into the treasury as deposits on my own account, I have generally accounted in my letter to the honorable the court of directors of the twenty-second of May, 1782, namely, that I either chose to conceal the first receipts from public curiosity by receiving bonds for the amount, or possibly acted without any studied design, which my memory, at that distance of time, could verify; and that I did not think it worth my care to observe the same means with the rest. It will not be expected that I should be able to give a more correct explanation of my intentions after a lapse of three years, having declared at the time, that many particulars had escaped my remembrance; neither shall I attempt to add more than the clearer affirmation of the facts implied in that report of them, and such inferences, as necessarily, or with a strong probability, follow them."

My lords, you see, as to any direct explanation, that he fairly gives it up; he has used artifice and stratagem, which he knows will not do, and at last attempts to cover the treachery of his conduct by the treachery of his memory. Frequent applications were made to Mr. Hastings upon this article from the company, —gentle hints, *gemitus columbae,*—rather little amorous complaints, that he was not more open and communicative; but all these gentle insinuations were never able to draw from him any further account till he came to England. When he came here, he left not only his memory, but all his notes and references, behind in India. When in India, the company could get no account of them, because he himself was not in England; and when he was in England, they could get no account, because his papers were in India. He then sends over to Mr. Larkins to give that account of his affairs, which he was not able to give himself. Observe, here is a man taking money privately, corruptly, and which was to be sanctified by the future application of it, taking false securities to cover it, and who, when called upon to tell whom he got the money from, for what ends, and on what occasion, neither will tell in India, nor can tell in England, but sends for such an account as he has thought proper to furnish.

I am now to bring before you an account of what I think much the most serious part of the effects of his system of bribery, corruption, and peculation. My lords, I am to state to you the astonishing and almost incredible means he made use of to lay all the country under contribution, to bring the whole into such dejection as should put his bribes out of the way of discovery. Such another example of boldness and contrivance I believe the world cannot furnish.

I have already shown amongst the mass of his corruptions, that he let the whole of the lands to farm to the banyans. Next, that he sold the whole Mahomedan government of that country to a woman. This was bold enough, one should think; but without entering into the circumstances of the revenue change in 1772, I am to tell your lordships, that he had appointed six provincial councils, each consisting of many members who had the ordinary administration of civil justice in that country, and the whole business of the collection of the revenues.

These provincial councils accounted to the governor-general and council, who, in the revenue department, had the whole management, control, and regulation of the revenue. Mr. Hastings did, in several papers to the court of directors, declare that the establishment of these provincial councils, which at first he stated only as experimental, had proved useful in the experiment. And on that use, and upon that experiment, he had sent even the plan of an act of Parliament to have it confirmed with the last and most sacred authority of this country. The court of directors desired that if he thought any other method more proper he would send it to them for their approbation.

Thus the whole face of the British government, the whole of its order and constitution, remained from 1772 to 1781. He had got rid some time before this period, by death, of General Clavering; by death, of Colonel Monson; and by vexation and persecution, and his consequent dereliction of authority, he had shaken off Mr. Francis. The whole council consisting only of himself and Mr. Wheler, he, having the casting vote, was in effect the whole council; and if ever there was a time when principle, decency, and decorum rendered it improper for him to do any extraordinary acts without the sanction of the court of directors, that was the time. Mr. Wheler was taken off, despair, perhaps, rendering the man, who had been in opposition futilely before, compliable. The man is dead. He certainly did not oppose him; if he had, it would have been in vain. But those very circumstances which rendered it atrocious in Mr. Hastings to make any change induced him to make this. He thought that a moment's time was not to be lost,—that the other colleagues might come,

of the plan, for which he destroyed the whole English administration in India. "The committee must have a dewan, or executive officer, call him by what name you please. This man in fact has all the revenue, paid at the presidency, at his disposal and can, if he has any abilities, bring all the renters under contribution. It is little advantage to restrain the committee themselves from bribery or corruption, when their executive officer has the power of practicing both undetected.

"To display the arts employed by a native on such occasions would fill a volume. He discovers the secret resources of the zemindars and renters, their enemies and competitors; and by the engines of hope and fear, raised upon these foundations, he can work them to his purpose. The committee, with the best intentions, best abilities, and steadiest application, must, after all, be a tool in the hands of their dewan."

Your lordships see what the opinion of the council was of their own constitution. You see for what it was made. You see for what purpose the great revenue trust was taken from the council-general, from the supreme council You see for what purposes the executive power was destroyed. You have it from one of the gentlemen of this commission, at first four in number, and afterwards five, who was the most active efficient member of it. You see it was made for the purpose of being a tool in the hands of Gunga Govin Sing; that integrity, ability, and vigilance, could avail nothing; that the whole country might be laid under contribution by this man, and that he could thus practice bribery with impunity. Thus, your lordships see the delegation of all the authority of the country, above and below, is given by Mr. Hastings to this Gunga Govin Sing. The screen, the veil spread before this transaction, is torn open by the very people themselves, who are the tools in it. They confess they can do nothing; they know they are instruments in the hands of Gunga Govin Sing; and Mr. Hastings uses his name and authority to make them such in the hands of the basest, the wickedest, the corruptest, the most audacious and atrocious villain ever heard of. It is to him all the English authority is sacrificed, and four gentlemen are appointed to be his tools and instruments. Tools and instruments for what? They themselves state, that, if he has the inclination, he has the power and ability to lay the whole country under contribution, that he enters into the most minute secrets of every individual in it, gets into the

when he might be overpowered by a majority again, and not able to pursue his corrupt plans. Therefore he was resolved,— your lordships will remark the whole of this most daring and systematic plan of bribery and peculation,—he resolved to put it out of the power of his council in the future to check or control him in any of his evil practices.

The first thing he did was to form an ostensible council at Calcutta for the management of the revenues, which was not effectually bound, except it thought fit, to make any reference to the supreme council. He delegated to them — that is, to four covenanted servants — those functions which, by act of Parliament and the company's orders, were to be exercised by the council-general; he delegated to four gentlemen, creatures of his own, his own powers, but he laid them out to good interest. It appears odd that one of the first acts of a governor-general, so jealous of his power as he is known to be, as soon as he had all the power in his own hands, should be to put all the revenues out of his own control. This, upon the first view, is an extraordinary proceeding. His next step was, without apprizing the court of directors of his intention, or without having given an idea of any such intention to his colleagues while alive, either those who died in India, or those who afterwards returned to Europe, in one day, in a moment, to annihilate the whole authority of the provincial councils, and to delegate the whole power to these four gentlemen. These four gentlemen had for their secretary an agent given them by Mr. Hastings; a name that you will often hear of, a name at the sound of which all India turns pale,—the most wicked, the most atrocious, the boldest, the most dexterous villain, that ever the rank of servitude of that country has produced. My lords, I am speaking with the most assured freedom, because there never was a friend of Mr. Hastings, there never was a foe of Mr. Hastings, there never was any human person, that ever differed on this occasion, or expressed any other idea of Gunga Govin Sing, the friend of Mr. Hastings, whom he intrusted with this important post. But you shall hear, from the account given by themselves, what the council thought of their functions, of their efficiency for the charge, and in whose hands that efficiency really was. I beg, hope, and trust, that your lordships will learn from the persons themselves, who were appointed to execute the office, their opinion of the real execution of it, in order that you may judge

bottom of their family affairs, and has a power totally to subvert and destroy them; and we shall show upon that head that he well fulfilled the purposes for which he was appointed. Did Mr. Hastings pretend to say that he destroyed the provincial councils for their corruptness or insufficiency, when he dissolved them? No; he says he has no objection to their competency, no charge to make against their conduct, but that he has destroyed them for his new arrangement. And what is his new arrangement? Gunga Govin Sing. Forty English gentlemen were removed from their offices by that change. Mr. Hastings did it, however, very economically; for all these gentlemen were instantly put upon pensions, and consequently burdened the establishment with a new charge. Well, but the new council was formed and constituted upon a very economical principle also. These five gentlemen, you will have it in proof, with the necessary expenses of their office, were a charge of £62,000 a year upon the establishment. But for great, eminent, capital services, £62,000, though a much larger sum than what was thought fit to be allowed for the members of the supreme council itself, may be admitted. I will pass it. It shall be granted to Mr. Hastings, that these pensions, though they created a new burden on the establishment, were all well disposed, provided the council did their duty. But you have heard what they say themselves,— they are not there put to do any duty, they can do no duty; their abilities, their integrity availed them nothing, they are tools in the hands of Gunga Govin Sing. Mr. Hastings, then, has loaded the revenue with £62,000 a year to make Gunga Govin Sing master of the kingdom of Bengal, Bahar, and Orissa. What must the thing to be moved be, when the machinery, when the necessary tools for Gunga Govin Sing, have cost £62,000 a year to the company? There it is; it is not my representation,—not the representation of observant strangers, of good and decent people that understand the nature of that service,—but the opinion of the tools themselves.

Now, did Mr. Hastings employ Gunga Govin Sing without a knowledge of his character? His character was known to Mr. Hastings; it was recorded long before, when he was turned out of another office. During my long residence, says he, in this country, this is the first time I heard of the character of Gunga Govin Sing being infamous. No information I have received, though I have heard many people speak ill of him, ever pointed to any particular act of infamy committed by Gunga Govin Sing. I have no intimate knowledge of Gunga Govin Sing. What I understand of his character has been from Europeans as well as natives. After—"He had many enemies at the time he was proposed to be employed in the company's service, and not one advocate among the natives who had immediate access to myself. I think, therefore, if his character had been such as has been described, the knowledge of it could hardly have failed to have been ascertained to me by the specific facts. I have heard him loaded, as I have many others, with general reproaches, but have never heard any one express a doubt of his abilities." Now, if anything in the world should induce you to put the whole trust of the revenues of Bengal, both above and below, into the hands of a single man, and to delegate to him the whole jurisdiction of the country, it must be that he either was, or at least was reputed to be, a man of integrity. Mr. Hastings does not pretend that he is reputed to be a man of integrity. He knew that he was not able to contradict the charge brought against him; and that he had been turned out of office by his colleagues, for reasons assigned upon record, and approved by the directors, for malversation in office. He had, indeed, crept again into the Calcutta committee; and they were upon the point of turning him out for malversation, when Mr. Hastings saved them the trouble by turning out the whole committee, consisting of a president and five members. So that in all times, in all characters, in all places, he stood as a man of a bad character and evil repute, though supposed to be a man of great abilities.

My lords, permit me for one moment to drop my representative character here, and to speak to your lordships only as a man of some experience in the world, and conversant with the affairs of men and with the characters of men.

I do then declare my conviction, and wish it may stand recorded to posterity, that there never was a bad man, that had ability for good service. It is not in the nature of such men: their minds are so distorted to selfish purposes, to knavish, artificial, and crafty means of accomplishing those selfish ends, that if put to any good service, they are poor, dull, helpless. Their natural faculties never have that direction,—they are paralytic on that side; the muscles, if I may use the expression, that ought to move it, are all dead. They know nothing, but how to

pursue selfish ends by wicked and indirect means. No man ever knowingly employed a bad man on account of his abilities, but for evil ends. Mr. Hastings knew this man to be bad; all the world knew him to be bad; and how did he employ him? In such a manner as that he might be controlled by others? A great deal might be said for him, if this had been the case. There might be circumstances, in which such a man might be used in a subordinate capacity. But who ever thought of putting such a man virtually in possession of the whole authority, both of the committee and the council-general, and of the revenues of the whole country?

I will do Mr. Hastings the justice to say, that if he had known there was another man more accomplished in all iniquity than Gunga Govin Sing he would not have given him the first place in his confidence. But there is another next to him in the country, whom you are to hear of by and by, called Debi Sing. This person in the universal opinion of all Bengal is ranked next to Gunga Govin Sing; and, what is very curious, they have been recorded by Mr. Hastings as rivals in the same virtues.

"Arcades ambo,
Et cantare pares, et respondere parati."

But Mr. Hastings has the happiest modes in the world; these rivals were reconciled on this occasion, and Gunga Govin Sing appoints Debi Sing, superseding all the other officers for no reason whatever upon record. And because, like champions, they ought to go in pairs, there is an English gentleman, one Mr. Goodlad, whom you will hear of presently, appointed along with him. Absolute strangers to the rajah's family, the first act they do is to cut off one thousand out of one thousand six hundred a month from his allowance. They state, though there was a great number of dependents to maintain, that six hundred would be enough to maintain him. There appears in the account of these proceedings to be such a flutter about the care of the rajah, and the management of his household—in short, that there never was such a tender guardianship as, always with the knowledge of Mr. Hastings, is exercised over this poor rajah, who had just given, if he did give, £40,000 for his own inheritance, if it was his due,—for the inheritance of others, if it was not his due. One would think he was entitled to some mercy; but probably, because the money could not otherwise be supplied, his establishment was cut down

by Debi Sing and Mr. Goodlad a thousand a month, which is just twelve thousand a year.

When Mr. Hastings had appointed those persons to the guardianship who had an interest in the management of the rajah's education and fortune, one should have thought, before they were turned out, he would at least have examined whether such a step was proper or not. No, they were turned out, without any such examination; and when I come to inquire into the proceedings of Gunga Govin Sing's committee, I do not find that the new guardians have brought to account one single shilling they received, appointed as they were by that council newly made to superintend all the affairs of the rajah.

There is not one word to be found of an account. Debi Sing's honor, fidelity, and disinterestedness, and that of Mr. Goodlad, is sufficient; and that is the way in which the management and superintendence of one of the greatest houses in that country is given to the guardianship of strangers. And how is it managed? We find Debi Sing in possession of the rajah's family, in possession of his affairs, in the management of his whole zemindary; and in the course of the next year he is to give him in farm the whole of the revenues of these three provinces. Now, whether the peshcush was received for the nomination of the rajah, as a bribe in judgment, or whether Mr. Hastings got it from Debi Sing, as a bribe in office, for appointing him to the guardianship of a family that did not belong to him, and for the dominion of three great, and once wealthy, provinces—which is best or worst I shall not pretend to determine. You find the rajah in his possession; you find his education, his household in his possession. The public revenues are in his possession; they are given over to him.

If we look at the records, the letting of these provinces appears to have been carried on by the new committee of revenue, as the course and order of business required it should. But by the investigation into Mr. Hastings's money transactions, the insufficiency and fallacy of these records is manifest beyond a doubt. From this investigation it is discovered that it was in reality a bargain secretly struck between the governor-general and Debi Sing, and that the committee were only employed in the mere official forms. From the time that Mr. Hastings newly modeled the revenue system, nothing is seen in its true shape. We now know, in spite of the fallacy of these records, who the

true grantor was; it will not be amiss to go a little further in supplying their defects, and to inquire a little concerning the grantee. This makes it necessary for me to inform your lordships who Debi Sing is.

[Mr. Burke here read the committee's recommendation of Debi Sing to the governor-general and council.]

Here is a choice, here is Debi Sing presented for his knowledge in business, his trust, and fidelity, and that he is a person against whom no objection can be made. This is presented to Mr. Hastings, by him recorded in the council books, and by him transmitted to the court of directors. Mr. Hastings has since recorded that he knew this Debi Sing,—though he here publicly authorizes the nomination of him to all that great body of trusts,—that he knew him to be a man completely capable of the most atrocious iniquities that were ever charged upon man. Debi Sing is appointed to all those great trusts through the means of Gunga Govin Sing, from whom he, Mr. Hastings, had received £30,000 as a part of a bribe.

Now, though it is a large field, though it is a thing that, I must confess, I feel a reluctance almost in venturing to undertake, exhausted as I am, yet such is the magnitude of the affair, such the evil consequences that followed from a system of bribery, such the horrible consequences of superseding all the persons in office in the country to give it into the hands of Debi Sing, that though it is the public opinion, and though no man that has ever heard the name of Debi Sing does not know that he was only second to Gunga Govin Sing, yet it is not to my purpose, unless I prove that Mr. Hastings knew his character at the very time he accepts him as a person against whom no exception could be made.

It is necessary to inform your lordship who this Debi Sing was, to whom these great trusts were committed, and those great provinces given.

It may be thought, and not unnaturally, that in this sort of corrupt and venal appointment to high trust and office, Mr. Hastings has no other consideration than the money he received. But whoever thinks so will be deceived. Mr. Hastings was very far from indifferent to the character of the persons he dealt with. On the contrary, he made a most careful selection; he had a very scrupulous regard to the aptitude of the men for the purposes for which he employed them, and was much guided by his experience of their conduct in those offices which had been sold to them upon former occasions.

Except Gunga Govin Sing, whom, as justice required, Mr. Hastings distinguished by the highest marks of his confidence, there was not a man in Bengal, perhaps not upon earth, a match for this Debi Sing. He was not an unknown subject; not one rashly taken up as an experiment. He was a tried man; and if there had been one more desperately and abandonedly corrupt, more wildly and flagitiously oppressive, to be found unemployed in India, large as his offers were, Mr. Hastings would not have taken this money from Debi Sing.

Debi Sing was one of those who, in the early stages of the English power in Bengal, attached himself to those natives who then stood high in office. He courted Mahomed Reza Khân, a Mussulman of the highest rank, of the tribe of Koreish, whom I have already mentioned, then at the head of the revenue, and now at the head of the criminal justice of Bengal, with all the supple assiduity, of which those who possess no valuable art or useful talent are commonly complete masters. Possessing large funds acquired by his apprenticeship and novitiate in the lowest frauds, he was enabled to lend to this then powerful man, in the several emergencies of his variable fortune, very large sums of money. This great man had been brought down by Mr. Hastings, under the orders of the court of directors, upon a cruel charge, to Calcutta. He was accused of many crimes, and acquitted, £220,000 in debt. That is to say, as soon as he was a great debtor, he ceased to be a great criminal.

Debi Sing obtained, by his services, no slight influence over Mahomed Reza Khân, a person of a character very different from his.

From that connection he was appointed to the farm of the revenue, and inclusively of the government of Purnea, a province of very great extent, and then in a state of no inconsiderable opulence. In this office he exerted his talents with so much vigor and industry, that in a very short time the province was half depopulated and totally ruined.

The farm, on the expiration of his lease, was taken by a set of adventurers in this kind of traffic from Calcutta. But when the new undertakers came to survey the object of their future operations and future profits, they were so shocked at the hideous

and squalid scenes of misery and desolation that glared upon them in every quarter, that they instantly fled out of the country, and thought themselves but too happy to be permitted, on the payment of a penalty of £12,000, to be released from their engagements.

To give in a few words as clear an idea as I am able to give of the immense volume which might be composed of the vexations, violence, and rapine of that tyrannical administration, the territorial revenue of Purnea, which had been let to Debi Sing at the rate of £160,000 sterling a year, was with difficulty leased for a yearly sum under £90,000, and with all rigor of exaction produced in effect little more than £60,000, falling greatly below one-half of its original estimate. So entirely did the administration of Debi Sing exhaust all the resources of the province. So totally did his baleful influence blast the very hope and spring of all future revenue.

The administration of Debi Sing was too notoriously destructive not to cause a general clamor. It was impossible that it should be passed over without animadversion. Accordingly, in the month of September 1772, Mr. Hastings, then at the head of the committee of circuit, removed him for maladministration, and he has since publicly declared on record, that he knew him to be capable of all the most horrid and atrocious crimes that can be imputed to man.

This brand, however, was only a mark for Mr. Hastings to find him out hereafter in the crowd; to identify him for his own; and to call him forth into action, when his virtues should be sufficiently matured for the services, in which he afterwards employed him through his instruments, Mr. Anderson and Gunga Govin Sing. In the meantime he left Debi Sing to the direction of his own good genius.

Debi Sing was stigmatized in the company's records, his reputation was gone, but his funds were safe. In the arrangement made by Mr. Hastings in the year 1773, by which provincial councils were formed, Debi Sing became deputy steward or secretary, soon in effect and influence principal steward, to the provincial council of Moorshedabad, the seat of the old government, and the first province of the kingdom; and to his charge were committed various extensive and populous provinces, yielding an annual revenue of one hundred and twenty lacs of rupees, or £1,500,000. This division of provincial council included

Rungpore, Edrackpore, and others, where he obtained such a knowledge of their resources as subsequently to get possession of them.

Debi Sing found this administration composed mostly of young men, dissipated and fond of pleasure, as is usual at that time of life, but desirous of reconciling those pleasures, which usually consume wealth, with the means of making a great and speedy fortune, at once eager candidates for opulence and perfect novices in all the roads that lead to it. Debi Sing commiserated their youth and inexperience, and took upon him to be their guide.

There is a revenue in that country, raised by a tax more productive than laudable. It is an imposition on public prostitutes, a duty upon the societies of dancing girls; those seminaries, from which Mr. Hastings has selected an administrator of justice and governor of kingdoms. Debi Sing thought it expedient to farm this tax, not only because he neglected no sort of gain, but because he regarded it as no contemptible means of power and influence. Accordingly, in plain terms, he opened a legal brothel, out of which he carefully reserved — you may be sure — the very flower of his collection for the entertainment of his young superiors; ladies recommended not only by personal merit, but, according to the Eastern custom, by sweet and enticing names, which he had given them. For, if they were to be translated they would sound:—Riches of my Life, Wealth of my Soul, Treasure of Perfection, Diamond of Splendor, Pearl of Price, Ruby of Pure Blood, and other metaphorical descriptions, that, calling up dissonant passions to enhance the value of the general harmony, heightened the attractions of love with the allurements of avarice. A moving seraglio of these ladies always attended his progress, and were always brought to the splendid and multiplied entertainments, with which he regaled his council. In these festivities, whilst his guests were engaged with the seductions of beauty, the intoxications of the most delicious wines of France, and the voluptuous vapor of perfumed India smoke, uniting the vivid satisfactions of Europe with the torpid blandishments of Asia, the great magician himself, chaste in the midst of dissoluteness, sober in the centre of debauch, vigilant in the lap of negligence and oblivion, attended with an eagle's eye the moment for thrusting in business, and at such times was able to carry without difficulty points of shameful enormity, which at

other hours he would not so much as have dared to mention to his employers, young men rather careless and inexperienced than intentionally corrupt. Not satisfied with being pander to their pleasures, he anticipated, and was purveyor to, their wants, and supplied them with a constant command of money; and by these means he reigned with an uncontrolled dominion over the province and over its governors.

For you are to understand that in many things we are very much misinformed with regard to the true seat of power in India. Whilst we were proudly calling India a British government, it was in substance a government of the lowest, basest, and most flagitious of the native rabble, to whom the far greater part of the English, who figured in employment and station, had from their earliest youth been slaves and instruments. Banyans had anticipated the period of their power in premature advances of money, and have ever after obtained the entire dominion over their nominal masters.

By these various ways and means, Debi Sing contrived to add job to job, employment to employment, and to hold, besides the farms of two very considerable districts, various trusts in the revenue; sometimes openly appearing; sometimes hid two or three deep in false names; emerging into light, or shrouding himself in darkness, as successful, or defeated crimes rendered him bold or cautious. Every one of these trusts was marked with its own fraud; and for one of those frauds committed by him in another name, by which he became deeply in balance to the revenue, he was publicly whipped by proxy.

All this while Mr. Hastings kept his eye upon him, and attended to his progress. But, as he rose in Mr. Hastings's opinion, he fell in that of his immediate employers. By degrees, as reason prevailed and the fumes of pleasure evaporated, the provincial council emerged from their first dependence, and, finding nothing but infamy attending the councils and services of such a man, resolved to dismiss him. In this strait and crisis of his power, the artist turned himself into all shapes. He offered great sums individually; he offered them collectively; and at last put a carte blanche on the table — all to no purpose! What! are you stones?—Have I not men to deal with?—Will flesh and blood refuse me?

When Debi Sing found that the council had entirely escaped, and were proof against his offers, he left them with a sullen and menacing silence. He applied where he had good intelligence that these offers would be well received, and that he should at once be revenged of the council, and obtain all the ends which through them he had sought in vain.

Without hesitation or scruple, Mr. Hastings sold a set of innocent officers; sold his fellow-servants of the company, entitled by every duty to his protection; sold English subjects, recommended by every tie of national sympathy; sold the honor of the British government itself; without charge, without complaint, without allegation of crime in conduct, or of insufficiency in talents. He sold them to the most known and abandoned character which the rank servitude of that clime produces. For him, he entirely broke and quashed the council of Moorshedabad, which had been the settled government for twelve years,—a long period in the changeful history of India,—at a time, too, when it had acquired a great degree of consistency, an official experience, a knowledge and habit of business, and was making full amends for early errors.

For now Mr. Hastings, having buried Colonel Monson and General Clavering, and having shaken off Mr. Francis, who retired half dead from office, began at length to respire; he found elbow-room once more to display his genuine nature and disposition, and to make amends in a riot and debauch of peculation for the forced abstinence to which he was reduced during the usurped dominion of honor and integrity.

It was not enough that the English were thus sacrificed to the revenge of Debi Sing. It was necessary to deliver over the natives to his avarice. By the intervention of bribe brokerage, he united the two great rivals in iniquity, who before, from an emulation of crimes, were enemies to each other, Gunga Govin Sing and Debi Sing. He negotiated the bribe and the farm of the latter through the former, and Debi Sing was invested in farm for two years with the three provinces of Dinagepore, Edrackpore, and Rungpore,—territories, making together a tract of land superior in dimensions to the northern counties of England, Yorkshire included.

To prevent anything which might prove an obstacle on the full swing of his genius, he removed all the restraints which had been framed to give an ostensible credit, to give some show of official order to the plans of revenue administration framed from time to time in Bengal. An officer, called a dewan, had been

established in the provinces, expressly as a check on the person who should act as farmer-general. This office he conferred along with that of farmer-general on Debi Sing, in order that Debi might become an effectual check upon Sing; and thus these provinces, without inspection, without control, without law, and without magistrates, were delivered over by Mr. Hastings, bound hand and foot, to the discretion of the man, whom he had before recorded as the destroyer of Purnea, and capable of every most atrocious wickedness that could be imputed to man.

Fatally for the natives of India, every wild project and every corrupt sale of Mr. Hastings, and those whose example he followed, is covered with a pretended increase of revenue to the company. Mr. Hastings would not pocket his bribe of £40,000 for himself without letting the company in as a sharer and accomplice. For the province of Rungpore, the object to which I mean in this instance to confine your attention, £7,000 a year were added. But lest this avowed increase of rent should seem to lead to oppression, great and religious care was taken in the covenant, so stipulated with Debi Sing that this increase should not arise from any additional assessment whatsoever on the country, but solely from improvements in the cultivation and the encouragement to be given to the landholder and husbandman. But as Mr. Hastings's bribe of a far greater sum was not guarded by any such provision, it was left to the discretion of the donor in what manner he was to indemnify himself for it.

Debi Sing fixed the seat of his authority at Dinagepore, where as soon as he arrived he did not lose a moment in doing his duty. If Mr. Hastings can forget his covenant, you may easily believe that Debi Sing had not a more correct memory, and, accordingly, as soon as he came into the province, he instantly broke every covenant which he had entered into, as a restraint on his avarice, rapacity, and tyranny, which, from the highest of the nobility and gentry to the lowest husbandman, were afterwards exercised with a stern and unrelenting impartiality upon the whole people. For, notwithstanding the province before Debi Sing's lease was, from various causes, in a state of declension, and in balance for the revenue of the preceding year, at his very first entrance into office he forced from the zemindars or landed gentry an enormous increase of their tribute. They refused compliance. On this refusal he threw the whole body of zemindars into prison, and thus in bonds and fetters compelled

them to sign their own ruin by an increase of rent, which they knew they could never realize.

Having thus gotten them under, he added exaction to exaction, so that every day announced some new and varied demand, until, exhausted by these oppressions, they were brought to the extremity to which he meant to drive them,—the sale of their lands.

The lands held by the zemindars of that country are of many descriptions. The first and most general are those that pay revenue. The others are of the nature of demesne lands, which are free and pay no rent to government. The latter are for the immediate support of the zemindars and their families, as from the former they derive their influence, authority, and the means of upholding their dignity. The lands of the former description were immediately attached, sequestered, and sold for the most trifling consideration. The rent-free lands, the best and richest lands of the whole province, were sold—sold for—what do your lordships think? They were sold for less than one year's purchase,—at less than one year's purchase, at the most underrated value; so that the fee simple of an English acre of rent-free land sold at the rate of seven or eight shillings. Such a sale on such terms strongly indicated the purchaser. And how did it turn out in fact? The purchaser was the very agent and instrument of Mr. Hastings, Debi Sing himself. He made the exaction; he forced the sale; he reduced the rate; and he became the purchaser at less than one year's purchase, and paid with the very money which he had extorted from the miserable vendors.

When he had thus sold and separated these lands, he united the whole body of them, amounting to about £7,000 a year (but according to the rate of money and living in that country equivalent to a rental in England of £30,000 a year); and then having raised in the new letting, as on the sale he had fraudulently reduced those lands, he reserved them as an estate for himself, or to whomsoever resembling himself Mr. Hastings should order them to be disposed.

The lands, thus sold for next to nothing, left, of course, the late landholder still in debt. The failure of fund, the rigorous exaction of debt, and the multiplication of new arbitrary taxes next carried off the goods. There is a circumstance attending this business, which will call for your lordships' pity. Most of the landholders or zemindars in that country happened at that

time to be women. The sex there is in a state certainly resembling imprisonment, but guarded as a sacred treasure with all possible attention and respect. None of the coarse male hands of the law can reach them; but they have a custom, very cautiously used in all good governments there, of employing female bailiffs, or sergeants, in the execution of the law, where that sex is concerned. Guards, therefore, surrounded the houses, and then female sergeants and bailiffs entered into the habitations of these female zemindars, and held their goods and persons in execution, nothing being left but, what was daily threatened, their life and honor. The landholders, even women of eminent rank and condition, for such the greater part of the zemindars then were, fled from the ancient seats of their ancestors and left their miserable followers and servants, who in that country are infinitely numerous, without protection and without bread. The monthly installment of Mr. Hastings's bribe was become due, and his rapacity must be fed from the vitals of the people.

The zemindars, before their own flight, had the mortification of seeing all the lands assigned to charitable and to religious uses, the humane and pious foundations of themselves and their ancestors, made to support infirmity and decrepitude, to give feet to the lame and eyes to the blind, and to effect which they had deprived themselves of many of the enjoyments of life, cruelly sequestered and sold at the same market of violence and fraud, where their demesne possessions and their goods had been before made away with. Even the lands and funds set aside for their funeral ceremonies, in which they hoped to find an end to their miseries, and some indemnity of imagination for all the substantial sufferings of their lives; even the very feeble consolations of death were by the same rigid hand of tyranny, a tyranny more consuming than the funeral pile, more greedy than the grave, and more inexorable than death itself, seized and taken to make good the honor of corruption and the faith of bribery pledged to Mr. Hastings or his instruments.

Thus it fared with the better and middling orders of the people. Were the lower, the more industrious, spared? Alas! as their situation was far more helpless, their oppression was infinitely more sore and grievous, the exactions yet more excessive, the demand yet more vexatious, more capricious, more arbitrary. To afford your lordships some idea of the condition of those who were served up to satisfy Mr. Hastings's hunger and thirst for bribes, I shall read it to you in the very words of the representative tyrant himself, Rajah Debi Sing. Debi Sing, when he was charged with a fraudulent sale of the ornaments of gold and silver of women, who, according to the modes of that country, had starved themselves to decorate their unhappy persons, argued on the improbability of this part of the charge, in these very words:—

"It is notorious," says he, "that poverty generally prevails amongst the husbandmen of Rungpore, more perhaps than in any other parts of the country. They are seldom possessed of any property, except at the time they reap their harvest; and at others, barely procure their subsistence. And this is the cause that such numbers of them were swept away by the famine. Their effects are only a little earthenware, and their houses only a handful of straw, the sale of a thousand of which would not perhaps produce twenty shillings."

These were the opulent people from whose superfluities Mr. Hastings was to obtain a gift of £40,000 over and above a large increase of rent, over and above the exactions by which the farmer must reimburse himself for the advance of the money, by which he must obtain the natural profit of the farm, as well as supply the peculium of his own avarice.

Therefore your lordships will not be surprised at the consequences. All this unhappy race of little farmers and tillers of the soil were driven like a herd of cattle by his extortioners, and compelled by imprisonments, by fetters, and by cruel whippings, to engage for more than the whole of their substance or possible acquisition.

Over and above this, there was no mode of extortion which the inventive imagination of rapacity could contrive, that was not contrived and was not put in practice. On its own day your lordships will hear with astonishment, detestation, and horror, the detail of these tyrannous inventions; and it will appear that the aggregate of these superadded demands amounted to as great a sum as the whole of the compulsory rent on which they were piled.

The country being in many parts left wholly waste, and in all parts considerably depopulated by the first rigors, the full rate of the district was exacted from the miserable survivors. Their burdens were increased as their fellow-laborers, to whose

joint efforts they were to owe the means of payment, diminished. Driven to make payments, beyond all possible calculation, previous to receipts and above their means, in a very short time they fell into the hands of usurers.

The usurers, who under such a government held their own funds by a precarious tenure, and were to lend to those whose substance was still more precarious,—to the natural hardness and austerity of that race of men,—had additional motives to extortion, and made their terms accordingly. And what were the terms these poor people were obliged to consent to, to answer the bribes and peshcush paid to Mr. Hastings? Five, ten, twenty, forty cent.? No! at an interest of six hundred per cent. per annum, payable by the day! A tiller of land to pay six hundred per cent., to discharge the demands of government! What exhaustless fund of opulence could supply this destructive resource of wretchedness and misery? Accordingly, the husbandman ground to powder between the usurer below and the oppressor above, the whole crop of the country was forced at once to market; and the market glutted, overcharged, and suffocated, the price of grain fell to the fifth part of its usual value. The crop was then gone, but the debt remained. A universal treasury extent, and process of execution, followed on the cattle and stock, and was enforced, with more or less rigor, in every quarter. We have it in evidence that in those sales five cows were sold for not more than seven or eight shillings. All other things were depreciated in the same proportion. The sale of the instruments of husbandry succeeded to that of the corn and stock. Instances there are, where, all other things failing, the farmers were dragged from the court to their houses in order to see them first plundered and then burned down before their faces. It was not a rigorous collection of revenue, it was a savage war made upon the country.

The peasants were left little else than their families and their bodies. The families were disposed of. It is a known observation that those who have the fewest of all other worldly enjoyments are the most tenderly attached to their children and wives. The most tender of parents sold their children at market. The most fondly jealous of husbands sold their wives. The tyranny of Mr. Hastings extinguished every sentiment of father, son, brother, and husband.

I come now to the last stage of their miseries; everything visible and vendible was seized and sold. Nothing but the bodies remained.

It is the nature of tyranny and rapacity never to learn moderation from the ill success of first oppressions; on the contrary, all oppressors, all men thinking highly of the methods dictated by their nature, attribute the frustration of their desires to the want of sufficient rigor. Then they redouble the efforts of their impotent cruelty, which producing, as they must ever produce, new disappointments, they grow irritated against the objects of their rapacity; and then rage, fury, and malice,—implacable because unprovoked,—recruiting and reinforcing their avarice, their vices are no longer human. From cruel men they are transformed into savage beasts, with no other vestiges of reason left but what serves to furnish the inventions and refinements of ferocious subtlety, for purposes of which beasts are incapable and at which fiends would blush.

Debi Sing and his instruments suspected, and in a few cases they suspected justly, that the country people had purloined from their own estates, and had hidden in secret places in the circumjacent deserts, some small reserve of their own grain to maintain themselves during the unproductive months of the year, and to leave some hope for a future season. But the under-tyrants knew that the demands of Mr. Hastings would admit no plea for delay, much less for subtraction of his bribe, and that he would not abate a shilling of it to the wants of the whole human race. These hoards, real or supposed, not being discovered by menaces and imprisonment, they fell upon the last resource, the naked bodies of the people. And here, my lords, began such a scene of cruelties and tortures as I believe no history has ever presented to the indignation of the world; such as I am sure, in the most barbarous ages, no politic tyranny, no fanatic persecution has ever yet exceeded. Mr. Patterson, the commissioner appointed to inquire into the state of the country, makes his own apology and mine for opening this scene of horrors to you, in the following words: "The punishments inflicted upon the ryots of Rungpore and Dinagepore for nonpayment were in many instances of such a nature that I would rather wish to draw a veil over them than shock your feelings by the detail. But however disagreeable the task may be to myself, it is absolutely necessary for the sake of justice, humanity, and the honor of

government that they should be exposed, to be prevented in future."

My lords, they began by winding cords round the fingers of the unhappy freeholders of those provinces, until they clung to and were almost incorporated with one another, and then they hammered wedges of iron between them, until, regardless of the cries of the sufferers, they had bruised to pieces and forever crippled those poor, honest, innocent, laborious hands, which had never been raised to their mouths but with a penurious and scanty proportion of the fruits of their own soil; but those fruits, denied to the wants of their own children, have for more than fifteen years past furnished the investment for our trade with China, and been sent annually out, and without recompense, to purchase for us that delicate meal with which your lordships, and all this auditory, and all this country, have begun every day for these fifteen years at their expense. To those beneficent hands that labor for our benefit, the return of the British government has been cords and hammers and wedges. But there is a place where these crippled and disabled hands will act with resistless power. What is it that they will not pull down when they are lifted to heaven against their oppressors? Then what can withstand such hands? Can the power that crushed and destroyed them? Powerful in prayer, let us at least deprecate, and thus endeavor to secure ourselves from the vengeance which those mashed and disabled hands may pull down upon us. My lords, it is an awful consideration. Let us think of it.

But to pursue this melancholy but necessary detail. I am next to open to your lordships, what I am hereafter to prove, that the most substantial and leading yeomen, the responsible farmers, the parochial magistrates, and chiefs of villages, were tied two and two by the legs together, and their tormentors, throwing them with their heads downwards over a bar, beat them on the soles of the feet with ratans until the nails fell from the toes, and then attacking them at their heads, as they hung downward, as before at their feet, they beat them with sticks and other instruments of blind fury until the blood gushed out at their eyes, mouths, and noses.

Not thinking that the ordinary whips and cudgels, even so administered, were sufficient to others,—and often also to the same, who had suffered as I have stated,—they applied, instead of ratan and bamboo, whips made of the branches of the bale tree, a tree full of sharp and strong thorns which tear the skin and lacerate the flesh far worse than ordinary scourges.

For others, exploring with a searching and inquisitive malice, stimulated by an insatiate rapacity, all the devious paths of nature for whatever is most unfriendly to man, they made rods of a plant highly caustic and poisonous, called *bechettea*, every wound of which festers and gangrenes, adds double and treble to the present torture, leaves a crust of leprous sores upon the body, and often ends in the destruction of life itself.

At night these poor innocent sufferers, these martyrs of avarice and extortion, were brought into dungeons; and in the season when nature takes refuge in insensibility from all the miseries and cares which wait on life, they were three times scourged, and made to reckon the watches of the night by periods and intervals of torment. They were then led out in the severe depth of winter, which there at certain seasons would be severe to any one, and to the Indians is most severe and almost intolerable,—they were led out before break of day, and, stiff and sore as they were with the bruises and wounds of the night, were plunged into water, and whilst their jaws clung together with the cold, and their bodies were rendered infinitely more sensible, the blows and stripes were renewed upon their backs; and then, delivering them over to soldiers, they were sent into their farms and villages to discover where a few handfuls of grain might be found concealed, or to extract some loan from the remnants of compassion and courage not subdued in those who had reason to fear that their own turn of torment would be next, that they should succeed them in the same punishment and that their very humanity, being taken as a proof of their wealth, would subject them—as it did in many cases subject them—to the same inhuman tortures. After this circuit of the day through their plundered and ruined villages, they were remanded at night to the same prison; whipped, as before, at their return to the dungeon, and at morning whipped at their leaving it; and then sent as before to purchase, by begging in the day, the reiteration of the torture in the night. Days of menace, insult, and extortion; nights of bolts, fetters, and flagellation succeeded to each other in the same round, and for a long time made up all the vicissitude of life to these miserable people.

But there are persons whose fortitude could bear their own suffering; there are men who are hardened by their very pains;

and the mind, strengthened even by the torments of the body, rises with a strong defiance against its oppressor. They were assaulted on the side of their sympathy. Children were scourged almost to death in the presence of their parents. This was not enough. The son and father were bound close together, face to face, and body to body, and in that situation cruelly lashed together, so that the blow, which escaped the father, fell upon the son, and the blow, which missed the son, wound over the back of the parent. The circumstances were combined by so subtle a cruelty, that every stroke, which did not excruciate the sense, should wound and lacerate the sentiments and affections of nature.

On the same principle and for the same ends, virgins, who had never seen the sun, were dragged from the inmost sanctuaries of their houses, and in the open court of justice, in the very place where security was to be sought against all wrong and all violence,—but where no judge or lawful magistrate had long sat, but in their place the ruffians and hangmen of Warren Hastings occupied the bench,—these virgins, vainly invoking heaven and earth, in the presence of their parents, and whilst their shrieks were mingled with the indignant cries and groans of all the people, publicly were violated by the lowest and wickedest of the human race. Wives were torn from the arms of their husbands, and suffered the same flagitious wrongs, which were, indeed, hid in the bottoms of the dungeons, in which their honor and their liberty were buried together. Often they were taken out of the refuge of this consoling gloom, stripped naked, and thus exposed to the world, and then cruelly scourged; and in order that cruelty might riot in all the circumstances that melt into tenderness the fiercest natures, the nipples of their breasts were put between the sharp and elastic sides of cleft bamboos. Here, in my hand, is my authority; for otherwise one would think it incredible. But it did not end there. Growing from crime to crime, ripened by cruelty for cruelty, these fiends, at length outraging sex, decency, nature, applied lighted torches and slow fire—I cannot proceed for shame and horror! These infernal furies planted death in the source of life, and where that modesty, which, more than reason, distinguishes men from beasts, retires from the view, and even shrinks from expression, there they exercised and glutted their unnatural, monstrous, and nefarious cruelty,—there, where the reverence of nature and the sanctity of justice dares not to pursue, nor venture to describe their practices.

These, my lords, were sufferings which we feel all in common in India and in England, by the general sympathy of our common nature. But there were in that province—sold to the tormentors by Mr. Hastings—things done, which, from the peculiar manners of India, were even worse than all I have laid before you, as the dominion of manners, and the law of opinion, contribute more to their happiness and misery than anything in mere sensitive nature can do.

The women thus treated lost their caste. My lords, we are not here to commend or blame the institutions and prejudices of a whole race of people, radicated in them by a long succession of ages, on which no reason or argument, on which no vicissitudes of things, no mixtures of men, or foreign conquest, have been able to make the smallest impression. The aboriginal Gentû inhabitants are all dispersed into tribes or castes; each caste born to an invariable rank, rights, and descriptions of employment, so that one caste cannot by any means pass into another. With the Gentûs certain impurities or disgraces, though without any guilt of the party, infer loss of caste; and when the highest caste, that of Brahmin, which is not only noble but sacred, is lost, the person who loses it does not slide down into one lower but reputable—he is wholly driven from all honest society. All the relations of life are at once dissolved. His parents are no longer his parents; his wife is no longer his wife; his children, no longer his, are no longer to regard him as their father. It is something far worse than complete outlawry, complete attainder, and universal excommunication. It is a pollution even to touch him; and if he touches any of his old caste, they are justified in putting him to death. Contagion, leprosy, plague, are not so much shunned. No honest occupation can be followed. He becomes an *Halichore*, if, which is rare, he survives that miserable degradation.

Upon those whom all the shocking catalogue of tortures I have mentioned could not make to flinch, one of the modes of losing caste for Brahmins, and other principal tribes, was practiced. It was to harness a bullock at the court door, put the Brahmin on his back, and lead him through the towns, with drums beating before him. To intimidate others, this bullock, with drums, the instruments according to their ideas of outrage, disgrace, and utter loss of caste, was led through the country, and as it advanced, the country fled before it. When

any Brahmin was seized he was threatened with this pillory, and for the most part he submitted in a moment to whatever was ordered. What it was may be thence judged. But when no possibility existed of complying with the demand, the people, by their cries, sometimes prevailed on the tyrants to have it commuted for cruel scourging, which was accepted as mercy. To some Brahmins this mercy was denied, and the act of indelible infamy executed. Of these men one came to the company's commissioner with the tale, and ended with these melancholy words: "I have suffered this indignity; my caste is lost; my life is a burden to me; I call for justice." He called in vain.

Your lordships will not wonder that these monstrous and oppressive demands, exacted with such tortures, threw the whole province into despair. They abandoned their crops on the ground. The people in a body would have fled out of its confines, but bands of soldiers invested the avenues of the province, and, making a line of circumvallation, drove back those wretches, who sought exile, as a relief, into the prison of their native soil. Not suffered to quit the district, they fled to the many wild thickets, which oppression had scattered through it, and sought amongst the jungles and dens of tigers a refuge from the tyranny of Warren Hastings. Not able long to exist here, pressed at once by wild beasts and famine, the same despair drove them back; and seeking their last resource in arms, the most quiet, the most passive, the most timid of the human race, rose up in a universal insurrection, and, what will always happen in popular tumults, the effects of the fury of the people fell on the meaner and sometimes the reluctant instruments of the tyranny, who, in several places, were massacred. The insurrection began in Rungpore, and soon spread its fire to the neighboring provinces which had been harassed by the same person with the same oppressions. The English chief in that province had been the silent witness, most probably the abettor and accomplice, of all these horrors. He called in first irregular, and then regular, troops, who, by dreadful and universal military execution, got the better of the impotent resistance of unarmed and undisciplined despair. I am tired with the detail of the cruelties of peace. I spare you those of a cruel and inhuman war and of the executions, which, without law or process, or even the shadow of authority, were ordered by the English revenue chief in that province.

It has been necessary to lay these facts before you,—and I have stated them to your lordships far short of their reality, partly through my infirmity, and partly on account of the odiousness of the task of going through things that disgrace human nature,—that you may be enabled fully to enter into the dreadful consequences which attend a system of bribery and corruption in a governor-general. On a transient view, bribery is rather a subject of disgust than horror; the sordid practice of a venal, mean, and abject mind; and the effect of the crime seems to end with the act. It looks to be no more than the corrupt transfer of property from one person to another; at worst a theft. But it will appear in a very different light when you regard the consideration for which the bribe is given, namely, that a governor-general, claiming an arbitrary power in himself, for that consideration delivers up the properties, the liberties, and the lives of a whole people to the arbitrary discretion of any wicked and rapacious person who will be sure to make good from their blood the purchase he has paid for his power over them. It is possible that a man may pay a bribe merely to redeem himself from some evil. It is bad, however, to live under a power whose violence has no restraint except in its avarice. But no man ever paid a bribe for a power to charge and tax others, but with a view to oppress them. No man ever paid a bribe for the handling of the public money, but to peculate from it. When once such offices become thus privately and corruptly venal, the very worst men will be chosen,—as Mr. Hastings has in fact constantly chosen the very worst,—because none but those who do not scruple the use of any means, are capable, consistently with profit, to discharge at once the rigid demands of a severe public revenue and the private bribes of a rapacious chief magistrate. Not only the worst men will be thus chosen, but they will be restrained by no dread whatsoever in the execution of their worst oppressions. Their protection is sure. The authority that is to restrain, to control, to punish them is previously engaged; he has his retaining fee for the support of their crimes. Mr. Hastings never dared, because he could not, arrest oppression in its course, without drying up the source of his own corrupt emolument. Mr. Hastings never dared, after the fact, to punish extortion in others, because he could not, without risking the discovery of bribery in himself. The same corruption, the same

11—51

oppression, and the same impunity will reign through all the subordinate gradations.

A fair revenue may be collected without the aid of wicked, violent, and unjust instruments. But when once the line of just and legal demand is transgressed, such instruments are of absolute necessity, and they comport themselves accordingly. When we know that men must be well paid—and they ought to be well paid—for the performance of honorable duty, can we think that men will be found to commit wicked, rapacious, and oppressive acts with fidelity and disinterestedness, for the sole emolument of dishonest employers? No; they must have their full share of the prey, and the greater share as they are the nearer and more necessary instruments of the general extortion. We must not therefore flatter ourselves, when Mr. Hastings takes £40,000 in bribes for Dinagepore and its annexed provinces, that from the people nothing more than £40,000 is extorted. I speak within compass, four times forty must be levied on the people; and these violent sales, fraudulent purchases, confiscations, inhuman and unutterable tortures, imprisonment, irons, whips, fines, general despair, general insurrection, the massacre of the officers of revenue by the people, the massacre of the people by the soldiery, and the total waste and destruction of the finest provinces in India, are things of course; and all a necessary consequence involved in the very substance of Mr. Hastings's bribery.

I therefore charge Mr. Hastings with having destroyed, for private purposes, the whole system of government by the six provincial councils, which he had no right to destroy.

I charge him with having delegated to others that power which the act of Parliament had directed him to preserve unalienably in himself.

I charge him with having formed a committee to be mere instruments and tools, at the enormous expense of £62,000 per annum.

I charge him with having appointed a person their dewan, to whom these Englishmen were to be subservient tools, whose name, to his own knowledge, was by the general voice of India, by the general recorded voice of the company, by recorded official transactions, by everything that can make a man known, abhorred, detested, and stamped with infamy, and with giving him the whole power, which he had thus separated from the council-general. and from the provincial councils.

I charge him with taking bribes of Gunga Govin Sing.

I charge him with not having done that bribe-service, which fidelity even in iniquity requires at the hands of the worst of men.

I charge him with having robbed those people of whom he took the bribes.

I charge him with having fraudulently alienated the fortunes of widows.

I charge him with having, without right, title, or purchase, taken the lands of orphans and given them to wicked persons under him.

I charge him with having removed the natural guardians of a minor rajah, and with having given that trust to a stranger, Debi Sing, whose wickedness was known to himself and all the world, and by whom the rajah, his family, and dependants, were cruelly oppressed.

I charge him with having committed to the management of Debi Sing three great provinces, and thereby with having wasted the country, ruined the landed interest, cruelly harassed the peasants, burned their houses, seized their crops, tortured and degraded their persons, and destroyed the honor of the whole female race of that country.

In the name of the Commons of England, I charge all this villainy upon Warren Hastings, in this last moment of my application to you.

My lords, what is it that we want here to a great act of national justice? Do we want a cause, my lords? You have the cause of oppressed princes, of undone women of the first rank, of desolated provinces, and of wasted kingdoms.

Do you want a criminal, my lords? When was there so much iniquity ever laid to the charge of any one? No, my lords, you must not look to punish any other such delinquent from India. Warren Hastings has not left substance enough in India to nourish such another delinquent.

My lords, is it a prosecutor you want? You have before you the Commons of Great Britain as prosecutors; and, I believe, my lords, that the sun, in his beneficent progress round the world, does not behold a more glorious sight than that of men, separated from a remote people by the material bounds and barriers of nature, united by the bond of a social and moral community,—all the Commons of England resenting, as their own, the

indignities and cruelties that are offered to all the people of India.

Do we want a tribunal? My lords, no example of antiquity, nothing in the modern world, nothing in the range of human imagination, can supply us with a tribunal like this. My lords, here we see virtually in the mind's eye that sacred majesty of the Crown, under whose authority you sit, and whose power you exercise. We see in that invisible authority, what we all feel in reality and life, the beneficent powers and protecting justice of his Majesty. We have here the heir apparent to the Crown, such as the fond wishes of the people of England wish an heir apparent of the Crown to be. We have here all the branches of the royal family in a situation between majesty and subjection, between the sovereign and the subject, offering a pledge in that situation for the support of the rights of the Crown and the liberties of the people, both which extremities they touch. My lords, we have a great hereditary peerage here; those, who have their own honor, the honor of their ancestors, and of their posterity, to guard, and who will justify, as they have always justified, that provision in the Constitution by which justice is made an hereditary office. My lords, we have here a new nobility, who have risen and exalted themselves by various merits, by great military services which have extended the fame of this country from the rising to the setting sun. We have those, who by various civil merits and various civil talents have been exalted to a situation, which they well deserve, and in which they will justify the favor of their sovereign and the good opinion of their fellow-subjects, and make them rejoice to see those virtuous characters, that were the other day upon a level with them, now exalted above them in rank, but feeling with them in sympathy what they felt in common with them before. We have persons exalted from the practice of the law, from the place in which they administered high, though subordinate, justice, to a seat here, to enlighten with their knowledge and to strengthen with their votes those principles which have distinguished the courts in which they have presided.

My lords, you have here also the lights of our religion; you have the bishops of England. My lords, you have that true image of the primitive church in its ancient form, in its ancient ordinances, purified from the superstitions and the vices which a long succession of ages will bring upon the best institutions.

You have the representatives of that religion which says that their God is love, that the very vital spirit of their institution is charity,— a religion, which so much hates oppression, that when the God whom we adore appeared in human form, he did not appear in a form of greatness and majesty, but in sympathy with the lowest of the people, and thereby made it a firm and ruling principle that their welfare was the object of all government, since the person, who was the Master of Nature, chose to appear himself in a subordinate situation. These are the considerations which influence them, which animate them, and will animate them against all oppression, knowing that he who is called first among them and first among us all, both of the flock that is fed and of those who feed it, made himself "the servant of all."

My lords, these are the securities which we have in all the constituent parts of the body of this House. We know them, we reckon, we rest upon them, and commit safely the interests of India and of humanity into your hands. Therefore, it is with confidence, that, ordered by the Commons,

I impeach Warren Hastings, Esquire, of high crimes and misdemeanors.

I impeach him in the name of the Commons of Great Britain in Parliament assembled, whose parliamentary trust he has betrayed.

I impeach him in the name of all the Commons of Great Britain, whose national character he has dishonored.

I impeach him in the name of the people of India, whose laws, rights, and liberties he has subverted; whose properties he has destroyed; whose country he has laid waste and desolate.

I impeach him in the name, and by virtue, of those eternal laws of justice which he has violated.

I impeach him in the name of human nature itself, which he has cruelly outraged, injured, and oppressed in both sexes, in every age, rank, situation, and condition of life.

AGAINST COERCING AMERICA

(From the Speech Moving Resolutions for Conciliation, House of Commons, March 22d, 1775)

AMERICA, gentlemen say, is a noble object. It is an object well worth fighting for. Certainly it is, if fighting a people be the best way of gaining them. Gentlemen in this respect will be led to their choice of means by their complexions and their habits. Those who understand the military art will, of course, have some predilection for it. Those who wield the thunder of the State may have more confidence in the efficacy of arms. But I confess, possibly for want of this knowledge, my opinion is much more in favor of prudent management than of force, considering force not as an odious, but a feeble, instrument for preserving a people so numerous, so active, so growing, so spirited as this, in a profitable and subordinate connection with us.

First, sir, permit me to observe, that the use of force alone is but temporary. It may subdue for a moment, but it does not remove the necessity of subduing again; and a nation is not governed which is perpetually to be conquered.

My next objection is its uncertainty. Terror is not always the effect of force; and an armament is not a victory. If you do not succeed you are without resource, for conciliation failing, force remains, but force failing, no further hope of reconciliation is left. Power and authority are sometimes bought by kindness, but they can never be begged as alms by an impoverished and defeated violence.

A further objection to force is, that you impair the object by your very endeavors to preserve it. The thing you fought for is not the thing which you recover; but depreciated, sunk, wasted, and consumed in the contest. Nothing less will content me than whole America. I do not choose to consume its strength along with our own, because in all parts it is the British strength that I consume. I do not choose to be caught by a foreign enemy at the end of this exhausting conflict, and still less in the midst of it. I may escape; but I can make no insurance against such an event. Let me add, that I do not choose wholly to break the American spirit, because it is the spirit that has made the country.

Lastly, we have no sort of experience in favor of force as an instrument in the rule of our colonies. Their growth and their utility have been owing to methods altogether different. Our ancient indulgence has been said to be pursued to a fault. It may be so; but we know, if feeling is evidence, that our fault was more tolerable than our attempt to mend it, and our sin far more salutary than our penitence.

These, sir, are my reasons for not entertaining that high opinion of untried force, by which many gentlemen, for whose sentiments in other particulars I have great respect, seem to be so greatly captivated.

But there is still behind a third consideration concerning this object, which serves to determine my opinion on the sort of policy which ought to be pursued in the management of America, even more than its population and its commerce,— I mean its temper and character. In this character of the Americans a love of freedom is the predominating feature, which marks and distinguishes the whole; and, as an ardent is always a jealous affection, your colonies become suspicious, restive, and untractable, whenever they see the least attempt to wrest from them by force, or shuffle from them by chicane, what they think the only advantage worth living for. This fierce spirit of liberty is stronger in the English colonies, probably, than in any other people of the earth, and this from a variety of powerful causes, which, to understand the true temper of their minds, and the direction which this spirit takes, it will not be amiss to lay open somewhat more largely.

First, the people of the colonies are descendants of Englishmen. England, sir, is a nation which still, I hope, respects, and formerly adored, her freedom. The colonists emigrated from you when this part of your character was most predominant; and they took this bias and direction the moment they parted from your hands. They are, therefore, not only devoted to liberty, but to liberty according to English ideas and on English principles. Abstract liberty, like other mere abstractions, is not to be found. Liberty inheres in some sensible object, and every nation has formed to itself some favorite point which, by way of eminence, becomes the criterion of their happiness. It happened you know, sir, that the great contests for freedom in this country were, from the earliest times, chiefly upon the question of taxing. Most of the contests in the ancient commonwealths turned

primarily on the right of election of magistrates, or on the balance among the several orders of the State. The question of money was not with them so immediate. But in England it was otherwise. On this point of taxes the ablest pens and most eloquent tongues have been exercised; the greatest spirits have acted and suffered. In order to give the fullest satisfaction concerning the importance of this point, it was not only necessary for those who in argument defended the excellence of the English constitution to insist on this privilege of granting money as a dry point of fact and to prove that the right had been acknowledged in ancient parchments and blind usages to reside in a certain body called the House of Commons. They went much further: they attempted to prove — and they succeeded — that in theory it ought to be so, from the particular nature of a House of Commons, as an immediate representative of the people, whether the old records had delivered this oracle or not. They took infinite pains to inculcate, as a fundamental principle, that, in all monarchies, the people must, in effect, themselves, mediately or immediately, possess the power of granting their own money, or no shadow of liberty could subsist. The colonies draw from you, as with their lifeblood, those ideas and principles, their love of liberty, as with you, fixed and attached on this specific point of taxing. Liberty might be safe or might be endangered in twenty other particulars, without their being much pleased or alarmed. Here they felt its pulse; and, as they found that beat, they thought themselves sick or sound. I do not say whether they were right or wrong in applying your general arguments to their own case. It is not easy, indeed, to make a monopoly of theorems and corollaries. The fact is, that they did thus apply those general arguments; and your mode of governing them, whether through lenity or indolence, through wisdom or mistake, confirmed them in the imagination that they, as well as you, had an interest in these common principles.

They were further confirmed in these pleasing errors by the form of their provincial legislative assemblies. Their governments are popular in a high degree; some are merely popular; in all, the popular representative is the most weighty; and this share of the people in their ordinary government never fails to inspire them with lofty sentiments and with a strong aversion from whatever tends to deprive them of their chief importance.

If anything were wanting to this necessary operation of the form of government, religion would have given it a complete effect. Religion, always a principle of energy, in this new people is in no way worn out or impaired; and their mode of professing it is also one main cause of this free spirit. The people are Protestants, and of that kind which is most averse to all implicit submission of mind and opinion. This is a persuasion not only favorable to liberty, but built upon it. I do not think, sir, that the reason of this averseness in the dissenting churches from all that looks like absolute government is so much to be sought in their religious tenets as in their history. Every one knows that the Roman Catholic religion is at least coeval with most of the governments where it prevails, that it has generally gone hand in hand with them, and received great favor and every kind of support from authority. The Church of England, too, was formed from her cradle under the nursing care of regular government. But the dissenting interests have sprung up in direct opposition to all the ordinary powers of the world, and could justify that opposition only on a strong claim to natural liberty. Their very existence depended on the powerful and unremitted assertion of that claim. All Protestantism, even the most cold and passive, is a kind of dissent. But the religion most prevalent in our northern colonies is a refinement on the principle of resistance; it is the dissidence of dissent, and the protestantism of the Protestant religion. This religion, under a variety of denominations, agreeing in nothing but in the communion of the spirit of liberty, is predominant in most of the northern provinces, where the Church of England, notwithstanding its legal rights, is in reality no more than a sort of private sect, not composing, most probably, the tenth of the people. The colonists left England when this spirit was high, and in the emigrants was the highest of all; and even that stream of foreigners which has been constantly flowing into these colonies has, for the greatest part, been composed of dissenters from the establishments of their several countries, and have brought with them a temper and character far from alien to that of the people with whom they mixed.

Sir, I can perceive by their manner that some gentlemen object to the latitude of this description, because in the southern colonies the Church of England forms a large body and has a regular establishment. It is certainly true. There is, however,

a circumstance attending these colonies, which, in my opinion, fully counterbalances this difference, and makes the spirit of liberty still more high and haughty than in those to the northward. It is that in Virginia and the Carolinas they have a vast multitude of slaves. Where this is the case in any part of the world, those who are free are by far the most proud and jealous of their freedom. Freedom is to them not only an enjoyment, but a kind of rank and privilege. Not seeing there that freedom, as in countries where it is a common blessing, and as broad and general as the air, may be united with much abject toil, with great misery, with all the exterior of servitude, liberty looks, among them, like something that is more noble and liberal. I do not mean, sir, to commend the superior morality of this sentiment, which has at least as much pride as virtue in it; but I cannot alter the nature of man. The fact is so; and these people of the southern colonies are much more strongly, and with a higher and more stubborn spirit, attached to liberty than those to the northward. Such were all the ancient commonwealths; such were our Gothic ancestors; such, in our days, were the Poles, and such will be all masters of slaves, who are not slaves themselves. In such a people the haughtiness of domination combines with the spirit of freedom, fortifies it, and renders it invincible.

Permit me, sir, to add another circumstance in our colonies, which contributes no mean part toward the growth and effect of this untractable spirit—I mean their education. In no country perhaps in the world is the law so general a study. The profession itself is numerous and powerful; and in most provinces it takes the lead. The greater number of the deputies sent to Congress were lawyers. But all who read, and most do read, endeavor to obtain some smattering in that science. I have been told by an eminent bookseller, that in no branch of his business, after tracts of popular devotion, were so many books as those on the law exported to the plantations. The colonists have now fallen into the way of printing them for their own use. I hear that they have sold nearly as many of Blackstone's 'Commentaries' in America as in England. General Gage marks out this disposition very particularly in a letter on your table. He states that all the people in his government are lawyers, or smatterers in law, and that in Boston they have been enabled, by successful chicane, wholly to evade many parts of one of your capital

penal constitutions. The smatterers of debate will say that this knowledge ought to teach them more clearly the rights of legislature, their obligations to obedience, and the penalties of rebellion. All this is mighty well. But my honorable and learned friend on the floor, who condescends to mark what I say for animadversion, will disdain that ground. He has heard, as well as I, that when great honors and great emoluments do not win over this knowledge to the service of the State, it is a formidable adversary to government. If the spirit be not tamed and broken by these happy methods, it is stubborn and litigious. *Abeunt studia in mores.* This study renders men acute, inquisitive, dexterous, prompt in attack, ready in defense, full of resources. In other countries, the people, more simple and of a less mercurial cast, judge of an ill principle in government only by an actual grievance. Here they anticipate the evil, and judge of the pressure of the grievance by the badness of the principle. They augur misgovernment at a distance, and snuff the approach of tyranny in every tainted breeze.

The last cause of this disobedient spirit in the colonies is hardly less powerful than the rest, as it is not merely moral, but laid deep in the natural constitution of things. Three thousand miles of ocean lie between you and them. No contrivance can prevent the effect of this distance in weakening government. Seas roll and months pass between the order and the execution, and the want of a speedy explanation of a single point is enough to defeat the whole system. You have, indeed, "winged ministers" of vengeance, who carry your bolts in their pouches to the remotest verge of the sea. But there a power steps in that limits the arrogance of raging passion and furious elements, and says: "So far shalt thou go, and no farther." Who are you, that should fret and rage, and bite the chains of nature? Nothing worse happens to you than does to all nations who have extensive empire; and it happens in all the forms into which empire can be thrown. In large bodies the circulation of power must be less vigorous at the extremities. Nature has said it. The Turk cannot govern Egypt and Arabia and Koordistan as he governs Thrace, nor has he the same dominion in Crimea and Algiers which he has at Broosa and Smyrna. Despotism itself is obliged to truck and huckster. The Sultan gets such obedience as he can. He governs with a loose rein, that he may govern at all, and the whole of the force and vigor of his authority in

his centre is derived from a prudent relaxation in all his borders. Spain, in her provinces, is, perhaps, not so well obeyed as you are in yours. She complies too; she submits; she watches times. This is the immutable condition, the eternal law, of extensive and detached empire.

PRINCIPLE IN POLITICS
(From the Speech to the Electors of Bristol)

THEY tell us that those of our fellow-citizens whose chains we had a little relaxed are enemies to liberty and our free Constitution,—not enemies, I presume, to their own liberty. And as to the Constitution, until we give them some share in it, I do not know on what pretense we can examine into their opinions about a business in which they have no interest or concern. But, after all, are we equally sure that they are adverse to our Constitution as that our statutes are hostile and destructive to them? For my part, I have reason to believe, their opinions and inclinations in that respect are various, exactly like those of other men. And if they lean more to the Crown than I, and than many of you think we ought, we must remember that he who aims at another's life is not to be surprised if he flies into any sanctuary that will receive him. The tenderness of the executive power is the natural asylum of those upon whom the laws have declared war; and to complain that men are inclined to favor the means of their own safety is so absurd that one forgets the injustice in the ridicule.

I must fairly tell you that, so far as my principles are concerned,—principles that I hope will depart only with my last breath,—I have no idea of a liberty unconnected with honesty and justice. Nor do I believe that any good constitutions of government or of freedom can find it necessary for their security to doom any part of the people to a permanent slavery. Such a constitution of freedom, if such can be, is in effect no more than another name for the tyranny of the strongest faction; and factions in republics have been, and are, fully as capable as monarchs, of the most cruel oppression and injustice. It is but too true, that the love, and even the very idea, of genuine liberty is extremely rare. It is but too true, that there are many, whose whole scheme of freedom is made up of pride, perverseness, and insolence. They feel themselves in a state of thraldom, they imagine that their souls are cooped and cabined in, unless they have some man, or some body of men, dependent on their mercy. This desire of having some one below them descends to those who are the very lowest of all — and a Protestant cobbler, debased by his poverty, but exalted by his share of the ruling church, feels a pride in knowing it is by his generosity alone, that the peer, whose footman's instep he measures, is able to keep his chaplain from a jail. This disposition is the true source of the passion which many men in very humble life have taken to the American War. Our subjects in America; our colonies; our dependants. This lust of party power is the liberty they hunger and thirst for; and this siren song of ambition has charmed ears that one would have thought were never organized to that sort of music.

This way of proscribing the citizens by denominations and general descriptions, dignified by the name of reason of state, and security for constitutions and commonwealths, is nothing better at bottom than the miserable invention of an ungenerous ambition, which would fain hold the sacred trust of power, without any of the virtues or any of the energies that give a title to it; a receipt of policy, made up of a detestable compound of malice, cowardice, and sloth. They would govern men against their will, but in that government they would be discharged from the exercise of vigilance, providence, and fortitude; and therefore, that they may sleep on their watch, they consent to take some one division of the society into partnership of the tyranny over the rest. But let government, in what form it may be, comprehend the whole in its justice, and restrain the suspicious by its vigilance; let it keep watch and ward; let it discover by its sagacity, and punish by its firmness, all delinquency against its power, whenever delinquency exists in the overt acts; and then it will be as safe as ever God and nature intended it should be. Crimes are the acts of individuals, and not of denominations, and therefore arbitrarily to class men under general descriptions, in order to proscribe and punish them in a lump for a presumed delinquency, of which perhaps but a part, perhaps none at all, are guilty, is indeed a compendious method, and saves a world of trouble about proof; but such a method, instead of being law, is an act of unnatural rebellion against the legal dominion of reason

and justice, and this vice, in any constitution that entertains it, at one time or other, will certainly bring on its ruin.

We are told that this is not a religious persecution, and its abettors are loud in disclaiming all severities on account of conscience. Very fine, indeed! then let it be so! they are not persecutors; they are only tyrants. With all my heart. I am perfectly indifferent concerning the pretexts upon which we torment one another; or whether it be for the constitution of the Church of England, or for the constitution of the State of England, that people choose to make their fellow-creatures wretched. When we were sent into a place of authority, you that sent us had yourselves but one commission to give. You could give us none to wrong or oppress, or even to suffer any kind of oppression or wrong, on any grounds whatsoever; not on political, as in the affairs of America; not on commercial, as in those of Ireland; not in civil, as in the laws for debt; not in religious, as in the statutes against Protestant or Catholic dissenters. The diversified but connected fabric of universal justice is well cramped and bolted together in all its parts; and depend upon it, I never have employed, and I never shall employ, any engine of power which may come into my hands, to wrench it asunder. All shall stand, if I can help it, and all shall stand connected. After all, to complete this work, much remains to be done; much in the East, much in the West. But great as the work is, if our will be ready, our powers are not deficient.

Since you have suffered me to trouble you so much on this subject, permit me, gentlemen, to detain you a little longer. I am, indeed, most solicitous to give you perfect satisfaction. I find there are some of a better and softer nature than the persons with whom I have supposed myself in debate, who neither think ill of the act of relief, nor by any means desire the repeal, not accusing but lamenting what was done, on account of the consequences, have frequently expressed their wish that the late act had never been made. Some of this description, and persons of worth, I have met with in this city. They conceive that the prejudices, whatever they might be, of a large part of the people, ought not to have been shocked; that their opinions ought to have been previously taken, and much attended to, and that thereby the late horrid scenes might have been prevented.

I confess my notions are widely different, and I never was less sorry for any action of my life. I like the bill the better, on account of the events of all kinds that followed it. It relieved the real sufferers; it strengthened the state; and, by the disorders that ensued, we had clear evidence that there lurked a temper somewhere, which ought not to be fostered by the laws. No ill consequences whatever could be attributed to the act itself. We knew beforehand, or we were poorly instructed, that toleration is odious to the intolerant; freedom to oppressors; property to robbers; and all kinds and degrees of prosperity to the envious. We knew that all these kinds of men would gladly gratify their evil dispositions under the sanction of law and religion, if they could; if they could not, yet, to make way to their objects, they would do their utmost to subvert all religion and all law. This we certainly knew. But knowing this, is there any reason, because thieves break in and steal, and thus bring detriment to you, and draw ruin on themselves, that I am to be sorry that you are in possession of shops, and of warehouses, and of wholesome laws to protect them? Are you to build no houses, because desperate men may pull them down upon their own heads? Or, if a malignant wretch will cut his own throat because he sees you give alms to the necessitous and deserving, shall his destruction be attributed to your charity, and not to his own deplorable madness? If we repent of our good actions, what, I pray you, is left for our faults and follies? It is not the beneficence of the laws, it is the unnatural temper which beneficence can fret and sour, that is to be lamented. It is this temper which, by all rational means, ought to be sweetened and corrected. If froward men should refuse this cure, can they vitiate anything but themselves? Does evil so react upon good, as not only to retard its motion, but to change its nature? If it can so operate, then good men will always be in the power of the bad; and virtue, by a dreadful reverse of order, must lie under perpetual subjection and bondage to vice.

As to the opinion of the people, which some think, in such cases, is to be implicitly obeyed, nearly two years' tranquillity, which followed the act and its instant imitation in Ireland, proved abundantly that the late horrible spirit was, in a great measure, the effect of insidious art and perverse industry and gross misrepresentation. But suppose that the dislike had been

much more deliberate and much more general than I am persuaded it was. When we know that the opinions of even the greatest multitudes are the standard of rectitude, I shall think myself obliged to make those opinions the masters of my conscience. But if it may be doubted whether Omnipotence itself is competent to alter the essential constitution of right and wrong, sure I am that such things as they and I are possessed of no such power. No man carries further than I do the policy of making government pleasing to the people. But the widest range of this politic complaisance is confined within the limits of justice. I would not only consult the interests of the people, but I would cheerfully gratify their humors. We are all a sort of children that must be soothed and managed. I think I am not austere or formal in my nature. I would bear, I would even myself play my part in, any innocent buffooneries to divert them. But I never will act the tyrant for their amusement. If they will mix malice in their sports I shall never consent to throw them any living, sentient creature whatsoever; no, not so much as a kitling to torment.

"But if I profess all this impolitic stubbornness, I may chance never to be elected into Parliament." It is certainly not pleasing to be put out of the public service. But I wish to be a member of Parliament, to have my share of doing good and resisting evil. It would, therefore, be absurd to renounce my objects in order to obtain my seat. I deceive myself, indeed, most grossly, if I had not much rather pass the remainder of my life hidden in the recesses of the deepest obscurity, feeding my mind even with the visions and imaginations of such things, than to be placed on the most splendid throne of the universe, tantalized with a denial of the practice of all which can make the greatest situation any other than the greatest curse. Gentlemen, I have had my day. I can never sufficiently express my gratitude to you for having set me in a place wherein I could lend the slightest help to great and laudable designs. If I have had my share in any measure giving quiet to private property and private conscience; if by my vote I have aided in securing to families the best possession, peace; if I have joined in reconciling kings to their subjects, and subjects to their prince; if I have assisted to loosen the foreign holdings of the citizen, and taught him to look for his protection to the laws of his country, and for his comfort to the good-will of his countrymen;—if I have thus taken my part with the best of men in the best of their actions, I can shut the book. I might wish to read a page or two more, but this is enough for my measure,—I have not lived in vain.

And now, gentlemen, on this serious day, when I come, as it were, to make up my account with you, let me take to myself some degree of honest pride on the nature of the charges that are against me. I do not here stand before you accused of venality, or of neglect of duty. It is not said, that, in the long period of my service, I have, in a single instance, sacrificed the slightest of your interests to my ambition, or to my fortune. It is not alleged that to gratify any anger or revenge of my own, or of my party, I have had a share in wronging or oppressing any description of men, or any one man in any description. No! the charges against me are all of one kind, that I have pushed the principles of general justice and benevolence too far; further than a cautious policy would warrant; and further than the opinions of many would go along with me. In every accident which may happen through life, in pain, in sorrow, in depression, and in distress, I will call to mind this accusation, and be comforted.

MARIE ANTOINETTE
(Born, 1755; beheaded, 1793. Burke saw her in 1773)

IT IS now sixteen or seventeen years since I saw the Queen of France, then the Dauphiness, at Versailles; and surely never lighted on this orb, which she hardly seemed to touch, a more delightful vision. I saw her just above the horizon, decorating and cheering the elevated sphere she had just begun to move in, glittering like the morning star, full of life and splendor and joy. O, what a revolution! and what a heart must I have, to contemplate without emotion that elevation and that fall! Little did I dream, when she added titles of veneration to those of enthusiastic, distant, respectful love, that she should ever be obliged to carry the sharp antidote against disgrace concealed in that bosom; little did I dream that I should have lived to see such disasters fallen upon her, in a nation of gallant men, in a nation of men of honor, and of cavaliers! I thought ten thousand swords must have leaped from their scabbards, to avenge even a look that threatened her with insult.

II—52

But the age of chivalry is gone; that of sophisters, economists, and calculators has succeeded, and the glory of Europe is extinguished forever. Never, never more, shall we behold that generous loyalty to rank and sex, that proud submission, that dignified obedience, that subordination of the heart, which kept alive, even in servitude itself, the spirit of an exalted freedom! The unbought grace of life, the cheap defense of nations, the nurse of manly sentiment and heroic enterprise is gone. It is gone, that sensibility of principle, that chastity of honor, which felt a stain like a wound, which inspired courage whilst it mitigated ferocity, which ennobled whatever it touched, and under which vice itself lost half its evil, by losing all its grossness.

ANSON BURLINGAME
(1820–1870)

FAMOUS as the principal negotiator of the Burlingame Treaty, the reputation of Anson Burlingame as an orator depends on a single speech, which because of its far-reaching consequences will always be memorable in American history. His denunciation of the assault on Senator Sumner by Preston S. Brooks, of South Carolina, gave him celebrity and opened for him the way to the prominence he afterwards achieved as a diplomat.

From 1850 until 1880, free speech in America illustrated its worst tendencies towards license. Vituperation was carried to an almost incredible extreme in the minor newspapers, which simply reflected the general demand for strong expressions of popular feeling. Public men, influenced by the same causes which controlled the press, often exhausted their intellectual resources in exaggerated invective. A marked change for the better both in the press and in public debate took place after the death of President Garfield. The sobering influence which that great calamity had upon the American people is likely to be a subject of careful consideration for the future historian. From it dates a change in the temper both of press and public, gradual but so great that it is difficult now to conceive how the personalities of such a debate as that over the Kansas-Nebraska Bill could have been possible in the Senate.

During the struggle over the admission of Kansas, Senator Sumner, of Massachusetts, had compared Senator Douglas, of Illinois, to "the noisome squat and nameless animal"—the American polecat—and again using the same comparison had said: "Mr. President, again the Senator has switched his tongue and again he fills the Senate Chamber with its offensive odor." Mr. Douglas, not himself guiltless of personalities, accepted vituperation and recrimination as a matter of course. But during the same debate, Mr. Sumner opening a very celebrated period by calling Senator Butler, of South Carolina, the Don Quixote and Senator Douglas, the Sancho Panza of chattel slavery, had exhausted the powers of his great intellect in the attempt to make them appear both detestable and absurd. A man of less intellectual force than Sumner might have brought condemnation upon himself by his daring climaxes, but Sumner carried his point, and in doing so, enraged Senator Butler's friends.

The assault by Preston S. Brooks, of South Carolina, followed and so stirred Massachusetts that the conservative element of its people was never afterwards at an advantage in attempting to check the extremists of both sections. It is not yet time and this is not the place to attempt a review of the history of that period, but Mr. Burlingame's references to Senator Douglas and others can be understood only by recalling the leading facts in the connection.

After the election of President Lincoln, Mr. Burlingame, who had been one of the active organizers of the Republican party, was sent to represent the United States in China. After the expiration of his term of service, he was employed by the Chinese government, and, gaining the confidence of its foreign office, he was sent to Washington and afterwards to Europe at the head of a numerous diplomatic retinue. One of the results of his visit was the Burlingame Treaty, the first marked concession willingly made by Chinese conservatism to the pressure of Caucasian civilization.

MASSACHUSETTS AND THE SUMNER ASSAULT
(Delivered in the House of Representatives, June 21st, 1856)

Mr. Chairman:—

THE House will bear me witness that I have not pressed myself upon its deliberations. I never before asked its indulgence. I have assailed no man; nor have I sought to bring reproach upon any man's State. But, while such has been my course, as well as the course of my colleagues from Massachusetts, upon this floor, certain members have seen fit to assail the State which we represent, not only with words, but with blows.

In remembrance of these things, and seizing the first opportunity which has presented itself for a long time, I stand here to-day to say a word for old Massachusetts—not that she needs it; no, sir; for in all that constitutes true greatness, in all that gives abiding strength, in great qualities of head and of heart, in moral power, in material prosperity, in intellectual resources and physical ability, by the general judgment of mankind, according to her population, she is the first State. There does not live the man anywhere, who knows anything, to whom praise of Massachusetts would not be needless. She is as far beyond that as she is beyond censure. Members here may sneer at her expense; they may praise her past at the expense of her present; but I say, with a full conviction of its truth, that Massachusetts, in her present performances, is even greater than in her past recollections. And when I have said this, what more can I say?

Sir, although I am here as her youngest and humblest Member, yet, as her representative, I feel that I am the peer of any man upon this floor. Occupying that high standpoint, with modesty, but with firmness, I cast down her glove to the whole band of her assailants. . . .

On the nineteenth of May, it was announced that Mr. Sumner would address the Senate upon the Kansas question. The floor of the Senate, the galleries, and avenues leading thereto, were thronged with an expectant audience, and many of us left our places in this House to hear the Massachusetts orator. To say that we were delighted with the speech we heard would but faintly express the deep emotions of our hearts awakened by it. I need not speak of the classic purity of its language, nor of the nobility of its sentiments. It was heard by many; it has been read by millions. There has been no such speech made in the Senate since the days when those Titans of American eloquence — the Websters and the Haynes — contended with each other for mastery.

It was severe, because it was launched against tyranny. It was severe as Chatham was severe when he defended the feeble colonies against the giant oppression of the mother country. It was made in the face of a hostile Senate. It continued through the greater portion of two days; and yet, during that time, the speaker was not once called to order. This fact is conclusive as to the personal and parliamentary decorum of the speech. He had provocation enough. His State had been called hypocritical. He himself had been called "a puppy," "a fool," "a fanatic," and "a dishonest man." Yet he was parliamentary from the beginning to the end of his speech. No man knew better than he did the proprieties of the place, for he had always observed them. No man knew better than he did parliamentary law, because he had made it the study of his life. No man saw more clearly than he did the flaming sword of the Constitution, turning every way, guarding all the avenues of the Senate. But he was not thinking of these things; he was not thinking then of the privileges of the Senate nor of the guaranties of the Constitution; he was there to denounce tyranny and crime, and he did it. He was there to speak for the rights of an empire, and he did it, bravely and grandly.

So much for the occasion of the speech. A word, and I shall be pardoned, about the speaker himself. He is my friend; for many and many a year I have looked to him for guidance and light, and I never looked in vain. He never had a personal enemy in his life; his character is as pure as the snow that falls on his native hills; his heart overflows with kindness for every being having the upright form of man; he is a ripe scholar, a chivalric gentleman, and a warm-hearted, true friend. He sat at the feet of Channing, and drank in the sentiments of that noble soul. He bathed in the learning and undying love of the great jurist Story, and the hand of Jackson, with its honors and its offices, sought him early in life, but he shrank from them with instinctive modesty. Sir, he is the pride of Massachusetts. His mother commonwealth found him adorning the highest walks of literature and law, and she bade him go and grace somewhat the rough character of political life. The people of Massachusetts, the old and the young and the middle-aged, now pay their full homage to the beauty of his public and private character. Such is Charles Sumner.

On the twenty-second day of May, when the Senate and the House had clothed themselves in mourning for a brother fallen in the battle of life in the distant State of Missouri, the Senator from Massachusetts sat in the silence of the Senate Chamber, engaged in the employments pertaining to his office, when a Member of this House, who had taken an oath to sustain the Constitution, stole into the Senate, that place which had hitherto been held sacred against violence, and smote him as Cain smote his brother.

Mr. Keitt, in his seat — That is false.

Mr. Burlingame — I will not bandy epithets with the gentleman. I am responsible for my own language. Doubtless he is responsible for his.

Mr. Keitt — I am.

Mr. Burlingame — I shall stand by mine. One blow was enough; but it did not satiate the wrath of that spirit which had pursued him through two days. Again and again, quicker and faster fell the leaden blows, until he was torn away from his victim, when the Senator from Massachusetts fell in the arms of his friends, and his blood ran down on the Senate floor. Sir, the act was brief, and my comments on it shall be brief also. I denounce it in the name of the Constitution it violated. I denounce

it in the name of the sovereignty of Massachusetts, which was stricken down by the blow. I denounce it in the name of humanity. I denounce it in the name of civilization which it outraged. I denounce it in the name of that fair play which bullies and prize-fighters respect. What! strike a man when he is pinioned — when he cannot respond to a blow? Call you that chivalry? In what code of honor did you get your authority for that? I do not believe that Member has a friend so dear who must not in his heart of hearts condemn the act. Even the Member himself, if he has left a spark of that chivalry and gallantry attributed to him, must loathe and scorn the act. God knows I do not wish to speak unkindly, or in a spirit of revenge; but I owe it to my manhood and the noble State I, in part, represent, to express my abhorrence of the act. But much as I reprobate the act, much more do I reprobate the conduct of those who were by and saw the outrage perpetrated. Sir, especially do I notice the conduct of that Senator recently from the free platform of Massachusetts, with the odor of her hospitality on him, who stood there, not only silent and quiet while it was going on, but, when it was over, approved the act. And worse; when he had time to cool, when he had slept on it, he went into the Senate Chamber of the United States, and shocked the sensibilities of the world by approving it. Another Senator did not take part because he feared that his motives might be questioned, exhibiting as extraordinary a delicacy as that individual who refused to rescue a drowning mortal because he had not been introduced to him. Another was not on good terms, and yet, if rumor be true, that Senator has declared that himself and family are more indebted to Mr. Sumner than to any other man; yet, when he saw him borne bleeding by, he turned and went on the other side. Oh, magnanimous Slidell! Oh, prudent Douglas! Oh, audacious Toombs!

Sir, there are questions arising out of this which far transcend those of a mere personal nature. Of those personal considerations I shall speak, when the question comes properly before us, if I am permitted to do so. The higher question involves the very existence of the government itself. If, sir, freedom of speech is not to remain to us, what is all this government worth? If we from Massachusetts, or any other State — Senators, or Members of the House — are to be called to account by some "gallant nephew" of some "gallant uncle," when we utter something

which does not suit their sensitive natures, we desire to know it. If the conflict is to be transferred from this peaceful, intellectual field to one where, it is said, "honors are easy and responsibilities equal," then we desire to known it. Massachusetts, if her sons and representatives are to have the rod held over them, if these things are to continue, the time may come — though she utters no threats — when she may be called upon to withdraw them to her own bosom, where she can furnish to them that protection which is not vouchsafed to them under the flag of their common country. But, while she permits us to remain, we shall do our duty, — our whole duty. We shall speak whatever we choose to speak, when we will, where we will, and how we will, regardless of all consequences.

Sir, the sons of Massachusetts are educated at the knees of their mothers, in the doctrines of peace and good-will, and, God knows, they desire to cultivate those feelings, — feelings of social kindness and public kindness. The House will bear witness that we have not violated or trespassed upon any of them; but, sir, if we are pushed too long and too far, there are men from the old commonwealth of Massachusetts who will not shrink from a defense of freedom of speech, and the honored State they represent, on any field where they may be assailed.

HORACE BUSHNELL

(1802–1876)

HORACE BUSHNELL illustrates a style of eloquence less suited than that of Henry Ward Beecher to subjects involving the emotions, but for many purposes equally effective. His «Discourse on the Dignity of Human Nature Shown from Its Ruins» is governed by the same idea which inspired Taine in his remarkable analysis of Shakespeare's purposes and methods. Whether or not the world is a «hospital for the sick of soul and mind,» as Bushnell thought and as Taine concludes that Shakespeare believed, there can be no question of the great power and extraordinary beauty of Bushnell's argument. It is perhaps his best example of sustained thought and eloquent expression, but his discourses abound in beauty and are generally characterized by power. When he surpasses himself, as he often does, he is equalled only by a very few among the most famous orators of the world.

He was born at Litchfield, Connecticut, April 14th, 1802. His pastorate at Hartford, which began in 1833, brought him continually increasing reputation. At a time when most pulpit reputations were made by sermons on politics, he devoted his mind to the elucidation of permanent truths, and, however far short of his best he may seem to fall at times, not a few of his characteristic passages are likely to live as long as the language. He died February 17th, 1876.

THE DIGNITY OF HUMAN NATURE

(From the «Discourse on the Dignity of Human Nature Shown from Its Ruins»)

THE great characters of the world furnish striking proof of the transcendent quality of human nature, by the dignity they are able to connect even with their littleness and meanness. On a small island of the southern Atlantic, is shut up a remarkable prisoner, wearing himself out there in a feeble mixture of peevishness and jealousy, solaced by no great thoughts and no heroic spirit; a kind of dotard before his time, killing and consuming himself by the intense littleness into which he has shrunk. And this is the great conqueror of the modern world, the man whose name is the greatest of modern names, or, some will say, of all the names the human world has pronounced; a man, nevertheless, who carried his greatest victories and told his meanest lies in close proximity, a character as destitute of private magnanimity, as he was remarkable for the stupendous powers of his understanding and the more stupendous and imperial leadership of his will. How great a being must it be, that makes a point of so great dignity before the world, despite of so much that is really little and contemptible.

But he is not alone. The immortal Kepler, piloting science into the skies, and comprehending the vastness of heaven, for the first time, in the fixed embrace of definite thought, only proves the magnificence of man as a ruin, when you discover the strange ferment of irritability and «superstition wild,» in which his great thoughts are brewed and his mighty life dissolved.

So, also, Bacon proves the amazing wealth and grandeur of the human soul only the more sublimely that, living in an element of cunning, servility, ingratitude, and dying under the shame of a convict, he is yet able to dignify disgrace by the stupendous majesty of his genius, and commands the reverence even of the world, as to one of its sublimest benefactors. And the poet's stinging line —

«The wisest, brightest, meanest of mankind,»

pictures, only with a small excess of satire, the magnificence of ruin comprehended in the man.

Probably no one of mankind has raised himself to a higher pitch of renown by the superlative attributes of genius displayed in his writings, than the great English dramatist; flowering out, nevertheless, into such eminence of glory, on a compost of fustian, buffoonery, and other vile stuff, which he so magnificently covers with splendor and irradiates with beauty, that disgust itself is lost in the vehemence of praise. And so we shall find, almost universally, that the greatness of the world's great men is proved by the inborn qualities that tower above the ruins of weakness and shame, in which they appear, and out of which, as solitary pillars and dismantled temples they rise.

But we must look more directly into the contents of human nature, and the internal ruin by which they are displayed. And here you may notice, first of all, the sublime vehemence of the passions. What a creature must that be, who, out of mere hatred,

or revenge, will deliberately take the life of a fellow man, and then dispatch his own to avoid the ignominy of a public execution. Suppose there might be found some tiger that, for the mere bitterness of his grudge against some other whelp of his mother, springs upon him in his sleep and rends him in pieces, and then deliberately tears open his own throat to escape the vengeance of the family. No tiger of the desert is ever instigated by any so intense and terrible passion, that, for the sweetness of revenge, it is willing afterward to rush on death itself. This kind of frenzy plainly belongs to none but a creature immortal, an archangel ruined, in whose breast a fire of hell may burn high enough and deep enough to scorch down even reason and the innate love of life. Or take the passion of covetousness, generally regarded as one essentially mean and degraded. After all, how great a creature must that be who is goaded by a zeal of acquisition so restless, so self-sacrificing, so insatiable. The poor, gaunt miser, starving for want, that he may keep the count of his gold — whom do we more naturally pity and despise. And yet he were even the greatest of heroes, if he could deny himself with so great patience, in a good and holy cause. How grand a gift that immortality, how deep those gulfs of want in the soul, that instigate a madness so desolating to character, a self-immolation so relentless, a niggard suffering so sublime. The same is even true of the licentious and gluttonous lusts and their loathsome results. No race of animals can show the parallel of such vices; because they are none of them instigated by a nature so insatiable, so essentially great in the magnificence of wants that find no good to satisfy their cravings. The ruin we say is beastly, but the beasts are clear of the comparison; it requires a mold vaster than theirs to burst the limits of nature in excesses so disgusting.

Consider again the wild mixtures of thought, displayed both in the waking life and the dreams of mankind. How grand! how mean! how sudden the leap from one to the other! how inscrutable the succession! how defiant of orderly control! It is as if the soul were a thinking ruin; which it verily is. The angel and the demon life appear to be contending in it. The imagination revels in beauty exceeding all the beauty of things, wails in images dire and monstrous, wallows in murderous and base suggestions that shame our inward dignity; so that a great part of the study and a principal art of life, is to keep our decency,

by a wise selection from what we think and a careful suppression of the remainder. A diseased and crazy mixture, such as represents a ruin, is the form of our inward experience. And yet, a ruin how magnificent, one which a buried Nineveh, or a desolated Thebes can parallel only in the faintest degree; comprehending all that is purest, brightest, most divine, even that which is above the firmament itself; all that is worst, most sordid, meanest, most deformed.

Notice, also, the significance of remorse. How great a creature must that be, that, looking down upon itself from some high summit in itself, some throne of truth and judgment which no devastation of order can reach, withers in relentless condemnation of itself, gnaws and chastises itself in the sense of what it is! Call it a ruin, as it plainly is, there rises out of the desolated wreck of its former splendor, that which indicates and measures the sublimity of the original temple. The conscience stands erect, resisting all the ravages of violence and decay, and by this, we distinguish the temple of God that was; a soul divinely gifted, made to be the abode of his spirit, the vehicle of his power, the mirror of his glory. A creature of remorse is a divine creature of necessity, only it is the wreck of a divinity that was.

So again you may conceive the greatness of man by the ruin he makes, if you advert to the dissonance and obstinacy of his evil will. It is dissonant as being out of harmony with God and the world, and all beside in the soul itself; *viz.*, the reason, the conscience, the wants, the hopes, and even the remembrances of the soul. How great a creature is it that, knowing God, can set itself off from God and resist him, can make itself a unit, separate from all beings beside, and maintain a persistent rebellion even against its own convictions, fears, and aspirations. Like a Pharaoh, it sits on its Egyptian throne, quailing in darkness, under the successive fears and judgments of life, relenting for the moment, then gathering itself up again to reassert the obstinacy of its pride, and die, it may be, in its evil. What a power is this, capable of a dominion how sublime, a work and sphere how transcendent! If sin is weak, if it is mean, little, selfish, and deformed, and we are ready to set humanity down as a low and paltry thing of nothing worth, how terrible and tragic in its evil grandeur does it appear, when we turn to look upon its defiance of God and the desperate obstinacy of its warfare. Who, knowing the judgment of God, that they which commit such things are worthy of death, not only do the same, but have pleasure in them that do them. Or, as we have it in the text—There is no fear of God before their eyes. In one view there is fear enough, the soul is all its life long haunted by this fear, but there is a desperation of will that tramples fear and makes it as though it were not.

Consider once more the religious aspirations and capacities of religious attraction that are garnered up and still live in the ruins of humanity. How plain it is, in all the most forward demonstrations of the race, that man is a creature for religion; a creature secretly allied to God himself, as the needle is to the pole, attracted toward God, aspiring consciously or unconsciously, to the friendship and love of God. Neither is it true that, in his fallen state, he has no capacity left of religious affection, or attraction, till it is first newly created in him. All his capacities of love and truth are in him still, only buried and stifled by the smoldering ruin in which he lies. There is a capacity in him still to be moved and drawn, to be charmed and melted by the divine love and beauty. The old affinity lives though smothered in selfishness and lust, and even proves itself in sorrowful evidence, when he bows himself down to a reptile or an idol. He will do his most expensive works for religion. There is a deep panting still in his bosom, however suppressed, that cries inaudibly and sobs with secret longing after God. Hence the sublime unhappiness of the race. There is a vast, immortal want stirring on the world and forbidding it to rest. In the cursing and bitterness, in the deceit of tongues, in the poison of asps, in the swiftness of blood, in all the destruction and misery of the world's ruin, there is yet a vast insatiate hunger for the good, the true, the divine, and a great part of the misery of the ruin is that it is so great a ruin; a desolation of that which cannot utterly perish, and still lives, asserting its defrauded rights and reclaiming its lost glories. And, therefore, it is that life becomes an experience to the race so tragic in its character, so dark and wild, so bitter, so incapable of peace. The way of peace we cannot know, till we find our peace, where our immortal aspirations place it, in the fullness and the friendly eternity of God.

verdict on his career and his character. He can be called everything and evidence of some kind can be adduced on every point — amounting nowhere to absolute proof except as it completely bars any one who can recognize almost unparalleled intellectual activity and subtlety from calling him a fool.

He was born in Deerfield, New Hampshire, November 5th, 1818. His father was a captain of dragoons who served under General Jackson at New Orleans. His mother, left a widow without adequate resources, supported herself for a time by keeping a boarding house in Lowell. Benjamin, however, was sent to Waterville College where he graduated in 1838, going very soon thereafter for a post-graduate course on his uncle's fishing schooner to the banks of Labrador. He was admitted to the bar in 1840, and, after ten years at Lowell, went to Boston. He served in the Massachusetts legislature as a Democrat and in 1860 was a delegate to the National conventions at Charleston and Baltimore. His enemies delighted to republish over and over, with all possible variations, the story of his championship of Jefferson Davis as a presidential candidate at Charleston. After the close of the war he was elected to Congress by the Massachusetts Republicans. Entering the House of Representatives in 1867, he left it in 1879 and in 1880 supported the Democratic party in the Hancock campaign. After several unsuccessful canvasses for governor he was elected by the Democrats in 1882 and during his term, especially in his management of the Tewkesbury Almshouse investigation, he seems to have enjoyed himself even more fully than he did while in military charge of New Orleans. That his great abilities in some other directions had been exercised at the expense of his judgment, especially as it involved ability to forecast results in politics, he showed in his candidacy for the Presidency, the result of which, however, seemed to occasion him neither humiliation, disappointment, nor regret. Perhaps history ought to disapprove him most in his radical fault of readiness to see the grotesque side of the desperate earnestness of others, but it is doubtful if any one who studies him impartially will ever be able to resist wholly the temptation to sympathize with him in his tendency to inward laughter at the suggestion of the absurd latent under the tragic.

He was chosen to open the case against Andrew Johnson at the impeachment trial and he did so with great ability, both as a lawyer and as an orator. Article Ten of the bill of impeachment dealt with what was known at the time as the "Swing Around the Circle" during which, in a series of public speeches, President Johnson arraigned Congress in very much the same style of free and unstudied invective he and "Parson" Brownlow had once employed in arraigning other Tennesseans for attempting to take the State out of the Union.

W. V. B.

BENJAMIN F. BUTLER

(1818–1893)

BENJAMIN F. BUTLER, one of the most picturesque characters in the history of any country, was, during the course of his long and intensely active life, "the best hated man in the United States"—and it is entirely characteristic of him that he enjoyed it. Involved in the bitterest civil struggle since the wars of the Stuarts, he probably came nearer living outside of it, if not above it, than any other man of his day. His extraordinary knowledge of human weakness, his remarkable ability to excite a white heat of anger in others without becoming angry himself, mark him as a man who belongs to a class of his own. Whether he is exciting the people of New Orleans to the deepest indignation by his acts as a military commander, or whether, as Governor of Massachusetts, he amuses himself by outraging the feeling of dignity and propriety which make the Massachusetts clergy the most respectable clerical body in the world, he seems to have derived the keenest enjoyment from every phase of his kaleidoscopic life. Perhaps rhetoric offers no finer example of apparent earnestness than the sentences in which he expressed the hope that the Massachusetts clergy who, temporarily at least, were almost unanimous in considering him "a child of hell," might find forgiveness from heaven for their rash and uncharitable judgment. He seems to have looked on dignity as "the starch of a shroud," and to have been always ready to sacrifice it in exercising his wonderful talents for inciting others to put on public record the qualities which excited his dislike or his derision. Below his great talents as a lawyer, his skill as a politician, his methods as a soldier, was a subtle sense of the humorous and the ridiculous, which was liable to govern him even at what his biographers must consider the most inopportune times. There is more than a suspicion of it even in the celebrated document in which he first called slaves "contraband of war," for he knew as a lawyer that the acceptance of that definition of their status must involve their continued recognition as property by those who were most anxious to repudiate that legal theory. He was by turns a Democrat, a Radical Republican, a Liberal Republican, a Democrat again, and finally a Butler Third Party man. "They have called me everything else," he said, "but no one ever called me a fool." His friends and his enemies alike accepted that epigrammatic sentence as the best possible

"ARTICLE TEN"

(Argument Impeaching Andrew Johnson, March 30th, 1868)

ARTICLE TEN alleges that, intending to set aside the rightful authority and powers of Congress, and to bring into disgrace and contempt the Congress of the United States, and to destroy confidence in and to excite odium against Congress and its laws, he, Andrew Johnson, President of the United States, made divers speeches set out therein, whereby he brought the office of President into contempt, ridicule, and disgrace.

To sustain these charges, there will be put in evidence the shorthand notes of reporters in each instance, who took these speeches, or examined the sworn copies thereof, and one instance where the speech was examined and corrected by the private secretary of the President himself.

To the charges of this article the respondent answers that a convention of delegates, of whom composed he does not say, sat in Philadelphia for certain political purposes mentioned, and appointed a committee to wait upon the respondent as President of the United States; that they were received, and by their chairman, the Hon. Reverdy Johnson, then and now a Senator of the United States, addressed the respondent in a speech, a copy of which the respondent believes from a substantially correct report is made part of the answer; that the respondent made a reply to the address of the committee. While, however, he gives us in his answer a copy of the speech made to him by Mr. Reverdy Johnson, taken from a newspaper, he wholly omits to give us an authorized version of his own speech, about which he may be supposed to know quite as much, and thus saved us some testimony. He does not admit that the extracts from his speech in the article are correct, nor does he deny that they are so.

In regard to the speech at Cleveland, he, again, does not admit that the extracts correctly or justly present his speech; but, again, he does not deny that they do so far as the same is set out.

As to the speech at St. Louis, he does not deny that he made it — says only that he does not admit it, and requires, in each case, that the whole speech shall be proved. In that, I beg leave to assure him and the Senate, his wishes shall be gratified to their fullest fruition. The Senate shall see the performance, so far as in our power to photograph the scene by evidence, on each of these occasions, and shall hear every material word that he said. His defense, however, to the Article is that "he felt himself in duty bound to express opinions of and concerning the public character, conduct, views, purposes, motives, and tendencies of all men engaged in the public service, as well in Congress as otherwise," "and that for anything he may have said on either of these occasions he is justified under the constitutional right of freedom of opinion and freedom of speech, and is not subject to question, inquisition, impeachment, or inculpation in any manner or form whatsoever;" he denies, however, that, by reason of any matter in said Article or its specifications alleged, he has said or done anything indecent or unbecoming in the Chief Magistrate of the United States, or tending to bring his high office into contempt, ridicule, or disgrace.

The issue, then, finally, is this: that those utterances of his, in the manner and form in which they are alleged to have been made, and under the circumstances and at the time they were made, are decent and becoming the President of the United States, and do not tend to bring the office into ridicule and disgrace.

We accept the issues. They are two:—

First. That he has the right to say what he did of Congress in the exercise of freedom of speech; and, second, That what he did say in those speeches was a highly gentlemanlike and proper performance in a citizen, and still more becoming in a President of the United States.

Let us first consider the graver matter of the assertion of the right to cast contumely upon Congress; to denounce it as a "body hanging on the verge of the government;" "pretending to be a Congress when in fact it was not a Congress;" "a Congress pretending to be for the Union when its every step and act tended to perpetuate disunion," "and make a disruption of the States inevitable;" "a Congress in a minority assuming to exercise power which, if allowed to be consummated, would result in despotism and monarchy itself;" "a Congress which had done everything to prevent the union of the States;" "a Congress factious and domineering;" "a radical Congress, which gave origin to another rebellion;" "a Congress upon whose skirts was every drop of blood that was shed in the New Orleans riots."

You will find these denunciations had a deeper meaning than mere expressions of opinion. It may be taken as an axiom in

III—53

the affairs of nations that no usurper has ever seized upon the legislature of his country until he has familiarized the people with the possibility of so doing by vituperating and decrying it. Denunciatory attacks upon the legislature have always preceded, slanderous abuse of the individuals composing it have always accompanied, a seizure by a despot of the legislative power of a country.

Two memorable examples in modern history will spring to the recollection of every man. Before Cromwell drove out by the bayonet the Parliament of England, he and his partisans had denounced it, derided it, decried it, and defamed it, and thus brought it into ridicule and contempt. He vilified it with the same name which it is a significant fact the partisans of Johnson, by a concerted cry, applied to the Congress of the United States when he commenced his memorable pilgrimage and crusade against it. It is a still more significant fact that the justification made by Cromwell and by Johnson for setting aside the authority of Parliament and Congress respectively was precisely the same, to wit: That they were elected by part of the people only. When Cromwell, by his soldiers, finally entered the hall of Parliament to disperse its members, he attempted to cover the enormity of his usurpation by denouncing this man personally as a libertine, that as a drunkard, another as the betrayer of the liberties of the people. Johnson started out on precisely the same course, but, forgetting the parallel, too early he proclaims this patriot an assassin, that statesman a traitor; threatens to hang that man whom the people delight to honor, and breathes out "threatenings and slaughter" against this man whose services in the cause of human freedom has made his name a household word wherever the language is spoken. There is, however, an appreciable difference between Cromwell and Johnson, and there is a like difference in the results accomplished by each.

When Bonaparte extinguished the legislature of France, he waited until, through his press and his partisans, and by his own denunciations, he brought its authority into disgrace and contempt; and when, finally, he drove the council of the nation from their chamber, like Cromwell, he justified himself by personal abuse of the individuals themselves as they passed by him.

That the attempt of Andrew Johnson to overthrow Congress has failed, is because of the want of ability and power, not of malignity and will.

We are too apt to overlook the danger which may come from words; we are inclined to say "that is only talk—wait till some act is done, and then it will be time to move." But words may be, and sometimes are, things—living, burning things that set a world on fire.

As a most notable instance of the power of words, look at the inception of the rebellion through which we have just passed. For a quarter of a century the nation took no notice of the talk of disunion and secession which was heard in Congress and on the "stump" until in the South a generation was taught them by words, and the words suddenly burst forth into terrible, awful war. Does any one think that if Jackson had hanged Calhoun in 1832 for talking nullification and secession, which was embryo treason, the cannon of South Carolina against Fort Sumter would ever have been heard with all their fearful and deadly consequences? Nay, more; if the United States officers, Senators, and Representatives had been impeached or disqualified from office in 1832 for advocating secession on the "stump," as was done in 1862 by Congress, then our sons and brothers, now dead in battle, or starved in prison, had been alive and happy, and a peaceful solution of the question of slavery had been found.

Does any one doubt that if the intentions of the respondent could have been carried out, and his denunciations had weakened the Congress in the affections of the people, so that those who had in the North sympathized with the rebellion could have elected such a minority even, of the Representatives to Congress as, together with those sent up from the governments organized by Johnson in the rebellious States, they should have formed a majority of both or either House of Congress, that the President would have recognized such body as the legitimate Congress, and attempted to carry out its decrees with the aid of the army and navy and the treasury of the United States, over which he now claims such unheard-of and illimitable powers, and thus lighted the torch of civil war?

In all earnestness, Senators, I call each one of you upon his conscience to say whether he does not believe, by a preponderance of evidence drawn from the acts of the respondent since he has been in office, that if the people had not been, as they ever have been, true and loyal to their Congress and themselves, such would not have been the result of these usurpations of power in the Executive?

Is it, indeed, to be seriously argued here that there is a constitutional right in the President of the United States, who, during his official life, can never lay aside his official character, to denounce, malign, abuse, ridicule, and contemn, openly and publicly, the Congress of the United States—a co-ordinate branch of the Government?

It cannot fail to be observed that the President (shall I dare say his counsel, or are they compelled by the exigencies of their defense?) have deceived themselves as to the *gravamen* of the charge in this article? It does not raise the question of freedom of speech, but of propriety and decency of speech and conduct in a high officer of the Government.

Andrew Johnson, the private citizen, as I may reverently hope and trust he soon will be, has the full constitutional right to think and speak what he pleases, in the manner he pleases, and where he pleases, provided always he does not bring himself within the purview of the common law offenses of being a common railer and brawler, or a common scold, which he may do, (if a male person is ever liable to commit this crime;) but the dignity of station, the proprieties of position, the courtesies of office, all of which are a part of the common law of the land, require the President of the United States to observe that gravity of deportment, that fitness of conduct, that appropriateness of demeanor, and those amenities of behavior which are a part of his high official functions. He stands before the youth of the country, the exemplar of all that is worthy in ambition, and all that is to be sought in aspiration; he stands before the men of the country as the grave magistrate who occupies, if he does not fill, the place once honored by Washington; nay, far higher and of greater consequence, he stands before the world as the representative of free institutions, as the type of man whom the suffrages of a free people have chosen as their chief. He should be the living evidence of how much better, higher, nobler, and more in the image of God, is the elected ruler of a free people than a hereditary monarch, coming into power by the accident of birth; and when he disappoints all these hopes and all these expectations, and becomes the ribald, scurrilous blasphemer, bandying epithets and taunts with a jeering mob, shall he be heard to say that such conduct is not a high misdemeanor in office? Nay, disappointing the hopes, causing the cheek to burn with shame, exposing to the taunts and ridicule of every nation the good name and fame of the chosen institutions of thirty millions of people, is it not the highest possible crime and misdemeanor in office, and, under the circumstances, the *gravamen* of these charges? The words are not alleged to be either false or defamatory, because it is not within the power of any man, however high his official position, in effect to slander the Congress of the United States, in the ordinary sense of that word, so as to call on Congress to answer as to the truth of the accusation. We do not go in, therefore, to any question of truth or falsity. We rest upon the scandal of the scene. We would as soon think, in the trial of an indictment against a termagant as a common scold, of summoning witnesses to prove that what she said was not true. It is the noise and disturbance in the neighborhood that is the offense, and not a question of a provocation or irritation which causes the outbreak.

At the risk of being almost offensive, but protesting that if so it is not my fault but that of the person whose acts I am describing, let me but faintly picture to you the scenes at Cleveland and St. Louis.

It is evening; the President of the United States on a journey to do homage at the tomb of an illustrious statesman, accompanied by the head of the army and navy and Secretary of State, has arrived in the great central city of the continent. He has been welcomed by the civic authorities. He has been escorted by a procession of the benevolent charitable societies and citizens and soldiers to his hotel. He has returned thanks in answer to addresses of the mayor and the citizens who have received him. The hospitality of the city has provided a banquet for him and his suite, when he is again expected to address the chosen guests of the city where all things may be conducted in decency and in order. While he was resting, as one would have supposed he would have wished to do, from the fatigue of the day, a noisy crowd of men and boys, washed and unwashed, drunk and sober, black and white, assemble in the street, who make night hideous by their bawling; quitting the drawing-room without the advice of his friends, the President of the United States rushes forth on to the balcony of the hotel to address what proves to have been a mob. And this he calls in his answer a "fit occasion on which he is held to the high duty of expressing opinions of and concerning the legislation of Congress, proposed or completed, in respect of its wisdom, expediency,

justice, worthiness, objects, purposes, and public and political motives and tendencies!"

Observe now, upon this "fit occasion," like in all respects to that at Cleveland, when the President is called upon by the constitutional requirements of his office to expound "the wisdom, expediency, justice, worthiness, objects, purposes, and tendencies of the acts of Congress," what he says and the manner in which he says it. Does he speak with the gravity of a Marshall when expounding constitutional law? Does he use the polished sentences of a Wirt? Or, failing in these, which may be his misfortune, does he, in plain homely words of truth and soberness, endeavor to instruct the men and youth before him in their duty to obey the laws and to reverence their rulers, and to prize their institutions of government? Although he may have been mistaken in the aptness of the occasion for such didactic instruction, still good teaching is never thrown away. He shows, however, by his language, as he had shown at Cleveland, that he meant to adapt himself to the occasion. He has hardly opened his mouth, as we shall show you, when some one in the crowd cries, "How about our British subjects?"

The Chief Executive, supported by his Secretary of State, so that all the foreign relations and diplomatic service were fully represented, with a dignity that not even his counsel can appreciate, and with an amenity which must have delighted Downing Street, answers: "We will attend to John Bull after awhile, so far as that is concerned." The mob, ungrateful, receive this bit of "expression of opinion upon the justice, worthiness, objects, purposes, and public and political motives and tendencies" of our relations with the kingdom of Great Britain, as they fall from the honored lips of the President of the United States, with "laughter," and the more unthinking with "cheers."

Having thus disposed of our diplomatic relations with the first naval and commercial nation on earth, the President next proceeds to "express his opinion in manner aforesaid, and for the purposes aforesaid," to this noisy mob, of the subject of the riot upon which his answer says, "it is the constitutional duty of the President to express opinions for the purposes aforesaid." A voice calls out "New Orleans, go on." After a graceful exordium the President expresses his high opinion that a massacre, wherein his pardoned and unpardoned rebel associates and friends deliberately shot down and murdered unarmed Union men, with-

out provocation, even Horton, the minister of the living God, as his hands were raised to the Prince of Peace, praying in the language of the great martyr, "Father, forgive them, for they know not what they do," was the result of the laws passed by the legislative department of your government, in the words following, that is to say:—

"If you will take up the riot at New Orleans and trace it back to its source, or to its immediate cause, you will find out who was responsible for the blood that was shed there."

"If you take up the riot at New Orleans and trace it back to the radical Congress"——

This, as we might expect, was received by the mob, composed, doubtless, in large part of unrepentant rebels, with great cheering and cries of "bully!" It was "bully," if that means encouraging for them to learn, on the authority of the President of the United States, that they might shoot down Union men and patriots, and lay the sin of murder upon the Congress of the United States; and this was another bit of "opinion" which the counsel say it was the high duty of the President to express upon the justice, the worthiness, objects, "purposes, and public and political motives, and tendencies of the legislation of your Congress."

After some further debate with the mob, some one, it seems, had called out "traitor." The President of the United States, on this fitting, constitutional occasion, immediately took this as personal, and replies to it, "Now, my countrymen, it is very easy to indulge in epithets, it is very easy to call a man a Judas, and cry out 'traitor,' but when he is called upon to give arguments and facts he is very often found wanting."

What were the "facts that were found wanting," which in the mind of the President prevented him from being a Judas Iscariot? He shall state the "wanting facts" in his own language on this occasion when he is exercising his "high constitutional prerogative."

"Judas Iscariot. There was a Judas once, one of the twelve Apostles. Oh, yes, the twelve Apostles had a Christ. [A voice, "and a Moses, too;" great laughter.] The twelve Apostles had a Christ, and he never could have had a Judas unless he had had the twelve Apostles. If I have played the Judas, who has been my Christ that I have played the Judas with? Was it Thad. Stevens? Was it Wendell Phillips? Was it Charles Sumner?"

If it were not that the blasphemy shocks us, we should gather from all this that it dwelt in the mind of the President of the United States that the only reason why he was not a Judas was that he had not been able to find a Christ toward whom to play the Judas.

It will appear that this bit of "opinion," given in pursuance of his constitutional obligation, was received with cheers and hisses. Whether the cheers were that certain patriotic persons named by him might be hanged, or the hissing was because of the inability of the President to play the part of Judas, for the reason before stated, I am sorry to say the evidence will not inform us.

His answer makes the President say that it is his "duty to express opinions concerning the public characters, and the conduct, views, purposes, objects, motives, and tendencies of all men engaged in the public service."

Now, as "the character, motives, tendencies, purposes, objects, and views" of Judas alone had "opinions expressed" about them on this "fit occasion," (although he seemed to desire to have some others, whose names he mentioned, hanged,) I shall leave his counsel to inform you what were the "public services" of Judas Iscariot, to say nothing of Moses, which it was the constitutional duty and right of the President of the United States to discuss on this particularly "fit occasion."

But I will not pursue this revolting exhibition any further.

I will only show you at Cleveland the crowd and the President of the United States, in the darkness of the night, bandying epithets with each other, crying, "Mind your dignity, Andy!" "Don't get mad, Andy!" "Bully for you, Andy!" I hardly dare shock, as I must, every sense of propriety by calling your attention to the President's allusion to the death of the sainted martyr, Lincoln, as the means by which he attained his office, and if it can be justified in any man, public or private, I am entirely mistaken in the commonest proprieties of life. The President shall tell his own story:—

"There was, two years ago, a ticket before you for the Presidency. I was placed upon that ticket with a distinguished citizen now no more. [Voices, "It's a pity;" "Too bad;" "Unfortunate."] Yes, I know there are some who say 'unfortunate.' Yes, unfortunate for some that God rules on high and deals in justice. [Cheers.] Yes, unfortunate. The ways of

Providence are mysterious and incomprehensible, controlling all who exclaim 'unfortunate.'"

Is it wonderful at all that such a speech, which seems to have been unprovoked and coolly uttered, should have elicited the single response from the crowd, "Bully for you"?

I go no further. I might follow this *ad nauseam*. I grant the President of the United States further upon this disgraceful scene the mercy of my silence. Tell me, now, who can read the accounts of this exhibition, and reflect that the result of our institutions of government has been to place such a man, so lost to decency and propriety of conduct, so unfit, in the high office of ruler of this nation, without blushing and hanging his head in shame as the finger of scorn and contempt for republican democracy is pointed at him by some advocate of monarchy in the Old World. What answer have you when an intelligent foreigner says, "Look, see, this is the culmination of the ballot unrestrained in the hands of a free people, in a country where any man may aspire to the office of President. Is not our government of a hereditary king or emperor a better one, where at least our sovereign is born a gentleman, than to have such a *thing* as this for a ruler?"

Yes, we have an answer. We can say this man was not the choice of the people for President of the United States. He was thrown to the surface by the whirlpool of civil war, and carelessly, we grant, elected to the second place in the government, without thought that he might ever fill the first.

By murder most foul he succeeded to the Presidency, and is the elect of an assassin to that high office, and not of the people. "It was a grievous fault, and grievously have we answered it;" but let me tell you, oh advocate of monarchy, that our form of government gives us a remedy for such a misfortune, which yours, with its divine right of kings, does not. We can remove him — as we are about to do — from the office he has disgraced, by the sure, safe, and constitutional method of impeachment; while your king, if he becomes a buffoon, or a jester, or a tyrant, can only be displaced through revolution, bloodshed, and civil war.

This, — this, oh monarchist, — is the crowning glory of our institutions, because of which, if for no other reason, our form of government claims precedence over all other governments of the earth.

faileth him, and he saith to every one that he is a fool. The other is, in the multitude of words there wanteth not sin.

As to the government of the tongue in respect to talking upon indifferent subjects: after what has been said concerning the due government of it in respect to the occasions and times for silence, there is little more necessary than only to caution men to be fully satisfied that the subjects are indeed of an indifferent nature; and not to spend too much time in conversation of this kind. But persons must be sure to take heed that the subject of their discourse be at least of an indifferent nature; that it be no way offensive to virtue, religion, or good manners: that it be not of a licentious, dissolute sort, this leaving always ill impressions upon the mind; that it be no way injurious or vexatious to others; and that too much time be not spent this way, to the neglect of those duties and offices of life which belong to their station and condition in the world. However, though there is not any necessity that men should aim at being important and weighty in every sentence they speak: yet since useful subjects, at least of some kinds, are as entertaining as others, a wise man, even when he desires to unbend his mind from business, would choose that the conversation might turn upon somewhat instructive.

The last thing is, the government of the tongue as relating to discourse of the affairs of others, and giving of characters. These are in a manner the same; and one can scarce call it an indifferent subject, because discourse upon it almost perpetually runs into somewhat criminal.

And, first of all, it were very much to be wished that this did not take up so great a part of conversation; because it is indeed a subject of a dangerous nature. Let any one consider the various interests, competitions, and little misunderstandings which arise amongst men; and he will soon see that he is not unprejudiced and impartial; that he is not, as I may speak, neutral enough to trust himself with talking of the character and concerns of his neighbor, in a free, careless, and unreserved manner. There is perpetually, and often it is not attended to, a rivalship amongst people of one kind or another in respect to wit, beauty, learning, fortune, and that one thing will insensibly influence them to speak to the disadvantage of others, even where there is no formed malice or ill-design. Since, therefore, it is so hard to enter into this subject without offending the first thing to be

JOSEPH BUTLER

(1692–1752)

JOSEPH BUTLER stands for a style of oratory which will always have the strongest attraction to minds addicted to directness of thought. In his sermons on "Human Nature," and still more in that on "The Government of the Tongue," he uses plain English as it never can be used except by one whom candor of thought has made its master. Those who hold that the use of language is to conceal thought rather than to express it, would be embarrassed if compelled to use either the language or the syntax of Butler's denunciation of lying, tattling, and slandering.

He was born in 1692 at Wantage in Berkshire, England, the youngest of the eight children of a linen-draper. His father was a Presbyterian who indulged him in his wish to enter the Church of England. Educated at Oxford, Butler, after entering the Church, became rector of Stanhope, where he published his celebrated work, "The Analogy of Religion, Natural and Revealed, to the Constitution and Course of Nature." The talent shown in this work recommended him to Queen Caroline, and after her death, in 1737, in fulfillment of her strongly expressed wish, he was made Bishop, first of Bristol, and afterwards of Durham. He died in 1752.

THE GOVERNMENT OF THE TONGUE

THE occasions of silence are obvious, and, one would think, should be easily distinguished by everybody: namely, when a man has nothing to say; or nothing but what is better unsaid: better, either in regard to the particular persons he is present with; or from its being an interruption to conversation itself; or to conversation of a more agreeable kind; or better, lastly, with regard to himself. I will end this particular with two reflections of the Wise Man; one of which, in the strongest manner, exposes the ridiculous part of this licentiousness of the tongue; and the other, the great danger and viciousness of it. When he that is a fool walketh by the wayside, his wisdom

observed is that people should learn to decline it; to get over that strong inclination most have to be talking of the concerns and behavior of their neighbor.

But since it is impossible that this subject should be wholly excluded conversation; and since it is necessary that the characters of men should be known: the next thing is that it is a matter of importance what is said; and, therefore, that we should be religiously scrupulous and exact to say nothing, either good or bad, but what is true. I put it thus, because it is in reality of as great imporance to the good of society, that the characters of bad men should be known, as that the characters of good men should. People who are given to scandal and detraction may indeed make an ill-use of this observation; but truths, which are of service towards regulating our conduct, are not to be disowned, or even concealed, because a bad use may be made of them. This, however, would be effectually prevented if these two things were attended to. First, That, though it is equally of bad consequence to society that men should have either good or ill characters which they do not deserve; yet, when you say somewhat good of a man which he does not deserve, there is no wrong done him in particular; whereas, when you say evil of a man which he does not deserve, here is a direct formal injury, a real piece of injustice done him. This, therefore, makes a wide difference; and gives us, in point of virtue, much greater latitude in speaking well than ill of others. Secondly, A good man is friendly to his fellow-creatures, and a lover of mankind; and so will, upon every occasion, and often without any, say all the good he can of everybody; but, so far as he is a good man, will never be disposed to speak evil of any, unless there be some other reason for it, besides, barely that it is true. If he be charged with having given an ill character, he will scarce think it a sufficient justification of himself to say it was a true one, unless he can also give some further account how he came to do so: a just indignation against particular instances of villainy, where they are great and scandalous; or to prevent an innocent man from being deceived and betrayed, when he has great trust and confidence in one who does not deserve it. Justice must be done to every part of a subject when we are considering it. If there be a man who bears a fair character in the world, whom yet we know to be without faith or honesty, to be really an ill man; it must be allowed in general that we shall do a piece of service to society by letting such a one's true character be known. This is no more than what we have an instance of in our Savior himself; though he was mild and gentle beyond example. However, no words can express too strongly the caution which should be used in such a case as this.

Upon the whole matter: If people would observe the obvious occasions of silence, if they would subdue the inclination to talebearing, and that eager desire to engage attention, which is an original disease in some minds, they would be in little danger of offending with their tongue; and would, in a moral and religious sense, have due government over it.

I will conclude with some precepts and reflections of the Son of Sirach upon this subject. Be swift to hear; and, if thou hast understanding, answer thy neighbor; if not, lay thy hand upon thy mouth. Honor and shame is in talk.

CAIUS JULIUS CÆSAR

(100–44 B. C.)

DOCTOR WILLIAM ROSE, the translator of Sallust, says that the speeches in the Senate, reported by Sallust as delivered by Cæsar and Cato during the conspiracy of Catiline "have been ranked as masterpieces of ancient composition and must not be considered as merely the production of the historian." He adds that both speeches were "addressed to the Senate in nearly such terms as those reported by Sallust." Doctor Rose believes that this is generally admitted, and it is easily credible at any rate.

Cæsar sympathized with Catiline and he was strongly suspected of complicity in the conspiracy. His enormous debts, his luxurious life, his great ambition and his recollections of the times of Marius, inclined him to look with favor on the overthrow of the Senatorial oligarchy which dominated Rome. He showed afterwards that in opposing the Senatorial order, he aimed at a dictatorship, supported by the masses of Rome and by the army, but at the time of the conspiracy of Catiline, his purposes, if already formulated, were not yet understood. When it was proposed to punish the associates of Catiline, Cæsar was placed in a position of great difficulty. He met it with characteristic promptness by protesting against extraordinary severity as unlawful. Silanus having voted for capital punishment, Cæsar, when called on to declare himself, delivered the celebrated oration preserved by Sallust.

ON THE CONSPIRACY OF CATILINE

(Delivered in the Roman Senate, 64 B. C.)

IT IS the duty of all men, Conscript Fathers, in their deliberations on subjects of difficult determination, to divest themselves of hatred and affection, of revenge and pity. The mind when clouded with such passions cannot easily discern the truth, nor has any man ever gratified his own headstrong inclination and at the same time answered any worthy purpose. When we exercise our judgment only, it has sufficient force, but when passion possesses us, it bears sovereign sway and reason is

of no avail. I could produce a great many instances of Kings and States pursuing wrong measures when influenced by resentment or compassion. But I had rather set before you the example of our forefathers, and show how they acted in opposition to the impulses of passion, but agreeably to wisdom and sound policy. In the war which we carried on with Perses, King of Macedonia, Rhodes, a mighty and flourishing city, which owed all its grandeur, too, to the Roman aid, proved faithless, and became our enemy: but when the war was ended, and the conduct of the Rhodians came to be taken into consideration, our ancestors pardoned them, that none might say the war had been undertaken more on account of their riches than of injuries. In all the Punic wars, too, though the Carthaginians, both in time of peace and even during a truce, had often insulted us in the most outrageous manner, yet our ancestors never improved any opportunity of retaliating; considering more what was worthy of themselves than what might in justice be done against them.

In like manner, Conscript Fathers, ought you to take care that the wickedness of Lentulus and the rest of the conspirators weigh not more with you than a regard to your own honor; and that, while you gratify your resentment, you do not forfeit your reputation. If a punishment, indeed, can be invented adequate to their crimes, I approve the extraordinary proposal made; but if the enormity of their guilt is such that human invention cannot find out a chastisement proportioned to it, my opinion is, that we ought to be contented with such as the law has provided.

Most of those who have spoken before me have in a pompous and affecting manner lamented the situation of the State; they have enumerated all the calamities of war, and the many distresses of the conquered; virgins and youths violated; children torn from the embraces of their parents; matrons forced to bear the brutal insults of victorious soldiers; temples and private houses plundered; all places filled with flames and slaughter; finally, nothing but arms, carcasses, blood, and lamentations to be seen.

But, for the sake of the immortal gods, to what purpose were such affecting strains? Was it to raise in your minds an abhorrence of the conspiracy, as if he whom so daring and threatening a danger cannot move, could be inflamed by the breath of eloquence? No; this is not the way: nor do injuries

appear light to any one that suffers them; many stretch them beyond their due size. But, Conscript Fathers, different allowances are made to different persons: when such as live in obscurity are transported by passion to the commission of any offenses, there are few who know it, their reputation and fortune being on a level: but those who are invested with great power are placed on an eminence, and their actions viewed by all; and thus the least allowance is made to the highest dignity. There must be no partiality, no hatred, far less any resentment or animosity, in such a station. What goes by the name of passion only in others, when seen in men of power, is called pride and cruelty.

As for me, Conscript Fathers, I look on all tortures as far short of what these criminals deserve. But most men remember best what happened last; and, forgetting the guilt of wicked men, talk only of their punishment, if more severe than ordinary. I am convinced that what Decius Silanus, brave and worthy man, said, was from his zeal to the State, and that he was neither biased by partiality nor enmity; such is his integrity and moderation, as I well know. But his proposal appears to me not, indeed, cruel, (for against such men what can be cruel?) but contrary to the genius of our government. Surely, Silanus, you were urged by fear, or the enormity of the treason, to propose a punishment quite new. How groundless such fear is it is needless to show; especially when, by the diligence of so able a consul, such powerful forces are provided for our security; and, as to the punishment, we may say, what indeed is the truth, that, to those who live in sorrow and misery, death is but a release from trouble; that it is death which puts an end to all the calamities of men, beyond which there is no room for care and joy. But why, in the name of the gods, did not you add to your proposal that they should be punished with stripes? Was it because the Porcian law forbids it? But there are other laws, too, which forbid the putting to death a condemned Roman, and allow him the privilege of banishment. Or was it because whipping is a more severe punishment than death? Can anything be reckoned too cruel or severe against men convicted of such treason? But if stripes are a lighter punishment, how is it consistent to observe the law in a matter of small concern, and disregard it in one that is of greater?

But you will say, "Who will find fault with any punishment decreed against traitors to the State?" I answer, time may, so may sudden conjectures; and fortune, too, that governs the world at pleasure. Whatever punishment is inflicted on these parricides will be justly inflicted. But take care, Conscript Fathers, how your present decrees may affect posterity. All bad precedents spring from good beginnings, but when the administration is in the hands of wicked or ignorant men, these precedents, at first just, are transferred from proper and deserving objects to such as are not so.

The Lacedæmonians, when they had conquered the Athenians, placed thirty governors over them; who began their power by putting to death, without any trial, such as were remarkably wicked and universally hated. The people were highly pleased at this, and applauded the justice of such executions. But when they had by degrees established their lawless authority, they wantonly butchered both good and bad without distinction; and thus kept the State in awe. Such was the severe punishment which the people, oppressed with slavery, suffered for their foolish joy.

In our own times, when Sylla, after his success, ordered Damasippus, and others of the like character, who raised themselves on the misfortunes of the State, to be put to death, who did not commend him for it? All agreed that such wicked and factious instruments, who were constantly embroiling the commonwealth, were justly put to death. Yet this was an introduction to a bloody massacre: for whoever coveted his fellow-citizen's house, either in town or country, nay, even any curious vase or fine raiment, took care to have the possessor of it put on the list of the proscribed.

Thus they who had rejoiced at the punishment of Damasippus were soon after dragged to death themselves; nor was an end put to this butchery till Sylla had glutted all his followers with riches. I do not, indeed, apprehend any such proceedings from M. Cicero, nor from these times. But in so great a city as ours there are various characters and dispositions. At another time, and under another consul, who may have an army too at his command, any falsehood may pass for fact; and when, on this precedent, the consul shall, by a decree of the Senate, draw the sword, who is to set bounds to it? who to moderate its fury?

Our ancestors, Conscript Fathers, never wanted conduct nor courage; nor did they think it unworthy of them to imitate the customs of other nations, if they were useful and praiseworthy.

III—54

From the Samnites they learned the exercise of arms, and borrowed from them their weapons of war; and most of their ensigns of magistracy from the Tuscans; in a word, they were very careful to practice whatever appeared useful to them, whether among their allies or their enemies; choosing rather to imitate than envy what was excellent.

Now, in those days, in imitation of the custom of Greece, they inflicted stripes on guilty citizens, and capital punishment on such as were condemned: but when the commonwealth became great and powerful, and the vast number of citizens gave rise to factions; when the innocent began to be circumvented, and other such inconveniences to take place; then the Porcian and other laws were made, which provided no higher punishment than banishment for the greatest crimes. These considerations, Conscript Fathers, appear to me of the greatest weight against our pursuing any new resolution on this occasion: for surely their share of virtue and wisdom, who from so small beginnings raised so mighty an empire, far exceeds ours, who are scarce able to preserve what they acquired so gloriously.—" What! shall we discharge the conspirators," you will say, " to reinforce Catiline's army? " By no means: but my opinion is this; that their estates should be confiscated; their persons closely confined in the most powerful cities of Italy; and that no one move the Senate or the people for any favor towards them, under the penalty of being declared by the Senate an enemy to the State and the welfare of its members.

DANIEL W. CAHILL

(1802–1864)

DANIEL W. CAHILL, D.D., celebrated as an American pulpit orator and lecturer on social, religious, and scientific subjects, had a remarkable command of fervid and picturesque eloquence. Born in Queens County, Ireland, in 1802, he studied at Carlow College and at Maynooth, where he was ordained a priest. He was for a time Professor of Natural History at Carlow College, and at another time editor of the Dublin Telegraph. He became a learned chemist and astronomer also, and, after living from 1851 to 1855 in England, came as a priest to America, where his labors gained for him a distinction that led to the publication of a large volume of his sermons and lectures after his death. He died in Boston October 24th, 1864.

THE LAST JUDGMENT

(From a Sermon Delivered by Very Rev. D. W. Cahill, D. D., in St. Peter's Church, Barclay Street, New York, on Sunday Evening, November 29th, 1863)

THERE was a time when there was no earth, no sun, no moon, no stars; when all the eye now beholds had no existence; when there was nothing,—all darkness, chaos,—when the Divinity reigned alone; when no created voice was heard through God's territories to break the silence of illimitable space. Six thousand years only have elapsed since he built the present world and peopled the skies with the myriad spheres that hang in the arched roof above us. The mere shell, the mere framework of this world may, perhaps, be somewhat older, but we know when Adam was created with the certainty of a parish register. It may be about six thousand years ago: and since that period the history of man is one unbroken page of wickedness and infidelity. Heaven once, in anger, nearly extirpated our race; and once, in mercy, forgave us. Yet, since, the earth is stained with guilt red as scarlet; and the patience of a God—

patience infinite—can alone bear it. Who can tell the amount of the crime of even one city for one day? But who can conceive the infinite guilt of all peoples, of all nations, and all ages, ascending and accumulating before God's throne since the beginning? God is great in power, great in goodness, great in mercy, great in wisdom; but he is more than great in patience, to bear the congregated offenses of countless millions, daily, hourly, provoking his anger and opposing his will.

But, as the hour of man's creation and man's redemption was arranged by God, and in due time occurred, so the moment for man's total extinction on earth is approaching, and when the time written in the records of heaven shall have arrived, that unerring decree will be executed. By one word he made this world; by one word he can destroy it. By one stroke of his omnipotent pencil he drew the present picture of creation; by one dash of the same brush he can blot it out again and expunge all the work of the skies. Who can limit his power? In one second he can reduce all things to their original chaos, and live again as he did before creation began. He can, when he pleases, destroy all things—the soul excepted. The soul he cannot annihilate. He made the world himself—of course, he can himself destroy it. But Christ is the redeemer of the soul, and, therefore, its immortal existence is as indestructible as the eternity of God. Redemption is a contract between the Father and the Son. That contract cannot be broken without ignoring the Cross. Hence, while God is at liberty to blot out his own creation, he cannot annihilate the work purchased with the blood of Christ. Hence, in the coming wreck, the soul cannot be destroyed. And this is the idea that renders that awful hour a source of joy unlimited to the blessed, and of terrors unspeakable to the wicked. Yet although no one can tell when this fatal day will arrive, still it may be fairly presumed to be at hand, when Christ's passion will be disregarded on earth; when vice will so predominate over virtue that the worship of God may be said to cease; when the destruction of the earth will be a mercy, a duty of justice which God owes to his own character and to the eternal laws of his kingdom. When this time shall have arrived, we may fairly expect the day of the general judgment. . . . .

Who can paint Omnipotent power pulling down firmaments, and suns, and stars, and moons: his will reversing his former creation; the earth trembling in desolation? How minutely graphic is Christ in this terrible description; and have you noticed his last words, where he says: "Have I not foretold all to you?" This single phrase is worth the entire history; since it stamps the terrors of this day with the certitude of any other truth of faith, any other fact of the Gospel.

St. Mark continues to detail the order of this terrible hour. Terror will follow on terror; curse upon curse, "till men will fall away with fear." The sun being not quite extinguished, fatal gloom will be spread over all things like a veil over the face of the dead: terrific signs are seen in the heavens, and all things announce that time is at an end. St. John says, that before God pronounces the final word there is silence in heaven; and voices are heard in the air, on the water, and on the earth. At length the skies open and he pours out the first vial of his anger. And the end is come. God speaks the command; and all nature trembles as if in agony. The seas swell, and boil, and rise, and lash the skies. The mountains nod and sink, and the poles collapse. The lightnings flash, and the moaning tempests sweep over the furious deep, piling up ocean upon ocean on the trembling globe. The earth reels in convulsion, and the whole frame of creation struggles.

A mighty conflagration bursts from the melting earth, rages like a hurricane roundabout, devouring all things in its storm and flood of fire, consuming the crumbling wreck of the condemned world. The heavens become terrible, as the kindling earth and seas show their overwhelming flashes on the crimson skies. The sun muffled, the moon black, the stars fallen, floating masses like clouds of blood sweep the skies in circling fury. The Omnipotence which, in the beginning of time, formed all creation, is now concentrated in a point; and, as it were, intensifies the infinity of his wrath, till his anger can swell no higher; and his voice is heard like thunder in the distance. With what eloquent terror does the Savior paint this scene in his own words: "Men fainting away with fear, running in wild distraction, calling on the ground to open and swallow them, and the rocks to fall on them and hide them from the face of the Lord." The earth on fire: the skies faded: the sun and the stars darkened or extinguished: mankind burning, dying: the angry voice of God coming to judge the world: and Jesus Christ describing the scene,—are realities which the history of God has never seen

before; and which never again will be repeated during the endless round of eternity.

Reason asks: Oh, who is God? and what is nature? and whence is man? and where is heaven? and why is hell? and what is our destiny? Was the world made in pleasure, moved for a moment in trial and suffering, and then blotted out in anger? In one revolution of the earth on fire it is a blank. Like a burning ship at sea, sinking to the bottom on fire, the earth vanishes into nonexistence under the blue vault, where it once careered in its brilliant circle. Not a vestige remains of its omnipotent path. Its wide territory is a tenantless, dark waste— the myriad lamps of the skies extinguished: all former existences crumbled: silent forever: all chaos: things are as if they had never been: the history of Earth and Time a mere record of the forgotten past: a mere hollow vault in the infinitude of space.

JOHN CAIRD

(1820-)

JOHN CAIRD'S 'University Addresses' represent the best thought of one of the strongest and clearest minds of the nineteenth century. In lucidity and directness and often in beauty of diction, they are models of their class. Though probably carefully prepared before their delivery, they often show the freedom and force of the extemporaneous speech. The address on the 'Art of Public Speaking' has compressed into it more thought than often goes to make an entire volume, and it has many periods of striking eloquence.

Caird was born at Greenock, Scotland, in 1820. Educated for the pulpit, he became Professor of Divinity at Glasgow University in 1862, and it was there that he delivered the addresses by which he is likely to be longest remembered. He is the author of numerous works on philosophy, metaphysics, and theology. He became Principal of the University in 1873, and is generally spoken of as Principal Caird.

THE ART OF ELOQUENCE

(From the address on the 'Art of Public Speaking,' delivered at the University of Glasgow, November 9th, 1889)

OF ALL intellectual agencies, the faculty of public speaking is that which, in proportion to its practical influence and importance, has received the least attention in our educational system. Of course, seeing that the first condition of good speaking is that the speaker should have something to say, indirectly all education is an education of the orator. External gifts of voice and manner, apart from more solid acquirements, may deceive and dazzle the unwary and make a slender stock of ideas go a long way with an uneducated or half-educated auditory. But such superficial qualities in the long run lose their effect, even on uncritical ears, and to the better instructed may even become offensive as a kind of tacit insult to their judgment. Knowledge and a disciplined intelligence therefore constitute the

first condition of effective speaking. But if it be true, as we must all admit, that the possession of knowledge does not imply the power of imparting it, that profound thinkers and ripe scholars may be poor and ineffective speakers; if experience proves that men who are strong in the study may be weak on the platform or in the pulpit, and that even men whose books evince a masterly grasp of their subject may be distanced as teachers or preachers or public speakers by persons of greatly inferior gifts and attainments—then it is obvious that something more than the possession of ideas goes to the making of the orator, and that that system of education is incomplete which confines itself to the acquirement of knowledge and neglects the art of oral expression.

Every one knows of the immense pains that were bestowed on the cultivation of this art in ancient times. "Ancient oratory," writes Professor Jebb, "is a fine art, an art regarded by its cultivators as analogous to sculpture, to poetry, to music." Already before the art of rhetoric had become an elaborate system, the orators were accustomed to prepare themselves for their task, first in composition, then in delivery. "Great is the labor of oratory," says Cicero, "as is its field, its dignity, its reward." And though it may be true that in this as in other arts, nature and original aptitude count for much, and the highest eminence is attainable by few, yet moderate success is not beyond the reach of average ability industriously and carefully cultivated. How then shall we explain the comparative neglect into which, in our modern educational system, this art has fallen; how shall we account for the fact that whilst every other art has its principles and methods, its long and laborious discipline, its assiduous study of the best models, the acquisition of this art is for the most part left to chance or to such proficiency as can be gained in course of time and at the expense of long-suffering audiences? How is it that in our schools and colleges everything is done for the attainment of knowledge, and nothing at all for the capacity of communicating it?

At first sight we might suppose that this neglect is to be ascribed to the diffusion of literature and the growing influence of the press. Oral teaching, we might naturally suppose, would count for more in times when there was almost no other access to the popular mind, and, with the spread of education and the multiplication of books, would gradually be superseded by instruction conveyed in a literary form. That the gift of eloquence should be rated high, and should be sedulously cultivated in an age before books existed in printed form, or when books were few and costly and readers a very limited class, and when for the great mass of men the preacher or public speaker was in himself all that books, newspapers, magazines, pamphlets, popular manuals, organs of political parties and religious sects, the vast and varied mass of publications that are constantly pouring forth from the press, are for us in the present day—that at such a period the faculty of oral address should be supremely important is only what we might expect. But as education advances, and ideas in the more exact and permanent form of printed matter, suited to every variety of taste and intelligence, become almost universally accessible, we might also expect that the speaker's function, if it did not become extinct, would fall into the background; and also that, in so far that it survived, the improved taste of society would tend at once to diminish the quantity and to raise the quality of public speaking.

How groundless such expectations would prove you need not be told. The vocation of the speaker has not only lost nothing, but has enormously gained in public consequence with the gradual diffusion of knowledge in printed form. There never was a time, in modern history at least, when it constituted so potent a factor in the national life as in our own day. There never was a time when the gift of oratory or the talent for debate brought so much influence, social, political, ecclesiastical, or when he who was endowed with it found the power of ready utterance so much in demand. In this country, at least, the man who can speak is under a perpetual pressure to exercise his gift. Lecture platforms, public meetings, associations for all sorts of objects; festivals, banquets, ceremonials, conferences, anniversaries, meetings to offer testimonials to retiring, or to organize memorials to departed, officials and celebrities, great and small—public occasions of all sorts, in short, create a perpetual call on his power of utterance. Nor is the demand confined to public occasions. The rage for oratory pursues him in his hours of relaxation and into the retreats of social and private life. In the pauses of a railway journey admiring auditors insist on a modicum of their favorite stimulant. At a private dinner or a garden party, the reporter, note-book in hand, is either openly or furtively introduced; and, sometimes, it must be confessed, not without his own connivance,

opportunity is afforded to the oratorical celebrity to give the world another taste of his quality.

Moreover, it is to be observed that, contrary to the natural anticipation I have just suggested, the public taste for public qualification does not become more fastidious with the progress of education. Public speaking, with rare exceptions, does not in our day improve in quality. The palmy days of oratory, when it was regarded as an art on a level with painting, and sculpture, and poetry, when the severest canons of criticism were applied to it, when the great speaker cultivated his gift by laborious and varied discipline, speaking seldom, and only on occasions worthy of his powers, and grudging no pains to meet the claims of an exacting but appreciative audience—these days are long passed away. How could it be otherwise? An epicure could not expect a chef in the culinary art to send up, day after day, at a moment's notice, a perpetual series of *recherche* viands; and from even men of the highest abilities it would be too much to ask for the production of off-hand, extempore, oratorical feasts. Hence we need not wonder if, when we examine the speeches of even the most renowned purveyors of modern oratory, political and other, we should find that, in the best qualities of eloquence, in clearness of thought, precision of aim, consecution of argument, force, aptitude, and elegance of expression, they fall miserably short of the best types of ancient oratory; and that loose, slipshod, and ambiguous phraseology, involved and interminable sentences, sounding but empty declamation, perplexed and inconclusive argument, and the cheap impressiveness of appeals to vulgar prejudice and passion, should be their too common characteristics.

There are, however, some considerations which may serve to abate the severity of the censure we pass on these and other defects of modern oratory. Much, of course, depends on our canons of criticism. We must consider how far the blemishes on which we animadvert arise, not from the incapacity or carelessness of the artist, but from the necessary limits and conditions of his art. It is obvious, for one thing, that we cannot apply the same standard, either as to matter or form, to written or spoken prose composition. It is even possible that the speaker who should aim at literary excellence would be going on a false quest, and that the qualities which made his work good as literature would mar or vitiate it as oratory. A reported speech, indeed, becomes

literature, but it is not to be judged of as such, but as a composition primarily addressed to the ear, and producing its effect, whether instruction or persuasion, whether intelligent conviction or emotion and action, under the condition of being rapidly spoken and rapidly apprehended. And this condition obviously implies that many qualities which are meritorious in a book or treatise—profundity or subtlety of thought, closeness and consecution of argument, elaborate refinement and beauty of style, expression nicely adapted to the most delicate shades of thought—would not only involve a waste of labor in a spoken address, but might mar or frustrate its effectiveness. A realistic painter who bestows infinite pains in copying the form and color of every pebble on the bank of brook or stream, and every reticulation of each leaf on the spray that overhangs it, not only squanders effort in achieving microscopic accuracy, but distracts by irrelevant detail the eye of the observer, and destroys the general idea or impression of the landscape. And a like result may attend elaboration of thought and fastidious nicety of form in a spoken composition. Such minute finish is either lost or unappreciated by the auditor, or, while he pauses to admire it, his attention is diverted, and he loses the thread of the discourse or argument.

Moreover, in studying a written composition, a reader has no right to complain of compression or conciseness, or, on the other hand, of the space occupied in the development of the thought. If the sense be not immediately obvious, or if he fails to catch it on a first reading, he can pause on a phrase or sentence; he can go back on a paragraph; if the matter sets his own mind aworking in a different track, he can suspend his reading to follow out the suggested train of thought, and then come back to take up the interrupted sequence of the author's argument; or again, if the strain on his attention or intelligence becomes too great, he can stop and resume his reading at will.

But an oral address admits of no such delays and interruptions. The meaning must be understood at a first hearing or not at all, the discourse must be so framed that the mind of the hearer can move on at least as fast as that of the speaker; and seeing you cannot, on many occasions at any rate, shut up a speaker as you can a book, there are limits of length to which every public address must conform. Obviously, therefore, oral composition not only admits, but requires, certain characteristics which

would not be only illegitimate, but positive blemishes in matter intended to be read. Hearers, of course, vary in quickness of apprehension, and no speaker is bound to be plain to auditors whose intelligence must be supplemented by a surgical operation. But though it is true that greater condensation is possible in addressing a select audience, an average audience cannot be fed with intellectual pemmican. To present the same thought in varied language or in diversified aspects, to make use of pictorial forms and abundant and familiar illustrations; to go at a slow pace in argument; to avoid rapid transitions and elliptical reasoning; to arrest wavering attention at the cost even of irrelevancy and digression; to be not over-scrupulous as to grammatical and dialectic proprieties or a telling roughness that jars on a fastidious ear; to make sure not merely that the ideas are there, but that they are so presented as to interest, strike, sustain the attention, and tell on the heart and soul of the hearers—these and such as these must be aims present to the mind of the public speaker and controlling the form and substance of his talk. But all this implies that a certain latitude must be conceded to oral, which is denied to written composition, and that the very effectiveness and success of a speech may be due to its offenses against the strict canons of literary criticism.

It is on this principle that we explain the fact that good speakers are often bad writers, good writers bad speakers, and that the instances are rare in which men attain to great and equal excellence as authors and as orators.

Following out a little further this comparison of speaking and writing, or of oral and written and prose composition, there is another characteristic by reason of which, at first sight at least, we must ascribe an inferior value to the former; *viz.*, its evanescence. Written or printed matter has the advantage not only of greater precision but of greater permanence. A great book is a treasure for all time. The thinker passes away, but the thoughts that are enshrined in the literature of the past live on for the instruction and delight of succeeding generations. It is of the very essence of oratory, on the other hand, to be ephemeral. Its most brilliant effects, like the finest aspects of nature, vanish in the very moment of observation. They can no more be arrested than the light of morning on the mountain summit, or the flashing radiance on the river's rippling waves, "a moment here, then gone forever." The words that touch us by their pathos, or rouse us by their lofty eloquence, pass away like the successive notes of a song in the very act of falling on the enraptured ear.

It may even be said that the best and noblest effects of oratory are more evanescent than those of music. The song may be sung, the great composer's work that delights us at a first hearing may be repeated with equal or higher artistic skill. But often the power of spoken words depends on a combination of circumstances that can never be reproduced. The speech of a great statesman in debate — say on some critical emergency when the vote is about to be taken that is to decide the fate of a ministry, or the passing of a measure of reform or of domestic or foreign policy on which the interests of millions are staked; or again, the speech spoken by an illustrious pleader in a great State trial, and before an audience composed of all the elements, social and intellectual, that stimulate to their very highest an orator's powers; or, to name no other instance, the words in which no one knows how to sympathize with and touch the hidden springs of human emotion, give expression to the sorrow of a community for departed greatness, or the proud reaction with which it rises to face some national calamity or peril — in these and in many similar instances the conditions of a great speech, and therefore the speech itself, can never recur. A song may be sung again by the same or other voice, but the speech can never be respoken even by the voice that uttered it; and that not merely because, under the inspiration of a great occasion, it may have reached the climax of its powers, but because the moving panorama of history never repeats itself, never revives again the circumstances that gave it its power to affect us. And when the eloquent voice has itself been silenced, unlike the song, no other voice can reproduce its music. On the lips of Æschines it may seem still instinct with power, but all his art cannot make us feel as we should have done, had we heard Demosthenes.

But if we reflect for a moment on this distinction between oral and written composition, may not the very fact of the evanescence of the former suggest to us that there is in good oratory an element of power which written or printed matter does not and cannot possess? Society will never, by reason of advancing culture and the diffusion of literature, outgrow the relish and demand for good speaking, for this, if for no other reason, that,

besides outward circumstances and accessories, there is something in what we call eloquent speech which by no effort or artifice can be produced in literary form. . . . There is a universal language which, long ere we have mastered the meaning of articulate words, carries with it for each and all of us its own interpretation, and with the potent aid of which the most consummate linguist can never dispense. Betwixt parent and child in all lands and climes, the light in the eye, the smile on the cheek, the tones of the voice, the thousand movements, touches, caresses of the enfolding arms, constitute a medium of communication intuitively understood, which not art but nature has taught. And this, too, is a language which we never outgrow, and which,, in the hands of one who knows how to use it, reinforces and in some measure transcends the capacities of oral address. The artifices of the printer, the notation of the musician, can no doubt do much to reduce this language of nature to formal expression. But even musical notation, though much more complete than any that could be adapted to speaking, leaves — as any one knows who has ever listened to a great artist and compared his singing or playing with that of an inferior and common-place performer — an almost boundless latitude of expression to individual taste and feeling.

And even more remarkable is this untaught and unteachable power in the case of the speaker. What ingenuity could invent a written or printed notation that would represent the infinite, nicely-discriminated, subtle shades of tone and accent which a great speaker instinctively employs, and which the ear and soul of a sympathetic auditory instinctively interprets. Even in deliberate speech, in exposition, narrative, calm and unimpassioned argument, there are innumerable subtle changes by which corresponding variations of thought are indicated. And when he rises to the region of emotion, has not nature wedded its own symbols to the whole gamut of feeling, — entreaty, passion, pathos, tenderness, grief subdued or unrepressed, remonstrance, anger, scorn, sarcasm, reverence, awe, aspiration, homage, the agony of the penitent, the hope and trust of the believer, the mystical rapture of the saint, — has not each of these and a thousand other varieties of feeling its own appropriate form of expression, so that, through the whole continuity of speech or sermon, a speaker can suffuse articulate language with this deeper, subtler, underlying and all-potent language of nature? Lacking this

organ of spiritual power a discourse may have every intellectual excellence, but it will fall short of the highest effect. For often

> "Words are weak and far to seek
>   When wanted fifty-fold,
> And so if silence do not speak,
> And trembling lip and tearful cheek,
>   There's nothing told."

In one word, the ultimate reason for the greater effectiveness of spoken than of written matter is simply this, that the latter is dead and silent, the former quick with the glow and vitality of intelligence and emotion. In certain scientific observations you must eliminate what is called the personal equation; but in good speaking, the personality of the speaker, instead of needing to be discounted, is that which lends its special value to the result. What reaches the auditor is not thought frozen into abstract form, but thought welling warm and fluent from a living source. In reading a book or report the whole burden of the process is thrown upon the reader. In listening to a spoken address more than half of the burden is borne by the speaker; or rather, activity and receptivity become almost indistinguishable. Charged alike with the electric force of sympathy, the minds of speaker and hearer meet and mingle in a common medium of intelligence and emotion.

JOHN C. CALHOUN

(1782-1850)

ALHOUN is one of the very few modern orators who actually represent the Attic school of the time of Demosthenes as closely as a majority of educated public speakers, consciously or unconsciously, represent that of Rome in the time of Cicero. Cicero's mind, like that of Burke, was at all times exuberant and the primary object of his art was to give it the freest and fullest possible expression. The primary object of Attic art, as it is illustrated not only in oratory, but in poetry, architecture, and sculpture, is chastity, — the rejection of everything but the fitting. In its logical extreme, this idea which created Greek civilization, gave the Spartans their biting wit and contempt for long speeches. Its loss, under the Persian influences which substituted Oriental moral and artistic standards for those of Greece, led to the complete corruption of later Greek poetry and brought about conditions under which Athens, though overflowing with wrangling and declamatory sophists, had not for generations a single orator of the first rank.

Imitating Demosthenes seemingly with the greatest pains and having the ability to appreciate his peculiar excellencies, Calhoun is, nevertheless, by the necessity of the case, an English orator — not a Grecian. The English language is by its genius as severe as the artistic intellect of Attica was in its processes, while on the other hand the Greek intellect expressed itself in a language of unequalled music. Exuberance of idea in a language so surpassing in its melody, would have been an intolerable excess, while, in a language so severe as English, the Attic severity of thought may often force its conscious imitator beyond the line of mere chastity into poverty of expression. It is on this side that Calhoun errs when he errs at all.

His tendency to excessive severity of expression is fully illustrated in his celebrated speech of February 15th and 16th, 1833, against the Force Bill. It is without rhetorical ornament and almost without metaphor. In it the attempt is made to supplant the graces of rhetoric with the impulses of force. It has at times a directness and intensity which are hardly compatible with any other style, and if there are many now who will hold with Thomas H. Benton that, considered as a whole, it is one of those characteristic productions of Calhoun's intellect which make almost intolerably hard reading, few will deny that it is necessary to read it in order to know American history, and to understand the logical method of a mind which, as much as any other intellect of that generation in Europe or America, worked to influence, if not to control, the course of events.

Nothing but the speech itself will show adequately what Calhoun stands for in American history, but at the close of the second day's speech, he came as near to a summary of his idea as it was possible to make. His argument there was that the States, in order to prevent the Constitution from becoming a dead letter, must exercise the functions of the Roman tribunes in "interposing their veto not only against the passage of laws but against their execution." As this theory was practically abandoned at Appomattox, it appeals for consideration now chiefly because of its influence on the history of the past.

Calhoun was born in the Abbeville district of South Carolina, March 18th, 1782. His father, Patrick Calhoun, a member of the South Carolina provincial legislature during the Revolution, held, as he told his son, that "the government is best which allows the largest amount of individual liberty compatible with good order and tranquillity," and that "improvement in political science will be found to consist in throwing off many of the restraints imposed by law and once deemed necessary to an organized society." Educated at Yale College and at the Litchfield (Conn.) Law School, John C. Calhoun was an intense student, with a power of concentration which is only attained as a habit by a small minority even of those who attempt to use their intellects habitually. It was a power which would have made him a leader in any epoch, but as he lived at a time when the reverence of the American people for great intellectual powers was almost idolatrous, it gave him influence over those who sympathized with him, so unbounded that he steadily forced out of leadership at the South the "Jacksonian Democrats" of the school represented in the Senate by his unyielding opponent, Benton.

After service in the South Carolina legislature, Calhoun entered Congress in 1811 and at once created a deep impression by his power as an orator. His strong support of the War party gave him the standing which made him Vice-President (from 1825 to 1832). When he resigned the Vice-Presidency in 1832 and entered the United States Senate, it was to take the place of Hayne who had shown himself an unequal match for Webster in the great debate precipitated by Calhoun's "Exposition of State Rights" published by the South Carolina legislature in 1829 as a preliminary definition of the same theory which he elaborated in his speech against the Force Bill. Under that bill, introduced by Mr. Wilkins, of Pennsylvania, it was proposed to give President Jackson power to coerce South Carolina or any other State resisting the collection of tariff duties or other Federal imposts. After the crisis was averted by Henry Clay's Compromise

III—55

Act, Calhoun's influence was greatly enhanced. He served as Secretary of State under Tyler and was afterwards re-elected to the Senate where he remained until his death March 31st, 1850. In summing up his character Webster said of him:—

"Sir, the eloquence of Mr. Calhoun, or the manner of his exhibition of his sentiments in public bodies, was part of his intellectual character. It grew out of the qualities of his mind. It was plain, strong, terse, condensed, concise; sometimes impassioned—still always severe. Rejecting ornament, not often seeking far for illustration, his power consisted in the plainness of his propositions, in the closeness of his logic, and in the earnestness and energy of his manner. These are the qualities, as I think, which have enabled him through such a long course of years to speak often, and yet always command attention. His demeanor as a Senator is known to us all—is appreciated, venerated by us all. No man was more respectful to others; no man carried himself with greater decorum, no man with superior dignity. . . . Mr. President, he had the basis, the indispensable basis, of all high character; and that was unspotted integrity—unimpeached honor and character. If he had aspirations, they were high, and honorable, and noble. There was nothing groveling, or low, or meanly selfish, that came near the head or the heart of Mr. Calhoun. Firm in his purpose, perfectly patriotic and honest, as I am sure he was, in the principles that he espoused, and in the measures that he defended, aside from that large regard for that species of distinction that conducted him to eminent stations for the benefit of the Republic, I do not believe he had a selfish motive, or selfish feeling."

Calhoun had been an active supporter of the annexation of Texas, and in 1850, the year in which he died, the questions presented by his speech on the Force Bill came to direct issue on the admission of California, the first State organized from the territory acquired as a result of the conquest of Mexico. This agitation provoked the spirit which resulted in William H. Seward's "Irrepressible Conflict" speech at Rochester in 1858—a speech in which, rather than in the always considerate eloquence of Webster, Calhoun's argument against the Force Bill was answered for the first time. W. V. B.

AGAINST THE FORCE BILL

(Delivered in the Senate of the United States, on the Fifteenth and Sixteenth Days of February, 1833)

Mr. President:—

I KNOW not which is most objectionable, the provisions of the bill, or the temper in which its adoption has been urged. If the extraordinary powers with which the bill proposes to clothe the Executive, to the utter prostration of the Constitution and the rights of the States, be calculated to impress our minds

with alarm at the rapid progress of despotism in our country, the zeal with which every circumstance calculated to misrepresent or exaggerate the conduct of Carolina in the controversy is seized on with a view to excite hostility against her, but too plainly indicates the deep decay of that brotherly feeling which once existed between these States, and to which we are indebted for our beautiful federal system, and by the continuance of which alone it can be preserved. It is not my intention to advert to all these misrepresentations; but there are some so well calculated to mislead the mind as to the real character of the controversy, and to hold up the State in a light so odious, that I do not feel myself justified in permitting them to pass unnoticed.

Among them one of the most prominent is the false statement that the object of South Carolina is to exempt herself from her share of the public burdens, while she participates in the advantages of the Government. If the charge were true—if the State were capable of being actuated by such low and unworthy motives, mother as I consider her, I would not stand up on this floor to vindicate her conduct. Among her faults,—and faults I will not deny she has,—no one has ever yet charged her with that low and most sordid of vices,—avarice. Her conduct on all occasions has been marked with the very opposite quality. From the commencement of the Revolution—from its first breaking out at Boston till this hour, no State has been more profuse of its blood in the cause of the country; nor has any contributed so largely to the common treasury in proportion to wealth and population. She has, in that proportion, contributed more to the exports of the Union—on the exchange of which with the rest of the world the greater portion of the public burden has been levied—than any other State. No; the controversy is not such as has been stated; the State does not seek to participate in the advantages of the Government without contributing her full share to the public treasury. Her object is far different. A deep constitutional question lies at the bottom of the controversy. The real question at issue is: Has this Government a right to impose burdens on the capital and industry of one portion of the country, not with a view to revenue, but to benefit another? And I must be permitted to say that, after the long and deep agitation of this controversy, it is with surprise that I perceive so strong a disposition to misrepresent its real character. To correct the impression which those misrepresentations are calculated to make, I

will dwell on the point under consideration for a few moments longer.

The Federal Government has, by an express provision of the Constitution, the right to lay on imposts. The State has never denied or resisted this right, nor even thought of so doing. The Government has, however, not been contented with exercising this power as she had a right to do, but has gone a step beyond it, by laying imposts, not for revenue, but protection. This the State considers as an unconstitutional exercise of power—highly injurious and oppressive to her and the other staple States, and has, accordingly, met it with the most determined resistance. I do not intend to enter, at this time, into the argument as to the unconstitutionality of the protective system. It is not necessary. It is sufficient that the power is nowhere granted; and that, from the journals of the convention which formed the Constitution, it would seem that it was refused. In support of the journals, I might cite the statement of Luther Martin, which has already been referred to, to show that the convention, so far from conferring the power on the Federal Government, left to the State the right to impose duties on imports, with the express view of enabling the several States to protect their own manufactures. Notwithstanding this, Congress has assumed, without any warrant from the Constitution, the right of exercising this most important power, and has so exercised it as to impose a ruinous burden on the labor and capital of the State, by which her resources are exhausted, the enjoyments of her citizens curtailed, the means of education contracted, and all her interests essentially and injuriously affected. We have been sneeringly told that she is a small State; that her population does not much exceed half a million of souls, and that more than one-half are not of the European race. The facts are so. I know she never can be a great State, and that the only distinction to which she can aspire must be based on the moral and intellectual acquirements of her sons. To the development of these much of her attention has been directed; but this restrictive system which has so unjustly exacted the proceeds of her labor, to be bestowed on other sections, has so impaired her resources that, if not speedily arrested, it will dry up the means of education, and with it deprive her of the only source through which she can aspire to distinction.

There is another misstatement as to the nature of the controversy, so frequently made in debate, and so well calculated to

mislead, that I feel bound to notice it. It has been said that
South Carolina claims the right to annul the Constitution and
laws of the United States; and to rebut this supposed claim the
gentleman from Virginia [Mr. Rives] has gravely quoted the Constitution, to prove that the Constitution, and the laws made in
pursuance thereof, are the supreme laws of the land—as if the
State claimed the right to act contrary to this provision of the
Constitution. Nothing can be more erroneous: her object is not
to resist laws made in pursuance of the Constitution, but those
made without its authority, and which encroached on her reserved powers. She claims not even the right of judging of the
delegated powers, but of those that are reserved, and to resist
the former when they encroach upon the latter. I will pause to
illustrate this important point.

All must admit that there are delegated and reserved powers,
and that the powers reserved are reserved to the States respectively. The powers, then, of the system are divided between the
General and the State governments; and the point immediately
under consideration is, whether a State has any right to judge as
to the extent of its reserved powers, and to defend them against
the encroachments of the General Government. Without going
deeply into this point at this stage of the argument, or looking
into the nature and origin of the Government, there is a simple
view of the subject which I consider as conclusive. The very
idea of a divided power implies the right on the part of the State
for which I contend. The expression is metaphorical when applied to power. Every one readily understands that the division
of matter consists in the separation of the parts. But in this
sense it is not applicable to power. What, then, is meant by a
division of power? I cannot conceive of a division, without giving an equal right to each to judge of the extent of the power
allotted to each. Such right I hold to be essential to the existence of a division; and that to give to either party the conclusive right of judging, not only of the share allotted to it, but of
that allotted to the other, is to annul the division and to confer
the whole power on the party vested with such right.

But it is contended that the Constitution has conferred on the
Supreme Court the right of judging between the States and the
General Government. Those who make this objection overlook, I
conceive, an important provision of the Constitution. By turning
to the tenth amended article, it will be seen that the reservation

of power to the States is not only against the powers delegated
to Congress, but against the United States themselves, and extends, of course, as well to the judiciary as to the other departments of the government. The article provides that all powers
not delegated to the United States, or prohibited by it to the
States, are reserved to the States respectively, or to the people.
This presents the inquiry: What powers are delegated to the
United States? They may be classed under four divisions: First,
those that are delegated by the States to each other, by virtue of
which the Constitution may be altered or amended by three-
fourths of the States, when, without which, it would have required
the unanimous vote of all; next, the powers conferred on Congress; then, those on the President; and, finally, those on the judicial department—all of which are particularly enumerated in
the parts of the Constitution which organize the respective departments. The reservation of powers to the States is, as I have
said, against the whole, and is as full against the judicial as it is
against the executive and legislative departments of the government. It cannot be claimed for the one without claiming it for
the whole, and without, in fact, annulling this important provision
of the Constitution.

Against this, as it appears to me, conclusive view of the subject, it has been urged that this power is expressly conferred on
the Supreme Court by that portion of the Constitution which provides that the judicial power shall extend to all cases in law and
equity arising under the Constitution, the laws of the United
States, and treaties made under their authority. I believe the
assertion to be utterly destitute of any foundation. It obviously
is the intention of the Constitution simply to make the judicial
power commensurate with the law-making and treaty-making
powers; and to vest it with the right of applying the Constitution, the laws, and the treaties, to the cases which might arise
under them, and not to make it the judge of the Constitution,
the laws, and the treaties themselves. In fact, the power of applying the laws to the facts of the case, and deciding upon such
application, constitutes, in truth, the judicial power. The distinction between such power and that of judging of the laws will be
perfectly apparent when we advert to what is the acknowledged
power of the court in reference to treaties or compacts between
sovereigns. It is perfectly established that the courts have no
right to judge of the violation of treaties; and that in reference

to them their power is limited to the right of judging simply of
the violation of rights under them; and that the right of judging
of infractions belongs exclusively to the parties themselves, and
not to the courts: of which we have an example in the French
treaty, which was declared by Congress null and void, in consequence of its violation by the government of France. Without
such declaration, had a French citizen sued a citizen of this
country under the treaty the court could have taken no cognizance of its infraction; nor, after such a declaration, would it have
heard any argument or proof going to show that the treaty had
not been violated.

The declaration, of itself, is conclusive on the court. But it
will be asked how the court obtained the power to pronounce a
law or treaty unconstitutional, when it comes in conflict with that
instrument. I do not deny that it possesses the right; but I can
by no means concede that it was derived from the Constitution.
It had its origin in the necessity of the case. Where there are
two or more rules established, one from a higher, the other from
a lower authority, which may come into conflict in applying
them to a particular case, the judge cannot avoid pronouncing in
favor of the superior against the inferior. It is from this necessity, and this alone, that the power which is now set up to overrule the rights of the States against an express provision of the
Constitution was derived. It had no other origin. That I have
traced it to its true source will be manifest from the fact that it
is a power which, so far from being conferred exclusively on the
Supreme Court, as is insisted, belongs to every court—inferior
and superior—State and general—and even to foreign courts.

But the Senator from Delaware [Mr. Clayton] relies on the
journals of the convention to prove that it was the intention of
that body to confer on the Supreme Court the right of deciding,
in the last resort between a State and the General Government.
I will not follow him through the journals, as I do not deem
that to be necessary to refute his argument. It is sufficient for
this purpose to state that Mr. Rutledge reported a resolution
providing expressly that the United States and the States might
be parties before the Supreme Court. If this proposition had
been adopted, I would ask the Senator whether this very controversy between the United States and South Carolina might not
have been brought before the court? I would also ask him
whether it can be brought before the court as the Constitution

now stands? If he answer the former in the affirmative, and
the latter in the negative, as he must, then it is clear, his elaborate argument to the contrary notwithstanding, that the report
of Mr. Rutledge was not, in substance, adopted as he contended,
and that the journals, so far from supporting, are in direct opposition to the position which he attempts to maintain. I might
push the argument much further against the power of the court,
but I do not deem it necessary, at least in this stage of the discussion. If the views which have already been presented be
correct, and I do not see how they can be resisted, the conclusion
is inevitable, that the reserved powers were reserved equally
against every department of the Government, and as strongly
against the judicial as against the other departments, and, of
course, were left under the exclusive will of the States.

There still remains another misrepresentation of the conduct
of the State, which has been made with the view of exciting
odium. I allude to the charge that South Carolina supported
the tariff of 1816, and is, therefore, responsible for the protective
system. To determine the truth of this charge, it becomes necessary to ascertain the real character of that law—whether it was
a tariff for revenue or for protection—and, as involved in this,
to inquire, What was, the condition of the country at the period?
The late war with Great Britain had just terminated, which, with
the restrictive system that preceded it, had diverted a large
amount of capital and industry from commerce to manufactures,
particularly to the cotton and woolen branches. There was a
debt at the same time of one hundred and thirty millions of
dollars hanging over the country, and the heavy war duties were
still in existence. Under these circumstances, the question was
presented, as to what point the duties ought to be reduced.
This question involved another—at what time the debt ought to
be paid? which was a question of policy, involving in its consideration all the circumstances connected with the then condition
of the country. Among the most prominent arguments in favor
of an early discharge of the debt was, that the high duties which
it would require to effect it would have, at the same time, the
effect of sustaining the infant manufactures, which had been
forced up under the circumstances to which I have adverted.
This view of the subject had a decided influence in determining
in favor of an early payment of the debt. The sinking fund
was, accordingly, raised from seven to ten millions of dollars,

with the provision to apply the surplus which might remain in the treasury as a contingent appropriation to that fund; and the duties were graduated to meet this increased expenditure. It was thus that the policy and justice of protecting the large amount of capital and industry which had been diverted by the measures of the Government into new channels, as I have stated, were combined with the fiscal action of the Government, and which, while it secured a prompt payment of the debt, prevented the immense losses to the manufacturers which would have followed a sudden and great reduction. Still, revenue was the main object, and protection but the incidental. The bill to reduce the duties was reported by the Committee of Ways and Means, and not of Manufactures, and it proposed a heavy reduction on the then existing rate of duties. But what of itself, without other evidence, is decisive as to the character of the bill is the fact that it fixed a much higher rate of duties on the unprotected than on the protected articles. I will enumerate a few leading articles only. Woolen and cotton above the value of twenty-five cents on the square yard, though they were the leading objects of protection, were subject to a permanent duty of only twenty per cent. Iron, another leading article among the protected, had a protection of not more than nine per cent. as fixed by the act, and of but fifteen as reported in the bill. These rates were all below the average duties as fixed in the act, including the protected, the unprotected, and even the free articles. I have entered into some calculation, in order to ascertain the average rate of duties under the act. There is some uncertainty in the data, but I feel assured that it is not less than thirty per cent. *ad valorem:* showing an excess of the average duties above that imposed on the protected articles enumerated of more than ten per cent., and thus clearly establishing the character of the measure — that it was for revenue and not protection.

Looking back, even at this distant period, with all our experience, I perceive but two errors in the act: the one in reference to iron, and the other the minimum duty on coarse cottons. As to the former, I conceive that the bill, as reported, proposed a duty relatively too low, which was still further reduced in its passage through Congress. The duty, at first, was fixed at seventy-five cents the hundredweight; but, in the last stage of its passage, it was reduced, by a sort of caprice, occasioned by an unfortunate motion, to forty-five cents. This injustice was

sense of injustice which the remarks of a Senator from Pennsylvania [Mr. Wilkins] excited for the moment, I hastily gave my pledge to defend myself against the charge which has been made in reference to my course in 1816: not that there will be any difficulty in repelling the charge, but because I feel a deep reluctance in turning the discussion, in any degree, from a subject of so much magnitude to one of so little importance as the consistency or inconsistency of myself, or any other individual, particularly in connection with an event so long since passed. But for this hasty pledge, I would have remained silent as to my own course on this occasion, and would have borne with patience and calmness this, with the many other misrepresentations with which I have been so incessantly assailed for so many years.

The charge that I was the author of the protective system, has no other foundation but that I, in common with the almost entire South, gave my support to the tariff of 1816. It is true that I advocated that measure, for which I may rest my defense, without taking any other, on the ground that it was a tariff for revenue, and not for protection, which I have established beyond the power of controversy. But my speech on the occasion, has been brought in judgment against me by the Senator from Pennsylvania. I have since cast my eyes over the speech; and I will surprise, I have no doubt, the Senator, by telling him that, with the exception of some hasty and unguarded expressions, I retract nothing I uttered on that occasion. I only ask that it may be judged, in reference to it, in that spirit of fairness and justice which is due to the occasion; taking into consideration the circumstances under which it was delivered, and bearing in mind that the subject was a tariff for revenue, and not for protection; for reducing, and not raising the duties. But, before I explain the then condition of the country, from which my main arguments in favor of the measure were drawn, it is nothing but an act of justice to myself that I should state a fact in connection with my speech, that is necessary to explain what I have called hasty and unguarded expressions. My speech was an *impromptu;* and, as such, I apologized to the House, as appears from the speech as printed, for offering my sentiments on the question without having duly reflected on the subject. It was delivered at the request of a friend, when I had not previously the least intention of addressing the House. I allude to Samuel D. Ingham, then and now, as I am proud to say, a personal and political

severely felt in Pennsylvania, the State, above all others, most productive of iron, and was the principal cause of that great reaction which has since thrown her so decidedly on the side of the protective policy. The other error was that as to coarse cottons, on which the duty was as much too high as that on iron was too low. It introduced, besides, the obnoxious minimum principle, which has since been so mischievously extended; and to that extent, I am constrained in candor to acknowledge, as I wish to disguise nothing, the protective principle was recognized by the Act of 1816. How this was overlooked at the time, it is not in my power to say. It escaped my observation, which I can account for only on the ground that the principle was then new, and that my attention was engaged by another important subject — the question of the currency, then so urgent, and with which, as chairman of the committee, I was particularly charged. With these exceptions, I again repeat, I see nothing in the bill to condemn; yet it is on the ground that the Members from the State voted for the bill, that the attempt is now made to hold up Carolina as responsible for the whole system of protection which has since followed, though she has resisted its progress in every stage. Was there ever greater injustice? And how is it to be accounted for, but as forming a part of that systematic misrepresentation and calumny which has been directed for so many years, without interruption, against that gallant and generous State? And why has she thus been assailed? Merely because she abstained from taking any part in the presidential canvass — believing that it had degenerated into a mere system of imposition on the people — controlled, almost exclusively, by those whose object it is to obtain the patronage of the government, and that without regard to principle or policy. Standing apart from what she considered a contest in which the public had no interest, she has been assailed by both parties with a fury altogether unparalleled; but which, pursuing the course which she believed liberty and duty required, she has met with a firmness equal to the fierceness of the assault. In the midst of this attack, I have not escaped. With a view of inflicting a wound on the State through me, I have been held up as the author of the protective system, and one of its most strenuous advocates. It is with pain that I allude to myself on so deep and grave a subject as that now under discussion, and which, I sincerely believe, involves the liberty of the country. I now regret that, under the

friend — a man of talents and integrity — with a clear head, and firm and patriotic heart; then among the leading Members of the House; in the palmy state of his political glory, though now for a moment depressed; — depressed, did I say? no! it is his State which is depressed — Pennsylvania, and not Samuel D. Ingham! Pennsylvania, which has deserted him under circumstances which, instead of depressing, ought to have elevated him in her estimation. He came to me, when sitting at my desk writing, and said that the House was falling into some confusion, accompanying it with a remark, that I knew how difficult it was to rally so large a body when once broken on a tax bill, as had been experienced during the late war. Having a higher opinion of my influence than it deserved, he requested me to say something to prevent the confusion. I replied that I was at a loss what to say; that I had been busily engaged on the currency, which was then in great confusion, and which, as I have stated, had been placed particularly under my charge, as the chairman of the committee on that subject. He repeated his request, and the speech which the Senator from Pennsylvania has complimented so highly, was the result.

I will ask whether the facts stated ought not, in justice, to be borne in mind by those who would hold me accountable, not only for the general scope of the speech, but for every word and sentence which it contains? But, in asking this question, it is not my intention to repudiate the speech. All I ask is, that I may be judged by the rules which, in justice, belong to the case. Let it be recollected that the bill was a revenue bill, and, of course, that it was constitutional. I need not remind the Senate that, when the measure is constitutional, all arguments calculated to show its beneficial operation may be legitimately pressed into service, without taking into consideration whether the subject to which the arguments refer be within the sphere of the Constitution or not. If, for instance, a question were before this body to lay a duty on Bibles, and a motion were made to reduce the duty, or admit Bibles duty free, who could doubt that the argument in favor of the motion — that the increased circulation of the Bible would be in favor of the morality and religion of the country, would be strictly proper? But who would suppose that he who adduced it had committed himself on the constitutionality of taking the religion or morals of the country under the charge of the Federal Government? Again: suppose the question to be, to raise the duty on silk, or any other article of luxury; and that it should be supported on the ground that it was an article mainly consumed by the rich and extravagant—could it be fairly inferred that in the opinion of the speaker, Congress had a right to pass sumptuary laws? I only ask that these plain rules may be applied to my argument on the tariff of 1816. They turn almost entirely on the benefits which manufactures conferred on the country in time of war, and which no one could doubt. The country had recently passed through such a state. The world was at that time deeply agitated by the effects of the great conflict which had so long raged in Europe, and which no one could tell how soon again might return. Bonaparte had but recently been overthrown; the whole southern part of this continent was in a state of revolution, and threatened with the interference of the Holy Alliance, which, had it occurred, must almost necessarily have involved this country in a most dangerous conflict. It was under these circumstances that I delivered the speech, in which I urged the House that, in the adjustment of the tariff, reference ought to be had to a state of war as well as peace, and that its provisions ought to be fixed on the compound views of the two periods—making some sacrifice in peace, in order that less might be made in war. Was this principle false? and, in urging it, did I commit myself to that system of oppression since grown up, and which has for its object the enriching of one portion of the country at the expense of the other?

The plain rule in all such cases is, that when a measure is proposed, the first thing is to ascertain its constitutionality; and, that being ascertained, the next is its expediency; which last opens the whole field of argument for and against. Every topic may be urged calculated to prove it wise or unwise: so in a bill to raise imposts. It must first be ascertained that the bill is based on the principles of revenue, and that the money raised is necessary for the wants of the country. These being ascertained, every argument, direct and indirect, may be fairly offered, which may go to show that, under all the circumstances, the provisions of the bill are proper or improper. Had this plain and simple rule been adhered to, we should never have heard of the complaint of Carolina. Her objection is not against the improper modification of a bill acknowledged to be for revenue, but that, under the name of imposts, a power essentially different from the taxing power is exercised—partaking much more of the character of a penalty

than a tax. Nothing is more common than that things closely resembling in appearance should widely and essentially differ in their character. Arsenic, for instance, resembles flour, yet one is a deadly poison, and the other that which constitutes the staff of life. So duties imposed, whether for revenue or protection, may be called imposts; though nominally and apparently the same, yet they differ essentially in their real character.

I shall now return to my speech on the tariff of 1816. To determine what my opinions really were on the subject of protection at that time, it will be proper to advert to my sentiments before and after that period. My sentiments preceding 1816, on this subject, are a matter of record. I came into Congress in 1812, a devoted friend and supporter of the then administration; yet one of my first efforts was to brave the administration, by opposing its favorite measure, the restrictive system—embargo, nonintercourse, and all—and that upon the principle of free trade. The system remained in fashion for a time; but, after the overthrow of Bonaparte, I reported a bill from the Committee on Foreign Relations, to repeal the whole system of restrictive measures. While the bill was under consideration, a worthy man, then a Member of the House [Mr. McKim, of Baltimore], moved to except the nonimportation act, which he supported on the ground of encouragement to manufactures. I resisted the motion on the very grounds on which Mr. McKim supported it. I maintained that the manufacturers were then receiving too much protection, and warned its friends that the withdrawal of the protection which the war and the high duties then afforded, would cause great embarrassment; and that the true policy, in the meantime, was to admit foreign goods as freely as possible, in order to diminish the anticipated embarrassment on the return of peace; intimating, at the same time, my desire to see the tariff revised, with a view of affording a moderate and permanent protection.

Such was my conduct before 1816. Shortly after that period I left Congress, and had no opportunity of making known my sentiments in reference to the protective system, which shortly after began to be agitated. But I have the most conclusive evidence that I considered the arrangement of the revenue, in 1816, as growing out of the necessity of the case, and due to the consideration of justice. But, even at that early period, I was not without my fears that even that arrangement would lead to abuse

and future difficulties. I regret that I have been compelled to dwell so long on myself; but trust that, whatever censure may be incurred, will not be directed against me, but against those who have drawn my conduct into the controversy; and who may hope, by assailing my motives, to wound the cause with which I am proud to be identified.

I may add, that all the Southern States voted with South Carolina in support of the bill: not that they had any interest in manufactures, but on the ground that they had supported the war, and, of course, felt a corresponding obligation to sustain those establishments which had grown up under the encouragement it had incidentally afforded; whilst most of the New England Members were opposed to the measure, principally, as I believe, on opposite principles.

I have now, I trust, satisfactorily repelled the charge against the State, and myself personally, in reference to the tariff of 1816. Whatever support the State has given the bill, originated in the most disinterested motives. There was not within the limits of the State, so far as my memory serves me, a single cotton or woolen establishment. Her whole dependence was on agriculture, and the cultivation of two great staples, rice and cotton. Her obvious policy was to keep open the market of the world, unchecked and unrestricted;—to buy cheap and to sell high: but from a feeling of kindness, combined with a sense of justice, she added her support to the bill. We had been told by the agents of the manufacturers that the protection which the measure afforded would be sufficient; to which we the more readily conceded, as it was considered a final adjustment of the question.

Let us now turn our eyes forward, and see what has been the conduct of the parties to this arrangement. Have Carolina and the South disturbed this adjustment? No; they have never raised their voice in a single instance against it, even though this measure, moderate, comparatively, as it is, was felt with no inconsiderable pressure on their interests. Was this example imitated on the opposite side? Far otherwise. Scarcely had the President signed his name, before application was made for an increase of duties, which was repeated, with demands continually growing, till the passage of the Act of 1828. What course now, I would ask, did it become Carolina to pursue in reference to these demands? Instead of acquiescing in them, because she had

acted generously in adjusting the tariff of 1816, she saw, in her generosity on that occasion, additional motives for that firm and decided resistance which she has since made against the system of protection. She accordingly commenced a systematic opposition to all further encroachments, which continued from 1818 till 1828; by discussions and by resolutions and by remonstrances and by protests through her legislature. These all proved insufficient to stem the current of encroachment: but, notwithstanding the heavy pressure on her industry, she never despaired of relief till the passage of the Act of 1828—that bill of abominations—engendered by avarice and political intrigue. Its adoption opened the eyes of the State, and gave a new character to the controversy. Till then, the question had been, whether the protective system was constitutional and expedient; but, after that, she no longer considered the question whether the right of regulating the industry of the States was a reserved or delegated power, but what right a State possesses to defend her reserved powers against the encroachments of the Federal Government: a question on the decision of which the value of all the reserved powers depends. The passage of the Act of 1828, with all its objectionable features, and under the circumstances connected with it, almost, if not entirely, closed the door of hope through the General Government. It afforded conclusive evidence that no reasonable prospect of relief from Congress could be entertained; yet, the near approach of the period of the payment of the public debt, and the elevation of General Jackson to the presidency, still afforded a ray of hope—not so strong, however, as to prevent the State from turning her eyes for final relief to her reserved powers.

Under these circumstances commenced that inquiry into the nature and extent of the reserved powers of a State, and the means which they afford of resistance against the encroachments of the General Government, which has been pursued with so much zeal and energy, and, I may add, intelligence. Never was there a political discussion carried on with greater activity, and which appealed more directly to the intelligence of a community. Throughout the whole, no address has been made to the low and vulgar passions; but, on the contrary, the discussion has turned upon the higher principles of political economy, connected with the operations of the tariff system, calculated to show its real bearing on the interests of the State, and on the structure of our political system; and to show the true character of the relations between the State and the General Government, and the means which the States possess of defending those powers which they reserved in forming the Federal Government.

In this great canvass, men of the most commanding talents and acquirements have engaged with the greatest ardor; and the people have been addressed through every channel — by essays in the public press, and by speeches in their public assemblies — until they have become thoroughly instructed on the nature of the oppression, and on the rights which they possess, under the Constitution, to throw it off.

If gentlemen suppose that the stand taken by the people of Carolina rests on passion and delusion, they are wholly mistaken. The case is far otherwise. No community, from the legislator to the plowman, were ever better instructed in their rights; and the resistance on which the State has resolved, is the result of mature reflection, accompanied with a deep conviction that their rights have been violated, and that the means of redress which they have adopted are consistent with the principles of the Constitution.

But while this active canvass was carried on, which looked to the reserved powers as the final means of redress if all others failed, the State at the same time cherished a hope, as I have already stated, that the election of General Jackson to the presidency would prevent the necessity of a resort to extremities. He was identified with the interests of the staple States; and, having the same interest, it was believed that his great popularity — a popularity of the strongest character, as it rested on military services — would enable him, as they hoped, gradually to bring down the system of protection, without shock or injury to any interest. Under these views, the canvass in favor of General Jackson's election to the presidency was carried on with great zeal, in conjunction with that active inquiry into the reserved powers of the States on which final reliance was placed. But little did the people of Carolina dream that the man whom they were thus striving to elevate to the highest seat of power would prove so utterly false to all their hopes. Man is, indeed, ignorant of the future; nor was there ever a stronger illustration of the observation than is afforded by the result of that election! The very event on which they had built their hopes has been turned against them; and the very individual to whom they

III—56

looked as a deliverer, and whom, under that impression, they strove for so many years to elevate to power, is now the most powerful instrument in the hands of his and their bitterest opponents to put down them and their cause!

Scarcely had he been elected, when it became apparent, from the organization of his cabinet and other indications, that all their hopes of relief through him were blasted. The admission of a single individual into the cabinet, under the circumstances which accompanied that admission, threw all into confusion. The mischievous influence over the President, through which this individual was admitted into the cabinet, soon became apparent. Instead of turning his eyes forward to the period of the payment of the public debt, which was then near at hand, and to the present dangerous political crisis, which was inevitable unless averted by a timely and wise system of measures, the attention of the President was absorbed by mere party arrangements, and circumstances too disreputable to be mentioned here, except by the most distant allusion.

Here I must pause for a moment to repel a charge which has been so often made, and which even the President has reiterated in his proclamation — the charge that I have been actuated, in the part which I have taken, by feelings of disappointed ambition. I again repeat that I deeply regret the necessity of noticing myself in so important a discussion; and that nothing can induce me to advert to my own course but the conviction that it is due to the cause, at which a blow is aimed through me. It is only in this view that I notice it.

It illy became the Chief Magistrate to make this charge. The course which the State took, and which led to the present controversy between her and the General Government, was taken as far back as 1828 — in the very midst of that severe canvass which placed him in power — and in that very canvass Carolina openly avowed and zealously maintained those very principles which he, the Chief Magistrate, now officially pronounces to be treason and rebellion. That was the period at which he ought to have spoken. Having remained silent then, and having, under his approval, implied by that silence, received the support and the vote of the State, I, if a sense of decorum did not prevent it, might recriminate with the double charge of deception and ingratitude. My object, however, is not to assail the President, but to defend myself against a most unfounded charge. The time alone when

that course was taken, on which this charge of disappointed ambition is founded, will of itself repel it, in the eye of every unprejudiced and honest man. The doctrine which I now sustain, under the present difficulties, I openly avowed and maintained immediately after the Act of 1828, that "bill of abominations," as it has been so often and properly termed. Was I, at that period, disappointed in any views of ambition which I might be supposed to entertain? I was Vice-President of the United States, elected by an overwhelming majority. I was a candidate for re-election on the ticket with General Jackson himself, with a certain prospect of the triumphant success of that ticket, and with a fair prospect of the highest office to which an American citizen can aspire. What was my course under these prospects? Did I look to my own advancement, or to an honest and faithful discharge of my duty? Let facts speak for themselves. When the bill to which I have referred came from the other House to the Senate, the almost universal impression was, that its fate would depend upon my casting vote. It was known that, as the bill then stood, the Senate was nearly equally divided; and as it was a combined measure, originating with the politicians and manufacturers, and intended as much to bear upon the presidential election as to protect manufactures, it was believed that, as a stroke of political policy, its fate would be made to depend on my vote, in order to defeat General Jackson's election, as well as my own. The friends of General Jackson were alarmed, and I was earnestly entreated to leave the chair in order to avoid the responsibility, under the plausible argument that, if the Senate should be equally divided, the bill would be lost without the aid of my casting vote. The reply to this entreaty was, that no consideration personal to myself could induce me to take such a course; that I considered the measure as of the most dangerous character, and calculated to produce the most fearful crisis; that the payment of the public debt was just at hand; and that the great increase of revenue which it would pour into the treasury would accelerate the approach of that period, and that the country would be placed in the most trying of situations — with an immense revenue without the means of absorption upon any legitimate or constitutional object of appropriation, and compelled to submit to all the corrupting consequences of a large surplus, or to make a sudden reduction of the rates of duties, which would prove ruinous to the very interests which were then

forcing the passage of the bill. Under these views I determined to remain in the chair, and if the bill came to me, to give my casting vote against it, and in doing so, to give my reasons at large; but at the same time I informed my friends that I would retire from the ticket, so that the election of General Jackson might not be embarrassed by any act of mine. Sir, I was amazed at the folly and infatuation of that period. So completely absorbed was Congress in the game of ambition and avarice — from the double impulse of the manufacturers and politicians — that none but a few appeared to anticipate the present crisis, at which all are now alarmed, but which is the inevitable result of what was then done. As to myself, I clearly foresaw what has since followed. The road of ambition lay open before me — I had but to follow the corrupt tendency of the times — but I chose to tread the rugged path of duty.

It was thus that the reasonable hope of relief through the election of General Jackson was blasted; but still one other hope remained: that the final discharge of the public debt — an event near at hand — would remove our burden. That event would leave in the treasury a large surplus: a surplus that could not be expended under the most extravagant schemes of appropriation, having the least color of decency or constitutionality. That event at last arrived. At the last session of Congress, it was avowed on all sides that the public debt, as to all practical purposes, was in fact paid, the small surplus remaining being nearly covered by the money in the treasury and the bonds for duties which had already accrued; but with the arrival of this event our last hope was doomed to be disappointed. After a long session of many months and the most earnest effort on the part of South Carolina and the other Southern States to obtain relief, all that could be effected was a small reduction in the amount of the duties; but a reduction of such a character, that, while it diminished the amount of burden, distributed that burden more unequally than even the obnoxious Act of 1828: reversing the principle adopted by the bill of 1816, of laying higher duties on the unprotected than the protected articles, by repealing almost entirely the duties laid upon the former, and imposing the burden almost entirely on the latter. It was thus that instead of relief — instead of an equal distribution of the burdens and benefits of the Government, on the payment of the debt, as had been fondly anticipated — the duties were so arranged as to be, in fact, bounties on one side and taxation on the other; thus placing the two great sections of the country in direct conflict in reference to its fiscal action, and thereby letting in that flood of political corruption which threatens to sweep away our Constitution and our liberty.

This unequal and unjust arrangement was pronounced, both by the administration, through its proper organ, the Secretary of the Treasury, and by the opposition, to be a permanent adjustment; and it was thus that all hope of relief through the action of the General Government terminated; and the crisis so long apprehended at length arrived, at which the State was compelled to choose between absolute acquiescence in a ruinous system of oppression, or a resort to her reserved powers—powers of which she alone was the rightful judge, and which only, in this momentous juncture, could save her. She determined on the latter.

The consent of two-thirds of her legislature was necessary for the call of a convention, which was considered the only legitimate organ through which the people, in their sovereignty, could speak. After an arduous struggle the State Rights party succeeded; more than two-thirds of both branches of the legislature favorable to a convention were elected; a convention was called —the ordinance adopted. The convention was succeeded by a meeting of the legislature, when the laws to carry the ordinance into execution were enacted: all of which have been communicated by the President, have been referred to the Committee on the Judiciary, and this bill is the result of their labor.

Having now corrected some of the prominent misrepresentations as to the nature of this controversy, and given a rapid sketch of the movement of the State in reference to it, I will next proceed to notice some objections connected with the ordinance and the proceedings under it.

The first and most prominent of these is directed against what is called the test oath, which an effort has been made to render odious. So far from deserving the denunciation which has been levelled against it, I view this provision of the ordinance as but the natural result of the doctrines entertained by the State, and the position which she occupies. The people of Carolina believe that the Union is a union of States, and not of individuals; that it was formed by the States, and that the citizens of the several States were bound to it through the acts of

their several States; that each State ratified the Constitution for itself, and that it was only by such ratification of a State that any obligation was imposed upon its citizens. Thus believing, it is the opinion of the people of Carolina that it belongs to the State which has imposed the obligation to declare, in the last resort, the extent of this obligation, as far as her citizens are concerned; and this upon the plain principles which exist in all analogous cases of compact between sovereign bodies. On this principle the people of the State, acting in their sovereign capacity in convention, precisely as they did in the adoption of their own and the Federal Constitution, have declared, by the ordinance, that the acts of Congress which imposed duties under the authority to lay imposts, are acts, not for revenue, as intended by the Constitution, but for protection, and therefore null and void. The ordinance thus enacted by the people of the State themselves, acting as a sovereign community, is as obligatory on the citizens of the State as any portion of the Constitution. In prescribing, then, the oath to obey the ordinance, no more was done than to prescribe an oath to obey the Constitution. It is, in fact, but a particular oath of allegiance, and in every respect similar to that which is prescribed, under the Constitution of the United States, to be administered to all the officers of the State and Federal Governments; and is no more deserving the harsh and bitter epithets which have been heaped upon it, than that, or any similar oath. It ought to be borne in mind that according to the opinion which prevails in Carolina, the right of resistance to the unconstitutional acts of Congress belongs to the State, and not to her individual citizens; and that, though the latter may, in a mere question of *meum* and *tuum*, resist, through the courts, an unconstitutional encroachment upon their rights, yet the final stand against usurpation rests not with them, but with the State of which they are members; and such act of resistance by a State binds the conscience and allegiance of the citizen. But there appears to be a general misapprehension as to the extent to which the State has acted under this part of the ordinance. Instead of sweeping every officer by a general proscription of the minority, as has been represented in debate, as far as my knowledge extends, not a single individual has been removed. The State has, in fact, acted with the greatest tenderness, all circumstances considered, towards citizens who differed from the majority; and in that spirit has directed the oath to be

administered only in case of some official act directed to be performed, in which obedience to the ordinance is involved.

It has been further objected that the State has acted precipitately. What! precipitately! after making a strenuous resistance for twelve years—by discussion here and in the other House of Congress—by essays in all forms—by resolutions, remonstrances, and protests on the part of her legislature—and, finally, by attempting an appeal to the judicial power of the United States? I say attempting, for they have been prevented from bringing the question fairly before the court, and that by an act of that very majority in Congress who now upbraid them for not making that appeal; of that majority who on a motion of one of the Members in the other House from South Carolina, refused to give to the Act of 1828 its true title—that it was a protective, and not a revenue Act. The State has never, it is true, relied upon that tribunal, the Supreme Court, to vindicate its reserved rights; yet they have always considered it as an auxiliary means of defense, of which they would gladly have availed themselves to test the constitutionality of protection, had they not been deprived of the means of doing so by the act of the majority.

Notwithstanding this long delay of more than ten years, under this continued encroachment of the Government, we now hear it on all sides, by friends and foes, gravely pronounced that the State has acted precipitately—that her conduct has been rash! That such should be the language of an interested majority, who, by means of this unconstitutional and oppressive system, are annually extorting millions from the South, to be bestowed upon other sections, is not at all surprising. Whatever impedes the course of avarice and ambition will ever be denounced as rash and precipitate; and had South Carolina delayed her resistance fifty instead of twelve years, she would have heard from the same quarter the same language; but it is really surprising that those who are suffering in common with herself, and who have complained equally loud of their grievances; who have pronounced the very acts which she has asserted within her limits to be oppressive, unconstitutional, and ruinous, after so long a struggle—a struggle longer than that which preceded the separation of these States from the mother-country—longer than the period of the Trojan war—should now complain of precipitancy! No, it is not Carolina which has acted precipitately; but her sister States, who have suffered in common with her, have acted

tardily. Had they acted as she has done; had they performed their duty with equal energy and promptness, our situation this day would be very different from what we now find it. Delays are said to be dangerous; and never was the maxim more true than in the present case, a case of monopoly. It is the very nature of monopolies to grow. If we take from one side a large portion of the proceeds of its labor and give it to the other, the side from which we take must constantly decay, and that to which we give must prosper and increase. Such is the action of the protective system. It exacts from the South a large portion of the proceeds of its industry, which it bestows upon the other sections in the shape of bounties to manufactures, and appropriations in a thousand forms; pensions, improvement of rivers and harbors, roads and canals, and in every shape that wit or ingenuity can devise. Can we, then, be surprised that the principle of monopoly grows, when it is so amply remunerated at the expense of those who support it? And this is the real reason of the fact which we witness, that all acts for protection pass with small minorities, but soon come to be sustained by great and overwhelming majorities. Those who seek the monopoly endeavor to obtain it in the most exclusive shape; and they take care, accordingly, to associate only a sufficient number of interests barely to pass it through the two Houses of Congress, on the plain principle that the greater the number from whom the monopoly takes, and the fewer on whom it bestows, the greater is the advantage to the monopolists. Acting in this spirit, we have often seen with what exact precision they count: adding wool to woolens, associating lead and iron, feeling their way, until a bare majority is obtained, when the bill passes, connecting just as many interests as are sufficient to ensure its success, and no more. In a short time, however, we have invariably found that this *lean* becomes a decided majority, under the certain operation which compels individuals to desert the pursuits which the monopoly has rendered unprofitable, that they may participate in those which it has rendered profitable. It is against this dangerous and growing disease that South Carolina has acted—a disease, whose cancerous action would soon have spread to every part of the system, if not arrested.

There is another powerful reason why the action of the State could not have been safely delayed. The public debt, as I have already stated, for all practical purposes, has already been paid;

and, under the existing duties, a large annual surplus of many millions must come into the treasury. It is impossible to look at this state of things without seeing the most mischievous consequences; and, among others, if not speedily corrected, it would interpose powerful and almost insuperable obstacles to throwing off the burden under which the South has been so long laboring. The disposition of the surplus would become a subject of violent and corrupt struggle, and could not fail to rear up new and powerful interests in support of the existing system, not only in those sections which have been heretofore benefitted by it, but even in the South itself. I cannot but trace to the anticipation of this state of the treasury the sudden and extraordinary movements which took place at the last session in the Virginia legislature, in which the whole South is vitally interested. It is impossible for any rational man to believe that that State could seriously have thought of effecting the scheme to which I allude by her own resources, without powerful aid from the General Government.

It is next objected that the enforcing acts have legislated the United States out of South Carolina. I have already replied to this objection on another occasion, and I will now but repeat what I then said: that they have been legislated out only to the extent that they had no right to enter. The Constitution has admitted the jurisdiction of the United States within the limits of the several States only so far as the delegated powers authorize; beyond that they are intruders and may rightfully be expelled; and that they have been efficiently expelled by the legislation of the State through her civil process, as has been acknowledged on all sides in the debate, is only a confirmation of the truth of the doctrine for which the majority in Carolina have contended.

The very point at issue between the two parties there, is, whether nullification is a peaceable and an efficient remedy against an unconstitutional act of the General Government, and may be asserted as such through the State tribunals. Both parties agree that the acts against which it is directed are unconstitutional and oppressive. The controversy is only as to the means by which our citizens may be protected against the acknowledged encroachments on their rights. This being the point at issue between the parties, and the very object of the majority being an efficient protection of the citizens through the State tribunals, the measures adopted to enforce the ordinance, of

course, received the most decisive character. We were not children, to act by halves. Yet for acting thus efficiently the State is denounced, and this bill reported, to overrule, by military force, the civil tribunals and civil process of the State! Sir, I consider this bill, and the arguments which have been urged on this floor in its support, as the most triumphant acknowledgment that nullification is peaceful and efficient, and so deeply intrenched in the principles of our system, that it cannot be assailed but by prostrating the Constitution, and substituting the supremacy of military force in lieu of the supremacy of the laws. In fact, the advocates of this bill refute their own argument. They tell us that the ordinance is unconstitutional; that it infracts the constitution of South Carolina, although to me, the objection appears absurd, as it was adopted by the very authority which adopted the constitution itself. They also tell us that the Supreme Court is the appointed arbiter of all controversies between a State and the General Government. Why, then, do they not leave this controversy to that tribunal? Why do they not confide to them the abrogation of the ordinance, and the laws made in pursuance of it, and the assertion of that supremacy which they claim for the laws of Congress? The State stands pledged to resist no process of the court. Why, then, confer on the President the extensive and unlimited powers provided in this bill? Why authorize him to use military force to arrest the civil process of the State? But one answer can be given: That, in a contest between the State and the General Government, if the resistance be limited on both sides to the civil process, the State, by its inherent sovereignty, standing upon its reserved powers, will prove too powerful in such a controversy, and must triumph over the Federal Government, sustained by its delegated and unlimited authority; and in this answer we have an acknowledgment of the truth of those great principles for which the State has so firmly and nobly contended.

Having made these remarks, the great question is now presented, Has Congress the right to pass this bill? which I will next proceed to consider. The decision of this question involves an inquiry into the provisions of the bill. What are they? It puts at the disposal of the President the army and navy, and the entire militia of the country; it enables him, at his pleasure, to subject every man in the United States, not exempt from militia duty, to martial law; to call him from his ordinary occupation to

the field, and under the penalty of fine and imprisonment, inflicted by a court-martial, to imbrue his hand in his brother's blood. There is no limitation on the power of the sword;—and that over the purse is equally without restraint; for among the extraordinary features of the bill, it contains no appropriation, which, under existing circumstances, is tantamount to an unlimited appropriation. The President may, under its authority, incur any expenditure, and pledge the national faith to meet it. He may create a new national debt, at the very moment of the termination of the former—a debt of millions, to be paid out of the proceeds of the labor of that section of the country whose dearest constitutional rights this bill prostrates! Thus exhibiting the extraordinary spectacle, that the very section of the country which is urging this measure, and carrying the sword of devastation against us, is, at the same time, incurring a new debt, to be paid by those whose rights are violated; while those who violate them are to receive the benefits in the shape of bounties and expenditures.

And for what purpose is the unlimited control of the purse and of the sword thus placed at the disposition of the Executive? To make war against one of the free and sovereign members of this confederation, which the bill proposes to deal with, not as a State, but as a collection of banditti or outlaws. Thus exhibiting the impious spectacle of this Government, the creature of the States, making war against the power to which it owes its existence.

The bill violates the Constitution, plainly and palpably, in many of its provisions, by authorizing the President, at his pleasure, to place the different ports of this Union on an unequal footing, contrary to that provision of the Constitution which declares that no preference shall be given to one port over another. It also violates the Constitution by authorizing him, at his discretion, to impose cash duties in one port, while credit is allowed in others; by enabling the President to regulate commerce, a power vested in Congress alone; and by drawing within the jurisdiction of the United States courts, powers never intended to be conferred on them. As great as these objections are, they become insignificant in the provisions of a bill which, by a single blow—by treating the States as a mere lawless mass of individuals—prostrates all the barriers of the Constitution. I will pass over the minor considerations, and proceed directly to the great

point. This bill proceeds on the ground that the entire sovereignty of this country belongs to the American people, as forming one great community, and regards the States as mere fractions or counties, and not as integral parts of the Union; having no more right to resist the encroachments of the Government than a county has to resist the authority of a State; and treating such resistance as the lawless acts of so many individuals, without possessing sovereignty or political rights. It has been said that the bill declares war against South Carolina. No. It decrees a massacre of her citizens! War has something ennobling about it, and, with all its horrors, brings into action the highest qualities, intellectual and moral. It was, perhaps, in the order of Providence that it should be permitted for that very purpose. But this bill declares no war, except, indeed, it be that which savages wage—a war, not against the community, but the citizens of whom that community is composed. But I regard it as worse than savage warfare—as an attempt to take away life under the color of law, without the trial by jury, or any other safeguard which the Constitution has thrown around the life of the citizen. It authorizes the President, or even his deputies, when they may suppose the law to be violated, without the intervention of a court or jury, to kill without mercy or discrimination!

It has been said by the Senator from Tennessee [Mr. Grundy] to be a measure of peace! Yes, such peace as the wolf gives to the lamb—the kite to the dove! Such peace as Russia gives to Poland, or death to its victim! A peace, by extinguishing the political existence of the State, by awing her into an abandonment of the exercise of every power which constitutes her a sovereign community. It is to South Carolina a question of self-preservation; and I proclaim it, that, should this bill pass, and an attempt be made to enforce it, it will be resisted, at every hazard—even that of death itself. Death is not the greatest calamity: there are others still more terrible to the free and brave, and among them may be placed the loss of liberty and honor. There are thousands of her brave sons, who, if need be, are prepared cheerfully to lay down their lives in defense of the State, and the great principles of constitutional liberty for which she is contending. God forbid that this should become necessary! It never can be, unless this Government is resolved to bring the question to extremity, when her gallant sons will stand prepared to perform the last duty—to die nobly.

I go on the ground that this Constitution was made by the States; that it is a federal union of the States, in which the several States still retain their sovereignty. If these views be correct, I have not characterized the bill too strongly: and the question is, whether they be or be not. I will not enter into the discussion of this question now. I will rest it, for the present, on what I have said on the introduction of the resolutions now on the table, under a hope that another opportunity will be afforded for more ample discussion. I will, for the present, confine my remarks to the objections which have been raised to the views which I presented when I introduced them The authority of Luther Martin has been adduced by the Senator from Delaware, to prove that the citizens of a State, acting under the authority of a State, are liable to be punished as traitors by this Government. Eminent as Mr. Martin was as a lawyer, and high as his authority may be considered on a legal point, I cannot accept it in determining the point at issue. The attitude which he occupied, if taken into view, would lessen if not destroy, the weight of his authority. He had been violently opposed in convention to the Constitution, and the very letter from which the Senator has quoted was intended to dissuade Maryland from its adoption. With this view, it was to be expected that every consideration calculated to effect that object should be urged; that real objections should be exaggerated; and that those having no foundation, except mere plausible deductions, should be presented. It is to this spirit that I attribute the opinion of Mr. Martin in reference to the point under consideration. But if his authority be good on one point, it must be admitted to be equally so on another. If his opinion be sufficient to prove that a citizen of a State may be punished as a traitor when acting under allegiance to the State, it is also sufficient to show that no authority was intended to be given in the Constitution for the protection of manufactures by the General Government, and that the provision in the Constitution permitting a State to lay an impost duty, with the consent of Congress, was intended to reserve the right of protection to the States themselves, and that each State should protect its own industry. Assuming his opinion to be of equal authority on both points, how embarrassing would be the attitude in which it would place the Senator from Delaware, and those with whom he is acting—that of using the

sword and bayonet to enforce the execution of an unconstitutional act of Congress. I must express my surprise that the slightest authority in favor of *power* should be received as the most conclusive evidence, while that which is, at least, equally strong in favor of right and *liberty*, is wholly overlooked or rejected.

Notwithstanding all that has been said, I may say that neither the Senator from Delaware [Mr. Clayton], nor any other who has spoken on the same side, has directly and fairly met the great question at issue: Is this a federal union? a union of States, as distinct from that of individuals? Is the sovereignty in the several States, or in the American people in the aggregate? The very language which we are compelled to use when speaking of our political institutions affords proof conclusive as to its real character. The terms union, federal, united, all imply a combination of sovereignties, a confederation of States. They are never applied to an association of individuals. Who ever heard of the United State of New York, of Massachusetts, or of Virginia? Who ever heard the term federal or union applied to the aggregation of individuals into one community? Nor is the other point less clear—that the sovereignty is in the several States, and that our system is a union of twenty-four sovereign powers, under a constitutional compact, and not of a divided sovereignty between the States severally and the United States. In spite of all that has been said, I maintain that sovereignty is in its nature indivisible. It is the supreme power in a State, and we might just as well speak of half a square, or of half a triangle, as of half a sovereignty. It is a gross error to confound the exercise of sovereign powers with sovereignty itself, or the delegation of such powers with the surrender of them. A sovereign may delegate his powers to be exercised by as many agents as he may think proper, under such conditions and with such limitations as he may impose; but to surrender any portion of his sovereignty to another is to annihilate the whole. The Senator from Delaware [Mr. Clayton] calls this metaphysical reasoning, which, he says, he cannot comprehend. If by metaphysics he means that scholastic refinement which makes distinctions without difference, no one can hold it in more utter contempt than I do; but if, on the contrary, he means the power of analysis and combination—that power which reduces the most complex idea into its elements,

which traces causes to their first principle, and, by the power of generalization and combination, unites the whole in one harmonious system—then, so far from deserving contempt, it is the highest attribute of the human mind. It is the power which raises man above the brute—which distinguishes his faculties from mere sagacity, which he holds in common with inferior animals. It is this power which has raised the astronomer from being a mere gazer at the stars to the high intellectual eminence of a Newton or a Laplace, and astronomy itself from a mere observation of insulated facts into that noble science which displays to our admiration the system of the universe. And shall this high power of the mind, which has effected such wonders when directed to the laws which control the material world, be forever prohibited, under a senseless cry of metaphysics, from being applied to the high purpose of political science and legislation? I hold them to be subject to laws as fixed as matter itself, and to be as fit a subject for the application of the highest intellectual power. Denunciation may, indeed, fall upon the philosophical inquirer into these first principles, as it did upon Galileo and Bacon when they first unfolded the great discoveries which have immortalized their names; but the time will come when truth will prevail in spite of prejudice and denunciation, and when politics and legislation will be considered as much a science as astronomy and chemistry.

In connection with this part of the subject, I understood the Senator from Virginia [Mr. Rives] to say that sovereignty was divided, and that a portion remained with the States severally, and that the residue was vested in the Union. By Union, I suppose the Senator meant the United States. If such be his meaning—if he intended to affirm that the sovereignty was in the twenty-four States, in whatever light he may view them, our opinions will not disagree; but according to my conception the whole sovereignty is in the several States, while the exercise of sovereign powers is divided—a part being exercised under compact, through this General Government, and the residue through the separate State governments. But if the Senator from Virginia [Mr. Rives] means to assert that the twenty-four States form but one community, with a single sovereign power as to the objects of the Union, it will be but the revival of the old question of whether the Union is a union between States as distinct communities, or a mere aggregate of the American people as a

mass of individuals; and in this light his opinions would lead directly to consolidation.

But to return to the bill. It is said that the bill ought to pass, because the law must be enforced. The law must be enforced! The imperial edict must be executed! It is under such sophistry, couched in general terms, without looking to the limitations which must ever exist in the practical exercise of power, that the most cruel and despotic acts ever have been covered. It was such sophistry as this that cast Daniel into the lions' den, and the three Innocents into the fiery furnace. Under the same sophistry the bloody edicts of Nero and Caligula were executed. The law must be enforced. Yes, the act imposing the "tea-tax must be executed." This was the very argument which impelled Lord North and his administration to that mad career which forever separated us from the British crown. Under a similar sophistry, "that religion must be protected," how many massacres have been perpetrated? and how many martyrs have been tied to the stake? What! acting on this vague abstraction, are you prepared to enforce a law without considering whether it be just or unjust, constitutional or unconstitutional? Will you collect money when it is acknowledged that it is not wanted? He who earns the money, who digs it from the earth with the sweat of his brow, has a just title to it against the universe. No one has a right to touch it without his consent, except his government, and this only to the extent of its legitimate wants; to take more is robbery, and you propose by this bill to enforce robbery by murder. Yes: to this result you must come by this miserable sophistry, this vague abstraction of enforcing the law, without a regard to the fact whether the law be just or unjust, constitutional or unconstitutional.

In the same spirit we are told that the Union must be preserved, without regard to the means. And how is it proposed to preserve the Union? By force? Does any man in his senses believe that this beautiful structure—this harmonious aggregate of States, produced by the joint consent of all—can be preserved by force? Its very introduction will be certain destruction to this Federal Union. No, no. You cannot keep the States united in their constitutional and federal bonds by force. Force may, indeed, hold the parts together, but such union would be the bond between master and slave—a union of exaction on one side and of unqualified obedience on the other. That obedience which, we are told by the Senator from Pennsylvania [Mr. Wilkins], is the Union! Yes, exaction on the side of the master; for this very bill is intended to collect what can be no longer called taxes — the voluntary contribution of a free people — but tribute — tribute to be collected under the mouths of the cannon! Your custom-house is already transferred into a garrison, and that garrison with its batteries turned, not against the enemy of your country, but on subjects (I will not say citizens), on whom you propose to levy contributions. Has reason fled from our borders? Have we ceased to reflect? It is madness to suppose that the Union can be preserved by force. I tell you plainly that the bill, should it pass, cannot be enforced. It will prove only a blot upon your statute book, a reproach to the year, and a disgrace to the American Senate. I repeat, it will not be executed; it will rouse the dormant spirit of the people, and open their eyes to the approach of despotism. The country has sunk into avarice and political corruption, from which nothing can arouse it but some measure on the part of the Government, of folly and madness, such as that now under consideration.

Disguise it as you may, the controversy is one between power and liberty; and I tell the gentlemen who are opposed to me that, as strong as may be the love of power on their side, the love of liberty is still stronger on ours. History furnishes many instances of similar struggles, where the love of liberty has prevailed against power under every disadvantage, and among them few more striking than that of our own Revolution; where, as strong as was the parent country, and feeble as were the colonies, yet, under the impulse of liberty and the blessing of God, they gloriously triumphed in the contest. There are, indeed, many and striking analogies between that and the present controversy. They both originated substantially in the same cause — with this difference — in the present case the power of taxation is converted into that of regulating industry; in the other, the power of regulating industry, by the regulations of commerce, was attempted to be converted into the power of taxation. Were I to trace the analogy further, we should find that the perversion of the taxing power, in the one case, has given precisely the same control to the northern section over the industry of the southern section of the Union, which the power to regulate commerce gave to Great Britain over the industry of the colonies in the other; and that the very articles in which the colonies were permitted to have a

III—57

free trade, and those in which the mother country had a monopoly, are almost identically the same as those in which the Southern States are permitted to have a free trade by the Act of 1832, and in which the Northern States have, by the same Act, secured a monopoly. The only difference is in the means. In the former, the colonies were permitted to have a free trade with all countries south of Cape Finisterre, a cape in the northern part of Spain; while north of that, the trade of the colonies was prohibited, except through the mother country, by means of her commercial regulations. If we compare the products of the country north and south of Cape Finisterre, we shall find them almost identical with the list of the protected and unprotected articles contained in the act of last year. Nor does the analogy terminate here. The very arguments resorted to at the commencement of the American Revolution, and the measures adopted, and the motives assigned to bring on that contest (to enforce the law), are almost identically the same.

But to return from this digression to the consideration of the bill. Whatever difference of opinion may exist upon other points, there is one on which I should suppose there can be none: that this bill rests on principles which, if carried out, will ride over State sovereignties, and that it will be idle for any of its advocates hereafter to talk of State rights. The Senator from Virginia [Mr. Rives] says that he is the advocate of State rights; but he must permit me to tell him that, although he may differ in premises from the other gentlemen with whom he acts on this occasion, yet, in supporting this bill, he obliterates every vestige of distinction between him and them, saving only that, professing the principles of 1798, his example will be more pernicious than that of the most open and bitter opponents of the rights of the States. I will also add, what I am compelled to say, that I must consider him [Mr. Rives] as less consistent than our old opponents, whose conclusions were fairly drawn from their premises, while his premises ought to have led him to opposite conclusions. The gentleman has told us that the new-fangled doctrines, as he chooses to call them, have brought State rights into disrepute. I must tell him, in reply, that what he calls new-fangled are but the doctrines of 1798; and that it is he [Mr. Rives], and others with him, who, professing these doctrines, have degraded them by explaining away their meaning and efficacy. He [Mr. Rives] has disclaimed, in behalf of Virginia, the

authorship of nullification. I will not dispute that point. If Virginia chooses to throw away one of her brightest ornaments, she must not hereafter complain that it has become the property of another. But while I have, as a representative of Carolina, no right to complain of the disavowal of the Senator from Virginia, I must believe that he [Mr. Rives] has done his native State great injustice by declaring on this floor, that when she gravely resolved, in 1798, that "in cases of deliberate and dangerous infractions of the Constitution, the States, as parties to the compact, have the right, and are in duty bound, to interpose to arrest the progress of the evil, and to maintain within their respective limits, the authorities, rights, and liberties, appertaining to them," she meant no more than to proclaim the right to protest and to remonstrate. To suppose that, in putting forth so solemn a declaration, which she afterwards sustained by so able and elaborate an argument, she meant no more than to assert what no one had ever denied, would be to suppose that the State had been guilty of the most egregious trifling that ever was exhibited on so solemn an occasion.

In reviewing the ground over which I have passed, it will be apparent that the question in controversy involves that most deeply important of all political questions, whether ours is a federal or a consolidated government; — a question, on the decision of which depend, as I solemnly believe, the liberty of the people, their happiness, and the place which we are destined to hold in the moral and intellectual scale of nations. Never was there a controversy in which more important consequences were involved; not excepting that between Persia and Greece, decided by the battles of Marathon, Platea, and Salamis — which gave ascendency to the genius of Europe over that of Asia — and which, in its consequences, has continued to affect the destiny of so large a portion of the world even to this day. There are often close analogies between events apparently very remote, which are strikingly illustrated in this case. In the great contest between Greece and Persia, between European and Asiatic polity and civilization, the very question between the federal and consolidated form of government was involved. The Asiatic governments, from the remotest time, with some exceptions on the eastern shore of the Mediterranean, have been based on the principle of consolidation, which considers the whole community as but a unit, and consolidates its powers in a central point.

The opposite principle has prevailed in Europe — Greece, throughout all her States, was based on a federal system. All were united in one common, but loose, bond, and the governments of the several States partook, for the most part, of a complex organization, which distributed political power among different members of the community. The same principles prevailed in ancient Italy; and, if we turn to the Teutonic race, our great ancestors — the race which occupies the first place in power, civilization, and science, and which possesses the largest and the fairest part of Europe — we shall find that their governments were based on federal organization, as has been clearly illustrated by a recent and able writer on the British constitution [Mr. Palgrave], from whose works I take the following extract: —

"In this manner the first establishment of the Teutonic States was affected. They were assemblages of septs, clans, and tribes; they were confederated hosts and armies, led on by princes, magistrates, and chieftains; each of whom was originally independent, and each of whom lost a portion of his pristine independence in proportion as he and his compeers became united under the supremacy of a sovereign, who was superinduced upon the State, first as a military commander and afterward as a king. Yet, notwithstanding this political connection, each member of the State continued to retain a considerable portion of the rights of sovereignty. Every ancient Teutonic monarchy must be considered as a federation; it is not a unit, of which the smaller bodies politic therein contained are the fractions, but they are the integers, and the State is the multiple which results from them. Dukedoms and counties, burghs and baronies, towns and townships, and shires, form the kingdom; all, in a certain degree, strangers to each other and separate in jurisdiction, though all obedient to the supreme executive authority. This general description, though not always strictly applicable in terms, is always so substantially and in effect; and hence it becomes necessary to discard the language which has been very generally employed in treating on the English constitution. It has been supposed that the kingdom was reduced into a regular and gradual subordination of government, and that the various legal districts of which it is composed, arose from the divisions and subdivisions of the country. But this hypothesis, which tends greatly to perplex our history, cannot be supported by fact; and, instead of viewing the constitution as a whole, and then proceeding to its parts, we must examine it synthetically, and assume that the supreme authorities of the State were created by the concentration of the powers originally belonging to the members and corporations of which it is composed."

Here Mr. Calhoun gave way for a motion to adjourn, and on the next day resumed:—

I have omitted at the proper place, in the course of my observations yesterday, two or three points, to which I will now advert before I resume the discussion where I left off. I have stated that the ordinance and acts of South Carolina were directed, not against the revenue, but against the system of protection. But it may be asked, if such was her object, how happens it that she has declared the whole system void — revenue as well as protection, without discrimination? It is this question which I propose to answer. Her justification will be found in the necessity of the case; and if there be any blame it cannot attach to her. The two are so blended, throughout the whole, as to make the entire revenue system subordinate to the protective, so as to constitute a complete system of protection, in which it is impossible to discriminate the two elements of which it is composed. South Carolina, at least, could not make the discrimination; and she was reduced to the alternative of acquiescing in a system which she believed to be unconstitutional, and which she felt to be oppressive and ruinous, or to consider the whole as one, equally contaminated through all its parts, by the unconstitutionality of the protective portion, and, as such, to be resisted by the act of the State. I maintain that the State has a right to regard it in the latter character, and that, if a loss of revenue follow, the fault is not hers, but of this Government, which has improperly blended together in a manner not to be separated by the State, two systems wholly dissimilar. If the sincerity of the State be doubted; if it be supposed that her action is against revenue as well as protection, let the two be separated — let so much of the duties as are intended for revenue be put in one bill, and the residue intended for protection be put in another, and I pledge myself that the ordinance and the acts of the State will cease as to the former, and be directed exclusively against the latter.

I also stated, in the course of my remarks yesterday, and I trust that I have conclusively shown, that the Act of 1816, with the exception of a single item, to which I have alluded, was in reality a revenue measure; and that Carolina and the other States, in supporting it, have not incurred the slightest responsibility in relation to the system of protection which has since grown up, and which now so deeply distracts the country. Sir,

I am willing, as one of the representatives of Carolina, and I believe I speak the sentiments of the State, to take that act as the basis of a permanent adjustment of the tariff, simply reducing the duties, in an average proportion, on all the items, to the revenue point. I make that offer now to the advocates of the protective system; but I must, in candor, inform them that such an adjustment would distribute the revenue between the protected and unprotected articles more favorably to the State, and to the South, and less to the manufacturing interest, than an average uniform *ad valorem*, and, accordingly, more so than that now proposed by Carolina through her convention. After such an offer, no man who values his candor will dare accuse the State, or those who have represented her here, with inconsistency in reference to the point under consideration.

I omitted, also, on yesterday, to notice a remark of the Senator from Virginia [Mr. Rives], that the only difficulty in adjusting the tariff grew out of the ordinance and the acts of South Carolina. I must attribute an assertion, so inconsistent with the facts, to an ignorance of the occurrences of the last few years in reference to this subject, occasioned by the absence of the gentleman from the United States, to which he himself has alluded in his remarks. If the Senator will take pains to inform himself, he will find that this protective system advanced with a continued and rapid step, in spite of petitions, remonstrances, and protests, of not only Carolina, but also of Virginia, and of all the Southern States, until 1828, when Carolina, for the first time, changed the character of her resistance, by holding up her reserved rights as the shield of her defense against further encroachment. This attitude alone, unaided by a single State, arrested the further progress of the system, so that the question from that period to this, on the part of the manufacturers, has been, not how to acquire more, but to retain that which they have acquired. I will inform the gentleman that, if this attitude had not been taken on the part of the State, the question would not now be how duties ought to be repealed, but a question as to the protected articles, between prohibition on one side and the duties established by the Act of 1828 on the other. But a single remark will be sufficient in reply to what I must consider the invidious remark of the Senator from Virginia [Mr. Rives]. The Act of 1832 which has not yet gone into operation, and which was passed but a few months since, was declared by the sup-

porters of the system to be a permanent adjustment, and the bill proposed by the Treasury Department, not essentially different from the act itself, was in like manner declared to be intended by the administration as a permanent arrangement. What has occurred since, except this ordinance, and these abused acts of the calumniated State, to produce this mighty revolution in reference to this odious system? Unless the Senator from Virginia can assign some other cause, he is bound, upon every principle of fairness, to retract this unjust aspersion upon the acts of South Carolina.

The Senator from Delaware [Mr. Clayton], as well as others, has relied with great emphasis on the fact that we are citizens of the United States. I do not object to the expression, nor shall I detract from the proud and elevated feelings with which it is associated; but I trust that I may be permitted to raise the inquiry, In what manner are we citizens of the United States? without weakening the patriotic feeling with which, I trust, it will ever be uttered. If by citizen of the United States he means a citizen at large, one whose citizenship extends to the entire geographical limits of the country, without having a local citizenship in some State or territory, a sort of citizen of the world, all I have to say is, that such a citizen would be a perfect nondescript; that not a single individual of this description can be found in the entire mass of our population. Notwithstanding all the pomp and display of eloquence on the occasion, every citizen is a citizen of some State or Territory, and, as such, under an express provision of the Constitution, is entitled to all privileges and immunities of citizens in the several States; and it is in this, and in no other sense, that we are citizens of the United States. The Senator from Pennsylvania [Mr. Dallas], indeed, relies upon that provision in the Constitution which gives Congress the power to establish a uniform rule of naturalization; and the operation of the rule actually established under this authority, to prove that naturalized citizens are citizens at large, without being citizens of any of the States. I do not deem it necessary to examine the law of Congress upon this subject, or to reply to the argument of the Senator, though I cannot doubt that he [Mr. Dallas] has taken an entirely erroneous view of the subject. It is sufficient that the power of Congress extends simply to the establishment of a uniform rule by which foreigners may be naturalized in the several States or territories,

without infringing, in any other respect, in reference to naturalization, the rights of the States as they existed before the adoption of the Constitution.

Having supplied the omissions of yesterday, I now resume the subject at the point where my remarks then terminated. The Senate will remember that I stated, at their close, that the great question at issue is, whether ours is a federal or a consolidated system of government; a system in which the parts, to use the emphatic language of Mr. Palgrave, are the integers, and the whole the multiple, or in which the whole is an unit and the parts the fractions. I stated, that on the decision of this question, I believed, depended not only the liberty and prosperity of this country, but the place which we are destined to hold in the intellectual and moral scale of nations. I stated, also, in my remarks on this point, that there is a striking analogy between this and the great struggle between Persia and Greece, which was decided by the battles of Marathon, Platea, and Salamis, and which immortalized the names of Miltiades and Themistocles. I illustrated this analogy by showing that centralism or consolidation, with the exception of a few nations along the eastern borders of the Mediterranean, has been the pervading principle in the Asiatic governments, while the federal system, or, what is the same in principle, that system which organizes a community in reference to its parts, has prevailed in Europe.

Among the few exceptions in the Asiatic nations, the government of the twelve tribes of Israel, in its early period, is the most striking. Their government, at first, was a mere confederation without any central power, till a military chieftain, with the title of king, was placed at its head, without, however, merging the original organization of the twelve distinct tribes. This was the commencement of that central action among that peculiar people which, in three generations, terminated in a permanent division of their tribes. It is impossible even for a careless reader to peruse the history of that event, without being forcibly struck with the analogy in the causes which led to their separation, and those which now threaten us with a similar calamity. With the establishment of the central power in the king commenced a system of taxation, which, under King Solomon, was greatly increased, to defray the expenses of rearing the temple, of enlarging and embellishing Jerusalem, the seat of the central government, and the other profuse expenditures of his magnificent reign. Increased taxation was followed by its natural consequences — discontent and complaint, which, before his death, began to excite resistance. On the succession of his son, Rehoboam, the ten tribes, headed by Jeroboam, demanded a reduction of the taxes; the temple being finished, and the embellishment of Jerusalem completed, and the money which had been raised for that purpose being no longer required, or, in other words, the debt being paid, they demanded a reduction of the duties — a repeal of the tariff. The demand was taken under consideration, and after consulting the old men, the counsellors of 1798, who advised a reduction, he then took the opinion of the younger politicians, who had since grown up, and knew not the doctrines of their fathers; he hearkened unto their counsel, and refused to make the reduction, and the secession of the ten tribes under Jeroboam followed. The tribes of Judah and Benjamin, which had received the disbursements, alone remained to the house of David.

But to return to the point immediately under consideration. I know that it is not only the opinion of a large majority of our country, but it may be said to be the opinion of the age, that the very beau ideal of a perfect government is the government of a majority, acting through a representative body, without check or limitation on its power; yet, if we may test this theory by experience and reason, we shall find that, so far from being perfect, the necessary tendency of all governments, based upon the will of an absolute majority, without constitutional check or limitation of power, is to faction, corruption, anarchy, and despotism; and this, whether the will of the majority be expressed directly through an assembly of the people themselves, or by their representatives. I know that, in venturing this assertion, I utter what is unpopular both within and without these walls; but where truth and liberty are concerned, such considerations should not be regarded. I will place the decision of this point on the fact that no government of the kind, among the many attempts which have been made, has ever endured for a single generation, but, on the contrary, has invariably experienced the fate which I have assigned to it. Let a single instance be pointed out, and I will surrender my opinion. But, if we had not the aid of experience to direct our judgment, reason itself would be a certain guide. The view which considers the community as an unit, and all its parts as having a similar interest, is

radically erroneous. However small the community may be, and however homogeneous its interests, the moment that government is put into operation — as soon as it begins to collect taxes and to make appropriations, the different portions of the community must, of necessity, bear different and opposing relations in reference to the action of the government. There must inevitably spring up two interests — a direction and a stockholder interest — an interest profiting by the action of the government, and interested in increasing its powers and action; and another, at whose expense the political machine is kept in motion. I know how difficult it is to communicate distinct ideas on such a subject, through the medium of general propositions, without particular illustration; and in order that I may be distinctly understood, though at the hazard of being tedious, I will illustrate the important principle which I have ventured to advance, by examples.

Let us, then, suppose a small community of five persons, separated from the rest of the world; and, to make the example strong, let us suppose them all to be engaged in the same pursuit, and to be of equal wealth. Let us further suppose that they determine to govern the community by the will of a majority; and, to make the case as strong as possible, let us suppose that the majority, in order to meet the expenses of the government, lay an equal tax, say of one hundred dollars, on each individual of this little community. Their treasury would contain five hundred dollars. Three are a majority; and they, by supposition, have contributed three hundred as their portion, and the other two (the minority), two hundred. The three have the right to make the appropriations as they may think proper. The question is, how would the principle of the absolute and unchecked majority operate, under these circumstances, in this little community? If the three be governed by a sense of justice — if they should appropriate the money to the objects for which it was raised, the common and equal benefit of the five, then the object of the association would be fairly and honestly effected, and each would have a common interest in the government. But, should the majority pursue an opposite course — should they appropriate the money in a manner to benefit their own particular interest, without regard to the interest of the two (and that they will so act, unless there be some efficient check, he who best knows human nature will least doubt), who does not see that the three and the two would have directly opposite

interests in reference to the action of the government? The three who contribute to the common treasury but three hundred dollars, could, in fact, by appropriating the five hundred to their own use, convert the action of the government into the means of making money, and, of consequence, would have a direct interest in increasing the taxes. They put in three hundred and take out five; that is, they take back to themselves all that they put in, and, in addition, that which was put in by their associates; or, in other words, taking taxation and appropriation together, they have gained, and their associates have lost, two hundred dollars by the fiscal action of the government. Opposite interests, in reference to the action of the government, are thus created between them: the one having an interest in favor of, and the other against the taxes; the one to increase, and the other to decrease the taxes; the one to retain the taxes when the money is no longer wanted, and the other to repeal them when the objects for which they were levied have been secured.

Let us now suppose this community of five to be raised to twenty-four individuals, to be governed, in like manner, by the will of a majority: it is obvious that the same principle would divide them into two interests — into a majority and a minority, thirteen against eleven, or in some other proportion; and that all the consequences which I have shown to be applicable to the small community of five would be applicable to the greater, the cause not depending upon the number, but resulting necessarily from the action of the government itself. Let us now suppose that, instead of governing themselves directly in an assembly of the whole, without the intervention of agents, they should adopt the representative principle; and that, instead of being governed by a majority of themselves, they should be governed by a majority of their representatives. It is obvious that the operation of the system would not be affected by the change, the representatives being responsible to those who chose them, would conform to the will of their constituents, and would act as they would do were they present and acting for themselves; and the same conflict of interest, which we have shown would exist in one case, would equally exist in the other. In either case, the inevitable result would be a system of hostile legislation on the part of the majority, or the stronger interest, against the minority, or the weaker interest; the object of which, on the part of the former, would be to exact as much as possible from the

latter, which would necessarily be resisted by all the means in their power. Warfare, by legislation, would thus be commenced between the parties, with the same object, and not less hostile than that which is carried on between distinct and rival nations — the only distinction would be in the instruments and the mode. Enactments, in the one case, would supply what could only be effected by arms in the other; and the inevitable operation would be to engender the most hostile feelings between the parties, which would merge every feeling of patriotism — that feeling which embraces the whole — and substitute in its place the most violent party attachment; and instead of having one common centre of attachment, around which the affections of the community might rally, there would in fact be two — the interests of the majority, to which those who constitute that majority would be more attached than they would be to the whole — and that of the minority, to which they, in like manner, would also be more attached than to the interests of the whole. Faction would thus take the place of patriotism; and, with the loss of patriotism, corruption must follow, and, in its train, anarchy, and, finally, despotism, or the establishment of absolute power in a single individual, as a means of arresting the conflict of hostile interests; on the principle that it is better to submit to the will of a single individual, who, by being made lord and master of the whole community, would have an equal interest in the protection of all its parts.

Let us next suppose that, in order to avert the calamitous train of consequences, this little community should adopt a written constitution, with limitations restricting the will of the majority, in order to protect the minority against the oppression which I have shown would necessarily result without such restrictions. It is obvious that the case would not be in the slightest degree varied, if the majority be left in possession of the right of judging exclusively of the extent of its powers, without any right on the part of the minority to enforce the restrictions imposed by the constitution on the will of the majority. The point is almost too clear for illustration. Nothing can be more certain than that, when a constitution grants power, and imposes limitations on the exercise of that power, whatever interests may obtain possession of the government, will be in favor of extending the power at the expense of the limitation; and that, unless those in whose behalf the limitations were imposed have, in some form or mode, the right of enforcing them, the power will ulti-mately supersede the limitation, and the government must oper-ate precisely in the same manner as if the will of the majority governed without constitution or limitation of power.

I have thus presented all possible modes in which a govern-ment founded upon the will of an absolute majority will be mod-ified; and have demonstrated that, in all its forms, whether in a majority of the people, as in a mere democracy, or in a majority of their representatives, without a constitution or with a consti-tution, to be interpreted as the will of the majority, the result will be the same: two hostile interests will inevitably be created by the action of the government, to be followed by hostile legis-lation, and that by faction, corruption, anarchy, and despotism.

The great and solemn question here presents itself: Is there any remedy for these evils? on the decision of which depends the question, whether the people can govern themselves, which has been so often asked with so much skepticism and doubt. There is a remedy, and but one, the effect of which, whatever may be the form, is to organize society in reference to this con-flict of interests, which springs out of the action of government; and which can only be done by giving to each part the right of self-protection; which in a word, instead of considering the com-munity of twenty-four a single community, having a common interest, and to be governed by the single will of an entire ma-jority, shall upon all questions tending to bring the parts into conflict, the thirteen against the eleven, take the will, not of the twenty-four as a unit, but of the thirteen and of the eleven sep-arately—the majority of each governing the parts, and where they concur, governing the whole—and where they disagree, ar-resting the action of the government. This I will call the con-curring, as distinct from the absolute majority. In either way the number would be the same, whether taken as the absolute or as the concurring majority. Thus, the majority of the thirteen is seven, and of the eleven six; and the two together make thir-teen, which is the majority of twenty-four. But, though the number is the same, the mode of counting is essentially differ-ent: the one representing the strongest interest, and the other, the entire interests of the community. The first mistake is, in supposing that the government of the absolute majority is the government of the people—that beau ideal of a perfect govern-ment which has been so enthusiastically entertained in every age

by the generous and patriotic, where civilization and liberty have made the smallest progress. There can be no greater error: the government of the people is the government of the whole com-munity—of the twenty-four—the self-government of all the parts—too perfect to be reduced to practice in the present, or any past stage of human society. The government of the abso-lute majority, instead of being the government of the people, is but the government of the strongest interests, and, when not efficiently checked, is the most tyrannical and oppressive that can be devised. Between this ideal perfection on the one side, and despotism on the other, no other system can be devised but that which considers society in reference to its parts, as differently affected by the action of the government, and which takes the sense of each part separately, and thereby the sense of the whole, in the manner already illustrated.

These principles, as I have already stated, are not affected by the number of which the community may be composed, but are just as applicable to one of thirteen millions—the number which composes ours—as of the small community of twenty-four, which I have supposed for the purpose of illustration; and are not less applicable to the twenty-four States united in one community, than to the case of the twenty-four individuals. There is, in-deed, a distinction between a large and a small community, not affecting the principle, but the violence of the action. In the smaller, the similarity of the interests of all the parts will limit the oppression from the hostile action of the parts, in a great degree, to the fiscal action of the government merely; but in the large community, spreading over a country of great extent, and having a great diversity of interests, with different kinds of labor, capital, and production, the conflict and oppression will ex-tend, not only to a monopoly of the appropriations on the part of the stronger interests, but will end in unequal taxes, and a general conflict between the entire interests of conflicting sec-tions, which, if not arrested by the most powerful checks, will terminate in the most oppressive tyranny that can be conceived, or in the destruction of the community itself.

If we turn our attention from these supposed cases, and direct it to our Government and its actual operation, we shall find a practical confirmation of the truth of what has been stated, not only of the oppressive operation of the system of an absolute ma-jority, but also a striking and beautiful illustration in the forma-

tion of our system, of the principle of the concurring majority, as distinct from the absolute, which I have asserted to be the only means of efficiently checking the abuse of power, and, of course, the only solid foundation of constitutional liberty. That our Government for many years has been gradually verging to consolidation; that the Constitution has gradually become a dead letter; and that all restrictions upon the power of government have been virtually removed, so as practically to convert the Gen-eral Government into a Government of an absolute majority with-out check or limitation, cannot be denied by any one who has impartially observed its operation.

It is not necessary to trace the commencement and gradual progress of the causes which have produced this change in our system; it is sufficient to state that the change has taken place within the last few years. What has been the result? Precisely that which might have been anticipated: the growth of faction, corruption, anarchy, and, if not despotism itself, its near approach, as witnessed in the provisions of this bill. And from what have these consequences sprung? We have been involved in no war. We have been at peace with all the world. We have been visited with no national calamity. Our people have been advanc-ing in general intelligence, and, I will add, as great and alarming as has been the advance of political corruption among the mer-cenary corps who look to government for support, the morals and virtue of the community at large have been advancing in improvement. What, I again repeat, is the cause? No other can be assigned but a departure from the fundamental principles of the Constitution, which has converted the Government into the will of an absolute and irresponsible majority, and which, by the laws that must inevitably govern in all such majorities, has placed in conflict the great interests of the country, by a system of hostile legislation, by an oppressive and unequal imposition of taxes, by unequal and profuse appropriations, and by rendering the entire labor and capital of the weaker interest subordinate to the stronger.

This is the cause, and these the fruits which have converted the Government into a mere instrument of taking money from one portion of the community to be given to another; and which has rallied around it a great, a powerful and mercenary corps of office-holders, office-seekers, and expectants, destitute of principle and patriotism, and who have no standard of morals or politics

but the will of the Executive—the will of him who has the dis-tribution of the loaves and the fishes. I hold it impossible for any one to look at the theoretical illustration of the principle of the absolute majority in the cases which I have supposed, and not be struck with the practical illustration in the actual opera-tion of our Government. Under every circumstance the absolute majority will ever have its American system (I mean nothing of-fensive to any Senator); but the real meaning of the American system is, that system of plunder which the strongest interest has ever waged, and will ever wage, against the weaker, where the latter is not armed with some efficient and constitutional check to arrest its action. Nothing but such a check on the part of the weaker interest can arrest it; mere constitutional limitations are wholly insufficient. Whatever interest obtains possession of the Government, will, from the nature of things, be in favor of the powers, and against the limitations imposed by the Con-stitution, and will resort to every device that can be imagined to remove those restraints. On the contrary, the opposite interest, that which I hear designated as the stockholding interests, the taxpayers, those on whom the system operates, will resist the abuse of powers, and contend for the limitations. And it is on this point, then, that the contest between the delegated and the reserved powers will be waged; but in this contest, as the inter-ests in possession of the Government are organized and armed by all its powers and patronage, the opposite interest, if not in like manner organized and possessed of a power to protect them-selves under the provisions of the Constitution, will be as inev-itably crushed as would be a band of unorganized militia when opposed by a veteran and trained corps of regulars. Let it never be forgotten that power can only be opposed by power, organization by organization; and on this theory stands our beau-tiful federal system of Government. No free system was ever further removed from the principle that the absolute majority, without check or limitation, ought to govern. To understand what our Government is, we must look to the Constitution, which is the basis of the system. I do not intend to enter into any minute examination of the origin and the source of its powers: it is sufficient for my purpose to state, as I do fearlessly, that it derived its power from the people of the separate States, each ratifying by itself, each binding itself by its own separate major-ity, through its separate convention.—the concurrence of the majorities of the several States forming the Constitution; — thus taking the sense of the whole by that of the several parts, representing the various interests of the entire community. It was this concurring and perfect majority which formed the Constitution, and not that majority which would consider the American people as a single community, and which, instead of representing fairly and fully the interests of the whole, would but represent, as has been stated, the interests of the stronger section. No candid man can dispute that I have given a correct description of the constitution-making power: that power which created and organized the Government, which delegated to it, as a common agent, certain powers, in trust for the common good of all the States, and which imposed strict limitations and checks against abuses and usurpations. In administering the delegated powers, the Constitution provides, very properly, in order to give promptitude and efficiency, that the Government shall be organized upon the principle of the absolute majority, or rather, of two absolute majorities combined: a majority of the States considered as bodies politic, which prevails in this body; and a majority of the people of the States, estimated in federal numbers, in the other House of Congress. A combination of the two prevails in the choice of the President, and, of course, in the appointment of Judges, they being nominated by the President and confirmed by the Senate. It is thus that the concurring and the absolute majorities are combined in one complex system: the one in forming the Constitution, and the other in making and executing the laws; thus beautifully blending the moderation, justice, and equity of the former, and more perfect majority, with the promptness and energy of the latter, but less perfect.

To maintain the ascendency of the Constitution over the law-making majority is the great and essential point on which the success of the system must depend. Unless that ascendency can be preserved, the necessary consequence must be that the laws will supersede the Constitution; and, finally, the will of the Executive, by the influence of his patronage, will supersede the laws — indications of which are already perceptible. This ascendency can only be preserved through the action of the States as organized bodies having their own separate governments, and possessed of the right, under the structure of our system, of judging of the extent of their separate powers, and of interposing their authority to arrest the unauthorized enactments of the General Government

within their respective limits. I will not enter, at this time, into the discussion of this important point, as it has been ably and fully presented by the Senator from Kentucky [Mr. Bibb], and others who preceded him in this debate, on the same side, whose arguments not only remain unanswered, but are unanswerable. It is only by this power of interposition that the reserved rights of the States can be peacefully and efficiently protected against the encroachments of the General Government — that the limitations imposed upon its authority can be enforced, and its movements confined to the orbit allotted to it by the Constitution.

It has, indeed, been said in debate that this can be effected by the organization of the General Government itself, particularly by the action of this body, which represents the States — and that the States themselves must look to the General Government for the preservation of many of the most important of their reserved rights. I do not underrate the value to be attached to the organic arrangement of the General Government and the wise distribution of its powers between the several departments, and, in particular, the structure and the important functions of this body; but to suppose that the Senate, or any department of this Government, was intended to be the only guardian of the reserved rights is a great and fundamental mistake. The Government, through all its departments, represents the delegated and not the reserved powers; and it is a violation of the fundamental principle of free institutions to suppose that any but the responsible representative of any interest can be its guardian. The distribution of the powers of the General Government and its organization were arranged to prevent the abuse of power in fulfilling the important trusts confided to it, and not, as preposterously supposed, to protect the reserved powers, which are confided wholly to the guardianship of the several States.

Against the view of our system which I have presented, and the right of the States to interpose, it is objected that it would lead to anarchy and dissolution. I consider the objection as without the slightest foundation; and that, so far from tending to weakness or disunion, it is the source of the highest power and of the strongest cement. Nor is its tendency in this respect difficult of explanation. The government of an absolute majority, unchecked by efficient constitutional restraints, though apparently strong is, in reality, an exceedingly feeble government. That tendency to conflict between the parts, which I have shown to be

inevitable in such governments, wastes the powers of the State in the hostile action of contending factions, which leaves very little more power than the excess of the strength of the majority over the minority. But a government based upon the principle of the concurring majority, where each great interest possesses within itself the means of self-protection, which ultimately requires the mutual consent of all the parts, necessarily causes that unanimity in council and ardent attachment of all the parts to the whole which give an irresistible energy to a government so constituted. I might appeal to history for the truth of these remarks, of which the Roman furnishes the most familiar and striking proofs. It is a well-known fact that, from the expulsion of the Tarquins to the time of the establishment of the tribunitian power, the government fell into a state of the greatest disorder and distraction, and, I may add, corruption. How did this happen? The explanation will throw important light on the subject under consideration. The community was divided into two parts — the Patricians and the Plebeians; with the power of the State principally in the hands of the former, without adequate checks to protect the rights of the latter. The result was as might be expected. The patricians converted the powers of the government into the means of making money to enrich themselves and their dependents. They, in a word, had their American system, growing out of the peculiar character of the government and condition of the country. This requires explanation. At that period, according to the laws of nations, when one nation conquered another, the lands of the vanquished belonged to the victor; and, according to the Roman law, the lands thus acquired were divided into two parts — one allotted to the poorer class of the people, and the other assigned to the use of the treasury — of which the patricians had the distribution and administration. The patricians abused their power by withholding from the plebeians that which ought to have been allotted to them, and by converting to their own use that which ought to have gone to the treasury. In a word, they took to themselves the entire spoils of victory, and had thus the most powerful motive to keep the State perpetually involved in war, to the utter impoverishment and oppression of the plebeians. After resisting the abuse of power by all peaceable means, and the oppression becoming intolerable, the plebeians at last withdrew from the city — they, in a word, seceded; and to induce them to reunite, the patricians conceded to them, as the means

of protecting their separate interests, the very power which I contend is necessary to protect the rights of the States, but which is now represented as necessarily leading to disunion. They granted to them the right of choosing three tribunes from among themselves, whose persons should be sacred, and who should have the right of interposing their veto, not only against the passage of laws, but even against their execution — a power which those who take a shallow insight into human nature would pronounce inconsistent with the strength and unity of the State, if not utterly impracticable; yet so far from this being the effect, from that day the genius of Rome became ascendant, and victory followed her steps till she had established an almost universal dominion. How can a result so contrary to all anticipation be explained? The explanation appears to me to be simple. No measure or movement could be adopted without the concurring assent of both the patricians and plebeians, and each thus become dependent on the other; and, of consequence, the desire and objects of neither could be effected without the concurrence of the other. To obtain this concurrence, each was compelled to consult the good-will of the other, and to elevate to office, not those only who might have the confidence of the order to which they belonged, but also that of the other. The result was, that men possessing those qualities which would naturally command confidence — moderation, wisdom, justice, and patriotism — were elevated to office; and the weight of their authority and the prudence of their counsel, combined with that spirit of unanimity necessarily resulting from the concurring assent of the two orders, furnish the real explanation of the power of the Roman State, and of that extraordinary wisdom, moderation, and firmness which in so remarkable a degree characterized her public men. I might illustrate the truth of the position which I have laid down by a reference to the history of all free States, ancient and modern, distinguished for their power and patriotism, and conclusively show, not only that there was not one which had not some contrivance, under some form, by which the concurring assent of the different portions of the community was made necessary in the action of government, but also that the virtue, patriotism, and strength of the State were in direct proportion to the perfection of the means of securing such assent.

In estimating the operation of this principle in our system, which depends, as I have stated, on the right of interposition on

the part of a State, we must not omit to take into consideration
the amending power, by which new powers may be granted, or
any derangement of the system corrected, by the concurring
assent of three-fourths of the States; and thus, in the same degree, strengthening the power of repairing any derangement occasioned by the eccentric action of a State. In fact, the power
of interposition, fairly understood, may be considered in the light
of an appeal against the usurpations of the General Government,
the joint agent of all the States, to the States themselves, to be
decided under the amending power, by the voice of three-fourths
of the States, as the highest power known under the system. I
know the difficulty, in our country, of establishing the truth of
the principle for which I contend, though resting upon the clearest reason, and tested by the universal experience of free nations. I know that the governments of the several States, which,
for the most part, are constructed on the principle of the absolute majority, will be cited as an argument against the conclusion
to which I have arrived; but, in my opinion, the satisfactory
answer can be given — that the objects of expenditure which fall
within the sphere of a State government are few and inconsiderable, so that, be their action ever so irregular, it can occasion but
little derangement. If, instead of being members of this great
confederacy, they formed distinct communities, and were compelled to raise armies, and incur other expenses necessary to
their defense, the laws which I have laid down as necessarily
controlling the action of a State where the will of an absolute
and unchecked majority prevailed, would speedily disclose themselves in faction, anarchy, and corruption. Even as the case is,
the operation of the causes to which I have referred is perceptible in some of the larger and more populous members of the
Union, whose governments have a powerful central action, and
which already show a strong moneyed tendency, the invariable
forerunner of corruption and convulsion.

But, to return to the General Government. We have now sufficient experience to ascertain that the tendency to conflict in its
action is between the southern and other sections. The latter
having a decided majority, must habitually be possessed of the
powers of the Government, both in this and in the other House;
and, being governed by that instinctive love of power so natural
to the human breast, they must become the advocates of the
power of government, and in the same degree opposed to

the limitations; while the other and weaker section is as necessarily thrown on the side of the limitations. One section is the
natural guardian of the delegated powers, and the other of the
reserved; and the struggle on the side of the former will be to
enlarge the powers, while that on the opposite side will be to
restrain them within their constitutional limits. The contest will,
in fact, be a contest between power and liberty, and such I consider the present — a contest in which the weaker section, with
its peculiar labor, productions, and institutions, has at stake all
that can be dear to freemen. Should we be able to maintain in
their full vigor our reserved rights, liberty and prosperity will be
our portion; but if we yield, and permit the stronger interest to
concentrate within itself all the powers of the Government, then
will our fate be more wretched than that of the aborigines whom
we have expelled. In this great struggle between the delegated
and reserved powers, so far from repining that my lot, and that
of those whom I represent, is cast on the side of the latter, I
rejoice that such is the fact; for, though we participate in but
few of the advantages of the Government, we are compensated,
and more than compensated, in not being so much exposed to its
corruptions. Nor do I repine that the duty, so difficult to be discharged, of defending the reserved powers against apparently
such fearful odds, has been assigned to us. To discharge it successfully requires the highest qualities, moral and intellectual;
and should we perform it with a zeal and ability proportioned to
its magnitude, instead of mere planters, our section will become
distinguished for its patriots and statesmen. But, on the other
hand, if we prove unworthy of the trust — if we yield to the
steady encroachments of power, the severest calamity and most
debasing corruption will overspread the land. Every southern
man, true to the interests of his section, and faithful to the
duties which Providence has allotted him, will be forever excluded from the honors and emoluments of this Government,
which will be reserved for those only who have qualified themselves, by political prostitution, for admission into the Magdalen
Aslyum.

DENOUNCING ANDREW JACKSON

(Delivered in the United States Senate During the Debate on the Expunging
Resolution, January, 1837)

THE gentleman from Virginia [Mr. Rives] says that the argument in favor of this expunging resolution has not been
answered. Sir, there are some questions so plain that they
cannot be argued. Nothing can make them more plain; and this
is one. No one, not blinded by party zeal, can possibly be insensible that the measure proposed is a violation of the Constitution. The Constitution requires the Senate to keep a journal;
this resolution goes to expunge the journal. If you may expunge a part, you may expunge the whole; and if it is expunged,
how is it kept? The Constitution says the journal shall be kept;
this resolution says it shall be destroyed. It does the very thing
which the Constitution declares shall not be done. That is the
argument, the whole argument. There is none other. Talk of
precedents? and precedents drawn from a foreign country? They
don't apply. No, sir. This is to be done, not in consequence of
argument, but in spite of argument. I understand the case. I
know perfectly well the gentlemen have no liberty to vote otherwise. They are coerced by an exterior power. They try, indeed,
to comfort their conscience by saying that it is the will of the
people, and the voice of the people. It is no such thing. We all
know how these legislative returns have been obtained. It is by
dictation from the White House. The President himself, with
that vast mass of patronage which he wields, and the thousand
expectations he is able to hold up, has obtained these votes
of the State legislatures; and this, forsooth, is said to be the
voice of the people. The voice of the people! Sir, can we forget the scene which was exhibited in this Chamber when that
expunging resolution was first introduced here? Have we forgotten the universal giving way of conscience, so that the Senator
from Missouri was left alone? I see before me Senators who
could not swallow that resolution; and has its nature changed
since then? Is it any more constitutional now than it was then?
Not at all. But executive power has interposed. Talk to me of
the voice of the people! No, sir. It is the combination of patronage and power to coerce this body into a gross and palpable
violation of the Constitution. Some individuals, I perceive, think

to escape through the particular form in which this act is to be
perpetrated. They tell us that the resolution on your records is
not to be expunged, but is only to be endorsed "Expunged."
Really, sir, I do not know how to argue against such contemptible sophistry. The occasion is too solemn for an argument of
this sort. You are going to violate the Constitution, and you get
rid of the infamy by a falsehood. You yourselves say that the
resolution is expunged by your order. Yet you say it is not expunged. You put your act in express words. You record it,
and then turn round and deny it.

But what is the motive? What is the pretext for this enormity? Why, gentlemen tell us the Senate has two distinct consciences — a legislative conscience, and a judicial conscience. As
a legislative body we have decided that the President has violated
the Constitution. But gentlemen tell us that this is an impeachable offense; and, as we may be called to try it in our judicial
capacity, we have no right to express the opinion. I need not
show how inconsistent such a position is with the eternal, imprescriptible right of freedom of speech, and how utterly inconsistent it is with precedents drawn from the history of our British
ancestors, where the same liberty of speech has for centuries
been enjoyed. There is a shorter and more direct argument in
reply. Gentlemen who take that position cannot, according to
their own showing, vote for this resolution; for if it is unconstitutional for us to record a resolution of condemnation, because
we may afterwards be called to try the case in a judicial capacity, then it is equally unconstitutional for us to record a resolution of acquittal. If it is unconstitutional for the Senate to
declare before a trial that the President has violated the Constitution, it is equally unconstitutional to declare before a trial that
he has not violated the Constitution. The same principle is
involved in both. Yet, in the very face of this principle, gentlemen are here going to condemn their own act.

But why do I waste my breath? I know it is all utterly
vain. The day is gone; night approaches, and night is suitable
to the dark deed we meditate. There is a sort of destiny in this
thing. The act must be performed; and it is an act which will
tell on the political history of this country forever. Other preceding violations of the Constitution (and they have been many
and great) filled my bosom with indignation, but this fills it only
with grief. Others were done in the heat of partisanship. Power

was, as it were, compelled to support itself by seizing upon new instruments of influence and patronage; and there were ambitious and able men to direct the process. Such was the removal of the deposits, which the President seized upon by a new and unprecedented act of arbitrary power; an act which gave him ample means of rewarding friends and punishing enemies. Something may, perhaps, be pardoned to him in this matter, on the old apology of tyrants—the plea of necessity. But here there can be no such apology. Here no necessity can so much as be pretended. This act originates in pure, unmixed, personal idolatry. It is the melancholy evidence of a broken spirit, ready to bow at the feet of power. The former act was such a one as might have been perpetrated in the days of Pompey or Cæsar; but an act like this could never have been consummated by a Roman senate until the times of Caligula and Nero.

REPLYING TO HENRY CLAY

(From the «Independent Treasury» Debate in the United States Senate, March, 1838)

I who have changed no opinion, abandoned no principle, deserted no party; I, who have stood still and maintained my ground against every difficulty, to be told that it is left to time to disclose my motive! The imputation sinks to the earth with the groundless charge on which it rests. I stamp it with scorn in the dust. I pick up the dart, which fell harmless at my feet. I hurl it back. What the Senator charges on me, unjustly, he has actually done. He went over on a memorable occasion, and did not leave it to time to disclose his motive.

The Senator next tells us that I bore a character for stern fidelity, which he accompanied with remarks implying that I had forfeited it by my course on the present occasion. If he means by stern fidelity a devoted attachment to duty and principle, which nothing can overcome, the character is, indeed, a high one, and, I trust, not entirely unmerited. I have, at least, the authority of the Senator himself for saying that it belonged to me before the present occasion, and it is, of course, incumbent on him to show that I have since forfeited it. He will find the task a Herculean one. It would be by far more easy to show the opposite; that, instead of forfeiting, I have strengthened my title to

I cannot retort on the Senator the charge of being metaphysical. I cannot accuse him of possessing the powers of analysis and generalization, those higher faculties of the mind (called metaphysical by those who do not possess them), which decompose and resolve into their elements the complex masses of ideas that exist in the world of mind, as chemistry does the bodies that surround us in the material world; and without which those deep and hidden causes which are in constant action, and producing such mighty changes in the condition of society, would operate unseen and undetected. The absence of these higher qualities of the mind is conspicuous throughout the whole course of the Senator's public life. To this it may be traced that he prefers the specious to the solid, and the plausible to the true. To the same cause, combined with an ardent temperament, it is owing that we ever find him mounted on some popular and favorite measure which he whips along, cheered by the shouts of the multitude, and never dismounts till he has ridden it down. Thus, at one time, we find him mounted on the protective system, which he rode down; at another, on internal improvement; and now he is mounted on a bank, which will surely share the same fate, unless those who are immediately interested shall stop him in his headlong career. It is the fault of his mind to seize on a few prominent and striking advantages, and to pursue them eagerly without looking to consequences. Thus, in the case of the protective system, he was struck with the advantages of manufactures; and, believing that high duties was the proper mode of protecting them, he pushed forward the system without seeing that he was enriching one portion of the country at the expense of the other; corrupting the one and alienating the other; and, finally, dividing the community into two great hostile interests, which terminated in the overthrow of the system itself. So, now, he looks only to a uniform currency, and a bank as the means of securing it, without once reflecting how far the banking system has progressed, and the difficulties that impede its further progress; that banking and politics are running together to their mutual destruction; and that the only possible mode of saving his favorite system is to separate it from the Government.

To the defects of understanding, which the Senator attributes to me, I make no reply. It is for others, and not me, to determine the portion of understanding which it has pleased the Author of my being to bestow on me. It is, however, fortunate

the character; instead of abandoning any principles, I have firmly adhered to them, and that, too, under the most appalling difficulties. If I were to select an instance in the whole course of my life on which, above all others, to rest my claim to the character which the Senator attributed to me, it would be this very one which he has selected to prove that I have forfeited it. I acted with the full knowledge of the difficulties I had to encounter and the responsibility I had to incur. I saw a great and powerful party, probably the most powerful in the country, eagerly seizing on the catastrophe which had befallen the currency and the consequent embarrassments that followed, to displace those in power against whom they had been long contending. I saw that to stand between them and their object I must necessarily incur their deep and lasting displeasure. I also saw that to maintain the administration in the position they had taken, to separate the Government from the banks, I would draw down on me, with the exception of some of the Southern banks, the whole weight of that extensive, concentrated, and powerful interest—the most powerful by far of any in the whole community; and thus I would unite against me a combination of political and moneyed influence almost irresistible. . . .

But the Senator did not confine his attacks to my conduct and motives in reference to the present question. In his eagerness to weaken the cause I support, by destroying confidence in me, he made an indiscriminate attack on my intellectual faculties, which he characterized as metaphysical, eccentric, too much of genius, and too little common sense, and of course wanting a sound and practical judgment.

Mr. President, according to my opinion, there is nothing of which those who are endowed with superior mental faculties ought to be more cautious, than to reproach those with their deficiency to whom Providence has been less liberal. The faculties of our mind are the immediate gift of our Creator, for which we are no farther responsible than for their proper cultivation, according to our opportunities, and their proper application to control and regulate our actions. Thus thinking, I trust I shall be the last to assume superiority on my part, or reproach any one with inferiority on his; but those who do not regard the rule, when applied to others, cannot expect it to be observed when applied to themselves. The critic must expect to be criticized, and he who points out the faults of others, to have his own pointed out.

for me, that the standard by which I shall be judged is not the false, prejudiced, and, as I have shown, unfounded opinion which the Senator has expressed, but my acts. They furnish materials, neither few nor scant, to form a just estimate of my mental faculties. I have now been more than twenty-six years continuously in the service of this Government, in various stations, and have taken part in almost all the great questions which have agitated this country during this long and important period. Throughout the whole I have never followed events, but have taken my stand in advance, openly and freely avowing my opinions on all questions, and leaving it to time and experience to condemn or approve my course.

SELF-GOVERNMENT AND CIVILIZATION

WE MAKE a great mistake in supposing all people capable of self-government. Acting under that impression, many are anxious to force free governments on all the people of this continent, and over the world, if they had the power. It has been lately urged, in a very respectable quarter, that it is the mission of this country to spread civil and religious liberty over all the globe, and especially over this continent, even by force, if necessary. It is a sad delusion. None but a people advanced to a high state of moral and intellectual excellence are capable, in a civilized condition, of forming and maintaining free governments; and, among those who are so far advanced, very few, indeed, have had the good fortune to form constitutions capable of endurance. It is a remarkable fact in the political history of man, that there is scarcely an instance of a free constitutional government which has been the work exclusively of foresight and wisdom. They have all been the result of a fortunate combination of circumstances. It is a very difficult task to make a constitution worthy of being called so. This admirable Federal Constitution of ours is the result of such a combination. It is superior to the wisdom of any or of all the men by whose agency it was made. The force of circumstances, and not foresight or wisdom, induced them to adopt many of its wisest provisions.

But of the few nations who have been so fortunate as to adopt a wise constitution, still fewer have had the wisdom long to preserve one. It is harder to preserve than to obtain liberty.

After years of prosperity, the tenure by which it is held is but too often forgotten; and I fear, Senators, that such is the case with us. There is no solicitude now for liberty. Who talks of liberty when any great question comes up? Here is a question of the first magnitude as to the conduct of this war; do you hear anybody talk about its effects upon our liberties and our free institutions? No, sir. That was not the case formerly. In the early stages of our Government, the great anxiety was, how to preserve liberty. The great anxiety now is for the attainment of mere military glory. In the one we are forgetting the other. The maxim of former times was, that power is always stealing from the many to give to the few; the price of liberty was perpetual vigilance. They were constantly looking out and watching for danger. Not so now. Is it because there has been any decay of liberty among the people? Not at all. I believe the love of liberty was never more ardent; but they have forgotten the tenure of liberty, by which alone it is preserved.

We think we may now indulge in everything with impunity, as if we held our charter by "right divine"—from heaven itself. Under these impressions we plunge into war, we contract heavy debts, we increase the patronage of the Executive, and we talk of a crusade to force our institutions of liberty upon all people. There is no species of extravagance which our people imagine will endanger their liberty in any degree. Sir, the hour is approaching, the day of retribution will come. It will come as certainly as I am now addressing the Senate; and, when it does come, awful will be the reckoning, heavy the responsibility somewhere.

INDIVIDUAL LIBERTY

(From a Speech Delivered in 1848)

SOCIETY can no more exist without government, in one form or another, than man without society. It is the political, then, which includes the social, that is his natural state. It is the one for which his Creator formed him, into which he is impelled irresistibly, and in which only his race can exist, and all his faculties be fully developed. Such being the case, it follows that any, the worst form of government is better than anarchy, and that individual liberty or freedom must be subordinate to whatever power may be necessary to protect society against anarchy

within or destruction from without; for the safety and well being of society are as paramount to individual liberty as the safety and well being of the race are to that of individuals; and, in the same proportion, the power necessary for the safety of society is paramount to individual liberty. On the contrary, government has no right to control individual liberty beyond what is necessary to the safety and well being of society. Such is the boundary which separates the power of government and the liberty of the citizen or subject in the political state, which, as I have shown, is the natural state of man, the only one in which his race can exist, and the one in which he is born, lives, and dies.

It follows from all this that the quantum of power on the part of the government, and of liberty on that of individuals, instead of being equal in all cases, must necessarily be very unequal among different people, according to their different conditions. For just in proportion as a people are ignorant, stupid, debased, corrupt, exposed to violence within and danger without, the power necessary for government to possess, in order to preserve society against anarchy and destruction, becomes greater and greater, and individual liberty less and less, until the lowest condition is reached, when absolute and despotic power becomes necessary on the part of the government, and individual liberty extinct. So, on the contrary, just as a people rise in the scale of intelligence, virtue, and patriotism, and the more perfectly they become acquainted with the nature of government, the ends for which it was ordered, and how it ought to be administered, and the less the tendency to violence and disorder within and danger from abroad, the power necessary for government becomes less and less, and individual liberty greater and greater. Instead, then, of all men having the same right to liberty and equality, as is claimed by those who hold that they are all born free and equal, liberty is the noblest and highest reward bestowed on mental and moral development, combined with favorable circumstances. Instead, then, of liberty and equality being born with man,—instead of all men, and all classes and descriptions, being equally entitled to them,—they are high prizes to be won; and are, in their most perfect state, not only the highest reward that can be bestowed on our race, but the most difficult to be won, and, when won, the most difficult to be preserved.

JOHN CALVIN

(1509-1564)

BEZA writes that Calvin "taught the truth not with affected eloquence but with such solid gravity of style, that there was not a man who could hear him without being ravished with admiration." One of his modern admirers says that he "preached ex tempore and that his style is like his character—plain, unartificial, transparent, and practical, verifying the remark of his biographer that the greatest genius is always the most simple."

He was born at Noyon in Picardy, July 10th, 1509, from a family whose real name was "Cauvin," which, after the fashion of his time, he Latinized into "Calvinus." He was educated at the College de la Marché at Paris and at the College Montaign, showing an extraordinary capacity for knowledge of all kinds with a special bent towards metaphysics, or, as it was then called, "philosophy." He studied law as well as theology, but his sympathy for the movement inaugurated by Luther determined his choice and the law lost a student whose eminently severe thinking and habits of persistence might have made him one of the most profound lawyers who ever lived. He settled in Geneva in 1536, engaging thereafter in one great controversy after another during the remainder of his life. The greatest of these was with Servetus, against whom, on his trial for heresy at Geneva in 1553, he appeared as accuser. Coleridge says, however, that the death of Servetus at the stake "was not Calvin's guilt especially, but the common opprobrium of all European Christendom" at a time when burning at the stake was a matter of course in the regulation of opinion.

Calvin's discourse "On the Necessity of Enduring Persecution" was delivered extemporaneously but was published by him at Geneva, and the argument here given from it on "The Necessity for Courage" may be accepted as representing him as nearly as the difference between English and the French in which it was delivered will allow. Beza, in whose arms he died May 27th, 1564, summed up his character in the words: "I have been a witness of him for sixteen years and I think I am fully entitled to say that in this man there was exhibited to all an example of the life and death of the Christian such as it will not be easy to depreciate, such as it will be difficult to emulate."

THE NECESSITY FOR COURAGE

(From a Discourse on Enduring Persecution, Geneva, 1552)

WHAT shall be done in order to inspire our breasts with true courage? We have, in the first place, to consider how precious the confession of our faith is in the sight of God. We little know how much God prizes it, if our life, which is nothing, is valued by us more highly. When it is so, we manifest a marvelous degree of stupidity. We cannot save our life at the expense of our confession, without acknowledging that we hold it in higher estimation than the honor of God and the salvation of our souls.

A heathen could say that "It was a miserable thing to save life by giving up the only things which made life desirable!" And yet he and others like him never knew for what end men are placed in the world, and why they live in it. It is true they knew enough to say that men ought to follow virtue, to conduct themselves honestly and without reproach; but all their virtues were mere paint and smoke. We know far better what the chief aim of life should be; namely, to glorify God, in order that he may be our glory. When this is not done, woe to us! And we cannot continue to live for a single moment upon the earth without heaping additional curses on our heads. Still we are not ashamed to purchase some few days to languish here below, renouncing the eternal kingdom by separating ourselves from him by whose energy we are sustained in life.

Were we to ask the most ignorant, not to say the most brutish persons in the world, Why they live? they would not venture to answer simply, that it is to eat, and drink, and sleep; for all know that they have been created for a higher and holier end. And what end can we find if it be not to honor God, and allow ourselves to be governed by him, like children by a good parent; so that after we have finished the journey of this corruptible life, we may be received into his eternal inheritance? Such is the principal, indeed the sole end. When we do not take it into account, and are intent on a brutish life, which is worse than a thousand deaths, what can we allege for our excuse? To live and not know why, is unnatural. To reject the causes for which we live, under the influence of a foolish longing for a respite of some few days, during which we are to live in the world, while separated from God — I know not how to name such infatuation and madness! . . .

It were easy, indeed, for God to crown us at once without requiring us to sustain any combats; but as it is his pleasure that until the end of the world Christ shall reign in the midst of his enemies, so it is also his pleasure that we, being placed in the midst of them, shall suffer their oppression and violence till he deliver us. I know, indeed, that the flesh kicks when it is to be brought to this point, but still the will of God must have the mastery. If we feel some repugnance in ourselves, it need not surprise us; for it is only too natural for us to shun the cross. Still let us not fail to surmount it, knowing that God accepts our obedience, provided we bring all our feelings and wishes into captivity, and make them subject to him.

When the Prophets and Apostles went to death, it was not without feeling within some inclination to recoil. "They will lead thee whither thou wouldst not," said our Lord Jesus Christ to Peter. When such fears of death arise within us, let us gain the mastery over them, or rather let God gain it; and meanwhile, let us feel assured that we offer him a pleasing sacrifice when we resist and do violence to our inclinations for the purpose of placing ourselves entirely under his command: This is the principal war in which God would have his people to be engaged. He would have them strive to suppress every rebellious thought and feeling which would turn them aside from the path to which he points. And the consolations are so ample, that it may well be said, we are more than cowards if we give way!

In ancient times vast numbers of people, to obtain a simple crown of leaves, refused no toil, no pain, no trouble; nay, it even cost them nothing to die, and yet every one of them fought for a peradventure, not knowing whether he was to gain or lose the prize. God holds forth to us the immortal crown by which we may become partakers of his glory: he does not mean us to fight at haphazard, but all of us have a promise of the prize for which we strive. Have we any cause then to decline the struggle? Do we think it has been said in vain, "If we die with Jesus Christ we shall also live with him?" Our triumph is prepared, and yet we do all we can to shun the combat.

III—59

THE CRISIS OF 1793

(From an Address in Convention July 11th, 1793, Reporting on the Condition of the Republic)

THE Committee of Public Safety having charged me to apprise you of the actual condition of the Republic, and of the operations it has conducted, I shall try to acquit myself of the duty.

You will recollect that, at the period of the establishment of the committee, the Republic was betrayed; Dumouriez had disorganized the armies of the North and the Ardennes, and there remained but about two thousand five hundred men in the garrisons of that whole frontier. The strongholds lacked provisions and munitions to sustain a siege, and this general, after having delivered to the Austrians the stores and arms for a considerable sum, would also have delivered up the fortifications without defense. You know that this general abandoned at Liege ten thousand guns and twenty-five thousand uniforms, which he placed in store for the benefit of our enemies, while the soldiers of the Republic were in need, and to deceive them as to his bent, he made this hall echo with his hypocritical plaints of the nakedness of the army, to the end to throw the blame upon this convention. The armies of the Rhine and the Moselle have been obliged to retreat and to abandon the environs of Mayence. They have sought frontier points and find themselves in a condition of disorganization which is the inevitable result of a forced retreat. The armies of the Alps and of Italy are tranquil since the snow in the mountains has separated them from the enemy. The Spaniards have attacked us in the direction of Bayonne and Perpignan. The armies of the Eastern and Western Pyrenees, of which we have heard much spoken, which were, it was frequently said, always on the point of organizing, are totally destitute. They need general officers, they have no cannon to take the field, hardly any ordnance for their siege guns, but little food stores, and few soldiers. The commissioners, Isnard, Aubry, and Despinassy, whom you sent to Perpignan, made you a reassuring report on the condition of that frontier; nevertheless the representatives of the people, who were there at the first invasion of the Spaniards, write you that it was totally abandoned; that the

PIERRE JOSEPH CAMBON

(1754–1820)

CAMBON has been called the greatest financier of the French Revolutionary period. Although he was practically responsible for the receipts and expenditures of the Republic during its stormiest times, the confidence of the Legislative Assembly, and of the Convention afterwards, in his honesty, was never shaken, not even during the Reign of Terror. From the first he was the ruling spirit and mouthpiece of the Financial Committee of both bodies. His expositions of the public situation to both are models of luminous and exhaustive statement.

Born into a wealthy bourgeois family in Montpellier, he was engaged in the grocery business in his native city when the beginning of the Revolution sent him to represent the *tiers etat* in the States General at Versailles in 1789. In 1791, after being elected first deputy for the department of Herault in the Legislative Assembly, he was placed at the head of its financial committee, where he soon became such an authority on financial matters that he was made the last President of the Assembly, elected first deputy for Herault to the Convention in 1792, and placed at the head of its financial committee also. He was made a member of the first Committee of Public Safety in 1793, but was left out of the second on account of his moderation. Although he co-operated in the overthrow of Robespierre, he was made one of the victims of the feeling against the first committee to such an extent that he was forced to return, a poorer man, to his business in Montpellier.

Here he was permitted to remain unmolested until the Bourbons, in 1815, included him with other alleged "regicides" in a decree of banishment. He died in exile at Brussels in 1820.

forts were nearly all dismantled; that most of the cannon found in the works lacked cartridges; that there were few if any stores, and that they were without food. As to our situation in the interior, fanatics having raised armies in La Vendee and adjoining departments, several strong cities came under the power of the rebels. It is hoped, however, that the courage of the Republicans will stifle this rebellion in its birth; and since it is impossible to send disciplined troops there, the object may be attained by the levies made by requisition on the spot and some small bodies of veteran troops. Unfortunately, as you know, intrigues have weakened the public spirit in part of the departments; the citizens fail to show the energy necessary to combat the fanatics, who have their own form of energy; the bravery of the soldiers was not seconded or else was paralyzed by the perfidy of their chiefs; we lost arms, cannon, and stores, which were used against us. Orders were then given to bring up battalions of the army; they were halted in their march; the committee ordered arms and supplies; the administration checked these in their passage; thenceforward there seemed to be no union in any operations; it might even be said that each administrator seemed occupied only in the defense of his own position; formed his own little army, and named his general, so that it was impossible that any comprehensive system of defense could be followed. At the same time we had to defend the ports of Brest and Cherbourg. There were but a few scattered troops in these garrisons. On the coasts of Brittany, where a revolt had broken out, there were hardly five thousand troops, a number not sufficient even to equip the ships of the line.

The coasts and seaports of the Republic did not present conditions reassuring those who hoped for their defense: everywhere cannon were being asked for, and calls were made for ammunition and men to man the redoubts. But little activity was displayed in fitting out the fleets of the Republic. The ports of Brest, Rochefort, and Lorient had but six vessels of the line fit to put to sea, and the Mediterranean fleet was being repaired at Toulon.

You had one hundred and seventy representatives of the people in the departments to excite the patriotism of the citizens for the enlistment of three hundred thousand men, or on diverse missions of recruiting; but one of the subterfuges of the enemy was to calumniate and discredit them. To check the success of their operations, nothing was left undone to decry them, to asperse their authority, and to create enemies for them. Everywhere a word was hurled at them which has since become the title of a party, they were called "Maratists"—a name invented by our enemies to decry the most energetic of our patriots. It was said that "Maratists" were assassins, the partisans of the Agrarian laws and of royalty for the Duke of Orleans. Very soon a portion of this assembly bore the same reproach. In spite of all these obstacles, the recruiting of three hundred thousand men was a success, but your commissioners had to have recourse to a few revolutionary acts necessitated by the resistance made by the aristocrats and moderates, in the endeavor to paralyze their efforts. Nevertheless I can say to France, without the mission of these commissioners, in place of the three hundred thousand men needed to defend France, you would hardly have had twenty thousand. Such was the condition of the Republic when the Committee of Public Safety was organized.

What has your committee done? It commenced by having from the Executive Council a full statement of the means they had adopted to save the public. But the Executive Council itself was paralyzed. The Minister of War had just been arrested, there was no force in the government, several of the ministers lacked the confidence of the public. The administrations were nullities, inapt and careless; everywhere were wanting men, arms, clothing, munitions of war, and food. At last demands came from all sections. Our political relations abroad felt the torpor into which our government had fallen.

Your committee felt they must take decided measures. They recognized that at such a critical moment, where all could not be foreseen or united at the centre, the power should be disseminated; that commissioners were needed to save the Republic, excite the zeal of the citizens, improvise armies, survey their equipment, and prevent treason.

They found that the one hundred and seventy commissioners sent into the departments depleted the convention too much. They proposed to you the recall of those whose missions were fulfilled, or whose duties were not essentially important.

The powers of your commissioners were unlimited, and frequently their purposes and operations crossed each other. The committee thought well to organize a surveillance; they proposed instructions which would definitely determine the power of the

representatives of the people. Here the malevolence which pursued all your decrees again sought to check the work of your new commissioners. Everywhere they were held up as disorganizers, "Maratists," "proconsuls," "dictators." Nevertheless, this surveillance, which you created by the law of the thirtieth of April last, has saved the Republic; it has provisioned the army and the forts; it has given activity even to the generals. Over three thousand deliberations have been held by these commissioners—not to commit arbitrary acts, but to organize, arm and equip the armies, which, without their aid, would still be in the most extreme disorder. Since this organization, complaints and demands for food, clothing, and forage have diminished; for the representatives of the people on the spot have neglected nothing to supply really pressing demands. Our enemies have felt this power, and, not wishing us to succeed in our defense, have, with the word "Marat," sought to stifle the energy of the patriots. Your committee thought also to excite the zeal of the administrators to co-operate for the common defense. When arms were wanting efforts were made, by letter and instruction, to create or perfect establishments for the manufacture of new and the repair of old guns; to equip fowling pieces with bayonets, and to use superfluous bells for the casting of field pieces. They superintended the manufacture of gunpowder and the casting of bullets, and urged on all to second in every way the representatives of the people in clothing and equipping the armies, in surveying the defenses of the seaports, forts, and coasts, and to prepare, as far as possible, for the formation of corps of cavalry, by the employment of the horses used in carriages and for pleasure.

ALEXANDER CAMPBELL

(1788–1866)

FROM about 1825 until the end of his active life, Alexander Campbell was one of the celebrities of the West as an orator, educator, and religious teacher. Crowded audiences attended wherever he spoke, and bulky volumes of his debates with the champions of doctrines other than his own were published. Besides being the organizer of "The Disciples of Christ," he was the founder and head of Bethany College, West Virginia, and he delivered many lectures and addresses on topics not involving religious controversy. He was a man of great intellectual force and a most impressive speaker. Born of Scottish ancestry in the County of Antrim, Ireland, September 12th, 1788, he came to America in 1809 and began in 1823 the publication of the Christian Baptist, which was merged into the Millennial Harbinger in 1830. He died at Bethany, West Virginia, March 4th, 1866.

MIND THE MASTER FORCE

(From an Address Delivered at Miami University in 1844)

As THERE is not one lawless atom in the material universe, so there is not one irresponsible agent in the social system.

The order of material nature is, indeed, the outward symbol of the order of spiritual nature, and that is the order of obedient dependence. We shall, then, enter the holy place of moral obligation by passing leisurely through the outer court of physical obligation.

In the material universe all the inferior masses are under law to the superior. One of the sublime designs of the Creator is, that all the central masses of the universe shall not only be the largest masses in their respective systems, but also radiating centres to their systems. Thus he has constituted the great masses perennial fountains of beneficence to all the subordinate masses that move round them. Our own bright orb, representative of all the suns of creation, is an unwasting fountain of life

to its own glorious system. No sooner does he show his radiant face than floods of life teem from his bosom upon some thirty attendant planets, which, in sublime majesty and in expressive silence, ceaseless move around him. Light, heat, life, and joy emanate from him. These are the sensible demonstrations of his bounty to his waiting retinue of worlds. What other emanations of goodness he vouchsafes to those who obey him are yet unknown, and perhaps unknowable to us while confined to this our native planet. In the purer and more elevated regions of ether he may perhaps generate and mature the ultimate and more recondite elements of the vital principle, which, combining with our atmosphere, quicken it with all the rudimental principles of animal existence.

In the realms of matter, so far as fact, observation, and analogy authenticate any conclusion, the law is universal; viz., that the minors must be subject to the majors; that the inferior masses shall depend on the superior for all that gives them life and comfort. But that the satellites of all systems and of all ranks requite their suns in some way by receiving from them their beneficence, and thereby maintaining, through their respective gravities, their central positions and perpetual quiescence, while they all move forward in one grand concert around the throne of the Eternal, in awful grandeur musing his praise, is not to be questioned or doubted by any one conversant with God's grand system of designs. On these sublime though simple principles are suspended the order, beauty, and felicity of the universe. Destroy this, and a scene of disorder, confusion, and destruction would instantly ensue, that would not leave an atom of the universe unscathed.

Such is also the order of the intellectual system. One great mind, nature's spiritual and eternal sun, constitutes the mighty centre around which, in their respective orbits, all pure minds, primary or secondary—angelic or human—revolve. In this system the great minds as certainly govern the inferior as in material nature the large masses govern the less. Now, as the power of mind consists of intelligence, educated mind must as certainly govern uneducated mind, and the more vigorous and talented the less favored, as the great material masses govern the inferior.

The beauty as well as the happiness of the universe requires inequality. Equal lines, smooth surfaces, and eternal plains have no beauty. We must have hill and dale, mountain and valley, sea and land, suns of all magnitudes, worlds of all sizes, minds of all dimensions, and persons and faces of divers casts and colors, to constitute a beautiful and happy world. We must have sexes, conditions, and circumstances — empires, nations, and families — diversities in person, mind, manners, in order to the communication and reception of happiness. Hence, our numerous and various wants are not only incentives to action, but sources of pleasure, both simple and complex — physical, intellectual, and moral.

Hence the foundation and the philosophy of unequal minds — unequal in power, in capacity, and in taste — unequal in intelligence, activity, and energy. The inequalities of mind are numerous and various as the inequalities of matter. One mind sports with worlds — another with atoms. One man perches himself on Mount Chimborazo and communes with the stars; another delves into the earth in search of hidden treasures, and buries himself in mines and minerals. One man moves along with the tardiness of the ox in the drudgery of life; another ascends in a balloon and soars above the clouds. Here we find a Newton measuring the comet's path, a Franklin stealing fire from heaven, a Columbus in search of a new world; and there a sportsman with his hounds in quest of a fox. One delights in his revelling and song, in riotous living and the giddy dance; another, in locking up his golden pelf in an iron chest. Talk we, then, of minds equally endowed by nature or improved by art! No such minds ever composed any community. Varieties, all manner of varieties, are essential to society. The world needs the rich and the poor, the young and the aged, the learned and the unlearned, the healthy and the infirm, the cheerful and the melancholic. These call forth all our energies, open channels for all the social virtues, lay the basis of our various responsibilities, and constitute much of the happiness of this life. They furnish opportunities for communicating and receiving benefits. . . .

To serve a society faithfully, whether as a scavenger of Rome or as a king of the French, is an honor to any man. But to serve society in any capacity promotive of its moral advancement is the highest style and dignity of man. True, indeed, that in the great category of moral improvement there are numerous departments, and consequently many offices. There are authors, teachers of all schools, ministers of all grades, missionaries of all

mercies, ambassadors of all ranks, employed as conservators, redeemers, and benefactors of men. These, in the tendencies and bearings of their respective functions, sweep the largest circles in human affairs. They extend not only to the individual first benefited, not only to those temporarily benefited by him, in a long series of generations, but breaking through the confines of time and space, those benefits reach into eternity and spread themselves over fields of blessings, waving with eternal harvests of felicity to multitudes of participants which the arithmetic of time wholly fails to compute, either in number or in magnitude. The whole vista of time is but the shaft of a grand telescope through which to see, at the proper angle, the teeming harvests of eternal blessedness flowing into the bosoms of the great moral benefactors of human kind. To choose a calling of this sort is superlatively incumbent on men of genius. As Wesley said of good music, so say we of good talents. The devil, said the reformer, shall not have all the good tunes; and we add, nor the law, nor politics, nor the stage, all the good talents.

If men are held responsible, not only for all the evil they have done, but also for all the good they might have done — as undoubtedly they will be; and if they are to be rewarded, not for having genius and talent, but for having *used* them in accordance with the Divine will and the dictates of conscience, then what immense and overwhelming interests are merged in the question, To what calling should men of great parts and of good education devote themselves? Taste, inclination, and talent are altogether, and always, to be taken into account in a matter of such thrilling interest. But we are speaking of men of genius in general, and not of a particular class. The historic painter may, like our great West, give us Bible characters and Bible scenes. We may as well have the patriarchal scenes, tabernacle and temple scenes, official personages and festivals upon the walls of our rooms and museums, as the island of Calypso, or the ruins of the Capitol, or the Pantheon, or the panorama of Mexico, Paris, or Waterloo. The poet may sing of Zion, and Siloam, of Jerusalem and its King, as well as of the wrath of Achilles, the siege of Troy, or the adventures of Æneas. An orator may as well plead for God as for man, for eternity as for time, for heaven as for earth; he may as well plead for man's salvation as for his political rights and immunities; and the same learning and eloquence that gain for a client a good inheritance

or a fair reputation might also have gained for him an unfading crown and an enduring inheritance. It depends upon the taste of the man of genius of any peculiar kind to what cause he may supremely devote it. It is his duty, however, to bring it to the best market and to consecrate it to the noblest and most exalted good.

But, finally, it is not only incumbent on men of genius that they cultivate their talents to the greatest perfection, and that they select the noblest and most useful calling, but that they also prosecute them with the greatest vigor, and devote themselves to them with the most persevering assiduity. It is not he that enters upon any career, or starts in any race, but he that runs well, and perseveringly, that gains the plaudits of others, or the approval of his own conscience.

Life is a great struggle. It is one splendid campaign, a race, a contest for interests, honors, and pleasures of the highest character and of the most enduring importance. Happy the man of genius who cultivates all his powers with a reference thereunto, who chooses the most noble calling, and who prosecutes it with all his might. Such a one, ultimately, secures to himself the admiration of all the great, the wise, the good. Such a one will always enjoy the approbation of his own judgment and conscience, and, better still, the approbation of his God and Redeemer. How pleasing to him who has run the glorious race, to survey from the lofty summit of his eternal fame the cumulative results of an active life, developed in the light of eternity! How transporting to contemplate the proximate and the remote, the direct and the indirect beatific fruits of his labors reflected from the bright countenances of enraptured myriads, beaming with grateful emotion to him as the honored instrument of having inducted them into those paths of righteousness which led them into the fruition of riches, honors, and pleasures boundless as the universe and enduring as the ages of eternity!

GEORGE CANNING

(1770-1827)

ANNING followed Pitt in protesting against the radical ideas of Revolutionary France, but he made a deliberate and often successful attempt to check himself and those he could influence in the tendency to go to the other extreme. He intended that his policies should represent the progress which at any given time is practicable, in spite of difficulties created by idealists, who insist on too much, and reactionists, who strive to take away what has already been gained. Outside of England he is apt to be remembered most gratefully for what he did to force the recognition and the independence of the Spanish-American republics, though in England itself he is chiefly regarded for his work in checking Napoleon. He was born in London, April 11th, 1770. After leaving the University, he entered public life under the patronage of Pitt. Elected to Parliament in 1794, he made the great reputation as an orator which still survives him, and is justified by many of his speeches even now, when the events which inspired them are no longer of living interest. He was Secretary for Foreign Affairs from 1807 to 1809; President of the Board of Control from 1816 to 1820; again Secretary for Foreign Affairs from 1822 to 1827, and Premier in 1827. He died in August 1827, not long after taking his place at the head of the cabinet.

The most admired of his orations — that delivered at Plymouth in 1823 — owes its reputation and its vitality to the single passage in which England in repose is compared to the fleet of men-of-war lying off Plymouth, seemingly inert, but representing at that time the greatest condensation of merely physical force in the politics of the world. Another celebrated speech on the affairs of Portugal is now obsolete. Canning believed that parliamentary eloquence ought to represent the conversational rather than the oratorical style, and where he seems to act consciously on his theory his speeches are often so matter of fact that their interest is merely historical. Often, however, he is moved by a strong idea to a forgetfulness of theory, and he then illustrates the strength of his intellect and the power of the genuine orator. He is often witty, and there are times when he comes dangerously near displaying the fatal gift of humor. It has been said of him, indeed, that he was capable of editing a comic paper or of directing the destinies of the greatest empire of the world. He could write verse with facility, but it is doubtful if he ever seriously attempted to achieve genuine poetry under metrical forms. His most poetical passages are to be found in his orations rather than in his verse.

ENGLAND IN REPOSE

(A Speech Delivered at Plymouth, in 1823, on Being Presented with the Freedom of the Town)

Mr. Mayor and Gentlemen:—

I ACCEPT with thankfulness, and with greater satisfaction than I can express, this flattering testimony of your good opinion and good-will. I must add, that the value of the gift itself has been greatly enhanced by the manner in which your worthy and honorable Recorder has developed the motives which suggested it, and the sentiments which it is intended to convey.

Gentlemen, your Recorder has said very truly, that whoever, in this free and enlightened State, aims at political eminence, and discharges political duties, must expect to have his conduct scrutinized, and every action of his public life sifted with no ordinary jealousy, and with no sparing criticism; and such may have been my lot as much as that of other public men. But, gentlemen, unmerited obloquy seldom fails of an adequate, though perhaps tardy, compensation. I must think myself, as my honorable friend has said, eminently fortunate, if such compensation as he describes has fallen to me at an earlier period than to many others; if I dare flatter myself (as his partiality has flattered me) that the sentiments that you are kind enough to entertain for me are in unison with those of the country; if, in addition to the justice done me by my friends, I may, as he has assured me, rely upon a candid construction, even from political opponents.

But, gentlemen, the secret of such a result does not lie deep. It consists only in an honest and undeviating pursuit of what one conscientiously believes to be one's public duty—a pursuit which, steadily continued, will, however detached and separate parts of a man's conduct may be viewed under the influence of partialities or prejudices, obtain for it, when considered as a whole, the approbation of all honest and honorable minds. Any man may occasionally be mistaken as to the means most conducive to the end which he has in view; but if the end be just

and praiseworthy, it is by that he will be ultimately judged, either by his contemporaries or by posterity.

Gentlemen, the end which I confess I have always had in view, and which appears to me the legitimate object of pursuit to a British statesman, I can describe in one word. The language of modern philosophy is wisely and diffusely benevolent; it professes the perfection of our species, and the amelioration of the lot of all mankind. Gentlemen, I hope that my heart beats as high for the general interest of humanity—I hope that I have as friendly a disposition towards other nations of the earth as any one who vaunts his philanthropy most highly; but I am contented to confess that in the conduct of political affairs the grand object of my contemplation is the interest of England.

Not, gentlemen, that the interest of England is an interest which stands isolated and alone. The situation which she holds forbids an exclusive selfishness; her prosperity must contribute to the prosperity of other nations, and her stability to the safety of the world. But, intimately connected as we are with the system of Europe, it does not follow that we are therefore called upon to mix ourselves on every occasion with a restless and meddling activity, in the concerns of the nations which surround us. It is upon a just balance of conflicting duties, and of rival, but sometimes incompatible advantages, that a government must judge when to put forth its strength, and when to husband it for occasions yet to come.

Our ultimate object must be the peace of the world. That object may sometimes be best attained by prompt exertions—sometimes by abstinence from interposition in contests which we cannot prevent. It is upon these principles that, as has been most truly observed by my worthy friend, it did not appear to the government of this country to be necessary that Great Britain should mingle in the recent contest between France and Spain.

Your worthy Recorder has accurately classed the persons who would have driven us into that contest. There were undoubtedly among them those who desired to plunge this country into the difficulties of war, partly from the hope that those difficulties would overwhelm the administration; but it would be most unjust not to admit that there were others who were actuated by nobler principles and more generous feelings, who would have rushed forward at once from the sense of indignation at aggres-

sion, and who deemed that no act of injustice could be perpetrated from one end of the universe to the other, but that the sword of Great Britain should leap from its scabbard to avenge it. But as it is the province of law to control the excess even of laudable passions and propensities in individuals, so it is the duty of government to restrain within due bounds the ebullition of national sentiment and to regulate the course and direction of impulses which it cannot blame. Is there any one among the latter class of persons described by my honorable friend (for to the former I have nothing to say), who continues to doubt whether the Government did wisely in declining to obey the precipitate enthusiasm which prevailed at the commencement of the contest in Spain? Is there anybody who does not now think that it was the office of the Government to examine more closely all the various bearings of so complicated a question, to consider whether they were called upon to assist a united nation, or to plunge themselves into the internal feuds by which that nation was divided—to aid in repelling a foreign invader, or to take part in a civil war. Is there any man who does not now see what would have been the extent of burdens that would have been cast upon this country? Is there any one who does not acknowledge that under such circumstances the enterprise would have been one to be characterized only by a term borrowed from that part of the Spanish literature with which we are most familiar—Quixotic; an enterprise, romantic in its origin, and thankless in the end?

But while we thus control even our feelings by our duty, let it not be said that we cultivate peace, either because we fear, or because we are unprepared for, war; on the contrary, if eight months ago the Government did not hesitate to proclaim that the country was prepared for war, if war should be unfortunately necessary, every month of peace that has since passed has but made us so much the more capable of exertion. The resources created by peace are means of war. In cherishing those resources, we but accumulate those means. Our present repose is no more a proof of inability to act than the state of inertness and inactivity in which I have seen those mighty masses that float in the waters above your town is a proof that they are devoid of strength and incapable of being fitted out for action. You well know, gentlemen, how soon one of those stupendous masses, now reposing on their shadows in perfect stillness,—how

soon, upon any call of patriotism, or of necessity, it would assume the likeness of an animated thing, instinct with life and motion,—how soon it would ruffle, as it were, its swelling plumage,—how quickly it would put forth all its beauty and its bravery, collect its scattered elements of strength, and awaken its dormant thunder. Such as is one of these magnificent machines when springing from inaction into a display of its might—such is England herself, while apparently passive and motionless she silently concentrates the power to be put forth on an adequate occasion. But God forbid that that occasion should arise! After a war sustained for nearly a quarter of a century—sometimes single-handed, and with all Europe arranged at times against her or at her side, England needs a period of tranquillity, and may enjoy it without fear of misconstruction. Long may we be enabled, gentlemen, to improve the blessings of our present situation, to cultivate the arts of peace, to give to commerce, now reviving, greater extension and new spheres of employment, and to confirm the prosperity now generally diffused throughout this island. Of the blessing of peace, gentlemen, I trust that this borough, with which I have now the honor and happiness of being associated, will receive an ample share. I trust the time is not far distant when that noble structure of which, as I learn from your Recorder, the box with which you have honored me, through his hands, formed a part, that gigantic barrier against the fury of the waves that roll into your harbor will protect a commercial marine not less considerable in its kind than the warlike marine of which your port has been long so distinguished as an asylum, when the town of Plymouth will participate in the commercial prosperity as largely as it has hitherto done in the naval glories of England.

CHRISTIANITY AND OPPRESSION

(From a Speech in Parliament, May 19th, 1826)

I HAVE before said, that theoretically true as it may be, that the spirit of slavery is repugnant to the spirit of the British Constitution, yet this country, blessed though she has been with a free Constitution herself, has encouraged in her colonies the practice of slavery, however alien to her own domestic institutions; and this, too, be it remembered, at a time when her councils were guided by men, the acknowledged and boasted friends of liberty. I will not stop to enter into a disquisition whether, at the time to which I refer, the duties of governments, and the rights of man, as man, were as fully understood as in the age in which we have the happiness to live; whether the freedom of England had then attained that moral maturity which it now exhibits. Be that as it may, the simple fact is, that this country, notwithstanding her free Constitution, did found and maintain, nay, more, did foster and prescribe a system, of which, not only was slavery an ingredient, but which required an annual influx of the black Stygian stream of slavery for its nutriment and sustentation.

But there was another part of the proposition put forth by the honorable Member for Weymouth, on the occasion to which the learned civilian has alluded, viz., that the state of slavery is repugnant to the principles of the Christian religion. To this, sir, I objected, not, certainly, meaning thereby to degrade the Christian religion by the imputation that it was tolerant of slavery, but meaning to free this country from the necessity which would result from the adoption of the honorable gentleman's doctrine — the necessity of proceeding, without pause or hesitation, not merely to the immediate modification and gradual abolition of slavery in the colonies, but to its instant and total extirpation. What I meant to deny in the honorable Member's proposition was that the Christian religion and slavery could not be in existence together. I said that the reverse is the fact — that they have co-existed from the very dawn of Christianity up to the present day. Neither, therefore, am I forced to admit that it is a principle of the Christian religion to sanction slavery. The course of the Christian religion has always been to adapt itself to the circumstances of the place and time in which it was seeking to make a progress; to accommodate itself to all stations of life, to all varieties of acting or of suffering; restraining the high, exalting the lowly, by precepts applicable to all diversities of situation; and alike contributing to the happiness of man, and providing for his welfare, whether connected with his highest destinies, or descending with him to his lowest degradation, — whether mounting the throne of the Cæsars, or comforting the captive in his cell.

But while Christianity has thus blessed and improved mankind, its operation has not been direct, precipitate, or violent. It has invaded no existing rights or relations, it has disturbed no

III—60

established modes of government or law. It has rendered and recommended obedience to temporal power, even where that power was exercised with no light hand, and administered through no mild or uncorrupted institutions. While the doctrines of Christianity were preaching in the streets of Rome, — servi cruciantur continued to be the ordinary form of process in the Forum, not for the punishment of the slave who had been convicted of a crime, but for extracting evidence from one produced as a witness.

Then, sir, it is not true that the Christian religion prescribes the extinction of slavery, with unsparing, uncompromising, indiscriminating haste. It is not true that Christianity ordains the extirpation of this great moral evil by other means than those which are consonant with the just spirit of the British Constitution, — means of equity and good faith, as well as of well-understood humanity; measures moderate in their character, and progressive in their operation.

Is there anything, then, sir, in what I have laid down to inculpate the spirit of Christianity or the principles of the British Constitution? If the British Government and the British Parliament have for a long series of years fostered that system upon which we all now look with abhorrence, what is the fair inference? Is it that we are to continue to foster and cherish it still? No, sir; that is not what I maintain: but I do maintain that we, having all concurred in the guilt of rearing and fostering the evil, are not to turn round upon the planters, and say, "You alone shall suffer all the penalty; — we determine to get rid of this moral pestilence, which infects our character as much as yours, which we have as much contributed to propagate as you; but you, as spotted lepers, shall be banished from our society and cast to utter ruin, to expiate our common crime."

HATE IN POLITICS

(From a Speech on Unlawful Societies in Ireland. — February 15th, 1825)

IN THE next place, are we prepared to say that these and other acts of the Catholic Association have no tendency to excite and inflame animosities? I affirm, without hesitation, that they have directly that tendency; and in support of this affirmation I must beg leave to recur, however solemnly warned against

the recurrence, to an expression which I was the first to bring to the notice of the House, but which has been since the subject of repeated animadversion; I mean the adjuration "by the hate you bear to Orangemen," which was used by the association in its address to the Catholics of Ireland.

Various and not unamusing have been the attempts of gentlemen who take the part of the association, to get rid of this most unlucky phrase, or at least to dilute and attenuate its obvious and undeniable meaning. It is said to be unfair to select one insulated expression as indicating the general spirit of the proceedings of any public body. Granted; — if the expression had escaped in the heat of debate, if it had been struck out by the collision of argument, if it had been thrown forth in haste, and had been upon reflection recalled: but if the words are found in a document which was prepared with care and considered with deliberation, — if it is notorious that they were pointed out as objectionable when they were first proposed by the framers of the address, but were nevertheless upon argument retained, — surely we are not only justified in receiving them as an indication at least of the animus of those who used them, but we should be rejecting the best evidence of that animus, if we passed over so well-weighed a manifestation of it.

Were not this felt by honorable gentlemen on the other side to be true, we should not have seen them so anxious to put forced and fanciful constructions on a phrase which is as plain in its meaning as any which the hand of man ever wrote or the eye of man ever saw. The first defense of this phrase was by an honorable Member from Ireland, who told us that the words do not convey the same meaning in the Irish language, which we in England naturally attach to them. I do not pretend to be conversant with the Irish language, and must therefore leave that apology to stand, for what it may be worth, on the honorable gentleman's erudition and authority. I will not follow every other gentleman who has strained his faculties to explain away this unfortunate expression, but will come at once to my honorable and learned friend [Sir James Mackintosh], the Member for Knaresborough, to whom the palm in this contest of ingenuity must be conceded by all his competitors. My honorable friend has expended abundant research and subtilty upon this inquiry, and having resolved the phrase into its elements in the crucible of his philosophical mind, has produced it to us purified and refined to a degree that must command the admiration of all who

take delight in metaphysical alchemy. My honorable and learned friend began by telling us, that, after all, hatred is no bad thing in itself. "I hate a Tory," says my honorable friend — "and another man hates a cat; but it does not follow that he would hunt down the cat, or I the Tory." Nay, so far from it, hatred, if it be properly managed, is, according to my honorable friend's theory, no bad preface to a rational esteem and affection. It prepares its votaries for a reconciliation of differences — for lying down with their most inveterate enemies, like the leopard and the kid, in the vision of the prophet.

This dogma is a little startling, but it is not altogether without precedent. It is borrowed from a character in a play which is, I dare say, as great a favorite with my learned friend as it is with me — I mean the comedy of 'The Rivals,' in which Mrs. Malaprop, giving a lecture on the subject of marriage to her niece (who is unreasonable enough to talk of liking as a necessary preliminary to such a union), says, "What have you to do with your likings and your preferences, child? Depend upon it, it is safest to begin with a little aversion. I am sure I hated your poor dear uncle like a blackamoor before we were married; and yet you know, my dear, what a good wife I made him." Such is my learned friend's argument to a hair.

But finding that this doctrine did not appear to go down with the house so glibly as he had expected, my honorable and learned friend presently changed his tack, and put forward a theory, which, whether for novelty or for beauty, I pronounce to be incomparable; and, in short, as wanting nothing to recommend it but a slight foundation in truth. "True philosophy," says my honorable friend, "will always contrive to lead men to virtue by the instrumentality of their conflicting vices. The virtues, where more than one exist, may live harmoniously together; but the vices bear mortal antipathy to one another, and therefore furnish to the moral engineer the power by which he can make each keep the other under control." Admirable! — but, upon this doctrine, the poor man who has but one single vice must be in a very bad way. No fulcrum, no moral power for effecting his cure. Whereas his more fortunate neighbor, who has two or more vices in his composition, is in a fair way of becoming a very virtuous member of society. I wonder how my learned friend would like to have this doctrine introduced into his domestic establishment. For instance, suppose that I discharge a servant because he is addicted to liquor, I could not venture to recommend him to my honorable and learned friend; it might be the poor man's only fault, and therefore clearly incorrigible, but if I had the good fortune to find out that he was also addicted to stealing, might I not, with a safe conscience, send him to my learned friend with a very strong recommendation, saying, "I send you a man whom I know to be a drunkard, but I am happy to assure you he is also a thief: you cannot do better than employ him: you will make his drunkenness counteract his thievery, and no doubt you will bring him out of the conflict a very moral personage." My honorable and learned friend, however, not content with laying down these new rules for reformation, thought it right to exemplify them in his own person, and, like Pope's *Longinus*, to be "himself the great sublime he drew." My learned friend tells us that Dr. Johnson was what he (Dr. Johnson himself) called a good hater; and that among the qualities which he hated most were two which my honorable friend unites in his own person — that of Whig and that of Scotchman. "So that," says my honorable friend, "if Dr. Johnson were alive, and were to meet me at the club, of which he was a founder, and of which I am now an unworthy member, he would probably break up the meeting rather than sit it out in such society." No, sir, not so. My honorable and learned friend forgets his own theory. If he had been only a Whig, or only a Scotchman, Dr. Johnson might have treated him as he apprehends; but being both, the great moralist would have said to my honorable friend, "Sir, you are too much of a Whig to be a good Scotchman; and, sir, you are too much of a Scotchman to be a good Whig." It is no doubt from the collision of these two vices in my learned friend's person, that he has become what I, and all who have the happiness of meeting him at the club, find him — an entirely faultless character.

For my own part, however, I must say that I cannot see any hope of obtaining the great moral victory which my learned friend has anticipated — of winning men to the practice of virtue by adjurations addressed to their peculiar vices. I believe, after all these ratiocinations and refinements, we must come back to the plain truth, which is felt even while it is denied — that the phrase, "by the hate you bear to Orangemen," is an indefensible phrase; that it is, at least, — what alone I am contending that it is, — incontestable evidence of the allegation that the Catholic Association does excite animosities in Ireland.

THOMAS CARLYLE

(1795-1881)

ON HIS election as rector of Edinburgh University, in 1866, Thomas Carlyle delivered, without notes or apparent preparation, an address on The Choice of Books. It had no more to do with the subject than, in his characteristic way, he thought necessary, but it gathered force in its progress until its closing passages became worthy of his great intellect. He was perhaps the most eloquent Englishman of the second half of the nineteenth century. His addresses on Heroes were delivered as lectures, but they are really orations in the same sense in which the carefully prepared speeches of Cicero and Demosthenes were orations. Many of his most admired essays, though never delivered from a platform, are really oratorical in form and spirit, and it is not unjust nor discreditable to his 'History of the French Revolution' to call it a series of orations, which come nearer complying with the classical requirements of oratorical composition than almost any English oration which has been prepared for actual delivery.

That in his Edinburgh address, Carlyle, the greatest and most incessant talker of his day, should eulogize silence as better than eloquence, and put the silent Phocion above Demosthenes, is eminently illustrative of his love of self-contradictory paradox. The address is illustrative of his mind in a much more important respect, for it is phosphorescent with ideas. They do not flash out of obscurity and increase the darkness after them, as it sometimes happens with his ideas. They grow steadily more luminous until the close. There Carlyle is at his simplest and best. If he ever equaled it elsewhere, it is hard to see how he or any one else, could have surpassed it.

He was born at Ecclefechan, Dumfriesshire, December 4th, 1795. After receiving a thoroughly Scottish education, consummated by his graduation at Edinburgh University, he began his after education with the study of German literature, which gave his mind its final bent. His style was probably influenced most largely by that of Richter, though Goethe undoubtedly influenced his thought more deeply than he was influenced by any other single writer. He died at Chelsea, London, February 4th, 1881, after a life of almost unparalleled intellectual activity.

THE EDINBURGH ADDRESS

(Delivered to the Students of the University of Edinburgh, April 2d, 1866)

Gentlemen :—

I HAVE accepted the office you have elected me to, and have now the duty to return thanks for the great honor done me.

Your enthusiasm towards me, I admit, is very beautiful in itself, however undesirable it may be in regard to the object of it. It is a feeling honorable to all men, and one well known to myself when I was in a position analogous to your own. I can only hope that it may endure to the end, — that noble desire to honor those whom you think worthy of honor, and come to be more and more select and discriminate in the choice of the object of it; for I can well understand that you will modify your opinions of me and many things else as you go on. [Laughter and cheers.] There are now fifty-six years gone last November since I first entered your city, a boy of not quite fourteen, — fifty-six years ago, — to attend classes here and gain knowledge of all kinds, I know not what, with feelings of wonder and awe-struck expectation; and now, after a long, long course, this is what we have come to. [Cheers.] There is something touching and tragic, and yet at the same time beautiful, to see the third generation, as it were,-of my dear old native land, rising up and saying, "Well, you are not altogether an unworthy laborer in the vineyard: you have toiled through a great variety of fortunes, and have had many judges." As the old proverb says, "He that builds by the wayside has many masters." We must expect a variety of judges; but the voice of young Scotland, through you, is really of some value to me, and I return you many thanks for it, though I cannot describe my emotions to you, and perhaps they will be much more conceivable if expressed in silence. [Cheers.]

When this office was proposed to me, some of you know that I was not very ambitious to accept it, at first. I was taught to believe that there were more or less certain important duties which would lie in my power. This, I confess, was my chief motive in going into it, — at least, in reconciling the objections felt to such things; for if I can do anything to honor you and my dear old *Alma Mater*, why should I not do so? [Loud cheers.] Well, but on practically looking into the matter when

the office actually came into my hands, I find it grows more and more uncertain and abstruse to me whether there is much real duty that I can do at all. I live four hundred miles away from you, in an entirely different state of things; and my weak health —now for many years accumulating upon me — and a total unacquaintance with such subjects as concern your affairs here, — all this fills me with apprehension that there is nothing worth the least consideration that I can do on that score. You may, however, depend upon it that if any such duty does arise in any form, I will use my most faithful endeavor to do whatever is right and proper, according to the best of my judgment. [Cheers.]

In the meanwhile, the duty I have at present — which might be very pleasant, but which is quite the reverse, as you may fancy — is to address some words to you on subjects more or less cognate to the pursuits you are engaged in. In fact, I had meant to throw out some loose observations, — loose in point of order, I mean, — in such a way as they may occur to me, — the truths I have in me about the business you are engaged in, the race you have started on, what kind of race it is you young gentlemen have begun, and what sort of arena you are likely to find in this world. I ought, I believe, according to custom, to have written all that down on paper, and had it read out. That would have been much handier for me at the present moment [a laugh], but when I attempted to write, I found that I was not accustomed to writing speeches, and that I did not get on very well. So I flung that away, and resolved to trust to the inspiration of the moment, — just to what came uppermost. You will therefore have to accept what is readiest, what comes direct from the heart, and you must just take that in compensation for any good order of arrangement there might have been in it.

I will endeavor to say nothing that is not true, as far as I can manage, and that is pretty much all that I can engage for. [A laugh.]

When the seven free Arts on which the old universities were based came to be modified a little, in order to be convenient for, or to promote the wants of, modern society, — though, perhaps, some of them are obsolete enough even yet for some of us, — there arose a feeling that mere vocality, mere culture of speech, if that is what comes out of a man, though he may be a great speaker, an eloquent orator, yet there is no real substance there,

—if that is what was required and aimed at by the man himself, and by the community that set him upon becoming a learned man. Maidservants, I hear people complaining, are getting instructed in the "ologies," and so on, and are apparently totally ignorant of brewing, boiling, and baking [laughter]; above all things, not taught what is necessary to be known, from the highest to the lowest,—strict obedience, humility, and correct moral conduct. O, it is a dismal chapter, all that, if one went into it!

What has been done by rushing after fine speech? I have written down some very fierce things about that, perhaps considerably more emphatic than I would wish them to be now; but they are deeply my conviction. [Hear, hear!] There is very great necessity, indeed, of getting a little more silent than we are. It seems to me the finest nations of the world—the English and the American—are going all away into wind and tongue. [Applause and laughter.] But it will appear sufficiently tragical by and by, long after I am away out of it. Silence is the eternal duty of a man. He won't get to any real understanding of what is complex, and, what is more than any other, pertinent to his interests, without maintaining silence. "Watch the tongue" is a very old precept and a most true one. I do not want to discourage any of you from your Demosthenes, and your studies of the niceties of language, and all that. Believe me, I value that as much as any of you. I consider it a very graceful thing, and a proper thing, for every human creature to know what the implement which he uses in communicating his thoughts is, and how to make the very utmost of it. I want you to study Demosthenes, and know all his excellencies. At the same time, I must say that speech does not seem to me, on the whole, to have turned to any good account.

Why tell me that a man is a fine speaker if it is not the truth that he is speaking? Phocion, who did not speak at all, was a great deal nearer hitting the mark than Demosthenes. [Laughter.] He used to tell the Athenians,—"You can't fight Philip. You have not the slightest chance with him. He is a man who holds his tongue; he has great disciplined armies; he can brag anybody you like in your cities here; and he is going on steadily with an unvarying aim towards his object; and he will infallibly beat any kind of men such as you, going on raging from shore to shore with all that rampant nonsense." Demosthenes said to him one day,—"The Athenians will get mad

some day and kill you." "Yes," Phocion says, "When they are mad; and you as soon as they get sane again." [Laughter.]

It is also told about him going to Messina on some deputation that the Athenians wanted on some kind of matter of an intricate and contentious nature, that Phocion went with some story in his mouth to speak about. He was a man of few words,—no unveracity; and after he had gone on telling the story a certain time there was one burst of interruption. One man interrupted with something he tried to answer, and then another; and, finally, the people began bragging and bawling, and no end of debate, till it ended in the want of power in the people to say any more. Phocion drew back altogether, struck dumb, and would not speak another word to any man; and he left it to them to decide in any way they liked.

It appears to me there is a kind of eloquence in that which is equal to anything Demosthenes ever said,—"Take your own way, and let me out altogether." [Applause.]

All these considerations, and manifold more connected with them,—innumerable considerations, resulting from observation of the world at this moment,—have led many people to doubt of the salutary effect of vocal education altogether. I do not mean to say it should be entirely excluded; but I look to something that will take hold of the matter much more closely, and not allow it to slip out of our fingers and remain worse than it was. For if a good speaker—an eloquent speaker—is not speaking the truth, is there a more horrid kind of object in creation? [Loud cheers.] Of such speech I hear all manner and kind of people say it is excellent; but I care very little about how he said it, provided I understand it, and it be true. Excellent speaker! but what if he is telling me things that are untrue, that are not the facts about it—if he has formed a wrong judgment about it—if he has no judgment in his mind to form a right conclusion in regard to the matter? An excellent speaker of that kind is, as it were, saying—"Ho, every one that wants to be persuaded of the thing that is not true, come hither." [Great laughter and applause.] I would recommend you to be very chary of that kind of excellent speech. [Renewed laughter.]

Well, all that being the too well-known product of our method of vocal education,—the mouth merely operating on the tongue of the pupil, and teaching him to wag it in a particular way

[laughter], it had made a great many thinking men entertain a very great distrust of this not very salutary way of procedure, and they have longed for some kind of practical way of working out the business. There would be room for a great deal of description about it if I went into it; but I must content myself with saying that the most remarkable piece of reading that you may be recommended to take and try if you can study is a book by Goethe,—one of his last books, which he wrote when he was an old man, about seventy years of age,—I think one of the most beautiful he ever wrote, full of mild wisdom, and which is found to be very touching by those who have eyes to discern and hearts to feel it. It is one of the pieces in 'Wilhelm Meister's Travels.' I read it through many years ago; of course, I had to read into it very hard when I was translating it [applause], and it has always dwelt in my mind as about the most remarkable bit of writing that I have known to be executed in these late centuries. I have often said there are ten pages of that which, if ambition had been my only rule, I would rather have written than have written all the books that have appeared since I came into the world. [Cheers.] Deep, deep is the meaning of what is said there. They turn on the Christian religion and the religious phenomena of Christian life,—altogether sketched out in the most airy, graceful, delicately-wise kind of way, so as to keep himself out of the common controversies of the street and of the forum, yet to indicate what was the result of things he had been long meditating upon. Among others, he introduces, in an aërial, flighty kind of way, here and there a touch which grows into a beautiful picture,—a scheme of entirely mute education, at least with no more speech than is absolutely necessary for what they have to do.

Three of the wisest men that can be got are met to consider what is the function which transcends all others in importance to build up the young generation, which shall be free from all that perilous stuff that has been weighing us down and clogging every step, and which is the only thing we can hope to go on with if we would leave the world a little better, and not the worse, for our having been in it for those who are to follow. The man who is the eldest of the three says to Goethe, "You give by nature to the well-formed children you bring into the world a great many precious gifts, and very frequently these are best of all developed by nature herself, with a very slight assistance,

where assistance is seen to be wise and profitable, and forbearance very often on the part of the overlooker of the process of education; but there is one thing that no child brings into the world with it, and without which all other things are of no use." Wilhelm, who is there beside him, says, "What is that?" "All who enter the world want it," says the eldest; "perhaps you yourself." Wilhelm says, "Well, tell me what it is." "It is," says the eldest, "reverence,—*Ehrfurcht*— Reverence! Honor done to those who are grander and better than you, without fear; distinct from fear." *Ehrfurcht*—"the soul of all religion that ever has been among men, or ever will be." And he goes into practicality. He practically distinguishes the kinds of religion that are in the world, and he makes out three reverences. The boys are all trained to go through certain gesticulations, to lay their hands on their breasts and look up to heaven, and they give their three reverences. The first and simplest is that of reverence for what is above us. It is the soul of all the pagan religions; there is nothing better in man than that. Then there is reverence for what is around us or about us,—reverence for our equals, and to which he attributes an immense power in the culture of man. The third is reverence for what is beneath us,— to learn to recognize in pain, sorrow, and contradiction, even in those things, odious as they are to flesh and blood,—to learn that there lies in these a priceless blessing. And he defines that as being the soul of the Christian religion,—the highest of all religions; a height, as Goethe says,—and that is very true, even to the letter, as I consider,—a height to which the human species was fated and enabled to attain, and from which, having once attained it, it can never retrograde. It cannot descend down below that permanently, Goethe's idea is.

Often one thinks it was good to have a faith of that kind— that always, even in the most degraded, sunken, and unbelieving times, he calculates there will be found some few souls who will recognize what that meant; and that the world, having once received it, there is no fear of its retrograding. He goes on then to tell us the way in which they seek to teach boys, in the sciences particularly, whatever the boy is fit for. Wilhelm left his own boy there, expecting they would make him a Master of Arts, or something of that kind; and when he came back for him he saw a thundering cloud of dust coming over the plain, of which he could make nothing. It turned out to be a tempest of wild horses, managed by young lads who had a turn for hunting with their grooms. His own son was among them, and he found that the breaking of colts was the thing he was most suited for. [Laughter.] This is what Goethe calls art, which I should not make clear to you by any definition unless it is clear already. [A laugh.] I would not attempt to define it as music, painting, and poetry, and so on; it is in quite a higher sense than the common one, and in which, I am afraid, most of our painters, poets, and music men would not pass muster. [A laugh.] He considers that the highest pitch to which human culture can go; and he watches with great industry how it is to be brought about with men who have a turn for it.

Very wise and beautiful it is. It gives one an idea that something greatly better is possible for man in the world. I confess it seems to me it is a shadow of what will come, unless the world is to come to a conclusion that is perfectly frightful; some kind of scheme of education like that, presided over by the wisest and most sacred men that can be got in the world, and watching from a distance,—a training in practicality at every turn; no speech in it except that speech that is to be followed by action, for that ought to be the rule as nearly as possible among them. For rarely should men speak at all, unless it is to say that thing that is to be done; and let him go and do his part in it, and to say no more about it. I should say there is nothing in the world you can conceive so difficult, *prima facie*, as that of getting a set of men gathered together—rough, rude, and ignorant people—gather them together, promise them a shilling a day, rank them up, give them very severe and sharp drill, and, by bullying and drill,—for the word "drill" seems as if it meant the treatment that would force them to learn,—they learn what it is necessary to learn; and there is the man, a piece of an animated machine, a wonder of wonders to look at. He will go and obey one man, and walk into the cannon's mouth for him, and do anything whatever that is commanded of him by his general officer. And I believe all manner of things in this way could be done if there were anything like the same attention bestowed. Very many things could be regimented and organized into the mute system of education that Goethe evidently adumbrates there. But I believe, when people look into it, it will be found that they will not be very long in trying to make some efforts in that direction; for the saving of human labor and the avoidance of human

misery would be uncountable if it were set about and begun even in part.

Alas! it is painful to think how very far away it is,—any fulfillment of such things; for I need not hide from you, young gentlemen,—and that is one of the last things I am going to tell you,—that you have got into a very troublous epoch of the world; and I don't think you will find it improve the footing you have, though you have many advantages which we had not. You have careers open to you, by public examinations and so on, which is a thing much to be approved and which we hope to see perfected more and more. All that was entirely unknown in my time, and you have many things to recognize as advantages. But you will find the ways of the world more anarchical than ever, I think. As far as I have noticed, revolution has come upon us. We have got into the age of revolutions. All kinds of things are coming to be subjected to fire, as it were; hotter and hotter the wind rises around everything.

Curious to say, now in Oxford and other places that used to seem to lie at anchor in the stream of time, regardless of all changes, they are getting into the highest humor of mutation, and all sorts of new ideas are getting afloat. It is evident that whatever is not made of asbestos will have to be burnt in this world. It will not stand the heat it is getting exposed to. And in saying that, it is but saying in other words that we are in an epoch of anarchy,—anarchy *plus* the constable. [Laughter.] There is nobody that picks one's pocket without some policeman being ready to take him up. [Renewed laughter.] But in every other thing he is the son, not of Kosmos, but of Chaos. He is a disobedient, and reckless, and altogether a waste kind of object, —a commonplace man in these epochs; and the wiser kind of man—the select of whom I hope you will be part—has more and more a set time to it to look forward, and will require to move with double wisdom; and will find, in short, that the crooked things that he has to pull straight in his own life, or round about, wherever he may be, are manifold, and will task all his strength wherever he may go.

But why should I complain of that either?—for that is a thing a man is born to in all epochs. He is born to expend every particle of strength that God Almighty has given him, in doing the work he finds he is fit for,—to stand it out to the last breath of life, and do his best. We are called upon to do that; and the

reward we all get—which we are perfectly sure of if we have merited it—is that we have got the work done, or, at least, that we have tried to do the work; for that is a great blessing in itself; and I should say there is not very much more reward than that going in this world. If the man gets meat and clothes, what matters it whether he have £10,000, or £10,000,-000, or £70 a year. He can get meat and clothes for that; and he will find very little difference intrinsically, if he is a wise man.

I warmly second the advice of the wisest of men,—"Don't be ambitious; don't be at all too desirous of success; be loyal and modest." Cut down the proud towering thoughts that you get into you, or see they be pure as well as high. There is a nobler ambition than the gaining of all California would be, or the getting of all the suffrages that are on the planet just now. [Loud and prolonged cheers.]

Finally, gentlemen, I have one advice to give you, which is practically of very great importance, though a very humble one.

I have no doubt you will have among you people ardently bent to consider life cheap, for the purpose of getting forward in what they are aiming at of high; and you are to consider throughout, much more than is done at present, that health is a thing to be attended to continually,—that you are to regard that as the very highest of all temporal things for you. [Applause.] There is no kind of achievement you could make in the world that is equal to perfect health. What are nuggets and millions? The French financier said, "Alas! why is there no sleep to be sold?" Sleep was not in the market at any quotation. [Laughter and applause.]

It is a curious thing that I remarked long ago, and have often turned in my head, that the old word for "holy" in the German language—*heilig*—also means "healthy." And so *Heilbronn* means "holy-well," or "healthy-well." We have in the Scotch "hale"; and I suppose our English word "whole"—with a "w"—all of one piece, without any hole in it—is the same word. I find that you could not get any better definition of what "holy" really is than "healthy—completely healthy." *Mens sana in corpore sano.* [Applause.]

A man with his intellect a clear, plain, geometric mirror, brilliantly sensitive of all objects and impressions around it, and imagining all things in their correct proportions,—not twisted up

into convex or concave, and distorting everything, so that he cannot see the truth of the matter without endless groping and manipulation,—healthy, clear, and free, and all round about him. We never can attain that at all. In fact, the operations we have got into are destructive of it. You cannot, if you are going to do any decisive intellectual operation—if you are going to write a book—at least, I never could—without getting decidedly made ill by it, and really you must if it is your business—and you must follow out what you are at—and it sometimes is at the expense of health. Only remember at all times to get back as fast as possible out of it into health, and regard the real equilibrium as the centre of things. You should always look at the *heilig*, which means holy, and holy means healthy.

Well, that old etymology,—what a lesson it is against certain gloomy, austere, ascetic people, that have gone about as if this world were all a dismal prison house! It has, indeed, got all the ugly things in it that I have been alluding to; but there is an eternal sky over it, and the blessed sunshine, verdure of spring, and rich autumn, and all that in it, too. Piety does not mean that a man should make a sour face about things, and refuse to enjoy in moderation what his Maker has given. Neither do you find it to have been so with old Knox. If you look into him you will find a beautiful Scotch humor in him, as well as the grimmest and sternest truth when necessary, and a great deal of laughter. We find really some of the sunniest glimpses of things come out of Knox that I have seen in any man; for instance, in his 'History of the Reformation,' which is a book I hope every one of you will read,—a glorious book.

On the whole, I would bid you stand up to your work, whatever it may be, and not be afraid of it,—not in sorrows or contradiction to yield, but pushing on towards the goal. And don't suppose that people are hostile to you in the world. You will rarely find anybody designedly doing you ill. You may feel often as if the whole world is obstructing you, more or less; but you will find that to be because the world is traveling in a different way from you, and rushing on in its own path. Each man has only an extremely good-will to himself—which he has a right to have—and is moving on towards his object. Keep out of literature as a general rule, I should say also. [Laughter.] If you find many people who are hard and indifferent to you in a world that you consider to be inhospitable and cruel,—as often, indeed, happens to a tender-hearted, stirring young creature,—you will also find there are noble hearts who will look kindly on you, and their help will be precious to you beyond price. You will get good and evil as you go on, and have the success that has been appointed to you.

I will wind up with a small bit of verse that is from Goethe also, and has often gone through my mind. To me it has the tone of a modern psalm in it in some measure. It is sweet and clear. The clearest of skeptical men had not anything like so clear a mind as that man had,—freer from cant and misdirected notion of any kind than any man in these ages has been. This is what the poet says:—

> The future hides in it
> Gladness and sorrow:
> We press still thorow;
> Nought that abides in it
> Daunting us,—Onward!
>
> And solemn before us,
> Veiled, the dark Portal,
> Goal of all mortal.
> Stars silent rest o'er us,—
> Graves under us, silent.
>
> While earnest thou gazest
> Comes boding of terror,
> Come phantasm and error
> Perplexes the bravest
> With doubt and misgiving.
>
> But heard are the voices,
> Heard are the sages,
> The Worlds and the Ages:
> "Choose well: your choice is
> Brief, and yet endless."
>
> Here eyes do regard you
> In Eternity's stillness;
> Here is all fullness,
> Ye brave, to reward you.
> Work, and despair not.

One last word. *Wir heissen euch hoffen,*—we bid you be of hope. Adieu for this time.

III—61

THE HEROIC IN HISTORY

(From the First Lecture on Heroes)

FAITH is loyalty to some inspired Teacher, some spiritual Hero. And what therefore is loyalty proper, the life-breath of all society, but an effluence of Hero-worship, submissive admiration for the truly great? Society is founded on Hero-worship. All dignities of rank, on which human association rests, are what we may call a *Hero*archy (Government of Heroes),—or a Hierarchy, for it is "sacred" enough withal! The Duke means *Dux*, Leader; King is *Kön-ning, Kan-ning,* Man that *knows* or *cans*. Society everywhere is some representation, not *in*supportably inaccurate, of a graduated Worship of Heroes;—reverence and obedience done to men really great and wise. Not *in*supportably inaccurate, I say! They are all as bank-notes, these social dignitaries, all representing gold;—and several of them, alas, always are *forged* notes. We can do with some forged false notes; with a good many even; but not with all, or the most of them forged! No: there have to come revolutions then; cries of Democracy, Liberty, and Equality, and I know not what:—the notes being all false, and no gold to be had for *them,* people take to crying in their despair that there is no gold, that there never was any!—"Gold," Hero-worship, *is* nevertheless, as it was always and everywhere, and cannot cease till man himself ceases.

I am well aware that in these days Hero-worship, the thing I call Hero-worship, professes to have gone out, and finally ceased. This, for reasons which it will be worth while some time to inquire into, is an age that, as it were, denies the existence of great men; denies the desirableness of great men. Show our critics a great man, a Luther for example, they begin to what they call "account" for him; not to worship him, but take the dimensions of him,—and bring him out to be a little kind of man! He was the "creature of the Time," they say; the Time called him forth, the Time did everything, he nothing—but what we, the little critic, could have done too! This seems to me but melancholy work. The Time call forth? Alas, we have known Times *call* loudly enough for their great man; but not find him when they called! He was not there; Providence had not sent him; the

---

Time, *calling* its loudest, had to go down to confusion and wreck because he would not come when called.

For if we will think of it, no time need have gone to ruin, could it have found a man great enough, a man wise and good enough: wisdom to discern truly what the time wanted, valor to lead it on the right road thither; these are the salvation of any time. But I liken common languid times, with their unbelief, distress, perplexity, with their languid doubting characters and embarrassed circumstances, impotently crumbling down into ever worse distress towards final ruin;—all this I liken to dry dead fuel, waiting for the lightning out of heaven that shall kindle it. The great man with his free force direct out of God's own hand is the lightning. His word is the wise healing word which all can believe in. All blazes round him now, when he has once struck on it, into fire like his own. The dry mouldering sticks are thought to have called him forth. They did want him greatly; but as to calling him forth—!—Those are critics of small vision, I think, who cry: "See, is it not the sticks that made the fire?" No sadder proof can be given by a man of his own littleness than disbelief in great men. There is no sadder symptom of a generation than such general blindness to the spiritual lightning, with faith only in the heap of barren dead fuel. It is the last consummation of unbelief. In all epochs of the world's history, we shall find the great man to have been the indispensable savior of his epoch;—the lightning, without which the fuel never would have burned. The history of the world, I said already, was the biography of great men.

Such small critics do what they can to promote unbelief and universal spiritual paralysis; but happily they cannot always completely succeed. In all times it is possible for a man to arise great enough to feel that they and their doctrines are chimeras and cobwebs. And what is notable, in no time whatever can they entirely eradicate out of living men's hearts a certain altogether peculiar reverence for great men; genuine admiration, loyalty, adoration, however dim and perverted it may be. Hero-worship endures forever while man endures. Boswell venerates his Johnson right truly even in the eighteenth century. The unbelieving French believe in their Voltaire, and burst out round him into very curious Hero-worship, in that last act of his life when they "stifle him under roses." It has always seemed to me extremely curious, this of Voltaire. Truly, if Christianity be the

---

highest instance of Hero-worship, then we may find here in Voltairism one of the lowest! He whose life was that of a kind of Antichrist does again on this side exhibit a curious contrast. No people ever were so little prone to admire at all as those French of Voltaire. Persiflage was the character of their whole mind; adoration had nowhere a place in it. Yet see! The old man of Ferney comes up to Paris; an old, tottering, infirm man of eighty-four years. They feel that he, too, is a kind of hero; that he has spent his life in opposing error and injustice, delivering Calases, unmasking hypocrites in high places;—in short that he, too, though in a strange way, has fought like a valiant man. They feel withal that, if persiflage be the great thing, there never was such a persifleur. He is the realized ideal of every one of them; the thing they are all wanting to be; of all Frenchmen the most French. He is properly their god,—such god as they are fit for. Accordingly, all persons, from the Queen Antoinette to the Douanier at the Porte St. Denis, do they not worship him? People of quality disguise themselves as tavern-waiters. The Maître de Poste, with a broad oath, orders his postilion, "*Va bon train;* thou art driving M. de Voltaire." At Paris his carriage is "the nucleus of a comet, whose train fills whole streets." The ladies pluck a hair or two from his fur, to keep it as a sacred relic. There was nothing highest, most beautiful, noblest in all France, that did not feel this man to be higher, more beautiful, nobler.

Yes, from Norse Odin to English Samuel Johnson, from the divine founder of Christianity to the withered Pontiff of Encyclopedism, in all times and places, the hero has been worshiped. It will ever be so. We all love great men—love, venerate, and bow down submissive before great men: nay, can we honestly bow down to anything else? Ah, does not every true man feel that he is himself made higher by doing reverence to what is really above him? No nobler or more blessed feeling dwells in man's heart. And to me it is very cheering to consider that no skeptical logic, or general triviality, insincerity, and aridity of any time and its influences can destroy this noble inborn loyalty and worship that is in man. In times of unbelief, which soon have to become times of revolution, much down-rushing, sorrowful decay and ruin is visible to everybody. For myself in these days, I seem to see in this indestructibility of Hero-worship the everlasting adamant lower than which the confused wreck of revolutionary things cannot fall. The confused wreck of things crumbling and even crashing and tumbling all round us in these revolutionary ages will get down so far; no farther. It is an eternal corner stone, from which they can begin to build themselves up again. That man, in some sense or other, worships heroes; that we all of us reverence and must ever reverence great men: this is, to me, the living rock amid all rushingsdown whatsover;—the one fixed point in modern revolutionary history, otherwise as if bottomless and shoreless.

LAZARE NICOLAS MARGUERITE CARNOT

(1753-1823)

OF THE prominent actors of the French Revolution who survived it, the one whose name is held in the highest honor in the existing Republic was the great organizer of the republican armies which suppressed insurrection at home and victoriously bore the tricolor wherever hostility to the Republic showed itself in Europe. "Carnot organized victory," said Napoleon. All the world stood amazed at the military resources of France as marshaled in battle array by him. He even commanded in person at Wattignies, and won the victory there by leading an infantry charge on foot.

He left to France not only a noble example of honest, unswerving, and patriotic Republicanism, but he left to her a line of descendants whose distinguished services and loyal adherence to his principles have kept alive French reverence for their ancestor. His eldest son, Nicolas Leonard Sadi Carnot, born in 1796, was a distinguished French scientist and author who, before his death from cholera in 1832, founded the modern science of thermodynamics, which revolutionized the study of physics. A younger son, Lazare Hippolyte Carnot, born in 1801, became Minister of Public Instruction in 1848, served in the Corps Legislatif from 1863 to 1867, was made a life Senator in 1875, and before he died in 1888 saw his son, Marie François Sadi Carnot, President of the Republic, after a long course of eminent public service.

The Carnot of the Revolution was born in Burgundy, May 13th, 1753, and after receiving a thorough education in mathematics and physics was placed in the corps of engineers by the influence of the Prince of Condé. He remained a scientist and strategist in the midst of responsibilities as a statesman which he had incurred through his zeal for the overthrow of monarchy and the substitution of popular self-government. Entering the Legislative Assembly in 1791 and the Convention in 1792, he was, in fact, when not always in name, the War Minister from that date till he resigned in disgust when Napoleon was made consul for life, seeing, as he did, behind that act, a monarchy triumphing over the Republic. As a member of the Committee of Public Safety, and of the Directory, he has been blamed for acts done without his advice or consent when his hands were full of other matters. Proscribed in 1797, he had to take refuge for a time in Germany, where he published the Memoire Justificatif, in which

he declared himself "the irreconcilable enemy of kings." After the downfall of the Directory, he returned home and resumed the position of War Minister. After resigning that, he remained a member of the Tribunate till it was abolished in 1806, when he retired to private life and devoted himself to science as an active member of the Institute.

After the Russian campaign, seeing that the independence of France depended upon the success of the Emperor, Carnot consented to serve under him again and was made governor of Antwerp which he defended till the abdication in 1814. He was still faithful to the Republic and his 'Memoire au Roi' did powerful service against the restoration of monarchy. During "The Hundred Days," he was Napoleon's Minister of War again. When Europe reimposed Bourbon rule upon France, he retired to Warsaw and subsequently to Magdeburg, where he died August 3d, 1823.

AGAINST IMPERIALISM IN FRANCE

(Delivered Against Making Napoleon Consul for Life in 1802)

Fellow-Citizens:—

AMONG the orators who have preceded me, and who have all touched on the motion of our colleague Curée, several have anticipated the objections that might be made to it, and have responded with as much talent as amenity; they have given an example of a moderation which I shall endeavor to imitate by proposing a few ideas which have apparently escaped them. And as to those whom I oppose, and thus render myself liable to that suspicion that my motives are merely personal, whoever would attribute such to me are ignorant of the character of a man entirely devoted to his country. In reply, I ask them to examine carefully my political conduct since the commencement of the revolution, and all the record of my private life.

I am far from desiring to diminish the praises accorded the First Consul; if we owed him but the code civil, his name would worthily be immortalized to posterity. But whatever the services a citizen has rendered his country, he must expect honors but in the extent of the national recognition of his work. If the citizen has restored public liberty, if he has been a benefactor to his country, would it be a proper recompense to offer him the sacrifice of that liberty? Nay! would it not be an annulment of his own work to convert that country into his private patrimony?

From the very moment it was proposed to the French people to vote to make the consulate an office for life, each easily judged there was a mental reservation, and saw the ulterior purpose and end of the proposal. In effect, there was seen the rapid succession of a series of institutions evidently monarchical; but at each move anxiety was manifested to reassure disturbed and inquiring spirits on the score of liberty, that these new institutions and arrangements were conceived only to procure the highest protection that could be desired for liberty.

To-day is uncovered and developed in the most positive manner the meaning of so many of these preliminary measures. We are asked to declare ourselves upon a formal proposition to re-establish the monarchical system, and to confer an imperial and hereditary dignity on the first consul.

At that time I voted against a life consulate; I shall vote now against any re-establishment of a monarchy, as I believe it my duty to do. But it is done with no desire to evoke partisanship; without personal feeling; without any sentiment save a passion for the public good, which always impels me to the defense of the popular cause.

I always fully submit to existing laws, even when they are most displeasing. More than once have I been a victim to my devotion to law, and I shall not begin to retrograde to-day. I declare, therefore, that while I combat this proposition, from the moment that a new order of things shall have been established, which shall have received the assent of the mass of our citizens, I shall be first to conform my actions; to give to the supreme authority all the marks of deference commanded by the constitutional oligarchy. Can every member of society record a vow as sincere and disinterested as my own?

I shall not force into the discussion my preference for the general merits of any one system of government over another. On these subjects there are numberless volumes written. I shall charge myself with examining in few words, and in the simplest terms, the particular case in which present circumstances place us. All the arguments thus far made for the re-establishment of monarchy in France are reduced to the statement that it is the only method of assuring the stability of the government and the public tranquillity, the only escape from internal disorder, the sole bond of union against external enemies; that the republican system has been vainly essayed in all possible manners; and that from all these efforts only anarchy has resulted. A prolonged and ceaseless revolution has reawakened a perpetual fear of new disorders, and consequently a deep and universal desire to see re-established the old hereditary government, changing only the dynasty. To this we must make reply.

I remark here that the government of a single person is no assurance of a stable and tranquil government. The duration of the Roman Empire was no longer than that of the Roman Republic. Their internecine troubles were greater, their crimes more multiplied. The pride of republicanism, the heroism, and the masculine virtues were replaced by the most ridiculous vanity, the vilest adulation, the boldest cupidity, the most absolute indifference to the national prosperity. Where was any remedy in the heredity of the throne? Was it not regarded as the legitimate heritage of the house of Augustus? Was a Domitian not the son of Vespasian, a Caligula the son of Germanicus, a Commodus the son of Marcus Aurelius? In France, it is true, the last dynasty maintained itself for eight hundred years, but were the people any the less tormented? What have been the internal dissensions? What the foreign wars undertaken for pretensions and rights of succession, which gave birth to the alliances of this dynasty with foreign nations? From the moment that a nation espouses the particular interest of one family, she is compelled to intervene in a multitude of matters which but for this would be to her of uttermost indifference. We have hardly succeeded in establishing a republic among us, notwithstanding that we have essayed it under various forms, more or less democratic. . . .

After the peace of Amiens, Napoleon had choice between the republican and monarchical systems; he could do as he pleased. He would have met but the lightest opposition. The citadel of Liberty was confided to him; he swore to defend it; and holding his promise, he should have fulfilled the desire of the nation which judged him alone capable of solving the grand problem of public liberty in its vast extent. He might have covered himself with an incomparable glory. Instead of that, what is being done to-day? They propose to make for him an absolute and hereditary property of a great power of which he was made the administrator. Is this the real desire and to the real interest of the first consul himself? I do not believe it.

It is true the State was falling into dissolution, and that absolutism pulled it from the edge of the abyss. But what do we

conclude from that? What all the world knows—that political bodies are subject to affections which can be cured but by violent remedies; that sometimes a dictator is necessary for a moment to save liberty. The Romans, who were so jealous of it, nevertheless recognized the necessity of this supreme power at intervals. But because a violent remedy has saved a patient, must there be a daily administration of violent remedies? Fabius, Cincinnatus, Camillus saved Rome by the exercise of absolute power, but they relinquished this power as soon as practicable; they would have killed Rome had they continued to wield it. Cæsar was the first who desired to keep this power: he became its victim; but liberty was lost for futurity. Thus everything that has ever been said up to this day on absolute government proves only the necessity for temporary dictatorships in crises of the State, but not the establishment of a permanent and irresponsible power.

It is not from the character of their government that great republics have lacked stability; it is because, having been born in the breasts of storms, it is always in a state of exaltation that they are established. One only was the labor of philosophy, organized calmly. That Republic, the United States of America, full of wisdom and of strength, exhibits this phenomenon, and each day their prosperity shows an increase which astonishes other nations. Thus it was reserved for the New World to teach the Old that existence is possible and peaceable under the rule of liberty and equality. Yes, I state this proposition, that when a new order of things can be established without fearing partisan influences, as the first consul has done, principally after the peace of Amiens, and as he can still do, it becomes much easier to form a republic without anarchy than a monarchy without despotism. For how can we conceive a limitation which would not be illusory in a government of which the chief had all the executive power in his hand and all the places to bestow?

They have spoken of institutions to produce all these good effects. But before we propose to establish a monarchy, should we not first assure ourselves and demonstrate to those who are to vote on the question, that these institutions proposed are in the order of possible things, and not metaphysical obstructions, which have been held a reproach to the opposite system? Up to this moment nothing has been successfully invented to curb supreme power but what are called intermediary bodies or privi-

leges. Is it, then, of a new nobility you would speak when you allude to institutions? But such remedies—are they not worse than the disease? For the absolute power of a monarch takes but our liberty, while the institution of privileged classes robs us at the same time of our liberty and our equality. And if even at the commencement dignities and ranks were but personal, we know they would finish always as the fiefs of other times, in becoming hereditary.

To these general principles I shall add a few special observations. I assume that all the French give assent to these proposed changes; but will it be the real free will and wish of Frenchmen which is produced from a register where each is obliged to individually sign his vote? Who does not know what is the influence in similar cases of the presiding authority? From all parties in France, it would be said, springs a universal desire of the citizens for the re-establishment of the hereditary monarchy; but can we not look suspiciously on an opinion, concentrated thus far almost exclusively among public functionaries, when we consider the inconvenience they would have to manifest any contrary opinion; when we know that the liberty of the press is so enfeebled that it is not possible to insert in any journal the most moderate and respectful protests?

Doubtlessly there will be no making any choice of the hereditary chief, if they declare it necessary to have one.

Is it hoped, in raising this new dynasty, to hasten the period of general peace? Will it not rather be a new obstacle? Are we assured that the other great powers of Europe will assent to this new title? And if they do not, do we take up arms to constrain them? Or after having sunk the title of First Consul in that of Emperor, will he be content to remain First Consul to the rest of Europe while he is Emperor only to Frenchmen, or shall we compromise by a vain title the security and the prosperity of the entire nation?

It appears, therefore, infinitely doubtful if the new order of things can give us the stability of the present state. There is for the government one method of consolidation and strength. It is to be just; that no favoritism or bias be of avail to influence its services; that there be a guarantee against robbery and fraud. It is far from me to desire to make any particular application of my language or to criticize the conduct of the government. It is against arbitrary power itself I appeal, and not

against those in whose hands this power may reside. Has liberty then been shown to man that he shall never enjoy it? Shall it always be held to his gaze as a fruit that when he extends the hand to grasp he must be stricken with death? And Nature, which has made liberty such a pressing need to us, does she really desire to betray our confidence? No! I shall never believe this good, so universally preferred to all others,— without which all others are nothing,—is a simple illusion. My heart tells me that liberty is possible, that its régime is easier and more stable than any arbitrary government, than any oligarchy.

MATTHEW HALE CARPENTER

(1824–1881)

GREAT jurist and orator, Judge Jeremiah S. Black, spoke of Carpenter as "the finest constitutional lawyer in the United States," after measuring swords with him in the McArdle case, brought before the United States Supreme Court to test the constitutionality of the Reconstruction Act of March 7, 1867. In many great cases before the courts and in the offhand discussions of measures before the Senate during his ten years of service in that body, as well as in his set speeches, he showed himself profoundly versed in the philosophy of law and republican government, ready and logical in debate, and master of the most pointed and forcible eloquence.

Studying law under Paul Dillingham of Vermont (afterwards governor, and his father-in-law), he spent a year after his admission to the bar in 1847 in the office of Rufus Choate, and then settled in Wisconsin. He gained his first distinction by winning a great land case against such lawyers as James R. Doolittle, Daniel Cady, and Abraham Lincoln, and in a *quo warranto* case for the removal of Governor Barston. His masterly management of the defense secured the acquittal of Secretary Belknap, when the latter was impeached. His first election to the Senate in 1869 was promoted by the influence of President-elect Grant and Secretary Stanton, exerted in gratitude for his services in supporting the Reconstruction Act.

He was a War Democrat who had opposed the Fugitive Slave Law, and as early as 1865 had advocated a strict governmental control of railroads and all semi-public corporations. He died in Washington, February 24th, 1881, two years after the beginning of his last term in the Senate.

pation of the serfs, and other great reforms in Russia, have commanded the admiration of the world and covered the present reigning dynasty with immortal renown. Both nations are young and have a future. While England is decaying and France distracted, and revolutions are threatening to wipe away everything established in both countries — and while it yet remains to be seen whether blessing or evil will result from the consolidation of the German States in the iron grasp of Prussia, Russia stands out before the world, full of the strength and resources of youth, and is just entering upon the great destiny Providence seems to have designed for her. In the immediate future the preponderance of Russia in the councils of Europe seems to be certain. Our own country presents, on this continent, much the same aspects. Slavery is abolished; rebellion, which threatened the life of the nation, is crushed; and the future supremacy of our country on this continent is as clear as any fact which rests on the future for its verification can be.

These two great nations — nations rejoicing in the strength and power of youth, with splendid opportunities before them — ought to be friends. In this idea, the friendship of two nations thus situated, how much of blessing for mankind is embodied!

The loves and friendships of individuals partake of the frail character of human life; and are brief and uncertain. The experience of a human life may be shortly summed up: A little loving and a good deal of sorrowing; some bright hopes and many bitter disappointments; some gorgeous Thursdays, when the skies are bright and the heavens blue, when Providence, bending over us in blessings, glads the heart almost to madness; many dismal Fridays, when the smoke of torment beclouds the mind, and undying sorrows gnaw upon the heart; some high ambitions and many Waterloo defeats, until the heart becomes like a charnel house filled with dead affections embalmed in holy but sorrowful memories; and then the chord is loosed, the golden bowl is broken, the individual life — a cloud, a vapor, passes away.

But, speaking relatively, a nation may count upon immortality on earth. Individuals rise and fall, generations come and go; but still the national unity is preserved, and a government constructed wisely with reference to the situation and wants of a nation may exist for centuries. Friendship between two nations may become a deeply cherished and hereditary principle, and two great nations, like America and Russia, may walk hand in

REPLYING TO THE GRAND DUKE ALEXIS

(Delivered January 7th, 1872, at a Banquet Given to the Grand Duke Alexis, Younger Son of Alexander II., of Russia, in Response to the Grand Duke's Toast, "To the President of the United States")

Mr. President:—

THE heart of every American citizen responds cordially to every compliment paid to the chief magistrate of our nation. Our people entertain for the great office first filled by Washington habitual respect and reverence; and of the present chief magistrate it is not too much to say that no President for many years has held a firmer or warmer place in popular affection. This occasion, which is eminently one in the interests of peace and national brotherhood, is one in which President Grant would take the liveliest interest. Though educated a soldier, and coming to the chief magistracy upon the reputation he had won as a leader of armies, no President, not even Washington himself, has manifested greater solicitude to manage our national affairs in the interests of peace with all the world.

We meet this evening to pay our respects to a member of the royal family of Russia; and we greet him, not as a prince merely, but as a man; not as an official representative of the Russian government, but as the son of the chief executive and head of a great nation which felt and showed warm sympathy for us in the greatest of our national trials. A mere diplomatic occasion means something or nothing, as the case may be, but this unofficial visit, this social journey of our distinguished guest, is, let us hope, an indication of the continued good feeling existing on the part of Russia toward the people of the United States.

In the situation of Russia and America there is much to draw us into international sympathy. The forms of government are totally different. But mere form of government is not so material as the manner of practical administration. A government which embodies all the elements and attributes of absolute sovereignty may be carried on with a spirit of liberality which will make it a blessing to the people; and free institutions in unworthy hands may be perverted to the worst ends of tyranny and oppression. The progress of liberal sentiments, the emanci-

hand through the brilliant career opened before them, and the blessings of brotherhood and peace reach countless generations.

God grant that such may be the relations between these two greatest among the nations forever.

THE LOUISIANA RETURNING BOARD

(From His Speech of February 13th, 1877, Before the Electoral Commission)

IF THE commission please to relieve some anxiety that exists in some parts of the country near my own home as to whom I appear for here, I desire to say in the first place that I do not appear for Samuel J. Tilden. He is a gentleman whose acquaintance I have not the honor of; with whom I have no sympathy; against whom I voted on the seventh of November last; and if this tribunal could order a new trial, I should vote against him again, believing as I do that the accession of the Democratic party to power in this country to-day would be the greatest calamity that could befall the people except one, and that one greater calamity would be to keep him out by fraud and falsehood. I appear here for ten thousand legal voters of Louisiana, who, without accusation or proof, indictment or trial, notice or hearing, have been disfranchised by four villains, incorporated with perpetual session, whose official title is "The Returning Board of Louisiana." I appear here for the next Republican candidate for the presidency, whoever he may be, whether he shall be one of my friends on this commission, or some other man, and insist that this court shall settle a rule here by which, in that campaign, if we carry Wisconsin by ten thousand majority for him, as I hope we shall be able to do, no board of returning officers can, by fraud or falsehood or bribery, be induced or be enabled to throw that State against him and against the voice and will of our people.

I beg your honors to pause a moment and consider the lesson you are to teach to the future politicians of this country by this day's work. This is no ordinary occasion, no ordinary tribunal, no ordinary cause. An emergency has arisen which has induced the two houses of Congress to create a tribunal never before known in this country; a tribunal made up of whatever is most distinguished in this country for integrity, for learning, for judicial and legislative experience, to tide the nation over a great crisis in its affairs. The decision which you pronounce upon this cause will stand as a landmark in all the future history of this country; and I ask you to pause and consider for a moment what you are asked to do here.

The honorable gentlemen from the House who have appeared here against us do not pretend that by the votes given on the seventh of November Mr. Hayes's electors were elected in Louisiana. No serious pretense of that kind is made. Now, if you are to decide in this case that, no matter how great and appalling were the frauds committed in the canvassing of their votes; that although it be true, as we shall offer to prove by record evidence, that they threw out of their count over ten thousand votes for the Tilden electors,—that nevertheless it is a matter you will not consider, might not every honorable member of this commission as well sit down and write his license to posterity to perpetrate all the frauds that ingenuity and self-interest can suggest?

Since the last election the Democrats have got possession of Florida. Say to them, by this decision to-day, that where clear proof is offered that a canvassing board has acted fraudulently in making up certificates, this high tribunal will take no notice of it, and if this tribunal will not, neither house of Congress ever can; for you have here all the power of each house and of both houses; and if those Democratic canvassers in Florida do not send up another ticket here by ten thousand majority, it will be because they have not improved upon the lesson given them. If it be true that a governor can certify a man as duly appointed elector of a State who has not received a single vote at the polls, and that to open the action of a canvassing board who have been bribed or coerced to throw away all the ballots cast and to certify a falsehood, known to the public mind, known to both houses of Congress from investigations they have carried on through their committees and the examination of witnesses under oath, who is so hopeful as to believe that there will ever be another President elected by anything but fraud? Why go through with all the tremendous labor of a political campaign? Why send your orators upon the stump, and spend thousands of dollars in circulating documents to convince the people that a certain candidate ought to be elected, when you can go with a third of that money and bribe a canvassing board and carry on an election without a vote?

III—62

more to carry the public mind to this commendable conclusion than the Senator from Oregon. And now, coming to the Chinese question, I would like to have that Senator show, if he can, how we are to escape the same dilemma. If all freemen subject to the law ought to have a vote, then the Chinaman is entitled to vote. And if he be not entitled to vote, it is because the theory of free government, "of the people, for the people, and by the people," is a delusion. Sir, for one, I propose to stand by our American principle of free government, and, applying it to the case before us, to say that the Chinaman who comes to reside among us, who conforms to our laws, shall be admitted to the rights of a citizen.

But, sir, suppose we were to make this admission to the monarchists of Europe, and confess that the dogma of self-government is a delusion, and that the Chinaman, although residing in our midst, and intelligent, industrious, and virtuous, ought not to have a voice in making the laws by which he is to be governed, by which his property is to be taxed, and by which his life is to be rendered happy or devoted to misery. Is it not certain that the Democrats, taking advantage of this admission, would press you again with their objections to the enfranchisement of the African? And do you clearly see how, after this admission, you could meet their objections? And where are you to stop? Will you enter upon a discussion of the property qualification, the test of intelligence, and all other anti-American standards by which the monarchists seek to measure the right of participation in government? While you stand upon our great principle of self-government, you have a ready answer against all objections. But, that principle surrendered, we are at sea, and nothing determined.

Sir, this American maxim, that all freemen bound by the law ought to have a voice in making the law, is either a truth or a falsehood. If it be a truth, the Chinaman is entitled to vote; if it be a falsehood, then you must call witnesses to prove that you are entitled to vote yourself.

Mr. Thurman — Is the Senator from Wisconsin in favor of woman suffrage?

Mr. Carpenter — I do not see the bearing of that question upon the subject before us, but I am happy to inform the Senator that I am in favor of citizen suffrage without distinction of sex, color, or birthplace.

Your honors will see that I am not overstating the case contended for. That would be a fraud a little more enormous, but not different in character from the one which is now before you for your consideration, and (I ought to apologize for saying) for your approval. You are expected to say by the decision to be rendered here to all the politicians of the Southern States and the Northern States and the East and the West, "No matter what frauds you commit, no matter how glaring and damnable, we see nothing." As the German colonel, when he went with a regiment from Illinois into Alabama, said to the boys, "Now, boys, I shuts my eyes; I opens them at three o'clock"; so this tribunal is expected to shut its eyes to all the frauds committed in the canvass of these votes, by which I will show your honors, not by declamation and assertion, but by argument which in any court of justice could not be gainsaid, that before this result was reached disfranchisement was imposed upon ten thousand legal voters by a tribunal which had no jurisdiction to exclude a vote. If these things can be done in the green tree, what may we not expect to see in the dry? If in the centennial year only of the life of our nation such frauds can pass unwhipped of justice, and not only pass unwhipped, but win the prizes, what may we not expect when the degeneracy of this nation shall come, as it has come to all nations, and must be expected some time to come to us?

IN FAVOR OF UNIVERSAL SUFFRAGE

(From a Speech in the Senate, March 1870)

Mr. President:—

EVERY candid man acknowledges that it was subjecting our American theory to a severe trial when we admitted the freedmen to citizenship; but there was no choice; we had to apply the principle that every freeman bound by the law was entitled to vote, or we had to say to the monarchists of Europe that their theory of government was right and ours was wrong; that it would not do to permit all men subject to the law to participate in the government; that there must be some limitations and some exclusions, and that the man who could not be trusted was the man who had a black skin. The latter view was so manifestly absurd that we determined to abide by our maxim and give the negro the benefit of it. And no man did

Mr. Thurman — That is satisfactory. The next question is, Is the Senator in favor of giving to the Indians of Alaska, who owe allegiance to our Government and obedience to our laws, the right of suffrage?

Mr. Carpenter — That is leaving the subject under consideration to deal with matters entirely foreign to it; but I can say to the Senator that if he should offer an amendment to this bill that no man born in Alaska should enjoy civil rights and political privileges, or any kindred amendment, I should vote against it. In other words, I am opposed to limiting principles geographically; I am opposed to saying that all men are created equal within certain parallels of latitude, but that God intended the people born north or south of those lines to be the subjects of despotism. A man is a man, no matter where he was born, no matter what may be the color of his skin, and he is entitled to be treated like a man, and to enjoy the rights, privileges, powers, and immunities of a man, under any government which professes to be founded upon the principle that all men are created equal.

ALEXANDER CARSON

(1776–1844)

A LONDON critic, explaining the great eminence of Doctor Carson as a public speaker, said: "He possessed the secret of making every subject interesting. There was great variety in all his addresses; but his chief glory was the Gospel theme. Here he shone out in full lustre; here all the powers of his mighty mind found ample scope; his manly eloquence was at home. Strangers who, from report, had formed high expectations, exclaimed: 'The half has not been told us'—such a torrent of magic thought would be poured forth in a style of burning, blazing, volcanic eloquence."

Doctor Carson was born in Tyrone County, Ireland, in 1776, of Scottish ancestry. Educated at Glasgow University, where he took the highest honors, he was ordained a Presbyterian minister at the age of twenty-two. In 1805 he became a Baptist, and thenceforward until his death, August 24th, 1844, he was a pastor in charge of a church in Tubbermore, founded by people who seceded with him from their former connection. He was an author of books on a wide range of subjects, scientific, philological, theological, and practical. His treatise, the 'Plenary Inspiration of the Scriptures,' was used by Doctor Chalmers as a text-book in his theological instructions, and commended in terms of admiration to his students.

THE GLORIES OF IMMORTALITY

WITH respect to the nature of the glory of the heaven of heavens, the Scriptures do not appear to afford much precise and specific information. It would appear in general, from the Book of Revelation, that the chief employments and happiness of the saints consist in the praises of their ever-blessed Redeemer. On earth, though they have not seen him, they love him above all things. But in heaven their happiness is perfect in the perfect love of him.

The representation of the new Jerusalem is evidently figurative, and therefore we are not warranted to say that any of the

specific objects mentioned in this description actually exist. We ought not to conceive heaven as being really a city, with such walls, gates, pavements, etc. This representation has no doubt an important meaning, but this importance would be infinitely diminished by supposing that it is a literal description. A city thus built would be the most glorious that the imagination could conceive to be made of earthly materials, but it is a faint figure of the glory of the true heaven.

Some have thought that the risen body will not possess any powers of sensation. With respect to sight and hearing this is manifestly false. How much of the pleasure of the heavenly inhabitants consists in the sweet and loved songs of praise to God and the Lamb! And for what is all the glory of heaven, if not to gratify the eye? Light is the most glorious object on earth, and the enjoyment of the light of heaven appears to be among the most eminent felicities.

The angels of heaven are called angels of light—as distinguished from the angels that kept not their first love, who are reserved in chains of everlasting darkness to the judgment of the great day. Now, it appears to me that the former are so called from the light in which they dwell, rather than from their knowledge, or from the nature of their works, as Macknight understands the passage. It would be difficult to point out a distinguishing ignorance in the fallen spirits, and angels of light would be a very indefinite and distant expression to denote that they are continually employed in promoting truth and virtue. Believers may be distinguished from the children of this world, as the children of light, because they are enlightened in that great truth of which the others are ignorant.

God is also said to dwell in light—"who only hath immortality, dwelling in the light which no man can approach unto; whom no man hath seen, nor can see." This light is so exceedingly glorious that no man in his present state can approach it. But the time will come when even the eyes of the saints will be able to bear that light, for "they shall see God." "Flesh and blood shall not inherit the kingdom of God," but the glorious spiritual bodies of the saints will enjoy it. What must be the brilliancy of the light of heaven when a glance of it now overpowers any of the human race? "At midday, O king, I saw in the way a light from heaven above the brightness of the sun, shining round about me and then which journied with me.

And when we were all fallen to the earth," etc. "And when I could not see for the glory of that light, being led by the hand of them that were with me," etc.

Some have supposed that God will never be visible and that the promise that we shall see God means only that we shall see the light in which he dwells. It is dangerous to advance too far on such a subject. But I am not willing even here to limit Scripture language by views of possibility. That one spirit may have a perception of another corresponding to what we call visible is surely not only possible but certain. If so, why may not our spirits have such a perception of God? And that it is impossible for the glorified eye of the saint to have a perception of God is more than I will say. Let it suffice us that "we shall see God." Let us leave the manner of this to himself. "Take heed," says Christ, "that ye despise not one of these little ones; for I say unto you that in heaven their angels do always behold the face of My Father which is in heaven." And if angels behold the face of God, it will not be impossible for us. To behold his face must imply to view him in his glory; we need not, therefore, confound ourselves by any subtle inquiries about the way of seeing a spirit. God is everywhere: it is possible to make us sensible of his presence, whatever part of space we may at any time occupy. This is an unfathomable subject, but though it represses arrogant inquiries beyond what is written, it opens up a boundless field of expectation to our future state. Having such a God as a father, what may we not expect? . . .

The reward of the saints is frequently exhibited with very animating effect, under the figure of the crowns of the victors in the Grecian games, and of the conquerors who obtain a triumph on their return to their country. In these games the greatest men of the times entered as competitors for the glory of victory, and even kings thought themselves honored by obtaining the prize. The victor was rewarded with a crown of leaves, and was received with unbounded honor by the vast multitudes assembled from all parts of Greece. Now, after all the self-denial of their former lives and unwearied diligence in preparatory exercises; after all the toils, dangers, and sufferings in the arduous struggle, they thought this crown of leaves a high recompense. It raised them upon a pinnacle of glory, to be viewed with admiration by all countries. Yet, as the Apostle says, they had in prospect only a corruptible crown; we have in our view an incorruptible crown.

Their crown was the greatest the world could bestow, but it was fading, and is already withered many a hundred years. The crown of the Christian flourishes on his head with unfading freshness, and will bloom through eternity. Its glory will be witnessed not by the people only of one age, but by all the principalities in heaven.

HAMPTON L. CARSON

(1852–)

AMPTON L. CARSON was born in Philadelphia, February 21st, 1852. His father, Dr. Joseph Carson, was professor of *materia medica* in the medical department of the University of Pennsylvania, and his family was a noted one in the colonial history of the State. He graduated from the University of Pennsylvania, taking his first degree in 1871, and from the law department of the University in 1874. He was admitted to the Philadelphia bar in 1874, and in 1896 was elected professor of law in the University of Pennsylvania. He is the author of 'The Law of Conspiracy as Shown in American Cases,' 'The History of the Hundredth Anniversary of the Framing of the Constitution of the United States,' and of 'A History of the Supreme Court of the United States.' He has delivered many addresses and orations on public occasions. The oration of July 4th, 1893, was delivered in Chicago on the invitation of that city and of the World's Fair Commission.

AMERICAN LIBERTY

(From the Oration Delivered at the World's Fair, Chicago, July 4th, 1893, on the Liberty Bell)

THE institutions established by our fathers we hold in trust for all mankind. It was the Pilgrim of Massachusetts, the Dutchman of New York, the Quaker of Pennsylvania, the Swede of Delaware, the Catholic of Maryland, the Cavalier of Virginia, and the Edict-of-Nantes man of South Carolina who united in building up the interests and in contributing to the greatness and the unexampled progress of this magnificent country. The blood of England, of Holland, and of France, wrung drop by drop by the agony of three frightful persecutions, was mingled by the hand of Providence in the alembic of America, to be distilled by the fierce fires of the Revolution into the most precious elixir of the ages. It is the glory of this era that we can stand here to-day and exclaim that we are not men of

Massachusetts, nor men of Pennsylvania, nor men of Illinois, but that we are Americans in the broadest, the truest, and the best sense of that word; that we recognize no throne, no union of Church and State, no domination of class or creed.

American liberty is composite in its character and rich in its material. Its sources, like the fountains of our Father of Waters, among the hills, are to be sought among the everlasting truths of mankind. All ages and all countries have contributed to the result. The American Revolution forms but a single chapter in the volume of human fate. From the pure fountains of Greece, before choked with dead leaves from the fallen tree of civilization; from the rude strength poured by barbaric transfusion into the veins of dying Rome; from the Institutes of Gaius and the Pandects of Justinian; from the laws of Alfred and the Magna Charta of King John; from the daring prows of the Norsemen and the sons of Rollo the Rover; from the precepts of Holy Writ and the teaching of him who was nailed to the cross on Calvary; from the courage of a Genoese and the liberality and religious fervor of a Spanish queen; from the enterprise of Portugal and the devoted labors of the French Jesuits; from the scaffolds of Russell and Sidney, and of Egmont and Horn; from the blood of martyrs and the visions of prophets; from the unexampled struggle of eighty years of the Netherlands for liberty, as well as from the revolution which dethroned a James; from the tongue of Henry, the pen of Jefferson, the sword of Washington, and the sagacity of Franklin; from the discipline of Steuben, the death of Pulaski and De Kalb, and the generous alliance of the French; from the Constitution of the United States; from the bloody sweat of France and the struggles of Germany, Poland, Hungary, and Italy for constitutional monarchy; from the arguments of Webster and the judgments of Marshall; from the throes of civil war and the failure of secession; from the Emancipation Proclamation and the enfranchisement of a dusky race; from the lips of the living in all lands and in all forms of speech; from the bright examples and deathless memories of the dead—from all these, as from ten thousand living streams, the lordly current upon which floats our Ship of State, so richly freighted with the rights of men, broadens as it flows through the centuries, past tombs of kings, and graves of priests, and mounds of buried shackles, and the charred heaps of human auction blocks, and the gray stones of perished institutions, out into the

boundless ocean of the Future. Upon the shores of that illimitable sea stands the Temple of Eternal Truth; not buried in the earth, made hollow by the sepulchres of her witnesses, but rising in the majesty of primeval granite, the dome supported by majestic pillars embedded in the graves of martyrs.

And thou, great bell! cast from the chains of liberators and the copper pennies of the children of our public schools, from sacred relics contributed by pious and patriotic hands, baptized by copious libations poured out upon the altar of a common country by grateful hearts, and consecrated by the prayers of the American people, take up the note of prophecy and of jubilee rung out by your older sister in 1776, and in your journey round the globe proclaim from mountain top and valley, across winding river and expansive sea, those tones which shall make thrones topple and despots tremble in their sleep, until all peoples and all nationalities, from turbaned Turks and Slavic peasants to distant islanders and the children of the Sun, shall join in the swelling chorus, and the darkest regions of the earth shall be illumed by the heaven-born light of Civil and Religious Liberty!

LEWIS CASS

(1782–1866)

EWIS CASS, of Michigan, was the first Northwestern Democrat nominated for President of the United States. That honor seemed to belong to Virginians and Massachusetts men exclusively, until the election of Andrew Jackson, of Tennessee, in 1828, disclosed the fact that the political centre of gravity had shifted towards the West. Jackson's great popularity enabled him at the end of his second term to make his Vice-President, Martin Van Buren, of New York, his successor, but, as the democratic nominee for a second term in 1840, Van Buren was beaten by William Henry Harrison, of Ohio, the Whig nominee. Then both parties nominated Southwestern men, Clay, of Kentucky, and Polk, of Tennessee, and the success of the latter, the second Democrat elected from the Southwest, gave the party nomination in 1848 to General Cass, of Michigan, at that time the most distinguished Democrat in the Northwest. He was beaten by the Whig nominee, General Zachary Taylor, the hero of the Mexican war and the last representative of the Southwest to be elected President during the nineteenth century. As the first distinctive representative of the Northwest in national politics, Cass has a very important place in history.

Born at Exeter, N. H., October 9th, 1782, he studied law under Governor Meigs at Marietta, Ohio, and as a member of the Ohio legislature drew up its memorial on the Burr movement. It attracted President Jefferson's attention, and he was made United States Marshal for Ohio in 1807, a place he held until he was made Colonel of the Third Ohio Volunteers in 1812. He took part in the battle of the Thames and for his services he was made a brigadier-general. Left at the close of the war in command of Michigan Territory, he was appointed its civil governor. Promoted to General Jackson's cabinet as Secretary of War (1832–36), he was latterly Minister to France (1836–42), and represented Michigan in the United States Senate (1845–57). He then entered Buchanan's cabinet as Secretary of State,—a post he resigned in 1860 on account of the President's refusal to reinforce Fort Sumter. He died in Detroit June 17th, 1866.

AMERICAN PROGRESS AND FOREIGN OPPRESSION

(From the Speech Delivered in the United States Senate, January 4th, 1850,
on the Motion to Suspend Diplomatic Relations with Austria)

Mr. President:—

I DO not mistake the true position of my country, nor do I seek to exaggerate her importance. I am perfectly aware that, whatever we may do or say, the immediate march of Austria will be onward in the course of despotism, with a step feebler or firmer, as resistance may appear near or remote, till she is stayed by one of those upheavings of the people, which is as sure to come as that man longs for freedom, and longs to strike the blow which shall make it his.

Pride is blind, and power tenacious; and Austrian pride and power, though they may quail before the signs of the times,— before barricades and fraternization, by which streets are made fortresses and armies revolutionists, new and mighty engines in popular warfare,—will hold out in their citadel till the last extremity. But many old things are passing away; and Austrian despotism will pass away in its turn. Its bulwarks will be shaken by the rushing of mighty winds—by the voice of the world, wherever its indignant expression is not restrained by the kindred sympathies of arbitrary power.

I desire, sir, not to be misunderstood. I do not mean that in all the revolutionary struggles which political contests bring on, it would be expedient for other governments to express their feelings of interest or sympathy. I think they should not; for there are obvious considerations which forbid such action, and the value of this kind of moral interposition would be diminished by its too frequent recurrence. It should be reserved for great events—events marked by great crimes and oppressions on the one side, and great exertions and misfortunes on the other, and under circumstances which carry with them the sympathies of the world, like the partition of Poland and the subjugation of Hungary. We can offer public congratulations, as we have done, to people crowned by success in their struggle for freedom. We can offer our recognition of their independence to others, as we have done, while yet the effort was pending. Have we sympathy only for the fortunate? Or is a cause less sacred or less dear

because it is prostrated in the dust by the foot of power? Let the noble sentiments of Washington, in his spirit-stirring reply to the French minister, answer these questions: "Born, sir, in a land of liberty; having early learned to estimate its value; having, in a word, devoted the best years of my life to its maintenance, I rejoice whensoever in any country I see a nation unfold the banner of freedom. To call your nation brave, were but common praise. Wonderful people! Ages to come will read with astonishment the history of your exploits."

I freely confess that I shall hail the day with pleasure when this Government, reflecting the true sentiments of the people, shall express its sympathy for struggling millions, seeking, in circumstances of peril and oppression, that liberty which was given to them by God, but has been wrested from them by man. I do not see any danger to the true independence of nations by such a course; and indeed I am by no means certain that the free interchange of public views in this solemn manner would not go far towards checking the progress of oppression and the tendency to war. Why, sir, the very discussion in high places and free places—and here is one of them—even when discussion is followed by no act, is itself a great element of retributive justice to punish it when an atrocious deed is done, and a great element of moral power to restrain it when such a deed is contemplated. I claim for our country no exemption from the decrees of these high tribunals; and when we are guilty of a tithe of the oppression and cruelty which have made the Austrian name a name of reproach through the world, I hope we shall receive, as we shall well merit, the opprobrium of mankind.

I anticipate with confidence the cordial support of the distinguished Senator from Kentucky in this effort. I will not doubt it; though I am afraid, from a somewhat playful remark he made the other day, that he is a more zealous disciple of the *stand still* school than he was some years since, when he proved himself the noble advocate of South American and of Grecian freedom. I have just renewed my recollection of what the honorable Senator said and did upon those memorable occasions; though, indeed, both the one and the other were deeply imprinted upon my memory as they are yet upon the hearts of his countrymen. Among the many splendid efforts, both as an orator and statesman, by which he will go down to posterity honored and applauded, there are none higher or holier than these:—

"I have no commiseration for princes," was his characteristic declaration. "My sympathies are reserved for the great mass of mankind." "Self-government is the natural government of man."

"It ought to animate us," he said upon another occasion, "to desire the redemption of the minds and bodies of unborn millions from the brutalizing effects of a system whose tendency is to stifle the faculties of the soul, and to degrade man to the level of beasts."

"Everywhere," he says at another time, "the interest in the Grecian cause is felt with the deepest intensity, expressed in every form, and increases with every new day and passing hour;" and he puts an emphatic question emphatically, which I repeat to him, and to every one, if there is any one who hesitates to keep "on a line," as Mr. Canning said, with the opinions of his countrymen: "And are the representatives of the people alone to be insulated from the common moral atmosphere of the world?" These sentiments have no connection with the recognition of independence, nor is their expression claimed as the right or the consequence of a mere political act. They belong to man, wherever he may be placed.

The honorable Senator describes in burning words the cruelties of Spanish and Turkish warfare; and in Murillo we have the very prototype of Haynau, and recent Austrian enormities may be read in the enormities powerfully portrayed almost thirty years ago; and this apostrophe comes to close the recapitulation: "Are we so mean, so base, so despicable, that we may not attempt to express our horror and our indignation at the most brutal and atrocious war that ever stained the earth or shocked high heaven?"

And I am happy, also, to anticipate the cordial co-operation of the distinguished Senator from Massachusetts, who, upon a recent occasion, expressed his sympathy for down-trodden Hungary, and his abhorrence of despotic sway, in a strain of indignant eloquence, which would have done honor to the elder Pitt, in the brightest days of his intellect. "We have had all our sympathies much interested," he truly said, "in the Hungarian effort for liberty. We have all wept at its failure. We thought we saw a more rational hope of establishing independence in Hungary than in any other part of Europe where the question has been in agitation within the last twelve months; but despotic power from abroad has intervened to suppress it."

And the honorable Senator, in scathing terms, which will touch a chord in the hearts of all his countrymen, rebukes the Russian Emperor for his insolent demand of the fugitives who had sought refuge within the Turkish frontier:—

"Gentlemen (he says), there is something on earth greater than arbitrary or despotic power. The lightning has its power; and the whirlwind has its power; and the earthquake has its power; but there is something among men more capable of shaking despotic power than lightning, whirlwind, or earthquake. That is the threatened indignation of the whole civilized world.

"The whole world will be the tribunal to try him [the Russian Emperor], and he must appear before it, and hold up his hand and plead, and abide its judgment.

"Nor let him, nor let any one imagine, that mere force can subdue the general sentiment of mankind; it is much more likely to extend that sentiment, and to destroy that power which he most desires to establish and secure.

"And now, gentlemen, let us do our part; let us understand the position in which we stand, as the great Republic of the world, at the most interesting era of the world; let us consider the mission and the destiny which Providence seems to have designed us for; and let us take care of our own conduct, that with irreproachable hands and hearts, void of offense, we may stand up, whenever and wherever called upon, and, with a voice not to be disregarded, say: This shall not be done—at least not without our protest."

These were noble words, and nobly spoken; and he who does not feel his blood course more rapidly through his veins as he reads them, has little in common with the freemen of this broad land. Well was the honorable Senator saluted with "tremendous cheerings," for he spoke to the hearts of his auditors when he said: "For my part, at this moment, I feel more indignant at recent events connected with Hungary than at all those which have passed in her struggle for liberty. I see that the Emperor of Russia demands of Turkey that the noble Kossuth and his companions shall be given up, and I see that this demand is made in derision of the law of nations." . . .

Hungary was an independent nation, having no political connection at all with Austria, except in the person of the sovereign who was common to both. The reigning Austrian family was called to the Hungarian throne by election, some three centuries ago; and we are told by a standard review—a high and neutral authority—that "the pedigree of their immunities, during that long space, continued unimpaired." The compact between the Hungarian people and their monarch declares that "Hungary is a country free and independent in her entire system of legislation and government; that she is not subject to any other people, or any other State; but that she should have her own separate existence and her own constitution, and should be governed by kings crowned according to her national laws and customs." This article the Austrian Emperor swore to preserve, as all his predecessors had done; and as late as the eleventh of April, 1848, he solemnly renewed his adhesion to it, with the guarantee of a ministry, responsible to the Diet—that plan, of English origin, by which European liberal politicians seek to reconcile the dogma of the personal independence of the sovereign with the direction of public affairs in conformity with the will of the nation. This was the constitution of Hungary, and thus was it secured. It guaranteed national independence, Hungarian laws and officers, and Hungarian administration of the affairs of the country. In these days of the violation of the most sacred rights, there has been no violation more signal or atrocious than the annihilation of the rights of this high-spirited people, once the bulwark of Christendom. A *charte octroyée*, the work of an Austrian cabinet, struck down their liberties at one stroke, and left them (as a kindred expedient—kindred in its objects though not in its form—left our fathers) no choice but submission or resistance.

These *chartes octroyées* are becoming quite fashionable in the world of arbitrary power, awakened from its long slumber by the thunder of popular indignation, and particularly since the restoration of the Bourbons—that family which was the very impersonation of the doctrine of the divine right of kings; and they mark significantly the utter contempt for the sovereignty of the people, which is engraved upon the hearts of all the lovers of the good old times, when there were but two classes in the world—those born to govern, and those born to be governed. We first heard of them as the foundation of national freedom, when the declaration of rights proposed by the provisional government of France, on the overthrow of Napoleon, was presented to Louis XVIII. for his solemn adhesion. He rejected this act of popular power, holding on to his divine right; but as the restoration would have been placed in hazard without some security for the liberties of

III—63

the French people, this plan of a *charte octroyée* was resorted to —a charter granted by the sovereign, emanating from his gracious benevolence, and giving to the nation certain rights, not because it was entitled to claim them, but because he was kindly disposed to limit his own hereditary authority, and to allow his beloved people to be a little less oppressed than they had been in the good old days of arbitrary power. And this is a *charte octroyée*, by which, when the fears of kings prompt them to make concessions to popular movements, their divine right is reserved for future use, and the sovereignty of the people practically rebuked and denied. The lesson was too precious to be lost, and Prussia and other States have followed the example; and human rights are *octroyée*, given, doled out, as the fears or caprice of a single man may dictate.

Well, sir, the Austrian ministry was seized with a passion for political unity; by which, at the sacrifice of all those feelings— prejudices, if you please—the growth of centuries, which separated the various races bound by ties feebler or stronger to the monarchy, they were to become one people, homogeneous in nothing but in an imperial decree. A *charte octroyée* was got up for the occasion, and by a kind of political legerdemain—if not as dexterous, at least as rapid as the feats of the necromancer— all the traits of nationality, cherished by the associated members of the monarchy, were swept away, and they all became Austrians by this act of arbitrary power, as offensive to their pride as it was subversive of their rights. Hungary was to disappear from the map of independent nations, and all its institutions were placed at the mercy of a foreign court; and while the empty form of a kind of representation was given to her, in a jarring assembly, divided by language, races, and interests, all substantial power was reserved to the Emperor and his cabinet.

But Kossuth has himself depicted the condition of his country in words of truth and power, which appeal to every heart:—

"Nothing but the most revolting treachery, the most tyrannical oppression and cruelties unheard of in the words of history—nothing but the infernal doom of annihilation to her national existence, preserved through a thousand years, through adversities so numerous, were able to arouse her to resist the fatal stroke, aimed at her very life, to enable her to repulse the tyrannical assaults of the ungrateful Hapsburgs, or accept the struggle for life, honor, and liberty, forced upon her."

She did accept it, and the Hungarian people rose as one man to resist these gross aggressions; and their gallant exertions would, in all probability, have been crowned by success, had not the common sympathy of despotism brought a new enemy into the field. The Russian scented the blood from afar, and Hungary fell, like Poland, before the Cossack and the Pandour—an everlasting reproach to the contemners of the laws of God and man, who accomplished these nefarious schemes.

The issue was made known to the Czar by his general, in a dispatch whose brevity Sparta might have envied: "Hungary lies at the feet of your Majesty." Memorable words, and to be remembered in all future time! The foot of one man upon ten millions of people! Imperial arrogance can go no further. He who does not instinctively and indignantly scorn such pretensions would have opposed the Declaration of Independence on this side of the water, and the great charter of King John on the other.

I have presented this brief review of Hungarian rights and wrongs, not as the direct motive for the adoption of this resolution—that I choose to put upon another ground, the ground of atrocious cruelty—but because I desire to take from Austrian advocates (if there are any in this country—I know there are none in this Senate) the last excuse for these violations of the common feelings of our nature, by showing that the attack upon Hungarian independence was as reckless and unjustifiable as were the cruelties inflicted upon the Hungarian people. . . .

This spirit of standing still—conservatism, I believe, is the fashionable name for it in England, and is becoming so here, while both the moral and physical world is giving evidence that change is one of the great laws of nature—little becomes a country like ours, which is advancing in the career of improvement with an accelerated pace unknown in the history of the world.

Standing still! Why, sir, you might as well attempt to follow the example of the Jewish leader, and say to the sun, "Stand thou still upon Gibeon, and thou moon in the valley of Ajalon," and expect to be obeyed, as to expect that this country would yield to this sentiment of immobility, and stand still in that mighty work of improvement, material and intellectual, which it has been doing for generations, and will be called upon to do for generations yet to come.

Let not the timid be alarmed; where there is free inquiry, there is no danger. There is a fund of practical good sense, as well as a deep moral and religious feeling, in the people of this country, which will hold on to our institutions, not with blind tenacity, but with a firm resolution to maintain them; and, while wisely admitting improvement, rejecting impracticable and dangerous projects, often originating in honest though mistaken views. Let us not fear the progress of opinion. The world is probably yet very far from its extreme point of improvement. Before that is reached, many a project will be proposed and rejected; many an experiment tried and failed; and a spirit of investigation will be abroad, dangerous only when met by force, instead of argument.

I am not going to reason with this feeling, which would have enjoined upon our fathers to stand still and suffer, instead of rushing into the danger of a revolution, not only because I am sure it is not a senatorial one, but because it is intrenched behind barriers which reason cannot overcome. To such, not here, but elsewhere, the example of the French Chamber may divest this proposition of half its terrors. The other half may be safely left to time. They will gradually learn that the great political truth of our day is contained in the sentiment recently announced by the distinguished Senator from Massachusetts— "We are in an age of progress."

EMILIO CASTELAR

(1832–1899)

AS PASSIONATE oratory, harnessed to rhyme and lyric measure, characterizes so much of Byron's poetry, so do poetic feeling, imagery, and modes of expression often make us hear a muffled tinkling of the lyre in the flow of Castelar's oratory. Fervid, sentimental, and florid, as his Spanish nativity presupposes, his poetic fancy asserts itself in his discussion of the most prosaic questions. But there is still enough of clear historic vision and grave reasoning to distinguish his statesman's mantle from the robes of the poet. As a Spanish Republican, striving earnestly to divorce his countrymen from monarchy and wed them to democracy, he has led a tempestuous life. More than once he was a fugitive in exile, once, at least, under sentence of death, yet once a cabinet minister, and at last President of a short-lived Spanish Republic.

He was born in Cadiz, September 8th, 1832, and became, when very young, the author of several novels and poems. He first distinguished himself politically by several stirring speeches at the Teatro del Oriente in Madrid against the misgovernment and vices of the court. He was made Professor of History and Philosophy in the University of Madrid in 1856, and by his lectures continued to increase his reputation. In 1864 he was deprived of his professorship on account of his connection with La Democracia, a journal established at that time under his direction. His connection with the disturbances of June 22d, 1866, led to the suppression of his journal; he was sentenced to death, and had to remain in exile till the flight of the royal family enabled him to return in 1868 and resume the professorship which was offered to him again. He was one of the few Republicans elected to the Cortes in 1869, and became more celebrated than ever for the part he took in the debates; opposing a regency, opposing monarchy, and in vain advocating a Republican constitution. The monarchy of Amadeus, limited by extreme constitutional restrictions, owed the brevity of its existence largely to Castelar's opposition, and in the provisional Republic which succeeded he became, first, Minister of Foreign Affairs, and next, President of the Executive.

But the Republicans were divided, some advocating a «Unitary Republic» while Castelar and his wing demanded a «Federal Republic,» «the United States of Spain» in «the United States of Europe,»

with an end of all wars. Insurrections in the Colonies and anarchy in Spain itself, made a burden too heavy for Castelar's strength; and «between the red demagogy of the Communists and the white demagogy of the Carlists,» he found the Cortes against him, and resigned in disgust, January 2d, 1874. For some time he remained the leader of the moderate faction of the Republicans, but in 1875 he resigned his professorship and in 1893 announced his retirement from politics, despairing of the Republican cause in Spain and regretting that he had not supported the limited monarchy of 1869 as the best thing the Spaniards of the present day are capable of appreciating.

Castelar is the author of a great number and variety of published books and of numerous lectures and speeches. He died May 25th, 1899.

A PLEA FOR REPUBLICAN INSTITUTIONS

(From a Speech in the Spanish Assembly, December 18th, 1869)

BEFORE replying to Minister Sagasta's speech of last Saturday, I desire to say that my public life forbids me to defend myself against personal attacks such as the gentleman seems to delight in. The Minister of Government was extremely kind in speaking of my address as a brilliant one and extremely severe when he declared that it was wanting in truth. Neither criticism was just. Gentlemen, I would not have to defend my own speeches if they had the resplendency and the beauty attributed to them by Mr. Sagasta. I would be content to let them shine, confident, with the most eloquent and greatest of ancient philosophers, that «Beauty is the resplendency of Truth.» After all, if there is any grand quality in this Assembly it is eloquence, the expressing of grand sentiments and sublime ideas in fervent language. I have heard such speeches come from every side of the Assembly and I would like to hear one, in the language of moderation, from the Government. Discussions carried on in that manner, with eloquence and good judgment, give us hope for the future, for the laws of history do not permit a dictatorship to fasten itself upon a people whose faces are lighted by the fires of eloquence,—a sure sign of grand apostolic work in social life.

I have said this, not being able to proceed without repelling a calumnious imputation directed against me by the Minister of Government. To a question of Mr. Oria relative to an attack

on property, the gentleman replied that it was the work of the Federalists. In what article, in what proclamation, in what program, in what bulletin, in what periodical, in what speech of a Federalist has the gentleman discovered that we attack property? Against the robbers are the courts and the judges, and it is an imposition on the Assembly and a calumny on our social conditions to charge us with such crimes and to seek to spatter this minority with the mud that bespatters all of you. This is not just.

Now, I must answer with calmness another slanderous imputation. The Minister of Government says that the Federal Republican party desired the dismemberment, the dissolution, the breaking up of this country. A party that aspires to a European confederation, a party that desires to see the abominable word «war» abolished, a party that desires to unite disunited people cannot seek the dismemberment of a country bound together by tradition and law. We desire that from Barcelona to Lisbon, from Irun to Cadiz, there shall be but one flag—a flag, however, under whose folds the citizen may have freedom, the municipality autonomy, and the province rights that belong to the whole country.

The accusation of the gentleman reminds me of the one concerning decentralization made by the Moderate party against the Progressive party, and the claim of the Moderates that with decentralization national unity was impossible. Notwithstanding this claim, it is generally believed to-day that people who suffer most in their independence have a centralized government, because it is enough to aim a blow at their head, like the blow aimed by the allied powers in Paris in 1815. The belief is general that those nations that have great internal dissensions are centralized nations, because they have an apoplectic head on a weak, stiff body. And so I say that, as centralization is believed in to-day, federation will be to-morrow—a federation the belief in which will result sooner or later in the organization of the United States of Spain within the United States of Europe.

Mr. Sagasta began to defend the dictatorship, and in defending it he drew an awful picture of our social condition, talking of crimes and criminals, and telling you that our education in the past was very bad, and that the corruption of to-day is very great. And what have the Republicans to see from that? For three centuries, yes, more than three centuries, our Church has been as an enemy to the human conscience. For many centuries

it has been inimical to the national will. Consequently, if there is anything very bad or vicious here to-day, it is owing to institutions with which we have nothing to do. And more, this evil, this viciousness, owe their existence to a lack of respect among the people for the law. And this lack of respect for the law is born of the systematic abuse of power by our arbitrary government. Judges nominated by a party and appointed to revise the electoral lists; schools, so called, for filling convents and military barracks; the jury outlawed; public life closed to the democracy; political corruption extending from above down in all directions —this is the product, and these the products, of the sore and wounded people painted by Mr. Sagasta; people who are the natural offspring of a long heredity of crime and error. It is impossible to cure the people if the system is not changed. . . .

Well, deputies, what form of government has come to Spain since the September revolution? The republican form has come and is still here. It so happens, that you have not been able yet to implant monarchical institution in its place. After having been fifteen days in power you declared yourselves for the monarchy. Did the monarchy come? After the elections you declared yourselves monarchists and us outlaws. Did you create the monarchy in the primaries? When the assembly convened, the monarchy was proposed; there we have had great battles. Has the monarchy been established? The Conservatives, although they have not said so, have, I believe, agreed upon a candidate; the Radicals, more loquacious, have told us theirs; but have you, separated or united, produced a monarchy?

The Conservatives have a candidate who really represents the latest privilege granted the middle classes. Why is it that they do not bring him here? Because they know that this is a democratic monarchy, based, as it is supposably, on universal suffrage, and because the candidate has not, never had, and never will have, the votes, the indorsement, the backing of the people. And you? You want a monarchy to keep up appearances, a monarchy in order that Europe may say, «See how prudent, how God-fearing, how wise, how intelligent are the Spaniards; they have a disguised republic!» After a provisional government and a provisional regency you want a provisional monarchy also. You do not expect or want to be strong in the right, in liberty, in the will of the people or in national sovereignty. All you want is a king who shall represent the predominance and the egotism of a party. You ought to know that as the candidate of the Conservatives cannot come here without the consent of the people your candidate cannot come without the consent of the Conservatives. Do you believe that your candidate will last if all the Conservative forces do not support him? Notwithstanding all that the Conservatives have declared to their representatives here, not one of them has said that he renounces his dynastic faith. Therefore, deputies, you cannot establish the monarchy.

On Saturday I pictured to you, in colors more or less vivid, the prestige which monarchical institutions have enjoyed in our country, and for this the Minister of State upbraided me without understanding my arguments. I ask you to concentrate your attention for a moment upon the parallel which I am going to present and which may be called a summary of this speech. I said the other afternoon, that to establish monarchical institutions it was necessary to possess monarchical faith and sentiment. One must have the poetry and the traditions of monarchy. I said this because I know that, although the assembly and the official authorities can make laws, they cannot decree ideas or sentiments, those real and solid foundations of institutions. Formerly, in other times, kings were representative of the national dignity, and now from those same benches we have heard that they sold their native soil to a foreigner and even prostrated themselves at his feet, the people in the meantime answering the enemy with the second of May and the siege of Saragossa. Formerly poetry, addressing the throne, exclaimed:—

"Oh! what a profound abyss
Of iniquity and malice
The mighty of the world
Have made of your justice!"

Formerly art sketched the apotheosis of Charles V. with Titian's brush, or the ladies-in-waiting of Philip VI. with the brush of Velasquez; now it sketches the image of the communists, of the victims of Charles V., or the ship in which the Puritans took the republic to the bosom of virgin America. Formerly, the gala days of the people were the birthdays of kings and the anniversaries of the beginning of their reigns. Now, the great days of celebration are the tenth of August, the thirtieth of July, the twenty-fourth of February, and the twenty-

ninth of September, days marking the expulsion of kings. Formerly, when a navigator landed in America, or an explorer went into the interior of a new country, the purest piece of gold, the largest pearl, the clearest diamond was reserved for the king. Now, your Minister of the Treasury claims from the king even the clasp which holds the royal mantle about his shoulders. I will not continue this parallel as the Chamber clearly sees the application.

What does this mean? What does it signify? If the throne has fallen, if the throne is broken, if the throne is dishonored, if the throne cannot be restored, Conservatives, Unionists, Progressists, Democrats, repeat with the poet:—

"Mankind, weep;
All of you laid your hands on him."

As there is no possibility of establishing the monarchy, as no candidate acceptable to all can be found, it is necessary, it is indispensable to get rid of the suspense, and I say that we should establish a republic. Have you not said that the forms of government are accidental? Gentlemen, you know the republic I want. It is a federal republic. I shall always defend the federal republic. I am a Federal, but, deputies, understand one thing, the republic is a form of government which admits many conditions, and which has many grades. From the republic of Venice to that of Switzerland there is an immense scale. Adjoining Mexico, where Church and State are separated, there is Guatemala, where the clergy have great power. Close to the decentralized and federal Agentine Republic is the Chilian Republic, another decentralized country enjoying great prosperity, its paper money being quoted in all the markets of Europe as high as that of England. Consequently, deputies, amidst this great affliction and this great trouble and this unstable equilibrium, which surrounds you, you can establish a form of government which is of the people and for the people, a form of government in harmony with the institutions you have proclaimed, and with the sentiment which all of you guard in the bottom of your hearts.

Have you not seen in history the inability of an assembly or any power to establish a form of government in conflict with great ideas? Remember the eighteenth century. Never had a monarchy attained more power, never was absolutism so strong, never was the destruction of obstacles in the way of kings more

complete. Philosophy ascended the throne with them, ascended with Charles III. and Aranda and Tombal. It ascended with Joseph I., with Frederick the Great, with Leopold of Tuscany. All seemed to conspire to establish the same idea, the idea of a philosophy and a liberalism. And did they succeed? No, they were the Baptists of the Revolution. They repented late and the philosophy they had thrown at the feet of the thrones came to naught. And what happened? Some were sentenced by the Assembly. The crowns of divine right were melted into cannon balls by the soldiers of the Revolution. What does this signify? That great powers cannot place absolutism above philosophy any more than you can build monarchical institutions on individual rights. Therefore, I beseech you to establish the republic. You are assured of our patriotism, our great interest in the country, our abnegation. Cato committed suicide because he found a Cæsar. Radicals of Spain, do not commit suicide because you cannot find a monarch. I have spoken.

IN THE CAMPO SANTO OF PISA

(An Example of Castelar's Prose Style)

Do you believe that death is the end of our being? I have never thought so. If it be, then the universe is created solely for destruction; and God is a child who has formed the world like a castle of cards, for the pleasure of overturning them.

The vegetable consumes the earth, the ox and the sheep graze upon the vegetable; we eat the ox and the sheep, and invisible agents which we call death or nothingness consume us. In the scale of existence some creatures serve only to destroy other creatures, and the universe is like an enormous polypus with a capacious stomach, or, if you desire a more classic image, a catafalque upon which burns a funeral torch, and is created the statue of fatal law. Some are patient because they have been born lymphatic; many are heroic because they have much blood; others are thinkers because they are bilious; more are poets because their nerves are sensitive; but all die of their own characteristics, and all live while their stomachs endure, while their hearts, their brains, their spines are sound. What we call virtues or vices are tendencies of organism; what we name faith

is but a few drops less blood in the veins, or some irritation of the liver, or some atoms of phosphorus in the bones, and what we term immortality is but an illusion. Death alone is real and certain, and human history is a procession of shadows passing like bats between day and night, all to drop, one behind the other, into that obscure, unfathomable abyss which is called nothing, the unique atmosphere of the universe.

Oh! No! No! I cannot believe it! Human wickedness can never so much affect me as to obscure divine truths in my soul. As I can distinguish good from evil, so can I separate death from immortality. I believe in the Almighty, and in a vision of the Almighty in another and better world.

I leave my body as armor which fatigues me by its weight, to continue my infinite ascension to the heaven of heavens, bathed in light eternal.

It is true that death exists, but true also that there is a soul; against Realism that would enshroud me with its leaden mantle I have the glow and fire of thought; and against Fatalism, that would confine me by its chain, I have the power and force of liberty.

History is a resurrection. Barbarians buried the ancient Grecian statues, but they live again here in this cemetery, producing immortal generations of artists with kisses from their cold lips of marble. Italy was as dead as Juliet. Each generation flung a handful of earth upon her corpse, and placed a flower in her mortuary crown; yet Italy is alive again!

To-day tyrants sing the 'Dies Iræ' on the field where unhappy Poland was divided. Yet soon humanity will approach, collect the bones, picked clean by the vultures of the Neva, and Poland will be reborn, standing like a statue of faith, with the cross in her arms and on her ancient altars.

I have always been impressed with the thought of immortality in cemeteries. But I felt it more than commonly in the Campo Santo of Pisa, filled with so much life; peopled by so many beings that give inspiration and consequently immortality, as the trunks of the trees distill honey when the bees have inhabited them. Insensibly the night falls. The grave-digger finishes his work, the noise of the shovel ceases, and I am asked to retire. But I prayed to remain another hour, in the bosom of night and of the shadows. I wish to submerge myself in the melancholy of nothingness, to anticipate my being in that place of silence and eternal repose, by long contemplation of the dust of the departed here where so many generations sleep forgotten.

There I remained leaning against a tomb, resting my forehead upon the marble, my eyes fixed on the picture of death and on the monsters of the Universal Judgment, illuminated by the last splendors of the expiring day, awaiting the greater sadness which the darkness of night would bring upon me.

But no! the fresh breeze of the sea comes to awaken me from my melancholy dreams; the sweet flowers of May raised their blossom before drooping; from the heat, a penetrating and intoxicating aroma, full of life and fragrance, diffused itself in the air; the winged glowworms began to hover between the shades of the cloister and the lines of the tombs like wandering stars, while the full moon rose above the horizon, floating majestically in ether, with her pale blue rays lighting up the faces of the funereal statues; and a nightingale, hidden in the thick branches of the highest cypress, chanted his song of love as a serenade to the dead and a supplication to the living.

CATO UTICENSIS

(95–46 B. C.)

AFTER Cæsar had spoken in the Roman Senate, protesting against the death penalty for the accomplices of Catiline, Cato, when called on by the Consul to speak, demanded that they be put to death under the ancient laws of the Republic which had been repealed by later enactments abolishing both the lash and the death penalty for Roman citizens. Sallust, in closing the report of the debate makes this celebrated parallel between Cato and Cæsar:—

«As to extraction, years, and eloquence, they were nearly equal. Both of them had the same greatness of mind, both the same degree of glory, but in different ways. Cæsar was celebrated for his great bounty and generosity; Cato for his unsullied integrity; the former became renowed by his humanity and compassion; an austere severity heightened the dignity of the latter. Cæsar acquired glory by a liberal, compassionate, and forgiving temper; as did Cato by never bestowing anything. In the one the miserable found a sanctuary; in the other the guilty met with certain destruction. Cæsar was admired for an easy, yielding temper; Cato for his immovable firmness. Cæsar, in a word, had formed himself for a laborious, active life; was intent on promoting the interest of his friends, to the neglect of his own; and refused to grant nothing that was worth accepting: what he desired for himself was, to have sovereign command, to be at the head of armies, and engaged in new wars, in order to display his military talents. As for Cato, his only study was moderation, regular conduct, and, above all, rigorous severity. He did not vie with the wealthy in riches, nor in turbulence with the factious; but, taking a nobler aim, he contended in valor with the brave; in modesty with the modest; in integrity with the upright; and was more desirous to be virtuous than appear so: so that the less he courted fame the more it followed him.»

Cato is called "Uticensis" to distinguish him from Cato the Censor. Failing by his virtue to save the liberties of a people already grown essentially servile, he committed suicide at Utica after Cæsar's victory at Thapsus rather than survive to witness the overthrow of the Republic. Lucan pays him what is, perhaps, the proudest compliment ever paid in history:—

«Victrix causa deis placuit, sed victa Catoni.»
«On the victor's side the gods abide, but with the conquered Cato.»

AGAINST THE ACCOMPLICES OF CATILINE

(Delivered in the Roman Senate, 64 B.C.)

[WHEN Cæsar had concluded, and the rest of the Senators, either by words or signs, approved or disapproved of the several propositions made, Cato, being asked his opinion, delivered it in the following strain:—Sallust.]

I AM very differently affected, Conscript Fathers, when I view our present situation and the danger we are in, and then consider the proposals made by some Senators who have spoken before me. They appear to me to have reasoned only about the punishment of those who have entered into a combination to make war on their country, on their parents, on religion, and private property; whereas, our present circumstances warn us rather to guard against them than to consider in what manner we shall punish them. You may take vengeance for other crimes after they are committed; but if you do not prevent the commission of this, when it is once accomplished, in vain will you have recourse to the tribunals. When the city is once taken, no resource remains to the conquered citizens.

Now, I conjure you, by the immortal gods! you who have always valued your splendid palaces, your pictures, your statues, more than the welfare of the State; if you are desirous to preserve these things which, whatever their real value be, you are so fond of; if you would have leisure for pursuing your pleasures; rouse for once out of your lethargy, and take on you the defense of the State. The debate is not about the public revenues, nor the oppression of our allies; no, our liberties, our lives are in danger.

Often, Conscript Fathers, have I spoken in this assembly; often have I complained of the luxury and avarice of our fellow-citizens; on which account I bear the enmity of many: I, who never indulged myself in any vice, nor even cherished the thought of any, could not easily pardon the crimes of others. And though you little regarded my remonstrances, yet the commonwealth remained firm; her native strength supported her even under the negligence of her governors. But the present debate is not about the goodness or depravity of our morals, nor about the greatness or prosperity of the Roman empire; no, it is whether this empire, such as it is, continue our own, or, together with ourselves, fall a prey to the enemy.

And, in such a case, will any one talk of gentleness or mercy? We have long since lost the true names of things. To give away what belongs to others is called generosity; to attempt what is criminal, fortitude; and thence the State is reduced to the brink of ruin. Let them, since such is the fashion of the times, be generous from the spoils of our allies; merciful to the plunderers of the treasury; but let them not be prodigal of our blood, and, by sparing a few bad citizens, destroy all the good.

Caius Cæsar has just now spoken, with great strength and accuracy, concerning life and death; taking for fictions, I doubt not, the vulgar notions of an infernal world, where the bad, separated from the good, are confined to dark, frightful, and melancholy abodes. Accordingly, his proposal is that their estates be confiscated and their persons confined in the corporate towns; from an apprehension, I imagine, that if they were kept at Rome they might be rescued by force, either by their fellow-conspirators or a mercenary mob; as if wicked and profligate persons were only to be found in this city, and not all over Italy; or as if there were not more encouragement to the attempts of the desperate where there is least strength to resist them.

This, then, is an empty proposal, if he fears any danger from them; but if, amid this so great and universal consternation, he alone is void of fear, so much the more does it concern me to be afraid, both for myself and you.

Hence, in determining the fate of Lentulus and the other prisoners, be assured that you likewise determine that of Catiline's army and all the conspirators. The more vigor and resolution you exert, so much the less spirit and courage will they have; but if they observe the least remissness in your proceedings, they will presently fall on you with fury.

Do not think it was by arms our ancestors raised the State from so small beginnings to such grandeur: if so, we should have it in its highest lustre; as having a greater number of allies and citizens, of arms and horses, than they had. But there were other things from which they derived their greatness, such as we are entirely without. They were industrious at home, and exercised an equitable government abroad; their minds were free in council, neither swayed by crimes nor passion. Instead of these virtues, we have luxury and avarice; poverty in the State, and great wealth in the members of it: we admire riches, and abandon ourselves to idleness; we make no distinction between the virtuous and the wicked; and all the rewards of virtue are possessed by ambition. Nor is it at all strange, while each of you pursues his separate interest; while you abandon yourselves to pleasure at home, and here in the Senate are slaves to money or favor, that attacks are made on the State when thus forsaken. But no more of this.

Romans of the highest quality have conspired to destroy their country, and are endeavoring to engage the Gauls, the sworn enemies of the Roman name, to join them. The commander of the enemy is hovering over us with an army, and yet at this very juncture you delay and hesitate how to proceed against such of the conspirators as are seized within your walls. Would you extend your compassion towards them? Be it so; they are young men only, and have offended through ambition: send them away armed, too; what would be the consequence of this gentleness and mercy? Why this; when they got arms in their hands, it would prove your utter ruin.

Our situation is indeed dangerous; but you are not afraid: yes, you are very much; only from effeminacy and want of spirit, you are in suspense, every one waiting the motions of another; trusting, perhaps, to the immortal gods, who have often saved this commonwealth in the greatest dangers. But assistance is not obtained from the gods by idle vows and supplications, like those of women; it is by vigilance, activity, and wise counsels that all undertakings succeed. If you resign yourselves to sloth and idleness, it will be in vain to implore the assistance of the gods; you will only provoke them to anger, and they will make you feel your unworthiness.

In the days of our ancestors, T. Manlius Torquatus, in a war with the Gauls, ordered his son to be put to death for having engaged the enemy without orders; and thus a young man of great hopes was punished for too much bravery. And do you demur about the doom of the most barbarous parricides?

Their present offense, perhaps, is unsuitable to their former character: show a tender regard then for the dignity of Lentulus, if you find that he himself ever showed any for his own chastity, for his honor, for gods or men; pardon Cethegus, in consideration of his youth, if this is not the second time of his making war on his country: for what need I mention Gabinius, Statilius, Cœparius? who, if they had possessed the least degree of

III—64

reflection, would never have embarked in such wicked designs against the State.

Finally, Conscript Fathers, were there any room for a wrong step on this occasion, I should suffer you to be corrected by the consequences, since you disregard my reasonings. But we are surrounded on all sides: Catiline is hovering over our heads with an army; we have enemies within the walls, and in the very heart of the city. No preparations can be made, no measures taken, without their knowledge: hence the greater reason for dispatch.

My opinion then is this: that since by a detestable combination of profligate citizens the State is brought into the greatest danger; since they are convicted, by the evidence of Volturcius, and the deputies of the Allobroges, and their own confession, to have entered into a conspiracy for destroying their fellow-citizens and native country, by slaughter, conflagration, and other unheard-of cruelties; they be put to death, according to the ancient usage, as being condemned by their own mouths.

CAMILLO BENSO COUNT DI CAVOUR

(1810–1861)

THE unification and redemption of Italy may well be considered a more wonderful achievement than the unification of Germany; and it is far more distinctly the achievement of Cavour than the existing German empire is the work of Bismarck. The latter had behind him the greatest military power in Europe and a mighty people to whom foreign domination had long been merely an ugly dream of the past. Cavour had only the feeble kingdom of Sardinia as a rallying point for heart-broken Italians, inhabiting provinces, which had known for centuries nothing but alien domination, cruel oppression, and savagely suppressed outbreaks. A long record of martyred aspirations for freedom and self-government naturally drove Italian patriotism into an extreme distrust with every monarchic power; into fierce outbreaks for a democracy which contiguous Europe would not tolerate, and into diverse conspiracies, and organizations of Carbonari. How Cavour, in private life, learned to mold all these elements to the uses of national unification; how he mastered the politics and the cabinet secrets of Europe, and with what sagacity and success, from his entrance into the Sardinian Parliament in 1848 until his death in 1861, he controlled the Sardinian King and his people, played the European powers against each other, and from the chaos of Italian revolutionary movements drew forth the Italy of to-day, united under a free representative government, "a free Church in a free State,"—all this is told in books and will be discussed in others without number.

Yet this greatest and noblest political feat of the century was accomplished in a brief public life of twelve years—and by a man whose speeches were said to be "not what is called eloquent," though, judged by their effect, they were the most moving orations men ever heard.

Count Cavour was born in Turin, August 10th, 1810. His family, descended from a Saxon ancestor of the time of Frederick Barbarossa, were known as the Bensi, and had a marquisate and an estate near Cavour, from which the title came. Camillo's father held a position at the court of Turin, and the babe was presented at the baptismal font by the beautiful Pauline Bonaparte, the Princess Borghese.

When made a page at court, Camillo scorned the uniform and menial service, and spoke his mind so freely that he was sent away to learn prudence. His tongue, again in 1831, made his position in the army untenable, and he retired to the family estate, which he successfully managed till his entrance into public life in 1848.

In the meantime he had been an active promoter of agriculture and public improvements, and withal, a close student and observer of politics, keeping himself aloof from conspiracies and revolutionary organizations, but more or less under suspicion of sympathizing with their aims. Entering the Sardinian Parliament in the exciting times of 1848, he became a member of the Cabinet in 1850 and Prime Minister in 1852, a post he held till he resigned in 1859, disgusted with the terms of peace his ally, Louis Napoleon, had conceded to Austria at Villa Franca. But he soon resumed his position, seeing in the Garibaldian movement a means of completing his work, which was practically done when he died—June 6th, 1861. During most of his premiership he was really a dictator, his will being a law alike to king, parliament, and people. Having no children, he left his property to the children of his elder brother.

ROME AND ITALY

(From a Speech on the Necessity of Having Rome for the Capital of United Italy)

ROME should be the capital of Italy. There can be no solution of the Roman question without the acceptance of this premise by Italy and by all Europe. If any one could conceive of a united Italy with any degree of stability, and without Rome for its capital, I would declare the Roman question difficult, if not impossible, of solution. And why have we the right, the duty of insisting that Rome shall be united to Italy? Because without Rome as the capital of Italy, Italy cannot exist.

This truth being felt instinctively by all Italians, being asserted abroad by all who judge Italian affairs impartially, needs no demonstration, but is upheld by the judgment of the nation.

And yet, gentlemen, this truth is susceptible of a very simple proof. Italy has still much to do before it will rest upon a stable basis; much to do in solving the grave problems raised by her unification; much to do in overcoming all the obstacles which time-honored traditions oppose to this great undertaking. And if this end must be compassed, it is essential that there be no cause of dissidence, of failure. Until the question of the capital of Italy is determined, there will be endless discords among the different provinces.

It is easy to understand how persons of good faith, cultured and talented, are now suggesting, some on historical, some on artistic grounds, and also for many other reasons, the advisability of establishing the capital in some other city of Italy. Such a discussion is quite comprehensible now, but if Italy already had her capital in Rome, do you think this question would be even possible? Assuredly not. Even those who are now opposed to transferring the capital to Rome, if it were once established there, would not dream of removing it. Therefore it is only by proclaiming Rome the capital of Italy that we can put an end to these dissensions among ourselves.

I am grieved that men of eminence, men of genius, men who have rendered glorious service to the cause of Italian unity, should drag this question into the field of debate, and there discuss it with (dare I say it) puerile arguments. The question of the capital, gentlemen, is not determined by climate, by topography, nor even by strategical considerations. If these things affected the selection, I think I may safely say that London would not be the capital of England, nor, perhaps, Paris of France. The selection of the capital is determined by great moral reasons. It is the will of the people that decides this question touching them so closely.

In Rome, gentlemen, are united all the circumstances, whether historic, intellectual, or moral, that should determine the site of the capital of a great State. Rome is the only city with traditions not purely local. The entire history of Rome from the time of Cæsar to the present day is the history of a city whose importance reaches far beyond her confines; of a city destined to be one of the capitals of the world. Convinced, profoundly convinced, of this truth, I feel constrained to declare it solemnly to you and to the nation, and I feel bound to appeal in this matter to the patriotism of every citizen of Italy, and to the representatives of her most eminent cities that discussions may cease, and that he who represents the nation before other powers may be able to proclaim that the necessity of having Rome as the capital is recognized by all the nation. I think I am justified in making this appeal even to those who, for reasons which I respect, differ with me on this point. Yet more; I can assume no Spartan

indifference in the matter. I say frankly that it will be a deep grief to me to tell my native city that she must renounce resolutely and definitively all hope of being the seat of government.

Yes, gentlemen, as far as I am personally concerned, it is no pleasure to go to Rome. Having little artistic taste, I feel sure that in the midst of the splendid monuments of ancient and modern Rome I will lament the plain and unpoetic streets of my native town. But one thing I can say with confidence; knowing the character of my fellow-citizens; knowing from actual facts how ready they have always been to make the greatest sacrifices for the sacred cause of Italy; knowing their willingness to make sacrifices when their city was invaded by the enemy and their promptness and energy in its defense; knowing all this, I have no fear that they will not uphold me when, in their name and as their deputy, I say that Turin is ready to make this great sacrifice in the interests of united Italy.

I am comforted by the hope — I may even say the certainty — that when Italy shall have established the seat of government in the eternal city, she will not be ungrateful to this land which was the cradle of liberty; to this land in which was sown that germ of independence which, maturing rapidly and branching out, has now reached forth its tendrils from Sicily to the Alps.

I have said and I repeat: Rome, and Rome only, should be the capital of Italy.

But here begin the difficulties of the problem. We must go to Rome, but there are two conditions: we must go there in concert with France, otherwise the union of Rome with the rest of Italy will be interpreted by the great mass of Catholics, within Italy and without, as the signal of the slavery of the Church. We must go, therefore, to Rome in such a way that the true independence of the Pontiff will not be diminished. We must go to Rome, but the civil power must not extend to spiritual things. These are the two conditions that must be fulfilled if this united Italy is to exist.

As to the first, it would be folly, in the present condition of affairs in Europe, to think of going to Rome in the face of the opposition of France. Yet more: even if, through events which I believe improbable and impossible, France were reduced to a condition which forbade material interference with our actions, we should none the less avoid uniting Rome to the rest of Italy, if, by so doing, we caused loss to our allies.

We have contracted a great debt towards France. I do not claim that the narrow moral code which affects individual actions should be applied *ad literam* to international relations. Still there are certain moral principles which even nations may not violate with impunity.

I know that many diplomats profess contrary views. I remember hearing a famous Austrian statesman applauded a few years ago when he laughingly declared that in a short time Austria would astound Europe by her ingratitude to Russia. As a matter of fact, Austria kept her word; you already know, and if you do not, I can testify to the fact, that at the Congress of Paris no power showed more hostility to Russia nor tried harder to aggravate the conditions of peace than Austria, whose sword had done nothing toward imposing peace upon her old ally. But, gentlemen, the violation of that great moral principle did not go unpunished. After a few years Russia had her revenge, and we should be glad of it, for I do not hesitate to attribute to the unforgotten ingratitude of Austria the facility with which friendly relations were established between Russia and ourselves, relations now unfortunately interrupted, but, I hope, without changing the feelings of Russia for Italy, and without any alteration of the sympathy for us which has always dwelt in the bosom of the Czar.

Gentlemen, we have an even graver motive for co-operating with France. When, in 1859, we invoked French aid, when the Emperor consented to descend into Italy at the head of his legions, he made no secret of his pledges to the court of Rome. We accepted his aid without protest against those pledges. Now, after reaping such advantages from that alliance, we can protest against the pledges only to a certain point. But then, you will object, the solution of the Roman question is impossible!

I answer: if the second of our conditions is fulfilled, the first will offer few obstacles. That is, if we can so act that the reunion of Rome to Italy does not cause alarm to Catholic society. By Catholic society I mean the great mass of people who profess religious belief from conviction and not for political ends, and who are free from vulgar prejudices. If, I say, we can persuade the great mass of Catholics that the uniting of Rome to Italy can be accomplished without sacrificing the liberty of the Church, the problem will, I think, be solved.

We must not deceive ourselves; there are many who, while not prejudiced against Italy nor against liberal ideas, yet fear that if Rome were united to Italy, the seat of Italian government established there and the King seated in the Quirinal, the Pontiff would lose both dignity and independence; they fear that the Pope instead of being the head of Catholicism would be reduced to the rank of grand almoner or head chaplain.

If these fears were well founded, if the fall of the temporal power would really have this consequence, I would not hesitate to say that the union of Rome to the Italian State would be fatal not only to Catholicism but to the existence of Italy itself. Yet, further, I can imagine no greater misfortune for a cultured people than to see in the hands of its rulers not only the civil but also the religious power.

The history of centuries proves to us that wherever this union was consummated, civilization immediately ceased to advance and, therefore, necessarily began to retrograde; the most detestable of despotisms followed, and this, whether a caste of priests usurped the temporal power or a caliph or sultan seized control of things spiritual. Everywhere this fatal union has produced the same result; God forbid that it should ever be so here! . . . .

When these doctrines have received the solemn sanction of the national Parliament, when it will be no longer lawful to doubt the feelings of Italians, when it is clear to the world that they are not hostile to the religion of their fathers, but wish to preserve this religion in their country, when it is no longer necessary to show them how to prosper and to develop their resources by combating a power which was an obstacle, not only to the reorganization of Italy but also to the spread of Catholicity, I believe that the greater part of Catholic society will absolve the Italians and will place where it belongs the responsibility of the fatal struggle which the Pope insists upon waging against the country in whose midst he lives.

But God avert this fatal chance! At the risk of being considered Utopian, I believe that when the proclamation of the principles which I have just declared, and when the indorsement of them that you will give are known and considered at Rome and in the Vatican, I believe, I say, that those Italian fibres which the reactionary party has, as yet, been unable to remove from the heart of Pius IX., will again vibrate, and there will be accomplished the greatest act that any people has yet performed. And so it will be given to the same generation to have restored a nation, and to have done what is yet greater, yet more sublime, an act of which the influence is incalculable, that is, to have reconciled the papacy with the civil power, to have made peace between Church and State, between the spirit of religion and the great principles of liberty. Yes, I hope that it will be given us to compass these two great acts which will most assuredly carry to the most distant posterity the worthiness of the present generation of Italians.

PAUL AMAND CHALLEMEL-LACOUR

(1827–1896)

AMONG the brilliant leaders under the existing Republic in France, one of the most cultivated and most honored has been Challemel-Lacour, so long the intimate friend and coadjutor of Gambetta, and latterly "one of the presidential possibilities" frequently considered. His first position after leaving the École Normale was the chair of French Literature at Zurich. But his ardent Republicanism soon drew him back to France and into journalism. In 1868 he joined Gambetta, Brisson, and Allain-Targé in founding the Revue Politique; became a member of the Chamber of Deputies in 1872 and a Senator in 1876. While a Senator he again joined Gambetta in founding a public journal, La République Française, of which, until appointed Minister Plenipotentiary at Berne, he was one of the principal writers. He was Ambassador to England from 1880 to 1882; became Minister of Foreign Affairs in 1883; was re-elected Senator in 1885, and was made President of the Senate in 1893.

HUMBOLDT AND THE TEUTONIC INTELLECT

(From the Oration on the Character and Work of Humboldt)

IT WOULD be impossible for a scientist to say that two molecules of matter can ever reach an absolute contact. It is almost as impossible that a French and a German spirit should ever, fully and reciprocally understand each other. Whoever will attempt to bring to the full comprehension of his fellows a man who represents the highest Germanic type will be tempted more than once to renounce his task. I do not deny I had several discouragements in studying William von Humboldt. All reasons which could explain and at the same time aggravate this difficulty were united in him. I shall note but two. We love to note the fame of a man by the works which survive him. "The worth of the work is the worth of the man" is a French proverb. If we did not expect to obtain positive results at least in proportion to our efforts, we should look upon all labor as a useless fatigue, which it would be absurd to impose.

When some day a Parisian, fired with literary ambition, passes along the quays meditating the work which shall be his masterpiece; if he realize that it will soon be on its way to that long necropolis which swallows indiscriminately the good and the bad, this is risking the work at once, for it might go up in smoke.

When in a moment of generous exaltation you are tempted to resign yourself to public affairs, a single reflection on all the lives uselessly expended in the public service will dampen your ardor, and you, I know, will repress a smile when you think of the public men confined to their tents after many fruitless conflicts, and after having seen effaced the last traces of their labor.

With these characteristics, it is not easy for us to understand those who, without disdaining success, seem to seek in labor only their own personal satisfaction; a philosopher delighting in his own system; a musician entranced day by day in his closet, as Sebastian Bach was for twenty years, hearing oratorios that no orchestra would ever execute, and masterpieces of harmony that no human ear would ever hear. This temperament can be recognized, unless I am much mistaken, in a more or less pronounced degree, in all Germans. We shall soon see the degree to which it dominated William von Humboldt.

Little is wanting to consign us to the specialization which is the inevitable tendency of modern civilization. Without doubt we touch on all things but as dilettanti; we rarely dare in an assembly to reason on everything, from theology to astronomy, without penetrating science with that light ignorance which seems to be one of the gracious moods of the French spirit. But we seem to decide at a comparatively early date, and with good grace, to be this or to be that; we are ambitious and are more flattered to be something than to be somebody, and when we have made a choice we consecrate ourselves to our part with the determination to succeed. We feel no regret at the sacrifices renounced in other lines, since these are the conditions of success, and consequently of wisdom.

To be frank, we must admit the surprise with which we observe the relative universality of certain Germans, and we explain it by saying there is much darkness in those vast brains over the Rhine, or try to persuade ourselves that this varied science is only superficial. Nevertheless, the desire to corral themselves in a separate corner of the intellectual world seems essentially to belong to the Germanic character. Only as a last

choice does the German lock himself up in a narrow and restricted corner. A German who has passed all four faculties before selecting a definite profession is no great rarity, and these are mastered not in a curious desire to effervesce in studies, but taken in hand seriously as a conscientious undertaking. Hence, in German writings we find the tendency to multiply the aspects of a subject; to follow it, not without some prolixity and confusion, through all its ramifications in the order of thought. Happily, then, sometimes to this desire to embrace the entire intellectual world is added the ardent desire to explore the forces of terrestrial realities.

I know that many Frenchmen, some of the greatest, including the Encyclopedists and Voltaire, have also addressed their minds to all the provinces of science, philosophy, history, and poetry. The writers of the eighteenth century asked no better examples, even if from time to time the Bastille assisted in restoring order or tempering their ardor. But all these men, it must be admitted, were seeking more to increase their influence than obeying a personal universal feeling. Without lacking respect for the genius of Voltaire, it may be said that the poetical and tragic inspiration with him was not very masterful; his poetry seems voluntary and measured, a sort of a popular philosophy. That which he pursued by all the routes of his intelligence was the conquest of minds, the reversal of prejudices, success, glory, revolution.

In the Germans, on the contrary, this aspiration, sometimes immoderate, for knowledge of universal science, is commonly manifested, and in William von Humboldt we recognize, in a pre-eminent degree, this trait of the national organization. Philosopher, translator, historian, publicist, humanitarian, linguist, poet, and statesman, he devoted himself carefully to the simultaneous culture of all his faculties; he permitted the withering of no single branch of his mighty spirit. When at last he had to adopt a specialty, as all must end there, he had become the first linguist in Europe. He made this science the one about which he carefully grouped all the others. His style breathes this tendency to be complete; he would reflect in every sentence all the aspects of the nature of things. It is not always easy to find one's self in the windings of his majestic style, limpid as air, changeable as Proteus, making a model for itself of the complex human brain as if it would reproduce it entirely. These peculiarities, it were useful to remember, for they explain in a great measure one side of our indifference towards those whom we have been unable to understand, the many intelligent Germans whom we should sincerely endeavor to understand.

It may be asked, Why not consider the fresh, living works instead of making the dead author our sole topic? The reply is that in not separating the man from his works I respectfully conform to what seems to be erected into a law in contemporary criticism. But there is another reply—the abstraction of the man would be a hindrance in effect to the understanding of the works. Singular as the statement may be and whatever the value of the works of William von Humboldt, it was first of all for himself and his own mental enjoyment that he produced them. It is a mistake to study him as if he works exclusively in view of public demand. This would not be just to the author. By its form as well as its quantity the labor of Humboldt is placed beyond the reach of the majority. The special scientists, who do not fail to recognize in him the equal of the greatest, admire his labor but do not unreservedly accept it. Besides, this work has never been made for the mass of readers, for the reason that in its progress it touches regions of which the masses know nothing. To them all knowledge which cannot be resolved into a palpable, common, and permanent utility, seems problematical, or under a shade of mysticism.

It is not altogether false to say that the works of Humboldt appear, in part, of a questionable, or at least a restricted, utility. They reveal a man of mind and thought, worthy of being known rather than one to teach a science, resolve a problem or present in a popular manner a certain number of truths. They testify to a high aspiration for moral advancement; they offer the varied developments, difficult to follow, of a strong intelligence, showing its strength by magnificent essays, rather than by works which could be profitably enjoyed without thought of their author. His pages show the studies of the man, nothing more, because all his works show himself, what he was—a man one would not rate as a politician, although William von Humboldt has been a diplomat and a minister and has taken part in the important movements of his time; nor as a philosopher, though he has agitated the capital questions of the philosopher; nor as a linguist, though he has been placed in the front rank of this science. We would simply credit him with the sustained efforts he made to prevent the

dulling of any of the powers which constituted the man: imagination, sentiment, reason, active energy. From this standpoint, Humboldt appears to me useful to study, for the methods of his work and for the extent to which he has succeeded.

Let me ask that no one attribute to me the desire to make a statue or even a bust. It would need an adept hand to sketch with truth such a moral figure, firmly established within itself, but with no one characteristic salient enough to define the man with a word. The sketch would be false if the details were not blended into each other in such equilibrium as to temper the impression of one by the other, and to impress rather by the general physiognomy than by the dominant effect of this or that accentuated trait.

THOMAS CHALMERS

(1780–1847)

SINCE the union with England, the most distinctive eloquence of Scotland has been that of the platform or pulpit rather than of the forum, and among Scottish pulpit orators Thomas Chalmers holds a first rank. He is hardly less distinguished as an author, for his works on astronomy, moral philosophy, political economy, theology, and other subjects, make over thirty considerable volumes. His discourses in the pulpit, as well as the 'Discourses on Astronomy' he published during his lifetime, achieved an extraordinary popularity. He was born at East Anstruther, Fifeshire, Scotland, March 17th, 1780; educated at St. Andrew's; and licensed as a minister of the Church of Scotland in his nineteenth year. He died at Morningside, near Edinburgh, March 30th, 1847.

WHEN OLD THINGS PASS AWAY

(From a Discourse, 'The Expulsive Power of a New Affection')

CONCEIVE a man to be standing on the margin of this green world, and that, when he looked toward it, he saw abundance smiling upon every field, with all the blessings which earth can afford scattered in profusion throughout every family, with the light of the sun sweetly resting upon all the pleasant habitations, and the joys of human companionship brightening many a happy circle of society—conceive this to be the general character of the scene upon one side of his contemplation, and that on the other, beyond the verge of the goodly planet on which he was situated, he could descry nothing but a dark and fathomless unknown. Think you that he would bid a voluntary adieu to all the brightness and all the beauty that were before him upon earth, and commit himself to the frightful solitude away from it? Would he leave its peopled dwelling-places and become a solitary wanderer through the fields of nonentity? If space offered him nothing but a wilderness, would he for it abandon the home-bred scenes of life and of cheerfulness that lay so near and exerted such a power of urgency to detain him?

Would not he cling to the regions of sense and of life and of society?—and shrinking away from the desolation that was beyond it, would not he be glad to keep his firm footing on the territory of this world and to take shelter under the silver canopy that was stretched over it?

But if, during the time of his contemplation, some happy island of the blest had floated by, and there had burst upon his senses the light of its surpassing glories, and its sounds of sweeter melody, and he clearly saw that there a purer beauty rested upon every field, and a more heartfelt joy spread itself among all the families, and he could discern there a peace and a piety and a benevolence which put a moral gladness into every bosom, and united the whole society in one rejoicing sympathy with each other and with the beneficent Father of them all; could he further see that pain and mortality were there unknown, and, above all, that signals of welcome were hung out, and an avenue of communication was made for him—perceive you not that what was before the wilderness would become the land of invitation, and what now the world would be the wilderness? What unpeopled space could not do can be done by space teeming with beatific scenes and beatific society. And let the existing tendencies of the heart be what they may to the scene that is near and visible around us, still if another stood revealed to the prospect of man, either through the channel of faith, or through the channel of his senses, then, without violence done to the constitution of his moral nature, may he die unto the present world, and live to the lovelier world that stands in the distance away from it.

WAR AND TRUTH

ON every side of me I see causes at work which go to spread a most delusive coloring over war and to remove its shocking barbarities to the background of our contemplations altogether. I see it in the history which tells me of the superb appearance of the troops and the brilliancy of their successive charges. I see it in the poetry which lends the magic of its numbers to the narrative of blood, and transports its many admirers, as by its images and its figures and its nodding plumes of chivalry it throws its treacherous embellishments over a scene of legalized slaughter. I see it in the music which represents the progress of the battle, and where, after being inspired by the trumpet-notes of preparation, the whole beauty and tenderness of a drawing-room are seen to bend over the sentimental entertainment; nor do I hear the utterance of a single sigh to interrupt the death-tones of the thickening contest and the moans of the wounded men, as they fade away upon the ear and sink into lifeless silence.

All, all, goes to prove what strange and half-sighted creatures we are. Were it not so, war could never have been seen in any other aspect than that of unmingled hatefulness; and I can look to nothing but to the progress of Christian sentiment upon earth to arrest the strong current of the popular and prevailing partiality for war. Then only will an imperious sense of duty lay the check of severe principle on all the subordinate tastes and faculties of our nature. Then will glory be reduced to its right estimate, and the wakeful benevolence of the Gospel, chasing away every spell, will be turned by the treachery of no delusion whatever from its simple but sublime enterprises for the good of the species. Then the reign of truth and quietness will be ushered into the world, and war — cruel, atrocious, unrelenting war — will be stripped of its many and its bewildering fascinations.

THE USE OF LIVING

THOUSANDS of men breathe, move, and live; pass off the stage of life, and are heard of no more. Why? They did not a particle of good in the world; and none were blest by them, none could point to them as the instrument of their redemption; not a line they wrote, not a word they spoke, could be recalled, and so they perished — their light went out in darkness, and they were not remembered more than the insects of yesterday. Will you thus live and die, O man immortal? Live for something. Do good, and leave behind you a monument of virtue that the storms of time can never destroy. Write your name by kindness, love, and mercy, on the hearts of the thousands you come in contact with year by year, and you will never be forgotten. No, your name, your deeds, will be as legible on the hearts you leave behind as the stars on the brow of evening. Good deeds will shine as bright on the earth as the stars of heaven.

III—65

boroughs returns 290 members, and a third population, also of 6,000,000, but residing in 16 great constituencies, only returns 36 members. The last of these 6,000,000 has only one-eighth of the political power which is conferred upon the 6,000,000 in the other boroughs; it has only about one-fourth of the political power which is conferred upon the 6,000,000 in the counties.

And why is this last population singled out and its representation minimized in this way? You know that it is the most active, the most intelligent part of the whole population of the Kingdom. The people who live in these great centres of the population enjoy an active political life which is not known elsewhere. They manage their own affairs with singular aptitude, discretion, and fairness. Why should not they be allowed to have their proportionate share in managing the affairs of the nation? Well, do you not think that the time has come when we should strive to substitute a real and honest representation of the people for this fraudulent thing which is called representation now? I will give you only one more illustration, and I will sit down — I will not go out of our own county. Warwick is an interesting place. It is generally in rather a dead-alive condition; but, twice a year, when Birmingham and its vast population is at a great expense and inconvenience to carry on its legal business, it awakens into a delusive animation. Warwick has a population of under 12,000 souls, less than the population of any one of the wards of this great borough. Warwick returns two members to Parliament, and if strict proportion were observed there are enough people in this hall to return six members to Parliament. As for Birmingham, our population is 400,000, and the annual increment of that population is so great that every two years we add another Warwick to our number. We return three members, and, lest you should be surfeited with this generous distribution of political power, you are only permitted to give two votes apiece, and so it happens that an elector of Warwick has thirty-four times the political power of every elector of Birmingham.

I have a great respect for the electors of Warwick; they seem to me to be modest and humble-minded men. They appear to feel they cannot lay claim to being six times as good, as virtuous, as intelligent as the electors of Birmingham, and consequently they return one Liberal and one Conservative, and so they deprive themselves of political power. Well, that is very public-spirited, and very self-denying, but why should they be

JOSEPH CHAMBERLAIN

(1836–)

FOR about fifteen years prior to 1886 Joseph Chamberlain stood next to John Bright as an orator, thinker, and leader of the English Radicals, and it was expected that he would wear Bright's mantle as an undisputed inheritance. But a rupture with Gladstone on the Irish Home Rule question in that year induced Chamberlain to organize the Liberal Unionist party, form a coalition between it and the Conservative party, and thus become a member of a Conservative Ministry and distinguish himself thenceforward rather by "jingoism" than by continuing the labors of John Bright. British Conservatives are no longer disturbed by Mr. Chamberlain's forcible and eloquent speeches advocating schemes akin to State socialism, or urging Church disestablishment, progressive income taxes, and the recovery of the "unearned increment" of land by land taxes. But, no matter which side of a question he takes, his speeches are always eloquent, plausible, and vigorous. He never fails to awaken and interest his hearers. He was born in London in July 1836, and was educated at the University School College. He afterwards became Mayor of Birmingham, Chairman of her School Board, and President of the School of Design. He began in 1876 his long service as a representative of Birmingham in the House of Commons, in which he soon became a power. In a Liberal Ministry he held the position of President of the Board of Trade (1880–85). He was made President of the Local Government Board in 1886, but soon afterwards resigned on account of his opposition to the Ministry's Home Rule measure. When the Salisbury Ministry asked his help he took the place of Colonial Secretary under it.

MANHOOD SUFFRAGE

(From a Speech at the Bright Celebration, in Birmingham, England, June 13th, 1883)

IN 1858 Mr. Bright told us that one-sixth of the electors returned half the House of Commons. At this moment, in 1883, one-fifth of the electors do the same. A population of 6,000,000 in the United Kingdom in 85 counties returns 136 members, and a similar population of exactly the same number in 217

forced to this alternative, which is very creditable to their good feeling, but very prejudicial to their political interests?

I need not dwell further upon these anomalies. If they were only anomalies I should not much care, but they are real obstacles to the legislation that is required in the interests of the people. Now, just let me sum up the situation. What does our Constitution do for us? First, it excludes from all political rights more than half the adult male population; and remember the class which is excluded is the most numerous class; but it is all one class, and every other class is represented to its last man. Well, then, in the next place, of the remainder four-fifths are out-voted by one-fifth, and so it happens that one-twelfth of what ought to be the whole constituency of the Kingdom returns a majority of the House of Commons. If the one-twelfth really represented the free voice of the people, it would not be of so much consequence; but you know, in many cases at all events, it only represents the influences of some great territorial family, or some local magnate.

Among the numerous discoveries which we owe to science, I was much interested some time ago in reading of one which I think was called the megaphone. Its province was to expand and develop the sounds which were intrusted to it. By its means a whisper becomes a roar. Well, at every general election you hear the roar of the parliamentary representative system, and some people are deceived; they think it the thunderous voice of the people to which they are listening. But if they would only trace it to its source they would find it was the whisper of some few privileged individuals swollen and expanded by the ingenious political megaphones which I have described to you. Do you wonder that in an arrangement like this every vested interest, every time-worn privilege, every ancient abuse, finds its account?

"Now a'nt this a system worth pains in preserving?
"When people finds joints and their friends does the carving."

I say it is time to make an effort to put the representation of the people upon a purer basis, and safer foundation. How shall we put the dots on the *i's*? What do we want?

We want, in the first place, a suffrage from which no man who is not disqualified by crime, or the receipt of relief, who is expected to fulfill the obligations of a citizen, shall be excluded.

We want equal electoral districts, in order that every vote may have an equal value, and we want, I think, the payment of members, in order that every man who has the capacity to serve his country, who has honesty, intelligence, and who is selected for that purpose by his fellow-countrymen, shall not be excluded for want of means.

That is what we want; what we shall get is another matter. We may have once more to take a composition. But mind, under my new bill, we will not give the debtor his discharge. This is a question in which Birmingham ought to take a foremost part. To Lancashire belongs the glory and the honor of the great struggle which freed the people's bread; from Yorktown came some of the most eloquent and able exponents of the principle of religious equality; to Birmingham it has twice been reserved to sound the trumpet note of parliamentary reform, to lead the van; and if we are faithful to our traditions, if we are true to the principles which we have inherited, we shall never cease, nor turn from the plow until we have completed the task which our forefathers commenced, until we have associated the whole people in the work of the Government, and until we have secured equal rights and equal privileges to every one who obeys the law and who contributes by his industry, his toil, or his intelligence to the true greatness and prosperity of the Empire.

ZACHARIAH CHANDLER

(1813–1879)

ZACHARIAH CHANDLER was a strong partisan, growing more intense as he grew older. Absolutely convinced of his own rectitude, it was not easy for him to be patient with those who combated his views. He was, moreover, one of those strong men who, not tolerating half-way measures, instinctively believe in the most thorough methods of demolishing opposition. It does not follow, and it is not true, that he was deficient in «the milk of human kindness» because he was «a good hater» and never in his life abated his political animosities, but his speeches in their strong expression of partisanship are valuable historically as expressions of the spirit of a period of violent political passion by which he himself was deeply moved.

He was born in Bedford, New Hampshire, December 10th, 1813; settled in Michigan; became a prosperous merchant, and in 1851 Mayor of Detroit; was defeated as the Whig nominee for Governor of Michigan in 1852; was active in the organization of the Republican party in 1854; succeeded Lewis Cass in the Senate in 1857; continued in the Senate until 1875; was Secretary of the Interior (1875–77); was re-elected Senator in 1879, and died in Chicago November 1st of the same year.

ON JEFFERSON DAVIS

(From the Debate in the United States Senate March 3d, 1879, on the Bill to Pension Veterans of the Mexican War)

Mr. President:—

TWENTY-TWO years ago to-morrow, in the old Hall of the Senate, now occupied by the Supreme Court of the United States, I, in company with Mr. Jefferson Davis, stood up and swore before Almighty God that I would support the Constitution of the United States. Mr. Jefferson Davis came from the Cabinet of Franklin Pierce into the Senate of the United States and took the oath with me to be faithful to this Government. During four years I sat in this body with Mr. Jefferson Davis and saw the preparations going on from day to day for

the overthrow of this Government. With treason in his heart and perjury upon his lips he took the oath to sustain the Government that he meant to overthrow.

Sir, there was method in that madness. He, in co-operation with other men from his section and in the Cabinet of Mr. Buchanan, made careful preparation for the event that was to follow. Your armies were scattered over all this broad land, where they could not be used in an emergency; your fleets were scattered wherever the winds blew and water was found to float them, where they could not be used to put down rebellion; your Treasury was depleted until your bonds bearing six per cent., principal and interest payable in coin, were sold for eighty-eight cents on the dollar for current expenses and no buyers. Preparations were carefully made. Your arms were sold under an apparently innocent clause in the Army Bill providing that the Secretary of War might, at his discretion, sell such arms as he deemed it for the interest of the Government to sell.

Sir, eighteen years ago last month I sat in these Halls and listened to Jefferson Davis delivering his farewell address, informing us what our constitutional duties to this Government were, and then he left and entered into the rebellion to overthrow the Government that he had sworn to support! I remained here, sir, during the whole of that terrible rebellion. I saw our brave soldiers by thousands and hundreds of thousands, aye, I might say millions, pass through to the theatre of war, and I saw their shattered ranks return; I saw steamboat after steamboat and railroad train after railroad train arrive with the maimed and the wounded; I was with my friend from Rhode Island [Mr. Burnside] when he commanded the Army of the Potomac, and saw piles of legs and arms that made humanity shudder; I saw the widow and the orphan in their homes, and heard the weeping and wailing of those who had lost their dearest and their best. Mr. President, I little thought at that time that I should live to hear in the Senate of the United States eulogies upon Jefferson Davis, living—a living rebel eulogized on the floor of the Senate of the United States! Sir, I am amazed to hear it; and I can tell the gentlemen on the other side that they little know the spirit of the North when they come here at this day and with bravado on their lips utter eulogies upon a man whom every man, woman, and child in the North believes to have been a double-dyed traitor to his Government.

WILLIAM ELLERY CHANNING

(1780–1842)

AFTER he had won the adoration and friendship of «the Lake Poets,» by a prolonged visit to them, Doctor Channing was described in 1823, by Samuel Taylor Coleridge, in a letter to Washington Alston, as one who had both «the love of wisdom and the wisdom of love.» Born in Newport, Rhode Island, April 7th, 1780, and educated at Harvard, he began preaching in 1802, and became pastor of the Federal Street Church in Boston in 1803. In defining the point of view from which he reasoned, he once said: «I wish to regard myself as belonging not to a sect, but to the community of lovers of truth and followers of Christ. . . . I desire to escape the narrow walls of a particular church and to stand under the open sky in the broad light, looking far and wide, seeing with my own eyes, hearing with my own ears, and following Truth meekly, but resolutely, however arduous or solitary be the path in which she leads.» This, indeed, was the chart by which he attempted to direct his whole course as a writer and orator. Always a philanthropist and reformer, discussing all current moral and social questions, he made himself especially prominent as a promoter of the agitation against slavery. He published a book against slavery as early as 1835 and in 1837 protested against the annexation of Texas, openly declaring that he preferred a dissolution of the Union to an extension of slave territory. Advanced and daring schemes for the relief and improvement of the poor were apt to find in him always an earnest and zealous supporter. He died October 2d, 1842, while on a journey at Bennington, Vermont, and a collection of his works published in this country has been republished in London.

THE MAN ABOVE THE STATE

A MAN, by his very nature, as an intelligent, moral creature of God, has claims to aid and kind regard from all other men. There is a grand law of humanity more comprehensive than all others, and under which every man should find shelter. He has not only a right, but is bound to use freely and improve the powers which God has given him, and other men, instead of obstructing, are bound to assist their development and exertion. These claims a man does not derive from the family or tribe in which he began his being. They are not the growth of a particular soil; they are not ripened under a peculiar sky; they are not written on a particular complexion; they belong to human nature. The ground on which one man asserts them all men stand on, nor can they be denied to one without being denied to all. We have here a common interest. We must all stand or fall together. We all have claims on our race, claims of kindness and justice, claims grounded on our relation to our common father, and on the inheritance of a common nature.

Because a number of men invade the rights of a fellow-creature and pronounce him destitute of rights, his claims are not a whit touched by this. He is as much a man as before. Not a single gift of God on which his rights rest is taken away. His relations to the rest of his race are in no measure affected. He is as truly their brother as if his tribe had not pronounced him a brute. If, indeed, any change takes place, his claims are enhanced, on the ground that the suffering and injured are entitled to peculiar regard. If any rights should be singularly sacred in our sight, they are those which are denied and trodden in the dust.

It seems to be thought by some that a man derives all his rights from the nation to which he belongs. They are gifts of the State, and the State may take them away if it will. A man, it is thought, has claims on other men, not as a man, but as an Englishman, an American, or a subject of some other State. He must produce his parchment of citizenship before he binds other men to protect him, to respect his free agency, to leave him the use of his powers according to his own will. Local, municipal law is thus made the fountain and measure of rights. The stranger must tell us where he was born, what privileges he enjoyed at home, or no tie links us to one another.

In conformity to these views, it is thought that when one community declares a man to be a slave other communities must respect this decree; that the duties of a foreign nation to an individual are to be determined by a brand set on him on his own shores; that his relations to the whole race may be affected by the local act of a community, no matter how small or how unjust.

This is a terrible doctrine. It strikes a blow at all the rights of human nature. It enables the political body to which we belong, no matter how wicked or weak, to make each of us an outcast from his race. It makes a man nothing in himself. As a man, he has no significance. He is sacred only as far as some State has taken him under its care. Stripped of his nationality, he is at the mercy of all who may incline to lay hold on him. He may be seized, imprisoned, sent to work in galleys or mines, unless some foreign State spreads its shield over him as one of its citizens.

This doctrine is as false as it is terrible. Man is not the mere creature of the State. Man is older than nations, and he is to survive nations. There is a law of humanity more primitive and divine than the law of the land. He has higher claims than those of a citizen. He has rights which date before all charters and communities; not conventional, not repealable, but as eternal as the powers and laws of his being.

This annihilation of the individual by merging him in the State lies at the foundation of despotism. The nation is too often the grave of the man. This is the more monstrous, because the very end of the State, of the organization of the nation, is to secure the individual in all his rights, and especially to secure the rights of the weak. Here is the fundamental idea of political association. In an unorganized society, with no legislation, no tribunal, no empire, rights have no security. Force predominates over right. This is the grand evil of what is called the state of nature. To repress this, to give right the ascendency over force, this is the grand idea and end of government, of country, of political constitutions. And yet we are taught that it depends on the law of a man's country, whether he shall have rights, and whether other States shall regard him as a man. When cast on a foreign shore, his country, and not his humanity, is to be inquired into, and the treatment he receives is to be proportioned to what he meets at home. Men worship power, worship great organizations, and overlook the individual; and few things have depraved the moral sentiment of men more, or brought greater woes on the race. The State, or the ruler in whom the State is embodied, continues to be worshiped, notwithstanding the commission of crimes which would inspire horror in the private man. How insignificant are the robberies, murders, piracies, which the law makes capital, in com-

parison with an unjust or unnecessary war, dooming thousands, perhaps millions, of the innocent to the most torturing forms of death, or, with the law of an autocrat or of a public body, depriving millions of all the rights of men! But these, because the acts of the State, escape the execrations of the world.

In consequence of this worship of governments it is thought that their relations to one another are alone important. A government is too great to look at a stranger, except as he is incorporated with some State. It can have nothing to do with political organizations like itself. But the humble stranger has a claim on it as sacred as another State. Standing alone, he yet has rights, and to violate them is as criminal as to violate the stipulations with a foreign power. In one view it is baser. It is as true of governments as of individuals, that it is base and unmanly to trample on the weak. He who invades the strong shows a courage which does something to redeem his violence; but to tread on the neck of a helpless, friendless fellow-creature is to add meanness to wrong.

If the doctrine be true that the character impressed on a man at home follows him abroad, and that he is to be regarded, not as a man, but as the local laws which he has left regard him, why shall not this apply to the peculiar advantages as well as disadvantages which a man enjoys in his own land? Why shall not he whom the laws invest with a right to universal homage at home receive the same tribute abroad? Why shall not he whose rank exempts him from the ordinary restraints of law on his own shores claim the same lawlessness elsewhere? Abroad these distinctions avail him nothing. The local law which makes him a kind of deity deserts him the moment he takes a step beyond his country's borders; and why shall the disadvantages, the terrible wrongs, which that law inflicts, follow the poor sufferer to the end of the earth?

I repeat it, for the truth deserves reiteration, that all nations are bound to respect the rights of every human being. This is God's law, as old as the world. No local law can touch it.

EDWIN HUBBELL CHAPIN

(1814–1880)

DOCTOR CHAPIN was one of the public men who divided with Beecher, Theodore Parker, and Wendell Phillips, the attention of his generation of Americans on the lecture platform at a time when that platform and the pulpit were doing far more than the politicians to influence the public mind on questions of political and social reform. He was born in Union Village, Washington County, New York, in 1814, and ordained at Utica as a Universalist minister in 1837. After having been tutor in a private family in Richmond, Virginia, and serving as pastor of a church in Charlestown, near Boston, the Second Universalist Church of the latter city made him associate pastor with Doctor Ballou. Here he became widely known as a lecturer on temperance, abolition of slavery, and universal peace. He became, in 1849, pastor of the Fourth Universalist Society in New York. His congregation soon outgrew its place of worship and kept on moving to larger and larger buildings until, in 1866, it occupied an immense edifice on the corner of Fifth Avenue and Forty-fifth Street, New York city. In 1872 he succeeded Doctor Emerson as editor of the Christian Leader. The Chapin Home, founded by his congregation, is a memorial of his work. He died December 27th, 1880.

THE SOVEREIGNTY OF IDEAS

IT IS sufficient that men have felt and enunciated the sublime doctrine that "knowledge is power;" that, as mind is superior to matter, so are ideas more potent and enduring than prodigies of physical might. Archimedes's thought is stronger than his lever. The mind that planned the pyramids was more powerful than the hands that piled them. The inventors of the mariner's compass and the telescope have outdone the Macedonian, and won new worlds. And the influence of the Cæsars seems mean and narrow beside the imperial dominion of the printing-press. Physical force is sectional, and acts in defined methods. But knowledge defies gravitation, and is not thwarted by space. It is miraculous in the wonder of its achievements, and in its independence of precedent and routine. "Knowledge is power!" Man gains wider dominion by his intellect than by his right arm The mustard-seed of thought is a pregnant treasury of vast results. Like the germ in Egyptian tombs, its vitality never perishes, and its fruit will spring up after it has been buried for long ages. To the superficial eye, the plain of modern history is merely an arena of battle and treaty, colonization and revolution. To the student, this modern history, so diversified and mutable, indicates more than this. Luther and Cromwell, Pilgrim Rock and the Declaration of Independence, are the results of an invisible but mighty power—a leveling and exalting power—a power which, with no mere Cyclopean effort, no fitful Ætna convulsion, but with silent throbbings, like some great tidal force in nature, is slowly undermining all falsehood, and heaving the mass of humanity upwards. But to dwell upon the power of knowledge, intellect, thought, is to run into trite declamation. The scholar who has wrung this power in toil and sacrifice knows it full well. He sees it, in secret places, distilling as the dew, and dropping as the gentle rain from heaven, and everywhere diffusing its potent spell. He experiences its superiority over nature and brute force. He knows its conquests in the past and in the future.

PEACEFUL INDUSTRY

WHO can adequately describe the triumphs of labor, urged on by the potent spell of money? It has extorted the secrets of the universe and trained its forms into myriads of powers of use and beauty. From the bosom of the old creation it has developed anew the creation of industry and art. It has been its task and its glory to overcome obstacles. Mountains have been leveled and valleys have been exalted before it. It has broken the rocky soil into fertile glades; it has crowned the hill tops with verdure, and bound round the very feet of ocean, ridges of golden corn. Up from the sunless and hoary deeps, up from the shapeless quarry, it drags its spotless marbles and rears its palaces of pomp. It steals the stubborn metals from the bowels of the globe, and makes them ductile to its will. It marches steadily on over the swelling flood and through the

Come, Howard, from the gloom of the prison and the taint of the lazar house, and show us what philanthropy can do when imbued with the spirit of Jesus. Come, Eliot, from the thick forest where the red man listens to the Word of Life;—come, Penn, from thy sweet counsel and weaponless victory,—and show us what Christian zeal and Christian love can accomplish with the rudest barbarians or the fiercest hearts. Come, Raikes, from thy labors with the ignorant and the poor, and show us with what an eye this faith regards the lowest and least of our race; and how diligently it labors, not for the body, not for the rank, but for the plastic soul that is to course the ages of immortality. And ye, who are a great number,—ye nameless ones,—who have done good in your narrow spheres, content to forego renown on earth, and seeking your record in the Record on High,—come and tell us how kindly a spirit, how lofty a purpose, or how strong a courage the religion ye professed can breathe into the poor, the humble, and the weak. Go forth, then, spirit of Christianity, to thy great work of reform! The past bears witness to thee in the blood of thy martyrs, and the ashes of thy saints and heroes; the present is hopeful because of thee; the future shall acknowledge thy omnipotence.

SCIENTIA LIBERATRIX

NO cause is so bound up with religion as the cause of political liberty and the rights of man. Unless I have read history backwards,—unless Magna Charta is a mistake, and the Bill of Rights a sham, and the Declaration of Independence a contumacious falsehood,—unless the sages and heroes and martyrs, who have fought and bled, were impostors,—unless the sublimest transactions in modern history, on Tower Hill, in the Parliaments of London, on the sea-tossed Mayflower,—unless these are all deceitful, there is no cause so linked with religion as the cause of Democratic liberty.

And, sir, not only are all the moral principles, which we can summon up, on the side of this great cause, but the physical movements of the age attend it and advance it. Nature is Republican. The discoveries of Science are Republican. Sir, what are these new forces, steam and electricity, but powers that are leveling all factitious distinctions, and forcing the world on to a

mountain clefts. It fans its way through the winds of ocean, tramples them in its course, surges and mingles them with flakes of fire. Civilization follows in its path. It achieves grander victories, it weaves more durable trophies, it holds wider sway than the conqueror. His name becomes tainted and his monuments crumble; but labor converts his red battlefields into gardens and erects monuments significant of better things. It rides in a chariot driven by the wind. It writes with the lightning. It sits crowned as a queen in a thousand cities, and sends up its roar of triumph from a million wheels. It glistens in the fabric of the loom; it rings and sparkles in the steely hammer; it glories in shapes of beauty; it speaks in words of power; it makes the sinewy arm strong with liberty, the poor man's heart rich with content, crowns the swarthy and sweaty brow with honor, and dignity, and peace.

THE SOURCE OF MODERN PROGRESS

THE great element of reform is not born of human wisdom, it does not draw its life from human organizations. I find it only in Christianity. "Thy kingdom come!" There is a sublime and pregnant burden in this prayer. It is the aspiration of every soul that goes forth in the spirit of reform. For what is the significance of this prayer? It is a petition that all holy influences would penetrate and subdue and dwell in the heart of man, until he shall think, and speak, and do good, from the very necessity of his being. So would the institutions of error and wrong crumble and pass away. So would sin die out from the earth; and the human soul living in harmony with the divine will, this earth would become like heaven. It is too late for the reformers to sneer at Christianity,—it is foolishness for them to reject it. In it are enshrined our faith in human progress,—our confidence in reform. It is indissolubly connected with all that is hopeful, spiritual, capable, in man. That men have misunderstood it, and perverted it, is true. But it is also true that the noblest efforts for human melioration have come out of it,—have been based upon it. Is it not so? Come, ye remembered ones, who sleep the sleep of the Just,—who took your conduct from the line of Christian philosophy,—come from your tombs, and answer!

noble destiny? Have they not already propelled the nineteenth century a thousand years ahead? What are they but the servitors of the people, and not of a class? Does not the poor man of to-day ride in a car dragged by forces such as never waited on kings, or drove the wheels of triumphal chariots? Does he not yoke the lightning, and touch the magnetic nerves of the world? The steam-engine is a Democrat. It is the popular heart that throbs in its iron pulses. And the electric telegraph writes upon the walls of Despotism, *Mene, mené, tekel, upharsin!* There is a process going on in the moral and political world,—like that in the physical world,—crumbling the old Saurian forms of past ages, the heritage of the absurd and unjust feudal system, under which serfs labored and gentlemen spent their lives in fighting and feasting. It is time that this opprobrium of toil were done away. Ashamed to toil, art thou? Ashamed of thy dingy workshop and dusty labor-field; of thy hard hand, scarred with service more honorable than that of war; of thy soiled and weather-stained garments, on which mother Nature has embroidered, midst sun and rain, midst fire and steam, her own heraldic honors? Ashamed of these tokens and titles, and envious of the flaunting robes of imbecile idleness and vanity? It is treason to Nature,—it is impiety to Heaven,—it is breaking Heaven's great ordinance. Toil, I repeat—toil, either of the brain, of the heart, or of the hand, is the only true manhood, the only true nobility.

RECTITUDE HIGHER THAN MORALITY

WHEN, from a right motive, with effort and sacrifice, I help a weak and poor man, I enrich my individual and spiritual being. If I bestow from a mere gush of feeling, I receive no permanent spiritual benefit; if from a bad motive, I impoverish my own heart. Acts, then, which appear the same thing in form, differ widely, considered in their religious bearings. There is the morality of impulse, the morality of selfishness, and the morality of principle, or religious morality. The motive of the first named we obey instantaneously, and it may do good, just as we draw our hands from the flame, and thereby obey a law of our physical nature, though we act without any consideration of that law. A great deal of the morality in the world is of this kind. It may do good, but has no reference to the law of rectitude. It is impulsive, and, therefore, does not indicate a steadfast virtue, or a deep religious life. For the very impulsiveness that leads to the gratification of the sympathies leads to the gratification of the appetites, and thus we often find generous and benevolent characteristics mixed with vicious conduct. Then, as I have said, there is the morality of selfishness. In this instance I may perform many good actions from sheer calculation of material profit. I may be benevolent, because it will increase my reputation for philanthropy. I may be honest, because "honesty is the best policy." But is this the highest, the religious sanction of morality? No; the morality of the religious man is the morality of principle. The motive in his case is not "I will," or "I had better," but "I ought." He recognizes morality as a law, impersonal, overmastering the dictates of mere self, and holding all impulses in subservience to the highest good. The morality of impulse is uncertain. The morality of policy is mean and selfish. The morality of religion is loyal, disinterested, self-sacrificing. It acts from faith in God, and with reference to God.

But another trait separates the religious from the merely formal moralist. It consists in the fact that with him, "morality," as we commonly employ the term, is not all. Piety has its place. His affections not only flow earthward, but turn heavenward. He not only loves his neighbor as himself, but he loves the Lord his God. He not only visits the widows and the fatherless in their affliction, but he keeps himself unspotted from the world. With him toil is prayer, and contentment is thanksgiving, but because he infuses into them a spirit of devotion, which he has cultivated by more solitary and special acts. With him it is a good thing to live honestly, industriously, soberly; but all life is not outward, is not in traffic and labor, and meat and drink. There is an inward world, to which his eyes are often introverted — a world of spiritual experience, of great realities, and everlasting sanctions — a world behind the veil — a holy of holies in his soul, where rests the Shecinah of God's more immediate presence; yea, where he meets God face to face. And it is this that directs his public conduct. The orderly and beautiful method of his life is not the huddled chance work of good impulses, is not the arithmetic of selfishness; but it is a serene and steady plan of being projected from the communion of the oratory, and the meditation of the closet.

III—66

Again, I say, let us not depreciate morality. Let us condemn that ostentatious piety which lifts up holy hands to God, but never stretches them out to help man — which anoints its head with the oil of sanctity, but will not defile its robes with the blood of the abused, or the contact of the guilty — which is loud in profession and poor in performance — which makes long prayers, but devours widows' houses. Let us condemn this, but remember that this is not real religion, only its form; as often, the kind deed, the honest method, is not true morality, only its form. Of both these departments of action let it be said: that these we have done, and not left the other undone. Let us recognize the perfect harmony, nay, the identity of religion and morality, in that One who came from the solitary conflict of the desert, to go about doing good, and who descended from the night-prayer on the mountain to walk and calm the troubled waves of the sea.

SALMON P. CHASE

(1808–1873)

WHEN Abraham Lincoln became President in 1861, he gave the treasury portfolio to Salmon Portland Chase, who had been among the foremost in organizing, in 1841, what was called at the time the "Liberal" or anti-slavery party of Ohio. He had also been for twenty years recognized as one of the wisest and most adroit directors, as well as one of the most devoted adherents of the antislavery movement.

Born in Cornish, New Hampshire, January 13th, 1808, and educated at Dartmouth College, he successfully conducted a classical school for boys in Washington, D. C., while he studied law under William Wirt. Beginning the practice of his profession in Ohio his talents and learning soon made him prominent. His antislavery fervor caused him to be known in Kentucky as "the Attorney-General of Runaway Negroes." Representing Ohio in the United States Senate from 1849 to 1855, he utilized every opportunity with his great stores of legal and historical learning to demonstrate that the antislavery sentiment was but a continuation of the sentiment of the Revolution, and that the antislavery movement was but the revival of a movement begun by the Revolutionary fathers of our government from all sections of the Thirteen Colonies. In fact he always claimed to be a disciple of Thomas Jefferson, separated from some other Democrats chiefly by their rejection of Jefferson's antislavery teachings.

His attitude and prominence made him one of the organizers of the Republican party, he having done much to clear the way for it by wrecking the Whig party. As the Republican nominee for Governor of Ohio he was elected in 1855 and re-elected in 1857 by great majorities. His administration of the Treasury during the great crisis from 1861 to 1864 is part of the country's history. He was appointed Chief-Justice of the Supreme Court in 1864 and presided at the impeachment trial of Andrew Johnson in 1868. It has been said that if, in this trial, he had made it impossible for any one to have suspected him of favoring acquittal, he would have been the Republican nominee for President in 1868. His opinions as recorded in the Supreme Court reports are the best monuments of his judicial fairness, integrity, and ability. Ill health forced him to resign in 1871, and he died in New York city, May 7th, 1873.

THOMAS JEFFERSON AND THE COLONIAL VIEW OF MANHOOD RIGHTS

(From a Speech in the Senate, March 26th, 1850)

IN SEPTEMBER 1774 the first Congress of the colonies met in Philadelphia. Had the opposition to slavery which had been previously manifested, and the desire for its extinction which had been so generally cherished, now become extinct? A decisive answer to this inquiry may be found in an extract from a singularly able exposition of the Rights of British America, prepared by Mr. Jefferson and laid before the convention of Virginia, which assembled in August 1774, for the purpose of appointing delegates to the proposed Congress. I will read this extract: —

"The abolition of domestic slavery is the greatest object of desire in these colonies, where it was unhappily introduced in their infant state. But, previous to the enfranchisement of the slaves, it is necessary to exclude further importations from Africa. Yet our repeated attempts to effect this by prohibitions, and by imposing duties which might amount to prohibition, have been hitherto defeated by his Majesty's negative; thus preferring the immediate advantage of a few African corsairs to the lasting interests of the American States and the rights of human nature, deeply wounded by this infamous practice." (Am. Archives, 4th series, Vol. i., p. 696.)

The Congress, which soon after assembled, shared these sentiments. Among its first acts was the framing of the celebrated Articles of Association which composed the Nonimportation, Nonexportation, and Nonconsumption Agreement. I will read the second of those articles: —

"That we will neither import nor purchase any slave imported after the first day of December next, after which time we will wholly discontinue the slave trade, and will neither be concerned in it ourselves, nor will we hire our vessels, or sell our commodities or manufactures to those who are concerned in it." (Am. Archives, 4th series, Vol. i., p. 914.)

There was another article in this agreement, which I will read: —

"Article 14. And we do further agree and resolve that we will have no trade, commerce, dealings, or intercourse whatever with any colony or province in North America which shall not accede to, or which shall hereafter violate, this association, but will hold them as unworthy of the rights of free men and as inimical to the liberties of this country." (Am. Archives, 4th series, Vol. i., p. 915.)

Well, sir, this solemn covenant, thus pledging every colony and every citizen to an entire abandonment and suppression of the slave trade, was signed by every delegate in Congress, Southern and Northern. Public sentiment on this subject was then unanimous, or next to unanimous, throughout the country. Among these signers we find the names of Rodney, McKean, and Read, of Delaware; Chase and Paca, of Maryland; Richard Henry Lee, of Virginia; Hooper and Hewes, of North Carolina; and Middleton, Rutledge, and Lynch, of South Carolina; all of whom subsequently subscribed the Declaration of Independence. We also find the names of George Washington and Patrick Henry.

Now, Mr. President, let it be remembered that these Articles of Association, entered into as a measure for obtaining a redress of grievances from the people and government of Great Britain, and to the faithful observance of which, in all their stipulations, the delegates of the colonies pledged themselves and their constituencies, "under the sacred ties of virtue, honor, and love of country"; let it be remembered, I say, that these articles constituted the first bond of American Union. The union thus constituted was, to be sure, imperfect, partial, incomplete; but it was still a union, a union of the colonies and of the people, for the great objects set forth in the articles. And let it be remembered also that, prominent in the list of measures agreed on in these articles, was the discontinuance of the slave trade, with a view to the ultimate extinction of slavery itself.

I say with a view to the ultimate extinction of slavery, and I have authority for saying so. I ask attention to an extract from the proceedings of a town meeting at Danbury, Connecticut, held on the twelfth of December, 1774:—

"It is with singular pleasure we notice the second article of the association, in which it is agreed to import no more negro slaves, as we cannot but think it a palpable absurdity so loudly to complain of attempts to enslave us while we are actually enslaving others." Am. Archives, 4th series, Vol. i., p. 1038.)

This was the Northern view. What was the Southern? We find it upon record in the proceedings of the Congress of the

Representatives of Darien, in the colony of Georgia. Acceding to the association, they declared their views in these words:—

"We, the representatives of the extensive district of Darien, in the colony of Georgia, being now assembled in Congress, by the authority and free choice of the inhabitants of said district, now freed from their fetters, do resolve."

Then follow several resolutions setting forth the grounds of complaint against the oppressions of Great Britain, closing with the emphatic declaration which I will now read:—

"To show to the world that we are not influenced by any contracted or interested motives, but by a general philanthropy for all mankind, of whatever climate, language, or complexion, we hereby declare our disapprobation and abhorrence of the unnatural practice of slavery in America (however the uncultivated state of our country or other specious arguments may plead for it)—a practice founded in injustice and cruelty, and highly dangerous to our liberties as well as lives, debasing part of our fellow-creatures below men, and corrupting the virtue and morals of the rest, and laying the basis of that liberty we contend for and which we pray the Almighty to continue to the latest posterity upon a very wrong foundation. We, therefore, resolve, at all times, to use our utmost endeavors for the manumission of our slaves in this colony upon the most safe and equitable footing for the masters and themselves." (Am. Archives, 4th series, Vol. i., p. 1135.)

That, sir, was the Southern view. At least it was the view of a large and intelligent and influential body of Southern men. And, with this understanding of their effects and tendency, the Articles of Association were adopted by colonial conventions, county meetings, and lesser assemblages throughout the country, and became the law of America—the fundamental constitution, so to speak, of the first American Union. It is needless to cite many resolutions of these meetings. They can be found in the American Archives by those who desire to investigate the subject. I will quote but two.

The first is a resolution of the convention of Maryland, held in November 1774, readopted by a subsequent convention, more fully attended, in December of the same year:—

"Resolved, That every member of this meeting will, and every person in the province should, strictly and inviolably observe and carry into executio. the association agreed on by the Continental Congress."

The other is the declaration adopted by a general meeting of the freeholders of James City County, Virginia, in November 1774, in these words:—

"The association entered into by Congress being publicly read, the freeholders and other inhabitants of the county, that they might testify to the world their concurrence and hearty approbation of the measures adopted by that respectable body, very cordially acceded thereto, and did bind and oblige themselves, by the sacred ties of virtue, honor, and love to their country, strictly and inviolably to observe and keep the same in every particular."

These, sir, are specimens of the formal and solemn declarations and engagements of public bodies. To show the sentiment which pervaded the masses of the people, I will read an extract from an eloquent paper, entitled "Observations Addressed to the People of America," printed at Philadelphia in November 1774:—

"The least deviation from the resolves of Congress will be treason; such treason as few villains have ever had an opportunity of committing. It will be treason against the present inhabitants of the colonies, against the millions of unborn generations who are to exist hereafter in America, against the only liberty and happiness which remain to mankind, against the last hopes of the wretched in every corner of the world; in a word, it will be treason against God. . . . We are now laying the foundations of an American constitution. Let us, therefore, hold up everything we do to the eye of posterity. They will most probably measure their liberties and happiness by the most careless of our footsteps. Let no unhallowed hand touch the precious seed of liberty. Let us form the glorious tree in such a manner, and impregnate it with such principles of life, that it shall last forever. . . . I almost wish to live to hear the triumphs of the jubilee in the year 1874; to see the medals, pictures, fragments of writings that shall be displayed to revive the memory of the proceedings of the Congress of 1774. If any adventitious circumstance shall give precedency on that day, it shall be to inherit the blood, or even to possess the name, of a member of that glorious assembly." (Am. Archives, 4th series, Vol. i., p. 976.)

In these various resolves and declarations, Mr. President, we have the first expressions of the public sentiment and will of the American people upon this subject of slavery. The earliest action of the associated colonies was antislavery action. The Union which they then formed was indeed, as I have said, incomplete; but it was complete enough to warrant the Congress

which represented it in declaring independence, in waging war, in contracting debts; in assuming, in short, many of the functions of nationality and sovereignty.

Well, sir, nearly two years passed by, and the grievances of the colonies remained unredressed. The war of the Revolution had begun, and the Declaration of Independence was promulgated. That instrument breathed the same spirit as the Articles of Association. The original draught, as it came from the hands of Jefferson, contained a clause reprobating in the strongest terms the traffic in men. I will read it:—

"He has waged cruel war against human nature itself, violating its most sacred rights of life and liberty in the persons of a distant people who never offended him; captivating and carrying them into slavery in another hemisphere, or to incur a miserable death in their transportation thither. This piratical warfare, the opprobrium of infidel powers, is the warfare of the Christian king of Great Britain. Determined to keep open a market where men should be bought and sold, he has prostituted his negative for suppressing every legislative attempt to prohibit or restrain this execrable commerce."

This clause was indeed omitted from the Declaration, not because it did not express the sentiments of the majority of Congress, but, as Mr. Jefferson informs us, in compliance to South Carolina and Georgia. He intimates also that some tenderness under these censures was manifested by Northern gentlemen, whose constituents had been somewhat largely engaged in the slave trade. But still the great fundamental truth, which constitutes the basis of all just government, and which condemns equally every form of oppression, was retained in the Declaration, and announced to the world as self-evident: the truth that "all men are created equal; that they are endowed by their Creator with certain inalienable rights; that among these are life, liberty, and the pursuit of happiness; that to secure these rights governments were instituted among men, deriving their just powers from the consent of the governed."

Thus we see that, in this second great act of the American people, the fundamental truth upon which the Articles of Association were based was reiterated; not as a "rhetorical flourish," not as an abstraction incapable of practical application in human affairs, but as a living principle, not to be disregarded, without fatal consequences, in the structure or the administration of government. That such was the view actually taken of the Declaration at that time is further evident from the language of the dispatches transmitting it to the authorities of the different colonies, and to the commander-in-chief of the army. I will quote a paragraph from the letter of the President of Congress, John Hancock, to the Convention of New Jersey.

"I do myself the honor to inclose, in obedience to the commands of Congress, a copy of the Declaration of Independence, which you will please to have proclaimed in your colony in such way and manner as you judge best. The important consequences resulting to the American States from this Declaration of Independence, considered as the ground and foundation of a future Government, will naturally suggest the propriety of proclaiming it in such a mode as that the people may be universally informed of it." (Am. Archives, 5th series, Vol. i., p. 11.)

Such were the principles, Mr. President, of the Government and the people during the struggle for independence. They were reiterated at the close of it. Very shortly after the treaty of peace was ratified in 1783, Congress issued an address to the States, drawn up by Mr. Madison, the main purpose of which was to persuade to the provision of a fund for the discharge of the public engagements. That address contains the clause which I will now read:—

"Let it be remembered, finally, that it has ever been the pride and boast of America that the rights for which she contended were the rights of human nature. By the blessing of the Author of these rights on the means exerted for their defense, they have prevailed against all opposition, and form the basis of thirteen independent States. No instance has heretofore occurred, nor can any instance be expected hereafter to occur, in which the unadulterated forms of republican government can pretend to so fair an opportunity of justifying themselves by their fruits. In this view, the citizens of the United States are responsible for the greatest trust ever confided to a political society." (Madison Papers, Appen. 11.)

This, sir, was the acknowledgment of 1783. That the War of the Revolution was waged, not to vindicate privileges, but rights; not the rights of any part or class of the people, but the rights of all men—"the rights of human nature."

It was not long before an occasion arose to test the sincerity of Congress in these various declarations; to determine whether or not Congress was prepared to carry the principles so solemnly

recognized into practical application, without respect to persons or sections. Nor was Congress wanting to the occasion.

On the first of March, 1784, Virginia ceded to the United States all her claim to the territory northwest of the Ohio. Much praise has been awarded to Virginia for this cession. I desire to detract nothing from it. Virginia, doubtless, confided fully in the validity of her title to the territory which she ceded. It is true that, acting under her authority, and in anticipation of an expedition ordered by Congress, the gallant George Rogers Clarke, at the head of a handful of brave Kentuckians, dispossessed the British authorities of that portion of the territory which they had occupied on the Wabash and Mississippi. But it is right to say, and I am bound to say, that the validity of the Virginia title was never recognized, was always contested, by Congress. Other States claimed interests in the same territory. New York claimed the whole; Connecticut claimed a part, and Massachusetts also advanced a claim. Against all these demands, Congress asserted a right, in behalf of the United States, to the entire trans-Alleghanian region, as Crown Lands, acquired from Great Britain by the common blood and treasure of all the States, and appealed to the claimant States to relinquish their pretensions. New York was the first to respond to this appeal, and her cession was accepted by Congress in 1782. Virginia had previously proposed to cede all her claim northwest of the Ohio on certain conditions; but, the conditions not being admitted, the cession was not accepted. Subsequently the contest was terminated by a satisfactory cession, made by Virginia and accepted by Congress. It was an arrangement, in fact, which involved concessions on both sides. Virginia yielded to the United States all her claims to territory northwest of the Ohio, and the United States tacitly surrendered to Virginia all claim to the territory southeast of that river, alleged to be within her chartered limits. I have thought it my duty to make these observations, as a Senator of a State whose rights and interests, as well as the rights and interests of her sister States of Pennsylvania, Indiana, and Illinois, are affected, to some extent, by the claim of exclusive title to the Western country which has been advanced in behalf of Virginia.

Whatever the title of Virginia may have been, however, it is certain that upon her cession, made, as I have said, on the first of March, 1784, the United States came into the undisputed ownership and sovereignty of the vast region northwest of the Ohio.

To dispose of the soil and to determine the political institutions of the Territory now became the duty of Congress; and the duty was promptly performed. On the very day of the cession, before the sun went down, Thomas Jefferson, in behalf of a committee, consisting of himself, Mr. Howell, of Rhode Island, and Mr. Chase, of Maryland, reported a plan for the government of the western territory—not that lying north of the Ohio merely, but of all, from the north line of Florida to the north line of the United States. This, sir, is a memorable document of our early history, and I propose to read portions of it to the Senate:—

"The territory ceded, or to be ceded, by the individual States to the United States, . . . shall be formed into distinct States. . . . The settlers . . . shall, either on their own petition or on the order of Congress, receive authority, with appointments of time and place, for their free males, of full age, to meet together for the purpose of establishing a temporary government. . . . Such temporary governments shall only continue in force, in any State, until it shall have acquired twenty thousand inhabitants; when, giving due proof thereof to Congress, they shall receive from them authority, with appointments of time and place, to call a convention of representatives to establish a permanent constitution and government for themselves: Provided, That both the temporary and permanent governments be established upon these principles as their basis."

Here follow sundry provisions, the last of which is as follows:

"That after the year 1800 of the Christian era there shall be neither slavery nor involuntary servitude in any of the said States, otherwise than in the punishment of crimes, whereof the party shall have been duly convicted to have been personally guilty." (Journals Cong. Confed., Vol. iv., p. 374.)

This, sir, was the plan and proviso of Jefferson. It met the approbation of the American people. It proved that the declaration of 1776 was not an empty profession, but a true faith. It proved that the spirit of the covenant of 1774 yet animated the heart of the nation. According to this grand and comprehensive scheme, the commencement of the nineteenth century was to witness the inauguration of freedom as the fundamental and perpetual law of the transmontane half of the American Republic.

Had this plan and proviso been adopted, we should not now be discussing the questions which embarrass us. The extension

of slavery would have been limited by the Alleghanies. No slave could ever have trodden a foot of the soil beyond. Unhappily, however, the proviso was not adopted; and, as I have already said that it met the approval of the people, I ask attention to the proceedings which resulted in its rejection. On the nineteenth of April, Mr. Spaight, of North Carolina, moved that the proviso be stricken out. Under the Articles of Confederation, which governed the proceedings of Congress, a majority of the thirteen States was necessary to an affirmative decision on any question; and the vote of no State could be counted, unless represented by at least two delegates.

The question upon Mr. Spaight's motion was put in this form:—

"Shall the words moved to be struck out stand?"

The vote stood—

For the proviso, six States, viz.: New Hampshire, Massachusetts, Rhode Island, Connecticut, New York, and Pennsylvania.

Against the proviso, three States, viz.: Virginia, Maryland, and South Carolina.

Delaware and Georgia were not represented. New Jersey, by Mr. Dick, voted aye, but her vote, only one delegate being present, could not be counted. The vote of North Carolina was divided—Mr. Williamson voting aye; Mr. Spaight, no. The vote of Virginia stood—Mr. Jefferson, aye; Messrs. Hardy and Mercer, no. Of the twenty-three delegates present and voting, sixteen voted for, and seven against, the proviso. Thus was the proviso defeated by a minority vote. The people were for it, the States were for it; but it failed in consequence of a provision which enabled the minority to control the majority. It so happened that Mr. Beatty, the colleague of Mr. Dick, had left Congress a day or two before and returned a day or two after. Had he been present, or had one of Mr. Jefferson's colleagues voted with him, the result would have been changed. How vast the consequences which, in this instance, depended on a single vote.

Well, sir, the Ordinance of 1784, thus maimed and otherwise mutilated, became the law of the land on the twenty-third of April following. In 1785 Mr. Jefferson went abroad as minister to France, and was out of the country until after the adoption of the Constitution. The agitation of the proviso, however, did not cease in consequence of his absence. In that same year (1785)

Mr. King, of Massachusetts, again moved the proviso in Congress, in a slightly modified form, as follows:—

« That there shall be neither slavery nor involuntary servitude in any of the States described in the resolves of Congress of the twenty-third of April, 1784, otherwise than in the punishment of crimes, whereof the party shall have been personally guilty; and that this regulation shall be an article of compact, and remain a fundamental principle of the constitutions between the thirteen original States and each of the States described in the said resolve of the twenty-third of April, 1784. » (Journals Cong. Confed., Vol. iv., p. 481.)

The resolution was ordered to be committed by the votes of New Hampshire, Massachusetts, Connecticut, Rhode Island, New York, New Jersey, Pennsylvania, and Maryland — eight; against the votes of Virginia, North Carolina, South Carolina, and Georgia — four. Delaware was not represented. The vote of Maryland was determined by two ayes against one no, while that of Virginia was determined by two noes against one aye. The decided favor shown to this resolution by the vote for its commitment was the more remarkable, inasmuch as it proposed the immediate prohibition of slavery, instead of prohibition after 1800, in all territory acquired and to be acquired.

No further action was had at this time; but in a little more than two years afterwards, the subject was brought for the third time before Congress, in connection, as before, with the government of the western territory. The Ordinance of 1784, from causes into which it is not material to inquire, had never been carried into practical operation. Settlements were about to commence in the Northwest, and the settlers needed protection and government. Congress, therefore, in 1787, resumed the consideration of the subject of western territory. These deliberations resulted in the celebrated Ordinance of 1787, the last great act, and among the greatest acts of the Congress of the Confederation; an act which received the unanimous votes of the States; and, with a single exception from New York, of all the delegates. This ordinance, in its sixth article of compact, expressly prohibited slavery and involuntary servitude, except for crime, throughout the Territory. It abolished existing slavery, and it forbade future slavery. It covered with this prohibition every inch of territory then belonging to the United States. It expressly declared the national policy which this prohibition and

kindred provisions contained in the articles of compact were meant to indicate and establish. This is its language:—

« For extending the fundamental principles of civil and religious liberty, whereon these republics, their laws and constitutions, are erected; to fix and establish those principles as the basis of all laws, constitutions, and governments, which forever hereafter shall be formed in the said territory: . . . Be it ordained and declared, etc. »

To guard against possible future departure from this policy, it was ordained that these articles should " forever remain unalterable, " unless altered by the " common consent of the original States, and the people and States in the Territory. "

It is hardly possible to conceive of a more explicit declaration of governmental policy than this. The state of public sentiment in regard to slavery, which resulted in this positive and unanimous exclusion of it from national territory, is well described in a letter of Mr. Jefferson to Dr. Price, who published about that time a book in favor of emancipation. The letter bears date Paris, August 7th, 1785. I will read an extract:—

« Southward of the Chesapeake, it will find but few readers concurring with it [Dr. Price's book] in sentiment on the subject of slavery. From the mouth to the head of the Chesapeake, the bulk of the people will approve it in theory, and it will find a respectable minority ready to adopt it in practice; a minority which, for weight and worth of character, preponderates against the greater number who have not the courage to divest their families of a property which, however, keeps their conscience uneasy. Northward of the Chesapeake, you may find here and there an opponent to your doctrine, as you may find here and there a robber or a murderer; but in no greater number. In that part of America, there being but few slaves, they can easily disencumber themselves of them; and emancipation is put into such a train that in a few years there will be no slaves northward of Maryland. In Maryland I do not find such a disposition to begin the redress of the enormity as in Virginia. This is the next State to which we may turn our eye for the interesting spectacle of justice in conflict with avarice and oppression; a conflict wherein the sacred side is gaining daily recruits from the influx into office of young men, grown and growing up. »

The general state of opinion is also well expressed by Mr. Jefferson in his 'Notes on Virginia,' where he says:—

« I think a change already perceptible since the origin of our present revolution. The spirit of the master is abating; that of the

slave is rising from the dust, his condition mollifying, and the way, I hope, preparing, under the auspices of heaven, for a total emancipation. »

In another place, declaring his own sentiments, he said:—

« Nobody wishes more ardently than I to see an abolition not only of the trade, but of the condition of slavery; and certainly nobody will be more willing to encounter any sacrifice for that object. »

Mr. President, I do not know that any monument has been erected over the grave of Jefferson, in Virginia.

Mr. Mason — There is — a granite obelisk.

Mr. Chase — I am glad to hear it. No monumental marble bears a nobler name.

Mr. Seward — The inscription is: " Here was buried Thomas Jefferson, Author of the Declaration of American Independence, of the Statute of Virginia for Religious Freedom, and Father of the University of Virginia. "

Mr. Chase — It is an appropriate inscription, and worthily commemorates distinguished services. But, Mr. President, if a stranger from some foreign land should ask me for the monument of Jefferson, I would not take him to Virginia and bid him look on a granite obelisk, however admirable in its proportions or its inscriptions. I would ask him to accompany me beyond the Alleghanies, into the midst of the broad Northwest, and would say to him:—

« Si monumentum quæris, circumspice! »

Behold, on every side, his monument. These thronged cities, these flourishing villages, these cultivated fields; these million happy homes of prosperous freemen; these churches, these schools; these asylums for the unfortunate and the helpless; these institutions of education, religion, and humanity; these great States, great in their present resources, but greater far in the mighty energies by which the resources of the future are to be developed; these, these are the monument of Jefferson. His memorial is over all our Western land —

« Our meanest rill, our mightiest river,
Rolls mingling with his fame forever. »

THREE GREAT ERAS

(From a Speech in the Senate, February 3d, 1854)

Mr. President:—

THREE great eras have marked the history of this country in respect to slavery. The first may be characterized as the Era of Enfranchisement. It commenced with the earliest struggles for national independence. The spirit which inspired it animated the hearts and prompted the efforts of Washington, of Jefferson, of Patrick Henry, of Wythe, of Adams, of Jay, of Hamilton, of Morris — in short, of all the great men of our early history. All these hoped for, all these labored for, all these believed in, the final deliverance of the country from the curse of slavery. That spirit burned in the Declaration of Independence, and inspired the provisions of the Constitution and the Ordinance of 1787. Under its influence, when in full vigor, State after State provided for the emancipation of the slaves within their limits, prior to the adoption of the Constitution. Under its feebler influence at a later period, and during the administration of Mr. Jefferson, the importation of slaves was prohibited into Mississippi and Louisiana, in the faint hope that those Territories might finally become free States. Gradually that spirit ceased to influence our public councils, and lost its control over the American heart and the American policy. Another era succeeded, but by such imperceptible gradations that the lines which separate the two cannot be traced with absolute precision. The facts of the two eras meet and mingle as the currents of confluent streams mix, so imperceptibly that the observer cannot fix the spot where the meeting waters blend.

This second era was the Era of Conservatism. Its great maxim was to preserve the existing condition. Men said: Let things remain as they are; let slavery stand where it is; exclude it where it is not; refrain from disturbing the public quiet by agitation; adjust all difficulties that arise, not by the application of principles, but by compromises.

It was during this period that the Senator tells us that slavery was maintained in Illinois, both while a Territory and after it became a State, in despite of the provisions of the ordinance. It is true, sir, that the slaves held in the Illinois country, under the French law, were not regarded as absolutely emancipated by the provisions of the ordinance. But full effect was given to the ordinance in excluding the introduction of slaves, and thus the Territory was preserved from eventually becoming a slave State. The few slaveholders in the Territory of Indiana, which then included Illinois, succeeded in obtaining such an ascendency in its affairs, that repeated applications were made, not merely by conventions of delegates, but by the Territorial legislature itself, for a suspension of the clause in the ordinance prohibiting slavery. These applications were reported upon by John Randolph, of Virginia, in the House, and by Mr. Franklin in the Senate. Both the reports were against suspension. The grounds stated by Randolph are specially worthy of being considered now. They are thus stated in the report:—

« That the committee deem it highly dangerous and inexpedient to impair a provision wisely calculated to promote the happiness and prosperity of the Northwestern country and to give strength and security to that extensive frontier. In the salutary operation of this sagacious and benevolent restraint, it is believed that the inhabitants of Indiana will, at no very distant day, find ample remuneration for a temporary privation of labor and of emigration.»

Sir, these reports, made in 1803 and 1807, and the action of Congress upon them, in conformity with their recommendation, saved Illinois, and perhaps Indiana, from becoming slave States. When the people of Illinois formed their State constitution, they incorporated into it a section providing that neither slavery nor involuntary servitude shall hereafter be introduced into this State. The constitution made provision for the continued service of the few persons who were originally held as slaves, and then bound to service under the Territorial laws, and for the freedom of their children, and thus secured the final extinction of slavery. The Senator thinks that this result is not attributable to the ordinance. I differ from him. But for the ordinance, I have no doubt slavery would have been introduced into Indiana, Illinois, and Ohio. It is something to the credit of the Era of Conservatism, uniting its influences with those of the expiring Era of Enfranchisement, that it maintained the Ordinance of 1787 in the Northwest.

The Era of Conservatism passed, also by imperceptible gradations, into the Era of Slavery Propagandism. Under the influences of this new spirit we opened the whole territory acquired

III—67

from Mexico, except California, to the ingress of slavery. Every foot of it was covered by a Mexican prohibition; and yet, by the legislation of 1850, we consented to expose it to the introduction of slaves. Some, I believe, have actually been carried into Utah and New Mexico. They may be few, perhaps, but a few are enough to affect materially the probable character of their future governments. Under the evil influences of the same spirit, we are now called upon to reverse the original policy of the Republic; to support even a solemn compact of the conservative period, and open Nebraska to slavery.

Sir, I believe that we are upon the verge of another era. That era will be the Era of Reaction. The introduction of this question here, and its discussion, will greatly hasten its advent. We, who insist upon the denationalization of slavery, and upon the absolute divorce of the General Government from all connection with it, will stand with the men who favored the compromise acts, and who yet wish to adhere to them, in their letter and in their spirit, against the repeal of the Missouri prohibition. But you may pass it here. You may send it to the other House. It may become a law. But its effect will be to satisfy all thinking men that no compromises with slavery will endure, except so long as they serve the interests of slavery, and that there is no safe and honorable ground for nonslaveholders to stand upon except that of restricting slavery within State limits, and excluding it absolutely from the whole sphere of Federal jurisdiction. The old questions between political parties are at rest. No great question so thoroughly possesses the public mind as that of slavery. This discussion will hasten the inevitable reorganization of parties upon the new issues which our circumstances suggest. It will light a fire in the country which may perhaps consume those who kindle it. . . .

CHÂTEAUBRIAND

(1768-1848)

RANÇOIS RENÉ AUGUSTE, VISCOUNT DE CHÂTEAUBRIAND, immortal in literature as the author of 'Atala,' 'René,' and 'The Genius of Christianity,' represents in political oratory the first strong reaction of "Bourbonism" against the ideas of the French Revolution. In 1823-24 he was Minister of Foreign Affairs under Louis XVIII., and helped to force what has been called a most unjustifiable war on Spain. In doing so he made the speech on Intervention, probably the most effective of his orations. In defining the causes of the assault on Spain, Lamartine, in his 'History of the Restoration of Monarchy in France,' says that "Spain was verging on a Republic and that a Republic proclaimed on the other side of the Pyrenees would sweep away the throne of the Bourbons in France."

From the reaction represented by this speech of Châteaubriand may be traced the great reactionary movement which gained such force in Europe during the last quarter of the century.

He was born at St. Malo, September 4th, 1768. In his youth a follower of Voltaire and the Encyclopedists, he changed his opinions and published his 'Genius of Christianity,' the work which has done most to give him an enduring reputation. His 'René,' 'Atala,' and 'Essay on Revolutions,' are of scarcely less celebrity than the 'Genius of Christianity,' though perhaps they are not so widely read outside of France. His appointment to the Cabinet under Louis XVIII. was due to a pamphlet, 'Bonaparte and the Bourbons,' which Louis said was worth a hundred thousand men to him. After his retirement from the ministry he was Ambassador to Rome under the Martignac administration. Resigning, he continued for a time in politics, representing under Louis Philippe "the principle of legitimacy." His residence in England strengthened his taste for English literature, and his translations of Milton, made after his retirement from politics, are among the last notable works of his later life. He died in 1848. His critics admire his brilliancy, but accuse him of overweening egotism. Richard Garnett calls him a "great rhetorician rather than a great poet, a great writer rather than a great man." Lamartine, who gives him credit for sincerity and earnestness, says, on the other hand, that "he saw far and saw correctly, going astray, when he erred at all, through passion and not from intellectual error."

HAS ONE GOVERNMENT THE RIGHT TO INTERVENE IN THE INTERNAL AFFAIRS OF ANOTHER?

(Delivered in the French Chamber of Deputies in 1823 on the Question of Intervening Forcibly in the Affairs of Spain)

Gentlemen:—

I SHALL at once set aside the personal objections, for private feelings must have no place here. I have no reply to make to mutilated pieces, printed by means unknown to me in foreign gazettes. I commenced my ministerial career with the honorable Member who spoke last, during the hundred days, when we each had a portfolio *ad interim*, he at Paris and I at Ghent. I was then writing a romance, he was employed on history; I still adhere to romance.

I am about to examine the series of objections presented at this tribune. These are numerous and diversified; but that I may not go astray in so vast a field, I shall arrange them under different heads.

Let us first examine the question of intervention. Has one government a right to intervene in the internal affairs of another government? This great question of public right has been resolved in opposite ways; those who have connected it with natural law, as Bacon, Puffendorf, Grotius, and all the ancients, are of opinion that it is permitted to take up arms, in the name of human society, against a people who violate the principles upon which general order is based, in the same manner as in private life we punish common disturbers of the peace. Those who look upon the question as a point of civil law maintain, on the contrary, that one government has no right to intervene in the affairs of another government. Thus, the former place the right of intervention in our duties, and the latter in our interests.

Gentlemen, I adopt the principle laid down by the civil law; I take the side of modern politicians, and I say with them, no government has a right to intervene in the internal affairs of another government. In fact, if this principle were not admitted, and especially by peoples who enjoy a free constitution, no nation could be free on its own soil; for the corruption of a minister, or the ambition of a king, would be sufficient to occasion an attack upon any State which should endeavor to improve its condition. To the various causes of war, already too numerous, you would thereby add a perpetual principle of hostility, a principle of which every man in possession of power would be the judge, because he would always have the right of saying to his neighbors: "Your institutions displease me; change them, or I shall declare war against you."

I hope my honorable opponents will acknowledge that I explain myself frankly. But in presenting myself in this tribune to maintain the justice of our intervention in the affairs of Spain, how am I to escape from the principle which I myself have enounced? You shall see, gentlemen.

When modern politicians had rejected the right of intervention, by quitting the natural, to place themselves within the civil law, they found themselves very much embarrassed. Cases occurred in which it was impossible to abstain from intervention without putting the State in danger. At the commencement of the Revolution it was said: "Let the colonies perish rather than a principle!" and the colonies accordingly perished. Was it right to say also: "Let social order perish rather than a principle"? That they might not be wrecked against the very rule they had established, they had recourse to an exception, by means of which they returned to the natural law, and said: "No government has a right to intervene in the internal affairs of a nation, unless in such a case as may compromise the immediate safety and essential interests of that government." I shall presently quote the authority from which I borrow these words.

The exception, gentlemen, does not appear to me more questionable than the rule; no State can allow its essential interests to perish, under the penalty of perishing itself as a State. Having reached this point of the question, the whole face of it is changed,— we find ourselves altogether upon different ground. I am no longer bound to contest the rule, but to prove that the case of exception has occurred for France.

Before I adduce the motives which justify your intervention in the affairs of Spain, I ought first, gentlemen, to support my statement on the authority of examples. I shall frequently have occasion in the course of my speech to speak of England, since my honorable opponents quote it every moment against us, in their extempore, as well as in their written and printed speeches. It was Great Britain alone who defended these principles at Verona, and it is she alone who now rises against the right of intervention; it is she who is ready to take up arms for the

cause of a free people; it is she that reproves an impious war, hostile to the rights of man,— a war which a little bigoted and servile faction wishes to undertake, to return on its conclusion to burn the French charter, after having rent to pieces the Spanish constitution. Is not that it, gentlemen? We shall return to all these points; but first let us speak of the intervention.

I fear that my honorable opponents have made a bad choice of their authority. England, say they, has set us a great example by protecting the independence of nations. Let England, safe amidst her waves, and defended by ancient institutions,— let England — which has not suffered either the disasters of two invasions or the disorders of a thirty years' revolution — think that she has nothing to fear from Spain, and feel averse to intervene in her affairs, nothing certainly can be more natural; but does it follow that France enjoys the same security, and is in the same position? When, under other circumstances, the essential interests of Great Britain have been compromised, did she not for her own safety, and very justly without doubt, derogate from the principles which are now invoked in her name?

England, on going to war with France, promulgated, in the month of November 1793 the famous declaration of Whitehall. Permit me, gentlemen, to read a passage of it for you. The document commences by recalling the calamities of the Revolution, and then adds:—

"The intentions set forth of reforming the abuses of the French government, of establishing upon a solid basis personal liberty and the rights of property, of securing to a numerous people a wise legislation, an administration, and just and moderate laws,— all these salutary views have unhappily disappeared; they have given place to a system destructive of all public order, maintained by proscriptions, by banishment, by confiscations without number, by arbitrary imprisonment and by massacres, the memory of which is frightful. The inhabitants of this unhappy country, so long deceived by promises of happiness, always renewed at the epoch of every fresh crime, have been plunged into an abyss of calamities without example.

"This state of affairs cannot subsist in France, without implicating in one common danger all the neighboring powers, without giving them the right, without imposing upon them the duty of arresting the progress of an evil which only exists by the successive violation of all laws and every sense of propriety, and by the subversion of the fundamental principles which unite men, by the ties of social life. His Majesty certainly does not mean to dispute with France

the right of reforming its laws; he would never wish to influence by external force the mode of government of an independent State: nor does he desire it now, but in so far as this object has become essential to the peace and security of other powers. Under these circumstances he demands of France, and his demand is based upon a just title, the termination at length of a system of anarchy which is only powerful in doing wrong, incapable of fulfilling towards the French people the first duty of government, to repress the disturbances and to punish the crimes which daily multiply in the interior of the country; but, on the contrary, disposing in an arbitrary manner of their lives and property, to disturb the peace of other nations, and to make all Europe the theatre of similar crimes and like calamities. He demands of France the establishment of a stable and legitimate government, founded on the recognized principles of universal justice, and calculated to maintain with other nations the customary relations of union and of peace. The King, on his part, promises beforehand a suspension of hostilities; friendship in so far as he may be permitted by events which are not at the disposal of the human will; and safety and protection to all those who, declaring themselves for a monarchical government, shall withdraw themselves from the despotism of an anarchy which has broken all the most sacred ties of society, rent asunder all the relations of civil life, violated all rights, confounded all duties; availing itself of the name of liberty to exercise the most cruel tyranny, to annihilate all property, to seize upon all estates, founding its power on the pretended consent of the people, and ruining whole provinces with fire and sword, for having reclaimed their laws, their religion, and their legitimate sovereign!"

Well, gentlemen, what think you of this declaration? Did you not imagine that you were listening to the very speech pronounced by the King at the opening of the present session; but that speech developed, explained, and commented upon with equal force and eloquence? England says she acts in concert with her allies, and we should be thought criminal in also having allies! England promises assistance to French royalists, and it would be taken ill if we were to protect Spanish royalists! England maintains that she has the right of intervening to save herself and Europe from the evils that are desolating France, and we are to be interdicted from defending ourselves from the Spanish contagion! England rejects the pretended consent of the French people; she imposes upon France, as the price of peace, the condition of establishing a government founded on

the principles of justice, and calculated to maintain the customary relations with other States, and we are to be compelled to recognize the pretended sovereignty of the people, the legality of a constitution established by a military revolt, and we are not to have the right of demanding from Spain, for our security, institutions legalized by the freedom of Ferdinand!

We must, however, be just: when England published this famous declaration, Marie Antoinette and Louis XVI. were no more. I acknowledge that Marie Josephine is, as yet, only a captive, and that nothing has yet been shed but her tears; Ferdinand, also, is at present only a prisoner in his palace, as Louis XVI. was in his, before he went to the Temple and thence to the scaffold. I do not wish to calumniate the Spaniards, but neither do I wish to estimate them more highly than my own countrymen. Revolutionary France produced a Convention, and why should not revolutionary Spain produce one also? Shall I be told that by accelerating the movement of intervention we shall make the position of the monarch more perilous? But did England save Louis XVI. by refusing to declare herself? Is not the intervention which prevents the evil more useful than that by which it is avenged? Spain had a diplomatic agent at Paris at the period of the celebrated catastrophe, and his prayers could obtain nothing. What was this family witness doing there? He was certainly not required to authenticate a death that was known to earth and heaven. Gentlemen, the trials of Charles I. and of Louis XVI. are already too much for the world, but another judicial murder would establish, on the authority of precedents, a sort of criminal right and a body of jurisprudence for the use of subjects against their kings.

LORD CHATHAM

(WILLIAM, VISCOUNT PITT AND EARL OF CHATHAM)

(1708–1778)

THE words with which the elder Pitt closed his reply to Lord Mansfield in arguing the Wilkes case in the House of Lords are at once the secret of his power as an orator and the explanation of his success as a statesman. "Where law ends, tyranny begins," he said as the final word of that great plea for the English constitution. It is for this idea that he stands in the history of England and of English-speaking people. "The higher law" to which appeal is made when impatience of wrong will not wait on prescription for reforms, he did not recognize,—or if he recognized it, combated it as a part of the tyranny which begins where prescription ends. What he dreaded most and opposed most strenuously for England was the arbitrary power, which in its own right of assumed superiority undertakes to decide the present without regard to the past, without the previously given consent of those who are affected, and without regard to those precedents and rules of procedure, which, whether or not they have been enacted as legislation, have the force of law because they stand for regularity, for order, for "due process," for the sanity, the reasonable consideration which every man in or out of power owes to every other. "We all know what the constitution is," said Chatham in the Wilkes case. "We all know that the first principle of it is that the subject shall not be governed by the *arbitrium* of any one man or body of men less than the whole legislature, but by certain laws to which he has virtually given his consent, which are open to him to examine and are not beyond his ability to understand."

That the weak, the "subject," the defenseless shall "not be governed by the *arbitrium* of any man," but only by the due and orderly processes of the justice which is necessary for their liberties and their defense—to hold that idea as Chatham held it, and to dare as much for it as he dared, would make any man great. Undoubtedly he was one of the greatest men of England. "I have sometimes seen eloquence without wisdom and often wisdom without eloquence," said Franklin in speaking of him, "but in him I have seen them united in the highest possible degree." No one who reads his speech in the Wilkes case in 1770 and after it the noble protest against the

attempt to subjugate America made by him in his speech on the address to the throne in November 1777 is likely to dissent from this verdict. He attacked the arbitrary action of the King as fearlessly as he had attacked that of Parliament. If the constitution was in danger, he did not stop to consider the rank, the dignity, the power of those who threatened it. He threatened them on his side in the name of that which he recognized as the greatest force in human affairs,—of the law, the love of order, the "due process," the justice and liberty which depend on due process under prescribed constitutional forms. If we wonder sometimes how the makers of the American constitution could have gained so much of that wisdom which comes from the hatred of disorderly power, we have only to read the speeches of Chatham, made in the face of the patriotic sentiment of England, in defiance of the royal prerogative, in contempt of all public opinion which supported arbitrary power, to understand that American love of liberty is an inheritance from the generations whose spirit inspired him, when in the House of Lords he said: "I rejoice that America has resisted. . . . I hope some dreadful calamity will befall this country which will open the eyes of the King."

He was not inconsistent in opposing American independence as he did in his last speech, delivered with what was almost literally his dying breath. He looked on Americans as Englishmen entitled to all their rights under the English constitution, and he was glad to see them fight for them if they could enforce them in no other way. But that as Englishmen they should join with France to free themselves from the constitution and laws he regarded with such reverence; that in doing so they should seek to "dismember the British Empire," seemed to him monstrous. Of the rights of humanity he seems to have had no governing conception. The rights of Englishmen were very dear to him, but it does not seem to have occurred to him that there was any compelling reason for respecting the rights of Frenchmen, of Spaniards, of Hindoos, or other foreigners whose interests seemed to antagonize those of the British Empire. It is possible, but by no means certain, that he could have warmed as Burke did to the strongest indignation against British oppression in India, but it is for British liberty under English law, not for human liberty under the laws of Nature or of God, that he stands distinctively. Yet taking him with all his limitations and weaknesses, with the pomposity which sometimes made him seem ridiculous, and the vehemence which often made him unreasonable, he is still one of the noblest figures in the history of modern England.

He was born at Westminster, November 15th, 1708. After studying at Oxford and serving in the army as a cornet of horse, he entered

Parliament in 1735, attracting immediate attention and winning the distinguished success of drawing the fire of Walpole, who complimented him by procuring his dismissal from the army because of his attacks on the administration. From this time until he was raised to the peerage in 1766, Pitt increased steadily in popular favor. He was called the "Great Commoner," and was in fact the first great popular parliamentary leader in English history. The most celebrated of his earlier speeches are only reported in fragments, but as a Commoner he could hardly have exceeded the fire of his denunciations of arbitrary power, when in the House of Lords he asserted the spirit of English liberty against the Tory policy towards America. He died May 11th, 1778, at Hayes, where he was removed after his collapse in the House of Lords, April 7th of the same year.

W. V. B.

THE ATTEMPT TO SUBJUGATE AMERICA

(On an Address to the Throne, in the House of Lords, November 18th, 1777)

I RISE, my lords, to declare my sentiments on this most solemn and serious subject. It has imposed a load upon my mind, which, I fear, nothing can remove; but which impels me to endeavor its alleviation, by a free and unreserved communication of my sentiments.

In the first part of the address, I have the honor of heartily concurring with the noble earl who moved it. No man feels sincerer joy than I do; none can offer more genuine congratulation on every accession of strength to the Protestant succession. I therefore join in every congratulation on the birth of another princess and the happy recovery of her Majesty. But I must stop here. My courtly complaisance will carry me no further. I will not join in congratulation on misfortune and disgrace. I cannot concur in a blind and servile address, which approves and endeavors to sanctify the monstrous measures which have heaped disgrace and misfortune upon us. This, my lords, is a perilous and tremendous moment! It is not a time for adulation. The smoothness of flattery cannot now avail; cannot save us in this rugged and awful crisis. It is now necessary to instruct the throne in the language of truth. We must dispel the delusion and the darkness which envelop it; and display, in its full danger and true colors, the ruin that is brought to our doors.

This, my lords, is our duty. It is the proper function of this noble assemblage, sitting, as we do, upon our honors in this house, the hereditary council of the crown. Who is the minister —where is the minister, that has dared to suggest to the throne the contrary, unconstitutional language this day delivered from it? The accustomed language from the throne has been application to Parliament for advice, and a reliance on its constitutional advice and assistance. As it is the right of Parliament to give, so it is the duty of the crown to ask it. But on this day, and in this extreme momentous exigency, no reliance is reposed on our constitutional counsels! no advice is asked from the sober and enlightened care of Parliament! but the crown, from itself and by itself, declares an unalterable determination to pursue measures—and what measures, my lords?—The measures that have produced the imminent perils that threaten us; the measures that have brought ruin to our doors.

Can the minister of the day now presume to expect a continuance of support, in this ruinous infatuation? Can Parliament be so dead to its dignity and its duty, as to be thus deluded into the loss of the one and the violation of the other?—To give an unlimited credit and support for the steady perseverance in measures not proposed for our parliamentary advice, but dictated and forced upon us—in measures, I say, my lords, which have reduced this late flourishing empire to ruin and contempt! —"But yesterday, and England might have stood against the world: now none so poor to do her reverence." I use the words of a poet; but, though it be poetry, it is no fiction. It is a shameful truth, that not only the power and strength of this country are wasting away and expiring; but her well-earned glories, her true honor, and substantial dignity are sacrificed. France, my lords, has insulted you; she has encouraged and sustained America; and whether America be wrong or right, the dignity of this country ought to spurn at the officious insult of French interference. The ministers and ambassadors of those who are called rebels and enemies are in Paris; in Paris they transact the reciprocal interests of America and France. Can there be a more mortifying insult? Can even our ministers sustain a more humiliating disgrace? Do they dare to resent it? Do they presume even to hint a vindication of their honor and the dignity of the State by requiring the dismission of the plenipotentiaries of America? Such is the degradation to which they have reduced the glories of England! The people whom they affect to call contemptible rebels, but whose growing power has at last obtained the name of enemies; the people with whom they have engaged this country in war, and against whom they now command our implicit support in every measure of desperate hostility: this people, despised as rebels, or acknowledged as enemies, are abetted against you, supplied with every military store, their interests consulted, and their ambassadors entertained, by your inveterate enemy! and our ministers dare not interpose with dignity or effect. Is this the honor of a great kingdom? Is this the indignant spirit of England, who, "but yesterday," gave law to the house of Bourbon? My lords, the dignity of nations demands a decisive conduct in a situation like this. Even when the greatest prince that perhaps this country ever saw filled our throne, the requisition of a Spanish general on a similar subject was attended to and complied with. For, on the spirited remonstrance of the Duke of Alva, Elizabeth found herself obliged to deny the Flemish exiles all countenance, support, or even entrance into her dominions; and the Count le Marque, with his few desperate followers, were expelled the kingdom. Happening to arrive at the Brille, and finding it weak in defense, they made themselves masters of the place: and this was the foundation of the United Provinces.

My lords, this ruinous and ignominious situation, where we cannot act with success, nor suffer with honor, calls upon us to remonstrate in the strongest and loudest language of truth, to rescue the ear of majesty from the delusions which surround it. The desperate state of our arms abroad is in part known: no man thinks more highly of them than I do. I love and honor the English troops. I know their virtues and their valor. I know they can achieve anything except impossibilities; and I know that the conquest of English America is an impossibility. You cannot, I venture to say it, you cannot conquer America. Your armies in the last war effected everything that could be effected; and what was it? It cost a numerous army, under the command of a most able general, now a noble lord in this house, a long and laborious campaign, to expel five thousand Frenchmen from French America. My lords, you cannot conquer America. What is your present situation there? We do not know the worst; but we know that in three campaigns we have done nothing and suffered much. Besides the sufferings, perhaps total

loss, of the Northern force, the best appointed army that ever took the field, commanded by Sir William Howe, has retired from the American lines. He was obliged to relinquish his attempt, and, with great delay and danger, to adopt a new and distant plan of operations. We shall soon know, and in any event have reason to lament, what may have happened since. As to conquest, therefore, my lords, I repeat, it is impossible. You may swell every expense and every effort still more extravagantly; pile and accumulate every assistance you can buy or borrow; traffic and barter with every little pitiful German prince that sells and sends his subjects to the shambles of a foreign prince; your efforts are forever vain and impotent: doubly so from this mercenary aid on which you rely. For it irritates, to an incurable resentment, the minds of your enemies—to overrun them with the mercenary sons of rapine and plunder; devoting them and their possessions to the rapacity of hireling cruelty! If I were an American, as I am an Englishman, while a foreign troop was landed in my country, I never would lay down my arms—never—never—never!

Your own army is infected with the contagion of these illiberal allies. The spirit of plunder and of rapine is gone forth among them. I know it, and notwithstanding what the noble earl, who moved the address, has given as his opinion of our American army, I know from authentic information, and the most experienced officers, that our discipline is deeply wounded. Whilst this is notoriously our sinking situation, America grows and flourishes; whilst our strength and discipline are lowered, hers are rising and improving.

But, my lords, who is the man that in addition to these disgraces and mischiefs of our army has dared to authorize and associate to our arms the tomahawk and scalping knife of the savage? To call into civilized alliance the wild and inhuman savage of the woods; to delegate to the merciless Indian the defense of disputed rights, and to wage the horrors of his barbarous war against our brethren? My lords, these enormities cry aloud for redress and punishment. Unless thoroughly done away, it will be a stain on the national character. It is a violation of the constitution. I believe it is against law. It is not the least of our national misfortunes, that the strength and character of our army are thus impaired. Infected with the mercenary spirit of robbery and rapine; familiarized to the horrid scenes of savage

cruelty, it can no longer boast of the noble and generous principles which dignify a soldier; no longer sympathize with the dignity of the royal banner, nor feel the pride, pomp, and circumstance of glorious war, "that make ambition virtue!" What makes ambition virtue?—the sense of honor. But is the sense of honor consistent with a spirit of plunder or the practice of murder? Can it flow from mercenary motives, or can it prompt to cruel deeds? Besides these murderers and plunderers, let me ask our ministers, What other allies have they acquired? What other powers have they associated to their cause? Have they entered into alliance with the king of the gipsies? Nothing, my lords, is too low or too ludicrous to be consistent with their counsels.

The independent views of America have been stated and asserted as the foundation of this address. My lords, no man wishes for the due dependence of America on this country more than I do. To preserve it, and not confirm that state of independence into which your measures hitherto have driven them, is the object which we ought to unite in attaining. The Americans, contending for their rights against arbitrary exactions, I love and admire. It is the struggle of free and virtuous patriots; but contending for independency and total disconnection from England, as an Englishman, I cannot wish them success. For, in a due constitutional dependency, including the ancient supremacy of this country in regulating their commerce and navigation, consists the mutual happiness and prosperity both of England and America. She derived assistance and protection from us; and we reaped from her the most important advantages. She was, indeed, the fountain of our wealth, the nerve of our strength, the nursery and basis of our naval power. It is our duty, therefore, my lords, if we wish to save our country, most seriously to endeavor the recovery of these most beneficial subjects; and in this perilous crisis, perhaps the present moment may be the only one in which we can hope for success. For in their negotiations with France they have, or think they have, reason to complain: though it be notorious that they have received from that power important supplies and assistance of various kinds, yet it is certain they expected it in a more decisive and immediate degree. America is in ill humor with France on some points that have not entirely answered her expectations. Let us wisely take advantage of every possible moment of reconciliation. Besides, the natural disposition of

America herself still leans towards England; to the old habits of connection and mutual interest that united both countries. This was the established sentiment of all the continent; and still, my lords, in the great and principal part, the sound part of America, this wise and affectionate disposition prevails; and there is a very considerable part of America yet sound—the middle and the southern provinces. Some parts may be factious and blind to their true interests; but if we express a wise and benevolent disposition to communicate with them those immutable rights of nature, and those constitutional liberties, to which they are equally entitled with ourselves; by a conduct so just and humane, we shall confirm the favorable and conciliate the adverse. I say, my lords, the rights and liberties to which they are equally entitled with ourselves, but no more. I would participate to them every enjoyment and freedom which the colonizing subjects of a free State can possess, or wish to possess; and I do not see why they should not enjoy every fundamental right in their property, and every original substantial liberty, which Devonshire or Surrey, or the county I live in, or any other county in England, can claim; reserving always, as the sacred right of the mother country, the due constitutional dependency of the colonies. The inherent supremacy of the State in regulating and protecting the navigation and commerce of all her subjects is necessary for the mutual benefit and preservation of every part, to constitute and preserve the prosperous arrangement of the whole empire.

The sound parts of America, of which I have spoken, must be sensible of these great truths and of their real interests. America is not in that state of desperate and contemptible rebellion which this country has been deluded to believe. It is not a wild and lawless banditti, who, having nothing to lose, might hope to snatch something from public convulsions. Many of their leaders and great men have a great stake in this great contest. The gentleman who conducts their armies, I am told, has an estate of four or five thousand pounds a year, and when I consider these things I cannot but lament the inconsiderate violence of our penal acts, our declarations of treason and rebellion, with all the fatal effects of attainder and confiscation.

As to the disposition of foreign powers, which is asserted to be pacific and friendly, let us judge, my lords, rather by their actions and the nature of things, than by interested assertions. The uniform assistance supplied to America by France suggests a different conclusion. The most important interests of France, in aggrandizing and enriching herself with what she most wants, supplies of every naval store from America, must inspire her with different sentiments. The extraordinary preparations of the house of Bourbon, by land and by sea, from Dunkirk to the Straits, equally ready and willing to overwhelm these defenseless islands, should rouse us to a sense of their real disposition, and our own danger. Not five thousand troops in England!—hardly three thousand in Ireland! What can we oppose to the combined force of our enemies? Scarcely twenty ships of the line fully or sufficiently manned, that any admiral's reputation would permit him to take the command of. The river of Lisbon in the possession of our enemies! The seas swept by American privateers! Our channel trade torn to pieces by them! In this complicated crisis of danger, weakness at home and calamity abroad, terrified and insulted by the neighboring powers, unable to act in America, or acting only to be destroyed, where is the man with the forehead to promise or hope for success in such a situation? or, from perseverance in the measures that have driven us to it? Who has the forehead to do so? Where is that man? I should be glad to see his face.

You cannot conciliate America by your present measures. You cannot subdue her by your present, or by any measures. What, then, can you do? You cannot conquer; you cannot gain; but you can address; you can lull the fears and anxieties of the moment into an ignorance of the danger that should produce them. But, my lords, the time demands the language of truth. We must not now apply the flattering unction of servile compliance or blind complaisance. In a just and necessary war to maintain the rights or honor of my country, I would strip the shirt from my back to support it. But in such a war as this, unjust in its principle, impracticable in its means, and ruinous in its consequences, I would not contribute a single effort, nor a single shilling. I do not call for vengeance on the heads of those who have been guilty; I only recommend to them to make their retreat. Let them walk off; and let them make haste, or they may be assured that speedy and condign punishment will overtake them.

My lords, I have submitted to you, with the freedom and truth which I think my duty, my sentiments on your present awful situation. I have laid before you the ruin of your power,

III—68

the disgrace of your reputation, the pollution of your discipline, the contamination of your morals, the complication of calamities, foreign and domestic, that overwhelm your sinking country. Your dearest interests, your own liberties, the constitution itself, totters to the foundation. All this disgraceful danger, this multitude of misery, is the monstrous offspring of this unnatural war. We have been deceived and deluded too long. Let us now stop short. This is the crisis—the only crisis of time and situation, to give us a possibility of escape from the fatal effects of our delusions. But if, in an obstinate and infatuated perseverance in folly, we slavishly echo the peremptory words this day presented to us, nothing can save this devoted country from complete and final ruin. We madly rush into multiplied miseries and "confusion worse confounded."

Is it possible, can it be believed, that ministers are yet blind to this impending destruction? I did hope that instead of this false and empty vanity, this overweening pride, engendering high conceits and presumptuous imaginations, that ministers would have humbled themselves in their errors, would have confessed and retracted them, and by an active, though a late repentance, have endeavored to redeem them. But, my lords, since they had neither sagacity to foresee, nor justice nor humanity to shun, these oppressive calamities; since not even severe experience can make them feel, nor the imminent ruin of their country awaken them from their stupefaction, the guardian care of Parliament must interpose. I shall, therefore, my lords, propose to you an amendment to the address to his Majesty, to be inserted immediately after the first two paragraphs of congratulation on the birth of a princess, to recommend an immediate cessation of hostilities and the commencement of a treaty to restore peace and liberty to America, strength and happiness to England, security and permanent prosperity to both countries. This, my lords, is yet in our power; and let not the wisdom and justice of your lordships neglect the happy, and, perhaps, the only opportunity. By the establishment of irrevocable law, founded on mutual rights, and ascertained by treaty, these glorious enjoyments may be firmly perpetuated. And let me repeat to your lordships, that the strong bias of America, at least of the wise and sounder parts of it, naturally inclines to this happy and constitutional reconnection with you. Notwithstanding the temporary intrigues with France, we may still be assured of their

ancient and confirmed partiality to us. America and France cannot be congenial. There is something decisive and confirmed in the honest American that will not assimilate to the futility and levity of Frenchmen.

My lords, to encourage and confirm that innate inclination to this country, founded on every principle of affection, as well as consideration of interest; to restore that favorable disposition into a permanent and powerful reunion with this country; to revive the mutual strength of the empire; again to awe the house of Bourbon, instead of meanly truckling, as our present calamities compel us, to every insult of French caprice and Spanish punctilio; to re-establish our commerce; to reassert our rights and our honor; to confirm our interests, and renew our glories forever, a consummation most devoutly to be endeavored! and which, I trust, may yet arise from reconciliation with America; I have the honor of submitting to you the following amendment, which I move to be inserted after the first two paragraphs of the address:—

"And that this house does most humbly advise and supplicate his Majesty, to be pleased to cause the most speedy and effectual measures to be taken, for restoring peace in America: and that no time may be lost in proposing an immediate cessation of hostilities there, in order to the opening of a treaty for the final settlement of the tranquillity of these invaluable provinces, by a removal of the unhappy causes of this ruinous civil war; and by a just and adequate security against the return of the like calamities in times to come. And this house desires to offer the most dutiful assurances to his Majesty, that it will, in due time, cheerfully co-operate with the magnanimity and tender goodness of his Majesty, for the preservation of his people, by such explicit and most solemn declarations, and provisions of fundamental and revocable laws, as may be judged necessary for the ascertaining and fixing forever the respective rights of Great Britain and her colonies."

[Lord Suffolk, having defended the employment of the Indians in war, as "a means that *God and nature put into our hands!*" Lord Chatham resumed:]—

I am astonished! shocked! to hear such principles confessed—to hear them avowed in this house, or in this country: principles **equally** unconstitutional, inhuman, and unchristian!

My lords, I did not intend to have encroached again upon your attention; but I cannot repress my indignation. I feel myself impelled by every duty. My lords, we are called upon as members of this house, as men, as Christian men, to protest against such notions standing near the throne, polluting the ear of majesty. "That God and nature put into our hand!" I know not what ideas that lord may entertain of God and nature; but I know that such abominable principles are equally abhorrent to religion and humanity. What! to attribute the sacred sanction of God and nature to the massacres of the Indian scalping knife—to the cannibal savage torturing, murdering, roasting, and eating; literally, my lords, eating the mangled victims of his barbarous battles! Such horrible notions shock every precept of religion, divine or natural, and every generous feeling of humanity. And, my lords, they shock every sentiment of honor; they shock me as a lover of honorable war and a detester of murderous barbarity.

These abominable principles, and this more abominable avowal of them, demand the most decisive indignation. I call upon that right reverend bench, those holy ministers of the Gospel and pious pastors of our church; I conjure them to join in the holy work, and vindicate the religion of their God. I appeal to the wisdom and the law of this learned bench, to defend and support the justice of their country. I call upon the bishops to interpose the unsullied sanctity of their lawn; upon the learned judges to interpose the purity of their ermine, to save us from this pollution. I call upon the honor of your lordships to reverence the dignity of your ancestors and to maintain your own. I call upon the spirit and humanity of my country to vindicate the national character. I invoke the genius of the constitution. From the tapestry that adorns these walls, the immortal ancestor of this noble lord frowns with indignation at the disgrace of his country. In vain he led your victorious fleets against the boasted Armada of Spain; in vain he defended and established the honor, the liberties, the religion, the Protestant religion, of this country, against the arbitrary cruelties of Popery and the Inquisition, if these more than popish cruelties and inquisitorial practices are let loose among us; to turn forth into our settlements, among our ancient connections, friends, and relations, the merciless cannibal, thirsting for the blood of man, woman, and child! to send forth the infidel savage—against whom? against your Protestant brethren; to lay waste their country, to desolate their dwellings, and extirpate their race and name, with these horrible hell-hounds of savage war!—hell-hounds, I say, of savage war. Spain armed herself with blood-hounds to extirpate the wretched natives of America; and we improve on the inhuman example even of Spanish cruelty; we turn loose these savage hell-hounds against our brethren and countrymen in America, of the same language, laws, liberties, and religion; endeared to us by every tie that should sanctify humanity.

My lords, this awful subject, so important to our honor, constitution, and our religion, demands the most solemn and effectual inquiry. And I again call upon your lordships, and the united powers of the State, to examine it thoroughly and decisively and to stamp upon it an indelible stigma of the public abhorrence. And I again implore those holy prelates of our religion to do away these inquities from among us. Let them perform a lustration; let them purify this house and this country from this sin.

My lords, I am old and weak, and at present unable to say more; but my feelings and indignation were too strong to have said less. I could not have slept this night in my bed, nor reposed my head on my pillow, without giving this vent to my eternal abhorrence of such preposterous and enormous principles.

THE ENGLISH CONSTITUTION

(A Speech Delivered in the House of Lords in Reply to Lord Mansfield in the Case of Wilkes, January 9th, 1770)

My Lords:—

THERE is one plain maxim, to which I have invariably adhered through life; that in every question in which my liberty or my property were concerned, I should consult and be determined by the dictates of common sense. I confess, my lords, that I am prone to distrust the refinements of learning, because I have seen the ablest and most learned men equally liable to deceive themselves and to mislead others. The condition of human nature would be lamentable indeed, if nothing less than the greatest learning and talents, which fall to the share of so small a number of men, were sufficient to direct our judgment and our conduct. But Providence has taken better care of our

happiness, and given us, in the simplicity of common sense, a rule for our direction, by which we can never be misled. I confess, my lords, I had no other guide in drawing up the amendment which I submitted to your consideration; and, before I heard the opinion of the noble lord who spoke last, I did not conceive that it was even within the limits of possibility for the greatest human genius, the most subtle understanding, or the acutest wit, so strangely to misrepresent my meaning, and to give it an interpretation so entirely foreign from what I intended to express, and from that sense which the very terms of the amendment plainly and distinctly carry with them. If there be the smallest foundation for the censure thrown upon me by that noble lord, if, either expressly, or by the most distant implication, I have said or insinuated any part of what the noble lord has charged me with, discard my opinions forever, discard the motion with contempt.

My lords, I must beg the indulgence of the House. Neither will my health permit me, nor do I pretend to be qualified to follow that learned lord minutely through the whole of his argument. No man is better acquainted with his abilities and learning, nor has a greater respect for them than I have. I have had the pleasure of sitting with him in the other House, and always listened to him with attention. I have not now lost a word of what he said, nor did I ever. Upon the present question I meet him without fear. The evidence which truth carries with it is superior to all argument; it neither wants the support nor dreads the opposition of the greatest abilities. If there be a single word in the amendment to justify the interpretation which the noble lord has been pleased to give it, I am ready to renounce the whole. Let it be read, my lords; let it speak for itself. [The amendment was read.] In what instance does it interfere with the privileges of the House of Commons? In what respect does it question their jurisdiction, or suppose an authority in this House to arraign the justice of their sentence? I am sure that every lord who hears me will bear me witness, that I said not one word touching the merits of the Middlesex election. So far from conveying any opinion upon that matter in the amendment, I did not even in discourse deliver my own sentiments upon it. I did not say that the House of Commons had done either right or wrong; but, when his Majesty was pleased to recommend it to us to cultivate unanimity among ourselves, I

thought it the duty of this House, as the great hereditary council of the Crown, to state to his Majesty the distracted condition of his dominions, together with the events which had destroyed unanimity among his subjects. But, my lords, I stated events merely as facts, without the smallest addition either of censure or of opinion. They are facts, my lords, which I am not only convinced are true, but which I know are indisputably true. For example, my lords, will any man deny that discontents prevail in many parts of his Majesty's dominions? or that those discontents arise from the proceedings of the House of Commons touching the declared incapacity of Mr. Wilkes? It is impossible. No man can deny a truth so notorious. Or will any man deny that those proceedings refused, by a resolution of one branch of the Legislature only, to the subject his common right? Is it not indisputably true, my lords, that Mr. Wilkes had a common right, and that he lost it in no other way but by a resolution of the House of Commons? My lords, I have been tender of misrepresenting the House of Commons. I have consulted their journals, and have taken the very words of their own resolution. Do they not tell us in so many words, that Mr. Wilkes, having been expelled, was thereby rendered incapable of serving in that Parliament? And is it not in their resolution alone which refuses to the subject his common right? The amendment says further, that the electors of Middlesex are deprived of their free choice of a representative. Is this a false fact, my lords? Or have I given an unfair representation of it? Will any man presume to affirm that Colonel Lutrell is the free choice of the electors of Middlesex? We all know the contrary. We all know that Mr. Wilkes (whom I mention without either praise or censure) was the favorite of the county, and chosen by a very great and acknowledged majority to represent them in Parliament. If the noble lord dislikes the manner in which these facts are stated, I shall think myself happy in being advised by him how to alter it. I am very little anxious about terms, provided the substance be preserved; and these are facts, my lords, which I am sure will always retain their weight and importance, in whatever form of language they are described.

Now, my lords, since I have been forced to enter into the explanation of an amendment, in which nothing less than the genius of penetration could have discovered an obscurity, and having, as I hope, redeemed myself in the opinion of the House,

having redeemed my motion from the severe representation given of it by the noble lord, I must a little longer entreat your lordships' indulgence. The Constitution of this country has been openly invaded in fact; and I have heard, with horror and astonishment, that very invasion defended upon principle. What is this mysterious power, undefined by law, unknown to the subject, which we must not approach without awe, nor speak of without reverence—which no man may question, and to which all men must submit? My lords, I thought the slavish doctrine of passive obedience had long since exploded; and, when our Kings were obliged to confess that their title to the Crown, and the rule of their government, had no other foundation than the known laws of the land, I never expected to hear a divine right, or a divine infallibility, attributed to any other branch of the Legislature. My lords, I beg to be understood. No man respects the House of Commons more than I do, or would contend more strenuously than I would to preserve to them their just and legal authority. Within the bounds prescribed by the Constitution, that authority is necessary to the well-being of the people. Beyond that line, every exertion of power is arbitrary, is illegal; it threatens tyranny to the people, and destruction to the State. Power without right is the most odious and detestable object that can be offered to the human imagination. It is not only pernicious to those who are subject to it, but tends to its own destruction. It is what my noble friend [Lord Lyttleton] has truly described it, *Res detestabilis et caduca*. My lords, I acknowledge the just power, and reverence the Constitution of the House of Commons. It is for their own sakes that I would prevent their assuming a power which the Constitution has denied them, lest, by grasping at an authority they have no right to, they should forfeit that which they legally possess. My lords, I affirm that they have betrayed their constituents, and violated the Constitution. Under pretense of declaring the law, they have made a law, and united in the same persons the office of legislator and judge!

I shall endeavor to adhere strictly to the noble lord's doctrine, which is, indeed, impossible to mistake, so far as my memory will permit me to preserve his expressions. He seems fond of the word jurisdiction; and I confess, with the force and effect which he has given it, it is a word of copious meaning and wonderful extent. If his lordship's doctrine be well founded, we must renounce all those political maxims by which our understandings have hitherto been directed, and even the first elements of learning taught in our schools when we were schoolboys. My lords, we knew that jurisdiction was nothing more than *jus dicere*. We knew that *legem facere* and *legem dicere* (to make law and to declare it) were powers clearly distinguished from each other in the nature of things, and wisely separated from each other by the wisdom of the English Constitution. But now, it seems, we must adopt a new system of thinking! The House of Commons, we are told, have a supreme jurisdiction, and there is no appeal from their sentence; and that, wherever they are competent judges, their decision must be received and submitted to as, *ipso facto*, the law of the land. My lords, I am a plain man, and have been brought up in a religious reverence for the original simplicity of the laws of England. By what sophistry they have been perverted, by what artifices they have been involved in obscurity, is not for me to explain. The principles, however, of the English laws are still sufficiently clear; they are founded in reason, and are the masterpieces of human understanding; but it is in the text that I would look for a direction to my judgment, not in the commentaries of modern professors. The noble lord assures us that he knows not in what code the law of Parliament is to be found; that the House of Commons, when they act as judges, have no law to direct them but their own wisdom; that their decision is law; and if they determine wrong, the subject has no appeal but to heaven. What then, my lords? Are all the generous efforts of our ancestors, are all those glorious contentions by which they meant to secure to themselves, and to transmit to their posterity, a known law, a certain rule of living, reduced to this conclusion, that, instead of the arbitrary power of a King, we must submit to the arbitrary power of a House of Commons? If this be true, what benefit do we derive from the exchange? Tyranny, my lords, is detestable in every shape, but in none so formidable as when it is assumed and exercised by a number of tyrants. But, my lords, this is not the fact; this is not the Constitution. We have a law of Parliament. We have a code in which every honest man may find it. We have Magna Charta. We have the Statute Book, and the Bill of Rights.

If a case should arise unknown to these great authorities, we have still that plain English reason left, which is the foundation

of all our English jurisprudence. That reason tells us that every judicial court and every political society must be invested with those powers and privileges which are necessary for performing the office to which they are appointed. It tells us, also, that no court of justice can have a power inconsistent with, or paramount to, the known laws of the land; that the people, when they choose their representatives, never mean to convey to them a power of invading the rights, or trampling on the liberties of those whom they represent. What security would they have for their rights, if once they admitted that a court of judicature might determine every question that came before it, not by any known positive law, but by the vague, indeterminate, arbitrary rule of what the noble lord is pleased to call the wisdom of the court? With respect to the decision of the courts of justice, I am far from denying them their due weight and authority; yet, placing them in the most respectable view, I still consider them, not as law, but as an evidence of the law. And before they can arrive even at that degree of authority, it must appear that they are founded in and confirmed by reason; that they are supported by precedents taken from good and moderate times; that they do not contradict any positive law; that they are submitted to without reluctance by the people; that they are unquestioned by the Legislature (which is equivalent to a tacit confirmation); and what, in my judgment, is by far the most important, that they do not violate the spirit of the Constitution. My lords, this is not a vague or loose expression. We all know what the Constitution is. We all know that the first principle of it is that the subject shall not be governed by the *arbitrium* of any one man or body of men (less than the whole Legislature), but by certain laws, to which he has virtually given his consent, which are open to him to examine, which are not beyond his ability to understand. Now, my lords, I affirm, and am ready to maintain, that the late decision of the House of Commons upon the Middlesex election is destitute of every one of those properties and conditions which I hold to be essential to the legality of such a decision. It is not founded in reason; for it carries with it a contradiction, that the representative should perform the office of the constituent body. It is not supported by a single precedent; for the case of Sir Robert Walpole is but a half precedent, and even that half is imperfect. Incapacity was indeed declared, but his crimes are stated as the ground of the resolution, and his oppo-

nent was declared to be not duly elected, even after his incapacity was established. It contradicts Magna Charta and the Bill of Rights, by which it is provided that no subject shall be deprived of his freehold, unless by the judgment of his peers or the law of the land; and that elections of members to serve in Parliament shall be free. So far is this decision from being submitted to the people, that they have taken the strongest measures, and adopted the most positive language to express their discontent. Whether it will be questioned by the Legislature will depend upon your lordships' resolution; but that it violates the spirit of the Constitution, will, I think, be disputed by no man who has heard this day's debate, and who wished well to the freedom of his country. Yet, if we are to believe the noble lord, this great grievance, this manifest violation of the first principles of the Constitution, will not admit of a remedy. It is not even capable of redress, unless we appeal at once to heaven! My lords, I have better hopes of the Constitution, and a firmer confidence in the wisdom and constitutional authority of this house. It is to your ancestors, my lords, it is to the English barons, that we are indebted for the laws and Constitution we possess. Their virtues were rude and uncultivated, but they were great and sincere. Their understandings were as little polished as their manners, but they had hearts to distinguish right from wrong; they had heads to distinguish truth from falsehood; they understood the rights of humanity, and they had the spirit to maintain them.

My lords, I think that history has not done justice to their conduct, when they obtained from their sovereign that great acknowledgment of national rights contained in Magna Charta; they did not confine it to themselves alone, but delivered it as a common blessing to the whole people. They did not say, these are the rights of the great barons, or these are the rights of the great prelates. No, my lords, they said, in the simple Latin of the times, *nullus liber homo* (no free man), and provided as carefully for the meanest subject as for the greatest. These are uncouth words, and sound but poorly in the ears of scholars; neither are they addressed to the criticism of scholars, but to the hearts of free men. These three words, *nullus liber homo*, have meaning which interests us all. They deserve to be remembered—they deserve to be inculcated in our minds— they are worth all the classics. Let us not, then, degenerate from the glorious example of our ancestors. Those iron barons

(for so I may call them when compared with the silken barons of modern days) were the guardians of the people; yet their virtues, my lords, were never engaged in a question of such importance as the present. A breach has been made in the Constitution—the battlements are dismantled—the citadel is open to the first invader—the walls totter—the Constitution is not tenable. What remains, then, but for us to stand foremost in the breach, and repair it, or perish in it?

Great pains have been taken to alarm us with the consequences of a difference between the two houses of Parliament; that the House of Commons will resent our presuming to take notice of their proceedings; that they will resent our daring to advise the Crown, and never forgive us for attempting to save the State. My lords, I am sensible of the importance and difficulty of this great crisis; at a moment such as this, we are called upon to do our duty, without dreading the resentment of any man. But if apprehensions of this kind are to affect us, let us consider which we ought to respect the most, the representative or the collective body of the people. My lords, five hundred gentlemen are not ten millions; and if we must have a contention, let us take care to have the English nation on our side. If this question be given up, the freeholders of England are reduced to a condition baser than the peasantry of Poland. If they desert their own cause, they deserve to be slaves! My lords, this is not merely the cold opinion of my understanding, but the glowing expression of what I feel. It is my heart that speaks. I know I speak warmly, my lords; but this warmth shall neither betray my argument nor my temper. The kingdom is in a flame. As mediators between a King and people, is it not our duty to represent to him the true condition and temper of his subjects? It is a duty which no particular respects should hinder us from performing; and whenever his Majesty shall demand our advice, it will then be our duty to inquire more minutely into the cause of the present discontents. Whenever that inquiry shall come on, I pledge myself to the house to prove that, since the first institution of the House of Commons, not a single precedent can be produced to justify their late proceedings. My noble and learned friend [the Lord Chancellor Camden] has pledged himself to the house that he will support that assertion.

My lords, the character and circumstances of Mr. Wilkes have been very improperly introduced into this question, not only here, but in that court of judicature where his cause was tried—I mean the House of Commons. With one party he was a patriot of the first magnitude; with the other, the vilest incendiary. For my own part, I consider him merely and indifferently as an English subject, possessed of certain rights which the laws have given him, and which the laws alone can take from him. I am neither moved by his private vices nor by his public merits. In his person, though he were the worst of men, I contend for the safety and security of the best. God forbid, my lords, that there should be a power in this country of measuring the civil rights of the subject by his moral character, or by any other rule but the fixed laws of the land! I believe, my lords, I shall not be suspected of any personal partiality to this unhappy man. I am not very conversant in pamphlets and newspapers; but from what I have heard, and from the little I have read, I may venture to affirm that I have had my share in the compliments which have come from that quarter. As for motives of ambition (for I must take to myself a part of the noble Duke's insinuation), I believe, my lords, there have been times in which I have had the honor of standing in such favor in the closet, that there must have been something extravagantly unreasonable in my wishes if they might not all have been gratified. After neglecting those opportunities I am now suspected of coming forward, in the decline of life, in the anxious pursuit of wealth and power which it is impossible for me to enjoy. Be it so! There is one ambition at least, which I ever will acknowledge, which I will not renounce but with my life. It is the ambition of delivering to my posterity those rights of freedom which I have received from my ancestors. I am not now pleading the cause of the individual, but of every freeholder in England. In what manner this house may constitutionally interpose in their defense, and what kind of redress this case will require and admit of, is not at present the subject of our consideration. The amendment, if agreed to, will naturally lead us to such an inquiry. That inquiry may, perhaps, point out the necessity of an act of the Legislature, or it may lead us, perhaps, to desire a conference with the other house; which one noble lord affirms is the only parliamentary way of proceeding, and which another noble lord assures us the House of Commons would either not come to, or would break off with indignation. Leaving their lordships to reconcile that matter between themselves, I shall

only say that, before we have inquired, we cannot be provided with materials; consequently, we are not at present prepared for a conference.

It is not impossible, my lords, that the inquiry I speak of may lead us to advise his Majesty to dissolve the present Parliament; nor have I any doubt of our right to give that advice, if we should think it necessary. His Majesty will then determine whether he will yield to the united petitions of the people of England, or maintain the House of Commons in the exercise of a legislative power which heretofore abolished the House of Lords and overturned the monarchy. I willingly acquit the present House of Commons of having actually formed so detestable a design; but they cannot themselves foresee to what excesses they may be carried hereafter; and, for my own part, I should be sorry to trust to their future moderation. Unlimited power is apt to corrupt the minds of those who possess it; and this I know, my lords, that where law ends, tyranny begins!

CHATHAM'S LAST SPEECH
(From Harsha, after Goodrich)

[On the seventh of April, 1778, Lord Chatham made his appearance, for the last time, in the House of Lords. It is a day memorable for the occurrence of one of the most affecting scenes ever witnessed in Parliament—a day when the great master of modern oratory was overwhelmed by the effort of his own powerful eloquence.

Lord Chatham was ignorant of the real state of feeling in America. He imagined that the colonies might be brought back to their former allegiance to the British Government. He did not wish to see the extensive dominion of old England rent in twain and the independence of America recognized. He could not endure these thoughts. He therefore heard «with unspeakable concern» that the Duke of Richmond intended, on the seventh of April, to move an address to the king, advising him to effect a conciliation with America, involving her independence. Such a measure he thought was disastrous and ruinous to the prosperity and happiness of England. He determined to take a bold stand against it, and, accordingly, was carried to the House of Lords, to raise his voice against the dismemberment of the empire. «He was led into the House of Peers by his son, the Honorable William Pitt, and his son-in-law, Lord Mahon. He was dressed in a rich suit of black velvet, and covered up to the knees in flannel. Within his large wig, little more of his countenance was seen than his aquiline nose and his penetrating eye, which retained all its native fire. He looked like a dying man, yet never was seen a figure of more dignity. He appeared like a being of a superior

species. The lords stood up and made a lane for him to pass to his seat, while, with a gracefulness of deportment for which he was so eminently distinguished, he bowed to them as he proceeded. Having taken his seat, he listened with profound attention to the Duke of Richmond's speech.» When Lord Weymouth had finished his reply in behalf of the ministry, Lord Chatham rose with slowness and great difficulty, and delivered the following speech. «Supported by his two relations, he lifted his hand from the crutch on which he leaned, raised it up, and, casting his eyes toward heaven, commenced as follows:»]

I THANK God that I have been enabled to come here to-day to perform my duty, and speak on a subject which is so deeply impressed on my mind. I am old and infirm. I have one foot—more than one foot—in the grave. I have risen from my bed to stand up in the cause of my country—perhaps never again to speak in this house.

[«The reverence, the attention, the stillness of the house,» said an eyewitness, «were here most affecting: had any one dropped a handkerchief, the noise would have been heard.»

As he proceeded, Lord Chatham spoke at first in a low tone, with all the weakness of one who is laboring under a severe indisposition. Gradually, however, as he warmed with the subject, his voice became louder and more distinct, his intonations grew more commanding, and his whole manner was solemn and impressive in the highest degree.]

«My lords,» he exclaimed, «I rejoice that the grave has not closed upon me; that I am still alive, to lift up my voice against the dismemberment of this ancient and most noble monarchy! Pressed down as I am by the hand of infirmity, I am little able to assist my country in this most perilous conjuncture; but, my lords, while I have sense and memory, I will never consent to deprive the offspring of the royal house of Brunswick, the heirs of the Princess Sophia, of their fairest inheritance. Shall we tarnish the lustre of this nation by an ignominious surrender of its rights and fairest possessions? Shall this great nation, that has survived, whole and entire, the Danish depredations, the Scottish inroads, the Norman Conquest—that has stood the threatened invasion of the Spanish Armada, now fall prostrate before the house of Bourbon? Surely, my lords, this nation is no longer what it was! Shall a people that seventeen years ago were the terror of the world now stoop so low as to tell their ancient inveterate enemy, Take all we have, only give us peace? It is impossible.

«In God's name, if it is absolutely necessary to declare either for peace or war, and the former cannot be preserved with honor, why is not the latter commenced without delay? I am not, I confess, well-informed as to the resources of this kingdom, but I trust it has still sufficient to maintain its just rights, though I know them not. But, my lords, any state is better than despair. Let us at least make one effort, and, if we must fall, let us fall like men!»

[When Lord Chatham had taken his seat Lord Temple said to him, «You have forgotten to mention what we have been talking about. Shall I get up?» «No,» replied Lord Chatham, «I will do it by and by.»

After the Duke of Richmond had concluded his speech, Lord Chatham made a strenuous attempt to rise, but after repeated efforts to regain an erect position, he suddenly pressed his hand to his heart and fell down in convulsions. The Duke of Cumberland, Lord Temple, Lord Stanford, and other peers caught him in their arms; and his son, the celebrated William Pitt, then a youth of seventeen, sprang forward to support him. The debate was immediately adjourned. Lord Chatham was conveyed in a state of insensibility from the house to his country residence at Hayes, where he lingered a few days, and expired on the eleventh of May, 1778, aged seventy years.]

DR. CHARLES CHAUNCY

(1705-1787)

A DISCOURSE of thanksgiving for the repeal of the Stamp Act must, from its historic associations, be interesting to Americans, and particularly so when some parts of it are found to be strikingly suggestive of passages in the speech delivered by Edmund Burke in the House of Commons three years later, showing that the utterances of the colonial clergymen in "the times that tried men's souls" were not without effect in England. Doctor Chauncy's remarks about the Stamp Act seem to have been in the mind of Burke when he made the speech referred to. In this discourse the reader will also find a clear and true statement of the aims of the Colonies up to the last moment when they were forced, in self-defense, to strike for independence. Till then they had no thought of anything but their inherited rights as Englishmen, and aimed at nothing more than some such system of local self-government as Canada now enjoys.

Doctor Chauncy's style is studiously plain, simple, and direct. The only ornamental expressions he allowed himself were apt quotations from the Bible. He was strongly opposed on principle to emotional or exciting oratory, and especially to such preaching as that of Whitefield with the attending religious excitement. He is even said to have expressed a wish that "somebody would translate Milton's 'Paradise Lost' into English," so that he could read it.

He was a descendant of the Charles Chauncy who was the second president of Harvard College. Born in Boston, January 1st, 1705, he was graduated from Harvard in 1721. Ordained soon afterwards, he became pastor of the First Church, Boston, and remained in charge of it until his death, February 10th, 1787.

III—69

GOOD NEWS FROM A FAR COUNTRY

(From a "Discourse Delivered on the Occasion of the Repeal of the Stamp Act on a Day of Thanksgiving Appointed by His Excellency the Governor of Massachusetts Bay in New England")

WHAT I have in view is to take occasion to call your attention to some of the important articles contained in the good news we have heard, which so powerfully fit it to excite a pungent sense of pleasure in the breasts of all that inhabit these American lands. The way will then be prepared to point out to you the wisest and best use we can make of these glad tidings "from a far country." . . .

In fine, this news is refreshing to us, "as cold waters to a thirsty soul," as it has affected an alteration in the state of things among us unspeakably to our advantage. There is no way in which we can so strikingly be made sensible of this as by contrasting the state we were lately in, and the much worse one we should soon have been in had the Stamp Act been enforced, with that happy one we are put into by its repeal.

Upon its being made certain to the colonies that the Stamp Act had passed both houses of Parliament and received the king's fiat, a general spirit of uneasiness at once took place, which, gradually increasing, soon discovered itself by the wiser sons of liberty in laudable endeavors to obtain relief; though by others in murmurings and complaints, in anger and clamor, in bitterness, wrath, and strife; and by some evil-minded persons, taking occasion herefor from the general ferment of men's minds, in those violent outrages upon the property of others, which, by being represented in an undue light, may have reflected dishonor upon a country which has an abhorrence of such injurious conduct. The colonies were never before in a state of such discontent, anxiety, and perplexing solicitude; some despairing of a redress, some hoping for it, and all fearing what would be the event. And, had it been the determination of the King and Parliament to have carried the Stamp Act into effect by ships of war and an embarkation of troops, their conditions, however unhappy before, would have been inconceivably more so. They must either have submitted to what they thought an insupportable burden, and have parted with their property without any will of their own, or have stood upon their defense; in either of

which cases their situation must have been deplorably sad. So far as I am able to judge from that firmness of mind and resolution of spirit which appeared among all sorts of persons, as grounded upon this principle, deeply rooted in their minds, that they had a constitutional right to grant their own moneys and to be tried by their peers, 'tis more than probable they would not have submitted unless they had been obliged to do it by superior power. Not that they had a thought in their hearts, as may have been represented, of being an independent people. They esteemed it both their happiness and their glory to be, in common with the inhabitants of England, Scotland, and Ireland, the subjects of King George III., whom they heartily love and honor, and in defense of whose person and crown they would cheerfully expend their treasure and lose even their blood. But it was a sentiment they had imbibed, that they should be wanting neither in loyalty to their King, or a due regard to the British Parliament, if they should not defend those rights which they imagined were inalienable, upon the footing of justice, by any power on earth. And had they, upon this principle, whether ill or well founded, stood upon their defense, what must have been the effect? There would have been opened on this American continent a most doleful scene of outrage, violence, desolation, slaughter, and, in a word, all those terrible evils that may be expected as the attendants on a state of civil war. No language can describe the distresses, in all their various kinds and degrees, which would have made us miserable. God only knows how long they might have continued, and whether they would have ended in anything short of our total ruin. Nor would the mother country, whatever some might imagine, have been untouched with what was doing in the colonies. Those millions that were due from this continent to Great Britain could not have been paid; a stop, a total stop, would have been put to the importation of those manufactures which are the support of thousands at home, often repeated. And would the British merchants and manufacturers have sat easy in such a state of things? There would, it may be, have been as much clamor, wrath, and strife in the very bowels of the nation as in these distant lands; nor could our destruction have been unconnected with consequences at home infinitely to be dreaded.

But the longed-for repeal has scattered our fears, removed our difficulties, enlivened our hearts, and laid the foundation of

future prosperity, equal to the adverse state we should have been in had the act been continued and enforced.

We may now be easy in our minds—contented with our condition. We may be at peace and quiet among ourselves, every one minding his own business. All ground of complaint that we are "sold for bondmen and bondwomen" is removed away, and, instead of being slaves to those who treat us with rigor, we are indulged the full exercise of those liberties which have been transmitted to us as the richest inheritance from our forefathers. We have now greater reason than ever to love, honor, and obey our gracious king, and pay all becoming reverence and respect to his two houses of Parliament; and may with entire confidence rely on their wisdom, lenity, kindness, and power to promote our welfare. We have now, in a word, nothing to "make us afraid," but may "sit every man under his vine and under his fig-tree," in the full enjoyment of the many good things we are favored with in the providence of God.

Upon such a change in the state of our circumstances, we should be lost to all sense of duty and gratitude, and act as though we had no understanding, if our hearts did not expand with joy. And, in truth, the danger is lest we should exceed in the expression of it. It may be said of these colonies, as of the Jewish people, upon the repeal of the decree of Ahasuerus, which devoted them to destruction, they "had light and gladness, joy and honor; and in every province, and in every city, whithersoever the king's commandment and his decree came, they had joy and gladness, a feast day, and a good day"; saying within themselves, "the Lord hath done great things for us, whereof we are glad." May the remembrance of this memorable repeal be preserved and handed down to future generations, in every province, in every city, and in every family, so as never to be forgotten.

We now proceed—the way being thus prepared for it—to point out the proper use we should make of this "good news from a far country," which is grateful to us "as cold waters to a thirsty soul."

We have already had our rejoicings, in the civil sense, upon the "glad tidings" from our mother country; and 'tis to our honor that they were carried on so universally within the bounds of a decent, warrantable regularity. There was never, among us, such a collection of all sorts of people upon any public occasion.

Nor were the methods in which they signified their joy ever so beautifully varied and multiplied; and yet, none had reason to complain of disorderly conduct. The show was seasonably ended, and we had afterwards a perfectly quiet night. There has, indeed, been no public disturbance since the outrage at Lieutenant-Governor Hutchinson's house. That was so detested by town and country, and such a spirit at once so generally stirred up, particularly among the people, to oppose such villainous conduct, as has preserved us ever since in a state of as great freedom from mobbish actions as has been known in the country. Our friends at home, it should seem, have entertained fears lest upon the lenity and condescension of the king and Parliament we should prove ourselves a factious, turbulent people; and our enemies hope we shall. But 'tis not easy to conceive on what the fears of the one or the hopes of the other should be grounded, unless they have received injurious representations of the spirit that lately prevailed in this as well as the other colonies, which was not a spirit to raise needless disturbances, or to commit outrages upon the persons or property of any, though some of those sons of wickedness which are to be found in all places might take occasion from the stand that was made for liberty, to commit violence with a high hand. There has not been, since the repeal, the appearance of a spirit tending to public disorder, nor is there any danger such a spirit should be encouraged or discovered, unless the people should be needlessly and unreasonably irritated by those, who, to serve themselves, might be willing we should gratify such as are our enemies, and make those so who have been our good friends. But, to leave this digression:

Though our civil joy has been expressed in a decent, orderly way, it would be but a poor, pitiful thing should we rest here, and not make our religious, grateful acknowledgments to the Supreme Ruler of the world, to whose superintending providence it is principally to be ascribed that we have had "given us so great deliverance." Whatever were the means or instruments in order to do this, that glorious being, whose throne is in the heavens, and whose kingdom ruleth over all, had the chief hand therein. He sat at the helm, and so governed all things relative to it as to bring it to this happy issue. It was under his allwise, overruling influence that a spirit was raised in all the colonies nobly to assert their freedom as men and English-born subjects —a spirit which, in the course of its operation, was highly serv-

iceable, not by any irregularities it might be the occasion of (in this imperfect state they will, more or less, mix themselves with everything great and good), but by its manly efforts setting forth the reasons they had for complaint in a fair, just, and strongly convincing light, hereby awakening the attention of Great Britain, opening the eyes of the merchants and manufacturers there, and engaging them, for their own interest as well as that of America, to exert themselves in all reasonable ways to help us. It was under the same all-governing influence that the late ministry, full of projections tending to the hurt of these colonies, was so seasonably changed into the present patriotic one, which is happily disposed, in all the methods of wisdom, to promote our welfare. It was under the same influence still that so many friends of eminent character were raised up and spirited to appear advocates in our behalf, and plead our cause with irresistible force. It was under the same influence, also, that the heart of our king and the British Parliament were so turned in favor to us as to reverse that decree which, had it been established, would have thrown this whole continent, if not the nation itself, into a state of the utmost confusion. In short, it was ultimately owing to this influence of the God of heaven that the thoughts, the views, the purposes, the speeches, the writings, and the whole conduct of all who were engaged in this great affair were so overruled as to bring into effect the desired happy event.

1095

LORD CHESTERFIELD

(PHILIP DORMER STANHOPE, FOURTH EARL OF CHESTERFIELD)

(1694–1773)

THAT history repeats itself, even in the matter of political agitations, is very plainly manifested in the speech on the Gin Act, delivered by Lord Chesterfield in the House of Lords in 1743. In it we find the arguments which have been made so familiar to the voters of America since the Prohibition movement began to figure in our politics more than fifty years ago. Lord Chesterfield on this occasion may have been more intent on harassing the ministry than on abolishing the liquor traffic, but no one has greatly improved upon his argument. He was a cultivated and trained statesman, a diplomat and man of affairs, as well as a man of fashion. He became Lord-Lieutenant of Ireland in 1744. Through his famous 'Letters to His Son,' which for more than a hundred years have been put into the hands of young persons going into society, his name has long been "a household word" in England and America, and all the world has read the famous letter written by him to Doctor Johnson. He was born in London, September 22d, 1694, and died March 24th, 1773.

AGAINST REVENUES FROM DRUNKENNESS AND VICE

(From the Speech on the Gin Act Delivered in the House of Lords, February 21st, 1743)

TO PRETEND, my lords, that the design of this bill is to prevent or diminish the use of spirits is to trample on common sense and to violate the rules of decency as well as of reason. For when did any man hear that a commodity was prohibited by licensing its sale, or that to offer and refuse is the same action?

It is indeed pleaded that it will be made dearer by the tax which is proposed, and that the increase of the price will diminish the number of the purchasers; but it is at the same time expected that this tax shall supply the expense of a war on the

Continent. It, is asserted, therefore, that the consumption of spirits will be hindered; and yet that it will be such as may be expected to furnish, from a very small tax, a revenue sufficient for the support of armies, or the re-establishment of the Austrian family, and the repressing of the attempts of France.

Surely, my lords, these expectations are not very consistent; nor can it be imagined that they are both formed in the same head, though they may be expressed by the same mouth. It is, however, some recommendation of a statesman, when, of his assertions, one can be found reasonable or true; and in this, praise cannot be denied to our present ministers. For though it is undoubtedly false that this tax will lessen the consumption of spirits, it is certainly true that it will produce a very large revenue—a revenue that will not fail but with the people from whose debaucheries it arises.

Our ministers will therefore have the same honor with their predecessors, of having given rise to a new fund; not indeed for the payment of our debts, but for much more valuable purposes; for the cheering of our hearts under oppression, and for the ready support of those debts which we have lost all hopes of paying. They are resolved, my lords, that the nation which no endeavors can make wise, shall, while they are at its head, at least be very merry; and, since public happiness is the end of government, they seem to imagine that they shall deserve applause by an expedient which will enable every man to lay his cares to sleep, to drown sorrow, and lose in the delights of drunkenness both the public miseries and his own.

Luxury, my lords, is to be taxed, but vice prohibited, let the difficulties in executing the law be what they will. Would you lay a tax on the breach of the ten commandments? Would not such a tax be wicked and scandalous; because it would imply an indulgence to all those who could pay the tax? Is not this a reproach most justly thrown by the Protestants upon the Church of Rome? Was it not the chief cause of the Reformation? And will you follow a precedent which brought reproach and ruin upon those that introduced it? This is the very case now before you. You are going to lay a tax, and consequently to indulge a sort of drunkenness, which almost necessarily produces a breach of every one of the ten commandments. Can you expect the reverend bench will approve of this. I am convinced they will not; and therefore I wish I had seen it full upon this occasion.

I am sure I have seen it much fuller upon other occasions, in which religion had no such deep concern.

We have already, my lords, several sorts of funds in this nation, so many that a man must have a good deal of learning to be master of them. Thanks to his Majesty, we have now among us the most learned man of the nation in this way. I wish he would rise up and tell us what name we are to give this new fund. We have already the Civil List Fund, the Sinking Fund, the Aggregate Fund, the South Sea Fund, and God knows how many others. What name we are to give this new fund I know not, unless we are to call it the Drinking Fund. It may, perhaps, enable the people of a certain foreign territory [Hanover] to drink claret, but it will disable the people of this kingdom from drinking anything else but gin; for when a man has, by gin drinking, rendered himself unfit for labor or business, he can purchase nothing else; and then the best thing for him to do is to drink on till he dies.

Surely, my lords, men of such unbounded benevolence as our present ministers deserve such honors as were never paid before; they deserve to bestride a butt upon every signpost in the city, or to have their figures exhibited as tokens where this liquor is to be sold by the license which they have procured. They must be at least remembered to future ages as the "happy politicians" who, after all expedients for raising taxes had been employed, discovered a new method of draining the last relics of the public wealth, and added a new revenue to the Government. Nor will those who shall hereafter enumerate the several funds now established among us, forget, among the benefactors to their country, the illustrious authors of the Drinking Fund.

May I be allowed, my lords, to congratulate my countrymen and fellow-subjects upon the happy times which are now approaching, in which no man will be disqualified from the privilege of being drunk; when all discontent and disloyalty shall be forgotten, and the people, though now considered by the ministry as enemies, shall acknowledge the leniency of that government under which all restraints are taken away?

But, to a bill for such desirable purposes, it would be proper, my lords, to prefix a preamble, in which the kindness of our intentions should be more fully explained, that the nation may not mistake our indulgence for cruelty, not consider their benefactors as their persecutors. If, therefore, this bill be considered and

amended (for why else should it be considered?) in a committee, I shall humbly propose that it shall be introduced in this manner: "Whereas the designs of the present ministry, whatever they are, cannot be executed without a great number of mercenaries, which mercenaries cannot be hired without money; and whereas the present disposition of this nation to drunkenness inclines us to believe that they will pay more cheerfully for the undisturbed enjoyment of distilled liquors than for any other concession that can be made by the Government; be it enacted by the King's most excellent Majesty, that no man shall hereafter be denied the right of being drunk on the following conditions."

The specious pretense on which this bill is founded, and, indeed, the only pretense that deserves to be termed specious, is the propriety of taxing vice; but this maxim of government has, on this occasion, been either mistaken or perverted. Vice, my lords, is not properly to be taxed, but suppressed; and heavy taxes are sometimes the only means by which that suppression can be attained. Luxury, my lords, or the excess of that which is pernicious only by excess, may very properly be taxed, that such excess, though not strictly unlawful, may be made more difficult. But the use of those things which are simply hurtful, hurtful in their own nature, and in every degree, is to be prohibited. None, my lords, ever heard, in any nation, of a tax upon theft or adultery, because a tax implies a license granted for the use of that which is taxed to all who shall be willing to pay it.

The noble lord has been pleased kindly to inform us that the trade of distilling is very extensive; that it employs great numbers; and that they have arrived at an exquisite skill, and therefore—note well the consequence—the trade of distilling is not to be discouraged.

Once more, my lords, allow me to wonder at the different conceptions of different understandings. It appears to me that since the spirits which the distillers produce are allowed to enfeeble the limbs and vitiate the blood, to pervert the heart and obscure the intellects, that the number of distillers should be no argument in their favor; for I never heard that a law against theft was repealed or delayed because thieves were numerous. It appears to me, my lords, that if so formidable a body are confederated against the virtue or the lives of their fellow-citizens, it is time

to put an end to the havoc, and to interpose while it is yet in our power to stop the destruction.

So little, my lords, am I afflicted with the merit of this wonderful skill which the distillers are said to have attained, that it is, in my opinion, no faculty of great use to mankind to prepare palatable poison; nor shall I ever contribute my interest for the reprieve of a murderer, because he has, by long practice, obtained great dexterity in his trade.

If their liquors are so delicious that the people are tempted to their own destruction, let us at length, my lords, secure them from these fatal draughts, by bursting the vials that contain them. Let us crush at once these artists in slaughter, who have reconciled their countrymen to sickness and to ruin, and spread over the pitfalls of debauchery such baits as cannot be resisted.

The noble lord has, indeed, admitted that this bill may not be found sufficiently coercive, but gives us hopes that it may be improved and enforced another year, and persuades us to endeavor a reformation of drunkenness by degrees, and, above all, to beware at present of hurting the manufacture.

I am very far, my lords, from thinking that there are, this year, any peculiar reasons for tolerating murder; nor can I conceive why the manufacture should be held sacred now, if it be to be destroyed hereafter. We are, indeed, desired to try how far this law will operate, that we may be more able to proceed with due regard to this valuable manufacture.

With regard to the operation of the law, it appears to me that it will only enrich the government without reforming the people; and I believe there are not many of a different opinion. If any diminution of the sale of spirits be expected from it, it is to be considered that this diminution will, or will not, be such as is desired for the reformation of the people. If it be sufficient, the manufacture is at an end, and all the reasons against the higher duties are of equal force against this; but if it be not sufficient, we have, at least, omitted part of our duty, and have neglected the health and virtue of the people. . . .

When I consider, my lords, the tendency of this bill, I find it calculated only for the propagation of diseases, the suppression of industry, and the destruction of mankind. I find it the most fatal engine that ever was pointed at a people; an engine by which those who are not killed will be disabled, and those who preserve their limbs will be deprived of their senses.

This bill, therefore, appears to be designed only to thin the ranks of mankind, and to disburden the world of the multitudes that inhabit it; and is perhaps the strongest proof of political sagacity that our new ministers have yet exhibited. They well know, my lords, that they are universally detested, and that, whenever a Briton is destroyed, they are freed from an enemy; they have therefore opened the flood gates of gin upon the nation that, when it is less numerous, it may be more easily governed.

Other ministers, my lords, who had not attained to so great a knowledge in the art of making war upon their country, when they found their enemies clamorous and bold, used to awe them with prosecutions and penalties, or destroy them like burglars, with prisons and with gibbets. But every age, my lords, produces some improvement; and every nation, however degenerate, gives birth, at some happy period of time, to men of great and enterprising genius. It is our fortune to be witnesses of a new discovery in politics. We may congratulate ourselves upon being contemporaries with those men who have shown that hangmen and halters are unnecessary in a State and that ministers may escape the reproach of destroying their enemies by inciting them to destroy themselves.

This new method may, indeed, have upon different constitutions a different operation; it may destroy the lives of some and the senses of others; but either of these effects will answer the purposes of the ministry, to whom it is indifferent, provided the nation becomes insensible, whether pestilence or lunacy prevails among them. Either mad or dead the greatest part of the people must quickly be, or there is no hope of the continuance of the present ministry.

For this purpose, my lords, what could have been invented more efficacious than an establishment of a certain number of shops at which poison may be vended—poison so prepared as to please the palate, while it wastes the strength, and only kills by intoxication? From the first instant that any of the enemies of the ministry shall grow clamorous and turbulent, a crafty hireling may lead him to the ministerial slaughterhouse and ply him with their wonder-working liquor till he is no longer able to speak or think, and, my lords, no man can be more agreeable to our ministers that he can neither speak nor think, except those who speak without thinking.

LANGDON CHEVES

(1776–1857)

WHAT we call "self-made" or "self-educated" men in America are very often the best-educated men of their generation. Such was Langdon Cheves, as were Benjamin Franklin, Horace Greeley, Abraham Lincoln, and so many others. A clerk in a mercantile house, he began to study law with very little education and very little encouragement from his friends. Nevertheless, in 1808, before he had been eleven years at the bar, his income from his practice exceeded twenty thousand dollars a year, a very remarkable achievement for a lawyer in South Carolina at that time. His manner of speaking must have been very impressive. After hearing him deliver a learned and eloquent speech in Congress in 1811, Washington Irving said it gave him, for the first time, a distinct idea of the manner in which the great Greek and Roman orators must have spoken.

He served in Congress as a "War Democrat" from 1811 to 1816, and was elected Speaker over Felix Grundy, January 19th, 1814, when Henry Clay was sent as a peace commissioner to Ghent. As Speaker he defeated Dallas's scheme to recharter the United States Bank. In 1819 when the bank had been ruined by mismanagement, Mr. Cheves became its president, restored its credit in three years, and resigned his position in 1822. Thenceforward until his death in 1857 he lived in retirement on his South Carolina plantation.

IN FAVOR OF A STRONGER NAVY

(From a Speech in Congress, January 1812)

IT HAS been said, by a strong and lively figure of rhetoric, that this country is a great land animal, which should not venture into the water. But if you look at its broad high back, the Alleghanies, and its great sides swelling to the east and to the west, where do you find its immense limbs terminate? Not on some great plain which has been formed for their reception, but in two great oceans, the Pacific on the one side and the Atlantic

thank any gentleman for this concession. The select committee conceived it to be their duty to bring the question fully before the House in the shape in which they have exposed it. Not to ask merely what it would do to assist by naval co-operation, in the first efforts of the contemplated struggle, but principally what it would do towards establishing and perpetuating a respectable naval force for the protection of those important rights of the people, which are, and must continue, exposed upon the ocean. Their determination was plainly, candidly, and boldly to speak to the House, and through it to the nation, on this great question, and leave its fate to the wisdom of the one and the good sense of the other.

That a respectable naval establishment affords the only effectual means of causing our commercial rights to be respected, will, as a general proposition, be denied by few persons, if any. But its adoption by us is deemed improper by those who oppose it, on the grounds of the enormous expense which, it is said, the establishment will necessitate, and the inability of the nation, by any force which it can provide, to resist with effect the immense naval power of Great Britain. Is it not surprising that so much prejudice should exist against this establishment on account of its expensiveness when it is ascertained that, during the whole eighteen years of its existence, from 1794 to 1811, inclusive, it has cost the Government only $27,175,695? I am afraid I shall be tedious, because the only way in which I hope to bring conviction home to the minds of the House is by entering, with minuteness and precision, into a dry detail of figures and statements; but the necessity of the case must be my apology for the course which I shall take. If the House shall have full confidence in my statements, much will be gained to the argument; for it will be difficult, if not impossible, for the hearer to follow me through an examination of these details as the argument proceeds. For this confidence, therefore, I will venture to hope. I believe the statements on which I rely to be accurate, as far as accuracy is material to the discussion. I will state them with candor, and, when I have concluded, I will put them into the hands of gentlemen who may wish to examine them for their own satisfaction, or to refute them. The average annual expense of this establishment, so much censured for its wasteful and improvident management, has but little exceeded $1,500,000, which is not much more than twice the amount of the usual annual

on the other. The figure explains the true interests of the country, in the inseparable union and necessary dependence of agriculture and commerce. The God of Nature did not give to the United States a coast of two thousand miles in extent, not to be used. No; it was intended by this bounty to make us a great commercial people; and shall we ungratefully reject the enjoyment of his unexampled beneficence? No; it has not and will not be neglected. A great portion of our people exists but upon the ocean and its fruits. It has been eloquently, and not less truly than eloquently, said, that "the ocean is their farm," and it must and will be protected. But how is this protection to be afforded? I will endeavor to prove that it can be done, and done most cheaply and effectually by a naval force; and if I succeed in this, I shall hope for the concurrence of the committee. No proposition appears to me more true or more obvious than that it is only by a naval force that our commerce and our neutral rights on the ocean can be protected. We are now going to war for the protection of these rights; but in what way, and under what circumstances? The mode is altogether accidental, and not founded on the permanent relations or means of the country. It is not my intention to condemn the course which has been taken. It has had my hearty concurrence, and my zealous, though feeble, support. I hope it may be altogether effectual; and I believe it will inflict a wound which will be felt with poignancy. But it is, notwithstanding, partial and accidental; for, if Great Britain had not the Canadas on our borders, how could we attack or resist her, armed as we are? If we possess ourselves of the Canadas, and this we shall certainly do in the event of war, how and where shall we then continue the war without a naval force? We shall suffer the evils of war, without inflicting any of them on the enemy. We cannot send our regulars or our volunteers on the ocean. Does it not then result, inevitably, as the dictate of common prudence, that we should, as soon as possible, commence our naval preparations? The Naval Establishment of the United States has been heretofore so much neglected that it is at present in a state of lamentable depression; and the question now is, whether we will suffer it to go down entirely, or attempt to raise it up to some degree of respectability. Some gentlemen say, "If you had asked for no more than the reparation of the frigates in ordinary, we might have granted your request." But, for myself, I would not

appropriation for our economical Civil List. It has been generally supposed that it has been much more expensive than the military establishment, but I will show that this is not really the case. The expense of the military establishment from 1791 to 1811, inclusive, has been $37,541,669, giving an annual average of $1,700,000 or $200,000 per annum more than that of the Navy. It thus appears that in the gross amount, as well as in the annual expenditure, the Army has been more expensive than the Navy. Compare, too, the services of the Army with those of the Navy, and it will be found that those of the latter have been most useful and most honorable to the nation. I know of no service of this character which the Army has performed, except the defeat of the Indians by General Wayne, and the late gallant affair on the Wabash. The Navy, in the contest with France in 1798, was victorious wherever it encountered the enemy, and probably laid the foundation of the subsequent accommodation with that nation. In the Mediterranean its exploits gave a name to the country throughout Europe; humbled, in an unexampled manner, the piratical and barbarous foe, and crowned itself with a reputation for intrepidity and heroism which had not been exceeded by the exploits of any nation and which must go down to a distant posterity. I mean not by this comparison to say anything injurious to the Army, but only to declare that preference to which I think the naval services of the country are entitled. Admitting, if it be desired, that the Navy has heretofore occasioned an expense not warranted by its force or its services,—and I cannot deny but that from a variety of causes the expense may have been unnecessarily great,—an argument cannot thence be fairly drawn against its future use—the contrary is the fair conclusion. Past errors lay the foundation of future improvement. It was thus the greatest orator and one of the greatest statesmen of antiquity reasoned. The great Athenian orator, when rousing his countrymen, by his impetuous eloquence, to resist the ambition of Philip, declared that it was on their past misconduct that he built his highest hopes; for, said he, "were we thus distressed, in spite of every vigorous effort which the honor of our State demanded, there were then no hopes of recovery." So may we reason in this case; for had these extraordinary expenses been the result of good economy, then, indeed, would their diminution be hopeless; but, as they have proceeded from a wasteful or unskillful expenditure, the remedy will be found in a reform of the abuse; to effect this reform is the duty of Congress. But it has not only been less expensive than the Army, but it may be proved, as the committee have declared in their report, that "a naval force within due limits and under proper regulations, will constitute the cheapest defense of the nation." This will be partly proved by a comparison between the expense of the permanent fortifications of our maritime frontier and that of an adequate naval defense. The experience of modern naval warfare has proved that no fortifications can prevent the passage of ships of war. The present fortifications of our maritime frontier, though they are more numerous and better than they have been at any other period in our history, cannot prevent an inconsiderable naval force from laying many of our towns in ashes. Indeed, it is believed that no fortifications which can be erected will afford a complete protection against such attacks, while their expense would be oppressive to the nation. The city of New York alone, if completely fortified, would require a further expenditure of three millions of dollars, and a garrison of ten thousand men, and then might be laid in ashes by four or five seventy-fours. But we have a coast of two thousand miles to protect, the expense of which could not be borne by the nation. A better defense would be furnished by such a naval force as would give you a mastery in the American seas, and at home much less expense. . . .

But, while it is contended by some that it will not be in the power of the nation to establish an effective naval force, there are others who are opposed to it, lest we become too great a naval power. They fear that our fleets will cover the ocean, and, seeking victory on all the opposite shores of the Atlantic, involve the nation in oppressive expenses and in wanton and habitual wars. Such objects are certainly not contemplated by the report of the committee, nor can such events possibly happen as long as we remain a free people. The committee have recommended such a Navy as will give to the United States an ascendency in the American seas and protect their ports and harbors. The people will never bear the establishment of a greater force than these objects require. The reasons which forbid Great Britain, or any other European power, to station large fleets on our seas will equally forbid us to cross the Atlantic or go into distant seas for the purpose of frequent or habitual wars.

ш—70

---

any point of his commission should cost him his life, and the exact performance of it be recompensed with as high a reward as were in the king's power to bestow upon him, can it be imagined that any man who believes this, and is in his right mind, can be so supinely and stupidly negligent of this charge, which so much imports him, as to oversee, through want of care, any one necessary article or part of his commission, especially if it be delivered to him in writing, and at his pleasure to peruse it every day? Certainly this absurd negligence is a thing without example, and such as peradventure will never happen to any sober man to the world's end; and, by the same reason, if we were firmly persuaded that this book doth indeed contain that charge and commission which infinitely more concerns us, it were not in reason possible but that to such a persuasion our care and diligence about it should be in some measure answerable. Seeing, therefore, most of us are so strangely careless, so grossly negligent of it, is there not great reason to fear that though we have professors and protesters in abundance, yet the faithful, the truly and sincerely faithful, are, in a manner, failed from the children of men? What but this can be the cause that men are so commonly ignorant of so many articles and particular mandates of it, which yet are as manifest in it as if they were written with the beams of the sun? For example, how few of our ladies and gentlewomen do or will understand that a voluptuous life is damnable and prohibited to them? Yet St. Paul saith so very plainly, "She that liveth in pleasure is dead while she liveth." I believe that this case directly regards not the sex: he would say he, as well as she, if there had been occasion. How few of the gallants of our time do or will understand that it is not lawful for them to be as expensive and costly in apparel as their means, or perhaps their credit, will extend unto? Which is to sacrifice unto vanity that which by the law of Christ is due unto charity; and yet the same St. Paul forbids plainly this excess, even to women —"Also let women (he would have said it much rather to men) array themselves in comely apparel, with shamefacedness and modesty, not with embroidered hair, or gold, or pearls, or costly apparel." And, to make our ignorance the more inexcusable, the very same rule is delivered by St. Peter also.

How few rich men are or will be persuaded that the law of Christ permits them not to heap up riches forever, nor perpetually to add house to house, and land to land, though by lawful

---

WILLIAM CHILLINGWORTH

(1602–1644)

ROBABLY the most famous preacher and author in the Church of England during the reign of Charles I. was William Chillingworth, pronounced by Tillotson "the glory of his age and nation," by Lord Mansfield "a perfect model of argumentation," and by Locke "a model of perspicuity and right reasoning." A native of Oxford, he was graduated in 1620, and obtained a Trinity College fellowship. The most famous of his works 'The Religion of Protestants a Safe Way to Salvation,' published in 1637, passed through two editions in less than five months, and brought him a succession of preferments the following year. His ardent loyalty carried him into the Royalist army at the beginning of the civil war. He was made a prisoner by Waller at Arundel Castle in December 1643, and died during the following January.

FALSE PRETENSES

LET a book that treats of the philosopher's stone promise never so many mountains of gold, and even the restoring of the Golden Age again, yet were it no marvel if few should study it; and the reason is, because few would believe it. But if there were a book extant, and ordinary to be had, as the Bible is, which men did generally believe to contain a plain and easy way for all men to become rich, and to live in health and pleasure, and this world's happiness, can any man imagine that this book would be unstudied by any man? And why, then, should I not believe that if the Scripture were firmly and heartily believed to be the certain and only way to happiness which is perfect and eternal, it would be studied by all men with all diligence? Seeing, therefore, that Christians are so cold and negligent in the study of it, prefer all other business, all other pleasures before it, is there not great reason to fear that many who pretend to believe it firmly believe it not at all, or very weakly and faintly? If the general of an army, or an ambassador to some prince or state, were assured by the king, his master, that the transgressing

---

means; but requires of them thus much charity at least, that ever, while they are providing for their wives and children, they should, out of the increase wherewith God hath blessed their industry, allot the poor a just and free proportion? And when they have provided for them in a convenient manner (such as they themselves shall judge sufficient and convenient in others), that then they should give over making purchase after purchase; but with the surplusage of their revenue beyond their expense, procure, as much as lies in them, that no Christian remain miserably poor. Few rich men, I fear, are or will be thus persuaded, and their daily actions show as much; yet, undoubtedly, either our Savior's general command, of loving our neighbors as ourselves, which can hardly consist with our keeping vainly, or spending vainly, what he wants for his ordinary subsistence, lays upon us a necessity of this high liberality: or his special command concerning this matter; *Quod superest date pauperibus,* "That which remains give to the poor:" or that which St. John saith reacheth home unto it: "Whosoever hath this world's good, and seeth his brother have need, and shutteth up the bowels of his compassion from him, how dwelleth the love of God in him?" Which is, in effect, as if he had said, He that keepeth from any brother in Christ that which his brother wants, and he wants not, doth but vainly think that he loves God; and therefore vainly hopes that God loves him.

JOSEPH HODGES CHOATE

(1832–)

WHEN an American acquires such a national reputation as an orator and publicist as to be chosen Ambassador to the Court of St. James, pending a war between the United States and Spain, the natural presumption is that he has made his reputation in Congress or in some other direct official connection with public affairs. But Joseph H. Choate had shunned office. It is the speeches he has made as a patriotic orator, and in famous cases at the bar, that have placed him in the front rank of our living speakers and public counselors. His style is clear and chaste but pregnant and pointed, characterized always by tact and good taste, and often by sallies of brilliant wit.

He was born at Salem, Massachusetts, January 24th, 1832. Graduated from Harvard in 1852, and at law in 1854, he has practiced his profession in New York since 1856. His connection with cases that attracted the attention of the whole country, and the New York habit of pressing his oratory into the public service on all great occasions, has made him President of the New England Society, President of the Union League Club, and at last Ambassador to London. His eulogy of the heroic record and traditions of our navy in the Farragut oration has been vindicated by more recent achievements of our squadrons.

FARRAGUT

(An Address Made at the Request of the Farragut Monument Association at the Unveiling of the Saint-Gaudens Statue, May 25th, 1881)

THE fame of naval heroes has always captivated and charmed the imaginations of men. The romance of the sea that hangs about them, their picturesque and dramatic achievements, the deadly perils that surround them, their loyalty to the flag that floats over them, their triumphs snatched from the jaws of defeat, and death in the hour of victory, inspire a warmer enthusiasm and a livelier sympathy than is awarded to equal deeds on land. Who can read with dry eyes the story of Nelson, in the supreme moment of victory at Trafalgar, dying in the cockpit of his flagship, embracing his beloved comrade with, " Kiss

Spanish race, which in all times has produced good fighters on sea and land. His mother must have been a woman fit to bear and suckle heroes, for his earliest recollection of her was upon the occasion when, ax in hand, in the absence of her husband, she defended her cottage and her helpless brood of little ones against an attack of marauding Indians who were seeking their scalps. Like all heroes then, he was born brave, and got his courage from his father's loins and his mother's milk. The death of the mother and the removal of the father to New Orleans, where he was placed by the Government in command of the naval station, introduced the boy to the very scenes where, more than half a century afterwards, some of the highest of his proud laurels were to be won, and led him, by a singular providence, to the final choice of his profession at an age when children generally are just beginning their schooling. The father of the renowned Commodore David Porter happened to fall ill and die under the roof of Farragut's father, and his illustrious son, whose heart o'erflowed with gratitude for the hospitable kindness which had welcomed his dying father, announced his intention to adopt a child of that house and to train him up in his own profession.

That happy conjunction of great merit with good fortune which attended the future admiral through his whole life was nowhere more signally marked than in the circumstance which thus threw together the veteran naval commander, already famous and soon to win a world-wide fame for skill and daring and enterprise and the boy who in his own last years was destined to eclipse the glory of his patron and to enchant the world with still more brilliant exploits.

The influence of such a spirit and character as Porter's on that of a dutiful, ardent, and ambitious boy like Farragut, cannot be overestimated. It was not a mere nominal adoption. Porter took him from his home and became his second father, and with him the boy lived and studied and cruised and fought. Having ever before him an example worthy of himself, no wonder that he aspired to place himself, at last, at the head of the profession into which his introduction had been under such auspices. Behold him, then, at the tender age of nine years the happy recipient of a midshipman's warrant in the United States navy, bearing date December 17th, 1810; and two years later, at the breaking out of the war with Great Britain, making his first cruise with his noble patron, who, as Captain Porter, now took

me, Hardy! Thank God I have done my duty," on his fainting lips, bidding the world good-night, and turning over like a tired child to sleep and wake no more? What American heart has not been touched by that kindred picture of Lawrence, expiring in the cabin of the beaten Chesapeake, with " Don't give up the ship" on his dying lips? What schoolboy has not treasured up in his memory the bloody fight of Paul Jones with the Serapis, the gallant exploits of Perry on Lake Erie, of McDonough on Lake Champlain, and the other bright deeds which have illuminated the brief annals of the American Navy.

We come together to-day to recall the memory and to crown the statue of one of the dearest of these idols of mankind — of one who has done more for us than all of them combined — of one whose name will ever stir, like a trumpet, the hearts of his grateful countrymen.

In the first year of the century, — at the very time when the great English admiral was wearing fresh laurels for winning in defiance of orders the once lost battle of the Baltic, the bloodiest picture in the book of naval warfare, — there was born on a humble farm in the unexplored wilderness of Tennessee a child who was sixty years afterwards to do for Americans what England's idol had just then done for her, to rescue her in an hour of supreme peril, and to win a renown which should not fade or be dim in comparison with that of the most famous of the sea kings of the old world. For though there were many great admirals before Farragut, it will be hard to find one whose life and fortunes combine more of those elements which command the enduring admiration and approval of his fellow-men. He was as good as he was great; as game as he was mild, and as mild as he was game; as skillful as he was successful; as full of human sympathy and kindness as he was of manly wisdom, and as unselfish as he was patriotic. So long as the Republic which he served and helped to save shall endure, his memory must be dear to every lover of his country; and so long as this great city continues to be the gateway of the nation and the centre of its commerce, it must preserve and honor his statue, which to-day we dedicate to the coming generations.

To trace the career of Farragut is to go back to the very infancy of the nation. His father, a brave soldier of the Revolution, was not of the Anglo-Saxon race for which we are wont to assert a monopoly of the manly virtues, but of that

command of the Essex, whose name he was to render immortal by his achievements under her flag. It was in this severe school of active and important service that Midshipman Farragut learned almost in infancy those first lessons in seamanship and war which he afterwards turned to practical account in wider fields and more dangerous enterprises. His faithful study of all the details of his profession, guided and inspired by that ever-present sense of duty, which was the most marked characteristic of his life, prepared him step by step for any service in the line of that profession which time or chance might happen to bring, and when at last in March 1814 the gallant little frigate met her fate in that spirited and bloody encounter with the British frigate Phebe and the ship of war Cherub, off the port of Valparaiso (a contest which brought new fame to the American navy as well as to all who bore a part in it), the boy of twelve, receiving an actual baptism of fire and blood, was found equal to the work of a man. He seems never to have known what fear was. If nerve makes the man, he was already as good as made. He thus describes this first of his great fights in his modest journal: —

" During the action, I was like Paddy in the Catharpins. A man on occasions, I performed the duties of captain's aid, quarter gunner, powder boy, and in fact did everything required of me. I shall never forget the horrid impression made upon me at the sight of the first man I had ever seen killed. It staggered and sickened me at first, but they soon began to fall all around me so fast, that it all appeared like a dream, and produced no effect on my nerves. I can remember well, while I was standing near the captain just abaft the mainmast, a shot came through the waterways and glanced upwards, killing four men who were standing by the side of the gun, taking the last one in the head and scattering his brains on both of us. But this awful sight did not affect me half as much as the death of the first poor fellow. I neither thought of nor noticed anything but the working of the guns."

He never was in battle again until forty-eight years afterwards, when he astounded the world by the capture of New Orleans; but who can doubt that that memorable day in the Essex, when her plucky commander fought her against hopeless odds, only lowering his colors when she was already sinking, with all but one of her officers and more than half of her crew on the list of killed and wounded, was a life-long inspiration to his courage and loyalty; that it planted forever in the heart of the boy that starry flag, which as an old man he was to bear, at last, through bloodier conflicts still to final victory. . . .

The traditions of the little American navy of that early day were proud and glorious ones, and well calculated to fire a youthful heart with generous enthusiasm. It had carried off the honors of the war, and on the lakes and on the ocean, in skill, pluck, and endurance; had coped successfully with the proud flag of England — the undisputed mistress of the seas — arrogant with the prestige of centuries, and fresh from the conquest of her ancient rivals. Its successful commanders were recognized as heroes alike by their grateful countrymen and by a generous foe, and furnished examples fit to be followed and imitated by the young and unknown midshipman, whose renown was one day to cast all theirs in the shade. It was neither by lucky accident nor political favor, nor simply by growing old in the service, that Farragut came in time to be the recognized head of his profession. From the first he studied seamanship and the laws of naval warfare as a science, and put his conscience into his work, as well in the least details as in the great principles of the business. So as he rose in rank he grew in power too, and never once was found unequal to any task imposed upon him. Self-reliance appears to have been the great staple of his character. Thrown upon his own exertions from the beginning, buoyed up by no fortune, advanced by no favor, he worked his way to the quarter-deck, and by the single-hearted pursuit of his profession was master of all its resources and ready to perform great deeds, if a day for the great deeds should ever come. Had that protracted and inglorious era of peace and compromise, which began with his early manhood and ended with the election of Lincoln, been continued for another decade, he would have passed into history without fame, but without reproach, as a brave and competent officer, but undistinguished in that bright catalogue of manly virtue and of stainless honor, which forms the muster roll of the American navy. But when treason reared its ugly head and by the guns of Fort Sumter roused from its long slumber the sleeping courage of the nation to avenge that insulted flag — that flag which from childhood to old age he had borne in honor over every sea and into the ports of every nation — his country found him ready and with his armor on, and found among all her champions no younger heart, no cooler

head, no steadier nerve, than in the veteran captain, who brought to her services a natural genius for fighting and a mind well stored with the rich experience of a well-spent life. And then, at last, all of that half century of patient waiting and of faithful study bore its glorious fruit.

Much as the country owes to Farragut for the matchless services which his brain and courage rendered in the day of her peril, she is still more indebted to him for the unconditional loyalty of his large and generous heart. Born, bred, and married in the South, with no friends and hardly an acquaintance except in the South, his sympathy must all have been with her. "God forbid," he said, "that I should have ever to raise my hand against the South." The approaching outbreak of hostilities found him on waiting orders at his home at Norfolk, surrounded by every influence that could put his loyalty to the test, in the midst of officers of the army and the navy all sworn, like him, to uphold the flag of the Republic, but almost to a man meditating treason against it. Could there have been a peaceful separation, could those erring sisters have been permitted, as at least one great Northern patriot then insisted they should, to depart in peace, he would doubtless have gone with his State, but with a heart broken by the rupture of his country. But when the manifest destiny of America forbade that folly, there was but one course for Farragut, and there is no evidence that his loyalty ever for a moment faltered. . . . At ten o'clock in the morning of the eighteenth of April, 1861, news came to Norfolk that the ordinance of secession had passed — and Farragut's mind was made up; he announced to his faithful wife that for his part, come what might, he was going to stick to the flag; and at five o'clock in the afternoon he had packed their carpetbags and taken the first steamboat for the North. That "Stick to the Flag" should be carved on his tombstone and on the pedestals of all his statues as it was stamped upon his soul. "Stick to the Flag" shall be his password to posterity, to the latest generations, for he stuck to it when all about him abandoned it. He was

> "Faithful found
> Among the faithless — faithful only he."

.   .   .   .

Never was a nation less prepared for a naval war than the United States in April 1861. Forty-two old vessels, many of

them unseaworthy, the remains only of a decrepit peace arrangement, constituted our entire navy: and all at once we had three thousand miles of exposed seacoast to blockade and defend, our own great seaports to protect, rebel cruisers to pursue, and American commerce to maintain, if possible. The last was utterly impossible, the merchant service took refuge under other flags and our own almost vanished from the seas, where it had so long, so proudly floated. But the same irresistible spirit of loyalty, the same indomitable will to preserve the imperiled union, which brought great armies into the field all equipped, soon created a fleet also, that commanded the respect of the world and placed the United States once more in the front rank of naval powers. The active services of such a man as Farragut could not long be spared, and when that great naval enterprise, the opening of the Mississippi, was planned, — an enterprise the like of which had never been attempted before, — he was chosen by the Government to lead it, by the advice of his superiors in rank and with the universal approval of the people, on the principle of choosing the best man for the service of the greatest danger; and he accepted it on his favorite maxim that the greatest exposure was the penalty of the highest rank. His experience was vast, but there was no experience that would of itself qualify any man for such a service. . . .

The sun would set upon us, if we were to undertake to tell this afternoon the story of the capture of New Orleans. The world knows it by heart, how when Farragut gave the signal at two o'clock in the morning the brave Bailey in the Cayuga led the way and how the great admiral in the Hartford in two short hours carried his wooden fleet in triumph through that storm of lightning from the forts, and scattered and destroyed the whole fleet of rebel gunboats and ironclads, and how it pleased Almighty God, as he wrote at sunrise to his wife, to preserve his life through a fire such as the world had scarcely known. Thus in a single night a great revolution in maritime warfare was accomplished, and a blow struck at the vitals of the Confederacy which made it reel to its centre. New Orleans, the key of the Mississippi, the queen city of the South, was taken never to be lost again, and the opening was made for all those great triumphs which soon crowned our arms in the West. But victory found our brave captain as modest and merciful as the conflict had proved him terrible, and history may be searched in vain for greater

clemency shown to a hostile city, captured after such a struggle, than that with which the Federal commander, under circumstances of the utmost aggravation and insult, treated New Orleans. . . .

"You know my creed," he says on the day after his gallant passage of the terrible batteries at Port Hudson. "I never send others in advance where there is a doubt, and being one on whom the country has bestowed its greatest honors, I thought I ought to take the risks which belong to them, and so I took the lead. I knew the enemy would try to destroy the old flagship, and I determined the best way to prevent that result was to try and hurt them the most." . . .

The battle at Mobile Bay has long since become a favorite topic of history and song. Had not Farragut himself set an example for it at New Orleans, this greatest of all his achievements would have been pronounced impossible by the military world, and its perfect success brought all mankind to his feet in admiration and homage. As a signal instance of one man's intrepid courage and quick resolve converting disaster and threatened defeat into overwhelming victory, it had no precedent since Nelson at Copenhagen, defying the orders of his superior officer and refusing to obey the signal to retreat, won a triumph that placed his name among the immortals.

When Nelson's lieutenant on the Elephant pointed out to him the signal of recall on the Commander-in-Chief, the battered hero of the Nile clapped his spyglass with his only hand to his blind eye and exclaimed: "I really do not see any signal. Keep mine for closer battle flying. That's the way to answer such signals. Nail mine to the mast!" and so he went on and won the great day.

When the Brooklyn hesitated among the fatal torpedoes in the terrible jaws of Fort Morgan, at the sight of the Tecumseh exploding and sinking with the brave Craven and his ill-fated hundred in her path, it was one of those critical moments on which the destinies of battle hang.

Napoleon said it was always the quarters of an hour that decided the fate of a battle; but here a single minute was to win or lose the day, for when the Brooklyn began to back, the whole line of Federal ships were giving signs of confusion, while they were in the very mouth of hell itself, the batteries of Fort Morgan making the whole of Mobile Point a living flame. It was the

supreme moment of Farragut's life. If he faltered all was lost.
If he went on in the torpedo-strewn path of the Tecumseh he
might be sailing to his death. It seemed as though Nelson himself were in the maintop of the Hartford. "What's the trouble?"
was shouted from the flagship to the Brooklyn. "Torpedoes!"
was the reply. "Damn the torpedoes," said Farragut. "Four
bells, Captain Drayton; go ahead full speed." And so he led his
fleet to victory. . . .

Van Tromp sailed up and down the British Channel in sight
of the coast with a broom at his masthead, in token of his purpose to sweep his hated rivals from the seas. The greatest of
English admirals, in his last fight, as he was bearing down upon
the enemy, hoisted on his flagship a signal which bore these
memorable words: "England expects every man to do his duty"
—words which have inspired the courage of Englishmen from
that day to this, but it was reserved for Farragut as he was
bearing down upon the death-dealing batteries of the rebels to
hoist nothing less than himself into the rigging of his flagship,
as the living signal of duty done, that the world might see that
what England had only expected America had fully realized, and
that every man, from the rear-admiral down, was faithful.

.   .   .   .

The golden days of peace have come at last, as we hope, for
many generations. The great armies of the Republic have long
since been disbanded. Our peerless navy, which at the close of
the war might have challenged the combined squadrons of the
world, has almost ceased to exist. But still we are safe from attack from within and from without. The memory of the heroes
is "the cheap defense of the nation, the nurse of manly sentiment and heroic enterprises forever." Our frigates may rot in
the harbor. Our ironclads may rust at the dock, but if ever
again the flag is in peril, invincible armies will swarm upon the
land, and steel-clad squadrons leap forth upon the sea to maintain it. If we only teach our children patriotism as the first
duty, and loyalty as the first virtue, America will be safe in the
future as in the past. When the War of 1812 broke out she had
only six little frigates for her navy, but the valor of her sons
eked out her scanty fleet and won for her the freedom of the
seas. In all the single engagements of that little war, with one
exception, the Americans were victors, and at its close the stars

and stripes were saluted with honor in every quarter of the
globe. So, when this War of the Rebellion came suddenly upon
us, we had a few ancient frigates, a few unseaworthy gunboats;
but when it ended our proud and triumphant navy counted
seven hundred and sixty vessels of war, of which seventy were
ironclads. We can always be sure then of fleets and armies
enough. But shall we always have a Grant to lead the one and
a Farragut to inspire the other? Will our future soldiers and
sailors share, as theirs almost to the last man shared, their devotion, their courage, and their faith? Yes, on this one condition;
that every American child learn from his cradle, as Farragut
learned from his, that his first and last duty is to his country,
that to live for her is honor, and to die for her is glory.

RUFUS CHOATE

(1799–1859)

AT THE unveiling of a statue of Rufus Choate in Boston, his
kinsman and former pupil, Joseph H. Choate, said: "Many
of his characteristic utterances have become proverbial, and
the flashing of his wit, the play of his fancy, and the gorgeous pictures of his imagination are the constant themes of reminiscence
wherever American lawyers assemble for social converse. . . . His
arguments, so far as they have been preserved, are text-books in the
profession. . . . His splendid and blazing intellect, fed and enriched by constant study of the best thoughts of the great minds of
the race, his all-persuasive eloquence, his teeming and radiant imagination, whisking his hearers along with it and sometimes overpowering
himself, his brilliant and sportive fancy, lighting up the most arid
subjects with the glow of sunrise, his prodigious and never-failing
memory, and his playful wit, always bursting forth with irresistible
impulse, have been the subjects of scores of essays and criticisms,
all struggling with the vain effort to describe and crystallize the
magical charm of his speech and his influence." Evidently he modeled his eloquence on that of Burke, of whom he wrote in a letter to
Charles Sumner: "Mind that Burke is the fourth Englishman—Shakespeare, Bacon, Milton, Burke;" and then, with a characteristic outburst of playful exaggeration, he added, "Out of Burke may be cut
50 Mackintoshes, 175 Macaulays, 40 Jeffreys, and 250 Sir Robert Peels,
and leave him greater than Pitt and Fox together."

Rufus Choate was born at Essex, Massachusetts, October 1st, 1799;
graduated from Dartmouth in 1819; admitted to the bar in 1823;
elected to Congress in 1830. Re-elected in 1832, he resigned before
the end of his term in 1834. While always ready to take an active
part in public affairs and to speak his mind freely, he shunned political promotion, and it was probably his desire to support his
friend, Daniel Webster, that induced him to take Webster's place in
the Senate from 1841 to 1845 while the latter was serving as Secretary of State, for he resigned and Webster was re-elected to the
Senate in 1845. To the day of his own death he was a staunch
defender of Webster's memory. In 1856, when the newly organized
Republican party was making its first campaign, he protested against
the "sixteen-starred flag" then sometimes seen in meetings addressed by orators who openly expressed a desire for the separation

of the free from the slave States. Speaking for the remnant of
Webster Whigs, he uttered a sentence that rang throughout the
Union and has since been heard a thousand times in every hamlet
of the land—"We join ourselves to no party that does not carry
the flag and keep step to the music of the Union."

He died at Halifax, Nova Scotia, July 13th, 1859, while on a voyage to Europe for the recovery of his health.

In him Burke had no unworthy pupil. His address of July 3d,
1845, before the Cambridge Law School, would give any man a sufficient title to immortality if he had no other claim upon it. Every
paragraph of it shows lifelong habits of incessant intellectual activity. No one can read it and mistake the fact that greatness of
mind is the first essential of greatness in oratory.

BOOKS AND CIVILIZATION IN AMERICA

(From a Speech on the Smithsonian Institute Delivered in the United States Senate)

IT IS easy to waste this money; it is easy to squander it in
jobs, salaries, quackeries; it is easy, even under the forms of
utility, to disperse and dissipate it in little rills and drops,
imperceptible to all human sense, carrying it off by an insensible
and ineffectual evaporation. But, sir, I take it that we all earnestly desire—I am sure the Senator from Ohio does desire—so
to dispense it as to make it tell. I am sure we all desire to see
it, instead of being carried off invisibly and wastefully, embody
itself as an exponent of civilization, permanent, palpable, conspicuous, useful. And to this end it has seemed to me, upon
the most mature reflection, that we cannot do a safer, surer,
more unexceptional thing with the income, or with a portion of
the income, perhaps twenty thousand dollars a year for a few
years, than to expend it in accumulating a grand and noble public library—one which for variety, extent, and wealth, shall be,
and be confessed to be, equal to any now in the world.

I say for a few years. Twenty thousand dollars a year, for
twenty-five years, are five hundred thousand dollars; and five
hundred thousand dollars discreetly expended, not by a biblioma-
niac, but by a man of sense and reading thoroughly instructed
in bibliography, would go far, very far, towards the purchase
of nearly as good a library as Europe can boast. I mean a

library of printed books, as distinct from manuscripts. Of course, such a sum would not purchase the number of books which some old libraries are reported to contain. It would not buy the 700,000 of the Royal Library at Paris, the largest in the world; nor the 500,000 or 600,000 of that of Munich, the largest in Germany; nor the 300,000 or 400,000 or 500,000 of those of Vienna and St. Petersburg, and the Vatican at Rome, and Copenhagen, and the Bodleian at Oxford. But mere numbers of volumes afford a very imperfect criterion of value. Those old libraries have been so long in collecting; accident and donation, which could not be rejected, have contributed so much to them; a general and indiscriminate system of accumulation gathers up, necessarily, so much trash; there are so many duplicates and quadruplicates, and so many books and editions, which become superseded, that mere bulk and mere original cost must not terrify us. *Ponderantur, non numerantur.* Accordingly the Library of the University at Göttingen, consisting perhaps of two hundred and fifty thousand or three hundred thousand volumes, but well chosen, selected, for the most part, within a century, and to a considerable extent by a single great scholar, Heyne, is perhaps to-day as valuable a collection of printed books as any in the world. Towards the accumulation of such a library, the expenditure of two-thirds of this income for a quarter of a century would make, let me say, a magnificent advance. And such a step taken, we should never have the work unfinished; yet when it should be finished, and your library should rival anything which civilization has ever had to show, there would still be the whole principal of your fund unexpended, yielding its income forever, for new and varying applications for increasing and diffusing knowledge in the world.

I hesitate, from an apprehension of being accused of entering too far into a kind of dissertation unsuited to this assembly of men of business, to suggest and press one-half the considerations which satisfy my mind of the propriety of this mode of expenditure. Nobody can doubt, I think, that it comes within the terms and spirit of the trust. That directs us to "increase and diffuse knowledge among men." And do not the judgments of all the wise; does not the experience of all enlightened states; does not the whole history of civilization, concur to declare that a various and ample library is one of the surest, most constant, most permanent, and most economical instrumentalities to increase and

Now there are very many among us, and every day we shall have more, who would feelingly adopt this language. Place within their reach the helps that guide the genius and labors of Germany and England, and let the genius and labors of Germany and England look to themselves! Our learned men would grow more learned and more able; our studies deeper and wider; our mind itself exercised and sharpened; the whole culture of the community raised and enriched. This is, indeed, to increase and diffuse knowledge among men.

If the terms of the trust, then, authorize this expenditure, why not make it? Not among the principal, nor yet the least of reasons for doing so, is, that all the while you are laying out your money, and when you have laid it out, you have the money's worth, the value received, the property purchased, on hand, to show for itself and to speak for itself. Suppose the professors provided for in the bill should gather a little circle of pupils, each of whom should carry off with him some small quotient of navigation, or horticulture, or rural economy, and the fund should thus glide away and evaporate in such insensible, inappreciable appropriations, how little there would be to testify of it! Whereas here, all the while, are the books; here is the value; here is the visible property; here is the oil, and here is the light. There is something to point to, if you should be asked to account for it unexpectedly; and something to point to, if a traveler should taunt you with the collections which he has seen abroad, and which gild and recommend the absolutisms of Vienna or St. Petersburg.

Another reason, not of the strongest, to be sure, for this mode of expenditure, is that it creates so few jobs and sinecures, so little salaried laziness. There is no room for abuses in it. All that you need is a plain, spacious, fireproof building, a librarian and assistants, an agent to buy your books, and a fire to sit by. For all the rest, he who wants to read goes and ministers to himself. It is an application of money that almost excludes the chances of abuses altogether.

But the decisive argument is, after all, that it is an application the most exactly adapted to the actual literary and scientific wants of the States and the country. I have said that another college is not needed here, because there are enough now, and another might do harm as much as good. But that which is wanted for every college, for the whole country, for

diffuse knowledge? There it would be—durable as liberty, durable as the Union; a vast storehouse, a vast treasury of all the facts which make up the history of man and of nature, so far as that history has been written; of all the truths which the inquiries and experiences of all the races and ages have found out; of all the opinions that have been promulgated; of all the emotions, images, sentiments, examples from all the richest and most instructive literatures; the whole past speaking to the present and the future; a silent, yet wise and eloquent teacher; dead, yet speaking—not dead! for Milton has told us that a "good book is not absolutely a dead thing—the precious lifeblood rather of a master spirit; a seasoned life of man embalmed and treasured up on purpose to a life beyond life." Is not that an admirable instrumentality to increase and diffuse knowledge among men? It would place within the reach of our mind, of our thinkers, and investigators, and scholars, all, or the chief intellectual and literary materials, and food and instruments, now within the reach of the cultivated foreign mind, and the effect would be to increase the amount of individual acquisition, and multiply the number of the learned. It would raise the standard of our scholarship, improve our style of investigation, and communicate an impulse to our educated and to the general mind. There is no library now in this country, I suppose, containing over fifty thousand volumes. Many there are containing less. But, from the nature of the case, all have the same works; so that I do not know, that of all the printed books in the world we have in this country more than fifty thousand different works. The consequence has been felt and lamented by all our authors and all our scholars. It has been often said that Gibbon's 'History' could not have been written here for want of books. I suppose that Hallam's 'Middle Ages,' and his 'Introduction to the Literature of Europe,' could not. Irving's 'Columbus' was written in Spain; Wheaton's 'Northmen' prepared to be written in Copenhagen. See how this inadequate supply operates. An American mind kindles with a subject; it enters on an investigation with a spirit and with an ability worthy of the most splendid achievement; goes a little way, finds that a dozen books —one book, perhaps—are indispensable, which cannot be found this side of Göttingen or Oxford; it tires of the pursuit, or abandons it altogether, or substitutes some shallow conjecture for a deep and accurate research. And there is the end!

every studious person, is a well-chosen library, somewhere among us, of three or four hundred thousand books. Where is such a one to be collected? How is it to be done? Who is to do it? Of the hundred and fifty colleges, more or less, distributed over the country, one has a library of perhaps fifty thousand volumes; others have good ones, though less; others smaller and smaller, down to scarcely anything. With one voice they unite, teacher and pupil, with every scholar and thinker, in proclaiming the want of more. But where are they to come from? No State is likely to lay a tax to create a college library, or a city library. No deathbed gift of the rich can be expected to do it. How, then, is this one grand want of learning to be relieved? It can be done by you and by you only. By a providential occurrence, it is not only placed within your constitutional power, but it has become your duty; you have pledged your faith; you have engaged to the dead and living that, without the charge of one dollar on the people, you will meet the universal and urgent demand by the precise and adequate supply. By such a library as you can collect here, something will be done, much will be done, to help every college, every school, every studious man, every writer and thinker in the country to just what is wanted most. Inquirers after truth may come here and search for it. It will do them no harm at all to pass a few studious weeks among these scenes. Having pushed their investigations as far as they may at home, and ascertained just what, and how much more, of helps they require, let them come hither and find it. Let them replenish themselves, and then go back and make distribution among the people! Let it be so that—

"Hither as to their fountains other stars
Repairing, in their golden urns, draw light."

I have no objection at all—I should rejoice rather—to see the literary representatives of an instructed people come hither, not merely for the larger legislation and jurisprudence, but for the rarer and higher knowledge. I am quite willing, not only that our "Amphyctionic council" should sit here, but that it should find itself among some such scenes and influences as surrounded that old renowned assembly; the fountain of purer waters than those of Castalia; the temple and the oracle of our Apollo! It will do good to have your educated men come to Washington for what has heretofore cost voyages to Germany. They will be of all parts of the country. They will become acquainted with each other. They will contract friendships and mutual regards. They will go away not only better scholars, but better Unionists. Some one has said that a great library molds all minds into one Republic. It might, in a sense of which he little dreamed, help to keep ours together.

I have intimated, Mr. President, a doubt whether a college or university of any description, even the highest, should be at present established here. But let it be considered by the enlightened friends of that object, if such there are, that even if your single purpose were to create such a university, you could possibly begin in no way so judiciously as by collecting a great library. Useful in the other modes which I have indicated, to a university it is everything. It is as needful as the soul to the body. While you are doubting, then, what to do, what you will have, you can do nothing so properly as to begin to be accumulating the books which you will require on whatever permanent plan of application you at last determine.

I do not expect to hear it said in this assembly that this expenditure for a library will benefit a few only, not the mass; that it is exclusive, and of the nature of monopoly. It is to be remembered that this fund is a gift; that we take it just as it is given; and that by its terms it must be disbursed here. Any possible administration of it, therefore, is exposed to the cavil that all cannot directly, and literally, and equally partake of it. How many and of what classes of youth from Louisiana, or Illinois, or New England, for example, can attend the lectures of your professor of astronomy? But I say it is a positive and important argument for the mode of application which I urge, that it is so diffusive. Think of the large absolute numbers of those who, in the succession of years, will come and partake directly of these stores of truth and knowledge! Think of the numbers without number who, through them, who by them indirectly, will partake of the same stores! Studious men will come to learn to speak and write to and for the growing millions of a generally educated community. They will learn that they may communicate. They cannot hoard if they would, and they would not if they could. They take in trust to distribute; and every motive of ambition, of interest, of duty, will compel them to distribute.

which other nations have not, shall we reject the knowledge which they have, and which we have not? Or will you not rather say, that, because we are free, therefore will we add to our freedom that deep learning and that diffused culture which are its grace and its defense?

THE NECESSITY OF COMPROMISES IN AMERICAN POLITICS

(On Friday, July 2d, 1841, the Senate Having Under Consideration the Amendment Proposed by Mr. Rives of Virginia to the Fiscal Bank Bill, Mr. Choate Spoke on the Necessity for Compromises Illustrating the Governing Theory of the First Half Century of National Politics. The Argument on the Bill Itself Is Here Omitted).

YOU see, sir, the nature and the effect of the proposed amendment. If it is adopted, instead of arming the corporation with the power of setting up branches all over the States, each possessing and exercising all the functions of a perfect bank, you empower it to do so only with the assent of the States. In the meantime, however, independently of, and prior to, any such assent, and even against their expressed dissent, if dissent they should happen to express, you empower it, by means of agencies distributed throughout the country, to perform everywhere all the business which a bank can perform, except to discount. That business, the loaning of money on local paper, itself in great measure a local and domestic one, and of inferior policy, it may not perform but with the consent of the States, within whose limits, for the benefit of whose inhabitants, and side by side with whose local banks, it is to be carried on. This is the whole of the amendment. The bill of the committee authorizes the bank to engross the local discount business of the States without their consent; the bill as amended authorizes it to do all things else which a bank can do: to deal in exchange; to issue a currency of its own notes; and to do all things else without their consent; but this one single power it permits to be exerted only on their application. It simply restores in this important feature the project furnished on our call by the Secretary of the Treasury, and which comes to us as an administration measure.

Now, sir, I do not vote for it from any doubt on the constitutional power of Congress to establish branches all over the

They buy in gross, to sell by retail. The lights which they kindle here will not be set under a bushel, but will burn on a thousand hills. No, sir; a rich and public library is no antirepublican monopoly. Who was the old Egyptian king who inscribed on his library the words, "The dispensary of the soul"? You might quite as well inscribe on it, "Armory and light and fountain of liberty!"

It may possibly be inquired what account I make of the library of Congress. I answer, that I think it already quite good and improving, but that its existence constitutes no sort of argument against the formation of such a one as I recommend. In the theory of it, that library is merely to furnish Congress and the Government with the means of doing their official business. In its theory it must be, in some sort, a professional library, and the expenditure we now make—five thousand dollars in a year, or, as last year, two thousand and five hundred—can never carry it up to the rank and enable it to fulfill the functions of a truly great and general public library of science, literature, and art. The value of books which could be added under the appropriations of the last year cannot greatly exceed twenty-one hundred dollars. Doubtless, however, in the course of forming the two, it would be expedient and inevitable to procure to a great extent different books for each.

I do not think, Mr. President, that I am more inclined than another to covet enviously anything which the older civilization of Europe possesses which we do not. I do not suppose that I desire, any more than you, or than any of you, to introduce here those vast inequalities of fortune, that elaborate luxury, that fantastic and extreme refinement. But I acknowledge a pang of envy and grief that there should be one drop or one morsel more of the bread of intellectual life tasted by the European than by the American mind. Why should not the soul of this country eat as good food and as much of it as the soul of Europe? Why should a German or an Englishman sit down to a repast of five hundred thousand books, and an American scholar who loves truth as well as he be put on something less than half allowance? Can we not trust ourselves with so much of so good a thing? Will our digestion be impaired by it? Are we afraid that the stimulated and fervid faculties of this young nation will be oppressed and overlaid? Because we have liberty

States, possessing the discounting function, directly and adversely against their united dissent. I differ in this particular wholly with the Senator who moves the amendment. I have no more doubt of your power to make such a bank and such branches anywhere than of your power to build a post office or a custom-house anywhere. This question, for me, is settled, and settled rightly. I have the honor and happiness to concur on it with all, or almost all, our greatest names: with our national judicial tribunal and with both the two great original political parties; with Washington, Hamilton, Marshall, Story, Madison, Monroe, Crawford, and with the entire Republican administration and organization of 1816 and 1817.

But it does not follow, because we possess this or any other power, that it is wise or needful, in a given case, to attempt to exert it. We may find ourselves so situated that we cannot do it if we would, for want of the concurrence of other judgments; and therefore a struggle might be as unavailing as it would be mischievous and unseemly. We may find ourselves so situated that we ought not to do it if we could. All things which are lawful are not convenient, are not practicable, are not wise, are not safe, are not kind. A sound and healing discretion, therefore, the moral coercion of irresistible circumstances, may fitly temper, and even wholly restrain, the exercise of the clearest power ever belonging to human government. Is not this your actual situation? . . .

Now I think the people ought not to be made to wait for the relief they have a right to demand. They ought not to be made to suffer while we argue one another out of the recorded and inveterate opinions of our whole lives. I say, therefore, for myself, that, anxious to afford them all the relief which they require, regretting that the state of opinion around me puts it out of my power to afford that relief in the form I might prefer, I accommodate myself to my position, and make haste to do all that I can by the shortest way that I can. Consider how much better it is to relieve them to some substantial extent by this means, at once, than not to relieve at all, than not to initiate a system or measure of relief at all, and then go home at the end of this session of Congress, weak and weary, and spend the autumn in trying to persuade them that it was the fault of some of our own friends that nothing was done. How poor a compensation for wrongs to the people will be the victories over our friends!

I am going now to give another reason for my vote, which you may say is scarcely suitable to the dignity of this place, on which I do not mean to dwell for a moment, but which the manliness of Senators will excuse my suggesting; and that is, that the adoption of the amendment will not only soonest effect the grand object of public relief, but will preserve the harmony and unity of the ascendant political party. Do not suppose I shall dwell for a moment on such a topic. I owe you, I owe especially the wakeful and powerful minority by which we are observed here, an apology for speaking of it. I address myself to the majority. You acknowledge the importance of united counsels and action. Subordinately to the larger offices of patriotism, or, rather, as the mode of fulfilling those offices, you acknowledge your duty to the party of relief and reform. Sir, in the language of the great philosophic orator on whose immortal and universal wisdom the Senator from Virginia drew so instructively yesterday, " in the way which men call party, worship we the Constitution of our country." Now, without entering in detail on the grounds of my opinion, I think we shall hold that party together longer; we shall do more good, and hinder more evil; we shall effect more relief and more reform; we shall carry out more of our great measures; we shall insure a longer succession of our great men by adopting than by rejecting the amendment. It was due to frankness and to honor to say so much. Decorum and custom forbid me to say more. See, however, if the keen and vigilant Opposition on this floor, who mark their objects and pursue them with the eyes of eagles, do not vote against the amendment in sufficient numbers to defeat it if we divide on it among ourselves. I speak not of motives, and I know nothing of actual intentions, but I reason from the obvious nature of the case, and I believe that, if they see that nothing else will, their party tactics will defeat it.

For my part I own that I wish the new administration to have the honor and the felicity of carrying successfully through this its first measure of relief. I wish it to relieve the country, and also to preserve itself. I wish to disappoint their prophecies who told us so often, during the late canvass, that our materials are discordant, that no common principles bind us together, and that our first attempt at a measure of government

would dissolve and dissipate us. I will not, if I can help it, have a hand in fulfilling such prophecies. But then, if we would hinder their inevitable fulfillment, remember that we must administer the power we have acquired with the same wise tolerance of the opinions of the widespread members of our party by which we acquired it. If you took up the candidate on one set of tests of political orthodoxy, will you try to destroy—will you destroy the incumbent by the application of different and stricter tests?

And, Mr. President, in a larger view of this matter, is it not in a high degree desirable to make such a charter that, while it secures to the people all that such kind of instrumentality as a bank can secure, we may still, in the mode and details of the thing, respect the scruples and spare the feelings of those who, just as meritoriously, usefully, and conspicuously as yourselves, are members of our political association, but who differ with you on the question of constitutional power? If I can improve the local currency, diffuse a sound and uniform national one, facilitate, cheapen, and systematize the exchanges, secure the safekeeping and transmission of the public money, promote commerce, and deepen and multiply the springs of a healthful credit by a bank, and can at the same time so do it as to retain the cordial, constant co-operation, and prolong the public usefulness of friends who hold a different theory of the Constitution, is it not just so much clear gain?

I was struck, in listening to the Senator from Virginia yesterday, with the thought how idle, how senseless, it is to spend time in deploring or being peevish about the inveterate constitutional opinions of the community he so ably represents. There the opinions are. What will you do with them? You cannot change them; you cannot stride over or disregard them. There they are; what will you do with them? Compromise the matter. Adjust it, if you can, in such sort that they shall neither yield their opinions nor you yield yours. Give to the people all the practical good which a bank can give, and let the constitutional question whether Congress can make a bank by its own powers or not stand over for argument on the last day of the Greek kalends, when the disputants may have the world all to themselves to wrangle it out in! Yes, sir, compromise it. Our whole history is but a history of compromises. You have compromised in larger things; do it in less; do it in this. You have done it

for the sake of the Union; do it for the sake of the party which is doing it for the sake of the Union. You never made one which was received with wider and sincerer joy than this would be. Do it, then. Do as your fathers did when they came together, delegates from the slave States and delegates from the free, representatives of planters, of mechanics, of manufacturers, and the owners of ships, the cool and slow New England men, and the mercurial children of the sun, and sat down side by side in the presence of Washington, to frame this more perfect Union. Administer the Constitution in the temper that created it. Do as you have yourselves done in more than one great crisis of your affairs, when questions of power and of administration have shaken these halls and this whole country, and an enlarged and commanding spirit, not yet passed away from our counsels, assisted you to rule the uproar and to pour seasonable oil on the rising sea. Happy, thrice happy for us all, if the Senator from Kentucky would allow himself to-day to win another victory of reconciliation!

Do not say that this is a mere question of power or no power, and that conciliatory adjustment is inapplicable and inadmissible. Do not say that we who believe that the General Government may establish a bank with branches in the States possessing the local discount function without their assent, do, by voting for this amendment, surrender our opinions, or strike out a particle of power from the Constitution. No, sir, we do neither. What we say and do, and all we say and do, is exactly this. We assert that the full power is in the Constitution. There we leave it, unabridged, unimpaired. We declared that, when, in our judgment, it is expedient to exert it, we will concur in exerting it in its whole measure, ourselves uncommitted, unembarrassed by the forbearance which we now advise and practice. But we say that all power is to be exercised with sound discretion in view of the time and circumstances; that contested constitutional power is pre-eminently so to be exercised; that it does not follow, because we possess a giant's strength, that we are therefore to put it all forth, with the blind and undistinguishing impulse of a giant; that, in this instance, deferring to temporary and yet embarrassing circumstances, to opinions, for the sake of harmonious and permanent administration, for the sake of conciliating and saving friends, for the sake of immediate relief to the vast, various, and sensitive business

interests of a great people, we do not think it needful or discreet to exercise the whole power over this subject which we find, assert, and cherish in the Constitution. We content ourselves with declaring that it is there, and that there we mean it shall remain. But perceiving that we can secure to the country all the practical good which it was introduced to secure without resorting to it; perceiving that, in the actual condition of things, we cannot now exert it if we would; perceiving that we can reconcile opinions, spare feelings, and insure a general harmony of useful administrative action, by abstaining from the use of it, we abstain from the use of it. Thus the Senator from Virginia understands this act, and thus do we. No broader, no other effect can be ascribed to it. If you inspect the bill itself, after it shall have received this amendment, you will find that it in truth assumes and asserts the constitutional power of the National Legislature to create a corporation which has authority to transact in every one of the States all the business of a bank except that of discounting. So much power it necessarily assumes and asserts. And then as to the business of making discounts, it neither asserts nor denies that you have the power to authorize it without the assent of the States; it just authorizes the corporation to do it with their assent, and there it leaves the matter. Both classes of expounders of the Constitution, certainly that to which I belong, may vote for such a bill without yielding any opinion, or changing in the least the sacred and awful text of the great Charter itself.

Let me say, sir, that to administer the contested powers of the Constitution is, for those of you who believe that they exist, at all times a trust of difficulty and delicacy. I do not know that I should not venture to suggest this general direction for the performance of that grave duty. Steadily and strongly assert their existence; do not surrender them; retain them with a provident forecast; for the time may come when you will need to enforce them by the whole moral and physical strength of the Union; but do not exert them at all so long as you can by other less offensive expedients of wisdom effectually secure to the people all the practical benefits which you believe they were inserted into the Constitution to secure. Thus will the Union last longest and do most good. To exercise a contested power without necessity on a notion of keeping up the tone of government is not much better than tyranny, and very improvident and impolitic tyranny, too. It is turning "extreme medicine into daily bread." It forgets that the final end of government is not to exert restraint, but to do good.

Within this general view of the true mode of administering contested powers, I think the measure we propose is as wise as it is conciliatory; wise because it is conciliatory; wise because it reconciles a sound and a strong theory of the Constitution with a discreet and kind administration of it. I desire to give the country a bank. Well, here is a mode in which I can do it. Shall I refuse to do it in that mode, because I cannot at the same time, and by the same operation, gain a victory over the settled constitutional opinions, and show my contempt for the ancient and unappeasable jealousy and prejudices of not far less than half of the American people? Shall I refuse to do it in that mode, because I cannot at the same time, and by the same operation, win a triumph of constitutional law over political associates, who agree with me on nine in ten of all the questions which divide the parties of the country; whose energies and eloquence, under many an October and many an August sun, have contributed so much to the transcendent reformation which has brought you into power? Shall I refuse to the people their rights, until and unless, by the mode of conferring those rights, I can also plant a wound in the side of one who has stood shoulder to shoulder with me in the great civil contest of the last ten years? Do you really desire that the same cloud of summer which pauses to pour out its treasures, long withheld, on the parched and dreary land, should send down a thunderbolt on the head of a noble and conspicuous friend? Certainly nobody here can cherish such a thought for a moment.

There is one consideration more which has had some influence in determining my vote. I confess that I think that a bank established in the manner contemplated by this amendment stands, in the actual circumstances of our time, a chance to lead a quieter and more secure life, so to speak, than a bank established by the bill. I think it worth our while to try to make, what never yet was seen, a popular National Bank. Judging from the past and the present, from the last years of the last bank, and the manner in which its existence was terminated; from the tone of the debate and of the press, and the general indications of public opinion, I acknowledge an apprehension that such an institution, created by a direct exertion of your power,

throwing off its branches without regard to the wishes or wants of the States, as judged of by themselves, and without any attempt to engage their auxiliary co-operation, diminishing the business and reducing the profits of the local banks, and exempted from their burdens—I confess that such an institution may not find so quiet and safe a field of operation as is desirable for usefulness and profit. I do not wish to see it standing like a fortified post on a foreign border—never wholly at peace, always assailed, always belligerent, not falling perhaps, but never safe, the nurse and the prize of implacable hostility. No, sir. Even such an institution, under conceivable circumstances, it might be our duty to establish and maintain in the face of all opposition and to the last gasp. But so much evil attends such a state of things, so much insecurity, so much excitement; it would be exposed to the pelting of such a pitiless storm of the press and of public speech; so many demagogues would get good livings by railing at it; so many honest men would really regard it as unconstitutional, and as dangerous to business and to liberty, that it is worth an exertion to avoid it. Why, sir, notice has been formally given us by the eloquent Senator from Ohio, that on the day you grant this charter he lays a resolution on your table to repeal it. Sir, I desire to see the Bank of the United States become a cherished domestic institution, reposing in the bosom of our law and of our attachments. Established by the concurrent action or on the application of the States, such might be its character. There will be a struggle on the question of admitting the discount power into the States; much good sense and much nonsense will be spoken and written; but such a struggle will be harmless and brief, and when that is over, all is over. The States which exclude it will hardly exasperate themselves further about it. Those which admit it will soothe themselves with the consideration that the act is their own, and that the existence of this power of the branch is a perpetual recognition of their sovereignty. Thus might it sooner cease to wear the alien, aggressive, and privileged aspect which has rendered it offensive, and become sooner blended with the mass of domestic interests, cherished by the same regards, protected by the same and by a higher law.

THE HEROISM OF THE EARLY COLONISTS

IF ONE were called on to select the most glittering of the instances of military heroism to which the admiration of the world has been most constantly attracted, he would make choice, I imagine, of the instance of that desperate valor, in which, in obedience to the laws, Leonidas and his three hundred Spartans cast themselves headlong, at the passes of Greece, on the myriads of their Persian invaders. From the simple page of Herodotus, longer than from the Amphyctionic monument, or the games of the commemoration, that act speaks still to the tears and praise of all the world.

Judge if, that night, as they watched the dawn of the last morning their eyes could ever see; as they heard with every passing hour the stilly hum of the invading host, its dusky lines stretched out without end, and now almost encircling them round; as they remembered their unprofaned home, city of heroes and the mother of heroes,—judge if, watching there, in the gateway of Greece, this sentiment did not grow to the nature of madness, if it did not run in torrents of literal fire to and from the laboring heart; and when morning came and passed, and they had dressed their long locks for battle, and when, at a little after noon, the countless invading throng was seen at last to move, was it not with a rapture, as if all the joy, all the sensation of life, was in that one moment, that they cast themselves, with the fierce gladness of mountain torrents, headlong in that brief revelry of glory?

I acknowledge the splendor of that transaction in all its aspects. I admit its morality too, and its useful influence on every Grecian heart, in that greatest crisis of Greece.

And yet, do you not think that whoso could, by adequate description, bring before you that winter of the Pilgrims,—its brief sunshine; the nights of storm, slow waning; the damp and icy breath, felt to the pillow of the dying; its destitutions, its contrasts with all their former experience in life, its utter insulation and loneliness, its deathbeds and burials, its memories, its apprehensions, its hopes; the consultations of the prudent; the prayers of the pious; the occasional cheerful hymn, in which the strong heart threw off its burden, and, asserting its unvanquished nature, went up, like a bird of dawn, to the skies;—do ye not think

that whoso could describe them calmly waiting in that defile, lonelier and darker than Thermopylæ, for a morning that might never dawn, or might show them, when it did, a mightier arm than the Persian raised as in act to strike, would he not sketch a scene of more difficult and rarer heroism? A scene, as Wordsworth has said, "melancholy, yea, dismal, yet consolatory and full of joy;" a scene even better fitted to succor, to exalt, to lead the forlorn hopes of all great causes, till time shall be no more!

I have said that I deemed it a great thing for a nation, in all the periods of its fortunes, to be able to look back to a race of founders, and a principle of institution, in which it might rationally admire the realized idea of true heroism. That felicity, that pride, that help, is ours. Our past, with its great eras, that of settlement, that of independence, should announce, should compel, should spontaneously evolve as from a germ, a wise, moral, and glowing future. Those heroic men and women should not look down on a dwindled posterity. That broad foundation, sunk below frost or earthquake, should bear up something more permanent than an encampment of tents, pitched at random, and struck when the trumpet of march sounds at next daybreak. It should bear up, as by a natural growth, a structure in which generations may come, one after another, to the great gift of the social life.

SAINT JOHN CHRYSOSTOM

(347–407)

OHN OF THE GOLDEN MOUTH» came to be the designation of the celebrated Father of the Greek Church, whose eloquence, pure life, and irrepressible fearlessness in the line of duty made him famous and raised him to an official eminence which he avoided as long as he could. As a preacher and prelate at Antioch, the capital of Syria, the fame of his piety and oratory led to his appointment as Archbishop of Constantinople under the Emperor Arcadius. He escaped the undesired promotion the first time by a stratagem, knowing, perhaps, that his conscience and sense of duty would sooner or later bring him under the ban of the court. On the archiepiscopal throne he persevered in his plain, abstemious mode of life, diligently applying to the support of hospitals the revenues his predecessors had consumed in pomp and luxury. The people of the city learned to love him, but the zeal and eloquence with which he opposed abuses in the Church and sin in high places arrayed against him many powerful enemies, both in court and Church, among them the notorious Empress Eudoxia. A synod packed with his enemies condemned him, on the grounds of contumacy, because he refused to appear before it to answer charges of heresy, and he was arrested and sent to Nicæa, in Bithynia. An uprising of the people so alarmed Eudoxia that he was recalled amid great popular rejoicings. He continued his assaults on the vices of the court, and after the city had been sufficiently garrisoned with barbarian legions to overawe the people, he was accused of insulting the Empress in a sermon with the words: "Herodias is again furious, Herodias again dances; she once more demands the head of John," and, though the accusation was false, it sealed his fate. He was sent a prisoner, first to a little village among the ridges of Mount Taurus, where it was hoped he would fall a victim to the hatred of the monasteries he had rebuked. But his influence still remaining formidable, an order was issued for his removal to the extreme desert of Pityus, and his guards so managed that he died at Comana in Pontus on the journey, September 4th, 407.

III—72

THE BLESSING OF DEATH

BELIEVE me, I am ashamed and blush to see unbecoming groups of women pass along the mart, tearing their hair, cutting their arms and cheeks—and all this under the eyes of the Greeks. For what will they not say? What will they not utter concerning us? Are these the men who philosophize about a resurrection? Indeed! How poorly their actions agree with their opinions! In words, they philosophize about a resurrection: but they act just like those who do not acknowledge a resurrection. If they fully believed in a resurrection, they would not act thus; if they had really persuaded themselves that a deceased friend had departed to a better state, they would not thus mourn. These things, and more than these, the unbelievers say when they hear those lamentations. Let us then be ashamed, and be more moderate, and not occasion so much harm to ourselves and to those who are looking on us.

For on what account, tell me, do you thus weep for one departed? Because he was a bad man? You ought on that very account to be thankful, since the occasions of wickedness are now cut off. Because he was good and kind? If so, you ought to rejoice; since he has been soon removed, before wickedness had corrupted him: and he has gone away to a world where he stands ever secure, and there is no room even to mistrust a change. Because he was a youth? For that, too, praise him who has taken him, because he has speedily called him to a better lot. Because he was an aged man? On this account, also, give thanks and glorify him that has taken him. Be ashamed of your manner of burial. The singing of psalms, the prayers, the assembling of the [spiritual] fathers and brethren—all this is not that you may weep and lament and afflict yourselves, but that you may render thanks to him who has taken the departed. For as when men are called to some high office, multitudes with praises on their lips assemble to escort them at their departure to their stations, so do all with abundant praise join to send forward, as to greater honor, those of the pious who have departed. Death is rest, a deliverance from the exhausting labors and cares of this world. When, then, thou seest a relative departing, yield not to despondency; give thyself to reflection; examine thy conscience; cherish the thought that after a

little while this end awaits thee also. Be more considerate; let another's death excite thee to salutary fear; shake off all indolence; examine your past deeds; quit your sins, and commence a happy change.

We differ from unbelievers in our estimate of things. The unbeliever surveys the heavens and worships it, because he thinks it a divinity; he looks to the earth and makes himself a servant to it, and longs for the things of sense. But not so with us. We survey the heaven, and admire him that made it; for we believe it not to be a god, but a work of God. I look on the whole creation, and am led by it to the Creator. He looks on wealth, and longs for it with earnest desire; I look on wealth, and contemn it. He sees poverty, and laments; I see poverty, and rejoice. I see things in one light; he in another. Just so in regard to death. He sees a corpse, and thinks of it as a corpse; I see a corpse, and behold sleep rather than death. And as in regard to books, both learned persons and unlearned see them with the same eyes, but not with the same understanding—for to the unlearned the mere shapes of letters appear, while the learned discover the sense that lies within those letters; so in respect to affairs in general, we all see what takes place with the same eyes, but not with the same understanding and judgment. Since, therefore, in all other things we differ from them, shall we agree with them in our sentiments respecting death?

Consider to whom the departed has gone, and take comfort. He has gone where Paul is, and Peter, and the whole company of the saints. Consider how he shall arise, with what glory and splendor.

THE HEROES OF FAITH

WHAT great labors did Plato endure, and his followers, discoursing to us about a line, and an angle, and a point, and about numbers even and odd, and equal unto one another and unequal, and such-like spiderwebs (for, indeed, those webs are not more useless to man's life, than were these subjects): and without doing good to any one great or small by their means, so he made an end of his life. How greatly did he labor, endeavoring to show that the soul is immortal! and even as he came he went away, having spoken nothing with certainty, nor persuaded any hearer. But the Cross wrought persuasion

by means of unlearned men; yea, it persuaded even the whole world: and not about common things, but in discourse of God and the godliness which is according to truth, and the evangelical way of life, and the judgment of the things to come. And of all men it made philosophers: the very rustics, the utterly unlearned. Behold how "the foolishness of God is wiser than men," and "the weakness stronger"! How, stronger? Because it overran the whole world, and took all by main force, and while men were endeavoring by ten thousands to quench the name of the Crucified, the contrary came to pass: that flourished and increased more and more, but they perished and wasted away; and the living, in war with the dead, had no power. So that when the Greek calls me foolish, he shows himself exceedingly above measure foolish: since I who am esteemed by him a fool evidently appear wiser than the wise. When he calleth me weak, then he showeth himself to be weaker. For the noble things which publicans and fishermen were able to effect by the grace of God, these, philosophers and rhetoricians and tyrants, and in short the whole world, running ten thousand ways here and there, could not even form a notion of. For what did not the Cross introduce? The doctrine concerning the Immortality of the Soul; that concerning the Resurrection of the Body; that concerning the contempt of things present; that concerning the desire of things future. Yea, Angels it hath made of men, and all, everywhere, practice self-denial, and show forth all kinds of fortitude.

But among them also, it will be said, many have been found contemners of death. Tell me who. Was it he who drank the hemlock? But if thou wilt, I can bring forward ten thousand such from within the Church. For had it been lawful when persecution befell them to drink hemlock and depart, all had become more famous than he. And besides, he drank when he was not at liberty to drink or not to drink; but willing or against his will he must have undergone it: no effect surely of fortitude, but of necessity, and nothing more. For even robbers and man-slayers, having fallen under the condemnation of their judges, have suffered things more grievous. But with us it is all quite the contrary. For not against their will did the martyrs endure, but of their will, and being at liberty not to suffer; showing forth fortitude harder than all adamant. This, then, you see is no great wonder, that he whom I was mentioning drank hemlock, it being no longer in his power not to drink, and also when he had arrived at a very great age. For when he despised life he stated himself to be seventy years old; if this can be called despising. For I for my part could not affirm it: nor, what is more, can any one else. But show me some one enduring firm in torments for godliness's sake, as I show thee ten thousand everywhere in the world. Who, while his nails were tearing out, nobly endured? Who, while his joints were wrenching asunder? Who, while his body was enduring spoil, member by member? or his head? Who, while his bones were being heaved out by levers? Who, while placed without intermission upon frying-pans? Who, when thrown into a caldron? Show me these instances. For to die by hemlock is all as one with a sleeping man's continuing in a state of sleep. Nay, even sweeter than sleep is this sort of death, if report say true. But if certain of them did endure torments, yet of these too the praise is gone to nothing. For on some disgraceful occasion they perished; some for revealing mysteries; some for aspiring to dominion; others detected in the foulest crimes; others again at random, and fruitlessly and ignorantly, there being no reason for it, made away with themselves. But not so with us. Wherefore of their deeds nothing is said; but these flourish and daily increase. Which Paul having in mind said, "The weakness of God is stronger than all men."

AVARICE AND USURY

THERE is nothing more cruel, nothing more infamous, than the usury so common amongst men.

The usurer traffics on the misfortunes of others; he enriches himself on their poverty, and then he demands his usury, as if they were under a great obligation to him.

He is heartless to his creditor, but is afraid of appearing so; when he pretends that he has every inclination to oblige, he crushes him the more and reduces him to the last extremity. He offers one hand, and with the other pushes him down the precipice.

He offers to assist the shipwrecked, and instead of guiding them safely into port he steers them among the reefs and rocks. Where your treasure is, there is your heart, says our Savior.

Perhaps you may have avoided many evils arising from avarice; but still, if you cherish an attachment to this odious vice, it will be of little use, for you will still be a slave, free as you fancy yourself to be; and you will fall from the height of heaven to that spot wherein your gold is hidden, and your thoughts will still complacently dwell on money, gains, usury, and dishonest commerce.

What is more miserable than such a state?

There is not a sadder tyranny than that of a man who is a willing subject to this furious tyrant, destroying all that is good in him, namely, the nobility of the soul.

So long as you have a heart basely attached to gains and riches, whatsoever truths may be told you, or whatsoever advice may be given to you, to secure your salvation — all will be useless.

Avarice is an incurable malady, an ever-burning fire, a tyranny which extends far and wide; for he who in this life is the slave of money is loaded with heavy chains and destined to carry far heavier chains in the life to come.

RANDOLPH HENRY SPENCER CHURCHILL

(1849-1895)

THREE HUNDRED MILLIONS of people, of diverse races, tongues, religions, and civilizations, occupying parts of all the continents and many remote islands, with not a single representative in the British House of Commons, yet ruled by that body which is itself ruled by the five million voters of the small United Kingdom — such is the picture of modern British imperialism portrayed by a Conservative leader and Minister, Lord Randolph Churchill, in his speech to an assemblage of Conservatives of the University Carlton Club at Oxford in June 1885. He says: "It is not difficult to understand that five millions of people may govern themselves with more or less success; but to what extent will these five millions be able to control and direct the destinies of the three hundred millions whom they have in their power?" This, he adds, "is a problem totally new"; but he faces it "with a firm belief in the ascertained and much-tried common sense which is the peculiarity of the English people." And he says: "That is the faith of the Tory democracy in which I shall ever abide."

In this speech we have a very lifelike political portrait of Lord Randolph Churchill, drawn by himself, and very distinctly differentiating the English Conservatives of to-day from those of even the preceding generation. Although a scion of a ducal house and a self-proclaimed "Tory," he was, as a party man, inclined to unruly and outspoken independence. He was withal a man of so much ability, so much alive to his own times, and so popular as an orator that a strong ministry could not be formed without including him while he remained active in politics.

He was born in London, February 13th, 1849, the second son of the Duke of Marlborough. He married Miss Jerome, of New York, in 1874, and entered Parliament the same year as Member for Woodstock, which he continued to represent till 1885, when he began to represent South Paddington. He was Secretary for India in Salisbury's first ministry, and in the second Salisbury ministry was Chancellor of the Exchequer and leader in the House. His health breaking down, he began to travel in Africa and Asia, but was never again well enough to resume active life. He died in London, January 24th, 1895.

THE AGE OF ACTION

(From an Address on Political Life and Thought in England. Delivered Before the University Carlton Club, at Cambridge, June 6th, 1885)

THIS is essentially an age of action. It does not appear to me to be an age of thought. I doubt very much whether, if Adam Smith, or even Mr. John Stuart Mill, had lived in these days, they would have been able to produce the works which they did produce. Railways and telegraphs, the steam printing machine, and shorthand writing have done their best to kill political thought. It is essentially an age of action, but action based rather on instinct than on logic, or reason, or experience. Look how very suddenly things occur, how very little anything is foreseen, and how very rapidly everything is forgotten. Take even such instances as the death of General Gordon, or the battle of Penj-deh, or even the vote of credit, and Mr. Gladstone's great war speech. These are events which caused intense and immeasurable excitement at the moment. That excitement lasted for about twenty-four hours; everybody chattered to everybody about that particular subject for that space of time, and then it was decently interred, for all practical political purposes, in the political cemetery of utter oblivion. Now, I do not think this at all an exaggerated or untrue picture of the manner in which we conduct our government and our political affairs; it is a very serious consideration. Yet, strange to say, I suppose there never was a time in the history of England when profound political thought and prolonged political study were more essential to the interests of England. The process of government has never approached even the nature of an exact science. It has always been purely empirical, and still continues to be so; and yet the difficulties of government now grow greater and greater every day, and experience seems to become less useful. I suppose there is not a man in England more experienced in the public service — I doubt whether there has ever been a man of greater experience in the public service — than Mr. Gladstone; and yet look at the extraordinary ill luck, to put it in the mildest way, which has attended his government every single day; there are a great many people — I dare say there are people in this university — who will tell you that, if you want to be able to judge the present, and forecast the future, you must study history. Well, I apprehend that the study of history in our present case is almost useless. The study of history to the Russian politician is very useful because it will tell him what must be the inevitable and speedy end of a grinding and cruel despotism. The study of history to the German may be useful, because it will tell him that a military oligarchy, acting under the semblance of a constitutional form, is a political system of ephemeral duration. The study of history to the Frenchman is useful, because it will tell him that the transition from a Republic to absolute and irrepressible power in one man is alike easy and regular. But, in our case, the study of history to an English politician affords very little guide whatever, because the state of things you have to deal with in England, at the present moment, is unparalleled in history.

What are the duties of the English government at the present moment? They have to provide for the security and, as best they can, to minister to the happiness of three hundred millions or more of human beings, and these three hundred millions are scattered over every quarter of the world, and they comprise every imaginable variety of the human race, of custom, of religion, of language and dialect. And what is the nature of the government which has to discharge these extraordinary and unparalleled duties? You have an hereditary monarchy, exercising an immense influence indirectly, but hardly any influence directly —almost precisely the reverse of what was the nature of hereditary monarchy two hundred years ago. You have an hereditary chamber possessing executive and legislative powers; and you have a representative chamber controlling these two forces and seeking to acquire, and gradually acquiring, into its own hands almost all executive and legislative authority. All these three institutions are institutions of extremely ancient origin, and they are all institutions intensely conservative in their constitution and their procedure. Because, mind you, if the House of Commons were to be elected in November, and were to be composed almost entirely of the Radical party, still, you may take it for certain, the spirit and the procedure of that House would be intensely conservative. Now, what is the foundation of this very curious and ancient structure? The foundation is totally new, purely modern, absolutely untried. You have changed the old foundation. You have gone to a new foundation. Your new foundation is a great seething and swaying mass of some five

million electors, who have it in their power, if they should so please, by the mere heave of the shoulders, if they only act with moderate unanimity, to sweep away entirely the three ancient institutions which I have described, and put anything they like in their place, and to profoundly alter, and perhaps for a time altogether ruin, the interests of three hundred million beings who are committed to their charge. That is, I say, a state of things unparalleled in history. And how do you think it will all end? Are we being swept along a turbulent and irresistible torrent which is bearing us towards some political Niagara, in which every mortal thing we now know will be twisted and smashed beyond all recognition? Or are we, on the other hand, gliding passively along a quiet river of human progress that will lead us to some undiscovered ocean of almost superhuman development? Who can tell? Is it not, gentlemen, an age—is not this a moment—when political thought is necessary? To what extent do you think these five million electors will be controlled or influenced, by law or custom, by religion or by reason? I can understand—it is not difficult to understand—that five million people may govern themselves with more or less success; but to what extent will these five million people be able to control and direct the destinies—and in what manner will they do so—of the three hundred millions whom they have in their power? and to what extent will the five million electors be exempt from the ordinary human influences of passion and caprice? This is a problem totally new. It is a problem upon which history throws no light whatever, and moreover it is a problem which comes at a time when the persons chiefly responsible for the government of our country are precluded by the very circumstances of their life from giving it the deep attention which it absolutely requires.

I believe that a club like yours can give much assistance in this direction. You are not yet drawn into that political machine which kills thought and stifles reflection. I dare say many of those whom I see before me soon will be, but some of you perhaps may not. At any rate, all I would say to you, filling the honorable position of president to which you have so kindly elected me, is to give time while you have time to political thought, and to the present consideration of these questions, and questions analogous to those, which I have tried to set before you. Discuss them and write about them, and endeavor in your

respective spheres to stimulate also political thought among the masses of your fellow-countrymen. But you can do more than this, because, by able summaries of statistical information, by precise investigation into sharply opposing arguments, and by original conclusions, all put together in an agreeable and attractive literary form, you may be able to do much to restrain politicians from acting hastily and heedlessly at critical moments and upon important subjects. In all probability you possess enormous advantages for this task. You represent the most perfect centre of higher education, practical and theoretical, which any country can show. You possess mental powers at the present moment in their highest degree of energetic efficiency. Because, depend upon it that the mental powers of a man at twenty-one for getting at the bottom of any very difficult question, or for arriving at the truth on any much-contested subject, are worth double and treble the mental powers of a man of thirty-five or forty, who, harassed and exhausted by ten or fifteen years of active political life, and by the circumstances of that life, is precluded from giving to the subject the concentrated attention you can do. Do you suppose that a man at thirty-five or forty could go in for the higher mathematics of this university with any chance of success? Why, he would be mad; every undergraduate in the schools would beat him hollow. And yet the difficulties of the extraordinary problems of higher mathematics are as nothing compared with the mystery, darkness, and confusion that surround some of our great political questions at the present day. I am quite certain that it is impossible for any one of you to overestimate the benefits you can confer upon society, and your country generally, by devoting and applying your best energies to the development and popularization of high and deep political thought.

I have shown—very cursorily indeed, but in a manner which your own intellects will fill up—the extraordinary, unparalleled, and complicated nature of the political problems with which political parties in England have to deal; and I have asked you, on my own behalf and on behalf of other politicians busily engaged, for your assistance. At the same time, gentlemen, I do not wish you to suppose for a moment that I am alarmed as to the future. My state of mind when these great problems come across me—which is very rarely—is one of wonder, or perhaps I should rather say of admiration and of hope, because the alter-

native state of mind would be one of terror and despair. And I am guarded from that latter state of mind by a firm belief in the essential goodness of life, and in the evolution, by some process or other which I do not exactly know and cannot determine, of a higher and nobler humanity. But, above all, my especial safeguard against such a state of mental annihilation and mental despair is my firm belief in the ascertained and much-tried common sense which is the peculiarity of the English people. That is the faith which, I think, ought to animate and protect you in your political future; that is the faith of the Tory democracy in which I shall ever abide; that is the faith which your club can, and I hope will, widely and wisely propagate; and that is the faith which, dominating our minds and influencing our actions on all occasions, no matter how dark and gloomy the horizon may appear to be, will contribute to preserve and adapt the institutions of our country and to guarantee and to consolidate the spreading dominions of the Queen.

GLADSTONE'S EGYPTIAN INCONSISTENCIES

(From an Address Delivered at Edinburgh Music Hall, December 18th, 1883)

THE other day the poor Egyptians were very near effecting a successful revolution; they were very near throwing off their suffocating bonds; but, unfortunately for us, Mr. Gladstone, the prime minister of Great Britain—Mr. Gladstone, the leader, the idol, the demigod of the Liberal party—Mr. Gladstone, the Member for Midlothian, came upon them with his armies and fleets, destroyed their towns, devastated their country, slaughtered their thousands and flung back these struggling wretches into the morass of oppression, back into the toils of their taskmasters. The revolution of Arabi was the movement of a nation; like all revolutions, it had its good side and its bad; you must never, for purposes of practical politics, criticize too minutely the origin, the authors, or the course of revolutions. Would you undo, if you could, the Revolution of 1688, which drove the Stuarts from the throne, because of the intrigues of the nobles and of the clergy? Would you undo the French Revolution because of the Reign of Terror? Would you undo the Revolution of Naples because Garibaldi might not be altogether a man of your mind? You know you would not; you know that those revolutions were justified by atrocious governments. I tell you, add together the misery of the French under the Bourbons, the terror this country labored under in the last year of James II., the atrocities committed by the ministry of Bomba, and you will arrive at an approximate estimate of what drove the Egyptians to the standard of Arabi Pasha. Since the Reform Bill of 1832, when first the people were admitted to a share in the government of this country, we have always been on the side of freedom against oppression; of constitutional government against arbitrary rule. Mr. Gladstone's gravest charge against the policy of the late government at the Congress of Berlin was that during those debates their influence had leaned to the side of despotism rather than to the side of freedom, which, he said, caused him the deepest shame and the bitterest regret. The charge could not be sustained by facts; but that made no matter Mr. Gladstone knew that even the insinuation of it from him would gravely injure the government in the minds of the liberty-loving English and Scotch. Never was any man so caught in his own toils; never was retribution so prompt or so terrible Within three years of his making that accusation he himself had to decide between an Oriental despotism on the one hand, and a struggling people on the other; he had to decide which he would favor; the lot was in his hands, his power was absolute, the whole responsibility was with him. Without a moment's hesitation, and for the wretched motive of concluding a commercial treaty with France, he joined hands with that country, and cast the whole weight and power of Britain against the struggling people, and on the side of, perhaps, the very worst ruler whom even centuries of Oriental abominations could produce, as I shall presently show you. A greater crime was never committed; a greater departure from our modern foreign policy cannot be conceived; a more detestable return to the evil foreign policy which preceded the great Reform Bill cannot be recorded. But I may be told, "In thus accusing Mr. Gladstone and his colleagues, you are in reality accusing us, the people of this great country, who allowed, and who may even be said to have approved, his policy."

I am not sure that the people have approved his policy. As far as by-elections can be said to go, they disapprove it. Manchester could not find a candidate to support it. York rejected it. The people of this country have not yet had an opportunity of giving judgment. Parliament may be said to have approved

the government policy, if you consider only the Liberal majority of the House of Commons. But is the approval of the Liberal majority of the House of Commons so very valuable or so very conclusive? If Mr. Gladstone were to stand on his head in Hyde Park, the Liberal majority would be ready to go into the lobby to record their opinion that it was the most marvelous feat of gymnastics ever performed; if Mr. Gladstone were to declare that black was white, which he very often does, the Liberal majority in the House of Commons would at once exclaim, "It is the voice of a god, not of a man." But in spite of these little weaknesses of the Liberal party, I will say this, that even if the approval of the Liberal majority were conclusive, even if the British people had sanctioned the entire Egyptian policy, the Liberal majority or the British people could not be held to be responsible if they were in error. For from first to last you have been systematically furnished with false information. You were told that Arabi was a military adventurer, and that his movement was a military rebellion. This was the first fabrication; no one will now deny that he was the leader of a nation, the exponent of a nation's woes, and that the military rebellion was the desperate struggle of a race. You were told that the British fleet was in danger from the forts of Alexandria; this was the second fabrication. In the first place, the British fleet might have sailed away, for there was hardly a European left who required protection. All the money-lending bloodsuckers and harpies, with their hordes of hangers-on, had fled panic-stricken before the wrath of an awakened and an aroused people. Some people would think — Mr. Gladstone most certainly would have thought when he was in Midlothian in 1880 — that the departure of the British fleet would have been preferable to the destruction of a great, ancient, and wealthy city; but the overwhelming proof that the British fleet was never in danger lies in the fact that, during an engagement of seven or eight hours, when the forts did all they knew, these terrible forts were unable to kill even half a dozen British seamen or to knock a hole in any one of your ironclad ships. You were told that the Suez Canal was in danger; this was fabrication number three. The Suez Canal was never in danger at any time except from the desperate genius of Lord Wolseley and M. de Lesseps. During the whole Egyptian difficulty commerce traversed the Suez Canal, with the exception of a period of forty-eight hours, when Lord Wolseley himself arrested it. You

were told that the Khedive Tewfik was an enlightened, constitutional, amiable prince. This was a most daring stretch of the imagination. I have proved him before the House of Commons to be one of the most despicable wretches who ever occupied an Eastern throne. At Mr. Gladstone's request — did I say request? — at his entreaty — I should say, in answer to his passionate challenge — I furnished him with documents, founded on the statements of irrefutable witnesses, and supported by official records, proving that the Khedive Tewfik was the author of the massacres of Alexandria when many British subjects were slaughtered, that he plotted those massacres for the purpose of ruining Arabi and of precipitating European intervention. He betrayed his country and his people to the foreigner, and verily he shall have his reward. Mr. Gladstone pledged himself most solemnly to examine those documents which I furnished him with, and to refute them if he could; his pledges, renewed twice and thrice, are recorded in black and white; but from the day in June when he received the papers, to this day, this eighteenth of December, no answer has he made, and no answer will he ever make — no answer can he make.

You will admit that, after all that has passed, if Mr. Gladstone and his Foreign Secretary could have crushed me — if they could have shown the public that I had been imposed upon, that I had made false accusations — they would not have spared me. Would they? No consideration for what might befall me in public estimation would have prevented them, if they could have done so, from whitewashing their miserable puppet Tewfik. But, instead of bringing about that happy event, they have preserved a blank silence; and you will not wonder at their silence when I tell you that one of my witnesses was Arabi Pasha himself, and that my official records were their own Blue-Books. Now, whatever may be said of Arabi Pasha, his bitterest enemies will not accuse him of being either a liar, a robber, or a murderer. From first to last all will admit that he has ever spoke candidly what was in his mind, that though for months he exercised supreme power in Egypt, a country whose records are dark with crime and assassination, though he was surrounded by violent opponents and desperate conspirators, he never took a human life, and that, though he could have made himself rich, as the expression goes, "beyond the dreams of avarice," he left Egypt with his family, an exile, without one single farthing. I say with confidence that

that man's evidence would be taken in any court of law against the statements of the Khedive Tewfik, who dethroned his own father, who robbed his own family, who banished from his native land his younger brother; who, although he professes to be anxious to suppress the slave trade, is himself a dealer and an owner of slaves; who practices magic and sorcery and every kind of the most debased superstition; whose most intimate friend will not believe a word he utters; who intrigued against his sovereign the Sultan, against his friends the British, against his friends the French, taking them up and betraying them one after another in turn; who plotted with Arabi against Riaz, with Sherif against Arabi, with that incomparable desperado, Omar Lutfi, against the European inhabitants of Alexandria; who ordered Arabi to fire on the British fleet which lay in the harbor for his protection, and who dared to proclaim Arabi a rebel and a traitor because he did not resist with fire and sword and carnage the occupation of Alexandria by the sailors of Lord Alcester. All this is written in Blue-Books; all this marvelous mass of wickedness and lying and plotting and conspiracy is as notorious in the East and as familiar to every Egyptian — aye, and to every English official — aye, and to Mr. Gladstone and his colleagues — as the incidents of the Midlothian campaign are to you.

This is the man — did I say man? — he is not a man; this is the being whom your army and navy supported against Arabi Pasha and the Egyptian people; this is the being to gratify whose frightful instincts Alexandria was bombarded and Tel-el-Kebir was fought; this is the being in whose name, and by whose power, Mr. Gladstone intends to give Egypt a fair start. I have not yet done with this Khedive Tewfik. But you may say to me, What is your object in bringing these accusations? What is the Khedive Tewfik to us, or he to me? I quite admit that he would be nothing either to you or me if the British army was not keeping him on his throne, and the British people responsible for all his acts. This is my object — to show you, the people, so that if you believe me you may intervene, that Great Britain, under the guidance of the stupendous genius of him whom the Liberals call the greatest man she ever produced, has gone astray, has commenced a hopeless task, and has entered upon a fatal course.

And this brings me to the last and greatest of all the fabrications which have been diligently crammed into your minds,

The Prime Minister has stated over and over again that we went to Egypt with no selfish aim or object, but only in the interests of Europe and for the benefit of the Egyptian people. Certainly Mr. Gladstone has a curious way of promoting the interests of Europe and of benefiting the people of Egypt. As the original inventor of the concert of Europe, he summoned Europe to Constantinople to deliberate upon Egyptian affairs; but no sooner had the Powers entered into conference than Mr. Gladstone seized upon Egypt with horse, foot, artillery, and dragoons, and the various powers, feeling extremely foolish, abandoned their deliberations in disgust. I do not think he will find it easy to collect them again. I do not think he will find it easy to appeal again to that concert of Europe to which, by so many pledges, he bound himself when he preached to you in Midlothian three years ago. He first struck a desperate blow at the commerce between Europe and the East by laying the city of Alexandria in ashes. He struck a second desperate blow at the same interests when he laid violent hands on the Suez Canal, which, since its construction, had been preserved sacred from the operations of war. He struck a third desperate blow at Eastern commerce when, for a period of three months and more, he put a stop to all commercial transactions over the whole land of Egypt; and the result of these three blows is that he has created a hatred of Europeans in general, and of the British in particular among the Egyptians, so bitter, so unappeasable, that for years to come the commercial interests of Europe in Egypt will hang upon a thread. The recent events in the Soudan are a fair indication of the feelings of Egypt for Europe. Turkey is only waiting for a chance of getting her finger in the pie; France is intriguing against us at Cairo with unceasing malignity; Germany and Austria are looking on with contemptuous ill-will; and Russia, whenever opportunity offers, stirs up the sparks of strife and jealousy among the powers. So much for the interests of Europe as promoted by Mr. Gladstone — so much for the attitude of the European concert, for which Mr. Gladstone took out his own special patent.

But now let us look at the Egyptian people, to whom Mr. Gladstone declares he only wished to do good. I will say no more about Alexandria. I will say nothing about the thousands of Egyptians who were slaughtered by his humane efforts; I will say nothing about the hundreds whom Mr. Gladstone's judges

have either hung or condemned to penal servitude or sentenced to a living death in the regions of the White Nile. All this I say nothing about, though the poor Egyptians might like to say something about it if you gave them the chance. I content myself with this, and I defy contradiction. We were sent to Egypt by the bondholders in the month of July 1882; we dispatched ships from Portsmouth and from Plymouth; we brought troops from Madras and from Bombay; we spent four millions of our own money; we sacrificed, one way and another, many British lives; we made two brand-new viscounts, and gave them each what was elegantly and eloquently called a "lump sum" for all the dangers they had so courageously encountered, and for all the glories they had so gloriously won. We distributed decorations and rewards so profusely that every man almost of that famous army is signalized forever. And what did we do to the Egyptians? Well, first we took them the cattle plague, which more than decimated the herds which were the wealth of the Delta of the Nile. The cattle plague, in consequence of the admirable sanitary laws which we taught the people, produced the cholera, and the cholera carried off fifty thousand lives; for wherever the cholera broke out we drew what was called a military cordon round the locality, which prevented a single soul from getting out or a single doctor from getting in. Then, when every Egyptian who had to die was dead, we made the country a handsome present of a dozen doctors, who arrived in time to assist at a great many funerals, when doctors are always so useful and so welcome. But we did a great deal more than this; we held elections for the Egyptian Parliament, which were so eagerly taken up by the people that hundreds of them fled to the officials begging and praying and bribing, in order that they might be excused the dignity and privilege of voting. But we did more; we had made the country a present of a dozen doctors; we now gave them in addition a dozen Dutch judges, who, at the present moment, are all on leave, endeavoring to learn the language from an elementary Arabic conversation-book, wandering about Europe, and waiting for their law courts to be built. We did not stop here; we created a Council of State, on which we placed Turks, French, Russians, Germans, and Greeks. More than this; having either slaughtered or frightened to death the old Egyptian army, we considered it our duty to form a magnificent new Egyptian army, the recruits for which are col-

lected by the bastinado and brought into barracks heavily chained — an army which is now brought to such an admirable degree of efficiency that they are made to do police duty at Cairo while the police are sent to fight the False Prophet, and who are warranted by those who know them best to cut the throats of Sir Evelyn Wood and other British officers whom we liberally quartered on Egypt, the moment the backs of the British troops were turned. In addition to all this largesse, this princely munificence, quite unprecedented in history from one nation to another, we generously added six millions to the Egyptian national debt; and to crown this splendid edifice, which is forever to be the grandest of the grand achievements of a "grand old man," we placed at the head the Khedive Tewfik, the conspirator against his father, the robber of his family, the banisher of his brother, the dealer in human flesh and blood, the betrayer of his allies, of his ministers, and of his country, the man of magic and of sorcery.

Now — so says Mr. Gladstone at the Guildhall — we, the Liberal Government, if only the False Prophet will keep quiet for a moment, are going to scuttle out of this pandemonium as soon as we can, and to all our former fabrications and imaginations we shall add by far the grossest and most audacious of all, for we shall tell Parliament, we shall tell the country, we shall tell Europe, that Egypt is pacified, and that the Egyptians are happy and free, although we know all the time, beyond the possibility of a doubt, that greater misery by far prevails in that country than before the battle of Telel-Kebir; that life and property are more insecure; that the people are more hopelessly burdened with debt; that justice is more frightfully corrupt than Scotchmen or Englishmen can well conceive; and that not one single real reform of any sort or kind has been set on foot, much less carried into effect. Plenty of shams, plenty of impostures, but genuine beneficial reform absolutely none. Such has been our work in Egypt; and for all this woe and misery that your government has wrought shall we expect the blessing of God upon our country? Shall we not rather, if we sanction such a work, if we do not without delay repair, as far as we can, so many errors, so many crimes — shall we not rather fear that retribution which sooner or later has never failed to overtake those who oppress the human race?

MARCUS TULLIUS CICERO

(106–43 B. C.)

N ORATORY and all forms of prose composition Cicero was for seventeen centuries the acknowledged master of the civilized world. So long as Latin remained the "vulgar tongue" of learning in Europe, every one who aspired to be heard beyond his own province studied and imitated the style of Cicero. As first the French and afterwards the English language began to be used in literature; as the great writers of Northern Europe, encouraged by the example of Dante, dared to employ the vernacular of the despised common people of their own countries, the style of Cicero passed from the Latin of the learned into literature which appealed to a wider circle of readers. In England, Bacon presents in his 'Essays' the first model of the later English prose which in the essays of Addison reasserts the right of the English language to be governed by its own laws rather than by those of any Latin, however elegant. In the main, however, the style of educated writers of English prose is Ciceronian, in spite of Addison, for Macaulay in the earlier years of the nineteenth century, and towards its close, the great Frenchman Taine, have strongly swayed the minds of English prose writers away from Saxon towards Ciceronian constructions.

If Cicero's influence over prose literature has been thus universal in English and other Teutonic tongues which have a "time" radically different from Latin and an accentuation which creates a sense of musical values in language greatly unlike that which made Latin intelligible as a spoken tongue,—if in spite of all differences of speech and of "ear" he has thus swayed the prose writing of Northern Europe, Teutonic as well as Latin, for so many centuries, we would naturally expect him to be the supreme arbiter of oratorical style. And this expectation has been fully realized. The Ciceronian construction of clauses, balancing each other in musical "time," and arranged to make possible the greatest cumulative force of idea, governs modern oratory still as it did that of the Middle Ages. During the last twenty-five years, we have seen a tendency to break away from it, towards a simpler construction, but it is far from its full realization. Whenever we say that this or that piece of prose is "oratorical" in its style, we mean simply that it approximates more or less the syntax of Cicero. If from the standpoint of the student of English who loves its mastering simplicity and admires its natural syntax because it tends to force the plain truth to be told, this seems unfortunate, there must have been a supreme and sufficient reason for it, or it could not have existed as it has done, the central fact in the oratory and the prose writing of so many centuries among so many people of diverse languages and habits of thought. Without doubt, this supreme reason is to be sought in the nice sense of time in language which Cicero has perhaps in a greater degree than any one else who ever wrote Latin prose. Unless an orator or a prose writer can develop this sense so that it will govern his composition as surely and as unconsciously as the feet of a skillful dancer are governed by the music of a waltz, his sentences must always be ragged and uneven, repellent to all whose intellects are sufficiently developed to give them an idea of order and a love of harmony. As this idea of order, this love of harmony, is the normal rule of the intellect, the speaker who offends through a defective ear for the time of the language in which he expresses himself must necessarily create an unfavorable impression. If, on the contrary, he has the sense of time as a governing factor in his constructions, if, when he adds a clause, his ear immediately impels him to give it its due balance with the next; if every period harmonizes and balances the time of every other; and if to this he adds such harmonies of tone as are illustrated in the Latin vowel successions of Cicero as they are in the English of Burke, he has a mode of expression worthy of the highest thought, and when used for the purpose of expressing great ideas, sure to compel permanent attention to them. This is the conclusion which every one must draw who studies the careful art of Cicero's constructions and considers in connection with it the permanent force it has given his ideas.

The art of oratory, as Cicero understood it, approximates in its technique the technical art of modern versification. Except that the time of balancing clauses must not be so exactly identical as to set them tripping, the oratory of Cicero makes demands on the ear for antithetical time in the government of its constructions almost if not quite as severe as does modern English blank verse of average regularity. Occasionally in classical oratory, the rythms of poetry were allowed; it was not considered a fault but rather a beauty that an orator, moved by his subject and speaking in cadenced periods, should occasionally break into a perfect hexameter, but as a rule the exactly identical time-balances of verse were avoided or disguised. The Greeks and Romans had a nice ear for time in language and were often conscious of it. Of course every one who speaks a modern language as a vernacular acquires, in learning to talk, the "natural" ear

for its time, but as a rule we never become conscious of the operations of this "ear" and so are ignorant of the first essentials of such art as governed Cicero's prose, as in its more nearly perfect measure it governed the verse of Horace and of Virgil.

To develop a consciousness of this sense of time without becoming self-conscious because of it is to have the A B C of Cicero's art as an orator. It has been said with truth that it was as nearly an exact art as poetry or sculpture, and for those who in seeking the artistic can avoid the always present and always imminent danger of the artificial it is likely to be not less a source of power in speaking than a knowledge of musical time is in the composition of verse.

In the politics of Rome, Cicero stands for the virtue of ancient aristocracy against the later imperialism through which one strong and masterful man after another sought supreme power by appealing to the fighting instincts of the lowest masses of the people. The later Roman republic was essentially an aristocratic and oligarchical institution, modified by mob law. It ended as aristocracies always end, in imperialism. In mediæval Europe, we have first the governing oligarchy of feudal barons with the king as their chief—*primus inter pares*. Next we have the struggle for supremacy between the one man and the oligarchy in which, by appealing to the previously unconsidered multitude, the one masterful man gets the better of the hundred who seek to master him and the masses. Thus in France we see established the absolutism which preceded the Revolution. Again after the Revolution, Napoleon followed the example of Marius and Cæsar in Rome, and of Cromwell in England, evoking the latent power of the many who are weak to overcome the few who are strong. Whenever an aristocracy or an oligarchy reaches a certain stage of corruption, this process becomes a part of the inevitable logic of events. First an oligarchy which has assumed to rule in the name and by the right of the people oppresses and defrauds them. Then some strong man appeals to the people as their champion and, winning their confidence, grasps the supreme power which first Catiline and then Cæsar strove for at Rome in the time of Cicero.

In his speeches against Verres, the plunderer of Sicily; in denouncing Catiline; in defending Milo for killing Clodius; in his Philippics against Antony, and in every public act to which he was impelled by his natural instincts, Cicero resists with all the strength of his great intellect the tendency of a corrupt Republic to surrender its last remnant of liberty to any and every desperate adventurer bold enough to grasp supremacy in the name of the people and use it for his own purposes of absolving himself from all restraint. When Cicero's head was sent to Rome; when Fulvia, the widow of Clodius and the wife of Antony, pierced with her needle the tongue

which had done more than any other for the perpetuation of all the good there was in Roman civilization, she paid him the highest compliment he ever received and illustrated in doing so the causes of his failure. He demanded disinterestedness from an oligarchy no longer capable of anything except the most extreme and immoral selfishness. Necessarily, he defeated himself, but he won in defeat a greater victory than that of any other man of his day—greater even than that of Cato, for out of his mental stress, the keen excitements of his struggles for the perpetuation of the republic, were born the Ciceronian oratory and literature of Rome and of all succeeding centuries until our own times.

He was born at Arpinum, January 3d, 106 B.C. A *novus homo*, a "new man," born from a family of plebeian origin, he forced his way to the first offices of the Republic. As Consul at the time of the conspiracy of Catiline, he saved Rome only to lose it, after Cæsar, suspected as an accomplice of Catiline, had been assassinated for his usurpation, by men who were mere antiquarians instead of the leaders they thought themselves. An antiquarian himself, Cicero had too great a reverence for antique virtue to win against the thoroughgoing scoundrelism of the triumvirate. Augustus, after encouraging him at least tacitly against Antony, consented at least tacitly to Antony's determination to have him assassinated. So on December 7th, 43 B.C., after Cicero's throat had been cut at the door of his Formian villa by a representative of the new order of things, his head and hands were sent to the triumvirs in witness that there was no longer a single living and formidable tongue to plead for the antique virtue, the ancient liberty, the republican glories of Rome.

W. V. B.

THE FIRST ORATION AGAINST CATILINE

(Delivered in the Roman Senate)

WHEN, O Catiline, do you mean to cease abusing our patience? How long is that madness of yours still to mock us? When is there to be an end of that unbridled audacity of yours, swaggering about as it does now? Do not the nightly guards placed on the Palatine Hill—do not the watches posted throughout the city—does not the alarm of the people, and the union of all good men—does not the precaution taken of assembling the Senate in this most defensible place—do not the looks and countenances of this venerable body here present have any effect upon you? Do you not feel that your plans are detected

Do you not see that your conspiracy is already arrested and rendered powerless by the knowledge which every one here possesses of it? What is there that you did last night, what the night before—where is it that you were—who was there that you summoned to meet you—what design was there which was adopted by you, with which you think that any one of us is unacquainted?

Shame on the age and on its principles! The Senate is aware of these things; the consul sees them; and yet this man lives. Lives! aye, he comes even into the Senate. He takes a part in the public deliberations; he is watching and marking down and checking off for slaughter every individual among us. And we, gallant men that we are, think that we are doing our duty to the republic if we keep out of the way of his frenzied attacks.

You ought, O Catiline, long ago to have been led to execution by command of the consul. That destruction which you have been long plotting against us ought to have already fallen on your own head.

What? Did not that most illustrious man, Publius Scipio, the Pontifex Maximus, in his capacity of a private citizen, put to death Tiberius Gracchus, though but slightly undermining the Constitution? And shall we, who are the consuls, tolerate Catiline, openly desirous to destroy the whole world with fire and slaughter? For I pass over older instances, such as how Caius Servilius Ahala with his own hand slew Spurius Mælius when plotting a revolution in the State. There was—there was once such virtue in this republic, that brave men would repress mischievous citizens with severer chastisement than the most bitter enemy. For we have a resolution of the Senate, a formidable and authoritative decree against you, O Catiline; the wisdom of the republic is not at fault, nor the dignity of this senatorial body. We, we alone,—I say it openly,—we, the consuls, are wanting in our duty.

The Senate once passed a decree that Lucius Opimius, the consul, should take care that the Republic suffered no injury. Not one night elapsed. There was put to death, on some mere suspicion of disaffection, Caius Gracchus, a man whose family had borne the most unblemished reputation for many generations. There were slain Marcus Fulvius, a man of consular rank, and all his children. By a like decree of the Senate the safety of the Republic was intrusted to Caius Marius and Lucius Valerius, the consuls. Did not the vengeance of the Republic, did not execution overtake Lucius Saturninus, a tribune of the people, and Caius Servilius, the prætor, without the delay of one single day? But we, for these twenty days, have been allowing the edge of the Senate's authority to grow blunt, as it were. For we are in possession of a similar decree of the Senate, but we keep it locked up in its parchment—buried, I may say, in the sheath; and according to this decree you ought, O Catiline, to be put to death this instant. You live,—and you live, not to lay aside, but to persist in your audacity.

I wish, O conscript fathers, to be merciful; I wish not to appear negligent amid such danger to the State; but I do now accuse myself of remissness and culpable inactivity. A camp is pitched in Italy, at the entrance of Etruria, in hostility to the Republic; the number of the enemy increases every day; and yet the general of that camp, the leader of those enemies, we see within the walls—aye, and even in the Senate—planning every day some internal injury to the Republic. If, O Catiline, I should now order you to be arrested, to be put to death, I should, I suppose, have to fear lest all good men should say that I had acted tardily, rather than that any one should affirm that I acted cruelly. But yet this, which ought to have been done long since, I have good reason for not doing as yet; I will put you to death then, when there shall be not one person possible to be found so wicked, so abandoned, so like yourself, as not to allow that it has been rightly done. As long as one person exists who can dare to defend you, you shall live; but you shall live as you do now, surrounded by my many and trusty guards, so that you shall not be able to stir one finger against the Republic; many eyes and ears shall still observe and watch you, as they have hitherto done, though you shall not perceive them.

For what is there, O Catiline, that you can still expect, if night is not able to veil your nefarious meetings in darkness, and if private houses cannot conceal the voice of your conspiracy within their walls;—if everything is seen and displayed? Change your mind; trust me; forget the slaughter and conflagration you are meditating. You are hemmed in on all sides; all your plans are clearer than the day to us; let me remind you of them. Do you recollect that on the twenty-first of October I said in the Senate, that on a certain day, which was to be the twenty-seventh of October, C. Manlius, the satellite and servant of

and to promise that very night, before daybreak, to slay me in my bed. All this I knew almost before your meeting had broken up. I strengthened and fortified my house with a stronger guard; I refused admittance, when they came, to those whom you sent in the morning to salute me, and of whom I had foretold to many eminent men that they would come to me at that time.

As, then, this is the case, O Catiline, continue as you have begun. Leave the city at last; the gates are open; depart. That Manlian camp of yours has been waiting too long for you as its general. And lead forth with you all your friends, or at least as many as you can; purge the city of your presence; you will deliver me from a great fear when there is a wall between me and you. Among us you can dwell no longer—I will not bear it, I will not permit it, I will not tolerate it. Great thanks are due to the immortal gods, and to this very Jupiter Stator, in whose temple we are, the most ancient protector of this city, that we have already so often escaped so foul, so horrible, and so deadly an enemy to the republic. But the safety of the commonwealth must not be too often allowed to be risked on one man. As long as you, O Catiline, plotted against me while I was the consul-elect, I defended myself not with a public guard, but by my own private diligence. When, in the next consular comitia, you wished to slay me when I was actually consul, and your competitors also, in the Campus Martius, I checked your nefarious attempt by the assistance and resources of my own friends, without exciting any disturbance publicly. In short, as often as you attacked me, I by myself opposed you, and that, too, though I saw that my ruin was connected with great disaster to the republic. But now you are openly attacking the entire republic.

You are summoning to destruction and devastation the temples of the immortal gods, the houses of the city, the lives of all the citizens; in short, all Italy. Wherefore, since I do not yet venture to do that which is the best thing, and which belongs to my office and to the discipline of our ancestors, I will do that which is more merciful if we regard its rigor, and more expedient for the State. For if I order you to be put to death, the rest of the conspirators will still remain in the republic; if, as I have long been exhorting you, you depart, your companions, those worthless dregs of the republic, will be drawn off from the city too. What is the matter, Catiline? Do you hesitate to do that when I order you, which you were already doing of your own

your audacity, would be in arms? Was I mistaken, Catiline, not only in so important, so atrocious, so incredible a fact, but, what is much more remarkable, in the very day? I said also in the Senate that you had fixed the massacre of the nobles for the twenty-eighth of October, when many chief men of the Senate had left Rome, not so much for the sake of saving themselves as of checking your designs. Can you deny that on that very day you were so hemmed in by my guards and my vigilance that you were unable to stir one finger against the Republic; when you said that you would be content with the flight of the rest, and the slaughter of us who remained? What? when you made sure that you would be able to seize Præneste on the first of November by a nocturnal attack, did you not find that that colony was fortified by my order, by my garrison, by my watchfulness and care? You do nothing, you plan nothing, you think of nothing which I not only do not hear, but which I do not see and know every particular of.

Listen while I speak of the night before. You shall now see that I watch far more actively for the safety than you do for the destruction of the Republic. I say that you came the night before (I will say nothing obscurely) into the Scythedealer's street, to the house of Marcus Lecca; that many of your accomplices in the same insanity and wickedness came there too. Do you dare to deny it? Why are you silent? I will prove it if you do deny it; for I see here in the Senate some men who were there with you.

O ye immortal gods, where on earth are we? in what city are we living? what constitution is ours? There are here,—here in our body, O conscript fathers, in this the most holy and dignified assembly of the whole world, men who meditate my death, and the death of all of us, and the destruction of this city, and of the whole world. I, the consul, see them; I ask them their opinion about the republic, and I do not yet attack, even by words, those who ought to be put to death by the sword. You were, then, O Catiline, at Lecca's that night; you divided Italy into sections; you settled where every one was to go; you fixed whom you were to leave at Rome, whom you were to take with you; you portioned out the divisions of the city for conflagration; you undertook that you yourself would at once leave the city, and said that there was then only this to delay you, that I was still alive. Two Roman knights were found to deliver you from this anxiety,

accord? The consul orders an enemy to depart from the city. Do you ask me, are you to go into banishment? I do not order it; but, if you consult me, I advise it.

For what is there, O Catiline, that can now afford you any pleasure in this city? for there is no one in it, except that band of profligate conspirators of yours, who does not fear you,—no one who does not hate you. What brand of domestic baseness is not stamped upon your life? What disgraceful circumstance is wanting to your infamy in your private affairs? From what licentiousness have your eyes, from what atrocity have your hands, from what iniquity has your whole body ever abstained? Is there one youth, when you have once entangled him in the temptations of your corruption, to whom you have not held out a sword for audacious crime, or a torch for licentious wickedness?

What? when lately by the death of your former wife you had made your house empty and ready for a new bridal, did you not even add another incredible wickedness to this wickedness? But I pass that over, and willingly allow it to be buried in silence, that so horrible a crime may not be seen to have existed in this city, and not to have been chastised. I pass over the ruin of your fortune, which you know is hanging over you against the ides of the very next month; I come to those things which relate not to the infamy of your private vices, not to your domestic difficulties and baseness, but to the welfare of the republic and to the lives and safety of us all.

Can the light of this life, O Catiline, can the breath of this atmosphere be pleasant to you, when you know that there is not one man of those here present who is ignorant that you, on the last day of the year, when Lepidus and Tullus were consuls, stood in the assembly armed; that you had prepared your hand for the slaughter of the consuls and chief men of the State, and that no reason or fear of yours hindered your crime and madness, but the fortune of the republic? And I say no more of these things, for they are not unknown to every one. How often have you endeavored to slay me, both as consul-elect and as actual consul? how many shots of yours, so aimed that they seemed impossible to be escaped, have I avoided by some slight stooping aside, and some dodging, as it were, of my body? You attempt nothing, you execute nothing, you devise nothing that can be kept hid from me at the proper time; and yet you do not cease to attempt and to contrive. How often already has that dagger of yours been wrested from your hands? how often has it slipped through them by some chance, and dropped down? and yet you cannot any longer do without it; and to what sacred mysteries it is consecrated and devoted by you I know not, that you think it necessary to plunge it in the body of the consul.

But now, what is that life of yours that you are leading? For I will speak to you not so as to seem influenced by the hatred I ought to feel, but by pity, nothing of which is due to you. You came a little while ago into the Senate: in so numerous an assembly, who of so many friends and connections of yours saluted you? If this in the memory of man never happened to any one else, are you waiting for insults by word of mouth, when you are overwhelmed by the most irresistible condemnation of silence? Is it nothing that at your arrival all those seats were vacated? that all the men of consular rank, who had often been marked out by you for slaughter, the very moment you sat down left that part of the benches bare and vacant? With what feelings do you think you ought to bear this? On my honor, if my slaves feared me as all your fellow-citizens fear you, I should think I must leave my house. Do not you think you should leave the city? If I saw that I was even undeservedly so suspected and hated by my fellow-citizens, I would rather flee from their sight than be gazed at by the hostile eyes of every one. And do you, who, from the consciousness of your wickedness, know that the hatred of all men is just and has been long due to you, hesitate to avoid the sight and presence of those men whose minds and senses you offend? If your parents feared and hated you, and if you could by no means pacify them, you would, I think, depart somewhere out of their sight. Now, your country, which is the common parent of all of us, hates and fears you, and has no other opinion of you, than that you are meditating parricide in her case; and will you neither feel awe of her authority, nor deference for her judgment, nor fear of her power?

And she, O Catiline, thus pleads with you, and after a manner silently speaks to you:—There has now for many years been no crime committed but by you; no atrocity has taken place without you; you alone unpunished and unquestioned have murdered the citizens, have harassed and plundered the allies; you alone have had power not only to neglect all laws and investigations, but to overthrow and break through them. Your former actions, though they ought not to have been borne, yet I did

consul though I be, in this very temple. But as to you. Catiline, while they are quiet they approve, while they permit me to speak they vote, while they are silent they are loud and eloquent. And not they alone, whose authority forsooth is dear to you, though their lives are unimportant, but the Roman knights too, those most honorable and excellent men, and the other virtuous citizens who are now surrounding the Senate, whose numbers you could see, whose desires you could know, and whose voices you a few minutes ago could hear,—aye, whose very hands and weapons I have for some time been scarcely able to keep off from you; but those, too, I will easily bring to attend you to the gates if you leave these places you have been long desiring to lay waste.

And yet, why am I speaking? that anything may change your purpose? that you may ever amend your life? that you may meditate flight or think of voluntary banishment? I wish the gods may give you such a mind; though I see, if alarmed at my words you bring your mind to go into banishment, what a storm of unpopularity hangs over me, if not at present, while the memory of your wickedness is fresh, at all events hereafter. But it is worth while to incur that, as long as that is but a private misfortune of my own, and is unconnected with the dangers of the republic. But we cannot expect that you should be concerned at your own vices, that you should fear the penalties of the laws, or that you should yield to the necessities of the republic, for you are not, O Catiline, one whom either shame can recall from infamy, or fear from danger, or reason from madness.

Wherefore, as I have said before, go forth, and if you wish to make me, your enemy as you call me unpopular, go straight into banishment. I shall scarcely be able to endure all that will be said if you do so; I shall scarcely be able to support my load of unpopularity if you do go into banishment at the command of the consul; but if you wish to serve my credit and reputation, go forth with your ill-omened band of profligates; betake yourself to Manlius, rouse up the abandoned citizens, separate yourself from the good ones, wage war against your country, exult in your impious banditti, so that you may not seem to have been driven out by me and gone to strangers, but to have gone invited to your own friends.

Though why should I invite you, by whom I know men have been already sent on to wait in arms for you at the forum Aurelium; who I know has fixed and agreed with Manlius upon

bear as well as I could; but now that I should be wholly occupied with fear of you alone, that at every sound I should dread Catiline, that no design should seem possible to be entertained against me which does not proceed from your wickedness, this is no longer endurable. Depart, then, and deliver me from this fear; that, if it be a just one, I may not be destroyed; if an imaginary one, that at least I may at last cease to fear.

If, as I have said, your country were thus to address you, ought she not to obtain her request, even if she were not able to enforce it? What shall I say of your having given yourself into custody? what of your having said, for the sake of avoiding suspicion, that you were willing to dwell in the house of Marcus Lepidus? And when you were not received by him, you dared even to come to me, and begged me to keep you in my house; and when you had received answer from me that I could not possibly be safe in the same house with you, when I considered myself in great danger as long as we were in the same city, you came to Quintus Metellus, the prætor, and, being rejected by him, you passed on to your associate, that most excellent man, Marcus Marcellus, who would be, I suppose you thought, most diligent in guarding you, most sagacious in suspecting you, and most bold in punishing you; but how far can we think that man ought to be from bonds and imprisonment who has already judged himself deserving of being given into custody?

Since, then, this is the case, do you hesitate, O Catiline, if you cannot remain here with tranquillity, to depart to some distant land, and to trust your life, saved from just and deserved punishment, to flight and solitude? Make a motion, say you, to the Senate (for that is what you demand), and if this body votes that you ought to go into banishment, you say that you will obey. I will not make such a motion, it is contrary to my principles, and yet I will let you see what these men think of you. Be gone from the city, O Catiline, deliver the republic from fear; depart into banishment, if that is the word you are waiting for. What now, O Catiline? Do you not perceive, do you not see the silence of these men; they permit it, they say nothing; why wait you for the authority of their words when you see their wishes in their silence?

But had I said the same to this excellent young man, Publius Sextius, or to that brave man, Marcus Marcellus, before this time the Senate would deservedly have laid violent hands on me,

a settled day; by whom I know that that silver eagle, which I trust will be ruinous and fatal to you and to all your friends, and to which there was set up in your house a shrine, as it were, of your crimes, has been already sent forward. Need I fear that you can long do without that which you used to worship when going out to murder, and from whose altars you have often transferred your impious hand to the slaughter of citizens?

You will go at last where your unbridled and mad desire has been long hurrying you. And this causes you no grief, but an incredible pleasure. Nature has formed you, desire has trained you, fortune has preserved you for this insanity. Not only did you never desire quiet, but you never even desired any war but a criminal one; you have collected a band of profligates and worthless men, abandoned not only by all fortune but even by hope.

Then what happiness will you enjoy, with what delight will you exult, in what pleasure will you revel, when in so numerous a body of friends you neither hear nor see one good man! All the toils you have gone through have always pointed to this sort of life; your lying on the ground not merely to lie in wait to gratify your unclean desires, but even to accomplish crimes; your vigilance, not only when plotting against the sleep of husbands, but also against the goods of your murdered victims, have all been preparations for this. Now you have an opportunity of displaying your splendid endurance of hunger, of cold, of want of everything; by which in a short time you will find yourself worn out. All this I effected when I procured your rejection from the consulship, that you should be reduced to make attempts on your country as an exile, instead of being able to distress it as consul, and that that which had been wickedly undertaken by you should be called piracy rather than war.

Now that I may remove and avert, O conscript fathers, any in the least reasonable complaint from myself, listen, I beseech you, carefully to what I say, and lay it up in your inmost hearts and minds. In truth, if my country, which is far dearer to me than my life,—if all Italy,—if the whole Republic were to address me, "Marcus Tullius, what are you doing? will you permit that man to depart whom you have ascertained to be an enemy? whom you see ready to become the general of the war? whom you know to be expected in the camp of the enemy as their chief, the author of all this wickedness, the head of the conspiracy, the instigator of the slaves and abandoned citizens, so that he shall seem not driven out of the city by you, but let loose by you against the city? Will you not order him to be thrown into prison, to be hurried off to execution, to be put to death with the most prompt severity? What hinders you? is it the customs of our ancestors? But even private men have often in this republic slain mischievous citizens. Is it the laws which have been passed about the punishment of Roman citizens? But in this city those who have rebelled against the republic have never had the rights of citizens. Do you fear odium with posterity? You are showing fine gratitude to the Roman people who have raised you, a man known only by your own actions, of no ancestral renown, through all the degrees of honor at so early an age to the very highest office, if from fear of unpopularity or of any danger you neglect the safety of your fellow-citizens. But if you have a fear of unpopularity, is that arising from the imputation of vigor and boldness, or that arising from that of inactivity and indecision most to be feared? When Italy is laid waste by war, when cities are attacked and houses in flames, do you not think that you will be then consumed by a perfect conflagration of hatred?"

To this holy address of the republic, and to the feelings of those men who entertain the same opinion, I will make this short answer:—If, O conscript fathers, I thought it best that Catiline should be punished with death, I would not have given the space of one hour to this gladiator to live in. If, forsooth, those excellent men and most illustrious cities not only did not pollute themselves, but even glorified themselves by the blood of Saturninus, and the Gracchi, and Flaccus, and many others of old time, surely I had no cause to fear lest by slaying this parricidal murderer of the citizens any unpopularity should accrue to me with posterity. And if it did threaten me to ever so great a degree, yet I have always been of the disposition to think unpopularity earned by virtue and glory, not unpopularity.

Though there are some men in this body who either do not see what threatens, or dissemble what they do see; who have fed the hope of Catiline by mild sentiments, and have strengthened the rising conspiracy by not believing it; influenced by whose authority many, and they not wicked, but only ignorant, if I punished him would say that I had acted cruelly and tyrannically. But I know that if he arrive at the camp of Manlius to which

III—74

he is going, there will be no one so stupid as not to see that there has been a conspiracy, no one so hardened as not to confess it. But if this man alone were put to death, I know that this disease of the republic would be only checked for a while, not eradicated forever. But if he banish himself, and take with him all his friends, and collect at one point all the ruined men from every quarter, then not only will this full-grown plague of the republic be extinguished and eradicated, but also the root and seed of all future evils.

We have now for a long time, O conscript fathers, lived among these dangers and machinations of conspiracy; but somehow or other, the ripeness of all wickedness, and of this long-standing madness and audacity, has come to a head at the time of my consulship. But if this man alone is removed from this piratical crew, we may appear, perhaps, for a short time relieved from fear and anxiety, but the danger will settle down and lie hidden in the veins and bowels of the republic. As it often happens that men afflicted with a severe disease, when they are tortured with heat and fever seem at first to be relieved if they drink cold water, but afterwards suffer more and more severely, so this disease which is in the republic, if relieved by the punishment of this man, will only get worse and worse, as the rest will be still alive.

Wherefore, O conscript fathers, let the worthless begone,—let them separate themselves from the good,—let them collect in one place,—let them, as I have often said before, be separated from us by a wall; let them cease to plot against the consul in his own house,—to surround the tribunal of the city prætor,—to besiege the Senate House with swords,—to prepare brands and torches to burn the city; let it, in short, be written on the brow of every citizen, what are his sentiments about the republic. I promise you this, O conscript fathers, that there shall be so much diligence in us the consuls, so much authority in you, so much virtue in the Roman knights, so much unanimity in all good men, that you shall see everything made plain and manifest by the departure of Catiline,—everything checked and punished.

With these omens, O Catiline, begone to your impious and nefarious war, to the great safety of the republic, to your own misfortune and injury, and to the destruction of those who have joined themselves to you in every wickedness and atrocity. Then do you, O Jupiter, who were consecrated by Romulus with the

same auspices as this city, whom we rightly call the stay of this city and empire, repel this man and his companions from your altars and from the other temples,—from the houses and walls of the city,—from the lives and fortunes of all the citizens; and overwhelm all the enemies of good men, the foes of the republic, the robbers of Italy, men bound together by a treaty and infamous alliance of crimes, dead and alive, with eternal punishments.

CATILINE'S DEPARTURE

(From the Second Oration Against Catiline)

AT LENGTH, O Romans, we have dismissed from the city, or driven out, or, when he was departing of his own accord, we have pursued with words, Lucius Catiline, mad with audacity, breathing wickedness, impiously planning mischief to his country, threatening fire and sword to you and to this city. He is gone, he has departed, he has disappeared, he has rushed out. No injury will now be prepared against these walls within the walls themselves by that monster and prodigy of wickedness. And we have, without controversy, defeated him, the sole general of this domestic war. For now that dagger will no longer hover about our sides; we shall not be afraid in the campus, in the forum, in the Senate House,—aye, and within our own private walls. He was moved from his place when he was driven from the city. Now we shall openly carry on a regular war with an enemy without hindrance. Beyond all question we ruin the man; we have defeated him splendidly when we have driven him from secret treachery into open warfare. But that he has not taken with him his sword red with blood as he intended,—that he has left us alive,—that we wrested the weapon from his hands,—that he has left the citizens safe and the city standing, what great and overwhelming grief must you think that this is to him! Now he lies prostrate, O Romans, and feels himself stricken down and abject, and often casts back his eyes towards this city, which he mourns over as snatched from his jaws, but which seems to me to rejoice at having vomited forth such a pest, and cast it out of doors.

But if there be any one of that disposition which all men should have, who yet blames me greatly for the very thing in which my speech exults and triumphs,—namely, that I did not

arrest so capital, so mortal an enemy rather than let him go,—that is not my fault, O citizens, but the fault of the times. Lucius Catiline ought to have been visited with the severest punishment, and to have been put to death long since; and both the customs of our ancestors, and the rigor of my office, and the republic, demanded this of me; but how many, think you, were there who did not believe what I reported? how many who out of stupidity did not think so? how many who even defended him,—how many who, out of their own depravity, favored him? If, in truth, I had thought that, if he were removed, all danger would be removed from you, I would long since have cut off Lucius Catiline, had it been at the risk, not only of my popularity, but even of my life.

But as I saw that, since the matter was not even then proved to all of you, if I had punished him with death, as he had deserved, I should be borne down by unpopularity, and so be unable to follow up his accomplices, I brought the business on to this point, that you might be able to combat openly when you saw the enemy without disguise. But how exceedingly I think this enemy to be feared now that he is out of doors, you may see from this,—that I am vexed even that he has gone from the city with but a small retinue. I wish he had taken with him all his forces. He has taken with him Tongillus, with whom he had been said to have a criminal intimacy, and Publicius, and Munatius, whose debts contracted in taverns could cause no great disquietude to the republic. He has left behind him others—you all know what men they are, how overwhelmed with debt, how powerful, how noble.

Therefore, with our Gallic legions, and with the levies which Quintus Metellus has raised in the Picenian and Gallic territory, and with these troops which are every day being got ready by us, I thoroughly despise that army composed of desperate old men, of clownish profligates, and uneducated spendthrifts; of those who have preferred to desert their bail rather than that army; and which will fall to pieces if I show them not the battle array of our army, but an edict of the prætor. I wish he had taken with him those soldiers of his whom I see hovering about the forum, standing about the Senate House, even coming into the Senate, who shine with ointment, who glitter in purple; and if they remain here, remember that that army is not so much to be feared by us as these men who have deserted the army. And they are the more to be feared, because they are aware that I know what they are thinking of, and yet they are not influenced by it.

I know to whom Apulia has been allotted, who has Etruria, who the Picenian territory, who the Gallic district, who has begged for himself the office of spreading fire and sword by night through the city. They know that all the plans of the preceding night are brought to me. I laid them before the Senate yesterday. Catiline himself was alarmed, and fled. Why do these men wait? Verily, they are greatly mistaken if they think that former lenity of mine will last forever.

What I have been waiting for, that I have gained,—namely, that you should all see that a conspiracy has been openly formed against the republic; unless, indeed, there be any one who thinks that those who are like Catiline do not agree with Catiline. There is not any longer room for lenity; the business itself demands severity. One thing, even now, I will grant,—let them depart, let them begone. Let them not suffer the unhappy Catiline to pine away for want of them. I will tell them the road. He went by the Aurelian road. · If they make haste, they will catch him by the evening. O happy republic, if it can cast forth these dregs of the republic! Even now, when Catiline alone is got rid of, the republic seems to me relieved and refreshed; for what evil or wickedness can be devised or imagined which he did not conceive? What prisoner, what gladiator, what thief, what assassin, what parricide, what forger of wills, what cheat, what debauchee, what spendthrift, what adulterer, what abandoned woman, what corrupter of youth, what profligate, what scoundrel can be found in all Italy, who does not avow that he has been on terms of intimacy with Catiline? What murder has been committed for years without him? What nefarious act of infamy that has not been done by him? . . .

Array now, O Romans, against these splendid troops of Catiline your guards and your armies; and first of all oppose to that worn-out and wounded gladiator ·your consuls and generals; then against that banished and enfeebled troop of ruined men lead out the flower and strength of all Italy: instantly the cities of the colonies and municipalities will match the rustic mounds of Catiline; and I will not condescend to compare the rest of your troops and equipments and guards with the want and destitution of that highwayman But if, omitting all these things in which

we are rich and of which he is destitute,—the Senate, the Roman knights, the people, the city, the treasury, the revenues, all Italy, all the provinces, foreign nations,—if, I say, omitting all these things, we choose to compare the causes themselves which are opposed to one another, we may understand from that alone how thoroughly prostrate they are. For on the one side are fighting modesty, on the other wantonness; on the one chastity, on the other uncleanness; on the one honesty, on the other fraud; on the one piety, on the other wickedness; on the one consistency, on the other insanity; on the one honor, on the other baseness; on the one continence, on the other lust; in short equity, temperance, fortitude, prudence, all the virtues contend against iniquity with luxury, against indolence, against rashness, against all the vices; lastly, abundance contends against destitution, good plans against baffled designs, wisdom against madness, well-founded hope against universal despair. In a contest and war of this sort, even if the zeal of men were to fail, will not the immortal gods compel such numerous and excessive vices to be defeated by these most eminent virtues?

THE CRUCIFIXION OF GAVIUS

(From the Oration Against Verres)

WHY should I speak of Publius Gavius, a citizen of the municipality of Cosa, O judges? or with what vigor of language, with what gravity of expression, with what grief of mind shall I mention him? But, indeed, that indignation fails me. I must take more care than usual that what I am going to say be worthy of my subject—worthy of the indignation which I feel. For the charge is of such a nature, that when I was first informed of it I thought I should not avail myself of it. For although I knew that it was entirely true, still I thought that it would not appear credible. Being compelled by the tears of all the Roman citizens who are living as traders in Sicily, being influenced by the testimonies of the men of Valentia, most honorable men, and by those of all the Rhegians, and of many Roman knights who happened at that time to be at Messana, I produced at the previous pleading only just that amount of evidence which might prevent the matter from appearing doubtful to any one. What shall I do now? When I have been speaking

for so many hours of one class of offenses, and of that man's nefarious cruelty,—when I have now expended nearly all my treasures of words of such a sort as are worthy of that man's wickedness on other matters, and have omitted to take precautions to keep your attention on the stretch by diversifying my accusations, how am I to deal with an affair of the importance that this is? There is, I think, but one method, but one line open to me. I will place the matter plainly before you, which is of itself of such importance that there is no need of my eloquence—and eloquence, indeed, I have none, but there is no need of any one's eloquence to excite your feelings. This Gavius whom I am speaking of, a citizen of Cosa, when he (among that vast number of Roman citizens who had been treated in the same way) had been thrown by Verres into prison, and somehow or other had escaped secretly out of the stone quarries, and had come to Messana, being now almost within sight of Italy and of the walls of Rhegium, and being revived, after that fear of death and that darkness, by the light, as it were, of liberty and of the fragrance of the laws, began to talk at Messana, and to complain that he, a Roman citizen, had been thrown into prison. He said that he was now going straight to Rome, and that he would meet Verres on his arrival there.

The miserable man was not aware that it made no difference whether he said this at Messana, or before the man's face in his own prætorian palace. For, as I have shown you before, that man had selected this city as the assistant in his crimes, the receiver of his thefts, the partner in all his wickedness. Accordingly, Gavius is at once brought before the Mamertine magistrates; and, as it happened, Verres came on that very day to Messana. The matter is brought before him. He is told that the man was a Roman citizen, who was complaining that at Syracuse he had been confined in the stone quarries, and who, when he was actually embarking on board ship, and uttering violent threats against Verres, had been brought back by them, and reserved in order that he himself might decide what should be done with him. He thanks the men and praises their good-will and diligence in his behalf. He himself, inflamed with wickedness and frenzy, comes into the forum. His eyes glared; cruelty was visible in his whole countenance. All men waited to see what steps he was going to take,—what he was going to do; when all of a sudden he orders the man to be seized, and to be

stripped and bound in the middle of the forum, and the rods to be got ready. The miserable man cried out that he was a Roman citizen, a citizen, also, of the municipal town of Cosa,—that he had served with Lucius Pretius, a most illustrious Roman knight, who was living as a trader at Panormus, and from whom Verres might know that he was speaking the truth. Then Verres says that he has ascertained that he had been sent into Sicily by the leaders of the runaway slaves, in order to act as a spy; a matter as to which there was no witness, no trace, nor even the slightest suspicion in the mind of any one. Then he orders the man to be most violently scourged on all sides. In the middle of the forum of Messana a Roman citizen, O judges, was beaten with rods; while in the meantime no groan was heard, no other expression was heard from that wretched man, amid all his pain, and between the sound of the blows, except these words, "I am a citizen of Rome." He fancied that by this one statement of his citizenship he could ward off all blows, and remove all torture from his person. He not only did not succeed in averting by his entreaties the violence of the rods, but as he kept on repeating his entreaties and the assertion of his citizenship, a cross—a cross, I say—was got ready for that miserable man, who had never witnessed such a stretch of power.

O the sweet name of liberty! O the admirable privileges of our citizenship! O Porcian law! O Sempronian laws! O power of the tribunes, bitterly regretted by, and at last restored to the Roman people! Have all our rights fallen so far, that in a province of the Roman people,—in a town of our confederate allies, —a Roman citizen should be bound in the forum, and beaten with rods by a man who only had the fasces and the axes through the kindness of the Roman people? What shall I say? When fire, and red-hot plates, and other instruments of torture were employed? If the bitter entreaties and the miserable cries of that man had no power to restrain you, were you not moved even by the weeping and loud groans of the Roman citizens who were present at that time? Did you dare to drag any one to the cross who said that he was a Roman citizen?

If you, O Verres, being taken among the Persians or in the remotest parts of India, were being led to execution, what else would you cry out but that you were a Roman citizen? And if that name of your city, honored and renowned as it is among all men, would have availed you, a stranger among strangers, among barbarians, among men placed in the most remote and distant corners of the earth, ought not he, whoever he was, whom you were hurrying to the cross, who was a stranger to you, to have been able, when he said that he was a Roman citizen, to obtain from you, the prætor, if not an escape, at least a respite from death by his mention of and claims to citizenship?

Men of no importance, born in an obscure rank, go to sea; they go to places which they have never seen before; where they can neither be known to the men among whom they have arrived, nor always find people to vouch for them. But still, owing to this confidence in the mere fact of their citizenship, they think that they shall be safe, not only among our own magistrates, who are restrained by fear of the laws and of public opinion, nor among our fellow-citizens only, who are united with them by community of language, of rights, and of many other things; but wherever they come they think that this will be a protection to them. Take away this hope, take away this protection from Roman citizens; establish the fact that there is no assistance to be found in the words, "I am a Roman citizen"; that a prætor, or any other officer, may with impunity order any punishment he pleases to be inflicted on a man who says that he is a Roman citizen, though no one knows that it is not true; and at one blow, by admitting that defense, you cut off from the Roman citizens all the provinces, and the kingdoms, all free cities, and indeed the whole world, which has hitherto been open most especially to our countrymen.

But why need I say more about Gavius? as if you were hostile to Gavius, and not rather an enemy to the name and class of citizens, and to all their rights. You were not, I say, an enemy to the individual, but to the common cause of liberty. For what was our object in ordering the Mamertimes, when, according to their regular custom and usage, they had erected the cross behind the city in the Pompeian road, to place it where it looked towards the strait; and in adding, what you can by no means deny, what you said openly in the hearing of every one, that you chose that place in order that the man who said that he was a Roman citizen might be able from his cross to behold Italy and to look towards his own home? And accordingly, O judges, that cross, for the first time since the foundation of Messana, was erected in that place. A spot commanding a view of Italy was picked out by that man for the express purpose that

the wretched man who was dying in agony and torture might see that the rights of liberty and of slavery were only separated by a very narrow strait, and that Italy might behold her son murdered by the most miserable and most painful punishment appropriate to slaves alone.

It is a crime to bind a Roman citizen; to scourge him is a wickedness; to put him to death is almost parricide. What shall I say of crucifying him? So guilty an action cannot by any possibility be adequately expressed by any name bad enough for it. Yet with all this that man was not content. "Let him behold his country," said he; "let him die within sight of laws and liberty." It was not Gavius, it was not one individual, I know not whom,—it was not one Roman citizen,—it was the common cause of freedom and citizenship that you exposed to that torture and nailed on that cross. But now consider the audacity of the man. Do not you think that he was indignant that he could not erect that cross for Roman citizens in the forum, in the comitium, in the very rostra? For the place in his province which was the most like those places in celebrity, and the nearest to them in point of distance, he did select. He chose that monument of his wickedness and audacity to be in the sight of Italy, in the very vestibule of Sicily, within sight of all passers-by as they sailed to and fro.

SUPERNATURAL JUSTICE

(From the Oration for Milo)

THIS investigation relates to the death of Publius Clodius. Imagine in your minds,—for our thoughts are free, and contemplate whatever they choose in such a manner that we do discern those things which we think we see;—place, therefore, before your mind's eye the image of this my condition if I were able to induce you to acquit Milo, but still only on condition of Publius Clodius being restored to life. What fear is it you show by your countenances? How would he affect you if alive, when even now that he is dead he has so agitated you by the bare thought of him? What? if Cneius Pompeius himself, who is a man of such virtue and such good fortune that he has at all times been able to do things which no one except him ever could have done,—if even he, I say, had been able, in

the same manner as he has ordered an investigation into the death of Publius Clodius to take place, so also to raise him from the dead, which do you think he would have preferred to do? Even if out of friendship he had been willing to raise him from the shades below, out of regard for the republic he would not have done it. You, then, are sitting now as avengers of the death of that man, whom you would not restore to life if you thought it possible that his life could be restored by you. And this investigation is appointed to be made into the death of a man who would never have seen such a law passed, if the law which ordered the inquiry had been able to restore him to life. Ought, then, the slayer of this man, if any such slayer there be, to have any reason, while confessing the deed, to fear punishment at the hand of those men whom he delivered by the deed?

Grecian nations give the honors of the gods to those men who have slain tyrants. What have I not seen at Athens? what in the other cities of Greece? What divine honors have I not seen paid to such men? What odes, what songs have I not heard in their praise? They are almost consecrated to immortality in the memories and worship of men. And will you not only abstain from conferring any honors on the savior of so great a people, and the avenger of such enormous wickedness, but will you even allow him to be borne off for punishment? He would confess,—I say, if he had done it, he would confess with a high and willing spirit that he had done it for the sake of the general liberty; a thing which would certainly deserve not only to be confessed by him, but even to be boasted of.

In truth, if he does not deny an action from which he seeks no advantage beyond being pardoned for having done it, would he hesitate to avow an action for which he would be entitled to claim rewards? Unless, indeed, he thinks it more pleasing to you to look upon him as having been the defender of his own life, rather than of you; especially as from that confession, if you were to choose to be grateful, he would reap the very highest honors. If his action were not approved of by you (although, how is it possible that any one should not approve of what secured his own safety?)—but still, if the virtue of a most gallant man had happened to be at all unpleasing to his fellow-citizens, then with a lofty and firm mind he would depart from an ungrateful city. For what could be more ungrateful than for all other men to be rejoicing, and for him alone to be mourning,

to whom it was owing that the rest were rejoicing? Although we have all at all times been of this disposition with respect to crushing traitors to our country,—that since the glory would be ours, we should consider the danger and the unpopularity ours also. For what praise should I have deserved to have given to me, when I showed so much courage in my consulship on behalf of you and of your children, if I had supposed that I could venture on the exploits which I was attempting without very great struggles and dangers to myself? What woman is there who would not dare to slay a wicked and mischievous citizen, if she was not afraid of the danger of the attempt? But the man who, though unpopularity, and death, and punishment are before his eyes, still ventures to defend the republic with no less alacrity than if no such evils threatened him, he deserves to be considered really a man.

It behooves a grateful people to reward those citizens who have deserved well of the republic; it is the part of a brave man, not to be so moved even by execution itself, as to repent of having acted bravely. Wherefore, Titus Annius may well make the same confession which Ahala made, which Nasica, which Opimius, which Marius, which we ourselves have made: and then, if the republic were grateful, he would rejoice; if ungrateful, then, though under the pressure of heavy misfortune, he would still be supported by his own conscience.

But, O judges, the fortune of the Roman people, and your felicity, and the immortal gods, all think that they are entitled to your gratitude for this service which has been thus done to you. Nor, indeed, can any one think otherwise except it be a man who thinks that there is no such thing at all as any divine power or authority—a man who is neither moved by the vastness of your empire, nor by that sun above us, nor by the motions of heaven and of the stars, nor by the vicissitudes and regular order of things, nor (and that is the greatest thing of all) by the wisdom of our ancestors; who both themselves cultivated with the most holy reverence the sacred rites and religious ceremonies and auspices, and also handed them down to us their posterity to be so cultivated by us.

There is—there is indeed, such a heavenly power! It is not the truth, that in these bodies and in this feebleness of ours there is something which is vigorous and endued with feeling, and nothing which is so in this vast and beautiful movement of nature. Unless, perhaps, some people think that there is no such thing in existence because it is not apparent, nor visible; just as if we were able to see our own mind,—that by which we are wise, by which we have foresight, by which we do and say these very things which we are doing and saying; or as if we could plainly feel what sort of thing it is, or where it is. That divine power, that very same divine power which has often brought incredible prosperity and power to this city, has extinguished and destroyed this mischief; by first of all inspiring it with the idea of venturing to irritate by violence and to attack with the sword the bravest of men, and so leading it on to be defeated by the man whom, if it had only been able to defeat, it would have enjoyed endless license and impunity. That result was brought about, O judges, not by human wisdom, nor even by any moderate degree of care on the part of the immortal gods. In truth, those very holy places themselves which beheld that monster fall appear to have been moved themselves and to have asserted their rights over him.

I implore you, I call you to witness,—you, I say, O ye Alban hills and groves, and you, O ye altars of the Albans, now overthrown, but nevertheless partners of and equals in honor with the sacred rites of the Roman people,—ye, whom that man with headlong insanity, having cut down and destroyed the most holy groves, had overwhelmed with his insane masses of buildings; it was your power then that prevailed, it was the divinity of your altars, the religious reverence due to you, and which he had profaned by every sort of wickedness that prevailed; and you, too, O sacred Jupiter of Latium, whose lakes and groves and boundaries he had constantly polluted with every sort of abominable wickedness and debauchery, you at last, from your high and holy mountain, opened your eyes for the purpose of punishing him; it is to you, to all of you, that those punishments, late indeed, but still just and well deserved, have been made an atonement for his wickedness.

CATO AND THE STOICS

(From the Oration Defending Lucius Murena Against a Charge of Bribery)

I COME now to Marcus Cato, who is the mainstay and prop of the whole prosecution; who is, however, so zealous and vehement a prosecutor, that I am much more afraid of the weight of his name than of his accusation. And with respect to this accuser, O judges, first of all I will entreat you not to let Cato's dignity, nor your expectation of his tribuneship, nor the high reputation and virtue of his whole life, be any injury to Lucius Murena. Let not all the honors of Marcus Cato, which he has acquired in order to be able to assist many men, be an injury to my client alone. Publius Africanus had been twice consul, and had destroyed those two terrors of this empire, Carthage and Numantia, when he prosecuted Lucius Cotta. He was a man of the most splendid eloquence, of the greatest good faith, of the purest integrity; his authority was as great almost as that of the Roman people itself, in that empire which had been mainly saved by his means. I have often heard old men say that this very extraordinarily high character of the accuser was of the greatest service to Lucius Cotta. Those wise men who then were the judges in that cause did not like any one to be defeated in any trial, if he was to appear overwhelmed only by the excessive influence of his adversary. What more shall I say? Did not the Roman people deliver Sergius Galba (the fact is preserved in the recollection of every one) from your grandfather, that most intrepid and prosperous man, Marcus Cato, who was zealously seeking his ruin? At all times in this city the whole people, and also the judges, wise men, looking far into futurity, have resisted the overweening power of prosecutors. I do not like an accuser bringing his personal power, or any predominant influence, or his own eminent authority, or his own excessive popularity, into a court of justice. Let all these things have weight to insure the safety of the innocent, to aid the weak, to succor the unfortunate. But in a case where the danger and ruin of citizens may ensue, let them be rejected. For if, perchance, any one should say that Cato would not have come forward as an accuser if he had not previously made up his mind about the justice of the cause, he will then be laying down a most unjust law, O judges, and establishing a miserable condition for men in their danger, if he thinks that the opinion of an

accuser is to have against a defendant the weight of a previous investigation legally conducted.

I, O Cato, do not venture to find fault with your intentions, by reason of my extraordinarily high opinion of your virtue; but in some particulars I may perhaps be able slightly to amend and reform them. "You are not very wrong," said an aged tutor to a very brave man; "but if you are wrong, I can set you right." But I can say with the greatest truth that you never do wrong, and that your conduct is never such in any point as to need correction, but only such as occasionally to require being guided a little. For nature has herself formed you for honesty and gravity and moderation and magnanimity and justice and for all the virtues required to make a great and noble man. To all these qualities are added an education not moderate, nor mild, but, as it seems to me, a little harsh and severe, more so than either truth or nature would permit. And since we are not to address this speech either to an ignorant multitude, or to any assembly of rustics, I will speak a little boldly about the pursuits of educated men, which are both well known and agreeable to you, O judges, and to me. Learn then, O judges, that all these good qualities, divine and splendid as they are, which we behold in Marcus Cato, are his own peculiar attributes. The qualities which we sometimes wish for in him are not all those which are implanted in a man by nature, but some of them are such as are derived from education. For there was once a man of the greatest genius, whose name was Zeno, the imitators of whose example are called Stoics. His opinions and precepts are of this sort: that a wise man is never influenced by interest; never pardons any man's fault; that no one is merciful except a fool and a trifler; that it is not the part of a man to be moved or pacified by entreaties; that wise men, let them be ever so deformed, are the only beautiful men; if they be ever such beggars, they are the only rich men; if they be in slavery, they are kings. And as for all of us who are not wise men, they call us runaway slaves, exiles, enemies, lunatics. They say that all offenses are equal; that every sin is an unpardonable crime; and that he does not commit a less crime who kills a cock, if there was no need to do so, than the man who strangles his father. They say that a wise man never feels uncertain on any point, never repents of anything, is never deceived in anything, and never alters his opinion.

All these opinions that most acute man, Marcus Cato, having been induced by learned advocates of them, has embraced; and that, not for the sake of arguing about them, as is the case with most men, but of living by them. Do the Publicans ask for any thing? "Take care that their influence has no weight." Do any suppliants, miserable and unhappy men, come to us? "You will be a wicked and infamous man if you do anything from being influenced by mercy." Does any one confess that he has done wrong, and beg pardon for his wrong-doing? "To pardon is a crime of the deepest dye." "But it is a trifling offense." "All offenses are equal." You say something. "That is a fixed and unalterable principle." "You are influenced not by the facts, but by your opinion." "A wise man never forms mere opinions." "You have made a mistake in some point." He thinks that you are abusing him. And in accordance with these principles of his are the following assertions: "I said in the Senate, that I would prosecute one of the candidates for the consulship." "You said that when you were angry." "A wise man never is angry." "But you said it for some temporary purpose." "It is the act," says he, "of a worthless man to deceive by a lie; it is a disgraceful act to alter one's opinion; to be moved by entreaties is wickedness; to pity any one is an enormity." But our philosophers (for I confess, O Cato, that I too, in my youth, distrusting my own abilities, sought assistance from learning), our philosophers, I say, men of the school of Plato and Aristotle, men of soberness and moderation, say that private interest does sometimes have weight even with a wise man. They say that it does become a virtuous man to feel pity; that there are different gradations of offenses, and different degrees of punishment appropriate to each; that a man with every proper regard for firmness may pardon offenses; that even the wise man himself has sometimes nothing more than opinion to go upon, without absolute certainty; that he is sometimes angry; that he is sometimes influenced and pacified by entreaty; that he sometimes does change an opinion which he may have expressed, when it is better to do so; that he sometimes abandons his previous opinions altogether; and that all his virtues are tempered by a certain moderation.

If any chance, O Cato, had conducted you, endowed with your existing natural disposition, to those tutors, you would not indeed have been a better man than you are, nor a braver one, nor more temperate, nor more just than you are (for that is not possible), but you would have been a little more inclined to lenity; you would not, when you were not induced by any enmity, or provoked by any personal injury, accuse a most virtuous man, a man of the highest rank and the greatest integrity; you would consider that as fortune had intrusted the guardianship of the same year to you and to Murena, that you were connected with him by some certain political union; and the severe things which you have said in the Senate you would either not have said, or you would have guarded against their being applied to him, or you would have interpreted them in the mildest sense. And even you yourself (at least that is my opinion and expectation), excited as you are at present by the impetuosity of your disposition, and elated as you are both by the vigor of your natural character and by your confidence in your own ability, and inflamed as you are by your recent study of all these precepts, will find practice modify them, and time and increasing years soften and humanize you. In truth, those tutors and teachers of virtue, whom you think so much of, appear to me themselves to have carried their definitions of duties somewhat further than is agreeable to nature; and it would be better if, when we had in theory pushed our principles to extremities, yet in practice we stopped at what was expedient. "Forgive nothing." Say rather, forgive some things, but not everything. "Do nothing for the sake of private influence." Certainly resist private influence when virtue and good faith require you to do so. "Do not be moved by pity." Certainly if it is to extinguish all impartiality; nevertheless, there is some credit due to humanity. "Abide by your own opinion." Very true, unless some other sounder opinion convinces you. That great Scipio was a man of this sort, who had no objection to do the same thing that you do; to keep a most learned man, a man of almost divine wisdom, in his house; by whose conversation and precepts, although they were the very same that you are so fond of, he was nevertheless not made more severe, but (as I have heard said by old men) he was rendered most merciful. And who was more mild in his manners than Caius Lælius? who was more agreeable than he? (devoted to the same studies as you); who was more virtuous or more wise than he? I might say the same of Lucius Philus and of Caius Gallus; but I will conduct you now into your own house. Do you think that there was any man more courteous,

III—75

ate whose interests were consulted, or against whose interests it was passed. Prove, then, that these actions have been done by Lucius Murena, and then I will grant to you that they have been done in violation of the law. . . .

But I must change my tone, for Cato argues with me on rigid and stoic principles. He says that it is not true that goodwill is conciliated by food. He says that men's judgments, in the important business of electing to magistracies, ought not to be corrupted by pleasures. Therefore, if any one, to promote his canvass, invites another to supper, he must be condemned. "Shall you," says he, "seek to obtain supreme power, supreme authority, and the helm of the republic, by encouraging men's sensual appetites, by soothing their minds, by tendering luxuries to them? Are you asking employment as a pimp from a band of luxurious youths, or the sovereignty of the world from the Roman people?" An extraordinary sort of speech! but our usages, our way of living, our manners, and the constitution itself, rejects it. For the Lacedæmonians, the original authors of that way of living and of that sort of language, men who lie at their daily meals on hard oak benches, and the Cretans, of whom no one ever lies down to eat at all, have neither of them preserved their political constitutions or their power better than the Romans, who set apart times for pleasure as well as times for labor; for one of those nations was destroyed by a single invasion of our army; the other only preserves its discipline and its laws by means of the protection afforded to it by our supremacy.

Do not, then, O Cato, blame with too great severity of language the principles of our ancestors, which facts, and the length of time that our power has flourished under them, justify. There was, in the time of our ancestors, a learned man of the same sect, an honorable citizen, and one of high rank, Quintus Tubero. He, when Quintus Maximus was giving a feast to the Roman people, in the name of his uncle Africanus, was asked by Maximus to prepare a couch for the banquet, as Tubero was a son of the sister of the same Africanus. And he, a most learned man and a Stoic, covered for that occasion some couches, made in the Carthaginian fashion, with skins of kids, and exhibited some Samian vessels, as if Diogenes the Cynic had been dead, and not as if he were paying respect to the obsequies of that godlike Africanus,—a man with respect to whom Maximus, when he was pronouncing his funeral panegyric on the day of his death,

more agreeable; any one whose conduct was more completely regulated by every principle of virtue and politeness, than Cato, your great-grandfather? And when you were speaking with truth and dignity of his virtue, you said that you had a domestic example to imitate. That, indeed, is an example set up for your imitation in your own family, and the similarity of nature ought rather to influence you who are descended from him than any one of us; but still that example is as much an object for my imitation as for yours. But if you were to add his courtesy and affability to your own wisdom and impartiality, I will not say that those qualities which are now most excellent will be made intrinsically better, but they will certainly be more agreeably seasoned.

Wherefore, to return to the subject which I began to speak of, take away the name of Cato out of the cause; remove and leave out of the question all mention of authority, which in courts of justice ought either to have no influence at all, or only influence to contribute to some one's safety; and discuss with me the charges themselves. What do you accuse him of, Cato? What action of his is it that you bring before the court? What is your charge? Do you accuse him of bribery? I do not defend bribery. You blame me because you say I am defending the very conduct which I brought in a law to punish. I punished bribery, not innocence. And any real case of bribery I will join you in prosecuting if you please. You have said that a resolution of the Senate was passed, on my motion, "that if any men who had been bribed had gone to meet the candidates, if any hired men followed them, if places were given men to see the shows of gladiators according to their tribes, and also, if dinners were given to the common people, that appeared to be a violation of the Calpurnian law." Therefore the Senate decides that these things were done in violation of the Calpurnian law, if they were done at all; it decides what there is not the least occasion for, out of complaisance for the candidates. For there is a great question whether such things have been done or not. That, if they have been done, they were done in violation of the law, no one can doubt. It is, therefore, ridiculous to leave that uncertain which was doubtful, but to give a positive decision on that point which can be doubtful to no one. And that decree is passed at the request of all the candidates, in order that it might be quite impossible to make out from the resolution of the Sen-

expressed his gratitude to the immortal gods for having caused that man to be born in this republic above all others, for that it was quite inevitable that the sovereignty of the world must belong to that state of which he was a citizen. At the celebration of the obsequies of such a man the Roman people were very indignant at the perverse wisdom of Tubero, and therefore he, a most upright man, a most virtuous citizen, though he was the grandson of Lucius Paullus, the sister's son, as I have said before, of Publius Africanus, lost the prætorship by his kid-skins.

The Roman people disapproves of private luxury, but admires public magnificence. It does not love profuse banquets, still less does it love sordid and uncivilized behavior. It makes a proper distinction between different duties and different seasons, and allows of vicissitudes of labor and pleasure. For as to what you say, that it is not right for men's minds to be influenced in appointing magistrates by any other consideration than that of the worth of the candidates, this principle even you yourself—you, a man of the greatest worth—do not in every case adhere to. For why do you ask any one to take pains for you, to assist you? You ask me to make you governor over myself, to intrust myself to you. What is the meaning of this? Ought I to be asked this by you, or should not you rather be asked by me to undertake labor and danger for the sake of my safety? Nay more, why is it that you have a nomenclator with you? for in so doing you are practicing a trick and a deceit. For if it be an honorable thing for your fellow-citizens to be addressed by name by you, it is a shameful thing for them to be better known to your servant than to yourself. If, though you know them yourself, it seems better to use a prompter, why do you sometimes address them before he has whispered their names in your ear? Why, again, when he has reminded you of them, do you salute them as if you knew them yourself? And why, after you are once elected, are you more careless about saluting them at all? If you regulate all these things by the usages of the city, it is all right; but if you choose to weigh them by the precepts of your sect, they will be found to be entirely wrong. Those enjoyments, then, of games and gladiators and banquets, all of which our ancestors desired, are not to be taken away from the Roman people, nor ought candidates to be forbidden the exercise of that kindness, which is liberality rather than bribery.

Oh, but it is the interest of the republic that has induced you to become a prosecutor. I do believe, O Cato, that you have come forward under the influence of those feelings and of that opinion. But you err out of ignorance. That which I am doing, O judges, I am doing out of regard to my friendship for Lucius Murena and to his own worth, and I also do assert and call you all to witness that I am doing it for the sake of peace, of tranquillity, of concord, of liberty, of safety—aye, even for the sake of the lives of us all.

FOR THE POET ARCHIAS

(Prosecuted on a Charge of Falsely Claiming to be a Roman Citizen)

IF THERE be any natural ability in me, O judges—and I know how slight that is; or if I have any practice as a speaker— and in that line I do not deny that I have some experience; or if I have any method in my oratory, drawn from my study of the liberal sciences, and from that careful training to which I admit that at no part of my life have I ever been disinclined; certainly, of all those qualities, this Aulus Licinius is entitled to be among the first to claim the benefit from me as his peculiar right. For as far as ever my mind can look back upon the space of time that is past, and recall the memory of its earliest youth, tracing my life from that starting-point, I see that Archias was the principal cause of my undertaking, and the principal means of my mastering, those studies. And if this voice of mine, formed by his encouragement and his precepts, has at times been the instrument of safety to others, undoubtedly we ought, as far as lies in our power, to help and save the very man from whom we have received that gift which has enabled us to bring help to many and salvation to some. And lest any one should, perchance, marvel at this being said by me, as the chief of his ability consists in something else, and not in this system and practice of eloquence, he must be told that even we ourselves have never been wholly devoted to this study. In truth, all the arts which concern the civilizing and humanizing of men have some link which binds them together, and are, as it were, connected by some relationship to one another.

And, that it may not appear marvelous to any one of you, that I, in a formal proceeding like this, and in a regular court

of justice, when an action is being tried before a prætor of the Roman people, a most eminent man, and before most impartial judges, before such an assembly and multitude of people as I see around me, employ this style of speaking, which is at variance, not only with the ordinary usages of courts of justice, but with the general style of forensic pleading, I entreat you in this cause to grant me this indulgence, suitable to this defendant, and as I trust not disagreeable to you—the indulgence, namely, of allowing me, when speaking in defense of a most sublime poet and most learned man, before this concourse of highly-educated citizens, before this most polite and accomplished assembly, and before such a prætor as him who is presiding at this trial, to enlarge with a little more freedom than usual on the study of polite literature and refined arts, and, speaking in the character of such a man as that, who, owing to the tranquillity of his life and the studies to which he has devoted himself, has but little experience of the dangers of a court of justice, to employ a new and unusual style of oratory. And if I feel that that indulgence is given and allowed me by you, I will soon cause you to think that this Aulus Licinius is a man who not only, now that he is a citizen, does not deserve to be expunged from the list of citizens, but that he is worthy, even if he were not one, of being now made a citizen.

For when first Archias grew out of childhood, and out of the studies of those arts by which young boys are gradually trained and refined, he devoted himself to the study of writing. First of all at Antioch (for he was born there, and was of high rank there), formerly an illustrious and wealthy city, and the seat of learned men and of liberal sciences; and there it was his lot speedily to show himself superior to all in ability and credit. Afterward, in the other parts of Asia, and over all Greece, his arrival was so talked of wherever he came, that the anxiety with which he was expected was even greater than the fame of his genius; but the admiration which he excited when he had arrived exceeded even the anxiety with which he was expected. Italy was at that time full of Greek science and of Greek systems, and these studies were at that time cultivated in Latium with greater zeal than they now are in the same towns; and here too at Rome, on account of the tranquil state of the republic at that time, they were far from neglected. Therefore, the people of Tarentum and Rhegium and Neapolis presented him

with the freedom of the city and with other gifts; and all men who were capable of judging of genius thought him deserving of their acquaintance and hospitality. When, from this great celebrity of his, he had become known to us, though absent, he came to Rome, in the consulship of Marius and Catulus. It was his lot to have those men as his first consuls, the one of whom could supply him with the most illustrious achievements to write about, the other could give him, not only exploits to celebrate, but his ears and judicious attention. Immediately the Luculli, though Archias was as yet but a youth, received him in their house. But it was not only to his genius and his learning, but also to his natural disposition and virtue, that it must be attributed that the house which was the first to be opened to him in his youth, is also the one in which he lives most familiarly in his old age. He at that time gained the affection of Quintus Metellus, that great man who was the conqueror of Numidia, and his son Pius. He was eagerly listened to by Marcus Æmilius; he associated with Quintus Catulus—both with the father and the sons. He was highly respected by Lucius Crassus; and as for the Luculli and Drusus and the Octavii and Cato and the whole family of the Hortensii, he was on terms of the greatest possible intimacy with all of them, and was held by them in the greatest honor. For, not only did every one cultivate his acquaintance who wished to learn or to hear anything, but even every one pretended to have such a desire.

In the meantime, after a sufficiently long interval, having gone with Lucius Lucullus into Sicily, and having afterward departed from that province in the company of the same Lucullus, he came to Heraclea. And as that city was one which enjoyed all the rights of a confederate city to their full extent, he became desirous of being enrolled as a citizen of it. And, being thought deserving of such a favor for his own sake, when aided by the influence and authority of Lucullus, he easily obtained it from the Heracleans. The freedom of the city was given him in accordance with the provisions of the law of Silvanus and Carbo: "If any men had been enrolled as citizens of the confederate cities, and if, at the time that the law was passed, they had a residence in Italy, and if within sixty days they had made a return of themselves to the prætor." As he had now had a residence at Rome for many years, he returned himself as a citizen to the prætor, Quintus Metellus, his most intimate friend. If we have nothing

else to speak about except the rights of citizenship, and the law, I need say no more. The cause is over. For which of all these statements, O Gratius, can be invalidated? Will you deny that he was enrolled, at the time I speak of, as a citizen of Heraclea? There is a man present of the very highest authority, a most scrupulous and truthful man, Lucius Lucullus, who will tell you not that he thinks it, but that he knows it; not that he has heard of it, but that he saw it; not even that he was present when it was done, but that he actually did it himself. Deputies from Heraclea are present, men of the highest rank. They have come expressly on account of this trial, with a commission from their city, and to give evidence on the part of their city; and they say that he was enrolled as a Heraclean. On this you ask for the public registers of the Heracleans, which we all know were destroyed in the Italian war, when the register-office was burned. It is ridiculous to say nothing to the proofs which we have, but to ask for proofs which it is impossible for us to have; to disregard the recollection of men, and to appeal to the memory of documents; and when you have the conscientious evidence of a most honorable man, the oath and good faith of a most respectable municipality, to reject those things which cannot by any possibility be tampered with, and to demand documentary evidence, though you say at the same moment that that is constantly played tricks with. "But he had no residence at Rome." What, not he who for so many years before the freedom of the city was given to him, had established the abode of all his property and fortunes at Rome? "But he did not return himself." Indeed he did, and in that return which alone obtains with the college of prætors the authority of a public document.

For as the returns of Appius were said to have been kept carelessly, and as the trifling conduct of Gabinius, before he was convicted, and his misfortune after his condemnation, had taken away all credit from the public registers, Metellus, the most scrupulous and moderate of all men, was so careful, that he came to Lucius Lentulus, the prætor, and to the judges, and said that he was greatly vexed at an erasure which appeared in one name. In these documents, therefore, you will see no erasure affecting the name of Aulus Licinius. And as this is the case, what reason have you for doubting about his citizenship, especially as he was enrolled as a citizen of other cities also? In truth, as men in Greece were in the habit of giving rights of citizenship to many men of very ordinary qualifications, and endowed with no talents at all, or with very moderate ones, without any payment, it is likely, I suppose, that the Rhegians and Locrians and Neapolitans and Tarentines should have been unwilling to give to this man, enjoying the highest possible reputation for genius, what they were in the habit of giving even to theatrical artists. What, when other men, who not only after the freedom of the city had been given, but even after the passing of the Papian law, crept somehow or other into the registers of those municipalities, shall he be rejected who does not avail himself of those other lists in which he is enrolled, because he always wished to be considered a Heraclean? You demand to see our own censor's returns. I suppose no one knows that at the time of the last census he was with that most illustrious general, Lucius Lucullus, with the army; that at the time of the preceding one he was with the same man when he was in Asia as quæstor; and that in the census before that, when Julius and Crassus were censors, no regular account of the people was taken. But, since the census does not confirm the right of citizenship, but only indicates that he, who is returned in the census, did at that time claim to be considered as a citizen, I say that, at that time, when you say, in your speech for the prosecution, that he did not even himself consider that he had any claim to the privileges of a Roman citizen, he more than once made a will according to our laws, and he entered upon inheritances left him by Roman citizens; and he was made honorable mention of by Lucius Lucullus, both as prætor and as consul, in the archives kept in the treasury.

You must rely wholly on what arguments you can find. For he will never be convicted either by his own opinion of his case, or by that which is formed of it by his friends.

You ask us, O Gratius, why we are so exceedingly attached to this man. Because he supplies us with food whereby our mind is refreshed after this noise in the forum, and with rest for our ears after they have been wearied with bad language. Do you think it possible that we could find a supply for our daily speeches, when discussing such a variety of matters, unless we were to cultivate our minds by the study of literature; or that our minds could bear being kept so constantly on the stretch if we did not relax them by that same study? But I

confess that I am devoted to those studies; let others be ashamed of them if they have buried themselves in books without being able to produce anything out of them for the common advantage, or anything which may bear the eyes of men and the light. But why need I be ashamed, who for many years have lived in such a manner as never to allow my own love of tranquillity to deny me to the necessity or advantage of another, or my fondness for pleasure to distract, or even sleep to delay my attention to such claims? Who then can reproach me, or who has any right to be angry with me, if I allow myself as much time for the cultivation of these studies as some take for the performance of their own business, or for celebrating days of festival and games, or for other pleasures, or even for the rest and refreshment of mind and body, or as others devote to early banquets, to playing at dice, or at ball? And this ought to be permitted to me, because by these studies my power of speaking and those faculties are improved, which, as far as they do exist in me, have never been denied to my friends when they have been in peril. And if that ability appears to any one to be but moderate, at all events I know whence I derive those principles which are of the greatest value. For if I had not persuaded myself from my youth upward, both by the precepts of many masters and by much reading, that there is nothing in life greatly to be desired, except praise and honor, and that while pursuing those things all tortures of the body, all dangers of death and banishment, are to be considered but of small importance, I should never have exposed myself, in defense of your safety, to such numerous and arduous contests, and to these daily attacks of profligate men. But all books are full of such precepts, and all the sayings of philosophers and all antiquity are full of precedents teaching the same lesson; but all these things would lie buried in darkness, if the light of literature and learning were not applied to them. How many images of the bravest men, carefully elaborated, have both the Greek and Latin writers bequeathed to us, not merely for us to look at and gaze upon, but also for our imitation! And I, always keeping them before my eyes as examples for my own public conduct, have endeavored to model my mind and views by continually thinking of those excellent men.

Some one will ask, "What? were those identical great men, whose virtues have been recorded in books, accomplished in all that learning which you are extolling so highly?" It is difficult

to assert this of all of them; but still I know what answer I can make to that question: I admit that many men have existed of admirable disposition and virtue, who, without learning, by the almost divine instinct of their own mere nature, have been, of their own accord, as it were, moderate and wise men. I even add this, that very often nature without learning has had more to do with leading men to credit and to virtue than learning when not assisted by a good natural disposition. And I also contend, that when to an excellent and admirable natural disposition there is added a certain system and training of education, then from that combination arises an extraordinary perfection of character; such as is seen in that godlike man, whom our fathers saw in their time, Africanus; and in Caius Lælius and Lucius Furius, most virtuous and moderate men; and in that most excellent man, the most learned man of his time, Marcus Cato the elder; and all these men, if they had been to derive no assistance from literature in the cultivation and practice of virtue, would never have applied themselves to the study of it. Though, even if there were no such great advantage to be reaped from it, and if it were only pleasure that is sought from these studies, still I imagine you would consider it a most reasonable and liberal employment of the mind: for other occupations are not suited to every time, nor to every age or place; but these studies are the food of youth, the delight of old age; the ornament of prosperity, the refuge and comfort of adversity; a delight at home, and no hindrance abroad; they are companions by night, and in travel, and in the country.

And if we ourselves were not able to arrive at these advantages, nor even taste them with our senses, still we should have admired them, even when we saw them in others. Who of us was of so ignorant and brutal a disposition as not lately to be grieved at the death of Roscius, who, though he was an old man when he died, yet, on account of the excellence and beauty of his art, appeared to be one who on every account ought not to have died? Therefore, had he by the gestures of his body gained so much of our affections, and shall we disregard the incredible movements of the mind and the rapid operations of genius? How often have I seen this man Archias, O judges (for I will take advantage of your kindness, since you listen to me so attentively while speaking in this unusual manner)—how often have I seen him, when he had not written a single word, repeat

extempore a great number of admirable verses on the very events which were passing at the moment! How often have I seen him go back, and describe the same thing over again with an entire change of language and ideas! And what he wrote with care and with much thought, that I have seen admired to such a degree as to equal the credit of even the writings of the ancients. Should not I, then, love this man? should not I admire him? should not I think it my duty to defend him in every possible way? And, indeed, we have constantly heard from men of the greatest eminence and learning, that the study of other sciences was made up of learning and rules and regular method, but that a poet was such by the unassisted work of nature, and was moved by the vigor of his own mind, and was inspired, as it were, by some divine wrath. Wherefore rightly does our own great Ennius call poets holy; because they seem to be recommended to us by some especial gift, as it were, and liberality of the gods. Let then, judges, this name of poet, this name which no barbarians even have ever disregarded, be holy in your eyes, men of cultivated minds as you all are. Rocks and deserts reply to the poet's voice; savage beasts are often moved and arrested by song; and shall we, who have been trained in the pursuit of the most virtuous acts, refuse to be swayed by the voice of poets? The Colophonians say that Homer was their citizen; the Chians claim him as theirs; the Salaminians assert their right to him; but the men of Smyrna loudly assert him to be a citizen of Smyrna, and they have even raised a temple to him in their city. Many other places also fight with one another for the honor of being his birthplace.

They, then, claim a stranger, even after his death, because he was a poet; shall we reject this man while he is alive,—a man who by his own inclination and by our laws does actually belong to us? especially when Archias has employed all his genius with the utmost zeal in celebrating the glory and renown of the Roman people? For, when a young man, he touched on our wars against the Cimbri, and gained the favor even of Caius Marius himself, a man who, as a rule, was proof against this sort of study. For there was no one so disinclined to the Muses as not willingly to endure that the praise of his labors should be made immortal by means of verse. They say that the great Themistocles, the greatest man that Athens produced, said, when some one asked him what sound or whose voice he took the greatest delight in hearing, "The voice of that by whom his own exploits were best celebrated." Therefore the great Marius was also exceedingly attached to Lucius Plotius, because he thought that the achievement which he had performed could be celebrated by his genius. And the whole Mithridatic war, great and difficult as it was, and carried on with so much diversity of fortune by land and sea, has been related at length by him; and the books in which that is sung of, not only make illustrious Lucius Lucullus, that most gallant and celebrated man, but they do honor also to the Roman people. For, while Lucullus was general, the Roman people opened Pontus, though it was defended both by the resources of the king and by the character of the country itself. Under the same general the army of the Roman people, with no very great numbers, routed the countless hosts of the Armenians. It is the glory of the Roman people that, by the wisdom of that same general, the city of the Cyzicenes, most friendly to us, was delivered and preserved from all the attacks of the kind, and from the very jaws, as it were, of the whole war. Ours is the glory which will be forever celebrated, which is derived from the fleet of the enemy which was sunk after its admirals had been slain, and from the marvelous naval battle off Tenedos; those trophies belong to us, those monuments are ours, those triumphs are ours. Therefore, I say that the men by whose genius these exploits are celebrated make illustrious at the same time the glory of the Roman people. Our countryman, Ennius, was dear to the elder Africanus; and even on the tomb of the Scipios his effigy is believed to be visible, carved in the marble. But undoubtedly it is not only the men who are themselves praised who are done honor to by those praises, but the name of the Roman people also is adorned by them. Cato, the ancestor of this Cato, is extolled to the skies. Great honor is paid to the exploits of the Roman people. Lastly, all those great men, the Maximi, the Marcelli, and the Fulvii, are done honor to, not without all of us having also a share in the panegyric.

Therefore our ancestors received the man who was the cause of all this, a man of Rudiæ, into their city as a citizen; and shall we reject from our city a man of Heraclea, a man sought by many cities, and made a citizen of ours by these very laws?

For if any one thinks that there is a smaller gain of glory derived from Greek verses than from Latin ones, he is greatly

mistaken, because Greek poetry is read among all nations, Latin is confined to its own natural limits, which are narrow enough. Wherefore, if those achievements which we have performed are limited only by the bounds of the whole world, we ought to desire that, wherever our vigor and our arms have penetrated, our glory and our fame should likewise extend. Because, as this is always an ample reward for those people whose achievements are the subject of writings, so especially is it the greatest inducement to encounter labors and dangers to all men who fight for themselves for the sake of glory. How many historians of his exploits is Alexander the Great said to have had with him; and he, when standing on Cape Sigeum at the grave of Achilles, said: "O happy youth, to find Homer as the panegyrist of your glory!" And he said the truth; for, if the Iliad had not existed, the same tomb which covered his body would have also buried his renown. What, did not our own Magnus, whose valor has been equal to his fortune, present Theophanes the Mitylenæan, a relator of his actions, with the freedom of the city in an assembly of the soldiers? And those brave men, our countrymen, soldiers and country-bred men as they were, still being moved by the sweetness of glory, as if they were to some extent partakers of the same renown, showed their approbation of that action with a great shout. Therefore, I suppose, if Archias were not a Roman citizen according to the laws, he could not have contrived to get presented with the freedom of the city by some general! Sylla, when he was giving it to the Spaniards and Gauls, would, I suppose, have refused him if he had asked for it! A man whom we ourselves saw in the public assembly, when a bad poet of the common people had put a book in his hand, because he had made an epigram on him with every other verse too long, immediately ordered some of the things which he was selling at the moment to be given him as a reward, on condition of not writing anything more about him for the future. Would not he who thought the industry of a bad poet still worthy of some reward have sought out the genius and excellence and copiousness in writing of this man? What more need I say? Could he not have obtained the freedom of the city from Quintus Metellus Pius, his own most intimate friend, who gave it to many men, either by his own request, or by the intervention of the Luculli? especially when Metellus was so anxious to have his own deeds celebrated in writing, that

he gave his attention willingly to poets born even at Cordova, whose poetry had a very heavy and foreign flavor.

For this should not be concealed, which cannot possibly be kept in the dark, but it might be avowed openly: we are all influenced by a desire of praise, and the best men are the most especially attracted by glory. Those very philosophers, even in the books which they write about despising glory, put their own names on the title-page. In the very act of recording their contempt for renown and notoriety, they desire to have their own names known and talked of. Decimus Brutus, the most excellent citizen and consummate general, adorned the approaches to his temples and monuments with the verses of Attius. And lately that great man Fulvius, who fought with the Ætolians, having Ennius for his companion, did not hesitate to devote the spoils of Mars to the Muses. Wherefore, in a city in which generals, almost in arms, have paid respect to the name of poets and to the temples of the Muses, these judges in the garb of peace ought not to act in a manner inconsistent with the honor of the Muses and the safety of poets.

And that you may do that the more willingly, I will now reveal my own feelings to you, O judges, and I will make a confession to you of my own love of glory — too eager perhaps, but still honorable. For this man has in his verses touched upon and begun the celebration of the deeds which we in our consulship did in union with you, for the safety of this city and empire, and in defense of the life of the citizens and of the whole republic. And when I had heard his commencement, because it appeared to me to be a great subject and at the same time an agreeable one, I encouraged him to complete his work. For virtue seeks no other reward for its labors and its dangers beyond that of praise and renown; and if that be denied to it, what reason is there, O judges, why in so small and brief a course of life as is allotted to us, we should impose such labors on ourselves? Certainly, if the mind had no anticipations of posterity, and if it were to confine all its thoughts within the same limits as those by which the space of our lives is bounded, it would neither break itself with such severe labors, nor would it be tormented with such cares and sleepless anxiety, nor would it so often have to fight for its very life. At present there is a certain virtue in every good man, which night and day stirs up the mind with the stimulus of glory, and reminds it that all

mention of our name will not cease at the same time with our lives, but that our fame will endure to all posterity.

Do we all who are occupied in the affairs of the State, and who are surrounded by such perils and dangers in life, appear to be so narrow-minded, as, though to the last moment of our lives we have never passed one tranquil or easy moment, to think that everything will perish at the same time as ourselves? Ought we not, when many most illustrious men have with great care collected and left behind them statues and images, representations not of their minds but of their bodies, much more to desire to leave behind us a copy of our counsels and of our virtues, wrought and elaborated by the greatest genius? I thought, at the very moment of performing them, that I was scattering and disseminating all the deeds which I was performing, all over the world for the eternal recollection of nations. And whether that delight is to be denied to my soul after death, or whether, as the wisest men have thought, it will affect some portion of my spirit, at all events I am at present delighted with some such idea and hope.

Preserve then, O judges, a man of such virtue as that of Archias, which you see testified to you not only by the worth of his friends, but by the length of time during which they have been such to him; and of such genius as you ought to think is his, when you see that it has been sought by most illustrious men. And his cause is one which is approved of by the benevolence of the law, by the authority of his municipality, by the testimony of Lucullus, and by the documentary evidence of Metellus. And as this is the case, we do entreat you, O judges, if there may be any weight attached, I will not say to human, but even to divine recommendation in such important matters, to receive under your protection that man who has at all times done honor to your generals and to the exploits of the Roman people, — who even in these recent perils of our own, and in your domestic dangers, promises to give an eternal testimony of praise in our favor, and who forms one of that band of poets who have at all times and in all nations been considered and called holy, so that he may seem relieved by your humanity, rather than overwhelmed by your severity.

The things which, according to my custom, I have said briefly and simply, O judges, I trust have been approved by all of you. Those things which I have spoken, without regarding the habits of the forum or judicial usage, both concerning the genius of the man and my own zeal in his behalf, I trust have been received by you in good part. That they have been so by him who presides at this trial, I am quite certain.

THE FOURTH PHILIPPIC
(Delivered to the People in the Roman Forum Against Antony)

THE great numbers in which you are here met this day, O Romans, and this assembly, greater than, it seems to me, I ever remember, inspires me with both an exceeding eagerness to defend the republic, and with a great hope of re-establishing it. Although my courage indeed has never failed, what has been unfavorable is the time; and the moment that that has appeared to show any dawn of light, I at once have been the leader in the defense of your liberty. And if I had attempted to have done so before, I should not be able to do so now. For this day, O Romans (that you may not think it is but a trifling business in which we have been engaged), the foundations have been laid for future actions. For the Senate has no longer been content with styling Antonius an enemy in words, but it has shown by actions that it thinks him one. And now I am much more elated still, because you too with such great unanimity and with such a clamor have sanctioned our declaration that he is an enemy.

And indeed, O Romans, it is impossible but that either the men must be impious who have levied armies against the consul, or else that he must be an enemy against whom they have rightly taken arms. And this doubt the Senate has this day removed—not indeed that there really was any; but it has prevented the possibility of there being any. Caius Cæsar, who has upheld and who is still upholding the republic and your freedom by his zeal and wisdom, and at the expense of his patrimonial estate, has been complimented with the highest praises of the Senate.

I praise you,—yes, I praise you greatly, O Romans, when you follow with the most grateful minds the name of that most illustrious youth, or rather boy; for his actions belong to immortality, the name of youth only to his age. I can recollect many things; I have heard of many things; I have read of many

III—76

things; but in the whole history of the whole world I have never known anything like this. For, when we were weighed down with slavery, when the evil was daily increasing, when we had no defense, while we were in dread of the pernicious and fatal return of Marcus Antonius from Brundusium, this young man adopted the design which none of us had ventured to hope for, which beyond all question none of us were acquainted with, of raising an invincible army of his father's soldiers, and so hindering the frenzy of Antonius, spurred on as it was by the most inhuman counsels, from the power of doing mischief to the republic.

For who is there who does not see clearly that if Cæsar had not prepared an army the return of Antonius must have been accompanied by our destruction? For, in truth, he returned in such a state of mind, burning with hatred of you all, stained with the blood of the Roman citizens, whom he had murdered at Suessa and at Brundusium, that he thought of nothing but the utter destruction of the republic. And what protection could have been found for your safety and for your liberty if the army of Caius Cæsar had not been composed of the bravest of his father's soldiers? And with respect to his praises and honors,— and he is entitled to divine and everlasting honors for his godlike and undying services,—the Senate has just consented to my proposals, and has decreed that a motion be submitted to it at the very earliest opportunity.

Now, who is there who does not see that by this decree Antonius has been adjudged to be an enemy? For what else can we call him, when the Senate decides that extraordinary honors are to be devised for those men who are leading armies against him? What? did not the Martial legion (which appears to me by some divine permission to have derived its name from that god from whom we have heard that the Roman people descended) decide by its resolutions that Antonius was an enemy before the Senate had come to any resolution? For if he be not an enemy, we must inevitably decide that those men who have deserted the consul are enemies. Admirably and seasonably, O Romans, have you by your cries sanctioned the noble conduct of the men of the Martial legion, who have come over to the authority of the Senate, to your liberty, and to the whole republic, and have abandoned that enemy and robber and parricide of his country. Nor did they display only their spirit and courage in

doing this, but their caution and wisdom also. They encamped at Alba, in a city convenient, fortified, near, full of brave men and loyal and virtuous citizens. The fourth legion imitating the virtue of this Martial legion, under the leadership of Lucius Egnatuleius, whom the Senate deservedly praised a little while ago, has also joined the army of Caius Cæsar.

What more adverse decisions, O Marcus Antonius, can you want? Cæsar, who has levied an army against you, is extolled to the skies. The legions are praised in the most complimentary language, which have abandoned you, which were sent for into Italy by you, and which, if you had chosen to be a consul rather than an enemy, were wholly devoted to you. And the fearless and honest decision of those legions is confirmed by the Senate, is approved of by the whole Roman people,—unless, indeed, you to-day, O Romans, decide that Antonius is a consul and not an enemy. I thought, O Romans, that you did think as you show you do. What? do you suppose that the municipal towns and the colonies and the prefectures have any other opinion? All men are agreed with one mind; so that every one who wishes the State to be saved must take up every sort of arms against that pestilence. What? I should like to know!—does the opinion of Decimus Brutus, O Romans, which you can gather from his edict, which has this day reached us, appear to any one deserving of being lightly esteemed? Rightly and truly do you say No, O Romans. For the family and name of Brutus has been by some especial kindness and liberality of the immortal gods given to the republic, for the purpose of at one time establishing, and at another of recovering, the liberty of the Roman people. What, then, has been the opinion which Decimus Brutus has formed of Marcus Antonius? He excludes him from his province. He opposes him with his army. He rouses all Gaul to war, which is already roused of its own accord, and in consequence of the judgment which it has itself formed. If Antonius be consul, Brutus is an enemy. Can we then doubt which of these alternatives is the fact?

And just as you now with one mind and one voice affirm that you entertain no doubt, so did the Senate just now decree that Decimus Brutus deserved excellently well of the republic, inasmuch as he was defending the authority of the Senate and the liberty and empire of the Roman people. Defending it against whom? Why, against an enemy. For what other sort of

defense deserves praise? In the next place the province of Gaul is praised, and is deservedly complimented in most honorable language by the Senate for resisting Antonius. But if that province considered him the consul, and still refused to receive him, it would be guilty of great wickedness. For all the provinces belong to the consul of right, and are bound to obey him. Decimus Brutus, imperator and consul-elect, a citizen born for the republic, denies that he is consul; Gaul denies it; all Italy denies it; the Senate denies it; you deny it. Who then thinks that he is consul except a few robbers? Although even they themselves do not believe what they say; nor is it possible that they should differ from the judgment of all men, impious and desperate men though they be. But the hope of plunder and booty blinds their minds; men whom no gifts of money, no allotment of land, nor even that interminable auction has satisfied; who have proposed to themselves the city, the properties, and fortunes of all the citizens as their booty; and who, as long as there is something for them to seize and carry off, think that nothing will be wanting to them; among whom Marcus Antonius (O ye immortal gods, avert, I pray you, and efface this omen) has promised to divide this city. May things rather happen, O Romans, as you pray that they should, and may the chastisement of this frenzy fall on him and on his friend. And, indeed, I feel sure that it will be so. For I think that at present not only men, but the immortal gods, have all united together to preserve this republic. For if the immortal gods foreshow us the future, by means of portents and prodigies, then it has been openly revealed to us that punishment is near at hand to him, and liberty to us. Or if it was impossible for such unanimity on the part of all men to exist without the inspiration of the gods, in either case how can we doubt as to the inclinations of the heavenly deities?

It only remains, O Romans, for you to persevere in the sentiments which you at present display.

I will act, therefore, as commanders are in the habit of doing when their army is ready for battle, who, although they see their soldiers ready to engage, still address an exhortation to them; and in like manner I will exhort you who are already eager and burning to recover your liberty. You have not—you have not, indeed, O Romans, to war against an enemy with whom it is possible to make peace on any terms whatever. For he does not now desire your slavery, as he did before, but he is angry now and thirsts for your blood. No sport appears more delightful to him than bloodshed and slaughter and the massacre of citizens before his eyes. You have not, O Romans, to deal with a wicked and profligate man, but with an unnatural and savage beast. And, since he has fallen into a well, let him be buried in it. For if he escapes out of it, there will be no inhumanity of torture which it will be possible to avoid. But he is at present hemmed in, pressed, and besieged by those troops which we already have, and will soon be still more so by those which in a few days the new consuls will levy. Apply yourselves then to this business, as you are doing. Never have you shown greater unanimity in any cause; never have you been so cordially united with the Senate. And no wonder. For the question now is not in what condition we are to live, but whether we are to live at all, or to perish with torture and ignominy.

Although nature, indeed, has appointed death for all men, yet valor is accustomed to ward off any cruelty or disgrace in death. And that is an inalienable possession of the Roman race and name. Preserve, I beseech you, O Romans, this attribute which your ancestors have left you as a sort of inheritance. Although all other things are uncertain, fleeting, transitory, virtue alone is planted firm with very deep roots. It cannot be undermined by any violence; it can never be moved from its position. By it your ancestors first subdued the whole of Italy; then destroyed Carthage, overthrew Numantia, and reduced the most mighty kings and most warlike nations under the dominion of this empire.

And your ancestors, O Romans, had to deal with an enemy who had also a republic, a Senate House, a treasury, harmonious and united citizens, and with whom, if fortune had so willed it, there might have been peace and treaties on settled principles. But this enemy of yours is attacking your republic, but has none himself; is eager to destroy the Senate, that is to say, the council of the whole world, but has no public council himself; he has exhausted your treasury, and has none of his own. For how can a man be supported by the unanimity of his citizens, who has no city at all? And what principles of peace can there be with that man who is full of incredible cruelty, and destitute of faith?

The whole, then, of the contest, O Romans, which is now before the Roman people, the conqueror of all nations, is with an

assassin, a robber, a Spartacus. For as to his habitual boast of being like Catilina, he is equal to him in wickedness, but inferior in energy. He, though he had no army, rapidly levied one. This man has lost that very army which he had. As, therefore, by my diligence, and the authority of the Senate, and your own zeal and valor, you crushed Catilina, so you will very soon hear that this infamous piratical enterprise of Antonius has been put down by your own perfect and unexampled harmony with the Senate, and by the good fortune and valor of your armies and generals. I, for my part, as far as I am able to labor and to effect anything by my care and exertions and vigilance and authority and counsel, will omit nothing which I may think serviceable to your liberty. Nor could I omit it without wickedness after all your most ample and honorable kindness to me. However, on this day, encouraged by the motion of a most gallant man, and one most firmly attached to you, Marcus Servilius, whom you see before you, and his colleagues also, most distinguished men, and most virtuous citizens; and partly, too, by my advice and my example, we have, for the first time after a long interval, fired up again with a hope of liberty.

CHAMP CLARK

(1850–)

UNDER the act of Congress which invites the States to present memorials of their most noted historical characters to be preserved in the Capitol, the busts of Thomas H. Benton and Francis P. Blair were presented by Missouri to the United States on February 4th, 1899. Congressman Champ Clark of the Ninth Missouri District, one of the orators selected to speak for the State, devoted his attention to Blair. As another volume of this work contains Blair's analysis of Benton's character, Mr. Clark's analysis of the qualities which made Blair himself a leader is here given.

Mr. Clark was born near Lawrenceburg, Kentucky, March 7th, 1850. He was educated at the Kentucky University, Bethany College, West Virginia, and at the Cincinnati Law School. In 1873–74 he was president of the first normal school established in West Virginia; and when he came to Missouri in 1875, it was to serve as principal of the High School at Louisiana. In 1876 he gave up teaching for the practice of law. He was elected to Congress in 1892 and has been re-elected at each succeeding election.

THE COURAGE OF LEADERSHIP

(From the Address Delivered February 4th, 1899, at the Presentation by Missouri to the United States of the Busts of Thomas H. Benton and Francis P. Blair)

IN THE outskirts of Louisiana, Missouri, stand four immense sugar trees, which, if the Druidical religion were in vogue in the Mississippi Valley, would be set aside as objects of worship by Democrats. They form the corners of a rectangle about large enough for a speaker's platform. Beneath their grateful shadow, with the Father of Waters behind him, the eternal hills in front of him, the blue sky above his head, in the presence of a great and curious concourse of people, Frank Blair made the first Democratic speech delivered in Missouri after the close of the Civil War. Excitement was intense. Armed men of all shades of opinion abounded on every hand. When Blair arose

to speak he unbuckled his pistol belt and coolly laid two navy revolvers on the table. He prefaced his remarks as follows:—

Fellow-citizens, I understand that I am to be killed here to-day. I have just come out of four years of that sort of business. If there is to be any of it here, it had better be attended to before the speaking begins.

That calm but pregnant exordium has perhaps no counterpart in the entire range of oratory.

"There was silence deep as death;
And the boldest held his breath
For a time."

He then proceeded with his speech, but had not been going more than five minutes until a man of gigantic proportions started toward him, shaking his huge fist and shouting: "He's an arrant rebel! Take him out! Take him out!" Blair stopped, looked the man in the face, crooked his finger at him, and said: "You come and take me out!" which put an end to that episode, for the man who was yelling "Take him out!" suddenly realized that Blair's index finger which was beckoning him on would soon be pressing the trigger of one of those pistols if he did go on, and he prudently declined Blair's invitation.

He got through that day without bloodshed, but when he spoke at Warrensburg, a little later, he had not proceeded a quarter of an hour before a prominent citizen sitting on the speaker's stand started toward Blair with a pistol in his hand and with a mighty oath, yelling: "That statement is a lie!" which instantly precipitated a free fight in which one man was killed and several severely wounded. Blair went on with his speech amid ceaseless interruptions. I know a venerable, mild-mannered, Christian statesman, now in this very Capitol, who for two mortal hours of that pandemonium stood with his hand upon his revolver ready to shoot down any man who assaulted Blair.

Afterwards Blair was advertised to speak at Marshall, in Saline County. On the day of his arrival an armed mob was organized to prevent him from speaking, and an armed body of Democrats swore he should. A collision occurred, resulting in a regular pitched battle in which several men lost their lives and others were badly injured. But Blair made his speech.

One night he was speaking in Lucas Market Place, in St. Louis, when a man in the crowd, not twenty feet from the stand, pointed a revolver directly at him. Friendly hands interposed to turn the aim skywards. "Let him shoot, if he dare," said Blair, gazing coolly at his would-be murderer; "if I am wrong I ought to be shot, but this man is not the proper executioner." The fellow was hustled from the audience.

Amid such scenes he toured the State from the Des Moines River to the Arkansas line, and from the Mississippi to the mouth of the "raging Kaw." The man who did that had a lion's heart in his breast.

The old Latin dictum runs: *Poeta nascitur, non fit.* The same is true of the leader of men — he is born, not made.

What constitutes the quality of leadership, Mr. Speaker? You do not know. I do not know. None of us knows. No man can tell.

Talent, genius, learning, courage, eloquence, greatness in many fields we may define with something approximating exactness; but who can inform us as to the constituent elements of leadership? We all recognize the leader the moment we behold him, but what entitles him to that distinction is and perhaps must forever remain one of the unsolved mysteries of psychology.

Talent, even genius, does not make a man a leader, for some men of the profoundest talents, others of the most dazzling genius, have been servile followers and have debased their rich gifts from God to the flattery of despots. Most notable among those was Lord Bacon, the father of the inductive philosophy, who possessed the most exquisite intellect ever housed in a human skull, with a spirit so abject, so groveling that he was not unjustly described in that blistering, scornful couplet by Alexander Pope: —

> "If parts allure thee, think how Bacon shin'd,
> The wisest, brightest, meanest of mankind!"

Courage is not synonymous with the quality of leadership, though necessary to it, for some of the bravest soldiers that ever met Death upon the battlefield and defied him to his face were amazingly lacking in that regard.

Learning does not render a man a leader, for some of the greatest scholars of whom history tells were wholly without influence over their fellow-men. Eloquence does not make a

leader, for some of the world's greatest orators, among them Cicero, have been the veriest cravens; and no craven can lead men.

Indeed, eloquence, learning, talents, genius, courage, all combined do not make a leader.

But whatever the quality is, people recognize it instinctively, and inevitably follow the man who possesses it.

Frank Blair was a natural leader.

Yet during his career there were finer scholars in Missouri than he, though he was an excellent scholar, a graduate from Princeton; there were more splendid orators, though he ranked with the most convincing and persuasive; there were profounder lawyers, though he stood high at the bar; there were better mixers, though he was of cordial and winning manners; there were men, perhaps, of stronger mental force, though he was amply endowed with brains, so good a judge of human nature as Abraham Lincoln saying of him, "He has abundant talents;" there were men as brave, though he was of the bravest; but as a leader he overtopped them all.

Believing sincerely that human slavery was wrong *per se* and that it was of most evil to the States where it existed, he fought it tooth and nail, not from sympathy for the negroes so much as from affection for the whites, and created the Republican party in Missouri before the Civil War — a most hazardous performance in that day and latitude. At its close, when, in his judgment, his party associates had become the oppressors of the people and the enemies of liberty, he left them, and lifting in his mighty arms the Democracy, which lay bleeding and swooning in the dust, he breathed into its nostrils the breath of life.

This man was of the stuff out of which martyrs are made, and he would have gone grimly, undauntedly, unflinchingly, and defiantly to the block, the scaffold, or the stake, in defense of any cause which he considered just. Though he was imperious, tempestuous, dogmatic, and impetuous, though no danger could swerve him from the path of duty, though he gave tremendous blows to his antagonists and received many of the same kind, he had infinite compassion for the helpless and the weak, and to the end his heart remained tender as a little child's.

CASSIUS MARCELLUS CLAY

(1810-)

AS A representative of the fierce devotion to the Union, which, antagonizing an equally fierce devotion to the South, made the Civil War in Kentucky so bloody, Cassius M. Clay was one of the most noted characters of the border States from the repeal of the Missouri Compromise to the surrender at Appomattox. He was born in Madison County, Kentucky, October 19th, 1810. His opposition to slavery and his absolute fearlessness in proclaiming his opinions in the face of an intensely hostile community gave him a standing in the Republican party which resulted in his selection as Minister to Russia during President Lincoln's administration. He lived to extreme age.

A RHAPSODY

I MAY be an enthusiast; but I cannot but give utterance to the conceptions of my own mind. When I look upon the special developments of European civilization; when I contemplate the growing freedom of the cities, and the middle class which has sprung up between the pretenders to divine rule on the one hand, and the abject serf on the other; when I consider the Reformation, and the invention of the press, and see, on the southern shore of the continent, an humble individual, amidst untold difficulties and repeated defeats, pursuing the mysterious suggestions which the mighty deep poured unceasingly upon his troubled spirit, till at last, with great and irrepressible energy of soul, he discovered that there lay in the far western ocean a continent open for the infusion of those elementary principles of liberty which were dwarfed in European soil, — I conceive that the hand of destiny was there!

When I see the immigration of the Pilgrims from the chalky shores of England, — in the night fleeing from their native home — so dramatically and ably pictured by Mr. Webster in his celebrated oration, — when father, mother, brother, wife, sister, lover, were all lost by those melancholy wanderers — "stifling," in the language of one who is immortal in the conception, "the mighty

hunger of the heart," and landing, amidst cold and poverty and death, upon the rude rocks of Plymouth, — I venture to think the will of Deity was there!

When I have remembered the Revolution of '76, — the Seven Years' War — three millions of men in arms against the most powerful nation in history, and vindicating their independence, — I have thought that their sufferings and death were not in vain! When I have seen the forsaken hearthstone, — looked upon the battlefield, upon the dying and the dead, — heard the agonizing cry, "Water, for the sake of God! water!" seeing the dissolution of being, — pale lips pressing in death the yet loved images of wife, sister, lover, — I have not deemed — I will not deem all these things in vain! I cannot regard this great continent, reaching from the Atlantic to the far Pacific, and from the St. John's to the Rio del Norté, as the destined home of a barbarian people of third-rate civilization.

Like the Roman who looked back upon the glory of his ancestors, in woe exclaiming,

> "Great Scipio's ghost complains that we are slow,
> And Pompey's shade walks unavenged among us,"

the great dead hover around me: — Lawrence, "Don't give up the ship!" — Henry, "Give me liberty or give me death!" — Adams, "Survive or perish, I am for the Declaration!" — Allen, "In the name of the living God, I come!"

Come then, thou Eternal, who dwellest not in temples made with hands, but who, in the city's crowd or by the far forest stream, revealest thyself to the earnest seeker after the true and right, inspire my heart; give me undying courage to pursue the promptings of my spirit; and, whether I shall be called in the shades of life to look upon as sweet and kind and lovely faces as now, or, shut in by sorrow and night, horrid visions shall gloom upon me in my dying hour — O, my country, mayest thou yet be free!

ASPIRATIONS FOR THE UNION

WHILE the Union lasts, amid these fertile, verdant fields, these ever-flowing rivers, these stately groves, this genial, healthful clime, this "old Kentucky land," — hallowed by the blood of our sires, endeared by the beauty of her daughters, illustrious by the valor and eloquence of her sons, the centre of a most glorious empire, guarded by a cordon of States garrisoned by freemen, girt round by the rising and setting seas,— we are the most blessed of all people. Let the Union be dissolved, let that line be drawn where it must be drawn, and we are a border State; in time of peace, with no outlet to the ocean, the highway of nations, a miserable dependency; in time of war the battle ground of more than Indian warfare — of civil strife and indiscriminate slaughter! And then, worse than Spanish provinces, we shall contend not for glory and renown, but, like the aborigines of old, for a contemptible life and miserable subsistence! Let me not see it! Among those proud courts and lordly coteries of Europe's pride, where fifty years ago we were regarded as petty provinces, unknown to ears polite, let me go forth great in the name of an American citizen! Let me point them to our statesmen and the laws and government of their creation, the rapid advance of political science, the monuments of their fame, now the study of all Europe! Let them look at our rapidly increasing and happy population, see our canals and turnpikes and railroads, stretching over more space than combined Britain and continental Europe have reached by the same means! Let them send their philanthropists to learn of our penitentiary systems, our schools, and our civil institutions! Let them behold our skill in machinery, in steamboat and ship-building! Let them hail the most gallant ship that breasts the mountain wave, and she shall wave from her flagstaff the stars and stripes! These are the images which I cherish; this the nation which I honor; and never will I throw one pebble in her track, to jostle the footsteps of her glorious march!

AMERICA AS A MORAL FORCE

How many, like the great Emmet, have died, and left only a great name to attract our admiration for their virtues, and our regret for their untimely fall, to excite to deeds which they would but could not effect! But what has Washington left behind, save the glory of a name? The independent mind, the conscious pride, the ennobling principle of the soul,— a nation of freemen. What did he leave? He left us to ourselves. This is the sum of our liberties, the first principle of government, the

Her productions are wafted to every shore; her flag is seen waving in every sea. She has wrested the glorious motto from the once queen of the sea, and high on our banner, by the stars and stripes, is seen:—

> « Columbia needs no bulwark,
> No towers along the steep,
> Her march is o'er the mountain wave,
> Her home is on the deep. »

power of public opinion, the only permanent power on earth. When did a people flourish like Americans? Yet where, in a time of peace, has more use been made of the pen, or less with the sword of power? When did a religion flourish like the Christian, since they have done away with intolerance? Since, men have come to believe that physical force cannot effect the immortal part, and that religion is between the conscience and the Creator only. He of 622, who with the sword propagated his doctrines through Arabia, and the greater part of the barbarian world, against the power of whose tenets the physical force of all Christendom was opposed in vain, under the effective operations of freedom of opinion, is fast passing the way of, all error. Napoleon, the contemporary of our Washington, is fast dying away from the lips of men. He who shook the whole civilized earth; who, in an age of knowledge and concert among nations, held the world at bay; — at whose exploits the imagination becomes bewildered,— who, in the eve of his glory, was honored with the pathetic appellation of "the last lone captive of millions in war,"— even he is now known only in history. The vast empire was fast tumbling to ruins while he yet held the sword. He passed away, and left no successor there! The unhallowed light which obscured is gone; but brightly beams yet the name of Washington!

This freedom of opinion, which has done so much for the political and religious liberty of America, has not been confined to this continent. People of other countries begin to inquire, to examine, to reason for themselves. Error has fled before it, and the most inveterate prejudices are dissolved and gone. Such an unlimited remedy has in some cases, indeed, apparently proved injurious, but the evil is to be attributed to the peculiarity of the attendant circumstances, or the ill-timed application. Let us not force our tenets upon foreigners. For, if we subject opinion to coercion, who shall be our inquisitors? No; let us do as we have done, as we are now doing, and then call upon the nations to examine, to scrutinize, and to condemn! No! they cannot look upon America, to-day, and pity; for the gladdened heart disclaims all woe. They cannot look upon her, and deride; for genius and literature and science are soaring above the high places of birth and pageantry. They cannot look upon us, and defy; for the hearts of thirteen millions are warm in virtuous emulation — their arms steeled in the cause of their country.

CLEMENT C. CLAY, Senior

(1789–1866)

As United States Senator from Alabama in 1837, Clement C. Clay opposed the financial policies advocated by Henry Clay, of Kentucky, and made what was considered at the time one of the most effective speeches during the debate on the Subtreasury Bill of that year. He was born in Halifax County, Virginia, December 17th, 1789. After his graduation at the University of East Tennessee, he was admitted to the bar and removed to Huntsville, Alabama, becoming prominent as a lawyer and public man. He served as a member of the Territorial Council of Alabama, as a Judge of the Circuit Court, as a Chief-Justice of Alabama, Speaker of the State Legislature, Member of Congress, Governor of Alabama, and as United States Senator from 1837 till 1842.

THE SUBTREASURY BILL OF 1837

(From a Speech in the United States Senate, October 4th, 1837)

Mr. President :—

I confess, sir, when this delicate and important subject was first brought forward, I had some hesitation, some doubt, as to its probable tendency; but the more I have reflected, deliberated, investigated the subject, the better I have become satisfied that its effects will be salutary, in regard to the immediate interests of the Government itself, and that they will not be pernicious, but, on the contrary, beneficial to the interests of the people — our constituents.

As the measure was at first proposed by the Committee on Finance, I apprehended the disconnection — divorce, if you choose — of the Government from the banks would be too sudden and would consequently cripple the banks and occasion a shock in the monetary affairs of the country generally. But, sir, these apprehensions have been obviated and removed by the amendment offered by the Senator from South Carolina [Mr. Calhoun], as it is now modified. Under that amendment, the bills of such banks as now pay specie, or as may think proper to resume specie payments, will be receivable in payment, and to the full amount, of all public dues, for customs, lands, etc., till the first of January, 1839; thereafter, three-fourths of such public dues, till the first of January, 1840; thereafter one-half till the first of January, 1841; and, thereafter one-fourth till the first of January, 1842.

Here, then, is inducement, held out to the banks now paying, to continue, and to such as have stopped, to resume, specie payments. We say to them, in effect: "We invite you to resume specie payments; show that you are solvent, that your notes are convertible into specie when desirable, and we will receive them in payment for public lands, and for all other revenue"; in the strong language of some of the gentlemen who have addressed us: "Do this, and we will indorse your notes." What stronger motive could be held out to such banking institutions as are solvent, honest, and desirous to effectuate the purposes of their creation? If the public interest and convenience be the object of bank directors, as legitimately they ought, would they not, by responding to this invitation and offer on our part, give greater value to their paper, give it a wider circulation, and adapt it to the use and interest of the community? And would not such banks as resumed, at once derive all the advantages of superior credit, furnish the circulating medium, and do the business of the country, to the exclusion of such as failed or refused to comply? The answer is palpable—no man can doubt on these questions.

Again, sir: The change in the mode of collecting the public revenue, in the kind of money receivable for it, will be so gradual as to occasion no shock whatever to the credit of the banks or to the commercial community. Before we entirely discontinue receiving bank paper, more than four years will have elapsed. All this time will be allowed for the banks and merchants to adapt their business to the new system contemplated and to conform their business to the new state of things. It will give time for the State legislatures to regulate their banking institutions, so as, in future, to prevent over-issues of paper; to restrain them from generating, or encouraging, a spirit of over-trading and inordinate speculation; to restrain them from making promises they cannot redeem, thus restoring to the country a sound circulating medium, the just equilibrium of trade, and business of every description.

III—77

Moreover, we ourselves shall have time to see how the new system works,—to check its velocity, if it be too great—or accelerate it, if it be too slow; and modify it, in all respects, as its results may indicate to be safe and expedient. As already shown, no change in the description of funds, receivable for public dues, will take place for the next fifteen months; for the year 1839, a reduction of one-fourth; for 1840, one-half may be paid in specie-paying bank paper; and so on to the consummation of the plan. If it be discovered that the policy operates injuriously, there will be ample time to amend or modify it.

But, sir, I have no apprehension that any injurious result will follow the adoption of this measure. The chief embarrassments of the community have arisen out of inordinate expansions of the circulating medium, excessive accommodations, begetting extravagance, and reckless speculations; and then sudden contractions, withdrawals of those enormous loans, reductions of the amount of circulation, and thus, almost in a moment, reducing the value of property one-third, sometimes one-half. The government deposits have, doubtless, heretofore, nurtured and increased this propensity of all banks to excessive issues and accommodations. They have loaned out the public money as if their own, and when called upon to pay it over, they have been necessarily compelled to press and coerce payments from their borrowers, who had, in their turn, treated this borrowed money as their own; and have thus occasioned embarrassment, the sacrifice of property, and, in too many instances, the impoverishment and ruin of their customers. To illustrate the correctness of these remarks, I need only refer you to the greater pecuniary distress and embarrassment of communities around any of the banks, which have been large depositaries of the public money, compared with those remote from such institutions. If they have no large sums of public money on general deposit, on which to grant accommodations, they will know and understand better the proper limits to prescribe to their liberality; they will have no fluctuations, no augmentations, no diminutions of capital to mislead them; their accommodations will be more uniform, and the amount of their circulation bear some relation to the amount of specie in their vaults. This being brought about, the value of produce, and property of all descriptions, will be more steady and uniform; we shall not have a negro, costing a thousand or fifteen hundred dollars to-day, sold twelve months hence to pay

half the amount of consideration—land at one time worth fifty dollars per acre, at another not more than twenty—and our great staple one while commanding twenty-five dollars, and then not worth eight.

Sir, the Government ought always to be able to command its funds and have them ever ready to meet any exigency. Experience has taught us that this cannot be expected while we rely on banks. Gentlemen tell us that, although the State banks have failed to meet our expectations, we ought to continue their agency. They ask us, would we discontinue the use of steamboats, because a boiler may sometimes explode and produce fatal results? By no means, sir, while care and skill may reasonably be expected to insure safety and prevent such calamities. But, were we to discover that the machinery is entirely uncontrollable, and the boiler liable to spontaneous combustion,—carrying universal misery and death among the passengers and crew, in despite of all the science, vigilance, and fidelity of the engineer, —would it be wise or prudent to trust ourselves on board? What would have been the situation of the country in May last, when the banks suspended specie payments, had we been involved in war with some powerful foreign enemy? Whatever might have been the emergency, we should not have been able to have commanded the resources of the nation. We might have been without a dollar for the pay or subsistence of an army to resist the invaders; our energies would have been crippled; and the most disastrous consequences might have followed. When we find that such is the unfortunate tendency of "the experiment," as gentlemen choose to call it, it is time we should abandon it, by whomsoever instituted or approved heretofore.

But, sir, was not the Bank of the United States an "experiment," and has not that also failed to answer just expectation? No other government but our own ever did employ such a fiscal agent, with powers of the same magnitude. It was, indeed, a fearful experiment, and well nigh fatal in its results. Yet, the recharter of the late United States Bank, or the establishment of a new one, is now announced as the only efficient remedy—the sovereign panacea—for existing evils. The Senator from Kentucky [Mr. Clay] has, to my astonishment, gone so far as to identify the establishment of such an institution with the permanency of the Union! It would seem the question of a national bank is always portentous—involving consequences of a most

alarming character. Shortly after the removal of the deposits from the late Bank of the United States, we were told, by the same distinguished gentleman, that we were then "in the midst of a revolution!" and the sentiment was responded to, by the presses and politicians of the opposition, from one end of the Union to the other. We were told, on the very floors of Congress, that the deposits must be restored, or a revolution was at hand. The same sentiment was announced, when two Members of Congress, during the same panic session, addressed an assembled multitude in Baltimore on Sunday. According to the newspapers of the day, it was said, by way of justification, "There were no Sabbaths in Revolutionary times!" Sir, the subject of a National or United States Bank cannot be touched without an attempt to produce excitement and agitation. It affords one of the most conclusive reasons against the establishment of such an institution, that it has the ability to produce such tremendous effects. The concentration of such an immense moneyed power in the hands of a few individuals is at war with our peace and quiet; too dangerous to our liberties. It would soon control all our elections, from the highest to the lowest, and direct the operations, nay, usurp the powers, of the Government itself.

HENRY CLAY

(1777–1852)

HENRY CLAY was born in Hanover County, Virginia, April 12th, 1777. He was called the "Mill Boy of the Slashes" by his political admirers, but he never really felt himself a member of the class at the South which produced Crockett in Tennessee and Lincoln in Kentucky. His family was poor and his early education was defective, but his reading in law and in general literature gave him the remarkable grasp of fact which co-operated with some undefined power of controlling language melodiously, to give him his great reputation as an orator. It has been said that his power as an orator lay so largely in the musical tones of his voice that his speeches are "not worth reading," but this is a radical mistake. A few of them are dull, and in none of them is there the systematic art which marshals every idea towards a final climax. Mr. Clay's climax is as apt to come in the middle of his speech as it is anywhere else; and after it is reached, it does strain the attention to go on following him through arguments on a lower plane than that to which he himself had elevated the mind. But when this is admitted, it still remains true that his best orations and hundreds of pages of others which are not his best easily command attention and excite warm admiration. He was greater as a statesman and political manager than he was as an orator, if oratory is to be judged by those severe classical standards of which he knew nothing. But he was eloquent by nature, a man of multitudinous ideas, of what Taine calls "thronging imaginations," with a poetical sense of the beautiful and with a musician's ear for the harmonies of language. The same training as a linguist which gave Erskine his sense of the order in language might have made Clay the greatest orator of modern times. If, as Macaulay and Choate agree, that honor belongs to Edmund Burke, it is nevertheless certain that Clay will always be studied and admired as one of the greatest of those great orators whose eloquence, if it did not give them a permanent supremacy in history, made them pre-eminent in their own generations, with an influence reaching far into the generations after them.

From the Compromise of 1850 until the close of the first two decades after the Civil War, it was not possible for justice to be done the fundamental idea Clay and Webster represented in their efforts

to maintain the Union without bloodshed. Perhaps it is not possible yet, but it is no longer possible to hear Webster called a traitor to liberty in New England, or Clay denounced as a coward at the South. Both believed that there was no necessity whatever for Americans to fight each other, and that every issue it was possible to imagine could be settled better by evolution and the slow processes of intellectual and moral development than it could possibly be by force. Both held to the doctrine of nonintervention and *laissez faire*, by which they meant that they were bound to trust the innate good in human nature to work out reforms and to insure continuous progress without violent attempts to accelerate it. This theory grew in popularity in England and America during the first quarter of the nineteenth century, but the Crimean War impaired its influence in England — while our own Civil War so weakened it that for nearly a generation it has been too much out of the public mind to be taken into general consideration as an explanation of the course followed by Clay and Webster in what have been denounced as their compromises of principle. In fact, compromise was with them a principle rather than a method. Those who hold that if the world is made freer it will become better; that they do most for progress who do most to keep the peace; that a policy of co-operation between neighboring States and countries without the "intervention" of one to correct the domestic abuses of the other, is the only mode of insuring evolutionary and steady development, necessarily believe in the continuous concessions which their theory forces, even when the question is not merely of the weakness but of the actual crimes of others beyond their jurisdiction.

The opponents of this idea in America asserted the jurisdiction of every man born into the world to interfere wherever wrong was perpetrated against weakness. "Are we not our brother's keeper?" they said, summing up their creed in the question.

The issue between two theories so antagonistic is not likely soon to be decided, but it must be understood before Clay's place in American history can be determined. From the time of the first Missouri Compromise, of which he has been called the chief designer, to the compromise tariff of 1833, and again up to the Compromise of 1850 and his death, Clay strove always to impress on the country his own governing idea that Americans of all sections were bound to tolerate each other in their mutual sins of ignorance, of lack of development, and of slowness to improve. Webster held with him, but in New England Webster was finally denounced as a renegade, and only a short time before the death of Clay, Mr. Jefferson Davis, listening to his pleas for the postponement of the crisis, concluded that it was cowardly for one generation to unload its responsibilities on the next, instead of meeting them at once.

It is seldom desirable to attempt a judgment of what events might have been had they been what they were not, but nothing which has occurred or is likely to occur can permanently obscure the fact that the great Americans who believed in the slow processes of growth were not mere cowards vacillating in the presence of every crisis, but were consistent followers of an ideal. Perhaps Clay was too consistent when his habit of compromising public questions led him to commit himself against himself in his presidential canvasses as he did when he lost the vote of New York and the Presidency by a partial recession from his position of resistance to war with Mexico. But it is hardly to be expected that a man who had in him so little of bitterness, so much of the genial, the tolerant, the charitable, as Clay had, could force any issue radically.

The ideas for which he stood as a constructive statesman were the use of all the powers of the Federal Government for internal improvements without being too strict in searching out constitutional objections; and after developing the internal trade of the country thus, to hold it against Europe, to give it commercial control of the hemisphere and, by excluding European products, to stimulate "competition in the home market." This he called "the American system," and his policy of supporting the South American countries against Europe seemed to him to be a part of it. He was, however, fundamentally opposed to coercive government where coercion could be avoided, and his denunciations of Andrew Jackson were the result of inherent intellectual tendencies, not of the mere prejudices created by rivalry. Clay believed in Republican institutions, but he believed government should be intrusted largely to those who shave regularly, bathe habitually, and do not ordinarily "expectorate" on the floor in public places. This made him the fit leader as it made him the idol of the "gentleman's party," and naturally enough it brought him into the strongest antagonism with Jackson who was accused by his enemies of smoking a corncob pipe, of sitting with his feet on the mantel, and of being a headstrong and violent advocate of the theory that "every one who did not interfere with his (Jackson's) own plans ought to be allowed the fullest liberty to interfere with those of other people." There was little of *laissez faire* in the policies of the man who hanged Arbuthnot and Ambruster first and considered the lawpoints involved afterwards. He came into collision with Clay as logically as he did with Calhoun and Webster. However else these three remarkable men differed, they agreed in detesting the theory of government which Jackson represented as a leader of what it is said Miss Nelly Custis once called the "dirty Democracy." It is fortunate for the reader that it is possible to see the element of humor in such antagonisms as this. Otherwise, such lives

as those of Clay and Webster, closing with the country on the verge of war and ending in what seemed complete failure, might seem sadder than they really were. For it is not yet demonstrated that they really did fail or that those who force radical issues to immediate settlement are more successful in improving the world than those who hold what Clay proclaimed and Webster practiced.

Clay entered national politics as United States Senator from Kentucky in 1806. After serving until 1807, he retired, and returned for another year of service in 1810. He was elected to the House of Representatives in 1811, and served, with an intermission of two years, until 1825. During twelve years of this period he was Speaker of the House. His candidacy for the Presidency in 1824 was followed by his acceptance of the Secretaryship of the State under John Quincy Adams and his long quarrel with Jackson, whose supporters accused him of a corrupt bargain with Adams, by which they alleged that their favorite was cheated out of the Presidency. From that period until his death Mr. Clay was charged with being, and probably was, continuously a candidate for the Presidency. In 1832, and again in 1844, he was the nominee of the Whig party, defeated, as some have said, by his own disposition to compromise, rather than by the inherent weakness of his party. He died in the city of Washington, June 29th, 1852, after being more enthusiastically admired in all sections of the Union than any other American had been since the time of Washington.

W. V. B.

DICTATORS IN AMERICAN POLITICS

(Denouncing Andrew Jackson, Delivered in the United States Senate on the Poindexter Resolution, April 30th, 1834)

NEVER, Mr. President, have I known or read of an administration which expires with so much agony, and so little composure and resignation, as that which now unfortunately has the control of public affairs in this country. It exhibits a state of mind, feverish, fretful, and fidgety, bounding recklessly from one desperate expedient to another, without any sober or settled purpose. Ever since the dog days of last summer, it has been making a succession of the most extravagant plunges, of which the extraordinary cabinet paper, a sort of appeal from a dissenting cabinet to the people, was the first; and the protest, a direct appeal from the Senate to the people, is the last and the worst.

A new philosophy has sprung up within a few years past, called Phrenology. There is, I believe, something in it, but not quite as much as its ardent followers proclaim. According to its doctrines, the leading passion, propensity, and characteristics of every man are developed in his physical conformation, chiefly in the structure of his head. Gall and Spurzheim, its founders, or most eminent propagators, being dead, I regret that neither of them can examine the head of our illustrious chief magistrate. But, if it could be surveyed by Dr. Caldwell, of Transylvania University, I am persuaded that he would find the organ of destructiveness prominently developed. Except an enormous fabric of executive power for himself, the President has built up nothing, constructed nothing, and will leave no enduring monument of his administration. He goes for destruction, universal destruction; and it seems to be his greatest ambition to efface and obliterate every trace of the wisdom of his predecessors. He has displayed this remarkable trait throughout his whole life, whether in private walks or in the public service. He signally and gloriously exhibited that peculiar organ when contending against the enemies of his country in the battle of New Orleans. For that brilliant exploit, no one has ever been more ready than myself to award him all due honor. At the head of our armies was his appropriate position, and most unfortunate for his fame was the day when he entered on the career of administration as the chief executive officer. He lives by excitement, perpetual, agitating excitement, and would die in a state of perfect repose and tranquillity. He has never been without some subject of attack, either in individuals, or in masses, or in institutions. I, myself, have been one of his favorites, and I do not know but that I have recently recommended myself to his special regard. During his administration this has been his constant course. The Indians and Indian policy, internal improvements, the colonial trade, the Supreme Court, Congress, the bank, have successively experienced the attacks of his haughty and imperious spirit. And if he tramples the bank in the dust, my word for it, we shall see him quickly in chase of some new subject of his vengeance. This is the genuine spirit of conquerors and of conquest. It is said by the biographer of Alexander the Great, that, after he had completed his Asiatic conquests, he seemed to sigh because there were no more worlds for him to subdue; and, finding himself without further employment for his valor or his

arms, he turned within himself to search the means to gratify his insatiable thirst of glory. What sort of conquest he achieved of himself, the same biographer tragically records.

Already has the President singled out and designated, in the Senate of the United States, the new object of his hostile pursuit; and the protest, which I am now to consider, is his declaration of war. What has provoked it? The Senate, a component part of the Congress of the United States, at its last adjournment left the Treasury of the United States in the safe custody of the persons and places assigned by law to keep it. Upon reassembling, it found the treasure removed; some of its guardians displaced; all, remaining, brought under the immediate control of the President's sole will; and the President having free and unobstructed access to the public money. The Senate believes that the purse of the nation is, by the Constitution and laws, intrusted to the exclusive legislative care of Congress. It has dared to avow and express this opinion, in a resolution adopted on the twenty-eighth of March last. That resolution was preceded by a debate of three months' duration, in the progress of which the able and zealous supporters of the Executive in the Senate were attentively heard. Every argument which their ample resources, or those of the members of the Executive, could supply was listened to with respect, and duly weighed. After full deliberation, the Senate expressed its conviction that the Executive had violated the Constitution and laws. It cautiously refrained, in the resolution, from all examination into the motives or intention of the Executive; it ascribed no bad ones to him; it restricted itself to a simple declaration of its solemn belief that the Constitution and laws had been violated. This is the extent of the offense of the Senate. This is what it has done to excite the Executive indignation and to bring upon it the infliction of a denunciatory protest.

The President comes down upon the Senate and demands that it record upon its journal this protest. He recommends no measure—no legislation whatever. He proposes no Executive proceeding on the part of the Senate. He requests the recording of his protest, and he requests nothing more nor less. The Senate has abstained from putting on its own record any vindication of the resolution of which the President complains. It has not asked of him to place it, where he says he has put his protest, in the archives of the Executive. He desires, therefore,

to be done for him, on the journal of the Senate, what has not been done for itself. The Senate keeps no recording office for protests, deeds, wills, or other instruments. The Constitution enjoins that "each House shall keep a journal of its proceedings." In conformity with this requirement, the Senate does keep a journal of its proceedings—not the proceedings of the Executive, or any other department of the government, except so far as they relate directly to the business of the Senate. The President sometimes professes to favor a strict construction of the Constitution, at least in regard to the powers of all the departments of the government other than that of which he is the chief. As to that, he is the greatest latitudinarian that has ever filled the office of President. Upon any fair construction of the Constitution, how can the Senate be called upon to record upon its journal any proceedings but its own? It is true that the ordinary messages of the President are usually inserted at large in the journal. Strictly speaking, it perhaps ought never to have been done; but they have been heretofore registered, because they relate to the general business of the Senate, either in its legislative or executive character, and have been the basis of subsequent proceedings. The protest stands upon totally distinct ground.

The President professes to consider himself as charged by the resolution with "the high crime of violating the laws and Constitution of my country." He declares that "one of the most important branches of the Government, in its official capacity, in a public manner, and by its recorded sentence, but without precedent, competent authority, or just cause, declares him guilty of a breach of the laws and Constitution." The protest further alleges that such an act as the Constitution describes "constitutes a high crime,—one of the highest, indeed, which the President can commit,—a crime which justly exposes him to an impeachment by the House of Representatives; and, upon due conviction, to removal from office, and to the complete and immutable disfranchisement prescribed by the Constitution." It also asserts: "The resolution, then, was an impeachment of the President, and in its passage amounts to a declaration by a majority of the Senate, that he is guilty of an impeachable offense." The President is also of opinion that to say that the resolution does not expressly allege that the assumption of power and authority which it condemns was intentional and corrupt, is

no answer to the preceding view of its character and effect. The act thus condemned necessarily implies volition and design in the individual to whom it is imputed; and, being lawful in its character, the legal conclusion is, that it was prompted by improper motives and committed with an unlawful intent." . . . "The President of the United States, therefore, has been, by a majority of his constitutional triers, accused and found guilty of an impeachable offense."

Such are the deliberate views, entertained by the President, of the implications, effects, and consequences of the resolution. It is scarcely necessary to say that they are totally different from any which were entertained by the Senate, or by the mover of the resolution. The Senate carefully abstained from looking into the quo animo, from all examination into the motives or intention with which the violation of the Constitution and laws was made. No one knows those motives and intentions better than the President himself. If he chooses to supply the omission of the resolution, if he thinks proper to pronounce his own self-condemnation, his guilt does not flow from what the Senate has done, but from his own avowal. Having cautiously avoided passing upon his guilt by prejudgment, so neither ought his acquittal to be pronounced by anticipation.

But, I would ask, in what tone, temper, and spirit does the President come to the Senate? As a great State culprit who has been arraigned at the bar of justice, or sentenced as guilty? Does he manifest any of those compunctious visitings of conscience which a guilty violator of the constitution and laws of the land ought to feel? Does he address himself to a high court with the respect, to say nothing of humility, which a person accused or convicted would naturally feel? No, no. He comes as if the Senate were guilty, as if he were in the judgment seat, and the Senate stood accused before him. He arraigns the Senate; puts it upon trial; condemns it; he comes as if he felt himself elevated far above the Senate, and beyond all reach of the law, surrounded by unapproachable impunity. He who professes to be an innocent and injured man gravely accuses the Senate, and modestly asks it to put upon its own record his sentence of condemnation! When before did the arraigned or convicted party demand of the court which was to try, or had condemned him, to enter upon their records a severe denunciation of their own conduct? The President presents himself before the Senate, not in the garb of suffering innocence, but in imperial and royal costume — as a dictator, to rebuke a refractory Senate; to command it to record his solemn protest; to chastise it for disobedience.

> « The hearts of princes kiss obedience,
> So much they love it; but to stubborn spirits
> They swell, and grow as terrible as storms. »

We shall better comprehend the nature of the request which the President has made of the Senate, by referring to his own opinions expressed in the protest. He says that the resolution is a recorded sentence, « but without precedent, just cause, or competent authority. » He « is perfectly convinced that the discussion and passage of the above-mentioned resolutions were not only unauthorized by the Constitution, but in many respects repugnant to its provisions, and subversive of the rights secured by it to other co-ordinate departments. » We had no right, it seems, then, even to discuss, much less express any opinion, on the President's proceedings encroaching upon our constitutional powers. And what right had the President to look at all into our discussions ? What becomes of the constitutional provision which, speaking of Congress, declares, « for any speech or debate in either house, they shall not be questioned in any other place » ?

The President thinks « the resolution of the Senate is wholly unauthorized by the Constitution, and in derogation of its entire spirit. » He proclaims that the passage, recording, and promulgation of the resolution affixes guilt and disgrace to the President, « in a manner unauthorized by the Constitution. » But, says the President, if the Senate had just cause to entertain the belief that the House of Representatives would not impeach him, that cannot justify « the assumption by the Senate of powers not conferred by the Constitution. » The protest continues: « It is only necessary to look at the condition in which the Senate and the President have been placed by this proceeding, to perceive its utter incompatibility with the provisions and the spirit of the Constitution, and with the plainest dictates of humanity and justice. » A majority of the Senate assume the function which belongs to the House of Representatives, and « convert themselves into accusers, witnesses, counsel, and judges, and prejudge the whole case. » If the House of Representatives shall consider

that there is no cause of impeachment, and prefer none, « then will the violation of privilege as it respects that House, of justice as it regards the President, and of the Constitution as it relates to both, be more conspicuous and impressive. » The Senate is charged with the « unconstitutional power of arraigning and censuring the official conduct of the Executive. » The people, says the protest, will be compelled to adopt the conclusion, « either that the Chief Magistrate was unworthy of their respect, or that the Senate was chargeable with calumny and injustice. » There can be no doubt which branch of this alternative was intended to be applied. The President throughout the protest labors to prove himself worthy of all respect from the people. Finally, the President says: « It is due to the high trust with which I have been charged, to those who may be called to succeed me in it, to the representatives of the people whose constitutional prerogative has been unlawfully assumed, to the people and to the States, and to the Constitution they have established, that I should not permit its provisions to be broken down by such an attack on the Executive department, without at least some effort ' to preserve, protect, and defend them.' »

These are the opinions which the President expresses in the protest, of the conduct of the Senate. In every form, and every variety of expression, he accuses it of violating the express language and spirit of the Constitution; of encroaching not only on his prerogatives, but those of the House of Representatives; of forgetting the sacred character and impartiality which belong to the highest court of justice in the Union; of injustice, of inhumanity, and of calumny. And we are politely requested to spread upon our own journal these opinions entertained of us by the President, that they may be perpetually preserved and handed down to posterity! The President respectfully requests it! He might as well have come to us and respectfully requested us to allow him to pull our noses, or kick us, or receive his stripes upon our backs. The degradation would not have been much more humiliating.

The President tells us, in the same protest, that any breach or violation of the Constitution and laws draws after it, and necessarily implies, volition and design, and that the legal conclusion is that it was prompted by improper motives and committed with an unlawful intent. He pronounces, therefore, that the Senate, in the violations of the Constitution which he deliberately

imputes to it, is guilty; that volition and design, on the part of the Senate, are necessarily implied; and that the legal conclusion is that the Senate was prompted by improper motives, and committed the violation with an unlawful intent. And he most respectfully and kindly solicits the Senate to overleap the restraint of the Constitution, which limits its journal to the record of its own proceedings, and place alongside of them his sentence of condemnation of the Senate.

That the President did not intend to make the journal of the Senate a medium of conveying his sentiments to the people is manifest. He knows perfectly well how to address to them his appeals. And the remarkable fact is established, by his private secretary, that, simultaneously with the transmission to the Senate of his protest, a duplicate was transmitted to the Globe, his official paper, for publication; and it was forthwith published accordingly. For what purpose, then, was it sent here ? It is painful to avow the belief, but one is compelled to think it was only sent in a spirit of insult and defiance.

The President is not content with vindicating his own rights. He steps forward to maintain the privileges of the House of Representatives also. Why? Was it to make the House his ally, and to excite its indignation against the offending Senate ? Is not the House perfectly competent to sustain its own privileges against every assault ? I should like to see, sir, a resolution introduced into the House, alleging a breach of its privileges by a resolution of the Senate, which was intended to maintain unviolated the constitutional rights of both houses in regard to the public purse, and to be present at its discussion.

The President exhibits great irritation and impatience at the presumptuousness of a resolution, which, without the imputation of any bad intention or design, ventures to allege that he has violated the Constitution and Laws. His constitutional and official infallibility must not be questioned. To controvert it is an act of injustice, inhumanity, and calumny. He is treated as a criminal, and, without summons, he is prejudged, condemned, and sentenced. Is the President scrupulously careful of the memory of the dead, or the feelings of the living, in respect to violations of the Constitution ? If a violation by him implies criminal guilt, a violation by them cannot be innocent and guiltless. And how has the President treated the memory of the immortal Father of his Country ? that great man, who, for purity of pur-

pose and character, wisdom and moderation, unsullied virtue and unsurpassed patriotism, is without competition in past history or among living men, and whose equal we scarcely dare hope will ever be again presented as a blessing to mankind. How has he been treated by the President? Has he not again and again pronounced that, by approving the bill chartering the first Bank of the United States, Washington violated the Constitution of his country? That violation, according to the President, included volition and design, was prompted by improper motives, and was committed with an unlawful intent. It was the more inexcusable in Washington, because he assisted and presided in the convention which formed the Constitution. If it be unjust to arraign, try unheard, and condemn as guilty, a living man filling an exalted office, with all the splendor, power, and influence which that office possesses, how much more cruel is it to disturb the sacred and venerated ashes of the illustrious dead, who can raise no voice and make no protests against the imputation of high crime!

What has been the treatment of the President towards that other illustrious man, yet spared to us, but who is lingering upon the very verge of eternity? Has he abstained from charging the Father of the Constitution with criminal intent in violating the Constitution? Mr. Madison, like Washington, assisted in the formation of the Constitution; was one of its ablest expounders and advocates; and was opposed, on constitutional ground, to the first Bank of the United States. But, yielding to the force of circumstances, and especially to the great principle, that the peace and stability of human society require that a controverted question, which has been finally settled by all the departments of Government by long acquiescence, and by the people themselves, should not be open to perpetual dispute and disturbance, he approved the bill chartering the present Bank of the United States. Even the name of James Madison, which is but another for purity, patriotism, profound learning, and enlightened experience, cannot escape the imputations of his present successor.

And, lastly, how often has he charged Congress itself with open violations of the Constitution? Times almost without number. During the present session he has sent in a message, in regard to the land bill, in which he has charged it with an undisguised violation. A violation so palpable, that it is not even disguised, and must, therefore, necessarily imply a criminal intent. Sir, the advisers of the President, whoever they are, deceive him and themselves. They have vainly supposed that, by an appeal to the people, and an exhibition of the wounds of the President, they could enlist the sympathies and the commiseration of the people—that the name of Andrew Jackson would bear down the Senate and all opposition. They have yet to learn, what they will soon learn, that even a good and responsible name may be used so frequently, as an indorser, that its credit and the public confidence in its solidity have been seriously impaired. They mistake the intelligence of the people, who are not prepared to see and sanction the President putting forth indiscriminate charges of a violation of the Constitution against whomsoever he pleases, and exhibiting unmeasured rage and indignation, when his own infallibility is dared to be questioned.

ON THE EXPUNGING RESOLUTIONS

(Peroration of the Speech of January 16th, 1837, Delivered in the United States Senate Against Andrew Jackson)

Mr. President:—

WHAT patriotic purpose is to be accomplished by this Expunging resolution? What new honor or fresh laurels will it win for our common country? Is the power of the Senate so vast that it ought to be circumscribed, and that of the President so restricted that it ought to be extended? What power has the Senate? None, separately. It can only act jointly with the other House, or jointly with the Executive. And although the theory of the Constitution supposes, when consulted by him, it may freely give an affirmative or negative response, according to the practice, as it now exists, it has lost the faculty of pronouncing the negative monosyllable. When the Senate expresses its deliberate judgment, in the form of resolution, that resolution has no compulsory force, but appeals only to the dispassionate intelligence, the calm reason, and the sober judgment, of the community. The Senate has no army, no navy, no patronage, no lucrative offices, no glittering honors, to bestow. Around us there is no swarm of greedy expectants, rendering us homage, anticipating our wishes, and ready to execute our commands.

How is it with the President? Is he powerless? He is felt from one extremity to the other of this vast republic. By means of principles which he has introduced, and innovations which he has made in our institutions, alas! but too much countenanced by Congress and a confiding people, he exercises, uncontrolled, the power of the State. In one hand he holds the purse, and in the other brandishes the sword of the country. Myriads of dependants and partisans, scattered over the land, are ever ready to sing hosannas to him, and to laud to the skies whatever he does. He has swept over the Government, during the last eight years, like a tropical tornado. Every department exhibits traces of the ravages of the storm. Take as one example the Bank of the United States. No institution could have been more popular with the people, with Congress, and with State Legislatures. None ever better fulfilled the great purposes of its establishment. But it unfortunately incurred the displeasure of the President; he spoke, and the bank lies prostrate. And those who were loudest in its praise are now loudest in its condemnation. What object of his ambition is unsatisfied? When disabled from age any longer to hold the sceptre of power, he designates his successor, and transmits it to his favorite! What more does he want? Must we blot, deface, and mutilate the records of the country, to punish the presumptuousness of expressing an opinion contrary to his own?

What patriotic purpose is to be accomplished by this Expunging resolution? Can you make that not to be which has been? Can you eradicate from memory and from history the fact that in March 1834 a majority of the Senate of the United States passed the resolution which excites your enmity? Is it your vain and wicked object to arrogate to yourselves that power of annihilating the past which has been denied to Omnipotence itself? Do you intend to thrust your hands into our hearts, and to pluck out the deeply rooted convictions which are there? Or is it your design merely to stigmatize us? You cannot stigmatize us.

«Ne'er yet did base dishonor blur our name.»

Standing securely upon our conscious rectitude, and bearing aloft the shield of the Constitution of our country, your puny efforts are impotent; and we defy all your power. Put the majority of 1834 in one scale, and that by which this Expunging

resolution is to be carried in the other, and let truth and justice, in heaven above and on earth below, and liberty and patriotism, decide the preponderance.

What patriotic purpose is to be accomplished by this Expunging resolution? Is it to appease the wrath and to heal the wounded pride of the Chief Magistrate? If he be really the hero that his friends represent him, he must despise all mean condescension, all groveling sycophancy, all self-degradation and self-abasement. He would reject, with scorn and contempt, as unworthy of his fame, your black scratches and your baby lines in the fair records of his country. Black lines! Black lines! Sir, I hope the Secretary of the Senate will preserve the pen with which he may inscribe them, and present it to that Senator of the majority whom he may select, as a proud trophy, to be transmitted to his descendants. And hereafter, when we shall lose the forms of our free institutions, all that now remain to us, some future American monarch, in gratitude to those by whose means he has been enabled, upon the ruins of civil liberty, to erect a throne, and to commemorate especially this Expunging resolution, may institute a new order of knighthood, and confer on it the appropriate name of «the Knights of the Black Lines.»

But why should I detain the Senate, or needlessly waste my breath in fruitless exertions? The decree has gone forth. It is one of urgency, too. The deed is to be done—that foul deed which, like the blood, staining the hands of the guilty Macbeth, all ocean's waters will never wash out. Proceed, then, to the noble work which lies before you, and, like other skillful executioners do it quickly. And when you have perpetrated it, go home to the people, and tell them what glorious honors you have achieved for our common country. Tell them that you have extinguished one of the brightest and purest lights that ever burned at the altar of civil liberty. Tell them that you have silenced one of the noblest batteries that ever thundered in defense of the Constitution, and bravely spiked the cannon. Tell them that, henceforward, no matter what daring or outrageous act any President may perform, you have forever hermetically sealed the mouth of the Senate. Tell them that he may fearlessly assume what powers he pleases, snatch from its lawful custody the public purse, command a military detachment to enter the halls of the Capitol, overawe Congress, trample down the Constitution, and raze every bulwark of freedom; but that the Senate must stand

mute, in silent submission, and not dare to raise its opposing voice. Tell them that it must wait until a House of Representatives, humbled and subdued like itself, and a majority of it composed of the partisans of the President, shall prefer articles of impeachment. Tell them, finally, that you have restored the glorious doctrine of passive obedience and nonresistance. And, if the people do not pour out their indignation and imprecations, I have yet to learn the character of American freemen.

ON THE SEMINOLE WAR

(From the Speech of January 19th, 1819, in the House of Representatives)

IF my recollection does not deceive me, Bonaparte had passed the Rhine and the Alps, had conquered Italy, the Netherlands, Holland, Hanover, Lubec, and Hamburg, and extended his empire as far as Altona, on the side of Denmark. A few days' march would have carried him through Holstein, over the two Belts, through Funen, and into the island of Zealand. What, then, was the conduct of England? It was my lot to fall into conversation with an intelligent Englishman on this subject. «We knew [said he] that we were fighting for our existence. It was absolutely necessary that we should preserve the command of the seas. If the fleet of Denmark fell into the enemy's hands, combined with his other fleets, that command might be rendered doubtful. Denmark had only a nominal independence. She was, in truth, subject to his sway. We said to her, Give us your fleet; it will otherwise be taken possession of by your secret and our open enemy. We will preserve it and restore it to you whenever the danger shall be over. Denmark refused. Copenhagen was bombarded, and gallantly defended, but the fleet was seized.» Everywhere the conduct of England was censured; and the name even of the negotiator who was employed by her, who was subsequently the minister near this Government, was scarcely ever pronounced here without coupling with it an epithet indicating his participation in the disgraceful transaction. And yet we are going to sanction acts of violence, committed by ourselves, which but too much resemble it! What an important difference, too, between the relative condition of England and of this country! She, perhaps, was struggling for her existence. She was combating, single-handed, the most enormous military power that the world has ever known. With whom were we contending? With a few half-starved, half-clothed, wretched Indians and fugitive slaves. And while carrying on this inglorious war, inglorious as it regards the laurels or renown won in it, we violate neutral rights, which the government had solemnly pledged itself to respect, upon the principle of convenience, or upon the light presumption that, by possibility, a post might be taken by this miserable combination of Indians and slaves.

.   .   .   .

I will not trespass much longer upon the time of the committee; but I trust I shall be indulged with some few reflections upon the danger of permitting the conduct on which it has been my painful duty to animadvert, to pass without the solemn expression of the disapprobation of this House. Recall to your recollection the free nations which have gone before us. Where are they now?

> « Gone glimmering through the dream of things that were,
> A schoolboy's tale, the wonder of an hour. »

And how have they lost their liberties? If we could transport ourselves back to the ages when Greece and Rome flourished in their greatest prosperity, and, mingling in the throng, should ask a Grecian if he did not fear that some daring military chieftain, covered with glory, some Philip or Alexander, would one day overthrow the liberties of his country, the confident and indignant Grecian would exclaim, No! no! we have nothing to fear from our heroes; our liberties will be eternal. If a Roman citizen had been asked if he did not fear that the conqueror of Gaul might establish a throne upon the ruins of public liberty, he would have instantly repelled the unjust insinuation. Yet Greece fell; Cæsar passed the Rubicon, and the patriotic arm even of Brutus could not preserve the liberties of his devoted country! The celebrated Madame de Staël, in her last and perhaps her best work, has said, that in the very year, almost the very month, when the president of the Directory declared that monarchy would never more show its frightful head in France, Bonaparte, with his grenadiers, entered the palace of St. Cloud, and dispersing with the bayonet the deputies of the people deliberating on the affairs of the State, laid the foundation of that vast fabric of despotism which overshadowed all Europe. I hope not to be misunderstood; I am far from intimating that General Jackson cherishes

any designs inimical to the liberties of the country. I believe his intentions to be pure and patriotic. I thank God that he would not, but I thank him still more that he could not if he would, overturn the liberties of the Republic. But precedents, if bad, are fraught with the most dangerous consequences. Man has been described, by some of those who have treated of his nature, as a bundle of habits. The definition is much truer when applied to governments. Precedents are their habits. There is one important difference between the formation of habits by an individual and by governments. He contracts only after frequent repetition. A single instance fixes the habit and determines the direction of governments. Against the alarming doctrine of unlimited discretion in our military commanders when applied even to prisoners of war, I must enter my protest. It begins upon them; it will end on us. I hope our happy form of government is to be perpetual. But, if it is to be preserved, it must be by the practice of virtue, by justice, by moderation, by magnanimity, by greatness of soul, by keeping a watchful and steady eye on the executive; and, above all, by holding to a strict accountability the military branch of the public force.

We are fighting a great moral battle for the benefit not only of our country, but of all mankind. The eyes of the whole world are in fixed attention upon us. One, and the largest portion of it, is gazing with contempt, with jealousy, and with envy; the other portion, with hope, with confidence, and with affection. Everywhere the black cloud of legitimacy is suspended over the world, save only one bright spot, which breaks out from the political hemisphere of the west, to enlighten and animate and gladden the human heart. Obscure that by the downfall of liberty here, and all mankind are enshrouded in a pall of universal darkness. To you, Mr. Chairman, belongs the high privilege of transmitting, unimpaired, to posterity the fair character and liberty of our country. Do you expect to execute this high trust by trampling, or suffering to be trampled down, law, justice, the Constitution, and the rights of the people? by exhibiting examples of inhumanity and cruelty and ambition? When the minions of despotism heard, in Europe, of the seizure of Pensacola, how did they chuckle, and chide the admirers of our institutions, tauntingly pointing to the demonstration of a spirit of injustice and aggrandizement made by our country, in the midst of an amicable negotiation! Behold, said they, the conduct of those

who are constantly reproaching kings! You saw how those admirers were astounded and hung their heads. You saw, too, when that illustrious man, who presides over us, adopted his pacific, moderate, and just course, how they once more lifted up their heads with exultation and delight beaming in their countenances. And you saw how those minions themselves were finally compelled to unite in the general praises bestowed upon our government. Beware how you forfeit this exalted character. Beware how you give a fatal sanction, in this infant period of our Republic, scarcely yet two-score years old, to military insubordination. Remember that Greece had her Alexander, Rome her Cæsar, England her Cromwell, France her Bonaparte, and that if we would escape the rock on which they split we must avoid their errors.

How different has been the treatment of General Jackson and that modest, but heroic young man, a native of one of the smallest States in the Union, who achieved for his country, on Lake Erie, one of the most glorious victories of the late war. In a moment of passion he forgot himself and offered an act of violence which was repented of as soon as perpetrated. He was tried, and suffered the judgment to be pronounced by his peers. Public justice was thought not even then to be satisfied. The press and Congress took up the subject. My honorable friend from Virginia, Mr. Johnson, the faithful and consistent sentinel of the law and of the Constitution, disapproved in that instance, as he does in this, and moved an inquiry. The public mind remained agitated and unappeased until the recent atonement so honorably made by the gallant commodore. And is there to be a distinction between the officers of the two branches of the public service? Are former services, however eminent, to preclude even inquiry into recent misconduct? Is there to be no limit, no prudential bounds to the national gratitude? I am not disposed to censure the President for not ordering a court of inquiry, or a general court-martial. Perhaps, impelled by a sense of gratitude, he determined, by anticipation, to extend to the general that pardon which he had the undoubted right to grant after sentence. Let us not shrink from our duty. Let us assert our constitutional powers, and vindicate the instrument from military violation.

I hope gentlemen will deliberately survey the awful isthmus on which we stand. They may bear down all opposition; they

may even vote the general the public thanks; they may carry him triumphantly through this House. But, if they do, in my humble judgment, it will be a triumph of the principle of insubordination, a triumph of the military over the civil authority, a triumph over the powers of this House, a triumph over the Constitution of the land. And I pray most devoutly to Heaven that it may not prove, in its ultimate effects and consequences, a triumph over the liberties of the people.

THE EMANCIPATION OF SOUTH AMERICA

(From the Speech Delivered March 24th, 1818, in the House of Representatives)

I RISE under feelings of deeper regret than I have ever experienced on any former occasion, inspired principally by the consideration that I find myself, on the proposition which I meant to submit, differing from many highly esteemed friends, in and out of this House, for whose judgment I entertained the greatest respect. A knowledge of this circumstance has induced me to pause; to subject my own convictions to the severest scrutiny, and to revolve the question over and over again. But all my reflections have conducted me to the same clear result; and, much as I value those friends, great as my deference is for their opinions, I cannot hesitate, when reduced to the distressing alternative of conforming my judgment to theirs, or pursuing the deliberate and mature dictates of my own mind. I enjoy some consolation for the want of their co-operation, from the persuasion that, if I err on this occasion, I err on the side of the liberty and happiness of a large portion of the human family. Another, and, if possible, indeed a greater source of the regret to which I refer is the utter incompetency which I unfeignedly feel to do anything like adequate justice to the great cause of American independence and freedom, whose interests I wish to promote by my humble exertions in this instance. Exhausted and worn down as I am, by the fatigue, confinement, and incessant application incident to the arduous duties of the honorable station I hold, during a four months' session, I shall need all that kind indulgence which has been so often extended to me by the House.

I beg, in the first place, to correct misconceptions, if any exist, in regard to my opinions. I am averse to war with Spain, or with any power. I would give no just cause of war to any power — not to Spain herself. I have seen enough of war, and of its calamities, even when successful. No country on earth has more interest than this in cultivating peace and avoiding war, as long as it is possible honorably to avoid it. Gaining additional strength every day; our numbers doubling in periods of twenty-five years; with an income outstripping all our estimates, and so great, as, after a war in some respects disastrous, to furnish results which carry astonishment, if not dismay, into the bosom of States jealous of our rising importance; we have every motive for the love of peace. I cannot, however, approve in all respects of the manner in which our negotiations with Spain have been conducted. If ever a favorable time existed for the demand, on the part of an injured nation, of indemnity for past wrongs from the aggressor, such is the present time. Impoverished and exhausted at home, by the wars which have desolated the peninsula; with a foreign war, calling for infinitely more resources, in men and money, than she can possibly command; this is the auspicious period for insisting upon justice at her hands in a firm and decided tone. Time is precisely what Spain now wants. Yet what are we told by the President, in his message at the commencement of Congress? That Spain has procrastinated, and we acquiesced in her procrastination. And the Secretary of State, in a late communication with Mr. Onis, after ably vindicating all our rights, tells the Spanish minister, with a good deal of sang-froid, that we had patiently waited thirteen years for a redress of our injuries, and that it required no great effort to wait longer. I would have abstained from thus exposing our intentions. Avoiding the use of the language of menace, I would have required, in temperate and decided terms, indemnity for all our wrongs; for the spoliations of our commerce; for the interruption for the right of depot at New Orleans, guaranteed by treaty; for the insults repeatedly offered to our flag; for the Indian hostilities, which she was bound to prevent; for belligerent use of her ports and territories by our enemy during the late war; and the instantaneous liberation of the free citizens of the United States, now imprisoned in her jails. Contemporaneously with that demand, without waiting for her final answer, and with a view to the favorable operation on her councils in regard to our own peculiar interests, as well as in justice to the cause itself, I would recognize any established government in Spanish

America. I would have left Spain to draw her own inferences from these proceedings as to the ultimate step which this country might adopt if she longer withheld justice from us. And if she persevered in her iniquity, after we had conducted the negotiation in the manner I have endeavored to describe, I would then take up and decide the solemn question of peace or war, with the advantage of all the light shed upon it, by subsequent events, and the probable conduct of Europe.

Spain has undoubtedly given us abundant and just cause for war. But it is not every cause of war that should lead to war. War is one of those dreadful scourges that so shakes the foundation of society, overturns or changes the character of governments, interrupts or destroys the pursuits of private happiness, brings, in short, misery and wretchedness in so many forms, and at last is, in its issue, so doubtful and hazardous, that nothing but dire necessity can justify an appeal to arms. If we are to have war with Spain, I have, however, no hesitation in saying that no mode of bringing it about could be less fortunate than that of seizing, at this time, upon her adjoining province. There was a time, under certain circumstances, when we might have occupied East Florida with safety; had we then taken it, our posture in the negotiation with Spain would have been totally different from what it is. But we have permitted that time, not with my consent, to pass by unimproved. If we were now to seize upon Florida, after a great change in those circumstances, and after declaring our intention to acquiesce in the procrastination desired by Spain, in what light should we be viewed by foreign powers, particularly Great Britain? We have already been accused of inordinate ambition, and of seeking to aggrandize ourselves by an extension, on all sides, of our limits. Should we not, by such an act of violence, give color to the accusation? No, Mr. Chairman; if we are to be involved in a war with Spain, let us have the credit of disinterestedness. Let us put her yet more in the wrong. Let us command the respect which is never withheld from those who act a noble and generous part. I hope to communicate to the committee the conviction which I so strongly feel, that the adoption of the amendment which I intend to propose would not hazard, in the slightest degree, the peace of the country. But if that peace is to be endangered, I would infinitely rather it should be for our exerting the right appertaining to every State, of acknowledging the independence

of another State, than for the seizure of a province, which, sooner or later, we must acquire.

In contemplating the great struggle in which Spanish America is now engaged, our attention is fixed first by the immensity and character of the country which Spain seeks again to subjugate. Stretching on the Pacific Ocean from about the fortieth degree of north latitude to about the fifty-fifth degree of south latitude, and extending from the mouth of the Rio del Norte (exclusive of East Florida), around the Gulf of Mexico and along the South Atlantic to near Cape Horn, it is about five thousand miles in length, and in some places nearly three thousand in breadth. Within this vast region we behold the most sublime and interesting objects of creation, the richest mines of the precious metals, and the choicest productions of the earth. We behold there a spectacle still more interesting and sublime — the glorious spectacle of eighteen millions of people struggling to burst their chains and to be free. When we take a little nearer and more detailed view, we perceive that nature has, as it were, ordained that this people and this country shall ultimately constitute several different nations. Leaving the United States on the north, we come to New Spain, or the viceroyalty of Mexico on the south; passing by Guatemala, we reach the viceroyalty of New Grenada, the late captain-generalship of Venezuela, and Guiana, lying on the east side of the Andes. Stepping over the Brazils, we arrive at the united provinces of La Plata, and crossing the Andes we find Chili on their west side, and, further north, the viceroyalty of Lima, or Peru. Each of these several parts is sufficient in itself in point of limits to constitute a powerful state; and, in point of population, that which has the smallest contains enough to make it respectable. Throughout all the extent of that great portion of the world which I have attempted thus hastily to describe, the spirit of revolt against the dominion of Spain has manifested itself. The revolution has been attended with various degrees of success in the several parts of Spanish America. In some it has been already crowned, as I shall endeavor to show, with complete success, and in all I am persuaded that independence has struck such deep root, that the power of Spain can never eradicate it. What are the causes of this great movement?

Three hundred years ago, upon the ruins of the thrones of Montezuma and the Incas of Peru, Spain erected the most

stupendous system of colonial despotism that the world has ever seen — the most vigorous, the most exclusive. The great principle and object of this system have been to render one of the largest portions of the world exclusively subservient, in all its faculties, to the interests of an inconsiderable spot in Europe. To effectuate this aim of her policy, she locked up Spanish America from all the rest of the world, and prohibited, under the severest penalties, any foreigner from entering any part of it. To keep the natives themselves ignorant of each other, and of the strength and resources of the several parts of her American possessions, she next prohibited the inhabitants of one viceroyalty or government from visiting those of another; so that the inhabitants of Mexico, for example, were not allowed to enter the viceroyalty of New Grenada. The agriculture of those vast regions was so regulated and restrained as to prevent all collision with the agriculture of the peninsula. Where nature, by the character and composition of the soil, has commanded, the abominable system of Spain has forbidden, the growth of certain articles. Thus the olive and the vine, to which Spanish America is so well adapted, are prohibited, wherever their culture can interfere with the olive and the vine of the peninsula. The commerce of the country, in the direction and objects of the exports and imports, is also subjected to the narrow and selfish views of Spain, and fettered by the odious spirit of monopoly, existing in Cadiz. She has sought, by scattering discord among the several castes of her American population, and by a debasing course of education, to perpetuate her oppression. Whatever concerns public law, or the science of government, all writings upon political economy, or that tend to give vigor and freedom and expansion to the intellect, are prohibited. Gentlemen would be astonished by the long list of distinguished authors, whom she proscribes, to be found in Depon's and other works. A main feature in her policy is that which constantly elevates the European and depresses the American character. Out of upwards of seven hundred and fifty viceroys and captains-general, whom she has appointed since the conquest of America, about eighteen only have been from the body of her American population. On all occasions, she seeks to raise and promote her European subjects, and to degrade and humiliate the Creoles. Wherever in America her sway extends, everything seems to pine and wither beneath its baneful influence. The richest regions of the earth; man, his happiness and his education, all the fine faculties of his soul, are regulated and modified and molded to suit the execrable purposes of an inexorable despotism.

Such is the brief and imperfect picture of the state of things in Spanish America, in 1808, when the famous transactions of Bayonne occurred. The King of Spain and the Indies (for Spanish America has always constituted an integral part of the Spanish empire) abdicated his throne and became a voluntary captive. Even at this day one does not know whether he should most condemn the baseness and perfidy of the one party, or despise the meanness and imbecility of the other. If the obligation of obedience and allegiance existed on the part of the colonies to the King of Spain, it was founded on the duty of protection which he owed them. By disqualifying himself for the performance of this duty, they became released from that obligation. The monarchy was dissolved, and each integral part had a right to seek its own happiness by the institution of any new government adapted to its wants. Joseph Bonaparte, the successor *de facto* of Ferdinand, recognized this right on the part of the colonies, and recommended them to establish their independence. Thus, upon the ground of strict right; upon the footing of a mere legal question, governed by forensic rules, the colonies, being absolved by the acts of the parent country from the duty of subjection to it, had an indisputable right to set up for themselves. But I take a broader and a bolder position. I maintain that an oppressed people are authorized, whenever they can, to rise and break their fetters. This was the great principle of the English revolution. It was the great principle of our own. Vattel, if authority were wanting, expressly supports this right. We must pass sentence of condemnation upon the founders of our liberty, say that they were rebels, traitors, and that we are at this moment legislating without competent powers, before we can condemn the cause of Spanish America. Our revolution was mainly directed against the mere theory of tyranny. We had suffered but comparatively little; we had, in some respects, been kindly treated; but our intrepid and intelligent fathers saw, in the usurpation of the power to levy an inconsiderable tax, the long train of oppressive acts that were to follow. They rose; they breasted the storm; they achieved our freedom. Spanish America for centuries has been doomed to the practical effects of an odious tyranny. If we were justified, she is more than justified.

I am no propagandist. I would not seek to force upon other nations our principles and our liberty, if they do not want them. I would not disturb the repose even of a detestable despotism. But, if an abused and oppressed people will their freedom; if they seek to establish it; we have a right, as a sovereign power, to notice the fact and to act as circumstances and our interest require. I will say, in the language of the venerated father of my country, "born in a land of liberty, my anxious recollections, my sympathetic feelings, and my best wishes, are irresistibly excited, whensoever, in any country, I see an oppressed nation unfurl the banners of freedom." Whenever I think of Spanish America, the image irresistibly forces itself upon my mind, of an elder brother, whose education has been neglected, whose person has been abused and maltreated, and who has been disinherited by the unkindness of an unnatural parent. And, when I contemplate the glorious struggle which that country is now making, I think I behold that brother rising, by the power and energy of his fine native genius, to the manly rank which nature, and nature's God, intended for him. . . .

In the establishment of the independence of Spanish America, the United States have the deepest interest. I have no hesitation in asserting my firm belief that there is no question in the foreign policy of this country, which has ever arisen, or which I can conceive as ever occurring, in the decision of which we have had or can have so much at stake. This interest concerns our politics, our commerce, our navigation. There cannot be a doubt that Spanish America, once independent, whatever may be the form of government established in its several parts, these governments will be animated by an American feeling, and guided by an American policy. They will obey the laws of the system of the new world, of which they will compose a part, in contradistinction to that of Europe. Without the influence of that vortex in Europe, the balance of power between its several parts, the preservation of which has so often drenched Europe in blood, America is sufficiently remote to contemplate the new wars which are to afflict that quarter of the globe, as a calm if not a cold and indifferent spectator. In relation to those wars, the several parts of America will generally stand neutral. And as, during the period when they rage, it will be important that a liberal system of neutrality should be adopted and observed, all America will be interested in maintaining and enforcing such a

system. The independence of Spanish America, then, is an interest of primary consideration. Next to that, and highly important in itself, is the consideration of the nature of their governments. That is a question, however, for themselves. They will, no doubt, adopt those kinds of governments which are best suited to their condition, best calculated for their happiness. Anxious as I am that they should be free governments, we have no right to prescribe for them. They are, and ought to be, the sole judges for themselves. I am strongly inclined to believe that they will in most, if not all parts of their country, establish free governments. We are their great example. Of us they constantly speak as of brothers, having a similar origin. They adopt our principles, copy our institutions, and, in many instances, employ the very language and sentiments of our revolutionary papers:

"Having then been thus impelled by the Spaniards and their king, we have calculated all the consequences, and have constituted ourselves independent, prepared to exercise the right of nature to defend ourselves against the ravages of tyranny, at the risk of our honor, our lives, and fortune. We have sworn to the only King we acknowledge, the supreme judge of the world, that we will not abandon the cause of justice; that we will not suffer the country which he has given us, to be buried in ruins, and inundated with blood, by the hands of the executioner, etc."

But it is sometimes said that they are too ignorant and too superstitious to admit of the existence of free government. This charge of ignorance is often urged by persons themselves actually ignorant of the real condition of that people. I deny the alleged fact of ignorance; I deny the inference from that fact, if it were true, that they want capacity for free government. And I refuse assent to the further conclusion if the fact were true, and the inference just, that we are to be indifferent to their fate. All the writers of the most established authority, Depons, Humboldt, and others, concur in assigning to the people of Spanish America great quickness, genius, and particular aptitude for the acquisition of the exact sciences, and others which they have been allowed to cultivate. In astronomy, geology, mineralogy, chemistry, botany, and so forth, they are allowed to make distinguished proficiency. They justly boast of their Abzate, Velasques, and Gama, and other illustrious contributors to science.

They have nine universities, and in the City of Mexico, it is affirmed by Humboldt, there are more solid scientific establishments than in any city even of North America. I would refer to the message of the supreme director of La Plata, which I shall hereafter have occasion to use for another purpose, as a model of fine composition of a State paper, challenging a comparison with any, the most celebrated, that ever issued from the pens of Jefferson or Madison. Gentlemen will egregiously err, if they form their opinions of the present condition of Spanish America from what it was under the debasing system of Spain. The eight years' revolution in which it has been engaged has already produced a powerful effect. Education has been attended to, and genius developed.

"As soon as the project of the revolution arose on the shores of the La Plata, genius and talent exhibited their influence; the capacity of the people became manifest, and the means of acquiring knowledge were soon made the favorite pursuit of the youth. As far as the wants or the inevitable interruption of affairs were allowed, everything has been done to disseminate useful information. The liberty of the press has indeed met with some occasional checks; but in Buenos Ayres alone, as many periodical works weekly issue from the press as in Spain and Portugal put together."

It is not therefore true, that the imputed ignorance exists; but, if it do, I repeat, I dispute the inference. It is the doctrine of thrones, that man is too ignorant to govern himself. Their partisans assert his incapacity, in reference to all nations; if they cannot command universal assent to the proposition, it is then demanded to particular nations; and our pride and our presumption too often make converts of us. I contend, that it is to arraign the dispositions of Providence himself, to suppose that he has created beings incapable of governing themselves, and to be trampled on by kings. Self-government is the natural government of man, and for proof I refer to the aborigines of our own land. Were I to speculate in hypotheses unfavorable to human liberty, my speculations should be founded rather upon the vices, refinements, or density of population. Crowded together in compact masses, even if they were philosophers, the contagion of the passions is communicated and caught, and the effect too often, I admit, is the overthrow of liberty. Dispersed over such an immense space as that on which the people of

Spanish America are spread, their physical, and I believe also their moral condition, both favor their liberty.

With regard to their superstition, they worship the same God with us. Their prayers are offered up in their temples to the same Redeemer whose intercession we expect to save us. Nor is there anything in the Catholic religion unfavorable to freedom. All religions united with government are more or less inimical to liberty. All, separated from government, are compatible with liberty. If the people of Spanish America have not already gone as far in religious toleration as we have, the difference in their condition from ours should not be forgotten. Everything is progressive; and, in time, I hope to see them imitating in this respect our example. But grant that the people of Spanish America are ignorant and incompetent for free government, to whom is that ignorance to be ascribed? Is it not to the execrable system of Spain, which she seeks again to establish and to perpetuate? So far from chilling our hearts, it ought to increase our solicitude for our unfortunate brethren. It ought to animate us to desire the redemption of the minds and the bodies of unborn millions from the brutifying effects of a system whose tendency is to stifle the faculties of the soul and to degrade man to the level of beasts. I would invoke the spirits of our departed fathers. Was it for yourselves only that you nobly fought? No, no! It was the chains that were forging for your posterity that made you fly to arms, and, scattering the elements of these chains to the winds, you transmitted to us the rich inheritance of liberty.

"THE AMERICAN SYSTEM" AND THE HOME MARKET

(Delivered in the United States Senate, February 2d, 1832 — Given by Benton as an Unabridged Report)

EIGHT years ago it was my painful duty to present to the House of Congress an unexaggerated picture of the general distress pervading the whole land. We must all yet remember some of its frightful features. We all know that the people were then oppressed and borne down by an enormous load of debt; that the value of property was at the lowest point of depression; that ruinous sales and sacrifices were everywhere made of real estate; that stop laws and relief laws and paper

IV—79

money were adopted to save the people from impending destruction; that a deficit in the public revenue existed, which compelled the Government to seize upon, and divert from its legitimate object, the appropriation to the sinking fund, to redeem the national debt; and that our commerce and navigation were threatened with a complete paralysis. In short, sir, if I were to select any term of seven years since the adoption of the present Constitution, which exhibited a scene of the most widespread dismay and desolation, it would be exactly that term of seven years which immediately preceded the establishment of the tariff of 1824.

I have now to perform the more pleasing task of exhibiting an imperfect sketch of the existing state of the unparalleled prosperity of the country. On a general survey, we behold cultivation extended, the arts flourishing, the face of the country improved, our people fully and profitably employed, and the public countenance exhibiting tranquillity, contentment, and happiness. And, if we descend into particulars, we have the agreeable contemplation of a people out of debt; land rising slowly in value, but in a secure and salutary degree; a ready, though not extravagant market for all the surplus productions of our industry; innumerable flocks and herds browsing and gamboling on ten thousand hills and plains, covered with rich and verdant grasses; our cities expanded, and whole villages springing up, as it were, by enchantment; our exports and imports increased and increasing; our tonnage, foreign and coastwise, swelling and fully occupied; the rivers of our interior animated by the perpetual thunder and lightning of countless steamboats; the currency sound and abundant; the public debt of two wars nearly redeemed; and, to crown all, the public treasury overflowing, embarrassing Congress, not to find subjects of taxation, but to select the objects which shall be liberated from the impost. If the term of seven years were to be selected of the greatest prosperity which this people have enjoyed since the establishment of their present Constitution, it would be exactly that period of seven years which immediately followed the passage of the tariff of 1824.

This transformation of the condition of the country from gloom and distress to brightness and prosperity has been mainly the work of American legislation, fostering American industry, instead of allowing it to be controlled by foreign legislation, cher-

ishing foreign industry. The foes of the American system, in 1824, with great boldness and confidence, predicted: 1st. The ruin of the public revenue, and the creation of a necessity to resort to direct taxation. The gentleman from South Carolina [Mr. Hayne], I believe, thought that the tariff of 1824 would operate a reduction of revenue to the large amount of eight millions of dollars. 2d. The destruction of our navigation. 3d. The desolation of commercial cities. And 4th. The augmentation of the price of objects of consumption, and further decline in that of the articles of our exports. Every prediction which they made has failed — utterly failed. Instead of the ruin of the public revenue, with which they then sought to deter us from the adoption of the American system, we are now threatened with its subversion, by the vast amount of the public revenue produced by that system. Every branch of our navigation has increased. As to the desolation of our cities, let us take, as an example, the condition of the largest and most commercial of all of them, the great northern capital. I have in my hands the assessed value of real estate in the city of New York, from 1817 to 1831. This value is canvassed, contested, scrutinized, and adjudged, by the proper sworn authorities. It is, therefore, entitled to full credence. During the first term, commencing with 1817, and ending in the year of the passage of the tariff of 1824, the amount of the value of real estate was, the first year, $57,799,435, and, after various fluctuations in the intermediate period, it settled down at $52,019,730, exhibiting a decrease, in seven years, of $5,779,705. During the year 1825, after the passage of the tariff, it rose, and, gradually ascending throughout the whole of the latter period of seven years, it finally, in 1831, reached the astonishing height of $95,716,485! Now, if it be said that this rapid growth of the city of New York was the effect of foreign commerce, then it was not correctly predicted, in 1824, that the tariff would destroy foreign commerce and desolate our commercial cities. If, on the contrary, it be the effect of internal trade, then internal trade cannot be justly chargeable with the evil consequences imputed to it. The truth is, it is the joint effect of both principles, the domestic industry nourishing the foreign trade, and the foreign commerce, in turn, nourishing the domestic industry. Nowhere more than in New York is the combination of both principles so completely developed. In the progress of my argument I will consider the effect upon the

price of commodities produced by the American system, and show that the very reverse of the prediction of its foes, in 1824, has actually happened.

Whilst thus we behold the entire failure of all that was foretold against the system, it is a subject of just felicitation to its friends, that all their anticipations of its benefits have been fulfilled, or are in progress of fulfillment. The honorable gentleman from South Carolina has made allusion to a speech made by me, in 1824, in the other house, in support of the tariff, and to which, otherwise, I should not have particularly referred. But I would ask any one, who could now command the courage to peruse that long production, what principle there laid down is not true? what prediction then made has been falsified by practical experience?

It is now proposed to abolish the system to which we owe so much of the public prosperity, and it is urged that the arrival of the period of the redemption of the public debt has been confidently looked to as presenting a suitable occasion to rid the country of the evils with which the system is alleged to be fraught. Not an inattentive observer of passing events, I have been aware that, among those who were most eagerly pressing the payment of the public debt, and, upon that ground, were opposing appropriations to other great interests, there were some who cared less about the debt than the accomplishment of other objects. But the people of the United States have not coupled the payment of their public debt with the destruction of the protection of their industry, against foreign laws and foreign industry. They have been accustomed to regard the extinction of the public debt as relief from a burden, and not as the infliction of a curse. If it is to be attended or followed by the subversion of the American system, and the exposure of our establishments and our productions to the unguarded consequences of the selfish policy of foreign powers, the payment of the public debt will be the bitterest of curses. Its fruit will be like the fruit

> "Of that forbidden tree, whose mortal taste
> Brought death into the world, and all our woe,
> With loss of Eden."

If the system of protection be founded on principles erroneous in theory, pernicious in practice — above all, if it be unconstitutional, as is alleged, it ought to be forthwith abolished, and not a vestige of it suffered to remain. But, before we sanction this sweeping denunciation, let us look a little at this system, its magnitude, its ramifications, its duration, and the high authorities which have sustained it. We shall see that its foes will have accomplished comparatively nothing, after having achieved their present aim of breaking down our iron foundries, our woolen, cotton, and hemp manufactories, and our sugar plantations. The destruction of these would undoubtedly lead to the sacrifice of immense capital, the ruin of many thousands of our fellow-citizens, and incalculable loss to the whole community. But their prostration would not disfigure, nor produce greater effect upon the whole system of protection, in all its branches, than the destruction of the beautiful domes upon the capitol would occasion to the magnificent edifice which they surmount. Why, sir, there is scarcely an interest, scarcely a vocation in society, which is not embraced by the beneficence of this system.

It comprehends our coasting tonnage and trade, from which all foreign tonnage is absolutely excluded.

It includes all our foreign tonnage, with the inconsiderable exception made by treaties of reciprocity with a few foreign powers.

It embraces our fisheries and all our hardy and enterprising fishermen.

It extends to all lower Louisiana, the delta of which might as well be submerged again in the Gulf of Mexico, from which it has been a gradual conquest, as now to be deprived of the protecting duty upon its great staple.

It affects the cotton planter himself, and the tobacco planter, both of whom enjoy protection.

Such are some of the items of this vast system of protection, which it is now proposed to abandon. We might well pause and contemplate, if human imagination could conceive the extent of mischief and ruin from its total overthrow, before we proceed to the work of destruction. Its duration is worthy, also, of serious consideration. Not to go behind the Constitution, its date is coeval with that instrument. It began on the ever-memorable fourth day of July—the fourth day of July, 1789. The second act which stands recorded in the statute book, bearing the illustrious signature of George Washington, laid the corner stone of the whole system. That there might be no mistake about the matter, it was then solemnly proclaimed to the American people

and to the world, that it was necessary, for "the encouragement and protection of manufactures," that duties should be laid. It is in vain to urge the small amount of the measure of protection then extended. The great principle was then established by the fathers of the Constitution, with the Father of his Country at their head. And it cannot now be questioned, that, if the Government had not then been new and the subject untried, a greater measure of protection would have been applied, if it had been supposed necessary. Shortly after, the master minds of Jefferson and Hamilton were brought to act on this interesting subject. Taking views of it appertaining to the departments of Foreign Affairs and of the Treasury, which they respectively filled, they presented, severally, reports which yet remain monuments of their profound wisdom, and came to the same conclusion of protection to American industry. Mr. Jefferson argued that foreign restrictions, foreign prohibitions, and foreign high duties, ought to be met, at home, by American restrictions, American prohibitions, and American high duties. Mr. Hamilton, surveying the entire ground, and looking at the inherent nature of the subject, treated it with an ability which, if ever equaled, has not been surpassed, and earnestly recommended protection.

The subject of the American system was again brought up in 1820, by the bill reported by the Chairman of the Committee on Manufactures, now a member of the bench of the Supreme Court of the United States, and the principle was successfully maintained by the representatives of the people; but the bill which they passed was defeated in the Senate. It was received in 1824, the whole ground carefully and deliberately explored, and the bill then introduced, receiving all the sanctions of the Constitution, became the law of the land. An amendment of the system was proposed in 1828, to the history of which I refer with no agreeable recollections. The bill of that year, in some of its provisions, was framed on principles directly adverse to the declared wishes of the friends of the policy of protection. I have heard (without vouching for the fact) that it was so framed, upon the advice of a prominent citizen, now abroad, with the view of ultimately defeating the bill, and with assurances that, being altogether unacceptable to the friends of the American system, the bill would be lost. Be that as it may, the most exceptional features of the bill were stamped upon it, against the earnest remonstrances of the friends of the system,

by the votes of Southern members, upon a principle, I think, as unsound in legislation as it is reprehensible in ethics. The bill was passed, notwithstanding it having been deemed better to take the bad along with the good which it contained than reject it altogether. Subsequent legislation has corrected very much the error then perpetrated, but still that measure is vehemently denounced by gentlemen who contributed to make it what it was.

Thus, sir, has this great system of protection been gradually built, stone upon stone, and step by step, from the fourth of July, 1789, down to the present period. In every stage of its progress it has received the deliberate sanction of Congress. A vast majority of the people of the United States has approved, and continues to approve it. Every Chief Magistrate of the United States, from Washington to the present, in some form or other, has given to it the authority of his name; and, however the opinions of the existing President are interpreted south of Mason and Dixon's Line, on the north they are, at least, understood to favor the establishment of a judicious tariff.

The question, therefore, which we are now called upon to determine is not whether we shall establish a new and doubtful system of policy, just proposed, and for the first time presented to our consideration, but whether we shall break down and destroy a long-established system, patiently and carefully built up, and sanctioned, during a series of years, again and again by the nation and its highest and most revered authorities. And are we not bound deliberately to consider whether we can proceed to this work of destruction without a violation of the public faith? The people of the United States have justly supposed that the policy of protecting their industry against foreign legislation and foreign industry was fully settled, not by a single act, but by repeated and deliberate acts of government performed at distant and frequent intervals. In full confidence that the policy was firmly and unchangeably fixed, thousands upon thousands have invested their capital, purchased a vast amount of real and other estate, made permanent establishments, and accommodated their industry. Can we expose to utter and irretrievable ruin this countless multitude without justly incurring the reproach of violating the national faith?

I shall not discuss the constitutional question. Without meaning any disrespect to those who raise it, if it be debatable, it has

been sufficiently debated. The gentleman from South Carolina suffered it to fall unnoticed from his budget; and it was not until after he had closed his speech and resumed his seat that it occurred to him that he had forgotten it, when he again addressed the Senate, and, by a sort of protestation against any conclusion from his silence, put forward the objection. The recent Free Trade Convention at Philadelphia, it is well known, were divided on the question; and although the topic is noticed in their address to the public, they do not avow their own belief that the American system is unconstitutional, but represent that such is the opinion of respectable portions of the American people. Another address to the people of the United States, from a high source, during the past year, treating this subject, does not assert the opinion of the distinguished author, but states that of others to be that it is unconstitutional. From which I infer that he himself did not believe it unconstitutional.

[Here the Vice-President [Mr. Calhoun] interposed, and remarked that if the Senator from Kentucky alluded to him, he must say that his opinion was that the measure was unconstitutional.]

When, sir [said Mr. Clay] I contended with you, side by side, and with perhaps less zeal than you exhibited, in 1816; I did not understand you then to consider the policy forbidden by the Constitution.

[The Vice-President again interposed, and said that the constitutional question was not debated at that time, and that he had never expressed an opinion contrary to that now intimated.]

I give way with pleasure [said Mr. Clay] to these explanations, which I hope will always be made when I say anything bearing on the individual opinions of the Chair. I know the delicacy of the position, and sympathize with the incumbent, whoever he may be. It is true, the question was not debated in 1816; and why not? Because it was not debatable; it was then believed not fairly to arise. It never has been made as a distinct, substantial, and leading point of objection. It never was made until the discussion of the tariff of 1824, when it was rather hinted at, as against the spirit of the Constitution, than formally announced as being contrary to the provisions of that instrument. What was not dreamt of before, or in 1816, and scarcely thought of in 1824, is now made by excited imaginations to assume the imposing form of a serious constitutional barrier.

And now, Mr. President, I have to make a few observations on a delicate subject, which I approach with all the respect that is due to its serious and grave nature. They have not, indeed, been rendered necessary by the speech of the gentleman from South Carolina, whose forbearance to notice the topic was commendable, as his argument throughout was characterized by an ability and dignity worthy of him and of the Senate. The gentleman made one declaration which might possibly be misinterpreted, and I submit to him whether an explanation of it be not proper. The declaration, as reported in his printed speech, is: "The instinct of self-interest might have taught us an easier way of relieving ourselves from this oppression. It wanted but the will to have supplied ourselves with every article embraced in the protective system, free of duty, without any other participation on our part than a simple consent to receive them."

[Here Mr. Hayne rose, and remarked that the passages which immediately preceded and followed the paragraph cited, he thought, plainly indicated his meaning, which related to evasions of the system by illicit introduction of goods, which they were not disposed to countenance in South Carolina.]

I am happy to hear this explanation. But, sir, it is impossible to conceal from our view the facts that there is great excitement in South Carolina; that the protective system is openly and violently denounced in popular meetings; and that the legislature itself has declared its purpose of resorting to counteracting measures—a suspension of which has only been submitted to for the purpose of allowing Congress time to retrace its steps. With respect to this Union, Mr. President, the truth cannot be too generally proclaimed nor too strongly inculcated, that it is necessary to the whole and to all the parts—necessary to those parts, indeed, in different degrees, but vitally necessary to each; and that threats to disturb or dissolve it, coming from any of the parts, would be quite as indiscreet and improper as would be threats from the residue to exclude those parts from the pale of its benefits. The great principle which lies at the foundation of all free government is that the majority must govern; from which there is or can be no appeal but to the sword. That majority ought to govern wisely, equitably, moderately, and constitutionally, but govern it must, subject only to that terrible appeal. If ever one, or several States, being a minority, can, by menacing a dissolution of the Union, succeed in forming an abandonment of

great measures deemed essential to the interests and prosperity of the whole, the Union from that moment is practically gone. It may linger on in form and name, but its vital spirit has fled forever! Entertaining these deliberate opinions, I would entreat the patriotic people of South Carolina—the land of Marion, Sumter, and Pickens—of Rutledge, Laurens, the Pinckneys, and Lowndes—of living and present names, which I would mention if they were not living or present—to pause, solemnly pause! and contemplate the frightful precipice which lies directly before them. To retreat may be painful and mortifying to their gallantry and pride, but it is to retreat to the Union, to safety, and to those brethren with whom, or with whose ancestors, they, or their ancestors, have won on fields of glory imperishable renown. To advance is to rush on certain and inevitable disgrace and destruction.

We have been told of deserted castles, of uninhabited halls, and of mansions, once the seats of opulence and hospitality, now abandoned and moldering in ruins. I never had the honor of being in South Carolina; but I have heard and read of the stories of its chivalry, and of its generous and open-hearted liberality. I have heard, too, of the struggles for power between the lower and upper country. The same causes which existed in Virginia, with which I have been acquainted, I presume, have had their influence in Carolina. In whose hands now are the once proud seats of Westover, Curles, Maycocks, Shirley, and others, on James River, and in lower Virginia? Under the operation of laws abolishing the principle of primogeniture, and providing the equitable rule of an equal distribution of estates among those in equal degree of consanguinity, they have passed into other and stranger hands. Some of the descendants of illustrious families have gone to the far West, whilst others, lingering behind, have contrasted their present condition with that of their venerated ancestors. They behold themselves excluded from their fathers' houses, now in the hands of those who were once their fathers' overseers, or sinking into decay; their imaginations paint ancient renown, the fading honors of their name, glories gone by; too poor to live, too proud to work, too high-minded and honorable to resort to ignoble means of acquisition, brave, daring, chivalrous, what can be the cause of their present unhappy state? The "accursed tariff" presents itself to their excited imaginations, and they blindly rush into the ranks of those who,

unfurling the banner of nullification, would place a State upon its sovereignty!

The danger to our Union does not lie on the side of persistence in the American system, but on that of its abandonment. If, as I have supposed and believe, the inhabitants of all north and east of the James River, and all west of the mountains, including Louisiana, are deeply interested in the preservation of that system, would they be reconciled to its overthrow? Can it be expected that two-thirds, if not three-fourths, of the people of the United States would consent to the destruction of a policy believed to be indispensably necessary to their prosperity? When, too, this sacrifice is made at the instance of a single interest which they verily believe will not be promoted by it? In estimating the degree of peril which may be incident to two opposite courses of human policy, the statesman would be shortsighted who should content himself with viewing only the evils, real or imaginary, which belong to that course which is in practical operation. He should lift himself up to the contemplation of those greater and more certain dangers which might inevitably attend the adoption of the alternative course. What would be the condition of this Union, if Pennsylvania and New York, those mammoth members of our confederacy, were firmly persuaded that their industry was paralyzed and their prosperity blighted by the enforcement of the British colonial system, under the delusive name of free trade? They are now tranquil and happy and contented, conscious of their welfare, and feeling a salutary and rapid circulation of the products of home manufactures and home industry throughout all their great arteries. But let that be checked, let them feel that a foreign system is to predominate, and the sources of their subsistence and comfort dried up; let New England and the West and the Middle States all feel that they too are the victims of a mistaken policy, and let these vast portions of our country despair of any favorable change, and then, indeed, might we tremble for the continuance and safety of this Union!

IN FAVOR OF A PATERNAL POLICY OF INTERNAL IMPROVEMENTS

(From the Speech of January 16th, 1824, in the House of Representatives on the Cumberland Road)

IT is said by the President that the power to regulate commerce merely authorizes the laying of imposts and duties. But Congress has no power to lay imposts and duties on the trade among the several States. The grant must mean, therefore, something else. What is it? The power to regulate commerce among the several States, if it has any meaning, implies authority to foster it, to promote it, to bestow upon it facilities similar to those which have been conceded to our foreign trade. It cannot mean only an empty authority to adopt regulations, without the capacity to give practical effect to them. All the powers of this Government should be interpreted in reference to its first, its best, its greatest object, the union of these States. And is not that union best invigorated by an intimate social and commercial connection between all the parts of the confederacy? Can that be accomplished, that is, can the federative objects of this Government be attained but by the application of federative resources?

Of all the powers bestowed on this Government, I think none are more clearly vested than that to regulate the distribution of the intelligence, private and official, of the country; to regulate the distribution of its commerce; and to regulate the distribution of the physical force of the Union. In the execution of the high and solemn trust which these beneficial powers imply, we must look to the great ends which the framers of our admirable Constitution had in view. We must reject as wholly incompatible with their enlightened and beneficent intentions that construction of these powers which would resuscitate all the debility and inefficiency of the ancient confederacy. In the vicissitudes of human affairs who can foresee all the possible cases in which it may be necessary to apply the public force, within or without the Union? This Government is charged with the use of it to repel invasions, to suppress insurrections, to enforce the laws of the Union; in short for all the unknown and undefinable purposes of war, foreign or intestine, wherever and however it may rage. During its existence may not Government, for its effectual prosecution, order a road to be made, or a canal to be cut, to relieve, for example, an exposed point of the Union? If, when the emergency comes, there is a power to provide for it, that power must exist in the Constitution, and not in the emergency. A wise, precautionary, and parental policy, anticipating danger, will provide beforehand for the hour of need. Roads and canals are in the nature of fortifications, since, if not the deposits of military resources, they enable you to bring into rapid action the military resources of the country, whatever they may be. They are better than any fortifications, because they serve the double purposes of peace and war. They dispense, in a great degree, with fortifications, since they have all the effect of that concentration at which fortifications aim. I appeal from the precepts of the President to the practice of the President. While he denies to Congress the power in question, he does not scruple, upon his sole authority, as numerous instances in the statute book will testify, to order at pleasure the opening of roads by the military, and then come here to ask us to pay for them.

. . . .

But, Mr. Chairman, if there be any part of this Union more likely than all others to be benefited by the adoption of the gentleman's principle, regulating the public expenditure, it is the west. There is a perpetual drain from that embarrassed and highly distressed portion of our country, of its circulating medium to the east. There, but few and inconsiderable expenditures of the public money take place. There we have none of those public works, no magnificent edifices, forts, armories, arsenals, dockyards, etc., which more or less are to be found in every Atlantic State. In at least seven States beyond the Alleghany, not one solitary public work of this Government is to be found. If, by one of those awful and terrible dispensations of Providence, which sometimes occur, this Government should be unhappily annihilated, everywhere on the seaboard traces of its former existence would be found, whilst we should not have, in the west, a single monument remaining on which to pour out our affections and our regrets. Yet, sir, we do not complain. No portion of your population is more loyal to the Union than the hardy freemen of the west. Nothing can weaken or eradicate their ardent desire for its lasting preservation. None are more prompt to vindicate the interests and rights of the nation from all foreign aggression. Need I remind you of the glorious scenes in which

they participated, during the late war—a war in which they had no peculiar or direct interest, waged for no commerce, no seamen of theirs. But it was enough for them that it was a war demanded by the character and the honor of the nation. They did not stop to calculate its cost of blood, or of treasure. They flew to arms; they rushed down the valley of the Mississippi, with all the impetuosity of that noble river. They sought the enemy. They found him at the beach. They fought; they bled; they covered themselves and their country with immortal glory. They enthusiastically shared in all the transports occasioned by our victories, whether won on the ocean or on the land. They felt, with the keenest distress, whatever disaster befell us. No, sir, I repeat it, neglect, injury itself, cannot alienate the affections of the west from this government. They cling to it, as to their best, their greatest, their last hope. You may impoverish them, reduce them to ruin, by the mistakes of your policy, yet you cannot drive them from you. They do not complain of the expenditure of the public money, where the public exigencies require its disbursement. But, I put it to your candor, if you ought not, by a generous and national policy, to mitigate, if not prevent, the evils resulting from the perpetual transfer of the circulating medium from the west to the east. One million and a half of dollars annually is transferred for the public lands alone, and almost every dollar goes, like him who goes to death—to a bourne from which no traveler returns. In ten years it will amount to fifteen millions; in twenty to—but I will not pursue the appalling results of arithmetic. Gentlemen who believe that these vast sums are supplied by emigrants from the east labor under great error. There was a time when the tide of emigration from the east bore along with it the means to effect the purchase of the public domain. But that tide has, in a great measure, now stopped. And as population advances farther and farther west, it will entirely cease. The greatest migrating States in the Union, at this time, are Kentucky first, Ohio next, and Tennessee. The emigrants from those States carry with them, to the States and territories lying beyond them, the circulating medium, which, being invested in the purchase of the public land, is transmitted to the points where the wants of government require it. If this debilitating and exhausting process were inevitable, it must be borne with manly fortitude. But we think that a fit exertion of the powers of this

Government would mitigate the evil. We believe that the Government incontestably possesses the constitutional power to execute such internal improvements as are called for by the good of the whole. And we appeal to your equity, to your parental regard, to your enlightened policy, to perform the high and beneficial trust thus sacredly reposed. I am sensible of the delicacy of the topic to which I have reluctantly adverted, in consequence of the observations of the honorable gentleman from Virginia. And I hope there will be no misconception of my motives in dwelling upon it. A wise and considerate government should anticipate and prevent, rather than wait for the operation of causes of discontent.

Let me ask, Mr. Chairman, What has this Government done on the great subject of internal improvements, after so many years of its existence, and with such an inviting field before it? You have made the Cumberland road, only. Gentlemen appear to have considered that a western road. They ought to recollect that not one stone has yet been broken, not one spade of earth has yet been removed in any western State. The road begins in Maryland and it terminates at Wheeling. It passes through the States of Maryland, Pennsylvania, and Virginia. All the direct benefit of the expenditure of the public money on that road has accrued to those three States. Not one cent in any western State. And yet we have had to beg, entreat, supplicate you, session after session, to grant the necessary appropriations to complete the road. I myself have toiled until my powers have been exhausted and prostrated, to prevail on you to make the grant. We were actuated to make these exertions for the sake of the collateral benefit only to the west; that we might have a way by which we should be able to continue and maintain an affectionate intercourse with our friends and brethren; that we might have a way to reach the capital of our country, and to bring our counsels, humble as they may be, to consult and mingle with yours in the advancement of the national prosperity.

Yes, sir, the Cumberland road has only reached the margin of a western State; and, from some indications which have been given during this session, I should apprehend it would there pause forever, if my confidence in you were not unbounded, if I had not before witnessed that appeals were never unsuccessful to your justice, to your magnanimity, to your fraternal affection.

But, sir, the bill on your table is no western bill. It is emphatically a national bill, comprehending all, looking to the interests of the whole. The people of the west never thought of, never desired, never asked, for a system exclusively for their benefit. The system contemplated by this bill looks to great national objects, and proposes the ultimate application to their accomplishment of the only means by which they can be effected, the means of the nation—means which, if they be withheld from such objects, the Union, I do most solemnly believe, of these now happy and promising States, may, at some distant (I trust a far, far distant) day, be endangered and shaken at its centre.

FOR «FREE TRADE AND SEAMEN'S RIGHTS»

(From a Speech on the War of 1812. Delivered in the House of Representatives, January 8th, 1813)

NEXT to the notice which the opposition has found itself called upon to bestow upon the French Emperor, a distinguished citizen of Virginia, formerly President of the United States, has never for a moment failed to receive their kindest and most respectful attention. An honorable gentleman from Massachusetts, Mr. Quincy, of whom, I am sorry to say, it becomes necessary for me, in the course of my remarks, to take some notice, has alluded to him in a remarkable manner. Neither his retirement from public office, his eminent services, nor his advanced age, can exempt this patriot from the coarse assaults of party malevolence. No, sir, in 1801 he snatched from the rude hand of usurpation the violated Constitution of his country, and that is his crime. He preserved that instrument in form and substance and spirit, a precious inheritance for generations to come, and for this he can never be forgiven. How vain and impotent is party rage directed against such a man! He is not more elevated by his lofty residence upon the summit of his own favorite mountain than he is lifted, by the serenity of his mind and the consciousness of a well-spent life, above the malignant passions and bitter feelings of the day. No! his own beloved Monticello is not more moved by the storms that beat against its sides than is this illustrious man by the howlings of the whole British pack set loose from the Essex kennel! When the gentleman to whom

I have been compelled to allude shall have mingled his dust with that of his abused ancestors; when he shall have been consigned to oblivion, or, if he lives at all, shall live only in the treasonable annals of a certain junto, the name of Jefferson will be hailed with gratitude, his memory honored and cherished as the second founder of the liberties of the people, and the period of his administration will be looked back to, as one of the happiest and brightest epochs of American history—an oasis in the midst of a sandy desert. But I beg the gentleman's pardon; he has indeed secured to himself a more imperishable fame than I had supposed. I think it was about four years ago that he submitted to the House of Representatives an initiative proposition for an impeachment of Mr. Jefferson. The House condescended to consider it. The gentleman debated it with his usual temper, moderation, and urbanity. The House decided upon it in the most solemn manner, and, although the gentleman had somehow obtained a second, the final vote stood, one for, and one hundred and seventeen against the proposition! The same historic page that transmitted to posterity the virtue and the glory of Henry the Great of France, for their admiration and example, has preserved the infamous name of the fanatic assassin of that excellent monarch. The same sacred pen that portrayed the sufferings and crucifixion of the Savior of mankind has recorded, for universal execration, the name of him who was guilty, not of betraying his country, but (a kindred crime!) of betraying his God.

In one respect there is a remarkable difference between the administration and the opposition; it is in a sacred regard for personal liberty. When out of power my political friends condemned the surrender of Jonathan Robbins; they opposed the violation of the freedom of the press in the Sedition Law; they opposed the more insidious attack upon the freedom of the person under the imposing garb of an Alien Law. The party now in opposition, then in power, advocated the sacrifice of the unhappy Robbins, and passed those two laws. True to our principles, we are now struggling for the liberty of our seamen against foreign oppression. True to theirs, they oppose a war undertaken for this object. They have, indeed, lately affected a tender solicitude for the liberties of the people, and talk of the danger of standing armies and the burden of taxes. But it must be evident to you, Mr. Chairman, that they speak in a foreign idiom. Their brogue evinces that it is not their vernacular tongue. What! the oppo-

seamen; because she had instigated the Indians to commit hostilities against us; and because she refused indemnity for her past injuries upon our commerce. I throw out of the question other wrongs. The war in fact was announced, on our part, to meet the war which she was waging on her part. So undeniable were the causes of the war, so powerfully did they address themselves to the feelings of the whole American people, that when the bill was pending before this House, gentlemen in the opposition, although provoked to debate, would not, or could not, utter one syllable against it. . . .

We are told by gentlemen in the opposition that Government has not done all that was incumbent on it to do to avoid just cause of complaint on the part of Great Britain; that, in particular, the certificates of protection, authorized by the act of 1796, are fraudulently used. Sir, Government has done too much in granting those paper protections. I can never think of them without being shocked. They resemble the passes which the master grants to his negro slave—"Let the bearer, Mungo, pass and repass without molestation." What do they imply? That Great Britain has a right to seize all who are not provided with them. From their very nature they must be liable to abuse on both sides. If Great Britain desires a mark by which she can know her own subjects, let her give them an ear-mark. The colors that float from the masthead should be the credentials of our seamen. There is no safety to us, and the gentlemen have shown it, but in the rule that all who sail under the flag (not being enemies) are protected by the flag. It is impossible that this country should ever abandon the gallant tars who have won for us such splendid trophies. Let me suppose that the genius of Columbia should visit one of them in his oppressor's prison and attempt to reconcile him to his forlorn and wretched condition. She would say to him, in the language of gentlemen on the other side: "Great Britain intends you no harm; she did not mean to impress you, but one of her own subjects; having taken you by mistake, I will remonstrate, and try to prevail upon her by peaceable means to release you; but I cannot, my son, fight for you." If he did not consider this mere mockery, the poor tar would address her judgment and say: "You owe me, my country, protection; I owe you in return obedience. I am no British subject, I am a native of old Massachusetts, where live my aged father, my wife, my children. I have faithfully

sition, who, in 1798 and 1799 could raise a useless army to fight an enemy three thousand miles distant from us, alarmed at the existence of one raised for a known and specified object—the attack of the adjoining provinces of the enemy! What! the gentleman from Massachusetts, who assisted by his vote to raise the army of twenty-five thousand, alarmed at the danger of our liberties from this very army! . . .

I omitted, yesterday, sir, when speaking of a delicate and painful subject, to notice a powerful engine which the conspirators against the integrity of the Union employ to effect their nefarious purposes—I mean Southern influence. The true friend to his country, knowing that our Constitution was the work of compromise, in which interests, apparently conflicting, were attempted to be reconciled, aims to extinguish or allay prejudices. But this patriotic exertion does not suit the views of those who are urged on by diabolical ambition. They find it convenient to imagine the existence of certain improper influences, and to propagate, with their utmost industry, a belief of them. Hence the idea of Southern preponderance; Virginia influence; the yoking of the respectable yeomanry of the North, with negro slaves, to the car of Southern nabobs. If Virginia really cherishes a reprehensible ambition, an aim to monopolize the chief magistracy of the country, how is such a purpose to be accomplished? Virginia, alone, cannot elect a President, whose elevation depends upon a plurality of electoral votes, and a consequent concurrence of many States. Would Vermont, disinterested Pennsylvania, the Carolinas, independent Georgia, Kentucky, Tennessee, Ohio, Louisiana, all consent to become the tools of inordinate ambition? But the present incumbent was designated to the office before his predecessor had retired. How? By public sentiment, —public sentiment which grew out of his known virtues, his illustrious services, and his distinguished abilities. Would the gentleman crush this public sentiment,—is he prepared to admit that he would arrest the progress of opinion?

The war was declared because Great Britain arrogated to herself the pretension of regulating our foreign trade, under the delusive name of retaliatory orders in council,—a pretension by which she undertook to proclaim to American enterprise,—"Thus far shalt thou go, and no farther,"—orders which she refused to revoke after the alleged cause of their enactment had ceased; because she persisted in the practice of impressing American

discharged my duty. Will you refuse to do yours?" Appealing to her passions, he would continue: "I lost this eye in fighting under Truxton with the Insurgente; I got this scar before Tripoli; I broke this leg on board the Constitution when the Guerriere struck." If she remained still unmoved, he would break out in the accents of mingled distress and despair:—

> "Hard, hard is my fate! once I freedom enjoyed,
> Was as happy as happy could be!
> Oh! how hard is my fate, how galling these chains!"

I will not imagine the dreadful catastrophe to which he would be driven by an abandonment of him to his oppressor. It will not be, it cannot be, that his country will refuse him protection. . . .

An honorable peace is attainable only by an efficient war. My plan would be to call out the ample resources of the country, give them a judicious direction, prosecute the war with the utmost vigor, strike wherever we can reach the enemy, at sea or on land, and negotiate the terms of a peace at Quebec or at Halifax.

We are told that England is a proud and lofty nation, which, disdaining to wait for danger, meets it half way. Haughty as she is, we once triumphed over her, and, if we do not listen to the counsels of timidity and despair, we shall again prevail. In such a cause, with the aid of Providence, we must come out crowned with success; but if we fail, let us fail like men, lash ourselves to our gallant tars, and expire together in one common struggle, fighting for free trade and seamen's rights.

THE GREEK REVOLUTION

(From the Speech of January 20th, 1824, in the House of Representatives, Supporting the Webster Resolution)

THERE is reason to apprehend that a tremendous storm is ready to burst upon our happy country—one which may call into action all our vigor, courage, and resources. Is it wise or prudent, in preparing to breast the storm, if it must come, to talk to this nation of its incompetency to repel European aggression, to lower its spirit, to weaken its moral energy, and to qualify it for easy conquest and base submission? If there be any reality in the dangers which are supposed to encompass us, should we not animate the people, and adjure them to believe, as I do, that our resources are ample; and that we can bring into the field a million of freemen, ready to exhaust their last drop of blood, and to spend the last cent in the defense of the country, its liberty, and its institutions? Sir, are these, if united, to be conquered by all Europe combined? All the perils to which we can possibly be exposed are much less in reality than the imagination is disposed to paint them. And they are best averted by an habitual contemplation of them, by reducing them to their true dimensions. If combined Europe is to precipitate itself upon us, we cannot too soon begin to invigorate our strength, to teach our heads to think, our hearts to conceive, and our arms to execute, the high and noble deeds which belong to the character and glory of our country. The experience of the world instructs us that conquests are already achieved, which are boldly and firmly resolved on, and that men only become slaves who have ceased to resolve to be free. If we wish to cover ourselves with the best of all armor, let us not discourage our people, let us stimulate their ardor, let us sustain their resolution, let us proclaim to them that we feel as they feel, and that, with them, we are determined to live or die like freemen.

Surely, sir, we need no long or learned lectures about the nature of government and the influence of property or ranks on society. We may content ourselves with studying the true character of our own people and with knowing that the interests are confided to us of a nation capable of doing and suffering all things for its liberty. Such a nation, if its rulers be faithful, must be invincible. I well remember an observation made to me by the most illustrious female* of the age, if not of her sex. All history showed, she said, that a nation was never conquered. No, sir, no united nation that resolves to be free can be conquered. And has it come to this? Are we so humbled, so low, so debased, that we dare not express our sympathy for suffering Greece, that we dare not articulate our detestation of the brutal excesses of which she has been the bleeding victim, lest we might offend some one or more of their imperial and royal majesties? If gentlemen are afraid to act rashly on such a subject, suppose, Mr. Chairman, that we unite in an humble petition, addressed to their majesties, beseeching them that of their gracious

*Madame de Staël.

succor Greece, and to invigorate her arms, in her glorious cause, while temples and senate houses were alike resounding with one burst of generous and holy sympathy;—in the year of our Lord and Savior, that Savior of Greece and of us—a proposition was offered in the American Congress to send a messenger to Greece to inquire into her state and condition, with a kind expression of our good wishes and our sympathies—and it was rejected!" Go home, if you can, go home, if you dare, to your constituents, and tell them that you voted it down; meet, if you can, the appalling countenances of those who sent you here, and tell them that you shrank from the declaration of your own sentiments—that you cannot tell how, but that some unknown dread, some indescribable apprehension, some indefinable danger, drove you from your purpose—that the spectres of scimeters and crowns and crescents gleamed before you and alarmed you; and that you suppressed all the noble feelings, prompted by religion, by liberty, by national independence, and by humanity. I cannot bring myself to believe that such will be the feeling of a majority of the committee. But, for myself, though every friend of the cause should desert it, and I be left to stand alone with the gentleman from Massachusetts, I will give to his resolution the poor sanction of my unqualified approbation.

THE NOBLEST PUBLIC VIRTUE

(Replying to Mr. Rives in the United States Senate, August 19th, 1841. Once Described by Mr. Clay Himself as His Most Effective Passage)

I ROSE not to say one word which should wound the feelings of President Tyler. The Senate says that, if placed in like circumstances, I would have been the last man to avoid putting a direct veto upon the bill, had it met my disapprobation; and he does me the honor to attribute to me high qualities of stern and unbending intrepidity. I hope that in all that relates to personal firmness, all that concerns a just appreciation of the insignificance of human life—whatever may be attempted to threaten or alarm a soul not easily swayed by opposition, or awed or intimidated by menace—a stout heart and a steady eye, that can survey, unmoved and undaunted, any mere personal perils that assail this poor, transient, perishing frame, I may, without disparagement, compare with other men. But there is a

condescension they would allow us to express our feelings and our sympathies. How shall it run? "We, the representatives of the free people of the United States of America, humbly approach the thrones of your imperial and royal majesties, and supplicate that, of your imperial and royal clemency,"—I cannot go through the disgusting recital—my lips have not yet learned to pronounce the sycophantic language of a degraded slave! Are we so mean, so base, so despicable, that we may not attempt to express our horror—to utter our indignation, at the most brutal and atrocious war that ever stained earth or shocked high heaven; at the ferocious deeds of a savage and infuriated soldiery, stimulated and urged on by the clergy of a fanatical and inimical religion, and rioting in all the excesses of blood and butchery, at the mere details of which the heart sickens and recoils!

If the great body of Christendom can look on calmly and coolly, whilst all this is perpetrated on a Christian people, in its own immediate vicinity, in its very presence, let us at least evince that one of its remote extremities is susceptible of sensibility to Christian wrongs, and capable of sympathy for Christian sufferings; that in this remote quarter of the world there are hearts not yet closed against compassion for human woes, that can pour out their indignant feelings at the oppression of a people endeared to us by every ancient recollection, and every modern tie. . . .

But, sir, it is not for Greece alone that I desire to see this measure adopted. It will give to her but little support, and that purely of a moral kind. It is principally for America, for the credit and character of our common country, for our own unsullied name, that I hope to see it pass. Mr. Chairman, what appearance on the page of history would a record like this exhibit? "In the month of January, in the year of our Lord and Savior 1824, while all European Christendom beheld, with cold and unfeeling indifference, the unexampled wrongs and inexpressible misery of Christian Greece, a proposition was made in the Congress of the United States, almost the sole, the last, the greatest depository of human hope and human freedom, the representatives of a gallant nation, containing a million of freemen ready to fly to arms, while the people of that nation were spontaneously expressing its deep-toned feeling, and the whole continent, by one simultaneous emotion, was rising, and solemnly and anxiously supplicating and invoking high heaven to spare and

sort of courage, which, I frankly confess it, I do not possess, a boldness to which I dare not aspire, a valor which I cannot covet. I cannot lay myself down in the way of the welfare and happiness of my country. That I cannot, I have not the courage to do. I cannot interpose the power with which I may be invested, a power conferred not for my personal benefit, nor for my aggrandizement, but for my country's good, to check her onward march to greatness and glory. I have not courage enough, I am too cowardly for that. I would not, I dare not, in the exercise of such a trust, lie down and place my body across the path that leads my country to prosperity and happiness. This is a sort of courage widely different from that which a man may display in his private conduct and personal relations. Personal or private courage is totally distinct from that higher and nobler courage which prompts the patriot to offer himself a voluntary sacrifice to his country's good.

Nor did I say, as the Senator represents, that the President should have resigned. I intimated no personal wish or desire that he should resign. I referred to the fact of a memorable resignation in his public life. And what I did say was, that there were other alternatives before him besides vetoing the bill, and that it was worthy of his consideration whether consistency did not require that the example which he had set when he had a constituency of one State should not be followed when he had a constituency commensurate with the whole Union. Another alternative was to suffer the bill, without his signature, to pass into a law under the provisions of the Constitution. And I must confess, I see, in this, no such escaping by the back door, no such jumping out of the window, as the Senator talks about.

Apprehensions of the imputation of the want of firmness sometimes impel us to perform rash and inconsiderate acts. It is the greatest courage to be able to bear the imputation of the want of courage. But pride, vanity, egotism, so unamiable and offensive in private life, are vices which partake of the character of crimes in the conduct of public affairs. The unfortunate victim of these passions cannot see beyond the little, petty, contemptible circle of his own personal interests. All his thoughts are withdrawn from his country and concentrated on his consistency, his firmness, himself. The high, the exalted, the sublime emotions of a patriotism, which, soaring toward heaven, rises far above all mean, low, or selfish things, and is absorbed by one soul-transporting thought of the good and the glory of one's country, are never felt in his impenetrable bosom. That patriotism, which, catching its inspirations from the immortal God, and leaving at an immeasurable distance below all lesser, groveling, personal interests and feelings, animates and prompts to deeds of self-sacrifice, of valor, of devotion, and of death itself — that is public virtue; that is the noblest, the sublimest of all public virtues!

SIXTY YEARS OF SECTIONALISM

(Closing Argument in Support of the Compromise of 1850, United States Senate, February 6th, 1850)

Mr. Mangum having offered to make a motion to adjourn, Mr. Clay said: «No, sir; no, sir; if the Senate will bear with me, I think I can go through with it better to-day than I could to-morrow.»

Mr. President:—

THIS Union is threatened with subversion. I desire to take a very rapid glance at the course of public measures in this Union presently. I wanted, however, before I did that, to ask the Senate to look back upon the career which this country has run from the adoption of the Constitution down to the present day. Was there ever a nation upon which the sun of heaven has shone which has exhibited so much of prosperity as our own? At the commencement of this Government, our population amounted to about four millions. It has now reached upwards of twenty millions. Our territory was limited chiefly and principally to that bordering upon the Atlantic Ocean, and that which includes the southern shores of the interior lakes of our country. Our territory now extends from the northern provinces of Great Britain to the Rio Grande and the Gulf of Mexico; from the Atlantic Ocean on the one side to the Pacific on the other — the largest extent of territory under one government existing upon earth, with only two solitary exceptions. Our tonnage, from being nothing, has risen to a magnitude and amount to rival that of the nation which has been proudly called the mistress of the ocean. We have gone through many wars; one with that very nation from whom in 1776, we broke off, as weak and feeble colonies, when we asserted our independence as a member of the family of nations. And, sir, we came out of that

struggle — unequal as it was, armed as she was at all points in consequence of the long struggles of Europe, and unarmed as we were at all points, in consequence of the habits and nature of our country and its institutions — we came out of that war without the loss of any honor whatever; we emerged from it gloriously. In every Indian war — we have been engaged in many of them — our arms have been triumphant. And without speaking at all as to the causes of the recent war with Mexico, whether they were right or wrong, and abstaining from the expression of any opinion as to the justice or propriety of the war when it commenced, all must unite in respect to the gallantry of our arms and the glory of our triumphs. There is no page — there are no pages of history which record more brilliant successes. With respect to the one in command of an important portion of our army, I need say nothing in praise of him who has been borne by the voice of his country to the highest station in it, mainly on account of his glorious military career. But of another military commander, less fortunate in other respects, I must take the opportunity of saying that for skill, for science, for strategy, for bold and daring fighting, for chivalry of individuals and of masses, that portion of the Mexican War which was conducted by the gallant Scott, as chief commander, stands unrivaled either by the deeds of Cortes himself or by those of any other commander in ancient or modern times.

Our prosperity is unbounded. Nay, Mr. President, I sometimes fear that it is the very wantonness of our prosperity that leads us to these threatening ills of the moment, that restlessness and these erratic schemes throughout the whole country, some of which have even found their way into legislative halls. We want, I fear, the chastising wand of Heaven to bring us back to a sense of the immeasurable benefits and blessings which have been bestowed upon us by Providence. At this moment, with the exception of here and there a particular department in the manufacturing business of the country, all is prosperous and happy — both the rich and poor. Our nation has grown to a magnitude in power and in greatness to command the respect, if it does not call for the apprehensions, of all the powers of the earth with which we can come in contact. Sir, do I depict with colors too lively the prosperity which has resulted to us from the operation of the Constitution under which we live? Have I exaggerated in any degree?

Now, let me go a little into detail as to the sway in the councils of the nation, whether of the North or of the South, during the sixty years of unparalleled prosperity that we enjoy. During the first twelve years of the administration of the government Northern councils rather prevailed, and out of them sprung the Bank of the United States; the assumption of the State debts; bounties to the fisheries; protection to the domestic manufactures — I allude to the Act of 1789; neutrality in the wars with Europe; Jay's Treaty; Alien and Sedition Laws; and a *quasi* war with France. I do not say, sir, that those leading and prominent measures which were adopted during the administration of Washington and the elder Adams were carried exclusively by Northern councils. They could not have been, but were carried mainly by the sway which Northern councils had obtained in the affairs of the country.

So, also, with the latter party for the last fifty years. I do not mean to say that Southern counsels alone have carried the measures which I am about to enumerate. I know they could not exclusively have carried them; but I say they have been carried by their preponderating influence, with co-operation, it is true, and large co-operation, in some instances, from the Northern section of the Union.

And what are those measures during the fifty years that Southern counsels have preponderated? The Embargo and other commercial restrictions of nonintercourse and nonimportation; war with Great Britain; the Bank of the United States overthrown; protection to domestic manufactures enlarged and extended (I allude to the passage of the Act of 1815 or 1816); the Bank of the United States re-established; the same bank put down; re-established by Southern counsels and put down by Southern counsels; Louisiana acquired; Florida bought; Texas annexed; war with Mexico; California and other Territories acquired from Mexico by conquest and purchase; protection superseded and free trade established; Indians removed west of the Missouri; fifteen new States admitted into the Union. I may very possibly have omitted some of the important measures which have been adopted during the latter period or time to which I have referred — the last fifty years; but these, I believe, are the most prominent.

I do not deduce from the enumeration of the acts of the one side or the other any just cause of reproach to the one side or

the other, although one side or the other has predominated in the two periods to which I have referred. It has been at least the work of both, and neither need justly reproach the other; but I must say in all candor and sincerity that least of all ought the South to reproach the North, when we look at the long list of measures we have had under our sway in the councils of the nation, and which have been adopted as the policy of the Government, when we reflect that even opposite doctrines have been prominently advanced by the South and carried at different times. A Bank of the United States was established under the administration of Mr. Madison, with the co-operation of the South. I do not, when I speak of the South or North, speak of the entire South or North — I speak of the prominent and larger proportions of the South or North. It was during Mr. Madison's administration that the Bank of the United States was established. The friend [Mr. Calhoun] whose sickness I again deplore, as it prevents us from having his attendance here upon this occasion, was the chairman of the committee of the House of Representatives, and carried the measure through Congress. I voted for it with all my heart, although I had been instrumental in putting down the old Bank of the United States. I had changed my mind; and I co-operated in the establishment of the bank of 1816. The same bank was again put down by Southern counsels, with General Jackson at their head, at a later period. Then, with respect to the policy of protection, the South, in 1815 — I mean the prominent and leading men of the South, Lowndes, Calhoun, and others — united in extending a certain measure of protection to the domestic manufacturers of the South, as well as of the North. You find, a few years afterwards, that the South opposes the most serious objection to this policy, at least one member of the Union staking upon that objection the dissolution of the Union.

Let us take another view; and of these several views no one is brought forward in any spirit of reproach, but in a spirit of conciliation — not to provoke or exasperate, but to quiet and produce harmony and repose, if possible. What have been the territorial acquisitions made by this country, and to what interests have they conduced? Florida, where slavery exists, has been introduced. All the most valuable parts of Louisiana have also added to the extent and consideration of the slaveholding portion of the Union; for although there is a large extent of that territory north of 36° 30′, yet, in point of intrinsic value and importance, I would not give the single State of Louisiana for the whole of it. All Louisiana, with the exception of what lies north of 36° 30′, including Oregon, to which we have obtained title mainly upon the ground of its being a part of the acquisition of Louisiana — all Texas, all the territories which have been acquired by the Government of the United States during the past sixty years of the operation of that Government, have been slave territories — theatres of slavery — with the exception I have mentioned lying north of the line of 36° 30′. But how was it in the case of a war made essentially by the South, growing out of the annexation of Texas, which was a measure pressed by the South upon the councils of the country, and which led to the war with Mexico? I do not say of the whole South; but a major portion of the South pressed the annexation of Texas upon the country, and that led to a war with Mexico, and to the ultimate acquisition of these territories which now constitute the bone of contention between the members of the confederacy. And now, when, for the first time, any free territory, — after these great acquisitions in Florida, Louisiana, and Texas had been made and redounded to the benefit of the South, — now, when, for the first time, free territories are attempted to be introduced, — territories without the institution of slavery, — I put it to the hearts of my countrymen of the South, if it is right to press matters to the disastrous consequences that have been intimated no longer ago than this very morning, upon the presentation of the resolutions from North Carolina.

[A Senator here offered to move an adjournment.]

Mr. President, I hope the Senate will only have the goodness, if I don't tire out their patience, to permit me to go on. I would prefer concluding to-day. I begin to see land. I shall pretty soon arrive at the end. I had much rather occupy half an hour now than leave what I have to say for to-morrow — to trespass upon the patience of the Senate another day.

Such is the Union, and such are its glorious fruits. We are told now, and it is rung throughout this entire country, that the Union is threatened with subversion and destruction. Well, the first question which naturally arises is, supposing the Union to be dissolved, — having all the causes of grievance which are complained of, — How far will a dissolution furnish a remedy

thousands would escape if the Union were severed in parts — I care not where nor how you run the line, if independent sovereignties were established.

Well, finally, will you, in a state of dissolution of the Union, be safer with your slaves within the bosom of the States than you are now? Mr. President, that they will escape much more frequently from the border States, no one will doubt.

But, I must take the occasion to say that, in my opinion, there is no right on the part of one or more of the States to secede from the Union. War and the dissolution of the Union are identical and inseparable. There can be no dissolution of the Union, except by consent or by war. No one can expect, in the existing state of things, that that consent would be given, and war is the only alternative by which a dissolution could be accomplished. And, Mr. President, if consent were given — if possibly we were to separate by mutual agreement and by a given line, in less than sixty days after such an agreement had been executed, war would break out between the free and slaveholding portions of this Union — between the two independent portions into which it would be erected in virtue of the act of separation. Yes, sir, sixty days — in less than sixty days, I believe, our slaves from Kentucky would be fleeing over in numbers to the other side of the river, would be pursued by their owners, and the excitable and ardent spirits who would engage in the pursuit would be restrained by no sense of the rights which appertain to the independence of the other side of the river, supposing it, then, to be the line of separation. They would pursue their slaves; they would be repelled, and war would break out. In less than sixty days war would be blazing forth in every part of this now happy and peaceable land.

But how are you going to separate them? In my humble opinion, Mr. President, we should begin at least with three confederacies — the Confederacy of the North, the Confederacy of the Atlantic Southern States (the slaveholding States), and the Confederacy of the Valley of the Mississippi. My life upon it, sir, that vast population that has already concentrated, and will concentrate, upon the headwaters and tributaries of the Mississippi, will never consent that the mouth of that river shall be held subject to the power of any foreign State whatever. Such, I believe, would be the consequences of a dissolution of the Union. But other confederacies would spring up, from time to

for those grievances? If the Union is to be dissolved for any existing causes, it will be dissolved because slavery is interdicted or not allowed to be introduced into the ceded territories; because slavery is threatened to be abolished in the District of Columbia, and because fugitive slaves are not returned, as in my opinion they ought to be, and restored to their masters. These, I believe, will be the causes, if there be any causes, which can lead to the direful event to which I have referred.

Well, now, let us suppose that the Union has been dissolved. What remedy does it furnish for the grievances complained of in its united condition? Will you be able to push slavery into the ceded Territories? How are you to do it, supposing the North — all the States north of the Potomac, and which are opposed to it — in possession of the navy and army of the United States? Can you expect, if there is a dissolution of the Union, that you can carry slavery into California and New Mexico? You cannot dream of such a purpose. If it were abolished in the District of Columbia, and the Union were dissolved, would the dissolution of the Union restore slavery in the District of Columbia? Are you safer in the recovery of your fugitive slaves, in a state of dissolution or of severance of the Union, than you are in the Union itself? Why, what is the state of the fact in the Union? You lose some slaves. You recover some others. Let me advert to a fact which I ought to have introduced before, because it is highly creditable to the courts and juries of the free States. In every case, so far as my information extends, where an appeal has been made to the courts of justice for the recovery of fugitives, or for the recovery of penalties inflicted upon persons who have assisted in decoying slaves from their masters and aiding them in escaping from their masters — as far as I am informed, the courts have asserted the rights of the owner, and the juries have promptly returned adequate verdicts in favor of the owner. Well, this is some remedy. What would you have if the Union were dissevered? Why, sir, then the severed parts would be independent of each other — foreign countries! Slaves taken from the one into the other would be then like slaves now escaping from the United States into Canada. There would be no right of extradition; no right to demand your slaves; no right to appeal to the courts of justice to demand your slaves which escape, or the penalties for decoying them. Where one slave escapes now, by running away from his owner, hundreds and

time, as dissatisfaction and discontent were disseminated over the country. There would be the Confederacy of the Lakes — perhaps the Confederacy of New England and of the Middle States.

But, sir, the veil which covers these sad and disastrous events that lie beyond a possible rupture of this Union is too thick to be penetrated or lifted by any mortal eye or hand.

Mr. President, I am directly opposed to any purpose of secession, of separation. I am for staying within the Union, and defying any portion of this Union to expel or drive me out of the Union. I am for staying within the Union, and fighting for my rights — if necessary, with the sword — within the bounds and under the safeguard of the Union. I am for vindicating these rights; but not by being driven out of the Union rashly and unceremoniously by any portion of this confederacy. Here I am within it, and here I mean to stand and die; as far as my individual purposes or wishes can go — within it to protect myself, and to defy all power upon earth to expel me or drive me from the situation in which I am placed. Will there not be more safety in fighting within the Union than without it?

Suppose your rights to be violated; suppose wrongs to be done you, aggressions to be perpetrated upon you; cannot you better fight and vindicate them, if you have occasion to resort to that last necessity of the sword, within the Union, and with the sympathies of a large portion of the population of the Union of these States differently constituted from you, than you can fight and vindicate your rights, expelled from the Union, and driven from it without ceremony and without authority?

I said that I thought that there was no right on the part of one or more of the States to secede from this Union. I think that the Constitution of the thirteen States was made, not merely for the generation which then existed, but for posterity, undefined, unlimited, permanent, and perpetual — for their posterity, and for every subsequent State which might come into the Union, binding themselves by that indissoluble bond. It is to remain for that posterity now and forever. Like another of the great relations of private life, it was a marriage that no human authority can dissolve or divorce the parties from; and, if I may be allowed to refer to this same example in private life, let us say what man and wife say to each other: "We have mutual faults; nothing in the form of human beings can be perfect. Let us then be kind to each other, forbearing, conceding; let us live in happiness and peace."

Mr. President, I have said what I solemnly believe—that the dissolution of the Union and war are identical and inseparable; that they are convertible terms.

Such a war, too, as that would be, following the dissolution of the Union! Sir, we may search the pages of history, and none so furious, so bloody, so implacable, so exterminating, from the wars of Greece down, including those of the Commonwealth of England, and the Revolution of France—none, none of them raged with such violence, or was ever conducted with such bloodshed and enormities, as will that war which shall follow that disastrous event—if that event ever happens—of dissolution.

And what would be its termination? Standing armies and navies, to an extent draining the revenues of each portion of the dissevered empire, would be created; exterminating wars would follow—not a war of two nor three years, but of interminable duration—an exterminating war would follow, until some Philip or Alexander, some Cæsar or Napoleon, would rise to cut the Gordian knot, and solve the problem of the capacity of man for self-government, and crush the liberties of both the dissevered portions of this Union. Can you doubt it? Look at history—consult the pages of all history, ancient or modern; look at human nature—look at the character of the contest in which you would be engaged in the supposition of a war following the dissolution of the Union, such as I have suggested—and I ask you if it is possible for you to doubt that the final but perhaps distant termination of the whole will be some despot treading down the liberties of the people?—that the final result will be the extinction of this last and glorious light, which is leading all mankind, who are gazing upon it, to cherish hope and anxious expectation that the liberty which prevails here will sooner or later be advanced throughout the civilized world? Can you, Mr. President, lightly contemplate the consequences? Can you yield yourself to a torrent of passion, amidst dangers which I have depicted in colors far short of what would be the reality, if the event should ever happen? I conjure gentlemen—whether from the South or the North, by all they hold dear in this world —by all their love of liberty—by all their veneration for their ancestors—by all their regard for posterity—by all their gratitude to him who has bestowed upon them such unnumbered

IV—81

blessings—by all the duties which they owe to mankind, and all the duties they owe to themselves—by all these considerations I implore them to pause—solemnly to pause—at the edge of the precipice before the fearful and disastrous leap is taken in the yawning abyss below, which will inevitably lead to certain and irretrievable destruction.

And, finally, Mr. President, I implore, as the best blessing which heaven can bestow upon me on earth, that if the direful and sad event of the dissolution of the Union shall happen, I may not survive to behold the sad and heart-rending spectacle.

1283

JOHN M. CLAYTON

(1796–1856)

OHN MIDDLETON CLAYTON, remembered chiefly because of his connection with the Clayton-Bulwer treaty, was a jurist and statesman whose leadership among the Whigs of his time was a concession to his talents rather than to the political importance of his State. Born in Sussex County, Delaware, July 24th, 1796, he was elected a United States Senator from Delaware as early as 1829 and remained in the Senate until he resigned in 1837 to serve as Chief-Justice of his State. After serving again in the Senate (1845-49) he became Secretary of State in President Taylor's cabinet in 1849. He held that office till he had concluded the negotiation of the Clayton-Bulwer treaty, and was then returned to the Senate (1851) where he zealously defended the treaty and continued to be prominent in the debates until his death at Dover, Delaware, November 9th, 1856.

THE CLAYTON-BULWER TREATY AND "EXPANSION"

(From a Speech in the United States Senate, March 18th, 1853)

ALL the objections of the Senator [Douglas] dwindle down at last, as I have said, to a single point—that the treaty ought to have been a treaty for the exclusive right of way across the isthmus; that the error of the treaty of 1850 is, that while it obtains protection from all nations, it makes a navigable highway for all nations on the same terms; and we see that if he had negotiated the treaty, he would have obtained an exclusive right; and he stood up here in defense of the treaty of Mr. Hise, which would have secured to this Government (if it had been ratified by Nicaragua and the United States) an exclusive right. What sort of an exclusive right is it that he demands? He thinks that the Government of the United States should have obtained the grant—the right to make a canal, and an exclusive right to navigate it; that forts should be built at both ends to protect it; and of course that we should protect it by every other means necessary. When the Government shall have made it,

and when the Government shall have established the forts, the canal, he says, will be open to everybody on the same terms; and thus he seeks the exclusive grant of a right of way! What does he want with it? Why does he prefer it to the plan adopted, of opening the canal to all nations on the same terms? The Senator says he would hold it as a rod—yes, a rod, to compel other nations to keep the peace! He would have no more settling of islands on the coast of Central America! If any government attempted it, he would shut his canal to them! He would also compel all foreign nations to treat us with all respect and regard, by means of the tremendous rod which he would hold in his hands! Let us look a little into the justice of this thing, as regards our own country.

It has been supposed that the construction of this great work will cost fifty or a hundred millions of dollars. I suppose we could not build a proper fortification at each end under less than a million of dollars for each fort. We would be compelled to maintain a garrison there; and, in the event of a war, to maintain a large navy, such a one as could resist the naval powers of the earth. If we were to go to war with France, or England, or any other great naval power, that, of course, would be one of the first points of attack. How convenient would it be for us to defend it at a distance of two thousand miles, and send troops to the different forts, and ships to protect our vessels that pass through the canal! We build it, and everybody is to have the benefit of the canal on the same terms, in time of peace! In war we alone are to defend it! The interest on a hundred millions would be six millions a year. The expenses of protecting and taking care of the canal and keeping it in good order would probably, when added to the interest, make an annual outlay from the Treasury of the United States, in that distant country, of not less than ten millions of dollars. Now, why should we make such an expenditure? Because we want a rod—a rod! Sir, I think it would prove to be a rod to inflict injuries upon ourselves. We want nothing but the right of way there. We proposed that no nation should go through that canal, unless she agreed to protect it. In case they agreed to protect it, we should want no forts, no garrisons, and no naval force to guard what none could attack. But, on the other hand, if we were to adopt the plan of the Senator, we should have to keep a standing army in that country to protect it, in the event of a war between us and foreign nations. What would be thought of a man who should purchase a farm, and then, after he had gone to the expense of putting it in order, invite everybody to come and till it, but should direct them to take care that they should pay no part of the expense of keeping up the repairs, nor any part of the taxes upon the land? I do not know that this or any other illustration can make his proposition seem more preposterous than it does on its own mere statement. . . .

The Senator from Illinois said "that treaties could not fetter or confine the limbs of this giant Republic." I do not know precisely the extent to which he meant to be understood; but the language and the manner in which the Senator applied it seemed to me to go to this extent: that we had a country exempt from the obligations of treaties, and that our limbs cannot be circumscribed by treaties. We were to disregard obligations of that description, being, like a "young giant," rising in power beyond anything that had been known in the history of the world before. The Senator made the same remark in reference to the treaty with Mexico. There is a clause in the treaty of Guadalupe Hidalgo to which the Senator made great objection at the time of its ratification, in effect, that without the consent of the governments of both countries, the line established by that treaty as the boundary between them, should be the *ultima thule* — the utmost limit of our territory. Yes, sir, we plighted our faith and honor in that treaty, confirmed as it was by more than two-thirds of the American Senate, that beyond that limit we would never go. Yet the Senator from Illinois says that the day is coming when we shall be compelled to violate the treaty — that treaties cannot fetter our limbs or restrict our limits. Sir, I regretted to hear it, because of the influence of that Senator in his party, as one of their standing candidates for the presidency. I should have regretted to have heard it from any Senator. We form the body that is to ratify all the treaties of the United States. We are the constitutional advisers of the President. We are a part of the treaty-making power.

Mr. Douglas — If it gives the Senator any regret that I stated that, I will explain to him what I did state, and thereby, I imagine, relieve him from all his regret. What I said was, that the steady, regular growth and expansion of this country would, in all probability, go ahead in the future as it has done in the past; that you might make as many treaties as you please, and

still they would not check our growth, and because they could not, it was useless to make treaties which must, of necessity, be violated; hence I argued against the making of treaties pledging our faith not to do that which inevitably would be done in the future. It was an argument in favor of the fidelity and observance of treaty stipulations, and that we should not, therefore, be so profuse in our pledges in cases where we could not fulfill them.

Mr. Clayton — An argument in favor of fidelity and observance of treaty stipulations, indeed! The idea is that we are incapable, from the nature of our institutions or our character as a people, of maintaining and observing treaties.

Mr. Douglas — No, sir.

Mr. Clayton (laughing) — We must grow, says the Senator. Our "manifest destiny," he means, is to extend our limits.

Mr. Douglas — The idea is, that some men are incapable of comprehending the growth of this nation. A few years ago, it was supposed that we could never extend beyond the Alleghanies. There were those who thought that —

Mr. Clayton — I have heard all that a dozen times.

Mr. Douglas — Then the Mississippi, then the Pacific was the boundary. I said that the same laws which have carried us forward must inevitably carry us further in the process of time, and that that growth will go on; and consequently it is unwise to make a treaty stipulation pledging ourselves not to do that which our interest may require us to do.

Mr. Clayton — I have given the Senator so many opportunities for explaining himself to me, as he terms it, that now I must be permitted to explain him to himself. . . . He insists upon it, that by some irresistible influence we are driven on in our course to such a degree of greatness that we shall be compelled to violate the treaties which we may make with foreign nations in regard to boundaries. We ought, he said, to nullify the treaty of 1850 at once. He now says that some men cannot comprehend the growth of this giant Republic. I do not know that there is any man of ordinary intelligence who does not comprehend it. There is no difficulty in understanding it. We have grown to such an extent already that we have a country greater than Rome possessed in her palmiest days. We cover a contiguous territory greater, perhaps, than ever was enjoyed by any civilized nation on earth. And yet we are told that we are not capable

of binding ourselves even by treaty stipulations to observe our plighted faith, and fulfill our solemn engagement of honor. I remonstrate against the declaration of such a principle, or rather of such a want of all principle. It is nothing more nor less than this, — let there be as many explanations on the part of the Senator from Illinois as he may choose to make, — that we are incapable of controlling our impulses and passions when our interests may lead us to violate our engagements. "Treaties cannot fetter us," says he. Sir, the plighted faith of every man of honor binds him at all times, no matter what his interest may be, and the plighted faith of nations equally binds them; and the last place from which a contrary principle should be promulgated is the Senate of the United States. Here, I repeat, we sit as the constitutional advisers of the President of the United States; and if foreign nations come to understand that the position is taken by members holding a prominent party position here, that treaties cannot be any restraint upon us, what foreign nation will ever make another treaty with us? If there be a country on earth that owes more than any other to treaties, it is ours. We owe our national existence to the old French treaties of 1778. Sir, within the limits of that great State which you in part represent on this floor [Mr. Cooper in the chair], Washington, in the darkest period of the Revolution, at Valley Forge, wintered with his suffering soldiers, when the intelligence reached them that France had entered into an alliance with us, and had guaranteed our independence. The glorious news ran through all the ranks of the American army, and the great "Father of his Country" stood up and waved his hat, and shouted for joy, in concert with his troops! Our destiny from that moment became fixed. Every American saw that we were free, whatever doubt he might have entertained about it before. We owe, I repeat, our national independence to treaties. And now, when we are becoming strong, shall we forget it? Shall not an American statesman adhere to treaties with as much fidelity as an Englishman, or a Frenchman, or one of any other nation? Shall he not rejoice that his country does stand by her honor? I trust that no idea of our growing importance, or of the necessity of our enlargement, will ever sink into the heart of any other American Senator, to induce him to abandon that principle without which our country would become a byword and a hissing among the nations.

If we must gain more territory, let us gain it honorably. The Senator from Illinois boasts that he opposed the treaty with Mexico. I recollect it very well, and I recollect the reason he gave for voting against it. It was the very reason which he assigned in the debate here for desiring to annul the treaty of 1850. He opposed that clause in the Mexican treaty which fixed the limits beyond which we could not go, and he cannot explain away his position, or shift it any longer. He then said the time would come when Mexico would become indispensable to our progress and our happiness. I would recall to the recollection of gentlemen who were present on the ninth day of February, 1847, the speech made by Mr. Calhoun, of South Carolina, on this very subject. In thrilling tones he gave utterance to views which seemed to carry conviction to the hearts of nine-tenths of those who heard him, and told us that Mexico was to us forbidden fruit. Whenever the day shall come that, in defiance of treaty limits or otherwise, we set about the business of annexing nine or ten millions of Mexicans to the United States, the days of our Republic will be numbered. The Mexican people are educated in the belief that no greater curse can befall a nation than that of slavery, and are said to be bound by treaty to abolish it. Could we permit them to take a part in the election of our Representatives and Senators in Congress? Could we admit them to assist in governing us? Sir, without any reference to that dangerous question to which I have barely alluded, there are many other questions on which they would have a powerful influence and an interest in deciding against us. I am utterly opposed to annexing them, and I do not hesitate to express that opposition now and at all times. The true policy of this Government is to build up Mexico as a republic, to sustain and cheer her by kind offices, and to teach her, by our example, the science of self-government. If we could annex other countries as England does, or as Rome did when she was triumphing over the world, the whole subject might receive another consideration. Whenever we annex, we make citizens of the people whom we unite to us. We do not enslave them. Other countries may make slaves of those whom they subdue, and never permit them to take any part in the government of their conquerors. If we annex Mexico, we are compelled, in obedience to the principles of our own Declaration of Independence, to receive her people as citizens. Yes! Aztecs, Creoles, Half-Breeds, Quadroons, Samboes, and I know not what else,—"ring-streaked and speckled,"—all will come in, and, instead of our governing them, they, by their votes, will govern us. Why do we want them or their territory? Are we cramped? Are we crowded? Have we more population than is necessary to fill the land which we already own? There is not a more sparsely populated country on earth which is inhabited by civilized men. We have hundreds of millions of acres of land upon which the foot of a white man never trod. When, in the lapse of time, all this shall be covered, then if we find men of our own race and class capable of sustaining our institutions and of self-government, in any contiguous territory which can be acquired without the violation of any principle of justice or humanity, I am not one that would stay the honorable progress of my country.

The day, however, will never come when an American Senator will be justified in the declaration that we intend to disobey treaties. No, sir; we have been, and mean to remain, faithful to treaties. We have often been accused of having violated them; but the honor of our country is yet dear to us, and it is worth more to the true American than all the land that Mexico and Central America contain.

The Senator objects to the treaty of 1850, because, under its provisions, we cannot annex the Central American States. Were there no such treaty, he could not annex them till he had first overrun Mexico, and broken the treaty of Guadalupe Hidalgo. Nay, he must first annex the West India Islands, and British Honduras, too. After "swallowing Mexico," he must take in all the other intermediate countries; and as Great Britain owns many of the islands and dependencies to be devoured, he must include the British Lion—a matter not quite so easy of digestion. What an intimation is it for us to make to the world, that we may some day annex these weak little sister Republics, thousands of miles away from us, with a population so different from ours, especially in laws, institutions, and usages! I would much rather other nations should know the fact that San Salvador, one of these very Central American States, once applied for admission into our Union, and that our Government not only declined to receive them, but treated the application as one not worthy of a moment's serious regard.

I heard with pleasure and admiration that passage in the inaugural address of the President which declared that his admin-

istration should leave no blot upon his country's record, and that no act within his constitutional control would be tolerated which could not challenge a ready justification before the tribunal of the civilized world. How great the difference between that and the sentiments of the Senator from Illinois! Let the President adhere to these principles, and he will thereby disarm opposition; he will make of those who have heretofore been strong political opponents some of the warmest friends he has in the world. I put this declaration in contrast with all these gigantic ideas [laughter] of breaking treaties, and going beyond the limits of the country in defiance of them. But if the President should, in opposition to all our hopes and belief, be induced to disregard the faith of treaties, he will hardly progress through half the period of his constitutional term before he will find the great heart of the American people, which is honest to the core, opposed to him, and the most sincere of his present friends will vindicate the justice of the sentence against him, while they sorrow for his fall.

JUSTICE THE SUPREME LAW OF NATIONS

(From a Speech on the Mexican War. United States Senate, January 11th and 12th, 1848)

I NEVER have been, and I am not now, willing to acquire one acre of ground from Mexico, or any other nation under heaven, by conquest or robbery. I hold that, in all our transactions with the other nations of the world, the great principle ought to be maintained by us that "Honesty is the best policy," and that an honorable reputation is of more value to a country than land or money. I hold that any attempt on our part, merely because we happen to possess superior strength, to compel a weaker nation to cede to us all that we choose, to demand as indemnity, while we at the same time admit that we ask for more than she owes us, is nothing else but robbery. If a man owe me a sum of money, and I meet him on the highway, and insist, with a pistol pointed at his breast, that he shall deliver to me a deed of his farm, at the estimate which I choose to put upon it, I think there could not be much difference of opinion as to the nature of that transaction. I should like to know how my friend from Maryland, who is an able lawyer,

would defend the man guilty of such conduct. Would it be any palliation, or excuse, or justification of the conduct of an offender in such a case, that some money was justly due him? Could there be found in Christendom a court and jury that would hesitate as to the verdict in such a case? And what, let me ask,—as a friend near me [Mr. Webster] suggests,—what would be the value of the deed obtained under such circumstances? If the possessor of it should even go "unwhipt of justice," would he not be the object to which the scornful finger of every honest man would be pointed, so long as he lived upon earth? I hold—and, however old-fashioned the notion may be, I shall maintain it so long as I have a seat here—that character is as valuable to a nation as it is to an individual; and inasmuch as I would scorn as a private citizen to despoil my neighbor of his property in these circumstances and with these avowals, so, as a public man, I never can sanction, in the slightest degree, such a course of conduct on the part of the government of the country.

We are one of the strongest nations of the earth. We have been amongst the weakest. In times gone by, we have suffered from the cruelty, the tyranny, and injustice of other nations, and have uttered loud complaints. We have now waxed strong and can put our foot upon the neck of a sister republic, and compel her to yield to the terms we ourselves dictate. The question now comes up, and it addresses itself to every genuine lover of his country, whether the acquisition of all this territory, under these circumstances, would compensate us for the loss of the reputation—that high national character which we have hitherto sustained?

JEREMIAH CLEMENS

(1814–1865)

WHEN the issues of sectional supremacy were so joined between the North and South as to make civil war or further concessions on both sides inevitable, it was believed by some that all inconvenient issues at home could be indefinitely postponed by forcing foreign war. In that connection, the annexation of Cuba, Porto Rico, the Central American States, Mexico, and Canada, were discussed as a part of what was called "the manifest destiny" of the Anglo-Saxon race in America. It was charged that this policy "originated with the Southern slave-owners," but one of the most effective protests ever made against it was the speech delivered in the United States Senate, February 7th, 1853, by Jeremiah Clemens, of Alabama. Mr. Clemens has not generally been classed among the greatest statesmen of his time, but no one will read a dozen of his sentences without seeing that he has the oratorical faculty highly developed. He was born in Huntsville, Alabama, December 28th, 1814. Educated at La Grange College and the University of Alabama, he studied law at the University of Transylvania, in Kentucky. Entering public life in 1838 as United States Attorney for the Northern District of Alabama, he served afterwards in the State Legislature, and in the Mexican War as a Lieutenant-Colonel. Returning in 1843, he was re-elected to the Legislature. From 1849 till 1853 he represented Alabama in the United States Senate. He died May 21st, 1865.

CUBA AND "MANIFEST DESTINY"

(From a Speech in the United States Senate, February 7th, 1853)

DANGER does not threaten us from abroad. In that quarter the skies are clear and bright. It is at home that the symptoms of an approaching hurricane are manifest. These symptoms are everywhere about us and around us. They may be found in the restless and disturbed state of the public mind; in the speeches of dinner orators, dignifying war with the name of "progress," and clothing wholesale robbery with the mantle of patriotism. They might have been seen in the frenzied enthusiasm which followed the footsteps of that sturdy beggar, Louis Kossuth and in the wild and reckless attempts of American citizens to take possession of the island of Cuba. Sir, I deplore their fate as much as any man can, and condemn as strongly the cruel and barbarous conduct of the Spanish governor. I but refer to them as evidence of a state of things to which all eyes ought to be directed. And last, sir, though not least, the signs of this danger may be found in the ill-regulated, but fierce and strenuous, efforts of "Young America" to bring about a war with anybody or upon any pretext.

All these things indicate that a spirit of change is abroad in the land. I may be told that word is written on every earthly thing. Perhaps it may be so; but justice, honor, mercy, are the children of God, and know no change. In the sublime morality of the Christian's creed we may find a guide for our footsteps which cannot lead to error: "Do unto others as ye would they should do unto you." It is not in the Book of Revelations that we are taught to covet the goods of our neighbors. It is not there we are encouraged to indulge a lawless spirit of war and conquest. We do not learn from thence the duty of progressing backward from a peaceful age to a period of barbarism, when the strong hand was the only law, and the steel blade the only arbiter of disputed questions.

Sir, I have heard much of this thing called progress. In the eyes of some gentlemen it covers all defects and makes atonement for every error. I am not its enemy, but I wish to know exactly what it means, and in what direction I am to progress. If it means that glorious spirit which sweeps abroad upon the wings of peace, shedding life and light and happiness on the land and on the sea; which sends the missionary among the heathen, and gathers the infidel and the unbeliever beneath the Gospel's ample shield; which doubles the productions of earth, and lays bare the treasures of ocean; which plants the church of God in the wilderness of the West, and substitutes the Sabbath bell for the howl of the panther; which carries literature and science to the log cabin of the pioneer, and connects every part of this wide Republic by links so strong, so close, that the traveler feels every spot he treads is home, and every hand he grasps a brother's hand,— if this be the progress which is meant, most gladly do I enlist under its banner.

But, sir, I am not permitted so to understand it. I understand progress, as interpreted by modern politicians, to be quite

a different thing. The first lesson they inculcate is a sort of general defiance to all mankind; an imitation of the worst practice of olden chivalry—the practice of hanging a glove in some public place as a challenge to every passer-by to engage in mortal combat—a practice, in no degree based upon wrongs to be redressed, or injuries to be avenged, but upon a pure, unmitigated love of blood and strife. They have borrowed also from the crusaders another vicious and indefensible habit—that of impoverishing themselves at home to raise the means of transportation to other lands to erect altars and inculcate principles by the edge of the sword. They propose to grasp the territory of an old and faithful ally, not only without the shadow of a claim, but without even the robber's plea of necessity; to hush the busy hum of commerce; to withdraw the artisan from his workshop, the laborer from his field, the man of science and the man of letters from their high pursuits; to convert the whole land into one vast camp, and impress upon the people the wild and fierce character of the followers of King Clovis.

Sir, I wish to indulge in no exaggerated statements, but let us, in the cant phraseology of the day, "establish a foreign policy." Let us set about convincing the world that we are indeed "a power upon earth." Let us rob Spain of Cuba, England of Canada, and Mexico of her remaining possessions, and this continent will be too small a theatre upon which to enact the bloody drama of American progress! Like the Prophet of the East, who carried the sword in one hand and the Koran in the other, American armies will be sent forth to proclaim freedom to the serf; but if he happen to love the land in which he was born, and exhibit some manly attachment to the institutions with which he is familiar, his own lifeblood will saturate the soil, and his wife and children be driven forth as houseless wanderers, in proof of our tender consideration for the rights of humanity. Sir, this is a species of progress with which Satan himself might fall in love.

Mr. President, there are in this connection still other lights in which the question before us may be presented. Look at America as she now is, prosperous in all things, splendid, magnificent, rich in her agriculture, rich in her commerce, rich in arts and sciences, rich in learning, rich in individual freedom, richer still in the proud prerogative of bending the knee to none but the God who made us, and of worshiping even in his tem-

ples according to the forms which conscience, not the law, has prescribed. Gaze upon that picture until your soul has drunk in all its beauty, all its glory, and then let me paint for you that which is offered as a substitute. Look upon a land where war has become a passion, and blood a welcome visitant; where every avenue to genius is closed save that which leads through a field of strife; where the widow and the orphan mingle unavailing tears for the husband and the father; where literature has become a mockery and religion a reproach; upon a people, strong indeed, but terrible in their strength, with the tiger's outward beauty and the tiger's inward fierceness; upon a people correctly described by the poet when he said:—

> "Religion, blushing, veils her sacred fires,
> And unawares morality expires;
> Nor public flame, nor private, dares to shine,
> Nor human spark is left, nor glimpse divine.
> Lo! thy dread empire, Chaos, is restored,
> Light dies before thy uncreating word;
> Thy hand, great Anarch, lets the curtain fall,
> And universal darkness buries all."

Let no one tell me that these are imaginary dangers. At the commencement of the French Revolution, if any one predicted the excesses to which it gave birth, he would have been regarded as a madman. What security have we against the occurrence of similar scenes? We are human, as they were. Our law of being is the same; and if we once depart from the plain path of prudence and of rectitude, no human wisdom can foresee the result.

The present acquisition of Cuba, in my opinion, in any way, is of questionable propriety; but if it is to come to us as the result of war and violence, instead of a blessing it will prove a deadly ill. When Caractacus was carried to Rome to grace the triumph of his conqueror, he gazed with wonder and awe upon the splendor and magnificence with which he was surrounded. Then, turning to the Emperor, he expressed his simple wonder that one so rich, so powerful, so blessed with the possession of everything that earth could bestow, should have envied him his humble cottage home in the forests of Britain. . . .

Mr. President, I need not say that I do not intend to vote for these resolutions. The one which announces our purpose not to

take possession of Cuba by fraud or violence is certainly, that far, in accordance with my own feelings; but I do not see the necessity of making the declaration. It seems to me to be both undignified and unmanly to be making constant protestations of our honesty. Let us show the world by our acts that we are honest, and leave all such declarations to those whose doubtful character requires some such bolstering. Nor do I think the reaffirmation of the Monroe Doctrine would add to its importance. Our policy has long ago been announced to the world, and this restless desire to reiterate it upon all occasions looks to me somewhat as if we doubted our own resolution, and required a few legislative resolves to keep up our courage.

The Senator from Michigan has expressed considerable surprise at what he terms our shrinking from meeting the questions raised by his resolutions. Sir, there may be other causes than fear which render us reluctant to vote for them. When a boy I read a story of the civil wars of England, which taught me a lesson not yet forgotten. An adherent of the Parliament had been cruelly treated by one of the opposite party. His houses had been burned down, and his fields made desolate. Some time afterwards he met an acquaintance to whom he told the story of his wrongs. It was done simply and plainly, without a single threat or execration. When he had finished, his friend asked him with surprise, "And did you not vow revenge?" "No," was the reply; "those who take the trouble to make vows are very certain that a time will come when they will need a vow to steady their purposes. I never doubted what I would do, and I made no vows." Sir, there was more danger in one such man than a whole regiment of noisy babblers. Silence is almost invariably the concomitant of determined resolution; and the world will be quite as likely to believe us in earnest, and will respect us as much for refusing to pass, year after year, a series of threatening resolutions.

Mr. President, I find that I am taxing my strength too much, and I must soon close. The pilgrim who, in obedience to a vision oftentimes repeated, seized his staff and set out in search of a land in which he had been promised all the joys of Paradise, after traversing many lands, steadily pursuing his dangerous way through forests, deserts, and jungles, reached at last the only mountain which shut out from his gaze the promised land. Slowly he commenced the ascent; then paused, overcome by contending emotions. If from that mountain top he should indeed look upon a valley, such as had appeared to him in his dreams, beautiful and glorious, where the flower had lost its thorn, where the sweetest melodies were continually poured into the ear, and the very air was redolent with perfume, how cheaply would it be purchased even by all the toils and dangers he had encountered. But then came the fear that his dream had deceived him; that he might find a barren waste of thorns and brambles, desert, cheerless, and inhospitable. Anxious to know the truth, yet dreading to have it revealed, he stood upon the mountain side unable to advance or to recede. Even such emotions, Mr. President, might now well swell the American bosom. We have reached the hillside from whose top the future of America may be viewed. But who can ascend it without a feeling of doubt and terror? Is it to be the America which all of us loved to paint in our boyish days — free, happy, and prosperous, inculcating by its precepts, and enforcing by its example, a deep love of law and order; offering a refuge and asylum to the fugitive from oppression; cultivating with assiduous care the arts of peace, and illustrating all the mild beauties of Christianity? Or is it to be that America which "progress," "manifest destiny," and "overruling necessity," are now seeking to make it, where freedom will be lost amid the clash of arms, and the wail of every good spirit will rise above the crushed and broken hope of man's capacity to govern himself? Sir, it is in our action that the answer must be found. Our country is at stake, and he who loves it as he ought should pause and ponder long and well before tampering, in any way, with so high and holy a trust.

IV—82

CLEON

(?)–422 B. C.

LEON has been called "the scorn and terror of all good men at Athens." Cicero characterizes him as turbulent, but eloquent, and he is generally classed as a typical Athenian demagogue. Perhaps much of his evil reputation is due to the comedies of Aristophanes, in which he was violently attacked. It is said that the poet had a private grudge against him, because of a complaint made to the Athenian Senate that the "Babylonians" held Athenian institutions up to ridicule. However this may be, Cleon, though the son of a tanner, and rude enough in his methods, was certainly not wholly a demagogue in the modern sense, for in his speech against the Mityleneans, reported by Thucydides, he begins by boldly questioning the fitness of the turbulent Athenian democracy to rule subject colonies. The date of Cleon's birth is uncertain. He became noted at Athens after the death of Pericles as the leader of the Athenian Democrats against the Aristocratic party under Nicias. In 425 B. C. he carrried on a successful campaign against the Spartans, but in 422 B. C., when put at the head of the expedition against Brasidas, the Lacedæmonian commander, he was defeated and killed at Amphipolis.

DEMOCRACIES AND SUBJECT COLONIES

(From the Speech Against Mitylene as Reported by Thucydides in the Third Book of the Peloponnesian War)

UPON many other occasions my own experience hath convinced me that a democracy is incapable of ruling over others, but I see it with the highest certainty now in this your present repentance concerning the Mityleneans. In security so void of terror, in safety so exempt from treachery, you pass your days within the walls of Athens, that you are grown quite safe and secure about your dependants. Whenever, soothed by their specious entreaties, you betray your judgment or relent in pity, not a soul amongst you reflects that you are acting the dastardly part, not in truth to confer obligations upon those dependants, but to endanger your own welfare and safety. It is then quite

remote from your thoughts, that your rule over them is in fact a tyranny, that they are ever intent on prospects to shake off your yoke — that yoke, to which they ever reluctantly submitted. It is not forgiveness on your part, after injuries received, that can keep them fast in their obedience, since this must be ever the consequence of your own superior power, and not of gratitude in them.

Above all, I dread that extremity of danger to which we are exposed, if not one of your decrees must ever be carried into act and we remain forever ignorant that the community which uniformly abides by a worse set of laws hath the advantage over another which is finely modeled in every respect except in practice; that modest ignorance is a much surer support than genius which scorns to be controlled, and that the duller part of mankind in general administer public affairs much better than your men of vivacity and wit. The last assume a pride in appearing wiser than the laws; in every debate about the public good they aim merely at victory, as if there were no other points sufficiently important wherein to display their superior talents; and by such conduct they generally subvert the public welfare; the former, who are diffident of their own abilities, who regard themselves as less wise than the laws of their country — though unable to detect the specious orator, yet being better judges of equity than champions in debate, for the most part enforce rational conduct. This beyond denial is our duty at present; we should scorn competitions in eloquence and wit, nor willfully and contrary to our own opinion mislead the judgment of this full assembly.

For my part, I persist in my former declarations, and I am surprised at the men who propose to have the affair of Mitylene again debated, who endeavor to protract the execution of justice, in the interest of the guilty more than of the injured. For by this means the sufferer proceeds to take vengeance on the criminal with the edge of his resentment blunted; when revenge, the opposite of wrong, the more nearly it treads upon the heels of injury, generally inflicts the more condign punishment. But I am more surprised at him, whoever he be, that shall dare to contradict, and pretend to demonstrate, that the injuries done by the Mityleneans are really for our service, and that our calamities are hardships on our dependants. He certainly must either presume upon his own eloquence, if he contends to prove that what was plainly decreed was never decreed; or, instigated by lucre,

will endeavor to seduce you by the elaborate and plausible artifice of words. In such contentions, the State, indeed, awards the victory to whom she pleaseth, but she sustains all the damage herself. You are answerable for this, Athenians — you, who fondly dote on these wordy competitions — you, who are accustomed to be spectators of speeches and hearers of actions. You measure the possibility of future effects by the present eloquence of your orators; you judge of actions already past, not by the certain conviction of your own eyes, but the fallible suggestions of your ears, when soothed by the inveigling, insinuating flow of words. You are the best in the world to be deceived by novelty of wit, and to refuse to follow the dictates of the approved judicious speaker, — slaves as you are to whatever trifles happen always to be in vogue, and looking down with contempt on tried and experienced methods. The most earnest wish that the heart of any of your body ever conceived is to become a speaker; if that be unattainable, you range yourselves in opposition against all who are so, for fear you should seem in judgment their inferiors. When anything is acutely uttered, you are ready even to go before it with applause, and intimate your own preconception of the point, at the same time dull at discerning whither it will tend. Your whole passion, in a word, is for things that are not in reality and common life; but of what passeth directly before your eyes you have no proper perception. And, frankly, you are quite infatuated by the lust of hearing, and resemble more the idle spectators of contending sophists than men who meet to deliberate upon public affairs. From such vain amusements, endeavoring to divert you, I boldly affirm that no one city in the world hath injured you so much as Mitylene. . . .

It is the usual effect of prosperity, especially when felt on a sudden, and beyond their hope, to puff up a people into insolence of manners. The successes of mankind, when attained by the rational course, are generally of much longer continuance than when they anticipate pursuit. And in a word, men are much more expert at repelling adversity than preserving prosperity. By this ought we long ago to have adjusted our conduct towards the Mityleneans, never distinguishing them above others with peculiar regard; and then they never would have been that insolent people we have found them now. For so remarkably perverse is the temper of man, as ever to contemn whoever courts him, and admire whoever will not bend before him. Let condign punishments therefore be awarded to their demerits. . . .

GROVER CLEVELAND

(1837-)

ROVER CLEVELAND was born at Caldwell, Essex County, New Jersey, March 18th, 1837. He was educated at the common schools, and admitted to the bar in 1859. His first public position was that of Assistant District Attorney in Erie County, New York, from 1863 till 1866. After being defeated as a candidate for District Attorney in 1865, he remained in private life until 1870, when he was elected Sheriff. In 1881 he was elected Mayor of Buffalo on the Democratic ticket, and the prominence he gained as a reformer during his administration resulted in his election as Governor of New York. Serving as Governor from 1883 till 1884, he was nominated by the Democrats for the Presidency and elected President in 1884. Defeated for a second term in 1888, he was renominated and re-elected in 1892. After the expiration of his term, in 1897 he retired to Princeton, New Jersey.

FIRST INAUGURAL ADDRESS

(Delivered March 4th, 1885)

Fellow-Citizens:—

IN THE presence of this vast assemblage of my countrymen, I am about to supplement and seal by the oath which I shall take the manifestation of the will of a great and free people. In the exercise of their power and right of self-government they have committed to one of their fellow-citizens a supreme and sacred trust, and he here consecrates himself to their service.

This impressive ceremony adds little to the solemn sense of responsibility with which I contemplate the duty I owe to all the people of the land. Nothing can relieve me from anxiety lest by any act of mine their interests may suffer, and nothing is needed to strengthen my resolution to engage every faculty and effort in the promotion of their welfare.

Amid the din of party strife the people's choice was made, but its attendant circumstances have demonstrated anew the

vail in which the Constitution had its birth. If this involves the surrender or postponement of private interests and the abandonment of local advantages, compensation will be found in the assurance that the common interest is subserved and the general welfare advanced.

In the discharge of my official duty I shall endeavor to be guided by a just and unstrained construction of the Constitution, a careful observance of the distinction between the powers granted to the Federal Government and those reserved to the States or to the people, and by a cautious appreciation of those functions which by the Constitution and laws have been especially assigned to the executive branch of the Government.

But he who takes the oath to-day to preserve, protect, and defend the Constitution of the United States only assumes the solemn obligation which every patriotic citizen — on the farm, in the workshop, in the busy marts of trade, and everywhere — should share with him. The Constitution which prescribes his oath, my countrymen, is yours; the Government you have chosen him to administer for a time is yours; the suffrage which executes the will of freemen is yours; the laws and the entire scheme of our civil rule, from the town meeting to the State capitals and the national capital, is yours. Your every voter, as surely as your Chief Magistrate, under the same high sanction, though in a different sphere, exercises a public trust. Nor is this all. Every citizen owes to the country a vigilant watch and close scrutiny of its public servants and a fair and reasonable estimate of their fidelity and usefulness. Thus is the people's will impressed upon the whole framework of our civil polity — municipal, State, and Federal; and this is the price of our liberty and the inspiration of our faith in the Republic.

It is the duty of those serving the people in public place to closely limit public expenditures to the actual needs of the Government economically administered, because this bounds the right of the Government to exact tribute from the earnings of labor or the property of the citizen, and because public extravagance begets extravagance among the people. We should never be ashamed of the simplicity and prudential economies which are best suited to the operation of a republican form of government and most compatible with the mission of the American people. Those who are selected for a limited time to manage public affairs are still of the people, and may do much by their example

strength and safety of a government by the people. In each succeeding year it more clearly appears that our democratic principle needs no apology, and that in its fearless and faithful application is to be found the surest guaranty of good government.

But the best results in the operation of a government wherein every citizen has a share largely depend upon a proper limitation of purely partisan zeal and effort and a correct appreciation of the time when the heat of the partisan should be merged in the patriotism of the citizen.

To-day the executive branch of the Government is transferred to new keeping. But this is still the Government of all the people, and it should be none the less an object of their affectionate solicitude. At this hour the animosities of political strife, the bitterness of partisan defeat, and the exultation of partisan triumph should be supplanted by an ungrudging acquiescence in the popular will and a sober, conscientious concern for the general weal. Moreover, if from this hour we cheerfully and honestly abandon all sectional prejudice and distrust, and determine, with manly confidence in one another, to work out harmoniously the achievement of our national destiny, we shall deserve to realize all the benefits which our happy form of government can bestow.

On this auspicious occasion we may well renew the pledge of our devotion to the Constitution, which, launched by the founders of the Republic and consecrated by their prayers and patriotic devotion, has for almost a century borne the hopes and the aspirations of a great people through prosperity and peace and through the shock of foreign conflicts and the perils of domestic strife and vicissitudes.

By the Father of his Country our Constitution was commended for adoption as "the result of a spirit of amity and mutual concession." In that same spirit it should be administered, in order to promote the lasting welfare of the country and to secure the full measure of its priceless benefits to us and to those who will succeed to the blessings of our national life. The large variety of diverse and competing interests subject to Federal control, persistently seeking the recognition of their claims, need give us no fear that "the greatest good to the greatest number" will fail to be accomplished if in the halls of national legislation that spirit of amity and mutual concession shall pre

to encourage, consistently with the dignity of their official functions, that plain way of life which among their fellow-citizens aids integrity and promotes thrift and prosperity.

The genius of our institutions, the needs of our people in their home life, and the attention which is demanded for the settlement and development of the resources of our vast territory, dictate the scrupulous avoidance of any departure from that foreign policy commended by the history, the traditions, and the prosperity of our Republic. It is the policy of independence, favored by our position and defended by our known love of justice and by our own power. It is the policy of peace suitable to our interests. It is the policy of neutrality, rejecting any share in foreign broils and ambitions upon other continents and repelling their intrusion here. It is the policy of Monroe, and of Washington, and of Jefferson — "Peace, commerce, and honest friendship with all nations; entangling alliance with none."

A due regard for the interests and prosperity of all the people demands that our finances shall be established upon such a sound and sensible basis as shall secure the safety and confidence of business interests and make the wages of labor sure and steady, and that our system of revenue shall be so adjusted as to relieve the people of unnecessary taxation, having a due regard to the interests of capital invested and workingmen employed in American industries, and preventing the accumulation of a surplus in the treasury to tempt extravagance and waste.

Care for the property of the nation and for the needs of future settlers requires that the public domain should be protected from purloining schemes and unlawful occupation.

The conscience of the people demands that the Indians within our boundaries shall be fairly and honestly treated as wards of the Government and their education and civilization promoted with a view to their ultimate citizenship, and that polygamy in the Territories, destructive of the family relation and offensive to the moral sense of the civilized world, shall be repressed.

The laws should be rigidly enforced which prohibit the immigration of a servile class to compete with American labor, with no intention of acquiring citizenship, and bringing with them and retaining habits and customs repugnant to our civilization.

The people demand reform in the administration of the Government and the application of business principles to public affairs. As a means to this end, civil service reform should be in good faith enforced. Our citizens have the right to protection from the incompetency of public employees who hold their places solely as the reward of partisan service, and from the corrupting influence of those who promise and the vicious methods of those who expect such rewards; and those who worthily seek public employment have the right to insist that merit and competency shall be recognized instead of party subserviency or the surrender of honest political belief.

In the administration of a government pledged to do equal and exact justice to all men, there should be no pretext for anxiety touching the protection of the freedmen in their rights or their security in the enjoyment of their privileges under the Constitution and its amendments. All discussion as to their fitness for the place accorded to them as American citizens is idle and unprofitable except as it suggests the necessity for their improvement. The fact that they are citizens entitles them to all the rights due to that relation and charges them with all its duties, obligations, and responsibilities.

These topics and the constant and ever-varying wants of an active and enterprising population may well receive the attention and the patriotic endeavor of all who make and execute the Federal law. Our duties are practical and call for industrious application, an intelligent perception of the claims of public office, and, above all, a firm determination, by united action, to secure to all the people of the land the full benefits of the best form of government ever vouchsafed to man. And let us not trust to human effort alone, but humbly acknowledging the power and goodness of Almighty God, who presides over the destiny of nations and who has at all times been revealed in our country's history let us invoke his aid and his blessing upon our labors.

DE WITT CLINTON

(1769–1828)

DE WITT CLINTON was the foremost man in the public life of New York during the first quarter of the nineteenth century, and he no doubt deserves to be called the chief of those whose sagacity and successful efforts lifted her to her position of "Empire State." He was the son of Gen. James Clinton of the Revolution, and nephew of another statesman and general, Gov. George Clinton, of New York, who was Vice-President of the United States from 1805 to 1812. Educated at Columbia College and admitted to the bar at the age of twenty in 1788, he became the secretary of his uncle, Governor Clinton, and one of the rising young men in the dominant Republican party. After serving in both houses of the State legislature, he became United States Senator in 1802. Besides being a Member of the State senate and Lieutenant-Governor [from 1811 to 1813], he was Mayor of the city of New York from 1803 to 1815, with the exception of two short intervals amounting to three years. In 1812 he was defeated as a candidate for the Presidency by James Madison. He then devoted himself to plans for internal improvement of which he had long been a distinguished advocate. The Federal Government having refused to undertake the proposed canals from the Hudson to Lake Erie and Lake Champlain, he presented a memorial which induced the State legislature to enter upon the preliminary steps. On this issue he was elected Governor in 1816, and re-elected in 1819, in 1824, and in 1826. He was born at Little Britain, Orange County, New York, March 2d, 1769, and died February 11th, 1828, at Albany.

FEDERAL POWER AND LOCAL RIGHTS

(Delivered in the New York Constitutional Convention of June 1788. From Elliot's Debates)

I RISE, Mr. Chairman, to make a few observations, with a view to obtaining information, and discovering on which side of this important question the truth rests. I have attended with pleasure to the gentlemen who have spoken before me. They appear, however, to have omitted some considerations, which have

tended to convince my mind that the representation in Congress ought to be more comprehensive and full than is proposed by this Constitution. It is said that the representation of this State in the legislature is smaller than the representation of the United States will be in the General Government. Hence it is inferred that the Federal Government, which, it is said, does not embrace more powers than that of the States, will be more favorable to the liberties of the people, on the principle that safety consists in numbers. This appears plausible at first view; but if we examine it we shall discover it to be only plausible. The cases, indeed, are so different as to admit of little comparison; and this dissimilarity depends on the difference of extent of territory. Each State is but a narrow district compared with the United States. The situation of its commerce, its agriculture, and the system of its resources, will be proportionably more uniform and simple. To a knowledge of these circumstances, therefore, every member of the State legislature will be in some degree competent. He will have a considerable share of information necessary for enacting laws which are to operate in every part of the State. The easy communication with a large number of representatives from the minute districts of the State will increase his acquaintance with the public wants. All the representatives, having the same advantages, will furnish a mass of information which will be the securest defense from error. How different will be the situation of the General Government! The body of the Legislature will be totally unacquainted with all those local circumstances of any particular State, which mark the proper objects of laws, and especially of taxation. A few men, possessed of but a very general knowledge of these objects, must alone furnish Congress with that information on which they are to act; and on these few men, in the most interesting transactions, must they rely. Do not these considerations afford reasons for enlargement of the representation?

Another argument may be suggested to show that there will be more safety in the State than in the Federal Government. In the State, the legislature, being generally known, and under the perpetual observation of their fellow-citizens, feel strongly the check resulting from the facility of communication and discovery. In a small territory, maladministration is easily corrected, and designs unfavorable to liberty frustrated and punished. But in large confederacies, the alarm excited by small and

gradual encroachments rarely extends to the distant members, or inspires a general spirit of resistance. When we take a view of the United States, we find them embracing interests as various as their territory is extensive. Their habits, their productions, their resources, and their political and commercial regulations, are as different as those of any nation upon earth. A general law, therefore, which might be well calculated for Georgia, might operate most disadvantageously and cruelly upon New York. However, I only suggest these observations for the purpose of hearing them satisfactorily answered. I am open to conviction, and if my objections can be removed, I shall be ready frankly to acknowledge their weakness. . . .

I declare, solemnly, that I am a friend to a strong and efficient government. But, sir, we may err in this extreme; we may erect a system that will destroy the liberties of the people. Sir, at the time some of these resolves were passed, there was a dangerous attempt to subvert our liberties, by creating a supreme dictator. There are many gentlemen present who know how strongly I opposed it. My opposition was at the very time we were surrounded by difficulties and danger. The people, when wearied with their distresses, will, in the moment of frenzy, be guilty of the most imprudent and desperate measures. Because a strong government was wanted during the late war, does it follow that we should now be obliged to accept of a dangerous one? I ever lamented the feebleness of the Confederation, for this reason, among others, that the experience of its weakness would one day drive the people into an adoption of a constitution dangerous to our liberties. I know the people are too apt to vibrate from one extreme to another. The effects of this disposition are what I wish to guard against. If the gentleman can show me that the proposed Constitution is a safe one, I will drop all opposition. The public resolves which have been read to you are only expressive of the desire that once prevailed to remove present difficulties. A general impost was intended, but it was intended as a temporary measure. I appeal to every gentleman present, if I have not been uniformly in favor of granting an impost to Congress. I confess that, seeing the manner in which that body proposed to exercise the power, I could not agree to it. I firmly believed, that, if it were granted in the form recommended, it would prove unproductive, and would also lead to the establishment of dangerous principles. I believed that granting the revenue, without giving the power of collection, or a control over our State officers, would be the most wise and prudent measure. These are and ever have been my sentiments.

AGAINST THE MILITARY SPIRIT

(From the Speech of February 23d, 1803, Protesting Against Forcing a War with Spain. Delivered in the United State Senate)

I SHALL not attempt to occupy your attention by threadbare declamation upon the evils of war, by painting the calamities it inflicts upon the happiness of individuals and the prosperity of nations. This terrible scourge of mankind, worse than famine or pestilence, ought not to be resorted to until every reasonable expedient has been adopted to avert it. When aggressions have been committed by the sovereign or representatives of the will of the nation, negotiation ought, in all cases, to be first tried, unless the rights of self-defense demand a contrary course. This is the practice of nations, and is enjoined by the unerring monitor which the God of nature has planted in every human bosom. What right have the rulers of nations to unsheathe the sword of destruction, and to let loose the demon of desolation upon mankind whenever caprice or pride, ambition or avarice, shall prescribe? And are there no fixed laws, founded in the nature of things, which ordain bounds to the fell spirit of revenge, the mad fury of domination, and the insatiable thirst of cupidity? Mankind have, not only in their individual character, but in their collective capacity as nations, recognized and avowed, in their opinions and actions, a system of laws calculated to produce the greatest happiness of the greatest number. And it may be safely asserted that it is a fundamental article of this code that a nation ought not to go to war until it is evident that the injury committed is highly detrimental, and that it emanated from the will of the nation, charged with the aggression, either by an express authorization in the first instance, or by a recognition of it when called upon for redress, and a refusal in both cases to give it. A demand of satisfaction ought to precede an appeal to arms, even when the injury is manifestly the act of the sovereign; and when it is the act of a private individual, it is not imputable to its nation until its government is called upon to explain and redress, and refuses; because the

evils of war are too heavy and serious to be incurred without the most urgent necessity; because remonstrance and negotiation have often recalled an offending nation to a sense of justice and a performance of right; because nations, like individuals, have their paroxysms of passion, and when reflection and reason resume their dominion, will extend that redress to the olive branch, which their pride will not permit them to grant to the sword; because a nation is a moral person, and as such is not chargeable with an offense committed by others, or where its will has not been consulted; the unauthorized conduct of individuals being never considered a just ground of hostility, until their sovereign refuses that reparation for which his right of controlling their actions and of punishing their misconduct necessarily renders him responsible. These opinions are sanctioned by the most approved elementary writers on the laws of nations. I shall quote the sentiments of some of them.

Vattel says: "Two things, therefore, are necessary to render it [an offensive war] just. First, a right to be asserted,—that is, that a demand made on another nation be important and well grounded; second, that this reasonable demand cannot be obtained otherwise than by force of arms. Necessity alone warrants the use of force. It is a dangerous and terrible resource. Nature, the common parent of mankind, allows of it only in extremity, and when all others fail. It is doing wrong to a nation to make use of violence against it, before we know whether it be disposed to do us justice, or to refuse it. Those, who, without trying pacific measures, on the least motive run to arms, sufficiently show that justificative reasons, in their mouths, are only pretenses; they eagerly seize the opportunity of indulging their passions and of gratifying their ambition under some color of right." It is subsequently stated by this admired writer, that "it is demonstrated in the foregoing chapter, that, to take arms lawfully, first, we have a just cause of complaint; second, that a reasonable satisfaction has been denied us, etc."

Burlamaqui says: "However just reason we may have to make war, yet as it inevitably brings along with it an incredible number of calamities, and often injustices, it is certain that we ought not to proceed too easily to a dangerous extremity, which may, perhaps, prove fatal to the conqueror himself. The following are the measures which prudence directs sovereigns to observe in these circumstances: First, supposing the reason of the war is just

in itself, yet the dispute ought to be about something of great consequence to us, since it is better even to relinquish part of our right, when the thing is not considerable, than to have recourse to arms to defend it. Second, we ought to have at least some probable appearance of success; for it would be a criminal temerity, and a real folly, wantonly to expose ourselves to certain destruction, and to run into a greater, in order to avoid a lesser evil. Lastly, there should be a real necessity for taking up arms; that is, we ought not to have recourse to force, but when we can employ no milder method of recovering our rights, or of defending ourselves from the evils with which we are menaced. These measures are agreeable not only to the principles of prudence, but also to the fundamental maxims of sociability, and the love of peace; maxims of no less force, with respect to nations, than individuals. By these a sovereign must, therefore, be necessarily directed; even the justice of the government obliges him to it, in consequence of the very nature and end of authority. For as he ought always to take particular care of the State, and of his subjects, consequently he should not expose them to all the evils with which war is attended, except in the last extremity, and when there is no other expedient left but that of arms." In addition to these great authorities, permit me to refer severally to the opinions of two more modern writers, Martens and Paley. The former says that all amicable means for redress must be tried in vain, before an appeal to arms, unless it is evident that it would be useless to try such means; and the latter is of opinion, that the only justifying causes of war are deliberate invasions of right, and maintaining the balance of power. It is not necessary to decide upon the justice of the last observation, because it does not apply to the case before us. But can any man lay his hand upon his heart, and declare that he believes the present case a deliberate invasion of right by the Spanish government? Can any man say that it would be fruitless to attempt amicable means of redress, and that the sword alone can restore us to our rights?

The opinions of these celebrated writers are corroborated by the general usage of nations. A demand of redress, before the application of force, has been almost uniformly practiced by the most barbarous, as well as the most civilized nations. Instances may, indeed, be found to the contrary, but they are to be considered as departures from established usage. The ancient Romans,

who were a military nation, and who marched to empire through an ocean of blood, always demanded satisfaction from the offending nation before they proceeded to war, and fixed upon a certain time in which the demand was to be complied with; at the expiration of which, if redress was still withheld, they then endeavored to obtain it by force. It has been the general practice of the civilized nations of Europe to promulgate manifestoes justificatory of their conduct, in resorting to arms. These manifestoes contain a full statement of their wrongs, and almost always declare that they had previously endeavored by negotiation to obtain a friendly adjustment of their complaints. What is this but a declaration that the law and the sense of nations demand this course? What is it but an appeal to the intuitive sense of right and wrong, which exists in every human bosom?

The practice of our government has been uniformly conformable to the principles I have endeavored to establish, and I trust I shall be excused for bestowing particular consideration on this subject. We have heard much of the policy of Washington; it has been sounded in our ears from all quarters, and an honorable gentleman from Delaware [Mr. White] has triumphantly contrasted it with that adopted by the present administration. I am not disposed to censure it in this case; on the contrary, I think it a high and respectable authority; but let it be properly understood, in order to be rightly appreciated, and it will be found that the United States, under his administration, and that of his successor, have received injuries more deleterious, insults more atrocious, and indignities more pointed than the present, and that the pacific measure of negotiation was preferred. If our national honor has survived the severe wounds it then received, it may surely outlive the comparatively slight attack now made upon it; but if its ghost only now remains to haunt the consciences of the honorable gentlemen, who were then in power, and who polluted their hands with the foul murder, let them not attempt to transfer the odium and the crime to those who had no hand in the guilty deed. They then stood high in the councils of their country; the reins of government were in their hands; and if the course they at that time pursued was diametrically opposite to that they now urge for our adoption, what shall we say of their consistency? What will they say of it themselves? What will their country say of it? Will it be believed that the tinkling sounds and professions of patriotism, which have been so vehemently pressed upon us, are the emanations of sincerity, or will they be set down to the account of juggling imposture?

. . . .

A vast augmentation of our national debt would be the certain consequence of this measure. It is a moderate estimate to say that our annual expenditures, over and above our surplus revenue, would be twenty millions of dollars; and we cannot reasonably expect that the war would continue a shorter period than five years. Hence one hundred millions would be added to our debt, and the great experiment, which we are now trying, of extinguishing it in fourteen years, would certainly fail — an experiment which has been defeated in Europe by war and prodigality; and for the success of which, in this country, every friend of republican government looks up with the greatest anxiety. But this is not all; heavy and oppressive taxation would be necessary in order to pay off the interest of the accumulating debt and to meet the other exigencies of government. We are now a happy nation in this respect. Neither the temper nor the habits of our citizens will patiently submit to severe burdens, and happily the posture of our financial arrangements does not require them. Give the rein, however, to chimerical notions of war — embrace the proposition now submitted to us, and the weight of your impositions will be felt in every nerve and artery of our political system. Excises, taxes on houses and lands, will be reintroduced, and the evils of former administrations will be multiplied upon us. But the mischief will not stop here. With the increasing calls for money from the people, their means to satisfy them will be diminished. The superior naval force of the enemy would cripple our commerce in every quarter of the globe. Great Britain and Spain hold the keys of the Mediterranean. We should, therefore, be entirely shut out of that sea, unless we could persuade the former to unite her exertions with ours. With the decay of our commerce, with our exclusion from foreign markets, the labors of our farmers would be palsied, the skill of our manufacturers would be rendered useless, and, with the fruits of their industry perishing on their hands, or greatly undersold, how would they be able to meet the augmented wants of government? What, in the meantime, would become of the claim of our merchants upon Spain, for at least five millions of dollars, and to what perils would your commercial cities be

exposed? These certain evils would be encountered without producing the least benefit to our Western brethren. The seizure of New Orleans would vest us with a place of deposit; but a place of deposit, without the free navigation of the Mississippi, would be entirely useless. As long as the enemy holds the country below New Orleans, and possesses a superior naval force, so long we will be excluded from the Mississippi. Suppose, however, this obstacle removed — suppose we are enabled to pass into the Gulf without molestation, is it not necessary for vessels to hug the island of Cuba on their passage to the Atlantic States? And will not this expose them to certain capture, as long as Spain retains that important possession? To secure the great object said to be aimed at by this resolution, and to establish beyond the reach of annoyance a free communication between the Atlantic and Western States, we must seize not only New Orleans, but the Floridas and Cuba; and we must immediately create a formidable navy. It is needless to mention that the Atlantic States are, with a few exceptions, the carriers of the Western produce. Three-fourths of that trade is managed by the merchants of the State I have the honor to represent. I therefore view this measure as pregnant with great mischief to the commerce of Atlantic America, and as a certain exclusion of the Western States from market as long as the war shall continue.

It is no slight objection in the minds of the sincere friends of republicanism that this measure will have a tendency to disadjust the balance of our government by strengthening the hands of the Executive, furnishing him with extensive patronage, investing him with great discretionary powers, and placing under his direction a large standing army. It is the inevitable consequence of war in free countries, that the power which wields the force will rise above the power that expresses the will of the people. The State governments will also receive a severe shock; those stately pillars which support the magnificent dome of our national government will totter under the increased weight of the superincumbent pressure. Nor will the waste of morals, the spirit of cupidity, the thirst of blood, and the general profligacy of manners, which will follow the introduction of this measure, be viewed by the great body of our citizens without the most fearful anxiety and the most heartfelt deprecation. And if there are any persons in this country, and I should regret if there are

any such in this House, who think that a public debt is a public blessing, and that heavy taxation is expedient in order to produce industry; who believe that large standing armies are essential to maintain the energy, and that extensive patronage is indispensable to support the dignity of government; who suppose that frequent wars are necessary to animate the human character, and to call into action the dormant energies of our nature; who have been expelled from authority and power by the indignant voice of an offended country, and who repine and suffer at the great and unexampled prosperity which this country is rapidly attaining under other and better auspices — such men, whoever they are, and wherever they be, will rally round the proposition now before us, and will extol it to the heavens as the model of the most profound policy, and as the offspring of the most exalted energy.

If I were called upon to prescribe a course of policy most important for this country to pursue, it would be to avoid European connections and wars. The time must arrive when we will have to contend with some of the great powers of Europe, but let that period be put off as long as possible. It is our interest and our duty to cultivate peace, with sincerity and good faith. As a young nation, pursuing industry in every channel, and adventuring commerce in every sea, it is highly important that we should not only have a pacific character, but that we should really deserve it. If we manifest an unwarrantable ambition, and a rage for conquest, we unite all the great powers of Europe against us. The security of all the European possessions in our vicinity will eternally depend, not upon their strength, but upon our moderation and justice. Look at the Canadas; at the Spanish territories to the south; at the British, Spanish, French, Danish, and Dutch West India Islands; at the vast countries to the west, as far as where the Pacific rolls its waves. Consider well the eventful consequences that would result, if we were possessed by a spirit of conquest. Consider well the impression, which a manifestation of that spirit will make upon those who would be affected by it. If we are to rush at once into the territory of a neighboring nation, with fire and sword, for the misconduct of a subordinate officer, will not our national character be greatly injured? Will we not be classed with the robbers and destroyers of mankind? Will not the nations of Europe perceive in this conduct the germ of a lofty spirit, and

an enterprising ambition, which will level them to the earth, when age has matured our strength, and expanded our powers of annoyance, unless they combine to cripple us in our infancy? May not the consequences be, that we must look out for a naval force to protect our commerce, that a close alliance will result, that we will be thrown at once into the ocean of European politics, where every wave that rolls, and every wind that blows, will agitate our bark? Is this a desirable state of things? Will the people of this country be seduced into it by all the colorings of rhetoric, and all the arts of sophistry — by vehement appeals to their pride, and artful addresses to their cupidity? No, sir. Three-fourths of the American people, I assert it boldly and without fear of contradiction, are opposed to this measure. And would you take up arms with a millstone hanging round your neck? How would you bear up, not only against the force of the enemy, but against the irresistible current of public opinion? The thing, sir, is impossible; the measure is worse than madness; it is wicked, beyond the powers of description.

HOWELL COBB

(1815–1868)

FROM December 4th, 1843, to March 3d, 1851, Howell Cobb was one of the most prominent of the Southern leaders in Congress. He was Speaker of the Thirty-First Congress, and Governor of Georgia from 1851 to 1853. He was again a Member of Congress from December 3d, 1855, to March 3d, 1857, when he became Mr. Buchanan's Secretary of the Treasury—an office in which he continued until his resignation, December 10th, 1860. He was President of the Montgomery convention which created the Confederate States Government. He was commissioned a Brigadier-General in the Confederate army in February 1862 and promoted to Major-General in September 1863. At the close of the war he surrendered at Macon, Georgia. He was born at Cherry Hill, Georgia, September 7th, 1815, and died in New York city, October 9th, 1868. His speech on the Oregon boundary question illustrates an issue which threatened war with England and caused great excitement in the United States.

«FIFTY-FOUR FORTY OR FIGHT!»

(From an Address of January 8th, 1846. Before a Committee of the House of Representatives Having Under Consideration the Oregon Boundary Question)

WHEN will this Government be prepared to maintain our just rights in the Oregon Territory? Will gentlemen who follow me in this debate be so good as to inform the country to what period of time they look forward when the United States will be in a proper condition to defend her national rights in Oregon? Where is the difficulty? Why are you not prepared to defend Oregon and your rights in the territory? Is it owing to the condition of your army or of your navy? So far as your army is concerned, it is a settled principle in the Government, if I understand and appreciate our people aright, that the Government shall never be dependent on a standing army for the protection of the rights of the people. You can

never induce, and I trust you will never desire to induce, this Government to create a large standing army in time of peace as preparatory to some future emergency which may require it. The bulwark of the defense of our country lies in the hearts and the spirit of the American people. It is to the citizen-soldier, and not the mercenary hireling, that the American people look for the defense of their rights in an emergency of this kind. Is your navy not prepared? Mr. Chairman, I am not prepared, nor should I detain you if I were prepared to go into a discussion of the condition and character of our navy. But tell me when we will be better prepared than we are now? Will it be at some future period? Are you prepared at once to make a heavy appropriation for the increase of your navy? Will this Government ever be prepared, in a time of peace, to pursue a policy of this kind? If so, it will differ widely from the history of the past or of congresses preceding. And those who are most anxious now for the settlement of the Oregon question, and those who are in favor of postponing it to a future period, many of them will be found on common ground in warfare upon our little navy—that gallant navy which needs no praise from me since its praise is written in the history of the country.

Mr. Chairman, I have exhausted more time upon the discussion of these one or two points than I had intended, and I fear I must pass by some others to which I had intended to refer. There was, however, one prominently brought forward in this discussion upon which I must bestow at least a passing thought. It is said by those who advocate it, that this is a peace measure, and by those who oppose it a war measure. Mr. Chairman, I am not prepared to go to the full extent with some who declare that the inevitable result of the passage of this notice will be to involve this country in a bloody and destructive war. Nor am I prepared, on the other hand, to go with those who fearlessly assert that there is no danger to result from our action in reference to Oregon. I plant myself on this ground, that the course which I propose to pursue is the one called for by the national faith and honor of my country; and I am in the prosecution of what I conceive to be the just rights of my Government, and am endeavoring to carry out the policy best calculated to secure this end. If peace be the result, I shall gladly welcome it. If war be the consequence, we must meet it. It is a crisis not to be avoided, not to be evaded, but to be met

with boldness, firmness, and decision. When we have discharged our duties, then, sir, it will be for another department of our Government, and for the Government with whom we are in collision upon this subject, to do what they may conceive to be their duty. If, Mr. Chairman, the result shall be inauspicious,—if it shall involve us in war,—I will have the consoling reflection left that I have pursued a course of policy dictated by the best interests of my country, as far as I have been enabled to appreciate those interests. That we should suffer from a war, I do not pretend to deny; that we shall lose the Oregon Territory by resorting to war is an idea I utterly repudiate. Whenever this Government shall be engaged in a conflict of this kind with the British Government, or with any other government on earth, peace will never be declared upon terms leaving one foot of territory which has ever been consecrated to American freedom and American principles, afterwards to be profaned by monarchical or despotic principles. No; Canada may be acquired. I do not dispute that position of gentlemen who have argued this proposition before the House; but that Oregon will ever be abandoned peacefully, or in the struggle of war, my mind has never been brought to conclude, nor will it be. Sir, upon this day, this memorable, glorious eighth of January, let it not be said by American statesmen, in an American Congress, that this Government can be injured, can be deprived, can be weakened in her just and unquestionable rights by a conflict with Great Britain, or with any other government. If war come, I venture the prediction that when it terminates we will have the consolation of knowing that not a British flag floats on an American breeze; that not a British subject treads on American soil. There is where war ought to terminate, if come it must; there is where I believe and trust in heaven it will terminate.

WILLIAM COBBETT

(1762–1835)

WILLIAM COBBETT reveled in the turmoil of controversy, and apparently was never happier than when undergoing prosecution for libelous or seditious utterances. Indeed, much of his work as editor and author was done in prison. His disposition to row against the current and to take the part of the "under dog" was conspicuous in his life in America as well as in England. A British soldier discharged in Canada, he began the publication of his Peter Porcupine Papers and his Porcupine Gazette in Wilmington, and in 1796 set up as a bookseller and publisher of his own writings in Philadelphia. Here he was as much against the government as he ever was against that of England after his return thither. His praises of Great Britain, his scorn of American institutions and attacks on American statesmen involved him in prosecutions for libel which in 1800 drove him back to England. There he was at first regarded as a loyal refugee, the champion of monarchy and order. He dined with Windham, was introduced to Pitt, and was offered a share in the True Briton. But he refused the gift, opened a bookshop in Pall Mall, and revived his Porcupine Gazette which was followed in 1802 by the Weekly Political Register. Ere long his windows were smashed by an angry mob, and by his personalities he again incurred heavy fines. In 1809 his comments on the flogging of several militia men exposed him to a fine of £1000 and two years' imprisonment. From his prison he continued the publication of the Political Register. By 1817 his debts and other difficulties compelled him to take refuge for a time in the United States, and it was here that he wrote his English grammar, of which ten thousand copies were sold in a month. He was a self-educated man, a vigorous if not a polished speaker and writer. His speeches and lectures in the principal cities of England and Scotland drew large audiences. He was born March 9th, 1762, in Surrey. In 1832 he was elected to the House of Commons, not long after the disagreement of a jury had delivered him from a prosecution for inciting rebellion. In 1834 he was reelected, but his health failed, and he died June 16th, 1835. A long list of his printed books can be found in the catalogue of any public library.

THE MAN ON THE TOWER

(Peroration of His Speech Before the Court of King's Bench, Defending Himself Against a Charge of Libel, in July 1831)

THE fact is, that I am the watchman, the man on the tower, who can be neither coaxed, nor wheedled, nor bullied; and I have expressed my determination never to quit my post until I obtain a cheap government for the country, and, by doing away with places and pensions, prevent the people's pockets from being picked. These men know that if I were to get into the House of Commons under a reformed Parliament, I should speedily effect that object, and therefore they are resolved to get rid of me by some means or 'other; but, thank God, gentlemen, you will not let them effect it on the present occasion.

I have little else to add, except to state what evidence I shall lay before you. The first witness I shall call will be the Lord Chancellor, and I will put in the letter to the Luddites, which by delivery to Lord Brougham for publication, I, in point of law, republished at the very time when I was said to be endeavoring to stir up the laborers to sedition and outrage. I will then call his lordship to prove the fact respecting the application for it, and he will tell you that I stipulated no terms, but that the whole of the letter should be published. I shall then call the Earl of Radnor, who knows me and all my sentiments well, and he will tell you whether I am a likely man to design and endeavor to do that which this false and malicious Whig indictment charges me with wishing to do. I shall also call several persons of the highest respectability from Kent, Sussex, and other parts of the country, to prove that I have not done anything to stir up disturbance, but that I have done a great deal to prevent it and to restore quiet. I shall then call Lord Melbourne to prove that the sentence on Goodman was not executed, but that he was sent out of the country, whereas Cook was put to death. When the jury shall have heard all this, and shall have read over the various publications, I have not the slightest doubt but that they will dismiss with scorn and contempt this groundless charge of the Whig Attorney-General. This is the second time in my life that I have been prosecuted by an Attorney-General, and brought before this court. I have been writing for thirty years, and only twice out of that long period

have I been brought before this court. The first time was by an apostate Whig. What, indeed, of evil have the Whigs not done? Since then, although there have been six Attorneys-General, all Tories, and although, were I a Crown lawyer, I might pick out plenty of libels from my writings, if this be a libel, yet I have never for twenty-one years been prosecuted until this Whig government came in. But the Whigs were always a most tyrannical faction; they always tried to make tyranny double tyranny; they were always the most severe, the most grasping, the most greedy, the most tyrannical faction whose proceedings are recorded in history. It was they who seized what remained of the Crown lands; it was they who took to themselves the last portion of Church property; it was they who passed the monstrous Riot Act; it was they also who passed the Septennial Bill. The Government are now acquiring great credit for doing away with the rotten boroughs; but if they deserve credit for doing them away, let it be borne in mind that the Whigs created them. They established an interest in the regulation, and gave consistency and value to corruption. Then came the excise laws, which were brought in by the Whigs; and from them, too, emanated that offensive statute by which Irish men and Irish women may be transported without judge or jury. There is, indeed, no faction so severe and cruel; they do everything by force and violence. The Whigs are the Rehoboam of England; the Tories ruled us with rods, but the Whigs scourge us with scorpions.

The last time I was brought before this court, I was sent out of it to two years' imprisonment among felons, and was condemned to pay, at the expiration of the two years, a fine of one thousand pounds sterling to the King, which the King took and kept. But this was not all; I was bound, too, in a penalty of five thousand pounds myself, and obliged to procure two sureties in two thousand five hundred pounds each to keep the peace for seven years. . . . I was carried seventy miles from my family and shut up in a jail, doubtless with the hope that I should expire from stench and mortification of mind. It pleased God, however, to bless me with health, and, though deprived of liberty, by dint of sobriety and temperance, I outlived the base attempt to destroy me. What crime had I committed? For what was it that I was condemned to this horrible punishment? Simply for writing a paragraph in which I expressed the indig-

nation I felt at an English local militiaman having been flogged under a guard of German bayonets! I only expressed the indignation I felt, and I should have been a base creature, indeed, if I had not expressed it. But now military flogging excites universal indignation. If there be at present any of the jury alive who found me guilty and sentenced me to that punishment, what remorse must they not feel for their conduct when they perceive that all the writers in every periodical of the present day, even including the favorite publication of the Whig Attorney-General, are now unanimous in deprecating the system of military flogging altogether! Yet, for expressing my disapprobation of that system I was tossed into a dungeon like Daniel into the lion's den. But why am I now tossed down before this court by the Attorney-General? What are my sins? I have called on the Government to respect the law; I have cautioned them that hard-hearted proceedings are driving the laborers to despair! That is my crime! If the Government really wish to avoid disturbances in the country, let them give us back the old laws; let them give the people the old game law, and repeal the new law; and let them do away with the other grinding laws that oppress the poor. I have read with horror which I cannot describe of a magistrate being accused to the Lord Chancellor of subornation of perjury; I have read of that magistrate being reinstated, and I have shuddered with horror at supposing that a poor starving laborer may be brought before such a man, and in conjunction with another such magistrate may be doomed to seven years' transportation for being out at night. And such a magistrate may be himself a game-preserver! This is a monstrous power, and certainly ought to be abolished. The ministry, however, will perhaps adopt the measures I have recommended, and then prosecute me for recommending them. Just so it is with parliamentary reform, a measure which I have been foremost in recommending for twenty years. I have pointed out and insisted upon the sort of reform that we must have; and they are compelled already to adopt a large part of my suggestions, and avowedly against their will. They hate me for this; they look upon it as I do, that they are married to Reform, and that I am the man who has furnished the halter in which they are led to church. For supplying that halter they have made this attack on me through the Attorney-General, and will slay me if they can. The Whigs know that my intention was not bad.

This is a mere pretense to inflict pecuniary ruin on me, or cause me to die of sickness in a jail, so that they may get rid of me, because they can neither buy nor silence me. It is their fears which make them attack me, and it is my death they intend. In that object they will be defeated, for, thank heaven, you stand between me and destruction. If, however, your verdict should be—which I do not anticipate—one that will consign me to death by sending me to a loathsome dungeon, I will with my last breath pray to God to bless my country and curse the Whigs; and I bequeath my revenge to my children and the laborers of England.

RICHARD COBDEN

(1804–1865)

ICHARD COBDEN sacrificed his life by leaving his sick room and hastening to London in the spring of 1865 to resist in the House of Commons the proposed fortification of Canada. His Free Trade agitation had always been subordinated to the high moral purpose of promoting peace on earth and good-will among men. As he considered free commerce between nations the surest means of avoiding wars and abolishing armies, the proposition to fortify Canada at a time of strained relations between the United States and England aroused him to undertake a journey which proved fatal. When his death was announced to the House of Commons, his character and public services were praised as "an honor to England" by his former political antagonists, and his old friend and co-adjutor, John Bright, overpowered by emotion after speaking a sentence or two in a tremulous voice, said he must leave to a calmer moment what he had to say "of the manliest and gentlest spirit that ever quitted or tenanted a human form."

In truth the production of men of the Cobden type is the greatest glory of modern England, and to the labors of such men she owes more of her greatness than to the splendid heroism of her warriors. A widow's son, with only such rudimentary education as could be obtained at a country grammar school, he found time in the midst of very assiduous and successful attention to commercial pursuits, to make himself one of the best informed and ablest teachers of his generation. After he had built up a business yielding him a profit of $40,000 a year, he turned aside from it and began to write the magazine articles and pamphlets which eventually revolutionized the politico-economic policy of England.

Omitting wholly the details of the great and incessant labors by which he forced Sir Robert Peel to repeal the Corn Laws in deference to public opinion, the barest mention can be made of his work as an international treaty reformer, and his remarkable series of peace congresses in the interest of arbitration as a substitute for war, as perhaps the most remarkable among many other distinguished services to his own country and to mankind. He became such a power in England that cabinet positions and even a baronetcy and seat in the Privy

Council were offered him by Lord Palmerston and refused. Throughout his long parliamentary career he was one of England's foremost debaters of political, economical, and commercial questions, while at the same time he was the writer of essays that are enduring text-books for the guidance of after generations.

He was born at his father's farmhouse near Midhurst in Sussex, June 3d, 1804, and died in London, April 2d, 1865.

FREE TRADE WITH ALL NATIONS

(Delivered at Manchester, January 15th, 1846)

I SHALL begin the few remarks which I have to offer to this meeting by proposing, contrary to my usual custom, a resolution; and it is, "That the merchants, manufacturers, and other members of the National Anti-Corn-Law League claim no protection whatever for the manufactured products of this country, and desire to see obliterated forever the few nominally protective duties against foreign manufactures, which still remain upon our statute books." Gentlemen, if any of you have taken the pains to wade through the reports of the Protectionist meetings, as they are called, which have been held lately, you would see that our opponents, at the end of seven years of our agitation, have found out their mistake, and are abandoning the Corn Laws; and now, like unskillful blunderers, as they are, they want to take up a new position, just as we are going to achieve the victory. Then they have been telling something very like fibs, when they claimed the Corn Laws as compensation for peculiar burdens. They say now that they want merely protection in common with all other interests, and they now call themselves the advocates of protection to native industry in all its branches; and, by way of making the appeal to the less-informed portion of the community, they say that the Anti-Corn-Law League are merely the advocates of Free Trade in corn, but that we want to preserve a monopoly in manufactures.

Now, the resolution which I have to submit to you, and which we will put to this meeting to-night — the largest by far that I ever saw in this room, and comprising men of every class and of every calling in this district — let that resolution decide, once and forever, whether our opponents can with truth lay that to our charge henceforth. There is nothing new in this proposi-

tion, for at the very beginning of this agitation — at the meeting of the Chamber of Commerce — when that faint voice was raised in that small room in King Street in December 1838, for the total and immediate repeal of the Corn Laws — when that ball was set in motion which has been accumulating in strength and velocity ever since, why, the petition stated fairly that this community wanted no protection for its own industry. I will read the conclusion of that admirable petition. It is as follows:—

"Holding one of the principles of eternal justice to be the inalienable right of every man freely to exchange the result of his labor for the productions of other people, and maintaining the practice of protecting one part of the community at the expense of all other classes to be unsound and unjustifiable, your petitioners earnestly implore your honorable House to repeal all laws relating to the importation of foreign corn and other foreign articles of subsistence, and to carry out to the fullest extent, both as affects agriculture and manufactures, the true and peaceful principles of Free Trade, by removing all existing obstacles to the unrestricted employment of industry and capital."

We have passed similar resolutions at all our great aggregate meetings of delegates in London ever since that was issued.

I don't put this resolution as an argument or as an appeal to meet the appeals made in the protection societies' meetings. I believe that the men who now, in this seventh year of our discussion, can come forth before their country, and talk as those men have done — I believe that you might as well preach to the deaf adder. You cannot convince them. I doubt whether they have not been living in their shells, like oysters; I doubt whether they know such a thing is in existence as a railroad, or as penny postage. They are in profound ignorance of everything, and incapable of being taught. We don't appeal to them, but to a very large portion of this community, who don't take a very prominent part in this discussion — who may be considered as important lookers-on. Many have been mislead by the reiterated assertions of our opponents; and it is at this eleventh hour to convince these men, and to give them an opportunity of joining our ranks, as they will do, that I offer this proof of disinterestedness and the fairness of our proposals. I don't intend to go into an argument to convince any man here that protection to all must be protection to none. If it takes from one man's pocket,

and allows him to compensate himself by taking an equivalent from another man's pocket, and if that goes on in a circle through the whole community, it is only a clumsy process of robbing all to enrich none, and simply has this effect, that it ties up the hands of industry in all directions. I need not offer one word to convince you of that. The only motive that I have for saying a word is, that what I say here may convince others elsewhere — the men who meet in protection societies. But the arguments I should adduce to an intelligent audience like this, would be spoken in vain to the Members of Parliament who are now the advocates of protection. I shall meet them in less than a week in London, and there I will teach the A B C of this protection. It is of no use trying to teach children words of five syllables, when they have not got out of the alphabet.

Well, what exhibitions these protectionists have been making of themselves! Judging from the length of their speeches, as you see them reported, you might fancy the whole community was in motion. Unfortunately for us, and for the reputation of our countrymen, the men who can utter the driveling nonsense which we have had exhibited to the world lately, and the men who can listen to it, are very few in number. I doubt exceedingly whether all the men who have attended all the protection meetings, during the last month, might not very comfortably be put into this hall. But these protection societies have not only changed their principles, but it seems they have resolved to change their tactics. They have now, at the eleventh hour, again resolved that they will make their body political, and look after the registration. What simpletons they must have been to have thought that they could have done any good without that! So they have resolved that their societies shall spend their money in precisely the same way that the League have been expending theirs. They have hitherto been telling us, in all their meetings and in all their newspapers, that the League is an unconstitutional body; that it is an infernal club which aims at corrupting, at vitiating, and at swamping the registrations; and now, forsooth, when no good can possibly come of it — when they most certainly should have wisely abstained from imitating it, since they cannot do any good, and have kept up the strain they formerly had, of calling the League an unconstitutional body, they resolve to rescind their resolution, and to follow his Grace, the Duke of Richmond's advice, and fight us with our own weapons. Now, I presume, we are a constitutional body. It is a fortunate thing that we have not got great dukes to lead us. But, now, of what force is this resolution? Like everything they do, it is farcical — it is unreal. The protection societies, from the beginning, have been nothing but phantoms. They are not realities. And what is their resolution — what does it amount to? They resolve that they will look after the registration. We all know that they have done their worst in that way already. We all know that these landlords may really make their acres a kind of electioneering property. We know right well that their land-agents are their electioneering agents. We know that their rent-rolls have been made their muster-rolls for fighting the battle of protection. These poor driveling people say that we buy qualifications, and present them to our friends; that we bind them down to vote as we please. We have never bought a vote, and we never intend to buy a vote or to give one. Should we not be blockheads to buy votes and give them, when we have ten thousand persons ready to buy them at our request?

But I suspect that our protectionist friends have a notion that there is some plan — some secret, sinister plan — by which they can put fictitious votes on the register. Now I beg to tell them that the League is not more powerful to create votes than it is to detect the flaws in the bad votes of our opponents; and they may depend on it, if they attempt to put fictitious voters on the register, that we have our ferrets in every county, and that they will find out the flaws; and when the registration time comes, we'll have an objection registered against every one of their fictitious qualifications, and make them produce their title-deeds, and show that they have paid for them. Well, we have our protectionist opponents; but how we may congratulate ourselves on the position which they have given to this question by the discussion that has been raised everywhere during the last few months! We cannot enter a steamboat or a railroad carriage — nay, we cannot even go into an omnibus, but the first thing that any man does, almost before he has deposited his umbrella, is to ask, "Well, what is the last news about the Corn Laws?" Now, we, who remember how difficult it was, at the beginning of our agitation, to bring men's minds to the discussion of this question, when we think that every newspaper is now full of it — the same broad sheet containing, perhaps, a report of this meeting, and of the miserable driveling of some hole-and-corner agricultural

IV—84

gathering — and when we think that the whole community is engaged in reading the discussion and pondering on the several arguments, we can desire no more. The League might close its doors to-morrow, and its work might be considered as done the moment it compels or induces people to discuss the question.

But the feeling I have alluded to is spreading beyond our own country. I am glad to hear that in Ireland the question is attracting attention. You have probably heard that my friend Mr. Bright and I have received a requisition, signed by merchants and manufacturers of every grade and party in Belfast, soliciting us to go there and address them; and I deeply regret that we cannot put our feet on Irish ground to advocate this question. To-day I have received a copy of a requisition to the mayor of Drogheda, calling a meeting for next Monday, to petition for the total and immediate repeal of the Corn Laws, and I am glad to notice at the head of that requisition the name of the Catholic Primate, Doctor Croly, a man eminent for learning, piety, and moderation; and that it is also headed by the rest of the Catholic clergy of that borough. I hope that these examples will not be without their due effect, in another quarter. We have, I believe, the majority of every religious denomination with us — I mean the dissenting denominations; we have them almost *en masse*, both ministers and laymen; and I believe the only body, the only religious body, which we may not say we have with us as a body, are the members of the Church of England.

On this point I will just offer this remark: The clergy of the Church of England have been placed in a most invidious, and, I think, an unfortunate position, by the mode in which their tithe commutation charge was fixed some years ago. My friend Colonel Thompson will recollect it, for he was in Parliament at the time, and protested against the way in which the tithe commutation rent-charge was fixed. He said, with the great foresight he had always shown in the struggle for the repeal of the Corn Laws, that it would make the clergy of the Church of England parties to the present Corn Law by fixing their tithe at a fixed quantity of corn, fluctuating according to the price of the last seven years. Let it be borne in mind, that every other class of the community may be directly compensated for the repeal of the Corn Laws — I mean every class connected with agriculture — except the clergy. The landlords may be compensated, if prices fall, by an increased

quantity of produce; so also may the farmer and the laborer; but the clergy of the Church of England receive a given number of quarts of wheat for their tithe, whatever the price may be. I think, however, we may draw a favorable conclusion, under all the circumstances, from the fact that I believe there has not been one clergyman of the Church of England at all eminent for rank, piety, or learning, who has come out, notwithstanding the strong temptation of personal interest, to advocate the existing Corn Law. I think that we may take this as a proof of the very strong appeal to justice which this question makes; and perhaps augur also that there is a strong feeling among the great body of the members of the Church of England in favor of Free Trade in corn.

Well, there is one other quarter in which we have seen the progress of sound principles — I allude to America. We have received the American President's message; we have had also the report of the Secretary of the Treasury, and both President Polk and Mr. Secretary Walker have been taking my friend Colonel Thompson's task out of his hands, and lecturing the people of America on the subject of Free Trade. I have never read a better digest of the arguments in favor of Free Trade than that put forth by Mr. Secretary Walker, and addressed to the Congress of that country. I augur from all these things that our question is making rapid progress throughout the world, and that we are coming to the consummation of our labors. We are verging now towards the session of Parliament, and I predict that the question will either receive its quietus, or that it will lead to the dissolution of this Parliament; and then the next will certainly relieve us of our burden.

Now, many people are found to speculate on what Sir Robert Peel may do in the approaching session of Parliament. It is a very hazardous thing, considering that in one week only you will be as wise as I shall, to venture to make a prediction on this subject. [A cry of "We are very anxious."] You are very anxious, no doubt. Well, let us see if we can speculate a little on futurity, and relieve our anxiety. There are three courses open to Sir Robert Peel. He may keep the law as it is; he may totally repeal it; or he may do something between the two by tinkering his scale again, or giving us a fixed duty. Now, I predict that Sir Robert Peel will either keep the law as it is, or he will propose totally to abolish it. And I ground my predic-

tion on this, because these are the only two things that anybody in the country wants him to do. There are some that want to keep protection as it is; others want to get rid of it; but nobody wants anything between the two. He has his choice to make, and I have this opinion of his sagacity, that, if he change at all, he will change for total repeal. But the question is, "Will he propose total and immediate repeal?" Now, there, if you please, I will forbear to offer a prediction. But I will venture to give you a reason or two why I think he ought to take total and immediate repeal. I don't think that any class is so much interested in having the Corn Law totally and immediately repealed as the farming class. I believe that it is of more importance to the farmers to have the repeal instantaneous, instead of gradual, than to any other class of the community. In fact, I observe, in the report of a recent Oxfordshire protection meeting, given in to-day's paper, that when Lord Norreys was alluding to the probability of Sir Robert Peel abolishing the Corn Laws gradually, a farmer by the name of Gillatt cried out, "We had better be drowned outright than ducked to death." Gentlemen, I used to employ another simile — a very humble one, I admit. I used to say that an old farmer had told me, that if he were going to cut off his sheep-dog's tail, it would be far more humane to cut it off all at once than a piece every day in the week. But now I think that the farmer's simile in Oxford is the newest and the best that we can use. Nothing could be more easy than to demonstrate that it is the true interest of the farmers, if the Corn Law is to be abolished, to have it abolished instantly. If the Corn Law were abolished to-morrow, my firm belief is, that instead of wheat falling, it would have a tendency to rise. That is my firm belief, because speculation has already anticipated Sir Robert Peel, and wheat has fallen in consequence of that apprehension. I believe that, owing to the scarcity everywhere, — I mean in all parts of Europe, — you could not, if you prayed for it, if you had your own wishing-cap on, and could make your own time and circumstances — I believe, I say, that you could never find such an opportunity for abolishing the Corn Laws totally and immediately as if it were done next week; for it so happens that the very countries from which, in ordinary times, we have been supplied, have been afflicted, like ourselves, with scarcity — that the countries of Europe are competing with us for the very small surplus existing in America. They have, in fact, anticipated us in that market, and they have left the world's markets so bare of corn, that, whatever your necessities may be, I defy you to have other than high prices of corn during the next twelve months, though the Corn Law was abolished to-morrow.

European countries are suffering as we are from the same evil. They are suffering from scarcity now, owing to the absurd legislation respecting the article of corn. Europe altogether has been corrupted by the vicious example of England in her commercial legislation. There they are, throughout the continent of Europe, with a population increasing at the rate of four or five millions a year; yet they make it their business, like ourselves, to put barriers in the way of a sufficiency of food to meet the demand of an increasing population.

I believe that if you abolish the Corn Law honestly, and adopt Free Trade in its simplicity, there will not be a tariff in Europe that will not be changed in less than five years to follow your example. Well, gentlemen, suppose the Corn Law be not abolished immediately, but that Sir Robert Peel bring in a measure giving you a duty of five shillings, six shillings, or seven shillings, and going down one shilling a year for four or five years, till the whole duty is abolished, what would be the effect on foreign countries? They will then exaggerate the importance of this market when the duty is wholly off. They will go on raising supplies, calculating that, when the duty is wholly off, they will have a market for their produce, and high prices to remunerate them; and if, as is very likely and consistent with our experience, we should have a return to abundant seasons, these vast importations will be poured upon our markets, probably just at the time when our prices are low; and they would come here, because they would have no other market, to swamp our markets, and deprive the farmer of the sale of his produce at a remunerating price. But, on the contrary, let the Corn Law be abolished instantly; let foreigners see what the English market is in its natural state, and then they will be able to judge from year to year and from season to season what will be the future demand from this country for foreign corn. There will be no extravagant estimate of what we want — no contingency of bad harvests to speculate upon. The supply will be regulated by the demand, and will reach that state which will be the best security against both gluts and famine. Therefore, for the farmer's sake,

parties or of ministers, shall ever make us swerve a hair's breadth. I am anxious to hear now, at the last meeting before we go to Parliament — before we enter that arena to which all men's minds will be turned during the next week — I am anxious, not merely that we should all of us understand each other on this question, but that we should be considered as occupying as independent and isolated a position as we did at the first moment of the formation of this League. We have nothing to do with Whigs or Tories; we are stronger than either of them; if we stick to our principles, we can, if necessary, beat both. And I hope we perfectly understand now, that we have not, in the advocacy of this great question, a single object in view but that which we have honestly avowed from the beginning. Our opponents may charge us with designs to do other things. No, gentlemen, I have never encouraged that. Some of my friends have said, "When this work is done you will have some influence in the country; you must do so and so." I said then, as I say now, "Every new political principle must have its special advocates, just as every new faith has its martyrs." It is a mistake to suppose that this organization can be turned to other purposes. It is a mistake to suppose that men, prominent in the advocacy of the principle of Free Trade, can with the same force and effect identify themselves with any other principle hereafter. It will be enough if the League accomplish the triumph of the principle we have before us. I have never taken a limited view of the object or scope of this great principle. I have never advocated this question very much as a trader.

But I have been accused of looking too much to material interests. Nevertheless, I can say that I have taken as large and great a view of the effects of this mighty principle as ever did any man who dreamt over it in his own study. I believe that the physical gain will be the smallest gain to humanity from the success of this principle. I look farther; I see in the Free Trade principle that which shall act on the moral world as the principle of gravitation in the universe, — drawing men together, thrusting aside the antagonism of race and creed and language, and uniting us in the bonds of eternal peace. I have looked even farther. I have speculated, and probably dreamt, in the dim future — aye, a thousand years hence — I have speculated on what the effect of the triumph of this principle may be. I believe that the effect will be to change the face of the world, so

I plead for the immediate abolition of this law. A farmer never can have a fair and equitable understanding or adjustment with his landlord, whether as respects rent, tenure, or game, until this law is wholly removed out of his way. Let the repeal be gradual, and the landlord will say to the farmer, through the land-agent, "Oh, the duty will be seven shillings next year; you have not had more than twelve-months' experience of the workings of the system yet"; and the farmer goes away without any settlement having been come to. Another year passes over, and when the farmer presents himself, he is told, "Oh, the duty will be five shillings this year; I cannot yet tell what the effect will be; you must stop awhile." The next year the same thing is repeated, and the end is, that there is no adjustment of any kind between the landlord and tenant. But put it at once on a natural footing, abolish all restrictions, and the landlord and tenant will be brought to a prompt settlement; they will be placed precisely on the same footing as you are in your manufactures.

Well, I have now spoken on what may be done. I have told you, too, what I should advocate; but I must say, that whatever is proposed by Sir Robert Peel, we, as Free Traders, have but one course to pursue. If he propose a total and immediate and unconditional repeal, we shall throw up our caps for Sir Robert Peel. If he propose anything else, then Mr. Villiers will be ready, as he has been on former occasions, to move his amendment for a total and immediate repeal of the Corn Laws. We are not responsible for what ministers may do; we are but responsible for the performance of our duty. We don't offer to do impossibilities; but we will do our utmost to carry out our principles. But, gentlemen, I tell you honestly, I think less of what this Parliament may do — I care less for their opinions, less for the intentions of the Prime Minister and the Cabinet, than what may be the opinion of a meeting like this and of the people out of doors. This question will not be carried by ministers or by the present Parliament; it will be carried, when it is carried, by the will of the nation. We will do nothing that can remove us a hair's breadth from the rock which we have stood upon with so much safety for the last seven years. All other parties have been on a quicksand, and floated about by every wave, by every tide, and by every wind — some floating to us; others, like fragments scattered over the ocean, without rudder or compass; whilst we are upon solid ground, and no temptation, whether of

as to introduce a system of government entirely distinct from that which now prevails. I believe that the desire and the motive for large and mighty empires — for gigantic armies and great navies — for those materials which are used for the destruction of life and the desolation of the rewards of labor — will die away; I believe that such things will cease to be necessary, or to be used, when man becomes one family and freely exchanges the fruits of his labor with his brother man. I believe that, if we could be allowed to reappear on this sublunary scene, we should see, at a far distant period, the governing system of this world revert to something like the municipal system; and I believe that the speculative philosopher of a thousand years hence will date the greatest revolution that ever happened in the world's history from the triumph of the principle which we have met here to advocate. I believe these things; but, whatever may have been my dreams and speculations, I have never obtruded them upon others. I have never acted upon personal or interested motives in this question; I seek no alliance with parties or favor from parties, and I will take none — but, having the feeling I have of the sacredness of the principle, I say that I can never agree to tamper with it. I, at least, will never be suspected of doing otherwise than pursuing it disinterestedly, honestly, and resolutely.

SMALL STATES AND GREAT ACHIEVEMENTS

(From a Speech Delivered at Rochdale, October 29th, 1862)

Now, gentlemen, coupled with this question is another upon which I must say a few words. We are placed in this tremendous embarrassment in consequence of the civil war that is going on in America. Don't expect me to be going to venture upon ground which other politicians have trodden, with, I think, doubtful success or advantage to themselves! Don't think that I am going to predict what is going to happen in America, or that I am going to set myself up as a judge of the Americans! What I wish to do is to say a few words to throw light upon our relations as a nation with the American people. I have no doubt whatever that, if I had been an American, I should have been true to my peace principles, and that I should have been amongst, perhaps, a very small number who had voted against, or raised my protest, in some shape or other, against this civil war in America. There is nothing in the course of this war that reconciles me to the brutality and havoc of such a mode of settling human disputes. But the question we have to ask ourselves is this: What is the position which, as a nation, we ought to take with reference to the Americans in this dispute? That is the question which concerns us. It is no use our arguing as to what is the origin of the war, or any use whatever to advise these disputants. From the moment the first shot is fired, or the first blow is struck, in a dispute, then farewell to all reason and argument; you might as well attempt to reason with mad dogs as with men when they have begun to spill each other's blood in mortal combat. I was so convinced of the fact during the Crimean War,—which you know I opposed,—I was so convinced of the utter uselessness of raising one's voice in opposition to war when it has once begun, that I made up my mind that as long as I was in political life, should a war again break out between England and a great power, I would never open my mouth upon the subject from the time the first gun was fired until the peace was made, because, when a war is once commenced it will only be by the exhaustion of one party that a termination will be arrived at. If you look back at our history, what did eloquence, in the persons of Chatham or Burke, do to prevent a war with our first American colonies? What did eloquence, in the persons of Fox and his friends, do to prevent the French Revolution or bring it to a close? And there was a man who at the commencement of the Crimean War, protested in terms of eloquence, in power and pathos and argument equal —in terms, I believe, fit to compare with anything that fell from the lips of Chatham and Burke—I mean your distinguished townsman, my friend Mr. Bright—and what was his success? Why, they burnt him in effigy for his pains!

Well, if we are here powerless as politicians to check a war at home, how useless and unavailing must it be for me to presume to affect in the slightest degree the results of the contest in America! I may say I regret this dreadful and sanguinary war; we all regret it; but to attempt to scold them for fighting, to attempt to argue the case with either, and to reach them with any arguments, while they are standing in mortal combat, a million of them standing in arms and fighting to the death; to think that, by any arguments here, we are to influence or be

heard by the combatants engaged on the other side of the Atlantic, is utterly vain. I have traveled twice through almost every free State in America. I know most of the principals engaged in this dreadful contest on both sides. I have kept myself pretty well informed of all that is going on in that country; and yet, though I think I ought to be as well informed on this subject as most of my countrymen,—Cabinet ministers included, —yet, if you were to ask me how this contest is to end, I confess I should find myself totally at a loss to offer an opinion worth the slightest attention on the part of my hearers. But this I will say: If I were put to the torture, and compelled to offer a guess, I should not make the guess which Mr. Gladstone and Earl Russell have made on this subject. I don't believe that if the war in America is to be brought to a termination, it will be brought to an end by the separation of the North and South. There are great motives at work amongst the large majority of the people in America, which seem to me to drive them to this dreadful contest rather than see their country broken in two. Now, I don't speak of it as having a great interest in it myself. I speak as to a fact. It may seem Utopian; but I don't feel sympathy for a great nation, or for those who desire the greatness of a people by the vast extension of empire. What I like to see is the growth, development, and elevation of the individual man. But we have had great empires at all times—Syria, Persia, and the rest. What trace have they left of the individual man? Nebuchadnezzar, and the countless millions under his sway,—there is no more trace of them than of herds of buffaloes, or flocks of sheep. But look at your little States; look at Greece, with its small territories, some not larger than an English county! Italy, over some of whose States a man on horseback could ride in a day,—they have left traces of individual man, where civilization has flourished, and humanity has been elevated. It may appear Utopian, but we can never expect the individual elevated until a practical and better code of moral law prevails among nations, and until the small States obtain justice at the hands of the great.

WILLIAM BOURKE COCKRAN

(1854–)

THE speech delivered by William Bourke Cockran at Madison Square Garden, New York, August 18th, 1896, represented the strong antagonism of a highly intelligent and powerful class to the speech made by William J. Bryan in the Democratic National Convention of 1896, commonly called his "Cross of Gold" oration. Mr. Bryan's speech was largely, if not wholly, extemporaneous. Mr. Cockran, who is one of the most facile extemporaneous speakers in the country, had time to consider his reply carefully, and doubtless did so; but there is none of the stiffness in it of a set speech. It moves easily and naturally, and is interesting even when it is dealing with questions of political economy in the abstract.

ANSWERING WILLIAM J. BRYAN

(From the Speech at Madison Square Garden, New York City, August 18th, 1896)

Mr. Chairman, Ladies and Gentlemen, Fellow-Democrats, All:—

WITH the inspiring strains of the national song still ringing in our ears, who can doubt the issue of this campaign. The issue has been well stated by your presiding officer. Stripped, as he says, of all verbal disguises, it is an issue of common honesty, an issue between the honest discharge and the dishonest repudiation of public and private obligations. It is a question as to whether the powers of the Government shall be used to protect honest industry or to tempt the citizen to dishonesty.

On this question honest men cannot differ. It is one of morals and justice. It involves the existence of social order. It is the contest for civilization itself. If it be disheartening to Democrats and to lovers of free institutions to find an issue of this character projecting into a presidential campaign, this meeting furnishes us with an inspiring truth of how that issue will be met

by the people. A Democratic convention may renounce the Democratic faith, but the Democracy remains faithful to the Democratic principles. Democratic leaders may betray a convention to the Populists, but they cannot seduce the footsteps of Democratic voters from the pathway of honor and justice. A candidate bearing the mandate of a Democratic convention may in this hall open a canvass leveled against the foundations of social order, but he beholds the Democratic masses confronting him organized for defense.

Fellow-Democrats, let us not disguise from ourselves the fact that we bear in this contest a serious and grave and solemn burden of duty. We must raise our hands against the nominee of our party, and we must do it to preserve the future of that party itself. We must oppose the nominee of the Chicago convention, and we know full well that the success of our opposition will mean our own exclusion from public life, but we will be consoled and gratified by the reflection that it will prove that the American people cannot be divided into parties on a question of simple morals or of common honesty. We would look in vain through the speech delivered here one week ago to find a true statement of the issue involved in this canvass. Indeed, I believe it is doubtful if the candidate himself quite understands the nature of the faith which he professes. I say this not in criticism of his ability but in justice to his morality. I believe that if he himself understood the inevitable consequences of the doctrines he preaches, his own hands would be the very first to tear down the platform on which he stands. But there was one statement in that speech which was very free from ambiguity, pregnant with hope and confidence to the lovers of order. He professes his unquestioned belief in the honesty of the American masses, and he quoted Abraham Lincoln in support of the faith that was in him. Well I don't believe that the faith of Abraham Lincoln was ever more significantly justified than in the appearance which Mr. Bryan presented upon this platform in the change that has come over the spirit and the tone of Populistic eloquence since the Chicago convention.

We must all remember that lurid rhetoric which glowed as fiercely in the Western skies as that sunlight which through the past week foretold the torrid heat of the ensuing day; and here upon this platform, we find that same rhetoric as mild, as insipid as the waters of a stagnant pool.

He is a candidate who was swept into the nomination by a wave of popular enthusiasm, awakened by appeals to prejudice and greed. He is a candidate who on his trip home, and in the initial steps of his trip eastward, declared that this was a revolutionary movement; who no sooner found himself face to face with the American feeling than he realized the fact that this soil is not propitious to revolution.

The people of this country will not change the institutions which have stood the tests and experiences of a century for institutions based upon the fantastic dreams of Populist agitators.

The American nation will never consent to substitute for the Republic of Washington, of Jefferson, and of Jackson the Republic of an Altgeld, a Tillman, or a Bryan. The power of public opinion which caused the vivid oratory of the Chicago platform to burn low and soft as the moonlight outside of this platform, which has already shown its power to control Populistic eloquence, will show the full extent of its wisdom, will give Abraham Lincoln's prophecy its triumphal vindication, when it crushes the seed of Populistic Socialism next November.

Now, my friends, I have said that there was one statement of great significance in Mr. Bryan's speech. There is another portion of it which is singularly free from any obscurity and that may be comprised within the two initial paragraphs when he talks, logically, consistently, plainly, the language of revolution. Whatever change may have come over his manner as a candidate, however much the vehemence of his eloquence may have been reduced, two things for which he stands remain unaltered. On this platform he defended the most revolutionary plank of the Chicago convention, in speech less vehement but not less earnest than that in which he supported their adoption. On this platform he defended the Populistic program of overthrowing the integrity of the Supreme Court. If there be any fruit which has grown for the benefit of all mankind, out of the establishment of this Republic, it has been the demonstration that it is possible by the organization of an independent tribunal to safeguard the rights of every citizen and protect those national privileges against any invasion from whatever source or however powerful might be the antagonistic elements. The very existence of that power presupposes the existence of an independent tribunal. Yet we have this Populistic convention, because a Populist measure

was condemned as unconstitutional, proposing not to amend the Constitution in the ordinary way prescribed by that instrument itself, but proposing to pack the court, to reorganize it (he used the language of the platform itself), so that it will pronounce those laws to be constitutional which the Constitution itself condemns,—a proposal to make the courts of law instruments of lawlessness; to violate that sacred pact between the States on which the security of this nation rests; to profane the temple erected for its protection by the hands of false priests who, though sworn to defend it, will be appointed to destroy it.

In the time to which I must confine myself to-night, I can do nothing but examine that one question, which Mr. Bryan himself declares to be the overshadowing issue of this campaign. I am a little puzzled when I read this speech to decide just exactly what Mr. Bryan himself imagines will be the fruit of a change in the standard of value throughout this country—I do not believe that any man can wholly agree with the speech, because if he dissent from one set of conclusions, he has to read but a few paragraphs and he will find another of a different variety. But I assume that it is fair in a discussion of this character, independently of what Mr. Bryan may say, or what Mr. Bryan himself may think he stands for, to examine the inevitable economic effects of a debasement of the coinage, of a change in the standard by which existing debts are to be measured to a baser measure of value. Now, I will imagine that Mr. Bryan himself may believe that in some way or other he is going to benefit the toilers of this country. He says that he is, but he declines to show us how. For my part I am willing to state here that if Mr. Bryan could show me that by any means known to heaven or known on earth, any means revealed to the comprehension of man, that wages could be increased, I will be ready to support him here and now. I do not make this statement through any pretense of special affection for the man who works with his hands. Such a pretense made in the heat of a presidential campaign would merely insult and discredit the intelligence to which it is addressed.

I repeat that I would support any measure calculated to increase the rate of wages, because I know of no test of prosperity absolutely infallible, except the rate of wages paid to laborers. When the rate of wages is high there must be prosperity; when the rate of wages is low, there must necessarily be distress.

If, then, Mr. Bryan can show me that by any enforcement of any portion of his program wages will be increased in this country, I will not only support him, but I will recognize him as the wisest orator that ever opened his mouth on a platform since the beginning of the world. I will be ready to confess that the rhetoric, which I do not now understand, is really the language of inspiration. I would regard the administration of the presidency as the kindling of a great light before the footsteps of man, showing him a broad pathway to endless happiness and measureless prosperity. But in searching through his speech, in reading through the whole reams of Populistic literature with which this country has been flooded for four years, I have never yet found the syllable which showed me how a Populist expected to increase the rate of wages. Now, in order to understand the significance of the remark that wages is the only test of prosperity, we have but to consider for a moment just what is meant by the term wages. Wages, as I suppose everybody here understands it, is that part of the laborer's product which is given to him, in compensation for his toil. If, for instance, I be engaged in the manufacture of chairs, and if I can make five chairs every day worth $20.00, and the rate of my wages is $4.00 per day, what I actually get is one chair out of the five I make. The other four chairs, the other four-fifths of my product, are devoted to the payment of all the other labor that has been expended in preparing the elements out of which the chair was made: to the man who felled the tree in the forest, the person who sawed it in the mill, the carrier who transported it, the workman who prepared its component parts, and the profit on the capital which set all this labor in motion. It is plain, however, that I could not take one chair home with me at night and attempt to settle my bills with it, for the moment I undertook to divide the chair among my creditors, that very moment it would lose its value; so instead of taking the chair which I cannot divide, I take its equivalent in money, which I can divide, but my wages all the time are fixed by the quantity of my own products. If, instead of five chairs I were able to make ten, and the rate of compensation remained the same, I would obtain for my wages two chairs or $8.00 per day; but instead of there being four chairs or $16.00 available for the payment of the other labor, there would be eight chairs at $32.00; and thus the larger my

wages, the larger my product, and the greater the prosperity in the chair-making industry.

Now, applying that principle to every other department of trade, we can see that the man who works on a tunnel cannot take part of the tunnel home with him for his wages, the man who paves the street cannot take part of the highway with him, but each one takes the money equivalent to that part of the product which is the result of his daily toil, and the laborer is the man who has the most vital interest in the character of the money which is paid to him. . . .

Nothing is more common than the mistake that money and property are identical. They are not. A redundancy of money does not prove any prosperity. There may be a very large amount of circulating medium and very great poverty. The issue of paper money simply is no more an increase of wealth than the issue by an individual of his promissory note would show an increase of his property. As a matter of fact, an increase in the coinage is no proof of an increase in property, but may be a strong proof of a decrease in wealth. . . . The volume of money plays but a small part even in the ordinary transactions of life. It is not the volume of money but the activity of money that counts. . . . Money never can circulate freely and actively unless there be absolute confidence in its value. If a man doubt whether the money in his pocket will be as valuable to-morrow as it is to-day, he will decline to exchange his commodity against it; and this Populistic agitation threatening the integrity of money has been the cause of the hard times through which this country is passing and from which it will not escape until the heel of popular condemnation is placed upon the Populistic agitation which undermines the foundation of our credit. . . .

In order that you should understand just how a change in the standard of value enables men to cheat their creditors, you have to consider the function which money plays in measuring debts. If I had paid $10.00 for ten yards of cloth to be delivered to me next week, and in the interim the Government should pass a law declaring that hereafter eighteen inches shall constitute a yard, and that all existing contracts shall be settled in that system of measure, I would be cheated of one-half the cloth for which I had paid. If, on the other hand, I owed a cloth merchant for ten yards of cloth which he had delivered to me, and which was payable next week, and in the meantime the Government would change the standard of value and cut down the unit of coinage one-half, then I would settle the debt with $5.00, and the cloth merchant would be cheated. . . .

Underlying the whole scheme of civilization is the confidence men have in each other, confidence in their integrity, confidence in their honesty, confidence in their future. If we went to a silver coinage to-morrow, if we even debased our standard of value, men say that you would still have the same property you have to-day, you would still have the same soil, you would still have the same continent. And it is true. But so did the Indians have the same rivers that roll past your cities and turn the wheels of commerce as they pass. So were the mountains piled full of mineral treasures four hundred years ago. The same atmosphere enwrapt this continent, the same soil covered the fields, the same sun shone in heaven, and yet there was none but the savage pursuing the pathway of war through the trackless forests, and the rivers bore no single living thing except the Indian in his canoe, pursuing a pathway of destruction. There was no industrial co-operation, because the Indian was a savage and did not understand the principle by which men aid each other, by taking from the bosom of the earth the wealth which makes life bearable and develops the intelligence which makes civilization. Anything that attacks that basis of human confidence is a crime against civilization and a blow against the foundations of social order. . . . We believe that the very essence of civilization is mutual interest, mutual forbearance, mutual co-operation. We believe the world has passed the time when men's hands are at each other's throats. We believe to-day that men stand shoulder to shoulder, working together for a common purpose, beneficial to all, and we believe that this attempt to assail wages, which means an attempt to attack the prosperity of all, will be resisted, not by a class, but by the whole nation. The dweller in the tenement house, stooping over his bench, who never sees a field of waving corn, who never inhales the perfume of grasses and of flowers, is yet made the participator in all the bounties of Providence in the fructifying influence of the atmosphere, in the ripening rays of the sun, when the product of the soil is made cheaper to him every day by the abundance of the harvest. It is from his share in this bounty that the Populists want to exclude the American

IV—85

workingman. To him we say, in the name of humanity, in the name of progress, you shall neither press a crown of thorns upon the brow of labor, nor place a scourge upon his back. You shall not rob him of any one advantage which he has gained by long years of study, of progress in the skill of his craft, and by the careful organization of the members who work with him at the same bench. You shall not obscure the golden prospect of a further improvement in his condition by a further appreciation of the cost of living as well as by a further cheapening of the dollar which is paid to him.

There can be no distress, there can be no hard times, when labor is well paid. The man who raises his hand against the progress of the workingman raises his hand against prosperity. He seeks to restrict the volume of production. He seeks to degrade the condition of the man who is steadily improving himself, and in his own improvement is accomplishing the improvement of all mankind. But this attempt will fail. I do not regret this campaign. I am glad this issue has arisen. The time has come when the people of this country will show their capacity for self-government. They will prove that the men who have led the world in the pathway of progress will be the jealous guardians of liberty and honor. They are not to be seduced by appeals to their cupidity or moved by threats of injury. They will forever jealously guard and trim the lamp of enlightenment, of progress. They will ever relentlessly press and crush under their heels the flaming torch of Populistic dscontent, Populistic agitation, and Populistic destruction. When this tide of Anarchy shall have receded, this tide of Populistic agitation, this assault upon common honesty and upon industry shall have abated forever, the foundations of this Republic will remain undisturbed. The Government will still shelter a people indissolubly wedded to liberty and order, jealously forbidding any distinction of burden or of privilege, conserving property, maintaining morality, resting forever upon the broad basis of American patriotism and American intelligence.

SIR EDWARD COKE

(1552-1634)

THE most celebrated of Sir Edward Coke's speeches, that in which he prosecuted Sir Walter Raleigh for treason, is grossly unjust to Raleigh, but it does equal violence to the true character of Coke himself. The speech shows a man insolent with the sense of authority, violent in his methods, and despotic in his habits of thought, while Coke, though in the case of Raleigh as in others he may have exceeded the brutality which seems to have been expected of a prosecuting attorney in his day, was essentially a Liberal in his construction of law and was so fearless in defending the common law of England and the liberties of the people against royal usurpation, that under Charles I. he was first imprisoned and then ordered into confinement at his house at Stoke Poges, "there to remain during his Majesty's pleasure." It has been said of Coke that he best represents among English lawyers that view of the common law which not only resulted in the resistance of the Commons to the Crown in England, but in the American Revolution against both Crown and Parliament. Such men as Samuel Adams and Jefferson are thought to have been largely indebted to Coke for views which did much to shape American institutions; and he is frequently put in antithesis to Blackstone as a representative of the liberal impulses of the common law.

Coke was born at Mileham, Norfolk, February 1st, 1552. He was Speaker of the House of Commons, 1592-93; Attorney-General, 1593-94; Chief-Justice of the Court of Common Pleas, 1606; and Chief-Justice of the King's Bench, 1613. As Chief-Justice of the King's Bench he fearlessly defended the common law against royal attempts to override it, and he was consequently removed November 15th, 1616. Elected to Parliament in 1620, he worked with Pym and Sir Robert Philips in favor of free speech, and was imprisoned with them in consequence. After his release he was one of those who drew up the Petition of Right. He died September 3d, 1634. His speech against Raleigh and his brutal diplomacy in forcing on his young daughter Frances a purely political marriage with Sir John Villiers are blots upon his reputation, but he is justly ranked as one of the greatest men of England and one of the greatest lawyers of modern times.

PROSECUTING SIR WALTER RALEIGH

(Delivered at the Trial of Sir Walter Raleigh for High Treason at Winchester, November 17th, 1603, Coke Being Then the King's Attorney-General)

I MUST first, my lords, before I come to the cause, give one caution, because we shall often mention persons of eminent places, some of them great monarchs; whatever we say of them we shall but repeat what others have said of them,— I mean the capital offenders in their confession. We professing law must speak reverently of kings and potentates. I perceive these honorable lords and the rest of this great assembly are come to hear what hath been scattered upon the wrack of report. We carry a just mind to condemn no man but upon plain evidence. Here is mischief, mischief *in summo gradu*, exorbitant mischief. My speech shall chiefly touch these three points: imitation, supportation, and defense. The imitation of evil ever exceeds the precedent; as, on the contrary, imitation of good ever comes short. Mischief cannot be supported but by mischief; yea, it will so multiply that it will bring all to confusion. Mischief is ever underpropped by falsehood or foul practices; and because all these things did occur in this treason, you shall understand the main, as before you did the bye. The treason of the bye consisteth in these points: first that the Lords Grey, Brook, Markham, and the rest, intended by force in the night to surprise the King's Court; which was a rebellion in the heart of the realm, yea, in the heart of the heart, in the Court. They intended to take him that is a sovereign to make him subject to their power, purposing to open the doors with muskets and cavaliers, and to take also the Prince and the Council; then under the King's authority to carry the King to the Tower, and to make a stale of the admiral. When they had the King there to extort three things from him: First, a pardon for all their treasons; second, a toleration of the Roman superstition, which their eyes shall sooner fall out than they shall ever see,— for the King hath spoken these words in the hearing of many: "I will lose the crown and my life before ever I will alter religion." And third, to remove counselors. In the room of the Lord Chancellor they would have placed one Watson, a priest, absurd in humanity and ignorant in divinity. Brook, of whom I will speak nothing, was to be Lord Treasurer. The great Secretary must be Markham, *oculus patriæ*. A hole must be found in my Lord Chief-Justice's coat. Grey must be Earl-Marshal, and Master of the Horse, because he would have a table in the Court; marry, he would advance the Earl of Worcester to a higher place. All this cannot be done without a multitude; therefore Watson, the priest, tells a resolute man that the King was in danger of Puritans and Jesuits—so to bring him in blindfold into the action, saying, That the King is no king until he be crowned; therefore every man might right his own wrongs. But he is *rex natus*, his dignity descends as well as yours, my lords. Then Watson imposeth a blasphemous oath, that they should swear to defend the King's person; to keep secret what was given them in charge, and seek all ways and means to advance the Catholic religion. Then they intend to send for the Lord Mayor and the aldermen in the King's name to the Tower, lest they should make any resistance, and then to take hostages of them, and to enjoin them to provide for them victuals and munition. Grey, because the King removed before midsummer, had a further reach, to get a company of sword-men to assist the action; therefore he would stay till he had obtained a regiment from Ostend or Austria. So you see these treasons were like Sampson's foxes which were joined in their tails, though their heads were severed.

Raleigh — You, gentlemen of the jury, I pray remember, I am not charged with the Bye, that being the treason of the priest.

Coke — You are not. My lords, you shall observe three things in the Treasons: 1. They had a watchword (the King's safety); their Pretense was *Bonum in se;* their Intent was *Malum in se.* 2. They avouched Scripture; both the priests had *Scriptum est;* perverting and ignorantly mistaking the Scriptures. 3. They avouched the common law to prove that he was no king until he was crowned, alleging a statute of 13 Elizabeth. This, by way of imitation, hath been the way of all traitors. In the 20th of Edward II, Isabella the Queen and the Lord Mortimer gave out that the King's person was not safe, for the good of the Church and the Commonwealth. The Bishop of Carlisle did preach on this text, "My head is grieved," meaning by the head the King; that when the head began to be negligent, the people might reform what is amiss. In the 3d of Henry IV., Sir Roger Clarendon, accompanied with two priests, gave out that Richard II.

was alive when he was dead. Edward III. caused Mortimer's head to be cut off for giving counsel to murder the King. Sir Henry Stanley found the crown in the dust and set it on the king's head; when Fitzwater and Garret told him that Edward V. was alive he said, "If he be alive, I will assist him." But this cost him his head. Edmund de la Pole, Duke of Suffolk, killed a man in the reign of Henry VII. for which the king would have him hold up his hand at the bar, and then pardoned him. Yet he took such an offense thereat that he sent to the noblemen to help to reform the Commonwealth, and then said he would go to France and get power there. Sir Roger Compton knew all the Treason, and discovered Windon and others that were attainted. He said there was another thing that would be stood upon, namely, that they had but one witness. Then he vouched one Appleyard's case, a traitor in Norfolk, who said a man must have two accusers. Helms was the man that accused him; but Mr. Justice Catlin said that that statute was not in force at that day. His words were, "Thrust her into the ditch." Then he went on speaking of accusers, and made this difference: an accuser is a speaker by report, when a witness is he that upon his oath shall speak his knowledge of any man. A third sort of evidence there is likewise, and this is held more forcible than either of the other two; and that is, when a man, by his accusation of another, shall, by the same accusation, also condemn himself, and make himself liable to the same fault and punishment. This is more forcible than many witnesses. So then so much by way of imitation. (Then he defined Treason. Treason in the heart, in the hand, in the mouth, in consummation; comparing that *in corde*, to the root of a tree; *in ore*, to the bud; *in manu*, to the blossom; and that which is *in consummatione*, to the fruit.) Now I come to your charge, you of the jury, the greatness of treason is to be considered in these two things: *determinatione finis*, and *electione mediorum*. This treason excelleth in both, for that it was to destroy the king and his progeny. These treasons are said to be *crimen læsæ majestatis;* this goeth further, and may be termed *crimen extirpandæ regiæ majestatis et totius progeniei suæ*. I shall not need, my lords, to speak anything concerning the King, nor of the bounty and sweetness of his nature, whose thoughts are innocent, whose words are full of wisdom and learning, and whose works are full of honor, although it be a true saying, *Nunquam nimis quod*

nunquam satis. But to whom do you bear malice? To the children?

Raleigh — To whom speak you this? You tell me news I never heard of.

Coke — Oh, sir, do I? I will prove you the notoriousest traitor that ever came to the bar. After you have taken away the King, you would alter religion: as you Sir Walter Raleigh, have followed them of the Bye in imitation; for I will charge you with the words.

Raleigh — Your words cannot condemn me; my innocency is my defense. Prove one of these things wherewith you have charged me, and I will confess the whole indictment, and that I am the horriblest traitor that ever lived, and worthy to be crucified with a thousand thousand torments.

Coke — Nay, I will prove all; thou art a monster; thou hast an English face, but a Spanish heart. Now you must have money; Aremberg was no sooner in England (I charge thee Raleigh) but thou incitedst Cobham to go unto him for money, to bestow on discontented persons, to raise rebellion on the kingdom.

Raleigh — Let me answer for myself.

Coke — Thou shalt not.

Raleigh — It concerneth my life.

The Lord Chief-Justice — Sir Walter Raleigh, Mr. Attorney is but yet in the general; but when the King's counsel have given the evidence wholly you shall answer every particular.

Coke — Oh, do I touch you?

Lord Cecil — Mr. Attorney, when you have done with this general charge, do you not mean to let him answer every particular?

Coke — Yes, when we deliver the proofs to be read. Raleigh procured Cobham to go to Aremberg, which he did by his instigation; Raleigh supped with Cobham before he went to Aremberg; after supper, Raleigh conducted him to Durham House; from thence Cobham went with Lawrency, a servant of Aremberg, unto him, and went in by a back way. Cobham could never be quiet until he had entertained this motion, for he had four letters from Raleigh. Aremberg answered: The money should be performed, but knew not to whom it should be distributed. Then Cobham and Lawrency came back to Durham House, where they found Raleigh. Cobham and Raleigh went

up, and left Lawrency below, where they had secret conference in a gallery; and after, Cobham and Lawrency departed from Raleigh. Your jargon was peace. What is that? Spanish invasion, Scottish subversion! And again, you are not a fit man to take so much money for procuring of a lawful peace, for peace procured by money is dishonorable. Then Cobham must go to Spain, and return by Jersey, where you were captain; and then, because Cobham had not so much policy, or at least wickedness, as you, he must have your advice for the distribution of the money. Would you have deposed so good a king, lineally descended from Elizabeth, eldest daughter of Edward IV.? Why then must you set up another? I think you meant to make Arabella a titular queen, of whose title I will speak nothing; but sure you meant to make her a stale. Ah, good lady you could mean her no good.

Raleigh — Did I ever speak with this lady?

Coke — I will track you out before I have done. Englishmen will not be led by persuasion of words, but they must have books to persuade.

Raleigh — The book was written by a man of your profession, Mr. Attorney.

Coke — I would not have you impatient.

Raleigh — Methinks you fall out with yourself, I say nothing.

Coke — By this book you would persuade men that he is not the lawful king. Now let us consider some circumstances. My lords, you know my Lord Cobham (for whom we all lament and rejoice; lament that his house, which hath stood so long unspotted, is now ruinated; rejoice, in that his treasons are revealed); Raleigh was both united in the cause with him, and therefore cause of his destruction. Another circumstance is the secret contriving of it. Humphry Stafford claimed sanctuary for treason. Raleigh in his Machiavelian policy hath made a sanctuary for treason. He must talk with none but Cobham; because, saith he, one witness can never condemn me. For Brook said unto Sir Griffith Markham, "Take heed how you do make my Lord Cobham acquainted; for whatsoever he knoweth, Raleigh, the witch, will get it out of him." As soon as Raleigh was examined on one point of treason concerning my Lord Cobham, he wrote to him thus: "I have been examined of you, and confessed nothing." Further, you sent to him by your trusty Francis Kemish, that one witness could not condemn; and therefore bade his lordship to be of good courage. Came this out of Cobham's quiver? No; but out of Raleigh's Machiavelian and devilish policy. Yea, but Cobham did retract it; why then did ye urge it? Now, then, see the most horrible practices that ever came out of the bottomless pit of the lowest hell. After that Raleigh had intelligence that Cobham had accused him, he endeavored to have intelligence from Cobham, which he had gotten by young Sir John Payton; but I think it was the error of his youth.

Raleigh — The lords told it me, or else I had not been sent to the Tower.

Coke — Thus Cobham, by the instigation of Raleigh, entered into these actions; so that the question will be whether you are not the principal traitor, and he would nevertheless have entered into it. Why did Cobham retract all that same? First, because Raleigh was so odious, he thought he should fare the worse for his sake. Second, he thought thus with himself: If he be free, I shall clear myself the better. After this Cobham asked for a preacher to confer with, pretending to have Doctor Andrews; but, indeed, he meant not to have him, but Mr. Galloway, a worthy and reverend preacher, who can do more with the king (as he said) than any other; that he, seeing his constant denial, might inform the king thereof. Here he plays with the preacher. If Raleigh could persuade the lords, that Cobham had no intent to travel, then he thought all should be well. Here is forgery. In the Tower, Cobham must write to Sir Thomas Vane, a worthy man, that he meant not to go into Spain; which letter Raleigh devised in Cobham's name.

Raleigh — I will wash my hands of the indictment, and die a true man to the king.

Coke — You are the absolutest traitor that ever was.

Raleigh — Your phrases will not prove it.

Coke — Cobham writeth a letter to my Lord Cecil, and doth will Mellis's man to lay it in a Spanish Bible, and to make as though he found it by chance. This was after he had intelligence with this viper, that he was false.

Lord Cecil — You mean a letter intended to me; I never had it.

Coke — No, my lord, you had it not. You, my masters of the jury, respect not the wickedness and hatred of the man, respect his cause; if he be guilty, I know you will have care of it, for

the preservation of the King, the continuance of the Gospel authorized, and the good of us all.

Raleigh — I do not hear yet, that you have spoken one word against me; here is no treason of mine done; if my Lord Cobham be a traitor, what is that to me?

Coke — All that he did was by thy instigation, thou viper; for I thou thee, thou traitor!

Raleigh — It becometh not a man of quality and virtue, to call me so; but I take comfort in it, it is all you can do.

Coke — Have I angered you?

Raleigh — I am in no case to be angry.

Chief-Justice Popham — Sir Walter Raleigh, Mr. Attorney speaketh out of the zeal of his duty, for the services of the king, and you for your life; be valiant on both sides!

JOHN DUKE COLERIDGE

(1820–1894)

JOHN DUKE COLERIDGE, Baron Coleridge, and Lord Chief-Justice of England, was born December 3d, 1820. His father, Sir John Taylor Coleridge, a nephew of the poet, was a Justice of the King's Bench and the editor of Blackstone's «Commentaries.» The son, John Duke Coleridge, soon rose to eminence at the bar. After becoming Queen's Counsel he was appointed Chief-Justice of the Court of Common Pleas in 1873, and in 1880 Lord Chief-Justice of England. In 1865 he appeared as counsel for the defendant in what was, at the time, a celebrated breach-of-promise case, tried before Lord Chief-Justice Cockburn in the Court of Queen's Bench, at Westminster. The position in which he was placed was difficult, not to say impossible, as after making an attack on the character of the lady plaintiff, the defendant had found himself unable to maintain it, and had been obliged to recede from it. It was in this connection that the future Lord Chief-Justice made the eloquent address on The Sacredness of Matrimony — which, however, did not prevent the jury from giving the injured lady, whom he condemned for taking advantage of the weakness of his client, a verdict of two thousand pounds. It is possible that even Curran, whose eloquence in similar cases was frequently at its best, might have fared no better had he been rash enough to appeal to a British jury against the woman in the case. Lord Chief-Justice Coleridge died June 14th, 1894.

THE SACREDNESS OF MATRIMONY

(Delivered in the Court of Queen's Bench, Westminster, 1865)

MAY it please your Lordship and Gentlemen of the Jury, the advocate of the defendant, in which character I appear before you to-day, has no doubt cast upon him a hard task. He has to defend a gentleman from the result of a breach of a contract which he, no doubt, deliberately entered into, and he has to do that after a very strong attack made upon his client by one of the ablest counsel in Westminster Hall [Mr. Bovill, Q. C.,

Counsel for the Plaintiff]. I am only giving you credit for the ordinary feelings of our common humanity, in supposing that you will not consider that a trivial or commonplace consideration would justify the defendant as a man of sense and a man of honor in not fulfilling his hasty and unnatural promise. These thoughts, no doubt, have already suggested themselves to your mind, if they have not been driven away by the somewhat vigorous vituperations to which my friend has subjected the defendant; but I cannot help thinking that if you bring to the consideration of this case, as I am sure you will, a calm and impartial understanding, you will see that the damages are of a very trivial character — that they are even nominal in amount, and that a nominal sum, at the most, is all the defendant ought to pay for having unquestionably broken a promise which he unquestionably made. The facts of this case are singularly few, undisputed, and simple, and I will try to make my comments on them correspondingly brief. It is idle to put before you considerations in the soundness of which I do not believe, and the fallacy of which your understandings would immediately detect. I am not going to say for one moment that there has not been a most deliberate promise of marriage made by the defendant. I am not here to contend before you that the promise so deliberately made has not, with a full view of all the circumstances attendant on it, been resolutely and deliberately broken; and therefore the question is, What damages, if any, has the defendant to pay for having brought himself within the perils of the law? Gentlemen, the questions really to consider in this case are: What is the contract made? Who were the parties to the contract? How came it to be made? and, under what circumstances was it departed from? Those are the simple and plain issues in the case. First of all, to begin with, What was the contract? The contract, as you will hear by and by, was a contract to assume the most solemn, the most touching, the most intimate relations in which one human being can possibly stand to another, so that they are «no more twain, but one flesh.» Respect, esteem, and love on both sides, are its true foundation. And, gentlemen, you will give me leave to say that those disgrace themselves and profane the sacred ordinance of marriage who enter upon it from bad motives or in an unworthy temper; and you will give me leave to say further, that those who seek to do so are not to be heard when they come into a court to claim damages which, from their own conduct, they are not entitled to. *Ex turpi causa non oritur actio*, or, to use the beautiful paraphase of Lord Mansfield, "Justice must be drawn from pure fountains." Who are the parties to the contract? One of them is a Colonel, not old in years, if you count by the calendar, but aged and enfeebled by a wasting disease,—crippled from the middle downwards, one leg entirely and the other partially, so that he is like the king in the 'Arabian Nights,' "half flesh and half marble"—heavily embarrassed in circumstances, but able to settle five hundred pounds a year on his wife. If I am not entitled to say he was intemperate in habits, he had habits which one of the witnesses said "he had not been weaned from," and which it was desirable he should be weaned from. Weakened and afflicted by the cruel and repeated assaults of his disorder, he was a person who could have had, in the eyes of a lady like the plaintiff, one recommendation and one only, namely, the fact that he could charge his estates in her favor.

Gentlemen, who is the other party to the contract? A woman in mature life also; only recently brought into the close and intimate relation in which you have heard she stood to the defendant. She was fully aware of his infirmities, and was trading in them, taking advantage of his weakness and of his temporary removal from all those friends who had surrounded him,—except the friends of her own immediate connection,—that she might drive with him her hard and disgusting bargain, and failing which she seeks to carry away the *spolia opima* of the diamond ring and the £5,000 damages. Not for her the pure sacred abandonment of self, which is the young virginity of affection. Not for her those loving and bright inspirations which lift us up above ourselves; which for a time hallow the worst of us, and elevate the most degraded. Nor for her those visions of a happy home, enlivened with bright children, circled in with its own sacred fence of love and joy, which is alike the brightest prospect of the bride and the dearest consolation of the widow. She was prepared to go to God's altar with totally different feelings—to assume the defendant's name and position to the injury of his family. For this purpose she was willing to subject herself to his caresses, and to undergo his paralytic embraces, setting herself up for sale in market overt like any other piece of merchandise; and for all these degrading compliances, money, and money only, was the miserable compensation. Gentlemen, in other

countries, where men are despots because women are slaves, women are treated as brute beasts, sold in the market like any other animal or chattel; and in such countries little is thought of the degradation, because it is the common lot. But in free and happy England, where a woman can marry for affection when she will,—marry on equal terms, marry with Christian dignity,—such a marriage contract as is sought to be here enforced is an indecency, an outrage, and a crime; and I trust you will not forget, when you look at the circumstances of this case, what was the contract the plaintiff strove to enter into with her intended husband. The defendant is a gentleman living in Wales, having a large place called Nant Eos, and also estates in other parts of the country. He had two other shooting boxes, which I suppose he reserved for his friends, as I presume he cannot himself shoot much out of his chair, in which it seems he is wheeled about. The defendant, early in this year, had a number of friends staying with him, among others the family of the plaintiff. A joke passed about leap year, the woman asking the man to marry her; and she appears to have asked him. I suppose the defendant's position may have been one that some women would desire to share, for it appears three women asked him, and amongst them was the plaintiff; and it appears that what passed at the time as a joke was considered as a serious matter in the mind of the defendant. . . .

At the same time, recollect who the defendant is, what the state of his mind and body has been proved to be. He is a man who has had nine or ten paralytic attacks, in London, since the last time he contested the county, which was in 1859; and that was known to Doctor King. Now, suppose for a moment he, having determined to break off this engagement, stated to a person perfectly unconnected with him, and perfectly trustworthy, the facts which he afterwards imported into the plea, and which he repeats. If it is a thing that can be proved, the way most people do is to state things when others have got to prove them,—they state them with a degree of confidence which, if they had to prove them themselves, and were responsible, they would not think of doing. Supposing a charge was made in the most perfect good faith, and the very nature of the charge would satisfy you that it was believed at the time, and under those circumstances the charge was first made, and afterwards persevered in, when it really comes to be looked into, it turns out there is not

a pretense for it, and that it never should have been suggested; what can a gentleman do more than what he has done—to write to the other attorney; take out a summons, to strike off the plea, and pay the expenses attending it, and to desire me to express his regret that it ever was pleaded? Gentlemen, although I am the defendant's advocate, I can see two sides to this question. As far as the plaintiff is concerned, she was not injured by it, if she is the person I believe her to be, and which I now state on the part of the defendant he believed her to be; stating such a charge as that and persevering in it might, no doubt, wound and distress some women, but, gentlemen, do forgive me for observing, we are not trying that. The question here to-day is whether the defendant broke his word, and if he broke it, what ought he to pay for having broken it. If he pleaded a plea for which there was no foundation, and put the plaintiff for some weeks to anxiety and inconvenience, still that is a matter now removed from your consideration. We have done all we possibly can do, we have withdrawn the plea, apologized for the plea, and have said there was no foundation for the plea, and that we were extremely sorry that ever the plea had found its way into the record. What further can a man do beyond saying he has made a mistake? As far as human language can go to rectify it, I express to you the most sincere regret that the mistake should have occurred. Any man may be subject to false information, and may make statements which he meant to prove. If he find he cannot prove them he ought to say so, and apologize, and make every reparation to the person whom he has unwittingly injured. Do not, when you come by and by to see what is the real issue in the case, and the real loss which the plaintiff has sustained, punish the defendant for a mistake which arose before the cause of action in this case of which she now complains, and for which the defendant has abundantly apologized. That seems to me nearly to exhaust the whole of the observations I have to make. You have got the case before you, and you have seen what the contract really was, the circumstances under which it was made, and how it was broken off. The question is, What are the real damages that the plaintiff has sustained in this case? Has she lost a marriage? It certainly can scarcely be called a marriage, to marry a man who could but be a husband in one sense. My friend does not suggest that there was anything like a shock or distress to her feelings on that account. He does not pretend

that there was anything like affection, esteem, or love to the defendant, or that the plaintiff's heart was wounded, in respect of which she is entitled to compensation. It is said that this is a monetary action for a money loss, as she might have had a settlement upon her; for monetary loss she is entitled to ask the jury for compensation. Putting aside the accusation which has been atoned for, it is quite true this is a monetary action, but an action in which, most justly and rightly, the character of the parties is always taken into account; and there is no general rule by which damages in a matter of this kind can be estimated. There was a case before my lord the other day when we were refreshed by hearing some of the tones of that great eloquence which used to ring high and clear not so very long ago from these same benches. In that case a girl had given herself up for life to be the affianced wife of a gentleman who had thrown her aside and discarded her, without reason and without redress. There the jury meted out damages with no niggard hand. But this is not that case: the plaintiff in this case is not that sort of plaintiff; you cannot give her special damages in this case, without, to some extent, approving of the conduct she pursued, and encouraging women in a like situation to follow in her steps; and, apart from idle declamation, and according to plain common sense, if you agree with me in the view of her conduct which I have endeavored to put before you, it will follow that you will agree with me when I say that she has forgotten the dignity of her sex, and by her conduct lowered our ideas of that which we most esteem, reverence, and admire in the character of woman. I sincerely trust that you twelve English gentlemen will pause before you do anything that will give the faintest shadow of countenance to conduct such as the plaintiff has pursued; and that, if you think a promise was made, and a promise broken, and that it must be followed by some damages, you will say they ought to be most trivial if not nominal in amount.

SCHUYLER COLFAX

(1823-1885)

CHUYLER COLFAX represented an Indiana district in Congress continuously from December 3d, 1855, to March 23d, 1869. During the last six years of this time, he was Speaker of the House. As editor and proprietor of the South Bend, Indiana, Register, he was one of the organizers of the Republican party, and from its first contests to the close of his public career, he was always in great demand as a campaign orator. He was elected Vice-President on the ticket with General Grant in 1868, and served until March 3d, 1873, when he retired to South Bend, and thereafter appeared in public only as a lecturer. He was born in New York city, March 23d, 1823. Going with his parents to Indiana in 1836, and receiving a common-school education, he began to take an active part in politics as soon as he was old enough to vote. He died of heart disease at Mankato, Minnesota, January 13th, 1885.

THE CONFISCATION OF REBEL PROPERTY

(From a Speech Delivered in the House of Representatives, April 23d, 1862)

THE bill that was laid on the table a short time ago would have left the matter in a very indefinite state, as I thought, in scanning its provisions after our adjournment last night. I was in favor of the first section of the bill, which declares that any man who shall hereafter willfully persist in the unholy rebellion against this Government shall be stripped of his property, of his stocks, of his money, and effects. But the second section provides that these proceedings shall be in the United States court, and that that court is to order this property to be sold. And when I recollected the decision of the Supreme Court of the United States made at one time in reference to "property," a decision which helped to inflame the South into demands for "rights" never before recognized, I felt it might possibly decide that the slaves of these rebels were "property," and that then we should be held up before the country and before the world

iv—86

---

as authorizing the slaves of rebels to be sold, and their proceeds to be paid into the Treasury. I do not myself, as the House knows, regard slaves as property. They are persons "held to labor," to use the language of the Constitution. But I have grave doubts as to what the Supreme Court would decide, and the bill just laid on the table having been under the previous question, and therefore not amendable, I prefer that we shall ourselves settle this important point indisputably by the details of whatever bill we may pass, and not leave it as a vague question of construction to the courts. . . .

The engineers of this rebellion—the Catilines who sat here in the council chambers of the Republic, and who, with the oath on their lips and in their hearts to support the Constitution of the United States, plotted treason at night, as has been shown by papers recovered at Florida, particularly the letter of Mr. Yulee, describing the proceedings of the midnight conclaves of these men to their confederates in the Southern States—should be punished by the severest penalties of the law, for they have added to their treason perjury, and are doubly condemned before God and man. Never, in any land, have there been men more guilty and more deserving of the extremest terrors of the law. The murderer takes but a single life, and we call him infamous. But these men wickedly and willfully plunged a peaceful country into the horrors of civil war, and inaugurated a régime of assassination and outrage against the Union men in their midst, hanging, plundering, and imprisoning, in a manner that throws into the shade the atrocities of the French Revolution. Not content with this, they aimed their blows at the life of the Republic itself; and on many a battlefield, in a carnival of blood, they sought not only to destroy the Union itself, but to murder its defenders. Plunging into even still darker crimes, they have bayoneted the wounded on the field of carnage, buried the dead that fell into their hands with every possible ignominy, and then, to gloat their revenge, dug up their lifeless remains from the tomb, where even savages would have allowed them to rest, and converted their skulls into drinking cups—a barbarism that would have disgraced the Visigoths of Alaric the barbarian, in the dark ages of the past. The blood of our soldiers cries out from the ground against them. Has not forbearance ceased longer to be a virtue? We were told a year ago that leniency would probably induce them to return to their allegiance, and to

---

cease this unnatural war; and what has been the result? Let the bloody battlefields of this conflict answer.

When I return home I shall miss many a familiar face that has looked in past years with the beaming eye of friendship upon me. I shall see those who have come home with constitutions broken down by exposure and wounds and disease to linger and to die. I shall see women whom I have met Sabbath after Sabbath leaning on beloved husbands' arms, as they went to the peaceful sanctuary, clothed now in widows' weeds. I shall see orphans destitute, with no one to train their infant steps into paths of usefulness. I shall see the swelling hillock in the graveyard—where, after life's fitful fever, we shall all be gathered—betokening that there, prematurely cut off by a rifle ball aimed at the life of the Republic, a patriot soldier sleeps. I shall see desolate hearthstones and anguish and woe on every side. Those of us here who come from Indiana and Illinois know too painfully the sad scenes that will confront us amid the circles of our constituents.

Nor need we ask the cause of all this suffering, the necessity for all these sacrifices. They have been entailed on us as part of the fearful cost of saving our country from destruction. But what a mountain of guilt must rest upon those who, by their efforts to destroy the Government and the Union, have rendered these terrible sacrifices necessary.

Standing here between the living and the dead, we cannot avoid the grave and fearful responsibility devolving on us. The people will ask us when we return to their midst: When our brave soldiers went forth to the battlefield to suffer, to bleed, and to die for their country, what did you civilians in the Halls of Congress do to cripple the power of the Rebels whom they confronted at the cannon's mouth? What legislation did you enact to punish those who are responsible, by their perjury and treason, for this suffering, desolation, and death? Did you levy heavy taxes upon us and our property to pay the expenses of a war into which we were unwillingly forced, and allow the men who are the guilty and reckless authors of it to go comparatively free? Did you leave the slaves of these Rebels to plant and sow and reap, to till their farms, and thus support their masters and the armies of treason, while they, thus strengthened, met us in the field? Did you require the patriots of the loyal States to give up business, property, home, health, life, and all for the

---

country, and yet hesitate about using the law-making power of the Republic to subject traitors to the penalties as to property and possessions which their crimes deserve? I would feel as if worthy of the severest condemnation for life, if I did not mete out to those who are the cause of all this woe and anguish and death, by the side of which all the vast expenses of the war dwindle into insignificance, the sternest penalties of the law while they still remain in arms in their parricidal endeavor to blot this country from the map of the world.

Why do we hesitate? These men have drawn the sword and thrown away the scabbard. They do not hesitate in punishing Union men within their power. They confiscate their property, and have for a year past, without any of the compunctions that trouble us here. They imprison John M. Botts for silently retaining a lingering love for the Union in his desolate home. They hang Union men in east Tennessee for bridge-burning, refusing them even the sympathy of a chaplain to console their dying hours. They persecute Brownlow because, faithful among the faithless, he refused, almost alone, in his outspoken heroism, to bow the knee to the Baal of their worship. Let us follow his counsel by stripping the leaders of this conspiracy of their possessions and outlawing them hereafter from the high places of honor and of trust they have heretofore enjoyed.

ROSCOE CONKLING

(1829–1888)

AFTER such leaders as Sumner and Seward had ceased to direct the course of the Republican party, Roscoe Conkling took, and long retained, national prominence as the leading representative of what finally came to be called its "stalwart" element. Between him and James G. Blaine, leader of the opposing element, there was a long-continued antagonism, first publicly developed during the celebrated debate in which Mr. Blaine compared Mr. Conkling to a turkey cock. The history of their time almost forces a comparison between the two men, each great in his own way. If Mr. Blaine had the broader intellect, the more extensive culture, the greater eloquence, the warmer sympathies, and the quicker apprehension, Mr. Conkling had in him a force which at times more than compensated for what would otherwise have been the overwhelming advantage of his rival. His strength of conviction, his decisiveness, his assured belief in his own cause, no matter what it was, his conviction that those whose errors he could see because their purposes conflicted with his own were "eternally wrong" gave him the one overwhelming element of strength which would have made Mr. Blaine irresistible had he possessed it in such a degree as adequately to represent the fiery passions and vindictive prejudices of the Civil War period. Something of the same contrast of character which exists between Conkling and Blaine is illustrated between Andrew Jackson and the great Kentuckian whom Mr. Blaine so admired. Mr. Conkling was hardly less assured of himself and of his cause, whatever it was at any given time, than was Andrew Jackson in his day. He became naturally the leader of the element which favored forcing the issues raised during the Civil War, until all opposition had been abandoned. He came thus into strong antagonism with members of his own party who wished to raise such new issues as that of Civil Service Reform. And as this same element was most strongly opposed to the nomination of President Grant for a third term, Mr. Conkling became a logical leader against them. His speech nominating Grant for a third term, delivered in the Republican National Convention in Chicago, in 1880, is perhaps the most celebrated nominating speech ever delivered in the country, and although it was apparently without immediate result, the impression it produced on

the convention doubtless had much to do with making Mr. Arthur Vice-President. Mr. Conkling was born October 30th, 1829, at Albany, New York. He was a Member of Congress from New York from 1859 to 1863, and from 1865 to 1867. Elected United States Senator in 1867, he resigned in 1881 as a result of a disagreement with President Garfield over the disposition of New York patronage. Defeated for re-election to the Senate, he retired from politics and practiced law with distinguished success up to the time of his death, April 18th, 1888.

NOMINATING GENERAL GRANT FOR A THIRD TERM

(Delivered in the National Republican Convention at Chicago, June 1880)

WHEN asked whence comes our candidate, we say from Appomattox. Obeying instructions I should never dare to disregard, expressing, also, my own firm conviction, I rise in behalf of the State of New York to propose a nomination with which the country and the Republican party can grandly win. The election before us will be the Austerlitz of American politics. It will decide whether for years to come the country will be "Republican or Cossack." The need of the hour is a candidate who can carry the doubtful States, North and South; and believing that he more surely than any other can carry New York against any opponent, and carry not only the North, but several States of the South, New York is for Ulysses S. Grant. He alone of living Republicans has carried New York as a presidential candidate. Once he carried it even according to a Democratic count, and twice he carried it by the people's vote, and he is stronger now. The Republican party with its standard in his hand is stronger now than in 1868 or 1872. Never defeated in war or in peace, his name is the most illustrious borne by any living man; his services attest his greatness, and the country knows them by heart. His fame was born not alone of things written and said, but of the arduous greatness of things done, and dangers and emergencies will search in vain in the future, as they have searched in vain in the past, for any other on whom the nation leans with such confidence and trust. Standing on the highest eminence of human distinction, and having filled all lands with his renown, modest, firm, simple, and self-poised, he has seen not only the titled but the poor and the lowly in the utmost ends of the world rise and uncover before him. He

has studied the needs and defects of many systems of government, and he comes back a better American than ever, with a wealth of knowledge and experience added to the hard common sense which so conspicuously distinguished him in all the fierce light that beat upon him throughout the most eventful, trying, and perilous sixteen years of the nation's history.

Never having had "a policy to enforce against the will of the people," he never betrayed a cause or a friend, and the people will never betray or desert him. Vilified and reviled, truthlessly aspersed by numberless presses, not in other lands, but in his own, the assaults upon him have strengthened and seasoned his hold upon the public heart. The ammunition of calumny has all been exploded; the powder has all been burned once, its force is spent, and General Grant's name will glitter as a bright and imperishable star in the diadem of the Republic when those who have tried to tarnish it will have moldered in forgotten graves and their memories and epitaphs have vanished utterly.

Never elated by success, never depressed by adversity, he has ever in peace as in war shown the very genius of common sense. The terms he prescribed for Lee's surrender foreshadowed the wisest principles and prophecies of true reconstruction.

Victor in the greatest of modern wars, he quickly signalized his aversion to war and his love of peace by an arbitration of international disputes which stands as the wisest and most majestic example of its kind in the world's diplomacy. When inflation, at the height of its popularity and frenzy, had swept both houses of Congress, it was the veto of Grant which, single and alone, overthrew expansion and cleared the way for specie resumption. To him, immeasurably more than to any other man, is due the fact that every paper dollar is as good as gold. With him as our leader we shall have no defensive campaign, no apologies or explanations to make. The shafts and arrows have all been aimed at him and lie broken and harmless at his feet. Life, liberty, and property will find a safeguard in him. When he said of the black man in Florida, "Wherever I am they may come also," he meant that, had he the power to help it, the poor dwellers in the cabins of the South should not be driven in terror from the homes of their childhood and the graves of their murdered dead. When he refused to receive Denis Kearney he meant that the lawlessness and communism, although it should dictate laws to a whole city, would everywhere meet a foe in

him, and, popular or unpopular, he will hew to the line of right, let the chips fly where they may.

His integrity, his common sense, his courage, and his unequaled experience are the qualities offered to his country. The only argument against accepting them would amaze Solomon. He thought there could be nothing new under the sun. Having tried Grant twice and found him faithful, we are told we must not, even after an interval of years, trust him again. What stultification does not such a fallacy involve? The American people exclude Jefferson Davis from public trust. Why? Because he was the arch traitor and would be a destroyer. And now the same people are asked to ostracize Grant and not trust him. Why? Because he was the arch preserver of his country; because, not only in war, but afterward, twice as a civic magistrate, he gave his highest, noblest efforts to the Republic. Is such absurdity an electioneering jugglery or hypocrisy's masquerade?

There is no field of human activity, responsibility, or reason in which rational beings object to Grant because he has been weighed in the balance and not found wanting, and because he has had unequaled experience, making him exceptionally competent and fit. From the man who shoes your horse to the lawyer who pleads your case, the officer who manages your railway, the doctor into whose hands you give your life, or the minister who seeks to save your soul, what now do you reject because you have tried him and by his works have known him? What makes the presidential office an exception to all things else in the common sense to be applied to selecting its incumbent? Who dares to put fetters on the free choice and judgment, which is the birthright of the American people? Can it be said that Grant has used official power to perpetuate his plan? He has no place. No official power has been used for him. Without patronage or power, without telegraph wires running from his house to the convention, without electioneering contrivances, without effort on his part, his name is on his country's lips, and he is struck at by the whole Democratic party because his nomination will be the deathblow to Democratic success. He is struck at by others who find offense and disqualification in the very service he has rendered and the very experience he has gained. Show me a better man. Name one and I am answered; but do not point, as a disqualification, to the very facts which make this man fit beyond all others. Let not experience disqualify or excellence impeach him. There is no third term in the case, and the pretense will die with the political dog-days which engendered it. Nobody is really worried about a third term except those hopelessly longing for a first term and the dupes they have made. Without bureaus, committees, officials or emissaries to manufacture sentiment in his favor, without intrigue or effort on his part, Grant is the candidate whose supporters have never threatened to bolt. As they say, he is a Republican who never wavers. He and his friends stood by the creed and the candidates of the Republican party, holding the right of a majority as the very essence of their faith, and meaning to uphold that faith against the common enemy and the charletans and the guerrillas who from time to time deploy between the lines and forage on one side or the other.

The Democratic party is a standing protest against progress. Its purposes are spoils. Its hope and very existence is a solid South. Its success is a menace to prosperity and order.

This convention, as master of a supreme opportunity, can name the next President of the United States and make sure of his election and his peaceful inauguration. It can break the power which dominates and mildews the South. It can speed the nation in a career of grandeur eclipsing all past achievements. We have only to listen above the din and look beyond the dust of an hour to behold the Republican party advancing to victory with its greatest marshal at its head.

THE STALWART STANDPOINT

(From a Speech in the United States Senate, April 24th, 1879)

WE ARE told that forty-five million people are in danger from an army nominally of twenty-five thousand men scattered over a continent, most of them beyond the frontiers of civilized abode. Military power has become an affrighting spectre. Soldiers at the polls are displeasing to a political party. What party? That party whose administration ordered soldiers, who obeyed, to shoot down and kill unoffending citizens here in the streets of Washington on election day; that party which has arrested and dispersed legislatures at the point of the bayonet; that party which has employed troops to carry elections to decide that a State should be slave and should not be free; that party

which has corraled courts of justice with national bayonets, and hunted panting fugitive slaves, in peaceful communities, with artillery and dragoons; that party which would have to-day no majority in either house of Congress except for elections dominated and decided by violence and fraud; that party under whose sway, in several States, not only the right to vote, but the right to be, is now trampled under foot.

Such is the source of an insulting summons to the Executive to become *particeps criminis* in prostrating wholesome laws, and this is the condition on which the money of the people, paid by the people, shall be permitted to be used for the purposes for which the people paid it.

Has the present national administration been officiously robust in checking the encroachments and turbulence of Democrats, either by the use of troops or otherwise? I ask this question because the next election is to occur during the term of the present administration. What is the need of revolutionary measures now? What is all this uproar and commotion, this daring venture of partisan experiment for? Why not make your issue against these laws, and carry your issue to the people? If you can elect a President and a Congress of your thinking, you will have it all your own way.

Why now should there be an attempt to block the wheels of government on the eve of an election at which this whole question is triable before the principals and masters of us all? The answer is inevitable. But one truthful explanation can be made of this daring enterprise. It is a political, a partisan manœuvre. It is a strike for party advantage. With a fair election and an honest count, the Democratic party cannot carry the country. These laws, if executed, insure some approach to a fair election. Therefore they stand in the way, and therefore they are to be broken down.

I reflect upon no man's motives, but I believe that the sentiment which finds expression in the transaction now proceeding in the two houses of Congress has its origin in the idea I have stated. I believe that the managers and charioteers of the Democratic party think that with a fair election and a fair count they cannot carry the State of New York. They know that with free course, such as existed in 1868, to the ballot box and count, no matter what majority may be given in that State where the green grass grows, the great cities will overbalance and swamp it. They

know that with the ability to give eighty, ninety, one hundred thousand majority in the county of New York and the county of Kings, half of it fraudulently added, it is idle for the three million people living above the Highlands of the Hudson to vote.

This is a struggle for power. It is a fight for empire. It is a contrivance to clutch the National Government. That we believe; that I believe.

The nation has tasted and drunk to the dregs the sway of the Democratic party, organized and dominated by the same influences which dominate it again and still. You want to restore that dominion. We mean to resist you at every step and by every lawful means that opportunity places in our hands. We believe that it is good for the country, good for every man North and South who loves the country now, that the Government should remain in the hands of those who were never against it. We believe that it is not wise or safe to give over our nationality to the dominion of the forces which formerly and now again rule the Democratic party. We do not mean to connive at further conquests, and we tell you that if you gain further political power you must gain it by fair means, and not by foul. We believe that these laws are wholesome. We believe that they are necessary barriers against wrongs, necessary defenses for rights; and so believing, we will keep and defend them even to the uttermost of lawful honest effort.

The other day, it was Tuesday I think, it pleased the honorable Senator from Illinois [Mr. Davis] to deliver to the Senate an address, I had rather said an opinion, able and carefully prepared. That honorable Senator knows well the regard not only, but the sincere respect in which I hold him, and he will not misunderstand the freedom with which I shall refer to some of his utterances. Whatever else his sayings fail to prove, they did, I think, prove their author, after Mrs. Winslow, the most copious and inexhaustible fountain of soothing syrup. The honorable Senator seemed like one slumbering in a storm and dreaming of a calm. He said there was no uproar anywhere,—one would infer you could hear a pin drop,—from centre to circumference. Rights, he said, are secure. I have his language here. If I do not seem to give the substance aright, I will stop and read it. Rights secure North and South; peace and tranquillity everywhere. The law obeyed and no need of special provisions or anxiety. It was in this strain that the Senator discoursed.

Are rights secure, when fresh-done barbarities show that local government in one portion of our land is no better than despotism tempered by assassination! Rights secure, when such things can be, as stand proved and recorded by committees of the Senate! Rights secure, when the old and the young fly in terror from their homes, and from the graves of their murdered dead! Rights secure, when thousands brave cold, hunger, death, seeking among strangers in a far country a humanity which will remember that—

> " Before man made them citizens,
> Great nature made them men!"

Read the memorial signed by Judge Dillon, by the Democratic mayor of St. Louis, by Mr. Henderson, once a Member of the Senate, and by other men known to the nation, detailing what has been done in recent weeks on the Southern Mississippi. Read the affidavits accompanying this memorial. Has anyone a copy of the memorial here? I have seen the memorial. I have seen the signatures. I hope the honorable Senator from Illinois will read it, and read the affidavits which accompany it. When he does, he will read one of the most sickening recitals of modern times. He will look upon one of the bloodiest and blackest pictures in the book of recent years. Yet the Senator says all is quiet. "There is not such faith no not in Israel." Verily, " order reigns in Warsaw."

Solitudinem faciunt, pacem appellant.

Mr. President, the Republican party everywhere wants peace and prosperity—peace and prosperity in the South as much and as sincerely as elsewhere. Disguising the truth will not bring peace and prosperity. Soft phrases will not bring peace. " Fair words butter no parsnips." We hear a great deal of loose flabby talk about " fanning dying embers," " rekindling smoldering fires," and so on. Whenever the plain truth is spoken, these unctuous monitions, with a Peter Parley benevolence, fall copiously upon us. This lullaby and hush has been in my belief a mistake from the beginning. It has misled the South and misled the North. In Andrew Johnson's time a convention was worked up at Philadelphia, and men were brought from the North and South for ecstasy and gush. A man from Massachusetts and a man from South Carolina locked arms and walked into the convention arm in arm, and sensation and credulity palpitated and clapped their hands, and thought a universal solvent had been found. Serenades were held at which "Dixie" was played. Later on, anniversaries of battles fought in the war of Independence were made occasions by men from the North and men from the South for emotional dramatic hugging ceremonies. General Sherman, I remember, attended one of them, and I remember also, that with the bluntness of a soldier and the wisdom and hard sense of a statesman, he plainly cautioned all concerned not to be carried away, and not to be fooled. But many have been fooled, and being fooled, have helped to swell the Democratic majorities which now display themselves before the public eye.

Of all such effusive demonstrations I have this to say: honest, serious convictions are not ecstatic or emotional. Grave affairs and lasting purposes do not express or vent themselves in honeyed phrase or sickly sentimentality, rhapsody, or profuse professions.

This is as true of political as of religious duties. The Divine Master tells us: "Not every one that saith unto me, Lord, Lord, shall enter into the kingdom of heaven; but he that doeth the will of my Father which is in heaven."

Facts are stubborn things, but the better way to deal with them is to look them squarely in the face.

The Republican party and the Northern people preach no crusade against the South. I will say nothing of the past beyond a single fact. When the war was over, no man who fought against his flag was punished even by imprisonment. No estate was confiscated. Every man was left free to enjoy life, liberty, and the pursuit of happiness. After the Southern States were restored to their relations in the Union, no man was ever disfranchised by national authority — not one. If this statement be denied, I invite any Senator to correct me. I repeat it. After the Southern State governments were rebuilded and the States were restored to their relations in the Union, by national authority, not one man for one moment was ever denied the right to vote, or hindered in the right. From the time that Mississippi was restored there never has been an hour when Jefferson Davis might not vote as freely as the honorable Senator in his State of Illinois. The North, burdened with taxes, draped in mourning, dotted over with newly-made graves tenanted by her bravest and

her best, sought to inflict no penalty upon those who had stricken her with the greatest, and, as she believed, the guiltiest rebellion that ever crimsoned the annals of the human race.

As an example of generosity and magnanimity, the conduct of the nation in victory was the grandest the world has ever seen. The same spirit prevails now. Yet our ears are larumed with the charge that the Republicans of the North seek to revive and intensify the wounds and pangs and passions of the war, and that the Southern Democrats seek to bury them in oblivion of kind forgetfulness.

AGAINST SENATOR SUMNER

(From the Debate in the United States Senate on Chinese Naturalization, March 1870)

THE Senator from Massachusetts says: "Let us have a recess." I fear the Greeks. He has no good-will for this bill; and if New York ever hold an honest election, it is to be in spite of the honorable Senator from Massachusetts, and not because he gives one ounce of aid to the Republican party in that State.

Mr. Sumner—I took the liberty of saying from my seat, "Have a recess." I said so sincerely. I am always in my place. I intended to be here to-night. I know not why the Senator from New York should strike back at me because I made that simple suggestion. He says that I gave no aid to his bill. I have voted for his bill from beginning to end on every proposition; and, as I now understand it, I shall to the end as faithfully as the Senator himself. But allow me to say that there is something higher than this bill; it is a great American principle which that Senator now, on the Fourth of July, declares his readiness to sacrifice. It shall not be sacrificed if I can save it.

Mr. Conkling—I shall never be able with the ostentation of the honorable Senator from Massachusetts to vaunt my great achievements in the cause of human progress, human equality, and human rights; yet when the volume is closed, though it should close with the now setting sun, I will put against the record of that Senator the humbler consistency of my own record from first to last. Nor do I fear that those who vote with

me, having some regard for common sense, and not alone for declamation, sensation, and high-sounding professions, will find "their ineffectual fires" paled before the blazing light of the distinguished Senator from Massachusetts.

I will vote to eliminate this amendment from the bill, and going to my constituents will say: "As the last sands were running out, when the time had come when, if ever, the protecting shield could be thrown around the ballot box, I had too much sincerity and too little regard for personal effect in the galleries and in the country to trample under foot a practical opportunity to do a good thing for the sake of a flourish of rhetoric or a vain and empty profession of love of human rights"; and pointing to the record of my votes, insignificant as that record may be, which has at least no vacant place where an entry might have been made in behalf of human progress and human rights, I will trust the intelligence and honesty of my constituents, by which they discern light from darkness, to discern also the difference between improving practically an occasion to do good and trifling it away by vaulting and hollow attempts which everybody knows can result in no good, and which mean nothing but popular pretension and striving after effect.

BENJAMIN CONSTANT

(1767–1830)

HENRI BENJAMIN CONSTANT DE REBECQUE was born October 25th, 1767, at Lausanne in Switzerland. In 1795 he removed to Paris, and attracting at once the attention of influential people, soon became prominent in the disturbed politics of that period. He was a member of the Tribunate from 1799 until 1802. Napoleon banished him, but he returned in 1814 and held office under Napoleon during the Hundred Days. As a result of the Bourbon victory he was again driven into exile, but returning in 1816 he was re-elected to the Chamber of Deputies, holding that position from 1819 to 1830. He published a number of works on political and ethical questions, at the head of which is generally ranked the 'Cours de Politique Constitutionnelle.' He died at Paris, December 8th, 1830. Constant stands in France for the advocacy of constitutional and representative government, such as that under which America and England have had their remarkable development. He has been admired for his earnestness and for his power of logical expression, but he had faults of delivery which impaired what might otherwise have been his commanding influence as an orator. It is said that his voice was dry and his manner stiff, and that his mind, though powerful, did not readily respond on the spur of the moment to demands made upon it for impromptus, so necessary for every one who aspires to political leadership.

FREE SPEECH NECESSARY FOR GOOD GOVERNMENT

(Delivered in the Chamber of Deputies at Paris, March 23d, 1820, Against Restricting the Liberty of the Press)

I WOULD ask the minister if he has reflected on the inevitable consequences incident to the suspension, temporary or otherwise, of the free circulation of our newspapers. It may render him ignorant of all that is passing in the cliques of parasites and flatterers at court. All governments, whether liberal or despotic (you see I eschew the words "foreign to the interests or rights of the people"), must rely for security on some means of knowing what is transpiring in the State. Even in Turkey the viziers are sometimes irritated at being deceived by their pashas as to the situation of the provinces, and perhaps much may be attributed to the inexact knowledge a neighbor prince had of the dispositions of his garrisons when he saw them declare against him. Now, gentlemen, I assert it as a fact, that in suspending the free circulation of newspapers, the Government condemns itself to know nothing, except from the advices of its salaried servants, that is to say, it will never know more than half the facts, and frequently it will believe the opposite of the true conditions. To prove this truth I shall not resort to reasoning. Reasoning is too near liberty to need to be availed of. I shall invoke only a few facts, because facts are always the same. As we have seen, the chartered rights of the people may be demolished, but the facts remain impregnable.

Well, then, gentlemen, will you remember the occurrence in Lyons in June 1817? France was then under the exceptional laws under which you had placed her. Individual liberty was then, as it again will be, at the mercy of a ministry, and the censor made of journalism what you will do here in a week, if you adopt this proposed law.

What was the result then, gentlemen? A real or a sham conspiracy resulted. The severest measures were taken. Many men were put to death, and for a long time persecution was a political method. Well! All this was done and the Government did not know just what it was agitating for. The Government saw its error itself, for after all these executions had taken place, when, as a result, the conditions were irreparable, a marshal of France was sent to the field of these bloody severities to enlighten the ministry on the true state of things. In the meanwhile, they incarcerated, judged, condemned, executed, and all without knowing wherefore; for had it not been felt necessary to inform them, the tardy mission of M. le Maréchal Marmont would not have been thought necessary. I shall not enter into this lugubrious history, nor judge between those who affirm or deny their authority in the conspiracy. Who is right or wrong, —this has no bearing on what I would prove. What is important is that for months the Government was in ignorance of the facts and they had to send a personal messenger to report eye-witness on which they could depend.

But, gentlemen, it might have been otherwise. If in the Department of the Rhone there had been a single liberal journal,

IV—87

importance the ministry attach to her requests by the lightness with which they treat them. I ask if they will do me the honor to reply, that they refute the example cited in the case of Lyons and not lose themselves in vague declamations in reply to the citation of a precise case.

Let us pass to another subject on which two words of explanation will be useful. To suspend the free circulation of the press is to place the newspapers in the hands of a minister, and to authorize the insertion in them of what he pleases.

Have you forgotten, gentlemen, what occurred when a law, similar to the one you would resurrect, gave to a cabinet minister this power? I would not speak of the elections. I should be ashamed to recapitulate facts so well known. It were idle almost to tell the damage caused, for in three successive elections, the minister discredited the official articles attacking the candidates. He only contributed to their election. On my part, I owe him gratitude in this respect and I pardon his intentions for their favorable results.

The facts I want you to consider are much more important. You will probably remember that in the summer of the year 1818 several individuals who had filled responsible functions were arrested because they were suspected of conspiracy. I am not called on to explain or to defend these individuals. Their innocence or their guilt has nothing to do with this matter. They were detained; they were ironed; they had yet to be judged; and as they were to be exposed to the rigors of justice, they had a rightful claim on its safeguards. General Canuel was among the number. Well, gentlemen, while General Canuel was incarcerated, what did the minister do? He selected a journal of which the editors were friendly to the inculpated, and in it inserted the most damaging articles, and as they related to a man who was untried and unconvicted, I call them the most infamous. These articles circulated throughout France, and he against whom they had been directed had not the power to respond with a line. Do you find in this ministerial usage of the press anything delicate, loyal, legitimate? It is this slavish use of the press they would solicit you to enact anew.

This condition can never be renewed. The constituency of our present ministry is a guarantee against it.

By a law against universal liberty, you place the rights of all citizens at the discretion of a ministry. By suspending the free-

this journal—Jacobin, Revolutionary, or whatever you would call it, might present things from a different point of view from the local authorities. The Government might hear the two sides. It should not commence by striking without reason, afterwards to send to find if it had any cause for striking.

I may be mistaken, but I think this side of the question has never been indicated, and that it is worth examination. In suspending the free circulation of newspapers, the ministry announce that they desire to hear or learn nothing save by their own agents,—that is to say if their agents are by imprudence, by any personal motives or passions, on a false route, they will learn from them only that which they think plausible to place their merit in evidence or to assure their justification. Is this to the interest of government? I ask the ministry to reflect. If at all times I treat this only from the standpoint of the interest of the ministry, it is because I would address them words they would hear. If it concerned them alone, I need not speak. All authority brings with it the penalties of its responsibilities, its vexations, and false measures; nothing can be more just and what the result would be to the ministry is to me indifferent.

But as the example at Lyons has shown us, the people resent this, and I would save the poor people a part of the sufferings towards which this new régime is inevitably conducting us. I call this a new régime, because it is different from what the charter had commenced to introduce in France. But I might as well and more justly call it the old régime, for it is the old régime which we are reconstructing piece by piece; *lettres de cachet*, censures, oligarchic elections—these are the bases of the edifice! The columns and the capitols will come later! I ask the ministry if they intend to govern France without knowing her. Will they adopt measures depending on events of which they are informed only by men whose interests are presumably to disguise them; to commit thus without profit to themselves much injustice which they can never repair? If this be their intent, the suspension of the liberty of the press is a sure method of its fulfillment. But if they find that the French people value the right of being heard before being condemned, and that twenty-eight million citizens should not be struck upon uncertain and possibly false reports, then the journals must be left free in their field of labor. Whatever the result, I am happy to have thus put the question. France will know if this be refused how much

dom of the press, you will place at their mercy all reputations. I shall not stop to examine the promises of the minister of the interior on this anodyne measure, which is to "stop personalities," to "encourage enlightenment," and to "leave writers free." What opinion have the censors?

Censors are to thought what spies are to innocence; they both find their gains in guilt, and where it does not exist they create it. Censors class themselves as lettered. Producing nothing themselves, they are always in the humor of their sterility. No writer who respects himself would consent to be a censor. The title of royal censor was almost a reproach under the ancient régime. Has it been rehabilitated under the imperial censorship? These men will bring into the monarchy all the traditions of the empire. They will treat the liberty of the press as they do the administration, and we shall be marching under the guidance of the errors of Bonaparte, without the prestige of his imperial glory and the quiet of its unity.

JOSEPH COOK

(1838–)

THE address on Ultimate America, delivered by Rev. Joseph Cook in New York city in 1884, is perhaps the most celebrated of those striking addresses which gave him his reputation, and at the same time caused him to be attacked as few other platform orators have been in the history of the country. Concerning the correctness of Mr. Cook's judgment on any given point, his opponents may find room to assert their own opinions as suit them best; but regardless of all such questions as they have raised against him, there is scarcely room for two opinions concerning his native ability as an orator. The facile expression which others have achieved at the expense of the greatest pains, he seems to have under some natural compulsion. To some men the effort of expressing themselves is always great and painful, while others, possessed by ideas which drive them into the arena of public debate, would have even greater trouble in refraining from expressing themselves. To this latter class Mr. Cook undoubtedly belongs. His address on Ultimate America, of which the exordium and peroration are here given complete with a verbatim extract from the body of the address, was delivered in New York city, July 4th, 1884. The verbatim report in the New York Independent of July 10th, 1884, has been authoritatively recommended and accordingly used for the purposes of this work.

ULTIMATE AMERICA

(From an Address Delivered in New York City, July 4th, 1884)

SIR CHARLES DILKE says that after he had seen cultured New England, he looked backward over his course of travel and did not seem to have seen America; and that after he had visited the torrid South and the spacious West and the brave Pacific Coast, he had no feeling that he had seen America; and that it was only after he had sailed on the Pacific out of sight of the continent and looked backward that he first, by a combination of all his impressions, obtained suddenly a conception of America and of the American character.

longest straight line that can be drawn inside the limits of the old Roman Empire will not reach from Boston to San Francisco.

Neither Cæsar's empire nor Alexander's had the vast and multiplex physical opportunity possessed by America. Gibraltar and London, Thebes and the frosty Caucasus were the four corners of imperial Rome, and Alexander ruled from the Adriatic to the Indus; but stretch your compasses on the globe from London to the Egyptian Thebes, or from Gibraltar to the Caucasian summits, or from the Macedonian Adriatic to the Indus at the foot of the Himalayas, and you have not opened them as far as you must separate them to span the green fields and steepled cities between the surf of the Bay of Fundy and the waterfalls of the Yosemite, or to touch, on the one side, the Florida Keys, and on the other, the continuous woods,

« Where rolls the Oregon and hears no sound
Save his own dashings. »

On the British Empire the sun never sets. In the short summer nights it never sets on the American Republic. San Francisco is the middle city in our territory. It is literally true that in August the sunset has not ceased to flash on the spears of the fishermen in the Aleutian Islands before it begins to glint and blaze on the axes of the woodsmen in the forests of Maine.

Roll up the map of New England! Unroll that of your whole country! How large is Texas? You could bury in it the German Empire, and have room enough left for England and Wales. How large is California? You could bury in it England, Scotland, Ireland, Wales, and have room enough left for Switzerland and Belgium. How large is Colorado? You could bury in it Norway and have room enough left for Denmark. How large is Iowa? You could bury in it Portugal and Switzerland. How large is Lake Superior? You could sink Scotland in it. How large is New York? You could bury in it Belgium and Switzerland and Greece. How large is the estimated area of arable land in the American Union? Half as large as the United States. How fully is this occupied? In 1880 the area occupied by the corn crop made a region only about as large as Kansas; that occupied by the wheat crop a space only as large as Alabama; that occupied by the cotton crop, a region less than half the size of Ohio.

This English baronet should have been yet more cautious. He should have floated in imagination above the lakes and the gulf, and have looked down on the continent when it shall have developed the capacities of its soil as fully as Europe now has those of hers. He should have asked what our population can be, and, therefore, probably will be. He should have seen how numerous and corrupt great cities may become—a London on the Hudson, a London on the Lakes, a London at the mouth of the Mississippi, a London on the Pacific Coast, tossing up, it may be, and playing with commonwealths in the giant arms of capital, as a conjuror tosses up and plays with his flying balls. He should have inquired how wide may ultimately become the separation between rich and poor, when the larger part of New England is a factory and half the West a rented farm, and the Pacific, on a hundred new lines of commerce, is vexed with unaccustomed keels. He should have estimated how far commercial and political vices will spread, and how much school and Church will do for the healing of the average millions, whose intelligence and virtue will probably not be, as they are now, in proportion to their political power. He should have breathed the air of the marshes as well as of the highlands and of the peaks with everlasting snowy tents in the spiritual landscapes of a new world, in which the formation of mountains and of marshes has but just begun. He should, in short, have taken counsel with Orion, as that constellation shall stand in the zenith, shaking his locks of sidereal fire above the Amazonian palms, when the stars have wheeled and burned above our good and evil another ten hundred years; for then, and then only, would he have seen Ultimate America!

When Edmund Burke was a young man he wrote a letter to a friend, stating that he had a plan of taking up his residence in Massachusetts for life. His reasons for this purpose were, that, in his opinion, the Western Continent was sure to have a great future; that it was in the infancy of momentous changes; and that it was, therefore, undoubtedly that quarter of the world in which right efforts, put forth early, would be the most certain of usefulness on a gigantic scale. Would this statesman and political philosopher hold a different opinion if alive to-day and young?

The Roman eagles, when their wings were strongest, never flew so far as from Plymouth Rock to the Golden Gate. The

How many countries of Europe must be put together to make a region equal in extent to that of the good arable soil of the United States? Austria, Germany, and France? These and more. Spain, Sweden, and Norway added? These and more. England, Scotland, and Ireland in addition? These and more. Portugal, the Netherlands, Greece, Switzerland, Denmark, and Belgium? All these sixteen regions must be thrown together to cover, not our territory as a whole, but that half of it which is good arable soil. These countries, with their good and poor soil, maintain two hundred millions of people. The good land of the United States will certainly sustain as many people as their good and poor land taken together. . . .

In 1870, the pivotal point or centre about which all the population of the United States would balance was a little east of Baltimore. It has been moving westward; in the year of Lincoln's election, for a divine sign it had crossed the Ohio and obtained secure lodgment on free soil; in 1870 it was near Cincinnati; and it is now in Indiana. If its position were, as it should be, marked by a blazing star at the summit of a monumental shaft, carried from time to time toward the setting sun, that shaft would move westward more than fifty feet in every twenty-four hours.

It is a narrow outlook that pauses at a time when a continent that can sustain a larger population than the Old World shall have one hundred million people. But at that date the popular imagination stops. North and South America will probably have one hundred millions of people before the twentieth century, whose upstretching auroras, already appearing at the rim of the sky, shall rise above the horizon of history. At the place where the popular foresight pauses I would begin. Daniel Webster said, when we had but twenty millions of people: "I do not know whose imagination is fertile enough, I do not know whose conjectures, I may almost say, are wild enough, to tell what may be the progress of wealth and population in the United States."

England and Prussia, two of the most thickly populated parts of Europe, now increase at the rate of more than one per cent. annually. But let our immigration fall away, let wars storm over our territory from time to time, who shall say that our rate of increase, now three per cent. annually, will, in a hundred or two hundred years, not be at least equal to that of suffocated England and Prussia to-day? Call it less, or only one per cent. annually after the year 2000. Even at that percentage of increase, we should double once each hundred years. Stand on this ocean shore. We see the curvature of a part of the surface of the sea; we know the law of the curve. Carry on the arc which we can measure; steady the imagination on the reason; project the majestic meridians, and bend them in and in, until they meet, eight thousand miles beneath your feet, and you feel the globe swim beneath you, afloat in the bosom of Omnipotence. This is the privilege and sublime duty of exact science.

Even at the far too cautious estimate that, after the year 2000, our population will increase only one per cent. annually, or less rapidly than that of England and Prussia to-day, and that in the year 2000 all America now having, or soon to have, 100,-000,000 will possess only 290,000,000 of inhabitants, we should have in 2100, 400,000,000; in 2200, 800,000,000; in 2300, 1,600,-000,000; in 2400, 3,200,000,000.

The capacity of the continent is supposed to be equal to the support of 3,600,000,000.

These figures, you say, represent a peculiarly American extravagance of hope. They represent German plodding. They are the outcome of Scotch sagacity. They are justified by haughty English condescension. It is certain that these calculations fall short of those which average German, Scottish, and English scholarship is now making as to the future of America. For thirty years the Encyclopædia Britannica has summarized the best investigation Europe has given to this topic by these amazing words: "If the natural resources of the American continent were fully developed, it would afford sustenance to 3,600,-000,000 of inhabitants,—a number nearly five times as great as the entire mass of human beings now existing upon the globe! What is even more surprising, it is not improbable that this prodigious population will be in existence within three, or at most four centuries." I think these numbers are not wisely chosen, but they represent the highest statistical authority. As early as 1853 the Encyclopædia Britannica said: "The great grandsons of those now in existence may live to see the New World contain a greater mass of civilized men than the Old."

I am aware of but three methods of estimating the future of our population. We may take as a standard of judgment either the capacity of our soil, or the law of growth ascertained by our own experience, or the law of increase exhibited by other parts

of the world. Two of these methods I have already used. But take the last, and to what astonishing results it leads! This was the standard employed by De Tocqueville. Europe, under the bayonet and the cannon wheel and the hoofs of war, charging in squadron after squadron; Europe which sent half of the population of Germany to death in the Thirty Years' War; Europe, staggering under a thousand impediments, inherited from the Middle Ages, and unknown and likely to remain unknown in America; Europe, from Charlemagne to Napoleon, smitten, seared, peeled, and sliced, has yet attained an average population of eighty inhabitants to the square mile. Will America have a harder fate in the next than Europe has had in the last ten centuries? What shall hinder all America from ultimately having as large an average population as all Europe? But we have fifteen millions of square miles and Europe only three. Look forward, then, to a population in the whole New World equal to the average of that of Europe; that is, to twelve hundred millions.

With whatever telescope I sweep the horizon I, for one, stand in awe. I set no dates; I seek to establish approximately no definite numbers. I assert only that America can sustain a larger population than Europe, Asia, and Africa taken together; that, since it can, probably, it ultimately will; that we may expect as large an average population as Europe now possesses; that America is, therefore, yet in its infancy; that for these immense numbers of the human family we stand in trust, and that the age, therefore, has not yet ceased to be a crisis.

It would have been worth something at Thermopylæ to have foreseen Salamis; and at Austerlitz, Sedan; and at Runnymede, America. It would have been worth something to Paul, when he went out of the Ostian gate to die, to have foreseen Constantine and Augustine and Luther, and churches on which the sun never sets. It would have been worth something at the parting from Delft Haven, or among the secreted graves on Plymouth Hill, to have foreseen the savages shut up behind the Mississippi, and church bells mingling their murmurs with the Pacific seas. But, undoubtedly, God's plans for the future are as majestic as those for the past; and so it ought to be worth something now to foresee what can be in America, and, therefore, probably will be, and to go out far in the dark beneath the wing under which infinities and eternities brood; for we know that the wing is there even in the dark. . . .

The American system of equality is the source of astonishing energy, and also of audacious and unscrupulous greed. Our greatest virtues and our greatest vices are both fostered by liberty.

> "Through spaces stretched from sea to sea,
> Our Maker and our Victim she."

Vastness of commercial opportunities and the value of success even in short courses tempt individuals, and especially corporations in America to unscrupulousness.

The absorption of citizens with their own exacting private enterprises leaves law with too lax execution. The preoccupation of the good is the opportunity of the bad. Plato said that there will be no ideal state until kings are philosophers and philosophers, kings. There will be no ideal Republic until active citizens are active Christians, and active Christians are active citizens.

Plutarch and Cicero take notice of a law of Solon which declared every man infamous who in civil discussions continued neutral. The able American citizen, however, except on great occasions, is absorbed in his personal business, and leaves that of the public to the political machine.

In America everything stimulates the will, and by no means everything the conscience. Our national character exhibits at its best the Anglo-Saxon strength and the Anglo-Saxon infirmity. But the American climate is producing a Latinized American temperament, and with the Latin temperament always goes *finesse*.

The magnetic pole of the world is in Boothia Felix, in the forehead of the North American Continent. Boston and Berlin are on the same climate line; but Berlin and Mexico are on the same magnetic line. On the American side of the Atlantic the auroral arch of the north rises higher and flames more intensely in electrical storms than on the European. Between the Old and New World is no contrast of physical conditions subtler in its influence than that of the electric. Our dry and stimulating climate has produced a distinctively American face, in which, as yet, I, for one, find more acuteness than elevation, more venturesomeness than veracity. But join Latin *finesse* to Anglo-Saxon daring, and you have the audacities of modern Anglo-Saxon dishonesty.

The ostrich buries her thin, willful head in the sand, and thinks her whole body covered. In circles, only half educated in morals, but aspiring, great is the American eagle, greater is the American peacock, and greatest is the American ostrich!

Charles Dickens wrote to his friend in England that a man with seven heads would attract less attention in Boston than a man who could not read and write. I wish the day to come, in American politics and average commerce, when a man with seven heads will attract less attention than one with seven faces.

"There are two nations in England," says Gasparin, "conscientious England and unscrupulous England."

The humiliations of the American Church in the conflict with slavery should make forever clear the fact that, under the voluntary system, the vices of the powerful part of society easily spread into the Church, and that most easy of all is the infection of the commercial vices.

But while there are fears, there are hopes. In 1800 the proportion of Church members to our whole population was as one to fifteen; now it is as one to five.

Competition encourages pretense, and also the exposure of pretense. In this work the higher American press, the best representative of the American people, has earned a good name for itself at home, and almost given the nation a bad one abroad. Publicity, in America, is the chief penalty of meanness and crime, not easily visited by legal punishment. Democratic manners are not dignified; but they are tolerably transparent, whether good or bad. We have carried our civilization more rapidly toward the setting sun than any nation has ever done before. In her settlements the question is whether a man is efficient, rather than whether he has blameless antecedents. Thus, standards of judgment as to character have been made lax while we have conquered the wilderness. Undoubtedly, when America is older, and the land fuller, society will be more exacting, for it will cost more to let thieves run.

The mobility of the upper and lower ranks in American society is such that, in our great cities, the dangerous classes do not become fixed and hereditary as in Europe. The United States has no ignorant peasantry in its rural districts. Aspiration marks the middle and lower orders of the American population, and this to a degree unknown among the middle and lower classes in Europe; and such aspiration favors religious and all other culture.

Church and State being separate from each other, the people do not hate the Church for political reasons as in Europe.

The Puritan religious ideals have established their national supremacy in a great civil war, abolishing the chief sin of the nation.

America has left behind it, in its passage over the ocean, the feudal system, hereditary aristocracy, primogeniture, entails, and the Established Church.

"There is nothing in the world," said Goldwin Smith, "so sound as American society, with its intimate union of all classes, its general diffusion of property, its common schools, and its free religion."

"Every American," said John Stuart Mill, "is in some sense a patriot and a person of cultivated intelligence. No such wide diffusion of the ideas, tastes, and sentiments of educated minds has ever been seen elsewhere or even conceived of as attainable."

"The people at large," Aristotle wrote, "however contemptible soever they may appear, when taken individually, are yet, when collectively considered, not perhaps unworthy of sovereignty. . . . The people at large are allowed to be the best judges of music and poetry."

Supply follows demand in history. As in recent ages, there has been a demand for the diffusion of liberty, property, and intelligence, there will be soon a demand for the diffusion of conscientiousness; and there will come slowly, and through much anguish of the ages, a supply! I foresee a great day for a scientific, biblical, and practical church. Wordsworth talked of an aristocracy. It will not come. Carlyle talks of a government of the best. It cannot be elected. Soon the Church and a true Church will be all the hope of the world. It will save the world by goodness and by truth; by practice and by doctrines also.

The Church needed by the American future must be scientific, biblical, and practical.

It must be scientific by a reasonable theology; by the absorption of all established science; by intellectual supremacy over rationalism; by mental primacy in literature and art; by indisputable authority in all philosophical research; by incisive triumph over popular crudity; by the courage to think syllogistically and on its knees and to the thirty-two points of the compass.

It must be biblical by the spirit of the founder of Christianity; by finding in the Holy Spirit a present Christ; by a sense that the nations are a theocracy and our Lord the world's Lord; by the doctrine of sin; by the doctrine of atonement; by the hope of immortality; by a far and fixed gaze on an eternal judgment.

It must be practical by carrying vital piety to every deathbed, every hearthstone, every cradle; by enlisting all believers in religious effort; by sleepless religious printing; by schools saturated by devout science; by making human legislation a close copy of natural law; by leadership in all just popular reforms; by righteousness as a river; by every-day integrity and holiness to the Lord, written on the bells of the horses, on bank vaults, and on the very dust of the streets, and by making of all secular pursuits spiritual avocations.

Cromwell and Hampden were once on shipboard in England for the purpose of coming to America for life. Their spirits seem to stand among those of our later martyrs.

Once in the blue midnight, in my study on Beacon Hill, in Boston, I fell into long thought as I looked out on the land and on the sea; and passing through the gate of dreams, I saw the angel having charge of America stand in the air, above the continent, and his wings shadowed either shore. Around him were gathered all who at Valley Forge and at Andersonville and the other sacred places suffered for the preservation of a virtuous Republic; and they conversed of what was and is and is to be. There was about the angel a multitude whom no man could number, of all nations and kindreds and tribes and tongues; and their voices were as the sound of many waters. And I heard thunderings and saw lightnings; but the face of the angel was above the brightness of the lightnings and the majesty of his words above that of the thunders.

Then came forth before the angel three spirits whose garments were as white as the light; and I saw not their faces, but I heard the ten thousand times ten thousand call them by names known on earth,—Washington and Lincoln and Garfield. And behind them stood Hampden and Tell and Miltiades and Leonidas and a multitude who had scars and crowns. And they said to the angel: "We will go on earth and teach the diffusion of liberty. We will heal America by equality." And the angel said: "Go. You will be efficient, but not sufficient."

Meanwhile, under emigrant wharves, and under the hovels of the perishing poor, and under crowded factories, and under the poisonous alleys of great cities, I heard, far in the subterranean depths, the black angels laugh.

Then came forward before the angel three other spirits, whose garments were white as the light; and I saw not their faces, but I heard the ten thousand times ten thousand call them by names known on earth,—Franklin and Hamilton and Irving. And behind them stood Pestalozzi and Shakespeare and Bacon and Aristotle and a multitude who had scrolls and crowns. And they said to the angel: "We will go on earth and teach the diffusion of intelligence. We will heal America by knowledge," and the angel said: "Go. You will be efficient, but not sufficient."

Meanwhile, under emigrant wharves and crowded factories, and under Washington, and under scheming conclaves of men acute and unscrupulous, and under many newspaper presses, and beneath Wall Street, and under the poisonous alleys of great cities, I heard the black angels laugh.

Then came forward before the angel three other spirits whom I heard the ten thousand times ten thousand call by names known on earth,—Adams and Jefferson and Webster. And behind them stood Chatham and Wilberforce and Howard and the Roman Gracchi and a multitude who had keys and crowns. And they said to the angel: "We will go on earth and teach diffusion of property. We will heal America by the self-respect of ownership." And the angel said, "Go. You will be efficient, but not sufficient."

Meanwhile under emigrant wharves and crowded factories, and beneath Wall Street, and under the poisonous alleys of suffocated great cities, I heard yet the black angels laugh.

Then came, lastly, forward before the angel three other spirits, with garments white as the light; and I saw not their faces, but I heard the ten thousand times ten thousand call them by names known on earth,—Edwards and Dwight and Whitefield. And behind them stood Wickliffe and Cranmer and Wesley and Luther and a multitude who had harps and crowns. And they said to the angel: "We will go on earth and teach the diffusion of conscientiousness. We will heal America by righteousness." Then the angel arose, and lifted up his far-gleaming hand to the heaven of heavens, and said: "Go. Not in the first three, but only in all four of these leaves from the tree of life, is to be

found the healing of the nations,—the diffusion of liberty, the diffusion of intelligence, the diffusion of property, the diffusion of conscientiousness. You will be more than very efficient, but not sufficient."

I listened, and under Plymouth Rock and the universities there was no sound; but under emigrant wharves and crowded factories, and under Wall Street, and in poisonous alleys of great cities, I heard yet the black angels laugh; but, with the laughter there came up now from beneath a clanking of chains.

Then I looked, and the whole firmament above the angel was as if it were one azure eye; and into it the ten thousand times ten thousand gazed; and I saw that they stood in one palm of a Hand of Him into whose face they gazed, and that the soft axle of the world stood upon the finger of another palm, and that both palms were pierced. I saw the twelve spirits which had gone forth, and they joined hands with each other and with the twelve hours, and moved perpetually about the globe; and I heard a Voice, after which there was no laughter: "Ye are efficient, but I am sufficient."

FRANCIS CORBIN

(1760–1821)

T IS probable that the principles of government have never been so earnestly and thoroughly discussed elsewhere as they were in the Virginia, New York, and Massachusetts conventions called in 1788 to ratify the Federal Constitution. It is a matter of curious interest to see how the orators in these conventions were carried forward into the history of the future and rendered prophetic by their adherence to one or the other of contending ideas of Federal or State sovereignty. Each side saw clearly that as ultimate sovereignty was left to reside with the State or was vested in the Federal Government, the history of the future would inevitably be controlled in the one direction or the other in spite of all that could be done after the Constitution was adopted. Patrick Henry, in Virginia, opposed, with all his force, the "nationalization" of the Government under the Constitution, as he had opposed the continuance of the federation. He wanted a "federal union" instead of a loosely joined confederation, but he was more hostile to a "national" government than he was to a confederacy. He declared, with vehemence, that under the Constitution, as proposed to the States, the Government would necessarily cease to be federal, and become national, as a result of the inherent force of principles which had been, as he thought, designedly introduced into the Constitution by those he believed were really opponents of the popular supremacy appealed to in the clause, "we, the people." Among the replies to his denunciation of what he considered the anti-federal principles of the Constitution, that of Francis Corbin is one of the ablest. Corbin argued openly that the National Government should have such power of coercion against the States as it was not possible for it to exercise under the confederation. He was far from being terrified by Henry's assertions that under a national government militarism and the coercion of the States, when they undertook to resist national authority, would become inevitable; in fact he seems to have been convinced that what Henry and others considered formidable was necessary and likely to be distinctly advantageous. Perhaps the very lucidity with which he expresses himself accounts for the fact that after the convention he disappeared almost completely from history. He was born in 1760 of one of the powerful colonial families of Virginia. After

IV—88

his return from England, where he was educated at Cambridge and in the Middle Temple, he was sent as a delegate to the constitutional convention, and though only twenty-eight years old he made one of the most notable speeches of the time. From 1787 to 1793 he represented Middlesex County, in the Virginia legislature. He died June 15, 1821.

ANSWERING PATRICK HENRY

(Delivered Saturday, June 7th, 1788, During the Debate on the Coercive Powers of the Federal Government, in the Virginia Convention Called to Ratify the Federal Constitution)

Mr. Chairman:—

PERMIT me to make a few observations on this great question. It is with great difficulty I prevail on myself to enter into the debate, when I consider the great abilities of those gentlemen who have already spoken on the subject. But as I am urged by my duty to my constituents, and as I conceive that the different manner of treating the subject may make different impressions, I shall offer my observations with diffident respect, but with firmness and independence. I will promise my acknowledgments to those honorable gentlemen who were in the Federal Convention, for the able and satisfactory manner in which they discharged their duty to their country. The introductory expression of "We, the people," has been thought improper by the honorable gentleman. I expected no such objection as this. Ought not the people, sir, to judge of that government whereby they are to be ruled? We are, sir, deliberating on a question of great consequence to the people of America, and to the world in general. We ought, therefore, to decide with extreme caution and circumspection; it is incumbent upon us to proceed without prejudice or prepossession. No member of the committee entertains a greater regard than myself for the gentleman on the other side, who has placed himself in the front of opposition. [Mr. Henry.] No man admires more than I do his declamatory talents; but I trust that neither declamation nor elegance of periods will mislead the judgment of any member here, and that nothing but the force of reasoning will operate conviction. He has asked, with an air of triumph, whether the Confederation was not adequate to the purposes of the Federal Government. Permit me to say, No. If, sir, perfection existed in

that system, why was the Federal Convention called? Why did every State except Rhode Island send deputies to that convention?

Was it not from a persuasion of its inefficacy? If this be not sufficient to convince him, let me call the recollection of the honorable gentleman to other circumstances. Let him go into the interior parts of the country and inquire into the situation of the farmers. He will be told that tobacco and other produce are miserably low, merchandise dear, and taxes high. Let him go through the United States. He will perceive appearances of ruin and decay everywhere. Let him visit the seacoast — go to our ports and inlets. In those ports, sir, where we had every reason to see the fleets of all nations, he will behold but a few trifling little boats; he will everywhere see commerce languish, the disconsolate merchant, with his arms folded, ruminating, in despair, on the wretched ruins of his fortune, and deploring the impossibility of retrieving it. The West Indies are blocked up against us. Not the British only, but other nations, exclude us from those islands: our fur trade has gone to Canada; British sentinels are within our own territories; our imposts are withheld. To these distresses we may add the derangement of our finances; yet the honorable gentleman tells us they are not sufficient to justify so radical a change. Does he know the consequences of deranged finances? What confusions, disorders, and even revolutions, have resulted from this cause, in many nations! Look at France at this time: that kingdom is almost convulsed; ministers of state, and first princes of the blood, banished; manufacturers and merchants become bankrupt, and the people discontented — all owing to the derangement of their finances.

The honorable gentleman must be well acquainted with the debts due by the United States, and how much is due to foreign nations. Has not the payment of these been shamefully withheld? How long, sir, shall we be able, by fair promises, to satisfy these creditors? How long can we amuse, by idle words, those who are amply possessed of the means of doing themselves justice? No part of the principal is paid to those nations, nor has even the interest been paid as honorably and punctually as it ought. Nay, we were obliged to borrow money last year to pay the interest. What! borrow money to discharge the interest of what was borrowed, and continually augment the amount of the public debt! Such a plan would destroy the richest country

on earth. What is to be done? Compel the delinquent States to pay requisitions to Congress? How are they to be compelled? By the instrumentality of such a scheme as was proposed to be introduced in the year 1784? Is this cruel mode of compulsion eligible? Is it consistent with the spirit of republicanism? This savage mode, which could be made use of under the Confederation, leads directly to civil war and destruction. How different is this from the genius of the proposed constitution! By this proposed plan, the public money is to be collected by mild and gentle means; by a peaceable and friendly application to the individuals of the community: whereas, by the other scheme, the public treasury must be supplied through the medium of the sword, by desolation and murder — by the blood of the citizens. Yet we are told that there is too much energy in this system. Coercion is necessary in every government. Justice, sir, cannot be done without it. It is more necessary in federal governments than any other, because of the natural imbecility of such governments.

The honorable gentleman is possessed of much historical knowledge. I appeal to that knowledge therefore. Will he not agree that there was a coercive power in the federal government of the Amphictyonics? The coercive power of the Amphictyonic Council was so great as to enable it to punish disobedience and refractory behavior in the most severe manner. Is there not an instance of its carrying fire and sword through the territories, and leveling to the ground the towns, of those who disobeyed it? [Here Mr. Corbin mentions particular instances.] Is there no coercion in the Germanic body? This body, though composed of three hundred different component sovereignties, principalities, and cities, and divided into nine circles, is controlled by one superintending power, the emperor. Is there no coercive power in the confederate government of the Swiss? In the alliance between them and France, there is a provision whereby the latter is to interpose and settle differences that may arise among them; and this interposition has been more than once used. Is there none in Holland? What is the stadtholder? This power is necessary in all governments; a superintending coercive power is absolutely indispensable. This does not exist under the present Articles of Confederation. To vest it with such a power, on its present construction, without any alteration, would be extremely dangerous, and might lead to civil war. Gentlemen must, before this, have been convinced of the necessity of an alteration. Our State vessel has sprung a leak; we must embark in a new bottom, or sink into perdition.

The honorable gentleman has objected to the Constitution on the old worn-out idea that a republican government is best calculated for a small territory. If a republic, sir, cannot be accommodated to an extensive country, let me ask, how small must a country be to suit the genius of republicanism? In what particular extent of country can a republican government exist? If contracted into as small a compass as you please, it must labor under many disadvantages. Too small an extent will render a republic weak, vulnerable, and contemptible. Liberty in such a petty state must be on a precarious footing; its existence must depend on the philanthropy and good nature of its neighbors. Too large an extent, it is said, will produce confusion and tyranny. What has been so often deprecated will be removed by this plan. The extent of the United States cannot render the government oppressive. The powers of the General Government are only of a general nature, and their object is to protect, defend, and strengthen the United States; but the internal administration of government is left to the State legislatures, who exclusively retain such powers as will give the States the advantages of small republics, without the danger commonly attendant on the weakness of such governments.

There are controversies even about the name of this government. It is denominated by some a federal, by others a consolidated government. The definition given of it by my honorable friend [Mr. Madison] is, in my opinion, accurate. Let me, however, call it by another name—a representative federal republic, as contradistinguished from a confederacy. The former is more wisely constructed than the latter; it places the remedy in the hands which feel the disorder: the other places the remedy in those hands which cause the disorder. The evils that are most complained of in such governments (and with justice) are faction, dissension, and consequent subjection of the minority to the caprice and arbitrary decisions of the majority, who, instead of consulting the interest of the whole community collectively, attend sometimes to partial and local advantages. To avoid this evil is perhaps the great desideratum of republican wisdom; it may be termed the philosopher's stone. Yet, sir, this evil will be avoided by this Constitution: faction will be removed by the

system now under consideration, because all the causes which are generally productive of faction are removed. This evil does not take its flight entirely; for were jealousies and divisions entirely at an end, it might produce such lethargy as would ultimately terminate in the destruction of liberty, to the preservation of which watchfulness is absolutely necessary. It is transferred from the State legislatures to Congress, where it will be more easily controlled. Faction will decrease in proportion to the diminution of counselors. It is much easier to control it in small than in large bodies. Our State legislature consists of upwards of one hundred and sixty, which is a greater number than Congress will consist of at first. Will not more concord and unanimity exist in one than in thirteen such bodies? Faction will more probably decrease, or be entirely removed, if the interest of a nation be entirely concentrated, than if entirely diversified. If thirteen men agree, there will be no faction. Yet if opposite, and of heterogeneous dispositions, it is impossible that a majority of such clashing minds can ever concur to oppress the minority. It is impossible that this Government, which will make us one people, will have a tendency to assimilate our situations, and is admirably calculated to produce harmony and unanimity, can ever admit of an oppressive combination by one part of the Union against the other.

A confederate government is, of all others, best calculated for an extensive country. Its component individual governments are, of all others, best calculated for an extensive country. Its component individual governments administer and afford all the local conveniences that the most compact governments can do; and the strength and energy of the confederacy may be equal to those of any government. A government of this kind may extend to all the Western World; nay, I may say, *ad infinitum*. But it is needless to dwell any longer on this subject; for the objection that an extensive territory is repugnant to a republican government applies against this and every State in the Union, except Delaware and Rhode Island. Were the objection well founded, a republican government could exist in none of the States, except those two. Such an argument goes to the dissolution of the Union, and its absurdity is demonstrated by our own experience.

But an objection is urged against this government because of its power of laying direct taxes. Let us ask the honorable gen-

tleman who opposes it on this ground, if he reflect whether this power be indispensable or not. Sir, if it be not vested with the power of commanding all the resources of the State, when necessary, it will be trifling. Wars are as much (and more) carried on by the length of the purse as by that of the sword. They cannot be carried on without money. Unless this power be given to Congress, foreign nations may crush you. The concession of this power is necessary to do Virginia justice, by compelling the delinquent States to pay as well as she. While she paid her quotas, and her citizens were much distressed to pay their taxes, other States most shamefully neglected or refused to pay their proportions. I trust gentlemen need not be alarmed on the subject of taxation, nor intimidated by the idea of double collectors, who, they tell us, will oppress and ruin the people. From our attention to our situation, we shall see that this mode of levying money, though indispensably necessary on great emergencies, will be but seldom recurred to. Let us attend to the finances of this country. . . .

The honorable gentleman declared in the most solemn manner, that, if he could see one single trait in that government to secure liberty, he would not object to it. I meet him on this ground. Liberty is secured, sir, by the limitation of its powers, which are clearly and unequivocally defined, and which are to be exercised by our own representatives freely chosen. What power is given that will endanger liberty? I consider all the traits of this system as having a tendency to the security of our liberty. I consider all its powers necessary, and only given to avoid greater evils; and if this conclusion of mine be well founded, let me ask if public liberty is not secured by bars and adamantine bolts—secured by the strongest guards and checks which human ingenuity can invent. Will this dread power of taxation render liberty insecure? Sir, without this power, other powers will answer no purpose. Government cannot exist without the means of procuring money. My honorable friend told us he considered this clause as the vitals of the Constitution. I will change the phrase, and say that I consider this part as the lungs of the Constitution. If it be sick, the whole system is consumptive, and must soon decay; and this power can never be dangerous if the principles of equal and free representation be fully attended to. While the right of suffrage is secured, we have little to fear. This Government, sir, fully secures us this noble privilege, on

the purest and simplest principles of equality. That number which, in any part of the country, has a right to send a representative, has the same right in another part. What does the Constitution say? That thirty thousand shall have one representative, no matter where. If this be not equal representation, what, in the name of God, is equal representation? But, says the honorable gentleman, the Constitution may be satisfied by one from each State. I conceive there is no fear of this. There is not a power to diminish the number. Does it not say that representatives shall be apportioned according to the number of the people, and that direct taxes shall be regulated by the same rules? Virginia, in the first instance, will have ten times as many as Delaware, and afterwards in proportion to their numbers. What is the criterion of representation? They have their wish: for the qualifications which the laws of the States require to entitle a man to vote for a State representative are the qualifications required by this plan to vote for a representative to Congress; and in this State, and most of the others, the possession of a freehold is necessary to entitle a man to the privilege of a vote. Do they wish persons to be represented? Here also they are indulged, for the number of representatives is determined by the number of people. This idea is so well attended to, that even three-fifths of those who are not free are included among those of whom thirty thousand shall have a right to elect one representative; so that, in either point of view, their wish is gratified. Is not liberty secured on this foundation? If it be not secured by one or the other mode, or by both, I am totally without reason. Liberty seems intrenched on this ground.

But the gentleman objects that the number is not sufficient. My opinion, with deference to that gentleman, and others who may be of different opinion from me, is that it is fully sufficient. Being delegated solely for general purposes, a few intelligent men will suffice; at least one from every thirty thousand, aided by the Senate, seems sufficient. Are combinations or factions so often formed in small as in numerous bodies? Are laws better made in large than in small assemblies? Is not the influence of popular declaimers less in small than in great bodies? Would not a more numerous representation be very expensive? Is economy of no consideration? We ought, sir, to attend to the situation of the people; and our measures should be as economical as possible, without extending, however, our parsimony to a dangerous length. Objections should be founded on just and real grounds, and ought not to be urged out of a mere obstinacy. Besides, it is by no means certain that a very numerous body is more independent, or upright, than a small one. Why should the number of our representatives be greater, Mr. Chairman? The county of Middlesex, in England, which includes the cities of London and Westminster, contains upwards of nine hundred and ninety thousand souls, and yet sends to Parliament no more than eight Members. Among all the clamors of the people there, it never entered the brain of any of them that these eight were not enough. They complain that the boroughs of Old Sarum, Newton, and Gatton, and other such places, should send each two Members to Parliament, although without houses or inhabitants, while the richest city sends but four. They also complain of the influence of the landed interest in some cases; that the county of Cornwall sends forty Members to Parliament, although it pays but eighteen parts, out of five hundred and thirteen, to the subsidy and land tax, when the county of Middlesex, which is calculated to pay two hundred and fifty parts out of five hundred and thirteen, sends but eight Members. In that country, it has been uniformly found that those Members, who are chosen by numerous respectable electors, make the greatest opposition to oppression and corruption, and signalize themselves for the preservation of liberty. The collective body of the Commons there have generally exerted themselves in the defense of freedom, and have been successful in their exertions, notwithstanding the inequality of their election. Our representatives are chosen in the fairest manner; their election is founded in absolute equality. Is the American spirit so degenerated, notwithstanding these advantages, that the love of liberty is more predominant and warm in the breast of a Briton than in that of an American? When liberty is on a more solid foundation here than in Britain, will Americans be less ready to maintain and defend it than Britons? No, sir; the spirit of liberty and independence of the people of this country, at present, is such that they could not be enslaved under any government that could be described. What danger is there, then, to be apprehended from a government which is theoretically perfect, and the possible blemishes of which can only be demonstrated by actual experience?

The honorable gentleman then urges an objection respecting the militia, who, he tells us, will be made the instruments of

tyranny to deprive us of our liberty. Your militia, says he, will fight against you. Who are the militia? Are we not militia? Shall we fight against ourselves? No, sir; the idea is absurd. We are also terrified by the dread of a standing army. It cannot be denied that we ought to have the means of defense, and be able to repel an attack.

If some of the community are exclusively inured to its defense, and the rest attend to agriculture, the consequence will be that the arts of war and defense and of cultivating the soil will be understood. Agriculture will flourish, and military discipline will be perfect. If, on the contrary, our defense be solely intrusted to militia, ignorance of arms and negligence of farming will ensue; the former plan is, in every respect, more to the interest of the State. By it we shall have good farmers and soldiers; by the latter we shall have neither. If the inhabitants be called out on sudden emergencies of war, their crops, the means of their subsistence, may be destroyed by it. If we are called in the time of sowing seed, or of harvest, the means of subsistence might be lost; and the loss of one year's crop might have been prevented by a trivial expense, if appropriated to the purpose of supporting a part of the community, exclusively occupied in the defense of the whole. I conceive that this idea, if it be a new one, is yet founded on solid and very substantial reasons. But, sir, we are told of the expediency and propriety of previous amendments. What end would it answer to attempt it? Will the States which have adopted the Constitution rescind their adopting resolutions? Had we adopted it, would we recede from it to please the caprice of any other State? Pride, sir, revolts at the idea. Admitting this State proposes amendments previous to her adoption, must there not be another Federal Convention? Must there not be also a convention in each State? Suppose some of our proposed conditions be rejected, will not our exclusion from the Union be the consequence? Or would other conventions again be called, and be eternally revolving and devising expedients, without coming to a final decision? The loss of the union, sir, must be the result of a pertinacious demand of precedent conditions. My idea is, that we should go hand in hand with Massachusetts; adopt it first, and then propose amendments of a general nature, for local ones cannot be expected. Consider the situation of Massachusetts, commanding the North, and the importance and respectability of Virginia to

the South. These, sir, are the two most populous, wealthy, and powerful States in the Union. Is it not very probable that their influence would have very great weight in carrying any amendments? Would any gentleman turn a deaf ear to their solicitations? By union alone can we exist; by no other means can we be happy. Union must be the object of every gentleman here. I never yet have heard any gentleman so wild and frantic in his opposition as to avow an attachment to partial confederacies. By previous adoption, the union will be preserved; by insisting on alterations previous to our adoption, the union may be lost, and our political happiness destroyed by internal dissensions. I trust, therefore, that this convention, after deliberate discussion, will not hesitate to determine on a previous ratification of a system which, even in its present form, seems competent to the perpetual preservation of our security and happiness.

THOMAS CORWIN

(1794-1865)

THE speech on the Mexican War, made in the United States Senate, February 11th, 1847, by Thomas Corwin, then a Senator from Ohio, is one of the most remarkable ever delivered in America. Seemingly futile, and apparently leaving Corwin almost in a minority of one among the public men of his day, it gave him an assured immortality and an influence that will endure in America as long as American institutions continue to be inspired by the love of justice which animated him in that supreme effort of his life. His prophecy of civil war as a result of the acquisition of territory by conquest from Mexico was literally fulfilled. In three years after the speech was delivered, the Civil War had virtually begun when lines were drawn on the admission of California, and, the influence of such conservatives as Clay and Webster being broken, the extremists of both sections gained such an overwhelming influence, that the maintenance of peace became impossible. It is sometimes supposed that the speech retired Corwin from politics, but this was not the case. Although he was left to make his stand alone, he was really representative in making it and he had the silent sympathy perhaps of a majority, and certainly, as the result shows, of a controlling balance of power, not only in Ohio, but in the country at large. The Whig party had been disorganized by the blunders, and the vacillation of its leaders on the questions of the tariff, of nullification, of the annexation of Texas, and of Slavery as a permanent institution, but the latent sentiment of repugnance to the conquest and dismemberment of Mexico, which Corwin represented, gave the party what has been called "a postmortem victory," the last it ever achieved in national politics. The Democratic party in administration had fought the war with almost no expense to the national treasury, had achieved a series of most remarkable victories, had marched triumphantly through the heart of the enemy's country, and had occupied their capital, and, without a single reverse to dim the military glory for which it had striven, had added to the country an immense domain, secured at a merely nominal price. Nevertheless, the immediate result was the defeat of the Democratic presidential ticket by the Whigs in the campaign immediately ensuing, and, hard on this reverse, the successful organization of the Republican party, whose radical sentiment was represented by James Russell Lowell, in his characteristic line, "You have got to get up airly if you hope to get 'round God." Corwin, after making his speech of 1847, and probably as a result of it, became Secretary of the Treasury in the Whig Cabinet, holding that place from 1850 to 1853, and thereafter working to assist the Republican party, which, as a result of the forces he represented in his speech of 1847, carried the election of 1860 and held power continuously for a quarter of a century. Corwin himself was elected to Congress from Ohio in 1859 and served to 1861, when President Lincoln appointed him United States Minister to Mexico, an office he held until 1864. He was born in Bourbon County, Kentucky, July 29th, 1794, and died at Washington, December 18th, 1865. In reading his impassioned protests against dismembering Mexico, it is often difficult to imagine what he lacked of the highest rank as an orator, but the speech, when read as a whole, suggests that he failed of leadership, not because of the courage and the compelling sense of justice which inspired him, but rather because of lacking the sustained force necessary for great achievement. He was content to go on record in a splendid outburst of impassioned protest against what his whole nature condemned as a wrong; and, being so content, he left to others the work of inflicting that retribution which he had seen so clearly was inevitable as a result of the operation of laws which govern human as they do universal nature. Doubtless, he lived more happily and died more contentedly than if it had been otherwise, but it is hard to see how any one who studies American history can impute his failure to maintain leadership to the speech which gave him so remarkable an opportunity for it.

W. V. B.

AGAINST DISMEMBERING MEXICO

(From a Speech in the United States Senate, February 11th, 1847)

You may wrest provinces from Mexico by war; you may hold them by the right of the strongest; you may rob her; but a treaty of peace to that effect with the people of Mexico, legitimately and freely made, you never will have! I thank God that it is so, as well for the sake of the Mexican people as ourselves; for, unlike the Senator from Alabama [Mr. Bagby], I do not value the life of a citizen of the United States above the lives of a hundred thousand Mexican women and children — a rather cold sort of philanthrophy in my judgment. For the sake of Mexico, then, as well as our own country, I rejoice that it is

an impossibility that you can obtain by treaty from her those territories, under the existing state of things.

I am somewhat at a loss to know on what plan gentlemen having charge of this war intend to proceed. We hear much said of the terror of your arms. The affrighted Mexican, it is said, when you have drenched his country in blood, will sue for peace, and thus you will indeed "conquer peace." This is the heroic and savage tone in which we have heretofore been lectured by our friends on the other side of the Chamber, especially by the Senator from Michigan [Mr. Cass]. But suddenly the Chairman of the Committee on Foreign Relations comes to us with the smooth phrase of diplomacy, made potent by the gentle suasion of gold. The Chairman of the Committee on Military Affairs calls for thirty millions of money and ten thousand regular troops; these, we are assured, shall "conquer peace," if the obstinate Celt refuses to treat till we shall whip him in another field of blood. What a delightful scene in the nineteenth century of the Christian era! What an interesting sight to see these two representatives of war and peace moving in grand procession through the Halls of the Montezumas! The Senator from Michigan [Mr. Cass], red with the blood of recent slaughter, the gory spear of Achilles in his hand, and the hoarse clarion of war at his mouth, blowing a blast "so loud and deep" that the sleeping echoes of the lofty Cordilleras start from their caverns and return to the sound, till every ear from Panama to Santa Fé is deafened with the roar. By his side, with "modest mien and downcast look," comes the Senator from Arkansas [Mr. Sevier], covered from head to foot with a gorgeous robe, glittering and embossed with three millions of shining gold, putting to shame "the wealth of Ormus or of Ind." The olive of Minerva graces his brow; in his right hand is the delicate rebeck, from which are breathed in Lydian measure notes "that tell of naught but love and peace." I fear very much that you will scarcely be able to explain to the simple mind of the half-civilized Mexican the puzzling dualism of this scene, at once gorgeous and grotesque. Sir, I scarcely understand the meaning of all this myself. If we are to vindicate our rights by battles — in bloody fields of war — let us do it. If that is not the plan, why, then, let us call back our armies into our own territory, and propose a treaty with Mexico, based upon the proposition that money is better for her and land for us. Thus we can treat Mexico like an equal, and

do honor to ourselves. But what is it you ask? You have taken from Mexico one-fourth of her territory, and you now propose to run a line comprehending about another third, and for what? I ask, Mr. President, for what? What has Mexico got from you, for parting with two-thirds of her domain? She has given you ample redress for every injury of which you have complained. She has submitted to the award of your commissioners, and, up to the time of the rupture with Texas, faithfully paid it. And for all that she has lost (not through or by you, but which loss has been your gain), what requital do we, her strong, rich, robust neighbor, make? Do we send our missionaries there "to point the way to heaven"? Or do we send the schoolmasters to pour daylight into her dark plans, to aid her infant strength to conquer, and reap the fruit of the independence herself alone had won? No, no; none of this do we. But we send regiments, storm towns, and our colonels prate of liberty in the midst of the solitudes their ravages have made. They proclaim the empty forms of social compact to a people bleeding and maimed with wounds received in defending their hearthstones against the invasion of these very men who shoot them down and then exhort them to be free. Your chaplains of the navy throw away the New Testament and seize a bill of rights. The Rev. Don Walter Colton, I see, abandons the Sermon on the Mount and betakes himself to Blackstone and Kent, and is elected a justice of the peace! He takes military possession of some town in California, and instead of teaching the plan of the atonement and the way of salvation to the poor ignorant Celt, he presents a Colt's pistol to his ear and calls on him to take "trial by jury and habeas corpus," or nine bullets in his head. Ah, Mr. President, are you not the light of the earth, if not its salt? You, you are indeed opening the eyes of the blind in Mexico with a most emphatic and exoteric power. Sir, if all this were not a mournful truth it would be the *ne plus ultra* of the ridiculous. But, sir, let us see what, as the Chairman of the Committee on Foreign Relations explains it, we are to get by the combined processes of conquest and treaty.

What is the territory, Mr. President, which you propose to wrest from Mexico? It is consecrated to the heart of the Mexican by many a well-fought battle with his old Castilian master. His Bunker Hills, and Saratogas, and Yorktowns are there! The Mexican can say, "There I bled for liberty! and shall I sur-

render that consecrated home of my affections to the Anglo-Saxon invaders? What do they want with it? They have Texas already. They have possessed themselves of the territory between the Nueces and the Rio Grande. What else do they want? To what shall I point my children as memorials of that independence which I bequeath to them, when those battlefields shall have passed from my possession?"

Sir, had one come and demanded Bunker Hill of the people of Massachusetts, had England's lion ever showed himself there, is there a man over thirteen and under ninety who would not have been ready to meet him? Is there a river on this continent that would not have run red with blood? Is there a field but would have been piled high with unburied bones of slaughtered Americans before these consecrated battlefields of liberty should have been wrested from us? But this same American goes into a sister Republic, and says to poor, weak Mexico, "Give up your territory, you are unworthy to possess it; I have got one-half already, and all I ask of you is to give up the other!" England might as well, in the circumstances I have described, have come and demanded of us, "Give up the Atlantic slope — give up this trifling territory from the Alleghany Mountains to the sea; it is only from Maine to St. Mary's — only about one-third of your Republic, and the least interesting portion of it." What would be the response? They would say we must give this up to John Bull. Why? "He wants room." The Senator from Michigan says he must have this. Why, my worthy Christian brother; on what principle of justice? "I want room!"

Sir, look at this pretense of want of room. With twenty millions of people, you have about one thousand millions of acres of land, inviting settlement by every conceivable argument, bringing them down to a quarter of a dollar an acre, and allowing every man to squat where he pleases. But the Senator from Michigan says we will be two hundred millions in a few years, and we want room. If I were a Mexican I would tell you, "Have you not room enough in your own country to bury your dead? If you come into mine, we will greet you with bloody hands, and welcome you to hospitable graves."

Why, says the Chairman of this Committee on Foreign Relations, it is the most reasonable thing in the world! We ought to have the Bay of San Francisco! Why? Because it is the best harbor on the Pacific! It has been my fortune, Mr. President, to have practiced a good deal in criminal courts in the course of my life, but I never yet heard a thief, arraigned for stealing a horse, plead that it was the best horse he could find in the country! We want California. What for? Why, says the Senator from Michigan, we will have it; and the Senator from South Carolina, with a very mistaken view, I think, of policy, says you can't keep our people from going there. I don't desire to prevent them. Let them go and seek their happiness in whatever country or clime it pleases them. All I ask of them is, not to require this government to protect them with that banner consecrated to war waged for principles — eternal, enduring truth. Sir, it is not meet that our old flag should throw its protecting folds over expeditions for lucre or for land. But you still say you want room for your people. This has been the plea of every robber chief from Nimrod to the present hour. I dare say when Tamerlane descended from his throne, built of seventy thousand human skulls, and marched his ferocious battalions to further slaughter, — I dare say he said, "I want room." Bajazet was another gentleman of kindred tastes and wants with us Anglo-Saxons — he "wanted room." Alexander, too, the mighty "Macedonian madman," when he wandered with his Greeks to the plains of India, and fought a bloody battle on the very ground where recently England and the Sikhs engaged in strife for "room," was, no doubt, in quest of some California there. Many a Monterey had he to storm to get "room." Sir, he made as much of that sort of history as you ever will. Mr. President, do you remember the last chapter in that history? It is soon read. Ah, I wish we could but understand its moral. Ammon's son (so was Alexander named), after all his victories, died drunk in Babylon! The vast empire he conquered to "get room," became the prey of the generals he had trained: it was dismembered, torn to pieces, and so ended. Sir, there is a very significant appendix; it is this: The descendants of the Greeks, Alexander's Greeks, are now governed by a descendant of Attila! Mr. President, while we are fighting for room, let us ponder deeply this appendix. I was somewhat amazed the other day to hear the Senator from Michigan declare that Europe had quite forgotten us, till these battles waked them up. I suppose the Senator feels grateful to the President for "waking up" Europe. Does the President, who is, I hope, read in civic as

iv—89

well as military lore, remember the saying of one who had pondered upon history long; long, too, upon man, his nature, and true destiny. Montesquieu did not think highly of this way of "waking up." "Happy," says he, "is that nation whose annals are tiresome."

The Senator from Michigan has a different view. He thinks that a nation is not distinguished until it is distinguished in war. He fears that the slumbering faculties of Europe have not been able to ascertain that there are twenty millions of Anglo-Saxons here, making railroads and canals, and speeding all the arts of peace to the utmost accomplishment of the most refined civilization! They do not know it! And what is the wonderful expedient which this democratic method of making history would adopt in order to make us known? Storming cities, desolating peaceful, happy homes; shooting men — ay, sir, such is war — and shooting women, too.

Sir, I have read in some account of your battle of Monterey, of a lovely Mexican girl who, with the benevolence of an angel in her bosom and the robust courage of a hero in her heart, was busily engaged during the bloody conflict — amid the crash of falling houses, the groans of the dying, and the wild shriek of battle — in carrying water to slake the burning thirst of the wounded of either host. While bending over a wounded American soldier, a cannon ball struck her and blew her to atoms! Sir, I do not charge my brave, generous-hearted countrymen who fought that fight with this. No, no. We who send them — we who know that scenes like this, which might send tears of sorrow "down Pluto's iron cheek," are the invariable, inevitable attendants on war — we are accountable for this; and this — this is the way we are to be made known to Europe. This — this is to be the undying renown of free, republican America; "she has stormed a city, killed many of its inhabitants of both sexes — she has room!" So it will read. Sir, if this were our only history, then may God in his mercy grant that its volume may speedily come to a close.

Why is it, sir, that we of the United States, a people of yesterday, compared with the older nations of the world, should be waging war for territory, for "room"? Look at your country extending from the Alleghany Mountains to the Pacific Ocean, capable itself of sustaining in comfort a larger population than will be in the whole Union for one hundred years to come.

Over this vast expanse of territory your population is now so sparse, that I believe we provided at the last session a regiment of mounted men to guard the mail from the frontier of Missouri to the mouth of the Columbia; and yet you persist in the ridiculous assertion, "I want room." One would imagine from the frequent reiteration of the complaint, that you had a bursting, teeming population, whose energy was paralyzed, whose enterprise was crushed, for want of space. Why should we be so weak or wicked as to offer this idle apology for ravaging a neighboring Republic! It will impose on no one, at home or abroad.

Do we not know, Mr. President, that it is a law, never to be repealed, that falsehood shall be short lived? Was it not ordained of old, that truth only shall abide forever? Whatever we may say to-day, or whatever we may write in our books, the stern tribunal of history will review it all, detect falsehood, and bring us to judgment before that posterity which shall bless or curse us as we may act now, wisely or otherwise. We may hide in the grave, which awaits us all! — in vain! We may hope to be concealed there, like the foolish bird that hides its head in the sand, in the vain belief that its body is not seen; yet, even there, this preposterous excuse of want of "room" shall be laid bare, and the quick-coming future will decide that it was a hypocritical pretense, under which we sought to conceal the avarice which prompted us to covet and to seize, by force, that which was not ours.

Mr. President, this uneasy desire to augment our territory has depraved the moral sense, and blighted the otherwise keen sagacity of our people. What has been the fate of all nations, who have acted upon the idea that they must advance thus? Our young orators cherish this notion with a fervid, but fatally-mistaken zeal. They call it by the mysterious name of "destiny." "Our destiny," they say, "is onward;" and hence they argue, with ready sophistry, the propriety of seizing upon any territory and any people that may lie in the way of our "fated" advance. Recently, these "progressives" have grown classical; some assiduous student of antiquities has helped them to a patron saint. They have wandered back into the desolated Pantheon, and there amongst the polytheistic relics of that "pale mother of dead empires," they have found a god whom these Romans, centuries gone by, baptized "Terminus."

Sir, I have heard much and read somewhat of this gentleman, Terminus. Alexander, of whom I have spoken, was a devotee of this divinity. We have seen the end of him and his empire. It was said to be an attribute of this god, that he must always advance, and never recede. So both republican and imperial Rome believed. It was, as they said, their destiny. And for a while it did seem to be even so. Roman Terminus did advance. Under the eagles of Rome, he was carried from his home on the Tiber to the farthest East, on the one hand, and to the far West, amongst the then barbarous tribes of western Europe, on the other. But at length the time came when retributive justice had become "a destiny." The despised Gaul cries out to the contemned Goth, and Attila, with his Huns, answers back the battle-shout to both. The "blue-eyed nations of the North," in succession, or united, pour forth their countless hosts of warriors upon Rome and Rome's always advancing god, Terminus. And now the battle-axe of the barbarian strikes down the conquering eagle of Rome. Terminus at last recedes, slowly at first, but finally he is driven to Rome, and from Rome to Byzantium. Whoever would know the further fate of this Roman deity, so recently taken under the patronage of American Democracy, may find ample gratification of his curiosity in the luminous pages of Gibbon's 'Decline and Fall.' Such will find that Rome thought, as you now think, that it was her destiny to conquer provinces and nations, and no doubt she sometimes said, as you say, "I will conquer a peace." And where now is she, the Mistress of the World? The spider weaves her web in her palaces, the owl sings his watch-song in her towers. Teutonic power now lords it over the servile remnant, the miserable memento of old and once omnipotent Rome. Sad, very sad, are the lessons which time has written for us. Through and in them all I see nothing but the inflexible execution of that old law, which ordains, as eternal, that cardinal rule, "Thou shalt not covet thy neighbor's goods, nor anything which is his." Since I have lately heard so much about the dismemberment of Mexico, I have looked back, to see how, in the course of events which some call "Providence," it has fared with other nations who engaged in this work of dismemberment. I see that in the latter half of the eighteenth century, three powerful nations — Russia, Austria, and Prussia — united in the dismemberment of Poland. They said, too, as you say, "It is our destiny." They "wanted room." Doubtless each of these thought, with his share of Poland, his power was too strong ever to fear invasion, or even insult. One had his California, another his New Mexico, and the third his Vera Cruz. Did they remain untouched and incapable of harm? Alas, no! Far, very far, from it! Retributive justice must fulfill its "destiny," too. A very few years pass, and we hear of a new man, a Corsican lieutenant, the self-named "armed soldier of Democracy"—Napoleon. He ravages Austria, covers her land with blood, drives the Northern Cæsar from his capital, and sleeps in his palace. Austria may now remember how her power trampled upon Poland. Did she not pay dear, very dear, for her California?

But has Prussia no atonement to make? You see this same Napoleon, the blind instrument of Providence, at work there. The thunders of his cannon at Jena proclaim the work of retribution for Poland's wrongs; and the successors of the great Frederick, the drill-sergeant of Europe, are seen flying across the sandy plain that surrounds their capital, right glad if they may escape captivity or death. But how fares it with the autocrat of Russia? Is he secure in his share of the spoils of Poland? No. Suddenly we see, sir, six hundred thousand armed men marching to Moscow. Does his Vera Cruz protect him now? Far from it. Blood, slaughter, desolation spread abroad over the land, and finally the conflagration of the old commercial metropolis of Russia closes the retribution; she must pay for her share in the dismemberment of her weak and impotent neighbor. Mr. President, a mind more prone to look for the judgments of heaven in the doings of men, than mine, cannot fail in this to see the Providence of God. When Moscow burned, it seemed as if the earth was lighted up that the nations might behold the scene. As that mighty sea of fire gathered and heaved, and rolled upwards, higher and yet higher, till its flames aspired the stars and lit the whole heavens, it did seem as though the God of nations was writing, in characters of flame on the front of his throne, the doom that shall fall upon the strong nation, which tramples in scorn upon the weak. And what fortune awaits him, the appointed executor of this work, when it was all done? He, too, conceived the notion that his "destiny" pointed onward to universal dominion. France was too small—Europe, he thought, should bow down before him. But as soon as this idea took possession of his soul, he,

too, became powerless. His terminus must recede, too. Right there, while he witnessed the humiliation, and doubtless meditated the subjugation of Russia, he who holds the winds in his fist, gathered the snows of the North and blew them upon his six hundred thousand men. They fled—they froze—they perished! and now the mighty Napoleon, who had resolved on universal dominion—he, too, is summoned to answer for the violation of that ancient law, "Thou shalt not covet anything which is thy neighbor's." How is the mighty fallen! He, beneath whose proud footstep Europe trembled,—he is now an exile at Elba, and now finally a prisoner on the rock of St. Helena. And there, on a barren island, in an unfrequented sea in the crater of an extinguished volcano,—there is the deathbed of the mighty conqueror! All his annexations have come to that! His last hour is now come, and he, "the Man of Destiny"; he who had rocked the world as with the throes of an earthquake, is now powerless and still. Even as the beggar dies, so he died. On the wings of a tempest that raged with unwonted fury, up to the throne of the only power that controlled him while he lived, went the fiery soul of that wonderful warrior, another witness to the existence of that eternal decree that they who do not rule in righteousness shall perish from the earth. He has found "room" at last. And France,—she, too, has found "room." Her "eagles" now no longer scream upon the banks of the Danube, the Po, and the Borysthenes. They have returned home to their old eyrie between the Alps, the Rhine, and the Pyrenees; so shall it be with your banners of conquest. You may carry them to the loftiest peaks of the Cordilleras, they may wave with insolent triumph in the Halls of the Montezumas, the armed men of Mexico may quail before them, but the weakest hand in Mexico, uplifted in prayer to the God of justice, may call down against you a Power, in the presence of which the iron hearts of your warriors shall be turned into ashes.

Mr. President, if the history of our race has established any truth, it is but a confirmation of what is written, "The way of the transgressor is hard." Inordinate ambition, wantoning in power, and spurning the humble maxims of justice ever has ended and ever shall end in ruin. Strength cannot always trample upon weakness; the humble shall be exalted; the bowed down will at length be lifted up. It is by faith in the law of strict justice, and the practice of its precepts, that nations alone can be

saved. All the annals of the human race, sacred and profane, are written over with this great truth in characters of living light. It is my fear, my fixed belief, that in this invasion, this war with Mexico, we have forgotten this vital truth. Why is it that we have been drawn into this whirlpool of war? How clear and strong was the light that shone upon the path of duty a year ago! The last disturbing question with England was settled. Our power extended its peaceful sway from the Atlantic to the Pacific: from the Alleghanies we looked upon Europe, and from the tops of the Stony Mountains we could descry the shores of Asia; a rich commerce with all the nations of Europe poured wealth and abundance into our lap on the Atlantic side, while an unoccupied commerce of three hundred millions of Asiatics waited on the Pacific for our enterprise to come and possess it. One hundred millions of dollars will be wasted in this fruitless war. Had this money of the people been expended in making a railroad from your northern lakes to the Pacific, as one of your citizens has begged of you in vain, you would have made a highway for the world between Asia and Europe. Your Capital then would be within thirty or forty days travel of any and every point on the map of the civilized world. Through this great artery of trade you would have carried through the heart of your own country the teas of China and the spices of India to the markets of England and France. Why, why, Mr. President, did we abandon the enterprises of peace and betake ourselves to the barbarous achievements of war? Why did we "forsake this fair and fertile field to batten on that moor"?

But, Mr. President, if further acquisition of territory is to be the result either of conquest or treaty, then I scarcely know which should be preferred, external war with Mexico, or the hazards of internal commotion at home, which last I fear may come if another province is to be added to our territory. There is one topic connected with this subject which I tremble when I approach, and yet I cannot forbear to notice it. It meets you in every step you take; it threatens you which way soever you go in the prosecution of this war. I allude to the question of slavery. Opposition to its further extension, it must be obvious to every one, is a deeply-rooted determination with men of all parties in what we call the non-slaveholding States. New York, Pennsylvania, and Ohio, three of the most powerful, have already sent their legislative instructions here. So it will be, I doubt

not, in all the rest. It is vain now to speculate about the reasons for this. Gentlemen of the South may call it prejudice, passion, hypocrisy, fanaticism. I shall not dispute with them now on that point. The great fact that it is so, and not otherwise, is what it concerns us to know. You and I cannot alter or change this opinion, if we would. These people only say, we will not, cannot consent that you shall carry slavery where it does not already exist. They do not seek to disturb you in that institution, as it exists in your States. Enjoy it if you will, and as you will. This is their language; this their determination. How is it in the South? Can it be expected that they should expend in common, their blood and their treasure, in the acquisition of immense territory, and then willingly forego the right to carry thither their slaves, and inhabit the conquered country if they please to do so? Sir, I know the feelings and opinions of the South too well to calculate on this. Nay, I believe they would even contend to any extremity for the mere right, had they no wish to exert it. I believe (and I confess I tremble when the conviction presses upon me) that there is equal obstinacy on both sides of this fearful question. If, then, we persist in war, which, if it terminates in anything short of a mere wanton waste of blood as well as money, must end (as this bill proposes) in the acquisition of territory, to which at once this controversy must attach—this bill would seem to be nothing less than a bill to produce internal commotion. Should we prosecute this war another moment, or expend one dollar in the purchase or conquest of a single acre of Mexican land, the North and the South are brought into collision on a point where neither will yield. Who can foresee or foretell the result! Who so bold or reckless as to look such a conflict in the face unmoved! I do not envy the heart of him who can realize the possibility of such a conflict without emotions too painful to be endured. Why, then, shall we, the representatives of the sovereign States of this Union,—the chosen guardians of this confederated Republic, why should we precipitate this fearful struggle, by continuing a war, the result of which must be to force us at once upon a civil conflict? Sir, rightly considered, this is treason, treason to the Union, treason to the dearest interests, the loftiest aspirations, the most cherished hopes of our constituents. It is a crime to risk the possibility of such a contest. It is a crime of such infernal hue, that every other in the catalogue of iniquity, when compared with it, whitens into virtue. Oh, Mr. President, it does seem to me, if hell itself could yawn and vomit up the fiends that inhabit its penal abodes, commissioned to disturb the harmony of this world, and dash the fairest prospect of happiness that ever allured the hopes of men, the first step in the consummation of this diabolical purpose would be, to light up the fires of internal war, and plunge the sister States of this Union into the bottomless gulf of civil strife. We stand this day on the crumbling brink of that gulf — we see its bloody eddies wheeling and boiling before us — shall we not pause before it be too late? How plain again is here the path, I may add the only way, of duty, of prudence, of true patriotism. Let us abandon all idea of acquiring further territory and by consequence cease at once to prosecute this war. Let us call home our armies, and bring them at once within our own acknowledged limits. Show Mexico that you are sincere when you say you desire nothing by conquest. She has learned that she cannot encounter you in war, and if she had not, she is too weak to disturb you here. Tender her peace, and, my life on it, she will then accept it. But whether she shall or not, you will have peace without her consent. It is your invasion that has made war; your retreat will restore peace. Let us then close forever the approaches of internal feud, and so return to the ancient concord and the old ways of national prosperity and permanent glory. Let us here, in this temple consecrated to the Union, perform a solemn lustration; let us wash Mexican blood from our hands, and on these altars, and in the presence of that image of the Father of his Country that looks down upon us, swear to preserve honorable peace with all the world, and eternal brotherhood with each other.

of Public Instruction in 1840, under Thiers. It is said that during the three years of his lectures after his return in 1828, "the Hall of the Sorbonne was crowded with auditors as the hall of no philosophical teacher in Paris had been since the days of Abélard." He died at Cannes, January 13th, 1867.

ELOQUENCE AND THE FINE ARTS

(From the Ninth Lecture on the True, the Beautiful, and the Good)

IT WILL, perhaps, seem strange that we rank among the arts neither eloquence, nor history, nor philosophy.

The arts are called the fine arts, because their sole object is to produce the disinterested emotion of beauty, without regard to the utility either of the spectator or the artist. They are also called the liberal arts, because they are the arts of free men and not of slaves, which affranchise the soul, charm and ennoble existence; hence the sense and origin of those expressions of antiquity, *artes liberales, artes ingenuæ.* There are arts without nobility, whose end is practical and material utility; they are called trades, such as that of the stove-maker and the mason. True art may be joined to them, may even shine in them, but only in the accessories and the details.

Eloquence, history, philosophy, are certainly high employments of intelligence. They have their dignity, their eminence, which nothing surpasses; but rigorously speaking, they are not arts.

Eloquence does not propose to itself to produce in the soul of the auditors the disinterested sentiment of beauty. It may also produce this effect, but without having sought it. Its direct end, which it can subordinate to no other, is to convince, to persuade. Eloquence has a client which, before all, it must save or make triumph. It matters little whether this client be a man, a people, or an idea. Fortunate is the orator if he elicit the expression: That is beautiful! for it is a noble homage rendered to his talent; unfortunate is he if he does not elicit this, for he has missed his end. The two great types of political and religious eloquence, Demosthenes in antiquity, Bossuet among the moderns, think only of the interest of the cause confided to their genius, the sacred cause of country and that of religion, whilst at bottom Phidias and Raphael work to make beautiful

VICTOR COUSIN

(1792-1867)

VICTOR COUSIN, celebrated both as a statesman and a philosopher, ranks with Guizot among the most eminent of the great platform orators of the nineteenth century. It is as a lecturer rather than as a political speaker that he is celebrated, and among his addresses delivered from the lecture platform are to be found most admirable examples of that class of oratory which has characterized the intellectual movement of the nineteenth century, as in another way it did that of the golden age of intellect at Athens and at Rome. The orations of Cicero and of Demosthenes were prepared in advance of delivery with the same care shown in the preparation of such addresses as those of Cousin and Guizot in France, Schlegel in Germany, Ruskin in England, Emerson in America, and the other great orators of the lecture platform who have forced issues for progress in every line during the nineteenth century, in advance of the great orators of the Forum and the Senate. Cousin's style is most attractive. While the tendencies of his mind are metaphysical and his reasoning abstract, he has what among philosophical thinkers is the rare faculty of clothing abstract thought in beauty of expression. His argument on some points of psychology frequently blossoms out into eloquent metaphors, which are never forced and never florid. His statement is always sustained and he is always master of his subject, of himself, and of the language in which he undertakes to give himself and his subject expression. He was born at Paris, November 28th, 1792; and at a time when the "fierce democracy" of France was attempting to stamp out every vestige of the Middle Ages, he won his first honors by a Latin oration, for which he was crowned in the Mediæval Hall of the Sorbonne, "in the presence of the general concourse of his school competitors." In 1815 he began at the Sorbonne those lectures for which he is so justly celebrated, but in 1820 he was proscribed by the Reactionist party under Louis XVIII., as was also Guizot. Leaving France for Germany, he was arrested and imprisoned at Berlin as a result of the same influence which had driven him from France. Released, and in 1828 restored to his position as teacher, he became a member of the Council of Public Instruction in 1830, peer of France in 1832, and Minister

things. Let us hasten to say, what the names of Demosthenes and Bossuet command us to say, that true eloquence, very different from that of rhetoric, disdains certain means of success. It asks no more than to please, but without any sacrifice unworthy of it; every foreign ornament degrades it. Its proper character is simplicity, earnestness. I do not mean affected earnestness, a designed and artful gravity, the worst of all deceptions; I mean true earnestness, that springs from sincere and profound conviction. This is what Socrates understood by true eloquence.

As much must be said of history and philosophy. The philosopher speaks and writes. Can he, then, like the orator, find accents which make truth enter the soul; colors and forms that make it shine forth evident and manifest to the eyes of intelligence? It would be betraying his cause to neglect the means that can serve it; but the profoundest art is here only a means, the aim of philosophy is elsewhere; whence it follows that philosophy is not an art. Without doubt, Plato is a great artist; he is the peer of Sophocles and Phidias, as Pascal is sometimes the rival of Demosthenes and Bossuet; but both would have blushed if they had discovered at the bottom of their souls another design, another aim than the service of truth and virtue.

History does not relate for the sake of relating; it does not paint for the sake of painting; it relates and paints the past that it may be the living lesson of the future. It proposes to instruct new generations by the experience of those who have gone before them, by exhibiting to them a faithful picture of great and important events, with their causes and their effects, with general designs and particular passions, with the faults, virtues, and crimes that are found mingled together in human things. It teaches the excellence of prudence, courage, and great thoughts profoundly meditated, constantly pursued, and executed with moderation and force. It shows the vanity of immoderate pretensions, the power of wisdom and virtue, the impotence of folly and crime. Thucydides, Polybius, and Tacitus undertake anything rather than procuring new emotions for an idle curiosity or a worn-out imagination. They doubtless desire to interest and attract, but more to instruct; they are the avowed masters of statesmen and the preceptors of mankind.

The sole object of art is the beautiful. Art abandons itself as soon as it shuns this. It is often constrained to make concessions to circumstances, to external conditions that are imposed upon it; but it must always retain a just liberty. Architecture and the art of gardening are the least free of arts; they are subjected to unavoidable obstacles; it belongs to the genius of the artist to govern these obstacles, and even to draw from them happy effects, as the poet turns the slavery of metre and rhyme into a source of unexpected beauties. Extreme liberty may carry art to a caprice which degrades it, as chains too heavy crush it. It is the death of architecture to subject it to convenience, to comfort. Is the architect obliged to subordinate general effect and the proportions of the edifice to such or such a particular end that is prescribed to him? He takes refuge in details, in pediments, in friezes, in all the parts that have not utility for a special object, and in them he becomes a true artist. Sculpture and painting, especially music and poetry, are freer than architecture and the art of gardening. One can also shackle them, but they disengage themselves more easily.

Similar by their common end, all the arts differ by the particular effects which they produce, and by the processes which they employ. They gain nothing by exchanging their means and confounding the limits that separate them. I bow before the authority of antiquity; but, perhaps, through habit and a remnant of prejudice, I have some difficulty in representing to myself with pleasure statues composed of several metals, especially painted statues. Without pretending that sculpture has not to a certain point its color, that of perfectly pure matter, that especially which the hand of time impresses upon it, in spite of all the seductions of a contemporaneous artist of great talent, I have little taste, I confess, for that artifice that is forced to give to marble the *morbidezza* of painting. Sculpture is an austere muse; it has its graces, but they are those of no other art. Flesh-color must remain a stranger to it. Nothing more would remain to communicate to it but the movement of poetry and the indefiniteness of music! And what will music gain by aiming at the picturesque, when its proper domain is the pathetic? Give to the most learned symphonist a storm to render. Nothing is easier to imitate than the whistling of the winds and the noise of thunder. But by what combinations of harmony will he exhibit to the eyes the glare of the lightning rending all of a sudden the veil of the night, and, what is most fearful in the tempest, the movement of the waves that now ascend like a mountain, now descend and seem to precipitate themselves into

bottomless abysses? If the auditor is not informed of the subject, he will never suspect it, and I defy him to distinguish a tempest from a battle. In spite of science and genius, sounds cannot paint forms. Music, when well guided, will guard itself from contending against the impossible; it will not undertake to express the tumult and strife of the waves and other similar phenomena; it will do more: with sounds it will fill the soul with the sentiments that succeed each other in us during the different scenes of the tempest. Haydn will thus become the rival, even the vanquisher of the painter, because it has been given to music to move and agitate the soul more profoundly than painting.

Since the 'Laocoon' of Lessing, it is no longer permitted to repeat, without great reserve, the famous axiom,—*Ut pictura poesis;* or, at least, it is very certain that painting cannot do everything that poetry can do. Everybody admires the picture of Rumor, drawn by Virgil; but let a painter try to realize this symbolic figure; let him represent to us a huge monster with a hundred eyes, a hundred mouths, and a hundred ears, whose feet touch the earth, whose head is lost in the clouds, and such a figure will become very ridiculous.

So the arts have a common end, and entirely different means. Hence the general rules common to all, and particular rules for each. I have neither time nor space to enter into details on this point. I limit myself to repeating that the great law which governs all others is expression. Every work of art that does not express an idea signifies nothing; in addressing itself to such or such a sense, it must penetrate to the mind, to the soul, and bear thither a thought, a sentiment capable of touching or elevating it. From this fundamental rule all the others are derived; for example, that which is continually and justly recommended, —composition. To this is particularly applied the precept of unity and variety. But, in saying this, we have said nothing so long as we have not determined the nature of the unity of which we would speak. True unity is unity of expression, and variety is made only to spread over the entire work the idea or the single sentiment that it should express. It is useless to remark, that between composition thus defined, and what is often called composition, as the symmetry and arrangement of parts according to artificial rules, there is an abyss. True composition is nothing else than the most powerful means of expression.

Expression not only furnishes the general rules of art, it also gives the principle that allows of their classification.

In fact, every classification supposes a principle that serves as a common measure.

Such a principle has been sought in pleasure, and the first of arts has seemed that which gives the most vivid joys. But we have proved that the object of art is not pleasure:—the more or less of pleasure that an art procures cannot, then, be the true measure of its value.

This measure is nothing else than expression. Expression being the supreme end, the art that most nearly approaches it is the first of all.

All true arts are expressive, but they are diversely so. Take music; it is without contradiction the most penetrating, the profoundest, the most intimate art. There is physically and morally between a sound and the soul a marvelous relation. It seems as though the soul were an echo in which the sound takes a new power. Extraordinary things are recounted of the ancient music. And it must not be believed that the greatness of effect supposes here very complicated means. No, the less noise music makes, the more it touches. Give some notes to Pergolese, give him especially some pure and sweet voices, and he returns a celestial charm, bears you away into infinite spaces, plunges you into ineffable reveries. The peculiar power of music is to open to the imagination a limitless career, to lend itself with astonishing facility to all the moods of each one, to arouse or calm, with the sounds of the simplest melody, our accustomed sentiments, our favorite affections. In this respect music is an art without a rival; however, it is not the first of arts. . . .

Between sculpture and music, those two opposite extremes, is painting, nearly as precise as the one, nearly as touching as the other. Like sculpture, it marks the visible forms of objects, but adds to them life; like music, it expresses the profoundest sentiments of the soul, and expresses them all. Tell me what sentiment does not come within the province of the painter? He has entire nature at his disposal, the physical world, and the moral world, a churchyard, a landscape, a sunset, the ocean, the great scenes of civil and religious life, all the beings of creation—above all, the figure of man, and its expression, that living mirror of what passes in the soul. More pathetic than sculpture, clearer

than music, painting is elevated, in my opinion, above both, because it expresses beauty more under all its forms, and the human soul in all the richness and variety of its sentiments.

But the art *par excellence*, that which surpasses all others, because it is incomparably the most expressive, is poetry.

Speech is the instrument of poetry; poetry fashions it to its use, and idealizes it, in order to make it express ideal beauty. Poetry gives to it the charm and power of measure; it makes of it something intermediary between the ordinary voice and music — something at once material and immaterial, finite, clear, and precise — like contours and forms the most definite, living and animated; like color pathetic, and infinite like sound. A word in itself, especially a word chosen and transfigured by poetry, is the most energetic and universal symbol. Armed with this talisman, poetry reflects all the images of the sensible world, like sculpture and painting; it reflects sentiment like painting and music, with all its varieties, which music does not attain, and in their rapid succession that painting cannot follow, as precise and immobile as sculpture; and it not only expresses all that; it expresses what is inaccessible to every other art,—I mean thought, entirely distinct from the senses and even from sentiment,—thought that has no forms,—thought that has no color, that lets no sound escape, that does not manifest itself in any way,—thought in its highest flight, in its most refined abstraction.

Think of it. What a world of images, of sentiments, of thoughts at once distinct and confused, are excited within us by this one word—country! and by this other word, brief and immense,—God! What is more clear and altogether more profound and vast!

Tell the architect, the sculptor, the painter, even the musician, to call forth also by a single stroke all the powers of nature and the soul! They cannot, and by that they acknowledge the superiority of speech and poetry.

They proclaim it themselves, for they take poetry for their own measure; they esteem their own works, and demand that they should be esteemed, in proportion as they approach the poetic ideal. And the human race does as artists do: a beautiful picture, a noble melody, a living and expressive statue, gives rise to the exclamation, How poetical! This is not an arbitrary comparison; it is a natural judgment which makes poetry the type of the perfection of all the arts,—the art *par excellence*, which comprises all others, to which they aspire, which none can reach.

When the other arts would imitate the works of poetry, they usually err, losing their own genius, without robbing poetry of its genius. But poetry constructs, according to its own taste, palaces and temples, like architecture; it makes them simple or magnificent; all orders, as well as all systems, obey it; the different ages of art are the same to it; it reproduces, if it please, the Classic or the Gothic, the beautiful or the sublime, the measured or the infinite. Lessing has been able, with the exactest justice, to compare Homer to the most perfect sculptor; with such precision are the forms which that marvelous chisel gives to all beings determined! And what a painter, too, is Homer! And, of a different kind, Dante! Music alone has something more penetrating than poetry, but it is vague, limited, and fugitive. Besides its clearness, its variety, its durability, poetry has also the most pathetic accents. Call to mind the words that Priam utters at the feet of Achilles while asking him for the dead body of his son, more than one verse of Virgil, entire scenes of the 'Cid' and the 'Polyeucte,' the prayer of Esther kneeling before the Lord, or the choruses of 'Esther' and 'Athalie.' In the celebrated song of Pergolese, 'Stabat Mater Dolorosa,' we may ask which moves most, the music or the words. The 'Dies Iræ, Dies Illa,' recited only, produces the most terrible effect. In those fearful words, every blow tells, so to speak; each word contains a distinct sentiment, an idea at once profound and determinate. The intellect advances at each step, and the heart rushes on in its turn. Human speech, idealized by poetry, has the depth and brilliancy of musical notes; it is luminous as well as pathetic; it speaks to the mind as well as to the heart; it is in that inimitable, unique, and embraces all extremes and all contraries in a harmony that redoubles their reciprocal effect — in which, by turns, appear and are developed, all images, all sentiments, all ideas, all the human faculties, all the inmost recesses of the soul, all the forms of things, all real and all intelligible worlds!

IV—90

LIBERTY AN INALIENABLE RIGHT

(From the Fourteenth Lecture on the True, the Beautiful, and the Good)

PASSIONS abandoning themselves to their caprices are anarchy. Passions concentrated upon a dominant passion are tyranny. Liberty consists in the struggle of will against this tyranny and this anarchy. But this combat must have an aim, and this aim is the duty of obeying reason, which is our true sovereign, and justice, which reason reveals to us and prescribes for us. The duty of obeying reason is the law of will, and will is never more itself than when it submits to its law. We do not possess ourselves as long as to the domination of desire, of passion, of interest, reason does not oppose the counterpoise of justice. Reason and justice free us from the yoke of passions, without imposing upon us another yoke. For, once more, to obey them is not to abdicate liberty, but to save it, to apply it to its legitimate use.

It is in liberty and in the agreement of liberty with reason and justice that man belongs to himself, to speak properly. He is a person only because he is a free being enlightened by reason.

What distinguishes a person from a simple thing is especially the difference between liberty and its opposite. A thing is that which is not free, consequently that which does not belong to itself, that which has no self, which has only a numerical individuality, a perfect effigy of true individuality, which is that of person.

A thing not belonging to itself belongs to the first person that takes possession of it and puts his mark on it.

A thing is not responsible for the movements which it has not willed, of which it is even ignorant. Person alone is responsible, for it is intelligent and free; and it is responsible for the use of its intelligence and freedom.

A thing has no dignity; dignity is only attached to person.

A thing has no value by itself; it has only that which person confers on it. It is purely an instrument whose whole value consists in the use that the person using it derives from it.

Obligation implies liberty; where liberty is not duty is wanting, and with duty right is wanting also.

It is because there is in me a being worthy of respect, that I have the duty of respecting it, and the right to make it respected by you. My duty is the exact measure of my right. The one is in direct ratio with the other. If I had no sacred duty to respect what makes my person, that is to say, my intelligence and my liberty, I should not have the right to defend it against your injuries. But as my person is inviolable and sacred in itself, it follows that, considered in relation to me, it imposes on me a duty, and, considered in relation to you, it confers on me a right.

I am not myself permitted to degrade the person that I am by abandoning myself to passion, to vice, and to crime, and I am not permitted to let it be degraded by you.

The person is inviolable; and it alone is inviolable.

It is inviolable not only in the intimate sanctuary of consciousness, but in all its legitimate manifestations, in its acts, in the product of its acts, even in the instruments that it makes its own by using them.

Therein is the foundation of the sanctity of property. The first property is the person. All other properties are derived from that. Think of it well. It is not property in itself that has rights, it is the proprietor, it is the person that stamps upon it, with its own character, its right and its title.

The person cannot cease to belong to itself, without degrading itself,—it is to itself inalienable. The person has no right over itself; it cannot treat itself as a thing, cannot sell itself, cannot destroy itself, cannot in any way abolish its free will and its liberty, which are its constituent elements.

Why has the child already some rights? Because it will be a free being. Why have the old man, returned to infancy, and the insane man still some rights? Because they have been free beings. We even respect liberty in its first glimmerings or its last vestiges. Why, on the other hand, have the insane man and the imbecile old man no longer all their rights? Because they have lost liberty. Why do we enchain the furious madman? Because he has lost knowledge and liberty. Why is slavery an abominable institution? Because it is an outrage upon what constitutes humanity. This is the reason why, in fine, certain extreme devotions are sometimes sublime faults, and no one is permitted to offer them, much less to demand them. There is no legitimate devotion against the very essence of right, against liberty, against justice, against the dignity of the human person.

THE FOUNDATIONS OF LAW

THERE is an education of liberty as well as our other faculties. It is sometimes in subduing the body, sometimes in governing our intelligence, especially in resisting our passions, that we learn to be free. We encounter opposition at each step. — the only question is not to shun it. In this constant struggle liberty is formed and augmented, until it becomes a habit.

Finally, there is a culture of sensibility itself. Fortunate are those who have received from nature the sacred fire of enthusiasm! They ought religiously to preserve it. But there is no soul that does not conceal some fortunate vein of it. It is necessary to watch it and pursue, to avoid what restrains it, to seek what favors it, and, by an assiduous culture, draw from it, little by little, some treasures. If we cannot give ourselves sensibility, we can at least develop what we have. We can do this by giving ourselves up to it, by seizing all the occasions of giving ourselves up to it, by calling to its aid intelligence itself; for the more we know of the beautiful and the good, the more we love it. Sentiment thereby only borrows from intelligence what it returns with usury. Intelligence in its turn finds, in the heart, a rampart against sophism. Noble sentiments, nourished and developed, preserve from those sad systems that please certain spirits so much only because their hearts are so small.

Man would still have duties, should he cease to be in relation with other men. As long as he preserves any intelligence and any liberty, the idea of the good dwells in him, and with it duty. Were we cast upon a desert island, duty would follow us thither. It would be beyond belief strange that it should be in the power of certain external circumstances to affranchise an intelligent and free being from all obligation towards his liberty and his intelligence. In the deepest solitude he is always and consciously under the empire of a law attached to the person itself, which, by obligating him to keep continual watch over himself, makes at once his torment and his grandeur.

If the moral person is sacred to me, it is not because it is in me—it is because it is the moral person. It is in itself respectable; it will be so, then, wherever we meet it.

It is in you as in me, and for the same reason. In relation to me it imposes on me a duty; in you it becomes the foundation of a right, and thereby imposes on me a new duty in relation to you.

I owe to you truth as I owe it to myself; for truth is the law of your reason as of mine. Without doubt there ought to be measure in the communication of truth,—all are not capable of it at the same moment and in the same degree. It is necessary to portion it out to them in order that they may be able to receive it; but, in fine, the truth is the proper good of the intelligence; and it is for me a strict duty to respect the development of your mind, not to arrest, and even to favor its progress towards truth.

I ought also to respect your liberty. I have not even always the right to hinder you from committing a fault. Liberty is so sacred that, even when it goes astray, it still deserves, up to a certain point, to be managed. We are often wrong in wishing to prevent too much the evil that God himself permits. Souls may be corrupted by an attempt to purify them.

I ought to respect you in your affections, which make part of yourself; and of all the affections there are none more holy than those of the family. There is in us a need of expanding ourselves beyond ourselves, yet without dispelling ourselves, of establishing ourselves in some souls by a regular and consecrated affection,—to this need the family responds. The love of men is something of the general good. The family is still almost the individual, and not merely the individual,—it only requires us to love as much as ourselves what is almost ourselves. It attaches one to the other, by the sweetest and strongest of all ties—father, mother, child; it gives to this sure succor in the love of its parents—to these hope, joy, new life, in their child. To violate the conjugal or paternal right is to violate the person in what is perhaps its most sacred possession.

I ought to respect your body, inasmuch as it belongs to you, inasmuch as it is the necessary instrument of your person. I have neither the right to kill you, nor to wound you, unless I am attacked and threatened; then my violated liberty is armed with a new right, the right of defense and even constraint.

I owe respect to your goods, for they are the product of your labor; I owe respect to your labor, which is your liberty itself in exercise; and, if your goods come from an inheritance, I still owe respect to the free will that has transmitted them to you.

penny, he would commit a crime. We here meet a new order of duties that do not correspond to rights. Man may resort to force in order to make his rights respected; he cannot impose on another any sacrifice whatever. Justice respects or restores; charity gives, and gives freely.

Charity takes from us something in order to give it to our fellow-men. If it go so far as to inspire us to renounce our dearest interests, it is called devotedness.

It certainly cannot be said that to be charitable is not obligatory. But this obligation must not be regarded as precise, as inflexible as the obligation to be just. Charity is a sacrifice; and who can find the rule of sacrifice, the formula of self-renunciation? For justice, the formula is clear,—to respect the rights of another. But charity knows neither rule nor limit. It transcends all obligation. Its beauty is precisely in its liberty.

TRUE POLITICS

TRUE politics does not depend on more or less well-directed historical researches into the profound night of a past forever vanished and of which no vestige subsists; it rests on the knowledge of human nature.

Wherever society is, wherever it was, it has for its foundations: 1st, The need that we have of our fellow-creatures, and the social instincts that man bears in himself; 2d, The permanent and indestructible idea and sentiment of justice and right.

Man, feeble and powerless when he is alone, profoundly feels the need that he has of the succor of his fellow-creatures in order to develop his faculties, to embellish his life, and even to preserve it. Without reflection, without convention, he claims the hand, the experience, the love of those whom he sees made like himself. The instinct of society is in the first cry of the child that calls for the mother's help without knowing that it has a mother, and in the eagerness of the mother to respond to the cries of the child. It is in the feelings for others that nature has put in us—pity, sympathy, benevolence. It is in the attraction of the sexes, in their union, in the love of parents for their children, and in the ties of every kind that these first ties engender. If Providence has attached so much sadness to solitude, so much charm to society, it is because society is indispen-

Respect for the rights of others is called justice; every violation of a right is an injustice.

Every injustice is an encroachment upon our person,—to retrench the least of our rights is to diminish our moral person, is, at least, so far as that retrenchment goes, to abase us to the condition of a thing.

The greatest of all injustices, because it comprises all others, is slavery. Slavery is the subjecting of all the faculties of one man to the profit of another man. The slave develops his intelligence a little only in the interest of another,—it is not for the purpose of enlightening him, but to render him more useful, that some exercise of mind is allowed him. The slave has not the liberty of his movements; he is attached to the soil, is sold with it, or he is chained to the person of a master. The slave should have no affection, he has no family, no wife, no children,—he has a female and little ones. His activity does not belong to him, for the product of his labor is another's. But, that nothing may be wanting to slavery, it is necessary to go further,—in the slave must be destroyed the inborn sentiment of liberty; in him must be extinguished all idea of right; for, as long as this idea subsists, slavery is uncertain, and to an odious power may respond the terrible right of insurrection, that last resort of the oppressed against the abuse of force.

Justice, respect for the person in every thing that constitutes the person, is the first duty of man towards his fellow-man. Is this duty the only one?

When we have respected the person of others, when we have neither restrained their liberty, nor smothered their intelligence, nor maltreated their body, nor outraged their family, nor injured their goods, are we able to say that we have fulfilled the whole law in regard to them? One who is unfortunate is suffering before us. Is our conscience satisfied, if we are able to bear witness to ourselves that we have not contributed to his sufferings? No; something tells us that it is still good to give him bread, succor, consolation.

There is here an important distinction to be made. If you have remained hard and insensible at the sight of another's misery, conscience cries out against you; and yet this man who is suffering, who, perhaps, is ready to die, has not the least right over the least part of your fortune, were it immense; and, if he used violence for the purpose of wresting from you a single

sable for the preservation of man and for his happiness, for his intellect and moral development.

But if need and instinct begin society, it is justice that completes it.

In the presence of another man, without any external law, without any compact, it is sufficient that I know that he is a man, that is to say that he is intelligent and free, in order to know that he has rights, and to know that I ought to respect his rights as he ought to respect mine. As he is no freer than I am, nor I than he, we recognize towards each other equal rights and equal duties. If he abuse his force to violate the equality of our rights, I know that I have the right to defend myself and make myself respected; and if a third party be found between us, without any personal interest in the quarrel, he knows that it is his right and his duty to use force in order to protect the feeble, and even to make the oppressor expiate his injustice by a chastisement. Therein is already seen entire society with its essential principles,—justice, liberty, equality, government, and punishment.

Justice is the guaranty of liberty. True liberty does not consist in doing what we will, but in doing what we have a right to do. Liberty of passion and caprice would have for its consequence the enslavement of the weakest to the strongest, and the enslavement of the strongest themselves to their unbridled desires. Man is truly free in the interior of his consciousness only in resisting passion and obeying justice; therein also is the type of true social liberty. Nothing is falser than the opinion that society diminishes our mutual liberty; far from that, it secures it, develops it; what it suppresses is not liberty, it is its opposite, passion. Society no more injures liberty than justice, for society is nothing else than the very idea of justice realized.

In securing liberty, justice secures equality also. If men are unequal in physical force and intelligence, they are equal in so far as they are free beings, and consequently equally worthy of respect. All men, when they bear the sacred character of the moral person, are to be respected, by the same title, and in the same degree.

The limit of liberty is in liberty itself; the limit of right is in duty. Liberty is to be respected, provided it injure not the liberty of another. I ought to let you do what you please, but on the condition that nothing which you do will injure my liberty. For then, in virtue of my right of liberty, I should regard myself as obligated to repress the aberrations of your will, in order to protect my own and that of others. Society guarantees the liberty of each one, and if one citizen attack that of another, he is arrested in the name of liberty. For example, religious liberty is sacred. You may, in the secret of consciousness, invent for yourself the most extravagant superstition; but if you wish publicly to inculcate an immoral worship, you threaten the liberty and reason of your citizens: such preaching is interdicted.

From the necessity of repressing, springs the necessity of a constituted repressive force.

Rigorously, this force is in us; for if I am unjustly attacked, I have the right to defend myself. But, in the first place, I may not be the strongest; in the second place, no one is an impartial judge in his own cause, and what I regard or give out as an act of legitimate defense may be an act of violence and oppression.

So the protection of the rights of each one demands an impartial and disinterested force, that may be superior to all particular forces.

This disinterested party, armed with the power necessary to secure and defend the liberty of all, is called government.

The right of government expresses the rights of all and each. It is the right of personal defense transferred to a public force, to the profit of common liberty.

Government is not, then, a power distinct from and independent of society; it draws from society its whole force. It is not what it has seemed to two opposite schools of publicists,—to those who sacrifice society to government,—to those who consider government as the enemy of society. If government did not represent society, it would be only a material, illegitimate, and soon powerless force; and without government, society would be a war of all against all. Society makes the moral power of government, as government makes the security of society. Pascal is wrong when he says that not being able to make what is just powerful, men have made what is powerful just. Government, in principle at least, is precisely what Pascal desired,—justice armed with force.

It is a sad and false political system that places society and government, authority and liberty, in opposition to each other, by making them come from two different sources, by presenting

them as two contrary principles. I often hear the principle of authority spoken of as a principle apart, independent, deriving from itself its force and legitimacy, and consequently made to rule. No error is deeper and more dangerous. Thereby it is thought to confirm the principle of authority; far from that, from it is taken away its solidest foundation. Authority—that is to say, legitimate and moral authority—is nothing else than justice, and justice is nothing else than the respect of liberty; so that there is not therein two different and contrary opinions, but one and the same principle, of equal certainty and equal grandeur, under all its forms and in all its applications.

SAMUEL SULLIVAN COX

(1824–1889)

LWAYS one of the readiest and most fluent, and often one of the most instructive and forcible speakers of his day, "Sunset" Cox, narrowly missed becoming a very great orator. He had every faculty which characterizes a great orator, in addition to one which no political orator can have and remain great,—a governing sense of humor. He was never safe from the temptation to become humorous at the expense of power. His speech of June 3d, 1879, against the "Ironclad Oath," might easily have become one of the great orations of Congress. Mr. Cox had mastered the entire literature of the subject, he was intensely in earnest, he looked beyond the passions of his day to the eternal verities, but arguing toward a climax in which he intended to appeal to the principles of "The Sermon on the Mount," he could not resist the temptation to stop, midway his triumphant progress towards great success, to convulse the House with the story of how Cornelius O'Flaherty "swore off" from drinking. In spite of his humor, and in a certain sense because of it, Mr. Cox exerted a wide influence during his generation, but so accustomed did the public grow to expecting humor from him, that the serious work of his life has never been fully recognized. Political life was a serious business for him, however, from the beginning,—so serious that his reactions into humor are not to be wondered at. He was born in Ohio, September 30th, 1824. When he entered Congress as a Member of the House of Representatives, elected from Ohio, he found himself as a Democrat almost completely isolated by the events which followed the fall of Fort Sumter. He was an earnest and logical supporter of the constitutional Union of the States, but his sympathies for all Americans, North and South, were strong. He was more actively a war Democrat than Vallandigham, or even than Pendleton, but the whole Civil War was a grief to him, and during the period of scarcely less violent political struggle which followed the cessation of actual hostilities, his efforts were directed to mollify prejudice, mitigate animosity, and restore as much as possible of the good-will between all Americans on which the American institutions he believed in were necessarily based. He entered politics as a Douglas Democrat, and one of the best of his earliest speeches was delivered on the death of Douglas in 1861. He served

in Congress as a representative from Ohio from 1857 to 1865. Removing to New York city, he was again elected to Congress as a Democrat in 1869, serving with an intermission of one term until 1885, when he was appointed United States Minister to Turkey. After his return in 1886, he was re-elected to Congress and again re-elected in 1888. He died in New York city, September 10th, 1889. Of his books, his 'Three Decades of Federal Legislation' is the most valuable, while his 'Diversions of a Diplomat' is the most characteristic and entertaining.

AGAINST THE IRONCLAD OATH

(From a Speech in the House of Representatives, June 3d, 1879)

THERE was a bitter contest in England after the revolution of 1640; it turned upon an oath. It was not merely prelacy, or the wearing of the surplice, or the use of a liturgy, or the Book of Common Prayer, or the sign of the cross which tried the soul of Richard Baxter and others like him, who would not conform to the Established Church. It was the *et cetera* oath. It had a clause from which it is named: "Nor will I ever give my consent to alter the government of the Church by archbishops, bishops, deans, and archdeacons, etc., as it stands now established and ought to stand." This was an oath promissory; an oath binding fallible men never to change opinions. It included in it an *et cetera*—no one knew what. An adjuration thus indefinite was like our ironclad, so indefinite as to be the essence of folly and despotism. [Applause.] Instead of helping the prelacy to be unchangeable, it roused up the Baxters of that day to resist; it became an advantage to the cause of dissent. The Long Parliament seized upon it, along with the ship-money question, to vindicate freedom and inflame the people against royalty. Puritanism thrived upon this insane proscription. It gave new truth to the French verse as to the English monarch:—

"Le roi d'Angleterre
Est le roi d'enfer."

Pym, Fiennes, Digby, and others of the Puritan heroes of Parliament, thundered against it. It was a part of the incitement which gave to the commonwealth its synod in spiritual and its Parliament for temporal matters.

After the restoration other oaths were enacted. Those in the service of the Church were required to promise subjection to the canons and abjure the solemn league and covenant. They were required to abjure the taking up of arms against the King and his officers. By this the English Church lost two thousand of its best ministers. Still another law was passed requiring of ministers an oath which, if they refused, they should not come within five miles of any city or corporation, or any place where they had lived or which sent burgesses to Parliament. This is the oath: —

I, A B, do swear that it is not lawful, upon any pretense whatsoever, to take arms against the King; and that I do abhor that traitorous position of taking arms by his authority against his person, or against those that are commissioned by him, in pursuance of such commission; and that I will not, at any time, endeavor any alteration of the government, either in Church or State.

Some took this oath, for they had no subsistence for their families among the strange country places to which they were expelled. "No severity," says Hallam, "comparable to this cold-blooded persecution has been inflicted by the late powers even in the ferment and fury of a civil war." All sorts of subterfuges and reservations were resorted to, to take the oath and not feel it binding in a certain sense. It was the fruitful source of prevarication and perjury.

In the persecutions under this oath, and while Sydney and others were falling under the ax of the despot, Richard Baxter, the leader of nonconformity, fell under the tender mercy of Jeffreys at Westminster. This judicial fiend was well selected to execute such laws, for never in the career of infamous judges is there anything to compare with his brutal treatment of this meek and just man. "Does your lordship think any jury will pass a verdict upon me upon such a trial?" asked the author of the Holy Commonwealth of this judge. "I'll warrant you," said Jeffreys; "don't you trouble yourself about that." The packed and corrupt jury, summoned to do the bidding of the obsequious tool of a licentious court, laid their heads together and found him guilty without leaving the box.

Out of the ordeal of these odious oaths and mock trials, sprang the noble army of nonconformist confessors whose labors and sufferings gave to them an immortalization on earth by the

fight for freedom against the King. It is known that many of them became more intolerant here than their persecutors had been in England. It is not for me to praise their burning of witches, their persecution of Catholics, their cutting out the tongues of Quakers, and their exile of the Baptists. Nor would it be proper to refer to their trade in slaves or their treatment of the Indians. Enough remains of the history of the Puritans of New England during the many years preceding our own Revolution to show that the spirit of Pym, Hampden, and Wentworth was instinct and alive in the Warrens, Adamses, and Hancocks of our elder day. But, alas, how have their descendants degenerated! They cannot read the history of these their own test oaths placed on our statute by them, even on "Revision," and the laws for the use of the army to control civil affairs and override by force local rights, without a blush. They were not merely the passive instruments of their enactment and execution, but the active instruments as well.

When Macaulay describes the Puritans of old England as "looking down upon the rich and the eloquent, upon nobles and upon priests, with contempt, esteeming themselves rich in a more enduring treasure, and eloquent in a more sublime language — nobles by the right of an earlier creation, and priests by the imposition of a mightier hand," could he have dreamed that out of a civil war in this land this domineering element, so proud and great, would fall so far as to keep on the statute tests, pains, and penalties which France, Turkey, Russia, and even Asiatic and African barbarians would be ashamed to defend?

Thus, when we follow this quasi-Puritan of this latter day, we find nothing of heroism to worship. It is like going into the old Egyptian temples; its priests are of grave aspect; its porticos and vestibules and groves beautiful; its walls resplendent with paintings, gems, silver, and amber; its adyta shaded with gold; but its god is a cat, a crocodile, or serpent, rolling upon purple coverlets. What history has not been written, what poems not sung, in praise of the heroic Puritan element, yet how ignoble their descendants seem when their proscription and bigotry are exposed. . . .

One of the peculiar features of the Ironclad is that it compels a person to swear that while he is taking the oath he is not forswearing himself, i. e., that he has no mental reservations, that he is playing no sleights with his conscience, no thimblerig with

muse of history, and gave to their immortality in heaven the beauty of holiness which was their "saints' rest" forever. It gave that grace and spirituality to the better part of the Puritan character, of which there is so much just boasting in our own country, and that, too, by men who have forgotten their shining example.

It is sad, almost savage satire on those who thus vaunt of these stanch men of spiritual faith and austere manners, that their "stalwart" descendants in the New World are the loud leaders in perpetuating the same system of proscriptive oath-taking and mock-jury trial which gave to England her revolution of 1688 and to America her earliest and bravest lovers of liberty. The lesson it teaches to New England is that—

"Those who on glorious ancestors enlarge,
Produce their debt, instead of their discharge." [Laughter.]

These very test oaths, sir, drove many a Puritan, Quaker, and Catholic to the New World. It was reserved for their descendants to re-enact them here in the noon of our century, not only to affect religion and State, but to inflict penalties and perpetuate hatred. Ah, where is that old Puritan spirit which led to the abolition of the Star Chamber, the High Commission, and the Council of York, which demanded the execution of Strafford and the King, and which always held to the "Petition of Right" as a palladium of English liberty? Where is that spirit of parliamentary courage which arrested the attempt of the King upon the Commons when he strove to suppress Wentworth and to arrest Hampden, Pym, Hollis, Hasselrig, and Strode for high treason, because they spoke for the great charter — the Petition of Right and the privileges of the Commons? Where is the Puritan nerve and spirit which resisted the attempt of the King when he came to the Commons to demand the five members, with his guard of pensioners and tories, exclaiming that he would not break their privileges, but that treason had no privilege? He found his birds had flown, and retreated ignominiously from the Commons, saluted with the cry, "Privilege! privilege!" This was at a time, too, when the ax hung over the heads of outspoken Puritans.

I would not derogate from the Puritan character nor unduly exalt it. It has been said that the Puritans who came to this country had not the heroism of those who remained at home to

words; or, in other words, he is sworn that while he is swearing he is not lying! I have here an illustration of a peculiar mode of swearing. It is an oath which reserves so many conditions and qualifications that it nullifies itself. Carlton publishes it of one of his Celtic characters. Being urged by his good priest to take a pledge against intemperance, the affiant went to the schoolmaster of his village and had the following drawn: —

Oath against liquor made by me, Cornelius O'Flaherty, philomath, on behalf of Misther Peter Connell, of the Cross-Roads, merchant, on one part, and of the soul of Mrs. Ellish Connell, now in purgatory, merchantess, on the other.

I solemnly, and meritoriously, and soberly swear that a single tumbler of whisky punch shall not cross my lips during the twenty-four hours of the day, barring twelve, the locality of which is as followeth: —

Imprimis — Two tumblers at home 2
Secundo — Two more ditto at my son Dan's 2
Tertio — Two more ditto behind my own garden 2
Quarto — One ditto at the Reverend Father Mulcahy's 1
Quinto — Two more ditto at Frank M'Carroll's, of Kilclay . . . 2
Sexto — One ditto wid ould Bartle Gorman, of Cargah 1
Septimo — Two more ditto wid honest Roger M'Gaugy, of Nurchasey 2
                                                              ——
                                                              12

N. B. — I except in case any docthor of physic might think it right and medical to ordher me more for my health; or in case I could get Father Mulcahy to take the oath off of me for a start, at a wedding, or a christening, or at any other meeting of friends where there's drink. [Applause and laughter.]

I do not know whether Congressmen would make these extensive reservations. [Laughter.] How would it affect my colleague [Mr. Chittenden] from the City of Churches? [Laughter.] He is our swearing member. [Laughter.] He could not take this oath after his orthodox apology. [Laughter.]

Gentlemen here know how recruits were sworn, and how they were prepared for the battles of the Republic. No customhouse officer ever administered a stressless oath with more haste and nonchalance than do some of our courts. Who feels their binding force? Who is not shocked by the irreverence and frivolity? When the captain of the Pinafore, in a hasty fit of temper, says "damme," the chorus of good sailors is horrified. The burlesque is equally applicable to other oaths. Such trivial and frequent swearing is no swearing at all; and by extremes, it comes near the Bible command, "Swear not at all." They remind one of the man who was swearing loudly to Hercules. His companion said: "Do not call so loud or the god may hear you." [Laughter.] Our statutes groan with oaths at every page, and, like the ghost in Hamlet, moan: "Swear! Swear!" They should evanish with the dawn. Governments condemn thugs, carbonari, kuklux, nihilists, and secret societies generally, for their mystic oaths. Let government set an example and abolish the custom. The wisest writers, like Bentham, hold them repugnant to the Christian religion. He wonders why, under such a religion, oaths should be so common. The answer is not complimentary to our civilization. In earlier days society was cemented by oaths. Liberty was assured, as in Switzerland, by an oath. Patriotism, perhaps, is nerved and obligations sanctified by it, when the bonds of society become loose and require tightening. But now what a farce is this constant swearing! . . .

I doubt if all the oaths ever recorded in sacred or classic lore, or propounded in any land, for political, religious, judicial, martial, or festive purposes; whether for jurors, witnesses, or officials; whether at customhouses or at marriage rites; whether to suspected patriots or supposed traitors; from Noah, who took the first oath, down to the cloud of investigation committee witnesses, can compare for one moment with what is known as our "Ironclad Oath" for the ridiculousness and variety of its application. There is one exception; and that, too, is in our country. It is to be found in the Missouri constitution made by the Republicans just before the end of the war.

That oath illustrates that there are some laws and some men who defy the everlasting order and congruity of things to carry out their grudges. It is enough to damn the party which made it to an eternity of infamy. Luckily the Supreme Court of the United States cut it up by the roots. Although it remained five years to blot the organic law of a great and growing State, and although its provisions again and again were used to give a small minority of the people of Missouri the ruling power, yet at last its authors hid from public execration, and the oath was stamped out by the decision of Mr. Justice Stephen J. Field, in an opinion which adds to his fame as an enlightened and liberal-minded jurist.

IV—91

Missouri, while toiling in the caverns of doubt and despair. In England and France the old test oaths which were so odious were limited to an opposition of the predominant government or religion. Their oath was directed against overt acts of hostility. It never reached the humiliation of punishing men for their heart-throbs and kinship.

Judge Field placed his heel upon this oath as if it were a viper. He found it not only to be in every sense a bill of attainder, but an *ex post facto* law. It was a law which imposed a punishment for an act not punishable at the time it was committed. He held that a deprivation of such offices and duties in life was in all senses a punishment, nor was it less a punishment because a way of escape from it was opened by an oath.

Well did those vile bigots of Missouri understand that whole classes would be unable to take the oath prescribed, and thereby become incapable of jury or any other duty to society or to the State. Hence, comforted and protected by the proscriptive bigotry and hate of Congress, with its "Ironclad," they disfranchised the majority of the State.

How was this law — if it were a law — executed? Certainly it was not in the ordinary sense a law. It had not the excuse of legislative inconsiderate haste. It was in the fundamental constitution of a great State. It had not even the flimsy excuse of Protestant bigotry against the Catholic faith. In some counties Methodists as well as Catholics were indicted, tried, and convicted for preaching Christ's gospel of love; because, like Richard Baxter, they would not commit perjury or conform to the oath. These men had been preaching for years; but no amount of work in the vineyard of the Lord saved them from the remorseless clutch of these self-righteous loyal Pharisees. True, this constitutional clause was not directed against the body. It did not use torture, rack, and thumbscrew. It was a radical ukase against the sacred conscience of men — a torture of the soul — a devilish plot against the ministrations of all religions and the teachings of all classes of mind. It was worse than barbaric.

In the recent wars of Europe the red-cross flag of Geneva upon the white ground of charity gave immunity to those who cared for the sick. It alleviated suffering and saved life. It earned the blessings and gratitude of all. It gave laws of kindness to war. But this infamous oath which stopped the physician

The decision was made in the case of Cummings *versus* The State of Missouri, 4 Wallace, page 277. The plaintiff was a Catholic priest. He was indicted and convicted of the crime of teaching and preaching the Christian religion without having first taken the oath required by the amended constitution of April 1865. He was fined $500. Refusing to pay it, he was committed to jail, and, like St. Paul, would not come out until by due process of the law which placed him there.

The Supreme Court of Missouri had the effrontery and ignorance to confirm that judgment. That oath was divided into more than thirty distinct tests. Some of the tests were never even offenses by the laws of the State, and some of them were not even blameworthy, but grew out of charity and affection. The affiant was required on oath to affirm not only that he had never been in armed hostility to the United States, but never by act or word manifested his adherence to the enemy or his desire or sympathy with those in rebellion, and had never harbored or aided or countenanced any person so engaged, and had never come into or left Missouri to avoid enrollment or draft or to escape his duty in the military service of the United States or the militia of the State, and had never indicated in any terms his disaffection.

Those who could not or did not take this "oath of loyalty," as it was called, within sixty days, were ousted from office, if in; and incapacitated from holding office, if out. They were debarred from all kinds of offices, even of corporations, public and private; they could not be supervisors, or even teachers of schools, nor hold real estate or property of any kind, in trust for any purpose. All such offices of trust became *ipso facto* vacant on the failure to take this many-headed, many-clawed oath. Nor could any one practice law, or be bishop, priest, deacon, elder, or other clergyman of any religious sect; neither could he teach, preach, or solemnize marriages. This oath is without precedent in history. This oath is without semblance among gods, prophets, saints, soldiers, men, women, or devils, and yet it remained five years! Besides, it required the fiat of our Supreme Court to tear it from the body-politic of Missouri.

The fourteenth section contained the penalty in which Cummings was amerced, as well as another penalty for false swearing. These were the devil-fish *tentacula*, grappling the people of

in his round of duty to the sick and dying, and the priest in his consolations, and that under the pressure of an oath to Almighty God, would have hauled down the red cross of Geneva. When it did not imprison the clergyman in his home, it did worse; it consigned him to the common jail. It was worse than the "five-mile act" of Episcopal bigotry against the Dissenters.

How was it executed? Let one instance illustrate. The radical ghouls of Cape Girardeau County, under this law, indicted the Sisters of Charity who taught in a convent. Three of these angels of mercy were dragged into court several times, indicted, and tried; and even the foreman of the grand jury sent his own child to the convent to be taught, so as to get proof of the teaching and so as to convict. They had not taken the oath. In their case, however, public opinion revolted, and the Titus Oateses of Missouri hid their heads for a time from public opinion, but not until they left for us lessons of their proscriptive meanness which, in degenerating from the days of Pym and Hampden, Baxter and De Foe, left imperishable evidence of their unfitness to live as generous co-workers for good in human society. Ah, if those Sisters of Charity and Mercy, the Florence Nightingales of our conflict, have passed from earth and found their beatitudes in the yonder azure sheen, where they walk white-handed in celestial light, singing the praises of the good Savior they served here among men,—with what pitying eye do they look down upon the foolish and spiteful human craftiness which sought to break the blessed utility and unity of their lives by relentless persecution. Language has no vehicle of expression, the mind no idea, fit to tell the burning shame which should blister forever the cowardice and cruelty of a test so odious and hateful. [Applause.]

Sergeant Talfourd in his 'Ion' exquisitely describes the solace and comfort of those who by benevolent endeavor mold their lives into benevolence: —

"'Tis a little thing
To give a cup of water; yet its draught
Of cool refreshment, drained by fevered lips,
May give a shock of pleasure to the frame
More exquisite than when nectarean juice
Renews the life of joy in happiest hours.

> It is a little thing to speak a phrase
> Of common comfort which by daily use
> Has almost lost its sense; yet on the ear
> Of him who thought to die unmourned 'twill fall
> Like choicest music."

But these radical constitution-makers and executors of infamous statutes would arrest and imprison the Sisters of Charity who have gladdened our sad world by their merciful ministrations. The names of this sisterhood are not sounded by the brazen trumpets of publicity, nor mingled with the notes of sectarian discord; but they are found on the criminal records of radical Missouri — the disgrace of our generation. [Applause.]

What execrations are not due to those who persecuted these loving laborers. From the earliest centuries after Christ when the noble Roman lady, Paula, took up her residence in Bethlehem to care for and comfort the sick; from the time she "laid their pillows aright," as the old chronicle tells us, and felt that the less service she did to the sick the less she did to God; from the time of this first sister of mercy down to our day, when the kind *Sœurs Hospitalières* of France, Béguines of Flanders, and the Sisters of Elizabeth in Germany, in their black gowns and white hoods, their complacent sweetness and holy living, gave to the striken their self-devotion so nobly illustrated by Florence Nightingale and her company of noble women, whose only prayer was to go where suffering and perils were greater, no one ever dared to lay secular or rude hands upon this sisterhood.

It was to have been hoped that, at the close of our Civil War, when the bugles had sounded the long truce, and war-broken soldiers were left stranded in the hospitals, there was no one in human shape who would be so regardless of those gentle and superior beings of the other sex — who had shown such self-abnegation — as to persecute them as outlaws of society. Had they not bent over the wounded and sick "when pain and anguish wrung the brow," and whispered low the words of peace, patience, and divine hope, while smoothing the pillow and holding the cup to the parched lip? Had they not aided the healing power with moral cheerfulness, and by their softening and purifying presence given good impulses and holy thoughts to the sick and dying? Why, even the Robespierres and Dantons and the very devils of the French Reign of Terror respected this

sisterhood. They were recalled by a special decree of the republic, which recited their boundless love and charity; and their faithful head, Citoyenne Duleau, was given new authority to practice that beautiful vocation, — as described in 'Lucille,'— the poetical counterpart of Florence Nightingale: —

> "The mission of genius on earth! To uplift,
> Purify, and confirm by its own gracious gift
> The world, in despite of the world's dull endeavor
> To degrade, and drag down, and oppose it forever.
> The mission of genius: to watch, and to wait,
> To renew, redeem, and to regenerate."

But had this sisterhood lived in Missouri and given their facile sympathy and good offices to the wounded rebels, fine and imprisonment would have been their punishment. The very fiends of the Reign of Terror put to shame these bigots of our day and generation! Spenser tells the story of three brothers; when one died he did not go to join Pluto's grizzly band, but his spirit entered into his brother, and when that brother died the joint spirit entered into the survivor. The Republicans of this Congress seem to have inherited the spirit of their brother radicals of Missouri. How long will they live?

THE SERMON ON THE MOUNT

(Peroration of the Speech of July 3d, 1879, in the House of Representatives)

Mr. Speaker :—

IT MAY be a fancy, but I sometimes think that the loftiest and purest thoughts come down to us from the mountain.

> "But in the mountains we do feel our faith.
> All things responsive to the writing there
> Breathed immortality, revolving life,
> And greatness still revolving; infinite;
> There littleness was not; the least of things
> Seemed infinite."

I hope it may not be presuming to say, Mr. Speaker, that I have been something of a traveler, and have been upon many mountains of our star. I would that my observations had been better utilized for duty. I have been upon the Atlas, whose

giant shoulders were fabled to have upheld the globe. I have learned from there, that even to Northern Africa the Goths brought their *fueros* or bills of right, with their arms, from the cold forests of the North to the sunny plains and rugged mountains of that old granary of the Roman world. I have been amid the Alps, where the spirit of Tell and liberty is always tempered with mercy, and whose mountains are a monument through a thousand of years of republican generosity. I have been among the Sierras of Spain, where the patriot Riego — whose hymn is the Marseillaise of the Peninsula — was hunted after he had saved constitutional liberty and favored amnesty to all,— the noblest examplar of patriotism since the days of Brutus. From the seven hills of Rome, down through the corridors of time, comes the story which Cicero relates from Thucydides; that a brazen monument was erected by the Thebans to celebrate their victory over the Lacedæmonians, but it was regarded as a memento of civil discord, and the trophy was abolished, because it was not fitting that any record should remain of the conflict between Greek and Greek. From the same throne of ancient power, come the words which command only commemoration of foreign conquests and not of domestic calamities; and that Rome, with her imperial grace, believed that it was wisest to erect a bridge of gold, that civil insurgents should pass back to their allegiance. From the Acropolis at Athens, there is the story of the herald at the Olympic games, who announced the clemency of Rome to the conquered, who had long been subjected to the privations and calamities imposed by the conqueror. The historian says that the Greeks, when the herald announced such unexpected deliverance, wept for joy at the grace which had been bestowed.

All these are but subordinate lights around the central light, which came from the mountain whence the great sermon was spoken. Its name is unknown; its locality has no geography. All we know is that it was "set apart."

The mountains of our Scriptures are full of inspiration for our guidance. Their teachings may well be carried into our political ethics. But it was not from Ararat, which lifted its head first above the flood and received the dove with its olive branch; not from Sinai, which looks proudly upon three nations and almost three countries and overlooks our kind with its great moral code; not from Horeb, where Jehovah with his fearful

hand covered his face that man might not look upon his brightness; not from Tabor, where the great transformation was enacted; not from Pisgah, where Moses made his farewell to the people he had delivered and led so long; not from Carmel, where the prayer of Elijah was answered in fire; not from Lebanon, whose cedars were the beauty of the earth; not from the Mount of Olives, which saw the agony of the Savior; not from Calvary, at whose great tragedy nature shuddered and the heavens were covered with gloom; not from one or all of these secular or sacred mountains that our best teaching for duty comes. It comes from that nameless mountain, set apart, because from it emanated the great and benignant truths of him who spake as never man spake. [Applause.] Here is the sublime teaching:

> "Ye have heard in the aforetime, that it hath been said, Thou shalt love thy neighbor and hate thine enemy.
> "But I say unto you, Love your enemies, bless them that curse you, do good to them that hate you, and pray for them that despitefully use you and persecute you.
> "That ye may be the children of your Father which is in heaven: for he maketh his sun to rise on the evil and on the good, and sendeth rain on the just and on the unjust."

The spirit of this teaching has no hospitality for test oaths, and asks no compensation for grace. [Applause.] Along with this teaching and to the same good end, are the teachings of history, patriotism, chivalry, and even economic selfishness. Yet these teachers are often blind guides to duty. They are but mole-hills compared with the lofty mountain whose spiritual grandeur brings peace, order, and civilization!

When these principles obtain in our hearts, then our legislation will conform to them. When they do obtain their hold in these halls, there will arise a brilliant day-star for America. When they do obtain recognition, we may hail a new advent of that Prince of Peace, whose other advent was chanted by the angelic choir!

In conclusion, sir, let me say that, in comparison with this celestial code, by which we should live and die, how little seem all the contests here about armies, appropriations, riders, and coercion, which so exasperate and threaten! Let our legislation be inspired by the lofty thought from that Judean mountain, and God will care for us. In our imperfections here as legislators, let us look aloft, and then "His greatness will flow around our incompleteness, and round our restlessness, his rest!" Then, measures which make for forgiveness, tranquillity and love, like the abolition of hateful oaths and other reminders of our sad and bloody strife, will rise in supernal dignity above the party passions of the day; and that party which vindicates right against might, freedom against force, popular will against Federal power, rest against unrest, and God's goodness and mercy, around and above all, will, in that sign, conquer. [Applause.]

To those in our midst who have the spirit of violence, hate, and unforgiveness, and who delight in pains, penalties, test oaths, bayonets, and force, and who would not replace these instruments of turbulence with love, gentleness, and forgiveness, my only curse upon such is, that God Almighty, in his abundant and infinite mercy may forgive them, for "they know not what they do." [Long-continued applause.]

STEPHEN A. DOUGLAS AND HIS PLACE IN HISTORY

(From a Speech in the House of Representatives, July 9th, 1861)

SCARCELY with any of our public men can Douglas be compared. The people like to compare him to Jackson, for his energy and honesty. He was like the great triumvirate,— Clay, Webster, and Calhoun,—but "like in difference." Like them in his gift of political foresight, still he had a power over the masses not possessed by them. Like Clay, in his charm to make and hold friends and to lead his party; like Webster, in the massive substance of his thought, clothed in apt political words; like Calhoun, in the tenacity of his purpose and the subtilty of his dialectics; he yet surpassed them all in the homely sense, the sturdy strength, and indomitable persistence with which he wielded the masses and electrified the Senate.

In the onslaught of debate he was ever foremost; his crest high and his falchion keen. Whether his antagonists numbered two or ten, whether the whole of the Senate were against him, he could "take a raking fire at the whole group." Like the shrouded Junius, he dared Commons, Lords, and King, to the encounter; but unlike that terrible Shadow, he sought no craven covert, but fought in the open lists, with a muscular and mental

might which defied the unreasoning cries of the mob and rolled back the thunders of the Executive anathema!

Douglas was no scholar, in the pedantic sense of the term. His reading was neither classical nor varied. Neither was he a sciolist. His researches were ever in the line of his duty, but therein they were thorough. His library was never clear from dust. His favorite volume was the book of human nature, which he consulted without much regard to the binding. He was skilled in the contests of the bar; but he was more than a lawyer—he easily separated the rubbish of the law from its essence. As a jurist, his decisions were not essays; they had in them something decisive, after the manner of the best English judges. As a legislator, his practicalness cut away the entanglements of theoretic learning and ancient precedent, and brought his mind into the presence of the thing to be done or undone. Hence he never criticized a wrong for which he did not provide a remedy. He never discussed a question that he did not propose a measure.

His style was of that plain and tough fibre which needed no ornament. He had a felicity in the use of political language never equaled by any public man. He had the right word for the right place. His interrogative method, and his ready and fit replies, gave dramatic vivacity to his debates. Hence the newspapers readily copied them and the people retentively remembered them. Gleams of humor were not infrequent in his speeches, as in his conversation. His logic had the reach of the rifled cannon, which annihilated while they silenced the batteries of his opponents.

Douglas was a partisan, but he never wore his party uniform when his country was in danger. His zeal, like all excess, may have had its defect; but to him who observes the symmetry and magnanimity of his life, it will appear that he always strove to make his party conservative of his country.

The tenacity with which he clung to his theory of territorial government, and the extension of suffrage, on local questions, from State to Territory, and the absolute nonintervention by Congress for the sake of peace and union, while it made him enemies, increased the admiration of his friends. His nature shines out with its loftiest grace and courage in his debates on these themes, so nearly connected as he thought them with the stability of the Republic.

If it be that every true man is himself a cause, a country, or an age; if the height of a nation is the altitude of its best men, then, indeed, are these enlarged liberalities, which are now fixed as American institutions, but the lengthened shadow of Stephen A. Douglas. This is the cause—self-government in State and Territory—with which he would love most to be identified in his country's history. He was ready to follow it to any logical conclusion, having faith in it as a principle of repose, justice, and union.

Placed at the head of the Territorial Committee, it was his hand which, on this basis, fashioned Territory after Territory, and led State after State into the Union. The latest constellation formed by California, Iowa, Oregon, Wisconsin, Minnesota, and I may add Kansas, received their charter to shine and revolve under his hand. These States, faithful to his fostering, will ever remain as monuments of his greatness!

His comprehensive forecast was exhibited in his speech on the Clayton and Bulwer treaty, on the fourth of March, 1853, wherein he enforced a continental policy suitable and honorable to the New World and its destiny, now so unhappily obscured. That speech was regarded by Judge Douglas as among the most valuable, as I think it the most finished and cogent speech of his life. His philippic against England, which to-day has its vindication in her selfish conduct towards us, will remind the scholar of Demosthenes, while his enlarged philosophy has the sweep and dignity of Edmund Burke. It was this speech which gave to Douglas the heart of Young America. He refused to prescribe limits to the area over which Democratic principles might safely spread. "I know not what our destiny may be." "But," he continued, "I try to keep up with the spirit of the age; to keep in view the history of the country; see what we have done, whither we are going, and with what velocity we are moving, in order to be prepared for those events which it is not in the power of man to thwart." He would not then see the limits of this giant Republic fettered by treaty; neither would he in 1861 see them curtailed by treachery. If he were alive to-day he would repeat with new emphasis his warning against England and her unforgiving spite, wounded pride, and selfish policy. When, in 1847, he advocated the policy of terminating her joint occupation with us of Oregon, he was ready to back it by military force; and if war should result, "we might drive Great Brit-

ain and the last vestiges of royal authority from the continent of North America, and make the United States an ocean-bound Republic!"

With ready tact and good sense, he brought to the fiscal and commercial problems of the country views suitable to this age of free interchange and scientific advancement.

His position on the Foreign Affairs Committee of the Senate gave him a scope of view abroad, which was enriched by European travel and historic research, and which he ever used for the advancement of our flag and honor among the nations. His knowledge of our domestic troubles, with their hidden rocks and horrid breakers, and the measures he proposed to remove them, show that he was a statesman of the highest rank, fit for calm or storm.

Some have lamented his death now as untimely and unfortunate for his own fame, since it has happened just at the moment when the politician was lost in the patriot, and when he had a chance to atone for past error by new devotion.

Mr. Speaker, men do not change their natures so easily. The Douglas of 1861 was the Douglas of 1850, 1854, and 1858. The patriot who denounced this great rebellion was the patriot in every fold and lineament of his character. There is not a page of his history that we can afford to blot. The words which escaped him in the delirium of his last days—when he heard the "battle afar off, the thunder of the captains, and the shouting"—were the keynote to a harmonious life.

Observant of the insidious processes North and South which have led us to this civil war, he ever strove, by adjustment, to avoid their disastrous effects. History will be false to her trust if she does not write that Stephen A. Douglas was a patriot of matchless purity, and a statesman who, foreseeing and warning, tried his utmost to avert the dangers which are now so hard to repress. Nor will she permit those who now praise his last great effort for the Union to qualify it, by sinister reflections upon his former conduct; for thus they tarnish the lustre of a life devoted, in peace and war, to the preservation of the Union. His fame never had eclipse. Its disk has been ever bright to the eye of history. It sank below the horizon, like the sun of the Morea, full-orbed, and in the full blaze of its splendor.

THOMAS CRANMER

(1489-1556)

ERHAPS in all English history there is nowhere else so striking an example of the sublimity of which human nature is capable in its utmost and most shameful weakness as that given by Cranmer in his speech at the stake. As a statesman he had vacillated and hesitated, sacrificing principle repeatedly for the sake of public policy or his own safety and immediate advantage. But it is hard to imagine a nobler death than his. In the full consciousness of his weakness, having put away completely his regard for public opinion, as well as what is generally considered self-respect, he used his last moments to exhort Englishmen who would survive him not to hate and hurt each other, and to entreat those who had «great substance and riches of this world,» to have mercy on the weak. Then when no longer allowed to speak, and when the fire had been lighted, he gave the memorable exhibition of self-mastery, which redeemed him from surviving in history as a mere weakling, and made him one of the great heroic figures of the English race. The scene after he was silenced is thus described by his biographer, John Strype, writing in 1693 on the authority of eye-witnesses:—

"And here, being admonished of his recantation and dissembling, he said, 'Alas, my Lord, I have been a man that all my life loved plainness, and never dissembled till now against the truth; which I am most sorry for.' He added thereunto, that, for the sacrament, he believed as he had taught in his book against the Bishop of Winchester. And here he was suffered to speak no more.

"So that his speech contained chiefly three points: love to God, love to the King, love to the neighbor. In the which talk he held men in very suspense, which all depended upon the conclusion; where he so far deceived all men's expectations, that, at the hearing thereof, they were much amazed; and let him go on awhile, till my Lord Williams bade him play the Christen man, and remember himself. To whom he answered that he so did; for now he spake truth.

"Then he was carried away; and a great number, that did run to see him go so wickedly to his death, ran after him, exhorting him while time was to remember himself. And one Friar John, a godly and well-learned man, all the way traveled with him to reduce him. But it would not be. What they said in particular I cannot tell, but the effect appeared in the end; for at the

stake he professed that he died in all such opinions as he had taught, and oft repented him of his recantation.

"Coming to the stake with a cheerful countenance and willing mind, he put off his garments with haste, and stood upright in his shirt; and a bachelor of divinity, named Elye, of Brazen-nose College, labored to convert him to his former recantation, with the two Spanish friars. But when the friars saw his constancy, they said in Latin one to another, 'Let us go from him; we ought not to be nigh him; for the Devil is with him.' But the bachelor of divinity was more earnest with him; unto whom he answered, that, as concerning his recantation, he repented it right sore, because he knew it was against the truth; with other words more. Whereupon the Lord Williams cried, 'Make short, make short.' Then the Bishop took certain of his friends by the hand. But the bachelor of divinity refused to take him by the hand, and blamed all others that so did, and said he was sorry that ever he came in his company. And yet again he required him to agree to his former recantation. And the Bishop answered (shewing his hand), 'This is the hand that wrote it, and therefore shall it suffer first punishment.'

"Fire being now put to him, he stretched out his right hand, and thrust it into the flame, and held it there a good space, before the fire came to any other part of his body; where his hand was seen of every man sensibly burning, crying with a loud voice, 'This hand hath offended.' As soon as the fire got up, he was very soon dead, never stirring or crying all the while."— (From 'Memorials of Thomas Cranmer,' by John Strype, M. A. 1693.)

Three centuries after the best and greatest man of any period has done his work, the world can look back upon it and see that it is not given to any man to be «eternally right» in anything whatever except in such renunciation and self-sacrifice as Cranmer, the martyr, showed at the last in his condemnation of Cranmer, the statesman, Cranmer the prelate, and Cranmer the politician.

He was born in Nottinghamshire, July 2d, 1489, and died at Oxford, March 21st, 1556. Educated at Cambridge, he became one of the most learned men of his day, and when, in 1529, he used his learning to enable Henry VIII. to divorce Catharine of Aragon, he came at once into high favor at court. Appointed the King's chaplain, he was sent in 1532 on a mission to Germany and in 1533 was appointed Archbishop of Canterbury. He used that position, as was expected, against the rights of Queen Catharine. Under Edward VI., in 1553, he was induced to sign a patent excluding Mary and Elizabeth from the succession in favor of Lady Jane Grey, and as a result, on the accession of Mary, daughter of Catharine of Aragon, he was sent to the tower for treason, and, subsequently, to the stake, on a charge of heresy; though, of course, as generally happened in such cases during that period, the motive back of the charge of spiritual error was purely one of politics. Cranmer had pledged himself to respect the will of Henry VIII., by which the succession devolved upon Mary, and his breach of faith in violating this pledge has been

called perjury, as his frequent shifting of position from the beginning of his political career up to the time when he collected all his faculties in his supreme effort at the stake has been called cowardice and lack of moral character. Macaulay denies, as others have done, his right to be called a martyr, but even if his life had been that of a coward in the last stages of moral infirmity up to the time when «with his hand seen by every one to be sensibly burning, he cried with a loud voice, 'This hand hath offended,'» and so died, his death would remain nevertheless one of the most admirable in history, so remarkable by reason of its very contrast with his life, that we can hardly imagine such strength possible for humanity, except as an antithesis to the extreme weakness, in repenting which Cranmer glorified himself and that common humanity of which his weaknesses were characteristic.

HIS SPEECH AT THE STAKE

(As Reported in 'The Memorials,' by John Strype, 1693)

GOOD people, I had intended indeed to desire you to pray for me; which because Mr. Doctor hath desired, and you have done already, I thank you most heartily for it. And now will I pray for myself, as I could best devise for mine own comfort and say the prayer, word for word, as I have here written it.

[And he read it standing; and afterwards kneeled down and said the Lord's Prayer, and all the people on their knees devoutedly praying with him. His prayer was thus:]—

O Father of heaven; O Son of God, redeemer of the world; O Holy Ghost, proceeding from them both, three persons and one God, have mercy upon me, most wretched caitiff and miserable sinner. I, who have offended both heaven and earth, and more grievously than any tongue can express, whither then may I go, or whither should I fly for succor? To heaven I may be ashamed to lift up mine eyes; and in earth I find no refuge. What shall I then do? shall I despair? God forbid. O good God, thou art merciful, and refusest none that come unto thee for succor. To thee, therefore, do I run. To thee do I humble myself saying, O Lord God, my sins be great; but yet have mercy upon me for thy great mercy. O God the Son, thou wast not made man, this great mystery was not wrought for few or small offenses. Nor thou didst not give thy Son unto death, O

God the Father, for our little and small sins only, but for all the greatest sins of the world, so that the sinner return unto thee with a penitent heart, as I do here at this present. Wherefore have mercy upon me, O Lord, whose property is always to have mercy. For although my sins be great, yet thy mercy is greater. I crave nothing, O Lord, for mine own merits, but for thy Name's sake, that it may be glorified thereby, and for thy dear Son, Jesus Christ's sake.

[Then rising, he said:] All men desire, good people, at the time of their deaths, to give some good exhortation that others may remember after their deaths, and be the better thereby. So I beseech God grant me grace that I may speak something, at this my departing, whereby God may be glorified and you edified.

First, it is an heavy case to see that many folks be so much doted upon the love of this false world, and so careful for it, that for the love of God, or the love of the world to come, they seem to care very little or nothing therefor. This shall be my first exhortation. That you set not overmuch by this false glozing world, but upon God and the world to come; and learn to know what this lesson meaneth, which St. John teacheth, that the love of this world is hatred against God.

The second exhortation is that next unto God you obey your King and Queen willingly and gladly, without murmur and grudging, and not for fear of them only, but much more for the fear of God, knowing that they be God's ministers, appointed by God to rule and govern you. And therefore whoso resisteth them, resisteth God's ordinance.

The third exhortation is, That you love altogether like brethren and sisters. For, alas! pity it is to see what contention and hatred one Christian man hath toward another; not taking each other as sisters and brothers, but rather as strangers and mortal enemies. But I pray you learn and bear well away this one lesson, To do good to all men as much as in you lieth, and to hurt no man, no more than you would hurt your own natural and loving brother or sister. For this you may be sure of, that whosoever hateth any person, and goeth about maliciously to hinder or hurt him, surely, and without all doubt, God is not with that man, although he think himself never so much in God's favor.

The fourth exhortation shall be to them that have great substance and riches of this world, that they will well consider and weigh those sayings of the Scripture. One is of our Savior Christ himself, who sayeth, It is hard for a rich man to enter into heaven; a sore saying, and yet spoken by him that knew the truth. The second is of St. John, whose saying is this, He that hath the substance of this world and seeth his brother in necessity, and shutteth up his mercy from him, how can he say he loveth God? Much more might I speak of every part; but time sufficeth not. I do but put you in remembrance of these things. Let all them that be rich ponder well those sentences; for if ever they had any occasion to show their charity they have now at this present, the poor people being so many, and victuals so dear. For though I have been long in prison, yet I have heard of the great penury of the poor. Consider that which is given to the poor is given to God; whom we have not otherwise present corporally with us, but in the poor.

And now, for so much as I am come to the last end of my life, whereupon hangeth all my life passed and my life to come, either to live with my Savior Christ in heaven in joy, or else to be in pain ever with wicked devils in hell; and I see before mine eyes presently either heaven ready to receive me, or hell ready to swallow me up; I shall therefore declare unto you my very faith, how I believe, without color or dissimulation; for now is no time to dissemble, whatsoever I have written in times past.

First, I believe in God the Father Almighty, maker of heaven and earth, and every article of the catholic faith, every word and sentence taught by our Savior Christ, his Apostles and Prophets, in the Old and New Testaments.

And now I come to the great thing that troubleth my conscience, more than any other thing that ever I said or did in my life; and that is, the setting abroad of writings contrary to the truth. Which here now I renounce and refuse, as things written with my hand, contrary to the truth which I thought in my heart, and writ for fear of death, and to save my life, if it might be; and that is, all such bills, which I have written or signed with mine own hand since my degradation, wherein I have written many things untrue. And forasmuch as my hand offended in writing contrary to my heart, therefore my hand shall be punished; for if I may come to the fire it shall be first burned. And as for the Pope, I refuse him as Christ's enemy and Antichrist, with all his false doctrine.

IV—92

FORGIVENESS OF INJURIES

(From a Sermon Preserved in Strype's 'Memorials')

THESE two may stand both well together; that we as private persons may forgive all such as have trespassed against us with all our heart, and yet that the public ministers of God may see a redress of the same trespasses that we have forgiven. For my forgiveness concerns only mine own person, but I cannot forgive the punishment and correction that by God's ordinance is to be ministered by the superior power. For in so much as the same trespass, which I do forgive, may be the maintenance of vice, not only of the offender, but also of others taking evil example thereby, it lies not in me to forgive the same. For so should I enterprise in the office of another, which by the ordinance of God be deputed to the same. Yea, and that such justice may be ministered to the abolishment of vice and sin, I may, yea and rather as the cause shall require I am bound to make the relation to the superior powers, of the enormities and trespasses done to me and others; and being sorry that I should have cause so to do, seek the reformation of such evil doers, not as desirous of vengeance, but of their amendment of their lives. And yet I may not the more cruelly persecute the matter, because the offense is peradventure done towards me; but I am to handle it as if it were done to any other, only for the use of the extirpation of sin, the maintenance of justice and quietness; which may right well stand with the ferventness of charity, as the Scripture testifieth. *Non oderis fratrem tuum in corde tuo, sed publice argue eum, ne habeas super illo peccatum.* Lev. xix. So that this may stand with charity, and also the forgiveness that Christ requireth of every one of us.

And yet in this doing, I must forgive him with all my heart, as much as lies in me; I must be sorry, that sin should have so much rule in him. I must pray to God to give him repentance for his misdeeds; I must desire God, that for Christ's sake he will not impute the sin unto him, being truly repentant, and so to strengthen him in grace, that he fall not again so dangerously. I think I were no true Christian man, if I should not thus do. And what other thing is this, that as much as lieth in me, with all my heart to remit the trespass? But I may by the laws

AGAINST THE FEAR OF DEATH

(From a Sermon preserved in Strype's 'Memorials')

IF DEATH of the body were to be feared, then them which have power to kill the body should we fear, lest they do their exercise over us, as they may at their pleasure. But our Savior forbids us to fear them, because when they have killed the body, then they can do no more to us. Wherefore it is plain that our Saviour would not that we should fear death. To die, saith St. John Chrysostom, is to put off our old garments, and death is a pilgrimage of the spirit from the body. (He means, for a time.) And a sleep, somewhat longer than the old custom. The fear of it, saith he, is nothing else than the fear of bugs, and a childish fear of that thing cannot harm thee. Remember holy St. Ambrose's saying, which St. Augustine, lying on his death-bed, ever had in his mouth, "I do not fear to die; for we have a good and merciful Lord and Master." Lactantius, the great learned man, confirms the saying of Cicero to be true, which said, "that no man can be right wise, which feareth death, pain, banishment, or poverty: and that he is the honest and virtuous man, which regardeth not what he suffers, but how well he doth suffer." Sedulius defineth death to be the gate, by which lieth the straight way unto our reign and kingdom. Basilius, who as in name, so both in virtue and learning, was great, thus he exhorteth us: "O man, saith he, shrink not to withstand your adversaries, to suffer labors; abhor not death, for it destroys not, nor makes an end of you, but it is the beginning and occasion of life. Nor death is the destruction of all things, but a departing, and a translation unto honors." And St. Hierom, the strong and stout champion of Almighty God, saith, declaring this saying of holy Job, "the day of death is better than the day of birth," that is, saith he, because either that by death it is declared what we are, or else because our birth doth bind our liberty of the soul with the body, and death do loose it."

require all that is due unto me of right. And as for the punishment and correction, it is not in my power to enterprise therein; but that only belongeth to the superior powers, to whom, if the grievousness of the cause shall require by the commandment, which willeth us to take away the evil from among us, we ought to show the offense and complain thereof. For he would not that we should take away the evil, but after a just and lawful means, which is only, by the ordinance of God, to show the same to the superior powers, that they may take an order in it, according to God's judgment and justice.

WILLIAM HARRIS CRAWFORD

(1772–1834)

ILLIAM H. CRAWFORD was one of the Presidential candidates in a contest which resulted in a reconstruction of parties and the evolution of an ultimately disastrous sectionalism. He had been chosen to fill an unexpired term in the United States Senate in 1807; had been re-elected in 1811; had been sent as Minister to France in 1813, and in 1816 had succeeded Alexander James Dallas as Secretary of the Treasury, a post he filled throughout the eight years of Monroe's two administrations, ending March 4th, 1825. During his service in the Senate he had taken a leading part, and had been in two duels, in one of which his opponent had fallen, while in the other he had himself been wounded. During the "era of good feeling" under Monroe, when old party lines had been practically effaced, there had been growing up a feeling that the Presidency should go to some State other than Virginia, which had been honored with it during thirty-two years out of thirty-six. Crawford, of Georgia, being a native of Virginia and a member of Monroe's cabinet, was the favorite of the Virginia party and became the nominee of the congressional caucus. But Jackson, of Tennessee; Clay, of Kentucky, and John Quincy Adams, of Massachusetts, all remained in the field as Republican candidates in spite of the caucus. Crawford received the electoral votes of Virginia and Georgia, and enough "scattering" to make 41, while Jackson received 99, Adams 84, and Clay 37. This threw the election into the House where the election of Adams, by the vote of Clay in the Kentucky delegation, brought about the new division of parties into Whigs and Democrats. After this contest Mr. Crawford retired from National politics, being in very poor health; he served, however, as Criminal Judge in Georgia from 1828 to 1831. He was born in Amherst County, Virginia, February 24th, 1772, and died in Elbert County, Georgia, September 15th, 1834

THE ISSUE AND CONTROL OF MONEY UNDER THE CONSTITUTION

(From a Speech in the United States Senate, February, 11th, 1812, on the Bank of the United States)

HEN I had the honor of addressing the Senate before I questioned the authority of the State governments to create banks, I then stated, and I again explicitly state, that it is with reluctance that I have felt it my duty to make any inquiry into the constitutional right of the State governments to incorporate banks. The State legislatures ought to have recollected the Spanish proverb, which says that those who live in glass houses ought not to throw stones. Before they undertook to question the constitutional authority of Congress, they ought to have thoroughly examined the foundation upon which their own right rested. The honorable gentleman from Virginia [Mr. Giles] says that the construction which I have given to that part of the Constitution which prohibits the States from emitting bills of credit would apply equally to promissory notes given by one individual to another under the laws of a State, as to a bank bill. Permit me to inquire of that gentleman whether he ever saw a law authorizing one man to give another his promissory note? He may search the pandects of Justinian; he may turn over the leaves of the musty volumes written upon the common law, from the days of Bracton and Fleta down to the present day, and his search will be in vain. For the right to make contracts, the right to give promissory notes, is antecedent to, and independent of all municipal law. The gentleman will find laws and decisions in abundance, regulating the effect of indorsements and other collateral circumstances, and prescribing the manner of enforcing the payment of promissory notes, but he will never find a law giving the right to execute the promissory note. But it is said that the bills of credit, which the States are prohibited from emitting, must be bills of credit emitted on the credit of the State. If this distinction should be well founded, many of the State banks are still subject to the charge of unconstitutionality, because in many of them the States are directly interested, and wherever that is the case, their bank bills are bills of credit emitted on the credit of the State. But the correctness of this distinction may well be denied, because the restriction is as gen-

eral as it could possibly be made. But it is said that this restriction applies only to bills of credit which are made a legal tender in the payment of debts; that bills of credit, designated in the Constitution, are *ex vi termini* a legal tender. For the correctness of this exposition, an appeal is made to the restriction which immediately follows it, which restrains the right of the States to make anything but gold and silver a legal tender in the payment of debts. It appears to me that the latter restriction excludes most emphatically the construction contended for. If the States be prohibited from emitting bills of credit, it would have been, to say the least of it, wholly nugatory to say they should not make them a legal tender. If the bills be not emitted, it is impossible that they can be made a legal tender. To suppose that the restriction upon the right of the States to make anything but gold and silver legal tender has any connection with or influence upon the restriction to emit bills of credit is as absurd as to suppose that the Decalogue, after having declared that "thou shalt do no murder," should have added, but, if you will murder, you shall not rob and strike the dead. The construction of the restraint upon the right to make anything but gold or silver a tender is that they shall not make specific articles, as tobacco or cotton, a tender, as was the case in some of the States.

But it is said that the history of the States will show that the bills of credit specified in the Constitution were those only which were a legal tender in the payment of debts. Let us examine this point, according to the rule of construction applied to another clause in the Constitution by a large majority of both houses of Congress during the present session. Another clause in the Constitution gives Congress the power to admit new States into the Union under two limitations: 1st. That no new State shall be formed within the limits of any State without the consent of the State; and, 2d. That no new State should be formed by the junction of two or more States without the consent of such States, and also of Congress. These limitations prove that the formation of new States, within the limits of the United States, was in view of the convention at the time that this clause was adopted; and the subsequent clause, which gives Congress the power to make rules for the government of its Territories, proves that these Territories were at that moment under consideration. In addition to these reasons for believing that the framers of the

Constitution had no idea of forming new States, beyond the limits of the United States, those who were opposed to the admission of Orleans as a State contended that the history of the United States proves that the power to erect new States and admit them into the Union was intended to be confined to new States within the limits of the United States at the formation of the Constitution, and that a different construction would disparage the rights of the original States, and, of course, be a violation of the Constitution. What reply did the majority of Congress give to this train of reasoning? They said that the right to admit new States cannot be subject to any other limitations or restrictions than those which are contained in the clause which gives the right, and as there is no restriction upon the right to erect new States without the then limits of the United States, Congress has an unlimited right to erect and admit them into the Union. Let us apply the same rule of construction to the restriction of the right of the States to emit bills of credit. The restriction is a general one; it has no exceptions, and every attempt to make exceptions ought to be repelled by the answer which was given to those who opposed the right of Congress to admit the Territory of Orleans into the Union as a State. The construction I have contended for gains additional weight when we consider the restriction which immediately precedes that under consideration: "No State shall coin money, emit bills of credit, etc." Bills of credit are but the representatives of money. The Constitution gives Congress the right to coin money, and to regulate its value. It takes from the States the right to coin money and to emit bills of credit. Why give to Congress the right to coin money and regulate its value? Because the interest of the Nation requires that the current coin of the Nation should be uniform both as to its species and value. If this be the true reason why the right of coining money and fixing its value was given to Congress, does not the right to issue that which is to be the representative of this coin; which, in fact, is to usurp its place; which is to be the real currency of the Nation, necessarily belong to Congress? Does not the right to create a bank, which shall issue this representative of money, come within the same reason? I think it does.

To the fervid imagination of my friend from Kentucky [Mr. Clay], this power to create a bank appears to be more terrific than was the lever of Archimedes to the frightened imagination of the Romans, when they beheld their galleys suddenly lifted up and whirled about in the air, and in a moment plunged into the bosom of the ocean. Are these apprehensions founded in reason, or are they the chimeras of a fervid and perturbed imagination? What limitation does the Constitution contain upon the power to lay and collect taxes, imposts, duties, and excises? None but that they shall be uniform, which is no limitation of the amount which they can lay and collect. What limitation does it contain upon the power to raise and support armies? None other than that appropriations shall not be made for a longer term than two years. What restriction is to be found in it upon the right to provide and maintain a navy? None. What upon the right to declare war and make peace? None, none. Thus the Constitution gives to the Government of the United States unlimited power over your purses — unlimited power to raise armies and provide navies — unlimited power to make war and peace, and you are alarmed; you are terrified at the power to create a bank to aid it in the management of its fiscal operations. Sir, nothing short of my most profound respect for honorable gentlemen, who have frightened themselves with this bugbear, could induce me to treat the subject seriously. Gentlemen have said that they are alarmed at the exercise of this power, and I am bound to believe them. Sir, after giving Congress the right to make war and peace; the right to impose taxes, imposts, duties, and excises, *ad libitum;* the right to raise and support armies without restriction as to number or term of service; the right to provide and maintain a navy without a limitation, I cannot bring myself to tremble at the exercise of a power incidental to only one of these tremendous grants of power.

FRANCESCO CRISPI

(1819–)

FRANCESCO CRISPI was born at Ribera, in Sicily, October 4th, 1819. He began his public career as a major under Garibaldi, with whom he served at Calatafimi in 1860, and a year later he was elected from Palermo to the first Italian Parliament. In 1876 he became President of the Chamber of Deputies, and in 1877 Minister of the Interior, an office he held for a single year. He became Prime Minister of Italy in 1887, holding the position until 1891, and again from 1893 to 1896. The Italy of his later public life has been so heavily taxed and the restrictions on the industrial and intellectual activities of its people have been so great, as a result of the attempt to keep up a display of militancy and give it a place with the "great powers," that the people have shown, from time to time, in the usual blind way in which ignorance asserts itself, their sense of the injustice they cannot define and the limitations they cannot understand. The result has been radical movements, which found in Crispi a strong Conservative opponent. More or less closely associated with the great financial and commercial interests which have succeeded the feudal nobility as the power behind the throne of European monarchy, his undoubted talents and his power as an orator, if they have not made him a heroic figure, have rendered great service to the Conservative interests, with the growing power of which, as shown through increased militancy and the substitution of the standing army for the justice-declaring spirit of civil law, he now seems most likely to be identified in Italian history.

His early sympathies with Garibaldi and his prominence in the Italian government made him the orator of the day when the Garibaldi monument was unveiled during the great fêtes of 1895. He was never a thorough sympathizer, however, either with Garibaldi or with Mazzini, and it is said that his dissent from Mazzini did much to perpetuate monarchy in Italy, preventing the establishment of the republic so many of Mazzini's followers had ardently hoped for.

AT THE UNVEILING OF GARIBALDI'S STATUE

(Delivered at Rome, September 20th, 1895)

THE twentieth of September, 1870, could not be better commemorated than by the inauguration in Rome of a monument to Garibaldi, the faithful and devoted friend of Victor Emmanuel, who in 1860 accepted the *plébiscite* in favor of the liberation of Rome. The citizens of Rome could not be the helots of unity, the slaves of cosmopolitan patriotism. Their servitude meant the restriction of the national sovereignty, which was Italy's due in mere virtue of her existence.

The day and the place remind us of the struggle against tyranny, so laborious, yet so fruitful of liberty. The years which elapsed between July 4th, 1849, and September 20th, 1870, were the last years of trial for the civil power. The Church, having shown that she was powerless to live by her own resources, had to rely upon foreign bayonets, of which she in her turn became completely the slave. It was here that on April 30th, after a bloody battle, Garibaldi repulsed the invader who, without provocation, had undertaken the barbarous mission of restoring tyranny. When hostilities were resumed, the defenders, although with right on their side, had to yield to force and await patiently the day of resurrection, the twentieth of September, 1870. . . .

The enemies of Italian unity have endeavored to prove that the present celebration is an insult to the head of the Catholic Church. Their object is to excite conscientious scruples against our country. But the common sense of the people is proof against such tricks, because we all know that Christianity is a Divine institution, which is not dependent upon earthly weapons for its existence. The religion of Christ preached by Paul and Chrysostom was able to subdue the world without the aid of temporal arms, and we cannot conceive that the Vatican should persist in wishing for temporal sovereignty to exercise its spiritual mission. The Gospel, as we all believe, is truth. If it has been disseminated by Apostolic teachings, such teachings are sufficient for its existence.

It is not really for the protection and prestige of religion that our adversaries demand the restoration of the temporal power of the Holy See, but for worldly reasons, from lust of power, and from earthly covetousness. They do not consider that temporal sovereignty cannot be saintly and above sin, that it cannot aspire

to celestial perfection in this world. Material weapons and legal violence, justified by reasons of State, should not belong to the Vicar of Christ on earth, who is to preach peace, to pray, and to pardon. Religion is not and it cannot be an affair of State. Its mission is to console believers with the hope of everlasting life, and to uphold the spirit of faith.

The Catholic Church has never enjoyed in any country so much freedom and respect as in Italy. We alone of all nations have renounced every claim to jurisdiction in ecclesiastical matters. It is a maxim of modern law that the State should have no influence in spiritual things which cannot be interfered with by the civil power without having recourse to violence. The spiritual autonomy which we protect and guarantee should be the stronghold of the Supreme Pontiff. In that stronghold he could not be assailed. Worldly matters elude his grasp, and it would be a virtue in him not to think of them. Souls are his kingdom, and he governs them so absolutely as to elicit the envy of other rulers of men. Protestant sovereigns and even princes who do not believe in Christ bow before him and reverently accept his judgments.

The Italians, by promulgating the law of May 1871, have solved a problem which seemed incapable of solution. In this country, where freedom of thought and of conscience is acknowledged, unlimited liberty has been granted to the head of the Church with reference to his sacred office and his irresponsibility and inviolability. In regard to his acts, the Pope is subject only to God, and no human potentate can reach him. He exercises a sovereign authority over all those who believe in him, and they are many millions, while he is surrounded by all the honors and privileges of royalty without the drawbacks of civil power, without the hatred, the resentment, and the penalties inseparable from such power. No earthly prince is in a similar position or on the same level. His position is unique. He has no territory to govern. Indeed, any extent of territory would be inadequate for his position, and yet all the world is subject to his spiritual empire. Were he a temporal prince his authority would be diminished, because it would be equal to that of other rulers, and he would cease to be pre-eminent. He would be exposed to continual struggles, as he has struggled for centuries to the detriment of the faith and of his spiritual authority. We have made him an independent sovereign, and as such he is superior to all other princes. In this lies his power. He exercises his office by virtue of his authority; he corresponds with all the world; he prays; he protects, without needing protection, because the Italian kingdom is his shield. Consequently, no earthly weapon can reach him, and the outrages inflicted upon Boniface VIII. cannot be repeated.

Catholics should be grateful to Italy for the services which we have rendered to the Roman Pontiff. Before September 20th, 1870, he was obliged to bow before the princes of the earth, and concordats were concessions of divine rights made to the prejudice of the Church. It was only when relieved of his temporal dominion that Pius IX. could cope with Bismarck and make that man of iron feel the power of spiritual arms. All this is our handiwork, the work of our Parliament and our King, and we are proud of the achievement. I will say more; it was the will of God, because the Almighty willed that Italy should gather her provinces together and become an equal of other nations.

We regret to say that those who oppose this evident will of the Creator call themselves his ministers on earth, but they will not prevail, because Italy is strong and self-reliant and will crush any effort at revolution. These men will not prevail, and perhaps they may grow wiser. They are aware that so long as they keep within lawful bounds and do not infringe the law, they are inviolable. But they ought to remember that if they rebel, if they revile their country and attack our national institutions, they will lose all the benefits which they have secured by our law of guarantees, which was granted to religion and for religion, and not for the personal advantage of any man. They know, or ought to know, that by inciting others to break the law they would help Anarchism, which denies both God and King, and they would not escape punishment. . . .

SOCIALISM AND DISCONTENT

(From a Speech Occasioned by the Revolutionary Outbreaks in Sicily)

WE HAVE before us a great social problem and one that must be solved. Not the problem which agitators love to pour out before an excited mob, advocating community of goods, the abolition of trustees, the destruction of all lawful

rights of ownership. To-day the right of spoliation is being dignified to the rank of a science; but none the less when attempts are made to realize such theories as I have referred to, a close approach is made to the domain of crime.

A favorite field with the agitator is the island of Sicily, but the field is ill chosen, for there the sentiments of life and property are strongly rooted. Glance at the scenes of our recent riots and you will not be able to say that they were caused by distress. In the Province of Trapani and in the communes of Palermo, where the riots were fiercest, the conditions of the people are unusually good. There are few large estates in the district, and land is distributed in small holdings among an industrious peasantry. The outbreaks in Sicily were the result of a well-organized conspiracy and the effects would have been even more dire had not a vigilant government taken wise precautions.

The country is thickly sown with socialistic clubs, which are well known as *Fasci dei Lavoratori*. Originally they seemed to be harmless organizations created for benevolent objects. A year later, in 1892, the National Exposition was held in Palermo. Far too promising to neglect was this opportunity for disseminating pernicious doctrines, and agitators from the mainland flocked to the island and took contagion with them. From that time onward, by means of congresses and other incitements from revolutionaries who lived abroad, the real organization of the *Fasci dei Lavoratori* as revolutionary societies began. The Fasci numbered one hundred and sixty-six and had two hundred and eighty-nine thousand members. The chiefs declared that they had no trust in the labors of Parliament, but put their confidence in revolution. This was made manifest by passages in letters which had been seized.

Unpatriotic, as revolutionists of this type are sure to be, they had endeavored to come to an understanding with clerical societies in Italy and elsewhere, and of this also we have the clearest proof. Finally, a meeting was held in Marseilles, and there it was decided that the "New Garibaldi of Anarchy" should go to Palermo.

It had been determined to rise in insurrection about the middle of February, but fearing that the government had been warned it was decided to anticipate the date originally fixed and there was a Fourth of April in which neither the "New Garibaldi" nor any of his friends took any part. The peasants had

been promised that during this year lands would be divided evenly among them, and the conspirators had planned to bring about a war by the help of Russia to which country it was intended to cede a port.

If you would understand the character of the movement, listen to this proclamation published in one commune. It describes the working classes as "Children of the Vespers," and closes with these words:—

"Do you sleep? Hasten to the prison to rescue your brethren. Death to the King. Death to employers. Down with taxes. Burn the mayoralty. Burn the Civilians' Club. Long live the Fascio. When the bells ring let us rush to the castle, for all is ready for liberty. Listen for the signal."

In the province of Massa Carrara the revolution burst forth in its worst forms. There as in Sicily martial law had to be proclaimed. . . .

The conditions in Sicily are precisely the same as those in the balance of Italy and the social laws which apply to the working classes on the mainland must apply to those on the island. The resources of Sicily are so great that the government desires to make use of them in repurchasing the *latifundia*, which it would divide among the people and so put an end to the injustices of the communal administrations, especially in regard to tithes. Concerning this we propose to ask for a magistrate specially detailed to readjust the rates.

Italy must consolidate and fortify herself, and for this, time and labor are still necessary. I ask you, therefore, to follow me in my program. Let us cleave to the King—the symbol of unity, the ark of salvation. I say now as I said in 1864, that the Monarchy alone guarantees unity and the future of the country. With this faith, which is the faith of the country, we must ward off dangers, oppose internal and external enemies, and carry Italy to the greatness to which we have aspired and without which she cannot exist.

JOHN JORDAN CRITTENDEN

(1787–1863)

JOHN J. CRITTENDEN represented, from 1850 to his death in 1863, the strong Union sentiment of the border States. He ranks with B. Gratz Brown and Frank P. Blair among the leaders of the determined band of Unionists who prevented Kentucky and Missouri from following their natural bent towards the Confederacy. His instincts, however, like those of Henry Clay, were conservative, and by the Crittenden Compromise of 1860-61, as well as by his work in the Peace Commission of 1861, which he was largely instrumental in organizing, he labored ineffectually to bring about reconciliation between the opposing sections. He was born in Woodford County, Kentucky, September 10th, 1787. A graduate of William and Mary College, he made a military record during the War of 1812, and thereafter held his position in public life securely until his death, July 26th, 1863. He was elected to the Kentucky legislature in 1816, and in 1817 was promoted to the United States Senate. He was Attorney-General under Harrison and Tyler, and in 1842 was again elected to the Senate. From 1848 to 1850 he served as Governor of Kentucky, leaving that office to become Attorney-General in the Cabinet of President Fillmore. Returning once more to the Senate in 1855, he served until 1861, when, the Whig party being now completely disorganized, he was elected a Member of the House of Representatives as a Unionist. His eulogy of Henry Clay is generally presented as the most representative of his many striking public speeches, but it scarcely equals, either in the dignity or the force of its eloquence, his speech of February 15th, 1859, delivered in the Senate, against the proposed acquisition of Cuba.

HENRY CLAY AND THE NINETEENTH-CENTURY SPIRIT

(Delivered in 1852)

I AM to address you in commemoration of the public services of Henry Clay, and in celebration of his obsequies. His death filled his whole country with mourning, and the loss of no citizen, save the Father of his Country, has ever produced such manifestations of the grief and homage of the public heart. His history has indeed been read "in a nation's eyes." A nation's tears proclaim, with their silent eloquence, its sense of the national loss. Kentucky has more than a common share in this national bereavement. To her it is a domestic grief;—to her belongs the sad privilege of being the chief mourner. He was her favorite son, her pride, and her glory. She mourns for him as a mother. But let her not mourn as those who have no hope nor consolation. She can find the richest and noblest solace in the memory of her son, and of his great and good actions; and his fame will come back, like a comforter, from his grave, to wipe away her tears. Even while she weeps for him, her tears shall be mingled with the proud feelings of triumph which his name will inspire; and Old Kentucky, from the depths of her affectionate and heroic heart, shall exclaim, like the Duke of Ormond, when informed that his brave son had fallen in battle, "I would not exchange my dead son for any living son in Christendom." From these same abundant sources we may hope that the widowed partner of his life, who now sits in sadness at Ashland, will derive some pleasing consolations. I presume not to offer any words of comfort of my own. Her grief is too sacred to permit me to use that privilege.

Henry Clay lived in a most eventful period, and the history of his life for forty years has been literally that of his country. He was so identified with the Government for more than two-thirds of its existence, that, during that time, hardly any act which has redounded to its honor, its prosperity, or its present rank among the nations of the earth, can be spoken of without calling to mind involuntarily the lineaments of his noble person. It would be difficult to determine whether in peace or in war, in the field of legislation or of diplomacy, in the springtide of his life or in its golden ebb, he won the highest honor. It can be no disparagement to any one of his contemporaries to say that, in all the points of practical statesmanship, he encountered no superior in any of the employments which his constituents or his country conferred upon him.

Henry Clay was indebted to no adventitious circumstances for the success and glory of his life. Sprung from a humble stock, "he was fashioned to much honor from his cradle"; and he achieved it by the noble use of the means which God and Nature had given him. He was no scholar, and had none of the advantages of collegiate education. But there was a "divinity that

IV—93

was his American system of policy. With inflexible patriotism he pursued and advocated it to his end. He was every inch an American. His heart, and all there was of him, were devoted to his country, to its liberty, and its free institutions. He inherited the spirit of the Revolution, in the midst of which he was born; and the love of liberty, and the pride of freedom were in him principles of action.

A remarkable trait in the character of Mr. Clay was his inflexibility in defending the public interest against all schemes for its detriment. His exertions were, indeed, so steadily employed and so often successful in protecting the public against the injurious designs of visionary politicians or party demagogues, that he may be almost said to have been, during forty years, the guardian angel of his country. He never would compromise the public interest for anybody, or for any personal advantage to himself.

He was the advocate of liberty throughout the world, and his voice of cheer was raised in behalf of every people who struggled for freedom. Greece, awakened from a long sleep of servitude, heard his voice, and was reminded of her own Demosthenes. South America, too, in her struggle for independence, heard his brave words of encouragement, and her fainting heart was animated and her arm made strong.

Henry Clay is the fair representative of the age in which he lived; an age which forms the greatest and brightest era in the history of man; an age teeming with new discoveries and developments, extending in all directions the limits of human knowledge,—exploring the agencies and elements of the physical world, and turning and subjugating them to the uses of man,—unfolding and establishing, practically, the great principles of popular rights and free government, and which, nothing doubting, nothing fearing, still advances in majesty, aspiring to and demanding further improvement and further amelioration of the condition of mankind.

With the chivalrous and benignant spirit of this great era Henry Clay was thoroughly imbued. He was, indeed, molded by it and made in its own image. That spirit, be it remembered, was not one of licentiousness, or turbulence, or blind innovation. It was a wise spirit, good and honest as it was resolute and brave; and truth and justice were its companions and guides.

stirred within him." He was a man of a genius mighty enough to supply all the defects of education. By its keen, penetrating observation, its quick apprehension, its comprehensive and quick conception, he gathered knowledge without the study of books;—he could draw it from the fountain head,—pure and undefiled; it was unborrowed; the acquisition of his own observation, reflection, and experiences, and all his own. It entered into the composition of the man, forming part of his mind, and strengthening and preparing him for all those great scenes of intellectual exertion or controversy in which his life was spent. His armor was always on, and he was ever ready for the battle.

This mighty genius was accompanied, in him, by all the qualities necessary to sustain its action, and to make it most irresistible. His person was tall and commanding, and his demeanor—

"Lofty and sour to them that loved him not;
But to those men that sought him, sweet as summer."

He was direct and honest, ardent and fearless, prompt to form his opinions, always bold in their avowal, and sometimes impetuous, or even rash, in their vindication. In the performance of his duties he feared no responsibility. He scorned all evasion or untruth. No pale thought ever troubled his decisive mind.

"Be just and fear not" was the sentiment of his heart and the principle of his action. It regulated his conduct in private and public life; all the ends he aimed at were his country's, his God's, and truth's.

Such was Henry Clay, and such were his talents, his qualities, and objects. Nothing but success and honor could attend such a character. For nearly half a century he was an informing spirit, a brilliant and heroic figure in our political sphere, marshaling our country in the way she ought to go. The "bright track of his fiery car" may be traced through the whole space over which, in his day, his country and its Government have passed in the way to greatness and renown. It will still point the way to further greatness and renown.

The great objects of his public life were to preserve and strengthen the Union; to maintain the Constitution and laws of the United States; to cherish industry; to protect labor; and to facilitate, by all proper national improvements, the communication between all parts of our widely extended country. This

These noble qualities of truth and justice were conspicuous in the whole public life of Henry Clay. On that solid foundation he stood erect and fearless; and when the storms of state beat around and threatened to overwhelm him his exclamation was still heard, "Truth is mighty, and public justice certain." What a magnificent and heroic figure does Henry Clay here present to the world! We can but stand before and look upon it in silent reverence. His appeal was not in vain;—the passions of party subsided, truth and justice resumed their sway, and his generous countrymen repaid him for all the wrong they had done him, with gratitude, affection, and admiration in his life, and tears in his death.

It has been objected to Henry Clay that he was ambitious. So he was. But in him ambition was virtue. It sought only the proper, fair objects of honorable ambition, and it sought these by honorable means only,—by so serving the country as to deserve its favors and its honors. If he sought office, it was for the purpose of enabling him, by the power it would give, to serve his country more effectually and pre-eminently; and, if he expected and desired thereby to advance his own fame, who will say that was a fault? Who will say that it was a fault to seek and desire office for any of the personal gratifications it may afford, so long as those gratifications are made subordinate to the public good?

That Henry Clay's object in desiring office was to serve his country, and that he made all other considerations subservient, I have no doubt. I knew him well,—I had full opportunity of observing him in his most unguarded moments and conversation,—and I can say that I have never known a more unselfish, a more faithful or intrepid representative of the people, of the people's rights, and the people's interests, than Henry Clay.

It was most fortunate for Kentucky to have such a representative, and most fortunate for him to have such a constituent as Kentucky; fortunate for him to have been thrown, in the early and susceptible period of his life, into the primitive society of her bold and free people. As one of her children, I am pleased to think that from that source he derived some of that magnanimity and energy which his after life so signally displayed. I am pleased to think that mingling with all his great qualities there was a sort of Kentuckyism (I shall not undertake to define it), which, though it may not have polished or refined, gave to them additional point and power, and free scope of action.

You all know Mr. Clay; your knowledge and recollection of him will present him more vividly to your minds than any picture I can draw of him. This I will add,— he was in the highest, truest sense of the term, a great man, and we shall never look upon his like again. He has gone to join the mighty dead in another and better world. How little is there of such a man that can die! His fame, the memory of his benefactions, the lessons of his wisdom, all remain with us,— over these death has no power.

How few of the great of this world have been so fortunate as he! How few of them have lived to see their labors so rewarded! He lived to see the country that he loved and served advanced to great prosperity and renown, and still advancing. He lived till every prejudice which at any period of his life had existed against him was removed, and until he had become the object of the reverence, love, and gratitude of his whole country. His work seemed then to be completed, and fate could not have selected a happier moment to remove him from the troubles and vicissitudes of this life.

Glorious as his life was, there was nothing that became him like the leaving of it. I saw him frequently during the slow and lingering disease which terminated his life. He was conscious of his approaching end, and prepared to meet it with all the resignation and fortitude of a Christian hero. He was all patience, meekness, and gentleness; these shone round him like a mild, celestial light, breaking upon him from another world—

> "And to add greater honors to his age
> Than man can give, he died in fear of God."

AGAINST WARRING ON THE WEAK

(From a Speech in the Senate, February 15th, 1859, on the Proposed Acquisition of Cuba)

IT was once the great policy of this Government to preserve amity and the kindest relations with all the States of North and South America; and we succeeded. A noble course of policy it was. I was here when they were springing into independence — emerging from that Spanish despotism into which they

had been immersed for so many ages. I remember the sensibility and the sympathy with which we all regarded the struggles going on in South America; and, as a Kentuckian, I remember with especial pride that it was the trumpet-toned voice of Henry Clay that led on this great subject of American policy and American sympathy. In South America, at that early day, nothing was so much cherished; and the speeches of Henry Clay in their behalf, proffering peace and friendship and kindness to them, and encouragement in their efforts, were read at the head of their armies, and hailed with shouts and enthusiasm. They came into the world as free nations, as it were, under our auspices; hailed, cheered on, and encouraged, by the voice of America. All their eyes were turned on us; we were an exemplar to them. What has become of that feeling? Where is it, you rulers of our people, where is it? or how is it that you have lost all these good feelings on their part? The good-will of a whole continent is a mighty fund of national strength; and we have lost it. The nations of South America were striving to establish such liberty as we had established; striving to connect themselves with us by all those bonds which unite republics, to take our stand against the great European world, and the great European system. That was the object of this policy.

At the close of the great wars of Europe, when Spain solicited assistance to resubjugate her South American colonies, when their menacing reached the ears of the rulers of this country, what was done? It was the mightiest question that had been presented to the world in this century — whether South America should be Europeanized and fall under the European system of government and policy, or whether it should be Americanized according to the American system of republics. What a mighty question was it! By kindness, by encouragement, by offers of unlimited kindness and protection, we won their hearts, and they fell into our system. They gave us all their sympathy; but now, where has it gone? Read the last message of the President, and consider the troubled state of our relations with these States which it depicts. There is not a state where we do not find enemies, where our citizens are free from violence, where their property is not taken from them. It seems that the persons and property of our citizens are exposed continually to daily violence in every State of South America with which we have relations. It is so, too, in Mexico and Guatemala and Costa Rica and the various States of Central America.

How has it been that this state of things has been brought about? How has it been that we have lost that mighty acquisition, — an acquisition, not of territory, but an acquisition of the hearts of men; an acquisition of the hearts of nations, ready to follow our lead; to stand by us in a common cause, to fight the world, if it were necessary? That great golden chain that bound freemen together from one end of the North to the end of the South American continent has been broken in a thousand pieces; and the message tells us the sad tale that we are everywhere treated with enmity and hostility, and that it is necessary for us to avenge it. We are gathering up little accounts with these nations; we are making quarrels with them. They have done some wrong; practiced some enmity against our citizens; taken some property that they ought not to have taken; and, besides, we have claims against them. From the Feejee Islands to the Spanish throne, we have demands to be urged; and I think we are coming to a very summary process of collection, where no congress is to sit to examine into the *casus belli*, but a ship of war, better than all the constables in the world, is to go around collecting, from the cannibals and others, whatever she is commissioned to say is due to us.

What peace can we have, what good-will can we have among men, if we are to depart from the noble course which governed our forefathers, who had no quarrels but those which they could make a fight out of, and ought to have made a fight out of, directly and at once, and be done with them? Do all these little clouds or specks of war that darken our horizon promise additional prosperity, or an increase of revenue to meet our debts? No, sir. If they portray anything, they portray the contrary — increased expenditures; for however summary your collections, however summarily you take vengeance on other nations, it costs always, and it will cost, a good deal. Fighting is an expensive luxury; luxury it may be considered, but there is cost in it. . . .

Here, in view of all this, we propose to let the President make war as he pleases. The Constitution says the Congress of the United States shall have the power to make war. Has anybody else the power to make war but we and the House of Representatives? Is it a little inferior jurisdiction that we can transfer and delegate to others? Did the Constitution intend that the President should exercise it? No; it gave it to us, and in the

balance of powers just as much denied it to the President as it gave it to us. We subvert the whole system of our Government; the whole constitutional framework of it is a wreck, if you take this most dangerous and most important of all powers and put it in the hands of the President of the United States. Can you abdicate this power which the people have given you as their trustees? You cannot do it. Does not this bill do it?

To be sure, it will be observed that the right of summary redress is limited to weak States. There seems to be some saving understanding upon the part of the framers of this policy that it would not be applicable to large States. Some trouble, some resistance, might be anticipated from them; but you can safely thunder it over the heads of these poor little South American States; you can make them tremble; you can settle the accounts, and make them pay your own balances. Sir, what sort of heroism is that for your country and my country, to triumph over the small and the weak? The bill on which I am commenting does not suppose that war is to require formal debate, but proposes, whenever it shall be made to appear to the President that an American citizen, in any of these countries, has been the subject of violence or depredation in his property, to allow the President, at his *ipse dixit*, to make war. Unheard, unquestioned, at once the will of a single man is to let loose the dogs of war against these small, weak nations. It is a violation of the spirit of the Constitution; and, besides, there is a pettiness about it that does not belong to our country. Surely it was in a thoughtless moment that the President intimated the necessity of such a measure, or that it was introduced into the Senate. There is nothing in it that can stand investigation. It is not more uncongenial to the Constitution of the United States than it is, I trust, to the magnanimous character of my countrymen, that they should be willing to hunt out the little and the weak and chastise them, and let the great go free, or leave them to the ordinary solemn course of proceeding, by treaty or by congressional legislation. No, sir; far better is the maxim of the old Roman — *debellare superbos*, to put down the proud.

DAVID CROCKETT

(1786–1836)

DUCATED and refined Americans of David Crockett's day refused to take him seriously, and it was only by dying in the angle of the Alamo, among the last of its defenders, that he escaped being remembered, if remembered at all, merely as a representative of the humor of the backwoods. He was a type of an uncultured but strong and persistent Americanism, which has done more, perhaps, than culture itself to give the country its possibilities of greatness. He won prominence among the backwoodsmen of what was then the West, by his fluency of speech and his humor. Sent to Congress as a representative of the West Tennessee District, he attracted immediate notice by his strong individuality and the raciness of his stories,—many of them the kind Lincoln loved so well. He was made much of in a semi-humorous way, until being at bottom entirely serious, he declined to be taken as a joke. Insisting on standing by his convictions, even against Andrew Jackson, he won much reputation and popularity in New England, where Jackson was then intensely unpopular. Unfortunately for his usefulness as a Tennessee Congressman, the New England view did not prevail with a majority of his constituents and he was retired from office. He left Tennessee disheartened, determined to make himself a new career in Texas. Finding the Alamo beleaguered by an overwhelming force of Mexicans, he managed, nevertheless, to make his way into the fort, where a few days later he was killed with the other riflemen whose courage and extraordinary marksmanship made the defense of the fort forever memorable. He was born at Limestone, Tennessee, August 17th, 1786. He served in Congress from 1827 to 1831 and from 1833 to 1835. His autobiography published in 1834 seems likely to keep a permanent place in American literature. His speech on the Buffalo and New Orleans Road Bill, reported by Benton, is characteristic, and it may be accepted as a sufficient illustration of his efforts at serious statesmanship.

Crockett approximates the perfect type of those pioneer stump-speakers whose rude eloquence had so much to do with making American history before the era of railroads and telegraphs; and being thus typical his place in the history of oratory is secure.

A RACCOON IN A BAG

(Delivered in March 1830 Before a Committee of the House of Representatives in Support of an Amendment to the Buffalo and New Orleans Road Bill)

WHEN I consider the few opportunities which I have had to obtain information on this important topic, I shrink at the idea of addressing so intelligent a body as this upon matters relating to it. My lips would be sealed in silence, were I not fully convinced that there has been in some instances a partial and improper legislation resorted to during the present session. I was elected from the Western District of Tennessee after declaring myself a friend to this measure; and I came here quite hot for the road—yes, the fever was upon me; but I confess I am getting quite cool on the subject of expending money for the gratification of certain gentlemen who happen to have different views from those I entertain. Let us inquire where this money comes from. It will be found that even our poor citizens have to contribute towards the supply. I have not forgotten how I first found my way to this House; I pledged myself to the good people who sent me here that I would oppose certain tariff measures, and strive to remove the duties upon salt, sugar, coffee, and other articles, which the poor as well as the rich are from necessity compelled to consume. The duties on these articles are felt to be oppressive by my fellow-citizens; and as long as I can raise my voice I will oppose the odious system which sanctions them.

Those who sustain the Government and furnish the means, have, by the illiberality of their servants, been kept in ignorance of the true cause of some of their sufferings. These servants, after the people intrust them with their confidence, too often forget the interest of their employers and are led away by some designing gentlemen, who, to gratify some wild notion, are almost willing to enslave the poorer class at least. I am one of those who are called self-taught men; by the kindness of my neighbors and some exertion of my own, I have been raised from obscurity without an education. I am therefore compelled to address the committee in the language of a farmer, which I hope will be understood. I do not mean to oppose internal improvements— my votes on that subject will show that I am an internal im-

provement man, though I cannot go, as the Kentuckian said, "the whole hog." I will only go as far as the situation of the country will admit—so far as not to oppress. I will not say that I will vote against the bill under all circumstances, yet at this moment I consider it a wild notion to carry the road to the extent contemplated, from Buffalo to this city, and from this to New Orleans. . . . I am astonished that certain of our Eastern friends have become so kind to us. They are quite willing to aid in distributing a portion of the national funds among us of the West. This was not so once. And if I am not deceived their present kindness is merely a bait to cover the hook which is intended to haul in the Western and Southern people; and when we are hooked over the barb we will have to yield. Their policy reminds me of a certain man in the State of Ohio, who, having caught a raccoon, placed it in a bag, and as he was on his way home he met a neighbor who was anxious to know what he had in his bag. He was told to put his hand in and feel, and in doing so he was bit through the fingers; he then asked what it was and was told that it was "only a bite." I fear that our good Eastern friends have a hook and a bite for us; and if we are once fastened, it will close the concern. We may then despair of paying the national debt; we may bid farewell to all other internal improvements; and, finally, we may bid farewell to all hopes of ever reducing duties on anything. This is honestly my opinion; and again I say I cannot consent to "go the whole hog." But I will go as far as Memphis. There let this great road strike the Mississippi where the steamboats are passing every hour in the day and night; where you can board a steamboat and in seven or eight days go to New Orleans and back; where there is no obstruction at any time of the year. I would thank any man to show this committee the use of a road which will run parallel with the Mississippi for five or six hundred miles. Will any man say that the road would be preferred to the river either for transportation or traveling? No, sir. Then, is not your project useless, and will it not prove an improper expenditure of the public funds to attempt to carry the road beyond Memphis?

OLIVER CROMWELL

(1599–1658)

ARLYLE says that Cromwell's speeches "excel human belief, in their unlikeness to all other speeches, in their utter disregard of all standards of oratory and logical sequence of thought. Some of them are certainly worthy to be called, as they have been called, "agglomerations of opaque confusions; of darkness on the back of darkness," when they are judged by our standards; but the time was when they had as much weight in England as the most polished orations of Demosthenes had in Athens. Unlike anything else in the history of oratory, they represent a time and mode of thought unlike anything else in the history of the world. The Cromwelian Puritan, Carlyle says, represents "a practical world based on belief in God." . . . "Our ancient Puritan reformers," he writes, "were,—as all reformers that will ever much benefit the earth are always, inspired by a heavenly purpose. To see God's own law, then, universally acknowledged for complete as it stood in the Holy Written Book, made good in this world; to see this, or the true unwearied aim and struggle towards this, was a thing worth living for and dying for. Eternal justice, that God's will be done on earth as it is in heaven—corollaries enough will flow from that, if that there be; it that be not there, no corollary good for much will flow. It was the general spirit of England in the seventeenth century. In other somewhat sadly disfigured form, we have seen the same immortal hope take practical form in the French Revolution and once more astonish the world."

This may be accepted as a correct characterization of Puritan eloquence in general, but those who read Cromwell's speech in reply to Whitlocke and the Committee of '99, when they offered him the crown, will readily understand that heroes are not always heroic. As a matter of fact, this speech, while it is one of the most characteristic Cromwell ever delivered, carefully refrains from announcing a definite conclusion, and is characteristic of Cromwell's great strength of intellect only in the skill with which he refrains from committing himself to any obligation which would have limited the absolute power he then exercised as Lord-Protector. Preferring the substance of power to its dignity, and remembering that he was in power himself but as a representative of the popular protest against royal prerogatives, he finally refused the crown and kept his historical consistency. As a speaker he is marvelous in his incomprehensibility. It is impossible to believe the assertions made by his enemies, that his speeches are the mere outpourings of an intellect in many respects radically disordered, but it does appear that he speaks extemporaneously with the utmost fluency without any idea of consistency of statement, or of the cohesiveness of thought which should have existed between the different parts of his speeches. His sentences are apt to grow interminable and he frequently despairs of completing them and wisely abandons them without even waiting to come to a semicolon. It has been pointed out that among modern speakers Bismarck shows the same mental bent towards involved utterances, but never fails to extricate himself, even where escape from the involutions of his extemporaneous style has grown seemingly impossible. Cromwell, trained as a soldier to force his way by main strength, ceases to rely on mere skill when it does not serve his purpose. When a sentence does not suit him, instead of attempting to mend it, he abandons it and begins afresh, appearing to speak simply from the suggestion of unco-ordinated ideas as they come into his mind, without making any great effort to control them. How such a style was possible for a great soldier who could marshal men as Cromwell did, it is not easy to imagine, but it is certain enough that only a Cromwell could afford to venture on it in any deliberative body of English-speaking people.

DEBATING WHETHER OR NOT TO BECOME KING OF ENGLAND

(From the Speech Delivered Monday, April 13th, 1657, at Whitehall, Before the Committee of Ninety-Nine, Addressing Whitlocke as Reporter of the Committee)

My Lord:—

I THINK I have a very hard task on my hand. Though it be but to give an account of myself, yet I see I am beset on all hands here. I say, but to give an account of myself: yet that is a business very comprehensive of others;—comprehending us all in some sense, and, as the Parliament have been pleased to shape it, comprehending all the interests of these three nations!

I confess I have two things in view. The first is, to return some answer to what was so well and ably said the other day on behalf of the Parliament's putting that title in the instrument

that it secures all who act under him." Truly these are the principal of those grounds that were offered the other day, so far as I do recollect.

I cannot take upon me to repel those grounds; they are so strong and rational. But if I am to be able to make any answer to them, I must not grant that they are necessarily conclusive; I must take them only as arguments which perhaps have in them much conveniency, much probability towards conclusiveness. For if a remedy or expedient may be found, they are not of necessity, they are not inevitable grounds: and if not necessary or concluding grounds, why, then, they will hang upon the reason of expediency or conveniency. And if so, I shall have a little liberty to speak; otherwise, I am concluded before I speak. Therefore, it will behoove me to say what I can, why these are not necessary reasons; why they are not—why it is not (I should say) so interwoven in the laws but that the laws may still be executed as justly, and as much to the satisfaction of the people, and answering all objections equally well, without such a title as with it. And then, when I have done that, I shall only take the liberty to say a word or two for my own grounds. And when I have said what I can say as to that latter point, I hope you will think a great deal more than I say.

Truly though Kingship be not a mere title, but the name of an office which runs through the whole of the law, yet it is not so *ratione nominis*, by reason of the name, but by reason of what the name signifies. It is a name of office plainly implying a supreme authority: is it more; or can it be stretched to more? I say, it is a name of office plainly implying the supreme authority; and if so, why, then, I should suppose,—I am not peremptory in anything that is matter of deduction or inference of my own,—but I should suppose that whatsoever name hath been or shall be the name under which the supreme authority acts,—why, I say, if it had been those four or five letters, or whatever else it had been, that signification goes to the thing, certainly it does; and not to the name. Why, then, there can no more be said but this: As such a title hath been fixed, so it may be unfixed. And certainly in the right of the authority, I mean the legislative power,—in the right of the legislative power, I think the authority that could christen it with such a name could have called it by another name. Therefore the name is only derived from that authority. And certainly they, the primary legislative authority, had the disposal of it, and might

of settlement. I hope it will not be expected I should answer everything that was then said, because I suppose the main things that were spoken were arguments from ancient constitutions and settlements by the laws, in which I am sure I could never be well skilled,—and therefore must the more ask pardon for what I have already transgressed in speaking of such matters, or shall now transgress, through my ignorance of them, in my present answer to you.

Your arguments, which I say were chiefly upon the law, seem to carry with them a great deal of necessary conclusiveness to enforce that one thing of kingship. And if your arguments come upon me to enforce upon me the ground of necessity,—why, then, I have no room to answer, for what must be must be! And therefore I did reckon it much of my business to consider whether there were such a necessity, or would arise such a necessity, from those arguments. It was said: "Kingship is not a title, but an office, so interwoven with the fundamental laws of this nation that they cannot, or cannot well, be executed and exercised without it,—partly, if I may say so, upon a supposed ignorance which the law hath of any other title. It knows no other; neither doth any know another. And, by reciprocation,—this said title, or name, or office, you were further pleased to say, is understood; in the dimensions of it, in the power and prerogatives of it, which are by the law made certain, and the law can tell when it keeps within compass and when it exceeds its limits. And the law knowing this, the people can know it also. And the people do love what they know. And it will neither be *pro salute populi*, nor for our safety, to obtrude upon the people what they do not nor cannot understand.

It was said also "that the people have always, by their representatives in Parliament, been unwilling to vary names,—seeing they love settlement and known names, as was said before.? And there were two good instances given of that: the one, in King James's time, about his desire to alter somewhat of the title; and the other in the Long Parliament, where they being otherwise, rationally moved to adopt the word "Representative" instead of "Parliament," refused it for the same reason. It was said, also, that "the holding to this word doth strengthen the new settlement; and hereby there is not anything *de novo* done, but merely things are revolved into their old current." It was said that "it is the security of the Chief Magistrate, and

have detracted from it, changed it:—and I hope it will be no offense to say to you, as the case now stands, So may you. And if it be so that you may, why, then, I say, there is nothing of necessity in your argument; and all turns on consideration of the expedience of it.

Truly I had rather, if I were to choose, if it were the original question,—which I hope is altogether out of the question,—I had rather have any name from this Parliament than any other name without it: so much do I value the authority of the Parliament. And I believe all men are of my mind in that; I believe the Nation is very much of my mind,—though it be an uncertain way of arguing, what mind they are of. I think we may say it without offense; for I would give none! Though the Parliament be the truest way to know what the mind of the Nation is, yet if the Parliament will be pleased to give me a liberty to reason for myself, and if that be one of your arguments, I hope I may urge against it that the reason of my own mind is not quite to that effect. But I do say undoubtingly, what the Parliament settles is what will run, and have currency, through the law; and will lead the thread of government through this land equally well as what hath been. For I consider that what hath been was upon the same account, by the same authority. Save that there hath been some long continuance of the thing, it is but upon the same account! It had its original somewhere! And it was with consent of the whole,—there is the original of it. And consent of the whole will still, I say, be the needle that will lead the thread through all; and I think no man will pretend right against it, or wrong!

And if so, then, under favor to me, I think these arguments from the law are all not as of necessity, but are to be understood as of conveniency. It is in your power to dispose and settle; and beforehand we can have confidence that what you do settle will be as authentic as the things that were of old,—especially as this individual thing, the name or title,—according to the Parliament's appointment. Is not this so? It is question not of necessity; we have power to settle it as conveniency directs. Why, then, there will (with leave) be way made for me to offer a reason or two to the other considerations you adduced; otherwise, I say my mouth is stopped!

There are very many enforcements to carry on this thing. But I suppose it will have to stand on its expediency. Truly I should have urged one consideration more which I forgot,—

namely, the argument not of reason only, but of experience. It is a short one, but it is a true one, and is known to you all in the fact of it. That the supreme authority going by another name and under another title than that of King hath been, why, it hath been already twice complied with! Twice: under the *Custodes Libertatis Angliæ*, and also since I exercised the place it hath been complied with. And truly I may say that almost universal obedience hath been given by all ranks and sorts of men to both. Now this, on the part of both these authorities, was a beginning with the highest degree of magistracy at the first alteration; and at a time when that Kingship was the name established; and the new name, though it was the name of an invisible thing, the very name I say was obeyed, did pass current, was received and did carry on the justice of the nation. I remember very well my lords the judges were somewhat startled; yet upon consideration,—if I mistake not,—I believe so,—they, there being among them as able and as learned as have sat there,—though they did, I confess, at first demur a little,—they did receive satisfaction, and did act, as I said before. And as for my own part, I profess I think I may say since the beginning of that change,—though I should be loath to speak anything vainly,—but since the beginning of that change to this day, I do not think there hath been a freer procedure of the laws, not even in those years called, and not unworthily, the "Halcyon Days of Peace," from the Twentieth of Elizabeth to King James's and King Charles's time. I do not think but the laws have proceeded with as much freedom and justice, and with less of private solicitation, since I came to the Government as they did in those years so named "Halcyon." I do not think, under favor, that the laws had a freer exercise, more uninterrupted by any hand of power, in those years than now; or that the judge has been less solicited by letters or private interpositions either of my own or other men's, in double so many years in all those times named "of peace!" And if more of 'my lords the judges were here than now are, they could tell us perhaps somewhat further. And, therefore, I say under favor: These two experiences do manifestly show that it is not a title, though never so interwoven with our laws, that makes the law to have its free passage and to do its office without interruption (as we venture to think it is now doing); and if a Parliament shall determine that another name run through the laws, I believe it will run

and the family that he blasted the very title. And you know when a man comes, *a parte post*, to reflect, and see this done, this title laid in the dust,—I confess I can come to no other conclusion. The like of this may make a strong impression upon such weak men as I am;—and perhaps upon weaker men (if there be any such) it will make a stronger. I will not seek to set up that which Providence hath destroyed and laid in the dust; I would not build Jericho again! And this is somewhat to me, and to my judgment and my conscience. This, in truth, it is this that hath an awe upon my spirit. And I must confess, as the times are,—they are very fickle, very uncertain, nay God knows you had need have a great deal of faith to strengthen you in your work, you had need look at settlement!—I would rather I were in my grave than hinder you in anything that may be for settlement of the Nation. For the Nation needs it, never needed it more! And therefore, out of the love and honor I bear you, I am forever bound, whatever becomes of me, to do what is best for that;—and I am forever bound to acknowledge you have dealt honorably and worthily with me, and lovingly, and have had respect for one who deserves nothing.

Indeed, out of the love and faithfulness I bear you, and out of the sense I have of the difficulty of your work, I would not have you lose any help that may serve you, that may stand in stead to you. I would willingly be a sacrifice, that there might be, so long as God shall please to let this Parliament sit, a harmony, and better and good understanding between all of you. And,—whatever any man may think,—it equally concerns one of us as another to go on to settlement: and where I meet with any that is of another mind, indeed I could almost curse him in my heart. And therefore, to deal heartily and freely I would have you lose nothing that may stand you in stead in this way. I would advise, if there be found any of a froward, unmannerly or womanish spirit.—I would not that you should lose them! I would not that you should lose any servant or friend who might help in this work; that any such should be offended by a thing that signifies no more to me than I have told you it does. That is to say: I do not think the thing necessary; I do not. I would not that you should lose a friend for it. If I could help you to many friends, and multiply myself into many, that would be to serve you in regard to settlement! And therefore I would not that any, especially any of these who

with as free a passage as this of King ever did. Which is all I have to say upon that head. . . .

I will now say something for myself. As for my own mind, I do profess it, I am not a man scrupulous about words, or names, or such things. I have not hitherto clear direction, but as I have the word of God, and I hope shall ever have, for the rule of my conscience, for my information and direction, so truly, if men have been led into dark paths through the providence and dispensations of God—why surely it is not to be objected to a man. For who can love to walk in the dark? But Providence doth often so dispose. And though a man may impute his own folly and blindness to Providence sinfully, yet this must be at a man's own peril. The case may be that it is the providence of God that doth lead men in darkness! I must needs say I have had a great deal of experience of providence; and though such experience is no rule without or against the Word, yet it is a very good expositor of the Word in many cases.

Truly the providence of God hath laid aside this title of King providentially *de facto:* and that not by sudden humor or passion; but it hath been by issue of as great deliberation as ever was in a Nation. It hath been by issue of ten or twelve years civil war, wherein much blood hath been shed. I will not dispute the justice of it when it was done, nor need I tell you what my opinion is in the case were it *de novo* to be done. But if it be at all disputable, and a man come and find that God in his severity hath not only eradicated a whole family, and thrust them out of the land, for reasons best known to himself, but also hath made the issue and close of that to be the very eradication of a name or title—! Which *de facto* is the case. It was not done by me, nor by them that tendered me the Government I now act in; it was done by the Long Parliament,—that was it. And God hath seemed providential, not only in striking at the family, but at the name. And, as I said before, it is blotted out: it is a thing cast out by an act of Parliament; it hath been kept out to this day. And as Jude saith, in another case, speaking of abominable sins that should be in the latter times,—he doth further say, when he comes to exhort the Saints, he tells them they should "hate even the garments spotted with the flesh."

I beseech you think not that I bring this as an argument to prove anything. God hath seemed so to deal with the persons

indeed, perhaps, are men that do think themselves engaged to continue with you, and to serve you, should be anywise disobliged from you.

I have now no more to say. The truth is, I did indicate this as my conclusion to you at the first, when I told you what method I would speak to you in. I may say that I cannot, with conveniency to myself, nor good to this service which I wish so well to, speak out all my arguments as to the safety of your proposal, as to its tendency to the effectual carrying on of this work. I say I do not think it fit to use all the thoughts I have in my mind as to that point of safety. But I shall pray to God Almighty that he would direct you to do what is according to his will. And this is that poor account I am able to give of myself in this thing.*

*The text of the speech here given is that edited by Carlyle, except that his peculiarities of capitalization and punctuation have not been followed.

SIR JOHN CULPEPER

(?–1660)

MONG the remarkable speeches reported by John Nalson in his 'Impartial Collection of Great Affairs of State' (London 1682), perhaps the most remarkable is that in which Sir John Culpeper (afterwards Lord Colepeper) denounced monopolies. Sir John Culpeper was elected to represent Kent in the Parliament of 1640, at a time when English eloquence was just beginning to develop its full powers under the stimulus of passion provoked by Charles the First's abuse of what he claimed as his divine right. In a speech delivered on the same day on which Culpeper spoke, Lord Digby defined the chief of these abuses as follows:—

1. The great and intolerable burthen of ship-money, touching the legality whereof they are unsatisfied.
2. The many great abuses in pressing the soldiers, and raising moneys concerning the same.
3. The multitude of monopolies.
4. The new canon, and the oath to be taken by lawyers, divines, etc.
5. The oath required to be taken by church officers according to articles new and unusual.

Culpeper's celebrated characterization of the monopolies under Charles I. has not had general currency as a quotation in later discussions of the same subject, but it is doubtful if it has been equaled, or even closely approached by the greater orators who have spoken since under the inspiration of the same ideas.

The fact that the "Sir John Culpeper" familiar to readers of Nalson appears in later history as "Colepeper" is significant. Elected to the Long Parliament in 1640, his speech against monopolies was probably the strongest of its kind delivered during the session. It marked Culpeper as a man capable of popular leadership, with force of character enough to direct the revolution. He figures in later history, however, on the side of the King. Leaving the opposition to monopoly to take care of itself, he became a member of the Privy Council and Chancellor of the Exchequer. The King made him "Lord Colepeper of Thoresway." After many vicissitudes in following Charles I. to his downfall, he went into exile and on the death of Cromwell was materially instrumental in winning over Monk and bringing about the restoration. He died June 11th, 1660.

---

relief by the name of benevolence, and to intermeddle with our freehold by suspensions and deprivation. This is a grievance of a high nature.

The next grievance is the ship-money; this cries aloud. I may say, I hope without offense, this strikes the firstborn of every family; I mean our inheritance; if the laws give the King power, in any danger of the kingdom, whereof he is judge, to impose what and when he please, we owe all that is left to the goodness of the King, not to the law, Mr. Speaker. This makes the farmers faint, and the plow go heavy.

The next is the great decay of clothing and fall of our wools; these are the golden mines of England which give a foundation to that trade which we drive with all the world. I know there are many stars concur in this constellation, I will not trouble you with more than one cause of it, which I dare affirm to be the greatest. It is the great custom and impositions laid upon our cloth and new draperies; I speak not this with a wish to lessen the King's revenues, so it be done by Parliament; I shall give my voice to lay more charge upon the superfluities, due regard being had to trade, which we import from all other nations; sure I am that all those impositions upon our native commodities are dangerous, give liberty to our neighbors to undersell; and I take it for a rule that besides our loss in trade, which is five times as much as the King receiveth, which is imposed upon our cloths, this is taken from the rent of our lands. I have but one grievance more to offer you; but this one compriseth many; it is a nest of wasps, or swarm of vermin, which have overcrept the land,—I mean the monopolies and polers of the people; these, like the frogs of Egypt, have gotten possession of our dwellings, and we have a room scarce free from them; they sup in our cup, they dip in our dish, they sit by our fire, we find them in the dye-vat, washbowl, and powdering tub. They share with the butler in his box; they have marked and sealed us from head to foot. Mr. Speaker, they will not bate us a pin; we may not buy our own clothes without their brokage; these are the leeches that have sucked the Commonwealth so hard that it is almost become hectical; and, Mr. Speaker, some of these are ashamed of their right names; they have a vizard to hide the brand made by that good law in the last Parliament of King James; they shelter themselves under the name of a Corporation; they make by-laws which serve their turns to

---

AGAINST MONOPOLIES

(Delivered in the English Parliament, November 9th, 1640)

Mr. Speaker:—

I STAND not up with a petition in my hand, I have it in my mouth, and have it in charge from them that sent me hither, humbly to present to the consideration of this House the grievances of the county of Kent; I shall only sum them up. They are these:—

First, the great increase of Papists by the remiss execution of those laws which were made to suppress them; the life of the law is execution; without this they become but a dead letter; this is wanting and a great grievance.

The second is the obtruding and countenancing of divers new ceremonies in matters of religion, as placing the Communion table Altar wise, and bowing and cringing towards it, and refusing the Holy Sacrament to such as refuse to come up to the rails,—these carry with them some scandal and much offense.

The third is military charges, and therein first coat and conduct money, required as a loan, or pressed as a due, and in each respect equally a grievance. The second is the enhancing the price of powder, whereby the trained bands are much discouraged in their exercising; however this may appear *prima facie*, upon due examination it will appear a great grievance. The third is more particular to our county; it is this: the last summer was twelve-month, ten thousand of our best arms were taken from the owners, and sent into Scotland; the compulsory way was this: "If you will not send your arms you shall go yourselves." Mr. Speaker, the train band is a militia of great strength and honor, without charges to the King, and deserves all due encouragement.

The fourth is the canons, I assign these to be a grievance; first, in respect of the matter, besides the oath. Secondly, in respect of the makers: they were chosen to serve in a convocation; that falling with the Parliament, the scene was altered; and the same men without any new election were shuffled into a sacred synod. Thirdly, in respect of the consequence, which in this age, when the second ill precedent becomes a law, is full of danger. The clergy, without confirmation of a Parliament, have assumed unto themselves power to make laws, to grant

---

squeeze us and fill their purses. Unface these and they will prove as bad cards as any in the pack; these are not petty chapmen, but wholesale men. Mr. Speaker, I have echoed to you the cries of the Kingdom, I will tell you their hopes: they look to heaven for a blessing upon this Parliament, they hang upon his Majesty's exemplary piety and great justice, which renders his ears open to the just complaints of his subjects; we have had lately a gracious assurance of it; it is the wise conduct of this, whereby the other great affairs of the kingdom and this our grievance of no less importance may go hand in hand in preparation and resolution; then, by the blessing of God, we shall return home with an olive branch in our mouths, and a full confirmation of the privileges which we received from our ancestors and owe to our posterity, and which every free-born Englishman hath received with the air he breathed in.

JOHN PHILPOT CURRAN

(1750–1817)

N<small>O ONE</small> is likely to argue against the proposition of Principal Caird that oratory, to be genuine, must have its mainspring in deep emotion, expressing itself through the processes of an habitually active intellect. The great thought or the deep emotion will always be painful to any one capable of it until he can find for it at least an approximately adequate expression. In this expression, the melody and rhythm of the language which embodies it will always co-ordinate with the thought which inspires it, in some definite, if indefinable, relation to the strength of the emotion which compels the thought. But there is a wide distinction of "personal equation." The question first of the nobility of the thought carries with it the secondary question of adequacy to express it, and that must be decided in each given moment by the whole of the speaker's past life, by the entire complex network of his intellectual processes, by every habit, moral as well as intellectual, which makes him what he is. We often see men of cold and unemotional natures transported out of themselves by some great event and moved by it from what may have been mere fluency of speech to genuine oratory, which, however badly sustained, is, for the time being, of the highest order. But between the mere fluency of the commonplace orator and the facility of speech habitual to such a man as Curran, there is a distinction which forces itself at once on attention. Curran, when he is speaking in his habitual manner, has the faculty of compelling language to sonorous music, so wedded to the thought, so much a part of the thought itself, so fully in harmony with the deep laws of the mind itself, that it delights us, unconsciously, merely as so much sound, without any regard whatever to the meaning of it; leaving us, however, unaware of the source of this pleasure and never distracting our attention from ideas to which, when noble, all nature, as it operates through the process of human expression, strives to give the noblest possible vehicle.

Such men as Curran master us first by mere expression that they may shackle us with their thought; they compel us with music that they may hold us with intellect; they take us captive through melody that they may compel our unwilling natures to suffer as they suffer all the pathos of the universal human life as its wrongs and

its sufferings take hold upon them. Of the sources of Curran's inspiration, his compatriot, Rev. R. M. Buckley writes:—

"There is an Irish school of oratory, and it was about Curran's time it came into vogue. When, indeed, was there such occasion for it? When the speaker's passions were roused by the contemplation of the cruelty with which his country was visited, and the sufferings his countrymen endured, the coldest nature should be eloquent, when speaking of those atrocious deeds. The grandest specimens of eloquence ever recorded in history were delivered in times of great social strife, great national upheaving, amid the ruins of a country, or over the cradle of a young revolution. It was towards the close of the Hebrew nationality that their prophets started up and proclaimed the ruin and captivity about to befall their fellow-countrymen. What eloquence can compare with that of Isaiah, sublime and impassioned? or with Jeremiah, wailing and despondent over the calamities of his race? Demosthenes flourished—the greatest orator the world ever saw—amid the crash of the Grecian republics. Cicero was the last orator of Rome: standing on the bridge that separated the prosperous Rome of the Consuls from the effete and degenerate Rome of the Cæsars. Mirabeau's eloquence flamed like a meteor amid the chaos of the French Revolution. So it was with Curran; he lived and spoke when his native land was steeped to the very lips in woe; when ('twas treason to love her, and death to defend.' Manifold were the thoughts that stirred his brain and quickened his tongue; the ancient glory of his country, the virtues of her children, their courage and constancy, through every peril and misfortune; the gleam of sunshine, short and transient, beaming from the Irish Parliament, and its sudden extinction in the Act of Union. Here was food for thought; here was fuel for the fire of eloquence, pride, passion, glory, hope, and, last of all, despair!"

Curran was born at Newmarket, County Cork, July 24th, 1750, and educated at Trinity College, Dublin, and the Middle Temple, London. He was admitted to the Irish bar in 1775, and although after his election to the Irish Parliament in 1783 he made many speeches supporting the patriotic party of which Grattan was the leader, it is only as a lawyer defending his countrymen against charges of libel, sedition, and treason preferred against them because of their determination to establish Irish nationality, that he is at his best. He defended the leaders of the Insurrection of 1798, and although he managed to remain sufficiently loyal to the English administration, to be appointed Master of the Rolls under Fox in 1806, a position from which, at the expiration of eight years, he retired with a pension of £3,000, his sympathy with Irish struggles for national individuality was so intense that the Union caused him the bitterest disappointment and made him contemplate voluntary exile from his country. A romantic incident of his biography was the attachment between his daughter and the celebrated Robert Emmett, at whose arrest Curran himself was examined before the privy council, which discharged him, as it appears, on his own evidence. After his retire-

ment as Master of the Rolls he spent several years in London in the society of such men as Sheridan, Erskine, Thomas Moore, and William Godwin. He died at Brompton, near London, October 14th, 1817. It was during his residence in London that Byron, speaking of Curran as "Longbow," made this famous comparison between him and "Strongbow," by whom Erskine is meant:—

> "There also were two wits, by acclamation,
> Longbow from Ireland, Strongbow from the Tweed,
> Both lawyers, and both men of education;
> But Strongbow's wit was of more polished breed.
> Longbow was rich in an imagination,
> As beautiful and bounding as a steed,
> But sometimes stumbling over a potato,
> While Strongbow's best things might have come from Cato.

> "Strongbow was like a new tuned harpsichord,
> But Longbow wild as an Æolian harp,
> With which the winds of heaven can claim accord,
> And make a music either flat or sharp.
> Of Strongbow's talk you would not change a word;
> At Longbow's phrases you would sometimes carp;
> Both wits—one born so, and the other bred—
> This by the heart, his rival by the head."

IN THE CASE OF JUSTICE JOHNSON—CIVIL LIBERTY AND ARBITRARY ARRESTS

(In the Cause of the King against the Justice Johnson, in the Court of Exchequer, Dublin, February 4th, 1805)

My Lords:—

I<small>T HAS</small> fallen to my lot, either fortunately or unfortunately, as the event may be, to rise as counsel for my client on this most important and momentous occasion. I appear before you, my lords, in consequence of a writ issued by his Majesty, commanding that cause be shown to this his court, why his subject has been deprived of his liberty; and upon the cause shown in obedience to this writ, it is my duty to address you on the most awful question, if awfulness is to be judged by consequences and events, on which you have been ever called upon to decide. Sorry am I that the task has not been confided to more adequate powers; but feeble as they are, they will at least not shrink from it. I move you, therefore, that Mr. Justice Johnson be released from illegal imprisonment.

I cannot but observe the sort of scenic preparation with which this sad drama is sought to be brought forward. In part I approve it; in part it excites my disgust and indignation. I am glad to find that the attorney and solicitor-general, the natural and official prosecutors for the State, do not appear; and I infer from their absence, that his excellency the lord-lieutenant disclaims any personal concern in this execrable transaction. I think it does him much honor; it is a conduct that equally agrees with the dignity of his character and the feelings of his heart. To his private virtues, whenever he is left to their influence, I willingly concur in giving the most unqualified tribute of respect. And I do firmly believe, it is with no small regret that he suffers his name to be even formally made use of, in avowing for a return of one of the judges of the land, with as much indifference and nonchalance as if he were a beast of the plow. I observe, too, the dead silence into which the public is frowned by authority for the sad occasion. No man dares to mutter; no newspaper dares to whisper that such a question is afloat. It seems an inquiry among the tombs, or rather in the shades beyond them.

Ibant sola sub nocte per umbram.

I am glad it is so—I am glad of this factitious dumbness; for if murmurs dared to become audible, my voice would be too feeble to drown them; but when all is hushed—when Nature sleeps—

Cum quies mortalibus ægris,

the weakest voice is heard—the shepherd's whistle shoots across the listening darkness of the interminable heath, and gives notice that the wolf is upon his walk; and the same gloom and stillness that tempt the monster to come abroad, facilitate the communication of the warning to beware. Yes, through that silence the voice shall be heard; yes, through that silence the shepherd shall be put upon his guard; yes, through that silence shall the felon savage be chased into the toil. Yes, my lords, I feel myself cheered and impressed by the composed and dignified attention with which I see you are disposed to hear me on the most important question that has ever been subjected to your consideration; the most important to the dearest rights of the human being; the most deeply interesting and animating that can beat in his heart, or burn upon his tongue—Oh! how recreating is it to feel that occasions may arise in which the soul of man may resume her pretensions; in which she hears the voice of Nature whisper to her, *Os homini sublime dedi cœlumque tueri;* in which even I can look up with calm security to the court, and down with the most profound contempt upon the reptile I mean to tread upon! I say reptile, because when the proudest man in society becomes so the dupe of his childish malice as to wish to inflict on the object of his vengeance the poison of his sting, to do a reptile's work he must shrink into a reptile's dimension; and so shrunk, the only way to assail him is to tread upon him. But to the subject:—this writ of *habeas corpus* has had a return. That return states that Lord Ellenborough, chief-justice of England, issued a warrant reciting the foundation of this dismal transaction: that one of the clerks of the crown-office had certified to him that an indictment had been found at Westminster, charging the honorable Robert Johnson, late of Westminster, one of the justices of his Majesty's court of common pleas in Ireland, with the publication of certain slanderous libels against the government of that country; against the person of his excellency Lord Hardwicke, lord-lieutenant of that country; against the person of Lord Redesdale, the chancellor of Ireland; and against the person of Mr. Justice Osborne, one of the justices of the court of king's bench in Ireland. One of the clerks of the crown-office, it seems, certified all this to his lordship. How many of those there are, or who they are, or which of them so certified, we cannot presume to guess, because the learned and noble lord is silent as to those circumstances. We are only informed that one of them made that important communication to his lordship. It puts me in mind of the information given to one of Fielding's justices: "Did not," says his worship's wife, "the man with the valet make his *fidavy* that you was *a vagram?*" I suppose it was some such petty bag officer who gave Lord Ellenborough to understand that Mr. Justice Johnson was indicted. And being thus given to understand and be informed, he issued his warrant to a gentleman, no doubt of great respectability, a Mr. Williams, his tipstaff, to take the body of Mr. Justice Johnson and bring him before a magistrate, for the purpose of giving bail to appear within the first eight days of this term, so that there might be a trial within the sittings after; and if, by the blessing of God, he should be convicted, then to appear on the return of the *postea*, to be dealt with according to law

Perhaps it may be a question for you to decide, whether that warrant, such as it may be, is not now absolutely spent; and, if not, how a man can contrive to be hereafter in England on a day that is past. And high as the opinion may be in England of Irish understanding, it will be something beyond even Irish exactness to bind him to appear in England, not a fortnight hence, but a fortnight ago. I wish, my lords, we had the art of giving time this retrograde motion. If possessed of the secret, we might be disposed to improve it from fortnights into years.

There is something not incurious in the juxtaposition of signatures. The warrant is signed by the chief-justice of all England. In music, the ear is reconciled to strong transitions of key by a preparatory resolution of the intervening discords; but here, alas! there is nothing to break the fall: the august title of Ellenborough is followed by the unadorned name of brother Bell, the sponsor of his lordship's warrant. Let me not, however, be suffered to deem lightly of the compeer of the noble and learned lord. Mr. Justice Bell ought to be a lawyer; I remember him myself long a crier, and I know his credit, too, with the State; he has had a *noli prosequi.* I see not, therefore, why it may not fairly be said *fortunati ambo!* It appears by his return, that Mr. Justice Bell indorses this bill of lading to another consignee, Mr. Medlicot, a most respectable gentleman. He describes himself upon the warrant, and he gives a delightful specimen of the administration of justice, and the calendar of saints in office; he describes himself a justice and a peace officer —that is, a magistrate and a catchpole:—so that he may receive informations as a justice. If he can write, he may draw them as a clerk; if not, he can execute the warrant as bailiff, and, if it be a capital offense, you may see the culprit, the justice, the clerk, the bailiff, and the hangman, together in the same cart; and, though he may not write, he may "ride and tie!" What a pity that their journey should not be further continued together! That, as they had been "lovely in their lives, so in their deaths they might not be divided!" I find, my lords, I have undesignedly raised a laugh; never did I less feel merriment. Let not me be condemned—let not the laugh be mistaken. Never was Mr. Hume more just than when he says that "in many things the extremes are nearer to one another than the means." Few are those events that are produced by vice and folly, that fire the heart with indignation, that do not also shake the sides with

laughter. So when the two famous moralists of old beheld the sad spectacle of life, the one burst into laughter, the other melted into tears: they were each of them right, and equally right.

Si credas utrique
Res sunt humanæ flebile ludibrium.

But these laughs are the bitter ireful laughs of honest indignation, or they are the laughs of hectic melancholy and despair.

It is stated to you, my lords, that these two justices, if justices they are to be called, went to the house of the defendant. I am speaking to judges, but I disdain the paltry insult it would be to them, were I to appeal to any wretched sympathy of situation. I feel I am above it. I know the bench is above it. But I know, too, that there are ranks and degrees and decorums to be observed; and, if I had a harsh communication to make to a venerable judge, and a similar one to his crier, I should certainly address them in a very different language indeed. A judge of the land, a man not young, of infirm health, has the sanctuary of his habitation broken open by these two persons, who set out with him for the coast, to drag him from his country, to hurry him to a strange land by the "most direct way!" till the king's writ stopped the malefactors, and left the subject of the king a waif dropped in the pursuit.

Is it for nothing, my lords, I say this? Is it without intention I state the facts in this way? It is with every intention. It is the duty of the public advocate not so to put forward the object of public attention, as that the skeleton only shall appear, without flesh, or feature, or complexion. I mean everything that ought to be meant in a court of justice. I mean not only that this execrable attempt shall be intelligible to the court as a matter of law, but shall be understood by the world as an act of state. If advocates had always the honesty and the courage, upon occasions like this, to despise all personal considerations, and to think of no consequence but what may result to the public from the faithful discharge of their sacred trust, these phrenetic projects of power, these atrocious aggressions on the liberty and happiness of men, would not be so often attempted: for, though a certain class of delinquents may be screened from punishment, they cannot be protected from hatred and derision. The great tribunal of reputation will pass its inexorable sentence upon their

crimes, their follies, or their incompetency; they will sink themselves under the consciousness of their situation; they will feel the operation of an acid so neutralizing the malignity of their natures, as to make them at least harmless, if it cannot make them honest. Nor is there anything of risk in the conduct I recommend. If the fire be hot, or the window cold, turn your back to either; turn your face. So, if you are obliged to arraign the acts of those in high station, approach them not in malice, nor favor, nor fear. Remember that it is the condition of guilt to tremble, and of honesty to be bold; remember that your false fear can only give them false courage; that while you nobly avow the cause of truth, you will find her shield an impenetrable protection; and that no attack can be either hazardous or inefficient, if it be just and resolute. If Nathan had not fortified himself in the boldness and directness of his charge, he might have been hanged for the malice of his parable.

It is, my lords, in this temper of mind, befitting every advocate who is worthy of the name, deeply and modestly sensible of his duty, and proud of his privilege, equally exalted above the meanness of temporizing or of offending, most averse from the unnecessary infliction of pain upon any man or men whatsoever, that I now address you on a question, the most vitally connected with the liberty and well-being of every man within the limits of the British Empire; which, if decided one way, he may be a freeman; which, if decided the other, he must be a slave. It is not the Irish nation only that is involved in this question: every member of the three realms is equally embarked; and would to God all England could listen to what passes here this day! They would regard us with more sympathy and respect, when the proudest Briton saw that his liberty was defended in what he would call a provincial court and by a provincial advocate. The abstract and general question for your consideration is this: My Lord Ellenborough has signed with his own hand a warrant, which has been indorsed by Mr. Bell, an Irish justice, for seizing the person of Mr. Justice Johnson in Ireland, for conveying his person by the most direct way, in such manner as these bailiffs may choose, across the sea, and afterwards to the city of Westminster, to take his trial for an alleged libel against the persons intrusted with the government of Ireland, and to take that trial in a country where the supposed offender did not live at the time of the supposed offense, nor, since a period of at least eighteen months previous thereto, has ever resided; where the subject of his accusation is perfectly unknown; where the conduct of his prosecutors, which has been the subject of the supposed libel, is equally unknown; where he has not the power of compelling the attendance of a single witness for his defense. Under that warrant he has been dragged from his family; under that warrant he was on his way to the water's edge: his transportation has been interrupted by the writ before you, and upon the return of that writ arises the question upon which you are to decide, the legality or illegality of so transporting him for the purpose of trial. I am well aware, my lords, of the limits of the present discussion; if the law were clear in favor of the prosecutors, a most momentous question might arise—how far they may be delinquents in daring to avail themselves of such a law for such a purpose—but I am aware that such is not the present question. I am aware that this is no court of impeachment; and therefore that your inquiry is, not whether such a power hath been criminally used, but whether it doth in fact exist. The arrest of the defendant has been justified by the advocates of the crown under the forty-fourth of his present majesty. I have had the curiosity to inquire into the history of that act, and I find that in the month of May 1804 the brother-in-law of one of the present prosecutors obtained leave to bring in a bill to "render more easy the apprehending and bringing to trial offenders escaping from one part of the united kingdom to another, and also from one county to another." That bill was brought in: it traveled in the caravan of legislation unheeded and unnoticed, retarded by no difficulties of discussion or debate, and in due fullness of season it passed into a law, which was to commence from and after the first of August, 1804.

This act, like a young Hercules, began its exploits in the cradle. In the November following, the present warrant was issued under its supposed authority. Let me not be understood to say that the act has been slided through an unsuspecting legislature, under any particular influence, or for any particular purpose; that any such man could be found, or any such influence exist, or any such lethargy prevail, would not, perhaps, be decent to suppose; still less do I question the legislative authority of Parliament. We all know that a Parliament may attaint itself, and that its omnipotence may equally extend in the same way to the whole body of the people. We know also that most unjust and

IV—95

from whose bourn no traveler returns," for of these wretched travelers how few ever did return. But of that flagrant abuse this statute has laid the ax to the root: it prohibits the abuse; it declares such detention or removal illegal; it gives an action against all persons concerned in the offense by contriving, writing, signing, countersigning such warrant, or advising or assisting therein. That you may form a just estimate of the rights which were to be secured, examine the means by which their infringement was in future to be prevented and punished. The injured party has a civil action against the offenders, but the legislature recollected that the sneaking unprincipled humility of a servile packed jury might do homage to ministerial power by compensating the individual with nominal damages. The statute does that, of which I remember no other instance. It leaves the jury at liberty to give damages to any extent above five hundred pounds, but expressly forbids them to find a verdict of damages below it. Was this sufficient? No. The offenders incur a *præmunire*. They are put out of the King's protection; they forfeit their lands and goods; they are disabled from bearing any office of trust or profit. Did the statute stop there?

The Legislature saw, in their prospective wisdom, that the profligate favorite, who had committed treason against the King by the oppression of his subjects, might acquire such a dominion over the mind of his master as by the exertion of prerogative to interrupt the course of justice and prevent the punishment of his crime. The king cannot pardon. Are bulwarks like these ever constructed to repel the incursions of a contemptible enemy? Was it a trivial and ordinary occasion which raised this storm of indignation in the Parliament of that day? Is the ocean ever lashed by the tempest to waft a feather or to drown a fly? Thus haughtily and jealously does this statute restrain the abuses that may be committed against the liberty of the subject by the judge, the jury, or the minister. One exception, and one exception only, does it contain: It excepts from its protection, by the sixteenth section, persons who may have committed "any capital offense" in Scotland or in Ireland. If the principle of that exception were now open to discussion, sure I am that much might be said against its policy. On the one side, you would have to consider the mischief of letting this statute protect a capital offender from punishment by prohibiting his transmission to that jurisdiction where his crime was committed, and where alone he

cruel acts of attainder have been obtained by corrupt men in bad times; and if I could bring myself to say, which I do not, that this act was contrived for the mere purpose of destroying an obnoxious individual, I should not hesitate to call it the most odious species of attainder that could be found upon the records of legislative degradation, because, for the simple purpose of extinguishing an individual, it would sweep the liberty of every being in the State into the vortex of general and undistinguishing destruction. But these are points of view upon which the minds of the people of Ireland and England may dwell with terror or indignation or apathy, according as they may be fitted for liberty or for chains, but they are not points for the court, and so I pass them by. The present arrest and detention are defended under the forty-fourth of the king. Are they warranted by that act? That is the only question for you to decide; and you will arrive at that decision in the usual course, by inquiring, first, how the law stood before upon the subject; next, what the imperfection or grievance of that law was; and third, what the remedy intended to be applied by the act in question.

First, then, how stood the law before? Upon this part it would be a parade of useless learning to go further back than the statute of Charles, the Habeas Corpus Act, which is so justly called the second Magna Charta of British liberty. What was the occasion of the law? The arbitrary transportation of the subject beyond the realm; that base and malignant war, which the odious and despicable minions of power are forever ready to wage against all those who are honest and bold enough to despise, to expose, and to resist them. Such is the oscitancy of man, that he lies torpid for ages under these aggressions, until at last some signal abuse, the violation of Lucrece, the death of Virginia, the oppression of William Tell, shakes him from his slumber. For years had those drunken gambols of power been played in England; for years had the waters of bitterness been rising to the brim; at last a single drop caused them to sleep—and what does that great statute do? It defines and asserts the right, it points out the abuse, and it endeavors to secure the right and to guard against the abuse by giving redress to the sufferer and by punishing the offender; for years had it been the practice to transport obnoxious persons out of the realm into distant parts under the pretext of punishment or of safe custody. Well might they have been said to be sent "to that undiscovered country

could be tried. On the other, you would have to weigh the danger to be feared from the abuse of such a power, which, as the Habeas Corpus Act stood, could not be resorted to in any ordinary way, but was confined to the sole and exclusive exercise of the advisers of the prerogative. You would have to consider whether it was more likely that it would be used against the guilty or the obnoxious; whether it was more likely to be used as an instrument of justice against the bad, or a pretext of oppression against the good; and finally, whether you might not apply to the subject the humane maxim of our law—that better it is that one hundred guilty men should escape than that one innocent, and, let me add, meritorious man should suffer. But our ancestors have considered the question; they have decided, and, until we are better satisfied than I fear we can be, that we have not degenerated from their virtue, it can scarcely become us to pass any light or hasty condemnation upon their wisdom. In this great statute then, my lords, you have the line of demarkation between the prerogative and the people, as well as between the criminal law and the subject, defined with all the exactness, and guarded by every precaution that human prudence could devise. Wretched must that legislature be whose acts you cannot trace to the first unchangeable principles of rational prerogative, of civil liberty, of equal justice! In this act you trace them all distinctly. By this act you have a solemn legislative declaration, "that it is incompatible with liberty to send any subject out of the realm, under pretense of any crime supposed or alleged to be committed in a foreign jurisdiction, except that crime be capital." Such were the bulwarks which our ancestors drew about the sacred temple of liberty—such the ramparts by which they sought to bar out the ever-toiling ocean of arbitrary power, and thought (generous credulity!) that they had barred it out from their posterity forever. Little did they foresee the future race of vermin that would work their way through those mounds and let back the inundation; little did they foresee that their labors were so like those frail and transient works that threatened for a while the haughty crimes and battlements of Troy, but so soon vanished before the force of the trident and the impulse of the waters; or that they were still more like the forms which the infant's finger traces upon the beach; the next breeze, the next tide erases them, and confounds them with the barren undistinguished strand. The ill-omened bird that lights upon it sees nothing to mark, to allure, or to deter, but finds all one obliterated unvaried waste:—

Et sola secum sicca spatiatur arena.

Still do I hope that this sacred bequest of our ancestors will have a more prosperous fortune, and be preserved by a more religious and successful care, a polar star to the wisdom of the legislator and the integrity of the judge.

As such will I suppose its principle not yet brought into disgrace; and as such, with your permission, will I still presume to argue upon that principle.

So stood the law till the two acts of the twenty-third and twenty-fourth of George II. which relate wholly to cases between county and county in England. Next followed the act of the thirteenth of his present Majesty, which was merely a regulation between England and Scotland. And next came the act of the forty-fourth of the present reign, upon which you are now called on to decide, which, as between county and county, is an incorporation of the two acts of George II.; and as between England, Scotland, and Ireland, is nearly a transcript of the thirteenth of the King.

Under the third and fourth sections of this last act the learned counsel for the learned prosecutors (for really I think it only candid to acquit the lord-lieutenant of the folly or the shame of this business, and to suppose that he is as innocent of the project from his temper as he must from his education be ignorant of the subject) endeavor to justify this proceeding. The construction of this act they broadly and expressly contend to be this: Firstly, they assert that it extends not only to the higher crimes, but to all offenses whatsoever; secondly, that it extends not only to persons who may have committed offenses within any given jurisdictions, and afterwards escaped or gone out of such jurisdictions, but to all persons whether so escaping or going out or not; thirdly, that it extends to constructive offenses, that is, to offenses committed against the laws of certain jurisdictions, committed in places not within them, by persons that never put their feet within them, but by construction of law committing them within such jurisdiction, and of course triable therein; fourthly, that it extends peculiarly to the case of libels against the persons intrusted with the powers of government, or with offices in

Lord Avonmore—No, Mr. Curran, you forget; it is not *præcentor*, it is *leguleius quidam cautus atque acutus, præco actionum, cantor formarum, anceps syllabarum*.

Mr. Curran—I thank you, my lord, for the assistance; and I am the more grateful, because, when I consider the laudable and successful efforts that have been made of late to make science domestic and familiar, and to emancipate her from the trammels of scholarship, as well as the just suspicion under which the harborers and abettors of those outlawed classics have fallen, I see at what a risk you have ventured to help me out. And yet see, my lord, if you are prudent in trusting yourself to the honor of an accomplice. Think, should I be prosecuted for this misprision of learning, if I could resist the temptation of escaping by turning evidence against so notorious a delinquent as you, my good lord, and so confessedly more criminal than myself, or perhaps than any other man in the empire.

To examine this act then, my lords, we must revert to the three English statutes of which it is a transcript. The first of these is the twenty-third of George II. cap. 26, § 11.

So much of the title as relates to our present inquiry is "for the apprehending of persons in any county or place upon warrants granted by justices of the peace in any other county or place."

See now section two that contains the preamble and enaction as to this subject:—

"And whereas it frequently happens that persons, against whom warrants are granted by justices of the peace for the several counties within this kingdom, escape into other counties or places out of the jurisdiction of the justices of the peace granting such warrants, and thereby avoid being punished for the offenses wherewith they are charged: For remedy whereof, be it enacted by the authority aforesaid, that from and after the twenty-fourth day of June, one thousand seven hundred and fifty, in case any person against whom a legal warrant shall be issued by any justice or justices of the peace for any county, riding, division, city, liberty, town, or place within this kingdom, shall escape or go into any other county, riding, division, city, liberty, town, or place out of the jurisdiction of the justice or justices granting such warrant as aforesaid, it shall and may be lawful for any justice of the peace of the county, riding, division, city, liberty, town, or place, to which such person shall have gone or escaped, to indorse such warrant, upon application made to him for

the State; and fifthly, that it extends not only to offenses committed after the commencement of the act, but also to offenses at any period, however remotely previous to the existence of the statute; that is, that it is to have an *ex post facto* operation. The learned prosecutors have been forced into the necessity of supporting these last monstrous positions, because, upon the return to the writ, and upon the affidavits, it appears, and has been expressly admitted in the argument—firstly, that the supposed libel upon these noble and learned prosecutors relates to the unhappy circumstances that took place in Ireland on the twenty-third of July, 1803, and of course must have been published subsequent thereto; and, secondly, that Mr. Justice Johnson from the beginning of 1802 to the present hour was never for a moment in England, but was constantly resident in Ireland; so that his guilt, whatever it may be, must arise from some act, of necessity committed in Ireland, and by no physical possibility committed or capable of being committed in England: these are the positions upon which a learned chancellor and a learned judge come forward to support their cause and to stake their character, each in the face of his country, and both in the face of the British Empire: these are the positions, which, thank God, it belongs to my nature to abhor, and to my education to despise, and which it is this day my most prompt and melancholy duty to refute and to resist—most prompt in obeying; most grieved at the occasion that calls for such obedience.

We must now examine this act of the forty-fourth of the king; and in doing so, I trust you will seek some nobler assistance than can be found in the principles or the practice of day-rules or side-bar motions; something more worthy a liberal and learned court, acting under a religious sense of their duty to their King, their country, and their God, than the feeble and pedantic aid of a stunted verbal interpretation, straining upon its tiptoe to peep over the syllable that stands between it and meaning. If your object were merely to see if its words could be tortured into a submission to a vindicate interpretation, you would have only to indorse the construction that these learned prosecutors have put upon it, and that with as much grave deliberation as Mr. Justice Bell has vouchsafed to indorse the warrant which my Lord Ellenborough has thought fit to issue under its authority. You would then have only to look at it, *ut leguleius quidam cautus atque acutus, præcentor.*

that purpose, and to cause the person against whom the same shall have been issued, to be apprehended and sent to the justice or justices who granted such warrant, or to some other justice or justices of the county, riding, division, city, liberty, town, or place, from whence such person shall have gone or escaped, to the end that he or she may be dealt with according to law, any law or usage to the contrary notwithstanding."

This act was amended by the twenty-fourth of the same reign, the title of which was:—

"An act for amending and making more effectual a clause in an act passed in the last session of Parliament for the apprehending of persons in any county or place upon warrants granted by justices of the peace of any county or place."

It then recites the eleventh section of the twenty-third of George II., and proceeds:—

"And whereas, such offender or offenders may reside or be in some other county, riding, division, city, liberty, town, or place, out of the jurisdictions of the justice or justices granting such warrant as aforesaid, before the granting such warrant, and without escaping or going out of the county, riding, division, city, liberty, town, or place, after such warrant granted."

I shall reserve a more particular examination of these two acts for that head of my argument that shall necessarily require it. At present I shall only observe: Firstly, that they are manifestly prospective; secondly, that they operate only as between county and county, in England; thirdly, that they clearly and distinctly go to all offenders whatsoever, who may avoid trial and punishment of their offenses by escaping from the jurisdiction in which they were committed, and were, of course, triable and punishable; and fourthly, that provision is made for bailing the persons so arrested in the place where taken, if the offenses charged upon them were bailable by law.

In the thirteenth of his present Majesty, it was thought fit to make a law with respect to criminals escaping from England to Scotland, and *vice versa:* of that act the present statute of the forty-fourth is a transcript. And upon this statute arises the first question made by the prosecutors; namely, whether, like the acts of the twenty-third and twenty-fourth of George II., which were merely between county and county, it extended indiscriminately to the lowest as well as the highest offenses, or whether the thirteenth and forty-fourth, which go to kingdom and kingdom, are not confined to some and to what particular species of offenses. The preamble to these two statutes, so far as they bear upon our present question, is contained in the third section of the forty-fourth, the act now under consideration. And there is not a word in it that is not most material. It says:—

"Whereas, it may frequently happen that felons and other malefactors in Ireland may make their escape into Great Britain, and also, that felons and other malefactors in Great Britain may make their escape into Ireland, whereby their crimes remain unpunished."

There being no sufficient provision by the laws now in force in Great Britain and Ireland, respectively, for apprehending such offenders and transmitting them into that part of the united kingdom in which their offenses were committed it is enacted "for remedy whereof," etc., that "if any person against whom a warrant shall be issued by any justice of the peace in Ireland, for any crime or offense against the laws of Ireland, shall escape, go into, reside, or be in any place in England or Scotland, it shall be lawful for any justice of the peace for the place, whither or where such persons shall escape, etc., to indorse his name on such warrant; which warrant so indorsed shall be a sufficient authority to the person bringing it to execute the same, by apprehending the person against whom it is granted, and to convey him by the most direct way into Ireland, and before a justice living near the place where he shall land, which justice shall proceed with regard to him as if he had been legally apprehended in such county of Ireland." The fourth section makes the same provision for escapes from England or Scotland into Ireland. The statute goes on and directs that the expenses of such removal shall be repaid to the person defraying the same, by the treasurer of the county in which the crime was committed, and the treasurer is to be allowed for it in his accounts.

To support the construction that takes in all possible offenses of all possible degrees, you have been told, and upon the grave authority of notable cases, that the enacting part of a statute may go beyond its preamble; that it cannot be restrained by the preamble, and still less by the title; that here the enacting clause was the words "any offense," and that "any offense" must extend to every offense, and of course to the offense in question.

If the question had been of a lighter kind, you might perhaps have smiled at the parade of authorities produced to establish what no lawyer ever thinks of denying. They would have acted with more advantage to the justice of the country, though perhaps not to the wishes of their clients, if they had reminded your lordships, that, in the construction of statutes, the preamble, and even the title itself, may give some assistance to the judge in developing its meaning and its extent; if they had reminded you that remedial laws are to be construed liberally, and penal laws with the utmost strictness and caution. And when they contend that a supposed libel is within the letter of this law, they would have done well to have added that it is a maxim that there may be cases within the letter of a statute, which, notwithstanding, the judge is bound to reject, from its operation being incompatible with its spirit. They would have done well in adding that the judge is bound so to construe all laws as not infringe upon any of the known rules of religion or morality, any of the known rules of distributive justice, any of the established principles of the liberties and rights of the subject, and that it is no more than a decent and becoming deference to the legislator to assume as certain, that whatever words he may have used, he could not possibly have meant anything that upon the face of it was palpably absurd, immoral, or unjust. These are the principles on which I am persuaded this court will always act, because I know them to be the principles on which every court of justice ought to act. And I abstain studiously from appealing to any judicial decisions in support of them, because to fortify them by precedent or authority would be to suppose them liable to be called in question. There is another rule which I can easily excuse the learned gentlemen from adverting to, and that is, that when many statutes are made in *pari materia*, any one of them is to be construed, not independently of the others, but with a reference to the entire code of which it is only a component part.

On these grounds, then, I say, the forty-fourth was not, and could not, be intended to go to all offenses whatsoever.

First, because the acts of twenty-third and twenty-fourth of George II. had already prescribed "all persons" by words of the most general and comprehensive kind. If the framers of the thirteenth and forty-fourth meant to carry these acts to the same length, they had the words of the former acts before their eyes,

and yet they have used very different words: a clear proof, in my mind, that they meant to convey a very different meaning. In these latter acts they use very singular words — "felons and other malefactors." That these words are somewhat loose and indefinite I make no difficulty of admitting, but will any man that understands English deny that they describe offenses of a higher and more enormous degree? You are told that felon does not necessarily mean a capital offender, because there are felonies not capital, the name being derived from the forfeiture, not of life, but of property. You are also told that malefactor means generally an ill-doer, and, in that sense, that every offender is a malefactor; but the thirteenth and forty-fourth states this class to be felons and malefactors, for whose transmission from kingdom to kingdom "no sufficient provision was made by the laws now in force." Now I think it is not unfair reasoning to say that this act extends to a class of offenders whose transmission was admitted to be not incompatible with the just liberty of the subject of England; but for whose transmission the legislature could not say there was no provision; but for whose transmission it was clear that there was not a sufficient provision, though there was some provision. If you can find any class so circumstanced, that is, exclusively liable by law to be so transmitted, the meaning of the words, "felons and other malefactors," becomes fixed, and must necessarily refer to such class.

Now that class is expressly described in the Habeas Corpus Act, because it declares the transmission of all persons to be illegal, except only persons charged with capital crimes; for their apprehension and transmission there was a provision, the *mandatum regis*, that is, the discretionary exercise of the prerogative. That power had therefore been used in cases of treason, as in Lundy's case; so in the case of Lord Sanchar; Carliel, the principal in the murder of Turner, committed in London by the procurement of Lord Sanchar, was arrested in Scotland, whither he had fled, by the order of King James I., and brought back to England, where he was executed for the crime, as was Lord Sanchar, the accessory before the fact; but such interference of the prerogative might be granted or withheld at pleasure, could be applied for only with great difficulty and expense, and therefore might well be called an insufficient provision. No provision for such a purpose can be sufficient, unless, instead of depending on the caprice of men in power, it can be resorted to in the ordinary

course of law. You have therefore, my lords, to elect between two constructions: one which makes an adequate provision for carrying the exception in the sixteenth section of the Habeas Corpus Act into effect; and the other, a complete and radical repeal of that sacred security for the freedom of Englishmen. But, further, the spirit and the letter of the Habeas Corpus law is that the party interested shall, without a moment's delay, be bailed, if the offense be bailable; but if misdemeanors are within this act, then an English subject, arrested under an Irish warrant, cannot be bailed within any part of the realm of England, but must be carried forward, in the custody of Irish bailiffs, to the seashore of his country, where he is to be embarked in such vessel as they think proper; and if it should be the good pleasure of his guardians to let him land alive in any part of Ireland, then, and not till then, may he apply to an Irish justice to admit him to bail in a foreign country, where he is a perfect stranger and where none but an idiot could expect to find any man disposed to make himself responsible for his appearance. Can you, my lords, bring your minds easily to believe that such a tissue of despotism and folly could have been the sober and deliberate intention of the legislature? but further, under the acts of George II., even from one county to the next, the warrant by the first justice must be authenticated upon oath, before it can be indorsed by the second; but, in this act, between, perhaps, the remotest regions of different kingdoms, no authentication is required; and upon the indorsement of, perhaps, a forged warrant, which the English justice has no means of inquiring into, a British subject is to be marched through England and carried over sea to Ireland, there to learn in the county of Kerry, or Galway, or Derry, that he had been torn from his family, his friends, his business, to the annihilation of his credit, the ruin of his affairs, the destruction of his health, in consequence of a mistake, or a practical joke, or an inhuman or remorseless project of vindictive malice; and that he is then at liberty to return if he be able; that he may have a good action at law against the worthy and responsible bailiff that abused him, if he be foolish enough to look for him, or unfortunate enough to find him. Can you, my lords, be brought seriously to believe that such a construction would not be the foulest aspersion upon the wisdom and justice of the legislature?

I said, my lords, that an Englishman may be taken upon the indorsement of a forged warrant. Let me not be supposed such a simpleton as to think the danger of forgery makes a shade of difference in the subject. I know too well that calendar of saints, the Irish justices; I am too much in the habit of prosecuting and defending them every term and every commission, not to be able to guess at what price a customer might have real warrants by the dozen; and, without much sagacity, we might calculate the average expense of their indorsement at the other side of the water. But, further yet, the act provides that the expense of such transmission shall be paid at the end of the journey by the place where the crime has been committed — but, who is to supply the expenses by the way? What sort of prosecutors do you think the more likely to advance those expenses, an angry minister, or a vindictive individual? I can easily see that such a construction would give a most effectual method of getting rid of a troublesome political opponent, or a rival in trade, or a rival in love, or of quickening the undutiful lingering of an ancestor that felt not the maturity of his heir; but I cannot bring myself to believe that a sober legislature, when the common rights of humanity seem to be beaten into their last entrenchment, and to make their last stand, I trust in God a successful one, in the British Empire, would choose exactly that awful crisis for destroying the most vital principles of common justice and liberty, or of showing to these nations that their treasure and their blood were to be wasted in struggling for the noble privilege of holding the right of freedom, of habitation, and of country, at the courtesy of every little irritable officer of state, or our worshipful Rivets and Bells and Medlicots and their trusty and well-beloved cousins and catchpoles.

But, my lords, even if the prosecutor should succeed, which for the honor and character of Ireland I trust he cannot, in wringing from the bench an admission that all offenses whatsoever are within this act, he will have only commenced his honorable cause; he will only have arrived at the vestibule of atrocity. He has now to show that Mr. Johnson is within the description of a malefactor, making his escape into Ireland, whereby his offense may remain unpunished, and liable to be arrested under a warrant indorsed in that place whither or where such person shall escape, go into, reside, or be. For this inquiry

you must refer to the twenty-third and twenty-fourth George II. The first of these, twenty-third, cap. 11, recites the mischief—"that persons against whom warrants are granted escape into other counties, and thereby avoid being punished." The enacting part then gives the remedy: "The justice for the place into which such person shall have gone or escaped shall indorse the original warrant, and the person accused shall thereunder be sent to the justice who granted it, to be by him dealt with, etc."

If words can be plain, these words are so; they extend to persons actually committing crimes within a jurisdiction, and actually escaping into some other after warrant granted, and thereby avoiding trial. In this act there were found two defects: Firstly, it did not comprehend persons changing their abode before warrant issued, and whose removing, as not being a direct flight from pursuit, could scarcely be called an escape; secondly, it did not give the second justice a power to bail. And here you see how essential to justice it was deemed that the person arrested should be bailed on the spot and the moment of arrest, if the charge were bailable.

Accordingly, the twenty-fourth of George II., cap. 55, was made. After reciting the former act and the class of offenders thereby described, namely, actual offenders actually escaping, it recites that "whereas such offenders may reside or be in some other county before the warrant granted, and without escaping or going out of the county after such warrant granted," it then enacts, "that the justice for such place where such person shall escape, go into, reside, or be, shall indorse, etc., and may bail if bailable, or transmit," etc.

Now the construction of these two acts taken together is manifestly this; it takes in every person, who, being in any jurisdiction and committing an offense therein, escaping after warrant, or without escaping after warrant, going into some other jurisdiction, and who shall there reside, that is permanently abide, or shall be, that is permanently, so as to be called a resident.

Now here it is admitted that Mr. Johnson was not within the realm of England, since the beginning of 1802, more than a year before the offense existed; and therefore you are gravely called upon to say that he is the person who made his escape from a place where he never was, and into a place which he had never left. To let in this wise and humane instruction, see what you are called upon to do: the statute makes such persons liable to

arrest if they shall have done certain things, to wit, if they shall escape, go into, reside, or be; but if the fact of simply being, i. e., existing in another jurisdiction, is sufficient to make them so liable, it follows, of course, that the only two verbs that imply doing anything, that is, escape or go into, must be regarded as superfluous; that is, that the legislature had no idea whatsoever to be conveyed by them when they used them, and therefore are altogether expunged and rejected.

Such, my lords, are the strange and unnatural monsters that may be produced by the union of malignity and folly. I cannot but own that I feel an indignant, and, perhaps, ill-natured satisfaction in reflecting that my own country cannot monopolize the derision and detestation that such a production must attract. It was originally conceived by the wisdom of the East; it has made its escape and come into Ireland under the sanction of the first criminal judge of the empire, where, I trust in God, we shall have only to feel shame or anger at the insolence of the visit, without the melancholy aggravation of such an execrable guest continuing to reside or to be among us. On the contrary, I will not dismiss the cheering expectation from my heart that your decision, my lords, will show the British nation that a country having as just and as proud an idea of liberty as herself is not an unworthy ally in the great contest for the rights of humanity; is no unworthy associate in resisting the progress of barbarity and military despotism, and in defending against its enemies that great system of British freedom in which we have now a common interest, and under the ruins of which, if it should be overthrown, we must be buried in a common destruction.

I am not ignorant, my lords, that this extraordinary construction has received the sanction of another court, nor of the surprise and dismay with which it smote upon the general heart of the bar. I am aware that I may have the mortification of being told in another country of that unhappy decision, and I foresee in what confusion I shall hang down my head when I am told it. But I cherish, too, the consolatory hope that I shall be able to tell them that I had an old and learned friend whom I would put above all the sweepings of their hall, who was of a different opinion, who had derived his ideas of civil liberty from the purest fountains of Athens and of Rome, who had fed the youthful vigor of his studious mind with the theoretic knowledge of their wisest philosophers and statesmen, and who had refined the the-

ory into the quick and exquisite sensibility of moral instinct, by contemplating the practice of their most illustrious examples; by dwelling on the sweet-souled piety of Cimon; on the anticipated Christianity of Socrates; on the gallant and pathetic patriotism of Epaminondas; on that pure austerity of Fabricius, whom to move from his integrity would have been more difficult than to have pushed the sun from his course. I would add that if he had seemed to hesitate, it was but for a moment; that his hesitation was like the passing cloud that floats across the morning sun and hides it from the view, and does so for a moment hide it by involving the spectator without even approaching the face of the luminary; and this soothing hope I draw from the dearest and tenderest recollections of my life, from the remembrance of those Attic nights, and those refections of the gods which we have spent with those admired and respected and beloved companions who have gone before us;—over whose ashes the most precious tears of Ireland have been shed; yes, my good lord, I see you do not forget them; I see their sacred forms passing in sad review before your memory; I see your pained and softened fancy recalling those happy meetings, when the innocent enjoyment of social mirth expanded into the nobler warmth of social virtue; and the horizon of the board became enlarged into the horizon of man; when the swelling heart conceived and communicated the pure and generous purpose,— when my slenderer and younger taper imbibed its borrowed light from the more matured and redundant fountain of yours. Yes, my lord, we can remember those nights without any other regret than that they can never more return, for—

> "We spent them not in toys, or lust, or wine;
> But search of deep philosophy,
> Wit, eloquence, and poesy,
> Arts which I lov'd; for they, my friend, were thine."

But, my lords, to return to a subject from which to have thus far departed, I think, may not be wholly without excuse. The express object of the forty-fourth was to send persons from places where they were not triable by law, back to the places that had jurisdiction to try them. And in those very words does Mr. Justice Blackstone observe on the thirteenth of the King, that it was made to prevent impunity by escape, by giving a power of "sending back" such offenders as had so escaped.

This topic of argument would now naturally claim its place in the present discussion. I mention it now that it might not be supposed that I meant to pretermit so important a consideration. And I only mention it, because it will connect itself with a subsequent head of this inquiry in a manner more forcibly applicable to the object; when, I think I may venture to say, it will appear to demonstration, that if the offense charged upon the defendant be triable at all, it is triable in Ireland and no where else; and of course that the prosecutors are acting in direct violation of the statute, when they seek to transport him from a place where he can be tried into another country that can have no possible jurisdiction over him.

Let us now, my lords, examine the next position contended for by those learned prosecutors. Having labored to prove that the act applies not merely to capital crimes, but to all offenses whatsoever; having labored to show that an act for preventing impunity by escape extends to cases, not only where there was no escape, but where escape in fact was physically impossible, they proceed to put forward boldly a doctrine which no lawyer, I do not hesitate to say it, in Westminster Hall would have the folly or the temerity to advance; that is, that the defendant may, by construction of law, be guilty of the offense in Westminster, though he should never have passed within its limits till he was sent thither to be tried. With what a fatal and inexorable uniformity do the tempers and characters of men domineer over their actions and conduct! How clearly must an Englishman, if by chance there be any now listening to us, discern the motives and principles that dictated the odious persecutions of 1794 reassuming their operations; forgetting that public spirit by which they were frustrated; unappalled by fear, undeterred by shame, and returning again to the charge; the same wild and impious nonsense of constructive criminality, the same execrable application of the ill-understood rules of a vulgar, clerk-like, and illiterate equity, to the sound and plain and guarded maxims of the criminal law of England,—the purest, the noblest, the chastest system of distributive justice that was ever venerated by the wise or perverted by the foolish, or that the children of men in any age or climate of the world have ever yet beheld; the same instruments, the same movements, the same artists, the same doctrines, the same doctors, the same servile and infuriate contempt of humanity, and persecution of freedom; the same shadows of

IV—96

the varying hour that extend or contract their length, as the beam of a rising or sinking sun plays upon the gnomon of self-interest! How demonstratively does the same appetite for mice authenticate the identity of the transformed princess that had once been a cat.

But it seems as if the whole order and arrangement of the moral and the physical world had been contrived for the instruction of man, and to warn him that he is not immortal. In every age, in every country, do we see the natural rise, advancement, and decline of virtue and of science. So it has been in Greece, in Rome; so it must be, I fear, the fate of England. In science, the point of its maturity and manhood is the commencement of its old age; the race of writers and thinkers and reasoners passes away and gives place to a succession of men that can neither write, nor think, nor reason. The Hales, the Holts, and the Somers shed a transient light upon mankind, but are soon extinct and disappear, and give place to a superficial and overweening generation of laborious and strenuous idlers,—of silly scholiasts, of wrangling mooters, of prosing garrulists, who explore their darkling ascent upon the steps of science, by the balustrade of cases and manuscripts, who calculate their depth by their darkness, and fancy they are profound because they feel they are perplexed. When the race of the Palladios is extinct, you may expect to see a clumsy hod-man collected beneath the shade of his shoulders,

ανηρ ηυεςτε μεγαστε
Εξοχος ανθρωπων κεφαλην και ευρεας ωμους,

affecting to fling a builder's glance upon the temple, on the proportion of its pillars; and to pass a critic's judgment on the doctrine that should be preached within them.

Let it not, my lords, be considered amiss, that I take this up rather as an English than an Irish question. It is not merely because we have no Habeas Corpus law in existence (the antiquarian may read of it, though we do not enjoy it); it is not merely because my mind refuses to itself the delusion of imaginary freedom, and shrinks from the meanness of affecting an indignant haughtiness of spirit that belongs not to our condition, that I am disposed to argue it as an English question; but it is because I am aware that we have now a community of interest and of destiny that we never had before—because I am aware,

that, blended as we now are, the liberty of man must fall where it is highest, or rise where it is lowest, till it find its common level in the common empire—and because, also, I wish that Englishmen may see that we are conscious that nothing but mutual benevolence and sympathy can support the common interest that should bind us against the external or the intestine foe; and that we are willing, whenever the common interest is attacked, to make an honest and animated resistance, as in a common cause, and with as cordial and tender anxiety for their safety as for our own.

Let me now briefly, because no subject can be shorter or plainer, consider the principle of local jurisdictions, and constructive crimes.

A man is bound to obedience, and punishable for disobedience of laws: Firstly, because, by living within their jurisdiction, he avails himself of their protection; and this is no more than the reciprocality of protection and allegiance on a narrower scale; and, secondly, because, by so living within their jurisdiction, he has the means of knowing them, and cannot be excused because of his ignorance of them I should be glad to know, upon the authority of what manuscript, of what pocket-case, the soundness of these principles can be disputed. I should be glad to know upon what known principle of English law, a Chinese or a Laplander can be kidnaped into England and arraigned for a crime which he committed under the pole, to the injury of a country which he had never seen—in violation of a law which he had never known, and to which he could not owe obedience—and, perhaps, for an act, the nonperformance of which he might have forfeited his liberty or his life to the laws of that country which he was bound to know and was bound to obey. Very differently did our ancestors think of that subject. They thought it essential to justice that the jurisdiction of criminal law should be local and defined; that no man should be triable but there, where he was accused of having actually committed the offense; where the character of the prosecutor, where his own character was known, as well as the characters of the witnesses produced against him; and where he had the authority of legal process to enforce the attendance of witnesses for his defense. They were too simple to know anything of the equity of criminal law. Poor Bracton or Fleta would have stared if you had asked them: "What, gentlemen, do you mean to say that such a crime as this

shall escape from punishment?" Their answer would have been, no doubt, very simple and very foolish. They would have said: "We know there are many actions that we think bad actions, which yet are not punishable, because not triable by law; and that are not triable, because of the local limits of criminal jurisdictions." And, my lords, to show with what a religious scrupulosity the locality of jurisdictions was observed, you have an instance in the most odious of all offenses, treason only excepted —I mean the crime of willful murder. By the common law, if a man in one county procured a murder to be committed which was afterwards actually committed in another, such procurer could not be tried in either jurisdiction, because the crime was not completed in either. This defect was remedied by the act of Edward VI. which made the author of the crime amenable to justice. But in what jurisdiction did it make him amenable? Was it there where the murder was actually perpetrated? By no means, but there only where he had been guilty of the procurement, and where alone his accessorial offense was completed. And here you have the authority of Parliament for this abstract position, that where a man living in one jurisdiction does an act, in consequence of which a crime is committed within another jurisdiction, he is by law triable only where his own personal act of procurement was committed, and not there where the procured or projected crime actually took effect. In answer to these known authorities of common law, has any statute, has a single decision or even dictum of a court, been adduced? Or, in an age when the pastry cooks and snuff-shops have been defrauded of their natural right to these compositions that may be useful without being read, has even a single manuscript been offered to show the researches of these learned prosecutors, or to support their cause? No, my lords; there has not.

I said, my lords, that this was a fruit from the same tree that produced the stupid and wicked prosecutions of 1794: let me not be supposed to say it is a mere repetition of that attempt, without any additional aggravation. In 1794, the design, and odious enough it was, was confined to the doctrine of constructive guilt, but it did not venture upon the atrocious outrage of a substituted jurisdiction; the Englishman was tried on English ground, where he was known, where he could procure his witnesses, where he had lived, and where he was accused of a crime, whether actual or constructive, but the locality of the trial defeated the infernal malice of those prosecutions. The speeches of half the natural day, where every juryman had his hour, were the knell of sleep, but they were not the knell of death. The project was exposed, and the destined victims were saved. A piece so damned could not safely be produced again on the same stage. It was thought wise, therefore, to let some little time pass, and then to let its author produce it on some distant provincial theatre for his own benefit, and at his own expense and hazard. To drag an English judge from his bench, or an English member of parliament from the Senate, and in the open day, in the city of London, to strap him to the roof of a mail coach, or pack him up in a wagon, or hand him over to an Irish bailiff, with a rope tied about his leg, to be goaded forward like an ox, on his way to Ireland, to be there tried for a constructive misdemeanor, would be an experiment, perhaps, not very safe to be attempted. These Merlins, therefore, thought it prudent to change the scene of their sorcery.

Modo Romæ, modo ponit Athenis!

The people of England might, perhaps, enter into the feelings of such an exhibition with an officiousness of sympathy, not altogether for the benefit of the contrivers—

Nec natos coram populo Medea trucidet—

and it was thought wise to try the second production before spectators whose necks were pliant, and whose hearts were broken; where every man who dared to refuse his worship to the golden calf would have the furnace before his eyes and think that it was at once useless and dangerous to speak, and discreet, at least, if it were not honest, to be silent. I cannot deny that it was prudent to try an experiment, that, if successful, must reduce an Englishman to a state of slavery more abject and forlorn than that of the helots of Sparta, or the negroes of your plantations—for see, my lords, the extent of the construction now broadly and directly contended for at your bar. The King's peace in Ireland, it seems, is distinct from his peace in England, and both are distinct from his peace in Scotland; and, of course, the same act may be a crime against each distinct peace, and severally and successively punishable in each country—so much more inveterate is the criminality of a constructive than of an actual offense. So that the same man for the same act against laws

that he never heard of may be punished in Ireland, be then sent to England by virtue of the warrant of Mr. Justice Bell, indorsed by my Lord Ellenborough, and, after having his health, his hopes, and his property destroyed for his constructive offenses against his Majesty's peace in Ireland, and his Majesty's peace in England, he may find that his Majesty's peace in the Orkneys has, after all, a vested remainder in his carcass; and, if it be the case of a libel, for the full time and term of fourteen years from the day of his conviction before the Scottish jurisdiction, to be fully completed and determined. Is there, my lords, can there be a man who hears me, that does not feel that such a construction of such a law would put every individual in society under the despotical dominion, would reduce him to be the despicable chattel of those most likely to abuse their power, the profligate of the higher, and the abandoned of the lower orders; to the remorseless malice of a vindictive minister, to the servile instrumentality of a trading justice? Can any man who hears me conceive any possible case of abduction, of rape, or of murder, that may not be perpetrated under the construction now shamelessly put forward? Let us suppose a case: By this construction a person in England, by procuring a misdemeanor to be committed in Ireland, is constructively guilty in Ireland, and, of course, triable in Ireland—let us suppose that Mr. Justice Bell receives, or says he receives, information that the lady of an English nobleman wrote a letter to an Irish chambermaid, counseling her to steal a row of pins from an Irish peddler, and that the said row of pins was, in consequence of such advice and counsel, actually stolen, against the Irish peace of our lord the King; suppose my Lord Ellenborough, knowing the signature, and reverencing the virtue of his tried and valued colleague, indorses this warrant; is it not clear as the sun that this English lady may, in the dead of night, be taken out of her bed and surrendered to the mercy of two or three Irish bailiffs, if the captain that employed them should happen to be engaged in any cotemporary adventure nearer to his heart, without the possibility of any legal authority interposing to save her, to be matronized in a journey by land and a voyage by sea, by such modest and respectable guardians, to be dealt with during the journey as her companions might think proper—and to be dealt with after by the worshipful correspondent of the noble and learned lord, Mr. Justice Bell, according to law? I can, without

much difficulty, my lords, imagine that after a year or two had been spent in accounts current, in drawing and redrawing for human flesh, between our worthy Bells and Medlicots on this side of the water, and their noble or their ignoble correspondents on the other, that they might meet to settle their accounts, and adjust their balances; I can conceive that the items might not be wholly destitute of curiosity:—Brother B., I take credit for the body of an English patriot. Brother E., I set off against it that of an Irish judge. Brother B., I charge you in account with three English bishops. Brother E., I set off Mrs. M'Lean and two of her chickens; petticoat against petticoat. Brother B., I have sent you the body of a most intractable disturber, a fellow that has had the impudence to give a threshing to Bonaparte himself; I have sent you Sir Sidney—Dearest brother E. But I see my learned opponents smile—I see their meaning. I may be told that I am putting imaginary and ludicrous, but not probable, and therefore, not supposable cases. But I answer, that reasoning would be worthy only of a slave, and disgraceful to a freeman. I answer, that the condition and essence of rational freedom is, not that the subject probably will not be abused, but that no man in the State shall be clothed with any discretionary power, under the color and pretext of which he can dare to abuse him. As to probability I answer that in the mind of man there is no more instigating temptation to the most remorseless oppression than the rancor and malice of irritated pride and wounded vanity. To the argument of improbability, I answer, the very fact, the very question in debate, nor to such answer can I see the possibility of any reply, save that the prosecutors are so heartily sick of the point of view into which they have put themselves by their prosecution, that they are not likely again to make a similar experiment. But when I see any man fearless of power, because it possibly, or probably, may not be exercised upon him, I am astonished at his fortitude; I am astonished at the tranquil courage of any man who can quietly see that a loaded cannon is brought to bear upon him, and that a fool is sitting at its touch-hole with a lighted match in his hand. And yet, my lords, upon a little reflection, what is it, after what we have seen, that should surprise us, however it may shock us? What have the last ten years of the world been employed in, but in destroying the landmarks of rights and duties and obligations; in substituting sounds in the place of sense; in substituting

a vile and canting methodism in the place of social duty and practical honor; in suffering virtue to evaporate into phrase, and morality into hypocrisy and affectation? We talk of the violations of Hamburg or of Baden; we talk of the despotical and remorseless barbarian who tramples on the common privileges of the human being; who, in defiance of the most known and sacred rights, issues the brutal mandate of usurped authority; who brings his victim by force within the limits of a jurisdiction to which he never owed obedience, and there butchers him for a constructive offense. Does it not seem as if it were a contest whether we should be more scurrilous in invective, or more atrocious in imitation? Into what a condition must we be sinking, when we have the front to select as the subjects of our obloquy, those very crimes which we have flung behind us in the race of profligate rivalry!

My lords, the learned counsel for the prosecutors have asserted that this act of the forty-fourth of the King extends to all offenses, no matter how long or previously to it they may have been committed. The words are: "That from and after the first day of August, 1804, if any person, etc., shall escape, etc." Now, certainly nothing could be more convenient for the purpose of the prosecutors than to dismiss, as they have done, the words, "escape and go into," altogether. If those words could have been saved from the ostracism of the prosecutors, they must have designated some act of the offenders, upon the happening or doing of which the operation of the statute might commence; but the temporary bar of these words they waive by the equity of their own construction, and thereby make it a retrospective law; and having so construed it a manifestly *ex post facto* law, they tell you it is no such thing, because it creates no new offense, and only makes the offender amenable who was not so before. The law professes to take effect only from and after the first of August, 1804. Now for eighteen months before that day, it is clear that Mr. Johnson could not be removed, by any power existing, from his country and his dwellings; but at the moment the act took effect, it is made to operate upon an alleged offense, committed, if at all, confessedly eighteen months before. But another word as to the assertion that it is not *ex post facto*, because it creates no new crime, but only makes the party amenable. The force of that argument is precisely this: If this act inflicted deportation on the defendant by way of punishment after his guilt had been established by conviction, that would, no doubt, be tyrannical, because *ex post facto;* but here he suffers the deportation, while the law is bound to suppose him perfectly innocent; and that only by way of process to make him amenable, not by way of punishment: and surely he cannot be so unreasonable as not to feel the force of the distinction.

How naturally, too, we find similar outrages resort to similar justifications! Such exactly was the defense of the forcible entry into Baden. Had that been a brutal violence, committed in perpetration of the murder of the unfortunate victim, perhaps very scrupulous moralists might find something in it to disapprove; but his imperial Majesty was too delicately tender of the rights of individuals and of nations to do any act so flagrant as that would be, if done in that point of view; but his imperial Majesty only introduced a clause of *ne omittas* into his warrant, whereby the worshipful Bells and Medlicots that executed it were authorized to disregard any supposed fantastical privilege of nations that gave sanctuary to traitors; and he did that from the purest motives; from as disinterested a love of justice as that of the present prosecutors, and not at all in the way of an *ex post facto* law, but merely as process to bring him in and make him amenable to the competent and unquestionable jurisdiction of the *Bois de Boulogne.* Such are the wretched sophistries to which men are obliged to have recourse, when their passions have led them to do what no thinking man can regard without horror; what they themselves cannot look at without shame; and for which no legitimate reasoning can suggest either justification or excuse. Such are the principles of criminal justice, on which the first experiment is made in Ireland; but I venture to pledge myself to my fellow-subjects of Great Britain, that if the experiment succeed, they shall soon have the full benefit of that success. I venture to promise them, they shall soon have their full measure of this salutary system for making men "amenable," heaped and running over into their bosoms.

There now remains, my lords, one, and only one topic of this odious subject, to call for observation. The offense here appears by the return and the affidavits to be a libel upon the Irish government, published by construction in Westminster. Of the constructive commission of a crime in one place by an agent, who, perhaps, at the moment of the act, is in another hemisphere, you have already enough; here. therefore, we will con-

sider it simply as an alleged libel upon the Irish government; and whether, as such, it is a charge coming within the meaning of the statute, and for which a common justice of peace in one kingdom is empowered to grant a warrant for conveying the person accused for trial into the other. Your lordships will observe that in the whole catalogue of crimes for which a justice of peace may grant a warrant, there is not one that imposes upon him the necessity of deciding upon any matter of law, involving the smallest doubt or difficulty whatsoever. In treason, the overt act; in felony, whether capital or not, the act; in misdemeanors, the simple act; the dullest justice can understand what is a breach of the peace, and can describe it in his warrant. It is no more than the description of a fact which the informer has seen and sworn to. But no libel comes within such a class, for it is decided over and over that a libel is no breach of the peace: and upon that ground it was that Mr. Wilkes in 1763 was allowed the privilege of parliament, which privilege does not extend to any breach of the peace.

See, then, my lords, what a task is imposed upon a justice of the peace, if he be to grant such a warrant upon such a charge; he no doubt may easily comprehend the allegation of the informer as to the fact of writing the supposed libel. In deciding whether the facts sworn amounted to a publication or not, I should have great apprehension of his fallibility, but if he got over those difficulties, I should much fear for his competency to decide what given facts would amount to a constructive publication. But even if he did solve that question, a point on which, if I were a justice, I should acknowledge myself most profoundly ignorant, he would then have to proceed to a labor in which I believe no man could expect him to succeed; that is, how far the paper sworn to was, in point of legal construction, libellous or not. I trust this court will never be prevailed upon to sanction, by its decision, a construction that would give to such a set of men a power so incompatible with every privilege of liberty or of law. To say it would give an irresistible power of destroying the liberty of the press in Ireland, would, I am aware, be but a silly argument, where such a thing has long ceased to exist; but I have for that very reason a double interest now, as a subject of the empire, in that noble guardian of liberty in the sister nation. When my own lamp is broken, I have a double interest in the preservation of my neighbor's. But if every man in Eng-

land, who dares to observe, no matter how honestly and justly, upon the conduct of Irish ministers, is liable to be torn from his family, and dragged hither by an Irish bailiff, for a constructive libel against the Irish government, and upon the authority of an Irish warrant, no man can be such a fool as not to see the consequence. The inevitable consequence is this: that at this awful crisis, when the weal, not of this empire only, but of the whole civilized world, depends on the steady faith and the consolidated efforts of these two countries; when Ireland is become the right arm of England; when everything that draws the common interest and affection closer gives the hope of life; when everything that has even a tendency to relax that sentiment is a symptom of death,—even at such a crisis may the rashness or folly of those intrusted with its management so act as to destroy its internal prosperity and repose, and lead it into the twofold, fatal error of mistaking its natural enemies for its friends, and its natural friends for its natural enemies; without any man being found so romantically daring as to give notice of the approaching destruction.

My lords, I suppose the learned counsel will do here what they have done in the other court; they will assert that this libel is not triable here; and they will argue that so false and heinous a production surely ought to be triable somewhere. As to the first position, I say the law is directly against them. From a very early stage of the discussion, the gentlemen for the prosecution thought it wise for their clients to take a range into the facts much more at large than they appeared on the return to the writ, or even by the affidavits that have been made; and they have done this to take the opportunity of aggravating the guilt of the defendant, and at the same time of panegyrizing their clients; they have therefore not argued upon the libel generally as a libel, but they thought it prudent to appear perfectly acquainted with the charges which it contains; they have therefore assumed that it relates to the transactions of the twenty-third of July, 1803, and that the guilt of the defendant was that he wrote that letter in Ireland, which was afterwards published in England, not by himself but by some other persons. Now, on these facts nothing can be clearer than that he is triable here. If it be a libel, and if he wrote it here, and it was published in England, most manifestly there must have been a precedent publication, not merely by construction of law, in Ireland, but a

publication by actual fact; and for this plain reason, if you for a moment suppose the libel in his possession (and if he did in fact write it, I can scarcely conceive that it was not, unless he wrote it perhaps by construction), there were no physical means of transmitting it to England that would not amount to a publication here; because, if he put it into the post office, or gave it to a messenger to carry thither, that would be complete evidence of publication against him; so would the mere possession of the paper in the hands of the witness who appeared and produced it, be perfect evidence, if not accounted for or contradicted, to charge him with the publication; so that really I am surprised how gentlemen could be betrayed into positions so utterly without foundation. They would have done just as usefully for their clients if they had admitted, what every man knows to be the fact, that is, that they durst not bring the charge before an Irish jury. The facts of that period were too well understood. The Irish public might have looked at such a prosecution with the most incredulous detestation; and if they had been so indiscreet as to run the risk of coming before an Irish jury, instead of refuting the charges against them as a calumny, they would have exposed themselves to the peril of establishing the accusation, and of raising the character of the man whom they had the heart to destroy because he had dared to censure them. Let not the learned gentlemen, I pray, suppose me so ungracious as to say that this publication, which has given so much pain to their clients, is actually true; I cannot personally know it to be so, nor do I say so, nor is this the place or the occasion to say that it is so. I mean only to speak positively to the question before you which is matter of law. But as the gentlemen themselves thought it meet to pronounce a eulogy on their clients, I thought it rather unseemly not to show that I attended to them; I have most respectfully done so; I do not contradict any praise of their virtues or their wisdom, and I only wish to add my very humble commendation of their prudence and discretion in not bringing the trial of the present libel before a jury of this country.

The learned counsel have not been contented with abusing this libel as a production perfectly known to them; but they have wandered into the regions of fancy. No doubt the other judges, to whom those pathetic flights of forensic sensibility were addressed, must have been strongly affected by them. The learned gentlemen have supposed a variety of possible cases. They have supposed cases of the foulest calumniators aspersing the most virtuous ministers. Whether such supposed cases have been suggested by fancy or by fact, it is not for me to decide; but I beg leave to say that it is as allowable to us as to them to put cases of supposition:—

—— *Cur ego si fingere pauca*
Possum, invidear?

Let me, then, my lords, put an imaginary case of a different kind. Let me suppose that a great personage, intrusted with the safety of the citadel (meaning and wishing perhaps well, but misled by those lacquered vermin that swarm in every great hall), leaves it so loosely guarded that nothing but the gracious interposition of Providence has saved it from the enemy. Let me suppose another great personage going out of his natural department, and, under the supposed authority of high station, disseminating such doctrines as tend to root up the foundation of society; to destroy all confidence between man and man; and to impress the great body of the people with a delusive and desperate opinion, that their religion could dissolve or condemn the sacred obligations that bind them to their country, and that their rulers have no reliance upon their faith, and are resolved to shut the gates of mercy against them.

Suppose a good and virtuous man saw that such doctrines must necessarily torture the nation into such madness and despair, as to render them unfit for any system of mild or moderate government; that if, on one side, bigotry or folly shall inject their veins with fire, such a fever must be kindled as can be allayed only by keeping a stream of blood perpetually running from the other, and that the horrors of martial law must become the direful but inevitable consequence. In such a case, let me ask you what would be his indispensable duty? It would be to avert such dreadful dangers by exposing the conduct of such persons, by holding up the folly of such bigoted and blind enthusiasm to condign derision and contempt, and painfully would he feel that on such an occasion he must dismiss all forms and ceremonies, and that to do his duty with effect he must do it without mercy. He should also foresee that a person so acting, when he returned to those to whom he was responsible, would endeavor to justify himself by defaming the country which he had abused—for calumny is the natural defense of the oppressor; he should, there-

fore, so reduce his personal credit to its just standard, that his assertions might find no more belief than they deserved. Were such a person to be looked on as a mere private individual, charity and good-nature might suggest not a little in his excuse. An inexperienced man, new to the world, and in the honeymoon of preferment, would run no small risk of having his head turned in Ireland. The people in our island are by nature penetrating, sagacious, artful, and comic—*natio comœda est*. In no country under heaven would an ass be more likely to be hoodwinked, by having his ears drawn over his eyes, and acquire that fantastical alacrity that makes dullness disposable to the purpose of humorous malice, or interested imposture. In Ireland, a new great man could get the freedom of a science as easily as of a corporation, and become a doctor, by construction, of the whole Encyclopædia, and great allowance might be made under such circumstances for indiscretions and mistakes, as long as they related only to himself; but the moment they become public mischiefs, they lose all pretensions to excuse—the very ambition of incapacity is a crime not to be forgiven, and however painful it may be to inflict, it must be remembered that mercy to the delinquent would be treason to the public.

I can the more easily understand the painfulness of the conflict between charity and duty, because at this moment I am laboring under it myself; and I feel it the more acutely, because I am confident that the paroxysms of passion that have produced these public discussions have been bitterly repented of. I think, also, that I should not act fairly if I did not acquit my learned opponents of all share whatsoever in this prosecution—they have too much good sense to have advised it; on the contrary, I can easily suppose Mr. Attorney-General sent for to give counsel and comfort to his patient; and after hearing no very concise detail of his griefs, his resentments, and his misgivings, methinks I hear the answer that he gives, after a pause of sympathy and reflection: "No, sir, don't proceed in such a business; you will only expose yourself to scorn in one country, and to detestation in the other. You know you durst not try him here, where the whole kingdom would be his witness. If you should attempt to try him there, where he can have no witness, you will have both countries upon your back. An English jury would never find him guilty. You will only confirm the charge against yourself; and be the victim of an impotent, abortive malice. If you should

have any ulterior project against him, you will defeat that also; for those that might otherwise concur in the design will be shocked and ashamed of the violence and folly of such a tyrannical proceeding, and will make a merit of protecting him and of leaving you in the lurch. What you say of your own feelings, I can easily conceive. You think you have been much exposed by those letters; but then remember, my dear sir, that a man can claim the privilege of being made ridiculous or hateful by no publications but his own.

Vindictive critics have their rights, as well as bad authors. The thing is bad enough at best; but if you go on, you will make it worse—it will be considered an attempt to degrade the Irish bench and the Irish bar; you are not aware what a nest of hornets you are disturbing. One inevitable consequence you don't foresee; you will certainly create the very thing in Ireland that you are so afraid of—a newspaper; think of that, and keep yourself quiet; and, in the meantime, console yourself with reflecting that no man is laughed at for a long time: every day will procure some new ridicule that must supersede him." Such, I am satisfied, was the counsel given; but I have no apprehension for my client, because it was not taken. Even if it should be his fate to be surrendered to his keepers, to be torn from his family; to have his obsequies performed by torch light; to be carried to a foreign land, and to a strange tribunal, where no witness can attest his innocence; where no voice that he ever heard can be raised in his defense; where he must stand mute, not of his own malice, but the malice of his enemies—yes, even so, I see nothing for him to fear. That all gracious Being that shields the feeble from the oppressor will fill his heart with hope and confidence and courage; his sufferings will be his armor, and his weakness will be his strength; he will find himself in the hands of a brave, a just, and a generous nation; he will find that the bright examples of her Russels and her Sidneys have not been lost to her children; they will behold him with sympathy and respect, and his persecutors with shame and abhorrence; they will feel, too, that what is then his situation may to-morrow be their own—but their first tear will be shed for him, and the second only for themselves; their hearts will melt in his acquittal; they will convey him kindly and fondly to their shore; and he will return in triumph to his country, to the threshold of his sacred home, and to the weeping welcome of his

delighted family; he will find that the darkness of a dreary and a lingering night hath at length passed away, and that joy cometh in the morning. No, my lords, I have no fear for the ultimate safety of my client. Even in these very acts of brutal violence that have been committed against him, do I hail the flattering hope of final advantage to him, and of better days and more prosperous fortune for this afflicted country—that country of which I have so often abandoned all hope, and which I have been so often determined to quit forever.

Sæpe vale dicto multa sum deinde locutus
Et quasi discedens oscula summa dabam,
Indulgens animo, pes tardus erat.

But I am reclaimed from that infidel despair—I am satisfied that while a man is suffered to live, it is an intimation from Providence that he has some duty to discharge, which it is mean and criminal to decline; had I been guilty of that ignominious flight, and gone to pine in the obscurity of some distant retreat, even in that grave I should have been haunted by those passions by which my life had been agitated—

Quæ cura vivos,
Eadem sequitur tellure repostos.

And, if the transactions of this day had reached me, I feel how my heart would have been agonized by the shame of the desertion; nor would my sufferings have been mitigated by a sense of the feebleness of that aid, or the smallness of that service which I could render or withdraw. They would have been aggravated by the consciousness that, however feeble or worthless they were, I should not have dared to thieve them from my country. I have repented; I have stayed; and I am at once rebuked and rewarded by the happier hopes that I now entertain. In the anxious sympathy of the public, in the anxious sympathy of my learned brethren, do I catch the happy presage of a brighter fate for Ireland. They see that within these sacred walls, the cause of liberty and of man may be pleaded with boldness and heard with favor. I am satisfied they will never forget the great trust, of which they alone are now the remaining depositaries. While they continue to cultivate a sound and literate philosophy, a mild and tolerating Christianity, and to make both the sources of a just and liberal and constitutional jurisprudence, I see everything for us to hope. Into their hands, therefore, with the most affectionate confidence in their virtue, do I commit these precious hopes. Even I may live long enough yet to see the approaching completion, if not the perfect accomplishment of them. Pleased shall I then resign the scene to fitter actors; pleased shall I lay down my wearied head to rest, and say: "Lord, now lettest thou thy servant depart in peace, according to thy word; for mine eyes have seen thy salvation."

FOR PETER FINNERTY AND FREE SPEECH

(From the Speech at the Trial of Finnerty for Libel, December 22d, 1797)

I TELL you, therefore, gentlemen of the jury, it is not with respect to Mr. Orr, or Mr. Finnerty, that your verdict is now sought. You are called upon, on your oaths, to say that the government is wise and merciful—the people prosperous and happy; that military law ought to be continued; that the constitution could not with safety be restored to Ireland; and that the statements of a contrary import by your advocates, in either country, are libellous and false.

I tell you these are the questions; and I ask you, if you can have the front to give the expected answer in the face of a community who know the country as well as you do. Let me ask you how you could reconcile with such a verdict, the gaols, the tenders, the gibbets, the conflagrations, the murders, the proclamations that we hear of every day in the streets, and see every day in the country. What are the prosecutions of the learned counsel himself, circuit after circuit? Merciful God! what is the state of Ireland, and where shall you find the wretched inhabitant of this land? You may find him, perhaps, in a gaol, the only place of security—I had almost said of ordinary habitation! If you do not find him there, you may see him flying with his family from the flames of his own dwelling—lighted to his dungeon by the conflagration of his hovel; or you may find his bones bleaching on the green fields of his country; or you may find him tossing on the surface of the ocean, and mingling his groans with those tempests, less savage than his persecutors, that drift him to a returnless distance from his family and his home, without charge, or trial, or sentence. Is this a foul misrepresentation? Or can you, with these facts ringing in your ears, and

IV—97

staring in your face, say, upon your oaths, they do not exist? You are called upon, in defiance of shame, of truth, of honor, to deny the sufferings under which you groan, and to flatter the persecution that tramples you under foot.

Gentlemen, I am not accustomed to speak of circumstances of this kind; and though familiarized as I have been to them, when I come to speak of them, my power fails me—my voice dies within me. I am not able to call upon you. It is now I ought to have strength; it is now I ought to have energy and voice. But I have none; I am like the unfortunate state of the country, —perhaps like you. This is the time in which I ought to speak, if I can, or be dumb forever; in which, if you do not speak as you ought, you ought to be dumb forever.

But the learned gentleman is further pleased to say that the traverser has charged the Government with the encouragement of informers. This, gentlemen, is another small fact that you are to deny at the hazard of your souls and upon the solemnity of your oaths. You are upon your oaths to say to the sister country that the government of Ireland uses no such abominable instruments of destruction as informers. Let me ask you honestly, What do you feel when, in my hearing, when, in the face of this audience, you are called upon to give a verdict that every man of us, and every man of you, know, by the testimony of your own eyes, to be utterly and absolutely false? I speak not now of the public proclamation for informers, with a promise of secrecy and of extravagant reward; I speak not of the fate of those horrid wretches who have been so often transferred from the table to the dock, and from the dock to the pillory; I speak of what your own eyes have seen, day after day, during the course of this commission, from the box where you are now sitting; the number of horrid miscreants who acknowledged upon their oaths that they had come from the seat of government—from the very chambers of the Castle—where they had been worked upon by the fear of death and the hope of compensation, to give evidence against their fellows; that the mild, the wholesome, and merciful councils of this government are holden over these catacombs of living death, where the wretch that is buried a man lies till his heart has time to fester and dissolve, and is then dug up a witness!

Is this a picture created by a hag-ridden fancy, or is it a fact? Have you not seen him, after his resurrection from that region

of death and corruption, make his appearance upon the table, the living image of life in death, and the supreme arbiter of both? Have you not marked when he entered how the stormy wave of the multitude retired at his approach? Have you not seen how the human heart bowed to the supremacy of his power, in the undissembled homage of deferential horror? how his glance, like the lightning of heaven, seemed to rive the body of the accused and mark it for the grave, while his voice warned the devoted wretch of woe and death—a death which no innocence can escape, no art elude, no force resist, no antidote prevent? There was an antidote—a juror's oath!—but even that adamantine chain that bound the integrity of man to the throne of eternal justice is solved and molten in the breath that issues from the informer's mouth; conscience swings from her moorings, and the appalled and affrighted juror consults his own safety in the surrender of the victim:—

Et quæ sibi quisque timebat,
Unius in miseri exitium conversa tulere.

Informers are worshiped in the temple of justice, even as the devil has been worshiped by Pagans and savages; even so in this wicked country is the informer an object of judicial idolatry; even so is he soothed by the music of human groans; even so is he placated and incensed by the fumes and by the blood of human sacrifices.

THE DIVERSIONS OF A MARQUIS

(From the Speech in Behalf of Rev. Charles Massy against the Marquis of Headford, who Eloped with Mrs. Massy; at the Ennis County Assizes, July 27th, 1804)

IN THE middle of the day, at the moment of Divine worship, when the miserable husband was on his knees, directing the prayers and thanksgiving of his congregation to their God, that moment did the remorseless adulterer choose to carry off the deluded victim from her husband, from her child, from her character, from her happiness, as if, not content to leave his crime confined to its miserable aggravations, unless he gave it a cast and color of factitious sacrilege and impiety. Oh! how happy had it been when he arrived at the bank of the river

with the ill-fated fugitive, ere yet he had committed her to that boat, of which, like the fabled barque of Styx, the exile was eternal—how happy at that moment, so teeming with misery and shame, if you, my lord, had met him, and could have accosted him in the character of that good genius which had abandoned him! How impressively might you have pleaded the cause of the father, of the child, of the mother, and even of the worthless defendant himself! You would have said, "Is this the requital that you are about to make for respect, and kindness, and confidence in your honor? Can you deliberately expose this young man, in the bloom of life, with all his hopes before him? Can you expose him, a wretched outcast from society, to the scorn of a merciless world? Can you set him a drift upon the tempestous ocean of his own passions, at this early season when they are most headstrong; and can you cut him out from the moorings of those domestic obligations by whose cable he might ride at safety from their turbulence? Think of, if you can conceive it, what a powerful influence arises from the sense of home, from the sacred religion of the hearth in quelling the passions, in reclaiming the wanderings, in correcting the discords of the human heart; do not cruelly take from him the protection of these attachments. But if you have no pity for the father, have mercy, at least, upon his innocent and helpless child; do not condemn him to an education scandalous or neglected; do not strike him into that most dreadful of all human conditions, the orphanage that springs not from the grave, that falls not from the hand of Providence, or the stroke of death, but comes before its time, anticipated and inflicted by the remorseless cruelty of parental guilt." For the poor victim herself,—not yet immolated, —while yet balancing upon the pivot of her destiny, your heart could not be cold, nor your tongue be wordless. You would have said to him, "Pause, my lord, while there is yet a moment for reflection. What are your motives, what your views, what your prospects from what you are about to do? You are a married man, the husband of the most amiable and respectable of women; you cannot look to the chance of marrying this wretched fugitive; between you and such an event there are two sepulchres to pass. What are your inducements? Is it love, think you? No; do not give that name to any attraction you can find in the faded refuse of a violated bed. Love is a noble and generous passion; it can be founded only on a pure and ardent friendship, on an exalted respect, on an implicit confidence in its object. Search your heart, examine your judgment, do you find the semblance of any one of these sentiments to bind you to her? What could degrade a mind to which nature or education had given port, or stature, or character, into a friendship for her? Could you repose upon her faith? Look in her face, my lord; she is at this moment giving you the violation of the most sacred of human obligations at the pledge of her fidelity. She is giving you the most irrefragable proof that, as she is deserting her husband for you, so she would, without a scruple, abandon you for another. Do you anticipate any pleasure you might feel in the possible event of your becoming the parents of a common child? She is at this moment proving to you that she is as dead to the sense of parental as of conjugal obligation; and that she would abandon your offspring to-morrow with the same facility with which she now deserts her own. Look then at her conduct, as it is, as the world must behold it, blackened by every aggravation that can make it either odious or contemptible, and unrelieved by a single circumstance of mitigation that could palliate its guilt or retrieve it from abhorrence." . . .

"Here is not the case of an unmarried woman, with whom a pure and generous friendship may insensibly have ripened into a more serious attachment, until at last her heart became too deeply pledged to be reassumed. If so circumstanced, without any husband to betray, or child to desert, or motive to restrain, except what related solely to herself, her anxiety for your happiness made her overlook every other consideration and commit her history to your honor; in such a case (the strongest and the highest that man's imagination can suppose), in which you at least could see nothing but the most noble and disinterested sacrifice; in which you could find nothing but what claimed from you the most kind and exalted sentiment of tenderness and devotion and respect, and in which the most fastidious rigor would find so much more subject for sympathy than blame,—let me ask you, could you, even in that case, answer for your own justice and gratitude? I do not allude to the long and pitiful catalogue of paltry adventures, in which it seems your time has been employed,—the coarse and vulgar succession of casual connections, joyless, loveless, and unendeared; but do you not find upon your memory some trace of an engagement of the character I have sketched? Has not your sense of what you would

owe in such a case, and to such a woman, been at least once put to the test of experiment? Has it not once at least happened that such a woman, with all the resolution of strong faith, flung her youth, her hope, her beauty, her talent, upon your bosom, weighed you against the world, which she found but a feather in the scale, and took you as an equivalent? How did you then acquit yourself? Did you prove yourself worthy of the sacred trust reposed in you? Did your spirit so associate with hers as to leave her no room to regret the splendid and disinterested sacrifice she had made? Did her soul find a pillow in the tenderness of yours, and support in its firmness? Did you preserve her high in your own consciousness, proud in your admiration and friendship, and happy in your affection? You might have so acted, and the man that was worthy of her would have perished rather than not so act, as to make her delighted with having confided so sacred a trust to his honor. Did you so act? Did she feel that, however precious to your heart, she was still more exalted and honored in your reverence and respect? Or did she find you coarse and paltry, fluttering and unpurposed, unfeeling, and ungrateful? You found her a fair and blushing flower, its beauty and its fragrance bathed in the dews of heaven. Did you so tenderly transplant it as to preserve that beauty and fragrance unimpaired? Or did you so rudely cut it as to interrupt its nutriment, to waste its sweetness, to blast its beauty, to bow down its faded and sickly head? And did you at last fling it like 'a loathsome weed away'? If then to such a woman, so clothed with every title that could ennoble, and exalt, and endear her to the heart of man, you would be cruelly and capriciously deficient, how can a wretched fugitive like this, in every point her contrast, hope to find you just? Send her then away. Send her back to her home, to her child, to her husband, to herself." Alas, there was none to hold such language to this noble defendant; he did not hold it to himself. But he paraded his despicable prize in his own carriage, with his own retinue, his own servants—this veteran Paris hawked his enamored Helen from this western quarter of the island to a seaport in the eastern, crowned with the acclamations of a senseless and grinning rabble, glorying and delighted, no doubt, in the leering and scoffing admiration of grooms and ostlers and waiters as he passed.

AGAINST PENSIONS

(Delivered in the Irish Parliament, March 13th, 1786, in Support of a Bill Limiting Pensions)

I OBJECT to adjourning this bill to the first of August, because I perceive in the present disposition of the House that a proper decision will be made upon it this night. We have set out upon our inquiry in a manner so honorable, and so consistent, that we have reason to expect the happiest success, which I would not wish to see baffled by delay.

We began with giving the full affirmative of this House, that no grievance exists at all; we considered a simple matter of fact, and adjourned our opinion; or rather, we gave sentence on the conclusion, after having adjourned the premises. But I do begin to see a great deal of argument in what the learned baronet has said, and I beg gentlemen will acquit me of apostasy, if I offer some reasons why the bill should not be admitted to a second reading.

I am surprised that gentlemen have taken up such a foolish opinion as that our Constitution is maintained by its different component parts, mutually checking and controlling each other; they seem to think, with Hobbes, that a state of nature is a state of warfare, and that, like Mahomet's coffin, the Constitution is suspended between the attraction of different powers. My friends seem to think that the Crown should be restrained from doing wrong by a physical necessity, forgetting that if you take away from man all power to do wrong, you, at the same time, take away from him all merit of doing right; and, by making it impossible for men to run into slavery, you enslave them most effectually. But if, instead of the three different parts of our Constitution drawing forcibly in right lines, in different directions, they were to unite their power, and draw all one way, in one right line, how great would be the effect of their force, how happy the direction of this union! The present system is not only contrary to mathematical rectitude, but to public harmony; but if, instead of Privilege setting up his back to oppose Prerogative, he were to saddle his back and invite Prerogative to ride, how comfortably they might both jog along! and therefore it delights me to hear the advocates for the royal bounty flowing

freely and spontaneously and abundantly as Holywell in Wales. If the Crown grant double the amount of the revenue in pensions, they approve of their royal master, for he is the breath of their nostrils.

But we shall find that this complaisance, this gentleness between the Crown and its true servants, is not confined at home; it extends its influence to foreign powers. Our merchants have been insulted in Portugal, our commerce interdicted; what did the British lion do? Did he whet his tusks? Did he bristle up, and shake his mane? Did he roar? No; no such a thing; the gentle creature wagged his tail for six years at the court of Lisbon; and now we hear from the Delphic Oracle on the treasury bench, that he is wagging his tail in London to Chevalier Pinto, who, he hopes soon to be able to tell us, will allow his lady to entertain him as a lapdog; and when she does, no doubt the British factory will furnish some of their softest woolens to make a cushion for him to lie upon. But though the gentle beast has continued so long fawning and couching, I believe his vengeance will be great as it is slow, and that posterity, whose ancestors are yet unborn, will be surprised at the vengeance he will take!

This polyglot of wealth, this museum of curiosities, the pension list, embraces every link in the human chain, every description of men, women, and children, from the exalted excellence of a Hawke or a Rodney, to the debased situation of the lady who humbleth herself that she may be exalted. But the lessons it inculcates form its greatest perfection; it teacheth that sloth and vice may eat that bread which virtue and honesty may starve for after they have earned it. It teaches the idle and dissolute to look up for that support which they are too proud to stoop and earn. It directs the minds of men to an entire reliance on the ruling power of the State, who feed the ravens of the royal aviary that continually cry for food. It teaches them to imitate those saints on the pension list that are like the lilies of the field,—they toil not, neither do they spin, and yet are arrayed like Solomon in his glory. In fine, it teaches a lesson which, indeed, they might have learned from Epictetus, that it is sometimes good not to be over-virtuous; it shows, that in proportion as our distresses increase, the munificence of the Crown increases also; in proportion as our clothes are rent, the royal mantle is extended over us.

Notwithstanding that the pension list, like charity, covers a multitude of sins, give me leave to consider it as coming home to the Members of this House,—give me leave to say that the Crown in extending its charity, its liberality, its profusion, is laying a foundation for the independence of Parliament; for hereafter, instead of orators or patriots accounting for their conduct to such mean and unworthy persons as freeholders, they will learn to despise them, and look to the first man in the State; and they will, by so doing, have this security for their independence, that while any man in the kingdom has a shilling, they will not want one.

Suppose at any future period of time the boroughs of Ireland should decline from their present flourishing and prosperous state —suppose they should fall into the hands of men who would wish to drive a profitable commerce, by having Members of Parliament to hire or let; in such a case a secretary would find great difficulty, if the proprietors of Members should enter into a combination to form a monopoly; to prevent which, in time, the wisest way is to purchase up the raw material, young Members of Parliament, just rough from the grass; and when they are a little bitted, and he has got a pretty stud, perhaps of seventy, he may laugh at the slave merchant; some of them he may teach to sound through the nose, like a barrel organ; some, in the course of a few months, might be taught to cry, "Hear! hear!" some, "Chair! chair!" upon occasion,—though those latter might create a little confusion, if they were to forget whether they were calling inside or outside of those doors. Again he might have some so trained that he need only pull a string, and up gets a repeating Member; and if they were so dull that they could neither speak nor make orations (for they are different things), he might have them taught to dance, *pedibus ire in sententia*. This improvement might be extended; he might have them dressed in coats and shirts all of one color; and, of a Sunday, he might march them to church two by two, to the great edification of the people and the honor of the Christian religion; afterwards, like ancient Spartans, or the fraternity of Kilmainham, they might dine altogether in a large hall. Good heaven! what a sight to see them feeding in public, upon public viands, and talking of public subjects, for the benefit of the public! It is a pity they are not immortal; but I hope they will flourish as a corporation, and that pensioners will beget pensioners, to the end of the chapter.

people. What is the fruit of a good government? The virtue and happiness of the people. Do four millions of people in this country gather those fruits from that government, to whose injured purity, to whose spotless virtue and violated honor, this seditious and atrocious libeler is to be immolated upon the altar of the Constitution? To you, gentlemen of the jury, who are bound by the most sacred obligation to your country and your God, to speak nothing but the truth, I put the question, Do the people of this country gather those fruits? Are they orderly, industrious, religious, and contented? Do you find them free from bigotry and ignorance, those inseparable concomitants of systematic oppression? . . .

This paper, gentlemen, insists upon the necessity of emancipating the Catholics of Ireland, and that is charged as a part of the libel. If they had waited another year, if they had kept this prosecution impending for another year, how much would remain for a jury to decide upon, I should be at a loss to discover. It seems as if the progress of public information was eating away the ground of the prosecution. Since the commencement of the prosecution, this part of the libel has unluckily received the sanction of the legislature. In that interval our Catholic brethren have obtained that admission, which it seems it was a libel to propose; in what way to account for this I am really at a loss. Have any alarms been occasioned by the emancipation of our Catholic brethren? Has the bigoted malignity of any individuals been crushed, or has the stability of the government, or that of the country been weakened? Or is it one million of subjects stronger than four millions? Do you think that the benefit they received should be poisoned by the sting of vengeance? If you think so, you must say to them, "you have demanded emancipation and you have got it; but we abhor your persons, we are outraged at your success, and we will stigmatize by a criminal prosecution, the adviser of that relief which you have obtained from the voice of your country." I ask you, do you think, as honest men, anxious for the public tranquillity, conscious that there are wounds not yet completely cicatrized, that you ought to speak this language at this time, to men who are too much disposed to think that in this very emancipation they have been saved from their own Parliament by the humanity of their sovereign? Or do you wish to prepare them for the revocation of these improvident concessions? Do you think it wise or humane at this

ENGLAND AND ENGLISH LIBERTIES—IN THE CASE OF ROWAN

(From the Speech in Behalf of Archibald Hamilton Rowan, Esq., for a Libel in the Court of King's Bench, Ireland, on the 29th of January, 1794)

I KNOW no case in which a jury ought to be more severe than where personal calumny is conveyed through a vehicle, which ought to be consecrated to public information; neither, on the other hand, can I conceive any case in which the firmness and the caution of a jury should be more exerted than when a subject is prosecuted for a libel on the State. The peculiarity of the British Constitution (to which in its fullest extent we have an undoubted right, however distant we may be from the actual enjoyment), and in which it surpasses every known government in Europe, is this: that its only professed object is the general good, and its only foundation the general will; hence the people have a right acknowledged from time immemorial, fortified by a pile of statutes, and authenticated by a revolution that speaks louder than them all, to see whether abuses have been committed, and whether their properties and their liberties have been attended to as they ought to be.

This is a kind of subject which I feel myself overawed when I approach; there are certain fundamental principles which nothing but necessity should expose to public examination; they are pillars, the depth of whose foundation you cannot explore without endangering their strength; but let it be recollected that the discussion of such topics should not be condemned in me, nor visited upon my client: the blame, if any there be, should rest only with those who have forced them into discussion. I say, therefore, it is the right of the people to keep an eternal watch upon the conduct of their rulers; and in order to that, the freedom of the press has been cherished by the law of England. In private defamation let it never be tolerated; in wicked and wanton aspersion upon a good and honest administration let it never be supported. Not that a good government can be exposed to danger by groundless accusation, but because a bad government is sure to find in the detected falsehood of a licentious press a security and a credit, which it could never otherwise obtain.

I said a good government cannot be endangered; I say so again, for whether it is good or bad it can never depend upon assertion; the question is decided by simple inspection; to try the tree, look at its fruit; to judge of the government, look at the

moment to insult them, by sticking up in a pillory the man who dared to stand forth as their advocate? I put it to your oaths; do you think that a blessing of that kind, that a victory obtained by justice over bigotry and oppression, should have a stigma cast upon it by an ignominious sentence upon men bold and honest enough to propose that measure? To propose the redeeming of religion from the abuses of the church, the reclaiming of three millions of men from bondage, and giving liberty to all who had a right to demand it; giving, I say, in the so much censured words of this paper, giving "Universal Emancipation!"

I speak in the spirit of the British law, which makes liberty commensurate with and inseparable from British soil; which proclaims even to the stranger and the sojourner, the moment he sets his foot upon British earth, that the ground on which he treads is holy, and consecrated by the genius of universal emancipation. No matter in what language his doom may have been pronounced; no matter what complexion incompatible with freedom, an Indian or an African sun may have burnt upon him; no matter in what disastrous battle his liberty may have been cloven down; no matter with what solemnities he may have been devoted upon the altar of slavery,—the first moment he touches the sacred soil of Britain the altar and the god sink together in the dust; his soul walks abroad in her own majesty; his body swells beyond the measure of his chains that burst from around him, and he stands redeemed, regenerated, and disenthralled by the irresistible genius of universal emancipation.

[Here Mr. Curran was interrupted by a burst of applause.]

Gentlemen, I am not such a fool as to ascribe any effusion of this sort to any merits of mine. It is the mighty theme, and not the inconsiderable advocate, that can excite interest in the hearer! What you hear is but the testimony which nature bears to her own character; it is the effusion of her gratitude to that power which stamped that character upon her.

And, permit me to say, that if my client had occasion to defend his cause by any mad or drunken appeals to extravagance or licentiousness, I trust in God I stand in that situation, that, humble as I am, he would not have resorted to me to be his advocate. I was not recommended to his choice by any connection of principle or party, or even private friendship; and saying this, I cannot but add that I consider not to be acquainted with such a man as Mr. Rowan a want of personal good fortune. But upon this great subject of reform and emancipation there is a latitude and a boldness of remark, justifiable in the people, and necessary to the defense of Mr. Rowan, for which the habits of professional studies and technical adherence to established forms have rendered me unfit. It is, however, my duty, standing here as his advocate, to make some few observations to you, which I conceive to be material.

Gentlemen, you are sitting in a country which has a right to the British Constitution, and which is bound by an indissoluble union with the British nation. If you were now even at liberty to debate upon that subject; if you even were not by the most solemn compacts, founded upon the authority of your ancestors and of yourselves, bound to that alliance, and had an election now to make; in the present unhappy state of Europe, if you had been heretofore a stranger to Great Britain, you would now say we will enter into society and union with you;

Una salus ambobus erit, commune periculum.

But to accomplish that union, let me tell you, you must learn to become like the English people. It is in vain to say you will protect their freedom, if you abandon your own. The pillar whose base has no foundation can give no support to the dome under which its head is placed; and if you profess to give England that assistance which you refuse to yourselves, she will laugh at your folly, and despise your meanness and insincerity. Let us follow this a little further; I know you will interpret what I say with the candor in which it is spoken. England is marked by a natural avarice of freedom, which she is studious to engross and accumulate, but most unwilling to impart; whether from any necessity of her policy, or from her weakness, or from her pride, I will not presume to say; but so is the fact. You need not look to the east, nor to the west, you need only look to yourselves.

In order to confirm this observation I would appeal to what fell from the learned counsel for the Crown, "that notwithstanding the alliance subsisting for two centuries past between the two countries, the date of liberty in one goes no further back than the year 1784."

If it required additional confirmation I should state the case of the invaded American, and the subjugated Indian, to prove

that the policy of England has ever been to govern her connections more as colonies than as allies; and it must be owing to the great spirit, indeed, of Ireland if she shall continue free. Rely upon it, she will ever have to hold her course against an adverse current; rely upon it, if the popular spring does not continue strong and elastic, a short interval of debilitated nerve and broken force will send you down the stream again, and reconsign you to the condition of a province.

THE LIBERTIES OF THE INDOLENT

(Exordium of the Speech on the Right of Election of Lord Mayor of the City of Dublin. Delivered before the Lord-Lieutenant and Privy Council of Ireland, 1790)

My Lords:—

I HAVE the honor to appear before you as counsel for the Commons of the corporation of the metropolis of Ireland, and also for Mr. Alderman Howison, who hath petitioned for your approbation of him as a fit person to serve as Lord Mayor in virtue of his election by the Commons to that high office; and in that capacity I rise to address you on the most important subject that you have ever been called upon to discuss. Highly interesting and momentous indeed, my lords, must every question be, that, even remotely and eventually, may affect the well-being of societies, or the freedom or the repose of nations; but that question, the result of which, by an immediate and direct necessity, must decide either fatally or fortunately the life or the death of that well-being, of that freedom, and that repose, is surely the most important subject on which human wisdom can be employed, if any subject on this side the grave can be entitled to that appellation.

You cannot, therefore, my lords, be surprised to see this place crowded by such numbers of our fellow-citizens; heretofore, they were attracted hither by a strong sense of the value of their rights, and of the injustice of the attack upon them; they felt all the magnitude of the contest, but they were not disturbed by any fear for the event; they relied securely on the justice of their cause, and the integrity of those who were to decide upon it. But the public mind is now filled with a fear of danger, the more painful and alarming because hitherto unforeseen; the pub-

lic are now taught to fear that their cause may be of doubtful merits and disastrous issue; that rights which they considered as defined by the wisdom and confirmed by the authority of written law may now turn out to be no more than ideal claims, without either precision or security; that acts of Parliament themselves are no more than embryos of legislation, or at best but infants, whose first labors must be, not to teach, but to learn; and which, even after thirty years of pupilage, may have thirty more to pass under that guardianship, which the wisdom of our policy has provided for the protection of minors. Sorry am I, my lords, that I can offer no consolation to my clients on this head, and that I can only join them in bewailing that the question, whose result must decide upon their freedom or servitude, is perplexed with difficulties of which we never dreamed before, and which we are now unable to comprehend. Yet surely, my lords, that question must be difficult, upon which the wisdom of the representative of our dread sovereign, aided by the learning of his chancellor and his judges, assisted also by the talents of the most conspicuous of the nobles and the gentry of the nation, has been twice already employed, and employed in vain. We know, my lords, that guilt and oppression may stand irresolute for a moment ere they strike, appalled by the prospect of danger, or struck with the sentiment of remorse; but to you, my lords, it were presumption to impute injustice; we must, therefore, suppose that you have denied your determination, not because it was dangerous, but because it was difficult to decide; and indeed, my lords, a firm belief of this difficulty, however undiscoverable by ordinary talents, is so necessary to the character which this august assembly ought to possess and to merit from the country, that I feel myself bound to achieve it by an effort of my faith if I should not be able to do so by any exertion of my understanding.

In a question, therefore, so confessedly obscure as to baffle so much sagacity, I am not at liberty to suppose that certainty could be attained by a concise examination. Bending then, as I do, my lords, to your high authority, I feel this difficulty as a call upon me to examine it at large; and I feel it as an assurance that I shall be heard with patience.

The Lord Mayor of this city hath from time immemorial been a magistrate, not appointed by the Crown, but elected by his fellow-citizens. From the history of the early periods of this

corporation and a view of its charters and by-laws, it appears that the Commons had from the earliest periods participated in the important right of election to that high trust; and it was natural and just that the whole body of citizens, by themselves or their representatives, should have a share in electing those magistrates who were to govern them, as it was their birthright to be ruled only by laws which they had a share in enacting.

The aldermen, however, soon became jealous of this participation, encroached by degrees upon the Commons, and at length succeeded in engrossing to themselves the double privilege of eligibility and of election; of being the only body out of which, and by which, the Lord Mayor could be chosen. Nor is it strange that in those times a board, consisting of so small a number as twenty-four members, with the advantages of a more united interest, and a longer continuance in office, should have prevailed, even contrary to so evident principles of natural justice and constitutional right, against the unsteady resistance of competitors, so much less vigilant, so much more numerous, and therefore so much less united. It is the common fate of the indolent to see their rights become a prey to the active. The condition upon which God hath given liberty to man is eternal vigilance; which condition if he break, servitude is at once the consequence of his crime and the punishment of his guilt.

HIS FAREWELL TO THE IRISH PARLIAMENT

(From the Speech Delivered May 15th, 1797, in Support of the Ponsonby Reform Resolution)

I CONSIDER this as a measure of justice, with respect to the Catholics and the people at large. The Catholics in former times groaned under the malignant folly of penal laws—wandered like herds upon the earth, or gathered under some threadbare grandee who came to Dublin, danced attendance at the Castle, was smiled on by the Secretary, and carried back to his miserable countrymen the gracious promise of favor and protection. They are no longer mean dependants but owners of their country, and claiming simply and boldly, as Irishmen, the national privileges of men and natives of their country. . . .

I now proceed to answer the objections to the measure. I was extremely shocked to see the agent of a foreign cabinet rise up in the assembly that ought to represent the Irish nation and oppose a motion that was made on the acknowledged and deplored corruption which has been imported from his country. Such an opposition is a proof of the charge, which I am astonished he could venture upon at so awful a crisis. I doubt whether the charge, or this proof of it, would appear most odious. However, I will examine the objections. It is said — It is not the time. This argument has become a jest in Ireland, for it has been used in all times; in war, in peace, in quiet, and in disturbance. It is the miserable, dilatory plea of persevering and stupid corruption, that wishes to postpone its fate by a promise of amendment, which it is resolved never to perform. Reform has become an exception to the proverb that says there is a time for all things; but for reform there is no time, because at all times corruption is more profitable to its authors than public virtue and propriety, which they know must be fatal to their views. As to the present time, the objections to it are a compound of the most unblushing impudence and folly. Forsooth it would seem as if the house had yielded through fear. Personal bravery or fear are inapplicable to a public assembly. I know no cowardice so despicable as the fear of seeming to be afraid. To be afraid of danger is not an unnatural sensation; but to be brave in absurdity and injustice, merely from fear of having your sense of honesty imputed to your own apprehension, is a stretch of folly which I have never heard of before. But the time is pregnant with arguments very different, indeed, from those I have heard; I mean the report of the Secret Committee and the dreadful state of the country. The allegation is that the people are not to have justice, because a rebellion exists within, and because we have an enemy at our gates — because, forsooth, reform is only a pretext, and separation is the object of the leaders. If a rebellion exist, every good subject ought to be detached from it. But if an enemy threaten to invade us, it is only common sense to detach every subject from the hostile standard and bring him back to his duty and his country.

The present miserable state of Ireland — its distractions, its distresses, its bankruptcy — are the effects of the war, and it is the duty of the authors of that war to reconcile the people by the most timely and liberal justice; the utmost physical strength should be called forth, and that can be done only by union. This is a subject so tremendous I do not wish to dwell on it; I

iv—98

a religious fanaticism being discarded by the good sense of mankind, instead of dying slowly by the development of its folly. And I am persuaded the hints thrown out this night to make the different sects jealous of each other will be a detected trick and will only unite them still more closely. The Catholics have given a pledge to their countrymen of their sincerity and their zeal, which cannot fail of producing the most firm reliance; they have solemnly disclaimed all idea of what is called emancipation, except as a part of that reform without which their Presbyterian brethren could not be free. Reform is a necessary change of mildness for coercion. The latter has been tried; what is its success? The convention bill was passed to punish the meetings at Dungannon and those of the Catholics; the Government considered the Catholic concessions as defeats that called for vengeance, and cruelly have they avenged them. But did that act, or those which followed it, put down those meetings? The contrary was the fact. It concealed them most foolishly. When popular discontents are abroad, a wise government should put them into a hive of glass. You hid them. The association at first was small; the earth seemed to drink it as a rivulet, but it only disappeared for a season. A thousand streams, through the secret windings of the earth, found their way to one course, and swelled its waters, until at last, too mighty to be contained, it burst out a great river, fertilizing by its exudations or terrifying by its cataracts. This is the effect of our penal code; it swelled sedition into rebellion. What else could be hoped from a system of terrorism? Fear is the most transient of all the passions; it is the warning that nature gives for self-preservation. But when safety is unattainable the warning must be useless, and nature does not, therefore, give it. Administration, therefore, mistook the quality of penal laws; they were sent out to abolish conventions, but they did not pass the threshold; they stood sentinels at the gates. You think that penal laws, like great dogs, will wag their tails to their masters and bark only at their enemies. You are mistaken; they turn and devour those they are meant to protect, and are harmless where they are intended to destroy.

I see gentlemen laugh; I see they are still very ignorant of the nature of fear; it cannot last; neither while it does can it be concealed. The feeble glimmering of a forced smile is a light that makes the cheek look paler. Trust me, the times are too humanized for such systems of government. Humanity will not

will therefore leave it; I will support a Reform on its own merits, and as a measure of internal peace at this momentous juncture. Its merits are admitted by the objection to the time, because the objection admits that at any other time it would be proper. For twenty years past there was no man of any note in England or Ireland who did not consider the necessity of it as a maxim; they all saw and confessed that the people are not represented, and that they have not the benefit of a mixed monarchy. They have a monarchy which absorbs the two other estates, and, therefore, they have the insupportable expense of a monarchy, an aristocracy, and a democracy, without the simplicity or energy of any one of those forms of government. In Ireland this is peculiarly fatal, because the honest representation of the people is swallowed in the corruption and intrigue of a cabinet of another country. From this may be deduced the low estate of the Irish people; their honest labor is wasted in pampering their betrayers, instead of being employed, as it ought to be, in accommodating themselves and their children. On these miserable consequences of corruption, and which are all the fatal effects of inadequate representation, I do not wish to dwell. To expatiate too much on them might be unfair, but to suppress them might be treason to the public. It is said that reform is only a pretense, and that separation is the real object of leaders; if this be so, confound the leaders by destroying the pretext, and take the followers to yourselves. You say there are one hundred thousand; I firmly believe there are three times the number. So much the better for you; if these seducers can attach so many followers to rebellion by the hope of reform through blood, how much more readily will you engage them, not by the promise, but the possession, and without blood? You allude to the British fleet; learn from it to avoid the fatal consequence that may follow even a few days' delay of justice. It is said to be only a pretext; I am convinced of the contrary — I am convinced the people are sincere, and would be satisfied by it. I think so from the perseverance in petitioning for it for a number of years; I think so, because I think a monarchy, properly balanced by a fair representation of the people, gives as perfect liberty as the most celebrated republics of old. But, of the real attraction of this object of reform, you have a proof almost miraculous; the desire of reform has annihilated religious antipathy and united the country. In the history of mankind it is the only instance of so fatal

execute them, but humanity will abhor them and those who wish to rule by such means. This is not theory; the experiment has been tried and proved. You hoped much, and, I doubt not, meant well by those laws; but they have miserably failed you; it is time to try milder methods. You have tried to force the people; the rage of your penal laws was a storm that only drove them in groups to shelter. Your convention law gave them that organization which is justly an object of such alarm; and the very proclamation seems to have given them arms. Before it is too late, therefore, try the better force of reason, and conciliate them by justice and humanity. The period of coercion in Ireland is gone, nor can it ever return until the people shall return to the folly and to the natural weakness of disunion. Neither let us talk of innovation; the progress of nature is no innovation. The increase of people, with the growth of the mind, is no innovation; it is no way alarming unless the growth of our minds lag behind. If we think otherwise, and think it an innovation to depart from the folly of our infancy, we should come here in our swaddling-clothes; we should not innovate upon the dress, more than the understanding of the cradle. As to the system of peace now proposed, you must take it on principles; they are simply two — the abolition of religious disabilities and the representation of the people. I am confident the effects would be everything to be wished. The present alarming discontent will vanish, the good will be separated from the evil-intentioned; the friends of mixed government in Ireland are many; every sensible man must see that it gives all the enjoyment of rational liberty if the people have their due place in the State. This system would make us invincible against a foreign or domestic enemy; it would make the empire strong at this important crisis; it would restore us to liberty, industry, and peace, which I am satisfied can never, by any other means, be restored. Instead, therefore, of abusing the people, let us remember that there is no physical strength but theirs, and conciliate them by justice and reason. I am censured heavily for having acted for them in the late prosecutions. I feel no shame at such a charge, except that, at such a time as this, to defend the people should be held out as an imputation upon a king's counsel, when the people are prosecuted by the State. I think every counsel is the property of his fellow-subjects. If, indeed, because I wore his Majesty's gown, I had declined my duty or done it weakly or treacherously; if I had made that gown a mantle of hypocrisy, and betrayed my client or sacrificed him to any personal view, I might, perhaps, have been thought wiser by those who have blamed me; but I should have thought myself the basest villain upon earth. The plan of peace, proposed by a reform, is the only means that I and my friends can see left to save us. It is certainly a time for decision, and not for half measures. I agree that unanimity is indispensable. The House seems pretty nearly unanimous for force; I am sorry for it, for I bode the worst from it. I will retire from a scene where I can do no good — where I certainly would interrupt that unanimity. I cannot, however, go without a parting entreaty that gentlemen will reflect on the awful responsibility in which they stand to their country and to their conscience, before they set the example to the people of abandoning the Constitution and the law, and resorting to the terrible expedient of force.

ON GOVERNMENT BY ATTACHMENT

(Delivered in the Irish Parliament, February 24th, 1785)

In 1784, Henry Reilly, Esq., Sheriff of the county of Dublin, summoned his bailiwick to elect members to a national congress. For this he was attached by the King's Bench on a Crown motion, and on the twenty-fourth of February, 1785, the Right Hon. William Brownlow moved a vote of censure on the judges of that court for the attachment. Curran's speech on the subject is still of interest in connection with contempt proceedings in political cases.

I HOPE I may say a few words on this great subject without disturbing the sleep of any right honorable member [the Attorney-General John Fitzgibbon had fallen asleep on his seat] and yet, perhaps, I ought rather to envy than blame the tranquillity of the right honorable gentleman. I do not feel myself so happily tempered as to be lulled to repose by the storms that shake the land. If they invite rest to any, that rest ought not to be lavished on the guilty spirit. I never more strongly felt the necessity of a perfect union with Britain, of standing or falling with her in fortune and Constitution, than on this occasion. She is the parent, the archetype of Irish liberty, which she has preserved inviolate in its grand points, while among us it has been violated and debased. I now call upon the house to

The power of attachment is wisely confined by the British laws and practiced within that limit. The Crown lawyers have not produced a single case where the King's Bench in England have gone beyond it. They have ranged through the annals of history; through every reign of folly and of blood; through the proud domination of the Tudors, and the blockhead despotism of the Stuarts, without finding a single case to support their doctrine.

I consider the office of sheriff as judicial and ministerial. Reilly's offense did not fall within any summary control, in either capacity. It was not a judicial act, it was not *colore officii*. An act *colore officii* must either be an act done by the actual exercise of an abused or of a usurped authority — neither of which can it be called; for where the sheriff summons his county, he does it by command, by authority, under pain of fine and imprisonment to those who disobey.

Was the appointment of a meeting any such active exertion of authority? Does any man suppose he was obliged to attend? that he would be fined if he refused to attend? No. Did the sheriff hold out any such colorable authority? Clearly not. The contrary: he explained the purpose of the intended meeting; he stated at whose instance he appointed such meeting; and thereby showed to every man in his senses that he was not affecting to convene them by color of any compulsive authority.

If, then, there was any guilt in the sheriff's conduct, it was not punishable by attachment. They who argue from its enormity are guilty of a shabby attempt to mislead men from the question, which is not whether he ought to be punished at all, but whether he had been punished according to law.

You have heard no man adduce a single case to support their assertion; but we have the uniform practice of the King's Bench in England in our favor, the uniform practice, both there and here, during these last years. Had they not meetings there and here? Did not the Crown receive petitions and addresses from such assemblies? Why, during that time, was there no motion for an attachment in either kingdom?

If an English attorney-general had attempted such a daring outrage on public liberty and law, he must have found some friend to warn him not to debase the court, and make it appear to all mankind as the odious engine of arbitrary power; not to put it into so unnatural a situation as that of standing between

consider the trust reposed in them as the Great Inquest of the people.

I respect judges highly. They ought to be respected, and feel their dignity and freedom from reprehension while they do what judges ought to do; but their stations should not screen them when they pass the limit of their duty. Whether they did or not is the question. This House is the judge of those judges, and it would betray the people to tyranny and abdicate their representation, if it does not act with probity and firmness.

In their proceedings against Reilly, I think they have transgressed the law, and made a precedent which, while it remains, is subversive of the trial by jury and, of course, of liberty. I regard the Constitution, I regard the judges, three of that court at least, and for their sakes I shall endeavor to undo what they have done.

The question is whether the court has really punished its own officer for a real contempt, or whether it has abused that power, for the illegal end of punishing a supposed offense against the State, by a summary proceeding without a trial by jury.

The question is plain, whether as a point of Constitution or as of law; but I shall first consider it in the former view. When I feel the Constitution rocking over my head, my first anxiety is to explore the foundation, to see if the great arches that support the fabric have fallen in; but I find them firm on the solid and massy principle of common law. The principle of legal liberty is that offense and trial and punishment should be fixed; it is sense, it is Magna Charta — a trial by jury as to fact, an appeal to judges as to law.

I admit attachment an exception to the general rule as founded in necessity for the support of courts, in administering justice, by a summary control over their officers acting under them; but the necessity that gave rise to it is also the limit. If it were extended further, it would reach to all criminal cases not capital; and in the room of a jury crimes would be created by a judge, the party accused by him, found guilty by him, punished by the utter loss of his liberty and property for life, by indefinite fine and imprisonment without remedy or appeal. If he did **not** answer, he was guilty; even if he did, the court might think, or say it thought, the answer evasive, and so convict him for imputed prevarication.

the people and the Crown, or between the people and their representatives.

I warn him not to bring public hatred on the Government, by the adoption of an illegal prosecution. If he show himself afraid of proceeding against offenders by the ordinary mode, then offenders will be exalted by arbitrary persecution of them; they will become suffering patriots, from being mere petty offenders; their cries will become popular. Let him be warned how he leads the court into an illegality, which the Commons can never endure. No honest representative can sacrifice his fame and his duty by voting in support of a proceeding subversive of liberty. I should shrink from the reproach of the most insignificant of my constituents if that constituent could say to me: "When thou sawest the thief of the Constitution, thou consentedst unto him."

Such would be the caution suggested to an English attorney-general; and, accordingly, we find no instance of his ever venturing on such a measure.

Without case, then, or precedent, or principle, what is the support of such a conduct here? — the distinction of a judge? And what is that distinction? It is different in different men; it is different in the same man at different times; it is the folly of a fool and the fear of a coward; it is the infamy of the young and the dotage of age; in the best man it is very weakness that human nature is subject to; and in the worst, it is very vice. Will you, then, tell the people that you have chosen this glorious distinction in the place of fixed laws, fixed offenses, and fixed punishments, and in the place of that great barrier between the prerogative and the people — trial by jury?

But it is objected that the resolution is a censure on the judges and a charge of corruption. I deny it and I appeal to your own acts.

[Mr. Curran then called to the clerk, who read from the journals a vote of censure passed upon Mr. Justice Robinson, for imposing a fine illegally in a county, when on circuit, without view or evidence.]

Was your resolution founded on any corruption of that judge? No; you would, if so, have addressed to remove him. I called for the resolution, therefore, not to charge him with guilt, — I am persuaded he acted merely through error, — but to vindicate him, to vindicate you, and to exhort you to be consistent. You thought a much smaller violation of the law was deserving your reprobation. Do not abandon yourselves and your country to slavery, by suffering so much a grosser and more dangerous transgression of the Constitution, to become a precedent forever. In tenderness even to the judges, interpose. Their regret, which I am sure they now feel, on reflection, cannot undo what they have done; their hands cannot wash away what is written in their records; but you may repair whatever has been injured,— if your friend had unwillingly plunged a dagger into the breast of a stranger, would you prove his innocence by letting the victim bleed to death? The Constitution has been wounded deeply, but, I am persuaded, innocently; it is you only who, by neglecting to interpose, can make the consequences fatal, and the wound ripen into murder.

I would wish, I own, that the liberty of Ireland should be supported by her own children; but if she be scorned and rejected by them, when her all is at stake, I will implore the assistance even of two strangers; I will call on the right honorable Secretary to support the principles of the British Constitution. Let him not render his administration odious to the people of Ireland by applying his influence in this House to the ruin of their personal freedom. Let him not give a pretense to the enemies of his friend in a sister country, to say that the son of the illustrious Chatham is disgracing the memory of his great father; that the trophies of his Irish administration are the introduction of an inquisition among us, and the extinction of a trial by jury; let them not say that the pulse of the Constitution beats only in the heart of the empire, but that it is dead in the extremities.

[Mr. Curraan concluded with declaring his hearty concurrence in the resolution proposed.]

[The Attorney-General, [Fitzgibbon] in a speech of much personality, opposed Curran's motion.]

[Mr. Curran in reply:]—

I thank the right honorable gentleman for restoring me to my good humor and for having, with great liberality and parliamentary decency, answered my arguments with personality. Some expressions cannot heat me, when coming from persons of a certain distinction. I shall not interrupt the right honorable gentleman in the fifth repetition of his speech. I shall prevent his arguments by telling him that he has not in one

instance alluded to Mr. Reilly. The right honorable gentleman said I had declared the judges guilty, but I said no such thing. I said, if any judge were to act in the manner I mentioned, it would be an aggravation of his guilt. The right honorable gentleman has said that the House of Commons had no right to investigate the conduct of judges; if so, I ask the learned sergeant why he sits in that chair. I ask why the resolution has been just read from the journals. The gentleman has called me a babbler; I cannot think that was meant as a disgrace, because, in another Parliament, before I had the honor of a seat in this House, but when I was in the gallery, I heard a young lawyer named Babbler. I do not recollect that there were sponsers at the baptismal font; nor was there any occasion, as the infant had promised and vowed so many things in his own name. Indeed, I find it difficult to reply, for I am not accustomed to pronounce panegyrics on myself; I do not know well how to do it; but since I cannot tell you what I am, I shall tell you what I am not: I am not a man whose respect in person and character depends upon the importance of his office; I am not a young man who thrusts himself into the foreground of a picture, which ought to be occupied by a better figure; I am not a man who replies with invective when sinking under the weight of argument; I am not a man who denied the necessity of a parliamentary reform, at the time he proved the expediency of it, by reviling his own constituents, the parish clerk, the sexton, and the grave digger; and if there be any man who can apply what I am not to himself, I leave him to think of it in the committee and to contemplate it when he goes home.

BENJAMIN ROBBINS CURTIS

(1809–1874)

THE most important question raised by the impeachment of President Johnson, and, in fact, the only one which obviously survives the politics of that period, is of the extent to which a President has the right to condemn publicly the acts of one of the co-ordinate departments of the Government. In defending President Johnson, Judge B. R. Curtis denied the right of a Congress holding itself aggrieved by a presidential criticism, to act as judge of its own cause. It was probably this consideration more than any other which prevented the President's conviction and removal.

Benjamin Robbins Curtis was born at Watertown, Massachusetts, November 4th, 1809. He died at Newport, Rhode Island, September 15th, 1874. He became eminent as a lawyer and left a number of works on American jurisprudence, among them a digest of the decisions of the United States Supreme Court, of which from 1851 to 1857 he was an associate justice. He was a brother of George Ticknor Curtis, author of 'History of the Constitution,' and other well-known works.

PRESIDENTIAL CRITICISMS OF CONGRESS — DEFENDING ANDREW JOHNSON

(From the Speech of April 9th, 1868, in Behalf of the President at the Impeachment Trial)

THE complaint is that the President made speeches against Congress. The true statement here would be much more restricted than that; for although in those speeches the President used the word "Congress," undoubtedly he did not mean the entire constitutional body organized under the Constitution of the United States; he meant the dominant majority in Congress. Everybody so understood it; everybody must so understand it. But the complaint is that he made speeches against those who governed in Congress. Well, who are the grand jury in this case? One of the parties spoken against. And who are the tryers? The other party spoken against. One would think there was some incongruity in this; some reason for giving pause

before taking any very great stride in that direction. The honorable House of Representatives sends its managers here to take notice of what? That the House of Representatives has erected itself into a school of manners, selecting from its ranks those gentlemen whom it deems most competent by precept and example to teach decorum of speech; and they desire the judgment of this body whether the President has not been guilty of indecorum, whether he has spoken properly, to use the phrase of the honorable manager. Now, there used to be an old-fashioned notion that although there might be a difference of taste about oral speeches, and, no doubt, always has been and always will be many such differences, there was one very important test in reference to them, and that is whether they are true or false; but it seems that in this case that is no test at all. The honorable manager, in opening the case, finding, I suppose, that it was necessary, in some manner, to advert to that subject, has done it in terms which I will read to you:—

"The words are not alleged to be either false or defamatory, because it is not within the power of any man, however high his official position, in effect to slander the Congress of the United States, in the ordinary sense of that word, so as to call on Congress to answer as to the truth of the accusation."

Considering the nature of our Government, considering the experience which we have gone through on this subject, that is a pretty lofty claim. Why, if the Senate please, if you go back to the time of the Plantagenets and seek for precedents there, you will not find so lofty a claim as that. I beg leave to read from two statutes, the first being 3 Edward I., cap. 34, and the second 2 Richard II., cap. 1. The statute, 3 Edward I., cap. 34, after the preamble, enacts—

"That from henceforth none be so hardy to tell or publish any false news or tales, whereby discord or occasion of discord or slander may grow between the King and his people, or the great men of the realm; and he that doeth so shall be taken and kept in until he hath brought him into court which was the first author of the tale."

The statute 2 Richard II., cap. 1, § 5, enacted with some alterations the previous statute. It commenced thus:—

"Of devisors of false news and of horrible and false lies of prelates, dukes, earls, barons, and other nobles and great men of the realm; and also of the chancellor, treasurer, clerk of the privy seal, steward of the King's house, justices of the one bench or of the other, and of other great officers of the realm."

The great men of the realm in the time of Richard II. were protected only against "horrible and false lies," and when we arrive in the course of our national experience during the war with France and the administration of Mr. Adams to that attempt to check, not free speech, but free writing, Senators will find that, although it applied only to written libels, it contained an express section that the truth might be given in evidence. That was a law, as Senators know, making it penal by written libels to excite the hatred or contempt of the people against Congress, among other offenses; but the estimate of the elevation of Congress, above the people was not so high but that it was thought proper to allow a defense of the truth to be given in evidence. I beg leave to read from this Sedition Act a part of one section and make a reference to another to support the correctness of what I have said. It is found in Statutes at Large, page 596:—

"That if any person shall write, print, utter, or publish, or shall cause or procure to be written, printed, uttered, or published, or shall knowingly and willingly assist or aid in writing, printing, uttering, or publishing any false, scandalous, and malicious writing or writings against the Government of the United States, or either house of the Congress of the United States, or the President of the United States, with intent to defame the said Government, or either house of the said Congress, or the said President, or to bring them, or either or any of them the hatred of the good people of the United States, or to stir up sedition within the United States, or to excite any unlawful combinations therein," etc.

Section three provides:—

"That if any person shall be prosecuted under this act for the writing or publishing any libel aforesaid, it shall be lawful for the defendant, upon the trial of the cause, to give in evidence in his defense the truth of the matter contained in the publication charged as a libel. And the jury who shall try the cause shall have a right to determine the law and the fact, under the direction of the court, as in other cases."

In contrast with the views expressed here, I desire now to read from the fourth volume of Mr. Madison's works, pages 542

and 547, passages which, in my judgment, are as masterly as anything Mr. Madison ever wrote, upon the relations of the Congress of the United States to the people of the United States, in contrast with the relations of the Government of Great Britain to the people of that island, and upon the necessity which the nature of our Government lays us under to preserve freedom of the press and freedom of speech:—

"The essential difference between the British Government and the American Constitution will place this subject in the clearest light.

"In the British Government the danger of encroachments on the rights of the people is understood to be confined to the Executive Magistrate. The Representatives of the people in the Legislature are not only exempt themselves from distrust, but are considered as sufficient guardians of the rights of their constituents against the danger from the Executive. Hence it is a principle that the Parliament is unlimited in its power, or, in their own language, is omnipotent. Hence, too, all the ramparts for protecting the rights of the people, such as their Magna Charta, their Bill of Rights, etc., are not reared against the Parliament, but against the royal prerogative. They are merely legislative precautions against Executive usurpations. Under such a government as this, an exemption of the press from previous restraint, by licensers appointed by the King, is all the freedom that can be secured to it.

"In the United States the case is altogether different. The people, not the Government, possess the absolute sovereignty. The Legislature, no less than the Executive, is under limitations of power. Encroachments are regarded as possible from the one as well as from the other. Hence, in the United States, the great and essential rights of the people are secured against legislative as well as against executive ambition. They are secured, not by laws paramount to prerogative, but by constitutions paramount to laws. This security of the freedom of the press requires that it should be exempt not only from previous restraint by the Executive, as in Great Britain, but from legislative restraint also; and this exemption, to be effectual, must be an exemption not only from the previous inspection of licenses, but from the subsequent penalty of laws."

One other passage on page 547, which has an extraordinary application to the subject now before you:—

"1. The Constitution supposes that the President, the Congress, and each of its houses may not discharge their trusts, either from defect of judgment or other causes. Hence they are all made responsible to their constituents at the returning periods of election;

and the President who is singly intrusted with very great powers, is, as a further guard, subjected to an intermediate impeachment.

"2. Should it happen, as the Constitution supposes it may happen, that either of these branches of the Government may not have duly discharged its trust, it is natural and proper that, according to the cause and degree of their faults, they should be brought into contempt or disrepute, and incur the hatred of the people.

"3. Whether it has, in any case, happened that the proceedings of either or all of those branches evince such a violation of duty as to justify a contempt, a disrepute, or hatred among the people, can only be determined by a free examination thereof, and a free communication among the people thereon.

"4. Whenever it may have actually happened that proceedings of this sort are chargeable on all or either of the branches of the Government, it is the duty, as well as the right, of intelligent and faithful citizens to discuss and promulge them freely, as well to control them by the censorship of the public opinion as to promote a remedy according to the rules of the Constitution. And it cannot be avoided that those who are to apply the remedy must feel, in some degree, a contempt or hatred against the transgressing party."

These observations of Mr. Madison were made in respect to the freedom of the press. There were two views entertained at the time when the Sedition Law was passed concerning the power of Congress over this subject. The one view was that when the Constitution spoke of freedom of the press it referred to the common-law definition of that freedom. That was the view which Mr. Madison was controverting in one of the passages which I have read to you. The other view was that the common-law definition could not be deemed applicable, and that the freedom provided for by the Constitution, so far as the action of Congress was concerned, was an absolute freedom of the press. But no one ever imagined that freedom of speech, in contradistinction from written libel, could be restrained by a law of Congress; for whether you treat the prohibition in the Constitution as absolute in itself or whether you refer to the common law for a definition of its limits and meaning, the result will be the same. Under the common law no man was ever punished criminally for spoken words. If he slandered his neighbor and injured him, he must make good in damages to his neighbor the injury he had done; but there was no such thing at the common law as an indictment for spoken words. So that this prohibition

in the Constitution against any legislation by Congress in restraint of the freedom of speech is necessarily an absolute prohibition; and therefore this is a case not only where there is no law made prior to the act to punish the act, but a case where Congress is expressly prohibited from making any law to operate even on subsequent acts.

What is the law to be? Suppose it is, as the honorable managers seem to think it should be, the sense of propriety of each Senator appealed to. What is it to be? The only rule I have heard—the only rule which can be announced—is that you may require the speaker to speak properly. Who are to be the judges whether he speak properly? In this case the Senate of the United States on the presentation of the House of Representatives of the United States; and that is supposed to be the freedom of speech secured by this absolute prohibition of the Constitution. That is the same freedom of speech, Senators, in consequence of which thousands of men went to the scaffold under the Tudors and the Stuarts. That is the same freedom of speech which caused thousands of heads of men and of women to roll from the guillotine in France. That is the same freedom of speech which has caused in our day more than once "order to reign in Warsaw." The persons did not speak properly in the apprehension of the judges before whom they were brought. Is that the freedom of speech intended to be secured by our Constitution? . . .

GEORGE WILLIAM CURTIS

(1824–1892)

HEN in the Republican national convention held at Chicago in June 1884, George William Curtis climbed on a chair to protest, on behalf of those who were afterwards called "mugwumps," against the Hawkins Resolution, the scene was one of the most dramatic in American history. Mr. Curtis had been one of those whose thorough-going earnestness had forced issues which had retired the Democratic party from power for twenty-five years. Under the Hawkins Resolution, he would have been bound to support the nominee of the convention, with the consent of his conscience or without it. He evidently felt himself in the presence of one of those great crises when the history of a nation may depend for years on the immediate and determined action of one man. When he climbed on his seat to speak, with his white hair thrown back from his face, and began: "Gentlemen of the convention, a Republican and a free man, I came into this convention; by the grace of God a Republican and a free man will I go out of this convention," his belief in the far-reaching importance of his action was immediately communicated to the thousands with whom the great hall was packed. The convention which so shortly before had been apparently an uncontrollable chaos of conflicting elements became breathlessly silent, and in making the speech which restored the Democratic party to power by inaugurating the independent Republican movement of 1884, Mr. Curtis had an audience which strained its ears to catch his every word. Perhaps there has not been in all American history a more striking example of the power of such oratory as is natural to any man of great and cultivated intellect, when he is deeply moved by a conscientious conviction of his duty. In his address on Wendell Phillips, delivered in April 1884, Mr. Curtis shows us his own ideal in his elucidation of the character of Phillips. He was not persistently intense in his modes of thought as Phillips was, but at a crisis he could call out wholly unsuspected reserves of power, as he did in his Chicago speech. He was a scholar rather than a statesman; a gentleman by instinct and habit; gracious in his demeanor, because of being essentially gracious; and seemingly unfitted for the rude and brawling contentions of practical politics; but such men as he have determined the course of events in America at every crisis,

IV—99

putting to confusion the merely professional politicians and asserting the omnipotent supremacy of that higher intellect which can begin and operate only under the direction of a sound and compelling conscience. Mr. Curtis was born at Providence, Rhode Island, February 24th, 1824. In his early life he was possessed by the ideas which moved a number of young transcendentalists to organize the Brook Farm community. After eighteen months of that celebrated failure to realize the ideal, he traveled in Europe, and returning, entered New York journalism, first on the daily press, and afterwards as the editor of weekly and monthly periodicals issued by well-known publishing houses. Of his numerous published books, the 'Potiphar Papers' are perhaps best, as they are best known to the general public. Mr. Curtis died at his home on Staten Island, August 31st, 1892.

HIS SOVEREIGNTY UNDER HIS HAT

(Delivered in the Republican National Convention, at Chicago, June 4th, 1884, on the Resolution Offered by Mr. Hawkins, of Tennessee: "*Resolved*, As the sense of this convention, That every member of it is bound in honor to support its nominee, whoever that nominee may be, and that no man should hold a seat here who is not ready to so agree")

Gentlemen of the Convention:—

A Republican and a free man I came into this convention; by the grace of God a Republican and a free man will I go out of this convention. Twenty-four years ago I was here in Chicago. Twenty-four years ago I took part with the men of this country who nominated the man who bears the most illustrious name in the Republican party, and the brightest ray in whose halo of glory and immortality is that he was the great emancipator. In that convention, sir, a resolution was offered in amendment of the platform. It introduced into that platform certain words from the Declaration of Independence. That man was voted down in that convention, and Joshua R. Giddings, of Ohio, rose from his seat and was passing out of the convention. As he went to pass by my chair, I, well nigh a boy and unknown to him, reached out my hand and said: "Sir, where are you going?" He said to me: "Young man, I am going out of this convention, for I find there is no place in a Republican convention for an original antislavery man like me." Well, gentlemen, after this he stopped and again took his seat, and before the convention concluded the Republican party declared no word, no deed, no sign should ever be made in a

Republican convention that in the slightest degree reflected upon the honor or the loyalty of the men who took part in that convention, and upon their adhesion to liberty. The gentleman who was last upon the floor dared any one upon this floor to vote against that resolution. I say to him in reply that the presentation of such a resolution in such a convention as this is a stigma, an insult, upon every man who stands here. The question is no question at all. Precisely the same motion was brought up at the last convention, and a man from West Virginia (I honor his name!) said in the face of the roaring galleries: "I am a Republican who carries his sovereignty under his own hat."

Now, Mr. Chairman, Mr. Campbell's position in that convention agreed with the wise reflection, the afterthought of the Republican convention of 1880, under the direction of that great leader whose face fronts us there, James A. Garfield, of Ohio. Under the lead of Garfield, I remind you, my friend from California, that convention, taking its action, induced the gentleman who presented the resolution to withdraw it from consideration. Now, sir, in the light of the character of the Republican party; in the light of the action of the last Republican convention, the first convention I have known in which such a pledge was required of the members; I ask this convention, mindful of all that hangs upon the wisdom, the moderation, the tolerance, and the patriotism of our action,—mindful of it all I beg this convention to remember Lincoln, to remember Garfield, to remember the most vital principle of the Republican party, and assume that every man here who is an honorable man will vote this resolution down, as something which should never have appeared in a Republican convention, and as unworthy to be ratified by the concourse of free men I see before me.

WENDELL PHILLIPS AS A HISTORY-MAKER

(From a Contemporary Stenographic Report of the Address Delivered in Tremont Temple, Boston, April 18th, 1884)

WHEN the war ended, and the specific purpose of his relentless agitation was accomplished, Phillips was still in the prime of his life. Had his mind recurred to the dreams of earlier years, had he desired, in the fullness of his fame and

the maturity of his powers, to turn to the political career which the hopes of the friends of his youth had forecast, I do not doubt that the Massachusetts of Sumner and of Andrew, proud of his genius and owning his immense service to the triumphant cause, although a service beyond the party line, and often apparently directed against the party itself, would have gladly summoned him to duty. It would, indeed, have been a kind of peerage for this great Commoner. But not to repose and peaceful honor did this earnest soul incline. "Now that the field is won," he said gaily to a friend, "do you sit by the camp-fire, but I will put out into the underbrush." The slave, indeed, was free, but emancipation did not free the agitator from his task. The client that suddenly appeared before him on that memorable October day was not an oppressed race alone; it was wronged humanity; it was the victim of unjust systems and unequal laws; it was the poor man, the weak man, the unfortunate man, whoever and whatever he might be. This was the cause that he would still plead in the forum of public opinion. "Let it not be said," he wrote to a meeting of his old Abolition friends, two months before his death, "that the old Abolitionist stopped with the negro, and was never able to see that the same principles claimed his utmost effort to protect all labor, white and black, and to further the discussion of every claim of humanity."

Was this the habit of mere agitation, the restless discontent that followed great achievement? There were those who thought so. But they were critics of a temperament which did not note that with Phillips agitation was a principle, and a deliberately chosen method to definite ends. There were still vast questions springing from the same root of selfishness and injustice as the question of slavery. They must force a hearing in the same way. He would not adopt in middle life the career of politics, which he had renounced in youth, however seductive that career might be, whatever its opportunities and rewards, because the purpose had grown with his growth and strengthened with his strength, to form public opinion rather than to represent it, in making or in executing the laws. To form public opinion upon vital public questions by public discussion, but by public discussion absolutely fearless and sincere, and conducted with honest faith in the people to whom the argument was addressed—this was the service which he had long performed, and this he would still perform, and in the familiar way.

His comprehensive philanthropy had made him, even during the antislavery contest, the untiring advocate of other great reforms. His powerful presentation of the justice and reason of the political equality of women, at Worcester, in 1857, more than any other single impulse launched that question upon the sea of popular controversy. In the general statement of principle, nothing has been added to that discourse. In vivid and effective eloquence of advocacy it has never been surpassed. All the arguments for independence echoed John Adams in the Continental Congress; all the pleas for applying the American principle of representation to the wives and mothers of American citizens echo the eloquence of Wendell Phillips at Worcester. His, also, was the voice that summoned the temperance voters of the Commonwealth to stand up and be counted; the voice which resolutely and definitely exposed the crime to which the busy American mind and conscience are at last turning — the American crime against the Indians. Through him the sorrow of Crete, the tragedy of Ireland, pleaded with America. In the terrible experience of the early antislavery debate, when the Church and refined society seemed to be the rampart of slavery, he had learned profound distrust of that conservatism of prosperity which chills human sympathy and narrows the conscience. So the vast combinations of capital, in these later days, with their immense monopolies and imperial power, seemed to him sure to corrupt the Government and to obstruct and threaten the real welfare of the people. He felt, therefore, that what is called the respectable class is often really, but unconsciously and with a generous purpose, not justly estimating its own tendency, the dangerous class. He was not a party politician; he cared little for party or for party leaders. But any political party which in his judgment represented the dangerous tendency was a party to be defeated in the interest of the peace and progress of all the people.

But his judgment, always profoundly sincere, was it not sometimes profoundly mistaken? No nobler friend of freedom and of man than Wendell Phillips ever breathed upon this continent, and no man's service to freedom surpasses his. But before the war he demanded peaceful disunion — yet it was the Union in arms that saved Liberty. During the war he would have superseded Lincoln — but it was Lincoln who freed the slaves. He pleaded for Ireland, tortured by centuries of misrule, and while every generous heart followed with sympathy the pathos and the

power of his appeal, the just mind recoiled from the sharp arraignment of the truest friends in England that Ireland ever had. I know it all; but I know also, and history will remember, that the slave Union which he denounced is dissolved; that it was the heart and conscience of the nation, exalted by his moral appeal of agitation, as well as by the enthusiasm of patriotic war, which held up the hands of Lincoln, and upon which Lincoln leaned in emancipating the slaves, and that only by indignant and aggressive appeals like his has the heart of England ever opened to Irish wrong.

No man, I say, can take a pre-eminent and effective part in contentions that shake nations, or in the discussion of great national policies, of foreign relations, of domestic economy and finance, without keen reproach and fierce misconception. "But death," says Bacon, "bringeth good fame." Then, if moral integrity remain unsoiled, the purpose pure, blameless the life, and patriotism as shining as the sun, conflicting views and differing counsels disappear, and firmly fixed upon character and actual achievement, good fame rests secure. Eighty years ago, in this city, how unsparing was the denunciation of John Adams for betraying and ruining his party, for his dogmatism, his vanity and ambition, for his exasperating impracticability — he, the Colossus of the Revolution! And Thomas Jefferson? I may truly say what the historian says of the Saracen mothers and Richard Cœur de Lion, that the mothers of Boston hushed their children with fear of the political devil incarnate of Virginia. But, when the drapery of mourning shrouded the columns and overhung the arches of Faneuil Hall, Daniel Webster did not remember that sometimes John Adams was imprudent and Thomas Jefferson sometimes unwise. He remembered only that John Adams and Thomas Jefferson were two of the greatest American patriots — and their fellow-citizens of every party bowed their heads and said, Amen. I am not here to declare that the judgment of Wendell Phillips was always sound, nor his estimate of men always just, nor his policy always approved by the event. He would have scorned such praise. I am not here to eulogize the mortal, but the immortal. He, too, was a great American patriot; and no American life — no, not one — offers to future generations of his countrymen a more priceless example of inflexible fidelity to conscience and to public duty; and no American more truly

than he purged the national name of its shame, and made the American flag the flag of hope for mankind.

Among her noblest children his native city will cherish him, and gratefully recall the unbending Puritan soul that dwelt in a form so gracious and urbane. The plain house in which he lived, — severely plain, because the welfare of the suffering and the slave were preferred to books and pictures and every fair device of art; the house to which the North Star led the trembling fugitive, and which the unfortunate and the friendless knew; the radiant figure passing swiftly through these streets, plain as the house from which it came, regal with a royalty beyond that of kings; the ceaseless charity untold; the strong sustaining heart of private friendship; the sacred domestic affections that must not here be named; the eloquence which, like the song of Orpheus, will fade from living memory into a doubtful tale; that great scene of his youth in Faneuil Hall; the surrender of ambition; the mighty agitation and the mighty triumph with which his name is forever blended; the consecration of a life hidden with God in sympathy with man — these, all these, will live among your immortal traditions, heroic even in your heroic story. But not yours alone! As years go by, and only the large outlines of lofty American characters and careers remain, the wide republic will confess the benediction of a life like this, and gladly own that if with perfect faith and hope assured America would still stand and "bid the distant generations hail," the inspiration of her national life must be the sublime moral courage, the all-embracing humanity, the spotless integrity, the absolutely unselfish devotion of great powers to great public ends, which were the glory of Wendell Phillips.

CALEB CUSHING

(1800–1879)

CALEB CUSHING represented a Massachusetts district in Congress from 1835 to 1843; was United States Commissioner to China from 1843 to 1844; was a Colonel and Brigadier-General in the Mexican War; Attorney-General under the Pierce administration from 1853 to 1857; Counsel for the United States before the Geneva Arbitration Tribunal from 1871 to 1872, and Minister to Spain from 1874 to 1877. He was nominated by President Grant for Chief-Justice in 1873, but the nomination was withdrawn. He was a great lawyer who aimed to make out his case by precedents, documentary proofs, historical evidence, and close reasoning, rather than by appeals to feeling or sentiment. But in his most studied efforts of this kind he would sometimes be carried off, apparently against his will, into bursts of passionate eloquence. Active as he was in public affairs and in the practice of his profession, he found time to write a number of books. He was born at Salisbury, Massachusetts, January 17th, 1800, and died at Newburyport, Massachusetts, January 2d, 1879.

The Defense of John Quincy Adams, delivered in the House of Representatives in 1837 by Mr. Cushing, soon ceased to be a mere plea for the rights of an individual, and became a defiant and most eloquent assertion of what he called, "the primordial rights of the universal people." "I disdain to hold these rights by any parchment title," he said. "The people of the Commonwealth of Massachusetts, the people of every State of this Union, came into it in the full possession of all these rights. . . . They are rights of heaven's own giving; we hold them by the supreme tenure of revolution; we hold them by the dread arbitrament of battle; we hold them by the concession of a higher and broader charter than all the constitutions in the land; the free donation of the eternal God, when he made us to be men." This is clearly an unpremeditated outburst of deep feeling, and if the periods of which it is a part were never afterwards equaled by Mr. Cushing, it is perhaps true that the expression they give the idea of the "Higher Law" has never been equaled by any one else.

THE PRIMORDIAL RIGHTS OF THE UNIVERSAL PEOPLE

(Delivered in the House of Representatives, February 7th 1837, against Censuring John Quincy Adams for "an Effort to Present a Petition from Slaves")

THIS House is called upon to punish my colleague for the alleged offense of speaking words in his place, and in the execution of his duty, which give color to the idea that slaves possess the right of petition. Was it an offense? And if so, in what text is the offense defined and the punishment prescribed? There is no such text. The proposition is to censure my colleague at the mere will of the House—its arbitrary will—for an act which offends a portion of its members, by raising the implication of an erroneous idea. Whither is this precedent to lead? Is it not utterly subversive of the freedom of debate? A Member is not to utter an opinion, or by words of inquiry insinuate an opinion, obnoxious to the rest of the House? I must express my surprise—I will not say my indignation, because that would infer reproach—that gentlemen who continually themselves exercise the privilege of debate in its widest latitude—who stretch it to the farthest verge—who do this in the utterance of opinions offensive to a majority of the House—my profound astonishment that such gentlemen should urge the arbitrary punishment of my colleague for a pretended abuse of the right of debate. Or do Members from the South conceive they are to have the privilege of speech exclusively to themselves? If so, it is time they should awake from their self-delusion.

Relying, however, very little on the merits of the question, gentlemen seek to justify their purpose by other considerations. To begin, they denounce in no measured terms the distinguishing opinions of Massachusetts on the subject of this great question of public liberty, incidental to the resolution before us. They err most egregiously, if they believe that such opinions are exclusively peculiar to Massachusetts or to New England. Those opinions prevail quite as extensively in the great States of New York, Pennsylvania, and Ohio, for example, as they do in New England. They are, indeed, opinions of elemental right lying at the very bottom of all the political institutions of the country. It may be that such opinions are more strongly held and more universally understood in New England than elsewhere in the

United States. I may not deny it. Deny it? I glory in the fact. It is the proof and the result of our old and persevering dedication to liberty.

Gentlemen talk to us of these our great fundamental rights—as the freedom of speech, of opinion, of petition—as if they were derived from the Constitution of the United States. I scout such a doctrine. If there were a drop in my veins that did not rebel against the sentiment, it would be bastard blood. Sir, I claim to be descended from the king-killing Roundheads of the reign of Charles I. through a race of men not unremembered in peace or war; never backward in the struggles of liberty; a family upon the head of a member of which the first price of blood was set by Great Britain, in revenge of his early devotion to the cause of independence. I venerate their character and their principles. I am ready to do as they did—to abandon all the advantages of country, home, fortune, station—to fly to some western wilderness—and to live upon a handful of parched corn and a cup of cold water, with God's blessing on honest independence—sooner than I will surrender one jot or tittle of those great principles of liberty which I have sucked in with my mother's milk. I disdain to hold these rights by any parchment title. The people of the Commonwealth of Massachusetts, the people of every State of this Union, came into it in the full possession and fruition of all these rights. We did not constitute this Government as the means of acquiring new rights, but for the protection of old ones which nature had conferred upon us; which the Constitution rightly regards as pre-existing rights, and as to which all the Constitution does is to provide that these rights neither you, nor any power on earth, shall alter, abrogate, or abridge. They are rights of heaven's own giving. We hold them by the supreme tenure of revolution. We hold them by the dread arbitrament of battle. We hold them by the concession of a higher and broader charter than all the constitutions in the land,—the free donation of the eternal God when he made us to be men. These, the cardinal principles of human freedom, he has implanted in us, and placed them before and behind and around us, for our guard and guidance, like the cloud by day and the pillar of fire by night, which led the Israelites through the desert. It is a liberty, native, inborn, original, underived, imprescriptible, and acknowledged in the Constitution itself as pre-eminently before and above the Constitution.

Now, in their denunciations of the North, it is these, the very primordial rights of the universal people of the United States. that gentlemen from the South assail. They strike at the freedom of opinion, of the press, and of speech, out of doors—and the right of petition and debate in this House.

It seems to be imputed as a crime, to a portion of the inhabitants of the nonslaveholding States, that they entertain sentiments condemned by a majority of this nation. But can it be a crime? I appeal once again to that portion of the Members from the South who are foremost in this debate—I mean the gentleman from South Carolina [Mr. Thompson] and his friends—who on certain subjects differ in opinion with a great majority of their countrymen; and I ask them whether they stand prepared to abide by and sustain the doctrine that opinions, unacceptable to the majority, are a moral or political crime. Will they apply to themselves the rule of judgment which they urge so vehemently against the people of the North? Will they deliberately sanction such an odious doctrine? I know they cannot. They must perceive that it is impossible by any act of the will to control the conclusions of the mind. It is our duty, in all the contingencies of life, to weigh well the facts and the reasonings upon which our judgments are to be formed; to apply to every question a conscientious desire to arrive at the truth; to spare no means to inform ourselves rightly as to the matters which the mind is to judge. But the result is not a thing within the scope of the will. And it is monstrous, therefore, to bring opinions to the bar of legal censure. It is a violation of the interior sanctuary of a man's own soul. It is the very acme of tyranny. The arbitrary power to condemn and punish opinion is that which gave birth to the Protestant reformation, and which has rendered the inquisition a byword of odium and reproach. It is that self-same thing from which our fathers fled,—the Puritans, the Catholics, the Quakers, the Huguenots,—when they left their native Europe to found an asylum for conscience in this New World. It is that which has nerved the arm and edged the sword, in every contest of liberty, which lightens along the history of civilized man.

As to speech and the press—I admit that here there is more difficulty than in the case of opinion. It is a practical problem, extremely difficult of solution, to determine always how much of liberty in this respect is possible to be maintained, without degenerating into licentiousness. And it is a practical question,

greatly dependent on times and circumstances. I shall not seek, in these cursory remarks, to solve the problem. It suffices for my present purpose to suggest the idea, that the suppression of political inquiry, while it is a thing hostile to the general spirit of our institutions, is hard of accomplishment, and apt enough to end in aggravating the evil it is designed to remedy.

I had occasion, the last winter, to express my views on the general subject of the right of petition. They remain without change. And I can but repeat my conviction, that this, like the liberty of conscience and the press, is not a right given by the Constitution, but an original right of the constituent people of the United States, and one which they never parted with, but in their compacts of political fellowship expressly saved from all abridgment and limitation forever. The right of the people to petition for a redress of grievances, and the duty of Congress to receive and consider such petitions, are in my estimation the correlative conditions of the right. A petition is the formal mode in which the people bring their wants or opinions to the direct notice of Congress. It is an essential ingredient of representative institutions. To forbid the citizen to prefer his wishes to Congress by petition would be to lop off one of the chief democratic features of our Government, and to convert it into an aristocracy of elective despotism. It would be a curtailment of the constitutional liberties of the people of the United States, to which they could not and should not submit.

Mr. Speaker, such are my sentiments in regard to these great fundamental rights of my fellow-citizens. I think they are, in the substance and the general outline, the sentiments of the bulk of the people of the North; and I had fondly imagined, until very recently, that they were sentiments co-extensive in prevalence with the jurisdiction of the Republic. Entertaining this belief, I have deeply regretted to see the dangerous topic of slavery mixed up with other questions, wholly foreign to it in principle.

Sir, I put it to gentlemen, in all directness and sincerity, do they suppose that angry attacks on the freedom of opinion, of speech, of the press, of petition, of debate, are likely to check the spread in the United States of that disapprobation of slavery, which is but another form, conversely considered, of the love of liberty? Do they deem it possible to smother the opinions and stifle the petitions of the free men of the United States? Aye, and of the free women, too? For I confess it seems to me a strange idea to uphold, in this enlightened age, that woman, refined, educated, intellectual woman, is to have no opinion, or no right to express that opinion. Do gentlemen soberly think their cause can be strengthened in the country, by bringing to the bar of the House for contempt, by subjecting to censure, by expelling, a Representative of one of the free States, because he may have given color to the idea that slaves can petition Congress?

The resolution before the House proposes to censure my colleague for the act of stating that he held a paper purporting to be a petition from slaves, and asking of the Speaker whether such a paper fall within a certain order of the House.

Now, as I have already said, I hold the right of petition to be an original and unalienated right of the people of the United States, secured to them by the Constitution, but not derived from it. I hold that the right appertains, not to the subject-matter of the petition, but to the person of the petitioner. I hold, also, that the obligation to receive a petition corresponds to the right of petitioning; since the right, without the duty, is a mere name, and not a substance. And there may be a power to receive a petition, without any obligation to receive it, or any right to insist upon its reception as a corresponding duty. For instance, Congress has the power to receive a petition of a foreigner, and yet Congress lies under no obligation to receive it, because the right of petition is guaranteed only to the people of the United States. Is it not, as a matter of constitutional law, just so in the case of a slave? The Constitution guarantees to the constituent people of the United States their natural rights of opinion, discussion, assembly, and petition, against all abridgment. Are slaves embraced within these guarantees of the Constitution? I think not. As to the natural right of the slave in these particulars, that, like his natural right of personal freedom, not being assured to him by the constitutional compact, is not a question within the constitutional competency of Congress.

But the inquiry whether Congress may receive the petition of a slave depends on other considerations. It is a question, not of the right of the petitioner, but of the discretion or power of the petitioned. And this appears to me to be just such a matter-of-fact question of common sense as might occur in the relations of private life. There is a multitude of supposable cases in which I could receive and grant the request — that is, the petition — of

a slave. I cannot infringe the legal rights of the master without becoming amenable to the law of the land; nay, to a higher forum, since I should be doing an act immoral and dishonorable as well as illegal. He is in the eye of the law the property of his master. But is he not also a human being? Does not the Constitution of the United States expressly call him a person, while making him an integral part of the basis of representation? Can he prefer no petition, no request, no prayer, in any circumstances? If I see him drowning in the canal, or about to be struck down by a stranger, and he cry to me for succor, may I not then listen to him? Suppose a memorial to come to me from a slave, setting forth by well-authenticated statements that he is in a foreign land, oppressed and wronged, and his master, a citizen of this country, does not know it, or cannot be found; may I not bring the matter before the Government, whether it be Congress or the Executive, whichever has the power to afford redress? What I mean to say is, that, in matters having nothing to do with Abolition, and not affecting in any other respect the legal rights of the master, it might be proper and reasonable to lend an ear to the petition of a slave. These, I know, are extreme cases; and they are suggested only as illustrations of my idea; for I would no more present a petition from slaves, in derogation of any of the constitutional rights of the South, than I would offer a deliberate insult to the Chair or to the House.

Having been at all times a strenuous advocate of the freedom of opinion, of the press, and of petition, I consider it my duty to state thus explicitly my views of the existing constitutional limitation of these immunities. It were unbecoming to be a stickler for the rights of one part of the country, and blind to the rights of another part. I resist the attempt to punish my colleague by a sort of *ex post facto* law, which in its tendency extinguishes the freedom of debate, and subjects every member to the arbitrary will of a majority. I defend the particular opinions of the North. I assert the freedom of opinion, speech, the press, petition, inherent in the people of the United States, and secured to them by the Constitution. But while I maintain the sanctity, the inviolability of these rights, as it befits a representative of Massachusetts to do, I will not practice here, nor countenance elsewhere, any encroachments on the constitutional rights of the South.

ENGLAND AND AMERICA IN CHINA

(In the House of Representatives, Monday March 16th, 1840, on the British and Chinese Question — Noninterference of the United States)

I BEG leave to put a question to the chairman of the Committee on Foreign Affairs [Mr. Pickens], in regard to a matter concerning which misapprehension exists abroad, and which, though it touches individually myself and a colleague of mine now absent on a sick-bed [Mr. Lawrence], I should not have troubled the House with, if it were not of great public importance to the welfare and reputation of the United States.

[No objection being made, Mr. Cushing proceeded to say:]

I proposed a resolution early in the session, calling on the Executive for information as to our relations with China, which resolution, being afterwards submitted to the Committee on Foreign Affairs, was by them reported to the House, and adopted; and to which the Executive has since responded, in a message now in the possession of the House. My colleague [Mr. Lawrence] also presented a memorial from the citizens of the United States in China, relative to the same matter. These papers are now under consideration in the Committee on Foreign Affairs. Meanwhile, I am somewhat disturbed to learn, through the intelligence brought by the Great Western, that these movements here are construed in England as indicating a disposition on the part of the American Government "to join heart and hand" — as the expression is in a paragraph of an English ministerial journal now before me — "to join heart and hand with the British Government, and endeavor to obtain commercial treaties from the authorities in China." Now, so far as regards myself, I wish to say that this is a great misconception, if it be not a willful perversion, of what is contemplated here. I have, it is true, thought that the present contingency, — when the Americans at Canton, and they almost or quite alone, have manifested a proper respect for the laws and public rights of the Chinese Empire, in honorable contrast with the outrageous misconduct of the English there — and when the Chinese Government, grateful for the upright deportment of the Americans, has manifested the best possible feeling towards them — I have thought that these circumstances

afforded a favorable opportunity to endeavor to put the American trade with China on a just and stable footing for the future. But, God forbid that I should entertain the idea of co-operating with the British Government in the purpose — if purpose it have — of upholding the base cupidity and violence and high-handed infraction of all law, human and divine, which have characterized the operations of the British, individually and collectively, in the seas of China. I disavow all sympathy with those operations. I denounce them most emphatically.

THE EXTERMINATION OF THE INDIANS

(Delivered in the House of Representatives, February 6th, 1837)

THE fate of the Indians in every part of the United States has been a deplorable one, from the first day of our intercourse with them to the present hour. In Maine, the tribes so conspicuous once in the wars of New England and of Canada are sunk to a community of humble fishermen. In Massachusetts, in Rhode Island, in Connecticut, the Mohicans, the Pequots, the Narragansetts, names of pride and power, have dwindled to a wretched remnant. In New York, how few survive of that great and famous confederacy of the Six Nations! The Delawares and their kindred tribes have disappeared from Pennsylvania and Virginia. In the newer States, we see that process of decay or of extinction now going on which is consummated in the old ones; the Seminoles in arms on their native soil, fighting not for life or land, but for vengeance, and vowed, it would seem, like the Pequots, to a war of self-extermination; the Creeks, hurrying, in broken bands, to the West; the Cherokees, the most cultivated of the Southern tribes, pausing over their doomed exile, like the waters of the cataract, which gather themselves on the edge of the precipice, ere they leap into the inevitable abyss.

Is there no responsibility devolved on us by this state of things? That we are wholly responsible for it, I can by no means admit. The condition in which we see the Indians has arisen from the fact that they are savages; that they are savages in contact with cultivated men; that they have not had the institutions of civilized life to guard their nationality and their property against the frauds and the vices of rapacious traders and land pirates, nor the arts of civilized life wherewith to gain subsistence. These are obstacles to their preservation, which we, as a people, in our efforts for their advantage, have perseveringly, but as yet vainly, endeavored to overcome. Wars between them and us have resulted almost inevitably from our contiguity. Yet those wars are not imputable to any general spirit of unkindness on our part; and we have strenuously endeavored to prevent their arming among themselves to protect them against the frauds and injustice of the lawless of our own people, and to impart to them the blessings of civilization.

Still, indirectly, it is clear, we have to answer for the present degradation of the Indians, since we sought them, not they us; and if no Europeans had come hither, the aboriginal inhabitants of the country would have retained their independence and their sovereignty. Abstractly considered, our conduct towards them, and the doctrines of public right which govern it, are marked by many traits of injustice. You take possession of their country by what you call "the right of discovery," or by conquest. "We pay them for it," do you say? Yes, you purchase land enough for the domicile of a nation with a string of beads. And it is impossible to adjust to the standard of abstract justice a dominion built on the bones and cemented with the blood of vanquished and extinguished tribes. You must offend against their natural rights, when your power could not otherwise stand. They feel as did the Indian described by Erskine: "Who is it," said the jealous ruler of the desert, encroached upon by the restless foot of transatlantic adventure—"who is it that causes this river to rise in the high mountains and to empty itself into the ocean? Who is it that makes the loud winds of winter to blow, and that calms them again in the summer? Who is it that rears up the shade of these lofty forests, and that blasts them with the quick lightning at his pleasure? The same Being who gave to you a country beyond the water, and gave ours to us!" "And by this title we will defend it," said the warrior, throwing down his tomahawk on the ground and raising the war cry of his nation. These are the feelings of subjugated men everywhere, civilized or uncivilized. These are the feelings which produce the scenes now occurring in Florida. They are the feelings in violation of which our empire in the New World was founded. Yet, will you abandon the land now by nativity yours, the homes of your kindred and your affection? You will not? But your dominion

IV—100

distraction, and half-dissolved by the contentions of rank, the competition of service, the criminations and recriminations which have sprung up in such rank abundance, like some noxious growth of the tropics, out of the soil of East Florida? and if the desperation of a few Seminoles, either by their own efforts or the contagion of their example, can excite a war that can summon regiment after regiment of troops, to the amount, it is reported to us first and last, of some twenty-five thousand men, what would be the consequence if injustice or mismanagement should kindle a similar flame among the Cherokees, the Creeks, and the great body of the emigrant Indians? God forbid that such a calamity should descend upon our beloved country!

Dictates of duty in this matter are not less imperative than arguments of policy. The Indians are in our hands. They have been sunk to what they are, if not by us, yet through us. We have assumed the guardianship of them, and have pledged ourselves by stipulation after stipulation to watch over their welfare. I invoke the faith of treaties, I appeal to the honor of the nation, I demand of its truth and justice, if there be any sense of right in civilized communities, that we act decidedly and promptly in the execution of some well-digested plan for the benefit of the Indians subject to our authority. Let us not speak to them only as conquerors and in the language of relentless vigor, but to the vigor that shall overawe and control, let us join the justice that shall command respect and the clemency that shall conciliate affection.

over the country has no root in abstract equity, and it is extended and upheld only by your superior strength and art, not by their gratitude or their attachment for benefits received. And it behooves you to make reparation for the injury your very existence here inflicts on the Indian by promoting, in all possible ways, his welfare, civilization, and peace.

Every consideration of policy calls upon us to conciliate, if we may, the Indians within our jurisdiction. We have compacted together in the West emigrant Indians from various quarters, tribes unfriendly, inimical to each other, sections of tribes reciprocally hostile, and all embittered, more or less, against us, by whom they have been driven from their own ancient abodes and stripped of their long-descended independence. Can savage warriors, the captives of battle, transported to the West, as chiefs of the hostile Creeks have recently been, as prisoners of war in irons—can such men, constituted as they are, fail to nourish the vindictive and jealous feelings which belong to their nature? Will we take no pains to remove or allay these feelings of irritation? Will we deal justly with them hereafter? Will our equity and our mercy be manifested as signally as our power? Will we secure these victims of our destiny in their new lands; guard them against the intrusion of our own people, and from hostility among themselves? Will we redeem our promise of protection and political fellowship? It is but the question whether we shall enjoy peace and prosperity on our western frontier, or whether the Indian shall send his yell into the heart of our settlements, ravage our lands, burn our dwellings, massacre our wives and children. Would you rally his tribes to the flaming sign of war? Would you see the thirsty prairies soaked with the mingling blood of the red man and the white? If not, be warned in time by the spectacle of desolation and carnage in the South.

Is not East Florida laid waste? Have not millions upon millions been expended already in the as yet unavailing endeavor to subdue a fragment of the Seminoles? But what do we care for money? It is the sufferings of our own fellow-citizens, the lives of the brave men of our army and militia, perishing amid the pestilential swamps of that fatal region, the destruction of the deluded Indians themselves, the tarnished honor of our country, and not the treasure exhausted in war, which I deplore. How many generals have left that field of war baffled, if not defeated. Nay, is not the whole army of the United States thrown into

CYPRIAN

(200–258)

THASCIUS CÆCILIUS CYPRIAN, Bishop of Carthage, beheaded in 258 A.D., during the Valerian persecution, began life as a teacher of rhetoric and oratory at Carthage. It is said that he was passionately fond of eloquence and, on being converted to Christianity at the age of forty-eight, he quickly attained eminence in the church at a time when it could easily mean martyrdom—as it did in his case. It is said that he did more than any other early writer except possibly Saint Augustine, "to give form and character to the doctrine and practice of the Latin Church." His style as an orator is characterized by earnestness and directness, rather than by ornament. He was born about the year 200.

UNSHACKLED LIVING

(From a Sermon on the Lord's Prayer)

IT is our prayer that the will of God may be done both in heaven and in earth; each of which bears toward the accomplishment of our health and salvation. Having a body from the earth, and a spirit from heaven, we are both earth and heaven; in both, that is, both in body and spirit, we pray that God's will may be done. Flesh and spirit have a strife between them, a daily encounter from their mutual quarrel, so that we cannot do the things that we would, because the spirit seeks things heavenly and divine, the flesh desires things earthly and temporal. Hence it is our earnest prayer that by God's help and aid a peace may be established between these two; that by the doing of God's will, both in the spirit and flesh, that soul may be preserved which has been born again through him. This the Apostle Paul, in distinct and manifest words, sets forth: "The flesh," saith he, "lusteth against the spirit, and the spirit against the flesh; and these are contrary the one to the other, so that ye cannot do the things that ye would. Now the works of the flesh are manifest, which are these, adulteries, fornications, uncleanness, lasciviousness, idolatry, witchcraft, murders, hatred, variance, emulations, wrath, strife, seditions, heresies, envyings, drunkenness, reveling, and such like, of the which I tell you before, as I have also told you in times past, that they which do such things shall not inherit the kingdom of God. But the fruit of the Spirit is love, joy, peace, magnanimity, goodness, faith, kindness, continence, chastity." For this cause we make it our daily, yea, our unceasing petition, that God's will in us may be done, both in heaven and earth; for this is the will of God, that the earthly should give way to the heavenly, that spiritual and divine things should become supreme. . . .

It were a self-contradicting and incompatible thing for us, who pray that the kingdom of God may quickly come, to be looking unto long life in the world below. Thus, also, the blessed Apostle instructs us, forming and establishing the steadfastness of our hope and faith: "We brought nothing into this world, and neither can we carry anything out. Having, therefore, food and raiment, let us herewith be content. But they that will be rich fall into temptation and a snare and into many and hurtful lusts which drown men in destruction and perdition. For the love of money is the root of all evil, which, while some coveted after, they have made shipwreck from the faith, and pierced themselves through with many sorrows." He teaches us that not only are riches despicable, but are also dangerous; that in them is the root of seductive evils, misleading the blindness of the human heart by a concealed deception. Wherefore also God judges that rich fool whose thoughts were for his earthly stores, and who boasted himself in the multitude of his abundant gathering: "Thou fool, this night thy soul shall be required of thee; then whose shall those things be which thou hast provided?" The fool made merry in his stores, even that night when he was to die; and while life was ceasing from his hand, life's multiplied provision still employed his thought. The Lord, on the other hand, teaches us that he becomes the perfect and accomplished Christian who, by selling all he has and giving to the poor, stores up for himself a treasure in heaven. That man, he says, it is that can follow him and imitate the glory of the Passion of the Lord, who unimpeded and close-girt, involved in no shackle of worldly possessions, is enabled in unrestraint and freedom himself to follow after these his possessions, which he has already sent before to God. In order that each of us may train himself to this, he may learn to offer a prayer corresponding to his doing

so, and may be taught from the standard which his prayer puts before him the manner of man that he ought to be. The just man can never be in want for his daily bread since it is written, "The Lord will not suffer the soul of the righteous to famish." And again, "I have been young, and now am old, yet have I not seen the righteous forsaken, nor his seed begging bread." The Lord also makes promise and says: "Take no thought, saying, what shall we eat, or what shall we drink, or wherewithal shall we be clothed? For after all these things do the Gentiles seek; for your Father knoweth that ye have need of all these things. Seek ye first the kingdom of God and his righteousness, and all these things shall be added unto you." He promises to those who seek God's kingdom and righteousness, that all other things shall be added. For since all things are of God, to him that has God there will nothing fail, if himself be not failing unto God. Thus Daniel had a meal miraculously provided, when he was shut up by the command of the king in the den of lions; and among wild beasts hungering, yet sparing him, the man of God was nourished. Thus Elijah received sustenance in his flight, and was fed through persecution by ravens that ministered to him in his solitude, and birds that bare him meat. And oh! the horrid cruelty of human wickedness! the wild beasts spare, and the birds give food, while it is men that lurk and rage. . . .

He has added the rule besides, binding us under the fixed condition and responsibility that we are to ask for our sins to be forgiven in such sort as we forgive them that are in debt to us, knowing that our entreaties for sin will have no acceptance unless we deal toward our debtors in like manner. Hence, in another place, he says, "With what measure ye mete, it shall be measured to you again;" and the servant who, after being forgiven all his debt by his Lord, refused to forgive his fellow-servant, was cast back into prison; on refusing to yield to his fellow-servant, he lost what his Lord had previously yielded to him. These things Christ still more impressively sets forth in his commandments, in the fuller force of his authority: "When ye stand praying, forgive if ye have aught against any, that your Father also which is in heaven may forgive you your trespasses. But if ye do not forgive, neither will your Father which is in heaven forgive your trespasses." No excuse will abide you in the day of judgment, when you will be judged by your own

sentence, and as you have dealt toward others will be dealt with yourself. For God commands us to be peacemakers, and dwell with one heart and one mind in his house; and what he made us by our second nativity, such he would have us continue when new-born, that having become sons of God, we may abide in God's peace, and partake as of one spirit, so of but one heart and one mind. Hence it is that God accepts not the sacrifice of the unreconciled, and commands him to return first and agree with his brother, that the prayers of the peacemaker may set him at peace with God. . . .

After these things, at the conclusion of the prayer, comes a sentence comprising shortly and collectively the whole of our petitions and desires. We end by saying, "Deliver us from evil," comprehending all adverse things which the enemy in this world devises against us; wherefrom we have a faithful and firm protection, if God deliver us, and grant his aid to our entreaties and complaints. But having said, "Deliver us from evil," there remains nothing beyond for us to ask for, after petition made for God's protection from evil; for that gained, we stand secure and safe against all things that the devil and the world work against us. What fear hath he from this life, who has God through life for his guardian? We need not wonder, dearest brethren, that this is God's prayer, seeing how his instruction comprises all our petitioning in one saving sentence. This had already been prophesied by Isaiah the prophet, when, filled with the Holy Spirit, he spoke concerning the majesty and mercy of God; "summing up and cutting short his word, in righteousness, because a short word will God make in the whole earth." For when the word of God, our Lord Jesus Christ, came unto all, and, gathering together alike the learned and the unlearned, did to every sex and age set forth the precepts of salvation, he made a full compendium of his instructions, that the memory of the scholars might not labor in the heavenly discipline, but accept with readiness whatsoever was necessary unto a simple faith. Thus, when he taught what is life eternal, he gathered the mystery of life within an especial and divine brevity. "This," said he, "is life eternal, that they might know thee, the only true God, and Jesus Christ whom thou hast sent." In like manner, when he gathered forth from the law and prophets what were the first and greatest commandments, he said, "Hear, O Israel, the Lord thy God is one God. And thou shalt love the Lord

thy God with all thy heart, and with all thy soul, and with all thy strength: this is the first and great commandment. And the second is like unto it, Thou shalt love thy neighbor as thyself. On these two commandments hang all the law and the prophets." And again, "Whatever good things ye would that men should do unto you, do ye even so to them; for this is the law and the prophets." . . .

Those who pray ought to come to God, not with unfruitful or naked prayers. Vainly we ask, when it is a barren petition that is given to God. For since "every tree not bringing forth good fruit is hewn down and cast into the fire," surely words also which bring no fruit must fail of favor with God, seeing they are joined with no productiveness in righteous deeds. Hence Divine Scripture instructs us, saying, "Prayer is good, with fasting and alms." For he who, in the day of judgment, will render to us a reward for our good works and alms is also a gracious listener to any that approach him in prayer, with the company of good works. Thus was it that the Centurion Cornelius, when he prayed, found a title to be heard. For he was one "that did many alms-deeds toward the people, and ever prayed to God." To him, when he was praying about the ninth hour, an angel came nigh, rendering testimony to his deeds, and saying, "Cornelius, thy prayers and thine alms are gone up in remembrance before God." Quickly do prayers go up to God, when the claims of our good works introduce them before him. Thus, also, the angel Raphael bare witness to the continual praying and continual alms-deeds of Tobias, saying, "It is honorable to reveal and confess the works of God. For when thou didst pray, and Sara, I did bring the remembrance of your prayers before the holiness of God. And when thou didst bury the dead, I was with thee likewise; and because thou didst not delay to rise up and leave thy dinner, to go and cover the dead, I was sent to prove thee; and now God hath sent me to heal thee and Jona, thy daughter-in-law. For I am Raphael, one of the seven holy angels, which go in and out before the glory of God." By Isaiah, likewise, the Lord admonishes and teaches us like things, thus testifying: "Loosen every knot of unrighteousness; release the oppression of contracts which have no power. Let the troubled go in peace, and break every unjust engagement. Deal thy bread to the hungry, and bring the poor that are cast out to thy house. When thou seest the naked, cover him, and

despise not them of thine own flesh. Then shall thy light break
forth in season, and thy raiment shall spring forth speedily, and
righteousness shall go before thee, and the glory of God shall
cover thee. Then shalt thou call, and God shall hear thee, and
while thou shalt yet speak, he shall say, Here I am." He promises that he is nigh, and hears and protects those who, loosening
the knots of unrighteousness from the heart, and giving alms
among the household of God, according to his commandment,
do, by hearkening to what God claims of them, themselves acquire a title to be heard of him. The blessed Paul, having been
assisted by the brethren in a needful time of pressure, declared
that good works performed were sacrifices to God. "I am full,"
saith he, "having received of Epaphroditus the things which
were sent from you, an odor of a sweet smell, a sacrifice acceptable, well-pleasing to God. For when one hath pity on the poor,
he lendeth to God"; and he that gives, even to the least, gives
to God, spiritually sacrificing to God an odor of a sweet smell.

CYRIL

(315–386)

CYRIL of Jerusalem bears translation into English much better
than many others of the celebrated pulpit orators of the
first centuries of the Christian era. In many of the sermons
of that period eloquence, which depends primarily on profound religious conviction, scarcely survives at all when deprived of its melodious expression in Greek or Latin. Cyril, however, has a poetry of
idea, which makes such sermons as that which he preached from the
second and third verses of the thirty-eighth chapter of Job, eloquent
in any language into which they are translated. He was born near
Jerusalem about 315 A. D. In 350 A. D. he succeeded to the bishopric of Jerusalem, from which seven years later he was deposed as
the result of a controversy with Acacius, the Arian Bishop of Cæsarea. Four years later he was restored to his see and held it until
his death in 386 A. D. His works were edited by Touttée in 1720.

THE INFINITE ARTIFICES OF NATURE

(From a Sermon on the Second and Third Verses of the Thirty-Eighth Chapter of Job)

WHAT! is there not much to wonder at in the sun, which, being small to look on, contains in it an intensity of power,
appearing from the east, and shooting his light even to
the west? The Psalmist describes his rising at dawn, when he
says, "Which is as a bridegroom coming out of his chamber."
This is a description of his pleasant and comely array on first
appearing to men; for when he rides at high noon we are wont
to flee from his blaze; but at his rising he is welcome to all, as
a bridegroom to look on. Behold, also, how he proceeds (or
rather not he, but one who has by his bidding determined his
course); how in summer time aloft in the heavens he finishes
off longer days, giving men due time for their works; while in
winter he straightens his course, lest the day's cold last too long,
and that the night's lengthening may conduce both to the rest
of men, and to the fruitfulness of the earth's productions. And

see, likewise, in what order the days correspond to each other, in
summer increasing, in winter diminishing, but in spring and autumn affording one another a uniform length; and the night
again in like manner. And as the Psalmist saith concerning
them, "Day unto day uttereth speech, and night unto night
showeth knowledge."

For to those who have no ears, they almost shout aloud, and
by their orders say there is no other God save their Maker
and the appointer of their bounds, him who laid out the universe. . . .

Those persons ought to have felt astonishment and admiration, not only at the sun and moon, but also at the well-ordered
choirs of the stars, their unimpeded courses, their respective risings
in due season; and how some are the signs of summer, others of
winter, and how some mark the time of sowing, others introduce
the season of sailing. And man, sitting in his ship, and sailing
on the boundless waves, looks at the stars and steers his vessel.
Well, says Scripture, concerning these bodies, "Let them be for
signs and for seasons, and for days and for years"; not for star-
gazing and vain tales of nativities. Observe, too, how consider-
ately he imparts the daylight by a gradual growth; for the sun
does not rise upon us while we gaze, all at once, but a little
light runs up before him, that by previous trial our eyeball may
bear his stronger ray; and again, how he has cheered the darkness of night by the gleam of moonlight.

Who is the father of rain; and who hath given birth to the
drops of dew? Who hath condensed the air into clouds, and bid
them carry the fluid mass of showers, at one time bringing from
the north golden clouds, at another giving these a uniform appearance, and then again curling them up into festoons and other
figures manifold? Who can number the clouds in wisdom? of
which Job saith, "He knoweth the balancings of the clouds, and
hath bent down the heaven to the earth; and he who numbereth
the clouds in wisdom; and the cloud is not rent under them."
For though measures of water ever so many weigh upon the
clouds, yet they are not rent, but with all order come down
upon the earth. Who brings the winds out of his treasures?
Who, as just now said, "hath given birth to the drops of dew?
Out of whose womb cometh forth the ice," watery in its substance, but like stone in its properties? And at one time the
water becomes snow like wool, at another it ministers to him

who scatters the hoar-frost like ashes; at another it is changed
into a stormy substance, since he fashions the waters as he will.
Its nature is uniform, its properties manifold. Water in the
vines is wine, which maketh glad the heart of man; and in the
olives oil, to make his face to shine; and is further transformed
into bread, which strengtheneth man's heart, and into all kinds
of fruits.

For such wonders was the great artificer to be blasphemed,
or rather worshiped? And, after all, I have not yet spoken of
that part of his wisdom which is not seen. Contemplate the
spring and the flowers of all kinds, in all their likeness, still
diverse from one another: the deep crimson of the rose, and the
exceeding whiteness of the lily. They come of one and the
same rain, one and the same earth. Who has distinguished, who
has formed them? Now do consider this attentively: The substance of the tree is one—part is for shelter, part for this or
that kind of fruit, and the artificer is one. The vine is one, and
part of it is for fuel, part for clusters. Again, how wondrously
thick are the knots which run round the reeds, as the artificer
hath made them! But of the one earth came creeping things,
and wild beasts and cattle and trees and food and gold and silver and brass and iron and stone. Water was but one nature;
yet of it comes the life of things that swim and of birds, and
as the one swims in the waters, so also the birds fly in the air.

And this great and wide sea, in it are things creeping innumerable. Who can tell the beauty of the fishes that are therein?
Who can describe the greatness of the whales, and the nature of
its amphibious animals? how they live both on dry land and in
the waters? Who can tell the depth and breadth of the sea, or
the force of its enormous waves? Yet it stays within its boundaries, because of him who said, "Hitherto shalt thou come, and
no further; and here shall thy proud waves be stayed." And to
show the decree imposed on it when it runs upon the land, it
leaves a plain line on the sands by its waves, declaring, as it
were, to those who see it, that it has not passed its appointed
bounds.

Who can understand the nature of the fowls of the air,—how
some have with them a voice of melody, and others have their
wings enriched with all manner of painting, and others soaring
on high stay motionless in the midst of the sky, as the hawk?
For by the Divine command, "the hawk, having spread out her

wings, stays motionless, looking down toward the south." Who of men can behold the eagle? But if thou canst not read the mystery of birds when soaring on high, how wouldst thou read the Maker of all things?

Who among men knows even the names of all wild beasts, or who can accurately classify their natures? But if we know not even their bare names, how should we comprehend their Maker? The command of God was but one, which said: "Let the earth bring forth wild beasts and cattle and creeping things, after their kinds"; and distinct natures sprang from one voice, at one command—the gentle sheep and carnivorous lion—also the various instincts of irrational creatures, as representations of the various characters of men. The fox is an emblem of men's craftiness, and the snake of a friend's envenomed treachery, and the neighing horse of wanton young men, and that busy ant to arouse the sluggish and the dull; for when a man passes his youth idly, then he is instructed by irrational creatures, being reproved by that Scripture which saith, "Go to the ant, thou sluggard; consider her ways and be wise," for when thou beholdest her in due season treasuring up food for herself, do thou copy her, and treasure up for thyself the fruits of good works for the world to come. And again, "Go to the bee, and learn how industrious she is"; how, hovering about all kinds of flowers, she culls the honey for thy use, that thou, also, ranging over Holy Scriptures, mayst lay hold on thy salvation, and, being satisfied with it, mayst say: "How sweet are thy words unto my taste; yea, sweeter than honey and the honeycomb unto my mouth."

Is not the Artificer, then, rather worthy to be glorified? For what, if thou know not the nature of everything, are the things, therefore, which he has made, without their use? For canst thou know the efficacy of all herbs? or canst thou learn all the advantage which comes of every animal? Even from poisonous adders have come antidotes for the preservation of men. But thou wilt say to me: "The snake is terrible." Fear thou the Lord, and it shall not be able to hurt thee. "The scorpion stings." Fear thou the Lord, and it shall not sting thee. "The lion is bloodthirsty." Fear thou the Lord, and he shall lie down beside thee, as by Daniel. And, truly, there is whereat to wonder, in the power even of the creatures; how some, as the scorpion, have their weapon in a sting, while the power of others is

in their teeth, and others, again, get the better by means of hoofs, and the basilisk's might is his gaze. Thus, from this varied workmanship, think of the Artificer's power.

But these things, perchance, thou art not acquainted with; thou hast nothing in common with the creatures which are without thee. Now, then, enter into thyself and consider the Artificer of thine own nature. What is there to find fault with in the framing of thy body? Master thine own self, and there shall nothing evil proceed from any of thy members. At the first, Adam, in Paradise, was without clothing, as was Eve; but it was not because of aught that he was that he was cast out. Naught that we are, then, is the cause of sin, but they who abuse what they are; but the Maker is wise. Who hath "fenced us with sinews and bones, and clothed us with skin and flesh"; and, soon as the babe is born, brings forth fountains of milk out of the breast? And how doth the babe grow to be a child, and the child to be a youth, and then to be a man, and is again changed into an old man, no one the while discerning exactly each day's change? How, also, does part of our food become blood, while another part is separated for the draught, and another is changed into flesh? Who is it that gives the never-ceasing motion to the heart? Who hath wisely guarded the tenderness of the eyes with the fence of the eyelids? for, concerning the complicated and wonderful contrivance of the eyes, scarcely do the ample rolls of physicians sufficiently inform us. Who, also, hath sent each breath we draw, through the whole body? Thou seest, O man, the Artificer; thou seest the wise Contriver.

GEORGE M. DALLAS

(1792–1864)

EORGE MIFFLIN DALLAS, of Philadelphia, Vice-President of the United States under the Polk administration (1845–49), represents in American history the practical politics of the period during which Pennsylvania was the "Keystone State." After Jackson, with the Southwest behind him, had destroyed the balance between Virginia and New England, there was a period of twenty years or more, ending with Buchanan and the Civil War, during which the question of the balance of power in national politics was between New York and Pennsylvania, with the advantage in favor of the latter State. In 1832 when Dallas spoke in the Senate against the position of South Carolina on the tariff, he defined the "Pennsylvania Idea" of his day by saying, "I am inflexible, sir, for nothing but adequate protection." Yet such are the compromises of politics that he was nominated for Vice-President on the ticket with Polk, of Tennessee, while it was under Buchanan, of Pennsylvania, that the country made its nearest approach to free trade.

Dallas was born in Philadelphia, July 10th, 1792. He was a graduate of Princeton, and his speeches show him to have been a man of superior education. His first political service was in Russia as an attaché of the American legation under Gallatin. Most of his life was spent in the public service. He was Mayor of Philadelphia, 1825; United States District-Attorney under Jackson, 1829; United States Senator, 1831–33; Ambassador to Russia under Van Buren, 1837–39; Vice-President of the United States, 1845–49; and Minister to England, 1856–61. He died at Philadelphia, December 31st, 1864.

«THE PENNSYLVANIA IDEA»

(From the Speech against South Carolina's Position on the Tariff—Delivered in the United States Senate, Monday, February 27th, 1832)

FIFTY-SIX years have ripened this confederated nation to a condition of unprecedented and incontestable greatness; greatness in extent; greatness in resources; greatness in moral and intellectual character; greatness in political structure and jurisprudence; greatness in the renown which follows just and successful wars; and greatness which results from the acquisition

of a before unknown sum of human contentment and freedom. Providence has smiled upon the work of our progenitors, and has blessed its progress. The whole civilized world has marked, with reiterated astonishment, the rapidity of our advancement; and, at this moment, from the Pisgah of Eastern eminence, exulting and longing myriads are pointing to our Western institutions as the objects towards which they have yet fruitlessly journeyed through a wilderness of ages and of wretchedness.

Who is there, sir, that, seeing this great result of our councils and forecast, can desire a change in the organic structure or practical legislation by which it has been effected? I have heard much on this floor of sectional divisions, sectional interests, sectional doctrines, sectional feelings, and sectional parties; of the East, the South, and the West; but I cannot adopt the language, and will not entertain the sentiments by which it is prompted. I claim no peculiar merit for the noble Commonwealth whose representative I am, for her uniform devotion to the union and democracy of these States, for her unwavering co-operation in all the efforts which have carried the nation to its present exaltation; she has done no more and no less than other portions of our Republic. But I will not recognize the right, claimed from what quarter it may be, to mar and deface the monument of our common labors; to tear down piecemeal, or at a blow, the structure which every hand has equaled and simultaneously contributed to erect; to prostrate and crumble into dust the fairest fabric ever yet reared by the energies and virtues of confederated freemen.

If, sir, in the picture I have sketched of the condition of our country, shades have been omitted which really exist, they ought to be introduced, they ought to be frankly met, and the assembled wisdom of the legislative bodies should anxiously devise remedies and relief. The impressive and gloomy description of the Senator from South Carolina [Mr. Hayne] as to the actual state and wretched prospects of his immediate fellow-citizens, awakens the liveliest sympathy and should command our attention. It is their right; it is our duty. I cannot feel indifferent to the sufferings of any portion of the American people; and esteem it inconsistent with the scope and purpose of the Federal Constitution that any majority, no matter how large, should connive at, or protract, the oppression or misery of any minority, no matter how small. I disclaim and detest the idea of making one part subservient to another; of feasting upon the extorted substance of my countrymen; of enriching my own region by draining the fertility and resources of a neighbor; of becoming wealthy with spoils which leave their legitimate owners impoverished and desolate. But, sir, I want proof of a fact, whose existence, at least as described, it is difficult even to conceive; and, above all, I want the true causes of that fact to be ascertained; to be brought within the reach of legislative remedy, and to have that remedy of a nature which may be applied without producing more mischiefs than those it proposes to cure. The proneness to exaggerate social evils is greatest with the most patriotic. Temporary embarrassment is sensitively apprehended to be permanent. Every day's experience teaches how apt we are to magnify partial into universal distress, and with what difficulty an excited imagination rescues itself from despondency. It will not do, sir, to act upon the glowing or pathetic delineations of a gifted orator; it will not do to become enlisted, by ardent exhortations, in a crusade against established systems of policy; it will not do to demolish the walls of our citadel to the sounds of plaintive eloquence, or fire the temple at the call of impassioned enthusiasm.

What, sir, is the cause of Southern distress? Has any gentleman yet ventured to designate it? Can any one do more than s ppose, or argumentatively assume it? I am neither willing nor competent to flatter. To praise the honorable Senator from South Carolina would be —

« To add perfume to the violet —
Wasteful and ridiculous excess.»

But if he has failed to discover the source of the evils he deplores, who can unfold it? Amid the warm and indiscriminating denunciations with which he has assailed the policy of protecting dome_tic manufactures and native produce, he frankly avows that he would not "deny that there are other causes besides the tariff, which have contributed to produce the evils which he has depicted." What are those "other causes"? In what proportion have they acted? How much of this dark shadowing is ascribable to each singly, and to all in combination? Would the tariff be at all felt, or denounced, if these other causes were not in operation? Would not, in fact, its influence, its discriminations, its inequalities, its oppressions, but for these "other causes," be

IV—101

shaken by the elasticity and energy and exhaustless spirit of the South, as "dewdrops from the lion's mane"? These inquiries, sir, must be satisfactorily answered before we can be justly required to legislate away an entire system. If it be the root of all evil, let it be exposed and demolished. If its poisonous exhalations be but partial, let us preserve such portions as are innoxious. If, as the luminary of day, it be pure and salutary in itself, let us not wish it extinguished, because of the shadows, clouds, and darkness, which obscure its brightness or impede its vivifying power.

Sir, there are "other causes" than the policy of protection, to which our Southern brethren might, and, in my opinion, ought to impute the deplored evils under which they suffer. Some of these are adequate to produce, and, if not providentially arrested in their progress, will unavoidably produce calamities far more extensive and desolating than any yet experienced. Every day, every hour, augments their force, enlarges their sphere, and manifests their agency. Nor is their onward march a sketch of fancy, or the conclusion of plausible argument; it is a fact, discernible to every eye, known to every well-informed man in the country, appreciated by every candid one, and disputed by none. The delusion and mistake lie in considering these "other causes" as secondary and slight, instead of primary and powerful; in visiting upon a subject of political dislike, consequences fairly and obviously attributable to specific, natural, social, or moral agencies; in fastening upon the tariff, as fanatics are apt to fasten upon their reputed conjurer or wizard, the storm of the elements, the barrenness of plantations, the debility arising from constitutional disease, and the mysterious operations of decay. . . .

I am inflexible, sir, as to nothing but adequate protection. The process of attaining that may undergo any mutation. Secure that to the home labor of this country, and our opponents shall have, as far as my voice and suffrage can give it to them, a *carte blanche* whereon to settle any arrangement or adjustment their intelligence may suggest. It might have been expected, not unreasonably, that they who desired change should tender their project; that they would designate noxious particulars, and intimate their remedies; that they would invoke the skill and assistance of practical and experienced observers on a subject with which few of us are familiar; and point with precision to such parts of the extensive system as can be modified without weak-

ening or endangering the whole structure. They have forborne to do this. They demand an entire demolition. Free trade is the burden of their eloquence, the golden fleece of their adventurous enterprise, the goal short of which they will not pause even to breathe. I cannot join their expedition for such an object. An established policy, coeval, in the language of President Jackson, with our Government; believed by an immense majority of our people to be constitutional, wise, and expedient, may not be abruptly abandoned by Congress without a treacherous departure from duty, a shameless dereliction of sacred trust and confidence. To expect it is both extravagant and unkind. But show us your scheme; call it one of revenue exclusively, if you will; names and epithets are immaterial; let it accommodate our policy with the new fiscal attitude of the nation and with your wishes; and, for one, I will give it the favorable hearing and consideration to which the purity of your motives and your alleged sufferings certainly entitle it. It is not impossible, sir (though I confess myself a very feeble instructor on this vast business), that some rational project may spring from sober and analytical inquiry to reconcile us all. I have heard intimated that new regulations in collecting the revenue might make the protection to manufactures even more effectual than it now is, and yet remove every cause of complaint. Let gentlemen set them forth for candid scrutiny. Shall it be by exacting the payment of duties in cash? By a system of licenses to auctioneers? By abolishing the assessment of duties on minimum values? Develop the scheme and enable us to judge. Do you prefer attaining your purpose by specific reductions of duty? On what articles, then? to what extent? by what gradual decrease? All we desire to enable us to prove our readiness to accommodate this entangling and distracting theme of legislation is that generalities may be relinquished; that an unconditional surrender to the Utopian theory of free trade may not be invoked; and that such modifications of the existing policy may be chalked out as will be useful to our opponents without being destructive to the policy itself.

I lament, Mr. President, having been obliged, in the discharge of a supposed duty, to trespass so long upon the indulgent attention of the Senate. I would close cheerfully, and forbear, in conformity with my original determination, adverting to any topic not directly connected with the subject of discussion. One mat-

ter, however, has been incidentally introduced, and has, in truth, been often vehemently urged upon our reflection, as to which I might be deemed a faithless and unfeeling representative were I to abstain from expressing the decided sense and anxious sentiments of the patriotic community who sent me here.

Sir, I have nothing so much and so deeply at heart as the maintenance of the harmony and perpetuity of this Union. Whatever may be the contrary and irreconcilable appearance of opinions, no danger is to be apprehended, and no difference can be contemned, while the preservation of our Constitution and the good of the country are the leading and paramount objects of us all. If there be any — certainly there are none upon this floor — who seek to distract the peace and dissolve the bonds of our federative Government; who would put at hazard, in pursuit of temporary projects, or to indulge ambitious aspirants, the repose and institutions of the Republic; who contemplate change and revolution; I beseech such men to extend their forecasting vision into the future, and to confront posterity. Let them be warned, by anticipating the judgment of that tribunal. The excitements of the day may be gratified; they may delude themselves into the belief that they are laboring to vindicate the Constitution, or to uphold the principles of human liberty; but if they recklessly involve the American people in the horrors, uncertainties, and fatal consequences of civil war, and of violent disruption, they must be content to receive, as a merited reward, an immortality of detestation. Their party and paltry pretexts will be forgotten; their refined discriminations in theory and their high-wrought declamation will be forgotten; even their virtuous passions will cease to extenuate their offense; and all posterity, struggling in vain to recombine the elements and to rebuild the edifice of our great and glorious and happy confederacy — amid the desolation of perpetual conflicts and in the darkness of sectional bondage — will doom them to loud, deep, and everlasting execration. Let no man, sir, seek elevation or renown, at the price of the National Union and tranquillity. He will never find it. Failing, he must rank during life among the few outcasts whom we have yet engendered; and if he achieve his country's ruin, when dead, the burning lava of universal hatred will roll hissing over his grave; and, though like "the aspiring youth who fired the Ephesian dome," he should acquire fame, it will be the fame of bitter and boundless abhorrence.

PETER DAMIANI

(1007–1072)

ST. PETER DAMIANI, poet, preacher, reformer, and flagellant, was born at Ravenna, Italy, in 1007. Such of his sermons as survive have all the characteristics of the Middle Ages before the Revival of Learning. That on the Last Journey of our Lord, in which he treats the untying of the ass on which Christ rode into Jerusalem as a parable, is a type of a class which illustrates the influence of the Northern races on oratory and literature. Damiani is an Italian by birth only, for in his style and modes of thought he represented the Gothic influences which in overthrowing Rome overthrew learning also. At the age of twenty-nine he became a hermit at Fonte Avellano in Umbria. He was noted for asceticism and self-inflicted scourgings. As a result, he became the head of an order of Flagellants, acquiring great influence which he used to put down the practice of simony and other abuses. He rose to the dignity of Bishop of Ostia and afterwards to that of Cardinal, with great influence at Rome. Besides his sermons, he left a number of poems, biographies of the saints, and other works.

THE SECRET OF TRUE GREATNESS

(From the Sermon, «The Presentation of Our Lord in the Temple»)

IT DELIGHTS the heart to celebrate the present, let us take pleasure also in expecting the coming festival. Let that teach us to render thanks to our Redeemer; let this kindle us to the love of the celestial country. In that let us learn how much God suffered for man; in this let us meditate to how great a height of glory man has ascended by God. In that the only-begotten Son of God was humbly presented in the Temple; in this his most blessed servant was elevated in glory to the palace of heaven. In that his parents carried our Redeemer to Jerusalem that they might present him to the Lord; in this the holy angels carried to the heavenly Jerusalem the soul of this blessed confessor that they might present it to the presence of the Divine Majesty. In that the Mediator of God and Man, after

his circumcision, was presented as an infant in the temple; in this, the confessor, after laying aside the load of his earthly body, ascended in freedom to heaven. In that he who owed nothing to the law paid the tribute of the law; in this, he, who was obnoxious to death, escaped the dominion of death. The one in his birth from his mother vouchsafed to become mortal; the other by his death in the flesh merited to become immortal. God, by coming into the world, took upon himself the form of a servant; Severus, by departing from the world, was raised to the dignity of angels. But, unless the one had descended, the other could in no wise have ascended. Unless God had assumed the form of man, man could never have attained to the glory of heaven. Unless God had been humbled beneath himself, man could never have been exalted above himself. And what more shall I say? Unless he, that is God and Man, had been made a little lower than the angels, he that is mere man could never have become the equal of the angels. Which equality the Truth set forth in the Gospel, saying, "In the Resurrection they neither marry nor are given in marriage, but are like the angels of God in heaven." To this height of most happy dignity, if, O man, thou desirest to be elevated, endeavor with thy whole strength to be prostrated in the dejection of true humility; if thou desirest to be exalted in Christ, be first cast down in thyself; subdue the pride of the flesh, and raise thyself to the altitude of the Creator; restrain whatever swells within thyself, and thou shalt soon be exalted far beyond thyself.

NEW TESTAMENT HISTORY AS ALLEGORY

(From the Sermon on «The Last Journey of Our Lord to Jerusalem»)

BUT when I consider thee, Lord Jesus, my admiration and my compassion increase. Why dost thou go to the Jews who lie in wait for thy soul? They are betrayers and murderers; trust not thyself to them for they love thee not; they will not pity thee; they will condemn thee to a most base death. Why dost thou hasten to endure such mocking, such scourging, such blaspheming? to be crowned with thorns, to be spit upon, to have vinegar given to thee to drink, to be pierced with the spear, to die, and to be laid in the sepulchre? In this thy resolution, in this thy design? My soul, when I consider it is over-

whelmed. I grieve with thee, Lord Jesus, over the miseries of thy passion. The advice of Peter, thy friend, is that which I should have given, who said, "Be it far from thee, Lord; this shall not happen unto thee. It is not meet that the Son of God should taste death." But this differs from thy counsel, who art determined to undergo thy passion. What then? Are we to follow the advice of Peter or Jesus? of the servant or of the Lord? of the disciple or of the Master? But the servant is not greater than his Lord, nor is the disciple more learned than his Master. We must acquiesce, therefore, in the determination of the Lord and Master who needs no other counsel; lest it be said to us with Peter, Get thee behind me, Satan; thou savorest not the things that be of God. For Peter knew not that Christ had from the beginning foreordained his passion, that by death he might destroy our death, and by rising again might restore our life.

That, then, which Divine Wisdom had foreordained he desired wisely to accomplish. He willed, according to the words of the prophet, to be humble and poor, to ride upon an ass, and so to enter into Jerusalem; as the Evangelist relates, saying: "When Jesus drew nigh to Jerusalem and was come to Bethphage and the Mount of Olives, then sent he two of his Disciples, saying: Go into the village over against you, and ye shall straightway find an ass tied and a colt with her; loose them, and bring them unto me." This village is the world, which rages against the Lord and his Disciples, not only by persecuting them with reproaches and injuries, but by inflicting on them a most cruel death. By the ass and the colt which were tied in the village are signified the people of the Jews, and that of the Gentiles, both of them in bondage to the chain of their sins. The ass, accustomed to the yoke, typifies the Jewish people that were subject to the yoke of the law. The colt that was wanton and unbridled denotes the Gentiles, who walked after the lusts of their own hearts. The two Disciples sent into the village are the preachers of the two Testaments, endued with twofold charity, the love of God and the love of our neighbor; or else Peter and Paul, of whom one was the Apostle of the Jews, and the other of the Gentiles. Whence the same Paul: "For he, who worked in Peter his apostleship, worked also with me among the Gentiles." These loosed both people from the error of infidelity, and, by the word of their preaching, brought them to the faith of Jesus Christ.

JOHN W. DANIEL

(1842–)

JOHN WARWICK DANIEL was born at Lynchburg, Virginia, September 5th, 1842. He was a boy at school when the Civil War began, but left his books to enlist as a private in the Stonewall Brigade. Wounded several times, he came out of the war a Major and went soon afterwards to the University of Virginia to complete his education. After studying law at the University, he was elected to the Virginia Legislature, and in the period between 1869 and 1881 served in both houses of that body, making such a reputation for oratory and general efficiency that the Democrats nominated him for Governor against Cameron. The "Readjuster" movement elected Cameron, but Mr. Daniel was elected to Congress in 1884 and a year later was chosen as the successor of General Mahone in the United States Senate. He has the reputation of being one of the most eloquent men in that body.

AT THE DEDICATION OF THE WASHINGTON MONUMENT

(From the Oration Delivered in the Hall of the House of Representatives, February 21st, 1885)

Mr. President of the United States, Senators, Representatives, Judges, Mr. Chairman, and My Countrymen:—

ALONE in its grandeur stands forth the character of Washington in history; alone like some peak that has no fellow in the mountain range of greatness.

"Washington," says Guizot, "Washington did the two greatest things which in politics it is permitted to man to attempt. He maintained by peace the independence of his country, which he had conquered by war. He founded a free government in the name of the principles of order and by re-establishing their sway." Washington did, indeed, do these things. But he did more. Out of disconnected fragments he molded a whole, and made it a country. He achieved his country's independence by the sword. He maintained that independence by peace as by war. He finally established both his country and its freedom in an enduring frame of constitutional government, fashioned to make liberty and union one and inseparable. These four things together constitute the unexampled achievement of Washington.

The world has ratified the profound remark of Fisher Ames, that "he changed mankind's ideas of political greatness." It has approved the opinion of Edward Everett, that he was "the greatest of good men, and the best of great men." It has felt for him, with Erskine, "an awful reverence." It has attested the declaration of Brougham that "he was the greatest man of his own or of any age." . . .

Conquerors who have stretched your sceptres over boundless territories; founders of empires who have held your dominions in the reign of law; reformers who have cried aloud in the wilderness of oppression; teachers who have striven to cast down false doctrine, heresy, and schism; statesmen whose brains have throbbed with mighty plans for the amelioration of human society; scar-crowned vikings of the sea, illustrious heroes of the land, who have borne the standards of siege and battle, come forth in bright array from your glorious fanes, and would ye be measured by the measure of his stature? Behold you not in him a more illustrious and more venerable presence? Statesman, soldier, patriot, sage, reformer of creeds, teacher of truth and justice, achiever and preserver of liberty, the first of men, founder and savior of his country, father of his people — this is he, solitary and unapproachable in his grandeur!

Oh, felicitous Providence that gave to America our Washington!

High soars into the sky to-day, higher than the pyramid or the dome of St. Paul's or St. Peter's — the loftiest and most imposing structure that man has ever reared — high soars into the sky to where —

"Earth highest yearns to meet a star,"

the monument which "We the people of the United States" have uplifted to his memory. It is a fitting monument, more fitting than any statue. For his image could only display him in some one phase of his varied character. So art has fitly typified his exalted life in yon plain, lofty shaft. Such is his greatness, that only by a symbol could it be represented. As Justice must be

blind in order to be whole in contemplation, so History must be silent that by this mighty sign she may disclose the amplitude of her story. . . .

It has seemed fitting to you, Mr. Chairman and gentlemen of the commission, that a citizen of the State which was the birthplace and the home of Washington; whose House of Burgesses, of which he was a member, made the first burst of opposition against the Stamp Act, although less pecuniarily interested therein than their New England brethren, and was the first representative body to recommend a general congress of the Colonies; of the State whose Mason drew that Bill of Rights which has been called the Magna Charta of America; whose Jefferson wrote, whose Richard Henry Lee moved, the Declaration that those Colonies be "free and independent States"; whose Henry condensed the Revolution into the electric sentence, "Liberty or death"; of the State which cemented union with the vast territorial dowry out of which five States have been carved, having now here some ninety Representatives; of that State whose Madison was named "the Father of the Constitution," and whose Marshall became its most eminent expounder; of the State which holds within its bosom the sacred ashes of Washington, and cherishes not less the principles which once kindled them with fires of Heaven descended — it has seemed fitting to you, gentlemen, that a citizen of that State should also be invited to deliver an address on this occasion.

Would with all my heart that a worthier one had been your choice. Too highly do I esteem the position in which you place me to feel aught but solemn distrustfulness and apprehension. And who, indeed, might not shrink from such a theatre when a Winthrop's eloquence still thrilled all hearts, with Washington the theme?

Yet, in Virginia's name I thank you for the honor done her. She deserved it. Times there are when even hardihood is virtue; and to such virtue alone do I lay claim in venturing to abide your choice to be her spokesman. . . .

No sum could now be made of Washington's character that did not exhaust language of its tributes and repeat virtue by all her names. No sum could be made of his achievements that did not unfold the history of his country and its institutions — the history of his age and its progress — the history of man and his destiny to be free. But, whether character or achievement be

regarded, the riches before us only expose the poverty of praise. So clear was he in his great office that no ideal of the leader or ruler can be formed that does not shrink by the side of the reality. And so has he impressed himself upon the minds of men, that no man can justly aspire to be the chief of a great free people who does not adopt his principles and emulate his example. We look with amazement on such eccentric characters as Alexander, Cæsar, Cromwell, Frederick, and Napoleon, but when Washington's face rises before us, instinctively mankind exclaims: "This is the man for nations to trust and reverence, and for rulers to follow."

Drawing his sword from patriotic impulse, without ambition and without malice, he wielded it without vindictiveness and sheathed it without reproach. All that humanity could conceive he did to suppress the cruelties of war and soothe its sorrows. He never struck a coward's blow. To him age, infancy, and helplessness were ever sacred. He tolerated no extremity unless to curb the excesses of his enemy, and he never poisoned the sting of defeat by the exultation of the conqueror.

Peace he welcomed as a heaven-sent herald of friendship; and no country has given him greater honor than that which he defeated; for England has been glad to claim him as the scion of her blood, and proud, like our sister American States, to divide with Virginia the honor of producing him.

Fascinated by the perfection of the man, we are loath to break the mirror of admiration into the fragments of analysis. But, lo! as we attempt it, every fragment becomes the miniature of such sublimity and beauty that the destructive hand can only multiply the forms of immortality.

Grand and manifold as were its phases, there is yet no difficulty in understanding the character of Washington. He was no Veiled Prophet. He never acted a part. Simple, natural, and unaffected, his life lies before us — a fair and open manuscript. He disdained the arts which wrap power in mystery in order to magnify it. He practiced the profound diplomacy of truthful speech — the consummate tact of direct attention. Looking over to the All-Wise Disposer of events, he relied on that Providence which helps men by giving them high hearts and hopes to help themselves with the means which their Creator has put at their service. There was no infirmity in his conduct over which charity must fling its veil; no taint of selfishness

from which purity averts her gaze; no dark recess of intrigue that must be lit up with colored panegyric; no subterranean passage to be trod in trembling lest there be stirred the ghost of a buried crime.

A true son of nature was George Washington — of nature in her brightest intelligence and noblest mold; and the difficulty, if such there be in comprehending him, is only that of reviewing from a single standpoint the vast procession of those civil and military achievements which filled nearly half a century of his life, and in realizing the magnitude of those qualities which were requisite to their performance — the difficulty of fashioning in our minds a pedestal broad enough to bear the towering figure, whose greatness is diminished by nothing but the perfection of its proportions. If his exterior — in calm, grave, and resolute repose — ever impressed the casual observer as austere and cold, it was only because he did not reflect that no great heart like his could have lived unbroken unless bound by iron nerves in an iron frame. The Commander of Armies, the Chief of a People, the Hope of Nations could not wear his heart upon his sleeve; and yet his sternest will could not conceal its high and warm pulsations. Under the enemy's guns at Boston he did not forget to instruct his agent to administer generously of charity to his needy neighbors at home. The sufferings of women and children, thrown adrift by war, and of his bleeding comrades, pierced his soul. And the moist eye and trembling voice with which he bade farewell to his veterans bespoke the underlying tenderness of his nature, even as the storm-wind makes music in its undertones.

Disinterested patriot, he would receive no pay for his military services. Refusing gifts, he was glad to guide the benefaction of a grateful State to educate the children of his fallen braves in the institution at Lexington which yet bears his name. Without any of the blemishes that mark the tyrant, he appealed so loftily to the virtuous elements in man, that he almost created the qualities of which his country needed the exercise; and yet he was so magnanimous and forbearing to the weaknesses of others, that he often obliterated the vices of which he feared the consequence. But his virtue was more than this. It was of that daring, intrepid kind that, seizing principle with a giant's grasp, assumes responsibility at any hazard, suffers sacrifice without pretense of martyrdom, bears calumny without reply, imposes superior will and understanding on all around it, capitulates to no unworthy triumph, but must carry all things at the point of clear and blameless conscience. Scorning all manner of meanness and cowardice, his bursts of wrath at their exhibition heighten our admiration for the noble passions which were' kindled by the aspirations and exigencies of virtue.

Invested with the powers of a Dictator, the country bestowing them felt no distrust of his integrity; he, receiving them, gave assurance that, as the sword was the last resort of Liberty, so it should be the first thing laid aside when Liberty was won. And keeping the faith in all things, he left mankind bewildered with the splendid problem whether to admire him most for what he was or what he would not be. Over and above all his virtues was the matchless manhood of personal honor, to which Confidence gave in safety the key of every treasure — on which Temptation dared not smile, on which Suspicion never cast a frown And why prolong the catalogue? "If you are presented with medals of Cæsar, of Trajan, or Alexander, on examining their features you are still led to ask what was their stature and the forms of their persons; but if you discover in a heap of ruin the head or the limb of an antique Apollo, be not curious about the other parts, but rest assured that they were all comfortable to those of a god." . . .

There can, indeed, be no right conception of Washington that does not accord him a great and extraordinary genius. I will not say he could have produced a play of Shakespeare or a poem of Milton; handled with Kant the tangled skin of metaphysics; probed the secrecies of mind and matter with Bacon; constructed a railroad or an engine like Stephenson; wooed the electric spark from heaven to earth with Franklin, or walked with Newton the pathways of the spheres. But if his genius were of a different order, it was of as rare and high an order. It dealt with man in the concrete — with his vast concerns of business stretching over a continent and projected into the ages; with his seething passions; with his marvelous exertions of mind, body, and spirit to be free. He knew the materials he dealt with by intuitive perception of the heart of man; by experience and observation of his aspirations and his powers; by reflection upon his complex relations, rights, and duties as a social being. He knew just where between men and States to erect the monumental mark to divide just reverence for authority from just resistance to its

abuse. A poet of social facts, he interpreted by his deeds the harmonies of justice. . . .

"Rome to America" is the eloquent inscription on one stone of your colossal shaft — taken from the ancient Temple of Peace that once stood hard by the Palace of the Cæsars. Uprisen from the sea of Revolution, fabricated from the ruins of battered Bastiles, and dismantled palaces of unrighteous, unhallowed power, stood forth now the Republic of republics, the Nation of nations, the Constitution of constitutions, to which all lands and times and tongues had contributed of their wisdom, and the priestess of Liberty was in her holy temple.

When Marathon had been fought and Greece kept free, each of the victorious generals voted himself to be first in honor, but all agreed that Miltiades was second. When the most memorable struggle for the rights of human nature of which time holds record was thus happily concluded in the muniment of their preservation, whoever else was second unanimous acclaim declared that Washington was first. Nor in that struggle alone does he stand foremost. In the name of the people of the United States, their President, their Senators, their Representatives, and their Judges do crown to-day with the grandest crown that veneration has ever lifted to the brow of glory him whom Virginia gave to America, whom America has given to the world and to the ages, and whom mankind with universal suffrage has proclaimed the foremost of the founders of empire in the first degree of greatness; whom liberty herself has anointed as the first citizen in the great Republic of Humanity.

Encompassed by the inviolate seas stands to-day the American Republic which he founded — a freer, Greater Britain — uplifted above the powers and principalities of the earth, even as his monument is uplifted over roof and dome and spire of the multitudinous city.

Long live the Republic of Washington! Respected by mankind, beloved of all its sons, long may it be the asylum of the poor and oppressed of all lands and religions — long may it be the citadel of that liberty which writes beneath the eagle's folded wings, "We will sell to no man, we will deny to no man, right and justice."

Long live the United States of America! Filled with the free, magnanimous spirit, crowned by the wisdom, blessed by the moderation, hovered over by the guardian angel of Washington's

example, may they be ever worthy in all things to be defended by the blood of the brave who know the rights of man and shrink not from their assertion; may they be each a column, and all together, under the Constitution, a perpetual Temple of Peace, unshadowed by a Cæsar's palace, at whose altar may freely commune all who seek the union of liberty and brotherhood.

Long live our country! Oh, long through the undying ages may it stand, far removed in fact as in space from the Old World's feuds and follies, alone in its grandeur and its glory, itself the immortal monument of him whom Providence commissioned to teach man the power of truth and to prove to the nations that their redeemer liveth.

WAS JEFFERSON DAVIS A TRAITOR?

(From the Oration on the Death of Jefferson Davis Delivered Before the General Assembly of Virginia, January 25th, 1890)

WHAT are the unities of our race? They are: First, aversion to human bondage; second, race integrity; third, thirst for power and broad empire; fourth, love of confederated union; fifth, assertion of local liberty, if possible, within the bounds of geographical and governmental union; sixth, but assertion of local liberty and individual right under all circumstances, at all times, and at any cost. These traits are so strong as to be the natural laws of the race. One or another of them has lost its balance in the conflict between interest and instinct, but only to reappear with renewed vigor when the suppressing circumstances were removed; and he who follows their operation will hold the key to the ascendency of Anglo-Saxon character, and to its wonderful success in grasping imperial domains and crowning freedom as their sovereign.

It will not do to dispute the existence of these natural laws of race, because they have been time and again overruled by greed, by ambition, or by the overwhelming influence of alien or hostile forces. As well dispute the courage of the race because now and then a division of its troops have become demoralized and broken in battle. Through the force of these laws this race has gone around the globe with bugles and swords, and banners and hymn books, and schoolbooks and constitutions, and codes and courts, striking down old-time dynasties to ordain free

principles; sweeping away barbaric and savage races that their own seed might be planted in fruitful lands; disdaining miscegenation with inferior races, which corrupts the blood and degenerates the physical, mental, and moral nature; widening the boundaries of their landed possessions, parceling them out in municipal subdivisions, and then establishing the maximum of local and individual privilege consistent with the common defense and general welfare of their grand aggregations; and then again rising in the supreme sovereignty of unfearing manhood against the oppressions of the tax-gatherer and the sword, recasting their institutions, flinging rulers from their high places, wrenching government by the mailed hand into consistency with their happiness and safety, and proclaiming above all the faith of Jefferson — "that liberty is the gift of God."

I shall maintain that the Southern people have been as true to these instincts as any portion of their race, and have made for them as great sacrifices; that the Southern Confederacy grew out of them, and only in a subsidiary degree in antagonism to any one of them; and I shall also maintain that Jefferson Davis is entitled to stand in the pantheon of the world's great men on a pedestal not less high than those erected for the images of Hampden, Sidney, Cromwell, Burke, and Chatham, of the Fatherland, and Washington and Hamilton, Jefferson and Adams, Madison and Franklin, of the New World, who, however varying in circumstances or in personality, were liberty-leaders and representatives of great peoples, great ideas, and great deeds.

On what ground will he be challenged? Did not the Southern folk show originally an aversion to slavery more manifestly even than those of the North? South Carolina protested against it as early as 1727, and as late as 1760. Georgia prohibited it by law. Virginia sternly set her face against it and levied a tax of ten dollars per head on every negro to prevent it. They were all overridden by the avarice of English merchants and the despotism of English ministers. "Do as you would be done by" is not yet the maxim of our race, which will push off on its weaker brethren what it will not itself accept; and thus slavery was thrust on the South; an uninvited — aye, a forbidden guest. Quickly did the South stop the slave trade. Though the Constitution forbade the Congress to prohibit it prior to 1808, when that year came every Southern State had itself prohibited it, Virginia leading the list. When Jefferson Davis was born it was gone altogether save in one State, South Carolina, where it had been revived under combination between large planters of the South and ship owners and slave traders of the north.

Fine exhibition, too, was that of unselfish Southern patriotism when in 1787 by Southern votes and Virginia's generosity, and under Jefferson's lead, the great Northwestern Territory was given to the Union and to freedom.

But the South yielded to slavery, we are told. Yes; but did not all America do likewise? Do we not know that the Pilgrim Fathers enslaved both the Indian and African race, swapping young Indians for the more docile blacks, lest the red slave might escape to his native forest?

Listen to this appeal to Governor Winthrop: "Mr. Endicott and myself salute you in the Lord Jesus. We have heard of a division of women and children and would be glad of a share—viz., a young woman or a girl and a boy if you think good."

Do we not hear Winthrop himself recount how the Pequods were taken "through the Lord's great mercy, of whom the males were sent to Bermuda and the females distributed through the Bay towns to be employed as domestic servants"? Did not the prisoners of King Philip's War suffer a similar fate? Is it not written that when one hundred and fifty Indians came voluntarily into the Plymouth garrison they were all sold into captivity beyond the seas? Did not Downing declare to Winthrop: "If upon a just war the Lord should deliver them [the Narragansetts], we might easily have men, women, and children enough to exchange for Moors, which will be more gainful pillage to us than we can conceive, for I do not see how we can thrive until we get in a stock of slaves sufficient to do all our business"? Were not choice parcels of negro boys and girls consigned to Boston from the Indies and advertised and sold at auction until after independence was declared? Was not the first slave ship in America fitted out by the Pilgrim colony? Was not the first statute establishing slavery enacted in Massachusetts in 1641, with a certain comic comprehensiveness providing that there should "never be any bond slavery unless it be of captives taken in just war, or of such as willingly sold themselves or were sold to them"? Did not the united colonies of New England constitute the first American confederacy that recognized slavery; and was not the first fugitive slave law originated at their bidding?

IV—102

All this is true. Speak slowly then, O man of the North, against the Southern slave owners, or the Southern chief, lest you cast down the images of your ancestors and their spirits rise to rebuke you for treading harshly on their graves. On days of public festival when you hold them up as patterns of patriotism, take care lest you be accused of passing the counterfeit coin of praise. Disturb not too rudely the memories of the men who defended slavery; say naught of moral obliquity lest the venerable images of Winthrop and Endicott be torn from the historic pages of the Pilgrim Land, and the fathers of Plymouth Rock be cast into outer darkness.

When Independence was declared at Philadelphia in 1776, America was yet a unit in the possession of slaves, and when the Constitution of 1787 was ordained, the institution still existed in every one of the thirteen States save Massachusetts only. True its decay had begun where it was no longer profitable, but every State united in its recognition in the federal compact, and the very fabric of our representative government was built upon it, as three-fifths of the slaves were counted in the basis of representation in the Congress of the United States, and property in it was protected by rigid provisions regarding the rendition of fugitive slaves escaping from one State to another.

Thus embodied in the Constitution, thus interwoven with the very integuments of our political system, thus sustained by the oath to support the Constitution, executed by every public servant and by the decisions of the supreme tribunals, slavery was ratified by the unanimous voice of the nation, and was consecrated as an American institution and as a vested right by the most solemn pledge and sanction that man can give.

Deny to Jefferson Davis entry to the Temple of Fame because he defended it? Cast out of it first the fathers of the Republic. Brand with the mark of condemnation the whole people from whom he inherited the obligation, and by whom was imposed upon him the oath to support their deed. America must prostrate herself in sackcloth and ashes, repent her history, and revile her creators and her being ere she can call recreant the man of 1861 who defended the heritage and promise of a nation.

There is a statue in Washington city of him who uttered the words, "Charity to all, malice to none," and he is represented in the act of breaking the manacles of a slave.

Suppose there were carved on its pedestal the words: "Do the Southern people really entertain fears that a Republican administration would directly or indirectly interfere with the slaves, or with them about their slaves?

"The South would be in no more danger in this respect than it was in the days of Washington."

This was his utterance December 22d, 1860, after South Carolina had seceded.

Carve again:—

"I have no purpose directly or indirectly to interfere with the institution of slavery in the States where it now exists. I believe I have no lawful right to do so, and I have no inclination to do so." These are the words of his Inaugural Address, March 4th, 1861.

Carve yet again:—

"*Resolved*, That this war is not waged upon our part with any purpose of overthrowing or interfering with the rights or established institutions of these States, but to defend and maintain the supremacy of the Constitution and to preserve the Union."

This resolution Congress passed (and he signed it) after the first battle of Manassas.

And yet once more:—

"I did not at any time say that I was in favor of negro suffrage. I declared against it. I am not in favor of negro citizenship."

This opinion he never changed.

These things show in the light of events—the Emancipation Proclamation, the Reconstruction Acts, the black suffrage, the anarchy that reigned—that the South read truly the signs of the irrepressible conflict.

They show further that by the right of revolution alone can Abraham Lincoln be defended in overthrowing the institution which he pledged himself to guard like Washington, and with it the Constitution which he had sworn "to defend and maintain." And if Jefferson Davis appealed to the sword and need the mantle of charity to cover him, where would Lincoln stand unless the right of revolution stretched that mantle wide, and a great people wrapped him in its mighty folds?

As time wore on, the homogeneous order of the American people changed. It was not conscience, but climate and soil,

which effected this change, or rather the instinct of aversion to bondage rose up in the North just in proportion as the temptation of interest subsided.

The inhospitable soil of New England repelled the pursuits of agriculture and compelled to those of commerce and the mechanic arts. In these the rude labor of the untutored African was unprofitable, and the harsh climate was uncongenial to the children of the Dark Continent translated from its burning suns to these frigid shores. Slavery there was an exotic; it did not pay and its roots soon decayed, like the roots of a tropic plant in the Arctic Zone.

In the fertile plantations of the sunny South there was employment for the unskilled labor of the African, and under its genial skies he found a fitting home. Hence, natural causes ejected him from the North and propelled him southward; and as the institution of slavery decayed in Northern latitudes, it thrived and prospered in the Southern clime.

The demand for labor in the North was rapidly supplied by new accessions of Europeans, and as the population increased their opinions were molded by the body of the society which absorbed and assimilated them as they came; while, on the other hand, the presence of masses of black men in the South, and the reliance upon them for labor, repelled in both social and economical aspects the European immigrants who eagerly sought for homes and employment in the New World. More than this, Northern manufacturers wanted high tariffs to secure high prices for their products in Southern markets, and Southern farmers wanted low tariffs that they might buy cheaply. Ere long it appeared that two opposing civilizations lay alongside of each other in the United States; and while the roof of a common government was over both of them, it covered a household divided against itself in the very structure of its domestic life, in the nature of its avocations, in the economies of its labor, and in the very tone of its thought and aspiration.

Revolution was in the air. An irrepressible conflict had arisen.

There were, indeed, two revolutions forming in the American Republic. The one was a Northern revolution against a Constitution which had become distasteful to its sentiments and unsuited to its needs. As the population of the east moved westward across the continent, the Southern emigrant to the new territories wished to carry with him his household servants, while the Northerner saw in the negro a rival in the field of labor, which cheapened its fruits and degraded, as he conceived, its social status.

Thus broke out the strife which raged in the territories of Northern latitudes, and as it widened it assailed slavery in every form, and denounced as "a covenant with death and with hell" the Constitution which had guaranteed its existence. . . .

Consider these grave words, which are but freshly written in the life of Webster, by Henry Cabot Lodge, who is at this time a Republican representative in Congress from the city of Boston, Massachusetts.

"When the Constitution was adopted by the votes of States at Philadelphia, and accepted by votes of States in popular conventions, it was safe to say there was not a man in the country, from Washington and Hamilton on the one side, to George Clinton and George Mason on the other, who regarded the new system as anything but an experiment entered upon by the States, and from which each and every State had the right to peaceably withdraw — a right which was very likely to be exercised."

Recall the contemporary opinions of Northern publicists and leading journals. The New York Herald considered coercion out of the question. On the ninth of November, 1860, the New York Tribune, Horace Greeley being the editor, said : —

"If the cotton States shall decide that they can do better out of the Union than in it, we insist on letting them go in peace. The right to secede may be a revolutionary one, but it exists nevertheless, and we do not see how one party can have a right to do what another party has a right to prevent. We must ever resist the asserted right of any State to remain in the Union and nullify or defy the laws thereof; to withdraw from the Union is quite another matter."

This was precisely the creed of Jefferson Davis. . . .

The United States have been unified by natural laws, kindred to those which unified the South in secession, but greater because wider spread. Its physical constitution in 1861 answered to the Northern mind the written Constitution and the traditions of our origin to which the South appealed. The Mississippi River, the natural outlet of a newborn empire to the sea, was a greater interpreter to it than the opinions of states-

men who lived when the great new commonwealths were yet in the wilderness, and before the great Republic spanned the Father of Waters.

The river seeking its bed as it rolls oceanward pauses not to consider whose are the boundaries of the estates through which it flows. If a mountain barrier stand in way, it forms a lake until the accumulated waters break through the impeding wall or dash over it in impetuous torrents. So nations in their great movements seem to be swept out of the grooves defined by the laws of man, and are oftentimes propelled to destinies greater than those conjured in their dreams.

The rivalry, not the harmony of sections, won the empire of the Union; its physical constitution proved more powerful than its written one; in the absence of a judge all appealed to the jury of the sword. We belong to a high-handed race and understand the law of the sword, for the men of independence in 1776 and 1861 were of the same blood as those who in each case cried, "Disperse, ye rebels." And were I of the North I would prefer to avow that it made conquest by the high hand than coin the great strife that marshaled over three millions of soldiers into police-court technicalities and belittle a revolution continent-wide into the quelling of an insurrection, and the vicarious punishment of its leader. The greatest conqueror proclaims his naked deed.

As we are not of the North but of the South, and are now, like all Americans, both of and for the Union, bound up in its destinies, contributing to its support and seeking its welfare, I feel that as he was the hero in war who fought the bravest, so he is the hero now who puts the past in its truest light, does justice to all, and knows no foe but him who revives the hates of a bygone generation.

If we lost by war a Southern union of thirteen States, we have yet a common part in a continental union of forty-two, to which our fathers gave their blood, and upon which they shed their blessings; and a people who could survive four years of such experience as we had in 1861–65, can work out their own salvation on any spot of earth that God intended for man's habitation. We are, in fact, in our father's home, and it should be, as it is, our highest aim to develop its magnificent possibilities and make it the happiest dwelling place of the children of men.

GEORGE JACQUES DANTON

(1759–1794)

DANTON, the greatest of the French Jacobins, and one of the most formidable figures in modern history, was born at Arcis-sur-Aube, October 28th, 1759, and he had not completed his thirty-fifth year when he went to the guillotine, declaring it better to live a poor fisherman than to have anything to do with the government of men.

No other man in modern times has so well and so reasonably embodied the latent fierceness of society. When the young French Republic was hemmed round with enemies; when all the forces of the world seemed leagued against the handful of radicals and fanatics who were attempting to make a constructive force out of the chaotic impulses of the Parisian mob, Danton gave the keynote of his own character and of the character of the great epoch which created him, in a single sentence: "To conquer we have need to dare, to dare again, always to dare; and France will be saved!" That sentence and yet another of Danton's overthrew Bourbonism. The other was: "Let France be free, though my name were accursed!" When a man of average abilities and average education so devotes himself to any cause that he accepts in advance, as a probable incident of his work, not merely death, but infamy, he has already more than half accomplished the possibilities of such achievement as made Danton the constructive power by virtue of which the French Republic of the last quarter of the nineteenth century developed out of the Reign of Terror. In the Arabian story those who attempt to climb an enchanted mountain to find the talisman of power at the top are assailed at every step of their upward progress by shrieks of execration from unseen enemies attacking them from behind with every imaginable calumny, every conceivable insult. Those who stop to answer or turn back to punish these intangible "conservative forces" are at once transformed to smooth, black stones, destined to remain inert under the power of obstruction until some one comes, so strong, so self-contained, so capable of maintaining a set purpose, that, like Danton, he will press forward to his object without fearing either the death or the infamy with which he is threatened. Then the smooth stones once more become men, and by virtue of the

strength of the one leader as they crowd around him, all their failures become a part of his success.

If the story were an allegory as it seems to be, it would come nearer than any biography of Danton can come to suggesting the secret of his success and of his overthrow. He was at once devoted and desperate. Threatened with everlasting infamy, he considered what it would mean, and took the risk. He saw certain death before him, and went forward to meet it, shrinking less from it for himself than he had done in inflicting it on others. It is doubtful if such a man could be created except through the very forces he so fiercely antagonized. The impulse of tyranny, of mastering men so as to compel them at their peril to accept the will of another, is shown in the life of Danton as it was in that of the other Attilas who are recognized by the generations after them as "Scourges of God." But neither an Attila nor a Danton could exist in a normal society. It is only when a civilization is effete that the strongest men become at once disorganizers and reorganizers. It is part of the theory of Pasteur that as soon as life leaves matter the same invisible organisms which operated to keep it alive begin to disintegrate it, that it may be reorganized into other, and in the sum of things into higher forms of life. We cannot study the life and work of such menacing and Titanic figures as Danton without seeing that in its economics and the conservation of its energies, nature is a unit, true to itself in what is greatest as in what is least.

Danton was a struggling young lawyer in Paris when the Revolution overtook him. In the Cordeliers Club he fitted himself for the popular leadership which came to him as a result of his fitness, when Mirabeau, the idol of the people, deserted them for the court. Called the "Mirabeau of the Sans-Culottes," Danton did not disdain the title. He accepted as an existing fact the wild desire of the populace of Paris to be free; their fierce determination to go to any extreme rather than return to the old order of things; and counting on it not only as a fact but as a force of the greatest possibilities, he attempted to use it first to demolish entirely the ruins of the monarchy and on the old foundations to build the splendid structure of his ideal Republic. His people were not fit for his ideal, nor was he himself. Loving justice, mercy, and liberty, he could still reconcile himself to shedding the blood of those he respected for their intentions, while he opposed their purposes. In his own death he foresaw and prophesied that of Robespierre. No doubt, he foresaw the guillotine for himself in the death of Vergniaud. It is certain that he was doomed when, regretting the "logic of the situation" which sent the Girondists to the scaffold, he did not oppose to it the same fiery energy that had saved the Republic from the Bourbons.

But his character shows always the same radical fault which appears in his oratory. He had for the time being the almost omnipotent power of passion, directed by intellect, but too intense to be sustained, and ending in inevitable reaction. It was in the impotence of such a reaction that on April 5th, 1794, Danton accepted the inevitable and went to the scaffold, leaving France and civilization "in a frightful welter," out of which were to come Napoleon, Hugo, Thiers, and Gambetta, Garrison, Phillips, Sumner, and Lincoln.

W. V. B.

TO DARE, TO DARE AGAIN; ALWAYS TO DARE

(Delivered in the National Assembly, September 2d, 1792, on the Defense of the Republic)

IT SEEMS a satisfaction for the ministers of a free people to announce to them that their country will be saved. All are stirred, all are enthused, all burn to enter the combat.

You know that Verdun is not yet in the power of our enemies and that its garrison swears to immolate the first who breathes a proposition of surrender.

One portion of our people will guard our frontiers, another will dig and arm the entrenchments, the third with pikes will defend the interior of our cities. Paris will second these great efforts. The commissioners of the Commune will solemnly proclaim to the citizens the invitation to arm and march to the defense of the country. At such a moment you can proclaim that the capital deserves the esteem of all France. At such a moment this National Assembly becomes a veritable committee of war. We ask that you concur with us in directing this sublime movement of the people, by naming commissioners to second and assist all these great measures. We ask that any one refusing to give personal service or to furnish arms shall meet the punishment of death. We ask that proper instructions be given to the citizens to direct their movements. We ask that carriers be sent to all the departments to notify them of the decrees that you proclaim here. The tocsin we shall sound is not the alarm signal of danger, it orders the charge on the enemies of France. [Applause.] To conquer we have need to dare, to dare again, always to dare! And France will be saved!

(*Pour les vaincre, il nous faut de l'audace; encore de l'audace, toujours de l'audace; et la France est sauvée.*)

«LET FRANCE BE FREE, THOUGH MY NAME WERE ACCURSED»

(On the Disasters on the Frontier—Delivered in Convention, March 10th, 1793)

THE general considerations that have been presented to you are true; but at this moment it is less necessary to examine the causes of the disasters that have struck us than to apply their remedy rapidly. When the edifice is on fire, I do not join the rascals who would steal the furniture, I extinguish the flames. I tell you therefore you should be convinced by the dispatches of Dumouriez that you have not a moment to spare in saving the Republic.

Dumouriez conceived a plan which did honor to his genius. I would render him greater justice and praise than I did recently. But three months ago he announced to the executive power, your General Committee of Defense, that if we were not audacious enough to invade Holland in the middle of winter, to declare instantly against England the war which actually we had long been making, that we would double the difficulties of our campaign, in giving our enemies the time to deploy their forces. Since we failed to recognize this stroke of his genius, we must now repair our faults.

Dumouriez is not discouraged; he is in the middle of Holland, where he will find munitions of war; to overthrow all our enemies, he wants but Frenchmen, and France is filled with citizens. Would we be free? If we no longer desire it, let us perish, for we have all sworn it. If we wish it, let all march to defend our independence. Your enemies are making their last efforts. Pitt recognizing he has all to lose, dares spare nothing. Take Holland, and Carthage is destroyed and England can no longer exist but for Liberty! Let Holland be conquered to Liberty; and even the commercial aristocracy itself, which at the moment dominates the English people, would rise against the government which had dragged it into this despotic war against a free people. They would overthrow this ministry of stupidity, who thought the methods of the *ancien régime* could smother the genius of Liberty breathing in France. This ministry once overthrown in the interests of commerce, the party of Liberty would show itself; for it is not dead! And if you know your duties, if your commissioners leave at once, if you extend the hand to the strangers

aspiring to destroy all forms of tyranny, France is saved and the world is free.

Expedite, then, your commissioners; sustain them with your energy; let them leave this very night, this very evening.

Let them say to the opulent classes, the aristocracy of Europe must succumb to our efforts, and pay our debt, or you will have to pay it! The people have nothing but blood,—they lavish it! Go, then, ingrates, and lavish your wealth! [Wild applause.] See, citizens, the fair destinies that await you. What! you have a whole nation as a lever, its reason as your fulcrum and you have not yet upturned the world! To do this we need firmness and character, and of a truth we lack it. I put to one side all passions. They are all strangers to me save a passion for the public good.

In the most difficult situations, when the enemy was at the gates of Paris, I said to those governing: "Your discussions are shameful, I can see but the enemy." [Fresh applause.] You tire me by squabbling in place of occupying yourselves with the safety of the Republic! I repudiate you all as traitors to our country! I place you all in the same line!" I said to them: "What care I for my reputation! Let France be free, though my name were accursed!" What care I that I am called "a blood-drinker"! Well, let us drink the blood of the enemies of humanity, if needful; but let us struggle, let us achieve freedom. Some fear the departure of the commissioners may weaken one or the other section of this convention. Vain fears! Carry your energy everywhere. The pleasantest declaration will be to announce to the people that the terrible debt weighing upon them will be wrested from their enemies or that the rich will shortly have to pay it. The national situation is cruel. The representatives of value are no longer in equilibrium in the circulation. The day of the workingman is lengthened beyond necessity. A great corrective measure is necessary! Conquerors of Holland reanimate in England the Republican party; let us advance France and we shall go glorified to posterity. Achieve these grand destinies; no more debates, no more quarrels, and the Fatherland is saved.

AGAINST IMPRISONMENT FOR DEBT

(Delivered in the Convention, March 9th, 1793)

BEYOND a doubt, citizens, the hopes of your commissioners will not be deceived. Yes, your enemies, the enemies of liberty shall be exterminated, for your efforts shall be relentless. You are worthy the dignity of regulating and controlling the nation's energy. Your commissioners, disseminated in all parts of the Republic, will repeat to Frenchmen that the great quarrel between despotism and liberty shall soon terminate. The people of France shall be avenged; it becomes us then to put the political world in harmony, to make laws in accord with such harmony. But before we too deeply entertain these grander objects, I shall ask you to make a declaration of a principle too long ignored; to abolish a baneful error, to destroy the tyranny of wealth upon misery.

If the measures I propose be adopted, then Pitt, the Breteuil of English diplomacy, and Burke, the Abbé Maury of the British Parliament, who are impelling the English people to-day against liberty, may be touched.

What do you ask? You would have every Frenchman armed in the common defense. And yet there is a class of men sullied by no crime, who have stout arms, but no liberty. They are the unfortunates detained for debt. It is a shame for humanity, it is against all philosophy, that a man in receiving money can pawn his person as security. I can readily prove that this principle is favorable to cupidity, since experience proves that the lender takes no pecuniary security, since he has the disposition of the body of his debtor. But of what importance are these mercantile considerations? They should not influence a great nation. Principles are eternal, and no Frenchman can be rightly deprived of his liberty unless he has forfeited it to society. The possessing and owning class need not be alarmed. Doubtless, some individuals go to extremes, but the nation, always just, will respect all the proprieties. Respect misery, and misery will respect opulence. [Applause.] Never wrong the unfortunate, and the unfortunate, who have more soul than the rich, will remain guiltless. [Loud applause.]

I ask that this National Convention declare that every French citizen imprisoned for debt shall be liberated, because such imprisonment is contrary to moral health, contrary to the rights of man, and to the true principles of liberty.

EDUCATION, FREE AND COMPULSORY

(From a Speech Delivered in the Convention, August 13th, 1793)

Citizens:—

AFTER having given liberty to France; after having vanquished her enemies, there can be no honor greater than to prepare for future generations an education in keeping with that liberty. This is the object which Lepeletier proposes: that all that is good for society shall be adopted by those who live under its social contract. . . . It has been said that paternal affection opposes the execution of such plans. Certainly we must respect natural rights even in their perversion. But even if we do not fully sustain compulsory schooling, we must not deprive the children of the poor of an education.

The greatest objection has been that of finding the means; but I have already said there is no real extravagance where the good result to the public is so great, and I add the principle that the child of the poor can be taught at the expense of the superfluities of the scandalous fortunes erected among us. It is to you who are celebrated among our Republicans that I appeal; bring to this subject the fire of your imagination, the energy of your character. It is the people who must endow national education.

When you commence to sow this seed of education in the vast field of the Republic, you must not count the expense of reaping the harvest. After bread, education is the first need of a people. [Applause.] I ask that the question be submitted, that there be founded at the expense of the nation establishments where each citizen can have the right to send his children for free public instruction. It is to the monks—it is to the age of Louis XIV., when men were great by their acquirements, that we owe the age of philosophy, that is to say, of reason, brought to the knowledge of the people. To the Jesuits, lost by their political ambitions, we owe an impetus in education evoking our admiration. But the Republic has been in the souls of our people,

twenty years ahead of its proclamation. Corneille wrote dedications to Montauron, but Corneille made the 'Cid,' 'Cinna'; Corneille spoke like a Roman, and he who said: "For being more than a king you think you are something," was a true Republican.

Now for public instruction; everything shrinks in domestic teaching, everything enlarges and ennobles in public communal instruction. A mistake is made in presenting a tableau of paternal affections. I, too, am a father, and more so than the aristocrats who oppose public education, for they are never sure of their paternities. [Laughter.] When I consider my rights relatively to the general good I feel elevated; my son is not mine. He belongs to the Republic. Let her dictate his duties that he can best serve her. It has been said it is repugnant to the heart of our peasantry to make such sacrifice of their children. Well, do not constrain them too much. Let there be classes, if necessary, that only meet on the Sabbath. Begin the system by a gradual adaptation to the manners of the people. If you expect the State to make an instant and absolute regeneration, you will never get public instruction. It is necessary that each man develop the moral means and methods he received from nature. Have for them all communal houses and faculties for instruction, and do not stop at any secondary considerations. The rich man will pay, and will lose nothing if he will profit for the instruction of his son.

I ask, then, that under suitable and necessary modifications you decree the erection of national establishments where children can be instructed, fed, and lodged gratuitously, and the citizens who desire to retain their children at home can send them there for instruction.

Convention, December 12th, 1793.—It is a proper time to establish the principle which seems misunderstood, that the youth belong to the Republic before they belong to their parents. No one more than myself respects nature, but of what avail the reasoning of the individual against the reason of the nation? In the national schools the child will suck the milk of Republicanism. The Republic is one and indivisible. Public instruction produces such a centre of unity. To none, then, can we accord the privilege of isolation from such benefits.

FREEDOM OF WORSHIP

(Delivered in the Convention, April 18th, 1793)

WE HAVE appeared divided in counsel, but the instant we seek the good of mankind we are in accord. Vergniaud has told us grand and immortal truths. The Constitutional Assembly, embarrassed by a king, by the prejudices which still enchain the nation, and by deep-rooted intolerance, has not uprooted accepted principles, but has done much for liberty in consecrating the doctrine of tolerance. To-day the ground of liberty is prepared and we owe to the French people a government founded on bases pure and eternal! Yes! we shall say to them: Frenchmen you have the right to adore the divinity you deem entitled to your worship: "The liberty of worship, which it is the object of law to establish, means only the right of individuals to assemble to render in their own way homage to the Deity." Such a form of liberty is enforcible only by legal regulations and the police, but you do not wish to insert regulating laws in your declaration of rights. The right of freedom of worship, a sacred right, will be protected by laws in harmony with its principles. We will have only to guarantee these rights. Human reason cannot retrograde; we have advanced too far for the people ever to believe they are not absolutely free in religious thought, merely because you have failed to engrave the principle of this liberty on the table of your laws. If superstition still seem to inhere in the movements of the Republic, it is because our political enemies always employ it. But look! everywhere the people, freed from malevolent espionage, recognize that any one assuming to interpose between them and their God is an impostor.

"SQUEEZING THE SPONGE"

(On Taxing the Rich—Delivered in the Convention, April 27th, 1793)

YOU have decreed "honorable mention" of what has been done for the public benefit by the Department De L'Hevault. In this decree you authorize the whole Republic to adopt the same measures, for your decree ratifies all the acts which have just been brought to your knowledge.

If everywhere the same measures be taken, the Republic is saved. No more shall we treat as agitators and anarchists the ardent friends of liberty who set the nation in motion, but we shall say: "Honor to the agitators who turn the vigor of the people against its enemies!" When the Temple of Liberty shall be reared, the people will know how to decorate it. Rather perish France than to return to our hard slavery. Let it not be believed we shall become barbarians after we shall have founded liberty. We shall embellish France until the despots shall envy us; but while the ship of State is in the stress of storm, beaten by the tempest, that which belongs to each, belongs to all.

No longer are Agrarian Laws spoken of! The people are wiser than their calumniators assumed, and the people in mass have much more sense than many of those who deem themselves great men. In a people we can no more count the great men than we can count the giant trees in the vast forest. It was believed that the people wanted the Agrarian Law, and this may throw suspicion on the measures adopted by the Department De L'Hevault. It will be said of them: "They taxed the rich"; but, citizens, to tax the rich is to serve them. It is rather a veritable advantage for them than any considerable sacrifice; and the greater the sacrifice, the greater the usufruct, for the greater is the guarantee to the foundation of property against the invasion of its enemies. It is an appeal to every man, according to his means, to save the Republic. The appeal is just. What the Department De L'Hevault has done, Paris and all France will do. See what resources France will procure. Paris has a luxury and wealth which is considerable. Well, by decree, this sponge will be squeezed! And with singular satisfaction it will be found that the people will conduct their revolution at the expense of their internal enemies. These enemies themselves will learn the price of liberty and will desire to possess it, when they will recognize that it has preserved for them their possessions.

Paris in making an appeal to capitalists will furnish her contingent, which will afford means to suppress the troubles in La Vendée; for, at any sacrifice, these troubles must be suppressed. On this alone depends your external tranquillity. Already, the Departments of the north have informed the combined despots that your territory cannot be divided; and soon you will probably learn of the dissolution of this formidable league of kings. For in uniting against you, they have not forgotten their ancient hatreds and respective pretensions; and if the Executive Council had had a little more latitude, the league might be already completely dissolved.

Paris, then, must be directed against La Vendée. All the men needed in this city to form a reserve camp should be sent at once to La Vendée. These measures once taken, the rebels will disperse, and, like the Austrians, will commence to kill each other. If the flames of this civil discord be extinguished, they will ask of us peace!

v—103

DAVID DAVIS

(1815–1886)

AVID DAVIS, celebrated for his independent position during a period of strong partisanship, was born in Cecil County, Maryland, March 9th, 1815, but he removed to Illinois at an age so early that, historically, he is completely identified with that State. He was a Republican, strongly supporting all the measures of that party for the restoration of the Union and the suppression of resistance to Federal authority, but after the war ended, without leaving the party, he asserted his right to use his individual judgment regardless of caucuses or of what he considered merely partisan policies. This attitude, well represented in his speech of April 22d, 1879, had a great influence on the politics of his time. He is supposed to have been the original type of the "Statesman on the Fence," but the jest of partisan paragraphers did not impair his usefulness or make him a less respectable figure, historically. He was Associate-Justice of the United States Supreme Court from 1862 to 1877; United States Senator from Illinois from 1877 to 1883, and from 1881 to 1883 acting Vice-President of the United States. He died at Bloomington, Illinois, June 26th, 1886.

ON APPEAL FROM THE CAUCUS

(From the Speech on Freedom of Elections, Delivered in the United States Senate, April 22d, 1879)

Mr. President: —

THE caucus is an important factor in American politics, and both the great parties of the country employ its agency. This is done on the theory that party action is most easily perfected by this method. I do not complain of the mode adopted to reach results, but as I have been for many years viewing public affairs from an independent standpoint, it does not help me to decide any question that may come before the Senate. Although usually preferring to give a silent vote, I cannot suffer this measure to be passed on without saying something on the subject.

The heat that has been manifested on the occasion of this debate has surprised me, if anything can surprise me in politics. A stranger unaccustomed to our modes of debate would suppose that the Union were in danger, and that the old questions, passions, prejudices, and purposes which it had been thought were laid aside forever were again revived. And this, too, fourteen years after the rebellion was conquered, and when there is no complaint from any quarter that the Federal compact presses too hard upon one section at the expense of another, and when the Federal Government is obeyed throughout the entire South.

There does not seem to be the least ground for the excitement and bitterness that have characterized the discussions in Congress at this session, and I should be amazed were it not that the record of all parties proves that majorities invariably commit legislative wrongs and minorities invariably protest against them. If it be true as charged that the success of one of the great parties of the country means revolution and ruin to constitutional liberty, of what value would be the securities of the Government, or, indeed, any other species of prosperity? In the nature of things, if a revolution were impending or there were any danger apprehended to free government or popular liberty, the Government would not be able to sell bonds at four per cent. interest, nor the stock market in New York to maintain its present high rate.

This charge, Mr. President, is mere fiction and has no foundation to rest on; but it produces infinite mischief and tends to demoralize the country and every material interest in it, alarms the thoughtless and timid, unsettles business and values, and produces a state of unrest in every community. It may succeed in winning elections, but it cannot restore prosperity. That great object can never be accomplished through a continuance of sectional strife and the violence that accompanies it, nor do I believe the people are in the mood for this kind of politics. They have had more than five years of harsh experience and they want to find some mode of relief from their present sufferings and impoverished condition. And they will honor the statesman who contributes to the stock of knowledge on this subject rather than the political leader who will not let the past alone.

I have no personal concern, Mr. President, in the rise and fall of parties, but I am deeply solicitous that the affairs of Government shall be so administered that labor seeking employ-

ment can obtain it; that all industrial pursuits will be suitably rewarded, and that heart be given to the people, North and South, to work out of their present embarrassments. We are one people, of the same blood and with the same destiny, and unity of feeling is essential to lift us out of the mire and to help us on the road to prosperity.

The different parts of our common country are so intimately connected in trade and commerce that, as a general rule, whatever injuriously affects one part has a corresponding effect on the other, and whatever benefits the one benefits the other.

It is, Mr. President, in my judgment, the imperative duty of the hour, instead of turning the attention of the people back into history with its animosities, to direct it to the troubled business interests of the country and the way to relieve them.

With the past buried and discussions on living issues, the people would soon regain confidence, which is essential in any plan for relieving the present hard times. It may be that such a course would affect the fortunes of parties — for both parties in Congress on any question of practical legislation fall to pieces — but it would have the most beneficial effect upon the fortunes of the country.

Without intending to reflect upon the patriotism of either party, it does appear to me that the speeches on the pending bill do not represent the wishes or opinions of the masses of the people of either section. Experience has taught them that legitimate business principles which lead to wealth and social happiness require a cessation from agitation on past subjects, and that sound policy dictates the cultivation of peace and good-will between the sections. The country, Mr. President, cannot be prosperous so long as the old conflict between the North and South is used at each recurring presidential election as an instrumentality of party success, and the statesman who shall rise equal to the occasion, and put it at rest, will receive the gratitude of a suffering people.

The bill before us is for the support of the Army for the ensuing fiscal year. It is attacked because the sixth section alters two provisions of the Revised Statutes. Section 2002 of these statutes reads as follows: —

"No military or naval officer, or other person engaged in the civil, military, or naval service of the United States, shall order, bring, keep, or have under his authority or control any troops or armed men at the place where any general or special election is held in any State, unless it be necessary to repel the armed enemies of the United States, or to keep the peace at the polls.»

And Section 5528 is in these words:—

«Every officer of the Army or Navy, or other person in the civil, military, or naval service of the United States who orders, brings, keeps, or has under his authority or control any troops or armed men at any place where a general or special election is held in any State, unless such force be necessary to repel armed enemies of the United States or to keep the peace at the polls, shall be fined not more than $5,000, and suffer imprisonment at hard labor not less than three months nor more than five years.»

These sections, though widely separated in the Revised Statutes, are parts of a general law passed on the twenty-fifth of February, 1865, "to prevent officers of the Army and Navy and other persons engaged in the service from interfering in elections in the States." (Statutes at Large, vol. xiii., page 437.)

The first section denounced the use of troops at elections except in two specified cases, and the second section provided the penalties for disobedience. The two excepted cases are when the troops were necessary to repel the armed enemies of the United States or to keep peace at the polls. The sixth section of the Appropriation Bill proposes to strike from both sections the words "or to keep the peace at the polls," and nothing more, so that the Army cannot be used hereafter at elections for any purpose. As an abstract proposition, can there be any rational objection to this? Ought the Army to be used at the polls when there has been profound peace for more than a decade? Does any one believe that such a law would ever have received the approval of the American Congress if it had been brought forward in a time of peace? It was passed when a formidable civil war was in progress, taxing to the utmost the resources of the country.

In the opinion of the patriots of that day the state of feeling in certain parts of the country was of such a character as to endanger peaceful elections while the war lasted, unless a military force was kept in readiness for any outbreak of popular commotion. This was the conviction that prompted the legislation, but I venture to say no one of the eminent men who voted for it

intended or expected that it would remain a part of the permanent law of the land. They were too well read in the lessons of history and the traditions of the Anglo-Saxon race to believe that a free people would tolerate—except on great emergencies like a war waged for the maintenance of the Union—the interference of the military in civic concerns. And they were men of principle and did not wish it to be otherwise.

It is no new thing in time of peace to repeal a law passed in time of war. Indeed, no wise statesman will hesitate to do it if the law be unsuitable to the changed condition of things. It is a part of the very nature of every man of our race to rebel against anything which interferes with the freedom of elections, and the days of the Republic are numbered if the people ever consent to place the ballot box under the protection of the bayonet.

But, Mr. President, this consent will never be obtained until they have forgotten the principles of constitutional liberty and the precedents set by the Commons of England. These precedents I refrain from referring to at length, but the preamble to an act passed in the time of George II. (1735), forbidding the presence of troops at elections, is so appropriate that I beg leave to read it:—

«WHEREAS, by the ancient common law of this land all elections ought to be free; and whereas by an act passed in the third year of the reign of King Edward I., of famous memory, it is commanded, upon great forfeiture, that no man, by force of arms, nor by malice or menacing, shall disturb any to make free election; and forasmuch as the freedom of elections of Members to serve in Parliament is of the utmost consequence to the preservation of the rights and liberties of this kingdom; and whereas it has been the usage and practice to cause any regiment, troop, or company, or any number of soldiers which hath been quartered in any city, borough, town or place where any election of Members to serve in Parliament hath been appointed to be made, to remove and continue out of the same during the time of such election, except in such particular cases as are hereinafter specified.»—'Pickering's Statutes,' vol. xvi.

And the 'History of Parliament' contains this incident:—

«The military having been called in to quell an alleged riot at Westminster election in 1741, it was resolved, December 22d, 'that the presence of a regular body of armed soldiers at an election of

Members to serve in Parliament is a high infringement of the liberties of the subject, a manifest violation of the freedom of elections, and an open defiance of the laws and constitution of this kingdom.' The persons concerned in this having been ordered to attend the House, received, on their knees, a very severe reprimand from the speaker."—'Parliament History,' vol. ix., page 326.

Can it be possible that a principle of common law—the right of the people to have an election free from the presence of troops—so dear to Englishmen one hundred years ago, is not equally dear to their descendants at the present day?

Mr. President, it will require some one now living to write accurately the history of these times, for the future historian will be slow to believe that there was any basis on which to rest such an inquiry in the Congress of the United States during the latter part of the nineteenth century. Why, then, should not the law of 1865 be altered in the manner proposed by this bill?

It is said that Mr. Lincoln signed it, and the inference is that it would reflect on his memory to change it. To say the least, this is a pretty strong presumption from such a predicate. No man loved Mr. Lincoln better or honors his memory more than I do, nor had any one greater opportunities to learn the constitution of his mind and character and his habits of thought. He was large-hearted, wiser than those associated with him, full of sympathy for struggling humanity, without malice, with charity for erring man, loving his whole country with a deep devotion, and intensely anxious to save it. Believing as I do that he was raised up by Providence for the great crisis of the War of the Rebellion, I have equal belief, had he lived, we would have been spared much of the strife of these latter days, and that we now would be on the highroad to prosperity. Such a man, hating all forms of oppression, and deeply imbued with the principle that induced the men of 1776 to resist the stamp tax, would never have willingly intrusted power to any one, unless war was flagrant, to send troops to oversee an election.

Why, then, I repeat, should not the proposed measure pass? There is no rebellion, nor any threatened, nor any domestic uproar anywhere. The Union is cemented by the blood that was shed in defense of its integrity; the laws are obeyed North and South, East and West, and our only real differences relate to the administration of the internal affairs of the Government. By the constitution of the human mind, there will of necessity be diverse

opinions among the people on the best way to manage their internal affairs, and Congress meets periodically to legislate for the people and to represent their views on the questions dividing them. But surely these differences, be they great or small, afford no justification for a departure from any of the principles that underlie republican government. If they do, the charter of our liberties will soon be frittered away. . . .

HENRY WINTER DAVIS

(1817–1865)

S A representative of Maryland who had opposed forcing issues on the abolition of slavery, Henry Winter Davis became one of the most prominent figures in national politics when in February, 1861, President Buchanan being still in office, he denounced the administration and demanded the use of any amount of force necessary to preserve "the unity of territory we have labored through three generations and spent millions to create and establish." This argument and others related to it, as he summarized them, were decisive against the idea of allowing the "erring sisters" to go in peace. The stand thus taken by Mr. Davis was maintained throughout the war. He reported the first "plan of reconstruction," proposed by the Republicans in 1864, and in his speech on that occasion summarized in a few sentences more clearly perhaps than they are presented elsewhere, the constitutional difficulties which were overcome in adopting the "Civil War amendments." He was born at Annapolis, August 16th, 1817, and died at Baltimore, December 30th, 1865. His biographers sometimes represent that at his first election to Congress in 1854 he was already a Republican, but in 1857 he made a speech denouncing that party as sectional, and declaring the "American" party to be the only really national party in existence. In 1859, when he voted for the Republican candidate for Speaker of the House of Representatives, the Maryland legislature adopted resolutions declaring that he had forfeited the confidence of the people. He replied in a speech on the floor of the House that the Maryland legislature could take their message back to their masters, for only to their masters the people was he responsible. He was re-elected to the House of Representatives as a Republican in 1862 and served until his death.

REASONS FOR REFUSING TO PART COMPANY WITH THE SOUTH

(From a Speech on the State of the Union, Delivered in the House of Representatives, February 7th, 1861)

Mr. Speaker:—

WE ARE at the end of the insane revel of partisan license, which, for thirty years, has, in the United States, worn the mask of government. We are about to close the masquerade by the dance of death. The nations of the world look anxiously to see if the people, ere they tread that measure, will come to themselves.

Yet in the early youth of our national life we are already exhausted by premature excesses. The corruption of our political maxims has relaxed the tone of public morals and degraded the public authorities from the terror to the accomplices of evil-doers. Platforms for fools — plunder for thieves — offices for service — power for ambition — unity in these essentials — diversity in the immaterial matters of policy and legislation — charity for every frailty — the voice of the people is the voice of God — these maxims have sunk into the public mind, have presided at the administration of public affairs, have almost effaced the very idea of public duty. The Government under their disastrous influence has gradually ceased to fertilize the fields of domestic and useful legislation, and pours itself, like an impetuous torrent, along the barren ravine of party and sectional strife. It has been shorn of every prerogative that wore the austere aspect of authority and power.

The President, no longer preceded by the fasces and the ax, — the emblems of supreme authority, — greets every popular clamor with wreathed smiles and gracious condescension, is degraded to preside in the palace of the nation over the distribution of spoils among wrangling victors, dedicates his great powers to forge or find arms to perpetuate partisan warfare at the expense of the public peace. The original ideas of the Constitution have faded from men's minds. That the United States is a government entitled to respect and command; that the Constitution furnishes a remedy for every grievance and a mode of redress for every wrong; that the States are limited within their spheres, are charged with no duties to each other, and bear no relation to the other States excepting through their common

head, the Government of the United States; that those in authority alone are charged with power to repress public disorder, and compose the public discontents, restrain the conduct of the people and of the States within the barriers of the Constitution — these salutary principles have faded from the popular heart with the great interests which the Government is charged to protect, and has gradually allowed to escape from its grasp. Congress has ceased to regulate commerce, to protect domestic industry, to encourage our commercial marine, to regulate the currency, to promote internal commerce by internal improvements — almost every power useful to the people in its exercise has been denied and abandoned, or so limited in its exercise as to be useless; its whole activity has been dedicated to expansion abroad and acquiring and retaining power at home, till men have forgotten that the Union is a blessing, and that they owe to the United States allegiance paramount to that to their respective States.

The consequence of this demoralization is that States, without regard to the Federal Government, assume to stand face to face and wage their own quarrels, to adjust their own difficulties, to impute to each other every wrong, to insist that individual States shall remedy every grievance, and they denounce failure to do so as cause of civil war between the States; and as if the Constitution were silent and dead, and the power of the Union utterly inadequate to keep the peace between them, unconstitutional commissioners flit from State to State, or assemble at the national capital to counsel peace or instigate war. Sir, these are the causes which lie at the bottom of the present dangers. These causes, which have rendered them possible and made them serious, must be removed before they can ever be permanently cured. They shake the fabric of our national Government. It is to this fearful demoralization of the Government and the people that we must ascribe the disastrous defections which now perplex us with the fear of change in all that constituted our greatness. The operation of the Government has been withdrawn from the great public interests, in order that competing parties might not be embarrassed in the struggle for power by diversities of opinion upon questions of policy; and the public mind, in that struggle, has been exclusively turned on the slavery question, which no interest required to be touched by any department of this Government. On that subject there are widely marked diversities of opinion and interest in the different

portions of the Confederacy, with few mediating influences to soften the collision. In the struggle for party power, the two great regions of the country have been brought face to face upon this most dangerous of all subjects of agitation. The authority of the Government was relaxed just when its power was about to be assailed; and the people, emancipated from every control, and their passions inflamed by the fierce struggle for the presidency, were the easy prey of revolutionary audacity.

Within two months after a formal, peaceful, regular election of the Chief Magistrate of the United States, in which the whole body of the people of every State competed with zeal for the prize, without any new event intervening, without any new grievances alleged, without any new menaces having been made, we have seen, in the short course of one month, a small portion of the population of six States transcend the bounds at a single leap at once of the State and the national constitutions; usurp the extraordinary prerogative of repealing the supreme law of the land; exclude the great mass of their fellow-citizens from the protection of the Constitution; declare themselves emancipated from the obligations which the Constitution pronounces to be supreme over them and over their laws; arrogate to themselves all the prerogatives of independent power; rescind the acts of cession of the public property; occupy the public offices; seize the fortresses of the United States confided to the faith of the people among whom they were placed; embezzle the public arms concentrated there for the defense of the United States; array thousands of men in arms against the United States; and actually wage war on the Union by besieging two of their fortresses and firing on a vessel bearing, under the flag of the United States, reinforcements and provisions to one of them. The very boundaries of right and wrong seem obliterated when we see a cabinet minister engaged for months in deliberately changing the distribution of public arms to places in the hands of those about to resist the public authority, so as to place within their grasp means of waging war against the United States greater than they ever used against a foreign foe; and another cabinet minister, still holding his commission under the authority of the United States, still a confidential adviser of the President, still bound by his oath to support the Constitution of the United States, himself a commissioner from his own State to another of the United States, for the purpose of organizing and extending another part of the same great scheme of rebellion; and the doom of the Republic seems sealed when the President, surrounded by such ministers, permits, without rebuke, the Government to be betrayed, neglects the solemn warning of the first soldier of the age, till almost every fort is a prey to domestic treason, and accepts assurances of peace in his time at the expense of leaving the national honor unguarded. His message gives aid and comfort to the enemies of the Union, by avowing his inability to maintain its integrity; and, paralyzed and stupefied, he stands amid the crash of the falling Republic, still muttering, "Not in my time, not in my time; after me the deluge!"

Sir, history, by her prophet Tacitus, has drawn his character for posterity — *Major privato visus dum privatus fuit, et consensu omnium capax imperii nisi imperasset.* Yes, sir, "*nisi imperasset*" James Buchanan might have passed to the grave as one of the men of the Republic equal to every station he filled and not incompetent for the highest. The acquisition of supreme power has revealed his incapacity and crowns him with the unenviable honor of the chief destroyer of his country's greatness.

We have, Mr. Speaker, this day to deal, in a great measure, with the consequences of his incapacity. Persons usurping power in six or seven States have thrown off their allegiance to the United States. It was fondly hoped that it was only temporary, possibly a desperate contrivance to restore the chief actors to power; but we are now authoritatively informed, by the response of South Carolina to the kindly messenger from Virginia, that their position is permanently fixed; that they desire to have, and will have, no further political connection with the United States; and a distinguished gentleman, until within one month a member of the Senate of the United States, recently elected president of the revolutionary convention at Montgomery, has informed us in his inaugural speech that it is their purpose finally to sever their connection with the United States and to take all the consequences of organizing an independent republic.

Mr. Speaker, we are driven to one of two alternatives; we must recognize what we have been told more than once upon this floor is an accomplished fact — the independence of the rebellious States — or we must refuse to acknowledge it, and accept all the responsibilities that attach to that refusal. Recognize them! Abandon the Gulf and coast of Mexico; surrender the forts of the United States; yield the privilege of free com-

merce and free intercourse; strike down the guarantees of the Constitution for our fellow-citizens in all that wide region; create a thousand miles of interior frontier to be furnished with internal customhouses, and armed with internal forts, themselves to be a prey to the next caprice of State sovereignty; organize a vast standing army, ready at a moment's warning to resist aggression; create upon our southern boundary a perpetual foothold for foreign powers, whenever caprice, ambition, or hostility may see fit to invite the despot of France or the aggressive power of England to attack us upon our undefended frontier; sever that unity of territory which we have spent millions, and labored through three generations, to create and establish; pull down the flag of the United States and take a lower station among the nations of the earth; abandon the high prerogative of leading the march of freedom, the hope of struggling nationalities, the terror of frowning tyrants, the boast of the world, the light of liberty — to become the sport and prey of despots whose thrones we consolidate by our fall — to be greeted by Mexico with the salutation: "Art thou also become weak as we? art thou become like unto us?" This is recognition.

Refuse to recognize! We must not coerce a State in the peaceful process of secession. We must not coerce a State engaged in the peaceful process of firing into a United States vessel, to prevent the reinforcement of a United States fort. We must not coerce States which, without any declaration of war, or any act of hostility of any kind, have united, as have Mississippi, Florida, and Louisiana, their joint forces to seize a public fortress. We must not coerce a State which has planted cannon upon its shores to prevent the free navigation of the Mississippi. We must not coerce a State which has robbed the United States Treasury. This is peaceful secession!

Mr. Speaker, I do not design to quarrel with gentlemen about words. I do not wish to say one word which will exasperate the already too much inflamed state of the public mind; but I say that the Constitution of the United States and the laws made in pursuance thereof must be enforced; and they who stand across the path of that enforcement must either destroy the power of the United States or it will destroy them.

CONSTITUTIONAL DIFFICULTIES OF RECONSTRUCTION

(From a Speech in the House of Representatives, March 22d, 1864)

Mr. Speaker: —

THE bill which I am directed by the committee on the rebellious States to report is one which provides for the restoration of civil government in States whose governments have been overthrown. It prescribes such conditions as will secure not only civil government to the people of the rebellious States, but will also secure to the people of the United States permanent peace after the suppression of the rebellion. The bill challenges the support of all who consider slavery the cause of the rebellion. . . . When military opposition shall have been suppressed, not merely paralyzed, driven into a corner, pushed back, but gone, the horrid vision of civil war vanished from the South, then call upon the people to reorganize in their own way, subject to the conditions that we think essential to our permanent peace, and to prevent the revival hereafter of the rebellion — a republican government in the form that the people of the United States can agree to.

Now, for that purpose there are three modes indicated. One is to remove the cause of the war by an alteration of the Constitution of the United States, prohibiting slavery everywhere within its limits. That, sir, goes to the root of the matter, and should consecrate the nation's triumph. But there are thirty-four States; three-fourths of them would be twenty-six. I believe there are twenty-five States represented in this Congress; so that we on that basis cannot change the Constitution. It is, therefore, a condition precedent in that view of the case that more States shall have governments organized within them. . . .

The next plan is that inaugurated by the President of the United States in the proclamation of the eighth of December, called the Amnesty Proclamation. That proposes no guardianship of the United States over the reorganization of the governments, no law to prescribe who shall vote, no civil functionaries to see that the law is faithfully executed, no supervising authority to control and judge of the election. But if in any manner by the toleration of martial law, lately proclaimed the fundamental law, under the dictation of any military authority, or under the prescription of a provost marshal, something in the form of a

government shall be presented, represented to rest on the votes of one-tenth of the population, the President will recognize that, provided it does not contravene the proclamation of freedom and the laws of Congress; and to secure that an oath is exacted. There is no guaranty of law to watch over the organization of that government. It may be recognized by the military power, and not recognized by the civil power, so that it would have a doubtful existence, half civil and half military, neither a temporary government by law of Congress nor a State government, something as unknown to the Constitution as the rebel government that refuses to recognize it. The only prescription is that it shall not contravene the provisions of the proclamation. Sir, if that proclamation be valid, then we are relieved from all trouble on that score. But if that proclamation be not valid, then the oath to support it is without legal sanction, for the President can ask no man to bind himself by an oath to support an unfounded proclamation or an unconstitutional law even for a moment, still less after it shall have been declared void by the Supreme Court of the United States.

By the bill we propose to preclude the judicial question by the solution of a political question. How so? By the paramount power of Congress to reorganize governments in those States, to impose such conditions as it thinks necessary to secure the permanence of republican government, to refuse to recognize any governments there which do not prohibit slavery forever. Aye, gentlemen, take the responsibility to say in the face of those who clamor for the speedy recognition of governments tolerating slavery, that the safety of the people of the United States is the supreme law; that their will is the supreme rule of law, and that we are authorized to pronounce their will on this subject. They take the responsibility to say that we will revise the judgments of our ancestors; that we have experience written in blood which they had not; that we find now what they darkly doubted, that slavery is really radically inconsistent with the permanence of republican governments; and that being charged by the supreme law of the land on our conscience and judgment to guarantee, that is to continue, maintain, and enforce, if it exist, to institute and restore, when overthrown, republican government throughout the broad limits of the Republic, we will weed out every element of their policy which we think incompatible with its permanence and endurance. The purpose of the bill is to preclude the judicial question of the validity and effect of the President's proclamation by the decision of the political authority in reorganizing the State governments. It makes the rule of decision the provisions of the State constitution, which, when recognized by Congress, can be questioned in no court; and it adds to the authority of the proclamation the sanction of Congress. If gentlemen say that the Constitution does not bear that construction, we will go before the people of the United States on that question, and by their judgment we will abide.

V—104

JEFFERSON DAVIS

(1808–1889)

A S A speaker, Jefferson Davis has a military directness of style in keeping with the West Point education which seems to have influenced his character more radically than any other single factor in its formation. He never hesitates for words to express his ideas, nor does he delay their flow to seek for ornament. His farewell to the Senate in 1861 and his inaugural as President of the Southern Confederacy have an unadorned simplicity which shows his consciousness of the importance of both occasions and his determination not to allow superfluous trope or forced metaphor to compromise him in the eyes of posterity. His speech against Clay in 1850, though less studied in its severity, shows the same characteristics. In less than half a dozen lines in this speech, Mr. Davis announced the end of the era of compromise and put himself at the head of those at the South who were in favor of meeting sectional issues without further postponement.

He was born in Christian County, Kentucky, June 3d, 1808. His family which removed to Mississippi in his infancy, sent him back to Transylvania University in Kentucky to be educated, but transferred him from it to West Point, where he graduated in 1828. From his graduation until 1835, he served in the Regular Army, resigning as a lieutenant of dragoons in that year to begin life on a plantation in Mississippi. He was active in the politics of his State from the period of his resignation from the army until the organization of the Confederacy. Elected to Congress in 1844, he resigned to take part in the Mexican War. Wounded at the battle of Buena Vista where he greatly distinguished himself, he was sent, while still on crutches, to represent Mississippi in the Senate. Serving in the Senate from 1847 to 1851, he was Secretary of War in the Cabinet of President Pierce from 1853 to 1857, and United States Senator a second time from 1857 to 1861. When he left the Senate after the secession of Mississippi, he was chosen President of the Confederacy without effort on his part to secure the place. Indeed, his severe ideas of personal dignity would never have allowed him to intrigue for any office. After the collapse of the Confederacy, he was confined for two years in Fortress Monroe, but was released without being brought to trial on the indictment for treason which

had been found against him. He died in New Orleans, December 6th, 1889. At the South the idea that he was individually or distinctively responsible for the Civil War, or for the action taken by the Southern States, has never gained acceptance. He has been regarded merely as a representative man, one of many such, obeying in public life the will of his constituency as far as it accorded with his own sense of propriety. This was his own theory of his position in history. From 1850 to 1860 in public and private he repeatedly asserted his devotion to the Union, coupling such assertions with warnings of the growing excitement among his constituents and with repeated enunciations of his determination to be governed by their will and their interests as a consideration paramount to all others. At the South from 1861 to 1865, he was often and hotly attacked, but from the surrender at Appomattox until his death, his friends and his enemies among ex-Confederates accepted him as the historical representative of the "Lost Cause" and defended him against all attack. While he lacked the faculty of inspiring the enthusiastic devotion which was a spontaneous tribute to such leaders as Robert E. Lee, he had the high regard of all who knew him intimately and the respect of all who sympathized with his views. Mr. Reagan, of Texas, a member of his Cabinet, called him "the most devout Christian I ever knew and the most self-sacrificing of men." W. V. B.

ANNOUNCING THE SECESSION OF MISSISSIPPI

(Delivered on Retiring from the United States Senate, January 21st, 1861)

I RISE, Mr. President, for the purpose of announcing to the Senate that I have satisfactory evidence that the State of Mississippi, by a solemn ordinance of her people in convention assembled, has declared her separation from the United States. Under these circumstances, of course my functions are terminated here. It has seemed to me proper, however, that I should appear in the Senate to announce that fact to my associates, and I will say but very little more. The occasion does not invite me to go into argument, and my physical condition would not permit me to do so if it were otherwise; and yet it seems to become me on an occasion so solemn as this.

It is known to Senators who have served with me here that I have for many years advocated, as an essential attribute of

State sovereignty, the right of a State to secede from the Union. Therefore, if I had not believed there was justifiable cause; if I had thought that Mississippi was acting without sufficient provocation or without an existing necessity, I should still, under my theory of the Government, because of my allegiance to the State of which I am a citizen, have been bound by her action. I, however, may be permitted to say that I do think she has justifiable cause, and I approve of her act. I conferred with her people before that act was taken, counseled them then that if the state of things which they apprehended should exist when the convention met, they should take the action which they have now adopted.

I hope none who hear me will confound this expression of mine with the advocacy of the right of a State to remain in the Union, and to disregard its constitutional obligations by the nullification of the law. Such is not my theory. Nullification and secession, so often confounded, are indeed antagonistic principles. Nullification is a remedy which it is sought to apply within the Union, and against the agent of the States. It is only to be justified when the agent has violated his constitutional obligation, and a State, assuming to judge for itself, denies the right of the agent thus to act, and appeals to the other States of the Union for a decision; but when the States themselves, and when the people of the States have so acted as to convince us that they will not regard our constitutional rights, then, and then for the first time, arises the doctrine of secession in its practical application.

A great man who now reposes with his fathers, and who has been often arraigned for a want of fealty to the Union, advocated the doctrine of Nullification, because it preserved the Union. It was because of his deep-seated attachment to the Union, his determination to find some remedy for existing ills short of a severance of the ties which bound South Carolina to the other States, that Mr. Calhoun advocated the doctrine of Nullification, which he proclaimed to be peaceful, to be within the limits of State power, not to disturb the Union, but only to be a means of bringing the agent before the tribunal of the States for their judgment.

Secession belongs to a different class of remedies. It is to be justified upon the basis that the States are sovereign. There was a time when none denied it. I hope the time may come again, when a better comprehension of the theory of our Government and the inalienable rights of the people of the States will prevent any one from denying that each State is a sovereign, and thus may reclaim the grants which it has made to any agent whomsoever.

I therefore say I concur in the action of the people of Mississippi, believing it to be necessary and proper, and I should have been bound by their action if my belief had been otherwise; and this brings me to the important point which I wish on this last occasion to present to the Senate. It is by this confounding of nullification and secession that the name of a great man, whose ashes now mingle with his mother earth, has been invoked to justify coercion against a seceded State. The phrase, "to execute the laws," was an expression which General Jackson applied to the case of a State refusing to obey the laws while yet a member of the Union. That is not the case which is now presented. The laws are to be executed over the United States, and upon the people of the United States. They have no relation to any foreign country. It is a perversion of terms, at least it is a great misapprehension of the case, which cites that expression for application to a State which has withdrawn from the Union. You may make war on a foreign State. If it be the purpose of gentlemen, they may make war against a State which has withdrawn from the Union; but there are no laws of the United States to be executed within the limits of a seceded State. A State finding herself in the condition in which Mississippi has judged she is, in which her safety requires that she should provide for the maintenance of her rights out of the Union, surrenders all the benefits (and they are known to be many), deprives herself of the advantages (they are known to be great), severs all the ties of affection (and they are close and enduring), which have bound her to the Union; and thus divesting herself of every benefit, taking upon herself every burden, she claims to be exempt from any power to execute the laws of the United States within her limits.

I well remember an occasion when Massachusetts was arraigned before the bar of the Senate, and when then the doctrine of coercion was rife and to be applied against her because of the rescue of a fugitive slave in Boston. My opinion then was the same that it is now. Not in a spirit of egotism, but to show that I am not influenced in my opinion because the case is my

own, I refer to that time and that occasion as containing the opinion which I then entertained, and on which my present conduct is based. I then said, if Massachusetts, following her through a stated line of conduct, chooses to take the last step which separates her from the Union, it is her right to go, and I will neither vote one dollar nor one man to coerce her back; but will say to her, God speed, in memory of the kind associations which once existed between her and the other States.

It has been a conviction of pressing necessity, it has been a belief that we are to be deprived in the Union of the rights which our fathers bequeathed to us, which has brought Mississippi into her present decision. She has heard proclaimed the theory that all men are created free and equal, and this made the basis of an attack upon her social institutions; and the sacred Declaration of Independence has been invoked to maintain the position of the equality of the races. That Declaration of Independence is to be construed by the circumstances and purposes for which it was made. The communities were declaring their independence; the people of those communities were asserting that no man was born—to use the language of Mr. Jefferson—booted and spurred to ride over the rest of mankind; that men were created equal—meaning the men of the political community; that there was no divine right to rule; that no man inherited the right to govern; that there were no classes by which power and place descended to families, but that all stations were equally within the grasp of each member of the body politic. These were the great principles they announced; these were the purposes for which they made their declaration; these were the ends to which their enunciation was directed. They have no reference to the slave; else, how happened it that among the items of arraignment made against George III. was that he endeavored to do just what the North has been endeavoring of late to do—to stir up insurrection among our slaves? Had the Declaration announced that the negroes were free and equal, how was the Prince to be arraigned for stirring up insurrection among them? And how was this to be enumerated among the high crimes which caused the colonies to sever their connection with the mother country? When our Constitution was formed, the same idea was rendered more palpable, for there we find provision made for that very class of persons as property; they were not put upon the footing of equality with white men—not even

upon that of paupers and convicts; but, so far as representation was concerned, were discriminated against as a lower caste, only to be represented in the numerical proportion of three-fifths.

Then, Senators, we recur to the compact which binds us together; we recur to the principles upon which our Government was founded; and when you deny them, and when you deny to us the right to withdraw from a Government which, thus perverted, threatens to be destructive of our rights, we but tread in the path of our fathers when we proclaim our independence, and take the hazard. This is done not in hostility to others, not to injure any section of the country, not even for our own pecuniary benefit, but from the high and solemn motive of defending and protecting the rights we inherited, and which it is our sacred duty to transmit unshorn to our children.

I find in myself, perhaps, a type of the general feeling of my constituents towards yours. I am sure I feel no hostility to you, Senators from the North. I am sure there is not one of you, whatever sharp discussion there may have been between us, to whom I cannot now say, in the presence of my God, I wish you well; and such I am sure is the feeling of the people whom I represent towards those whom you represent. I therefore feel that I but express their desire when I say I hope, and they hope, for peaceful relations with you, though we must part. They may be mutually beneficial to us in the future, as they have been in the past, if you so will it. The reverse may bring disaster on every portion of the country; and if you will have it thus, we will invoke the God of our fathers, who delivered them from the power of the lion, to protect us from the ravages of the bear; and thus, putting our trust in God and in our own firm hearts and strong arms, we will vindicate the right as best we may.

In the course of my service here, associated at different times with a great variety of Senators, I see now around me some with whom I have served long; there have been points of collision, but whatever of offense there has been to me, I leave here; I carry with me no hostile remembrance. Whatever offense I have given which has not been redressed, or for which satisfaction has not been demanded, I have, Senators, in this hour of our parting, to offer you my apology for any pain which in heat of discussion I have inflicted. I go hence unencumbered of the remembrance of any injury received, and having discharged the

duty of making the only reparation in my power for any injury offered.

Mr. President and Senators, having made the announcement which the occasion seemed to me to require, it only remains for me to bid you a final adieu.

INAUGURAL ADDRESS OF 1861

(Delivered at Montgomery, Alabama, Monday, February 18th, 1861)

Gentlemen of the Congress of the Confederate States of America, Friends and Fellow-Citizens:—

CALLED to the difficult and responsible station of Chief Executive of the provisional government which you have instituted, I approach the discharge of the duties assigned to me with a humble distrust of my abilities, but with a sustaining confidence in the wisdom of those who are to guide and aid me in the administration of public affairs, and an abiding faith in the virtue and patriotism of the people.

Looking forward to the speedy establishment of a permanent government to take the place of this, and which, by its greater moral and physical power, will be better able to combat with the many difficulties which arise from the conflicting interests of separate nations, I enter upon the duties of the office to which I have been chosen with the hope that the beginning of our career, as a Confederacy, may not be obstructed by hostile opposition to our enjoyment of the separate existence and independence which we have asserted, and, with the blessing of Providence, intend to maintain. Our present condition, achieved in a manner unprecedented in the history of nations, illustrates the American idea that governments rest upon the consent of the governed, and that it is the right of the people to alter or abolish governments whenever they become destructive of the ends for which they were established.

The declared purpose of the compact of union from which we have withdrawn was "to establish justice, insure domestic tranquillity, provide for the common defense, promote the general welfare, and secure the blessings of liberty to ourselves and our posterity"; and when in the judgment of the sovereign States now composing this Confederacy it had been perverted from the purposes for which it was ordained, and had ceased to answer the ends for which it was established, a peaceful appeal to the ballot box declared that so far as they were concerned, the Government created by that compact should cease to exist. In this they merely asserted a right which the Declaration of Independence of 1776 had defined to be inalienable. Of the time and occasion for its exercise, they as sovereigns were the final judges, each for itself. The impartial and enlightened verdict of mankind will vindicate the rectitude of our conduct, and he, who knows the hearts of men, will judge of the sincerity with which we labored to preserve the government of our fathers in its spirit. The right solemnly proclaimed at the birth of the States and which has been affirmed and reaffirmed in the bills of rights of States subsequently admitted into the Union of 1789, undeniably recognizes in the people the power to resume the authority delegated for the purposes of government. Thus the sovereign States, here represented, proceeded to form this Confederacy, and it is by abuse of language that their act has been denominated a revolution. They formed a new alliance, but within each State its government has remained, and the rights of person and property have not been disturbed. The agent, through whom they communicated with foreign nations, is changed; but this does not necessarily interrupt their international relations.

Sustained by the consciousness that the transition from the former Union to the present Confederacy has not proceeded from a disregard on our part of just obligations, or any failure to perform any constitutional duty; moved by no interest or passion to invade the rights of others; anxious to cultivate peace and commerce with all nations, if we may not hope to avoid war, we may at least expect that posterity will acquit us of having needlessly engaged in it. Doubly justified by the absence of wrong on our part, and by wanton aggression on the part of others, there can be no cause to doubt that the courage and patriotism of the people of the Confederate States will be found equal to any measures of defense which honor and security may require.

An agricultural people, whose chief interest is the export of a commodity required in every manufacturing country, our true policy is peace and the freest trade which our necessities will permit. It is alike our interest, and that of all those to whom we would sell and from whom we would buy, that there should be the fewest practicable restrictions upon the interchange of commodities. There can be but little rivalry between ours and

any manufacturing or navigating community, such as the northeastern States of the American Union. It must follow, therefore, that a mutual interest would invite good-will and kind offices. If, however, passion or the lust of dominion should cloud the judgment or inflame the ambition of those States, we must prepare to meet the emergency, and to maintain, by the final arbitrament of the sword, the position which we have assumed among the nations of the earth. We have entered upon the career of independence, and it must be inflexibly pursued. Through many years of controversy with our late associates, the Northern States, we have vainly endeavored to secure tranquillity and to obtain respect for the rights to which we are entitled. As a necessity, not a choice, we have resorted to the remedy of separation; and henceforth our energies must be directed to the conduct of our own affairs and the perpetuity of the Confederacy which we have formed. If a just perception of mutual interest shall permit us peaceably to pursue our separate political career, my most earnest desire will have been fulfilled; but if this be denied to us, and the integrity of our territory and jurisdiction be assailed, it will but remain for us, with firm resolve, to appeal to arms and invoke the blessings of Providence on a just cause.

As a consequence of our new condition, and with a view to meet anticipated wants, it will be necessary to provide for the speedy and efficient organization of branches of the Executive Department, having special charge of foreign intercourse, finance, military affairs, and the postal service.

For purposes of defense, the Confederate States may, under ordinary circumstances, rely mainly upon the militia; but it is deemed advisable in the present condition of affairs that there should be a well-instructed and disciplined army, more numerous than would usually be required on a peace establishment. I also suggest that for the protection of our harbors and commerce on the high seas a navy adapted to those objects will be required. These necessities have doubtless engaged the attention of Congress.

With a Constitution differing only from that of our fathers in so far as it is explanatory of their well-known intent, freed from the sectional conflicts which have interfered with the pursuit of the general welfare, it is not unreasonable to expect that States from which we have recently parted may seek to unite their fortunes with ours under the Government which we have

instituted. For this your Constitution makes adequate provision; but beyond this, if I mistake not the judgment and will of the people, a re-union with the States from which we have separated is neither practicable nor desirable. To increase the power, develop the resources, and promote the happiness of the Confederacy, it is requisite that there should be so much homogeneity that the welfare of every portion shall be the aim of the whole. Where this does not exist, antagonisms are engendered which must and should result in separation.

Actuated solely by the desire to preserve our own rights and promote our own welfare, the separation of the Confederate States has been marked by no aggression upon others and followed by no domestic convulsion. Our industrial pursuits have received no check; the cultivation of our fields has progressed as heretofore; and even should we be involved in war, there would be no considerable diminution in the production of the staples which have constituted our exports, and in which the commercial world has an interest scarcely less than our own. This common interest of the producer and consumer can only be interrupted by an exterior force, which should obstruct its transmission to foreign markets — a course of conduct which would be as unjust towards us as it would be detrimental to manufacturing and commercial interests abroad. Should reason guide the action of the Government from which we have separated, a policy so detrimental to the civilized world, the Northern States included, could not be dictated by even the strongest desire to inflict injury upon us; but if otherwise, a terrible responsibility will rest upon it, and the suffering of millions will bear testimony to the folly and wickedness of our aggressors. In the meantime, there will remain to us, besides the ordinary means before suggested, the well-known resources for retaliation upon the commerce of the enemy.

Experience in public stations of subordinate grades to this which your kindness has conferred has taught me that care and toil and disappointment are the price of official elevation. You will see many errors to forgive, many deficiencies to tolerate, but you shall not find in me either a want of zeal or fidelity to the cause that is to me highest in hope and of most enduring affection. Your generosity has bestowed upon me an undeserved distinction — one which I neither sought nor desired. Upon the continuance of that sentiment, and upon your wisdom and patri-

otism I rely to direct and support me in the performance of the duty required at my hands.

We have changed the constituent parts but not the system of our Government. The Constitution formed by our fathers is that of these Confederate States in their exposition of it; and in the judicial construction it has received, we have a light which reveals its true meaning.

Thus instructed as to the just interpretation of the instrument, and ever remembering that all offices are but trusts held for the people and that delegated powers are to be strictly construed, I will hope by due diligence in the performance of my duties, though I may disappoint your expectations, yet to retain, when retiring, something of the good-will and confidence which welcomed my entrance into office.

It is joyous, in the midst of perilous times, to look around upon a people united in heart, where one purpose of high resolve animates and actuates the whole — where the sacrifices to be made are not weighed in the balance against honor and right and liberty and equality. Obstacles may retard — they cannot long prevent — the progress of a movement sanctified by its justice and sustained by a virtuous people. Reverently let us invoke the God of our fathers to guide and protect us in our efforts to perpetuate the principles which, by his blessing, they were able to vindicate, establish, and transmit to their posterity; and with a continuance of his favor, ever gratefully acknowledged, we may hopefully look forward to success, to peace, and to prosperity.

AGAINST CLAY AND COMPROMISE

(From a Speech Delivered in the Senate, February 14th, 1850, "The Senate Having in Committee of the Whole the Resolutions Submitted by Mr. Clay" on the Admission of California)

IF, SIR, the spirit of sectional aggrandizement, or, if gentlemen prefer, this love they bear the African race, shall cause the disunion of these States, the last chapter of our history will be a sad commentary upon the justice and the wisdom of our people. That this Union, replete with blessings to its own citizens and diffusive of hope to the rest of mankind, should fall a victim to a selfish aggrandizement and a pseudo philanthropy, prompting one portion of the Union to war upon the domestic rights and peace of another, would be a deep reflection on the good sense and patriotism of our day and generation. But, sir, if this last chapter in our history shall ever be written, the reflective reader will ask, Whence proceeded this hostility of the North against the South? He will find it there recorded that the South, in opposition to her own immediate interests, engaged with the North in the unequal struggle of the Revolution. He will find again that when Northern seamen were impressed, their brethren of the South considered it cause for war, and entered warmly into the contest with the haughty power then claiming to be mistress of the seas. He will find that the South, afar off, unseen and unheard, toiling in the pursuits of agriculture, had filled the shipping, and supplied the staple for manufactures, which enriched the North. He will find that she was the great consumer of Northern fabrics — that she not only paid for these their fair value in the markets of the world, but that she also paid their increased value, derived from the imposition of revenue duties. And if, still further, he seek for the cause of this hostility, it at last is to be found in the fact that the South held the African race in bondage, being the descendants of those who were mainly purchased from the people of the North. And this was the great cause. For this the North claimed that the South should be restricted from future growth — that around her should be drawn, as it were, a sanitary cordon to prevent the extension of a moral leprosy; and if for that it shall be written the South resisted, it would be but in keeping with every page she has added to the history of our country.

It depends on those in the majority to say whether this last chapter in our history shall be written or not. It depends on them now to decide whether the strife between the different sections shall be arrested before it has become impossible, or whether it shall proceed to a final catastrophe. I, sir — and I speak only for myself — am willing to meet any fair proposition; to settle upon anything which promises security for the future; anything which assures me of permanent peace; and I am willing to make whatever sacrifice I may properly be called on to render for that purpose. Nor, sir, is it a light responsibility. If I strictly measured my conduct by the late message of the Governor and the recent expressions of opinion in my State, I should have no power to accept any terms save the unqualified admission of the

equal rights of the citizens of the South to go into any of the Territories of the United States with any and every species of property held among us. I am willing, however, to take my share of the responsibility which the crisis of our country demands. I am willing to rely on the known love of the people I represent for the whole country and the abiding respect which I know they entertain for the Union of these States. If, sir, I distrusted their attachment to our Government, and if I believed they had that restless spirit of disunion which has been ascribed to the South, I should know full well that I had no such foundation as this to rely upon — no such great reserve in the heart of the people to fall back upon in the hour of accountability.

Mr. President, is there such incompatibility of interest between the two sections of this country that they cannot profitably live together? Does the agriculture of the South injure the manufactures of the North? On the other hand, are they not their life-blood? And think you if one portion of the Union, however great it might be in commerce and manufactures, were separated from all the agricultural districts, that it would long maintain its supremacy? If any one so believes, let him turn to the written history of commercial States; let him look upon the moldering palaces of Venice; let him ask for the faded purple of Tyre, and visit the ruins of Carthage; there he will see written the fate of every country which rests its prosperity on commerce and manufactures alone. United we have grown to our present dignity and power — united we may go on to a destiny which the human mind cannot measure. Separated, I feel that it requires no prophetic eye to see that the portion of the country which is now scattering the seeds of disunion to which I have referred, will be that which will suffer most. Grass will grow on the pavements now worn by the constant tread of the human throng which waits on commerce, and the shipping will abandon your ports for those which now furnish the staples of trade. And we who produce the great staple upon which your commerce and manufactures rest, will produce those staples still; shipping will fill our harbor; and why may we not found the Tyre of modern commerce within our own limits? Why may we not bring the manufacturers to the side of agriculture, and commerce, too, the ready servant of both?

But, sir, I have no disposition to follow this subject. I certainly can derive no pleasure from the contemplation of anything

which can impair the prosperity of any portion of this Union; and I only refer to it that those who suppose we are tied by interest or fear should look the question in the face, and understand that it is mainly a feeling of attachment to the Union which has long bound, and now binds the South. But, Mr. President, I ask Senators to consider how long affection can be proof against such trial and injury and provocation as the South is continually receiving.

The case in which this discrimination against the South is attempted, the circumstances under which it was introduced, render it especially offensive. It will not be difficult to imagine the feeling with which a Southern soldier during the Mexican War received the announcement that the House of Representatives had passed that odious measure, the Wilmot Proviso; and that he, although then periling his life, abandoning all the comforts of home, and sacrificing his interests, was, by the legislature of his country, marked as coming from a portion of the Union which was not entitled to the equal benefits of whatever might result from the service to which he was contributing whatever power he possessed. Nor will it be difficult to conceive of the many sons of the South whose blood has stained those battle-fields, whose ashes now mingle with Mexican earth, that some, when they last looked on the flag of their country, may have felt their dying moments embittered by the recollection that that flag cast not an equal shadow of protection over the land of their birth, the graves of their parents, and the homes of their children so soon to be orphans. Sir, I ask Northern Senators to make the case their own — to carry to their own fireside the idea of such intrusion and offensive discrimination as is offered to us — realize these irritations, so galling to the humble, so intolerable to the haughty, and wake before it is too late, from the dream that the South will tamely submit. Measure the consequences to us of your assumption, and ask yourselves whether, as a free, honorable, and brave people, you would submit to it.

It is essentially the characteristic of the chivalrous that they never speculate upon the fears of any man, and I trust that no such speculations will be made upon the idea that may be entertained in any quarter that the South, from fear of her slaves, is necessarily opposed to a dissolution of this Union. She has no such fear; her slaves would be to her now, as they were in the Revolution, an element of military strength. I trust that no

speculations will be made upon either the condition or the supposed weakness of the South. They will bring sad disappointments to those who indulge them. Rely upon her devotion to the Union, rely upon the feeling of fraternity she inherited and has never failed to manifest; rely upon the nationality and freedom from sedition which has in all ages characterized an agricultural people; give her justice, sheer justice, and the reliance will never fail you.

Then, Mr. President, I ask that some substantial proposition may be made by the majority in regard to this question. It is for those who have the power to pass it to propose one. It is for those who are threatening us with the loss of that which we are entitled to enjoy to state, if there be any compromise, what that compromise is. We are unable to pass any measure, if we propose it; therefore, I have none to suggest. We are unable to bend you to any terms which we may offer; we are under the ban of your purpose; therefore, from you, if from anywhere, the proposition must come. I trust that we shall meet it and bear the responsibility as becomes us; that we shall not seek to escape from it; that we shall not seek to transfer to other places, or other times, or other persons, that responsibility which devolves upon us; and I hope the earnestness which the occasion justifies will not be mistaken for the ebullition of passion, nor the language of warning be construed as a threat. We cannot, without the most humiliating confession of the supremacy of faction, evade our constitutional obligations, and our obligations under the treaty with Mexico, to organize governments in the Territories of California and New Mexico. I trust that we will not seek to escape from the responsibility, and leave the country unprovided for unless by an irregular admission of new States; that we will act upon the good example of Washington in the case of Tennessee, and of Jefferson in the case of Louisiana; that we will not, if we abandon those high standards, do more than come down to modern examples — that we will not go further than to permit those who have the forms of government under the Constitution to assume sovereignty over territory of the United States; that we may at least, I say, assert the right to know who they are, how many they are, where they voted, how they voted, and whose certificate is presented to us of the fact before it is conceded to them to determine the fundamental law of the country and to prescribe the conditions on which other citizens of the United States may enter it. To reach all this knowledge, we must go through the intermediate stage of territorial government.

How will you determine what is the seal, and who are the officers of a community unknown as an organized body to the Congress of the United States? Can the right be admitted in that community to usurp the sovereignty over territory which belongs to the States of the Union? All these questions must be answered before I can consent to any such irregular proceeding as that which is now presented in the case of California.

Mr. President, thanking the Senate for the patience they have shown towards me, I again express the hope that those who have the power to settle this distracting question — those who have the ability to restore peace, concord, and lasting harmony to the United States — will give us some substantial proposition, such as magnanimity can offer, and such as we can honorably accept. I, being one of the minority in the Senate and the Union, have nothing to offer, except an assurance of co-operation in anything which my principles will allow me to adopt, and which promises permanent substantial security.

v—105

MICHAEL DAVITT

(1846–)

MICHAEL DAVITT has been one of the most forceful men of his generation, made so by the intensity of his hatred of oppression. He was born in the village of Straide, County Mayo, Ireland, in 1846. His father belonged to the humblest class of Irish tenant-farmers and Michael's career was determined by the eviction of the family from their holding. This forced them to emigrate to England where Michael, while still a boy, lost his arm in a Lancashire cotton factory. As he could not support himself by manual labor, his family managed to give him the rudiments of an education — for a mind like his, enough to serve as the key to all knowledge. He went from school to a printing office, and in 1866 began in the Fenian movement the career which has made him celebrated all over the English-speaking world. He has been without doubt the most effective Irish Nationalist of his generation and has paid for his effectiveness by undergoing repeated imprisonment. One of his convictions was for "treason-felony," and he served over seven years of the fifteen-year sentence through which it was sought to silence his eloquent protests against abuses.

IRELAND A NATION, SELF-CHARTERED AND SELF-RULED

(From the Address in Mechanics' Hall, Boston, December 8th, 1878)

WHEN we appeal to mankind for the justice of our cause, we must assume the attitude of a united, because an earnest, people, and show reason why we refuse to accept our political annihilation. We can only do this by the thoroughness of purpose which should actuate, and the systematic exertions which alone can justify, us in claiming the recognition due to a country which has never once acquiesced in its subjugation, nor abandoned its resolve to be free. Viewing that country then, as she presents herself to-day, the problem of her redemption may be put in this formula: Given the present social and political condition of Ireland, with the spirit, national tendencies, physical

---

and moral forces of her people — together with the power, influence, and policy arrayed against them — to indicate what should be the plans pursued, and action adopted, whereby the condition of our people could be materially improved, in efforts tending to raise them to their rightful position as a Nation.

I confess to the difficulty of solving such a problem, but not so much as to the putting it into practice if theoretically demonstrated; but —

> "Right endeavor's not in vain —
> Its reward is in the doing;
> And the rapture of pursuing,
> Is the prize the vanquished gain."

Let us see if we can discover a key to the difficulty of the Irish question. I will assume that there are certain matters or contingencies important to or affecting the Irish race which are of equal interest to its people (irrespective of what differences of opinion there may be amongst them on various other concerns), — such as the preservation of the distinctive individuality of the race itself among peoples; the earning for it that respect and prestige to which it is by right and inheritance entitled, by striving for its improvement, physically and morally, and its intellectual and social advancement, revival of its ancient language, etc.; and that there are past occurrences and sectional animosities which all classes must reasonably desire to prevent in future, for the honor and welfare of themselves and country, — such as religious feuds and provincial antipathies. I will also assume that the raising of our peasant population from the depths of social misery to which it has been sunk by an unjust land system would meet with the approval of most classes in Ireland, and receive the moral co-operation of Irishmen abroad, as would also the improvement of the dwellings of our agricultural population, which project, I also assume, would be accepted and supported by all parties in Irish political life. Without particularizing any further measures for the common good of our people, for which political parties cannot refuse to mutually co-operate, if consistent with their *raison d'être* as striving for their country's welfare, I think it will be granted that Nationalists (pronounced or quiescent), Obstructionists, Home Rulers, Repealers, and others, could unite in obtaining the reforms already enumerated by concerted action on and by whatever means the present existing state of

---

affairs in Ireland can place within their reach. Such concerted action for the general good would necessitate a centripetal platform, as representing that central principle or motive which constitutes the hold and supplies the influence that a country's government has upon the people governed.

A race of people, to preserve itself from destruction by a hostile race, or by partisan spirit and factious strife internally, or absorption by a people among which it may be scattered, absolutely requires some central idea, principle, or platform of motives of action, by which to exercise its national or race individuality and strength, with a view to its improvement and preservation. A people's own established government supplies this need, of course, but where, as in Ireland, there is no government of or by the people, and the dominant power is but a strong executive faction, the national strength is wasted: 1. By the *divide et impera* policy of that dominant English faction; 2. By desperate attempts to overthrow that power; and 3. By hitherto fruitless agitation to win a just rule, or force remedial legislation from an alien assembly by means repugnant to the pride of the largest portion of our people; while here, in this great shelterland of peoples, the Irish race itself is fast disappearing in the composite American. If, therefore, a platform be put forth embodying resistance to every hostile element pitted, or adverse influence at work, against the individuality of Ireland and its people, and a program of national labor for the general welfare of our country be adopted, resting upon those wants and desires which have a first claim upon the consideration of Irishmen — such a platform, if put forth, not to suit a particular party, but to embrace all that is earnest and desirous among our people for labor in the vineyard of Ireland's common good, a great national desire would be gratified, and an immense stride be taken towards the goal of each Irishman's hopes. . . .

It is showing a strange want of knowledge of England's hatred and jealousy of Ireland to suppose that a government formed from any of the English parties would ever concede all that could satisfy the desires of the Irish people; and to ground an apprehension upon such an improbable contingency is a mistake.

Again, the supposition that the spirit of Irish nationality, which has combated against destruction for seven centuries, only awaits a few concessions from its baffled enemy to be snuffed out thereby, does not speak highly for those who hold that opinion of its frailty. In my opinion, we may expect to hear no more of "the cause" when the genius of Tipperary shall carve the Rock of Cashel into a statue of Judge Keogh, and Croagh Patrick shall walk to London to render homage to the Duke of Connaught. Every chapter of our history, every ensanguined field upon which our forefathers died in defense of that cause, every name in the martyrology of Ireland, from Fitzgerald to Charles McCarthy, proclaim the truth of Meagher's impassioned words: "From the Irish mind the inspiring thought that there once was an Irish nation self-chartered and self-ruled can never be effaced; the burning hope that there will be one again can never be extinguished."

With these convictions, 'and the consummation of such hopes predestined by an indestructible cause and imperishable national principles, Irish Nationalists can, without fear of compromising such principles, grapple with West-Britonism on its own ground, and strangle its efforts to imperialize Ireland. The popular party in Ireland has a right to participate in everything concerning the social and political condition of the country; to compete with the constitutional and other parties who cater for public support, and stamp in this manner its Nationalist convictions and principles upon everything Irish, from a local board of poor-law guardians to a (by circumstances compulsory) representation in an alien parliament.

No party has a right to call itself National which neglects resorting to each and every justifiable means to end the frightful misery under which our land-crushed people groan. It is exhibiting a callous indifference to the state of social degradation to which the power of the landlords of Ireland has sunk our peasantry to ask them to "plod on in sluggish misery from sire to son, from age to age," until we, by force of party and party selfishness, shall free the country. It is playing the part of the Levite who passed by the man plundered by thieves. It is seeing a helpless creature struggling against suffocation in a ditch, and making no immediate effort to save him. If we refuse to play the part of the Good Samaritan to those who have fallen among robber landlords, other Irishmen will not. The cry has gone forth, "Down with the land system that has cursed and depopulated Ireland"; and this slogan cry of war has come from the Constitutionalists.

In the name of the common good of our country, its honor, interests, social and political, let the two great Irish parties agree to differ on party principles, while emulating each other in service to our impoverished people. Let each endeavor to find points upon which they can agree, instead of trying to discover quibbles whereon to differ. Let a centre platform be adopted, resting on a broad, generous, and comprehensive Nationalism, which will invite every earnest Irishman upon it. The manhood strength of Ireland could then become an irresistible power, standing ready at its post, while the whole Irish race, rallying to the support of such a platform, would cry:—

> "We want the land that bore us!
> We'll make that want our chorus;
>   And we'll have it yet, tho' hard to get,
> By the heavens bending o'er us."

HENRY LAURENS DAWES

(1816-)

ENRY LAURENS DAWES represented a Massachusetts district in the House of Representatives from 1857 to 1875. From 1875 to 1893 he was United States Senator from Massachusetts. He supported the policies of the Republican party from its organization, but immediately after the war it was believed for a time that he would take a determined stand against giving the ballot at once to the newly emancipated slaves. This expectation was not realized. During the Reconstruction period and the decade following, the Democratic party strongly insisted on a revision of the "War Tariff," and as there was a theory among economists regardless of party that the protection given by tariff taxes should be equal to the difference in cost of raw material and labor cost, the result was the Tariff Commission, supported by Mr. Dawes in 1880. He was born at Cummington, Massachusetts, October 13th, 1816.

THE TARIFF COMMISSION OF 1880

(Delivered in the Senate, May 10th, 1880, on the Bill to Provide for a Tariff Commission)

Mr. President:—

I AM in favor of the bill reported by the Committee on Finance because I am in favor of a revision and reform of the tariff.

Great inconsistencies and incongruities exist in the tariff. A great many excessive duties remain upon the statute-book. Many dutiable articles should be on the free list, and many of the provisions of the tariff have become obsolete and inoperative. The present is a favorable time for such a revision. The increased prosperity of the country and of all business in it has so increased the receipts of the Government, both from sources of internal revenue and from customs duties, as to render such a revision desirable and possible, keeping in view first the primary object of the imposition of duties, a revenue for the maintenance of the Government, and keeping that revenue as near as possible to its current and necessary expenses. There is an opportunity

to revise and reform not only the duties but the methods of enforcing the law and collecting them. Some of the circumstances justifying this course have sprung up without any reference to legislation. Changes in business, changes in the relations of industries to each other as well as changes in the sources of revenue to the Government, require the Government to look now to one quarter and now to another from which little was expected or received in former times. We should conform our legislation to the changes going on all the time in the methods of business as well as in the sources of revenue. All these invoke at our hands attention to the question whether we shall permit the revenue system of the Government to remain as it is or address ourselves to the best method of producing out of it a state of things that shall answer as well the demands of the Government as the expectations and necessities and claims of those under the Government without affecting whose business pursuits it is impossible to reform the revenue laws.

If I desired the continuance of the present state of things, if I wished to perpetuate these incongruities and these excesses and these defects, I should desire that the ideas submitted on Friday last by the Senator from Kentucky [Mr. Beck] should prevail; for it is by the attempt to enforce just such ideas in the past that has come this condition of things. Since the tariff of 1846, before the tariff of 1846, yea, before from the time of the tariff of 1842, the effort has been made to establish a tariff system by precisely the same means as those suggested by the Senator from Kentucky. All the industries of the land affected by the imposition of duties, or by the relief of industries from their imposition, have been summoned before committees from 1842 to to-day in precisely the same manner suggested by him. They have been in a great measure also under the control of party organizations.

Sir, I am not about to discuss the comparative claim of one of the two parties to the confidence and support of the people on this question of the tariff. I am not here now to say that to the Democratic party or to the Republican party the country may most safely turn for relief or for reform. I do not think that it is a part of my duty, resulting from the conviction of an experience in this matter somewhat extended, to undertake at this time to stake the great question involved in the bill and the substitute before the Senate upon the merits of either party. Out of these contests of parties have come the evils of which we complain. We have had the struggle of the one party or the other to take to itself and appropriate the work of so adjusting the tariff in this country between the Government and those affected by it as to seek and obtain from the people some support that the adversary should not be entitled to; and out of that has come the shifting from party to party of this question and these measures; and the Government on the one hand and the many industries of the country on the other have suffered in this conflict of party. It is only from the possibility now presented that the wise men of both parties can take up this question without reference to its effect upon political parties, and determine it upon its merits, that anything like permanency, built upon justice and fairness, will ever result from legislation.

A duty for the purpose of revenue must be imposed in one of two ways: indifferently, at haphazard, by blind folly; or with discrimination. I take it that neither the Senator from Kentucky nor any other Senator proposes to impose duties for revenue blindly and indiscriminately, without regard to what will be the effect either upon the revenue or upon the subject-matter upon which the duty is imposed. Then it must be imposed with discrimination. And one other question arises immediately and settles the whole matter; it must either be imposed upon the raw material or upon the manufactured article, and no man can address himself one moment to the consideration of this question, but must settle at the threshold the point whether he will impose that duty upon the raw material or upon the manufactured article.

These men represent the manufactured article who are invited before a committee of Congress, by the side of whom in the proposition of the Senator from Arkansas two or three experts are invited to take seats. They are producers in this land. According to the census of 1860 their products amounted to $1,800,000,000, and in 1870 to $4,000,000,000, an increase in value of 102 per cent. in ten years. Making all due allowance for the disturbance of prices by inflation, in actual quantity during those ten years the increase had been 52 per cent. Fifty-two per cent. more in actual quantities was produced at the end of that decade. According to that rate of increase, well-nigh eight billion dollars' worth of fabrics will have been produced and developed in the year 1880, as shown by the census. This is represented by men who must appear before this committee. This is the

The question is all summed up in this single aphorism: To the American laborer belongs the labor which is to be performed for Americans; whatever is to be performed for us should be done here among us. I desire for one to see an effort made to frame a revenue tariff upon this principle. See to it that the Government is supplied; take that which it is necessary to levy upon production and levy it upon manufactured articles, so distributed upon each and every article as well as you may until you bring up our own producers to a level in cost with the foreign competition, and let the raw material come in free. Sir, to that work, involving the growth and prosperity and development of this country, all men of all parties, the wisest and the most discreet and expert, ought to be invited. No one party can accomplish it. The doctrine thus developed does not exist in this or that party exclusively. It has come to be every day more and more the common sentiment and conviction of economists throughout the country.

production in this land consumed here, made here for our own people, under such an adjustment of duties as the Government was under the necessity of imposing, so imposed that they could be produced here rather than brought here already produced; for where the production is, there is the manufacture, there are the people whose hands fashion these fabrics; and where the people are whose hands manufacture these fabrics, there is the capital which moves the thousand busy fingers of industry, and there is the town built up by those whose time is employed in these productions; and where the town is, there is the schoolhouse and there is the Church and there is the State.

These are productions which, under a proper adjustment of the tariff, as I conceive, every Senator I apprehend would say it were better should be on this side of the Atlantic than on the other. The men who appear before these committees are citizens of the United States, part and parcel of the body politic, having all sorts of politics and political affiliations, with their thoughts turned to the productions of these industries which are required for consumption by the people of this land. They furnish employment for the people, the thousands and tens of thousands and millions of people who find employment in these establishments, fashioning for our own people the fabrics our own people consume. They are those most interested in this question. They furnish employment.

Sir, the condition of things which I have described renders a revision of the tariff not only possible, but necessary. We have arrived at that condition in production that puts it in our power to take off these large and excessive duties, for I hold that, keeping to the idea that revenue is the object and purpose in laying the duty upon the manufactured article as against the raw material, that should never rise one penny above a perfect equality with this. Put the American producer, in levying your duties, simply upon an equality with the foreign producer; make up the difference between the interest on his money, the cost of his living, and the wages he pays; just even them up and no more; lift up and not pull down; for if you desire an interchange of produce, he who can manufacture the cheapest will in the end triumph over his neighbor. On any other basis, if you maintain these industries in this land, you must cut down the pay of the laborer to a level with the pay of him with whom you compete, or you cannot compete with him.

WILLIAM L. DAYTON

(1807-1864)

N HIS opposition to the Mexican War and to the acquisition of Mexican territory by conquest or forced sale, William L. Dayton, of New Jersey, represented a large body of Whigs in the Northern States, who deprecated agitation for the immediate abolition of slavery, but foresaw that the organization of new territory would force issues. His speeches of 1847 and 1850 are among the most important historically of the two decades. He was born at Baskingridge, New Jersey, February 17th, 1807. Educated at Princeton, he became eminent at the bar of his native State and was Associate Justice of its supreme court from 1838 to 1842. From 1842 to 1851 he represented New Jersey in the United States Senate. A Whig during this period, the dissolution of that party as a result of the slavery agitation forced him to act with the new Republican party. He was a candidate for Vice-President in 1856, and in 1861 President Lincoln appointed him Minister to France. He died at Paris, December 1st, 1864.

ARRAIGNING PRESIDENT POLK

(From a Speech on the Mexican War, January 28th, 1847)

THE annexation of Texas, and the subsequent order of the President, placing our armies on the Rio Grande (pointing your guns to rake the streets of the city of Matamoras), were the obvious and immediate causes of this war. Without such annexation and orders, it can scarcely be pretended that the remote grievances complained of could have produced war; with such annexation and orders, it can scarcely be pretended that the want of such grievances would have prevented it.

But, sir, suppose it be all true, how does it help the President in his vindication? Who gave him the right to involve his country in war for any cause? How does he possess himself of that power which the Constitution invests in Congress alone? Sir, the President has not gone far enough to make good a justification, admitting that all he says is true.

But we are told that there was just cause for war, and that it will be prosecuted to obtain peace and indemnity for expenses and the pecuniary demands of our citizens against Mexico. Sir, will any gentleman on that or this side of the Chamber tell me the effect of this very war upon the pecuniary demands referred to? Does not the declaration of war of itself cancel all treaty stipulations, all binding obligations to pay this money? Where now is the argument of those gentlemen who so stoutly resisted the payment of the claims of our citizens for French spoliations prior to 1800? The whole groundwork of that opposition was based on the *quasi* state of war between this country and France, after those claims accrued. Sir, miserable as was the condition of these claims on Mexico prior to this war, by reason of the poverty and distraction of that Government, I hold them tenfold worse now. If we cancel a treaty stipulation by war, it would be the duty of the Government to make good to the claimants their wrong. But where is the man connected with this administration who thinks of assuming the payment of these debts, now or hereafter; unless, perchance, in the result of the war we may receive them? Then, perhaps, after years of delay, after the original claimants shall have died, after speculators shall have bought up the claims, after a long and weary haggling about the amount due, some kind of half payment by the Government may be agreed upon. This, sir, if we may judge the future from the past, is about the best we can anticipate for these claimants; this, for them, will be the result, at best, of the war.

But, Mr. President, my object was to speak not so much of the origin as of the object and conduct of this war.

The President, although not the war-making, is the war-conducting power of our Government. He asks aid for an existing war. He has the means now to prosecute it in one way, and declares that he will prosecute it. He seems not to think of settling this question in reference to the original controversy — the proper boundary of Texas. Sir, I believe the President has made this war, made it without right and against right — still, he has made it; it is upon us and, as it seems to me, we have no alternative but to aid in its prosecution, or suffer our arms to be disgraced in the face of the world. If our army were this side of the Rio Grande, with my present knowledge I would not vote the President one dollar or one man; but we are

in a position where a kind of necessity controls us — a fate hurries us on blindly, we know not where. To withdraw our troops now would look like a retreat before a superior force, or a tacit acknowledgment, at least, that we could do nothing. To take up a line of extended positions within and across the Mexican territory, and hold them, would require a vast expenditure and force to be continued for an indefinite time. Sir, I know not whether we will better ourselves by its direct prosecution, but that is the recommendation of the Executive — the constitutional commander-in-chief of our armies — who is responsible for the conduct of this war, and I will sustain him, at least with all adequate supplies. But, while I do this, I shall claim the right freely, but respectfully, to express my opinions. What, then, has the President recommended? What has he done? . . .

What have we seen? The plan of campaign is accomplished. Our soldiers have crossed the far prairies; they have overrun New Mexico and California; they have occupied their towns and cities; they have gained, against odds unknown in modern warfare, two pitched battles; they have carried Monterey by storm and yet *cui bono?* Sir, the days of Quixotism have passed. I do not depreciate the value of that reputation which comes of a " well foughten field "; but nations do not, in our day, fight simply for renown. What other profit have we of this campaign? Mexico has suffered less by her defeats than we have by our victories. Our losses to hers have been as five to one. Already by battle and climate we have lost from one thousand five hundred to two thousand men! Our army expenses have been millions per month; hers, by one of her late official documents, are $368,789 only. And where is it to end? Who can see that end in the dim future? . . .

Sir, the whole secret of this miserable plan of campaign is here. It was not a campaign formed primarily to bring us peace. Peace, "an honorable peace," as they phrase it, was sought, not as an end, but as a means to an end. Acquisition was the end, peace but the means to attain it. I have regretted this manifestation on the part of the Executive; one wrong was scarcely accomplished, when another was begun. Through all the clouds and darkness which have covered this administration, shutting out from its view the pathway of its future, one single star has glimmered in the distance; seen, watched by it, as the star of its hope and its destiny. Sir, this is a war, not for

peace, but for California! Aye, California! and a strip of country connecting us is its grand object and end. The conduct of the administration and the documents prove this, in spite of all official disavowals. From the beginning, it has been pursued with a boldness, a shamelessness, without parallel. Heretofore, we have affected some hesitation, a little maiden coyness, about appropriating that which did not belong to us; even Texas was at first declined! Alas, sir, each sin but hardens the sinner!

ISSUES AGAINST SLAVERY FORCED BY THE MEXICAN WAR

(From a Speech Delivered in the Senate of the United States, March 22d, 1850)

Mr. President: —

THE war with Mexico has brought with it much territory and much trouble. This result was early foreseen. It was not only foreseen, but it was strongly deprecated. We now have a national estate beyond our national wants or means of enjoyment, and yet not less the subject of contention among the heirs. Some gentlemen on this side of the chamber, in anticipation of the difficulties which now surround us, never assented to the treaty by which this territory was acquired; they preferred the hazard of a continuance of the war with Mexico rather than a peace which should bring territory along with it. There were a few upon this side of the chamber, and I was of the number, who preferred, as an alternative, peace, upon the terms then offered, rather than a continuance of the war, with the chances of a larger amount of territory, further south, at its close. I do not now, Mr. President, regret my action upon that subject; it is easy to appreciate difficulties which are around us and upon us, but it is hard to say what these difficulties would have been had that war been continued by defeating the treaty, and, as a probable consequence, had the Whig party been defeated at the ensuing election. I hesitate not to believe that the conclusion of that war under the auspices of a Democratic administration would have brought with it an additional amount of territory, further south, and better appropriated to slave labor. It would have increased rather than diminished the difficulties which now surround us. But, Mr. President, the acquisition of this territory

was emphatically the act, the policy of the South. This matter, either for good or for evil, has been forced upon the North, not only against our will, but against our remonstrance and fears, ofttimes expressed in this chamber. But the territory is here, and the next step in the progress of this matter is as to the disposition which is to be made of it. That the citizens of the two sections of the Confederacy have equal rights there, no man can dispute. But that very equality of right repels the idea that the minority in interest shall have an absolute control. " Equality is equity "; but a system which shall give to the few (having a lesser interest) the control of the many is neither equality nor equity.

There is no controversy, then, in regard to the principle that our Southern friends have with us, politically and personally, equal rights in the Territories; but they are no more than equal. It is the application of this principle of equality which makes the issue between them and us. The first difficulty grows out of California. That country has accomplished what, at the last session, I did not suppose could be accomplished within so brief a space. Her condition must have been misunderstood or misrepresented. There have been, it would seem, but few, comparatively, of her population engaged during the past season in the mines and washings. Others have met in convention and formed a constitution which her people have adopted. They have appointed Senators and elected Representatives in the usual forms; and they are now here asking admission for California as one of the States of the Union. The question then occurs, Why shall not the request be granted? California was not at the last session a State, and that, though not the whole, was a principal objection to her admission then. That she is now a State *de facto* no man can dispute. But, sir, they have incorporated, it seems, an antislavery clause in their State constitution. This, however, I understand distinctly from our friends of the South is, to their minds, no objection to the admission of California into the Union. I understand that they stand now, as they ever have, upon the principle of nonintervention; and the fact of the incorporation of this principle into the California constitution forms of itself no objection in their minds to the admission of the State into the Union. That being so, it narrows very much the ground of opposition. We get rid in this way of those sources of excitement which have pervaded the country from North to South. The matter is thus brought to stand, not upon a question of right, or honor, or power, but as a mere question of political expediency. . . .

I hold that slavery is not a political institution of the Federal Government; that it is not an institution of this Government at all; it does not exist through or by its action; it has no control over it in the States to save or abolish it; and that consequently the Constitution of the Federal Government cannot carry it where it had not a prior existence. These questions I have argued before. My opinions are on record, and I do not intend to repeat them now.

Mr. President, I concur in the sentiment which has been expressed, that it is time the North and South should understand each other upon these questions. I desire, therefore, to say that, as far as I know, the sentiment of the North in reference to the extension of slavery to free territory is settled, fixed, determined in its opposition. Its representatives here may sit in quiet while the South is tempest-tossed; while Southern feeling rolls in on us here, like foam on the crest of the billow; but, when the storm shall have passed, when its fury shall have spent itself, the North will be found just where it was in the beginning—calm, settled, determined in its opposition to the extension of slavery to free territory. That is my view of the feelings of the North. This feeling may be sought to be carried out by different persons through different means. One may be content only with a positive law passed to prohibit slavery there; another may content himself with laws of Mexico as they are; and yet another may say that God has decreed against it, and that it is useless to re-enact his decrees; but they all have the same object, the same purpose. He who used this last expression [Mr. Webster], which has been much carped at both in this chamber and by the press, used it, I presume, not in reference to the re-enactment of the moral laws of God, but of those laws which God had stamped upon the physical condition, upon the outward form of the universe, and to which the laws of man could add no sanction. But I may add, in passing, that it is not customary for human codes to re-enact God's other laws. I believe no one of us has ever seen the Ten Commandments re-enacted. Who has seen a statute saying, "Thou shalt not kill, or

v—106

upon us for greater sacrifices; they could call upon us to sacrifice everything to their safety. But, sir, in reference to the extension of slavery to these distant territories, this claim has no support; it is rather matter of sentiment upon the part of the South; and if it were sentiment on both sides, the propriety of concession, and how much, would depend upon the value of the sentiment advocated by the parties respectively. But the vivid picture portrayed by the distinguished Senator of a servile insurrection, burning dwellings, shrieking wives and children, as applicable to these distant territories, has no place; or, if a place, the picture must serve but as a warning, telling us to beware in season how we transfer to a soil now free institutions pregnant with such anticipated horrors. They warn us in time of the responsibility which we incur to posterity if we plant slavery where it is not. We are about now to lay the foundations of other commonwealths; the North says it is our duty, as statesmen and as men, to lay their foundations in such wise that our children and our children's children, to the remotest generation, "may rise up and call us blessed!"—that they may not at some distant day say of us, in bitterness and in sorrow, "The stone which the builder did refuse," the same should have been "the chief of the corner." This is the origin of Northern feeling; it is no sickly sentiment, but judgment, a sound discretion which induces the feeling of the North upon these questions. Sir, draw the slave and free line from the ocean to the Mississippi, and mark the difference between the two sides. "Comparisons are odious." I have no wish to make them, but I know the magnanimity of Kentucky will excuse me. Kentucky, in 1790, had a free population of sixty thousand souls. The sun shines upon no better soil, or stronger hands or stouter hearts than her own. Ohio, her neighbor, with no better soil, if so good, and no superior facilities then or now, was then an unbroken, howling wilderness. Fifty years have rolled round. Kentucky has a free population of less than six hundred thousand. Ohio has a free population of one million and a half! The same difference exists in reference to their productions, agricultural, mechanical, and manufactured. I ask, whence comes the difference? It comes, sir, from the single fact that Kentucky carries dead weight. She has been paralyzed in her efforts by the crushing influence of one institution. I do not wonder that her people are attached to it; he who has been

steal, or bear false witness." The human law does not create, but recognizes these as crimes, and merely attaches the penalty. But this is digression. I add that, while we are opposed to the extension of slavery, we are disposed to carry out these views only in good feeling and in what we believe to be the spirit of the Constitution. It has been a leading principle with the Whig party at the North from the beginning (both in and out of Congress) to oppose the admission of slavery to Territories now free But, very unfortunately I must say for us, a party—no, not a party, but a sect, a political sect—has sprung up in our midst, that, taking advantage of a good principle in itself, has pushed it to extremes, connected it with abolition in all its phases, and has, I fear, done more hurt to us and the cause of human freedom than they ever have or ever will do to our adversaries and the system of slavery.

Mr. Underwood—That is true, no doubt.

Mr. Dayton—Members of that party declaim with great unction against slavery and with slavery all it comprises; they deprecate as an unworthy thing that half-and-half virtue which leads us to tolerate it for a moment, or tamper with it at all; they denounce it as weakness, cowardice, because we see the right, and yet dare not pursue it. Mr. President, I always suspect, not the motives, but the moral and mental perceptions of that class of men who, forgetting the possible infirmities of their own little sect of one idea, hold up their one principle, their single light, perhaps a farthing candle, with which to view and pronounce upon the opinions of all mankind. The Whig party North have other principles besides free-soil; and, without depreciating this, I trust that the party will live and flourish North and South when free-soilism and abolitionism, as mere party tests, shall have found one common grave. It has other and high principles of conservatism, which ultimately must regulate and control its destiny.

But, sir, this free-soil feeling at the North has not been, I am persuaded, as mere matter of sentiment, as the Senator from Kentucky [Mr. Clay] seemed to intimate at an early stage in this debate. He said that he thought he might fairly ask of the North a greater sacrifice than was claimed in his compromise resolutions. That with the North it was "sentiment, sentiment, sentiment," while with the South it was a question of domestic security. Sir, if that were so, I grant that the South could call

bred in its midst, nursed by the slave in infancy, followed by him in manhood, looked after by him in age—he may be unwilling to give up the comforts which attend this kind of domestic servitude. But, sir, when we are laying the foundation of empires, the question is not how a few may live in ease, but the question is, how the many shall best live, increase, beautify, and fructify the earth.

DEMOSTHENES

(384–322 B.C.)

HE Oration on the Crown has been called the greatest oration of the world's greatest orator. If it be so, it is because Demosthenes is defending civilization in defending himself as the champion of Athenian autonomy and liberty. The Athens of his day represented all that was highest in intellect, and in the application of intellect to art, to science, to philosophy, to moral force in government. Against it, threatening its overthrow, was the blind desire of empire, the primitive instinct of coercion, the savage pride in dominating the strong and subjugating the weak, represented by Philip and his Macedonians. Athens, a small State, forced to rely almost wholly on intellectual resources, had by virtue of them become the most conspicuous nation in Europe. Athenian diplomacy, the subtle, intangible, all-pervading forces of mind which Demosthenes and his work enable later generations to understand as essentially Attic qualities, influenced not only the policies of Greece, but those of every civilized people in the known world.

The Greece which produced and energized Demosthenes had been itself energized by two great ideas — the ideals of Athens and of Sparta. The one was of grace, the other of strength. The Athenian believed that he ought to develop all his faculties and enjoy them. The Spartan held life useless unless it developed character at the expense of enjoyment. The Athenian was incredibly quick, subtle, æsthetic. The Spartan was strong, simple, self-denying. So opposite in their virtues they had the same fundamental weakness — a defective sense of justice. Of the Athenian character as it had reached its logical climax in the time of Demosthenes, Rufus Choate shows a just appreciation when he writes:—

"Whether Republics have usually perished from injustice need not be debated. One there was, the most renowned of all, that certainly did so. The injustice practiced by the Athens of the age of Demosthenes upon its citizens, and suffered to be practiced by one another, was as marvelous as the capacities of its dialect, as the eloquence by which its masses were regaled, and swayed this way and that as clouds, as waves,—marvelous as the long banquet of beauty in which they reveled,—as their love of Athens, and their passion for glory. There was not one day in the whole public life of Demosthenes when the fortune, the good name, the civil existence of any considerable man was safer there than it would have been at Constantinople or Cairo

Dionysian festival, at the performance of the new tragedies, announcing that Demosthenes was rewarded by the people with a golden crown for his integrity, for the good-will which he had invariably displayed towards the Greeks and towards the people of Athens, and also for his magnanimity, and because he had ever both by word and deed promoted the interests of the people and been zealous to do all the good in his power."

Rallying behind Æschines, the Macedonian party attacked Ktesiphon as a means of ruining Demosthenes. They alleged that the measure he proposed was unlawful; first, because it was unlawful to make a false allegation in any public document; second, that it was unlawful to vote a crown to any official who had still a report to make of his official conduct; and third, that the Dionysian festival was not lawfully the place for presenting crowns. Of course, the case turned on the question of whether or not Ktesiphon in moving to crown Demosthenes as a patriot and public benefactor had moved to place a lie in the archives of Athens. Demosthenes was thus put on trial for his Philippics, for his Olynthaics, for all the other orations he had delivered against Philip and the Macedonian movement since he began his crusade twenty years before (351–352 B.C.). After the accusation had been preferred against Ktesiphon, it was allowed to rest seven years (until 330 B.C.). When trial was forced, Philip was dead, and Alexander being at the height of his successes, the cause of Demosthenes seemed hopeless. Nevertheless, all Greece, understanding that the prosecution was not against Ktesiphon, but against Demosthenes as the representative of the old Greek idea of small independent states in friendly alliance, watched the case with breathless interest. When Demosthenes won it, Æschines went into exile, but in 324 Demosthenes was himself exiled by the Macedonian party, and in 322 he took poison to escape death at their hands.

He was born at Pæania, Attica, 384 (385?), B.C., and died at Calauria in the Temple of Neptune where he had taken sanctuary from Macedonian pursuit, 322 B.C. He was not a philosopher or an essayist like Cicero, whose all-embracing mind considered nothing in the visible or invisible universe foreign to it. He was a patriot, a statesman, a great thinker, because his sympathies with his country and what it stood for made him so. His style may seem unadorned, but that is merely another way of calling it Attic. Indeed, it was objected by one of his contemporaries that he allowed himself more ornament than the laws of good taste warranted. No one in modern times will make such a complaint of his direct and rapid sentences, compelled as they are by the earnestness of one of the greatest intellects in the history of the world.

under the very worst forms of Turkish rule. There was a sycophant to accuse, a demagogue to prosecute, a fickle, selfish, necessitous court — no court at all, only a commission of some hundreds or thousands from the public assembly sitting in the sunshine, directly interested in the cause — to pronounce judgment. And he who rose rich and honored might be flying at night for his life to some Persian or Macedonian outpost, to die by poison on his way in the Temple of Neptune."

This is the central truth in the life of Greece as it is in that of the greatest Greek orator and statesman. It must be kept in mind in reading every period of the 'Oration on the Crown,' that then, as always when he spoke on public affairs, the patriot staked fortune, honor, life, on his words. Between Æschines, the rival of Demosthenes, and Demosthenes himself, the issue is always possibly one of life and death — certainly of exile for the loser. But with Demosthenes, it is infinitely higher and broader. He feels that in controling Athens he is moving Greece and the world. He is staking everything for his country and braving for his countrymen the certainty of ingratitude, treachery, and persecution to save them and their civilization from being overcome by encircling and menacing barbarism.

As he came forward to deliver the 'Oration on the Crown,' Demosthenes stood for fruitless patriotism, defeated by the injustice of those it would save. Neither Sparta nor Athens was longer competent to lead Europe. The Macedonians, half Greek, half barbarian, represented the logic of the situation created by the fraud and force of the long struggle for the "hegemony" of Greece. The sovereignty of intellect which Athens might have held against the world was challenged. It was now a question of the Macedonian phalanx against oratory addressed to a people so æsthetic as to be capable of protesting loudly against the use of a grave accent in place of an acute, but with none of that governing public conscience through which alone moral force can exercise itself.

The 'Oration on the Crown' seems to be largely personal and in some measure egotistical, but in defending himself Demosthenes, attacked by the Macedonian party at Athens, feels that he is still defending Athens against Macedon, liberty against Philip, civilization against barbarism. In this feeling he was justified. He had led Athenian opposition to the aggressions of Macedon from the first, and in 338 B.C., when Philip of Macedon so disastrously defeated the Athenians and their allies at Chæronea, Demosthenes, one of the officials in charge of the walls of Athens, had used his own money freely to repair them. After the panic following the battle was over, Ktesiphon, on behalf of the friends of Demosthenes and the opponents of Philip, moved that the orator "should be presented with a golden crown and that a proclamation should be made in the theatre at the great

THE ORATION ON THE CROWN

(Delivered at Athens, 330 B.C., in Defense of Ktesiphon — from the Translation of Kennedy. Following the plan of the work under which the 'World's Best Orations' are published in full, the 'Oration on the Crown' is given complete, as are also the Second Olynthaic, the Second Philippic, and the 'Oration on the Peace.')

I BEGIN, men of Athens, by praying to every god and goddess that the same good-will which I have ever cherished toward the commonwealth and all of you, may be requited to me on the present trial. I pray likewise — and this specially concerns yourselves, your religion, and your honor — that the gods may put it in your minds not to take counsel of my opponent touching the manner in which I am to be heard,— that would indeed be cruel! — but of the laws and of your oath, wherein (besides the other obligations) it is prescribed that you shall hear both sides alike. This means not only that you must pass no pre-condemnation, not only that you must extend your good-will equally to both, but also that you must allow the parties to adopt such order and course of defense as they severally choose and prefer.

Many advantages hath Æschines over me on this trial; and two especially, men of Athens. First, my risk in the contest is not the same. It is assuredly not the same for me to forfeit your regard, as for my adversary not to succeed in his indictment. To me — but I will say nothing untoward at the outset of my address. The prosecution, however, is play to him. My second disadvantage is the natural disposition of mankind to take pleasure in hearing invective and accusation, and to be annoyed by those who praise themselves. To Æschines is assigned the part which gives pleasure; that which (I may fairly say) is offensive to all is left for me. And if, to escape from this, I make no mention of what I have done, I shall appear to be without defense against his charges, without proof of my claims to honor; whereas, if I proceed to give an account of my conduct and measures, I shall be forced to speak frequently of myself. I will endeavor, then, to do so with all becoming modesty; what I am driven to by the necessity of the case will be fairly chargeable to my opponent who has instituted such a prosecution.

I think, men of the jury, you will all agree that I, as well as Ktesiphon, am a party to this proceeding, and that it is a matter of no less concern to me. It is painful and grievous to be deprived of anything, especially by the act of one's enemy; but your good-will and affection are the heaviest loss, precisely as they are the greatest prize to gain.

Such being the matters at stake in this cause, I conjure and implore you all alike to hear my defense to the charge in that fair manner which the laws prescribe — laws to which their author, Solon, a man friendly to you and to popular rights, thought that validity should be given, not only by the recording of them, but by the oath of you the jurors; not that he distrusted you, as it appears to me; but, seeing that the charges and calumnies, wherein the prosecutor is powerful by being the first speaker, cannot be got over by the defendant unless each of you jurors, observing his religious obligation, shall with like favor receive the arguments of the last speaker, and lend an equal and impartial ear to both, before he determines upon the whole case.

As I am, it appears, on this day to render an account both of my private life and my public measures, I would fain, as in the outset, call the gods to my aid, and in your presence I implore them, first, that the good-will which I have ever cherished toward the commonwealth and all of you may be fully requited to me on the present trial; next, that they may direct you to such a decision upon this indictment as will conduce to your common honor and to the good conscience of each individual.

Had Æschines confined his charge to the subject of the prosecution, I, too, would have proceeded at once to my justification of the decree. But since he has wasted no fewer words in the discussion of other matters, in most of them calumniating me, I deem it both necessary and just, men of Athens, to begin by shortly adverting to these points that none of you may be induced by extraneous arguments to shut your ears against my defense to the indictment.

To all his scandalous abuse of my private life, observe my plain and honest answer. If you know me to be such as he alleged — for I have lived nowhere else but among you — let not my voice be heard, however transcendent my statesmanship! Rise up this instant and condemn me! But if, in your opinion and judgment, I am far better and of better descent than my adversary; if (to speak without offense) I am not inferior, I or mine, to any respectable citizen, then give no credit to him for

his other statements, — it is plain they were all equally fictions, — but to me let the same good-will, which you have uniformly exhibited upon many former trials, be manifested now. With all your malice, Æschines, it was very simple to suppose that I should turn from the discussion of measures and policy to notice your scandal. I will do no such thing; I am not so crazed. Your lies and calumnies about my political life I will examine forthwith; for that loose ribaldry I shall have a word hereafter, if the jury desire to hear it.

The crimes whereof I am accused are many and grievous: for some of them the laws enact heavy — most severe penalties. The scheme of this present proceeding includes a combination of spiteful insolence, insult, railing, aspersion, and everything of the kind; while for the said charges and accusations, if they were true, the state has not the means of inflicting an adequate punishment, or anything like it. For it is not right to debar another of access to the people and privilege of speech; moreover, to do so by way of malice and insult — by heaven! is neither honest, nor constitutional, nor just. If the crimes which he saw me committing against the state were as heinous as he so tragically gave out, he ought to have enforced the penalties of the law against them at the time — if he saw me guilty of an impeachable offense, — by impeaching and so bringing me to trial before you; if moving illegal decrees, by indicting me for them. For surely, if he can prosecute Ktesiphon on my account, he would not have forborne to indict me myself, had he thought he could convict me. In short, whatever else he saw me doing to your prejudice, whether mentioned or not mentioned in his catalogue of slander, there are laws for such things, and punishments, and trials, and judgments, with sharp and severe penalties; all of which he might have enforced against me: and had he done so — had he thus pursued the proper method with me, his charges would have been consistent with his conduct. But now he has declined the straightforward and just course, avoided all proofs of guilt at the time, and, after this long interval, gets up, to play his part withal, a heap of accusation, ribaldry, and scandal. Then he arraigns me, but prosecutes the defendant. His hatred of me he makes the prominent part of the whole contest; yet, without having ever met me upon that ground, he openly seeks to deprive a third party of his privileges. Now, men of Athens, besides all the other arguments that may be urged in Ktesiphon's

behalf, this, methinks, may very fairly be alleged — that we should try our own quarrel by ourselves; not leave our private dispute, and look what third party we can damage. That surely were the height of injustice.

It may appear from what has been said, that all his charges are alike unjust and unfounded in truth. Yet I wish to examine them separately, and especially his calumnies about the peace and the embassy, where he attributed to me the acts of himself and Philocrates. It is necessary also, and perhaps proper, men of Athens, to remind you how affairs stood at those times, that you may consider every single measure in reference to the occasion.

When the Phocian War had broken out, — not through me, for I had not then commenced public life, — you were in this position: you wished the Phocians to be saved, though you saw they were not acting right — and would have been glad for the Thebans to suffer anything, with whom for a just reason you were angry, for they had not borne with moderation their good fortune at Leuctra. The whole of Peloponnesus was divided: they that hated the Lacedæmonians were not powerful enough to destroy them, and they that ruled before by Spartan influence were not masters of the States. Among them, as among the rest of the Greeks, there was a sort of unsettled strife and confusion. Philip, seeing this, — it was not difficult to see, — lavished bribes upon the traitors in every State, embroiled and stirred them all up against each other; and so, by the errors and follies of the rest, he was strengthening himself and growing up to the ruin of all. But when every one saw that the then overbearing, but now unfortunate, Thebans, harassed by so long a war, must of necessity have recourse to you, Philip, to prevent this and obstruct the union of the States, offered to you peace, to them succor. What helped him then almost to surprise you in a voluntary snare? The cowardice, shall I call it? or ignorance — or both — of the other Greeks; who, while you were waging a long and incessant war, and that too for their common benefit, as the event has shown, assisted you neither with money nor men, nor anything else whatsoever. You, being justly and naturally offended with them, lent a willing ear to Philip. The peace then granted was through such means brought about, not through me, as Æschines calumniously charged. The criminal and corrupt practices of these men during the treaty will be found on fair examination to be the cause of our present

condition. The whole matter I am for truth's sake discussing and going through; for, let there appear to be ever so much criminality in these transactions, it is surely nothing to me. The first who spoke and mentioned the subject of peace was Aristodemus, the actor; the seconder and mover, fellow-hireling for that purpose with the prosecutor, was Philocrates the Agnusian — your associate, Æschines, not mine, though you should burst with lying. Their supporters — from whatever motives — I pass that by for the present — were Eubulus and Cephisophon. I had nothing to do with it.

Notwithstanding these facts, which I have stated exactly according to the truth, he ventured to assert — to such a pitch of impudence had he come — that I, besides being author of the peace, had prevented the country making it in a general council with the Greeks. Why you — I know not what name you deserve! — when you saw me robbing the state of an advantage and connection so important as you described just now, did you ever express indignation? Did you come forward to publish and proclaim what you now charge me with? If, indeed, I had been bribed by Philip to prevent the conjunction of the Greeks, it was your business not to be silent, but to cry out, to protest, and inform the people. But you never did so; your voice was never heard to such a purpose; and no wonder; for at that time no embassy had been sent to any of the Greeks; they had all been tested long before, and not a word of truth upon the subject has Æschines spoken.

Besides, it is the country that he most traduces by his falsehoods. For, if you were at the same time calling on the Greeks to take arms, and sending your own embassadors to treat with Philip for peace, you were performing the part of an Eurybatus, not the act of a commonwealth, or of honest men. But it is false, it is false. For what purpose could ye have sent for them at that period? For peace? They all had it. For war? You were yourselves deliberating about peace. It appears, therefore, I was not the adviser or the author of the original peace; and none of his other calumnies against me are shown to be true.

Observe again, after the state had concluded the peace, what line of conduct each of us adopted. Hence, you will understand who it was that co-operated in everything with Philip; who that acted in your behalf, and sought the advantage of the commonwealth.

I moved in the council that our embassadors should sail instantly for whatever place they heard Philip was in, and receive his oath; they would not, however, notwithstanding my resolution. What was the effect of this, men of Athens? I will explain. It was Philip's interest that the interval before the oaths should be as long as possible; yours, that it should be as short. Why? Because you discontinued all your warlike preparations, not only from the day of swearing peace, but from the day that you conceived hopes of it; a thing which Philip was from the beginning studious to contrive, believing—rightly enough—that whatever of our possessions he might take before the oath of ratification, he should hold securely, as none would break the peace on such account. I, men of Athens, foreseeing and weighing these consequences, moved the decree to sail for whatever place Philip was in, and receive his oath without delay, so that your allies, the Thracians, might be in possession of the places which Æschines ridiculed just now (Serrium, Myrtium, and Ergisce), at the time of swearing the oaths; and that Philip might not become master of Thrace by securing the posts of vantage, nor provide himself with plenty of money and troops to facilitate his further designs. Yet this decree he neither mentions nor reads, but reproaches me, because, as councilor, I thought proper to introduce the embassadors. Why, what should I have done? Moved not to introduce men who were come for the purpose of conferring with you? or ordered the manager not to assign them places at the theatre? They might have had places for their two obols if the resolution had not been moved. Was it my duty to guard the petty interests of the state, and have sold our main interests like these men? Surely not. Take and read me this decree, which the prosecutor, knowing it well, passed over. Read.

THE DECREE

"In the archonship of Mnesiphilus, on the thirteenth of Hecatombæon, in the presidency of the Pandionian tribe, Demosthenes, son of Demosthenes of Pæania, moved,—Whereas Philip has sent embassadors for peace, and hath agreed upon articles of treaty, it is resolved by the Council and People of Athens, in order that the peace voted in the first assembly may be ratified, to choose forthwith from the whole body of Athenians five embassadors; and that the persons elected do repair, without any delay, wheresoever they shall ascertain that Philip is, and as speedily as may be exchange oaths with him,

according to the articles agreed on between him and the Athenian people, comprehending the allies of either party. For embassadors were chosen, Eubulus of Anaphlestus, Æschines of Cothocidæ, Cephisophon of Rhamnus, Democrates of Phlya, Cleon of Cothocidæ."

Notwithstanding that I had passed this decree for the advantage of Athens, not that of Philip, our worthy embassadors so little regarded it as to sit down in Macedonia three whole months, until Philip returned from Thrace after entirely subjugating the country, although they might in ten days, or rather in three or four, have reached the Hellespont and saved the fortresses, by receiving his oath before he reduced them: for he would never have touched them in our presence, or we should not have sworn him; and thus he would have lost the peace, and not have obtained both the peace and the fortresses.

Such was the first trick of Philip, the first corrupt act of these accursed miscreants, in the embassy: for which I avow that I was and am and ever will be at war and variance with them. But mark another and still greater piece of villainy immediately after. When Philip had sworn to the peace, having secured Thrace through these men disobeying my decree, he again bribes them not to leave Macedonia, until he had got all ready for his expedition against the Phocians. His fear was, if they reported to you his design and preparation for marching, you might sally forth, sail round with your galleys to Thermopylæ as before, and block up the strait: his desire, that, the moment you received the intelligence from them, he should have passed Thermopylæ, and you be unable to do anything. And in such terror and anxiety was Philip, lest, notwithstanding he had gained these advantages, if you voted succor before the destruction of the Phocians, his enterprise should fail; he hires this despicable fellow, no longer in common with the other embassadors, but by himself individually, to make that statement and report to you, by which everything was lost.

I conjure and beseech you, men of Athens, throughout the trial to remember this, that, if Æschines in his charge had not traveled out of the indictment, neither would I have spoken a word irrelevant; but since he has resorted to every species both of accusation and calumny, it is necessary for me to reply briefly to each of his charges.

What, then, were the statements made by Æschines, through which everything was lost? That you should not be alarmed

by Philip's having passed Thermopylæ—that all would be as you desired, if you kept quiet; and in two or three days you would hear he was their friend to whom he had come as an enemy, and their enemy to whom he had come as a friend—it was not words that cemented attachments (such was his solemn phrase), but identity of interest; and it was the interest of all alike, Philip, the Phocians, and you, to be relieved from the harshness and insolence of the Thebans. His assertions were heard by some with pleasure, on account of the hatred which then subsisted against the Thebans. But what happened directly, almost immediately, afterward? The wretched Phocians were destroyed, their cities demolished; you that kept quiet, and trusted to Æschines, were shortly bringing in your effects out of the country, while Æschines received gold; and yet more—while you got nothing but your enmity with the Thebans and Thessalians, Philip won their gratitude for what he had done. To prove what I say, read me the decree of Callisthenes, and the letter of Philip, from both of which these particulars will be clear to you. Read.

THE DECREE

"In the archonship of Mnesiphilus, an extraordinary assembly having been convened by the Generals, with the sanction of the Presidents and the Council, on the twenty-first of Mæmacterion, Callisthenes, son of Eteonicus of Phalerum, moved:—No Athenian shall on any pretense sleep in the country, but all in the city and Piræus, except those who are stationed in the garrisons; and they shall every one keep the posts assigned to them, without absenting themselves by night or day. Whosoever disobeys this decree, shall be amenable to the penalties of treason, unless he can show that some necessity prevented him; the judges of such necessity shall be the General of Infantry, and he of the Finance Department, and the Secretary of the Council. All effects shall be conveyed out of the country as speedily as may be; those that are within a hundred and twenty furlongs into the city and Piræus, those that are beyond a hundred and twenty furlongs to Eleusis and Phyle and Aphidna and Rhamnus and Sunium. On the motion of Callisthenes of Phalerum."

Was it with such expectations you concluded the peace? Were such the promises this hireling made you? Come, read the letter which Philip sent after this to Athens.

THE LETTER OF PHILIP

"Philip, king of Macedonia, to the Council and People of Athens, greeting. Ye know that we have passed Thermopylæ, and reduced Phocis to submission, and put garrisons in the towns that opened their gates; those that resisted we took by storm, and razed to the ground, enslaving their inhabitants. Hearing, however, that ye are preparing to assist them, I have written unto you, that ye may trouble yourselves no farther in the business. For it seems to me, ye are acting altogether unreasonably; having concluded peace, and nevertheless taking the field, and that too when the Phocians are not comprehended in our treaty. Wherefore, if ye abide not by your engagements, ye will gain no advantage but that of being the aggressors."

You hear how plainly, in his letter to you, he declares and asserts to his own allies—"all this I have done against the will of the Athenians, and in their despite; therefore if ye are wise, ye Thebans and Thessalians, ye will regard them as enemies, and put confidence in me"; not writing in such words, but meaning so to be understood. And by these means he carried them away with him, insomuch that they had neither foresight nor sense of the consequences, but suffered him to get everything into his power; hence the misfortunes under which those wretched people at present are. The agent and auxiliary who helped to win for him such confidence,—who brought false reports here and cajoled you,—he it is who now bewails the sufferings of the Thebans and dilates upon them so pathetically, he himself being the cause both of these calamities, and those in Phocis, and all the rest which the Greeks have sustained. Truly must you, Æschines, grieve at these events, and compassionate the Thebans, when you hold property in Bœotia and farm their lands; and I rejoice at a work whose author immediately required me to be delivered into his hands.

But I have fallen upon a subject which it may be more convenient to discuss by and by. I will return then to my proofs, showing how the iniquities of these men have brought about the present state of things.

When you had been deceived by Philip through the agency of these men, who sold themselves in the embassies, and reported not a word of truth to you—when the unhappy Phocians had been deceived and their cities destroyed—what followed? The despicable Thessalians and stupid Thebans looked on Philip as a friend, a benefactor, a savior: he was everything with them — not a syllable would they hear from any one to the contrary. You, though regarding his acts with suspicion and anger, still observed the peace; for you could have done nothing alone. The rest of the Greeks, cheated and disappointed like yourselves, gladly observed the peace, though they also had in a manner been attacked for a long time. For when Philip was marching about, subduing Illyrians and Triballians and some also of the Greeks, and gaining many considerable accessions of power, and certain citizens of the states (Æschines among them) took advantage of the peace to go there and be corrupted, all people then, against whom he was making such preparations, were attacked. If they perceived it not, that is another question, no concern of mine. I was forever warning and protesting, both at Athens and wheresoever I was sent. But the States were diseased; one class in their politics and measures being venal and corrupt, while the multitude of private men either had no foresight, or were caught with the bait of present ease and idleness; and all were under some such influence, only they imagined each that the mischief would not approach themselves, but that by the peril of others they might secure their own safety when they chose. The result, I fancy, has been that the people, in return for their gross and unseasonable indolence, have lost their liberty: the statesmen, who imagined they were selling everything but themselves, discovered they had sold themselves first; for, instead of friends, as they were named during the period of bribery, they are now called parasites and miscreants and the like befitting names. Justly. For no man, O Athenians, spends money for the traitor's benefit, or, when he has got possession of his purchase, employs the traitor to advise him in future proceedings: else nothing could have been more fortunate than a traitor. But it is not so — it never could be — it is far otherwise! When the aspirant for power has gained his object, he is master also of those that sold it; and then — then, I say, knowing their baseness, he loathes and mistrusts and spurns them.

Consider only — for though the time of the events is past, the time for understanding them is ever present to the wise: Lasthenes was called the friend of Philip for a while, until he betrayed Olynthus; Timolaus for a while, until he destroyed Thebes; Eudicus and Simus of Larissa for a while, until they brought

v—107

the people crown Demosthenes, son of Demosthenes of Pæania, with a golden crown, on account of his virtue, and of the good-will which he has constantly cherished toward all the Greeks as well as toward the people of Athens, and of his integrity, and because he has constantly by word and deed promoted the advantage of the people, and is zealous to do whatever good he can: all which clauses are false and illegal; the laws enacting: firstly, that no false allegations shall be entered in the public records; secondly, that an accountable officer shall not be crowned (but Demosthenes is a conservator of the walls, and has charge of the theoric fund); thirdly, that the crown shall not be proclaimed in the theatre at the Dionysian festival, on the new exhibition of tragedies, but if the council confer a crown, it shall be published in the council-hall, if the people, in the Pnyx at the assembly. Penalty, fifty talents. Witnesses to the summons, Cephisophon, son of Cephisophon of Rhamnus, Cleon, son of Cleon of Cothocidæ."

The clauses of the decree which he prosecutes are these, men of Athens. Now from these very clauses I think I shall immediately make it clear to you that my whole defense will be just; for I shall take the charges in the same order as my adversary, and discuss them all one by one, without a single intentional omission.

With respect to the statement, "that I have constantly by word and deed promoted the advantage of the people, and am zealous to do whatever good I can," and the praising me on such grounds, your judgment, I conceive, must depend on my public acts; from an examination of which it will be discovered whether what Ktesiphon has alleged concerning me is true and proper, or false. As to his proposing to give the crown without adding "when he has passed his accounts," and to proclaim the crown in the theatre, I imagine that this also relates to my political conduct, whether I am worthy of the crown and the public proclamation, or not. However, I deem it necessary to produce the laws which justified the defendant in proposing such clauses.

Thus honestly and simply, men of Athens, have I resolved to conduct my defense. I now proceed to my own actual measures. And let no one suppose that I wander from the indictment, if I touch upon Grecian questions and affairs: he who attacks that clause of the decree, "that by word and deed I have promoted your good" — he who has indicted this for being false — he, I say, has rendered the discussion of my whole policy pertinent and necessary to the charge. Moreover, there being many de-

Thessaly under Philip's power. Since then the world has become full of traitors expelled and insulted and suffering every possible calamity. How fared Aristratus in Sicyon? how Perilaus in Megara? Are they not outcasts? Hence, one may evidently see, it is the vigilant defender of his country, the strenuous opponent of such men, who secures to you traitors and hirelings, Æschines, the opportunity of getting bribes; through the number of those that oppose your wishes you are in safety and in pay, for had it depended on yourselves you would have perished long ago.

Much more could I say about those transactions, yet methinks too much has been said already. The fault is my adversary's, for having spurted over me the dregs, I may say, of his own wickedness and iniquities, of which I was obliged to clear myself to those who are younger than the events. You, too, have probably been disgusted, who knew this man's venality before I spoke a word. He calls it friendship, indeed, and said somewhere in his speech — "the man who reproaches me with the friendship of Alexander." I reproach you with the friendship of Alexander! Whence gotten, or how merited? Neither Philip's friend nor Alexander's should I ever call you; I am not so mad; unless we are to call reapers and other hired laborers the friends of those who hire them. That, however, is not so — how could it be? It is nothing of the kind. Philip's hireling I called you once, and Alexander's I call you now. So do all these men. If you disbelieve me, ask them; or rather I will do it for you. Athenians! is Æschines, think ye, the hireling or the friend of Alexander? You hear what they say.

I now proceed to my defense upon the indictment itself, and to the account of my own measures, that Æschines may hear, though he knows already, on what I found my title both to these which have been decreed and to far greater rewards. Take and read me the indictment itself.

THE INDICTMENT

"In the archonship of Chærondas, on the sixth of Elaphebolion, Æschines, son of Atrometus of Cothocidæ, preferred before the archon an indictment against Ktesiphon, son of Leosthenes of Anaphlystus, for an illegal measure: for that he proposed a decree against law, to wit, that it was right to crown Demosthenes, son of Demosthenes of Pæania, with a golden crown and to proclaim in the theatre at the great Dionysian festival, at the exhibition of the new tragedies, that

partments of political action, I chose that which belonged to Grecian affairs: therefore, I am justified in drawing my proofs from them.

The conquests which Philip had got and held before I commenced life as a statesman and orator, I shall pass over, as I think they concern not me. Those that he was baffled in from the day of my entering on such duties, I will call to your recollection, and render an account of them; premising one thing only — Philip started, men of Athens, with a great advantage. It happened that among the Greeks — not some, but all alike — there sprang up a crop of traitors and venal wretches, such as in the memory of man had never been before. These he got for his agents and supporters: the Greeks, already ill-disposed and unfriendly to each other, he brought into a still worse state, deceiving this people, making presents to that, corrupting others in every way; and he split them into many parties, when they had all one interest, to prevent his aggrandizement. While the Greeks were all in such a condition, — in such ignorance of the gathering and growing mischief, — you have to consider, men of Athens, what policy and measures it became the commonwealth to adopt, and of this to receive a reckoning from me; for the man who assumed that post in the administration was I.

Ought she, Æschines, to have cast off her spirit and dignity, and, in the style of Thessalians and Dolopians, helped to acquire for Philip the dominion of Greece, and extinguished the honors and rights of our ancestors? Or, if she did not this, — which would indeed have been shameful, — was it right that what she saw would happen if unprevented, and was for a long time, it seems, aware of, she should suffer to come to pass?

I would gladly ask the severest censurer of our acts, with what party he would have wished the commonwealth to side, — with those who contributed to the disgraces and disasters of the Greeks, the party, we may say, of the Thessalians and their followers, or those who permitted it all for the hope of selfish advantage, among whom we may reckon the Arcadians, Messenians, and Argives? But many of them, or rather all, have fared worse than ourselves. If Philip after his victory had immediately marched off and kept quiet, without molesting any either of his own allies or of the Greeks in general, still they that opposed not his enterprises would have merited some blame and reproach. But when he has stripped all alike of their dignity, their authority, their liberty,—nay, even of their constitutions, where he was able,—can it be doubted that you took the most glorious course in pursuance of my counsels?

But I return to the question—What should the commonwealth, Æschines, have done, when she saw Philip establishing an empire and dominion over Greece? Or what was your statesman to advise or move?—I, a statesman at Athens?—for this is most material—I who knew that from the earliest time, until the day of my own mounting the platform, our country had ever striven for precedency and honor and renown, and expended more blood and treasure for the sake of glory and the general weal than the rest of the Greeks had expended on their several interests?—who saw that in the strife for power and empire, Philip himself, with whom we were contending, had had his eye cut out, his collar bone fractured, his hand and leg mutilated, and was ready and willing to sacrifice any part of his body that fortune chose to take, provided he could live with the remainder in honor and glory? Hardly will any one venture to say this—that it became a man bred at Pella, then an obscure and inconsiderable place, to possess such inborn magnanimity as to aspire to the mastery of Greece and form the project in his mind, while you, who were Athenians, day after day in speeches and in dramas reminded of the virtue of your ancestors, should have been so naturally base as of your own free will and accord to surrender to Philip the liberty of Greece. No man will say this!

The only course then that remained was a just resistance to all his attacks upon you. Such course you took from the beginning, properly and becomingly; and I assisted by motions and counsels during the period of my political life·—I acknowledge it. But what should I have done? I put this question to you, dismissing all else: Amphipolis, Pydna, Potidæa, Halonnesus—I mention none of them: Serrium, Doriscus, the ravaging of Peparethus, and any similar wrongs which the country has suffered—I know not even of their occurrence. You, indeed, said that by talking of these I had brought the people into a quarrel, although the resolutions respecting them were moved by Eubulus and Aristophon and Diopithes—not by me, you ready utterer of what suits your purpose! Neither will I speak of these now. But I ask—the man who was appropriating to himself Eubœa, and making it a fortress against Attica, and attempting Megara, and seizing Oreus, and razing Porthmus, and setting

up Philistides as tyrant in Oreus, Clitarchus in Eretria, and subjugating the Hellespont, and besieging Byzantium, and destroying some of the Greek cities, restoring exiles to others—was he by all these proceedings committing injustice, breaking the truce, violating the peace, or not? Was it meet that any of the Greeks should rise up to prevent these proceedings, or not? If not—if Greece were to present the spectacle (as it is called) of a Mysian prey, while Athenians had life and being, then I have exceeded my duty in speaking on the subject—the commonwealth has exceeded her duty, which followed my counsels—I admit that every measure has been a misdeed, a blunder of mine. But if some one ought to have arisen to prevent these things, who but the Athenian people should it have been? Such, then, was the policy which I espoused. I saw him reducing all men to subjection, and I opposed him: I continued warning and exhorting you not to make these sacrifices to Philip.

It was he that infringed the peace by taking our ships; it was not the state, Æschines. Produce the decrees themselves, and Philip's letter, and read them one after another. From an examination of them it will be evident who is chargeable with each proceeding. Read.

THE DECREE

"In the archonship of Neocles, in the month Boedromion, an extraordinary assembly having been convened by the generals, Eubulus, son of Mnesitheus of Cytherus, moved: Whereas the generals have reported in the assembly that Leodamas the admiral, and the twenty vessels dispatched with him to the Hellespont for the safe conduct of the corn, have been carried to Macedonia by Philip's general, Amyntas, and are detained in custody, let the presidents and the generals take care that the council be convened, and embassadors to Philip be chosen, who shall go and treat with him for the release of the admiral, vessels, and troops; and if Amyntas has acted in ignorance, they shall say that the people make no complaint against him; if the admiral is found wrongfully exceeding his instructions, that the Athenians will make inquiry and punish him as his negligence deserves: if it be neither of these things, but a willful trespass on the part of him who gave or him who received the commission, let them state this also, that the people, being apprised, may deliberate what course to take."

This decree Eubulus carried, not I. The next, Aristophon; then Hegesippus, then Aristophon again, then Philocrates, then

Cephisophon, then the rest. I had no concern in the matter. Read the decree.

THE DECREE

"In the archonship of Neocles, on the last day of Boedromion, at the desire of the council, the presidents and generals introduced their report of the proceedings of the assembly, to wit: that the people had resolved to appoint embassadors to Philip for the recovery of the ships, and to furnish them with instructions and with the decrees of the assembly; and they appointed the following: Cephisophon, son of Cleon of Anaphlystus; Democritus, son of Demophon of Anagyrus; Polycritus, son of Apemantus of Cothocidæ. In the presidency of the Hippothoontian tribe, on the motion of Aristophon of Colyttus, committeeman."

Now then, as I produce these decrees, so do you, Æschines, point out what decree of my passing makes me chargeable with the war. You cannot find one; had you any, there is nothing you would sooner have produced. Why, even Philip makes no charge against me on account of the war, though he complains of others. Read Philip's own letter.

THE LETTER OF PHILIP

"Philip, king of Macedon, to the Council and People of Athens, greeting. Your embassadors, Cephisophon, Democritus, and Polycritus, came to me and conferred about the release of the galleys which Laomedon commanded. Upon the whole, I think you must be very simple if you imagine I do not see that those galleys were commissioned, under the pretense of conveying corn from the Hellespont to Lemnos, to relieve the Selymbrians, whom I am besieging, and who are not included in the friendly treaty subsisting between us. And these instructions were given, without leave of the Athenian people, by certain magistrates and others who are not now in office, but who are anyways desirous for the people to exchange our present amity for a renewal of war, and are far more anxious for such a consummation than to relieve the Selymbrians. They suppose it will be a source of income to themselves; however, I scarcely think it is for your advantage or mine. Wherefore I release you the vessels carried into my port; and for the future, if, instead of allowing your statesmen to adopt malignant measures, you will punish them, I too will endeavor to maintain the peace. Farewell."

Here is no mention by him of Demosthenes, or any charge against me. Why, then, while he complains of the others, makes

he no mention of my acts? Because he must have noticed his own aggressions, had he written aught concerning me; for on these I fixed myself—these I kept resisting. And first I proposed the embassy to Peloponnesus, when into Peloponnesus he began to steal; next that to Eubœa, when on Eubœa he was laying his hands; then the expedition (no longer an embassy) to Oreus, and that to Eretria, when he established rulers in those cities. Afterward I dispatched all the armaments, by which Chersonesus was preserved, and Byzantium, and all our allies; whence to you there accrued the noblest results—praises, eulogies, honors, crowns, thanks from those you succored; while the people attacked—those that trusted you then obtained deliverance, those that disregarded you have had often to remember your warnings and to be convinced that you were not only their friends, but wise men also and prophets: for all that you predicted has come to pass.

That Philistides would have given a great deal to keep Oreus —Clitarchus a great deal to keep Eretria—Philip himself a great deal to have these vantage-posts against you, and in other matters to avoid exposure, and any inquiry into his wrongful acts in general—no man is ignorant, and least of all you. For the embassadors who came here then from Clitarchus and Philistides lodged with you, Æschines, and you were their host. The commonwealth regarded them as enemies, whose offers were neither just nor advantageous, and expelled them; but they were your friends. None of their designs then were accomplished; you slanderer—who say of me that I am silent when I have got something, and bawl when I have spent it! That is not your custom. You bawl when you have something, and will never stop, unless the jury stop you by disfranchisement to-day.

When you crowned me then for those services, and Aristonicus drew up the same words that Ktesiphon here has now drawn up, and the crown was proclaimed in the theatre,—for this now is the second proclamation in my favor,—Æschines, being present, neither opposed it, nor indicted the mover. Take this decree now and read it.

THE DECREE

"In the archonship of Chærondas, son of Hegemon, on the twenty-fifth of Gamelion, in the presidency of the Leontian tribe, Aristonicus of Phrearrii moved: Whereas Demosthenes, son of Demosthenes of

Pæania, hath rendered many important services to the people of Athens, and to divers of her allies heretofore, and hath also on the present occasion aided them by his decrees, and liberated certain of the cities in Eubœa, and perseveres in his attachment to the people of Athens, and doth by word and deed whatever good he can for the Athenians themselves and the rest of the Greeks: It is resolved by the Council and People of Athens, to honor Demosthenes, son of Demosthenes of Pæania, with public praise and a golden crown, and to proclaim the crown in the theatre at the Dionysian festival at the new tragedies, and the proclamation of the crown shall be given in charge to the presiding tribe and the prize-master. On the motion of Aristonicus of Phrearrii.»

Is there one of you that knows of any disgrace falling on the state by reason of this decree, or any scorn or ridicule — consequences which this man now predicts, if I be crowned? It is when acts are recent and notorious that, if good, they obtain reward, if the contrary, punishment; and it appears that I then obtained reward, not blame or punishment. So, up to the period of those transactions, I am acknowledged on all occasions to have promoted the interests of the state — because my speeches and motions prevailed in your councils — because my measures were executed, and procured crowns for the commonwealth and for me and all of you — because you have offered sacrifices and thanksgivings to the gods for their success.

When Philip therefore was driven out of Eubœa, with arms by you, with councils and decrees — though some persons there should burst! — by me, he sought some new position of attack upon Athens. Seeing that we use more foreign corn than any people, and wishing to command the passage of the corn trade, he advanced to Thrace; the Byzantines being his allies, he first required them to join in the war against you, and when they refused, saying (truly enough) that they had not made alliance on such terms, he threw up intrenchments before the city, planted batteries, and laid siege to it. What course hereupon it became you to take, I will not ask again; it is manifest to all. But who was it that succored the Byzantines and rescued them? Who prevented the alienation of the Hellespont at that crisis? You, men of Athens. When I say you, I mean the commonwealth. But who advised, framed, executed the measures of state, devoted himself wholly and unreservedly to the public business? — I! — What benefits thence accrued to all, you need no further to be told;

you have learned by experience. For the war which then sprang up, besides that it brought honor and renown, kept you in a cheaper and more plentiful supply of all the necessaries of life than does the present peace, which these worthies maintain to their country's prejudice in the hope of something to come. Perish such hope! Never may they share the blessings for which you men of honest wishes pray to the gods, nor communicate their own principles to you!

Read them now the crowns of the Byzantines, and those of the Perinthians, which they conferred upon the country as a reward.

THE BYZANTINE DECREE

«In the presbytership of Bosporichus, Damagetus moved in the assembly, having obtained permission of the Council: Whereas the people of Athens have ever in former times been friendly to the Byzantines and their allies, and to their kinsmen the Perinthians, and have rendered them many signal services, and also, on the present occasion, when Philip of Macedon attempted by invasion and siege to exterminate the Byzantines and Perinthians, and burned and ravaged their country, they succored us with a hundred and twenty ships and provisions and weapons and soldiers, and rescued us from grievous perils, and preserved our hereditary constitution, our laws, and our sepulchres; it is resolved by the people of Byzantium and Perinthus to grant unto the Athenians the right of intermarriage, citizenship, purchase of land and houses, the first seat at the games, first admission to the council and people after the sacrifices, and exemption from all public services to such as wish to reside in the city; and that three statues of sixteen cubits be erected in the harbor, representing the people of Athens crowned by the people of Byzantium and Perinthus; and deputations sent to the general assemblies of Greece, — the Isthmian, Nemean, Olympian, and Pythian, — to proclaim the crowns wherewith the people of Athens hath been honored by us, that all the Greeks may know the virtue of the Athenians and the gratitude of the Byzantines and Perinthians.»

Now read the crowns given by the people of Chersonesus.

THE DECREE

«The Chersonesites, inhabitants of Sestus, Eleus, Madytus, and Alopeconnesus, crown the Council and People of Athens with a golden crown of the value of sixty talents, and build an altar to Gratitude

and the Athenian People, because that people hath helped the Chersonesites to obtain the greatest of blessings, by rescuing them from the power of Philip, and restoring their country, their laws, their liberty, their sanctuaries; and in all future time they will not fail to be grateful, and do what service they can. Decreed in general council.»

Thus the saving of Chersonesus and Byzantium, the preventing Philip's conquest of the Hellespont, and the honors therefore bestowed on this country, were the effects of my policy and administration; and more than this — they proved to all mankind the generosity of Athens and the baseness of Philip. He, the ally and friend of the Byzantines, was before all eyes besieging them — what could be more shameful or outrageous? You, who might justly on many grounds have reproached them for wrongs done you in former times, instead of bearing malice and abandoning the oppressed, appeared as their deliverers, — conduct which procured you glory, good-will, honor from all men. That you have crowned many of your statesmen, every one knows; but through what other person (I mean what minister or orator) besides myself, the commonwealth has been crowned, no one can say.

To prove now, the malignity of those calumnies, which he urged against the Eubœans and Byzantines, reminding you of any unkindness which they had done you — prove it I shall, not only by their falsehood, which I apprehend you know already, but (were they ever so true) by showing the advantages of my policy — I wish to recount one or two of the noble acts of your own state, and to do it briefly; for individuals, as well as communities, should ever strive to model their future conduct by the noblest of their past.

Well, then, men of Athens, when the Lacedæmonians had the empire of land and sea, and held the country round Attica by governors and garrisons, Eubœa, Tanagra, all Bœotia, Megara, Ægina, Cleonæ, the other islands; when our state possessed neither ships nor walls, you marched out to Haliartus, and again not many days after to Corinth; albeit the Athenians of that time had many causes of resentment against both Corinthians and Thebans for their acts in the Decelean war; but they showed no resentment, none. And yet neither of these steps took they, Æschines, for benefactors, nor were they blind to the danger; but they would not for such reasons abandon people who sought their protection; for the sake of renown and glory they willingly

exposed themselves to peril. Just and noble was their resolve! For to all mankind the end of life is death, though one keep oneself shut up in a closet; but it becomes brave men to strive always for honor, with good hope before them, and to endure courageously whatever the Deity ordains.

Thus did your ancestors, thus the elder among yourselves. For, though the Lacedæmonians were neither friends nor benefactors, but had done many grievous injuries to our state, yet when the Thebans, victorious at Leuctra, sought their destruction, you prevented it, not fearing the power and reputation then possessed by the Thebans, nor reckoning up the merits of those whom you were about to fight for. And so you demonstrated to all the Greeks that, however any people may offend you, you reserve your anger against them for other occasions; but should their existence or liberty be imperiled, you will not resent your wrongs or bring them into account.

And not in these instances only hath such been your temper. Again, when the Thebans were taking possession of Eubœa, you looked not quietly on, you remembered not the wrongs done you by Themison and Theodorus in the affair of Oropus, but assisted even them. It was the time when the volunteer captains first offered themselves to the state, of whom I was one; but of this presently. However, it was glorious that you saved the island, but far more glorious that, when you had got their persons and their cities in your power, you fairly restored them to the people who had ill-used you, and made no reckoning of your wrongs in an affair where you were trusted.

Hundreds of cases which I could mention I pass over — sea fights, land marches, campaigns, both in ancient times and in your own, all of which the commonwealth has undertaken for the freedom and safety of the Greeks in general. Then, having observed the commonwealth engaging in contests of such number and importance for the interests of others, what was I to urge, what course to recommend her when the question in a manner concerned herself? To revive grudges, I suppose, against people who wanted help, and to seek pretenses for abandoning everything. And who might not justly have killed me, had I attempted even by words to tarnish any of the honors of Athens? For the thing itself, I am certain, you would never have done — had you wished, what was to hinder you? any lack of opportunity? — had you not these men to advise it?

I must return to the next in date of my political acts; and here again consider what was most beneficial for the state. I saw, men of Athens, that your navy was decaying, and that, while the rich were getting off with small payments, citizens of moderate or small fortunes were losing their substance, and the state, by reason thereof, missing her opportunities of action. I therefore proposed a law, by which I compelled the one class (the rich) to perform their duty, and stopped the oppression of the poor; and — what was most useful to the country — I caused her preparations to be made in time. And being indicted for it, I appeared on the charge before you, and was acquitted; and the prosecutor did not get his portion of the votes. But what sums, think ye, the chief men of the boards, or those in the second and third degrees, offered me, first, not to propose that law, second, when I had recorded it, to drop it on the abatement oath ? Such sums, men of Athens, as I should be afraid to tell you. And no wonder they did so; for under the former laws they might divide the charge between sixteen, spending little or nothing themselves, and grinding down the needy citizens; whereas under my law every one had to pay a sum proportioned to his means, and there was a captain for two ships, where before there was a partner with fifteen others for one ship — for they were calling themselves not captains any longer, but partners. They would have given anything then to get these regulations annulled, and not be obliged to perform their duties. Read me, first, the decree for which I appeared to the indictment, then the service rolls, that of the former law, and that under mine. Read.

THE DECREE

"In the archonship of Polycles, on the sixteenth of Boedromion, in the presidency of the Hippothoontian tribe, Demosthenes, son of Demosthenes of Pæania, introduced a law for the naval service, instead of the former one under which there were the associations of joint captains; and it was passed by the council and people. And Patrocles of Phlyus preferred an indictment against Demosthenes for an illegal measure, and, not having obtained his share of the votes, paid the penalty of five hundred drachms."

Now produce that fine roll.

THE ROLL

"Let sixteen captains be called out for every galley, as they are associated in the companies, from the age of twenty-five to forty, defraying the charge equally."

Now for the roll under my law.

THE ROLL

"Let captains be chosen according to their property by valuation, taking ten talents to a galley: if the property be valued at a higher sum, let the charge be proportionate, as far as three ships and a tender; and let it be in the same proportion for those whose property is less than ten talents, joining them in a partnership to make up ten talents."

Think ye I but slightly helped the poor of Athens, or that the rich would have spent but a trifling sum to escape the doing what was right ? I glory, however, not only in having refused this compromise, and having been acquitted on the indictment, but because my law was beneficial, and I have proved it so by trial. For during the whole war, while the armaments were shipped off according to my regulations, no captain ever appealed to you against oppression, or took sanctuary at Munychia, or was imprisoned by the clearing officers; no galley was lost to the state by capture abroad, or left behind from unfitness to go to sea. Under the former laws all these things happened — because the burden was put upon the poor, and therefore difficulties frequently arose. I transferred the charge from the poor to the wealthy, and then every duty was done. For this itself, too, I deserve praise, that I adopted all such measures as brought glory and honor and power to the state: there is no envy, spite, or malice in any measure of mine, nothing sordid or unworthy of Athens. The same character is apparent in my home and in my foreign policy. At home, I never preferred the favor of the wealthy to the rights of the many: abroad, I valued not the presents or the friendship of Philip above the general interests of Greece.

I conceive it remains for me to speak of the proclamation and the accounts: for that I acted for the best — that I have

throughout been your friend and zealous in your service, is proved abundantly, methinks, by what I have said already. The most important part of my policy and administration I pass by, considering that I have in regular course to reply to the charge of illegality; and besides — though I am silent as to the rest of my political acts — the knowledge you all have will serve me equally well.

As to the arguments which he jumbled together about the counter-written laws, I hardly suppose you comprehend them — I myself could not understand the greater part. However I shall argue a just case in a straightforward way. So far from saying that I am not accountable, as the prosecutor just now falsely asserted, I acknowledge that I am all my life accountable for what as your statesman I have undertaken or advised; but for what I have voluntarily given to the people out of my own private fortune, I deny that I am any day accountable, — do you hear, Æschines? — nor is any other man, let him even be one of the nine archons. For what law is so full of injustice and inhumanity as to enact that one who has given of his private means and done an act of generosity and munificence, instead of having thanks, shall be brought before malignants, appointed to be the auditors of his liberality? None. If he says there is, let him produce it, and I will be content and hold my tongue. But there is none, men of Athens. The prosecutor in his malice, because I gave some of my own money when I superintended the theoric fund, says, "The council praised him before he had rendered his account." Not for any matters of which I had an account to render, but for what I spent of my own, you malignant!

"Oh, but you were a Conservator of Walls!" says he. Yes; and for that reason was I justly praised, because I gave the sums expended and did not charge them. A charge requires auditing and examiners; a donation merits thanks and praise; therefore the defendant made this motion in my favor.

That this is a settled principle in your hearts as well as in the laws, I can show by many proofs easily. First, Nausicles has often been crowned by you for what he expended out of his own funds while he was general. Secondly, Diotimus was crowned for his present of shields; and Charidemus too. Again, Neoptolemus here, superintendent of divers works, has been honored for his donations. It would, indeed, be cruel if a man holding an

office should either, by reason of his office, be precluded from giving his own money to the state, or have, instead of receiving thanks, to render an account of what he gave. To prove the truth of my statements, take and read me the original decrees made in favor of these men.

A DECREE

"Archon, Demonicus of Phlyus. On the twenty-sixth of Boedromion, with the sanction of the council and people, Callias of Phrearrii moved: That the council and people resolve to crown Nausicles, general of foot, for that, there being two thousand Athenian troops of the line in Imbrus, for the defense of the Athenian residents in that island, and Philo of the Finance Department being by reason of storms unable to sail and pay the troops, he advanced money of his own and did not ask the people for it again; and that the crown be proclaimed at the Dionysian festival, at the new tragedies."

ANOTHER DECREE

"Callias of Phrearrii moved, the presidents declaring it to be with the sanction of the council: Whereas Charidemus, general of foot, having been sent to Salamis, he and Diotimus, general of horse, after certain of the troops had in the skirmish by the river been disarmed by the enemy, did at their own expense arm the young men with eight hundred shields: It hath been resolved by the council and people to crown Charidemus and Diotimus with a golden crown, and to proclaim it at the great Panathenaic festival, during the gymnastic contest, and at the Dionysian festival, at the exhibition of the new tragedies: the proclamation to be given in charge to the judges, the presidents, and the prize masters."

Each of these men, Æschines, was accountable for the office which he held, but not accountable for the matters in respect of which he was crowned. No more then am I; for surely I have the same rights, under the same circumstances, as other men. Have I given money? I am praised for that, not being accountable for what I gave. Did I hold office? Yes; and I have rendered an account of my official acts, not of my bounties. Oh, but I was guilty of malpractices in office! And you, present when the auditors brought me up, accused me not?

To show you that he himself bears testimony to my having been crowned for what I had no account to render of, take and read the whole decree drawn up in my favor. By the portions of the bill which he never indicted it will appear that his prosecution is vexatious. Read.

THE DECREE

"In the archonship of Euthycles, on the twenty-second of Pyanepsion, in the presidency of the Œneian tribe, Ctesiphon, son of Leosthenes of Anaphlystus, moved: Whereas Demosthenes, son of Demosthenes of Pæania, having been superintendent of the repair of the walls, and having expended on the works three additional talents out of his own money, hath given that sum to the people; and whereas, having been appointed treasurer of the theoric fund, he hath given to the theoric officers of the tribes a hundred minas toward the sacrifices, the council and people of Athens have resolved to honor Demosthenes, son of Demosthenes of Pæania, with public praise for the goodness and generosity which he has shown throughout on every occasion toward the people of Athens, and to crown him with a golden crown, and to proclaim the crown in the theatre, at the Dionysian festival, at the performance of the new tragedies: the proclamation to be given in charge to the prize master."

These were my donations; none of which have you indicted; the rewards which the council says I deserve for them are what you arraign. To receive the gifts then you confess to be legal; the requital of them you indict for illegality. In the name of heaven! what sort of person can a monster of wickedness and malignity be, if not such a person as this?

Concerning the proclamation in the theatre, I pass over the fact that thousands of thousands have been proclaimed, and I myself have been crowned often before. But by the gods! are you so perverse and stupid, Æschines, as not to be able to reflect that the party crowned has the same glory from the crown wherever it be published, and that the proclamation is made in the theatre for the benefit of those who confer the crown? For the hearers are all encouraged to render service to the state, and praise the parties who show their gratitude more than the party crowned. Therefore has our commonwealth enacted this law. Take and read me the law itself.

THE LAW

"Whensoever any of the townships bestow crowns, proclamations thereof shall be made by them in their several townships, unless
v—108

Since, therefore, the righteous and true verdict is made clear to all; but I must, it seems,—though not naturally fond of railing, yet on account of the calumnies uttered by my opponent,—in reply to so many falsehoods, just mention some leading particulars concerning him, and show who he is, and from whom descended, that so readily begins using hard words—and what language he carps at, after uttering such as any decent man would have shuddered to pronounce. Why, if my accuser had been Æacus, or Rhadamanthus, or Minos, instead of a prater, a hack of the market, a pestilent scribbler, I don't think he would have spoken such things, or found such offensive terms, shouting, as in a tragedy, "O Earth! O Sun! O Virtue!" and the like; and again appealing to intelligence and education, by which the honorable is distinguished from the base:—all this you undoubtedly heard from his lips. Accursed one! What have you or yours to do with virtue? How should you discern what is honorable or otherwise? How were you ever qualified? What right have you to talk about education? Those who really possess it would never say as much of themselves, but rather blush if another did: those who are destitute like you, but make pretensions to it from stupidity, annoy the hearers by their talk, without getting the reputation which they desire.

I am at no loss for materials concerning you and your family, but am in doubt what to mention first—whether how your father Tromes, being servant to Elpias, who kept a reading-school in the temple of Theseus, wore a weight of fetters and a collar; or how your mother, by her morning spousals in the cottage by Hero Calamites, reared up you, the beautiful statue, the eminent third-rate actor!

But all know without my telling these things; or how the galley piper Phormio, the slave of Dion of Phrearrii, removed her from that honorable employment. But, by Jupiter and the gods! I fear, in saying what is proper about you, I may be thought to have chosen topics unbecoming to myself. All this, therefore, I shall pass by, and commence with the acts of his own life; for, indeed, he came not of common parents, but of such as are execrated by the people. Very lately,—lately do I say?—it is but yesterday that he has become both an Athenian and an orator—adding two syllables, he converted his father from Tromes to Atrometus, and dignified his mother by the name of Glaucothea, who (as every one knows) was called Em-

where any are crowned by the people of Athens or the council; and it shall be lawful for them to be proclaimed in the theatre at the Dionysian festival."

Do you hear, Æschines, the law distinctly saying—"unless where any are voted by the people or the council"; such may be proclaimed? Why, then, wretched man, do you play the pettifogger? Why manufacture arguments? Why don't you take hellebore for your malady? Are you not ashamed to bring on a cause for spite and not for any offense? to alter some laws and to garble others, the whole of which should in justice be read to persons sworn to decide according to the laws? And you that act thus describe the qualities which belong to a friend of the people, as if you had ordered a statue according to contract, and received it without having what the contract required; or as if friends of the people were known by words, and not by acts and measures! And you bawl out, regardless of decency, a sort of cart-language, applicable to yourself and your race, not to me.

Again, men of Athens, I conceive abuse to differ from accusation in this, that accusation has to do with offenses for which the laws provide penalties, abuse with the scandal which enemies speak against each other according to their humor. And I believe our ancestors built these courts, not that we should assemble you here and bring forth the secrets of private life for mutual reproach, but to give us the means of convicting persons guilty of crimes against the state. Æschines knew this as well as I, and yet he chose to rail rather than to accuse.

Even in this way he must take as much as he gives; but before I enter upon such matters, let me ask him one question—Should one call you the state's enemy or mine, Æschines? Mine, of course. Yet, where you might, for any offense which I committed, have obtained satisfaction for the people according to the laws, you neglected it—at the audit, on the indictments and other trials; but where I in my own person am safe on every account, by the laws, by time, by prescription, by many previous judgments on every point, by my never having been convicted of a public offense—and where the country must share, more or less, in the repute of measures which were her own—here it is you have encountered me. See if you are not the people's enemy, while you pretend to be mine!

pusa; having got that title (it is plain) from her doing and submitting to anything—how else could she have got it? However, you are so ungrateful and wicked by nature, that after being raised through the people from servitude to freedom, from beggary to affluence, instead of returning their kindness, you work against them as a hireling politician.

Of the speeches, which it may possibly be contended he has made for the good of the country, I will say nothing: of the acts which he was clearly proved to have done for the enemy, I will remind you.

What man present but knows of the outcast Antiphon, who came into the city under promise to Philip that he would burn your arsenal? I found him concealed in Piraeus, and brought him before the Assembly; when this mischief-maker, shouting and clamoring that it was monstrous in a free state that I should ill-treat unfortunate citizens, and enter houses without warrant, procured his release. And had not the Council of Areopagus, discovering the fact, and perceiving your ill-timed error, made search after the man, seized and brought him before you, a fellow like that would have been rescued, would have slipped through the hands of justice, and been sent out of the way by this declaimer. As it was, you put him to torture and to death, as you ought this man also. The Council of Areopagus were informed what Æschines had done, and therefore, though you had elected him for your advocate on the question of the Delian temple, in the same ignorance by which you have sacrificed many of the public interests, as you referred the matter to the council, and gave them full powers, they immediately removed him for his treason, and appointed Hyperides to plead; for which purpose they took their ballots from the altar, and not a single ballot was given for this wretch. To prove the truth of my statements, call me the witnesses.

WITNESSES

We, Callias of Sunium, Zenon of Phlyus, Cleon of Phalerum, Demonicus of Marathon, testify for Demosthenes in the name of all, that, the people having formerly elected Æschines for their advocate before the Amphictyons on the question of the Delian temple, we in council determined that Hyperides was more worthy to plead on behalf of the state, and Hyperides was commissioned."

Thus, by removing this man when he was about to plead, and appointing another, the council pronounced him a traitor and an enemy.

Such is one of this boy's political acts, similar — is it not? — to what he charges me with. Now let me remind you of another. When Philip sent Python of Byzantium, together with an embassy from all his own allies, with the intention of putting our commonwealth to shame, and proving her in the wrong, then — when Python swaggered and poured a flood of abuse upon you — I neither yielded nor gave way; I rose and answered him, and betrayed not the rights of the commonwealth. So plainly did I convict Philip of injustice that his very allies rose up and acknowledged it; while Æschines fought his battle, and bore witness, aye, false witness, against his own country.

Nor was this enough. Again, some time afterward, he was found meeting Anaxinus the spy at Thraso's house. A man, I say, who had a private meeting and conference with an emissary of the foe must himself have been a spy by nature and an enemy to his country. To prove these statements, call me the witnesses.

WITNESSES

"Teledemus, son of Cleon, Hyperides, son of Callæschrus, Nicomechus, son of Diophantus, testify for Demosthenes, as they swore before the generals, that Æschines, son of Atrometus of Cothocidæ, did, to their knowledge, meet by night in Thraso's house, and confer with Anaxinus, who was adjudged to be a spy of Philip. These depositions were returned before Nicias, on the third of Hecatombæon."

A vast deal besides that I could say about him I omit. For thus (methinks) it is. I could produce many more such cases, where Æschines was discovered at that period assisting the enemy and harassing me. But these things are not treasured up by you for careful remembrance or proper resentment. You have, through evil custom, given large license to any one that chooses to supplant and calumniate your honest counselors, exchanging the interest of the state for the pleasure and gratification of hearing abuse; and so it is easier and safer always to be a hireling serving your enemies than a statesman attached to you.

That he should co-operate openly with Philip before the war was shocking — O heaven and earth! could it be otherwise? — against his country! Yet allow him if you please, allow him

this. But when the ships had openly been made prize, Chersonesus was ravaged, the man was marching against Attica, matters were no longer doubtful, war had begun — nothing that he ever did for you can this malicious iambic-mouther show — not a resolution has Æschines, great or small, concerning the interests of the state. If he assert it, let him prove it now while my water-glass is running. But there is none. He is reduced to an alternative; either he had no fault to find with my measures and therefore moved none against them, or he sought the good of the enemy and therefore would not propose any better.

Did he abstain from speaking as well as moving when any mischief was to be done to you? Why, no one else could speak a word. Other things, it appears, the country could endure, and he could accomplish without detection; but one last act he achieved, O Athenians, which crowned all he had done before; on which he lavished that multitude of words, recounting the decrees against the Amphissian Locrians in hopes of distorting the truth. But the thing admits it not. No! never will you wash yourself clean from your performances there — talk as long as you will!

In your presence, men of Athens, I invoke all the gods and goddesses to whom the Attic territory belongs, and Pythian Apollo, the father god of our State; and I implore them all! As I shall declare the truth to you, as I declared it in your assembly at the time, the very moment I saw this wretch putting his hand to the work, — for I perceived, instantly perceived it, — so may they grant me favor and protection! If from malice or personal rivalry I bring a false charge against my opponent, may they cut me off from every blessing!

But wherefore this imprecation, this solemn assurance? Because, though I have documents lying in the public archives, from which I shall clearly prove my assertions, though I know you remember the facts, I fear this man may be considered unequal to the mischiefs which he has wrought; as before happened, when he caused the destruction of the unhappy Phocians by his false reports to you.

The Amphissian war, I say, — which brought Philip to Elatea, which caused him to be chosen general of the Amphictyons, which ruined everything in Greece, — was this man's contrivance. He is the single author of all our heaviest calamities. I protested at the time, and cried out in the assembly: "You are

bringing a war, Æschines, into Attica, an Amphictyonic war" — but his packed party would not let me be heard; the rest wondered, and supposed that I was bringing an idle charge against him out of personal enmity. However, the real character of those transactions, the purpose for which they were got up, the manner in which they were accomplished, hear ye now, men of Athens, as ye were prevented then. You will see that the thing was well concerted, and it will help you much to get a knowledge of public affairs, and what craftiness there was in Philip you will observe.

Philip could neither finish nor get rid of the war with Athens, unless he made the Thebans and Thessalians her enemies. Though your generals fought against him without fortune or skill, yet from the war itself and the cruisers he suffered infinite damage. He could neither export any of the produce of his country, nor import what he needed. He was not then superior to you at sea, nor able to reach Attica, unless the Thessalians followed him and the Thebans gave him a passage; so that, while he overcame in war the generals whom you sent out, — such as they were — I say nothing about that, — he found himself distressed by the difference of your local position and means. Should he urge either Thessalians or Thebans to march in his own quarrel against you, none, he thought, would attend to him: but should he, under the pretense of taking up their common cause, be elected general, he trusted partly by deceit and partly by persuasion to gain his ends more easily. He sets to work therefore — observe how cleverly — to get the Amphictyons into a war and create a disturbance in the congress. For this he thought they would immediately want him. Now, if any of the presbyters commissioned by himself or any of his allies brought it forward, he imagined that both Thebans and Thessalians would suspect the thing and would all be on their guard; whereas, if the agent were an Athenian and commissioned by you his opponents, it would easily pass unnoticed. And thus it turned out.

How did he effect his purpose? He hires the prosecutor. No one (I believe) was aware of the thing or attending to it, and so — just as these things are usually done at Athens — Æschines was proposed for Pylæan deputy, three or four held up their hands for him, and his election was declared. When clothed with the dignity of the state he arrived among the Amphictyons, dismissing and disregarding all besides, he hastened to execute what

he was hired for. He makes up a pretty speech and story, showing how the Cirrhæan plain came to be consecrated; reciting this to the presbyters, men unused to speeches and unsuspicious of any consequences, he procures a vote from them to walk round the district, which the Amphissians maintained they had a right to cultivate, but which he charged to be parcel of the sacred plain. The Locrians were not then instituting any suit against us, or any such proceeding as Æschines now falsely alleges. This will show you it was impossible (I fancy) for the Locrians to carry on process against our commonwealth without a citation. Who summoned us then? In whose archonship? Say who knows — point him out. You cannot. Your pretense was flimsy and false.

When the Amphictyons at the instance of this man walked over the plain, the Locrians fell upon them and well-nigh speared them all; some of the presbyters they carried off captive. Complaints having followed, and war being stirred up against the Amphyssians, at first Cottyphus led an army composed entirely of Amphictyons; but as some never came, and those that came did nothing, measures were taken against the ensuing congress by an instructed gang, the old traitors of Thessaly and other States, to get the command for Philip. And they had found a fair pretext: for it was necessary, they said, either to subsidize themselves and maintain a mercenary force and fine all recusants, or to elect him. What need of many words? He was thereupon chosen general; and immediately afterward collecting an army, and marching professedly against Cirrha, he bids a long farewell to the Cirrhæans and Locrians, and seizes Elatea. Had not the Thebans, upon seeing this, immediately changed their minds and sided with us, the whole thing would have fallen like a torrent upon our country. As it was, they for the instant stopped him; chiefly, O Athenians, by the kindness of some divinity to Athens, but secondly, as far as it could depend on a single man, through me. Give me those decrees, and the dates of the several transactions, that you may know what mischief this pestilent creature has stirred up with impunity. Read me the decrees.

THE DECREE OF THE AMPHICTYONS

"In the priesthood of Clinagoras, at the spring congress, it hath been resolved by the deputies and councilors of the Amphictyons, and by the assembly of the Amphictyons, seeing that the Amphissians trespass upon the sacred plain and sow and depasture it with cattle, that the deputies and councilors do enter thereupon and define the boundaries with pillars, and enjoin the Amphissians not to trespass for the future."

ANOTHER DECREE

"In the priesthood of Clinagoras, at the spring congress, it hath been resolved by the deputies and councilors of the Amphictyons and by the assembly of the Amphictyons, seeing that the people of Amphissa have partitioned among themselves the sacred plain and cultivate and feed cattle upon the same, and on being interrupted have come in arms, and with force resisted the general council of the Greeks, and have wounded some of them; that Cottyphus, the Arcadian, who hath been elected general of the Amphictyons, be sent embassador to Philip of Macedon, and do request him to come to the aid of Apollo and the Amphictyons, that he may not suffer the god to be insulted by the impious Amphissians; and do announce that the Greeks who are members of the Amphictyonic Council appoint him general with absolute powers."

Now read the dates of these transactions. They correspond with the time when Æschines was deputy. Read.

DATES

"Mnesithides archon, on the sixteenth of the month Anthesterion."

Now give me the letter which, when the Thebans would not hearken to Philip, he sends to his allies in Peloponnesus, that you may plainly see even from this how the true motives of his enterprise, his designs against Greece and the Thebans and yourselves were concealed by him, while he affected to be taking measures for the common good under a decree of the Amphictyons. The man who furnished him with these handles and pretexts was Æschines. Read.

THE LETTER OF PHILIP

"Philip, King of Macedon, to the magistrates and councilors of the confederate Peloponnesians and to all the other allies greeting. Whereas the Locrians surnamed Ozolian, dwelling in Amphissa, commit sacrilege against the temple of Apollo at Delphi, and coming with arms despoil the sacred plain, I propose, with your assistance,

return. I say, when Æschines had excited the war in Amphissa, and his coadjutors had helped to establish enmity with Thebes, Philip marched against us,—that was the object for which these persons embroiled the states,—and had we not roused up a little in time we could never have recovered ourselves; so far had these men carried matters. In what position you then stood to each other, you will learn from the recital of these decrees and answers. Here, take and read them.

DECREE

"In the archonship of Heropythus, on the twenty-fifth of the month Elaphebolion, in the presidency of the Erechtheian tribe, by the advice of the council and the generals: Whereas Philip hath taken possession of certain neighboring cities, and is besieging others, and finally is preparing to advance against Attica, setting our treaty at nought, and designs to break his oaths and the peace in violation of our common engagements: the council and people have resolved to send unto him embassadors, who shall confer with him, and exhort him above all to maintain his relations of amity with us and his convention, or if not, to give time to the Commonwealth for deliberation, and conclude an armistice until the month Thargelion. These have been chosen from the council: Simus of Anagyrus, Euthydemus of Phlyus, Bulagoras of Alopece."

ANOTHER DECREE

"In the archonship of Heropythus, on the last day of the month Munychion, by the advice of the Polemarch: Whereas Philip designs to put the Thebans at variance with us, and hath prepared to advance with his whole army to the places nearest to Attica, violating the engagements that subsist between us, the council and people have resolved to send unto him a herald and embassadors, who shall request and call upon him to conclude an armistice, so that the people may take measures according to circumstances; for now they do not purpose to march out in the event of anything reasonable. Nearchus, son of Sosinomus and Polycrates, son of Epiphron, have been chosen from the council; and for herald, Eunomus of Anaphlystus from the people."

Now read the answers:—

TO THE ATHENIANS

"Philip, King of Macedon, to the Council and People of Athens, greeting. Of the part which you have taken in reference to me

to avenge the god, and to chastise people who violate any part of our recognized religion. Wherefore meet me with arms in Phocis, bringing provisions for forty days, in the ensuing month of Lous, as we style it, Boedromion as the Athenians Panemus as the Corinthians. Those who do not meet us with all their forces, we shall visit with punishment. Farewell."

You see, he avoids all private pleas and has recourse to an Amphictyonic. Who was it, I say, that helped him to this contrivance—that lent him these excuses? Who is most to blame for the misfortunes which have happened? Surely Æschines. Then go not about saying, "O Athenians, that one man has inflicted these calamities on Greece!" Heaven and earth! It was not a single man, but a number of miscreants in every state. Æschines was one of them; and, were I obliged to speak the truth without reserve, I should not hesitate to call him the common pest of all that have since been ruined, men, places, cities: for whoever supplies the seed, to him the crop is owing. I marvel, indeed, you turned not your faces away the moment you beheld him. But there is a thick darkness, it seems, between you and the truth.

The mention of this man's treasonable acts brings me to the part which I have myself taken in opposition to him. It is fair you should hear my account of it for many reasons, but chiefly, men of Athens, because it would be a shame, when I have undergone the toil of exertions on your behalf, that you should not endure the bare recital of them.

When I saw that the Thebans, and I may add the Athenians, were so led away by Philip's partisans and the corrupt men of either state, as to disregard and take no precaution against a danger which menaced both and required the utmost precaution (I mean the suffering Philip's power to increase), and were readily disposed to enmity and strife with each other, I was constantly watchful to prevent it, not only because in my own judgment I deemed such vigilance expedient, but knowing that Aristophon, and again Eubulus, had all along desired to bring about that union, and, while they were frequently opposed upon other matters, were always agreed upon this. Men whom in their lifetime—you reptile!—you pestered with flattery, yet see not that you are accusing them in their graves; for the Theban policy that you reproach me with is a charge less affecting me than them who approved that alliance before I did. But I must

from the beginning I am not ignorant, nor what exertions you are making to gain over the Thessalians and Thebans, and also the Bœotians. Since they are more prudent and will not submit their choice to your dictation, but stand by their own interest, you shift your ground, and, sending embassadors and a herald to me, you talk of engagements and ask for an armistice, although I have given you no offense. However, I have given audience to your embassadors, and I agree to your request and am ready to conclude an armistice if you will dismiss your evil counselors and degrade them as they deserve. Farewell."

TO THE THEBANS

"Philip, King of Macedon, to the Council and People of Thebes, greeting. I have received your letter wherein you renew peace and amity with me. I am informed, however, that the Athenians are most earnestly soliciting you to accept their overtures. I blamed you at first for being inclined to put faith in their promises and to espouse their policy. But since I have discovered that you would rather maintain peace with me than follow the counsels of others, I praise you the more on divers accounts, but chiefly because you have consulted in this business for your safety, and preserve your attachment to me, which I trust will be of no small moment to you if you persevere in that determination. Farewell."

Philip having thus disposed the States toward each other by his contrivances, and being elated by these decrees and answers, came with his army and seized Elatea, confident that, happen what might, you and the Thebans could never again unite. What commotion there was in the city you all know; but let me just mention the most striking circumstances.

It was evening. A person came with a message to the presidents, that Elatea was taken. They rose from supper immediately, drove off the people from their market-stalls, and set fire to the wicker-frames; others sent for the generals and called the trumpeter, and the city was full of commotion. The next morning at daybreak the presidents summoned the council to their hall, and you went to the assembly, and before they could introduce or prepare the question, the whole people were up in their seats. When the council had entered, and the presidents had reported their intelligence and presented the courier, and he had made his statement, the crier asked: "Who wishes to speak?" and no one came forward. The crier put the question repeatedly—still no man rose, though all the generals were present and all the orators, and our country with her common voice called for some one to speak and save her — for when the crier raises his voice according to law, it may justly be deemed the common voice of our country. If those of greatest wealth, the three hundred — if those who were both friendly to the state and wealthy, the men who afterward gave such ample donations; for patriotism and wealth produced the gift, — if those who desired the salvation of Athens were the proper parties to come forward, all of you and the other Athenians would have risen and mounted the platform; for I am sure you all desired her salvation. But that occasion, that day, as it seems, called not only for a patriot and a wealthy man, but for one who had closely followed the proceedings from their commencement, and rightly calculated for what object and purpose Philip carried them on. A man who was ignorant of these matters, or had not long and carefully studied them, let him be ever so patriotic or wealthy, would neither see what measures were needful, nor be competent to advise you.

Well, then, I was the man called for upon that day. I came forward and addressed you. What I said I beg you for two reasons attentively to hear; firstly, to be convinced that of all your orators and statesmen I alone deserted not the patriot's post in the hour of danger, but was found in the very moment of panic speaking and moving what your necessities required; secondly, because at the expense of a little time you will gain large experience for the future in all your political concerns.

I said those who were in such alarm under the idea that Philip had got the Thebans with him did not, in my opinion, understand the position of affairs; for I was sure, had that really been so, we should have heard not of his being at Elatea, but upon our frontiers; he was come, however, I knew for certain, to make all right for himself in Thebes. "Let me inform you," said I, "how the matter stands. All the Thebans whom it was possible either to bribe or deceive he has at his command; those who have resisted him from the first, and still oppose him, he can in no way prevail upon; what, then, is his meaning and why has he seized upon Elatea? He means, by displaying a force in the neighborhood, and bringing up his troops, to encourage and embolden his friends, and to intimidate his adversaries, that they may either concede from fear what they now refuse, or be compelled. Now," said I, "if we determine on the present occasion to remember any unkindness which the Thebans have done us, and to

regard them in the character of enemies with distrust, in the first place, we shall be doing just what Philip would desire; in the next place, I fear his present adversaries embracing his friendship and all Philippizing with one consent, they will both march against Attica. But if you will hearken to me, and be pleased to examine (not cavil at) what I say, I believe it will meet your approval, and I shall dispel the danger impending over Athens. What, then, do I advise? First, away with your present fear; and rather fear all of ye for the Thebans; they are nearer harm than we are; to them the peril is more immediate. Next, I say, march to Eleusis, all the fighting men and the cavalry, and show yourselves to the world in arms, that your partisans in Thebes may have equal liberty to speak up for the good cause, knowing that as the faction who sell their country to Philip have an army to support them at Elatea, so the party that will contend for freedom have your assistance at hand if they be assailed.

"Further, I recommend you to elect ten embassadors and empower them in conjunction with the generals to fix the time for going there and for the out-march. When the embassadors have arrived at Thebes, how do I advise that you should treat the matter? Pray attend particularly to this. Ask nothing of the Thebans (it would be dishonorable at this time); but offer to assist them if they require it, on the plea that they are in extreme danger, and we see the future better than they do. If they accept this offer and hearken to our counsels, so shall we have accomplished what we desire, and our conduct will look worthy of the state; should we miscarry, they will have themselves to blame for any error committed now, and we shall have done nothing dishonorable or mean."

This and more to the like effect I spoke and left the platform. It was approved by all; not a word was said against me. Nor did I make the speech without moving, nor make the motion without undertaking the embassy, nor undertake the embassy without prevailing on the Thebans. From the beginning to the end, I went through it all; I gave myself entirely to your service to meet the dangers which encompassed Athens.

Produce me the decree which then passed. Now, Æschines, how would you have me describe you, and how myself, upon that day? Shall I call myself Batalus, your nickname of reproach, and you not even a hero of the common sort, but one of those upon the stage, Cresphontes or Creon, or the Œnomaus

whom you execrably murdered once at Colyttus? Well, upon that occasion, I, the Batalus of Pæania, was more serviceable to the state than you, the Œnomaus of Cothocidæ. You were of no earthly use; I did everything which became a good citizen. Read the decree.

THE DECREE OF DEMOSTHENES

"In the archonship of Nausicles, in the presidency of the Æantian tribe, on the sixteenth of Scirophorion, Demosthenes, son of Demosthenes of Pæania, moved: Whereas, Philip, King of Macedon, hath in time past been violating the treaty of peace made between him and the Athenian people, in contempt of his oaths and those laws of justice which are recognized among all the Greeks, and hath been annexing unto himself cities that no way belong to him, and hath besieged and taken some which belong to the Athenians without any provocation by the people of Athens, and at the present time he is making great advances in cruelty and violence, forasmuch as in certain Greek cities he puts garrisons and overturns their constitution, some he razes to the ground and sells the inhabitants for slaves, in some he replaces a Greek population with barbarians, giving them possession of the temples and sepulchres, acting in no way foreign to his own country or character, making an insolent use of his present fortune, and forgetting that from a petty and insignificant person he has come to be unexpectedly great; and the people of Athens, so long as they saw him annexing barbarian or private cities of their own, less seriously regarded the offense given to themselves, but now that they see Greek cities outraged and some destroyed, they think it would be monstrous and unworthy of their ancestral glory to look on while the Greeks are enslaved:

"Therefore it is resolved by the council and people of Athens, that having prayed and sacrificed to the gods and heroes who protect the Athenian city and territory, bearing in mind the virtue of their ancestors, who deemed it of greater moment to preserve the liberty of Greece than their own country, they will put two hundred ships to sea, and their admiral shall sail up into the straits of Thermopylæ, and their general and commander of horse shall march with the infantry and cavalry to Eleusis, and embassadors shall be sent to the other Greeks, and first of all to the Thebans, because Philip is nearest their territory, and shall exhort them without dread of Philip to maintain their own independence and that of Greece at large, and assure them that the Athenian people, not remembering any variance which has formerly arisen between the countries, will assist them with troops and money and weapons and arms, feeling that for them

(being Greeks) to contend among themselves for the leadership is honorable, but to be commanded and deprived of the leadership by a man of foreign extraction is derogatory to the renown of the Greeks and the virtue of their ancestors: further, the people of Athens do not regard the people of Thebes as aliens either in blood or race; they remember also the benefits conferred by their ancestors upon the ancestors of the Thebans; for they restored the children of Hercules who were kept by the Peloponnesians out of their hereditary dominion, defeating in battle those who attempted to resist the descendants of Hercules; and we gave shelter to Œdipus and his comrades in exile; and many other kind and generous acts have been done by us to the Thebans: wherefore now also the people of Athens will not desert the interests of the Thebans and the other Greeks: And let a treaty be entered into with them for alliance and intermarriage, and oaths be mutually exchanged. Embassadors: Demosthenes, son of Demosthenes of Pæania, Hyperides, son of Cleander of Spettus, Mnesithides, son of Antiphanes of Phrearrii, Democrates, son of Sophilus of Phlyus, Callæschrus, son of Diotimus of Cothocidæ."

That was the commencement and first step in the negotiation with Thebes: before then the countries had been led by these men into discord and hatred and jealousy. That decree caused the peril which then surrounded us to pass away like a cloud. It was the duty of a good citizen, if he had any better plan, to disclose it at the time, not to find fault now. A statesman and a pettifogger, while in no other respect are they alike, in this most widely differ. The one declares his opinion before the proceedings, and makes himself responsible to his followers, to fortune, to the times, to all men: the other is silent when he ought to speak; at any untoward event he grumbles.

Now, as I said before, the time for a man who regarded the commonwealth, and for honest counsel, was then: however, I will go to this extent — if any one now can point out a better course, or, indeed, if any other were practicable but the one which I adopted, I confess that I was wrong. For if there be any measure now discovered, which (executed then) would have been to our advantage, I say it ought not to have escaped me. But if there is none, if there was none, if none can be suggested even at this day, what was a statesman to do? Was he not to choose the best measures within his reach and view? That did I, Æschines, when the crier asked, "Who wishes to speak?" — not, "Who wishes to complain about the past or to guarantee the future?"

While you on those occasions sat mute in the assembly, I came forward and spake. However, as you omitted then, tell us now. Say, what scheme that I ought to have devised, what favorable opportunity was lost to the state by my neglect?—what alliance was there, what better plan, to which I should have directed the people? But no! The past is with all the world given up; no one even proposes to deliberate about it: the future it is, or the present, which demands the action of a counselor. At the time, as it appeared, there were dangers impending, and dangers at hand. Mark the line of my policy at that crisis; don't rail at the event. The end of all things is what the Deity pleases: his line of policy it is that shows the judgment of the statesman. Do not then impute it as a crime to me that Philip chanced to conquer in battle: that issue depended not on me, but on God. Prove that I adopted not all measures that according to human calculation were feasible—that I did not honestly and diligently and with exertions beyond my strength carry them out—or that my enterprises were not honorable and worthy of the state, and necessary. Show me this, and accuse me as soon as you like. But if the hurricane that visited us hath been too powerful, not for us only, but for all Greece besides, what is the fair course? As if a merchant, after taking every precaution, and furnishing his vessel with everything that he thought would insure her safety, because afterward he met with a storm and his tackle was strained or broken to pieces, should be charged with the shipwreck! "Well, but I was not the pilot," he might say, just as I was not the general. "Fortune was not under my control: all was under hers."

Consider and reflect upon this—If, with the Thebans on our side, we were destined so to fare in the contest, what was to be expected, if we had never had them for allies, but they had joined Philip, as he used every effort of persuasion to make them do? And if, when the battle was fought three days' march from Attica, such peril and alarm surrounded the city, what must we have expected, if the same disaster had happened in some part of our territory? As it was (do you see?) we could stand, meet, breathe; mightily did one, two, three days, help to our preservation: in the other case—but it is wrong to mention things of which we have been spared the trial by the favor of some deity, and by our protecting ourselves with the very alliance which you assail.

V—109

to Philip. Why, had we resigned without a struggle that which our ancestors encountered every danger to win, who would not have spit upon you? Let me not say, the commonwealth or myself! With what eyes, I pray, could we have beheld strangers visiting the city, if the result had been what it is, and Philip had been chosen leader and lord of all, but other people without us had made the struggle to prevent it; especially when in former times our country had never preferred an ignominious security to the battle for honor? For what Grecian or what barbarian is ignorant that by the Thebans, or by the Lacedæmonians who were in might before them, or by the Persian king, permission would thankfully and gladly have been given to our commonwealth, to take what she pleased and hold her own, provided she would accept foreign law and let another power command in Greece?

But, as it seems, to the Athenians of that day such conduct would not have been national, or natural, or endurable; none could at any period of time persuade the commonwealth to attach herself in secure subjection to the powerful and unjust: through every age has she persevered in a perilous struggle for precedency and honor and glory. And this you esteem so noble and congenial to your principles that among your ancestors you honor most those who acted in such a spirit; and with reason. For who would not admire the virtue of those men who resolutely embarked in their galleys and quitted country and home rather than receive foreign law, choosing Themistocles who gave such counsel for their general, and stoning Cyrsilus to death who advised submission to the terms imposed—not him only, but your wives also stoning his wife? Yes, the Athenians of that day looked not for an orator or a general who might help them to a pleasant servitude; they scorned to live, if it could not be with freedom. For each of them considered that he was not born to his father or mother only, but also to his country. What is the difference? He that thinks himself born for his parents only, waits for his appointed or natural end: he that thinks himself born for his country also, will sooner perish than behold her in slavery, and will regard the insults and indignities, which must be borne in a commonwealth enslaved, as more terrible than death.

Had I attempted to say that I instructed you in sentiments worthy of your ancestors, there is not a man who would not

All this, at such length, have I addressed to you, men of the jury, and to the outer circle of hearers; for, as to this contemptible fellow, a short and plain argument would suffice.

If the future was revealed to you, Æschines, alone, when the state was deliberating on these proceedings, you ought to have forewarned us at the time. If you did not foresee it, you are responsible for the same ignorance as the rest. Why, then, do you accuse me in this behalf, rather than I you? A better citizen have I been than you in respect of the matters of which I am speaking (others I discuss not at present), inasmuch as I gave myself up to what seemed for the general good, not shrinking from any personal danger, nor taking thought of any; while you neither suggested better measures (or mine would not have been adopted), nor lent any aid in the prosecuting of mine: exactly what the basest person and worst enemy of the state would do, are you found to have done after the event; and at the same time Aristratus in Naxos and Aristolaus in Thasos, the deadly foes of our state, are bringing to trial the friends of Athens, and Æschines at Athens is accusing Demosthenes. Surely the man who waited to found his reputation upon the misfortunes of the Greeks deserves rather to perish than to accuse another; nor is it possible that one who has profited by the same conjunctures as the enemies of the commonwealth can be a well-wisher of his country. You show yourself by your life and conduct, by your political action, and even your political inaction. Is anything going on that appears good for the people? Æschines is mute. Has anything untoward happened or amiss? Forth comes Æschines; just as fractures and sprains are put in motion, when the body is attacked by disease.

But since he insists so strongly on the event, I will even assert something of a paradox: and I beg and pray of you not to marvel at its boldness, but kindly to consider what I say. If, then, the results had been foreknown to all, if all had foreseen them, and you, Æschines, had foretold them and protested with clamor and outcry,—you that never opened your mouth,—not even then should the commonwealth have abandoned her design, if she had any regard for glory, or ancestry, or futurity. As it is, she appears to have failed in her enterprise, a thing to which all mankind are liable, if the Deity so wills it: but then—claiming precedency over others, and afterward abandoning her pretensions—she would have incurred the charge of betraying all

justly rebuke me. What I declare is that such principles are your own. I show that before my time such was the spirit of the commonwealth; though certainly in the execution of the particular measures I claim a share also for myself. The prosecutor, arraigning the whole proceedings, and embittering you against me as the cause of our alarms and dangers, in his eagerness to deprive me of honor for the moment, robs you of the eulogies that should endure forever. For should you, under a disbelief in the wisdom of my policy, convict the defendant, you will appear to have done wrong, not to have suffered what befell you by the cruelty of fortune. But never, never can you have done wrong, O Athenians, in undertaking the battle for the freedom and safety of all! I swear it by your forefathers—those that met the peril at Marathon, those that took the field at Platæa, those in the sea fight at Salamis, and those at Artemisium, and many other brave men who repose in the public monuments, all of whom alike, as being worthy of the same honor, the country buried, Æschines, not only the successful or victorious! Justly! For the duty of brave men has been done by all, their fortune has been such as the Deity assigned to each.

Accursed scribbler! you, to deprive me of the approbation and affection of my countrymen, speak of trophies and battles and ancient deeds, with none of which had this present trial the least concern; but I!—Oh, you third-rate actor!—I, that rose to counsel the state how to maintain her pre-eminence! in what spirit was I to mount the hustings? In the spirit of one having unworthy counsel to offer?—I should have deserved to perish! You yourselves, men of Athens, may not try private and public causes on the same principles: the compacts of every-day life you are to judge of by particular laws and circumstances; the measures of statesmen, by reference to the dignity of your ancestors. And if you think it your duty to act worthily of them, you should every one of you consider, when you come into court to decide public questions, that, together with your staff and ticket, the spirit of the commonwealth is delivered to you.

But in touching upon the deeds of your ancestors, there were some decrees and transactions which I omitted. I will return from my digression.

On our arrival at Thebes, we found embassadors there from Philip, from the Thessalians and from his other allies; our friends in trepidation, his friends confident. To prove that I am not asserting this now to serve my own purposes, read me the letter which we embassadors dispatched on the instant. So outrageous is my opponent's malignity, that, if any advantage was procured, he attributes it to the occasion, not to me; while all miscarriages he attributes to me and my fortune. And according to him, as it seems, I, the orator and adviser, have no merit in results of argument and counsel, but am the sole author of misfortunes in arms and strategy. Could there be a more brutal calumniator or a more execrable? Read the letter. [The letter is read.]

On the convening of the assembly, our opponents were introduced first, because they held the character of allies. And they came forward and spoke in high praise of Philip and disparagement of you, bringing up all the hostilities that you ever committed against the Thebans. In fine, they urged them to show their gratitude for the services done by Philip, and to avenge themselves for the injuries which you had done them, either—it mattered not which—by giving them a passage against you, or by joining in the invasion of Attica; and they proved, as they fancied, that by adopting their advice the cattle and slaves and other effects of Attica would come into Bœotia, whereas by acting as they said we should advise, Bœotia would suffer pillage through the war. And much they said besides, tending all to the same point. The reply that we made I would give my life to recapitulate, but I fear, as the occasion is past, you will look upon it as if a sort of deluge had overwhelmed the whole proceedings, and regard any talk about them as a useless troubling of you. Hear, then, what we persuaded them and what answer they returned. Take and read this:— [The answer of the Thebans is read.]

After this they invited and sent for you. You marched to their succor, and—to omit what happened between—their reception of you was so friendly, that, while their infantry and cavalry were outside the walls, they admitted your army into their houses and citadel, among their wives and children and all that was most precious. Why, upon that day three of the noblest testimonies were before all mankind borne in your favor by the Thebans, one to your courage, one to your justice, one to your good behavior. For when they preferred fighting on your side to fighting against you, they held you to be braver and juster in your demands than Philip; and when they put under your charge what they and all men are most watchful to protect, their wives

and children, they showed that they had confidence in your good behavior. In all which, men of Athens, it appeared they had rightly estimated your character. For after your forces entered the city, not so much as a groundless complaint was preferred against you by any one, so discreetly did you behave yourselves; and twice arrayed on their side in the earlier battles, that by the river and the winter battle, you proved yourselves not irreproachable only, but admirable in your discipline, your equipments, and your zeal, which called forth eulogies from other men to you, sacrifice and thanksgiving from you to the gods. And I would gladly ask Æschines—while these things were going on, and the city was full of enthusiasm and joy and praise, whether he joined with the multitude in sacrifice and festivity, or sat at home sorrowing and moaning and repining at the public success. For if he were present and appeared with the rest, is not his conduct monstrous, or rather impious, when measures, which he himself called the gods to witness were excellent, he now requires you to condemn—you that have sworn by the gods? If he were not present, does he not deserve a thousand deaths for grieving to behold what others rejoiced at? Read me now the decrees. [The decrees for sacrifice are read.]

We thus were engaged in sacrifice; the Thebans were in the assurance that they had been saved through us, and it had come about that a people, who seemed likely to want assistance through the practices of these men, were themselves assisting others in consequence of my advice which you followed. What language Philip then uttered, and in what trouble he was on this account, you shall learn from his letters which he sent to Peloponnesus. Take and read them, that the jury may know what my perseverance and journey and toils and the many decrees which this man just now pulled to pieces accomplished.

Athenians, you have had many great and renowned orators before me; the famous Callistratus, Aristophon, Cephalus, Thrasybulus, hundreds of others; yet none of them ever thoroughly devoted himself to any measure of state; for instance, the mover of a resolution would not be embassador, the embassador would not move a resolution; each one left for himself some relief, and also, should anything happen, an excuse. How, then, it may be said, did you so far surpass others in might and boldness as to do everything yourself? I don't say that; but such was my conviction of the danger impending over us, that I considered it left

no room or thought for individual security; a man should have been only too happy to perform his duty without neglect. As to myself, I was persuaded, perhaps foolishly, yet I was persuaded, that none would move better resolutions than myself, none would execute them better, none as embassador would show more zeal and honesty. Therefore I undertook every duty myself. Read the letters of Philip. [The letters are read.]

To this did my policy, Æschines, reduce Philip. This language he uttered through me, he that before had lifted his voice so boldly against Athens! For which I was justly crowned by the people; and you were present and opposed it not, and Diondas who preferred an indictment obtained not his share of the votes. Here, read me the decrees which were then absolved, and which this man never indicted. [The decrees are read.]

These decrees, men of Athens, contain the very words and syllables which Aristonicus drew up formerly, and Ctesiphon the defendant has now. And Æschines neither arraigned these himself, nor aided the party who preferred an indictment. Yet, if his present charge against me be true, he might then have arraigned Demomeles the mover and Hyperides with more show of reason than he can the defendant. Why? Because Ktesiphon may refer to them, and to the decisions of the courts, and to the fact of Æschines not having accused them, although they moved the same decrees which he has now, and to the laws which bar any further proceedings in such a case, and to many points besides:—whereas then the question would have been tried on its own merits, before any such advantages had been obtained. But then, I imagine, it would have been impossible to do what Æschines now does—to pick out of a multitude of old dates and decrees what no man knew before, and what no man would have expected to hear to-day, for the purpose of slander—to transpose dates and assign measures to the wrong causes instead of the right, in order to make a plausible case. That was impossible then. Every statement must have been according to the truth, soon after the facts, while you still remembered the particulars and had them almost at your fingers' ends. Therefore it was that he shunned all investigation at the time, and has come at this late period; thinking, as it appears to me, that you would make it a contest of orators, instead of an inquiry into political conduct; that words would be criticized, and not interests of state.

Then he plays the sophist, and says you ought to disregard the opinion of us which you came from home with—that, as when you audit a man's account under the impression that he has a surplus, if it cast up right and nothing remain, you allow it, so should you now accept the fair conclusion of the argument. Only see how rotten in its nature (and justly so) is every wicked contrivance! For by this very cunning simile he has now acknowledged it to be your conviction that I am my country's advocate and he is Philip's. Had not this been your opinion of each, he would not have tried to persuade you differently. That he has, however, no reasonable ground for requiring you to change your belief, I can easily show, not by casting accounts,—for that mode of reckoning applies not to measures,—but by calling the circumstances briefly to mind, taking you that hear me both for auditors and witnesses.

Through my policy which he arraigns, instead of the Thebans invading this country with Philip, as all expected, they joined our ranks and prevented him; instead of the war being in Attica, it took place seven hundred furlongs from the city on the confines of Bœotia; instead of corsairs issuing from Eubœa to plunder us, Attica was in peace on the coast-side during the whole war; instead of Philip being master of the Hellespont by taking Byzantium, the Byzantines were our auxiliaries against him. Does this computation of services, think you, resemble the casting of accounts? Or should we strike these out on a balance, and not look that they be kept in everlasting remembrance? I will not set down that of the cruelty, remarkable in cases where Philip got people all at once into his power, others have had the trial; while of the generosity, which, casting about for his future purposes, he assumed toward Athens, you have happily enjoyed the fruits. I pass that by.

Yet this I do not hesitate to say: that any one desirous of truly testing an orator, not of calumniating him, would never have made the charges that you advanced just now, inventing similes, mimicking words and gestures; (doubtless it hath determined the fortune of Greece, whether I spoke this word or that, whether I moved my hand one way or the other!) no! he would have examined the facts of the case, what means and resources our country possessed, when I entered on the administration, what, when I applied myself to it, I collected for her, and what was the condition of our adversaries. Then, if I had lessened her resources, he would have shown me to be guilty; if I had greatly increased them, he would not have calumniated me. However, as you have declined this course, I will adopt it. See if I state the case fairly.

For resources, our country possessed the islanders,—not all, but the weakest, for neither Chios, nor Rhodes, nor Corcyra was with us; subsidies she had amounting to five-and-forty talents, and they were anticipated; infantry or cavalry, none besides the native. But what was most alarming and wrought most in favor of the enemy, these men had got all our neighbors to be hostile rather than friendly to us—Megarians, Thebans, Eubœans. Such were the circumstances of our state; no man can say anything to the contrary; look now at those of Philip, whom we had to contend with. In the first place, he ruled his followers with unlimited sway, the most important thing for military operations; in the next place, they had arms always in their hands; besides, he had plenty of money and did what he pleased, not giving notice by decrees, not deliberating openly, not brought to trial by calumniators, not defending indictments for illegal measures, not responsible to any one, but himself absolute master, leader, and lord of all. I, who was matched against him,—for it is right to examine this,—what had I under my control? Nothing. Public speech, for instance, the only thing open to me—even to this you invited his hirelings as well as myself; and whenever they prevailed over me (as often happened for some cause or other), your resolutions were passed for the enemy's good. Still, under these disadvantages, I got you for allies Eubœans, Achæans, Corinthians, Thebans, Megarians, Leucadians, Corcyræans, from whom were collected fifteen thousand mercenaries and two thousand horse, besides the national troops. Of money, too, I procured as large a contribution as possible.

If you talk about just conditions with the Thebans, Æschines, or with the Byzantines or Eubœans, or discuss now the question of equal terms, first, I say, you are ignorant that of those galleys formerly which defended Greece, being three hundred in number, our commonwealth furnished two hundred, and never (as it seemed) thought herself injured by having done so, never prosecuted those who advised it or expressed any dissatisfaction, —shame on her if she had!—but was grateful to the gods, that when a common danger beset the Greeks, she alone furnished double what the rest did for the preservation of all. Besides, it

is but a poor favor you do your countrymen by calumniating me. For what is the use of telling us now what we should have done?—Why, being in the city and present, did you not make your proposals then; if, indeed, they were practicable at a crisis when we had to accept not what we liked but what the circumstances allowed? Remember, there was one ready to bid against us, to welcome eagerly those that we rejected, and give money into the bargain.

But if I am accused for what I have actually done, how would it have been, if, through my hard bargaining, the states had gone off and attached themselves to Philip, and he had become master at the same time of Eubœa, Thebes, and Byzantium? What, think ye, these impious men would have said or done? Said doubtless, that the states were abandoned — that they wished to join us and were driven away — that he had got command of the Hellespont by the Byzantines, and become master of the corn trade of Greece — that a heavy neighbor war had by means of the Thebans been brought into Attica — that the sea had become unnavigable by the excursion of pirates from Eubœa! All this would they have said sure enough, and a great deal besides. A wicked, wicked thing, O Athenians, is a calumniator always, every way spiteful and fault-finding. But this creature is a reptile by nature, that from the beginning never did anything honest or liberal; a very ape of a tragedian, village Œnomaus, counterfeit orator! What advantage has your eloquence been to your country? Now do you speak to us about the past? As if a physician should visit his patients, and not order or prescribe anything to cure the disease, but on the death of any one, when the last ceremonies were performing, should follow him to the grave and expound, how, if the poor fellow had done this and that, he never would have died! Idiot! do you speak now?

Even the defeat — if you exult in that which should make you groan, you accursed one!—by nothing that I have done will it appear to have befallen us. Consider it thus, O Athenians. From no embassy on which I was commissioned by you did I ever come away defeated by the embassadors of Philip — neither from Thessaly, nor from Ambracia, nor from the kings of Thrace, nor from Byzantium, nor from any other place, nor on the last recent occasion from Thebes; but where his embassadors were vanquished in argument, he came with arms and carried the day. And for this you call me to account, and are not ashamed to

jeer the same person for cowardice, whom you require single-handed to overcome the might of Philip—and that too by words! For what else had I at my command? Certainly not the spirit of each individual, nor the fortune of the army, nor the conduct of the war, for which you would make me accountable; such a blunderer are you!

Yet understand me. Of what a statesman may be responsible for, I allow the utmost scrutiny; I deprecate it not. What are his functions? To observe things in the beginning, to foresee and foretell them to others — this I have done. Again, wherever he finds delays, backwardness, ignorance, jealousies, vices inherent and unavoidable in all communities, to contract them into the narrowest compass, and, on the other hand, to promote unanimity and friendship and zeal in the discharge of duty. All this, too, I have performed; and no one can discover the least neglect on my part. Ask any man by what means Philip achieved most of his successes, and you will be told by his army and by his bribing and corrupting men in power. Well; your forces were not under my command or control; so that I cannot be questioned for anything done in that department. But by refusing the price of corruption I have overcome Philip; for as the offerer of a bribe, if it be accepted, has vanquished the taker, so the person who refuses it and is not corrupted has vanquished the person offering. Therefore is the commonwealth undefeated as far as I am concerned.

These, and such as these (besides many others), are the grounds furnished by myself to justify the defendant's motion in my behalf. Those which you, my fellow-citizens, furnished, I will proceed to mention. Immediately after the battle, the people, knowing and having witnessed everything which I did, in the very midst of their alarm and terror, when it would not have been surprising if the great body of them had even treated me harshly, passed my resolutions for the safety of the country; all their measures of defense, the disposition of the garrisons, the trenches, the levies for our fortifications, were carried on under my decrees; and further, upon the election of a commissioner of grain, they chose me in preference to all. Afterward, when those who were bent to do me a mischief conspired and brought indictments, audits, impeachments, and the rest of it against me, not at first in their own persons, but in such names as they imagined would most effectually screen themselves (for you surely

know and remember that every day of that first period I was arraigned, and neither the desperation of Sosicles, nor the malignity of Philocrates, nor the madness of Diondas and Melantus, nor anything else was left untried by them against me); on all those occasions, chiefly through the gods, secondly through you and the other Athenians, I was preserved. And with justice! Yes, that is the truth, and to the honor of the juries who so conscientiously decided. Well, then; on the impeachments, when you acquitted me and gave not the prosecutors their share of the votes, you pronounced that my policy was the best; by my acquittal on the indictments, my counsels and motion were shown to be legal; by your passing of my accounts, you acknowledged my whole conduct to have been honest and incorruptible. Under these circumstances, what name could Ktesiphon with decency or justice give to my acts? [What could he give if not] that which he saw the people give, which he saw the jurors give, which he saw truth establish to the world?

Aye, says he, that was a fine thing of Cephalus, never to have been indicted. Yes, and a lucky one, too. But why should a man, who has often been charged, but never convicted of crime, be a whit the more liable to reproach? However, men of Athens, against my opponent I have a right to use the boast of Cephalus, for he never preferred or prosecuted any indictment against me; therefore I am a citizen as good as Cephalus, by his admission.

From many things one may see his unfeelingness and malignity, but especially from his discourse about fortune. For my part, I regard any one who reproaches his fellow-man with fortune as devoid of sense. He that is best satisfied with his condition, he that deems his fortune excellent, cannot be sure that it will remain so until the evening; how, then, can it be right to bring it forward, or upbraid another man with it? As Æschines, however, has on this subject (besides many others) expressed himself with insolence, look, men of Athens, and observe how much more truth and humanity there shall be in my discourse upon fortune than in his.

I hold the fortune of our commonwealth to be good, and so I find the oracles of Dodonæan Jupiter and Pythian Apollo declaring to us. The fortune of all mankind, which now prevails, I consider cruel and dreadful: for what Greek, what barbarian, has not in these times experienced a multitude of evils? That

Athens chose the noblest policy, that she fares better than those very Greeks who thought, if they abandoned us, they should abide in prosperity, I reckon as part of her good fortune: if she suffered reverses, if all happened not to us as we desired, I conceive she has had that share of the general fortune which fell to our lot. As to my fortune (personally speaking) or that of any individual among us, it should, as I conceive, be judged of in connection with personal matters. Such is my opinion upon the subject of fortune, a right and just one, as it appears to me, and I think you will agree with it. Æschines says that my individual fortune is paramount to that of the commonwealth, the small and mean to the good and great. How can this possibly be?

However, if you are determined, Æschines, to scrutinize my fortune, compare it with your own, and, if you find my fortune better than yours, cease to revile it. Look, then, from the very beginning. And I pray and entreat that I may not be condemned for bad taste. I do not think any person wise who insults poverty, or who prides himself on having been bred in affluence; but by the slander and malice of this cruel man I am forced into such a discussion, which I will conduct with all the moderation which circumstances allow.

I had the advantage, Æschines, in my boyhood, of going to proper schools and having such allowance as a boy should have who is to do nothing mean from indigence. Arrived at man's estate I lived suitably to my breeding; was choir master, ship commander, rate payer; backward in no acts of liberality, public or private, but making myself useful to the commonwealth and to my friends. When I entered upon state affairs, I chose such a line of politics that both by my country and many people of Greece I have been crowned many times, and not even you, my enemies, venture to say that the line I chose was not honorable. Such, then, has been the fortune of my life: I could enlarge upon it, but I forbear, lest what I pride myself in should give offense.

But you, the man of dignity, who spit upon others, look what sort of fortune is yours compared with mine. As a boy you were reared in abject poverty, waiting with your father on the school, grinding the ink, sponging the benches, sweeping the room, doing the duty of a menial rather than a freeman's son. After you were grown up you attended your mother's initiations, reading her books and helping in all the ceremonies; at night

wrapping the novitiates in fawn skin, swilling, purifying, and scouring them with clay and bran, raising them after the lustration, and bidding them say, "Bad I have scaped, and better I have found"; priding yourself that no one ever howled so lustily —and I believe him! for do not suppose that he who speaks so loud is not a splendid howler! In the daytime you led your noble orgiasts, crowned with fennel and poplar, through the highways, squeezing the big-cheeked serpents and lifting them over your head, and shouting Evœ Sabœ, and capering to the words Hyes Attes, Attes Hyes, saluted by the beldames as leader, conductor, chest bearer, fan bearer, and the like, getting as your reward tarts and biscuits and rolls; for which any man might well bless himself and his fortune.

When you were enrolled among your fellow-townsmen,—by what means I stop not to inquire,—when you were enrolled, however, you immediately selected the most honorable of employments, that of clerk and assistant to our petty magistrates. From this you were removed after a while, having done yourself all that you charge others with; and then, sure enough, you disgraced not your antecedents by your subsequent life, but hiring yourself to those ranting players, as they were called, Simylus and Socrates, you acted third parts, collecting figs and grapes and olives like a fruiterer from other men's farms, and getting more from them than from the playing, in which the lives of your whole company were at stake, for there was an implacable and incessant war between them and the audience, from whom you received so many wounds, that no wonder you taunt as cowards people inexperienced in such encounters.

But passing over what may be imputed to poverty, I will come to the direct charges against your character. You espoused such a line of politics (when at last you thought of taking to them), that, if your country prospered, you lived the life of a hare, fearing and trembling and ever expecting to be scourged for the crimes of which your conscience accused you, though all have seen how bold you were during the misfortunes of the rest. A man who took courage at the death of a thousand citizens— what does he deserve at the hands of the living? A great deal more that I could say about him I shall omit; for it is not all I can tell of his turpitude and infamy which I ought to let slip from my tongue, but only what is not disgraceful to myself to mention.

Contrast now the circumstances of your life and mine, gently and with temper, Æschines, and then ask these people whose fortune they would each of them prefer. You taught reading, I went to school; you performed initiations, I received them; you danced in the chorus, I furnished it; you were assembly clerk, I was a speaker; you acted third parts, I heard you; you broke down, and I hissed; you have worked as a statesman for the enemy, I for my country. I pass by the rest; but this very day I am on my probation for a crown, and am acknowledged to be innocent of all offense, while you are already judged to be a pettifogger, and the question is, whether you shall continue that trade or at once be silenced by not getting a fifth part of the votes. A happy fortune, do you see, you have enjoyed, that you should denounce mine as miserable!

Come, now, let me read the evidence to the jury of public services which I have performed. And by way of comparison do you recite me the verses which you murdered:—

"From Hades and the dusky realms I come."

And

"Ill news, believe me, I am loth to bear."

Ill betide thee, say I, and may the gods, or at least the Athenians, confound thee for a vile citizen and a vile third-rate actor! Read the evidence. [The evidence is read.]

Such has been my character in political matters. In private, if you do not all know that I have been liberal and humane and charitable to the distressed, I am silent; I will say not a word; I will offer no evidence on the subject, either of persons whom I ransomed from the enemy, or of persons whose daughters I helped to portion, or anything of the kind. For this is my maxim. I hold that the party receiving an obligation should ever remember it, the party conferring should forget it immediately, if the one is to act with honesty, the other without meanness. To remind and speak of your own bounties is next door to reproaching. I will not act so; nothing shall induce me. Whatever my reputation is in these respects, I am content with it.

I will have done then with private topics, but say another word or two upon public. If you can mention, Æschines, a single man under the sun, whether Greek or barbarian, who has not suffered by Philip's power formerly and Alexander's now,

well and good; I concede to you that my fortune, or misfortune (if you please), has been the cause of everything. But if many that never saw me or heard my voice have been grievously afflicted, not individuals only but whole cities and nations, how much juster and fairer is it to consider that to the common fortune apparently of all men, to a tide of events overwhelming and lamentable, these disasters are to be attributed. You, disregarding all this, accuse me whose ministry has been among my countrymen, knowing all the while that a part (if not the whole) of your calumny falls upon the people, and yourself in particular. For if I assumed the sole and absolute direction of our counsels, it was open to you, the other speakers, to accuse me; but if you were constantly present in all the assemblies, if the State invited public discussion of what was expedient, and if these measures were then believed by all to be the best, and especially by you (for certainly from no good-will did you leave me in possession of hopes and admiration and honors, all of which attended on my policy, but doubtless because you were compelled by the truth and had nothing better to advise); is it not iniquitous and monstrous to complain now of measures, than which you could suggest none better at the time?

Among all other people I find these principles in a manner defined and settled—Does a man willfully offend? He is the object of wrath and punishment. Hath a man erred unintentionally? There is pardon instead of punishment for him. Has a man devoted himself to what seemed for the general good, and without any fault or misconduct been in common with all disappointed of success? Such a one deserves not obloquy or reproach, but sympathy. These principles will not be found in our statutes only; Nature herself has defined them by her unwritten laws and the feelings of humanity. Æschines, however, has so far surpassed all men in brutality and malignity, that even things which he cited himself as misfortunes he imputes to me as crimes.

And besides,—as if he himself had spoken everything with candor and good-will,—he told you to watch me, and mind that I did not cajole and deceive you, calling me a great orator, a juggler, a sophist, and the like: as though, if a man say of another what applies to himself, it must be true, and the hearers are not to inquire who the person is that makes the charge. Certain am I that you are all acquainted with my opponent's character, and believe these charges to be more applicable to him than to me. And of this I am sure, that my oratory,—let it be so: though, indeed, I find that the speaker's power depends for the most part on the hearers; for according to your reception and favor it is that the wisdom of a speaker is esteemed,—if I however possess any ability of this sort, you will find it has been exhibited always in public business on your behalf, never against you or on personal matters; whereas that of Æschines has been displayed not only in speaking for the enemy, but against all persons who ever offended or quarreled with him. It is not for justice or the good of the commonwealth that he employs it. A citizen of worth and honor should not call upon judges impaneled in the public service to gratify his anger or hatred or anything of that kind; nor should he come before you upon such grounds. The best thing is not to have these feelings; but, if it cannot be helped, they should be mitigated and restrained.

On what occasions ought an orator and statesman to be vehement? Where any of the commonwealth's main interests are in jeopardy, and he is opposed to the adversaries of the people. Those are the occasions for a generous and brave citizen. But for a person who never sought to punish me for any offense, either public or private, on the state's behalf or on his own, to have got up an accusation because I am crowned and honored, and to have expended such a multitude of words—this is a proof of personal enmity and spite and meanness, not of anything good. And then his leaving the controversy with me, and attacking the defendant, comprises everything that is base.

I should conclude, Æschines, that you undertook this cause to exhibit your eloquence and strength of lungs, not to obtain satisfaction for any wrong. But it is not the language of an orator, Æschines, that has any value, nor yet the tone of his voice, but his adopting the same views with the people, and his hating and loving the same persons that his country does. He that is thus minded will say everything with loyal intention: he that courts persons from whom the commonwealth apprehends danger to herself rides not on the same anchorage with the people, and therefore has not the same expectation of safety. But—do you see? —I have: for my objects are the same with those of my countrymen; I have no interest separate or distinct. Is that so with you? How can it be—when immediately after the battle you went as embassador to Philip, who was at that period the author

V—110

were then avowedly such. They thought it right, also, that the person who was to speak in honor of the fallen and celebrate their valor should not have sat under the same roof or at the same table with their antagonists; that he should not revel there and sing a pæan over the calamities of Greece in company with their murderers, and then come here and receive distinction; that he should not with his voice act the mourner of their fate, but that he should lament over them with his heart. This they perceived in themselves and in me, but not in any of you: therefore they elected me, and not you. Nor, while the people felt thus, did the fathers and brothers of the deceased, who were chosen by the people to perform their obsequies, feel differently. For having to order the funeral banquet (according to custom) at the house of the nearest relative to the deceased, they ordered it at mine. And with reason: because, though each to his own was nearer of kin than I was, none was so near to them all collectively. He that had the deepest interest in their safety and success had upon their mournful disaster the largest share of sorrow for them all.

Read him this epitaph, which the state chose to inscribe on their monument, that you may see even by this, Æschines, what a heartless and malignant wretch you are. Read.

> "These are the patriot brave, who side by side
> Stood to their arms, and dash'd the foeman's pride,
> Firm in their valor, prodigal of life,
> Hades they chose the arbiter of strife;
> That Greeks might ne'er to haughty victors bow,
> Nor thraldom's yoke, nor dire oppression know;
> They fought, they bled, and on their country's breast
> (Such was the doom of heaven) these warriors rest.
> Gods never lack success, nor strive in vain,
> But man must suffer what the fates ordain."

Do you hear, Æschines, in this very inscription, that "gods never lack success, nor strive in vain"? Not to the statesman does it ascribe the power of giving victory in battle, but to the gods. Wherefore, then, execrable man, do you reproach me with these things? Wherefore utter such language? I pray that it may fall upon the heads of you and yours!

Many other accusations and falsehoods he urged against me, O Athenians, but one thing surprised me more than all, that.

of your country's calamities, notwithstanding that you had before persisted in refusing that office, as all men know?

And who is it that deceives the state? Surely the man who speaks not what he thinks. On whom does the crier pronounce a curse? Surely on such a man. What greater crime can an orator be charged with than that his opinions and his language are not the same? Such is found to be your character. And yet you open your mouth, and dare to look these men in the faces! Do you think they don't know you?—or are sunk all in such slumber and oblivion as not to remember the speeches which you delivered in the assembly, cursing and swearing that you had nothing to do with Philip, and that I brought that charge against you out of personal enmity, without foundation? No sooner came the news of the battle than you forgot all that; you acknowledged and avowed that between Philip and yourself there subsisted a relation of hospitality and friendship—new names these for your contract of hire. For upon what plea of equality or justice could Æschines, son of Glaucothea the timbrel player, be the friend or acquaintance of Philip? I cannot see. No! You were hired to ruin the interests of your countrymen; and yet, though you yourself have been caught in open treason, and been informed against yourself after the fact, you revile and reproach me for things which you will find any man is chargeable with sooner than I.

Many great and glorious enterprises has the commonwealth, Æschines, undertaken and succeeded in through me; and she did not forget them. Here is the proof. On the election of a person to speak the funeral oration immediately after the event, you were proposed, but the people would not have you, notwithstanding your fine voice, nor Demades, though he had just made the peace, nor Hegemon, nor any other of your party—but me. And when you and Pythocles came forward in a brutal and shameful manner (O merciful heaven!) and urged the same accusations against me which you now do, and abused me, they elected me all the more. The reason—you are not ignorant of it—yet I will tell you. The Athenians knew as well the loyalty and zeal with which I conducted their affairs, as the dishonesty of you and your party; for what you denied upon oath in our prosperity, you confessed in the misfortunes of the republic. They considered, therefore, that men who got security for their politics by the public disasters had been their enemies long before, and

when he mentioned the late misfortunes of the country, he felt not as became a well-disposed and upright citizen; he shed no tear, experienced no such emotion; with a loud voice exulting, and straining his throat, he imagined apparently that he was accusing me, while he was giving proof against himself that our distresses touched him not in the same manner as the rest. A person who pretends, as he did, to care for the laws and constitution, ought at least to have this about him, that he grieves and rejoices for the same cause as the people, and not by his politics to be enlisted in the ranks of the enemy, as Æschines has plainly done, saying that I am the cause of all, and that the commonwealth has fallen into troubles through me, when it was not owing to my views or principles that you began to assist the Greeks; for, if you conceded this to me, that my influence caused you to resist the subjugation of Greece, it would be a higher honor than any that you have bestowed upon others. I myself would not make such an assertion—it would be doing you injustice—nor would you allow it, I am sure; and Æschines, if he acted honestly, would never, out of enmity to me, have disparaged and defamed the greatest of your glories.

But why do I censure him for this when with calumny far more shocking has he assailed me? He that charges me with Philippizing—O heaven and earth!—what would he not say? By Hercules and the gods! if one had honestly to inquire, discarding all expression of spite and falsehood, who the persons really are on whom the blame of what has happened may by common consent fairly and justly be thrown, it would be found they are persons in the various states like Æschines, not like me—persons who, while Philip's power was feeble and exceedingly small, and we were constantly warning and exhorting and giving salutary counsel, sacrificed the general interests for the sake of selfish lucre, deceiving and corrupting their respective countrymen, until they made them slaves—Daochus, Cineas, Thrasylaus, the Thessalians; Cercidas, Hieronymus, Eucampidas, the Arcadians; Myrtis, Teledamus, Mnaseas, the Argives; Euxitheus, Cleotimus, Aristæchmus, the Eleans; Neon and Thrasylochus, sons of the accursed Philiades, the Messenians; Aristratus, Epichares, the Sicyonians; Dinarchus, Demaratus, the Corinthians; Ptœodorus, Helixus, Perilaus, the Megarians; Timolaus, Theogiton, Anemœtas, the Thebans; Hipparchus, Clitarchus, Sosistratus, the Eubœans. The day will not last me to recount the names of the traitors. All these, O Athenians, are men of the same politics in their own countries as this party among you,—profligates and parasites and miscreants, who have each of them crippled their fatherlands; toasted away their liberty, first to Philip and last to Alexander; who measure happiness by their belly and all that is base, while freedom and independence, which the Greeks of olden time regarded as the test and standard of well-being, they have annihilated.

Of this base and infamous conspiracy and profligacy,—or rather, O Athenians, if I am to speak in earnest, of this betrayal of Grecian liberty,—Athens is by all mankind acquitted, owing to my counsels; and I am acquitted by you. Then do you ask me, Æschines, for what merit I claim to be honored? I will tell you. Because, while all the statesmen in Greece, beginning with yourself, have been corrupted formerly by Philip and now by Alexander, me neither opportunity, nor fair speeches, nor large promises, nor hope, nor fear, nor anything else, could tempt or induce to betray aught that I considered just and beneficial to my country. Whatever I have advised my fellow-citizens, I have never advised like you men, leaning as in a balance to the side of profit; all my proceedings have been those of a soul upright, honest, and incorrupt; intrusted with affairs of greater magnitude than any of my contemporaries, I have administered them all honestly and faithfully. Therefore do I claim to be honored.

As to this fortification, for which you ridiculed me, of the wall and fosse, I regard them as deserving of thanks and praise, and so they are; but I place them nowhere near my acts of administration. Not with stones nor with bricks did I fortify Athens, nor is this the ministry on which I most pride myself. Would you view my fortifications aright, you will find arms and states and posts and harbors and galleys and horses and men for their defense. These are the bulwarks with which I protected Attica as far as was possible by human wisdom; with these I fortified our territory, not the circle of Piræus or the city. Nay, more; I was not beaten by Philip in estimates or preparations; far from it; but the generals and forces of the allies were overcome by his fortune. Where are the proofs of this? They are plain and evident. Consider.

What was the course becoming a loyal citizen—a statesman serving his country with all possible forethought and zeal and fidelity? Should he not have covered Attica on the seaboard

with Eubœa, on the midland frontier with Bœotia, on the Peloponnesian with the people of that confine? Should he not have provided for the conveyance of corn along a friendly coast all the way to Piræus? preserved certain places that belonged to us by sending off succors, and by advising and moving accordingly,—Proconnesus, Chersonesus, Tenedos? brought others into alliance and confederacy with us,—Byzantium, Abydus, Eubœa? cut off the principal resources of the enemy, and supplied what the commonwealth was deficient in? All this has been accomplished by my decrees and measures; and whoever will examine them without prejudice, men of Athens, will find they were rightly planned and faithfully executed; that none of the proper seasons were lost or missed or thrown away by me; nothing which depended on one man's ability and prudence was neglected. But if the power of some deity or fortune, or the worthlessness of commanders, or the wickedness of you that betrayed your countries, or all these things together, injured and eventually ruined our cause, of what is Demosthenes guilty? Had there been in each of the Greek cities one such man as I was in my station among you, or, rather, had Thessaly possessed one single man, and Arcadia one, of the same sentiments as myself, none of the Greeks either beyond or within Thermopylæ would have suffered their present calamities; all would have been free and independent, living prosperously in their own countries with perfect safety and security, thankful to you and the rest of the Athenians for such manifold blessings through me.

To show you that I greatly understate my services for fear of giving offense, here—read me this—the list of auxiliaries procured by my decrees. [The list is read.]

These and the like measures, Æschines, are what become an honorable citizen (by their success—O earth and heaven!—we should have been the greatest of people incontestably, and deserved to be so: even under their failure the result is glory, and no one blames Athens or her policy: all condemn fortune that so ordered things); but never will he desert the interests of the commonwealth, nor hire himself to her adversaries, and study the enemy's advantage instead of his country's; nor on a man who has courage to advise and propose measures worthy of the state, and resolution to persevere in them, will he cast an evil eye, and, if any one privately offend him, remember and treasure it up; no, nor keep himself in a criminal and treacherous retirement, as you so

often do. There is, indeed, a retirement just and beneficial to the state, such as you, the bulk of my countrymen, innocently enjoy: that, however, is not the retirement of Æschines; far from it. Withdrawing himself from public life when he pleases,—and that is often,—he watches for the moment when you are tired of a constant speaker, or when some reverse of fortune has befallen you, or anything untoward has happened (and many are the casualties of human life): at such a crisis he springs up as an orator, rising from his retreat like a wind; in full voice, with words and phrases collected, he rolls them out audibly and breathlessly, to no advantage or good purpose whatsoever, but to the detriment of some or other of his fellow-citizens and to the general disgrace.

Yet from this labor and diligence, Æschines, if it proceeded from an honest heart, solicitous for your country's welfare, the fruits should have been rich and noble and profitable to all—alliances of states, supplies of money, conveniences of commerce, enactment of useful laws, opposition to our declared enemies. All such things were looked for in former times,—and many opportunities did the past afford for a good man and true to show himself,—during which time you are nowhere to be found, neither first, second, third, fourth, fifth, nor sixth—not in any rank at all—certainly on no service by which your country was exalted. For what alliance has come to the state by your procurement? What succors, what acquisition of good-will or credit? What embassy or agency is there of yours, by which the reputation of the country has been increased? What concern domestic, Hellenic, or foreign, of which you have had the management, has improved under it? What galleys? what ammunition? what arsenals? what repair of walls? what cavalry? What in the world are you good for? What assistance in money have you ever given, either to the rich or the poor, out of public spirit or liberality? None. But, good sir, if there is nothing of this, there is at all events zeal and loyalty. Where? when? You infamous fellow! Even at a time when all who ever spoke upon the platform gave something for the public safety, and last Aristonicus gave the sum which he had amassed to retrieve his franchise, you neither came forward nor contributed a mite—not from inability—no! for you have inherited above five talents from Philo, your wife's father, and you had a subscription of two talents from the chairmen of the boards for what you did to cut up the

navy law. But, that I may not go from one thing to another and lose sight of the question, I pass this by. That it was not poverty prevented your contributing, already appears; it was, in fact, your anxiety to do nothing against those to whom your political life is subservient. On what occasions, then, do you show your spirit? When do you shine out? When aught is to be spoken against your countrymen!—then it is you are splendid in voice, perfect in memory, an admirable actor, a tragic Theocrines.

You mention the good men of olden times; and you are right so to do. Yet it is hardly fair, O Athenians, that he should get the advantage of that respect which you have for the dead, to compare and contrast me with them,—me who am living among you; for what mortal is ignorant that toward the living there exists always more or less of ill-will, whereas the dead are no longer hated even by an enemy? Such being human nature, am I to be tried and judged by the standard of my predecessors? Heaven forbid! It is not just or equitable, Æschines! Let me be compared with you, or any persons you like of your party who are still alive. And consider this—whether it is more honorable and better for the state, that because of the services of a former age, prodigious though they are beyond all power of expression, those of the present generation should be unrequited and spurned, or that all who give proof of their good intentions should have their share of honor and regard from the people. Yet, indeed,—if I must say so much,—my politics and principles, if considered fairly, will be found to resemble those of the illustrious ancients, and to have had the same objects in view, while yours resemble those of their calumniators; for it is certain there were persons in those times who ran down the living, and praised people dead and gone, with a malignant purpose like yourself.

You say that I am nothing like the ancients. Are you like them, Æschines? Is your brother, or any of our speakers? I assert that no one is. But pray, my good fellow (that I may give you no other name), try the living with the living and with his competitors, as you would in all cases—poets, dancers, athletes. Philammon did not, because he was inferior to Glaucus of Carystus and some other champions of a bygone age, depart uncrowned from Olympia, but, because he beat all who entered the ring against him, was crowned and proclaimed conqueror. So I ask you to compare me with the orators of the day, with yourself, with anyone you like: I yield to none. When the commonwealth was at liberty to choose for her advantage, and patriotism was a matter of emulation, I showed myself a better counselor than any, and every act of state was pursuant to my decrees and laws and negotiations; none of your party was to be seen, unless you had to do the Athenians a mischief. After that lamentable occurrence, when there was a call no longer for advisers, but for persons obedient to command, persons ready to be hired against their country and willing to flatter strangers, then all of you were in occupation, grand people with splendid equipages; I was powerless, I confess, though more attached to my countrymen than you.

Two things, men of Athens, are characteristic of a well-disposed citizen,—so may I speak of myself and give the least offense:—In authority, his constant aim should be the dignity and pre-eminence of the commonwealth; in all times and circumstances his spirit should be loyal. This depends upon nature; power and might upon other things. Such a spirit, you will find, I have ever sincerely cherished. Only see. When my person was demanded—when they brought Amphictyonic suits against me—when they menaced—when they promised—when they set these miscreants like wild beasts upon me—never in any way have I abandoned my affection for you. From the very beginning I chose an honest and straightforward course in politics, to support the honor, the power, the glory of my fatherland, these to exalt, in these to have my being. I do not walk about the market place gay and cheerful because the stranger has prospered, holding out my right hand and congratulating those whom I think will report it yonder, and on any news of our own success shudder and groan and stoop to the earth, like these impious men who rail at Athens, as if in so doing they did not rail at themselves; who look abroad, and if the foreigner thrive by the distresses of Greece, are thankful for it, and say we should keep him so thriving to all time.

Never, O ye gods, may those wishes be confirmed by you! If possible, inspire even in these men a better sense and feeling! But if they are, indeed, incurable, destroy them by themselves; exterminate them on land and sea; and for the rest of us, grant that we may speedily be released from our present fears, and enjoy a lasting deliverance!

THE SECOND OLYNTHIAC

(Delivered at Athens 349, B. C.)

ON MANY occasions, men of Athens, one may see the kindness of the gods to this country manifested, but most signally, I think, on the present. That here are men prepared for a war with Philip, possessed of a neighboring territory and some power, and (what is most important) so fixed in their hostility as to regard any accommodation with him as insecure, and even ruinous to their country; this really appears like an extraordinary act of divine beneficence. It must then be our care, Athenians, that we are not more unkind to ourselves than circumstances have been; as it would be a foul, a most foul reproach, to have abandoned not only cities and places that once belonged to us, but also the allies and advantages provided by fortune.

To dilate, Athenians, on Philip's power, and by such discourse to incite you to your duty, I think improper: and why? Because all that may be said on that score involves matter of glory for him, and misconduct on our part. The more he has transcended his repute, the more is he universally admired; you, as you have used your advantages unworthily, have incurred the greater disgrace. This topic, then, I shall pass over. Indeed, Athenians, a correct observer will find the source of his greatness here, and not in himself. But of measures, for which Philip's partisans deserve his gratitude and your vengeance, I see no occasion to speak now. Other things are open to me, which it concerns you all to know, and which must, on a due examination, Athenians, reflect great disgrace on Philip. To these will I address myself.

To call him perjured and treacherous, without showing what he has done, might justly be termed idle abuse. But to go through all his actions and convict him in detail, will take, as it happens, but a short time, and is expedient, I think, for two reasons: Firstly, that his baseness may appear in its true light; secondly, that they, whose terror imagines Philip to be invincible, may see he has run through all the artifices by which he rose to greatness, and his career is just come to an end. I myself, men of Athens, should most assuredly have regarded Philip as an object of fear and admiration, had I seen him exalted by honorable

conduct; but observing and considering, I find that in the beginning, when certain persons drove away the Olynthians who desired a conference with us, he gained over our simplicity by engaging to surrender Amphipolis, and to execute the secret article once so famous; afterward he got the friendship of the Olynthians, by taking Potidæa from you, wronging you, his former allies, and delivering it to them; and lastly now the Thessalians, by promising to surrender Magnesia, and undertake the Phocian war on their behalf. In short, none who have dealt with him has he not deceived. He has risen by conciliating and cajoling the weakness of every people in turn who knew him not. As, therefore, by such means he rose, when every people imagined he would advance their interest, so ought he by the same means to be pulled down again, when the selfish aim of his whole policy is exposed.

To this crisis, O Athenians, are Philip's affairs come; or let any man stand forward and prove to me, or rather to you, that my assertions are false, or that men whom Philip has once overreached will trust him hereafter, or that the Thessalians who have been degraded into servitude would not gladly become free.

But if any among you, though agreeing in these statements, think that Philip will maintain his power by having occupied forts and havens and the like, this is a mistake. True, when a confederacy subsists by good-will, and all parties to the war have a common interest, men are willing to co-operate and bear hardships and persevere. But when one has grown strong, like Philip, by rapacity and artifice, on the first pretext, the slightest reverse, all is overturned and broken up. Impossible is it,—impossible, Athenians,—to acquire a solid power by injustice and perjury and falsehood. Such things last for once, or for a short period; maybe, they blossom fairly with hope; but in time they are discovered and drop away. As a house, a ship, or the like, ought to have the lower parts firmest, so in human conduct, I ween, the principle and foundation should be just and true. But this is not so in Philip's conduct.

I say, then, we should at once aid the Olynthians (the best and quickest way that can be suggested will please me most), and send an embassy to the Thessalians, to inform some of our measures and to stir up the rest; for they have now resolved to demand Pagasæ, and remonstrate about Magnesia. But look to

this, Athenians, that our envoys shall not only make speeches, but have some real proof that we have gone forth as becomes our country, and are engaged in action. All speech without action appears vain and idle, but especially that of our commonwealth; as the more we are thought to excel therein, the more is our speaking distrusted by all. You must show yourselves greatly reformed, greatly changed, contributing, serving personally, acting promptly, before any one will pay attention to you. And if ye will perform these duties properly and becomingly, Athenians, not only will it appear that Philip's alliances are weak and precarious, but the poor state of his native empire and power will be revealed.

To speak roundly, the Macedonian power and empire is very well as a help, as it was for you in Timotheus's time against the Olynthians; likewise for them against Potidæa the conjunction was important; and lately it aided the Thessalians in their broils and troubles against the regnant house: and the accession of any power, however small, is undoubtedly useful. But the Macedonian is feeble of itself, and full of defects. The very operations which seem to constitute Philip's greatness, his wars and his expeditions, have made it more insecure than it was originally. Think not, Athenians, that Philip and his subjects have the same likings. He desires glory, makes that his passion, is ready for any consequence of adventure and peril, preferring to a life of safety the honor of achieving what no Macedonian king ever did before. They have no share in the glorious result; ever harassed by these excursions up and down, they suffer and toil incessantly, allowed no leisure for their employments or private concerns, unable even to dispose of their hard earnings, the markets of the country being closed on account of the war. By this, then, may easily be seen how the Macedonians in general are disposed to Philip. His mercenaries and guards, indeed, have the reputation of admirable and well-trained soldiers, but, as I heard from one who had been in the country, a man incapable of falsehood, they are no better than others. For if there be any among them experienced in battles and campaigns, Philip is jealous of such men and drives them away, he says, wishing to keep the glory of all actions to himself,—his jealousy (among other failings) being excessive. Or if any man be generally good and virtuous, unable to bear Philip's daily intemperances, drunkenness, and indecencies, he is pushed aside and accounted as nobody. The rest about him are brigands and parasites and men of that character, who will get drunk and perform dances which I scruple to name before you. My information is undoubtedly true; for persons whom all scouted here as worse rascals than mountebanks, Callias the town-slave and the like of him, antic-jesters and composers of ribald songs to lampoon their companions, such persons Philip caresses and keeps about him. Small matters these may be thought, Athenians, but to the wise they are strong indications of his character and wrong-headedness. Success, perhaps, throws a shade over them now; prosperity is a famous hider of such blemishes; but on any miscarriage they will be fully exposed. And this (trust me, Athenians) will appear in no long time, if the gods so will and you determine. For as in the human body, a man in health feels not partial ailments, but, when illness occurs, all are in motion, whether it be a rupture or a sprain or anything else unsound, so with states and monarchs, while they wage eternal war, their weaknesses are undiscerned by most men, but the tug of a frontier war betrays all.

If any of you think Philip a formidable opponent because they see he is fortunate, such reasoning is prudent, Athenians. Fortune has, indeed, a great preponderance—nay, is everything in human affairs. Not but that, if I had the choice, I should prefer our fortune to Philip's, would you but moderately perform your duty. For I see you have many more claims to the divine favor than he has. But we sit doing nothing; and a man idle himself cannot require even his friends to act for him, much less the gods. No wonder, then, that he, marching and toiling in person, present on all occasions, neglecting no time or season, prevails over us delaying and voting and inquiring. I marvel not at that; the contrary would have been marvelous, if we, doing none of the duties of war, had beaten one doing all. But this surprises me that formerly, Athenians, you resisted the Lacedæmonians for the rights of Greece, and rejecting many opportunities of selfish gain, to secure the rights of others, expended your property in contributions, and bore the brunt of the battle; yet now you are loath to serve, slow to contribute, in defense of your own possessions, and, though you have often saved the other nations of Greece collectively and individually, under your own losses you sit still. This surprises me, and one thing more, Athenians, that not one of you can reckon how long your war with Philip has lasted, and what you have been doing while the

time has passed. You surely know that while you have been delaying, expecting others to act, accusing, trying one another, expecting again, doing much the same as ye do now, all the time has passed away. Then are ye so senseless, Athenians, as to imagine that the same measures which have brought the country from a prosperous to a poor condition will bring it from a poor to a prosperous? Unreasonable were this and unnatural; for all things are easier kept than gotten. The war now has left us nothing to keep; we have all to get, and the work must be done by ourselves.

I say, then, you must contribute money, serve in person with alacrity, accuse no one, till you have gained your objects; then, judging from facts, honor the deserving, punish offenders; let there be no pretenses or defaults on your own part; for you can not harshly scrutinize the conduct of others, unless you have done what is right yourselves. Why, think you, do all the generals whom you commission avoid this war and seek wars of their own? (For of the generals, too, must a little truth be told.) Because here the prizes of the war are yours; for example, if Amphipolis be taken, you will immediately recover it; the commanders have all the risk and no reward. But in the other case the risks are less, and the gains belong to the commanders and soldiers; Lampsacus, Sigeum, the vessels which they plunder. So they proceed to secure their several interests: you, when you look at the bad state of your affairs, bring the generals to trial; but when they get a hearing and plead these necessities, you dismiss them. The result is that, while you are quarreling and divided, some holding one opinion, some another, the commonwealth goes wrong. Formerly, Athenians, you had boards for taxes; now you have boards for politics. There is an orator presiding on either side, a general under him, and three hundred men to shout; the rest of you are attached to the one party or the other. This you must leave off; be yourselves again; establish a general liberty of speech, deliberation, and action. If some be appointed to command as with royal authority, some to be ship captains, tax payers, soldiers by compulsion, others only to vote against them, and help in nothing besides, no duty will be seasonably performed; the aggrieved parties will still fail you, and you will have to punish them instead of your enemies. I say, in short, you must all fairly contribute, according to each man's ability: take your turns of service till you have all been

afield; give every speaker a hearing, and adopt the best counsel, not what this or that person advises. If ye act thus, not only will ye praise the speaker at the moment, but yourselves afterward, when the condition of the country is improved.

THE ORATION ON THE PEACE

(Delivered at Athens 346, B. C.)

I SEE, men of Athens, our affairs are in great perplexity and confusion, not only because many interests have been sacrificed, and it is useless to make fine speeches about them, but because, for preserving what remains, you cannot agree upon any single expedient, some holding one opinion, and some another. And besides, perplexing and difficult as deliberation of itself is, you, Athenians, have rendered it far more so. For other men usually hold counsel before action, you hold it after; the result of which during all the time of my remembrance has been that the censurer of your errors gets repute and credit as a good speaker, while your interests and objects of deliberation are lost. Yet, even under these circumstances, I believe, and I have risen with the persuasion, that if you will desist from wrangling and tumult, and listen as becomes men on a political consultation of such importance, I shall be able to suggest and advise measures by which our affairs may be improved and our losses retrieved.

Well as I know, Athenians, that to talk before you of one's self and one's own counsels is a successful artifice with unscrupulous men, I think it so vulgar and offensive that I shrink from it even in a case of necessity. However, I think you will better appreciate what I shall say now, by calling to mind a little that I said on former occasions. For example, Athenians, when they were advising you in the troubles of Eubœa to assist Plutarch, and undertake a discreditable and expensive war, I, and I alone, stood forward to oppose it, and was nearly torn to pieces by the men who for petty lucre have seduced you into many grievous errors. A short time later, when you incurred disgrace and suffered what no mortals ever did from parties whom they assisted, you all acknowledged the worthlessness of their counsels who misled you and the soundness of mine. Again, Athenians, when I saw that Neoptolemus the actor, privileged under color of

his profession, was doing serious mischief to the state, managing and directing things at Athens on Philip's behalf, I came and informed you, not from any private enmity or malice, as subsequent occurrences have shown. And herein I shall not blame the advocates of Neoptolemus (for there were none), but you yourselves; for had you been seeing a tragedy in the temple of Bacchus, instead of it being a debate on the public weal and safety, you could not have heard him with more partiality, or me with more intolerance. But I suppose you all now understand that he made his journey to the enemy in order (as he said) to get the debts there owing to him, and defray thereout his public charges at home; and, after urging this argument, that it was hard to reproach men who brought over their effects from abroad as soon as he obtained security through the peace, he converted into money all the real estate which he possessed here, and has gone off with it to Philip. Thus two of my warnings, justly and rightfully pronounced in accordance with the truth, testify in my favor as a counselor. A third, men of Athens, I will mention, this one only, and straight proceed to the subject of my address. When we embassadors, after receiving the oaths on the peace, had returned, and certain men were promising that Thespiæ and Platæa would be repeopled; that Philip, if he got the mastery, would save the Phocians, and disperse the population of Thebes; that Oropus would be yours, and Eubœa given as compensation for Amphipolis, with more of the like hopes and delusions which led you on, against policy, equity, and honor, to abandon the Phocians; you will find I neither aided in any of these deceits, nor held my tongue. I warned you, as you surely remember, that I knew not of these things nor expected them, and deemed it all idle gossip.

These instances, wherein I have shown greater foresight than others, I mention not by way of boast, nor ascribe, Athenians, to any sagacity of my own, nor will I pretend to discover or discern the future from any but two causes, which I will state: Firstly, men of Athens, through good fortune, which I observe beats all the craft and cleverness of man; secondly, because I judge and estimate things disinterestedly, and no one can show that any lucre is attached to my politics or my speeches. Therefore, whatever be your true policy as indicated by the circumstances, I have a correct view of it; but when you put money on one side as in a balance, it carries away and pulls down the judgment with it, and he that does so can no longer reason upon anything justly or soundly.

The first thing which I maintain to be necessary is this: Whether you seek to obtain allies or contribution or aught else for the state, do it without disturbing the present peace; not that it is very glorious or worthy of you, but, whatever be its character, it had better suited our interests never to have made peace than to break it ourselves, for we have thrown away many advantages which would have rendered the war then safer and easier for us than it can be now. Secondly, Athenians, we must take care that these people assembled and calling themselves Amphictyons are not by us necessitated or furnished with a plea to make a common war against us. I grant, if we renewed the war with Philip on account of Amphipolis or any such private quarrel in which Thessalians, Argives, and Thebans are not concerned, none of them would join in it, and least of all—hear me before you cry out—the Thebans; not that they are kindly disposed to us or would not gratify Philip, but they see clearly, stupid as one may think them, that, if they had a war with you, the hardships would all be theirs, while another sat waiting for the advantages. Therefore, they would not throw themselves into it, unless the ground and origin of the war were common. So if we again went to war with the Thebans for Oropus or any private cause, I should fear no disaster, because our respective auxiliaries would assist us or them, if either country were invaded, but would join with neither in aggression. Such is the spirit of alliances that are worth regard, and so the thing naturally is. People are not friendly either to us or the Thebans to the extent of equally desiring our safety and our predominance. Safe they would all have us for their own sakes; dominant, so as to become their masters, they would not have either of us. What then, say I, is the danger? What is to be guarded against, lest in the coming war there be found a common plea, a common grievance for all? If Argives, and Messenians, and Megalopolitans, and some of the other Peloponnesians, who are in league with them, are hostile to us on account of our negotiating with the Lacedæmonians and seeming to take up some of their enterprises; if the Thebans are (as they say) our enemies, and will be more so, because we harbor their exiles and in every way manifest our aversion to them; Thessalians again, because we harbor the Phocian exiles, and Philip, because we oppose his admission

V—III

more beneficial than strife and contest about such questions. It were folly then and utter absurdity after dealing thus with each party singly on matters of vital moment to ourselves, to battle now with them all for a shadow at Delphi.

THE SECOND PHILIPPIC

(Delivered at Athens 344, B. C.)

IN ALL the speeches, men of Athens, about Philip's measures and infringements of the peace, I observe that statements made on our behalf are thought just and generous, and all who accuse Philip are heard with approbation; yet nothing (I may say) that is proper, or for the sake of which the speeches are worth hearing, is done. To this point are the affairs of Athens brought, that the more fully and clearly one convicts Philip of violating the peace with you, and plotting against the whole of Greece, the more difficult it becomes to advise you how to act. The cause lies in all of us, Athenians, that, when we ought to oppose an ambitious power by deeds and actions, not by words, we men of the hustings shrink from our duty of moving and advising, for fear of your displeasure, and only declaim on the heinousness and atrocity of Philip's conduct; you of the assembly, though better instructed than Philip to argue justly, or comprehend the argument of another, are totally unprepared to check him in the execution of his designs. The result is inevitable, I, imagine, and perhaps just. You each succeed better in what you are busy and earnest about; Philip in actions, you in words. If you are still satisfied with using the better arguments, it is an easy matter, and there is no trouble: but if we are to take measures for the correction of these evils, to prevent their insensible progress and the rising up of a mighty power, against which we could have no defense, then our course of deliberation is not the same as formerly; the orators, and you that hear them, must prefer good and salutary counsels to those which are easy and agreeable.

First, men of Athens, if any one regard without uneasiness the might and dominion of Philip, and imagine that it threatens no danger to the state, or that all his preparations are not aimed against you, I marvel, and would entreat you every one to hear briefly from me the reasons why I am led to form a contrary expectation, and wherefore I deem Philip an enemy; that, if I appear

to the Amphictyonic body; I fear that, each incensed on a private quarrel, they will combine to bring war upon you, setting up the decrees of the Amphictyons, and be drawn on (beyond what their single interests require) to battle it with us, as they did with the Phocians. For you are surely aware that now the Thebans and Philip and the Thessalians have co-operated, without having each exactly the same views. For example, the Thebans could not hinder Philip from advancing and occupying the passes, nor yet from coming last and having the credit of their labors. True, in respect of territorial acquisition, something has been done for them; but in regard to honor and reputation, they have fared wretchedly; since, had Philip not stepped in, they would (it seems) have got nothing. This was not agreeable to them, but having the wish without the power to obtain Orchomenos and Coronea, they submitted to it all. Of Philip, you know, some persons venture to say that he would not have given Orchomenos and Coronea to the Thebans, but was compelled to do so. I wish them joy of their opinion, but thus far I believe that he cared not so much about that business as he desired to occupy the passes and have the glory of the war, as being determined by his agency and the direction of the Pythian games. Such were the objects of his ambition. The Thessalians wished not either Philip or Thebes to be aggrandized, since in both they saw danger to themselves, but sought to obtain these two advantages, the synod at Thermopylæ, and the privileges at Delphi; for which objects they aided the confederacy. Thus you will find that each party has been led into many acts unwillingly: and against this danger being such as I describe, you must take precautions.

Must we, then, do as we are bidden for fear of the consequences? and do you recommend this? Far from it. I advise you so to act as not to compromise your dignity, to avoid war, to prove yourselves right-thinking, just-speaking men. With those who think we should boldly suffer anything and do not foresee the war, I would reason thus. We permit the Thebans to have Oropus; and if one ask us why, and require a true answer, we should say, To avoid war. And to Philip now we have ceded Amphipolis by treaty, and allow the Cardians to be excepted from the other people of the Chersonese; and the Carian to seize the islands Chios, Cos, and Rhodes, and the Byzantines to detain our vessels; evidently because we think the tranquillity of peace

to have the clearer foresight, you may hearken to me; if they, who have such confidence and trust in Philip, you may give your adherence to them.

Thus, then, I reason, Athenians. What did Philip first make himself master of after the peace? Thermopylæ and the Phocian state. Well, and how used he his power? He chose to act for the benefit of Thebes, not of Athens. Why so? Because, I conceive, measuring his calculations by ambition, by his desire of universal empire, without regard to peace, quiet, or justice, he saw plainly that to a people of our character and principles nothing could he offer or give that would induce you for self-interest to sacrifice any of the Greeks to him. He sees that you, having respect for justice, dreading the infamy of the thing, and exercising proper forethought, would oppose him in any such attempt as much as if you were at war: but the Thebans, he expected (and events prove him right), would, in return for the services done them, allow him in everything else to have his way, and, so far from thwarting or impeding him, would fight on his side if he required it. From the same persuasion he befriended lately the Messenians and Argives, which is the highest panegyric upon you, Athenians; for you are adjudged by these proceedings to be the only people incapable of betraying for lucre the national rights of Greece, or bartering your attachment to her for any obligation or benefit. And this opinion of you, that (so different) of the Argives and Thebans, he has naturally formed, not only from a view of present times, but by reflection on the past. For assuredly he finds and hears that your ancestors, who might have governed the rest of Greece on terms of submitting to Persia, not only spurned the proposal, when Alexander, this man's ancestor, came as herald to negotiate, but preferred to abandon their country and endure any suffering, and thereafter achieved such exploits as all the world loves to mention,—though none could ever speak them worthily, and therefore I must be silent, for their deeds are too mighty to be uttered in words. But the forefathers of the Argives and Thebans, they either joined the barbarian's army, or did not oppose it; and therefore he knows that both will selfishly embrace their advantage, without considering the common interest of the Greeks. He thought then, if he chose your friendship, it must be on just principles; if he attached himself to them, he should find auxiliaries of his ambition. This is the reason of his preferring them to you both then and now. For certainly he does not see them with a larger navy than you, nor has he acquired an inland empire and renounced that of the sea and the ports, nor does he forget the professions and promises on which he obtained the peace.

Well, it may be said, he knew all this, yet he so acted, not from ambition or the motives which I charge, but because the demands of the Thebans were more equitable than yours. Of all pleas, this now is the least open to him. He that bids the Lacedæmonians resign Messene, how can he pretend, when he delivered Orchomenos and Coronea to the Thebans, to have acted on a conviction of justice?

But, forsooth, he was compelled,—this plea remains,—he made concessions against his will, being surrounded by Thessalian horse and Theban infantry. Excellent! So of his intentions they talk; he will mistrust the Thebans; and some carry news about, that he will fortify Elatea. All this he intends and will intend, I dare say; but to attack the Lacedæmonians on behalf of Messene and Argos he does not intend; he actually sends mercenaries and money into the country, and is expected himself with a great force. The Lacedæmonians, who are enemies of Thebes, he overthrows; the Phocians, whom he himself before destroyed, will he now preserve?

And who can believe this? I cannot think that Philip, either if he were forced into his former measures, or if he were now giving up the Thebans, would pertinaciously oppose their enemies; his present conduct rather shows that he adopted those measures by choice. All things prove to a correct observer that his whole plan of action is against our state. And this has now become to him a sort of necessity. Consider. He desires empire: he conceives you to be his only opponents. He has been for some time wronging you, as his own conscience best informs him, since, by retaining what belongs to you, he secures the rest of his dominion: had he given up Amphipolis and Potidæa, he deemed himself unsafe at home. He knows, therefore, both that he is plotting against you, and that you are aware of it; and, supposing you to have intelligence, he thinks you must hate him· he is alarmed, expecting some disaster, if you get the chance, unless he hastes to prevent you. Therefore he is awake, and on the watch against us; he courts certain people, Thebans, and people in Peloponnesus of the like views, who from cupidity, he

thinks, will be satisfied with the present, and from dullness of understanding will foresee none of the consequences. And yet men of even moderate sense might notice striking facts, which I had occasion to quote to the Messenians and Argives, and perhaps it is better they should be repeated to you.

Ye men of Messene, said I, how do ye think the Olynthians would have brooked to hear anything against Philip at those times, when he surrendered to them Anthemus, which all former kings of Macedonia claimed, when he cast out the Athenian colonists and gave them Potidæa, taking on himself your enmity, and giving them the land to enjoy? Think ye they expected such treatment as they got, or would have believed it if they had been told? Nevertheless, said I, they, after enjoying for a short time the land of others, are for a long time deprived by him of their own, shamefully expelled, not only vanquished, but betrayed by one another and sold. In truth, these too close connections with despots are not safe for republics. The Thessalians, again, think ye, said I, when he ejected their tyrants, and gave back Nicæa and Magnesia, they expected to have the decemvirate which is now established? or that he who restored the meeting at Pylæ would take away their revenues? Surely not. And yet these things have occurred, as all mankind may know. You behold Philip, I said, a dispenser of gifts and promises: pray, if you are wise, that you may never know him for a cheat and a deceiver. By Jupiter, I said, there are manifold contrivances for the guarding and defending of cities, such as ramparts, walls, trenches, and the like: these are all made with hands, and require expense; but there is one common safeguard in the nature of prudent men, which is a good security for all, but especially for democracies against despots. What do I mean? Mistrust. Keep this, hold to this, preserve this only, and you can never be injured. What do ye desire? Freedom. Then see ye not that Philip's very titles are at variance therewith? Every king and despot is a foe to freedom, an antagonist to laws. Will you not beware, I said, lest, seeking deliverance from war, you find a master?

They heard me with a tumult of approbation; and many other speeches they heard from the embassadors, both in my presence and afterward; yet none the more, as it appears, will they keep aloof from Philip's friendship and promises. And no wonder that Messenians and certain Peloponnesians should act contrary

to what their reason approves; but you, who understand yourselves, and by us orators are told, how you are plotted against, how you are inclosed! you, I fear, to escape present exertion, will come to ruin ere you are aware. So doth the moment's ease and indulgence prevail over distant advantage.

As to your measures, you will in prudence, I presume, consult hereafter by yourselves. I will furnish you with such an answer as it becomes the assembly to decide upon. [Here the proposed answer was read.]

It were just, men of Athens, to call the persons who brought those promises on the faith whereof you concluded peace. For I should never have submitted to go as embassador, and you would certainly not have discontinued the war, had you supposed that Philip, on obtaining peace, would act thus; but the statements then made were very different. Aye, and others you should call. Whom? The men who declared—after the peace, when I had returned from my second mission, that for the oaths, when, perceiving your delusion, I gave warning and protested, and opposed the abandonment of Thermopylæ and the Phocians — that I, being a water-drinker, was naturally a churlish and morose fellow, that Philip, if he passed the straits, would do just as you desired, fortify Thespiæ and Platæa, humble the Thebans, cut through the Chersonese at his own expense, and give you Oropus and Eubœa in exchange for Amphipolis. All these declarations on the hustings I am sure you remember, though you are not famous for remembering injuries. And, the most disgraceful thing of all, you voted in your confidence that this same peace should descend to your posterity,—so completely were you misled. Why mention I this now, and desire these men to be called? By the gods, I will tell you the truth frankly and without reserve. Not that I may fall a-wrangling to provoke recrimination before you, and afford my old adversaries a fresh pretext for getting more from Philip, nor for the purpose of idle garrulity. But I imagine that what Philip is doing will grieve you hereafter more than it does now. I see the thing progressing, and would that my surmises were false; but I doubt it is too near already. So when you are able no longer to disregard events, when, instead of hearing from me or others that these measures are against Athens, you all see it yourselves, and know it for certain, I expect you will be wrathful and exasperated. I fear then, as your embassadors have concealed the purpose for

which they know they were corrupted, those who endeavor to repair what the others have lost may chance to encounter your resentment; for I see it is a practice with many to vent their anger, not upon the guilty, but on persons most in their power. While, therefore, the mischief is only coming and preparing, while we hear one another speak, I wish every man, though he knows it well, to be reminded who it was persuaded you to abandon Phocis and Thermopylæ, by the command of which Philip commands the road to Attica and Peloponnesus, and has brought it to this, that your deliberation must be, not about claims and interests abroad, but concerning the defense of your home and a war in Attica, which will grieve every citizen when it comes, and indeed it has commenced from that day. Had you not been then deceived there would be nothing to distress the state. Philip would certainly never have prevailed at sea and come to Attica with a fleet, nor would he have marched with a land force by Phocis and Thermopylæ; he must either have acted honorably, observing the peace and keeping quiet, or been immediately in a war similar to that which made him desire the peace. Enough has been said to awaken recollection. Grant, O ye gods, it be not all fully confirmed! I would have no man punished, though death he may deserve, to the damage and danger of the country.

CHAUNCEY M. DEPEW

(1834–)

AKING his first reputation for oratory by the facility and grace of his "after-dinner speeches," Chauncey Mitchell Depew has gradually enlarged his field until, during the last decade of the nineteenth century, he has been easily first among New York orators, with a reputation which has become international and has made his speeches as welcome in London as they are in New York. He was born at Peekskill, New York, April 23d, 1834. Graduating at Yale in 1856, he studied law and entered public life as a member of the New York Assembly (1861–62); from 1863 to 1865, he was Secretary of State for New York, and in 1869 he formed a connection with the New York Central Railroad as its counsel, which determined his future career. He became president of the road in 1885. In 1898 was elected to the United States Senate.

THE COLUMBIAN ORATION

(Delivered at the Dedication Ceremonies of the World's Fair at Chicago, October 21st, 1892)

THIS day belongs not to America, but to the world. The results of the event it commemorates are the heritage of the peoples of every race and clime. We celebrate the emancipation of man. The preparation was the work of almost countless centuries; the realization was the revelation of one. The cross on Calvary was hope; the cross raised on San Salvador was opportunity. But for the first, Columbus would never have sailed; but for the second, there would have been no place for the planting, the nurture, and the expansion of civil and religious liberty. Ancient history is a dreary record of unstable civilizations. Each reached its zenith of material splendor, and perished. The Assyrian, Persian, Egyptian, Grecian, and Roman empires were proofs of the possibilities and limitations of man for conquest and intellectual development. Their destruction involved a sum of misery and relapse which made their creation rather a curse than a blessing. Force was the factor in the government

of the world when Christ was born, and force was the source and exercise of authority both by Church and State when Columbus sailed from Palos. The Wise Men traveled from the East towards the West under the guidance of the Star of Bethlehem. The spirit of the equality of all men before God and the law moved westward from Calvary with its revolutionary influence upon old institutions, to the Atlantic Ocean. Columbus carried it westward across the seas. The emigrants from England, Ireland, Scotland, and Wales, from Germany and Holland, from Sweden and Denmark, from France and Italy, from Spain and Portugal, under its guidance and inspiration, moved west, and again west, building states and founding cities until the Pacific limited their march. The exhibition of arts and sciences, of industries and inventions, of education and civilization, which the Republic of the United States will here present, and to which, through its Chief Magistrate, it invites all nations, condenses and displays the flower and fruitage of this transcendent miracle.

The anarchy and chaos which followed the breaking up of the Roman Empire necessarily produced the feudal system. The people, preferring slavery to annihilation by robber chiefs, became the vassals of territorial lords. The reign of physical force is one of perpetual struggle for the mastery. Power which rests upon the sword neither shares nor limits its authority. The king destroyed the lords, and the monarchy succeeded feudalism. Neither of these institutions considered or consulted the people. They had no part but to suffer or die in this mighty strife of masters for the mastery. But the throne, by its broader view and greater resources, made possible the construction of the highways of freedom. Under its banner, races could unite and petty principalities be merged, law substituted for brute force and right for might. It founded and endowed universities, and encouraged commerce. It conceded no political privileges, but unconsciously prepared its subjects to demand them.

Absolutism in the State and intolerance in the Church shackled popular unrest, and imprisoned thought and enterprise in the fifteenth century. The divine right of kings stamped out the faintest glimmer of revolt against tyranny, and the problems of science, whether of the skies or of the earth, whether of astronomy or geography, were solved or submerged by ecclesiastical decrees. The dungeon was ready for the philosopher who proclaimed the truths of the solar system, or the navigator who

would prove the sphericity of the earth. An English Gladstone. or a French Gambetta, or a German Bismarck, or an Italian Garibaldi, or a Spanish Castelar, would have been thought a monster, and his death at the stake, or on the scaffold, and under the anathemas of the Church, would have received the praise and approval of kings and nobles, of priests and peoples. Reason had no seat in spiritual or temporal realms. Punishment was the incentive to patriotism, and piety was held possible by torture. Confessions of faith extorted from the writhing victim on the rack were believed efficacious in saving his soul from fires eternal beyond the grave. For all that humanity to-day cherishes as its best heritage and choicest gifts, there was neither thought nor hope.

Fifty years before Columbus sailed from Palos, Guttenberg and Faust had forged the hammer which was to break the bonds of superstition and open the prison doors of the mind. They had invented the printing press and movable types. The prior adoption of a cheap process for the manufacture of paper at once utilized the press. Its first service, like all its succeeding efforts, was for the people. The universities and the schoolmen, the privileged and the learned few of that age, were longing for the revelation and preservation of the classic treasures of antiquity, hidden, and yet insecure in monastic cells and libraries. But the firstborn of the marvelous creation of these primitive printers of Mayence was the printed Bible. The priceless contributions of Greece and Rome to the intellectual training and development of the modern world came afterwards, through the same wondrous machiné. The force, however, which made possible America and its reflex influence upon Europe was the open Bible by the family fireside. And yet neither the enlightenment of the new learning, nor the dynamic power of the spiritual awakening, could break through the crust of caste which had been forming for centuries. Church and State had so firmly and dexterously interwoven the bars of privilege and authority that liberty was impossible from within. Its piercing light and fervent heat must penetrate from without.

Civil and religious freedom are founded upon the individual and his independence, his worth, his rights, and his equal status and opportunity. For his planting and development a new land must be found where, with limitless areas for expansion, the avenues of progress would have no bars of custom or heredity,

of social orders or privileged classes. The time had come for the emancipation of the mind and soul of humanity. The factors wanting for its fulfillment were the new world and its discoverer.

God always has in training some commanding genius for the control of great crises in the affairs of nations and peoples. The number of these leaders is less than the centuries, but their lives are the history of human progress. Though Cæsar and Charlemagne and Hildebrand and Luther and William the Conqueror and Oliver Cromwell and all the epoch-makers prepared Europe for the event, and contributed to the result, the lights which illumine our firmament to-day are Columbus the discoverer, Washington the founder, and Lincoln the savior.

Neither realism nor romance furnishes a more striking and picturesque figure than that of Christopher Columbus. The mystery about his origin heightens the charm of his story. That he came from among the toilers of his time is in harmony with the struggles of our period. Forty-four authentic portraits of him have descended to us, and no two of them are the counterfeits of the same person. Each represents a character as distinct as its canvas. Strength and weakness, intellectuality and stupidity, high moral purpose and brutal ferocity, purity and licentiousness, the dreamer and the miser, the pirate and the Puritan, are the types from which we may select our hero. We dismiss the painter, and piercing with the clarified vision of the dawn of the twentieth century the veil of four hundred years, we construct our Columbus.

The perils of the sea in his youth upon the rich argosies of Genoa, or in the service of the licensed rovers who made them their prey, had developed a skillful navigator and intrepid mariner. They had given him a glimpse of the possibilities of the unknown beyond the highways of travel, which roused an unquenchable thirst for adventure and research. The study of the narratives of previous explorers and diligent questionings of the daring spirits who had ventured far towards the fabled West gradually evolved a theory which became in his mind so fixed a fact that he could inspire others with his own passionate beliefs. The words, "That is a lie," written by him on the margin of nearly every page of a volume of the travels of Marco Polo, which is still to be found in a Genoese library, illustrate the skepticism of his beginning, and the first vision of the New World the fulfillment of his faith.

To secure the means to test the truth of his speculations, this poor and unknown dreamer must win the support of kings and overcome the hostility of the Church. He never doubted his ability to do both, though he knew of no man living who was so great in power, or lineage, or learning, that he could accomplish either. Unaided and alone he succeeded in arousing the jealousies of sovereigns, and dividing the councils of the ecclesiastics. "I will command your fleet and discover for you new realms, but only on condition that you confer on me hereditary nobility, the Admiralty of the Ocean and the Vice-Royalty and one-tenth the revenues of the New World," were his haughty terms to King John of Portugal. After ten years of disappointment and poverty, subsisting most of the time upon the charity of the enlightened monk of the Convent of Rabida, who was his unfaltering friend, he stood before the throne of Ferdinand and Isabella, and, rising to imperial dignity in his rags, embodied the same royal conditions in his petition. The capture of Granada, the expulsion of Islam from Europe, and the triumph of the Cross, aroused the admiration and devotion of Christendom. But this proud beggar, holding in his grasp the potential promise and dominion of El Dorado and Cathay, divided with the Moslem surrender the attention of sovereigns and of bishops. France and England indicated a desire to hear his theories and see his maps while he was still a suppliant at the gates of the camp of Castile and Aragon, the sport of its courtiers, and the scoff of its confessors. His unshakable faith that Christopher Columbus was commissioned from heaven, both by his name and by Divine command, to carry "Christ across the sea" to new continents and pagan peoples lifted him so far above the discouragements of an empty purse and a contemptuous court that he was proof against the rebuffs of fortune or of friends. To conquer the prejudices of the clergy, to win the approval and financial support of the State, to venture upon that unknown ocean, which, according to the beliefs of the age, was peopled with demons and savage beasts of frightful shape, and from which there was no possibility of return, required the zeal of Peter the Hermit, the chivalric courage of the Cid, and the imagination of Dante. Columbus belonged to that high order of "cranks" who confidently walk where "angels fear to tread," and often become the benefactors of their country or their kind.

he was unconsciously making for the port of civil and religious liberty. Thinkers who believed men capable of higher destinies and larger responsibilities, and pious people who preferred the Bible to that union of Church and State where each serves the other for the temporal benefit of both, fled to these distant and hospitable lands from intolerable and hopeless oppression at home. It required three hundred years for the people thus happily situated to understand their own powers and resources and to break bonds which were still revered or loved, no matter how deeply they wounded or how hard they galled.

The nations of Europe were so completely absorbed in dynastic difficulties and devastating wars, with diplomacy and ambitions, that, if they heard of, they did not heed the growing democratic spirit and intelligence in their American colonies. To them these provinces were sources of revenue, and they never dreamed that they were also schools of liberty. That it exhausted three centuries under the most favorable conditions for the evolution of freedom on this continent demonstrates the tremendous strength of custom and heredity when sanctioned and sanctified by religion. The very chains which fettered became inextricably interwoven with the habits of life, the associations of childhood, the tenderest ties of the family, and the sacred offices of the Church from the cradle to the grave. It clearly proves that if the people of the Old World and their descendants had not possessed the opportunities afforded by the New for their emancipation, and mankind had never experienced and learned the American example, instead of living in the light and glory of nineteenth-century conditions they would still be struggling with mediæval problems.

The northern continent was divided among England, France, and Spain, and the southern between Spain and Portugal. France, wanting the capacity for colonization, which still characterizes her, gave up her western possessions and left the English, who have the genius of universal empire, masters of North America. The development of the experiment in the English domain makes this day memorable. It is due to the wisdom and courage, the faith and virtue of the inhabitants of this territory, that government of the people, for the people, and by the people was inaugurated and has become a triumphant success. The Puritan settled in New England and the Cavalier in the South. They represented the opposites of spiritual and temporal life

It was a happy omen of the position which woman was to hold in America that the only person who comprehended the majestic scope of his plans and the invincible quality of his genius was the able and gracious Queen of Castile. Isabella alone of all the dignitaries of that age shares with Columbus the honors of his great achievement. She arrayed her kingdom and her private fortune behind the enthusiasm of this mystic mariner, and posterity pays homage to her wisdom and faith.

The overthrow of the Mohammedan power in Spain would have been a forgotten scene in one of the innumerable acts in the grand drama of history had not Isabella conferred immortality upon herself, her husband, and their dual crown, by her recognition of Columbus. The devout spirit of the Queen and the high purpose of the explorer inspired the voyage, subdued the mutinous crew, and prevailed over the raging storms. They covered with the divine radiance of religion and humanity the degrading search for gold and the horrors of its quest, which filled the first century of conquest with every form of lust and greed.

The mighty soul of the great admiral was undaunted by the ingratitude of princes and the hostility of the people by imprisonment and neglect. He died as he was securing the means and preparing a campaign for the rescue of the Holy Sepulchre at Jerusalem from the infidel. He did not know what time has revealed, that while the mission of the crusades of Godfrey of Bouillon and Richard of the Lion Heart was a bloody and fruitless romance, the discovery of America was the salvation of the world. The one was the symbol, the other the spirit; the one death, the other life. The tomb of the Savior was a narrow and empty vault, precious only for its memories of the supreme tragedy of the centuries, but the new continent was to be the home and temple of the living God.

The rulers of the Old World began with partitioning the New. To them the discovery was expansion of empire and grandeur to the throne. Vast territories, whose properties and possibilities were little understood, and whose extent was greater than the kingdoms of the sovereigns, were the gifts to court favorites and the prizes of royal approval. But individual intelligence and independent conscience found here haven and refuge. They were the passengers upon the caravels of Columbus, and

and opinions. The processes of liberty liberalized the one and elevated the other. Washington and Adams were the new types. Their union in a common cause gave the world a Republic both stable and free. It possessed conservatism without bigotry, and liberty without license. It founded institutions strong enough to resist revolution, and elastic enough for indefinite expansion to meet the requirements in government of ever-enlarging areas of population and the needs of progress and growth. It was nurtured by the toleration and patriotism which bound together in a common cause the Puritans of New England and the Catholics of Maryland, the Dutch Reformers of New York and the Huguenots of South Carolina, the Quakers and Lutherans of Pennsylvania and the Episcopalians, Methodists, Presbyterians, Baptists, and religionists of all and of opposite opinions in the other colonies.

The Mayflower, with the Pilgrims, and a Dutch ship laden with African slaves were on the ocean at the same time, the one sailing for Massachusetts, and the other for Virginia. This company of saints and first cargo of slaves represented the forces which were to peril and rescue free government. The slaver was the product of the commercial spirit of Great Britain, and the greed of the times to stimulate production in the colonies. The men who wrote in the cabin of the Mayflower the first charter of freedom, a government of just and equal laws, were a little band of Protestants against every form of injustice and tyranny. The leaven of their principles made possible the Declaration of Independence, liberated the slaves, and founded the free commonwealths which form the Republic of the United States.

Platforms of principles, by petition or protest or statement, have been as frequent as revolts against established authority. They are a part of the political literature of all nations. The Declaration of Independence proclaimed at Philadelphia, July 4th, 1776, is the only one of them which arrested the attention of the world when it was published and has held its undivided interest ever since. The vocabulary of the equality of man had been in familiar use by philosophers and statesmen for ages. It expressed noble sentiments, but their application was limited to classes or conditions. The masses cared little for them, nor remembered them long. Jefferson's superb crystallization of the popular opinion that "all men are created equal, that they are endowed by their Creator with certain inalienable rights, that among these are life, liberty, and the pursuit of happiness," had its force and effect in being the deliberate utterance of the people. It swept away in a single sentence kings and nobles, peers and prelates. It was Magna Charta and the Petition of Rights planted in the virgin soil of the American wilderness and bearing richer and riper fruit. Under its vitalizing influence upon the individual, the farmer left his plow in the furrow, the lawyer his books and briefs, the merchant his shop, and the workman his bench, to enlist in the patriot army. They were fighting for themselves and their children. They embodied the idea in their Constitution in the immortal words with which that great instrument of liberty and order began: —

"We, the people of the United States, do ordain."

The scope and limitations of this idea of freedom have neither been misinterpreted nor misunderstood. The laws of nature in their application to the rise and recognition of men according to their mental, moral, spiritual, and physical endowments are left undisturbed. But the accident of birth gives no rank and confers no privilege. Equal rights and common opportunity for all have been the spurs of ambition and the motors of progress. They have established the common schools and built the public libraries. A sovereign people have learned and enforced the lesson of free education. The practice of government is itself a liberal education. People who make their own laws need no lawgivers. After a century of successful trial, the system has passed the period of experiment, and its demonstrated permanency and power are revolutionizing the governments of the world. It has raised the largest armies of modern times for self-preservation, and at the successful termination of the war returned the soldiers to the pursuits of peace. It has so adjusted itself to the pride and patriotism of the defeated that they vie with the victors in their support of and enthusiasm for the old flag and our common country. Imported anarchists have preached their baleful doctrines, but have made no converts. They have tried to inaugurate a reign of terror under the banner of the violent seizure and distribution of property only to be defeated, imprisoned, and executed by the law made by the people and enforced by juries selected from the people, and judges and prosecuting officers elected by the people. Socialism finds disciples only among those who were its votaries before they were

V—112

in the support of a nation of newspaper readers. The humblest and poorest person has, in periodicals whose price is counted in pennies, a library larger, fuller, and more varied than was within the reach of the rich in the time of Columbus.

The sum of human happiness has been infinitely increased by the millions from the Old World who have improved their conditions in the New, and the returning tide of lesson and experience has incalculably enriched the Fatherlands. The divine right of kings has taken its place with the instruments of mediæval torture among the curiosities of the antiquary. Only the shadow of kingly authority stands between the government of themselves, by themselves, and the people of Norway and Sweden. The union in one empire of the States of Germany is the symbol of Teutonic power and the hope of German liberalism. The petty despotisms of Italy have been merged into a nationality which has centralized its authority in its ancient capitol on the hills of Rome. France was rudely roused from the sullen submission of centuries to intolerable tyranny by her soldiers returning from service in the American revolution. The wild orgies of the Reign of Terror were the revenges and excesses of a people who had discovered their power, but were not prepared for its beneficent use. She fled from herself into the arms of Napoleon. He, too, was a product of the American experiment. He played with kings as with toys and educated France for liberty. In the processes of her evolution from darkness to light, she tried Bourbon and Orleanist and the third Napoleon, and cast them aside. Now in the fullness of time, and through the training in the school of hardest experience, the French people have reared and enjoy a permanent republic. England of the Mayflower and of James II., England of George III. and of Lord North, has enlarged suffrage and is to-day animated and governed by the democratic spirit. She has her throne admirably occupied by one of the wisest of sovereigns and best of women, but it would not survive one dissolute and unworthy successor. She has her hereditary peers, but the House of Lords will be brushed aside the moment it resists the will of the people.

The time has arrived for both a closer union and greater distance between the Old World and the New. The former indiscriminate welcome to our prairies and the present invitation to these palaces of art and industry mark the passing period. Unwatched and unhealthy immigration can no longer be permitted

forced to fly from their native land, but it does not take root upon American soil. The State neither supports nor permits taxation to maintain the Church. The citizen can worship God according to his belief and conscience, or he may neither reverence nor recognize the Almighty. And yet religion has flourished, churches abound, the ministry is sustained, and millions of dollars are contributed annually for the evangelization of the world. The United States is a Christian country and a living and practical Christianity is the characteristic of its people.

Benjamin Franklin, philosopher and patriot, amused the jaded courtiers of Louis XVI. by his talks about liberty, and entertained the scientists of France by bringing lightning from the clouds. In the reckoning of time, the period from Franklin to Morse, and from Morse to Edison is but a span, and yet it marks a material development as marvelous as it has been beneficent. The world has been brought into contact and sympathy. The electric current thrills and unifies the people of the globe. Power and production, highways and transports have been so multiplied and improved by inventive genius, that within the century of our independence sixty-four millions of people have happy homes and improved conditions within our borders. We have accumulated wealth far beyond the visions of the Cathay of Columbus or the El Dorado of De Soto. But the farmers and freeholders, the savings banks and shops illustrate its universal distribution. The majority are its possessors and administrators. In housing and living, in the elements which make the toiler a self-respecting and respected citizen, in avenues of hope and ambition for children, in all that gives broader scope and keener pleasure to existence, the people of this Republic enjoy advantages far beyond those of other lands. The unequaled and phenomenal progress of the country has opened wonderful opportunities for making fortunes, and stimulated to madness the desire and rush for the accumulation of money. Material prosperity has not debased literature nor debauched the press; it has neither paralyzed nor repressed intellectual activity. American science and letters have received rank and recognition in the older centres of learning. The demand for higher education has so taxed the resources of the ancient universities as to compel the foundation and liberal endowment of colleges all over the Union. Journals, remarkable for their ability, independence, and power, find their strength, not in the patronage of government, or the subsidies of wealth, but

to our shores. We must have a national quarantine against disease, pauperism, and crime. We do not want candidates for our hospitals, our poorhouses or our jails. We cannot admit those who come to undermine our institutions and subvert our laws. But we will gladly throw wide our gates for, and receive with open arms, those who by intelligence and virtue, by thrift and loyalty, are worthy of receiving the equal advantages of the priceless gift of American citizenship. The spirit and object of this exhibition are peace and kinship.

Three millions of Germans, who are among the best citizens of the Republic, send greeting to the Fatherland their pride in its glorious history, its ripe literature, its traditions and associations. Irish, equal in number to those who still remain upon the Emerald Isle, who have illustrated their devotion to their adopted country on many a battlefield, fighting for the Union and its perpetuity, have rather intensified than diminished their love for the land of the shamrock and their sympathy with the aspirations of their brethren at home. The Italian, the Spaniard, and the Frenchman, the Norwegian, the Swede, and the Dane, the English, the Scotch, and the Welsh, are none the less loyal and devoted Americans because in this congress of their kin the tendrils of affection draw them closer to the hills and valleys, the legends and the loves associated with their youth.

Edmund Burke, speaking in the British Parliament with prophetic voice, said: "A great revolution has happened — a revolution made, not by chopping and changing of power in any of the existing states, but by the appearance of a new state, of a new species, in a new part of the globe. It has made as great a change in all the relations and balances and gravitations of power as the appearance of a new planet would in the system of the solar world." Thus was the humiliation of our successful revolt tempered to the motherland by pride in the state created by her children. If we claim heritage in Bacon, Shakespeare, and Milton, we also acknowledge that it was for liberties guaranteed Englishmen by sacred charters our fathers triumphantly fought. While wisely rejecting throne and caste and privilege and an Established Church in their newborn state, they adopted the substance of English liberty and the body of English law. Closer relations with England than with other lands, and a common language rendering easy interchanges of criticisms and epithet, sometimes irritate and offend, but the heart of republican America beats with responsive pulsations to the hopes and aspirations of the people of Great Britain.

The grandeur and beauty of this spectacle are the eloquent witnesses of peace and progress. The Parthenon and the cathedral exhausted the genius of the ancient, and the skill of the mediæval architects, in housing the statue or spirit of Deity. In their ruins or their antiquity they are mute protests against the merciless enmity of nations, which forced art to flee to the altar for protection. The United States welcome the sister republics of the Southern and Northern continents, and the nations and peoples of Europe and Asia, of Africa and Australia, with the products of their lands, of their skill and of their industry, to this city of yesterday, yet clothed with royal splendor as the Queen of the Great Lakes. The artists and architects of the country have been bidden to design and erect the buildings which shall fitly illustrate the height of our civilization and the breadth of our hospitality. The peace of the world permits and protects their efforts in utilizing their powers for man's temporal welfare. The result is this park of palaces. The originality and the boldness of their conceptions, and the magnitude and harmony of their creations, are the contributions of America to the oldest of the arts and the cordial bidding of America to the peoples of the earth to come and bring the fruitage of their age to the boundless opportunities of this unparalleled exhibition.

If interest in the affairs of this world is vouchsafed to those who have gone before, the spirit of Columbus hovers over us to-day. Only by celestial intelligence can it grasp the full significance of this spectacle and ceremonial.

From the first century to the fifteenth counts for little in the history of progress, but in the period between the fifteenth and the twentieth is crowded the romance and reality of human development. Life has been prolonged, and its enjoyment intensified. The powers of the air and the water, the resistless forces of the elements, which in the time of the Discoverer were the visible terrors of the wrath of God, have been subdued to the service of man. Art and luxuries which could be possessed and enjoyed only by the rich and noble, the works of genius which were read and understood only by the learned few, domestic comforts and surroundings beyond the reach of lord or bishop, now adorn and illumine the homes of our citizens. Serfs are sovereigns and the people are kings. The trophies and splendors

of their reign are commonwealths, rich in every attribute of great States, and united in a Republic whose power and prosperity and liberty and enlightenment are the wonder and admiration of the world.

All hail, Columbus, discoverer, dreamer, hero, and apostle! We here, of every race and country, recognize the horizon which bounded his vision and the infinite scope of his genius. The voice of gratitude and praise for all the blessings which have been showered upon mankind by his adventure is limited to no language, but is uttered in every tongue. Neither marble nor brass can fitly form his statue. Continents are his monument, and unnumbered millions present and to come, who enjoy in their liberties and their happiness the fruits of his faith, will reverently guard and preserve, from century to century, his name and fame.

LIBERTY ENLIGHTENING THE WORLD

(Peroration of the Address, Delivered October 28th, 1886, at the Dedication of the Bartholdi Statue of Liberty in New York Harbor)

AMERICAN liberty has been for a century a beacon light for the nations. Under its teachings and by the force of its example, the Italians have expelled their petty and arbitrary princelings and united under a parliamentary government; the gloomy despotism of Spain has been dispelled by the representatives of the people and a free press; the great German race has demonstrated its power for empire and its ability to govern itself. The Austrian monarch, who, when a hundred years ago Washington pleaded with him across the seas for the release of Lafayette from the dungeon of Olmutz, replied that "he had not the power," because the safety of his throne and his pledges to his royal brethren of Europe compelled him to keep confined the one man who represented the enfranchisement of the people of every race and country, is to-day, in the person of his successor, rejoicing with his subjects in the limitations of a Constitution which guarantees liberties, and a Congress which protects and enlarges them. Magna Charta, won at Runnymede for Englishmen, and developing into the principles of the Declaration of Independence with their descendants, has returned to the mother country to bear fruit in an open Parlia-

ment, a free press, the loss of royal prerogative, and the passage of power from the classes to the masses.

The sentiment is sublime which moves the people of France and America, the blood of whose fathers, commingling upon the battlefields of the Revolution, made possible this magnificent march of liberty and their own Republics, to commemorate the results of the past and typify the hopes of the future in this noble work of art. The descendants of Lafayette, Rochambeau, and De Grasse, who fought for us in our first struggle, and Laboulaye, Henri Martin, De Lesseps, and other grand and brilliant men, whose eloquent voices and powerful sympathies were with us in our last, conceived the idea, and it has received majestic form and expression through the genius of Bartholdi.

In all ages the achievements of man and his aspirations have been represented in symbols. Races have disappeared and no record remains of their rise or fall, but by their monuments we know their history. The huge monoliths of the Assyrians and the obelisks of the Egyptians tell their stories of forgotten civilizations, but the sole purpose of their erection was to glorify rulers and preserve the boasts of conquerors. They teach sad lessons of the vanity of ambition, the cruelty of arbitrary power, and the miseries of mankind. The Olympian Jupiter enthroned in the Parthenon expressed in ivory and gold the awful majesty of the Greek idea of the king of the gods; the bronze statue of Minerva on the Acropolis offered the protection of the patron goddess of Athens to the mariners who steered their ships by her helmet and spear; and in the Colossus of Rhodes, famed as one of the wonders of the world, the Lord of the Sun welcomed the commerce of the East to the city of his worship. But they were all dwarfs in size and pigmies in spirit beside this mighty structure and its inspiring thought. Higher than the monument in Trafalgar Square, which commemorates the victories of Nelson on the sea; higher than the Column Vendome, which perpetuates the triumphs of Napoleon on the land; higher than the towers of the Brooklyn bridge, which exhibit the latest and grandest results of science, invention, and industrial progress, this Statue of Liberty rises toward the heavens to illustrate an idea which nerved the three hundred at Thermopylæ and armed the ten thousand at Marathon; which drove Tarquin from Rome and aimed the arrow of Tell; which charged with Cromwell and his Ironsides and accompanied Sidney to the block; which fired the

farmer's gun at Lexington and razed the Bastile in Paris; which inspired the charter in the cabin of the Mayflower and the Declaration of Independence from the Continental Congress.

It means that with the abolition of privileges to the few and the enfranchisement of the individual; with the equality of all men before the law and universal suffrage; with the ballot secure from fraud and the voter from intimidation; with the press free and education furnished by the State for all; with liberty of worship and free speech; with the right to rise and equal opportunity for honor and fortune, the problems of labor and capital, of social regeneration and moral growth, of property and poverty, will work themselves out under the benign influences of enlightened law-making and law-abiding liberty, without the aid of kings and armies, or of anarchists and bombs.

Through the Obelisk, so strangely recalling to us of yesterday the past of twenty centuries, a forgotten monarch says, "I am the Great King, the Conqueror, the Chastiser of Nations," and except as a monument of antiquity it conveys no meaning and touches no chord of human sympathy. But, for unnumbered centuries to come, as Liberty levels up the people to higher standards and a broader life, this statue will grow in the admiration and affections of mankind. When Franklin drew the lightning from the clouds, he little dreamed that in the evolution of science his discovery would illuminate the torch of Liberty for France and America. The rays from this beacon, lighting this gateway to the continent, will welcome the poor and the persecuted with the hope and promise of homes and citizenship. It will teach them that there is room and brotherhood for all who will support our institutions and aid in our development, but that those who come to disturb our peace and dethrone our laws are aliens and enemies forever. I devoutly believe that from the unseen and the unknown two great souls have come to participate in this celebration. The faith in which they died fulfilled, the cause for which they battled triumphant, the people they loved in the full enjoyment of the rights for which they labored and fought and suffered, the spirit voices of Washington and Lafayette join in the glad acclaim of France and the United States to Liberty Enlightening the World.

THE MILITARY SPIRIT IN AMERICA

(Delivered at the Banquet to Gen. Nelson A. Miles, Given at the Waldorf-Astoria, New York City, November 11th, 1898)

Mr. President and Gentlemen:—

NEW YORK gives cordial greeting to the commanding general of the American army. New York's welcome is the applause of the United States. This metropolis is more than a great city. It surpasses all other cities in the representative character of its population. The sons of every State in the Union are living in our midst, while our foreign population is larger than many of the cities in the lands from which they came. New York is the second largest city in the world within its own corporate limits. If we add the population which naturally belongs to it, across the North River, on the shores of New Jersey, it is the largest city in the world. Within this room are gathered gentlemen from the North and the South, from the East and the West, and from the Pacific Slope. So better and more significantly than would be possible under any other circumstances, this great Republic honors to-night her foremost soldier.

So many governors are here, and they have spoken with such boastfulness of their several commonwealths that my frankness as a New Yorker compels me to speak plainly. The governor of Massachusetts in his eloquent address, after claiming for the Pilgrim State the origin of most of the institutions which make our country free and great, says, with a deprecating gesture, " Massachusetts does not claim everything." He evidently does not know the tendencies of his own State. The governor of Ohio having told us that all the men who have been generals, or would have been if they had had an opportunity, and all the men who have been Presidents or ought to have been, and all the greatness in every department of public life, hail from Ohio, compels me to repeat what I said many years ago at an Ohio dinner after hearing its orators, that if Shakespeare had written his famous plays in our time he would have said: " Some men are born great and some in Ohio."

We meet to-night in honor of a soldier. It has been only once in a generation that the fame and services of a soldier have commanded the attention of our people. This is the first

time since the Civil War, which closed thirty-three years ago, that the soldier has been sufficiently in evidence to receive decoration and applause. We are fond in our literature and our oratory of drawing sharp contrasts between the Old World and the New. We compare the governments of Europe with that of the United States, and the peoples of Europe with the citizens of our country. In these comparisons we always find much that is gratifying to our pride and our patriotism. The difference is widest in the military conditions and military and naval preparations of America and Europe. With the exception of Great Britain, in every European nation every man is a soldier for the first three years of his majority, and by conscription, while here we have nothing but voluntary enlistment. The peace establishment of Europe is 8,000,000 men; that of the United States, with 70,000,000 population, is only 27,000.

A meeting of American sovereigns, where every voter is recognized as a sovereign, would be a phenomenal gathering. A few years ago there was a meeting of the crowned heads of Europe. It was small, select, and brilliant. The sovereigns were attended by the great officers of their armies and their statesmen, who had also been, or were at the time, soldiers. The Czar of Russia proposed as the one sentiment of the evening, " To Our Order, the Soldier." The toast was both accurate and comprehensive. Every throne in the Old World has been carved by the sword. With the exception of Great Britain's, they rest upon bayonets, while the Chief Magistrate of the United States, is the choice of 14,000,000 independent citizen voters, and at the end of four years surrenders his place and power to the people.

When General Grant made his famous tour of the world, he was received at every court with the most distinguished consideration, not as an ex-President of the United States, but as a great captain who had commanded larger armies and won more victories than any other soldier of that period. He became weary of the continued pomp and ceremony, and when the day arrived for a presentation to the King of Sweden he escaped somehow from the American minister, the royal coach, with its gorgeously appareled horses, its outriders, and its royal guard, and appeared at the palace in his tourist costume—the costume of an American tourist at that. He paralyzed the flunkies in attendance by figuratively ringing the front door bell and sending in his card. The King received him as if he had come in

royal state. This very sensible sovereign said afterward, " General Grant, as the foremost soldier of his age, is the chief of our order, and therefore whatever ceremony he prescribes for his own reception is the right and proper method of according to him our hospitality."

I was in London last summer during the Jubilee days of Queen Victoria. I saw that wonderful and historic pageant, which illustrated the devotion of her people and the glories of her marvelous reign. The kings and princes, the generals and statesmen of the world were in that procession. Brilliant beyond language were the costumes, the uniforms, and the decorations which they wore,—all except our own embassador, who, by the regulations framed during a primitive period of isolation and provincialism, was compelled to appear in the early morning in this brilliant throng in a dress suit. If the regulations prescribed that he should appear as Daniel Webster always did, in a blue frock coat with brass buttons, and a buff vest, that would be an American uniform; or if they should prescribe that he appear in the close-buttoned frock coat, black " pants," and high standing collar, which is the traditional uniform of the American orator on state occasions, that would be American. But the dress suit in the morning is in touch with no American habit of the club, the drawing-room, the farm, the ranch, the mine, the business office, the social function, or the state ceremony. However, the regulations of the State Department do not apply to the officers of our army and navy. General Miles, in the full and effective uniform of the commanding general of the American army, rode among princes in the procession and sat his horse amid the royalties and marshals and generals of Europe at the review at Aldershot. His commanding figure and soldierly presence filled every American with honest pride both for our little army and that it had such a distinguished and admirable representative on this famous occasion. A Russian grand duke whom I knew came up to me in great excitement and fairly shouted,—though shouting is very bad form in Europe,—not anything about the parade or the procession or the significance of the event, but simply, " I have seen your American general." Here to-night, on this side of the ocean, we also show with our cheers that we are glad to see our American general.

Our wars have come but once in each generation since the formation of our Government. The hero of our Revolutionary

War, which closed in 1783, was General Washington. The gratitude of the people made him twice President of the United States, and he lives with imperishable and growing fame in the affections of his countrymen. The hero of the next war, which closed in 1814, was General Jackson, who was also twice President of the United States and is the titular saint of the Democratic party. Between 1814 and 1848 the country was at peace. The soldier was unknown in our civil life. It became fashionable to deride the army and to speak slightingly of the navy as of no use to a country situated like ours. The humorist, the caricaturist, and the satirist selected for their subjects training day and the State militia. The service was dropping into contempt. The War with Mexico developed instantly the military spirit of the Republic. The whole country was filled with warlike enthusiasm and anxiety to participate in the fight. We had two heroes from that war—General Scott and General Taylor. General Scott missed the presidency because of his unfortunate letter of acceptance of the nomination beginning, " I have just risen from a hasty plate of soup." From that line has become crystallized into a phrase that situation in American public life when a man has tumbled by his own folly into political defeat or oblivion, that he has " fallen into the soup." General Taylor became President of the United States.

Another generation passed, and we had the Civil War, which closed in 1865. This contest was a supreme demonstration that peace does not decrease the military ardor, the vigor, or the patriotism of the American citizen. It was a battle of Americans against Americans, in which a million volunteers lost their lives. The hero of that war was General Grant, who became twice President of the United States. Then we had long peace from 1865 to 1898. The American jingoes, who are perpetually seeking occasions for war, when no better reason offers, base their action upon the argument that the virility and manhood of a people degenerate unless kept alive by conditions which compel them to fight frequently for the honor and the flag of their country. Some of them have insisted for years that this period had arrived, that patriotism and self-sacrificing courage were yielding to gross materialism, and unless we had our war we would speedily see the decadence of the nation. But no sooner had war been declared against Spain than a generation which knew nothing of scars or of the battles the glories or the fury of the fighting of the Civil War, rushed to the recruiting offices to enlist as volunteers in numbers ten times beyond what was named in the call for troops. Napoleon said: "Scratch a Russian and you find a Tartar." Scratch an American and you find a fighter. The inheritors of an ancestry which for generations have never yielded to a foe, have avenged wrongs, have vindicated right, have fought and died for their own liberty, and, more, have fought and died for the liberty of others, have to-day, as they will have under the inspiring spirit of liberty for all time, that dominant spirit which makes their country powerful, keeps their institutions pure and permanent and enlarges their own freedom.

I am delighted with the tribute which our governor-elect, Colonel Roosevelt, has paid to-night to the regular army. We never fail to give a full and deserved measure of applause and recognition to the volunteer soldiers. We have not sufficiently recognized the superb service and fidelity of our regular army. During the civil strife it was this small and invincible army which prevented the Government from being overthrown until the volunteers had been drilled into soldiers. They held aloft the standard which never fell, never retreated, and around which rallied the raw troops. At the close of the Civil War this army, which was always at the front, had dwindled by losses in battle to scarcely a regiment. At frontier posts, at forts on the coast, and in encampments, the regular army is always drilling and working. It becomes and remains the most complete fighting machine in the world. The intelligence of its soldiers puts the man behind the gun, who in all emergencies, where commands fail because commanders are shot, can take the initiative and hold the field or rush the battery. We must give more care and more skilled attention to this great arm of our service and raise it to the standard required by the conditions of our country and the numbers of our population. I do not mean a great standing army, but I do mean one which will be universally recognized by our people as a reasonable and respectable size and efficiency.

A singular illustration of the importance of the navy in the new conditions forced upon us by the victories it has won and its conquests in the Western Hemisphere and the Pacific Ocean is furnished by comparing the consideration it received in former wars and its present prominence. While Washington lives forever as the hero of the first war, Paul Jones is seldom men-

tioned; while General Jackson lives as the hero of our second war, we hear little of Decatur and Perry and the other great naval commanders; while Grant lives as the embodiment of our Civil War, we hear little of Farragut, Porter, or Paulding, but the historian of this war is likely to put the navy ahead of the army, and in the popular imagination of the future which will crystallize the war in its heroes, Dewey will stand beside Miles. The fame of Miles will live because of his brilliant record in the Civil War and campaigns against the Indians, and because the military successes which we had in the war with Spain were largely due to his plan of campaign and his broad and comprehensive strategy.

ENGLAND AND AMERICA SINCE THE SPANISH WAR

(Delivered at the Lotos Club Banquet to Lord Herschel, New York, November 5th, 1898)

Gentlemen:—

WHEN an American has enjoyed the cordial hospitality of an English home, he is ever after craving an opportunity to reciprocate in his own country. He discovers that the traditional icy reserve and insular indifference with which the Englishman is popularly credited are only the shield and armor which protect the inhabitants of the centre and capital of the activities of the Old World from the frauds and fools of the whole world. When once thawed out, our kin across the sea can be as demonstrative and, in their own way, as jocose as the untamed natives of these Western wilds. An eminent medical authority, in a learned essay on heredity and longevity, advanced this theory: That the emigrant from the British Isles to our shores, under the influence of our dry and exciting atmosphere, becomes, in a few generations, abnormally nervous, thin, and dyspeptic. Between forty and fifty he can arrest the speed with which he is hurrying to an untimely grave, if he will move over to England. The climate there will work upon his ancestral tendencies, and he will develop backward to the original type. Instead of his restless spirit reading the epitaph upon his tombstone in the United States, he will be enjoying life in the old country in the seventies and eighties, be taking his daily gospel from the Times, and, on gouty days, lamenting modern degeneracy. The con-

verse must be equally true, and the Englishman who has passed his climacteric and is afflicted with inertia and adipose, will find in the sunshine and champagne air of America the return of the energy and athletic possibilities of his youth. Thus the two countries, in the exchange, will exhibit a type which, once safely past the allotted line of life, in their new environment, will keep going on forever. None of us want to quit this earthly scene so long as we can retain health and mind. The attractions of the heavenly city are beyond description, but residence there runs through such countless ages that a decade, more or less, before climbing the golden stairs, is a loss of rich experience this side, and not noticed on the other.

It is a singular fact that the United States has known England for nearly three hundred years, and England has known little about the United States until within the past ten years. Eight years ago Mr. Gladstone asked me about the newspapers in this country. I told him that the press in nearly all of our large cities had from a half to a whole column of European cables daily, and three columns on Sunday, and two-thirds of it was about English affairs. He expressed surprise and pleasure, and great regret that the English press was not equally full of American news. From ten to fifty lines on our markets was all the information British readers had about our interests, unless a lynching, a railroad smash-up, or a big corporation suddenly gone bankrupt commanded all the space required and gave a lively picture of our settled habits. English statesmen of all parties have been as well known and understood by our people for a quarter of a century as those of our own country, while beyond Lincoln, Grant, and Garfield, the British public never heard of our party leaders and public men. Such is the power and educational value of the press.

With the advent of Smalley, Norman, and others, sending full dispatches from the United States to the English newspapers, our press relations have become reciprocal. The American in England is as much in touch each morning with the happenings at home as the Englishman is in America with the affairs of Europe. This daily interchange of information as to the conditions, the situation, the opinions, and the mutual interests of the two countries has been of incalculable benefit in bringing about a better acquaintance and more cordial sentiments between these two great English-speaking nations. The better we know each

other, the riper grows our friendship. The publication of Bryce's 'American Commonwealth' was the dawn of a clearer understanding and closer relations. In my schooldays the boys of the village still played "Fee, fi, fow, fum, I smell the blood of an Englishman; dead or alive I will have some."

An East Tennessee Union farmer, coming into Knoxville in the early days of the Civil War, heard of Mason and Slidell, the Confederate commissioners, who were passengers for Europe on an English merchant vessel, having been taken off by force by an American cruiser and brought back prisoners to this country, and that Great Britain had demanded their release. "What?" he said in great astonishment, "Is that blasted old English machine going yet?" Now, and especially since the practical friendship shown to us by England during our war with Spain, the villagers cheer the *entente cordiale* between the two countries, and the Tennessee mountaineers and the Rugby colonists join in celebrating the Queen's birthday and the Fourth of July.

We have been for a hundred years evoluting toward the mutual understanding of each other and the intelligent friendship which existed between the greatest of Americans, George Washington, and a great Englishman, Lord Shelburne. Shelburne, beyond all of his countrymen, appreciated the American conditions and position in the Revolutionary War, and was the first of foreigners to form that estimate of Washington, as the foremost man of the world, which is now universally accepted. It was for him that Washington sat for a full-length portrait, which now holds the place of honor in the house of another great and brilliant English statesman and warm friend of the United States, Lord Rosebery. On Washington's initiative, and Shelburne's co-operation, the two countries made their famous Jay Treaty of 1796.

The Government of the United States is, and always has been, a lawyers' government. All but three of our Presidents were lawyers, and four-fifths of our Cabinet Ministers, and a large majority of both houses of Congress, have always been members of the bar. The embassador who framed and negotiated this treaty was that eminent jurist, John Jay, the first Chief-Justice of the Supreme Court of the United States. In this treaty, for the first time, I think, among nations, appeared the principle of the settlement by arbitration of disputes between nations. Such was the temper of the period, however, one hundred years ago, and such the jealous and hostile feelings between

America and England, that it required a long time, with all the influence of Washington, to have the treaty ratified by the Senate. Jay was burned in effigy by indignant mobs all over our country, and Lord Granville, the British Foreign Minister, was denounced by the opposition — England — as having been duped by Chief-Justice Jay, and the charge was one of the causes which led to the overthrow of the ministry of which he was a member. While that treaty has received little public notice, yet under it many cases which might have led to serious irritation have been settled, and notably, and most significant of all, the Geneva arbitration of the Alabama claims under the presidency, and with the cordial support of the greatest soldier of our Republic, General Grant. The Bench and the Bar of the United States have always approved and supported the principle of the Jay Treaty.

The common law and the interchangeable decisions of the courts of the United States and Great Britain have been a continuing and refreshing bond of union between the lawyers of the two countries. It was my privilege, in the midst of the Venezuelan excitement, to deliver the annual address before the State Bar Association of the State of New York. The subject I chose was 'International Arbitration,' and as a result of the discussion, this powerful body, with the calmness and judicious candor characteristic of the profession, unanimously adopted a memorial in favor of settling all disputes between Great Britain and the United States by arbitration and in favor of the establishment of an international court of dignity and power. This action received substantially the unanimous approval of the Bench and the Bar of the United States, and was met with equal warmth by our kin across the sea.

One of the best signs of our times, tending more to peace, humanity, and civilization than even the famous proclamation of the Russian Czar, has been, and is, the warm and increasing friendship between the great electorate — the democracy of Great Britain and the people of the United States. Sir Henry Irving told me, last summer, a story full of significance. It demonstrated that when the people of Great Britain and the people of the United States understood one another, they are, in many respects, one people. One of the most brilliant and eloquent platform orators the world has ever known was Henry Ward Beecher. During the time of our Civil War, when the press and the upper classes of Great Britain were largely hostile to us, Beecher went

abroad as a popular embassador from the people of the United States to the people of England. Irving said that when Beecher spoke at Manchester, the feeling among the operatives and artisans of that great manufacturing town was that if the North succeeded, the rebellion was put down, and the Union was preserved, in some way the cotton of the Southern States would be diverted, and their employment gone.

We are not unfamiliar with that sort of politics by misrepresentation in the United States. Irving said that at that time he was a young actor in a stock company in Manchester. Having secured a good position in the hall, he saw a maddened mob struggling to get hold of a handsome young man upon the platform, with the evident purpose of tearing him to pieces. The young man, Mr. Beecher, was protected by the leading citizens of Manchester and the police. It was half an hour before the crowd would listen to a word. The first five minutes of Beecher's speech set them wild again, and then Irving thought that Beecher would certainly be dragged from the platform and killed. By the exertions, however, of the gentlemen about the orator, a hearing was finally secured, and Beecher developed in his own masterly way the common language, the literature, and the ties of the two countries, the common origin of their liberty, and the common freedom of their people, the interest which every man had for himself and his children in the perpetuity and strength of free government in the American Republic. The first half-hour was silence, the second half-hour was tumultuous applause, the next hour was unanimous and enthusiastic approval, and at the close the crowd insisted upon bearing upon their shoulders and carrying in triumph to his lodgings the orator, whose cause they then understood.

The men of letters who write and speak in the English tongue have always been mutually appreciative, and always friends. It began with the father of American literature, Washington Irving, who was held by the British critic as a second Addison. Longfellow and Hawthorne of a recent period, and Mark Twain of to-day, find appreciation and applause,—find equal recognition and pride on both sides of the Atlantic.

It was not until we became involved in a war with a European power that Americans appreciated the extent and depth of this feeling of kinship among the English-speaking peoples across the Atlantic. A famous Scotch divine told me that when on the

one hand Emperor William had sent his telegram encouraging Kruger in South Africa to fight England, and on the other the Venezuelan message of President Cleveland was interpreted on the part of the United States as a challenge for a fight, he preached a sermon to a Scotch congregation. There are no other people so devoted and undemonstrative in the world inside the church as the Scotch Presbyterians. "But," said the preacher, "when I said that under no conditions would the people of Great Britain fight their kin in the United States, and that if there was to be fighting it must all be from the Americans, there was wild applause, but when I said that if the German Emperor moved one step further in the hostile action indicated by his telegram, the British fleet would sweep his vessels from the oceans, and British arms would capture all his colonies inside of sixty days, the congregation rose and gave cheers."

The war with Spain threatened the equilibrium of that delicate instrument known as the European balance of power, an instrument so delicate that it requires eight millions of soldiers and the waters of the globe covered with navies, to keep it from getting out of trim. Every consideration of the associations of ambitions in the East impelled the continental powers to sympathize with Spain. They proposed that all Europe should intervene, as was done in the Turko-Grecian War. Great Britain said: "No; we will take no part in any international action which is hostile to the United States." It was then proposed by the continental powers that they should intervene and Great Britain remain neutral. The reply of Great Britain was: "In that case England will be on the side of the United States." That ended the subject of interference in our Spanish War. That action promoted the peace of the world. That sentiment, flashed across the ocean, electrified the American people. That position, unanimously approved in Great Britain by the masses and by the classes, received such a recognition in the United States as only a great and generous people can give for a great and generous friendship. That action sent the current of the blood of English-speaking people flowing in like channels, and was the beginning of the era of good fellowship which is to have the most marked influence upon the story of nations and of peoples in the future history of the world.

Our guest, Lord Herschel, typifies that career common to all Americans, and which Americans delight to honor. He is the

architect of his own career, and by the greatest qualities of brain and character has successfully climbed to the highest office by which his country can honor and decorate a lawyer. The mission which brings him to this side is worthy of his great acquirements and his broad and catholic judgment. With the irritations and vexations which naturally arise between Canada and ourselves permanently removed, there is no spot on earth where the United States and Great Britain can seriously clash. With our possessions stretching at intervals of two thousand miles for harbors and coaling stations, for six thousand miles across the Pacific, we face the doors of the various gateways of the Orient, closed by the great powers of the world, except Great Britain, and we hail the open door which she offers for the entrance into China and the East for the products of our farms and our factories.

But yesterday there were four great powers governing the world, dividing territories of barbarous or semi-civilized peoples, and ruling the destinies of mankind. They were Great Britain, France, Germany, and Russia. To-day there are five. The last has come into this concert of nations by the unprecedented successes and marvelous victories of its hundred days of war. Two of the five, the United States and Great Britain, with the ties of common language and common law and like liberties, will work together naturally in this international development. They will not be, and they cannot be, bound or limited by a hard and fast alliance, offensive and defensive, like that which marks the Dreibund or the unknown relations between Russia and France. But there are relations, there are ties which are stronger than parchment treaties based upon selfishness, greed, or fear. They are the ties of blood, of language, and of common aims for the loftiest purposes for which peoples work and governments exist.

POETRY AND POLITICS IN BRITAIN

(Delivered in Chickering Hall, March 14th, 1885, after a Visit to England)

IN THE early morning we leave behind the great town, and in a few hours are sailing over Loch Lomond, the queen of the Scottish lakes. The vast expanse of water, the beautiful islands, the mountains rising peak on peak till lost in the clouds, the beetling crags which meet the waves make this one of the few sights which fulfill expectations. Through the passes surrounding this lake, the Highland chieftains and their clans raided the Lowland farms. The Celtic warriors of the olden time followed the golden rule of the day:—

> « The good old rule, the simple plan,
> That they do take who have the power,
> And they do keep who can. »

The McGregors, the McFarlanes, the Colquhouns, here had their lairs, and fought those bloody battles which have given to literature some of its best poetry and romance. It was over these mountains that the fire signals flashed from peak to peak, calling the clansman to resist the invader, and it was through these glens that Roderick Dhu sent his fiery cross, while bold Rob Roy McGregor defied here his enemies, and far up above the beach you see the cave which was his shelter and retreat. But with all that nature has done for Scotland, and she has been very lavish, the country owes the magic charm with which her hills and vales are invested for all the world to the genius of three men — Sir Walter Scott, Robert Burns, and John Knox.

I never shall forget the feelings of reverence and gratification with which I entered Abbotsford. It is a great, irregular house on the banks of the Tweed, designed by Sir Walter Scott to meet his passion for the age of chivalry. It is filled with objects suggestive of themes upon which he loved to write. In the armory are suspended from the walls the suits of mail, the lances and claymores which had belonged to many gallant knights and border chiefs, and in battle, in foray, and in the tournament had done bloody and glorious work. In the library were the twenty thousand volumes he knew so well, and upon the walls, among famous pictures, one of Queen Mary's severed head. Kings and queens and heroes had paid homage to his genius, and here are gifts from Napoleon, George IV., the Duke of Wellington, Admiral Nelson, and the Pope! Those he prized most were relics of Queen Mary, the dagger and pouch of Rob Roy, the sword of Bruce, the brooch of Flora McDonald, and the chair of Wallace. But it is when you enter his study that you seem to be communing with him in the flesh. Everything is undisturbed and ready for his return. His desk, his pen and inkstand, all the paraphernalia of his work, are there just as when they were the

and he did it magnificently. He attacked members of the opposition fiercely and personally; he charged into every opening they offered. He was pathetic, eloquent, argumentative, and sarcastic. The Conservative leaders tried their best to prevent the younger men from being tempted by him into side discussions, and to confine him to a defense of his mistakes. But they failed, and the debate closed in a grand burst of oratory from the Premier, who had never touched a dangerous topic.

instruments of his wonderful creations. The attendant takes his coat and hat from the closet, and brings out his cane, and you almost gasp for breath, so realistic is the impression, that as you have pictured him, so he will come in, to resent this intrusion on his privacy.

[From Scotland, Mr. Depew passed into England, and told his audience of the condition of the people, of the architectural wonders of the English cathedrals, and something of English politics. The following is his description of a debate he witnessed in the House of Commons:] —

When the debate opened, both sides were present in force. Facing each other, sat those fierce enemies and rising leaders of their respective parties — Mr. Chamberlain and Lord Randolph Churchill. Both are seeking to ride into power as the friends of the working man, and their success enforces Puck's apothegm: «What fools we mortals be!» Lord Randolph Churchill is the son of the Duke of Marlborough, and loyal to his class. His audacity is unbounded, and he is a veritable little gamecock of the House. But he is not and never will be a statesman. Mr. Chamberlain is a humbug and a demagogue, and in dress so much of a dandy as to be almost a dude over here. Even Mr. Justus Schwab would not follow him. He possesses immense wealth acquired as a manufacturer, and by drying up and driving out small dealers and reducing the wages of his workmen to the last penny they will bear; and then he seeks the workingmen's votes by proposing to confiscate the land. Bah, brother! Take the beam out of your own eye first.

Sir Stafford Northcote started the ball by an indictment of the Government. Though usually the dullest of speakers, this time he was so strong, direct, and incisive, that he made it exceedingly lively. Of course, he skipped over all the merits like a lawyer presenting his side, and bunched in most glaring colors the defects. Mr. Gladstone rose to reply, and we all felt that he knew the occasion demanded all his powers. In facility of speech, depth and breadth of information, and powers of presentation, I do not believe he has an equal in the world. He knew that the French had outgeneraled him in the East; Bismarck had stolen a march on him in Australia and Africa; his Egyptian policy had ended in a fiasco; Gordon was shut up in Khartoum, and commerce and trade were in dreadful straits. His efforts were to avoid meeting these issues and create false ones,

DERBY, EDWARD G. F. STANLEY, EARL OF

(1799–1869)

THE politics of the United States, during the whole of the nineteenth century, were deeply affected by the movement begun by Wilberforce in England for the manumission of British slaves. The movement originated in Revolutionary America, gathered fresh impetus from the speeches of French orators during the Revolution, and was urged on by the Liberals in the English parliament, not only as a humanitarian, but as a political measure. The English Conservatives could not maintain opposition to it, but they did secure gradual and compensated emancipation. It was for this that Edward Geoffrey Smith-Stanley, afterwards Earl of Derby, spoke in the House of Commons, May 14th, 1833.

He was born at Knowsley, Lancashire, March 29th, 1799. Entering Parliament in 1820, he became Chief Secretary for Ireland in 1830, and Colonial Secretary in 1833. In 1844, he became Baron Stanley, and in 1851 he succeeded to the Earldom of Derby. He was Premier of England in 1852, 1858–59, and 1866–68. His translation of the 'Iliad' is well known. He died October 23d, 1869.

THE EMANCIPATION OF BRITISH NEGROES

(From a Speech on Gradual Emancipation in the West Indies, Delivered in the House of Commons, May 18th, 1833)

A SLAVE proprietor, who was examined before the committee last year (I forget his name), told us that if a slave only looked his master in the face, he might order him to receive thirty-nine lashes. Is this the way to teach him to respect law, and prepare him for the immunities of a free man? Is it thus he is to be raised to a level with other men?

In 1826, Mr. Canning, talking of the dignity of man, quoted the lines:—

> ——— « cælumque tueri
> jussit, et erectos ad sidera tollere vultus. »

But how can you tell the negro that he shall look up as a free man — how can you talk of hopes, encouragement, preparation for individual freedom, and general emancipation, when even at this moment the slave dares not to raise his eyes to his master's face without the risk of receiving thirty-nine lashes? I do not speak of the actual exercise of any such power,—I do not believe it could be exercised,—but that such a power exists there can be no doubt. In case of unjust infliction the slave must go before two magistrates, themselves slave masters; and if he can persuade them to believe him, the master is to be prosecuted, and if found guilty by a jury, subjected to fine and imprisonment; but if the magistrates think the evidence insufficient, without any malicious motive on the part of the slave, he is to be subjected to a second flogging for having made the complaint. This is the practical working in Jamaica of the law in favor of the slave. But there is a further punishment:—in case aggravated, overwhelming cruelty be proved against a master, if a jury find that it has been atrocious, then an addition is to be made to the fine and imprisonment; and what is it? That the slave may be sold and the money handed over to the criminal master. This is the punishment inflicted on masters in Jamaica for conduct which is called atrocious. . . .

I am afraid I may disgust the House by details of the punishments inflicted; but they are a part of the system, and I must refer to them. I find that in 1829, when the slave population was 61,627, the number of punishments returned to the protectors was no less than 17,359; in the next year, when the population was 59,547, the punishments were increased to 18,324,—the number of lashes in that time amounting to 194,744. In the year 1831, the population being then only 58,000, the number of punishments were 21,656, the lashes being 199,500.

This was the official record of the punishments supplied to the protectors of slaves by the owners themselves; it did not include any punishments inflicted under judicial authority; not one of those inflicted by direction of a magistrate; but those domestic punishments alone, which, in the present state of the law, are sanctioned; and this return also, let it be recollected, is confined to the Crown colonies, and represents the domestic, irresponsible punishments which the owners of slaves have inflicted by their own authority. I will not impute any guilt to the owners of the slaves—I will not impute to them anything more than that perversion of moral feeling which it is one of the greatest curses of slavery, that it entails and impresses upon the mind of the

enslaver—I will not impute any want of the ordinary feelings of humanity, further than that they are perverted by prejudice and rendered callous by custom and habit—but I call upon the House to consider where punishments are unrecorded, where no check is interposed by the legal authority, where no remedy or no efficient remedy is given to the slave by authority of the law—to consider if, in this comparatively free state of Demerara, this be the amount of punishment inflicted in one year, what must be the nature of the system which is carried on in other colonies where there are no checks? What must be the degradation of the system under which the other colonies of the British Empire at this moment labor? What is the amount of unredressed injustice,—what is the amount of fatal oppression and cruel tyranny which calls upon this House to regulate, by interposing its solemn authority between this dreadful system of oppression and that which Mr. Canning called "the abstract love of the cart-whip"! . . .

There is also another object on which I am sure his Majesty's government will not appeal in vain to the House or to the country. I feel perfect confidence in calling upon this House to pledge itself, whether in aid of the local legislatures of the colonies, or without any aid from those legislatures, to establish a religious and moral system of education for the negroes. We are about to emancipate the slaves; the old, after a trial of their industrious and other good qualities—the young immediately. With the young, therefore, our responsibility will immediately commence. If we place them in a state of freedom, we are bound to see that they are fitted for the enjoyment of that state; we are bound to give them the means of proving to themselves that the world is not for merely animal existence, that it is not the lot of man merely to labor incessantly from the cradle to the grave, and that to die is not merely to get to the end of a wearisome pilgrimage. We must endeavor to give them habits and to imbue them with feelings calculated to qualify them for the adequate discharge of their duties here; and we must endeavor to instil into them the conviction that when those duties shall be discharged they are not "as the brutes that perish."

Sir, I have now gone through the various points to which I think it necessary to call the attention of the House. I know the difficulties, the almost insurmountable obstacles, which attend almost any plan with reference to this subject; and I know the

peculiar disadvantages under which I bring forward the present plan. But I entertain a confident hope that the resolutions which I shall have the honor to submit to the House contain a germ, which, in the process of time, will be matured, by better judgment and knowledge, into a perfect fruit; and that from the day on which the act passes there will be secured to the country, to the colonies, and to all classes of his Majesty's subjects, the benefit of a virtual extinction of all the horrors attendant on a state of slavery; and that, at no very distant period, by no uncertain operation, but by the effect of that machinery which the proposed plan will put in motion, the dark stain which disfigures the fair freedom of this country will be wholly wiped out. Sir, in looking to this most desirable object, it is impossible not to advert to those who first broached the mighty question of the extinction of slavery, the earliest laborers in that cause, the final triumph of which they were not destined to see. They struggled for the establishment of first principles—they were satisfied with laying the foundation of that edifice which they left it to their successors to rear; they saw the future, as the prophets of old saw "the days that were to come," but they saw it afar off, and with the eye of faith. It is not without the deepest emotion, I recollect, that there is yet living one of the earliest, one of the most religious, one of the most conscientious, one of the most eloquent, one of the most zealous friends of this great cause, who watched it in its dawn. Wilberforce still remains to see, I trust, the final consummation of the great and glorious work which he was one of the first to commence, and to exclaim, like the last of the prophets to whom I have already alluded: "Lord, now let thy servant depart in peace."

Sir, it is with great regret that I have felt it necessary to detain the House so long; but on a subject of so much difficulty it was imperative upon me to do so. I will now, however, after thanking the House for the patience and attention with which they have been so good as to listen to me, conclude with offering up an ardent prayer that by the course which they may adopt they will for a second time set the world a glorious example of a commercial nation, weighing commercial advantages light in the balance against justice and religion; that they will achieve the great object of extinguishing slavery, gradually, safely, but at the same time completely,—a result the more to be desired, if accomplished by a yielding on one side and the other,

which may make both sides forget extreme opinion, and which will exhibit a great and proud example of a deliberative assembly, reconciling conflicting interests, liberating the slave without inflicting hardship on his master, gratifying the liberal and humane spirit of the age, without harming even those who stand in its way, and vindicating their high functions moderately, but with determination, and in a manner honorable to the people of whom they are the representatives, and acting in a manner on this important question which will afford a sure pledge of a successful termination of the glorious career on which they are about to enter.

SIR EDWARD DERING

(1598-1644)

IR EDWARD DERING was Member from Kent and Chairman of the Committee on Religion in the Long Parliament. A graduate of Cambridge and a man of scholarly tastes, he was inclined to sympathize strongly with the people in their grievances against abuses in Church and State, but when he attempted to hold a middle course between the Puritans and the extreme advocates of a political episcopacy, he failed so signally that the Puritan element impeached him for treason. His speeches in favor of a modified episcopacy and an educated clergy separated him from the popular party and forced him to side with the King for whom he fought after he escaped the process of Parliament. He was born in the Tower of London, January 28th, 1598, his father being at that time deputy-lieutenant of the Tower. He died June 22d, 1644. Among the various works left by him were a volume of his speeches prepared and published by himself. It was this volume which excited the anger of the Puritans against him. It was burned by order of the House of Commons, and he was sent to the Tower because of it.

FOR THE ENCOURAGEMENT OF LEARNING

(Delivered in the English Parliament, November 22d, 1841, Against Passing the Remonstrance)

Mr. Speaker:—

THIS has been a very accusative age; yet have I not heard any superstition, much less idolatry, charged, much less proved, upon the several Bishops of London, Winchester, Chester, Carlisle, Chichester.

Parcite paucorum crimen diffundere in omnes. Not for love unto the persons of the Bishops, but for honor to our religion, although the times of late have been somewhat darkened, yet let us not make the day blacker in report than it is in truth.

In the last place I observe a promise in general words: That learning shall be rather advanced than discouraged: *Sed quid verbe audio, cum facta videam.*

enough in half their work; very few do or can travel the whole circle round.

Some one in an age, perhaps, may be found, who, as Sir Francis Drake about the terrestrial globe, may have traveled the celestial orb of theological learning, both for controversial and instructive divinity.

The incomparable primate of Ireland deserves first to be named. Bishop Morton, whom I mentioned before, is another reverend worthy and hath highly deserved of our Church in both capacities. Jewel, of pious memory, is another Bishop never to be forgotten. Some few others I could name, able and active both for pulpit and the pen. But, sir, these be *raræ aves*, and there are very few of them.

The reason is evident. For whilst one man doth chiefly intend the pulpit exercises, he is thereby disabled for polemic discourses; and whilst another indulgeth to himself the faculty of his pen, he thereby renders himself the weaker for the pulpit. Some men aiming at eminency in both have proved but mean proficients in either. For it is a rule and a sure one:—

Pluribus intentus minor est ad singula.

Now, sir, such a way, such a temper, of Church government and of Church revenue, I must wish, as may best secure unto us both; both for preaching to us at home, and for convincing such as are abroad.

Let me be always sure of some champions in our Israel, such as may be ready and able to fight the Lord's battle against the Philistines of Rome, the Socinians of the North, the Arminians and Semi-Pelagians of the West, and generally against heretics and atheists everywhere. God increase the number of his laborers within his vineyard, such as may plentifully and powerfully preach faith and good life among us. But never let us want some of these watchmen also about our Israel, such as may from the Everlasting Hills (so the Scriptures are called) watch for us, aud destroy the common enemy, which way soever he shall approach. Let us maintain both pen and pulpit. Let no Ammonite persuade the Gileadite to fool out his right eye, unless we be willing to make a league with destruction and to wink at ruin, whilst it comes upon us.

Learning, sir, it is invaluable; the loss of learning, it is not in one age recoverable. You may have observed that there

Great rewards do beget great endeavors; and certainly when the great basin and ewer are taken out of the lottery, you shall have few adventures for small plate and spoons only.

If any man could cut the moon out all into little stars, although we might still have the same moon, or as much in small pieces, yet we shall want both light and influence.

To hold out the golden ball of honor and of profit is both policy and honesty, and will be operative upon the best natures and the most pious minds.

But, Mr. Speaker, if I observe aright, learning (I mean religious learning) in this remonstrance is for one-half thereof utterly unthought on. And because I hear often speech of one-half, but seldom mention of the other, give me leave, I beseech you, in this theme a little to enlarge myself; if your remonstrance once pass, it will too late, I fear, to enter this plea.

It is, I dare say, the unanimous wish, the concurrent sense of this whole House to go such a way as may best settle and secure an able, learned, and fully sufficient ministry among us. This ability, this sufficiency, must be of two several sorts.

It is one thing to be able to preach and to fill the pulpit well; it is another ability to confute the perverse adversaries of truth, and to stand in that breach. The first of these gives you the wholesome food of sound doctrine; the other maintains it for you, and defends it from such harpies as would devour or else pollute it. Both of these are supremely necessary for us and for our religion.

Both are of divine institution. The holy Apostle requireth both. Both to call and to convince. First to preach, that he be able with sound doctrine to exhort; and then to convince the gainsayers. For, saith he, there are many deceivers whose mouths must be stopped.

Now, sir, to my purpose; these double abilities, these several sufficiencies, may perhaps sometime meet together in one and the same man, but seldom, very seldom, so seldom that you scarce can find a very few among thousands rightly qualified in both.

Nor is this so much infelicity of our time, or any times, as it is generally the incapacity of man, who cannot easily raise himself up to double excellencies.

Knowledge in religion doth extend itself into so large, so vast a sphere, that many do out-cross the diameter, and find weight

hath been a continual spring, a perpetual growth of learning, ever since it pleased God first to light Luther's candle; I might have said Wickliff's, and justly so I do, for even from that time unto this day and night and hour, this light hath increased; and all this while our better cause hath gained by this light, which doth convince our *Miso-musists* and doth evict that learning and religion, by their mutual support, are like hypocrite twins,—they laugh and mourn together.

But, sir, notwithstanding all this so long increase of learning, there is *terra incognita*, a great land of learning not yet discovered; our adversaries are daily trading, and we must not sit down and give over, but must encourage and maintain and increase the number of our painful adventurers for the Golden Fleece; and except the fleece be of gold, you shall have no adventurers.

RELIGIOUS CONTROVERSY IN PARLIAMENT

(From a Speech on the State of the Kingdom, November 20th, 1641)

Mr. Speaker:—

MUCH has been said and attempted to be done to regulate the exterior part of our religion; but, sir, we bleed inwardly.

Much endeavor hath been to amend the deformed shape we were in, and to new govern the government; yet, sir, this is but the leaves of good religion, fit, I confess notwithstanding, to be taken care of for beauty and for ornament. Nay, some leaves are fit and necessary to be preserved for shadow and for shelter to the blossoms and the fruit.

The fruit of all is good life, which you must never expect to see, unless the blossoms be pure and good; that is, unless your doctrines be sound and true.

Sir, I speak it with full grief of heart, whilst we are thus long pruning and composing of the leaves, or rather whilst some would pluck all leaves away, our blossoms are blasted; and whilst we sit here in cure of government and ceremonials, we are poisoned in our doctrinals. And at whose door will the guilt and sin of all this lie?

Qui non vetat peccare cum potest, jubet.

It is true that this mischief grows not by our consent; and yet I know not by what unhappy fate there is at present such an all-daring liberty, such a lewd licentiousness, for all men venting their several senses — senseless senses — in matter of religion, as never was in any age or in any nation until this Parliament were met together.

Sir, it belongs to us to take heed that our countenance, the countenance of this honorable House, be not prostituted to sinister ends by bold offenders. If it be in our power to give a remedy, a timely and seasonable remedy, to these great and growing evils, and if we, being also put in mind, shall neglect to do it, we then do pluck their sins upon our own heads.

Alienum qui fert scelus, facit suum.

Shall I be bold to give you a very few instances? one for a hundred, wherewith our pulpits do groan?

Mr. Speaker, there is a certain newborn, unseen, ignorant, dangerous, desperate way of independence. Are we, sir, for this independent way? Nay, are we for the elder brother of it, the presbyterial form? I have not yet heard any one gentleman within these walls stand up and assert his thoughts here for either of these ways, and yet we are made the patrons and protectors of these so different, so repugnant innovations; witness the several dedications to us. . . .

One absurdity leads to a thousand, and when you are down the hill of error there is no bottom but in hell, and that is bottomless too. Shall I be bold to give you one (and but one) instance more? Much clamor now there is against our public liturgy, though hallowed with the blood of some of the first composers thereof. And surely, sir, some parts of it may be well corrected. But the clamors now go very high. Impudence and ignorance are now grown so frontless that it is loudly expected by many that you should utterly abrogate all forms of public worship, and at least if you have a short form yet not to impose the use of it. Extirpation of episcopacy, that hope is already wallowed, and now the same men are as greedy for the abolition of the liturgy, that so the Church of England in her public prayers may hereafter turn a babbler at all adventure — a brainless, stupid, and ignorant conceit of some. . . .

I might have added in due place above a mention of: (1) Frequent schismatical conventicles. (2) That tailors, shoemakers, braziers, feltmakers do climb our public pulpits. (3) That several odd irregular fasts have been held for partial venting of private

flatteries of some; slanders of other members of this house. (4) That the distinction of the clergy and laity is popish and anti-Christian and ought no longer to remain. (5) That the Lord's Prayer was not taught us to be used. (6) That no national Church can be a true Church of God. (7) That the visible Church of anti-Christ did make the King head of the Church. (8) That supreme power in Church affairs is in every several congregation. (9) That a presbytery without a Bishop was in the world before it was at Geneva. (10) That it is a heinous sin to be present when prayers are read out of a book. (11) That to communicate in presence of a profane person is to partake of his profaneness. (12) That Christ's kingdom hath been a candle under a bushel, whilst anti-Christ hath outreigned him for one thousand six hundred years together.

Many more instances at little leisure I can gather, which together have begotten a general increase of open Libertinism, secret Atheism, bold Arminianism, desperate Socinianism, stupid Anabaptism, and with these the new Chiliastes, and the willfulness of Papists strangely and strongly confirmed by these distractions.

Good God! look down and direct our consultations, the best issue whereof, I think, would be to debate the whole debate of religion out of our doors, by putting it into a free synod, whereupon I doubt not but we should grow unanimous in all our other works.

RAYMOND DESEZE

(1748–1828)

RAYMOND DESEZE (who after the Bourbon Restoration was known as Raymond, Count de Seze) has been greatly admired for his boldness in defending Louis XVI. before the Convention of 1792–93, which condemned and ordered him to the scaffold. The peroration of his speech in behalf of Louis represents the whole so fully, and is so fully characteristic of the speaker, that the reader will have no great difficulty in deciding the extent to which Deseze impressed the Terrorists around him as an uncompromising and dangerous opponent of their methods. He was born in Bordeaux in 1748. Practicing at the Paris bar, he had already become celebrated as an advocate when Malesherbes asked him to undertake the King's defense before the Convention. The result was a foregone conclusion and it might be unjust to expect from Deseze a more burning zeal than he shows for the interests of his royal client. He does show dignified and manly adherence as a lawyer to the cause of a client who had no other friend, and that is much. After the Restoration, he was rewarded for the speech by being made President of the Court of Cassation and a peer of France. He died in 1828. Napoleon once denounced him as an English agent. This is said to be unjust; and even if it were true, it would not be a reproach to a Royalist attempting to restore the Bourbons through the influence of their foreign allies.

DEFENDING LOUIS XVI.

(Delivered in the French Convention, December 12th, 1792)

Representatives of the Nation: —

THAT moment is at length arrived when Louis, accused in the name of the French people, appears, surrounded by his own council, in order to exhibit his conduct to the eyes of mankind. A celebrated republican hath said that the calamities of kings always inspire the minds of those men with sympathy and tenderness who have lived under a monarchical form of government. If this maxim be true, who can invoke it with more justice than Louis, whose misfortunes are unbounded, and whose

losses and calamities cannot be calculated? You have called him to your bar, and he appears before you with calmness and with dignity, fortified in the consciousness of his own innocence and in the goodness of his intentions. These are testimonies which must console, these are testimonies of which it is impossible to bereave him. He can only declare to you his innocence; I appear here in order to demonstrate it; and I shall adduce the proofs before that very people in whose name he is now accused.

The present silence demonstrates to me that the day of justice has at length succeeded to the days of prejudice. The misfortunes of kings have something in them infinitely more affecting than those of private men; and he who formerly occupied the most brilliant throne in the universe ought to excite a still more powerful interest in his behalf.

I wish that I now spoke before the whole nation; but it will be sufficient to address myself to its representatives. Louis well knows that the eyes of all Europe are fixed upon this prosecution; but his mind is entirely occupied with France. He is sure that posterity will carefully collect and examine the charges and proofs adduced against him, but he thinks only of his contemporaries; and it is the first wish of his heart to undeceive them. If I were only addressing myself at this moment to his judges, I should say: " Royalty is abolished, and you cannot now pronounce any other sentence against him "; but I am speaking to the people. I shall therefore examine the situation of Louis previous to the abolition of royalty and the situation of Louis at its abolition.

Nations are sovereigns; they are at liberty to assume any species of government that appears most agreeable to themselves. After having recognized and discovered the badness of their ancient form, they may enact for themselves a new one; this is a position which one of the council of Louis procured the insertion of in the constitutional code. But the whole nation cannot exercise the sovereignty; it is necessary, therefore, that it should delegate the exercise of it.

In 1789 the people of France demanded a monarchical form of government; now a monarchical government requires the inviolability of the chief, and this inviolability was established, not in behalf of the king, but of the nation.

Much has been said on this subject. Some have pretended that it is not a synallagmatic contract, but a delegation. It is.

however, a contract until it is revoked; but let it be called a mandate if you please! Let it be recollected, however, that the mandatory is not obliged to submit to any other conditions, or any other penalties, than those expressed in the letter of the compact. I open the book of the Constitution, and in the second chapter, which has by way of title "Royalty," I there find that the king is inviolable; there is not any exception in, nor any modification of, this article, but certain circumstances may occur, when the first public functionary may cease to enjoy this character of inviolability. The following is the first instance.

ART. V. "If the king shall not take the oath, or, after having taken it, he retract, he shall be considered as having abdicated the royalty."

The nation here hath foreseen a crime and enacted a forfeiture, but there is not a single word to be found concerning either trial or judgment. However, as, without retracting an oath, a king might betray and favor criminal and hostile principles against the State, the nation hath been aware of this, and the Constitution hath provided against it.

ART. VI. "If the king place himself at the head of an army and direct the forces against the nation, or if he doth not oppose himself, by a formal act, to any enterprise of this kind made in his name, he shall be considered as having abdicated the throne."

I beseech you to reflect on the heinous nature of this offense; there cannot be a more criminal one. It supposes all the machinations, all the perfidies, all the treasons, all the horrors, all the calamities of bloody civil war; and yet what does the constitution pronounce? The presumption of having abdicated the throne!

ART. VII. "If the king, having left the kingdom, shall not return immediately after an invitation made to him by the legislative body, then, etc."

What does the Constitution pronounce upon this occasion? The presumption of having abdicated the throne.

ART. VIII. says, "that after an abdication, either express or implied, the king shall then be tried in the same manner as all other citizens, for such crimes as he may commit after his abdication."

CAMILLE DESMOULINS

(1760-1794)

WHEN the ill-fated Louis XVI. dismissed Necker, Camille Desmoulins, hearing the news in a café in the Palais Royal, leaped on a table, defied the police, and with a pistol in each hand, made the speech which precipitated the actual Revolution. He called the people to arms, declaring that the action of the King was "the tocsin for the Bartholomew of the patriots." From that time until he was executed with the Dantonists in April 1794, Desmoulins was one of the great forces of the Revolution. He was born at Guise, in Picardy, March 2d, 1760. His father, who was Lieutenant-General of the bailiwick of Guise, educated him carefully, and Camille acquired a familiarity with the classics which, as editor of the Vieux Cordelier, he made use of to show the advantage of republics over monarchies, of democracies over aristocracies. He stammered so painfully that, as a rule, his great eloquence found vent only at the point of his pen. His street speeches were made only when he was transported out of himself by excitement, and only scraps of them are reported. It is said that in his great speech of July 12th, 1789, on the dismissal of Necker, the stammering habit which usually kept him silent in public assemblages, lost its hold on him, and that he spoke with the utmost fluency. The extract, 'Live Free or Die,' translated from the Vieux Cordelier, is characteristic both of his style and of his habit of thought. He is always classical. It was through too frequent illustrations from Tacitus that he aroused the anger of Robespierre, which sent him to the guillotine.

LIVE FREE OR DIE

(February 1788)

ONE difference between the monarchy and the republic, which alone should suffice to make the people reject with horror all monarchical rule and make them prefer the republic regardless of the cost of its establishment, is that in a democracy, though the people may be deceived, yet, at least, they love virtue. It is merit that they believe they put in power in place

Louis is accused of sundry offenses. He is accused in the name of the nation. Now, either these offenses have been foreseen by the constitutional act, and then the corresponding punishment is to be applied to them, or they have not; and if so, it follows that no punishment can follow from their commission. But I say that the most atrocious of all possible offenses hath been foreseen — that of a cruel war against the nation; and this surely includes all inferior crimes, and consequently points out the extent of all constitutional punishment.

I know that royalty being now abolished, deprivation cannot at present be applied. But has not Louis a right to exclaim: "What! will you, because you have abolished royalty, inflict a punishment on me, not mentioned in the constitutional code? Because no existing law can punish me, will you create one expressly on purpose? You possess every degree of power, it is true, but there is one species which you dare not execute, that of being unjust."

It has been said that Louis ought to be condemned as an enemy, but is he a greater enemy than if he had put himself at the head of an army in order to act against the nation? And you all know that in such a case, he could not have incurred more than a forfeiture of the crown! But if you take away from Louis the prerogative of being inviolable as a king, you cannot deprive him of the right of being tried as a citizen. And I here demand of you, where are those propitiatory forms of justice? Where are those juries which are so many hostages, as it were, for the lives and honor of citizens? Where is that proportion of suffrages which the law has so wisely required? Where is that silent scrutiny which in the same urn incloses the opinion and the conscience of the judge?

I now speak with the frankness becoming a freeman; it is in vain that I look around and search among you for judges — I can see none but accusers. You wish to pronounce upon the fate of Louis, and yet you have accused him! Will you decide his doom after having already expressed your opinion on his conduct?

of the rascals who are the very essence of monarchies. The vices, the concealments, and the crimes which are the diseases of republics are the very health and existence of monarchies. Cardinal Richelieu avowed openly in his political principles, that "the King should always avoid using the talents of thoroughly honest men." Long before him Sallust said: "Kings cannot get along without rascals. On the contrary, they should fear to trust the honest and the upright."

It is, therefore, only under a democracy that the good citizen can reasonably hope to see a cessation of the triumphs of intrigue and crime; and to this end the people need only to be enlightened.

There is yet this difference between a monarchy and the republic; the reigns of Tiberius, of Claudius, of Nero, of Caligula, of Domitian, had happy beginnings. In fact, all reigns make a joyous entry, but only as a delusion. Therefore the Royalists laugh at the present state of France as if its violent and terrible entry under the republic must always last.

Everything gives umbrage to a tyrant. If a citizen have popularity, he is becoming a rival to the prince. Consequently, he is stirring up civil strife, and is a suspect. If, on the contrary, he flee popularity and seclude himself in the corner of his own fireside, this retired life makes him remarked, and he is a suspect. If he is a rich man, there is an imminent peril that he corrupt the people with his largesses, and he is a suspect. Are you poor? How then! Invincible emperors, this man must be closely watched; no one so enterprising as he who has nothing. He is a suspect! Are you in character sombre, melancholy, or neglectful? You are afflicted by the condition of public affairs, and are a suspect.

If, on the contrary, the citizen enjoy himself and have resultant indigestion, he is only seeking diversion because his ruler has had an attack of gout, which made his Majesty realize his age. Therefore he is a suspect. Is he virtuous and austere in his habits? Ah! he is a new Brutus with his Jacobin severity, censuring the amiable and well-groomed court. He is a suspect. If he be a philosopher, an orator, or a poet, it will serve him ill to be of greater renown than those who govern, for can it be permitted to pay more attention to the author living on a fourth floor than to the emperor in his gilded palace. He is a suspect.

Has one made a reputation as a warrior—he is but the more dangerous by reason of his talent. There are many resources with an inefficient general. If he is a traitor he cannot so quickly deliver his army to the enemy. But an officer of merit like an Agricola—if he be disloyal, not one can be saved. Therefore, all such had better be removed and promptly placed at a distance from the army. Yes, he is a suspect.

Tacitus tells us that there was anciently in Rome a law specifying the crimes of "Lese-Majesté." That crime carried with it the punishment of death. Under the Roman Republic treasons were reduced to but four kinds, viz., abandoning an army in the country of an enemy; exciting sedition; the maladministration of the public treasury; and the impairment by inefficiency of the majesty of the Roman people. But the Roman emperors needed more clauses, that they could place cities and citizens under proscription.

Augustus was the first to extend the list of offenses that were "Lese-Majesté" or revolutionary, and under his successors the extensions were made until none were exempt. The slightest action was a State offense. A simple look, sadness, compassion, a sigh, even silence was "Lese-Majesté" and disloyalty to the monarch. One must needs show joy at the execution of their parent or friend lest they would perish themselves. Citizens, liberty must be a great benefit, since Cato disemboweled himself rather than have a king. And what king can we compare in greatness and heroism to the Cæsar whose rule Cato would not endure? Rousseau truly says: "There is in liberty as in innocence and virtue a satisfaction one only feels in their enjoyment and a pleasure which can cease only when they are lost."

SIR SIMON D'EWES

(1602–1650)

IR SIMON (SIMONDS?) D'EWES, the celebrated antiquary, was a Member of the Long Parliament and helped by his eloquence to make it celebrated among the deliberative bodies of the world. Of the three of his speeches of 1640 which are preserved in verbatim reports, that on the 'Antiquity of Cambridge' is the most characteristic of the man and of the learning of the educated classes of a time when education, devoting itself to what Raleigh called "tickle points of niceness," was rendering its possessors foreign to the great body of the English people. On the eve of one of the greatest revolutions of history, D'Ewes took advantage of the fact that the name of Cambridge appeared above that of Oxford in a document under consideration by the House to make a learned and interesting speech—at which, under the circumstances, posterity cannot fail to wonder.

He was born at Coxden, in Dorsetshire, December 18th, 1602, and died April 8th, 1650. He collected the journals of the Parliaments held during the reign of Elizabeth, and his manuscripts sold after his death to Sir Robert Harley are now among the treasures of the British Museum.

THE ANTIQUITY OF CAMBRIDGE

(Delivered in Parliament, January 21st, 1640)

I STAND up to persuade, if it may be, the declining of the present question and the further dispute of this business. Yesterday we had long debate about the putting out of a word, and now we are fallen upon the dispute of putting one word before another. I account no honor to Cambridge that it got the precedency by voices at the former committee, nor will it be any glory to Oxford to gain it by voices here, where we all know the multitudes of borough towns of the western parts of England do send so many worthy Members hither, that if we measure things by number, and not by weight, Cambridge is

sure to lose it. I would therefore propound a more noble way and means for the decision of the present controversy than by question, in which, if the University of Oxford (which for my own part I do highly respect and honor) shall obtain the prize, it will be far more glory to it than to carry it by multitude of voices, which, indeed, can be none at all. Let us therefore dispute it by reason, and not make an idol of either place, and if I shall be so convinced I shall readily change my vote, wishing we may find the same ingenuity in the Oxford men.

There are two principal respects, besides others, in which these famous universities may claim precedency each of the other.

Firstly, in respect of their being, as they were places of note in the elder ages.

Secondly, as they were ancient nurseries and seed plots of learning. If I do not, therefore, prove that Cambridge was a renowned city at least three hundred years before there was a house of Oxford standing, and whilst brute beasts fed, or corn was planted on that place, where the same city is now seated, and that Cambridge was a nursery of learning before Oxford was known to have a Grammar School in it, I will yield up the bucklers. If I should lose time to reckon up the vain allegations produced for the antiquity of Oxford by Twyne, and of Cambridge by Cajus, I should but repeat *deliria senum*, for I account the most of that they have published in print to be no better. But I find my authority without exception, that in the ancient catalogue of cities of Britain, Cambridge is the ninth in number, where London itself is but the eleventh, and who would have thought that ever Oxford should have contended for precedency with Cambridge, which London gave it above twelve hundred years. This I find in 'Gildas Albanius,' his British story, who died about the year 520, being the ancientest domestic monument we have (page 60); and in a Saxon anonymous story in Latin, touching the Britons and Saxons (page 39), who saith of himself that he lived in the days of Penda, King of the Mercians, in the tenth year of his reign, and that he knew him well, which falls out to be near the year 620. And lastly, I find the catalogue of the said British cities, with some little variation, to be set down in 'Nennius,' his Latin story of Britain (page 38), and he wrote the same, as he says of himself, in the year 880. They all call it "Cair-grant,"—the word "Cair" in the old Celtic tongue signifying city.

These three stories are exotic, and rare monuments, remaining yet only in ancient manuscripts amongst us not known to many; but the authority of them is irrefragable and without exception. The best and most ancient copies that I have seen of 'Gildas Albanius' and 'Nennius' remain in the University library of Cambridge, being those I have vouched, and the 'Saxon Anonymous' in a library we have near us. This Cairgrant is not only expounded by Alfred of Beverley to signify Cambridge, but also by William de Ramsey, Abbot of Croyland, in his manuscript story of the life of 'Guthlacas,' ignorantly in those elder days reputed a Saint, the said William goes further, and says it was so called *a granta flumine*. This place remained still a city of fame and repute a long time under the reign of the English Saxons, and is called in divers of the old manuscript Saxon annals "Grantecearten." And notwithstanding the great devastations it suffered with other places, by reason of the Danish incursions, yet in the first tome or volume of the book of 'Domes Dei' (for now I come to cite records) it appears to have been a place of considerable moment, having in it *decem custodias* and a castle of great strength and extent, and so I have done with Cambridge as a renowned place.

And now I come to speak to it, as it hath been a nursery of learning, nor will I begin higher with it than the time of the learned Saxon monarch King Alfred, because I suppose no man will question or gainsay but that there are sufficient testimonies of certain persons that did together in Cambridge study the arts and sciences much about that time. And it grew to be a place so famous for learning about the time of William I., the Norman, that he sent his younger son Henry thither to be there instructed, who himself being afterwards King of England, by the name of Henry I., was also surnamed Beauclerk, in respect of his great knowledge. If I should undertake to allege and vouch the records and other monuments of good authority, which assert and prove the increase and flourishing estate of this University in the succeeding ages, I should spend more time than our great and weighty occasions at this present will permit; it shall therefore suffice to have added, that the most ancient and first endowed college of England was Valence College in Cambridge, which after the foundation thereof, as appears by one of our Parliament Rolls remaining upon record in the Tower of London, received the new name or appellation of Pembroke Hall; it is in Rota. Parliam. de Anno 38 H. 6 num. 31. It appearing therefore so evidently by all that I have said, that Cambridge is in all respects the elder sister (which I speak not to derogate from Oxford), my humble advice is, that we lay aside the present question, as well to avoid division amongst overselves as to intomb all further emulation between the two sisters, and that we suffer the present bill to pass as it is now penned; and the rather, because I think Oxford had the precedence in the last bill of this nature that passed this House.

ORVILLE DEWEY

(1794–1882)

ORVILLE DEWEY, one of the favorite platform and pulpit orators of the second quarter of the nineteenth century, was born at Sheffield, Massachusetts, 1794, and died there, March 21st, 1882. He had a style of admirable lucidity, and his addresses show that he joined habits of logical thinking to sound scholarship. He was by profession a clergyman, and his sermons, addresses, and works of a general character, keep their place in public libraries.

THE GENIUS OF DEMOSTHENES

THE favorite idea of a genius among us is of one who never studies, or who studies nobody can tell when, — at midnight, or at odd times and intervals, — and now and then strikes out, "at a heat," as the phrase is, some wonderful production. "The young man," it is often said, "has genius enough, if he would only study." Now, the truth is, that the genius will study; it is that in the mind which does study; that is the very nature of it. I care not to say that it will always use books. All study is not reading, any more than all reading is study.

Attention is the very soul of genius; not the fixed eye, not the poring over a book, but the fixed thought. It is, in fact, an action of the mind which is steadily concentrated upon one idea, or one series of ideas; which collects, in one point, the rays of the soul, till they search, penetrate, and fire the whole train of its thoughts. And while the fire burns within, the outside may be indeed cold, indifferent, negligent, absent in appearance; he may be an idler or a wanderer, apparently without aim or intent, but still the fire burns within. And what, though "it bursts forth" at length, as has been said, "like volcanic fires, with spontaneous, original, native force"? It only shows the intense action of the elements beneath. What though it break forth like lightning from the cloud? The electric fire had been collecting in the firmament through many a silent, clear, and

calm day. What though the might of genius appear in one decisive blow, struck in some moment of high debate, or at the crisis of a nation's peril?

That mighty energy, though it may have heaved in the breast of Demosthenes, was once a feeble, infant thought. A mother's eye watched over its dawnings. A father's care guarded its early youth. It soon trod, with youthful steps, the halls of learning, and found other fathers to wake and to watch for it, even as it finds them here. It went on, but silence was upon its path, and the deep strugglings of the inward soul silently ministered to it. The elements around breathed upon it, and "touched it to finer issues." The golden ray of heaven fell upon it and ripened its expanding faculties. The slow revolutions of years slowly added to its collected energies and treasures, till, in its hour of glory, it stood forth embodied in the form of living, commanding, irresistible eloquence. The world wonders at the manifestation, and says: "Strange, strange that it should come thus unsought, unpremeditated, unprepared!" But the truth is, there is no more a miracle in it than there is in the towering of the pre-eminent forest tree, or in the flowing of the mighty and irresistible river, or in the wealth and waving of the boundless harvest.

THE RUST OF RICHES

AH! THE rust of riches! — not that portion of them which is kept bright in good and holy uses — "and the consuming fire" of the passions which wealth engenders! No rich man — I lay it down as an axiom of all experience — no rich man is safe who is not a benevolent man. No rich man is safe, but on the imitation of that benevolent God who is the possessor and dispenser of all the riches of the universe. What else mean the miseries of a selfish, luxurious, and fashionable life everywhere? What mean the sighs that come up from the purlieus and couches and most secret haunts of all splendid and self-indulgent opulence? Do not tell me that other men are sufferers too. Say not that the poor and destitute and forlorn are miserable also. Ah! just Heaven! thou hast in thy mysterious wisdom appointed to them a lot hard, full hard, to bear. Poor houseless wretches! who "eat the bitter bread of penury, and

drink the baleful cup of misery"; the winter's winds blow keenly through your "looped and windowed raggedness"; your children wander about unshod, unclothed, untended; I wonder not that ye sigh. But why should those who are surrounded with everything that heart can wish, or imagination conceive — the very crumbs that fall from whose table of prosperity might feed hundreds — why should they sigh amidst their profusion and splendor? They have broken the bond that should connect power with usefulness and opulence with mercy. That is the reason. They have taken up their treasures, and wandered away into a forbidden world of their own, far from the sympathies of suffering humanity; and the heavy night-dews are descending upon their splendid revels; and the all-gladdening light of heavenly beneficence is exchanged for the sickly glare of selfish enjoyment; and happiness, the blessed angel that hovers over generous deeds and heroic virtues, has fled away from that world of false gaiety and fashionable exclusion.

SAMUEL DEXTER

(1761–1816)

N THE fourth of August, 1806, Thomas O. Selfridge, an attorney at law, shot and killed Charles Austin on the public Exchange in Boston. There had been a newspaper controversy between Selfridge and Austin's father, and when the case came to trial, the celebrated Samuel Dexter, who defended Selfridge, had to meet a charge that his client had "armed himself and sought a quarrel, after first calling the father of his victim opprobrious names in the newspapers." The defense was handled with great skill by an eloquent appeal to a "higher law" which, though some have questioned its morality, made it a model for defenses in similar cases in all parts of the Union. This appeal, made in the peroration of the speech delivered at the trial of the defendant in Boston, resulted in the defendant's acquittal.

Dexter was born in Boston, May 14th, 1761. As a young man he became distinguished for his rebellious attitude towards the English government. After the Revolution he was elected to Congress, serving in both House and Senate. He was Secretary of War under the administration of John Adams, and Secretary of the Treasury during a part of that of Jefferson. After leaving the Cabinet, he took up the practice of law in Boston and made even a greater reputation at the bar than he had already made in public life.

«THE HIGHER LAW» OF SELF-DEFENSE

(Peroration of the Speech in the Case of Selfridge)

I HAVE hitherto admitted that the publication in the newspaper was a fault in the defendant, nor am I disposed entirely to justify it; yet circumstances existed which went far to extenuate it. He had been defamed on a subject, the delicacy of which, perhaps, will not be understood by you, as you are not lawyers, without some explanation. Exciting persons to bring suits is an infamous offense, for which a lawyer is liable to indictment, and to be turned away from the bar. It is so fatal to the reputation of a lawyer, that it is wounding him in the

---

nicest point, to charge him with it. It is the point of honor; and charging him with barratry, or stirring up suits, is like calling a soldier a coward. Mr. Austin, the father, had accused the defendant publicly of this offense, respecting a transaction in which his conduct had been punctiliously correct. The defendant first applied to him in person, and with good temper, to retract the charge; afterwards, in conversations with Mr. Welsh, Mr. Austin acknowledged the accusation to be false, and promised to contradict it as publicly as he had made it. Yet he neglected to do it; again he said he had done it,—but the fact appeared to be otherwise. This induced the defendant to demand a denial of it in writing. Though Mr. Austin privately acknowledged he had injured Mr. Selfridge, yet he refused to make him an adequate recompense when he neglected to make the denial as public as the charge. This was a state of war between them upon this subject, in which the more the defendant annoyed his enemy, the less power he had to hurt him. It was, therefore, a species of self-defense; and Mr. Austin, who had first been guilty of defamation, perhaps had little cause to complain. To try the correctness of this, we will imagine an extreme case.

Suppose a man should have established his reputation as a common slanderer and calumniator by libeling the most virtuous and eminent characters of his country, from Washington and Adams down through the whole list of American patriots; suppose such a one to have stood for twenty years in the kennel, and thrown mud at every well-dressed passenger; suppose him to have published libels until his style of defamation had become as notorious as his face,—would not every one say that such conduct was some excuse for bespattering him in turn?

I do not apply this to any individual; but it is a strong case to try a principle. And if such conduct would amount almost to a justification of him who should retaliate, will not the slander of Mr. Austin against Mr. Selfridge furnish some excuse for him?

It has also been stated to you, gentlemen, and some books have been read to prove it, that a man cannot be justified or excused in killing another in his own defense, unless a felony were attempted or intended. Some confusion seems to have been produced by this, which I will attempt to dissipate. It has been settled that if a felony be attempted, the party injured may kill the offender, without retreating as far as he safely can; but that

---

if the offense intended be not a felony, he cannot excuse the killing in his own defense, unless he so retreat, provided circumstances will permit. On this principle, all the books that have been read on this point may easily be reconciled. But the position contended for by the opposing counsel is in direct contradiction to one authority which they themselves have read. In the fourth volume of Blackstone's 'Commentaries,' page 185, the law is laid down as follows: "The party assaulted must therefore flee as far as he conveniently can, either by reason of some wall, ditch, or other impediment, or as far as the fierceness of the assault will permit him: for it may be so fierce as not to allow him to yield a step, without manifest danger of his life, or enormous bodily harm; and then, in his defense, he may kill his assailant instantly. And this is the doctrine of universal justice, as well as of the municipal law."

Also in 1 Hawkin's Pleas of the Crown, chap. 29, § 13, the law on this point is stated thus: "And now I am to consider homicide *se defendendo*, which seems to be, where one, who has no other possible means of preserving his life from one who combats with him on a sudden quarrel, or of defending his person from one who attempts to beat him (especially if such attempt be made upon him in his own house), kills the person by whom he is reduced to such an inevitable necessity."

From these two highly respectable authorities, it appears that, though nothing more be attempted than to do great bodily injury, or even to beat a man, and there be no possibility of avoiding it but by killing the assailant,- it is excusable so to do.

When the weight and strength of the cane, or rather cudgel, which the deceased selected is considered, and the violence with which it was used, can it be doubted that great bodily harm would have been the consequence, if Selfridge had not defended himself? The difference between this weapon and the pistol made use of by the defendant, perhaps, is greatly exaggerated by the imagination. The danger from the former might be nearly as great as from the latter. When a pistol is discharged at a man, in a moment of confusion and agitation, it is very uncertain whether it will take effect at all; and if it should, the chances are, perhaps, four to one, that the wound will not be mortal. Still further, when the pistol is once discharged, it is of little or no use; but with a cane, a man, within reach of his object, can hardly miss it; and if the first blow should prove ineffectual, he can repeat his strokes until he has destroyed his enemy.

---

fectual, he can repeat his strokes until he has destroyed his enemy.

If it were intended to excite contempt for the laws of the country, a more effectual method could hardly be taken than to tell a man, who has a soul within him, that if one attempt to rob him of a ten-dollar bill, this is a felony, and therefore esteemed by the law an injury of so aggravated a nature that he may lawfully kill the aggressor; but that if the same man should whip and kick him on the public Exchange, this is only a trespass, to which he is bound to submit rather than put in jeopardy the life of the assailant; and the laws will recompense him in damages.

Imagine that you read in a Washington newspaper that on a certain day, immediately on the rising of Congress, Mr. A, of Virginia, called Mr. B, of Massachusetts, a scoundrel for voting against his resolution, and proceeded deliberately to cut off his ears. Mr. B was armed with a good sword cane, but observed that his duty as a citizen forbade him to endanger the life of Mr. A, for, that cutting off a man's ear was by law no felony; and he had read in law books that courts of justice were the only proper *vindices injuriarum*, and that he doubted not that, by means of a lawsuit, he should obtain a reasonable compensation for his ears. What are the emotions excited in your breasts at this supposed indignity and exemplary patience of the representative of your country? Would you bow to him with profound respect on his return? or rather would not his dignity and usefulness, by universal consent, be lost forever?

We have now taken a view of the facts and the positive rules of law that apply to them; and it is submitted to you with great confidence that the defendant has brought himself within the strictest rules, and completely substantiated his defense by showing that he was under a terrible necessity of doing the act, and that by law he is excused. It must have occurred to you, however, in the course of this investigation, that our law has not been abundant in its provisions for protecting a man from gross insult and disgrace. Indeed, it was hardly to be expected that the sturdy hunters who laid the foundations of the common law would be very refined in their notions. There is, in truth, much intrinsic difficulty in legislating on this subject. Laws must be made to operate equally on all members of the community; and such is the difference in the situations and feelings of men that no general rule on this subject can properly apply to all. That which is an irreparable injury to one man, and which he would feel himself bound to repel even by the instantaneous death of the aggressor, or by his own, would be a very trivial misfortune to another. There are men in every civilized community whose happiness and usefulness would be forever destroyed by a beating which another member of the same community would voluntarily receive for a five-dollar bill. Were the laws to authorize a man of elevated mind and refined feelings of honor to defend himself from indignity by the death of the aggressor, they must at the same time furnish an excuse to the meanest chimney sweeper in the country for punishing his sooty companion, who should fillip him on the cheek, by instantly thrusting his scraper into his belly. But it is too much to conclude from this difficulty in stating exceptions to the general rule, that extreme cases do not furnish them. It is vain, and worse than vain, to prescribe laws to a community which will require a dereliction of all dignity of character, and subject the most elevated to outrages from the most vile. If such laws did exist, the best that could be hoped would be that they would be broken. Extreme cases are, in their nature, exceptions to all rules; and when a good citizen says that, the law not having specified them, he must have a right to use his own best discretion on the subject, he only treats the law of his country in the same manner in which every Christian necessarily treats the precepts of his religion. The law of his Master is, " Resist not evil "; " If a man smite thee on one cheek, turn to him the other also." No exceptions to these rules are stated; yet does not every rational Christian necessarily make them ? I have been led to make these observations, not because I think them necessary in the defense of Mr. Selfridge, but because I will have no voluntary agency in degrading the spirit of my country. The greatest of all public calamities would be a pusillanimous spirit that would tamely surrender personal dignity to every invader. The opposing council have read to you from books of acknowledged authority that the right of self-defense was not given by the law of civil society, and that that law cannot take it away. It is founded, then, on the law of nature, which is of higher authority than any human institution. This law enjoins us to be useful in proportion to our capacities; to protect the powers of being useful, by all means that nature has given us, and to secure our own happiness, as well as that of

others. These sacred precepts cannot be obeyed without securing to ourselves the respect of others. Surely, I need not say to you that the man who is daily beaten on the public Exchange cannot retain his standing in society by recurring to the laws. Recovering daily damages will rather aggravate the contempt that the community will heap upon him; nor need I say that when a man has patiently suffered one beating he has almost insured a repetition of the insult.

It is a most serious calamity for a man of high qualifications for usefulness, and delicate sense of honor, to be driven to such a crisis, yet should it become inevitable, he is bound to meet it like a man, to summon all the energies of the soul, rise above ordinary maxims, poise himself on his own magnanimity, and hold himself responsible only to his God. Whatever may be the consequences, he is bound to bear them; to stand like Mount Atlas,

> "When storms and tempests thunder on its brow,
> And oceans break their billows at his feet."

Do not believe that I am inculcating opinions tending to disturb the peace of society. On the contrary, they are the only principles that can preserve it. It is more dangerous for the laws to give security to a man disposed to commit outrages on the persons of his fellow-citizens than to authorize those who must otherwise meet irreparable injury to defend themselves at every hazard. Men of eminent talents and virtues, on whose exertions in perilous times the honor and happiness of their country must depend, will always be liable to be degraded by every daring miscreant, if they cannot defend themselves from personal insult and outrage. Men of this description must always feel that to submit to degradation and dishonor is impossible. Nor is this feeling confined to men of that eminent grade. We have thousands in our country who possess this spirit; and without them we should soon deservedly cease to exist as an independent nation. I respect the laws of my country and revere the precepts of our holy religion; I should shudder at shedding human blood; I would practice moderation and forbearance to avoid so terrible a calamity; yet should I ever be driven to that impassable point where degradation and disgrace begin, may this arm shrink palsied from its socket if I fail to defend my own honor.

It has been intimated that the principles of Christianity con-

demn the defendant. If he is to be tried by this law, he certainly has a right to avail himself of one of its fundamental principles. I call on you, then, to do to him, as in similar circumstances you would expect others to do to you; change situations for a moment and ask yourselves what you would have done if attacked as he was. And instead of being necessitated to act at the moment, and without reflection, take time to deliberate. Permit me to state for you your train of thought. You would say: This man who attacks me appears young, athletic, active, and violent. I am feeble and incapable of resisting him; he has a heavy cane, which is undoubtedly a strong one, as he had leisure to select it for the purpose; he may intend to kill me; he may, from the violence of his passion, destroy me without intending it; he may maim or greatly injure me; by beating me he must disgrace me. This alone destroys all my prospects, all my happiness, and all my usefulness. Where shall I fly when thus rendered contemptible ? Shall I go abroad ? Every one will point at me the finger of scorn. Shall I go home ? My children — I have taught them to shrink from dishonor; will they call me father ? What is life to me after suffering this outrage ? Why should I endure this accumulated wretchedness, which is worse than death, rather than put in hazard the life of my enemy ?

Ask yourselves whether you would not make use of any weapon that might be within your power to repel the injury; and if it should happen to be a pistol, might you not, with sincere feeling of piety, call on the Father of Mercies to direct the stroke ?

While we reverence the precepts of Christianity, let us not make them void by impracticable construction. They cannot be set in opposition to the law of our nature; they are a second edition of that law; they both proceed from the same Author.

Gentlemen, all that is dear to the defendant in his future life is by the law of his country placed in your power. He cheerfully leaves it there. Hitherto he has suffered all that his duty as a good citizen required with fortitude and patience; and if more be yet in store for him, he will exhibit to his accusers an example of patient submission to the laws. Yet permit me to say in concluding his defense that he feels full confidence that your verdict will terminate his sufferings.*

* The jury returned a verdict of " Not Guilty."

PORFIRIO DIAZ

(1830-)

AT THE Monterey banquet of 1898, President Diaz of Mexico outlined the policy he has pursued in developing the resources of his country — a policy modeled on that of Jefferson and involving as fundamental principles the utmost possible hospitality to immigration. Though he does not speak habitually in public, President Diaz has a style of 'the greatest ease and flexibility, illustrating in every sentence the suavity of intellect which has enabled him to establish a stable government in Mexico where so many others who were mere soldiers had failed. Perhaps no other living Latin-American has more of the faculty of pleasing than President Diaz shows in complimenting Monterey for its achievements of peaceful progress.

He was born at Oaxaca, September 15th, 1830. He received a liberal education, but his enlistment when the United States invaded Mexico in 1847 made him a soldier rather than the lawyer he might have been. He served against Santa Anna in 1854; against Marquez in 1861 ; and against Maximilian and the French from 1863 to 1867. In 1876 he drove out Lerdo, and the following year he became President of Mexico, an office which he has held or controlled ever since. The Constitution has been changed to allow him to succeed himself, and if Mexico prosper under him in the future as it has done in the past, he is likely to remain its President until he dies or refuses to serve.

MEXICAN PROGRESS

(Delivered at the Banquet Given in His Honor at Monterey, December 21st, 1898)

Mr. Governor and Gentlemen: —

IN THE eloquent toast that we have just heard, there are thoughts expressed so beautifully and with so pronounced a spirit of friendship, that I can only accept them as a sign of the fully reciprocated regard with which the author honors me. However little I may deserve them, they nevertheless demand acknowledgment.

Hence, in replying, I must begin by thanking you most cordially. In the name of my fellow-guests, and in my own, I also thank this attractive and beautiful city for the splendid welcome with which it has honored us.

The impression made on us by its munificence is so pleasant and so great that we do not know what to admire most and what to be most thankful for,—whether for the charming hospitality, elegance, and good taste shown in receiving us, or for the striking exhibition of improvements we already knew by hearsay and that now they are so kind as to show us in review.

If the hospitality and attentions extended to us make us happy during the days we spend with our amiable hosts of Nuevo Leon, the exhibition of their improvements gives us good reason for knowing, appreciating, and admiring with proper national pride the abundant, varied, and worthy results of the spirit of enterprise animating capital and industry, when governed by a scrupulous honesty, supported by the good name which this invaluable virtue perpetuates by its presence, and firmly protected by a government which, with firm hand and clear and just conscience, guarantees the life, the property, the liberty, the honor, and all natural and civil rights of the man and of the citizen.

Sixteen years, more or less, of intelligent work under direction of the great principles of prosperity we have just enumerated, have been sufficient to awaken and put into productive action the industrial intelligence and noble ambition of the citizens of Nuevo Leon, while the well-deserved fame of the satisfactory results achieved has attracted, and is still attracting, from all quarters, the capital, the industry, the energy, and all other faculties belonging to that genius which, when stimulated amongst themselves and competing in worthy initiative and noble strength, has extended, improved, and beautified every day this great and typical display of the industrial progress of Nuevo Leon, which, with well-founded and noble pride its beautiful capital offers us.

It is certain that this magnificent picture is the objective demonstration and measure of the present prosperity and advanced civilization of this intelligent and industrious people. But this is not all; for after this, there is something which claims all our attention,—so much the more imperiously, since this something tends to prepare a future still more prosperous. Nevertheless, I am not surprised at this, for it is only natural that a

people which has created men like Zaragoza and produced them like Zuazua and Escobedo, Treviño, Naraujo, and so many nameless heroes, should accomplish its high destiny as soon as it was allowed to apply in peace the energy that moved it in war.

And thus we see that as soon as this invaluable advantage of peace has been established and government representation normalized in the State, government, fulfilling one of its first and most necessary duties, becomes an educator, wishing that the large and desirable population attracted to Monterey on account of the industries of the city should not make merely a short stay in this favored land, but that willingly they should decide to leave their bones among us in return for the generosity their activity, their work, and their talent has prompted. So the city provides intelligently and generously for instruction to their children in primary, secondary, and high schools, so that without the inconvenience that their absence in quest of instruction would cause to their families, and especially to the mothers, children may be educated here at home. Thus, here at home, they may get practical knowledge and become wise, if they wish it, at the side of their parents, with the generation to which they belong, a part of the society in which they live, if they decide to adopt altogether this hospitable home, which is willing to receive them with all the motherly love she bears to her own sons, recognizing their merits, without distinction between her own and her adopted children.

Finally, gentlemen, now that I have the great satisfaction of seeing around me the most prominent business men of this nation, as well as those of foreign countries, and government officers who, uniting their manly and intelligent action, have elevated Monterey to the height of which she is rightly proud—now that I have the pleasure of breaking bread with them at the same table and toasting with them their well-deserved prosperity, I am pleased to be able to say to them in accordance with a conscience which has never deceived me: "You who toil for the progress of Nuevo Leon, natives and foreigners—you are worthy of this Republic whose national wealth and habits of industry you have cultivated and increased with your own well-earned private wealth!"

As for the governor, who inspires, encourages, and represents the administrative staff, I shall remind him that eighteen years ago, in promoting him from colonel to brigadier-general in

reward of a very distinguished service, I said to him: "This is the way the weapons with which the country honors us ought to be used. This is the way a dutiful and honorable soldier fulfills his promise to defend his flag." And now, after eighteen years, and after having studied carefully the great advantages that under his intelligent and firm government this brave and intelligent State has attained, I consider it just to say to you, condensing all the praises with which his deeds have inspired me: "General Reyes, this is the way to govern; this is the way to respond to the sovereign will of the people."

Gentlemen, I drink to the increasing prosperity of Nuevo Leon and to the well-deserved honor it bestows on its authors.

MAHLON DICKERSON

(1769–1853)

MATTHEW LYON, the Member of Congress whose vote made Thomas Jefferson President, had been prosecuted under the Sedition Law passed during the administration of John Adams. After his retirement from Congress he presented a petition, setting forth that the law under which he had been fined was unconstitutional, and asking to have the money returned to him. This put Congress in the position of reviewing the action of the federal courts. The case was a very celebrated one, as it involved not only this principle, but a leading point in the "practical politics" of the great political revolution of 1800. The claim remained before Congress until 1840, when the sum of $1,060.90, with interest from 1799, was ordered paid as compensation for the enforcement of an unconstitutional act. When the case was before the Senate in 1821, Mahlon Dickerson, of New Jersey, urged the claims of Lyon very strongly. Senator Dickerson, who was born in New Jersey in 1769, was long one of its leading public men. He was judge of its Supreme Court and governor before his election to the United States Senate (1817). He was Secretary of the Navy in the Cabinets of Jackson and Van Buren. He died in Morris County, New Jersey, October 5th, 1853.

THE ALIEN AND SEDITION ACTS OF THE ADAMS ADMINISTRATION

(From the Speech in the Case of Matthew Lyon, United States Senate, January 19th, 1821)

I HAVE never doubted that the Sedition Act, so far as it respects the printing and publishing of libels, was a direct, open, and unequivocal breach of the Constitution. And, although I do not hold the United States responsible for all the losses sustained under that act, I would not willingly retain in our Treasury a single dollar of the money iniquitously acquired under it. The whole forms but a small sum, but if it were large, it should be returned to those from whom it was taken. I should not stop to inquire whether it were a thousand or a hundred thousand dollars.

To ascertain how far this act was an abridgment of the liberty of the press, let us examine a little further into its practical operation. It is unnecessary to add anything to what has already been said upon the trial of Matthew Lyon. The trial of Thomas Cooper in 1800, in the Circuit Court of the United States, for the Pennsylvania District, will furnish a complete illustration of the views of those who made and of those who administered this law.

I select this case because I was a witness of the whole trial; a trial which, at the time, filled my mind with horror and indignation. I saw a man whom it was my pride then, as it is now, to call my friend; a man of the most honorable feelings; a man whose name is identified with science and literature; the constant study of whose life it has been to render himself useful to his fellow-beings; I saw this man dragged before a criminal court, arraigned, tried, and punished, for publishing words which nothing but the violence and blindness of party rage could have construed into crime. In the year '97 Mr. Cooper had asked of the President, Mr. Adams, to be appointed an agent for American claims; the request was made through Doctor Priestly directly to Mr. Adams, with a frankness warranted on the part of the Doctor by the intimacy which had long existed between them. As the application was thus personal, it was supposed to be confidential. It was unsuccessful, and there it should have rested. But, by some means never explained, two years afterwards this application was made public, and afforded the editor of a paper in Reading an opportunity of inserting a scurrilous paragraph against Mr. Cooper. Irritated at being thus held up as a subject of ridicule, Mr. Cooper, in justification of his own conduct, published the address for which he was indicted. The words contained in the indictment, stripped of the innuendoes, are the following: —

"Nor do I see any impropriety in making this request of Mr. Adams; at that time he had just entered into office; he was hardly in the infancy of political mistake; even those who doubted of his capacity, thought well of his intentions. Nor were we yet saddled with the expense of a permanent navy, or threatened, under his auspices, with the existence of a standing army. Our credit was not yet reduced quite so low as to borrow money at eight per cent. in time of peace, while the unnecessary violence of official expressions might justly have provoked a war. Mr. Adams had not yet projected his

embassies to Prussia, Russia, and the Sublime Porte, nor had he yet interfered, as President of the United States, to influence the decisions of a court of justice,—a stretch of authority which the monarch of Great Britain would have shrunk from; an interference without precedent, against law, and against mercy! The melancholy case of Jonathan Robbins, a native citizen of America, forcibly impressed by the British, and delivered up, with the advice of Mr. Adams, to the mock trial of a British court-martial, had not yet astonished the Republican citizens of this free country; a case too little known, but which the people ought to be fully apprised of before the election, and they shall be."

I have the highest veneration for the exalted statesman and revolutionary patriot against whom this censure was leveled; but he was not infallible—much less so were those around him, by whose advice, at this particular period, he was too much influenced. But, however exalted his station, he had accepted it with a full knowledge that it was the disposition and practice, and a salutary one, too, in this country, to examine and censure. with great freedom, the conduct of those in power. To be censured freely, and sometimes unjustly, is a tax which every one must pay who holds the highest station in our Government. Laws which should completely prevent this would as completely prostrate the liberties of the people.

However much Mr. Adams might have been hurt at the asperity of the language applied to him, I am confident he never intimated a wish in favor of a prosecution. Most probably this took place in consequence of the advice of those who advised that Robbins should be given up. About this time Mr. Adams thought proper to repress the zeal of his political friends by pardoning Fries, who had been guilty of a misdemeanor, but was convicted of treason, and by other acts evincing a disposition to pursue a more moderate system than that which had prevailed for two preceding years. It will also be remembered that not long after this period he dismissed some of his advisers, in whom he had probably placed too much confidence.

At the present time of good feelings it seems incredible that what Mr. Cooper said of the expenses of a permanent navy,—of the standing army,—the eight per cent. loan, and the projected embassies to Prussia, Russia, and the Sublime Porte, should have been considered as the subject of indictment. What was said as to the case of Jonathan Robbins, otherwise called Thomas Nash,

was of a more serious character, and should have been answered, if it could have been answered, by a true history of that transaction—not by punishing Mr. Cooper; for, if this interference on the part of the President were without precedent against law and against mercy, fining and imprisoning Mr. Cooper could not make it otherwise.

The friends of the Sedition Act say that Congress were authorized to pass it as a law necessary and proper for carrying into effect the powers vested by the Constitution in the Government, under the eighth section of the first article of the Constitution.

This part of the Constitution is very elastic, and some gentleman discovered that under it Congress may do what they please, by simply making the word "necessary" mean "convenient." But I cannot imagine what power vested by the Constitution in the Government it was necessary to carry into effect by the Sedition Act. That no such necessity as is alleged did exist is evident from this circumstance, that the Government went on very well before that act passed, and quite as well since it has expired. However convenient, therefore, the law might have been, it certainly was not necessary. If it were necessary in the meaning of the Constitution, it was indispensably necessary—not partly necessary. If necessary then it must be necessary now, and Congress must, of course, be neglecting their duty in not reviving that law.

We are now in effect to declare this act to have been constitutional or unconstitutional. If we do the latter we correct not the errors of the court but of Congress. If the law was not constitutional when passed, the decisions of the court could not make it so. Probably the court did not think that a question for them to decide. The act was a legislative construction of the Constitution expressly. It was opposed and supported on constitutional grounds, and is a declaration of the three branches of the legislature of the meaning of the Constitution in this particular. And it is not yet ascertained that, in construing the Constitution, Congress is subordinate to the judiciary. Probably the first decisive experiment upon this subject will prove the contrary.

I do not think it necessary to search for precedents to justify us in the measure now proposed. If we have no precedent let us make one that may be a memento to dominant parties not to abuse their power. But if precedents were necessary we may

find enough in the history of England, not in that of our own country; for, fortunately for us, our history affords but a few instances of the abuse of power. For such precedents we need not go back to the heavy time of York and Lancaster, when the triumphant party constantly reversed all that had been done by the party subdued. We may look into a later period when the Stuarts and their immediate successors were upon the throne, when the principles of liberty were much better understood than practiced.

The attainder of the Earl of Stafford, who had been treacherously given up by a cowardly king to the indignation of Parliament, was reversed.

The attainders against Algernon Sidney and against Lord Russell were reversed.

The attainder against Alderman Cornish was reversed, as also that against Lady Lisle and many others. In these cases it is true the Parliament only reversed their own proceedings. But they sometimes reversed the proceedings of other courts, as in the case of Bastwick, Burton, and Prynne, who were tried in the court of Star Chamber for libels, and sentenced to lose their ears, to pay a fine of five thousand pounds each and to be imprisoned for life. This is a very strong case, and in point; for the Parliament not only reversed the sentence, but remitted the fine, and ordered satisfaction for damages to the parties injured.

I must ask the indulgence of the Senate while I read a few passages from the proceedings in this extraordinary case. I shall read them for the edification of those who are, who have been, or who hereafter may be, in favor of a Sedition Act.

Dr. Bastwick, Mr. Burton, and Mr. Prynne had written some religious books, in which were contained some reflections on the Bishops, which were deemed libelous. Mr. Prynne, three years before this time, had written a book in which he censured stage plays, music, and dancing, for which he was punished by the loss of his ears. Between eight and nine o'clock in the morning, the fourteenth of June [1637], the lords being set in their places, in the said court of Star Chamber, and casting their eyes at the prisoners, then at the bar, Sir John Finch, Chief-Justice of the Commons Pleas, began to speak after this manner: —

I had thought Mr. Prynne had no ears, but methinks he hath ears; which caused many of the lords to take a stricter view of him;

and, for their better satisfaction, the usher of the court was commanded to turn up his hair and show his ears; upon the sight whereof, the lords were displeased that they had been formerly no more cut off, and cast out some disgraceful words of him.

To which Mr. Prynne replied, "My lords, there is never a one of your honors but would be sorry to have your ears as mine are."

The lord keeper replied again, "In good faith, he is somewhat saucy."

"I hope," said Mr. Prynne, "your honors will not be offended; I pray God to give you ears to hear."

"The business of the day," said the lord keeper, "is to proceed on the prisoner at the bar."

Mr. Prynne then humbly desired the court to give him leave to make a motion or two; which being granted, he moves:—

First, that their honors would be pleased to accept of a cross-bill against the prelates, signed with their own hands, being that which stands with the justice of the court, which he humbly craved, and so tendered it.

Lord Keeper—As for your cross-bill, it is not the business of the day; hereafter if the court should see just cause, and that it savor not of libeling, we may accept of it; for my part I have not seen it, but have heard somewhat of it.

Mr. Prynne—I hope your honors will not refuse it, being, as it is, on his Majesty's behalf. We are his Majesty's subjects, and therefore require the justice of the court.

Lord Keeper—But this is not the business of the day.

Mr. Prynne—Why then, my lords, I have a second motion, which I humbly pray your honors to grant, which is, that your lordships will please to dismiss the prelates, here now sitting, from having any voice in the censure of this cause, being generally known to be adversaries, as being no way agreeable with equity or reason, that they who are our adversaries should be our judges; therefore I humbly crave they may be expunged out of the court.

Lord Keeper—In good faith it is a sweet motion; is it not? Herein you are become libelous; and if you should thus libel all the lords and reverend judges as you do the reverend prelates, by this your plea, you would have none to pass sentence upon you for your libeling, because they are parties.

The whole trial is very interesting. I proceed to the sentence.

Thus, the prisoners, desiring to speak a little more for themselves, were commanded to silence. And so the lords proceed to censure.

v—116

defenders of the people against the oppressions of the Government. From what I witnessed in the years 1798, 1799, and 1800, I never shall, I never can, consider our judiciary as the bulwark of the liberties of the people. The people must look out for other bulwarks for their liberties. I have the most profound respect for the learning, talents, and integrity of the honorable judges who fill our Federal bench. But, if those who carried into effect the Sedition Act are to be called the people's defenders, it must be for nearly the same reason that the Fates were called *Parcæ — quia non parcebant.*

The Lord Cettington's censure: "I condemn these three men to lose their ears in the palace yard at Westminster, to be fined five thousand pounds a man to his Majesty, and to perpetual imprisonment in three remote places in the kingdom, namely, the castles of Caernarvon, Cornwall, and Lancaster."

The Lord Finch added to this censure:—

"Mr. Prynne to be stigmatized in the cheeks with two letters, S and L, for seditious libeler." To which all the lords agreed.

I omit what is said of the punishment of Dr. Bastwick and Mr. Burton, which was inflicted with great cruelty, but that of Mr. Prynne deserves a particular notice:—

Now, the executioner being come to sear him and cut off his ears, Mr. Prynne said these words to him: "Come, friend, come burn me, cut me; I fear not; I have learned to fear the fire of hell, and not what man can do unto me. Come, sear me, sear me; I shall bear in my body the marks of the Lord Jesus"; which the bloody executioner performed with extraordinary cruelty, heating his iron twice to burn one cheek, and cut one of his ears so close that he cut off a piece of his cheek. At which exquisite torture he never moved with his body, or as much as changed his countenance, but still looked up as well as he could towards Heaven, with a smiling countenance, even to the astonishment of all the beholders, and uttering, as soon as the executioner had done, this heavenly sentence: "The more I am beaten down, the more I am lift up."

What protection was afforded to these wretched men by the common law, the law in which they lived and moved and had their being?

The honorable gentleman from Georgia admonishes us not to destroy the independence of the judiciary, the bulwark of the liberties of the people. We shall not, in the measure now proposed, in the slightest degree interfere with the independence of the judiciary. It must be a matter of indifference to them what we do with the Sedition Act; it cannot affect their emoluments. I have understood that the independency of the judiciary was regulated by the greater or less permanency in the tenure of their office, and the greater or less certainty in the payment of their fixed salaries.

But I must beg leave to differ from the honorable gentleman when he informs us that our independent judiciary is the bulwark of the liberties of the people. By which he must mean,

DANIEL S. DICKINSON

(1800–1866)

DANIEL S. DICKINSON represented New York in the United States Senate from 1844 to 1851, and during the great debates over the slavery question he made a number of speeches against Sectionalism, which gave him a national reputation and great popularity as an orator. Extracts from his orations in favor of the Union were published in the school speakers and often declaimed by the young orators of his generation. He was born in Connecticut, September 11th, 1800, but his family removed to New York when he was only six years old, and as a result of his own efforts in educating himself and pushing himself at the bar, he rose to eminence both as a lawyer and a public man. He retired from politics after leaving the Senate. In 1861, however, he made a number of speeches in favor of maintaining the Union at any cost, and in 1864 he was a delegate to the Baltimore convention.

REBUKING SENATOR CLEMENS OF ALABAMA

(From a Speech in the United States Senate, January 12th, 1850)

I AM for maintaining the Union in spirit as well as in form; and I have deprecated the assaults which I have seen made upon the Constitution occasionally in the nonslaveholding States, in the refusal to deliver fugitives from service according to a solemn provision of that instrument. But this, sir, I look upon as a matter which must be reformed at home, as it will be by a sound and healthy public opinion, when it shall set a just estimate upon the interference of political agitators, and condemn a morality that is purer than the fundamental law. But I will not even dwell upon the alleged errors of any section of my country. If she has ever been astray, rather than contemplate it, I would, like the son of the erring patriarch, walk backward and cast the mantle of concealment over it. I desire to preserve in all its vigor the glorious inheritance which our fathers gave us; to see the South secure in the full possession and enjoyment of their constitutional rights. I have stood by them when I thought them right, regardless of peril, and will now aid in shielding them from unjust and improper aggressions upon their institutions. In this struggle numerically they are the weaker party, and when I have seen them unjustly assaulted and assailed, my sympathies have been with them, and I have exposed and denounced not only the sectional agitators, but have warned those against excitement whose views and intentions are just, but who have been provoked to retaliation by just such wholesale sectional assaults as are now heaped upon the North by the Senator from Alabama [Mr. Clemens]. Sir, crimination begets recrimination; and although men may put on the garb of philosophy for an occasion, they are yet liable to be betrayed by impulse and excitement; and when they hear distinguished Southern men day after day making sectional appeals, grouping all together and condemning all in gross, without stint or exception, they in their turn will make other declarations, and thus the work goes on. One sectional agitator begets another—a blow given brings a blow in return, and thus sectional agitation makes the meat it feeds on. I have already said I regretted that this subject has been introduced. Allow me to say that I do not regret that it is about to reach its culminating point. I care not how soon this may be the case. I believe that the great mass of the people of the South are honest, just, and generous, and that all they desire is to remain secure in the possession of their rights. I believe, too, sir, that the great mass of the people of the North are equally just and equally generous, and true to the Constitution, and that they too desire nothing more than what they deem to be their rights, and the rights of the whole people, and best calculated to advance the honor of the Confederacy and the interest and happiness of mankind. When reviled, I will not revile again. I will by no means repudiate the Southern Democracy. They have too often proved themselves worthy of the name they bear. Nor, sir, upon the question of this Union, much and radically as I differ with them upon other questions, will I repudiate the patriotic among our opponents. This question shoots too deep and stretches too high to be measured by political parties; and when the day of trial comes, if come it does, every patriotic man will breast himself for the shock, and sectional agitators will be foiled. The Constitution throws its broad ægis over this

mighty Republic, and its people worship at its shrine with more than an Eastern devotion. They have contemplated the priceless value of the Union. They have thought of the blood and tears by which it was purchased. They see the proud vessel bearing majestically onward, and they exclaim in the language of the poet:—

> "Thou, too, sail on, O Ship of State!
> Sail on, O UNION, strong and great!
> Humanity with all its fears,
> With all the hope of future years,
> Is hanging breathless on thy fate!
> We know what master laid thy keel,
> What workmen wrought thy ribs of steel,
> Who made each mast, and sail, and rope,
> What anvils rang, what hammers beat,
> In what a forge and what a heat
> Were shaped the anchors of thy hope!"

They will cheer on this noble ship; they will stand by this Constitution; they will adhere to this Union; and although the Northern people are opposed to the institution of slavery, the great mass of them have no intention or disposition to trench improperly upon the constitutional rights of the South; and this they will prove, should the occasion arise, even though they should sell their lives in her defense. Sir, if it should come to the worst, as it never will, so firmly are the Northern people devoted to the Constitution, that if armed incendiarism, foreign or domestic, should push her mad crusade against the South, and she be placed in peril, I am free to declare, I would, and so I believe would every patriotic man of the free States who had a sword to draw, draw it in defense of their Southern brethren and of the rights guaranteed to them by a common compact, and stand by them to the death. But, sir, they will only stand by her when she is right; and so long as she is so, no sword will be called into requisition, except against a foreign and a common foe. The very heat, natural and artificial, to which sectional agitation has attained, will work its own cure. It will burn itself out. Northern agitators and Southern agitators will find themselves side by side in their errand of mutual mischief, and the great mass of the American people will look upon this

Union as it is, and upon Southern rights and Northern rights as they are, and will stand by them and protect them.

These territorial questions, this District of Columbia question, the question of jurisdiction in forts and dock yards, arsenals and navy yards, and so forth, are mostly questions temporary in their character, and, together with the question of fugitives from service, would be soon settled by the good sense of the right-minded, were it not for the wholesale denunciations of men grouped together in whole communities and States, on one hand denouncing the North, the North, the North, and on the other hand the South, the South, the South. This provokes the greater part of this struggle; and I would suggest whether it would not be more wise if gentlemen would exercise a little forbearance, always remembering the saying, "Let him that is without sin cast the first stone." I am willing to admit that the great mass of our Southern friends treat this question as it should be treated; and I am pleased to see them stand up boldly as they do for their right of being let alone. I am gratified to hear them, in a proper spirit, stand by their institutions and defend them, for it serves to show, what some seem practically to forget, that this Confederacy is a sisterhood of free and independent States associated for a few common purposes, and not a consolidated Federal Government. The North and the South stand together upon one great constitutional platform, and neither has a right to claim superiority over the other. The people of the South have institutions that are sensitive and that can be endangered by agitation in the North, and in opposing such agitation I have been willing to throw myself into the breach to turn it aside. I have attempted to call the attention of the Northern people—nay, of the whole American people—to the danger of agitating this question, and I would say in all kindness to my friend from Alabama that he gives more food in one speech for the nourishment of the Abolition movement than all the Garrisons, Wendell Phillipses, and Abby Folsoms, and all the speeches of all the "Free Soil" agitators and abolition demagogues put together. He does more to provoke assaults upon the institutions of the South than all that Abolitionism has ever been able to accomplish in the hour of its most fiendish triumphs. I beg of that honorable Senator when he has anything to say hereafter—unless he is impelled by a strong sense of duty—that he will not attempt to foment and carry on this sectional agitation. To what end and

to whose good will result the dissolution of this Union, from the contemplation of which every patriotic mind instinctively recoils with horror?

I sing no hosannas to a Union without a constitution. I admit that when the life and spirit have departed, the framework will be valueless and will tumble to decay. But the spirit has not yet departed—the life is not yet gone. It is true it has received many assaults, but it is capable of receiving and sustaining many more. Let those who are disposed to indulge in agitation ask for the rights guaranteed by the Constitution only; but when they ask for these let them not ask for what the Constitution does not guarantee. Let them not provoke assaults themselves, while decrying the assaults they invite.

The honorable Senator from Alabama repudiates and casts off the Northern Democracy. They will, however, do no such thing with him. They will retain him in full membership, but endeavor to teach him some instructive and useful lessons. And upon this subject of reading out the entire Democracy of fifteen States of this Union, they will request my young friend from Alabama to tarry a while at Jericho until his beard shall have grown. [Laughter.]

JOHN DICKINSON

(1732–1808)

JOHN DICKINSON, of Pennsylvania, was the author of the 'Declaration on Taking Up Arms,' read in the Continental Congress in June 1775, and adopted July 6th of the same year. A year later he opposed the Declaration of Independence as premature, but he vindicated his patriotism by enlisting as a private soldier and marching against the British forces in New Jersey. He was a member of the Colonial Congress of 1765; of the Continental Congress of 1774; and from 1782 to 1785 he was President of Pennsylvania. He was a member of the Constitutional Convention of 1787, elected as a delegate from Delaware. Born in Maryland, November 13th, 1732, he died in Delaware, February 14th, 1808.

THE DECLARATION ON TAKING UP ARMS

(Read Before Congress on the Sixth of July, 1775)

IF IT were possible for men who exercise their reason to believe that the Divine Author of our existence intended a part of the human race to hold an absolute property in and an unbounded power over others, marked out by his infinite goodness and wisdom as the objects of a legal domination never rightfully resistible, however severe and oppressive, the inhabitants of these colonies might at least require from the Parliament of Great Britain some evidence that this dreadful authority has been granted to that body. But a reverence for our great Creator, principles of humanity, and the dictates of common sense must convince all those who reflect upon the subject, that government was instituted to promote the welfare of mankind, and ought to be administered for the attainment of that end. The legislature of Great Britain, however, stimulated by an inordinate passion for a power, not only unjustifiable, but which they know to be peculiarly reprobated by the very constitution of that kingdom, and desperate of success in any mode of contest where regard should be had to truth, law, or right, have at length, deserting

though so recently and amply acknowledged in the most honorable manner by his Majesty, by the late King and by Parliament, could not save them from the meditated innovations. Parliament was influenced to adopt the pernicious project, and, assuming a new power over them, has, in the course of eleven years, given such decisive specimens of the spirit and consequences attending this power, as to leave no doubt concerning the effects of acquiescence under it. They have undertaken to give and grant our money without our consent, though we have ever exercised an exclusive right to dispose of our own property; statutes have been passed for extending the jurisdiction of courts of admiralty and vice-admiralty beyond their ancient limits; for depriving us of the accustomed and inestimable privilege of trial by jury in cases affecting both life and property; for suspending the legislature of one of the colonies; for interdicting all commerce to the capital of another, and for altering fundamentally the form of government established by charter and secured by acts of its own legislature, solemnly confirmed by the Crown; for exempting the "murderers" of colonists from legal trial, and, in effect, from punishment; for erecting in a neighboring province, acquired by the joint arms of Great Britain and America, a despotism dangerous to our very existence, and for quartering soldiers upon the colonists in time of profound peace. It has also been resolved in Parliament that colonists charged with committing certain offenses shall be transported to England to be tried.

But why should we enumerate our injuries in detail? By one statute it is declared that Parliament can, "of right, make laws to bind us in all cases whatsoever." What is to defend us against so enormous, so unlimited a power? Not a single man of those who assume it is chosen by us, or is subject to our control or influence; but, on the contrary, they are all of them exempt from the operation of such laws, and an American revenue, if not diverted from the ostensible purposes for which it is raised, would actually lighten their own burdens, in proportion as they increase ours. We saw the misery to which such despotism would reduce us. We, for ten years, incessantly and ineffectually besieged the throne as supplicants; we reasoned, we remonstrated with Parliament in the most mild and decent language.

The Administration, sensible that we should regard these oppressive measures as freemen ought to do, sent over fleets and armies to enforce them. The indignation of the Americans was roused,

those, attempted to effect their cruel and impolitic purpose of enslaving these colonies by violence, and have thereby rendered it necessary for us to close with their last appeal from reason to arms. Yet, however blinded that assembly may be, by their intemperate rage for unlimited domination, so to slight justice and the opinion of mankind, we esteem ourselves bound by obligations of respect to the rest of the world, to make known the justice of our cause.

Our forefathers, inhabitants of the island of Great Britain, left their native land to seek on these shores a residence for civil and religious freedom. At the expense of their blood; at the hazard of their fortunes; without the least charge to the country from which they removed; by unceasing labor and an unconquerable spirit, they effected settlements in the distant and inhospitable wilds of America, then filled with numerous and warlike nations of barbarians. Societies or governments, vested with perfect legislatures, were formed under charters from the Crown, and a harmonious intercourse was established between the colonies and the kingdom from which they derived their origin. The mutual benefits of this union became in a short time so extraordinary as to excite astonishment. It is universally confessed that the amazing increase of the wealth, strength, and navigation of the realm arose from this source; and the minister who so wisely and successfully directed the measures of Great Britain in the late war, publicly declared that these colonies enabled her to triumph over her enemies. Towards the conclusion of that war, it pleased our sovereign to make a change in his counsels. From that fatal moment, the affairs of the British Empire began to fall into confusion, and gradually sliding from the summit of glorious prosperity, to which they had been advanced by the virtues and abilities of one man, are at length distracted by the convulsions that now shake its deepest foundations. The new ministry finding the brave foes of Britain, though frequently defeated, yet still contending, took up the unfortunate idea of granting them a hasty peace and of then subduing her faithful friends.

These devoted colonies were judged to be in such a state as to present victories without bloodshed, and all the easy emoluments of statutable plunder. The uninterrupted tenor of their peaceable and respectful behavior from the beginning of colonization; their dutiful, zealous, and useful services during the war,

it is true, but it was the indignation of a virtuous, loyal, and affectionate people. A congress of delegates from the united colonies was assembled at Philadelphia, on the fifth day of last September. We resolved again to offer an humble and dutiful petition to the King, and also addressed our fellow-subjects of Great Britain. We have pursued every temperate, every respectful measure; we have even proceeded to break off our commercial intercourse with our fellow-subjects, as the last peaceable admonition that our attachment to no nation upon earth should supplant our attachment to liberty. This, we flattered ourselves, was the ultimate step of the controversy, but subsequent events have shown how vain was this hope of finding moderation in our enemies.

Several threatening expressions against the colonies were inserted in his Majesty's speech; our petition, though we were told it was a decent one, and that his Majesty had been pleased to receive it graciously, and to promise laying it before his Parliament, was huddled into both houses, among a bundle of American papers, and there neglected. The Lords and Commons in their address, in the month of February, said that "a rebellion at that time actually existed within the province of Massachusetts Bay, and that those concerned in it had been countenanced and encouraged by unlawful combinations and engagements, entered into by his Majesty's subjects in several of the other colonies; and, therefore, they besought his Majesty that he would take the most effectual measures to enforce due obedience to the laws and authority of the supreme legislature." Soon after, the commercial intercourse of whole colonies with foreign countries and with each other was cut off by an act of Parliament; by another, several of them were entirely prohibited from the fisheries in the seas near their coasts, on which they always depended for their subsistence, and large re-enforcements of ships and troops were immediately sent over to General Gage.

Fruitless were all the entreaties, arguments, and eloquence of an illustrious band of the most distinguished peers and commoners, who nobly and strenuously asserted the justice of our cause, to stay, or even to mitigate the heedless fury with which these accumulated and unexampled outrages were hurried on. Equally fruitless was the interference of the city of London, of Bristol, and many other respectable towns, in our favor. Parliament adopted an insidious manœuvre, calculated to divide us, to establish a perpetual auction of taxations, where colony should bid against colony, all of them uninformed what ransom would redeem their lives, and thus to extort from us, at the point of the bayonet, the unknown sums that should be sufficient to gratify, if possible to gratify, ministerial rapacity, with the miserable indulgence left to us of raising, in our own mode, the prescribed tribute. What terms more rigid and humiliating could have been dictated by remorseless victors to conquered enemies? In our circumstances, to accept them would be to deserve them.

Soon after the intelligence of these proceedings arrived on this continent, General Gage, who, in the course of the last year, had taken possession of the town of Boston, in the province of Massachusetts Bay, and still occupied it as a garrison, on the nineteenth day of April sent out from that place a large detachment of his army, who made an unprovoked assault on the inhabitants of the said province at the town of Lexington, and as appears by the affidavits of a great number of persons, some of whom were officers and soldiers of that detachment, murdered eight of the inhabitants, and wounded many others. From thence the troops proceeded, in warlike array, to the town of Concord, where they set upon another party of the inhabitants of the same province, killing several and wounding more, until, compelled to retreat by the country people, suddenly assembled to repel this cruel aggression. Hostilities, thus commenced by the British troops, have been since prosecuted by them, without regard to faith or reputation. The inhabitants of Boston being confined within that town by the general, their governor, and having, in order to procure their dismission, entered into a treaty with him, it was stipulated that the said inhabitants having deposited their arms with their own magistrates, should have liberty to depart, taking with them their other effects. They accordingly delivered up their arms, but in open violation of honor, in defiance of the obligation of treaties, which even savage nations esteem sacred, the governor ordered the arms deposited as aforesaid, that they might be preserved for their owners, to be seized by a body of soldiers, detained the greatest part of the inhabitants in the town, and compelled the few who were permitted to retire, to leave their most valuable effects behind.

By this perfidy, wives are separated from their husbands, children from their parents, the aged and the sick from their

most solemnly, before God and the world, declare that, exerting the utmost energy of those powers which our beneficent Creator has graciously bestowed upon us, the arms we have been compelled by our enemies to assume, we will, in defiance of every hazard, with unabating firmness and perseverance, employ for the preservation of our liberties,—being with one mind resolved to die freemen rather than to live slaves.

Lest this declaration should disquiet the minds of our friends and fellow-subjects in any part of the empire, we assure them that we mean not to dissolve that union which has so long and so happily subsisted between us, and which we sincerely wish to see restored. Necessity has not yet driven us into that desperate measure, or induced us to excite any other nation to war against them. We have not raised armies with ambitious designs of separating from Great Britain and establishing independent States. We fight not for glory or for conquest. We exhibit to mankind the remarkable spectacle of a people attacked by unprovoked enemies, without any imputation or even suspicion of offense. They boast of their privileges and civilization, and yet proffer no milder conditions than servitude or death.

In our own native land, in defense of the freedom that is our birthright, and which we ever enjoyed till the late violation of it—for the protection of our property, acquired solely by the honest industry of our forefathers and ourselves, against violence actually offered, we have taken up arms. We shall lay them down when hostilities shall cease on the part of the aggressors, and all danger of their being renewed shall be removed, and not before.

With an humble confidence in the mercies of the Supreme and impartial Judge and Ruler of the universe, we most devoutly implore his divine goodness to protect us happily through this great conflict, to dispose our adversaries to reconciliation on reasonable terms, and thereby to relieve the empire from the calamities of civil war.

relations and friends, who wish to attend and comfort them, and those who have been used to live in plenty, and even elegance, are reduced to deplorable distress.

The general, further emulating his ministerial masters, by a proclamation bearing date on the twelfth day of June, after venting the grossest falsehoods and calumnies against the good people of these colonies, proceeds to "declare them all, either by name or description, to be rebels and traitors, to supersede the course of common law, and instead thereof to publish and order the use and exercise of the law martial." His troops have butchered our countrymen; have wantonly burnt Charlestown, besides a considerable number of houses in other places; our ships and vessels are seized; the necessary supplies of provisions are intercepted; and he is exerting his utmost power to spread destruction and devastation around him.

We have received certain intelligence that General Carleton, the Governor of Canada, is instigating the people of that province, and the Indians, to fall upon us; and we have but too much reason to apprehend that schemes have been formed to excite domestic enemies against us. In brief, a part of these colonies now feel, and all of them are sure of feeling, as far as the vengeance of administration can inflict them, the complicated calamities of fire, sword, and famine. We are reduced to the alternative of choosing an unconditional submission to the tyranny of irritated ministers, or resistance by force. The latter is our choice. We have counted the cost of this contest, and find nothing so dreadful as voluntary slavery! Honor, justice, and humanity forbid us tamely to surrender that freedom which we received from our gallant ancestors, and which our innocent posterity have a right to receive from us. We cannot endure the infamy and guilt of resigning succeeding generations to that wretchedness which inevitably awaits them, if we basely entail hereditary bondage upon them.

Our cause is just. Our union is perfect. Our internal resources are great, and, if necessary, foreign assistance is undoubtedly attainable. We gratefully acknowledge, as signal instances of Divine favor towards us, that his providence would not permit us to be called into this severe controversy, until we were grown up to our present strength, had been previously exercised in warlike operations, and possessed the means of defending ourselves. With hearts fortified by these animating reflections, we

PÈRE DIDON

(1840–)

ENRI DIDON, one of the most celebrated thinkers and orators of contemporary France, stands distinctively for the axiom that between the different phases of truth there can be no real conflict. His lifework has been to align the Catholic Church in France with the modern spirit of experimentalism in science and of criticism in the investigation of religious records. He was born at Touvet, March 17th, 1840, and in 1862 identified himself with the Dominican order. He has described himself as "a spiritual son of Lacordaire." Holding that there is nothing in the creed of the Church opposed to true science, he has also attempted to demonstrate that the Democratic movement of modern times is the delayed fruit of Christian teachings. In 1879, he took grounds on the question of divorce, which his superiors condemned, and was temporarily "silenced," but after his return from Corsica, to which he was retired, he was restored to favor, and in 1890 became director of the college of Albert the Great at Arcueil.

CHRIST AND HIGHER CRITICISM

JESUS CHRIST is the greatest name of history. There are others for which men have died. His is the only one worshiped among all peoples of all races in all ages.

He who bears it is known of all the earth. Among savages of the most degenerate tribes of the human species, missionaries go incessantly to announce his death on the Cross and the sacrifice made for the human race which is saved by loving him. The most indifferent in the modern world have been obliged to admit that nothing has ever helped the weak and the suffering more than Christianity.

The most glorious geniuses of the past will be obscured. Whether in monuments, palaces, obelisks, or tombs; whether in written encomiums, papyrus or parchment, bricks or medallions,— only reminiscences of them have been preserved for us. Jesus will live forever in the conscience of his faithful people. Here in this great manifestation of his power is his indestructible monument.

The Church founded by him fills with his name all time and all places. The Church knows him, loves him adores him! As he lives in her, so she lives in him. . . . In a few simple words the Church teaches that the greatest event which ever occurred to humanity was the arrival of Christ, and that God loves man, since God saves him from the penalty of the law; that God would save him from harm by giving him aid; that charity is the supreme duty, since by his charity and goodness the Savior was brought to the Cross; that the Christian must be vigilant in the good because his Master will be the judge; that he need not fear death because his Master conquered it and because he himself is destined to eternal life.

The man who accepts these instructions and believes in Christ can walk uprightly in life. He is armed for defense and for growth. Nothing can arrest his progress. The disciple of Jesus Christ has become the conqueror of the world—not from the standpoint of materialism and brutality, for violence is not in the spirit of the crucified Master, but in the sense of goodness, of abnegation, of sacrifice, and of moral dignity. In sowing these virtues as seeds of life, he prepares and enriches the human soil until it is capable of all culture and of all harvests.

But since believers in their intelligence seek to find reasons for elementary dogmas, it is necessary that we explain to them, in the measure of our imperfect and always limited knowledge, the facts and details of the human and divine life of Jesus, the words he spoke, the laws he formulated, his manner of teaching, evangelizing, combating, suffering, and dying. The history of Jesus is the foundation of faith. Evangelical doctrine, moral Christianity, culture, hierarchy, Church dignities, all rest on him. Thanks to the work of educated teachers, the doctrine of Jesus, his moralities, his faith, and his Church, have become little by little the object of distinct science, perfected, organized, responding to the legitimate aspirations of believers who would be men of faith and men of science; equally, the life of Jesus Christ must in its detail meet the exigencies of history.

The partisans of those called the critical school will say: The Christ of dogma and of tradition, the Christ of the Apostles and the evangelists, interpreted according to the doctrines of the Church, is not and cannot be the Christ of history. This ideal

V—117

ridiculed his doctrines, calling them absurd, and his Cross he called infamous. Origen refuted him and proclaimed with his mighty voice the divinity of his master. Since then the ages have advanced; the Crucified One has grown, destroying paganism, absorbing philosophy, dethroning empires, conquering the earth, civilizing the barbarian, creating a new world!

With what reason, then, did the Jews anathematize Jesus and kill him! Pagans, like Tacitus, Suetonius, and the honest proconsul of Bithynia, Pliny the younger, disdained him, and looked upon his Disciples as a detestable sect. Philosophers like Celsus, bore him down with their wisdom, while the Apostles adored in him the Son of God.

If Jesus was, indeed, but the wretch despised by Jews and Pagans, how has he carved on earth such a pathway? How has he founded a religion that dominates the earth? Were he merely human, the achievements would be inexplicable, and it is the popular proof that Jesus is what the Church affirms him to be.

We must not confound criticism with history. Though inseparable from each other, they must remain distinct. In its general sense criticism is the exercise of the judgment, a faculty essential in all reasonable beings. To criticize and to judge are synonomous terms. For judgment as criticism first tries to discern the true from the false. This is the first right and the most necessary duty of the mind. Whatever the domain it explores, religion, philosophy, science, literature, æsthetics, even in mathematics, reason must be attentive to discern the real from the apparent, the true, sometimes unapparent, from the false which is frequently most plausible.

Criticism, therefore, cannot be a special science. It is rather a condition of all science. It enters into the logical rules which determine how men shall think fairly and judge justly. These simple considerations demonstrate the vanity of those who would arrogate a monopoly of criticism. The school of criticism is the school of all the world. Each has a right to claim and to exercise it. The most ordinary temptation of the cultivated mind is to desire to criticize too much, to overjudge, to criticize even that of which he knows nothing. The sage moderates this intemperance. He learns to judge only what he knows, never forgetting that his knowledge is limited and his ignorance immeasurable.

Christ, God in man, Spirit Incarnate, conceived by an unknown miracle, calling himself the only Son of God, in the absolute and metaphysical sense, multiplying miracles, speaking as the fourth Evangelist makes him speak, rising again three days after death, ascending to the heavens in the face of his Disciples, after forty days,—such a man is not real! He exists only in the pious fancy of his believers who have created him piecemeal. The true Jesus, the Jesus of history, was born as are all other men; he lived like them; he did no more miracles than they! He taught a purer morality, and founded a religion less imperfect than others. Like all reformers, as a rule, he succumbed to the jealousies of his contemporaries. Becoming the victim of Jewish hatred and dying as we die, he has neither ascended to heaven nor is he living with God!

I revolted (pardon the phrase) not only in my Christian faith, but in my impartiality as a man, at this contradiction. Convinced that Jesus was the invisible God in a human form resembling our own, I, as a historian, regard him as still living, such as he was in this double nature.

The question of his Divinity has divided the greatest minds since the advent of Christ, and it will create division to the end. It is already a strange phenomenon that Jesus alone disposed of a problem that never sleeps in the consciousness of humanity,— a problem that always excites the emotions. I shall permit myself here to make a simple historical reflection addressed to unprejudiced men, to true critics with open minds.

This violent contradiction and contention of which Jesus is the object was prophesied. It shall last as long as the world; it afflicts the Christian, but it does not astonish or trouble him; he sees the signs of his Master. It is the product of living the life of Christ.

While his Disciples in reply to the question said: "You are the Christ, the Son of the living God," the Jews said: "He is but a prophet"; others, blinder, called him a blasphemer and a conspirator.

After he had left the earth and while his Apostles preached in the Jewish synagogues, the Messiah, God and man, filled with the wisdom and goodness of God, the first sectaries, the Nazarenes and Ebionites, would see in him nothing but a man.

The contention on this point continued for centuries. A Pagan philosopher, Celsus, without denying the miracles of Christ,

One may be a good critic in philosophy and a very poor judge of religion or history. Certain human sciences demand, not only the speculative mind, but a long experience.

Moral doctrines are much better criticized even by the ignorant who have experimented with virtue than by the skeptic who doubts the austere joys of sacrifice.

The saints who lived on the word of Jesus will always understand him better than the exacting Pharisees who repelled him and knew not the Savior. A delicate taste distinguishes shadings which escape the chemist.

As applied to history, the critic has a well-defined duty. The object of history is to state facts. That is, the facts of the past being known to us but by documents, and the documents being the records of witnesses, more or less immediate, to the facts themselves, the critic should examine the documents, facts, and witnesses together.

Some facts are absurd; the critic discards them. Some documents are altered or suspected; the critic notices and amends. If some witnesses are unworthy of belief, he unmasks and confounds them.

In all that concerns the life of Christ, the critic has the right and the duty to inspect the documents and the witnesses we adduce. To judge the life, the antiquity, and the authenticity of one, the value as testimony of the other, they should examine the nature of the facts in the documents as reported by the witnesses.

LORD GEORGE DIGBY

(1612-1676)

ORD GEORGE DIGBY, son of John Digby, Earl of Bristol, was one of the most notable orators of the Parliamentary party under Charles I., and had he been more thoroughgoing as a reformer, he might have easily become one of the greatest historical characters of the period. Clarendon says that he was "of great eloquence and becoming in discourse," but after opposing the attempt of the King to dispense with Parliament and make himself absolute, he went over to the court and so virtually disappeared from history. The occasion of the change was his refusal to join in compassing the death of Strafford. Appointed one of the committee of impeachment he made a speech declaring that the House of Commons, without the lords and the King, had no right to pass a bill of attainder, involving a death sentence. He advised that the bill be laid aside and another substituted such as would secure the State from Lord Strafford, "saving only life." For this advice he was finally expelled from Parliament after his speech had been ordered burned by the hangman. The King made him a baron, and in 1641-42 he was accused of high treason in Parliament. The next year he was Secretary of State to the King. During the Commonwealth he went into exile, and, returning after the Restoration, was made a Knight of the Garter.

"GRIEVANCES AND OPPRESSIONS" UNDER CHARLES I.

(Delivered in Parliament, November 9th, 1640, on Moving the Remonstrance to the King)

Mr. Speaker:—

YOU have received now a solemn account from most of the shires of England of the several grievances and oppressions they sustain, and nothing as yet from Dorsetshire. Sir, I would not have you think that I serve for a land of Goshen, that we live there in sunshine, whilst darkness and plagues overspread the rest of the land; as little would I have you think that being under the same sharp measure as the rest, we are either

---

insensible or benumbed, or that the shire wanteth a servant to represent its sufferings boldly.

It is true, Mr. Speaker, the county of Dorset hath not digested its complaints into that formal way of petition which others (I see) have done, but have intrusted them to my partners and my delivery of them by word of mouth unto this honorable House. And there was given unto us in the county court, the day of our election, a short memorial of the heads of them, which was read in the hearing of the freeholders there present, who all unanimously with one voice signified upon each particular, that it was their desire that we should represent them to the Parliament, which, with your leave, I shall do, and these they are:—

1. The great and intolerable burden of Ship-Money, touching the legality whereof they are unsatisfied.

2. The many great abuses in pressing of soldiers, and raising money concerning the same.

3. The multitude of monopolies.

4. The new canon, and the oath to be taken by lawyers, divines, etc.

5. The oath required to be taken by Church officers according to articles new and unusual.

Besides this there was likewise presented to us by a very considerable part of the clergy of that county a note of remonstrance containing these two particulars:—

Firstly, the imposition of a new oath required to be taken by all ministers and others, which they conceive to be illegal, and such as they cannot take with a good conscience.

Secondly, the requiring of a pretended benevolence, but in effect a subsidy, under the penalty of suspension, excommunication, and deprivation, all benefit of appeal excluded.

This is all we had particularly in charge, but that I may not appear a remiss servant of my country and of this House, give me leave to add somewhat of my own sense.

Truly, Mr. Speaker, the injurious sufferings of some worthy Members of this House, since the dissolution of the last two Parliaments, are so fresh in my memory that I was resolved not to open my mouth in any business wherein freedom and plain dealing were requisite, until such time as the breach of our privileges was vindicated and the safety of speech settled.

But since such excellent Members of our House thought fit the other day to lay aside that caution and to discharge their souls so freely in the way of zeal to his Majesty's service and their country's good, I shall interpret that confidence of theirs for a lucky omen to this Parliament, and with your permission license my thoughts, too, a little.

Mr. Speaker, under those heads which I proposed to you as the grievances of Dorsetshire, I suppose are comprised the greatest part of the mischiefs which have of late years laid battery either to our estates or consciences.

Sir, I do not conceive this the fit season to search and ventilate particulars, yet I profess I cannot forbear to add somewhat to what was said the last day by a learned gentleman of the long robe, concerning the acts of that reverend new synod, made of an old convocation. Doth not every Parliament man's heart rise to see the prelates thus usurp to themselves the grand preeminence of Parliament? The granting of subsidies, and that under so preposterous a name as of a benevolence, for that which is a malevolence, indeed; a malevolence I am confident in those that granted it against Parliaments, and a malevolence surely in those that refuse it, against those that granted it,— for how can it incite less when they see wrested from them what they are not willing to part with, under no less a penalty than the loss of both heaven and earth: of heaven by excommunication, and of the earth by deprivation,— and this without redemption by appeal? What good Christian can think with patience on such an ensnaring oath as that which is by the new canons enjoined to be taken by all ministers, lawyers, physicians, and graduates in the universities, where, besides the swearing such an impertinence, as that things necessary to salvation are contained in discipline; besides the swearing those to be of divine right, which, amongst the learned, never pretended to it as the arch things in our hierarchy; besides the swearing not to consent to the change of that which the State may, upon great reason, think fit to alter; besides the bottomless perjury of an "*et cetera,*"— besides all this, Mr. Speaker, men must swear that they swear freely and voluntarily what they are compelled unto; and, lastly, that they swear that oath in the literal sense, whereof no two of the makers themselves that I have heard of, could ever agree in the understanding?

In a word, Mr. Speaker, to tell you my opinion of this oath, it is a covenant against the King, for bishops and the hierarchy; as the Scottish covenant is against them, only so much worse than the Scottish, as they admit not of the supremacy in ecclesiastical affairs, and we are sworn unto it.

Now, Mr. Speaker, for those particular heads of grievances whereby our estates and properties are so radically invaded, I suppose (as I said before) that it is no season now to enter into a strict discussion of them; only this much I shall say of them, with application to the country for which I serve, that none can more justly complain, since none can more fully challenge exemption from such burdens than Dorsetshire, whether you consider it a country subsisting much by trade, or as none of the most populous, or as exposed as much as any to foreign invasion.

But alas, Mr. Speaker, particular lamentations are hardly distinguishable in universal groans.

Mr. Speaker, it hath been a metaphor frequent in Parliament, and, if my memory fail me not, was made use of in the lord keeper's speech at the opening of the last, that what money kings raised from their subjects, they were but as vapors drawn up from the earth by the sun, to be distilled upon it again in fructifying showers. The comparison, Mr. Speaker, hath held of late years too unluckily; what hath been raised from the subject by those violent attractions hath been formed, it is true, into clouds. But how? To darken the sun's own lustre! And it hath fallen again upon the land only in hailstones and mildews, to batter and prostrate still more and more our liberties, to blast and wither our affections, had the latter of these been still kept alive by our King's own personal virtues, which will ever preserve him, in spite of all ill counselors, a sacred object, both of our admiration and love.

Mr. Speaker, it hath been often said in this House, and I think it can never be too often repeated, that the kings of England can do no wrong; but though they could, Mr. Speaker, yet princes have no part in the ill of those actions which their judges assure them to be just, their counselors that they are prudent, and their divines that they are conscientious.

This consideration, Mr. Speaker, leadeth me to that which is more necessary far, at this season, than any further laying open of our miseries,— that is, the way to the remedy, by seeking to remove from our Sovereign, such unjust judges, such pernicious counselors, and such disconscient divines, as have of late years, by their wicked practices, provoked aspersions upon the government of the graciousest and best of kings.

Mr. Speaker, let me not be misunderstood, I level at no man with a forelaid design. Let the faults, and those well proved, lead us to the men; it is the only true parliamentary method and the only fit one to incline our Sovereign. For it can no more conflict with a gracious and righteous prince to expose his servants, upon irregular prejudices, than with a wise prince to withhold malefactors, how great soever, from the course of orderly justice.

Let me acquaint you, Mr. Speaker, with an aphorism in Hypocrates, no less authentic, I think, in the body politic than in the natural. Thus it is, Mr. Speaker, "bodies to be thoroughly and effectually purged must have their humors first made fluid and movable."

The humors that I understand to have caused all the desperate maladies of this nation are the ill ministers. To purge them away clearly they must first be loosened, unsettled, and extenuated, which can no way be affected with a gracious master, but by truly representing them unworthy of his protection.

And this leadeth me to my motion, which is, that a select committee may be appointed to draw out of all that hath here been represented, such a remonstrance as may be a faithful and lively representation unto his Majesty of the deplorable estate of this Kingdom, and such as may happily discover unto his clear and excellent judgment the pernicious authors of it. And that this remonstrance being drawn, we may with all speed repair to the lords, and desire them to join with us in it; and this is my humble motion.

THE ARMY IN DOMESTIC POLITICS

(Delivered in the House of Commons, April 21st, 1641, on the Bill of Attainder against Strafford)

WE ARE now upon the point of giving, as much as in us lies, the final sentence unto death or life, on a great minister of state and peer of this kingdom, Thomas, Earl of Strafford, a name of hatred in the present age for his practices, and fit to be made a terror to future ages by his punishment.

able in a prosecutor. Judges we are now, and must, therefore, put on another personage. It is honest and noble to be earnest in order to the discovery of truth; but when that hath been brought so far as it can be to light, our judgment thereupon ought to be calm and cautious. In prosecution upon probable grounds we are accountable only for our industry or remissness; but in judgment we are deeply responsible to Almighty God for its rectitude or obliquity. In cases of life, the judge is God's steward of the party's blood, and must give a strict account of every drop.

But, as I told you, Mr. Speaker, I will not insist long upon this ground of difference in me from what I was formerly. The truth of it is, sir, the same ground whereupon I, with the rest of the few to whom you first committed the consideration of my Lord Strafford, brought down our opinion that it was fit he should be accused of treason — upon the same ground, I was engaged with earnestness in his prosecution; and had the same ground remained in that force of belief in me, which till very lately it did, I should not have been tender in his condemnation. But truly, sir, to deal plainly with you, that ground of our accusation — that which should be the basis of our judgment of the Earl of Strafford as to treason — is, to my understanding, quite vanished away.

This it was, Mr. Speaker, — his advising the King to employ the army in Ireland to reduce England. This I was assured would be proved before I gave my consent to his accusation. I was confirmed in the same belief during the prosecution, and fortified most of all in it after Sir Henry Vane's preparatory examination, by assurances which that worthy Member, Mr. Pym, gave me, that his testimony would be made convincing by some notes of what passed in the Junto (Privy Council) concurrent with it. This I ever understood would be of some other counselor; but you see now, it proves only to be a copy of the same secretary's notes, discovered and produced in the manner you have heard; and those such disjointed fragments of the venomous parts of discourses — no results, no conclusions of councils, which are the only things that secretaries should register, there being no use of the other but to accuse and bring men into danger.

But, sir, this is not that which overthrows the evidence with me concerning the army in Ireland, nor yet that all the rest of the Junto remember nothing of it; but this, sir, which I shall

I have had the honor to be employed by the House in this great business, from the first hour it was taken into consideration. It was a matter of great trust; and I will say with confidence that I have served the House in it, not only with industry, according to my ability, but with most exact faithfulness and justice.

And as I have hitherto discharged my duty to this House and to my country in the progress of this great cause, so I trust I shall do now, in the last period of it, to God and to a good conscience. I do wish the peace of that to myself, and the blessing of Almighty God to me and my posterity, according as my judgment on the life of this man shall be consonant with my heart, and the best of my understanding in all integrity.

I know well that by some things I have said of late, while this bill was in agitation, I have raised some prejudices against me in the cause. Yea, some (I thank them for their plain dealing) have been so free to tell me, that I have suffered much by the backwardness I have shown in the bill of attainder of the Earl of Strafford, against whom I have formerly been so keen, so active.

I beg of you, Mr. Speaker, and the rest, but a suspension of judgment concerning me, till I have opened my heart to you, clearly and freely, in this business. Truly, sir, I am still the same in my opinion and affections as to the Earl of Strafford. I confidently believe him to be the most dangerous minister, the most insupportable to free subjects, that can be charactered. I believe that his practices in themselves to have been as high and tyrannical as any subject ever ventured on; and the malignity of them greatly aggravated by those rare abilities of his, whereof God hath given him the use, but the devil the application. In a word, I believe him to be still that grand apostate to the Commonwealth, who must not expect to be pardoned in this world till he be dispatched to the other.

And yet let me tell you, Mr. Speaker, my hand must not be to that dispatch. I protest, as my conscience stands informed, I had rather it were off.

Let me unfold to you the mystery, Mr. Speaker: I will not dwell much upon justifying to you my seeming variance at this time from what I was formerly, by putting you in mind of the difference between prosecutors and judges — how misbecoming that fervor would be in a judge which, perhaps, was commend-

tell you, is that which works with me, under favor, to an utter overthrow of his evidence as touching the army of Ireland. Before, while I was prosecutor, and under tie of secrecy, I might not discover (disclose) any weakness of the cause, which now, as Judge, I must.

Mr. Secretary Vane was examined thrice upon oath at the preparatory committee. The first time he was questioned as to all the interrogatories; and to that part of the seventh which concerns the army of Ireland, he said positively these words: "I cannot charge him with that"; but for the rest, he desired time to recollect himself, which was granted him. Some days after, he was examined a second time, and then deposed these words concerning the King's being absolved from rules of government, and so forth, very clearly. But being pressed as to that part of the Irish army, he said he could say "nothing to that." Here we thought we had done with him, till divers weeks after, my Lord of Northumberland, and all others of the Junto, denying to have heard anything concerning those words of reducing England by the Irish army, it was thought fit to examine the secretary once more; and then he deposed these words to have been spoken by the Earl of Strafford to his Majesty: "You have an army in Ireland, which you may employ here to reduce [or some word to that sense] this kingdom." Mr. Speaker, these are the circumstances which I confess with my conscience, thrust quite out of doors that grand article of our charge concerning his desperate advice to the King of employing the Irish army here.

Let not this, I beseech you, be driven to an aspersion upon Mr. Secretary, as if he should have sworn otherwise than he knew or believed. He is too worthy to do that. Only let this much be inferred from it, that he, who twice upon oath, with time of recollection, could not remember anything of such a business, might well, a third time, misremember somewhat; and in this business the difference of one word "here" for "there," or "that" for "this," quite alters the case; the latter also being the more probable, since it is confessed on all hands that the debate then was concerning a war with Scotland. And you may remember that at the bar he once said, "employ there." And thus, Mr. Speaker, have I faithfully given you an account what it is that hath blunted the edge of the hatchet, or bill, with me, toward my Lord Strafford.

This was that whereupon I accused him with a free heart; prosecuted him with earnestness; and had it to my understanding been proved, should have condemned him with innocence; whereas now I cannot satisfy my conscience to do it. I profess I can have no notion of any body's intent to subvert the laws treasonably, but by force; and this design of force not appearing, all his other wicked practices cannot amount so high with me. I can find a more easy and natural spring from whence to derive all his other crimes than from an intent to bring in tyranny, and make his own posterity, as well as us, slaves; viz., from revenge, from pride, from passion, and from insolence of nature. But had this of the Irish army been proved, it would have diffused a complexion of treason over all. It would have been a withe, indeed, to bind all those other scattered and lesser branches, as it were, into a fagot of treason.

I do not say but the rest of the things charged may represent him a man as worthy to die, and perhaps worthier than many a traitor. I do not say but they may justly direct us to enact that they shall be treason for the future. But God keep me from giving judgment of death on any man, and of ruin to his innocent posterity, upon a law made *à posteriori*. Let the mark be set on the door where the plague is, and then let him that will enter, die.

I know, Mr. Speaker, there is in Parliament a double power of life and death by bill, a judicial power, and a legislative. The measure of the one is what is legally just; of the other, what is prudentially and politically fit for the good and preservation of the whole. But these two, under favor, are not to be confounded in judgment. We must not piece out want of legality with matter of convenience, nor the defailance of prudential fitness with a pretense of legal justice.

To condemn my Lord of Strafford judicially, as for treason, my conscience is not assured that the matter will bear it, and to do it by the legislative power, my reason consultively cannot agree to that, since I am persuaded that neither the lords nor the King will pass this bill; and, consequently, that our passing it will be a cause of great divisions and contentions in the state.

Therefore, my humble advice is, that, laying aside this bill of attainder, we may think of another, saving only life, such as may secure the state from my Lord of Strafford, without endangering

it as much by division concerning his punishment as he hath endangered it by his practices.

If this may not be hearkened unto, let me conclude in saying that to you all which I have thoroughly inculcated upon mine own conscience, on this occasion. Let every man lay his hand upon his own heart and seriously consider what we are going to do with a breath; either justice or murder — justice on the one side, or murder, heightened and aggravated to its supremest extent, on the other! For, as the casuists say, he who lies with his sister commits incest, but he that marries his sister sins higher, by applying God's ordinance to his crime; so, doubtless, he that commits murder with the sword of justice, heightens that crime to the utmost.

The danger being so great and the case so doubtful that I see the best lawyers in diametrical opposition concerning it, let every man wipe his heart as he does his eyes, when he would judge of a nice and subtle object. The eye, if it be pretinctured with any color, is vitiated in its discerning. Let us take heed of a blood-shotten eye in judgment. Let every man purge his heart clear of all passions. I know this great and wise body politic can have none; but I speak to individuals from the weakness which I find in myself. Away with personal animosities! Away with all flatteries to the people, in being the sharper against him because he is odious to them! Away with all fears, lest by sparing his blood they may be incensed! Away with all such considerations, as that it is not fit for a Parliament that one accused by it of treason should escape with life! Let not former vehemence of any against him, nor fear from thence that he cannot be safe while that man lives, be an ingredient in the sentence of any one of us.

Of all these corruptives of judgment, Mr. Speaker, I do, before God, discharge myself to the utmost of my power; and do now, with a clear conscience, wash my hands of this man's blood by this solemn protestation, that my vote goes not to the taking of the Earl of Strafford's life.

SIR CHARLES WENTWORTH DILKE, Bart.

(1843–)

THE distinguished author of 'Greater Britain' was born at Chelsea, September 4th, 1843. His father, the late Sir Charles Wentworth Dilke, was prominent in the intellectual life of his day, and his 'Papers of a Critic,' edited by his son, keep their place in the libraries of England and America.

After his graduation from Trinity Hall, Cambridge, in January 1866, as "Senior Legalist," Sir Charles was called to the bar at the Middle Temple. Soon afterwards he made the celebrated tour of the world which resulted in the production of "Greater Britain"—a work which is believed to have had a larger sale than any other "first book" of its class ever printed in English. Sir Charles traveled in the United States, Canada, Australia, India, and other countries which either acknowledge English authority or represent the "Anglo-Saxon" tradition. Studying the influence of race on institutions, and of climatic and geographical conditions on race, he presented new problems for consideration, and forced his work on public attention as one which showed marked originality and great intellectual activity.

Returning to England, Sir Charles, who has always been a Radical in politics, was elected to Parliament from the new borough of Chelsea, which he continued to represent until his defeat in 1886. When re-elected, it was for Forest of Dean in Gloucestershire, which he now represents.

Among the numerous achievements of his parliamentary career, was the abolition of "drawing and quartering," which still remained a legal method of punishment in England until he compelled the attention of the House of Commons to it. Another was the reform through which school boards are elected by the rate-payers. In May 1880 he became Under Secretary of State for Foreign Affairs in the Gladstone ministry. In 1881–82 he was chairman of the Royal Commission for Negotiating a Commercial Treaty with France; in December 1892 he was appointed President of the Local Government Board with a seat in the Cabinet, and the following year he took charge of and carried the Unreformed Corporation Bill. In 1884 he was chairman of the Royal Commission for Housing the Poor, and in 1885 he took charge of and carried the Diseases Prevention Act.

At the beginning of his parliamentary career he openly declared that he preferred a republic to a constitutional monarchy, and one of his speeches on the expense of monarchy prompted a celebrated response in favor of aristocracy from Disraeli. As a speaker, Sir Charles is forcible and direct. Few men in English public life have spoken more effectively, but as he does not prepare his speeches by writing them in advance, some of his best and most representative efforts are reported only in synopsis. Without doubt he has been more effective in a practical way as a speaker than as an author, but since it is as the author of 'Greater Britain' and works on related subjects that he first made his international reputation, a rule of the World's Great Orations is suspended in his case, and the examples of his style here given are from his 'Greater Britain' rather than from his speeches. He is the author of other notable works besides 'Greater Britain'—among them 'The Present Position of European Politics (1887)'; 'The British Army'; 'Problems of Greater Britain'; and 'The Fall of Prince Florestan of Monaco,' a satire which, when he published it anonymously in 1874, had a great run in England, and was translated into French.

Sir Charles is generally recognized as the ablest living opponent of English Conservatism. As a Radical he is eminently practical. There is nothing destructive or emotional in his theories of government, and the parliamentary debates show that on all questions of the greatest moment,—especially on those affecting England's foreign policy and the condition of her city populations,—he has been one of the most efficient constructive statesmen of his day. He has had the Premiership of England in reach, and if English Liberals had the courage of their convictions, they might have in him now a leader capable of giving Liberalism a meaning it has lost since the death of Gladstone.

In 1898, Sir Charles in a public statement which was cabled to this country, reiterated his well-known views on America and the possibilities of achievement in its future. As a result, he was asked to take the premiership of the Advisory Council of the World's Best Orations. When the idea of the work was explained to him, he promptly accepted the position, and has greatly contributed — as have all other members of the Council — to the success of the work.

AMERICA

WE ARE coasting again, gliding through calm, blue waters, watching the dolphins as they play, and the boobies as they fly, stroke and stroke, with the paddles of the ship. On the right, mountains rise through the warm, misty air, and form a long towering line upon the upper skies. Hanging high above us are the volcano of fire and that of water — twin menacers of Guatemala city. In the sixteenth century the watermountain drowned it; in the eighteenth it was burnt by the fire-hill. Since then the city has been shaken to pieces by earthquakes, and of sixty thousand men and women, hardly one escaped. Down the valley, between the peaks, we have through the mahogany groves an exquisite distant view toward the city. Once more passing on, we get peeps, now of West Honduras, and now of the island coffee plantations of Costa Rica. The heat is terrible. It was just here, if we are to believe Drake, that he fell in with a shower so hot and scalding that each drop burnt its hole through his men's clothes as they hung up to dry. « Steep stories,» it is clear, were known before the plantation of America.

Now that the time has come for a leave-taking of the continent, we can begin to reflect upon facts gleaned during visits to twenty-nine of the forty-five Territories and States — twenty-nine empires the size of Spain.

A man may see American countries, from the pine wastes of Maine to the slopes of Sierra; may talk with American men and women, from the sober citizens of Boston to Digger Indians in California; may eat of American dishes, from jerked buffalo in Colorado to clambakes on the shores near Salem; and yet, from the time he first « smells the molasses » at Nantucket light-ship to the moment when the pilot quits him at the Golden Gate, may have no idea of an America. You may have seen the East, the South, the West, the Pacific States, and yet have failed to find America. It is not till you have left her shores that her image grows up in the mind.

The first thing that strikes the Englishman just landed in New York is the apparent Latinization of the English in America; but before he leaves the country he comes to see that this is at most a local fact, and that the true moral of America is

v—118

the vigor of the English race — the defeat of the cheaper by the dearer peoples, the victory of the man whose food costs four shillings a day over the man whose food costs four pence. Excluding the Atlantic cities, the English in America are absorbing the Germans and the Celts, destroying the Red Indians, and checking the advance of the Chinese.

The Saxon is the only extirpating race on earth. Up to the commencement of the now inevitable destruction of the Red Indians of Central North America, of the Maories, and of the Australians by the English colonists, no numerous race had ever been blotted out by an invader. The Danes and Saxons amalgamated with the Britons, the Goths and Burgundians with the Gauls; the Spaniards not only never annihilated a people, but have themselves been all but completely expelled by the Indians in Mexico and South America. The Portuguese in Ceylon, the Dutch in Java, the French in Canada and Algeria, have conquered but not killed off the native peoples. Hitherto it has been nature's rule that the race that peopled a country in the earliest historic days should people it to the end of time. The American problem is this: Does the law, in a modified shape, hold good, in spite of the destruction of the native population? Is it true that the negroes, now that they are free, are commencing slowly to die out — that the New Englanders are dying fast, and their places being supplied by immigrants? Can the English in America, in the long run, survive the common fate of all migrating races? Is it true that, if the American settlers continue to exist, it will be at the price of being no longer English, but Red Indian? It is certain that the English families long in the land have the features of the extirpated race; on the other hand, in the negroes there is at present no trace of any change, save in their becoming dark brown instead of black.

The Maories — an immigrant race — were dying off in New Zealand when we landed there. The Red Indians of Mexico — another immigrant people — had themselves undergone decline, numerical and moral, when we first became acquainted with them. Are we English in turn to degenerate abroad, under pressure of a great natural law forbidding change? It is easy to say that the English in Old England are not a native, but an immigrant race; that they show no symptoms of decline. There, however, the change was slight, the distance short, the difference of climate small.

The rapidity of the disappearance of physical type is equaled at least, if not succeeded, by that of the total alteration of the moral characteristics of the immigrant races — the entire destruction of eccentricity, in short. The change that comes over those among the Irish who do not remain in the great towns is not greater than that which overtakes the English hand-workers, of whom some thousands reach America each year. Gradually settling down on land, and finding themselves lost in a sea of intelligence, and freed from the inspiring obstacles of antiquated institutions and class prejudice, the English handicraftsman, ceasing to be roused to aggressive Radicalism by the opposition of sinister interests, merges into the contented homestead settler or adventurous backwoodsman. Greater even than this revolution of character is that which falls upon the Celt. Not only is it a fact known alike to physiologists and statisticians, that the children of Irish parents born in America are, physically, not Irish, but Americans, but the like is true of the moral type; the change in this is at least as sweeping. The son of Fenian Pat and bright-eyed Biddy is the normal, gaunt American, quick of thought, but slow of speech, whom we have begun to recognize as the latest production of the Saxon race, when housed upon the Western prairies, or in the pine woods of New England.

For the moral change in the British workmen it is not difficult to account; the man who will leave country, home, and friends, to seek new fortunes in America, is essentially not an ordinary man. As a rule, he is above the average in intelligence, or, if defective in this point, he makes up for lack of wit by the possession of concentrativeness and energy. Such a man will have pushed himself to the front in his club, his union, or his shop, before he emigrates. In England he is somebody; in America he finds all hands contented, or, if not this, at all events too busy to complain of such ills as they profess to labor under. Among contented men, his equals both in intelligence and ambition, in a country of perfect freedom of speech, of manners, of laws, and of society, the occupation of his mind is gone, and he comes to think himself what others seem to think him — a nobody; a man who no longer is a living force. He settles upon land; and when the world knows him no more, his children are happy corn-growers in his stead.

The shape of North America makes the existence of distinct peoples within her limits almost impossible. An upturned bowl,

with a mountain rim, from which the streams run inward toward the centre, she must fuse together all the races that settle within her borders, and the fusion must now be in an English mold.

There are homogenous foreign populations in several portions of the United States; not only the Irish and Chinese, at whose prospects we have already glanced, but also Germans in Pennsylvania, Spanish in Florida, French in Louisiana and at Sault de Ste. Marie. In Wisconsin there is a Norwegian population of over a hundred thousand, retaining their own language and their own architecture, and presenting the appearance of a tough morsel for the English to digest; at the same time, the Swedes were the first settlers of Delaware and New Jersey, and there they have disappeared.

Milwaukee is a Norwegian town. The houses are narrow and high, the windows many, with circular tops ornamented in wood or dark-brown stone, and a heavy wooden cornice crowns the front. The churches have the wooden bulb and spire which are characteristic of the Scandinavian public buildings. The Norwegians will not mix with other races, and invariably flock to spots where there is already a large population speaking their own tongue. Those who enter Canada generally become dissatisfied with the country, and pass on into Wisconsin or Minnesota, but the Canadian Government has now under its consideration a plan for founding a Norwegian colony on Lake Huron. The numbers of this people are not so great as to make it important to inquire whether they will ever merge into the general population. Analogy would lead us to expect that they will be absorbed; their existence is not historical, like that of the French in Lower Canada.

From Burlington, in Iowa, I had visited a spot the history of which is typical of the development of America — Nauvoo. Founded in 1840 by Joe Smith, the Mormon city stood upon a bluff overhanging the Des Moines Rapids of the Mississippi, presenting on the land-side the aspect of a gentle, graceful slope surmounted by a plain. After the fanatical pioneers of English civilization had been driven from the city and their temple burned, there came Cabet's Icarian band, who tried to found a new France in the desert; but in 1856 the leader died, and his people dispersed themselves about the States of Iowa and Missouri. Next came the English settlers, active, thriving, regardless of tradition, and Nauvoo is entering on a new life as the capital of a wine-growing country. I found Cabet and the Mormons alike forgotten. The ruins of the temple have disappeared, and the huge stones have been used up in cellars, built to contain the Hock — a pleasant wine, like Zeltinger.

The bearing upon religion of the gradual destruction of race is of great moment to the world. Christianity will gain by the change; but which of its many branches will receive support is a question which only admits of an imperfect answer. Arguing *a priori*, we should expect to find that, on the one hand, a tendency toward unity would manifest itself, taking the shape, perhaps, of a gain of strength by the Catholic and Anglican Churches; on the other hand, there would be a contrary and still stronger tendency toward an infinite multiplication of beliefs, till millions of men and women would become each of them his own church. Coming to the actual cases in which we can trace the tendencies that commence to manifest themselves, we find that in America the Anglican Church is gaining ground, especially on the Pacific side, and that the Catholics do not seem to meet with any such success as we should have looked for; retaining, indeed, their hold over the Irish women and a portion of the men, and having their historic French branches in Louisiana and in Canada, but not, unless it be in the cities of New York and Philadelphia, making much way among the English.

Between San Francisco and Chicago, for religious purposes the most cosmopolitan of cities, we have to draw distinctions. In the Pacific city, the disturbing cause is the presence of New Yorkers; in the metropolis of the Northwestern States, it is the dominance of New England ideas; still, we shall find no two cities so free from local color, and from the influence of race. The result of an examination is not encouraging; in both cities there is much external show in the shape of Church attendance; in neither does religion strike its roots deeply into the hearts of its citizens, except so far as it is alien and imported.

The Spiritualist and Unitarian Churches are both of them in Chicago extremely strong; they support newspapers and periodicals of their own, and are led by men of remarkable ability and energy, but they are not the less Cambridge Unitarianism, Boston Spiritualism; there is nothing of the Northwest about them. In San Francisco, on the other hand, Anglicanism is prospering, but it is New York Episcopalianism, sustained by immigrants and money from the East; in no sense is it a Californian Church.

This strange religion has long since left behind the rappings and table-turnings in which it took its birth. The secret of its success is that it supplies to every man the satisfaction of the universal craving for the supernatural in any form in which he will receive it. The Spiritualists claim two millions of active believers and five million "favorers" in America.

The presence of a large German population is thought by some to have an important bearing on the religious future of America, but the Germans have hitherto kept themselves apart from the intellectual progress of the nation. They for the most part withdraw from towns, and, retaining their language and supporting local papers of their own, live out of the world of American literature, politics, and thought, taking, however, at rare intervals, a patriotic part in national affairs, as was notably the case at the time of the last rebellion. Living thus by themselves, they have even less influence upon American religious thought than have the Irish, who, speaking the English tongue, and dwelling almost exclusively in towns, are brought more in contact with the daily life of the republic. The Germans in America are in the main pure materialists under a certain show of deism; but hitherto there has been no alliance between them and the powerful Chicago Radical Unitarians — difference of language having thus far proved a bar to the formation of a league which would otherwise have been inevitable.

On the whole, it would seem that for the moment religious prospects are not bright; the tendency is rather toward intense and unhealthily developed feeling in the few, and subscription to some one of the Episcopalian Churches — Catholic, Anglican, or Methodist — among the many, coupled with real indifference. Neither the tendency to unity of creeds nor that toward infinite multiplication of beliefs has yet made that progress which abstract speculation would have led us to expect. So far as we can judge from the few facts before us, there is much likelihood that multiplication will in the future prove too strong for unity.

After all, there is not in America a greater wonder than the Englishman himself, for it is to this continent that you must come to find him in full possession of his powers. Two hundred and fifty millions of people speak or are ruled by those who speak the English tongue and inhabit a third of the habitable globe; but at the present rate of increase, in sixty years there will be two hundred and fifty millions of Englishmen dwelling

Throughout America the multiplication of churches is rapid, but, among the native-born Americans, Supernaturalism is advancing with great strides. The Shakers are strong in thought, the Spiritualists in wealth and numbers; Communism gains ground, but not Polygamy — the Mormon is a purely European Church.

There is just now progressing in America a great movement, headed by the "Radical Unitarians," toward "free religion," or Church without creed. The leaders deny that there is sufficient security for the spread of religion in each man's individual action; they desire collective work by all free-thinkers and liberal religionists in the direction of truth and purity of life. Christianity is higher than dogma, we are told; there is no way out of infinite multiplication of creeds but by their total extirpation. Oneness of purpose and a common love for truth form the members' only tie. Elder Frederick Evans said to me, "All truth forms part of Shakerism"; but these free religionists assure us that in all truth consists their sole religion.

The distinctive feature of these American philosophical and religious systems is their gigantic width; for instance, every human being who admits that disembodied spirits may in any way hold intercourse with dwellers upon earth, whatever else he may believe or disbelieve, is claimed by the Spiritualists as a member of their Church. They tell us that by "Spiritualism they understand whatever bears relation to spirit"; their system embraces all existence, brute, human, and divine; in fact, "the real man is a spirit." According to these ardent proselytizers, every poet, every man with a grain of imagination in his nature, is a "Spiritualist." They claim Plato, Socrates, Milton, Shakespeare, Washington Irving, Charles Dickens, Luther, Melanchthon, Paul, Stephen, the whole of the Hebrew prophets, Homer, and John Wesley, among the members of their Church. They have lately canonized new saints; St. Confucius, St. Theodore (Parker), St. Ralph (Waldo Emerson), St. Emma (Hardings), all figure in their calendar. It is a noteworthy fact that the saints are mostly resident in New England.

The tracts published at the Spiritual Clarion Office, Auburn, New York, put forward Spiritualism as a religion, which is to stand toward existing churches as did Christianity toward Judaism, and announce a new dispensation to the people of the earth "who have sown their wild oats in Christianity." But they spell "supersede" with a "c."

in the United States alone. America has somewhat grown since the time when it was gravely proposed to call her "Alleghania," after a chain of mountains which, looking from this western side, may be said to skirt her eastern border, and the loftiest peaks of which are but half the height of the very passes of the Rocky Mountains.

America is becoming, not English merely, but world-embracing in the variety of its type; and as the English element has given language and history to that land, America offers the English race the moral directorship of the globe, by ruling mankind through Saxon institutions and the English tongue. Through America, England is speaking to the world.

OMPHALISM

DASHING through a grove of cottonwood trees draped in bignonia and ivy, we came out suddenly upon a charming scene; a range of huts and forts crowning a long, low hill seamed with many a timber-clothed ravine, while the clear stream of the Republican Fork wreathed itself about the woods and bluffs. The blockhouse over which floated the Stars and Stripes was Fort Riley, the Hyde Park Corner from which continents are to measure all their miles; the "capital of the universe," or "centre of the world." Not that it has always been so. Geographers will be glad to learn that not only does the earth gyrate, but that the centre of its crust also moves; within the last ten years it has removed westward into Kansas from Missouri, from Independence to Fort Riley. The contest for centreship is no new thing. Herodotus held that Greece was the very middle of the world, and that the unhappy Orientals were frozen, and the yet more unfortunate Atlantic Indians baked every afternoon of their poor lives in order that the sun might shine on Greece at noon; London plumes herself on being the "centre of the terrestrial globe"; Boston is the "hub of the hull universe," though the latter claim is less physical than moral, I believe. In Fort Riley, the Western men seem to have found the physical centre of the United States, but they claim for the Great Plains as well the intellectual as the political leadership of the whole continent. These hitherto untrodden tracts, they tell you, form the heart of the empire, from which the lifeblood must be driven to the extremities. Geographical and political centres must ultimately coincide.

Connected with this belief is another Western theory — that the powers of the future must be "Continental." Germany, or else Russia, is to absorb all Asia and Europe except Britain. North America is already cared for, as the gradual extinction of the Mexicans and absorption of the Canadians they consider certain. As for South America, the Californians are already planning an occupation of western Brazil, on the ground that the continental power of South America must start from the head waters of the great rivers and spread seaward down the streams. Even in the Brazilian climate they believe that the Anglo-Saxon is destined to become the dominant race.

The success of this omphalism, this government from the centre, will be brought about, in the Western belief, by the necessity under which the natives on the head waters of all streams will find themselves of having the outlets in their hands. Even if it be true that railways are beating rivers, still the railways must also lead seaward to the ports, and the need for their control is still felt by the producers in the centre countries of the continent. The Upper States must everywhere command the Lower, and salt-water despotism find its end.

The Americans of the Valley States, who fought all the more heartily in the Federal cause from the fact that they were battling for the freedom of the Mississippi against the men who held its mouth, look forward to the time when they will have to assert, peaceably but with firmness, their right to the freedom of their railways through the North Atlantic States. Whatever their respect for New England, it cannot be expected that they are forever to permit Illinois and Ohio to be neutralized in the Senate by Rhode Island and Vermont. If it go hard with New England, it will go still harder with New York, and the Western men look forward to the day when Washington will be removed, Congress and all, to Columbus or Fort Riley.

The singular wideness of Western thought, always verging on extravagance, is traceable to the width of Western land. The immensity of the continent produces a kind of intoxication; there is moral dram-drinking in the contemplation of the map. No Fourth of July oration can come up to the plain facts contained in the land commissioner's report. The public domain of the United States still consists of one thousand five hundred millions

of acres; there are two hundred thousand square miles of coal-lands in the country, ten times as much as in all the remaining world. In the Western Territories not yet States, there is land sufficient to bear, at the English population rate, five hundred and fifty millions of human beings.

It is strange to see how the Western country dwarfs the Eastern States. Buffalo is called a "Western city"; yet from New York to Buffalo is only three hundred and fifty miles, and Buffalo is but seven hundred miles to the west of the most eastern point in all the United States. On the other hand, from Buffalo we can go two thousand five hundred miles westward without quitting the United States. "The West" is eight times as wide as the Atlantic States, and will soon be eight times as strong.

The conformation of North America is widely different to that of any other continent on the globe. In Europe the glaciers of the Alps occupy the centre point, and shed the waters toward each of the surrounding seas; confluence is almost unknown. So it is in Asia; there the Indus flowing into the Arabian Gulf, the Oxus into the Sea of Aral, the Ganges into the Bay of Bengal, the Yangtse Kiang into the Pacific, and the Yenesei into the Arctic Ocean, all take their rise in the central table-land. In South America the mountains form a wall upon the West, whence the rivers flow eastward in parallel lines. In North America alone are there mountains on each coast, and a trough between, into which the rivers flow together, giving in a single valley twenty-three thousand miles of navigable stream to be plowed by steamships. The map proclaims the essential unity of North America. Political geography might be a more interesting study than it has yet been made.

JOHN A. DIX

(1798–1879)

JOHN A. DIX was born at Boscawen, New Hampshire, July 24th, 1798, and educated partly in the schools of his native State and partly in a French college at Montreal. He served in the War of 1812, and returning was admitted to the bar of New York. Becoming interested in politics he held various State offices until 1845, when he was elected to the United States Senate, where he served four years. He was Postmaster of New York city and Secretary of the Treasury under President Buchanan. In 1861 he became a Major-General of volunteers, and afterwards served with the same rank in the regular army. From 1866 to 1869 he was Minister to France, and from 1873 to 1875 Governor of New York. He died in New York city, April 21st, 1879. While he is more noted as a soldier and man of affairs than as a speaker, some passages from his addresses have become celebrated. Among the most often quoted is that on the Influence of Christianity on Politics, here reproduced from 'Munn's American Orator' (Boston 1853).

CHRISTIANITY AND POLITICS

THE influence of Christianity upon the political condition of mankind, though silent and almost imperceptible, has doubtless been one of the most powerful instruments of its amelioration. The principles and the practical rules of conduct which it prescribes; the doctrine of the natural equality of men, of a common origin, a common responsibility, and a common fate; the lessons of humility, gentleness, and forbearance, which it teaches, are as much at war with political as they are with all moral injustice, oppression, and wrong. During century after century, excepting for brief intervals, the world too often saw the beauty of the system marred by the fiercest intolerance and the grossest depravity. It has been made the confederate of monarchs in carrying out schemes of oppression and fraud. Under its banner armed multitudes have been banded together and

led on by martial prelates to wars of desolation and revenge. Perpetrators of the blackest crimes have purchased from its chief ministers a mercenary immunity from punishment.

' But nearly two thousand years have passed away, and no trace is left of the millions who, under the influence of bad passions, have dishonored its holy precepts, or of the far smaller number who, in seasons of general depravation, have drunk its current of living water on the solitary mountain or in the hollow rock. Its simple maxims, outliving them all, are silently working out a greater revolution than any which the world has seen; and long as the period may seem since its doctrines were first announced, it is almost imperceptible when regarded as one of the divisions of that time which is of endless duration. To use the language of an eloquent and philosophical writer: —

"The movements of Providence are not restricted to narrow bounds; it is not anxious to deduce to-day the consequences of the premises it laid down yesterday. It may defer this for ages, till the fullness of time shall come. Its logic will not be less conclusive for reasoning slowly. Providence moves through time as the gods of Homer through space; it makes a step, and years have rolled away. How long a time, how many circumstances, intervened before the regeneration of the moral powers of man by Christianity exercised its great, its legitimate function upon his social condition! Yet who can doubt or mistake its power?"

ALBERT B. DOD

(1805-1845)

ALBERT B. DOD was born at Medham, New Jersey, March 24th, 1805. A graduate of Princeton University, he was identified with it during the whole of his brilliant career. Graduating a doctor of divinity he filled the chair of mathematics at Princeton, lectured on architecture, political economy, and other subjects, and contributed to the reviews, besides preaching sermons which are ranked as pulpit classics. He died November 20th, 1845, at the height of his usefulness. "As a teacher," writes one of his biographers, "the genius of Professor Dod enkindled the enthusiasm of all who came under his instructions, and made him eminent in his profession. As a champion for the truth, he was earnest, able, and successful. He appeared before the public much more frequently as a literary and scientific man than as a preacher. But when speaking from the pulpit he never failed to command the most marked attention and fix deep in the mind the truth under discussion."

THE VALUE OF TRUTH

(From a Sermon on the Responsibility of Man for His Beliefs)

IT IS evident that the happiness of man was intended to be derived chiefly from his own internal dispositions. External circumstances are but secondary and inferior sources of enjoyment or suffering. In the heart itself is hid the secret fountain which refreshes or saddens us with its sweet or bitter waters. We can conceive of a heart so filled with pure affections, so informed with knowledge and strengthened by love, so thoroughly fortified by acquiescence —

> "In the will Supreme
> For time and for eternity; by Faith,
> Faith absolute in God, including Hope,"

and the defense that lies in boundless love of his perfections, that the darts of anguish, though they may strike upon that

only agency by which a principle of good can be implanted and nourished in our own hearts, or in others. It is as inseparable from virtue as virtue itself is from happiness. In all our modes of education and our attempts to improve the character of individuals or communities, we proceed upon this principle. We never think of working a permanent good in any other way than by instilling the truth; nor do we ever dream that error would answer our purpose equally well, if we could only succeed in making it pass for truth. Any man would spurn the shameless effrontery of the scorner who should tell him that the good of society and of its individual members would be equally well promoted by teaching them to lie and steal and murder, provided we could only persuade them that these things were right. That men can be elevated in their moral character, or in any way benefited by being taught to receive error as truth, is as monstrous an absurdity and as palpable a contradiction to all the lessons of experience as can be conceived. Man is so made as to be swayed to good only by the truth. His moral nature can not respond to any other influence.

heart and wound it, cannot fix or rankle there. Upon the ruin of all its expectations such a heart may gaze with subdued calmness; through all the disasters of life it may pass untroubled, or at least,

> "With only such degree of sadness left,
> As may support longings of pure desire
> And strengthen love, rejoicing secretly,
> In the sublime attractions of the grave."

So, too, we can conceive of a heart so weak that it can withstand the presence of no external evil — so ignorant that, in the blank and solitude of things, it is robbed of all enjoyment — so depraved that in the midst of all external advantages it is preyed upon by hatred, malice, envy, and all disturbing passions; it is within the compass of moral excellence to produce the one of these states — and the other does not transcend the capabilities of vice. The obvious tendency of virtue, in whatever degree it be cultivated, is to produce happiness; and vice, by an equally obvious and indissoluble connection, is the parent of misery. The man who disobeys his reason, or violates his conscience, in his search after happiness, grasps at a good at the expense of the very appetite which is to relish it. To injure his moral nature is to waste and wear away his only capability of happiness. If we take the constitution of man to pieces, as we would a watch or other piece of mechanism, to ascertain the object for which it was constructed, we see evident marks in every part that virtue was the end for which its Maker designed it. And if we then inquire further how this end is to be gained, that is, how men are to become virtuous, we find equally strong reasons for concluding that it can only be through a belief of the truth. The essence of virtue consists in its principle; and every moral principle has its root in truth. Error may be productive of some partial and transient good, as when a crying child is stilled, or a refractory one frightened into obedience, by a belief in some nursery fiction; but no one doubts that this trivial good is purchased at a lamentable sacrifice. Every honest man knows that whenever he uses deception and falsehood to promote even a good end, he is sacrificing the law of reason to the dictates of a low and short-sighted policy, and that he gains his end only as he would gain the sword which he should purchase with the loss of the arm that is to wield it. Truth is the

JOHN DONNE

(1573-1631)

JOHN DONNE, poet and preacher, "carried some of his hearers to heaven in holy raptures and enticed others by a sacred art and persuasiveness to amend their lives." Born in London in 1573, he was educated at Oxford first and afterwards at Cambridge. Appointed chaplain in ordinary to James I., he became a royal favorite, perhaps more for his poetry than for his sermons, though both have been much admired. His theological indorsers decline to give their unqualified approval to his verse, which they say is "tainted by the vice of his age," but he retains, nevertheless, the reputation of sincere piety, profound learning, and wonderful persuasiveness as a pulpit orator. He died March 1st, 1631, like the "sated guest" of Horace, his last words being "I were miserable if I could not die."

MAN IMMORTAL, BODY AND SOUL

(From a Sermon on the Resurrection)

TO CONSTITUTE a man there must be a body as well as a soul. Nay, the immortality of the soul will not so well lie in proof, without a resuming of the body. For, upon those words of the Apostle, "If there were no resurrection we were the miserablest of all men," the school reasons reasonably: naturally the soul and body are united; when they are separated by death, it is contrary to nature, which nature still affects this union; and consequently the soul is the less perfect for this separation: and it is not likely that the perfect natural state of the soul, which is to be united to the body, should last but three or four score years, and in most much less, and the unperfect state, this is, the separation, should last eternally, forever: so that either the body must be believed to live again, or the soul believed to die.

Never, therefore, dispute against thine own happiness; never say, God asks the heart, that is, the soul, and therefore rewards the soul, or punishes the soul, and hath no respect to the body.

Says Tertullian: "Never go about to separate the thoughts of the heart from the college, from the fellowship of the body; all that the soul does, it does in, and with, and by the body." And therefore, says he also, the body is washed in baptism, but it is that the soul might be made clean; in all unctions, whether that which was then in use in baptism, or that which was in use at our transmigration and passage out of this world, the body was anointed that the soul might be consecrated. Says Tertullian still, the body is signed with the cross, that the soul might be armed against temptations; and again, "My body received the body of Christ, that my soul might partake of his merits." He extends it into many particulars, and sums up all thus, "These two, body and soul, cannot be separated forever, which, while they are together, concur in all that either of them do." "Never think it presumption," says St. Gregory, "to hope for that in thyself which God admitted when he took thy nature upon him." "And God hath made it," says he, "more easy than so for thee to believe it, because not only Christ himself, but such men as thou art did rise at the resurrection of Christ." And therefore when our bodies are dissolved and liquefied in the sea, putrefied in the earth, resolved to ashes in the fire, macerated in the air, make account that all the world is God's cabinet, and water, and earth, and fire, and air, are the proper boxes in which God lays up our bodies for the resurrection. Curiously to dispute against our own resurrection is seditiously to dispute against the dominion of Jesus, who is not made Lord by the resurrection, if he have no subjects to follow him in the same way. We believe him to be Lord, therefore let us believe his and our resurrection.

This blessed day, which we celebrate now, he rose; he rose so as none before did, none after ever shall rise; he rose, others are but raised. "Destroy this temple," says he, "and I will raise it"; I, without employing any other architect. "I lay down my life," says he; the Jews could not have killed him when he was alive; if he were alive here now, the Jesuits could not kill him except his being made Christ and Lord, an anointed King, have made him more open to them. "I have power to lay it down," says he, "and I have power to take it up again."

This day we celebrate his resurrection; this day let us celebrate our own. . . . Fulfill, therefore, that which Christ says, "The hour is coming, and now is, when the dead shall hear the voice of the Son of God, and they that hear shall live." Be this

v—119

that hour, be this thy first resurrection. Bless God's present goodness for this now, and attend God's leisure for the other resurrection hereafter. He that is "the first fruits of them that slept," Christ Jesus is awake; he dies no more, he sleeps no more. He offered a sacrifice for thee, but he had that from thee that he offered for thee; he was the first fruits, but the first fruits of thy corn; doubt not of having that in the whole crop which thou hast already in thy first fruits; that is, to have that in thyself which thou hast in thy Savior. And what glory soever thou hast had in this world, glory inherited from noble ancestors, glory acquired by merit and service, glory purchased by money and observation, what glory of beauty and proportion, what glory of health and strength soever thou hast had in this house of clay, "the glory of the latter house shall be greater than that of the former." To this glory, the God of this glory, by glorious or inglorious ways, such as may most advance his own glory, bring us in his time, for his Son Christ Jesus's sake. Amen.

JAMES R. DOOLITTLE

(1815-1897)

JAMES R. DOOLITTLE was one of the Northwestern Republicans who helped to decide the issues of 1860-61 for war, and of 1866-70 for reconciliation with the South. They held with Stephen A. Douglas that the South had constitutional rights which ought to be respected, but that these rights were not to be considered at all as against the political unity of the Mississippi Valley. Senator Doolittle represented what this element considered the logic of the situation in declaring that "by every law, human and divine, the same national jurisdiction and the same flag should and must govern the lower and the upper Mississippi."

Born at Hampton, New York, in 1815, Mr. Doolittle graduated at Geneva (now Hobart) College and removed to Wisconsin (1851) where he was elected judge of the first judicial circuit and in 1856 United States Senator. He remained in the Senate from 1857 to 1869, and was one of the readiest and strongest speakers in it. He was a member of the peace convention of 1861 and opposed all compromises with the South, but as soon as the war was over, he advocated all compromise measures, led the Northwest in the Greeley movement, and made one of the most effective speeches in the Democratic convention which nominated Samuel J. Tilden. He died July 27th, 1897.

THE ATTITUDE OF THE WEST IN THE CIVIL WAR

(From a Speech Delivered in the United States Senate, February 24th, 1862, Against Admitting Benjamin Stark as Senator from Oregon)

MR. STARK appears with a record under the seal of the State of Oregon, giving him *prima facie* a right to a seat; he is conceded to have the requisite age, residence, and citizenship; but several of his constituents, said to be respectable citizens, charge that he is an open and avowed secessionist, and that the Governor who appointed him is a secessionist; and they have forwarded their memorials to this body, accompanied by *ex parte* statements upon oath to show that he has on various

occasions declared that if there were to be war he would go and help the South to fight; that Davis was fighting in a good cause; that on occasions he has expressed sympathy with secessionists; and on one occasion, on hearing of the news of the repulse of the Union forces at Bull Run, he drank a toast to Beauregard, as a witness believed. To all these charges he replies, in substance, that they are made by his bitter political opponents, and that in many important particulars the declarations of his assailants are false, without specifying wherein. . . .

If I understand this matter, he not only, as it would appear from the declaration of witnesses, has advocated the doctrine that States may constitutionally secede from the Union; but in this letter he declared that nine States then, on the fifth of June, 1861, had already seceded; that our jurisdiction over them had ceased; and, in substance, that we could only get back our jurisdiction over those States by some negotiation. The nine States referred to are, I suppose, South Carolina, Georgia, Alabama, Mississippi, Louisiana, Florida, Texas, North Carolina, and Tennessee. Now, he avows his loyalty and offers to take the oath to support the Constitution of the United States. Loyalty to what? What does he mean by the Constitution of the United States? What does he mean by the United States? Does he mean to embrace all the States, or only such as Jefferson Davis and his confederates have left us, only such as they have not usurped to govern by military depotism? Does the flag he is willing to support bear for him only twenty-five stars, or is it still full high advanced, bearing upon its ample folds thirty-four stars—a star for every State? When he raises his hand before Almighty God, and swears to support the Federal Constitution, does he mean to support that Constitution and its supremacy over Florida and Louisiana as well as over Oregon—at Pensacola and at New Orleans, as well as at the mouth of the Columbia?

We purchased Florida, gave $5,000,000 to get rid of a foreign power between us and the Gulf of Mexico, and we have expended $40,000,000 to conquer and remove the Seminoles. Does he mean to assert the national jurisdiction there? We purchased Louisiana of France, giving $15,000,000 to get control of the Mississippi River and the Gulf of Mexico. Jefferson made the purchase because he knew that if the mouth of that river were held by a foreign power, it would be our eternal enemy. In swearing to support the Constitution, does he mean to assert and maintain its authority at New Orleans and to the mouth of the Mississippi River? Does the lower valley of that river belong to the United States, whose Constitution he will swear to support, or does it belong to some foreign government? That is the question.

I speak earnestly, because I feel deeply on this question. I belong to the great West. We know and feel the interests and the necessities of our position. It is not only because our instincts for empire are strong, and because our men are hardy and brave, that we go into this struggle so earnestly. It is because we know the grand design of this infernal conspiracy, so long plotting the destruction of the Union, was first to set up a military despotism over the States of the Gulf and on the lower Mississippi; second, to compel the border slave States to join them; and, third, by appealing to the Buchanan Democracy of Pennsylvania, and offering to make that State their manufacturing State, to persuade her to join them according to what was believed to be a pledge given by a Pennsylvanian in the convention which nominated Buchanan in 1856. The traitors believed they could accomplish all this, and then the great West would be cut off from the East and from the South at the same time, and by the same conspiracy, and be compelled to submit to their dictation.

Sir, I repeat, we know our interests and our necessities. It is not that our sons are any braver or our instincts for freedom any stronger, that they go so earnestly into this struggle. They know it is for existence. It is for them like a death struggle. They know that by every law, human or divine, the same national jurisdiction and the same flag should govern and must govern the lower and the upper Mississippi — the flag of liberty and Union, or the flag of rebellion and despotism. There is and there can be no neutrality or compromise. The one or the other must prevail. We believe that justice, law, reason, and constitutional liberty itself are all staked upon the issue of the struggle. We go into it, therefore, with all the power and energy which God has given us.

IN FAVOR OF RE-UNION

(From a Speech Delivered in the National Democratic Convention — St. Louis, June 28th, 1876)

I BELIEVE, as much as I believe in my existence, that if ever a great responsibility rested upon a convention, it rests upon this convention now and here. That responsibility is to take such measures, to lay down such a platform, and to put upon it such candidates as will make our success certain in the overthrow of the party in power.

This party in power is a great and powerful party. Do not let us deceive ourselves by supposing that it is weak. I know that party. I have known it long and well. I have fought with it, and I have fought against it. I know it inside and out, through and through, and I tell you, gentlemen, that that party for the last fifteen years has been a war party, imbued with the spirit, accustomed to use the methods and practices which surround military encampments, not only during the war, but after the war had ended, in the reconstruction of the South. Guided by that spirit, this party in power, after the war had closed,—three years after the war had closed, almost,—I saw them take, in the Senate of the United States and in the House of Representatives, such action and such proceedings as could only be justified by military ideas, acting not as civilians in the administration of law, but as the leaders of military forces in the organization of the States of the South, in order to gain an unlimited control of both houses of Congress by a two-thirds' majority, which could overrule the veto of the President. I saw in the Senate of the United States, by the domination and despotic exercise of this power, a gentleman upon the floor of this convention was driven from the Senate (I refer to Mr. Stockton of New Jersey), and in order to get the vote which was necessary to obtain that two-thirds majority and accomplish that purpose, I saw one Senator, who from the committee reported in favor of Mr. Stockton, break his pair with the colleague of the Senator from New Jersey, confined by sickness at home.

By that act of revolution against law and all the usages of the Senate, they usurped that two-thirds majority which has ruled this country with military and despotic power from that day to the present moment. Having acquired this two-thirds

majority in both houses, trampling under its feet all the pledges it made, and by which it obtained its lease of power, I saw that party trample the Constitution under its feet. I saw them pass military reconstruction acts by which ten States in this Union and ten millions of people were robbed of every civil right of liberty and property, and I saw them subjected to the absolute unqualified domination of military dictators in time of peace.

You remember with what despotic and unrelenting power it undertook to depose the President and put in his place a man who would be more pliable to execute the behests of this despotic power at Washington. You know, too, how they persecuted those Senators who preferred to obey their oaths rather than obey the behests of this party. You saw, gentlemen, that same party by telegraphic decrees entering with the regular army State legislatures and organizing them against the law of the people. [Applause.] But I will not dwell on these things. I have said this only for the purpose of making one further remark — that is, that if any man in this country supposes that because this party lately at Cincinnati, instead of putting forward its great recognized leaders, have put forward Mr. Hayes, of Ohio, and Mr. Wheeler, of New York,—who are very respectable gentlemen in the States where they live, but are not much known elsewhere,—that this party has changed its spirit, its genius, its ambitions, its despotic centralizing tendencies, he is utterly mistaken. That party which could crush Trumbull and Schurz and Henderson, and even Sumner when he would not obey its behests, will take Hayes and Wheeler in its hands like things of wax. They cannot resist nor refuse to obey what that party shall decree. Therefore the responsibility rests upon you, gentlemen, and upon me, in our action here, to put forward such a platform and such candidates that we can wrest this Government from the hands of despotism and centralization and extravagance and corruption, such as makes the heart sick — corruption such as is our shame abroad and our disgrace and humiliation at home.

I say, gentlemen, if we would do it, we must act here wisely, not in the heat of passion. We must look beyond this chamber, and all the heat and excitement of the present hour; we must look beyond the excited crowds at the Lindell, the Southern, and other hotels in this city. We must look to the great field where the battle is to be fought and lost or won. As I said in the beginning, gentlemen, I have been laboring hard to keep myself

cool, both inside and out, in order that if I have any judgment to give, any opinion to express, or any advice to offer upon this great and important question, it may come as the opinion and advice and suggestion of a brain that is cool and a breast that is excited with nothing but love for the Union and love for the country. [Cheers.] Gentlemen, let me say, in my brief period in public affairs,—and not so very brief, either, for this is the tenth presidential canvass in which I have taken and am to take an active part [Applause],—I have learned — and learned what I did not know in the beginning — that when conventions assemble in great numbers, and the friends of candidates are excited, they believe for the moment, when the result is announced, that the victory is already won. I have sadly found myself mistaken when we came to the field of battle. Four times, fellow-citizens, four times have I attended a convention since the close of the war — conventions which had the same purpose and spirit which we now have — I mean to restore the Union of the States upon the platform of fraternity, liberty, and equality to all the States and to all the citizens of the States, to restore that Union, not only the Union which we established by our conquering, but to establish that Union in our heart of hearts [Applause], away down deep in all the affections and interests and aspirations of the whole people, North and South, black and white. Well do I remember the first at Philadelphia in 1866. I recognize here many familiar faces which met me there on that great occasion. They came together at Philadelphia ten years ago, from all the States of the Union. It was the first reunion after the Civil War. They came to shake hands together literally over the "bloody chasm," and when their united thanks went up to Almighty God that the war was over, that peace had come, that no more sons and fathers and brothers were to go down to battle and to death, that sweet peace had come, and come to stay [Cheers], there was a joy in that convention unutterable. Ten thousand men and women — strong men — in that convention, filled with an exultation which words could not express, gave way to every demonstration of joy. They wept, they embraced, and then, recovering themselves, they cheered and shouted — such cheers and shouts as go up from conquering armies when great fields are won. [Cheers.] But, fellow-citizens, though the object with which we met, the ideas to which we gave utterance, the platform we adopted, and all that was done to restore the former—and let me say to you in a single word, we failed in my opinion because at the city of New York we did not properly organize the forces for the victory. [Applause.] So badly was the Democratic party beaten in 1868 that in 1872, as if by unanimous consent, they gave out their word to the Liberal Republicans,—such Senators as Trumbull, Schurz, and others,—that if they would take the lead, if they would lay down a platform consistent with the constitutional views entertained by the great Democratic party and put candidates upon it, that party pledged its honor that, when assembled in convention, it would indorse and sustain them and aid them in the contest. You remember how well that pledge was kept, and I say to the Liberal Republicans, if there are any within the sound of my voice, or if anything that I say here shall reach them elsewhere—I say to the Liberal Republicans, and to all the Liberal Republicans, that they have been placed under a debt and obligation of gratitude to the Democratic party [Cheers] that they ought never to forget, and which they can never so well repay as by uniting with the Democratic party now in the coming contest. [Cheers.]

IN FAVOR OF SLITTING PRYNNE'S NOSE

(Delivered in the Star Chamber in February 1634, against William Prynne, for Writing and Publishing 'Histrio-Mastix, or a Scourge for Stage-Players')

SUCH swarms of murmurers as this day disclose themselves— are they not fearful symptoms of this sick and diseased time? Ought we not rather with more justice and fear apprehend those heavy judgments which this minor prophet Prynne hath denounced against this land for tolerating different things, to fall upon us for suffering them, like those mutineers against Moses and Aaron, as not fit to breathe? My lords, it is high time to make a lustration to purge the air. And will justice ever bring a more fit oblation than this Achan? Adam, in the beginning, put names on creatures correspondent to their natures. The title he hath given this book is "Histrio-Mastix," or, rather, as Mr. Secretary Cook observed, "Anthropo-mastix"; but that comes not home; it deserves a far higher title—"Damnation," in plain English, of prince, prelacy, peers, and people. Never did Pope in Cathedra, assisted with the spirit of infallibility, more positively and more peremptorily condemn heretics and heresy than this doth mankind. Lest any partial auditor may think me transported with passion, to judge of the base liveries he bestoweth upon court and courtiers, I shall do that which a judge ought to do, viz., assist the prisoner at the bar. Give me leave to remember what Mr. Attorney let fall the other day.—I will take hold of it for the gentleman's advantage,—that this gentleman had no mission; if he had had a mission it would have qualified the offense. Our blessed Savior, when he conversed in this world, chose Apostles whom he sent after him into the world, saying: "Ite, prædicate," to show the way of salvation to mankind. Faith, hope, and charity were the steps of this Jacob's ladder to ascend heaven by. The devil, who hates every man upon earth, played the divine, cited books, wrought miracles; and he will have his disciples, too, as he had his confessors and martyrs. My lords, this contempt, disloyalty, and despair are the ropes which this emissary lets down to his great master's kingdom for a general service. My lords, as the tenor of their commission was different, so are their ways. These holy men advanced their

THE EARL OF DORSET

(1591-1652)

THE age of Shakespeare, Bacon, and Raleigh, of Cromwell, Hampden, and Milton, is one of the most extraordinary in history—the most remarkable in the history of England, and, excepting only the revolutionary periods of France and America, the most significant in modern times. It has not yet been explained scientifically, and it may not be for another century to come. But when it is explained, such speeches as that made by the Earl of Dorset against Prynne will be understood as indexes of the times and arguments of the future. In the eloquence of his denunciation of Prynne, in his biting sarcasm, in the delicacy of the irony with which he works his way towards his climax—a climax in which, as one of the lords of the Star Chamber, he announced his vote in favor of branding Prynne in the forehead, cropping his ears, and slitting his nose, Dorset stood for everything which sent Charles I. to the block, as Prynne, for the time being at least, represented fully all the forces of reaction against the æstheticism and tyrannical spirit of the court.

There is no question of the corruption against which Prynne protested in his 'Histrio-Mastix, or a Scourge for Stage-Players,' but the corruption of the stage was only an incident of that general loss of moral sense among the governing classes which in its reactions forced Puritanism among those who, while they were making intellectual and moral progress, were as yet but at the beginning of both. Dorset stands for the highest culture of the court. He was one of the literary Sackvilles, æsthetes who were shocked by the vulgarity and bad taste of such Puritans as Prynne. Cromwell himself from their standpoint was a mere vulgarian, and Dorset would undoubtedly have voted to pillory him and slit his nose had he stood in Prynne's place. But it was only a few years until reaction against all that Dorset stood for had produced Milton and Cromwell. It is always so in history for those who having taken the coat demand the cloak also. Had not Prynne's ears been cropped in the pillory, there might never have been a Milton or a Cromwell. Yet it is said that Milton's contempt for Prynne was as great as that of Dorset, and that he sneered at him for the marks of his martyrdom.

cause in former times by meekness, humility, patience to bear with the weakness and infirmities of their brethren; they taught obedience to magistracy, even for conscience' sake; they divided not their estates into factions; they detracted from none; they sought the salvation of men's souls, and guided their bodies and affections answerably; they gave to Cæsar the things that were Cæsar's; if princes were bad, they prayed for them; if good, they praised God for them; however, they bore with them. This was the doctrine of the primitive Church, and this they did. I appeal to my lords, they that have read this book, if Mr. Prynne has not, with breach of faith, discharged his great Master's end. My lords, when God had made all his works, he looked upon them and saw that they were good.

This gentleman, the devil having put spectacles on his nose, says that all is bad; no recreation, vocation, no condition good; neither sex, magistrate, ordinance, custom, divine and human, things animate, inanimate, all, my lords, wrapt up in massa damnata, all in the ditch of destruction. Here, my lords, we may observe the great prudence of this prince of darkness, a soul so fraught with malice, so void of humanity, that it gorgeth out all the filth, impiety, and iniquity that the discontent of this age doth contract against the State and Church. But it may be that some follower of his will say it was the pride and wickedness of the times that prompted him to this work, and set his zeal, through tenderness of conscience, to write this book. My lords, you may know an unclean bird by his feathers; let him be unplumed, unmasked, pull off the deceitful wizard, and see how he appeareth: this brittle-conscienced brother, that perhaps starts at the sight of the corner-cap, sweats at the surplus, swoons at the sign of the cross, and will rather die than put on woman's apparel to save his life; yet, he is so zealous for the advancement of his babel, that he invents legions, coins new statutes, corrupts and misapplies texts with false interpretations, dishonors all men, defames all women, equivocates lies! And yet this man is a holy man, a pillar of the Church! Do you, Mr. Prynne, find fault with the "court and courtiers' habit, silk and satin divines"? I may say of you, you are all purple within, all pride, malice, and all disloyalty. You are a tumbler, who is commonly squint-eyed; you look one way and run another way; though you seemed by the title of your book to scourge stage-plays, yet it was to make people believe that there was an apostasy in the magistrates. But, my lords, admit all this to be venial and pardonable, this pigmy groweth a giant, and invades the gods themselves. Where we enjoy this felicity under a gracious prince, with so much advantage as to have the light of the Gospel, whilst others are kept in darkness, the happiness of the recreations to the health of the body, the blessed government we now have. When did ever Church so flourish, and State better prosper? And since the plagues happened, none have been sent among us such as this caterpillar is. What vein hath opened his anger? Or, who hath let out his fury? When did ever man see such a quietus as in these days? Yet in this golden age is there not a Shimei amongst us, that curseth the anointed of the Lord? So puffed with pride, now can the beams of the sun thaw his frozen heart, and this man appeareth yet. And now, my lords, pardon me, as he hath wounded his Majesty in his head, power, and government, and her Majesty, his Majesty's dear consort, our royal Queen, and my gracious mistress, I can spare him no longer, I am at his heart. Oh! *quantum!* If any cast infamous aspersions and censures on our Queen and her innocency, silence would prove impiety rather than ingratitude in me, that do daily contemplate her virtues; I will praise her for that which is her own; she drinks at the springhead, whilst others take up at the stream. I shall not alter the great truth that hath been said, with a heart as full of devotion, as a tongue of eloquence, the other day, as it came to his part [meaning Sir John Finch]. My lords, her own example to all virtues, the candor of her life, is a more powerful motive than all precepts, than the severest of laws; no hand of fortune nor of power can hurt her; her heart is full of honor, her soul of chastity; majesty, mildness, and meekness are so married together, and so impaled in her, that where the one begetteth admiration, the other love; her soul of that excellent temper, so harmoniously composed; her zeal in the ways of God unparalleled; her affections to her Lord so great, if she offend him it is no sunset in her anger; in all her actions and affections so elective and judicious, and a woman so constant for the redemption of all her sex from all imputations, which men (I know not how justly) sometimes lay on them; a princess, for the sweetness of her disposition, and for compassion, always relieving some oppressed

soul, or rewarding some deserving subject; were all such saints as she, I think the Roman Church were not to be condemned: on my conscience, she troubleth the ghostly father with nothing, but that she hath nothing to trouble him withal. And so when I have said all in her praise, I can never say enough of her excellency; in the relation whereof an orator cannot flatter, nor poet lie: yet is there not Doeg among us, notwithstanding all the tergiversations his counsel hath used at the bar? I can better prove that he meant the King and Queen by that infamous Nero, etc., than he proves players go to hell. But Mr. Prynne, your iniquity is full, it runs over, and judgment is come; it is not Mr. Attorney that calls for judgment against you, but it is all mankind; they are the parties grieved, and they call for judgment.

Mr. Prynne, I do declare you to be a schism maker in the Church, a sedition sower in the commonwealth, a wolf in sheep's clothing; in a word, *omnium malorum nequissimus.* I shall fine you ten thousand pounds sterling, which [addressing the other lords] is more than he is worth, yet less than he deserveth; I will not set him at liberty no more than a plagued man or a mad dog, who though he cannot bite, he will foam; he is so far from being a sociable soul that he is not a rational soul; he is fit to live in dens with such beasts of prey as wolves and tigers like himself. Therefore, I do condemn him to perpetual imprisonment as those monsters that are no longer fit to live among men, nor to see light. Now for corporal punishment, my lords, whether I should burn him in the forehead, or slit him in the nose? He that was guilty of murder was marked in a place where he might be seen, as Cain was. I should be loath he should escape with his ears, for he may get a periwig, which he now so much inveighs against, and so hide them, or force his conscience to make use of his unlovely love-locks on both sides. Therefore, I would have him branded in the forehead, slit in the nose, and his ears cropped too. My lords, I now come to this ordure; I can give no better term to it, to burn it, as it is common in other countries, or otherwise we shall bury Mr. Prynne and suffer his ghost to walk. I shall, therefore, concur to the burning of the book; but let there be a proclamation made, that whosoever shall keep any of the books in his hands and not bring them to some public magistrate to be burnt in the fire, let them fall under the

sentence of this court; for if they fell into wise men's hands, or good men's hands, that were no fear, but if among the common sort, and into weak men's hands, then tenderness of conscience will work something. Let this sentence be recorded, and let it be sent to the library of Sion [meaning a college in London], whither a woman, by her will, will allow Mr. Prynne's work to be sent.

[The sentence against Prynne was executed the seventh and tenth days of May following.]

DANIEL DOUGHERTY

(1826–1892)

DANIEL DOUGHERTY was for almost a generation one of the favorite orators of Philadelphia. He was a Democrat in politics and made the speech nominating Hancock, which fixed on him the title of "Hancock the Superb." He also put Cleveland in nomination at the St. Louis convention of 1888. He died September 5th, 1889. His reputation as an orator was national, but his speeches have never been collected, and as he did not attempt a congressional career, it is possible that he will become one more addition to the already long list of those who are praised as "silver-tongued" by their generation, without transmitting themselves adequately to posterity.

"HANCOCK THE SUPERB"

(Delivered in the Democratic National Convention at Cincinnati, June 1880, Nominating Winfield Scott Hancock for the Presidency)

I PROPOSE to present to the thoughtful consideration of the convention the name of one who, though on the field of battle he was styled the "The Superb," won still nobler renown as a military governor, whose first act when in command of Louisiana and Texas was to salute the Constitution by proclaiming that military rule shall ever be subservient to the civil power. The plighted word of the soldier was made good by the acts of the statesman. I nominate one whose name, suppressing all factions, will be alike acceptable to the North and to the South — a name that will thrill the Republic; the name of a man who, if nominated, will crush the last embers of sectional strife — a man whose name will be hailed as the dawning of a day of perpetual brotherhood. With him we can fling away our shields, and wage an aggressive war. We can appeal to the supreme tribunal of the American people against the corruption of the Republican party and its untold violations of constitutional liberty. With him as our chieftain, the bloody banner of the

Republicans will fall from their palsied grasp. Oh, my countrymen, in this supreme moment the destinies of the Republic are
at stake and the liberties of the people are imperiled. The people hang breathless on your deliberation. Take heed! Make no
misstep! I nominate one who can carry every Southern State,
and who can carry Pennsylvania, Indiana, Connecticut, New Jersey, and New York—the soldier statesman, with a record as
stainless as his sword, Winfield Scott Hancock, of Pennsylvania.
If elected, he will take his seat.

V—120

FREDERICK DOUGLAS

(1817–1895)

REDERICK DOUGLAS gained prominence at a time when it was
still supposed by many that any considerable infusion of
African blood would prevent intellectual development. It
might be inferred, therefore, that his reputation as an orator gained
under such circumstances is due in part to the false idea that he
was a prodigy rather than to the merits of his oratory. If this be
true, it is not largely true, for in such speeches as his 'Plea for Free
Speech,' in Boston, he shows not merely deep feeling, but ability to
master it completely; to give it sustained, connected, and calm expression, and in his climax to exhibit himself, not as the special
advocate of a race, but as the champion of humanity. He was born
in Maryland in 1817. His father was a white man, but his mother
was a negro slave, and, following the condition of his mother, he was
a slave also. He escaped from his master in 1838, and in 1841 made
a speech before the Antislavery Society of Massachusetts, at Nantucket, so eloquent that he was employed to lecture as the society's
agent. He had learned to read while a slave, and at this period
was a man of considerable education. Between 1850 and 1860 he was
not in harmony with the Garrison abolitionists, and the paper he published at Rochester is frequently mentioned with disapproval in the
Liberator. After the Civil War he held office as United States Marshal and Recorder of Deeds for the District of Columbia, and as
Minister to Hayti. He died February 20th, 1895.

A PLEA FOR FREE SPEECH IN BOSTON

(Delivered in Music Hall, Boston, in 1860—Reported in the Liberator of
December 4th, 1860)

OSTON is a great city—and Music Hall has a fame almost
as extensive as that of Boston. Nowhere more than here
have the principles of human freedom been expounded.
But for the circumstances already mentioned, it would seem
almost presumption for me to say anything here about those

principles. And yet, even here, in Boston, the moral atmosphere
is dark and heavy. The principles of human liberty, even if
correctly apprehended, find but limited support in this hour of
trial. The world moves slowly, and Boston is much like the
world. We thought the principle of free speech was an accomplished fact. Here, if nowhere else, we thought the right of
the people to assemble and to express their opinion was secure.
Dr. Channing had defended the right, Mr. Garrison had practically asserted the right, and Theodore Parker had maintained
it with steadiness and fidelity to the last.

But here we are to-day contending for what we thought was
gained years ago. The mortifying and disgraceful fact stares us
in the face, that though Faneuil Hall and Bunker Hill Monument stand, freedom of speech is struck down. No lengthy
detail of facts is needed. They are already notorious; far more
so than will be wished ten years hence.

The world knows that last Monday a meeting assembled to
discuss the question: "How Shall Slavery Be Abolished?" The
world also knows that that meeting was invaded, insulted, captured, by a mob of gentlemen, and thereafter broken up and
dispersed by the order of the mayor, who refused to protect it,
though called upon to do so. If this had been a mere outbreak
of passion and prejudice among the baser sort, maddened by
rum and hounded on by some wily politician to serve some immediate purpose,—a mere exceptional affair,—it might be allowed
to rest with what has already been said. But the leaders of the
mob were gentlemen. They were men who pride themselves
upon their respect for law and order.

These gentlemen brought their respect for the law with them
and proclaimed it loudly while in the very act of breaking the
law. Theirs was the law of slavery. The law of free speech
and the law for the protection of public meetings they trampled
under foot, while they greatly magnified the law of slavery.

The scene was an instructive one. Men seldom see such a
blending of the gentleman with the rowdy, as was shown on that
occasion. It proved that human nature is very much the same,
whether in tarpaulin or broadcloth. Nevertheless, when gentlemen approach us in the character of lawless and abandoned
loafers,—assuming for the moment their manners and tempers,—
they have themselves to blame if they are estimated below their
quality.

No right was deemed by the fathers of the Government more
sacred than the right of speech. It was in their eyes, as in the
eyes of all thoughtful men, the great moral renovator of society
and government. Daniel Webster called it a homebred right, a
fireside privilege. Liberty is meaningless where the right to
utter one's thoughts and opinions has ceased to exist. That, of
all rights, is the dread of tyrants. It is the right which they
first of all strike down. They know its power. Thrones, dominions, principalities, and powers, founded in injustice and wrong,
are sure to tremble, if men are allowed to reason of righteousness, temperance, and of a judgment to come in their presence.
Slavery cannot tolerate free speech. Five years of its exercise
would banish the auction block and break every chain in the
South. They will have none of it there, for they have the
power. But shall it be so here?

Even here in Boston, and among the friends of freedom, we
hear two voices: one denouncing the mob that broke up our
meeting on Monday as a base and cowardly outrage; and another, deprecating and regretting the holding of such a meeting,
by such men, at such a time. We are told that the meeting was
ill-timed, and the parties to it unwise.

Why, what is the matter with us? Are we going to palliate
and excuse a palpable and flagrant outrage on the right of
speech, by implying that only a particular description of persons should exercise that right? Are we, at such a time, when
a great principle has been struck down, to quench the moral indignation which the deed excites, by casting reflections upon
those on whose persons the outrage has been committed? After
all the arguments for liberty to which Boston has listened for
more than a quarter of a century, has she yet to learn that the
time to assert a right is the time when the right itself is called
in question, and that the men of all others to assert it are the
men to whom the right has been denied?

It would be no vindication of the right of speech to prove
that certain gentlemen of great distinction, eminent for their
learning and ability, are allowed to freely express their opinions
on all subjects—including the subject of slavery. Such a vindication would need, itself, to be vindicated. It would add insult to
injury. Not even an old-fashioned abolition meeting could vindicate that right in Boston just now. There can be no right of
speech where any man, however lifted up, or however humble,

however young, or however old, is overawed by force, and compelled to suppress his honest sentiments.

Equally clear is the right to hear. To suppress free speech is a double wrong. It violates the rights of the hearer as well as those of the speaker. It is just as criminal to rob a man of his right to speak and hear as it would be to rob him of his money. I have no doubt that Boston will vindicate this right. But in order to do so, there must be no concessions to the enemy. When a man is allowed to speak because he is rich and powerful, it aggravates the crime of denying the right to the poor and humble.

The principle must rest upon its own proper basis. And until the right is accorded to the humblest as freely as to the most exalted citizen, the government of Boston is but an empty name, and its freedom a mockery. A man's right to speak does not depend upon where he was born or upon his color. The simple quality of manhood is the solid basis of the right—and there let it rest forever.

STEPHEN A. DOUGLAS

(1813-1861)

HENRY CLAY hoped he might never live to see the Civil War, and died seeing it inevitable. Stephen A. Douglas, who attempted to take his place as a pacificator, lived to see it begin, and died, sternly determined to accept for himself and for all those he could influence the issues he had striven to avoid.

To go over the measures of home and foreign policy by which it was sought to postpone the crisis of the struggle for sectional supremacy will never be a pleasant duty, and it is only necessary to point out here that as Clay stood for the traditional foreign policy of Washington and Jefferson,—the maintenance of our "splendid isolation" and the development of the nation from within,—Douglas stood for the distraction of attention from domestic affairs to expansion and aggressive advance abroad. When Clay's influence as the representative of what had been a "pivotal border State" waned after the fruitless Compromise of 1850, Douglas, as the representative of the growing power of the "border States" north of the Ohio, forced himself into leadership as the spokesman of "Young America" and of progressive ideas, which were interpreted by some of his followers to mean the conquest of the territory remaining to Mexico, the seizure of Cuba and the Central American States, and the annexation of Canada. These exuberances of the theory of "Manifest Destiny" Douglas repudiated, but for a time it was hoped by some that in the discussion of them there would be a cessation of the agitation for disunion, now carried on by both the Secessionists of the Gulf States and the terribly determined idealists of New England. Any one who reads now the burning words in which Wendell Phillips, under the promptings of a genius as fiery as that of Desmoulins and as stern as that of Danton, denounced "the league with death and the covenant with hell," will see how sadly futile was the hope that Douglas entertained—that Buchanan expressed in one of his messages at a time when civil war had virtually begun—the hope that any mere "policy" can change the logic of events or alter the reality of "manifest destiny" involved in the accumulation of moral and intellectual forces from generation to generation, from country to country, from age to age.

Douglas was hailed by enthusiastic thousands as a very great man. He will always be remembered as one of the leading actors in the

prologue of the greatest tragedy of American history. But the only verdict possible on his career as a whole is that he mistook the logic of history and so failed, in spite of his great powers, to control the logic of events.

He was a man of remarkable natural ability, hardly surpassed as a political debater, yet an unequal match for Lincoln, because of a lack of the subtlety which is the most characteristic of all Lincoln's qualities. In the great debate of 1858, Mr. Lincoln, by his knowledge of the underlying forces of politics, was able to force issues far more radically and effectively through the speeches of Mr. Douglas than through his own. Lincoln's masterly habit of self-suppression was hardly suspected at the time, and few then could have supposed that Douglas, accustomed to use language to express his thoughts, was matched against a greater politician than Talleyrand,—one who knew the last great secret of politics—that of going twain willingly with those who had compelled him to go an unwilling mile.

Born in Vermont and bred to the trade of a cabinet maker, Douglas removed to Illinois in his youth and educated himself to such advantage that after giving up his trade and being admitted to the bar, he soon became recognized as one of the most effective lawyers of the State. He was elected Judge of the Supreme Court of Illinois in 1841. From 1843 to 1847 he served in the House of Representatives, and in the United States Senate from 1847 to 1861. He began to come into prominence just as Webster, Clay, Calhoun, and Benton were yielding their places at the front. Lewis Cass had been discredited by defeat, and Douglas easily took his place as the Western leader and Presidential candidate of those Democrats who still hoped to postpone the issue against slavery. As the representative of these, Douglas appealed for the Presidency on a theory which his opponents called "squatter sovereignty"—the doctrine that the people of a territory had a right to decide for themselves in adopting their constitution, whether they would have slavery or any other institution not prohibited by the Federal Constitution. The logic of this position seemed to be irrefragable, but it left William Lloyd Garrison and Wendell Phillips out of consideration, and so in his last speeches, made in 1860 and 1861, Mr. Douglas declared against the extreme logic of "local self-government" and in favor of any force necessary to prevent the Gulf States from establishing a confederation to control the Lower Mississippi and the ports of the Gulf of Mexico. Without doubt, the "Douglas Democrats" of 1861 held the decisive balance of power, and it is hardly too much to say of him that, defeated and heartbroken, Douglas did no less to prevent the success of the Southern States in their attempt at secession than Mr. Lincoln himself. W. V. B.

REPLY TO LINCOLN

(In the Joint Debate, at Freeport, Illinois, June 17th, 1858)

Ladies and Gentlemen:—

I AM glad that at last I have brought Mr. Lincoln to the conclusion that he had better define his position on certain political questions to which I called his attention at Ottawa. He there showed no disposition, no inclination, to answer them. I did not present idle questions for him to answer merely for my gratification. I laid the foundation for those interrogatories by showing that they constituted the platform of the party whose nominee he is for the Senate. I did not presume that I had the right to catechise him as I saw proper, unless I showed that his party, or a majority of it, stood upon the platform and were in favor of the propositions upon which my questions were based. I desired simply to know, inasmuch as he had been nominated as the first, last, and only choice of his party, whether he concurred in the platform which that party had adopted for its government. In a few moments I will proceed to review the answers which he has given to these interrogatories; but in order to relieve his anxiety, I will first respond to these which he has presented to me. Mark you, he has not presented interrogatories which have ever received the sanction of the party with which I am acting, and hence he has no other foundation for them than his own curiosity.

First, he desires to know if the people of Kansas shall form a constitution by means entirely proper and unobjectionable, and ask admission into the Union as a State, before they have the requisite population for a Member of Congress, whether I will vote for that admission. Well, now, I regret exceedingly that he did not answer that interrogatory himself before he put it to me, in order that we might understand, and not be left to infer on which side he is. Mr. Trumbull, during the last session of Congress, voted from the beginning to the end against the admission of Oregon, although a free State, because she had not the requisite population for a Member of Congress. Mr. Trumbull would not consent, under any circumstances, to let a State, free or slave, come into the Union until it had the requisite population. As Mr. Trumbull is in the field fighting for Mr. Lincoln, I would like to have Mr. Lincoln answer his own question, and tell me whether he is fighting Trumbull on that issue or not. But I will answer his question. In reference to Kansas, it is my opinion that as she has population enough to constitute a slave State, she has people enough for a free State. I will not make Kansas an exceptionable case to the other States of the Union. I hold it to be a sound rule of universal application to require a Territory to contain the requisite population for a Member of Congress before it is admitted as a State into the Union. I made that proposition in the Senate in 1856, and I renewed it during the last session in a bill providing that no Territory of the United States should form a constitution and apply for admission, until it had the requisite population. On another occasion I proposed that neither Kansas or any other territory should be admitted until it had the requisite population. Congress did not adopt any of my propositions containing this general rule, but did make an exception of Kansas. I will stand by that exception. Either Kansas must come in as a free State, with whatever population she may have, or the rule must be applied to all the other territories alike. I therefore answer at once, that it having been decided that Kansas has people enough for a slave State, I hold that she has enough for a free State. I hope Mr. Lincoln is satisfied with my answer; and now I would like to get his answer to his own interrogatory—whether or not he will vote to admit Kansas before she has the requisite population. I want to know whether he will vote to admit Oregon before that territory has the requisite population. Mr. Trumbull will not, and the same reason that commits Mr. Trumbull against the admission of Oregon commits him against Kansas, even if she should apply for admission as a free State. If there is any sincerity, any truth, in the argument of Mr. Trumbull in the Senate against the admission of Oregon, because she had not 93,420 people, although her population was larger than that of Kansas, he stands pledged against the admission of both Oregon and Kansas, until they have 93,420 inhabitants. I would like Mr. Lincoln to answer this question. I would like him to take his own medicine. If he differ with Mr. Trumbull, let him answer his argument against the admission of Oregon, instead of poking questions at me.

The next question propounded to me by Mr. Lincoln is: Can the people of the territory in any lawful way, against the wishes of any citizen of the United States, exclude slavery from their

limits prior to the formation of a State constitution? I answer emphatically, as Mr. Lincoln has heard me answer a hundred times from every stump in Illinois, that in my opinion the people of a territory can, by lawful means, exclude slavery from their limits prior to the formation of a State constitution. Mr. Lincoln knew that I had answered that question over and over again. He heard me argue the Nebraska Bill on that principle all over the State in 1854, in 1855, and in 1856, and he has no excuse for pretending to be in doubt as to my position on that question. It matters not what way the Supreme Court may hereafter decide as to the abstract question whether slavery may or may not go into a territory under the Constitution; the people have the lawful means to introduce it or exclude it as they please, for the reason that slavery cannot exist a day or an hour anywhere, unless it is supported by local police regulations. Those police regulations can only be established by the local legislature; and if the people are opposed to slavery, they will elect representatives to that body who will by unfriendly legislation effectually prevent the introduction of it into their midst. If, on the contrary, they are for it, their legislation will favor its extension. Hence, no matter what the decision of the Supreme Court may be on that abstract question, still the right of the people to make a slave Territory or a free Territory is perfect and complete under the Nebraska Bill. I hope Mr. Lincoln deems my answer satisfactory on that point.

In this connection, I will notice the charge which he has introduced in relation to Mr. Chase's amendment. I thought that I had chased that amendment out of Mr. Lincoln's brain at Ottawa, but it seems that still haunts his imagination, and he is not yet satisfied. I had supposed that he would be ashamed to press that question further. He is a lawyer, and has been a Member of Congress, and has occupied his time and amused you by telling you about parliamentary proceeding. He ought to have known better than to try to palm off his miserable impositions upon this intelligent audience. The Nebraska Bill provided that the legislative power and authority of the said Territory should extend to all rightful subjects of legislation, consistent with the organic act and the Constitution of the United States. It did not make any exception as to slavery, but gave all the power that it was possible for Congress to give without violating the Constitution to the territorial legislature, with no exception or

limitation on the subject of slavery at all. The language of that bill which I have quoted gave the full power and the full authority over the subject of slavery, affirmatively and negatively, to introduce it or exclude it, so far as the Constitution of the United States would permit. What more could Mr. Chase give by his amendment? Nothing. He offered his amendment for the identical purpose for which Mr. Lincoln is using it, to enable demagogues in the country to try and deceive the people.

His amendment was to this effect. It provided that the legislature should have the power to exclude slavery; and General Cass suggested: "Why not give the power to introduce as well as exclude?" The answer was: "They have the power already in the bill to do both." Chase was afraid his amendment would be adopted if he put the alternative proposition, and so make it fair both ways, but would not yield. He offered it for the purpose of having it rejected. He offered it, as he has himself avowed over and over again, simply to make capital out of it for the stump. He expected that it would be capital for small politicians in the country, and that they would make an effort to deceive the people with it; and he was not mistaken, for Lincoln is carrying out the plan admirably. Lincoln knows that the Nebraska Bill, without Chase's amendment, gave all the power which the Constitution would permit. Could Congress confer any more? Could Congress go beyond the Constitution of the country? We gave all a full grant with no exception in regard to slavery one way or the other. We left that question, as we left all others, to be decided by the people for themselves, just as they pleased. I will not occupy my time on this question. I have argued it before all over Illinois. I have argued it in this beautiful city of Freeport; I have argued it in the North, the South, the East, and the West, avowing the same sentiments and the same principles. I have not been afraid to avow my sentiments up here for fear I would be trotted down into Egypt.

The third question which Mr. Lincoln presented is: "If the Supreme Court of the United States shall decide that a State of this Union cannot exclude slavery from its own limits, will I submit to it?" I am amazed that Lincoln should ask such a question. "A schoolboy knows better." Yes, a schoolboy does know better. Mr. Lincoln's object is to cast an imputation upon the Supreme Court. He knows that there never was but one man in America, claiming any degree of intelligence or decency,

who ever for a moment pretended such a thing. It is true that the Washington Union, in an article published on the seventeenth of last December, did put forth that doctrine, and I denounced the article on the floor of the Senate in a speech which Mr. Lincoln now pretends was against the President. The Union had claimed that slavery had a right to go into the free States, and that any provisions in the Constitution or laws of the Free States to the contrary were null and void. I denounced it in the Senate, as I said before, and I was the first man who did. Lincoln's friends, Trumbull and Seward and Hale and Wilson and the whole black Republican side of the Senate were silent. They left it to me to denounce it. And what was the reply made to me on that occasion? Mr. Toombs, of Georgia, got up and undertook to lecture me on the ground that I ought not to have deemed the article worthy of notice and ought not to have replied to it; that there was not one man, woman, or child south of the Potomac, in any slave State, who did not repudiate any such pretension. Mr. Lincoln knows that that reply was made on the spot, and yet now he asks this question. He might as well ask me: "Suppose Mr. Lincoln should steal a horse, would you sanction it?" and it would be as genteel in me to ask him, in the event he stole a horse, what ought to be done with him. He casts an imputation upon the Supreme Court of the United States by supposing that they would violate the Constitution of the United States. I tell him that such a thing is not possible. It would be an act of moral treason that no man on the bench could ever descend to. Mr. Lincoln himself would never in his partisan feelings so far forget what was right as to be guilty of such an act.

The fourth question of Mr. Lincoln is: "Are you in favor of acquiring additional territory, in disregard as to how such acquisition may affect the Union on the slavery question?" This question is very ingeniously and cunningly put.

The Black Republican creed lays it down expressly, that under no circumstances shall we acquire any more territory unless slavery is first prohibited in the country. I ask Mr. Lincoln whether he is in favor of that proposition. Are you [addressing Mr. Lincoln] opposed to the acquisition of any more territory, under any circumstances, unless slavery is prohibited in it? That he does not like to answer. When I ask him whether he stands up to that article in the platform of his party he turns, Yankee fashion, and, without answering it, asks me whether I am in favor of acquiring territory without regard to how it may affect the Union on the slavery question. I answer that whenever it becomes necessary, in our growth and progress, to acquire more territory, that I am in favor of it, without reference to the question of slavery; and when we have acquired it, I will leave the people free to do as they please, either to make it slave or free territory, as they prefer. It is idle to tell me or you that we have territory enough. Our fathers supposed that we had enough when our territory extended to the Mississippi River, but a few years' growth and expansion satisfied them that we needed more, and the Louisiana Territory, from the west branch of the Mississippi to the British possessions, was acquired. Then we acquired Oregon, then California and New Mexico. We have enough now for the present, but this is a young and a growing nation. It swarms as often as a hive of bees; and as new swarms are turned out each year, there must be hives in which they can gather and make their honey. In less than fifteen years, if the same progress that has distinguished this country for the last fifteen years continue, every foot of vacant land between this and the Pacific Ocean owned by the United States will be occupied. Will you not continue to increase at the end of fifteen years as well as now? I tell you, increase and multiply and expand is the law of this nation's existence. You cannot limit this great Republic by mere boundary lines, saying: "Thus far shalt thou go, and no further." Any one of you gentlemen might as well say to a son twelve years old that he is big enough, and must not grow any larger, and in order to prevent his growth put a hoop around him to keep him to his present size. What would be the result? Either the hoop must burst and be rent asunder, or the child must die. So it would be with this great nation. With our natural increase, growing with a rapidity unknown in any other part of the globe, with the tide of emigration that is fleeing from despotism in the Old World to seek refuge in our own, there is a constant torrent pouring into this country that requires more land, more territory upon which to settle; and just as fast as our interests and our destiny require additional territory in the North, in the South, or on the islands of the ocean, I am for it, and when we acquire it, will leave the people, according to the Nebraska Bill, free to do as they please on the subject of slavery and every other question.

I trust now that Mr. Lincoln will deem himself answered on his four points. He racked his brain so much in devising these four questions that he exhausted himself, and had not strength enough to invent the others. As soon as he is able to hold a council with his advisers, Lovejoy, Farnsworth, and Fred Douglas, he will frame and propound others. ["Good, good!"] You Black Republicans who say good, I have no doubt think that they are all good men. I have reason to recollect that some people in this country think that Fred Douglas is a very good man. The last time I came here to make a speech, while talking from the stand to you, people of Freeport, as I am doing to-day, I saw a carriage, and a magnificent one it was, drive up and take a position on the outside of the crowd; a beautiful young lady was sitting on the box-seat, whilst Fred Douglas and her mother reclined inside, and the owner of the carriage acted as driver. I saw this in your own town. ["What of it?"] All I have to say of it is this, that if you, Black Republicans, think that the negro ought to be on a social equality with your wives and daughters, and ride in a carriage with your wife, whilst you drive the team, you have a perfect right to do so. I am told that one of Fred Douglas's kinsmen, another rich black negro, is now traveling in this part of the State making speeches for his friend Lincoln as the champion of black men. ["What have you to say against it?"] All I have to say on that subject is, that those of you who believe that the negro is your equal and ought to be on an equality with you socially, politically, and legally, have a right to entertain these opinions, and, of course, will vote for Mr. Lincoln.

"EXPANSION" AND CO-OPERATION WITH ENGLAND

(From the Debate in the Clayton Bulwer Treaty — United States Senate, March 14th, 1853)

I HAVE a word or two to say in reply to the remarks of the Senator from Delaware upon so much of my speech as related to the pledge in the Clayton and Bulwer Treaty, never to annex any portion of that country. I objected to that clause in the treaty, upon the ground that I was unwilling to enter into a treaty stipulation with any European powers, in respect to this continent, that we would not do, in the future, whatever our duty, interest, honor, and safety might require in the course of

events. The Senator infers that I desire to annex Central America, because I was unwilling to give a pledge that we never would do it. He reminded me that there was a clause in the treaty with Mexico containing the stipulation that in certain contingencies we would never annex any portion of Mexico. Sir, it was unnecessary that he should remind me of that provision. He has not forgotten how hard I struggled to get that clause out of the treaty where it was retained in opposition to my vote. Had the Senator given me his aid then to defeat that provision in the Mexican Treaty, I would be better satisfied now with his excuse for having inserted a still stronger pledge in his treaty. But having advocated that pledge then, he should not attempt to avoid the responsibility of his own act by citing that as a precedent. I was unwilling to bind ourselves by treaty for all time to come never to annex any more territory. I am content for the present with the territory we have. I do not wish to annex any portion of Mexico now. I did not wish to annex any part of Central America then, nor do I at this time.

But I cannot close my eyes to the history of this country for the last half century. Fifty years ago the question was being debated in this Senate whether it was wise or not to acquire any territory on the west bank of the Mississippi River, and it was then contended that we could never, with safety, extend beyond that river. It was at that time seriously considered whether the Alleghany Mountains should not be the barrier beyond which we should never pass. At a subsequent date, after we had acquired Louisiana and Florida, more liberal views began to prevail, and it was thought that perhaps we might venture to establish one tier of States west of the Mississippi; but in order to prevent the sad calamity of an undue expansion of our territory, the policy was adopted of establishing an Indian Territory, with titles in perpetuity, all along the western border of those States, so that no more new States could possibly be created in that direction. That barrier could not arrest the onward progress of our people. They burst through it, and passed the Rocky Mountains, and were only arrested by the waters of the Pacific. Who, then, is prepared to say that in the progress of events, having met with the barrier of the ocean in our western course, we may not be compelled to turn to the north and to the south for an outlet? How long is it since the gentleman from Delaware himself thought that a time would never arrive when we would want

California? I am aware that he was of that opinion at the time we ratified the treaty, and annexed it.

Mr. Clayton — How?

Mr. Douglas — By his voting for Mr. Crittenden's resolutions declaring that we did not want any portion of Mexican territory. You will find your vote in this volume which I hold in my hand. I am aware that he belonged to that school of politicians who thought we had territory enough. I have not forgotten that a respectable portion of this body but a few years ago thought it would be preposterous to bring a country so far distant as California, and so little known, into the Union. But it has been done, and now since California has become a member of the Confederacy, with her immense commerce and inexhaustible resources, we are told that the time will never come when the territory lying halfway between our Atlantic and Pacific possessions will be desirable. Central America is too far off, because it is halfway to California, and on the main, direct route, on the very route upon which you pay your Senators and Representatives in Congress their mileage in coming to the capital of the nation. The usual route of travel, the public highway, the halfway house from one portion of the country to the other, is so far distant that the man who thinks the time will ever come when we will want it is deemed a madman.

Mr. Clayton — Does the Senator apply those sentiments to me? I did not think so.

Mr. Douglas — I simply say that such an opinion was indicated by the vote of the gentleman on the resolution of Mr. Crittenden.

Mr. Clayton — The Senator is entirely mistaken on that point.

Mr. Douglas — In order to save time I waive the point as to the Senator's vote, although it is recorded in the volume before me, and he can read it at his leisure. But I am not mistaken in saying that the Senator on yesterday did ridicule the idea that we were ever to want any portion of Central America. He was utterly amazed, and in his amazement inquired where were these boundaries ever to cease. He wanted to know how far we were going and if we were going to spread over the entire continent. I do not think we will do it in our day, but I am not prepared to prescribe limits to the area over which Democratic principles may safely spread. I know not what our destiny may be. I try to keep up with the spirit of the age, to keep in view the history of the country, see what we have done, whither we are going, and with what velocity we are moving, in order to be prepared for those events which it is not in the power of man to thwart.

You may make as many treaties as you please to fetter the limits of this giant Republic, and she will burst them all from her, and her course will be onward to a limit which I will not venture to prescribe. Why the necessity of pledging your faith that you will never annex any more of Mexico? Do you not know that you will be compelled to do it; that you cannot help it; that your treaty will not prevent it, and that the only effect it will have will be to enable European powers to accuse us of bad faith when the act is done, and associate American faith and Punic faith as synonymous terms? What is the use of your guarantee that you will never erect any fortifications in Central America; never annex, occupy, or colonize any portion of that country? How do you know that you can avoid doing it? If you make the canal, I ask you if American citizens will not settle along its line; whether they will not build up towns at each terminus; whether they will not spread over that country and convert it into an American State; whether American principles and American institutions will not be firmly planted there? And I ask you how many years you think will pass away before you will find the same necessity to extend your laws over your own kindred that you found in the case of Texas? How long will it be before that day arrives? It may not occur in the Senator's day, nor mine. But so certain as this Republic exists, so certain as we remain a united people, so certain as the laws of progress which have raised us from a mere handful to a mighty nation shall continue to govern our action, just so certain are these events to be worked out, and you will be compelled to extend your protection in that direction.

Sir, I am not desirous of hastening the day. I am not impatient of the time when it shall be realized. I do not wish to give any additional impulse to our progress. We are going fast enough. But I wish our public policy, our laws, our institutions, should keep up with the advance in science, in the mechanic arts, in agriculture, and in everything that tends to make us a great and powerful nation. Let us look the future in the face, and let us prepare to meet that which cannot be avoided. Hence, I was unwilling to adopt that clause in the treaty guaranteeing that neither party would ever annex, colonize, or occupy

v—121

any portion of Central America. I was opposed to it for another reason. It was not reciprocal. Great Britain had possession of the island of Jamaica. Jamaica was the nearest armed and fortified point to the terminus of the canal. Jamaica at present commands the entrance of that canal; and all that Great Britain desired was, inasmuch as she had possession of the only place commanding the canal, to procure a stipulation that no other power would ever erect a fortification nearer its terminus. That stipulation is equivalent to an agreement that England may fortify, but that we never shall. Sir, when you look at the whole history of that question, you will see that England, with her far-seeing, sagacious policy, has attempted to circumscribe and restrict and restrain the free action of this Government. When was it that Great Britain seized the possession of the terminus of this canal? Just six days after the signing of the treaty which secured to us California! The moment that England saw that, by the pending negotiations with Mexico, California was to be acquired, she collected her fleets and made preparations for the seizure of the port of San Juan, in order that she might be gate-keeper on the public highway to our own possessions on the Pacific. Within six days from the time we signed the treaty, England seized by force and violence the very point now in controversy. Is not this fact conclusive as to her motives? Is it not clear that her object was to obstruct our passage to our new possessions? Hence I do not sympathize with that feeling which the Senator expressed yesterday, that it was a pity to have a difference with a nation so friendly to us as England. Sir, I do not see the evidence of her friendship. It is not in the nature of things that she can be our friend. It is impossible she can love us. I do not blame her for not loving us. Sir, we have wounded her vanity and humbled her pride. She can never forgive us. But for us, she would be the first power on the face of the earth. But for us, she would have the prospect of maintaining that proud position which she held for so long a period. We are in her way. She is jealous of us, and jealously forbids the idea of friendship. England does not love us; she cannot love us, and we do not love her either. We have some things in the past to remember that are not agreeable. She has more in the present to humiliate her that she cannot forgive.

I do not wish to administer to the feeling of jealousy and rivalry that exists between us and England. I wish to soften

and smooth it down as much as possible; but why close our eyes to the fact that friendship is impossible while jealousy exists? Hence England seizes every island in the sea and rock upon our coast where she can plant a gun to intimidate us or to annoy our commerce. Her policy has been to seize every military and naval station the world over. Why does she pay such enormous sums to keep her post at Gibraltar, except to keep it *in terrorem* over the commerce of the Mediterranean? Why her enormous expense to maintain a garrison at the Cape of Good Hope, except to command the great passage on the way to the Indies? Why is she at the expense to keep her position on that little barren island Bermuda, and the miserable Bahamas, and all the other islands along our coast, except as sentinels upon our actions? Does England hold Bermuda because of any profit it is to her? Has she any other motive for retaining it except jealousy which stimulates hostility to us? Is it not the case with all of her possessions along our coast? Why, then, talk about the friendly bearing of England towards us when she is extending that policy every day? New treaties of friendship, seizure of islands, and erection of new colonies, in violation of her treaties, seem to be the order of the day. In view of this state of things, I am in favor of meeting England as we meet a rival; meet her boldly, treat her justly and fairly, but make no humiliating concession even for the sake of peace. She has as much reason to make concessions to us as we have to make them to her. I would not willingly disturb the peace of the world; but, sir, the Bay Island Colony must be discontinued. It violates the treaty.

Now, Mr. President, it is not my purpose to say another word upon our foreign relations. I have only occupied so much time as was necessary to put myself right in respect to the speech made by the Senator from Delaware. He advocates one line of policy in regard to our foreign relations, and I have deemed it my duty to advocate another. It has been my object to put the two systems by the side of each other, that the public might judge between us.

KANSAS AND "SQUATTER SOVEREIGNTY"
(From the Speech Delivered at Springfield, Illinois, June 12th, 1857)

Mr. President, Ladies, and Gentlemen: —

I APPEAR before you to-night, at the request of the grand jury in attendance upon the United States Court, for the purpose of submitting my views upon certain topics upon which they have expressed a desire to hear my opinion. It was not my purpose when I arrived among you to have engaged in any public or political discussion; but when called upon by a body of gentlemen so intelligent and respectable, coming from all parts of the State, and connected with the administration of public justice, I do not feel at liberty to withhold a full and frank expression of my opinion upon the subjects to which they have referred, and which now engrosses so large a share of the public attention. . . .

Of the Kansas question but little need be said at the present time. You are familiar with the history of the question and my connection with it. Subsequent reflection has strengthened and confirmed my convictions in the soundness of the principles and the correctness of the course I have felt it my duty to pursue upon that subject. Kansas is about to speak for herself through her delegates assembled in convention to form a constitution, preparatory to her admission into the Union on an equal footing with the original States. Peace and prosperity now prevail throughout her borders. The law under which her delegates are about to be elected is believed to be just and fair in all its objects and provisions. There is every reason to hope and believe that the law will be fairly interpreted and impartially executed, so as to insure to every *bona fide* inhabitant the free and quiet exercise of the elective franchise. If any portion of the inhabitants, acting under the advice of political leaders in distant States, shall choose to absent themselves from the polls, and withhold their votes, with a view of leaving the Free-State Democrats in a minority, and thus securing a Pro-Slavery Constitution, in opposition to the wishes of a majority of the people living under it, let the responsibility rest on those who, for partisan purposes, will sacrifice the principles they profess to cherish and promote. Upon them, and upon the political party for whose benefit and under the direction of whose leaders they act, let the blame be visited of fastening upon the people of a new State institutions repugnant to their feelings and in violation of their wishes. The organic act secures to the people of Kansas the sole and exclusive right of forming and regulating their domestic institutions to suit themselves, subject to no other limitation than that which the Constitution of the United States imposes. The Democratic party is determined to see the great fundamental principles of the organic act carried out in good faith. The present election law in Kansas is acknowledged to be fair and just, the rights of the voters are clearly defined, and the exercise of those rights will be efficiently and scrupulously protected. Hence, if the majority of the people of Kansas desire to have it a free State (and we are told by the Republican party that nine-tenths of the people of that Territory are free State men), there is no obstacle in the way of bringing Kansas into the Union as a free State, by the votes and voice of her own people, and in conformity with the principles of the Kansas-Nebraska Act, provided all the free State men will go to the polls and vote their principles in accordance with their professions. If such is not the result, let the consequences be visited upon the heads of those whose policy it is to produce strife, anarchy, and bloodshed in Kansas, that their party may profit by slavery agitation in the Northern States of this Union. That the Democrats in Kansas will perform their duty fearlessly and nobly, according to the principle they cherish, I have no doubt; and that the result of the struggle will be such as will gladden the heart and strengthen the hopes of every friend of the Union, I have entire confidence.

The Kansas question being settled peacefully and satisfactorily, in accordance with the wishes of her own people, slavery agitation should be banished from the halls of Congress, and cease to be an exciting element in our political struggles. Give fair play to that principle of self-government which recognizes the right of the people of each State and Territory to form and regulate their own domestic institutions, and sectional strife will be forced to give place to that fraternal feeling which animated the fathers of the Revolution and made every citizen of every State of this glorious confederacy a member of a common brotherhood.

THE JOHN BROWN RAID

(From a Speech Delivered in the Senate, January 16th, 1860, Supporting a Bill «to Protect the States against Invasion»)

I PRESUME there will be very little difference of opinion that it will be necessary to place the whole military power of the Government at the disposal of the President, under proper guards and restrictions against abuse, to repel and suppress invasion when the hostile force shall be actually in the field. But, sir, that is not sufficient. Such legislation would not be a full compliance with this guaranty of the Constitution. The framers of that instrument meant more when they gave the guaranty. Mark the difference in language between the provision for protecting the United States against invasion and that for protecting the States. When it provided for protecting the United States, it said Congress shall have power to "repel invasion." When it came to make this guaranty to the States, it changed the language and said the United States shall "protect" each of the States against invasion. In the one instance the duty of the Government is to repel; in the other, the guaranty is that they will protect. In other words, the United States are not permitted to wait until the enemy shall be upon your borders; until the invading army shall have been organized and drilled and placed in march with a view to the invasion; but they must pass all laws necessary and proper to insure protection and domestic tranquillity to each State and Territory of this Union against invasion or hostilities from other States and Territories.

Then, sir, I hold that it is not only necessary to use the military power when the actual case of invasion shall occur, but to authorize the judicial department of the Government to suppress all conspiracies and combinations in the several States with intent to invade a State, or molest or disturb its government, its peace, its citizens, its property, or its institutions. You must punish the conspiracy, the combination with intent to do the act, and then you will suppress it in advance. There is no principle more familiar to the legal profession than that wherever it is proper to declare an act to be a crime it is proper to punish a conspiracy or combination with intent to perpetrate the act. Look upon your statute books, and I presume you will find an enactment to punish the counterfeiting of the coin of the United

States; and then another section to punish a man for having counterfeit coin in his possession with intent to pass it; and another section to punish him for having the molds or dies or instruments for counterfeiting, with intent to use them. This is a familiar principle in legislative and judicial proceedings. If the act of invasion is criminal, the conspiracy to invade should also be made criminal. If it is unlawful and illegal to invade a State and run off fugitive slaves, why not make it unlawful to form conspiracies and combinations in the several States with intent to do the act? We have been told that a notorious man, who has recently suffered death for his crimes upon the gallows, boasted in Cleveland, Ohio, in a public lecture, a year ago, that he had then a body of men employed in running away horses from the slaveholders of Missouri, and pointed to a livery stable in Cleveland which was full of the stolen horses at that time.

I think it is within our competency, and consequently our duty, to pass a law making every conspiracy or combination in any State or Territory of this Union to invade another with intent to steal or run away property of any kind, whether it be negroes or horses or property of any other description, into another State, a crime, and punish the conspirators by indictment in the United States courts and confinement in the prisons and penitentiaries of the State or Territory where the conspiracy may be formed and quelled. Sir, I would carry these provisions of law as far as our constitutional powers will reach. I would make it a crime to form conspiracies with a view of invading States or Territories to control elections, whether they be under the garb of Emigrant Aid Societies of New England or Blue Lodges of Missouri. In other words, this provision of the Constitution means more than the mere repelling of an invasion when the invading army shall reach the border of a State. The language is, it shall protect the State against invasion; the meaning of which is, to use the language of the preamble to the Constitution, to insure to each State domestic tranquillity against external violence. There can be no peace, there can be no prosperity, there can be no safety in any community unless it is secured against violence from abroad. Why, sir, it has been a question seriously mooted in Europe, whether it was not the duty of England, a power foreign to France, to pass laws to punish conspiracies in England against the lives of the princes of France. I shall not argue the question of comity between

foreign States. I predicate my argument upon the Constitution by which we are governed and which we have sworn to obey, and demand that the Constitution be executed in good faith so as to punish and suppress every combination, every conspiracy, either to invade a State or to molest its inhabitants, or to disturb its property, or to subvert its institutions and its government. I believe this can be effectually done by authorizing the United States courts in the several States to take jurisdiction of the offense, and punish the violation of the law with appropriate punishments.

It cannot be said that the time has not yet arrived for such legislation. It cannot be said with truth that the Harper's Ferry case will not be repeated, or is not in danger of repetition. It is only necessary to inquire into the causes which produced the Harper's Ferry outrage, and ascertain whether those causes are yet in active operation, and then you can determine whether there is any ground for apprehension that that invasion will be repeated. Sir, what were the causes which produced the Harper's Ferry outrage? Without stopping to adduce evidence in detail, I have no hesitation in expressing my firm and deliberate conviction that the Harper's Ferry crime was the natural, logical, inevitable result of the doctrines and teachings of the Republican party, as explained and enforced in their platform, their partisan presses, their pamphlets and books, and especially in the speeches of their leaders in and out of Congress. . . .

And, sir, inasmuch as the Constitution of the United States confers upon Congress the power coupled with the duty of protecting each State against external aggression, and inasmuch as that includes the power of suppressing and punishing conspiracies in one State against the institutions, property, people, or government of every other State, I desire to carry out that power vigorously. Sir, give us such a law as the Constitution contemplates and authorizes, and I will show the Senator from New York that there is a constitutional mode of repressing the "irrepressible conflict." I will open the prison doors to allow conspirators against the peace of the Republic and the domestic tranquillity of our States to select their cells wherein to drag out a miserable life as a punishment for their crimes against the peace of society.

THE ISSUES OF 1861

(From an Address to the Illinois Legislature, April 25th, 1861)

WHENEVER our government is assailed, when hostile armies are marching under rude and odious banners against the government of our country, the shortest way to peace is the most stupendous and unanimous preparation for war. The greater the unanimity the less blood will be shed. The more prompt and energetic is the movement, and the more important it is in numbers, the shorter will be the struggle.

While all the States of this Union, and every citizen of every State, has a priceless legacy dependent upon the success of our efforts to maintain this Government, we in the great valley of the Mississippi have peculiar interests and inducements to the struggle. What is the attempt now being made? Seven States of this Union choose to declare that they will no longer obey the behest of the United States, that they will withdraw from the government established by our fathers, that they will dissolve, without our consent, the bonds that have united us together. But, not content with that, they proceed to invade and obstruct our dearest and most inalienable rights, secured to us by the Constitution. One of their first acts is to establish a battery of cannon upon the banks of the Mississippi, on the dividing line between the States of Mississippi and Tennessee, and require every steamer that passes down the river to come to under a gun, to receive a customhouse officer on board to prescribe where the boat may land, and upon what terms it may put out a barrel of flour or a cask of bacon, to cut off our freedom of trade upon the river and on the borders of those States.

We are called on to sanction this policy. Before consenting to their right to commit such acts, I implore you to consider that the same principle which will allow the cotton States to exclude us from the ports of the Gulf would authorize the New England States and New York and Pennsylvania to exclude us from the Atlantic, and the Pacific States to exclude us from the ports of that ocean. Whenever you sanction this doctrine of secession, you authorize the States bordering on the Atlantic and Pacific Oceans to withdraw from us, form alliances among themselves, and exclude us from the markets of the world and from communication with all the rest of Christendom. Not only

this, but there follows a tariff of duties on imports, the levying of taxes on every pound of tea and coffee and sugar and every yard of cloth that we may import for our consumption; the levying, too, of an export duty upon every pound of meat and every bushel of corn that we may choose to send to the markets of the world to pay for our imports. Bear in mind that these very cotton States, who in former times have been so boisterous in their demands for free trade, have, among their first acts, established an export duty on cotton for the first time in American history.

It is an historical fact, well known to every man who has read the debates of the convention which framed the Constitution of the United States, that the Southern States refused to become parties to the Constitution unless there was an express provision in the Constitution forbidding Congress to levy an export duty on any product of the earth. No sooner have these cotton States seceded than an export duty is levied; and, if they will levy it on their cotton, do you not think that they will levy it on our pork, and our beef, and our corn, and our wheat, and our manufactured articles, and on all we have to sell? Then what is the proposition? It is to enable the tier of States bordering on the Atlantic and Pacific, and on the Gulf, surrounding us on all sides, to withdraw from our Union, form alliances among themselves, and then levy taxes on us without our consent, and collect revenue without giving us any just proportion of all the amount collected. Can we submit to taxation without representation? Can we permit nations foreign to us to collect revenues out of our produce, out of the fruit of our industry? I ask the citizens of Illinois, I ask every citizen in the great basin between the Rocky Mountains and the Alleghanies, in the valleys of the Ohio, the Mississippi, and the Missouri, to tell me whether he is willing to sanction a line of policy that may isolate us from the markets of the world, and make us provinces dependent on the powers that thus choose to isolate us?

I warn you, my countrymen, that, whenever you permit this to be done in the Southern States, New York will very soon follow their example. New York, that great port, where two-thirds of our revenue are collected, and whence two-thirds of our goods are exported, will not long be able to resist the temptation of taxing fifteen millions of people in the great West, when she can thus monopolize their resources, and release her own people

from any taxation whatever. . . . I am not prepared to take up arms, or to sanction a policy of our government to take up arms, to make any war on the rights of the Southern States, on their institutions, on their rights of person or property, but, on the contrary, would rush to their defense and protect them from assault; but, while that is the case, I will never cease to urge my countrymen to take arms to fight to the death in defense of our indefeasible rights. Hence, if a war does come, it is a war of self-defense on our part. It is a war in defense of our own just rights; in defense of the government which we have inherited as a priceless legacy from our patriotic fathers; in defense of our great rights of freedom of trade, commerce, transit, and intercourse from the centre to the circumference of this great continent. . . .

My friends, I can say no more. To discuss these topics is the most painful duty of my life. It is with a sad heart, with a grief that I have never before experienced, that I have to contemplate this fearful struggle; but I believe in my conscience that it is a duty we owe to ourselves, our children, and our God, to protect this Government and that flag from every assailant, be he who he may.

LORENZO DOW, JUNIOR

(1777–1834)

FEW subjects are of greater scientific interest than that of the extent to which the human mind, when not habitually governed in its operations by the will, is liable to be influenced by such musical suggestion as influences the ear of a composer in making an instrumental melody, or of a versifier in rhyming. It is certain that this unconscious suggestion is a factor in the pleasing expression of thought and that in disordered intellects it is liable to operate independently of the will. In its extreme manifestations it is recognized as a mark of insanity and is treated as a disease by alienists. In its healthy development, however, it has a great deal to do with the modes of thought and expression of those who are called "natural orators." To this class Lorenzo Dow belongs. Had he been carefully educated, so that his sense of humor and his ear for melody would not have co-operated in impelling him continually to precipitate himself from the sublime into the ridiculous, he might have been one of the greatest orators of America. As it is, he is remarkable among speakers in English because of the misfortune of humor and the complete fluency which illustrates the results of unrestrained ability to give melodious expression to everything that is liable to come into the mind of a speaker in sympathy with the average intellect of his times. He was born at Coventry, Connecticut, October 16th, 1777. Inspired by the example of Wesley, but without Wesley's education, he became an evangelist, unconventional in his ideas and eccentric in his methods. After making himself celebrated in America, he went as a missionary to England and Ireland, attracting much attention there. He died in Washington, February 2d, 1834. His journals and miscellaneous writings have been published, and are still in print.

IMPROVEMENT IN AMERICA

My Dear Friends:—

I MEAN to speak of the spirit of improvement in general terms, as relating to enlightenment, the advancement of knowledge and progress in the arts and sciences. In this respect it is like the rolling avalanche, that leaves detached portions of its bulk by the way, and yet keeps augmenting in its circumvolutionary course. Hardy Enterprise first goes forward as a pioneer in the untracked wilderness, and commences fight with the mighty trees of the forest, cutting them off, some in the prime of life, and others in a green old age, and compelling them to spill their sap upon their country's soil. Then walks Agriculture into them 'ere diggins, with spade, harrow, and hoe, and scatters the seed of promise hither and thither, assuring the hopeful settler that his children's children shall sop their hard-earned crumbs in the real gravy of the land. The handmaid Art then comes forward, erects edifices of splendor, and leaves her ornaments of skill on every side — builds studios for the scholars of science, and throws facilities in their way for increasing their wisdom, or for making egregious fools of themselves.

Such, my hearers, is the spirit of improvement. Like the overflowing of a stream that covers and enriches the valley, it betters the natural and social condition of man, opens wide the avenues to the temple of reason, and expands the young buds of prosperity. Brush away the fog of a couple of centuries, and take a look at this, our native land, as it then appeared. Here, upon the Atlantic shore, the scream of the panther arose on the midnight air with the savage war whoop, and the pale-faced pilgrim trembled for the safety of his defenseless home. He planted his beans in fear, and gathered them in trouble; his chickens and his children were plundered by the foe, and life itself was in danger of leaking out from between the logs of his hut, even if it was fortified with three muskets, a spunky wife, and a jug of whisky. Yes, my friends, this was then a wild, gloomy, and desolate place. Where the Indian squaw hung her young papoose upon the bough, and left it to squall at the hush-a-bye of the blast, the Anglo-Saxon mother now rocks the cradle of her delicate babe on the carpet of peace, and in the gay parlor of fashion. The wild has been changed to a blooming

sinking over head in the mud of despondency, for despair is never quite despair. No, my friends, it never comes quite up to the mark in the most desperate cases. I know the prospects of man are sometimes most tormentingly conglomerous; but the clouds eventually clear away, and his sky again becomes clear and quiescent as a basin of potato starch. His sun of ambition may be darkened, his moon of memory turned to blood, and the star of his peace blotted from the firmament of his — I don't know what; but he is not entirely a gone goose even in this situation. Those semi-celestial angels of light and loveliness, Hope and Fancy, will twine the sweetest of roses round his care-wrinkled brow; and while one whispers in his ear, "Don't give up the ship," the other dresses up for him a bower of future happiness, and festoons it with the choicest of Elysian flowers. The very darkest cell of despair always has a gimlet hole to let the glory of hope shine in, and dry up the tears of the poor prisoner of woe.

garden, and its limits are expanding with the mighty genius of Liberty. On Erie's banks the flocks are now straying o'er thymy pastures, and a few Dutchmen (but no shepherds) are already piping there. The yells of fierce savages now faintly echo from beyond the waters of the Mississippi, and the time is not far off when the last Indian will leave his bones to bleach on the rock-bound coast of the Pacific.

HOPE AND DESPAIR

THE whitest foam dances upon the darkest billow, and the stars shine the brightest when surrounded by the blackest of thunder clouds, even as a diamond pin glistens with the greatest effulgence when fastened upon the ebony bosom of an Ethiopian wench. So hope mirrors its most brilliant rays in the dark wave of despair, and happiness is never so complete as when visited occasionally by the ministers of misery. These ups and downs in the pathway of man's existence are all for the best, and yet he allows them to vex and torment his peace till he bursts the boiler of his rage, and scalds his own toes. I have no doubt but the common run of people would like to have a railroad built from here to the grave, and go through by steam, but if they all worked as easy in life's galling collar as I do, they would have things just as they are,— some ups and some downs, some sweet and some bitter, some sunshine and some storm,— because they constitute a variety. I wouldn't give a shinplaster penny to have the road of existence perfectly level; for I should soon become tired of a dull sameness of prospect, and make myself miserable in the idea that I must experience no material change, either for better or for worse. Plum pudding is most excellent stuff to wind off a dinner with; but all plum pudding would be worse than none at all. So you see, my friends, the troubles and trials of life are absolutely necessary to enable us to judge rightly of genuine happiness, whenever it happens to enliven the saturnine region of the heart with its presence.

If we never were to have our jackets and shirts wet with the cold rain of misfortune, we could never know how good it feels to stand out and dry in the warm rays of comfort. You need not hesitate ever to travel through swamps of trouble for fear of

CHARLES D. DRAKE

(1811–1892)

CHARLES D. DRAKE plays an important part in the history of the Reconstruction period as a representative of what was contemporaneously called its extreme "radicalism." He represented an element which intended to play and did play the rôle of "Root and Branch Men," demanding the complete eradication of the political power of the former slave-holders. As the putative father of the "Drake Constitution" in Missouri, he became celebrated, and is likely to keep a place in history in connection with that instrument — scarcely if at all less important in its connection than the Missouri Compromise was to the issue of the territorial extension of slavery. He was born in Cincinnati in 1811. In 1827 he served in the navy as a midshipman, but left the service, studied law, was admitted to the bar in Cincinnati, and in 1834 removed to St. Louis. He served in the Missouri Legislature of 1859–60; was Vice-President of the Constitutional Convention which adopted the "Drake Constitution" of 1865; was United States Senator for Missouri from 1867 till 1870; and was Presiding Justice of the Court of Claims from 1870 to 1885.

AGAINST "COPPERHEADS"

(From a Speech Delivered in Chicago, September 1st, 1864)

MUCH has been said in the last three years about the cause of this war. I have my own views of what caused it, which I will give presently; but let us now see what the Copperheads have said in Chicago on that subject. A Mr. Ben Allen, from somewhere on the face of the globe,— I don't know where,— tells us what was not the cause — tells us that "slavery was not the cause of the war!" and so all the rest would have said, had they spoken on that point. I never saw a rebel, a Copperhead, or a Democrat, who would admit that slavery had anything to do with the war. Oh, no, "the peculiar institution" is as innocent of that as a lamb of stirring up strife with a wolf!

Then he goes on to say that "the Abolitionists were the cause of the war"; and every rebel, traitor, Copperhead, and Democrat in the North would say Amen! if he were called to respond to that sentiment. He then says that "if you would remove the cause of the war, you must remove the Abolitionists"; and to that sublime proposition every rebel, traitor, Copperhead, and Democrat in the land would cry, Glory, Hallelujah! But if they undertook to remove all the Abolitionists which this infernal war has made, who were never Abolitionists before, they would have a jolly time of it. That is Mr. Ben Allen's explanation of the cause of the war, and that is the Democratic explanation of it.

Then comes Vallandigham with his explanation and says: "We resorted to arms to compel a people to submission when they simply wanted a redress of grievances." My friends, of all the falsehoods which traitors, North or South, have uttered in defense of the Rebellion, there is not one more black than that. If there is anything certain, it is that the old "Father of Lies" has made Chicago his particular abode since Friday last. He no doubt thought that a Democratic convention was the very place where he would be at home; and now that his body is gone, I trust, for your sake, he has gone too.

But look at these explanations of the cause of the war in one point of view. They are exponents of Democratic opinion and sentiment, and I ask you to note that they impute the whole blame of the war to the North and utter not one word of blame to the South. Who can doubt that the men who can so express themselves know better? Do they not willfully lie, by the suppression of the truth, as well as by the expression of falsehood? They know, as well as they know they live, that the war was begun by the South with but one object, and that was to establish a great empire of slavery upon the shores of the Gulf of Mexico. That is my explanation of the cause of the war, and before God it is the only true one. I would be glad to give you the evidence of it, as I have on former occasions given it to the people of Missouri, but I fear I have already detained you too long. Well, my friends, if you are willing to listen, I will present to you such expressions from Southern leaders, in 1860 and 1861, as will not fail, I think, to demonstrate the irrefragable truth of my views on this subject. I do it the more willingly, because I think that such matter should everywhere be brought out and always kept before the people.

V—122

throughout the civilized world, and pass down, we trust, to the remotest ages. We ask you to join us in forming a Confederacy of Slaveholding States."

Senator Brown, of Mississippi, said:—

"I want Cuba; I want Tamaulipas, Potosi, and one or two other Mexican States; and I want them all for the same reason—for the planting and spreading of slavery. And a footing in Central America will wonderfully aid us in acquiring those other States. Yes, I want those countries for the spread of slavery. I would spread the blessings of slavery, like the religion of our Divine Master, to the uttermost ends of the earth. . . . Whether we can obtain the territory while the Union lasts, I do not know; I fear we cannot, but I would make an honest effort, and if we failed I would go out of the Union and try it there."

Ex-Governor Call, of Florida, said:—

"Slavery cannot be stopped in its career of usefulness to the whole world. It cannot be confined to its present limits. Dire and uncontrollable necessity will compel the master and the slave to cut their way through every barrier which may be thrown around it, or perish together in the attempt. . . . It may be in the providence of God that the American Union, which has cheered the whole world with its promises, like the star which stood for a time over the cradle of Bethlehem, may fall and lose its light forever. It may be, in his dispensation of human events, that the great American family shall be divided into many nations. But divided or united, the path of destiny must lead the Anglo-Saxon race to the mastery of this whole continent. And if the whole column shall not advance, this division of the race will, with the institution of African slavery, advance from the banks of the Rio Grande to the line under the sun, establishing the waymarks of progress, the altars of the reformed religion, the temples of a higher civilization, a purer liberty, and a better system of human government."

There, my friends, you have the open avowal of that empire of slavery which the South was to build upon the ruins of the Union, the broken ramparts of the Constitution, and the grave of Liberty. For such a cause as that the war was begun, for such a cause it is prosecuted, and to such an end it will go, if the Democracy can carry it there, even if the country go into the very jaws of hell. It is for the loyal men of the North, and for them alone, to say whether that cause shall triumph.

Senator Iverson, of Georgia, said:—

"There is but one path of safety for the South, but one mode of preserving her institution of domestic slavery, and that is, a confederacy of States having no incongruous and opposing elements—a confederacy of slave States alone, with homogeneous language, laws, interests, and institutions. Under such a Confederate Republic, with a constitution that should shut out the approach and entrance of all incongruous and conflicting elements, which should protect the institution from change, and keep the whole nation bound to its preservation by an unchangeable fundamental law, the fifteen slave States, with their power of expansion, would present to the world the most free, prosperous, and happy nation on the face of the earth."

Mr. Brooks, Representative from South Carolina, said:—

"We have the issue upon us now; and how are we to meet it? I tell you from the bottom of my heart, that the only mode which I can think available for meeting it is just to tear the Constitution of the United States and to trample it underfoot, and form a Southern Confederacy, every State of which shall be a slaveholding State."

The South Carolina convention thus addressed the people of the slave States:—

"People of the slaveholding States of the United States: Circumstances beyond our control have placed us in the van of the great controversy between the Northern and Southern States. We would have preferred that other States should have assumed the position we now occupy. Independent ourselves, we disclaim any intention or design to lead the counsels of the other Southern States. Providence has cast our lot together by extending over us an identity of purpose, interests, and institutions. South Carolina desires no destiny separate from yours. To be one of a great slaveholding confederacy, stretching its arms over a territory larger than any power in Europe possesses—with a population four times greater than that of the whole United States when they achieved their independence of the British Empire—with productions which make our existence more important to the world than that of any other people who inhabit it—with common institutions to defend and common danger to encounter, we ask your sympathy and your confederation. . . .

"United together, and we must be the most independent, as we are the most important among the nations of the world. United together, and we require no other instrument to conquer peace than our beneficent productions. United together, and we must be a great, free, and prosperous people, whose renown must be spread

HENRY DRUMMOND

(1851–1897)

PROFESSOR HENRY DRUMMOND'S address, 'The Greatest Thing in the World,' has probably been circulated more extensively than any other address of the nineteenth century, and its place as one of the great classics of the language is already assured. This is partly due to the masterly simplicity of its style, but there is a deeper reason. After a quarter of a century of wrangling between the "dons" of science and the doctors of theology, Drummond came to "speak with authority and not as the scribes." From the publication of Darwin's 'Origin of Species,' until Drummond, as thorough-going an evolutionist as Darwin himself, published his 'Natural Law in the Spiritual World,' not a few supposed that a great conflict was in progress between Religion and Science. Under the influence of Drummond's work, this idea lost its popularity, and when, some time after its delivery, his address, 'The Greatest Thing in the World,' was published, it had an unprecedented circulation,—a circulation which resulted in quieting the fears of the religious world, until then greatly apprehensive of what was called "Darwinism."

Drummond was born at Stirling, Scotland, in 1851. As professor of biology in the Free Church College of Glasgow, he was brought into close touch with such great evolutionists as Spencer and Huxley; and as fully as they, he accepted the conclusion that all the forces of nature work continually to develop the higher forms of life from the lower. This central thought of evolution seemed to him to be in the fullest harmony with the central thought of Christianity, and he found in it an inspiration which gave him an almost prophetic earnestness in pleading with his generation to hold to its old ideals and realize them through what he looked on as the new manifestations of their power in controlling the human mind and bringing it into closer touch with the order and harmony of nature.

An ordained minister in the Free Church of Scotland, Professor Drummond diversified his work as a scientist by not less zealous work as an evangelist. He was a friend and pupil of Moody, but his greatest work has been in influencing the intellect of those who had become skeptical because changes in language and habits of expression had made unintelligible or even repulsive to them what their ancestors had regarded with veneration as the deepest truths the human mind is capable of conceiving. It was in translating into modern forms these antique expressions of principle that Drummond most excelled. The ability to do this and at the same time to translate "scientific ideas into common English" was, without doubt, the chief source of his power. His address, 'The Greatest Thing in the World,' is by some considered the masterpiece of its class.

THE GREATEST THING IN THE WORLD

EVERY one has asked himself the great question of antiquity as of the modern world: What is the *summum bonum*—the supreme good? You have life before you. Once only you can live it. What is the noblest object of desire, the supreme gift to covet?

We have been accustomed to be told that the greatest thing in the religious world is Faith. That great word has been the keynote for centuries of the popular religion, and we have easily learned to look upon it as the greatest thing in the world. Well, we are wrong. If we have been told that, we may miss the mark. I have taken you, in the chapter which I have just read, to Christianity at its source, and there we have seen "The greatest of these is love." It is not an oversight. Paul was speaking of faith just a moment before. He says: "If I have all faith, so that I can remove mountains, and have not love, I am nothing." So far from forgetting, he deliberately contrasts them, "Now abideth Faith, Hope, Love," and without a moment's hesitation the decision falls: "The greatest of these is Love."

And it is not prejudice. A man is apt to recommend to others his own strong point.

Love was not Paul's strong point. The observing student can detect a beautiful tenderness growing and ripening all through his character as Paul gets old; but the hand that wrote: "The greatest of these is Love," when we meet it first, is stained with blood.

Nor is this letter to the Corinthians peculiar in singling out love as the *summum bonum*. The masterpieces of Christianity are agreed about it. Peter says, "Above all things have fervent love among yourselves." Above all things. And John goes further, "God is love." And you remember the profound remark which Paul makes elsewhere, "Love is the fulfilling of the law."

Did you ever think what he meant by that? In those days men were working their passage to Heaven by keeping the Ten Commandments and the hundred and ten other commandments which they had manufactured out of them. Christ said, I will show you a more simple way. If you do one thing, you will do these one hundred and ten things without ever thinking about them. If you love, you will unconsciously fulfill the whole law. And you can readily see for yourselves how that must be so. Take any of the commandments: "Thou shalt have no other gods before me." If a man love God, you will not require to tell him that. Love is the fulfilling of that law. "Take not his name in vain." Would he ever dream of taking his name in vain, if he loved him? "Remember the Sabbath Day to keep it holy." Would he not be too glad to have one day in seven to dedicate more exclusively to the object of his affection? Love would fulfill all these laws regarding God. And so, if he loved man, you would never think of telling him to honor his father and mother. He could not do anything else. It would be preposterous to tell him not to kill. You could only insult him if you suggested that he should not steal—how could he steal from those he loved? It would be superfluous to beg him not to bear false witness against his neighbor. If he loved him, it would be the last thing he would do.

And you would never dream of urging him not to covet what his neighbors had. He would rather they possessed it than himself. In this way, "Love is the fulfilling of the law." It is the rule for fulfilling all rules, the new commandment for keeping all the old commandments, Christ's one secret of the Christian life.

Now Paul had learned that; and in this noble eulogy he has given us the most wonderful and original account extant of the *summum bonum*. We may divide it into three parts: In the beginning of the short chapter we have Love contrasted; in the heart of it we have Love analyzed; toward the end we have Love defended as the supreme gift.

Paul begins by contrasting Love with other things that men in those days thought much of. I shall not attempt to go over those things in detail. Their inferiority is already obvious.

He contrasts it with eloquence. And what a noble gift it is, the power of playing upon the souls and wills of men, and rousing them to lofty purposes and holy deeds. Paul says: "If I

speak with the tongues of men and of angels, and have not love, I am become as sounding brass, or a tinkling cymbal." And we all know why. We have all felt the brazenness of words without emotion, the hollowness, the unaccountable unpersuasiveness, of eloquence behind which lies no Love.

He contrasts it with prophecy. He contrasts it with mysteries. He contrasts it with faith. He contrasts it with charity. Why is Love greater than faith? Because the end is greater than the means. And why is it greater than charity? Because the whole is greater than the part. Love is greater than faith, because the end is greater than the means. What is the use of having faith? It is to connect the soul with God. And what is the object of connecting man with God? That he may become like God. But God is Love. Hence Faith, the means, is in order to Love, the end. Love, therefore, obviously is greater than faith. It is greater than charity, again, because the whole is greater than a part. Charity is only a little bit of Love, one of the innumerable avenues of Love, and there may even be, and there is, a great deal of charity without Love. It is a very easy thing to toss a copper to a beggar on the street; it is generally an easier thing than not to do it. Yet Love is just as often in the withholding. We purchase relief from the sympathetic feelings roused by the spectacle of misery, at the copper's cost. It is too cheap—too cheap for us, and often too dear for the beggar. If we really loved him, we would either do more for him, or less.

Then Paul contrasts it with sacrifice and martyrdom. And I beg the little band of would-be missionaries—and I have the honor to call some of you by this name for the first time—to remember that though you give your bodies to be burned, and have not Love, it profits nothing—nothing! You can take nothing greater to the heathen world than the impress and reflection of the Love of God upon your own character. That is the universal language. It will take you years to speak in Chinese, or in the dialects of India. From the day you land, that language of Love, understood by all, will be pouring forth its unconscious eloquence. It is the man who is the missionary, it is not his words. His character is his message. In the heart of Africa, among the great lakes, I have come across black men and women who remembered the only white man they ever saw before—David Livingstone; and as you cross his footsteps in

that dark continent, men's faces light up as they speak of the kind doctor who passed there years ago. They could not understand him; but they felt the Love that beat in his heart. Take into your new sphere of labor, where you also mean to lay down your life, that simple charm, and your lifework must succeed. You can take nothing greater, you need take nothing less. It is not worth while going if you take anything less. You may take every accomplishment; you may be braced for every sacrifice; but if you give your body to be burned, and have not Love, it will profit you and the cause of Christ nothing.

After contrasting Love with these things, Paul, in three verses, very short, gives us an amazing analysis of what this supreme thing is. I ask you to look at it. It is a compound thing, he tells us. It is like light. As you have seen a man of science take a beam of light and pass it through a crystal prism, as you have seen it come out on the other side of the prism broken up into its component colors—red and blue and yellow and violet and orange, and all the colors of the rainbow—so Paul passes this thing, Love, through the magnificent prism of his inspired intellect, and it comes out on the other side broken up into its elements. And in these few words we have what one might call the Spectrum of Love, the analysis of Love. Will you observe what its elements are? Will you notice that they have common names; that they are virtues which we hear about every day; that they are things which can be practiced by every man in every place in life; and how, by a multitude of small things and ordinary virtues, the supreme thing, the *summum bonum*, is made up?

The Spectrum of Love has nine ingredients:—

Patience, "Love suffereth long."
Kindness, "And is kind."
Generosity, "Love envieth not."
Humility, "Love vaunteth not itself, is not puffed up."
Courtesy, "Doth not behave itself unseemly."
Unselfishness, "Seeketh not her own."
Good Temper, "Is not easily provoked."
Guilelessness, "Thinketh no evil."
Sincerity, "Rejoiceth not in iniquity, but rejoiceth in the truth."

Patience; kindness; generosity; humility; courtesy; unselfishness; good temper; guilelessness; sincerity—these make up the supreme gift, the stature of the perfect man. You will observe that all are in relation to men, in relation to life, in relation to the known to-day and the near to-morrow, and not to the unknown eternity. We hear much of love to God; Christ spoke much of love to man. We make a great deal of peace with heaven; Christ made much of peace on earth. Religion is not a strange or added thing, but the inspiration of the secular life, the breathing of an eternal spirit through this temporal world. The supreme thing, in short, is not a thing at all, but the giving of a further finish to the multitudinous words and acts which make up the sum of every common day.

There is no time to do more than make a passing note upon each of these ingredients. Love is *Patience*. This is the normal attitude of Love; Love passive, Love waiting to begin; not in a hurry; calm; ready to do its work when the summons comes, but meantime wearing the ornament of a meek and quiet spirit. Love suffers long; beareth all things; believeth all things; hopeth all things. For Love understands, and therefore waits.

Kindness. Love active. Have you ever noticed how much of Christ's life was spent in doing kind things — in merely doing kind things? Run over it with that in view, and you will find that he spent a great proportion of his time simply in making people happy, in doing good turns to people. There is only one thing greater than happiness in the world, and that is holiness; and it is not in our keeping, but what God has put in our power is the happiness of those about us, and that is largely to be secured by our being kind to them.

"The greatest thing," says some one, "a man can do for his Heavenly Father is to be kind to some of his other children." I wonder why it is that we are not all kinder than we are? How much the world needs it. How easily it is done. How instantaneously it acts. How infallibly it is remembered. How superabundantly it pays itself back — for there is no debtor in the world so honorable, so superbly honorable, as Love. "Love never faileth." Love is success. Love is happiness. Love is life. "Love," I say with Browning, "is energy of life."

> "For life, with all it yields of joy or woe
> And hope and fear,
> Is just our chance o' the prize of learning love,—
> How love might be, hath been indeed, and is."

the ploughman-poet. It was because he loved everything — the mouse, and the daisy, and all the things, great and small, that God had made. So with this simple passport he could mingle with any society, and enter courts and palaces from his little cottage on the banks of the Ayr. You know the meaning of the word "gentleman." It means a gentle man — a man who does things gently with Love. And that is the whole art and mystery of it. The gentle man cannot, in the nature of things, do an ungentle and ungentlemanly thing. The ungentle soul, the inconsiderate, unsympathetic nature cannot do anything else. "Love doth not behave itself unseemly."

Unselfishness. "Love seeketh not her own." Observe: Seeketh not even that which is her own. In Britain, the Englishman is devoted, and rightly, to his rights. But there come times when a man may exercise even the higher right of giving up his rights. Yet Paul does not summon us to give up our rights. Love strikes much deeper. It would have us not seek them at all, ignore them, eliminate the personal element altogether from our calculations. It is not hard to give up our rights. They are often external. The difficult thing is to give up ourselves. The more difficult thing still is not to seek things for ourselves at all. After we have sought them, bought them, won them, deserved them, we have taken the cream off them for ourselves already. Little cross, then, to give them up. But not to seek them, to look every man not on his own things, but on the things of others — *id opus est*. "Seekest thou great things for thyself"? said the prophet; "seek them not." Why? Because there is no greatness in things. Things cannot be great. The only greatness is unselfish love. Even self-denial in itself is nothing, is almost a mistake. Only a great purpose or a mightier love can justify the waste. It is more difficult, I have said, not to seek our own at all, than, having sought it, to give it up. I must take that back. It is only true of a partly selfish heart. Nothing is a hardship to Love, and nothing is hard. I believe that Christ's "yoke" is easy. Christ's "yoke" is just his way of taking life. And I believe it is an easier way than any other. I believe it is a happier way than any other. The most obvious lesson in Christ's teaching is that there is no happiness in having and getting anything, but only in giving. I repeat, there is no happiness in having or in getting, but only in giving. And half the world is on the wrong scent in pursuit of happiness.

Where Love is, God is. He that dwelleth in Love dwelleth in God. God is Love. Therefore love. Without distinction, without calculation, without procrastination, love. Lavish it upon the poor, where it is very easy; especially upon the rich, who often need it most; most of all upon our equals, where it is very difficult, and for whom, perhaps, we each do least of all. There is a difference between trying to please and giving pleasure. Give pleasure. Lose no chance of giving pleasure. For that is the ceaseless and anonymous triumph of a truly loving spirit. "I shall pass through this world but once. Any good thing therefore that I can do, or any kindness that I can show to any human being, let me do it now. Let me not defer it or neglect it, for I shall not pass this way again."

Generosity. "Love envieth not." This is Love in competition with others. Whenever you attempt a good work, you will find other men doing the same kind of work, and probably doing it better. Envy them not. Envy is a feeling of ill-will to those who are in the same line as ourselves, a spirit of covetousness and detraction. How little Christian work even is a protection against un-Christian feeling. That most despicable of all the unworthy moods which cloud a Christian's soul assuredly waits for us on the threshold of every work, unless we are fortified with this grace of magnanimity. Only one thing truly need the Christian envy, the large, rich, generous soul which "envieth not."

And then, after having learned all that, you have to learn this further thing, *Humility* — to put a seal upon your lips and forget what you have done. After you have been kind, after Love has stolen forth into the world and done its beautiful work, go back into the shade again, and say nothing about it. Love hides even from itself. Love waives even self-satisfaction. "Love vaunteth not itself, is not puffed up."

The fifth ingredient is a somewhat strange one to find in this *summum bonum: Courtesy*. This is Love in society, Love in relation to etiquette. "Love doth not behave itself unseemly" Politeness has been defined as love in trifles. Courtesy is said to be love in little things. And the one secret of politeness is to love. Love cannot behave itself unseemly. You can put the most untutored persons into the highest society, and if they have a reservoir of Love in their hearts, they will not behave themselves unseemly. They simply cannot do it. Carlyle said of Robert Burns that there was no truer gentleman in Europe than

They think it consists in having and getting, and in being served by others. It consists in giving, and in serving others. He that would be great among you, said Christ, let him serve. He that would be happy, let him remember that there is but one way — it is more blessed, it is more happy, to give than to receive.

The next ingredient is a very remarkable one: *Good Temper*. "Love is not easily provoked." Nothing could be more striking than to find this here. We are inclined to look upon bad temper as a very harmless weakness. We speak of it as a mere infirmity of nature, a family failing, a matter of temperament, not a thing to take into very serious account in estimating a man's character. And yet here, right in the heart of this analysis of Love, it finds a place; and the Bible again and again returns to condemn it as one of the most destructive elements in human nature.

The peculiarity of ill-temper is that it is the vice of the virtuous. It is often the one blot on an otherwise noble character. You know men who are all but perfect, and women who would be entirely perfect, but for an easily ruffled, quick-tempered, or "touchy" disposition. This compatibility of ill-temper with high moral character is one of the strangest and saddest problems of ethics. The truth is there are two great classes of sins — sins of the Body, and sins of the Disposition. The Prodigal Son may be taken as a type of the first, the Elder Brother of the second. Now, society has no doubt whatever as to which of these is the worse. Its brand falls, without a challenge, upon the Prodigal. But are we right? We have no balance to weigh one another's sins, and coarser and finer are but human words; but faults in the higher nature may be less venial than those in the lower, and to the eye of him who is Love, a sin against Love may seem a hundred times more base. No form of vice, not worldliness, not greed of gold, not drunkenness itself, does more to un-Christianize society than evil temper. For embittering life, for breaking up communities, for destroying the most sacred relationships, for devastating homes, for withering up men and women, for taking the bloom of childhood, in short, for sheer gratuitous misery-producing power, this influence stands alone. Look at the Elder Brother, moral, hard-working, patient, dutiful — let him get all credit for his virtues — look at this man, this baby, sulking outside his own father's door. "He was angry," we read, "and would not go in." Look at the effect upon the father, upon the servants, upon the happiness of the guests. Judge of the effect upon the Prodigal—and how many prodigals are kept out of the Kingdom of God by the unlovely character of those who profess to be inside? Analyze, as a study in Temper, the thundercloud itself as it gathers upon the Elder Brother's brow. What is it made of? Jealousy, anger, pride, uncharity, cruelty, self-righteousness, touchiness, doggedness, sullenness—these are the ingredients of this dark and loveless soul. In varying proportions, also, these are the ingredients of all ill-temper. Judge if such sins of the disposition are not worse to live in, and for others to live with, than sins of the body. Did Christ, indeed, not answer the question himself when he said: "I say unto you that the publicans and the harlots go into the kingdom of Heaven before you." There is really no place in Heaven for a disposition like this. A man with such a mood could only make Heaven miserable for all the people in it. Except, therefore, such a man be born again, he cannot, he simply cannot, enter the Kingdom of Heaven. For it is perfectly certain—and you will not misunderstand me—that to enter Heaven a man must take it with him.

You will see, then, why temper is significant. It is not in what it is alone, but in what it reveals. This is why I take the liberty now of speaking of it with such unusual plainness. It is a test for love, a symptom, a revelation of an unloving nature at bottom. It is the intermittent fever which bespeaks unintermittent disease within; the occasional bubble escaping to the surface which betrays some rottenness underneath; a sample of the most hidden products of the soul dropped involuntarily when off one's guard; in a word, the lightning form of a hundred hideous and un-Christian sins. For a want of patience, a want of kindness, a want of generosity, a want of courtesy, a want of unselfishness, are all instantaneously symbolized in one flash of temper.

Hence it is not enough to deal with the temper. We must go to the source and change the inmost nature, and the angry humors will die away of themselves. Souls are made sweet not by taking the acid fluids out, but by putting something in—a great Love, a new spirit, the spirit of Christ. Christ, the spirit of Christ interpenetrating ours, sweetens, purifies, transforms all. This only can eradicate what is wrong, work a chemical change, renovate and regenerate and rehabilitate the inner man. Will power does not change men. Time does not change men. Christ does.

joiceth not in unrighteousness, but rejoiceth with the truth," a quality which probably no one English word—and certainly not Sincerity—adequately defines. It includes, perhaps more strictly, the self-restraint which refuses to make capital out of others' faults; the charity which delights not in exposing the weakness of others, but, "covereth all things"; the sincerity of purpose which endeavors to see things as they are, and rejoices to find them better than suspicion feared or calumny denounced.

So much for the analysis of Love. Now the business of our lives is to have these things fitted into our characters. That is the supreme work to which we need to address ourselves in this world, to learn Love. Is life not full of opportunities for learning Love? Every man and woman every day has a thousand of them. The world is not a playground; it is a schoolroom. Life is not a holiday, but an education. And the one eternal lesson for us all is how better we can love. What makes a man a good cricketer? Practice. What makes a man a good artist, a good sculptor, a good musician? Practice. What makes a man a good linguist, a good stenographer? Practice. What makes a man a good man? Practice. Nothing else. There is nothing capricious about religion. We do not get the soul in different ways, under different laws, from those in which we get the body and the mind. If a man does not exercise his arm, he develops no biceps muscle; and if a man does not exercise his soul, he acquires no muscle in his soul, no strength of character, no vigor of moral fiber, nor beauty of spiritual growth. Love is not a thing of enthusiastic emotion. It is a rich, strong, manly, vigorous expression of the whole round Christian character—the Christlike nature in its fullest development. And the constituents of this great character are only to be built up by ceaseless practice.

What was Christ doing in the carpenter's shop? Practicing. Though perfect, we read that he learned obedience, and grew in wisdom and in favor with God. Do not quarrel therefore with your lot in life. Do not complain of its never-ceasing cares, its petty environment, the vexations you have to stand, the small and sordid souls you have to live and work with. Above all, do not resent temptation; do not be perplexed because it seems to thicken round you more and more, and ceases neither for effort nor for agony nor prayer. That is your practice. That is the practice which God appoints you; and it is

Therefore, "Let that mind be in you which was also in Christ Jesus." Some of us have not much time to lose. Remember, once more, that this is a matter of life or death. I cannot help speaking urgently, for myself, for yourselves. "Whoso shall offend one of these little ones which believe in me, it were better for him that a millstone were hanged about his neck and that he were drowned in the depth of the sea." That is to say, it is the deliberate verdict of the Lord Jesus that it is better not to live than not to love. It is better not to live than not to love.

Guilelessness and *Sincerity* may be dismissed almost with a word. Guilelessness is the grace for suspicious people. And the possession of it is the great secret of personal influence. You will find, if you think for a moment, that the people who influence you are people who believe in you. In an atmosphere of suspicion men shrivel up; but in that atmosphere they expand, and find encouragement and educative fellowship. It is a wonderful thing that here and there in this hard, uncharitable world there should still be left a few rare souls who think no evil. This is the great unworldliness. Love "thinketh no evil," imputes no motive, sees the bright side, puts the best construction on every action. What a delightful state of mind to live in! What a stimulus and benediction even to meet with it for a day! To be trusted is to be saved. And if we try to influence or elevate others, we shall soon see that success is in proportion to their belief of our belief in them. For the respect of another is the first restoration of the self-respect a man has lost; our ideal of what he is becomes to him the hope and pattern of what he may become.

"Love rejoiceth not in iniquity, but rejoiceth in the truth." I have called this Sincerity from the words rendered in the Authorized Version by "rejoiceth in the truth." And, certainly, were this the real translation, nothing could be more just. For he who loves will love truth not less than men. He will rejoice in the truth—rejoice not in what he has been taught to believe; not in this church's doctrine or in that; not in this ism or in that ism; but "in the Truth." He will accept only what is real; he will strive to get at facts; he will search for truth with a humble and unbiased mind, and cherish whatever he finds at any sacrifice. But the more literal translation of the Revised Version calls for just such a sacrifice for truth's sake here. For what Paul really meant is, as we there read, "Re-

having its work in making you patient, and humble, and generous, and unselfish, and kind, and courteous. Do not grudge the hand that is molding the still too shapeless image within you. It is growing more beautiful, though you see it not, and every touch of temptation may add to its perfection. Therefore keep in the midst of life. Do not isolate yourself. Be among men, and among things, and among troubles, and difficulties, and obstacles. You remember Goethe's words: "*Es bildet ein Talent sich in der Stille, Doch ein Charakter in dem Strom der Welt.*" (Talent develops itself in solitude; character in the stream of life.) Talent develops itself in solitude—the talent of prayer, of faith, of meditation, of seeing the unseen; character grows in the stream of the world's life. That chiefly is where men are to learn love.

How? Now, how? To make it easier, I have named a few of the elements of Love. But these are only elements. Love itself can never be defined. Light is a something more than the sum of its ingredients—a glowing, dazzling, tremulous ether. And Love is something more than all its elements—a palpitating, quivering, sensitive, living thing. By synthesis of all the colors, men can make whiteness, they cannot make light. By synthesis of all the virtues, men can make virtue, they cannot make Love. How, then, are we to have this transcendent living whole conveyed into our souls? We brace our wills to secure it. We try to copy those who have it. We lay down rules about it. We watch. We pray. But these things alone will not bring Love into our nature. Love is an effect. And only as we fulfill the right condition can we have the effect produced. Shall I tell you what the cause is?

If you turn to the Revised Version of the First Epistle of John, you will find these words: "We love because he first loved us." "We love," not "We love him." That is the way the old version has it, and it is quite wrong. "We love—because he first loved us." Look at that word "because." It is the cause of which I have spoken. "Because he first loved us," the effect follows that we love, we love him, we love all men. We cannot help it. Because he loved us, we love, we love everybody. Our heart is slowly changed. Contemplate the love of Christ, and you will love. Stand before that mirror, reflect Christ's character, and you will be changed into the same image from tenderness to tenderness. There is no other way. You cannot love to order. You can only look at the lovely object, and fall in love with it, and grow into likeness to it. And so look at this Perfect Character, this Perfect Life. Look at the great Sacrifice as he laid down himself, all through life, and upon the Cross of Calvary, and you must love him. And loving him, you must become like him. Love begets love. It is a process of induction. Put a piece of iron in the presence of an electrified body, and that piece of iron for a time becomes electrified. It is changed into a temporary magnet in the mere presence of a permanent magnet, and as long as you leave the two side by side, they are both magnets alike. Remain side by side with him who loved us, and gave himself for us, and you, too, will become a permanent magnet, a permanently attractive force; and like him you will draw all men unto you, like him you will be drawn unto all men. That is the inevitable effect of Love. Any man who fulfills that cause must have that effect produced in him. Try to give up the idea that religion comes to us by chance, or by mystery, or by caprice. It comes to us by natural law, or by supernatural law, for all law is Divine. Edward Irving went to see a dying boy once, and when he entered the room he just put his hand on the sufferer's head, and said, " My boy, God loves you," and went away. And the boy started from his bed, and called out to the people in the house, " God loves me! God loves me!" It changed that boy. The sense that God loved him overpowered him, melted him down, and began the creating of a new heart in him. And that is how the love of God melts down the unlovely heart in man, and begets in him the new creature, who is patient and humble and gentle and unselfish. And there is no other way to get it. There is no mystery about it. We love others, we love everybody, we love our enemies, because he first loved us.

Now I have a closing sentence or two to add about Paul's reason for singling out Love as the supreme possession. It is a very remarkable reason. In a single word it is this: it lasts. " Love," urges Paul, " never faileth." Then he begins again one of his marvelous lists of the great things of the day, and exposes them one by one. He runs over the things that men thought were going to last, and shows that they are all fleeting, temporary, passing away.

" Whether there be prophecies, they shall fail." It was the mother's ambition for her boy in those days that he should

become a prophet. For hundreds of years God had never spoken by means of any prophet, and at that time the prophet was greater than the King. Men waited wistfully for another messenger to come, and hung upon his lips when he appeared as upon the very voice of God. Paul says: " Whether there be prophecies, they shall fail." This book is full of prophecies. One by one they have " failed"; that is, having been fulfilled, their work is finished; they have nothing more to do now in the world except to feed a devout man's faith.

Then Paul talks about tongues. That was another thing that was greatly coveted. " Whether there be tongues, they shall cease." As we all know, many, many centuries have passed since tongues have been known in this world. They have ceased. Take it in any sense you like. Take it, for illustration merely, as languages in general — a sense which was not in Paul's mind at all, and which, though it cannot give us the specific lesson, will point the general truth. Consider the words in which these chapters were written — Greek. It has gone. Take the Latin — the other great tongue of those days. It ceased long ago. Look at the Indian language. It is ceasing. The language of Wales, of Ireland, of the Scottish Highlands, is dying before our eyes. The most popular book in the English tongue at the present time, except the Bible, is one of Dickens's works, his 'Pickwick Papers.' It is largely written in the language of London street life, and experts assure us that in fifty years it will be unintelligible to the average English reader.

Then Paul goes further, and with even greater boldness adds: " Whether there be knowledge, it shall vanish away." The wisdom of the ancients, where is it? It is wholly gone. A schoolboy to-day knows more than Sir Isaac Newton knew. His knowledge has vanished away. You put yesterday's newspaper in the fire. Its knowledge has vanished away. You buy the old editions of the great encyclopædias for a few pence. Their knowledge has vanished away. Look how the coach has been superseded by the use of steam. Look how electricity has superseded that, and swept a hundred almost new inventions into oblivion. One of the greatest living authorities, Sir William Thompson, said the other day: " The steam engine is passing away." " Whether there be knowledge, it shall vanish away." At every workshop you will see, in the back yard, a heap of old iron, a few wheels, a few levers, a few cranks, broken and eaten with rust. Twenty

years ago that was the pride of the city. Men flocked in from the country to see the great invention; now it is superseded, its day is done. And all the boasted science and philosophy of this day will soon be old. But yesterday, in the University of Edinburgh, the greatest figure in the faculty was Sir James Simpson, the discoverer of chloroform. The other day his successor and nephew, Professor Simpson, was asked by the librarian of the University to go to the library and pick out the books on his subject that were no longer needed. And his reply to the librarian was this: " Take every text-book that is more than ten years old, and put it down in the cellar." Sir James Simpson was a great authority only a few years ago; men came from all parts of the earth to consult him; and almost the whole teaching of that time is consigned by the science of to-day to oblivion. And in every branch of science it is the same. " Now we know in part. We see through a glass darkly."

Can you tell me anything that is going to last? Many things Paul did not condescend to name. He did not mention money, fortune, fame; but he picked out the great things of his time, the things the best men thought had something in them, and brushed them peremptorily aside. Paul had no charge against these things in themselves. All he said about them was that they would not last. They were great things, but not supreme things. There were things beyond them. What we are stretches past what we do, beyond what we possess. Many things that men denounce as sins are not sins; but they are temporary. And that is a favorite argument of the New Testament. John says of the world, not that it is wrong, but simply that it " passeth away." There is a great deal in the world that is delightful and beautiful; there is a great deal in it that is great and engrossing; but it will not last. All that is in the world, the lust of the eye, the lust of the flesh, and the pride of life, are but for a little while. Love not the world therefore. Nothing that it contains is worth the life and consecration of an immortal soul. The immortal soul must give itself to something that is immortal. And the only immortal things are these: " Now abideth faith, hope, love, but the greatest of these is love."

Some think the time may come when two of these three things will also pass away — faith into sight, hope into fruition. Paul does not say so. We know but little now about the conditions of the life that is to come. But what is certain is that Love must

last. God, the eternal God, is Love. Covet, therefore, that everlasting gift, that one thing which it is certain is going to stand, that one coinage which will be current in the universe when all the other coinages of all the nations of the world shall be useless and unhonored. You will give yourselves to many things, give yourself first to Love. Hold things in their proportion. Hold things in their proportion. Let at least the first great object of our lives be to achieve the character defended in these words, the character — and it is the character of Christ — which is built round Love.

I have said this thing is eternal. Did you ever notice how continually John associates love and faith with eternal life? I was not told when I was a boy that " God so loved the world that he gave his only-begotten Son that whosoever believeth in him should have everlasting life." What I was told, I remember, was, that God so loved the world that if I trusted in him I was to have a thing called peace, or I was to have rest, or I was to have joy, or I was to have safety. But I had to find out for myself that whosoever trusteth in him — that is, whosoever loveth him, for trust is only the avenue to Love — hath everlasting life. The Gospel offers a man life. Never offer men a thimbleful of Gospel. Do not offer them merely joy, or merely peace, or merely rest, or merely safety; tell them how Christ came to give men a more abundant life than they have, a life abundant in love, and therefore abundant in salvation for themselves, and large in enterprise for the alleviation and redemption of the world. Then only can the Gospel take hold of the whole of a man, body, soul, and spirit, and give to each part of his nature its exercise and reward. Many of the current Gospels are addressed only to a part of man's nature. They offer peace, not life; faith, not Love; justification, not regeneration. And men slip back again from such religion because it has never really held them. Their nature was not all in it. It offered no deeper and gladder life-current than the life that was lived before. Surely it stands to reason that only a fuller love can compete with the love of the world.

To love abundantly is to live abundantly, and to love forever is to live forever. Hence, eternal life is inextricably bound up with Love. We want to live forever for the same reason that we want to live to-morrow. Why do you want to live to-morrow? It is because there is some one who loves you, and whom you want to see to-morrow, and be with, and love back. There is no other reason why we should live on than that we love and are beloved. It is when a man has no one to love him that he commits suicide. So long as he has friends, those who love him and whom he loves, he will live, because to live is to love. Be it but the love of a dog, it will keep him in life; but let that go and he has no contact with life, no reason to live. He dies by his own hand. Eternal life also is to know God, and God is Love. This is Christ's own definition. Ponder it. " This is life eternal, that they might know thee, the only true God, and Jesus Christ whom thou hast sent." Love must be eternal. It is what God is. On the last analysis, then, Love is life. Love never faileth, and life never faileth, so long as there is Love. That is the philosophy of what Paul is showing us; the reason why, in the nature of things, Love should be the supreme thing—because it is going to last; because, in the nature of things, it is an eternal life. It is a thing that we are living now, not that we get when we die; that we shall have a poor chance of getting when we die, unless we are living now. No worse fate can befall a man in this world than to live and grow old alone, unloving and unloved. To be lost is to live in an unregenerate condition, loveless and unloved; and to be saved is to love; and he that dwelleth in love dwelleth already in God. For God is Love.

Now I have all but finished. How many of you will join me in reading this chapter once a week for the next three months? A man did that once, and it changed his whole life. Will you do it? It is for the greatest thing in the world. You might begin by reading it every day, especially the verses which describe the perfect character. " Love suffereth long, and is kind; love envieth not; love vaunteth not itself." Get these ingredients into your life. Then everything that you do is eternal. It is worth doing. It is worth giving time to. No man can become a saint in his sleep; and to fulfill the condition required demands a certain amount of prayer and meditation and time, just as improvement in any direction, bodily or mental, requires preparation and care. Address yourselves to that one thing; at any cost have this transcendent character exchanged for yours. You will find as you look back upon your life that the moments that stand out, the moments when you have really lived, are the moments when you have done things in a spirit of love. As memory scans the past, above and beyond all the transitory

other charge than lovelessness shall be preferred. Be not deceived. The words which all of us shall one day hear sound not of theology, but of life; not of churches and saints, but of the hungry and the poor; not of creeds and doctrines, but of shelter and clothing; not of Bibles and prayer-books, but of cups of cold water in the name of Christ. Thank God the Christianity of to-day is coming nearer the world's need. Live to help that on. Thank God, men know better, by a hair's breadth, what religion is, what God is, who Christ is, where Christ is. Who is Christ? He who fed the hungry, clothed the naked, visited the sick. And where is Christ? Where?—whoso shall receive a little child in my name receiveth me. And who are Christ's? Every one that loveth is born of God.

PREPARATION FOR LEARNING

BEFORE an artist can do anything, the instrument must be tuned. Our astronomers at this moment are preparing for an event which happens only once or twice in a lifetime; the total eclipse of the sun in the month of August. They have begun already. They are making preparations. At chosen stations, in different parts of the world, they are spending all the skill that science can suggest upon the construction of their instruments; and up to the last moment they will be busy adjusting them; and the last day will be the busiest of all, because then they must have the glasses and the mirrors polished to the last degree. They have to have the lenses in place and focused upon this spot before the event itself takes place.

Everything will depend upon the instruments which you bring to this experiment. Everything will depend upon it; and therefore fifteen minutes will not be lost if we each put our instrument into the best working order we can. I have spoken of lenses, and that reminds me that the instrument which we bring to bear upon truth is a compound thing. It consists of many parts. Truth is not a product of the intellect alone; it is a product of the whole nature. The body is engaged in it, and the mind, and the soul.

The body is engaged in it. Of course, a man who has his body run down, or who is dyspeptic, or melancholy, sees every-

pleasures of life, there leap forward those supreme hours when you have been enabled to do unnoticed kindnesses to those round about you, things too trifling to speak about, but which you feel have entered into your eternal life. I have seen almost all the beautiful things God has made; I have enjoyed almost every pleasure that he has planned for man; and yet as I look back I see standing out above all the life that has gone, four or five short experiences when the love of God reflected itself in some poor imitation, some small act of love of mine, and these seem to be the things which alone of all one's life abide. Everything else in all our lives is transitory. Every other good is visionary. But the acts of Love which no man knows about, or can ever know about—they never fail.

In the book of Matthew, where the Judgment Day is depicted for us in the imagery of One seated upon a throne and dividing the sheep from the goats, the test of a man then is not, " How have I believed?" but " How have I loved?" The test of religion, the final test of religion, is not religiousness, but Love. I say, the final test of religion at that great day is not religiousness, but Love; not what I have done, not what I have believed, not what I have achieved, but how I have discharged the common charities of life. Sins of commission in that awful indictment are not even referred to. By what we have not done, by sins of omission, we are judged. It could not be otherwise. For the withholding of love is the negation of the spirit of Christ, the proof that we never knew him, that for us he lived in vain. It means that he suggested nothing in all our thoughts, that he inspired nothing in all our lives, that we were not once near enough to him to be seized with the spell of his compassion for the world. It means that—

" I lived for myself, I thought for myself,
     For myself, and none beside —
Just as if Jesus had never lived,
     As if he had never died."

It is the Son of Man before whom the nations of the world shall be gathered. It is in the presence of Humanity that we shall be charged. And the spectacle itself, the mere sight of it, will silently judge each one. Those will be there whom we have met and helped; or there, the unpitied multitude whom we neglected or despised. No other witness need be summoned. No

thing black, and distorted, and untrue. But I am not going to dwell upon that. Most of you seem in pretty fair working order, so far as your bodies are concerned; only it is well to remember that we are to give our bodies a living sacrifice—not a half-dead sacrifice, as some people seem to imagine. There is no virtue in emaciation. I don't know if you have any tendency in that direction in America, but certainly we are in danger of dropping into it now and then in England, and it is just as well to bear in mind our part of the lens—a very compound and delicate lens—with which we have to take in truth.

Then comes a very important part: the intellect—which is one of the most useful servants of truth; and I need not tell you as students, that the intellect will have a great deal to do with your reception of truth. I was told that it was said at these conferences last year, that a man must crucify his intellect. I venture to contradict the gentlemen who made that statement. I am quite sure no such statement could ever have been made in your hearing—that we were to crucify our intellects. We can make no progress without the full use of all the intellectual powers that God has endowed us with.

But more important than either of these is the moral nature—the moral and spiritual nature. Some of you remember a sermon of Robertson of Brighton entitled, 'Obedience the Organ of Spiritual Knowledge.' A very startling title!—'Obedience the Organ of Spiritual Knowledge.' The Pharisees asked about Christ: " How knoweth this man letters, never having learned?" How knoweth this man, never having learned? The organ of knowledge is not nearly so much mind as the organ that Christ used, namely, obedience; and that was the organ which he himself insisted upon when he said: " He that willeth to do his will shall know of the doctrine whether it be of God." You have all noticed, of course, that the words in the original are: " If any man will to do his will, he shall know of the doctrine." It doesn't read: " If any do his will," which no man can do perfectly; but if any man be simply willing to do his will,—if he has an absolutely undivided mind about it,—that man will know what truth is and know what falsehood is; a stranger will he not follow. And that is by far the best source of spiritual knowledge on every account—obedience to God—absolute sincerity and loyalty in following Christ. " If any man do his will, he shall know " —a very remarkable association of knowledge, a thing which is usually considered quite intellectual, with obedience, which is moral and spiritual.

But even although we use all these three different parts of the instrument, we have not at all got at the complete method of learning. There is a little preliminary that the astronomer has to do before he can make his observation. He has to take the cap off his telescope. Many a man thinks he is looking at truth when he is only looking at the cap. Many a time I have looked down my microscope and thought I was looking at the diatom for which I had long been searching, and found I had simply been looking at a speck of dust upon the lens itself. Many a man thinks he is looking at truth, when he is only looking at the spectacles he has put on to see it with. He is looking at his own spectacles. Now, the common spectacles that a man puts on,—I suppose the creed in which he has been brought up,—if a man looks at that, let him remember that he is not looking at truth; he is looking at his own spectacles. There is no more important lesson that we have to carry with us than that truth is not to be found in what I have been taught. That is not truth. Truth is not what I have been taught. If it were so, that would apply to the Mormon, it would apply to the Brahman, it would apply to the Buddhist. Truth would be to everybody just what he had been taught. Therefore, let us dismiss from our minds the predisposition to regard that which we have been brought up in as being necessarily the truth. I must say it is very hard to shake oneself free altogether from that. I suppose it is impossible.

But you see the reasonableness of giving up that as your view of truth when you come to apply it all around. If that were the definition of truth, truth would be just what one's parents were—it would be a thing of hereditary transmission and not a thing absolute in itself. Now, let me venture to ask you to take that cap off. Take that cap off now and make up your minds you are going to look at truth naked—in its reality, as it is, not as it is reflected through other minds, or through any theology, however venerable.

Then there is one thing I think we must be careful about, and that is, besides having the cap off and having all the lenses clean and in position, to have the instrument rightly focused. Everything may be right, and yet when you go and look at the object, you see things altogether falsely. You see things not

only blurred, but you see things out of proportion. And there is nothing more important we have to bear in mind in running our eye over successive theological truths, or religious truths, than that there is a proportion in those truths, and that we must see them in their proportion, or we see them falsely. A man may take a dollar or a half-dollar and hold it to his eye so closely that he will hide the sun from him. Or he may so focus his telescope that a fly or a bowlder may be as large as a mountain. A man may hold a certain doctrine very intensely—a doctrine which has been looming upon his horizon for the last six months, let us say, and which has thrown everything else out of proportion, it has become so big itself. Now, let us beware of distortion in the arrangement of the religious truths which we hold. It is almost impossible to get things in their true proportion and symmetry, but this is the thing we must be constantly aiming at. We are told in the Bible to "add to your faith virtue, and to virtue knowledge, and to knowledge balance," as the word literally means—"balance." It is a word taken from the orchestra, where all the parts—the sopranos, the basses, the altos, and the tenors, and all the rest of them—must be regulated. If you have too much of the bass, or too much of the soprano, there is want of harmony. That is what I mean by the want of proper focus—by the want of proper balance—in the truths which we all hold. It will never do to exaggerate one truth at the expense of another, and a truth may be turned into a falsehood very, very easily, by simply being either too much enlarged or too much diminished. I once heard of some blind men who were taken to see a menagerie. They had gone around the animals, and four of them were allowed to touch an elephant as they went past. They were discussing afterward what kind of a creature the elephant was. One man, who had touched its tail, said the elephant was like a rope. Another of the blind men, who had touched his hind limb, said: "No such thing! the elephant is like the trunk of a tree." Another, who had felt its sides, said: "That is all rubbish. An elephant is a thing like a wall." And the fourth, who had felt its ear, said that an elephant was like none of those things; it was like a leather bag. Now, men look at truth at different bits of it, and they see different things, of course, and they are very apt to imagine that the thing which they have seen is the whole affair—the whole thing. In reality, we can only see a very little bit at a time,

and we must, I think, learn to believe that other men can see bits of truth as well as ourselves. Your views are just what you see with your own eyes; and my views are just what I see; and what I see depends on just where I stand, and what you see depends on just where you stand; and truth is very much bigger than an elephant, and we are very much blinder than any of those blind men, as we come to look at it.

Christ has made us aware that it is quite possible for a man to have ears and hear nothing, and to have eyes and see not. One of the Disciples saw a great deal of Christ, and he never knew him. "Have I been so long time with you, Philip, and yet hast thou not known me?" "He that hath seen me hath seen the father also." Philip had never seen him. He had been looking at his own spectacles, perhaps, or at something else, and had never seen him. If the instrument had been in order, he would have seen Christ. And I would just add this one thing more: the test of value of the different verities of truth depends upon one thing: whether they have or have not a sanctifying power. That is another remarkable association in the mind of Christ—of sanctification with truth—thinking and holiness—not to be found in any of the sciences or in any of the philosophies. It is peculiar to the Bible. Christ said, "Sanctify them through thy truth. Thy Word is truth." Now, the value of any question—the value of any theological question—depends upon whether it has a sanctifying influence. If it has not, don't bother about it. Don't let it disturb your minds until you have exhausted all truths that have sanctification within them. If a truth make a man a better man, then let him focus his instrument upon it and get all the acquaintance with it he can. If it is the profane babbling of science, falsely so called, or anything that has an injurious effect upon the moral and spiritual nature of a man, it is better let alone. And above all, let us remember to hold the truth in love. That is the most sanctifying influence of all. And if we can carry away the mere lessons of toleration, and leave behind us our censoriousness, and criticalness, and harsh judgments upon one another, and excommunicating of everybody except those who think exactly as we do, the time we shall spend here will not be the least useful parts of our lives.

A TALK ON BOOKS

(An Address Delivered in New York City in 1887)

MY OBJECT at this time is to give encouragement and help to the "duffers," the class of "hopeful duffers." Brilliant students have every help, but second-class students are sometimes neglected and disheartened. I have great sympathy "with the duffers," because I was only a second-rate student myself. The subject of my talk with you is 'Books.'

A gentleman in Scotland, who has an excellent library, has placed on one side of the room his heavy sombre tomes, and over those shelves the form of an owl. On the other side of the room are arranged the lighter books, and over these is the figure of a bird known in Scotland as "the dipper." This is a most sensible division. The "owl books" are to be mastered,—the great books, such as Gibbon's 'Rome,' Butler's 'Analogy,' Dorner's 'Person of Christ,' and text-books of philosophy and science. Every student should master one or two, at least, of such "owl books," to exercise his faculties, and give him concentrativeness. I do not intend to linger at this side of the library, but will cross over to the "dipper books," which are for occasional reading—for stimulus, for guidance, recreation. I will be autobiographical.

When I was a student in lodgings, I began to form a library, which I arranged along the mantelshelf of my room. It did not contain many books; but it held as many as some students could afford to purchase, and, if wisely chosen, as many as one could well use. My first purchase was a volume of extracts from Ruskin's works, which then, in their complete form, were very costly. Ruskin taught me to use my eyes. Men are born blind as bats or kittens, and it is long before men's eyes are opened; some men never learn to see as long as they live. I often wondered, if there was a Creator, why he had not made the world more beautiful. Would not crimson and scarlet colors have been far richer than green and brown? But Ruskin taught me to see the world as it is, and it soon became a new world to me, full of charm and loveliness. Now I can linger beside a ploughed field and revel in the affluence of color and shade which are to be seen in the newly-turned furrows, and I gaze in wonder at the liquid amber of the two feet of air above the brown earth.

Now the colors and shades of the woods are a delight, and at every turn my eyes are surprised at fresh charms. The rock which I had supposed to be naked I saw clothed with lichens — patches of color — marvelous organisms, frail as the ash of a cigar, thin as brown paper, yet growing and fructifying in spite of wind and rain, of scorching sun and biting frost. I owe much to Ruskin for teaching me to see.

Next on my mantelshelf was Emerson. I discovered Emerson for myself. When I asked what Emerson was, one authority pronounced him a great man; another as confidently wrote him down a humbug. So I silently stuck to Emerson. Carlyle I could not read. After wading through a page of Carlyle, I felt as if I had been whipped. Carlyle scolded too much for my taste, and he seemed to me a great man gone delirious. But in Emerson I found what I would fain have sought in Carlyle; and, moreover, I was soothed and helped. Emerson taught me to see with the mind.

Next on my shelf came two or three volumes of George Eliot's works, from which I gained some knowledge and a further insight into many philosophical and social questions. But my chief debt to George Eliot at that time was that she introduced me to pleasant characters, — nice people, and especially to one imaginary young lady whom I was in love with one whole winter, and it diverted my mind in solitude. A good novel is a valuable acquisition, and it supplies companionship of a pleasant kind.

Amongst my small residue of books, I must name Channing's works. Before I read Channing I doubted whether there was a God; at least I would rather have believed that there was no God. After becoming acquainted with Channing, I could believe there was a God, and I was glad to believe in him, for I felt drawn to the good and gracious Sovereign of all things. Still, I needed further what I found in F. W. Robertson, the British officer in the pulpit, — bravest, truest of men, — who dared to speak what he believed at all hazards. From Robertson I learned that God is human; that we may have fellowship with him because he sympathizes with us.

One day as I was looking over my mantelshelf library, it suddenly struck me that all these authors of mine were heretics — these were dangerous books. Undesignedly I had found stimulus and help from teachers who were not credited by orthodoxy.

us? And shall we not think a little, and pay a little, for the clothing and adorning of the imperishable mind? This private library may begin, perhaps, with a single volume, and grow at the rate of one or two a year; but these, well-chosen and well-mastered, will become such a fountain of strength and wisdom that each shall be eager to add to his store. A dozen books accumulated in this way may be better than a whole library. Do not be distressed if you do not like time-honored books, or classical works, or recommended books. Choose for yourself; trust yourself; plant yourself on your own instincts; that which is natural for us, that which nourishes us, and gives us appetite, is that which is right for us. We have all different minds, and we are all at different stages of growth. Some other day we may find food in the recommended book, though we should possibly starve on it to-day. The mind develops and changes, and the favorities of this year, also, may one day cease to interest us. Nothing better, indeed, can happen to us than to lose interest in a book we have often read; for it means that it has done its work upon us, and brought us up to its level, and taught us all it had to teach.

And I have since found that much of the good to be got from books is to be gained from authors often classed as dangerous, for these provoke inquiry and exercise one's powers. Towards the end of my shelf I had one or two humorous works, chief amongst them all being Mark Twain. His humor is peculiar; broad exaggeration, a sly simplicity, comical situations, and surprising turns of expression; but to me it has been a genuine fund of humor. The humorous side of a student's nature needs to be considered, and where it is undeveloped it should be cultivated. I have known many instances of good students who seemed to have no sense of humor.

I will not recommend any of my favorite books to another; they have done me good, but they might not suit another man. Every man must discover his own books; but when he has found what fits in with his tastes, what stimulates him to thought, what supplies a want in his nature, and exalts him in conception and feelings, that is the book for the student, be it what it may. This brings me to speak of the friendship of books.

To fall in love with a good book is one of the greatest events that can befall us. It is to have a new influence pouring itself into our life, a new teacher to inspire and refine us, a new friend to be by our side always, who, when life grows narrow and weary, will take us into his wider and calmer and higher world. Whether it be biography, introducing us to some humble life made great by duty done; or history, opening vistas into the movements and destinies of nations that have passed away; or poetry, making music of all the common things around us, and filling the fields, and the skies, and the work of the city and the cottage, with eternal meanings — whether it be these, or story books, or religious books, or science, no one can become the friend even of one good book without being made wiser and better. Do not think I am going to recommend any such book to you. The beauty of a friend is that we discover him. And we must each taste the books that are accessible to us for ourselves. Do not be disheartened at first if you like none of them. That is possibly their fault, not yours. But search and search till you find what you like. In amazingly cheap form, — for a few pence indeed, — almost all the best books are now to be had; and I think every one owes it as a sacred duty to his mind to start a little library of his own. How much do we not do for our bodies? How much thought and money do they not cost

TIMOTHY DWIGHT

(1752–1817)

TIMOTHY DWIGHT, a grandson of Jonathan Edwards, inherited his ability as an orator and writer. He was born at Northampton, Massachusetts, May 14th, 1752. Educated for the Congregational ministry, he rose to great eminence as an author, preacher, and educator. He was President of Yale College from 1795 to 1817, dying at New Haven, Connecticut, January 11th of the latter year. In addition to theological works and a book of travels, he wrote several poems.

THE PURSUIT OF EXCELLENCE

(From a Sermon on the Sovereignty of God, Jeremiah x. 23)

HUMAN life is ordinarily little else than a collection of disappointments. Rarely is the life of man such as he designs it shall be. Often do we fail of pursuing at all the business originally in our view. The intentional farmer becomes a mechanic, a seaman, a merchant, a lawyer, a physician, or a divine. The very place of settlement, and of residence through life, is often different and distant from that which was originally contemplated. Still more different is the success which follows our efforts. . . .

A principal design of the mind in laboring for these things is to become superior to others. But almost all rich men are obliged to see, and usually with no small anguish, others richer than themselves; honorable men, others more honorable; voluptuous men, others who enjoy more pleasure. The great end of the strife is therefore unobtained, and the happiness expected never found. Even the successful competitor in the race utterly misses his aim. The real enjoyment existed, although it was unperceived by him, in the mere strife for superiority. When he has outstripped all his rivals, the contest is at an end, and his spirits, which were invigorated only by contending, languish for want of a competitor.

Besides, the happiness in view was only the indulgence of pride, or mere animal pleasure. Neither of these can satisfy or endure. A rational mind may be, and often is, so narrow and groveling, as not to aim at any higher good, to understand its nature, or to believe its existence. Still, in its original constitution, it was formed with a capacity for intellectual and moral good, and was destined to find in this good its only satisfaction. Hence, no inferior good will fill its capacity or its desires. Nor can this bent of its nature ever be altered. Whatever other enjoyment, therefore, it may attain, it will, without this, still crave and still be unhappy. . . .

There are two modes in which men seek happiness in the enjoyments of the present world. "Most persons freely indulge their wishes, and intend to find objects sufficient in number and value to satisfy them." A few "aim at satisfaction by proportioning their desires to the number and measures of their probable gratifications." . . . Desires indulged grow faster and further than gratifications extend. Ungratified desire is misery. Expectations eagerly indulged and terminated by disappointment are often exquisite misery. But how frequently are expectations raised only to be disappointed, and desires let loose, only to terminate in distress! The child pines for a toy; the moment he possesses it he throws it by, and cries for another. When they are piled up in heaps around him, he looks at them without pleasure, and leaves them without regret. He knew not that all the good which they could yield lay in expectation, nor that his wishes for more would increase faster than toys could be multiplied, and is unhappy at last for the same reason as at first; his wishes are ungratified. Still indulging them and still believing that the gratification of them will furnish the enjoyment for which he pines, he goes on, only to be unhappy.

Men are merely taller children. Honor, wealth, and splendor are the toys for which grown children pine; but which, however accumulated, leave them still disappointed and unhappy. God never designed that intelligent beings should be satisfied with these enjoyments. By his wisdom and goodness they were formed to derive their happiness from virtue.

Moderated desires constitute a character fitted to acquire all the good which this world can yield. He, who is prepared, in whatever situation he is, therewith to be content, has learned effectually the science of being happy, and possesses the alchymic stone,

v—124

which will change every metal into gold. Such a man will smile upon a stool, while Alexander at his side sits weeping on the throne of the world.

The doctrine of the text teaches you irresistibly that, since you cannot command gratifications, you should command your desires, and that, as the events of life do not accord with your wishes, your wishes should accord with them. Multiplied enjoyments fall to but few men, and are no more rationally expected than the highest prize in a lottery. But a well-regulated mind, a dignified independence of the world, and a wise preparation to possess one's soul in patience, whatever circumstances may exist, is in the power of every man, and is greater wealth than that of both Indies, and greater honor than Cæsar ever acquired. . . .

GEORGE F. EDMUNDS

(1828)

FOR many years Senator George F. Edmunds, of Vermont, was recognized as the best constitutional lawyer on the Republican side of the Senate chamber, and his presentation of the Constitutional Principles of the Electoral Commission was generally accepted as an authoritative expression of the views of his party. He was born at Richmond, Vermont, February 1st, 1828. Elected to the Senate in 1866, he held his place until 1891, and he might have held it indefinitely had he not preferred to retire. He was the author of the Edmunds Bill abolishing polygamy, and was, perhaps, more prominently identified with that measure than with any other, though he was largely instrumental in the settlement of the contested election of 1876, and was a member of the Electoral Commission.

THE CONSTITUTION AND THE ELECTORAL COMMISSION

(From a Speech Delivered in the United States Senate, January 20th, 1877)

TO DO an act which the Constitution commands is one thing; to decide a dispute is an entirely different thing. Whatever the Constitution commands, you are to do. Whatever the Constitution commands the Executive, he is to do. Whatever the Constitution authorizes to be decided, the Judiciary, or some other tribunal fixed by law or by the Constitution itself, is to decide. Those are the only three ways in which Government can express itself. So that whatever you are to do, whatever the claims at the other end of the Capitol may be that they have a right to do, whatever the Vice-President may say that he has a right to do under the Constitution when the President has not been elected, whatever you, the President of the Senate, have a right to do when both of them are unable to perform the duties of their office, there still remains behind it all, in the very essence of government, the necessity of having a power that binds you all at the same time to determine when and under what circumstances each of you shall bring your forces

into play; and as the Constitution has not fixed that tribunal, it has declared that Congress shall pass every law which shall carry into execution every power that is vested anywhere in the Government.

The question may be asked, Why did not the Constitution say so, then? It did not say so because after having defined the range of powers and their nature for every department of the Government, commanded what should be done, it left, as all constitutions in all civilized governments everywhere have done and must do forever, to the law-making power from time to time to carry all these great powers into effect by the regular measure of legislative procedure. I can scarcely state that so well—I am sure I cannot—as it is stated by the Supreme Court of the United States itself more than sixty years ago, when, just as now, and just as always in governments, there arise great disputes touching the powers of government. This was a question of State rights, of the right of the Supreme Court of the United States to disregard and set aside the judgment of the supreme court of the great State of Virginia; and when arguments similar to those that I have been putting forward as what might be suggested against this bill and about the language of the Constitution were made, the court answered them in this way:—

"The Constitution, unavoidably, deals in general language. It did not suit the purposes of the people, in framing this great charter of our liberties, to provide for minute specifications of its powers, or to declare the means by which those powers should be carried into execution—

Mark the words, Mr. President—"or to declare the means by which those powers should be carried into execution."

"It was foreseen that this would be a perilous and difficult, if not impracticable task. The instrument was not intended to provide merely for the exigencies of a few years, but was to endure through a long lapse of ages, the events of which were locked up in the inscrutable purposes of Providence. It could not be foreseen what new changes and modifications of power might be indispensable to effectuate the general objects of the charter; and restrictions and specifications, which at the present might seem salutary, might, in the end, prove the overthrow of the system itself. Hence, its powers are expressed in general terms, leaving to the Legislature, from time to time, to adopt its own means to effectuate legitimate objects, and to mold and model the exercise of its powers, as its own wisdom and the public interests should require.»—Martin *versus* Hunter's Lessee, 1 Wheaton 326.

If there is any one principle of constitutional law that is settled as deep as the foundations of the Government itself, it is that which I have just read. There is scarcely one, in fact I only remember one provision of the Constitution of the United States, that has been said to execute itself, and for which it was not necessary or proper that there should not be the provisions of legislation to carry it into effect and to regulate the methods and manners by which results should be arrived at. I believe it was said in the case of Prigg *versus* The Commonwealth of Pennsylvania, on the subject of fugitive slaves, that as the Constitution recognized a slave as property and as the fugitive clause in the Constitution gave the master the right to his property if it should have escaped from him, that clause in the Constitution did execute itself, so far as the right of the master was concerned, to recapture his property anywhere he could find it, if he could do so without violence and without a breach of the peace. That was put upon the ground that it was simply a recognition of the right of property, just as at the common law, as under the laws of most of the States, no doubt, a man would be entitled, if he could do it without violence or a breach of the peace, to recapture his children or his wife who were illegally detained from him. But beyond that I say I know of no instance in this wide variety of powers, legislative, executive, and judicial, anywhere, where there is not the fit necessity for legislative action to regulate and carry on the great objects of the exertion of the powers that are not by implication, but expressly, vested in some one of the departments of the Government; and even in that case to which I have alluded, where the court said that the Constitution did execute itself, they nevertheless held that that also was the proper subject of legislative action of Congress, and that Congress might regulate, as it had regulated, the manner in which and the means by which the owner of the slave should assert his right to his property. The President of the United States, by the express language of the Constitution, is the Commander-in-Chief of the armies and navies of the Republic; and yet from the beginning until now, without question by anybody as to the constitutional propriety of such legislation,

the judgment of whatever tribunal should have ascertained that fact for you, because it is only an act which you are to do, not a decision that you are to render. . . .

So, then, Mr. President, it cannot be maintained that this bill is unconstitutional upon the ground that it takes away from the President of the Senate or the House of Representatives a power which the Constitution has vested in them free from limit and free from guide, and free from regulation, to be exercised according to their own opinion of what may be the public propriety of the occasion.

Having said so much, Mr. President, for the present, I dismiss the subject, in the hope that the Senate will carefully consider whether it is wise, by stimulating doubts in their own minds, or by allowing their wishes to outrun their judgment, to send this Republic on the first Thursday in February, or the second Wednesday in that month, like the mountains that the poet has spoken of that were—

«Toppling evermore
Into seas without a shore,»

or whether it is better that in the fair course of equal law a dispute shall be justly settled.

the manner in which and the means by which he shall exercise the power of Commander-in-Chief of the Army has been regulated by law. The Constitution of the United States vests judicial powers in one Supreme Court and in such inferior courts as Congress from time to time may establish; and yet one of the very first acts that the Congress under this Constitution ever passed was an act that regulated and guided and controlled, from top to bottom, the exercise of those powers that were clearly and expressly delegated to the judicial branch; and no man ever suspected that Congress was exceeding its power in providing by law for the means and the ways of the performance of the great judicial functions — which, least of all, it would be safe for a republic to permit to be unduly meddled with.

So, Mr. President, it does appear to us, without my enlarging upon this branch of the discussion, and for the very few reasons that I have so feebly stated, that the idea that this bill can be assailed as an unconstitutional measure, even if you say that the Constitution has vested the power of performing the executive or ministerial function of counting the votes which the Constitution says the person having the greatest number of shall be President, is not at all maintainable. You have only done in this bill what in respect to every other branch of the Government, and for all time, year by year, you have been daily doing with the acceptance of everybody. It only provides for ascertaining in a regular and lawful way what is the subject upon which this executive function of counting the vote, finding out who has the highest number, rests. It might be contended with considerable force, even if the duty, as far as I have heard it claimed for you, Mr. President, rested in that chair, that we have only furnished you the means of justly performing that duty; and that would be true unless it should be contended that the Constitution had reposed in you the functions of Congress and of the Judiciary to hear, try, and determine all questions of law and fact once for all, as in a given case whether you should be President of the United States or not. If the pretension goes as far as that, of course this bill is against it. But if it only goes to the point that you are to exercise a commanded ministerial duty of counting a vote, then upon the principles that I have stated it would be entirely competent, and the absolute duty of Congress to provide you a means of finding out what is the vote that you are to count, and compelling you, as it does courts, presidents, everybody, to follow

JONATHAN EDWARDS

(1703–1758)

T IS said that when Jonathan Edwards preached his sermon, 'Sinners in the Hands of an Angry God,' the hearers "groaned and shrieked convulsively," and that their outcries drowned the preacher's voice. At the climax of the discourse, a brother clergyman, no longer able to restrain himself, cried out: "Mr. Edwards, Mr. Edwards, is not God merciful, too?"

That question has been asked ever since, by all readers of Edwards's sermons. The last words the great painter of "hell-torments" ever uttered on earth were: "Trust in God, and ye need not fear!" But this dying message to the world did not break the force of such sermons as have made him one of the great revolutionary forces of modern theology. The reaction against his ideas, which set in during his life, became especially strong in New England, but perhaps it never reached its climax until Mivart wrote his celebrated disquisition on 'Happiness in Hell.' Dante saw in justice and "primal love" the necessity for a terrible punishment for those who wrong and oppress the helpless. With the same thought and scarcely an inferior eloquence, the great Puritan preacher depicts the horrors of the Inferno which it seemed to him was inevitable for all who stubbornly invited retribution.

Jonathan Edwards was born at East Windsor, Connecticut, October 5th, 1703. His father was a minister of the Gospel, and it is said of his mother that she was a philosopher and metaphysician without knowing it. From her and from John Locke, whose works he read when a boy, Jonathan Edwards acquired the logical faculty which is so strikingly apparent in his discourses. He graduated at Yale College before he was seventeen years old, and soon afterwards began the career as a preacher and teacher which immortalized him. The work for which he is most celebrated was done in New England, but in 1758 he became President of Princeton College, and died there March 22d of the same year. One of his biographers says of him:—

«As a preacher Edwards has been rarely, if ever, excelled since the days of the Apostles. His manner was not oratorical, and his voice was feeble; but this was of little account with so much directness and richness of thought, and such overwhelming power of argument, pressed home upon the conscience and the heart. In vain did any one attempt to escape from falling a prey under his mighty appeal. It was in the application of his subject that he specially excelled. The part of the sermon before this was only preparatory. Here was the stretching out of the arms of the discourse, to borrow a figure, upon the hearts and lives of his audience. 'It was a kind of moral inquisition; and sinners were put upon argumentative racks, and beneath screws, and, with an awful revolution of the great truth in hand, evenly and steadily screwed down and crushed.'"

ETERNITY OF HELL TORMENTS

(From a Sermon Preached from the Text, "These shall go away into everlasting punishment," Matthew xxv. 46)

B E ENTREATED to consider attentively how great and awful a thing eternity is. Although you cannot comprehend it the more by considering, yet you may be made more sensible that it is not a thing to be disregarded. Do but consider what it is to suffer extreme torment forever and ever; to suffer it day and night, from one day to another, from one year to another, from one age to another, from one thousand ages to another, and so adding age to age and thousands to thousands, in pain, in wailing and lamenting, groaning and shrieking, and gnashing your teeth; with your souls full of dreadful grief and amazement, with your bodies and every member full of racking torture, without any possibility of getting ease; without any possibility of moving God to pity by your cries; without any possibility of hiding yourselves from him; without any possibility of diverting your thoughts from your pain; without any possibility of obtaining any manner of mitigation, or help, or change for the better any way.

Do but consider how dreadful despair will be in such torment. How dismal will it be, when you are under these racking torments, to know assuredly that you never, never shall be delivered from them; to have no hope: when you shall wish that you might be turned into nothing, but shall have no hope of it; when you shall wish that you might be turned into a toad or a serpent, but shall have no hope of it; when you would rejoice, if you might but have any relief, after you shall have endured these torments millions of ages, but shall have no hope of it; when after you shall have worn out the age of the sun, moon, and stars, in your dolorous groans and lamentations, without

any rest day or night, or one minute's ease, yet you shall have no hope of ever being delivered; when after you shall have worn out a thousand more such ages, yet you shall have no hope, but shall know that you are not one whit nearer to the end of your torments, but that still there are the same groans, the same shrieks, the same doleful cries, incessantly to be made by you, and that the smoke of your torment shall still ascend up forever and ever, and that your souls, which shall have been agitated with the wrath of God all this while, yet will still exist to bear more wrath; your bodies, which shall have been roasting and burning all this while in these glowing flames, yet shall not have been consumed, but will remain to roast through an eternity yet, which will not have been at all shortened by what shall have been past.

You may, by considering, make yourselves more sensible than you ordinarily are; but it is a little you can conceive of what it is to have no hope in such torments.

How sinking would it be to you to endure such pain as you have felt in this world without any hopes, and to know that you never should be delivered from it, nor have one minute's rest! You can now scarcely conceive how doleful that would be. How much more to endure the vast weight of the wrath of God without hope! The more the damned in hell think of the eternity of their torments, the more amazing will it appear to them; and alas! they are not able to avoid thinking of it, they will not be able to keep it out of their minds. Their tortures will not divert them from it, but will fix their attention to it. Oh, how dreadful will eternity appear to them after they shall have been thinking on it for ages together, and shall have had so long an experience of their torments! The damned in hell will have two infinites perpetually to amaze them and swallow them up; one is an infinite God, whose wrath they will bear, and in whom they will behold their perfect and irreconcilable enemy. The other is the infinite duration of their torment.

If it were possible for the damned in hell to have a comprehensive knowledge of eternity, their sorrow and grief would be infinite in degree. The comprehensive view of so much sorrow which they must endure would cause infinite grief for the present. Though they will not have a comprehensive knowledge of it, yet they will doubtless have a vastly more lively and strong

apprehension of it than we can have in this world. Their torments will give them an impression of it. A man in his present state, without any enlargement of his capacity, would have a vastly more lively impression of eternity than he has if he were only under some pretty sharp pain in some member of his body, and were at the same time assured that he must endure that pain forever. His pain would give him a greater sense of eternity than other men have. How much more will those excruciating torments which the damned will suffer have this effect!

Besides, their capacity will probably be enlarged, their understandings will be quicker and stronger in a future state; and God can give them as great a sense and as strong an impression of eternity as he pleases, to increase their grief and torment.

Oh, be entreated, ye that are in a Christless state and are going on in a way to hell, that are daily exposed to damnation, to consider these things. If you do not, it will surely be but a little while before you will experience them, and then you will know how dreadful it is to despair in hell; and it may be before this year or this month or this week is at an end; before another Sabbath, or ever you shall have the opportunity to hear another sermon.

WRATH UPON THE WICKED TO THE UTTERMOST

(From a Sermon on 1 Thessalonians ii. 16)

W HEN those that continue in sin shall have filled up the measure of their sin, then wrath will come upon them to the uttermost.

There is a certain measure that God hath set to the sin of every wicked man. God says concerning the sin of man, as he says to the raging waves of the sea, "Hitherto shalt thou come, and no further." The measure of some is much greater than of others. Some reprobates commit but a little sin in comparison with others, and so are to endure proportionably a smaller punishment. There are many vessels of wrath; but some are smaller, and others greater vessels; some will contain comparatively but little wrath, others a greater measure of it. Sometimes, when we see men go to dreadful lengths, and become very heinously wicked, we are ready to wonder that God lets them

alone. He sees them go on in such audacious wickedness, and keeps silence, nor does anything to interrupt them, but they go smoothly on, and meet with no hurt. But sometimes the reason why God lets them alone is, because they have not filled up the measure of their sins. When they live in dreadful wickedness, they are but filling up the measure which God hath limited for them. This is sometimes the reason why God suffers very wicked men to live so long; because their iniquity is not full. "The iniquity of the Amorites is not yet full." For this reason, also, God sometimes suffers them to live in prosperity. Their prosperity is a snare to them, and an occasion of their sinning a great deal more. Wherefore God suffers them to have such a snare, because he suffers them to fill up a larger measure. So, for this cause, he sometimes suffers them to live under great light, and great means and advantages, at the same time to neglect and misimprove all. Every one shall live till he hath filled up his measure.

While men continue in sin, they are filling the measure set them. This is the work in which they spend their whole lives; they begin in their childhood; and, if they live to grow old in sin, they still go on with this work. It is the work with which every day is filled up. They may alter their business in other respects; they may sometimes be about one thing, and sometimes about another; but they never change from this work of filling up the measure of their sins. Whatever they put their hands to, they are still employed in this work. This is the first thing that they set themselves about when they awake in the morning, and the last thing they do at night. They are all the while treasuring up wrath against the day of wrath, and the revelation of the righteous judgment of God. It is a gross mistake of some natural men, who think that when they read and pray they do not add to their sins, but, on the contrary, think they diminish their guilt by these exercises. They think that, instead of adding to their sins, they do something to satisfy for their past offenses; but, instead of that, they do but add to the measure by their best prayers, and by those services with which they themselves are most pleased.

When once the measure of their sins is filled up, then wrath will come upon them to the uttermost. God will then wait no longer upon them. Wicked men think that God is altogether such an one as themselves, because, when they commit such wickedness, he keeps silence. "Because judgment against an evil work is not executed speedily, therefore the heart of the children of men is fully set in them to do evil." But when once they shall have filled up the measure of their sins, judgment will be executed; God will not bear with them any longer. Now is the day of grace, and the day of patience, which they spend in filling up their sins; but when their sins shall be full, then will come the day of wrath, the day of the fierce anger of God. God often executes his wrath on ungodly men in a less degree, in this world. He sometimes brings afflictions upon them, and that in wrath. Sometimes he expresses his wrath in very sore judgments; sometimes he appears in a terrible manner, not only outwardly, but also in the inward expressions of it on their consciences. Some, before they died, have had the wrath of God inflicted on their souls in degrees that have been intolerable. But these things are only forerunners of their punishment, only slight foretastes of wrath. God never stirs up all his wrath against wicked men while in this world; but when once wicked men shall have filled up the measure of their sins, then wrath will come upon them to the uttermost; and that in the following respects.

Wrath will come upon them without any restraint or moderation in the degree of it. God doth always lay, as it were, a restraint upon himself; he doth not stir up his wrath; he stays his rough wind in the day of his east wind; he lets not his arm light down on wicked men with its full weight. But when sinners shall have filled up the measure of their sins, there will be no caution, no restraint. His rough wind will not be stayed nor moderated. The wrath of God will be poured out like fire. He will come forth, not only in anger, but in the fierceness of his anger; he will execute wrath with power, so as to show what his wrath is, and make his power known. There will be nothing to alleviate his wrath; his heavy wrath will lie on them, without anything to lighten the burthen, or to keep off, in any measure, the full weight of it from pressing the soul. His eye will not spare, neither will he regard the sinner's cries and lamentations, however loud and bitter. Then shall wicked men know that God is the Lord; they shall know how great that majesty is which they have despised, and how dreadful that threatened wrath is which

they have so little regarded. Then shall come on wicked men that punishment which they deserve. God will exact of them the uttermost farthing. Their iniquities are marked before him; they are all written in his book; and in the future world he will reckon with them, and they must pay all the debt. Their sins are laid up in store with God; they are sealed up among his treasures; and them he will recompense, even recompense into their bosoms. The consummate degree of punishment will not be executed till the day of judgment; but the wicked are sealed over to this consummate punishment immediately after death; they are cast into hell, and there bound in chains of darkness to the judgment of the great day, and they know that the highest degree of punishment is coming upon them.

SINNERS IN THE HANDS OF AN ANGRY GOD

(From a Sermon on Deuteronomy xxxii. 35, Preached at Enfield, Connecticut, July 8th, 1741)

THE God that holds you over the pit of hell much as one holds a spider or some loathsome insect over the fire abhors you, and is dreadfully provoked; his wrath towards you burns like fire; he looks upon you as worthy of nothing else but to be cast into the fire; he is of purer eyes than to bear you in his sight; you are ten thousand times as abominable in his eyes as the most hateful and venomous serpent is in ours. You have offended him infinitely more than ever a stubborn rebel did his prince, and yet it is nothing but his hand that holds you from falling into the fire every moment; it is ascribed to nothing else that you did not go to hell the last night that you were suffered to awake again in this world, after you closed your eyes to sleep; and there is no other reason to be given why you have not dropped into hell since you arose in the morning, but that God's hand has held you up; there is no other reason to be given why you have not gone to hell, since you have sat here in the house of God provoking his pure eye by your sinful, wicked manner of attending his solemn worship; yea, there is nothing else that is to be given as a reason why you do not this very moment drop down into hell.

O sinner! consider the fearful danger you are in; it is a great furnace of wrath, a wide and bottomless pit, full of the fire of

wrath that you are held over in the hands of that God whose wrath is provoked and incensed as much against you as against many of the damned in hell; you hang by a slender thread, with the flames of Divine wrath flashing about it, and ready every moment to singe it and burn it asunder, and you have no interest in any mediator, and nothing to lay hold of to save yourself, nothing to keep off the flames of wrath, nothing of your own, nothing that you have ever done, nothing that you can do to induce God to spare you one moment. . . .

It would be dreadful to suffer this fierceness and wrath of Almighty God one moment; but you must suffer it to all eternity: there will be no end to this exquisite, horrible misery: when you look forward, you shall see along forever a boundless duration before you, which will swallow up your thoughts, and amaze your soul; and you will absolutely despair of ever having any deliverance, any end, any mitigation, any rest at all; you will know certainly that you must wear out long ages, millions of millions of ages in wrestling and conflicting with this Almighty, merciless vengeance; and then when you have so done, when so many ages have actually been spent by you in this manner, you will know that all is but a point to what remains, so that your punishment will indeed be infinite. Oh! who can express what the state of a soul in such circumstances is! All that we can possibly say about it gives but a very feeble, faint representation of it; it is inexpressible and inconceivable: for "who knows the power of God's anger!"

How dreadful is the state of those that are daily and hourly in danger of this great wrath and infinite misery! But this is the dismal case of every soul in this congregation that has not been born again, however moral and strict, sober and religious they may otherwise be. Oh! that you would consider it, whether you be young or old! There is reason to think that there are many in this congregation now hearing this discourse, that will actually be the subjects of this very misery to all eternity. We know not who they are, or in what seats they sit, or what thoughts they now have—it may be they are now at ease, and hear all these things without much disturbance, and are now flattering themselves that they are not the persons, promising themselves that they shall escape. If we knew that there was one person, and but one, in the whole congregation, that was to

be the subject of this misery, what an awful thing it would be to think of! If we knew who it was, what an awful sight it would be to see such a person! How might all the rest of the congregation lift up a lamentable and bitter cry over him! But, alas! instead of one, how many is it likely will remember this discourse in hell! And it would be a wonder, if some that are now present should not be in hell in a very short time, before this year is out. And it would be no wonder if some persons that now sit here in some seats of this meetinghouse, in health, and quiet and secure, should be there before to-morrow morning'

SIR JOHN ELIOT

(1592–1632)

THE 'Petition of Right' adopted by the English Parliament in 1628 is one of the great landmarks of modern history. It declared the sovereignty of the people represented in Parliament as against the King, and as a logical result of it, Charles I., resisting popular supremacy, was impeached for treason, and executed. The fundamental question involved in the 'Petition of Right' is that of the right of the producer to own and control his product. In adopting the bill, Parliament declared that "no freeman shall be required to give any gift, loan, benevolence, or tax, without common consent, by act of Parliament." Other declarations of the Petition were that "no freeman be imprisoned or detained contrary to the law of the land;" that soldiers or mariners be not billeted on private houses; and that "commissions to punish soldiers and sailors by martial law be revoked and no more issued."

Sir John Eliot, one of the most eloquent men of his day, gave his full power to the support of the Petition, which was drawn by the celebrated Coke. Born April 20th, 1592, Eliot, after graduating at Oxford and studying law in London, entered Parliament in 1625. He became one of the leaders of an Opposition which boasts such great names as Coke, Pym, and Hampden. In 1626, in company with Sir Dudley Digges, he was seized by Charles I. and hurried to the Tower, but Parliament asserted its prerogative with such vigor that the King was compelled to surrender his prisoners. The 'Petition of Right,' adopted in the third Parliament under Charles I., though drawn in the form of a petition to the throne, was really so bold an assertion of popular rights that Eliot's share in it was never forgiven. On the dissolution of Parliament in 1629, he was arrested, sentenced to pay a fine of £2,000 and to remain in prison until he should acknowledge himself guilty of conspiracy against the King. He died in the Tower, November 27th, 1632. Goodrich compares Eliot's style to that of Demosthenes. It is severe in expression but admirable in its directness, with a cumulative force that is seen only in the speeches of men of great intellect.

V—125

ON THE PETITION OF RIGHT

(Delivered in the House of Commons, June 3d, 1628)

Mr. Speaker:—

WE SIT here as the great Council of the King, and in that company it is our duty to take into consideration the state and affairs of the kingdom, and, when there is occasion, to give a true representation of them by way of counsel and advice, with what we conceive necessary or expedient to be done.

In this consideration I confess many a sad thought hath affrighted me, and that not only in respect of our dangers from abroad (which yet I know are great, as they have been often pressed and dilated to us), but in respect of our disorders here at home, which do enforce those dangers and by which they are occasioned. For I believe I shall make it clear to you that both at first the cause of these dangers were our disorders, and our disorders now are yet our greatest dangers; that not so much the potency of our enemies as the weakness of ourselves doth threaten us; so that the saying of one of the Fathers may be presumed by us, "*Non tam potentia sua quam negligentia nostra*" (Not so much by our power as by our neglect). Our want of true devotion to Heaven; our insincerity and doubting in religion; our want of councils; our precipitate actions; the insufficiency or unfaithfulness of our generals abroad; the ignorance or corruption of our ministers at home; the impoverishing of the sovereign; the oppression and depression of the subject; the exhausting of our treasures; the waste of our provisions; consumption of our ships; destruction of our men;—these make the advantage to our enemies, not the reputation of their arms; and if in these there be not reformation, we need no foes abroad; time itself will ruin us.

To show this more fully, I believe you will all hold it necessary that what I say should not seem an aspersion on the state or imputation on the government, as I have known such motions misinterpreted. But far is this from me to propose, who have none but clear thoughts of the excellency of the King; nor can I have other ends but the advancement of his Majesty's glory. I shall desire a little of your patience extraordinary, as I lay

open the particulars, which I shall do with what brevity I may, answerable to the importance of the cause and the necessity now upon us; yet with such respect and observation to the time, as I hope it shall not be thought troublesome.

1. For the first, then, our insincerity and doubting in religion is the greatest and most dangerous disorder of all others. This hath never been unpunished; and of this we have many strong examples of all states and in all times to awe us. What testimony doth it want? Will you have authority of books? Look on the collections of the Committee for Religion; there is too clear an evidence. See there the commission procured for composition with the Papists of the North! Mark the proceedings thereupon, and you will find them to little less amounting than a toleration in effect; the slight payments, and the easiness of them, will likewise show the favor that is intended. Will you have proofs of men? Witness the hopes, witness the presumptions, witness the reports of all the papists generally. Observe the dispositions of commanders, the trust of officers, the confidence in secretaries to employments in this kingdom, in Ireland, and elsewhere. These will all show that it hath too great a certainty. And to this add but the incontrovertible evidence of that All-Powerful Hand, which we have felt so sorely, that gave it full assurance; for as the heavens oppose themselves to our impiety, so it is we that first opposed the heavens.

2. For the second, our want of councils, that great disorder in a state under which there cannot be stability. If effects may show their causes (as they are often a perfect demonstration of them), our misfortunes, our disasters, serve to prove our deficiencies in council, and the consequences they draw with them. If reason be allowed in this dark age, the judgment of dependencies and foresight of contingencies in affairs do confirm my position. For, if we view ourselves at home, are we in strength, are we in reputation, equal to our ancestors? If we view ourselves abroad, are our friends as many? Are our enemies no more? Do our friends retain their safety and possessions? Do not our enemies enlarge themselves, and gain from them and us? To what council owe we the loss of the Palatinate where we sacrificed both our honor and our men sent thither, stopping those greater powers appointed for the service, by which it might have been defended? What council gave direction to the late action, whose wounds are yet bleeding? I mean the expedition to

Rhé, of which there is yet so sad a memory in all men. What design for us or advantage to our state could that impart?

You know the wisdom of your ancestors, and the practice of their times, how they preserved their safeties. We all know, and have as much cause to doubt (*i. e.*, distrust or guard against) as they had, the greatness and ambition of that kingdom, which the Old World could not satisfy. Against this greatness and ambition we likewise know the proceedings of that princess, that never-to-be-forgotten, excellent Queen Elizabeth, whose name, without admiration, falls not into mention even with her enemies. You know how she advanced herself, and how she advanced the nation in glory and in state; how she depressed her enemies, and how she upheld her friends; how she enjoyed a full security, and made those our scorn who now are made our terror.

Some of the principles she built on were these, and if I mistake, let reason and our statesmen contradict me:—

First, to maintain, in what she might, a unity in France, that the kingdom, being at peace within itself, might be a bulwark to keep back the power of Spain by land.

Next, to preserve an amity and league between that State and us, that so we might come in aid of the Low Countries (Holland), and by that means receive their ships, and help them by sea.

This triple cord, so working between France, the States (Holland), and England, might enable us, as occasion should require, to give assistance unto others. And by this means, as the experience of that time doth tell us, we were not only free from those fears that now possess and trouble us, but then our names were fearful to our enemies. See now what correspondency our action had with this. Try our conduct by these rules. It did induce, as a necessary consequence, a division in France between Protestants and their king, of which there is too woeful and lamentable experience. It hath made an absolute breach between that State and us, and so entertains us against France, and France in preparation against us, that we have nothing to promise to our neighbors, nay, hardly to ourselves. Next, observe the time in which it was attempted, and you shall find it not only varying from those principles, but directly contrary and opposite to those ends; and such, as from the issue and success, rather might be thought a conception of Spain than begotten here with us.

You know the dangers of Denmark, and how much they concern us; what in respect of our alliance and the country; what in the importance of the sound; what an advantage to our enemies the gain thereof would be! What loss, what prejudice to us by this disunion; we breaking in upon France, France enraged by us, and the Netherlands at amazement between both! Neither could we intend to aid that luckless King (Christian IV., of Denmark), whose loss is our disaster.

Can those (the King's ministers) that express their trouble at the hearing of these things, and have so often told us in this place of their knowledge in the conjunctures and disjunctures of affairs—can they say they advised in this? Was this an act of council, Mr. Speaker? I have more charity than to think it; and, unless they make confession of it themselves, I cannot believe it.

3. For the next, the insufficiency and unfaithfulness of our generals (that great disorder abroad), what shall I say? I wish there were not cause to mention it; and but for the apprehension of the danger that is to come, if the like choice hereafter be not prevented, I could willingly be silent. But my duty to my sovereign, my service to this House, and the safety and honor of my country, are above all respects; and what so nearly trenches to the prejudice of these, must not, shall not be forborne.

At Cadiz, when in that first expedition we made, when we arrived and found a conquest ready,—the Spanish ships I mean,—fit for the satisfaction of a voyage, and of which some of the chiefest then there themselves have since assured me that the satisfaction would have been sufficient, either in point of honor, or in point of profit—why was it neglected? Why was it not achieved, it being granted on all hands how feasible it was?

Afterwards when, with the destruction of some of our men and the exposure of others, who (though their fortune since has not been such), by chance, came off safe—when, I say, with the loss of our serviceable men, that unserviceable fort was gained, and the whole army landed, why was there nothing done? Why was there nothing attempted? If nothing was intended, wherefore did they land? If there was a service, wherefore were they shipped again? Mr. Speaker, it satisfies me too much (i. e., I am over-satisfied) in this case—when I think of their dry and hungry march into that drunken quarter (for so the soldiers termed it) which was the period of their journey—that divers

The exchequer, you know, is empty, and the reputation thereof gone; the ancient lands are sold; the jewels pawned; the plate engaged; the debt still great; almost all charges, both ordinary and extraordinary, borne up by projects! What poverty can be greater? What necessity so great? What perfect English heart is not almost dissolved into sorrow for this truth?

6. For the oppression of the subject, which, as I remember, is the next particular I proposed, it needs no demonstration. The whole kingdom is a proof; and, for the exhausting of our treasures, that very oppression speaks it. What waste of our provisions, what consumption of our ships, what destruction of our men there hath been? Witness that expedition to Algiers; witness that with Mansfeldt; witness that to Cadiz; witness the next— witness that to Rhé; witness the last (I pray God we may never have more such witnesses!)—witness, likewise, the Palatinate; witness Denmark, witness the Turks, witness the Dunkirkers, witness all! What losses we have sustained! How we are impaired in munitions, in ships, in men!

It is beyond contradiction that we were never so weakened, nor ever had less hope how to be restored.

These, Mr. Speaker, are our dangers, these are they who do threaten us, and these are, like the Trojan horse, brought in cunningly to surprise us. In these do lurk the strongest of our enemies, ready to issue on us; and if we do not speedily expel them, these are the signs, these are the invitations to others! These will so prepare their entrance that we shall have no means left of refuge or defense; for if we have these enemies at home, how can we strive with those that are abroad? If we be free from these, no other can impeach us. Our ancient English virtue (like the old Spartan valor) cleared from these disorders— our being in sincerity of religion and once made friends with heaven; having maturity of councils, sufficiency of generals, incorruption of officers, opulency in the King, liberty in the people, repletion in treasure, plenty of provisions, reparation of ships, preservation of men—our ancient English virtue, I say, thus rectified, will secure us; and unless there be a speedy reformation in these, I know not what hopes or expectations we can have.

These are the things, sir, I shall desire to have taken into consideration; that as we are the great council of the kingdom, and have the apprehension of these dangers, we may truly represent them unto the King, which I conceive we are bound to do

of our men being left as a sacrifice to the enemy, that labor was at end.

For the next undertaking at Rhé, I will not trouble you with much, only this in short. Was not that whole action carried against the judgment and opinion of those officers that were of the council? Was not the first, was not the last, was not all in the landing, in the intrenching, in the continuance there, in the assault, in the retreat, without their assent? Did any advice take place of such as were of the council? If there should be made a particular inquisition thereof, these things will be manifest and more. I will not instance the manifest that was made, giving the reason of these arms; nor by whom, nor in what manner, nor on what grounds it was published, nor what effects it hath wrought, drawing, as it were, almost the whole world into league against us. Nor will I mention the leaving of the wines, the leaving of the salt, which were in our possession, and of a value, as it is said, to answer much of our expense. Nor will I dwell on that great wonder (which no Alexander or Cæsar ever did), the enriching of the enemy by courtesies when our soldiers wanted help; nor the private intercourse and parleys with the fort, which were continually held. What they intended may be read in the success; and upon due examination thereof, they would not want their proofs.

For the last voyage to Rochelle, there need be no observations; it is so fresh in memory; nor will I make an inference or corollary on all. Your own knowledge shall judge what truth or what sufficiency they express.

4. For the next, the ignorance and corruption of our ministers, where can you miss of instances? If you survey the court, if you survey the country; if the Church, if the city be examined; if you observe the bar, if the bench, if the ports, if the shipping, if the land, if the seas,—all these will render you variety of proofs, and that in such measure and proportion as shows the greatness of our disease to be such that if there be not some speedy application for remedy, our case is almost desperate.

5. Mr. Speaker, I fear I have been too long in these particulars that are past, and am unwilling to offend you; therefore in the rest I shall be shorter; and as to that which concerns the impoverishing of the King, no other arguments will I use than such as all men grant.

by a triple obligation—of duty to God, of duty to his Majesty, and of duty to our country.

And therefore I wish it may so stand with the wisdom and judgment of the House that these things may be drawn into the body of remonstrance, and in all humility expressed, with a prayer to his Majesty that, for the safety of himself, for the safety of the kingdom, and for the safety of religion, he will be pleased to give us time to make perfect inquisition thereof, or to take them into his own wisdom, and there give them such timely reformation as the necessity and justice of the case doth import.

And thus, sir, with a large affection and loyalty to his Majesty, and with a firm duty and service to my country, I have suddenly (and it may be with some disorder) expressed the weak apprehensions I have; wherein if I have erred, I humbly crave your pardon, and so submit myself to the censure of the House.

OLIVER ELLSWORTH

(1745–1807)

OLIVER ELLSWORTH, Chief-Justice of the United States during the administration of John Adams, was an orator of exceptional power. It is said that though his imagination was cold and colorless, his eloquence was nevertheless irresistible—a result due, no doubt, to such masterly handling of facts as is illustrated in his address to the Connecticut State Convention, when the question of coercing the States was under consideration. No one else, perhaps, has presented the logic of coercion so forcibly—certainly not Hamilton, who is much less direct. Ellsworth shows a strength of conviction on this point, which it is necessary to understand before it is possible to understand the forces which made American history from 1850 to 1870. His address on Coercion is one of the most important historical documents in American archives.

He was born at Windsor, Connecticut, April 29th, 1745. From 1789 to 1796 he was United States Senator for Connecticut. In 1796 he left the Senate to become Chief-Justice of the United States. In 1799 he went as envoy to France, and, during his absence, resigned as Chief-Justice. Returning to America he served as a member of the State Council of Connecticut from 1802 to 1807, dying November 26th, 1807.

UNION AND COERCION

(Delivered at the Opening of the Debates on the Federal Constitution, in the Convention of the State of Connecticut, January 4th, 1788)

Mr. President:—

IT is observable that there is no preface to the proposed Constitution; but it evidently presupposes two things: one is, the necessity of a federal government; the other is the inefficiency of the old Articles of Confederation. A union is necessary for the purposes of a national defense. United, we are strong; divided, we are weak. It is easy for hostile nations to sweep off a number of separate States one after another. Witness the States in the neighborhood of ancient Rome. They were suc-

cessively subdued by that ambitious city, which they might have conquered with the utmost ease, if they had been united.

Witness the Canaanitish nations whose divided situation rendered them an easy prey. Witness England, which, when divided into separate States, was twice conquered by an inferior force. Thus it always happens to small States, and to great ones, if divided. Or if, to avoid this, they connect themselves with some powerful State, their situation is not much better. This shows us the necessity of combining our whole force, and, as to national purposes, becoming one State.

A union, sir, is likewise necessary, considered with relation to economy. Small States have enemies, as well as great ones. They must provide for their defense. The expense of it, which would be moderate for a large kingdom, would be intolerable to a petty State. The Dutch are wealthy; but they are one of the smallest of the European nations, and their taxes are higher than in any other country of Europe. The taxes amount to forty shillings per head, when those of England do not exceed half that sum.

We must unite in order to preserve peace among ourselves. If we be divided, what is to prevent wars from breaking out among the States? States, as well as individuals, are subject to ambition, to avarice, to those jarring passions which disturb the peace of society. What is to check these? If there be a parental hand over the whole, this, and nothing else, can restrain the unruly conduct of members.

Union is necessary to preserve commutative justice between the States. If divided, what is to prevent the large States from oppressing the small? What is to defend us from the ambition and rapacity of New York, when she has spread over that vast territory which she claims and holds? Do we not already see in her the seeds of an overbearing ambition? On our other side, there is a large and powerful State. Have we not already begun to be tributaries? If we do not improve the present critical time,—if we do not unite,—shall we not be like Issachar of old, a strong ass crouching down between two burdens? New Jersey and Delaware have seen this, and have adopted the Constitution unanimously.

A more energetic system is necessary. The present is merely advisory. It has no coercive power. Without this, government is ineffectual, or rather is no government at all. But it is said:

« Such a power is not necessary. States will not do wrong. They need only to be told their duty, and they will do it. » I ask, sir, what warrant is there for this assertion? Do not States do wrong? Whence come wars? One of two hostile nations must be in the wrong. But, it is said: "Among sister States, this can never be presumed." But do we not know that, when friends become enemies, their enmity is the most virulent? The seventeen provinces of the Netherlands were once confederated; they fought under the same banner. Antwerp, hard pressed by Philip, applied to the other States for relief. Holland, a rival in trade, opposed and prevented for the needy, succors. Antwerp was made a sacrifice. I wish I could say there were no seeds of similar injustice springing up among us. Is there not in one of our States injustice too barefaced for Eastern despotism? That State is small; it does little hurt to any but itself. But it has a spirit which would make a Tophet of the universe. But some will say: "We formerly did well without any union." I answer, Our situation is materially changed. While Great Britain held her authority, she awed us. She appointed governors and councils for the American provinces. She had a negative upon our laws. But now our circumstances are so altered that there is no arguing what we shall be from what we have been.

It is said that other confederacies have not had the principle of coercion. Is this so? Let us attend to those confederacies which have resembled our own. Some time before Alexander, the Grecian States confederated together. The Amphictyonic Council, consisting of deputies from these States, met at Delphos, and had authority to regulate the general interests of Greece. This council did enforce its decrees by coercion. The Bœotians once infringed upon a decree of the Amphictyons. A mulct was laid upon them. They refused to pay it. Upon that, their whole territory was confiscated. They were then glad to compound the matter. After the death of Alexander, the Achæan League was formed. The decrees of this confederacy were enforced by dint of arms. The Ætolian League was formed by some other Grecian cities, in opposition to the Achæan; and there was no peace between them until they were conquered and reduced to a Roman province. They were then obliged to sit down in peace under the same yoke of despotism.

How is it with respect to the principle of coercion in the Germanic body? In Germany there are about three hundred

principalities and republics. Deputies from these meet annually in the general Diet, to make regulations for the empire. But the execution of these is not left voluntarily with the members. The empire is divided into ten circles, over each of which a superintendent is appointed, with the rank of a major-general. It is his duty to execute the decrees of the empire with a military force.

The Confederation of the Swiss Cantons has been considered as an example. But their circumstances are far different from ours. They are small republics about twenty miles square, situated among the Alps, and inaccessible to hostile attacks. They have nothing to tempt an invasion. Till lately, they had neither commerce nor manufactures. They were merely a set of herdsmen. Their inaccessibleness has availed them. Four hundred of those mountaineers defeated fifteen thousand Austrians, who were marching to subdue them. They spend the ardor of youth in foreign service; they return old, and disposed for tranquillity. Between some of the cantons and France, there has long subsisted a defensive treaty. By this treaty, France is to be a mediator to settle differences between the cantons. If any one be obstinate, France is to compel a submission to reasonable terms.

The Dutch Republic is an example that merits attention. The form of their Constitution, as it is on paper, admits not of coercion. But necessity has introduced it in practice. This coercive power is the influence of the stadtholder, an officer originally unknown to their Constitution. But they have been necessitated to appoint him, in order to set their unwieldy machine of government in motion. He is commander-in-chief of their navy and of their army, consisting of forty or fifty regiments. He appoints the officers of the land and naval forces. He presides in the States-General and in the States of every province; and, by means of this, he has a great opportunity to influence the elections and decisions. The province of Holland has ever been opposed to the appointment of a stadtholder, because by its wealth and power, being equal to all the other provinces, it possesses the weight and influence of the stadtholder, when that office is vacant. Without such an influence, their machine of government would no more move than a ship without a wind, or a clock without weights.

But to come nearer home. Mr. President, have we not seen and felt the necessity of such a coercive power? What was the consequence of the want of it during the late war, particularly towards the close? A few States bore the burden of the war. While we and one or two more of the States were paying eighty or a hundred dollars per man to recruit the Continental Army, the regiments of some States had scarcely men enough to wait on their officers. Since the close of the war, some of the States have done nothing towards complying with the requisitions of Congress. Others, who did something at first, seeing that they were left to bear the whole burden, have become equally remiss. What is the consequence? To what shifts have we been driven? To the wretched expedient of negotiating new loans in Europe, to pay the interest of the foreign debts. And what is still worse, we have been obliged to apply the new loans to the support of our own civil Government at home.

Another ill consequence of this want of energy is that treaties are not performed. The treaty of peace with Great Britain was a very favorable one for us. But it did not happen perfectly to please some of the States, and they would not comply with it. The consequence is, Britain charges us with the breach, and refuses to deliver up the forts on our northern quarter.

Our being tributaries to our sister States is in consequence of the want of a federal system. The State of New York raises sixty thousand or eighty thousand pounds a year by impost. Connecticut consumes about one-third of the goods upon which this impost is laid, and consequently pays one-third of this sum to New York. If we import by the medium of Massachusetts, she has an impost, and to her we pay a tribute. If this is done when we have the shadow of a national government, what shall we not suffer when even that shadow is gone?

If we go on as we have done, what is to become of the foreign debt? Will sovereign nations forgive us this debt, because we neglect to pay? or will they levy it by reprisals, as the laws of nations authorize them? Will our weakness induce Spain to relinquish the exclusive navigation of the Mississippi or the territory which she claims on the east side of that river? Will our weakness induce the British to give up the northern posts? If a war break out, and our situation invite our enemies to make war, how are we to defend ourselves? Has Government the means to enlist a man or to buy an ox? Or shall we rally the remainder of our old army? The European nations I believe to be not friendly to us. They were pleased to see us disconnected

from Great Britain; they are pleased to see us disunited among ourselves. If we continue so, how easy is it for them to canton us out among them, as they did the kingdom of Poland! But supposing this is not done, if we suffer the Union to expire, the least that may be expected is that the European powers will form alliances, some with one State and some with another, and play the States off one against another, and that we shall be involved in all the labyrinths of European politics. But I do not wish to continue the painful recital; enough has been said to show that a power in the General Government to enforce the decrees of the Union is absolutely necessary.

The Constitution before us is a complete system of legislative, judicial, and executive power. It was designed to supply the defects of the former system; and I believe, upon a full discussion, it will be found calculated to answer the purposes for which it was designed.

RALPH WALDO EMERSON

(1803–1882)

THE profoundest thinker of the America of his day, Ralph Waldo Emerson is, by that right, one of its greatest orators. It is doubtful if any one else has spoken in America, in whose sentences ideas crowd each other as they do in his. His training as an orator preceded the practice which made him a great essayist; and though, for the most part, he gave up professional public speaking on leaving the pulpit, his addresses and lectures express his lofty genius better, perhaps, than it is expressed in any equal number of his essays. He is a genuine poet, as well as an orator and essayist, but his eloquence is that of the great thinker rather than of the great poet. He does not amplify under the influence of his ear for melody. His address on the death of Lincoln is a model of brevity as it is of condensed and compacted truthfulness. Instead of putting Lincoln in "apotheosis," he humanizes him. The Lincoln of Beecher and of Phillips Brooks might have come from Utopia. Emerson's Lincoln certainly came from Illinois, and Emerson demonstrates him a greater man than any Utopia has yet produced.

Born in Boston, May 25th, 1803, Emerson graduated at Harvard in 1821, and from 1827 to 1832 filled the pulpit of a Unitarian Church in Boston. In 1833 he began lecturing and producing the works which immortalized him. He has been charged with having a defective ear as a poet, but if so, the defect is in his sense of metre, rather than of melody. His oratory, though completely dominated by idea, is always melodious in tone, and it is not necessarily to its discredit that it will not break up into blank verse. Emerson died at Concord, April 27th, 1882. His was the greatest mind of New England. The world has produced few greater.

THE GREATNESS OF A PLAIN AMERICAN

(Delivered at Concord, Massachusetts, on the Occasion of the Funeral Services in Honor of Mr. Lincoln, 1865)

WE MEET under the gloom of a calamity which darkens down over the minds of good men in all civilized society, as the fearful tidings travel over sea, over land, from country to country, like the shadow of an uncalculated eclipse over

the planet. Old as history is, and manifold as are its tragedies, I doubt if any death has caused so much pain to mankind as this has caused, or will cause, on its announcement; and this not so much because nations are by modern arts brought so closely together, as because of the mysterious hopes and fears which, in the present day, are connected with the name and institutions of America. In this country, on Saturday, every one was struck dumb, and saw, at first, only deep below deep, as he meditated on the ghastly blow. And, perhaps, at this hour, when the coffin which contains the dust of the President sets forward on its long march through mourning States, on its way to his home in Illinois, we might well be silent, and suffer the awful voices of the time to thunder to us. Yes, but that first despair was brief; the man was not so to be mourned. He was the most active and hopeful of men, and his work had not perished, but acclamations of praise for the task he had accomplished burst out into a song of triumph, which even tears for his death cannot keep down. The President stood before us a man of the people. He was thoroughly American, had never crossed the sea, had never been spoiled by English insularity or French dissipation; a quiet, native, aboriginal man, as an acorn from the oak; no aping of foreigners, no frivolous accomplishments; Kentuckian born, working on a farm, a flatboatman, a captain in the Blackhawk War, a country lawyer, a representative in the rural legislature of Illinois — on such modest foundations the broad structure of his fame was laid. How slowly, and yet by happily prepared steps, he came to his place! All of us remember — it is only a history of five or six years — the surprise and disappointment of the country at his first nomination at Chicago. Mr. Seward, then in the culmination of his good fame, was the favorite of the Eastern States. And when the new and comparatively unknown name of Lincoln was announced (notwithstanding the report of the acclamations of that convention), we heard the result coldly and sadly. It seemed too rash, on a purely local reputation, to build so grave a trust, in such anxious times; and men naturally talked of the chances in politics as incalculable. But it turned out not to be chance. The profound good opinion which the people of Illinois and of the West had conceived of him, and which they had imparted to their colleagues, that they also might justify themselves to their constituents at home, was not rash, though they did not begin to know the richness of his worth. A plain man of the people, an extraordinary fortune attended him. Lord Bacon says: "Manifest virtues procure reputation; occult ones, fortune." He offered no shining qualities at the first encounter: he did not offend by superiority. He had a face and manner which disarmed suspicion, which inspired confidence, which confirmed good-will. He was a man without vices. He had a strong sense of duty which it was very easy for him to obey. Then he had what farmers call a long head; was excellent in working out the sum for himself, in arguing his case and convincing you fairly and firmly. Then it turned out that he was a greater worker, and that, having prodigious faculty of performance, he worked easily. A good worker is so rare; everybody has some one disabling quality. But this man was found to the very core, cheerful, persistent, all right for labor, and he liked nothing so well. Then he had a vast good nature, which made him tolerant and accessible to all; fair-minded, leaning to the claim of the petitioner, affable, and not sensible to the affliction which the innumerable visits paid to him, when President, would have brought to any one else. And how this good nature became a noble humanity in many a tragic case which the events of the war brought to him, everyone will remember, and with what increasing tenderness he dealt when a whole race was on his compassion. The poor negro said of him, on an impressive occasion, "Massa Linkum am eberywhere." Then his broad good humor, running easily into jocular talk, in which he delighted and in which he excelled, was a rich gift to this wise man. It enabled him to keep his secret, to meet every kind of man and every rank in society, to take off the edge of the severest decisions, to mask his own purpose and sound his companion, and to catch with true instinct the temper of each company he addressed. And, more than all, such good nature is to a man of severe labor, in anxious and exhausting crises, the natural restorative, good as sleep, and is the protection of the overdriven brain against rancor and insanity. He is the author of a multitude of good sayings, so disguised as pleasantries that it is certain that they had no reputation at first but as jests; and only later, by the acceptance and adoption they find in the mouths of millions, turn out to be the wisdom of the hour. I am sure if this man had ruled in a period of less facility of printing, he would have become mythological in a few years, like Æsop or Pilpay, or one of the

Seven Wise Masters, by his fables and proverbs. But the weight and penetration of many passages in his letters, messages, and speeches, hidden now by the very closeness of their application to the moment, are destined hereafter to wide fame. What pregnant definitions; what unerring common sense; what foresight; and on great occasions, what lofty and more than natural, what humane tone! His occupying the chair of State was a triumph of the good sense of mankind and of the public confidence. This middle-class country has got a middle-class President at last. Yes, in manners, sympathies, but not in powers, for his powers were superior. His mind mastered the problem of the day; and, as the problem grew, so did his comprehension of it. Rarely was man so fitted to the event. In the midst of fears and jealousies, in the babel of counsels and parties, this man wrought incessantly with all his might and all his honesty, laboring to find what the people wanted, and how to obtain that. It cannot be said there is any exaggeration of his worth. If ever a man was fairly tested, he was. There was no lack of resistance, nor of slander, nor of ridicule. The times have allowed no State secrets; the nation has been in such a ferment, such multitudes had to be trusted, that no secret could be kept. Every door was ajar, and we know all that befell. Then what an occasion was the whirlwind of the war! Here was place for no holiday magistrate, no fair-weather sailor; the new pilot was hurried to the helm in a tornado. In four years—the four years of battle-days—his endurance, his fertility of resources, his magnanimity, were sorely tried and never found wanting. There, by his courage, his justice, his even temper, his fertile counsel, his humanity, he stood, an heroic figure in the centre of an heroic epoch. He is the true history of the American people in his time. Step by step, he walked before them; slow with their slowness, quickening his march by theirs; the true representative of this continent; an entirely public man; father of his country, the pulse of twenty millions throbbing in his heart, the thought of their minds articulated by his tongue. Adam Smith remarks that the ax which in Houbraken's portraits of British kings and worthies is engraved under those who have suffered at the block adds a certain lofty charm to the picture. And who does not see, even in this tragedy so recent, how fast the terror and ruin of the massacre are already burning into glory around the victim? Far happier this fate than to have lived to be wished away; to have

watched the decay of his own faculties; to have seen—perhaps, even he—the proverbial ingratitude of statesmen; to have seen mean men preferred. Had he not lived long enough to keep the greatest promise that ever man made to his fellow-men—the practical abolition of slavery? He had seen Tennessee, Missouri, and Maryland emancipate their slaves. He had seen Savannah, Charleston, and Richmond surrendered; had seen the main army of the Rebellion lay down its arms. He had conquered the public opinion of Canada, England, and France. Only Washington can compare with him in fortune. And what if it should turn out, in the unfolding of the web, that he had reached the term; that this heroic deliverer could no longer serve us; that the rebellion had touched its natural conclusion, and what remained to be done required new and uncommitted hands—a new spirit born out of the ashes of the war; and that Heaven, wishing to show the world a completed benefactor, shall make him serve his country even more by his death than his life. Nations, like kings, are not good by facility and complaisance. "The kindness of kings consists in justice and strength." Easy good nature has been the dangerous foible of the Republic, and it was necessary that its enemies should outrage it, and drive us to unwonted firmness, to secure the salvation of this country in the next ages.

THE AMERICAN SCHOLAR
(From the Oration Delivered August 31st, 1837, at Cambridge)

I HEAR with joy whatever is beginning to be said of the dignity and necessity of labor to every citizen. There is virtue yet in the hoe and the spade, for learned as well as for unlearned hands. And labor is everywhere welcome; always we are invited to work; only be this limitation observed, that a man shall not for the sake of wider activity sacrifice any opinion to the popular judgments and modes of action.

I have spoken of the education of the scholar by nature, by books, and by action. It remains to say somewhat of his duties.

They are such as become Man Thinking. They may all be comprised in self-trust. The office of the scholar is to cheer, to raise, and to guide men by showing them facts amidst appearances. He plies the slow, unhonored, and unpaid task of observ-

ation. Flamsteed and Herschel, in their glazed observatories, may catalogue the stars with the praise of all men, and, the results being splendid and useful, honor is sure. But he, in his private observatory, cataloguing obscure and nebulous stars of the human mind, which as yet no man has thought of as such,—watching days and months, sometimes, for a few facts; correcting still his old records,—must relinquish display and immediate fame. In the long period of his preparation, he must betray often an ignorance and shiftlessness in popular arts, incurring the disdain of the able who shoulder him aside. Long he must stammer in his speech; often forego the living for the dead. Worse yet, he must accept,—how often! poverty and solitude. For the ease and pleasure of treading the old road, accepting the fashions, the education, the religion of society, he takes the cross of making his own, and, of course, the self-accusation, the faint heart, the frequent uncertainty and loss of time, which are the nettles and tangling vines in the way of the self-relying and self-directed; and the state of virtual hostility in which he seems to stand to society, and especially to educated society. For all this loss and scorn, what offset? He is to find consolation in exercising the highest functions of human nature. He is one who raises himself from private considerations, and breathes and lives on public and illustrious thoughts. He is the world's eye. He is the world's heart. He is to resist the vulgar prosperity that retrogrades ever to barbarism, by preserving and communicating heroic sentiments, noble biographies, melodious verse, and the conclusions of history. Whatsoever oracles the human heart, in all emergencies, in all solemn hours, has uttered as its commentary on the world of actions,—these he shall receive and impart. And whatsoever new verdict Reason from her inviolable seat pronounces on the passing men and events of to-day,—this he shall hear and promulgate.

These being his functions, it becomes him to feel all confidence in himself, and to defer never to the popular cry. He, and he only, knows the world. The world of any moment is the merest appearance. Some great decorum, some fetish of a government, some ephemeral trade, or war, or man, is cried up by half mankind and cried down by the other half, as if all depended on this particular up or down. The odds are that the whole question is not worth the poorest thought which the scholar has lost in listening to the controversy. Let him not quit his belief that a popgun is a popgun, though the ancient and honorable of the earth affirm it to be the crack of doom. In silence, in steadiness, in severe abstraction, let him hold by himself; add observation to observation, patient of neglect, patient of reproach; and bide his own time,—happy enough, if he can satisfy himself alone, that this day he has seen something truly. Success treads on every right step. For the instinct is sure that prompts him to tell his brother what he thinks. He then learns that, in going down into the secrets of his own mind, he has descended into the secrets of all minds. He learns that he who has mastered any law in his private thoughts is master to that extent of all men whose language he speaks, and of all into whose language his own can be translated. The poet, in utter solitude remembering his spontaneous thoughts and recording them, is found to have recorded that which men in crowded cities find true for them also. The orator distrusts at first the fitness of his frank confessions,—his want of knowledge of the persons he addresses,—until he finds that he is the complement of his hearers; that they drink his words because he fulfills for them their own nature; the deeper he dives into his privatest, secretest presentiment, to his wonder he finds this is the most acceptable, most public, and universally true. The people delight in it; the better part of every man feels, This is my music, this is myself.

In self-trust, all the virtues are comprehended. Free should the scholar be,—free and brave. Free even to the definition of freedom, "without any hindrance that does not arise out of his own constitution." Brave; for fear is a thing which a scholar, by his very function, puts behind him. Fear always springs from ignorance. It is a shame to him if his tranquillity, amid dangerous times, arise from the presumption that, like children and women, his is a protected class; or if he seek a temporary peace by the diversion of his thoughts from politics or vexed questions, hiding his head like an ostrich in the flowering bushes, peeping into microscopes, and turning rhymes, as a boy whistles to keep his courage up. So is the danger a danger still; so is the fear worse. Manlike let him turn and face it. Let him look into its eye and search its nature, inspect its origin,—see the whelping of this lion, which lies no great way back; he will then find in himself a perfect comprehension of its nature and extent; he will have made his hands meet on the other side, and can henceforth defy it, and pass on superior. The world is

his, who can see through its pretension. What deafness, what stone-blind custom, what overgrown error you behold, is there only by sufferance,—by your sufferance. See it to be a lie, and you have already dealt it its mortal blow.

Yes, we are the cowed,—we the trustless. It is a mischievous notion that we are come late into nature; that the world was finished a long time ago. As the world was plastic and fluid in the hands of God, so it is ever to so much of his attributes as we bring to it. To ignorance and sin, it is flint. They adapt themselves to it as they may; but in proportion as a man has anything in him divine, the firmament flows before him and takes his signet and form. Not he is great who can alter matter, but he who can alter my state of mind. They are the kings of the world who give the color of their present thought to all nature and all art, and persuade men by the cheerful serenity of their carrying the matter, that this thing which they do is the apple which the ages have desired to pluck, now at last ripe, and inviting nations to the harvest. The great man makes the great thing. Wherever Macdonald sits, there is the head of the table. Linnæus makes botany the most alluring of studies, and wins it from the farmer and the herb-woman; Davy, chemistry; and Cuvier, fossils. The day is always his who works in it with serenity and great aims. The unstable estimates of men crowd to him whose mind is filled with a truth, as the heaped waves of the Atlantic follow the moon.

For this self-trust, the reason is deeper than can be fathomed,—darker than can be enlightened. I might not carry with me the feeling of my audience in stating my own belief. But I have already shown the ground of my hope, in adverting to the doctrine that man is one. I believe man has been wronged; he has wronged himself. He has almost lost the light that can lead him back to his prerogatives. Men are become of no account. Men in history, men in the world of to-day are bugs, are spawn, and are called "the mass" and "the herd." In a century, in a millenium, one or two men; that is to say, one or two approximations to the right state of every man. All the rest behold in the hero or the poet their own green and crude being,—ripened; yes, and are content to be less, so that may attain to its full stature. What a testimony, full of grandeur, full of pity, is borne to the demands of his own nature, by the poor clansman, the poor partisan, who rejoices in the glory of his chief. The poor

and the low find some amends to their immense moral capacity, for their acquiescence in a political and social inferiority. They are content to be brushed like flies from the path of a great person, so that justice shall be done by him to that common nature which it is the dearest desire of all to see enlarged and glorified. They sun themselves in the great man's light, and feel it to be their own element. They cast the dignity of man from their downtrod selves upon the shoulders of a hero, and will perish to add one drop of blood to make that great heart beat, those giant sinews combat and conquer. He lives for us and we live in him.

Men such as they are very naturally seek money or power; and power because it is as good as money,—the "spoils," so called, "of office." And why not? for they aspire to the highest, and this, in their sleep-walking, they dream is highest. Wake them, and they shall quit the false good and leap to the true, and leave governments to clerks and desks. This revolution is to be wrought by the gradual domestication of the idea of culture. The main enterprise of the world for splendor, for extent, is the upbuilding of a man. Here are the materials strewn along the ground. The private life of one man shall be a more illustrious monarchy,—more formidable to its enemy, more sweet and serene in its influence to its friend, than any kingdom in history. For a man, rightly viewed, comprehendeth the particular natures of all men. Each philosopher, each bard, each actor, has only done for me, as by a delegate, what one day I can do for myself. The books which once we valued more than the apple of the eye, we have quite exhausted. What is that but saying that we have come up with the point of view which the universal mind took through the eyes of one scribe; we have been that man and have passed on. First, one; then, another; we drain all cisterns, and, waxing greater by all these supplies, we crave a better and more abundant food. The man has never lived that can feed us ever. The human mind cannot be enshrined in a person who shall set a barrier on any one side to this unbounded, unboundable empire. It is one central fire, which, flaming now out of the lips of Etna, lightens the capes of Sicily; and now out of the throat of Vesuvius, illuminates the towers and vineyards of Naples. It is one light which beams out of a thousand stars. It is one soul which animates all men.

MAN THE REFORMER

(Peroration of the Address before the Mechanics' Apprentices' Library Association, Boston, January 25th, 1841)

WHAT is a man born for but to be a Reformer, a Re-maker of what man has made; a renouncer of lies; a restorer of truth and good, imitating that great Nature which embosoms us all, and which sleeps no moment on an old past, but every hour repairs herself, yielding us every morning a new day, and with every pulsation a new life? Let him renounce everything which is not true to him, and put all his practices back on their first thoughts, and do nothing for which he has not the whole world for his reason. If there are inconveniences, and what is called ruin, in the way, because we have so enervated and maimed ourselves, yet it would be like dying of perfumes to sink in the effort to reattach the deeds of every day to the holy and mysterious recesses of life.

The power, which is at once spring and regulator in all efforts of reform, is the conviction that there is an infinite worthiness in man which will appear at the call of worth, and that all particular reforms are the removing of some impediment. Is it not the highest duty that man should be honored in us? I ought not to allow any man, because he has broad lands, to feel that he is rich in my presence. I ought to make him feel that I can do without his riches, that I cannot be bought,—neither by comfort, neither by pride,—and though I be utterly penniless, and receiving bread from him, that he is the poor man beside me. And if, at the same time, a woman or a child discover a sentiment of piety, or a juster way of thinking than mine, I ought to confess it by my respect and obedience, though it go to alter my whole way of life.

The Americans have many virtues, but they have not Faith and Hope. I know no two words whose meaning is more lost sight of. We use these words as if they were as obsolete as Selah and Amen. And yet they have the broadest meaning, and the most cogent application to Boston in 1841. The Americans have no faith. They rely on the power of a dollar; they are deaf to a sentiment. They think you may talk the north wind down as easily as raise society; and no class more faithless than the scholars or intellectual men. Now, if I talk with a sincere, wise man, and my friend with a poet, with a conscientious youth who is still under the dominion of his own wild thoughts, and not yet harnessed in the team of society to drag with us all in the ruts of custom, I see at once how paltry is all this generation of unbelievers, and what a house of cards their institutions are, and I see what one brave man, what one great thought executed might effect. I see that the reason of the distrust of the practical man in all theory is his inability to perceive the means whereby we work. Look, he says, at the tools with which this world of yours is to be built. As we cannot make a planet with atmosphere, rivers, and forests, by means of the best carpenter's or engineer's tools, with chemist's laboratory and smith's forge to boot, so neither can we ever construct that heavenly society you prate of out of foolish, sick, selfish men and women, such as we know them to be. But the believer not only beholds his heaven to be possible, but already to begin to exist,—not by the men or materials the statesman uses, but by men transfigured and raised above themselves by the power of principles. To principles something else is possible that transcends all the power of expedients.

Every great and commanding moment in the annals of the world is the triumph of some enthusiasm. The victories of the Arabs after Mahomet, who, in a few years, from a small and mean beginning, established a larger empire than that of Rome, is an example. They did they knew not what. The naked Derar, horsed on an idea, was found an overmatch for a troop of Roman cavalry. The women fought like men, and conquered the Roman men. They were miserably equipped, miserably fed. They were Temperance troops. There was neither brandy nor flesh needed to feed them. They conquered Asia and Africa and Spain on barley. The Caliph Omar's walking-stick struck more terror into those who saw it than another man's sword. His diet was barley bread; his sauce was salt; and oftentimes, by way of abstinence, he ate his bread without salt. His drink was water; his palace was built of mud; and when he left Medina to go to the conquest of Jerusalem, he rode on a red camel, with a wooden platter hanging at his saddle, with a bottle of water and two sacks, one holding barley and the other dried fruits.

But there will dawn ere long on our politics, on our modes of living, a nobler morning than that Arabian faith, in the senti

ment of love. This is the one remedy for all ills, the panacea of nature. We must be lovers, and at once the impossible becomes possible. Our age and history, for these thousand years, has not been the history of kindness but of selfishness. Our distrust is very expensive. The money we spend for courts and prisons is very ill laid out. We make by distrust the thief and burglar and incendiary, and by our court and jail we keep him so. An acceptance of the sentiment of love throughout Christendom for a season would bring the felon and the outcast to our side in tears, with the devotion of his faculties to our service. See this wide society of laboring men and women. We allow ourselves to be served by them, we live apart from them, and meet them without a salute in the streets. We do not greet their talents, nor rejoice in their good fortune, nor foster their hopes, nor in the assembly of the people vote for what is dear to them. Thus we enact the part of the selfish noble and king from the foundation of the world. See, this tree always bears one fruit. In every household the peace of a pair is poisoned by the malice, slyness, indolence, and alienation of domestics. Let any two matrons meet, and observe how soon their conversation turns on the troubles from their "help," as our phrase is. In every knot of laborers, the rich man does not feel himself among his friends, —and at the polls he finds them arrayed in a mass in distinct opposition to him. We complain that the politics of masses of the people are controlled by designing men, and led in opposition to manifest justice and the common weal, and to their own interest. But the people do not wish to be represented or ruled by the ignorant and base. They only vote for these because they were asked with the voice and semblance of kindness. They will not vote for them long. They inevitably prefer wit and probity. To use an Egyptian metaphor, it is not their will for any long time " to raise the nails of wild beasts, and to depress the heads of the sacred birds." Let our affection flow out to our fellows; it would operate in a day the greatest of all revolutions. It is better to work on institutions by the sun than by the wind. The state must consider the poor man, and all voices must speak for him. Every child that is born must have a just chance for his bread. Let the amelioration in our laws of property proceed from the concession of the rich, not from the grasping of the poor. Let us begin by habitual imparting. Let us understand that the equitable rule is, that no one should take

more than his share, let him be ever so rich. Let me feel that I am to be a lover. I am to see to it that the world is the better for me and to find my reward in the act. Love would put a new face on this weary old world in which we dwell as pagans and enemies too long, and it would warm the heart to see how fast the vain diplomacy of statesmen, the impotence of armies and navies and lines of defense would be superseded by this unarmed child. Love will creep where it cannot go, will accomplish that by imperceptible methods,—being its own lever, fulcrum, and power,—which force could never achieve. Have you not seen in the woods, in a late autumn morning, a poor fungus or mushroom,—a plant without any solidity, nay, that seemed nothing but a soft mush or jelly,—by its constant, total, and inconceivably gentle pushing, manage to break its way up through the frosty ground, and actually to lift a hard crust on its head? It is the symbol of the power of kindness. The virtue of this principle in human society in application to great interests is obsolete and forgotten. Once or twice in history it has been tried in illustrious instances, with signal success. This great, overgrown, dead Christendom of ours still keeps alive at least the name of a lover of mankind. But one day all men will be lovers; and every calamity will be dissolved in the universal sunshine.

Will you suffer me to add one trait more to this portrait of man the reformer? The mediator between the spiritual and the actual world should have a great prospective prudence. An Arabian poet describes his hero by saying:—

> "Sunshine was he
> In the winter day;
> And in the midsummer
> Coolness and shade."

He who would help himself and others should not be a subject of irregular and interrupted impulses of virtue, but a continent, persisting, immovable person,—such as we have seen a few scattered up and down in time for the blessing of the world; men who have in the gravity of their nature a quality which answers to the fly-wheel in a mill, which distributes the motion equably over all the wheels, and hinders it from falling unequally and suddenly in destructive shocks. It is better that joy should be, spread over all the day in the form of strength than that it should

be concentrated into ecstasies, full of danger and followed by reactions. There is a sublime prudence which is the very highest that we know of man, which, believing in a vast future,—sure of more to come than is yet seen,—postpones always the present hour to the whole life; postpones talent to genius, and special results to character. As the merchant gladly takes money from his income to add to his capital, so is the great man very willing to lose particular powers and talents, so that he gain in the elevation of his life. The opening of the spiritual senses disposes men ever to greater sacrifices, to leave their signal talents, their best means and skill of procuring a present success, their power and their fame,—to cast all things behind, in the insatiable thirst for divine communications. A purer fame, a greater power rewards the sacrifice. It is the conversion of our harvest into seed. As the farmer casts into the ground the finest ears of his grain, the time will come when we, too, shall hold nothing back, but shall eagerly convert more than we now possess into means and powers, when we shall be willing to sow the sun and the moon for seeds.

USES OF GREAT MEN

(Delivered in 1850, as the First of a Series of Seven Addresses on Representative Men)

IT is natural to believe in great men. If the companions of our childhood should turn out to be heroes, and their condition regal, it would not surprise us. All mythology opens with demigods, and the circumstance is high and poetic; that is, their genius is paramount. In the legends of the Gautama, the first men ate the earth, and found it deliciously sweet.

Nature seems to exist for the excellent. The world is upheld by the veracity of good men; they make the earth wholesome. They who lived with them found life glad and nutritious. Life is sweet and tolerable only in our belief in such society; and actually or ideally we manage to live with superiors. We call our children and our lands by their names. Their names are wrought into the verbs of language, their works and effigies are in our houses, and every circumstance of the day recalls an anecdote of them.

The search after the great is the dream of youth, and the most serious occupation of manhood. We travel into foreign parts to find his works,—if possible, to get a glimpse of him. But we are put off with fortune instead. You say the English are practical; the Germans are hospitable; in Valencia the climate is delicious; and in the hills of the Sacramento there is gold for the gathering. Yes, but I do not travel to find comfortable, rich, and hospitable people, or clear sky, or ingots that cost too much. But if there were any magnet that would point to the countries and houses where are the persons who are intrinsically rich and powerful, I would sell all and buy it and put myself on the road to-day.

The race goes with us on their credit. The knowledge that in the city is a man who invented the railroad raises the credit of all the citizens. But enormous populations, if they be beggars, are disgusting, like moving cheese, like hills of ants, or of fleas—the more, the worse.

Our religion is the love and cherishing of these patrons. The gods of fable are the shining moments of great men. We run all our vessels into one mold. Our colossal theologies of Judaism, Christism, Buddhism, Mahometism, are the necessary and structural action of the human mind. The student of history is like a man going into a warehouse to buy cloths or carpets. He fancies he has a new article. If he go to the factory, he shall find that his new stuff still repeats the scrolls and rosettes which are found on the interior walls of the pyramids of Thebes. Our Theism is the purification of the human mind. Man can paint, or make, or think nothing but man. He believes that the great material elements had their origin from his thought. And our philosophy finds one essence collected or distributed.

If now we proceed to inquire into the kinds of service we derive from others, let us be warned of the danger of modern studies, and begin low enough. We must not contend against love, or deny the substantial existence of other people. I know not what would happen to us. We have social strengths. Our affection towards others creates a sort of vantage or purchase, which nothing will supply. I can do that by another which I cannot do alone. I can say to you what I cannot first say to myself. Other men are lenses through which we read our own minds. Each man seeks those of different quality from his own, and such as are good of their kind; that is, he seeks other men, and the *otherest*. The stronger the nature, the more it is reactive. Let us have the quality pure. A little genius let us leave

health, eternal youth, fine senses, arts of healing, magical power, and prophecy. The boy believes there is a teacher who can sell him wisdom. Churches believe in imputed merit. But, in strictness, we are not much cognizant of direct serving. Man is endogenous, and education is his unfolding. The aid we have from others is mechanical, compared with the discoveries of nature in us. What is thus learned is delightful in the doing, and the effect remains. Right ethics are central, and go from the soul outward. Gift is contrary to the law of the universe. Serving others is serving us. I must absolve me to myself. "Mind thy affair," says the spirit; "coxcomb, would you meddle with the skies, or with other people?" Indirect service is left. Men have a pictorial or representative quality, and serve us in the intellect. Behmen and Swedenborg saw that things were representative. Men are also representative—first, of things, and secondly, of ideas.

As plants convert the minerals into food for animals, so each man converts some raw material in nature to human use. The inventors of fire, electricity, magnetism, iron, lead, glass, linen, silk, cotton; the makers of tools; the inventor of decimal notation; the geometer; the engineer; the musician,—severally make an easy way for all, through unknown and impossible confusions. Each man is, by secret liking, connected with some district of nature, whose agent and interpreter he is, as Linnæus, of plants; Huber, of bees; Fries, of lichens; Van Mons, of pears; Dalton, of atomic forms; Euclid, of lines; Newton, of fluxions.

A man is a centre for nature, running out threads of relation through everything, fluid and solid, material and elemental. The earth rolls; every clod and stone comes to the meridian; so every organ, function, acid, crystal, grain of dust, has its relation to the brain. It waits long, but its turn comes. Each plant has its parasite, and each created thing its lover and poet. Justice has already been done to steam, to iron, to wood, to coal, to loadstone, to iodine, to corn, and cotton; but how few materials are yet used by our arts! The mass of creatures and of qualities are still hid and expectant. It would seem as if each waited, like the enchanted princess in fairy tales, for a destined human deliverer. Each must be disenchanted, and walk forth to the day in human shape. In the history of discovery, the ripe and latent truth seems to have fashioned a brain for itself. A magnet must be made man, in some Gilbert, or Swedenborg,

alone. A main difference betwixt men is, whether they attend their own affair or not. Man is that noble endogenous plant which grows, like the palm, from within, outward. His own affair, though impossible to others, he can open with celerity and in sport. It is easy to sugar to be sweet, and to nitre to be salt. We take a great deal of pains to waylay and entrap that which of itself will fall into our hands. I count him a great man who inhabits a higher sphere of thought, into which other men rise with labor and difficulty; he has but to open his eyes to see things in a true light, and in large relations; whilst they must make painful corrections, and keep a vigilant eye on many sources of error. His service to us is of like sort. It costs a beautiful person no exertion to paint her image on our eyes; yet how splendid is that benefit! It costs no more for a wise soul to convey his quality to other men. And every one can do his best thing easiest. *Peu de moyens, beaucoup d'effét.* He is great who is what he is from nature, and who never reminds us of others.

But he must be related to us, and our life receive from him some promise of explanation. I cannot tell what I would know; but I have observed there are persons who, in their character and actions, answer questions which I have not skill to put. One man answers some question which none of his contemporaries put, and is isolated. The past and passing religions and philosophies answer some other question. Certain men affect us as rich possibilities, but helpless to themselves and to their times, —the sport, perhaps, of some instinct that rules in the air; they do not speak to our want. But the great are near; we know them at sight. They satisfy expectation, and fall into place. What is good is effective, generative; makes for itself room, food, and allies. A sound apple produces seed; a hybrid does not. Is a man in his place, he is constructive, fertile, magnetic, inundating armies with his purpose, which is thus executed. The river makes its own shores, and each legitimate idea makes it own channels and welcome,—harvests for food, institutions for expression, weapons to fight with, and disciples to explain it. The true artist has the planet for his pedestal; the adventurer, after years of strife, has nothing broader than his own shoes.

Our common discourse respects two kinds of use or service from superior men. Direct giving is agreeable to the early belief of men; direct giving of material or metaphysical aid, as of

or Oersted, before the general mind can come to entertain its powers.

If we limit ourselves to the first advantages;—a sober grace adheres to the mineral and botanic kingdoms which, in the highest moments, comes up as the charm of nature,—the glitter of the spar, the sureness of affinity, the veracity of angles. Light and darkness, heat and cold, hunger and food, sweet and sour, solid, liquid, and gas, circle us round in a wreath of pleasures, and, by their agreeable quarrel, beguile the day of life. The eye repeats every day the first eulogy on things—"He saw that they were good." We know where to find them; and these performers are relished all the more after a little experience of the pretending races. We are entitled, also, to higher advantages. Something is wanting to science until it has been humanized. The table of logarithms is one thing, and its vital play in botany, music, optics, and architecture, another. There are advancements to numbers, anatomy, architecture, astronomy, little suspected at first, when, by union with intellect and will, they ascend into the life, and reappear in conversation, character, and politics.

But this comes later. We speak now only of our acquaintance with them in their own sphere, and the way in which they seem to fascinate and draw to them some genius who occupies himself with one thing all his life long. The possibility of interpretation lies in the identity of the observer with the observed. Each material thing has its celestial side—has its translation, through humanity, into the spiritual and necessary sphere, where it plays a part as indestructible as any other. And to these, their ends, all things continually ascend. The gases gather to the solid firmament: the chemic lump arrives at the plant and grows; arrives at the quadruped, and walks; arrives at the man, and thinks. But also the constituency determines the vote of the representative. He is not only representative, but participant. Like can only be known by like. The reason why he knows about them is that he is of them; he has just come out of nature, or from being a part of that thing. Animated chlorine knows of chlorine, and incarnate zinc of zinc. Their quality makes his career, and he can variously publish their virtues because they compose him. Man, made of the dust of the world, does not forget his origin; and all that is yet inanimate will one day speak and reason. Unpublished nature will have its whole secret told. Shall we say that quartz mountains will **pulverize** into innumerable Werners, Von Buchs, and Beaumonts, and the laboratory of the atmosphere holds in solution I know not what Berzeliuses and Davys?

Thus we sit by the fire and take hold on the poles of the earth. This *quasi* omnipresence supplies the imbecility of our condition. In one of those celestial days when heaven and earth meet and adorn each other, it seems a poverty that we can only spend it once; we wish for a thousand heads, a thousand bodies, that we might celebrate its immense beauty in many ways and places. Is this fancy? Well, in good faith, we are multiplied by our proxies. How easily we adopt their labors! Every ship that comes to America got its chart from Columbus. Every novel is a debtor to Homer. Every carpenter who shaves with a fore-plane borrows the genius of a forgotten inventor. Life is girt all round with a zodiac of sciences—the contributions of men who have perished to add their point of light to our sky. En-gineer, broker, jurist, physician, moralist, theologian, and every man, in as much as he has any science, is a definer and map-maker of the latitudes and longitudes of our condition. These road-makers on every hand enrich us. We must extend the area of life, and multiply our relations. We are as much gainers by finding a new property in the old earth as by acquiring a new planet.

We are too passive in the reception of these material or semi-material aids. We must not be sacks and stomachs. To ascend one step we are better served through our sympathy. Activity is contagious. Looking where others look, and conversing with the same things, we catch the charm which lured them. Napo-leon said: "You must not fight too often with one enemy, or you will teach him all your art of war." Talk much with any man of vigorous mind, and we acquire very fast the habit of looking at things in the same light, and on each occurrence we anticipate his thought.

Men are helpful through the intellect and the affections. Other help, I find a false appearance. If you affect to give me bread and fire, I perceive that I pay for it the full price, and at last it leaves me as it found me, neither better nor worse. But all mental and moral force is a positive good. It goes out from you whether you will or not, and profits me whom you never thought of. I cannot even hear of personal vigor of any kind, great power of performance, without fresh resolution. We are emulous of all that man can do. Cecil's saying of Sir Walter

gence. This honor, which is possible in personal intercourse scarcely twice in a lifetime, genius perpetually pays; contented, if now and then, in a century, the proffer is accepted. The indi-cators of the values of matter are degraded to a sort of cooks and confectioners, on the appearance of the indicators of ideas. Genius is the naturalist or geographer of the supersensible re-gions, and draws their map; and, by acquainting us with new fields of activity, cools our affection for the old. These are at once accepted as the reality, of which the world we have con-versed with is the show.

We go to the gymnasium and the swimming-school to see the power and beauty of the body; there is the like pleasure, and a higher benefit, from witnessing intellectual feats of all kinds; as feats of memory, of mathematical combination, great power of abstraction, the transmutings of the imagination, even versatility, and concentration, as these acts expose the invisible organs and members of the mind, which respond, member for member, to the parts of the body. For we thus enter a new gymnasium, and learn to choose men by their truest marks, taught, with Plato, "to choose those who can, without aid from the eyes, or any other sense, proceed to truth and to being." Foremost among these activities are the somersaults, spells, and resurrec-tions, wrought by the imagination. When this wakes, a man seems to multiply ten times or a thousand times his force. It opens the delicious sense of indeterminate size, and inspires an audacious mental habit. We are as elastic as the gas of gun-powder, and a sentence in a book or a word dropped in conver-sation sets free our fancy, and instantly our heads are bathed with galaxies, and our feet tread the floor of the pit. And this benefit is real, because we are entitled to these enlargements, and, once having passed the bounds, shall never again be quite the miserable pedants we were.

The high functions of the intellect are so allied that some imaginative power usually appears in all eminent minds, even in arithmeticians of the first class, but especially in meditative men of an intuitive habit of thought. This class serve us, so that they have the perception of identity and the perception of reac-tion. The eyes of Plato, Shakespeare, Swedenborg, Goethe, never shut on either of these laws. The perception of these laws is a kind of metre of the mind. Little minds are little, through fail-ure to see them.

Raleigh, "I know that he can toil terribly," is an electric touch. So are Clarendon's portraits,—of Hampden, "who was of an in-dustry and vigilance not to be tired out or wearied by the most laborious, and of parts not to be imposed on by the most subtle and sharp, and of a personal courage equal to his best parts,"— of Falkland, "who was so severe an adorer of truth that he could as easily have given himself leave to steal as to dissemble." We cannot read Plutarch without a tingling of the blood, and I ac-cept the saying of the Chinese Mencius: "A sage is the instructor of a hundred ages. When the manners of Loo are heard of, the stupid become intelligent, and the wavering determined."

This is the moral of biography; yet it is hard for departed men to touch the quick like our own companions, whose names may not last as long. What is he whom I never think of? whilst in every solitude are those who succor our genius and stimulate us in wonderful manners. There is a power in love to divine another's destiny better than that other can, and, by heroic en-couragements, hold him to his task. What has friendship so signal as its sublime attraction to whatever virtue is in us? We will never more think cheaply of ourselves or of life. We are piqued to some purpose, and the industry of the diggers on the railroad will not again shame us.

Under this head, too, falls that homage, very pure, as I think, which all ranks pay to the hero of the day, from Coriolanus and Gracchus down to Pitt, Lafayette, Wellington, Webster, Lamar-tine. Hear the shouts in the streets! The people cannot see him enough. They delight in a man. Here is a head and a trunk! What a front! what eyes! Atlantean shoulders, and the whole carriage heroic, with equal inward force to guide the great machine! This pleasure of full expression to that which, in their private experience, is usually cramped and obstructed, runs, also, much higher, and is the secret of the reader's joy in literary genius. Nothing is kept back. There is fire enough to fuse the mountain of ore. Shakespeare's principal merit may be con-veyed in saying that he, of all men, best understands the Eng-lish language, and can say what he will. Yet these unchoked channels and floodgates of expression are only health or fortunate constitution. Shakespeare's name suggests other and purely in-tellectual benefits.

Senates and sovereigns have no compliment, with their medals, swords, and armorial coats, like the addressing to a human being thoughts out of a certain height, and presupposing his intelli-

Even these feats have their surfeit. Our delight in reason degenerates into idolatry of the herald. Especially when a mind of powerful method has instructed men, we find the examples of oppression. The dominion of Aristotle, the Ptolemaic astronomy, the credit of Luther, of Bacon, of Locke,—in religion, the his-tory of hierarchies, of saints, and the sects which have taken the name of each founder, are in point. Alas! every man is such a victim. The imbecility of men is always inviting the impudence of power. It is the delight of vulgar talent to dazzle and to bind the beholder. But true genius seeks to defend us from itself. True genius will not impoverish, but will liberate, and add new senses. If a wise man should appear in our village, he would create in those who conversed with him a new conscious-ness of wealth by opening their eyes to unobserved advantages; he would establish a sense of immovable equality, calm us with assurances that we could not be cheated, as every one would dis-cern the checks and guaranties of condition. The rich would see their mistakes and poverty, the poor their escapes and their resources.

But nature brings all this about in due time. Rotation is her remedy. The soul is impatient of masters, and eager for change. Housekeepers say of a domestic who has been valuable, "She had lived with me long enough." We are tendencies, or, rather, symptoms, and none of us complete. We touch and go, and sip the foam of many lives. Rotation is the law of nature. When nature removes a great man, people explore the horizon for a successor; but none comes, and none will. His class is extin-guished with him. In some other and quite different field, the next man will appear; not Jefferson, not Franklin, but now a great salesman; then a road-contractor; then a student of fishes; then a buffalo-hunting explorer, or a semi-savage western gen-eral. Thus we make a stand against our rougher masters; but against the best there is a finer remedy. The power which they communicate is not theirs. When we are exalted by ideas, we do not owe this to Plato, but to the idea, to which, also, Plato was debtor.

I must not forget that we have a special debt to a single class. Life is a scale of degrees. Between rank and rank of our great men are wide intervals. Mankind have, in all ages, attached themselves to a few persons, who, either by the quality of that idea they embodied, or by the largeness of their reception, were entitled to the position of leaders and law-givers. These teach us the qualities of primary nature,—admit us to the constitution of things. We swim, day by day, on a river of delusions, and are effectually amused with houses and towns in the air, of which the men about us are dupes. But life is a sincerity. In lucid intervals we say: "Let there be an entrance opened for me into realities; I have worn the fool's cap too long." We will know the meaning of our economies and politics. Give us the cipher, and, if persons and things are scores of a celestial music, let us read off the strains. We have been cheated of our reason; yet there have been sane men, who enjoyed a rich and related existence. What they know, they know for us. With each new mind, a new secret of nature transpires; nor can the Bible be closed, until the last great man is born. These men correct the delirium of the animal spirits, make us considerate, and engage us to new aims and powers. The veneration of mankind selects these for the highest place. Witness the multitude of statues, pictures, and memorials which recall their genius in every city, village, house, and ship:—

> "Ever their phantoms arise before us,
> Our loftier brothers, but one in blood;
> At bed and table they lord it o'er us,
> With looks of beauty, and words of good."

How are we to illustrate the distinctive benefit of ideas, the service rendered by those who introduce moral truths into the general mind? I am plagued, in all my living, with a perpetual tariff of prices. If I work in my garden and prune an apple tree, I am well enough entertained, and could continue indefinitely in the like occupation. But it comes to mind that a day is gone and I have got this precious nothing done. I go to Boston or New York and run up and down on my affairs; they are sped, but so is the day. I am vexed by the recollection of this price I have paid for a trifling advantage. I remember the *peau d'ane*, on which whoso sat should have his desire, but a piece of the skin was gone for every wish. I go to a convention of philanthropists. Do what I can, I cannot keep my eyes off the clock. But if there should appear in the company some gentle soul who knows little of persons or parties, of Carolina or Cuba, but who announces a law that disposes these particulars, and so certifies me of the equity which checkmates every false player, bankrupts

most ill-used people alive, and never get over their astonishment at the ingratitude and selfishness of their contemporaries. Our globe discovers its hidden virtues, not only in heroes and archangels, but in gossips and nurses. Is it not a rare contrivance that lodged the due inertia in every creature, the conserving, resisting energy, the anger at being waked or changed? Altogether independent of the intellectual force in each is the pride of opinion, the security that we are right. Not the feeblest grandame, not a mowing idiot, but uses what spark of perception and faculty is left, to chuckle and triumph in his or her opinion over the absurdities of all the rest. Difference from me is the measure of absurdity. Not one has a misgiving of being wrong. Was it not a bright thought that made things cohere with this bitumen, fastest of cements? But, in the midst of this chuckle of self-gratulation, some figure goes by, which Thersites, too, can love and admire. This is he that should marshal us the way we were going. There is no end to his aid. Without Plato, we should almost lose our faith in the possibility of a reasonable book. We seem to want but one, but we want one. We love to associate with heroic persons, since our receptivity is unlimited; and, with the great, our thoughts and manners easily become great. We are all wise in capacity, though so few in energy. There needs but one wise man in a company, and all are wise, so rapid is the contagion.

Great men are thus a collyrium to clear our eyes from egotism and enable us to see other people and their works. But there are vices and follies incident to whole populations and ages. Men resemble their contemporaries even more than their progenitors. It is observed in old couples, or in persons who have been housemates for a course of years, that they grow alike; and, if they should live long enough, we should not be able to know them apart. Nature abhors these complaisances, which threaten to melt the world into a lump, and hastens to break up such maudlin agglutinations. The like assimilation goes on between men of one town, of one sect, of one political party; and the ideas of the time are in the air, and infect all who breathe it. Viewed from any high point, this city of New York, yonder city of London, the western civilization, would seem a bundle of insanities. We keep each other in countenance, and exasperate by emulation the frenzy of the time. The shield against the stingings of conscience is the universal practice of our contempo-

every self-seeker, and apprises me of my independence on any conditions of country, or time, or human body, that man liberates me; I forget the clock. I pass out of the sore relation to persons. I am healed of my hurts. I am made immortal by apprehending my possession of incorruptible goods. Here is great competition of rich and poor. We live in a market where is only so much wheat, or wool, or land; and if I have so much more, every other must have so much less. I seem to have no good, without breach of good manners. Nobody is glad in the gladness of another, and our system is one of war, of an injurious superiority. Every child of the Saxon race is educated to wish to be first. It is our system; and a man comes to measure his greatness by the regrets, envies, and hatreds of his competitors. But in these new fields there is room; here are no self-esteems, no exclusions.

I admire great men of all classes, those who stand for facts and for thoughts; I like rough and smooth, "Scourges of God," and "Darlings of the human race." I like the first Cæsar and Charles V. of Spain, and Charles XII. of Sweden, Richard Plantagenet, and Bonaparte in France. I applaud a sufficient man, an officer equal to his office; captains, ministers, senators. I like a master standing firm on legs of iron, well-born, rich, handsome, eloquent, loaded with advantages, drawing all men by fascination into tributaries and supporters of his power. Sword and staff, or talents sword-like or staff-like, carry on the work of the world. But I find him greater when he can abolish himself and all heroes by letting in this element of reason, irrespective of persons; this subtilizer and irresistible upward force into our thought, destroying individualism; the power so great that the potentate is nothing. Then he is a monarch who gives a constitution to his people; a pontiff who preaches the equality of souls and releases his servants from their barbarous homages; an emperor who can spare his empire.

But I intended to specify, with a little minuteness, two or three points of service. Nature never spares the opium or nepenthe; but, wherever she mars her creature with some deformity or defect, lays her poppies plentifully on the bruise, and the sufferer goes joyfully through life, ignorant of the ruin, and incapable of seeing it, though all the world point their finger at it every day. The worthless and offensive members of society, whose existence is a social pest, invariably think themselves the

raries. Again; it is very easy to be as wise and good as your companions. We learn of our contemporaries what they know, without effort, and almost through the pores of the skin. We catch it by sympathy, or as a wife arrives at the intellectual and moral elevations of her husband. But we stop where they stop. Very hardly can we take another step. The great, or such as hold of nature and transcend fashions, by their fidelity to universal ideas, are saviors from these federal errors, and defend us from our contemporaries. They are the exceptions which we want, where all grows alike. A foreign greatness is the antidote for cabalism.

Thus we feed on genius, and refresh ourselves from too much conversation with our mates, and exult in the depth of nature in that direction in which he leads us. What indemnification is one great man for populations of pigmies! Every mother wishes one son a genius, though all the rest should be mediocre. But a new danger appears in the excess of influence of the great man. His attractions warp us from our place. We have become underlings and intellectual suicides. Ah! yonder in the horizon is our help:—other great men, new qualities, counterweights and checks on each other. We cloy of the honey of each peculiar greatness. Every hero becomes a bore at last. Perhaps Voltaire was not bad-hearted, yet he said of the good Jesus, even: "I pray you, let me never hear that man's name again." They cry up the virtues of George Washington,—"Damn George Washington!" is the poor Jacobin's whole speech and confutation. But it is human nature's indispensable defense. The centripetence augments the centrifugence. We balance one man with his opposite; and the health of the state depends on the seesaw.

There is, however, a speedy limit to the use of heroes. Every genius is defended from approach by quantities of unavailableness. They are very attractive, and seem at a distance our own; but we are hindered on all sides from approach. The more we are drawn, the more we are repelled. There is something not solid in the good that is done for us. The best discovery the discoverer makes for himself. It has something unreal for his companion, until he too has substantiated it. It seems as if the Deity dressed each soul which he sends into nature in certain virtues and powers not communicable to other men, and, sending it to perform one more turn through the circle of beings, wrote, "Not transferable," and "Good for this trip only," on these garments of the soul. There is something deceptive about the intercourse of minds. The boundaries are invisible, but they are never crossed. There is such good will to impart, and such good will to receive, that each threatens to become the other; but the law of individuality collects its secret strength: you are you, and I am I, and so we remain.

For Nature wishes everything to remain itself; and, whilst every individual strives to grow and exclude, and to exclude and grow, to the extremities of the universe, and to impose the law of its being on every other creature, Nature steadily aims to protect each against every other. Each is self-defended. Nothing is more marked than the power by which individuals are guarded from individuals, in a world where every benefactor becomes so easily a malefactor, only by continuation of his activity into places where it is not due; where children seem so much at the mercy of their foolish parents, and where almost all men are too social and interfering. We rightly speak of the guardian angels of children. How superior in their security from infusions of evil persons, from vulgarity and second thought! They shed their own abundant beauty on the objects they behold. Therefore, they are not at the mercy of such poor educators as we adults. If we huff and chide them, they soon come not to mind it, and get a self-reliance; and if we indulge them to folly, they learn the limitation elsewhere.

We need not fear excessive influence. A more generous trust is permitted. Serve the great. Stick at no humiliation. Grudge no office thou canst render. Be the limb of their body, the breath of their mouth. Compromise thy egotism. Who cares for that, so thou gain aught wider and nobler? Never mind the taunt of Boswellism: the devotion may easily be greater than the wretched pride which is guarding its own skirts. Be another: not thyself, but a Platonist; not a soul, but a Christian; not a naturalist, but a Cartesian; not a poet, but a Shakesperean. In vain, the wheels of tendency will not stop, nor will all the forces of inertia, fear, or of love itself, hold thee there. On, and forever onward! The microscope observes a monad or wheel-insect among the infusories circulating in water. Presently, a dot appears on the animal, which enlarges to a slit, and it becomes two perfect animals. The ever-proceeding detachment appears not less in all thought, and in society. Children think they cannot live without their parents. But, long before they

are aware of it, the black dot has appeared, and the detachment taken place. Any accident will now reveal to them their independence.

But "great men": — the word is injurious. Is there caste? is there fate? What becomes of the promise to virtue? The thoughtful youth laments the superfœtation of nature. "Generous and handsome," he says, "is your hero; but look at yonder poor Paddy, whose country is his wheelbarrow; look at his whole nation of Paddies." Why are the masses, from the dawn of history down, food for knives and powder? The idea dignifies a few leaders, who have sentiment, opinion, love, self-devotion; and they make war and death sacred; — but what for the wretches whom they hire and kill? The cheapness of man is every day's tragedy. It is as real a loss that others should be low, as that we should be low; for we must have society.

Is it a reply to these suggestions to say society is a Pestalozzian school; all are teachers and pupils in turn? We are equally served by receiving and by imparting. Men who know the same things are not long the best company for each other. But bring to each an intelligent person of another experience, and it is as if you let off water from a lake by cutting a lower basin. It seems a mechanical advantage, and great benefit it is to each speaker, as he can now paint out his thought to himself. We pass very fast, in our personal moods, from dignity to dependence. And if any appear never to assume the chair, but always to stand and serve, it is because we do not see the company in a sufficiently long period for the whole rotation of parts to come about. As to what we call the masses and common men — there are no common men. All men are at last of a size; and true art is only possible on the conviction that every talent has its apotheosis somewhere. Fair play and an open field, and freshest laurels to all who have won them! But heaven reserves an equal scope for every creature. Each is uneasy until he has produced his private ray unto the conclave sphere, and beheld his talent, also, in its last nobility and exaltation.

The heroes of the hour are relatively great; of a faster growth; or they are such in whom, at the moment of success, a quality is ripe which is then in request. Other days will demand other qualities. Some rays escape the common observer, and want a finely adapted eye. Ask the great man if there be none greater. His companions are; and not the less great but the

more, that society cannot see them. Nature never sends a great man into the planet, without confiding the secret to another soul.

One gracious fact emerges from these studies, — that there is true ascension in our love. The reputations of the nineteenth century will one day be quoted to prove its barbarism. The genius of humanity is the real subject whose biography is written in our annals. We must infer much, and supply many chasms in the record. The history of the universe is symptomatic and life is mnemonical. No man, in all the procession of famous men, is reason or illumination, or that essence we were looking for, but is an exhibition, in some quarter, of new possibilities. Could we one day complete the immense figure which these flagrant points compose! The study of many individuals leads us to an elemental region wherein the individual is lost, or wherein all touch by their summits. Thought and feeling that break out there cannot be impounded by any fence of personality. This is the key to the power of the greatest men, — their spirit diffuses itself. A new quality of mind travels by night and by day in concentric circles from its origin, and publishes itself by unknown methods; the union of all minds appears intimate; what gets admission to one cannot be kept out of any other; the smallest acquisition of truth or of energy, in any quarter, is so much good to the commonwealth of souls. If the disparities of talent and position vanish when the individuals are seen in the duration which is necessary to complete the career of each, even more swiftly the seeming injustice disappears when we ascend to the central identity of all the individuals, and know that they are made of the substance which ordaineth and doeth.

The genius of humanity is the right point of view of history. The qualities abide; the men who exhibit them have now more, now less, and pass away; the qualities remain on another brow. No experience is more familiar. Once you saw phœnixes: they are gone; the world is not therefore disenchanted. The vessels on which you read sacred emblems turn out to be common pottery; but the sense of the pictures is sacred, and you may still read them transferred to the walls of the world. For a time, our teachers serve us personally, as metres or milestones of progress. Once they were angels of knowledge, and their figures touched the sky. Then we drew near, saw their means, culture, and limits, and they yielded their places to other geniuses. Happy, if a few names remain so high, that we have not been

able to read them nearer, and age and comparison have not robbed them of a ray. But, at last, we shall cease to look in men for completeness, and shall content ourselves with their social and delegated quality. All that respects the individual is temporary and prospective, like the individual himself, who is ascending out of his limits, into a catholic existence. We have never come at the true and best benefit of any genius, so long as we believe him an original force. In the moment when he ceases to help us as a cause, he begins to help us more as an effect. Then he appears as an exponent of a vaster mind and will. The opaque self becomes transparent with the light of the First Cause.

Yet, within the limits of human education and agency, we may say, great men exist that there may be greater men. The destiny of organized nature is amelioration, and who can tell its limits? It is for man to tame the chaos; on every side, whilst he lives, to scatter the seeds of science and of song, that climate, corn, animals, men, may be milder, and the germs of love and benefit may be multiplied.